MEDIEVAL MANUSCRIPTS
IN BRITISH LIBRARIES

MEDIEVAL MANUSCRIPTS IN BRITISH LIBRARIES

BY N. R. KER

II

ABBOTSFORD–KEELE

OXFORD

AT THE CLARENDON PRESS

1977

Oxford University Press, Walton Street, Oxford OX2 6DP

OXFORD LONDON GLASGOW NEW YORK
TORONTO MELBOURNE WELLINGTON CAPE TOWN
IBADAN NAIROBI DAR ES SALAAM LUSAKA ADDIS ABABA
KUALA LUMPUR SINGAPORE JAKARTA HONG KONG TOKYO
DELHI BOMBAY CALCUTTA MADRAS KARACHI

ISBN 0 19 818162 0

© Oxford University Press 1977

Printed in Great Britain
at the University Press, Oxford
by Vivian Ridler
Printer to the University

PREFACE

IN the preface to volume I, I expressed the hope that 'Aberdeen–Liverpool' and 'Maidstone–York' would 'fit into volumes of about the same size as the present volume'. In fact, volume II ends at Keele and is twice as thick as volume I. This is partly because much space is taken up by descriptions of manuscripts at Eton College. In 1969 I thought that Eton would be treated like Westminster Abbey and that I should describe only the few manuscripts which M. R. James had not catalogued. But James's *Westminster* (1909) is different from his Eton (1895). Eton was his first catalogue and the qualities which made him a great cataloguer are only just apparent. James's love of medieval manuscripts began early. It grew, no doubt, because his home was a few miles from Bury St. Edmunds and his school was Eton. Before he was seventeen[1] he was able to explore the old books of the parish library of St. James's Church at Bury, then kept in the Guildhall. As for College Library at Eton, 'Henry Babington Smith and I succeeded in wheedling the keys out of Vice-Provost Dupuis, and for the first time we were able to handle actual manuscripts' (M. R. James, *Eton and Kings*, p. 23). In a letter home in February 1881 he reported that the library had 'an excellent Apuleius with most spirited pen and ink drawings, an early MS. of the Decretals, some handsome Bibles (all Vulgates), a copy of Adelard of Bath's natural history, some Ovids and a little Cicero'. Probably his descriptions of the manuscripts, although not printed until 1895, were substantially finished by 1887, when he became a fellow of King's College, Cambridge. By the time of his death, 12 June 1936, he knew a great deal about the collection and had recorded it in interleaved copies of his catalogue. Any time after 1918, when he became Provost of Eton, would have been a good time for a new edition, but he never made one. I can only hope that pp. 628–798 are a worthy contribution to the history of the library which he knew best and loved best and in which I spent happy Sunday afternoons some forty-five years after James, K. S. Unlike James, I did not see the manuscripts.[2]

Twenty-two of the 'larger' collections mentioned in the preface to volume I are in the A–K section of the alphabet. They are (besides Eton): Cambridge University Library; the National Libraries of Scotland and Wales; the cathedrals at Canterbury, Durham, and Hereford; the universities of Aberdeen, Durham, Edinburgh, and Glasgow; ten Cambridge

---

[1] See his letter in *The Academy*, 26 July 1879. Dr. A. C. de la Mare tells me that the fragments of Bruni's translation of Plutarch in question here are in the hand of the Florentine notary Ser Giovanni di Piero da Stia, *c.* 1440.

[2] This paragraph owes much to Dr. R. W. Pfaff.

colleges; the Fitzwilliam Museum, Cambridge. I am concerned with these collections here only in so far as there are uncatalogued manuscripts at Canterbury Cathedral and Durham Cathedral, at the four universities, and at six of the ten Cambridge colleges, and in so far as it seemed necessary to supplement Woodruffe's Canterbury descriptions with 'abbreviated descriptions' of my own and to help users of the *Handlist of Manuscripts in the National Library of Wales* and the National Library of Scotland's *Catalogue of Manuscripts acquired since 1925*: the medieval manuscripts are not easy to find in these publications.

Most of the 'smaller collections of fewer than fifty . . . manuscripts' in the A–K section belong to institutions of six kinds: cathedrals; Benedictine abbeys; universities; colleges of Cambridge University; theological colleges; public libraries, art galleries, and museums. The cathedrals are Bangor, Bristol, Carlisle, Chester, Chichester, Edinburgh (Episcopal), Ely, Exeter, and Gloucester. The abbeys are Ampleforth, Douai, Downside, and Fort Augustus. The universities are Birmingham, Hull, and Keele. The Cambridge colleges are Clare, Christ's, King's, Newnham, Queens', St. Catharine's, Selwyn, and Trinity Hall. The theological colleges are the Baptist College in Bristol, Selly Oak Colleges in Birmingham, Blairs College, St. Peter's College, Cardross, St. Augustine's College, Canterbury, and New College, Edinburgh. The public libraries,[1] art galleries, and museums are at Barnard Castle (the Bowes Museum), Bath, Birmingham, Blackburn, Brighton, Bristol, Cardiff, Carlisle, Colchester, Dunfermline, Edinburgh, Evesham, Glasgow, Hartlepool, and Ipswich. With eight exceptions, these smaller collections have not been described in print until now, or not in a generally accessible publication, or only very briefly, and I have dealt with them in the way referred to on pp. vii–xiii of the preface to volume I. The exceptions are:

> Christ's College, Clare College, King's College, Queens' College, St. Catharine's College, and Trinity Hall, Cambridge. Catalogued by James. Additions at Christ's and King's catalogued here.
> Bristol Central Public Library, MSS. 1–10. Catalogued by Mathews. Abbreviated descriptions here.
> Ipswich Central Public Library, MSS. 1–9. Catalogued by James. Abbreviated descriptions here.

Some space has been taken up in this volume by descriptions of binding fragments found in the capitular and diocesan records of Canterbury, Chichester, Durham, Ely, Gloucester, and Hereford. There seemed to me to be a case for including localizable material of this kind, some of which came certainly or probably from the medieval libraries in these places.

---

[1] I have used the term 'public library' for what is now usually called 'central library'; cf. the 'List of Libraries', pp. xiii–xxxv.

One small collection which would have been listed in volume II was dispersed in 1971. One of the four medieval manuscripts belonging to Bury St. Edmunds Cathedral was then sold to the Wellcome Historical Medical Library in London. The other three manuscripts were sold at Sotheby's on 12 July, lots 35A, 36, 37, and are now respectively in the Bibliothèque Royale in Brussels, the Huntington Library at San Marino, California, and Leiden University Library.

The collections are of many kinds. Some have been where they now are since the Middle Ages: Canterbury Cathedral; Eton College; Exeter Cathedral. Some were formed between the last years of the sixteenth century and 1800: Blickling Hall; Bristol Baptist College; Bristol Public Library; the Hunter Collection at Durham Cathedral; the General Collection at Glasgow University; Gloucester Cathedral; Ipswich Public Library. Some, the majority, are nineteenth- and twentieth-century collections. They include specialist collections of alchemy in Glasgow University (Ferguson) and astronomy and astrology at the Edinburgh Royal Observatory (Crawford) and of illuminated manuscripts at Blackburn (Hart) and Edinburgh University (White), and collections made by enterprising librarians with not much money to spend at Birmingham University and Cardiff Public Library. The manuscripts in the Bowes Museum are French, because of the interests of the donor. At Ampleforth there are manuscripts from Hildesheim, because of historical links with that city. Books of Hours abound and there are many Bibles. Three of the Bibles belong to the churches to which they belonged in the Middle Ages (Appleby, near Leicester; St. Thomas, Bristol; Buckingham: cf. St. Mary, Colchester).

I add here some further remarks in amplification of what is said in the paragraphs numbered 1, 2, 10, 12, 14 on pp. vii–xiii of volume I.

1. In volume I the second sentence reads 's.xiii by itself denotes the middle of the thirteenth century'. I think now that it was a bad mistake to have left out the word 'med.' when assigning dates to manuscripts written probably in the middle of a century. To make the paragraph applicable to volume II, the second sentence should be cancelled and the first sentence should read 's.xiii in., s.xiii^1, s.xiii med., s.xiii^2, s.xiii ex., s.xiii/xiv denote respectively the beginning, first half, middle, second half, end, and turn of the thirteenth century'.

2. *Contents.* **Bibles.** In volume I, Lambeth Palace 1364 was taken as the example of a common type of Bible, common that is in France, but not in England, in which the number of books and their order does not vary and in which there are sixty-four prologues in a particular order. In the present volume, Bristol Public Library 15 is taken as the example. In 'The Soissons Bible paintshop in thirteenth-century Paris', *Speculum* xliv (1969), 13–34, R. Branner discusses a particular group of these

Bibles: he lists the sixty-four prologues on p. 24. **Books of Hours.** The formula 'hours of B.V.M. of the use of', followed by a place-name within brackets, indicates that the use is deduced from the antiphon and capitulum at prime and none, as set out by F. Madan in *Bodleian Quarterly Record*, iii (1923), 40–4. This test is not wholly satisfactory, but in most cases what one finds by looking at Madan's list is confirmed by evidence from calendar and litany.

10. *Quire signatures and leaf signatures.* On 'ad hoc' signatures see P. J. G. Lehmann, *Erforschung des Mittelalters*, iii (1960), 13, 33–4. A variant of the normal late medieval system of marking by serial letter and serial number is to begin with 'a' on the *second* quire; the first quire is either unmarked or marked '+'. John Malberthorpe is a known scribe (cf. Eton College 47) whose 'a 1' is regularly on the first leaf of the second quire. The practice is a tiresome one, if one wishes to calculate how many leaves are missing from the beginning of a manuscript.

12. *Script.* On **anglicana** see now M. B. Parkes, *English Cursive Book Hands*, 1969, pp. xiv–xviii, xxii–xxiv.[1] Volume I contained no example, I think, of the bastard German script in which Aberdeen 245 and Glasgow, Ferguson 104 are written. This resembles the usual book-hand form of anglicana in having minims made in separate strokes, ascenders with heads, two-compartment *a*, looped *d*, *f* and *s* as descenders, everything in fact except the typically English long-tailed *r*, a feature which writers of the most formal kind of anglicana tended to avoid (Parkes, pls. 6 (ii), 8 (i)). It is a common type of hand, but it did not achieve the status of anglicana as a book-hand and has not often been reproduced in facsimile.[2] The corresponding Italian script of Eton College 112 is well known because of its use for manuscripts of Dante.[3]

On **secretary** see now Parkes, op. cit., pp. xix–xxi. Thomas Rud (†1732) used the word as a name for the script we call secretary in his catalogue of the manuscripts of Durham Cathedral: thus he says of B. III. 29 that it is written 'literis mediocribus acutis quas Secretarias vocant'.

14. **Decoration.** In measuring pictures the height is given before the width. A 'full-page' picture is one which occupies all the written space. For 'cadels' see B. Kruitwagen, *Paleografica*, 1942, p. 16, and W. de Vreese, 'Over handschriften en handschriftenkunde', *Tijdschrift voor Nederl. taal en letterkunde*, li (Leiden, 1932), pp. 29–31.

Aids to cataloguing which have appeared since 1969 include 'Dondaine and Shooner' for Aquinas (in progress), '*SOPMA*' (in progress), Dole-

[1] As in vol. I, 'anglicana' without qualification means non-current anglicana, as in vol. I, pls. 7, 8.

[2] *Manuscrits datés*, II, pl. xlviii*b*, written in 1334. J. van den Gheyn, *Album belge de paléographie*, 1908, pl. 21, written about 1373.

[3] E. Crous and J. Kirchner, *Die gotischen Schriftarten*, 1928, pl. 10. J. Kirchner, *Scriptura gothica libraria*, 1966, pl. 39. *Manuscrits datés*, I, pl. xliii, written about 1345.

zalek's *Verzeichnis* of manuscripts of Roman law, J. B. Schneyer's *Reper-torium* of sermons, and the Italian, British, Spanish, and Polish sections of *Die handschriftliche Überlieferung der Werke des heiligen Augustinus* sponsored by the Austrian Academy of Sciences. An English speciality, registers of writs, can now be described adequately, thanks to 'de Haas and Hall': most of my descriptions were made before it appeared and have been only partially revised.

The last paragraph of the preface to volume I applies also to volume II. It did not express sufficiently how much I owe to librarians, especially librarians in places where I have spent a long time. I should like to mention particularly Patrick Strong at Eton College and Anne Oakley at Canterbury Cathedral. The Canterbury binding fragments gave us both a good deal of work and I could not have done my share of it without her help. At Durham I have had much help from Ian Doyle and Alan Piper. Because of its greater size, volume II owes even more than volume I to Andrew Watson, who read the proofs.

CONTENTS

	page
LIST OF LIBRARIES AND MANUSCRIPTS	xiii
SIGNS AND ABBREVIATIONS	xxxvii
MANUSCRIPTS: ABBOTSFORD–KEELE	I
ADDENDA	997

LIST OF LIBRARIES AND MANUSCRIPTS

s before the short title shows that the name of the scribe or illuminator of all or part of the manuscript is known. The country or place of origin is noted after the date, and also, in italics, the provenance, if the manuscript belonged to a particular institution in the Middle Ages or was then in a particular part of a country or was in a country different from that in which it originated. Bold type shows that a manuscript was both written in (or for) and belonged to a particular institution. An asterisk before a short title or pressmark shows that the manuscript in question is kept in a library other than that to which it belongs.

In this list and in the text 'Netherlands' is used in its older, wider sense of 'Low Countries'.

ABBOTSFORD, Melrose, Roxburghshire. Scott Collection

'The Haye Manuscript' (in Scots). s. xv ex. Scotland.

ABERDEEN. UNIVERSITY LIBRARY

109. *s*Comment. in Physica Aristotelis. A.D. 1467. Louvain.
110. *s*Comment. in libros naturalium Aristotelis. *c.* A.D. 1467. Louvain.
115. De oculo morali. s. xv ex. France (?).
123. Miscellanea (partly in English). s. xv. England (Cheshire).
134. *s*Mirror of Our Lady (in English). s. xv ex. England. *Syon, Ord. Brig.*
195. *s*H. Retherus, Super titulo de verborum obligationibus, etc. A.D. 1433. Louvain. *Aberdeen, King's College.*
196. *s*Comment. in jus civile. *c.* A.D. 1433. Louvain. *Aberdeen, King's College.*
197. *s*J. Grosbek et R. de Turnaco, Comment. in jus civile. A.D. 1433. Louvain. *Aberdeen, King's College.*
199. Comment. in Decretales. s. xv². Netherlands (?).
200. 'Lectura super Clementinas'. s. xv². Louvain (?). *Aberdeen, King's College.*
201. J. de Imola, In Constitutiones Clementinas. s. xv. Netherlands (?). *Aberdeen, King's College.*
202. Decisiones Rotae Romanae, etc. s. xv. Netherlands. *Aberdeen, King's College.*
245. Compendium theologicae veritatis, etc. s. xiv ex. N. Germany.
257. Comment. in Decretales. s. xv². Netherlands.
264. Johannes de Irlandia. s. xv². Netherlands (?). *Aberdeen, King's College.*
679. Petrarch, Trionfi (in Italian). s. xv med. Florence.
987. Receptae medicinales. s. xv. Germany (?).

ABERYSTWYTH, Dyfed. NATIONAL LIBRARY OF WALES. See pp. 21–3.

AMPLEFORTH ABBEY (Benedictine Abbey of St. Lawrence), near York

8. Tractatus de superstitionibus, etc. s. xv. Netherlands (?).
14, pp. 1–31. J. de Lineriis. s. xv/xvi. Germany.
15. Gerhardus de Monte; Thomas Aquinas, Opuscula; etc. s. xv². Germany.
16. De modo legendi abbreviaturas. s. xv. Germany.
17. Pius II, Bulla; etc. s. xv². Germany (Hildesheim?).
178. P. Riga, Aurora. s. xiii in. Italy. *Mantua, S. Maria Gratiarum.*
180. G. de Cauliaco, etc. s. xv. Italy.

182. Malogranatum. A.D. 1459. **Hildesheim, nuns 'Sancte Marie Magdalene prope et extra muros'.**
183. 'Materia passionis Domini'. s. xv ex. Germany. *Hildesheim* (?).
184. Jacobus de Jueterbogk. s. xv/xvi. Germany.
185. Caesarius Arelatensis, Sermones; etc. s. xv. Germany. *Hildesheim, Luchtenhof.*
187. Horae B.V.M. (Sarum). s. xiv ex. France.
188. Psalterium, etc. s. xv. Netherlands (?).
190. Horae B.V.M. (Paris). s. xv². France.
191. Sermones, etc. s. xiii–xiv. Germany. *Hildesheim, S. Godehard, O.S.B.*
192. Horae B.V.M. s. xv². England.
192a. Horae B.V.M. (Rome). s. xv². Italy.
193. Breviarium. s. xv² (A.D. 1499?). Germany (?), for O.C.
274. Horae B.V.M. (Le Mans). s. xv in. France.
275. Horae B.V.M. (Rouen). s. xv². France.
276. Horae B.V.M. (Paris). s. xv ex. France.
277. Horae B.V.M. (Sarum). s. xv in. Netherlands.
281. Biblia (fragm.). s. xii¹. England.

APPLEBY, Cumbria. APPLEBY GRAMMAR SCHOOL

1. Petrus de Crescentiis. s. xv. England.

APPLEBY MAGNA, Leicestershire. PARISH CHURCH

*Biblia. s. xiii². England (?).

BAMBURGH, Northumberland. BAMBURGH CASTLE, LIBRARY OF THE TRUSTEES OF LORD CREWE'S CHARITY

*Sharp Collection, Select 6. Psalterium, etc. s. xii/xiii. Scotland (?), for O.S.A.
*Sharp Collection, Select 23. Psalterium, etc. (Sarum). s. xv. Netherlands.

BANGOR, Gwynedd. CATHEDRAL

'Liber pontificalis Aniani episcopi'. s. xiv in. Wales or England, for Anianus (II?) of Bangor.

BARNSTAPLE, Devon. NORTH DEVON ATHENAEUM.

1618. Guido Faba. s. xiv/xv. England (Oxford?).
3960. Logica, etc. s. xv¹. England (Oxford).

BATH, Avon. PUBLIC LIBRARY (**Bath Central Library**), Queen Sq.

Horae B.V.M. (Nantes). s. xv². France.

BIRMINGHAM, West Midlands

ART GALLERY, Congreve St.

*s*Horae B.V.M. (Rome). s. xv in. France. *Les-Saintes-Maries-de-la-Mer; Arles* (?).

PUBLIC LIBRARY (**Central Libraries**)

091/MED/1. Psalterium. s. xiii¹. Germany, for O.C. (?).
091/MED/2. Missale (Sarum). s. xiii med. England.
091/MED/3. Hugo de S. Victore, Opera. s. xiii². France. *Palazzuolo* (O.C.?); *Assisi, O.F.M.*

091/MED/4. Biblia. s. xiii². France.
091/MED/5. Horae B.V.M. (in Netherlandish: Utrecht). s. xv. Netherlands.
091/MED/6. Horae B.V.M. (Rome). s. xv². France. *Paris.*
091/MED/7. Psalterium. s. xv². Italy.
091/MED/8. *s*Horae B.V.M. (in Netherlandish: Utrecht). A.D. 1502 (?). Netherlands.

SELLY OAK COLLEGES, Bristol Rd.

Ital. 1. Lives of saints (in Italian). s. xv². Italy.
Lat. 1. Breviarium. s. xv. Italy (Padua?).
    2. M. Meldensis, Distinctiones super Psalterium. s. xiii in. N. France (?). *Palazzuolo (O.C.?); Assisi, O.F.M.*
    4. Breviarium. s. xiv. Italy.
    5. Jeronimus, Vita Malchi, etc. (fragm.). s. xv ex. Italy.
    7. Regula S. Augustini, etc. s. xv/xvi. Germany.
    8. *s*Antoninus Florent., Confessionale; etc. A.D. 1473. Italy. *Siena, Ord. Carm.* (?).
Fragm. B. 16. Poenitentiale (fragm.). s. xiii. in.

UNIVERSITY OF BIRMINGHAM

BARBER INSTITUTE OF FINE ART

Acc. no. 313. Horae B.V.M. (Metz). s. xiv. France (Metz?).
       397. Horae B.V.M. (Rome). s. xv². N. Italy.

UNIVERSITY LIBRARY

5/vi/2. Augustinus de Ascolo. s. xiii/xiv. Italy.
5/vi/12. Pseudo-Augustinus, Sermones; etc. s. xv. Italy.
6/i/19. Horae B.V.M. (Rome). s. xv in. NE. France.
6/ii/18. Hugo de S. Victore. s. xv². Germany. *Cologne* (?).
6/iii/14. Psalterium, etc. s. xv in. Italy, for O.S.B.
6/iii/15. 'Manuale notarii'. A.D. 1456–7. Bourg St. Andéol (Ardèche).
6/iii/19. 'Collationes'. s. xiii/xiv. Italy.
6/iii/20. Plautus. s. xv. Italy.
6/iii/25. Horae B.V.M. (Rome). s. xv. Italy (Florence?).
6/iii/26. Vetus Testamentum. s. xiii med. England.
6/iii/36. Innocentius III, De miseria humanae conditionis (*bis*). (A) s. xiv. France. [. . . .], *Ord. Carth.* (B) s. xiii ex. Italy (?).
6/iv/17. W. de S. Theodorico. s. xv. Italy.
6/iv/26. Missae. s. xiv. Italy.
6/iv/27. Ordinances of a lay company (in Italian). s. xv². Florence.
6/iv/28. Horae B.V.M. (Rome). s. xv. Italy.
7/i/12. Fabulae. s. xv. Germany.
7/i/18. W. Peraldus, De vitiis; etc. s. xiii². Italy.

BLACKBURN, Lancashire. MUSEUM AND ART GALLERY

091.20865. Horae B.V.M. (Paris). s. xv in. France, *Brittany.*
091.20884. Horae B.V.M. (Rome). s. xv/xvi. French Flanders (?).
091.20918. *s*Missale Romanum. A.D. 1400. Trisulto, Ord. Carth.
091.20927. Horae B.V.M. (Paris). s. xv². France.
091.20932. Horae B.V.M. (Rome). s. xv². Paris.
091.20954. Horae B.V.M. (Rome). s. xvi¹. France, for Germaine d'Alençon (?).
091.20960. (Pictures only). s. xiii. N. France.

091.20961. Psalterium, etc. A.D. 1500. Italy, for O.E.S.A. (?).
091.20966. Horae B.V.M. (Rome). s. xv ex. Italy.
091.20984. Horae B.V.M. (fragm.). s. xv². France.
091.20989. Evangelia, etc. s. xv in.–xv ex. Italy; France.
091.21001. Psalterium, etc. s. xiii². England.
091.21002. Horae B.V.M. (Rome). s. xvi in. France.
091.21004. Psalterium, s. xiii ex. France, for O.S.B.
091.21018. Horae B.V.M. (Sarum). s. xv. England. *Cambridgeshire.*
091.21035. Horae B.V.M. (Sarum). s. xv med. Flanders.
091.21037. Horae B.V.M. (Paris). s. xv ex. France.
091.21038. Biblia. s. xiii. England. *London, Ord. Carth.*
091.21039. Cicero, Paradoxa. s. xv med. Italy (Florence).
091.21040. Horae B.V.M. (Sarum). s. xv med. England. *Malling, O.S.B. nuns.*
091.21041. Bonaventura, Vita S. Francisci. s. xiii². S. France (?).
091.21117. Psalterium, etc. s. xiii¹. France. *Diocese of Langres.*
091.21195. Breviarium. s. xv. England, for **London, Ord. Carth.**

BLAIRS COLLEGE, Kincardineshire.

*1. Horae B.V.M. (Sarum). s. xv. France, for Bethune of Balfour.
*2. Horae B.V.M. s. xv. France, for Marie de Rieux.
*3. Horae B.V.M. s. xv ex. France.
*4. sHorae B.V.M. (Autun). s. xv. France.
*5. Memoriae sanctorum, etc. s. xv/xvi. Scotland.
*6. Horae B.V.M. (Sarum). s. xv med. England.
*7. Horae B.V.M. (Paris). s. xv². France.
*8. Floriger ex libris S. Augustini, etc. s. xv². Netherlands (?).
*9. Arma Christi (in English). s. xv. England.

BLICKLING HALL, Aylsham, Norfolk

6844. Orationes et Epistolae. s. xv²–xvi¹. Germany.
6849. 'Flosculus ex prato', etc. s. xv²–xv/xvi. France.
6855. Biblia. s. xiii. Germany (?).
6864. Gregorius, Dialogi; etc. s. xii/xiii–xiii in. SE. (?) England.
6867. sStella clericorum, etc. s. xv; A.D. 1439. Münster, Westphalia (in part).
        Köningsfeld, Ord. Praem.
6881. Dictys Cretensis, etc. s. xv. N. Germany or Netherlands.
6892. P. Langtoft (in French), etc. s. xiv¹. England.
6898. Juvenalis. s. xv². Italy.
6899. Ovidius, Heroides; etc. A.D. 1466. Italy.
6910. Bonaventura, Breviarium; Sermones; etc. s. xiii². England.
6917. sSuetonius. A.D. 1452 (?). Italy (Ferrara?), for Borso d'Este.
6931. Faits des romains (in French). s. xiii. France.

BLOXHAM, Oxfordshire. BLOXHAM SCHOOL

1. sOrationes, etc. s. xv. Germany. *Erfurt, Ord. Carth.*
2. Antiphonale. s. xiii/xiv. N. Italy.

BOSTON, Lincolnshire. PARISH CHURCH

Augustinus. s. xii med. England. *Pontefract, Ord. Clun.*

BOWES MUSEUM, Barnard Castle, co. Durham

091/MED/1. Missale. s. xiv². France, for use in diocese of Mende.
091/MED/2. Antiphonale. s. xv. Germany (?), for O.S.A.
091/MED/3. Processionale. s. xv. France, for O.P.
091/MED/4. Horae B.V.M. (Rome). s. xv/xvi. France.
091/MED/5. Horae B.V.M. (Tours). s. xv in. France.
091/MED/6. Horae B.V.M. (Rome). s. xv². S. Netherlands (?).
091/MED/7. Horae B.V.M. s. xv in. France.
091/MED/8. Horae B.V.M. (O.P.). A.D. 1471. France. *Poissy. O.P. nuns.*
091/MED/9. Horae S. Spiritus, etc. (in Netherlandish). s. xv. Netherlands.

BRAILES, Warwickshire. PRESBYTERY. See p. 996 (Addenda)

BRECHIN, Angus. DIOCESAN LIBRARY

*1. Psalterium. s. xv in. Italy.
*2. Horae B.V.M. (Tournai). s. xv. S. Netherlands (?).
*3. sSermones dominicales Veni domine jesu. A.D. 1435. Germany (Wendel-
    stein). *Erfurt, Ord. Carth.*

BRIDGNORTH, Salop. PARISH CHURCH OF ST. LEONARD

*1. Adalbertus Levita, Speculum Moralium. s. xii¹. England.
*2. Statuta Angliae; Registrum brevium. s. xiv in. England (Northamptonshire?).
    Great Doddington (?).

BRIDPORT, Dorset. CORPORATION

*2644. sStatuta Angliae; Registrum brevium. s. xiv¹. England (Bridport?).
    Bridport.

BRIGHTON, East Sussex. PUBLIC LIBRARY **(Central Library)**

 1. Biblia. s. xiii. France.
 2. Horae B.V.M. (Paris). s. xv². France.
 3. Horae B.V.M. s. xv in. France.
 4. Pseudo-J. de Garlandia. s. xiv in. France (?).
 5. Antiphonale. s. xiv. Italy, for Ord. Carth.
 6. Horae B.V.M. (Tournai). s. xv. S. Netherlands (?).
 8. Plinius Secundus, etc. A.D. 1468. Italy.
 9. 'Devotorum precordiale', etc. s. xvi in. S. Germany, for O.S.B. nuns.
10. Psalterium, etc. s. xv in. S. Netherlands (?).

BRISTOL, Avon

PARISH CHURCH OF ALL SAINTS

1. sW. Peraldus, Sermones; etc. s. xv¹. England. *Bristol.*
2. G. Zerbolt, De spiritualibus ascensionibus; etc. s. xv¹. England.
3. Augustinus, De Trinitate; etc. A.D. 1465. *Kempen, O.F.M. nuns.*

BAPTIST COLLEGE, Woodlands Rd.

Z.c. 17. Biblia. s. xiii/xiv. England.
Z.c. 18. Biblia. s. xiii in. England (?). *England.*
Z.c. 20. Eulogium historiarum, lib. 5. s. xiv ex. England.
Z.c. 23. sPsalterium, etc. s. xii². England. *Harrold, O.S.A. nuns.*

Z.d. 5. Regula S. Augustini, etc. s. xiv med. England. *Lanthony, O.S.A.*
Z.d. 37. New Testament (in English). s. xv. England.
Z.d. 38. Horae B.V.M. (Rome), etc. s. xv. England, for O.F.M.
Z.d. 39. Biblia. s. xiii. Portugal (?). *England, O.P.; Oxford.*
Z.d. 40. Processionale. s. xv–xvi¹. England, for Syon, Ord. Brig.
Z.d. 41. Biblia. s. xiii. England (?).
Z.d. 42. Horae B.V.M. (Paris). s. xv. France.
Z.e. 37. Preces privatae (partly in English). s. xvi¹. **Syon, Ord. Brig.** (?).
Z.e. 38. Biblia. s. xiii. France. *Crowland, O.S.B.*
Z.f. 38. Matthew and Acts (in English). s. xiv/xv. England.

CATHEDRAL

Graduale (fragm.). s. xiv². England.

PUBLIC LIBRARY **(Bristol Central Libraries),** College Green

1–10. See pp. 201–4.
11. Horae B.V.M. (Sarum). A.D. 1479. England, for P. Ringeston of Bristol.
12. Psalterium, etc. s. xii². England. *Kingswood, O.C.*
13. Missale (Sarum). s. xvi¹. England.
14. Horae B.V.M. (Sarum). s. xv in. England, for Isabel Ruddock (of Bristol?).
15. Biblia. s. xiii². France. *Avignon, Ord. Celest.*

PARISH CHURCH OF ST. THOMAS THE MARTYR

* Biblia. s. xiv/xv. England.

UNIVERSITY LIBRARY

DM 14. Medulla grammaticae (in Latin and English). s. xv². England.
268. Innocentius III. s. xiv. S. France (?). *Rodez, O.F.M.,* in s. xvi.

BUCKINGHAM. PARISH CHURCH

Biblia. s. xiv in. England. *Buckingham Ch.*

BURY ST. EDMUNDS, Suffolk

BURY ST. EDMUNDS AND WEST SUFFOLK RECORD OFFICE

A/8/1. Chronicon Angliae, etc. s. xiii ex. England (Bury St. Edmunds?).

BURY ST. EDMUNDS SCHOOL

*1. Psalterium, etc. s. xiv/xv–xv ex. England, for **Bury St. Edmunds O.S.B.**
*2. Prudentius, etc. s. xv/xvi. N. Germany (?).

CAMBRIDGE.

CHRIST'S COLLEGE

Rouse 251. *s*Ovidius. A.D. 1482–3. Italy.
256. Terentius. s. xv. Italy.
257. Cicero. s. xv². Italy.
258. R. Higden, Polychronicon. s. xiv². England.
270. *s*Lucanus. s. xv. Italy.
271. Cicero. s. xv. Italy.
274. Cicero, etc. s. xv/xvi. France (?).

CORPUS CHRISTI COLLEGE

540. Horae B.V.M. (Rome). s. xiv ex. France.
544. W. Lyndwood. s. xv². England.

FITZWILLIAM MUSEUM. See p. 228.

GONVILLE AND CAIUS COLLEGE

455/393. 'Excepta ex decretis romanorum pontificum'. s. xii². England.

KING'S COLLEGE

43. Genealogia regum anglorum. s. xv¹. England.
47. Feoda militum, etc. s. xv in. England (Cambridgeshire).
50. J. de Voragine, Quadragesimale; etc. s. xiv/xv. Germany.
51. Psalterium Romanum. s. xv in. Italy (**Potenza**).
52. Juvenalis. s. ix/x. NE. France. *Germany* (?); *Italy* (?).

MAGDALENE COLLEGE

F. 4. 34.+Pepys Collection, 2124. Ovid (in English: 2 vols.). s. xv ex. England.
Pepys Collection, 911. Bernardus Sylvestris, etc. s. xiii². England.

NEWNHAM COLLEGE

1. Biblia. s. xiii. France. *Caen, O.F.M.*
2. Horae B.V.M. (Sarum). s. xv in. England.
3. Missale (Sarum). s. xv med. England.
4. Piers Plowman, etc. (in English). s. xv. England.
5. Christine de Pisan, Othea (in French). s. xv. France.
6. Horae B.V.M. (Rouen). s. xvi in. France.
7. Preces, etc. s. xv. Italy.
8. Horae B.V.M. (Tours). s. xv². France.

PEMBROKE COLLEGE

309. W. Lyndwood. s. xv ex. England. *London, Ord. Carth.*
313. Fragments. See pp. 245–7.

RIDLEY HALL

RH 1. Epistolae Pauli. s. xv. Italy.
   2. Biblia. s. xiii. England.
   3. Preces et meditationes per annum. s. xv ex. Netherlands, for O.S.B. nuns.

ST. JOHN'S COLLEGE

103**. Psalterium. s. xiv¹. England.
137**. Nova officia, etc. s. xv¹. England (**St. Albans, O.S.B.**).
137***. Biblia. s. xiii. France (?).
524. Biblia. s. xiii. France (?). *Southwark, O.S.A.*
581. Decretales Gregorii IX, etc. s. xiii. Italy. *Germany.*
602. Anselmus, Proslogion. s. xii². France. *Vézelay, O.S.B.* (?).

SELWYN COLLEGE

108. K. 1. Augustinus, De doctrina Christiana. s. xv. England.
108. K. 2. Biblia, I; etc. s. xv. Germany. *Erfurt, Ord. Carth.*
108. K. 3. Biblia, II, III; etc. A.D. 1460. Germany (Smoll). *Erfurt, Ord. Carth.*
108. L. 19. New Testament (in English). s. xv in. England.

TRINITY COLLEGE

B. 11 extra 1. Evangelia glosata. s. xiii. England (?).
O. 10a. 26.   Breviarium (Sarum). s. xiv. England.

O. 10a. 27.   Horae B.V.M. s. xv/xvi. France, for diocese of Coutances.
O. 11. 11.   Brut Chronicle (in English). s. xv². England.
R. 15. 38.   Verses (in Italian). s. xv. Italy.
R. 17. 22.   Missale. s. xvi in. France.
R. 17. 23.   Augustine, De civitate Dei, bks. 11–22 (in French). s. xv². France.

UNIVERSITY LIBRARY. See p. 265.

CANTERBURY

CATHEDRAL

Lit. A. 1–E. 25. See pp. 265–89.
Lit. E. 42, ff. 1–68, 75–81 +Maidstone, Kent County Archives Office, S/Rm. Fae. 2.
          Passionale (fragm.). s. xii¹. **Canterbury Cathedral Priory, O.S.B.**
Lit. E. 42, ff. 69–74. Vitae Sanctorum (fragm.). s. xv². **Canterbury Cathedral Priory, O.S.B.**
HH L. 3. 2.   Horae B.V.M. (Paris). s. xv in. France.
HH L. 3. 3.   Horae B.V.M. (Paris). s. xv. France.
HH L. 3. 4.   Preces, etc. s. xv². England.
HH N. 2. 1.   Biblia. A.D. 1432–8. Bohemia (?).
HH O. 9. 1.   N. de Lyra, In Psalmos. s. xv. Netherlands (?).
HH O. 9. 2.   Commentary on parts of Exodus, etc. (in Netherlandish). s. xv. Netherlands.
Add. 6.   Breviarium. s. xiv². **Canterbury Cathedral Priory, O.S.B.**
      17.   Chronicle (fragm.: in French). s. xiii ex. England.
      18.   Prognostications (in French), etc. s. xiii/xiv.
      23.   Epistola Salvatoris, etc. s. xiii. England.
      38.   Biblia. s. xiii. Spain (?).
      40.   Lectionarium. s. xiii. Italy, for O.C. (?).
      66.   Comment. in Matthaeum. s. xiv². England.
      68.   sDescriptio civitatis Romae, etc. (in Latin and English). s. xv². England.
      75.   Breviarium. s. xiv². Southern Netherlands or NE. France.
     118.   Psalmi, etc. s. xv². Netherlands.
Chart. Antiq. A. 42. Vitae paparum et archiepiscoporum Cantuariae. s. xiii ex. *Canterbury Cathedral Priory, O.S.B.*
Fragments in Add. 16, 20, 25, 32, 127–9. See pp. 312–30.

ST. AUGUSTINE'S COLLEGE
Missale (Sarum). s. xv. England (Kent?).

CARDIFF, South Glamorgan. PUBLIC LIBRARY **(Central Library)**, The Hayes.

1. 217.   Sermones, etc. s. xv. Germany. *Hildesheim, S. Godehard, O.S.B.*
1. 218.   Theologica. s. xv². England.
1. 362, 363. See p. 333.
1. 366.   Horae B.V.M. (Sarum). s. xiv/xv. England.
1. 367.   Horae B.V.M. s. xv ex. France.
1. 368.   Horae B.V.M. (Paris). s. xv. France.
1. 369.   Horae B.V.M. (Rouen). s. xv². N. France.

1. 370. Horae B.V.M. (O.P.). s. xv². Netherlands.
1. 371. Horae B.V.M. (Utrecht: in Netherlandish). s. xv. S. Netherlands.
1. 372. Horae B.V.M. (Rome). A.D. 1431. Italy.
1. 373. sHorae B.V.M. (Rome), etc. (partly in Italian). A.D. 1477. Milan.
1. 375, ff. 149–53. 'La vie saint iohan baptiste' (in French). s. xv. France.
1. 376. Officium mortuorum. s. xv. Italy.
1. 377. Psalterium, etc. s. xii–xiv. Italy (Tuscany?).
1. 378. Breviarium. s. xv². Italy.
1. 379. Breviarium. s. xiv/xv. Italy.
1. 380. Officia pontificalia, etc. s. xiv. For **Oliva, O.C.**
1. 381, ff. 1–80. Vita S. Winwaloi. s. xiii in. England. *Dover, O.S.B.*
1. 381, ff. 81–146. Vitae sanctorum. s. xii in.–xii med. England, for **Barking, O.S.B. nuns.**
1. 382. Biblia. s. xiii. France (?).
1. 384. Weichbildchronik (in German). s. xiv. Germany.
1. 385. Statuta Angliae; Leges et consuetudines de Montgomery. s. xiv¹–xv. England; Wales. *Mid Wales.*
1. 704. W. Lyndwood, etc. s. xv. England.
2. 2. sSpeculum Regis, etc. s. xv–xv/xvi. England; Wales.
2. 7. See p. 355.
2. 81. See p. 356.
2. 385. Apocalypsis cum glosa; Cantica Canticorum cum glosa. s. xii¹. France. *Metz, O.P.*
2. 386. Conradus de Saxonia, Speculum Mariae; etc. s. xiv. Germany or Austria. *Waldhausen, O.S.A.*
2. 611. G. Monemutensis, etc. s. xiii/xiv. Wales or England.
2. 636. 'Livre des fortunes et infortunes' (in French). s. xv/xvi. France.
2. 637. Breviarium. s. xv. France, for use in Poitiers diocese.
2. 638. Ordo sepeliendi mortuos. s. xv. Italy, for use in Lodi diocese.
2. 641. Legenda aurea (in Netherlandish). s. xv. Netherlands.
2. 801. Pseudo-Cicero, Rhetorica ad Herennium. s. xv. Italy.
2. 874. Pauline Epistles, etc. (in Netherlandish). A.D. 1486. Netherlands.
2. 878. Nova Statuta Angliae. s. xv in. England.
3. 46. See p. 362.
3. 174. J. de Bromyard, etc. s. xv¹. England.
3. 175. Epistolarium. s. xv¹. N. England.
3. 236. J. de Mandevilla, etc. s. xv. England.
3. 242+5. 99, nos. i–vi. Medical texts, etc. (mostly in Welsh). s. xiv/xv. Wales and England.
3. 244. Ubertinus de Casali. s. xiv. Italy.
3. 516. Versus grammaticales. s. xv. England. *N. Somerset.*
3. 717. Missale. s. xiv/xv. France, for use in Lyons diocese.
3. 833. Defensor, etc. s. xiii². England. *Barking, O.S.B. nun* (?).
4. 234. Ludolphus de Saxonia (fragm.). s. xv². Netherlands.
4. 271. sExpositio in Psalterium; J. Gerson, Opuscula; etc. A.D. 1455. Germany.
4. 332. Pontificale Romanum. s. xv. Italy (Tuscany?).
4. 333. Cicero, De inventione rhetorica. s. xv. Italy.
4. 586. Missale cum notis (Sarum). s. xiv. England.

CARDROSS, Dumbartonshire. COLLEGE OF ST. PETER
1. Horae B.V.M. (Rome). 1490. W. Flanders (?).

CARLISLE, Cumbria

CATHEDRAL

1. Lives of Saints, etc. (in French). s. xiii. N. France.
2. Roman de la Rose (fragm.: in French). s. xiv in. France.

ST. MARY'S CATHOLIC CHURCH, Warwick Bridge
*Missale (Sarum). s. xv. England. *Caldbeck Ch.*

TULLIE HOUSE, PUBLIC LIBRARY
Augustinus, Epistolae, etc. s. xiii[1]. England.

CARMARTHEN. CARMARTHENSHIRE RECORD OFFICE
Psalterium, etc. s. xiii. England or Wales.

CHELTENHAM, Gloucestershire. CHELTENHAM LADIES' COLLEGE
*Breviarium. s. xiii ex. France, for use in Arras diocese.

CHESTER. CATHEDRAL

1. Biblia. s. xiii. England.
2. R. Higden, Polychronicon. s. xv. England.
3. Horae B.V.M. s. xv. NE. France (?).

CHICHESTER, West Sussex

CATHEDRAL

Med. 1. Augustinus. s. xiii in. England.
      2. Missale; Manuale. s. xiii[2]. England for **Kenilworth, O.S.A.**
      3. 'Distinctiones Groningen'. A.D. 1442. Ghent. *Erfurt, St. Peter, O.S.B.*
      4. Crispus, Sermones, s. xv. Germany. *Erfurt, Ord. Carth.*
      5. Ordo missae, etc. A.D. 1481. Germany.
Fragments. See p. 395.

DIOCESAN RECORD OFFICE
Fragments. See pp. 396–400.

COLCHESTER, Essex

CASTLE SOCIETY
*Evangelia. s. xii[1]. England.

COLCHESTER AND ESSEX MUSEUM

213. 32. Breviarium (Sarum). s. xv in. England.
214. 32. Bartholomaeus de S. Concordio. s. xv. Italy. *Padua, Santa Justina, O.S.B.*
215. 32. Statuta Angliae. s. xiv[1]. England. *Devon.*
216. 32. Horae S. Crucis, etc. s. xv in. France.
218. 32. Missale. s. xv/xvi. France, for use in Langres diocese.
219. 32A. Dieta Salutis. s. xv[1]. England.
219. 32B. Pore Caitif (in English). s. xv[1]. England.
221. 32. Officia cum notis. A.D. 1462 and s. xvi. **Polirone, O.S.B.**
222. 32. Antiphonale. s. xiii ex. Italy, for O.F.M.

PARISH CHURCH OF ST. MARY
Biblia. s. xiii. England.

COVENTRY, West Midlands. CORPORATION RECORD OFFICE
Acc. 325/1. Hoccleve, etc. (in English). s. xv. England.

DOUAI ABBEY (Benedictine Abbey of Our Lady and St. Edmund), Upper
Woolhampton, Reading

3. Biblia. s. xiii. France.
4. Breviarium, etc. s. xiii². England, for O.S.A., York diocese.
5. Psalterium, etc. s. xiv–xv. France.
6. Psalterium, etc. s. xv. England, for O.S.B.
7. Prick of Conscience (in English). s. xiv/xv. England.
8. Horae B.V.M. (Tournai). s. xv. S. Netherlands.
9. Officium mortuorum (Sarum). s. xiv/xv. England.
10. Antiphonale. s. xvi. Spain (?).
11. Versarius (fragm.). s. xii¹. England, Ord. Clun. **(Reading, Ord. Clun.?).**

DOWNSIDE ABBEY (Benedictine Abbey of St. Gregory), Stratton on the
Fosse, Somerset

21722. Pontificale. s. xv. Germany, for use in Paderborn diocese.
26524. Missale (Sarum). s. xv. England.
26525. Missale Romanum. s. xiv in. Germany.
26526. Breviarium. s. xv ex. Italy, for O.S.B., Congregation of St. Justina.
26527. Breviarium. s. xiv. Italy (Perugia?).
26528. Breviarium. s. xiii/xiv. N. Germany.
26529. Horae B.V.M. (Sarum). s. xv in. Netherlands.
26530. Horae B.V.M. (Sarum). s. xiv/xv. Netherlands.
26531. Horae B.V.M. (Rome). s. xv². France.
26532. Liber precum. s. xvi in. Netherlands (?).
26533. Horae B.V.M. (Sarum), Psalterium, etc. s. xiv. England, for use in
    Suffolk (?).
26534. sOfficium mortuorum, etc. A.D. 1439. England.
*26536. Pontificale. s. xiv²–xv. France, for Lyons diocese (?). *Diocese of Moustiers
    en Tarentaise.*
26537. sHymnarium, etc. s. xv ex. and A.D. 1498. Vienna.
26539. Antiphonale. s. xv. Italy, for Vicenza, Ordo Servorum.
26540. Medulla Grammaticae, etc. s. xv. England.
26542. Pricking of Love, etc. (mainly in English). s. xv². England. *Dartford,
    O.P. nuns.*
26543. Horae B.V.M. s. xv. **Winchester Cathedral Priory, O.S.B.**
26547. Bullarium Franciscanum. s. xiv in. France, for O.F.M.
26549. Vitalis Blesensis, etc. s. xvi in. France (?).
26619. J. de Guytrode, etc. A.D. 1476 (?). Germany for Ord. Carth. *Buxheim,
    Ord. Carth.*
33553. Horae B.V.M. (Rome). s. xv ex. Italy (Florence?).
33554. Horae B.V.M. (Sarum). s. xv in. Netherlands.
36212. Breviarium cum notis. s. xii. Italy, for O.S.B. (Ravenna, San Apollinaris?).
40190. Collectarius, etc. A.D. 1506. **Stavelot, O.S.B.**
45857. Bernardus Ayglerius, In Regulam S. Benedicti. s. xv. England.
48242 (Clifton 1). Missale Romanum. s. xv. Italy. *Bassano.*

48243 (Clifton 2). *s*Missale. s. xv in. England (Hereford?). *Herefordshire.*
48244 (Clifton 3). Breviarium (Sarum). s. xv[1]. England.
48245 (Clifton 4). Preces, etc. s. xv/xvi. Germany (Regensburg?), for O.S.B.
48246 (Clifton 5). Misc. theol. s. xv[1] (art. 2, A.D. 1428). Germany. *Erfurt, Ord. Carth.*
48247 (Clifton 6). Misc. theol. s. xv. Germany. *Erfurt, Ord. Carth.*
48248 (Clifton 7). De imitatione Christi, etc. s. xv. Germany. *Huysburg, O.S.B.*
48249 (Clifton 8). *s*Sermones et exempla. A.D. 1411; s. xv[1]. Germany. *Erfurt, St. Peter, O.S.B.*
48250 (Clifton 9). Libri sapientiales; Armandus de Bellovisu, O.P.; etc. s. xv. Germany. *Hamm, O.F.M.*
48251 (Clifton 10). T. Ebendorfer, etc. s. xv[2]. Germany. *Erfurt, St. Peter, O.S.B.*
48252 (Clifton 11). Horae B.V.M. (Sarum). s. xv. England.
48253 (Clifton 12). Pseudo-Augustinus, Meditationes; etc. s. xv. England. *London, Ord. Carth.*
58254 Modus orandi, etc. See p. 476.

DUNFERMLINE, Fife. PUBLIC LIBRARY (Abbey View Branch).

1. *s*Missale. s. xv med. Münster (Westphalia), Fraterhaus, for diocese of Münster.
2. Antiphonale. s. xiii. Italy, for O.C.
3. Horae B.V.M. (Rome). s. xv. Italy.
4. Horae B.V.M. (Bourges). s. xv in. France.
5. Horae B.V.M. (Rome). s. xvi in. Italy.
6. Graduale. s. xiv[2]. Italy.

DURHAM

CATHEDRAL

A. III. 36.   Petrus Cantor, etc. s. xii/xiii–xiii[1]. England.
A. IV. 33.   Uthredus de Boldon. s. xv[1]. England.
A. IV. 34, 35. See p. 486.
A. IV. 36.   Simeon Dunelmensis, etc. s. xiii in. England. *Durham Cathedral Priory, O.S.B.*
B. III. 33.   Laurentius Dunelmensis, etc. s. xii/xiii. France or Netherlands. *Orval, O.C.*
B. III. 34.   Kalendarium, etc. s. xiv/xv. England.
C. III. 20.   See p. 488.
C. III. 22.   Biblia. s. xiii[1]. England. *Durham Cathedral Priory, O.S.B. Stamford, O.S.B., cell of Durham.*
C. III. 24.   Hermannus Contractus. s. xii[1]. England.
C. III. 25.   Bernardus Dorna, etc. (fragm.). s. xiii. France (?). *Durham Cathedral Priory, O.S.B.* (?).
C. III. 26.   Damasus, Brocarda (fragm.). s. xiii. France (?). *Durham Cathedral Priory, O.S.B.* (?).
C. III. 27.   Dictionarium (fragm.). s. xiv. England.
C. III. 28.   Miscellanea (fragm.). s. xiv[1]. England.
Hunter 15, pt. 1. P. Comestor. s. xiii[1]. England.
      15, pt. 2. Three Kings of Cologne, etc. (in English). s. xv in. England.
      30.   Defensor, etc. s. xiv[2]. France (?). *N. England.*
      57.   Augustinus. s. xii[1]. England (?). *Hexham, O.S.A.*
      58.   Exceptiones patrum, etc. s. xiv. England. *Durham Cathedral Priory, O.S.B.* (?).

59.   J. Bury, Gladius Salomonis. s. xv². England.
67, item 10. De oratione. s. xv ex. NW. Germany (?).
97.   Registrum brevium. s. xiv¹. England.
98.   Horae B.V.M. (Sarum). s. xv. Netherlands (?).
99.   Officium mortuorum, etc. s. xv in. England.
100, 101. See p. 504.
102.   Sermones, etc. s. xiii¹. England.
103.   Officium mortuorum, etc. s. xv. England.
123.   L. Lazzarellus. *c.* A.D. 1468. Padua, for J. Chedworth.
Inc. 7, item 2. T. Aquinas, etc. A.D. 1482. Louvain. *Frankfurt am. Maine, O.P.*
Binding fragments. See pp. 507–11.

UNIVERSITY OF DURHAM
ST. CHAD'S COLLEGE
1. Antiphonale. s. xiii. Veneto, for O.C.
2. Horae B.V.M. (Rome). s. xv. Italy.

UNIVERSITY LIBRARY
Cosin Collection. See p. 513.
Cosin V. IV. 9. Historia trium regum, etc. s. xv med. England.
Mickleton and Spearman 27. Statuta Angliae. s. xiv/xv. England (Coventry?).
Mickleton and Spearman 57. Statuta Collegii de N. Cadbury. A.D. 1428.
Mickleton and Spearman 89. De oculo morali. s. xiii ex. England. *Durham Cathedral Priory, O.S.B.*
S.R. 2 B. 3, item 2. Sermones, etc. A.D. 1480 and s. xv². Germany (Huysburg, O.S.B.?). *Huysburg, O.S.B.*
S.R. 3 A. 4. P. Dorlandus, Viola animae. A.D. 1497. *Liège, St. Jacques, O.S.B.*
Add. 189. 4B7. Bonaventura, Breviloquium. s. xv in. England.

EASTBOURNE, East Sussex. PARISH CHURCH
*Horae B.V.M. (Bayeux). s. xv². France.

EDINBURGH
COLUMBA HOUSE, 16 Drummond Place. SCOTTISH CATHOLIC ARCHIVES
J. de Fordun, Chronicon, cum continuatione. s. xv ex.–1509. Scotland.
Psalterium. s. xiii. Germany (?).

FACULTY OF ADVOCATES. See p. 524.

NATIONAL GALLERIES OF SCOTLAND. See p. 525.

NATIONAL LIBRARY OF SCOTLAND. See pp. 526–30.

NEW COLLEGE
Med. 1. Jeronimus; Augustinus. s. xv. Spain.
    2. Athanasius; Vigilius Tapsensis. s. xv. Italy (Florence?).
    3. Bonaventura, etc. s. xiii ex. England. *Canterbury, St. Augustine's, O.S.B.* (?).
    4. Augustinus, Soliloquia; Preces. s. xv. Italy.
    5. *s*De tripartita domo Dei, etc. s. xiii¹. France.

PUBLIC LIBRARY (Central Library), George IV Bridge

32746. Graduale. s. xv/xvi. Italy.
32747. Antiphonale. A.D. 1535 (?). Germany (Cologne?).

ROYAL COLLEGE OF PHYSICIANS, Queen St.

Cursor Mundi; Northern Homily Cycle (in English). s. xiv[1]. England (Yorkshire?).

ROYAL COLLEGE OF SURGEONS OF EDINBURGH, Nicolson St.

1. Horae B.V.M. (Rouen). s. xv[1]. France.
2. Horae B.V.M. (Rouen). s. xv[2]. France.

ROYAL OBSERVATORY, Blackford Hill. Crawford Collection.

Cr. 1. 2.	J. de Sacrobosco, De sphaera; etc. s. xv. England.
Cr. 1. 27.	Jordanus de Nemore, etc. s. xiii med. France. *Paris, Sorbonne.*
Cr. 2. 2.	sJ. de Rupescissa. A.D. 1476. Budapest.
Cr. 2. 3.	J. de Sacrobosco, etc. s. xiv[2]–xv[2] and A.D. 1462. Germany (Hildesheim?). *Hildesheim, St. Michael, O.S.B.*
Cr. 2. 5.	Tabulae astronomicae. s. xiii. N. Italy.
Cr. 2. 20/1.	Kalendarium inrotulatum. s. xiv (A.D. 1339?). France (?), for O.C.
Cr. 2. 20/2.	Almanac. s. xv[2]. England.
Cr. 2. 20/3.	Almanac. s. xv[2]. England.
Cr. 2. 98.	sJ. de Sacrobosco, De sphaera; etc. A.D. 1468. Italy.
Cr. 2. 119.	J. de Muris. A.D. 1443. Germany.
Cr. 2. 123.	J. Dancko, Tabulae astronomicae; etc. A.D. 1482 (?). Nuremberg (?).
Cr. 3. 2.	sAlcabitius (in German). A.D. 1474. Salzburg.
Cr. 3. 3.	Alhacen, Optica; De crepusculo. s. xiii. Spain (?).
Cr. 3, 4.	Astrologica. s. xv. England.
Cr. 3. 5, ff. 17–25.	'Liber fatorum'. s. xv[2]. France (?).
Cr. 3. 9.	Tabulae Alphonsinae; etc. s. xv[2]. N. Italy.
Cr. 3. 12.	Messahala, De astrolabio; etc. s. xiv in. Italy.
Cr. 3. 13.	sJ. de Gerson. A.D. 1474. Germany.
Cr. 3. 14.	Astrologica, etc. s. xv. France.
Cr. 3. 23.	Michael Scotus, etc. s. xiv[2]. England.
Cr. 3. 25.	Tabulae astronomicae. s. xv[1]. Italy; France.
Cr. 3. 28.	Prosdocimus de Beldomandis, etc. s. xv[2]. Italy.
Cr. 3. 29.	Thebit, etc. A.D. 1317 and s. xiv in. Italy.
Cr. 4. 3.	Guido Bonatus. s. xv[1]. Italy.
Cr. 4. 5.	Soloneus; Bartholomaeus de Usingen; etc. s. xv/xvi. Germany (Leipzig?).
Cr. 4. 6.	Astrological, etc., texts (in German). s. xv[2]. E. Swabia (Augsburg?).
Cr. 4. 11.	J. de Ashenden, etc. s. xv. Germany.
Cr. 5. 3A.	Kalendarium. s. xv/xvi. N. Germany (?), for Ord. Brig.
Cr. 5. 10.	Book of fate (in German). s. xv. S. Germany (?).
Cr. 5. 14.	Aristoteles, etc. s. xiii[2]. Italy. *Assisi, O.F.M.*
Cr. 7. 76.	sJ. de Sacrobosco. A.D. 1496 (?). Strasbourg.

ST. MARY'S EPISCOPAL CATHEDRAL, Palmerston Pl.

Horae B.V.M. (Sarum). s. xv/xvi. Netherlands.

SCOTTISH RECORD OFFICE, H.M. General Register House

PA 5/1 ('Berne Manuscript'). R. de Glanvilla, etc. s. xiii[2]. N. England or S. Scotland. *Roxburghshire* (?).

PA 5/2 ('Ayr Manuscript'). Leges burgorum Scotiae, etc. s. xiv. S. Scotland.

SOCIETY OF ANTIQUARIES OF SCOTLAND. See p. 587.

UNIVERSITY OF EDINBURGH

REID SCHOOL OF MUSIC

D. 25. Officia liturgica. s. xv. Germany. *Marienberg, O.S.A. nuns.*

UNIVERSITY LIBRARY

300. Decretales Gregorii IX et Innocentii IV. s. xiii. France. *Custody of Rodez, O.F.M.*
301. Psalterium. s. xv in. Germany, for Ord. Carth. *Erfurt, Ord. Carth.*
302. Horae B.V.M. (Paris). s. xv in. France.
303. Horae B.V.M. (Sarum). s. xv. England (?).
304. Horae B.V.M. (Rouen). s. xv/xvi. France.
305. Horae B.V.M. (Rome). s. xv². S. Netherlands.
306. Horae B.V.M. (Rouen). s. xv/xvi. France.
307. Horae B.V.M. (Troyes). s. xv. France.
308. Horae B.V.M. (Sarum). s. xv. England.
309. Horae B.V.M. (Rome). s. xv ex. France (Paris?).
310. Horae B.V.M. (Paris). s. xv¹. France.
311. Horae B.V.M. (Beauvais). s. xv/xvi. France, for use at Senlis (?).
312. Horae B.V.M. (Rome). s. xv². Flanders.
313. Biblia. s. xiii. France.
314. A. de Cermisono, Cirurgia. s. xv. N. Italy.
315. Statuta Edwardi III, etc. s. xiv². England.
318. sDe musica. s. xv/xvi. Germany.
320. sP. de Pergula, Logica. A.D. 1455. Padua, S. Johannes in Viridario, O.S.A.
321. P. de Pergula, Logica; etc. s. xv. Italy.
322. R. de S. Victore, Beniamin minor. s. xv. Italy.
324. Gesta Alexandri Magni, etc. s. xv². Italy.
326. Pius II, Gesta concilii Basiliensis. s. xv. Germany.
328. Miscellanea Franciscana. s. xv². Netherlands, for O.F.M.
329. sMacer, Ortolf von Bayerlant, etc. (in German). A.D. 1463–4; s. xv ex. S. Germany or Austria.
331. Misc. theol. A.D. 1431, 1433, and s. xv¹. Germany (Erfurt, Ord. Carth.?). *Erfurt, Ord. Carth.*

ELY, Cambridgeshire

CATHEDRAL

*Liber Eliensis. s. xii ex. **Ely, O.S.B.**
*Binding fragments. See p. 625.

DIOCESAN RECORD OFFICE, University Library, Cambridge

F/5/32. Formularium juris canonici. s. xv². N. England (York?).
F/5/33. Formularium juris canonici, etc. s. xv in. York (?). *Worcester.*
Binding fragments. See pp. 627–8.

ETON COLLEGE, Berkshire.

1, 2. Biblia. s. xiii¹. England (?). *Eton College.*
3. Bible historiale (in French). s. xiv². France.
4. Dictionarium; P. Comestor, Allegoriae. s. xiv/xv–xv. England.

5.   Ambrosius, In Ps. 118. s. xii². *Eton College.*
6.   Augustinus, In Psalmos 1–50. s. xv. England. *Eton College.*
7.   Augustinus, In Psalmos 51–100. s. xii². England.
8.   R. Grosseteste, In Psalmos 1–100. s. xv. England.
9.   P. Lombardus, In Psalmos. s. xiii¹. England.
10.   R. Rolle, On Psalms and Canticles (in English). s. xv. England.
12.   Gregorius Magnus, In Job, II. s. xiii¹. England.
13.   Gregorius Magnus, In Job. s. xiii med. England. *Eton College.*
14, 16, 19.   P. Cantor; Gilbertus Autissiodorensis. s. xii/xiii. England. *Quarr, O.C. Eton College.*
15.   Radulphus Flaviacensis. s. xii ex. England. *Eton College.*
17.   Hugo de S. Caro, In libros Salomonis. s. xiii². England (?). *Eton College.*
18.   R. Holcot, In Sapientiam Salomonis. s. xiv/xv. England. *Bristol. Eton College.*
20.   Haimo, In Isaiam; A. de Essebie, Liber festivalis. s. xii ex. England. *Eton College.*
21.   Jeronimus, In Danielem et Prophetas Minores; etc. s. xii med. England. *Peterborough, O.S.B.*
22.   Jeronimus, In Prophetas Minores. s. xiii med. England. *Eton College.*
23.   Prophetae Minores glossatae. s. xiii. England. *Eton College.*
24.   *s*Apocalypsis (Latin and English), etc. A.D. 1455. Woodhouse, Isle of Wight. *Eton College.*
25.   Biblia. s. xiii². Italy.
26.   Biblia. s. xii/xiii. England. *St. Albans, O.S.B. Eton College.*
27.   Biblia. s. xiii in. England.
28, 29.   Vetus Testamentum cum comment. Hugonis de S. Caro. s. xiii². France (?). *Eton College.*
30.   J. de Athon, Septuplum. s. xv. England. *Eton College* (?).
32, ff. ii, 1–96.   Misc. theol. s. xiii². England. *Eton College.*
32, ff. 97–216.   T. Wallensis, In Psalterium. s. xv. England. *Eton College.*
33.   Gregorius Magnus, Dialogi; etc. s. xii/xiii. England. *Monk Sherborne, O.S.B. Eton College.*
34.   *s*Gregorius Magnus, Homiliae in Ezekielem; Fasciculus Morum. s. xv; A.D. 1443. England. *Eton College.*
35+219, pp. 51–4.   Thomas Aquinas. s. xiii ex. England.
36.   Martinus Polonus, Aquinas, etc. s. xiii/xiv. England. *Eton College.*
37.   Gregorius Magnus, Dialogi, etc. s. xii/xiii. England or Wales. *De Valle Crucis, O.C. Eton College.*
38.   Sermones, etc. s. xii med. England (Gloucester?). *Oxford. Eton College.*
39.   Bernardus (etc.), Sermones. s. xiii in. England. *Eton College.*
41.   Homiliae in Evangelia. s. xi/xii. France (?). *Eton College.*
42.   *s*Pseudo-Chrysostomus, In Matthaeum. s. xv in. England. *Eton College.*
43.   Matthaeus glosatus. s. xii/xiii. England. *Otham, Ord. Praem.*
44.   Albertus Magnus, In Lucam et Marcum. c. A.D. 1481. Oxford. *Eton College.*
45.   P. Comestor; Allegoriae in Bibliam. s. xiii¹. England.
46.   *s*Ambrosius; Faustus Reiensis. s. xv. Italy.
47.   *s*Augustinus, etc. s. xv. England (Oxford or Eton?).
48, ff. 1–96.   Augustinus. s. xii¹. England. *Eton College.*
48, ff. 97–106.   Prosper, Sententiae. s. xii/xiii. England.
48, ff. 107–240.   Notulae in Bibliam. s. xii ex. England. *Belvoir, O.S.B.*
74.   J. de Voragine, Sermones dominicales. s. xv. England. *Eton College* (?).

76, ff. 1–40,+82. Jeronimus, In Danielem; W. de Monte. s. xii–xiii in. England. *Eton College.*

76, ff. 41–132. Berengaudus, In Apocalypsin. s. xiv ex. England. *Eton College.*

77. 'Glosule Mathei'. s. xii ex. England.

78. Psalterium, etc. s. xiii in. **Canterbury Cathedral Priory, O.S.B.** (?).

79. P. de Palma, In Parabolas Salomonis. s. xiv/xv–xvi¹. France (?), and England, for W. Horman. *Eton College.*

80. Jeronimus, Contra Jovinianum; etc. s. xii in. **Rochester Cathedral Priory, O.S.B.** *Eton College.*

81. Gregorius Magnus, Liber pastoralis; etc. s. xii med. England. *Eton College.*

83, ff. 1–83. Paschasius Radbertus, etc. s. xii in. Germany (?).

83, ff. 84–199. P. Cantor. s. xiii. England (?). *Eton College.*

84. A. de Insulis, Distinctiones theologicae. s. xiv². England.

87. Plautus. s. xv. Italy.

88. Germanicus Caesar. s. xv². Italy.

89. Seneca. s. xiii. Germany (?). *England.*

90. Cicero, etc. s. xii/xiii. England. *Haverfordwest, O.P.*

91. Ovidius. s. xiii. France (?). *Canterbury Cathedral Priory, O.S.B.* (?). *Winchester College.*

96. Chronicon. s. xiii med. England **(Glastonbury, O.S.B.?).**

97. Decreta Romanorum Pontificum, etc. s. xii in. Exeter Cathedral (?). *Exeter Cathedral. Eton College.*

98. W. Lyndwood. s. xv¹. England. *Eton College.*

99. P. Calo de Clugia, Legenda Sanctorum, II. s. xiv/xv. France. *Eton College.*

101, ff. i, 1–182. Augustinus, In Johannem. s. xiv². England. *Eton College.*

101, ff. 183–328. Gregorius Magnus, Homiliae in Evangelia, etc. s. xiii ex. *Eton College.*

102. N. de Gorran, In Lucam. A.D. 1450. England (?). *Eton College.*

103. Pseudo-Gorran, In Epistolas Pauli. s. xv¹. **St. Albans, O.S.B.** *Eton College.*

104. Pseudo-Hugo de S. Caro, In Epistolas Pauli. s. xv. England.

105. Augustinus, Epistolae, etc. s. xiii in. England. *Eton College.*

106. Augustinus, De verbis Domini; etc. s. xii. France (?). *Eton College.*

107. Augustinus, De civitate Dei. s. xiii in. England. *Eton College.*

108, ff. 1–111. Augustinus, De Trinitate. s. xiii/xiv. France (?). *England. Eton College.*

108, ff. 112–87. Tabula in N. de Lyra, etc. s. xv in. England. *Eton College.*

109. Eusebius, Historia ecclesiastica; etc. s. xiii in. England. *Eton College* (?).

110. Seneca, Tragoediae. s. xiv. Italy.

112. Dante, Divina commedia (in Italian). s. xiv. Italy.

114. P. Lombardus, Sententiae. s. xiii². England. *Eton College.*

115. Jacopo della Lana, Commentary on Dante (in Italian). s. xv. Italy.

116+219 pp. 27–50. T. Aquinas, Summa, I. s. xiii/xiv. England (?). *Eton College.*

117. R. Grosseteste; J. Ridevall; etc. s. xiv–xiv/xv. England. *Eton College.*

118. Bartholomaeus de Pisis, Vita S. Francisci. s. xv². Italy. *Brescia, San Apollonio.*

119. Gregorius Magnus, Registrum; etc. s. xiii in.–xv. England. *Ford, O.C. Eton College.*

120. Augustinus, etc. s. xiv. England. *Launde, O.S.A. Eton College.*

122. Eustrathius (*et al.*), In Ethica Aristotelis. s. xiii ex. England. *O.F.M.* (?). *Eton College.*

123. Flores historiarum. s. xiii ex.–xiv in. *Merton, O.S.A.*
124. Johannes Diaconus, Vita S. Gregorii. s. xi/xii. Italy (Farfa, Ord. Clun.?). Farfa, Ord. Clun.
125+219, pp. 71–8. P. Comestor. s. xii/xiii. France (?).
126. Johannes filius Serapionis. s. xiii ex. France (?). *Eton College.*
127. Articella, etc. s. xiii ex. France (?). *Eton College.*
128. L. B. Albertus, De re aedificatoria. s. xv². Italy.
129. Aristoteles, Ethica, etc. s. xiii ex. Italy and England (?). *England.*
130. Porchetus; Petrus, prior S. Trinitatis; T. Aquinas. s. xiii²–xiv¹. England.
131. Cassiodorus, Historia tripartita; Martinus Polonus; Vegetius. s. xiv med.– xiv ex. England. *Eton College.*
132. Galenus. s. xiii². France (?). *Eton College.*
133. Orosius; Epistola Alexandri. s. xii med. England.
134. Robertus Crikeladensis. s. xii². England. *Oxford* (?). *Eton College* (?).
135. Seneca, Epistolae. s. xii. Italy.
136. *s*Seneca, Letters, etc. (in Italian). s. xiv/xv. Florence.
137. Vitruvius. s. xiv/xv. Italy.
140. Cl. Ptolemaeus, Cosmographia. s. xv ex. Italy.
145. Ambrosius. s. xii. England. *Eton College.*
147. Apuleius. s. xv in. Italy.
149. *s*Cicero, De officiis. A.D. 1497/8. Rome.
150. Theodulus, etc. s. xi. S. Italy.
151. Baptista Mantuanus. s. xv/xvi. Italy, for B. Bembo (?).
152. Juvenalis. s. xv. Italy.
153. *s*Juvenalis; Persius. s. xv. Florence.
154. Comment. in Persium. s. xv/xvi. Italy.
155. Eutropius et Paulus Diaconus. s. xv. Netherlands.
156. P. Marsus. s. xv². Italy, for B. Bembo.
157. Naldus Naldii. s. xv². Italy, for B. Bembo.
158. J. Boccaccius, De mulieribus claris. s. xv. Italy.
160. W. de Conchis. s. xiii. France. *Canterbury, St. Augustine's, O.S.B.*
161. Adelardus Bathoniensis. s. xii. England. *Canterbury, St. Augustine's, O.S.B.*
165. M. Vegius. s. xv. Italy.
169. P. Riga. s. xiii in. France (?). *England.*
170. Pharetra sacramenti. s. xvi¹. England.
171. N. de Gorran, Fundamentum aureum. s. xiii/xiv. England.
172. J. de Dondis, Opus Planetarii. s. xv med. N. Italy.
176. H. de Bracton. s. xiii ex.–xiii/xiv. England.
177, pt. 1. Figurae Bibliorum. s. xiii. England.
177, pt. 2. Apocalypsis, cum figuris. s. xiii. England.
178. 'The Eton Choirbook'; Biblia (fragm.). s. xii in.–xvi in. England. *Eton College.*
179. Biblia. s. xiii. England.
181. Horae B.V.M. (Troyes). s. xv.
191. Chronicon Angliae inrotulatum. s. xvi¹. England.
196. Beda, In Lucam (fragm.). s. xii ex. England.
202. Alexander de Villa Dei. s. xiv. Italy.
203. J. de Voragine, Legenda aurea. s. xiv. France. *Angers, S. Aubin, O.S.B.*
204. Apuleius Barbarus, etc. s. xii. Germany.
208–12. Binding fragments. See pp. 781–2.
213. R. Higden, Polychronicon. s. xvi¹. England. Witham, Ord. Carth.

218. Bernardus, In Cantica Canticorum (fragm.). s. xii med. England.
219–21. Binding fragments. See pp. 785–90.
223. Breviarium (fragm.). s. xiv in. England (**Glastonbury, O.S.B.?**).
225. Jeronimus, In Prophetas Minores et Danielem. s. xii med. England.
226. Gregorius Magnus, Moralia in Job, I. s. xii med. England (Reading, Ord. Clun.?). *Reading, Ord. Clun.*
246. G. Monemutensis. s. xiii². England or Wales.
265. Horae B.V.M. (Rome). s. xv/xvi. Netherlands.
266. Horae B.V.M. (Paris). s. xv. France.
267. Horae B.V.M. (Rome). s. xv/xvi. France.
268. Julius Caesar. s. xv². Italy (Ferrara?).
280. Binding fragments. See p. 798.

EVESHAM, Hereford and Worcester. ALMONERY MUSEUM

Psalterium. s. xiv¹. **Evesham, O.S.B.**

EXETER, Devon. CATHEDRAL

3500. Exon Domesday. A.D. 1086 (?). England.
3501, ff. o, 1–7. Manumissions, etc. (in English and Latin). s. xi²–xii. **Exeter Cathedral.**
3501, ff. 8–130. 'The Exeter Book' (in English). s. x². England. *Exeter Cathedral.*
3502. Ordinale. s. xv². **Exeter Cathedral.**
3503. Euclides, etc. s. xiii². England. *Exeter Cathedral.*
3504. Legenda Exon. (Temporale). s. xiv. **Exeter Cathedral.**
3505. Legenda Exon. (Sanctorale). s. xiv. **Exeter Cathedral.**
3505B. Legenda Exon. (Sanctorale). s. xiv ex. Exeter (?). *Exeter Cathedral.*
3506. sJ. de Gadesden, etc. s. xiv². England. *Oxford, All Souls College.*
3507. Rabanus Maurus, etc. s. x². England. *Exeter Cathedral.*
3508. Psalterium, etc. s. xiii¹. England (Worcester?). *Worcester, Church of St. Helen* (?). *Exeter Cathedral.*
3509. R. Higden, Polychronicon. s. xiv². England. *Exeter Cathedral.*
3510. Missale. s. xiii². England. *Exeter Cathedral.*
3511. J. de Voragine, Sermones. s. xiv. England. *Exeter, Hospital of St. John Baptist.*
3512. 'Excerpta ex decretis romanorum pontificum', etc. s. xii in. England (Exeter Cathedral?). *Exeter Cathedral.*
3513. Pontificale. s. xiv/xv. England. *Exeter Cathedral.*
3514. G. Monemutensis; H. Huntendonensis; etc. s. xiii med.–xiii². England or Wales.
3515. Missale cum notis. s. xiii in.–xv. England. *Exeter, Chapel of St. Anne.*
3516. W. Woodford; R. Ullerston. s. xv¹. England. *Exeter Cathedral.*
3517. 'Catholicon'. A.D. 1431. France, for R. Lugon.
3518. Martyrologium Ecclesiae Exon. s. xii¹. **Exeter Cathedral.**
3519. Medica, etc. s. xv in. England.
3520. Anselmus, Opera; Ambrosius, etc; Misc. theol. s. xii in.–xii¹. France (?) and England. *Exeter Cathedral.*
3521. J. Seward, etc. s. xiv med.–xv¹. England (arts. 1, 4, 5, Ottery St. Mary?). *Ottery St. Mary Collegiate Ch.*
3522, etc. Constitutiones P. de Quivil. s. xv. See p. 834.
3525. Misc. theol. s. xii in. England.
3526. J. de S. Paulo. s. xiii¹. England (?).

3529. J. Boccaccius, Genealogiae Deorum. s. xv². England. *Canterbury, St. Augustine's, O.S.B.*

3533. Formularium, etc. s. xv med.–xv ex. England (Gloucestershire?).

3548A–C, F. Binding fragments. See pp. 839–41.

3549B. Isidorus, Seneca, etc. s. xiii. England.

3549G. Horae B.V.M. (Sarum). s. xv in. England.

FMS/1–3; Misc. 1/2. Binding fragments. See pp. 845–6.

FORT AUGUSTUS, Inverness-shire. THE ABBEY (Benedictine Abbey of St. Benedict).

Rat. 1. *s*Patristica. A.D. 1080–3. **Regensburg, S. Jakob, O.S.B.**

Rat. 2. *s*Regula S. Benedicti, cum expositione B. Ayglerii. s. xv. Germany. *Regensburg, S. Jakob, O.S.B.*

A. 2.   Horae B.V.M. (Rome). s. xv ex. France.

A. 3.   Horae B.V.M. (Thérouanne). s. xv in. NE. France.

A. 4.   Bernardus, etc. s. xv. Germany.

GLASGOW

ART GALLERY AND MUSEUM

*Psalterium, etc. s. xiv. Italy.

Burrell Collection, 1. P. Lombardus, Sententiae. s. xiii. France (?).

        2. Horae B.V.M. s. xv–xv². France (Brittany?).

        3. Horae B.V.M. (Rome?). s. xv. France.

MITCHELL LIBRARY, North St.

185666. Gratiae congr. S. Georgii in Alga concessae. s. xv ex. Italy.

308857. Horae B.V.M. (Rome). s. xiv². France, for Rodez diocese.

308858. Horae B.V.M. (Utrecht: in Netherlandish). s. xv. Netherlands.

308859. Horae B.V.M. (Rouen). s. xv/xvi. France.

308876. J. de Fordun, Chronicon, cum continuatione. s. xv/xvi. Scotland. *Newbattle, O.C.*

308892. Institutiones patrum Praemonstratensium. s. xiii¹–xiv². France.

308893. Statuta Angliae. s. xiv¹. England.

308894. Antiphonale. s. xv ex. **Arezzo, SS. Flora e Lucilla, O.S.B.**

309758. Registrum brevium. s. xiv in. England.

309759. Psalterium. s. xii². England.

UNIVERSITY

HUNTERIAN MUSEUM. See p. 871.

UNIVERSITY LIBRARY

Euing 1.   Biblia. s. xiii². Italy.

    2.   P. Riga. s. xiii¹. England (?)

    3.   Horae B.V.M. (Rome). s. xv². S. Netherlands.

    4.   Horae B.V.M. (Thérouanne). s. xv¹. NE. France.

    7.   Officium Missae, etc. s. xv ex. Netherlands.

    9.   Psalterium, etc. s. xv. France, for Arras diocese.

   10.   *s*Psalterium, etc. A.D. 1502. Germany, for O.F.M. nuns.

   26.   Missale (fragm.). s. xiv ex. England, for London, Ord. Carm.

   29.   Missale. s. xvi in. **Grammont, O.S.B.**

Euing Music Collection, R. d. 56. Antiphonale, etc. s. xv. Germany, for O.F.M.

Euing Music Collection, R. d. 57. Hymnale, etc. s. xv/xvi. Netherlands (?), for
 O.C.
Ferguson 13. L. Rigius. A.D. 1492 (?). Italy.
  32. Macer, etc. s. xv. England.
  39. Geber, etc. s. xiii/xiv. France (?).
  63. sTurba philosophorum, etc. A.D. 1470, A.D. 1495, and s. xv². Veneto (?).
  76. sR. Bacon, etc. s. xv² and A.D. 1492. Veneto (?).
  80. Geber. s. xv². Italy.
  83. R. Lullius. A.D. 1469. Italy.
  104. s'Dicta Bartholomei', etc. A.D. 1364 or 1365. N. (?) Germany.
  106. sJ. de Rupescissa, etc. A.D. 1469/70 and s. xv ex. Italy.
  116. J. Platearius. s. xiii¹. England (?). *England.*
  135. sGeber. s. xv². Veneto (?).
  147. Antidotarium Nicholai, etc. (in English). s. xv in. England.
  153. Guielmo Sadacense, Ord. Carm., De alchimia (in Italian). s. xvi in. Italy.
  192. sR. Lullius, etc. s. xv². Veneto (?).
  205. J. de Rupescissa, etc. (in English). s. xv². England.
  209. Isaac Judeus, etc. s. xiv in. Italy.
  234. Bartholomaeus Anglicus. s. xv. Netherlands.
  241. Dialogue of Placides and Timeo, etc. (in French). s. xv ex. France.
  259. Recepta alchimica, etc. s. xv² and A.D. 1474. Germany.
  263. Albertus Magnus, etc. s. xiii ex. Germany.
Gen. 1. Horae B.V.M. s. xv². France.
  2. Horae B.V.M. (Sarum: partly in Netherlandish). s. xv. S. Netherlands and England.
  6. Vegetius, etc. s. xv. France.
  7. Biblia. s. xiii. England (?).
  193. Diodorus Siculus. s. xv. Italy.
  212. Florus. s. xv. Italy.
  216. Juvenalis; Persius. s. xv². Italy.
  223. Clement of Lanthony, etc. (in English). s. xv in. England.
  235. Juvenalis. s. xv². Italy.
  288. Psalterium, etc. s. xv. NE. France (?).
  324. Ambrosius, De officiis. s. xv ex. Italy.
  327. Lactantius. s. xv. France.
  333. J. de Fordun, Chronicon, cum continuatione. s. xv². Dunfermline, O.S.B., for W. Schevez.
  334. Cicero. s. xv². France.
  335. 'Compendiosa abstraccio super octo libros phisicorum', etc. s. xv ex. England. *Reading, Ord. Clun.*
  336. Statuta Angliae. s. xiv¹. England.
  337. Boethius. s. xv². Spain (?).
  338. Lactantius. A.D. 1444. Basel.
  339. R. de Peniaforti, etc. s. xiii. France (?).
  482. Horae B.V.M. (Sarum). s. xv. Netherlands. *Scotland.*
  999. Graduale (fragm.). s. xv. Italy (?).
  1053. Processus Scotiae (in Latin and French). s. xiv/xv. England.
  1060. Biblia, I. s. xv. Italy.
  1111. J. de Voragine, Legenda Sanctorum. s. xv¹. S. Netherlands. *Piacenza* (?).

1115. Euclides, etc. A.D. 1480. France.
1116. Palladius. s. xv¹. Spain.
1119. *s*Biblia, II. A.D. 1446. Netherlands.
1125. Terentius. s. xv. France.
1126. Biblia. s. xiii². England (?). *Cambuskenneth, O.S.A.*
1130. Nicholas Love, Mirror (in English); etc. s. xv med. England.
1184. Seneca, Tragoediae. s. xv ex. Italy.
1189. Terentius. s. xv. Italy.
1228. Alex. Trallianus. s. xv². France (?).
1357. Pseudo-Aristoteles, Secreta secretorum; etc. s. xv. Spain (?).

Hamilton 8.   Leonardo Bruni (in Italian). s. xv². Italy.
    11.   'Commentum super Macrobium'. s. xii². France.
    22.   Ambrosius, De officiis. s. xv². Netherlands (?).
    26.   R. Lull, etc. (in French). s. xv/xvi. France.
    79.   *s*P. de Pergula. A.D. 1431. Italy.
   137.   J. Dorp. s. xv. Germany.
   138.   Ars moriendi. s. xv ex. Germany or Netherlands.
   141.   Aegidius Romanus, De regimine principum. s. xv. S. (?) France. *England.*

Hepburn 1.   Biblia. s. xiii. France.
Murray 504.   A. de Butrio, Reportorium juris civilis et canonici. s. xv¹. Italy (Bologna?). *Parc. Ord. Praem.*
   657.   Sextus liber decretalium, etc. s. xiv. Spain (?). *Spain.*

GLOUCESTER

CATHEDRAL

  1. Vitae sanctorum. s. xiii in. England. *Leominster, Ord. Clun.* (?).
  2. Pseudo-Athanasius, etc. s. xii² and s. xv/xvi. England.
  3. Augustinus, De civitate Dei. s. xiii ex. England. *Eton College.*
  5. J. Lydgate, Siege of Troy (in English). s. xv. England.
  6. Gilbertus Anglicus. s. xiii/xiv. England (?).
  7. G. de Cauliaco. s. xv. England.
 12. Legenda sanctorum (in English). s. xv. England.
 14. Sermones, etc. s. xiii/xiv. England (O.S.A.?).
 16. Medica. s. xiii ex.–xv in. England.
 17. Galenus, etc. s. xiii ex. England.
 18. Medica. s. xiii in.–xiii ex. England (?). *England.*
19+23, f. 1. H. Daniel (in English). s. xv. England.
 21. *s*Astrologica, etc. s. xv². England.
 22. Sermons, etc. (in English). s. xv. England.
 23, ff. 2–238. *s*Harmonia Evangeliorum, etc. s. xvi in. England (art. 6, Winchester?).
 25. Medica, etc. s. xiii. England. *Worcester Cathedral Priory, O.S.B.*
 27. Theologica. s. xiii ex.–xv. England.
 28. W. de Conchis, etc. s. xv. England.
 29. M. de Hungaria. s. xv. England.
 33. Registrum brevium; Statuta Angliae; etc. s. xv in. N. (?) England.
 34. Historia monasterii Glouc.; Macer; etc. s. xv in. England (Gloucester?).
 35, 36. Binding fragments. See p. 969.

DIOCESAN RECORD OFFICE

Binding fragments. See pp. 969–73.

GUILDFORD, Surrey. SURREY ARCHAEOLOGICAL SOCIETY
*Registrum brevium. s. xiv¹. England.

HARROW, Greater London. HARROW SCHOOL
11 AA. Cicero, Epistolae. s. xv. Italy.
Sine numero. Horae B.V.M. (Rouen). s. xv². France.

HARTLEBURY CASTLE, Hereford and Worcester. HURD EPISCOPAL
LIBRARY
Biblia. s. xiii med. England.

HARTLEPOOL, Cleveland. PUBLIC LIBRARY (Central Library)
Psalmi, hymni, etc. s. xv/xvi. **Reggio d'Emilia, San Prospero, O.S.B.**

HAWARDEN, Clwyd. ST. DEINIOL'S LIBRARY
1. Breviarium. A.D. 1514. S. (?) Germany, for O.P. nuns.
2. Horae eternae sapientiae, etc. s. xv/xvi. SE. Germany or Bohemia.
5. Horae B.V.M. (Paris). s. xv. France.

HEREFORD
CATHEDRAL. See p. 984.
DIOCESAN RECORD OFFICE, The Old Barracks, Harold St.
Binding fragments. See pp. 984–5.

HODNET, Salop. PARISH CHURCH
Horae B.V.M. (Sarum). s. xv¹. France (?). *England.*

HORNBY, Lancashire. ST. MARY'S CATHOLIC CHURCH
1. Breviarium (Sarum). s. xiv/xv. England.
2. Breviarium (Sarum). s. xiv. England.

HULL, Humberside. UNIVERSITY
F. 1300. sPaulus Venetus, Logica. A.D. 1434. Italy.

HUNTINGDON, Cambridgeshire. ARCHDEACONRY LIBRARY
*Biblia. s. xiii. France.
*Formularium. s. xv¹. Lincolnshire (?). *Norfolk (?).*

IPSWICH, Suffolk. PUBLIC LIBRARY (Central Library).
1–9. See pp. 990–3.
Suffolk Collection, 1. sAlbertus de Saxonia, Sophismata. A.D. 1402. Siena.
Mantua, O.F.M.

KEELE, Staffordshire. UNIVERSITY
1. Hugo de S. Victore, etc. s. xiii¹–xiv. Italy.

SIGNS AND ABBREVIATIONS

In quotations from the manuscripts: round brackets are used to show editorial additions; square brackets are used where the text is illegible as a result of damage or where the space for an initial letter has not been filled and no guide-letter is to be seen; caret marks, ` ´, are used to show words or letters added to the text after it was written.

AFH	*Archivum Franciscanum Historicum.*
AFP	*Archivum Fratrum Praedicatorum.*
AGM	*Archiv für Geschichte der Medizin.*
AH	*Analecta Hymnica Medii Aevi*, ed. G. M. Dreves *et al.* 1886–1922. 55 vols.
Anal. Boll.	*Analecta Bollandiana.*
Ancient Libraries	M. R. James, *Ancient Libraries of Canterbury and Dover.* 1903.
Andrieu, *Ord. Rom.*	*Les Ordines Romani*, ed. M. Andrieu. 5 vols. Spicilegium Sacrum Lovaniense, 11, 23, 24, 28, 29. 1931–61.
Andrieu, *Pont. Rom.*	M. Andrieu, *Le Pontifical romain au moyen âge.* 4 vols. (Studi e Testi, 86–8, 99.) 1938–42.
Aristoteles Latinus	G. Lacombe *et al.*, *Aristoteles Latinus*: Codices. Pars prior, Rome, 1939. Pars posterior, Cambridge, 1955.
ASOC	*Analecta Sacri Ordinis Cisterciensis.*
Axters, *BDNM*	S. G. Axters, O.P., *Bibliotheca dominicana Neerlandica manuscripta.* Bibliothèque de la Revue d'histoire ecclesiastique, fasc. 49. Louvain, 1970.
Bale, *Index*	J. Bale, *Index Britanniae Scriptorum*, ed. R. L. Poole and M. Bateson. Anecdota Oxoniensia, Mediaeval and Modern Series, 9. Oxford, 1902.
BGPTM	*Beiträge zur Geschichte der Philosophie und Theologie des Mittelalters.*
BHL	*Bibliotheca Hagiographica Latina.* Ediderunt Socii Bollandiani. 1898–1901.
Biblia Sacra	*Biblia Sacra iuxta Latinam vulgatam versionem . . . iussu Pii PP XI . . . edita.* Rome, 1926– (in progress).
B.L.	British Library.
Bloomfield	M. W. B. Bloomfield, 'A preliminary list of incipits of Latin works on the virtues and vices', *Traditio*, xi (1955), 259–379.
BLR	*Bodleian Library Record.*
B.M.	British Museum.
BMC	*Catalogue of books printed in the fifteenth century now in the British Museum.* 1908– (in progress).
B.N.	Bibliothèque Nationale.
Brev. ad usum Sarum	*Breviarium ad usum Sarum*, ed. F. Procter and C. Wordsworth. 3 vols. Cambridge, 1882–6.

Carmody, 1956	F. J. Carmody, *Arabic Astronomical and Astrological Sciences in Latin Translation*. Berkeley, 1956.
Cat. of Romances	H. L. D. Ward and J. A. Herbert, *Catalogue of Romances in the Department of Manuscripts in the British Museum*. 3 vols. 1883–1910.
Catt. Vett.	*Catalogi Veteres Librorum Ecclesiae Cathedralis Dunelm*. Surtees Society, vii. 1838.
CC	*Corpus Christianorum*.
Clavis	E. Dekkers, *Clavis Patrum Latinorum*. Sacris Eruditi, iii, 1951. 2nd edn. 1961.
CMA	(E. Bernard) *Catalogi Manuscriptorum Angliae et Hiberniae*. Oxford, 1697.
CSEL	*Corpus Scriptorum Ecclesiasticorum Latinorum*.
Davis, *MC*	G. R. C. Davis, *Medieval Cartularies of Great Britain*, 1958.
Dearden	J. S. Dearden, 'John Ruskin, the Collector', *The Library*, 5th series, xxi (1966), 124–54.
de Bruyne, *Préfaces*	(D. de Bruyne) *Les Préfaces de la Bible*. Namur, 1920.
de Bruyne, *Sommaires*	(D. de Bruyne) *Sommaires, divisions, et rubriques de la Bible latine*. Namur, 1914.
de Haas and Hall	E. de Haas and G. D. G. Hall, *Early Registers of Writs*. Selden Society, lxxxvii. 1970.
de Morenas	H. Jougla de Morenas, *Grand armorial de France*. 6 vols. 1934–49. *Supplément*, 1952.
DNB	*Dictionary of National Biography*.
Dolezalek	G. Dolezalek, *Verzeichnis der Handschriften zum römischen Recht bis 1600*. 4 vols. Frankfurt-am-Main, 1972.
Dondaine and Shooner	H. F. Dondaine and H. V. Shooner, *Codices manuscripti operum Thomae de Aquino*. Rome, 1967– (in progress).
EBSB	J. B. Oldham, *English Blind-Stamped Bindings*. Cambridge, 1952.
EETS	Early English Text Society.
EHR	*English Historical Review*.
Emden, *BRUC*	A. B. Emden, *A Biographical Register of the University of Cambridge to 1500*. Cambridge, 1963.
Emden, *BRUO*	A. B. Emden, *A Biographical Register of the University of Oxford to A.D. 1500*. 3 vols. Oxford, 1957–9.
Emden, *Donors*	A. B. Emden, *Donors of Books to S. Augustine's Abbey, Canterbury*. Oxford Bibliographical Society, Occasional Publication, no. 4. Oxford, 1968.
Foedera	T. Rymer, *Foedera*. Ed. 1704–35 (20 vols.).
Forshall and Madden	*The Holy Bible made from the Latin vulgate by John Wycliffe and his followers*, ed. J. Forshall and F. Madden. 4 vols. 1850.
Frere	H. Frere *et al.*, *Bibliotheca Musico-Liturgica*.

	Plainsong and Medieval Music Society. 2 vols. 1901–32.
GKW	*Gesamtkatalog der Wiegendrucke.* 1925– (in progress).
Glorieux	P. Glorieux, *Répertoire des maîtres en théologie de Paris au xiiie siècle.* 2 vols. Études de philosophie médiévale, xvii, xviii. 1933–4.
Goff	F. R. Goff, *Incunabula in American Libraries.* New York, 1964.
Haebler	C. Haebler, *Rollen- und Plattenstempel des xvi. Jahrhunderts.* 2 vols. Leipzig, 1928–9.
Hain	L. Hain, *Repertorium Bibliographicum.* 2 vols. 1826–38.
Hauréau	Initia operum scriptorum latinorum collecta a B. Hauréau (B.N., MSS. nouv. acq. lat. 2392–2402: photostat in Students' Room, Department of MSS. of B. L., and Bodleian Library).
Haymo	*Ordines of Haymo of Faversham.* Henry Bradshaw Society, lxxxv. [1961].
HBS	Henry Bradshaw Society.
HMC	Historical Manuscripts Commission.
Holdsworth	W. S. Holdsworth, *A History of English Law.* All references are to vol. 2 (1903).
Horae Ebor.	*Horae Eboracenses,* ed. C. Wordsworth. Surtees Society, cxxxii. 1920.
Hoskins	E. Hoskins, *Horae Beatae Mariae Virginis.* 1901. Republished, 1969.
IMEV	C. Brown and R. H. Robbins, *Index of Middle English Verse.* New York, 1943. *Supplement* by R. H. Robbins and J. L. Cutler, Lexington, 1965.
JBAA	*Journal of the British Archaeological Association.*
Jolliffe	P. S. Jolliffe, *A Check-list of Middle English Prose Writings of Spiritual Guidance.* Pontifical Institute of Mediaeval Studies, Toronto, Subsidia Mediaevalia, ii. Toronto, 1974.
Ker, *MLGB*	N. R. Ker, *Medieval Libraries of Great Britain.* Royal Historical Society, Guides and Handbooks, No. 3. 2nd edn. 1964.
Ker, *Pastedowns*	N. R. Ker, *Pastedowns in Oxford Bindings.* Oxford Bibliographical Society, new series, v. Oxford, 1954.
Klebs	A. C. Klebs, 'Incunabula scientifica et medica', *Osiris,* iv, pt. 1 (1938).
Långfors	A. Långfors, *Les incipit des poèmes français anterieurs au xvie siècle.* 1917.
Leroquais	V. Leroquais, *Les Livres d'heures manuscrits de la Bibliothèque Nationale.* 2 vols., plates, and supplement. 1927–43.
Lieftinck, *Maatschappij*	*Codices 168–360 Societatis cui nomen Maatschappij der Nederlandsche Letterkunde descripsit G. I. Lieftinck. Bibliotheca Universitatis Leidensis. Codices Manuscripti, V. i.* Leiden, 1948.

Lyell Cat.	A. de la Mare, *Catalogue of the Collection of Medieval Manuscripts bequeathed to the Bodleian Library, Oxford, by James P. R. Lyell.* Oxford, 1971.
MacKinney	L. MacKinney, *Medical Illustrations in Medieval Manuscripts.* Publications of the Wellcome Historical Medical Library, new series, v. 1965.
McRoberts	D. McRoberts, *Catalogue of Scottish Medieval Liturgical Books and Fragments.* 1953.
Manuale Sarum	*Manuale ad usum percelebris ecclesie Sarisburiensis,* ed. A. J. Collins. Henry Bradshaw Society, xci. 1960.
MBDS	*Mittelalterliche Bibliothekskataloge Deutschlands und der Schweiz,* ed. P. Lehmann *et al.* Munich, 1918– (in progress).
Mearns, *Canticles*	J. Mearns, *The Canticles of the Christian Church, eastern and western.* Cambridge, 1914.
Mearns, *Hymnaries*	J. Mearns, *Early Latin Hymnaries.* Cambridge, 1913.
Meertens	M. Meertens, *De Godsvrucht in de Nederlanden,* pts. i–iii, vi. 1930–4.
MGH	Monumenta Germaniae Historica.
Missale Romanum	*Missale Romanum Mediolani 1474,* ed. R. Lippe. 2 vols. Henry Bradshaw Society, xvii, xxxiii (1899, 1907).
Missale Westm.	*Missale ad usum ecclesie Westmonasteriensis,* ed. J. W. Legg. 3 vols. Henry Bradshaw Society, i, v, xii (1891–7).
MMBL	N. R. Ker, *Medieval Manuscripts in British Libraries.*
N.L.S.	National Library of Scotland.
N.L.W.	National Library of Wales.
NLWJ	*National Library of Wales Journal.*
Notices et extraits	*Notices et extraits des manuscrits de la Bibliothèque du Roi* (or *Impériale,* or *Nationale*). 1787–1938. 42 vols.
NT	New Testament.
O.C.	Ordo Cisterciensis.
OED	*The Oxford English Dictionary.*
O.E.S.A.	Ordo Eremitarum Sancti Augustini.
O.F.M.	Ordo Fratrum Minorum.
Oldham	The context shows whether the reference is to J. B. Oldham, *English Blind-Stamped Bindings,* Cambridge, 1952, or to J. B. Oldham, *Blind Panels of English Binders,* Cambridge, 1958.
O.P.	Ordo Fratrum Praedicatorum.
Ord. Brig.	Ordo Brigittanorum.
Ord. Carm.	Ordo Carmelitarum.
Ord. Carth.	Ordo Carthusiensium.
Ord. Clun.	Ordo Cluniacensium.
Ord. Praem.	Ordo Praemonstratensium.
O.S.A.	Ordo Sancti Augustini.
O.S.B.	Ordo Sancti Benedicti.
OT	Old Testament.

PCC	Prerogative Court of Canterbury.
PG	J. P. Migne, *Patrologia Graeca.*
PL	J. P. Migne, *Patrologia Latina.*
PLS	*Patrologia Latina, Supplementum.*
PMLA	*Publications of the Modern Language Association of America.*
Pont. Rom.-Germ.	*Le Pontifical Romano-Germanique du dixième siècle,* ed. C. Vogel and R. Elze. Studi e Testi, 226–7. 2 vols. 1963.
Potthast	A. Potthast, *Regesta Pontificum Romanorum.* 2 vols. 1874–5.
PRM	P. Glorieux, *Pour revaloriser Migne.* Supplement to *Mélanges de Sciences Religieuses,* ix. 1952.
P.R.O.	Public Record Office.
PSAS	*Proceedings of the Society of Antiquaries of Scotland.*
Renzi	S. de Renzi, *Collectio Salernitana.* 5 vols. Naples, 1852–9.
RH	U. Chevalier, *Repertorium Hymnologicum.* 6 vols. 1892–1921.
Rietstap	J.-B. Rietstap, *Armorial général.* 2nd edn., 1884–7. Plates, 1903–26 and Supplements, 1926–51, by V. Rolland and H. Rolland.
Römer	F. Römer, *Die handschriftliche Überlieferung der Werke des heiligen Augustinus,* II, *Grossbritannien und Irland.* (2 vols.: (1) Werkverzeichnis; (2) Verzeichnis nach Bibliotheken.) Österreichische Akademie der Wissenschaften, Phil.-Hist. Klasse, Sitzungsberichte 276, 281. Vienna, 1972.
RTAM	*Recherches de théologie ancienne et médiévale.*
SAO	*Sancti Anselmi Opera,* ed. F. S. Schmitt. 6 vols. 1946–61.
Sarum Missal	*The Sarum Missal, edited from three early manuscripts,* ed. J. W. Legg. Oxford, 1916.
Saxl and Meier	F. Saxl and H. Meier, *Verzeichnis astrologischer und mythologischer illustrierter Handschriften des lateinischen Mittelalters.* 3 vols. 1915–53.
SBO	*Sancti Bernardi Opera,* ed. J. Leclercq *et al.* 1957– (in progress).
Schenkl	H. Schenkl, *Bibliotheca Patrum Latinorum Britannica.* 3 vols. 1891–1908.
Schneyer	J. B. Schneyer, *Wegweiser zu lateinischen Predigtreihen des Mittelalters.* Munich, 1965.
Schneyer, *Rep.*	J. B. Schneyer, *Repertorium der lateinischen Sermones des Mittelalters.* 5 vols. Beiträge zur Geschichte des Mittelalters, xliii. 1969–74.
Schulte	J. F. von Schulte, *Die Geschichte der Quellen und Literatur des canonischen Rechts.* 3 vols. Stuttgart, 1875–80.
Shirley, *Cat.*	W. W. Shirley, *Catalogue of the Original Works of John Wyclif.* 1865.

Singer and Anderson	D. W. Singer and A. Anderson, *Catalogue of Latin and Vernacular Alchemical Manuscripts in Great Britain and Ireland.* 3 vols. Brussels, 1928–31.
Singer and Anderson, 1950	D. W. Singer and A. Anderson, *Catalogue of Latin and Vernacular Plague Texts in Great Britain and Eire.* Collection de Travaux de l'Académie Internationale d'Histoire des Sciences, No. 5. 1950.
SMRL	S. J. P. van Dijk, *Sources of the Modern Roman Liturgy.* 2 vols. Studia et Documenta Franciscana, i, ii. 1963.
Sonet	J. Sonet, *Répertoire d'incipit de prières en ancien français.* Société de publications romanes et françaises, liv. Geneva, 1956.
SOPMA	T. Kaeppeli, *Scriptores ordinis Praedicatorum Medii Aevi.* 1970– (in progress).
SR	*Statutes of the Realm.* References are to ed. 1810–28.
STC	A. W. Pollard and G. R. Redgrave, *A Short-title Catalogue of Books printed 1475–1640.* 1926.
Stegmüller	F. Stegmüller, *Repertorium Biblicum Medii Aevi.* In progress (7 vols. published). Madrid, 1950–.
Stegmüller, *Sent.*	F. Stegmüller, *Repertorium Commentariorum in Sententias Petri Lombardi.* 2 vols. Würzburg, 1947.
STS	Scottish Text Society.
Sum. Cat.	*Summary Catalogue of Western Manuscripts in the Bodleian Library.* 7 vols. 1895–1953.
Talbot and Hammond	C. H. Talbot and E. A. Hammond, *The Medical Practitioners in medieval England.* 1965.
Thomson, *Grosseteste*	S. H. Thomson, *The Writings of Robert Grosseteste.* Cambridge, 1940.
Thorndike and Kibre	L. Thorndike and P. Kibre, *A Catalogue of Incipits of Mediaeval Scientific Writings in Latin.* 2nd edn. 1963.
Trésors	*Trésors des Bibliothèques d'Écosse.* Bibliothèque Albert Iᵉʳ, Catalogue no. 12. Brussels, 1963.
TSPES	*Transactions of the St. Paul's Ecclesiological Society.*
VCH	*Victoria County History*
Walther	H. Walther, *Initia carminum ac versuum medii aevi posterioris Latinorum.* Carmina Medii Aevi Posterioris Latina, i. Göttingen, 1959.
Walther, *Sprichwörter*	H. Walther, *Lateinische Sprichwörter und Sentenzen des Mittelalters.* Carmina Medii Aevi Posterioris Latina, ii. 5 vols. Göttingen, 1963–7.
Weale	W. H. J. Weale, *Bookbindings and Rubbings of Bindings in the National Art Library, South Kensington Museum.* 1898.
Wells, *Manual*	J. E. Wells, *A Manual of the Writings in Middle English 1050–1400.* New Haven, 1916. With nine supplements, 1919–51.
Wickersheimer	E. Wickersheimer, *Dictionnaire biographique des médecins en France au moyen âge.* 1936.

Wordsworth and White	*Novum Testamentum . . . Latine,* ed. J. Wordsworth, H. J. White, *et al.* Oxford, 1889–1954.
Zetzner	L. Zetzner, *Theatrum chemicum.* 6 vols. ed. Strasbourg, 1659–61.
Zumkeller	A. Zumkeller, *Manuskripte von Werken der Autoren des Augustiner-Eremiten-Ordens in mitteleuropäischen Bibliotheken.* Cassiciacum, xx, 1966.

ABBOTSFORD. THE SCOTT COLLECTION

'The Haye Manuscript' (in Scots)[1] s. XV ex.

1–3. Three translations from the French: (1) ff. 1ᵛ–85, 'the buke of the law of armys'; (2) ff. 85–103ᵛ, 'the buke of the order of knychthede'; (3) ff. 103ᵛ–129ᵛ, 'the buke of the gouernaunce of princis'.

Gilbert of the Haye's Prose Manuscript, ed. J. H. Stevenson, Scottish Text Society, xliv (1901) and lxii (1916). Vol. 1 contains art. 1 on pp. 1–303. Vol. 2 contains art. 2 on pp. 1–70 and art. 3 on pp. 71–165. A description of the manuscript and facsimiles of three water-marks and of part of f. 1ᵛ are in vol. 1, pp. xvi–xxiii.

Art. 1 is a translation of the Arbre des Batailles of Honoré Bonet, prior of Salon, O.S.B., made 'be me Gilbert of the Haye knycht' at the request of William, Lord Sinclair, at Roslin Castle in 1456. Art. 2 is translated from the Livre de Chevalerie and art. 3 from the Secret des Secrets, presumably by the same person. For French texts of all three works see *Catalogue of Royal and King's MSS. in the British Museum* (1921), descriptions of MSS. 20 C. viii, 14 E. ii, and 20 B. v. f. 1ʳ was left blank.

4. The blank space at the end of quire 11 was filled in s. xvi²: (*a*) f. 130ʳᵛ Heir followis ye ordoʳ of the processioun and bering 'of' ye sacrament in Antuarpe the first day of Iunii ye ʒeir of god iᵐ vᶜ lxii; (*b*) ff. 131–2ᵛ A letter from Thomas (Tulloch), bishop of Orkney, and his chapter, 1 June 1440, to the king of Norway about the right of the Sinclair family to the earldom of Orkney, 'Translatit out of latin into Scott*is* be me Deine Thomas Gwld munk of Newbothill at ye request of . . . Williame santclar baroun of Roislin' in 1554.

(*a*) and (*b*) are in one hand, that of Sir William Sinclair, third of Roslin, †1585, who also wrote notes against arts. 1–3 and especially art. 1: cf. edn. 1. viii, xxi, xl–xlii. (*b*) is printed in *Bannatyne Miscellany*, iii (1845), 65.

ff. i+132+i. Paper. 390×280 mm. Written space 265×175 mm. 42–9 long lines, the number varying from page to page. Frame ruling with pencil. Collation: 1–11¹². Catch-words are written immediately below the end of the last line of writing in each quire. Written in cursiva of a French kind by the same skilled Scotch scribe as wrote Bodleian, Arch. Selden B. 24 (*Sum. Cat.*, 3354), ff. 1–209ᵛ, during the reign of James IV (1488–1513): cf. J. Norton-Smith in *The Times Literary Supplement*, 4 June 1971, p. 649, and the fac-simile of a page of the Selden manuscript by M. B. Parkes, *English Cursive Book Hands 1250–1500* (1969), pl. 13 (ii).[2] Contemporary binding of wooden boards covered with calf

---

[1] I am grateful to the Trustees of the Scott Collection and Mrs. Maxwell-Scott of Abbotsford for permission to describe this manuscript.

[2] George Neilson's suggestion (*Athenaeum*, 1899, ii. 835) that the Selden manuscript was written by James Graye has been accepted, but seems to have little or nothing in its favour. Neilson thought that one and the same person must have written the inscriptions 'Natiuitatis principis nostri Iacobi quarti anno domini Mᵐᵒ iiiiᶜ lxxiiᵒ xvii die mensis marcii videlicet in festo sancti patricii confessoris. In monasterio sancte crucis prope Edinburgh' (Selden, f. 120) and 'Princeps Iacobus 4ᵗᵘˢ natus Ed' in die sancti patricii Anno domini iᵐ iiiiᶜ lxxii' (N.L.S., Adv. 34. 7. 3, f. 22ᵛ). The hands are as alike as those of two contemporary Scotch scribes might be expected to be. The *e* with a *c*-like second element used almost always in the Abbotsford and Selden manuscripts does not occur in Adv. Much of Adv. was written by James Graye who describes himself in one place as

B

bearing thirty-three different stamps, three of which make up the sentence 'Patricius/Lowes me/ligauit': five bands: repaired. The binding is described by J. H. Stevenson in *Transactions of the Edinburgh Bibliographical Society*, vi (1906), 77–82, and by G. D. Hobson, ibid. xiv (1930), 89–97. Facsimiles of the back cover by Stevenson and of the front cover, reduced, by Hobson, who considered it 'very unlikely that the Lowes' binding is earlier than 1480 and it may well be 10 or 15 years later' (p. 95) and showed that Lowes got his stamps from Cologne.

Written in Scotland, probably for Oliver Sinclair of Roslin, the second son of William, Lord Sinclair: his name is on ff. 1ᵛ, 133. Belonged to his son William, his grandson William,[1] and his great-grandson William, all of whom wrote their names in the book, and later to members of the Curry family, to George Mackenzie (†1725) in 1722, to James Mackenzie, and to John Sinclair of Sinclair, †1750, by gift of James Mackenzie: cf. Stevenson, I. xxxviii–xlix. A damaged book-plate of Sinclair, s. xviii, inside the cover, is discussed by Stevenson, pp. xlvii–xlix: immediately below it is the shelfmark B.b.24, with 'P' in front of 'B', 'S' in front of 'b', and 'N' in front of '24'. Catalogued as part of the Abbotsford Library in 1838—six years after the death of Sir Walter Scott—and recognized then by David Laing as a book which George Mackenzie had mentioned in 1722. Formerly in Press Z, shelf 1, at Abbotsford.

ABERDEEN. UNIVERSITY LIBRARY

M. R. James, *A Catalogue of the Medieval Manuscripts in the University Library, Aberdeen*, Cambridge, 1932, omits the seventeen volumes listed below and MSS. 13, 14 (not 15, 16, as stated on p. 18), two volumes of a five-volume set of Panormitanus (MSS. 12–16). L. Macfarlane describes MSS. 12–17, 184, 195–8, 201, 202, 222, 262 in 'William Elphinstone's Library', *Aberdeen University Review*, xxxvii (1958), 253–71.

109. *Comment. in Physica Aristotelis*   1467

Circa inicium primi libri phisicorum arist. Queritur quid est phisica specialiter dicta . . . (f. 267) motor non est quantus. Et sic est finis octaui libri phisicorum per me georgium de morauia. (f. 267ᵛ) Expliciunt copulata phisice completa per

notary public and priest of the diocese of Dunblane and in another as secretary to Archbishop Schevez. He may be the person who wrote 'Et per me Iacobum Graye' in red immediately after the words 'per me Magnum Makculloch' in black at the end of bk. 2 of the Scotichronicon which Makculloch wrote in Edinburgh in 1480 and which is now in the Scottish Record Office on indefinite loan from Lord Dalhousie. A later hand added 'illuminatus' after 'Graye', rightly, since it is evident that Graye's part was to add the red chapter headings throughout most of the manuscript.

The record of the birth of James IV in Adv. is one of a collection of historical memoranda. The entry in Selden looks more like a colophon to art. 2c than a casual memorandum in a blank space. It seems likely that the scribe finished writing this piece on the king's birthday.

[1] The second William wrote 'W. sancclair of Roislin anno lxv' inside the front cover. These words are in the same hand as 'W. sancclair of Roislin knecht anno lxv' on sign. a. ii of a copy of Hector Boece, *Historia Scotorum*, in the library of New College, Edinburgh (J. Durkan and A. Ross, *Early Scottish Libraries* (1961), p. 144). The spelling 'sancclair' is used in all signatures by this Sir William in the Haye manuscript.

manus georgii de morauia alias lychon: lecta per uenerabilem virum in artibus magistrum regentem necnon legentem in scolis fancultatis arcium magistrum gisbertum de busco ducis louanii in petagogio lylii Anno domini M° cccc° sexagesimo septimo vicesimo sexto die mensis maii inter sextam et septimam horas laus et gloria deo ac eius intacte genitrici marie uirgini.

Bk. 2, f. 52; 3, f. 96; 4, f. 142; 5, f. 191; 6, f. 211; 7, f. 227; 8, f. 240. Bk. 1 ends with a colophon, f. 51, 'Et sic est finis primi libri phisicorum per me georgium de morauia studentem louanii in lilii petagogio': below, a student in a red hat and gown holds a scroll, 'Explicit primus phisicorum'. Drawings in three other blank spaces: f. 51ᵛ, a class-room with a lecturing master seated in a chair before a reading-desk on which is an open book: eight students sit on the floor, with three books among them: four books, one open, on a wall shelf; f. 95, a master and reading-desk, with open book on it, displaying the *explicit* of bk. 2 and the incipit of bk. 3; f. 190ᵛ, a dressy scholar holding scrolls, 'Explicit quartus liber phisicorum' and 'Incipit quintus liber phisicorum aristotilis' and 'Lilii sub venerabili regente ac legente magistro gisberto de bussco ducis laus et gloria deo eiusque intacte genitrici marie virgini'. The picture on f. 51ᵛ is reproduced in *Medium Aevum*, xxxix (1970), opposite p. 33, and all four pictures in *Academische Tijdingen* (Leuven), vii, no. 6 (1971), 24–7.

The commentary is followed by a table in the main hand giving the first proposition in each book of the *Physics*, *De celo*, *De generatione*, *Meteora*, and *De anima*, ff. 268ᵛ–269. Blank spaces and f. iiᵛ contain notes, most of them probably in Lichton's later hand: cf. MS. 110.

ff. ii+269+ii. Paper, except f. 271, a thick parchment leaf, no doubt part of the original cover (cf. MS. 110). 213×143 mm. Written space *c.* 148×95 mm. *c.* 35 long lines. Frame ruling in pencil. Collation: quires 2–4, 6, 8–17, 19–22 twelves, quires 1, 5, 7, 18 tens with an added singleton (ff. 11, 48, 74, 202), quire 23 a nine. Written in very current hybrida. A framed red initial at the beginning of each book: the corners of the frames contain shields or other drawings and on f. 191 the letters MO RA VI A. Nearly contemporary binding of wooden boards covered with brown leather, repaired: central clasp missing.

Written at Louvain in 1467: for the scribe see above and MS. 110. 'Liber magistri roberti anderson regentis collegii sancti saluatoris', f. 1, s. xvi: for two printed books so inscribed see Durkan and Ross, p. 69. 'Liber Collegii Regii Aberdonensis' and pressmark θ. 2. 21, f. 1.

110. *Comment. in libros naturalium Aristotelis*   *c.* 1467

A companion volume to MS. 109.

1. ff. 1–58ᵛ Short commentaries on (*a*) ff. 1–25ᵛ De celo et mundo, bks. 1, 3, 4, (*b*) ff. 27–48ᵛ Meteora, (*c*) ff. 49–56ᵛ De sensu, (*d*) ff. 57–58ᵛ De memoria.

(*a*). Bk. 3, f. 12; 4, f. 23. (*b*). Bk. 2, f. 33; 3, f. 39ᵛ. The incipits are: (*a*) Summa cognicionis nature et sciencie. Iste est 2ᵘˢ liber de principiis (?) tocius philosophie naturalis in quo; (*b*) De primis quidem igitur . . . Iste est liber metheororum aristotelis in quo determinat de corpore mobili; (*c*) Quoniam autem de annima . . . Presens liber de sensu et sensato . . .; (*d*) Iste est liber de memoria et reminiscentia in quo p. determinat. f. 26 has diagrams of zodiacal signs, the four elements, and the planets: the verso is blank. f. 59 has writing in the ink of the text, but it has been written over later (see below): the verso is blank.

2. ff. 60–237 Commentaries on (*a*) ff. 60–155ᵛ De celo et mundo, bks. 1, 2 (f. 105), 4 (f. 141), (*b*) ff. 156–217ᵛ Meteora, (*c*) ff. 218–223ᵛ De sensu, (*d*) ff. 224–7

De memoria, (e) ff. 227ᵛ–237 De somno, each beginning with the words 'Circa inicium'.

The incipits are: (a) Circa inicium primi libri de celo et mundo Queritur quotus est liber de celo et mundo inter libros aristotelis naturalis philosophie. dicitur quod est 2ᵘˢ; (b) Circa Inicium primi libri metheororum aristotelis Queritur quotus est liber metheororum inter libros naturalis philosophie. dicendum quod est quartus; (c) Circa inicium libri de sensu et sensato. Queritur de quo determinatur in libro de sensu et sensato dicendum est quod de ipsa anima; (d) Circa inicium libri de memoria et re. Secundus liber paruorum naturalium qui est liber de memoria et reminiscentia; (e) Circa inicium libri de sompno. Iste est liber de sompno et vigilia qui diuiditur in tres libros.

Pieces have been cut aimlessly from ff. 31, 32, 226–8. f. 237ᵛ was left blank. It and f. 59ʳᵛ contain notes in writing like that of the ex-libris on f. 237ᵛ. The scribe of the text made a memorandum on f. 238: '[. . .] xvi die mensis Iulii nos dominus alexander scrimgeor andreas de dunde georgius de morauia terminatiue[1] soluimus pro tempore preterito domestico nostro de anno tertio (?) et 1ᵘˢ terminus esset in festo beate katerine uirginis et martiris pro quo termino teneremur pro vnoquoque nostrorum trium xviii s'.

ff. ii+237+ii. Paper, except ff. ii, 238, thick parchment which, no doubt, formed the covers before the present binding was put on: cf. MS. 109. Size, ruling, and hand as for MS. 109. Collation: 1¹⁰ 2–18¹² (f. 154 is an inserted slip in quire 13) 19 eight (ff. 216–23) 20 five (ff. 224–8) 21⁸+1 leaf after 8. Decoration as in MS. 109, save for the use of blue for the C, f. 156: a gallows with a corpse hanging on it is in one corner of the frame on f. 33 and bagpipes in another corner. Binding as for MS. 109, but with a title label under horn and framed in metal (six nails) on the front cover, 'De celo et mundo etc' '.

The scribe names himself in MS. 109, q.v., but not here. He is identifiable with the Georgius de Moravia, Scotus, who matriculated at Louvain, 26 Aug. 1463 (Matricule de l'Université de Louvain, II. ii (1946), 117), and probably with the George Lichton who wrote on f. 237ᵛ, 'Iste est liber fratris georgii lichton olim abbatis de kylloss'. Ex-libris of Robert Anderson, as in MS. 109. 'Liber Collegii Regii Aberdonensis' and pressmark θ. 2. 22.

115. De oculo morali   s. XV ex.

Si diligenter voluerimus in lege domini meditari . . . et illuc eriguntur. Ad illud regnum nos perducat qui . . . secula amen.

Petrus Limovicensis, De oculo morali (cf. Durham, Univ. Libr. Mickleton and Spearman 89), here anonymous. Fifteen chapters.

ff. iii+75+iii. Paper. 195×140 mm. c. 140×85 mm. 25–33 long lines. Frame ruling in pencil. Collation: 1–8⁸ 9 eleven (ff. 65–75). Written in a mixed cursiva-hybrida, with elaborately footed r. Initials 2-line, blue with red ornament or red without ornament. The red initials, if A or I, are of elaborate knotwork. Capital letters in the ink of the text touched with red. Bound by Douglas Cockerell in 1938. Secundo folio crucea seccione.

Written probably in France. 'Liber Coll. Regii Aberdonensis' in the usual hand, mark '5. 23' and eighteenth-century title 'Tractatus Physico-Theologicus de Oculo et V[. . . .] repertus ab Joanne [. . .]ker [. . . .]' on f. 1.

123. Miscellanea (partly in English)   s. XV

1. ff. 1–7ᵛ (begins imperfectly) volens singulis satisfacere . . . prudencium reprobabo etc.

---

[1] Read for me by Mr. Colin MᶜLaren.

Paragraphs numbered (33)–64 of a collection of moralized tales, etc. The first clearly legible number is 38 on f. 2, where a tale begins 'Contigit quod canis voluit facere rusticitatem suam'. No. 56 (?) begins 'Quidam simplices ut dicuntur anglice Wylekey' (f. 4ᵛ). Nos. 44–51 are missing with the leaf after f. 2.

2. ff. 39ʳᵛ, 10 Tria sunt principia operacionis . . . preclarus et erectus.

Eight questions and answers about liturgical practices and five other theological notes. The last piece begins 'Interrogandum est unde factus est homo Respondendum est de octo partibus mundi'.

3. ff. 10ᵛ–23ᵛ, 25ʳᵛ, 24ʳᵛ, 26–30ᵛ Bred and mylk for chyldryn. Lytyl lowys my sone . . . is þe naddyr of þe 6 etc. Explicit liber qui vocatur bred and mylk.

Chaucer, Treatise on the Astrolabe, ed. W. W. Skeat, *Works of Chaucer*, iii (1894), 175–218/18. The text on f. 26 is all torn away except for a few words of sect. 25 of pt. 2: the leaf contained sects. 24/1–26/5. Sects. 37–45 of pt. 2 are not in this copy.

4. (a) ff. 31–35ᵛ Hic incipit Seneca de quattuor virtutibus cardinalibus. Quattuor virtutum series . . . deficientem puniat ignauiam. Explicit Seneca de virtutibus. (b) ff. 35ᵛ–38 Incipit Seneca de moribus. Omne peccatum accio voluntaria est . . . quod odium ostendit. Explicit Seneca de moribus.

(a). Martin of Braga, Formula honestae vitae. *Martini episcopi Bracarensis opera omnia*, ed. C. W. Barlow, 1950, pp. 237–50. (b). Pseudo-Seneca, Apophthegmata, printed by J. C. Orellius, *Opuscula graecorum veterum sententiosa et moralia*, 1819, pp. 269–76, and often earlier. The last three sentences here, 'Cum iudicaueris amare non cum amaueris iudicare', 'Mira racio est que non vult predicari quod gaudet intelligi', and 'Agnosci amat quod odium ostendit', are in place of nos. 145–6 in the edition.

5. ff. 40–86ᵛ A miscellany of mainly computistical, astronomical, and astrological pieces, partly in English.

(a) f. 40 Diagram of a quadrant.

(b) f. 41 Table to show the length of daylight by a series of numbers from 15 to 61. The solstices are marked at 9 June and 10 Dec.

(c) f. 41ᵛ Latitudes and longitudes of forty-eight places, the first eighteen of them in England.

(d) ff. 42–43ᵛ For to make a quadrant. Take a plate of cop*ur* or of laton . . . in yᵉ tabyl of the diuercite of yᵉ sone. Explicit canon quadrantis. (e) f. 43ᵛ Quadrus in quadrante sic fit. yus sall' yu make yi quadrus . . . lyne of A.C. etc. Explicit composicio quadrantis. (f) f. 44 Tables 'of þo diuersite of þo heght of þo sonne' to go with (d, e). (g) f. 44ᵛ Diagram. (h) ff. 44ᵛ–46ᵛ Composicio nauis. [F]irst make a cercle and diuide hym by A.C. and B.D. diametres . . .

The 'inscripcion of monethis in þo figure . . . schal be wroght be þo newe calendar made of frere Ion Som*er*' (f. 46ᵛ).

(i) ff. 47–48ᵛ Calendar, September to December only, including Thomas of Hereford at 2 Oct.

(j) ff. 49–50 Table, four months to a page, to show (1) gradus solis in signis, (2) altitudo meridiane solis, (3) littere feriales mensium.

(k) f. 51 Kings of England, William I –Henry VI, with additions by a later hand, 'xxxix' as the regnal years of Henry VI and the names 'Eduard the iiii' and 'Thomas of lancaster', with regnal years 'xxiii' and 'xxxvi' respectively.

(*l*) f. 51ᵛ Verses, including 'Armis gunfe de calathos . . .' (four lines: Walther, no. 1496), 'Poto ligna cremo de vite superflua demo . . .' (four lines on the occupations of the months: Walther, no. 14374), and couplets on the ransom of King Richard, the fine of King John, and the date of Arthur's death and burial at Glastonbury.

(*m*) f. 52 Table of cardinal, ordinal, distributive, adverbial, and ponderal numbers.

(*n*) ff. 52ᵛ–53 Table of a great cycle, 1140–1571, in which a word represents each year, the whole forming the set of verses 'Virgo deum pariens venie spes maxima sola' (Walther, no. 20500).

(*o*) ff. 54–5 A few brief annals from the year 1 to the death of Henry I.

Entries at 1106, 'intrauerunt canonici in ecclesiam sancte marie de Sudwerch', at 1114, 'Tamisia exsiccata est', and at 1135 on the burning of Paul's suggest a London source.

(*p*) f. 57 Filius esto dei celum bonus accipe gratis . . . (18 lines).

(*q*) f. 57ʳᵛ Cisio ianus epi lucianus et hil fe mav mar sul . . . (26 lines).

(*r*) ff. 57ᵛ–58ᵛ 'Centum quinta tenet . . .' and other computistical verses.

(*p, q*). Walther, nos. 6525, 2808. C. Wordsworth, *Ancient Kalendar of the University of Oxford*, pp. 161, 166–8. (*q*) occurs again at f. 84. (*r*) includes Walther nos. 9785 and 8678 and has forty-two lines in all.

(*s*) f. 58ᵛ Tables of epacts and concurrents.

(*t*) ff. 58ᵛ–59ᵛ Verses by which to remember the dates of the battle of Agincourt, the capture of Rouen, the murder of St. Thomas (Walther, no. 1165), and the battle of Hastings, a couplet, 'Tres quinquagenos . . . canit ille', giving the number of psalms and verses in the Psalter, two couplets of weather lore, 'Martini magni translacio si pluuiam det Quadraginta dies continuare solet. Si pluat in festo processi et martiniani Grandys erit pluuia et suffocacio grani' (Walther, nos. 10719, 17853), verses on the liberal arts, 'Gramatica. Quicquid agunt artes ego semper . . .' (Walther, no. 15973), a note of the death of 'sanctus confessor Ricardus Cayster' in 1420, and commonplaces 'secundum Eulogium cronic'' and 'secundum cestrensem'.

(*u*) ff. 60–1 Table of a great cycle 1437–1968, preceded by a 'Canon tabule sequentis' in English, beginning 'Thys tabyl folowyng ys callyd þe tabyll of Estyr'.

(*v*) f. 61ᵛ Verses on computus, including four lines referring to the year 1417, four lines on the 'annus magnus platonis', and Walther no. 2169 ascribed to St. Augustine.

(*w*) f. 62 The thirty-two 'dies periculose'. (*x*) f. 62ᵛ The seven 'dies congrui ad minuendum sanguinem' and prognostications according to the month of birth, 'Qui natus fuit . . . in Ianuario necligens erit . . .'

(*y*) f. 63 A square of figures to show multiplication up to 10 × 10.

(*z*) ff. 63ᵛ–64ᵛ Table showing the size of a 'ferthyng wast*ell*', a 'halpeny whyte lofe', a 'halpeny wheten lofe', and a 'halpeny horslofe' for prices of wheat from 1*s*. a quarter to 20*s*. a quarter, preceded by an introduction, 'Thys tabull ys of the syse of bred as corn heyith and lowyth in þe market so þe weyt moreth and lassyth'.

(*aa*) f. 65 Volvellum solis et lune. A diagram with two turning pointers.

(*ab*) ff. 66–68ᵛ Instrumentum per quod sciuntur hore diei per vmbram . . . volueris fabricare Describe . . . (f. 66ᵛ) To make a Instrument to knowe ye ourys of ye day by þo vmbre . . .

Instructions in Latin and English, followed by diagrams.

(*ac*) f. 68ᵛ Table of numbers in looking-glass writing.

(*ad*) ff. 69–70 Planetary tables and text in Latin and English.

(*ae*) f. 70ᵛ Table of great cycle, 1386–1917.

(*af*) f. 71 Table to show the sign of the zodiac in each month.

(*ag*) ff. 71ᵛ–72, 75 Diagrams of solar and lunar eclipses with descriptive text.

(*ah*) f. 72ᵛ Prognostications of weather according to the sign of the zodiac which the sun is entering.

(*ai*) f. 73ᵛ Diagram showing thirty-two points of the compass, with the names in English.

(*aj*) f. 74 Diagram showing months and signs of the zodiac, with two turning pointers. (*ak*) ff. 75ᵛ–77ᵛ Texts and diagrams relating to the signs of the zodiac.

(*al*) f. 77 'Complexions' of the four seasons in Latin and of four divisions of the day in English.

(*am*) ff. 78–83ᵛ Astrological calendar.

(*an*) ff. 84–86ᵛ Cisioianus (as on f. 57) and other mnemonic verses on computus.

Includes the verses Altitonans . . ., Dat crux . . ., Fortis es . . ., Largus . . ., Si per quin-denos . . . (Walther, nos. 869, 4055, 6805, 10131, 17839) and couplets on the golden num-ber, Cantus lux . . ., Astra beans . . ., and on the solstice. Interlinear glosses, some in English.

(*ao*) f. 85ᵛ A man of signs and text, 'Imago signorum. Aries. Caue ab inscisione in capite . . .'.

6. f. 87ʳᵛ Secundum vsum romanum Triplex est stilus dictaminis. scilicet spondaicus . . . et varietate distinccionum etc.

7. f. 87ᵛ Model inventory 'omnium bonorum Georgii coluel inuentorum in domo mansionis eius apud C die quo obiit videlicet quinto maii Anno domini mᵒ ccccᵐᵒ xiiiᵒ'.

8. ff. 88–94ᵛ Seven formulary letters. The first letter begins 'Ordo iuris expos-tulat vt amicorum alter alterius precibus'. The others are under the headings 'Exempla contra inuidos et detractores', 'Exempla a filiis', 'Exemplum de con-solacione pro morte amici', 'Exempla contra prelatos', 'Exempla dominorum', and 'Exempla subditorum'.

(1) The writer excuses himself to a superior for having failed to do what he was asked to do. (3) A son asks for money. (5) The writer is unable to help a bishop 'Cum terra nostra tota sit posita in scandalo maximo et ruina'.

9. ff. 95–116 De compoto et de kalendario et de pertinentibus ad [. . .]. Quoniam sicut ait beatus Augustinus Sacerdotes compotum scire tenentur . . . pro peccatis meis deuotas oraciones effundant amen Explicit compotus.

10. Fourteen formulary letters: (a) f. 116ᵛ, of confraternity, Stephen, carmelite provincial prior, to William Whyte and Katherine, his wife, 'Dat' in domo nostra Couentrie', 8 July 1412; (b) ff. 116ᵛ–117, of confraternity, William, minister of the Friars Minor, to William Whyte, Oxford, 13 Nov. 1410; (c) f. 117, John Seynell, 'miles' of the hospital of St. John of Jerusalem and proctor 'indulgencie Castri sancti Petri', in favour of William Whyte and Katherine, his wife, Temple Bruern, 1420; (d) f. 117, three lines of thanks to a lady; (e) f. 117ᵛ, a monk of Lenton (Ord. Clun.) writes to his prior, then at Leicester, about a letter to the prior from the Duke of Gloucester; (f) f. 117ᵛ, written at Sutton to a lady, asking that she should not pay attention to reports that the schoolmaster 'non proficit diligenciam suam michi sicut et aliis scolaribus'; (g) f. 118, a scribe writes to another scribe 'docenti in mansione Iohannis Empyngham' inviting him to a writing match in which they are to write 'sine regularum caract' ut mos est plurimorum scriptorum qui propter suas honores scripturas sic lineatas penitus excludant'; (h) f. 118, a fragment; (i) f. 118ʳᵛ, W. G., patron of 'heley parua', Essex, to Richard (Clifford), bishop of London, about an exchange of benefices, 5 May 10 Henry V (sic); (j) f. 118ᵛ, prioress and convent of St. Michael, Stamford (O.S.B.), to Philip (Repingdon), bishop of Lincoln, 17 Apr. 1411, about the presentation of Richard N. of Peterborough, clerk, to the title of the house; (k) ff. 118ᵛ–119, the same to Henry (sic), archbishop of Canterbury, 30 May 1410, about the presentation of John Jamys of Peterborough, clerk, to the title of the house; (l) f. 119, appointment of Richard Paple of Peterborough, acolyte, to the title of the prioress and convent of St. Michael, Stamford, on the occasion of a visitation at Spalding, 6 June 1430, by Thomas (sic), archbishop of Canterbury; (m) f. 119ᵛ, Philip, bishop of Lincoln, anno 7, ordination of Richard Oxney of Peterborough, subdeacon, after his appointment to the title of the prioress and convent of St. Michael, Stamford, by Bishop William Sulton at Liddington, 19 Dec. 1431; (n) ff. 119ᵛ–120, resignation of the vicarage of Lullington (Derbyshire), to William (Heyworth), bishop of Coventry and Lichfield, by William de Catton, O.S.A., canon of Gresley, 11 Aug. 1428 'in aula prioris prioratus de Grysley', William Arderne of Overton, notary public, attesting.

11. f. 120ᵛ Clerici accusati . . . in curia domini regis.

The nine points 'pro quibus moriebatur sanctus Thomas archiepiscopus Cantuarie'.

12. f. 121 (a) Be it knowen to all crysten men þat I am kyng of all kynges. lord of all lordes. Souden of Surry . . . I send gretyng and gode loue to all sondry and namly to herry 30ᵘʳ kyng and he will wed my do3ter I schall becom crysten . . . (b) Reply by 'harry . . . kyng of Inglond' (etc.) that he will think about this until 1441 and then give answer. (a) is crossed out.

13. f. 121ᵛ Invitations to an exchange of verses and a meeting for learned discussion, 'Et quia ad presens index mee manus dextere est Iesus ideo vobis cancellaui cum manu sinistra'.

14. ff. 122–31 Orthographiam scribendi rite sophiam Hec presens pueris pagina dat teneris . . . Sunt autem figure litterarum vt dicit precianus . . . nulla sit questio. Explicit arte pia scribentis orthographia.

Goes through the alphabet in prose and verse (Walther, no. 13499). W is included with V and exemplified by the names Willelmus, Walterus, Wulstanus.

15. ff. 131ᵛ–132 (a) Menskful and myȝty in mynde. modyr of maries iii . . . Zachary hyr knew in hast And scho consayued ful fast. Ion þo baptist. Explicit stirps Anne beate. (b) Anna solet . . . (3 lines). (c) Prima parit cristum . . . (3 lines). (d) Ascolonita necat . . . (2 lines).

(a). Sixty-four lines. *IMEV*, no. 2153. 5. (b–d) are additions at the foot of the pages.

16. Texts relating to St. Ursula: (a) ff. 132ᵛ–133ᵛ A hermit writes 'venerabili patri nostro Arundell Archiepiscopo Cantuarie pro eo quod forum siue mercatum tentum in die dominica in tempore autumpni mutasset in diem sabbatum dum stetit cum Rege': he has been sent a marvellous sign; (b) f. 133ᵛ Hic incipit oracio que sancta vrsula docuit Iohannem heremitam de Warwyk . . .; (c) ff. 134–135ᵛ Account of a miracle of John, hermit of Warwick, with help of St. Ursula, at Langley in Shropshire, Palm Sunday A.D. 1411, preceded by a vouching letter from Robert Lee, armiger, of Roden and Langley, and Petronella, his wife;[1] (d) ff. 135ᵛ–136 The writer has been charged by St. Ursula 'certificare inter magnatos ecclesiasticos et milites quod nisi cessarent corroboracionem false fidei et mercatum in die dominica illi qui sunt extra fidem illos predictos fidedignos fortiter obstarent': he was once captured by Lollards at Havering: he ends 'Mercatum dominicale heresis est et perdicio veritatis pro istis maxime laboro. Explicit'.

17. ff. 136ᵛ–137ᵛ O monachi diabolici pensate quid est/ Vos estis deus est testis vilissima pestys . . . Passio cuiusdam monachi secundum luxuriam. In maligno tempore . . . sponsus ad vxorem suam. Explicit passio de quodam nigro monacho.

Substantially the text printed by Feifalik in *Sitzungsberichte der kaiserl. Akademie der Wissenschaften*, Phil. hist. kl. xxxvi (Vienna 1861), 173–4: cf. P. Lehmann, *Die Parodie im Mittelalter*, 1922, p. 172.

18. f. 138 Prophecia hermerici. Notandum est quod hermericus est in historia alemannorum sicut merlinus in historia britonum. Lilium in meliori parte . . .

Cf. *Cat. of Romances*, i. 314.

19. ff. 138ᵛ–139 Hic sequuntur hereses et errores vita et interitus Iohannis Oldcastell militis et heretici qui misit pragum illum maledictum petrum toti orbi. Martino quinto cecinit constancia vitis . . . Qua veteris castri testa cremata datur. Explicit.

Fifty-two lines of verse, mainly as Thomas Elmham, *Liber metricus de Henrico Quinto* (RS xi, 1858), lines 1196–1275. Printed by H. Hargreaves in *Medium Aevum*, xlii (1973), 141–3.

20. f. 139ʳᵛ O rex mi domine metra suscipe que tibi pango . . . Hec memorare precor. hic tibi dixit ita.

Thirty-six lines of verse. *Political Poems and Songs*, ed. T. Wright (RS xiv, 1861), ii. 118–19 (Thomas Elmham to Henry V).

[1] For the Lee family see Eyton, *Antiquities of Shropshire*, vi. 41.

21. ff. 140ᵛ–141 A table in French setting out on a double opening the descent of Henry VI from St. Louis.

22. ff. 141ᵛ–143ᵛ Saturnus ys ye hyest planete and ye wykkydest . . . (143) Be almagest in centiloqui of tholomy ilk lym of maɳnus body ys rulyd by a certeyn sygne of þe zodyac . . .

Influences of the planets and the signs of the zodiac.

23. ff. 145ᵛ–146 Tables of measurement.

24. ff. 146ᵛ–149 Laudes abrade si scriptas videris ade . . . Verbis demollit te dum tullia tollit Per predictam patet fraus muliere latet.

One hundred and sixty-five lines of scurrilous verse, three against each of fifty-five women in alphabetical order from Ada to Tullia.

25. ff. 149ᵛ–152ᵛ Thow þᵗ has cast iii sixes her' Shalt haue þy desyr þˢ same ȝere . . .

Forty-seven out of fifty-six four-line stanzas, each a prognostication from throwing three dice, ending imperfectly at three threes. *IMEV*, no. 3694. 3.

26. ff. 153–4 Here tellyth þe dyetyng of blode letyng of man or woman in euery monyth yn þe ȝere. In þe monyth of Ienyuer . . .

Rules for health in each month and lists of dangerous days for bloodletting and (f. 154) of 'lunares periculosi'.

27. f. 154ᵛ Prognostications from wind and sun during the twelve nights and days before Christmas.

28. ff. 155–8 Fistulat hec duplici celer astat glos feriendi . . . Gloria fine datur cristo bellantibus augur.

Twenty-eight three-line stanzas: Walther, no. 6561. Each stanza consists of nineteen words and each word represents by its initial letter one year of a great cycle of 532 years beginning at 1140. Events are noted between the lines in English or Latin, all in red ink, except the last, the coronation of Queen Margaret, 30 May 1445. '1444' is written against the first word of stanza 17. The verses are followed on f. 156ᵛ by an explanation in red ink, 'Cum in plerisque dubiis que in nostro kalendario . . .'.

29. ff. 158ᵛ–159 Thyse ben þe namys of þe kyng*is* of all Crystendom . . .

A table in English of the arms borne by twenty-four kings and by the emperor and the sultan.

30. Miscellaneous pieces in hands of s. xv med. include: (a) f. 38ᵛ A note of the price of wheat, peas, beans, etc., in 1438; (b) f. 38ᵛ A note of the great storm, 27–8 Jan. 1439–40; (c) f. 72ᵛ A note of the decollation of Thomas of Lancaster in 1321; (d) f. 72ᵛ A couplet, 'M bis C semel L. X ter subdendo nouemque / . . . nato criste fundatus erat locus iste', and beside it 'domus fratrum augustinenc' de Werynton fundata fuit anno domini 1289'; (e, f) f. 74ᵛ Two calligraphic scribbles, 'Henricus dei gracia . . . vicecomitibus Cestr' salutem supplicauit nobis Bartholomeus Norwych ut cum ipse de vita mutillacione membrorum suorum' and 'In domino confundo et non erubescam quod Ricardus Ham bonus puer de Cestr' '; (g) f. 136 O bone feodum lex . . ., a piece of nonsense mentioning 'homo de meridionali venella Cestr' '; (h) f. 137ᵛ A similar piece, '. . . Rogans illam

obuiare michi in nemore per Walterum latus . . .' (the water side?); (*i*) f. 161ᵛ
A charm in English to cure a lame horse, a recipe 'for to destroy flees', Latin
verses 'O deus in quantis . . .', 'Diligo te non propter te . . .', 'Mutnegra cum
murua . . .' (Walther, *Sprichwörter*, nos. 19445, 5786, 15813), and the words 'As
fortune will Trebrech' (repeated) and 'Thomas Hemelyr'.

31. Later pieces mainly in the very current hand, s. xv², which added to art.
5, including: (*a*) f. 38ᵛ Horoscope of King Henry VII, born 28 Jan. 1457;
(*b*) f. 55ᵛ Fifteen more or less faded lines in Netherlandish (?); (*c*) f. 56 A charm
to make a thief confess; (*d*) f. 56 The gifts of the devil to his nine sons; (*e*) f. 144
Note of the birth of 'dom. R. Chbmbfrwrþ', 14 Mar. 1421; (*f*) f. 144 chyer herry
bord est cordelyer de saynte croes et esscocoes natyf et ne fra Iames bien a vustre
Noble persone ne a vustre Royalme; (*g*) ff. 159ᵛ–161 Charms 'ad inueniendum
furem' and 'ad ligandum furem' and to get rid of rats and mice.

ff. ii+161+ii. Paper and (ff. 1, 2, 8, 9, 16, 17, 24, 25, 32, 39, 40, 44, 65, 73, 74, 87, 96,
97, 105 which are or may be presumed to have been the outside and middle sheets of
quires) parchment. ff. 9, 26 are small fragments. *c.* 220×150 mm. Written space
c. 160×105 mm. *c.* 30 long lines. Ruling, if any, with a hard point, usually the frame
only. Probably twelve quires: the first three are ff. 1–8 (1¹⁶ wants 1–7, 10), ff. 39, 10–23,
25 (2¹⁶), ff. 24, 26–38, 9 (3¹⁴+1 leaf after 7); after this ff. 46–7, 58–9, 73–4, 83–4, 96–7,
113–14, 129–30, a missing leaf and 146, 157–8 are middle sheets of quires and ff. 87, 105
are the outside sheet of a quire; a leaf missing after f. 152. Written in several current
hands in a mixture of secretary and anglicana. Red initials, 2-line and 1-line. Capital
letters in the ink of the text sometimes lined with red. Rebound by Maltby, Oxford, s. xx¹:
nearly all the paper leaves were repaired at this time.

Written in England, *c.* 1440 (cf. arts. 12*b*, 28, 30*a*, *b*) and in the neighbourhood of Chester
(cf. art. 30*f*, *g*). The hand which wrote art. 30*d* (at the Augustinian convent of Warring-
ton?) appears to be one of the main hands of the manuscript. 'William fitton with my hand'
is scribbled on f. 98ᵛ: for the family at Gawsworth, Cheshire, see Ormerod, *History of
Cheshire*, iii. 547. 'Hunc librum Collegio Regio Universitatis Aberdonen' Dono dedit
Robertus Barclay de Urie 1723', f. 8ᵛ.

134. *Mirror of Our Lady* (*in English*) s. xv ex.

(f. 2) Viderunt eam filie syon et beatissimam predicauerunt. Thes wordes are
wrytt in holy scripture . . . (f. 135ᵛ) Per eundem. By þᵉ same our lord Crist
Amen. Here endethe the Story on sonday And that is sufficient for this halff of
our*e* Ladyes myrro*ʳ*. Love drede and pray (*these four words in red ink*) Your
symple seruaunt R Tailour.

The first of two volumes, the second being Bodleian, Rawlinson C. 941. No other manuscript is known, but the text was printed in London in 1530, and thence by J. H. Blunt,
EETS, Extra Series, xix (1873), who printed also, p. lx, the first two pages of Aberdeen
134. A full description by H. Hargreaves in *Aberdeen University Review*, xlii (1968), 267–
80, with facsimile of f. 99ᵛ. See also *The Bridgettine Breviary of Syon Abbey*, ed. A. J.
Collins (HBS xcvi, 1969), pp. xxxv–xl.

Two prologues are followed on ff. 8–9 by a table of the twenty-four chapters of pt. 1,
which follows on ff. 9–51ᵛ. Pt. 2 begins on f. 51ᵛ and the 'story and service of the Sonday'
on f. 56ᵛ. f.1ʳᵛ is blank, except for the title 'The myrrour of our Lady' on the recto.

ff. vi+140+ii, foliated i–vi, 1–31, 31, 32–141. Paper. ff. iii–vi are contemporary flyleaves, iii backed by modern paper. 213×150 mm. Written space *c.* 150×85 mm. 24–6 long lines. Frame ruling. Collation: 1–8¹⁶ 9¹². Clearly written in a mixture of anglicana and secretary: medial *v* is usual. No decoration, apart from a few red initials. Binding of s. xix. The mark from the strap-and-pin fastening of a former binding shows on ff. 125–39.¹ *Secundo folio of eny thinge.*

Written in England by R. Tailour. 'Thys booke belongyth to syster Elyzabeth Monton' ', f. 135ᵛ: Elizabeth Mou*n*ton is in the Sion Martiloge at 17 July, Elizabeth Mountayn was a nun of Syon in 1518 and Elizabeth Mountague a nun in 1539 (Aungier, *History and Antiquities of Syon*, 1840, pp. 81, 89). 'Brought from the Cape of Good Hope and presented to the University by Mʳ William Robertson A.M. April 1828', f. 1.

195. *H. Retherus, Super titulo de verborum obligationibus, etc.*

1433

Lectures on the Digest by Henry Rether, professor of civil law at Louvain, as taken down by a student, William Elfynston. Noticed, together with MSS. 196, 197, by L. Macfarlane in *Aberdeen University Review*, xxxvii (1958), 264–6. Elfynston matriculated at Louvain in 1431 (*Matricule de l'Université de Louvain*, ed. E. Reusens, i. 49) and may be identical with the man of this name who was canon of Glasgow in 1441. In view of the descent of his books he was no doubt a relative and almost certainly the father of the man of the same name—but spelling it with *ph* instead of *f*—who was bishop of Aberdeen from 1483 to 1514 and founded Aberdeen University in 1494/5.

1. ff. 1–122ᵛ [Inci]pit liber xlv digesti De uerborum obligacionibus Willelmus elfynston... legentium in vniversitate louan script' per Willelmum Elfynston. Relata Domini Henrici Reteri Legum Doctoris super titulo de v' obligat' fenita anno domini mcccc xxxiiiⁱᵒ quinta die decembris.

On bk. 45. 'quod Elfynston' and the like is written in at least nine places in art. 1. The last eighteen lines on f. 74ᵛ and the whole of f. 75ʳ are in another hand. In a partly blank line (75/17) Elfynston wrote 'Hoc non scripsit gillelmus Elfynston'.

2. (*a*) ff. 123–59, on bk. 24, tit. 3. (*b*) ff. 159–64, on bk. 25, tit. 1. (*c*) ff. 165–221ᵛ, on bk. 28, titt. 1–3 (2, f. 180; 3, f. 211ᵛ). (*d*) ff. 221ᵛ–240, on bk. 29, tit. 2. (*e*) ff. 241–297ᵛ, on bk. 30, tit. 1.

(*a*) ends 'finis de isto titulo de soluto matrimonio secundum lecturam venerabilis et magne sciencie viri domini henrici retere (*sic*) in legibus doctoris exemei ordinarie legentis lowanii post prandium secundum scripturam diuersorum videlicet in principio magistri michaelis colas' in artibus magistri et in iure canonico bacalarii et in fine M' Willelmi Elfynston in artibus magistri pro tunc in legibus studentis Louain. Explicit ista Rubrica quod W de E':² Elfynston did not write ff. 123–46ᵛ. (*b*) ends 'quod Willelmus Elfynston'. (*d*) begins 'Sequitur modo Rubrica de acquirenda uel auertenda hereditate omissis aliis intermediis titulis quod Willelmus Elfynston'. (*e*) begins 'Incipit liber viᵘˢ inforciati qui intitulatur De legatis Primo an(n)o domini Mᵐᵒ cccc xxxiiiⁱᵒ Elfynston'. ff. 164ᵛ, 240ᵛ blank. 'Digestum inforciatum Reteri' at the head of f. 123.

3. Notes and scribblings by Elfynston on f. 122ᵛ, legible by ultra-violet light, include 'Iste quem doctor noster allegat pro domino suo est dominus pe de

---

¹ The Bodleian manuscript is in binding with Oldham's panel HE 23 on both covers. The last leaves show the mark from the strap-and-pin fastening.

² Professor Robert Feenstra kindly told me of this colophon.

Unsutio ordinarius pagine' and 'Vinum scriptori tradatur de meliori Sed quia credo mori potebo de meliori. Viuat in eternum qui dat michi tale falernum Qui michi dat villum mala passio torqueat illum Willelmus Elfynston'.

ff. ii+297+ii. Paper, damp-stained. 295×215 mm. Written space *c.* 260×110 mm. and (ff. 123–46) *c.* 260×165 mm. *c.* 47 long lines. No ruling: a fold makes a bounding crease. Collation impracticable after mending, but catchwords on versos of ff. 22, 34, 46, 58, 70, 82, 94, 106, 134, 178, 190, 202, 238, 252, 264, 276 show that the quires were mostly twelves. Written in current cursiva, all by one hand, except ff. 123–146ᵛ (two quires?). The main hand uses long tailed *r.* No decoration. Bound by Maltby, Oxford, *c.* 1930. Secundo folio illegible by me.

Written in 1433 at Louvain, mostly (see above) by William Elfynston, senior. 'Liber magistri Willelmi de Elphinston', f. 297ᵛ, is the ex-libris of the bishop of Aberdeen: no doubt he gave or bequeathed this and other manuscripts which had belonged to William Elfynston senior.

196. *Commentaria in jus civile* *c.* 1433

1. ff. 1–39ᵛ Rubrica de accionibus.

H. de Piro[1] on Justinian, Institutes, bk. 4, tit. vi. Louvain is mentioned on f. 14.

2. ff. 40–160ᵛ In nomine domini nostri Ihesu cristi codicis domini Iustiniani sacratissimi principis perpetui etc.

Notes on bks. 1, 2 (ff. 76–132ᵛ), 3 (ff. 133–160ᵛ), 6 (ff. 161–207), 7 tits. xxxii–xxxv (ff. 208–27). Elfynston writes his name in colophons or after rubrics: on ff. 79, 157, 'quod Willelmus Elfynston'; on f. 115ᵛ, his name and 'Vinum scriptori tradatur de Meliore Qui legit hunc uersum sciat se stercure mersum': line 2 is Walther, *Sprichwörter*, no. 24173; on f. 132ᵛ, his name and ten lines of verse, 'Qui vult seruare sanctorum singula festa . . . Si discas leges in nullo tempore deges. Nam mundum reges et subduntur tibi reges': here lines 1–7 are in Walther, *S.*, nos. 24961, 20654, 29012a, lines 1, 3, 4, and line 8 is the first line of Walther, *Init.*, no. 11884. Cf. MS. 197 for another of these law-school jingles. ff. 75ᵛ, 179, 207ᵛ, 227ᵛ blank. A legal note by Elfynston on f. 228ʳᵛ.

3 (added). f. 161, upside-down. Verses, not in Elfynston's hand, beginning 'Venus' and ending 'Allac yat euer scho bewte bar yat now is went me fra. scho has mad my hart full sar Allace qwy did scho sa'. As Mr. Macfarlane pointed out to me, some of the words are Netherlandish.

ff. ii+228+ii. Paper. Format and written space as MS. 195. As there, the parts written by Elfynston are in shorter lines (*c.* 110 mm.) than the rest and the bounding line was made by folding the paper. Collation: 1–3¹² 4 three 5–9¹² 10¹⁶ (ff. 100–15): from this point doubtful, except that catchwords show that quires ended on ff. 151, 219. Several hands: Elfynston himself wrote ff. 76–160ᵛ, 208–27, and ff. 40–75 appear to be by the same scribe as MS. 195 ff. 123–46ᵛ. Binding like MS. 195.

Written about the same time as MS. 195 and partly by the same scribes. 'Liber magistri Willelmi de elphinston', f. 227. Acquired at the same time as MS. 195, no doubt.

[1] I owe the identification of the author of MS. 196, art. 1, to Professor Robert Feenstra.

197. J. Grosbek et R. de Turnaco, Commentaria in jus civile 1433

A volume of the same set as MSS. 195, 196.

1. ff. 1–186 Incipit liber xii De rebus creditis . . . Explicit Rubrica notabilis de Rei vendicacione secundum lecturam venerabilis licenciati in legibus magistri Ricardi de Turnaco qui dictum titulum legit ordinarie post leccionem domini Iohannis grosbek doctoris de mane in vniuersitate louain' scriptum et fenitum per gillelmum Elfynston' scotum Anno domini m^mo cccc^mo xxxiii immediate ante nouum ordinarium. Quid queris quid eges ut non egeas lege leges. Legibus insiste labor utilis est labor iste.

Notes on Digestum Vetus, bks. 12 (ff. 1–144), 13, titt. i–iii (ff. 144–54) and 6, tit. i (ff. 155–86). 'Finis duodecimi libri per dominum Io grosbek pro tunc rectore vniuersitatis louanii script' per V elfynston' ', f. 144. The notes on bk. 13 begin, f. 144, 'Sequitur modo Rubrica de condicione furtiua que Rubrica incipiebatur a domino doctore 2⁰ die decembris anno etc xxxiii', and end, f. 154, 'Relata domini Io grosbek legum doctoris ordinarius de mane in facultate legum in vniuersitate louan' Elfynston' '. The notes on bk. 6 were taken from Grosbek's and R. de Tournai's lectures in the summer of 1433, as appears from Elfynston's note on f. 177, written probably soon after 31 Aug., on which day Grosbek became rector of the University: cf. N. R. Ker in *Medium Aevum*, xxxix (1970), 32. f. 186^v was left blank.

2. ff. 188–234 Incipiunt constituciones feudorum et primo de hiis qui feudum dare possunt et qualiter acquira*ntur*. Non continuatur hec Rubrica . . .

Notes on Liber feudorum, as far as bk. 2, tit. xv, after which there is only the heading of tit. xvi and the words 'Guillelmus Elfinstoun Studens louain''. ff. 187^rv and 234^v were left blank. The notes on bk. 1, tit. iv are nearly complete: at the point where they end, f. 202^v, are the words 'Sequitur modo alia rubrica quia ista nimis fetigauit me Willelmus Elfynston'. Bk. 1, tit. xxi was left out on f. 212^v and added in the blank space on f. 187^v, together with a note on f. 212^v referring to it, 'set inuenies in primo folio primi sisterni in 2⁰ latere'.

ff. ii+234+ii. Paper. 297×210 mm. Written space *c.* 270×210 mm. *c.* 50 long lines. No ruling. Collation: twelves, except 4^14, 6^14, 13^6 (ff. 149–54), 16 eight (ff. 179–86), 17^16 (ff. 187–202), 20 eight (ff. 227–34). Written wholly in Elfynston's hand, except ff. 187^v–210, which are by the same scribe as MS. 195, ff. 123–46, and MS. 196, ff. 40–75. Binding like MSS. 195, 196.

Written by William Elfynston at Louvain in 1433. 'Liber magistri Willelmi de elphynston', f. 234: cf. MS. 195. Acquired at the same time as MS. 195, no doubt.

199, 199.2. Commentarium in Decretales Gregorii IX s. xv²

De presumpcionibus Rubrica. Continuatur hec Rubrica ad precedentem in hunc modum quia supra visum est de probacionibus in genere et postea de aliquibus speciebus probacionum . . . Nota bene istam glo que wlt (*ends imperfectly*).

A commentary on Decretals, bk. 2, from tit. xxiii. 1 to tit. xxx. 8, now bound in two volumes.

ff. ii+218+ii (MS. 199). ff. ii+224+ii (MS. 199.2). Foliated continuously, flyleaves apart, 1*,¹ 1–439: single leaves have been missed after ff. 61, 81, 144, and the number 188

¹ This leaf was found by Dr. Leslie Macfarlane in 1962.

was passed over. Paper. 295 × 220 mm. Written space *c.* 200 × 110 mm. 32–9 long lines. No ruling: the leaves were folded to make a bounding crease. Written in hybrida, but after f. 248 ascenders are often looped: a new hand at f. 272ᵛ. Collation: 1 ten (ff. 1*, 1–9) 2¹² 3 eleven (ff. 22–32) 4–24¹² (ff. 33–282): thenceforward uncertain, owing to damage (ff. 1*, 1–10, 354–439 are mounted on modern paper). No decoration apart from paragraph marks, strokes on capital letters, and underlinings in red. Rebound by Maltby, Oxford, *c.* 1930: the division is after the fifth leaf of quire 19. Secundo folio *supra de proba.*

Written probably in the Netherlands. '[. . .] archidia' sanctiandree', in a hand of s. xv/xvi, is legible by ultra-violet light at the head of f. 1. It suggests ownership by an archdeacon of St. Andrews.[1] 'Liber Coll. Regii Aberd.' and the King's College mark *θ.* 1. 7 on f. 1*.

200. '*Lectura super clementinas*' s. xv²

(*Preface*) . . . dei auxilio et gloriose virginis marie sue matris ac omnium ciuium celestium instanter inuocat' quia nonnulli cupiunt ut in librorum auspiciis enum[erentur] hi qui super eisdem libris conscripserunt et hunc obsequar sciendum quod inter omnes commentatores . . . sequar pro vt melius potero. Iohannes episcopus seruus. Glosa non summat hoc exordium . . . (*ends in commentary on bk. 5. tit. iii*).

A commentary on the Clementine Constitutions. In the preface fifteen writers on the Clementines are named, the three latest in date being Petrus de Anchorano (†1416), Franciscus de Zabarellis (†1417), and Johannes de Imola (Schulte, ii. 278, 283, 296). Of William de Monte Lauduno and Gesselinus (de Cassanis) the writer says 'hii ambo scripserunt in studiis citra montanis habentes respectum ad locum presentem videlicet louanium'. 'Nota pro rege scocie' is in the margin of f. 136ᵛ against the commentary on 'Ut illud . . . promulgata' in ii. xi. 2 (ed. Friedberg, col. 1152).

ff. ii+293+ii. Paper. 295 × 220 mm. Written space *c.* 220 × 155 mm. 29–45 long lines. No ruling, but a margin is made by creasing the paper. Collation: 1¹⁴ 2¹² 3¹⁶ 4–5¹² 6¹⁴ 7¹² 8¹⁴ 9¹² 10¹⁸ 11¹⁴ 12–15¹² 16¹⁰ 17–18¹² 19¹² wants 1 before f. 233 20¹² 21¹⁴ 22–23¹². Quires numbered at the beginning, except the first, and at the end, except the last. Written in cursiva, ff. 129–35 better than the rest: the main hand is difficult: *r* is often long. No decoration. Contemporary Netherlandish binding of wooden boards covered with stamped brown leather: stamps of four patterns, with a different design on each cover: two clasps: 'restored by Maltby, Oxford'. Secundo folio *Circa primam.*

Written probably at Louvain. No doubt given as MS. 195. 'Liber Coll. Regii Aberdonensis' and the King's College pressmark *θ.* 1. 14, f. 1, s. xviii.

201. *Johannes de Imola, In Constitutiones Clementinas* s. xv med.

[A]bbates. glo' summat et diuidit. cle' diuiditur in duas partes quia primo duplex prohibicio . . . (f. 367) per intercessionem virginis gloriose nos collocet cum electis Amen. Deo gracias Mᵒ cccc iiii die sabbati xxi Iunii etc. Habetis cle expeditam cum apparatu suo . . . (f. 373ᵛ) bona fides etc. Et sic est finis huius cle et per consequens tocius libri clementinarum. Deo gracias Amen. Explicit liber clementinarum editus per utriusque iuris doctorem. d. Io de ymola peritissimum.

Schulte, ii. 298. Completed in 1404 and printed in 1475 and later. ff. 367–373ᵛ contain a summary. f. 374ʳᵛ blank.

[1] Of persons listed in Durkan and Ross, *Early Scottish Libraries*, William Schevez and Alexander Inglis held this office at about the right date.

ff. iii+374+i. Paper. 288×215 mm. Written space 212×155 mm. 2 cols. 39–49 long lines. Frame ruling with pencil or hard point: no ruling on ff. 21–5. Written in a good set hybrida, apart from ff. 2–15ᵛ which are in a current hand using long-tailed *r*. Spaces for initials remain blank. Binding of wooden boards, covered with stamped leather, 'Restored by Maltby, Oxford': a triple border formed by fillets encloses a flower stamp and an eagle stamp: one of two clasps remains and fastens from the front cover to the back cover. Secundo folio *est verbum*.

Written probably in the Netherlands. 'Liber magistri Wilelmi de Elphinstoun' ', f. 1: cf. f. 373ᵛ. 'Liber Coll. Regii Aberdonensis' and a King's College pressmark, θ. 1. 15, on f. 1, s. xviii.

202. *Decisiones Rotae Romanae, etc.*   s. xv med.

1. ff. 1–39 Notes on canon law, principally De Matrimonio. ff. 7–8ᵛ, 15ᵛ–17ᵛ are blank.

2. ff. 40–159 In nomine domini Anno a natiuitate eiusdem 1376 die mercurii 30ᵃ mensis Ianuarii . . . Ego Wilhelmus horborch . . . vsque ad annum domini 1381 ad mensem maii et hoc sub correctione et emendacione omnium predictorum dominorum meorum et aliorum subuenientium melius sencientium. Prima est quod attemptata appellatione . . . dilecti de excep.

The Decisiones novae collected by William Horborch for the years 1376–81, often printed in decretal order, but here chronologically as in New College, Oxford, MS. 214, and in *GKW* 8196. The decisions are in 450 numbered paragraphs.

3. f. 159ʳᵛ Casus talis est papa reseruauit beneficia . . . Et aliam que incipit Item tu obtinens prebendam Colonien' etc.

4. ff. 160–162ᵛ A list of the words in art. 5.

5. ff. 163–428 A law dictionary, Absens–Vxor, the second entry beginning 'Absens in seruicio pape an habeatur pro presente et residente'. Before this, 'Aequebitur accio ex contractu . . .' seems out of place. The last entry is 'Vxori An debeantur alimenta ab heredibus viro mortuo vide sub verbo alimenta que miseracionis causa etc' '.

Six leaves have been cut out after f. 351: traces on the stub after f. 351 show that the first of these leaves began with the words which now begin f. 356. Scribes beginning work wrote the tags 'In nomine trino hoc opus incipio' (f. 318), 'Plasmator rerum doceat me scribere verum' (ff. 162ᵛ, 335). f. 428ᵛ is blank. Notes and scribbles on f. 429ʳᵛ include 'Quo die procurator domini Iohannis Ray . . .' and 'Cum pium et meritorium sit testimonium perhibere pro veritate hinc est quod Iohannes dalgles canonicus glasguen' volens'.

6. f. iii, once the pastedown, is from a document, s. xiv, which has been folded and is hard to read. It includes a long list of churches and the date 31 Oct. 1340 and describes a bull of Eugenius, then pope, 'factum et concessum dicto monasterio sancte marie quod Bauduxie situm erat' (line 5).

ff. iii+433+ii, foliated 1–22, 22*, 23–32, 32*, 33–226, 226*, 227–347, 347*, 349–429. ff. 40–158 have a medieval foliation 1–119. For f. iii see above. Paper. 281×218 mm. Written space of art. 2 215×125 mm.; of art. 4, *c*. 180×140 mm. *c*. 45 long lines (art. 2) and *c*. 39 (art. 4). Collation: 1¹⁶+1 leaf after 16 2²⁴ 3–14¹⁰ (ff. 40–159) 15²⁰ 16–17¹² 18¹⁸ 19 twenty-three (ff. 222–43) 20–23¹⁶ 24¹² wants 11, 12, probably blank after f. 317 25¹² 26⁶ wants 6, blank, 27¹² 28 ten (ff. 347–55: cf. above, art. 5) 29⁶ 30 fifteen (ff. 362–76) 31⁸ 32¹²

33^{16} 9 cancelled after f. 404 34^{18}. Frame ruling from f. 192 (17^1): little or no ruling before this, but the edge was sometimes folded to make a boundary. Several hands, writing for the most part a neat current hybrida. Art. 1 is mainly in W. de Elphinston's scribble hand, which occurs also in marginalia elsewhere, e.g. on ff. 191^v, 207. No decoration. Binding of s. xix, 'restored by Maltby, Oxford', s. xx.

Written in the Netherlands. 'Liber Wilelmi de Elphinstoune', f. 163. 'Liber magistri Willelmi de elphinston', f. 428. Probably Elphinston had the manuscript in his Glasgow period: cf. art. 5 and the inscription on f. iii, 'Detur . . . magistro Roberto Penven': one of this name was incorporated in the Glasgow University law faculty in 1452.[1] Given or bequeathed as MS. 195. Usual King's College ex-libris and pressmark θ. 2. 18, f. 1.

245. *Compendium Theologicae Veritatis, etc.*   s. XIV ex.

1. ff. 2–33 Ueritatis theologice sublimitas . . . recipiet sine fine per cristum dominum nostrum amen. Explicit compendium theologye. Explicit.

In seven books of which 3–5 and parts of 2 and 6 are missing in a gap after f. 17. Now attributed to Hugh of Strasbourg, O.P.: here anonymous. Printed often among the works of St. Albert and St. Thomas Aquinas (cf. Glorieux, i. 75, 103). f. 1^{IV} contains a table of chapters of each book.

2. Notes: (*a*) f. 33^{rv} beginning 'Nota quod aliter deus videtur a bonis in terris et aliter a beatis in celis'; (*b*) ff. 33^v–34 on the seven deadly sins, beginning 'Nota septem sunt vicia capitalia ut ait augustinus'.

3. ff. 34–38^v Hic incipiunt exposiciones eorum que dicuntur in missa que vocantur speculum ecclesie. Dicit apostolus ad ephesios vi^o. Induite vos armatura dei . . . esse cum filiis hominum. Explicit commentum hugonis cardinalis super missam totam.

Hugh of St. Cher. For manuscripts and printed editions cf. Glorieux, i. 48.

4. ff. 39–69^v 'De institucione sacramentorum'. Samaritanus. Queritur an sacramenta debeant institui. Solucio. triplici racione . . . subtilitatem quam habet (*ends imperfectly*).

Questions on bk. 4 of the Sentences of Peter Lombard. The last now remaining is 'si corpus gloriosum possit simul esse cum altero glorioso corpore'.

5. The pastedown on the front cover is formed of two documents: (*a*) certifying that the seven 'consules' of the city of 'Golnaw' (Gollnow, near Stettin, now Goleniów, Poland) grant an annual life payment 'Monete stetynensis' to John Denekens, and after his death to two relatives, 29 Sept. 1365, in return for a loan to the city by him; (*b*) a blurred sheet bearing the notarial mark of Gerhardus de Beceman, clerk and notary public by imperial authority, and beginning 'In nomine domini amen anno natiuitatis eiusdem m^o ccc^o sexagesimo quinto . . . in Golnow in domo habitacionis Gerhardi beceman'.

ff. iii+68+ii, foliated (i, ii), 1–69 (70, 71). 285 × 208 mm. Written space c. 220 × 160 mm. 2 cols. 45–54 lines. Quire 5 is fully ruled: the rest has frame ruling. Collation of ff. 2–69: 1–2^8 3^8 wants 7, 8 after f. 23 4^{12} 5^6 wants 4–6 blank after f. 38 6–7^8 8^8 wants 1 before f. 55 9^8. Written in a modified textura or semi-cursive script (feet to minims often, loops to *d* and ascenders) by several hands. Red initials, 3-line, 2-line, and 1-line. Capital

---

[1] Information from Dr. Leslie Macfarlane.

letters in the ink of the text touched with red. Contemporary binding of wooden boards covered with white leather, rebacked and repaired by Douglas Cockerell: two strap-and-pin fastenings. Secundo folio *m^{am} ut cum dicitur.*

Written probably in the Stettin region to judge from the general similarity of the script to that of the pasted-down documents. 'Cam. Cod. 4' inside cover. Bought in 1952 from Mr. Boleslaw Zerzecki.

257. *Commentarium in Decretales*   s. xv²

Incipit liber tercius decreta(lium). Rubrica de vi. et honesta. cle. Rubrica ista ymo et totus iste liber potest continuari ad precedentem in hunc modum . . . (*ends imperfectly in commentary on 3. xxiv. 6*).

The author was from the diocese of Liège and brings in references to it and to Brussels: f. 157^v (on 3. v. 28), a question 'an capelle sancti gaugerici et sancti nicholai opidi bruxellen' sint beneficia curata vel non'; f. 201 (on 3. vii. 6), 'id est Rectores ecclesiarum Iuxta vulgare anglicorum quia Rectores ecclesiarum ibi vocantur persone sicut eciam vocantur in istis partibus in diocesi leodiense'; f. 200^v (on 3. vii. 4), 'ut eciam videmus per experienciam in archidiaconis ecclesie leodiensis'.

ff. i+417+i. Paper. 295×220 mm. Written space 212×120 mm. *c.* 42 long lines. No ruling, but the edge of the paper was sometimes folded to make a bounding line. Collation: 1–4¹² 5–7⁶ 8–18¹² 19¹²+an added slip after 10 (f. 209) 20–36¹². Written in a mixture of cursiva and hybrida. The only decoration is a red and black *I* with red ornament, f. 1. Rebound in s. xx, but the old brown leather covers have been pasted on: they are divided by fillets into lozenges, each of which contains a small round stamp of an eagle: two clasps missing. Secundo folio *du^m an liceat.*

Written probably in the southern Netherlands. The usual King's College ex-libris and pressmark *θ.* 1. 17 are on f. 1.

264. *Johannes de Irlandia*   s. xv²

1. ff. 1–118^v Circa inicium 3^i libri Queritur primo vtrum possibile fuerit uerbum diuinum . . . et sancti frequenter libere sustinuerunt.

2. ff. 119–252^v Circa principium huius 4^{ti} in quo agitur de sacramentis noue legis que sunt vasa gracie . . . ad racionem autem oppositum questionis patet solucio ex dictis. 'Scriptum magistri Ihoannis de Irlandia supra quartum sentenciarum parisius'.

1, 2. John of Ireland on the third and fourth books of the Sentences of Peter Lombard, the only known copy: cf. *The Meroure of Wyssdome by Johannes de Irlandia*, pt. 2, ed. F. Quinn (Scottish Text Society, 4th series, 2, 1965), p. xix.

3 (added, s. xvi in.). Two questions about mass: (*a*) ff. 253–254^v Queritur primo vtrum sacerdos obligatus ad dicendum missam pro vno obligatus eciam ad dicendum missam pro alio . . .; (*b*) ff. 254^v–255^v Sequitur de 2° articulo. Querit doctor noster vnam questionem Tu dixisti quod missa . . . (*ending perhaps imperfectly*).

ff. ii+255+i. f. ii is a contemporary flyleaf. Paper. 284×215 mm. Written space *c.* 250×185 mm. *c.* 44 long lines. No ruling. Collation: 1¹² wants 4, 5 damaged (ff. 1–11)

2–9¹² 10¹² wants 12, probably blank, after f. 118, 11¹² 12¹⁴ 13–18¹² 19¹⁶ 20¹² 21¹² wants 12. Arts. 1, 2 all in one current mixed cursiva and hybrida. No decoration beyond red paragraph marks. Binding of modern boards covered with old brown leather bearing a pattern of intersecting fillets: two clasps missing. Secundo folio *vnitum denominatur*.

Written in the Netherlands (?). Given by Hector Boece, †1537: 'Scripta magistri nostri Io de Irlandia sacre theologie professoris scoti parisiensis super tercium et 4ᵐ sentenciarum. Collegii aberdonen' dono magistri hectoris boetii primi primarii eiusdem', f. ii, s. xvi in. 'pro magistro Iohanne de Irlandia' and 'A Gallouay' (†*c.* 1552), f. 1, at top. King's College pressmark θ. 1. 18, f. ii.

679. *Petrarch, Trionfi (in Italian)* s. xv med.

1. ff. 1–46 CLARISSIMI VIRI DOMINI FRANCISCI PETRARCAE POETAE LAUREATI FLORENTINI LIBER TRIVMPHORVM INCIPIT TRIVMPHVS AMORIS Nel tempo che rinnuoua i miei sospiri . . . Orche fia adunque riuederla in cielo. FRANCISCI PETRARCE AETERNITATIS TRIVMPHORVM VI ET LIBER VNICVS FELICITER EXPLICIT VALE QVI LEGERIS.

Fully described by N. Mann, *Petrarch manuscripts in the British Isles* (Italia medioevale e umanistica, xviii), 1975, pp. 149–50. Three lines on f. 43 are supplied in the excellent hand of arts. 2, 3.

2. ff. 46ᵛ–47 Tabula triumphorum . . . . *Τέλος*.

Gives the first line of each part of the Triumphus amoris, Triumphus pudicitiae, Triumphus mortis, Triumphus famae, Triumphus temporis, and Triumphus aeternitatis, fourteen in all.

3. ff. 47ᵛ–48 Scriptum manu propria domini francisci Petrarcae poetae Laureati in quodam eius Virgilio uisum est. Laurea propriis virtutibus illustris: et meis longum celebrata carminibus . . . acriter ac uiriliter cogitanti. *Τέλος*. ff. 48ᵛ–50ᵛ blank.

Petrarch on Laura, lines first printed after the Triumphi in the Rome edition of 1473 from the Virgil 'in papiensi biblyotheca reperta', now Milan, Ambrosiana, MS. S.P. Arm. 10 scaf. 27 (formerly A. 49 inf.).

ff. i+50+i. 226×125 mm. Written space 168×70 mm. 24 long lines. Ruling with a hard point. The first line of writing is above the top ruled line. Collation: 1–5¹⁰. Quires numbered at the end. Art. 1 is in humanistica with a slight backward slope, by the same scribe as Balliol College, Oxford, 140.[1] Initials: (i) f. 1, gold on a blue ground, decorated in red and white; (ii) 3-line, blue. Binding of s. xvii (?). Secundo folio *Vna ombra*.

Written in Florence. Damaged armorial shields in the lower margin of f. 1. Book-plate of James Curle, LL.D., Priorwood, Melrose. His gift in 1925.

987. *'Recepte' P. de Tussignano, G. de Foligno, etc.* s. xv med.

1. ff. 2–7 (*Begins imperfectly*) Iste sunt medicine decocciones laxatiue patris mei cum quibusdam positis superius in medicinis cerebri communiter. Nunc ponam quasdam alias . . . fiat ungentum. Expliciunt recepte quas extraxi de quodam receptario patris mei magistri Antonii et magistri Bartholomei doctorum medicine.

---

[1] Information from Dr. A. de la Mare.

Nine leaves preceded f. 2. Of these, f. 1, now mostly illegible, remains. The running title 'Decocciones solutiue' shows that it came immediately before f. 2 (cf. art. 6).

2. ff. 7–31ᵛ Incipiunt quedam Recepte ordinate per reuerendum patrem meum magistrum Nicholaum de sancta sophia et primo ponam syrupos. Primus syrupus est . . .

Thorndike and Kibre. The series of recipes is interrupted on ff. 19ᵛ–22ᵛ by consilia under four headings: 'magistri vgutionis de padua'; 'magistri nicholai'; 'nescio cuius'; 'magistri Alberti de Zanchariis bononiensis doctoris physice facultatis. Consilium ordinatum pro domino Marchione spineta'.

3. ff. 32–45ᵛ Incipiunt Recepte super nonum Almansoris secundum Ghirardum etc. Item primo circa passiones capitis et primo in materia calida sanguinea. Recipe prunorum dalmaseni . . . cum medicina vomitu vel cristerei(?).

Followed on f. 46 by a 'Registrum receptarum super nono Almansoris 2ᵐ Giraldum et primo circa passiones capitis'. f. 46ᵛ, left blank, contains Latin and German verses added in s. xvi.

4. ff. 47–89ᵛ Hic est tractatus pulcherrimus assumens receptas bonas et vtiles a capite vsque ad pedes . . . conpilatus per eggregium arcium et medicine doctorem M. Iohannem [blank] 1385 tempore quo legat nonum Almansorem in Vrbe. In descripcione medicinarum seu receptarum conueniencium . . . Tractatus primus. Incipiamus primo a colera. Medicine simplices digestiue colere sunt hec viola rosa . . . (f. 88ᵛ) et applicetur membro dolenti et sic est finis huius tractatus.

Thorndike and Kibre (Petrus de Tussignano). Printed after Rhases, Nonus liber Almansoris, in ed. 1483 and later. The nine tractates are listed on f. 88ᵛ. The ninth, ff. 51ᵛ–88ᵛ, 'De egritudinibus a capite usque ad pedes 2ᵐ ordinem almansoris', has ninety-three chapters, listed on ff. 88ᵛ–89ᵛ. Two lines of verse after the text, f. 88ᵛ, 'Fallere flere nere statuit deus in muliere' and 'Femina fallere falsaque dicere quando carebit': Walther, Sprichwörter, nos. 8751, 9048.

5. ff. 89ᵛ–92 Notes and recipes, beginning with a note on electuaries and unguents.

6 (added, s. xv ex). ff. 92ᵛ–94 A table of contents of ff. '1–40', i.e. of the present ff. 1–32 and the eight missing leaves. f. 94ᵛ blank.

7. ff. 95–170 Incipiunt quedam consilia gentilis de fuligno doctoris eximii et incipiunt a capite . . . Sirupus pro fratre angelo . . . Isto modo curam in propria forma ponit Guilbertus anglicus. Et finiuntur hic consilia probissimi Gentilis. deo gracias.

Twenty chapters. Thorndike and Kibre. Cf. GKW 6515, etc.

8. ff. 170ᵛ–171ᵛ Hic secuntur quedam Cyrugicalia et descripciones quarundam medicinarum nominatarum in consiliis predictis etc. Ad apostemata et vlcera . . . (ends imperfectly).

ff. ii+172+ii, foliated (i, ii) 1–156, 156*, 157–71 (172–3). A foliation probably of s. xvi in. is '10–54' on ff. 2–46 and '61–185' on ff. 47–170. Paper. 305 × 210 mm. Written space 220 × 145 mm. 2 cols. 39–46 lines. Frame ruling in pencil. Collation: 1 four (no doubt 1¹² wants 1–8) 2–4¹² 5 six (ff. 41–6: no doubt 5¹² wants 7–12, perhaps blank) 6–15¹² 16 eight (ff. 164–71). Strengthening strips of parchment laid down the centres of quires 2–8 are cut across a bifolium of a grammatical (?) manuscript of s. xiii. Written in cursiva, arts. 4, 5 by one hand, art. 3 by another and arts. 1, 2, 7, and the index to art. 3 by a third: *i* is dotted. Red initials, 3-line, 2-line, and 1-line. Bound by Maltby, Oxford, in 1934. Written probably in Germany.

ABERYSTWYTH. NATIONAL LIBRARY OF WALES

The library was founded in 1909.

Catalogues. **1.** *Report on manuscripts in the Welsh language*, HMC 1898–1905, 2 vols. **2.** J. H. Davies, *Catalogue of 'Additional' Manuscripts in the Collections of Sir John Williams, Bart.*, 1921. **3.** *Handlist of Manuscripts in the National Library of Wales*, 1940– (in progress).

1 includes over eighty medieval or very early sixteenth-century manuscripts now in the National Library: about sixty-five (Hengwrt-)Peniarth manuscripts in Welsh and a few (Peniarth 28, 42, 43, 119, 162i) in Latin, listed in i. 297–1124; Mostyn MSS. 88, 116, 117, 184 (now N.L.W. 3026, 3035, 3036, 3063), listed in i. 16, 56, 62, 274; Llanstephan MSS. 1–4, 6, 10, 27–9, 116, 175, 176, 196, 199 (these last four in Latin),[1] 200, listed in ii. 419–793. These came to the National Library in 1909, 1918, and 1909 respectively. The manuscripts listed in **2** are N.L.W., 1–446: only 1A,[2] 76A, 423D (s. xv²), 442D, 443D, 444D, 445D, 446E are earlier than 1500. Thirty-one parts of **3** have been published. Parts 1–21 make three volumes, each with title-page, pagination, and indexes; vol. 1 (pts. 1–6), 1943; vol. 2 (pts. 7–12), 1950; vol. 3 (pts. 13–21), 1961. Considerable numbers of medieval manuscripts are listed only in pts. 1, 7, 8, forty-one on pp. 1–9, 18, 26–7 of pt. 1, which covers Peniarth 328–532 (**1** ends with MS. 327)[3] and N.L.W., 447–500, and thirty-eight in pts. 7, 8 among the 148 (MSS. 5001–148) from the collection formed by F. W. Bourdillon (1851–1921): most of these Bourdillon manuscripts are in French.

Outside part 1 and the Bourdillon collection the following medieval manuscripts are listed in the *Handlist*.

572D. s. xv². Medical recipes and a herbal (Agnus Castus) in English, Latin, and Welsh.

733B. s. xv. Piers Plowman. See *NLWJ* ii. 48.

735C. s. xi¹–xi². Astronomia. See *NLWJ* xviii. 197.

---

[1] **175.** Chronicon Angliae, etc. s. xiv. Belonged to Edward Dering. Ashburnham App. 104. Sale 1 May 1899, lot 53. **176.** Glanville, Register of writs, Geoffrey of Monmouth. s. xiii². Phillipps MS. 9162. **196.** Geoffrey of Monmouth. s. xv. Belonged to W. Bowyer in 1555. **199.** Abbo of Fleury, Vita S. Edmundi, and Samson, Super miraculis S. Edmundi, with marginalia in Welsh. s.xiii in.

[2] The letters A–F after National Library numbers show that the height measured on the outside of the bindings is under 181, 229, 281, 335, 429 mm and over 429 mm respectively.

[3] The history of the Peniarth collection is in pt. 1, pp. i–xxiii. Peniarth MSS. 366, 386, 388, 481 are described in *NLWJ*: i. 105; i. 119; xviii. 87; ii. 38.

1222D. s. xv. Cassianus, De coenobiorum institutis, etc. From St. Maynulf, Paderborn. See *NLWJ* ii. 4. Römer, ii. 20.

1478C. s. xiv. W. Brito, Vocabularium Bibliae. Phillipps MS. 12308.

1609D,iv. s. xv. Comment. in Metaphysica Aristotelis (fragm.: ff. 6).

1610F,i. s. xiii². Petrus Pictaviensis, Chronicon (fragm., Esau-St. Joseph: ff. 4).

1611E. s. xiii ex. Expositiones Canonis Missae Innocentii III, Odonis Cameracensis, Ricardi de Wedinghausen, etc.

2050B. s. xv. Quaestiones in libros Aristotelis de anima; Ars algorismi; etc.

3020E. s. xv–xvi. Descriptio Angliae, etc. Mostyn MS. 172. HMC, *4th Report*, App. p. 354.

3024C. s. xiv ex. Giraldus Cambrensis. Mostyn MS. 83. See *NLWJ* ii. 7; HMC, *4th Report*, App. p. 350.

3074D. s. xiii. Giraldus Cambrensis. Mostyn MS. 264. HMC, *4th Report*, App. p. 362.

3090C. s. xiv¹–xiv². W. Brito, Vocabularium Bibliae (abbrev.), etc.

4874E. s. xii ex.-xv. Fragmenta. Römer, ii. 20, notices a leaf and twenty-six initials of Augustine, In Psalmos, s. xiv ex.

4920E. s. xv. Lactantius. Phillipps MS. 4086.

4997C. s. xiii ex. Epistolae Pauli.

5266B. s. xiii. Geoffrey of Monmouth (in Welsh: 'Brut Dingestow').

5267B. s. xv. Miscellaneous prose in Welsh.

5667E. s. xiv. Les Aventures de Tristran (in French).

6133–6B. s. xv. J. Diest, Spirituale Granarium Psalmorum (4 vols.). From the Augustinian priory of Groenendael, near Brussels.

6680C. s. xiv–xv. Poems in Welsh.

6985E. A.D. 1457. Boccaccio (in Italian). Written by Ambrugio Spezzaferro d'Archi.

7006D. s. xiv–xv. 'The Black Book of Basingwerk' (in Welsh).

7851D. s. xiii–xvi. Cartularium Abbatiae S. Petri de Salopesberia. Davis, *MC*, no. 895.

7855A. s. xv. New Testament (fragm.: Matthew 6: 4–13: 4) in the later Wycliffite version.

8431B. s. xv. R. Holcot, Moralitates.

9852C. s. xv. Kalendarium. From the collegiate church of St. John, Beverley.

11330D. s. xiv. J. de Voragine, Legenda aurea (fragm.: ff. 22). Leaves taken from the bindings of notebooks of William Lloyd, 1627–1717: see *NLWJ* xi. 174–6.

11611C. s. xii ex. Gesta Alexandri Magni, etc. Duke of Newcastle (Clumber) sale at Sotheby's, 14 Feb. 1938, lot 1201: facsimile in the sale catalogue.

12389E. A.D. 1454. Genealogia Regum Anglorum ad Henricum VI. Phillipps MS. 3835.

13052E. s. xiii. G. Monemutensis. Phillipps MS. 32.

The following acquired before 1974 are not yet recorded in the *Handlist*.[1]

13210D. s. xiii. G. Monemutensis. From the abbey of Robertsbridge, O.C. Phillipps MS. 26233. Sale at Sotheby's, 30 Nov. 1971, lot 499.

15536E. s. xiv. Missale (Sherbrooke Missal: Yates Thompson, 94).

15537C. s. xv. Horae (de Grey Hours: Yates Thompson, 27).

16147A. s. xv. Breviarium.

16338C. s. xi/xii. Missale (fragm.: ff. 2).

16347A A.D. 1510–11. Compilationes fratris Petri de Moguntia.

16983B. s. xiii. Sermones. Phillipps MS. 12313.

16986A. s. xiv. Statuta Angliae.

17110E. s. xii. 'Liber Landavensis'.

See W. Davies, 'Liber Landavensis: its construction and credibility', *EHR* lxxxviii (1973), 335–51.

17430B. s. xv. R. Higden, Polychronicon (excerpta).

17520A. s. xiv ex. Horae (Llanbeblig (Caernarvon) Hours). Dyson Perrins MS. 15 (G. F. Warner, *Descriptive Catalogue*, p. 59): sale at Sotheby's, 29 Dec. 1960, lot 115.

18951C. s. xv. Gesta Romanorum.

18952C. s. xiv. W. Brito, Vocabularium Bibliae (abbrev.). Belonged to Lord Somers, 1651–1716: Th. 15 in his collection. Sale at Sotheby's, 7 Dec. 1964, lot 147.

20143A. s. xiv. Welsh Laws (in Welsh).

20541E. s. xiv. Antiphonale.

AMPLEFORTH ABBEY

Brief notices of MSS. 8, 14, 16, 17, 182–4, 187, 190–1 are in Joseph Stevenson's report, HMC, *Second Report* (1874), App., p. 109, nos. 7, 2, 5, 4, 10, 6, 3, 8, 12, 11, 9. Descriptions of MSS. 274–7 by Father Justin McCann are in *Ampleforth*

[1] I am most grateful to Mr. B. G. Owens and Mr. Daniel Huws for information about these manuscripts and other help with this notice.

Journal, li (1946), 112–16.[1] MSS. 8, 14–17, 184 may have the same recent history as MS. 183, that is to say, they may have been bound up with printed books until some time in s. xix[2].

Ampleforth probably owes its manuscripts and early printed books from religious houses in Hildesheim to Fr. Adrian Towers who was a monk of the English Benedictine house of Lamspring, near Hildesheim, until its dissolution in 1802, and subsequently of Ampleforth.

8. *Tractatus de superstitionibus; F. de Mayronis, De indulgentiis*

s. xv med.

1. ff. 1–75ᵛ Incipit tractatus de supersticionibus. Utrum ydolatrie peccatum sit peccatorum grauissimum arguitur quod non peccatum ydolatrie nichil est igitur non est peccatum grauissimum . . . semper et presupposicione diuine voluntatis etc amen. Explicit tractatus de supersticionibus deo G.

2 (filling the quire). ff. 76–83 [Q]uodcumque ligaueris super terram erit ligatum et in celis . . . Beatus aug' xxi et xxii de ci dei duos fines ultimos . . . horror inhabitat a quo nos defendat . . . Amen. Explicit tractatus de indulgenciis editus a fratre francisco de maronis fratrum minorum sacre theologie doctore.

Printed as the sermon for Chains of Peter, but with a different ending: ed. Basel 1498, ff. xciii–c.

ff. i+83+i. Paper. 308×220 mm. Written space *c.* 235×140 mm. 2 cols. 46 lines. Frame ruling. Collation: 1–6¹² 7¹⁰+1 leaf after 10. Cursiva: the hand changes at f. 76. 4-line red initial *U*, f. 1. Binding as on MS. 183.
Written perhaps in the Netherlands.

14, pp. 1–31. *J. de Lineriis*

s. xv/xvi

1. pp. 1, 2 Tabula sinus.

2. pp. 3–17 Canon primus. Cuiuslibet arcus propositi sinum rectum inuenire. Sinus rectus est medietas corde portionis arcus . . . ex parte aquilonis.

Thorndike and Kibre (J. de Lineriis). Forty-four canons. pp. (iii), 18–31 blank.

A quire of sixteen leaves of paper. The pagination begins on the verso of the first leaf. 298×217 mm. Written space 245×170 mm. 2 cols. 60 lines. Bound up before twelve

---

[1] Two manuscripts a little too late for *MMBL* are: 278, sixty-nine leaves with prayers in Netherlandish, one of them indulgenced by Pope Leo X (1513–21), followed by the penitential psalms and a litany in Latin: book-plate of Henry Curwen; 279, a quire of twelve leaves containing an 'Ordo ad reconciliandum hereticum' written in Spain. For the Caldbeck missal deposited at Ampleforth see under Carlisle, St. Mary's Catholic Church.
I am grateful to Fr. Barnabas Sandeman, O.S.B., and Fr. Placid Spearritt, O.S.B., for the help they have given me in making these descriptions.

leaves containing Paulus Germanus de Middelburgo, Compendium correctionis Calen-
darii pro recta pasche celebratione (pp. 32–40), a letter of Pope Leo X to the emperor
Maximilian (pp. 40, 41) and other texts, s. svi in. Hybrida. Binding uniform with that of
MS. 183.
Written in Germany.

15. *Gerhardus de Monte; T. Aquinas, Opuscula; etc.*   s. xv²

1. pp. 1–70 [I]nsignis peripo*tetic*e veritatis interpres doctor sanctus nedum
adultos prouehere . . . institui prelibare. Queritur itaque primo vtrum de ente et
essencia sit aliqua sciencia . . . set luc*is* eternaliter amen.

Gerhardus de Monte. Printed at Cologne, *c.* 1485: Goff, G. 169. The colophon of the
printed edition calls it a 'Commentatio . . . compilata circa compendium de quidditatibus
rerum. quod edidit Sanctus Thomas de Aquino'.

Arts. 2–14 are short pieces mostly printed among the philosophical works of St.
Thomas. Except 5, 13, 14 they follow art. 1 in the same order in Munich, Univ.
2° 49, ff. 108–203ᵛ. 2, 3, 5–13 are Glorieux, no. 14*di, dn, cn, ce, ch, dm, br, g,
dl, cd, ds*.¹

2. pp. 71–93 [Q]uoniam omnis creatura generis limitibus . . . ille a deo sunt qui
est super omnia benedictus amen.

De natura generis.

3. pp. 93–4 Sequitur tr(actatus) de principio indiuiduationis. [Q]uoniam due
sunt potentie cognoscitiue . . .

Ends imperfectly in the sentence beginning 'Hoc autem non': ed. M. de Maria, 1886,
ii. 258/11. There is a large gap here, as the Munich manuscript shows.

4. pp. 95–6 (*begins imperfectly*) efficiens semper quia ad principium . . . ab eo
qui est super omnia benedictus in secula amen.

The end of the De productione formae substantialis in esse of Thomas Sutton (Emden,
BRUO, p. 1824), as Vatican, Ottob. lat. 198, ff. 222ᵛ–223.

5. pp. 96–7 Sequitur epistola b(eati) th(ome) ad dominam ducem (*sic*) brabancie
de iudiciis astrorum. [Q]uia petisti ut tibi scriberem . . . iudiciis astrorum vti.

6. pp. 97–8 Sequitur tr(actatus) b(eati) th(ome) de commixtion(e) ele(men-
torum). [D]ubium apud multos esse solet . . . uirtus illorum.

7. pp. 98–101. Se(quitur) libellus b(eati) thom(e) de perpetuitate mundi.
[S]upposito secundum fidem katholicam . . . afferre. Et hec de eternitate mundi
sufficiunt pro presenti.

8. pp. 102–8 [Quoniam omnem duratio]nem comitatur . . . a quo omnia alia
sunt et omnia bona cuius bonitatis particeps nos faciat filius virginis ihesus
cristus amen.

De instantibus.

9. pp. 108–11 [Q]uoniam in quibusdam naturalibus corporibus . . . procedentes.
Et hec de operibus et accionibus occultis nature ad presens dicta sufficiunt.

---

¹ I owe the identification of arts. 4 and 15 and the reference to the Munich manuscript
to the Revd. H. Dondaine, O.P.

10. pp. 111–17 [Q]uoniam quoddam potest esse licet non sit . . . sunt principia ceterorum.

De principiis naturae.

11. pp. 117–30 Sequitur de natura materie. [P]ostquam sermo completus est de principiis nature remansit plenius . . . ut dicitur in primo phisicorum.

12. pp. 131–3. [Q]uoniam omne quod mouetur . . . calesit et infrigidatur.
De motu cordis.

13. p. 134 [C]irca consideracionem ca^i cōm vniuersalis oportet te scire quare sensus sit singularium . . . set non est sensus. hec de vniuersali et singulari sufficiunt.

De sensu respectu singularium et intellectu respectu universalium.

14. pp. 133–40 Sequitur t(ractatus). [Q]ueritur de natura vniuersalis et quod vniuersale esse habeat satis planum est . . . et differencia constare dicit. Et ideo intencionem (*ends imperfectly*).

Tractatus de Universalibus attribuito a San Tommaso d'Aquino, ed. C. Ottaviano, Rome, 1932, pp. 35–50/14. Half the text is missing.

15. pp. 183–204, 141–82 (*begins imperfectly*) hec autem indicatiua . . . superueniamus (*ends imperfectly*).

Aristotle, Ethics, vi. 8–vii. 8, vii. 14–x. 1: ed. *Aristoteles Latinus*, xxvi. 485/16–507/3, 516/26–564/24. pp. 205–6 blank.

ff. i+103+i, paginated (i, ii), 1–(208). Paper. 293 × 200 mm. Written space c. 230 × 145 mm. 2 cols. c. 50 lines (art. 15, c. 25 long lines). Collation: 1–2¹² 3¹² wants 12, probably blank, after p. 70 4–5¹² 6¹² wants 12 after p. 140 7¹² (pp. 183–206) 8¹² wants 1–3 before p. 141 9¹²: quires missing between quires 4 and 5 and between quires 6 and 7. Arts. 1–14 in a very current hand. Art. 15 in larger script and better written. Coloured initials not filled in. Bound like MS. 183.

Written in Germany.

16. *De modo legendi abbreviaturas in utroque jure*   s. xv med.

Incipit liber dans modum legendi abbreuiaturas in vtroque iure. Quia preposterus ordo et prius . . . siue vsus feudorum habet titulos lxxxi. Explicit libellus dans modum studendi et legendi contenta ac abbreuiata vtriusque iuris deo laus sit per infinita secula seculorum amen.

Printed often: Goff, M. 741–60. The end here agrees with ed. 1488 (Goff, M. 748). f. 44^{rv} blank.

ff. i+44+i. Paper. 285 × 200 mm. Written space 245 × 140 mm. c. 41 long lines. Frame ruling. Collations: 1–3¹² 4 eight. Red and green initials. Binding as MS. 183.
Written in Germany.

17. *Pius II, Bulla; etc.*   s. xv²

(*a*) ff. 1^v–7^v Pius episcopus seruus seruorum dei . . . Ezechielis prophete magni sentencia est venientem gladium . . . (*b*) f. 1 Pius papa ii. Venerabilis frater salutem . . . Mittet ad fraternitatem tuam ex mandato nostro tuus Metropolita exemplum autenticum litterarum apostolicarum quas nuper edidimus. Per eas videbis . . . . (c) f. 1ʳᵛ Venerabili fratri Episcopo Hildensemen' Adolffus dei gracia Electus et Confirmatus Magunt' etc' Sacri Romani Imperii Princeps Elector Reuerendo in cristo patri domino Ernesto Episcopo hildem' Consanguineo nostro Carissimo. Post sinceram . . . Recipimus paucis effluxis diebus certas litteras apostolicas . . .

(a) is the bull of Pope Pius II of Oct. 1463, urging action against the Turks: *Opera*, ed. 1551, pp. 914–23 (Ep. 412). (b) and (c) are short explanatory letters designed to accompany (a), (b) from the Pope, 10 Nov. 1463, and (c) from Adolf von Nassau, archbishop of Mainz, to Bishop Ernst von Schaumburg of Hildesheim, 31 Jan. 1464.

ff. i+7. 283 × 210 mm. Written space *c.* 210 × 150 mm. *c.* 40 long lines. Collation: 1⁸ wants 8. The third sheet, ff. 3, 6, is in a different hand from the rest. Spaces for initials not filled. Binding as MS. 183.

Written in Germany (Hildesheim?).

178. *P. Riga, Aurora* s. XIII in.

The 'second edition' of the Aurora, as set out in the edition by P. E. Beichner, 1965, p. xviii, except that the Recapitulationes follow Maccabees.

f. 1, Preface, 'Frequens sodalium . . . illuxit'. f. 1 Genesis. f. 17ᵛ Exodus. f. 32ᵛ Leviticus. f. 40ᵛ Numbers. f. 47 Deuteronomy. f. 50 'Liber yosue'. f. 52ᵛ Judges. f. 56 Ruth. f. 56ᵛ 1 Kings. f. 62 2 Kings. f. 66 3 Kings. f. 70ᵛ 4 Kings. f. 71ᵛ Tobit, ending with line 508, 'Explicit expositio bede presbiteri super tobiam' and lines 509–11. f. 76ᵛ Daniel. f. 85 Judith. f. 87 Esther. f. 90 1, 2 Maccabees. f. 94ᵛ Verses 'sine a', etc. f. 99ᵛ 'Incipiunt nomina antiquorum patrum', followed by lines 469–74. f. 99ᵛ 'Finito de patribus antiquis. Incip' de nouis', followed by lines 475–82. f. 100 Gospels, ending on f. 131ᵛ, 'Dat finem petrus finit et ipse suum Explicit [. . . . . .].

Headings on ff. 4, 6ᵛ, 8 show that bks. 2, 3, 4 begin at lines 285, 521, 707 respectively: cf. ed., p. xvii. Spaces for heading have not been filled in quire 5. 'Usque ad locum istum est emendatum' in the margin, f. 94ᵛ, opposite Maccabees, line 446: the emendation includes notes of absent verses in the margins of f. 39, 'Hic carent xiiii [. . .]', f. 40ᵛ 'Hic deficiunt decem', f. 94ᵛ 'Hic desi. xxxi linee'.

ff. v+131+iv. ff. v, 132, 133 are medieval parchment end-leaves. 235 × 145 mm. Written space *c.* 180 mm high. 49–51 long lines. Writing above top ruled line. Collation: 1–6⁸ 7⁶ 8⁸ 9 three (ff. 63–5) 10¹⁰ 11–17⁸. Quires 1–3 numbered at the beginning. Hand changes at f. 66. Initials: (1) f. 1, a dragon of red, green, and blue penwork; (2) 2-line, red or blue, with ornament of the other colour. The capital letter beginning each line has been marked with red only on ff. 17–32ʳ. Russia binding of s. xix: see below. Secundo folio *Hos latices*.

Written in Italy. Erasures on ff. 1, 131ᵛ, 'Iste liber est [. . . . . .] dioc' ' (s. xiv). Ex-libris of St. Mary of Graces, near Mantua, f. v, s. xv: 'Biblia in metro loci Sancte Marie g[ra]cia]rum extra Mantuam'. 'Aurora petri sex flor' et o' ', f. 131ᵛ, s. xiv. 'Q. 3 of Rodd, 1840 bound by Gough. T.' in ink on f. iii, and below in pencil '4905'. The relevant slip from an English catalogue of s. xix is pasted to f. vᵛ. Armorial book-stamp of Edmund Macrory (†1904) on the covers.

180. *G. de Cauliaco, etc.* s. xv med.

1. ff. 1–33ᵛ In dei nomine incipit inuentorium seu collectorium in parte cyrurgicali medicine compilatum et completum Anno domini Mᵒ cccᵒ lxiiiᵒ per gwidonem de cahulhiaco cyrurgicum magistrum in medicina in preclaro studio montispessulani. Postquam prius gracias egero deo largienti vitam perpetuam animarum . . . propter virtutem epatis seruandam esset melius (*ends abruptly*).

Guy de Chauliac, Cyrurgia. The last words here are the last of the third section, De duritia hepatis, of Doct. II, cap. 6 (ed. 1585, p. 109/34). ff. 33*–34ᵛ blank.

2. ff. 35–42ᵛ (*text*) Vita breuis ars longa . . . (*commentary*) Iste liber est amphorismorum ypocratis In quo ostendit ypocras non vniuersaliter .... (*text*) hiis humectantur.

Hippocrates, Aphorismi, intended for a surrounding commentary, but only one leaf of commentary was completed and the headings cease on f. 37.

3. f. 43ʳᵛ [*blank*] alteratus in corde ad id quod est preter naturam . . . Differunt eciam ista duo (*ends imperfectly*).

On fevers. The scribe left a space for the rubricator to put in the first word in colour, but he never did so.

ff. i+44+i, foliated (i), 1–33, 33*, 34–43, (44). Paper. 400×275 mm. Written space 265×160 mm. 2 cols. 60 lines. Ruling with a hard point in arts. 1, 2. Collation: 1–3¹⁰ 4¹⁰ wants 7–10 (ff. 31–3, 33*, 34, 43) 5⁸ (ff. 35–42). Worm-holes show that f. 43 has long been where it now is. Written in hybrida of two sizes. Red initials of several sizes. After f. 15 the spaces for initials have only been filled on f. 35. Binding like that of MS. 183. Secundo folio *a pluribus.*

Written in Italy. 'Iste liber pertinet magistro [. . . . .]' scratched on f. 42ᵛ.

182. *Tertia pars Malogranati* 1459

1. (f. 2ᵛ) Incipit liber tercius malogranati tractans de statu perfectorum in quibus consistit status perfectorum. Cap' primum. Filius. Postquam informatus sum a te o pater . . . (f. 225) Ad que inenarrabilia bona eterne glorie perducat nos dominus noster ihesus cristus qui . . . Amen. Explicit liber qui intitulatur malogranatum.

Bk. 3 of the Malgranatum attributed by Trithemius to Gallus, abbot of Königsaal, O.C., Bohemia. Preceded by a table of fifty-one chapters, headed, f. 2, 'Incipit Registrum in librum tercium Malogranati'. ff. 1ʳᵛ, 225ᵛ–226ᵛ were left blank.

2. The pastedowns are leaves cclxxx and cclxxxv of a missal of s. xiv in. in two columns of thirty lines and with a written space of 257×180 mm. They contain votive masses and masses for the dead.

ff. i+226, foliated 1–168, 168*, 169–226. 315×225 mm. Written space 220×145 mm 2 cols. 37 lines. Frame ruling in ink. Writing above the top ruled line. Collation: 1–28⁸ 29². The quires, except the last, are signed a–z, ꝫ, ÷, –, ꝩ, con. Written in set hybrida. In spite of the absence of ruling, apart from the frame, the scribe maintained a level line and the same number of lines to the page throughout. Punctuation includes the flex (7). Black ink. Initials: (i) f. 2ᵛ, 8-line, red and blue, with ornament of both colours and a partial filling of olive-green; (ii, iii) 3-line and 2-line, red or blue; (iv) in capitula, f. 2^{rv}, 1-line, red. Capital letters in the ink of the text are marked with red. Contemporary binding of wooden boards, covered with brown leather, rebacked, no doubt Hildesheim work (cf. MSS. 183, 185): horizontal and vertical fillets form a border and diagonal fillets subdivide the enclosed panel: stamps of the four evangelists, one in each corner of the border, and stamps of nine different patterns elsewhere, three, one of them inscribed 'maria', in the side borders, three, one of them inscribed 'ihesus', in the borders at head and foot, and three within the panel: metal tips at the corners: five bosses on each cover and two clasps now missing. Secundo folio *one eos.*

Written in 1459 for the use of the nuns of St. Mary Magdalene, Hildesheim: 'Anno domini millesimo quadringentesimo quiquagesimo nono presens liber scriptus est et datus pro vtilitate sororum sancte Marie Magdalene prope et extra muros hilden'. Orate ergo pro huius datoribus vt nomina eorum in libro vite scribantur Hoc est sine fine viuant', f. 1.

183. *'Materia passionis domini'* s. XV ex.

Passio domini nostri ihesu ad quinque principalia puncta siue articulos reduci potest. Et sunt hec. prodicio detestabilis . . . ille nos dignetur perducere qui . . . amen. Explicit materia passionis domini nostri ihesu cristi.

Five parts: 2, p. 26; 3, p. 36; 4, p. 45; 5, p. 58. pp. iii, iv, the first leaf of quire 1, left blank.

ff. i+31+i, paginated (i–iv), 1–60, (61, 62). Paper. 305×215 mm. Written space *c.* 240×160 mm. 2 cols. *c.* 42–9 lines. No ruling. Collation: 1–2^{10} 3^{10}+1 leaf after 10. Written in hybrida. Bound in s. xix^2.

Written in Germany. Formerly, until 1870, bound in front of C. V. 30, Durandus, Rationale diuinorum, Nuremberg 1481 (*GKW* 9123). The printed book is in contemporary binding of wooden boards covered with brown leather with stamps of eight patterns arranged in a typically Hildesheim pattern: the Ihesus stamp at the foot and the Maria stamp at the side are smaller than the corresponding stamps on the binding of MS. 182, but larger than those on MS. 185. 'prepositus in esscherde nec non plebanus in vallens' est possessor huius libri', p. iii.

184. *Jacobus de Jueterbogk, Ord. Carth., De restitutione ablatorum* s. XV/XVI

1. ff. 1–60^v Incipit liber de resticucione ablatorum domini doctoris Iacobi Carthusiensis. Attollens mentis oculos in latissimum alueum tocius orbis contemplor . . . et ad viam proficiant salutis Amen Deo gracias.

Fourteen chapters, subdivided in the margins by letter-marks which are used also as a means of reference in the table on ff. 60^v–64, 'Absenti . . . Cristianus . . . Explicit Registrum'. For a long list of works, including De Restitucionibus, by this Erfurt Carthusian see *MBDS* ii. 708–11.

2. f. 64^{rv} Nota quod bellare est licitum laycis.et non clericis et quare. Circa bellum consideranda sunt tria . . . sint irregulares. Hec beatus thomas. secunda secunde q xl arti. ii cor. 9 et in solucione iiii.

An abbreviation and rearrangement of Aquinas, *Secunda Secundae*, q. 40, art. 2.

ff. i+68+i. Paper. 295×200 mm. Written space 230×140 mm. 2 cols. 31–6 lines.

Frame ruling. Collation: 1–5¹² 6⁸. Written in hybrida. Metallic red initials, 5-line and 3-line. Capital letters in the ink of the text marked with red. Binding of s. xix², like that of MS. 183. Secundo folio *penas*.

Written in Germany.

185. *Caesarius Arelatensis, Sermones; etc.* s. xv med.

1. ff. i^v, 1–97 Incipiunt exhortaciones beati Cesarii arelatensis episcopi. Ad monachos Sermo primus de prelatorum sollicitudine et subditorum instancia. (f. 1) Vereor in cristo venerabiles filii ne dum vobis pro seruanda quiete . . .

Thirty-two pieces, the first sixteen (ff. 1–51), nos. 1, 5, 7–13, 15–17, 20–2, 18 of Morin's Collectio C and the second sixteen (ff. 51–97^v), nos. 1–3, 6, 7, 10, 8, 13, 14, 16, 18, 19, 34–7 of Morin's Collectio A: cf. G. Morin, *Sancti Caesarii Arelatensis Sermones* (Corpus Christianorum, ciii), pp. xl–xliii, xlv–li. The title, written here on an otherwise blank leaf, is like that noted by Morin, pp. xli, xlii, from several Netherlandish manuscripts. The first sermon is conflated, as in Morin's C. 1 and other late copies. The first sixteen sermons, i.e. those of Collectio C, are, with one exception, numbered: the series runs 1–8, 10, 11, 9, 12, 13, no number, 14, 15.

2. ff. 97–8^v Sermo exhortacionis. Ammonet nos beatus apostolus ut de dormientibus . . . spiritaliter amant.

PL xxxviii. 936–7 (Augustine, sermo 172). Follows Collectio A in several manuscripts: cf. Morin, pp. xlix, l, 956.

3. ff. 98^v–100 Sermo. Scire debet vestra fraternitas dilectissimi fratres in domino quod sicut homo ex carne . . . et patriam . . .

4. ff. 100–1 Sermo de sacerdotibus. Pauci sunt fratres in plebe ista qui intelligant . . . saluemini quod ipse . . .

5. ff. 101–2 Sermo de eodem. Timeo fratres periculum meum et vestrum si . . . liberabitis.

6. ff. 102–4 De dignitate clericorum. Audite fratres qui clerici vocamini et vos maxime . . . atque amanda . . .

7. ff. 104–6 Item sermo. Videte fratres quid dicimini. cristiani enim vocamini . . . ascendere. quod ipse . . .

8. ff. 106–8 Item sermo de operibus misericordie. Volumus vos fratres karissimi perfecte instruere in quantum . . . implendo. quod ipse . . .

9. ff. 108–12^v De septem capitalibus viciis. Nosse debet vestra fraternitas karissimi quod omnia opera in tribus diuisionibus . . . misericors dominus.qui . . . ff. 113–114^v blank.

10. The pastedown at the end is the last leaf of a collection of eighty-three sermons written in 1456: the text ends 'diligens et dilectus ihesus cristus dominus noster qui est super omnia deus benedictus in secula Amen. Explicit sermo lxxxiii^us Anno domini M° cccc° lvi [. . . .] Qui in contemplacione proficere uoluerit hunc librum attente perstudeat. [. . . . .].'

ff. i+114. 196×138 mm. Written space 138×83 mm. 28 long lines. Frame ruling with
double lines. Collation: 1–10⁸ 11¹⁰ 12–14⁸. Quires 1–11 signed a–l. Written in a good set
hybrida and black ink. Initials: (i) f. 1, 8-line, red and blue with red and green ornament,
partly on a ground of green; (ii) 2-line, red or blue. Capital letters in the ink of the text
marked with red. Contemporary (?) binding of wooden boards covered with pigskin
bearing stamps of six patterns: the design is like that on MS. 182 and three of the stamps
are common to both bindings (cf. also 183): central clasp.

Written in Germany. Belonged to the convent of brethren of the common life 'in horto
luminum' near Hildesheim, which existed from 1425 to 1538: 'Liber presbiterorum et
clericorum in orto luminum 'yn dem luchthoue' beate marie virginis prope hildensem in
brulone', f. i and f. 114ᵛ, s. xv.[1] Later, s. xviii, the ex-libris of the Benedictine abbey of
St. Michael, Hildesheim, was entered on f. iᵛ: 'Liber Monasterii S. Michaelis'.

187. *Horae*   s. XIV ex.

1. pp. i–iv Calendar in French in red and black, November and December only.

'Saint luis euesque', 13 Nov., and 'S' Ladre martir', 17 Dec., are in red.

2 (added). Prayers: (*a*) p.v, Domine ihesu criste qui hanc sacratissimam carnem
. . .; (*b*) p. vi, Dulcis domina adoro te et benedico beatissimos illos pedes . . .

3. pp. 1–95 Hours of B.V.M. of the use of (Sarum), with hours of the Cross and
hours of the Holy Spirit worked in.

Prime ends imperfectly on p. 48. Sext begins on p. 49. p. 96 is blank.

4. 97–132 Penitential psalms and (p. 119) litany.

Confessors are only ten, Martin, Martial, Gregory, Ambrose, Augustine, Jerome, Nicholas,
Benedict, Columbanus, and Julian.

5. pp. 133–96 Office of the dead.

6. pp. 197–203 Obsecro te . . .

7. pp. 203–9 Oracio beate marie. O intemerata . . . orbis terrarum. de te
enim . . .

Masculine forms: cf. art. 11.

8. pp. 209–12 Passio domini nostri ihesu cristi secundum Iohannem. Apprehendit pilatus ihesum . . . testimonium eius. Deo gracias. Deus qui manus
tuas . . .

9. pp. 212–13 Cruci corone spinee clauique . . .

A memoria of three Instruments of the Passion. Cf. *RH*, no. 3986 and Leroquais, *Livres
d'heures*, i. 186.

10. p. 213 Benedicatur hora qua deus homo natus est . . .

Cf. Leroquais, i. 150.

11. pp. 214–15 Sancte cristofore martir dei preciose rogo te per nomen conditoris tui . . .

A memoria of St. Christopher. Feminine forms.

[1] Cf. B. Kruitwagen, *Paleografica*, 1942, p. 77 and pl. opposite p. 78, no. VI; also R.
Doebner, *Annalen und Akten der Brüder des gemeinsamen Lebens in Luchtenhofe zu Hildesheim*, 1903.

12. pp. 218–20 Inicium sancti euangelii secundum iohannem. In principio . . .
(p. 220) Protector in te sperantium . . .

St. John 1: 1–14 and the prayer which commonly goes with it.

13 (added). pp. 221–4 Domine sancte pater eterne deus. In illa sancta custodia
. . .

ff. i+115+v. Paginated, flyleaves apart, i–vi, 1–224. 180×135 mm. Written space
105×75 mm. 15 long lines. Collations: 1 three 2–4⁸ 5⁸ wants 1 and 8 (pp. 49–60) 6–7⁸ 8²
(pp. 93–6) 9–15⁸ 16⁶ 17². A full-page St. Christopher on p. 217 after art. 11. Nineteen
stiff, but attractive 11-line pictures in rectangular frames and usually on chequered grounds,
eleven in art. 3, one before each of arts. 4, 5, and one after art. 10 (p. 214), but illustrating
art. 9 (Christ rises from the tomb: instruments of the Passion): in art. 3 there is no picture
before lauds of B.V.M. and the Visitation illustrates prime, shepherds sext, flight none,
kings vespers, and Presentation compline: terce is missing. The sets for Holy Cross and
Holy Spirit should have seven pictures each, but in each, prime and terce are missing.
Initials: (i) in colour, patterned in white, on gold and coloured grounds, the colour patterned in white and the gold decorated with oak leaves: prolongations in gold and colours
form continuous borders topped by grotesques; (ii) 2-line, gold on coloured grounds
patterned in white, with sprays into the margins; (iii) 1-line, as (ii), but no sprays, or blue
with red ornament. Capital letters in the ink of the text filled with yellow. Line fillers in
patterned red and blue and gold. Binding of s. xix. The old limp parchment binding is
kept separately: on the spine 'Heures Gothiques sur parchemin avec figures. Nº 5': as
lining part of two leaves of a document in French, s. xvi/xvii.

Written in France.

188. *Psalterium, Cantica, etc.*   s. xv med.

1. ff. 1–143 Psalms 1–150.

2. ff. 143–157ᵛ Six ferial canticles, Te deum, Benedicite, Benedictus, Magnificat, Nunc dimittis, Quicunque vult.

3 (added, s. xvi in.). (*a*) ff. iiiᵛ–ivᵛ Prayers of the litany. (*b*) f. ivᵛ Benedictiones
lectionum. (*c*) ff. v–xiiᵛ Twenty-nine hymns of the temporale from Advent to
Pentecost. (*d*) ff. 158–9 Eight hymns of the common of saints. (*e*) ff. 159–160ᵛ
Antiphons for each day of the week. (*f*) ff. 160ᵛ–161 Sequuntur preces et
Oraciones xxv psalmorum tempore xlᵐⁱ. Intret oracio nostra et cetera . . .

(*c*) includes the hymn Nuntium vobis (*AH* l. 283) at Epiphany. f. 161 is more than half
torn away: the verso blank.

ff. iii+171+iv, foliated (one unnumbered leaf), i–xii, 1–165. 170×112 mm. Written
space 110×70 mm. 22 long lines. Collation of ff. iii–xii, 1–161: 1² (ff. iii, iv) 2⁸ (ff. v–xii)
3–10⁸ 11⁸+1 leaf after 2 (f. 67) 12–15⁸ 16⁶ (ff. 106–11) 17–22⁸ 23² (ff. 161–2). Art. 3 in
hybrida by one hand. Initials in arts. 1, 2: (i) f. 1, in colour, patterned in white, on
decorated gold ground; (ii) 3-line, red and blue; (iii, iv) 2-line and 1-line, blue or red.
A border on two sides of f. 1. Binding of s. xviii, rebacked. Secundo folio (f. 2) *re.*
Apprehendite. Written in the Netherlands (?). In England by s. xviii. 'Robert Benson',
ff. 163ᵛ, 164ᵛ.

190. *Horae* s. xv²

1. ff. 1–12ᵛ Nearly full calendar in French, in red and black.

2. ff. 13–18 Sequentiae of the Gospels, with the prayer 'Protector in te sperantium . . .' after the extract from St. John.

3. ff. 18–21ᵛ Oracio valde deuota. Obsecro te . . .

4. ff. 21ᵛ–24ᵛ Oracio. O intemerata . . . orbis terrarum de te enim . . .

5. ff. 25–82 Hours of B.V.M. of the use of (Paris). f. 82ᵛ blank.

6. ff. 83–6 Hours of Holy Cross.

7. ff. 86ᵛ–89ᵛ Hours of Holy Spirit.

8. ff. 90–106 Penitential psalms and litany.

Thirteen confessors: . . . (3) Remigi . . . (5) Germane . . . (11–13) Ludouice. Fiacri. Anthoni. Genovefa eighth of 12 virgins. f. 106ᵛ blank.

9. ff. 107–42 Office of the dead.

10. ff. 142–146ᵛ Oracio valde deuota. Doulce dame de misericorde mere de
pitie . . .

Sonet, no. 458.

11. ff. 146ᵛ–149 Oracio ualde deuota. Doulx dieu doulx pere saincte trinite.

Sonet, no. 504.

12. f. 149 Saincte vraie croix aouree . . .

Sonet, no. 1876. f. 149ᵛ blank.

ff. i+149+iv. 162×113 mm. Written space 90×56 mm. 16 long lines. Collation:
1¹² 2⁸ 3⁴ (ff. 21–4) 4–18⁸ 19⁶ wants 6, blank. A 12-line picture before arts. 5–9 (6, Christ
bears his Cross; 8, David and Bathsheba; 9, hermit in front of his cave, and corpse). Four
smaller pictures in art. 2. Initials: (i) patterned mauve on grounds of colour and gold paint,
decorated with flowers; (ii, iii) 2-line and 1-line, gold on coloured grounds patterned in
white. Line fillers of patterned blue and red broken with blobs of gold. Compartmented
floral borders, partly on grounds of gold paint, surround pages with larger pictures, are on
three sides of the picture pages in art. 2, and run the height of the written space on the
outside of pages with initials of type (ii). Olive morocco binding, s. xvii, stamped all over
with double λ and double B, the bows of the Bs facing one another and interlacing (see
below). Secundo folio (f. 14) *qui credunt*.

Written in France. That the owner in s. xvii was Léon Bouthillier, Comte de Chavigny,
1618–52, is noted in a hand of s. xx on f. 150ᵛ, with a reference to J. Guigard, *Nouvel
armorial du bibliophile*, ii (1890), 84–5.

191. *Sermones, etc.* s. xiii med.–xiv med.

1 (quires 1–9). ff. 1–105ᵛ De natiuitate. Paruulus natus est nobis etc. B'.
Tanta est karissimi dominice natiuitatis sollempnitas . . .

Fifty-two sermons, according to the list on f. 106 (s. xiv), but the two last there, both 'De beata virgine', are missing. Nos. 1–24 (ff. 1–51ᵛ) are of the temporale from Christmas to the 18th Sunday after Pentecost, in the order of the church year.

2 (quire 10). ff. 107–114ᵛ In fide et lenitate sanctum fecit illum Ecc.xlv. (4) Duo sunt que hominem beatificant ut dicitur in uerbo preposito . . .

Seven sermons for unspecified occasions.

3 (quire 11). ff. 115–122ᵛ Habrahe dicte sunt . . . gala. iiii (Gal. 3: 16). In ewangelio istius dominice agitur de dileccione . . .

Sermons on epistle and gospel of the 13th to 16th Sundays after Pentecost, the last ending imperfectly.

4 (quires 12, 13). (a) ff. 123–131ᵛ Quasi stella matutina in medio nebule id est peccatorum proprie huius stelle matutine possunt referri ad quemlibet doctorum . . . Peremptorium iacere. Miris. Explicit stella clericorum. (b) ff. 132–8 Assit principio sancta maria meo. Dixerunt fratres eius ad eum transi hinc et vade in iudeam (John 7: 3). In hoc ewangelio reliquid nobis cristus magnum humilitatis exemplum . . . (c) ff. 138ᵛ–139, 141ᵛ–143 Miscellaneous notes for sermons, etc. (d) ff. 139ᵛ–141ᵛ Non est sine causa fratres karissimi quod preceptorum legis dei numerus . . . (e) f. 143ʳᵛ Verses: (1) Inuidus iratus elatus . . . (2 lines); (2) Gustus olfactus auditus . . . (2 lines); (3) Vnum crede deum nec iures . . . (4 lines); (4) Inpugnans verum desperans . . . (2 lines); (5) Ars amor et pietas . . . (2 lines); (6) Ordo coniugium fons . . . (2 lines); (7) Colligo cibo poto . . . (2 lines); (8) Iussio consilium confessus . . . (2 lines); (9) Clamitat in celis vox sanguinis . . . (2 lines). (f) f. 143ᵛ Virtutes principales. fides . . . (g) f. 143ᵛ De his debet fieri predicacio. Sacra fides vicium laus virtus penitencia pena.

(a). Popular in Germany and printed often (Hain 15060–80). (b). Six sermons, the first on the gospel for Tuesday in the 5th week of Lent and the others assigned to Friday in the 5th week of Lent, Palm Sunday, Holy Thursday (2), and Easter. (d). On the ten command-ments. (e). Commonplace verses, (1–3) on the seven sins, five senses, and ten command-ments, (4) 'In spiritum sanctum', (5–7) on the seven gifts, seven sacraments, and seven works of mercy, (8) on the 'ix peccata que rogant vindiciam', and (9) on the 'peccata que rogant vindiciam', mostly printed in copies of *Peniteas cito* and *Hortulus anime*: cf. for (1, 2) Walther, *Sprich-wörter*, nos. 12800, 10503, for (3, 6, 7) Walther, *Init.*, nos. 19669, 13452, 3031, and for (9) Walther, *S.*, no. 2786. (f, g) are in one hand.

5 (quire 14). ff. 144–154ᵛ [S]alomon rex irsahel (*sic*) in cuius pectore dominus benignissimus sui verbi potenciam ostendens . . . (f. 145) dei pietatem. . . (*list of fifteen chapters*) . . . (f. 145ᵛ) [I]ncipit prohemium siue excepciones quas magnus apollonius ad erudicionem omnium scienciarum . . . [E]go igitur apollonius omnium arcium magister . . . sciens ad eius exposissionem [........]

Thorndike and Kibre. Ends abruptly. A later hand, s. xvi in. (?), wrote at the head of f. 144 'Caueas tibi ab his oracionibus que sunt lacrime cocodrilli'. f. 155ʳᵛ blank.

6 (quire 15). ff. 156–160ᵛ Osculeter me osculo oris sui. vbi est aduertendum quantum igitur ad hystoriam . . .

A commentary on Song of Songs, ending abruptly in the exposition of 1:9. f. 161ʳᵛ blank. The quire is palimpsest, the underwriting perhaps of s. xii.

7 (quire 16). ff. 162–173ᵛ (*begins imperfectly*) nobis ucuales pro uilibus mercibus . . . sauc(i)ati vinum (*ends imperfectly*).

Nine sermons on the gospels of the temporale, the first and last incomplete. Nos. 2–9 are for Ascension Day, the Sunday following, and the 3rd, 4th, 8th, 9th, 11th, and 14th Sundays after Pentecost. No. 2 begins 'Duo occurrunt hic notanda. primum est quare dominus in celum assumptus esse dicatur'. No. 9 begins 'In presenti ewangelio iiii principalia sunt notanda. De primo nota quod per hominem istum quilibet homo cristi'. Sermons usually end with 'Rogate (*or* Rogamus) ergo dominum . . . ut . . .'. Cf. the sermons of Pseudo-Albertus Magnus listed by Schneyer and printed in *Alberti Magni Opera*, ed. Borgnet, xiii. 3–304: the last words here are in edn., p. 261/10.

8 (quire 17). (*a*) ff. 174–177ᵛ (*begins imperfectly*) illum. Exemplum huius cum beatus nycolaus videret sibi finem appropinquare . . . numquam de cetero (*ends imperfectly*). (*b*) ff. 178–181ᵛ Fourteen tales.

(*a*). Three sermons, only one of them complete. The gospel texts of nos. 2, 3 are for the 7th and 16th Sundays after Pentecost: no. 2 begins 'In hoc ewangelio duo possunt notari. Primo motus ire', and no. 3 'Quidam homo erat qui per industriam suam multa bona'. (*b*). No. 2 begins 'Narrat petrus damianus quod duo fuerunt simul in deserto' and no. 12 'Tempore beati bernhardi abbatis quidam decanus diues': 30,000 died on one day, of whom two, St. Bernard and the deacon, went to heaven, three to purgatory, and the rest to hell.

9 (quire 18). ff. 182–193ᵛ (*begins imperfectly*) eius. q.d. quia sapienter . . .

Notes and sermons, including one for the Annunciation (f. 184) and one for Philip and James (f. 192ᵛ) which ends imperfectly.

10 (quire 19). (*a*) ff. 194–7 (*begins imperfectly*) precepit inquid eis ab ierosolimis . . . (*b*) ff. 197–202ᵛ Tribus temporibus in anno seu festiuitatibus filii israhel debebant . . .

(*a*). On the Ascension and (f. 196) De operibus trinitatis. (*b*). The events of Holy Week, in badly faded ink and imperfect at the end.

11. The end-leaves, ff. i, ii, 203–4, a conjoint pair at each end of the book, are from a noted hymnal, s. xiv. Only the upper part of each leaf remains, on which there are the beginnings of ten hymns: (f. iʳᵛ) Deus tuorum militum sors et corona and Quem terra pontus; (f. iiʳᵛ) Pange lingua gloriosa prelium certaminis, Salue festa dies, and Quod chorus vatum; (f. 203ʳᵛ) Rex gloriose martirum, Urbs beata iherusalem, and Martir dei qui unicum; (f. 204ʳᵛ) Virginis proles and Gloria laus et honor tibi sit rex criste.

ff. ii+202+ii. ff. i and 204 were pasted down. Medieval foliation of ff. 1–105 i–cvᵐ in ink (also 1–015 (*sic*) in red ink). 155 × 115 mm. Written space *c*. 120 × 90 mm. 2 cols. and (quires 12–15, 17, 19) long lines. 33–4 lines (art.1). Collation: 1–8¹² 9 ten (ff. 97–106) 10⁸ 11¹⁰ wants 9, 10 after f. 122 12¹⁴ 13¹⁰ 1–3 cancelled before f. 137 14¹² 15⁸ wants 6, 7 blank 16¹² 17⁸ 18¹² 19¹⁰ wants 3 after f. 195. Quires 1–9 numbered at beginning or end. Many hands, the latest, arts. 4, 5, of s. xiv. Art. 5 is the most carefully written. Initials: in art. 1, 3-line (f. 1) and 2-line, blue with red ornament or without ornament; elsewhere, red initials or spaces left blank. Binding of s. xv: brown leather over wooden boards, the upper cover decorated with fillets and small stamps of four patterns, the lower cover plain: central strap and pin fastening. Secundo folio *derat predestinendo*.

Written in Germany. From the Benedictine abbey of St. Godehard, Hildesheim: 'Liber monasterii sancti Godehardi prope hildens' ordinis sancti Benedicti. Sermones de tempore 'et de aliquibus sanctis' et Stella clericorum', f. iᵛ, s. xv. A scribbler wrote on f. 172ᵛ 'dy dyt buch het gescreben den hezset hemze' and on f. 107 'dy dit buch henze', s. xv.

192. *Horae*   s. xv med.

1. pp. 1–40 Hours of B.V.M., beginning imperfectly.

Only the special forms of office in Advent, etc., remain.

2. pp. 40–76 In commemoracione omnium sanctorum hoc modo fiet seruicium secundum sarum ecclesie vsum. Ad vesperas super psalmos a'. Sancti dei omnes . . .

Differs much from *Brev. ad usum Sarum*, iii. 969–80, especially in psalms, capitula, and lessons. The psalms at matins after the hymn Jesu salvator are 1, 8, 10, 14, 18, 33, 83, 96, 98. In Jesu salvator stanza 4 begins with the word *Monachorum* not *Clericorum*.

3. pp. 76–83 Antiphons and benedictions in feasts of B.V.M. p. 84 blank.

4. pp. 85–112 Penitential psalms, beginning imperfectly.

5. pp. 112–38 Quindecim psalmi.

6. pp. 138–77 Letania.

A litany for each week-day as in *Brev. ad usum Sarum*, ii. 250–60. p. 178 blank. The name of St. Thomas erased in the Tuesday list, p. 161. p. 178 blank.

7. pp. 179–230 Office of the dead, beginning and ending imperfectly.

ff. vi+115+v, paginated i–xii, 1–240. 95 × 66 mm. Written space 59 × 38 mm. 14 long lines. Collation of pp. 1–178: 1 two (pp. 1–4) 2–6⁸ 7⁸ wants 1 before p. 85 8–12⁸: the rest uncertain. Well written. Initials: (i) missing; (ii) 2-line, gold on red and blue grounds, patterned in white, with sprays of green and gold into the margins; (iii) 1-line, blue with red ornament or gold with slate-grey ornament. Line fillers in litany only: gold or blue. Bound by Maltby, Oxford, s. xx.

Written in England. A scribble on p. 115, s. xvi: [. . . .]nt est possessor huius libri vell huic libro. si quis furauerit deabolus. 'W. Middelton 1833' above an armorial shield, p. xi. 'G. Manley Jun.' stamped on p. v.

192a. *Horae*   s. xv²

1. pp. 1–24 Calendar in red and black.

Feasts in red include Victor (15 May), Bernardine (20 May), Visitation of B.V.M. (2 July), 'Sancte Marthe hospite cristi' (29 July), Crescentius (12 Oct.), Savinus (30 Oct.), and Ansanus (1 Dec.).

2. pp. 25–251 Incipit offitium beate uirginis marie secundum consuetudinem romane curie.

3. pp. 251–4 Ant'. Aue regina celorum. Aue domina angelorum . . . Omnipotens sempiterne deus qui gloriose uirginis . . .

RH, no. 2070.

4. pp. 255–69 Incipit offitium crucis compositum per dominum papam iohannem uigesimo secundo . . . Patris sapientia . . .

The heading conveys 'singulis deuote dicentibus pro qualibet uice . . . unum annum in remissionem peccatorum'.

5. pp. 269–72 Conmemoratione di sancto sebastiano laquale e molto utile a dire contra la peste. Ant'. O sancte sebastiane miles . . .

6. pp. 273–361 Incipiunt septem psalmos penitentiales. . . . (p. 318) Letanie.

Martyrs: Innocents, Stephen, Laurence, Vincent, Ansanus, Blasius, Fabian, Sebastian. Monks and hermits: Antony, Onuphrius, Benedict, Dominic, Francis.

7. pp. 362–502 Incipit offitium mortuorum. pp. 503–4 blank.

ff. iv+246+iv. paginated i–viii, 1–329, 340–510. pp. vii, viii, 503–4 are parchment flyleaves ruled like the rest of the book. 94×61 mm. Written space 45×33 mm. 11 long lines. Collation: 1¹² 2–10¹⁰ 11⁸ 12¹⁰ 13–14⁸ 15–25¹⁰. Punctuation includes the flex ?) occasionally. Initials: (i) pp. 25, 256, 273, 363, 5-line or 6-line, in colours on gold and coloured grounds historiated with half-length figure (B.V.M. and Child, p. 25) and with a skull (p. 363); (ii) as (i), but decorated, instead of historiated; (iii, iv) 2-line and 1-line, blue or red, with ornament of the other colour. Capital letters in the ink of the text filled with yellow. Framed floral borders on pages with initials of types (i, ii). Binding of s. xix. Secundo folio (p. 27) *erat in principio*.

Written in Italy: Ansanus (arts. 1, 6) suggests Siena. A roundel in the lower border on p. 25 probably contained arms, now obliterated. A strip from an English sale catalogue, s. xix, is attached to p. ii. 'G. N. Romanes from Mother 1930', p. iii.

193. *Breviarii pars autumnalis*   s. xv² (A.D. 1499?)

1. ff. 1–29ᵛ Antiphons and OT lections of the temporale for September, October, and November, beginning with Job 1: 1.

2. ff. 30–54ᵛ Homilies on the Gospels for the 9th to 25th Sundays after Pentecost.

3. ff. 55–166ᵛ Sanctorale from Decollation of John to Chrysanthus and Darias (29 Aug.–1 Dec.) with Katherine, 24 Nov., out of place at the end.

Twelve lessons for Lambert (ff. 77ᵛ–83), Maurice, Denis, 11,000 Virgins, and Malachi, among others.

4. ff. 167–176ᵛ Hymns: (a) at the hours; (b) of the sanctorale, 29 Aug.–30 Nov.; (c) of the common of saints; (d) of the dedication of a church.

The Cistercian collection printed in *Hymnarium Parisiense* (i.e. of Pairis, near Colmar), ed. C. Weinmann, 1905: (a) nos. 1–7, 9, 8; (b) nos. 39, 35–7, 18–20, 42–7; (c) nos. 48–51; (d) no. 52. Iesu corona (*HP*, no. 50) is also here (cue only) for St. Luke and Aeterna Christi munera (*HP*, no. 48) at nocturns of Exaltation of Cross and All Saints.

5. ff. 176ᵛ–180 Monastic canticles.

The same sets—less, of course, Christmas, Easter, and Holy Crown—as in St. Paul's Cathedral 15 (*MMBL* i. 257: Mearns, *Canticles*, pp. 87–92, *Sundays* (1), *Apostles, etc.*, 8, 1, *Virgins* 2), followed, as in the St. Paul's manuscript, by cues of canticles for Holy Cross and Dedication agreeing with those noted by Mearns, p. 89 from B.L., Add. 34750 (G. a).

6. ff. 180–2 'Ordo priuatis diebus' from the octave of Pentecost to Advent. '1499' in red at the end. f. 182ᵛ blank.

Begins with the antiphon 'Rector decet' (first nocturn on Monday) and ends with the collect at none on Saturday, Dies nostros quesumus domine.

ff. i+182+i. ff. 55–166 are foliated in red I–CXII. 170×118 mm. Written space 105×
75 mm. 22 long lines. Collation: 1–6⁸ 7⁶ (ff. 49–54) 8–28⁸. Written in an expert sloping
hybrida. Initials: (i) ff. 1, 55, 133 (All Saints), red and blue with red ornament; (ii, iii)
2-line and 1-line, red or blue. Capital letters in the ink of the text marked with red.
Binding of red morocco, s. xix. Secundo folio *Vtinam.*

Written in a Germanic area for Cistercian use.

274. *Horae*   s. xv in.

1. pp. 1–24 Calendar in red and black.

The entries are at first in French, but after 15 Jan. in Latin. Feasts in red include: Juliani
episcopi cenoman', 27 Jan.; Ludouici regis francie, 26 Aug; Francisci episcopi (!), 4 Oct.

2. pp. 25–120 Hours of B.V.M. of the use of (Le Mans). Hours of Cross and
of Holy Spirit worked in.

3. pp. 121–57 Penitential psalms and litany.

Julian is the fourth and Louis, Dompnolus, and Yvo the last three of fifteen confessors.
The first two virgins are Mary Magdalene and Anne.

4. pp. 157–64 Oracio beate marie. Obsecro te . . .

Feminine forms.

5. pp. 165–224 Office of the dead, ending imperf.

The end was supplied on pp. 225–8 in imitative script, s. xvi (?).

ff. 114+iii, paginated 1–234. 155×112 mm. Written space 80×57 mm. 14 long lines.
Collation: 1–2⁶ 3–11⁸ 12⁶ (pp. 153–64) 13–15⁸ 16⁸ wants 7, 8 after p. 224 17² (a later supply).
Four 10- or 11-line pictures, pp. 25, 67 (Crucifixion), 121 (Christ on the rainbow), 165,
except the second on chequered backgrounds. Initials: (i) 3- or 4-line, in colour patterned
in white on decorated gold grounds; (ii, iii) 2-line and 1-line, gold on coloured grounds
patterned in white. Floral borders—much gold ivy leaf—continuous on picture pages and
on three sides (*not* the outer margin) or one side (p. 157) of pages with initials of type (i).
Line fillers in red and blue picked out with gold. All the gold is thin and worn. Capital
letters in the ink of the text filled with yellow. Brown morocco, s. xviii, bearing gilt
interlaced Ms (see below). Secundo folio (p. 27) *eius in.*

Written in France for use in the diocese of Le Mans. 'Amen. M. J. Lounet', p. 228, perhaps by the writer of pp. 225–8. 'Je partiens a madelene de Mailloc Je luy ay este donnee
par fren's'choy Achar que lon ne me presne pas comme bien aultre chose quy luy avet
donne que lon luy a cruellement aute', on pastedown in front, s. xviii. Book-plate with
printed 'J. Hamilton-Leigh Ex libris', s. xix, pasted to p. 229. Given in 1946 by Miss
Norah Dawson of Holme Park, Ashburton.

275. *Horae*   s. xv²

1. pp. 1–24 Full calendar in French in gold, blue, and red, the two colours
alternating for effect.

Among entries in gold are Gervais, Eloy, Sauueur, Denis, Romain (19, 25 June, 6 Aug.,
9, 23 Oct.).

2. pp. 25–36 Sequentiae of the gospels.

The extract from St. John is followed by two prayers, Protector in te sperantium and Ecclesiam tuam quesumus.

3. pp. 37–44 Obsecro te . . . Masculine forms.

4. pp. 44–51 Alia oracio. O intemerata . . . orbis terrarum. De te enim . . . Masculine forms. p. 52 blank.

5. pp. 53–153 Hours of B.V.M. of the use of (Rouen). Memoriae of B.V.M., Holy Spirit, and SS. John Baptist, Laurence, Nicholas, and Margaret follow lauds. p. 154 blank.

6. pp. 155–88 Penitential psalms and litany.

In the litany Romanus is seventh of ten confessors and Honorina ninth of twelve virgins.

7. pp. 189–95 Hours of Holy Cross. p. 196 blank.

8. pp. 197–203 Hours of Holy Spirit. p. 204 blank.

9. pp. 205–61 Office of the dead. p. 262 blank.

10. pp. 262–73 Doulce dame de misericorde mere de pitie . . .

Sonet, no. 458.

11. pp. 274–9 Doulx dieu doulx pere saincte trinite . . .

Sonet, no. 504.

12. p. 280 Saincte vraie croix aouree . . .

Sonet, no. 1876. pp. 281, 282 blank.

---

ff. ii + 141 + iii, paginated i–iv, 1–288. 185 × 135 mm. Written space 92 × 65 mm. 15 long lines. Collation: 1–2⁶ 3⁸ 4⁶ (pp. 41–52) 5–10⁸ 11 three (pp. 149–54) 12⁸ 13⁸+1 leaf after 8 (pp. 187, 188) 14–18⁸ 19⁸ wants 8 blank. Fourteen skilful 12-line pictures, eight in art. 5 and one before each of arts. 2 (four compartments, an evangelist writing in each), 6, 7, 8, 9 (burial), 10 (B.V.M. and Child: angels crown her: a woman in a red dress and black head-dress kneels before her). Art. 1 has the signs of the zodiac on rectos, but no occupations. Initials: (i) usually 3-line, blue, patterned in white on decorated gold grounds: three of the initials, those beginning arts. 3, 4, and 11, are historiated (the dead Christ on the lap of B.V.M.; B.V.M. and Child; Trinity); (ii), as (i), but 2-line; (iii) 1-line, gold on blue and red grounds patterned in white, the blue and red alternately inside and outside the initial. Line fillers blue and red patterned in white and picked out with gold. Capital letters in the ink of the text filled with pale yellow. Floral borders, the flowers often in gold hat-like tubs on grounds of gold paint: (i) continuous and framed on f. 1 and on pages with initials of type (i), the ornament including grotesques, cherubs, a naked woman pursued by a devil (pp. 1, 205), and a begging fox contemplated by a duck, a cock, and a hen (p. 263); (ii) the height of the written space on two sides of rectos containing initials of type (ii); (iii) in the outer margin of all other pages. French binding of s. xviii, with gilt centrepiece of the crucifixion and cornerpieces. Secundo folio (p. 27) *lux uera*.

Written in France for use in the diocese of Rouen. 'Mʳ Wittinoom' inside the cover, s. xix. Book-plate of James Cazalet, Halsted, Kent, s. xix: motto 'Spero meliora'. No. 289 in a catalogue of Bernard Halliday, 1 King Richard's Rd., Leicester. Given as MS. 274.

276. *Horae* s. XV ex.

1. pp. 1–24 Full calendar in French, in red and black.

2. pp. 25–32 Sequentiae of the gospels, ending imperfectly in the extract from Mark. The prayer 'Protector in te sperantium . . .' follows John.

3. pp. 33–6 Obsecro te, beginning imperfectly 'litatem in qua respondisti archangelo gabrieli'. Masculine forms.

4. pp. 36–42 Alia oratio. O intemerata . . . orbis terrarum. De te enim . . .

5. pp. 43–95 Hours of B.V.M. of the use of (Paris).

The first leaf of every hour except prime is missing. p. 96 was left blank: cf. art. 19c.

6. pp. 97–118 The penitential psalms, beginning imperfectly, and (f. 112ᵛ) litany, ending imperfectly.

Denis 'cum sociis' eighth of eighteen martyrs. Agatha second, Anne third, Genovefa tenth of fourteen virgins.

7. pp. 119–22 Hours of the Cross, beginning imperfectly.

8. pp. 122–7 Sequuntur hore de sancto spiritu.

9. pp. 127–68 Ensuit loffice des mors.

The first nocturn only and lauds. Cf. art. 19 (i).

10. pp. 168–73 Legitur cum beatus thomas archiepiscopus cartusiensis septem gaudia temporalia beate marie virginis cum nimia cordis exultacione diceret beata virgo sibi apparuit eique dixit Cur de gaudiis . . . Quicumque deuotote (*sic*) cum istis gaudiis venerabitur me in extremis diebus videbit me et ego eum secure presentabo in conspectu dei filii mei de predictis gaudiis in eterna gloria perpetuo mecum gauiisurus. Ensuiuent les sept ioies nostre dame esperituelles que composa monʳ saint thomas daquin. Gaude flore virginali honoreque spirituali (*sic*). . . . (*and prayer*) Domine ihesu criste fili dei viui qui beatam gloriosam benignam . . .

RH, no. 6809. For the heading cf. Leroquais, *Livres d'heures*, ii. 90.

11. pp. 173–4 Sancta maria mater dei miserere me (*sic*) . . .

Seven misereres.

12. (*a*) p. 174 Aue caro cristi sanctissima . . . (*b*) pp. 174–5 Aue verum corpus natum . . . (*c*) p. 175 Aue sanguis domini nostri ihesu cristi . . . (*d*) pp. 175–6 Anima cristi sanctifica me . . .

(*a*). In verse. Leroquais, *Livres d'heures*, ii. 122. (*b, d*). *RH*, nos. 2175, 1090.

13. pp. 176–7 Salue regina . . . Oratio. Omnipotens sempiterne deus qui gloriose virginis . . .

14. (*a*) p. 177 Aue regina celorum. Aue domina angelorum. Salue . . . cristum exora. Amen. (*b*) pp. 177–8 Aue regina celorum mater regis angelorum . . . (*c*) p. 178 Regina celi letare Alleluya . . . Oratio. Concede nos famulos tuos quesumus domine deus perpetua mentis . . .

(*a–c*). *RH*, nos. 2070, 2072, 17170.

15. (*a*) pp. 178–80 O bone et dulcissime ihesu. per tuam misericordiam esto michi ihesus . . . (*b*) p. 180 Oratio. O beatissime domine ihesu criste respicere digneris super miserum . . .

Leroquais, *Livres d'heures*, ii. 123; i. 154.

16. pp. 180–1 Domine ihesu criste adoro te in cruce pendentem . . .

Five Oes, nos. 1–4, 7 of the set printed by Leroquais, *Livres d'heures*, ii. 346. Nos. 5, 6 were added in the margins of pp. 182–3, s. xvi.

17. p. 181–4 O sancte sebastiane. Semper vespere et mane . . .

RH, no. 13708.

18. pp. 184–7 Passio domini nostri ihesu cristi. Secundum Iohannem. Apprehendit pylatus ihesum . . . et verum est testimonium eius. Deo gracias Per euangelica dicta . . . Deus qui manus tuas . . .

19 (added in s. xvi). (*a*) pp. i–iv Prayers to the Trinity and the Godhead individually. (*b*) pp. iv–vi Deuota contemplacio beate marie. Stabat mater . . . (*c*) p. 96 Quant vn veult Receuoir le corps nostre seigneur. Domine non sum dignus . . . (*d*) pp. 187–91 Les sept vers saint bernard. O bone Iesu illumina oculos meos . . . (*e*) pp. 192–3 Les dix comandement de la loi. Vng seul dieu tu adoreras Et aymeras parfaictement . . . (*f*) p. 193 Les cinq commandement de leglise. Les dimanches messe orras . . . (*g*) pp. 194–5 Oraison tres deuote a la glorieuse vierge marie. [A]ue stella matutina. Mundi princeps et regina . . . (*h*) pp. 195–8 Deus propicius esto michi peccatori . . . (*i*) pp. 195–208 The parts of art. 9 omitted there.

(*c*.) Leroquais, *Livres d'heures*, i. 176. (*d*). Not the usual text. (*e, f*). Sonet, nos. 2287, 1060. (*g*). *RH*, no. 2134.

ff. iii + 107 + iii, paginated (three unnumbered leaves), i–vi, 1–214. 140 × 100 mm. Written space 88 × 55 mm. 20 long lines. Written in *lettre bâtarde*. Collation of pp. i–vi, 1–208: 17 quires, 1, 4, 9, and 17 of three, two, two, and two leaves respectively (pp. i–vi, 39–42, 93–6, 205–8), 2 of 12 (pp. 1–24), and the rest of 8 with the following losses: 3⁵ after p. 32, 5¹ before p. 43, 5⁸ after p. 54, 7², ⁵, ⁷ after pp. 72, 76, 78, 8², ⁷ after pp. 82, 90, 10¹ before p. 97, 11⁵ after p. 118. Initials: (i) 3-line, blue patterned in white or red patterned in gold paint on similarly patterned grounds of the other colour; historiated on p. 25 (St. John); (ii) 2-line, gold on red grounds decorated in gold paint; (iii) 1-line, as (ii), or on blue grounds patterned in white. Line fillers blue or red decorated with gold paint. Capital letters in the ink of the text filled with gold paint. Framed floral borders, compartmented, the grounds of gold paint or white, but only three remain, pp. 25, 123, 128. English binding of red morocco, gilt, s. xviii. Secundo folio (p. 27) *mus o beata*.

Written in France (Paris?). 'Randall Druce', f. i, s. xx. Given as MS. 274.

277. *Horae* s. xv in.

Additions apart, this book of hours conforms to the common type of hours written abroad for the English market (cf. *MMBL* i. 46), but art. 3 has been reduced from the usual ten to four saints.

1. pp. 3–12 Calendar in red and black, lacking January and February.

The word 'pape' and feasts of St. Thomas of Canterbury crossed out.

2. pp. 13–20 The Fifteen Oes of St. Bridget.

3. pp. 21–7 Memoriae of four saints, one to a page: George (Georgi martir inclite . . .), Katherine (Gaude virgo katherina qua doctores . . .), John Baptist (Gaude iohannes baptista qui maternali cista . . .), Mary Magdalene (Gaude xpristi que lauisti . . .).

RH, nos. 7242, 6991, 26987, 6726. pp. 22, 24, 26, 28 left blank.

4. (added). p. 22 Gaude virgo mater cristi que per aurem concepisti . . .

RH, no. 7017.

5. pp. 29–72 Hours of B.V.M. of the use of (Sarum), with hours of the Cross worked in.

The memoriae after lauds are sixteen, as in *MMBL* i. 47: Holy Spirit; Holy Trinity; Holy Cross; Michael; John Baptist; Peter and Paul; Andrew; Stephen, Laurence; Thomas of Canterbury (Tu per thome sanguinem . . ., cut with scissors, but without hurting any letter); Nicholas; Mary Magdalene; Katherine; Margaret; All Saints; peace. pp. 58, 62, 66 blank.

6. (a) pp. 72–3 Antiphona. Salve regina, followed by the set of versicles O virgo mater ecclesie . . . and prayer Omnipotens sempiterne deus qui gloriose uirginis . . . (b) pp. 75–81 Has uideas laudes . . . . salutando mariam. Salue. Salue uirgo uirginum stella matutina . . .

(a). RH, nos. 18147, 21818. (b). RH, nos. 7687, 18318. p. 74 was left blank.

7 (added). pp. 73–4 Gaude flore virginali honoreque speciali . . .

RH, no. 6809.

8. pp. 81–3 Oracio. O intemerata . . . orbis terrarum. Inclina mater . . .
For male use.

9. pp. 83–6 Oracio bona et deuota. Obsecro te . . . For masculine use.

10. p. 86 Quicumque hec septem gaudia in honore beate marie uirginis semel in die dixerit centum dies indulgenciarum obtinebit a domino papa clemente qui hec septem gaudia proprio stilo composuit. Uirgo templum trinitatis . . . (*ends imperfectly*).

RH, no. 21899.

11. pp. 87–9 Omnibus consideratis, beginning imperfectly.

AH xxxi. 87–9. RH, no. 14081 (etc.).

12. pp. 89–92 Oracio uenerabilis bede presbiteri de septem uerbis . . . preparatam. Domine ihesu criste . . . Oracio. Precor te piissime domine . . .

13. (a) p. 92 Oracio bona. Aue domine ihesu criste uerbum patris . . . (5 aves) (b) p. 92 Oracio. Aue corpus uerum natum . . . (c) pp. 92–3 Oracio. Aue caro cristi cara . . . (d) p. 93 Oracio. Anima cristi sanctifica me . . . (e) pp. 93–4 Omnibus confessis et contritis hanc oracionem dicentibus . . . dominus papa

(*half erased*) bonifacius concessit duo milia annorum ad supplicacionem philippi regis francie. Domine ihesu criste qui hanc sacratissimam carnem . . .

(*b–d*). RH, nos. 2175, 1710, 1090.

14 (added). p. 94 Stella celi extirpauit . . .
RH, no. 19438.

15. pp. 95–109 Penitential psalms, gradual psalms (cues only of the first twelve), and litany.

Of two leaves missing, the second, after p. 104, contained most of the litany: for Edith the scribe wrote 'edicha'.

16 (added, s. xvi). pp. 109–10 O bone Iesu. O dulcis Iesu . . .

17. pp. 111–36 Office of the dead.

18. pp. 137–50 Incipiunt commendaciones animarum.

19. pp. 151–63 Incipit psalterium sancti iheronimi.

p. 164, once blank, has later text now erased.

ff. iii+81+iii, paginated (i–vi), 3–164 (165–70). 188 × 132 mm. Written space 128 × 80 mm. 24 long lines. Collation: 1⁶ wants 1 2–5⁸ 6 nine (pp. 77–94) 7⁸ wants 2 after p. 96 and 7 after p. 104 8–9⁸ 10 six (pp. 139–50) 11 seven (pp. 151–64). Initials: (i) usually 8-line, blue or brick red on gold and coloured grounds, decorated with oak leaves: the colours patterned in white; (ii) 2-line, gold on coloured grounds patterned in white; (iii) 1-line, blue with red ornament or gold with slate-grey ornament. Bound by Rivière and Son, s. xix/xx. Secundo folio (p. 15) *amarissimi*.

Written in the Netherlands for English use. Arts. 4, 6, 14, 16 added in England, s. xv, xvi. An alphabet and the words 'By me Francys Feton Amen' pencilled on p. 62 and 'by me francis feton gentelman of the quense pryue cha[mber]' on p. 61. 'Elyzabethe Davemport', p. 62. No. 366 in an English bookseller's catalogue, s. xx. Given as MS. 274.

281. *Biblia* (*fragm.*) s. xii¹

Five strips cut from a bifolium of a large Bible in a handsome English hand. The recto of the first leaf of the bifolium contained capitula of 1 Maccabees, the last eight of which remain from 'De scripto pacis ad symonem ab sparciatis' to 'Vbi ptolomeus . . . cum filiis suis'. Parts of 1 Maccabees 1: 3–62 remain on the recto and verso of the first leaf and parts of 1 Maccabees 4: 18–5: 23 on the recto and verso of the second leaf.

Enough remains to show that the dimensions of a leaf were at least 438 × 310 mm, that the written space was 310 × 208 mm, and that the text was in two columns of forty-one lines. Strips 4+5 together form an all but complete outer column of the second leaf and strips 1+2 contain all the text in the first eleven lines over both columns of the first leaf.

Written in England. Used in the binding of a three-volume book.

APPLEBY (CUMBRIA). GRAMMAR SCHOOL

1. *Petrus de Crescentiis*[1]   s. xv med.

1. Incipit liber ruralium comodorum a petro de crescenciis ciue Bononie ad honorem dei omnipotentis. et ad vtilitatem omnium gencium compilatus. Prohemium. Cum ex uirtute prouidencie . . . communi. Capitulum primum. Liber iste Ruralium comodorum dicitur . . . (f. 140) atque visco capiuntur. Explicit. Venerabili in cristo patri et domino speciali . . . fratri Aymerico de placencia . . . multa iocunda. Epistola eiusdem ad serenissimum Regem karolum. Excellentissimo principi domino karolo secundo . . . et mandatis. (ff. 140^v–142^v) Incipiunt rubrice . . .

The twelve books of the Liber Ruralium Commodorum of Petrus de Crescentiis of Bologna, *c.* 1316, followed by his letters to Aymeric of Piacenza, O.P., and King Charles II of Jerusalem and Sicily and by tables of contents of each book. Printed in s. xv (*GKW*, nos. 7820–5) and later. ff. 123–30 should be the fifth quire, after f. 40, but was already misbound in its present position as quire 13 when the quires were numbered in s. xv. The ink ran on f. 28 and the recto and lines 1–18 on the verso were recopied by the main hand on an added leaf, f. 131: a direction to the binder, 'ponatur istud folium in quarto (*sic for* tercio) quaterno in Capitulo de Faba', is on f. 131^v. In the margins of bk. 6 some plant-names are written in Latin and English, for example on f. 73, 'fungus agaryk' and 'Gramen lytellwald'.

f. 143^{rv}, originally blank, has on the recto a commendation of cheese, including verses, 'Ignari medici me dicunt esse nociuum' (ten lines: Walther, no. 8666) and two recipes in English 'Ad remouendum talpas'.

2. ff. i, ii, 144–5 are from a roll of accounts on parchment: ff. i^r, 145^v were pasted down. The accounts relate to the Clifford estates in Westmorland and Cumberland and are datable in 1408:[2] for the Cliffords of Appleby and Brough cf. Nicolson and Burn, *History of Westmorland*, i. 274–304 and *Complete Peerage*, iii. 290.

ff. ii+143+ii. Paper, except ff. 1, 5, 6, 10, and the end-leaves (see above). 294 × 213 mm. Written space *c.* 215 × 160 mm. *c.* 40 lines, the number varying from page to page. Frame ruling at first; sometimes none later. Collation: 1–6^{10} 7^{12} 8–12^{10} 13^8+1 leaf after 8 (f. 131) 14^{12}. Quires numbered 'Primus quaternus'—'xiiii^{us} quaternus' in red at the top of the first recto of each quire. The script is a current mixture of secretary and anglicana. Red initials, 3-line (f. 1) and 2-line. Contemporary binding of wooden boards covered with brown leather, now gone from the front board: five bands, the two upper pairs set V-shaped into the front board and the two lower pairs V-shaped into the lower board: central strap-and-pin fastening now missing. Secundo folio *et humidus*.

Bound probably in Westmorland. 'Robertus Sewell' is scribbled on f. 137^v and 'Iohn Sewell' on f. 143, s. xvi: the name was common in Appleby. Old Grammar School press-marks, Θ 17 (f. ii^v), Y 22 and G 3 (f. i). The first mark is that in the catalogue of 1656

---

[1] On deposit in the library of the University of Newcastle upon Tyne, BAI MS 1.
[2] I owe the date to Mrs. V. J. C. Rees, who used the accounts for her Manchester M.Litt. thesis, 'The Cliffords in the later Middle Ages', 1973.

printed in *Cumberland and Westmorland Antiquarian and Archaeological Society*, N.S. xxxix (1939), 246–60: see there p. 247.[1] The second and third marks are those of the catalogues of 1782 and 1847 respectively.

APPLEBY MAGNA (LEICS.). PARISH CHURCH

Biblia[2]   s. xiii[2]

1. ff. 1–491. A Bible in the usual order,[3] except that 1, 2 Thessalonians precede Colossians, and with the common set of sixty-four prologues,[3] except that Stegmüller's nos. 510, 515 do not occur, 468, 487, 707, 715, 728 have been added, and two prologues to Romans, not of the common set, 670 and 674, precede 677.

Tobit, Proverbs, 1 Maccabees, and Matthew begin on new quires, ff. 193, 243, 373, 395. A stichometric note at the end of 2 Maccabees: Explicit liber machabeorum secundus. uersus habens mille octingentos. ff. 491ᵛ–494ᵛ were left blank: cf. art. 3.

2. ff. 495–531. Aaz apprehendens . . . consiliatores eorum.

The usual dictionary of Hebrew names. ff. 531ᵛ–533 were left blank: cf. art. 4.

3. (added, s. xiii ex., in the blank space at the end of art. 1). (*a*) f. 491ʳᵛ A table of Gospel and Epistle lections of the temporale for the year. (*b*) ff. 492–494ᵛ Tables of biblical texts suitable for feast days and special occasions. The occasion is indicated in the heading of each table: Advent, Andrew, Christmas, Stephen, John Evangelist, Innocents, Thomas the Martyr, Circumcision, Epiphany, Agnes, Vincent, Conversion of Paul, Purification, Chair of Peter, Matthew, Ash Wednesday, Holy Thursday, Good Friday, Annunciation, Easter, Rogationtide, Mark, Ascension, Philip and James, Invention of Cross, Pentecost, Barnabas, John Baptist, Peter, Paul, Peter and Paul, Margaret, Mary Magdalene, James, Chains of Peter, Laurence, Assumption of B.V.M., Bartholomew, Decollation of John Baptist, Nativity of B.V.M., Exaltation of Cross, Matthew, Michael, Francis, Luke, Simon and Jude, All Saints, All Souls, Martin, Edmund king and martyr, Clement, Katherine, Common of Saints under 11 heads, Dedication of church, Translation of saint, 'Ad claustrales', 'Ad moniales', 'Ad uiuentes solitarie', 'In synodo', 'Ad ordinandos', 'Ad episcopos consecrandos', 'Ad magistros et scolares', 'Ad curiales', 'Ad pauperes', 'Ad peregrinos'.

(*b*). The number of texts under any one heading varies from about 40 to about 6. For Francis there are 36 and for Edmund 6. This and the similar series in the Bible at Perth Museum may be derived from one in use by the friars of Babwell, near Bury St. Edmunds. The series in Bodleian Auct. D. 4. 9 (*Sum. Cat.* 1968) is rather different, but also presumably Franciscan. References are to chapter-numbers and the subdivisions of chapters by letters *a–f*, as in the *Concordantiae Sancti Jacobi*; the letters themselves have not been entered in the margins of art. 1.

4 (added in s. xiv in the blank space at the end of art. 2). ff. 531ᵛ–533 A table like art. 3*a*, but Advent to Easter only.

[1] The 1656 catalogue records also a now missing 'Ovid Metamorph: cum notis MS' and an unidentified and probably missing 'Directiones Scholasticae MS'. The Ovid may have been a printed book with manuscript scholia.

[2] On deposit in the care of the Leicestershire Record Office, New Walk, Leicester.

[3] Cf. Bristol Public Library, MS. 15, below.

ff. ii+533. 153×110 mm. Written space 103×72 mm. 2 cols. 50 lines. Collation: 1–6²⁰ 7²² 8²⁰ 9¹⁸ 10² (ff. 191–2) 11²⁴ 12²⁶ (ff. 217–42) 13²⁰ 14²⁰ wants 16, 17 after f. 277 15–17²⁰ 18¹⁸ 19¹⁴ (ff. 359–72) 20²⁰ 21² (ff. 393–4) 22–24²⁰ 25²⁴ 26¹⁶ (ff. 479–94) 27²⁰ 28²⁰ wants 20 probably blank: 19 is pasted to the cover. Written in a very small hand. Initials: (i) to books and the usual eight divisions of the Psalter, red and blue with ornament in red and green-blue; (ii) to prologues, sometimes as (i) and sometimes as (iii); (iii) to chapters, 2-line, red with green-blue ornament or blue with red ornament; (iv) to verses of psalms and in art. 2, 1-line, red or blue. Binding of s. xvi/xvii, with gilt centrepiece. Secundo folio *lipsi septem*.

Written probably in England. In English and probably Franciscan ownership in s. xiii ex. 'E Libris Jos: Waldron', f. 2. Given by John Mould 'in usum Ecclesie de Appleby', 8 Feb. 1701/2, according to the inscription on f. iᵛ: cf. J. Nichols, *History of Leicestershire*, iv, pt. 2 (1811), p. 434.

BAMBURGH CASTLE. LIBRARY OF THE TRUSTEES OF LORD CREWE'S CHARITY

Sharp Collection, Select 6. *Psalterium, etc.*[1]   s. xii/xiii

Described by A. I. Doyle, 'A Scottish Augustinian Psalter', *Innes Review*, viii (1957), 75–85, with a reduced facsimile of f. 9 and facsimiles of the initials on ff. 34ᵛ, 47ᵛ, 57ᵛ, 69ᵛ (pls. I–III).

1. ff. 3–8ᵛ Graded calendar in red, green, and black, the first two colours alternating for effect.

Printed and discussed by Doyle. 'Transfiguratio domini iii lc' ' in green, 26 July. 'Translatio sancti Thome martiris (*entry erased*) Et dedicatio ecclesie Glasg' ' added in red in a hand of s. xiii, 7 July. The word 'pape' erased.

2. ff. 9–116 Psalms 1–150.

3. ff. 116ᵛ–125ᵛ Six ferial canticles, Te deum (headed 'Cant' Romane ecclesie'), Benedicite, Benedictus, Quicumque vult, Magnificat.

4. Prayers: (*a*) f. 126 Domine sancte spiritus. deus omnipotens. qui coequalis coeternus et consubstancialis . . .; (*b*) f. 126 Ad sanctam trinitatem. Sancta trinitas atque indiuisa unitas. omnipotens eterne deus. spes unica mundi . . .'; (*c*) f. 126ʳᵛ Orationes ad crucem omni die. Domine ihesu criste gloriosissime conditor mundi. qui cum sis splendor . . .; (*d*) f. 126ᵛ Domine ihesu criste adoro te in cruce ascendentem . . . in cruce uulneratum.' deprecor te ut ipsa uulnera remedium sint (*ends imperfectly*).

(*c*, *d*) cancelled in pencil. Printed from other copies by L. Gjerløw, *Adoratio crucis*, 1961, pp. 27, 26.

5. f. 1, the first of a pair of leaves pricked like ff. 3–8, but not ruled, has preliminaries to the Psalter added in s. xiii/xiv: (*a*) (*begins imperfectly*) prophetatas.

---

[1] Deposited in Durham University Library in 1958. For the library, see A. I. Doyle in *The Book Collector*, viii (1959), 14–24.

Incarnacionem quoque . . . (*the three last lines only*); (*b*) Oracio ante phalterium. Suscipere dignare deus omnipotens has spalmos consecratos et has oraciones quas ego indignus . . .; (*c*) Item. Suscipe eciam domine hos spalmos et preces non tantum pro me . . .; (*d*) Inmense et misericors deus pater omnipotens qui per os dauid electi tui . . .; (*e*) Salua me domine ihesu criste Rex glorie quia potes saluare . . .; (*f*) Oracio ante psalterium. Suscipere digneris omnipotens deus hos psalmos consecratos quos ego indignus . . .; (*g*) Or' post psalterium. Maiestatem tuam suppliciter deprecor omnipotens et misericors deus ut placabilis et acceptabilis sit tibi hec mea modulacio psalmorum . . .

The list of saints in honour of whom (*f*) is said ends with five confessors and ten virgins: 'Benedicti Martini Nicholai Yuonis Cuthberti . . . Cecilie Agathe Agnetis Lucie Scolastice Katerine Margarite Albe (*sic*) . . . Marie Magdalene . . . Marie Egipciace'.

ff. 122, foliated wrongly 1–40, 45–126. 298 × 205 mm. Written space *c.* 210 × 137 mm. 23 long lines. Collation: 1 eight (ff. 1, 2 are a bifolium and ff. 3–6 are two bifolia) 2–15⁸ 16 two (ff. 125–6). Traces of signatures *i–s* on quires 6–15 suggest that the present quire 2, the first of the Psalter, was marked *e*. Initials: (i) beginning the eight liturgical divisions and Pss. 51, 101, in colour on decorated grounds of gold and colour, edged with green: cf. Doyle's description and his five facsimiles; (ii) 2-line, gold, edged with green and filled with pale-brown curled-leaf ornament on a dark-red ground; (iii) 1-line, blue or red. Line-fillers in red: cf. Doyle, p. 76. Binding of medieval wooden boards, recovered in s. xix: cf. Doyle, p. 75. Secundo folio (f. 10) *gunt*.

Written probably in Scotland. The calendar is Augustinian and an origin at Holyrood and transfer in s. xiii to the house at Blantyre, founded *c.* 1240, would suit with the facts it provides: cf. Doyle, pp. 78–9. The obit of 'Agnes de leth' (Leith?), 4 Jan., is early. The private prayer, art. 5*f*, is Benedictine and comes in its present form probably from Colding-ham, where Cuthbert and Abba were the local saints, but the error *Albe* for *Abbe* suggests that Abba was not familiar to the writer. A gift to the church of St. Michael le Belfry, York, in 1558: 'Ex dono perceualli crawfurth Ciuitatis Ebor. 22 Augusti 1558 ad vsum Ecclesie sancti Michaelis de Berefrido eiusdem ciuitatis' inside the cover: cf. Doyle, p. 79. 'Iohn Commyn', s. xvi/xvii, f. 68ᵛ. No Sharp book-plate.

Sharp Collection, Select 25. *Psalterium, etc.*[1]   s. xv med.

1. ff. 1–150 Psalms 1–150.

Pss. 80: 9–81: 2 were omitted on f. 83. The place was marked by the word 'vacat' and the text supplied later on f. 82: cf. art. 5.

2. ff. 150–164ᵛ Six ferial canticles, Benedicite, Benedictus, Magnificat, Nunc dimittis, Te deum, Quicumque vult.

3. ff. 164ᵛ–169 Litany.

Eighteen martyrs . . . (17, 18) cypriane elyzabeth (*sic*). Ten confessors: (7–10) gildarde medardi eusebi vrine (cf. Sarum use).

4. ff. 170–175ᵛ Incipiunt uigilie defunctorum.

Office of the dead, with lessons in full and, for the rest, cues.

5. f. 176, containing Pss. 80: 9–81: 2 is apparently a supply leaf rejected in favour of f. 82: cf. art. 1. f. 177ʳᵛ blank.

[1] Deposited in Durham University Library in 1958.

ff. ii+177+ii. 180×125 mm. Written space 105×70 mm. 21 long lines. Collation: 1–10⁸ 11⁸+1 leaf inserted after 1 (f. 82) 12–17⁸ 18⁶ 19–21⁸, 22¹⁰ wants 9, 10, probably blank, 23² (ff. 176–7). Initials: (i) f. 1, 10-line Beatus *B*, blue, patterned in white and decorated gold, historiated; (ii) of the usual seven psalms (Ps. 26, etc.), 5-line, blue or pink, patterned in white, historiated; (iii) f. 170, as (ii), but 3-line and decorated, not historiated; (iv) of Ps. 101, 5-line, gold on ground of blue and red patterned in white; (v) as (iv), but 2-line; (vi) 1-line, gold with grey-green ornament or blue with red ornament. Line fillers blue and red, with gold roundels, one or two according to length. Binding of wooden boards, recovered, but the old covers have been pasted on: they are badly rubbed, but probably bear Oldham's roll FP. f. 7 (London, s. xvi/xvii) as a double border and lozenges within it: two clasps. Secundo folio *Seruite*.

Written in the Netherlands for English use. In England by s. xvi/xvii. Book-plate of 'T. Sharp, DD. Prebendary of Durham and Archdeacon of Northumberland' inside the cover: Thomas Sharp, † 1758, held both these preferments from 1732.

BANGOR. CATHEDRAL

'Liber pontificalis Aniani episcopi'   s. XIV in.

Thirty-three offices are listed in a numbered table on f. 6, which is now so badly damaged that only fourteen titles remain (17–27, 31–3). Corresponding numbers are in the top right corner of each leaf. I keep this numbering and call the two unnumbered pieces 34 and 35. The volume was on loan to William Maskell in 1847 (cf. f. ii^v) and is described by him in his *Monumenta ritualia ecclesiae Anglicanae*, i (1846), cxvi–cxviii. It is described also by W. G. Henderson, *Liber pontificalis Chr. Bainbridge* (Surtees Soc. lxi), pp. xxxv–xxxvii. Maskell printed or collated some of its offices and Henderson printed all or part of arts. 9–13, 22b, 23, 24, 26, 27, 31, 34 in his *York Missal* and *York Manual* (Surtees Soc. lx, lxiii). In *Pontifical offices used by David de Bernham*, 1885, Christopher Wordsworth attempted a reconstruction of the table on f. 6 (pp. 85–91) and printed arts. 22b, 24, 30e, f, 33, 36a and part of art. 16. A description by J. Endell Tylor, 2 Sept. 1840, is bound in as ff. 1–3. ff. 59^v–60 are in facsimile, reduced, in M. L. Clarke, *Bangor Cathedral*, 1969, pl. opposite p. 97, and the same opening and f. 8^v, reduced, are in G. Richards, *Bangor Cathedral, A souvenir booklet*. 2nd edn., 1971.

1. ff. 9–15^v (*begins imperfectly*) ad la[udem] . . .

Noted office of consecration of an altar. The first three leaves are fragments. The remaining text corresponds to *Liber pontificalis of Edmund Lacy*, ed. R. Barnes, 1847, pp. 20/4–23/5, but is fuller.

2. ff. 16–18 Ordo quomodo reliquie ponende sunt in altari. . . . Oratio. Aufer a nobis . . .

Full noted office. Cf. *Lacy*, pp. 32–4.

3. ff. 18–20 Post hec pontifex preparat se ad missam . . .

Full office of dedication of an altar. *Lacy*, p. 34, has only collect, secret, and postcommunion.

4. ff. 20–26ᵛ In dedicacione altaris sine ecclesia procedimus in hunc modum. Primo dicimus psalmos Iudica me deus . . .

Cf. *Lacy*, pp. 23–32. The formulas 'Consecrare . . . Singulare illud . . . in tabulis' on f. 23 are those which have already occurred in art. 1, ff. 12–13. *Singulare* is in Andrieu, *Pont. Rom.*, iii. 470 (pontifical of Durandus, 1293–5).

5. (a) ff. 26ᵛ–29 Reliquiarum collocacio fiat hoc modo. In primis uadat pontifex . . . Aufer a nobis . . . (b) f. 29 In dedicacione altaris portatilis idem facimus officium quam in dedicacione altaris immobilis quando altare sine ecclesia . . . in sacrario.

(a) repeats art. 2. (b). Heading only.

6. ff. 29ᵛ–33ᵛ [I]n dedicacione cimiterii procedimus in hunc modum. Primo dicimus istos psalmos. Iudica me deus . . .

Cf. *Lacy*, pp. 42–6. Ends with a 'Benedictio poliandri secundum Romam. Domine sancte pater omnipotens eterne deus locorum omnium sanctificator . . .' (Andrieu, *Pont. Rom.* ii. 440).

7. ff. 33ᵛ–43 In reconciliacione altaris . . . seu cimiterii . . .

Cf. *Lacy*, p. 46. Repeats the exorcisms of salt and water and the blessings of salt, water, ashes, and wine in art. 4 and repeats art. 3.

8. ff. 43–53ᵛ [. . . . .] accedant qui ordinandi sunt ostiarii . . .

Cf. *Lacy*, pp. 79–92. Lectores, f. 43ᵛ, Exorciste, f. 44, Acoliti, f. 44ᵛ, Subdiaconi, f. 45ᵛ, Diaconi et sacerdotes, f. 46ᵛ.

9. ff. 53ᵛ–54ᵛ [B]enedictio candelarum in purificatione s. marie. Benedic domine ihesu criste hanc creaturam cere . . .

Cf. *Manuale Sarum*, pp. 7–9. *York Missal*, ii. 325.

10. ff. 55–56ᵛ [O]rdo ad dandam penitenciam. Cum uenerit penitens ad sacerdotem. primo inquiratur . . . Kyrieleison . . . Exaudi domine preces nostras . . .

Ash Wednesday. Cf. ibid., pp. 9–11. *York Missal*, ii. 325–7.

11. ff. 56ᵛ–57ᵛ [Dominica] in palmis. Exorcismus florum et frondium. Exorcizo te creatura florum . . .

Cf. ibid., pp. 13, 14. *York Missal*, ii. 327–8.

12. Masses: (a) f. 58ʳᵛ Missa de trinitate. [B]enedicta sit sancta trinitas . . .; (b) ff. 58ᵛ–59 Missa de sancto spiritu; (c) ff. 59ᵛ–60 Missa de cruce; (d) f. 60ʳᵛ De sancta maria; (e) ff. 60ᵛ–61ᵛ Missa de sancta maria in aduentu domini; (f) f. 62ʳᵛ In natiuitate domini de sancta maria; (g) ff. 62ᵛ–64ᵛ Missa pro defunctis.

York Missal, ii. 328–31.

13. (a) ff. 65–69ᵛ Noted prefaces of mass and prayer 'Infra canonem. Communicantes . . .', from Christmas to Trinity, for the common of apostles, for Holy Cross, and for feasts of B.V.M., ending imperfectly in the common preface. (b) ff. 70–73ᵛ Canon of mass, beginning imperfectly at the words 'tis. Sixti Cornelii'.

York Missal, ii. 331–5.

14. ff. 74–7 [I]n consecracione sancte crucis. primum letanie agantur. Deinde dicat . . .

15. ff. 77–9 Ad signum ecclesie benedicendum.' primo letanie agantur et deinde . . .

Maskell, i. 156.

16. ff. 79–108 Incipiunt benedictiones per anni circulum. Dominica prima aduentus domini. Deus cuius unigeniti aduentu . . . Expliciunt benedicciones pontificales per anni circulum.

A series of 200 benedictions, 193 of which are in *Lacy*, pp. 152–205, where they are said to be 'edite' by Archbishop Pecham. The seven which occur here and not there are for Michael 'in monte tumba' after no. (126), translation of Francis after no. (127), Anthony confessor after no. (129), Dominic after no. (140), Clare after no. (142), Bernard after no. (144), and Francis after no. (152). These and the benediction for Thomas of Canterbury are printed by Wordsworth, pp. 78–80. *Lacy*, nos. (87–91), (111–22) are missing here, owing to the loss of leaves in quires 12, 13.

17. f. 108ʳᵛ In intronizacione archiepiscopi quando ipse archiepiscopus defert pallium a sede romana . . . Deus qui de excelso . . . Omnipotens sempiterne deus qui cum sis . . . Omnipotens sempiterne deus qui est summo . . .

Maskell, iii. 292–3. Collect, secret, and postcommunion only.

18. ff. 108ᵛ–109ᵛ In consecracione archiepiscopi . . . Domine deus pater omnipotens qui sola . . .

19. ff. 109ᵛ–116ᵛ Secretum (*sic*) quod clerus et populus firmare debet pro electo episcopo. [U]enerando sancte cantuariensis ecclesie metropolitano N clerus et populus ecclesie N . . . (f. 110) Incipit examinacio ordinandi episcopi . . . Antiqua sanctorum patrum institucio . . .

Cf. Andrieu, *Pont. Rom.* i. 142. Maskell, iii. 238, 292.

20. ff. 117–121ᵛ [C]onsecracio uirginum que in diebus dominicis uel in apostolorum sollempnitatibus . . . cantando antiphonam. Amo cristum in cuius thalamum . . .

21. ff. 121ᵛ–122ᵛ (*a*) Benedictio eukaristialis uasculi. (*b*) Benedictio turibuli. (*c*) Consecracio thumiamatis uel incensi.

Cf. *Lacy*, pp. 222–3.

22. (*a*) ff. 122ᵛ–131ᵛ In cena domini primo mane custodes ecclesie ordinent omnia que ad consecraciones oleorum . . . (*b*) f. 131ʳᵛ Benediccio ignis de silice excusa feria sexta parasceues uel sabbato sancto . . . Oremus. Domine sancte pater omnipotens eterne deus . . .

(*a*). Cf. *Lacy*, pp. 60–74. (*b*). Cf. *Manuale Sarum*, p. 20. Printed in *York Missal*, ii. 337, and by Wordsworth, p. 92.

23. ff. 131ᵛ–135ᵛ Incipit benediccio foncium. [O]mnipotens sempiterne deus adesto . . .

Blessing of font and office of baptism. *Manuale Sarum*, pp. 33/18–37/20. *York Manual*, pp. 150*–151*.

24. ff. 135ᵛ–138 [R]econciliacio penitencium in cena domini. . . . Adest o uenerabilis pontifex tempus acceptum . . .

York Missal, ii. 337–8. Wordsworth, pp. 93–5.

25. ff. 138–40 Ad scrinium uel archam. uel capsam benedicendam.' primum letanie agantur. Deinde dicat episcopus . . .

Cf. *Lacy*, pp. 231–3.

26. (*a*) f. 140ʳᵛ [O]rdo ad communicandum infirmum . . . Dominus ihesus cristus qui dixit discipulis . . . (*b*) ff. 140ᵛ–142ᵛ Ordo ad unguendum infirmum. (*c*) ff. 142ᵛ–145ᵛ Ordo commendacionis.

(*c*) includes a short litany, 'In primis fiant letanie breues in hunc modum . . .', in which the named saints are Peter, Paul, Andrew, Stephen, Silvester, Francis, Benedict, Paul first hermit, and Lucy. (*a*–*c*). *York Manual*, pp. 194*–199*.

27. ff. 146—149ᵛ [O]rdo ad sepeliendum corpus . . . Non intres in iudicium . . .

York Manual, pp. 199*–203*.

28. Blessings of persons and things: (*a*) ff. 149ᵛ–152 In abbatis ordinacione . . . [E]cclesie N. pater electus . . .; (*b*) f. 152 Specialis benediccio abbatisse. Domine deus . . .; (*c*) f. 152ʳᵛ Benediccio uestium monachalium; (*d*) f. 152ᵛ Benediccio ueli uirginalis; (*e*) ff. 152ᵛ–153 Benediccio lapidis pro fundanda ecclesia; (*f*) f. 153 Benediccio lintheaminum; (*g*) f. 153 Item benediccio ad lintheamina et alia que opus fuerint in sacro ministerio. Exaudi domine . . .; (*h*) f. 153ʳᵛ Benediccio patene consecrande; (*i*) f. 153ᵛ Benediccio calicis consecrandi; (*j*) ff. 153ᵛ–154 Benediccio corporalium; (*k*) f. 154 Benediccio incensi; (*l*) f. 154ʳᵛ Benediccio planete. dalmatice stole et aliarum uestium sacerdotalium ac leuitarum. Oracio. Omnipotens sempiterne deus qui per moysen . . .

(*a*) is for a Benedictine abbot: *Lacy*, pp. 103–7. (*b*). *Lacy*, pp. 113–14.

29. f. 154ᵛ Ordo ad consignand' pueros. Omnipotens sempiterne deus qui regenerare . . .

Manuale Sarum, p. 167.

30. Blessings: (*a*) f. 155 Benediccio panis in ecclesia populo distribuendi; (*b*) f. 155 Benediccio agni et aliarum carnium; (*c*) f. 155ʳᵛ Benediccio casei. lactis. et mellis in pascha; (*d*) f. 155ᵛ Benediccio noue domus; (*e*) f. 155ᵛ Benediccio cilicii. (*f*) ff. 155ᵛ–156 Benediccio cineris. Deus indulgencie deus pietatis . . .

(*e*, *f*). Wordsworth, p. 95.

31. ff. 156–157ᵛ [O]rdo ad facienda sponsalia. primo dicatur . . . huius uersu. Ps' Manda deus . . .

York Manual, pp. 162*–163*.

32. ff. 158–63 Cum portatur corpus ad ecclesiam cantetur hoc *Responsorium*. [S]ubuenite sancti dei . . .

33. f. 163ʳᵛ Benedictio super ymaginem uel ymagines. Dominus uobiscum. [D]eus cuius omnipotencie placere . . . Deus omnis bone actionis . . .

Wordsworth, p. 95.

34. ff. 163ᵛ–164ᵛ Collect, secret, and postcommunion: (*a*) De sancto spiritu; (*b*) Pro semetipso; (*c*) Pro iter agentibus.

Cf. *York Missal*, pp. 338–9.

35. ff. 7–8 Litany.

f. 7, badly damaged, has martyrs in the second column of the recto, lam[berte] uincen[ti] eadmun[de] albane thoma aelphege, and virgins in the second column of the verso. f. 8 is complete. For f. 8ᵛ see below, decoration.

36 (added on flyleaves). (*a*) f. 5 In festo Corporis cristi. [D]eus qui corpus suum in perenne memoriale . . . (*b*) f. 166 Letter of John, bishop of Bangor, excommunicating Thomas ap Howell ap Gron'. (*c*) f. 166 Letter of Anianus, bishop of Bangor, 'minister humilis', giving ten days' relaxation of penance to all who pray at Clare (O.E.S.A., Suffolk) for the soul of Richard Cristeshale. Dated at Clare, 25 Apr. 1279. (*d*) f. 166 Similar letter of Bishop Anianus giving twenty days' relaxation of penance to all who give to the repairs, etc., of the house of Clare. Dated at Clare, 24 Apr. 1279. (*e*) f. 166 'Constituciones domini Aniani Episcopi Bangoren' . . . (*heading only*). (*f*) f. 166ᵛ 'Ego Willelmus de Colnaham deaconus . . .', diocese of Coventry and Lichfield: he swears not to annoy Anianus, bishop of Bangor, or his successors; (*g*) f. 166ᵛ 'Ego Willelmus de Hertwell' diaconus . . .', Lincoln diocese, swears not to annoy A., bishop of Bangor, or his successors. Dated 'Sabbato quo cantatur offic' scicient', A.D. 1324.

(*a*). s. xv. Printed by Wordsworth, p. 78. (*b*–*g*). Cf. Wordsworth, p. 92. (*b*). s. xv. (*c*–*e*). s. xv, in one hand. (*g*) is contemporary and (*f*) looks a little earlier than (*g*) and is likely to have been written before it, because of its position on the page. A transcript of (*c*–*e*) by Alfred Stowe, M.A., Wadham College, Oxford, A.D. 1868, is on f. 165, a modern leaf. The pattern of worm-holes on ff. 166–7 is to be seen also on f. 164 (20⁸).

ff. vii+159+v, foliated (i, ii), 1–167 (168–9). For ff. 5, 166, 167 see above, art. 36: f. 5 is a bit of a medieval flyleaf pasted to a leaf of later parchment. 258×175 mm. Written space 185×115 mm. 27 long lines or 9 long lines and music, except in art. 13 (25 long lines or 8 long lines and music) and in art. 35 (2 cols.). Collation of ff. 6–164: 1 three 2–8⁸ 9 nine (ff. 65–73) 10–11⁸ 12 five (ff. 90–4) 13 six (ff. 95–100) 14–21⁸. The ink has faded on ff. 91–94ᵛ, 96–97/24, at which point the scribe got new ink, and the red ink has often faded badly in headings. A full-page picture on f. 8ᵛ, 165×100 mm within the frame: a bishop before a church: his staff in his left hand: he sprinkles water with his right hand: punched gold ground. Initials: (i) pink, patterned in white, on decorated blue and gold grounds, with prolongations into the margins, except for the letter *I* which is regularly a pink and blue dragon; (ii) f. 69ᵛ, *P* of *Per omnia* and *U* of *Uere dignum*; (iii) 2-line, blue with red ornament or red with green-blue ornament; (iv) 1-line, blue or red. An initial of type (i) probably began each numbered section, except 13, 21, 29, 30, but many have been cut out: the initial of art. 8 seems to have been larger than the others. Rebound at Aberystwyth in 1939: according to a note on f. ivᵛ 'this cover (*the previous cover*) was put on by Dean Jones . . . collated 1696'.

Written for the use of Bishop Anianus of Bangor, probably Anianus II, 1309–28, to judge from the hand, rather than Anianus I, 1267–1305 or 1306: 'Iste liber est pontificalis domini aniani bangor' episcopi', f. 164ᵛ, in the main hand. Probably handed down from bishop to bishop until the time of Bishop Ednam, 1465–94: 'Iste liber est pontificalis Fratris Ricardi Ednam Bangor' Episcopi quem librum predictus Ricardus episcopus dedit Ecclesie sue Cathedrali Bangorie Anno domini Millesimo quadringentesimo Octuagesimo quinto Et sue Consecracionis Anno vicesimo primo', f. 164ᵛ. Probably alienated (in s.xvi?) and given back by Bishop Humphreys: 'C 65 Sum Decani et Capituli Ecclesiæ Cathedralis Bangor. ex dono Humphredi Humphreys S.T.P. Episcopi Bangoriensis Anno Domini 1701', f. 4.

BARNSTAPLE. NORTH DEVON ATHENAEUM

1618. *Guido Faba, 'Exordia Senece'* s. XIV/XV

1. ff. 1–14^v Incipiunt exordia Senece cum conclusionibus sequentibus que multum exornant epistolare dictamen et primo inter socios et amicos. Ordo rationis expostulat vt amicorum precibus . . . in talem disciplinam semat disciplina.

For seven other manuscripts in English libraries see N. Denholm-Young in *Oxford Essays presented to H. E. Salter*, 1934, p. 96, and H. G. Richardson in *Formularies which bear on the history of Oxford*, ed. H. E. Salter, W. A. Pantin, H. G. Richardson, Oxford Historical Soc. n.s. iv, v (1942), 28. The heading here on f. 1 and the titles of the eight main divisions are closely similar to those added in Oxford, Bodleian, Laud. misc. 402, ff. 16–28^v. The title *Exordia Senece* occurs also in Longleat 37 f. 29, in Bodleian, Laud misc. 402, f. 16, and in Clare College, Cambridge, 14.

2. ff. 15–16^v Miscellaneous additions including grammatical verses, 'Vertex pars capitis vertigo girus habetur . . .', and a couplet 'Me male rodentes coram me blandi loquentes Sunt detractores sunt demone deteriores'. The name of Oxford occurs in a phrase on f. 16 and in one on f. 16^v ('. . . equis nostris intendentium oxoniam declinare. . . .').

ff. 16. Paper. 220 × 145 mm. Written space 168 × 100 mm. 35 long lines. One quire of 16 leaves. A piece of parchment as strengthening in the gutter of the central opening has the name 'Wyllelmus Knyght' on it. No ornament. No binding. Written in England (Oxford ?).

3960. *Logica, etc.* s. XV[1]

Noticed by J. R. Chanter and T. Wainwright, *Reprint of the Barnstaple Records*, ii (1900), 44–6, and by H. E. Salter, 'An Oxford Hall in 1424', *Essays in history presented to R. L. Poole*, 1927, pp. 421–35.

1. Notes on logic, beginning (f. 1) 'Vtrum tantum 5 sint vniuersalia'.

Headings are: f. 3^v, De specie; ff. 5–6, De differencia; f. 8, De proprio; f. 8^v, De accidente; ff. 14^v–16, De quantitate; f. 17^v, De relatiuis; ff. 19^v–23, De substantia; ff. 27–8, De ente et substantia; f. 29, De qualitate; f. 35, De quantitate. Written in short paragraphs, one of which begins (f. 18) 'Nota secundum burley sic. Si natura vox esset'. Part of each quire was left blank: (quire 1) ff. 9^v–10^v; (2) ff. 13^v–14, 16^v–17, 18^v; (3) ff. 23^v–26^v; (4) ff. 30–31^v, 32^v–34^v; (5) ff. 36^v–42^v.

2. The blank spaces of art. 1 were partly filled, s.xv[1]. A few of the additions are on logic, for example, f. 18^v, but most of them are memoranda about moneys received and paid out by Mr John Arundell (fellow of Exeter College, Oxford, 1420, †1477: cf. Emden, *BRUO*), whose name occurs on ff. i, 10^{rv}, 43^v.

Salter showed that the memoranda are mainly about money received by Arundell as principal of a hall, possibly St Mildred's Hall, Oxford, and spent by him on behalf of his
pupils: thus, for example, we have on f. 10 a memorandum of the money received from
Thomas Russell 'pro filio suo Iohanne' in 1424 (this is the only date) and on f. 37 a note
of the 'partiales expense pro I Russell'. Of two dozen pieces seven are printed and most
of the others noticed by Salter. An edition by Dr. J. M. Fletcher is in preparation.

3. The conjugate pair of parchment flyleaves, ff. i, 43, and the inside of the
cover at the back contain grammatical notes, perhaps in Arundell's hand.

For example, (f. 43) Nota quod tria sunt genera loquendi . . . Nota quod transmutacio
litterarum est duplex videlicet substancialis et accidentalis . . .

ff. i+40+i, together with a slip, ff. 4, 7. Paper, except the flyleaves. 150×115 mm.
Written space c. 135×87 mm. Long lines, varying in number: many pages not full.
Frame ruling open at the foot. Collation: 1–5⁸ (ff. 1–3, 5, 6, 8–42: 4+7 is a slip): 4⁴, f. 30,
is a small fragment only. Art. 1 in neat current anglicana. No ornament. Limp parchment cover, the quires attached to it by string at four points or (quire 1) by a narrow
strip of rolled up parchment at two points.

  Written in England (Oxford ?). Used for notes by John Arundell in and about 1424:
see art. 2.

BATH. PUBLIC LIBRARY

Horae   s. xv²

1. ff. 1–72ᵛ Hours of B.V.M. of the use of (Nantes), beginning imperfectly.
Hours of Cross and of Holy Spirit are worked in.

2. ff. 73–6 Deus propicius esto michi peccatori . . . A prayer to guardian angels.

3. ff. 76–77ᵛ Versus sancti Bernardi.

4. ff. 78–99ᵛ Penitential psalms, beginning imperfectly, and litany.

5. ff. 100–63 Office of the dead.

6. ff. 163ᵛ–168ᵛ Deuota oracio de nostra domina. O intemerata . . . orbis
terrarum. De te enim . . .

7. ff. 169–170ᵛ Aue cuius concepcio . . . *RH*, no. 1744.

8. ff. 170ᵛ–173 Septem gaudia spiritualia nostre domine. Gaude flore virginali
. . . *RH*, no. 6809.

9. ff. 173–4 Oracio Recommendacionis. Sancta maria mater domini . . .

10. ff. 174–7 De nostra domina oracio lamentatiua. Stabat mater dolorosa . . .,
and prayer 'Intemerata pro nobis . . .'.

11. ff. 177–183ᵛ Prayers, etc., at mass: (*a*) f. 177 Domine ihesu criste qui
hanc sacratissimam carnem . . .; (*b*) f. 177ᵛ Anima cristi sanctifica me . . .;
(*c*) f. 178 Oracio. O bone ihesu, o piissime ihesu . . .; (*d*) f. 180 Aue verum

corpus natum . . . (*RH*, no. 2175); (*e*) f. 180 Alia oracio. O beatissime domine
ihesu criste. Respicere digneris super me miserum peccatorem . . .; (*f*) f. 181
Aue ihesu . . .; (*g*) f. 181ᵛ Salue sancta caro dei . . . (*RH*, no. 18175); (*h*) f. 182ᵛ
Quando volueris recipere corpus domini. Domine ihesu criste fili dei uiui te
supplex queso . . .; (*i*) Post recepcionem corporis cristi. Vera suscepcio corporis . . .

12. ff. 184–91 Deus pater qui creasti . . . *RH*, no. 4477: fifty 4-line stanzas.

13. ff. 191–192ᵛ Passio domini nostri ihesu cristi. Secundum Iohannem. In
illo tempore. Apprehendit Pylatus . . . Et qui ista vidit (*ends imperfectly*).

Mainly from John 19: cf. *Lyell Cat.*, pp. 65–6.

ff. ii+192+i. 108×85 mm. Written space 53×38 mm. 14 long lines. Collation:
26 quires, all originally eights, except quire 2 (seven: ff. 6–12) and quire 22 (seven:
ff. 156–62), but fourteen leaves are missing, as follows: 1¹⁻³, 3¹ before f. 13, 5¹ before f. 28,
6³ after f. 36, 7³ after f. 43, 8² after f. 49, 9¹ before f. 56, 10⁴ after f. 65, 12¹ before f. 78,
14⁸ after f. 99, 26⁷, ⁸ after f. 192. Written in *lettre bâtarde*. All leaves with principal
decoration (pictures?) removed. Initials: (i, ii) 5-line and 2-line, in colour on gold grounds,
decorated; (iii) 1-line, gold on coloured grounds. A border in colours and gold on three
sides of pages with initials of type (i)—now only those on which Hours of Cross and Holy
Spirit begin. A similar border the height of the written space on pages with initials of
type (ii). Binding of s. xix.

Written in France. Book-plate, dated 1700, of Pembroke College, Cambridge. Given by
Cedric Chivers in 1929.

BIRMINGHAM. CITY ART GALLERY

Horae B.V.M. s. xv in.

1 (added, s. xv¹). Memoriae: (*a*) ff. 3–4, Antiphona de maria iacobi et salome.
O felix prosapia . . .; (*b*) ff. 5–6, of Barbara.

(*a*). A collect asks for the intercession 'marie iacobi et marie salome. Quarum corpora
in presenti requiescunt ecclesia'. (*b*). Barbara is invoked 'ut ab orrando fulgore et a clade
tonitrui nos serues' and 'a grandine et in die iudicii a pena et a iudice'. ff. 1–2ᵛ (see below,
art. 26), 4ᵛ, 6ᵛ were left blank.

2. ff. 7–18 Calendar in red and black.

'Obiit beatus petrus de lucembourg' in red at 5 July. Conceptio B.V.M. in red, 8 Dec.
Additions, s. xv²: 'Sancti honoraty' (of Arles), 16 Jan.; 'ludouici cardinalis arel' ', 17 Sept.
(Cardinal Louis Aleman, †16 Sept. 1450, beatified in 1527).

3. ff. 19–25 Sequentiae of the Gospels.

4. ff. 25–29ᵛ Deuota oracio beate marie uirginis. Obsecro te . . . Masculine
forms.

5. ff. 29ᵛ–32ᵛ Alia deuota oracio beate marie uirginis et beati iohannis euuange-
liste. O intemerata . . . orbis terrarum. Inclina . . .

6. ff. 32ᵛ–100ᵛ Incipit officium beate marie uirginis secundum usum romane ecclesie.

Tuesday and Friday psalms, f. 82. Wednesday and Saturday psalms, f. 86. Advent office, f . 91.

7. ff. 101–4 Incipit officium sancte trinitatis.

Hours of Holy Trinity. The hymn is Quicumque vult animam, *RH*, no. 16566; *AH* xxx. 10.

8. ff. 105–108ᵛ Hours of the Cross. Hymn, Patris sapiencia.

9. ff. 108ᵛ–112 Hours of the Holy Spirit. Hymn, Nobis sancti spiritus.

10. ff. 112ᵛ–137 Hic incipiunt septem psalmi penitenciales . . .: the litany follows on f. 126.

The order of monks and hermits is Benedict, Francis, Anthony, Dominic. Nineteen virgins: . . . (14) Genouefa.

11. ff. 137–174ᵛ Incipit officium defunctorum.

12 (added, s. xv, in hand of art. 24). ff. 174ᵛ–175ᵛ Ceste oroison qui sensuit composa pape boniface a la requeste de philip iadis roy de france et octroya a tous ceulx qui la diront deuotement entre la leuacion du corps nostres' et le tiers agnus dei. deux Mille ans de vray pardon. [D]omine ihesu criste fili dei qui hanc carnem sacratissimam . . . f. 176ʳᵛ blank.

13. Deuote salutaciones dicende in eleuacione corporis xpisti. (*a*) f. 177ʳᵛ Aue domine ihesu criste uerbum patris . . . (*b*) ff. 177ᵛ–180 Salue sancta caro dei per quam salui fiunt rei . . . et da michi sedem iustorum per cuncta secula seculorum: antiphons follow. (*c*) f. 180ʳᵛ Salue corpus domini nostri ihesu cristi salue uictima deo patri oblata . . .

(*a*). Five aves. (*b*). Fourteen couplets followed by prose antiphons.

14. (*a*) ff. 180ᵛ–182 Deuota oracio beate marie uirginis. Sancta maria filia dei patris mater ihesu xpisti amica spiritus sancti . . . (*b*) ff. 182–3 Alia oracio beate marie uirginis. Aue maria gracia plena dominus tecum ita tu mecum sis . . .

15. ff. 183–185ᵛ Passio domini nostri ihesu cristi secundum iohannem. In illo tempore. Apprehendit pilatus . . . quia uerum est testimonium eius. Deo gracias. Deus qui manus tuas . . .

See *Lyell Cat.*, pp. 65–6.

16. ff. 185ᵛ–186ᵛ Ymnus de sancto spiritu. Ueni creator spiritus mentes tuorum uisita . . .

17. ff. 186ᵛ–189 Saint leon pape de romme escript ce brief et lenuoya au roy charles . . . lequel lange lui apporta du ciel . . . tantost sans peril. +(M)essias +sother . . .

Thirty-one holy names and, after further directions in red, six and four names, followed by the names of the Three Kings, +Gaspar fert mirram . . . (Walther, no. 2535), and the names of the apostles. The rubric notes the virtues of the letter for those who are lost, ill, etc.

18. ff. 189–212 Secuntur aliqua suffragia sanctorum et primo de resurrectione domini.

Memoriae of the Resurrection, Corpus Christi, Michael, John Baptist, Peter, Paul, Andrew, John Evangelist, James and Philip, James the greater, Thomas apostle, Simon and Jude, Bartholomew, Barnabas (Barnaba celi sydus . . .), Matthew, Matthias, Mark, Luke, all apostles, all evangelists, Stephen, Sebastian, Blasius (Aue presul honestatis . . .: *RH*, no. 2056), Christopher, Cosmas and Damian, Laurence, all martyrs, Martin, Nicholas, Anthony hermit, all confessors, Mary Magdalene, Anne, Katherine, all virgins, All Saints.

19. ff. 212–213^{v} Bonifacius papa viii^{us} concessit cuilibet dicenti hanc oracionem xxx^{a} diebus continuatis ut esset absolutus omnium peccatorum ore confesso et corde contricto. et ita scriptum est in ecclesia sancti pauli urbis rome ad pedes cuiusdam crucifixi qui est ad latus maioris. Deus qui uoluisti pro redemptione mundi nasci . . .

Cf. *Lyell Cat.*, p. 64.

20. ff. 213^{v}–215 Sequentem oracionem constituit bonifacius papa viii^{us} et concessit omnibus dicentibus eam qualibet die corde contricto ut esset absolutus a pena et culpa et ab omnibus peccatis suis: oracio. Stabat uirgo iuxta crucem. Videns . . .

Thirty-three lines. *RH*, no. 19423.

21. f. 215^{rv} Quando surgis de lecto. Domine ihesu xpiste nostrorum operum peruigil . . .

22. ff. 215^{v}–217^{v} Sequitur uersus beati bernardi quos qui cotidie dixerit numquam dampnabitur ut dyabolus sibi retulit prout in uita beati bernardi legitur et continetur. [O] bone ihesu. Illumina . . .

Ten, instead of (as usual) eight verses, Illumina . . ., In manus . . ., Locutus sum . . ., Et numerum . . ., Dirripuisti . . ., Periit . . ., Clamaui . . ., Fac mecum . . ., Signatum est . . ., Dixi confitebor . . ., each preceded by a holy name in red, O bone ihesu—O raboni. The usual prayer follows, 'Omnipotens sempiterne deus qui ezechie . . .' and finally in a new line are the words 'Ita est Prepositi' and a paraph.

23. ff. 217^{v}–219 Memoriae 'De sancto petro de lucemburgo', of Symphorianus, and of Lucy.

24 (added, s. xv, in the hand of art. 12). ff. 219^{v}–221 Pappe benedic de lordre de citeaux composa ceste oroison et octroia a tous . . . Precor te piissime domine ihesu criste propter illam caritatem qua tu rex celestis pendebas in cruce . . .

The indulgence is of 5555 days, equal to the number of Christ's wounds.

25 (added, s. xv). ff. 221^{v}–223^{v} Memoriae of: (*a*) Honoratus; (*b*) Restitutus, confessor and pontiff, who 'a multorum oculis dolorem sanas et uisum clarificas'.

26. Three of four blank pages in quire 1 were filled by one current hand with entries recording the births of (f. 2) Honoré, (f. 2^{v}) Agnes, and (f. 1) Anthoine de la Tour on, respectively, 26 Jan. 1470, 13 Dec. 1479 and 26 Feb. 1481, their baptism in the parish of St. Laurence, and the names of godparents.

The least difficult entry is on f. 2^{v}: 'Lan mil iiii^{c} lxxix e le xiiie de desenbre es nada agna de latour e la fach bategar lo primer paure que es veni gut a la porte nomat bennet verpillat e estada (?) la mayrina katarinna Rycauda de marsselia e fou bategada en la perocha de monsenher sant laurens dieux par la sainta mysericordia ly don longua via amen'.

27. The pastedown in front is a leaf from a prayer-book written in *lettre bâtarde*, s. xv². The text appears to be the final prayer of a memoria of St. Martha.

ff. 223+iii. 115×77 mm. Written space 77×50 mm. 13 long lines. Collation: 1⁶ 2¹²
3–12⁸ 13⁶ (ff. 99–104) 14–27⁸ 28⁶+1 leaf after 6. One full page picture, f. 104ᵛ. Four
8-line pictures, ff. 33, 102, 113 (the Pentecost picture for art. 9 placed by the illuminator
in front of art. 10), 137ᵛ. Initials: (i) 4-line, patterned blue or pink on gold grounds,
decorated: a blue flower with usually four petals projects to the left from each initial;
(ii) 2-line, gold on grounds of patterned blue and pink; (iii) 1-line, blue with red ornament
or gold with slate-grey ornament. Borders, mainly ivy-leaf, are continuous on picture
pages and partial on other pages with initials of type (i). Line fillers in litany gold and
blue. Capital letters in the ink of the text filled with yellow. French binding of red gilt
morocco, s. xviii.

Written in France, perhaps by a scribe named Prévost (art. 22). Belonged in s. xvᴵ to an
inhabitant of Les-Saintes-Maries-de-la-Mer (art. 1a) and in s. xv² to a member of the
Latour family, perhaps in Arles (arts. 2, 25, 26). 'George [. . .]n Lancaster 1846', a brief
description, and the number 'M. 26' are on a piece of blue paper attached to f. 1. Numbers,
s. xix, on the pastedown: 8 (on a round label), 25, and (in pencil) 225.

BIRMINGHAM. PUBLIC LIBRARY

091/MED/1. *Psalterium* s. XIII¹

1. ff. 1–72ᵛ Pss. 47: 13 te syon et complectimini eam—150.

Ps. 101 is headed 'Oratio pauperis in angustia'. Antiphons (not noted) and a few scholia
added in s. xv; also a few glosses in German, s. xv. Probably thirty-two leaves are missing
before f. 1.

2. ff. 72ᵛ–83ᵛ Six ferial canticles, Benedicite, Benedictus, Magnificat, Nunc
dimittis, Pater noster, Credo in deum patrem, Te Deum, Quicumque vult.

German glosses more frequent than in art. 1, for example (f. 76ᵛ), 'dz werck des oley baums
wirt liegen oder felen' above 'Mentietur opus oliue' (Habakkuk 3: 17) and (f. 78) 'ist es nit'
over 'Nonne' (Deuteronomy 32: 34).

3. ff. 83ᵛ–86ᵛ Cant' dominicis. et de sancto michaele. Domine miserere nostri
te enim . . . Aliud. Audite qui longe estis . . . Aliud. Miserere domine plebi
tue . . . In nat' domini. Cant' et in purif'. Populus qui ambulabat . . . Aliud.
Letare ierusalem . . . Vrbs fortitudinis nostre . . . custodiens veritatem (*ends
imperfectly*, f. 85ᵛ). (*begins imperfectly*, f. 86) in uoce labiorum . . . Aliud.
Gaudens gaudebo . . . Aliud. Non uocaberis ultra . . . laudem in terra.

Monastic canticles for Sundays and Christmas (Mearns' 'first set' in each case) and, after
a gap, for the common of virgins (Mearns' 'second set'): cf. J. Mearns, *Canticles eastern
and western*, pp. 87, 92.

4. Pastedowns, now missing, have left offset traces: in front, of a document, s.
xiv, mentioning a prebend and church of St. Thomas; at the end, of a service
book (?).

ff. xii+86+xxiv. 313×225 mm. Written space 215×145 mm. 20 long lines. Collation: 1–10⁸ 11 six. Quires 1–10 numbered Vᵘˢ–XIIIIᵘˢ in the bottom left corner of versos. The first line of writing below the top ruled line. Hands of twelfth-century type, with occasional bitings, for example, f. 52/7. Added flex punctuation (7) until f. 83, after which a new hand uses punctus elevatus, flex, and, instead of a simple point, a point with a vertical stroke above and to the right of it. Initials: (i) of Ps. 51, 9-line, in outline, with red and black patterning, on a blue and red ground, decorated with curving branches in white; of Ps. 101, 9-line, blue and red with ornament of both colours; (ii) of other principal psalms, more or less as Ps. 101, but smaller; (iii) 2-line, blue or red with ornament of the other colour; (iv) 1-line, red. Contemporary binding of white leather over wooden boards which show signs of use the other way round: three bands: the leather on the back cover extends over the fore-edge and is attached by two straps to pins on the front cover.

Written in Germany, for monastic (Cistercian?) use. Obtained in or before 1928: an inserted description is dated 19 Dec. 1928.

091/MED/2. *Missale* s. XIII med.

Disordered fragments, twenty-seven bifolia in all, of a small noted Sarum missal described by W. H. Frere, *Graduale Sarisburiense*, 1894, p. liii.

1. One complete quire and parts of five other quires of the temporale.

Quire 1 (pp. 13–36). Complete. *Sarum Missal*, pp. 38/19–58/30. Quire 2 (pp. 93–108). Leaves 1–3, 5, 8, 10–12 of a quire of 12. *SM*, pp. 58/30–78/15, with three gaps. Quire 3 (pp. 77–84). Leaves 4, 5, 8, 9 of a quire of 12. *SM*, pp. 100/27–110/5, with one gap. Quire 4 (pp. 37–52). Leaves 2, 4–9, 11 of a quire of 12. *SM*, pp. 138/31–159/6, with two gaps. Quire 5 (pp. 53–64). Leaves 4–9 of a quire of 12. *SM*, pp. 171/2–181/33. Quire 6 (pp. 65–8, 73–6). Leaves 5–8 of a quire of 12. *SM*, pp. 198/26–192/21: the order agrees with Legg's MS. B.

2. Parts of two quires of the sanctorale.

Quire 7 (pp. 1–12). Leaves 4–9 of a quire of 12. *SM*, pp. 247/11–276/14 (2 Feb.–14 June). Quire 8 (pp. 85–92). Leaves 2, 4, 9, 11 of a quire of 12. *SM*, pp. 286/5 (2 July)–347, footnote, line 2 of postcommunion of office of Anianus (17 Nov.), as in Legg's MS. B. The offices in *SM*, pp. 331, 335, 347 (Francis, Wulfran, and Edmund of Canterbury) do not occur.

3. Part of a quire of the common of saints.

Quire 9 (pp. 69–72). Leaves 5, 8 of a quire of 12. *SM*, pp. 361/12–370/13, with a gap.

ff. ii+54+ii. 168×106 mm. Written space 112×78 mm. 2 cols. 54 lines. Collation: probably all twelves (see above). Quires 1, 2 are numbered II, III at the end. Written in a very small hand. A small picture in the margin of p. 2, 22×15 mm, shows the Presentation on a gold ground. 2-line initials, red or blue, with ornament of the other colour. Binding of s. xix.

Written in England. Transferred from the City Museum and Art Gallery in 1951.

091/MED/3. *Hugo de Sancto Victore, Opera* s. XIII²

A corpus of the works of Hugh of St. Victor. Each quire is marked 'Cor' ' at beginning and end. A description supplied by the British Museum in 1922 is attached to f. (214).

1. ff. 1–35ᵛ (*a*) Incipit expositio super prologum Ieronimi in Pentateucum quem dirigit ad desiderium quendam amicum suum. cuius rogatu quinque libros moysi de hebreo in latinum transtulit. Desiderius proprium nomen est ... (f. 1ᵛ) greca. (*b*) Qui scripture merito diuine appellari debent. Lectorem ... (f. 6ᵛ) Iudei. (*c*) De nuncupatione Genesis. Liber iste ... (f. 16ᵛ) super genua. Expliciunt note ad litteram de genesi. (*d*) Incipiunt note de exodo. Locus in quo stas ... (f. 24ᵛ) redimi. Explicit leuiticus. (*e*) Incipit Iudicum. Liber iudicum ... (f. 34ʳᵇ/25) destruam. (*f–k*) Quis fecit os hominis? ... potest in hoc seculo.

Notes on Jerome's prologue, the Pentateuch, Judges, and 1–4 Kings corresponding to the text printed in *PL* clxxv. 29–114, but in a different order: (*a*) 29–32; (*b*) 9–24 (chapters 1–17); (*c*) 32–61/7; (*d*) 62A–84C, with small omissions (see below, *f*); (*e*) 87–114, with an omission (see below, *j*); (*f*) *sparsim* between 62D and 84B, notes on Exodus and Leviticus; (*g*) 84D–85D, notes on Numbers; (*h*) 86A–D, notes on Deuteronomy; (*i*) 85D–86A, notes on Numbers 24: 21, 22; (*j*) 95D–96D, notes on 1 Kings 3: 2–4; (*k*) 61/10–28, notes on Genesis 49. The last part of (*e*) from 'Cumque uenisset dies' (4 Kings 8) and all (*f–k*) are in a single paragraph. (*f*) begins at f. 34ʳᵇ/25, (*g*) at f. 34ᵛᵇ/4, (*h*) at f. 35ʳᵃ/38, (*i*) at f. 35ʳᵇ/45, (*j*) at f. 35ᵛᵃ/13, (*k*) at f. 35ᵛᵃ/35. (*a, c, k*) Stegmüller, no. 3793; (*d*) 3796–7; (*e*) 3801, 3803–7; (*g, i*) 3798; (*h*) 3799. The one note on Ruth (Stegm., no. 3803: *PL* clxxv. 96) follows Judges without break or mark of punctuation or capital letter, f. 28ʳᵃ/7.

2. ff. 35ᵛ–37 Presens seculum distinguitur in duos status ... Tempore achaz regis iuda.

Notes on OT history and ancient kingdoms, especially Assyria, with lists of names.

3. ff. 37ᵛ–38ᵛ Multa in scriptura sacra occurrunt ... interfecit. *PL* clxxv. 25–8.

4. ff. 38ᵛ–39ᵛ Proportiones rerum ... (f. 39) Libra attica. lxxv dragmas. Mensurarum in liquidis. Coclear ... Culleus. Duo cori. Mensurarum agrestium ... Leuga. Miliare et dimidium.

Three paragraphs on weights and measures. Also in Douai 366, f. 76ᵛ.

Arts. 5–26 are very nearly identical with and in the same order as Paris, Mazarine 717, ff. 124–212ᵛ, arts. 11–115 of the description by R. Baron in *Scriptorium*, x (1956), 184–9: for differences see arts. 9, 26.

5. ff. 40–54ᵛ De uanitate rerum mundanarum. O munde inmunde ... non mutetur. *PL* clxxvi. 703–40.

6. ff. 54ᵛ–65ᵛ Incipit liber de tribus diebus pro ea que in meditacione constat speculatio rerum et post lectionem secunda. Verbum bonum ... ad resurrectionem. *PL* clxxvi. 811–38.

7. ff. 65ᵛ–72ᵛ Incipit prologus in soliloquium de arra anime. Dilecto fratri G ... concupisco. *PL* clxxvi. 951–70.

8. ff. 72ᵛ–75 Incipit prologus de laude karitatis. Seruo cristi petro H. Gustare et videre ... secula seculorum amen. *PL* clxxvi. 969–76.

9. f. 75 Incipit de substantia dilectionis. Cotidianum de dilectione ... riuos infundit.

Ten lines only. *PL* clxxvi. 15/3–9. Cf. art. 27. Maz. has the whole text, ff. 151ᵛ–152ᵛ, and follows it with De virtute orationis, ff. 152ᵛ–155ᵛ, but Baron notes that 'ff. 152–6 ont été refaits au xvᵉ s.'

10. ff. 75–76ᵛ Meditatio est frequens cogitatio . . . apprehendat.

PL clxxvi. 993–8. Ed. R. Baron, *Hugues de Saint-Victor, Six opuscules spirituels*, 1969, pp. 44–58.

11. ff. 76ᵛ–79 Spiritalis diiudicat omnia . . . natura.

PL clxxvii. 469–77.

12. ff. 79–80 Omnia per sapientiam dei . . . Magnificat anima mea dominum etc'. *PL* clxxvii. 320–4. (De verbo incarnato, Collatio III).

13. ff. 80–1 Egredietur uirga de radice iesse . . . Hodie fratres karissimi impletum est . . . et mortuus pro nobis amen.

Ed. R. Baron in *Revue ascétique et mystique*, cxxiii (1955), 269–71.

14. f. 81ʳᵛ Maria porta cristi . . . et coroneris. Sixteen lines only.

15. ff. 81ᵛ–82 Verbum caro factum est. Quod uerbum dei . . . non persona. *PL* clxxvii. 318–20 (De verbo incarnato, Collatio II).

16. ff. 82–83ᵛ Queris de uoluntate dei . . . uiuit deo. *PL* clxxvi. 841–6.

17. ff. 83ᵛ–85 De cibo emanuelis. De cibo emanuelis magna questio est quare butyrum . . . non est appetenda. Per dominum nostrum. *PL* clxxvii. 477–81.

18. ff. 85–89 Incipit prologus de sapientia cristo et sapientia cristi. Prudenti ac religioso . . . presumere. Vale. *PL* clxxvi. 845–56.

19. ff. 89–97 De uirginitate beate marie. Sancto pontifici G. . . . sanciatur. *PL* clxxvi. 857–76.

20. ff. 97–8. Dum medium silentium tenerent omnia. Tria sunt silencia . . . ab initio seculi. Amen. *PL* clxxvii. 315–18 (De verbo incarnato, Collatio I).

21. ff. 98–9 Quod natum est ex carne . . . sciendum facit. *PL* clxxvii. 285–9.

22. ff. 99ᵛ–116. Cum esset ihesus annorum xii etc'. Sicut mundus iste . . . est in retributione.

Eighty-three paragraphs, all but two of them forming part of bk. 1 of the Miscellanea in *PL* clxxvii: nos. 81–91, 106, 92, (f. 102ᵛ) In peccato duo sunt. Vitium et culpa . . . contra pietatem (5 lines), 93–6, 99, 97, 98, 100–3, 105, 106 lines 1–5 *preterita* (here attached to no. 105), 104, 107–17, 62, (f. 110) Queritur etiam de potestate dei . . . Sed presciuit (*PL* clxxvi. 839–42), 118–58. Set out in detail from Maz. 717, op. cit., pp. 185–9.

23. ff. 116–132ᵛ Excerpta de libro psalmorum. Quosdam tibi psalmiste . . . iudic(i)um deus.

Eighty-two paragraphs, all forming part of bk. 2 of the Miscellanea in *PL* clxxvii: prologue, nos. 1–4, 6–43, 45, 44, 46, 48, 47, 49–68, 70, 69, 71–7, 79–81, 78, 82. Stegmüller, no. 3810.

24. ff. 132ᵛ–134 Audi israel deus tuus . . . id quod est. *PL* clxxvi. 9–14/43 (*ends abruptly*).

25. ff. 134–6 Quinque septena in sacra scriptura . . . memento mei. Gracia dei sit tecum amen. *PL* clxxv. 405–10. Ed. Baron, 1969 (op. cit.), pp. 100–18.

26. ff. 136–8 Semel locutus est deus. quia unum verbum . . . circumdati sunt.

PL clxxvii. 289–94, the latter part of De unione corporis et spiritus (art. 21). Maz. 717 ends imperfectly.

27. ff. 138–44 Quando pater coeternum . . . sed inordinata cupiditas.

Fourteen paragraphs, all but the end of the last one forming nos. 159–73 of bk. 1 of the Miscellanea in *PL* clxxvii. The last paragraph goes with no. 173 as far as 'et est amor bonus' (ed., col. 571/5) and continues (f. 143ʳᵇ/34), without punctuation after *bonus*, 'amor mundi cupiditas . . . inordinata cupiditas', which is all but the first lines of De substantia dilectionis (*PL* clxxvi. 15/9–18 (end): ed. Baron, 1969 (op. cit.), pp. 82–92): cf. above, art. 9.

28. ff. 144–8 Incipit prologus. Domino et patri th. H. Munusculum . . . cordis adoletur.

PL clxxvi. 977–88 (De modo orandi). For this text in Maz. cf. above, art. 9.

29. ff. 148–9 Hugo Ranulfo de Mauriaco. Feruor caritatis . . . dampnabile non sit. *PL* clxxvi, 1011–14 (Epistola II). In Maz., f. 74 (art. 7).

30. ff. 149–75 Due precipue res sunt . . . finem accepit. Didascalon Hugonis de studio legendi. Primus liber de origine artium. Omnium expetendorum . . . a persis venit.

PL clxxvi. 741–812. Ed. Buttimer, 1939, pp. 2–133. Only the second section, 'Qui doctrine . . .', of bk. 3, cap. 8 occurs here, f. 160. In Maz., f. 74ᵛ (art. 8).

31. ff. 175–9 Epytoma dindimi in philosophiam. Sepe nobis indaleti Frater dindimus iste noster . . . (f. 178ᵛ) liber euadet.

Ed. R. Baron, *Opera propaedeutica*, 1966, pp. 187–206. In Maz., f. 51 (art. 5). A table of the divisions of philosophy under the four main heads Logica, Ethica, Theorica, Mechanica, follows (ff. 178ᵛ–179): cf. ed., after p. 163, the plate from Maz.

32. ff. 179–192ᵛ De grammatica. Sosthenes. Quid est grammatica? . . . Secundus secundam et cetera (*ends abruptly*).

Ibid., pp. 76–135/17 (line 1808). In Maz., f. 54 (art. 6). The scribe wrote in the lower margin of f. 192ᵛ, 'Hic defecit scriptori exemplar'.

33. ff. 193–203ᵛ Practicam geometrie nostris tradere conatus sum . . . circulis reseruamus.

Ibid., pp. 15–64. In Maz., f. 41 (art. 4).

34. ff. 203ᵛ–211ᵛ Primum in planitie ubi archam . . . prouocet. Sit deus benedictus per cuncta seculorum secula. amen.

PL clxxvi. 681–704 (De arca Noe mystica). In Maz., f. 1 (art. 1). f. 212ʳᵛ blank.

ff. ii+212+ii. Medieval foliation. 320×200 mm. Written space 215×138 mm. 2 cols. 49 lines. Collation: 1–26⁸ 27⁴. In s.xiv a quire number was added on the first recto and last verso of each quire: for this distinctive marking used by the Franciscans of Assisi see below, Birmingham, Selly Oak Colleges, Lat. 2. Initials: (i) blue and red, with ornament of both colours; (ii) 3-line, blue or red, with ornament of the other colour; (iii) 1-line, blue or red. Capital letters in the ink of the text touched with red. Binding of 1903 by Douglas Cockerell. Secundo folio *Sed membra*.

Written in France. An erasure at the foot of f. 1. A faint inscription at the head of f. 1, s. xiv: 'Istum librum emit dominus P. Card' a mon[asterio sancte Marie] de P[al]azolo' (cf. below, Birmingham, Selly Oak Colleges, Lat. 2).[1] The number '6' is to the left of it. Belonged to the Franciscans of Assisi by 1381. Their catalogue entry is 'Didascolus eiusdem ugonis. cum pluribus aliis tractatibus. cum postibus et cathena. Cuius principium est Desiderius proprium nomen est. Finis vero Sit deus benedictus per cuncta secula seculorum Amen. In quo libro omnes quaterni sunt xxvii. K' (L. Alessandri, *Inventario dell'antica biblioteca del S. Convento di S. Francesco in Assisi compilato nel 1381*, 1906, p. 18, no. lxxx of the Bibliotheca pubblica). Michael Tomkinson sale at Sotheby's, 3 July 1922, lot 1495.

091/MED/4. *Biblia*   s. XIII²

1. ff. 1–400 A 'normal' Bible, no doubt, as in Bristol, Public Library, 15, but now lacking all before Numbers 36: 6 'gata est. Nubant' and probably seventeen other leaves.

Daniel and Matthew begin on new quires. The gaps after ff. 86, 126, 195, 200, 220 contained from 4 Kings 24: 15 to near the end of the prologue to 1 Chronicles, 2 (3) Ezra 8: 47–Tobit 2: 10, Ecclesiasticus 10: 25–21: 36; Ecclesiasticus 38: 18–Isaiah 13: 20, and Jeremiah 15: 6–22: 1. The prologues are sixty of the common set of sixty-four set out below under Bristol, Public Library, 15; the other four came on missing leaves. The prologue to 1 Timothy ends 'scribens ei a laodicia ab urbe roma'. Guide letters for the rubricator written in the lower margins remain on ff. 183ᵛ–190.

2. f. 400ʳᵛ Incipiunt interpretaciones. Aaz apprehendens . . .

The usual list of Hebrew names, ending here in Abisay.

ff. v+400+vi. 158×110 mm. Written space 118×77 mm. 2 cols. 51 lines. Collation: 1 six 2–4²⁴ 5²⁴ wants 9 after f. 86 6²⁴ (21 damaged) 7²⁴ wants 2, 3 after f. 126 8–9²⁴ 10 thirteen (ff. 196–208) 11²⁴ wants 13–15 after f. 220 12²⁸ wants 28 blank after f. 256 13–18²⁴. Initials: (i) red and blue, with saw-pattern and other ornament of both colours; (ii) red or blue, with ornament of both colours or one of them; (iii) in art. 2, 1-line, red or blue. Capital letters in the ink of the text stroked with red. Rebound in 1950 in green morocco. Written in France. 'Basill Brokes', f. 321ᵛ in a fancy hand. 'Charles Wayland', f. ivᵛ, s. xix. Notes, s. xix, about the family of Brewer on ff. iv, 402 may have been taken over in part from older flyleaves. Acquired in or before 1923 when a description was supplied by Dr. Eric Millar of the British Museum (f. 401).

091/MED/5. *Horae (in Netherlandish)*   s. xv med.

1. pp. 1–24 Full calendar in red and black. Ponciaen, Gheertruud, Pancraes, Servaes, Bonifaes, Odulphus, Lebuyn (June and Nov.), Geroen, Lambert, Remigius ende Bavo, Willebroert in red. Includes the Visitation of B.V.M. A leaf at the beginning and a leaf at the end were left blank: see below, collation.

2. pp. 25–92 Hier begint die vrouwen ghetide. Use of (Utrecht).

3. pp. 173–4, 93–130 Hours of the Cross, in the long form.

4. pp. 131–71 Hours of the Holy Spirit, in the long form, beginning imperfectly. p. 172 and the next two pages were left blank: see below, collation.

[1] Letters in brackets are derived from the British Museum description.

5. pp. 175–202 Penitential psalms (*beginning imperfectly*) and (p. 189) litany.

Twenty-six confessors: . . . (13–26) Baue, Franciscus, Dominicus, Eusebius, Galle, Hubert, Seuerus, Lebuyn, Odulf, Seruaes, Symon, Felix, Hubert, Seueryn.

6. pp. 203–67 Office of the dead: use of (Utrecht).

7. pp. 267–74 Dit ghebet salstu lesen alstu dat heilighe sacrament selste ontfaen. O ouerste priester ende waer bisscop . . . pp. 275–6 blank.

ff. iii+141. Paginated i–viii, 1–276.[1] 175 × 120 mm. Written space 88 × 62 mm. 21 long lines. Collation: 1⁸ (pp. vii, viii, 1–14) 2⁶ (pp. 15–26) 3⁸ (pp. 25–40) 4–6⁸ 7⁸ (pp. 89–92, 173–4, 93–102) 8⁸ 9⁸ wants 7, 8 after p. 130 10–11⁸ 12⁶ (pp. 163–74) 13⁸ wants 1 before p. 175 14⁸ wants 8 after p. 202 15⁸ wants 1 before p. 203 16–18⁸ 19⁶: 2⁶ and 3¹ have been made into one leaf, pp. 25, 26, by cutting round the edges of the text on 3¹, the first leaf of art. 2, and attaching it to the blank leaf 2⁶, in which a hole of corresponding size was made: 12⁶, a blank leaf, and 7³, the first leaf of art. 3, were similarly treated and the composite leaf so formed was treated as though it were the first leaf of art. 5, pp. 173–4. Initials: (i) pp. 25, 173, blue, patterned in white, on decorated gold grounds; (ii) 4-line or 3-line, in two styles, either (*a*) gold on grounds of red and blue patterned in white, with or without ornament in red and green, or (*b*) blue with red and green ornament or red with violet and green ornament; (iii, iv) 2-line and 1-line, red or blue. The border on p. 25 has been removed, but that on p. 173 remains: flowers in colours and gold, with peacock and grotesques. Gold and blue line fillers in the litany only. Capital letters in the ink of the text are stroked with red. Binding of s. xviii, lettered on the spine 'Getydenboek M.S.'.

Written probably in the southern Netherlands. 'Dit bouck hoort toe Machtelt van der Burch 1593', p. vi. 'G. Sumner, Woodmansey, 1848. Chest L. 13', p. i. Lent and later given by S. Jevons to the City Museum and Art Gallery, whence it was transferred in 1951.

091/MED/6. *Horae*   s. xv²

A book of hours either acquired or written[2] in Paris in 1497. For art. 27 and the headings to arts. 21, 22, 26, 30 cf. BN, lat. 10561 (Leroquais, *Livres d'heures*, ii. 23).

1. pp. 1–12 Full calendar in French in gold, red, and blue, the two colours alternating for effect.

One month to a page, set out in two columns. Forty-nine feasts in gold, among them Anne, Denis, Eligius, Thomas of Canterbury.

2. pp. 13–24 Sequentiae of gospels.

3. pp. 21–7 Oratio de beata maria. Obsecro te . . . For male use.

4. pp. 27–30 Oratio de beata maria. O intemerata . . . orbis terrarum. Inclina mater . . . For male use.

5. pp. 31–123 Hours of B.V.M. of the use of (Rome).

The Tuesday and Friday psalms begin on p. 103, the Wednesday and Saturday psalms on p. 109, and the special office for Advent on p. 114. p. 124 blank.

---

[1] The leaves numbered as pp. 25, 26, 173, 174 are each made up of bits of two leaves of the original manuscript: see below, collation.

[2] The illegible word on p.v. could be either *achetees* or *escriptes*.

6. pp. 125–54 Penitential psalms and (p. 142) litany.

Fifteen confessors: . . . (14) Leobine. Twelve virgins: . . . (9) Genouefa.

7. pp. 154–9 Sensuiuent les heures de le croix qui se doiuent dire tous les vendrediz . . . Hymnus. Patris sapiencia . . .

8. pp. 160–5 Sensuiuent les heures du saint esperit qui se doiuent dire tous les mardis . . . Hymnus. Nobis sancti spiritus . . . p. 166 blank.

9. pp. 167–226 Office of the dead.

10. pp. 227–36 Memoriae of Holy Trinity, John Baptist, Peter and Paul, Sebastian, Nicholas, Anthony (Anthoni pastor inclite . . .: *RH*, no. 1203), Anne, Mary Magdalene, Katherine, Barbara, one to a page.

11. pp. 237–40 Oroison de monseigneur sainct ladre. Sancte lazare martir dei . . . Ideo ego N famula tua peccatrix indigna . . .

12. pp. 240–8 Sensuiuent les heures de la trinite q[ui] se doiuent dire le dimenche. . . . Ymnus. Quicumque vult firmiter . . .

The hymn is *RH*, no. 16566; *AH* xxx. 10.

13. pp. 248–55 Sensuiuent les heures des mors qui se doiuent dire le lundi. . . . Ymnus. Deitatis paternitas . . .

The hymn is *RH*, no. 4335; *AH* xxx. 173.

14. pp. 255–61 Sensuiuent les heures de tous les saintz qui se doiuent dire le me(r)credi. . . . Hymnus. Sancta dei genitrix flos virginitatis . . .

The hymn is *RH*, no. 18373; *AH* xxx. 143.

15. pp. 261–7 Sensuiuent les heures du saint sacrement que le pape benedic fist et donna a tous ceulx qui les diront deuotement iii^c et xvii xl^es Et leur relaiche la vii^e partie de leur penitence enioincte. . . . Ymnus. Ihesus donat dominus in diebus singulis . . .

The hymn is *RH*, no. 28656; *AH* xxx. 30.

16. pp. 267–73 Sensuiuent les heures nostre dame qui se doiuent dire tous les samedis. . . . Ymnus. Deus qui primum hominem de limo terre . . .

The hymn is *RH*, no. 4496; *AH* xxx. 123.

17. pp. 273–9 Sensuiuent les heures saincte anne. . . . Ymnus. Gaude nobilissima sancta sancta parens anna . . .

18. pp. 279–88 Sensuit la messe nostre dame.

19. pp. 288–91 Inicium sancti euangelii secundum matheum. Gloria tibi domine. Liber generationis . . . qui vocatur cristus. Matthew 1. 1–16.

20. pp. 291–7 La letanie de la uierge marie.

21. pp. 297–300 Nous trouuons es escriptures que nostre benoit saulueur ihesucrist sapparut une foiz a monseigneur saint gregoire . . . lequel . . . donna xiiii mille ans de vray pardon a tous vrays confes et repentans . . .

D

The Seven Oes of St. Gregory. According to the heading, the indulgence was increased by later popes to 46000 years 'ou enuiron'.

22. pp. 300–3 Deuota contemplacio beate marie uirginis iuxta crucem filii sui lacrimantis et ad compassionem saluatoris singulos inuitantis. Stabat mater dolorosa . . . *RH*, no. 19416.

23. pp. 303–5 Sequens oratio data fuit beato bernardo ab angelo qui et dixit sicut aurum est preciosissimum metallum sic ista oratio precellit alias orationes. Aue maria ancilla trinitatis humilima . . .

24. pp. 305–6 Oratio ad beatam virginem. Aue maria gratia plena dominus tecum: ita et tu sis mecum . . .

25. pp. 306–11 Prayers before and after confession and before and after mass, with headings in French: (*a*) Per sanctorum angelorum . . . merita . . .; (*b*) Domine deus meus antequam terra cum datham et abirum me absorbeat . . .; (*c*) Domine ihesu criste filii (*sic*) dei viui te supplex queso . . .; (*d*) Domine ihesu criste non sum digna ut intres . . .; (*e*) Uera perceptio corporis et sanguinis . . . (*b*), (*d*). Feminine forms.

26. pp. 311–18 Sensuiuent cinq belles oroisons que monseigneur saint iehan leuangeliste fist en lonneur de la uierge marie dont nostre seigneur donne aucuns benefices . . .

The long heading is followed by the prayers Mediatrix . . ., Auxiliatrix . . ., Reparatrix . . ., Illuminatrix . . . and Alleuiatrix . . ., each of which begins with a letter of the word MARIA.

27. Prayers and a form of confession in French (except *g*), in the same order as in B.N., lat. 10561, ff. 101ᵛ–105, which has one more after (*c*) and lacks (*g*): (*a*) pp. 318–20 Oroison a dieu le pere laquelle se doit dire par maniere de protestation deuote. O dieu createur redempteur conseruateur . . .; (*b*) pp. 320–1 Oraison a iesucrist. Doulz iesucrist ie proteste deuant toy . . .; (*c*) pp. 321–2 Les xii articles de la foy. Ie croy en dieu le pere tout puissant . . .; (*d*) pp. 322–3 Oraison a tous les sains. Ie vous supplie tous anges . . .; (*e*) pp. 323–5 Oroison tres deuote a dieu pour prier pour son amy . . . Ie te command N. a dieu . . .; (*f*) pp. 325–7 Oraison de la croix a dire come celle de deuant. La saincte croix soit deuant toy . . .; (*g*) p. 327 Loraison saint charlemaigne. Domine iesu criste pastor bone iustos conserua . . .; (*h*) pp. 327–30 Oraison a iesucrist. Mon benoit dieu ie croy de cueur et confesse de bouche . . .; (*i*) pp. 330–2 Oraison a iesucrist. Doulx iesucrist filz de dieu redempteur . . .; (*j*) pp. 332–4 Aultre oraison. Nostre seigneur iesucrist filz de dieu le pere vif par la uertu . . .

(*a–f, h–j*) are Sonet, nos. 1314, 524, 794, 932, 837, 1020, 1150, 521, 1259.

28. p. 334 Quiconques dira en leleuation du corps nostre seigneur ceste oroison qui sensuit si apres escripte il aura trois cens ans de indulgences. Aue uerum corpus natum ex maria uirgine . . . *RH*, no. 2175.

29. pp. 334–6 Benoist pape xiiᵉ composa lorayson cy apres escripte et donna a tous ceulx qui la diront deuotement a la messe entre leleuation du corps nostre seigneur et le pater noster. autant de iours de indulgences que nostre seigneur

eut de plaies le iour de sa passion la somme des indulgences quinze ans. Precor te amantissime et piissime domine iesu criste creator celi . . .

30. pp. 336–7 Pape boniface a donne a tous ceulx qui diront deuotement ceste oroison qui sensuit entre leleuation du corps nostre seigneur et le dernier agnus dei deux mille ans de vray pardon. Oratio. Domine iesu criste qui hanc sacratissimam carnem . . .

31. pp. 337–8 Prayers at mass, with headings in French: (*a*) Sancta caro xpisti cara immolata . . .; (*b*) Spiritus sancti gracia illustret . . .; (*c*) Domine non sum dignus vt intres . . .

(*a*). *RH*, no. 1710.

32. (*a*) pp. 338–41 On treuue en la saincte escripture que la glorieuse uirge marie sapparut a saint thomas de canturbie . . . La premiere ioye que iay . . .
(*b*) pp. 341–4 Sensuiuent les sept gaude nostre dame. Gaude flore uirginali. Que honore speciali . . .

The Seven Joys of B.V.M. in prose and verse (*RH*, no. 6810).

33. pp. 344–7 Sensuiuent les sept parolles que nostre seigneur dist en la croix le iour de sa passion. Domine iesu criste qui septem verba . . .

34. pp. 347–50 Prayers with headings in French, on getting up, on going out, on entering church, on taking holy water, on beginning any business, and on going to bed: (*a*) Gratias ago tibi domine . . .; (*b*) Vias tuas . . .; (*c*) Introibo in domum . . .; (*d*) Aqua benedicta . . .; (*e*) Ihesu pie iesu bone . . .; (*f*) Ore tuo xpriste benedictus . . .

35. pp. 350–64 Memoriae with headings in French 'du bon ange' (O mi sancte angele . . .) and of Michael, angel, John Evangelist, James, Joseph (Euge ioseph singularis . . .), apostles, martyrs, Margaret, Clare (Salue sponsa dei uirgo sacra plena minorum . . .: *RH*, no. 18240), Eleven thousand virgins, Stephen, Leger, 'Des seurs nostre dame', 'Des cinq sains priuilegies' (Dyonisi radius grecie . . .: *RH*, no. 4707), 'Des v sainctes preuilegies' (Katherina tyrannum superans . . .: *RH*, no. 2691), Claude, and (added) Ten thousand martyrs.

36. p. 364 Passio domini nostri ihesu cristi secundum iohannem.
The heading only.

ff. iii + 182 + ii, paginated (i–vi), 1–364 (365–8). For pp. v, vi see below. 182 × 125 mm. Written space 107 × 62 mm. 21 long lines. Collation: 1⁶ 2–23⁸. In each quire of 8 the first five rectos are signed at the head, an unusual position. A new hand at p. 237 (16¹). Twenty 17-line pictures, eight in art. 5 and one before each of arts. 2, 6, 7, 8, 9 (Death on a brown horse carries three arrows: one man dead and one about to die), 12 (Christ ascending), 13 (raising of Lazarus), 14 (four saints, Francis, who receives the stigmata, Clare, Dominic, and a Dominican lady holding a fruit), 15 (Christ washes the feet of the disciples), 16 (a tree of Jesse), 17 (B.V.M. on the steps of the temple: Anne and Joachim), 18 (Augustus and the Sybil: in the sky B.V.M. and the Child, who holds a cross). Fifteen smaller pictures, ten in art. 10, three in art. 2, and one before each of arts. 3 (Pietà), 4 (B.V.M. and Child). The occupation of the month and sign of the zodiac at the head of each page of art. 1. Initials: (i, ii) 3-line and 2-line, white and violet on decorated grounds of gold paint; (iii) 1-line, gold on grounds of red and blue patterned in white. Continuous compartmented floral borders on pages with 17-line pictures. Borders on three sides of pages with smaller pictures. Line fillers in blue and red patterned in white and decorated with blobs of gold. Headings usually in blue ink. Capital letters in the ink of the text filled with pale yellow. Binding of s. xix. Secundo folio (p. 15) *qui credunt.*

Bought (?) in Paris in 1497 for the use of sister Anne Dorge, as appears from a fifteen-line inscription in red on p. v: 'Ie seure anne dorge loue et remercie le createur et sa glorieuse mere qui tant donneur et de grace ma fait que de mauoir appellee en ceste saincte diuine magnifique et deuote maison au seruice de ces poures et moy indigne fus receupe le xxiiᵉ iour de nouembre. vng dimenche qui estoit la feste de saincte cecile lam mil iiii cens lxxii nostre seigneur me doient grace de il perceueres de bien en mieulx iusques a la fin. A.M.E.N. Cestes presentes heures furent [. . . .]es a paris lam mil quatre cens quatre xx et xvii'. Armorial bookplate of William Constable, Esq., F.R.S. and F.S.A., p. iv: not apparently in his sale, 24 June 1889. Transferred from the City Museum and Art Gallery in 1951.

091/MED/7. *Psalterium*   s. xv²

A liturgical psalter, with noted antiphons and hymns. Ps. 1 (f. 1) is preceded by (ff. i–iiᵛ) the invitatories Venite exultemus, Preoccupemus faciem, Quoniam deus magnus, In manu tua domine, Venite adoremus, Dominum qui fecit nos, Adoremus dominum and (ff. iiᵛ–ivᵛ) the hymns Nocte surgentes and Primo dierum omnium. Nunc dimittis is followed by (f. 257) Antiphona. Salua nos domine . . . Postea dicitur secreto. Pater noster . . . Postea dicitur. Credo in deum patrem . . . Oremus. Visita quesumus domine habitacionem istam . . . Deinde dicitur Salue regina . . . Oratio. Omnipotens sempiterne deus: qui gloriose uirginis matris marie corpus . . . (f. 258ᵛ) Simbolum in dominicis diebus. Credo in unum deum . . . (f. 259) Ymnus. Te deum laudamus . . . (f. 260ᵛ) Ymnus Angellorum. Gloria in excelsis deo . . . in gloria dei patris. amen. finis. f. 261ᵛ blank.

ff. 267, foliated i–iv, 1–204, 204 (bis), 205–13, 213 (bis), 214–61. 543 × 372 mm. Written space 340 × 260 mm. 18 long lines. Collation: 1–26¹⁰ 27⁸ wants 8 blank. Large round hand: minims are 10 mm high. The flex (?) is used on ff. 94–142 and is often set in the margin beside the place where it comes in the text. Initials: (i) f. 1, *B* of *Beatus*, blue patterned in white on a gold ground, historiated: a hilly landscape: David kneels, clasping his harp: above, God the Father and the heavenly choir look down; (ii) of principal psalms, ff. 65ᵛ, 89, 106ᵛ, 123ᵛ, 149ᵛ, 171ᵛ, 214, 5–8 line, red and blue on gold grounds decorated in red, blue, green, brown, and gold; (iii) of antiphons and hymns and (iv) of psalms, 3-line and 2-line, red or blue, patterned in white, with ornament of the other colour; (v) of verses of psalms, 1-line, red or blue. A border inhabited by cherubs on three sides of f. 1. Contemporary (?) binding of thick wooden boards covered with brown leather, bearing a pattern of fillets: of two metal centrepieces and eight metal cornerpieces, only the centrepiece on the back cover and one cornerpiece on the front cover remain, the former with a rectangular lamb-and-flag stamp in the middle and eight circular lamb-and-flag stamps round the edge, and the latter with stamps of B.V.M. and Child, lamb and flag (2), and 'ihesus': two clasps fasten from front to back: studs projected from the edges of the boards, but only one remains: a framed label on the back cover 'Salterio intiero Notturno e Diurno'. Secundo folio *terre.*

Written in Italy. A shield in the lower margin of f. 1 bears the Medici arms, or eight torteaux, two, three, two, one (Rietstap, *Planches*, iv. clxxvi).

091/MED/8. *Horae (in Netherlandish)* s. xv/xvi

A book of hours noticed by J. W. Bradley, *Dictionary of Miniaturists*, iii (1889), 258, under Nicholas Spierinc, but the illuminator is more probably his son Jan, under whose name F. Lyna lists this and eight other manuscripts in Thieme-Becker, *Allgemeines Lexicon der bildenden Künstler*, xxxi. 373.

1. ff. 1–12 Full calendar in red and black. 'Drie coninghen' in red at 6 Jan.; also the saints listed above, 091/MED/5, except that Remigius is the only name at 1 Oct.

2. ff. 14–47 Hier beghint die vrouwe ghetide. Use of (Utrecht).

Arts. 3–11 are devotions to B.V.M.

3. ff. 47–8 Dit sijn die droeuenissen van onser lieuer vrouwen. O moeder vol van rouwen . . .

4. ff. 48–9 Dit sijn drie gebeden van onser vrouwen marien die si leerde eenre deuoter nonnen die mechtelt ghenoemt was. aue. O gloriose maget ende coninghinne maria gheliker wijs als god . . .

Three Aves of Mechtild von Hackeborn.

5. f. 49ᵛ Hier beghint een beuelinghe van onser vrouwen marien. aue maria. O vrouwe der glorien . . .

Lieftinck, p. 158.

6. ff. 49ᵛ–54ᵛ Hier begint een suuerlic ghebet van marien dat men gheerne lesen sal in haer hoechtiden of op wat tiden dat die mensche in druck ende tribulacie is. O edel coninghinne der hemelen ende reyne maget maria moeder alre ontfarmhertichheit Om die bitteren rouwen . . .

Lieftinck, p. 158.

7. Three prayers: (a) ff. 54ᵛ–55ᵛ Hier beghinnen die droeffenisse die maria hadde onder cruce aue. O moeder vol van rouwen bi den cruce . . .; (b) f. 55ᵛ Een schoen suuerlic gebet van marien. O vrouwe der glorien ende coninghinne der vrolicheit O fonteine . . .; (c) f. 56ʳᵛ Een ander ghebet van onser vrouwe. Weest ghegruet coninghinne der hemelen. Weest ghegruet . . .

8. ff. 56ᵛ, 58 Item sixtus die vierde (1471–84) heeft ghegheuen allen den . . . Weest ghegruet alre heilichste maria moeder gods coninghinne des hemels poerte des paradiis . . .

The heading conveys an indulgence of 11000 years to those saying this prayer 'voer dat beelde onser lieuer vrouwen in die sonne'. Lieftinck, p. 209.

9. ff. 58–60 Item dese nae bescreuen seuen blijscappen heeft ghemaect die heilighe aerwaerdighe (?) biscop sinte thomas van cantellenberch ter eeren der moeder goeds marien. Verblijdt v heilige maria . . .

The Seven Joys. Lieftinck, p. 164.

10. ff. 60–1 Dit nauolgende ghebet was vertoent den heiligen man ende doctoer

sinte bernaert van den heiligen enghel . . . Weest gegruet alre oetmoedichste dienstmaecht . . .

Lieftinck, p. 124.

11. ff. 61–62ᵛ Een suuerlic ghebet van maria ende van sinte iohannes. O onbeulecte maget . . .

12. ff. 62ᵛ–66ᵛ Hier beghinnen seer suuerlike gebeden van die passie ons heren die men gaerne lesen sal alle daghe. ende bisonder alle vridaghe nae die manier van den seuen getiden. O here ihesu criste om dat wredelike starcke antasten . . .

Hours of the Passion. Lieftinck, p. 156.

13. ff. 66ᵛ–68ᵛ Item eer du dat heilighe sacrament ontfanghen selste so les dit nauolgende ghebet. O here ihesu criste ic gae voert . . .: followed by two other prayers at mass.

14. ff. 68ᵛ–69 Van dinen heiligen enghel. O mijn alre liefste engel claerblenckende sterre . . . Lieftinck, p. 208.

15. ff. 69–73ᵛ Memoriae of Peter, Paul, apostle, martyr, Anthony, Agatha, All Saints and for peace.

16. ff. 75–76ᵛ O here ihesu criste ic aenbede di in den cruce hangende . . .

Nine oes and notice at the end of indulgence of 92 years, 24 quadragenes, and 80 days. Lieftinck, p. 162. S. Axters, 'Adoro te', *Studia eucharistica*, 1946, p. 289.

17. ff. 77–8 Ic bidde di alre minlicste here ihesu criste om der groten caritaten willen . . .

18. f. 78ʳᵛ A memoria of Holy Cross.

19. ff. 80–97ᵛ Seven penitential psalms and (f. 90ᵛ) litany.

Twenty-one confessors: . . . (12–21) seruaes, willibroert, benedictus, gielijs, bernaert, franciscus, dominicus, seuerijn, lebuijn odulphus.

20. ff. 97ᵛ–103ᵛ, 105 Hier beghint die metten van den cruus getiden. . . . Des vaders wijsheit . . . The short hours of the Cross.

21. ff. 105–125ᵛ Hier beghint die uighelie van den doden.

Three lessons. Lauds, f. 115.

22. ff. 125ᵛ–128 Dit ghebet is gheheten dat gulden ghebet voer alle gelouige sielen. O heer vader ende ghenadige god want du een troester . . .: followed by two more prayers for the dead.

23. ff. 128–30 Eight short prayers at mass, the first 'O siele cristi heilich mi . . .'.

24. ff. 130–138ᵛ Hier beghint der prologus van mariencrans. Hier begint een sonderlinge deuote manier om te lesen marien rosencrans welc een deuote broeder van der cathuser oerden woenachtich int cathuser cloester van triere . . . (f. 132ᵛ) Weest gegruet maria vol van genaden . . . ihesus cristus. Die eerste artikel. Dien du aldersuuerste maget ouermits . . . A prayer after the rosary begins (f. 138) 'God gruet v goedertiren maria een venster . . . een dore . . . ende licht . . .'.

ff. i+139+ii, foliated (i, ii), 1–138, (139, 140). 175 × 120 mm. Written space 97 × 67 mm. 20 long lines. Collation: 1⁶ (ff. ii, 1–5) 2⁸ wants 8, perhaps blank, 3–16⁸ 17⁸+1 leaf after 8 (f. 138), together with six singletons, ff. 13, 57, 74, 79, 98, 104, with pictures on the versos, and blank rectos, in front of arts. 2, 8 (Augustus and the Sybil on the left and an angel and scribe on the right: above, B.V.M. and Child), 16 (vision of Pope Gregory), 19 (Christ on the rainbow, B.V.M. and St. John below, and at the foot on the left, the good, and on the right the damned, one of whom is being thrown by a devil into the jaws of hell), 20, 21. Initials: (i) in colours on gold grounds, historiated: f. 14, B.V.M. and Child; f. 61, B.V.M., Christ, and St. John; f. 75, Christ risen from the tomb, his left hand on a blue shield bearing lamb and flag; (ii) 4-line or 3-line, as (i), but smaller, or in gold on grounds of red and blue, the red patterned in gold paint and the blue in white; (iii) red and blue, with red and green ornament; (iv) 2-line, blue with red and green ornament or red with violet and green ornament; (v) in the litany only, 1-line, blue with red ornament or gold with violet ornament; (vi) 1-line, red or blue. Capital letters in the ink of the text stroked with red. Continuous framed floral borders on picture pages and on pages facing them contain figures, etc.: 'sperinc 502' is in the lower border on ff. 14, 58, 75, 105, and 'sperinc 503' in the lower border on f. 57ᵛ.[1] Floral borders spattered with gold stars above and below the written space on f. 1 and on pages with initials of type ii: the lady with the unicorn on f. 38. Contemporary binding of wooden boards covered with brown leather bearing Weale's Image of Pity panel stamp, R. 388, on the front and his 'Flemish animals' panel stamp, R. 408, on the back,[2] each surrounded by a border formed of fillets in which are small stamps of five patterns: two clasps.

Written in the Netherlands, probably in 1502, when (Jan?) Sperinc signed four borders. Bought for Aston Manor Public Reference Library from Mr. W. Downing for fifteen guineas about 1880–1 and transferred later to the Central Public Library.

BIRMINGHAM. SELLY OAK COLLEGES

Ital. 1. *Lives of saints (in Italian)* s. xv²

Lives of Abram, Eufrosina, Marina, Margaret called Pelagius, Theodora, and Pelagia in Italian, derived from Vitas Patrum and from Legenda aurea.

1. ff. 1–15 Comenza la vita di sancto Abram romito. Lo sanctissimo abram essendo fiolo di parenti richissimi . . . Cf. *PL* lxxiii. 283.

2. ff. 15–24ᵛ De Sancta Eufrosina ditto frate smeraldo. Fue nella citade dalexandria un gentil homo . . . Cf. *PL* lxxiii. 643.

3. ff. 24ᵛ–27 De sancta Marina vergene. Vno buono home secolare. morta che fo la moglie . . . Cf. *PL* lxxiii. 691.

4. ff. 27–9 De sancta Margarita ditta Pellagio. Margarita ditta Pellagio uergene

---

[1] Bradley, op. cit., misread these figures which stand, presumably, for 1502 and 1503. According to him a border is dated 1498, but this I have not found.

[2] The inscription on R. 388 is 'O vos omnes qui transitis | per viam attendite | et videte si est dolor similis | sicut dolor meus'. The inscriptions on R. 408 are 'Omnia si perdas | famam seruare memento | qua semel | amissa nula reuisio erit' and 'De profundis | clamaui ad te domine | domine | exaudi vocem meam'. Weale knew these panels from a book of hours in Dutch in the archiepiscopal museum at Utrecht.

bellissima riccha e nobile. con tanta sollecitudine . . . Cf. *Legenda aurea* (ed. Graesse), no. cli.

5. ff. 29–34 De sancta Theodora. Al tempo zenone imperadore fo ne la cita dalexandria . . . Cf. *Legenda aurea*, no. xcii.

6. ff. 34–40ᵛ De sancta Pellagia. Vna fiata louescouo de antiochia per certa caxone . . . Cf. *PL* lxxiii. 663.

f. iiᵛ contains a note of contents in the main hand.

ff. ii+40+i. Contemporary foliation 1–40: another, later, at foot of rectos, 258–98, includes f. ii. Paper. f. ii is a medieval flyleaf. 141 × 103 mm. Written space 95 × 71 mm. *c.* 28 long lines. Frame ruling. Collation: 1–4¹⁰. Written in an informal text hand. Red initials. Binding of s. xix. Secundo folio *in meglio*.

Written in Italy. 'Iste liber est dn̄i Bartholamei de coltis e (?) fratribus. n° 32' (f. 1, s. xv ex.). No doubt once part of the collection of M. L. Canonici, 1727–1805; foliation in the same hand as that at the foot of the rectos occurs in many Canonici manuscripts in the Bodleian, e.g. Canon misc. 220. Bookplate of Walter Sneyd (who bought the residue of the Canonici collection in 1835), but not identifiable in the Sneyd sale, 16 Dec. 1903. 'Bought from H. H. Peach, Bookseller 37 Belvoir Street Leicester, Oct. 1904 10/' (W. C. Braithwaite's note). Given by J. B. Braithwaite.

Lat. 1. *Breviarium*   s. xv med.

1. pp. 1–12 Calendar in red and black. No gradings, apart from 'duplex' (30 feasts) and 'semiduplex' (4 feasts).

Feasts in red include the translation of Augustine, Antony of Padua, 'Marie niuis' (duplex), Augustine (duplex), Prosdocimus (28 Feb., 13 June, 5, 28 Aug., 7 Nov.). The Franciscan saints, Louis (duplex), Francis, and Clare are in black.

2. pp. 15–339 Temporale for the year from Advent. In the Ash Wednesday litany, Francis, Antony, and Dominic follow Benedict. The first leaf and six other leaves are missing.

3. pp. 340–3 Aduentus domini celebratur . . . scilicet O sapientia.

The *Rubrice generales* printed in *Haymo*, pp. 100–5, and *SMRL* ii. 114–21. p. 344 is blank.

4. pp. 347–456 Liturgical psalter. The ferial canticles are worked in. The first leaf is missing.

5. pp. 456–62 Benedicite, Benedictus, Ecce nunc benedicite, Te lucis ante terminum, Nunc dimittis, 'Laus edita a doctoribus' (Te Deum), Gloria, 'Symbolum ecclesie' (Credo in unum Deum), Salve regina, 'Symbolum apostolorum' (Credo in Deum), Pater noster, Ave Maria.

6. pp. 463–78 Hymns for the year, temporale, beginning imperfectly at Lent, sanctorale, common of saints, and In dedicatione ecclesie.

The first leaf is missing. The temporale includes Corpus Christi. The sanctorale (p. 470) has proper hymns for Conversion of Paul, Chair of Peter, John Baptist, Peter and Paul, Mary Magdalene, Chains of Peter, Michael, All Saints.

7. pp. 479–753 Incipit proprium sanctorum de breuiario per totum annum.

Saturninus—Katherine. Sixteen leaves are missing, including the doubtless illuminated leaf before p. 712, on which the office of St. Francis began. The nine lessons for Louis of Toulouse are headed (p. 669) 'Incipit legenda et canonizatio sancti ludouici episcopi et confessoris de ordine fratrum minorum sicut habetur subulla (*sic*) domini Iohannis pape xxii': cf. Wadding, *Annales Minorum*, ed. 3, vi (1931), 327–32.

8. pp. 753–82 Common of saints.

9. pp. 782–8 Dedication of church, ending imperfectly.

10. pp. 789–95 Office of B.V.M., the first leaf missing.

11. pp. 795–800 Incipit officium in agenda mortuorum . . . secundum con-suetudinem romane curie. Notandum est quod officium . . .

12. pp. 800–2 Ordo ad ungendum infirmum. Cum peruenerit sacerdos . . .

13. pp. 802–6 Ordo commendacionis anime. Primum fiant . . .

Cf. *SMRL* i. 390–2. In the litany Francis precedes Benedict.

14. pp. 806–8 Ordo ad tumulandum defunctum. Dum portatur ad ecclesiam . . .

15. pp. 808–11 Incipit ordo ad benedicendam mensam per totum annum. *SMRL* i. 199–203, and *Haymo*, pp. 171–4.

ff. ii+385+ii. The modern pagination, 1–812, allows for some but not all the missing leaves. Fine, soft parchment. 340 × 240 mm. Written space 203 × 143 mm. 2 cols. 32 lines. Collation: 43 quires, all tens, except 1^6, 43^4, but 30 leaves of text are missing (2^1, 4^1, $5^{5, 8}$, 12^1, $13^{3, 9}$, $14^{4, 6}$, 19^1, 21^3, 22^4, 25^1, 26^5, 27^9, 29^5, $30^{5, 6}$, 31^5, 33^7, 35^1, 36^6, $37^{6, 10}$, 39^{8-10}, 40^1, 43^4) and 5 probably blank leaves (24^{8-10} after p. 462, 25^{10} after p. 478, and 43^4). Flex punctuation is used occasionally. Initials: (i) in colour on gold and coloured grounds, historiated, or with portrait busts of apostles and saints, including Louis of Toulouse (p. 669), and with prolongations into the margins in colours, mainly dark green, and gold: 33 remain; (ii) as (i), but decorated, without figures; (iii) 2-line, blue with red ornament or red with pale-pink or blue ornament; (iv) for verses of psalms and hymns, 1-line, as (iii) or, from p. 479, plain blue or red. A continuous border on p. 479. Binding of s. xix.

Written in Italy, perhaps in the Padua region: cf. art. 1, Prosdocimus. Bookplate of Alfred Higgins, F.S.A.: his sale, 2 May 1904, lot 22 (?). Bought by W. C. Braithwaite from H. H. Peach of Leicester. Given by J. B. Braithwaite.

Lat. 2. *Michael Meldensis, Distinctiones super Psalterium* s. XIII in.

1. ff. 1–129^v De triplici ordine librorum ueteris testamenti. Sciendum quod hebrei hesdra auctore libros ueteris testamenti secundum numerum suarum litterarum . . . (f. 129^v/22) accipit brauium. Duo consideranda in sacra pagina precipue . . . De naturis ut fisica pertractat. Explicit.

The commentary on the Psalms by Michael of Meaux, †1199, printed among the works of St. Bonaventura (ed. 1588, i. 90–208), but reworked, as a rule by shortening, but some-times by extension, apparently in order to convert the work into a set of Distinctions. The divisions between the psalms are not shown and subject headings are set out in the margins in prominent red letters, for example on f. 1^v, 'De triplici prerogatiuia dauid',

'De anno iubeleo'. The text is written without break until f. 129ᵛ. The new paragraph beginning at this point, 'Duo consideranda . . .', is part of the preface in the printed edition (p. 90). The same variant form of the commentary is in Monte Cassino MS. 238, pp. 205–300 (Stegmüller, no. 5640). The red headings cease at f. 66, 'De infirmitate'. The work is called 'Distinctiones noui et ueteris testamenti' in titles of s. xiv ex. (?) on ff. 147, 155.

Arts. 2, 3 are binding fragments which formed a protective pad at each end of art. 1.

2. ff. 130–42, formerly the pad at the end, as appears from the marks of rust on f. 142 which coincide with marks on f. 155, a quire of sixteen leaves, wanting 14–16: 248×175 mm., written space 175×110 mm., 2 cols., 46 lines, s. xiii in. Sermons: (*a*) f. 130 Orietur stella ex Iacob (Numbers 24: 17). Inter ornamenta mulieris satis decens eam ornamentum est uitta . . .; (*b*) f. 132 Mundare. Consuetudo est quod cum aliquis uult aliquid subtile . . .; (*c*) f. 134 Fecit deus duo magna luminaria (Genesis 1: 16) . . . Consuetudo est quod bene obsequentes famuli . . .; (*d*) f. 136ᵛ Maria. Duo sunt qui me ad predicandum hodie. facilius induxerunt . . . (on St. Mary Magdalene); (*e*) f. 129 Egredietur virga (Isaiah 11: 1) . . . Oremus dominum ihesum quod meritis matris sue . . .; (*f*) in another hand, f. 141ᵛ, Iob. Unde ergo uenit sapientia (Job 28: 20) . . . Duas interrogationes proponit . . . (*ends imperfectly*).

3. ff. 143–54, formerly the pad at the beginning, as appears from the stained and wormholed condition of f. 147, and formerly in the order 147–54, 143–6, as appears from the pattern of wormholes which only disappears finally after f. 145, two quires, one of eight leaves (147–54) and one of four (143–6): 260×190 mm., written space 220×160 mm., at first closely written in two columns of 56 lines, later widely spaced in two columns of 29–39 lines; current writing, s. xii/xiii. (*a*) ff. 147–50 Cum te ipsum et omnia quecumque habes homo . . . affabilitate et familiaritate sua. (*b*) ff. 150–1ᵛ Theological notes. (*c*) ff. 152–4ᵛ, 143–6ᵛ Primum quidem sermonem feci (Acts 1: 1) . . . Quoniam deo cura est de hominibus et plus animarum curam gerit quam corporum . . . et cum palma ad regnum perueniemus. Qui nobis prestare dignetur. etc.

(*a*). On penitence. In (*c*) the rules of grammar and dialectic (f. 153ᵛ, Sequitur de dialectica) are applied to the exposition of scripture. St. Bernard is quoted. On ff. 152ᵛ–153 is 'quod solet in gallico cantari et li tens senuait et ie nai ren fait'. How the 'avis Sancti Martini' breaks shellfish is told on f. 146ᵛ.

ff. i+129+xxvi. For ff. 130–54 see above, arts. 2, 3. f. 155 was pasted to a former binding. 270×190 mm. Written space 195×110 mm. 27–8 long lines. Collation: 1–8⁸ 9–10¹⁰ 11–13¹² 14¹² wants 10–12 after f. 129. Quires 1–14 are numbered at beginning and end in the centre of the lower margin (s. xiv?). The quire forming a binding pad at the end (see above, art. 2) is similarly numbered XV at the beginning, and the number is preceded by the words 'In isto libro. omnes quaterni. sunt'. Each number has a short vertical stroke above and below it and a short horizontal stroke on each side of it and there are three dots, respectively red, black, and red between each horizontal and vertical stroke. For this form of quire-numbering see G. Mercati, 'Codici del Convento di S. Francesco in Assisi nelle bibliotece vaticane', *Studi e testi*, xli (1924), 83–127, with facsimile.[1] Art. 1 is in two good hands, changing at f. 121. Red initials. Binding of s. xix. Secundo folio *tenario*.

[1] I owe the reference to Professor Bernard Peebles.

Written in northern France (?), but in Italy early in s. xiii, when arts. 2, 3 were added as part of the binding and the last thirty-three words of art. 1 were supplied in a current hand in the lower margin of f. 129ᵛ (the following leaf having been scrapped?). 'Psalterium sancte marie de palazolis' (f. 147, s. xiii/xiv), perhaps the Cistercian house of this name south east of Rome. Belonged in s. xiv ex. to the Franciscan convent of Assisi, as appears from the distinctive quire-numbering (see above) and from an entry in the catalogue printed by L. Alessandri, *Inventario dell'antica biblioteca del S. Convento di S. Francesco in Assisi compilato nel 1381*, Assisi, 1906, p. 66 (no. cxi of the Libraria secreta): 'Distinctiones novi et veteris testamenti. Cum postibus. Cuius principium est. Sciendum quod ebrei auctore. Finis vero. Naturis et fisica pertractat Explicit. In quo libro omnes quaterni sunt xv. H'. On the pastedown at the beginning is 'Henry Bachelor Walker Esq. J.P. The Gables New Romney'. Given by J. B. Braithwaite.

Lat. 4. *Breviarium* s. XIV med.

1. ff. 2–161 Temporale for the year from Advent. The first leaf and ten other leaves are missing.

2. (*a*) ff. 161–3 The rubric beginning 'Aduentus domini celebratur'. (*b*) ff. 163–165ᵛ A table for finding anthems before Christmas. (*c*) ff. 165ᵛ–166 Tabula de dominicis que uenerint post pentecosten ut non errentur. (*d*) f. 166ʳᵛ Tabula ista est de ystoriis septembris quando imponuntur.

(*a*). Cf. MS. Lat. 1, art. 3. Only sect. 1–23 occur here: *Haymo*, pp. 100–4 and *SMRL* ii. 114–20. A reader noted 'alie rubrice sunt in fo. ii', but they are now missing. (*b*). The *Tabula Parisiensis*, *SMRL* ii. 401–8. (*c*). Cf. *SMRL* i. 142, 244. (*d*). Cf. *SMRL* i. 244.

3. ff. 168–174ᵛ Hymns for the year, temporale, sanctorale, common of saints, De dedicatione, and the hymn Nocte surgentes.

Nearly as MS. Lat. 1, art. 6, except for the absence of Corpus Christi hymns and the presence of Nocte surgentes at the end. The first leaf and the last leaf are missing.

4. ff. 176 (modern foliation '175')–231ᵛ Liturgical psalter.

The first leaf and five other leaves are missing.

5. ff. 231ᵛ–237 The six ferial canticles, Te deum, Benedicite, Benedictus, Magnificat, Pater noster, Nunc dimittis, Credo in deum, Gloria, Credo in unum deum, Quicumque vult.

6. ff. 237–238ᵛ Litany.

The five monks and hermits are Benedict, Bernard, Francis, Antony, Dominic.

7 (added). ff. 239–240ᵛ Office 'in festo Niuis sancte marie virginis'.

8. ff. 242 (modern foliation '241')–319. Sanctorale, lacking the first leaf, a leaf after f. 309, and all from All Saints.

Six lessons for Francis, f. 315, and six for his translation, f. 269.

ff. ii+301+ii. The medieval foliation is followed here. It runs 2, 9–20, 24–89, 91–9, 101–66, 168–74, 176–94, 196–205, 207–10, 213–40, 242–79, 279–309, 311–19 and was made before nineteen leaves were lost. The figures are partly cut off, and have been supplied, not always correctly, in a modern hand. 150 × 105 mm. Written space *c.* 100 × 75 mm. 2 cols. 29 lines. Collation: 33 quires, all originally tens, except 17 six (ff. 161–6) and

25 four (ff. 237–40), but 1^1, 3^{-8}, 3^1, 3, 9^{10}, 10^{10}, 18^1, 9, 20^9, 21^{10}, 22^{5}, 6, 26^1, 33^1 are missing. Initials: (i) in colour on decorated coloured grounds, the decoration including a little gold; (ii) 2-line, blue with red ornament, or red with blue or violet ornament; (iii) for verses of hymns and psalms, 1-line, blue or red.   Binding of s. xix ex.

Written in Italy. Bought by W. C. Braithwaite from H. H. Peach, Leicester, in 1904. Given by J. B. Braithwaite.

Lat. 5. *Jeronimus, Vita Malchi, etc.* s. XV ex.

A quire of a larger manuscript containing Jerome's lives of Malchus and Paul (*Clavis*, nos. 619, 617): (1) ff. 1–5 Diuus Hieronymus. Malchi Monachi captiui vita feliciter incipit. Qui nauali praelio dimicaturi sunt . . . posse superari; (2) ff. 5^v–11 Beati Pauli primi heremitæ vita incipit feliciter. Inter multos saepe dubitatum est . . . quam regum purpuras cum regnis suis. Explicit feliciter.

PL xxiii. 53–60; 17–28.

ff. 11. Paper. A foliation, in the same hand as that in MS. Ital. 1 runs from 48 to 58. 202 × 140 mm. Written space 146 × 90 mm. Long lines. A quire of 12 leaves, lacking 12, probably blank. Written in sloping humanistica. One red initial, f. 5^v. No binding.

Written in Italy. No doubt once part of the Canonici collection: cf. above, MS. Ital. 1. Bought for 5s. at the same time as Ital. 1.

Lat. 7. *Regula S. Augustini, etc.* s. XV/XVI

A fragment of a larger manuscript.

1. ff. 1–13^v Ante omnia fratres charissimi diligatur deus ? deinde proximus: quia ista precepta . . . non inducatur. Explicit regula.

The rule of St. Augustine: *PL* xxxii. 1377–84. *Clavis*, no. 1839.

2. ff. 13^v–17^v Sermo beati Augustini de Obedientia. Si premia vite eterne volumus promereri. precepta dei . . . pro nobis obediuit xpristus.

PL xl. 1344–5, no. 61 of the Sermones ad fratres in eremo.

3. ff. 17^v–20^v Sequitur de Obedientia. Deuotus subditus quitquid sibi per prelatum . . . de corporibus sed clamantes.

Quotes 'Bernhardus'.

ff. 20. 200 × 143 mm. Written space 140 × 100 mm. 16 long lines. Collation: 1 six 2^8 3^8 wants 7, 8. Written in a large service-book type of hybrida. Punctuation by flex (?), colon (:) and point (.). The two initials are blue on gold (f. 1) and blue on pink (f. 14): parti-coloured frames. Capital letters in the ink of the text touched with red. Binding of wooden boards covered with tooled pigskin, German work, s. xvi: a roll bears heads in medallions inscribed TVR and HEI. Metal cornerpieces and centrepiece. Two clasps.

Written in Germany. Given by Dr. R. Hingston Fox.

Lat. 8. *Antoninus, Confessionale; etc.* 1473

1. ff. 1–83 (*begins imperfectly*) causam et quod adducit ad hoc aduertentur . . . premium uite eterne amen.

The 'secundus tractatus' of the Confessionale of St. Antoninus, archbishop of Florence, in three parts: pt. 2, f. 15ᵛ; pt. 3, f. 33ᵛ. Often printed: the text here corresponds to edn. 1564, pp. 173–386. f. 83ᵛ is blank.

2. ff. 84–138 Extracts from classical and other writers, 'Macrobius Saturnalium' (f. 84ᵛ), Lucius Apuleius (ff. 86ᵛ–87), Terence (ff. 87ᵛ–88), Variae of Cassiodorus (ff. 88ᵛ–105), etc., followed by florilegia on particular subjects, e.g. peace and justice, mainly from patristic writings (ff. 109–133ᵛ) and by excerpts from the Bible (ff. 133ᵛ–138). ff. 138ᵛ–157ᵛ are blank.

ff. 157. Paper. 145 × 110 mm. Written space 92 × 63 mm. *c.* 25 long lines in art. 1 and *c.* 35 long lines in art. 2. Frame ruling. Collation: 1¹⁰ wants 1–3 2–6¹² 7¹⁶ (ff. 68–83) 8–12¹² 13⁸ 14⁸ wants 7, 8, blank. Narrow strips of blank parchment lie in the central opening of quires and between quires. Written in an informal textura, all by one scribe. No coloured initials in art. 2. In art. 1 the spaces for them remain blank. Capital letters in the ink of the text touched with red. Contemporary binding of wooden boards covered with white skin, over part of which is a flowered paper.

Written by fr. Antonio Cenni of Siena, a carmelite, partly at least in 1473: 'Iste liber est mei fratris Antonii Cenni de senis fratrum ordinis beate Marie carmelo. Quem propria manu scripsi in anno domini Mᵒ.ccccᵒ.lxxiii. die xxix Maii. Finito libro referamus gracia cristo', f. 83. Bookplate of William le Queux. Belonged to Dr. R. Hingston Fox in 1913: given by him.

Fragm. B. 16. *Poenitentiale* s. XIII in.

Vt in capite quadragesime omnes publice penitentes in ciuitatem ueniant et ante fores ecclesie nudis pedibus et cilio induti episcopo suo se representant. In capite quadragesime omnes publice penitentes. qui publicam suscipiunt penitentiam . . .

The first quire of a penitential, beginning with the 'ordo' on Ash Wednesday. Forty-one numbered chapters remain and the barely legible heading of ch. 42. Ch. 41 begins 'Non nulli ideo poscunt penitentiam ut statim sibi reddi communionem uelint', as Gratian, Decretum, De pen., I. 55. From ch. 7 the source of each chapter is given in front of its heading. The sources are said to be: (7–23) works of Augustine; papal decrees, (24–6) of Gregory VII, (27–35) of Leo, (36, 37) of Julius, (38, 39) of Innocent; (40, 41) works of Ambrose. Most, if not all, occur in the collections of Ivo and Gratian.

ff. 8. 145 × 100 mm. Written space 105 × 65 mm. 27 long lines. The first line of writing above the top ruled line. Pricks in both margins to guide ruling. A quire of eight leaves, signed 'I' at the end. Initials alternately red and blue. Kept in a folder.

No. 16 of a collection of fragments. No. 551 in a catalogue, *c.* 1920 (?), of R. Atkinson, 97 Sunderland Rd., Forest Hill, London, S.E., who marked it as coming from the Dunn sale: the relevant page of the catalogue is kept with it. Given by Dr. R. Hingston Fox.

BIRMINGHAM. UNIVERSITY OF BIRMINGHAM, BARBER INSTITUTE OF FINE ART

Acc. no. 313. *Horae* s. xiv[1]

A book of hours of the use of Metz, fully described by G. F. Warner, *Descriptive catalogue of illuminated manuscripts in the library of C. W. Dyson Perrins*, 1920, no. 35 and pl. XLIb.

In the calendar 'The number of bishops of Metz (ten) makes a Metz provenance certain': cf. also f. 151ᵛ. The antiphon and capitulum at prime are Sub tuum presidium and Hec est virgo and at none Beata mater and Per te dei.

Bought at the Dyson Perrins sale, 1 Dec. 1959, lot 67.

Acc. no. 397. *Horae* s. xv[2]

1. ff. 2–13ᵛ Calendar in gold, red, and black.

'Anthonii abbatis', 17 Jan., is the only entry in gold.

2. ff. 16–81ᵛ Incipit officium intemerate uirginis.

Use of (Rome). Compline is followed by 'Canticum beate marie uirginis. Salue regina . . .' (f. 64ᵛ), and the special psalms for use on Tuesdays and Fridays (f. 65ᵛ) and on Wednesdays and Saturdays (f. 70). The Advent office begins without break on f. 73ᵛ.

3. ff. 84–105ᵛ Incipiunt septem psalmi penitenciales. Litany follows, f. 95.

Eleven martyrs: . . . (6) Donate . . . The monks and hermits are Paul, Anthony, Benedict, Bernard, Dominic, Francis, Leonard. ff. 106–107ᵛ blank.

4. ff. 108–113ᵛ Incipit officium sancte crucis.

5. ff. 116–61 Incipit officium mortuorum. f. 161ᵛ blank.

6. ff. 162–72 Psalmi graduales cum uersiculis et orationibus annotatis. ff. 172ᵛ–173ᵛ blank.

7. ff. 174–96 Incipit psalterium abbreuiatum beati hieronymi quod ideo abbreuiatum est . . .

A 25-line heading and prayers, 'Sother tetragramaton . . .' and 'Deus qui ecclesie tue in exponendis . . .', before the psalter, which begins on f. 176ᵛ. After the psalter, prayers, 'Suscipere digneris domine deus hos psalmos consecratos: quos ego indignus peccator . . .', 'Liberator animarum et mundi redemptor . . .', and 'Omnipotens sempiterne deus clementiam tuam . . .' (ff. 194–6).

8 (in the hand of art. 1). (*a*) ff. 196–8 De Spe erigenda ad deum. Ego autem creatura tua sub umbra alarum tuarum . . . (*b*) ff. 198–9 Orauit Hester ad dominum dicens Domine deus Rex omnipotens in ditione tua . . . ora canentium domine deus noster. (*c*) f. 199ʳᵛ Ecce+Crucem domini fugite partes aduerse . . . Saluator mundi salua me Dominicum . . . Libera me Dominicum de morte maligna . . . (*d*) ff. 199ᵛ–200 Oratio. Domine mi Iesu christe qui sanctam elisabeth cum precursore . . . (*e*) f. 200ʳᵛ Commemoratio ad sanctum Anthonium

de Padua. antiphona. Si queris miracula mors error Calamitas . . . (*f*) ff. 200ᵛ–
201 Oratio ad dominum iesum christum. Domine mi iesu christe filii (*sic*) dei uiui
non sum dignus . . . et prosperitate corporis mei Dominici . . .

(*b*). Esther 13: 9–17. (*e*). *RH*, no. 18886. f. 201ᵛ blank.

9. ff. 202–207ᵛ Oratio S. Augustini. Domine deus omnipotens qui es trinus et
unus . . .

Cf. A. Wilmart, *Auteurs spirituels*, pp. 573–7. *PL* xl. 938–40.

10. ff. 207ᵛ–211ᵛ Pro itinerantibus antiphona. In uiam pacis . . .

Includes Benedictus dominus, the prayer 'Deus qui filios israel . . .' and six other prayers.

11. ff. 212–22, 223–225ᵛ Passio D. N. Iesu Christi secundum Iohannem.
Egressus est dominus iesus . . . posuerunt iesum. . . . Oratio. Deus qui manus
tuas . . .

John 18: 1–19: 42 in nine sections, the last (19: 31–42) placed after art. 12.

12. f. 222ʳᵛ Septem uersus S. Bernardi. Illumina oculos meos . . .

13 (on flyleaves). (*a*) f. 226, s. xvi. Descent of the male members of the family of
della Rovere through five generations from Rainerius and notes of the births of
Martinus, Violantis, and Dominicus in 1430, 1437, and 1442 respectively.
(*b*) f. 227, s. xv². '2 febr' 1478 obiit frater/11 februarii 1478 creatus fui e[. .]
cardinalis'.

ff. iv+224+v, foliated (i–iii), 1–227, (228–30). ff. iv, 1, 226–7 are conjoint pairs, pastedown and flyleaf, flyleaf and pastedown, taken over from a former binding. 140×89 mm.
Written space 85×47 mm. 15 long lines. Ruling with hard point. Collation of ff. 2–225:
1¹² 2–8⁸ 9¹⁰ (ff. 72–81) 10–11⁸ 12–13⁶ (ff. 100–5, 108–13) 14–18⁸ 19⁶ (ff. 156–61) 20¹⁰ 21²
(192–3) 22¹⁰ 23⁸ 24⁶ 25⁴ (ff. 198–201) 26¹⁰ 27⁸ 28⁶, together with four bifolia without text,
ff. 14–15, 82–3, 106–7, 114–15. Written in humanistic script, arts. 1, 8 in a fine hand. Full-
page pictures before arts. 2–5, ff. 15ᵛ, 83ᵛ, 107ᵛ, 115ᵛ (raising of Lazarus). Pictures containing initials in front of arts. 6 (B.V.M. on the steps of the temple), 9 (God the Father),
10 (Tobias and the angel), 12 (Bernard) and in front of each section of art. 11 to form a
passion series: the initial is of type (iii) or (iv) and is set in a corner of the picture. Initials:
(i) 6-line or more, gold paint on red or blue patterned grounds or, less commonly, in colour,
usually red, on grounds of gold paint, historiated, at each hour of art. 2 (B.V.M. and Child
at matins opposite the Annunciation picture) and on ff. 65ᵛ (a man, half-length, reading)
and 70 (choristers at a lectern); also beginning arts. 3, 4 (head of Christ crowned with
thorns), 5 (skull), 7 (Jerome); (ii) in art. 4 and on f. 174ʳᵛ, 4-line or 3-line, gold paint on
grounds of red, blue, or green, patterned in gold paint; (iii, iv) 2-line and 1-line, gold paint
on grounds of red, blue, or green, the larger size patterned. Full borders on first pages of
arts. 2–7, 9 and at each hour in art. 2. A border in the inner margin of other pages with
pictures or initials of type (i). Facsimiles in the Sotheby sale catalogue, pl. 39, show the
picture on f. 15ᵛ, the initial of type (i) and border on f. 16 and the initials of types (iii) and
(iv) on ff. 51ᵛ–52. Binding of s. xix. Secundo folio (f. 17) *eius in confessione*.

Written in northern Italy. Belonged to Cardinal Domenico della Rovere (1442–1501),
who wrote art. 13*b* and for whom arts. 1, 8 were written. His (?) arms in a full-page
heraldic achievement, f. 1ᵛ, azure a cross counter-compony sable and or, and in six
borders. The motto 'Soli deo' on five pages and the motto 'Adroit' on four. 'E. and F.
Hunt', f. 1. Western MS. 121 in the A. Chester Beatty collection. Sale at Sotheby's,
24 June 1969, lot 67.

BIRMINGHAM. UNIVERSITY OF BIRMINGHAM, UNIVERSITY LIBRARY

5/vi/2. *Augustinus de Ascolo, Sermones dominicales*   s. xiii/xiv

[S]tudiosis uiris et religiosis sibique in cristo fratribus studentibus ordinis here-mitarum sancti Augustini in studio paduano Frater Augustinus de Esculo eiusdem ordinis salutem . . . (f. 1ᵛ) Erunt signa etc. Luc' xxi. Inter ceteras questiones . . . (f. 96) vado ad eum qui (*ends abruptly*).

Schneyer, p. 250. The series ends here in the course of the sermon on John 16: 5 for the fourth Sunday in Lent, beginning 'Tria dumtaxat sunt'. The title, s. xvii, at the foot of f. 1 is 'Sermones ab aduentu usque ad Pasqua fratris Augustini de Esculo ordinis Eremi-tarum'. f. 52 should precede f. 51 and f. 69 should precede f. 68. There is a break before the Ash Wednesday sermon which begins (f. 23) '[C]um ieiunatis . . . Secundum quod homo est ex duplici compositus substancia . . . (Schneyer, p. 117, without author's name). ff. 96ᵛ–97ᵛ are blank.

ff. i+97+i. 242×170 mm. Written space 148×118 mm. 2 cols. 35 lines. Collation: 1¹² 2¹⁰ 3–4¹² 5¹⁰ 6–9⁸ 10¹² wants 9, 10, 12, blank. In quires 5 and 7 the central sheets are bound the wrong way round. Quires signed early k, g, a–f, h, i, but the present order is right. Initials: (i) the spaces for *S* on f. 1 and *C* on f. 23 remain blank; (ii) 2-line, red with violet ornament or blue with red ornament. Continental binding, s. xix. Secundo folio *est thesaurus*.

Written in Italy. Bought from Hammond's Bookshop in 1957.

5/vi/12. *Pseudo-Augustinus, Sermones; etc.*   s. xv med.

1. ff. 1–48ᵛ, 51–77 'Incipiunt sermones sancti augustini ad heremitas et nonnulli ad sacerdotes suos et ad aliquos alios Et primo de institutione regularis uite. Sermo primus.' Fratres mei et lętitia cordis mei . . .

Forty-three sermons. (*a*). Forty sermons from the series Ad fratres in eremo. *PL* xl. 1233 sqq., nos. 1–18, 26 (part), 19–29, 31, 46, 32–5, 30, 36, 47, 37, 43. Römer, i. 353. The first copy of no. 26, De murmuratione, extends only to 'miseria positi estis. Amen' (f. 28ᵛ: ed. 1278/37). It occurs again on ff. 38ᵛ–41ᵛ with an added heading 'De murmuratione habetur etiam iste sermo ut supra. sed non ita completus ut hic'. No. 29, ff. 47ᵛ–48, is in the hand which added headings throughout, over erasure of forty-five lines of verse in the main hand. (*b*). ff. 55ᵛ–57, after no. 46 of (*a*): Petentibus¹ discipulis fratres karissimi qualiter esset orandum respondit eis doctor veritatis . . . intermissione orare semper. Amen. On the Pater Noster. (*c*). ff. 72–73ᵛ, after no. 37 of (*a*): Sanctam ac uenerabilem et desiderabilem . . . peruenire. Ideo stante (*sic*) domino nostro . . . Amen. *PL* clxxi. 388–90. For Christ-mas. (*d*). ff. 73ᵛ–75, after (*c*): Hodierna die fratres karissimi apparuit benignitas et humani-tas saluatoris nostri gaudeamus. Hodie stella duxit magos . . . colocare digneris. Amen. For Christmas.

2. (*a*) f. 48ᵛ 'Calixtus de conuersione sancti augustini episcopi.' Magnus ille doctor et egregius Augustinus . . . deus attendit. Hec Calixtus de Augustini (*sic*). (*b*) f. 48ᵛ 'Sigisbertus in epistola ad Macedonium de beato augustino.' Tempore Theodosii senioris. Augustinus uir accutissimus . . . scolas liberalium

¹ MS. Netentibus.

(*ends imperfectly*). (*c*) ff. 49–50ᵛ (*begins imperfectly*) sinum collocabat . . . in nouissimo die. Amen.

(*a, b*) on St. Augustine and (*c*) on St. Monica are printed in old editions of *Opera Augustini,* for example in the Basel edition of 1569, x. 1439–42.

ff. i+77+i. Paper. 222×195 mm. Written space 192×110 mm. 35 long lines. Ruling with a hard point. Collation: 1–4¹⁰ 5¹⁰ wants 9 after f. 48 6–7¹⁰ 8 eight (ff. 70–7). Humanistic script in which *f* and *s* are descenders. Initials: (i) ff. 1, 48ᵛ, 51, gold on blue, red, and green grounds, decorated with vine stems and white dots in groups of three; (ii) 3-line, red or blue. Bound by Charles Lewis, probably in 1827 (see below). Secundo folio *infidelibus.*

Written in Italy. 'De me Carlo A[. . . . .]gi' scratched through at foot of f. 1, s. xvi. 'H. Drury. 1827 comp. C. Lewis', f. 1. 'Phillipps MS. 3375'. Phillipps sale, 5 June 1899, lot 82, to Thomas for 16s. 0d. Given by Mrs. A. F. Dauglish in 1957.

6/i/19. *Horae*   s. xv in.

1. ff. 1–2 Exaudi quesumus . . ., Deus qui non mortem . . ., Ecclesie tue . . ., Deus a quo sancta desideria . . ., Omnipotens deus qui viuorum . . .

These are prayers to follow a litany. No doubt leaves containing the penitential psalms and litany are missing before them. The position, before instead of after hours of B.V.M., is unusual.

2. ff. 2–20ᵛ Hours of B.V.M. of the use of (Rome).

From prime on the hours are abbreviated. Headings in French: spellings are 'lechon', 'capitiel', 'tierche', 'noene'.

3. ff. 21–5 Les commandises pour les trespases. Subuenite . . .

Nearly as *Manuale Sarum*, pp. 118–21.

4. ff. 25–33ᵛ Vigile des mors . . .

The ninth lesson is 'Audiui uocem . . . sequntur illis' (Apoc. 14: 13). The last three lines on f. 33ᵛ have been erased.

ff. iii+33+iii. 143×97 mm. Written space 77×53 mm. 17 long lines. Collation: 1–4⁸ 5 one (f. 33). Initials: (i) beginning arts. 2–4, gold on blue and red grounds patterned in white; (ii, iii) 2-line and 1-line, red or blue. Capital letters in the ink of the text filled with pale yellow. Binding of red velvet, s. xx.

Written in north-eastern France or French Flanders. Armorial 'Ex libris Gertrude Tomkinson'. Given by Mrs. A. F. Dauglish in 1964.

6/ii/18. *Hugo de Sancto Victore*   s. xv²

1. ff. 1–152 Que de libro salomonis qui ecclesiastes dicitur nuper coram vobis disserui . . . profutura sint ignorat.

Hugh of St. Victor on Ecclesiastes. Stegmüller, no. 3812. *PL* clxxv. 113–256.

2. ff. 152–79 Incipit argumentum in Opusculum domini hugonis de operibus trium dierum. Invisibilia dei a creatura mundi . . . Tria sunt inuisibilia . . .

pertinet ad resurrectionem. Explicit tractatus domini Hugonis de opere trium dierum.

PL clxxvi. 811–38. ff. 179ᵛ–180ᵛ blank.

ff. iv+180+iii. Paper. f. iv is a contemporary flyleaf. 215×145 mm. Written space 140 ×85 mm. 25–7 long lines. Frame ruling in pencil. Fifteen twelves, signed a-p. Written in clear hybrida and black ink. Initials: (i) f. 1, 5-line, red with violet ornament; (ii) 2-line, metallic red, ff. 1ᵛ, 2ᵛ, 152ᵛ–153 only, the rest omitted. Binding of s. xx by J. P. Gray & Son, Cambridge. Secundo folio *simul et.*

Written in Germany. Probably from the Cologne region, to judge from: (*a*) 'Liber Mauricii Comitis de Spegelberch prepositi Embricensis Capellarii Coloniensis 'donatus ab eodem nobis oretur pro eo", s. xvi in., f. iv, below an excised ex-libris and (*b*) 'Nᵒ 126 MSS. Van Ess', f. iv (cf. A. N. L. Munby, *Phillipps Studies*, iii. 29).[1] 'Phillipps MS. 511': sale, Sotheby's, 6 June 1910, lot 449, to Dobell. 'Walter W. Greg Trin: Coll: Camb. 1911', f. i. Bookplate of James P. R. Lyell inside the cover. In catalogue 699 of Bernard Quaritch Ltd. (1952), no. 85 (£25). Bought from Quaritch.

6/iii/14. Psalterium, etc.   s. xv in.

1. ff. 1–6ᵛ Calendar in red and black.

Among many entries in red are: 'Dedicatio s' sauini', 24 Feb.; 'Sancti Miniatis cum sociis suis', 25 Oct.; 'S' fridiani episcopi et confessoris', 18 Nov.; 'Sancti sauini episcopi et martyris et s' ambrosii', 7 Dec. 'S' iocund'' added at 27 Nov., s. xvi (?).

2. ff. 7–11 Litany.

As art. 5, except that Pontianus among martyrs and Symeon among confessors are absent. Benedict is doubled. ff. 11ᵛ–12ᵛ blank.

3. ff. 13–153 Liturgical psalter.

4. ff. 153–167ᵛ Six ferial canticles, Benedicite, Te deum (headed 'Hymnus sancti Nicetis'), Benedictus, Magnificat, Nunc dimittis, Pater noster, Credo, Quicumque vult.

5. ff. 167ᵛ–171ᵛ Litany.

Twenty-nine martyrs: . . . (16) Sauine, (17) Pontiane. Nineteen confessors: . . . (8) Fridiane . . . (10) Benedicte, (11) Symeone. Twenty virgins: . . . (13–19) Reparata, Flora, Lucilla, Brigida, Orsula, Margarita, Barbara; the next and last name has been erased in favour of Jocunda (s. xvi?), as in art. 2. The *P* of *Pontiane*, *B* of *Benedicte* and *S* of *Symeone* are touched with red. Anne does not occur.

6. ff. 171ᵛ–213 Incipit commune plurimorum sanctorum per totum annum. Twelve lessons.

7 (added). ff. 213–214ᵛ Canticles: (*a*) Domine miserere nostri . . .; (*b*) Audite qui longe estis . . .; (*c*) Miserere dominus plebi tue . . .

The first set of monastic canticles for nocturns on Sundays in Mearns, *Canticles*, p. 87. f. 215ʳᵛ blank.

---

[1] Dr. Sigrid Krämer tells me that of seven manuscripts known to her as having belonged to Moritz von Spiegelberch, three passed into the possession of Cologne Cathedral, Darmstadt, LB, 2151, 2190, and Cologne, Diözesanbibl. 200.

8 (added). ff. 216–233ᵛ Incipit offitium mortuorum. ff. 224–225ᵛ left blank.

9. f. i Part of a leaf of a breviary of s. xv, used in binding: office of Epiphany.

ff. i+225. 112×80 mm. Written space 78×55 mm. 20 long lines. Collation: 1–17¹² 18¹² wants 12, blank, after f. 214 19¹⁰. Arts. 3–6 are in a different hand from arts. 1, 2. Initials: (i) f. 13, 14-line, pink on gold and blue ground, historiated (God the Father is in the upper loop of the B and David in the lower loop); (ii) 3-line, in colour on blue grounds; (iii) 2-line, red with violet ornament or blue with red ornament; (iv) 1-line, red or blue. Sewn on three bands: no covers. Secundo folio (f. 14) *turbabit eos.*

Written in Italy for use in a Benedictine house dedicated to St. Sabinus of Spoleto. Bought from Hammond's Bookshop in 1957.

6/iii/15. '*Manuale notarii*' 1456–7

The day-book of Pierre Riffard, notary, from 14 Aug. 1456 (f. xxv) to 16 Mar. 1456/7 (f. ciiᵛ).

A heading on f. ciiᵛ, 'Hec est rubrica presentis libri anni quinquagesimi sexti In qua rubricabuntur omnes note et libri scripte et recitate per me petrum Riffard notarium auctoritate episcopali uiuar' exceptis aliquibus notis . . .', is followed by a list of 109 pieces, of which the first twenty-nine were on the twenty-four leaves now missing at the beginning. Most of the pieces have against them 'Alibi est ad plenum', often with a reference to 'Liber D', for example, f. lxviii, 'Alibi est ad plenum libro D f° cxlvii'. They each have a heading beginning with such words as *Emptio, Obligatio, Compromissum, Novum accapitum, Remissio, Testimonium.* Riffard's place of work was evidently Bourg St. Andéol in the diocese of Viviers. The title on the outside of the front cover is 'Manuale notarii anno millesimo quattergesimo quinquagesimo sexto. 'Riffard 1456''.

ff. 84, foliated xxv–cviii. Paper. 200×148 mm. Collation: 1²⁴ 2³² 3²⁸. More or less scribbly cursiva by Pierre Riffard. The three quires are sewn at two points to a parchment cover cut from a document of 4 Feb. 14[.]3, when Charles (VII) was king of France and John (de Linières, 1407–42) was bishop of Viviers. The blank dorse forms the outside of the cover.

Written at Bourg St. Andéol, Ardèche.[1] 'Acheté à Paris en 1843, dans la vente des livres de la Biblᵠᵘᵉ de feu Mʳ Noisy, N° 698 10 *livres* les 2 vol.' inside the cover.

6/iii/19. '*Collationes*' s. XIII/XIV

'Collationes' on various subjects, the first, listed in the table of contents as 'De confessione collatio prima', beginning imperfectly at the words 'Confessio parum ualet Cum enim contraria contrariis curentur'. Other pieces are 'De coreis' (f. 102ᵛ), 'De ornatu' (five), on the life of Christ (twelve), 'De mortuis' (ff. 201–32) and 'De consiliariis' (ff. 232–234ᵛ). ff. 234ᵛ–243ᵛ contain thirty-one stories which the older table of contents calls 'Miracula', the first beginning 'In ciuitate ferrarie fuit quidam miles nobilis et potens nomine aldigerius de fontana precipuus pater minorum fratrum' and the last about a friar minor who left out the words 'Placeat tibi sancta trinitas' at the end of mass: it ends 'et ait frater ad

---

[1] For notarial registers of Bourg St. Andéol in the Archives Nationales see A. Gouron in *Recueil de mémoires et travaux publiés par la Société d'histoire du droit* (Université de Montpellier), v (1966), 51. I owe the reference to Professor C. R. Cheney.

socium ueritatem locutus est demon quia oracionem illam per incuriam obmisi et cetera. Expliciunt collaciones'.

Outside the final section there are a good number of stories in the text. 'Exemplum' in the margin draws attention to them. The author was evidently Franciscan. The old foliation and the collation show that the first two leaves are missing and four leaves elsewhere.

A table of f. 243^{rv} in the main hand does not correspond with the actual contents or order of the text here. A second table was added later on ff. 243^v–244^v. It provides leaf numbers and covers the contents of ff. 1–234^v: ninety-one heads.

ff. ii+238. The medieval foliation 3–244 takes account of 6 missing leaves. 180 × 130 mm. Written space 130 × 92 mm. 2 cols. 33 lines. Collation: 1^{12} wants 1, 2 2–5^{12} 6^{12} wants 11 after f. 70 7–9^{12} 10^{12} wants 3 after f. 110 11–13^{12} 14^{12} wants 7 after f. 162 15–16^{12} 17^{12} wants 3 after f. 194 18–20^{12} 21^4. Quires, except the last three, numbered at the end, and marked by catchwords. 3-line initials, blue or red, with ornament of the other colour. Binding much repaired: the back cover is calf, s. xv ex., with stamps of three patterns, rosette, quatrefoil, and honeycomb: rebacked and the spine lettered, absurdly, 'Cassiani collationes patrum ægyptus. sæc. xv'.

Written in Italy. 'ex Archivio collegiatu (?) Castiglionis' on the parchment pastedown at the end, s. xvii (?). 'This M.S. was brought from Italy about 1745 by a member of an aristocratic family (Sir D. Norries) in this county. Two or three Irish gentlemen were making what was then termed the "Grand Tour" considered then to be requisite for an educated gentleman. They visited the Library of a Monastry near Milan, when they expressed their astonishment at the beauty and perfection of the ancient MSS which were set before them for their inspection. One of the party (Mr. Norries) was so grateful for the attention shown him that he offered a sum to help the hospital which was in connection and presented the abbot with it. The abbot not wishing to be out done in generosity presented the donor with this MS. on his departure as a memento of his gratitude. It is remarkable for its beauty and diversity of the scroll work with which the capitals are adorned', f. i. Armorial book-plate of 'Joseph Bennett. Blair Castle', s. xix: motto 'Virtute et fidelitate'. Bought in 1955–6.

6/iii/20. *Plautus* s. xv med.

Eight comedies of Plautus in the common order: 'Amphitrio'; 'Asinaria', f. 21^v; 'Captiui', f. 39; 'Curgulio', f. 57^v; 'Cassina', f. 71; 'Cistellaria', f. 85^v; 'Epidicus', f. 94; 'Aularia', f. 105^v, ending 'feres a me' and in the margin 'Deficit'.

Lines 149–202 of Cistellaria are here at the beginning, immediately after the Argumentum. The flyleaf, f. v, has in a hand of s. xv: (*a*) Eusebius de origine et conditione plauti. Plautus ex umbria . . .; (*b*) Epigramma plauti. Postquam est morte . . . (three lines: Aulus Gellius, Noct. Att. i. 24). ff. 121–122^v blank.

ff. v+122+iii. ff. iv, v are flyleaves ruled like the text. 230 × 170 mm. Written space 145 mm high. 28 long lines. Collation: 1–11^{10} 12^{12}. Ruling of verticals with a hard point and of horizontals with a light pencil. Strips of a late manuscript in Greek lie down the centres of the quires (see at ff. 35^v–6). Written in humanistic hands, changing at f. 91 (10^1). The first scribe writes his catchwords vertically, the second horizontally. 2-line spaces for initials not filled. Binding of s. xix. The marks of five bosses on the old covers show on ff. iv and 122.

Written in Italy. T. Thorpe's catalogue for 1836, item 1008. 'Phillipps MSS. 9445': not in the Phillipps sales, unless it is 17 May 1897, lot 609. Acquired before 1950.

6/iii/25. *Horae*   s. XV med.

1. ff. 1–70^v Incipit offitium beate uirginis secundum consuetudinem Curie Romane.

Leaves were lost by s. xvi, when the beginning of sext and the whole of none and vespers were supplied on ff. 35^{rv}, 39–45^v. Terce, sext, and compline end imperfectly, ff. 34^v, 38^v, 49^v. f. 50 begins in a commemoration of B.V.M., 'filii tui habitaculum effici . . .'. It is followed on ff. 50–70^v by the special psalms for use on particular days of the week and the special forms for use at particular seasons.

2. ff. 71–96^v Incipiunt septem psalmi penitentiales. A litany follows.

In the litany Romulus is last of nine martyrs and the monks and hermits are Benedict, Bernard, Anthony, Leonard, John Gualbert (the founder of Vallombrosa), Francis and Dominic. Eleven virgins: . . . (10, 11) Reparata Elizabeth.

3. ff. 97–148 Incipit offitium mortuorum. . . . Deo gratias. Domnus Iohannes Monachus scripsit. Orate pro eum (*sic*).

ff. 133 and 134 are supply-leaves, s. xvi. f. 148^v blank.

ff. vi+148+iii. ff. iv–vi are medieval parchment end-leaves: iv was pasted down. 112 × 80 mm. Written space 63 × 42 mm. 14 long lines. Collation: 1–3^{10} 4 eight (ff. 31–8: f. 35 is a supply leaf) 5^6+1 leaf before 1 (ff. 39–45, all supplied), 6 five (ff. 46–50) 7–12^{10} 13^8 14^{10} 15^{10} wants 5, 6, supplied in s. xvi (ff. 133–4) 16^{10}. Initials: (i) of arts. 1–3, 8-line and 7-line, in colour on gold grounds, historiated (B.V.M. and Child (1), a saint (2), a skull (3)): continuous borders; (ii) 4-line, in colour on gold and coloured decorated grounds; (iii) 2-line, blue with red ornament or red with violet ornament; (iv) 1-line, blue or red. Binding of s. xix. Secundo folio *Venite*.

Written in Italy (Florence?: cf. art. 2) by a named scribe. Bought from Hammond's Bookshop in 1957.

6/iii/26. *Vetus Testamentum*   s. XIII med.

The Old Testament in the order Genesis–4 Kings, Tobit, Judith, Esther (ends imperfectly at 9: 31), 1, 2 Chronicles, Ezra, Nehemiah (ends at the foot of f. 189^v, a few lines from the end of the book: f. 190^r is blank), Job, five Sapiential Books (Ecclesiasticus begins 'Omnis sapientia', not 'Multorum nobis'), Isaiah, Jeremiah, Lamentations, Baruch, Ezekiel, Daniel, Minor Prophets, 1, 2 Maccabees.

Esther and 1 Chronicles begin on new quires, ff. 141, 144. The only prologues are of the common set: Stegmüller, nos. 323, 332, 335, 341, 327 (to 1 Chronicles), 330, 344, 457, 482, 487. There are many nearly contemporary references in the margins, often a dozen or more on one page, to other books of the Bible by chapter and letter, for example at Genesis 31: 7 'N 14 d. Job 19 a' (Numbers 14: 22, Job 19: 3).

ff. iii+321+iii. 143 × 97 mm. Written space 112 × 75 mm. 2 cols. 46–52 lines. Collation impracticable: mainly in sixteens. Several hands: changes at ff. 144, 191. Initials: (i) of books, blue and red with ornament in both colours; (ii) of prologues, as (i) or in one colour only, with ornament in both colours; (iii) of chapters, 2-line, blue or red, with ornament of the other colour. Capital letters in the ink of the text touched with red. Bound in red morocco, gilt, s. xviii. Secundo folio *custos*.

Written in England. A scribble 'Henry Hulloke', f. 145, s. xvi. Lot 126 in a sale, s. xx:

the relevant cutting from the catalogue is inserted loose. Bought probably in 1952 from Francis Edwards.

6/iii/36. *Innocentius III, De miseria humanae conditionis* (*2 copies*)
s. xiv med.; s. xiii ex.

A. 1. ff. 1–47ᵛ Incipiunt capitula libri lotharii de uilitate conditionis humane . . . (f. 3) Incipit liber lotharii de uilitate conditionis humane. prologus. Domino patri karissimo. P. portuen' Episcopo Lotharius . . . exaltetur. De miserabili conditionis humane ingressus. Quare de wlua . . . et ignis ardens sine fine. a quibus omnibus liberet nos deus qui est benedictus in secula seculorum amen. Explicit iste liber.

Ed. M. Maccarrone, 1955; *PL* ccxvii. 701–46. The table on ff. 1–2ᵛ lists three books of 28, 37, and 18 chapters, but the text is not divided into books, but into 88 paragraphs, including the prologue, with headings to the first thirteen only.

2. f. 47ᵛ Nota Bernardus. Illi qui peccatis acquiescunt . . . et misericordia cruciandi. Quotes St. Bernard. f. 48ʳᵛ blank.

Written space 108 × 75 mm. 22 long lines. Collation: 1–5⁸ 6⁸ wants 8, blank. Initials: (i) f. 1, red and blue, with ornament of both colours; (ii) f. 3, blue, with red ornament; (iii) 2-line, red or blue. Secundo folio (f. 4) *luto.De.*

Written in France. 'Iste liber pertinet cartusiens' prope Pa[. . . .]' ('Parisios' is suggested in a nineteenth-century note on f. iᵛ, perhaps rightly), f. 1, s. xv. A large '.9.' on f. 47ᵛ, s. xv (?).

B. 1. f. 48ʳᵛ . . . in sanguine virtute verborum.

The end of a short treatise on the mass. A paragraph begins De secunda parte misse dicendum est.

2. (*a*) f. 48ᵛ A recipe, s. xiv, 'Subsequens vnguentum valet ad collendam omnem scabiem . . .' (*b*) Lists, s. xvi, of six 'Occasiones peccandi' and of the twelve 'abusiones claustri secundum Bernardum'. (*c*) f. 49ᵛ A table of chapters of art. 3, 74 in all, s. xv.

Additions in the blank space between art. 1 and art. 3.

3. ff. 50–67ᵛ Domino patri karissimo P. portuen' Episcopo Lotharius . . . et ignis ardens in secula seculorum. Explicit summa de miseria condicionis humane quam composuit papa Innocencius. `iste liber vocatur lotharius a nomine compilatoris qui postea fuit papa innocencius cuius anima requiescat in pace amen.´

Divided after the prologue into three books of 30, 41, and 19 paragraphs. Cf. art. 2c. A note, s. xiv, 'Miror de clericis . . .', headed 'Bernardus', fills the space left blank on f. 67ᵛ.

4. ff. 48–67 are palimpsest, the underwriting probably from an unfinished law text, s. xiv, with wide blank margins. The running red and blue book-numbers of this text, 'L' I' and 'L' II', have not been erased and appear at intervals in the upper margins.

Written space 130 × 67 mm. ff. 50–67 have a medieval foliation 1–18. 42 long lines. One quire of twenty leaves. Two-line red initials. Secundo folio (f. 51) *runt vuam.*
Written in Italy (?).

(A+B). ff. i+67+i. 153×105 mm. (A) at least has been much cut down by the binder, as appears from f. 2, where the full width, 120 mm., has been kept for the sake of notes running into the margin. Binding of s. xviii.

Phillipps MS. 2866: sale 21 Mar. 1895, lot 602, to Nichols for 5s. Armorial 'Ex libris Gertrude Tomkinson'. Given by Mrs. A. F. Dauglish in 1961.

6/iv/17. *Willelmus de S. Theodorico*   s. xv med.

1. ff. 1–12 Bernardi clareualensis abbatis de amore dei feliciter incipit. Uenite ascendamus ad montem domini: et ad domum dei . . . adoramus et benedicimus: tibi gloria in secula seculorum amen. *PL* clxxxiv. 367–80.

2. ff. 12–37 Ars est artium ars amoris . . . et nouissimi primi. Explicit feliciter de amore dei. *PL* clxxxiv. 379–408.

3. ff. 37ᵛ–40ᵛ were left blank and are so, except for six lines of verse on f. 40ᵛ, s.xv ex.: (*a*) four lines 'Non est enim pondus uere uirtutis insensibilitas cordis . . .'; (*b*) two lines, 'Petrus asspiciat petrum . . .'.

ff. ii+40+ii. 140×95 mm. Written space 96×70 mm. 26 long lines. Collation: 1–5⁸. Humanistic script. Initials: (i) ff. 1, 12, red on gold and blue grounds historiated (f. 1, St. Bernard?), with sprays of gold and colour in the margins; (ii) 2-line, red or blue. Binding of s. xix in., described in the 1843 sale catalogue as 'blue morocco gilt leaves by Lewis'. Secundo folio *in quo ut*.

Written in Italy. Book-plates of John Trotter Brockett, F.S.A. (†1842: his sale, 16 June 1843, lot 43), J. Cresswell, and 'E. H.'. Lot 104 in a sale, s. xx: the relevant cutting is pasted inside the cover. Given by Mrs. A. F. Dauglish in 1955.

6/iv/26. *Missae*   s. xiv med.

1. ff. 1–4ᵛ Prefaces and canon of mass.

2. Masses: (*a*) ff. 4ᵛ–5 In honore sancte Marie; (*b*) ff. 5–7 of SS. Philip and James and St. James; (*c*) ff. 7–8ᵛ Missa mortuorum; (*d*) f. 8ᵛ Missa dedicationis; (*e*) ff. 8ᵛ–9 of Holy Trinity, Holy Spirit, and Holy Cross; (*f*) ff. 10–11 of the dead; (*g*) ff. 11–19 of the common of saints; (*h*) f. 19ʳᵛ In anniuersario dedicationis ecclesie; (*i*) ff. 19ᵛ–22 of Holy Trinity, Holy Spirit, and Holy Cross; (*j*) ff. 22–24ᵛ In commemoratione beate marie uirginis; (*k*) ff. 24ᵛ–25 Missa pro peccatis; (*l*) ff. 25–7 of SS. Andrew, Nicholas, Gregory, Anthony confessor, John Baptist, Laurence, Bartholomew, Michael, Francis, Martin, Catherine; (*m*) ff. 27–9 Ad poscenda suffragia sanctorum, Pro persecutoribus ecclesie, Pro pace, Pro iter agentibus, Pro infirmis, Pro se ipso sacerdote, Pro temptatione carnis, Pro amico, Pro deuotis amicis, Ad pluuiam postulandam, Pro serenitate; (*n*) f. 29ʳᵛ Missa generalis sancti augustini pro uiuis et defunctis. Omnipotens sempiterne deus qui uiuorum . . . Alia missa generalis. Pietate tua . . .

(*d–f, l–n*). Collect, secret, and postcommunion only. (*c*). *SMRL* ii. 327, no. 63a, i, o. (*e*). ibid. 318, nos. 2 (Holy Trinity) and 4 (Holy Cross) and for Holy Spirit the collect, secret, and post communion as in Van Dijk's MSS. F, G, H. (*h*). ibid. 317. (*j*). ibid. 319–20. (*m*). ibid. 321–4, nos. 9–11, 13, 14, 17, 24, 30, 33–5. (*n*). ibid. 324, nos. 37, 38.

3. ff. 9–10 Benediccio salis et aque.

4. f. 30 Table of arts. 1–3, with leaf references.

5. ff. i^{rv}, 31^{rv} Part of a bifolium of a lawyer's journal, s. xiv, cut in two and formerly used as pastedowns. Entries are headed: (a) f. 31, die xvi Iunii; (b) f. i^v, die xx Iunii. (a) begins 'Hec est inquisitio que fit et fieri intendit [. . . .] tochul' de tridento generalem v[. . . . . .]: three cases follow. Side notes show the decisions: (i) S. Fati condempnetur Iulli xiii scilicet ll' x pro spada et ll' iii pro tangeta; (ii) contra dulzamicum non proceditur quia clericus est; (3) P. michael condempnetur. pro [. . . .]. The name 'Guentinum (?) de tochul' de tri[. . . .]' can just be made out in the first line of (b). Other cases of 23 and 24 June 'in palc' episcopali' are on f. i^v.

ff. i+30+i. Medieval foliation i–xxx. 228×153 mm. Written space 145×115 mm. 26 long lines. Three tens. Well written. Punctuation with flex occasionally, for example, f. 29/18. 2-line red initials. Binding of thick wooden boards, bare of leather: three bands. Secundo folio *Per omnia*.

Written in Italy. Bought from Hammond's Bookshop in 1957.

6/iv/27. *Ordinances of a lay company (in Italian)*   s. xv²

1. ff. 2–18^v, 21 Al nome s[. .] della sanctissima e indiuidua trinita padre figliuolo e spirito sancto . . . amen. Lo spirito sancto parlla parlla bocha del propheta dauid dicendo. Declina a malo . . .

Two preliminary paragraphs, followed by ordinances in twenty-two chapters. The second preliminary paragraph is historical. It states that the company was founded on 15 Aug. 1471 'in sancto piero ghattolino' (Florence) and that the decision to draw up ordinances was taken on 20 Dec. 1472, and ends with the words 'Considerando questi essere confermati parlla autorita del nostro padre messere arciuescouo di firenze o altri ueschoui o di messerllo uicario di detto arciueschouo'. f. 1^v contains a table of chapters. ff. 1, 21^v blank.

2. ff. 19–20^v Aue maria gratia plena. Dominus tecum. Venite exultemus domino . . . in requiem meam.

For the Assumption of B.V.M. Ps. 94 and (cues only) Pss. 18, 19, 62, Benedicite, and Ps. 148 and hymns, Quem terra pontus and O gloriosa domina.

ff. 21. 270×190 mm. Written space 168×98 mm. 25 long lines. Collation: 1⁸ (ff. 2–5, 7–10)+1 leaf after 4 (f. 6) 2¹⁰ (ff. 11–18, 21, 1)+a bifolium inserted after 8 (ff. 19, 20): 2¹⁰ has been folded back round quire 1 to form f. 1 Initials: (i) f. 2, pink on blue, green, and gold ground, historiated (assumption of B.V.M. above crossed keys); (ii) 2-line, blue or red, with ornament of the other colour. Capital letters in the ink of the text filled with pale yellow. A pen-and-ink drawing in the lower margin of f. 2: two surpliced masked figures hold scrolls: the only colour is an oval of red on the back of each surplice. Contemporary (?) binding of wooden boards covered with stamped brown leather: 4 out of 8 bosses remain and 1 of 2 clasps. A now-damaged picture like that in the initial on f. 2 is secured by nails to the centre of the front cover and once, perhaps, had the protection of a piece of horn.

Written in Florence, probably in 1473. Bought from Hammond's Bookshop in 1957.

6/iv/28. *Horae* s. xv med.

1. ff. 1–57, 123–131ᵛ Incipit offitium beate uirginis marie. secundum ordinem romane curie.

At first writing the text lacked the special psalms for particular days of the week which usually come before the special forms of service at particular seasons. These psalms were supplied by the main hand on ff. 123ᵛ–131ᵛ, together with a second copying on f. 123ʳ of the part of the text on f. 57ʳ. Presumably f. 57 was meant to be a reject and it shows signs of having been used in binding: the verso is blank.

2 (in the blank space at the end of quire 18). f. 132 Decem precepta legis. f. 132ᵛ is blank.

3. ff. 58–77 Incipiunt viiᵉᵐ psalmi penitentiales cum letaniis eorum.

The monks and hermits are Benedict, Francis, Anthony, Dominic. Nine virgins: . . . (8, 9) Clare, Elizabeth.

4. ff. 77–80 Incipit officium sancte crucis.

5. ff. 80–6 Incipit officium sancti spiritus.

ff. 86ᵛ–87ᵛ were left blank. 87 has an invocation of B.V.M. in Italian, s. xvi.

6. ff. 88–120 Incipit offitium mortuorum.

ff. 120ᵛ–122ᵛ were left blank, and are blank, except for scribbles.

ff. 132. 82 × 68 mm. Written space 55 × 40 mm. 15 long lines. Collation: 1–7⁸ 8 one (f. 57: see above) 9⁸ 10⁶ 11–16⁸ 17⁴ wants 4, blank, after f. 122 18¹² wants 11, 12, blank: this supplementary quire should follow quire 7 (see above). Initials: (i) f. 1, 7-line or 8-line, deep red patterned in white on grounds of gold paint, historiated (f. 1, B.V.M. and Child; elsewhere in art. 1, saints: at sext John Baptist is surrounded by a scroll 'ecce agnus dei ecce . . . peccata mundi'; altar-cross at art. 3; Dove at art. 4; skull at art. 5) and with blue and green or red and blue tails into the margins; (ii, iii) 2-line and 1-line, blue or red. f. 1 has a border in colours and gold, with a blank gold shield centred in the lower margin. Binding probably of s. xvii. Secundo folio *sunt omnes*.

Written in Italy. 'Nᵒ 18', f. 132. Bought in 1958.

7/i/12. *Fabulae* s. xv med.

1. ff. 1–26 [G]recia disciplinarum . . . moraliter concludit. Gallus dum escas . . . in plena potestate dare.

The 'Dérivé complet du Romulus Anglo-Latin', printed by L. Hervieux, *Fabulistes latins*, 2nd edn., ii. 564–649, and discussed ibid., i. 775–93. The chapters here are 1–6, 8–59, 61–86, 88, 89, 87, 90–136. The 'Moralitas' is often longer than that printed by Hervieux, for example at chapters 22, 24, 64 (cf. Hervieux, i. 790). In this respect and in the omission of chapters 7 and 60 it resembles Göttingen, theol. 140.

2. ff. 26–32 Rustica quedam habuit filium qui assiduis flectibus . . . Expedit insignem promeruisse necem.

The 'Anonymi Avianicae Fabulae' printed ibid., iii. 319–52 and discussed iii. 159–71. Forty-two chapters, nos. 1–18, 20–1, 19, 22–41, 45, as in Göttingen, theol. 140. The scribe left a space of eight lines on f. 26 for a heading, which has not been filled in.

3. ff. 32–3 De gallo et iaspide . . . arboribus. Expliciunt capitula de esopo.
Capitula de animo (? *sic for* auiano). De rustica et filio . . . Quomodo hedus
noluit credere lupo. Expliciunt capitula de a*ni*mo.

A table of chapters of arts. 1, 2.

4. f. 33 Ceneca de remediis fortuitorum. Licet cunctorum poetarum carmina
. . . (*ends abruptly: one column only*).

Only the introduction and the twelve dicta beginning *Morieris* (in the order 1–7, 10, 11, 8,
12, 9) followed by the words 'De collacione': ed. Haase, iii. 446–7. f. 33ᵛ blank.

ff. ii+33+i. f. ii is a contemporary blank leaf perhaps taken from the end of quire 3.
Paper. 290×215 mm. Written space 245×160 mm. 2 cols. 38–42 lines. Frame ruling.
Collation: 1–2¹² 3¹² wants 10–12, probably blank. Written in very current cursiva.
3-line (f. 1) and 2-line spaces for initials remain blank. Binding probably German, s. xix.

Written in Germany. Printed visiting card of 'Mr Robert Hare Hutchinson' pasted inside
the cover. 'To "Giuseppe" from' is written before the name and 'and family, with much
love, R.H.H.' after it, and below it, on the cover, 'York: Sept. 1932'.[1] Bought from the
Marchmont Bookshop, 39 Bruton St., London, in 1974.

7/i/18. *W. Peraldus, De vitiisi; etc.*   s. XIII²

1. (*a*) ff. 5–10 Titulus. Incipit tractatus moralis de vii viciis capitalibus et
peccato lingue. Tractatus iste continet viii partes. Prima pars continet de hiis
que . . . sit reprehensibilis 'in prelatis'. Expliciunt capitula in tractatu de peccato
lingue xpisto gloria qui perfecit amen. 'De tarditate loquendi et silentio clau-
stralium et commendatione silentii et bo(n)is ex eo prouenientibus.' (*b*) f. 10ᵛ Hic
incipiunt exempla omnia que in presenti summa continentur. Exempla de
luxuria . . . (*c*) ff. 11–189 Dicturi de singulis uiciis cum oportunitas se offeret . . .
penituit tacere n*o*n (*sic: expunged*) numquam. Explicit. Explicit summa de
uiciis. (*d*) ff. 189–93 Hic incipiunt rubrice et notabilia omnia que sunt in ista
summa per alfabetum ordinata et conposita sicut decet. Aggrauare x a . . .
zelus xliiii c cl a

Many manuscripts and printed editions: cf. A. Dondaine in *AFP* xviii (1948), 184–97.
(*a, c, d*) are furnished with leaf numbers and letters a, b, c, d, referring to the four columns
on each leaf.

2. ff. 193–5 Incipit uita et modus uiuendi qualiter religiosus se debeat habere
coram deo et hominibus. De amore et desiderio dei . . . De reprehensione
(*36 heads*). Incipit uita (*etc.*). [S]unt alique necessaria inter uirtutes et mores
illis qui sunt uinculo ordinis deputati . . . ut recipias gloriam quam preparauit
deus diligentibus se quem nobis concedat . . . in secula seculorum amen.

3 (added early). f. 195ᵛ Item si sanguinis stilla cadat super terram . . . On
accidents at mass.

4. ff. 195ᵛ–196ᵛ, 1–4 Heads of sermons, among them John Evangelist, Stephen,
and Thomas the apostle, added in a current hand, s. xiv, on quires 1, 19 and on
flyleaves.

[1] A piece of paper bearing a 'promise to pay' Thomas Richardson Esq. £100, 31 Aug.
1772, lies loose in the book. Presumably it only got there much after this date.

ff. ii+194, foliated 1–196. ff. 11–188 have a medieval foliation in red i–clxxviii. 150×
110 mm. Written space 102×72 mm. 2 cols. (3 cols., ff. 10ᵛ, 189–193ᵛ). 40 lines. ff. 11–88
are ruled in red with three lines against the first column on each page and three lines
between the columns. Collation: 1⁴ (ff. 3–6) 2⁴ (ff. 7–10) 3–17¹² (ff. 11–190) 18⁴ (ff. 191–4)
19². Small hand. Initials: (i) of each part, red and blue, with ornament of both colours;
(ii) 2-line, red or blue, with ornament of the other colour; (iii) in art. 1d, 1-line, red or
blue. Medieval wooden boards on which a few scraps of leather remain: five bands: two
clasps. Secundo folio (f. 12) *corporis*.

Written in Italy. Bought from L. Olschki in 1974.

BLACKBURN. MUSEUM AND ART GALLERY

Twenty-two manuscripts, all except 21195, were bequeathed by Mr. R. E. Hart
in 1946. Sixteen of them and a fragment of a Greek gospel book are listed as
nos. 1–17 of *Illustrated Manuscripts and Early Printed Books from the Hart
Collection*, issued by the Public Library in (1964), which contains also reduced
facsimiles of 20918, ff. 139ᵛ, 233ᵛ (pls. 4, 5), 21040, ff. 7ᵛ–8 (pl. 6) and 21117,
ff. 7ᵛ, 8, 14ᵛ–15 (pls. 1, 3, 2). The numbers in brackets are those of this list.
Eleven manuscripts (20865, 20884, 20918, 20932, 20960, 20966, 20984, 21001,
21018, 21040, 21117) were exhibited at the Whitworth Art Gallery, University
of Manchester, in 1976 and described by Dr. J. J. G. Alexander in the catalogue *Medieval and Early Renaissance Treasures in the North West*, with
facsimiles, pls. 2, 5a, 6, 11, 13, 15 and colour pl. 1. The collection was transferred from the Public Library in 1974.

091.20865. (14). *Horae*   s. xv in.

1. ff. 1–12ᵛ Full calendar in French, in gold, blue, and red, the two colours
alternating.

Genevieve, Mor, Yves, Eloy, Loys, 'S. Leu. S. Gille', Denis are in gold.

2. ff. 13–19 Sequentiae of the Gospels.

3. ff. 19–21 Passio domini nostri ihesu cristi secundum iohannem. In illo
tempore apprehendit pylatus . . . testimonium eius. Per euangelica dicta deleantur nostra delicta Amen . . . Oracio. Deus qui manus tuas et pedes tuos . . .

The catena mainly from John 19: cf. *Lyell Cat.*, pp. 65–6.

4. ff. 21ᵛ–25ᵛ Valde bona oracio de beata maria. Obsecro te . . .

Masculine forms, as in art. 5: cf. arts. 14, 15.

5. ff. 26–28ᵛ O intemerata . . . orbis terrarum. Inclina aures . . .

6. ff. 29–104ᵛ Hours of B.V.M. of the use of (Paris).

7. ff. 105–27 Penitential psalms and (f. 120) litany.

Twenty-six confessors: (1–3) Siluester Yuo Tutguale . . . (16–26) Heruee Albine Corentine Paule Guillerme Macloui Briace Maudethe Maiole Theobalde Verane.

8. ff. 127–135ᵛ Incipiunt hore sancte crucis. The short hours.

9. ff. 136–43 Hours of the Holy Spirit. The short hours.

10. ff. 143–149ᵛ Cy apres commencent les xv ioyes nostre dame. Doulce dame de misericorde mere de pitie . . . Sonet, no. 458.

11. ff. 150–153ᵛ Quiconques ueult estre bien conseilles . . . Doulx dieu doulx pere . . . The seven Requests. Sonet, no. 504.

12. f. 154 Sainte uraye croix aouree . . . Sonet, no. 1876.

13. ff. 154ᵛ–208 Ad vesperas mortuorum.
Office of the dead. f. 208ᵛ blank.

14. ff. 209–27 Thirty-eight memoriae in the order of the church year: Circumcision, Genovefa, Epiphany, Maur, Fabian and Sebastian, Agnes, Vincent, Paul, Julian, Purification of B.V.M., Peter, Matthew, Gregory, Benedict, Annunciation of B.V.M., George, Mark, Philip and James, Holy Cross, John Evangelist, Nicholas, Urban, Germanus, Barnabas, Gervase, John Baptist, Eligius, Peter, Martin, Margaret, Mary Magdalene, James, Christopher, Stephen, Laurence, Denis, Anne, Katherine.

15. ff. 228–229ᵛ Oracio coram sacrosancto corpore (et) sanguine domini. In presencia corporis et sanguinis tue domine ihesu xpiste commendo tibi me miseram famulam tuam . . .

16. ff. 229ᵛ–231 Oracio ad corpus et sanguinem domini nostri ihesu xpisti. Per inestimabile sacramentum corporis et sanguinis tui . . . miserere michi peccatrici . . .

17. ff. 231–3 Oracio ad sanctam crucem. O crux benedicta redempcio nostra. Redemptrix nostra . . .

18. f. 233ʳᵛ Oracio ad angelum cui homo committitur. Sancte angele dei minister . . .

19. ff. 234–236ᵛ Prayers: Domine rex omnipotens in illa sancta custodia . . . commendo hodie . . .; Omnipotens sempiterne deus qui sedes in throno . . .; Euge in nobis domine per intercessionem beate marie semper uirginis . . . uirtutem fidei . . .

20. ff. 236ᵛ–237 O gloriose uirginis (sic) cum angelis iam diuites . . .
A memoria of Ursula and 11,000 virgins. f. 238ʳᵛ blank.

ff. ii+238+ii. 200×140 mm. Written space 100×64 mm. 14 long lines. Collation: 1¹²
2–12⁸ 13⁴ (ff. 101–4) 14–28⁸ 29¹⁴. Fifteen 9-line pictures, eight in art. 8, and one before
each of arts. 2, 7–11, 13. In art. 1 the occupations of the months and signs of the zodiac
are in roundels at the foot of each page. Initials: (i, ii) 3-line and 2-line, in colours on gold
grounds; (iii) 1-line, gold on coloured grounds. Borders containing figures, grotesques,
etc., on three sides of pages with initials of type i. Frames of oak leaf and ivy leaf surround
all other pages. Capital letters in the ink of the text are filled with yellow. Rebound in
s. xx: the new covers have pasted on them the old covers of brown leather, elaborately
tooled in gold, French work of s. xvi.

Written in France, for the use of a woman (arts. 15, 16). The litany is Breton. Cartouches on the covers bear respectively the names 'IEHANNE' and 'CAMEL' in gold letters.

091.20884. (16). *Horae*   s. xv/xvi

A lavishly ornamented book of hours.

1. ff. 2–13ᵛ Calendar in red and black.

The marriage of Eugène de Noyelles, 'Comte de Marle, Baron de Rossignol etc.', in the castle of Limbourg, 21 Oct. 1629, and the births of his two daughters, 14 Oct. 1640 at Brussels and 17 Feb. 1647/8 at St. Omer, are recorded in the lower margins of ff. 1ᵛ–5. f. 14ʳᵛ blank.

2. ff. 15–21 Sequentiae of the Gospels. The prayer 'Protector in te sperantium . . .' after John. f. 21ᵛ blank.

3. ff. 22–30 Passion according to St. John (18: 1–19: 42) and prayer 'Deus qui manus tuas . . .'.

4. ff. 30ᵛ–32 Deuotissima oratio de septem verbis domini nostri ihesu xpristi in cruce pendentis. Domine ihesu xpriste qui septem uerba . . .

5. f. 32ʳᵛ Deuota oratio dicenda post eleuationem corporis cristi ante tercium agnus dei . . . Domine ihesu xpriste qui hanc sacratissimam carnem . . .

The heading conveys an indulgence of 2,000 years from Pope Boniface VI, 'qui eam composuit'.

6. ff. 34–9 Incipiunt hore sancte crucis . . . Hymnus. Patris sapiencia . . .

7. ff. 41–45ᵛ Hore de sancto spiritu . . . Hymnus. Nobis sancti spiritus . . .

8. ff. 47–105ᵛ Hore beate marie virginis: use of (Rome).

Advent office, f. 99. f. 106ʳᵛ blank.

9. ff. 108–24 Penitential psalms and (f. 116ᵛ) litany.

Eight pontiffs and confessors: . . . (8) ludouice. Six doctors: francisce, benedicte, anthoni, dominice, ludouice, bernardine. Eight virgins: . . . (8) clara. f. 124ᵛ blank.

10. ff. 126–160ᵛ Office of the dead. f. 161ʳᵛ blank.

11. ff. 162–165ᵛ De sancta trinitate. Antiphona. Te inuocamus . . . Oratio. Omnipotens sempiterne deus qui dedisti famulis tuis . . .

A memoria of Holy Trinity. Prayers follow: Domine ihesu criste rogo te amore illius gaudii . . .; Precor te piissime domine ihesu criste per illam nimiam caritatem . . .; O bone ihesu o piissime ihesu . . . (of the name of Jesus).

12. ff. 166–167ᵛ Orationes beati gregorii pape. O domine ihesu xpriste adoro te in cruce pendentem . . . Seven Oes.

13. ff. 168–71 Deuota oratio ad mariam. Obsecro te . . . For male use.

14. ff. 171–4 Alia oratio ad virginem mariam. O intemerata . . . orbis terrarum. De te enim . . .

15. ff. 174–6 Alia oratio ad eandem virginem. O intemerata ... orbis terrarum. inclina mater misericordie ...

16. ff. 176ᵛ–178 Pia contemplatio beate marie virginis iuxta crucem. Stabat mater ...

17. f. 179ʳᵛ Pulcherrima oratio de conceptione marie virginis. Aue maria virgo o mater dei sine peccato ...

A memoria of the Conception.

18. ff. 181–186ᵛ Deuota oratio ad mariam. Missus est gabriel angelus ...

19. ff. 187–205ᵛ Memoriae of sixteen saints: Michael, John Baptist, James (O lux et decus . . .: *RH*, no. 30580), Guillermus (O guillerme naufragantes respexisti laborantes . . .), Christopher, Adrian (Pie martir et modeste . . .: *RH*, no. 31655), Sebastian (O quam mira refulsit . . .: *RH*, no. 30904), Antony confessor, Hubert, Anne (O gloriosa mater anna . . .: *RH*, no. 13052), Katherine, Barbara (Gaude barbara beata . . .: *RH*, no. 6911), Margaret, Agatha, Apollonia, Mary Magdalene. ff. 206–208ᵛ blank.

ff. ii+207+i, foliated i, 1–209. ff. i, 1, 209 are flyleaves of contemporary parchment. 160×115 mm. Written space 92×62 mm. 19 long lines. Ruling in red ink. Collation of ff. 2–208: 1⁶ 2⁶+1 leaf after 6 (f. 14) 3–5⁸ 6⁶ 7–13⁸ 14⁴ (ff. 103–6) 15–16⁸ 17⁸+1 leaf after 7 (f. 132) 18–20⁸ 21⁴ (ff. 158–61) 22–26⁸ 27⁶, together with five singleton picture pages, ff. 33, 40, 107, 125, 180. Catchwords are written vertically. A set round script based on cursiva and approaching *lettre bâtarde*. Full-page pictures on versos before arts. 6, 7, 9, 10, 18: the rectos are blank. Thirty-nine 14-line pictures, sixteen in art. 19, eight in art. 8, four in art. 2, and one before each of arts. 3 (Christ risen from the tomb), 6, 7, 9–13, 16–18 (17, God with scroll 'Tota pulcra es . . .', looks down on B.V.M. and two saints: she carries two scrolls, they one scroll each). Initials: (i, ii) 5-line and 2-line, in grisaille on grounds of gold paint, (iii) 1-line, gold on red or dark-green grounds. All pages with pictures or with initials of type (i) have continuous or partial framed borders, usually on grounds of gold paint and sometimes including scenes, for example (f. 34), soldiers playing dice, (f. 108) David and Goliath. Capital letters in the ink of the text are touched with pale yellow. Binding of wooden boards covered with stamped leather, s. xvi: the stamps, in vertical rows, are hardly distinguishable.

Written probably in French Flanders. The family of de Noyelles (cf. art. 1) owned another hours of the use of Rome, now Cambridge, Fitzwilliam Mus., 108. Bought at St. Omer in 1801 by 'Duval', according to a note on the pastedown at the beginning.

091.20918. (5). *Missale romanum* 1400

A missal written by a named Dutch scribe and completed by him at the Charterhouse of Trisulti, near Rome, on 24 July 1400, presumably to the order of Cardinal Serra.

1. ff. 2–6ᵛ Incipit ordo quando episcopus parat se ad celebrandum missam in pontificalibus ... O dilecta tabernacula tua ...

2. ff. 6ᵛ–9ᵛ Incipit ordo ad catetizandum infantes ... Quid uenisti ad ecclesiam querere ... R'. Fidem cristi ...

3. ff. 10–14ᵛ Calendar in red and black, lacking January and February. Principal feasts marked 'Duplex': no other gradings.

All entries in the calendar printed in *SMRL* ii. 365 are here, except the octave of Francis (Margaret is 14 not 20 July), and seven others, 'Sancte Marie ad niues Duplex' in red before Dominic, 5 Aug., and the Conception of B.V.M. 'Duplex' in red at 8 Dec., and five in black, Herculanus, Thomas Aquinas O.P., Petrus Martyr O.P., Petrus confessor, 11,000 virgins (1, 7 Mar., 29 Apr., 19 May, 21 Oct.).

4. ff. 15–133ᵛ Temporale from Advent to Easter Eve, the first leaf missing.

5. ff. 133ᵛ–148 Ordinary, noted prefaces, and (f. 143) canon of mass.

6. ff. 148–198ᵛ Temporale from Easter to the 24th Sunday after Pentecost.

7. ff. 198ᵛ–249ᵛ Sanctorale from Andrew to Katherine.

8. ff. 249ᵛ–273 Incipit commune sanctorum de missali.

9. ff. 273–4 In anniuersario dedicationis ecclesie.

10. ff. 274–89 Votive masses.

Nos. 1–5, 9–16, 6–8, 17–20, 23–46, 48–60, 62 of the series in *SMRL* ii. 318–27, together with a full office, 'Missa pro peccatis', in sixth place.

11. ff. 289–94 In agenda mortuorum.

SMRL ii. 327–31, nos. 63a, b, d–p, s, 64, 65.

12. ff. 294–295ᵛ Incipit ordo ad faciendum aquam benedictam.

13. ff. 295ᵛ–297 Missa uel actio nuptialis pro sponso et sponsa.

ff. ii+296+i, foliated (i, ii), 2–297, (298). 325 × 240 mm. Written space 205 × 148 mm. 2 cols. 31 lines. Collation: 1⁶+2 leaves after 6 (ff. 8, 9) 2⁶ wants 1 3⁸ wants 1 before f. 15 4–35⁸ 36⁶ 37⁸ 38⁶. Written in a rotonda script: reduced facsimiles of ff. 233ᵛ, 139ᵛ in *Hart Collection*, pls. 4, 5. The double opening 142ᵛ–143 has a full-page Crucifixion facing a large historiated *T* of *Te igitur*. Continuous borders in art. 3 include the signs of the zodiac and occupations of the months. Initials: (i) in colours, historiated, on gold grounds, with border ornament, including birds and beasts and a few figures; (ii), as (i), but usually smaller and not historiated; (iii, iv) 2-line and 1-line, blue with red ornament or red with violet ornament. Capital letters in the ink of the text are filled with yellow. Binding of red morocco, s. xix in.

'Explicit missale secundum consuetudinem romane curie scriptum per manus iohannis de berlandia presbiteri traiectensis dyocesis sub anno domini millesimo quatricentesimo indictione octaua pontificatus sanctissimi in cristo patris et domini nostri domini bonifatii diuina prouidentia pape noni anno undecimo die uero uicesimo quarto mensis iulii in monasterio sancti bartholomei de trisulto ordinis cartusientium alatrine diocesis', f. 297ᵛ. Arms on ff. 2, 143, surmounted by a cardinal's hat are azure a mullet or, on a chief gules a bend checky of argent and azure. These are the arms of Cardinal Petrus Serra, created 1397, †1404: cf. A. Ciaconius, *Vitae pontificum*, edn. 1677, ii. 739. From the library of the Duke of St. Albans, according to R. E. Hart. A ticket at the end: 'Exhibition Italian Art Reg. Nᵒ 24/4'.

091.20927. (13). *Horae* s. xv²

1. ff. 1–12ᵛ Full calendar in French in gold, blue, and red.

Genevieve, Mor, Eloy, Loys, Denis are in gold.

2. ff. 13–18 Sequentiae of the Gospels.

3. ff. 18–21^v Oratio. Obsecro te . . . For male use.

4. ff. 22–25^v Oratio beate marie uirginis. O intemerata . . . orbis terrarum de te enim . . . f. 26^{rv} blank.

5. ff. 27–92^v Hours of B.V.M. of the use of (Paris). A leaf missing after f. 44.

6. ff. 93–108^v Penitential psalms and (f. 103^v) litany.

Eleven confessors: . . . (3–5) remigy maglori ludouice.

7. ff. 109–13 Hours of the Cross. Patris sapiencia . . .

8. ff. 113^v–116^v Hours of the Holy Spirit. Nobis sancti spiritus . . .

9. ff. 117–162^v Office of the dead. f. 163^{rv} blank.

10. ff. 164–169^v Doulce dame de misericorde. mere de pitie . . .

The Fifteen Joys of B.V.M. Sonet, no. 458.

11. ff. 170–3 Doulx dieu doulx pere saincte trinite . . .

The Seven Requests. Sonet, no. 504.

12. f. 173 Sainte vraye crois aouree . . . Sonet, no. 1876.

13. ff. 173^v–179^v Memoriae of Barbara (Virgo fide sana . . .: *RH*, no. 34601), Margaret, Genovefa (O felix ancilla dei . . .: *RH*, no. 30425), Katherine (Virgo sancta Katherine grecie gemma . . .: *RH*, no. 34646), Christopher, Sebastian.

ff. i+179+i. 172 × 126 mm. Written space 95 × 65 mm. 15 long lines. Ruling in red ink. Collation: 1^{12} 2^8 3^6 (ff. 21–6) 4–5^8 6 six (ff. 43–8) 7 nine (ff. 49–57) 8–11^8 12^2 (ff. 90–1) 13–23^8. Eighteen 11-line pictures, eight in art. 5, three in art. 13 (Barbara, Margaret, Genovefa and a kneeling woman), and one before each of arts. 2, 6–11. Initials: (i, ii) 3-line and 2-line, in colours on gold grounds; (iii) 1-line, gold on coloured grounds. Line fillers in pink, blue, and gold. Continuous framed borders on pages with pictures: they include scenes within roundels at arts. 5–9. A border the height of the written space on all other pages. Capital letters in the ink of the text filled with pale yellow. Contemporary (?) French binding of thin wooden boards covered with brown leather: a branch stamp as frame encloses five vertical rows of eagle (?) and fleur-de-lis stamps.

Written in France. Belonged to W. Wix in 1791, to R. H. E. Wix in 1881, and to H. E. Wix in 1893. In Tregaskis's catalogue 856, 22 May 1922, item 1 at £175, with facsimile of f. 271. 'Tregaskis 24.6.22' is inside the cover (cf. 21018).

091.20932. (12). *Horae*   s. xv^2

1. ff. 1–12^v Full calendar in French, in gold, red, and blue, the two colours alternating for effect.

Genevieve, Loys, 'S. Leu S. Gile', Denis are in gold at 3 Jan., 25 Aug., 1 Sept., 9 Oct.

2. ff. 13–20 Sequentiae of the Gospels.

3. ff. 20^v–25 Oratio ad uirginem. Obsecro te . . . Masculine forms.

4. ff. 25ᵛ–29ᵛ Oratio ad uirginem. O intemerata . . . orbis terrarum.
De te enim . . . Masculine forms.

5. ff. 30–117ᵛ Hours of B.V.M., of the use of (Rome). Hours of the Cross and
the Holy Spirit worked in.

6. ff. 118–38 Penitential psalms and (f. 131) litany.
Valeria is third of eleven virgins.

7. ff. 138ᵛ–188 Incipiunt vigilie mortuorum. Office of the dead.

8. ff. 188–197ᵛ Memoriae of SS. Michael, Peter, Paul, Bartholomew (Bartholomei meritis . . .), James, Sebastian, Anthony, Nicholas, Louis king and confessor,
Katherine, Barbara, Apollonia, Margaret. Headings in French.

9 (added early). ff. 198–199ᵛ Les sept oraisons S. Gregoire. O domine ihesu
criste adoro te in cruce pendentem . . .

10 (added early). ff. 199ᵛ–201ᵛ Memoriae of Barbara, Gaude barbara beata . . .,
and Roche, Aue roche sanctissime nobili natus . . . *RH*, nos. 6711, 2078.

ff. ii+201+ii. 173 × 112 mm. Written space 95 × 56 mm. 17 long lines. Ruling with red
ink. Collation: 1¹² 2⁸ 3¹⁰ wants 10, blank, after f. 29 4–24⁸ 25⁴. Profuse and good decoration. Eighteen 13-line pictures, four in art. 2 (the first, St. John in the cauldron; the last,
St. Mark, is reproduced in the sale catalogue), ten in art. 5 (Innocents at vespers), and
one before each of arts. 3, 4 (Pietà), 6 (reproduced in the sale catalogue), 7. Sixteen small
pictures, thirteen in art. 8, two in art. 10, and one before art. 9. Occupations of the
months and signs of the zodiac in art. 1, at the foot of each page. Initials: (i) 3-line, white
on decorated grounds of gold paint and colours; (ii, iii) 2-line and 1-line, gold paint on
decorated blue or red grounds. The pages with larger pictures have a continuous framed
border in which four miniatures alternate with floral designs on grounds of gold paint.
All other pages have a framed floral border the height of the written space in the outer
margin: the grounds are in compartments partly of gold paint and partly of dark colours,
black, purple, or brown. Line fillers are of gold paint simulating cut branches or are
rectangles of red or blue patterned with gold paint. Capital letters in the ink of the text
are filled with yellow. Binding of s. xx by Trautz-Bauzonnet.

Written in France (Paris). 'Ex musæo Huthii' book-stamp inside the cover. Huth sale at
Sotheby's, 17 June 1913, lot 3808, to Francis Edwards (£360).

091.20954. (15). *Horae*   s. xvi¹

1. ff. 1–12ᵛ Full calendar in French, in gold, red, and blue, the two colours
alternating for effect.

Sebastian, George, Denis in gold. Forty-eight lines of French verse, 'Les six premiers ans
que vit lhomme au monde . . .', are in the lower margin of each page, four lines to a page.

2. ff. 13–16 Sequentiae of the Gospels.

3. ff. 16ᵛ–22 Passio domini nostri iesu christi secundum iohannem.

John 18: 1–19: 42, followed by 'Deo gratias. Per euangelica dicta deleantur omnia nostra
delicta . . . Deus qui manus tuas . . .'.

4. ff. 23–66ᵛ Heures/de nostre da (*sic*)/dame tout au long/sans requerir a lusaige de/Romme.

The heading in five lines of gold. Hours of Cross and Holy Spirit are worked in. Terce, sext, and none are followed by a 'Rondeau de nostre dame': (*a*) f. 44ᵛ Dame dhonneur et Royne de renom . . . (13 lines); (*b*) f. 48ᵛ Sans finesse et a tousiour mais . . . (5 lines); (*c*) f. 52ᵛ A tousiour mais et Sans finesse . . . (13 lines).

5. ff. 68–79 'Les sept pseaumes' and (f. 73ᵛ) litany.

Twenty-three confessors: . . . (23) Ioseph. Seventeen virgins: . . . (13) Rosa.

6. ff. 80–100ᵛ A vespres de mors. Office of the dead.

7. ff. 102–4 Memoriae of Holy Trinity, including prayers to Father, Son and Holy Spirit severally, Holy Face (Salue sancta facies . . .: *RH*, no. 18189) and Holy Cross.

8. ff. 104ᵛ–108 Prayers, with headings in French: (*a*) Deus propitius esto michi peccatori . . .; (*b*) Conditor celi et terre . . .; (*c*) O bone iesu O dulcissime iesu . . .

9. ff. 108–112ᵛ Les quinze oraisons de saincte Brigide. Qui sont de la passion nostre seigneur. O suauitas et requies . . .

10. ff. 112ᵛ–114 Les sept oraisons sur chascune heure de la passion nostre seigneur. A Matines. Domine iesu criste qui hora matutinali . . .

11. ff. 114–116ᵛ Autre oraison a nostre seigneur iesuscrist. O dulcissime domine iesu criste verus deus . . .

12. ff. 116ᵛ–117 Les vers sainct Gregoire. O domine iesu criste adoro te . . . The Seven Oes.

13. f. 117ʳᵛ Les sept vers sainct bernard. Illumina oculos meos . . .

14. ff. 117ᵛ–118ᵛ Oraison a nostre saulueur iesus crist. Mon benoist dieu ie croy de cueur et confesse de bouche . . . Sonet, no. 1150.

15. ff. 118ᵛ–119 Du sainct sacrament de lautel. A memoria.

16. ff. 120–121ᵛ Les heures de limmaculee conception de la vierge marie.

17. Prayers to B.V.M.: (*a*) f. 121ᵛ Salutation a la vierge marie. Aue cuius conceptio . . . (*RH*, no. 1744); (*b*) f. 122 Salutation a nostre dame. Aue regina celorum . . .; (*c*) f. 123 Oraison de nostre dame de laurette. Aue sanctissima maria mater dei regina celi . . .; (*d*) f. 123ʳᵛ Salutation et priere a nostre dame. Aue maria ancilla trinitatis . . .; (*e*) ff. 123ᵛ–124 Autre oraison a nostre dame. O illustrissima et excellentissima gloriosa uirgo . . .

18. ff. 125–126ᵛ Autre oraison a nostre dame. Obsecro te . . . Masculine forms.

19. ff. 126ᵛ–127 Oraison a nostre dame et a sainct Iehan leuangeliste. O intemerata . . . orbis terrarum. Inclina mater . . . Masculine forms.

20. f. 128 Deuote contemplation et oraison sur les douleurs de la vierge marie. Stabat mater . . .

21. ff. 128^v–131^v Les cinq oraisons de saincte Brigide a la vierge marie. Mediatrix omnium et fons viuus . . . Auxiliatrix . . . Reparatrix . . . Illuminatrix . . . Alleuiatrix . . .

22. ff. 131^v–145^v Sensuyuent les suffrages et oraisons de plusieurs sainctz et sainctes. Memoriae of SS. Michael, Gabriel, John Baptist, John Evangelist, Peter and Paul, Andrew, James the greater, Philip and James, All apostles, Stephen, Laurence, Christopher, Sebastian, All martyrs, Nicholas, Claude, Anthony hermit, Anthony of Padua, Francis, Germanus, Martin, Denis, Roche, Jerome, Blaise, All confessors, Anne, Mary Magdalene, Margaret, Katherine, Barbara, Apollonia, Geneviève, Martha, Avia. f. 146^v blank.

ff. ii+146+iii. f. ii is a parchment flyleaf, s. xvi(?). 177 × 120 mm. Written space 115 × 65 mm. 22 long lines. Collation doubtful. Written in a very clear print-like humanistic hand. Sixteen full-page pictures, one facing the first picture of art. 4 (f. 22^v, a woman suppliant dressed in black, with a bishop and SS. Barbara and Christopher behind her: facsim. in 1909 sale-catalogue), ten in art. 4 (facsim. of the first, f. 23, in 1909 sale-catalogue) and one before each of arts. 5 (David and Bathsheba), 6, 7, 16 (the Virgin surrounded by thirteen emblems, as in London, Oratory MS. 12546 (*MMBL* i. 168), but rose and lily are absent: above, God the Father and scroll 'Tota pulcra es amica mea et macula non est in te'), 17c (a woman suppliant in black before Virgin and Child). Two nearly full-page pictures before arts. 2, 3. Forty-one smaller pictures, three in art. 2, two in art. 7, thirty-three in art. 22 and one before each of arts. 8, 9, 15. The full-page pictures have inscriptions in capital letters round the edges, e.g. f. 29, Visitatio tua custodiet spiritum meum. In seven pictures a small female figure, sometimes called a sybil, stands in a corner holding an inscribed scroll, e.g. f. 23 (matins: facsim. in sale-catalogue), f. 38 (prime) La sibille Samne de dixhuyt ans / Lenfant ne de vierge pourette . . . Initials: (i) white on decorated gold-paint grounds; (ii, iii) 2-line and 1-line, gold paint on red or blue grounds. Headings in blue or gold. Line fillers in red and gold. Binding of s. xix.

Written in France. Evidence of origin and early history comes from: (i) the motto 'A tourioursmais' (*sic*) and monogram of SNB (?) on f. 22; (ii) initials GB in the margins of ff. 13^v, 22^v, 23, 29, 38, 122^v; (iii) initials CG in the margins of ff. 29, 35^v, 49^v, 58^v, 67^v, 101^v, 119^v; (iv) arms in the picture on f. 22^v (cf. facsim.). P. Gélis-Didot noted on ff. 147–8, Paris, 15 Feb. 1886, that the book was made for Germaine, daughter of Nicholas Balue of Villepreux (†1506) and wife of Charles d'Alençon (†1545), the arms being parted per pale, azure three lilies or, on a border gules eight besants or for Alençon and argent a chevron azure between three lion heads gules for Balue: see *Dictionnaire de biographie française*, i. 1421, v. 19. 'Ce presant liure appartient a Renée Villefeu presente au manz fait au manz ce 17 marz 1719' (f. ii). Advertised in a French catalogue, s. xix, from which a cutting is pasted inside the cover. Sale at Sotheby's, 6 May 1909, lot 47.

091.20960.   s. XIII med.

Four leaves each containing a picture measuring 110 × 85 mm. The subjects are: (1) the Adoration of the Three Kings; (2) the Presentation in the Temple; (3) The Flight into Egypt; (4) the Baptism of Christ. In an accompanying note S. C. Cockerell points out that these pictures closely resemble those in New York, Pierpont Morgan Library, M. 74, for which cf. *Illustrated Catalogue of Illuminated Manuscripts* (Burlington Fine Arts Club, 1908), no. 124 and pl. 83.

ff. 4, one side of each leaf pasted down and presumably blank. Northern French. Hastings sale at Sotheby's, 20 July 1931, lot 6; the sale catalogue has facsimiles of all four pictures.

091.20961. (17). *Psalterium, etc.*   1500

1. Liturgical psalter: ff. 1–127, matins and lauds; 127–145^v, prime, terce, sext, none; 146–167^v, vespers; 167^v–170, compline.

2. ff. 170^v–171 Aue maria, Pater noster, and Credo in deum patrem.

3. ff. 171^v–172^v Incipit canticum graduum absolute. in feriali officio tantum. Gradual psalms, abbreviated.

4. ff. 172^v–181 Penitential psalms, abbreviated, and (f. 173^v) litany.

Pantalemon fourth of ten martyrs. Sixteen confessors: . . . (3) Sancte pater augustine . . . (15, 16) Sancte nicholae de tollentino Sancte guilerme. Thirteen virgins: . . . (10) Sancte mater monicha.

5. ff. 181–192^v Incipit officium mortuorum.

6. ff. 192^v–193^v Oratio ad summam trinitatem. Tibi ago laudes et gratias. O summa sanctissima . . .

7. 193^v–194^v Dominus Gregorius papa concessit omnibus infrascriptam orationem dicentibus septem annos indulgentiarum. que fuit data sancto Bernardo ab angelo . . . Tibi domina dilectissima. mater domini nostri yesu christi . . .

8. Prayers: (*a*) ff. 194^v–196 Oratio sancti Hieronimi dicenda est in mane. Mane cum surrexero intende ad me . . .; (*b*) ff. 196–197^v Alia oratio pro tribulatione. Miserere domine miserere pie . . .; (*c*) f. 197^v Oratio multum deuota ad angelum. Queso et obsequenter rogo sancte angele dei . . .; (*d*) ff. 197^v–198 Qui dixerit hanc orationem tres annos habet in indulgentiam. Domine yesu christe fili uirginis marie da mihi in te . . .; (*e*) f. 198 Oratio ualde utilis. Signore mio amoroso yesu cristo te prego. dona me scientia . . . f. 198^v blank.

ff. i+198+i. 154×95 mm. Written space 88×52 mm. 17 long lines. Collation: 1–16^{10} 17^8 18–20^8. Initials: (i) of Ps. 1, 5-line, violet on blue and gold ground, with continuous border; (ii) of the other nineteen principal psalms, 3-line, blue with red ornament or red with greenish-brown ornament; (iii, iv) 2-line and 1-line, red or blue. Green morocco binding, blind-tooled, s. xvi.

Written in Italy in 1500, probably by an Austin friar (art. 4): 'Fratris *Victorini de Crema* opus completum fuit an(n)o 1499 die 16 Februarii hora vespertina', f. 170, in the main hand, except the words in italics. Erased ex-libris, s. xvii, at the head of f. 1 and 'Visus est f 17 g' at the foot. A strip from a French bookseller's catalogue and the armorial bookplate of Willett Lawrence Adye inside the cover.

091.20966. *Horae*   s. xv ex.

1. ff. 1^v–13 Calendar in gold and blue.

Among feasts in gold are Thomas Aquinas, Petrus Martyr, Bernardinus, Honofrius confessor, Dominic, Nicholas de Tolentino, Francis (7 Mar., 29 Apr., 20 May, 12 June, 5 Aug., 10 Sept., 4 Oct.) and the 'Dedicatio sancti saluatoris' and 'Dedicatio basilice apostolorum petri et pauli' (9, 18 Nov.). ff. 1^r, 13^v blank.

2. ff. 145–164ᵛ, 15–66ᵛ Hours of B.V.M. of the use of (Rome), beginning imperfectly in matins.

The psalms at matins on (*a*) Tuesdays and Fridays and (*b*) Wednesdays and Saturdays follow lauds (ff. 160–164ᵛ, 15–19ᵛ). Prime begins imperfectly, f. 20.

3. ff. 68–73ᵛ Missa in honore sancte marie uirginis.

4. ff. 74–81ᵛ Hours of the Cross, beginning imperfectly.

5. ff. 83–105ᵛ Seven penitential psalms and (f. 95ᵛ) litany.

Eight doctors: . . . (7, 8) Dominice Francisce.

6. ff. 107–144ᵛ Incipit officium mortuorum. Ends imperfectly.

ff. iii + 164 + iii. 164 × 116 mm. Written space 95 × 55 mm. 16 long lines. Collation: 1¹⁴ wants 14, probably blank, 2¹⁰ (ff. 145–54) 3⁸ (ff. 155–8, 160–3) 4⁸ wants 7 after f. 19 (ff. 164, 15–20) 5–7¹⁰ 8⁸ wants 6 after f. 56 (ff. 51, 53–8) 9¹⁰ 10⁶ wants 6 after f. 73 11⁸ 12⁸ wants 2 after f. 83 13–14⁸ 15–17¹⁰ 18¹⁰ wants 9, 10 after f. 144, together with five singleton picture leaves, ff. 159, 14, 52, 82, 106. Eleven full-page pictures, two of them nineteenth-century, ff. 52ᵛ Crucifixion, 159ᵛ Baptism in Jordan. The others are in art. 2 (ff. 147ᵛ, 14ᵛ, 24ᵛ, 30ᵛ, 36ᵛ, 42ᵛ), and on versos before arts. 3 (Assumption of B.V.M.), 5 (David and Goliath), 6 (Death in an ox cart). Initials: (i) in colours, usually historiated, on gold grounds; (ii, iii) 2-line and 1-line, gold or blue with violet ornament. Continuous framed borders on pages with initials of type (i), usually including a fancy picture at the foot: a hart, f. 14ᵛ. Binding of s. xix (?), covered with mauve velvet: gilt clasps.

Written in Italy. Or a hart gules on a rock of six points azure in the lower margin, f. 83. The numbers '42' on f. iᵛ and 'N 720' on f. ii are modern.

091.20984. *Horae* s. XVI in.

Leaves from a book of hours arranged as a picture book with a picture on each recto. A foliation of s. xvii made when the manuscript was complete shows the correct order of leaves in arts. 1–7. pp. 3, 7, 9, 10, 11, 17, 20, 23, 25, 27, 30, 31 are the wrong way round.

1. ff. 15–18 (formerly '1', '10', '17', '26') The Passion according to each of the four evangelists. Each first leaf remains.

2. ff. 4, 3, 1, 2, 20 (formerly '32'–'36') Sequentiae of the Gospels.'

The prayer 'Protector in te sperantium . . .' follows John. The end of Mark is on the verso, formerly the recto, of f. 20.

3. f. 20 (formerly '36') Sequuntur oraciones beate marie virginis. Obsecro te . . . Ends imperfectly.

4. f. 22 (formerly '39') O intemerata . . . orbis terrarum. Inclina . . . For male use. Ends imperfectly.

5. ff. 5–11, 21. Hours of B.V.M.

The first leaf of each hour. f. 21 (compline) was formerly '60'.

6. f. 19 (formerly '73') Hours of the Holy Cross. Patris sapiencia . . . The first leaf.

7. f. 12 (formerly '7[.]')' Hours of the Holy Spirit. Nobis sancti spiritus ... The first leaf.

8. f. 14 Office of the dead. The first leaf of matins.

9. Memoriae of saints on ten leaves: f. 24 *Michael* (complete) and heading for John Baptist; f. 13 *John Baptist* (complete), John Evangelist; f. 28 *Peter and Paul* (complete) and heading for James; f. 29 *James* (complete) and heading for Stephen; f. 26 *Laurence* (complete) and heading for Christopher; f. 30 Christopher (end), *Sebastian* (beginning); f. 27 Denis (end), martyrs (complete), *Nicholas* (beginning); f. 25 Anthony hermit (end), *George* (beginning: Fideles hic attendite, *RH*, no. 6293); f. 31 George (end), *Francis* (beginning: Salve sancte pater, *RH*, no. 40727); f. 23 Jerome (end) and *Anne* (beginning).

ff. 24, 13 are consecutive leaves and so are ff. 28, 29 and ff. 25, 31. Italics show the saints depicted. Pictures of Stephen, Christopher, Denis, Anthony hermit, and Jerome once existed, no doubt.

ff. iii+31+iv. 186 × 130 mm. Written space 108 × 68 mm. 24 long lines. Written in a sloping cursiva formata, approaching *lettre batârde*. Thirty-one 21-line pictures: Pietà before art. 3 and B.V.M. and Child before art. 4. Initials: (i) blue on gold grounds; (ii) blue on grounds of gold paint and red; (iii) gold paint on red or blue grounds. Capital letters in the ink of the text are touched with red. Bound by F. Bedford.

Written in France. The pictures are in the style of the Rouen school. Belonged to Mrs. Simpson Rostron, South Warnborough Manor, Basingstoke: sale 20 June 1922, lot 433.

091.20989. (9). *Evangelia, etc.*   s. xv in., xv ex.

1. ff. 1–109 The four Gospels, without prologues.

2 (not foliated). The sequentiae of the Gospels taken from a book of hours and broken up so as to act as the frontispiece to each Gospel, before ff. 1, 33, 52, 85. Each leaf contains the evangelist's portrait, followed by the usual extract from his Gospel.

ff. i+113+i. 149 × 105 mm. Written space 110 × 75 mm. 29 long lines. Collation of art. 1: 1–10^{10} 11^{10} wants 10, probably blank. Initials (i) of Gospels, 6-line, red and blue with ornament of both colours; (ii) of chapters, 2-line, red or blue, with ornament of the other colour. Capital letters in the ink of the text are touched with yellow. Art. 2 is in *lettre batârde*, s. xv ex.: continuous framed borders on each recto contain animals, flowers, etc., on grounds of colour and gold paint. Binding of s. xix. Secundo folio *ego ueniens*.

Written in Italy and (art. 2) France. An erasure at the foot of f. 1. Notes in English, s. xviii and s. xix, on f. i, the later signed 'E.C.'. The relevant cutting from a Sotheby sale catalogue, s. xx in. (?), is attached to f. i.

091.21001. (4). *Psalterium, etc.*   s. xiii^2

1. ff. 1–6^v Twelve full-page pictures: Manger, Magi, Presentation in the Temple, Entry into Jerusalem, Peter cutting off ear, Scourging of Christ, Christ

bearing his Cross, Crucifixion, Resurrection, Ascension, Pentecost, Christ and B.V.M.

2. ff. 7–12ᵛ Calendar in blue, red, and black. Feasts in blue include Augustine of England (26 May), translation of Thomas of Canterbury (7 July), Edward, king and confessor (13 Oct.), Edmund, archbishop (16 Nov.), and Thomas of Canterbury (29 Dec.). Feasts in red include Edward, king and confessor (17 Mar.), Dunstan (19 May), Osith (3 June), Swithun (2 July), Frideswide (19 Oct.). The feasts of St. Thomas of Canterbury have not been cancelled.

3. ff. 13–128ᵛ Psalter, lacking Pss. 104: 17–105: 37 after f. 104, verses 95–139 of Ps. 118 after f. 119, Pss. 118: 160–128: 5 after f. 120 and all after 'tabernaculum deo iacob' (131: 5).

ff. i+121+i. 212×140 mm. Written space 126×74 mm. 23 long lines. Collation: 1–2⁶ 3–11¹⁰ 12¹⁰ wants 3, 4, after f. 104, and 10, probably blank, after f. 109, 13¹⁰ 14 two (ff. 120–1, a bifolium). Twelve pictures (see above). Initials: (i) of Pss. 1, 26, 38, 51, 52, 68, 80, 97, 101, 109, in colours on gold and coloured grounds framed in gold, with framed border ornament carrying grotesques, cranes, etc.; (ii) to other psalms, 2-line, gold with blue ornament or blue with red ornament; (iii) to verses of psalms, 1-line, red or blue, with ornament of the other colour. Line fillers in red and blue. Red velvet binding, s. xix. Secundo folio (f. 14) *Et nunc.*

Written in England. Book-plate, s. xix, of Eugène Marcel, Havre de Grace, 'Loviers il franc', with number '17' added in manuscript.

091.21002. (11). *Horae*   s. XVI in.

1. ff. 1–6ᵛ Full calendar in French, in gold, blue, and red, the two colours alternating for effect. 'S. Leu. S. Gille' in gold, 1 Sept.

2. ff. 7–11 Sequentiae of the Gospels.

3. ff. 12–14 Oratio valde deuotissima ad beatissimam virginem mariam. Obsecro te . . . For male use.

4. ff. 14–15ᵛ Alia oratio ad beatam Virginem. O intemerata . . . orbis terrarum. Inclina . . . For male use.

5. ff. 16–21ᵛ Passion according to St. John (John 18: 1–19: 42), beginning imperfectly at 18: 9, and prayer 'Deus qui manus tuas . . .'.

6. ff. 22–3 Stabat mater . . .

7. ff. 24–78 Hours of B.V.M. of the use of (Rome).

Hours of the Cross and of the Holy Spirit are worked in; also memoriae: of the Visitation, Acceleratur ratio in puero . . ., after matins; of the Annunciation, Aue stella matutina . . . (*RH*, no. 2135), after lauds; of the Five Joys, Gaude virgo mater cristi (*RH*, no. 7017), after prime.

8. ff. 79–91 Penitential psalms and (f. 86ᵛ) litany. Julian is first of twelve confessors.

9. ff. 92–119^v Office of the dead.

10. ff. 119^v–132^v Memoriae of Holy Trinity (Te inuocamus . . . Oratio. Omni-potens sempiterne deus qui dedisti famulis tuis . . ., followed by prayers to each Person individually, as in 20954), Michael, John Baptist, John Evangelist, James, Christopher, Nicholas, Lupus (of Troyes: Aue presul honestatis . . .), Claude, Anthony hermit, Sebastian, Laurence, Adrian (Aue sancte adriane qui martirium in mane . . .), Roche (Aue roche sanctissime . . .), Anne, Mary Magdalene, 'De sororibus beate marie', Katherine, Barbara (Gaude barbara beata . . .), Agnes, Margaret, Genovefa.

RH, nos. 35676 (Lupus), 2106 (Adrian), 2078 (Roche), 6711 (Barbara).

11. ff. 133–135^v O doulce croix signe resplendissant . . . Tant que les lermes en yssent de nos yeulx. Sonet, no. 1330.

ff. iv+135+iv. 190×120 mm. Written space 120×60 mm. 25 long lines. Ruling in red ink. Mainly in eights (1^6), the leaves with full-page pictures mostly singletons: single leaves missing before ff. 16, 70. Written in humanistica (rounded *d*). Profusely decorated. Eight full-page pictures, ff. 11^v (B.V.M. and Child in glory), 23^v (tree of Jesse), 36^v, 55^v, 59^v, 78^v (David gives a letter to a kneeling knight: inscribed 'Ne reminiscaris domine'), 91^v (man and woman at table: inscribed 'Placebo domine'), 97^v (man and woman and two children at table). Ten 21-line pictures, six in art. 7 and one before each of arts. 2, 8 (David and Bathsheba), 9 (a naked man is dragged to hell by devils), 11 (a woman and a male saint kneel before a cross). Thirty-one small pictures, twenty-four in art. 10, three in art. 2, one before each of arts. 3 (a woman kneels in prayer), 4 (Pietà), 6 (Pietà), and one in art. 10 (f. 98, Job on his dunghill). Occupations of the months and signs of the zodiac in the margins of art. 1. Initials: (i) pink on grounds of gold paint, in several sizes; (ii) 1-line, gold paint on coloured grounds. Line fillers of gold paint, either together with blue or red, or in the form of cut branches. Framed compartmented borders round picture pages, except on the pages where the picture covers the whole page, and in the outer margins of all other pages. Binding of red morocco, s. xvii.

Written in France. An armorial shield on f. 24 has been painted over. 'Ce presant liu(r)e apartien a Monsieur lenoir apotigere Demourant a orleans', f. 139^v, s. xvii. 'Ex libris F. G. H. Culemann/Hannoverae/1862', f. i: not identifiable in his sale at Sotheby's, 7 Feb. 1870. 'N° 286', f. i. 'Amy E. R. Jarvis (?) Easter 1895', f. i.

091.21004. Psalterium   s. XIII ex.

1. ff. 1–69^v Psalms 1–150.

Larger initials distinguish sixteen psalms: 1, 20, 26, 32, 38, 45, 52, 59, 68, 73, 79, 85, 95, 101, 105, 109. Pss. 9, 36, 67, 68, 77, 105, 143 are divided at verses 20, 27, 16, 19, 36, 32, and 9 respectively. Antiphons were added in the margins in s. xv and a red 'G' was put against every other psalm.

2. ff. 69^v–72 Six ferial canticles and Benedicite, ending imperfectly.

Audite celi is divided at Ignis succensus est (Deuteronomy 32: 22).

ff. iii+72+iii. 160×110 mm. Written space 122×85 mm. 2 cols. 27 lines. Collation: 1–6^{12}. Punctuation with the flex (?) is partly original and partly added. Initials: (i) brick red on grounds of blue and pink and occasionally gold: eight out of sixteen are historiated (Pss. 1, 26, 32, 38, 52, 68, 95, 109); (ii) 2-line, red or blue with ornament of both colours running the height of the written space; (iii) of psalm verses, 1-line, blue or red. French binding, s. xix. Secundo folio *Meum. Intende*.

Written in France. 'Adrienne Moullart', f. 1, s. xvii. Book-plate of s. xix, inscribed 'Bibliothèque De Renier Chalon' and 'Liber cum libris'.

091.21018. (8). *Horae*   s. xv med.

1. ff. 1–6ᵛ Calendar in red and black. The feasts of St. Thomas of Canterbury have not been cancelled. Entries by one hand, s. xvi, record the births of four children: John, 25 Aug. 1515, 'a Wykyn'; Robert, 23 Aug. 1522, 'a grantcester'; Anne, 24 Aug. 1526, 'at Iselham in the vicaredge'; Richard, 1 Feb. 1529, 'at Iselham'.

2. ff. 7–35ᵛ Hours of the B.V.M. of the use of (Sarum). Memoriae in lauds are of Holy Spirit, Holy Trinity, Holy Cross, SS. Michael, John Baptist, Peter and Paul, Thomas of Canterbury (crossed out), martyrs, Nicholas, Katherine, virgins, relics, All Saints, Pro pace terre. Hours of the Cross are worked in.

3. ff. 35ᵛ–42 Penitential psalms.

4. ff. 42–4 Quindecim psalmi (first words only of the first twelve psalms).

5. ff. 44–9 Litany.

6. ff. 49–68ᵛ Vigilie mortuorum.

7. ff. 69–79 Commendation of Souls (Pss. 118, 138).

8. ff. 79ᵛ–83ᵛ Psalmi de Passione.

9. f. 83ᵛ (added in s.xvi) A prayer made by the most noble prynce Charles the fyfthe (in English).

10. ff. 84–91ᵛ Psalter of St. Jerome, beginning imperfectly.

11. f. 92ʳᵛ (added in s. xv) Devotions based on Missus est angelus.

ff. ii+91+iii. f. 92 is a medieval flyleaf. 245 × 170 mm. Written space 125 × 87 mm. 18 long lines. Collation: 1⁶ 2–4⁸ 5⁸ wants 1, 2 before f. 31 6–10⁸ 11⁸ wants 8 after f. 83 12⁸. Initials: (i) in colours on gold grounds; (ii) 2-line, gold on coloured grounds; (iii) 1-line, gold with violet ornament or blue with red ornament. Nine type (i) initials are historiated, five in art. 2 (Annunciation and four Passion scenes: no historiation at lauds: none and vespers began on leaves now missing), and one before each of arts. 3 (Christ on the rainbow), 6, 7 (Christ takes up three naked figures to heaven in a sheet), 8 (Christ stands in the tomb). Borders all round or on three sides of pages with initials of type (i). Line fillers in art. 5 are gold or blue. English binding, s. xviii. Secundo folio (f. 8) *adorant*.

Written in England. Wicken, Isleham, and Grantchester (art. 1) are in Cambridgeshire. Tregaskis, catalogue 856, 22 May 1922, item 2, with facsimile of f. 23 (prime). 'Tregaskis 24/6/22' is inside the cover (cf. 20927).

091.21035. (7). *Horae*   s. xv med.

A Sarum book of hours of the kind produced abroad for English use (cf. *MMBL* i. 46), abnormal only in art. 3 and in art. 4 (three instead of ten memoriae).

1. ff. 2–7^v Calendar in red and black.

'Translacio riquardi' (Richard of Chichester) in red, 16 June. 'Obitus agnetis Thornbrugh' added at 16 Nov., s. xv/xvi.

2. ff. 8–12 The Fifteen Oes of St Bridget.

3. f. 13^{rv} Te adoro deum patrem et filium et spiritum Sanctum misericordia (*sic for* unam) diuinitatem . . . in hac hora amen.

Cf. *Lyell Cat.*, p. 399.

4. ff. 14–16^v Memoriae of Christopher (Gaude martir cristofore. qui curasti seruus ore . . .), Anne (Gaude felix anna que concepisti prolem . . .) and Barbara (Gaude barbara serena uerbo patris quam effrena . . .). *RH*, nos. 37534, 6773, 6715.

5. ff. 17–43^v Hore uirginis marie Secundum usum Sarum.

Memoriae in lauds of Holy Spirit, *Holy Trinity*, Holy Cross, *Michael*, John Baptist, Peter and Paul, Andrew, Stephen, *Thomas of Canterbury* (cancelled lightly), Nicholas, *Mary Magdalene, Katherine, Margaret*, and *All Saints*. Hours of the Cross are worked in. Single leaves are missing after ff. 33, 41.

6. ff. 43^v–47^v Has videas laudes . . . (*in red*), followed by the farcing of Salve regina with Salve virgo virginum. *RH*, nos. 7687, 18147, 18318.

7. ff. 47^v–48^v Deuotissima oracio ad virginem mariam et ad beatum Iohannem apostolum et ewangelistam virginem. O intemerata . . . orbis terrarum. Inclina mater . . . Masculine forms.

8. ff. 48^v–50 Ad idem uirginem mariam. Oracio. Obsecro te . . . Masculine forms.

9. ff. 50–52 Quicumque hec septem gaudia . . . Virgo templum trinitatis . . .

The Seven Joys (*RH*, no. 21899), with heading conveying an indulgence of 100 days.

10 ff. 52^v–54^v Ad ymaginem crucifixi. Omnibus consideratis . . .

AH xxxi. 87–9. *RH*, no. 14081 (etc.).

11. (*a*) ff. 54^v–55^v Oracio uenerabilis bede . . . Domine ihesu criste qui septem uerba . . . (*b*) ff. 55^v–56 Precor te piissime domine ihesu criste . . .

12. f. 56^{rv} Gratias tibi ago domine ihesu criste qui uoluisti pro redemptione mundi . . .

13. ff. 56^v–58 Salutationes ad sacramentum. (*a*) Aue domine ihesu criste uerbum patris . . . (*b*) Aue principium nostre creationis . . . (*c*) Aue uerum corpus domini nostri ihesu cristi . . . (*d*) Aue caro cristi cara . . . (*e*) Domine ihesu criste qui hanc sacratissimam carnem . . ., with heading lightly cancelled conveying a 2,000-year indulgence of Pope Boniface VI. (*f*) Anima cristi sanctifica me . . .

(*a, b, d, f*). *RH*, nos. 1778, 2059, 1710, 1090.

14. f. 58^{rv} Deus propicius esto michi peccatori et custos mei . . .

15. (*a*) ff. 59–62^v Penitential psalms, beginning imperfectly: one leaf missing.

(*b*) ff. 62ᵛ–66 Quindecim psalmi . . . (cues only of the first twelve). (*c*) ff. 66–9 Letania sanctorum.

Spellings in (*c*) are 'dinistane' (Dunstan), 'botulpe' (Botulph), 'ossatha' (Osyth).

16. ff. 69ᵛ–87 Vigilie defunctorum. Office of the dead. f. 70 should come before f. 69.

17. ff. 87ᵛ–94ᵛ Commendationes animarum.

18. ff. 94ᵛ–100 Psalmi de passione.

19. ff. 100–107ᵛ Beatus ieronimus psalterium sic abbreuiauit . . . Dicant cotidie sequentem psalterium. et possidebunt regnum eternum. This heading is followed by the Psalter of St. Jerome, 'Uerba mea auribus percipe . . .', and it by the prayer 'Omnipotens sempiterne deus clementiam tuam suppliciter deprecor . . .'.

ff. iii+106+iii, foliated i, ii, 1–108 (109, 110). f. 1 is a medieval flyleaf. 265 × 183 mm. Written space 165 × 94 mm. 24 long lines. Collation of ff. 2–107: 1⁶ 2¹⁰ wants 10, perhaps blank, after f. 16 3–4⁸ 5⁸ wants 2 after f. 33 6⁸ wants 3 after f. 41 7⁸ 8¹² wants 5 after f. 58 9–12⁸ 13¹⁰. Eighteen out of twenty-one 17-line pictures remain, six in art. 5 (terce and compline missing), three in art. 4, and one before each of arts. 2, 3, 6, 9, 10, 16–19. 12-line pictures illustrate the memoriae italicized in art. 5: the three ladies are fitted into one picture. Seventeen small pictures, seven in art. 5 illustrating the hours of the Cross and ten in art. 10. Initials: (i) in colours on gold grounds; (ii) 3-line, gold on coloured grounds; (iii) 1-line, gold with blue-grey ornament or blue with red ornament. Red and blue line fillers in the litany. Capital letters in the ink of the text are touched with red. Continuous borders on pages with initials of type (i) contain grotesques, birds, etc. Borders on pages with initials of type (ii) are at head and foot, the width of the written space, and extend half-way down the outer margin. Gilt binding, s. xix in. Secundo folio (f. 9) *arundine*.

Written in Flanders for England. The obit in the calendar and the memorandum on f. 1ᵛ of the birth of John Cotton, 24 June 1545, may give the names of owners. Lot 207 in a Sotheby sale.

091.21037. (10). *Horae*   s. XV ex.

1. ff. 1–5ᵛ Sequentiae of the Gospels.

2. f. 6ʳᵛ (*a*) Domine ihesu criste adoro te in cruce pendentem . . . (*b*) O domine ihesu criste pater dulcissime. rogo te ut amore istius gaudii . . .

(*a*). Five oes, nos. 1, 2, 4, 7, 3 of the Seven Oes of St. Gregory printed by Leroquais, *Livres d'heures*, ii. 346.

3. ff. 7–9 Obsecro te . . . For male use.

4. ff. 9–10ᵛ O intemerata . . . orbis terrarum. Inclina . . . For male use.

5. ff. 10ᵛ–12ᵛ Memoriae of Michael, John Baptist, Peter and Paul, Christopher (O martir cristofore. pro saluatoris honore . . .: *RH*, no. 29471), Genovefa, Mary Magdalene, Katherine, Barbara.

6. ff. 13–35ᵛ, 44ʳᵛ, 36–43ᵛ Hours of B.V.M. of the use of (Paris).

Prime, sext, and compline begin imperfectly, ff. 31, 36, 42: single leaves missing. Nine lessons in matins.

7. ff. 45–53ᵛ Penitential psalms, beginning imperfectly, and (f. 50ᵛ) litany.

Thirteen virgins: (1) Genovefa . . . (10) Clotildis . . .

8. f. 54ʳᵛ Short hours of the Cross, beginning imperfectly.

9. ff. 55–56ᵛ Short hours of the Holy Spirit, beginning imperfectly.

10. ff. 57–80 Office of the dead.

11. Prayers (?) added in the margins of ff. 77ᵛ–79ᵛ in faded, yellow-brown ink, s. xvi.

ff. i+80+i. 125 × 84 mm. Written space 69 × 45 mm. 23 long lines. Collation: 1–10⁸ 11⁶+1 leaf after 6 originally, but 4⁵,⁸, 5⁶, 6⁶, 7¹, 8³,⁵ are missing after ff. 28, 30, 35, 41, 45, 53, 54 respectively. Twelve out of eighteen 19-line pictures remain, five in art. 6, four in art. 1, and one before each of arts. 2 (Christ seated, wearing a crown of thorns and holding a forked branch), 3, 10. Initials: (i) pink and white on grounds of gold paint and red; (ii, iii) 2-line and 1-line, gold paint on red grounds. Line fillers in gold paint and red. Framed borders, continuous on picture pages and the height of the written space in the outer margin of all other pages, contain beasts, birds, grotesques, etc., on grounds of colour and gold paint. Binding of s. xviii ex.

Written in France. A handsome armorial book-plate, s. xviii: party per pale sable three rosettes argent and gules on a chevron or three leopard heads: motto 'Deo cari nihillo carent': the background is a quay with figures and barrels and beyond it a ship at sea. Book-plate of Henry Godwin, F.S.A., at the end: not it seems in his sale, 15 July 1875.

091.21038. (1). *Biblia*   s. XIII med.

1. ff. 1–298ᵛ, 327–342ᵛ A Bible with the usual contents,[1] save for the absence of the Prayer of Manasses and 3 Ezra, and in the usual order, except that the psalter (Hebrew version: Pss. 1–151) is now at the end, after art. 2. Four leaves are missing.

The psalter was once no doubt in its proper place: Job ends on one quire and Proverbs begins on another, f. 141. Words of psalms are often shortened, for example 'm.' for *mea*, 'abho.' for *abhominabiles*: the whole book is fitted into one 16-leaf quire. The prologues are thirty-eight of the usual set and fifteen others, shown here by *: Stegmüller, nos. 284, 285, 311, 323, 328, 330, 332, 335, 341+343, 344, 457, 482, 487, 491, 492, 494, 500, 507, Ioel incipiens interpretatur . . . sepultus*, Amos honustus . . . set uerbum*, 516,* 522*, 525*, 527*, 529*, 532*, 535*, 540*, 544*, 551, 590, 607, 620, 624, 675*, 685 to 793 as usual (765, 1 Tim., . . . scribens Nichapoli . . .), prologue to Acts ending as 640, 'proficeret medicina', but beginning 'Lucas plenus sancto spiritu spiritu sancto instigante . . .'*, 631*, 809, 829*, second prologue to Apocalypse, 'Asia minor est ista non magna illa . . . quam docuerat scripsit euangelium'*.

2. ff. 299–326ᵛ Aaz apprehendens . . . consiliatores eorum.

The usual dictionary of Hebrew names.

3. Notes mainly of s. xiv on the flyleaves include one on Jerome's three versions of the psalter (f. 343), a list of the books of the Bible in this copy (f. 343ᵛ), and the verses 'Anna solet dici tres concepisse marias . . .' (f. 344: Walther, no. 1060).

[1] Cf. Bristol Public Library, 15.

ff. v+342+vii. ff. ii–v, 343–8 are medieval parchment end-leaves: 348 was pasted down. 157×105 mm. Written space 108×71 mm. 2 cols. 50 lines. Collation originally 1–8¹⁶, 9¹⁴ (ff. 127–40), 10–20¹⁶, 21¹² (315–26), 22¹⁶, but 13, 15 are missing from quire 4 (after ff. 60, 61) and 8, 9 from quire 18 (after f. 275). Written in more than one very small hand. Initials: (i) f. 3, the six days of Creation; (ii) of books, blue and red with ornament of both colours or blue with red ornament; (iii) of prologues, red or blue with ornament of the other colour; (iv) of chapters, 2-line, as (iii); (v) in art. 2, 1-line, red or blue. Binding of s. xviii, with silver clasps and cornerpieces. Secundo folio *moabitidis*.

Written in England. From the London Charterhouse: 'Liber domus salutacionis matris dei ord' cart' prope London per Edmundum storour eiusdem loci monachum', f. 347, s. xv/xvi. An erased inscription, s. xv, on f. 326ᵛ contained a date. 'Sum Hugonis Vaghan et amicorum', f. 346, s. xvi: cf. f. iii. 'Bound for Richard D. Sanderson who died 1775' is in a hand of s. xix inside the cover: the initials 'RDS' are on the metalwork of the binding.

091.21039. *Cicero, Paradoxa* s. xv med.

M.T.C. Paradoxarum liber Incipit feliciter. Animaduerti brute sepe catonem . . . existimandi sunt. M.T.C. Paradoxarum liber explicit.

Running title DE/P. Part of a larger book: see below.

ff. i+24+i, foliated in modern pencil 53–76. 160×115 mm. Written space 106×57 mm. 20 long lines. Collation: 1¹⁰ wants 1, 2 2¹⁰ 3¹⁰ wants 7–10. Written in humanistica. Initials: (i) f. 1, gold with white vine decoration; (ii) 3-line, blue. Parchment binding, s. xx. Written in Italy (Florence, *c.* 1440–50).¹ The rest of the book, ff. 1–52, Cicero, De amicitia, belongs to Mrs. Andrew Jackson of New York.¹

091.21040. (6). *Horae* s. xv med.

1. ff. 1–6ᵛ Calendar in gold (December feasts only), red, and black. 'pape' and feasts of St. Thomas erased. 'Natiuitas R. Tanffeld' Iunioris', 3 Edw. IV, added at 28 July. Later, records were entered of the birth and death of Margaret Nevile (1520–75), of the deaths of her father and mother, children, and first husband, Robert Southwell (†1559), and of her second marriage to William Plumbe in 1561. These entries and one on f. 184 recording Plumbe's second marriage, 4 June 1579, to Elizabeth Gresham, in the parish church of Fulham, are printed by F. J. Furnivall in *Notes and Queries*, 4th series, ii (1868), 577–8.

2. ff. 8–52ᵛ Hours of B.V.M. of the use of (Sarum). Memoriae in lauds are of Holy Spirit, Holy Trinity, Holy Cross, SS. Michael, John Baptist, John Evangelist, Peter, Andrew, Thomas of Canterbury (scratched out), Stephen, Laurence, Nicholas, Mary Magdalene, Katherine, Margaret, relics, All Saints, and for peace. Hours of the Cross are worked in.

3. ff. 51–2 Salue regina and prayer Omnipotens sempiterne deus qui gloriose virginis ac matris marie . . .

4. ff. 53–62 Penitential psalms.

¹ I owe the date and my knowledge of the whereabouts of ff. 1–52 to Dr. A. de la Mare.

5. ff. 62–64^v Quindecim psalmi penitenciales (only the first words of the first twelve psalms).

6. ff. 64^v–72 Litany.

7. ff. 73–107^v Vigilie mortuorum.

8. ff. 108–121^v Commendacio animarum (Pss. 118, 138).

9. ff. 122–133^v Psalmi de passione.

10. ff. 133^v–134^v Psalter of St. Jerome, beginning imperfectly (f. 135), preceded by the prayer 'Suscipere dignare domine deus . . .' and the heading 'Beatus ieronimus in hoc modo disposuit hoc psalterium sicut angelus domini docuit eum cum spiritum sanctum (*sic*)'

11. ff. 149^v–158^v Fifteen Oes of St. Bridget.

12. ff. 159–160^v Salutations to the Holy Face: (*a*) Salue sancta facies nostri redemptoris . . . ; (*b*) Aue facies preclara . . . *RH*, nos. 18189, 1787.

13. ff. 160^v–162 Oracio venerabilis bede . . . Domine ihesu qui septem verba . . .

14. ff. 162^v–166 Ad ymaginem crucifixi. Omnibus consideratis paradisus voluptatis . . . *RH*, no. 14081.

15. f. 166^{rv} Salutaciones ad eleuacionem corporis cristi. (*a*) Aue ihesu criste uerbum patris . . . (5 aves). (*b*) Aue uerum corpus natum . . . *RH*, no. 2175.

16 (in another hand). ff. 167–83 Olde and yonge I pray yow nowe . . .

A life of St. Margaret in 644 lines of verse: *IMEV*, no. 2672. Furnivall printed the first and last lines of this copy, loc. cit., p. 578, and K. Horstmann printed the whole text from MS. Bodley 779 in *Archiv für das Studium der neueren Sprachen*, lxxix (1887), 411–19.

17. Added devotions, s. xv ex., at beginning and end: (*a*) f. i Domine Ihesu criste qui me creasti redimisti . . . ; (*b*) f. 183^v Saluator mundi salua nos omnes . . . Domine deus noster multiplica super nos misericordiam tuam . . .

(*b*) asks for the intercession of saints: Christopher and Erasmus are the named martyrs.

ff. ii+183+ii. Flyleaves of medieval parchment. 210×150 mm. Written space 132–120 ×85–76 mm. 17 long lines and (ff. 167–83) 20 long lines. Collation: 1^6 2^8+1 leaf before 1 3–8^8 9^8+1 leaf after 8 (f. 72) 10–13^8 14^2+1 leaf after 2 (f. 107) 15–17^8 18^8 wants 4 after f. 134 19–20^8 21^{12} wants 11, 12, perhaps blank, 22^8 23^8+1 leaf after 8 (f. 183). One full-page Annunciation picture, f. 7^v. Twelve 8-line pictures, seven in art. 2 (a Passion series) and one before each of arts. 4, 7, 8 (angels carry three naked figures in a sheet to heaven), 9 (Christ stands in the tomb), 11 (Arma Christi). Initials: (i, ii) 6-line or 5-line and 2-line, in colours on gold grounds; (iii) 1-line, gold on coloured grounds, and, often, sprays into the margin. Gold, blue, and red line fillers in the litany. Borders of acanthus and gold ivy leaves go all round pages with pictures and initials of type (i) and on three sides of pages with initials of type (ii). Parchment binding, s. xvii. Secundo folio (f. 9) *cia plena*.

Written in England. Bequeathed by Elizabeth Hull, abbess of Malling, to her godchild, Margaret Nevile, according to an inscription on f. 7. Later in the possession of Margaret Nevile's second husband, William Plumbe (see above, art. 1), and of Henry Percy, Earl of Northumberland, † 1632, as appears from the binding, which bears a Percy badge intermediate in size between the two badges reproduced in *The Library*, 5th series, xv (1960), pl. opp. p. 254. Described in HMC, *Sixth Report*, Appendix, p. 288, among the manuscripts of Lord Leconfield at Petworth House. Leconfield sale at Sotheby's, 23 Apr. 1928, lot 65, to Francis Edwards: facsimiles of ff. 7ᵛ–8 in the sale catalogue. Bought from Edwards by R. E. Hart in 1944.

091.21041. *Bonaventura, Vita Sancti Francisci*   s. xiii²

1. ff. 1–45 Incipit prologus in uitam beati francisci. Apparuit gratia dei saluatoris . . . uirtutis altissimi cui . . . Explicit uita beati francisci.

Ed. Quaracchi, viii. 504–49.

2. ff. 45–61ᵛ Incipiunt quedam de miraculis . . . Ad omnipotentis dei honorem . . . serui sui francisci.' ad laudem et gloriam . . . amen. Expliciunt miracula.' post transitum beati francisci hostensa.

Ed. cit., viii. 549–64.

ff. i+61+i. 210×155 mm. Written space 140×100 mm. 2 cols. 34 lines. Collation: 1–3¹⁶ 4¹² 5 one (f. 61). Initials: (i) historiated *A* on f. 1 (a sleeping figure, sword and shield above him on a gold ground) and on f. 45 (angel and saint); (ii) 3-line, blue with red ornament or red with violet ornament. Capital letters in the ink of the text touched with red. Binding of s. xviii.

Written probably in southern France. 'Ex libris Ludouici-Cosmæ-Damianis Rolandin, Massiliensis' printed on a label inside the cover, s. xix in.

091.21117. (2). *Psalterium, etc.*   s. xiii¹

1. ff. 1–6ᵛ Calendar in blue and red, the two colours alternating. Many additions in red and black.

Among original entries: Mammertus, 11 May; Mammes, 17 Aug.; Bernard, 20 Aug.; Sequanus, 19 Sept.; Andochius, Tyrsus, and Felix, 24 Sept.; Columbanus, 21 Nov.: no gradings.

Among additions, s. xiv, in red: 'Dedicacio ecclesie sancti mammetis', 26 Aug.; 'Inuentio sanctorum ferreoli et ferrucii', 5 Sept.; Marcharius abbot, 12 Aug.; Privatus martyr, 20 Aug.; Eleopas martyr, 25 Sept.; Translation of Mammes 'ix liccons', 10 Oct.; Vinardus confessor 'ix liccons', 11 Oct.; Girardus confessor 'ix liccons', 13 Oct.; Bassolus confessor 'ix liccons', 15 Oct.; in black: 'Translacio sanctorum ferreoli et ferruci', 30 May.

2 (added in s. xiv). Sequentiae of the Gospels of Mark and Luke on the originally blank f. 7 and in the margin of f. 7ᵛ.

3. The second quire, ff. 7–13, is arranged so that every other double opening contains a picture on each side. The third picture, now missing, faced f. 9. Each picture is in two compartments: (1) Annunciation and Visitation; (2) Manger and Kings; (3) missing; (4) Temptation and Scourging; (5) Crucifixion and Descent from Cross; (6) Three Marys at the Sepulchre and Christ appearing to Mary Magdalene (reproduced in sale catalogues of 1927 and 1937: see below); (7) Ascension and Pentecost; (8) Christ in Majesty and Day of Judgement. Contemporary captions in French are partly cut off. ff. 7, 8ᵛ, 9ᵛ, 10, 11ᵛ, 12, 13ᵛ blank.

4. ff. 14^v–104^v Psalms, ending imperfectly at 'flabit', 147:7.

Seven leaves are missing before this point. ff. 33–8 are misplaced: they belong after f. 23.
Larger initials mark the usual eight liturgical divisions and Pss. 51, 101. Antiphons added
in the margins, s. xiv/xv. f. 14 was left blank.

ff. ii+104+ii. 272 × 192 mm. Written space 172 × 110 mm. 24 long lines. Writing above
top ruled line. Collation: 1⁸ wants 1, 2 2⁸ wants 3 after f. 8 3⁸+1 before 1 (f. 14) 4⁸
(ff. 23, 33–8, 24) 5–8⁸ 9⁸ wants 4, 5 after f. 65 10⁸ wants 5 after f. 72 and 7 after f. 73
11–13⁸ 14⁸ wants 5, 6 after f. 102 and 8 after f. 103 15 one (f. 104). Good round hand.
For the full-page pictures, see above art. 3. Occupations of the months and signs of the
zodiac in the side margins of art. 1. Initials: (i) f. 14^v, a full-page Beatus *B*; (ii) of nine
psalms, in colours on gold and coloured grounds, historiated or (Ps. 51) decorated: facsimiles in the sale catalogues of 1927 (Pss. 38, 97) and 1937 (Ps. 80); (iii) of other psalms,
3-line, gold on coloured grounds; (iv) of verses, 1-line, gold or blue. Line fillers alternately blue and gold. Occasional streamers into the margins. Binding of s. xix by Rapar-
lier. Secundo folio (f. 15) *qui non abiit.*

Written in France. In use in s. xiv and probably earlier in the diocese of Langres (art. 1).
Given by Jean Doroz, Prince-bishop and Count of Lausanne, on 6 June 1604, to the
convent of nuns of the third order of St. Francis newly founded at Vercel (Doubs), on
which day a bell, to be called Jeanne Chrestienne Susanne, was blessed: the long inscription to this effect on f. 14. Belonged later to the Jesuits of Osnaburg: 'Otto Comes à
Bronckhorst in Gron[. . .] Eberstein etc 'donat Collegio societatis Jesu Osnabrugi", on a
parchment strip attached to the pastedown. Book-plates of (*a*) Jonathan Peckover, (*b*) Algerina Peckover, (*c*) William Harrison Woodward. Algerina Peckover sale at Sotheby's,
12 Dec. 1927, lot 138 (£3,500). W. H. Woodward sale at Sotheby's, 16 June 1937, lot 506
(£1,050).

091.21195. *Breviarium*   s. xv med.

1. ff. 1–6^v Calendar in red and black, graded.

Includes: Erkenwald 'Missa tantum', 30 Apr.; translation of Hugh of Lincoln 'xii lc'', in
red, 6 Oct.; 'Dedicacio ecclesie Cartus' Lond' Cand'', 26 Oct.; 'Festum reliquiarum.
Cand'', 8 Nov.; 'Anniuersarium generale. Miss'', 17 Nov. 'Obitus Walteri Mawny fundatoris huius domus' is an addition at 15 Jan.

2. ff. 7–37^v Psalms. Two leaves are missing.

3. ff. 38–109^v Temporale from Advent.

4. ff. 109^v–111 In dedicacione ecclesie.

5. ff. 111–117^v Hymns.

Twenty-two hymns: (1–9) at the hours, Deus creator, Eterne rerum, Splendor paterne,
Iam lucis, Nunc sancte, Rector potens, Rerum deus, Criste qui lux; (10) in Advent, Veni
redemptor (divided); (11) in Lent, Audi benigne; (12) at Easter, Hic est dies verus
(divided); (13) at Ascension, Optatus uotis (divided); (14, 15) at Pentecost, Veni creator
and Impleta gaudet uiscera; (16, 17) for B.V.M., Aue maris stella and Uere gracia plena es;
(18, 19) for St. John Baptist, Ut queant laxis and O nimis felix; (20) for Exaltation of Cross,
Crux fidelis; (21, 22) in feasts of twelve lessons, Criste redemptor and Ihesu saluator
seculi.

6. ff. 117^v–148^v Sanctorale, Andrew to Saturninus.

The English saints are Thomas of Canterbury, Edward king and martyr, Edmund (Rich)
and Hugh of Lincoln. The Feast of Relics follows All Saints. After Saturninus a rubric 'In
festis sanctorum xii lc' . . . et altera ad vi^a'.

7. ff. 148ᵛ–155ᵛ Common of Saints.

8. ff. 155ᵛ–156 Memoriae of Holy Cross, John Baptist, and All Saints at vespers and matins.

9. Additions in several hands, s. xv: (*a*) ff. 156–7 Psalms at compline, 'de die' and 'de domina'; (*b*) f. 157ᵛ Alma redemptoris mater que peruia . . . (*RH*, no. 861); (*c*) ff. 157ᵛ–158ᵛ Office 'ferialibus diebus infra oct' visitacionis beate marie'; (*d*) ff. 158ᵛ–159 Hymns for Passion Sunday, Vexilla regis and Arbor decora; (*e*) f. 159 a prayer, 'valde deuota post horas canonicas dicenda. Domine ihesu criste fili dei viui pone passionem . . . gaudia paradisi. Amen'; (*f*) f. iiiʳᵛ Directions for services, beginning 'In die cene domini et duorum dierum sequentibus . . .'.

ff. ii+161, foliated i–iii, 1–160. ff. i, ii are parchment flyleaves. 143 × 100 mm. Written space 102 × 63 mm. 23 long lines. Collation of ff. iii, 1–156: 1⁸+1 leaf after 8 (f. 8) 2–4⁸ 5⁶ wants 3, 4 after f. 34+1 leaf after 6 (f. 37) 6–8⁸ 9⁶ + 1 leaf after 2 (f. 64) 10–20⁸ 21⁴. Blue initials with red ornament. Binding by John Reynes, s. xvi in.: the lower cover has Oldham's BIB 17, Christ's Baptism, the upper his ST 9, St. George, badly worn. Secundo folio (f. 8) *lauabo per singulas*.

Written in England for use at the London Charterhouse (art. 1). 'Charterhouse. London', f. i, s. xvi. 'Thomas Scherman', f. 159ᵛ, 'Constat Colyns nullus nessit dycere contrarium. Testantibus Calond Cranfyld Cosyn Wynsore Clarke', f. 160, 'R. Richard', f. ii, 'Hatton Lincolnes Inne', f. ivᵛ, are perhaps all post-Dissolution, although the first two look rather earlier. 'Ph: Mainwaringe pre: 15 s', f. ii, s. xvii in. Found in Bank Top County Primary School. Given by Mr. John B. Sudworth of Lower Darwen, headmaster of the Junior School of Bank Top, in 1954.

BLAIRS COLLEGE[1]

HMC, *Second Report* (1874), Appendix, cols. 201–3, notices MSS. 1 (22), 2 (23), 8 (8) and 9 (13).

1. *Horae*   s. xv med.

A book of hours closely related to Fitzwilliam Museum, Cambridge, MSS. Add. 176 and 177, both of which were fully described by M. R. James when they were H. Y. Thompson's MSS. 83 and 84.[2] No. 689 in the *Memorial Catalogue* (Edinburgh, 1892) of the heraldic exhibition held in Edinburgh in 1891. Of the

---

[1] The manuscripts are on deposit in the National Library of Scotland, Edinburgh.
[2] *A Descriptive Catalogue of the Second Series of Fifty Manuscripts*, 1902, pp. 218–38. The English in these manuscripts tends to be even more corrupt than it is in the Blairs manuscript.

thirty-six pieces forming arts. 10–23 all but one (14*a*) are in Add. 176, but not in quite the same order:

10*a*	Add. 176, f. 50	17	Add. 176 f. 60 *bis*
10*b*	50^v	18*a*	60 *ter*
11*a*	49	*b*	61
b	50^v	19*a*	64
c	50^v	*b*	64^v
d	51	*c*	64^v
12	52	20*a*	65^v
13	52^v	*b*	67
14*b*	48	*c*	67^v, 69^{v3}
15*a*	47$^{vi, 2}$	*d*	71
b	47^{vi}	*e*	71^v
c	58^1	*f*	71^v
d	58^1	21*a*	68
e	58^{vi}	*b*	68^v
f	58^{vi}	22	69^v
g	58^{v,1} 53	23	49^v
h	53^v		
i	54^v		
16	55^v–57^v, 59–60^v		

1. ff. 1–3^v Sarum calendar in red and black, two months to a page. ff. 3*^{rv} and 4^r blank.

2. ff. 5–39 Pss. 1–150.

3. ff. 39^v–42^v Ferial canticles, Te Deum, Benedicite, Benedictus, Magnificat, Nunc dimittis, Quicumque vult.

4. ff. 42^v–44^v Litany. Thomas and Edward are the only English martyrs and Cuthbert is the only English confessor.

5. ff. 45–56 Hours of B.V.M. (of Sarum use). Hours of the Cross are worked in. A long series of memoriae after lauds: Holy Spirit, Holy Trinity, Holy Cross, John Baptist, John Evangelist, Peter, Andrew, James, all apostles and evangelists, George, Denis, Louis, Christopher, Leonard, Gaucherus, Anthony hermit, Francis, confessors, martyrs (naming Blaise, Christopher, George, Denis, Vincent, Katherine and Margaret), virgins (Katherina Margareta virgines sacratissime . . .), Sebastian, Innocents, Stephen, Laurence, Vincent, Thomas of Canterbury, Blaise, Edmund (Aue rex gentis angelorum (*sic*) miles regis angelorum eadmunde flos martirum . . .), one martyr, all martyrs, Nicholas, Martin, Leonard, one confessor, Anne, Mary Magdalene, Katherine, Margaret, Anastasia, Barbara, virgins, relics, All Saints, peace. Cf. *RH* nos. 23809–10 and *AH* xxviii. 292 (Edmund).

---

[1] ff. 47 and 58 are misbound. They should come between f. 52 and f. 53.
[2] See the footnote to art. 15.
[3] See the footnote to art. 20.

6. f. 56 Salue regina . . . Virgo clemens virgo pia . . .

RH, nos. 18147, 34577.

7. f. 56 Gaude virgo mater xpisti que per aurem concepisti . . .

RH, no. 7017. 56ᵛ blank.

8. ff. 57–61 Penitential psalms and litany agreeing with art. 4.

9 (added). f. 61ʳᵛ De sancta trinitate ad matutinas in die dominica.

Abbreviated hours.

10. f. 62 (*a*) The blissing of god fader and son and yᵉ holy gost . . . (*b*) Lorde Ihesucrist here me and haue mercy upon me today and eueri day . . .

11. Prayers to the crucified Christ: (*a*) f. 62 Oratio. Benedicat me imperialis maiestas. + Protegat me . . .; (*b*) f. 62 Oratio. Sanctifica me domine signacula sancte crucis + ut sis michi . . .; (*c*) f. 62 Oratio. Obsecro te domine ihesu xpiste fili dei viui per sanctam + crucem tuam . . .; (*d*) f. 62ʳᵛ Domine ihesu xpiste pro sancta cruce + tua . . .

12. f. 62ᵛ De quinque festis beate marie. Aue cuius concepcio solenni plena gaudio . . . Oracio. Sancta maria virgo virginum. sancte trinitatis sacrarium . . .

The antiphon is *RH*, no. 1744.

13. f. 62ᵛ Dominus noster ihesus xpistus qui es summus sacerdos et verus pontifex . . .

A form of absolution.

14. Prayers for protection: (*a*) ff. 62ᵛ–63 Oracio. Deus qui in celis est ducat me in viam rectam . . .; (*b*) f. 63 Oracio. Deus tu propicius esto michi peccatori et custos omnibus diebus . . .

15. (*a*) f. 63ʳᵛ 'Quiconques Regardera ceste remembrance de Ihesucrist en la Remembrance de sa deuote passion il aura xl iours de veray pardon. de par leon apostole de Romme' below a picture of the Holy Face. (*b*) f. 63ᵛ 'Cest la mesure de la playe du coste de nostre seigneur ihesucrist' below a picture of the Wound and before the prayer 'Beau tres doulx ihesucrist ie vous viens aourer . . .' (*c*) ff. 63ᵛ –64 'Vng philosophe estoit et disoit en ce Iour en ceste maniere. Le monde define en ce Iour. ou le dieu de nature a souffert mort le quel philosophe ne congnoissoit pas nostre sire ihesucrist puis il fu conuerti par la predicacion saint pol. et dit on que ce fut Saint denis en france' below a picture of Christ sitting on the tomb. (*d*) f. 64 'Cest la memoire de la souffrance nostre seigneur ihesucrist. Li beaulx escu signifie le corps Ihesucrist' below a picture of the Holy Face and Arma Christi. (*e*) f. 64 De hospitali pauperum cristi quod fuit apertum quinque portis videlicet vulneribus cristi. Quinque portis est apertum. sed a multis est desertum hospitale pauperum . . . (*f*) f. 64ʳᵛ Oracio. Tu agne dei pro salute humani generis immolatus es . . . (*g*) f. 64ᵛ Oracio sancti augustini. Salua me rex glorie qui potes saluare . . . (*h*) ff. 64ᵛ–65 Hec sunt septem verba . . . Domine ihesu xpiste qui in sancta cruce pendens . . . (*i*) f. 65 In honore corone spinee de qua ihesus xpistus coronatus fuit. Oracio. O redemptor

mundi qui spineam coronam. . . .: prayers in honour of the wounds of hands, feet, and side follow.[1]

(c). Sonet, no. 212. (h). Seven paragraphs, each beginning thus.

16. ff. 65–7 And also oure lord seiþe he þat seiþe þe ose (sic) oroisonnes hor herteli hem he scal se myne body and receyue hyt xv dayes before hys deþ. O domine ihesu xpiste eterna dulcedo . . .

The Fifteen Oes of St. Bridget.

17. ff. 67–8 Ad matutinas de Sancto spiritu.

Hours of Holy Spirit, RH, no. 12022.

18. (a) ff. 68–9 Ad matutinas de Sancta Katherina . . . Ympnus. Castitatis lilium virgo Katherina . . . (b) ff. 69–70 Sequitur prosa Sancte Katherine. Katherina regia Virgo mater egregia . . . (146 lines).

(a). Hours of St. Katherine, RH, no. 2672. (b). RH, no. 2690.

19. (a) f. 70^{rv} De sancta maria magdalene. Te sanctam mariam magdalenam laudamus . . . (b) f. 70^{v} Sequitur antyphona que dicitur loco de Salue regina misericordie. O magdalena nobilis. insignita miraculis . . . (c) ff. 70^{v}–71 Secuntur septem gaudia eiusdem marie. Gaude pia magdalena Spes salutis vite vena . . .

(a, c). RH, nos. 20229, 6895.

20. Prayers, etc., in need: (a) f. 71^{rv} Oracio valde bona pro tribulacione. O dulcissime domine ihesu xpiste vere deus qui de sinu dei patris . . .; (b) ff. 71^{v}–72 Alia oracio valde bona ad ihesum xpistum. Domine rex in illa sancta custodia in qua commendasti . . .; (c) f. 72^{rv} Psalmus. Exurget deus et dissipentur . . .; (d) f. 72^{v} Memoria of St. Michael; (e) f. 72^{v} Psalmus. Deus in nomine tuo saluum me fac . . .; (f) ff. 72^{v}–73 Oracio. O bone ihesu. O piissime ihesu . . .[2]

(c, e). Pss. 68, 53.

21. (a) f. 73 Gaude flore virginali. que honore speciali . . . Oremus. Oracio. Domine ihesu criste fili dei viui qui beatam gloriosam . . . (b) f. 73^{v} Gaude felix maria. tota plena gracia . . .

(a, b). RH, nos. 6810, 26951.

22. f. 73^{v} Oracio ad ihesum xpistum. Aue domine ihesu xpiste uerbum patris . . . (five aves).

23. (a) ff. 73^{v}–74 Oracio. Domine ihesu criste fili dei miserere mei et deffende me . . . (b) f. 74 Cruci corone spinee flagellis clauis lancee . . .

(a). Gives thirty-four names of Christ and after them the words '+Crux bona+Crux digna+lignum super omnia ligna+me tibi designa+Redimens a morte maligna. +Crux

---

[1] Art. 15 is in this order in Add. 177. In Add. 176 the (c) picture precedes the (a) caption in first place and the (a) picture precedes the (c) caption in third place.

[2] In Add. 176 the scribe: (1) wrote 20a, b and as much of 20c as would fit on f. 67; (2) erased 20c and replaced it with a memoria of St. Mellon which continues on f. 68 and is followed by a memoria of St. Romanus; (3) wrote 21ab, 22 and 20c–f in that order on ff. 68–71^{v}. In Add. 177 20c ends imperfectly.

fugat omne malum+Crux est reparacio rerum. +Per crucis hoc signum fugiat procul omne malignum. +Et per idem signum saluetur quoque benignum. +Per signum crucis de inimicis . . .', and the names of the twelve apostles. Cf. Walther, *Sprichwörter*, nos. 3814, 3823, 21192. (*b*). Cf. *RH*, no. 3986.

24. f. 74ʳᵛ De sancto Herasme Martire. Herasme flos decoris Honestatis et honoris . . .

25. f. 74ᵛ Two memoriae of Barbara.

26. ff. 74ᵛ–75 Ad pedes crucif'. Adoramus te criste . . .

Ends with the prayer 'Domine ihesu criste fili dei viui in honore et in memoria trium sanctissimarum oracionum . . .'.

27. f. 75 Secuntur octo versus Sancti Bernardi. Illumina oculos meos . . . consolatus es me.

28. ff. 76–81ᵛ Office of the dead.

29. ff. 82–84ᵛ An'. Requiem. Beati immaculati . . .

The commendatory psalms.

30. ff. 86–90 Prefaces, ordinary, and canon of mass.

31. ff. 90ᵛ–95 Sequitur officium de beata maria . . .: followed on f. 91 by masses of Holy Trinity, Holy Spirit, Holy Cross, St. George, the Holy Name and St. Gabriel.

32. ff. 96–98ᵛ Glorieux crosse that with the holy blood . . . mercy calle.

IMEV, no. 914. In Add. 176, f. 81.

33. ff. 100–13 Domine labia mea Apperi car volente a Mon cuer danoncier par la bouche . . .

Hours of B.V.M. in French verse. Sonet, no. 452.

34. ff. 113ᵛ–115ᵛ Glorieuse vierge Royne Qui par la vertu diuine . . .

285 lines. Sonet, no. 695. The final 8-line stanza here, 'En paradis par ta priere . . .', is not in MS. 2, art. 3.

35. ff. 115ᵛ–116ᵛ Vierge doulce et debonnaire. . . . Sonet, no. 2313.

36. ff. 116ᵛ–117ᵛ Royne des cieulx glorieuse. Fille et mere de dieu precieuse. . . Sonet, no. 1793.

37 (added in blank spaces). Sets of hours: (*a*) f. 75ᵛ [P]ro cunctis fidelibus . . . [.]ietatis paternitas . . .; (*b*) f. 85ʳᵛ [S]ancta dei genitrix mater pietatis . . .; (*c*) f. 95 [D]eus qui proprium (*sic*) hominem de limo terre creauit . . .; (*d*) f. 95ᵛ De passione Domini nostri ihesu xpisti. Matris cor uirgineum totum triuit . . .; (*e*) f. 99 Corpus (*sic*) mysterium pange gloriosi . . .; (*f*) f. 99ᵛ Patris sapientia . . . (*ends abruptly*).

(*a–f*). Hours of the dead, of All Saints, of B.V.M., of the Compassion of B.V.M., of Corpus Christi, and of the Cross: *AH* xxx. 173 (Deitatis paternitas), 143, 123, 106, 29, 32. Cf. art. 9.

38 (added). ff. 118–19 O domine ihesu criste adoro te in cruce pendentem . . .

Nine oes and the prayer 'Domine Ihesu criste fili dei viui qui sanctissime tue misterium . . .'.
f. 119ᵛ blank.

ff. ii+121+ii. The foliation (i), 1–119, (120–1) omits the blank leaf at the beginning and the blank leaf after f. 3. ff. ii, 120 are parchment flyleaves. 224×90 mm. Written space 143×46 mm. 68 long lines. Collation: 1⁶ 2–7⁸ (ff. 5–52) 8⁸+1 leaf after 8 (f. 61) 9¹⁰ (both ff. 65–6 and ff. 67–8 are bifolia) 10⁴ (ff. 72–5) 11⁸ 12² (ff. 84–5) 13⁸ 14² (ff. 94–5) 15⁴ 16–17⁸ 18⁴. Written in skilful *lettre bâtarde*. Twenty-three pictures, 25-line or less, sixteen in art. 32, four in art. 15, one before *Te igitur* in art. 30, and one before arts. 2 and 33. Initials: (i) in colour, patterned in white, on coloured grounds, historiated: eight in art. 2, eight in art. 5, and one before each of arts. 17, 18, 28, 29 (burial); (ii) in colour patterned in white on decorated gold grounds; (iii, iv) 4-line and 2-line, gold on grounds of red and blue, patterned in white; (v) 1-line, blue with red ornament or gold with slate-grey ornament. A continuous border on picture pages, mainly sprays of gold ivy leaves, and a border as tall as the written space on all other pages. Binding of s. xix, but the old covers have been laid on: each bears four repetitions of Oldham's panel AN. 17.[1] Secundo folio (f. 6) *iustus*.

An adaptation of a Talbot book of hours—but not copied from either of the manuscripts now in the Fitzwilliam Museum—made apparently in France for a member of the family of Bethune of Balfour. f. 4ᵛ, reproduced together with f. 5 in the *Memorial Catalogue* (see above), pl. xliv, has: (1) in the upper part, a picture of B.V.M. and the Child, accompanied by two standing saints and by a kneeling man and woman, both of them young and he bearing the Talbot arms on his tabard; (2) in the lower part, a floral design including two identical shields of arms, 1st and 4th azure a fess between three mascles or (for Bethune), 2nd and 3rd argent on a chevron sable an otter's head erased of the first (for Balfour); (3), below (2), two badges; (4), below (3), the letters IB linked in a love knot. Bound in London, c. 1500: see above. 'Maroun (Marown) skot', three times on f. ii, s. xvi (?). 'Ex bibliotheca Collegii Scotorum Paris' and 'Ex libris Scholæ Aquortisiensis 1824', f. 1.[2]

2. *Horae* s. xv med.

The last sixty-eight leaves of a book of hours. Paris, BN, lat. 1170, seventy-three leaves, is another part of it: cf. V. Leroquais, *Livres d'heures manuscrits de la Bibliothèque Nationale*, i. 97–9. Yet another part was Tours, Bibliothèque Municipale, 217, sixty-one leaves, destroyed in the Second World War. On all three parts cf. L. Delisle, *Les grandes heures de la reine Anne de Bretagne*, 1912, pp. 55–61. Cf. also Delisle, *Le Cabinet des manuscrits de la Bibliothèque impériale* (later *nationale*), 1868–81, ii. 336. No. 27 in *Trésors*.

1. ff. 2–6 Doulce dame de misericorde mere de pitie . . .

The Fifteen Joys of B.V.M. Sonet, no. 458.

---

[1] Oldham knew this panel only from a book at Lambeth Palace (1494.6: *STC* 15875) printed by de Worde and probably bound soon after it was printed. Another example of it is on a Sarum book of hours, Bodleian, Arch. B. e. 37, printed in Paris in 1506 (*STC* 15903): cf. H. S. Herbruggen in *Festschrift für Edgar Mertner*, 1969, p. 113 and pls. 5, 6. On Arch. B. e. 37 the panel is accompanied by stamps of the 'Caxton bindery', Oldham's 234, 243.

[2] The present Blairs College was at Aquhorthies, near Inverurie, Aberdeenshire, from 1799 until 1829.

2. ff. 6–8ᵛ Sensuiuent les sept requestes a nostre seigneur. Doulz dieu doulz pere sainte ternite . . .

Sonet, no. 504.

3. ff. 8ᵛ–17 Cy ampres sensuit lorayson theophile. Glorieuse uierge royne En qui par la uertu diuine . . .

Forty-six 6-line stanzas. Sonet, no. 695.

4. ff. 17–19ᵛ Orayson de nostre dame. Stabat mater dolorosa . . .

RH, no. 19416. The prayer 'Interueniat pro nobis quesumus domine . . .' follows.

5. ff. 19ᵛ–20ᵛ Cy ampres sensuiuent lez vers saint bernart. Illumina oculos meos . . .

The prayer 'Omnipotens sempiterne deus qui ezechie regi . . .' follows.

6. ff. 20ᵛ–53ᵛ Cy apres sensuiuent lez suffrages de sains. Et premier de la ternite. . . . Memoriae, illustrated by pictures, of *Holy Trinity*, Holy Spirit, Veronica, Michael (heading only: picture (?) and text are missing on a leaf after f. 22), *John Baptist*, *John Evangelist*, *Peter and Paul*, *James*, *Stephen*, Laurence, Vincent, *George*, Eustace, *Blaise*, Thomas of Canterbury, *Sebastian*, Cosmas and Damian, Julian, Denis, Peter Martyr, *Christopher*, martyrs, Martin, Gatien, *Nicholas*, Éloi, Gobrianus, Hilary, Giles, *Anthony hermit*, Leonard, Maturin, Fiacre, Ives, *Francis*, Avertinus, *Louis bishop and confessor*, *Louis king and confessor*, Peter of Luxembourg, *Mary Magdalene*, Anne, *Katherine*, *Apollonia*, *Margaret*, *Lucy*, Barbara, *Susanna*, Avia, 11,000 Virgins, All Saints, 'De cincq sains' (Denis, George, Christopher, Blaise, Giles), 'De cincq saintes vierges' (Katherine, Margaret, Martha, Christina, Barbara).[1]

Metrical antiphons are Fideles hic attendite (George: RH, no. 6293), Aue presul honestatis (Blaise: 2056), O petre martyr inclite predicatorum gloria (Peter Martyr: cf. 30815), Martir dei cristofore (Christopher: 29471), O lux clara turonorum (Gatien), Copiose caritatis (Nicholas: 3864), Aue gemma sacerdotum eligi norma uirtutum (Éloi), Sancte francisce propere (Francis: 18465), Aue gemma claritatis (Katherine: 1807), Virgo martyr egregia pro nobis appolonia (Apollonia), Dyonisi radius grecie (five saints: 4707), Katherina tyrannum superans (five virgins: 2691).

7. ff. 53–54ᵛ Sensuiuent lez sept principales ioyez de nostre dame. Gaude flore uirginali . . .

RH, no. 6809.

8. ff. 54ᵛ–57 Sensuiuent lez cincq grans douleurs de nostre dame. A long introduction in French, 'Selon ce que lon treuue es fais monseigneur saint iehan leuuangeliste . . . confes et repentans', followed by five prayers, 'Mediatrix . . .', 'Auxiliatrix . . .', 'Reparatrix . . .', 'Illuminatrix . . .', 'Alleuiatrix . . .'.

9. ff. 59–60 Sensuiuent les douze articles de la foy . . .

The apostles' creed, each clause attributed to one of the twelve, followed by the prayer, 'Deus propicius esto michi peccatrici . . .'.

10. f. 60ʳᵛ Orayson a ihesu crist. O pie rex criste propter tua quinque vulnera tu miserere mei peccatricis penitentis . . .

---

[1] Italics show the memoriae with pictures.

11. ff. 60^v–61 Miserere mei domine: et exaudi oracionem meam. Miserere mei domine quoniam infirma sum . . .

12. f. 61 Sensuit le vers saint patrice. Ihesu criste fili dei viui redemptor mundi miserere mei.

13. ff. 61–2 Sensuit la maniere dempetrer les vii dons du saint esperit contre les sept peches mortelx. Le don de la sapience contre le peche dorgueil. Cor mundum crea in me deus . . .

14. f. 62^{rv} Hymne de nostre dame. Ad honorem marie uirginis psallat hec concio . . .

RH, no. 22365.

15. ff. 62^v–63 Pour pere et mere et freres et seurs orayson. Pietate tua quesumus domine absolue . . .

16. f. 63^{rv} Memoire et orayson a dire pour celuy a qui on a especiale deuocion en aucune aduersite. Antienne. Doleo super te frater mi ionatha . . .

17. ff. 63^v–64^v Prayers: (*a*) Pour les desconfortes; (*b*) Pour ceulx qui sont assambles pour faire aucune grant besoingne; (*c*) Item pour ceulx a qui on a especiale deuocion; (*d*) Pour impetrer quelconque chose necessaire quon veult auoir iustement.

18 (in another hand). ff. 65–9 Abbreviated hours of B.V.M. of the use of (Paris). f. 69^v blank.

19 (added in s. xvii). f. 1^v Arms and mottoes of Louis XII and Anne of Brittany, as in the Paris and Tours manuscripts.

ff. i+68+i, foliated 1–70. For f. 1, supplied in s. xvii, see above art. 19. 214 × 180 mm. Written space 122 × 90 mm. 17 long lines and in art. 18, 20. Ruling with red ink. Collation of ff. 2–69: 1–2^8 3^8 wants 6 after f. 22 4–8^8 9^6 wants 6, probably blank. 26 good three-quarter-page pictures, 22 in art. 6 and 1 before each of arts. 1–4: (1) B.V.M. and Child, who stretches for cherries offered by an angel; (2) Christ in glory showing His wounds; (3) B.V.M. seated and Child; (4) The dead Christ in the arms of B.V.M.: three angels attend Him and one of them writes with the blood of His left hand. Initials on ff. 2–64: (i, ii) 3-line and 2-line, in colour, patterned in white, on decorated gold grounds; (iii) 1-line, gold on coloured grounds patterned in white. Initials on ff. 65–9: (i) f. 65, 3-line, blue and dark red; (ii, iii) 2-line and 1-line, dark red or blue. Capital letters in the ink of the text filled with pale yellow. Line fillers in red, blue, and gold. Continuous floral borders on all pages, except 65–69^v. Red morocco binding for Philippe de Béthune, with his armorial centrepiece and crowned double P within a wreath as cornerpieces and in the compartments of the back-strip: cf. Delisle, *Cabinet* (op. cit.), p. 267.

Written in France for Marie de Rieux, †1466, wife of Louis d'Amboise: cf. Leroquais, op. cit., p. 99. The complete manuscript, Paris+Tours+Blairs, was bound in three volumes for Philippe, Comte de Béthune, †1649, and, as Delisle and Leroquais showed, furnished with ornamental pages, one in each volume, to suggest ownership by Louis XII and his queen: cf. art. 19. 'Ex libris Scholæ Aquortisiensis 1824', ff. 1, 64^v.

3. *Horae* s. XV ex.

1. ff. 1–12ᵛ Calendar in red and black. 'Mayoli abbatis' in red, 11 May.

2. ff. 13–14ᵛ John 1: 1–14 (beginning imperfectly) and prayer, 'Protector in te sperantium . . .'.

3. ff. 15–20 Obsecro te . . . Masculine forms.

4. ff. 21–83ᵛ Hours of B.V.M., beginning imperfectly.
The antiphon and capitulum at prime are Ave maria and Virgo dei genitrix and at none Ortus conclusus and Felix namque.

5. ff. 84–7 Hours of the Cross, beginning imperfectly. f. 87ᵛ blank.

6. ff. 88–92ᵛ Hours of the Holy Spirit.

7. ff. 92ᵛ–94ᵛ Oroison a nostre seignur. Mon benoit dieu ie croy de cueur et confesse de bouche . . . Sonet, no. 1150.

8. ff. 94ᵛ–98 Memoriae of the dead and of SS. John Baptist, John Evangelist, and Katherine. f. 98ᵛ blank.

9. ff. 99–121 Penitential psalms, beginning imperfectly, and (f. 114) litany.
Thirteen martyrs: (1, 2) stephane cirice . . . Seven monks and hermits: benedicte paule dominice francisce anthoni fiacri guillerme. f. 121ᵛ blank.

10. ff. 122–158ᵛ Office of the dead, beginning imperfectly. Three lessons only.

ff. ii+158+ii. 205 × 140 mm. Written space 98 × 64 mm. 14 long lines. Ruling in red ink. Collation: 1–2⁶ 3⁸ wants 1 before f. 13+1 leaf after 8 (f. 20) 4⁸ wants 1 before f. 21 5–11⁸ 12⁸ wants 1 before f. 84 13⁸ 14⁸ wants 1 before f. 99 15–16⁸ 17⁸ wants 1 before f. 122 18–20⁸ 21⁸ wants 7, 8, probably blank. Only two three-quarter-page pictures remain, one before art. 3 (B.V.M. and Child in glory) and one before art. 6. Initials: (i, ii) 3-line and 2-line, in colours patterned on white on gold grounds decorated with flowers; (iii) 1-line, gold on coloured grounds. Capital letters in the ink of the text filled with pale yellow. Line fillers in pink, blue, and gold. Framed borders in colours, partly on grounds of gold paint, continuous on ff. 15, 88 and on three sides of pages with initials of type (i). Borders the height of the written space in the outer margins of many other pages, including all with initials of type (ii). Binding of s. xviii.
Written in France. 'Ex libris Scholæ Aquortisiensis 1824', ff. 2, 158ᵛ.

4. *Horae* s. XV med.

1. ff. 1–12ᵛ Calendar in French, in red and black.
Feasts in red include Medard and Andocheus (8 June, 24 Sept.).

2. ff. 13–62ᵛ Hours of B.V.M. of the use of (Autun), with hours of the Cross worked in. Headings in French.

3. ff. 62ᵛ–63ᵛ John 1: 1–14.

4. ff. 64–81ᵛ Penitential psalms, beginning imperfectly, and (f. 74) 'La letanie'.
Three 'discipuli': lazare marcialis saturnine. Thirty-six martyrs: (2, 3) nazari et celse

leodegari . . . Twenty-seven confessors: . . . (9–27) simplici macute albine germane remigi amator simplice primati eptadi brixi auiane nicholae bonefaci benedicte philiberte columbane sequane anthoni theobalde.

5. ff. 81ᵛ–85 Papa Innocentius hanc oracionem conposuit et concessit omnibus uere penitentibus et confessis qui eam cothidie dixerunt centum dies indulgencie. Obsecro te . . . Masculine forms. f. 85ᵛ blank.

6. ff. 86–113ᵛ Office of the dead, beginning imperfectly.

The ninth lesson is 'Quare lacero . . . arguam' (Job 13: 14–15).

7. ff. 114–17 Le francois de aue maria. Dame ie te rens le salut . . . leurs ames deffens et deliure. Amen.

Ten stanzas of eight lines each: Sonet, no. 320 (nine stanzas). ff. 117ᵛ–118ᵛ left blank: cf. below.

ff. 118. 202 × 150 mm. Written space 105 × 73 mm. 14 long lines. Ruling in red ink. Collation: 1¹² 2–4⁸ 5⁸ wants 3 after f. 39 6–7⁸ 8⁶ (ff. 58–63) 9⁸ wants 1 before f. 64 10⁸ 11⁸ wants 8, perhaps blank, after f. 85 12⁸ wants 1 before f. 86 13–14⁸ 15⁶ wants 6, probably blank, after f. 113 17⁸ wants 5–7, probably blank, after f. 117. An 11-line picture before art. 2 and before art. 7 (B.V.M. and Child: an angel gives a basket of cherries). Initials: (i, ii) 3-line and 2-line, blue or red patterned in white on decorated gold grounds; (iii) 1-line, gold on coloured grounds patterned in white. Capital letters in the ink of the text filled with yellow. Line-fillers in red, blue, and gold. Borders are continuous on picture pages and on three sides of pages with initials of type (i). Binding of wooden boards covered with part of a leaf of a noted service book.

Written for use in the diocese of Autun (cf. arts. 2, 4) probably by or for someone of the name 'Anbry': this name is written in the line filler opposite the words 'Sancte simplice' in the litany, f. 77, instead of the usual white patterning. 'Jhean de la chaussee' inside the cover, s. xvi. 'Jehanne de foissy 1568' and verses in French, beginning 'Celle quy ses heurs vous donne', on f. 118. 'marie bansims (?) demeurant a sousance et mon[. . . .]', f. 117, s. xvi. Erased inscriptions on ff. 1 (dated 1717?), 85 (dated 1723?) and a cancelled inscription on f. 12ᵛ. The red wax impression of an armorial seal is on top of an obliterated book-plate inside the cover and above the name 'François Lambert Baron Varicourt': the arms are those of Rouph, barons of Varicourt (created in 1808), as given by Rietstap, *Armorial général*, p. 1070. The bookplate has the name '[. . . .] Hacqu[. . . .]' above a coat of arms, azure three roses argent: for these arms used by 'Michel François Hacquebec, curé de Dieppe près Verdun' see the *Supplément* to Rietstap, ii. 3. 'To Mrˢ Kyle with Capt. Anderson's kindest respects', f. 1. Book-plate of John James Kyle, canon of Aberdeen, s. xix.

5. *Memoriae sanctorum, etc.* s. XV/XVI

A volume fully described by W. J. Anderson, 'Andrew Lundy's Primer', *Innes Review*, xi (1960), 39–51, with six facsimiles, pls. x–xv.

1. ff. 1–4 Calendar in blue, red, and black, written without break, save for one line between the months, beginning imperfectly at 24 June.

Printed by Anderson, pp. 42–3. His pl. x shows ff. 3ᵛ–4 (16 Nov.–31 Dec.), reduced. 'Niniani episcopi' and 'Medani episcopi' in black, 16 Sept. and 4 Dec. 'Egidii abbatis' added in red, 1 Sept. f. 4ᵛ was left blank: cf. art. 2.

2 (added in s. xvi). f. 4ᵛ O my souerayne lorde Ihesus The weray sone of almyghty god . . . ' (*ends abruptly*).

Printed by Anderson, p. 44.

3. f. 5ʳᵛ Adoro te domine Iesu criste in cruce pendentem . . . anima tua nobilissima (*ends imperfectly*).

The Seven Oes of St. Gregory, ending in no. 7.

4. ff. 6–16ᵛ Psalms of the Passion (Pss. 21–30), beginning imperfectly at Ps. 21, verse 9, and lacking two leaves after f. 8. The versicle 'Cristus factus est . . .' and prayer 'Respice quesumus super hanc familiam tuam . . .' follow.

5. ff. 16ᵛ–17ᵛ Oracio ad beatam mariam in sole. tociens quociens aliquis dixerit habebit xi milia annorum indulgenciarum. Aue sanctissima Maria mater dei regina celi . . .

Cf. Anderson, pp. 44–5, and pls. xii, xiv, showing f. 17ʳᵛ.

6. ff. 18–19 Secundum Lucam. In illo tempore. Missus est gabriel . . . Fiat michi secundum uerbum tuum. Deo gracias. Luke 1: 26–38.

7. ff. 19–23 Oracio deuota ad virginem mariam. Obsecro te . . .

Masculine forms, with feminine interlined in the same ink.

8. f. 23ʳᵛ Oracio deuotissima ad beatam uirginem mariam. O domina mea sancta maria me in tuam benedictam fidem . . .

9. ff. 23ᵛ–24ᵛ Alexander papa sextus (1492–1503) concessit x milia annorum pro mortalibus et xx pro venialibus dicenti trina vice hanc oracionem coram imagine sancte anne ac beate virginis et filio eius quas proprio ore promulgauit. Aue mar[ia gracia] plena dominus t[e]cum tua gracia . . .

Printed by Anderson, pp. 45–6. His pl. xiii shows f. 24 which has a piece cut out of it.

10. ff. 24ᵛ–25ᵛ Dominus raymundus cardinalis concessit omnibus istam oracionem coram predict' ymag' (dicentibus) tociens quociens c di[es] indulgenciarum. Quotquot maris sunt gutte et are[ne t]erre . . .

Cf. Anderson, p. 46.

11. Memoriae of SS. Anne and Martha: (*a*) ff. 25ᵛ–26 Oracio deuota ad beatam annam. Anna pia mater aue . . .; (*b*) f. 26ᵛ Exultet urbs bethania . . .

(*a, b*). The antiphons, *RH*, nos. 1109, 5911, printed by Anderson, p. 46.

12. Memoriae: (*a*) f. 28ʳᵛ De sancto Niniano episcopo. A'. Stirpe regalis que vita floruit . . .; (*b*) f. 28ᵛ De sancto symione sene, ending imperfectly.

(*a*) as in the Aberdeen breviary. Anderson, pl. xv, shows ff. 27ᵛ–28, reduced.

13. ff. 29–72 Eighty-two memoriae in the order of the church year, beginning imperfectly at 21 Jan. (Agnes) and ending at 31 Dec. (Sylvester).

Listed, except Anne (26 July) and Stephen (26 Dec.), by Anderson, pp. 47–50, where also the antiphons of SS. Joseph (not in *RH*), Mary of Egypt, George, and Christopher are printed: the last includes the words 'michi famule tue N'. Metrical antiphons are: (Charlemagne) O spes afflic*torum* timor hostibus hostia . . .; (Gregory) Aue sanctitatis organum dignissimum . . .; (Anthony) O proles hyspanie . . . (*RH*, no. 13448); (Visitation of B.V.M.)

Adiutrix visitacio et frequens ministracio . . .; (Roche) Aue roche sanctissime . . (*RH*, no. 2078); (Adrian) Aue sancte adriane qui martirium immane . . . (*RH*, no. 3106); (Francis) Salue pater patrie lux forma minorum. . . . There are no Scotch, nor, apart from Thomas of Canterbury, English saints.

14. ff. 72–3 Memoriae of B.V.M. in Advent and of Holy Trinity. f. 73^v blank.

15. ff. 74–92 Psalter of St. Jerome and concluding prayer, 'Dona michi queso omnipotens deus ut per hanc sacrosanctam psalterii celestis melodiam . . .'.

Anderson, pl. xi, shows f. 74.

16. ff. 92–3 Oratio ad Sanctum Iheronimum. Aue amator quam famose . . .

A memoria of St. Jerome, the antiphon printed by Anderson, p. 50. f. 93^v blank.

ff. iii+93+ii. 167 × 100 mm. Written space 108 × 55 mm. 16 long lines (23 on f. 5^{rv}; 33 in art. 1). Collation: 1^8 wants 1–3 2^8 wants 1, 5, 6 (ff. 6–10) 3–4^8 5^8 wants 2, 3 after f. 28+1 leaf before 1 (f. 27) 6–12^8 13 four. Written in a formal but unskilled cursiva. One full-page picture (f. 27^v, St. Ninian) and four *c.*10-line pictures: f. 17 B.V.M. in glory; f. 17^v, Annunciation; f. 24, B.V.M., Child, and St. Anne; f. 74, St. Jerome: all five are shown by Anderson, pls. xii, xiv, xiii, xv, xi. Initials: (i) 2-line, gold with blue or red ornament and (ff. 17–24 only) gold on coloured grounds; (ii) 1-line, blue or red with ornament of the other colour. Three type (i) initials have been cut out, ff. 25, 26, 27. Framed borders of flowers, etc., on picture pages and on f. 18. Binding of s. xviii, lettered 'Old Manuscrip(t)'.

Doubtless written in Scotland, perhaps for female use, in view of arts. 7, 13. 'Andrew Lundy wth my hand In my defens god me defend', f. 4, s. xvi: for the east of Scotland family of Lundy and their connections with the family of Forbes of Fintray, Aberdeenshire, see Anderson, pp. 40–1: the church at Fintray was dedicated to St. Giles and possessed, according to tradition, the head of St. Modan. 'R.C.', f. 1. 'A.G.' inside the cover and on f. 1, s. xviii: Anderson suggests Alexander Geddes, 1737–1802. Formerly in the library of the catholic archbishop of St. Andrews and Edinburgh, as appears from the cross stamped on f. iii: cf. Anderson, p. 40. Transferred to Blairs College, *c.* 1930.

6. *Horae* (*including some English*)　　　　　　s. xv med.

1. ff. 1–6^v Calendar in red and black.

'pape' is cancelled and feasts of St. Thomas of Canterbury have been erased.

2. ff. 7–8 Diagrams showing 'eclipses solis pro duobus ciclis' on seventeen occasions between 28 Aug. 1448 and 11 June 1462. f. 7 is damaged, with loss of five diagrams.

3. ff. 9–10 Rules for finding Easter, etc., with mnemonic verses, 'Quinque bis. inde dias . . .' (1 line), and 'Post cineres. post pen . . .' (2 lines).

4. ff. 10^v–12 Advice about eating and drinking and blood-letting in each month, in English, beginning 'Ianuarius. In þis moneth of Ianuere whyte is gode to drynke'.

5. f. 12 A note on blood-letting ascribed to Bede, 'vnde versus Ultima lunaris Aprilis . . .' (2 lines).

6. f. 12^v Prognostications of weather, according to the day of the week on which the first day of the month falls.

7. ff. 12ᵛ–13 'Tabula ad sciendum pro qualibet hora quis planeta regnet' and 'Tabula ad inueniendum locum lune et moram eius sub quolibet signo'.

8. ff. 13ᵛ–15 Prayers for protection: (a) 'In presencia sacrosancti et ineffabilis sacramenti . . .'; (b) 'Deus propicius esto michi peccatori . . .'.

9. ff. 15–16ᵛ Mary mayden wel þow be . . . þat I be neuer takyn þere inne. Amen.

Fifty-two lines of verse. *IMEV*, no. 2119.

10. ff. 17–50 Hours of B.V.M. of the use of (Sarum).

After lauds are a series of twenty-two memoriae, all but the last two illustrated by a picture (ff. 27–37ᵛ): Holy Spirit, Holy Trinity, B.V.M., SS. John Baptist, Peter and Paul, Andrew, John Evangelist, Christopher, Laurence, Sebastian, Blaise, Three Kings, Hugh confessor and bishop, Giles, Anne, Katherine, Margaret, Barbara, Mary Magdalene, Etheldreda, eight martyrs and eight virgins (George, Denis, Christopher, Eustace, Blaise, Giles, Anthony, Wynwaloe; Anne, Martha, Katherine, Margaret, Radegund, Barbara, Gertrude, Ursula), peace. The rhymed antiphons are Stella celi extirpauit . . . (B.V.M.: *RH*, no. 19438), Salue martir nostra saluacio. salue nos in mundi naufragio . . . (Blaise: cf. *RH*, no. 33128), Gaude felix anna . . . (*RH*, no. 6773), Gaude barbara regina . . . (*RH*, no. 6714), Aue gemma preciosa uirgo decens et formosa (Etheldreda: not in *RH*). The collect of St. Giles ends imperfectly: one leaf missing. Hours of the Cross and the 'Memoria de lamentacione beate marie. Matris cor uirgineum trena totum triuit . . .' (*RH*, no. 29551) are worked in.

11. f. 50ʳᵛ Salue regina . . .

12. ff. 51–63ᵛ Penitential psalms, (f. 57) gradual psalms (cues only of the first twelve), and (f. 58ᵛ) litany.

Swithun, Birin, and Edith are the only English saints. In the absence of St. Thomas of Canterbury an earnest blotter-out removed the name of St. Thomas the apostle.

13. f. 64ʳᵛ Confiteor domino deo celi et terre . . . Masculine forms.

14. ff. 64ᵛ–65ᵛ Domine ihesu criste qui septem uerba . . .

The prayer of Christ's seven words from the Cross, without heading.

15. Prayers: (a) ff. 65ᵛ–66 Domine ihesu criste qui hanc sacratissimam carnem . . .; (b) f. 66 Aue uerum corpus natum . . .; (c) f. 66 Aue principium nostre creacionis . . .; (d) f. 66ʳᵛ Deus qui uoluisti pro redempcione mundi . . .; (e) f. 66ᵛ Dirupisti domine uincula mea . . .; (f) ff. 66ᵛ–67 Auxilientur michi domine ihesu criste omnes passiones tue . . .; (g) f. 67 O bone ihesu duo in me agnosco naturam quam tu fecisti. et peccatum quod ego adieci . . .; (h) ff. 67–68ᵛ Domine ihesu criste fili dei uiui te deprecor per sacratissimam carnem . . .; (i) f. 68ᵛ Domine ihesu criste fili dei uiui saluator mundi rex glorie pone passionem . . .; (j) f. 69 Aue domine ihesu criste uerbum patris . . . (five aves).

(b, c, j). *RH*, nos. 2175, 2059, 1778.

16. f. 69ʳᵛ Omnipotens sempiterne deus respice propicius ad preces nostras . . .

17. ff. 69ᵛ–71 Crux frutex saluificus . . .

RH, no. 25085.

18. ff. 71–2 O bone ihesu o piissime o dulcissime ihesu . . .

19. ff. 72–73^v O intemerata . . . orbis terrarum. inclina aures tue pietatis . . .

20. f. 73^v Domine ihesu criste fili dei uiui qui in cruce sancta pendens . . .

21. ff. 73^v–74^v Gaude flore uirginali honor(e)que speciali . . .

RH, no. 6809 (Seven Joys).

22. Prayers: (a) ff. 74^v–75 Sancte michael archangele domini nostri ihesu cristi . . .; (b) f. 75^{rv} Omnipotens deus et misericors pater et bone domine miserere michi peccatori . . .; (c) ff. 75^v–77^v Deus inmense misericordie deus ineffabilis pietatis . . .; (d) ff. 77^v–78 Domine deus meus qui offencione mea non uinceris . . .

23. f. 78^{rv} O ihesu criste eterna dulcedo te amantium . . .

The first of the Fifteen Oes of St. Bridget. No doubt the others were on the leaves missing after f. 78.

24. ff. 79–85 Psalms 21–30 (psalms of the Passion).

25. ff. 85^v–86 Hec est oracio deuota ad dicendum ad libitum. Gracias tibi ago domine ihesu criste qui passionem tuam . . .

26. ff. 86–87^v Stabat mater dolorosa . . .: the heading conveys an indulgence of Pope Boniface of 1,000 years.

27. ff. 87^v–88^v Passio domini nostri ihesu cristi secundum Iohannem. In illo T. Apprehendit Pilatus Ihesum . . . uerum est testimonium eius.

Extracted mainly from John 1: 1–35. The prayer 'Deus qui manus tuas . . .' follows. Cf. Lyell Cat., pp. 65, 66.

28. ff. 88^v–90^v Domine ihesu criste rex glorie qui es uerus agnus in ara crucis . . ., and ten other short prayers to the crucified Christ, each beginning 'Domine ihesu criste'.

29. ff. 90^v–91 Aue precium (sic) nostre creacionis . . . Longer than art. 15c.

30. f. 91^{rv} Nota quod papa Urbanus quintus misit Imperatori vnum Agnus dei cum istis versibus subsequentibus. Balsamus et munda cera cum crismate vnda . . .

RH, no. 24055.

31. ff. 92–119^v Hic incipiunt vigilie mortuorum. f. 120^{rv} was left blank.

32. ff. 121–129^v Hic incipit commendacio animarum . . . Beati immaculati . . .

33. ff. 130–132^v Aue uirgo gloriosa. stella sole clarior . . .

One hundred lines. RH, no. 23969.

34. Prayers: (a) ff. 132^v–133 Aue et gaude gloriosa uirgo . . .; (b) f. 133 Omnipotens sempiterne deus qui gloriose uirginis . . .; (c) f. 133^{rv} Te deprecor domina dulcissima et beatissima uirgo maria . . .; (d) ff. 133^v–134 O dulcis domina o beata uirgo maria porta uite . . .; (e) f. 134^{rv}, as art. 15h.

35. ff. 134^v–135^v A deuout prayer for all maner of tribulacions if a man or

woman þies masses und*ur* writen synge for hymself or for any other of hys frendes. In qwatt nede or tribulacion or seknes þᵗ þei be in. þe(i) schall be deliuered by grace of god wᵗ oute doute wᵗ in x days. or in þe same maner for to deliuer þe saule of þi frende oute of þe peyn for þise thingis er preuid. Do synge a masse on þe sonday in þe wirchip of þe trinite and alighte iii candels . . .

Directions in English for masses and candles and feeding the poor on each day of the week.

36. Blank spaces, some margins, and f. 136ʳᵛ contain later additions in faded ink. The last is a litany of the Holy Name, as Mr. C. A. Martin tells me.

ff. i+135+ii. ff. i and 137 were formerly pasted down. 150 × 108 mm. Written space 93 × 72 mm. 18 long lines. Ruling in ink. Collation: 1–4⁸ 5⁸ wants 1 before f. 33. 6–9⁸ 10⁸ wants 8 after f. 78 11⁸ wants 1–3 before f. 79 12–15⁸ 16⁴ (ff. 116–19) 17–18⁸. The hand changes at f. 92 (art. 29). Pictures: full-page mass of St. Gregory, f. 8ᵛ; 14-line B.V.M. and Child, f. 16ᵛ, after art. 9; twenty-two smaller pictures, mostly 8-line, twenty in art. 10 illustrating the memoriae, one before art. 31, and one before art. 33 (B.V.M. and Child in glory). Initials: (i) in colours patterned in white on decorated gold grounds: prolongations form continuous borders; (ii) 2-line, gold on blue and red grounds patterned in white; (iii) 1-line, blue with red ornament or gold with pink ornament (a pink under-colour where the gold has flaked, as it often has). Line fillers in blue and gold. Contemporary binding of dark-brown limp leather: four bands: two ties missing.

Written in England. 'Reddendus Edwardo Willoughby Armigero de Aspley in Comitatu Nottinghamensi', f. iᵛ, s. xviii.

7. *Horae* s. xv²

1. ff. 2–7ᵛ Full calendar in French in blue, red, and black.

geneuiefue, eloy, loys, s' leu s' gile, denis, iue, marcel, thomas (of Canterbury) in blue. ff. 1ʳᵛ, 8ʳᵛ blank.

2. ff. 9–12ᵛ Sequentiae of the Gospels.

3. ff. 12ᵛ–15 Obsecro te . . . Masculine forms. ff. 15ᵛ–16ᵛ blank.

4. ff. 17–49ᵛ Hours of B.V.M. of the use of (Paris). ff. 50–52ᵛ were ruled, but left blank.

5. ff. 53–63ᵛ Penitential psalms and (f. 60ᵛ) litany.

In the litany Genovefa and Avia are fifth and sixth of ten virgins.

6. ff. 63ᵛ–66 Les heures de la croix.

7. ff. 66ᵛ–69 Les heures du saint esperit.

8. ff. 69–89 Incipiunt vigilie mortuorum.

9. ff. 89ᵛ–106 Commendationes animarum pro defunctis. An'. Subuenite . . .

10. ff. 106–10 Incipit officium beate marie virginis. abreuiatum a beato anselmo compositum. Eya mea labia nunc annunciate laudes et preconia virgini beate . . . o dulcis maria.

Hours of the Conception of B.V.M. *RH*, no. 5307. *AH* xxx. 93.

11. ff. 110–120ᵛ Passio domini nostri ihesu cristi. secundum Iohannem. In illo tempore. Egressus est ihesus . . . (f. 117) monumentum posuerunt ihesum. Oratio. O dulcissime domine ihesu criste uere deus qui de sinu dei patris . . .

12. Prayers: (a) ff. 120ᵛ–121 Oratio ad cristum. Domine ihesu criste. qui hanc sacratissimam carnem . . .; (b) f. 121ʳᵛ Oratio. O bone et dulcissime ihesu per tuam magnam misericordiam . . .; (c) ff. 121ᵛ–122 Oratio. O beatissime domine ihesu criste respice digneris super me miserum peccatorem . . .

13. f. 122 De cruce. Antyphona. Cruci corone spinee. sacroque ferro lancee . . .
A memoria of Holy Cross. Cf. *RH*, no. 3986.

14. ff. 122–3 Oratio. Aue ihesu criste verbum patris filius virginis . . . (five aves: *RH*, no. 1778). V' Omnis terra . . . R' Et psallat . . . Deus qui in sancta cruce pendens . . .

15. (a) f. 123 Oroison quant on lieue le corps nostreseigneur. Aue uerum corpus natum . . . (b) f. 123ʳᵛ Oroison quant on celebre le corps de nostreseigneur. Anima cristi sanctifica me . . . (c) ff. 123ᵛ–124 Oratio. Domine ihesu criste qui hanc sacratissimam carnem . . .
(a, b). *RH*, nos. 2175, 1090. (c). As art. 12a.

16. f. 124ʳᵛ Les vii vers saint bernard. Illumina oculos meos . . . Oratio. Omnipotens sempiterne deus qui ezechie regi . . .

17 (added in s. xvi). ff. 125–6 Ma priere glaude sainct confesseur amy de dieu . . .
Four stanzas, each with the refrain 'Ie te Requiers donne moy Reconfort'. ff. 126ᵛ–140ᵛ are ruled, but without writing.

ff. i+140. 130×90 mm. Written space 82×48 mm. 24 long lines. Collation: 1–5⁸ 6⁴ (ff. 41–4) 7–9⁸ 10⁴ (ff. 69–72) 11–16⁸ 17–18⁶ 19⁸. Written in a good *lettre bâtarde*. A larger picture, 18-line or 19-line, introduces arts. 4–7, 8 (Death leads pope, cardinal, and bishop). Eight smaller pictures, *c.* 30×30 mm., one before art. 2 and seven in art. 4. Initials: (i) blue-grey on grounds of gold paint and red; (ii–iv) 4-line, 2-line, and 1-line, gold paint on coloured grounds patterned in gold paint. Pages with larger pictures and f. 9 have continuous floral borders, the grounds compartmented (except f. 9) and partly of gold paint. Binding of wooden boards, covered with brown leather, s. xvi: 3 rolls laid vertically in six rows, 1, 2, 3, 3, 2, 1: two clasps and metal cornerpieces and centrepieces missing. Secundo folio (f. 10) *In illo tempore*.

Written in France. '[. .]don de lan[. . .]est de [. .] de voyyenon et de lugny (*or* Cugny) Ianuier 1608', inside the front cover. 'Ex libris Scholæ Aquortisiensis. 1824', f. 49ᵛ.

8. *Floriger ex libris Augustini, etc.*   s. xv²

1. ff. 1–62ᵛ Incipiunt extractiones de diuersis libris beati Augustini. Quorumdam gloriosi et incomparabilis doctoris augustini librorum tractatus percurrentes vt pigri lectores . . . sic aperietur te prestante. Qui viuis . . . Amen. Explicit floriger extractus ex diuersis libris beati Augustini.

An often-copied anthology from St. Augustine in twenty-six chapters, beginning, after the prologue, 'Da michi domine scire': cf. the catalogue descriptions of BL, Royal 5 B. xi and Bodleian, Hatton 101 (*Sum. Cat.* 4048), and Römer, i. 373–4.

2. ff. 63–127ᵛ Incipiunt capitula extractionis sequentis. De indiscreto feruore . . . (*table of eleven chapters*) . . . (f. 64) Prologus. Rationabile sit obsequium vestrum . . . (f. 64ᵛ) vertitur in vitium. De indiscreto feruore Capitulum primum. Indiscretus feruor quodammodo vitium oppositum est . . .

Of the eight remaining 'chapters' three are sermons, one is called a 'Soliloquium' and one a 'Meditatio': (2) f. 75ᵛ Quomodo deus diligendus sit et quare et ex quanto. Primo considerandum est modus diligendi . . .; (3) f. 83 Soliloquium de septem venis anime et christi. Consolator hominum homo christus ihesus. videns animam . . .; (4) f. 92ᵛ Sermo beati bernardi. De guerra inter regem Iherusalem. Et babylonis. Inter regem iherusalem et babilonis nulla pax est . . . caritatis decem milia. Explicit; (5) f. 100 Magister hugo de sex idriis. Iohannis quinto capitulo. Erant ibi posite sex ydrie . . . Intelligamus has sex ydrias . . . vt ex seruo proueharis ad filium; (6) f. 107 De hiis que impediunt confessionem. Quatuor sunt que impediunt confessionem. Pudor timor spes et desperatio . . .; (7) f. 109 Sermo de arbore palme . . . Dixi ascendam in palmam . . . In sacra scriptura aliquando per palmam . . .; (8) f. 123 Meditatio saluberrima omni claustrali incipienti. Ut nulla hora tediose uel otiose viuas . . . Cum in aliquo grauaris statim (*ends imperfectly*). The table on f. 63ᵛ shows that (9–11) were 'Exhortatio de conuersatione et vnde fasciculus mirre colligitur'; 'Qualis monachus debeat esse. Quid factum sit de columba . . .'; 'De temptacionibus et de modis temptandi'.

ff. i+127. 100×71 mm. Written space 60×45 mm. 16 long lines. Collation: 1⁸ wants 3 2–10⁸ 11⁶+1 leaf after 1 (f. 81) 12⁸+1 leaf before 1 (f. 87) 13–16⁸. Initials: (i, ii) 4-line (f. 65 only) and 2-line, red or blue. Capital letters in the ink of the text filled with pale yellow. No cover.

Written probably in the Netherlands, for monastic use. 'William Brown', f. 72, s. xviii. 'Eastern District' on a printed stamp, f. 1.[1]

9. *Arma Christi* (*in English*) s. xv med.

(*a*) O veronicle I honoure him in the . . . Ihesu crist vs þiþer seende Amen. (*b*) I thanke þe lord þat þou me wroȝt . . . Derworþe lord for þi pite Amen. (*c*) These armis of crist boþe god and man . . . of paradon these popes ȝeue þe. Anime eorum et omnium fidelium defunctorum per misericordiam tuam domine requiescant in pace amen. A.M.E.N.

The Arma Christi in (*a*) 142, (*b*) 42, and (*c*) 34 lines of verse. *IMEV*, nos. 2577 and 1370. (*a*) is illustrated by pictures of the twenty-four arms, Veronica, Cultellus, Pellicanus . . . Sepulcrum: cf. the edition by R. Morris, *Legends of the Holy Rood; Symbols of the Passion and Cross Poems* (EETS xlvi), pp. 170–93. (*c*) is in red ink. The dorse is blank.

A roll of four membranes, 2,220 mm in length and 127 mm in width. The pictures are ranged in a 25 mm wide strip down the left side opposite the verses which go with them: from the point where they cease the margin has been cut off. Headings (Veronica, etc.) in gold. Initials: (i) 2-line *O* in gold on faded ground; (ii) 2-line, blue with red ornament or gold with violet ornament. Line fillers in gold and blue.

Written in England.

[1] The Scottish Vicariate-Apostolic was divided into Eastern, Western, and Northern Districts in the Period from 1827 to 1878.

BLICKLING HALL

The library was assembled by Sir Richard Ellys (1688–1742), of Nocton, Lincolnshire, and catalogued for him by Michael Maittaire (1668–1747). It was moved to Blickling Hall in s. xviii. Maittaire made his catalogue by using the blank rectos of a huge repertory of books written in a Germanic hand, s. xviii in., and bound in ten volumes. The repertory originated evidently in Zürich and may be the work of Johann Baptist Ott (1661–1742) mentioned by H. J. Leu, *Supplement zum Helvetischen Lexicon*, iv (1789), 412: '*Conradus Gesnerus* redivivus et multiplicatus, seu Lexicon omnium autorum juxta alphabetum, 50 Vol. in 4'.[1] No copy of this work has been traced.

Probably eight of Ellys's manuscripts were sold in the Marquess of Lothian sale, New York (Anderson Galleries), 27 Jan. 1932, lots 1 (Blickling Psalter), 2 (Blickling Homilies), 3 (Bible, now New York, Pierpont Morgan 791), 5 (cf. below, 6855), 16, 19, 20 (now Princeton, U.L. 89), 21. Blickling Hall and its contents became the property of the National Trust in 1940.

6844. *Orationes et epistolae*   s. xv²–xvi¹

Sixty-two leaves bound after (J. Sacranus), *Errores atrocissimorum Ruthenorum* (ff. 4, Cologne 1507?) and before Paulus de Roma, O.P., *Tractatus in favorem religionis Ierusolimitan'* (ff. 12: *BMC* i. 42) and two Zell quartos of writings of pope Pius II (Goff, P. 696, P. 656). Arts. 2–5, 8, 10, 11 are concerned with events of 1452–60. Arts. 9, 12 are later additions.

1. ff. 1–3 Iohannis auruspi viri eloquentissimi in allexandri hanibalis et Scipionis comparacionem e greco in latinum conuersum prohemium feliciter Incipit. Cum in rebus bellicis . . . neque hic quidem spernendus est.

Giovanni Aurispa's translation of Lucian's dialogue was printed at (Padua) in 1482 (Hain 10276; *BMC* vii. 926).

2. Letters of John of Capistrano, O.F.M.: (*a*) ff. 3ᵛ–10 Copia litterarum destinatarum per fratrem Iohannem de Capestrano ad omnes Barones Nobiles et famosos Bohemie. qui prage debent conuenire pro quadam eorum dieta celebranda secunda feria post octabas pasche. Oracio profecta et luculenta probatissimisque argumentis referta. Credo magnifici ac preclarissimi barones . . . Ex ponto in Regno Bohemie xvᵃ aprelis 1452°; (*b*) ff. 10ᵛ–11 and (*c*) ff. 11ᵛ–12ᵛ Letters to Pope Calixtus III, 24 July and 17 Aug. 1456, after the victory over the Turks at Belgrade.

(*a*). Against the Hussites: cf. J. Hofer, *Johannes Kapistran*, edn. 1964–5, ii. 121–6, who refers to a printed text in A. Hermann, *Capistranus triumphans*, 1700, pp. 371–8. (*b*, *c*). Printed in Wadding, *Annales Minorum* (ed. 3, 1932), xii. 796–8 and 430–2. (*b*) has been noticed hitherto only in a Salzburg manuscript: cf. *AFH* xix. 63–75.

3. (*a*) ff. 12ᵛ–13 Missiua Regis ladislai ad papam Calistum in facto Turcorum. Beatissime pater et domine post debitam subiectionem . . . Legatum et visita-

[1] I owe this suggestion to Dr. Bodmer of the Centralbibliothek, Zürich.

cionem apostolice gracie . . .: Prag, 26 Jan. (*b*) f. 13ʳᵛ Ladislaus to the emperor Frederick III, 'Detulerunt ad audienciam nostram comites de Segina . . . conseruentur', Prag, 9 Febr.

(*a*) is about his legate and (*b*) about restoring castles to Bonatus.

4. ff. 14–16ᵛ Ad serenissimum d. ladislaum Vngarie et Bohemie regem etc. Iohannis de Castilio Episcopi Papien' legati apostolici exhortacio in Turcos. Tametsi nichil dubitet summus et maximus pontifex noster lugubrem . . . qui te felicem faciat etc.

Giovanni de Castigliano's letter written after the capture of Constantinople by the Turks 'ante hos plurimos dies', so shortly after 28 May 1453.

5. ff. 16ᵛ–20 Iam pridem audita et reddita est sermonis vicissitudo Reuerendissime pater . . . Cuius pedibus se iterum recommendat etc.

To the Pope on the matter of the Turks.

6. ff. 20–24ᵛ Leonardi Iustiniani Veneti viri patricii oracio habita in funere clarissimi viri Caroli zeno in celestibus. Maximum et amplissimum manus . . . ac opere declaremus.

L. Giustiniani, †1446. Printed often. *Orationes funebres*, ed. 1613, pp. 140–9.

7. ff. 25–9 Ad Regem ladislaum Vngarie Bohemieque Per Reuerendum in cristo patrem D Episcopum Caphensem In sacra Theologia magistrum ordinis fratrum predicatorum. Sacra regiaque maiestas peractis a sede apostolica michi commissis in partibus armenie inferioris . . . quibus nunc labor durus esse uidetur Amen.

A report on Armenia by Jacobus Campora of Genoa: *SOPMA*, no. 2064 (cf. 2063); Emden, *BRUO*, p. 344. Printed, with some omissions, by N. Iorga, *Notes et extraits pour servir à l'histoire des croisades*, 4th series, Bucarest, 1915, 57–63.

8. ff. 29–34ᵛ Iohannes de Castiliano Episcopus papien' Sanctissimi domini nostri pape legatus ad dietam franckfordien' Exhortacio in Turchos. Pollicitus sum hoc tempore mee legacionis . . . qui est vera salus dominus et deus noster Amen.

Cf. art. 4. The diet was in Oct. 1454.

9 (quire fillers, s. xvi in.). (*a*) f. 35 Questio mota in consilio Constan' cum Iohannes Huyss allegabat sibi saluum conductum datum a rege Rhomanorum. Vtrum liciat alicui dare heretico saluum conductun . . ., followed by Gerson's 'Determinatio' under six heads, '1ᵃ conclusio. Rex potest licite . . .'. (*b*) ff. 35ᵛ–36ᵛ Letter of Pope (Leo X) to King (Francis I of France?), Rome, 4 Jan. 1517, 'Charissimo etc. Quod scripsimus superioribus diebus maiestati tue de rumoribus victorie Turcarum tiranni contra sultanum egypti dominum . . .'.

(*b*). At the end the date is followed by the words 'Reseruatum apud nos pro copia'.

10. (*a*) ff. 37–9 Infrascriptos articulos dederunt domini Ambasiatores . . . in factis Turcorum. (*b*) ff. 39ᵛ–40ᵛ Etsi in omnem terram Reuerendissime in cristo pater et domine metuendissime . . . felicem non posse habere exitum arbitrantur principes et domini nostri predicti.

(*a*). Ten articles presented by the ambassadors of Frederic III at the diet of Mantua

(1459) 'in factis Turcorum' and the reply to them in nine paragraphs, 'In primis oblaciones nostras . . . possit et certificet'. (b). Refers to the diet.

11. Speeches: (a) ff. 40ᵛ–46ᵛ Reuerendissime in cristo pater . . . Censebant magnifici venerabiles et spectabiles oratores . . . non relinquatur; (b) ff. 47–9 Reuerendissime in cristo pater et domine michi metuendissime . . . per organum Reuerendissimi in cristo patris domini Archiepiscopi Sepontini . . . non possunt tute; (c) ff. 49ᵛ–50 Vellem prestantissimi oratores . . . secuturam intelligerem; (d) ff. 50ᵛ–60 Responsio domini legati ad responsionem dominorum oratorum et fraterna correctio atque exhortacio. Multa quidem et ante hac . . . vnanimi consilio decernemus; (e) ff. 60ᵛ–61 Putabamus grata . . . postulamus et depreca-mur. B Episcopus thusculanus Cardinalis Nycenus per germaniam apostolice sedis legati; (f) f. 61ʳᵛ Neque nobis grati sunt. neque fuerunt . . . ostendere presumatis.

(a). Partly printed by H. C. Senckenberg, *Selecta iuris* (1738), iv. 347–57. (b). Ibid. 334–47. (c–f) are from the time when Cardinal Bessarion was papal legate in Germany, 1460–1, and are printed by L. Mohler, *Kardinal Bessarion*, iii (Quellen und Forschungen aus dem Gebiete der Geschichte, xxiv, 1942), 399–401, 384–98, 401–2, 403. All four occur in Vat. lat. 4037.

12 (added, s. xvi in.). Letters of Beatrix of Cordova to her lover Matthew: (a) f. 62ʳᵛ Iucundissime citra omnem . . .; (b) Gratissime fuerunt littere tue . . .; (c) Diu tacitam percutiens amor tuus . . .

(a) is dated Rome, 12 Dec. 1511. (b, c) in the same hand as (a) are on the two blanks at the end of Goff, P. 656. After (a) the scribe wrote 'Collationata est presens Copia ex vero suo originali per me Iohannem de borcfren ipsa die Conuersionis sancti pauli anno etc. 1517' and after (c) 'Collacionate sunt presentes epistole ex suo vero originali decima nona decembris Anno etc. xvii Per me Iohannem Darp de borcfren concordantque cum suo originali de verbo ad verbum quod protestor manu mea propria'.

ff. 62. 205 × 140 mm. Written space c. 165 × 90 mm. c. 34 long lines. No ruling, but folds to make margins. Collation: 1–4¹² 5¹⁴. Written, except arts. 9, 12, in a neat cursiva by one hand. No coloured initials. German binding, s. xvi¹, covered with brown leather bearing a roll with heads in medallions (IVDIT, VERVS, HESTER) and a cartouche containing the date 1538, not, it seems, listed by Haebler.

Written in Germany and bound with printed texts in or before 1517, perhaps for the writer of arts. 9, 12, Johannes Darp of 'Borcfren'. 'Henricus ab Horuel Epeus (?) Anno 1568' is on the title-page of Sacranus. Entered in Maittaire's catalogue under *Rutheni*.

6849. *'Flosculus ex prato', etc.*   s. xv²–xv/xvi

1. ff. 1–83ᵛ Incipit hic series descripta parabolarum. flosculus Ex prato dem-ptarum legitur ut flos. Plurimis ex liberis (sic) titulatim et ordine scriptis. sed salomon primo quem dauid genuit israhel Rex uenit in ritum. fundens prouerbia siue parabolas quidem audi quod protulit idem. Audiens sapiens sapientior erit . . . confici nequeat. Explicit.

A numbered series¹ of extracts: from Proverbs, Ecclesiastes, Wisdom, Ecclesiasticus (1–4); 'de exortacionibus ysocratis ad dunonitum (?sic)' (5, ff. 10ᵛ–12); 'de exordiis summe gui-

¹ 80 and 81 are omitted from the numbering. I have supplied the numbers 99 and 122 and made changes where the scribe wrote 74 instead of 72 and 84 instead of 87.

donis fabe' (6, ff. 12–15ᵛ); from Valerius Maximus, Sallust, and Vegetius (7–9); from Cassiodorus (10–12); from Cicero and Seneca (13–29, 30–45); from bks. 1–5 of an unnamed work on natural history (46: the first excerpt begins 'Auaricia quicquid omnibus astulit'); from Terence, Boethius, Fulgentius, and Quintilian (47–52, 53–64, 65, 66); from 'De discalone (*sic*)' and 'Compendium philosophie' of Hugh of St. Victor (67, 68); from the De amore of Andreas Capellanus (69: the first excerpt begins 'Res imperfecte modica turbatione deficiunt'); from Isidore and Lactantius (70, 71); 'socratis' (72, 74); from Pliny the Younger (73); 'de libro epistolarum synodii qui dictus est salmanus' (75); 'beati Enodii episcopi papiensis' (76); from Deuteronomy and Psalms (77, 78); from Jerome's letters (79); from Isaiah, Gospels, Catholic Epistles, and Pauline Epistles (82, 83–6, 87–9, 90–7); 'de libris legalibus digestis' (98); from Codex Justiniani, Institutes, and Authentica (99–101); from Aristotle (102–21: the texts of Metheora, De sensu et sensato, and De historia animalium are noted as being 'secundum nouam translacionem'); 'de libro primo policrationis compilati a iohanne solobmense anglico' (122). f. 84ʳᵛ blank.

2. ff. 85–92ᵛ Partes oracionis quot sunt? Octo. Que? Cognicio substancie ... vbi uero sunt gaudia amen. Et sic est finis donati spiritualis.

Printed in du Pin's edition of Gerson (1706), iv. 835–44.

3. ff. 93–125ᵛ Incipit prefacio soliloquiorum sancti ysidori hyspaniensis episcopi. In subsequenti hoc libro qui nuncupatur sinonima ... Anima mea in angustiis est ... penitencie esse noscuntur. Explicit liber soliloquiorum (*etc.*).

PL lxxxiii. 825–65/2 dignitate prelatus, followed by fourteen lines, 'Sicut septem sunt capitalia vicia ...'. Bk. 2, f. 108ᵛ.

4. ff. 125ᵛ–165ᵛ Domino et patri carissimo petro portuen' episcopo lotharius indignus ... exaltetur. Liber primus et continet ad quid miser homo nascatur. Et primo ponit de miseria hominis iheremias. Quare de vulua ... et ignis ardens in secula seculorum. Amen. Explicit liber de miseria humane condicionis uel contemptu mundi quem edidit Innocentius papa tercius. cum adhuc esset sanctorum Sergii et Bachi diachonus cardinalis.

Ed. M. Maccarrone, 1955; PL ccxvii. 701–46. Text in paragraphs, with headings, but without numbers. Bk. 3, f. 157. The beginning of bk. 2 is not indicated.

5. ff. 165ᵛ–167ᵛ Ad agendum penitenciam mouentur quatuor de quibus bernardus. Nimis durum ... et opere per laborem.

Six paragraphs, the first and last on penitence, and the fifth on the seven heavens, quoting 'Rabi maximus philosophus'.

6. ff. 168–72 Quoniam multi errant in loquendo ... ideo ego breuem doctrinam sub dicendis et tacendis ... utiliter applicari etc. Explicit libellus de forma loquendi bonus et vtilis.

A commentary on the verses 'Quis cui quid dicas cur quomodo quando requiras' (Walther, *Sprichwörter*, no. 25428).

7. ff. 172ᵛ–189 Incipiunt meditaciones beati augustini. Eya nunc homuncio fuge paululum ... et ignis ardens. Expliciunt meditaciones beati Augustini.

For this text cf. below, Edinburgh, New College, Med. 3, art. 10, and Römer, i. 377. ff. 189ᵛ–193ᵛ were left blank.

8 (added, s. xvi). f. 193 'die sabbato viiᵃ mensis Ianuarii xiᵃ hora post meridiem natus est ludouicus fumee quem leuauit de sacro fonte baptismatis reuerendus in theologia magister dominus tesaurarius ecclesie metropolitane turonensis

magister Iohannes brette et arnolfus ruse generalis monetarum cum sorore
sua kathelina et erat luna in aquario'.

ff. i+193. f. i is a medieval parchment leaf. 210×142 mm. Written space 150×90 mm.
31–2 long lines. Collation: 1–7¹² 8–20⁸ 21⁶ wants 6, blank, and probably now f. i. Written
in current hybrida, arts. 1, 2 in a good hand. In art. 1 catchwords are written vertically.
Initials: (i) f. 1, 3-line, blue patterned in white on a decorated gold ground: prolongations
in colour and gold ivy leaf form a border on three sides; (ii) f. 85, 2-line, gold on red and
blue ground, patterned in white; (iii) 2-line, blue or red. Binding of s. xviii. Secundo
folio *letificat*.

Written in France. 'A[..] lucas fumee chanoine de tours prieur de sainct martin lez bourges',
f. 189, s. xvi: cf. ff. 83ᵛ, 165ᵛ. 'Ludouicus fumee Iunior. Ex domino (?) Tho. Ruze', f. 193,
s. xvi: cf. art. 8. A shield flanked by symbols of the evangelists at the foot of f. 126, s. xvi:
azure two fesses or accompanied by six besants argent 3 2 1.¹ 'R' on the fore-edge at the
head and 'G' on the tail. 'B. Schroder kost 19 mark 14ˢ' inside the end cover. Entered in
Maittaire's catalogue: 'Flores Parabolarum Salomonis ... MS. in Pergameno, in 4ᵗᵒ
penes Illustr. D. D. Rich. Ellys'.

6855. *Biblia*   s. XIII med.

1. ff. 1–458ᵛ A Bible in the usual order and with 62 of the 64 common prologues
(cf. Bristol Public Library, 15): the prologue to Wisdom is absent, as not in-
frequently in otherwise regular Bibles, and the prologue to Philippians came on
a leaf now missing after f. 424.

A new chapter begins on a new line from f. 16ᵛ (Genesis 36): before this the text is written
without breaks. f. 197 is torn and the end of Esther lost. A new scribe began Job on a new
quire, f. 198; the first prologue of Job, Cogor ..., was copied twice, on f. 197ᵛ and on f.
198. Psalms are numbered in the margin in an early hand. After Apocalypse is 'Explicit
iste liber 'Alberti''. Corrections to the text are often in carefully shaped red frames in the
margins, for example on ff. 44, 47ᵛ, 49ᵛ, 61.

2. ff. 459–495ᵛ Aaz apprehendens ... Zance. ista requies etc' (*ends imperfectly*).

The usual dictionary of Hebrew names, the last leaf missing and ff. 493–5 damaged.

ff. iii+495+iii. 190×135 mm. Written space *c.* 135×95–85 mm. 2 cols. 52 lines.
Collation: 1¹⁶ 2²⁴ 3–7¹⁶ 8²⁴ 9–11¹⁶ 12 five (ff. 193–7) 13–18¹⁶ 19¹⁴ 20–26¹⁶ 27¹⁶ wants 7 after
f. 424 28¹⁶ 29⁸ (ff. 451–8) 30–31¹⁶ 32⁶ wants 6. Several hands: the scribe who began at
f. 198 got more on a page although he left a wider space between the columns. Initials:
(i) of books and prologues and the usual eight principal psalms, red and blue with ornament of both colours; (ii) of psalms, 3-line, and chapters, 2-line, red or blue, with ornament of the other colour; (iii) of psalm verses, Genesis 2–35, and in art. 2, 1-line, red or
blue. Capital letters in the ink of the text are filled with red. German binding of brown
leather over wooden boards, s. xvi: three rolls, the outermost and broadest including
St. George and the dragon, a bearded head in medallion, and a double-headed eagle.
Secundo folio *cum legeret*.

Written perhaps in Germany. A (to me) difficult inscription in German at the foot of f. 2
begins 'Anno domini 1545 vmb eyn kyndtlein dage (?)' and records the death of 'goes in

¹ According to the *Grand armorial*, iv. 78, the arms of Fumée are 'D'az. a 2 fasces dor
accomp. de 6 besans du mesme pose en orle 3.2.1'.

der hallen (?)': the same hand wrote occasionally in the margins, for example on f. 283. Probably the quarto Bible recorded in Maittaire's catalogue.[1]

6864. *Gregorius, Dialogi; etc.*   s. xii/xiii–xiii in.

1. ff. 1–34ᵛ 'Capitulum primum'. De honorato puero . . . a morte suscitauit (*table of 36 chapters*). Quadam die nimis . . . hostia ipsi fuerimus.

Gregory, Dialogues. *PL* lxxvii. 150–429. An imperfect copy lacking all between 'quod postulabat', the last words of ch. '43' of bk. 4, and 'calciamenta abstraheret' in ch. '65' of bk. 4 (ed. 308ᴀ–417ᴀ) in a gap of probably sixteen leaves after f. 32. Bk. 2 (39 chapters), f. 9; 3 (47 chapters), f. 18ᵛ; 4 (73 chapters), f. 33. A table of chapters in front of bks. 1–3.

The scribe began quires 1, 2 by writing 'In nomine patris et filii et spiritus sancti' in the upper margin. 'loke' on f. 4ᵛ and 'loke de sancto paulo' on f. 26ᵛ by a reader of s. xiii.

Arts. 2 (s. xii/xiii) and 3 (s. xiii) fill the space remaining in quire 5.

2. (*a*) f. 34ᵛ Qualiter Processiones et letanie fiant in quadragesima. Omni quarta feria et sexta fiat processio hoc ordine. Prius aspergatur . . . et pergit processio ad altare Sancti Iacobi. uel ad altare sancti Iohannis . . . Vt aeris serenitatem uel temperiem nobis tribuere dign'. Te Ro*gamus*. (*b*) f. 35 Litanies for Tuesday to Saturday set out in five columns. (*c*) f. 35 Ich geleue on þane fader alweldende . . . 7 þat eche lif amen. (*d*) f. 35 [E]cclesię tuę quesumus domine uota benignus intende et.' beate uirginis tuę Ætheldrithe intercedentibus meritis ab omnibus nos absolue peccatis. per.

Three saints of each class are named in the litanies of (*a*) and (*b*) and the third martyr, confessor, and virgin is English, except once. The saints in (*a*) are: (apostles) Petre Paule Iohannes; (martyrs) Stephane Line Albane; (confessors) Siluester Iuliane Augustine cum sociis tuis; (virgins) Maria Magdalena Felicitas Ositha. The third saints in (*b*) are: (Tuesday) *M.* Oswalde, *C.* Eorkenwalde, *V.* Adelburga; (Wednesday) *M.* Thomas, *C.* Mellite, *V.* Adeldritha; (Thursday) *M.* Eadmunde, *C.* Benedicte, *V.* Wihtburga; (Friday) *M.* Alphege *C.* Dunstane, *V.* Sexburga; (Saturday) *M.* Adelberte, *C.* Cuthberte, *V.* Eormenilda. (*c*). The Lord's Prayer in English ('Kentish dialect') printed hence by A. S. Napier in *Modern Language Notes*, iv (1889), 137. Wyn is used, not *w*. (*d*) Collect of St. Etheldreda.

3. f. 35ᵛ Sententia anathematis post trinam denunciacionem. Ex auctoritate dei omnipotentis patris et filii . . . et satisfaccionem peruenerint. fiat amen.

4 (s. xiii in.). ff. 36–46 Incipit regula sancti Benedicti. De generibus uel vita Monachorum. [M]onachorum quatuor esse genera.' manifestum est . . . regna patebunt superna.

CSEL lxxv. 17–165. *Clavis*, no. 1852. The prologue is absent.

5 (s. xiii in.). ff. 46–8 Incipit regula sancti Augustini de uita clericorum quid precipue sit obseruandum in monasterio constitutis (?) ut nichil dicatur proprium et ut unusquisque a preposito uictum regimentumque accip'i'at. [A]nte omnia fratres karissimi diligatur deus . . . et in temptacionem non inducatur. Amen.

PL xxxii. 1377–84. *Clavis*, no. 1839. The outer half of f. 48 has been cut off. The verso

---

[1] Maittaire listed three manuscript Bibles, one in folio, one in quarto, and one in octavo 'Penes Ill. D. Ric. Ellys, Bar.'. The first of these was lot 3 and the last probably lot 5 in the Lothian sale.

was left blank and contains scribbles of s. xiv, one giving the number of Christ's wounds (5475) and another beginning 'Anno regni Regis E[dwardi] tercii post conquestum [. . .]'. f. 49, a flyleaf, or perhaps a leaf of the last quire, is now only a small fragment preserved for the sake of a table of contents, s. xiv in., listing arts. 1, 3, 4 and pasted to the recto of the modern flyleaf.

ff. i+48+i. 258×170 mm. Written space 197×120 mm. 2 cols. 41 or 42 lines. Collation: 1–4⁸ 5⁴ wants 4, blank, after f. 35 6⁸ 7 five. Quires 1–5 numbered at the beginning 1–4, 7: see above for the gap after quire 4. Art. 2, in a good round hand, must have been written after art. 1 but the script looks earlier and like a hand of s. xii. Initials of art. 1: blue and red, with ornament of one colour or both colours; (ii) f. 1, blue D, with a red ground outside and red ornament inside; (iii) 2-line, red or blue with ornament of the other colour; (iv) in tables of chapters, 1-line, red or blue. Initials omitted in arts. 4, 5. Binding of s. xix. Secundo folio *ceperunt*.

Written in England, probably in the south-east: cf. art. 2 *a–c*.

6867. *Stella clericorum, etc.* s. xv med.; 1439.

One hundred and eighty-one leaves bound after J. Brugman, *Vita alme virginis Lydwine de Schiedam*, printed in 1498 (*GKW* 5579).

1 (quires 1–3). (*a*) ff. 1–9 'Incipit vitas patrum sanctorum'. Benedictus deus qui wlt omnes homines saluos fieri . . . (f. 2) Primum igitur tamquam vere fundamentum . . . que facere alios dotes (*ends abruptly*). (*b*) ff. 9ᵛ–47ᵛ Exempla, etc., in short paragraphs, interrupted by (*c*), ff. 27ᵛ–28ᵛ mnemonic verses, and (*d*), ff. 32ᵛ–38 a moralizing piece on the twelve signs of the zodiac, beginning 'Sole intrante signum geminorum tunc herbe et flores'. (*e*) f. 38 Two lines of verse, 'Post tres sepe dies vilescit piscis et hospes . . .': Walther, *Sprichwörter*, no. 22066.

(*b*) begins with eighteen miracles of B.V.M., no. 3 about a canon of St. Gereon, Cologne, 'nomine habderadus', and nos. 16, 18 about Cistercians. (*c*). Seventeen sets of verses: (1) Ten commandments, 'Sunt precepta decem moysi que contulit almus . . .' (4 lines); (2) eight beatitudes, 'Pauper et in spiritu mitis . . .' (5 lines); (3) Seven gifts of the Holy Spirit, 'Sap. intel. . . . collige dona'; (4) Seven works of corporal mercy, 'Visito poto cibo . . .' (2 lines); (5) Seven works of spiritual mercy, 'Corripe suade doce . . .' (4 lines); (6, 7) Seven sacraments, 'Docens crisma dolor . . . (2 lines) vel aliter Abluo firmo cibo dolet . . .' (3 lines); (8, 9) Four cardinal and three theological virtues; (10) Seven articles of faith, 'Nascitur abluitur . . .' (2 lines); (11) Seven mortal sins, 'Monstrat siligia . . .' (2 lines); (12) Nine sins, 'Iussio consilium . . .' (3 lines); (13) Seven sins against the Holy Spirit, 'Inuidus impugnans . . .' (2 lines); (14) Five senses, 'Gustus odoratus . . .' (2 lines); (15) Seven keys of wisdom, 'Sis humilis rogitans . . . claues sapienter' (4 lines); (16) Pains of hell, 'Vermes et tenebre . . .' (3 lines); (17) Sins crying to heaven, 'Clamitat in celum vox . . .' (2 lines). Nos. 2–5, 12, 17 occur in editions of *Peniteas cito*, for example, ed. 1491 (Goff, M. 769), sign. D. iiiᵛ–D. iv. Nos. 5, 7, 10–13, 16, 17: Walther, nos. 3368, 177, 11568, 11195, 9990, 9552, 20207, 2821. Nos. 4, 10, 11, 14, 16, 17: Walther, *Sprichwörter*, nos. 33805, 15894a, 15032c, 10504a, 33159b, 2786. No. 5: cf. Walther, *S.*, no. 33805.

2 (quires 4–6). (*a*) ff. 48–59ᵛ De trinitate hoc tenendum est quod in vna substancia sunt tres persone . . . pro salute generis humane. (*b*) ff. 59ᵛ–69ᵛ Incipiunt auctoritates omnium doctorum. Sapiens dicit. Pauper vbi diuitem ceperit imitari perit. Sic monasteria depauperantur . . . vero superbie timor. (*c*) ff. 69ᵛ–83 Miscellaneous short theological pieces, including (f. 77ʳᵛ) a series

of thirty-eight sayings headed 'Incipiunt auctoritates', the first 'Plus valet cordis contriccio quam tocius mundi peregrinacio Aug.', (ff. 77ᵛ–81) twenty-seven 'mirabilia' under the heading 'De natiuitate domini nostri ihesu cristi et de diuersis miraculis in die natiuitatis', and (f. 82ʳᵛ) a note on the holy places, 'Ab oriente est introitus iherusalem . . .'. f. 83ᵛ blank.

3 (quire 7). (*a*) ff. 84–94ᵛ Incipit stella clericorum. Quasi stella id est peccatorum proprietates . . . et semper ve et sic est finis. Explicit tractatulus cuius stella clericorum extat titulus. Amen scriptum monasterii per manus cristiani de quaelbart'. (*b*) f. 95ʳᵛ Nota septem elemosinis dandis. Prima elemosina est quod homo . . . (*c*) f. 95ᵛ Five couplets: (1) Qui vult stare choro . . .; (2) Cum domino psallas psallendo . . .; (3) Nunc lege nunc ora . . .; (4) Mors tua mors cristi fraus mundi . . .; (5) Qui psalmos resecat et verba . . .

(*a*). Printed often: Hain 15060–80. (*c*, 1, 2, 4, 5). Walther, *Sprichwörter*, nos. 24965, 4128, 15210, 24574. (*c*, 3). Cf. Walther, *S.*, nos. 19347a–50.

4 (quire 8). ff. 96–99ᵛ Doctores theologie. Vt populus domini simus . . .

As above, art. 2*c*, ff. 81ᵛ–82, but continuing further. Aquinas and 'Magister in compendio' are quoted.

5 (quire 9). ff. 100–107ᵛ Miraculum de sancto andrea. Episcopus quidam religiosus agens vitam . . .

Miracles of ten saints, in the order of the church year, of Holy Cross, and of B.V.M.

6 (quire 10). (*a*, *b*) Lives of Sts. Martha, 'Martha hospita cristi 'siro patri' matre eucharia . . .' (ff. 108–111ᵛ), and Ludger, bishop of Münster, 'Beatus ludgerus ex patre thiadgrimo . . . et sic est finis secundum passionale' (ff. 111ᵛ–114). (*c*, *d*) Collecta de martha . . . Collecta de karolo magno . . . (f. 114ᵛ). (*e*) Five exempla added later in the space left blank on ff. 114ᵛ–115ᵛ.

(*a*, *b*). *BHL*, nos. 5548, 4946.

7 (quires 11–16). ff. 116–180ᵛ Memorare nouissima tua . . . Dicit beatus augustinus in libro suarum meditacionum . . . et intellegerent et nouissima prouiderent. Explicit liber finitus et completus anno domini mᵒ ccccᵒ xxxixᵒ die quinta post festum omnium sanctorum hora xiiᵃ in prandio. f. 181ʳᵛ blank.

Printed often: *GKW* 7469–7510 (Cordiale quattuor novissimorum).

8. The pastedown at each end is from a theological manuscript, s. xiv. Sections on Castitas and Contemplacio are at the front and on Avaricia, Ambulare, Anima, and Caro at the back.

ff. 181. Paper, except ff. 1, 6, 7, 12. A contemporary foliation of art. 2*a* '62'–'73'. 207 × 140 mm. Written space 190 × 120 mm. and in art. 7 140 × 90 mm. Frame ruling, except in art. 1*a*. 24–38 long lines. Collation: 1–2¹² 3²²+1 leaf after 22 (f. 47) 4–7¹² 8⁴ (ff. 96–9) 9–10⁸ 11–15¹² 16¹⁰ wants 7–10, blank; inserted slips, ff. 17*, 46*. Written in cursiva, current hybrida, and (art. 1*a*), textura by several hands. Initials in art. 7, 5-line and 2-line, red. Late fifteenth-century Netherlandish binding of wooden boards covered with brown leather decorated with a pattern of vertical, horizontal, and diagonal fillets, with small rosettes at the intersections: 'repaired at Cambridge in 1955'.

Art. 7 was written in 1439 and art. 3*a* by a named scribe at Münster, Westphalia. Bound with a printed book of 1498 at about that date. A table of contents on the flyleaf at the beginning, s. xv/xvi, covers the printed book and arts. 1–7 and is followed in the same hand by an ex-libris of the Premonstratensian abbey of Koningsveld: 'Liber Monasterii campi regis prope delft'. Entered in Maittaire's catalogue: 'Lydwinæ Virginis vita . . .'.

6881. *Dictys Cretensis, etc.*   s. xv med.

1. ff. 1–35 Incipit Prologus Troiane Hystorie A dicte Cretens. Conscripte. Dictis cretensis genere. gnoso urbe isdem temporibus . . . textus ostendit. Incipit liber primus. Cuncti reges qui minois . . . Neque tamen inualidus uirium. Ed. W. Eisenhut, 1958. Bk. 2, f. 5ᵛ; 3, f. 16; 4, f. 21ᵛ; 5, f. 26ᵛ; 6, f. 31ᵛ. f. 35ᵛ blank.

2. ff. 36–7 Excerpta ex agellio noctium atticarum. Tarentinus architas dum se pytagore . . . atque esse. ut uiuerent. (*blank 5-line space*) Exagerat quis culpam. propellit gratiam dum merita iactat.

Twenty paragraphs. The last four are from the beginning of bk. 16, xvi. 4. *1*, xvi. 15. 1, and xix. 2. 7.

ff. ii+37+ii. Paper. 287×210 mm. Written space *c.* 210×120 mm. 44 long lines. Collation: 1–2¹² 3¹⁴ wants 14 probably blank. Catchwords run vertically. Written in hybrida. Initials: (i) red with blue ornament or blue patterned in white with red ornament; (ii) 4-line or 3-line, blue or red; (iii) in art. 2, 2-line, blue or red. Capital letters in the ink of the text stroked with red. Gilt morocco binding, s. xviii. Secundo folio *menelaus*.

Written in northern Germany or the Netherlands. Probably once part of a larger book. Listed in Maittaire's catalogue: 'Dictys Cretensis . . . MS. apud Illustr. D. Ric. Ellys'.

6892. *P. Langtoft, Chronicle (in French); etc.*   s. xiv¹

1. (*a*) ff. 1–5 A descent of the nine kings of England from William I (f. 1) to Edward I (f. 5), one king to each page, which contains (1) a Latin couplet about the king, (2) a head-and-shoulders portrait of him, (3), except on ff. 1ᵛ, 2ᵛ, 3ᵛ, roundels in which are set the names of descendants of William I, Henry I, II, John, and Edward I, (4) on ff. 1ᵛ, 2ᵛ, 3ᵛ, seventy-two Latin verses, twenty-four to a page, forming a brief chronicle from the death of William II to the death of Richard I, 'Nota canunt gesta Ruffum . . . Regem Ricardum cristus teneat sibi care. Et velit Edwardum iuuenem sibi consimulare', and (5) notes of the length of reign and place of burial of each king. (*b*) f. 5ᵛ contains (1) a couplet, 'Princeps Edwarde non sit tua lancea tarde . . .', (2) a space (for a picture?), (3) twenty lines of verse, 'O rex anglorum dux et princeps populorum . . . Noli tardare Scotos miseros superare', and (4) four erased lines.

The verses and descents in (*a*) and (*b*) are in Bodleian, Laud misc. 637, ff. 75–6, and, except (*b*3), in B.L., Royal 20 A. ii, ff. 5ᵛ–10.¹ (*a*1). The first couplet begins 'Dux normannorum Willelmus vi validorum'. (*a*3). The roundels on f. 5 containing the names of the four eldest sons of Edward I are inscribed 'Iohannem qui obiit', 'Henricum qui viuit (*altered to* obiit)', 'Edwardum qui uiuit', and 'Alfurnum qui obiit'.

¹ But some text has been erased, Royal, f. 10, below the picture of Edward II and verses in French, 'En temps dyuer . . .', substituted.

2. ff. 6–100ᵛ Deu le tut pussant qe ciel e tere creayt . . . Le feu gregeys encountre et Rich' va percer (*ends imperfectly*: *catchword* Dal beke sa galeye).

Langtoft's French verse chronicle, ed. T. Wright, RS (47), 1866–7, 2 vols. The last words
here are in ed. ii. 72/23. Nine leaves are missing before this point, one after f. 37 with the
text in edn. i. 188/9–194/7 and eight after f. 60 with the text in edn. i. 338/3–380/10. The
Latin verses 'Finito Bruto . . . Anglis aliena' are in this copy as in Wright's D (f. 50:
edn. i. 264).

ff. i+100+i. 240×155 mm. Written space 195–175 mm high. 30–4 long lines. Collation:
1⁶ wants 6, perhaps blank, 2–5⁸ 6⁸ wants 1 before f. 38 7–13⁸. Quires 2–13 numbered at the
beginning (top of first recto) i–vii, ix–xiii. Written in anglicana of a slightly 'business'
type: *u* is current, *n* not. Capital letters in the ink of the text filled with yellow-brown.
Initials, 4-line (f. 6) and 2-line, not filled in. Binding of s. xvi², rebacked. Secundo folio
Suffra (f. 7) or *Henrici* (f. 2).

Written in England. In art. 1, *a* and *b*1—not in the same hand as *a*—appear to have been
written before the accession of Edward II. *b*2, 3 are in the hand of art. 2.

6898. *Juvenalis*   s. xv²

Semper ego auditor . . . omnes et torquibus omnes. Finis deo gracias amen.

Satires 1–16 in five books, as usual (1–5, 6, 7–9, 10–12, 13–16). Forty-four and a half lines,
'Sudauit clipeis . . . Sic pretextatos' (II. 126–70), were copied in error on ff. 7–8 after 'in
agris' (II. 79), crossed out, and marked 'vacat': they occur again in their proper place.
On the other hand thirty-one lines, 'Perditus . . . abstulit odo' (VIII. 212–42) copied in
error on f. 51ʳᵛ after 'et nos' (VIII. 163) remain out of place: VIII. 211 is the last line on
f. 52ᵛ and VIII. 243 the first line on f. 53. Many corrections in and above the line. Space
for the Greek after 'Sollicitent' (IX. 37) not filled.

An argumentum in a single line or in two lines of verse is placed before each satire except
the first and last,[1] Carpitura . . ., Odisti quia rhoma . . ., Crispini . . ., Quot mala . . ., Haec
satira . . ., Mendicant . . ., Notabilitas . . ., Concubitus . . ., Arguit hec hominum . . .,
Leuta reprehenduntur . . ., Arguit hec auidos . . ., Mens cruciat . . ., Imbuit . . ., Im-
manes . . . : cf. B. L., King's 29. They are marked in the margin 'de rosso', or 'de roso', or
'rosso' or 'ro'.

ff. ii+93+ii. Paper. 212×145 mm. Written space 145 mm. high. 21 long lines. Ruling
with a hard point. Collation: 1–4¹² 5 eleven (ff. 49–59) 6–7¹² 8¹⁰. Written in humanistica,
current except for three lines on f. 25ᵛ, eleven lines on f. 26ᵛ and the two last lines of the
text. Spaces for initials, 5-line on f. 1, and 2-line elsewhere, have not been filled. Binding
of s. xix. Secundo folio *Vnciolam*.

Written in Italy. Listed in Maittaire's catalogue under Juvenal as 'MS. Antiquum in
Charta. Penes. Ill. D. Ric. Ellys Bar.'.[2]

6899. *Ovidius, Heroides; etc.*   1466

1. ff. 1–68 Hanc tua penelope . . . Quos uereor paucos ne uelit esse michi.
Explicit Liber Ouidii Epistolarum Deo gratia amen 1466 die 23 mensis agusti
etc'.

---

[1] But the lines belonging to sat. VI, XI, XIII are written before the explicits of sat.
V, X, XII.

[2] Maittaire edited Juvenal in 1716.

Heroides, Epp. I–XIV, XVI–XX, XXI. 1–12. The scribe left out lines 39–142 of Ep. XVI on f. 45ᵛ and lines 35–86 of Ep. XVIII on f. 56, perhaps because an exemplar with twenty-six lines to the page lacked three leaves. Fairly numerous interlinear glosses and some scholia were added rather later in the margins, but not after f. 45ᵛ. f. 68ᵛ blank.

2 (added in the space remaining blank in quire 7). (*a*) f. 69ʳᵛ Parue pulex et amara lues . . . quam sibi me socium. (*b*) ff. 69ᵛ–70 Philomela. Dulcis amica ueni . . . sorte cecinit anas. (*c*) f. 70ᵛ Eight lines of Italian verse.

(*a*, *b*) in three hands, s. xv². (*a*). 38 lines. Walther, nos. 13745, 13752. (*b*). Walther, no. 4796; Riese, *Anthologia Latina*, no. 762, lines 1–22. (*c*) is of s. xvi¹.

ff. ii+70+ii. Paper. 315 × 145 mm. Written space 150 mm high. 25 long lines. Collation: 1–7¹⁰. Written in poor fere-humanistica. Rough initials: (i) f. 1, 5-line, red and green; (2) 2-line, red with red ornament. The first letter of each line is stroked with red. Binding of s. xix. Secundo folio *Si maneo*.

Written in Italy. Maittaire's description is pasted inside the cover. The entry in his catalogue under Ovid is 'Epistolæ. MS. in Charta. Penes Ill. D. Ric. Ellys Bar.'.

6910. *Breviarium Bonaventurae; Sermones; etc.*   s. XIII²

1. ff. 1–2 De eucharistia sciendum quod ad hoc quod conficeatur (*changed to* -iatur) exigitur ex necessitate ordo sacerdocii et materia panis . . .

Four paragraphs on the eucharist.

2. ff. 2ᵛ–51 [F]lecto genua mea . . . in gaudium dei mei qui est trinus et vnus deus benedictus in secula seculorum amen. 'Explicit breuiarium bonauenture domini albanensis fratris minoris'.

Quaracchi ed. v (1891), 201–91. A leaf missing after f. 12.

3. ff. 51–60ᵛ Si quis reginam anglie in sui custodia positam corrumperet . . .

At first, short paragraphs mainly containing exempla, for example (f. 57) 'Philomena dum cantat de nocte ponit se inter spinas ne capiatur a bubone sic est de penitentibus qui se affligunt in nocte presentis seculi et variis asperitatibus ut cilicio vigiliis Ieiuniis ne capiantur a diabolo'. They end on f. 58ᵛ, 'et non retinent', after which a small hand which has added extracts from Vitas patrum, etc., in the margins, continues in the text space with extracts from Bede, Historia ecclesiastica, and lives of saints, including Cuthbert and Guthlac. ff. 61–63ᵛ were left blank.

4. (*a*) ff. 64–142 Veniet desideratus cunctis gentibus . . . aggai ii. wlgo dicitur che mut greue ki atent prouerb' xiii spes que differtur affligit animam . . . Nota et expone. (*b*) ff. 142–169ᵛ Incipit proprium sanctorum. De sancto andrea. Suspendium elegit anima . . . Iob vii. ad laudem beati andree apostoli qui sicut hodie legitur. . . . Isti expoliant se tunica qua sunt induti ut Ionathas (*ends imperfectly*). (*c*) ff. 170–194ᵛ (*begins imperfectly*) est in iusticia scilicet operis . . . ne nudus ambulet et videant nuditatem eius (*ends imperfectly*).

(*a*–*c*). Sermons of (*a*) temporale, (*b*) sanctorale, and (*c*) common of saints: cf. Schneyer, pp. 501, 474, 480 (Petrus de S. Benedicto, O.F.M.). (*b*) is for fourteen feasts now, Andrew, Nicholas, Conversion of Paul, Purification of B.V.M., Annunciation of B.V.M. (2), Mark, Invention of Cross, Philip and James, Peter and Paul, Mary Magdalene, Chains of Peter, Laurence, Assumption of B.V.M., Bartholomew. (*c*) begins in the sermon for apostles before that beginning 'Tollite iugum . . . Cum quis diu . . .' (Schneyer, p. 480) and ends in a sermon for virgins, 'Que parate intrauerant . . . M^t 25. quod satis patet in hac virginum conuersacione . . .' (Schneyer, *Rep.*, iv. 799). Eight leaves are missing after f. 169. 'scribatur hic sermo de mulieri cananea' in red, f. 99, against unfilled space, f. 99^{rv}. 'istud non scribatur' in pencil at the foot of f. 142. Some pencillings in English in margins are hard to read: f. 71^v, 'from misdede . . .'; f. 95, 'þe blisse þat þou ast lorn . . .'.

5. ff. 195–199^v A projected index (to art. 4?) was laid out with red letters A–X at the head of the pages. Rather later, the hand which added to art. 3 filled part of the space with patristic extracts.

ff. i+199+i. A medieval foliation of art. 4, 1–139, takes account of the missing leaves. On ff. 64–74 rectos are lettered *a* and versos *b* and on ff. 86–169 the columns of each leaf are numbered *a–d* and the lines of each page *a–f* or *a–e* at intervals of eight or nine lines: letters and numbers are in red ink. 182 × 130 mm. Written space 130 × 95 mm. 37 or 38 lines, long lines on ff. 52–75 and two columns elsewhere. Collation: 1^{10} wants 1 2^{12} wants 4 after f. 12 3–5^{12} 6^8 wants 7, blank, after f. 62 7^{12} 8^{10} 9–15^{12} 16 three (ff. 170–2) 17^{12} 18^{12} wants 11, 12 after f. 194 19^6 wants 5 after f. 198. Written in current anglicana. Spaces for 2-line initials remain blank, except for a red *D* and a red *S* on f. 1. Binding of s. xix, uniform with that of MS. 6864. Secundo folio *recondantur*.

Written in England.

6917. *Suetonius*   s. xv med. (1452?)

1. ff. 1–175 (*begins imperfectly*) ab rhodo quo pertenderat . . . insequentium principum. (*blank*) Caesarum liber xii explicit.

Suetonius, Lives of the Caesars, lacking single leaves at the beginning—f. 1 begins at Jul. 4. 2—, between f. 56 which ends 'atque recita' (Aug. 101. 1) and f. 57 which begins 'uero (*sic for* Nero) aduenientem' (Tib. 2. 1), and between f. 168, which ends 'pene iustarum clas' (Dom. 4. 2) and f. 169 which begins 'domum quidem' (Dom. 7. 1). Blank spaces here and there for Greek words and other words: for example *lamie* is omitted at Dom. 1. 3 and *erarium* at Dom. 9. 2. Marginalia in the main hand in pink ink cease at f. 67^v.

2. ff. 175^v–176 (*a*) [C]aesareos proceres in quorum regna secundis . . . obitumque peregit. (*b*) Primus regalem . . . sua roma neronem. (*c*) [I]ulius ut perhibent . . . frater habenis. (*d*) [E]xegit penas . . . quos tenet imperii.

5+12+12+14 lines. (*a–c*). *PL* xix. 865–6. MGH, *Auct. Antiq.*, v. 2 (1883), 112–19. *Clavis*, no. 1406 (Ausonius). (*d*). Walther, no. 6055.

ff. iv+176+iii. f. iv is a parchment flyleaf. 300 × 210 mm. Written space 175 × 110 mm. 27 long lines. Ruling with a hard point: 29 horizontals, the first *and last* not being used to write on. Collation: 18 tens, wanting 1^1, 6^8, 18^1 and 18^{10}, a blank. Catchwords have ⸵. before and .⸵ after them. Upright humanistic script, apparently that of John of Mainz (see below): brown ink: *g* is conspicuous from about f. 40 with its large closed tail, a narrow oval about 4 mm long stuck on the vertical stalk descending from the upper part of the *g*: a capital letter if it comes at the beginning of a line is placed in the margin close to the outer of the two vertical bounders. Initials: (i) beginning each life (ten out of twelve remain), 10-line, usually gold on grounds of blue, red, and green, densely patterned with white interlace: some of the decoration has a heavier effect because of the extensive use of gold or gold paint: on f. 23^v, the most elaborate page, the gold is punched and the border ornament runs out into points of gold or colour; (ii) 1-line, pink: they cease with the marginalia; (iii) in art. 2, 1-line spaces not filled. Pages with initials of type (i) have a border on the left nearly the height of the written space and, either within the border or separate from it, a side-face portrait of the emperor in a square or round frame: the offset of a missing border shows on f. 57. Binding of s. xvi, calf with gilt centrepiece, corner-pieces and anglepieces: earlier the binding was apparently 'Braxilio rubeo cum quinque Brochis magnis super unaque alba et quattuor azuliis deauratis' (see below). Secundo folio (f. 1) *ab rhodo*.

Written in Italy (Ferrara?). Arms in the border on f. 23^v are of Este, 1, 4 azure three fleur-de-lis or 2, 3 azure an eagle displayed argent: cf. D. Fava and M. Salmi, *I manoscritti miniati della biblioteca estense di Modena*, 1950, pl. 41. Identifiable almost certainly with no. 29 in the Este catalogue of 1467 printed by G. Bertoni, *La biblioteca estense*, 1903, p. 216: Gaius Suetonius Tranquillus de Vita Caesarum nouus et pulcher in (c)art. membranis in forma mediocri littera antiqua cum principiis deauratis ad formam antiquam cum Armis et deuisis Ill^{m1} d.n. ducis Borsii in prima facie istius libri. Cohopert. Braxilio (*etc. as noted above*) Cart. in totum 168'. The number of leaves is not 168, but this is the number given in an inscription on f. iv, '[. . .]mi [. . .]e fortuna [. . .]gua n° 33 cartarum 168'. Presumably the Suetonius for which Borso d'Este owed four gold ducats in 1452 to 'Iohanni de Maguntia scriptori', 'pro residuo mercedis sue quia scripsit unum suetonium praef° Domino Nostro' (Bertoni, p. 255).[1] 'Caius Suetonius de Vitis Duodenis Caesaribus. Volumen CCV. non Petavianus', f. iv: for the marking of the non-Petau manuscripts in the collection of Queen Christina (1626–89) at Antwerp in 1655 with inscriptions like this see A. Wilmart, *Codices Reginenses Latini*, i (1937), ix. According to Wilmart, Isaac Voss was not a faithful curator and some manuscripts went astray at this time. 'Nicolai Heinsii', f. 1: for manuscripts in Queen Christina's collection belonging to Nicholaus Heinsius (1620–81), see Vatican, Reg. lat. 71, 161, 219. '307' and an erasure, f. iv. Entered in Maittaire's catalogue.

6931. *Faits des romains (in French)*   s. XIII med.

Quant diex ot fait le ciel et la terre et les iaues douces et salees . . . estoit nule qui grammment fust greuable par trestout le monde.

The *Faits des romains* (no title here), twenty-nine manuscripts of which are described by P. Meyer, *Romania*, xiv. 36–63. Larger initials and headings divide the text into thirteen main divisions: f. 45, Ci coumence de thebes; f. 58, Ci coumence de ceus dathenes . . .; f. 60^v, Ci coumence la uraie estoire de troie; f. 71, Que li grezois . . .; f. 82^v, Des assyriens . . .; f. 83^v, Ci commence de lestoirement de la cite de roume; f. 109, De nectanabris . . .; f. 127, Que cil de tarante . . .; f. 130^v, Ci commence la bataille entres ceus de rome et ceus de cartaige; f. 140^v, Que Hannibal assambla . . .; f. 152, Ci recoumence des macedoniens; f. 158, Ci coumence la destruction de la cite de cartage. Maittaire wrote a title on f. ii: 'Histoire ou Chronique generale du Monde, jusqu'au tems de Pompée le Grand.'

ff. iii+190+iii. Foliation of s. xvi. 330 × 250 mm. Written space 242 × 185 mm. 2 cols. 40 lines. Collation: 1–23^8 24^8 wants 7, 8, blank. Two 12-line pictures, *c*. 70 × 75 mm, on gold grounds framed in blue, each divided into four compartments; f. 4, the ark and its making; f. 24^v, Jacob and Esau. Initials: (i) f. 1, a damaged 13-line *Q* in pink on a ground of blue and gold, historiated (Creation); (ii) at main divisions, as set out above, 8–5 line, blue and red with ornament of both colours; (iii) 2-line, blue or red with ornament of the other colour. Binding of s. xviii lettered 'Histoires/de la creat/du monde'. Secundo folio *et uouloient*.

Written in France. 'N° lxxi' (?), f. 1, s. xvi. Entered in Maittaire's catalogue under the heading 'Histoire': 'MS. en velin Penes Ill. D. Ric. Ellys'. 'd:y:2', f. i^v.

[1] A manuscript of Livy, lot 29 in the A. Chester Beatty sale at Sotheby's, 3 Dec. 1968, was written by Johannes de Maguntia for the Este family. It is in the same hand as the Blickling Suetonius, to judge from the facsimile in the sale catalogue.

BLOXHAM SCHOOL

1. *Orationes, etc.* s. xv

A miscellany of prayers, two parts, ff. 1–93 and ff. 94–193, put together in s. xv.
The table of contents, eleven heads, on the end pastedown picks out arts. 1, 2,
23, 24, 28–30, 32, 46c for special mention and covers arts. 3–22, and 33 sqq. in
general terms. It ends with the words 'Alie oraciones hic habentur que per
singula tedet scribere'. A little German occurs in the margins (arts. 26, 36b).

1. Tracts on dictamen: (a) ff. 1–6ᵛ Ornatus oracionis elegancia composicione ac
dignitate conficitur elegancia facit latinitatem puram . . . sub compendio videa-
mus. Quid sit repeticio. Repeticio est . . . expresse declarantur; (b) ff. 7–17
[V]niuersis tabellionibus Ciuitatis bononiensis . . . magister de aquilegia Salutem
. . . iusticia dicitur esse iuris. Salutaciones ad summum pontificem . . . Quot
sunt virtutes tot ego remitto salutes. Explicit practica siue vsus dictaminis
Magistri Laurencii de aquilegia edita Bonon' etc.; (c) ff. 17ᵛ–19 Refulsit sol in
clipeos aureos . . . [C]um ergo ut dictum est rethorica est sciencia pauperes . . .
Sequitur de statu (ends abruptly); (d) ff. 19ᵛ–22 [H]omo albus est bonum latinum
est quare quia . . . (ends abruptly); (e) ff. 22ᵛ–23 (added). Notes from the Ethics,
the Bible, and 'Boicius de disciplina scolarium', and four couplets: (1) 'Non
sine labore . . .'; (2) Ordo natura . . .; (3) Continuo stude ne perdes tempora
lusu . . .; (4) In choro laycos. prohibet scriptura sedere . . .

(a). Sixty definitions, each with its heading. (b). Formulas for use in letter-writing. For
Laurence of Aquilegia, c. 1300, cf. L. Rockinger, *Briefsteller und Formelbücher des eilften bis
vierzehnten Jahrhunderts* (Quellen und Forschungen zur Bayerischen und Deutschen
Geschichte, ix, 1863), p. 952; H. Bresslauer, *Handbuch der Urkundenlehre*, 2nd edn., 1931,
pp. 260–1. This copy ends, as many do, with nine lines of verse, 'Quot generum species
Quot res sunt nomina rerum . . .'. (e1). Headed 'Pauper hinricus': cf. *PL* cciv. 858C,
Henricus Septimellensis (or Pauper), De diversitate fortunae, III. 92–3, and Walther,
Sprichwörter, nos. 18463, 18464a. (e2). Walther, *S.*, no. 20371. ff. 23ᵛ–24ᵛ blank.

2. ff. 25–35ᵛ Primo de percepcione sacramenti. In disposicione prioris est
utrum conuersi uel alii . . . et ne nos aperta inferi etc. (ends imperfectly).

Carthusian customs. 'Expliciunt multe declaraciones ordinis carth'' is on f. 33ᵛ, but
further customs follow, the first forbidding the reading of any but St. Jerome's prologues
to the Bible in church or refectory.

3. 36–7 [D]omine ihesu criste qui septem verba die ultimo vite tue dixisti . . .
Si quis hanc oracionem de die in diem flexis genubus deuote dixerit . . . sine dubio
apparebit.

Cf. Wilmart in *RB* xlvii. 273–4.

4. 37ʳᵛ [D]omine deus pater omnipotens creator celi et terre . . .

5. ff. 37ᵛ–38 [D]omine ihesu criste in tuam proteccionem me indignum famulum
heinricum hodie et in omni tempore . . .

6. f. 38ʳᵛ [G]racias ago domine tibi ihesu criste pro sexaginta et quinquies mille
wlneribus tuis . . .

7. ff. 38ᵛ–39ᵛ (*a*) [S]alue sancta facies nostri saluatoris . . . (*b*) Salue wltus reuerende nunc et semper inquirende . . . (*c*) Aue facies preclara. que pro nobis in crucis ara . . . (*d*) Deus qui nobis signatum lumen . . .

(*a*). *RH*, no. 18191. Occurs again below, art. 30*e*. (*c*). *RH*, no. 1787.

8. Prayers at mass: (*a*) ff. 39ᵛ–39* [D]omine ihesu criste qui hanc sacratissimam carnem . . .: followed by an indulgence of 2,000 years from Pope Boniface; (*b*) ff. 39*–40 [O]mnipotens et misericors deus Ecce accedo ad sacramentum vnigeniti filii tui . . .; (*c*) f. 40 [E]ya nunc oro ut sit michi piissime deus hoc dulcissimum sacramentum . . .; (*d*) ff. 40–1 [C]onsciencia domine ihesu criste trepidus (*sic*) accedo ad sumendum . . . Istam oracionem composuit dominus vrbanus papa quintus et concessit cuilibet deuote dicenti decem annos venialium peccatorum et tres annos mortalium peccatorum et septem karenas indulgenciarum.

(*d*). At first as art. 26*b*.

9. f. 41ᵛ Serenissima ac inclita mater domini nostri ihesu cristi Maria virgo . . .

10. ff. 41ᵛ–42ᵛ Celestis agricola deus pater omnipotens da nobis per ihesum cristum filium tuum dominum nostrum agrum mentis nostre sic colere . . .

11. ff. 42ᵛ–43ᵛ [A]ue crux gloriosissima et splendidissima . . .

12. ff. 43ᵛ–44ᵛ [P]atris sapiencia veritas diuina . . .
RH, no. 14726.

13. Devotions to B.V.M.: (*a*) ff. 45–48ᵛ [O] beatissima mea sancta Maria perpetua virgo virginum mater summe Benignitatis . . .; (*b*) ff. 48ᵛ–50ᵛ Quicumque hanc oracionem ante ymaginem beate Marie . . . . (*indulgence of 400 years from Pope Innocent IV*). Aue mundi spes Maria aue mitis . . .; (*c*) ff. 50ᵛ–51ᵛ [S]tabat mater dolorosa iuxta crucem lacrimosa . . . Hanc oracionem composuit et confirmauit leo papa et donauit omnibus vere confitentibus contritis et confessis eam deuote dicentibus septem annos indulgenciarum et tot karenas. (*d*) f. 51ᵛ Sequitur alia. [S]ancta maria rogo te per sanctam crucem in qua . . .; (*e*) ff. 51ᵛ–52 [C]ongaudete omnes mecum qui diligitis me . . .; (*f*) ff. 52–3 [S]aluto te sanctissima virgo Maria eadem salutacione qua te Gabriel . . .; (*g*) ff. 53–4 Cuidam sancto viro septem gaudia beate Marie sepius dicenti apparuit beata virgo dicens Cur fili mi . . . [G]aude uirgo mater cristi tu que sola meruisti . . .; (*h*) ff. 54ᵛ–56ᵛ Legitur postquam Beata virgo assumpta fuit in celum et Beatus Iohannes multum gemens fuit . . .

(*b*, *c*). *RH*, nos. 1974, 19416. (*g*). *RH*, no. 7023. (*h*). The annotator notes that there is a more perfect copy at f. '90' (art. 46*c*).

14. ff. 56ᵛ–57 [A]ue sanctissima caro cristi super omnia dulcedo. Aue celestis potus . . .

15. Prayers to angels: (*a*) ff. 57ᵛ–57* [S]ancte Michael archangele domini nostri ihesu cristi qui venisti in adiutorium . . .; (*b*) f. 57* [O]bsecro vos sancte Michahel sancte Gabriel sancte Raphahel . . .; (*c*) f. 57*ʳᵛ Sancte minister celestis imperii tibi deus omnipotens mei custodiam deputauit . . .; (*d*) ff. 57*ᵛ–58

Sancte angele dei ab omnipotenti deo . . .; (e) f. 58 [C]ustodi me sanctissime custos meos (sic) et ab omni inpugnacione . . .; (f) f. 58ᵛ Angele bone qui es michi datus . . .

16. Prayers invoking St. John Baptist and apostles: (a) ff. 58ᵛ–60ᵛ [S]alue felix o baptista veritatis euphonista . . .; (b) ff. 60ᵛ–66 [S]ancte Iohannes apostole dei et Ewangelista. qui es virgo electus . . .; (c) ff. 61ᵛ–62 [S]anctissime Petre apostole et dilecte dei qui confessus es . . .; (d) f. 62 [S]anctissime Paule vas eleccionis qui a cristo de celo . . .; (e) f. 62ᵛ Iste est sanctus qui amore contempsit minas hominum . . . martir Bartholomeus . . .; (f) f. 62ᵛ [O]mnipotens sempiterne deus qui hanc Ecclesiam venerandam in Beati apostoli Bartholomei veneracione . . . construxisti in qua eius suum corpus sanctissimum . . .; (g) f. 63ʳᵛ [B]artholomee apostole dei dilectissime qui modis multivariis tuis fulsisti miraculis . . .; (h) ff. 63ᵛ–64 [D]eus qui beatum Bartholomeum dilectum apostolum tuum Indiam visitare voluisti . . .; (i) f. 64 [A]postoli cristi et ab ipso electi vasa ecclesie . . .; (j) f. 64ʳᵛ [D]eus qui nos per beatos apostolos tuos Symonem et Iudam . . .; (k) f. 64ᵛ [S]ancti apostoli dei vos elegit dominus in salutem populi sui . . .

17. Prayers invoking martyrs and confessors: (a) ff. 65–6 O Beatissime Nicolae confessor domini et pontifex venerande . . .; (b) f. 66ʳᵛ Tu ihesus es testis. ubi cristoforus nominatur . . .; (c) ff. 66ᵛ–67ᵛ [S]ancte Herasme preciose martir. et pontifex cristi . . .; (d) ff. 67ᵛ–68 [P]rotector et propagator et amator omnium in te sperancium et credencium domine deus pater gloriose qui beatum herasmum . . .; (e) f. 68ʳᵛ [D]eus qui beati herasmi martiris tui atque pontificis barbe extraccionem . . .; (f) f. 68ᵛ [Q]uicumque in pericula uel in infirmitates ceciderint et nomen serui tui blasii . . .; (g) ff. 68ᵛ–69 [M]artires sanctissimi milites et (sic) victissimi Hermolae Achacie Allexandri et Marce . . .; (h) f. 69ʳᵛ O pastor eterne o martir egregie . . .; (i) f. 69ᵛ [D]eus qui preclara merita sanctorum decem milia martirum . . .

(b). RH, no. 34108. (h). RH, no. 13355. AH v. 93. Hermolaus.

18. Invocations of virgins: (a) f. 70ʳᵛ [A]ue virgo katherina Aue martir et regina . . .; (b) ff. 70ᵛ–71 [G]aude virgo katherina. Qua doctores lux diuina . . .; (c) f. 71ʳᵛ [G]aude virgo Katherina te refecit lux diuina . . .; (d) ff. 71ᵛ–72 O pia virgo katherina martir sancta et Regina. Electa mea specialis . . .; (e) f. 72ʳᵛ [A]ue virgo gloriosa Barbaraque generosa . . .; (f) ff. 73–74ᵛ [V]irgo sancta katherina amica dei dilectissima meum corpus et animam . . .; (g) ff. 74ᵛ–75 [V]irgo sancta Barbara quanta meruisti munera apud deum vnigenitum . . .; (h) ff. 75ᵛ–76 Barbara preclara cristi venerabilis ara . . .; (i) ff. 76–7 [A]ue uirgo Margareta. dei gracia repleta . . .; (j) f. 77ʳᵛ [A]ue gemma virtuosa. Dorochea graciosa mundi (sic) vite patens glosa . . .; (k) f. 78ʳᵛ [N]obilis et iusta mitis uirgo Dorochea . . .; (l) ff. 78ᵛ–79 'De sancta gerdrudi.' Domine ihesu criste qui ut errantem gregem . . .; (m) f. 79 [A]ue gerdrudis uirgo grata. Ex regali stirpe nata . . .; (n) ff. 79ᵛ–80 [S]alue sancta dorochea. audi queso vota mea. propter . . .; (o) f. 80ʳᵛ [G]aude pia Magdalena spes salutis vite vena . . .

(a–c). RH, nos. 2180, 6991, 6993. (e). RH, no. 2204. (h). RH, no. 2306. (j, k). RH, nos. 1824, 29887. (m–o). RH, nos. 1825, 18186, 6895.

19 (added in blank space at end of quire 7). f. 80ᵛ Verses: (a) Peccata in spiritum sanctum. In sanctum pneuma peccat . . . (3 lines); (b) Octo beatitudines. Mitis pacificis . . . (2 lines); (c) Clamitant ad deum vox sangwinis . . .

(c). Walther, *Sprichwörter*, no. 2786.

20 (added after art. 19). f. 81ʳᵛ Collects of Severus, Augustine, Holy Cross, and Cendo (?: . . . intercedente beato Cendone . . .).

21. Fifteen pieces, mostly prayers to Holy Spirit and B.V.M., in a new and skilled hand, filling quire 8 and ending imperfectly: (a) ff. 83–4 [S]piritus sancte omnipotens coessencialis et coeternus patri . . .; (b) ff. 84–5 [S]ancte spiritus assit nobis gracia. Que corda nostra sibi faciat habitaculum . . .; (c) f. 85ʳᵛ Veni sancte spiritus et emitte celitus . . .; (d) ff. 86–87ᵛ [L]auda syon saluatorem lauda ducem . . .; (e) ff. 87ᵛ–88ᵛ [P]neuma eukaristiarum terram rigans viniarum . . .; (f) f. 88ᵛ [V]eni rerum conditor illustra nostras mentes . . .; (g) ff. 88ᵛ–90 Vtherus virgineus tronus est eburneus . . .; (h) f. 90 Puellari (?) eleganter triumphale reuerenter . . .; (i) f. 90ʳᵛ Virgo en mater deifica post partum manens castissima . . .; (j) ff. 90ᵛ–91 Preconia etroclita tripudia reciproca . . .; (k) ff. 91–2 Salue mater saluatoris dulcedo cordis fauus oris . . .; (l) f. 92ʳᵛ [P]residiorum erogatrix . . .; (m) ff. 92ᵛ–93ᵛ Veni sancte spiritus reple tuorum corda fidelium . . . Deus in adiutorium meam intende . . . Veni creator spiritus mentes tuorum visita . . .; (n) f. 93ᵛ Quam dilecta tabernacula tua . . . (*ends imperfectly*).

(c, d, g, m). *RH*, nos. 21242, 10222, 21086, 21204. (n). Psalm 83.

22. f. 94ʳᵛ Aue ihesu nobis natus . . . Quicumque hanc oracionem Aue ihesu deuote dixerit: tria milia annorum venalium et tria milia annorum penitencialium a domino papa Iohanne XXII obtinebit.

RH, no. 23555.

23. ff. 94ᵛ–95ᵛ Septem gaudia beate virginis marie. Gaude felix anna nata. stirpe dauid generata . . .

24. (a) ff. 95ᵛ–104 Incipit dulceloquium beati bernardi de beata virgine maria . . . Gaude plaude clara rosa . . . (b) f. 104ʳᵛ Vite premonstratensis claustri steynuelnensis humi coloniensis. et lingwe rinensis. fuit quidam presbiter Iosephus vocatus . . .

(a). *RH*, no. 6898. *AH* xxxii. 92–9, where Hermann Joseph, monk of Steinfeld, is suggested as the author. A pen-and-ink drawing of B.V.M., Child, and a suppliant monk in the margin of f. 96.

25. (a) ff. 104ᵛ–105ᵛ Missa de facie domini. (b) f. 106 Prefacio de sancta cruce.

26. Prayers at mass, etc.: (a) ff. 106–7 Omnipotens et misericors deus. ecce ad sacramentum corporis et sangwinis . . .; (b) ff. 107–108ᵛ Conscientia domine ihesu criste trepida accedo . . .; (c) ff. 108ᵛ–110ᵛ Hic incipit oracio que sic genua flectendo debet dici. Pater noster. Aue maria. Domine ihesu criste fili dei viui per desolacionem qua derelictus es . . .; (d) ff. 110ᵛ–111 Oracio bona de quinque mille cccc et lxv vulneribus. Domine sancte pater omnipotens eterne deus qui ex nimia caritate . . .; (e) ff. 111ᵛ–112 'De domina nostra.' Memento

obsecro dulcissima mater et domina illius venerande stacionis . . .; (f) f. 112ʳᵛ
De tribus regibus oracio bona. Rex iaspar. Rex melchior . . .; (g) ff. 112ᵛ–113
'Pro vita bona. Et fine bona.' O gloriosissima domina sanctissima virgo maria . . .;
(h) f. 113ʳᵛ 'Pro fine bona.' Oracio. O virgo virginum et pia secundum magnam
misericordiam tuam . . .; (i) ff. 113ᵛ–114 Oracio serotina bona. Lege in sero.
Domine sancte pater omnipotens eterne deus, quicquid in hac die . . .; (j)f. 114ʳᵛ
Deprecor te sanctissima maria mater dei. pietate plenissima . . . Quicumque
hanc oracionem Deprecor te sanctissima deuote legerit. habet trecentas dies
indulgenciarum; (k) ff. 114ᵛ–115 Saluator mundi saluum me fac . . .; (l) f. 115ʳᵛ
Domine deus rex celi et terre pater clementissime. ante conspectum tuum . . .;
(m) f. 115ᵛ Innocencius papa dat septem annos indulgencie ad eleuacionem
hostie sancte dicenti in eleuacione. Aue principium nostre creacionis . . .

(c). A prayer of fifteen Pater Nosters and fifteen Ave Marias. German notes in the
margins of (d) and (f) and a reference to 'Vita cristi fol. 170 col. secunda' in the margin
of (d). (m). RH, no. 2059.

27. ff. 115ᵛ–116ᵛ De sancto Georgio. Georgii admirabilis victor in tormentis . . .
A memoria of St. George, RH, no. 27340.

28. ff. 116ᵛ–127ᵛ Incipit psalterium gloriosissime virginis marie. Quisque
hoc psalterium semel in die deuote dixerit. sciat certissime quod virgo decora
largissime sibi succurret in hora sue mortis. Aue beatissima origo conditoris . . .
(118ᵛ) Prima quinquagena. Hic incipit. Aue miseratrix tibi restat supplicare . . .
RH, no. 1702. A litany of B.V.M. begins at f. 123. f. 121 is mostly torn away.

29. ff. 127ᵛ–145ᵛ Hic incipiunt septem hore de sancta cruce . . . In passione
domini. qua salus datur homini . . .
RH, no. 8722. Hours of the passion of B.V.M. are added in the margins of all pages.

30. Prayers of the passion of Christ. (a) ff. 145ᵛ–146ᵛ Sequntur oraciones alie
de passione domini. Primo videlicet de corona capitis sui. O redemptor mundi
qui spineam coronam . . . (b) ff. 146ᵛ–147ᵛ Quicumque hanc sequentem
oracionem intimo corde recitauerit trecentos dies indulgenciarum ab Innocencio
papa quinto. misericorditer consequetur . . . Gracias ago tibi domine ihesu
criste pro sexaginta 'quinque' et quadringentis et quinquies mille uulneribus. . . .
(c) ff. 147ᵛ–148ᵛ Quicumque arma ista. siue insignia domini nostri ihesu cristi
deuote inspexerit. a summis pontificibus subscriptam indulgenciam consequetur. His qui arma ihesu cristi. quibus nos . . . (d) ff. 148ᵛ–150 Alia oracio.
Domine ihesu criste fili dei viui per sanctam carnem tuam . . . (e) f. 150ʳᵛ Hanc
oracionem Egydius magnus composuit et dominus Iohannes papa xxiiᵘˢ ipsam
centum dierum indulgenciis dedicauit. Salue sancta facies nostri redemptoris . . .
(f) ff. 150ᵛ–151ᵛ Beatus gregorius papa omnibus vere penitentibus et confessis.
veronicam intuentibus deuote hanc subscriptam oracionem dicentibus centum
dies indulgencie donauit. Omnis terra adoret 'te' . . . (g) ff. 151ᵛ–152 Sequentem
oracionem conposuit (altered to composuit) beatus augustinus. affirmans quicumque eam flexis genibus singulis diebus dixerit. numquam in peccatis
morietur. Aspice ad me infelicem pietas immensa . . . (h) f. 152ʳᵛ Hanc
oracionem dicentibus deuote. dat Iohannes papa xxiiᵘˢ ccc dies indulgencie.

'Sed Bonifacius eam composuit et vii annis dedicauit'. Fremuit (*sic*) ihesus spiritu . . .

(*b*). Notes in the margin refer to 'Vita hugonis patroni nostri' and to a 'libellus ubi habes oraciones de omnibus apostolis fol. 94, 95, 96'. (*c*, *e*). *RH*, nos. 27682, 18189. Prayers added in the margins of ff. 147–53.

31. f. 152ᵛ Deus qui per spiritus sancti graciam almani virginem odiliam ab oculorum cecitate . . .

32. ff. 152ᵛ–155 Hanc si cottidie vigili cantabis amore. Auxiliatricem domini sanctam genitricem. ante diem mortis presentem letus habebis. Hoc fore dico ratum. quia constat sepe probatum. O clementissima. O piissima. o dulcissima virgo maria . . .

Nearly all f. 154 torn away.

33. f. 155ʳᵛ Quicumque sequentem oracionem cum mentis puritate. et cordis deuocione. quinquies in die dixerit sine dubio beatam virginem in fine suo letus videbit. O maria virgo virginum Rogo te per patrem . . .

34. ff. 155ᵛ–159ᵛ Prayers at and after mass: (*a*) Aue principium creacionis nostre . . .; (*b*) Aue verum corpus domini nostri ihesu cristi. natum . . .; (*c*) Eya deus meus. misericordia mea remicte michi indigno sacerdoti . . .; (*d*) Huic sacramento corporis et sangwinis tui custodiendo committo animam meam . . .; (*e*) Ego gracias ago tibi piissime deus quia me ad ordinem presbiteratus . . .; (*f*) Gracias ago tibi domine deus meus qui me indignum peccatorem . . .; (*g*) Serenissima et inclita mater . . . pia et perpetua virgo . . .; (*h*) Gracias ago tibi omnipotens deus graciarum actione . . .

(*b*) is indulgenced with 300 days. The annotator added 'Innocencius papa dat tres annos'.

35. ff. 160–2 O maria virgo virginum que genuisti dominum. triumphatorem zabuli . . . *RH*, no. 11152.

36. (*a*) ff. 162ᵛ–163 Angele qui meus es custos pietate superna. . . . (*b*) added on a slip, f. 162a, by the hand which occurs in the margins. O myn lieber enghel zcart . . .

(*a*). *RH*, no. 22954. *AH* xxxiii. 24.

37. (*a*) ff. 163–4 O insignes excelsi regis milites et apostoli domini nostri ihesu cristi symon et iudas qui in cultu . . . (*b*) f. 164ᵛ Sancte symon apostole dei . . .

38. ff. 165–166ᵛ Oracio beati augustini. quam qui . . . exspirare. et sic incipit. Domine ihesu criste fili dei viui. qui in hunc mundum propter nos . . .

39. ff. 166ᵛ–168 Si quis infrascriptam oracionem deuote dixerit habebit a papa Iohanne tria milia dierum indulgenciarum de peccatis mortalibus et mille annos indulgenciarum de peccatis venialibus quas indulgencias papa predictus regine vngarie destinauit. O beatissima anima cristi sanctifica me . . .

40. ff. 168–9 Papa benedictus composuit infrascriptam oracionem . . . Deprecor te piissime domine ihesu criste fili dei viui propter illam eximiam caritatem . . .

The heading conveys an indulgence of Pope Benedict of the 5,465 wounds of Christ in days. The annotator notes in the margin that Pope John XXII indulgenced it with 6,640 years and gives a notice of Pope John.

41. Devotions to B.V.M.: (a) ff. 169ᵛ–170 Quidam cristianus in partibus occidentalibus natus deuocione egregius . . . dictaret. Gaude mundi gaudium maria laus virginum . . .; (b) f. 170ᵛ Aue maria mitis et pia gracia plena . . .; (c) ff. 170ᵛ–171ᵛ Beatus ambrosius scribit in exameron de quodam clerico . . . soluta est. Incipit autem oracio sic gaude maria dei genitrix uirgo immaculata; (d) f. 171ᵛ Gaude uirgo graciosa verbum verbo concepisti . . .

(d). *RH*, no. 7006.

42. (a) ff. 171ᵛ–172ᵛ Gaude pia magdalena spes salutis. vite vena . . . (b) 172ᵛ–174 Gaude pia magdalena mater sancta. lux serena spes salutis. vite vena . . .

(a). *RH*, no. 6895. (b) is an amplified form of (a).

43. Devotions to B.V.M.: (a) f. 174ʳᵛ O gloriosa virgo virginum et piissima sancta maria . . .; (b) ff. 174ᵛ–176 Aue dei genitrix et immaculata . . .; (c) f. 176 Iure coronata stellis es uirgo beata . . . (6 lines).

(b). *RH*, no. 1761.

44 (added by the annotator). ff. 176ᵛ–177ᵛ Seven prayers, the first 'Aue virgo mater cristi speciosa virgo admirabilis . . .' (*RH*, no. 23965). Headings of three of the others are 'Ut deus det tibi bonum finem', 'Quando in nocte habuisti grauia sompnia', and 'Quando vis sanguinem minuere'.

45 (added like art. 44). ff. 177ᵛ–178ᵛ In conspectu diuine maiestatis tue omnipotens et misericors deus . . .

46. Devotions to B.V.M.: (a) ff. 178ᵛ–182 Papa Innocencius concessit cuilibet dicenti sequentem oracionem virginis marie cottidie Centum dies indulgencie . . . Obsecro te domina sancta maria mater dei pietate plenissima . . .; (b) f. 182ʳᵛ O maria piissima. stella maris clarissima . . .; (c) ff. 182ᵛ–188 Scriptum reperi quod beatus iohannes ewangelista postquam virgo maria fuisset assumpta in celum . . . (f. 184ᵛ) Explicit prologus. Incipit oracio. Venite exultemus . . . Domina sancta maria . . . (*six prayers begin thus*); (d) f. 188ʳᵛ Oracio sancti bernardi de beata virgine maria. Aue sydus lux dierum Aue gemma mulierum . . .; (e) ff. 188ᵛ–190 Hanc oracionem beatus Bernardus composuit ad laudem gloriose virginis et incipit sic. Loquar ad cor tuum o maria loquar ad cor tuum . . .; (f) f. 190ʳᵛ Ad beatam virginem oracio. Tu es porta paradysi. tu ianua celi. tu templum domini . . .; (g) ff. 190ᵛ–191ᵛ Saluto te beatissima dei genitrix virgo maria regina celorum . . .; (h) ff. 191ᵛ–192 Deus qui de beate marie virginis utero . . .; (i) f. 192 Suscipiat pietas tua dei genitrix uirgo semper maria . . .; (j) f. 192ʳᵛ Gaude virgo gloriosa verbum verbo concepisti . . . (6 lines).

(a). The vision of an abbess is related in the heading. (b). *RH*, no. 13213. (d). The annotator says that this prayer is indulgenced with forty days. *RH*, no. 2115. (j). *RH*, no. 7006.

47. f. 193, an added slip, has 'O anima cristi sanctifica me . . .' (*RH*, no. 1090) with a reference to f. '74', now f. 167, where a farced version, art. 39, occurs.

48. The end-leaves, ff. i, ii, are two consecutive parchment leaves of a small

manuscript of sermons (?) in a good hand, s. xiii, with a written space of *c.* 100 ×
70 mm and 28 long lines to the page. A text begins 'Tulerunt ergo lapides'
(John 8: 9).

ff. ii+196, foliated i, ii, 1–15, 15*, 16–29, 29*, 30–9, 39*, 40–57, 57*, 58–192. ff. 94–192
have a contemporary foliation 1–99. For the flyleaves, i, ii, see art. 48. Paper. 150 ×
115 mm. Written space *c.* 110 × 80 mm. Long lines, *c.* 35 (arts. 1, 2) and *c.* 20. Frame
ruling or verticals only. Collation: 1¹² 2²⁰ wants 13–17 after f. 23 and 19, 20 after f. 24
3–8¹² (ff. 25–93) 9–17¹⁰ wants 10. Slips, ff. 162a, 193, inserted after 15⁹ and 18⁹. Nearly
all 11⁹ and 15¹ torn away (ff. 121, 154). Arts. 1–20 in current cursiva and the rest in a sort
of fere-textura. Flex punctuation (?) is used now and then. A few red initials (6-line,
f. 1). In arts. 2, 21–46 capital letters in the ink of the text are filled or touched with
metallic red. Binding of contemporary (?) wooden boards half covered with brown leather.
Secundo folio *quod duobus.*

Written in Germany. Two parts joined in s. xv. The second part, which begins at f. 94,
was much annotated by the main scribe of the first part, a Carthusian whose first name
was Heinrich (art. 5). 'Hic libellus est fratrum carth' in Errford' and—in red—'F 39',
f. ii. Entered as F. 39 primo in the late fifteenth-century catalogue of the Erfurt Charterhouse, *MBDS* ii. 352. Given by Mrs. Hinde, daughter of the Revd. P. Egerton, *c.* 1940.

2. *Antiphonale* s. XIII/XIV

Thirteen leaves, ff. (276)–288, from the winter part of an antiphonal containing
offices of the proper and common of saints: ff. (276)–280, Chair of St. Peter
(22 Feb.); ff. 280ᵛ–287ᵛ, In annunciacione beate uirginis marie (25 Mar.);
ff. 287ᵛ–288ᵛ, beginning of the common.

Cf. the texts in *SMRL* ii. 130, 132–3, 173–4.

ff. 13, foliated (276)–288 in s. xviii (?): f. (276) is framed and the recto side covered over.
460 × 330 mm. Written space 385 × 245 mm. 8 long lines and music. Collation: 1⁸
2 five. Letters are 7 mm high. Long-tailed *r* is used in headings occasionally. Initials:
(i) *c.* 105 × 90 mm, in colour patterned in white on grounds of gold and colour, historiated:
f. 276ᵛ, Christ and Peter; f. 281, Christ and B.V.M., and a kneeling woman in white head-
dress and red dress, holding a distaff; (ii) 1-line, in colour on coloured grounds; (iii) 1-line,
blue or red, with ornament of both colours.

Written in northern Italy.

BOSTON. PARISH CHURCH

Augustinus s. XII med.

1. ff. 1–133 Per idem tempus . . . bipertita est. Liber Beati Augustini In Genesim. Omnis scriptura diuina bipertita est . . . fine concludimus. Explicit exameron sancti Augustini episcopi liber xii.

In Genesim, preceded by the appropriate passage from the Retractationes. *PL* xxxiv.
245–486.

2. ff. 133ᵛ–156ᵛ Si eligerent manichei quos deciperent . . . que mihi uidebantur. Exposui.

De Genesi contra Manicheos. *PL* xxxiv. 173–220.

3. ff. 157–159ᵛ Licet multi ac probatissimi uiri diuerso quidem stilo . . . Aug'. Clarificata carne (*ends imperfectly*).

Pseudo-Augustine, Dialogus quaestionum lxv. *PL* xl. 733–8. Römer, i. 60.

ff. ii+159. f. ii is a medieval end-leaf, now backed with paper and probably once pasted down. 303×210 mm. Written space 220×145 mm. 2 cols. 33 lines. Ruling with a hard point: not only the first two and last two, but also the fifth and sixth and twenty-eighth and twenty-ninth lines on each page are prolonged into the margins and across the space between the columns. Collation: 1–5⁸ 6⁸ wants 3 7–20⁸. Moderate hand. Gay initials to each book of art. 1 in red, blue, green, and brown: those to bks. 1, 7, 11 include animals and animal heads. Medieval and probably contemporary binding of thick wooden boards now bare of leather, repaired and rebacked: the boards are cut square and are flush with the edges of the leaves: central strap (restored) and pin (missing). Secundo folio *intelligamus*.

Written in England. From the Cluniac priory of Pontefract: 'Iste liber pertinet Monasterio beati Iohannis apostoli et Ewang' de pontefracto', f. iiᵛ, s. xv. 'The gift of Mʳ Wᵐ Skelton Mʳ of Artes and Rector of Consby', f. iiᵛ: William Skeltons, rectors of Coningsby, Lincolnshire, †1602, 1660, and 1679.

BOWES MUSEUM

The Bowes Museum was founded at Barnard Castle in the second half of the nineteenth century by John and Josephine Bowes of Streatlam Castle, co. Durham. It has been administered by the County Council of Durham since 1956.

091/MED/1. *Missale* s. xiv²

1. ff. 1–5ᵛ Te igitur . . . Canon of mass: music on ff. 3–4. f. 6ʳᵛ blank.

2. ff. 7–28 Sanctorale, beginning imperfectly at Matthew (21 Sept.) and ending at Thomas the Apostle (21 Dec.).

The old foliation shows that seventy-three leaves are missing between f. 6 and f. 7. A cross reference to the feast of the Conception (8 Dec.: art. 7*i*) is in the margin of f. 27: Quere prope finem sub numero sequenti cccxxxv. Romanus and Theofredus (of Lérins, 18 Nov.) are added in November.

3. ff. 28–41 Common of saints.

4. ff. 41–2 In dedicatione ecclesie altaris sancti petri.

5. ff. 42–5 Masses of: angels; Holy Trinity; Holy Spirit; Holy Cross.

6. ff. 45–7 Mass of B.V.M.

7. 47–54 Masses: (*a*) of the Five Wounds; (*b*) Pro peccatis; (*c*) Pro mortalitate uitanda. quam dominus clemens papa sextus (1342–52) fecit . . . Et concessit . . .

ccxl dies indulgencie et uenie. Et omnes prefatam missam audientes debent portare in manu unam candelam ardentem et hoc per quinque dies continuos et eis mors subitanea et pestifera nocere non poterit. Et fuit probatum in auinione et in partibus occitanis officium. Recordare domine testamenti tui . . .; (d) Pro quacumque tribulatione; (e) Pro infirmis; (f) Apostolica sede uacante; (g) Pro peccatis; (h) In transfiguratione domini; (i) In conceptione beate marie.

8. ff. 55–61ᵛ Collect, secret, and postcommunion ('oratio', 'oblata' (or 'oblatum'), 'conplendum') of thirty-six masses: beati petri; pro omnibus sanctis; ad suffragia sanctorum postulanda; pro seipso; pro temptatione carnis (two forms); pro petitione lacrimarum; ad postulandam gratiam sancti spiritus; ad postulandam sapienciam; pro karitate; pro fideli amico; pro amico; contra paganos; pro apostolico; pro familiaribus; pro congregatione; sanctorum quorum reliquie in ecclesia continentur; pro concordia fratrum; pro principibus; pro peste animalium; pro peccatis; in tempore belli; pro pace; pro quacumque tribulacione; pro contencione; contra iudices male agentes; ad pluuiam postulandam; pro serenitate; pro tempestate; pro infirmis; pro salute uiuorum; pro iter agentibus; pro stabilitate loci; pro uiuis et defunctis; pro episcopo; pro sacerdotibus.

9. ff. 61ᵛ–66 Masses of the dead.

10. (a) f. 66 Missa sede apostolica uacante. (b) f. 66ᵛ Festum reliquiarum ecclesie et dyocesis mimatens'. quod semper celebratur post xvᶜⁱᵐ dies festi omnium sanctorum. (c) f. 67 Officium in festo reliquiarum ecclesie mimaten' et dyocesis.

(a). As art. 7f. (b) and (c) are different forms for the feast of relics. The collect of (b) asks for the intercession of B.V.M., SS. Michael, John Baptist, Peter and Paul, and SS. Privatus, Fredaldus, Firminus, Ylerus, Severianus, Ylarius, and Lupus 'huius ecclesie pontificum'.[1]

11. ff. 67–77 Incipiunt prose tocius anni.

Thirty-three hymns for principal feasts from Christmas to St. Nicholas (1–25), the common of saints (26–30), dedication of church (31), and B.V.M. (32, 33). Eleven are not listed in RH and three (28–30), printed in AH xlviii. 319–21, were known to Dreves only from the 1495 edition of the Uzès missal, where they are attributed to the Languedoc canonist, William de Mandagot, †1312.

1. Nat. Dom.	Promissa mundo gaudia . . .		RH 15617
2. Stephanus	Prioris martirio martiris celorum summo desiderio . . .		
3. Joh. Evang.	Trinitatem reserat . . .		20574
4. Innoc.	Celsa pueri . . .		2747
5. Circ.	Replet noua dies . . .		17315 (Epiph.).
6. Epiph.	Letabundus exultet . . .		10012
7. Purif. B.V.M.	Formam monstrans et exemplum . . .		
8. Blasius	Nardus mundus blasius datus est diuinitus . . .		
9. Annunc. B.V.M.	Aue maria gracia plena . . .		1879
10. Pasch.	Victime paschalis . . .		21505
11. Inv.	Salue lignum saluificum crucifixique . . .		
12. Asc.	Rex omnipotens die hodierna . . .		17479

[1] Of these seven bishops of Mende, Lupus is not recorded by Gams, Series Episcoporum. He is at 21 Aug. in a Mende calendar (Leroquais, Sacramentaires, ii. 29).

13.	Pent.	Veni sancte spiritus et emitte . . .	21242
14.	Corp. Christi	Corpus nostri saluatoris . . .	25026
15.	Joh. Bapt.	Helizabeth zacharie . . .	5353
16.	Petrus	Gaude roma caput mundi . . .	6928
17.	Maria Magd.	Demoniis septem plena. fuit primo magdalena . . .	
18.	Jacobus	Ad honorem hodiernum conuenite populi . . .	
19.	Assumpt. B.V.M.	A rea virga . . .	16
20.	Nativ. B.V.M.	Nativitas marie virginis . . .	11881
21.	Michael	Ad superne monarchie laudes cunctis in hac die . . .	
22.	Omn. SS.	Superne matris gaudia . . .	19822
23.	Katherina	Gratuletur cum canore presens chorus in honore . . .	
24.	Andreas	Andree festiuitas celebratur hodie . . .	
25.	Nicholaus	Salue presul morum flore . . .	
26.	Evang.	Iocundare plebs fidelis . . .	9843
27.	Apost.	Celi solem 'h'imitantes . . .	3513
28.	Mart.	Cristum regem immortalem . . .	3200
29.	Conf.	Gloriosi confessoris digne . . .	7346
30.	Virg.	Virgo prudens et decora . . .	21861
31.	In Ded. Eccl.	Clara chorus uoce pangat . . .	3297
32.	B.V.M.	Admiranda nouitas descendit diuinitas . . .	
33.	B.V.M.	Salue mater saluatoris uas . . .	18051

12. ff. 77–78ᵛ, 82 Incipiunt benedictiones episcopales tocius anni.

Leaves missing after f. 78. The benedictions before the gap are for dedication, Christmas, Stephen, John Evangelist and octave, Epiphany, Purification of B.V.M., Palm Sunday, and Holy Thursday; after the gap, for Holy Trinity (Omnipotens trinitas unus et uerus deus . . .) and the common of an apostle.

13. f. 82ʳᵛ Office 'In festo sancti Iohannis euangeliste. ad missam matutinalem'. A leaf or more missing after f. 82.

Arts. 14–16 were added in s. xiv ex.

14. f. 79ʳᵛ Office at the blessing of candles, beginning imperfectly. f. 80ʳ is blank.

15. ff. 80ᵛ–81 Gloria and Credo, noted.

16. (a) f. 81 Incipit absolucio clamdestine cum suis precibus. . . . Et ego auctoritate domini nostri ihesu cristi absoluo uos a sententia excommunicationis qua ligati estis ratione clamdestine contraxionis et restituo uos . . . (b) f. 81ʳᵛ Benedictio arrarum cum suis precibus. Hostende nobis domine . . . Oratio. Benedic domine arras istas quas hodie . . . (c) ff. 81ᵛ, 83ʳᵛ Benediction of persons 'qui coniungendi sunt', beginning 'Postquam autem sacerdos communicauerit'.

ff. iii+6+xii+77+viii. The twelve leaves of blank paper inserted after f. 6 are not numbered. f. 84 is a medieval binding leaf and was pasted down. ff. 1–80 are foliated in a contemporary hand ccix–ccxiiii, cclxxxvii[i]–ccclvi, ccclviii–ccclx, ccclxvi, ccclxvii. f. 82 belongs in the gap after 'ccclx', but it does not bear a visible number. 327 × 240 mm. Written space 225 × 156 mm. 2 cols. 27 lines. Collation: 1⁶ 2–10⁸ 11 five (ff. 82, 79–81, 83: ff. 80, 81 are a bifolium). Initials: (i, ii) in colour on coloured or gold and coloured grounds, decorated and with border prolongations in colours and gold: a blue cross on a red and black ground in the T on f. 1 and a monstrous bagpipe-player as the I on f. 7ᵛ;

(iii, iv), 2-line and 1-line, red with violet ornament or blue with red ornament. Capital letters in the ink of the text are touched with yellow-brown. Binding of s. xix.

Written in France, for use in the diocese of Mende (art. 10). 'No. 10. 1525' at the beginning and '1958. 2519' at the end are modern marks.

091/MED/2. *Antiphonale*   s. xv med.

The winter part of an antiphonal. Probably more than fifty leaves are missing. The text was often altered and added to much later, s. xvii ex. (?), by writing in the margins and in blank spaces and sometimes by pasting pieces of paper over the original text, for example on f. 71ᵛ where the last five words of 'Commendemus nosmetipsos in multa paciencia per arma iusticie uirtutis dei' have been changed to 'in ieiuniis multis per arma iustitie'. On ff. 117ᵛ, 118 'Concepcio' has been changed to 'Desponsatio'.

1. ff. 1–101ᵛ Ecce dies veniunt dicit dominus . . . Temporale, Advent–Easter Eve.

2. ff. 102–41 Sanctorale, 30 Nov.–25 Mar.

Ten feasts, Andrew, Conception of B.V.M., Lucy, Agnes, Conversion of Paul, Purification of B.V.M., Agatha, Chains of Peter, Annunciation of B.V.M.

3. ff. 141ᵛ–157ᵛ Sequitur commune sanctorum.

Ends imperfectly in the common of virgins.

4. f. 158 (*begins imperfectly in office of B.V.M.*) premimur et non est qui adiuuet . . . Antiphona. Sub tuam protectionem confugimus.

5. ff. 158–9 Suffragia dicenda ab octauis epyph[anie usque] ad caput ieiunii: of Holy Cross, B.V.M., St. Augustine, and All Saints at vespers and matins.

The forms for St. Augustine are 'Letare mater nostra iherusalem . . .', 'Factus Augustinus presbyter . . .', and as an addition of s. xviii (?) at the foot of f. 159, 'Presul sanctissime Augustine via morum . . .'.

6. f. 159ʳᵛ Eight settings of Gloria. f. 160ʳᵛ blank, the verso formerly pasted down.

ff. 160. 360 × 270 mm. Written space 285 × 178 mm. 10 long lines and music. Collation uncertain: seven complete quires remain and are all eights, ff. 5–12, 13–20, 21–8, 60–7, 93–100, 102–9, 110–17. Black ink. Initials: (i) in colour, usually blue, patterned in white, with attractive penwork ornament in red and a little green and yellow: only six remain, ff. 1, 29ᵛ, 31, 102, 113, 137; (ii) f. 107ᵛ, blue with red ornament; (iii) red or blue. Cadels and capital letters in the ink of the text are touched with red. Binding of thick wooden boards covered with dark velvet.

Written probably in Germany for the use of Augustinian canons. In liturgical use still in s. xviii. A printed label stuck on the binding bears the words 'Algemene Expeditie-Onderneming Van Gend & Loos', s. xix. '282' is on a small round paper label on the spine.

091/MED/3. *Processionale*   s. xv med.

1. Processional offices for eleven feasts: (*a*) f. 1 Palm Sunday, Pueri hebreorum . . .; (*b*) f. 8 Holy Thursday: (*c*) f. 26 Good Friday; (*d*) f. 31 Ascension

Day; (e) f. 35 Purification of B.V.M.; (f) f. 40 Corpus Christi; (g) f. 43 St. Dominic; (h) f. 46 Assumption of B.V.M.; (i) ff. 50ʳᵛ, 57–60 St. Louis, king and confessor; (j) ff. 60ʳᵛ, 52–54ᵛ St. John Baptist; (k) ff. 54ᵛ, 51ʳᵛ, 55–56ᵛ Nativity of B.V.M.

(b). A rubric on f. 17ᵛ is 'Hic ponantur antiphone. versiculi. et orationes de sanctis secundum disposicionem altarium in quolibet conuentu'.

2 (added, s. xvi). (a) ff. 61ᵛ–65 Fulget sponsus ecclesiæ in thalamo uirgineo . . . (b) ff. 65ᵛ–67 Summe trinitati simplici deo . . . (c) f. 67 Felix namque es sacra virgo maria . . .

ff. iv+67+ii. 122 × 90 mm. Written space 85 × 63 mm. 5 long lines and music. 15 long lines on pages without music. Collation: 1–6⁸ 7⁸ (ff. 49, 50, 57–60, 52, 53) 8 four (ff. 54, 51, 55, 56) 9⁴ 10 three (ff. 65–7). Initials are blue with red ornament or red with slate-grey ornament. Capital letters and cadels in the ink of the text are touched with pale yellow. Binding of s. xix. Secundo folio *te in castellum.*

Written in France for Dominican use.

091/MED/4. *Horae*   s. XV/XVI

1. ff. 1–12ᵛ Full calendar in French in red and black.

'Saint leu saint gile' in red, 1 Sept.

2. ff. 13–14ᵛ Sequentiae of the Gospels, John 1: 1–11 and Mark 16: 14–20 only, as a result of loss of leaves after f. 13.

3. ff. 15–54 Hours of B.V.M. of the use of (Rome).

Salve regina after compline f. 54ᵛ blank. The special offices in Advent, etc., are absent: they were presumably on leaves now missing after f. 54.

4. ff. 55–8 O intemerata . . . orbis terrarum. De te enim . . .

5. ff. 58–60ᵛ Oracio. Obsecro te . . . Et michi famulo tuo N . . .

6. Further devotions to B.V.M.: (a) ff. 61–3 Alia oracio. O gloriosissima dei genitrix maria . . .; (b) ff. 63–69ᵛ Oracio beate marie valde deuota. Auxiliatrix michi sis sancta dei genitrix . . .; (c) ff. 69ᵛ–70ᵛ Oracio beate marie. Aue maria gracia plena dominus tecum. martir cum martiribus transgladiata . . .; (d) ff. 70ᵛ–71ᵛ Gaude virgo mater cristi que per aurem . . .; (e) ff. 71ᵛ–72ᵛ Aue mundi spes maria aue mitis aue pia . . .

(d, e). *RH*, nos. 7017, 1974.

7. f. 72ᵛ Cy apres sens' le credo en francoys et autres oroisons: (a) f. 73ʳᵛ Ie croy en dieu le pere tout puissant . . .; (b) ff. 73ᵛ–74 Alia oracio de sancta cruce en francoys. Saincte vraye croix aouree . . .; (c) f. 74ʳᵛ Oracion de nostre dame en francoys. O glorieuse vierge marie a toy me rens . . .; (d) ff. 74ᵛ–75 Pour guerir des fieures. Le iour du grant vendredi. Ihesu crist en la croix fut mis Et les iuifs lui bouterent . . .

(a–c). Sonet, nos. 794, 1876, 675. (d). Cf. Sonet, no. 1044.

8. f. 76ʳᵛ Hours of the Cross, imperfect at both ends.

9. ff. 77–78ᵛ (*begins imperfectly*) haberemus . . . iocundari et commorari.
The prayer of the Seven Words.

10. ff. 78ᵛ–81 Passio domini nostri Ihesu cristi secundum Iohannem. In illo tempore apprehendit pylatus . . .
A catena consisting of John 19: 1–3, Matthew 27: 30, John 19: 16 Susceperunt—18, 28–30, Matthew 27: 51–4, John 19: 34, 35, with many variations from the Vulgate text, followed by the prayers 'Deus qui manus tuas . . .', 'Omnipotens sempiterne deus qui pendens . . .', and 'Domine ihesu criste fili dei viui qui pro redimendo hominem . . .'.

11. ff. 81ᵛ–85 Hours of the Holy Spirit.

12. Prayers: (*a*) f. 85ʳᵛ Oracio, Pater in manus tuas commendo spiritum meum . . .; (*b*) ff. 85ᵛ–86ᵛ Recommendacio ad deum patrem. Deus propicius esto michi peccatori et sis custos . . .; (*c*) ff. 86ᵛ–87 Alia oracio. Domine sancte pater omnipotens qui permanes in trinitate . . .; (*d*) f. 87 Ure igne sancti spiritus . . .; (*e*) ff. 87–92 Oracio ad patrem. Domine deus omnipotens qui es trinus et vnus . . .; (*f*) ff. 92–4 Oracio beati thome de acquino ad dominum. Concede michi misericors deus que tibi placita sunt . . .; (*g*) ff. 94–95ᵛ Oracio dicenda ante corpus cristi. In presencia corporis et sanguinis tui domine . . .; (*h*) ff. 95ᵛ–96ᵛ Preparacio ad recipiendum corpus cristi. Omnipotens et misericors deus ecce accedo . . .

(*b, e, g, h*). Cf. *Lyell Cat.*, 'Index of Incipits'. (*f*). Ed. A. I. Doyle, 'A Prayer attributed to St. Thomas Aquinas', *Dominican Studies*, i (1948), 229–38.

13. ff. 96ᵛ–97ᵛ Versus beati bernardi. Illumina oculos meos . . .
Seven verses and prayer. f. 98ʳᵛ is blank.

14. ff. 99–114 Penitential psalms and (f. 108ᵛ) litany.
Eighteen confessors: . . . (9, 10) . . . dominice thoma . . .

15. ff. 114ᵛ–149ᵛ Office of the dead.

16. ff. 150–60 Memoriae of Holy Trinity, Corpus Christi, Angels, SS. John Baptist, John Evangelist, Peter, Paul, James, Andrew, all apostles, SS. Stephen, Denis, Laurence, Christopher, Peter Martyr, all martyrs, SS. Nicholas, Martin, Anthony abbot, Fiacre, Dominic, all confessors, SS. Mary Magdalene, Katherine, Margaret, Agnes, Cecilia, Barbara, all virgins, All Saints, Holy Cross.

17. ff. 160ᵛ–166ᵛ Hore de sancta Katherina. Domine labia mea aperies . . .
The hymns of these hours are printed in *AH* xlvi, no. 248: *RH*, no. 23129.

18. ff. 166ᵛ–167 Quinque gaudia beate katherine. Gaude dulcis katherina virgo martir et regina. fulgens sub maxentio . . . *RH*, no. 26923.

19. ff. 167ᵛ–173 Deus pater qui creasti mundum et illuminasti . . . *RH*, no. 4477.

ff. iii+173+ii. 160×116 mm. Written space 105×68 mm. 19 long lines. Too tightly bound to collate: mainly eights. Written in *lettre bâtarde*. Illustrated—not skilfully—by thirteen 15-line pictures, eight in art. 3, and one before each of arts. 2, 11, 14, 15, 17 (a man kneels before St. Katherine), a smaller picture, corpse on tomb, before Verba mea auribus in art. 15 (f. 122), and occupations of the months on rectos and signs of the zodiac on versos of art. 1. Initials: (i) blue or rarely pink, patterned in white, on gold grounds decorated in colours and, f. 69ᵛ (art. 6c), historiated (Pietà); (ii, iii) 2-line and 1-line, gold on coloured grounds. Line fillers of blue, pink, and gold. Borders, including figures and animals and on f. 99 David and Goliath, on three sides of picture pages, in the upper and lower margins of other pages with initials of type (i), and in the outer side margin of all other pages. Binding of s. xix.

Written in France under Dominican influence. The name Segur can just be read on f. 1 and in an erased inscription on f. 121ᵛ, 'Ses heures sont [. . . .] segur noʳᵉ [. . .]' (s. xvi/xvii?).

091/MED/5. *Horae*   s. XV in.

1. ff. 1–12ᵛ Nearly full calendar in French in red and black.
St. Gatien added in blue at 18 Dec.

2. ff. 13–45ᵛ Hours of B.V.M. of the use of (Tours), beginning and ending imperfectly and with many gaps.

3. ff. 46–47ᵛ Hours of the Cross, beginning imperfectly.

4. ff. 47ᵛ–49ᵛ Hours of the Holy Spirit, ending imperfectly.

5. ff. 50–64ᵛ Penitential psalms, beginning imperfectly, and (f. 60) litany.
Thirteen confessors: . . . (5) iuliane . . . (9) gaciane . . .

6. ff. 64ᵛ–65ᵛ St. John 1: 1–14 and prayer 'Protector in te sperancium . . .'.

7. 66–9 Obsecro te . . . Et michi famulo tuo . . . ff. 69ᵛ–71ᵛ were left blank.

8. ff. 72–104ᵛ Office of the dead, beginning imperfectly. f. 105ʳᵛ blank.

ff. iii + 105 + iii. 152 × 112 mm. Written space 102 × 69 mm. 15 long lines. Collation: 1¹² 2⁸ wants 1 and 8 (ff. 13–18) 3⁸ wants 3 and 6 (ff. 19–24) 4⁸ wants 3 and 6 (ff. 25–30) 5 two (ff. 31–2) 6⁸ wants 3 and 7 (ff. 33–8) 7⁸ wants 5 (ff. 39–45) 8 four (ff. 46–9) 9⁸ wants 1 and 8 (ff. 50–5) 10–11⁸ 12⁸ wants 1 before f. 72 13–15⁸ 16 three (ff. 103–5). Initials: (i) only two remain, ff. 47ᵛ, 66, pink patterned in white on gold grounds, decorated in colour; (ii, iii) 2-line and 1-line, blue with red ornament or gold with slate-grey ornament. The longer line fillers are blue and red, picked out with red, and the shorter a gold-centred quatrefoil. A border on three sides of f. 47ᵛ and in the upper and lower margins of f. 66. Binding of s. xix.

Written in France. Belonged in 1630 and 1768 to members of the Boudard family: 'Ce liure á couté trois Louis á monsieur de boue. qui me la donné a moi Nicolas boudard 1630', f. 71ᵛ; 'cet liure apartiens a moy Gabriel boudard 1768', f. 70. One of the name wrote 'Du péron à Paris De Paris jusqu'à Rome Le plus sot Animal A mon avis C'est l'homme (Boil. Saty.) Boudard' on f. 69, s. xviii.

091/MED/6. *Horae*   s. XV²

1. ff. 1–6ᵛ Calendar in red and black.

Feasts in red include 'Basilii episcopi' and 'Donaciani episcopi' (14 June, 14 Oct.). Many new saints added in s. xvii, among them Francis Xavier, François de Sales, and Charles Borromeus, and a notice of the capture of Ostende on 22 Sept. 1604.

2. ff. 7–11ᵛ Incipiunt hore de sancta cruce.

3. ff. 13–16ᵛ Incipiunt hore de sancto spiritu.

4. ff. 18–21ᵛ Incipit missa beate marie virginis.

5. ff. 22–25ᵛ Sequentiae of the Gospels.

6. ff. 26–28ᵛ Ad gloriosam uirginem mariam. Obsecro te . . . Et michi famule tue . . .

7. ff. 29–30ᵛ Oracio bona de sancta maria. O intemerata . . . orbis terrarum. Inclina . . . Et esto michi peccatrici. . . .

8. ff. 31–36ᵛ Memoriae, one to a page, of SS. Michael, John Baptist, Peter, Paul, Andrew, Stephen, Laurence, Nicholas, Mary Magdalene, Katherine, Barbara, Margaret.

9. ff. 38–90 Incipiunt hore beate marie uirginis secundum usum romane curie.

Salve regina follows compline. The office in Advent begins on f. 85. f. 90ᵛ blank.

10. ff. 92–105ᵛ Penitential psalms and (f. 100) litany.

11. ff. 106–134ᵛ Incipiunt vigilie mortuorum. Ends imperfectly.

12. Many additional prayers were added in s. xvii in blank spaces and in the margins, where little of them is left, thanks to the binder.

ff. iii+134+iii. 148×100 mm.: the margins much cropped by a binder. Written space 110×70 m. 21 long lines. Too tightly bound to collate: probably leaves are missing at the end and the leaves with full-page pictures are inserted singletons, since the rectos are blank. Much decorated, but not well. Nine full-page pictures, six in art. 9 (ff. 37ᵛ, 51ᵛ, 60ᵛ, 73ᵛ before vespers with slaughter of Innocents, 79ᵛ before compline with flight into Egypt, 84ᵛ before Advent office with Coronation of B.V.M.: no picture now before terce, sext, or none), and one before each of arts. 3, 4, 10 (Christ on the rainbow in judgement). Seventeen small pictures, c. 45×40 mm., twelve in art. 8, four in art. 5, and one before art. 6. Initials: (i) pink or blue, patterned in white, on gold grounds decorated in colours; (ii, iii), 2-line and 1-line, gold on grounds of pink and blue patterned in white. Continuous framed borders, badly cropped, on each side of double openings, if the left-hand side had a full-page picture. On all other pages a bar of gold and pink or rarely gold and blue, with spray termination, is in the outer margin. Binding of s. xix.

Written for female use (arts. 6, 7), probably in the southern Netherlands (art. 1). Later at Dole: 'Appartenant au procuʳ de Dole', f. 1, s. xvii; 'A Pierre Roy procur' a la cour 1662', f. 134; 'J: H: Brocard', f. 134ᵛ; notice of the death 'Le Iour duy', 17 Apr. 17[07], of '[mon]sieur Brocard ap[res] son nom de batem[e] (Claude antoine Ieane babtiste roy [. . .] son pere iean batist[e] Brocard cler (?) iuré [. . .] cour du roy) 'brocard' chiru[. . .] iuré a dole le [. . .] aprilis 1707 il fut enterre le mesme mois [. . .]', f. 73; 'J'appartiens a Jeanne Francoise Chappuis de Dole usufruit reserue a sa mere', f. 2, s. xviii.

091/MED/7. *Horae*   s. xv in.

1. ff. 1–16ᵛ Calendar in red and black, three pages to a month, beginning imperfectly at 22 Jan. and lacking 12–28 Feb.

Entries in red include Blaise and Claude (3 Feb., 6 June). Feasts are marked for nine lessons and some principal feasts have also 'col' ' and/or 'qui' against them, for example 'Natiuitas beati iohannis ix lc' col'. qui oct qui'. 'Cleophe apostoli qui' added at 25 Sept.

2. ff. 17–71ᵛ, 132ʳᵛ, 72–5 Hours of B.V.M.

Seven leaves are missing. No antiphon provided at prime and none. The capitulum is Ab inicio at prime and Quasi cedrus at none. ff. 28ᵛ, 65ᵛ, 75ᵛ were left blank.

3. ff. 76–101 Penitential psalms and (f. 91ᵛ) litany.

Twenty-five martyrs: . . .(3) genesii . . . Confessors divided into pontiffs and doctors (16: . . .(4) fulciane) and monks and hermits (9: . . . (6–9) columbane guillerme roberte geralde). f. 101ᵛ was left blank.

4. ff. 102–131ᵛ, 133–141ᵛ Office of the dead, beginning and ending imperfectly.

ff. iii+141+ii. 105 × 75 mm. Written space 53 × 35 mm. 13 long lines. Collation: 1⁶ wants 1 and 3 2–3⁶ 4⁸ wants 1 before f. 17 5⁴+1 leaf after 4 (f. 28) 6–8⁸ 9⁶ wants 2 after f. 53 10⁴ 11¹⁰ wants 1 before f. 62 and 5, 6 after f. 64+1 leaf now missing after f. 66 12⁸ wants 5 before f. 72: 4 is misbound as f. 132 13–15⁸ 16² (ff. 100, 101) 17⁸ wants 1 before f. 102 18–21⁸ (ff. 109–31, 133–41). Arts. 2–4 have a medieval foliation made before eight leaves were lost: the highest legible number is 'cvii' on f. 115. Three 10-line pictures remain, two in art. 2 (ff. 29, 58: Visitation, Shepherds) and one before art. 3. Initials: (i) ff. 29, 58, 76, blue patterned in white on gold grounds decorated in colour; (ii, iii) 2-line and 1-line, gold on coloured grounds. Capital letters in the ink of the text are touched with yellow. Borders on three sides of the picture pages. Binding of s. xix.

Written in France. Arms in the lower border on f. 76: or between a chevron vert (?) three choughs (?) sable.

091/MED/8. *Horae* 1471

1. ff. 1–12ᵛ Calendar in red and black of Dominican use, graded.

2. ff. 23–40ᵛ, 14ʳᵛ, 13ʳᵛ, 41–61ᵛ Hours of B.V.M. of (Dominican) use, beginning imperfectly.

3. ff. 62–74 Memoriae of SS. Margaret, Yvo, Holy Cross, SS. John Baptist, John Evangelist (Ave gemma claritatis . . .: *RH*, no. 1810), Dominic, Peter Martyr, Thomas Aquinas, Vincent confessor, Katherine of Siena (preceded by 'Oratio de beata Katherina de senis', ff. 68–70), Peter (O beate martir petre . . .: *RH*, no. 12694), Katherine.

4. ff. 74–76ᵛ Oratio multum deuota ad beatam uirginem. Aue lumen gratie . . .
Mostly erased. *RH*, no. 1866.

5. ff. 76ᵛ–78ᵛ Sanctus gregorius papa sequentem orationem composuit de planctu beate marie iuxta crucem et concessit omnibus eam deuote dicentibus septem annos indulgenciarum. Stabat mater dolorosa . . . *RH*, no. 19416.

6. Prayers in Latin and French: (a) f. 79ʳᵛ Crucem tuam adoramus et veneramur . . ., with rubric conveying indulgence of 300 days of Pope Innocent, confirmed by Pope Clement VI; (b) f. 80ʳᵛ Oratio dicenda ante communionem. Ecce ihesu benigne quod cupiui . . .; (c) ff. 80ᵛ–81 Aue sanctissimum corpus nostri saluatoris . . .; (d) f. 81ʳᵛ Oratio dicenda post communionem. Gratias

tibi ago domine deus meus . . .; (e) ff. 81ᵛ–82ᵛ Alia oratio. Non de meritorum qualitate confidens . . . (feminine forms); (f) ff. 82ᵛ–84 the Seven Verses of St. Bernard; (g) ff. 84–85ᵛ Oratio dicenda ante confessionem. Misericordissime deus qui pro salute generis humani . . .; (h) f. 85ᵛ Cy apres ensuit vne oroison que on appelle. fons sapiencie. Vray dieu et vray seigneur ihesu crist nostre salueur et redempteur qui es la parole de dieu . . . (ends imperfectly); (i) f. 86 Alia oratio. Sire nous te prions que ce que de bouche . . .; (j) f. 86 Alia oratio deuota. La reception du corps et du sanc . . .

(h–j) are prayers before communion not recorded by Sonet. Two leaves are missing after f. 85.

7. ff. 86ᵛ–88 O sancte Sebastiane Semper vespere et mane . . . *RH*, no. 13708.

8. ff. 88–92ᵛ Sequitur pulcherima oratio ad filium dei et matrem eius. Summe summ(i) tu patris vnice . . . *RH*, no. 19710.

9. ff. 92ᵛ–93 De trinitate. antyphona. Benedicta sit creatrix . . .

10. (a) ff. 93–4 De sancto spiritu. hympnus. Veni creator spiritus mentes tuorum visita . . . (b) ff. 94ᵛ–95 Prosa. Veni sancte spiritus et emitte celitus . . . *RH*, nos. 21204, 21242.

11. ff. 95–97ᵛ (a) De nostra domina. antiphona. Beata dei genitrix maria . . . (b) Gaude virgo mater cristi . . . (c) De nostra domina. Aue uirgo gratiosa Virgo mater gloriosa . . .

(b, c). *RH*, nos. 7017, 2217.

12. ff. 97–99ᵛ, 16–18ᵛ Memoriae of SS. Peter and Paul, Matthew, Nicholas, Fiacre, Eustace, Angels, SS. Katherine, Mary Magdalene, Barbara, Christina, All Saints, and 'Pro amico speciali et pro se ipso'.

13. ff. 18ᵛ–20 De sero ante dormitionem hympnus. Christe qui lux es et dies . . . *RH*, no. 2934.

14. ff. 20–22ᵛ, 15ʳᵛ, 100–111ᵛ Incipiunt quedam deuote sequencie de beata uirgine.

Sequences (1–7) for the Annunciation, Christmas, the Purification, Assumption and Nativity of B.V.M., Advent, Easter, and (8–18) of B.V.M. 'A festo trinitatis usque aduentum', ending imperfectly: (1–7) Aue maria, Letabundus, Inuiolata, Saluatoris mater salue, Natiuitas marie, Verbum bonum, Virgini marie (*RH*, nos. 1879, 10012, 9093, 18051, 11881, 21343, 21656): (8–18) Hodierne lux, Aue mundi spes, Iubilemus in hac die, Tibi cordis, Stella maris, Aue uirgo uirginum, Mater patris, Salue sancta, Aue virgo gratiosa, Aue virgo gloriosa, Saluatoris mater pia (*RH*, nos. 7945, 1974, 9813, 20459, 19456, 2261, 11350, 18178, 2217, 2205, 17821).

15. ff. 112–130ᵛ Penitential psalms and (f. 122ᵛ) litany, in which B.V.M., Matthew, Dominic, Louis, and Katherine are in gold and Margaret is in blue.

16. ff. 131–71 Office of the dead, beginning imperfectly. f. 171ᵛ blank.

ff. iv+171+ii. For f. iv see below. 98×72 mm. Written space 54×36 mm. 16 long lines. Collation: 1–2⁶ 3⁸ wants 1 before f. 23 4⁸ 5⁸ (ff. 38–40, 14, 13, 41–3) 6–7⁸ 8¹⁰ 9–10⁸ 11⁸ wants 1, 2 before f. 86 12⁸ (f. 92–9) 13⁸ (ff. 16–22, 15) 14⁸ (ff. 100–7) 15⁸ wants 7, 8 after f. 111 16–17⁸ 18⁴ wants 4 after f. 130 19⁸ wants 1 before f. 131 20–22⁸ 23¹⁰. Neat script and decoration. Initials: (i) in colours, patterned in white, on gold grounds decorated in colours; (ii) 2-line, gold on coloured grounds; (iii) 1-line, red or blue. Line fillers in red (in litany only). Capital letters in the ink of the text touched with pale yellow. A floral side border on pages with initials of type (i). Binding of s. xix, inside which the leather covers of a French binding, s. xvi in., have been pasted: one cover bears a panel of the mass of St. Gregory and the other a panel of the baptism of Christ.

Written for a nun of the Dominican convent of Poissy (Seine-et-Oise) in 1471, as appears from an inscription, probably in the main hand, on the recto of f. iv, a leaf intended for use in the manuscript, as the ruling shows, but left blank and used as a flyleaf instead: Ce liure escript en lan mil iiii^e soixante et xi apartient a seur marguerite de la chaussee humble professe ou royal monastere de pouessy qui le trouuera sy luy rende [. . . . .]. Non remittitur peccatum nisi presens restituatur ablatum. An inscription below this in faded ink, s. xvi, reads 'Seur marie de pardieu est ce presant liure et la enuoie de paradis a sa petite niepce de catenale (?) e la charge que tous les iours lira ces sept pseaulme pour elle. Requiescant in pace'.

091/MED/9. *Hours of the Holy Spirit, etc. (in Netherlandish)*
s. xv med.

1. (a) ff. 2–26 Hier beghinnen die ghetiden van den heiligen geest. (b) f. 26^{rv} Antifen. Regina celi letare. Verblide v coninghinne des hemels . . .

(a). *Het getijdenboek van Geert Grote*, ed. N. van Wijk, Leiden, 1940, pp. 71–86. (b). A memoria of B.V.M.

2. ff. 28–48^v Hier beghinnen die ewighe wijsheit getide.

Op. cit., pp. 92–112. Axters, *BDNM*, p. 216, lists this copy.

3. Prayers: (a) ff. 49–51 Hier beghint een suuerlic ghebet van onser lieuer vrouwen. Sancta maria. O suete maria moeder gods vol alre goedertierenheit . . .; (b) f. 51^{rv} Hier beghint een gebet van die geboerten ons heren. Verbliden wi ons in den here wi ballinghe . . .; (c) f. 51^v Oracio. O ewighe wijsheit woert des vaders . . .; (d) ff. 51^v–52 Oracio. Ghebenedijt si die sone des vaders . . .; (e) f. 52^{rv} Oracio. Lof ende eer si den coninc der glorien . . .; (f) f. 53^{rv} Een deuoet ghebet tot onsen lieuen here. O almechtich god vader in der ewicheit di si lof ende eer . . .; (g) ff. 54–5 Maria die moeder gods leerden . . . (*an 8-line heading*). O alre heilichste maghet maria Ic loue ende eer u ghebenedide oren . . .; (h) ff. 55^v–56 Een deuoet ghebet van onser lieuer vrouwen. O maria moeder ende reyne maghet ghebendijt soe si dijn heilighe ombesmette lichaem . . .

(b). Meertens, vi. 151. (g). Eleven oes, all but one in praise of a part of the body of B.V.M., ending with the heart.

4. ff. 56–62^v Memoriae of SS. John Evangelist, John Baptist, Jerome, Mary Magdalene, Mary of Egypt, All Saints, All Souls, and B.V.M.

5. ff. 62^v–65^v Een mynlijc ghebet van onser lieuer vrouwen. God gruet v heilighe maria coninghinne der hemelen salighe vruchbarighe wortel van yesse . . .

Nine paragraphs, each beginning with the same five words. Meertens, vi. 30.

6. Prayers: (a) f. 65^{rv} O heer ihesu xpriste moghende prince om dat mynnentlike vanden . . .; (b) f. 66^{rv} Van ons heren verrisenis oraci(o). O heer ihesu xpriste om dat verrisen . . .; (c) ff. 66^v–67 Van der vertonighen ons liefs heren. O here ihesu xpriste om dat vertonen . . .; (d) f. 67^{rv} Van den heilighen geeste. O suete heilighe gheest here god ewighe mynne . . .; (e) ff. 67^v–68 Van den toecomende

oerdale Oracio. O ihesu xpriste here coninc der coninghen . . . ; (*f*) f. 68ʳᵛ Van der vertoningen der apostolen. O heer ihesu xpriste om dat vertonen dat ghi v vertoemde . . . ; (*g*) f. 68ᵛ Van ons heren hemeluaert. O heer ihesu xpriste. om dat gloriose opuaren . . . (*ends imperfectly*).

7. f. 69ʳᵛ A memoria of St Erasmus, imperfect at both ends.

8. ff. 70–78ᵛ Prayers at and after communion: (*a*) ff. 70–3 Ouerste priester ende waer bisscop . . . ; (*b*) f. 73 Oracio. O here ihesu xpiste ic gruete dijn vleesche . . . ; (*c*) ff. 73–74ᵛ O here allenne der enghelen glorie . . . ; (*d*) ff. 74ᵛ–76 Dit sal men lesen als men dat heilighe sacrament ontfanghen heeft. O heer ihesu xpiste lof si dine onsprekelike minnenliche goedertierenheit . . . ; (*e*) ff. 76–7 Oracio. O mynnentlike ende alre suetste heer ihesu xpriste . . . ; (*f*) f. 77 Here ihesu xpriste leuende gods sone. Ic en ben niet weerdich . . . ; (*g*) f. 77ʳᵛ Aye here vader van hemelrijck hoe sal ic arme sondighe mensche . . . ; (*h*) ff. 77ᵛ–78 Willecome ihesu xpriste leuende gods sone . . . ; (*i*) f. 78ʳᵛ Oracio. Coem heilighe gheest ende seynt ons dijn schijn . . .

(*a–d*). Lieftinck, p. 142. Meertens, vi. 9, 89, 107, 49. (*f, g*). Meertens, vi. 191.

9. (*a*) ff. 78ᵛ–80ᵛ God groet di maria o gloriose heilighe hoechgheboren ioncfrou ende maghet . . . ; (*b*) ff. 80ᵛ–83ᵛ Ghebenedijt moestu sijn . . .

(*a*). Thirteen sections, each beginning 'God gruet di (*or* v)'. Meertens, vi. 140. (*b*). Fourteen sections, each beginning 'Ghebenedijt moestu sijn . . .'. Ends imperfectly. Lieftinck, p. 110. f. 84ʳᵛ blank.

10. ff. 85–86ᵛ Calendar, not full, for 1 Jan. to 15 Mar. only, in red and black.

ff. 86. 160×120 mm. Written space 108×74 mm. 20 long lines. Collation: 1–2⁸ 3¹⁰ (ff. 17–26) 4–5⁸ 6⁶ (ff. 43–8) 7⁸ wants 1 before f. 49 8⁸ 9⁸ wants 6 after f. 68 and 8 after f. 69 10⁸ 11⁸ wants 7, 8 after f. 83 12 three (ff. 84–6). Full-page pictures before arts. 1, 2 and in art. 4 (ff. 1ᵛ, 27ᵛ, the Son on the lap of the Father, 59ᵛ, All Saints). Initials: (i) in colours on gold grounds, historiated, one beginning each of arts. 1–3, 8, six in art. 4 and two in art. 6 (f. 66, Resurrection; f. 68ᵛ Ascension); (ii) 4-line or 3-line, in colours on gold grounds, or vice versa, decorated; (iii, iv) 2-line and 1-line, gold on coloured grounds. Capital letters in the ink of the text are touched with red. Continuous borders on pages with initials of types (i, ii). Decorated bars of gold and blue or gold and pink in the left margin of pages with initials of type (iii). Sewn, but not now covered.

Written in the Netherlands. 'Edouard Coopez', f. 43. 'Livinus Burrik (?) tot Liedekerkie' wrote a note of ownership dated 18 Sept. 1812, ff. 83ᵛ, 84.

BRECHIN. DIOCESAN LIBRARY[1]

1. *Psalterium*   s. xv in.

The psalter part of a breviary, ending abruptly in compline at the word 'conpungimini' (Ps. 4: 5: f. 52ᵛ). The rest of f. 52ᵛ and ff. 53ᵛ–57ᵛ are ruled, but blank.

[1] The library is on permanent deposit in Dundee University Library.

ff. i+57. f. i is a parchment flyleaf. 240×180 mm. Written space 178×128 mm. 2 cols. 36 lines. Ruling in ink. Collation: 1–5¹⁰ 6⁶+1 leaf after 1 (f. 52). A point before and after the catchword. Initials: (i) 10-line or less, to Primo dierum (f. 1) and Pss. 1, 26, 38, 52, 68, 80, 97, 109, pink patterned in white on decorated blue and gold grounds; (ii, iii) 2-line and 1-line, red or blue. Binding of s. xix.

Written in Italy. Book-plate and (f. i) stamp: 'Ex Bibliotheca almæ Ecclesiæ Brechinensis'.

2. *Horae* s. xv med.

1. ff. 1–12ᵛ (quires 1, 2) Calendar in red and black.

Eleutherius (20 Feb.), 'Dedicatio beate marie tornac'' (9 May), 'Remigii confessoris. Pyati martyris' (1 Oct.) in red.

2. ff. 13–19ᵛ (quire 3) Hours of the Trinity. . . . Quicunque uult animam . . . (*RH*, no. 16566).

3. ff. 20–25ᵛ (quire 4) Hore sancti spiritus Incipiunt hic. . . . Nobis sancti spiritus . . . (*RH*, no. 12022).

4. ff. 26–32 (quire 5) Hours of the Cross. . . . Patris sapientia . . . (*RH*, no. 14725). f. 32ᵛ blank.

5. ff. 33–64 (quires 6–10) Hours of B.V.M. of the use of (Tournai), each hour on a separate quire, matins (f. 33), lauds (f. 42), prime (f. 51), terce (f. 56), compline (f. 60): sext, none, and vespers are missing. Salve regina follows compline (f. 64ʳᵛ).

6. ff. 65–80 (quires 11, 12) Penitential psalms and (f. 75) litany.

Twenty-three confessors: . . . (8–10) Ambrose, Eleutherius, Jerome. f. 80ᵛ blank.

7. ff. 81–105ᵛ (quires 13–15) Office of the dead. Three lessons, not nine.

ff. iv+105+iii. 160×120 mm. Written space 100×72 mm. 16 long lines. Ruling in red ink. Collation: 1–5⁶ 6–7⁸ 8–10⁴ 11⁸ 12⁶+1 leaf after 6 (f. 80) 13–15⁸, together with single leaves in front of quires 3, 5–8, 10, 11, 13. 12-line pictures on the eight singletons and on ff. 20, 56 in a strongly marked style (except f. 20), with long thin figures, five (out of eight) in art. 5 and one before each of arts. 2–4, 6, 7. Initials: (i, ii) 4-line and 2-line, in colour on decorated gold grounds; (iii) 1-line, gold on coloured grounds patterned in white. Initials of type ii, if the letter *I*, are placed outside the written space. Capital letters in the ink of the text filled with yellow. Pages with initials of type (i)—the picture pages—have continuous borders and all other pages have a border in the outer margin as high as the written space. A binding of pasteboard covered with red velvet, s. xviii (?), lettered 'Missal'¹ on the spine, was replaced by a Douglas Cockerell and Son binding of red morocco in 1968.

Written for use in the diocese of Tournai. 'Edinburgh 24ᵗʰ Novembʳ 1802 / Presented / by / Sir William Forbes / of / Pitsligo / to / Miss Mary Drummond / as a mark of his regard', f. ivᵛ. 'Frances F. Forbes. / given to me by / Miss Mary Drummond / on her death bed. / May 1831', f. iiiᵛ. The Brechin book-plate, as in MS. 1, has been raised from the old binding and is kept separately.

¹ See below, Brighton Public Library, 6, footnote.

3. 'Lucas', Sermones dominicales Veni domine ihesu 1435

Veni domine ihesu apo^a vlt^o. In hoc verbo exprimitur desiderium anime . . . (f. 197^v) requies defunctis amen. Expliciunt sermones luce tam de epistolis quam de ewangeliis dominicarum per circulum anni. Scripti per manus conr' plũmlein plebani in wendelstein sub anno domini 1435to completi feria 4^a post letare. amen.

Sermons from Advent to the twenty-fifth Sunday after Pentecost, usually three to a Sunday, listed by Schneyer, *Rep.* iv. 87–94, nos. 145–301, and attributed doubtfully to Lucas de Padua, O.F.M., †1287. The third sermon (Schneyer, no. 147) was omitted in its place and added in the main hand on ff. 197^v–198^v. A note was added later at the foot of f. 198^v; 'hic est defectus quem quere in alio libro vbi sub eodem titulo habentur iidem sermones 'scilicet O 90' (*the addition in red ink*)'. f. 199^{rv} blank.

On the pastedown in front is 'Contenta. Sermones dominicales Veni domine ihesu per totum annum super epistolas et euangelia. Et est hic defectus in fine sermonum solempnitatum. Et eciam Registri. Que omnia plena habentur in alio libro pergameneo 'scilicet O 90' in bona littera qui eodem titulo intitulatur. scilicet Sermones dominicales Veni domine ihesu. 'Set videntur nisi exerpta. et ibi habetur Registrum alphabeticum' (*the additions in red ink*)'.

Pasted down binding strips are from a fourteenth-century theological manuscript on parchment.

ff. 199. Paper, with a parchment strip down the centre of each quire as strengthening. 214 × 152 mm. Written space 165 × 103 mm. 2 cols. *c.* 38 lines. Frame ruling in ink. Collation: 1–16^{12} 17 seven (ff. 193–9). Quires numbered at the beginning. Upright textura, with some cursive forms: *i* has a dot, not a stroke, over it. 3-line (f. 1) and 2-line red initials and touching of capital letters with red on ff. 1–5, 119–20 only: elsewhere spaces for initials remain blank. Contemporary binding of wooden boards covered with pigskin: two strap-and-pin fastenings from the back to the front cover and five bosses on each cover are missing: a label on the front cover bears a title like that on the pastedown. Secundo folio *qui nunc in spiritu.*

Written by the 'plebanus' of Wendelstein (near Nuremberg?) and finished on 21 Mar. 1435/6. The references to another copy of these sermons with the pressmark O 90 show that this is a manuscript from the Charterhouse of Erfurt and, no doubt, the one described in the medieval Erfurt catalogue under the pressmark O 89, 'Sermones dominicales Veni domine ihesu super epistolis et euangeliis tocius anni. Eciam habetur alibi. scil. hic in proximo' (*MBDS* ii. 503). At the end of the description of the next item, O 90, the cataloguer noted 'Hi sermones videntur esse Lucii magistri Winensis'. '66' on a fairly old label on the spine. 'Robert Kilgour Thom to the Brechin Diocesan Library Aug. 5th 1863' inside the cover: Thom was rector of Drumlithie, Kincardineshire.

BRIDGNORTH. ST. LEONARD'S PARISH CHURCH, STACKHOUSE LIBRARY

1. Adalbertus Levita, Speculum Moralium[1] s. XII^1

(*Begins imperfectly*) tur.' non exaudiunt. quia consentire contempnunt. XXXIII. De concordi retributione iustorum et de uera libertate seruorum. Hinc nanque

[1] Deposited in the Parochial Libraries Collection, County Library, Shrewsbury.

per beatum iob dicitur . . . Discite a me quia mitis sum (*ends imperfectly in ch. 191*).

Excerpts from Gregory's Moralia in Job by Adalbertus Levita. Three quires are missing at the beginning and a few leaves at the end. The text corresponds to that in B.L., Royal 5 F.v, ff. 10ᵛ–77ᵛ. Among scribbles in the margins, s. xvi, is one in a good humanistic hand: 'Londini in edibus Thome Berthelet: voluntas omnipotentis dei et domini nostri Ihesu cristi'.

ff. i+136+i. 253×160 mm. Written space 185×118 mm. 30 long lines. Ruling with a hard point. Collation: 1–17⁸: 3 and 6 in quire 16 are half-sheets. Quires 3–17 are signed at the end VI–XX. Written in several fairly good hands. Green, blue, or metallic red initials, mostly monochrome. Unusual *I*, ff. 100ᵛ, 110, and *T*, f. 120ᵛ. Binding of s. xix.

Written in England. Part of the collection bequeathed by Hugh Stackhouse, †1743, to the Society of Clergymen in and around Bridgnorth.

2. *Statuta Angliae, etc.*[1]   s. XIV in.

1. ff. 1–4ᵛ Numbered tables of chapters of arts. 2–6, 10, 24, 9, in that order.

2. ff. 4ᵛ–8ᵛ Incipit Magna carta de libertatibus Anglie. Edwardus dei gracia . . . Pro hac autem concessione . . . pro nullo habeatur. Teste etc. Cf. *SR* i. 114.

3. ff. 8ᵛ–10 Incipit de Foresta. Henricus dei gracia . . . etc' omnia vt supra 'vt' in mangna carta.

4. ff. 10–13 Provisions of Merton. *SR* i. 1.

5. ff. 13–20 Statute of Marlborough. *SR* i. 19.

6. ff. 20–32ᵛ Statute of Westminster I. In French. *SR* i. 26.

7. ff. 32ᵛ–34 Incipit Statutum de Finibus. Quia fines . . . *SR* i. 128.

8 (added early). f. 34ʳᵛ Incipit Statuta (*sic*) de Recongnitoribus factis ad Turrim lond'. Pur ceo que nostre seyngnur le Rey . . . en la greue merci le Rey. Explicit statut' de R'.

9. ff. 35–51ᵛ Statute of Westminster II. *SR* i. 71.

10. ff. 51ᵛ–53ᵛ Statute of Gloucester, beginning with a short introduction, 'Pur les grauns meschef . . .'. In French. *SR* i. 45.

11. ff. 53ᵛ–55 Incipit Statut' de Mercatoribus. In French. *SR* i. 53.

12. f. 55ʳᵛ Incipit de Iustic' Assingn'. In French. *SR* i. 44.

13. f. 56ʳᵛ Incipit Assisa de Foresta de Tempore henrici filii Matill'. Hec est assisa Domini Regis H. filii Matild' in Angl' . . . facta apud Wodestok. Primo precepit Rex quod nullus ei forisfaciat de venacione . . . negotia facienda in Com'. Explicit assisa foreste.

As Hoveden, *Chronica*, ed. RS, ii. 245, ch. i–ix, xiv, xiii, xii, xv, x, xi.

[1] Deposited in the Parochial Libraries Collection, County Library, Shrewsbury.

14. ff. 57–62ᵛ Articuli in Itinere. Ici comencent les veus et nouuelez plez de la Corone en Eyre dez Iustices. Cf. *SR* i. 233 (in Latin).

15. ff. 62ᵛ–64 Incipiunt Articuli Corone. In Primes ausitost que les Corounerz eient maundement . . . Cf. *SR* i. 40 (in Latin).

16. f. 64ʳᵛ Incipit Tractatus de Antiquo Dominico Corone. Licet in antiquo dominico . . . ingnoro etc.

Ed. A. J. Horwood, *Year Books 20–21 Edward I* (RS, 1866), pp. xviii–xix.

17. f. 64ᵛ Incipit Statut' de Anno Bisextili. Edwardus dei gracia . . . anno regni nostri xviii. Cf. *SR* i. 7 (40 Henry III).

18. f. 65 Incipit Statutum de Gauelet. *SR* i. 222.

19. ff. 65–67ᵛ Incipit Statut' de Scaccario. In French. *SR* i. 197.

20. ff. 67ᵛ–68 Incipiunt Distrincciones eorundem. In French. *SR* i. 197*b*.

21. f. 68ʳᵛ Incipit Statut' Religiosorum. *SR* i. 51.

22. f. 68ᵛ Incipit Westm' Tercium. Quia emptores . . . *SR* i. 106.

23. ff. 68ᵛ–69 Incipit Statut' contra Prohibiciones. Edwardus dei gracia etc'. Circumspecte agatis . . . licet porigatur. Sub qua forma . . . Regia prohibicio est. *SR* i. 101.

24. ff. 69ᵛ–71 Incipit Statut' Wynton. In French. *SR* i. 96.

25. ff. 71–72ᵛ Incipit Statut' Exon. In French. *SR* i. 210.

26. ff. 72ᵛ–75ᵛ Incip(i)unt Articuli Exonie. In French. *SR* i. 211.

27. ff. 75ᵛ–76 Incipit Visus Francipl'. Inquirendum est si omnes capitales plegii . . . et per quantum tempus. Cf. B.L., Royal 9 A. vii, art. 53, and 11 A. viii, art. 29.

28. ff. 76–77 Incipit Extenta Manerii. De domibus cuiuslibet (m)anerii et hameletti et commoditibus earum . . . nundinarum et passagiorum.

Thirty-five heads. Not as *SR* i. 242.

29. f. 77ʳᵛ Incipit Assisa Panis. *SR* i. 200.

30. ff. 77ᵛ–78 Incipit Modus faciendi homagium. Quando liber homo faciet homagium . . . beysera le liure.

In French, except the first sentence. Cf. *SR* i. 227.

31. f. 78ʳᵛ Incipiunt Dies Communes in Banco. Si breue venerit a die Pasche in xv dies . . .

As *SR* i. 208, but beginning at Easter.

32. f. 78ᵛ Incipiunt Dies Communes in placito Dotis. Si breue venerit in quind' Pasche . . .

As *SR* i. 208, but beginning at Easter.

33. ff. 78ᵛ–79 Incipit Statutum de Conspiratoribus. The writ follows. *SR* i. 216.

34. f. 79 Incipit Statutum de Schaumpart. In French. *SR* i. 216.

35. f. 79ᵛ Incipit Lucrum Pistoris. E(t) sciendum est . . . et bene possunt.
SR i. 200 (Lucrum Pistoris and De Cervisia).

36. ff. 79ᵛ–80ᵛ Tractatus Soke et Sake. Sok.ᵉ hoc est secta . . . reficiendos etc. Expliciunt Interpretaciones Nomina libertat'.
Thirty-one terms, Sok–Brigebote. Cf. B.L., Royal 9 A. ii, art. 34.

37. ff. 80ᵛ–81 Incipit Composissio mone(te) et ponderibus. *SR* i. 204–5.

38. ff. 81ᵛ–84 Incipiunt dampna in triplo. Dampna in triplo vt in vasto . . . vt in eisdem statutis Capitulo viii. Expliciunt dampna.
With reference to statutes, mainly Westminster I and II. Bodleian, Lat. misc. d. 82, ff. 78–80, is another copy.

39. ff. 84–5 Incipit Difinicio Breuis de Recto. Circa breue de Recto expresse notemus quid sit breue . . . sicut breuia de transgressione.
Bodleian, Douce 98, f. 138ᵛ, is another copy.

40. ff. 85ᵛ–92ᵛ Incipit Detencio Namii. Detenue de Naam. pur fer' detresces . . . et si seyt fet de semblable chose. Explicit de vetito Nameo.

41 (added early). f. 92ᵛ Incipit Statutum nouum quo waranto. *SR* i. 107.

42. ff. 93–102 Fet a sauer. a concement . . . en la forme que desus est.
Ed. G. E. Woodbine, *Four thirteenth century law tracts*, 1910, pp. 53–115.

43. ff. 102–117ᵛ Incipit Magnum hengham.
Ed. W. S. Dunham, *Radulphi de Hengham Summae*, 1932, pp. 1–50.

44. ff. 117ᵛ–121ᵛ Incipit Curia Baronum. Cely que veut estre tenu pur sage . . . tot dreit a tel our'.

45. ff. 121ᵛ–127ᵛ Incipiunt diuersa Interrogaciones. En quant de maners passe le bref de Mordancestr' . . . garde sun corps est . . .
Cf. *Casus Placitorum*, ed. W. H. Dunham (Selden Soc. lxix, 1950), p. 4.

46. ff. 127ᵛ–135ᵛ Incipit Summa Paruus Hengham.
Ed. W. S. Dunham, *Radulphi de Hengham Summae*, pp. 52–171.

47. ff. 135ᵛ–141 Incipit Summa Bastardie. Nota quod Bastardus clamando . . . encountre ly. Partly in French.

48. ff. 141–147ᵛ Incipit Cadit assisa. Rex vic' salutem. Si A fecerit . . . loco suo vt predictum est.

49. ff. 147ᵛ–148ᵛ Incipit summa de tenuris diuersorum tenementorum. Tenementorum aliud tenetur per seruicium militare . . . vel per modum donacionis obseruetur.

50. f. 148^v Incipit Modus Calumpniandi Esson'. Esson' non iacet quia terra . . .
SR i. 217.

51. ff. 149–53 Excepciones contra breuia. Ceo est ordre de excepcion . . . ly est
aloyne.

Ed. Woodbine, op. cit., 163–81. Ends as Woodbine's C.

52. f. 153^{rv} Incipit Quot modus dicitur Excepcio. Notandum quod quatuor
modus (*sic*) . . . ad aliam resortire responsionem. 9 lines.

53. ff. 153^v–157^v Incipit modus Componendi Breuia. Cum sit necessarium . . .

Ed. Woodbine, op. cit., 143–62.

54. ff. 157^v–163 Incipit iudicium Essoniarum. Primum capitulum de difficultate . . . discrecionem.

Ed. Woodbine, op. cit., 116–42.

55. ff. 163^v–164 La Nature des Assoygnes. La nature des assoynes . . . de tere.
Vt patet ante excepciones contra breuia.

Cf. B.L., Royal 10 A. v, art. 40.

56. A register of writs in 180 chapters (ff. 168–235), preceded in the same hand
by a numbered table of chapters (ff. 164^v–167). The first chapter is De recto and
begins with a writ dated 'apud N', 4 Feb., 28 Edw. (I). The last chapter is De
conspiratoribus. The order is not that of any of the registers analysed in
Holdsworth, ii. 606–39. The sections marked Rubrica are underlined.

57. f. 235^{rv} Three writs: (*a*) De homine replegiando, addressed to the sheriff
of Northampton, 1 Nov. 1303; (*b*) De aueriis replegiandis post Returnum
factum; (*c*) De Returno aueriorum habendo, 24 Feb., 1305, beginning 'Si
Robertus de Grendon et cristiana vxor eius'.

58 (added early). (*a*) f. 236 A table to show what so much a day comes to in
a week, a month, and a year, e.g. 'iid xiiiid iiiis viiid lxs viiid'. (*b*) ff. 235^v–236.
Field names, headed on one page '[. . .]dington magna' and on the other
'Dodingt' '. (*c*) ff. 236^v–237 Names of fields and their extents in virgates and
fractions thereof, in three sections, headed 'Primo anno', 'Secundo anno', and
'Tercio anno'.

59 (added early). ff. 237^v–238^v (*a–h*) Eight model letters, (*a*) and (*b*) from and
(*e*) to the official of the archdeacon of Northampton, (*c*) dated in 1303, (*g*) beginning 'In dei nomine amen Intellecto nuper quod vos Adam de Holcute Rector
ecclesie de G. et R. tuus capellanus parochialis ad vestrum mandatum me Robertum de G. in quem nullum habetis iurisdiccionem', and (*h*) beginning 'In dei
nomine amen fama referente quod henricus keylemers' and mentioning the
mayor of Northampton, Robert de [. . . .]. f. 238^v is stained from exposure.

ff. i+238+i. 183 × 120 mm. Written space *c.* 150 × 85 mm. 27–30 long lines. Collation:
1^{10} 2–4^{12} 5^{10} 6–10^{12} 11–12^{10} 13^{12} 14^8 (ff. 149–56) 15^{12} wants 12, blank, after f. 167 16^{16}
17–20^{12} 21^8 wants 8. Quires 1–20 are signed at the beginning b–x. Written in several

business hands. Initials: (i) red and blue, with ornament of both colours; (ii) blue, with red ornament. Binding of s. xix. Secundo folio *capitulum vi.*

Written in England, probably in Northamptonshire (art. 57). The owner in s. xiv in. had a special interest (art. 58*b*) in Great Doddington in the valley of the Nene, near Wellingborough, and three miles from Grendon where Adam de Holcute (art. 59*f*) was rector, 1290–1315. Bequeathed by Hugh Stackhouse, †1743.

BRIDPORT. CORPORATION

2644. *Statuta Angliae, etc.*¹   s. xiv¹

Described in HMC, *Sixth Report*, App., p. 475, and by Thomas Wainwright, *The Bridport Records and Ancient Manuscripts*, 1900, pp. 1, 2. I omit the local Bridport material in arts. 47, 62.

1. pp. 8–15 Edwardus dei gracia . . . Testibus etc. Anno regni n' Edwardi ix. Explicit carta de libertatibus Anglie. *SR* i. 114 (25 Edward I).

2. pp. 15–18 Incipit carta de Foresta. *SR* i. 120.

3. pp. 18–19 Sentencia lata super cartas. *SR* i. 6.

4. pp. 19–21 Hic incipit Assisa foreste. Si quis forestarius . . . possit pati vt fiat exitus porcorum. *SR* i. 243–244/36.

5. pp. 21–4 Provisions of Merton. *SR* i. 1.

6. pp. 24–35 Statuta de Marlebergh. *SR* i. 19.

7. pp. 35–56 Statuta Westm' primi. In French. *SR* i. 26.

8. pp. 57–62 Incipit statuta Gloucestrie. In French. *SR* i. 45.

9. pp. 62–3 Incipiunt explanaciones eorundem. *SR* i. 50.

10. pp. 63–98 Incipiunt statuta Westm' secundi. *SR* i. 71.

11. pp. 98–9 Incipiunt statuta Westm' tercii. *SR* i. 106.

12. pp. 99–102 Incipit statut' quia fines in Cur'. *SR* i. 128.

13. pp. 102–3 Hic incipit statuta de Religiosis. *SR* i. 51.

14. pp. 103–6 Hic incipit statut' de Religiosis alieginis. *SR* i. 150.

15. pp. 106–7 Hic incipit statut' Circumspecte agatis. *SR* i. 101.
Two paragraphs, the second beginning 'Sub qua forma laici'.

16. pp. 107–8 Incip' stat' de vocat' ad war'. *SR* i. 108.

17. pp. 108–10 Si quis ponatur in assisis. *SR* i. 113.

¹ Deposited in the County Record Office, Dorchester, B3/G1.

18. p. 110 Incipit statut' de Champart. In French. *SR* i. 216.

19. p. 110 Incipit statut' de mensur' et ponderibus. Per discrecionem tocius Angl' fuit mensura . . . octaua pars quarterii. *SR* i. 200, footnote 2.

20. pp. 110–12 Incipit statut' de Tonsura Monete. De tonsura monete tam de iudeis quam de cristianis est inquirendum primo de his qui tradiderunt denarios suos retonsoribus . . . in quid et cui et quomodo.

21. pp. 112–13 Incipit statuta de militibus. *SR* i. 229.

22. pp. 113–15 Hic incipit statut' de mercatoribus. In French. *SR* i. 98.

23. pp. 115–18 Hic incipit statuta Wyntonye. In French. *SR* i. 96.

24. pp. 119–21 Incipit statut' Eboracum. facta ibidem in tribus septimanis sancti Michaelis Anno Regni Regis E fil' E xii. In French. *SR* i. 177.

25. pp. 121–7 Hic incipit statuta Exon'. In French. *SR* i. 210.

26. pp. 127–31 Hic incipit statuta de scaccario. In French. *SR* i. 197.

27. pp. 132–3 Incipit Districciones Eorundem. In French. *SR* i. 197*b*.

28. pp. 133–4 Hic incipit statuta de Bigamis. *SR* i. 42.

29. pp. 134–6 Hic incipit Statut' de communi feoffamento. *SR* i. 145.

30. p. 137 Hic incipit tractatus de antiquo dominico corone. Licet in antiquo . . . consuetudinem manerii. Cf. above, Bridgnorth 2, art. 16.

31. pp. 137–40 Hic incipit articuli monete. In French. *SR* i. 219.

32. pp. 140–1 Hic incipit Stat' de Wardis et Releuiis. In French. *SR* i. 228.

33. pp. 141–2 Hic incipit Statut' de quo Warento. *SR* i. 107.

34. p. 142 Hic incipit de Calumpniend' Essonium. *SR* i. 217.

35. p. 143 Sequitur dies communes in Banco. *SR* i. 208.

36. pp. 143–4 Sequitur dies communes de dote. *SR* i. 208.

37. pp. 144–6 Hic incipit officium coronatoris. *SR* i. 40.

38. pp. 146–7 Hic incipit visus Franciplegii. Inquirendum est si omnes . . . nomen habebit ad Rectum. Cf. B.L., Royal 11 A. viii, art. 29.

39. pp. 147–8 Hic incipit assisa panis. *SR* i. 199.

40. p. 148 Hic incipit lucrum pistoris. *SR* i. 200.

41. p. 148 Hic incipit assisa seruicie. *SR* i. 200.

42. p. 149 Hic incipit iudicium pistor' et Braciatrices. Si pistor . . . molendini coligant. *SR* i. 201/1–16.

43. pp. 149–50 A noster seygn^r le Roy et a soun counsail monstre la commune de la terre qe com nadgerres . . . (*ends abruptly*).

Rot. Parl. ii. 7, items 1–3/10 (petition from the commonalty to Edward III, a.d. 1326/7). p. 151 is blank.

44 (added, s. xiv[1]): (*a*) p. 152 a form of release; (*b*) pp. 152–7 Quod principi placuit leges habe(n)t vigorum et magnat' tocius regni consensu(m) ad fidelitatem obseruandam vt iura siue leges monete mensur' pondera et assi(s)e prouisa sunt et . . . per eandem cedulam.

A treatise on money, the assize of bread and beer, and forestallers. p. 157 is hard to read, as a result of rubbing.

45. pp. 158–287 A register of writs, beginning with a writ of right of 19 Edward (II?).

The running title is 'Registrum'. There are side headings and a few headings in larger script in the text, but no obvious divisions or coloured initials. Two leaves are missing before p. 254. The order agrees sometimes with that of the manuscript of the time of Edward I analysed in Holdsworth, ii. 613–15: groups 7 and 8 there are here on pp. 257–65 and groups 11–13 on pp. 267–87. In Novel Disseisin the limitation is 'post primam transfretacionem domini h Regis patris nostri in Vascon''.

46. pp. 287–9 Three pieces included under the running title of art. 45, but not properly part of it: (*a*) p. 287 Breue de conspiratoribus (cf. *SR* i. 216 and de Haas and Hall, p. cxxxiv); (*b*) p. 288 Breue de finibus atturnat' et statutis. Cum nuper . . . obseruari. Teste me ipso apud Ca(r)liolum in octabis sancti Hilarii anno regni nostri trices(i)mo quinto (ibid., i. 215); (*c*) p. 289 A letter to the archdeacon of Dorset, 19 June 1326, bidding him pronounce sentence of excommunication against persons unknown who had maltreated R. de C., clerk.

47. pp. 289–313 Documents relating to Bridport added on the last leaf of quire 15 and on quire 16, mainly in a hand resembling the main hand.

48. pp. 313*–329 Hic incipit Natura Breuium. Bref de nouel disseyne est la ou . . . est pleyd' com br' de Trepas. Hic explicit Natura Breuium. Thirty-two paragraphs.

49. pp. 329–68 Et incipit Curia Baronum. Chequune maner' de Trepas . . . auerer les poutz iugg*es*, etc. Expliciunt placita Curie Baronis.

For the incipit cf. B.L., Royal 9 A. vii, art. 51, and Egerton 656 f. 188[v].

50. pp. 368–77 Incipiunt excepciones contra Breuia. Ceo est order' de excepcion . . . seyt atteynt a garde.

Ed. G. E. Woodbine, *Four thirteenth century texts*, pp. 163 sqq: ends differently.

51. pp. 377–403 Hic incipit Summa [. . .]. Fet a sauer . . . ibi hoc breue. Explicit feit a sauer. Ibid., 53–115.

52. pp. 403–11 Sequitur summa Bastardie. Nota quod si bastardus se clamando . . . dum fuerit in custodia. Nota si vn home . . . a court le Roy. Explicit Summa Bastardie. Only the last four lines are in French.

53. pp. 411–23 Sequitur cadit assisa. Rex vic' salutem. Si A. fecerit te securum

. . . mort' antecessorum. Cadit assisa si petatur . . . loco suo vt predictum est. Expliciunt cadit assisa.

Cf. ibid., p. 1, note 4.

54. pp. 424–31 Sequitur modus componendi Breuia. Cum sit necessarium . . . fuerit disseysitus. Explicit summa que vocatur modus componendi breuia.

Ed. ibid., pp. 143–159/27.

55. pp. 431–47 Sequitur paruum hengham. Notandum est quod quinque . . . quod est legatum. Explicit summa que vocatur paruum Hengham.

Ed. W. H. Dunham, *Radulphi de Hengham Summae*, 1932, pp. 52–71, but the last five lines here are not in the printed text.

56. pp. 447–57 Hic incipit de iudiciis Essoniorum. Primum quidem capitulum de difficultate esson' circa viros et mulieres . . . eorum districcionem etc. Explicit summa Iudicium Essoniorum.

Ed. Woodbine, op. cit., pp. 116–42.

Arts. 57–60 are noticed in some detail in HMC.

57. pp. 457–93 Hic incipit modus cartarum. Quit est carta. scriptum sigillatum de re immobili . . . et vendicionibus vti poterunt. Explicit modus cartarum obligat' Et aliorum script'.

58. pp. 493–6 Hic incipit In(uen)torium Cuiusdam Magnate. Modo videndum est quomodo debent inbreuiari et ordinari . . . ad reddend' Mesur' Bacorum et cetera. Explicit Modus ordinandi Inuentorium. Dated in 20 Edw. II.

59. pp. 496–500 Hic incipit Testamentum general' cuiusdam Mag'. In nomine patris . . . Item in expensis clerico scribent' testamentum et compotum iii s'. Summa totus. Explicit testamentum generalis cuiusdam Magnati.

Model will and inventory, 19 Sept. 1326. No books.

60. pp. 500–4 Hic incipit extenta Manerii cuiusdam Magnati. Extenta Manerii I. de C. de forma . . . Summa vi li' x s. ix d. Explicit exstenta Manerii. Dated in 20 Edw. II.

61. pp. 505–6 A multiplication table.

62 (added in hand of art. 46). Documents relating to Bridport.

63. Notes about weights and measures on the pastedown, p. 512.

64. pp. 1–6 A table of chapters of arts. 1, 2, 5–8, 10.

p. 1 is the exposed side of the pastedown. p. 7 is blank, except for a note in a hand like the main hand recording the birth of Laurence, second son of Richard and Petronilla Laur*ence*, 30 May 1338.

ff. 260, paginated on versos, beginning with the pastedown, 1–71, 73, 73**, 75–191, 191**, 193–201, 201**, 203–313, 313**, 315–431, 435–511, (513). 188 × 115 mm. Written space c. 140 × 95 mm. c. 37 long lines. Collation: 1¹⁰ (1 pasted down) 2–13¹⁰ 14¹⁰ wants 1, 2 before p. 254 15¹⁰ 16¹² 17–25¹⁰ 26¹⁰ (10 pasted down). Written in current anglicana. Initials: (i) red and blue with ornament of both colours or red; (ii) 2-line, blue with red ornament. Contemporary binding of wooden boards covered with dark leather: two strap-and-pin fastenings missing. Secundo folio *faciat quod.*

Written probably in and shortly after 1326 (cf. arts. 43, 35, 58–60) and perhaps at Bridport, since arts. 47, 62, although additions, are in writing like the main hand (cf. also art. 45), as is the note on p. 7, art. 64, which suggests that the writer may have been Richard Laurence, bailiff in 1350.

BRIGHTON. PUBLIC LIBRARY

Brighton Public Libraries. Catalogue of Manuscripts and Printed Books before 1500 (1962), pp. 5–7, contains brief descriptions of MSS. 1–10.[1]

1. *Biblia*   s. XIII med.

1. ff. ix–xii, 1–663ᵛ A Bible in the usual order, lacking Psalms, but otherwise with the usual contents, including the Prayer of Manasses.[2]

Matthew and Pauline Epistles begin on new quires, ff. 519, 583. Proverbs begins on a new page, but not a new leaf, f. 324ᵛ. The prologues are 63 of the usual 64 (there is no prologue to 2 Chronicles), together with eight to Minor Prophets, each of which follows the usual prologue or prologues: Stegmüller, nos. 516, 522, 525, 527, 529, 535, 540, 545. Stegmüller, nos. 519 and 517 are not run together, as usual, but treated as two separate prologues.

2. ff. 664–686ᵛ Aaron mons fortis . . . Zorobabe(l) . . . expositus.

For copies of the dictionary of Hebrew names, Aaron mons fortis–Zorobabel, see *Sum. Cat.*, Index, p. 213, and B.L., Royal 1 A. i, 1 A. vii, 1 B. viii, 1 D. iv.

3. (*a*) ff. 686ᵛ–687 Ista non inueniuntur in interpretationibus aliiquibus (*sic*) nec beati ieronimi. Aadama i esdre viii b.c . . . Zebdiel i mach' xi b. (*b*) f. 687 Notandum quod preter ista nomina hic supra nomina que non inueniuntur in interpretationibus aliquibus nec in interpretationibus beati ieronimi sunt plura in istis interpretationibus posita secundum beatum ieronimum que in aliiquibus (*sic*) interpretationibus non sunt. Notandum etiam in hiis interpretationibus quod h non ponitur pro littera sed quere dictamen que incipit per h in littera que sequitur immediate h.

(*a*). Twenty-seven names, not interpreted, but furnished, as entries in art. 2 are not, with chapter-numbers and letter-marks subdividing chapters.

ff. viii+689+vii. Foliated (i–xii), 1–49, 49*, 50–193, 193*, 194–387, 389–434, 436–516, 518–64, 564*, 565–667, 667*, 668–72, 672*, 673–87, (688–94). 150×110 mm. Written space 110×72 mm. 2 cols. 42 lines. Collation: 1–13²⁴ 14⁶+1 leaf after 2 (f. 309) 15¹⁰ (ff. 314–23) 16–24²⁴ 25²⁰+3 leaves after 20 (ff. 563, 564, 564*) 26¹⁸ 27–29²⁴ 30 twenty-three (ff. 655–75) 31¹². Changes of hand at ff. 211 (10¹), 583 (27¹), 608. Initials: (i) of books and Jerome's general prologue, 7-line or more, in colour on red and blue grounds, historiated

[1] MS. 7, not described here, contains the institution and statutes of the Order of the Golden Fleece in French, s. xvi.
[2] See Bristol Public Library, 15.

and framed in gold; (ii) of many prologues, red and blue, with ornament of both colours; (iii) of chapters and some prologues, 2-line, red or blue, with ornament of the other colour; (iv) in art. 2, 1-line, blue or red. Capital letters in the ink of the text touched with red. Binding of red morocco, s. xviii. Secundo folio *ruditis posse*.

Written in France. 'Achepte de maistre Louys Libraire a Beauvais L'an 1587', f. 663ᵛ. 'J. B. Vranckix', f. iᵛ. 'Church Congress Exhibition 157' on a label inside the cover. Given by the Misses Gurney in May 1903.

2. *Horae*   s. xv²

1. ff. 1–9ᵛ Full calendar, March–October, and December, in French in gold, red, and blue, the two colours alternating for effect.

'denis' in gold, 9 Oct.

2. ff. 10–13ᵛ Sequentiae of the Gospels, beginning and ending imperfectly.

3. ff. 14–17ᵛ Obsecro te, beginning imperfectly. Masculine forms.

4. ff. 18–21ᵛ O intemerata, beginning imperfectly. Masculine forms.

5. Prayers and salutations to B.V.M.: (*a*) f. 22ʳᵛ De nostre dame. oroison. Sancta maria mater domini nostri ihesu cristi in manus filii tui . . .; (*b*) f. 23ʳᵛ Sancta maria mater immaculata miserere michi indigno famulo tuo . . .; (*c*) ff. 23ᵛ–24 Antiphona. Aue regina celorum mater regis angelorum . . .; (*d*) ff. 24–25ᵛ Oracio. Aue maria gracia plena dominus tecum ita tu mecum . . .; (*e*) ff. 25ᵛ–28 Gaude flore uirginali honoreque spirituali (*sic*). Transcendens . . .; (*f*) f. 28ᵛ Sancta maria mater dei miserere mei et tocius populi cristiani . . .; (*g*) f. 29ʳᵛ Gaude uirgo mater cristi. Que per aurem concepisti . . .; (*h*) ff. 29ᵛ–30ᵛ Salut. Aue cuius concepcio Solenni plena gaudio . . .; (*i*) f. 31 Alia. Ad te confugio mater misericordie domina sancta maria . . .; (*j*) ff. 31ᵛ–32 Benedicta sit illa sacratissima hora in qua deus homo . . .; (*k*) f. 32ʳᵛ Alia Oracio. Maria uirgo uirginum rogo te per patrem cuius uirtus . . .; (*l*) ff. 32ᵛ–34ᵛ Alia. Stabat mater dolorosa . . .; (*m*) ff. 34ᵛ–37ᵛ Alia deuota oracio. Aue uirgo gloriosa. Stella sole clarior . . . (13 stanzas).

(*c, e, g, h, l, m*). *RH*, nos. 2072, 6810, 7017 (Five Joys), 1744, 19416, 2215.

6. ff. 38–81ᵛ Hours of B.V.M. of the use of (Paris)

Each hour begins imperfectly. Nine lessons in matins.

7. ff. 82–100ᵛ Penitential psalms, beginning imperfectly, and (f. 94) litany.

Denis 20th of martyrs. Genovefa does not occur.

8. ff. 101–103ᵛ De sancta cruce.

Hours of the Cross, beginning imperfectly. The heading is on f. 100ᵛ.

9. ff. 104–106ᵛ De sancto spiritu.

Hours of the Holy Spirit, beginning imperfectly. The heading is on f. 103ᵛ.

10. ff. 107–139ᵛ Office of the dead, beginning imperfectly.

The heading 'In vigilia mortuorum' is on f. 106ᵛ.

11. ff. 140–3 De sancta trinitate. memoria. O beata et benedicta et gloriosa

trinitas . . . Oremus. Sancta trinitas atque indiuisa vnitas . . . Oremus. Oracio. Omnipotens sempiterne deus qui dedisti famulis tuis in confessione. etc'.

12. Prayers to the Son: (a) ff. 143–4 Alia oracio. Criste fili dei miserere nobis . . . Oremus. Oracio. Domine ihesu criste fili dei viui lux vera qui . . .; (b) 144^{rv} Oracio. O beatissime domine ihesu criste respicere digneris super me miserum peccatorem oculis . . .; (c) ff. 144^v–145 Oracio. Domine ihesu criste distilla in corde meo . . . (d) f. 145^{rv} Te domine ihesu criste supplice corde . . .; (e) ff. 145^v–146 Domine ihesu criste fili dei viui cuius passio modo recollitur. . . .; (f) ff. 146^v–147 Corpus domini nostri ihesu cristi veni veni veni in animam meam . . .; (g) ff. 147–8 Oracio. Domine ihesu criste et redemptor animarum. Te deprecor . . .; (h) ff. 148–9 Alia oracio. Domine ihesu criste adoro te in cruce descendentem . . .; (i) ff. 149–150^v Oracio. Aue domine ihesu criste verbum patris filius virginis . . . vita perennis . . . Oremus. Domine ihesu criste redemptor bone eam confessionem . . .; (j) ff. 150^v–153^v Domine ihesu criste fili dei uiui qui septem uerba die ultimo . . .; (k) ff. 153^v–154^v Oracio. Domine ihesu criste qui celum et terram fecisti . . .; (l) ff. 154^v–155^v Alia oracio. Domine misericors da michi contricionem cordis . . .; (m) f. 155^v Alia oracio. Domine ihesu criste misericors deus da michi dilectionem tuam . . .; (n) f. 156 Domine ihesu criste misericors deus dilectionem proximi da michi . . .

(h). A corrupt version of the Seven Oes. (i). Five Aves. (j). Prayer of the Seven Words.

13. f. 156^{rv} Oracio ad deum patrem. Domine sancte pater omnipotens eterne deus qui manes in trinitate . . .

14. ff. 156^v–157 Uisita quesumus domine habitacionem istam . . .

15. f. 157 Oracio. Domine ihesu criste da michi amare quod amas . . .

16. f. 157^v Domine misericors deus da michi ad renunciacionem peccatorum . . .

17. ff. 157^v–159 Les viii vers saint bernard. Illumina . . . Oracio. Omnipotens sempiterne deus qui ezechie regi . . .

18. f. 159^{rv} Requeste. Sire dieu ihesu crist mon dieu mon createur mon pere . . .

19. f. 160^{rv} Suscipere digneris domine deus pater omnipotens hos psalmos consecratos. et has oraciones quas ego indignus et miser peccator . . .

20. Memoriae: (a) f. 161^{rv} De sanctissimo sacramento. a'. O quam suauis est domine spiritus tuus . . .; (b) ff. ff. 161^v–162^v De sancta cruce memoria. O crux splendidior cunctis astris . . .

21. ff. 163–175^v Memoriae of Holy Cross (beginning imperfectly), angels, (angel) O mi sancte angele deus michi dedit te . . ., A son ange. Angele qui meus es . . ., John Baptist, Peter, Paul, Andrew, John Evangelist, James, Bartholomew, Matthew, Thomas apostle, Philip and James, Simon and Jude, Luke, of peace and of All Saints.

22. ff. 175^v–177 Prayers: (a) quant on ist de sa chambre. Vias tuas domine . . .; (b) intrando ecclesiam. Introibo in domum tuam . . .; (c) quant on prent leaue

benoite. Aqua benedicta . . .; (*d*) oracio dicenda ante crucifixum. Salue sancta crux speciosa . . .

23. ff. 177–194ᵛ Memoriae of SS. Apollonia, Margaret, Mary Magdalene, Barbara, Anne, Mary Magdalene, Katherine, Genovefa, Christopher, Sebastian, John Evangelist, 'De sancto glaudio' (Claude), Nicholas.

f. 194ᵛ is rubbed from exposure. Its last line bears an illegible heading after the memoria of Nicholas.

ff. ii+194+ii. 122×80 mm. Written space *c.* 65×43 mm. 15 long lines. Collation: 1¹² wants 1, 2, 11, followed by 25 quires, probably nearly all eights once, from which about eighteen leaves have been removed. Written in *lettre bâtarde*. Initials: (i) removed; (ii, iii) 2-line and 1-line, blue with red ornament or gold with blue-grey ornament. Line fillers red and blue or gold and blue. Capital letters in the ink of the text filled with pale yellow. Binding of s. xx by L. Broca.

Written in France. 'Bought 1933 from collection of Lady Thomas Stanford', inside cover.

3. *Horae*   s. xv in.

A book of hours from which many leaves are missing. Arts. 3, 4, 6, 7*a* are imperfect at both ends, arts. 1*a*, 5 at the beginning and art. 2 at the end.

1 (quire 1). (*a*) ff. 3–5ᵛ Sequentiae of the Gospels, the first two leaves missing. (*b*) ff. 6–7ᵛ, 2ʳᵛ Obsecro te . . .: masculine forms.

2 (quire 2). ff. 1ʳᵛ, 8–9ᵛ O intemerata . . . orbis terrarum. De te enim . . .

3 (quires 3–7). ff. 10–35ᵛ Hours of B.V.M.

Very imperfect. Memoriae of Holy Spirit, Nicholas, and Katherine after lauds are followed by a blank page, f. 24ᵛ.

4 (quires 8, 9). ff. 36–44ᵛ Penitential psalms.

5 (quire 10). ff. 45–46ᵛ Hours of Holy Spirit.

6 (quires 11–13). ff. 47–69ᵛ Office of the dead.

7 (quire 14). (*a*) ff. 70–72ᵛ The Fifteen Joys. (*b*) ff. 73–74ᵛ The Seven Requests. (*c*) f. 74ᵛ Saincte uraie crois aouree . . .

In French, Sonet, nos. 458, 504, 1876. Ten Joys of (*a*) are complete.

8. Insertions and paste-ons: (i) part of a leaf of a psalter (?), s. xv, with beginning of Te Deum, is pasted to f. 2ᵛ; (ii) borders and a woodcut are pasted to ff. 24ᵛ, 46ᵛ; (iii) twelve paper leaves with texts in English and drawings, s. xvii/xviii, have been inserted: the main theme is mortality.

ff. ii+74+ii. 190×138 mm. Written space 110×80 mm. 16 long lines. Collation: 14 quires, mainly eights (5², 10⁴, 14⁴), but all except 5 (ff. 23, 24), 12 are imperfect. Initials: (i) ff. 1, 6, 28, 31ᵛ, blue patterned in white on decorated gold grounds; (ii, iii) 2-line and 1-line, gold on red and blue grounds patterned in white. Capital letters in the ink of the text are filled with pale yellow. A framed floral border on three sides of ff. 1, 6, 28, 31ᵛ. Binding of carved oak, s. xix.

Written in France. Belonged to J. P. Dowse, s. xix. Book-plate of Leonard Lionel Bloomfield, dated 1908. Bequeathed by him in 1917.

4. *Pseudo-J. de Garlandia*[1]   s. XIV in.

1. ff. 1–19ᵛ Cartula nostra tibi mandat dilecte salutes . . .

822 lines. Walther, no. 2521. This version is more than twice as long as the one printed in *PL* clxxxiv. 1307–14 (371 lines). It is not the version printed in *Auctores octo*, edn. 1538, etc.

(1) ff. 1–12 Lines 1–495, Hoc tibi det munus qui regnat trinus et unus. Mostly as in *PL*, but 110 lines on ff. 8–10ᵛ come here between lines 301 and 302 in *PL*.

(2) ff. 12–16ᵛ Lines 496–690, Sit caro lubrica et (?) tibi celica lex fit amara . . . Quod bene quod iuste quod item feceris ipse.

(3) ff. 16ᵛ–19ᵛ Lines 691–815, Tu quis (*sic*) amas mundum tibi prospice qualis eundum (cf. Walther, no. 17910, Si quis amat . . .) . . . Quo non [. . . . . .] et non deitate [. . . .].

(4) f. 19ᵛ Lines 816–22, Finito libro sit laus et gloria xpristo Hic liber est scriptus qui scripsit sit benedictus Scripsit yardinus pro scripto sit sibi pignus Scriptor scripsisset melius si uoluisset Maxima nam summi non est data copia nummi Est hec scriptura sine forma littera pura Et michimet tristi donetur gratia xpristi. Explicit contemptus mundi.

Red initial letters begin (1), (2), and (3) and occur within (1) at lines 11, 82, 202, 252 in *PL* and on f. 9, line 366, at the line 'Regnum celorum requies est plena bonorum' (cf. Walther, no. 16542).

2. ff. 19ᵛ–20 Sicut ait sapiens sciencia moralis est de expulsione viciorum . . . philosophie. Ad litteram curramus. Cartula nostra tibi. De iusticia. de prudencia de temperancia et fortitudine (*ends abruptly*).

The beginning of a commentary on art. 1. f. 20ᵛ blank.

ff. ii+20+i. 153 × 110 mm. Written space 112 mm high. 22 long lines, each between a pair of ruled lines. Two quires of ten leaves each. Initials red, 3-line, 2-line, and 1-line. Binding of s. xix, the cover stamped with the words 'J. de Gallandia Liber de contunptu mundi MS du xiii siecle'. Secundo folio *Illa ferit*.

Written in France (?). A note in French on f. iᵛ is followed by the words 'Ce note me parais etre de l'Abbé Tersin (?) de S. Leger' and in another paragraph '[Ce MSS] vient de l'Abbé de Tersan [à la vente] duquel je l'ai achete. [D.L.]':[2] the owner was therefore Charles-Philippe Campion de Tersan, 1736–1819, for whose sale in 1819 cf. Delisle, *Cabinet des Manuscrits*, ii. 285. Thomas Thorpe's catalogue for 1836, item 492. Phillipps MS. 9169: in sale 10 June 1896, lot 569, to Quaritch for £4. 18s. '£5. 0. 0', f. iᵛ. Given as MS. 3.

5. *Antiphonale*   s. XIV med.

1. ff. 1–196ᵛ Temporale from Advent to the twenty-fifth Sunday after Pentecost.

The office for the twenty-fifth Sunday ends on f. 182ᵛ and is followed by the heading 'Antiphone in sabbatis ad vesperas de libris regum'. The series of antiphons (etc.) continues to f. 196ᵛ and ends imperfectly in the 'Antiphone de machabeis' at the versicle 'Mementote mirabilium eius'. Nineteen leaves are missing between 'i' and 'cxcvi'.

---

[1] A facsimile in the Bodleian Library, Oxford, MS. Facs. e. 41.
[2] The words in brackets, now illegible, are derived from the 1896 sale catalogue.

2. ff. 202–37 Sanctorale, beginning imperfectly.

Nine feasts: John Baptist, Peter and Paul, Paul, Mary Magdalene, Assumption of B.V.M., Decollation of John Baptist, Exaltation of Cross, Michael, All Saints. A note in the lower margin, f. 236ᵛ, In festo reliquiarum omnia dicuntur sicut in festo omnium sanctorum excepto quod ad ultimas vesperas dicitur paruulum responsum. 'In festo sancti hugonis in primis vesperiis [. . . .].' A cross reference on f. 235 to art. 9a.

3. ff. 237–66 Common of saints.

4. ff. 266–268ᵛ In dedicacione ecclesie.

5. ff. 268ᵛ–270 In annunciacione dominica quando post pascha celebratur. Ad vesperas antiphona super psalmos. Missus est gabriel . . .

6. ff. 270–1 Responses of the common of saints, each followed by Alleluia.

7. f. 271 Antiphons in commemorations of Holy Cross, B.V.M., John Baptist, and All Saints, Nos autem oportet, Tota pulcra es, Inter natos mulierum, Fulgebunt iusti, and 'Ite missa est' (etc.), 'tempore paschali'.

8. ff. 271ᵛ–272 Differencia primi toni . . .

Eight tones of Gloria patri.

9 (added, s. xiv). f. 272ᵛ (a) In festo xi mil' virginum ad primas vesperas R' Audi filia . . . (b) in upper margin and partly cut off, 'Ego iohannes de [. . . .] talem societatem fecimus inter nos scilicet quod unus pro altero dicat [. . . .] missas quando dei uoluntas de nobis ordinauerit'.

10 (added, s. xvii). (a) f. 272 Cues for St. Joseph and a cross reference to the office of St. Anne 'quod inuenies in supplemento antiphonarii in libro hymnorum'. (b) ff. 273–291ᵛ Offices of the Holy Name, Transfiguration (ff. 278, 287), and Holy Trinity (f. 282). f. 292ʳᵛ blank.

11. f. vi is part of a notarial document, s. xv, used in binding, the recto blank, the verso with faded writing, 'Reuerendo in cristo . . .'.

ff. xiv+263+xi. Arts. 1–8 have a medieval foliation on versos, I–CCLXXI, to which I have adhered. It takes into account the thirty missing leaves of text, 2–5, 7, 8, 39, 100, 140–1, 150–1, 162, 174–7, 184–5, 197–202, 252–5, 261, and is in error by marking two successive leaves CLXXXX and CXC at the point where a new foliator began work. For ff. vi and 273–91 see above, arts. 10, 11. 250 × 180 mm. Written space 190 × 120 mm. 9 long lines and music. The collation of ff. 1–272 was 1–15¹⁰ 16–17¹² 18¹⁰+1 leaf in the first half of the quire 19–26¹⁰ (ff. 186–264) 27⁸: for the thirty missing leaves, see above. Initials: (i) f. 1ᵛ, A of Aspiciebam red and green with ornament in red, green, and violet; (ii) red and green, with ornament of both colours or in red and violet; (iii) red with violet ornament, or green with red ornament; (iv) 1-line, red or green. A yellow wash over cadels. Binding of wooden boards, with leather backstrip, s. xx¹.

Written in Italy for Carthusian use. The relevant slip from an English sale catalogue, s. xix, is pasted to f. vi. Given as MS. 3.

6. Horae   s. xv med.

1. ff. 1–6ᵛ Calendar in French in red and black, rather empty.

Spellings vinchent, leurent, bettremieu, brixe.

2. ff. 7–11^v Hours of Holy Cross.

3. ff. 11^v–12 De sainte barbe. ant'. Aue troni lucifera post mariam flos virginum . . . A memoria of St. Barbara. f. 12^v blank.

4. ff. 13–17 Hours of Holy Spirit.

5. Memoriae: (a) f. 17^{rv} Hymne du saint esperit. Veni creator spiritus . . .;
(b) ff. 17^v–18^v De nostre dame ant'. Salue regina . . .

RH, nos. 21204, 18150.

6. ff. 18^v–19^v Les viii vers saint bernard. Illumina . . . Oremus. Omnipotens
sempiterne deus qui ezechie regi . . .

7. ff. 19^v–20^v Memoriae of SS. Nicholas, Sebastian, and Anthony hermit.

8. ff. 21–65^v Hours of B.V.M. of the use of (Tournai).

The Brighton catalogue, op. cit., pl. 1, shows ff. 34^v–35 reduced. f. 43^{rv} blank after lauds.

9. ff. 66–77^v Penitential psalms and (f. 74) litany.

Nine confessors: . . . (9) amande. f. 78^{rv} blank.

10. ff. 79–99 Office of the dead.

Three lessons only. ff. 99^v–100^v blank.

ff. ii + 100 + ii. 158 × 115 mm. Written space 100 × 75 mm. 16 long lines. Collation: 1^6 2^8
3^6 (ff. 15–20) 4–9^8 10^{10} (ff. 69–78) 11–12^8 13^6. Twelve 12-line pictures, eight in art. 8 (Presentation at sext, Kings at none, Innocents at vespers, Flight at compline) and one before
each of arts. 2, 4, 9, 10 (Death holding a coffin and a spear stands on a naked man: a
woman sits in the background). Initials: (i) blue, patterned in white on grounds of gold
and red, the latter patterned in gold paint; (ii) 2-line, gold on red and blue grounds,
patterned in white; (iii) 1-line, red or blue. Red or blue line fillers in litany. Framed
floral borders on three sides of picture pages. Capital letters in the ink of the text filled
with pale yellow. English binding, s. xix, labelled 'Missal'.[1] Secundo folio (f. 8) *giri digneris.*
Written for use in the diocese of Tournai (Belgium). 'of Leighton £42. 0. 0' and 'N°
1580' inside the cover. Given as MS. 3.

8. *Plinius Secundus, etc.*   1468

1. ff. 1–24^v Gaii plinii secundi oratori Veronensis de viris illustribus liber
incipit. P.R.C.X. Rex albanorum Amulium et Numitorem filios habuit. quibus
regnum . . . cremandum curauit. Finis. laus deo. expletum die Sabbatiant'
H. 16 aprilis 1468. Gaii plinii secundi oratoris veronensis de viris illustribus
liber explicit.

Pseudo-Pliny, the younger. Ed. often, by itself and after the Epistolae and Panegyricus.
A scholium on Aesculapius, f. 8, quotes Aristophanes in neatly written Greek.

2. ff. 5–47 M.T.C. De amicicia. Liber incipit. Quintus Mutius augur sceuola
multa narrare de Lelio . . . prestabilius esse putetis. Explicit liber M. tulii

---

[1] Books of Hours were commonly so called. The word is probably equivalent to
'Service book of the Roman Catholic Church'.

ciceronis de amicicia. feliciter amen xxiiii° augusti 1468. Felix qui meruit tranquillam ducere uitam Et letos stabili claudere fine dies. f. 47ᵛ blank.

3. ff. 48–60 Bertho*lomе*i facii ad carulum Vintimilium. Virum clarissimum. de origine inter gallos et britanos belli Historia foeliciter Incipit. Quod me rogasti Carole generose inter multas ac uarias curas . . . prope exhausta est. Finis. Laus deo patri.

Printed in the supplement to A. Ciaconius, *Bibliotheca* (ed. Amsterdam 1744, pp. 893–902).

4. ff. 60–5 M. tuli ciceronis oratio priusquam iret in exilium. Si quando inimicorum impetum propulsare . . . uirtute conseruetis. Explicit M.T.C. oracio habita pridie quem iret in exilium. f. 65ᵛ blank.

Pseudo-Cicero. Teubner edn., iii. iv (1898), 425–34.

ff. ii+65+ii. 212×142 mm. Written space *c.* 135×78 mm. 27 long lines. Collation: 1–2¹⁰ 3⁸ 4–6¹⁰ 7⁸ wants 8, blank. Pencil ruling, ff. 1–48ᵛ, then ink. Writing above top ruled line. Written in a small sloping fere-humanistica (rounded *d*; 2-shaped *r* in all positions; some bitings). Initials: (i) 3-line, gold on red and blue grounds, patterned crudely in white; (ii) 2-line, blue or red. English binding, s. xix in. Secundo folio *centum*. Written in Italy. 'Henry Drury. Harrow. 1821', f. i. Phillipps MS. 3365: Phillipps sale, 15 June 1908, lot 614. '18/11/09 £28', f. i. Given as MS. 3.

9. *'Devotorum precordiale'*, etc.   s. XVI in.

1. ff. 1ᵛ–13 Calendar in red and black, graded.

In red: Udalrici episcopi, Aurely episcopi, Galli abbatis, Conradi episcopi (4 July, 14 Sept., 16 Oct., 26 Nov.), marked, except at 14 Sept., for twelve lessons. In black: Com' abbatum, 6 Jan.; Com' fratrum, 7 Feb., 7 May, 4 Aug., 3 Oct.; Com' benefactorum, 3 Mar., 6 June, 4 Sept., 2 Dec.; Com' fundatorum, 6 Apr.; Com' parentum, 7 July. 'Walpurge virginis natal'' added at 26 Feb. ff. 1ʳ, 13ᵛ blank.

2. ff. 14–86ᵛ Deuotorum precordiale excitatiuum in diuinis et extra cum frequenti exercitatione obseruandum. Omnes nos manifestari oportet ante tribunal christi[1] . . . (f. 17) Hunc ergo presentem libellum ob deuotionis incrementum ac orationis studium frequenter inspice . . .

The 'precordiale' seems to extend at least to f. 86ᵛ and probably further. On ff. 17ᵛ–86ᵛ main headings are: (*a*) f. 17ᵛ Sequuntur quedam generalia de quotidiana exercitatione religiosi breuiter excerpta et annotanda; (*b*) f. 25ᵛ De horis canonicis nunc dicendum et de locatione psalmorum singulorum in singulis digitis . . .; (*c*) f. 30ᵛ Sequitur fructuosa exercitatio de passione domini . . .; (*d*) f. 44 Sequitur exercitatio qualiter te debeas habere post omnes horas canonicas; (*e*) f. 45ᵛ Sequitur nunc de horis canonicis quando dicuntur in priuato; (*f*) f. 51 Nota de suffragiis ad beatam virginem siue alios speciales patronos; (*g*) f. 56 Sequitur de exercitatione habenda de passione domini seu specialiter de quinque vulneribus christi; (*h*) f. 60ᵛ De ministerio misse et aliis astantibus ibidem; (*i*) f. 69ᵛ Exercitacio circa cibum potum balneum colloquium seu aliud commodum corporale habenda; (*j*) f. 70ᵛ De amore solitudinis commendatione celle et monastica conuersatione breuiter nota que sequuntur; (*k*) f. 83 Formula breuis danda nouiciis in conuersionis inicio; (*l*) f. 85 Formula breuis viuendi danda religiosis. Cross references by the main hand in red ink are to leaf numbers of this manuscript.

[1] *Christus* is commoner than *cristus* in this manuscript and, I think, *oratio* than *oracio*. I have expanded abbreviations to *chr-* and *-tio*.

Feminine forms here and there, e.g., ff. 19, 47ᵛ. (*j*) includes the five vows 'tue professionis' and meditations for each day of the week, ff. 74ᵛ–82. f. 87ʳ blank.

3. ff. 87ᵛ–109 Sequuntur orationes deuote propter earum efficaciam et indulgentias sepius dicende causa deuotionis et exercitacionis et cetera. (*a–c*) Oracio dominica . . ., Aue maria . . ., Credo in deum patrem . . . (*d*) f. 88ᵛ Sequitur oratio dicenda de sancta Trinitate pro graciarum actione dicenda. Omnipotens sempiterne deus ineffabilis clemens . . . (*e*) f. 92 Oratio Sixti pape quarti contra pestilenciam cum quadraginta diebus indulgenciarum. Per signum thau . . . (*f*) f. 92ᵛ Orationes deuote ante ymaginem pietatis dicende . . . O domine iesu christe adoro te . . . (*g*) f. 93ᵛ Sequuntur salutaciones ad omnia membra christi . . . Salue tremendum cunctis potestatibus . . . (*h*) f. 95ᵛ Oratio sequens tot dies in purgatorio suspendit penales quot christus pertulit vulnera . . . Domine iesu christe fili dei viui propter tuam innocenciam . . . (*i*) f. 96 Oratio alia satis efficax . . . ante crucifixi ymaginem flexis genibus dicenda. Precor te amantissime domine Iesu christe fili dei viui propter illam eximiam charitatem . . . (*j*) f. 97 Ad veronicam sanctam . . . Salue sancta facies . . . (*k*) f. 99 Alia oratio ad faciem . . . O facies christi que quondam te tribuisti . . . (*l*) f. 99 Versus alii ad christi faciem. Aue facies omnipotentis: in throno iudicis . . . (*m*) f. 99ᵛ Notice of the indulgences attached to Arma passionis christi. (*n*) f. 100 Sequitur Rosarium beate Marie virginis cum versibus ex textu Sancti euangelii compositum . . . Aue maria gracia plena . . . (*o*) f. 105ᵛ Sixtus papa quartus . . . Aue sanctissima Maria mater dei . . . (*p*) f. 106 Sequitur oratio alia breuis et bona ad beatam virginem. Salue virgo egregia mater eterni solis . . . (*q*) f. 106ᵛ Celestinus papa dedit trecentos dies indulgenciarum dicentibus orationem . . . Per illud dulce osculum . . . (*r*) f. 107 Sequuntur Versus beati Anselmi episcopi contra carnis tentaciones . . . Fluat stilla de mamilla . . . (*s*) f. 107ᵛ Sequitur de sancta Anna . . . Anna pia mater aue cuius nomen est suaue . . . (*t*) f. 108ᵛ Allexander papa sextus dedit omnibus orationem sequentem coram ymagine sancte Anne dicentibus decem milia mortalium . . . Aue Maria gratia plena dominus tecum . . . et benedictus fructus ventris tui. Iesus Christus Quem tu virgo sanctissima . . . f. 109ᵛ blank.

(*d*). Feminine forms. (*f*). Seven oes. Feminine forms. (*g*). Indulgenced with 300 days for each Salve and Ave. (*j*). *RH*, no. 18189. (*n*). Fifty paragraphs, each followed by Aue maria. (*o*). Indulgenced by Pope Sixtus IV. (*s*). *RH*, no. 1109.

4. ff. 110–26 Penitential psalms and (f. 119) litany.

In the litany the last five lines on f. 119 have been erased: the passage began 'Sancte angele mi custos et director' and ended 'omnes sancti beatorum spirituum ordinis Orate'. On f. 119ᵛ the names of eighteen patriarchs have been erased. Twenty apostles, evangelists, and disciples: (1) ioachim et anna, (2) ioseph, (3–5) caspar baltasar melchior . . . (18–20) lazare martha veronica. Thirty-five confessors: . . . (8–10) aureli conrade vdalrice . . . Twenty-two virgins: (1–3) scolastica walpurga katherina . . . (14) fenagaria . . . (17, 18) reiswinda otilia.

5. ff. 127–30 Prayers for the dead.

6. ff. 130ᵛ–133 Sequuntur notabilia optima de variis indulgenciis.

Thirty-two indulgences of Pope John XXII are listed on ff. 131–3. f. 133ᵛ blank.

7. ff. 134–165ᵛ Incipit passio domini nostri Iesu christi ex concordancia quatuor

euangelistarum de verbo ad verbum diligenter collecta. In illo tempore: dixit Iesus discipulis suis Scitis quia post biduum . . . habeatis in nomine ipsius Amen.

8. ff. 166–169ᵛ Sequitur ordo miraculorum que saluator noster in ebdomada palmarum pro salute nostra operari dignatus est. In die palmarum . . . Et mane facto in die ramis palmarum . . . pro die festo procurasset etc.

Divided for Sunday–Wednesday in Holy Week.

9. f. 170ʳᵛ Sequitur oracio efficacissima de passione domini maximis dotata indulgenciis. edita a beato Augustino episcopo. Domine Iesu christe fili dei viui qui pro redemptione nostra nasci . . . latronem. Qui viuis . . . Amen.

10. ff. 170ᵛ–173 Oracio deuota de Sancta Scolastica virgine cristi sorore sancti Benedicti abbatis. O sanctissima et gloriosa virgo scolastica sponsa. . . .

A memoria.

11. ff. 173–4 Notandum quod diebus infrascriptis habentur staciones speciales in ecclesiis vrbis Rome. Omnibus dominicis . . .

12. ff. 174ᵛ–175ᵛ Sequitur tenor indulgenciarum quas christifideles consequi valent fideliter cum aqua benedicta se aspergentes. Notum sit cunctis christifidelibus. quod Alexander papa quintus . . . indulgenciam consequetur. Sex operatur aqua . . . (4 lines).

The verses at the end are Walther, *Sprichwörter*, no. 28208, with a differing fourth line: here it is 'Quot guttas sentis. tot tollit crimina mentis'.

ff. 179, including the pastedowns. A medieval foliation in red I–XCVI covers arts. 2, 3. 97 × 75 mm. Written space 63 × 43 mm. 18 long lines. Frame ruling in red ink. Collation: 1⁶ (pastedown and ff. 1–5) 2–22⁸ 23⁶ wants 6 (ff. 174–8: 178 pasted down). Written in hybrida. Initials: (i) red, with ornament in the ink of the text; (ii–iv) 3-line, 2-line, and 1-line, red. Capital letters in the ink of the text marked with red. Contemporary(?) binding of wooden boards covered with red leather: only the metal pieces of a central clasp remain: each cover had a metal centrepiece and metal cornerpieces, now missing.

Written in southern Germany for Benedictine and female use. Book-plate of George Dunn of Woolley Hall, Maidenhead: his sale, 14 Feb. 1913, lot 623.

10. *Psalterium, etc.* s. xv in.

1. ff. 2–235ᵛ Psalter.

Catalogue, pl. 2, shows ff. 182ᵛ–183, reduced. ff. 1ʳ, 182ʳ blank.

2. ff. 235ᵛ–257ᵛ Six ferial canticles, Benedicite, Benedictus, Magnificat, Nunc dimittis, Quicumque vult. f. 258ʳᵛ left blank.

3 (added in s. xvi ex., xvii in.). Records of birth, deaths, and a marriage: ff. ii–iiiᵛ, 'Memoire pour les eages de mes enffans . . .', dates of birth and godparents of eight children, 1586–96; f. iiiᵛ, death of their father, Franchois de Pollinchoue, 6 Nov. 1602, aged about 42 years; f. iv, death of their mother, Honorinne de Bonnieres, 20 Aug. 1626, aged 72 years; f. v, marriage of 'mademoiselle Isabeau

de polinchoue fille (*the fourth child*) de Messire franchois Chevalier et Sieur de Westoutre et de dame Honorinne de Bonnieres' to 'Messire Ian le liepure Chevalier Sieur de Noeuuille', 17 Feb. 1620; ff. v–vi, births of their two children, 13 Feb. 1621 and 12 Feb. 1623; f. vi, death of Isabel, 21 Jan. 1626; f. vi^v, death of Jan de Liepure, 23 Dec. 1641.

Charles, the eldest son of Franchois and Honorinne was 'ne et baptize a Steenworde'.

4 (added in s. xvii). (*a*) f. 258^v Notice of the death of Isabel de Saintomer, wife of the 'Sieur de Neville', 22 Mar. 1610, aged 62. (*b*), on a paper slip fastened inside the back cover, notice of the mother of Honorinne de Bonnieres, dame de Westoutre.

ff. iii+258+iii, foliated ii–iv, 1–258, v–vii. 200 × 150 mm. Written space 110 × 75 mm. 16 long lines. Ruling with violet ink. Collation: 1^8+1 leaf before 1 2–22^8 23^4 (ff. 178–81) 24^4+1 leaf before 1 (f. 182) 25–33^8. Quires 25–33 signed 7, Ɔ, (a), b–g. Two full-page pictures on striking backgrounds of gold and red (f. 1^v) and gold and blue (f. 182^v): f. 1^v, Pietà; f. 182^v, a woman in black kneels before St. Agnes. Initials: (i) f. 2, 8–line, blue patterned in white, historiated (David); (ii) 6-line, 4-line (Pss. 51, 101) and 3-line (beginning art. 2), blue or red, patterned in white, on decorated gold grounds, with prolongations into the margins; (iii, iv) 2-line and 1-line, blue with red ornament or gold with blue-green ornament. Continuous borders on picture pages and on f. 2. Capital letters in the ink of the text filled with pale yellow. Line fillers in gold and blue. Binding of wooden boards covered with brown leather, s. xv/xvi, rebacked: on the front cover a triple border of stamps, (1) eagle, (2) fleur-de-lis, and (3) lamb and flag, encloses three rows of stamps of two patterns, (4) a winged creature and (5) facing birds: the cross-section is 1, 2, 3, 4, 5, 4, 3, 2, 1. The back cover has the same pattern, except that the four lower lamb-and-flag stamps in the lower horizontal row are replaced by a stamp inscribed 'ia gontier'.[1] Two clasps missing. Secundo folio *pes conuenerunt*.

Written in French Flanders (?). 'Marie de Bonnieres' inside the front cover and 'Jespere et crains M. Bonnieres' inside the back cover, s. xvi. 'Ce Liuere appertient a mesire Charles de bonnieres cheualier sieur et baron dauchy et at este donne a sa fille honorinne de bonnyeres chanonyesse de Maubouge pour prier dieu pour luy Le xviii doctobre 15lxxiii', f. iii. For the next owners, see above, art. 3. Presumably 'Las apas l'on passe Paul van der Dussen anno 1603 xxviii vii' on f. vii^v does not denote ownership. Belonged to Sir C. T. Stanford. No. 130 in the Burlington Fine Arts Club Exhibition in 1936.

BRISTOL. ALL SAINTS CHURCH

1. *W. Peraldus, Sermones; etc.*   s. xv¹

1. ff. 1^v–2^v Decem promouentia ad ascendendum in scala virtutum. [V]t homo possit amplius proficere . . . terminet suum appetitum. Amen. Expliciunt decem promouentia ad ascendendum in scala virtutum.

2. ff. 3–14 Hic incipit tractatus beati Augustini de visitacio[ne infirmorum].

---

[1] The same pattern and four of the stamps, including the 'ia gontier' stamp, are on the binding of a Vienna manuscript owned in French Flanders in 1498. It is reproduced in facsimile by T. Gottlieb, *K. K. Hofbibliothek Bucheinbände*, Vienna, 1911, pl. 35.

[V]isitacionis gracia nepoti meo . . . iustificatus ab ipso qui . . . seculorum. Explicit 'ii^us' tractatus beati Augustini doctoris vocatus de visitacione infirmorum quod TRAMENT.

PL xl. 1147–58. Cf. below, Eton College 120, art. 22.

3. ff. 14–24^v Liber beati Augustini de vita cristiana. [V]t ego peccator . . . conferamus absentes. Explicit liber de doctrina cristiana.

PL xl. 1031–46. *Clavis*, no. 730 (Pelagius).

4. ff. 24^v–28 Notandum est quod quamuis cristus apostoli ecciam et doctores aliqui auten^ti nominauerunt hoc sacramentum nomine panis . . . eciam si tante rei sacramentum ad iudicium sibi manducat et bibit. hec a' isti. On the Host.

5. f. 28^rv Beatus bernardus ad monachos montis dei in libro ii^o sic dicit de anima. Anima est res incorporea . . . et promouemur per spem. et figimur per amorem.

From the treatise of William of St. Thierry, commonly ascribed to St. Bernard, *PL* clxxxiv. 340–1.

6. ff. 28^v–30 [C]lamat dominus per os ysaie prophete cuntis cristi sacerdotibus sed precipue aliorum curam gerentibus dicens ys. lviii^o Clama ne cesses . . . Et qui taliter 'salubriter' vult agere in sequenti opusculo per assiduitatem legendi possit adiscere.

7. ff. 30–188^v Epistule dominicales secundum doctorem parisien[sem]. [H]ora est iam nos de sompno surgere roman' tercio decimo. Hoc tempus tempus dicitur aduentus . . . Apoc' 21 Non intrabit in eam inquinatum etc. 3^m (*ends abruptly*).

For manuscripts and printed editions of these sermons on the Sunday Epistles see A. Dondaine, 'Guillaume Peyraut', *AFP* xviii (1948), 204–5. Schneyer, p. 302. The last words here are in the middle of a sentence of the sermon for the fourth Sunday after Trinity: ed. Lyon 1576, f. 98^v. Occasionally subdivided by letters in the margins.

f. 189^rv blank. f. 190, left blank, has a recipe 'ad faciendum cementum' on the recto and a note, 'due macule sunt in ecclesia mea. Vna est quod pauci absoluuntur nisi pecunia precedente 2^a est quod parochiales sacerdotes non aude[. . .]', on the verso, s. xv.

8. The inside of the old parchment cover, now f. iii^v and f. 191^r, and the recto of f. 1, originally blank, contain memoranda, partly legible by ordinary light, of the affairs of a Bristol merchant trading with Ireland, s. xv^I, for example, f. 1, 'be hit in mynd þ^t Rechard olfe hath resseuid of my maister Water Pouer (?) at brystow'. Personal and place-names are 'Wylliam Lincoll' at Clonmell (?)', 'John Slater at Lymryke', 'geffrey mayow at water[ford]' and 'Nycollas Serche'. A bond in Latin in which William More of Bristol acknowledges a debt owing to Edward Leycetre of Gloucester, f. 191, may be rather later.

For persons named Walter Power, William Lincoln, and William More, s. xiv ex.-xv in., see E. M. Carus-Wilson, *The Overseas Trade of Bristol*, Bristol Record Society, vii, 1937.

ff. iii+190+iii, foliated (i–iii), 1–19, 19*, 20–110, 112–191, (192–3). For ff. iii, 191 see above. Paper. 220×142 mm. Written space *c.* 170×115 mm. 25–35 long lines, varying in number from page to page. No ruling: sometimes a vertical bounder was made by folding the edge of the paper. Collation: 1^{16} wants 3, perhaps blank, after f. 2 2–3^{16} 4^{12}+2 leaves after 12 (ff. 59, 60) 5^{24} 6^{16} 7^{22} 8–9^{16} 10–11^{12} 12^{12} wants 11, probably blank, after f. 189. Written in two current hands mainly of anglicana type, changing at f. 68. 2-line spaces left for initials have not been filled. Capital letters in the ink of the text touched with red on ff. 18^{v}–32. Binding of s. xx: the old wrapper preserved (see above). Secundo folio *vigilancia*.

Written in England, ff. 1^{v}–2, 3–25 and perhaps other leaves by a scribe named Trament. In Bristol in s. xv, probably: cf. art. 8. The names Johannes Bysseth and Margareta Thomas are in one hand on f. 2.

2. G. Zerbolt, *De spiritualibus ascensionibus; etc.*   s. xv^{1}

1. ff. 1–44 Incipit deuotus tractatulus De spiritualibus ascensionibus. Capitulum primum de quinque necessariis in hiis ascensionibus proficere disponenti. Beatus vir cuius est auxilium abs te. Ascensiones in corde suo disposuit in valle lacrimarum. in loco quem posuit. Noui homo quod ascensionum sis cupidus . . . incessabiliter curant. hec Gregorius. Deo gracias.

Gerard Zerbolt of Zutphen, †1398, De spiritualibus ascensionibus. Printed often, last in 1936: for manuscripts and printed editions see J. van Rooji, *Gerard Zerbolt van Zutphen*, 1936, pp. 287–313, 358–9.

Art. 2, in the main hand, and arts. 3, 4, in other hands, fill the end of quire 3.

2. f. 44^{rv} Regula aurea. Silentium teneas quod secundum Ysodorum Custos est omnium virtutum . . . In omnibus exhibere Fiat. Fiat. Sic In dei nomine Amen.

3. ff. 44^{v}–45^{v} Tot video gentes que sunt peruersa loquentes . . . (line 40) Perdere vim mentis. sed tradere talia ventis.

Walther, no. 19326. Printed by H. Walther in *Studien zur lateinischen Dichtung des Mittelalters, Ehrengabe für Karl Strecker*, 1931, pp. 197–8. f. 46^{r} is blank.

4. f. 46^{v} A list of fifteen books, among them two service-books, a psalter and a breviary of Roman use, together with secundo-folio references. Two books are marked as sold on 16 Oct. 1432. Except for the notices of sale, the whole list has been lined through.

5. ff. 47–54 (quire 4) Miscellanea: (*a*) f. 47 The fifteen twelves prefigured in scripture, the first 'xii apostoli' and the last 'xii stelle in corona sponse'; (*b*) f. 47 Seven lines of English verse, 'These xii apostles vnd*ur* figure I shal declare in short manere . . .; (*c*) ff. 48^{v}–52^{v} Incipit genealogia cristi. Sicut primus liber Moysi genesis vocatur . . .; (*d*) ff. 51^{v}–52 A list of seventy sequences of Sarum use, thirty-four of the temporale and thirty-six of the sanctorale, including Eya gaudens for St. Alban and Testamento veteri for St. Anne; (*e*) f. 54 The fifteen signs before the Day of Judgement.

(*b*). *IMEV*, no. 3559.5. (*d*) was written before (*c*).

ff. iii+54+iii. For ff. iii, 55 see below. Paper, except ff. iii, 1, 14, 55. *c.* 220×145 mm. Written space 147×80 mm. 27 long lines. Frame ruling and, after f. 30, no ruling. Collation: 1^{14} 2–3^{16} 4 eight (ff. 47–54). Arts. 1–3 by two hands in current anglicana. Arts. 4, 5 added in several more or less current hands, s. xv^{1}, art. 4 before 16 Oct. 1432. 3-line initials in red. Capital letters in the ink of the text touched with yellow-brown.

Binding of s. xx, uniform with MS. 1: the old parchment wrapper is preserved as ff. iii, 55. Secundo folio *ductiua ita.*

Written in England. 'Iohn kolern in povlys cherche' inside the old cover, f. iii^v, s. xv ex. (?), suggests local ownership: Colerne is sixteen miles east of Bristol. A large capital *A* is on the outside of the wrapper, f. iii.

3. *Augustinus, De Trinitate; etc.* 1465

1. ff. 1–152 In nomine domini nostri ihesu cristi incipiunt libri augustini aurelii de trinitate sunt numero xv. Incipiunt capitula libri primi. De triplici causa erroris . . . Prefacio augustini ad aurelium. Domino et sincerissima caritate venerando sancto fratri et consacerdoti pape aurelio augustinus . . . (f. 1^v) poni iubeas. Ora pro me. Explicit prefacio. Incipit liber de trinitate primus Aurelii Augustini. de sancta trinitate. Lecturus hec que de trinitate . . . et tu ignosce et Tui. Explicit liber de sancta trinitatis fide.

PL xlii. 817–1098. *CC* xvi, where, pp. 3–23, the capitula, here before each book, are printed. The beginning of each book is shown by a parchment tab.

2. ff. 152–3 Sermo leonis pape. Post miraculum virginei partus . . . post sepulchra victores.

Printed from Monte Cassino MS. 12 in *Bibliotheca Casinensis, Florilegium,* i. 149–51. f. 153^v blank.

ff. i+153+i. Paper. 298 × 210 mm. Written space 200 × 144 mm. 2 cols. 36–9 lines. Frame ruling. Collation: 1–12^12 13^10 wants 10, probably blank. Quires signed A–N in the usual late medieval style. Fairly current German cursiva: punctuation includes the flex (?). Initials: (i) 7-line, blue or metallic red, or both blue and metallic red, patterned in white, with well-drawn ornament in red or violet or both colours; (ii) 2-line, red. Capital letters in the ink of the text touched with red. Contemporary binding of wooden boards covered with brown leather bearing a pattern of fillets: two clasps now missing fastened from the back to the front cover: 'Augustinus de trinitate' on the front cover. Secundo folio *Qui autem putat.*

Written at the convent of nuns of the third order of St. Francis at Kempen (near Crefeld, Rheinland) in 1465: 'Scriptum et consummatum apud sorores tercii ordinis francisci Conuentus sancte Anne in kempen Anno domini m° cccc°.lxv° de quo sit benedictus sancta trinitas et inseparabilis vnitas diuine maiestatis et infinite virtutis Amen', f. 152, after art. 1, in the hand of the scribe. 'Liber sororum 3^i ordinis Anne sancte in kemp'', f. 153, after art. 2, in the hand of the scribe. 'F. Jurlitt' (*or* 'Gurlitt'), f. 1, s. xix in. A note about the manuscript, signed 'H. Rogers 1844 Bristol', is inside the cover.

BRISTOL. BAPTIST COLLEGE

Z.c. 17. *Biblia* s. XIII/XIV

1. ff. 1–511^v The Bible in the order Genesis–2 Chronicles+Prayer of Manasses, Ezra, Nehemiah (the running title changes from 'Esdre II' to 'Neemie' at ch. 8), Tobit, Judith, Esther, Job, Psalter (Gallican version: running title 'Spalterium'),

Psalter (Hebrew version: running title 'Spalterium Ieroni'), five Sapiential Books, Isaiah, Jeremiah, Lamentations, Baruch, Ezekiel, Daniel, Minor Prophets, 1, 2 Maccabees, Gospels, Pauline Epistles (including the Epistle to the Laodiceans after 2 Thessalonians, without title), Acts, Catholic Epistles, Apocalypse.

The prologues are 42 of the common set of 64[1] and 18 others (as marked by *): Stegmüller, nos. 284, 285, 311, 315*, 323, 332, 335, 341 + 343, 344, 414*, 430*, 443*, 429*, 457, 468, 482, 491, 492, 494, 507, 500, 511, 512, 516*, brief preface to Obadiah, Arguuntur illi . . . referuntur*, 522*, 525*, 527*, 529*, 532*, 535*, 540*, 544*, 551, 590, 607, 620, 624, 677 and 13 more as usual to 793 (765 . . . ab urbe roma), 640, 631*, 809, 818*, 834*.

The beginning of Genesis is on a missing leaf. Tobit and Proverbs begin new quires and are preceded by blank spaces. Psalms are numbered. 1 Maccabees ends with a stichometric note, '. . . habens uersus ii° milia trecentos'. A few marginalia, s. xiv. A list of the books of the Bible, s. xv, is on f. iv^v.

2. ff. 512–543^v Hec sunt interpretationes hebraicorum nominum. Aaz apprehendens . . . consiliatores eorum.

The usual dictionary of Hebrew names.

ff. iv + 543 + iii. f. iv is medieval (cf. above, art. 1). Thin soft parchment: total thickness, 66 mm. 303 × 202 mm. Written space 188 × 112 mm. 2 cols. 51 lines. Collation: 1^16 wants 4 after f. 3 2–11^16 12^10 13–14^16 15^18 16^16 17^10 18–32^16 33^10 34–35^16. Well written in a—for a Bible—large hand. Initials: (i) of books and the usual eight divisions of the Psalms, in colours, on decorated gold and coloured grounds framed in gold, with prolongations into the margins forming bars of colour picked out with gold: the decoration includes a few grotesques: the initial of Genesis was on the missing leaf; (ii) of prologues and Pss. 51, 101, as (i) but smaller, and not prolonged; (iii) of chapters, 2-line, blue, with red and blue ornament running down the page; (iv) in art. 2, 1-line, blue or red, with ornament of the other colour. Capital letters in the ink of the text are touched with yellow-brown. Running titles flanked by horizontal streamers in red and blue. Red and blue ornament falls from the chapter numbers in the margins. Binding of s. xviii. Secundo folio *commemorat*.

Written in England. Bequeathed by Andrew Gifford, †1784: his armorial book-plate inscribed 'A. Gifford D.D. of the Museum' inside the cover.

Z.c. 18. *Biblia* s. XIII in.

ff. 19–306 A Bible in the order Genesis–2 Chronicles, Ezra, Nehemiah, Tobit, Judith, Esther, 1, 2 Maccabees, Isaiah, Jeremiah, Baruch, Ezekiel, Daniel, Minor Prophets, Job, Psalms (numbered in three fifties), five Sapiential Books, Gospels, Pauline Epistles, Acts, Catholic Epistles, Apocalypse.

Genesis begins on the second leaf of a quire: the first leaf, f. 18^rv, is blank, except for pencilled notes. Ezekiel begins a new quire (18^1: f. 163). Six leaves (?) are missing after f. 42 with the end of Leviticus and the beginning of Numbers. Quires 6 and 7 are bound in the wrong order: ff. 45–54 should follow ff. 55–64. Psalms apart, the books are written continuously, the only paragraphing being in the first half of John.

The only prologues on ff. 19–306 are three of the common set,[1] to Matthew, Mark, and John (Stegmüller, nos. 590, 607, 624) and three not of the common set, to 1, 2 Peter and Apocalypse (Stegmüller, nos. 812, 818, 834). Other prologues and capitula of Genesis to Ruth were collected at the end on six and a half leaves of the quire on which the Apocalypse ended and on a quire following it. By a change of order in s. xiii^1 these leaves were removed

[1] See Bristol Public Library, 15.

to the beginning of the manuscript and part of the Apocalypse was copied out afresh on the present quire 33. The first three of the old leaves were scrapped and the fourth was made into the front pastedown, now f. 1. The capitula and prologues, ending imperfectly at Colossians, occupy ff. 1ᵛ–17ᵛ. The capitula to the Heptateuch (ff. 4–8) appear to be those printed as 'Series *A*, forma a' in *Biblia Sacra*, i. 91–101, ii. 27–51, 302–12, iii. 13–38, 302–317, iv. 18–27, 199–203, 365–6. The prologues are on ff. 1ᵛ–4, 8–17ᵛ, 39 of the common set[1] and fifteen others, shown here by *: Stegmüller, nos. 284, 285, 311, 323, 328, 330, 332, 335, 341+343, 547, 482, 487, 492, 494, 500, 507, 511, 510, 515, 512, 513, 517+ 519, 524, 521, 526, 528 (. . . demonstrabitur), 531, 534, 538+535*, 539, 543, 345*, 344+ 349* (joined by the words 'Fuit hic additum est') +a prologue to Job, Quedam hystorie hic dicuntur allegorice et moraliter . . . qui in eo loquitur*, a prologue to Job, In typa ecclesie . . . operatur deo gracias*, 457, 470*, 590, 607, 620, 628*, 624, 671*, a prologue to 1 Corinthians, Hanc epistolam scripsit . . . salutationem dicens*,[2] a prologue to 2 Corinthians, Hanc item epistolam . . . se nominat dicens*,[2] 707+a prologue to Galatians, Hanc epistolam . . . personam suam dicens*,[2] a prologue to Ephesians, Hanc epistolam . . . significans ait*,[2] a prologue to Philippians, Hanc epistolam . . . salutationem ait*,[2] a prologue to Colossians, Hanc epistolam . . .* (*ends imperfectly*).[2]

ff. ii+305+ii, foliated (i, ii), 1–34, 36–231, 233–68, 268*, 269–306, (307, 308). ff. 1, 306ᵛ were pasted down to a former binding. 284×200 mm. Written space *c.* 210×120 mm. 2 cols. 58 or 59 lines. Pricks in both margins to guide ruling. The first line of writing above the top ruled line. Collation: 1¹⁰ wants 1–3 (ff. 1–4, 6, 5, 7) 2¹⁰ 3¹² 4¹⁰ 5 four (ff. 41–4, two outer bifolia) 6–16¹⁰ 17⁸ (ff. 155–62) 18–32¹⁰ 33⁴: for the original position of quires 1, 2 see above. Within quires, the first verso and the second, third, fourth, and fifth rectos are signed in pencil; the mark on the first verso is the same as that on the second recto. Several small and rather inexpert hands. Initials: (i) of Genesis, Exodus, Leviticus (ff. 19, 29, 39), in colours on gold grounds, the frames edged with green: Genesis historiated in seven roundels strung on the *I*: a sketch only for Deuteronomy (f. 58); (ii) of books other than the first four, and prologues and ten psalms (i.e. Pss. 51, 101, as well as the usual eight), red and blue with ornament in red and green or red and blue; (iii) of Psalms, other than those referred to under (ii), and chapters of John, 2-line, blue with red ornament or red with green ornament; (iv) of verses of psalms and chapters of all books, except John, 1-line, red or blue. Binding of s. xviii: 'GIFFORD' in gold letters at the foot of the spine.[3] Secundo folio (f. 20) *aque super faciem* or (f. 2) *intellectum*.

Probably written in England. Medieval and sixteenth-century notes are in English hands. Bequeathed as Z.c. 17.

Z.c. 20. *Eulogium Historiarum, liber 5* s. XIV ex.

De ueteri eciam et de nouo testamento . . . uidit per magnum spacium episcopum . . . (*ends imperfectly*).

Bk. 5 of the Eulogium historiarum, ending with the death of St. Edmund Rich in 1240: ed. Haydon (RS ix, 1858), ii. 202–iii. 118/26. '[Incipit liber 5 de] historiis britonum' at the head of f. 1 in red. A quire is missing after f. 15 and a leaf after f. 10 and ff. 1ʳ, 63ᵛ are damaged from exposure. The story of Havelok the Dane is on f. 36. The text is divided for reference purposes into roughly equal portions numbered in red in a single series from 1 to 76 and these portions are further subdivided by letters in red, a–d, at intervals of about seventeen lines. Marginalia of s. xv in. and s. xvi.

ff. ii+63+ii. A medieval foliation begins at 156 and runs, with errors, to 238: it takes account of leaves now missing after ff. 10 and 15. 287×190 mm. Written space 215×127

---

[1] See Bristol Public Library, 15.
[2] These prologues are taken from Peter Lombard's introductions to the Pauline Epistles.
[3] So too on the spines of Z.c. 23, Z.d. 5, Z.d. 37, and Z.d. 41.

mm. 37 long lines. Collation: 1⁸ 2⁸ wants 3 after f. 10 3–8⁸. Poor textura. Initials: (i) ff. 1, 10, gold with violet ornament; (ii) 2-line, blue or red with ornament of the other colour; (iii) 1-line, blue or red. Capital letters in the ink of the text are touched with red. Binding of s. xviii.

Written in England. Price-mark, '2–10–0', f. 1. Bequeathed by Andrew Gifford in 1784.

Z.c. 23. *Psalterium, etc.* s. XII²

1. (*a*) ff. 2–7ᵛ A calendar in red, green, and blue, the colours alternating for effect; (*b*) ff. 1ᵛ, 8 Computistical tables, including on f. 8 'Versus Lanfranci de iiiiᵒʳ legitimis ieiuniis. Ebdomada prima martis ieiunia prima . . . quam par sibi cesserat ordo' (5 lines: Walther, no. 5057).

(*a*). Nearly the same as the Christ Church, Canterbury, calendar printed by F. Wormald, *English Benedictine Kalendars after A.D. 1100* (Henry Bradshaw Soc., lxxvii, 1938), pp. 68–79, but with the translation of St. Andrew, 9 May, and without the feast of the Conception of B.V.M., 8 Dec. The dedication of Christ Church is at 4 May, with octave, and the 'Passio sancti Thome archiepiscopi et martiris' at 29 Dec. No grading. Before the end of s. xii two obits were added in one hand: 'Obitus Simonis sacerdotis qui fecit librum hunc', 4 July; 'Obitus iuonis filii ade de cerringes (Charing, Kent)', 18 Feb.

As Gifford noted on the front pastedown, the twelve verses on the 'Dies mali', one at the head of each month, are an unusual set: the line for January is 'Lux prior undena nocet hora. septima sena' and the line for December 'Septima dat primam. sextam dat sena nociuam'. Of the versions recorded by R. Steele, 'Dies Aegyptiaci', *Proceedings of the Royal Society of Medicine*, xii (1919), *Section of the History of Science*, pp. 108–21, that in Harley 1804 (*not* Harley 863: Steele, p. 119) is most like the version here.

2. ff. 9–128 Psalter. Three leaves missing after f. 89 and single leaves after ff. 40, 100.

3. ff. 128–39 The six ferial canticles, 'Ymnus sancti Ambrosii' (Te Deum), Benedicite, Benedictus, Quicumque vult, Magnificat, Nunc dimittis.

4. ff. 139–143ᵛ Litany and prayers.

5 (added, s. xiii in.). ff. 143ᵛ–145ᵛ Documents concerning the claim of the priory of Harrold to the church of Stevington, Beds.

Printed from this manuscript by C. R. Cheney, 'Harrold Priory: a twelfth century dispute', *Bedfordshire Historical Record Soc.*, xxxii (1952), 11–26.

6 (added, s. xv). A note about the Harrold property at Milton Ernest, Beds. Printed by Cheney, loc. cit., p. 2.

7. f. i and the pastedown at the beginning are two bifolia, laid sideways, of a theological manuscript (sermons?) in a rather current English hand, s. xiii ex. The pages are numbered in red 18–21 and 26–9.

8. (*a*) ff. ii–iii An original letter of confraternity in favour of the rector of Northill, Beds., issued by Simon (Tunstede), provincial of the Friars Minor at the Bristol chapter in 1363. (*b*) in the space below (*a*), a presentation to the vicarage of Harrold in 1415.

(*a*). Printed by D. W. Whitfield in *Franciscan Studies*, xiv (1954), 388–9; not in the list in *BLR*, v (1954), 21. (*b*). See Cheney, loc. cit., p. 2.

ff. iii+146. For ff. i–iii see above, arts. 7, 8. 255 × 185 mm. Written space 185 × 107 mm.
21 long lines. Collation: 1–5⁸ 6⁸ wants 1 before f. 41 7–11⁸ 12⁸ wants 3–5 after f. 89 13⁸ 14⁸
wants 1 before f. 101 15–18⁸ 19⁸ wants 8, probably blank. A backward-sloping hand.
Initials in art. 2: (i) of Pss. 1, 26, 51, 52, 68, 80—the probably similar initials of Pss. 38, 97,
101 and 109 were on now missing leaves—, blue or gold on grounds of gold, blue, or pale
pink, decorated mainly with spirals and foliage in gold, green, blue, and yellow-brown;
(ii) of other psalms, red or blue, with ornament in one or more colours; (iii) of psalm verses,
red, blue, or green. Binding of s. xv: wooden boards covered with brown leather bearing
a pattern of fillets and a small stamp in the spaces formed by the fillets: rebacked: central
strap and pin missing. Secundo folio (f. 10) *Postula a me*.

Written in England after 1170, by or for a priest, Simon, in Kent (art. 1). Belonged by s.
xiii in. to the priory of Augustinian nuns at Harrold, Beds., where arts. 5, 6, 8*b* were
added. 'Huius libri possessor Iohannes Sunnyng vicarius de luswe (?)', f. 143ᵛ, s. xvi².
Theol. MS. 3 in the catalogue of the manuscripts of Sir James Ware printed at Dublin
in 1648. Bequeathed by Andrew Gifford in 1784.

Z.d. 5. Regula S. Augustini, cum expositione; etc.   s. xiv med.

1. pp. 1–95 De uita clericorum cum expositione. Regula. Hec sunt que . . .
constituti. Expositio. Ad hoc nobis diuina precepta leguntur . . . non inducatur.
Explicit exposicio. regule sancti augustini de uita clericorum.

The Rule of St. Augustine with the commentary on it by Hugh of St. Victor, printed in
PL clxxvi. 881–924. Marginalia of s. xv/xvi.

2 (in another hand). p. 96 Incipit exposicio breuissima oracionis dominice.
Pater.' quia speramus nos a te . . .

3. pp. 97–101, 104 Extracts concerning St. Augustine from (*a*) sermons of
Peter Comestor beginning 'Tolle filium tuum' and 'Melior est', (*b*) 'Petrus de
Sancto Remigio in libro suo de claustrali disciplina' and the same 'de disciplina
apostolica', and (*c*) Prosper, De vita contemplatiua, with quotations from the
Confessions and from the Bible.

(*b*). *PL* cci. 1097–1146 (Petrus Cellensis): chapter 2 is 'De apostolica disciplina'.

4. p. 102 Nomina fundatorum ecclesie beate Marie Lanthon' extra Gloucestr'
defunctorum et in domo capitulari ibidem quiescentium videlicet . . .

Names of sixteen persons buried at Lanthony priory, Gloucester, beginning with Milo,
the founder.

5. p. 103 Nomina progenitorum et fundatorum ecclesie beate Marie Lanthon'
extra Gloucestr' et eorum heredum Comitum Hereford' et constabular'
Anglie.

Names of Milo, Earl of Gloucester, and his children, and the descent of the Bohuns through
eleven generations to Humphrey de Bohun, Earl of Northampton, †16 Jan. 1372/3.

6. pp. ii–iv Succession of the constables of England from the Conquest to the
time of Thomas of Woodstock, Duke of Gloucester (1355–97), husband of
Eleanor, the elder daughter of Humphrey de Bohun, Earl of Northampton.

ff. ii+48+iv, paginated (i–iv), 1–104. The flyleaves are medieval. 226 × 136 mm.
Written space 160 × 98 mm. 26 long lines. Collation of pp. 1–96: 1 three (pp. 1–6) 2¹² 3¹⁰

4^{12} 5^{12} wants 12 after p. 96. Arts. 1, 2 in two sizes of textura and arts. 3–6 in current anglicana. Initials: (i) p. 1, *H* in blue patterned in white on a silver ground framed in pink, historiated: a bishop writes (?) in a book, the open pages of which bear the first 12½ words of the Rule, 'ante omnia . . . sunt princi'; (ii) p. 1, gold *A* on blue and pink ground patterned in white; (iii, iv) 2-line and 1-line, red or blue with ornament of the other colour. Capital letters in the ink of the text touched with red. Binding of s. xviii.

Written in England. Probably part of a larger manuscript, the first three leaves being the last three of a broken quire. No doubt from the Augustinian priory of Lanthony at Gloucester (arts. 4, 5), but not no. 175 in the medieval Lanthony catalogue, ed. T. W. Williams in *Trans. Bristol and Gloucestershire Arch. Soc.*, xxxi (1908), 148, which is to be identified with Lambeth Palace MS. 151 ff. 210–335. An erasure at the head of f. 1. An inscription on the pastedown of gift from Richard Graves (of Mickleton, Gloucestershire, 1677–1729) to John Anstis, Garter. Lot 130 in the Anstis sale, 12 Dec. 1768. Blyke sale, 11 May 1776, MS. no. 10 in the sale catalogue, p. 114, sold for 8*s*. 6*d*.[1] Bequeathed by Andrew Gifford in 1784.

Z.d. 37. *Part of the New Testament (in English)* s. xv med.

(begins imperfectly in Romans 6: 13) ʒou silf to god.as þei þ^t lyuen of deede men.

Pauline Epistles, Acts, Catholic Epistles, Apocalypse in the later Wycliffite version, with the usual prologues. The Epistle to the Laodiceans follows Colossians, ff. 65^v–66. Not listed by Forshall and Madden. Part of 2 Corinthians 3, 4 missing on a leaf after f. 30. Chapters are subdivided occasionally by letters in the margins. f. 172^v blank.

ff. vii + 172 + ii. For f. iii see below. 210 × 150 mm. Written space 146 × 95 mm. 2 cols. 28 lines. Collation: 1–3^8 4^8 wants 7 after f. 30 5–21^8 22^6 wants 6, probably blank. Quire signatures begin with 'b' on quire 1. Slightly sloping textura. Initials: (i) of books, 4-line, red and blue with ornament of both colours; (ii) of chapters, 2-line blue with red ornament. Capital letters in the ink of the text are touched with red. Binding of s. xviii.

'Thomas Martin 1718', f. 1: he wrote on f. iv 'I think it is Wickliff's Translation'. 'Parted with this MS. to Dr Gifford for Fourteen shillings Augt. 24th 1779. T. D. Harriott of Newgate Street', f. 1. Gifford added to this 'which was rather a gift than a Sale, as 'tis worth 5 times ye money' and wrote against Martin's name 'who was my particular friend' and against Martin's note on f. iv 'and so does also A. Gifford Mus. Br. 1779'. f. iii added by Gifford contains his notes on Harleian manuscripts of Wycliffe, Rolle, and Trevisa written on the back of an invitation to him to dine with Mr. and Mrs. Rempel, 28 Oxford St. (London)', on 12 June 1777 'about two o'clock according to Promise'.

Z.d. 38. *Horae, etc.* s. xv med.

1. ff. 1–6^v Kalendar of Franciscan use in red and black, graded.

Some English saints, but only three of them in red, Thomas of Canterbury (7 July, erased, and 29 Dec.), Winefred, 3 Nov., and Edmund, 20 Nov. Later additions include: Bernardinus, 20 May, in red, with octave; Sampson, 27 July; 'Dedicacio sancte marie de portiuncula. festum duplex', 2 Aug.; 'Festum sacrorum stigmatum', 17 Sept.; Eleazar, 27 Sept. Obits in red added in one hand: Henry Cornewalleys, 29 Aug. 1469; Katherine Bassyngborne, 4 Oct. 1463: 'dompne Margarete Haseley minoresse', 14 Oct. 1462;[2] Philippa Cornewalleys, 19 Oct. 1472.

---

[1] Bodleian MS. Lat. misc. c. 26 has the same Blyke–Gifford history.

[2] Margaret Haseley was of the London convent and the owner of a copy of Pore Caitiff untraced since the J. Meade Falkner sale at Sotheby's, 12 Dec. 1932, lot 387 to Tregaskis.

2. ff. 7–49 Hours of B.V.M. of the use of (Rome).

Headings in French. Each hour ends with a memoria of All Saints. ff. 49ᵛ–50ᵛ blank.

3. ff. 51–71 Penitential psalms, litany (f. 58) and Quindecim psalmi (f. 64).

The litany includes Francis, Clare, and Elizabeth. Thomas of Canterbury is the only English saint.

4. ff. 71ᵛ–100ᵛ Office of the dead.

The last two of eight prayers at the end for the dead on special occasions, 'In die deposicionis' and 'In die iiiᵒ vel viiᵒ vel tricesimo', are for the use of a woman. A leaf (or three leaves) missing after f. 77. f. 101ʳᵛ blank.

5. f. 102ʳᵛ Incipiunt benedicciones per totum annum.

Ends imperfectly, one leaf missing.

6. ff. 103–110ᵛ Capitula through the year.

Begins imperfectly at the third Sunday in Advent. A leaf missing after f. 104.

7. ff. 110ᵛ–120ᵛ Thirty-two antiphons 'De sancta maria'.

8. f. 121ʳᵛ Gloria patri, spaced for music, but no music entered. ff. 122–123ᵛ blank.

9. ff. 124–177ᵛ Omnibus diebus dominicis ad iᵃᵐ ympnus Iam lucis orto . . .

Sunday and weekday offices for prime, terce, sext, none, vespers, and compline.

10. ff. 178–233ᵛ Incipit officium commune sanctorum.

11. ff. 234–42 Memoriae of apostles and of four Franciscan saints, Francis (Franciscus vir catholicus . . .: RH, no. 6544), Anthony, Louis, and Clare (Iam sancte clare claritas . . .: RH, no. 9372).

12. Offices of: (a) ff. 242ᵛ–245ᵛ Louis; (b) ff. 246–259ᵛ Invention and Exaltation of Cross; (c) ff. 259ᵛ–260 'In festo stigmatum beati francisci'; (d) f. 260ᵛ 'In festo sancti [thome] martyris'.

(a). The antiphon is 'Aurea sacro torida . . .' (RH, no. 23290). At the end is 'Spero. Ihesu miserere. gaudium' in red, probably in the hand which wrote the obits in the calendar, s. xv². (c). A leaf or more missing after f. 259. (d). Only 3½ lines remain and these have been erased, 'Pastor cesus in gregis medio . . .' (RH, no. 16426).

13 (added, s. xviii). f. ivᵛ Description of a triptych at Hengrave, near Bury St. Edmunds: 'Reuerendus Pater frater Cornwalleys Ordinis fratrum Minorum sacerdos, natus anno domini 1511. Vti videre licet in effigie ipsius depicta in valuis tabulæ imaginis B. Marie virginis Hengraui pendentis in cubiculo Dominæ. in dextra est imago S. Francisci in læva supradicti Patris cum insignib(us) familiæ Cornewallis et hac inscriptione. anno ætatis suæ 66 anno Domini 1577'.

ff. v+260+iii. ff. iv, v are medieval parchment end-leaves. 198×143 mm. Written space c. 126×73 mm. 19–20 long lines. Collation: 1⁶ 2–6⁸ 7⁴ (ff. 47–50) 8–10⁸ 11 five (ff. 75–9) 12⁸ 13⁶ 14⁸ 15⁸ wants 2 after f. 102 and 5 after f. 104 16–17⁸ 18⁶ 19–23⁸ 24⁶ (ff. 170–5) 25 two (ff. 176–7) 26–29⁸ 30⁶ 31–33⁸ 34⁶ 35¹⁰ 36 five (ff. 256–60). Initials: (i) f. 7, blue and pink on gold ground; (ii) gold on grounds of blue and dark red patterned in white; (iii) 2-line, as (ii), but smaller; (iv) 1-line, blue with red ornament or gold with blue-grey ornament. Line fillers in blue and gold. A continuous border on f. 7. Binding of s. xx. Secundo folio (f. 8) *errant*.

Written in England for Franciscan use. Arms of Cornwallis in the initial on f. 7: sable goutty d'eau on a fess argent three Cornish choughs proper. 'Thomas Crokwell', f. 260ᵛ, s. xviii. Price-mark 'o–15–o', f. 260ᵛ. 'Tenet A. Gifford 1764', f. ivᵛ. Bequeathed by Andrew Gifford in 1784.

Z.d. 39. *Biblia*   s. XIII med.

1. pp. 1–503 A Bible in the order Genesis–2 Chronicles+Prayer of Manasses, Isaiah, Jeremiah, Lamentations, Baruch, Ezekiel, Daniel, Minor Prophets, Job, Psalms (running title DAVID), five Sapiential Books, Tobit, Judith, Esther, Ezra, Nehemiah, 2 (= 3 Ezra), 1, 2 Maccabees, Gospels, Pauline Epistles, Acts, Catholic Epistles, Apocalypse. The prologues are 33 of the common set of 64,[1] Stegmüller nos. 285, 311, 323, 328, 482, 487, 492, 494, 500, 526, 468, 332, 330, 590, 607, 620, 624, 677 and 13 more as usual to 793 (765 ends *a laodicea*), 640, 809, together with 831, instead of 839, to Apocalypse and 284 as a contemporary addition on flyleaves at the beginning (pp. x–xii).

Books, except Psalms, are written continuously. The preface to Ezra follows Esther without break (p. 370) and the three books of Ezra are written as one. 3 Ezra, 'Et egit iosias pascha . . . et magnifice enim exultabant in sermonibus quibus docti sunt et iterum conuenerunt' (pp. 380–5) is hard to read, but appears not to be the 'versio altera' printed by Sabatier (Stegmüller, no. 94, 2). The twenty-five chapter numbers in the margins of 3 Ezra were reduced by a later scribe to nine. Job begins on a new quire. p. 504 was left blank. Much of the text is disfigured by added paragraph marks of triangular shape. Corrections of s. xiii and s. xiv.

2 (added, s. xiv). A table of epistle and gospel lections of the temporale.

Probably in John Lisbon's hand: see below.

3. pp. 505–40 Aaz apprehendens . . . consiliatores eorum. Finito libro sit laus et gloria cristo.

The usual dictionary of Hebrew names.

ff. viii+270+v, paginated (one unnumbered leaf), i–xiv, 1–547, (548–50). pp. iii–xiv, 541–8 are medieval flyleaves. Smooth and, for a Bible of this size and date, thick parchment. 190×138 mm. Written space 138×95 mm. 2 cols. and (art. 3) 3 cols. 60 lines. Some quires are pricked in both margins. Collation: 1–7¹² 8¹⁰ 9–20¹² 21¹⁴ 22¹² 23 six. Written in a very small hand and in more or less faded brown ink. Initials: (i) of books and prologues and the usual eight divisions of the Psalms, red and blue, usually ornamented in red and sometimes filled in pale yellow or green: the style is unusual; (ii) of chapters, but only if the chapter chances to begin at the beginning of a line, so that the initial can be placed in the margin or between the columns, red or blue with ornament of the other colour. Binding of s. xviii. Secundo folio *nomen eius dictus*.

Not English script or decoration. 'Hec biblia est de' in one line and 'fratrum predica-(torum)' in the next is all that remains of an ex-libris, s. xiii ex., on p. v: the outer portion of the leaf has gone. 'Ista biblia est fratris Vᶜⁱ Ihoannis Vlixbon' de ordine predicatorum' and 'Constitit centum libras', p. vii, in one hand, s. xiv. A pressmark, E. 3, on p. iii and annotations of *c.* 1400 are in English hands. Deposited in the Celton loan chest at Oxford, as a pledge, 3 Apr. 1400: 'Caucio m. Nicholai herry et Iohannis Vyfyan exposita in cista

[1] See Bristol Public Library, 15.

sulton' pro iiii marcis anno domini m^{mo} cccc^{mo} die sancti Ric' episcopi et habet supplementum portiforium 2° fo honor virtus', p. 542. For Vicente de Lisboa, O.P., lector at Oxford in 1376, †1401, Nicholas Henry, fellow of Oriel in 1394 and, later, provost, and John Vyfyan see Emden, *BRUO*, pp. 1151, 910, 1952. Owned later by William Bromley (p. 542, s. xvi/xvii) and 'Rob. Brentt' (p. xiv, s. xvii). Acquired by Andrew Gifford 'July 5. 79. From T. P.' (p. vii) and bequeathed by him in 1784. Gifford's book-plate is inside the cover and the book-plate of the 'Bristol Education Society Museum' on p. ii.

Z.d. 40. *Processionale*   s. xv med.–xvi[1]

A Bridgettine processional.

1. pp. 1–113 Processional offices for twelve feasts: Visitation of B.V.M.; Relics; Nativity of Bridget; Anne; Chains of Peter; Assumption and Nativity of B.V.M.; Michael; dedication of church; canonization of Bridget; All Saints; Conception of B.V.M. p. (xv) is blank.

2. pp. 113–40 Letania.
Fourteen virgins: (1, 2) Anna Birgitta . . .

3. pp. 140–67 Antiphone . . . in cena domini.
Eleven antiphons at the washing of feet.

4. pp. 167–74 Office 'In die professionis'.
Profession of nun or nuns.

5. pp. 174–6 Rubrics for Ash Wednesday and Good Friday.

6. pp. 176–8 Ut sorores monasterii sancti saluatoris de syon tam presentes quam future a consciencia scrupulosa remoueantur intuentes in hac processionario . . .
Dispensation by John Kemp, bishop of London (1421–5). p. 179 blank.

7. pp. 180–94 Antiphons after compline on Sunday and weekdays, as in *The Bridgettine Breviary of Syon Abbey*, ed. A. J. Collins (HBS xcvi, 1969), pp. 113–14.
RH, nos. 861, 2070, 2072, 12991, 2135, 18150 and on Friday the non-metrical Mundi domina celi regina . . .

8. pp. 195–211 Antiphons: (*a*) In tempore pascali. Virgo mater ecclesie eterna porta glorie . . .; (*b*) in Advent, 'De te uirgo nasciturum mundi saluatorem . . .'; (*c*) at Christmas, 'Gaudendum nobis est . . .'; (*d*) at Easter, 'Regina celi letare . . .'.
(*a*). *RH*, no. 21818. (*b*–*d*). *Bridgettine Breviary*, pp. 111–12.

9 (added, s. xv ex.). pp. 212–16 Miles cristi gloriose Augustine sanctissime . . .
Office of St. Augustine. p. 217 blank.

10 (added, s. xvi¹). pp. 218–20* In die apostolorum petri et pauli ad processionem . . .

11 (added, s. xvi¹). pp. 220**–31 In the feste of the most holy name of Iesu. in

processyon. prose. Salue festa dies toto uenerabili euo qua resonante Iesu . . .
In enteryng into yᵉ quere . . . Versicle . . . Answer. . . .

12 (added in 1776). pp. (233–8) Copies of the Sunday and Monday antiphons of
art. 7 and of art. 8*d* in the hand of 'Josephus Dorion Musicæ scriptor et Antiquæ
Musicæ Versificator et Transpositor In stradâ Wardorianâ N⁰ 78 apud Sᵗᵃᵐ
Annam Soho. Iᵃ die Mai 1776 Londini'. No writing on pp. 232, 239.

13 (added in 1776). pp. (240–60) Notes made by Edward O'Reilly, 11 May
1776, about the present manuscript, Syon Abbey, etc.

ff. vii+117+xix. The paginator of ff. 1ᵛ–117ᵛ missed an opening after 220: it is now 220*,
220**. For fifteen of the nineteen leaves at the end see arts. 12, 13. pp. vii–xiv, 262–5 are
medieval end-leaves. 191 × 127 mm. Written space 130 × 76 mm. 5 long lines and music.
Collation of pp. (xv), 1–(231): 1² 2–14⁸ 15² 16¹⁰ wants 10, probably blank. Art. 11 is in
very large textura, broken, seriffed, and adorned with hair-lines: cf. MS. Z.e. 37. Initials:
(i) blue with red ornament; (ii) 1-line, blue or red. Cadels and capital letters in the ink
of the text are touched with yellow-brown. Line fillers in blue and red (art. 2 only).
Recently rebound: when I first saw it the binding was of wooden boards covered with
brown leather, s. xv, the central strap and pin missing. Secundo folio (p. 2) *zabeth*.

Written in England for the use of the Bridgettine nuns of Syon Abbey. 'Anne dyngue
O mater dei memento mei Anne Amarson O mater dei obliuiscere me' is in a hand of s.
xvi in. on p. vi, formerly the exposed side of the pastedown: for Anne Amersham, nun
of Syon in 1518, see G. J. Aungier, *Syon Monastery*, 1840, p. 82. Presumably bequeathed
as Z.c. 17.

Z.d. 41. *Biblia*   s. XIII med.

1. ff. 1–432ᵛ A Bible in the order Genesis–2 Chronicles, Ezra, Nehemiah,
Judith, Esther, Tobit, Job, Psalms, five Sapiential Books, Isaiah, Jeremiah,
Lamentations, Baruch (ends at 5: 9 *que est ex ipso*), Ezekiel, Daniel, Minor
Prophets, 1, 2 Maccabees, Gospels, Pauline Epistles, Acts, Catholic Epistles,
Apocalypse.

The prologues are 50 of the common set of 64 and 11 others, shown here by *: Stegmüller,
nos. 284, 323, 328, 330, 335, 341+343, 332, 344, 457, 468, 482, 487, 491, 492, 500 (. . .
monstratur), 511+510+509*, 515, 512, 513, 519+517, 524, 522*, 526, 525*, 528, 527*,
530*, 529*, 534, 532*, 538 (Moriente dario rege medorum . . .), 535*, 539, 540*, prologue
to Malachi, Ultimum xii prophetarum . . . uenit in ierusalem*, 545*, 544, 551, 590, 589,
607, 620, 624, 677 and twelve more as usual to 793 (no prologue to 2 Corinthians), 640.

A set of capitula is attached to the second prologue to Matthew (589): De natiuitate cristi.
Magi cum muneribus ueniunt . . . et doctrina eius de baptismo. Wordsworth and White
print this from Codex Cavensis on pp. 18–38.

A stichometric note follows 2 Maccabees: Versus habens Mille Octingentos. Proverbs
and Matthew begin on new quires, ff. 209, 335. A form of shorthand below the running
titles seems to give the names of the books. Marginalia to John are many, s. xv. Elsewhere
there are few.

2. ff. 433–440ᵛ The dictionary of Hebrew names 'Aaron mons fortis . . . confusionis'.

Cf. *Sum. Cat.*, Index, p. 213, for Bodleian copies of *Aaron mons fortis*.

3. ff. 441–2 A tabular concordance of the Gospels under 226 heads. The first and last entries are:

	Math.	Mar.	Lu.	Io.
De genealogia ihesu cristi	1a		3d	
De assensione domini saluatoris nostri ihesu cristi		16g	24g	

The numbers here refer to chapters and the letters a–g to subdivisions of chapters. Corresponding letters are not entered in art. 1.[1]

ff. i+442+i. 176×135 mm. Written space 140×85 mm. 2 cols. (art. 2, 3 cols.). 53–6 lines. Collation: 1–15¹⁶ 16¹⁴ 17–26¹⁶ 27¹⁸ 28¹² wants 11, 12, probably blank. Written mainly in one small and not very good hand. Initials: (i) of books, prologues, the usual eight divisions of the Psalms and Ps. 51 (but not Ps. 101), mostly 6-line, red and blue, with ornament of both colours; (ii) of chapters, 1-line, red or blue, with ornament of the other colour; (iii) of verses of psalms and in arts. 2, 3, 1-line, red or blue. English gilt-tooled, olive-green morocco, s. xvii. Secundo folio *gari longius*.

Probably written in England. Marginalia of s. xiv and s. xv are in English hands. Bequeathed by Andrew Gifford in 1784.

Z.d. 42. *Horae*   s. xv med.

1. ff. 1–12ᵛ Full calendar in French, in gold, blue, and red, the two colours alternating for effect. Geneuiefue, Denis, Leu are in gold.

2. ff. 13–19 Sequentiae of the Gospels.

3. ff. 19–23ᵛ Oroison de notre dame. Obsecro te . . . michi famule tue N . . .

4. ff. 23ᵛ–27ᵛ Oroison de la benoite uierge marie. O intemerata . . . orbis terrarum. de te enim . . .

5. (a) ff. 27ᵛ–28 Memoire de saint spire (*Exuperius*). (b) f. 28ʳᵛ Memoire des deux suers nostre dame. O sorores egregie . . .

6. ff. 29–112 Hours of B.V.M. of the use of (Paris), with hours of Cross and Holy Spirit worked in.

7. ff. 113–30 Penitential psalms and litany.

8. ff. 131–177ᵛ Office of the dead.

9. ff. 178–92 Passion according to St. John (18: 1–19: 42), followed by (ff. 189–90) the hymn Vexilla regis, (ff. 190–191ᵛ), John 19: 1–35, abbreviated, and (ff. 191ᵛ–192), the prayer 'Deus qui manus tuas . . .'.

10. (a) ff. 192–198ᵛ Oroison de notre seigneur. Domine ihesu criste qui in hunc mundum propter nos peccatores . . . (*ends imperfectly*). (b) f. 199ʳᵛ (*begins imperfectly*) reprobari. a iuda traditore osculo tradi . . .

a). '. . . (f. 196) de me miserrime famule tue N . . .'. SS. George, Denis, and Agatha are

---

[1] Few Bibles have these letters. Presumably the system of dividing chapters was well understood and readers worked it by eye, looking for a, b references near the beginning, for f, g references near the end and for c, d, e references in the middle of a chapter.

invoked on f. 196^v. (*b*). The prayer beginning *Deus qui voluisti pro redemptione mundi a iudeis reprobari*.

11. ff. 200–3 Oroison de nostre dame. Stabat mater . . .

12. ff. 203–7 Pseaume de la trinite. Quicumque uult . . .

13. (*a*) ff. 207–8 Deuant que on recoyue nostre seigneur. Salue sancta cara dei... (*b*) f. 208^{rv} Quant on veult recepuoir nostre s. Domine ihesu criste fili dei uiui non sum dignus . . . (*c*) ff. 208^v–209 Apres la recepcion oroison. Vera susceptio corporis . . . (*d*) f. 209 Gratias ago tibi domine . . .

(*a*). *RH*, no. 18175.

14. ff. 209^v–210 Salutation a nostre dame. Aue cuius concepcio . . . *RH*, no. 1744.

15. ff. 210^v–212 Les vii uers saint bernard. Eight verses.

16. ff. 212–14 Les vii gaudes nostre dame. Gaude flore uirginali . . . *RH*, no. 6809.

17. ff. 214–215^v Les v ioyes nostre dame. Gaude uirgo mater cristi . . . *RH*, no. 7017.

18. (*a*) ff. 215^v–216^v Hymne du saint esperit. Veni creator spiritus... (*b*) ff. 216^v–217^v Hymne. Pange lingua gloriosi corporis misterium . . . (*c*) ff. 217^v–218 Criste qui lux es . . .

RH, nos. 21204, 14467, 2934.

19. ff. 218^v–223 La messe du saint esperit.

20. ff. 223–225^v La messe de nostre dame.

21. ff. 225^v–231 La messe du saint sacrement.

22. ff. 231–4 Au ieudi les heures du saint sacrement . . . Corporis misterium pange gloriosi. Atque cristi . . . *RH*, no. 3936. *AH* xxx. 29.

23. ff. 234–239^v La messe de requiem.

24. ff. 239^v–240 Quant on lieuue nostre seignur. Domine ihesu criste qui hanc sacratissimam carnem . . .

25. ff. 240–241^v Oroison a la uierge marie. Diuina uirgo flos nubes . . .

The first part of this prayer consists of some seventy names applicable to B.V.M.

26. f. 241^v Aue sanctissima cristi caro . . . f. 242^{rv} blank.

27. ff. 243–282^v Memoriae of Holy Spirit, Trinity, B.V.M. (Salue regina . . .), Christmas, Circumcision, Epiphany, 'De pasques fleuries', 'Au iour du grant vendredi', Pentecost, Holy Sacrament, Ascension, Angels, John Baptist, Peter and Paul, Paul, Andrew, James, John Evangelist, Thomas, James and Philip, Bartholomew, Matthew, Simon and Jude, Barnabas, Luke, Stephen, Innocents, Vincent, Sebastian, Christopher, Laurence, Denis, Eustace, Vincent, Fiacre, Nicholas, Eutrope, George, Germain, Maur, Maturin, Antony abbot, Leonard,

martyrs, Francis, Claude, Conception of B.V.M., Purification of B.V.M., Assumption of B.V.M., Nativity of B.V.M., Katherine, Margaret, Agnes, Agatha, Apollonia, Barbara, Gemma, virgins, Anne, Yves, Augustine, Francis, Antony of Padua, Bernardine, All Saints.

Rhymed antiphons for Sebastian, 'O sancte sebastiane. Semper uespere et mane . . .' (*RH*, no. 13708), Fiacre, 'O tu qui cuncta fabricasti . . .', Gemma, 'Aula regnans ethera . . .', Francis, 'Salue sancte pater patere (*sic*) lux . . .' (40727), Bernardine, 'Gaudeat ordo minorum . . .' (7095).

ff. iv+283+iv, foliated (i–iv), 1–160, 160*, 161–282, (283–6). 175 × 122 mm. Written space 82 × 58 mm. 15 long lines. Collation: 1¹² 2–13⁸ 14⁴ (ff. 109–12) 15–16⁸ 17² 18–25⁸ 26⁸ wants 6 after f. 198 27–30⁸ 31². 12-line pictures with distinctive flower-patterned broad gold frames, two in art. 2 (John and Luke), ten in art. 6 (one before each hour and the Betrayal and Pilate washing his hands before matins of the Cross and of the Holy Spirit respectively) and one before each of arts. 3, 7 (Christ on the rainbow, flanked by B.V.M. and St. John: below, the resurrection), 8 (a corpse laid out), 9 (Crucifixion), 11 (Pietà). Initials: (i, ii) 3-line and 2-line, in colour on gold grounds, decorated; (iii) 1-line, gold on coloured grounds patterned in white. Capital letters in the ink of the text touched with pale yellow. Line fillers in blue, red, and gold. Continuous framed floral borders on picture pages and framed borders on three sides of all other pages. Olive morocco binding, s. xviii, lettered on the spine 'Office de leglise': gilt armorial centrepiece. Secundo folio *de lumine* (f. 14).

Written in France. The armorial on the cover is of Anne-Gabriel-Henri Bernard de Boulainvilliers, 1724–c. 1765: cf. J. Guigard, *Armorial du bibliophile*, 1870, p. 88. Andrew Gifford's bookplate on f. iv^v is preceded by the words 'Mʳ Handasyd Nᵒ 4 East Street presented this Book to' and followed by the date 'Decʳ 8 1777' and the words 'I desire my Friend Dʳ Gifford will present this Book to the Baptist Museum at Bristol. T. B. Handasyd Septʳ 16ᵗʰ 1780'. Book-plate of the 'Bristol Education Society 1786' and number 'A.d. 13' inside the cover.

Z.e. 37. *Preces privatae* (*partly in English*)   s. xvi[1]

Prayers in Latin and prayers and directions for prayer in English, for the use of a woman. For many of these, see Hoskins, pp. 383–444.

1. A preliminary quire, partly blank, has: (*a*) ff. 3–4 O dulcis maria benedicta sis tu . . . electi gaudent; (*b*) f. 5ʳᵛ A devowtt prayer to the passyon of oure lorde Iesu. And fyrst beholdyng the fete devouwtly and say Adoramus te criste . . .

(*a*). Marked as 'li. 4 ca 18'. (*b*). Directions only.

2. f. 9 In the nyght or in the mornyng when thow rysest commend the bothe sowle and body vnto me thankyng me for thy kepyng . . . Gracias ago tibi omnipotens deus pro proteccione diuina . . .

From this point to f. 58ᵛ the text is in over sixty paragraphs, most of them forming independent pieces. They include: (*a*) ff. 20–3 O Blessyd trynyte father sonne and holy gost. thre persons and one very god. I beleue wyth my hartt . . .; (*b*) ff. 23–24ᵛ O blessyd god almyghty. all seyng. all thyngys knowyng. wysdome and sapyence of all: I poore synner make thys day yn the dyspytt of þᵉ fende of hell: protestacyon . . .; (*c*) ff. 24–8 Sancta maria regina celi et terre. mater domini nostri . . .; (*d*) f. 28ʳᵛ Angele qui meus es custos pietate . . . assignaris. (*e*) ff. 28ᵛ–32 O vos omnes sancti et electi dei . . .; (*f*) ff. 32–37ᵛ Dominator domine deus omnipotens qui es trinitas. in patre et filio et spiritu sancto . . .; (*g*) ff. 41–42ᵛ Domine Iesu criste fac quod amem te . . .; (*h*) ff. 43ᵛ–48

O domine mea sancta maria. me in tuam benedictam fidem . . . Lord Ihesu cryste thys day I beseche the to lyghten my hart . . .; (*i*) f. 48 Salue regina . . .

For (*a*, *b*) see *Horae Ebor.*, pp. 86–8 and *MMBL* i. 414. (*h*) is a series of seven prayers to B.V.M. in Latin, each followed by a prayer to her Son in English.

3. (*a*) ff. 58ᵛ–66ᵛ [A]lso after complyne. Afore matens and yn the mornyng Take gode hede how thow haste gouernyd thy self . . . (f. 60ᵛ) Say then as present in hys syght of his fyue wounds. Ad dexterum pedem. Dulcissime iesu in hoc vulnere . . . Goode lord I appeer here afore the . . . (*b*) ff. 66ᵛ–68ᵛ Aue cuius concepcio. solenni plena gaudio . . . (*c*) ff. 68ᵛ–70ᵛ Oro te beatissima virgo maria ut sicut deus . . .

(*a*). Directions in English and a prayer in Latin to each of the five wounds, each followed by a prayer in English. (*b*). *RH*, no. 1744.

4. Prayers to the guardian angel: (*a*) ff. 70ᵛ–72ᵛ Obsecro te angelice spiritus cui ego indigna peccatrix . . .; (*b*) ff. 72ᵛ–73ᵛ Omnipotens et misericors deus. qui hominem ad imaginem tuam . . .

5. f. 73ᵛ Laudo benedico et glorifico et saluto dulcissimum cor tuum . . .

From here to f. 107 is in forty-two paragraphs and consists mainly of prayers to God the Son.

6. ff. 107–24 Devotions to B.V.M., including: (*a*) ff. 107–111ᵛ O intemerata . . . orbis terrarum. Inclina . . .; (*b*) ff. 111ᵛ–117 Obsecro te . . .; (*c*) f. 117 O domina mea dulcissima virgo maria per omnia illa gaudia . . .; (*d*) ff. 117ᵛ–120 O pre-excellentissima maria . . . per illum dolorem . . .

(*d*). Prayers of the five sorrows of B.V.M.

7. ff. 124–5 Confiteor tibi domine deus omnipotens. creator celi et terre . . .

8. ff. 123–35 O iesu dulcissime. iesu dilectissime tu mecum queso maneas. hac nocte . . .

Prayers on going to bed, in sixteen paragraphs.

9. ff. 135–144ᵛ Nine paragraphs of prayers, the first 'Saluto te o sancta virgo maria domina celorum . . .'.

10. The paper quire added at the end, ff. 145–9, includes on f. 146 verses 'Pro fidei meritis vocitatur iure beatus . . .' (12 lines: Walther, no. 14749; *AH* xvii. 19) and 'Sponsus vt e thalamo . . .' (6 lines).

ff. iv+149+iv. Stout parchment and (quires 1, 19) paper. f. 1 has been pasted down. 155×110 mm. Written space 108×64 mm. 14 long lines. Collation: 1–16⁸ 17⁶+1 leaf before 6 (f. 135) 18⁸+1 leaf after 8 (f. 144) 19 five (ff. 145–9). Large broken textura, with serifs and hair-lines depending from them, apparently the same hand as Z.d. 40, art. 11. 2-line initials, blue or red. Capital letters in the ink of the text filled with pale yellow. Binding of s. xx, with pasted-on leather bearing panel stamps: on one side the 'Lucresia' panel reproduced by E. P. Goldschmidt, *Gothic and Renaissance Bookbindings*, 1928, pl. 64 (Weale, R. 433, from his no. 177), which he assigns probably to Louvain, *c.* 1550; on the other an (unrecorded?) head-in-medallion panel, with I P immediately above the head.

Written in England for a woman who was, probably, a nun of Syon: cf. Z.d. 40. 'James Dawson 1640', f. 2. 'March 31 1731', f. 1.[1]

Z.e. 38. *Biblia*   s. XIII med.

1. ff. 1–514ᵛ A Bible in the usual order and with the common set of 64 prologues, as in Bristol Public Library 15, q.v.

2. ff. 515–61 Aaz apprehendens . . . consiliatores eorum.
The usual dictionary of Hebrew names.

3 (added early). ff. 561ᵛ–562 Mnemonic verses, beginning abruptly: (*a*) [. . . .] tribuit. signum pharisei . . . et cum transisset. marchi ultima fiet; (*b*) Lucas. Zacharie gabriel uenit inde marie . . . Valde diluculo pro summa parte . . .; (*c*) [. . . .] In principio testis baptista probatur . . .

(*a–c*) cover Mark, from 8: 11 (29 lines), Luke (81 lines) and John (much damaged). Presumably the rest of the verses were on a now missing flyleaf at the beginning. f. 562ᵛ has writing on it, but hardly legible, within compartments.

ff. iii+562+iii. 142 × 93 mm. Written space 105 × 66 mm. 2 cols. 50 lines. Collation hardly practicable: quires mainly of 24 leaves probably. A very small hand. Initials: (i) of books and the usual eight divisions of the Psalms, blue or pink on grounds of the other colour, historiated; (ii) of prologues, as (i), but decorated, not historiated; (iii) of chapters, 2-line, blue or red with ornament of the other colour; (iv) of verses of psalms and in art. 2, 1-line, blue or red. English dark-green morocco binding, s. xviii. Secundo folio *personaret ignorabat*.

Written in France. 'Ric' Slefurth' Monachus Croylandie', f. 561ᵛ, s. xv/xvi. Acquired by John Curcon (?) in 1552 in exchange for a 'biblia anglicana', f. 1. Bequeathed by Andrew Gifford in 1784.

Z.f. 38. *Matthew and Acts (in English)*   s. XIV/XV

St. Matthew (ff. 1–80ᵛ) and Acts (ff. 81–168ᵛ) in the earlier Wycliffite version, with prologues 'Mathew of iewrye born . . .' and 'Luke of sirie by nacion . . .'. Acts ends three verses from the end '7 þei schulen here'.

Not listed by Forshall and Madden. The missing end of Acts was extant in s. xvi and was copied then on f. 169 by a scribe who added the words 'here enden the dedes of the apostles whilke I put to mathew and here followen in order marke Luke and Ihon'. Alternative readings in the text are underlined in red, for example 'on þe nol *or necke*', 'bitoken *or auen*', 'soulis *or lyues*' (Acts 15:10 and 26). Throughout Acts 1–19 rubrics show the occasion on which a text should be read and the word 'eende' in red in the margin shows where a lection ends.

ff. v+168+vii. ff. iii–v, 169–72 are parchment flyleaves, probably of s. xvi. 108 × 71 mm. Written space 75 × 50 mm. 19–23 long lines. Collation: 1–21⁸. Signatures a–k on quires 1–10 and a–l on quires 11–21. 2-line blue initials with red ornament. Binding of gilt red morocco, s. xviii, rebacked. Secundo folio *him for*.

Written in England. The descent of the manuscript to eight owners during a period of a

---

[1] The binding and later history of this book are accounted for if its owner was a Syon nun who went into exile in 1539 and returned to Syon in Mary's reign.

hundred years is given in an inscription three times added to on f. v[v]: '(1) fitzhenry alias harrison 1564 (2) Gyven by him to the Lorde William Cobham: by whome it was willed to his Son M[r] George Brooke and by him gyven to William Lambarde (3) who willed itt to his sonne S[r] Multon Lambard who by will gave itt to his sonne Thomas Lambard who hath given itt to his Brother in Law Ben: Madox this 10th of June 1635 (4) who willed it to his son S[r] Benjamin Maddox'. (2) is in William Lambard's hand: he wrote his name, 'willeham lam[w]yrte' and the date 1596 on f. 1. 'J. West 1732', f. v. '1-1-0 1779 A. Gifford', f. v. Bequeathed by Andrew Gifford in 1784.

BRISTOL. CATHEDRAL

Graduale (fragment)   s. xiv[2]

Eight bifolia from the temporale of a handsome Sarum gradual, with fragments of offices from the fourth Sunday in Advent to Passion Sunday.

Fully described by G. F. Browne (Bishop of Bristol, 1897–1914) in *Archaeologia*, lxviii (1917), 127–60, with reduced facsimiles of eight pages, and in *Transactions of the Clifton Antiquarian Club*, vi (1908), 163–71, with a reduced facsimile of f. 10. The office of St. Thomas of Canterbury on ff. 3–4[v] has been lined through lightly. On f. 10 the *P* of 'Passer inuenit . . .', the communio of the third Sunday in Lent, has in it the words 'Be wel war' lest y[u] fayle': cf. Browne, 1917, p. 135. The correct order of leaves is 1–5, 8, 7, 6, 9–16.

ff. ii+16+ii. 464×315 mm. Written space 305×210 mm. 2 cols. 12 lines and music. Fragments of six quires: (1) ff. 1, 2, the outer bifolium; (2) ff. 3, 4, the central bifolium; (3) ff. 5, 8; (4) ff. 7, 6; (5) ff. 9–12, the two central bifolia; (6) ff. 13–16, the two central bifolia. Initials: (i) of officia, sequences, and tracts, blue with red ornament; (ii) of collects and lections, blue; (iii) of verses of sequences, red or blue. Elaborate cadels (cf. Browne, 1917, pp. 132–3): (i) of grails, offertories, and communiones, fishes, animals, etc., bent to form letters in pale green with red ornament; (ii) of versicles and psalms, black with pale-green ornament. Repaired and bound by Eyre & Spottiswoode, British Museum: their bill for £2. 2s. dated 28 Mar. 1907 is attached to f. i.

Written in England. Used to wrap accounts of the Cathedral of the years 1557–68, as appears from dated headings on each bifolium: '1557' on ff. 1, 2; '1559' on ff. 3, 4; '1561' on ff. 5, 8; '1562' on ff. 6, 7; '1563' on ff. 9, 12; '1564' on ff. 10, 11; '1567' on ff. 13, 16; '1568' on ff. 14, 15. Bishop Browne wrote on f. i, 'I paid Hooper, the dealer in antiquities, £2. 10. 0 for the 32 pages, Jan[ry] 1907. G. F. B.'. His gift in 1912.

BRISTOL. PUBLIC LIBRARY

John Reade's brief catalogue in *CMA* ii. 40 records fifteen manuscripts: no. 1, Bateman upon Bartol. a Natural and Political History. Imperf. Fol.', probably an erroneous description of MS. 9; nos. 2, 5, 6, 8–10, 12, 13, identifiable with MSS. 8, 2, 5, 10, 7, 4, 6, 1 respectively; nos. 3, 4, 7, 11, 14, 15 not found. The manuscripts which appear to be missing are:

3. Additiones ad Speculum Juris cum Allegationibus a Lapide Castiovocho. fol.
4. Nicolai Trivetti Ordinis Praedicatorum Comment. in Senecae Tragoedias. fol.
7. Poema de Regibus Angliae ab Aluredo ad Henricum IV. Historia Ecclesiastica et Politica ab Adamo usque ad Coronationem Edvardi III Regis Angliae, incerti Auctoris. fol.
11. Liber de Medicina incerti Auctoris.
14. S. Biblia Lat. 8vo
15. Julii Solini Epistolae. Sidonii Epistolae et Poemata.

MSS. 1–10 are described by N. Mathews, *Early Printed Books and Manuscripts in the City Reference Library, Bristol*. Bristol, 1899, pp. 59–70.

1. s. xiii in. Biblia. ff. 279. Written space *c*. 248 × 157 mm. Written in England (?). Transferred from the Chamberlain's Office of Bristol Corporation to the Public Library in 1785.[1]

Books in the usual order:[2] two gaps, one after f. 139 from Job 31: 7 to Ps. 77: 54, and the other after f. 149 from Proverbs 15: 12 to Ecclesiasticus 1: 2; Hebrews, Acts, Catholic Epistles, and Apocalypse missing at the end. Fifty-five prologues, all of the common set of 64 and in the usual order:[2] the absentees are the prologues to 2 Chronicles, Romans, and 2 Corinthians (Stegmüller, nos. 327, 677, 707) and the prologues of six now missing books. A table of chapters precedes each book: if there is a prologue, the table follows it.

2 cols. 58 lines. Pricks in both margins to guide ruling. The first line of writing above the top ruled line. Good script and decoration: Mathews, pls. 3–5, shows, on a reduced scale, the beginning of Numbers, the beginning of 1 Ezra, and the prologue, capitula, and beginning of John.

2. s. xv^{1}. Missale. ff. 153. Written space 225 × 155 mm. Written in England for the use of the Augustinian (Victorine) abbey of St. Augustine, Bristol.

Described by E. G. C. F. Atchley, 'Notes on a Bristol manuscript missal', *Transactions of the St. Paul's Ecclesiological Society*, iv (1900), 277–92. He prints the sequence for St. John Baptist, Assit cristus sanctorum gloria (f. 2^{v}), the sequence for St. Thomas of Canterbury, Ad honorem (f. 4), the rubric for Good Friday (ff. 62^{v}–63), and the office of St. Cadoc (f. 146^{rv}) and lists the sequences. The office of St. Thomas of Canterbury (f. 4^{rv}) is cancelled by large Xs which do not make it less legible. Reduced facsimiles of ff. 67, 78, and of part of f. 95^{v} by Mathews, pls. 6–8, and by Atchley.

3. s. xiii^{1}. 1. ff. 3–52 Isidore, Sententiae. 2. ff. 52–65^{v} Isidore, Synonima. 3. ff. 67–85^{v} Augustine, Contra Adimantum. 4. ff. 85^{v}–112^{v} Augustine, Contra epistolam Parmeniani. 5. ff. 112^{v}–113 Ex dialogo contra Parmenianum Augustinus. Dominus declarauit . . . aliena peccata. ff. 112. Written space 220 × 155 mm. Written in England. Given by Joscelyn, bishop of Bath and Wells, †1242, to the Franciscan convent at Bristol. Its pressmarks 'F. 19 ysidorus' and 'F. 24' on ff. 1, 3.

---

[1] This early thirteenth-century Bible is of special interest because it combines new with old, the contents and order and very nearly the prologues of the Paris Bible with the tables of chapters which were still commonly copied about the turn of the century, but form no part of the Paris Bible.   [2] See MS. 15.

1–4. *Clavis*, nos. 1199, 1203, 319, 331. **3, 4**. Römer, i. 26, 81. He lists only one other copy of **3** in England. Reduced facsimiles of ff. 3 and 85^v (part) by Mathews, pls. 9, 10.

4. s. xii². P. Lombardus, Sententiae. ff. 105. Written space 192×135 mm. Written in France (?).

An early copy, without author's name. The scribe was much concerned to save space and uses many abbreviations. He left at most one blank line for chapter headings which he added later in the ink of the text, overflowing into the margins. His *quod* sign, q with a v-like mark attached to the top of the back, is unusual. Careful punctuation. Puncta in text, but not in margins. ff. 1–4, unnumbered tables of chapters of all four books, Omnis . . . gloriam, written in the main hand on a preliminary quire. f. 5, prologue, Cupientes . . . premisimus. f. 5, bk. 1, Veteris ac noue . . . non uoluit. Hic finitur liber primus de misterio trinitatis. f. 38, bk. 2, Incipit liber secundus de rerum creatione et formatione corporalium et spiritualium et aliis pluribus eis pertinentibus. Que ad misterium . . . (f. 41^v) et amenus (*ends imperfectly in vi. 3*). f. 42, bk. 3, (*begins imperfectly in xiv. 2*) et ideo non equatur . . . (f. 60^v) fere occidantur. Explicit liber tercius. His tractatis que ad doctrinam rerum pertinent. quibus fruendum est et quibus utendum est. et que fruuntur et utuntur. ad doctrinam signorum accedamus. f. 61, bk. 4, Incipit quartus. Samaritanus . . . usque peruenit. Distinction numbers added later in pencil.

2 cols. 40 lines. Quires of 8 (1⁴) numbered at the end. The last three leaves of quire 6 and all the next five quires are missing after f. 41. Facsimile of part of f. 41^v by Mathews, pl. 11.

5. s. xiv/xv. Jacobus de Voragine, Sermones quadragesimales. ff. 102. Written space 210×135 mm. Written in England. From the Benedictine abbey of Glastonbury: 'Liber monasterii beate marie glastonie', f. 2; 'Liber glastonie', f. 9.

Schneyer, p. 278. Ends imperfectly in sermon 98, Stetit ihesus . . . A flyleaf at the end, f. 103, contains an inspeximus of Thomas Arundel, archbishop of Canterbury, dated at Lambeth 25 July 1408. Facsimile of part of f. 1 by Mathews, pl. 12.

Quires of 8, lacking 12³ and 13⁸. Secretary script.

6. A.D. 1502. (1–3) Expositions of the Sarum sequences (ff. 3–47) and of difficult words of the missal (ff. 47^v–109^v) and psalter (ff. 110–19) in Latin are followed by **(4–10)** short pieces in English and **(5)** Latin: **(4)** ff. 119^v–120^v and in the lower margins of ff. 120^v, 121 Tribulacyon is the best thyng that any man may haue yn thys world . . .; **(5)** ff. 120^v–121^v Da pauperibus vnum denareum in vita tua cum bona voluntate . . .; **(6)** ff. 121^v–127^v Her ys a tretys techyng vs to knowe the dyuersytes of temptacyons and to chose that ys good and leue the euyle. For as much as the apostle sayth wythouten feyth . . .; **(7)** ff. 127^v–133^v Here begynneth a profytable ynformacyon techyng a man to knowe the kynd of spyrytys whych ben good and whych not. For bycause that ther ben dyuerse kyndis of spyritys . . .; **(8)** ff. 134–137^v Benedicite Dominus (*sic*). Confiteor deo beate marie omnibus sanctis et vobis peccaui mea culpa I knowlege and yeld me gylty to god all myghty . . .; **(9)** ff. 137^v–140^v Thyes are the notable rewles of the lyfe heremiticalle as they folow here after made be pope celestyne . . . How be yt that the state of heremytes ys not cananizit . . .; **(10)** f. 140^v Thes ben þe veertues of þe Rosemarye ful precyous . . . (*ends imperfectly: catchword* also drye). ff. 140. Written space 160×110 mm. **1** is dated at the end 13 Sept. 1502 and **3** was finished in the hospital of St. Mark, Bristol, 31 Oct. 1502. 'Sancte Marce ora pro nobis. Ihesus Maria Iohannes' at the end of **8**.

2 begins 'Dominica prima aduentus domini et cetera. Ihesus hebrayce grece sother'. **3** begins 'Beatus vir et cetera. Cathedra breuiatur componitur a catha'. **4, 6, 8, 9.** Jolliffe, J. 14, K. 8b, C. 21, H. 10a. **8** is for use by a woman. **9** is the rule of hermits of St. Augustine doubtfully ascribed to Richard Rolle: H. E. Allen, *Writings ascribed to Richard Rolle*, p. 331.

7. s. xiii med. Huguitio, Derivationes, beginning with the preface 'Cum nostri prothoplasti . . .' and ending imperfectly in *Spondeo*. ff. 180. Written space 220 × 145 mm. Written in England.

2 cols. 46 lines. Leaves numbered on rectos, top centre. Columns numbered a, b on rectos and c, d on versos. Line numbering by fives, 5 10 5 20 5 30 5 40 5. These numbers and letters are used for cross references in the margins of the text and in the index where, for example, 'caupo 27 d 29' refers to f. 27ᵛ, col. 2, line 29. Reduced facsimile of f. 1 by Mathews, pl. 13.

8. s. xv med. Lydgate, Siege of Troy, in English. ff. 120. Written space 290 × 205 mm. Scribbled in in s. xvi/xvii by someone interested in the family of Vaux, Lord Harrowden.

The text in EETS, Extra Series, xcvii, ciii, cvi. Anglicana script.

9. s. xv/xvi. Bartholomaeus Anglicus, De proprietatibus rerum, in the English translation of John Trevisa. ff. 137. Written space 318 × 205 mm.

A damaged copy. Written in a set upright script, basically secretary, but with textura forms for ascenders and *a* and without linking of minim strokes. Reduced facsimiles of part of f. 58 and part of f. 122 by Mathews, pls. 14, 15.[1]

10. s. xv med. **1.** ff. 1–5ᵛ Incipit practica astrolabii. De nominibus instrumentorum astrolabii. Nomina instrumentorum sunt hec primum est armilla . . . stature tue ad planiciem. Explicit. **2.** ff. 16–272ᵛ Guido de Cauliaco, Inventarium seu collectarium in parte cirurgicali medicine . . . Postquam prius gracias egero. . . . **3.** ff. 272ᵛ–279ᵛ Circa istam materiam est intelligendum quod natura dierum creticorum sumitur a simplici radice . . . **4.** ff. 280–1 Quia secundum sentenciam tholomei in suo centilogio . . . **5.** ff. 282–4 A Latin-English glossary, Amnus. is. id est anglice a broke . . . **6.** ff. 284–6 A Latin-Latin glossary arranged alphabetically C–V. **7.** f. 287ᵛ Notes, including a charm using almonds, printed by Mathews. ff. 288. Paper. Written space 232 × 140 mm. Written in England.

1–4. Thorndike and Kibre. **2** was used by M. S. Ogden, *The Cyrurgie of Guy de Chauliac*. EETS 1971. The skilful drawings which illustrate it are described by Mathews, with facsimiles of those on f. 16 (reduced) and f. 161 (enlarged), and by MacKinney. **3.** The Astrology of Guy de Chauliac printed in *Comptes rendus du deuxième congrès international d'histoire de la médecine*, Evreux, 1922, pp. 168–76. The 'secunda pars' begins on f. 276. **4.** Nicholas of Lynn, Canon pro minutionibus et purgationibus recipiendis. **5** is probably imperfect at the beginning: leaves have been cut out before f. 282.

The script is anglicana under secretary influence.

11. *Horae*   1479

1. ff. 1–46 Hours of B.V.M. of the use of (Sarum), with hours of the Cross worked in. Memoriae after lauds of Holy Spirit, Holy Trinity, Holy Cross,

[1] The top two lines on pl. 9 belong to f. 59, not f. 58.

Angels, John Baptist, Peter and Paul, Andrew, Laurence, Thomas of Canterbury (Tu per thome sanguinem . . .), Nicholas, Mary Magdalene, Katherine, Margaret, All Saints, and of peace.

2. ff. 46–47ᵛ Ant'. Salve regina . . .: followed by the set of versicles, 'Virgo mater ecclesie . . .'.

RH, nos. 18147, 21818. Horae Ebor., pp. 62–3.

3. (a) ff. 47ᵛ–48ᵛ Antiphona. Gaude uirgo mater cristi . . . (b) ff. 48ᵛ–51 Alia antiphona. Gaude flore uirginali . . .

Five Joys and Seven Joys of B.V.M. RH, nos. 7017, 6810. Horae Ebor., pp. 63–5.

4. ff. 51–6 Has uidere (sic) laudes . . . sic salutando mariam: followed by 'Salue uirgo uirginum . . .', a farcing of Salve regina.

RH, nos. 7687, 18318.

5. ff. 56–9 Item oracio de sancta maria. O intemerata . . . orbis terrarum. Inclina . . . For male use.

6. ff. 59–62 Oratio. Obsecro te . . . For male use.

7. ff. 62–66ᵛ Incipiunt letanie gloriosissime uirginis marie.

Seventy-nine 'Sancta . . .' invocations, all but the first three 'Sancta mater . . .' (no. 4, 'Sancta mater dei . . .'; no. 79, 'Sancta mater hylaritatis . . .').

8. (a) ff. 67–85 (after an 8-line heading in red erased) Sancta dei genitrix dulcis et decora. Regem morti traditur pro nobis exora. Ad matut'. Domine labia mea . . . (b) ff. 85–86ᵛ Hec antiphona cum or' dicetur in loco Salue regina. Planctus ante nescia planctu lassor anxia . . .

(a). Hours of the Compassion of B.V.M. The metrical pieces are at matins, Psalmus. Venite mares et femine . . . (RH, no. 34405: AH xxxi. 155), hymn, Imperatrix clemencie . . . (no. 8483) three lessons, Prolem in cruce . . ., Cum de cruce positus . . ., Filii presencia . . . (nos. 15565, 4064, 6324), Canticum. Te deum laudamus qui carnem induisti . . . (no. 20085: AH xxxi. 51); at lauds, prime, and vespers, hymns, O gloriosa domina que tot cruciamina . . ., Ihesu nate de uirgine . . ., Caste parentis uiscera . . . (nos. 13047, 9578, 2663); at compline, hymn, Qui iacuisti mortuus . . . (no. 16432: AH l. 570, compline of Bonaventura's hours of the Cross). For (2–5, 7–9) see F. Mone, Hymni latini medii aevi, ii (1854), 139–44. (b). RH, no. 14850.

9. ff. 87–91 Ad imaginem crucifixi. Omnibus consideratis . . .

RH, no. 14081 (etc.). AH xxxi. 87–9.

10. ff. 91–4 Oracio uenerabilis Bede . . . Domine ihesu criste qui septem uerba . . . Horae Ebor., pp. 141–2.

11. ff. 94–95ᵛ Oracio beati ricardi. O bone ihesu O piissime ihesu O dulcissime ihesu . . . dulce quod est ihesus amen.

Prayer of the Holy Name. Horae Ebor., p. 179. For the ascription to Richard Rolle see H. E. Allen, Writings ascribed to Richard Rolle, 1927, pp. 314–17.

12. ff. 95ᵛ–106 Summa indulgencie . . . contritus. O domine ihesu criste eterna dulcedo . . .

The Fifteen Oes of St. Bridget, the heading damaged. Horae Ebor., pp. 76–80.

13. (a) ff. 106ᵛ–109ᵛ In nomine domini nostri ihesu cristi et in ueneracione quinque plagarum eius . . . Salue gloriosissima et splendidissima sancta crux . . . (b) f. 109ᵛ Oracio. Domine ihesu criste qui sepultus es. et qui des– (ends imperfectly).

(a). Five salutations to the Cross, each with its prayer.

14. ff. 110–111ᵛ (a) (begins imperfectly) in eadem carne libera me . . . preteritis et futuris. (b) Oracio. Aue uerum corpus domini nostri ihesu cristi natum de maria uirgine . . . (c) Alia oracio. Anima cristi sanctifica me . . . (d) Oracio. Aue domine ihesu criste uerbum incarnatum . . .

(a). The end of the prayer Domine Jesu Christe qui hanc sacratissimam carnem. (c). RH, no. 1090. (d). Five aves.

15. ff. 111ᵛ–113 Oracio Sancti Augustini. Deus propicius esto michi peccatori . . .

Römer, i. 374.

16. Memoriae of SS. John Baptist, Gaude iohannes baptista qui in maternali cista . . ., Christopher, Tu ihesus es testis . . ., and Katherine, Gaude dulcis katerina uirgo mater et regina . . . RH, nos. 26987, 34108, 26924.

17. f. 117ʳᵛ De sancto spiritu.Ympnus. Veni creator spiritus mentes tuorum visita . . . RH, no. 21204.

18. f. 118ʳᵛ Octo uersus sancti Barnardi. Et quicumque hos uersus dixerint (sic) quotidie. numquam dampnabitur. Primus . . .

19. ff. 119–150ᵛ Hic incipiunt vigilie mortuorum.

20. ff. 151–68 Hic incipiunt commendaciones animarum. Ps. Beati inmaculati . . . Horae Ebor., pp. 111–13.

21. ff. 168ᵛ–189 Penitential psalms, 'Quindecim psalmi' (cues only of the first twelve), and (f. 181ᵛ) litany.

22. ff. 189ᵛ–196ᵛ Hic incipiunt psalmi passionis. Deus deus meus . . . Horae Ebor., pp. 114–16.

23. ff. 196ᵛ–207ᵛ Beatus ieronimus papa hoc per spiritum sanctum abreuiauit psalterium . . . cantet assidue. Suscipe domine . . . (f. 197ᵛ) Incipit psalterium. Verba mea auribus . . . (f. 207) Deus cui proprium est . . . clementer indulge. Per . . . Amen.

Psalter of St. Jerome. The psalms in Horae Ebor., pp. 116–22, but not the heading nor the prayers Suscipe and Deus cui.

24 (added). f. 208 (a) Disparibus meritis pendent tria corpora ramis . . . (5 lines). (b) Iasper fert mirram. thus melchior. baltazar aurum. (c) In camo et freno maxillas eorum . . . (Ps. 31: 9). Oremus. Hostium nostrorum quesumus. . . .

(a). Walther, no. 4582. (b). Walther, Sprichwörter, no. 2456 (3 lines: Caspar fert . . .). (c). Against enemies.

ff. v+208+v. The end-leaves iv, v, 209, 210 seem to be rejects from the text, the writing carefully erased. 175 × 128 mm. Written space 118 × 61 mm. 16 long lines, ruled in red ink. Collation: 1–13⁸ 14 five (ff. 105–9) 15⁸+1 leaf after 8 (f. 118) 16–25⁸ 26¹⁰. Well written. Initials: (i) red and blue, with ornament of both colours; (ii) 2-line, blue with red ornament; (iii) 1-line, plain blue or red. Capital letters in the ink of the text filled with yellow-brown. Important pages have narrow continuous borders in red and blue. Catchwords inside well-drawn scrolls: the head and shoulders of a man wearing a hat with a feather in it beside the scroll on f. 24ᵛ. English binding, s. xix: 'MISSAL' on the spine. Secundo folio *aridam.*

Written in England for Philip Ringeston, merchant of Bristol: 'Quod Philippus Ryngeston Mercator Ville Bristoll' Qui istum librum fecit fieri Anno domini Millesimo Septuagesimo Nono. littera dominicalis C', in red and blue, f. 207ᵛ; 'Quod Philippus Ringeston', above a rebus of two rings and a tun, f. 118ᵛ, after art. 17.[1] The births of the two eldest sons of John Snyg are entered on f. v: Thomas, 2 Sept. 1509; George, 9 Sept. 1510. Armorial book-plate of Sir Godfrey Webster, Bt., s. xix. Price-mark '6.6.0', f. iii. Bequeathed by G. W. Brakenridge in Apr. 1908: a note followed by his initials is on f. iii.

12. *Psalterium, etc.*   s. XII²

1. ff. 1–111ᵛ Psalms 1–150, each followed by a collect.

Ps. 109 begins on a new quire (f. 85: 12¹). The original f. 17 had been lost by s. xv, when the text was supplied on a new leaf. 'Gloria' is written in the margins of the longer psalms at a point before the end, to mark division, for example at Pss. 68: 16 and 77: 36. 'Explicit hic dauid rex qui cristum generauit / Versus ter mille sexcentos sex canit ille', f. 111ᵛ, s. xv.

The collects are the 'Romana series' printed by L. Brou, *The Psalter Collects*, HBS lxxxiii (1949), 174–227. They usually have the DN text, but with further editing. The collect to Ps. 117 is not *Consolatio*, but 'Bonitatis et iusticie solus largitor . . . reddere mereamur' (f. 89ᵛ).[2] The twenty-two collects of Ps. 118 are: nos. 1–10, as Brou, nos. 1–10 (but the first five words of no. 2 are 'Deus qui custodieris uitam adolescentium'); no. 11, 'Deus cuius eloquium mentis . . .', which Brou notes (p. 248) in Paris, Ste Geneviève 1177; nos. 12–22, as Brou, nos. 11–21 (but no. 22 begins 'Introducatur domine oratio nostra'). Brou's no. 22 is absent.[2]

2. ff. 112–116ᵛ The canticles Confitebor, Ego dixi, Exultauit, Cantemus domino, Domine audiui, Audite celi, the last ending imperfectly at the words 'Mea est ultio et' (Deuteronomy 32: 35).

ff. 116. 265 × 182 mm. Written space 195 × 110 mm. 25 long lines. Ruling with a hard point, but flesh sides and sometimes hair sides have been gone over again with pencil. Collation: 1–2⁸ 3⁸ wants 1, supplied in s. xv (f. 17), 4–10⁸ 11⁴ (ff. 81–4) 12–15⁸. The hand has a slight backward slope. Flex punctuation (?) added. Initials: (i) f. 1, a 21-line *Beatus B* in outline, patterned in gold and on a gold ground decorated with dragon coils in blue, red and green: one dragon's head bites the top and another the bottom of the *B*;[3] (ii) of Pss. 26, 38, 51, 52, 68, 80, 97, 101, 109, and of art. 2, in gold, red, or blue on a pale-pink ground with 'bristly-brush' and other decoration in two or three of the colours green, red, and blue; (iii) of other psalms, 3-line, usually monochrome, red, blue, green, or brown; (iv) of verses, 1-line, red, green, or brown. Early sixteenth-century binding of wooden boards covered with brown leather bearing Oldham's roll SV. a. 7 and ornament

---

[1] These inscriptions written by the scribe of the text show that 'Quod . . .' is not always written by the person whose name follows.

[2] At these points this psalter differs from any psalter known to Dom Brou.

[3] This initial was at one time cut out and has been sewn back on to f. 1.

A. 4 and a small triangular stamp of a sprig of foliage not recorded by Oldham. For evidence that SV. a. 7 (= Gibson, *Early Oxford Bindings*, roll II) was used at Oxford see N. R. Ker, *Pastedowns in Oxford Bindings*, 1954, p. 203. No pastedowns. A central strap now missing, but the pin for it remains on the back cover. Secundo folio *conturbabit*.

Written in England. From the Cistercian abbey of Kingswood, Gloucestershire: 'LIBER MONACHORVM SANCTE MARIE *DE KINGESWDE*' in large red and black capitals at the head of f. 1, s. xii/xiii: letters in italics cannot now be read. Similar inscriptions are in Trinity College, Oxford, MS. 34, and other manuscripts. Lent, *c.* 1934, and later given by William Jane, after having been long in his family, according to tradition.

13. *Missale*   s. xv[1]

A Sarum missal described by E. G. C. F. Atchley in *Transactions of the St. Paul's Ecclesiological Soc.* iv (1900), 293–6. Probably six whole quires and more than twenty other leaves are missing (see below).

1. ff. 1–123ᵛ Temporale, Advent to Easter Eve, preceded by a general rubric which now begins imperfectly 'pentecost. tunc autem dalmatica et tunica induantur'. The secret for the second Sunday after Epiphany is Placare domine (f. 25ᵛ).

2. ff. 123ᵛ–145 Ordinary and canon of mass.

Introductory rubrics, 'Ad missam dicendam executor officii . . . manuum ablucione', occupy ff. 123ᵛ–131. f. 145ᵛ blank.

3. ff. 146–210 Temporale, Easter to 'Sabbato iiijᵒʳ temporum'.

4. ff. 210–13 Dedication of church.

5 (added, s. xv). Office of St. Winefred.

Printed by Atchley, loc. cit.; the sequence 'Salue uirgo decollata . . .' also in *AH*, xl. 318.

6. ff. 214–62 Sanctorale, ending imperfectly at 31 Oct.

7. ff. 263–79 Common of saints.

8. ff. 279–284ᵛ Mass of B.V.M.

9. ff. 284ᵛ–303 Forty-three votive masses.

The votives are thirty-eight of the set of forty printed in *Sarum Missal*, pp. 384–7, 392–412, together with five others: edn., nos. (1–3); De angelis (edn., p. 459); edn., nos. (4, 8, 25, 24, 40, 23, 12, 13, 20, 14, 15, 31, 22, 28, 30, 34, 36, 16, 17); Item alie oraciones pro infirmo (edn., p. 410, footnote); edn., nos. (32, 26, 39, 27, 7, 6, 9, 11, 10, 18, 19, 21, 29, 33, 35); Contra paganos (edn., p. 406, footnote); De incarnacione domini nostri ihesu cristi; Ad memoriam de sanctis katerina. margareta et maria magdalene; edn., no. (5). Edn., nos. (37, 38), Pro benefactoribus and Contra aduersantes, are absent.

10. ff. 303–12 Mass of the dead.

11. f. 312ʳᵛ Ordo trigintalis.

12. ff. 312ᵛ–316 Ordo ad catechuminum faciendum.

13. ff. 316–319ᵛ Ordo ad faciendum sponsalia.

The English formulas are printed by Atchley, loc. cit.

14. ff. 320–321ᵛ Visitation of the sick, ending imperfectly.

15. ff. 322–325ᵛ Burial office, beginning and ending imperfectly.
The offset of a border shows on f. 325ᵛ.

ff. iii+325+ii, foliated (i–iii), 1–232, 234–326 (327, 328). 235 × 160 mm. Written space
148 × 105 mm. 2 cols. 31 lines and, in the canon (ff. 137–45), 27 lines. Forty-four quires,
all originally eights, except 28⁶ (ff. 208–13) and perhaps 44 (now four leaves). Quires 1–14
are signed e–s (ff. 1–106) and quires 29–42 b–h, k–q (ff. 214–315). The missing leaves are:
1¹⁻³, ⁶, ⁸; 4² after f. 20; 18¹ before f. 131; 19⁸ after f. 145, blank; 22² after f. 162; 23⁸ after
f. 175; 29⁴ after f. 216 and 29⁶ after f. 217; 31⁴ after f. 231 and 31⁶ after f. 232; 32⁶ after
f. 239; 33⁴ after f. 244; 34³ after f. 251; 35⁸ after f. 262; 36⁴, ⁵ after f. 265; 37⁸ after f.
275; 43⁷, ⁸ after f. 321. A full-page crucifixion picture on the verso of a leaf inserted into
quire 18. Initials: (i) 4–6 line, in colours on decorated gold grounds and prolonged into
borders which are continuous on ff. 1, 15, 21ᵛ, 146, 167, 210, 236, 312ᵛ; (ii) 2-line, gold
on coloured grounds patterned in white, with ornament of green and gold sprays into
the margin; (iii) 1-line, blue with red ornament or gold with grey-brown ornament.
Capital letters in the ink of the text are filled with pale yellow. Binding of s. xviii, repaired.
Written in England. A scribble on f. 70ᵛ, s. xvi: 'Iohannes Maunot est nomen Meus'.
Given by Benjamin Rotch to the Bristol Museum in 1825 and transferred thence in 1952.

14. *Horae*   s. xv in.

1. ff. 4–9ᵛ Calendar in red and black.
The word 'pape' and entries of St. Thomas of Canterbury erased. The birth of Walter
Pym in 1462 added at 24 Aug.

2. ff. 10–11 In illo tempore: quo beatus Gregorius . . . Et hoc est in capella
beate marie de ierusalem et hoc registratur in Roma. Domine ihesu criste fili dei
uiui qui pendens in cruce . . .
A picture of the wounded Christ rising from the tomb, surrounded by instruments of the
Passion, precedes the heading which conveys: (*a*) an indulgence of Pope Gregory of
1,400 years to those kneeling before the picture and saying five pater nosters and five
aves; (*b*) indulgences of later popes amounting to 20,006 years and thirty-six days. The
prayer asks forgiveness of sins 'malefactoribus meis'.

3. f. 12ʳᵛ A memoria of St. Christopher, 'Tu ihesus es testis . . .'.
RH, no. 34108. f. 11ᵛ contains a full-page picture of St. Christopher, the Christ Child,
hermit, and dog.

4. ff. 13–14 (*begins imperfectly*) cuta sum et illud corpus tuum . . .
Prayers before and after mass. A heading in French, f. 13ᵛ, 'Apres que uous auez receu
. . .'. The forms are feminine.

5. ff. 15–45 Hours of B.V.M. of the use of (Sarum), with hours of the Cross
worked in. Memoriae in lauds of Holy Spirit, Holy Trinity, Holy Cross,
SS. Michael, Peter and Paul, John Baptist, John Evangelist, Stephen, Laurence,
Katherine, All Saints (two forms) and for peace.

6. f. 45ᵛ Salutacio de Sancta Maria. Salue regina . . .

7. f. 46 Domine deus omnipotens pater et filius et spiritus sanctus da michi

Issabelle Ruddok famule tue uictoriam contra omnes inimicos meos . . . libera me Issabellam Ruddok ab omnibus peccatis . . . dignare me Issabellam Ruddok famulam tuam ab omni malo presenti preterito et futuro. Amen.

8. ff. 47–60ᵛ Penitential psalms, Quindecim Psalmi (cues only of the first twelve) and (f. 57) litany.

The litany is brief and without English saints. 'Egidi' repeated.

9. ff. 61–82ᵛ Office of the dead.

10. ff. 83–93 Commendatory psalms (Pss. 118, 138), beginning and ending imperfectly.

Manuale Sarum, pp. 142–4.

11 (added, s. xv). (*a*) f. 2 Benedicite domino. Confiteor deo celi . . . I knowliche me gylty to god almy3ty and to oure lady synt mary . . . (*b*) f. 2ᵛ Gaude virgo mater cristi . . . (*RH*, no. 7017).

(*a*). An English form of confession, rehearsing the deadly sins and their branches, pride in full. Jolliffe, C. 22. The text breaks off in the third line of envy. A similar piece in MS. 6, ff. 134–137ᵛ, goes through all the sins: Jolliffe, C. 21.

ff. v+90+ii, foliated (i, ii), 1–93, (94, 95). ff. 1–3 are medieval flyleaves. 188 × 128 mm. Written space 130 × 78 mm. 18 long lines. Collation of ff. 4–93: 1⁶ 2⁴ wants 4 after f. 12 3² 4–11⁸ 12⁸ wants 5 after f. 82 13⁸. Full-page pictures before arts. 2 and 3 (see above) and 5. Initials: (i) in colours on gold and coloured grounds, historiated on ff. 15 (B.V.M. and Child), 47 (Trinity), 61 (bier) and decorated elsewhere; (ii) 2-line, gold on coloured grounds patterned in white; (iii) 1-line, red or gold with violet ornament or blue with red ornament. Continuous borders on the ten pages with initials of type (i). English gilt-tooled red morocco binding, s. xviii. Secundo folio (f. 11) *dierum*.

Written in England for the use of Isabel Ruddok (art. 7), who may be Isabel Ruddok or Clive of St. Thomas the Martyr, Bristol, †1434 (will, P.C.C. 22 Luffenam).¹ 'Iohannes Somere de Stowe (*or* Stave)', f. 3ᵛ, s. xv. See also art. 1. Given to the Bristol Museum by Hart (?) in 1784. Transferred thence in 1952.

15. *Biblia*   s. xiii²

1. ff. 1–504 A Bible in the usual order,² Genesis–2 Chronicles+Prayer of Manasses, Ezra, Nehemiah, 2 Ezra (= 3 Ezra: Stegmüller, no. 94, 1), Tobit, Judith, Esther, Job, Psalms, Proverbs, Ecclesiastes, Song of Songs, Wisdom, Ecclesiasticus (without the Prayer of Solomon at the end), Isaiah, Jeremiah, Lamentations, Baruch, Ezekiel, Daniel, Minor Prophets, 1, 2 Maccabees, Gospels, Pauline Epistles, Acts, Catholic Epistles, Apocalypse. Proverbs begins on a new quire, f. 250. The first leaf is missing. The prologues are the common set of 64.³

¹ I owe this suggestion to Dr. Ian Doyle.

² By usual order I mean the order of books commonly found in manuscripts written in France in s. xiii: see above p. vii and the preface to vol. i, p. vii.

³ The number of prologues is sixty-four, both in the Bibles and by Stegmüller's reckoning. In the Bibles, Stegmüller's nos. 343 and 517 are not separated from nos. 341 and 519, and, on the other hand, two biblical texts, the introduction to Ecclesiasticus, *Multorum nobis* . . ., and Luke 1: 1–4, are considered as prologues. The latter usually precedes prologue no. 620, but in this Bible it follows it.

Stegmüller no.

1	284	General prologue	Frater Ambrosius
2	285	Pentateuch	Desiderii mei
3	311	Joshua	Tandem finito
4	323	1 Kings	Viginti et duas
5	328	1 Chronicles	Si Septuaginta
6	327	2 Chronicles	Quomodo Graecorum
7	330	1 Ezra	Utrum difficilius
8	332	Tobit	Mirari non desino
9	335	Judith	Apud Hebraeos
10+11	341+343	Esther	Librum Esther+Rursum
12	344	Job	Cogor per singulos
13	357	Job	Si aut fiscellam
14	457	Proverbs	Iungat epistola
15	462	Ecclesiastes	Memini me
16	468	Wisdom	Liber Sapientiae
17	482	Isaiah	Nemo cum prophetas
18	487	Jeremiah	Ieremias propheta
19	491	Baruch	Liber iste
20	492	Ezekiel	Ezechiel propheta
21	494	Daniel	Danielem prophetam
22	500	Minor Prophets	Non idem ordo est
23	507	Hosea	Temporibus
24	511	Joel	Sanctus Ioel
25	510	Joel	Ioel filius Phatuel
26	515	Amos	Ozias rex
27	512	Amos	Amos propheta
28	513	Amos	Hic Amos
29+30	519+517	Obadiah	Iacob Patriarcha+Hebraei
31	524	Jonah	Sanctum Ionam
32	521	Jonah	Ionas columba
33	526	Micah	Temporibus Ioathae
34	528	Nahum	Nahum prophetam
35	531	Habakkuk	Quattuor prophetae
36	534	Zephaniah	Tradunt Hebraei
37	538	Haggai	Ieremias propheta
38	539	Zechariah	In anno secundo
39	543	Malachi	Deus per Moysen
40	547	1 Maccabees	Cum sim promptus
41	553	1 Maccabees	Memini me
42	551	1 Maccabees	Maccabaeorum libri
43	590	Matthew	Matthaeus ex Iudaeis
44	589	Matthew	Matthaeus cum primo
45	607	Mark	Marcus evangelista
46	620	Luke	Lucas Syrus
47	624	John	Hic est Iohannes
48	677	Romans	Romani sunt
49	685	1 Corinthians	Corinthii sunt
50	699	2 Corinthinas	Post actam
51	707	Galatians	Galatae sunt
52	715	Ephesians	Ephesii sunt
53	728	Philippians	Philippenses sunt
54	736	Colossians	Colossenses et hi
55	747	1 Thessalonians	Thessalonicenses sunt
56	752	2 Thessalonians	Ad Thessalonicenses
57	765	1 Timothy	Timotheum instruit
58	772	2 Timothy	Item Timotheo

Stegmüller no.

59	780	Titus	Titum commonefacit
60	783	Philemon	Philemoni familiares
61	793	Hebrews	In primis dicendum
62	640	Acts	Lucas natione Syrus
63	809	Catholic Epistles	Non idem ordo est
64	839	Apocalypse	Omnes qui pie[1]

2. ff. 504–44 Incipiunt interpretaciones hebraicorum nominum. Aaz apprehendens . . . consiliatores eorum.

The common dictionary of Hebrew names, Stegmüller, no. 7709, usually anonymous,
sometimes attributed to Remigius.

ff. ii+544+iii. Thin parchment. 122 × 82 mm. Written space 82 × 57 mm. 2 cols.
48 lines. Collation: 1²⁴ wants 1 2²⁶ 3²⁴ 4²⁶ 5–7²⁴ 8–9²⁶ 10²⁸ wants 28, blank, after f. 250
11–13²⁴ 14²²+1 leaf after 12 (f. 335) 15–21²⁴ 22³⁰+1 leaf after 17 (f. 531). Very small hand.
Initials: (i) of books and the usual eight divisions of the Psalms, 6-line, in colours on
coloured grounds, historiated; (ii) of prologues, as (i), but 4-line and decorated, not
historiated; (iii) of chapters, 2-line, blue or red with ornament of the other colour; (iv) of
verses of psalms and in art. 2, 1-line, red or blue. Binding of red morocco, s. xviii. Secundo
folio *Quanti* (f. 1).

Written in France. Belonged in s. xvi to the convent of Celestines at Avignon: 'Cele-
stinorum Auenionis', f. 544ᵛ. 'P. M. Benza M.D. Siculus emit 1815', f. 544ᵛ. Given to
the Bristol Museum by 'Mr. Marsh pr. G. Cumberland Esq' in 1832. Transferred thence
in 1952.

BRISTOL. PARISH CHURCH OF ST. THOMAS
THE MARTYR

Biblia[2]

s. XIV/XV

1. ff. 4–305 A Bible with the usual contents in the usual order,[3] except that
(1) the prayer of Manasses is not after 2 Chronicles, but an addition in the blank
space after Ecclesiasticus (f. 181ᵛ), (2) the prayer of Solomon follows Ecclesiasticus without break, (3) Colossians comes after 2 Thessalonians instead of after
Philippians.

The first forty or so leaves were seriously damaged by damp in the Second World War.
A missing leaf contained Apoc. 7–12 and parts of Apoc. 6 and 13. Books are written
continuously: a blue initial in the text shows where a new chapter begins and the chapter
number is written opposite to it. Isaiah begins on a new quire.

The prologues are 52 of the common set of 64 and 16 others shown here by *: Stegmüller,
nos. 284, 285, 311, 323, 328, 330, 332, 335, 341+343, 357, 349* (Job), 430* (Psalms),
457, 456* (. . . esse regem: as prologue to Ecclesiastes, not Proverbs), 455* (as prologue to
Wisdom, not Proverbs), 482, 487, 491 (not distinguished from the text of Baruch, which

---

[1] I follow Stegmüller's spellings and wording. The manuscripts read *Iona* not *Ionas*
at no. 521, *Iudea* not *Iudeis* at 590, and *ita* not *idem* at no. 809.
[2] Deposited in the Bristol Record Office, Council House, Bristol, as P/St. T/PB/1.
[3] See Bristol Public Library, 15.

follows), 492, 494, 500, 504*, prologue to Joel, 'Ioel qui interpretatur . . . quando et
micheas'*, 510, 511, 512, 515, 516*, 519, 522*, 524, 525*, 526, 527*, 528, 529*, 530*,
532*, 534, 535*, 538 (Moriente dario rege medorum . . .), 540*, 539 (. . . fuisse describun-
tur), 544* 551, 590, 589, 607, 620, 624, 677 and thirteen more as usual to 793 (765, 1
Timothy, . . . ab urbe roma), 640, 809, 839. Prologues 284, 285 are on the last two leaves
of the preliminary quire, perhaps so that a new quire could begin with the decorated
page of Genesis (f. 6ʳ). f. 305ᵛ was left blank.

2. ff. 306–329ᵛ The usual dictionary of Hebrew names, 'Aaz apprehendens . . .',
lacking the last leaf.

3, in front of prologue 284. (*a*) ff. 1–3 A table of epistle and gospel lections of
temporale, sanctorale, and common of saints. (*b*) f. 3 A list of books of the Bible,
numbered 1–74, with the number of chapters in each book. (*c*) f. 3 Versus de
ordine librorum contentorum in biblia. Geneseos. ex. le. . . . iud. apocalipsis
(9 lines).

(*a*). Written continuously. (*b*). Colossians after 2 Thessalonians, as in art. 1. f. 3ᵛ was
left blank.

ff. 329. 425 × 295 mm. Written space 330 × 220 mm. 2 cols. 60 lines, ink-ruled. Collation, as far as the break after Ecclesiasticus: 1⁴+1 leaf after 2 (ff. 1–5) 2–13⁸ 14⁴+2 leaves
before 1 (ff. 102–7) 15–17⁸ (ff. 108–31) 18¹²+2 leaves after 9 (ff. 132–45) 19–22⁸ 23⁴
(ff. 178–81) 24⁸+2 leaves before 1 (ff. 182–91) 25–37⁸ 38⁸+1 leaf after 1 (ff. 296–304)
39–41⁸ 42 one (f. 329). Written in more than one hand. Letters in the top line are sometimes elongated upwards and ornamented with faces, etc. Art. 3 is in anglicana. A long
narrow six-compartment picture of the Creation in the inner margin of f. 6. Initials:
(i) of the first Psalm and Matthew in colours on decorated gold grounds and of Genesis
in gold on a coloured ground; (ii) of books and the main divisions of Psalms, usually
4-line or more, red and blue with ornament of both colours and violet running the height of
the written space; (iii–v) of prologues, psalms, and chapters, 3-line, 2-line, and 1-line,
blue with red ornament; (vi) of verses of psalms and in art. 2, 1-line, red or blue. Continuous or three-quarter borders in colours and gold on the three pages with initials of
type (i). At present loose in quires within a rough-calf binding stamped with an ex-libris
on the upper cover: 'This / manuscript bible / belongs to / Sᵗ Thomas Church / Bristol /
repair'd and new bound 1745'. Secundo folio (f. 5) *qui in psalterio*.

Written in England. 'Restored' to St. Thomas's in 1567 and rebound in that year, according
to inscriptions: (f. 5ᵛ) 'Thys booke was Restored to yᵉ Chirche of Sᵗ Thomas yᵉ apostollᴵ
the xx of octobr' 1567 at wyche time Mʳ Soudly and thomas pallmar made ther acontt';
(f. 3ᵛ) 'Mʳ Mycahell Sodley sett this boke to by(n)dyng and browghtt hym in to chyrche
of st thomas in the chyrchhows as aperith by his acontt in anno 1567'; (f. 305, after
Apocalypse, in capital letters) 'S' Thomas Chirche Boke Anno 1568 repared and brought
in bi master Sowdley in anno 15(6)7'. The names of churchwardens, s. xvii and s. xviii,
occur here and there.

BRISTOL. UNIVERSITY LIBRARY

DM 14. *Medulla grammaticae*   s. xv²

1. ff. 1–4 Huius facultatis secunda pars prosodia dicitur . . . duobus accentibus
proferuntur etc.

On accentuation.

ᴵ The church was St. Thomas the Martyr's until the reformation.

2. ff. 4ᵛ–85ᵛ Hec est regula generalis pro toto libro omnia nomina verbalia et participia . . . sub breuitate. Incipit liber intitulatus medulla gramatice. Alma id est virgo abscondita vel absconsio virginitatis . . . pomorum locus ludi pomerium anglice orchard pomentum idem.

For the Medulla, a dictionary in which many interpretations are in English, and the manuscripts, see *Promptorium Parvulorum*, ed. A. Way (Camden Soc., 1865), pp. i–liv.¹ This copy ends in the letter P. The last leaf is in a looser hand than the rest, bears scribbles of s. xv/xvi, and has probably long been at the end, if not always. f. 43ᵛ ends with Exceptorius and f. 44 begins with Exortor instead of Excerpo: Excerpo–Exhillero were duly copied, but out of place on f. 50 after words beginning with Fo- and before words beginning with Fr-. Eighteen words missed by the scribe on f. 76ᵛ were added on an attached slip, f. 76ʙ. 'versus' marks metrical lines. Notes in the hand of Francis Douce here and there.

ff. i+85+i. Paper. *c.* 305 × 220 mm. Written space *c.* 230 × 150 mm. 2 cols. *c.* 45 lines. Collation: 1⁸ 2¹² 3⁸ 4¹² 5¹²+1 leaf after 12 (f. 53) 6¹² 7 twenty (ff. 66–85: probably a quire of 14 leaves with a quire of 6 leaves, ff. 77–82, inserted into it). Written in legal anglicana. Spaces for coloured initials were not filled. Secundo folio *Interrogacio*.

Written in England. Belonged to Roger Wilbraham in s. xix in. A letter to him from Francis Douce, 1757–1834, and a note by Douce about the manuscript are kept with it. The letter, dated 'Friday morning', refers to a sale at Evans's on the following Monday in which lot 303 was 'Ubaldino with the plates': this, Douce thought, Wilbraham should buy. Book-plate of George Wilbraham, s. xix. Mentioned in HMC, *Third Report* (1872), App., p. 293, as the property of George F. Wilbraham, Delamere House, Cheshire.² Bought from Thomas Thorp, 93 St. Martin's Lane, London, 20 Sept. 1928.

DM 268. *Innocentius III*³   s. xiv med.

Domino patri karissimo P. dei gracia portuen' episcop[o] loth[arius] indignus diachonus 'cardinalis sanctorum sergi et bachi' gracia[m in presenti] et gloriam . . . exaltetur. Incipit primus liber de miserabili humane condicionis ingressu. Quare de uulua . . . (f. 56) sulphur et ignis ardens. in secula seculorum Amen. Explicit liber de uita et morte a domino lotario compositus. qui tunc sanctorum sergii et bachi erat diaconus. et non post multos annos in [. . . .] est electus.

Ed. M. Maccarrone, 1955; *PL* ccxvii. 701–46. No division into books, apart from a small 'liber ii' in the margin, f. 21, and no chapter numbers. Headings to chapters nearly as in edn. 1955. Bk. 3, ch. 2, 3, 8 omitted: a reader noted in the margin opposite the end of ch. 1, f. 44ᵛ, 'Hic defficit capitulum . . . .'. Headings in red often precede quotations from the

---

¹ Way did not know of the Bristol copy nor of those now at Shrewsbury School and Stonyhurst College. For a leaf at Gloucester see below, p. 972.
   A fragment of three leaves, now Bristol University DM 1, appears to be also from Medulla Grammaticae. It contains part of C and the end of D and is described and printed by P. Haworth in *Trans. Bristol and Gloucestershire Archaeological Society*, xlv (1923), 253–75, with two facsimiles. Written space *c.* 232 × 150 mm. 2 cols. 45 lines. Used apparently in the binding of a volume of Buckinghamshire wills, s. xvi. The title 'Liber test' bucks (?) sacerdotis magistri Ric' Edmunds anno 1569 xxix decembris' is on f. 3 and the names of some testators, Thomas Gayts of Coleshill, Ralph Wright of Olney and John Haward of Chesham Wooburn, are on f. 1.
   ² Information from Mr. James Sledd.
   ³ Professor Robert Lewis kindly told me of this manuscript.

Bible, for example 'In Iob', 'Psalmista', 'Ezechiel' (edn. 9/20, 9/23, 11/17). f. 56ᵛ left blank: a current medieval hand added a table, 'Meditaciones Bernardi / Ricardus de sancto victore / de bona voluntate / . . .': from the third line the entries are noted as 'capitula'.

ff. ii + 56. Medieval foliation. 175 × 120 mm. Written space 120 × 83 mm. 20 long lines. Collation: 1–7⁸. Initials: (i) f. 1, red and blue with red ornament; (ii) 2-line, blue with red ornament or red with violet ornament. French red morocco binding s. xviii: spine gilt: f. ii is part of the parchment cover (?) of an account book, '[. . . .] de Recette Grains Et fourages', dated 1773.

Written probably in southern France. Ex-libris of the Franciscans of Rodez, ff. 1, 56, s. xvi: 'Ex bibliotheca conuentus Ruthenæ de obseruantia Sᵗⁱ Francisci fratrum minorum. Anathema furanti'. Coloured armorial book-plate of Douin de la Motte inside the cover. Numbers on f. iᵛ include '261', which is also on a green label on the spine, s. xix. Bought from R. C. Hatchwell, 11 Apr. 1956.

BUCKINGHAM. PARISH CHURCH

Biblia   s. xiv in.

1. A Bible in the order Genesis–2 Chronicles, Ezra, Nehemiah, Tobit, and thence as usual,[1] except that Catholic Epistles precede Pauline Epistles. Many books are imperfect and the whole of 1 Maccabees is missing, and all after 1 Corinthians 11 : 13, through loss of several quires and of, probably, forty-one leaves in the quires that remain. The gaps are after ff. 20, 63, 85, 91, 115, 156, 159, 168, 188, 196, 204, 213, 230, 250, 251, 287, 291.

The remaining prologues are 21 of the common set of 64[2] and 14 others shown here by *: Stegmüller, nos. 284, 285, 307*, 315, 323, 328, 327, 326* (all three to 1 Chronicles), 330, 329*, 332, 335, 336*, 342, 344, 349*, 457, 482, 487, 491, 492, an 'Argumentum' to Ezekiel from Isidore, De ortu patrum, *PL* lxxxiii. 143, sect. 75, 'Ezechiel sacerdos . . . in sepulchro semzarphaxath'*, 500, 510 (. . . continetur), 513, prologue to Obadiah, 'Abdias quanto breuior . . . quibusdam uerbis'*, 521, prologue to Micah, 'Sermo dei qui semper . . . imposita sunt'*, 530*, 532*, 535*, 540*, 544*, 551, prologue to Catholic Epistles from Isidore, Proemia, *PL* lxxxiii. 178, sect. 100–4, 'Iacobus frater domini scripsit unam epistolam . . . et ad penitenciam cohortatur'*.

Thomas Hearne's description of this Bible, made when he visited Whaddon Hall in May 1716, is printed in *Letters written by Eminent Persons . . . from the originals in the Bodleian Library and Ashmolean Museum*, 1813, ii. 182–3 and in *Remarks and Collections of Thomas Hearne*, v (Oxford Historical Society, xlii, 1901), 350.

2. ff. iii, iv, binding leaves, are from the sanctorale of a breviary written in England, s. xiv.

Lessons for Andrew, Conception of B.V.M., and Lucy. 2 cols. 51 lines.

ff. iv + 295 + ii. For ff. iii, iv see above. 284 × 185 mm. Written space 222 × 135 mm. 2 cols. 51 lines. Collation: 1–28¹², less the following missing leaves: 2⁹, ¹⁰, 6⁶, 8⁵, ¹², 11¹, ², 14⁸, ¹², 15¹, ², ¹², 17¹, ², ¹¹, ¹², 18¹⁻⁴, 19¹, ¹⁰, 20⁸, 22²⁻¹¹, 24⁸, ¹⁰⁻¹², 28¹, ⁶, ⁷, ¹².

[1] See Bristol Public Library, 15.

Initials: (i) of books and to mark the usual liturgical divisions of Psalms, red and blue; (ii, iii) of prologues and chapters, 4-line and 3-line, red or blue; (iv) of verses of psalms, 1-line, red or blue. Running titles and chapter numbers are in black and headings and colophons are in the hand and ink of the text, except in Psalms. Binding of wooden boards, probably medieval, recovered in s. xviii. Secundo folio *est enim*.

Written in England, perhaps all by one scribe. 'Sancti spiritus assit nobis gracia. quod pyers', f. 4, is probably not in the scribe's hand. Given by John Rudyng (Emden, *BRUO*, p. 1603: Archdeacon of Lincoln 1471; †1481): 'Hunc librum dedit Magister Iohannes Rudyng'. Archidiaconus Lincoln' cathenandum in principali disco infra Cancellum ecclesie sue prebendalis de Buckyngham ad vsum Capellanorum et aliorum ibidem in eodem studere uolencium quamdiu durauerit. 'Hic magister Ruding fundavit Cancellum ecclesie de Buck'", f. 3 at foot: the addition is of s. xvi. Rudyng's name is scribbled in pencil on f. 263 and his armorial shield, gules a crescent argent between six mullets of the same, with motto 'All may god amend', is on f. 268. Given to Browne Willis (of Whaddon Hall, Bucks., 1682–1760) 'to preserve', as he noted on f. 1 (cf. his *History of Buckingham*, 1755, p. 57): his ex-libris is on f. iii. Robert Fleming sale at Christie and Manson, 20 July 1849, lot 190, to Thomas Kerslake, bookseller of Bristol, and from him to H. Roundell, vicar of Buckingham, in 1855: a letter from Kerslake to Roundell, 10 Feb. 1855, is on the pastedown at the beginning. Given by Roundell's widow after his death in 1883.

BURY ST. EDMUNDS.
BURY ST. EDMUNDS AND WEST SUFFOLK
RECORD OFFICE

A. 8/1.[1] *Chronicon Angliae, etc.*   s. XIII ex.

A chronicle from the beginning of the world to 1283 (art. 6) and other historical pieces, all of which occur with the chronicle in College of Arms, Arundel 30. Described by A. Gransden, *The Chronicle of Bury St. Edmunds 1212–1301*, 1964, pp. xlii, xliii.

1. ff. 1–14 Incipit gesta britonum a sapiente gilda edita. A principio mundi usque ad diluuium anni ii. cc. xl. ii. A diluuio usque ad abraham . . . solus in extremis finibus cosmi. Explicit gesta britonum a sapiente Gilda edita.

As Arundel 30, art. 38. Nennius, Historia Britonum, ed. T. Mommsen, MGH, Auct. Antiq., xiii, 145–218 (sect. 1–75). f. 14ᵛ blank.

2. f. 15ʳᵛ De regno Ca(n)tuariorum. Woden a quo Wechta . . . Hic genuit Kerdich' primum Regem Westsaxonum.

As Arundel 30, art. 40. Lists of the kings of Kent, the East Angles and East Saxons, Mercia, Deira, Bernicia, and the West Saxons.

3. ff. 15ᵛ–16 Hec est descripcio Hybernie secundum libros ueteres terram describentes. Lagenia id est Leniestere . . . Clokorensis id est Archid'.

As Arundel 30, art. 41.

---

[1] Kept at Moyses Hall, Bury St. Edmunds.

4. ff. 16ᵛ–21ᵛ Regna pristina Anglie et eorum Episcopatus.

As Arundel 30, art. 42. Lists of archbishops and bishops of English sees, many reaching only to the second quarter of s. xii. Written after the accession of Richard (de Gravesend) to London in 1280. The names of Thomas (of Ingoldsthorpe), John (of Kirkby), and Ralph (of Walpole) who became bishops of Rochester, Ely, and Norwich in 1283, 1286, and 1289 respectively, have been added.

5. ff. 22–27ᵛ Quibus terminis regna a regnis olim in Anglia distinguebantur. Reges Cancie proprie regnabant in Cancia . . . rediens coronatus est.

As Arundel 30, art. 43. Ends at the coronation of Edward I. ff. 28–29ᵛ blank.

6. ff. 30–104ᵛ Fructuosum arbitror seriem temporum transactorum huic pagine inserere . . . spem satorum in viridi: delusit in arido.

As Arundel 30, art. 54 (ff. 97–204), which, however, continues further: the last words here belong to 1283 (Ar., f. 171ᵛ/18).[1] From 1212 collated by Gransden, op. cit. At f. 84ᵛ (1255) 'Hic attonsus fuit' is in the text: cf. Ar., f. 148ᵛ, 'Hic attonsus fui', added in a blank space. Ascribed by Bale, who used Arundel 30, to John de Everesdene, cellarer at Bury, but groundlessly, as Luard first noticed: in the present copy 'Iohannes Eueresdene monacus de buri S. Edmondi' is in a hand of s. xvi at the head of f. 30. f. 91ᵛ ends with the annal for 1268, '. . . conuentus sancti Edmundi secundum formam prescriptam' (Ar., f. 155); 91ᵛ/18–36 was left blank and the next leaf has been excised. On f. 92 the first eighteen lines have been erased and the text recommences in line 19 with 'Isto anno die Apostolorum Symonis et Iude' (Ar., f. 157/8). Probably the account of the taxation of 1268 at Bury, matter of purely local interest filling Ar., ff. 155ᵛ–157/8, has been removed. ff. 105–106ᵛ are blank and without ruling.

ff. ii+106. 210×145 mm. Written space 160×90 mm. 36 long lines. Collation: 1–7¹² 8¹² wants 7 after f. 91 9¹² wants 12, blank. Admirably written, apparently by the same (professional?) scribe as wrote Pembroke College, Cambridge, 32, ff. 1–108, from the abbey of Bury St. Edmunds.[2] Initials: (i) f. 1, blue and lake on a gold ground, framed in green, historiated; (ii) f. 48, 5-line, red and blue with ornament of both colours; (iii) 2-line, blue or red with ornament of the other colour; (iv) 1-line, blue or red. Well drawn grotesques in the lower margins of ff. 60ᵛ, 61, 72ᵛ, 73, 84, 84ᵛ. Capital letters in the ink of the text filled with yellow. Bound by D. Cockerell in 1950: the previous binding was red morocco. Secundo folio *rat. et.*

Written in England, probably by a scribe working at Bury St. Edmunds in or soon after 1283. A copy of Arundel 30 from the abbey of Bury (see above, f. 84ᵛ), but not a direct copy: Mrs. Gransden notes that there are important differences in the readings after 1268.[3] 'W. Fletewoode 1580', f. 1, at the top. Armorial book-plates, s. xviii, xix: (1) of Edward Browne, A.M.; (2) of Thomas Somers Cocks; (3) of C. L. C(ocks), inscribed 'Treverbyn dean'. Bought at Sotheby's 9 Feb. 1948, lot 222.

---

[1] Arundel appears to have been written all at one time to 1268 and at intervals thereafter.

[2] Gransden, p. xlii, who considers Arundel 30, annals for 1268–85, as also the work of this scribe. It seems to me, however, less good writing by a scribe who places his hyphens differently. I am indebted to Mrs. Gransden for the loan of photographs.

[3] p. xliii.

BURY ST. EDMUNDS. SCHOOL

1. *Psalterium, etc.*[1]   S. XIV/XV–XV ex.

A psalter described by E. S. Dewick, 'On a MS. Psalter formerly belonging to the Abbey of Bury St. Edmunds', *Archaeologia*, liv (1895), 399–410, and more briefly by M. R. James, *On the Abbey of St. Edmund at Bury*, Cambridge Antiq. Soc. 8° publications, xxviii (1895), 93–5.

1. ff. (iii–viii^v) Sarum calendar in blue, red, and black, adapted for use in the diocese of Norwich.

Dewick shows (p. 400) that the calendar is not an original part of the volume, but it is of the same date and size. The word 'pape' and feasts of St. Thomas of Canterbury have been erased.

2. ff. 1–112 Pss. 1–150.
Benedictine divisions: cf. Dewick, p. 401.

3. ff. 112–23 The six ferial canticles followed by Te deum, Benedicite, Benedictus, Magnificat, Nunc dimittis, and Quicumque vult.

4. ff. 123–127^v Litany of Bury St. Edmunds discussed and printed by Dewick, pp. 403–5, 407–10.

5. ff. 128–130^v Office of the dead, ending imperfectly in the seventh lesson at matins.

6. ff. 133–139^v Monastic canticles for Advent, Christmas, Lent, Easter, Corpus Christi, and the common of saints, beginning imperfectly in the first Advent canticle 'ulcionem retribucionis' (Isaiah 35: 4).

Cf. Mearns, *Canticles*, pp. 83–92, where this manuscript is referred to as 4, and J. B. L. Tolhurst, *Monastic Breviary of Hyde Abbey*, vi (HBS lxxx, 1942), 182–4. The Corpus Christi canticles are Lauda ierusalem, Confitebor (cues only of these two), and Beatus vir qui in sapientia.

7. ff. 139^v–166^v A noted hymnal, ending imperfectly in the hymn for All Saints, Festiua seclis colitur.

Cf. Mearns, *Hymnaries*; he refers to this manuscript as E. 7. O mundi pater unice for the translation of St. Edmund king and martyr (f. 150), and O mater preclarissima anna deo gratissima (f. 163^v) are recorded here only: Dewick prints O mundi pater, p. 406.

8. ff. 169–72 Noted hymns for the common of saints, added s. xv ex.
Begins imperfectly in the hymn for martyrs.

9. ff. 172–184^v Noted antiphons, etc., for the offices of the Visitation of B.V.M. and (f. 179^v) the Holy Name, added in s. xv ex. The latter ends imperfectly.

ff. ii+136+ii+36+ii+16. Thick parchment. The foliation 1–184, s. xvii?, begins with art. 2, takes account of the two leaves now missing after f. 130 and the two leaves now missing after f. 166, and passes over two leaves after f. 149 (ff. 149*, 149**). The four

[1] Deposited in the Bury St. Edmunds and West Suffolk Record Office, E. 5/9/608.7.

missing leaves are now represented by unnumbered blanks. 442 × 305 mm. Written space 315 × 210 mm. 2 cols. and (ff. 180–4) long lines. 22–4 lines. Collation of ff. (iii–viii), 1–184: 1⁶ (ff. iii–viii) 2–16⁸ 17⁸ wants 8, probably blank, after f. 127 18⁸ wants 4, 5, after f. 130 19–22⁸ 23 one (f. 166) 24–25⁸. Arts. 2–7 are in a large hand, the minims about 9 mm high. Initials of arts. 2–7: (i) in colours on gold and coloured grounds, historiated, with continuous or partial borders in gold and colours: they begin the eight liturgical divisions of art. 2 and, in smaller size, Ps. 51: cf. Dewick, pp. 401–3 and pls. xxix, xxx, and James, op. cit.; (ii) in colours on decorated gold grounds, with border prolongations, beginning arts. 5, 7. (iii) of Ps. 101, gold on coloured ground; (iv) of psalms (except as above) and divisions of psalms, canticles, and hymns, blue with red ornament or gold with pink ornament; (v) of verses of psalms, etc., blue with red ornament or red with violet ornament. Initials of arts. 8, 9: (i) gold on pink and blue grounds; (ii) red or blue. Cadels with olive-green ornament in art. 9. Binding of s. xix ex.: cf. Dewick, p. 399. Secundo folio (f. 2) *maui? et.*

Written in England, for use in the abbey of Bury St. Edmunds, O.S.B. John Myldenall (myldhyll) scribbled his name on ff. 127, 169. 'Hunc librum olim Jacobi Cobs Armigeri Dedit nobis in Bibliotheca Scholæ Buriensis seruandum Jacobus Harvy Jurisconsultus ejus ex Filia Nepos et hujus Scholæ aliquando Alumnus An. Domini 1706', f. (iii), at foot.

2. *Prudentius, etc.*[1]   S. XV/XVI

A brief description in *The Library*, 3rd series, i (1910), 329. ff. 276ᵛ, 278 contain a contemporary table of contents.

1. ff. 1–262 Aurelii prudentii clementis poete lirici prefatio in libros suos. Metrum tricolon tristrophon. Nam primus uersus dicitur glicomus . . . et pirrhichio. Prefatio. Per quinquennia iam decem . . .

Prefatio (f. 1ʳᵛ), Cathemerinon (ff. 2–41ᵛ), Peristephanon 1, 3, 9, 7, 2, 10, 11, 13, 12, 14, 4, 6, 5, 8 (ff. 42–132ᵛ), Epilogus, under the heading 'Curocheus prudentii de toto veteri et nouo testamento personis excerptis . . .' (f. 133ʳᵛ), Tituli historiarum (ff. 133ᵛ–139), Psychomachia (ff. 139ᵛ–163), Apotheosis (ff. 163ᵛ–190ᵛ), Hamartigenia (ff. 191–214ᵛ), Contra Symmachum in two books (ff. 215–62). Many scholia and glosses in minute writing in Latin and German.

2. The dispute over the removal of the altar of victory in the time of the emperor Valentinian II, A.D. 384. (*a*) ff. 262–265ᵛ Ambrosius episcopus principi christianissimo imperatori ualentiniano iuniori scribit. Cum omnes homines . . . intelligis profuturum. (*b*) ff. 265ᵛ–269 Relatio symmachi prefecti urbis romane ad imperatorem ualentinianum iuniorem de reparanda ara uictorie. Ubi primum senatus . . . non fuisse. (*c*) ff. 269–76 Finitus relatio symmachi epistola beati ambrosii contra ipsam relacionem symmachi. ad imperatorem valentinianum iuniorem . . . Cum uir clarissimus . . . iudicas conuenire. Deo gracias. (*d*) f. 276ʳᵛ Ambrosius de obitu valentiniani iunioris . . . Miserat propter recuperanda . . . Pectoris ex ymo manibus pro uicibus auctum.

(*a–c*). PL xvi. 961–6, 966–71, 972–82 (Epp. 17, 17*a*, 18). Cf. *Clavis*, no. 160. (*d*). Cf. PL xvi. 1365, 1375–6.

ff. ii + 276 + ii. Paper and (16, 7, 12 in each quire) parchment. Contemporary flyleaves, an outer parchment leaf and an inner paper leaf at each end: the conjugate halves of the paper leaves emerge after ff. 12, 264. Medieval foliation. 128 × 90 mm. Written

---

[1] Deposited in the Bury St. Edmunds and West Suffolk Record Office, E. 5/9/608. 1.

space *c.* 92 mm high. Collation: 1–23¹². The central opening of each quire is strengthened by two small pieces of parchment taken from a service-book (?). Small set cursiva. Initials: (i) f. 1, blue with red ornament; (ii) blue or red. Bound in a strip of stiff parchment. Secundo folio *Primus himnus.*

Written probably in northern Germany. 'M. Coe clericus dedit M.SS', f. ii^v: according to the Donors' Book the gift of Moses Coe (†1727) was in 1684.

CAMBRIDGE

Catalogues by M. R. James of western manuscripts in all Cambridge colleges, except Newnham and Selwyn, were published between 1895 and 1925: Christ's, 1905 (8 medieval manuscripts); Clare, 1905 (25); Corpus Christi, 1912 (2 vols.: 201+250); Emmanuel, 1904 (92); Gonville and Caius, 1907–14 (3 vols.: 314+147 +13); Jesus, 1895 (75); King's, 1895 (32); Magdalene, 1909 (24); Magdalene, Pepysian Library, 1923 (36); Pembroke, 1905 (289); Peterhouse, 1899 (276); Queens', 1905 (18); St. Catharine's, 1925 (8); St. John's, 1913 (256); Sidney Sussex, 1895 (61); Trinity, 1900–4 (3 vols., text, and 1 vol., index and plates: 326+135+231); Trinity Hall, 1907 (24).

The French manuscripts in three colleges are described by P. Meyer, 'Les manuscrits français de Cambridge', *Romania*, viii (1879), 305–42 (St. John's); xxxii (1903), 18–118 (Trinity); xxxvi (1907), 481–542 (Gonville and Caius).

CAMBRIDGE. CHRIST'S COLLEGE

Rouse 251. *Ovidius* 1482–3

1. ff. 1–93^v [T]empora cum causis . . . increpuitque lyra. Finis die prima aprilis M CCCC lxxxiii° per me F ueloci calamo.

Fasti. Bk. 2, f. 14^v; 3, f. 31; 4, f. 47^v; 5, f. 65; 6, f. 78^v. f. 94^rv blank. Some interlinear glosses at first, but seldom after f. 14.

2. ff. 95–137^v P. Nasonis Ouidii De arte amandi Liber foeliciter incipit. [S]i quis in hoc artem . . . Naso magister erat. Pii Ouidii Sulmonensis De arte amandi liber Tertius et ultimus foeliciter explicit per me F.A. die xxviij mensis ottobris M° cccc lxxxii Laus deo. Amen. Τελωσ.

Divided into *four* books: bk. 2 begins at i. 163. The scribe left blank spaces here and there, for example at ii. 725, iii. 101. ff. 138–141^v blank.

3. ff. 142–3 P. Nasonis Ouidii Sulmonensis De psitaco libellus foeliciter Incipit. [P]sitacus eois . . . par sibi carmen habet. Τελωσ.

Amores, ii. 6, lines 1–60.

4. f. 143^{rv} P. Ouidii Nasonis Sulmonensis liber De anulo Foeliciter Incipit. [A]nule formose . . . sentiat esse fidem. Τελωσ.

Amores, ii. 15.

5. ff. 143^{v}–144^{v} P. Nasonis Ouidii Sulmonensis De aurora Liber foeliciter incipit. [I]am super oceanum . . . tardior ora dies. Τελωσ Amen.

Amores, i. 13.

6. ff. 144^{v}–145 P. Ouidii S. de somno liber foeliciter Incipit. [N]ox erat et somnus . . . nox stetit alta meos.

Amores, iii. 5.

7. f. 145^{rv} P. Ouidii N.S. De medicamine aurium. foeliciter incipit. [N]ec tibi displiceam quod sic sim corpore paruus . . . patiens assummat in aurem. Τελωσ.

Ed. C. Pascal, *Poesia latina medievale*, 1907, pp. 101–2. Walther, no. 11675.

8. ff. 145^{v}–146^{v} P. Nasonis Ouidii S. De lumaca L. foeliciter incipit. Venerat ad segetes . . . causidici ueniant. Τελωσ amen.

Pseudo-Ovid, De lumaca et Lombardo, ed. H. Sedlmayer in *Wiener Studien*, vi (1884), 151–2. Walther, no. 20072.

9. ff. 147–8 Dulcis amica ueni . . . siue sonare queant.

Pseudo-Ovid, De philomena, ed. A. Riese, *Anthologia Latina*, i, no. 762.

10. ff. 148–50 Discite quæ faciem . . . illineretque genis.

Medicamina faciei.

11. ff. 150–153^{v} Nux ego iuncta uie . . . perficiatis iter.

Nux. The scribe wrote the first two lines straight on from art. 10 and then, seeing his mistake, repeated them, leaving space for an initial *N*.

12. ff. 153^{v}–154 Parue pulex: et amara lues inimica puellis . . . quam sibi me socium. Finis Amen.

Pseudo-Ovid. *Poetae Latini minores*, ed. Lemaire, vii. 275. Walther, no. 13745.

13. ff. 154–155^{v} Visa diu foelix . . . quae dedit una duos.

Consolatio ad Liviam, lines 1–82. ff. 156–157^{v}, 158–162^{v} blank.

14 (added). (*a*) f. 157^{v} Aspice sudantes uenerando pondere fratres . . . palluit ore color. (*b*) ff. 163–4 De his que continentur in primo L. fatorum . . .

(*a*) Six couplets. (*b*). An index to art. 1, ending with the heading 'Liber quintus Maius'. ff. 164^{v}–167^{v} blank.

ff. iii+167+iii. ff. 1–94 have or had a foliation of s. xvi. Paper. 210×140 mm. Written space *c.* 150 mm high. 25–7 long lines. Ruling with a hard point, the horizontal lines only. Collation: 1–3^{10} 4^{8} 5–8^{10} 9^{12} 10^{4} (ff. 91–4) 11–14^{10} 15–16^{6} (ff. 135–46) 17^{10}+1 leaf after 10 (f. 157) 18^{10}. ff. 1–24^{v} in quite good sloping humanistica; the rest in an untidy, ugly, and difficult current hand, basically humanistic. Spaces for 3-line and 2-line initials remain blank. English binding, s. xix. Secundo folio *Nam simul*.

Written in Italy. '1876 £8. 18. 6', f. ii. 'W. H. D. Rouse 'Presented to the library July 3rd 1940", f. iv.

Rouse 256. *Terentius* s. xv med.

Six plays of Terence, 'Andria' beginning at line 6 (f. 3), 'Eunuchus' (f. 22), 'Heautontumerumenos' (f. 45ᵛ), 'Adelphos' (f. 69), 'Phormio' (f. 91), and 'Hechira' (f. 113ᵛ), with argumenta, prologues, and the subscriptions of Calliopius. f. 133 ends 'Terentii Afri Comici Poetæ Echira feliciter Explicit Finis'. f. 133ᵛ blank.

The argumenta are: (Eunuchus) 'Meretrix . . . illuditur' before and 'Sororem . . . ephebo' after the title; (Heauton.) 'In militiam . . . accipit'; (Adelphi) 'Duos cum . . . duro Domea'; (Phormio) 'Ex duobus . . . subuenisset' before 'Cremetis . . . agnitam'; (Hecyra) 'Adolescens qui . . . nascitur' before 'Vxorem . . . cum filio'. Heavily annotated in s. xvii, when also a bifolium was added at the beginning, the second leaf of which (f. 2) contains the argumentum 'Sororem falso . . . coniugem', the title, the prologue, and the first five lines of Andria.

ff. iv+131+ii, foliated i, ii, 1–(135). For ff. 1, 2 see above. 216×130 mm. Written space 135×72 mm. 27 long lines. Ruling with a hard point. Collation of ff. 3–133: 1¹⁰ wants 1 2¹⁰ 3¹⁰+1 leaf before 1 (f. 22) 4–12¹⁰ 13⁸ 14⁴ wants 4, blank. Written in good upright humanistica. Initials: (i) 3-line, gold on grounds of pink, blue, and green or of pink and one of the other colours, patterned in white; (ii) 2-line, blue. English binding, s. xvii/xviii. Secundo folio (f. 3) *Sed his*.

Written in Italy. An armorial shield of two Florentine families, f. 1, s. xvii: Soldani impales Aldobrandini and a scroll is labelled 'Iacobi Soldani' (1579–1641: cf. *Dictionnaire de biographie universel*). 'E libris Caroli Scott 1698', f. ii. 'N. Bacon Vicar: Coddenh:' and 'E Libris Bibliothec: Vicari: Coddenham: dedit Vir rever: Nich: Bacon' inside the cover: Bacon was vicar of Coddenham, Suffolk, 1768–97. The ex-libris shows that this book is a stray from the still existing parochial library for which see J. A. Fitch in *Proc. Suffolk Inst. of Archaeology*, xxx (1965), 77–83. Priced at '12. 12. o', f. i. 'W. H. D. Rouse Cambridge. 1902' inside the cover: his gift, 10 June 1940.

Rouse 257. *Cicero* s. xv²

1. ff. 1–28ᵛ M. TVLLI CICERONIS DE AMICITIA LIBER FOELICITER INCIPIT. Quintus Mutius Augur Sceuola multa narrare . . . prestabilius putetis.

2. ff. 29–41ᵛ M. TVLLI CICERONIS PARADOXA LIBER FOELICITER INCIPIT. Animaduerti Brute saepe Catonem . . . existimandi sunt.

The Greek neatly written in red. A few variant readings are entered in the margin preceded by 'aliter'.

3. ff. 42–8 M. TVLLI CICERONIS DE SOMNO SCIPIONIS LIBELLVS FOELICITER INCIPIT. Cum in Aphricam venissem . . . e somno solutus sum.

ff. 48ᵛ–50ᵛ blank.

4. ff. 51–78 'M. Tulli ciceronis de senetute feliciter incipit.' O Tite si quid ego... probare possitis. FINIS DE SENECTVTE.

f. 78ᵛ blank, except for later scribbles.

ff. i+78+i. 195×130 mm. Written space 125×70 mm. 23 long lines. Double vertical bounders. No horizontal lines project beyond the written space. Collation: 1–7¹⁰ 8⁸. Written in one current humanistic hand. Initials: 3-line (ff. 1, 51) and 2-line, gold on coloured grounds: the grounds are usually quartered into squares or triangles, two coloured blue, one green, and one red. Binding of s. xviii. Secundo folio *memorabilem*. Written in Italy. Arms in a pointed oval in the lower margin of f. 1 erased. Arms of Michael Wodhull (*DNB* †1816) on the front cover. J. E. Severne sale, 11 Jan. 1886, lot 725.[1] Given by W. H. D. Rouse in 1940.

Rouse 258. *R. Higden, Polychronicon* s. xiv[2]

Fragments of bks. 1–5 of an AB text of the Polychronicon, including forty-two out of forty-five consecutive leaves from bks. 1–3 (pp. 5–86, 95–6). Book 2 lacks only one leaf.

The following portions of the Rolls Series edition by C. Babington, 1865–86, remain here: i. 188/19–230/2 (pp. 1–4); i. 332/10–ii. 226/1 (pp. 5–34); ii. 244/21–iii. 104, title of bk. 3 (pp. 35–64, 85–6, 65–6); iii. 126/9–196/9 (pp. 67–72); iii. 220/15–370/2 (pp. 73–84, 95–6); iv. 436/10–v. 44/19 (pp. 89–94); v. 68/11–166/10 (pp. 97–100, 87–8, 101–2); v. 236/7–336/8 (pp. 103–4, 107, 105–6, 108–10); v. 360/11–408/13 (pp. 111–14). After writing a recto (p. 107), the scribe forgot to turn over, but instead began another recto (p. 105). When he had finished the verso of this leaf (p. 106) he went back to the verso of the previous leaf (p. 108). The dislocated passage is 'longum . . . dicitur' (ed. v. 296/6–308/5). Signes de renvoi at the foot of p. 106, 'Reuerte ad proximum folium . . .', and at the foot of p. 108, 'Procedas ultra ad secundum folium ad istud signum', refer to the disorder. The scribe wrote 'Cum dei laude amen' after the title of each book (2, 3, 5).

ff. i+57 (paginated 1–114)+i. Paper. 290 × 200 mm. Written space 225 × 150 mm. 48 long lines. Collation impossible: catchwords on pp. 48, 66, 94, 110. Written in current anglicana. Initials: (i) 3-line, blue or (p. 104, beginning bk. 5) blue and red; (ii) 2-line, blue. A yellow wash, for emphasis, covers headings, the first letter of each line of verse on pp. 10–13, and references to authorities. Binding of s. xix.

Written in England. A scribbled copy of the heading of the audit and compotus of John Adams, bailiff of the king 'ibidem', 35–6 Henry VIII '. . . et recessit Quietus', is in the margin of p. 22. 'J. Harland from Rev. T. E. Poynting. Fragments of a MS. Copy of Higden's Polychronicon Recovered about 1 year from the Waste Paper used for wrapping butter, bacon, cheese, etc. etc. in a Provision Shop at Bath . . . J. Harland 1864', f. i. Given by W. H. D. Rouse in 1933.

Rouse 270. *Lucanus* s. xv med.

1. ff. 1–116 Corduba me genuit . . . coma placet. Bella per emathios . . . callantem męnia magnum. Finis.

Lucan, Pharsalia, preceded, as often, by the four-line epigram on Lucan, Walther, no. 3329. Bk. 2, f. 11; 3, f. 21ᵛ; 4, f. 32; 5, f. 44; 6, f. 55ᵛ; 7, f. 67ᵛ; 8, f. 80; 9, f. 92ᵛ; 10, f. 108ᵛ. Some interlinear glosses and marginal scholia in a small hand and some variants introduced by 'aliter', for example at x. 387, 'aliter ictus'. x. 132–92 omitted in error on f. 110 were added at the end by another hand, ff. 115ᵛ–16.

2 (added). f. 116ᵛ S. Augustini oratio dicenda in extremo vite nostre. Deus meus deus meus misericordia mea: et refugium meum: te desidero: ad te confugio . . .

ff. ii+116+ii. Paper. 296 × 208 mm. Written space 205 mm high. 35 long lines. In the

[1] The marked catalogue in the Bodleian has 'Lost at £21' against this entry.

ruling no horizontals project into the margins. Collation: 1–3¹⁰ 4–9¹² 10¹⁴. Several upright humanistic or mixed hands, changing at ff. 15ᵛ, 30, 43, and probably elsewhere: two-compartment *a* and *v* for *u* in all positions is common from about f. 80. 5-line, 3-line, and 2-line initials, plain red or roughly ornamented. The first letter of each verse usually has a yellow wash over it as far as f. 25ʳ. Binding of s. xviii. Secundo folio *Solicitare*.

Written in Italy. 'Sigismondus buc'h'us dum ageret tertium et decimum annum hunc Lucanum propria manu transcripsit legente illum Nicolao botano illius preceptore', f. 116ᵛ.¹ Acquired by Sir Thomas Phillipps from the Abbé Celotti: 'Phillipps MS. 951', f. i. Phillipps sale 10 June 1896, lot 840, to Leighton for £3. 6s: the slip from the sale catalogue is pasted inside the cover. Priced at '10. 10. –', f. i. Given by W. H. D. Rouse in 1933.

Rouse 271. *Cicero*   s. xv med.

1. ff. 1–84ᵛ 'Tulius De oratore Incipit Feliciter'. Cogitanti mihi sepenumero ... curamque laxemus. LAVS DEO AC VIRGINVM VIRGINI PECCATORVM ADVOCATĘ MISERICORDI AC SVMMĘ. M.T.C. ARPI. DE ORATORE LIBER TERTIVS EXPLICIT.

Bk. 2, f. 29ᵛ; 3, f. 65. An annotator, s. xv ex., began to write long notes in the margins, but did not get further than f. 1ᵛ. Some variant readings in the margins preceded by 'aliter'. The main scribe wrote 'Iesus sit mihi adiutor propitius' at the head of f. 1.

2. ff. 85–94ᵛ Studeo mi pater ... maius expecto. LAVS DEO. AC VIRGINVM VIRGINI EIVS MATRI CELORVM REGINĘ.

De partitione oratoria.

3. ff. 95–112ᵛ M. T. Ciceronis de optimo genere dicendi ad Brutum liber primus Incipit. Vtrum mihi difficilius ... impudentiam suscepisse. LAVS DEO AC GLORIOSAE VIRGINI MARIAE EXCELSAE SVPER OMNEM CAELICAE GENTIS CHORVM. A'C' SVPERNORVM CIVIVM. AMEN. Finis operis Ciceronis inscripti de optimo genere dicendi.

Orator. 'Iesus' and 'Alius titulus est De perfecto oratore. ad marcum brutum' at the head of f. 95.

ff. i+113+i. Paper. 285 × 205 mm. Written space 180–195 mm × 115–130 mm. 37–40 long lines. On ff. 1–96 only vertical bounding lines are ruled and from f. 97 there is no ruling. Collation: 1–9¹² 10⁴+1 leaf before 1 (f. 109). Written in a non-current upright humanistic hand. Red 4-line or 2-line initials: rough ornament, f. 1: spaces left blank, ff. 29ᵛ, 65. Binding of paper-covered pasteboard, s. xviii (?). Secundo folio *In qua*. Written in Italy. 'yhesus Liber Damiani Maroti v scholaris' f. 113ᵛ, s. xvi. A label on the spine, s. xix, '123 Cartaceo ... Secolo xv'. '611' inside the cover. 'Phillipps MS. 16296' inside the cover: Phillipps sale, 10 June 1896, lot 289, to Quaritch for £1. 17s. Given by W. H. D. Rouse in 1940.

Rouse 274. *Cicero, etc.*   s. xv/xvi

1. ff. 1–62ᵛ Marcii Tulii Ciceronis Ad Marcum Filium Liber de officiis Primus Feliciter Incipit. Ihesus xpistus Marie f. etc. [Q]uamquam te Marce fili ...

¹ Mr. Andrew Watson tells me of a rather similar inscription in B.L., Egerton 1119, f. 48, naming Nicholas de Botanis (*or* Betanis) and dated at Lucca, 25 June 1463.

preceptisque letabere. Excellitant cunctos hii libros philosophorum / Libri quos fecit tres Tullius offitiorum etc. Amen. Io. hir. de Bur. ar. bar. wie, etc.

Bk. 2, f. 26ᵛ; 3, f. 43ᵛ. Scholia and interlinear glosses in a very small hand.

2. (*a*) ff. 63–75 [C]ahos vt cliodus iudicat . . . secure promittit. (*b*) ff. 75ᵛ–78 . . . Epilogus digesti operis. Laus Deo Pax Viuis Requiem Eternam Defunctis. (*c*) ff. 89–91ᵛ In noua fert animus. Ponit ouidius primo et ante omnia quod postquam mundus . . . iuxta fluminem nili vbi (*ends abruptly*).

(*a*) is an epitome of, (*b*) a table of chapters of, and (*c*) a commentary on Ovid, Metamorphoses. In (*b*) the chapters of bks. 1–5 are numbered 1–60; of bks. 6–10, 1–68; of bks. 11–15, 1–53. (*c*) ends in bk. 1, in the first sentence of a paragraph beginning '[Y]o amica Iouis'. ff. 78ᵛ–88ᵛ, 92ʳᵛ blank.

ff. vi+92. Paper. 293 × 215 mm. Written space 175 × 120 mm. 26 or 27 long lines and (art. 2) 2 cols. of *c*. 50 lines. Collation: 1–4¹⁰ 5¹² 6–9¹⁰. Written in hybrida. Initials in art. 1: (i) f. 43ᵛ, red with ornament in the ink of the text; ff. 1, 26ᵛ, omitted; (ii) 3-line or 2-line, red. In art. 2 the spaces for initials have not been filled. Capital letters in the ink of the text stroked with red as far as f. 56. Contemporary binding of bare wooden boards, rebacked: two clasps fasten from the front cover to the back cover: the metal on the back cover is stamped 'yh*esus*'. Secundo folio *uelint*.

Written in France (?). The subscription to art. 1 may be in the main hand. 'Dr Hirst sale 10. 10. 0 1878 H. W.', f. i. Given by W. H. D. Rouse in 1940.

CAMBRIDGE. CORPUS CHRISTI COLLEGE

540. *Horae*   s. XIV ex.

1. ff. 4–15ᵛ Calendar in red and black.

'Antonii abbatis' in red, 17 Jan. 'Anno domini mᵒ ccᵒ xxiiᵒ fuit edificatum castrum de Cordua albigesii per comitem tholosanum', f. 14 (7 Nov.), perhaps in the main hand. f. 16ʳᵛ blank.

2. ff. 17–21 Sequentiae of the Gospels.

3. f. 21ᵛ Quicumque hos versus cotidie deuote dixerit in honore beate marie uirginis non morietur sine confessione. [M]ater digna dei uenie . . .

RH, no. 11335.

4. ff. 22–84 Hours of B.V.M. of the use of (Rome). The leaves beginning lauds, prime, none, vespers, and compline, on which there were pictures, are missing. Salve regina as a memoria after compline. Advent office, f. 77ᵛ.

5. ff. 84ᵛ–86 Missa de beata maria. Introitus. Salue sancta parens enixa puerpera regem . . .

RH, no. 18197.

6. ff. 86ᵛ–89 Legitur quod cum beatus thomas martir ecclesie cantuariensis archiepiscopus preesset deuotissimus septem gaudia . . . Explicit reuelacio.

Incipiunt gaudia per dictum sanctum super hiis ordinata. Gaude flore uirginali . . .

RH, no. 6809.

7. ff. 89–90ᵛ Passio domini nostri ihesu cristi secundum iohannem. In illo tempore. Apprehendit pylatus . . . testimonium eius. Oracio. Deus qui manus tuas . . . *Horae Ebor.*, p. 123.

8. ff. 91–108 Penitential psalms and (f. 103) litany.

9. ff. 108ᵛ–117ᵛ Masses of Holy Trinity, Holy Spirit, Holy Cross, and (f. 115) Missa pro defunctis.

10. (*a*) ff. 117ᵛ–118 Iste salutaciones dicuntur ad eleuacionem corporis cristi. Aue domine ihesu criste uerbum patris . . . (five aves). (*b*) f. 118ᵛ In presencia corporis cristi oracio. Domine ihesu criste qui hanc sacratissimam carnem . . .

11. ff. 119–154ᵛ Hours of the Cross.

The office attributed to Bonauentura: Quaracchi edn., viii. 152–8; *AH* l. 568–71.

12. ff. 155–8 Hours of the Cross. Patris sapientia . . . f. 158ᵛ blank.

13. ff. 159–62 Hours of the Holy Spirit. Nobis sancte spiritus . . . f. 162ᵛ blank.

14. ff. 163–166ᵛ Hours of St. Katherine.

(f. 163ᵛ) *Antifona.* Castitatis lilium . . .: *RH*, no. 2672; *AH* xxx. 15.

15. ff. 167–209 Office of the dead, beginning imperfectly. f. 209ᵛ blank.

16. ff. 210–212ᵛ Incipit officium mortuorum in breui compendio. Exaudi domine . . . Hymnus. Salutiferis meritis matutinalis . . . (prime) Hora prima qua fuisti . . . (terce) Crux mortuos foueat . . . (sext) Membrorum concussio . . . (none) Mors tua nos saciet . . . (vespers) Te recordor vesperis . . . (compline) Nunc hora completorii . . .

17 (added early). ff. 212ᵛ–213 Nota quod octo merita attribuuntur homini. propter uisionem cristi. Primo. necessaria uite illa die . . .

18 (added early). ff. 213ᵛ–216ᵛ Missa pro morte euitanda a domino papa data anno domini millesimo cccᵒ xlviiiᵒ et concessit omnibus ipsam missam deuote audientibus ducentos et decem dies de indulgencia . . . Introitus misse. Recordare domine testamenti tui . . .

19 (added). (*a*) ff. 1–2ᵛ Si quis uult clemenciam altissimi saluatoris exorare pro peccatis uel pro qualibet necessitate legitur quod cum dominus papa innocentius quartus uoluisset a domino petere consilium stetit in oracionem tresdecim diebus et confessus dixit has missas sequentes . . . Incipiunt misse. Prima missa est de aduentu domini. Officium Ad te leuaui . . . (*b*) f. 3ʳᵛ Memoria of St. Sebastian 'et ualet contra epidimiam'.

(*a*). Titles and cues of thirteen masses.

ff. i+216+ii. f. 217, a parchment leaf, was pasted down to an earlier binding. 160×112 mm. Written space 90×55 mm. 17 long lines. Collation of ff. 4–216: 1–3⁶ 4⁸ 5⁸ wants 3 after f. 31 6⁸ wants 7 after f. 42 8⁸ wants 5 after f. 55 9⁸ wants 1 before f. 59 and 8 after f. 64 10–11⁸ 12¹⁰ (ff. 81–90) 13–14⁸ 15¹² (ff. 107–18) 16–21⁸ 22⁸ wants 1 before f. 167 23–27⁸ 28 three. Eight out of thirteen 13-line pictures remain, three in art. 4 (matins, terce, sext) and one before each of arts. 8, 11 (Instruments of the Passion, Christ standing in the tomb, B.V.M. and St. John), 12–14. Five pictures are missing from art. 2 and one in front of art. 15. Initials: (i) 3-line, in colour on gold and coloured grounds, decorated in colours and framed in gold, with prolongations forming a continuous border on picture pages; (ii) 2-line, gold on coloured grounds patterned in white, with ivy-leaf sprays into the margin; (iii) 1-line, as (ii), but without the sprays. Line fillers in red and blue, patterned in white and picked out with bars or roundels of gold. Binding of s. xix. Secundo folio (f. 18) *eius gloriam*.

Written in France. Was probably in the region of Albi (art. 1). Given by A. H. Paget (Lord Queenborough) in 1923.

544. *W. Lyndwood, Provinciale*   s. xv²

1. Constituciones prouinciales. De summa trinitate et fide catholica. Rubrica. Ignorancia sacerdotum et infra. Ne quis per ignoranciam . . . et aliis solempnitatibus prout decet. Finis.

This and other copies listed by C. R. Cheney, *The Jurist*, xxi (1961), 433–4. No apparatus. Notices of feasts of St. Thomas, etc., erased, for example on f. 18.

2. ff. 97–9 Leaves from an early fourteenth-century copy of the commentary of Robert Grosseteste on the Posterior Analytics of Aristotle taken over from an older binding of art. 1, as scribbles show.[1]

Conclusio 9, 'Explanatis autem omnibus modis . . .' (bk. 1, ch. 14) is on f. 97: ed. Ven., 1504, f. 13. One complete leaf folded in two (ff. 98, 99) and the upper half of a second leaf. Written space 245×180 mm. 2 cols. 50 lines. Pricks in both margins. Written in England.

ff. ii+96+vi. 210×140 mm. Written space 118×75 mm. 2 cols. 29 long lines. Collation: 1–12⁸. Written throughout in one secretary hand. Initials: (i) f. 1, blue shaded to white on gold ground, with ornament in colours, including green, extending round three sides of the written space; (ii) gold on blue and red grounds patterned in white, with sprays of green and gold into the margins; (iii) 2-line, blue with red ornament; (iv) 1-line, red. Additional ornament was added in the margins in s. xviii (?). Secundo folio *sub specie*.

Written in England. 'W. Stukely: C C Colleg in Cantabr' (*these words over erasure*) me iure tenet', f. 1; also 'Ed. Hall. Donum amicissimi Gull. Stukely M.B.'. Stukely, †1765, was admitted at Corpus in 1703.

Belonged to the Revd. P. Hookins, of Great Barford (Oxfordshire), who bequeathed it to his housekeeper, Mrs. Lively, from whom Messrs. Walford and Cambray, High St., Banbury, obtained it. Bought from them by the Revd. C. J. Bowen, St. John's Catholic Church, Banbury, 21 July 1893. Bought by Corpus Christi College for £10 in 1932. These facts emerge from pieces kept with the manuscript: a newspaper article about it written by Bowen in July 1893; Messrs. Walford and Cambray's certificate as to its provenance; two letters from John Johnson, printer to the University of Oxford, written in 1932, recommending the purchase.

[1] I owe the identification to Dr. L. Minio-Paluello.

CAMBRIDGE. FITZWILLIAM MUSEUM

Catalogues. **1.** M. R. James, *A Descriptive Catalogue of the Manuscripts in the Fitzwilliam Museum*, 1895. 19 plates. **2.** M. R. James, *A Descriptive Catalogue of the McClean Collection of Manuscripts in the Fitzwilliam Museum*. 1912. 108 plates. **3.** F. Wormald and P. M. Giles, 'A handlist of the Additional Manuscripts in the Fitzwilliam Museum', *Transactions of the Cambridge Bibliographical Society*, i. 197–207, 297–309, 365–375, ii. 1–13, iv. 173–8, vi. 243–51. **4.** F. Wormald and P. M. Giles, *Illuminated Manuscripts in the Fitzwilliam Museum*, 1966. 32 plates. **5.** *Heraldry at the Fitzwilliam*, 1970. **6.** P. M. Giles, 'A handlist of the Bradfer-Lawrence Manuscripts deposited on loan at the Fitzwilliam Museum', *Transactions of the Cambridge Bibliographical Society*, vi, pt. 2 (1973), 86–99.

1. 184 medieval manuscripts.[1] **2.** 175 medieval manuscripts.[1] The McClean collection was bequeathed in 1904. **3.** Six parts: I–IV, 1951–4 (pt. IV is an index); V, 1966; VI, 1975. 142 medieval manuscripts,[1] not counting single leaves and cut-out miniatures (18)[2] and a collection of binding fragments.

CAMBRIDGE. GONVILLE AND CAIUS COLLEGE

455/393. *'Excepta ex decretis romanorum pontificum'*[3]   s. xii[2]

Excepta ex decretis romanorum pontificum. Quoniam quorundam romanorum decretalia pontificum synodalibus . . . In hora ultima confessione (*ends imperfectly*).

Z. N. Brooke, *The English Church and the Papacy*, 1931, pp. 92, 93, 242–3 (Collectio Trium Partium). Ends in the section De penitencia of part 3.

ff. ii+188+ii. 288 × 190 mm. Written space *c.* 205 × 135 mm. 2 cols. 34 lines. Collation: 1–5[12] 6–7[10] 8–16[12]. Quires numbered at the end. Green, blue, and red initials, the larger ones decorated in a distinctive style. Running titles are lined through in red. Secundo folio *ita ut ne*.

Written in England. 'Joh. Banister liber ex dono Josiæ Lambert Avunculi mei 1608', f. 1.

[1] Including service books, s. xvi[1].
[2] The large Marlay collection of cuttings is not described: see **3** (*TCBS* i. 297) and, for cuttings G. 4 and G. 9, 4, pls. 5, 25.
[3] Temporarily mislaid when James was cataloguing the manuscripts. He reproduced the description in the 1849 catalogue.

CAMBRIDGE. KING'S COLLEGE

43. *Genealogia regum anglorum* s. xv[1]

A genealogical roll resembling Oxford, Bodleian, Bodley Rolls 10 (*Sum. Cat.* 2967) and B.L., Lansdowne Rolls 2. Characteristics of these three rolls are that they start from Noah, not Adam, that they have against Edward the Confessor the prophecy 'Arbor quelibet viridis . . .' and the 'Exposicio prophecie. Arbor hec anglorum regnum . . . quasi lapis factus angularis', and that they have at the end, in place of any notice of Henry IV, Henry V, or Henry VI, a piece about the newly quiet character of the Welsh, 'Primo anno henrici quarti surrexit . . . falleratus dicior hec ille', taken mainly from Higden, Polychronicon (edn. RS, i. 410–12), but applied to the reign of Henry V when 'seperunt (*sic, King's 43*) Wallenses more anglorum viuere'. The last king is Henry VI and this form of the royal genealogy was probably made early in his reign.

All but a segment of the roundel which in Bodley Rolls 10 contains a drawing of the ark has been cut off and the first two paragraphs of text are damaged. Below this point two of the three pictures in Bodley Rolls 10 are present, a crowned head in the Lucius roundel, with 'Iste erat primus rex cristianus in hoc regno' beside it, and the head and shoulders of a bishop above the point in the left-hand margin where the line of archbishops of Canterbury starts with Augustine: the picture of the Nativity in a roundel a little above and to the left of Lucius does not occur here. The line of archbishops runs, as in Lansdowne Rolls 2, to 'Robertus' (Winchelsey): in Bodley Rolls 10 it is brought down to Henry Chicheley (archbishop 1414–43). The latest names in roundels are 'Ricardus Comes Sar'' (Richard Neville, Earl of Salisbury 1429) and 'Robertus Episcopus Sar'' (Robert Neville, bishop of Salisbury 1427), as in Lansdowne Rolls 2: Bodley Rolls 10 has these two and also three more of the grandsons of John of Gaunt by Joan, Countess of Westmorland. The main stem ends with 'Henricus Sextus', not in a roundel, but in red within a large green and white *H* decorated with white interlace. The dorse is blank.

A roll of seven membranes, measuring *c.* 5250 × 295 mm. Written in a neat hand of mixed, but mainly secretary character. Two penwork pictures: see above. Spaces for small coloured initials not filled. Red (for the main line), brown, and green strokes connect roundels.

Written in England. No. 1 at £30 in J. and J. Leighton's catalogue 13 (new series). A small label on the dorse of two membranes has 'Royal Archaeological Institute' printed on it and bears the number 50. Given by Mrs. G. Mackay in 1948.

47. *Feoda militum, etc.* s. xv in.

1. ff. 1–14ᵛ (*begins imperfectly*) Gilling' Theob' de lek tenet . . .

A return of knights' fees for the hundreds of Cambridgeshire and Huntingdonshire agreeing with that printed by J. W. Clark, *Liber Memorandorum Ecclesie de Bernewelle*, 1907, pp. 238–72, but defective owing to loss of leaves. The remains correspond to Clark's edition as follows: f. 1ʳᵛ, Yelling–Catworth, pp. 265/28–267/25; ff. 2–3ᵛ, Graffham–Somersham, and Fordham and Badlingham, pp. 269/20–272, 261/5–14; ff. 4–11, Landbeach–Hinxton, pp. 241/14–256/6; ff. 12–14ᵛ, Cheveley–Hinton, and Fordham and Badlingham, pp. 259/15–261/4, 261/15–263, 261/5–14. In the manuscript Clark used Fordham and Badlingham were out of place after Somersham. Here they occur twice, out of place on f. 14ᵛ and in place on f. 3ᵛ, and are referred to in the margin of f. 12ᵛ, 'Fordham Require in secundo folio sequente'. A leaf is missing before and after f. 1 and probably three leaves are missing before f. 4 and two leaves after f. 11. Presumably the leaves were once in the order 4–14, 1–3, but the present order is medieval, since the catchword on f. 14^v refers to f. 15.

For the date of the return, 1236–8, see W. Farrer, *Feudal Cambridgeshire*, p. vi. William Cole copied it in 1747 from 'an ancient Roll of Parchment' in the Archives of Corpus Christi College (B.L., Add. 5838, ff. 58^v–71^v) and in Apr. 1748 he collated his copy with the present manuscript which he referred to as 'C' (cf. art. 3).

2. ff. 15–19 In comitatibus Cantebrig' et Huntedon' de visu franciplegii . . .

A view of frankpledge and (ff. 18^v–19) sheriff's aid for Cambridgeshire and Huntingdon-shire. Printed by Clark, op. cit., pp. 273–80.

3. ff. 19^v–29 Trippelawe pro viii hyd' se defendit . . . Childresleya pro x hyd' . . . de feodo Regis.

The Domesday return for Cambridgeshire arranged by hundreds under localities. f. 29^v was left blank. A note about Domesday at the foot of f. 19^v is in the same good hand of s. xvi as occurs on ff. 4, 19, and 29^{rv}. Copied by William Cole in B.L., Add. 5838, ff. 72^v–82^v. Cole dated his copy 31 Mar. 1748 and noted on f. 72^v that it was 'procured for me by Mr. Ames 'Secretary to the Antiquary Society' 'From Mr Chandler''.

ff. 29+ii. 203 × 165 mm. Written space 150 × 108 mm. 26 long lines. Collation as now bound (see above): 1 three (ff. 1–3: 2, 3 are a bifolium) 2^8 wants 1–3 before f. 4 3^8 wants 4, 5 after f. 11 4^8 5^8 wants 8, blank. Written in anglicana (with secretary g and r). No coloured initials. Bound in a limp parchment cover, s. xviii (?).

'moyun', a roughly drawn shield and 'il port argent. La [. . . . .] est gules', f. 16, s. xv ex. 'George Billingham', f. 4, is a scribble. Lent to William Cole in 1748, as appears from a note in Cole's hand on a piece of paper kept with MS. 47 referring to a manuscript at Corpus Christi College, Cambridge, and the subsequent addition in another hand 'From Mr Willm Cole of King's College Cambridge (to whom I had Lent the Book) in March 1748 (in a letter to Dr Jos. Ames Dated Apr. 11 1748)'. The 'I' in this sentence is presumably Chandler.[1] Bought in Aug. 1961.

50. *Jacobus de Voragine, Quadragesimale; etc.*   s. xiv/xv

1. Incipit xl^e Iacobi sermo primus. Filia populi mei induere cilicio . . . Ierem vi(:26). Quamuis solempnitas quadragesimalis . . . (f. 85^v) consortium angelorum. Rogemus etc.

Printed often. Goff, J. 186, 198–202.

2. The space left blank at the end of the last quire is filled with miscellaneous pieces. (*a*) ff. 85^v–86 Isti sunt denuncciandi. excommunicati a papa. Primo inuasores ecclesiarum et cimiteriorum . . . (*6 heads*). Isti sunt excommunicati ab episcopo. Primo sacrilegii. Kyrchprichil . . . (*52 heads*). Hiis omnibus sacra communio supradictis est interdicenda nisi confiteantur et peniteant. (*b*) f. 86^{rv} De nouo sacerdote. Hodie incipiam te exaltare . . . Iosue iii^o. Hoc verbum quondam dominus dixit Iosue duci . . . de purgatorio liberacio. Rogemus et cetera. (*c*) ff. 86^v–87 Notes on fasting, etc. (*d*) f. 87^v Tables to find the golden number and Sunday letter, with explanations. (*e*) f. 87^v Domine quis credidit auditui nostro . . .

(*a*, *b*) in the main hand. (*a*). A few words in German. (*b*). A sermon. (*d*). Two passages

[1] See above, art. 3.

contain dates: 'Cum aureum numerum invenire volueris tolle ab annis incarnacione (*sic*) domini M° ccc° nonagesimo secundo residuo computa . . .'; 'Tolle m° ccc° lxxxxii°. residuum computa incipiens ab a grosso . . .'. (*e*). Isaiah 53: 1–12.

3. A bifolium of a paper manuscript of biblical history (2 cols., 43 lines) in German cursiva, s. xiv, is pasted inside the covers. A paragraph is headed 'Ioseph'.

ff. 87. Paper. 302 × 225 mm. Written space *c*. 232 × 162 mm. 2 cols. *c*. 48 lines. Frame ruling. Collation: 1–3¹² 4¹² wants 8 after f. 43 5¹² 6–7¹⁴. A strip of parchment as strengthening in the middle of each quire. Quires numbered at the end. Written in cursiva. 2-line metallic red initials. Capital letters in the ink of the text touched with red. Contemporary binding of limp parchment, with leather back strip through which the strings are brought at four points, at the head, above and below the mid point, and at the foot: in all there are twenty holes, ten above and ten below the mid point. The leather was also pierced with four horizontal holes at the mid point, but the parchment below it has not been pierced. Secundo folio *caput eius*.

Written in Germany. Bequeathed by D. H. Beves and received '23 Aug. 1961'.

51. *Psalterium*   s. xv in.

1. Incipit psalterium ordinatum secundum (usum) curie romane. et est conuentus potencie. Inuitatoria. Uenite . . .

A liturgically arranged psalter, with canticles, hymns, etc., in their places.

2. Leaves used in binding: (*a*) f. 81 a leaf of Digestum Novum (bk. 47, tit. 2) in an Italian hand, s. xiv; (*b*) the pastedown at the end, the lower half of a leaf containing on the exposed side Numbers 1: 32–6 and 45–50 in an Italian hand, s. xii.

(*b*) is the last twelve lines of a page of a large two-column manuscript with a written space 230 mm wide.

ff. i+80+i. For f. 81 see above. 272 × 203 mm. Written space 170 × 125 mm. Collation: 1–10⁸. Initials: (i) red and blue patterned in white, with violet ornament; (ii) 2-line, blue with red ornament or red with violet ornament; (iii) 1-line, blue or red. Binding of wooden boards, s. xvi?, with leather patterned with fillets over some 55 mm of each cover and the spine: two clasps, one missing. Secundo folio *et in lege*.

Written in Italy for and perhaps in the convent of Potenza. No. 601 [348] in a bookseller's catalogue, s. xix, at £21. Bequeathed as MS. 50.

52. *Juvenalis*   s. ix/x

1. f. 1ᵛ (*a*) Iuuenalis satyr'ic'us aquinates fuit. id est de aquino oppido. Hic suo tempore . . . damnatus est. (*b*) Hoc autem opus . . . plenum sit.

(*a*, *b*) printed from this copy by S. G. Owen, 'The Phillipps Manuscripts of Juvenal', *Journal of Philology*, xxxiii (1914), 239. (*a*) is 'Vita vii', ed. Jahn, p. 386. (*b*) a scholium is run on with (*a*). (*a*, *b*) are in the main hand of scholia in the margin of a blank page.

2. ff. 2–61ᵛ Decimi iunii iuuenalis Satyrarum liber primus incipit. Semper ego

auditor . . . et torquibus omnes. Decimi iunii iuuenalis satyrarum liber quintus explicit.

Bk. 2, f. 16^v; 3, f. 27; 4, f. 37^v; 5, f. 48^v. For the text, cf. Owen, loc. cit. 238–64. Nearly contemporary scholia, thick at first, are mostly in alphabetical series, beginning usually with A on each new page.[1] The first under A on f. 2 begins 'Cum inquit omnes luxurientur in scribendis libris'. The last lettered scholium is under N on f. 56^v, the last page of quire 7, 'Quondam homines in templo martis . . . galeam abstulerant': it refers to xiv. 261. There are few scholia after this point. Some marginalia in good rustic capitals. Old High German glosses on ff. 1, 29, 45^v, 46, 47, 48^v, 50^{rv}: points stand for vowels.

3. ff. 61^v–62^v Quęstiunculam mihi datam a uestra reuerentia. his diebus attulit familiaris noster fredilo in qua requirebantur . . . his que efferenda sunt iuste damnari. Finit [. . . . .]s.

An answer attributed to Lupus Servatus to a question on the meaning of Ceroma (Sat. vi. 246). Edited from this and six other copies in MGH, Epp. vi (1925), 115–17: collated as I.

4. Additions in blank spaces at either end. (a) f. 1, s. x, glosses, Ciclops id est gigas . . . Serracum. carpentum. plaustrum. (b) f. 1, s. xiii, verses, Presul ana-gnine pandulfe polum sine fine . . . (4 lines). (c) f. 1, s. xiii, verses, Ostia presule te gaudet bene nupta. set et te . . . (4 lines). (d) f. 1, s. xiii, verses, Aspera passa satis non edibus usa paratis . . . fueris clerdona fidelis (6 lines). (e–g) f. 62^v, s. xi/xii: (e) Parua culix (uel culex *interlined*) pecudum . . . pro munere reddit (2 lines); (f) Nocte pluit tota . . . cum ioue cesar habet (2 lines); (g) Hos ego versiculos . . . uellera fertis oues (3 lines). (h) f. 62^v, s. xiii in., `Incipit ars algorismi de numero'. Numerorum alius digitus alius articulus alius compositus ex digito et articulo . . . quam ipsa non habet.

(b). Pandulf, bishop of Anagni, 1237. (e–g) in a good hand, s. xi/xii. (e). Virgil, *Culex*, lines 413–14. (f, g) ed. Riese, *Anthologia Latina*, nos. 256, 257.

ff. ii+63+ii. 285 × 190 mm. Written space c. 217 mm high and (art. 3) 90 mm wide. 32 long lines. Collation: 1–7^8 8^8 wants 7 or 8. Quires 1–7 numbered at the end and quire 8 at the beginning: catchwords added, s. xii (?). The script has open a, ra, and ro ligatures (an elaborate ro ligature in the scholia-writing hand) and occasionally a form of t closed on the left side (see f. 37) and broken-backed forms of c and e which may have been taken over from the exemplar. Each satire, except the fourth, is preceded by a heading in red or green rustic capitals and each, except the fourth, begins with a small red or green initial. There is a heading also at vii. 17 and an initial after a 1-line space at iii. 17. No break between satires 3 and 4. On f. 52^v a dog forms the back of the P of *Plurima* (xiv. 1) and holds the two ends of the bow in his mouth and paws. A binding with the arms of King's College made by W. H. Smith for John Hely-Hutchinson in 1949 replaces one said to have been of s. xix. Secundo folio *Et multum*.

Written in north-east France or south Belgium, perhaps in the Valenciennes or Stavelot region, according to a letter from Bernhard Bischoff, 24 Apr. 1949, kept with the manuscript: Bischoff saw it in Cheltenham in 1934. Glossed in a Germanic region. Probably later in Italy: cf. art. 4b, c, and a scribble on f. 1, s. xv, 'domnus leonardus de patrica habet senecam meum'. Libri sale, 25 July 1862, lot 305. Phillipps 16395. Bought by John Hely-Hutchinson of Chippenham Lodge, Ely, before 30 Oct. 1947: bequeathed by him and received in 1954. Schenkl, no. 2029.

[1] The unit is the page on ff. 2–31^v, the leaf on f. 32^{rv}, and the double opening on ff. 33^v–34.

CAMBRIDGE. MAGDALENE COLLEGE

F. 4. 34+Pepys 2124. *Ovid, Metamorphoses (in English)* s. xv ex.

Caxton's translation of Ovid, Metamorphoses, in two volumes, bks. i–ix in vol. 1 and bks. x–xv in vol. 2. Both volumes were reproduced in facsimile in 1968 by George Braziller, New York, in association with Magdalene College, Cambridge.

vol. 1, ff. 1–9ᵛ Table of the fifteen books. f. 10 Prohemye. Scyence hath many enemyes . . . (15ᵛ) glorye and lawde Amen. And thus endeth the prohemye. f. 16 Here begynneth the booke Intituled Ovyde of Methamorphoseos. whiche conteyneth in somme xv bookes. And first begynneth the prologue. Alle scriptures and wrytyngis ben they good or evyll . . . (vol. 2, f. 206ᵛ) can be knowen and rehercd. Amen. Thus endeth Ouyde hys booke of Methamorphose translated and fynyshed by me William Caxton at Westmestre the xxii day of Apryll. the yere of our' lord m¹ iiiiᶜ iiiixx And the xx yere of the Regne of Kynge Edward' the fourth.

ff. iii+272+ii (vol. 1). ff. iii+206+ii (vol. 2). Paper. 312×215 mm (vol. 1). 287×205 mm (vol. 2). Written space *c.* 200×140 mm. 30 long lines. Ruling in red ink. Written by one hand in skilled secretary. A space, usually 19-line, was left for a picture in front of each book, but only the first four pictures were executed, ff. 16, 39ᵛ, 71ᵛ (mostly torn away), 98ᵛ. Initials: (i) of books, 4-line, blue or red and blue, usually with red ornament; (ii) of chapters, 3-line, blue or red; (iii) subdividing chapters, 2-line, as (ii). Capital letters in the ink of the text stroked with red. Bindings: (vol. 1) morocco by the British Museum bindery, 1969; (vol. 2) s. xvii².

'A frynde is to hys frynd a nother hym sylfe' (cf. *Dictionary of English Proverbs*, p. 227) is scribbled on f. 143 above the name 'Tamesyn Audeleye', s. xvi. Other names, s. xvi, in vol. 2: 'Rychard Wastffeld', f. 127, 'Audley Seeley', f. 206ᵛ. Vol. 2 was part of the library bequeathed by Samuel Pepys, †1703. Earlier it belonged to Lord Lumley, †1609: his name at the foot of f. 1: not entered in his catalogue.¹ Vol. 1, from the collection of Sir Thomas Phillipps (no Phillipps number), was sold at Sotheby's, 27 June 1966, lot 318 (£90,000). Acquired finally for Magdalene College in 1970: cf. R. F. Bennett, 'Caxton Retained', *Magdalene College Magazine and Record*, N.S. xi (1966–7), 19–23, and A. N. L. Munby in Munby and Towner, *The Flow of Books and Manuscripts*, University of California, William Andrews Clark Memorial Library Seminar Paper, 1969, pp. 3–8.

Pepys 911. Bernardus Sylvester, etc. s. xiii²

Arts. 1–4, 6, 7 are also in Bodleian, Ashmole 304, admirably described in Black's catalogue, arts. 2, 5, 6, 7, 8, 4 (misnumbered 3). Pages of Ashmole corresponding to ff. 14, 19, 30ᵛ and 63 of MS. 911 are reproduced in *Trans. Cambr. Bibl. Soc.* i, pl. 16b, by F. Wormald, 'More Matthew Paris Drawings', *Walpole Soc.* xxxi (1946), pl. xxviii (1, 2), and by R. Vaughan, *Matthew Paris*, 1958, pl. xxi b.

1. ff. 2–18ᵛ Materia huius libelli est [. . .]tus² et efficacia lune . . . reuelat euidenciam. Utilitas autem . . . (f. 2ᵛ) indicem inuenerunt. Hic incipit

---

¹ Cf. S. Jayne and F. R. Johnson, *The Lumley Library*, 1956, p. 300.
² A blotted word which does not look quite like 'effectus'. The reading of Ashm. 'virtus' was interlined above it, s. xvii (?).

experimentarius. Bernardi. Siluestris in astronomia. Titulus uero talis est. Experimentarius bernardi siluestris . . . interpres. Prima regula. Iaciantur primo puncta . . . Inuocato semper spiritu sancto. (f. 3) Tabula questionum . . . (f. 3ᵛ) Tabula secunda responsionum . . . (f. 4) Tabula tercia . . . (f. 4ᵛ) Tabula quarta Legationum . . . (f. 5) Almazane. Tuum indumentum durabit tempore longo . . . Opta que dei sunt fauebit dominus ipse. Explicit.

In Ashm., ff. 2ʳ, 3–16ᵛ (incomplete). Cf. Thorndike, *History of Magic and Experimental Science*, ii. 122–3. Each page, ff. 5–18ᵛ, has twenty-eight lines of verse below the name of the answering judge. A 'Turris astrorum' is at the foot of f. 3 and seven towers are in the outer margin of f. 3ᵛ. A volvel applying to art. 1 was added in s. xv and is now attached to f. viᵛ.

2. ff. 19ᵛ–29ᵛ 'I' Si puer viuet *Vade ad columbam*[1] i . . . (f. 20) '36' Si amissio per latronem inuenietur *Vade ad arpharperet*[1] xxxvi. (f. 20ᵛ) Columba. Iudex iᵘˢ. Iste puer uiuet satis et prosperabitur in diebus suis . . . (f. 29ᵛ) Dilucidatio precedentium. Sint tibi bis sena . . . capitalis obortam.

In Ashm., ff. 42ᵛ–52 (art. 5), except the fourteen lines of verse headed Dilucidatio. On ff. 20ᵛ–29 twelve lines are assigned to each of thirty-six judges. As in Ashm., the words 'Non computentur rubrice' are written in red against the beginning of the text. Drawings of the birds (35 and 'vespertilio') in the margins. f. 30 blank. For f. 19ʳ see below, decoration.

3. ff. 30ᵛ–33ᵛ De cogitatione.Responde. Quere in libro prophecie Iude . . . (f. 31) Indas iudex id est Regalis confitens ueritatem. Uelle dei nosse . . . mens tua credit.

In Ashm., ff. 52ᵛ–55ᵛ (art. 6). The twelve patriarchs occupy the head of f. 30ᵛ, as on the corresponding page of Ashm. On ff. 31–33ᵛ one 12-line stanza is assigned to each patriarch. 'Non computentur rubrice' is in the margin against the beginning of the text. f. 34 blank.

4. ff. 34ᵛ–44ᵛ i. De infante si viuet. Quid erit dic. Quere in primo gradu Arietis . . . (f. 35) A Gradus primus Redii Responde Vade ad Iudicem questionis Gosal iᵘˢ . . . (f. 35ᵛ) Gosal. Iudex primus. Qui prisagus uel primicerius interpretatur. Sub facis uita fiet diuturna beata . . . (f. 44) quamuis ueteranus. (f. 44ᵛ) Documentum experimenti retrogradi. Dato numero primitiuo . . . que in capite pagine est.

Ashm., ff. 56–63ᵛ (art. 7: nine leaves, two marked '56'), contain the thirty-six 12-line stanzas here on ff. 35ᵛ–44. The pages of questions and answers under thirty-six heads, ff. 34ᵛ, 35, are headed, respectively, 'abula' and 'almadati'.

5. The last two leaves of quire 6 were left blank, except for (a) f. 45, twenty words 'Lucrum Consilium . . . Captus', each with a serial number attached to it, running from i to xx. Later, s. xiii/xiv, (b) a hand was added on each page and filled with French and (f. 45) Latin explanations of the lines in palmistry, and, s. xiv, (c) a recipe, 'glist'.Recipe violariam maluam . . .', on f. 46ᵛ.

6. (a) ff. 47–48ᵛ Five pairs of roundels on each page, twenty birds on the left and sun, moon, five planets, serpent, and twelve signs of the zodiac on the right. Connecting words between each pair of roundels: i. Pauo mittit te ad solem . . . xx. Dugo te mittit ad pisces. (b) ff. 49–58ᵛ Mittam te ad amicum et dicet tibi uerum. Sol. Certe tibi dico prope est . . . a deo paratum est.

[1] Underlined in red in the manuscript.

Each page of (*b*) consists of one line spoken by the bird and twenty lines in reply spoken by one of the heavenly bodies. In Ashm., ff. 64–70ᵛ (art. 8), (*a*) is missing and the last six zodiacal signs in (*b*).

7. ff. 59–68 An erit bonum ire extra domum uel non . . . Grauida pariet filiam de qua bonum erit.

The Pronosticon Socratis Basilei (no title here): in Ashm., ff. 32–40ᵛ (art. 4, misnumbered 3 in the catalogue: ten leaves, two marked '33'), except for the twenty-four verses on f. 60ᵛ, 'Puncta saxas tibi fige decem pro limite summo . . . Hic de socraticis constant excerpta libellis'. Cf. also below, Eton College 132, art. 14.

8 (added, s. xiv). f. 68ʳᵛ Recipes in French for making colours, 'Ki vout sauer e conoytre la ma`ne're des colours Ici les pora sauer. Si tou voys fere blaunk de plumb . . .'.

9. Fragments of a copy of Compilatio prima of the Decretals, s. xiiiⁱ, used in binding.

The lower part of a bifolium folded to make four thicknesses at the beginning (ff. iv–vi: vi is double). The upper part of one of these same leaves is at the end (f. vii).

Fragments of bk. 3. The leaves at the beginning contain parts of: xi. 4, 5; xi. 8; xii. 1, 2; xiv. 1, 2; xv. 3, 4; xvi. 2, 3; xvii. 3; xviii. 1, 2; xviii. 4, 5; xx. 2, 3. The leaf at the end has xvii. 1–3 on the verso and xviii. 2–4 on the recto. Cf. A. Friedberg's edition, pp. 30–2.

ff. vi+67+ii. The modern foliation i–vi, 2–68, vii, (viii), includes the pastedown, (i), and takes account of the leaf missing from quire 1. ff. iv–vii were taken over from an older binding: see above. 168×118 mm. Written space 133×73 mm. 21–8 long lines and (ff. 67, 68) 2 cols. of 30 lines. Collation: 1⁸ wants 1 2⁸ 3⁸ (3 and 6 are half-sheets) 4⁶ wants 6, blank, after f. 29 5⁸ +1 leaf before 1 (f. 32) 6⁸ 7² (ff. 47, 48) 8–9¹⁰. Arts. 5*b*, 8 in anglicana. The full-page picture of 'Pithagoras' on f. 19 is very similar in design to that by Matthew Paris in Ashm.: it and the picture on f. 30ᵛ are on punched gold grounds. The grounds of the roundels on ff. 47–48ᵛ are alternately gold and blue and the frames alternately red and green. Initials: (i) 2-line, blue with red ornament or red with pale-blue or green-blue ornament; (ii) 1-line, blue or red. Binding for Samuel Pepys. Secundo folio *Tabula*.

Written in England. 'Thomas Harriots', f. iv, 'Thomas Harriotus', f. v, and 'Mʳ Rees Thomas esquire', f. 62ᵛ, are of s. xvi. Belonged to John Maitland, Duke of Lauderdale, †1682: his sale, 25 Jan. 1692, lot 84. Part of the library bequeathed by Samuel Pepys, †1703. Old numbers 543ᴅ and 583 crossed out on f. ii. *CMA* 6779.

CAMBRIDGE. NEWNHAM COLLEGE

1. *Biblia*   s. xiii med.

1. ff. 1–453ᵛ A Bible with the usual contents (see Bristol, Public Library, 15), save for the absence of Psalms, and in the usual order, save that 1 Thessalonians was omitted in its place: it follows Hebrews. Acts 6: 11–7: 53, omitted on f. 433ᵛ, was added on a supply leaf, f. 434, s. xiii. Proverbs begins a new quire, f. 219.

The prologues are fifty-three of the common set and sixteen others, shown here by *:
Stegmüller, nos. 284, 285, 311, 328, 327 (. . . non legant. Nota quod iste prologus in

principio libri ponendus est et legendus), 330, 332, 341+342*, 344+349*+350* (. . . ipse et non alius), 357, 457, 462, 482, 487, 491, 492, 500, 507, 511, 510, 509*, prologue to Joel, 'Fathuel propheta pater ioel prophete . . . id est locutum est uerbum ad prophetam'* ('vacat' against it), 515, 512, 513, 519+517, prologue to Obadiah, 'Abdias quanto breuior . . . mutatis quibusdam uerbis'*, 524, 521, 526, prologues to Micah, 'Sermo dei qui semper . . . sunt imposita'* and 'Mycheas secundum hebraicam ueritatem . . . continere mysteria'* ('vacat' against them), 528, prologue to Nahum, 'Cum ionas et naum . . . denuntiat'*, 531, 530* ('vacat' against it), 534, prologue to Zephaniah, 'In tytulo generacio prophete . . . erant ab assyriis'* ('vacat' against it), 538, prologues to Haggai, 'Cum cyrus rex . . . prohibentibus'* and 'Darius interpretatur generaciones . . . ad unitatem dei'* ('vacat' against the latter), 540* ('vacat' against it), 539 (. . . per noctem profectus est), 543, 590, 589, 607, 620 (after Luke 1: 1–4), 624, 674 and usual prologues to Pauline Epistles (none, however, to 1 Thessalonians; 765, 1 Timothy, . . . de Laodicia), 809, 651*, 670*, 834*. ff. 218ᵛ, 454ʳᵛ blank.

Arts. 2–5 were added later.

2. ff. 455–60 [A]lma. uirgo abscondita . . . Zorobabel . . . iste magister confusionis.

An unusual list of Hebrew names.

3. f. 460ᵛ List of books of this Bible and the number of chapters each book contains.

4. f. 460ᵛ Verses: (a) Sunt genes ex le nu de . . .; (b) Intrat in egiptum Genesis liber exodus exit . . .; (c) Anna solet dici tres concepisse marias . . .

(a, b). Mnemonic verses, Walther, nos. 18824, 9505. (c). Walther, no. 1060.

5. Tables: (a) f. 462ᵛ, of the five *termini* over nineteen years, with an introduction (f. 461) beginning '[P]rima terminorum tabula dicitur quoniam in ista termini mobilium festorum per ordinem inueniuntur'; (b) f. 463, of a great cycle, 1044–1575, headed 'Tabula principalis gerlandi', with an introduction (f. 461ʳᵛ) beginning '[S]ecunda tabula principalis Gerlandi dicitur'; (c) f. 463ᵛ Tabula secunda Gerlandi et est contratabula.

(b, c). Cf. B.L., Royal 12 C. xvii, art. 2. f. 462ʳ blank.

ff. i+463+ii. 190×127 mm. Written space c. 125×75 mm. 2 cols. 51–8 lines. Collation doubtful: mainly twelves (18¹⁴, ff. 205–18). Initials: (i) of books, red and blue with ornament of both colours and often a yellow-brown filling; (ii, iii) of prologues, 3-line, and of chapters, 2-line, blue or red with ornament of the other colour; (iv) in art. 2, 1-line, red. Binding of s. xix: marks from the binding in use before arts. 2–5 were added show on f. 454. Secundo folio *rio absconditus*.

Written in France. The ex-libris of the Franciscan convent at Caen, s. xiv, and records of two sales are on f. 460: (a) Ista biblia est de conuentu [. . . .] cadomensi 'et est de librario' [. . . . .] deo gracias; (b) Ista biblia est fratri tho[. . . . .] Monachi [. .]g[. .] 'et emit eam a gardiano fratrum minorum cadomensium anno m° ccc50 (?) die lune ante conuercionem sancti pauli Et constitit in toto x scuta auri'; (c) Istam bibliam emit dompnus vducus chabordat capellanus a nycodo girard mercat' de paterniaco precio xx scutorum seu xxiii l' et xii solid' bone monetis Inclusis vi solidis pro vino in expensis datis viiᵃ die mensis octob' anno domini m° cccclv°. The dates 1382 and 1386 are in a damaged note at the head of f. 461ᵛ. In an English sale catalogue, s. xxˡ: the relevant slip is attached to f. iᵛ. Book-plate of Harold Edgar Young: his gift in 1931.

2. *Horae*

1. ff. 1–12 Calendar in red and black on versos facing tables on rectos.

The calendar for January is missing. Feasts in red include Erkenwald, 30 Apr., Edward king and martyr, 18 Mar., 20 June, and Edward confessor, 13 Oct. 'pape' is erased and the feasts of St. Thomas at 7 July and 29 Dec. are half erased. A column is provided for the day of the month and another for the length of each day in hours and minutes.

The tables are of conjunction and opposition of sun and moon. The four headings on each page are 'Ciclus coniunccionis tercius', 'Ciclus opposicionis tercius', 'Ciclus coniunccionis quartus', 'Ciclus opposicionis quartus'. f. 12ᵛ blank.

2. ff. 14–63ᵛ Hours of B.V.M. of the use of (Sarum).

Memoriae in lauds of Holy Spirit, Holy Trinity, Holy Cross, SS. Michael, John Baptist, Peter and Paul, John Evangelist, Andrew, Stephen, Laurence, Thomas of Canterbury (Tu per thome sanguinem . . .), lightly erased, George (Petit cristum carceratus . . .), Christopher (Martir cristofore pro saluatoris honore . . .: *RH*, no. 29471), Fabian and Sebastian, Nicholas, Anne (Hec est radix anna pia . . .), Katherine, Margaret, Mary Magdalene, Barbara (Gaude barbara regina summa pollens . . .: *RH*, no. 6714), Etheldreda, De reliquiis, All Saints, of peace. Hours of the Cross worked in.

3. ff. 63ᵛ–65ᵛ An'. Salue regina . . . V'. Virgo mater ecclesie . . . (five stanzas). Or'. Omnipotens sempiterne deus qui gloriosissime virginis et matris marie corpus et animam . . .

RH, nos. 18147 and 21818.

4. f. 65ᵛ Ant'. Aue regina celorum . . .

5. ff. 65ᵛ–67 Pro fidelibus defunctis. De profundis . . .

6. ff. 67–78 vii psalmi.

7. ff. 78–81 xv psalmi.

Cues only of the first twelve psalms.

8. ff. 81–91 Litany.

Thomas of Canterbury, second of martyrs, is lightly erased.

9. ff. 91–2 Gaude uirgo mater cristi que per aurem concepisti . . . Or'. Deus qui beatissimam uirginem mariam in conceptu . . .

RH, no. 7017. ff. 92ᵛ–93ᵛ left blank.

10. ff. 95–125ᵛ Vigilie mortuorum.

Manuale Sarum, pp. 132–141/18.

11. ff. 126–43ᵛ Incipiunt commendaciones animarum. Beati inmaculati . . .

The final prayer, 'Tibi domine commendamus . . .', is longer than in *Manuale Sarum*, p. 144.

ff. iii + 143 + iii. 90 × 60 mm. Written space 55 × 35 mm. 17 long lines. Collation: ff. 13–141 are sixteen eights, with one leaf, a blank (?), missing after f. 125, and two inserted singletons, ff. 13 and 94. Two full-page pictures, f. 13ᵛ, the dead Christ on the lap of the Virgin, and f. 94, the vision of St. Gregory, with borders: rectos blank. Initials: (i) in colours on decorated gold grounds, with continuous borders in gold and colours, including green; (ii) 2-line, gold on coloured grounds patterned in white; (iii) 1-line, gold with violet ornament or blue with red ornament. Line fillers in gold and blue in art. 8. Binding of s. xx. Secundo folio (f. 15) *fundauerunt*.

Written in England. Belonged probably to William Copwood or to 'Ane brokett his wiffe', the birth of whose daughter Margaret 'wiche whas ye first day of October in the xxix yere of ye Rayng of King Henry the viii^th' is recorded on f. 92^v: both Copwood and Brockett are Hertfordshire family names. Book-plate of M. A. Elton. Given by Miss J. P. Strachey, principal 1923–41.

3. *Missale*   s. xv med.

A carefully corrected Sarum missal.[1] The corrections were first written in the margin in pencil and then incorporated into the text in the ugly black hand which added art. 15. Music occurs only in the offices for the vigil of Christmas, Epiphany, Easter Eve, and the Purification of B.V.M. and in the prefaces, art. 3.

1. ff. 1–6^v Calendar in red and black.

'pape' and feasts of St. Thomas of Canterbury erased lightly. The grading 'duplex' marks principal feasts including, of English saints, those of Thomas, the translation and deposition of Osmund, 16 July, 3 Dec., and the translation of Edward, king and confessor, 13 Oct.

2. ff. 9–14^v, 17–98^v Temporale to Easter Eve, beginning at the first Sunday of Advent.

In the first quire the first and last leaves are missing.

3. ff. 98^v–109^v Gloria, Credo, prefaces, ordinary, and canon of mass.

4. ff. 109^v–154 Temporale from Easter to Sabbato quatuor temporum.

5. ff. 154–6 In dedicacione ecclesie.

6. ff. 156^v–169 Common of saints.

7. ff. 169–171^v Mass of B.V.M.

8. ff. 171^v–174 Masses of the Trinity, Holy Spirit, Cross, Angels, and 'Pro fratribus et sororibus'.

9. ff. 174–178^v Collect, secret, and postcommunion: (1) De omnibus sanctis; (2) Pro penitentibus; (3) Pro uniuersali ecclesia; (4) Pro pace; (5) Pro rege; (6) Pro rege et regina; (7) In commemoracione de sancto spiritu; (8) Pro semetipso sacerdote; (9) Pro postulandum donum sancti spiritus; (10) Pro penitentibus; (11) Pro inspiracione diuine sapiencie; (12) Pro tribulacione cordis; (13) Pro quacumque tribulacione; (14) Pro infirmo; (15) Pro salute amici; (16) Item alia oracio pro amico; (17) Item alia oracio pro proximo; (18) Pro serenitate; (19) Ad pluuiam postulandam; (20) Pro tempore belli; (21) Pro eo qui in vinculis detinetur; (22) Pro contra (*sic*) mortalem (*sic*) hominum; (23) Pro iter agentibus; (24) Pro [papa]; (25) Pro episcopo; (26) Item alia pro episcopo; (27) Pro prelatis et subditis; (28) Contra temptacionis (*sic*) carnis; (29) Contra malas cogitaciones; (30) Pro peticione lacrimarum; (31) Contra aeres potestates; (32) Contra inuasores ecclesie; (33) Pro nauigantibus; (34) Pro benefactoribus; (35) Contra

[1] But the corrector did not bother with headings: cf. art. 9.

aduersantes; (36) Missa de incarnacione domini nostri ihesu cristi; (37) Ad memoriam de sanctis Katerina margareta et maria magdalena.

Sarum Missal has all but nos. 17, 36, 37 on pp. 394–412, but in the order 1, 24, 3, 4, 25, 27, 26, 5, 6, 10, 15, 16, 28, 29, 7, 30, 2, 13, 19, 18, 22, 23, 10, 31, 11, 9, 21, 32, 12, 33, 14, 34, 35, 20. No. 17 is in *S.M.*, p. 410, note 8. Nos. 36, 37 occur commonly in early printed Sarum missals.

10. ff. 178ᵛ–180 Missa in die sponsalis de sancta trinitate. Benedicta sit sancta trinitas . . .

Manuale Sarum, p. 50. The reference to second marriages (cf. ibid., pp. 54, 55) is here on f. 179ᵛ: Caueat sacerdos de ista clausula Deus qui tam excellenti ne dicitur eam in secundis nupciis usque Deus per quem ut patet inferius post finem istius.

11. ff. 180–184ᵛ Ad missam pro defunctis. Requiem eternam . . .

12. ff. 184ᵛ–185ᵛ Oracio generalis.

Four forms, as in *Sarum Missal*, p. 460. Most of the second form is *secunda manu* over faded (?) writing.

13. ff. 185ᵛ–186 Pro trentale.

Sarum Missal, p. 460, but the collect here is Deus summa spes nostre redempcionis.

14. ff. 186ᵛ–235 Sanctorale. ff. 235ᵛ–237ᵛ left blank.

15 (added). f. 235ᵛ Office of St Winefred.

ff. iii+233+i, together with four inserted blanks, ff. 7, 8, 15, 16. *c.* 328 × 228 mm. Written space 228 × 145 mm. 2 cols. 36 lines (33 lines on ff. 100–109ʳ). Collation of ff. 1–6, 9–14, 17–237: 1⁶ 2⁸ wants 1 and 8 (ff. 9–14) 3–11⁸ 12⁶+1 leaf before 1 (ff. 89–95) 13–29⁸ 30⁶ (ff. 232–7). Signatures mostly cut off. A full-page crucifixion picture, f. 104ᵛ. Initials: (i) in colours on gold grounds handsomely decorated in colours and with prolongations forming continuous and sometimes framed borders; (ii) in art. 3, 3-line or 2-line, gold on coloured grounds patterned in white, with sprays into the margin; (iii) 2-line, blue with red ornament; (iv) in art. 3, 1-line, gold with violet ornament or blue with red ornament; (v) 1-line, blue or red. Brown morocco binding by Riviere for 'Harold E. Young, Sandgate, Blundellsands': in 1929 it was 'old calf'. Secundo folio *aque* (f. 9).

Written in England. From the collection of W. V. Campbell-Wyndham-Long, Corhampton House, Bishop's Waltham, Hants, sold at Sotheby's, 3 June 1929, lot 492, to H. E. Young (£62): his gift, as MS. 1.

4. *Piers Plowman, etc.*   s. xv med.

1. ff. 1–104 In a somer seson . . . till I gan awake. Explicit hic dialagus Petri Plowman.

B text. Listed as no. xvi and collated as Y by W. W. Skeat, *Piers the Plowman*, 1886.

2. ff. 104ᵛ–109ᵛ Man or woman þat wol ler' A masse deuouly for to her' . . . of whom we spek of when we say our' crede.

IMEV, no. 3507. Printed as F by T. F. Simmons, *The Lay Folk's Mass Book*, EETS lxxi (1879), 3–60: cf. pp. lxx, lxxi.

3. f. 109ᵛ *gracias*. God that his brede brake at his mawde whanne he sate⸴

Amongis his postyllis twelue He bles our' brede and our' ayl.' þat we haw and haw schal.' and be with vs him selwe. In nomine patris et filii et spiritus sancti Amen. *IMEV*, no. 620. Printed by Simmons, op. cit., p. 60.

ff. ii+109+ii. 295×185 mm. Written space 210 mm high. 40 long lines. The scribe left a blank line after each paragraph, for example on f. 1^{rv} (Passus I) after lines 10, 22, 24, 30, 45, 52, 57, 67. Collation: 1–13^8 14 five (ff. 105–9: 107–8 are a bifolium). Signatures cut off after 'l', f. 81. Quires 10 and 12 numbered after the catchwords 'x quaternus' and 'xii'. Written in anglicana, arts. 2, 3 in a different hand from art. 1. Initials: (i) f. 1, blue patterned in white on decorated gold ground, with prolongations forming a continuous border; (ii) ff. 35, 68^v, 98^v, beginning the Dowel, Dobet, and Dobest passus (8, 15 and 20), 4-line, gold with violet ornament; (iii) 4-line or 3-line, blue with red ornament. Binding of s. xix. Secundo folio *Lewed men*.

On the four main pages (see above) the lower margin contains an eagle with a red *L* on its breast, standing, wings out, on grass, s. xv. 'Inherited from Jos. B. Yates 1856' on a label inside the cover. 'H. Yates Thompson, Thingwall, Liverpool, 1856', f. i. 'Presented to the Newnham College Library by H. Y. Thompson May 16th 1906' inside the cover.

5. *Christine de Pisan, Othea (in French)*   s. xv med.

Ci commence lespitre que Othea la deesse enuoia a Hector de Troye quant il estoit en laage de xv ans. Othea deesse de prudence . . . Qui destre aoure le reprist.

One of forty-three manuscripts listed by G. Mombello in *Studi francesi*, lxxiv (1964), 403. No dedication. 'Texte' in a central column, 530 lines of verse, flanked by prose 'Glose' on the left and prose 'Alegorie' on the right. From line 151, 'Avec des inclinacions . . .', the arrangement is four lines to a page below a picture (ff. 4^v–51^v). This copy is described and the hundred pictures listed by H. Y. Thompson, *Descriptive Catalogue of Twenty Illuminated Manuscripts*, nos. lxxv–xciv, 1907, pp. 33–8 (no. lxxix), and in *Illustrations from One Hundred Manuscripts in the Library of Henry Yates Thompson*, 1918, pp. 16–18 and pls. lxi, lxii.[1] f. 52^{rv} blank.

ff. ii+52+ii. 295×220 mm. Written space 170 mm wide and at most (ff. 1–4) 200 mm high. Collation: 1–6^8 7^4. Written in two sizes of cursiva, the larger broken and not current. Except on ff. 1^v, 3^r, there is a picture on each page in a frame measuring *c.* 70× 65 mm. Initials: 3-line (f. 1) and 2-line, gold on blue and red grounds, patterned in white. Binding of gilt red morocco, s. xviii. Secundo folio *louenge*.

Written in France. '41' and a paragraph at the foot of f. 1, s. xviii (?). Two labels inside the cover: (i) printed 'Ex Musæo Henrici Yates Thompson', to which is added in manuscript 'lxxix' and 'M.G.e.e. Ed. Rahir 13 March 1904'; (ii) 'Given to Newnham College Library in memory of Henry Yates Thompson 1838–1928'.

6. *Horae*   s. xvi in.

1. ff. 1–6^v Calendar in French in gold, blue and red, the two colours alternating for effect.

In October (9, 18, 23) Denis, Ivo, and Romanus are in gold.

[1] For the hundred pictures in Harley 4431 and Bodley 421 see Saxl and Meier, iii. 176–85, 296–309.

2. ff. 7–11ᵛ Sequentiae of the gospels, and, after John, the prayers 'Protector in te sperantium . . .' and 'Ecclesiam tuam . . .'.

3. ff. 11ᵛ–13ᵛ Oratio deuotissima ad beatissimam virginem mariam. Obsecro te . . .

4. (a) ff. 13ᵛ–15ᵛ Alia oratio deuota ad beatam mariam: et sanctum iohannem euangelistam. O intemerata . . . orbis terrarum. Inclina . . . (b) ff. 15ᵛ–16 O beatissime domine iesu christe respicere digneris supe(r) miserum peccatorem . . .

5. ff. 16ᵛ–52 Hore Intemerate virginis marie. Ad Vsum Rothom'.

f. 16ᵛ is blank, except for the title. Hours of Cross and Holy Spirit are worked in.

6. ff. 52ᵛ–65 Penitential psalms and litany.

Martial is last among apostles: then 'Sancte Ursine or'. Omnes sancti discipuli domini orate'. Fourteen confessors: . . . (6, 7) mellone.romane . . . Ten virgins: . . . (6) austreberta. . .

7. ff. 65ᵛ–88ᵛ Secuntur vigilie mortuorum.

f. 65ᵛ is blank, except for the title.

8. (a) ff. 88ᵛ–89ᵛ Deuota contemplatio beate marie virginis iuxta crucem filii sui lachrymantis. [Stabat mater], beginning imperfectly in stanza 5 'Fac ut ardeat cor meum': the prayer 'Interueniat pro nobis quesumus domine . . .' follows. (b) ff. 89ᵛ–90ᵛ Alia salutatio ad beatam virginem mariam. Aue cuius conceptio . . .: the prayer 'Deus qui nos conceptionis . . .' follows. (c) ff. 90ᵛ–91 Alia oratio de beata maria. Aue domina sancta maria mater dei regina celi . . . (d) f. 91 Alia oratio deuota. Salue regina misericordie vita dulcedo et spes nostra salue . . . (e) ff. 91–2 Deuota oratio de beata maria. Inuiolata integra et casta es maria . . .: the prayer 'Omnipotens sempiterne deus qui gloriose virginis . . .' follows.

(a, b, d, e). RH, nos. 19416, 1744, 18150, 9094.

9. ff. 92–94ᵛ Memoriae of SS. Michael, John Baptist, John Evangelist, Peter, Nicholas, Anne, Katherine.

The scribe wrote 'Laus deo' at the end.

ff. ii+93+ii, foliated i, ii, 1–77, 79–96. 187 × 117 mm. Written space 115 × 62 mm. 21 long lines. Ruling with red ink. Collation: 1⁶ 2⁸ 3² (ff. 15, 16) 4–11⁸ 12⁸ wants 8 after f. 88 13⁶. Written in hybrida: 2-compartment g. Thirteen pictures, c. 125 × 90 mm within the frame, each containing three lines of the text of the manuscript on a scroll at the foot: ten pictures in art. 5 and one before each of arts. 2 (St. John, with eagle carrying a roll-container in his beak), 6, 7 (Christ in judgement seated on the orb). Smaller pictures of the occupations of the months and signs of the zodiac in the borders flanking the text of art. 1. Decorated initials in shaded grey on grounds of gold paint, 3-line, 2-line, and 1-line. The thirteen picture pages have framed borders in the lower margin in which are circling branches closing to a jewel-like centre which sometimes holds a 'cameo' head. All other pages have in the outer margin a framed floral border on gold-paint ground the height of the written space. Capital letters in the ink of the text filled with yellow. The line fillers are red or blue flowers on grounds of gold paint. Binding like MS. 3. Secundo folio (f. 8) et sui.

Written in France for use in the diocese of Rouen. A strip from an English sale catalogue, s. xx, and the book-plate of Harold Edgar Young inside the cover. Given as MS. 1.

7. *Preces, etc.*

s. xv med.

1. ff. 1–13 Incipit oratio Sancti Ambrosii episcopi. Summe sacerdos et uere pontifex . . .

A text of the B type, but continuing after 'in eternum' (f. 11ᵛ/10: ed. A. Wilmart, *Auteurs spirituels*, p. 124, line 148) with a prayer for the aid and intercession of B.V.M., apostles, martyrs, confessors, angels, and virgins, 'Et ut hec efficax mea sit deprecatio beate marie semper uirginis suffragium peto . . . te miserante et donante. Qui . . .'.

2. ff. 13–15ᵛ Oratio sancti thome de aquino. Concede michi misericors deus. que tibi placita sunt . . . in patria perfrui per gloriam qui . . .

Printed often. Ed. A. I. Doyle, 'A prayer attributed to St. Thomas Aquinas', *Dominican Studies*, i (1948), 229–38.

3. ff. 16–41 Quando pontifex preparat se ad missam. quis ordo et per quos seruari debeat. qui uersiculi. que antifone. qui psalmi et orationes et hore dicantur. Rubrica. Quando preparat se ad missam pontifex. dicit terciam . . .

Directions, psalms, prayers, etc., for the use of a celebrating bishop, before, during, and after communion, beginning with Pss. 83, 84, 85, 115, 129 and seven prayers (cf. Andrieu, *Pont. Rom.* iii. 143), after which, ff. 24ᵛ–25ᵛ, is a long vesting rubric, 'Dum autem premissas dixerit oraciones induat se uestibus que sequuntur . . .' and a series of prayers at vesting and devesting, ending with 'Actiones nostras . . .'.

4. ff. 41–48ᵛ Finita missa sacerdos sine casula cum ministris. Subdiaconus cum cruce. et omnes alii . . . stent in circuitu feretri in modum rote . . . Oratio. Non intres in iudicium cum seruo tuo . . . Postea cantor incipiat Responsorium Subuenite . . .

Office of burial, ending with the prayer 'In ea potestate uel auctoritate fidentes . . .'.

5. ff. 48ᵛ–52 Blessing and four prayers: (*a*) Benedictio super sponsum et sponsam. 'et' eorum subarratio. Bene+dic domine has arras quas hodie . . .; (*b*) Alia oratio. Exaudi nos omnipotens et misericors deus ut quod nostro ministratur officio . . .; (*c*) Alia oratio. Quesumus omnipotens deus institutor prouidentie tue . . .; (*d*) Alia oratio. Propitiare domine supplicationibus nostris et institutis tuis . . .; (*e*) Alia oratio. Deus qui potestate uirtutis tue de nichilo . . .

Cf. Andrieu, *Pont. Rom.* i. 260–2, sect. 3, 14, 11, 12.

6. (*a*) ff. 52–3 De benedictione agni et aliarum carnium in pascate. fit hoc modo. V'. Adiutorium . . . Deus uniuerse carnis . . . (*b*) ff. 53–4 De benedictione casei.lactis ouorum et mellis. V'. Adiutorium . . . Bene+dic domine has creaturas . . . Et aspergantur aqua benedicta.

(*a, b*). Cf. Durand's pontifical (ed. Andrieu, *Pont. Rom.* iii), II. 25, 26. f. 54ᵛ blank.

ff. ii+54+ii. 281 × 192 mm. Written space 165 × 115 mm. 13 long lines (25 lines in the rubric on f. 25). Double vertical bounders. No horizontal lines project beyond the written space. Collation: 1–5¹⁰ 6 four (ff. 51–4). A handsome black hand, the minims 'sine pedibus'. Initials: (i–iii) 4-line (ff. 1, 16ᵛ), 3-line (f. 13ᵛ) and 2-line, in colours, including green, on decorated grounds of blue, patterned in white, buff—as an internal frame—and gold, with short projections into the margins, except on f. 1; (iii) 1-line, blue or red. The continuous border on f. 1 has landscape in the lower edge in which angels support an armorial shield. Capital letters in the ink of the text are filled with yellow. Binding of red velvet over wooden boards, s. xix. Secundo folio *dotale*.

Written in Italy. Arms in the border, f. 1: bendy of six sable and argent over all a lion rampant gules: a mitre above the shield. Belonged to the congregation and monastery of St. Justina, Padua: 'Iste liber est Monasterii congregationis Sancte Iustine de padua. monasterio Sancte Iustine deputatus signatusque numero 5[. .]',[1] f. 1, at foot, s. xv/xvi. 'This volume formerly in the Library of . . . Joseph Brooks Yates Esqre of West Dingle Liverpool was presented to the Library of Newnham College Cambridge in the year 1902 by Henry Yates Thompson, his grandson . . . H. Y. T.', f. i.

8. *Horae*   s. xv^2

A complete, but seriously disarranged book of hours.

1. ff. 1–12^v Full calendar in gold, blue, and red, the two colours alternating for effect.

Feasts in gold include Fabian and Sebastian (20 Jan.), George (23 Apr.), 'Gaciani archiepiscopi' (2 May), Urban (25 May), 'Ludouici francorum regis' (25 Aug.), 'Lydorii archiepiscopi' (13 Sept.), 'Francisci confessoris' (4 Oct.), 'Martini archiepiscopi' (11 Nov.), 'Gaciani archiepiscopi' (18 Dec.).

2. ff. 21–28^v Sequentiae of the Gospels.

A prayer after each Gospel, (John) 'Protector in te sperantium . . .', (Luke) 'Deus qui de beate marie . . .', (Matthew) 'Deus qui unigenitum tuum . . .', (Mark) 'Concede quesumus omnipotens deus . . .'.

3. ff. 28^v–33 Oratio deuotissima ad beatam uirginem mariam. Obsecro te . . . Masculine forms.

4. ff. 33^v–34^v Memoria de quinque festiuitatibus beate marie virginis. Aue cuius concepcio . . . *RH*, no. 1744.

5. ff. 34^v–46^v Passio domini nostri ihesu cristi secundum iohannem. In illo tempore. Egressus est ihesus . . . posuerunt ihesum . . . Respice quesumus domine super hanc familiam tuam . . .

6. Recto and verso of ff. 13–20, 47–81, 83, 82, 84–6, 123–5, 121, 130, 126–9, 134, 135, 131, 136, 132, 133, 122, 87, 137–42, 96 Hours of B.V.M. of the use of (Tours). Hours of the Cross and of the Holy Spirit are worked in.

7. ff. 97–120^v, 94^{rv} Penitential psalms and (f. 110) litany.

Twenty-seven confessors: (1–3) Silvester Gaciane Lydori . . . Twenty-eight virgins: . . . (28) Castitas.

8. Recto and verso of ff. 94, 95, 93, 92, 91, 90, 88, 89, 144–51, 143, 161–6, 152–60, 171–4, 167–70, 175–85 Office of the dead.

A feminine form, f. 144. f. 186^{rv} blank.

9. ff. 187–194^v Memoriae of Holy Trinity, Michael, John Baptist, Sebastian, Maurice, Gatian, Martin, Mary Magdalene, Katherine, Barbara (O pulchra precipuum . . .: *RH*, no. 30857), Apollonia (Virgo martir egregia pro nobis appolonia . . .), Martha, All Saints.

---

[1] Possibly 562, which appears to be the number on a later roundel pasted to the inner lower corner of f. 1.

10. (*a*) ff. 194ᵛ–195 De beata maria Antiphona. Salue regina. . . . (*b*) ff. 195–6 Alia antiphona De beata maria. Alma redemptoris mater que preuia celi porta . . . (*c*) f. 196ʳᵛ De beata maria in tempore paschali a'. Regina celi letare . . . (*a–c*). *RH*, nos. 18147, 861, 17170.

11 (additions, s. xv/xvi). (*a*) ff. 196ᵛ–198 Seven Oes of St. Gregory. (*b*) f. 198ʳᵛ Auete omnes anime fideles . . . (*c*) ff. 198ᵛ–199 Domine iesu christe salus et liberator . . . (*d*)f. 199ʳᵛ O domine iesu christe adoro te ad iudicium uenientem . . .

ff. ii+199+ii. 153 × 117 mm. Written space 95 × 55 mm. 17 long lines. Ruling with red ink. Collation: 1–2⁶ 3–5⁸ (ff. 21–44) 6 two (ff. 45, 46) 7–24⁸ (ff. 13–20, 47–182) 25⁴ 26¹⁰ 27 three (ff. 197–9): for the dislocations in quires 12 (ff. 79–86), 13 (ff. 121, 123–8, 130), 14 (ff. 122, 129, 131–6), 15 (ff. 87, 96, 137–42), 19 (ff. 88–95), 21 (ff. 143, 152, 161–6), 23 (ff. 167–74) see above. Catchwords in cursiva. Seven 13-line pictures: three in art. 6 (ff. 13, 63, Crucifixion, 65, Pentecost) and one before each of arts. 3 (Pietà), 5 (Gethsemane), 7 (Bathsheba, clothed, bathes her feet; David stands by the fountain, gesticulating), 8 (Job and his comforters). A 12-line picture before art. 11. Initials in arts. 2–10: (i, ii) 3-line and 2-line, in colour on decorated gold grounds; (iii) 1-line, gold on red and blue grounds patterned in white. Capital letters in the ink of the text filled with yellow. Full framed floral borders on picture pages, the grounds all or partly of gold paint. Binding of red velvet, s. xix, perhaps over older wooden boards. Secundo folio (f. 22) *Qui non*.

Written in France, for use in the diocese of Tours. A strip from the relevant English sale catalogue, s. xix/xx, inside the cover. Book-plate of H. E. Young. Given as MS. 1.

CAMBRIDGE. PEMBROKE COLLEGE

309. *W. Lyndwood, Provinciale*　　　　　　s. xv ex.

1. ff. 2–373 Reuerendissimo in cristo . . . gaudere et quiescere mereamur. AMEN.

The Provinciale, with commentary in a smaller size of script. For the manuscripts, apart from this one, see C. R. Cheney in *The Jurist*, xxi (1961), 433–4. Bk. 2, f. 94; 3, f. 136; 4, f. 301ᵛ; 5, f. 307ᵛ. The beginnings of books are not shown, except at f. 307ᵛ, 'Hic incipit liber terciu(s) (*altered later to* Quintus)'.

2. ff. 373–94 A Hec monasillaba . . .

An index to art. 1, ending abruptly in Redditus. ff. 394ᵛ–397ᵛ blank.

ff. i+396+v, foliated 1–402. 440 × 305 mm. Written space *c.* 285 × 185 mm. 2 cols. of 46–59 lines. Frame ruling from f. 49. Collation: 1–33⁸ 34–44¹²: 'xxxxiiij quaterni', f. 1ᵛ. Three hands changing at f. 42 col. 1/40 and at f. 268 col. 1/5. All write the 'straight-ascenders' variant of the secretary hand, but the second scribe, who was unskilful, only gradually learned to write the larger size of secretary which distinguishes text and lemmata from commentary: up to f. 188ᵛ he was often helped by more competent writers and many of the spaces for lemmata remain blank.[1] Spaces for initials remain blank, 7-line (f. 2), 4-line (from f. 268), and 3-line. Contemporary binding by the 'greyhound binder', wooden

---

[1] Text and lemmata are in poor textura by scribe 2 on ff. 43–5. After this they are in secretary, but not, I think, by scribe 2 until f. 83ᵛ.

boards covered with brown leather bearing Oldham's stamps 138 and 142 (cf. *EBSB*, p. 21, G. D. Hobson, *Bindings in Cambridge Libraries*, p. 49 and pl. xv, G. D. Hobson, *English Bindings before 1500*, p. 24 and pl. 53): six bands: two clasps. Secundo folio *circa legem*.

'Thys Booke gyven by Elizabeth Colles xii^{mo} die Sep(t)embris Anno xxix^{no} R' H viii to fader Bartholomewe Burgoyn' monke of the Charterhouse in london', f. 402^{v}. Savile sale, 6 Feb. 1860, lot 48, to Sir Thomas Phillipps (£25). Phillipps 25257: sale 17 June 1908, lot 499, to Leighton (£44. 5s.). 'Ex dono H. W. Underdown Aug. 8° 1908', inside cover.

313. *Covers and end-leaves from manuscripts*

Many manuscripts were still in their medieval bindings until shortly before James catalogued them in 1905. On rebinding, the leather covers or such part of them as remained, were preserved. These pieces of leather, together with one wooden board and some end-leaves, either pieces of plain parchment or pieces taken from medieval manuscripts, have been assembled as MS. 313. On many of them E. H. Minns wrote notes to show where they came from. Identification marks are in the form 313/5: the number after the stroke is that of the Pembroke manuscript to which the piece belongs.

Pieces from the following manuscripts are in MS. 313: 5*, 7*(?), 9 (red leather), 10, 17, 20*, 23 (or 24), 24*, 25*, 26, 29, 30**, 33, 34**, 39*, 40*, 54, 62*, 63**, 65, 66, 68, 75, 77, 80, 82*, 83, 84, 88, 91, 94, 95, 96, 99, 108, 122, 124, 127*, 130, 134*(?), 139, 140*, 142, 149(?), 156**, 158, 161**, 164*, 170, 174, 176, 179**, 189, 192, 194*, 195, 212, 238**, 239 (pink leather), 256, 276, 286, 291, 300*.[1]

Complete leather covers. MSS. 10, 17, 34 (two thicknesses, the upper forming a chemise), 54, 75, 80, 94, 96, 108, 239, 276, 286. MSS. 10, 17, 54, 95, were 'half leather bindings', that is to say the wooden boards were covered by a piece of leather which extended over the spine and part of each board only, as still on MSS. 47, 69, 70. For MS. 10 the leather was obtained by taking the 'whole leather' binding of a smaller manuscript (cf. below, *Titles and pressmarks*) and turning it sideways: cf. Bodleian, Laud misc. 233, from Bury, where the 'half leather' was obtained by cutting it from what seems to have been the cover of Bodleian, e Mus. 31.

Titles and pressmarks.[2] MS. 10: 'B 30 BIBL. VERSIFIC' ' on what was the spine of the manuscript from which the leather for MS. 10 was obtained: see above. MS. 17: 'Iheronimus super Isaiam prophetam ab viii usque ad xl[. . .] I 6', s. xiii/xiv, on the spine. MS. 30: 'Robertus Krichelandensis' on the pastedown. MS. 34: 'IIII senten' tho cum al'. T 7' on the leather under the chemise, running from the back cover to the front cover. MS. 77: '[B] 204' on the front cover, sideways. MS. 80: 'B 225' on the front cover, sideways, and title on the spine. MS. 88: 'Eglo[. . . . .]' on the spine. MS. 91: 'I 3' on the back cover, sideways. MS. 94: 'O 2' and 'Origenes[. . .]' on the spine. MS. 176: '[Gregor]ii moralia' on the spine. MS. 239: 'Gawyn' and 'Distincciones' on the back cover.

[1] One asterisk shows that the pieces are end-leaves, not covers. Two asterisks show that they are both covers and end-leaves.

[2] I note medieval marks only. Many covers have on them the later Pembroke College mark consisting of a capital letter and number. These marks are recorded in the eighteenth-century catalogue attributed to Clement Chevallier. James does not note them.

A *label* was formerly on the back cover of MSS. 122, 170, 239.

Marks of *chaining*. MS. 30: head and foot of front cover. MS. 75: head of front cover. MS. 80: foot of front cover. MSS. 82, 122, 174, 179, 212: staplemark on back cover. MS. 170: staplemark on front cover.

Marks of *bosses* at the corners. MSS. 88, 130, 174.

Number of *bands*. Nine on MS. 33. Eight on MS. 192. Seven on MS. 194. Six on MS. 122. Three on MSS. 83, 94.

A *wooden board*, square cut at the edges, was the front board of MS. 83. On the inside of it there is offset from the Anglo-Saxon text on the flyleaf: cf. James, *Catalogue*, p. 73.

Fragments of *manuscript* used as end-leaves. Probably from MS. 7, from Bury St. Edmunds: four leaves from the end of a handsome Italian copy of Codex Justiniani, s. xii, with a late medieval foliation 189–[192], described by James, *Catalogue*, p. xl, (*a*).[1] Other leaves of the same manuscript were used in binding Corpus Christi College, Cambridge, 149, and Gonville and Caius College, Cambridge, 285.[2] From MS. 20, from Bury: from the front, two leaves, a central bifolium, of a pontifical in a handsome English hand, s. xi/xii, with text corresponding closely to that in *Pontifical of Magdalen College* (HBS xxxix, 1910), pp. 154/1–156/19: written space 217×115 mm: 28 long lines; from the back, a bifolium of canon law, s. xiii/xiv. From MSS. 24, 62, 63, all from Bury: leaves, fourteen in all, of Digestum novum, s. xiii: 2 cols. 51 lines. From MS. 25, from Bury: sixteen leaves, eight from Bury accounts, s. xiv[1], and eight from a manuscript of s. xiii, described by James, *Catalogue*, pp. xxxix–xl, nos. I, II. From MS. 30, from Bury: a bifolium, blank except for one page which contains a list, s. xiv in., of the signs written in the margins of the text of MS. 30 (Robert of Cricklade, Homilies on Ezechiel) and their meaning, homily by homily, for example 'Omelia xxxi Nota ibi de temptacione cristi ⊹ Item de . . .'.[3] From MS. 82, from Tynemouth: four leaves (two bifolia) three from a lawbook in an Italian hand, s. xiii, and one blank, except for a poem in English, s. xv in., beginning '[A]s I welk thorow a garthyn grene': five eight-line stanzas, rhyming ababbcbc, the last line of each stanza being 'Verbum caro factum est'.[4] From MS. 127; three leaves from the first and second books of Digestum novum, s. xiii: written space *c.* 170×110 mm.: 2 cols. 39 lines.[5] From MS. 238: three leaves of 'notulae' (or the like) on the Bible in an English hand, s. xiii/xiv.

[1] The pieces described by James, *Catalogue*, p. xl, (*b–e*), are from the bindings of printed books and are now kept in MS. 312C. MSS. 312A–C and 314 are a large collection of fragments taken from the bindings of printed books.

[2] Possibly 'Postilla B 231' was written in error on the Pembroke fragment in s. xix, since the last leaf has an obvious staplemark in the middle of it: Pembroke college books were chained from this position, but Bury books were not. The staplemark may, however, be evidence that this copy of Codex Justiniani was chained in a Cambridge college library before it was given over to a (Cambridge?) binder as waste. That the Bury monks had books bound in Cambridge at the end of the Middle Ages is very probable.

[3] This piece is now kept separately as MS. 30*.

[4] A transcript by E. H. Minns is kept with the original.

[5] The five bifolia at beginning and end of Vatican, Ottoboni lat. 188 (Aquinas, Secunda secundae), and the two bifolia at beginning and end of lat. 202 (Aquinas, Prima secundae) are from this same manuscript of the New Digest. MS. 127, Aquinas, Quaestiones

Pieces from unidentified manuscripts.

An end-leaf bearing the names 'Thomas Cambregge' and 'Iohannes Cranewys', s. xv. The latter is probably the Bury monk who bought Pembroke College MS. 31. 313/A.

Two fragments of accounts noticed by James, *Catalogue*, p. xl, (f). 313/B,C.

Part of a large notarial document folded to make a pastedown and flyleaf. It is thought to be from the binding of MS. 134, but this seems very doubtful. The document is part of the process of provision to a canonry and expectancy of a prebend of Wells, of Thomas Hakelut, drawn up by a notary public by apostolic authority, Stephen Trippe, in July 1330.[1] Used in binding by s. xv, when a pledge note, 'Supplementum [. . . .] cuius principale [. . . .]', was entered on the dorse. 313/D.

The upper part of a large leaf, s. xiv, with the beginning of Nicholas de Lyra's commentary on the Song of Moses (Exodus 15: 1), 'Tunc cecinit moyses. Hic consequenter ponitur . . .'. 313/E.

Eight blank pieces, two of them bits of covers. 313/F–M.

CAMBRIDGE. RIDLEY HALL

R.H. 1. *Epistolae Pauli*   s. xv med.

P[aulus seruus iesu] christi uocatus a[.]postolus . . . gratia cum omnibus uobis Amen finis.

Romans begins on f. 1/4, below two erased lines and one blank line. Colossians follows 2 Thessalonians. No chapter numbers. The text is in paragraphs which are more numerous than the modern chapters; for example there are twenty-two in 2 Corinthians. The prologues are Stegmüller, nos. 685, 699 (. . . emendatos ostendit scribit a philippis), 707 (. . . ab epheso scripta a macedonia), 715, 728, 747, 752, 736 (. . . et honesimum acolitum ab urbe roma), 765 (. . . de Nicopoli), 772 (. . . ab urbe roma scripta de liodicie), 780 (. . . scribit a nichapoli scripta de laudicia), 783. Two leaves are missing, one in 1 Corinthians and one in 2 Corinthians, also the prologue to Romans.

ff. ii+103+ii. The foliation, s. xviii (?), (i, ii), 1–31, 33–8, 40–105 takes account of the two leaves now missing. 230 × 145 mm. Written space *c.* 143 × 75 mm. 26 long lines. Ruling with a hard point, the first line of writing above the first ruled line. Collation: 1–3¹⁰ 4¹⁰ wants 2 after f. 31 and 9 after f. 38 5–6¹⁰ 7⁸ 8–10¹⁰ 11¹⁰ wants 8–10, perhaps blank. Written in good slightly backward-sloping humanistica. Initials: (i) f. 1, 6-line gold *P* on a ground of pink, blue, and green, historiated (St. Paul) and decorated with white vine interlace prolonged into a three-sided border in colours picked out with gold stars: in the lower edge winged cherubs support an empty shield; (ii) 4-line, gold on blue, pink, and green ground, the pink patterned in black, the blue in white, and the green in gold paint; (iii) 3-line, blue, for prologues; (iv) blue, 1-line in size, but placed in the margins, beginning paragraphs within books. Calf binding of s. xviii, rebacked. Secundo folio *glorificauerunt*.

Written in Italy. Probably once part of a larger manuscript: cf. f. 1. 'To Ridley Hall in memory of a long and happy connection from Arthur Bernard Cook 20 April 1947', f. ii.

Disputatae, may, therefore, have the same provenance, the Cambridge Austin Friars, as lat. 202. The convent was immediately to the north of Pembroke College, on the other side of the present Downing Street.

[1] I owe the description to Professor C. R. Cheney.

R.H. 2. *Biblia*   s. XIII med.

The Old Testament is in the usual[1] order, except that Psalms, on two independent quires, comes at the end, ff. 364–81 (quires 36, 37): as compared with a
'normal'[1] Bible, this copy lacks 3 Ezra and the prayer of Manasses. The New
Testament is in the unusual order Gospels, Acts, Catholic Epistles, Pauline
Epistles, Apocalypse.

Very defective, lacking all (fourteen leaves) before Genesis 26: 7 'iugio reputans', and
probably fifty-four leaves of text after this point. Stichometric notes after Leviticus and
2 Kings: 'Explicit... habens uersus' 2300; 'Explicit... habens uersus' 2200. Within books
there is no paragraphing, but coloured initials in the text and numbers opposite them show
where a new chapter begins. The divisions seem to be the ones now in use.

The remaining prologues are 28 of the normal set of 64[1] and 8 others shown here by *:
Stegmüller, nos. 311, 330, a prologue to Tobit, 'Tobias filius ananihel ex tribu neptalim...
lumen claritatis promeruit'*, 332, 341 + 342*, 344, 462, 482, 487, 491, 492, 500, a prologue to Joel, 'Iohel qui interpretatur... quando et micheas'*,[2] 515, 519+517, 524, 526,
528, 530*, 534 (... neque elati sunt oculi mei), 545*, 551, 607, 620, 624, 640, 809, 807*,
806*, 677, 685, 780, 783, 835*. Amos has only the one prologue, 515.

f. 381ᵛ, left blank after Psalms, contains notes in anglicana, s. xiii ex. Notes in English,
s. xvi, on Hebrew measures are in the margins of ff. 297ᵛ, 325.

f. iii+421+ii, foliated (i–iii), 15–474 (475–6). This foliation, s. xvi, takes account of all
missing leaves, except one after f. 157 and one probably blank after f. 361: it does not
include the numbers 1–14, 20, 27, 44, 72, 95, 107, 121, 168, 187, 194, 215, 223, 228, 229,
256, 316, 336, 362–3, 365–7, 370, 374, 376–7, 382, 452–63, 465; it passes over the leaf now
numbered 172*. 185×125 mm. Written space 127×75 mm. 2 cols. 48–50 lines.
Originally 47 quires, all but probably 6 of them quires of ten leaves: the first quire, a ten,
and the forty-sixth, a twelve, are now missing and many quires lack one or more leaves.
Quires are numbered at the end up to XVII (f. 169ᵛ). Initials: (i) blue and bright red or
blue only, patterned in white, on grounds of purple and dark red, decorated: green edging
sometimes, and sometimes, for example on f. 415ᵛ, purple knobs projecting from the
straight edges of the ground; (ii) 4-line, blue with red ornament; (iii) of psalms, as (ii),
but 2-line; (iv) 1-line, blue or red, plain or with ornament of the other colour. Capital
letters in the ink of the text filled with red. Thick wooden boards, rebacked: a little of
the brown leather covers, with a pattern of fillets, s. xvi (?), remains on the back board:
a central clasp missing.

Written in England. 'James docsey is the trwe possessor of this boke', f. 381, s. xvi. 'William massye of Ipstones (Staffordshire) Owithe this boke god make him a good mahounde
and send him draffe ynought for charitie', f. 430, s. xvi. A strip from a sale catalogue,
s. xix ex. (?), is pasted inside the cover. Said by F. W. B. Bullock, *History of Ridley Hall*,
1953, ii. 227, to have been the gift of A. B. Cook, †1952: cf. MS. 1.

R.H. 3. *Preces et meditationes per annum*   s. XV ex.

A long series of prayers and meditations for feasts of the temporale and sanctorale, incomplete and divisible now into four main sections: (1: quires 1–12)
Christmas (ff. 2–59ᵛ), within the octave of Christmas (ff. 59–65), Circumcision
(ff. 65ᵛ–74), Epiphany (ff. 74ᵛ–88); (2: quires 13–26) Easter (ff. 93ᵛ–117),
Ascension (ff. 118–163ᵛ), Pentecost (ff. 164ᵛ–191ᵛ), Monday after Pentecost

[1] See Bristol Public Library, 15.
[2] de Bruyne printed this not-in-Stegmüller, but fairly common prologue.

(ff. 191ᵛ–192ᵛ), Trinity (ff. 193–215); (3: quires 27–36) Cena Domini (ff. 217–44), Dedication of church (ff. 244ᵛ–295ᵛ); (4) Simon and Jude (ff. 296ᵛ–311ᵛ: quires 37, 38), Cecilia (ff. 312–330ᵛ: quires 39–41), All Saints (ff. 336–57: quires 42–4).

(1) begins imperfectly 'sie ac pro vniuersis peccatoribus': probably only one leaf is missing. f. 65ᵛ begins 'In vigilia circumcisionis reuoca ad mentem quid sit factum inter deum et te'. Probably nine quires are missing in the gap after f. 88. f. 56 is torn at the foot. The right order of ff. 2–33 is 2–7, 9, 8, 10–24, 26–33, 25.

(2) begins 'In gloriosissima ac letissima Vigilia Pasche vade sponsa cristi electa ad sepulchrum'. f. 118 begins 'O fidelis anima si nunc usque facta diuini sponsi tui diligenter attendisti debes in eius recessu corporali verba et facta eius diligenter obseruare'. ff. 204ᵛ–213 contain meditations 'de beneficiis dei' for use 'post prandium vel quando tempus adest' and ff. 213–15 the Twelve Joys of B.V.M. 'quem habuit singulariter ex speciali dotacione sancte trinitatis'. ff. 93ʳ, 117ᵛ, 164ʳ, 215ᵛ are blank.

(3) begins imperfectly (one leaf missing) 'nignissime deus altissime pater'. f. 224ᵛ begins 'In die desiderabili cene vltime in qua nobis dei filius'. f. 244ᵛ begins 'O homo cristiane qui gaudes te esse membrum'. Prayers begin (f. 247) 'Saluto vos ego indigna peccatrix', (f. 247ᵛ) 'Salue o venerabilis pater sancte Benedicte dignare venire et intrare habitacionem monasterii nostri', and (f. 275) 'Ego indigna famula'.

(4) begins 'In preclara vigilia sanctissimorum apostolorum'. f. 312 begins 'O fidelis anima in hac valle lacrimarum' and f. 336 'O fidelis anima adueniente solempni festo omnium sanctorum'. On f. 323ᵛ a prayer to Cecilia, 'O du eddele schinende gemme . . .', is partly in Netherlandish. ff. 296ʳ, 331–332ᵛ and 357ᵛ–358 blank.

ff. ii+345+i. The modern foliation (i, ii), 2–358, (359) takes account of thirteen leaves presumed to be lost and therefore omits the numbers 1, 16 (nothing missing here), 87, 89–92, 216, 294–5, 333–5. 205 × 145 mm. Written space c. 130 × 85 mm. 24–6 long lines. Collation: 1⁸ wants 1 (ff. 2–7, 9), 2⁸ want 8 (ff. 8, 10–15) 3⁸ (ff. 17–24) 4⁸ wants 6 after f. 30 5⁸ wants 2 and 7 (ff. 33, 25, 34–8), 6⁸ wants 2 and 7 (ff. 39–44) 7–11⁸ 12 three (ff. 85, 86, 88) 13⁸ (ff. 93–100) 14 nine (ff. 101–9) 15–21⁸ 22¹⁰ 23⁸+2 leaves after 2 (ff. 178–9) 24–26¹⁰ 27⁸ wants 1 before f. 217 28–35⁸ 36⁸ wants 7, 8 probably blank after f. 293 37–40⁸ 41⁸ wants 6–8 blank after f. 332 42–43⁸ 44⁸ wants 8, blank, after f. 358. Quires 2–26, 32–8 appear to have been marked in a continuous series from a to z and from aa to ss: probably quire 12 was marked l and quire 13 x, and, if so, nine quires are missing here. Quires 27–31 (ff. 217–55) are not marked with letters, but the first four leaves of each quire are numbered in a single series from i to xx. Quires 39–44 are not marked. Two main hands, changing often: both occur for example on the double opening 122ᵛ–123. Initials: (i) patterned vermilion or vermilion and blue, with blue and red ornament forming borders: from f. 306ᵛ pigeons are frequent in the borders and there are a few owls: Simon and Jude are in the U on f. 307ᵛ and Cecilia in the O on f. 323ᵛ, the figures in outline, with gold haloes and gold edges to their robes; (ii) 4-line, as (i), but with less extensive ornament or in blue, patterned in white, with red ornament; (iii) 2-line, blue or red, patterned in white, the blue letters sometimes with red ornament; (iv) 1-line, red alternating with capital letters in the ink of the text stroked with red. Perhaps contemporary binding of bare wooden boards, rebacked: three bands: two clasps. Secundo folio (f. 2) sie ac.

Written in the Netherlands for the use of Benedictine nuns: see above. 'A.D. (?) possidet', f. ii, s. xvi in. 'A. B. pertinet', f. iiᵛ, s. xvi in.

CAMBRIDGE. ST. JOHN'S COLLEGE

103** (D. 30). *Psalterium* s. xiv¹

1. ff. 1–6ᵛ Calendar in gold, blue, red, and black. A few gradings.

Sarum calendar, with a few Ely feasts. Feasts in gold include Etheldreda and Edmund, king and martyr (23 June, 20 Nov.); in red, Ermenilda, 'Sancti francisci non sarum', translation of Etheldreda (13 Feb., 4, 17 Oct.); in black, Wihtburga and her translation (17 Mar., 8 July). Feasts of St. Thomas of Canterbury and the word 'pape' erased.

2. ff. 7–136ᵛ Pss. 1–150.

Ps. 109 begins on a new leaf. Corrections written in the margins in current anglicana and pale ink have been neatly incorporated into the text, for example on ff. 33ᵛ, 53, 68ᵛ. Facsimile of f. 7 in the Sotheby sale catalogue: see below.

3. f. 136ᵛ (no break in text)–149ᵛ Six ferial canticles, Benedicite, Benedictus, Te Deum, Magnificat, Nunc dimittis, Quicumque vult.

4. ff. 149ᵛ, 152–154ᵛ Litany.

f. 149ᵛ ends with the third entry, 'Fili redemptor mundi . . .', after which two leaves are missing: f. 152 begins 'Ab inmundis cogitationibus'. The prayer 'Fidelium deus omnium conditor . . .' and the first lines of 'Pietate tua quesumus . . .' have been crossed out on f. 154.

5. ff. 154ᵛ–160ᵛ In commemoracione animarum. a'. Placebo . . .

Office of the dead. The prayer 'Fidelium deus omnium conditor . . .' has been crossed out on ff. 155 and 160, together with the four prayers which precede it on ff. 159ᵛ–160, 'Deus indulgenciarum . . .', 'Inclina domine . . .', 'Deus qui nos patrem et matrem . . .', and 'Quesumus domine pro tua pietate miserere anime famule tue et a contagiis mortalitatis exutata in eterne saluacionis partem restitue'.

ff. ii+158+ii. The modern foliation 1–149, 152–60 allows for the two missing leaves. 305 × 195 mm. Written space 205 × 112 mm. 22 long lines. Collation: 1⁶ 2–5⁸ 6⁴ (ff. 39–42) 7⁶ (ff. 43–8) 8–14⁸ 15² (ff. 105–6) 16–19⁸ 20⁶ 21⁸ wants 6, 7 after f. 149 (ff. 145–9, 152) 22⁸. Signatures b–f in the usual late medieval manner on quires 10–14. Probably written in one hand, except ff. 153–154ᵛ/5. ff. 7–38 (quires 2–5) and ff. 107–14 (quire 16) are more elaborately and finely decorated than the rest,¹ but probably not earlier, as the Sotheby cataloguer suggested they were. Initials: of Pss. 1, 26, 38, 52, 68, 80, 97, 109, 7-line or 6-line, in colour, mainly blue, on gold and blue or gold and pink grounds, historiated; so too the *P* of *Placebo* on f. 154ᵛ (art. 5: four nuns beside a coffin); (ii) 2-line, as (i), but decorated, not historiated: prolongations in gold and colours the height of the written space often curl round into upper and lower margins; (iii) 1-line, gold on pink and blue grounds patterned in white. Line fillers in blue, red, and gold. Continuous borders on pages with initials of type i: on f. 7, a hunting scene at the head of the page and David and Goliath, dog, hare, and squirrel at the foot. Binding of s. xix. Secundo folio (f. 8) *Cum exarserit*.

Written in England. Arms of Montacute, argent three fusils conjoined in fess gules within a bordure bendy or and azure, between David and Goliath on f. 7. They and the Ely entries in the calendar suggest that this psalter may have been made for Simon de Montacute, bishop of Ely, †1345: a woman's soul is prayed for in art. 5. 'Thomas Moyle Prayer Book', f. 1, s. xviii. 'H. Zouch 1781—This Book was given me by the last will of Thomas

¹ Dr. J. J. G. Alexander tells me that the same artist decorated MS. Astor Dep. A. 1, deposited in the Bodleian Library.

Moyle of Wakefield, Glazier; who by a long course of honest industry had accumulated a fortune to the amount of several thousand pounds', f. ii. Passed with the rest of the library of the Revd. Henry Zouch, rector of Swillington, Yorkshire, †1795, to his nephew, William Lowther, first Earl of Lonsdale. Lonsdale sale, Sotheby's, 12 July 1937, lot 462, to Francis Edwards Ltd. (£360). No. 245 in an Edwards catalogue. Bought by H. P. W. Gatty, fellow, 12 Nov. 1945, and bequeathed by him in 1948.

137** (E. 36). *Nova officia, etc.*   s. xv[1]

1. ff. 1–27 In transubstanciacione corporis cristi ad iᵃ ves 'A'. Memoria mea in generacione seculorum . . .

Office of Corpus Christi: twelve lessons at matins; office of mass, f. 15ᵛ; within the octave, Friday (f. 18ᵛ), Saturday (f. 20), Sunday (f. 20ᵛ), Monday (f. 22ᵛ), Tuesday (f. 23), Wednesday (f. 24); 'In octauis' (eight lessons), ff. 24ᵛ–27.

2. ff. 27–44 In festo sancte Anne matris gloriose uirginis dei genitricis marie.

Twelve lessons at matins; office of mass, f. 42.

3. ff. 44–54 In festo sancti Oswyni . . . A'. O sancte oswyne . . . (f. 45ᵛ) Lec' i. Anno incarnationis . . .

Proper office, 11 Mar. Twelve lessons, 1–8 nearly as in Surtees Soc. viii (1838), 11–13/1 *potuisset.*

4. ff. 54–61 In passione sancti Oswyni festum minus principale . . .

20 Aug. Proper collect, commemorations of B.V.M. and St. Philibert, twelve lessons, 'Translato ad celestia . . .' (lesson 8 ends 'Quod factum fuit die tercia decima kalendarum septembrium. anno domini secentesimo primo'), and gospel, Matthew 10: 34–42; for the rest, cues.

5. ff. 61–63ᵛ Cues for office within the octave of St. Oswyn and three lessons, 'Quoniam humilitas . . . ex hac vita rapiendum', as in Surtees Soc. viii. 5/10–6/7.

6. ff. 63ᵛ–70ᵛ Duodecimo kl' nouembris. Passio sanctarum vndecim Milium uirginum. festum iii lc'.

The hymn is the rare 'O felix chorus' (*RH*, no. 12958). Two leaves missing after f. 67 which ends 'A'. 'Virgines sancte dei orate . . . Ps. Laudate': f. 68 begins 'exultacione. Ps. Eructauit'. Office of mass, f. 68.

7. ff. 70ᵛ–75 In nomine ihesu omne genu . . .

Mass of the Name of Jesus, the heading not filled in. *Brev. ad usum Sarum*, ii. 548–53.

8. ff. 75–77ᵛ Sciendum est uero quod sequenti modo debet trigintale quod dicitur sancti gregorii celebrari. Quod quotidie per annum dicatur Placebo et Dirige cum nouem psalmis . . .

Collect, secret, and postcommunion, as Sarum (Burntisland edn., col. 883*).

9. ff. 77ᵛ–80 Rubrica de sex missis quarum quinque debent legi de sancta cruce. et vna de resurrectione domini. Quas si quis . . .

Long rubric and (f. 78ᵛ) a prayer for each day of the week, Tuesday–Sunday, each beginning 'Domine ihesu criste fili dei viui rogo te': the first is '. . . rogo te per innocentem captiuitatem . . .'.

10. ff. 80–1 Pro muliere in articulo pariendi. or'. Omnipotens sempiterne deus qui beatissimam uirginem . . .

Collect, secret (Suscipe quesumus domine preces . . .) and postcommunion (Adesto domine supplicationibus . . .).

11. ff. 81–3 *Dompnus* papa Iohannes vicesimus secundus. istud euangelium quod sequitur diligenter composuit . . . In illo tempore apprehendit pilatus ihesum . . . uerum est testimonium eius. Deus qui manus tuas . . .

The heading conveys indulgence of 300 days. For it and this catena from John and Matthew and the prayer see *Lyell Catalogue*, p. 65. ff. 83ᵛ–84ᵛ blank, except for a scribble and inscription; for the latter and the costing note on f. 83, see below.

ff. vi+84+ii, foliated i–iii, 1*–3*, 1–84 (85, 86). ff. 1*–3* are medieval parchment endleaves: 1* was pasted down. 215 × 150 mm. Written space 115 × 87 mm. 15 long lines. Collation: 1–8⁸ 9⁸ wants 4, 5 after f. 67 10⁸ wants 7, 8, probably blank. Usual late medieval quire and leaf signatures. Initials: (i) 2-line, blue with red ornament; (ii) 1-line, red or blue. Their cost and other expenses are noted on f. 83 in the margin: de magnis littere i c' dᶜ xiiiiᴵ / de paruis littere ii c' / Summa totalis xᵈ / Item for yᵉ byndyng xiiᵈ / Item for yᵉ custodiis iᵈ / Item a quayr of mater iiᵈ ob'. / Summa totalis iiˢ iᵈ ob'. The present binding is of s. xx. Secundo folio *sacrificium*.

Written in England, for use at the Benedictine abbey of St. Albans. 'Liber de infirmitorio sancti Albani', f. 1, s. xv. 'Iste liber pertenet aud (*or* and) infirmitorium', f. 84ᵛ, s. xv/xvi. 'Charles Fotherby given by Cha: Fothe: Esq.', f. 1, at foot. Armorial book-plate of Osmund Beauvoir, f. iᵛ. 'Edw. S. Dewick', f. ii. Given by his son, the Revd. E. S. Dewick, in 1950.

137*** (E. 37). *Biblia*   s. XIII med.

1. pp. 5–1046 The usual books of the Bible in the usual order.[2]

Proverbs begins on a new quire, p. 527. Psalms are numbered. The text breaks off in Isaiah 22: 20 (p. 626) and begins again in Jeremiah 18: 11: one quire is missing. The prologues were originally, no doubt, the common set of 64,[2] together with a third prologue to Obadiah after nos. 519 and 517 (which are, here, separate prologues and not, as usual, run together), but Jerome's general prologue, no. 284, and the prologue to Jeremiah, no. 487, are missing: p. 5 begins 'ramus. Illi interpretati' near the end of the prologue to Desiderius (no. 285). The third prologue to Obadiah is 'Esau filius ysaac frater iacob . . . loquitur hic propheta', as in Douai Abbey, 3. pp. 1047–8 blank.

2. pp. 1049–1178 Interpretationes hebraicorum nominum . . . Aaz apprehendens . . . (*ends imperfectly*).

The usual dictionary of Hebrew names. The last remaining entry is Zabadei, the fifth under letter Z.

ff. ii+587, paginated (1–4), 5–99, 90–433, 444–1046, (1047–1178). 160 × 110 mm. Written space 102 × 77 mm. 2 cols. 45 lines. Collation: 1²² wants 1, 2, 2²⁶ 3²⁴ 4²⁶ 5–7²⁴ 8²⁶ 9–10²⁴ 11²⁰ wants 20 blank after p. 526 12²² 13²⁸ 14²⁶ 15 twenty-three (679–724) 16²⁴ 17²⁶ 18²⁴ 19²⁶ 20³⁰ 21²⁶ 22⁶ (pp. 1037–48) 23–24²⁴ 25²⁰ wants 18–20. *Ad hoc* signatures in red, quires 12–25. A new hand begins at p. 527 (12ᴵ). Initials: (i) of books, in colour patterned in white on decorated—often zoomorphic—coloured grounds picked out with a little gold;

---

[1] I reckon 158. Probably there were six 2-line letters on the leaves missing after f. 67.
[2] See Bristol Public Library, 15.

(ii) at the main divisions of the psalms, red and blue, flourished in both colours; (iii) of prologues, as (ii), but smaller (4-line); (iv) of chapters, 2-line, red or blue, flourished in both colours; (v) of psalm verses and in art. 2, 1-line, red or blue. Saw-pattern and feather-work borders with initials of types ii–iv. Capital letters in the ink of the text touched with red. Binding of s. xix.

Written probably in France. In England by s. xvi when 'Anthony Pethwyn' was written on p. 984. Cancelled name and price and the date 1694 on p. 5. Given by G. U. Yule in 1951.

524 (N. 11). *Biblia* s. XIII med.

1. ff. 1–553 A Bible with the usual contents in the usual order.[1]

The prologues are 63 of the common set of 64 (all but the prologue to Wisdom, Stegmüller, no. 468) and 8 others, Stegm., nos. 516, 522, 525, 527, 529, 532, 535, 540, which come after nos. 517, 521, 526, 528, 531, 534, 538, 539 respectively. No. 327 is not in its place, but was added by the main hand in the space between Job and Psalms (f. 248), followed by the words 'Hic prologus debet legi ante secundum librum paralipomenon': a corresponding notice in red is on the page on which 2 Chronicles begins. No. 517 is not, as it usually is, one prologue with no. 519, but is preceded by the heading 'Item alius prologus'. No. 589 is divided in two by 'Item alius prologus' before 'Matheus in homine intelligitur'.

Psalms and Proverbs begin new quires, ff. 249, 277. ff. 247^v–248^v were left blank.

2. ff. 553^v–594 Incipiunt interpretationes. Aaz apprehendens . . . consiliatores eorum. Expliciunt interpretationes deo gracias. f. 594^v blank.

ff. iii+594+iii. 120×80 mm. Written space 78×56 mm. 2 cols. (3 cols. in art. 2). 46 lines. Collation: 1–9^{24} 10^{20} 11^{12} (ff. 237–48) 13–21^{24} 22^{30} 23–25^{24} 26^{26} 27^{22}. *Ad hoc* signatures in red in quire 6. Initials: (i) of books and prologues, 3-line or more, red and blue with ornament of both colours; (ii) of chapters, 2-line, red or blue, with ornament of both colours; (iii) of verses of psalms and in art. 2, 1-line, red or blue. The ornament in the margins runs the full length of the page and is partly saw-pattern, if the initial is of type (ii). Capital letters in the ink of the text are filled with red. Binding of s. xix. Secundo folio *paulus sapientiam*.

Written in France (?). From the Augustinian priory of Southwark: 'Liber beate ouerey in suthwerke', f. 247^v, s. xv. Bequeathed by H. H. Hughes, fellow, in 1884.

581 (A. 23). *Decretales Gregorii noni, etc.* s. XIII med.

1. The five books of Gregory's Decretals: bk. 1, f. 1; 2, f. 60; 3, f. 114; 4, f. 174^v; 5, ff. 196^v–251^v . . . compellatur. Testu finito sit laus et gloria cristo. The apparatus is in various hands and not continuous.

Begins imperfectly at ed. Friedberg, p. 7/20: the first leaf is missing. The word 'GREGORIVS' is in elongated blue and red letters either before or after the *explicit* of each book.

Marginalia, s. xiii², include: f. 69, 'hoc nota pro causa prepositi de Moyk' at II. x. 2; f. 189^v 'hanc glosam nota contra comitissam flandren*sem* que Iohannem de Auena filium comitis esse negabat' at IV. xvii. 3; f. 227, 'Nota hoc contra superbiam prepositorum de hungr' qui uolunt archid' preferre' at V. xxxi. 15; f. 241, Nota contra Nicholaum et alios fautores ipsius' at V. xxxix. 14. 'Magister Ber' ' is often referred to.

ff. i^v–ii^v contain an alphabetical list of tituli, 'Apostatis . . . vt infra certum tempus', s. xiii.

[1] See Bristol Public Library, 15.

A table of rubrics of bks. 1–4, s. xv, is on the paper pastedown at the end. For f. i^r see art. 3.

2. Decrees, headed as a rule 'Innocentius iiii^{us} in concilio lugdunensi', together with their apparatus, were added, one of them in duplicate, by several hands, s. xiii, in the wide margins and on four added leaves (254–7). All but one were included in the Sextus liber decretalium: I. vi. 1 on f. 17^v; I. vi. 2 on f. 18; I. viii. 1 on f. 29; I. xiii. 1 on f. 39; I. xiv. 1 on f. 46^v; I. xv. 1 on f. 48; I. xvi. 1 on f. 49; II. i. 1 on f. 61^v; II. ii. 1 on f. 62; II. iii. 1 on f. 64^v; II. vi. 1 on f. 75^v; II. vii. 1 on f. 76; II. ix. 1 on f. 77; II. x. 2 on f. 85 (Innocentius iiii' struck through); II. x. 3 on f. 85; II. v. 1 on f. 100; II. xii. 1 on f. 100^v; II. xiv. 1 on f. 102^v; II. xv. 1 on f. 111^v; II. xv. 2 on f. 112; II. xv. 3 on f. 113^v; III. ix. 1 on f. 129; III. xx. 1 on f. 162^v; V. iv. 1 on f. 215^v; V. vii. 1 on f. 226^v; V. ix. 1 on f. 237^v; V. x. 1 on f. 239^v; V. xi. 1 on f. 241; V. xi. 2 on f. 242^v; V. xi. 3 on f. 243^v; V. xi. 4 on f. 244 (including the addition printed in edn., p. 1095, footnote); V. xi. 5 on f. 246^v; V. xi. 6 on f. 249; I. viii. 2 on f. 252; V. xii. 1 on f. 252^v (marked 'vacat'); I. vi. 16 on f. 254; II. xiv. 2 on ff. 254^v–257^v; V. xii. 1 on f. 257^v, a repetition of the text on f. 252^v. The one decree not in the Sext is on ff. 252^v, 254 where it is marked 'vacat': 'Venerabilium fratrum . . . processerit uoluntatem' (Gregory IX: Potthast 10698; Auvray, *Reg.*, nos. 4708–9).[1] f. 253 is a corner only of a leaf which seems to have been left blank.

3. Scraps of verse in the margins and among legal notes on the flyleaves include: (*a*) f. 33 Septem sunt dona que sunt baptismate clara . . . (6 lines); (*b*) f. 39^v Consensus negligit . . . (2); (*c*) f. 98 Hostis scisma minor . . . (5); (*d*) f. 138 Debita quarta datur . . . (14); (*e*) f. 174^v Error condicio . . . (4); (*f*) f. 197 Non ligat ad penam . . . (4); (*g*) f. i, s. xiv in. Si quis cordis et oculi . . . (28); (*h*) f. i Dum bipedem supra tripodem . . . (2); (*i*) f. i Quadrupedis dente felice plus esuriente . . . (4); (*j*) f. i Virgo iohannes auis . . . (4).

(*d*, *e*, *g*, *j*). Walther, *Initia*, nos. 4195, 5520, 17915 (P. de Grève), 20508. (*b*). Walther, *Sprichwörter*, no. 3125.

4. Tituli secundi libri decretalium. Iudicium forus libellus mutuumque peto . . . (10 lines).

Mnemonic verses written in a German hand, s. xv, on the paper pastedown inside the front cover.

ff. ii + 257. Paper pastedowns, s. xv. 330 × 220 mm. Written space *c*. 185 × 95 mm. 2 cols. 45–7 lines. Collation of ff. 1–253: 1^{10} wants 1 2–6^{10} 7^8 8–10^{10} 11–12^8 13–26^{10}. The initials, red or blue, with ornament of the other colour, lie outside the written space. Binding of s. xvi: wooden boards covered with white leather: four bands: bosses, five on each cover, and a pair of clasps missing: two of eight metal corner-strips remain on the edges of the boards. Secundo folio (f. 1) *desiisset*.[2]

Written in Italy. Probably north of the Alps by s. xiii[2] (cf. art. 1) and in Germany in s. xv: 'Decretales Ecclesie [. . . .] Mutuate Doctori Kalmo (?) de Ratisbona Anno cristi etc. mcccc' inside the front cover. Bought from T. Thorp, St. Martin's Lane, London, in 1929 for £18: see Minutes of the Library Committee, 29 July 1929.

[1] I owe the references to Professor Stephan Kuttner.
[2] *desiisset* is right but the scribe probably wrote *clesiis set*, misreading *d* as *cl*.

602 (N. 18*). *Anselmus, Proslogion* s. xii²

'Incipit liber augustini. de inquirendo et videndo deo.' Eya nunc homuntio. Fuge paululum . . . donec intrem in gaudium domini nostri. qui est trinus et unus deus benedictus in secula amen.

SAO i. 97–122. Not divided into chapters. The attribution to Augustine is in an early and perhaps contemporary hand in the lower margin of f. 1: cf. edn., p. 97. Listed by Römer, i. 377, ii. 72, but the text here is not the catena found in Blickling 6849 and other manuscripts. The lower part of f. 8 contains a set of red squares with patterned fillings, placed diagonally within a frame. f. 8ᵛ blank.

ff. 8. Medieval foliation, I–VIII. 135 × 98 mm. Written space 94 × 65 mm. 26 long lines. One quire of eight leaves. The 4-line initial *E* on f. 1 may be a later addition. Parchment binding, s. xx in. Secundo folio *Liceat michi*.

Written in France. A scribble in the lower margin of f. 5ᵛ, s. xiii: 'I. diuina miseratione abbas virzeliacn' G. priori Sancti Remigii procuratori prioratus de Melloto'. Saint-Rémyl'Abbaye and Mello, Oise, were priories dependent on the abbey of Vézelay, O.S.B. This is perhaps part of a Vézelay book, therefore. 'Ex libris Ronaldi Coates Anno Salutis MDCXIV' inside the cover. Given by G. U. Yule, fellow, in 1931.

CAMBRIDGE. SELWYN COLLEGE

108. K. 1. *Augustinus, De doctrina Christiana* s. xv med.

1. ff. 3–83ᵛ Sentencia beati Augustini de libro Retractationum pertinens ad hunc librum. Libros de doctrina cristiana . . . phylosophia scripsit. Aurelii Augustini doctoris prefacio in libro de doctrina cristiana incipit. Sunt precepta quedam . . . facultate disserui. Aurelii Augustini eximii doctoris liber Quartus de doctrina cristiana Explicit.

PL xxxiv. 15–122, preceded by the relevant passage of Retractationes. ff. 1–2ᵛ, 84ʳᵛ left blank.

2 (added in the main hand). f. 2ᵛ Tabular 'Divisiones beati Augustini in libro de doctrina cristiana', as in B.L., Royal 5 B. xii.

3. f. ii 'Natos mactatos tu criste cruore beatos (renatos *interlined*) . . .' and other couplets and triplets on the Holy Blood.

ff. ii+84+i. f. ii, a medieval parchment end-leaf, was formerly pasted down. *c.* 240 × 165 mm. Written space *c.* 175 × 115 mm. 25 long lines at first, increasing to 43 on f. 83. No ruling. Collation: 1–3⁸ 4⁸ wants 1 5–10⁸ 11⁶ wants 5, blank. Written in clumsy, but legible current anglicana. Initials omitted, apart from a 3-line *Q* on f. 17 and a 4-line *H* on f. 64 in red. Binding of s. xviii: the marks of the five bands and two strap-and-pin fastenings of an older binding show on ff. ii, 84. Secundo folio *ut sibi* (f. 4).

Written in England. A letter-mark (?) 'B' on f. 1. 'The Right Honᵇˡᵉ Phillip Lord Viscount Wenman His Book April the 22ᵈ 1708', f. 1. 'Bought with several other MSS. and Books at the Sale of the last Viscount Wenman (†1800) at Thame Park. W. Mavor LLD

(†1837)', f. 1. 'Sale of Dʳ Mavor's books at Oxon' 1838 £[. . .]', f. i, refers to the sale of 5 June 1838, when this manuscript was lot 107. 'E libris Gul' Selwyn S.T.B. (†1875) . . . ex dono J. A. Jeremie (†1872)' inside the cover, above Selwyn's armorial book-plate. College book-plate inscribed 'The Gift of Mʳ William Selwyn', f. i.

108. K. 2. *Biblia sacra, Prima pars; etc.* s. xv med.

1. ff. 1–13ᵛ Quomodo biblia habuit ortum et ueritatem. Ecclesiastica hystoria libro 5ᵗᵒ . . . Tocius biblie sunt septuaginta duo libri ut habetur luculenter per uersus subscriptos. Et quot capitula vnumquodque habet habetur in glosa desuper consignata. (f. 1ᵛ) Ge Ex Le Nu Deu Io Iu Rut Re qua Para duo . . . Iu Apochalipsis (9 lines). Licet sufficienti elucidacioni subtillisima sagacitatis indagine . . . (f. 3) vltimus versus vnum capitulum designat. Genesis. Astra polum cuncta . . . Assunt sex opera . . . Bisseni fructus adora. Expliciunt uersiculi siue versificature tocius biblie septuaginta duorum librorum . . . sunt mille ccc octaginta octo etc.

The verses are Walther, nos. 7141, 1641. In 'Astra polum . . .' single lines in red summarize the contents of each book of the Bible, each line beginning with the appropriate letter in an alphabetical series in which A stands for Genesis, B for Exodus, etc.: the series runs in three twenties, A–V, A–V, A–V, and then A–N (Apocalypse).[1] The lines in black make up similar alphabets summarizing the contents of each chapter of each book, A denoting the first chapter, B the second, etc.: the final line begins with B because Apocalypse has twenty-two chapters. The author of the table of contents on f. iᵛ, s. xv ex., doubted the usefulness of art. 1 and remarks that it has in it 'multa pro memoria beneficio et forte magis pro eius confusione et destructione': cf. *MBDS* ii. 273. ff. 14–17ᵛ are blank.

2. ff. 18–86ᵛ Incipiunt concordancie biblie distincte per quinque libros . . . Prima pars libri incipit de peccato et eius effectibus. 1 de peccato simpliciter. Iob 26e . . . gaudio. Et est finis quinque librorum concordanciarum super bibliotecam. Pro quo deus sit benedictus in secula seculorum. Amen.

For more details see *MBDS* ii. 274 and cf. Stegmüller, no. 1382. ff. 87–95ᵛ blank.

3. ff. 96–513ᵛ Genesis to Job in the usual order,[2] including the prayer of Manasses.

Begins imperfectly in Jerome's general prologue: two leaves are missing before f. 96. Ruth begins on a new quire, f. 290. The prologues are the usual thirteen,[2] but Stegmüller, no. 327 is here the second prologue to 1 Chronicles and not the prologue to 2 Chronicles.

4. ff. 514–605 Incipiunt distincciones exemplorum noui et ueteris testamenti abbreuiate et reducte ad diuersas materias secundum ordinem alphabeti per fratrem Bindonem de Senis fratrum heremitarum ordinis sancti agostini. De Abstinencia et Ieiunio. Abstinencia est meriti augmentiua . . . persequeretur cristianos Actuum xiii Deo gracias amen.

Stegmüller, no. 1765. A table of the distinctions follows the text on ff. 605ᵛ–606, furnished with leaf numbers i–lxxix which do not suit this copy. ff. 606ᵛ–609ᵛ are blank.

---

ff. i+609. Paper, except f. i. 310 × 215 mm. Written space 235 × 130 mm. 2 cols. 43 lines and (quire 47, ff. 500–13) 36 long lines. Frame ruling with a hard point for horizontals and

[1] I is used twice in these alphabets and K is left out.
[2] See Bristol Public Library, 15.

ink for verticals, except on ff. 500–13 where there is full ruling in ink. Collation: 55 quires, all twelves, except $8^{10}+1$ leaf after 10 (f. 95), 9^{12} wants 1, 2 before f. 96, 25^4 (ff. 286–9), 46^{18}, 47^{14}, 51^{14}, 55^{12} wants 11, 12, blank. A new series of quire numbers begins at quire 30, f. 290. Strips of parchment taken from manuscripts at the quire centres as strengthening: a Hebrew manuscript was used for quires 1 and 55. Written in cursiva, ff. 500–13 by a hand different from the rest. Initials 2-line or more in metallic red, but many spaces remain blank. Capital letters in the ink of the text marked with a stroke of red. Contemporary binding of wooden boards covered with stamped pigskin: an 'aue maria' stamp forms a continuous border: five bands: ten bosses, five from each cover, and five out of eight metal cornerpieces missing: two clasps missing. Secundo folio *liber*.

Written in Germany (Erfurt?). 'Istud volumen est domu[. . . . .]sis prope erford ob salutis anime domini iodoci cristen lega*tum* Anno nouiciatis sui 1465 ipsa die katherine virginis', f. i, at top, partly cut off, is the ex-libris of the charterhouse of Erfurt, which possessed when the catalogue was made, *c.* 1475, two 2-volume Bibles with the same contents as 108. K. 2–3, B. 15–16 and B. 17–18, the latter 'ligate in albo corio porcino', and the former 'rubea'. Presumably the present volume is identical with B. 17. Bülow sale, 10 Oct. 1836, lot 155. 'G. Sumner, Woodmansey, 1855/Case B/X', f. i: his sale, Beverley, 31 Oct. 1877, lot 528.

108. K. 3. *Biblia sacra, Secunda et tertia pars; etc.* 1460

1. ff. 1–490^v Proverbs to Apocalypse in the usual order.[1] Ecclesiasticus ends with the prayer of Solomon, 'Et inclinauit . . . vir in te. Explicit ecclesiasticus' (f. 73).

Five of the usual prologues[1] are omitted, the three to Maccabees, Stegmüller no. 590 to Matthew, and 839 to Apocalypse. The prologue to Haggai is no. 539 and the prologue to Zechariah no. 538, instead of the other way round. The nine prologues not of the common set are 532 to Zephaniah before 534, 806, 815 (first eight words only), 818, 822, 823, 824, 825 before each of the seven Catholic Epistles, and 834 before Apocalypse. 'Explicit secunda pars biblie Anno domini MCCCC sexagesimo' after Maccabees, f. 287. Matthew and Romans begin on new quires. ff. 287^v–288^v, 383–384^v after John, and 491–494^v blank.

2. ff. 495–596^v Incipit mammetractus. Ambrosius frater in fide perferens id est portans fidem . . . translati ad requiem de labore et cetera et cetera. Finita . . . (*see below*).

Stegmüller, nos. 4776–7 (Johannes Marchesinus, O.F.M.). ff. 597–602^v left blank. The order here is Genesis–Job, Proverbs–Apocalypse, Psalter, De mensibus hebreorum and other short sections on biblical subjects, Antiphons (f. 584^v), Hymns (f. 589). ff. 597–602^v were left blank.

ff. 602. Paper. 305 × 220 mm. Written space 225 × 135 mm. 35–6 long lines. Ruling as in 108. K. 2, except on ff. 385–420 (quires 33–5) where it is all in ink, and on ff. 421–34 (quire 36) where there is no ruling. Collation: 50 quires, all twelves, except 36^{14} (ff. 421–34). Strips of manuscript as strengthening, as in 108. K. 2. Written in cursiva by several hands, changing at ff. 193/3, 289 (first hand again), 385. Initials: (i) red, sometimes with green ornament; (ii) red. The red is usually metallic. Capital letters in the ink of the text marked with red. Contemporary binding of wooden boards covered with stamped calf: a border stamp encloses a panel filled with repetitions of a 'yh̄s' stamp within rectangular hatched fillets: four bands: metal cornerpieces and two clasps missing. Secundo folio *meo et*.

[1] See Bristol Public Library, 15.

'Finita est ista pars biblie in toto Anno domini mcccclx die lune xxviii mensis Iulii Scripta in smoll' ', f. 596ᵛ, in the hand of art. 2: cf. above, art. 1. 'Iste liber pertinet [. . . .] prope erff'. continens prophetas cum nouo testamento et Mammetrecton Cum notabilibus multis Et est valde utilis pro communitate in libraria', inside the cover, is presumably the ex-libris of the charterhouse of Erfurt: for the entries in the medieval catalogue see above, 108. K. 2. This was B. 16 at Erfurt:[1] Bülow sale, 10 Oct. 1836, lot 158. 'G. Sumner, Woodmansey, 1855/Case B/Y', f. i: his sale, Beverley, 31 Oct. 1877, lot 530.

108. L. 19. *Part of the New Testament* (*in English*)   s. xv in.

The New Testament, except Mark, Luke, John, and Apocalypse, in English: ff. 1–12ᵛ God made mankynde . . . in þe furste moneþ of (*a preface, ending abruptly*); 13–32, Catholic Epistles; 33–85, Pauline Epistles; 85ᵛ–133, Acts; 133–9, Matthew 1: 1–6: 13.

The basis of the edition by A. C. Paues, *A Fourteenth Century English Biblical Version*, 1904, and called *S* by her: cf. especially, pp. xi, xii. She points out that the short quire 5, except the first leaf, and quires 13–19 (ff. 29–32, 86–139) are in a Midland dialect and the rest in a Southern dialect. Chapter numbers and headings were added in s. xv. 'Maria Ihesus Iohannes' at the head of f. 1, as in the copy now Corpus Christi College, Cambridge, MS. 434. ff. 32ᵛ, 139ᵛ–140ᵛ were left blank.

ff. iii+140+iii. 180×135 mm. Written space *c.* 150×90 mm. 27–9 long lines. Collation: 1⁸ 2⁴ 3–4⁸ 5⁴ 6–11⁸ 12 five (ff. 81–5) 13–18⁸ 19⁸ wants 7, blank. Written in textura with some anglicana forms mixed in, but of these only the long-tailed *r* persists to the end. The hand varies in size, but is probably the same throughout; there is no evident change at ff. 29, 33, and 86 (see above). 2-line initials in red in quire 13: elsewhere the spaces for initials remain blank. Binding of s. xviii. Secundo folio *forsoken*.

Written in England, 'B/g' and 'Mʳ Aspley' (s. xvii), f. 140ᵛ. Book-plate of William Cooke, canon of Chester: his gift of 500 volumes, mostly of patristic literature, was in 1891 (*Selwyn College Calendar 1894*, p. 28) and he added further volumes by bequest in 1895.

CAMBRIDGE. TRINITY COLLEGE

B. 11 extra 1. *Quatuor Evangelia glosata*   s. xiii med.

The four Gospels flanked by commentary in smaller writing: Matthew, f. 1; Mark, f. 91; Luke, f. 147; John, f. 248, ending imperfectly at 20: 13 Dicunt ei illi. The prologues in the same size of writing as the text of the Gospels are Stegmüller, nos. 590, 607, 620, 624. Those in smaller writing are no. 589 on the left of no. 590 and no. 628, Omnibus diuine scripture . . ., flanking no. 624.

Two leaves, probably, are missing between f. 296 which ends 'Dixerunt ergo ex dis' (John 16: 17) and f. 297 which begins 'que dedisti michi' (John 17: 7). Chapter numbers in the margins. f. 247ᵛ left blank after Luke.

Marginalia in an English hand, s. xiv ex., refer to 'Aug. in sermone de martiribus sermo 7ᵘˢ' (f. 39ᵛ), 'Augustinus in sermone de sancto cipriano de hoc et est sermo 73' (f. 181: cf. f. 43)

---

[1] The *MBDS* identification of B.16 with the present Berlin, lat. fol. 506, is wrong, as Dr. Sigrid Krämer tells me.

and to William of Auxerre on bk. 3 of the Sentences of Peter Lombard (f. 181ᵛ). A pencil sketch of the evangelist's symbol on the first page of each gospel, top right: John's eagle has been cut out, except one edge. The line, 'Mucro cruor sauli liber est conuersio pauli' (Walther, *Sprichwörter*, no. 15337a: Mucro furor . . .) is written large at the foot of f. 1, s. xiv ex. A note on f. iiᵛ, 'Ignis significat caritatem . . .', s. xiii.

ff. iii+303+ii. ff. ii, iii are medieval parchment end-leaves: iiʳ was pasted down. 325 × 205 mm. Written space c. 205 × 123 mm. Collation: 1⁸ 2–6¹² 7⁸+2 leaves after 8 (ff. 77, 78) 8–12¹² 13⁸ 14–20¹² 21¹⁶+1 leaf after 16 (f. 247) 22–25¹² 26¹² wants 2, 3 after f. 296 and 11, 12 after f. 303. In quires 6 and 25 the first six leaves are marked in pencil on rectos with from one to six vertical strokes, but in quire 8 the marking is in red ink on versos beginning with six strokes on the first verso (f. 79ᵛ) and ending with one stroke on the sixth verso. In some quires a cross made in one stroke (and therefore resembling a medieval 4) is on the recto of the central opening at the foot. Initials: (i) beginning each Gospel, red and blue with ornament of both colours; (ii) at Luke 22: 1 and Mark 14: 1, blue with red ornament. The letters after the first of *Marcus* (f. 91), *Initium euangelii* (f. 92), *Hic est Iohannes* (f. 248), *In principio erat* (f. 248) are elongated and coloured red or blue. Capital letters in the ink of the text marked with red. Binding of wooden boards recovered in 1970 by D. Cockerell and Son, whose note on a leaf fastened inside the back cover records 'evidence of there having been four strap clasps to four studs on the back board. Studs and straps missing'; also 'Old boards repaired and replaced. Covered with alumed Italian sheepskin. Remains of old sides replaced'. Secundo folio *utile est*.

Written probably in England. An erased inscription on f. iiᵛ seems to begin with 'Liber', after which are seven (?) illegible words and the date 'Anno domini Mᵒ ccl Quinto'. Given in 1970 by J. U. Todd of Redgrave, Diss, Norfolk.

O. 10a. 26. *Breviarium* s. XIV med.

1. Fragments of a small noted Sarum breviary, beginning imperfectly in the memoria of B.V.M. of the Monday ferial office (*Brev. ad usum Sarum*, ii. 93). The remains are: (*a*) ff. 1–82ᵛ, temporale; (*b*) ff. 82ᵛ–88ᵛ, In dedicatione ecclesie; (*c*) ff. 89–131, psalter; (*d*) ff. 131–135ᵛ, six ferial canticles, followed by Te deum, Benedicite, and Benedictus (*ends imperfectly*); (*e*) f. 136, part of an addition to (*b*) (?).

(*a*) f. 9ᵛ ends at 'Ps. Benedictus' at the end of the Friday ferial office (ii. 169). f. 10 begins in Septuagesima Sunday 'ram et spiritus' (i. ccclxxxvi/8). f. 79ᵛ ends in Easter Monday, 'Dicat nunc israel quoni-' followed by the catchword 'am bonus' (i. dcccxxviii). f. 80 begins in the twentieth Sunday after Trinity 'rant non fuerunt' (i. mccccxxxix/3). (*b*) ends imperfectly 'iacob erigebat lapidem in' (i. mccccclxxxii/47). (*c*) begins at Ps. 17: 49. f. 100ᵛ ends at Ps. 49: 9. f. 101 begins in Ps. 73: 7. Antiphons noted. (*e*) 'eam redemptori . . . pandere dignatus sit' (i. mcccclxxii/15–22). f. 136ᵛ left blank.

2 (added in a current hand, s. xv). f. 136ᵛ (*a*) Alma virgo virginum Intercede pro nobis ad dominum . . . (*b*) Pura pudica pia miseris miserere maria . . . det nobis gaudia vite (9 lines).

ff. ii+136+ii. 165 × 105 mm. Written space c. 112 × 70 mm. 2 cols. 33 lines. Twenty-three quires, all perhaps eights, except 11⁶, but only quires 2, 4, 11, and 22 are now complete (ff. 2–9, 17–24, 63–68, 122–9). Initials: (i) on now missing leaves; (ii) ff. 20ᵛ, 24, 37, 74ᵛ, 4-line, pink patterned in white on blue grounds patterned in white and decorated in gold and colours; (iii) 2-line, gold on blue and pink grounds patterned in white, but the letter *I* tends to be a dragon or monster or fish in colours with a touch of gold on the back;

(iv) 1-line, gold with pale-blue ornament or blue with red ornament. Almost every column has ornament down its length, even where there is not an initial of types (ii) or (iii) to which it can be attached: ivy leaf, oak leaf, or acorn terminals, and here and there a grotesque. Capital letters in the ink of the text stroked with red. Dark-brown calf by D(ouglas) C(ockerell), dated 1902.

Written in England. 'Thomas Oseley os thys boke', f. 136ᵛ, s. xv ex. 'By me Francis Mathewes', f. 39. 'Be(r)nardus Mathewes', 'Dundalke', and a man and horse, f. 136, all of s. xvi/xvii. 'R. Ranshaw', f. i, s. xix/xx. Bequeathed by A. G. W. Murray, librarian 1913–19.

O. 10a. 27. *Horae*   s. xv/xvi

1. ff. 1–6ᵛ Calendar in gold, blue, red, and black, the three colours alternating for effect.

'Sancti laudi episcopi. Mat' ' and 'Dyonisii episcopi' in gold, 21 Sept. and 9 Oct. 'Dedicacio ecclesie Const' ', 12 July. 'Reliquiarum constan' ', 30 Sept., with octave. Each month is laid out in two columns and occupies the last seventeen lines on the page. The upper 55 mm on each page were probably intended for a double picture of the occupation of the month and sign of the zodiac, but remain blank.

2. ff. 7–9ᵛ Sequentiae of the Gospels.

The prayer 'Protector in te sperantium . . .' follows John.

3. ff. 9ᵛ–14 Passio domini nostri iesu cristi. Secundum Iohannem. Egressus est . . . posuerunt iesum. Deo gracias. Oremus. Deus qui manus tuas . . .

St. John, chapters xviii, xix. ff. 14–16ᵛ were left blank.

4. ff. 17–37ᵛ Hours of B.V.M., beginning imperfectly and lacking many leaves. Hours of the Cross are worked in.

5. ff. 38–48ᵛ Penitential psalms and (f. 43ᵛ) litany.

Ursinus is listed as a disciple. Twenty-two confessors: . . . (6–9) Sanson germane audoene gerobolde. The lists of martyrs, confessors, and virgins end with three blanks, only 'Sancte' ('Sancta') being written.

6. ff. 48ᵛ–66ᵛ Office of the dead.

7. ff. 67–9 Memoriae of Holy Trinity, Holy Face (Salue sancta facies . . .: *RH*, no. 18189) and Holy Cross.

8. ff. 69–70ᵛ Obsecro te . . . For male use.

9. ff. 70ᵛ–72ᵛ O intemerata . . . orbis terrarum. De te enim . . . For male use.

10. ff. 74–86ᵛ Memoriae of SS. Michael, John Baptist, John Evangelist, Peter and Paul, James, N. and N. apostles, Stephen, Laurence, Christopher, Sebastian, Denis, Eustace (O eustachi princeps milicie . . .), Cosmas and Damian, N. and N. martyrs, Martin, Nicholas, Claude, Anthony hermit (Anthoni pastor inclite qui cruciatos reficis . . .: *RH*, no. 1203), Laudus, Julian, Eloi, Maur, Fiacre, Germain, N. and N. confessors, Anne, Maria Jacobi and Maria Salome (O nobile ternarium sanctarum sororum trium . . .: *RH*, no. 13323; *AH* xv. 233), Mary Magdalene, Katherine, Margaret, Barbara (Gaude barbara beata summe

pollens in doctrina . . .: *RH*, no. 6711), Appolonia, Susanna, Genovefa, Avia.
ff. 87–88ᵛ left blank.

11. Three of the pieces added in s. xvi in blank spaces on ff. 14–16ᵛ, 66ᵛ, 86ᵛ–88ᵛ
are in French: (*a*) f. 87ʳᵛ Vierge dousce vierge benigne vierge saincte vierge
tres digne . . .; (*b*) f. 87ᵛ Ie te salue marie tressaincte mere de dieu . . .; (*c*) f. 88ᵛ
Iesus soit en ma teste et en mon entendement . . .

(*a*). 28 lines for Geneviève: Sonet, no. 2314. (*c*). 5 lines: Sonet, no. 991.

ff. iii+88+iii. ff. ii, iii, 89, 90 are parchment end-leaves: see below. 200×182 mm.
Written space *c*. 127×72 mm. 23 long lines. Ruling with red ink. Collation: 1⁶ 2¹⁰ 3⁸
wants 1 (ff. 17–23) 4⁸ wants 1 before f. 24 and 7, 8, perhaps blank, after f. 28 5 three (ff. 29–
31) 6 six (ff. 32–7) 7⁸ 8⁸ wants 6 after f. 50 9–12⁸ 13⁴. Written in *lettre bâtarde*. 16-line
pictures intended, but not executed, before arts. 3, 5, 6 (ff. 10, 38, 48ᵛ) and before the
memoria of St. Martin on f. 79; so too, smaller pictures before the other memoriae (arts. 7,
10) and before art. 8 (cf. also art. 1). Initials: (i–iii) 3-line, 2-line, and 1-line, in grisaille
on grounds of decorated gold paint. A broad framed floral border the height of the written
space in the outer margin of all pages where there was to be a picture and on some other
pages: twenty-eight of them remain. Binding of s. xviii. Secundo folio (f. 8) *in seculum*.

Written in France for use in the diocese of Coutances. Inscribed in s. xvi: 'Matines a
lusage de Coustance', f. iii; 'Ces heures sont et appartiennent a Madamoiselle de la
Blondeliere 1595', f. iii; 'Iste liber ad dominum dorual attinet', f. iii; 'Pour damoiselle
guillemette michel', ff. 89ᵛ, 90. Armorial book-plate of Bulman, s. xix, inside the cover:
motto 'Patienter'. Bequeathed as O. 10a. 26.

O. 11. 11. *Brut Chronicle (in English)* s. xv²

How this lond was first callid Albion and of whom it hadde that name ye shall
here as foloweth aftirward. In þe yeer fro þe begynnyng of þe worlde mˡmˡmˡ ixᶜ
lxxxx there was in the noble lond of grece a worthi kyng and a myghty and a
man of greet Renoun that was callid Dioclician . . . (f. 3ᵛ) In the noble Cite of
grete Troie . . . (f. 130ᵛ) wherof vii were dedly 'y dar say no mor''.

An abbreviated Brut Chronicle (ed. Brie, EETS 131, 136, 1906–8), ending with the murder
of James I of Scotland in 1437. Chapter numbers begin with 'I' on f. 3ᵛ and cease with
'CXXVI' on f. 103ᵛ (edn., ch. 242). After ch. 54, death of Arthur, a page, f. 37ʳ, was left
blank, and from f. 60ᵛ, accession of William II, a new reign always begins on a new page.
f. 68ᵛ ends in ch. 95, 'to the kyng prayyng him in goodly' (cf. edn., p. 158) and f. 69 begins
with the first words of the story of Henry III: probably seven leaves are missing in the gap.
One leaf is missing between f. 88 which ends 'þe kyng of Cipris' (edn., p. 315/20) and f. 89
which begins 'vndertook þe quarell' (cf. edn., p. 319/13). The story of Henry V is much
shortened, taking only eight leaves (120ᵛ–128ᵛ). f. 129ᵛ begins 'Aftir the noble and vic-
torious prince kyng Harri þe v regned his sone' (cf. edn., p. 563).

The blank space on f. 130 bears doodles and a note of s. xvi, 'Thys same (?) dyd master
Iohn ardyns sunⁿs honde at bartylmatyde (*cancelled*) wrytyng of henly (?) at bartyll-
madyde'. ff. 131ᵛ–132ᵛ are blank, except for a prayer and a 'thanksgiueing for Deliverance
from any Danger', s. xvi/xvii.

ff. iii+132+iii. 260×180 mm. Written space *c*. 173×100 mm. 28 long lines. Collation:
1–8⁸ 9⁸ wants 5–8 after f. 68 10⁶ wants 1–3 before f. 69 11–12⁸ 13⁸ wants 2 after f. 88
14–16⁸ 17⁸ wants 7, 8, blank. Traces of signatures suggest that the series began with *a* on

quire 2.[1] Written in a secretary hand, the same throughout. 2-line blue initials with red ornament. Binding of s. xviii. Secundo folio *mende*.

Written in England. 'Catal. A N° 170 (*altered to* 109)' and 'N. 26' inside the cover, both of s. xix. Loscombe sale, 19 June 1854, lot 1146, to Upham and Bête (£16) and sold by them to Lord Ashburnham. Ashburnham Appendix 109 in his 1897 catalogue: 'Appendix' sale, 1 May 1899, lot 58 to Leighton (£5. 10s.). Label of George Dunn, of Woolley Hall, near Maidenhead, inside the cover: his sale, 11 Feb. 1913, lot 443. Bequeathed as O. 10a. 26.

R. 15. 38. *Verses in Italian*   s. xv med.

O increata maestra diddio / o infinita eterna potenza . . . beni di uita eterna.

244 8-line stanzas on the Passion, four to a page, rhyming *ababab cc*. Probably three leaves are missing. f. 31ᵛ blank.

ff. ii+31+ii. Paper. Traces of a contemporary foliation, preceded by *C* (for *Carta*). 278×208 mm. Written space *c.* 260 mm high. Collation: ff. 18–27 is a 10 and ff. 28–31 a 6, wanting 5 and 6; the presence of a parchment strip between f. 4 and f. 5 and formerly between f. 12 and f. 13, a catchword on f. 9ᵛ, and the fact that the only distinctly legible old leaf number is '25' on f. 22, show that ff. 1–17 (which have been mended) were two 10s, the first wanting one leaf in the first half and the second one leaf in each half. Written in a round cursiva. Initial *O* on f. 1, 4-line, blue, patterned in white, with red ornament. Binding of s. xviii.

Written in Italy. '4566' top left of f. 1, s. xviii. Said in a modern note to have belonged to Robert Bridges, 1658–1725, and to be from (the collection of Sir F. S. Powell Bt. at) Horton Old Hall, Bradford.[2] Given by the Revd. C. L. Hulbert Powell, Hon. Canon of Ely, in Sept. 1941.

R. 17. 22. *Missale*   s. xvi in.

1. ff. 1–6ᵛ Calendar in red and black, not graded.

Feasts in red include 'Dedicatio ecclesie beate marie', Benedict, 'Claudii abbatis', 'Translatio sancti Martini', 'Translatio sancti benedicti abbatis' (14 Feb., 21 Mar., 6 June, 4, 11 July).

2. f. 7ʳᵛ Sequitur quomodo induitur sacerdos primum ad amictum oracio. Pone domine galeam salutis in capite meo . . . in conspectu domini.

Nineteen prayers by the officiating priest before and during mass, the last 'Vertendo ad populum'.

3. ff. 8–145ᵛ Temporale from Advent to the twenty-fourth Sunday after the octave of Pentecost.

The litany on ff. 84–5 is not subdivided under apostles, martyrs, etc., but in one single list. Thirty-two martyrs and confessors: . . . (4–8) babila foca fructuose alexander yppipodi . . . Nine virgins: petronilla simphorosa eugenia basilla domitilla dorotea anthonia emilia leonilla. 'correctum est' in pencil at the end of some quires.

---

[1] The series +, a . . . is not uncommon. Cf. *MMBL*, i. 427, and below, Eton College, 117.

[2] Manuscripts and printed books from Horton Old Hall were sold at Sotheby's, 16 Dec. 1929, lots 664–832.

4. ff. 146–7 Gloria in excelsis and Credo in unum deum.

Three versions of Gloria, the second having additional phrases referring to B.V.M., and the third the additional phrases 'Saluatio nostra Christe benigne qui hortaris ut precemur' and 'Munda corda accende in te desideria nostra qui regnas'. f. 147ᵛ blank.

5. ff. 150–163ᵛ Noted prefaces, including one of St. Andrew, and canon of mass.

6. ff. 163ᵛ–164 Six settings of Gloria in excelsis. f. 164ᵛ blank.

7. ff. 165–210ᵛ Incipiunt misse sanctorum tocius anni. Et primo de sanctis qui ueniunt in decembri post natiuitatem domini. In nat' sancti stephani. . . .

Thirty-four proper offices ending with Thomas the apostle. Includes Claude (f. 187ᵛ), Benedict (f. 181ᵛ), and the translation of Benedict (f. 193ᵛ): cf. art. 1.

8. ff. 211–19 Incipit commune sanctorum.

9. ff. 219–22 Mass of B.V.M.

10. f. 222ʳᵛ Missa de cruce.

11. ff. 222ᵛ–228ᵛ In agenda mortuorum.

12. ff. 228ᵛ–235ᵛ Votive masses (collect, secret, and postcommunion only) of SS. Martin (two forms) and Benedict (two forms), for peace, of a confessor, of SS. John Baptist, Mary Magdalene, All Saints, Ad sancti spiritus graciam postulandam, Pro temptacione carnis, Pro sacerdote (two forms), Pro abbate uel pro congregacione sibi commissa, Pro salute viuorum (two forms), Pro iter agentibus, Pro pace, In tempore belli, Pro inimicis ecclesie, Pro peticione lacrimarum, De quacumque tribulatione, Ad pluuiam postulandam, Pro infirmis, Pro patre et matre, Pro amico deffuncto, Pro hiis qui in cimitterio requie(scant).

13. ff. 235ᵛ–236ᵛ Mass 'tempore pestis et epidimie'.

14 (added, s. xvi in.). f. 237 Collect, secret, and postcommunion for the soul 'famule tue'. ff. 237ᵛ, 238ʳᵛ blank.

---

ff. 238. A medieval foliation in red I–CXXXVIII on ff. 8–145 and CXXXIX–CCX[I] on ff. 165–237. 465 × 320 mm. Written space 285 × 190 mm. 2 cols. 26 lines (long lines on ff. 7, 150–64). Collation: 1⁸ wants 8, perhaps blank 2–18⁸ 19–21² (ff. 144–9) 22–23⁶ (ff. 150–61) 24⁴ wants 4, blank, after f. 164 25–28⁸ 29⁶ (ff. 197–202) 30–33⁸ 34⁶ wants 4, 5: 6, f. 238, is pasted down. Signatures begin with a on f. 8 and with aa (?) on f. 165. Two full-page pictures form a double opening, ff. 148ᵛ–149: on the verso the Crucifixion and on the recto God the Father enthroned, backed by the heavenly host, flanked by evangelists and, above, angels playing musical instruments. Seventeen smaller pictures, mostly c. 140 × 84 mm, nine in art. 3 before Advent, Christmas, Epiphany, Palm Sunday, Easter, Ascension, Pentecost, Trinity, Corpus Christi (procession), seven in art. 7 before Stephen, Purification of B.V.M., Benedict, Annunciation of B.V.M., John Baptist, Assumption of B.V.M., Martin, and one before art. 8. Initials: (i) f. 158ᵛ, historiated *T* of *Te igitur*; (ii–iv) 4-line, 3-line, and 2-line, in colours and gold paint on grounds of the same or of gold,¹ showing much variation and invention: heads often peep from between broken branches. Line fillers red or blue, or of both colours, patterned in gold paint. Capital letters in the ink of the text stroked with pale yellow. Continuous borders on

¹ Gold is used mainly as a background to blue initials.

picture pages, sometimes on compartmented grounds. Short borders beside initials of types (ii, iii). Binding of s. xviii, pale-green leather with gilt fillets and cornerpieces. Secundo folio (f. 9) *dictus qui*.

Written in France for a church of B.V.M. Art. 14 suggests female use. Arms in the border of four picture pages, 8, 17ᵛ, 22, 86ᵛ, and on f. 156 are sable a Latin cross or, a crozier behind.[1] A strip cut from the foot of ff. 1, 15. 'Presented by Dame Maria Newberry to her kinsman Edmund Kershaw, Clerk in Holy Orders, M.A. Trin.: Coll: Cam: June 1865', inside the cover. 'The gift of the Revᵈ Edmund Dickie Kershaw M.A. late of Trinity College', but the actual transference to Trinity was in 1909 after Mrs. Kershaw's death, 'in accordance with her husband's desire', as appears from a letter of W. J. Jeaffreson dated 30 Mar. 1909: this letter and another from Jeaffreson, 22 June 1909, are kept with the manuscript.

R. 17. 23. *Augustine, De Civitate Dei, bks. 11–22 (in French)*

s. xv²

Cy commence la seconde (*cancelled*) partie de la translacion et exposicion du liure de monseigneur saint augustin de la cite de dieu translate et expose par maistre Raoul de praelles scelon et par la maniere que contenu est en son pro-logue sur la premiere partie. Combien que au commencement. . . . (f. 424ᵛ) et que nostre mere sainte eglise en tient. Ceste Translacion et exposicion fu com-mencee par maistre Raoul de praelles a la tous sains lan de grace mil ccc lxxi. Et fu acheuee le premier Iour de septembre lan de grace mil lxxv. deo gracias.

Printed in 1486 (*GKW* 2891). A table of 'Rubriches' precedes each book. Bks. 16, 17 are imperfect at the end and bks. 17, 18 at the beginning, as a result of the loss of four leaves. ff. 425–428ᵛ blank. The binder misplaced the paper leaves of quire 8 in quire 11 and vice versa. *Signes de renvoi* on ff. 97ᵛ, 102, 122, 125ᵛ and notices on f. 97ᵛ 'faulte de relier queres oulc' xxiiii feulles a cel signe' and on f. 125ᵛ 'retournes xxiiii arriere a tel figur', draw atten-tion to this mistake.

ff. i+426+i, foliated 1–282, 285–(428). Paper, except the outermost and central bifolia in quires 2–36 and the two outermost bifolia and the central bifolium in quire 1. 493 × 285 mm. Written space *c.* 290 × 195 mm. 2 cols. *c.* 46 lines. Frame ruling. Collation: 1–11¹² 12¹⁴ 13¹⁰ 14–15¹² 16¹² wants 6, 7 after f. 185 17–18¹² 19¹² wants 6, 7 after f. 219 20–23¹² 24¹⁰ 25–29¹² 30¹⁴ 31–35¹² 36¹² wants 7, 12, blanks. Written in current hybrida. A picture before each book and before the prologue in front of part 2 (f. 1): the size is *c.* 200 × 195 mm on f. 2ᵛ (bk. 11) and elsewhere *c.* 120 × 90 mm (column width). On ff. 1, 2ᵛ St. Augustine is at work. The scribe managed so that all the pictures came on parch-ment leaves and most of them at the head of a column, where they could be given a rounded top. Initials: (i) 6-line, blue patterned in white on decorated gold grounds; (ii) 2-line, blue with red ornament or gold with violet ornament. Capital letters in the ink of the text filled with yellow. A continuous framed floral border in gold and colours on picture pages. Binding uniform with R. 17. 22: 'Manuscript tres precieux' and '1023' on the spine in gold. Secundo folio *felicite*.

Written in France. 'Pour nostre dame' in gold at the foot of f. 1, s. xv (?). The relevant cutting from a French sale catalogue, s. xviii, is pasted to a piece of writing paper laid down on f. iᵛ, on which E. D. Kershaw wrote a note dated 30 June 1865: '. . . In 1793 it was bought at Lord Hardwick's sale and has recently come into my possession . . .'. Bequeathed as R. 17. 22.

[1] The arms of the Cistercian nunnery of Ounans, Jura, were sable a Latin cross or, according to J. Meugey, *Armorial de l'Église de France*, 134.

CAMBRIDGE. UNIVERSITY LIBRARY

Catalogues, etc.

Charles Hardwick and H. R. Luard, *A Catalogue of the Manuscripts preserved in the Library of the University of Cambridge.* 5 vols. and an index vol. 1856–67.

J. C. T. Oates and H. L. Pink, 'Three Sixteenth-century Catalogues of the University Library', *Transactions of the Cambridge Bibliographical Society*, i (1953), 310–40.

Manuscripts in French are described by P. Meyer in *Romania*, xv (1886), 236–357.

C. Sayle, *Annals of Cambridge University Library*, 1916.

The Hardwick–Luard catalogue contains descriptions of just over 1,000 medieval western manuscripts, excluding Greek manuscripts. After its publication a new series of Additional Manuscripts was begun in 1859. At present this series contains over 350 medieval western manuscripts, excluding Greek manuscripts and collections of binding fragments. Descriptions of Additional Manuscripts by M. R. James and others are available on application to the staff and are being currently revised for eventual publication.

CANTERBURY. CATHEDRAL

C. E. Woodruff, *Catalogue of the Manuscript Books in the Library of Christ Church, Canterbury*, 1911.

Catalogue of the Books both Manuscript and Printed . . . in the Library of Christ Church, Canterbury. 1802.[1]

HMC, *Ninth Report*, pt. 1 (1883), App., pp. 125–8, refers to Lit. B. 4, 7, 8, 12, 13 (in with 7), D. 8, 10, E. 9, 13, 18.

Lit. A. 1 (65). s. xiii/xiv. Richard of Middleton on the fourth book of the Sentences of Peter Lombard (Stegmüller, *Sent.*, no. 722). ff. 190, foliated 3–192. Written space *c.* 305 × 180 mm. 2 cols. *c.* 70 lines. Collation: 1–15^{12} 16^{10}. Secundo folio *gracie uisibilis*.

Written in England. Belonged to Christ Church, Canterbury: no. 22 in Ingram's list of the chained library, A.D. 1508 (*Ancient Libraries*, p. 153). The words 'de perquisito fratris I de Fro' follow the colophon, f. 192^{v}: the donor was perhaps John de Frome, professed in 1337.

---

[1] The copy at St. Augustine's College, Canterbury, was given by H. J. Todd (1763–1845), who notes in it that the catalogue of the manuscripts (pp. 111–31) was his work in 1793 and the catalogue of the printed books mainly the work of David Wilkins (1685–1745).

Lit. A. 2 (11). s. xv. **1.** ff. 1–124 Notes and questions on canon law. **2.** ff. 126–144^v Alexander de S. Elpidio, O.E.S.A., Opusculum de ecclesiastica potestate, ending imperfectly. ff. 143. Paper. Written space *c.* 280 × 185 mm. Mainly in twelves (9–10^{14}, 12^{12} wants 8–12). Written in cursiva in Germany or the Netherlands. Secundo folio *appellabit ut nota*: identifiable, therefore, with the Christ Church, Canterbury, book called 'Noue questiones Iuris in paupiro', no. 242 in Ingram's list (*Ancient Libraries*, p. 161).[1]

1. Begins 'Prima nota quod ubi aliquis tenuit duo beneficia'. Up to f. 58 each paragraph begins 'Item nota'. A break at f. 119. Ends with two decrees: (f. 123) on leper hospitals, 'Quamuis super reformacione . . . Dat' Auinion' v kl' Septembris Anno Secundo. Sumpto de Registris domini Vrbani pape quinti (1362–70) existentibus in Archiuio palacii apostolici per me Iohannem de Baro'; (ff. 123–4) 'Gregorius . . . Ad futuram Rei memoriam nuper attendens quod sit nobis . . .', Avignon, 8 Jan. anno primo (Gregory XI: 1371). ff. 124^v–125^v blank. **2.** Zumkeller, no. 88. Printed in 1494 and later. B.L., Royal 7 E. x is another copy in England. The author was bishop of Melfi, 1325–8. The last words here are 'celebrandi hunc ordinem sacerdotalem', near the beginning of Tractatus 3.

Lit. A. 4 (16). s. xiv^1. (S. de Monte Calvo) Abbreviatio decretalium. ff. 140, foliated 3–142. Written space 295 × 175 mm by the first hand and *c.* 285 × 210 mm by the second. 2 cols. 70 lines. Eleven quires of 12 and a final 8. Written in England. The hand changes from a black textura to a brown anglicana at f. 75 (7^1), but the decoration remains the same. Secundo folio *factus fuit iustinianus*: identifiable, therefore, with the 'Sampson de Caluo Monte' at Christ Church, Canterbury, no. 250 in Ingram's list (*Ancient Libraries*, p. 161). Probably the 'Sampsonus de Calvo Monte' given by Thomas Chillenden (*Ancient Libraries*, p. 151).[2]

'Licet lectura domini hostiensis . . . In iiii vltimis C. e quod alii etc. Amen. Explicit iste liber sit scriptor a crimine liber. scripto Natiuitate cristi. Amen. Amen. Deo gracias etc. quod Io.'. For the compiler cf. Schulte, ii. 203. f. 143 is a binding leaf from Digestum Infortiatum, s. xiii ex. 2 cols. 51 lines.

Lit. A. 5–7 (45). s. xiii^1. Stephen Langton, Moralia on Isaiah, Jeremiah, Lamentations, Ezekiel (A. 5), Joshua, Judges, Ruth, 1–3 Kings, Esther, 1 Ezra, Nehemiah, 1, 2 Maccabees (A. 6), Minor Prophets (A. 7). ff. 56+62+48. Written space *c.* 265 × 165 mm. 2 cols. *c.* 87 lines. The first line of writing above the top ruled line. Collation: (A. 5) 1–2^{10} 3–6^8 7 seven; (A. 6, ff. 2–63) 1–2^8 3–4^{10} 5^8 6^{10} 7^8; (A. 7) 1^8 2–3^{10} 4^8 5^{12}. Written in England in a very small hand. 'Liber Willelmi Caperun' on the versos of the flyleaves in front of A. 5, 6: the former is now misplaced as f. 57. Three of the five volumes of Langton listed under the heading 'Libri Willelmi Capun (*sic*)' in the early fourteenth-century catalogue of Christ Church, Canterbury, and identifiable by the secundo folios *tamen martyr* (A. 5), *u(i)uant prelati* (A. 6), and *dicitur in trenis* (A. 7) with

[1] James gives the secundo folio of no. 242 wrongly as *appellabit ut uocant*.

[2] All but three of twenty-three books of canon law given by Chillenden (†1411: Emden, *BRUO*, p. 415) are probably identifiable in Ingram's list. They had a special claim to be among the books selected for chaining in the library room which prior Chillenden built in 1408. The only known survivors are the present volume and one at Sion College (*MMBL* i. 285), together with eight flyleaves in Trinity College, Cambridge, 154, and part of a leaf in Bodleian, Lat. misc. b. 12, f. 8.

entries in Ingram's list (*Ancient Libraries*, p. 107, nos. 1214–18; p. 154, nos. 37–9).

A. 5. Stegmüller, nos. 7817 (but the last words are 'in die quo noui'), 7829, 7832 (ending 'iacet prostratus'), 7834.

A. 6. Stegmüller, nos. 7749–54, 7776, 7759, 7760, 7778, 7780. 3 Kings (7754) ends imperfectly, f. 45ᵛ, and 4 Kings, Tobit, and Judith, all listed in the table of contents on f. 1ᵛ, are missing at this point. Another gap between quires 6 and 7 contained the end of Nehemiah, and the beginning of 1 Maccabees. Esther and 1, 2 Maccabees seem to be in the versions recorded by Stegmüller from Vienna 1466.

A. 7. Stegmüller, nos. 7843, 7844 (ends 'fuisse mundus'), 7845–6, 7847 (ends 'quod fiat sermo de dicto'), 7848 (?: ends abruptly in the lemma 'racemos uindemie', Micah 7: 1), 7856–61.

A new book often begins on a new page. A. 5 f. 28ᵛ, A. 6 ff. 9ʳ, 16ᵛ–17ᵛ, A. 7 f. 26ᵛ are blank.

The commentaries appear to correspond exactly with those in Peterhouse, Cambridge, MSS. 112, 119, as Miss Smalley noted of A. 6 in *Archives d'histoire doctrinale et littéraire du moyen âge*, v (1930), 174. In Peterhouse 119 the commentary on Micah only goes to the end of chapter 6, which suggests that it is derived from A. 7 rather than the other way round.

Lit. A. 8 (68). s. xii in. Augustinus, Sermones. ff. 152. Written space 260 × 190 mm. 2 cols. 43 lines. Nineteen quires of 8 leaves, lettered at the end. Secundo folio (f. 4) *tuus sermo*. From St. Augustine's, Canterbury, and probably written there: 'Augustinus de uerbis domini. ⸍cum B'. and 'liber sancti Augustini Cant' cum [. . .] Dist' iiii Gᵃ iii', f. 1ᵛ. The hand is excellent. *Ancient Libraries*, p. 222, no. 349.

Ninety-one sermons. 1–89 are 1–89 of the collection of ninety-nine genuine and supposititious sermons of St. Augustine known as De verbis Domini and De verbis Apostoli, which was put together not later than s. viii: cf. *RB* lvii. 109. This collection (1–23 on St. Matthew; 24–37 on St. Luke; 38 on 2 Corinthians 5: 10; 39–65 on St. John; 66, Contra Arrianos; 67–99 on Pauline Epistles) is set out by P. Verbraken in *RB* lxxvii. 27–32.[1] Sermon 90, 'Lectio diuina . . .', and sermon 91, 'Meminisse debet . . .' are *PL* xxxviii. 814 and 819 (sermons 151, 152): they follow sermons 1–89 also in B.L., Royal 5 C. viii, from Rochester.

ff. 1ʳᵛ, 152ᵛ were left blank. A table of the ninety-one sermons, misnumbered 1–93, is in the main hand on ff. 2–3. A late medieval foliation begins on f. 3 and the sermons were then numbered correctly 1–91. The main initials, on blue or purple grounds, are on ff. 3ᵛ, 41ᵛ, 56ᵛ (sermons 1, 24, 39).

Lit. A. 9 (75). s. xiii/xiv. Johannes Duns Scotus, Scriptum super primum librum Sententiarum Petri Lombardi. ff. 146. Written space 260 × 170 mm. 2 cols. 53 lines. Collation: 1–11¹² 12¹⁴. Belonged to Christ Church, Canterbury, and identifiable by the secundo folio *quod ex ente* with no. 29 in Ingram's list (*Ancient Libraries*, p. 153). Listed also in Ingram's binding record in MS. C.

---

[1] Verbraken lists 68 manuscripts. 29 of them lack the last 10 of the 99 sermons. Of these 29 manuscripts 7 are on the continent and 22 in England. Only 3 manuscripts now in England have sermons 90–9, Eton College 106 (q.v.), Harley 3028 (s. xii), and Bodleian, Rawlinson C. 88 (s. xv).

11 (27), f. 102^v: it was 'new bownd new bordyd short clasp' in or soon after 1508. 'Hic liber constat dompno Thome Humfrey custodi collegii Cantuariensis in Oxonia' (c. 1473–8: Emden, BRUO, p. 983).

Ordinatio I. Used for the Vatican edition where it is referred to as I and described in vol. i (1950), 37*–38*.

Lit. A. 12 (42). s. xiii^2. Hugh of St. Cher, Scriptum super quatuor libros Sententiarum Petri Lombardi. ff. 153. Written space 248×158 mm. 2 cols. 50–9 lines. Collation: 1^{12} 2^{14} 3^2 4–7^{12} 8–9^8 10^4 11–13^{12} 14^8 15^{14} wants 14, probably blank. Secundo folio *personarum. quomodo.* Written in France, probably. Belonged to Christ Church, Canterbury: 'Liber iste est Magistri Martini de Clyue Monachi ecclesie cristi Cant' (†1301) quem perquisiuit et eidem ecclesie dedit. Et est scriptum satis bonum super . . .', f. iii^v. No. 1597 in Eastry's catalogue and no. 20 in Ingram's (*Ancient Libraries*, pp. 132, 153).

Stegmüller, *Sent.*, no. 372. Glorieux, no. 2a. Bk. 2, f. 29; 3, f. 61; 4, f. 97. One scribe wrote bks. 2, 3 and from f. 107^v in bk. 4, another wrote bk. 1, and a third the first 10½ leaves of bk. 4.

Lit. A. 13 (74). s. xiv^1. 1. ff. 6–118^v Scotus on the first book of Sentences of Peter Lombard. 2. ff. 118^v–125 Scotus on bk. 1, dist. 26, repeating ff. 93^v–96^v. 3. ff. 125–127^v 'Questio Magistri Henrici de Herkley de operibus sex dierum.' Utrum mundus totus quantum ad omnes partes . . . (and, f. 127^v, a question, 'Utrum in creatura fuit idem esse et essencia'). 4. ff. 128–175^v Scotus on bk. 3, ending imperfectly. 5. ff. 2–5 Utrum paradisus terrestris sit locus conueniens habitacioni hominum. arguitur primo quod non. locus ille . . . (*ends abruptly?: f. 5^v left blank*). 6. ff. 176–9, flyleaves, s. xii^2, canticles of the psalter, with a commentary. ff. iv+175+iv. Written space c. 260×155 mm. 2 cols. 62 lines. ff. 6–175 are fourteen quires of 12, together with two leaves at the end of quire 10 (ff. 126–7). Secundo folio (f. 7) *Ad confirmacionem.*

Written in England. 'Scotus' (*over erasure*) super primum librum et tercium Sentenciarum cum collacionibus eiusdem 'domini Iacobi de Oxeney' (*over erasure*) doctoris sacre pagine. '[. . .] Henrici de hark' quondam cancellarii oxonie De operibus sex dierum et de relaci[. . . .] pret' xx^{ti} et vnius solidorum', f. 5^v. The original part of the inscription is in a handsome hand, s. xiv^1: for Oxney, monk of Christ Church, Canterbury, c. 1361 and evidently not the first owner, see Emden, BRUO, p. 1416. No. 27 in Ingram's list (*Ancient Libraries*, p. 153).

1, 4. Ordinatio I, III. Used for the Vatican edition and referred to as C: described in vol. i (1950), 30*–31*. 2. Cf. edn. at d. 26. A reader noted at the foot of f. 93^v in s. xv 'Istam questionem bene correctam require in fine primi libri'. 3. The first question is Harkley's q. 19 in MS. Borghes. 171 (*Studi e Testi*, xxxvii. 326). 5. On bk. 2, d. 17? 6. Confitebor, Ego dixi, Exultauit, Cantemus, as far as 'submersi sunt', Audite celi, from 'ac nouissima', Quicumque uult, as far as 'inmensus spiritus sanctus'. The commentary is usually that in Eadwine's Psalter, f. 262^v onwards, and the script is of the same sort as Eadwine's, but a bit later.

Damp has affected the leaves at the head. Damaged text on ff. 128–37 was restored in s. xv/xvi.

Lit. B. 1(73). s. xiii ex. **1.** Scotus, Ordinatio super quartum librum Sententiarum Petri Lombardi. **2.** f. 124 Scocia plange quia periit tua gloria clara . . . quem sic tulit equor. ff. 125, foliated 2–126. Written space 240×170 mm. 2 cols. 58 lines. Collation: 1–6¹⁰ 7⁸+1 leaf before 1 8–12¹⁰ 13⁶. Secundo folio *intendendo*.

Written in England (?). Ex-libris, s. xiv, of the Cistercian abbey of Whalley lightly cancelled, f. 1ᵛ: 'Iste liber procuratus fuit Monasterio de Whalleye per fratrem Willelmum de Singleton quondam scolarem dicti loci. quem quicumque a dicta domo alienauerit anathema sit amen'. Alienated by s. xv and pledged in Oxford loan chests in 1455, 1457, and 1465 (f. 125: cf. Emden, *BRUO*, under James Harington and Robert Paslew) and together with three supplements for five marks in [. . . .] and 1473 (f. 126ᵛ): the supplements were Augustine, De civitate Dei, the Prima secunde of St. Thomas and Questiones de potencia et malo. 'Liber magistri Thome Dryffeld qui debet dompno Roberto Estry monacho ecclesie cristi Cant' liii s' iiii d' ', f. 1ᵛ: Dryffeld and Estry were both at Oxford in 1474–6 (cf. *BRUO*, pp. 597, 621) and it seems possible that this book came to Estry as part payment of the debt.

1. The colophon, f. 124, is 'Expliciunt questiones super 4ᵐ sentenciarum disputate a subtili doctore fratre Io. Scoto ordinis fratrum Minorum. Deo gracias'. The scribe wrote 'Principium medium finem regat alma Maria' at the head of f. 1.

Lit. B. 3 (15). s. xiii². **1.** ff. 3–49 Incipit liber primus . . . Gregorius episcopus etc. In hoc prologo assignat dominus papa iiiiᵒʳ causas . . . (f. 49) quis homagium compellatur. Explicit summa nouarum decretalium . . . (f. 49ᵛ) Expliciunt decretalium tituli domini gregorii noni. **2.** ff. 50–180 Summa domini goffredi de trano super rubricis decretalium. Glosarum diuersitas . . . ff. 181, foliated 3–183. Written space *c.* 235×140 mm. 2 cols. 57–61 lines. Collation: 1–3¹² 4¹⁰ 5–10¹² 11¹²+2 leaves inserted after 10 to mend an omission in bk. 3 (ff. 132–3) 12–15¹². f. 32 is an added slip. Secundo folio *Significauit*.

Written in England. Belonged to Christ Church, Canterbury: 'Summa decretalium cum summa Gaufredi H. de Depham' and 'Secunde demonstracionis' on the flyleaf, f. 1. No. 1493 in Eastry's catalogue and no. 217 in Ingram's (*Ancient Libraries*, pp. 125, 160).

1. B.L., Royal 11 A. ii, art. 3, is another copy of this summary of the Decretals of Gregory IX. Verses, 'Pars prior officia . . .' (5 lines) and 'Quatuor hiis verbis . . .' (2 lines) and a note beginning 'Iste consuetudines et decretales sciri debent ab omnibus regularibus scilicet . . .' are in a blank space on f. 49ᵛ. **2.** G. de Trano, †1245. Schulte, ii. 88. Often printed.

A new hand at f. 37 and at f. 50 (5¹). The scribe wrote at the end 'Gloria sit cristo. de cuius munere sisto'.

Lit. B. 4 (13). s. xiv. **1.** ff. 1–66 Incipit apparatus Iohannis de Aton' super constitucionibus Othonis. Ad succindendos palmites pestiferos . . . vlt' in constitucione cle. **2.** ff. 67–126 Incipit glosa Iohannis de Aton' super constitucionibus Ottoboni. Mandata dei et lex altissimi . . . ecclesiastici vndecimo capitulo. . . . Explicit expliciat labore scriptor eat. ff. 126. Written space

215×145 mm. 50 long lines. Fifteen quires, eights except 8¹⁰ (ff. 57–66), 15¹². Written in anglicana. Identifiable by the secundo folio *legitur et notatur* with no. 221 in Ingram's list of the chained library of Christ Church, Canterbury (*Ancient Libraries*, p. 160): cf. also below.

Texts of the constitutions of 1237 and 1268 (Wilkins, *Concilia* (1737), i. 649, ii. 1), with the commentaries of J. de Athona (Emden, *BRUO*, p. 11, Acton) printed after Lyndwood, Oxford 1679, and earlier. f. 126ʳᵛ has a table of rubrics preceded by ten lines of verse, 'Vt triples sensum quem gestant dicte figure / Dic cephas vsum glosantis Aton' memorari . . .'. Added running titles and rubric numbers 1–29 in art. 1 and 1–45 in art. 2: on f. 126, beside the last number, is 'per I. Wodnysbergh' cotacio fit totalis' (cf. Emden, *BRUO*, p. 2074: professed 1413, †1457). Many marginalia in art. 1, among them 'War thys' (f. 25), 'Loke' (f. 26), 'Loke thys' (f. 28). f. 66ᵛ blank.

Lit. B. 6 (4). s. xiii in. **1.** ff. 2–29ᵛ Incipit Solatium fidelis anime. Rerum subtilium fugas . . . **2.** ff. 30–405 Bible. **3.** ff. 1ᵛ, 333ʳᵛ, 405ᵛ Verses added on the flyleaf and in blank spaces. ff. 404, foliated 2–405. Written space: of **1**, 233 × 163 mm in 2 cols. of 40 lines; of **2**, 190×128 mm in 2 cols. of 46–53 lines. Writing above top ruled line. Collation: 1–3⁸ 4 four (ff. 26–9) 5–17¹² 18¹⁰ 19¹⁰ wants 8 blank after f. 204 20–29¹² 30¹⁰ wants 8 blank after f. 333 31–36¹². Secundo folio *eiusdem* (f. 3) or *or eius* (f. 31).

Written in England. 'Biblia Thome de Banchest*er* cum c. D. 1 Gᵃ 2', on f. 1ᵛ, formerly the verso of the pastedown, shows that this is no. 17 in the late medieval catalogue of St. Augustine's, Canterbury (*Ancient Libraries*, p. 197: Biblia Thome Bransester et in eodem tractatus moralis super Genesim 2° fo in textu *or eius*. D. 1 G. 1, *altered to* 2). Given by Sir John Wilde, s. xvii.

1. A commentary on Genesis 1: 1–2: 15: only this copy known to Stegmüller (no. 8987). **2.** The order is Genesis–2 Chronicles, Job, Psalms, five sapiential books, Isaiah–Malachi, Ezra, Nehemiah, Tobit, Judith, Esther, 1, 2 Maccabees, Gospels, Acts, Pauline Epistles, Catholic Epistles, Apocalypse. Psalms, Proverbs, and Matthew begin new quires, ff. 186, 205, 334: ff. 185ᵛ, 203–204ᵛ, 331ᵛ–333ᵛ were left blank. **3.** The main piece is on f. 333ʳᵛ, 148 lines on the Gospels, chapter by chapter, beginning 'Matheus non ut lucas fert ordine recto' and ending 'prandent amo set sic'. Short pieces are: f. 1ᵛ Quinque libros moysi . . . (5: Walther, no. 16027); f. 405ᵛ Regula prima caput . . . (7: W., no. 16552), Totum per partes uel summa . . . (3), Argue quadratim . . . (6), Auctores uarios confer . . . (2), Apta metafora . . . (5), Quadruplicem sensum si litera postulet adde . . . (5), Effectus causas quod . . . (2).

Lit. B. 7 (57, ii). s. xi/xii. Diversorum patrum sentencie de primatu Romanę ecclesię. Si difficile et ambiguum. apud te iudicium esse . . . cui obedire contempnis. ff. 91, foliated 1–41, 43–92. Written space 180×115 mm. 38 long lines. Collation: 1–11⁸ 12⁴ wants 4, probably blank. Secundo folio *precedente*. Written in French hands.

As far as f. 73ᵛ this is a collection in four books, of which 1–3 are an augmented rearrangement of the text ed. J. T. Gilchrist, *Diversorum patrum sententiae, sive collectio in lxxiv itulos digesta*, Mon. jur. can., Series B, Corpus Collectionum, vol. 1, 1973: twelve copies known. A quotation from Isidore and sixteen lines beginning 'De uindicta non proibenda in nouo testamento' are on the last leaf in two possibly English hands, s. xii in.

Lit. B. 8 (50). A.D. 1465. R. Lull, etc. **1.** ff. 2–8ᵛ Deus cum virtute tua . . . Protinus ut ars et sciencia transmutatoria quam in precedenti libro . . . **2.** ff. 9–26

Incipit tractatus de questionibus figure . . . **3**. ff. 26ᵛ–29 Sequuntur questiones pauline et olimpiadis. **4**. ff. 29–32ᵛ Sequuntur disputaciones inter Raymundum et monachum. Cum Raymundus . . . **5**. ff. 33–53 . . . Anima artis transmutatorie . . . Fulgeat regis dyadema . . . **6**. ff. 53ᵛ–112ᵛ . . . Incipit liber de famulatu philosophie pauperibus euangelicis viris erogatus. Dixit Salomon. Sapienc' capitulo 7°. Deus dedit . . . **7**. ff. 113–17 Composicio balsami rectissimi artificialis. Recipe mirre . . . **8**. ff. 119ᵛ–127 Incipit kalendare iudiciale de hominis natiuitate. prohemium. Secundum philosophorum ducem primo metheororum . . . (f. 127) Hic incipit canon predicti kalendarii. Si fiat questio de natiuitate viri . . . (f. 127) De fortitudine planetarum. Nunc autem de signis. quedam fortitudines . . . (f. 129) De natura et motibus planetarum. Septem sunt planete . . . virtutem contrariam habentis. Anno domini 1465. Explicit liber de signis et planetis cum eorum kalendario. **9**. ff. 132–7 Si quis cupit habere colloquium cum angelo suo bono . . . Explicit angelicum volumen. **10**. f. 137ʳᵛ Recipes 'pro scabie' and a charm 'Pro spasmo' added early. **11**. ff. 32ᵛ, 117ᵛ–119, 120ᵛ, 131ᵛ, 138ʳᵛ Recipes and (ff. 118–19) 'Proprietates auri potabilis' added in s. xv/xvi.
ff. 138. Paper and parchment. Written space 195 × 115 mm. 27 long lines. Quires of 10 leaves (12 nine (ff. 111–19): wants 14¹⁰, probably blank), signed +, a–l, l, m. Written in England in fere textura. For colophons see below.

'Iste liber vocatur. Liber maioris voluminis secretorum. et cetera', f. 1. Table of contents printed by Woodruff, f. 1ᵛ. **1–6** are alchemical texts listed by Singer and Anderson: (1) no. 255. xiv; (2) nos. 255. xx, 1111. xlvi; (3) no. 60; (4) no. 255. iv; (5) no. 253. xi; (6) no. 292. ix (J. de Rupescissa, De consideratione quintae essentiae, ascribed here to Lull: bk. 2 begins on f. 95ᵛ). **8**. Cf. Thorndike and Kibre. The calendar (Sarum) is on ff. 121–126ᵛ, but is empty after July. **9**. Prayers to the guardian angel and for protection by angels and (f. 135) a prayer reciting the holy names, 'Rogo te agyos pater luminum . . .'. **11**. The pieces on ff. 117ᵛ–119 and the figures of alchemical apparatus on f. 131ᵛ are Singer and Anderson, nos. 475, 447ᴬ.

Arts. **1, 2, 4–6, 8** are dated at the end 1465: **4** was completed on 30 July and **5** on 8 Aug. The scribe names himself three times, f. 32, 'per D.R.' and ff. 95, 112ᵛ 'per manus D. R.': Mrs. Singer suggests that he is 'David Ragor Cambrensis nacionis' whose name is in the text on f. 94 of B.L., Add. 15449. A memorandum on f. 138ᵛ of fourteen books 'of my maisters laft at hillysdon at his departing' is printed by Woodruff: the present volume is perhaps one of the 'v bokis of Raymunde'.

Lit. B. 9 (104). s. xiv in. A 'postilla' (notes and sermons) on Isaiah, chapter by chapter, with a brief introduction beginning 'Sustulit me in spiritu in montem mangnum et altum.et cetera . . . nota quod per sacram scripturam tanquam per speculum possumus considerare'. ff. 517, including flyleaves, 1, 516, 517, and four slips, 157, 196, 199, 420, which are omitted from a medieval foliation 1–510. The parchment varies in size, and many sheets, but not usually the outside sheet of each quire, are faulty. Written space c. 180 × 140 mm in 28–35 long lines. Collation of ff. 2–515, excluding the four numbered slips: 1⁶ 2–6⁸ 7¹² 8¹⁶ 9¹⁰ 10–12⁸ 13¹² 14–17⁸ 18¹² 19–20⁸ 21¹² 22–23⁸ 24⁶ 25–27⁸ 28–31¹² 32–34⁸ 35⁶ 36¹⁰ 37¹² 38⁶ 39⁸ 40¹² 41¹⁰ 42¹² wants 8, blank after f. 386 43 nine (ff. 390–8) 44¹² 45–51⁸ 52¹⁶ 53–56⁸. Secundo folio *cellam*.

Written in England in a broken-down textura, except ff. 84ᵛ–92 and some other pages and parts of pages, which are in a good business hand. 'Lectura super ysayam W. de Northwico', f. 1, s. xiv in.: identifiable, therefore, with the 'Lectura super Isaiam', no. 7 of nineteen 'Libri W. de Northwico' listed as an early addition to Eastry's catalogue of the books at Christ Church, Canterbury (*Ancient Libraries*, p. 141, no. 1810).

Home-made looking. W. de Northwico, †1328, may have been donor, author, and scribe. Some leaves, for example 102, 159, 227, seem to have been covered at first with now half-erased pencillings. A flyleaf and blank spaces contain added lists and an index: f. 1ᵛ, a list of nine sermons headed 'Nota sermones infra contentos'; f. 384, a list numbered 1–73 and headed 'Incipiunt themata sermonum in presenti postilla contentorum': each entry refers to one of the seventy-three leaves on which the word 'collatio' appears at the point where a 'thema' begins; a select index, A–T on ff. 515ᵛ–517ᵛ and V, X on f. 384, headed 'Incipit tabula super hanc postillam saltim quantum ad eius notabilia . . .'.

Lit. B. 10 (37). s. xiv¹. **1.** ff. 1–2ᵛ Incipiunt diuersi tractatus penitencie in vnum redacti secundum Magistrum Robertum grossi capitis. In principio huius libri admonet auctor . . . x dies peniteas. Explicit diuersitas penitencie secundum Robertum grossi capitis. **2.** (*a*) ff. 3–4 Hic incipit tabula de summa sequente que uocatur Chabham et incipit sic Cum sint miseraciones . . . (*b*) ff. 5–68 Cum sint miseraciones . . . peccabit uir iustus. Explicit expliceat ludere scriptor eat. qui scripsit carmen sit benedictus amen. **3.** f. 68 Articuli super quibus in visitacione sua dominus archiepiscopus inquirit scilicet de ministris ecclesie de titulis . . . obligat' ad ea. **4.** Miscellaneous pieces added in s. xiv¹, partly by the main hand in blank spaces and on the inside of the cover. ff. 68. 230 × 140 mm. *c.* 52 long lines. Frame ruling. Collation: 1⁴ 2–9⁸. Written in current anglicana. Contemporary limp parchment cover, the quires attached to it in two places only, near the head and near the foot: a bookmarker at f. 18. Secundo folio *si mulier*.

Written in England. 'Liber M. Willelmi Blankpayn Rectoris de Oreseta' inside the cover: he exchanged Orsett (Essex) for Ickham (Kent) in 1386 (Emden, *BRUO*, p. 199). 'R. Chelmynton' monachus Ecclesie cristi Cant' 1452' inside the front cover: cf. ff. 36ᵛ, 68ᵛ and the outside of the back cover.

1. Thomson, *Grosseteste*, p. 126. **2.** 'Magistri Thome Chabham' is in the margin, f. 68. This copy mentioned in edn. by F. Broomfield, *Analecta Mediaevalia Namurcensia*, xxv (1968). **4.** (*a*) f. 2ᵛ A note, 'Quatuor sunt quadragene . . .'. (*b*) f. 4ᵛ Statuta Bonefacii Archiepiscopi Cantuar'. Quoniam propter diuersas consuetudines in petendo decimas . . . modo puniendi: printed as Winchelsea's in Lyndwood, *Provinciale*, bk. 3, together with a final paragraph not here. (*c*) f. 4ʳᵛ Constitutiones Ottonis legati de minutis decimis. Inter ecclesiarum Rectores . . . cum reliquis non concurret. (*d*) f. 68ᵛ Questions on canon law. (*e*) inside the cover at both ends. Extracts from the Fathers. (*f*) inside the front cover. Twenty-six lines of French verse in rhyming couplets, hard to read, but, it seems, on eating and drinking: lines 13–15 are 'Benoi soit li bon [r]eisyn Qi nous doint (?) payn et vyn E la dame del hostal'. (*g*) inside the front cover. Thirty-seven lines of verse, 'Ecclesia dormire caue non pilliolatum . . .': Walther, no. 5178, referring to Bodleian, Rawlinson C. 552, f. 20. (*h*) inside the back cover. Verses: Vt quantum quamuis vt qualiter equeuocabis . . . (2 lines); Mittite promissum michi per puerum tibi missum . . . (4 lines); Ingenium mores . . .: Walther, *Sprichwörter*, no. 12372; Mars xvii dextris Aper vndecimoque sinistris . . . (3 lines on bloodletting).

Lit. B. 11 (1). s. xv in. **1.** ff. 4–153ᵛ Aegidius Romanus, De regimine principum. **2** (added, s. xv). f. 154ʳᵛ Epistola Bernardi ad quemdam militem de cura et modo rei familiaris vtilius gubernande. Glorioso et felici Militi Raymundo domino Castri Ambrosii Bernardus in senium ductus. salutem. Doceri petisti a nobis. . . . **3.** ff. 155–161ᵛ . . . Explicit tabula super Egidium de regimine principum per I.S. **4.** The pastedown in front is from a volume of legal distinctions (?), s. xiv. ff. iii+158+i, foliated 1–162. Written space *c.* 200×130 mm. Frame ruling. 2 cols. *c.* 43 lines. Collation of ff. 4–161: 1–19⁸ 20⁶. Written in anglicana and, from f. 128ᵛ, a mixture of anglicana and secretary. Contemporary binding of wooden boards covered with white leather, with a chemise of white leather over all: five bands: two clasps missing: the mark of a chain near the top of the front cover. Secundo folio *Nam sicut in speculabilibus.*

Written in England. 'Liber Magistri Iohannis Kynton Monachi Xⁱ Cantuarie' (†1416: Emden, *BRUO*, p. 1076), f. 3ᵛ. In Ingram's list of the chained library at Christ Church, Canterbury (*Ancient Libraries*, p. 162, no. 269).

2. *PL* clxxxii. 647–51 (Pseudo-Bernard). **3.** Runs from Abhominacio to Zelotopia. References are to book, part, and chapter. **4.** On Absolutio.

Lit. B. 12 (100). s. xiv med. 'Tabula Speculi Historialis'. ff. 171. Written space *c.* 220×135 mm. 2 cols. 42 lines. Collation: 1–14¹² 15². Secundo folio *Acon.* Written in fere-textura in England. In Ingram's list of the chained library at Christ Church, Canterbury (*Ancient Libraries*, p. 157, no. 141).

Ingram's list shows that in 1508 the Speculum historiale of Vincent of Beauvais lay on the first side of the eighth desk on the south side of the library and this extensive index to the Speculum faced it on the second side of the seventh desk. References are by book and chapter and the letters *a–f* show divisions of chapters. The main index is followed by another on ff. 169–170ᵛ, 'Quoniam in principali tabula precedenti . . . Iacobi de uictriaco x et sequentibus. vsque ad li. Explicit secunda Tabula'.

Lit. B. 13 (57, iii). s. xiii in. Sermones, etc. ff. 78. Written space 170×115 mm. 2 cols. 32 lines. The first line of writing above the top ruled line. Collation of ff. 3–78: 1–5⁸ 6⁴ (ff. 43–6) 7–10⁸. Quires 1–5, 7–10 numbered ix–xiii, i–iiii. Secundo folio (f. 4) *pro gloria.* Written in England. 'Sermones Sanctificamini 'D xiiiiᵃ gra iiiᵃ' 'Rogerii Noreys'', f. 1, s. xiv. From Christ Church, Canterbury, the only known survivor of more than sixty books entered in Eastry's catalogue as 'Libri Rogeri Noreis' (prior 1189–90, †1223: *Ancient Libraries*, p. 102, no. 1122): twenty-four of them are collections of sermons distinguished usually, as here, by the opening word or words of the first sermon.

The sermons, all anonymous, are in one hand perhaps, but ff. 47–78 look later than ff. 3–46. They are numbered i–xxii on ff. 3–46 and xxxiii–xlvii on ff. 47–78 in the hand of the table of contents. The table, s. xiii, on ff. 1–2 lists the ten missing pieces: xxiii hildebertus cenomanensis episcopus de missa. uersifice; xxiiii Oraciones ad patrem et filium et spiritum s.; xxv De fide catholica et spacio penitencie; xxvi Compendiosum cronicum de regibus francorum; xxvii De regibus anglie; xxviii De momentis et horis; xxix De libris ueteris et noui testamenti; xxx De palleo archiepiscopi; xxxi De simonia; xxxii Moralis instructio.

1. Nos. i–vii, x, xi, xiiii (ff. 3–16, 20–23ᵛ). Ten sermons of St. Bernard printed in *SBO* and in *PL* clxxxiii: Vig. Nat. 5, 6, Asc. 4, Quad. 7 (ending in ¶4 'deus deorum in Syon'), Cap. Jejun. 3, Circ. 3 ¶1–4, Circ. 3 ¶5–11, De Diversis 4, 31, 19.

2. Nos. ix, xiii (De sancta genofefa), xv (In quadragesima), xvi, xlii–xliiii (ff. 18–20, 23ᵛ–30, 73ᵛ–76ᵛ). Seven sermons printed in *PL* clxxi and cxcviii (Petrus Comestor): cxcviii. 1741, clxxi. 895, 639, cxcviii. 1749, clxxi. 695, cxcviii. 1768, 1811. The last three vary greatly from the printed text.

3. Nos. xxxiii–xxxix, xxxix*,[1] xxxix**, xl (ff. 47–72). Ten sermons, eight of them to be found in the collection of sermons of Alexander Nequam in Bodleian, Wood empt. 13, and the other two copied immediately before Nequam sermons in Merton College 180: xxxiii–xxxv, Wood empt. 13, ff. 18ᵛ, 76ᵛ, 67ᵛ; xxxvi, xxxvii, Merton 180, ff. 159, 160; xxxviii–xl (five sermons), Wood empt. 13, ff. 53, 1, 4ᵛ, 7, 112ᵛ. Nos. xxxiii, xl are here assigned 'quando volueris'. The other eight are for Good Friday, Easter, Vigil of Christmas, St. John Evangelist, Assumption of B.V.M. and three for Advent, all included under the number xxxix.

4. No. viii (ff. 16–18). In festo omnium sanctorum. Vidit iacob scalam . . . Triplex est uisio . . . coronant. Amen. Cf. Hauréau, *Notices et extraits*, i. 28.

No. xii (ff. 23ᵛ–24ᵛ). De spiritu sancto. Veni sancte spiritus . . . Spiritus deus est . . . misericors deus. Cf. Paris, B.N., lat. 2952, f. 2.

No. xvii (ff. 30ᵛ–38). Melior est obedientia quam uictime . . . Quantum sit obedientie bonum . . . percipiamus. Prestanti . . . amen.

No. xviii (ff. 38–40). Postquam consummati sunt dies octo etc. Caro verbi fratres karissimi de superfluo . . . ex ratione conditionis.

No. xix (ff. 40–1). De resurrectione domini. Et dixit ad me dominus. Fili hominis putasne . . . Vt ait apostolus. Caro et sanguis . . . ossa arida. quia custodit (*ends abruptly*).

No. xxi (ff. 41–43ᵛ). In purificatione beate uirginis. Adorna thalamum tuum . . . Ecce quod audistis spiritus sancti edictum est . . . deo patri.

No. xxii (ff. 43ᵛ–46ᵛ). Sermo ad uincula. Nunc scio uere etc'. Huius historie ueritatem iuxta moralem sensum . . . sine discrimine transitur (*ends imperfectly*).

No. xli (ff. 72–73ᵛ). Sermo de beata uirgine. Ego quasi libanus . . . Quoniam instat nostre redemptionis desiderata festiuitas . . . exhibite. Quod prestare dignetur.

No. xlv (ff. 76ᵛ–77ᵛ). In pascali tempore. Cantate Deo psalmum . . . Ammonemur karissimi in hiis festis paschalibus . . . accipiamus in gloria. Quod prestare dignetur etc.

No. xlvi (ff. 77ᵛ–78ᵛ). Sermo quando uolueris. Ait Moyses ad Aaron. Tolle turribulum . . . Omnis scriba doctus in regno celorum . . . gaudia perfruamur. Eo prestante . . .

5. Nos. xxi, xlvii (ff. 41, 78ᵛ). Two short notes on the virtue of obedience, added early in blank spaces: (xxi) De obedientia. Adam periit quia . . .; (xlvii) Que sint necessaria ut conseruetur obedientia . . .

6. Nequam's second advent sermon, 'Tu exurgens . . .', no. xxxix* (above, art. 3), ends abruptly on f. 68 at the words *dolis armatus* after which the scribe left a blank space of 10½ lines. A signe de renvoi and the words 'quere hoc signum in scedula' are written in the space. The reference is to a piece of parchment inserted between the third and fourth sheets of quire 9. The part of it lying after f. 65 (f. 65a) has the end of the sermon. The part of it lying after f. 67 (f. 67a) has an explanatory letter (to Roger Noreys?), written in the same neat hand as f. 65a: Dilecto sibi in cristo et amico karissimo R. capellano archi-episcopi. suus W. de Melida. Salutem et se ipsum. Mitto uobis finem sermonis illius qui sic incipit. Tu exurgens misereberis syon. Rogo etiam uos quatinus notetis in quadam cedula omnium sermonum principia quos habetis penes uos et mittatis michi per primum nuntium quem inuenire poteritis. Inueni enim postquam recessistis a me sicut uoluntas dei fuit quosdam sermones magistri Alex' [. . . . .][2] ubi continentur alii eius sermones quos penes uos non habetis. et quia memoriter non retineo omnes quos penes uos habetis omnium principia michi mittite. ut sic sermones illos quos non habetis scribere faciam. Valete. The writer was a canon of Cirencester, where Nequam was

---

[1] See below, art. 6.
[2] A dozen words erased.

abbot.[1] The form of the line mark of punctuation on f. 65a is in the form found in Ciren-cester manuscripts.[2]

7. Verses and some proverbial sayings were added early in the lower margins of many pages. Later, all or part of what had been written on ff. 5[rv], 6[rv], 15[rv], 16[rv], 19, 27[rv], 30[rv], 33[rv] was cut out. The remaining pieces are:

1. f. 3 Versus nigelli monachi. ne pudor aut pena . . . prandeo.ceno meum (2 lines).
2. ff. 3[v]–4 Persius, *Satirae*: 3. 94, 95 (reduced to one line); 4. 7–9; 5. 152–3; 5. 144–5.
3. ff. 6–8 Ovid, *Remedium amoris*: lines 91, 92, 94, 589–90, 615–16, 729–30, 746, 808.
4. ff. 8[v]–12[v] Ovid, *De arte amatoria*: 1. 239–40, 359–60, 443–4; 2. 13, 107, 113–14, 277–8, 389–90, 437–8, 603–4, 732.
5. f. 13 Ingenii sapiens . . . Walther, *Sprichwörter*, no. 12352.
6. f. 13[v] Factis non uerbis . . . Ibid., no. 8708.
7. f. 14 Quidam sapiens ait. nouerca pacis est dissimilitudo. e contra ad connectandas amicicias.' tenacissimum uinculum est morum similitudo.
8. ff. 17[v]–20 Ovid, *Epistulae*: 2. 61–4, 85–6; 17. 97–8.
9. ff. 20[v]–24 Ovid, *Amores*: 1. 8. 49–50, 104; 2. 2. 9–10, 28; 1. 10. 48; 2. 9. 41–2; 3. 4. 17–18; 3. 11. 35–6.
10. f. 25 Denigrat meritum . . . Walther, *Sprichwörter*, no. 5376.
11. f. 25[v] Dulcia sunt cupido (?) lucrosa pericula.
12. f. 26 Vis dare . . . A variant of Walther, *Sprichwörter*, no. 33768.
13. f. 26[v] Alternam requiem numquam . . . sitim (2½ lines).
14. f. 27 Insipidum scire est . . . (2).
15. f. 27[v] O male felices . . . (4: Walther, *Sprichwörter*, no. 19487a).
16. f. 28 Pauperis haut numquam . . . (4: ibid., no. 20990a).
17. f. 29[v] Cura quidem cunctis . . . transformat in unum (5).
18. f. 30 Animo fortuna uirili omnis leta uenit.
19. f. 31 Qui flet in aduersis . . . aduersa dolor (2½).
20. f. 31[v] Nec redimunt nec dampna leuant qui dampna queruntur.
21. f. 31[v] Rem male prouisam dubius manet exitus.
22. f. 32 Tarda uenit subitus . . . tractanda more (2½).
23. f. 34 Exiguus labor est. set merces . . . fine carent (2).
24. f. 34[v] Maria egipciaca. Vt quid peccaui. qua . . . de fornice tristi (2).
25. f. 35 Sis memor . . . credas. Horace, *Satirae*, 2. 2. 71–3 reversed.
26. f. 36 oracius. suaue est de magno tollere aceruo.
27. f. 51[v] De quodam archiepiscopo qui duos diuites. duobus anulis aureis ditauit. ter-cium pauperem socium. neglexit. Dicia diuitibus . . . solutum (2).

Lit. C. 1 (36). s. xiv[2]. Decretals of Gregory IX surrounded by the apparatus (of Bernardus de Botone) beginning 'In huius libri principio quinque sunt pre-cipue prenotanda': ends imperfectly at bk. 3. xxxix. 13. ff. 210. Written space *c*. 270×170. Eighteen quires, twelves, except 8[10] 13[8]. Secundo folio (in textu) *omnium uisibilium*; (in glosa) *voluntaria certitudo*. Written in England.

Only a fragment of 1[11] (f. 11) remains. Titulus xli of bk. 1 ends with the chapter 'Idem in eodem. Ecclesia que ad retractandam sentenciam . . . conuentum', crossed out and marked 'vacat' (f. 83).

Lit. C. 12 (14). s. xiv[2]. 1. ff. 1–32 A commentary on Decretals, bk. 3. i–v, xxx. 2. ff. 34–41 Tabula 6[ti] libri secundum ordinem alphabeti 'ex glosis card*inalis* archidiaconi et Io an'. 3. ff. 41–50 A table of the Sext and Clementines. 4. ff. 50–

---

[1] As Dr. R. W. Hunt tells me.
[2] Cf. N. R. Ker, *English manuscripts in the century after the Norman Conquest*, 1960, p. 48 and pl. 20b.

65. Incipit alia tabula. A. de ista diccione a notatur . . . Explicit A littera istius tabule. **5.** ff. 65–69ᵛ Incipit summa bartholomei in casibus non placuit michi inserere prohemium. Abbas conferre potest suis subditis . . . (*ends imperfectly in Approbacio*). **6.** ff. 70–79ᵛ Incipiunt casus clementinarum. Rubrica. de etate et qualitate. Cum ecclesie . . . est satis planus. Expliciunt casus clementinarum per W. de C. **7.** ff. 80–151 Sequitur prohemium clementinarum et reportorium post magistrum thomam de Walkynton doctorem decretorum anno domini Millesimo cccᵐᵒ septuagessimo septimo. Paulus dicit hic in prohemio quod hec compilacio . . . (f. 150) secundum canones. Incipiunt extrauagan*cia* clementinarum. Suscepti regiminis cristi ministrorum. . . . (f. 151) Explicit. Explicit materia Clementinarum cum extrauaganciis. **8.** ff. 151ᵛ–152 Questions on cases. **9.** f. 152ʳᵛ Tabula sancti thome de alquino super compendium theologie. Absolucio . . . (*ends imperfectly in letter C*). **10.** Binding leaves: (*a*) f. iii, a bifolium of a grammatical text, s. xiv; (*b*) f. iv, part of a papal(?) document, s. xiv, mostly illegible, the verso blank and used in s. xiv for a table listing arts. 1–9. ff. 153 and two medieval binding leaves (ff. iii, iv). Paper and (the outside and middle sheets of each quire) parchment. A medieval foliation i–clvi takes account of the five missing leaves: 'cxxi' is repeated. Written space *c.* 225 × 160 mm. 2 cols. and long lines, the number varying. Collation: 1¹⁰ 2¹² 3¹² wants 11 blank after f. 32 4–6¹² 7¹⁰ (ff. 70–9) 8¹² 9¹² wants 12 after f. 102 10¹² wants 1 before f. 103 11–13¹² 14¹⁰ wants 2–4, 7–9 (ff. 150–3: 10, f. 153, was pasted down). Written in current anglicana. Secundo folio *in minoribus*.

Written in England. 'W. Molasshe pri(*or*)', f. ivᵛ: he was prior of Christ Church, Canterbury, 1428–38. In Ingram's list of the Christ Church chained library (*Ancient Libraries*, p. 161, no. 235).

1 begins 'In isto tercio libro decretalium de vita et honestate clericorum'. Probably several quires are missing after f. 22, with the commentary on tituli vi–xxix. **3.** Two couplets against women in the margin, f. 49ᵛ: Ad libitum canis mingit mulier lacrimatur. Pro tali luctu nullus sapiens moueatur (cf. Walther, *Sprichwörter*, no. 375a); Ius est ut faueat . . . (ibid., no. 13427). **5.** Bartholomaeus de Sancto Concordio, Summa de casibus conscientiae (Schulte, ii. 429). Printed often. **7.** For Walkynton see Emden, *BRUO*, p. 1964. The extravagant on f. 150 is of John XXII (Extrav. Comm. 3. 3). The commentary on it ends imperfectly: three leaves are missing. 'Est optimus liber qui dicitur Kyngishom' is written in the upper margin of f. 150.

Lit. C. 15 (30). s. xv². Cicero, Epistolae. ff. 215. Paper. Written space 180 × 110 mm. 33 long lines. Eighteen quires of 12: 18¹² blank, cut out. Cursiva. A handsome floral border, f. 2. Secundo folio *sine exercitu*. Written in France. 'This booke I Edmond Withrpoll found in the lybrary of owre ladyes church in bulleyn (*Boulogne*) the xxvᵗⁱ day of September in Anno Domini 1544', f. 1. 'Guliel: Kingsley 1667', f. 2: presumably of his gift.

Letters in sixteen books. The first leaf is blank and the text begins on f. 2 'Marci tullii Ciceronis ad publium lentulum et ad alios liber primus feliciter incipit. C publio lentulo s.d.p. (*thus far in gold*) Ego omni officio . . .'. The last letter is [M]irificam mihi verberationem . . . dissuauiabo. Me ama vale'. 'EPIST CICERONIS' in handsome capitals on the fore-edge. Quire centres were strengthened with strips of manuscript now removed: cf. after f. 210.

In s. xvii in. a bookseller used blank space on f. 214ᵛ to write '3 lubartus magnus / 6 Cristall

Ius Sinogoge / To M[r] Will Cox in Sinmarye hall lands (?) 1616 bill / 1 bibell in octauo o. 6. 8 / 3 qrto bibles o. 1. 8 / 3 follio bibles 10. o. o'.

Lit. D. 2 (88). s. xv. Hec [est regula generalis pro toto] libro . . . medulla gramatice intitulatur. Alma. id est virgo abscondita . . . Zezimus. a. n̄. id est viuax vel viuidus. ff. 140. Paper. Written space *c.* 220×145 mm. 2 cols. 48 lines. Collation: $1–17^{8}$ 18^{4}. Written in current anglicana. Secundo folio *Abusio.* Written in England.

For other copies see above, Bristol, University Library, DM 14. The English interpretations are in red ink. Somner (?) added many Anglo-Saxon forms. f. 1 is torn at the top. 'This is Gieles Winston his boke' and the scribbled names of Giles and Thomas Winston of the parish of St. Dunstan (Canterbury) on f. 130, s. xvi.

Lit. D. 5 (49). s. xiii ex. **1.** ff. 3–86 Logica vetus. **2.** ff. 85^{v}–88^{v} Incipit liber de articulis fidei. Demens (*sic*)[1] papa cuius rem nominis . . . Hee quoque sunt ad probacionem sequentium introducte. Hic ponit descriptiones. Causa est per quam aliquid habet esse . . . iudicandis homo iudex. Explicit de articulis fidei. **3.** ff. 89–146 Priscianus minor. **4.** ff. 146^{v}–151^{v} Littera est nota elementi que cum scribitur . . . ut pape. euax. Explicit accent'. **5.** ff. 152–153^{v} Littera est minima pars uocis composite . . . Opusculum breue precedere debet breuis prologus . . . offendiculo facias. finito prologo incipit principale propositum a uocalibus. Uersus facturo versus tibi vertere curo . . . Tu puer aduertas istis ut carmina vertas. **6.** ff. 154–158^{v} Barbarismus est una . . . uexit ad urbes. Explicit barbarismus donati. ff. 155 and a slip (f. 141). Written space 120×72 mm. 28 long lines and (art. 1) 26 long lines and (art. 2) 2 cols. of 64 lines. Very wide margins. Collation of ff. 3–158: $1–3^{12}$ 4^{12}+1 leaf after 12 (f. 51) 5^{12}+1 leaf before 1 (f. 52) $6–7^{12}$ $8–9^{8}$ 10^{10} 11^{12} 12^{8} 13^{10}, a slip (f. 141) after 6 14^{12}+1 leaf after 7 (f. 143). Secundo folio *inuicem.*

Written in England. One of many books given to St. Augustine's, Canterbury, by John of London, for whom cf. A. B. Emden, *Donors of Books to S. Augustine's Abbey Canterbury*, Oxford Bibliographical Soc., Occasional Publications, no. 4, 1968, pp. 11, 12 and pls. iii–v: Liber Iohannis de Lond' de Librario sancti Augustini Cant' ', f. 2^{v} and f. 3. Entered in the late medieval catalogue of St. Augustine's (*Ancient Libraries*, p. 350, no. 1286).

1. The six pieces are in the usual order, Isagoge, Praedicamenta, Periermenias, Liber sex principiorum, Liber divisionum, Topica Boetii, as in thirteen other copies once at St. Augustine's (*Ancient Libraries*, nos. 1279–85, 1287–92). This copy described in *Aristoteles Latinus*, i. 362, no. 264. **2.** A quire filler. Glorieux, no. 107a (Nicholas of Amiens), listing twenty-nine copies, but not this one or Oxford, Bodleian Library, Digby 28 and 154. As *PL* ccx. 595–618, but continuing further after 'puniendi sunt pena' (f. 88) with fourteen chapters, the first six on power, wisdom, and goodness, and the rest on the Trinity, beginning 'Potentia est uis factis aliquando motum operari'. **3.** Bks. 17, 18. **4.** On accentuation. **5.** Called 'Quedam Regule versificandi' in the St. Augustine's catalogue. The part in verse consists of forty-eight lines on f. 152 ending 'ista reuoluit' and 121 lines on f. 153^{v} beginning 'Sillaba longatur'. **6.** *Grammatici Latini*, ed. H. Keil, iv (1864), 392–402. The St. Augustine's catalogue lists 'Duo libri ethicorum' in last place. Only the heading remains, 'Incipit primus liber etycorum', f. 158^{v}.

[1] 'clemens papa' in the margin as a guide to the rubricator, who misread *cl* as *d*.

Lit. D. 6 (34). s. xii ex. **1.** Preliminaries to **2. 2.** ff. 6–118 Matheus glosatus.
3. Additions after **2.** ff. i+119+i, foliated 1–121. **2** is a central column of text
185 mm high, in seventeen lines, with apparatus flanking it on specially ruled
lines. Collation of ff. 6–120: 1–10⁸ 11⁸+1 leaf after 6 (f. 92) 12–13⁸ 14¹⁰.
Secundo folio (f. 5) *nationem cristi* or (f. 7) *manassen*. Written in England.
'D. III Gᵃ III (*altered to* I) / Matheus glo. cum C / Liber sancti Augustini
Cant' ' f. 2, s. xiii². Listed in the late medieval catalogue of St. Augustine's,
Canterbury (*Ancient Libraries*, p. 206, no. 157). 'Guliel: Kingsley. Anno
domini 1667', f. 2.

1. (*a*) ff. 2ᵛ–3 Incipiunt capitula super matheum. Natiuitas cristi magi . . . et de baptismo
(twenty-eight paragraphs). (*b*) f. 4 [C]um multi scripsisse euangelia . . . compassionem.
(*c*) f. 4ᵛ [M]atheus in hac uita que iiii . . . et aquila. (*d*) ff. 4ᵛ–5ᵛ [N]omen libri euangelium
grece . . . operamur. (*e*) f. 5ᵛ. Matheus cum primum . . . recepta sunt (Stegmüller, no. 589).
2. 'Cuius sit generatio . . .' are the first words of the apparatus. **3.** (*a*) ff. 119–120ᵛ Three
paragraphs: Prima sabbati diluculo sicut omnes consentiunt . . .; Plures quidem fuerunt
apparitiones . . .; Homo id est deus habuit duos filios iiᵒˢ populos. iudeos et gentes . . .
(*b*) on the flyleaf, f. 121, s. xii/xiii, [T]anta dignitas humane conditionis est . . .

f. 2, left blank, contains four lines of verse, s. xiii, 'Hic homo cerne quid es . . .'. Three
lines of Hebrew on the flyleaf, f. 1ᵛ, record the pledging of this book, s. xiii med.: the
inscription is discussed and shown in reduced facsimile by C. Roth, *The Library*, 5th
series, xix (1964), 196–200.

Lit. D. 7 (67). s. xiii med. Sermones. ff. i+177. Written space *c.* 190×130 mm.
2 cols. 39–48 lines. The first line of writing above the top ruled line on ff. 1–96
(after which a new hand begins), 111–15, 163–78. Collation of ff. 2–178: 1¹⁰+1
leaf after 10 (f. 12) 2–4⁸ 5–6¹⁰ 7¹⁰ wants 10, perhaps blank after f. 65 8 two
(ff. 66, 67) 9¹⁰ wants a leaf in the second half (ff. 68–76) 10⁸+a leaf after 2 (f. 79)
11–12⁸ 13⁸+3 leaves after 8 (ff. 110–12) 14¹⁰ 15–21⁸. Many hands. Written in
France (?). 'Liber sermonum Collectio de multis 'R. prioris de Sancto Elphego'',
f. 1ᵛ: identifiable, perhaps, with the third of nine books listed under the name of
R(ichard) of St. Elphege (prior, 1258–63) in the medieval catalogue of Christ
Church, Canterbury, 'Liber Sermonum cum notabilibus sacre Scripture'
(*Ancient Libraries*, p. 68, no. 577).

114 sermons, most of them attributed to particular authors, notably fr. Jordan (of Saxony,
O.P.: 33 sermons), Philip the Chancellor (16 sermons), and the subdean of Salisbury
(Thomas of Chabham?: 14 sermons), listed by T. Kaeppeli, 'Un recueil de sermons
prêchés à Paris et en Angleterre', *AFP* xxvi (1956), 161–91. For Alardus, the author of a
sermon on ff. 161ᵛ–162ᵛ, see T. Kaeppeli, *SOPMA* i. 26. Divisible into thirteen booklets:
quire 1; quire 2; quire 3 (numbered v); quire 4 (numbered vii); quires 5–7; quire 8; quire 9
(a note pencilled at the foot of the first leaf, f. 68, 'Dominus Alex' perficiet iii quinternos
'de exemplis' pro iiii s' vi d' et si bene fecerit erunt plene v s' '); quire 10; quires 11–13;
quire 14; quires 15–18; quire 19; quires 20, 21. The parchment is sometimes defective,
for example, ff. 117, 149, 151.

Lit. D. 8 (53). s. xiv in. A miscellany mainly of canon law described by Woodward, *Cat.*, pp. 26–8: I keep his numbering of arts. **1–13. 1, 12.** ff. 7–58, 95–
102. Formularium iuris canonici. **2.** (*a*) ff. 59–73 Consuetudines curie
cant*uariensis* et obseruationes que experimento qʳ seruata fuisse noscuntur. Aut
aliquid est attemptatus . . . (*b*) ff. 73ᵛ–74ᵛ Tractus super appellacionibus tam

directis quam tuitoriis secundum consuetudinem curie cantuar*iensis*. Quando appellatur ad curiam Cant' . . . **3.** ff. 73ᵛ–79 Statuta curie cant' edita per R. de Winch' Cantuar' archiepiscopi Anno infrascripto ad finem. Robertus. Ad viam nostri regiminis . . . ac beato Thoma martire. Amen. **4.** f. 79 Statutum Gregorii. **5.** ff. 79ᵛ–84 Constituciones fratris Iohannis de Pecham edite in concilio Lamheth' vii die Octobris anno gracie Mᵒ ccᵒ lxxxᵐᵒ primo. Ab exordio . . . et consecracionis nostre Tercio. **6.** ff. 84ᵛ–87ᵛ Tractus super formis eleccionum cum Instrumentis ad ipsarum formam spectantibus. Tres sunt forme eleccionum . . . **7.** ff. 88–89ᵛ Carta magna communium libertatum Anglie. Dated 12 Oct., 25 Edward I. **8.** ff. 89ᵛ–90ᵛ Carta de Libertatibus Foreste in Anglia. Same date as **7**. **9.** ff. 90ᵛ–91. Vocacio prelatorum ad Concilium pro corroboracione dictarum Cartarum et pro remediis contra quasdam oppressiones ecclesie ordinandis. Robertus permissione diuina . . . Transacti temporis . . . Dated 12 Apr. 1302. **10.** f. 91ʳᵛ Littera Executoria super ordinatis in Concilio. R. Cantuar' Archiepiscopus . . . Frequenter exigit . . . seriem continentes. Otford, 15 July 1298. **11** (added). f. 92 Walterus permissione diuina . . . Si subtili . . . Dover, 9 Mar. 1324. **12.** See **1**, above. **13.** ff. 107–215ᵛ Oculus sacerdotis, ending imperfectly. **14.** ff. 1–4 A table of contents covering **1–11**. **15.** f. 216 A binding leaf taken from a theological manuscript, s. xiv: the subject appears to be 'tribulatio'.

ff. 216+iv (ff. 216–19). Written space of **1–12**, *c.* 195 × 130 mm in 53 long lines; of **13**, *c.* 175 × 112 mm. in 2 cols. of 33–7 lines. Collation of ff. 1–215, 220: 1⁶ 2¹⁶ 3–9¹² (ff. 23–106) 10–18¹² 19 two (ff. 215, 220, the outside bifolium). Medieval binding of pasteboard covered with white leather: two ties. Secundo folio *copiamque*. Written in England, arts. **1–12** in current anglicana (a new hand at **4**) and art. **13** in textura by several hands. From Christ Church, Canterbury: 'Pertinet ad dompnum W. Inggrame penitenciarium ecclesie cristi Cant' ', f. iᵛ; 'Liber dompni Willelmi londone. E dono', f. iᵛ.

1. Put together and copied very soon after 1300. The first piece is a letter of Pope Boniface (VIII), Lateran, 15 May 'anno viii'. A piece on f. 50 is dated in 1300. Bishop Baldock's letter asking for Grosseteste's canonization, 9 June 1307, is an addition on f. 56. ff. 57–58ᵛ blank. **2.** Cf. B. L. Woodcock, *Medieval ecclesiastical courts in the diocese of Canterbury*, 1952, p. 66. An edition by Dr. F. D. Logan is in preparation. **3.** Statutes of 1295, Wilkins, *Concilia*, ii. 204–13. **4.** Assessment of Peter's pence in fifteen English dioceses: see Woodruff. The text is crossed through. Attributed in Lit. C. 14, f. 1, to Gregory V, A.D. 997. **5.** Wilkins, *Concilia*, ii. 50. **7, 8.** *SR* i. 114, 120. **9, 10.** Wilkins, *Concilia*, ii. 272–3, 240–1. **11.** Woodruff, *Cat.*, p. 27. **13.** Cf. Lit. D. 9, art. 1. The last words here are in the Dextra pars and occur in D. 9 at f. 55/34. **14.** Gives leaf references: 'a' indicates the recto and 'b' the verso.

Lit. D. 9 (54). s. xiv med. **1.** ff. 1–88ᵛ Hic incipit pars oculi sacerdotum. [C]um ecclesie . . . Explicit summa que vocatur sinistra pars oculi. Qui scripsit carmen benedictus erit amen. **2.** f. 89 Memento homo quod cinis es . . . Fratres karissimi legimus in Euangelio domini dicentem. Qui audit verba mea . . . **3.** ff. 90–147 Qui bene presunt presbiteri . . . (*ends abruptly*). **4.** ff. 148–171ᵛ Incipiunt instituciones beati gregorii. Quomodo uenerandi sunt sancti. Festiuitates sanctorum apostolorum seu martirum. antiqui patres . . . (*ends imperfectly*).

5, flyleaf additions, include: (*a*) f. 172 Hec sunt festa obseruanda in prouincia Cantuarie iuxta ordinacionem domini Symonis cant' archiepiscopi. In primis sacrum diem dominicum . . . Thome apostoli; (*b–g*) f. 172 Verses; (*h*) f. 173 A memorandum of Henry V's expedition against Harfleur in 1415. ff. 171 and two medieval binding leaves, ff. 172–3. Written space: of **1**, *c.* 185 × 115 mm in 38–56 long lines; of **2–4**, 152–72 × 105 mm in 36–9 long lines, rising to 185 × 135 mm in 44 long lines in quires 21, 22, to save parchment. Collation: 1–2⁸ 3⁴ 4⁸ 5¹⁰ 6–7⁸ 8⁶ 9–10⁸ 11¹² (ff. 77–88) 12 five (ff. 89–93) 13–18⁸ 19⁸ wants 7 and 8: a scrap of parchment, f. 147*, is attached to 6, 20–22⁸. Art. **1** in anglicana, current from f. 12ᵛ. Secundo folio *ad mitem*. Written in England. Belonged 'domino Iohanni Germyn' and by gift of (*blank*) Jacks, 10 Dec. 1500, to Thomas Richardson 'ad orandum pro anima domini Ioh' Germyn'.

1. W. de Pagula. This copy and Lit. D. 8, art. 13, listed by L. Boyle in *Transactions of the Royal Historical Society*, 5th series, v (1955), 84–110: Dextra pars, f. 31; Sinistra pars, f. 59. The worn condition of f. 88 suggests that **1** was long separate from **2–4**. **3.** A common text: cf. *MMBL* i. 43. f. 147ᵛ blank. **4.** In the order of the church year from Advent, ending now at All Saints. Includes English saints, Thomas of Canterbury, Cuthbert, Elphege, Dunstan, Augustine of England, Mildred, Kenelm, Frideswide. **5***a*. Simon Islep. Lyndwood, *Provinciale*, edn. 1679, pp. 101–3 (bk. 2, tit. 3. 3). *b*. Ecce flat hoc anno Maurus in orbe tonans: m°ccc° lxi *interlined*. *c*. Rex Francus siccum captus fuit aspice cliccum: m° ccc°lvi° *interlined*. *d*. Vinum lacte laua...(2). *e*. Transit ad ethera virgo puerpera . . . (2). *f*. Lumine solari vitrum nessit violari . . . (2). *g*. Post dunstanum post tempus meridianum vixi c cuculum terremotum tibi dixi: mccclxxxii *interlined*. *h*. Printed, inexactly, by Woodruff, *Catalogue*.

Lit. D. 10 (54*), ff. 1–30. s. xiii ex. (*begins imperfectly*) Cerui dicti apotay ceraton id est a cornibus . . . ff. 30, foliated in s. xv 114–16, 118–24, 126–32, 134–46. 180 × 122 mm. 35 long lines. Collation: 1¹⁰ wants 4 2⁸ wants 2 3⁸ wants 2 4¹⁰ wants 8–10, perhaps blank. Written in current anglicana.

An imperfect copy of an illustrated bestiary of the 'Second Family', listed as no. 30 by M. R. James, *The Bestiary* (Roxburghe Club 176, 1928), p. 19. Begins with Ceruus, Caper, Caprea. The first twelve or so beasts are missing, Leo–Satyrus, and single leaves after ff. 3, 10, 17. Fifty-five drawings of beasts, birds, etc., remain. Some spaces for drawings not filled. An excision f. 22. Part of a larger book, now bound with later pieces.

Lit. D. 11 (17). s. xiii. **1**. ff. 5–93 Johannes de Deo, Casus Decretalium. **2**. ff. 96–143 (Bernardus de Botone, Apparatus Decretalium Gregorii IX), ending abruptly in the first words of the commentary on bk. 1. xxii. **2**. **3**. ff. 144–51 Creacionem rerum insinuans etc. Cassiodorus. Tota sacra scriptura aut est de creatrice essencia . . . sic non habuerunt gratuita (*ends abruptly*). **4**, added on flyleaves and in blank spaces: see below. ff. 149 and four medieval binding leaves, ff. 1–4. Written space: of **1**, *c.* 183 × 103 mm in 2 cols. of 62 lines; of **2**, *c.* 185 × 140 mm in 2 cols. of 49 lines; of **3**, *c.* 175 × 115 mm in 2 cols. of 46 lines. The first line of writing below the top ruled line. Collation of ff. 5–153: 1–5¹² 6⁸ (ff. 65–72) 7¹² 8¹² wants 12, blank, after f. 95 9–12¹² (ff. 96–143) 13¹⁰. **1** in very small script. Secundo folio *Ex parte* (f. 6).

Written in England. A gift to Christ Church, Canterbury, from Adam (de Chillenden), prior (1264–74): 'Casus decretalium.Ade prioris secundum Iohan-

nem hyspanum', f. 1. 'Liber ecclesie cristi Cant' ' and 'de prima monstra(cione)',
f. 1. In Eastry's catalogue among prior Adam's gifts (*Ancient Libraries*, p. 71,
nos. 628–9).[1] In Ingram's list, A.D. 1508 (ibid., p. 161, no. 237).[2]

1. Schulte, ii. 97. A new hand begins at bk. 5, f. 73: ff. 68^v–72^v were left blank. **2.** The
commentary beginning 'In huius libri principio quinque sunt prenotanda'. It often surrounds the text of the decretals. **3.** A commentary on bk. 2 of the Sentences of Peter
Lombard, ending in dist. 3. **4a.** ff. 2^v–4 Tituli of the decretals of Gregory IX in ink (f. 3^{rv})
and pencil. **b.** f. 68^v Commentary on bk. 1, v. 1, 'Ad hec in beato petro . . .'. **c.** ff. 69^v–70^v
A scholastic piece on the soul, 'Ignoras te o pulcherima mulierum . . . Tibi anima racionalis
proponitur . . .'. **d.** Pencilled notes in a large hand on ff. 70^v, 71^{rv}, 94^{rv}, 143^{rv}, 152^v include:
(94) a letter of Thomas (de Ringmere), prior—he succeeded Adam de Chillenden—datable
1281–4 (cf. Woodruff, *Catalogue*, p. 11); (152^v) a formulary letter about a debt of £2. 5s.
'[C]oram vobis domine iudex propono ego talis . . .', in which the words 'talis', 'talem',
and 'talis' have been changed in the same hand to 'Iohannes de Sandwico', 'Rogerum de
la thihe', and 'Adam le large' respectively.

Lit. D. 13 (66). s. xiv med. Prick of Conscience, in English. ff. 144. Thick paper.
Written space *c.* 170 mm high. 26–9 long lines. Collation: 1^{12} 2^{10} 3–11^{12} 12^{12}
wants 3–10 13^{10}. Written in current anglicana. Secundo folio *To louy him.*
Scribbles, s. xv ex., on flyleaves, ff. ii–iv (ii is a parchment leaf), include 'Iste
liber constat domino Rectori de Borton' and suggest ownership by Nicholas
Moyn or Mayne, the beginning of whose will is on f. iv^v: he asks for burial in
the church of North Morton. Verses on f. ii^v have the name 'Willelmus Mayne'
against them. 'Iste liber constat henri Sadeler', f. ii, s. xvi. Given to William
Kingsley by Roger Shopswell (?), 10 Nov. 1672.

Printed by Richard Morris in 1863. Lines 7558–7996 are missing in a gap after f. 132.

Lit. D. 14 (76). s. xv med. Fasciculus morum. ff. 236. Paper. Written space
153 × 90 mm. 29 long lines. Frame ruling. Collation: 1 four 2–18^{12} 19^{14} 20^8 21^8
wants 7, 8. Secretary hand. Written in England. Belonged to Richard Turner
in s. xvi (f. 237).

Begins imperfectly in the first of the seven 'particulae' at the words 'oracione clamorosa':
probably eight leaves are missing before this. Ends on f. 222, 'et sic terminatur iste libellus. Finis sermonum. fit hec collectio morum' (cf. MS. Bodley 410). An index follows
(ff. 223–235^v) and verses 'Si tetigit tetigit . . .' headed 'Versus iste sequentes excerpte sunt
de diuersis particulis huius libri. vt patebit. inferius. singillatim' (ff. 235^v–236^v, ending
imperfectly in Particula 4). For copies in Oxford libraries see the indexes to *Sum. Cat.*,
the Laud and Rawlinson Catalogues, and Coxe's catalogue of the college collections, under
Fasciculus Morum and Silk (Robert).

Lit. D. 16 (58). s. xiv/xv. 1. ff. 3–7 . . . Explicit Correctorium tocius Biblie.
traditum a domino Roberto Grostede episcopo Lincolniensi. 2. ff. 11–109^v N. de
Hanapis, O.P., Liber exemplorum sacre scripture: preceded by tables, ff. 7^v–10^v.
3. ff. 110–123^v (Higden, Polychronicon), part of bk. 1, abbreviated: ends

---

[1] The cataloguer called **2** 'Constituciones Romanorum Pontificum et decretales Epistole'. Perhaps he was misled by **4a.**
[2] In Ingram's manuscript *Hyspanie* follows *Iohannem.* The word is out of place in
Ancient Libraries.

imperfectly. **4.** f. 124^r A world map, with about 100 names. ff. 124 and five medieval binding leaves, ff. i, 1, 2, 127–8. Paper, except f. 124, and the binding leaves. Written space *c.* 180×110 mm. *c.* 40 long lines. Frame ruling. Collation of ff. 3–126: 1^8 2^{10} 3^{10}, 5 or 6 cancelled, 4–11^{10} 12^6+1 leaf after 4 (f. 124). Written in current anglicana. Secundo folio *aspiratur*.

Written in England. From St. Augustine's, Canterbury, 'De adquisicione I. Prestone liber rarus et bonus', f. i^v. An addition to the late medieval catalogue[1] (*Ancient Libraries*, p. 217, no. 300).

1. Thomson, *Grosseteste*, p. 127. The title on f. 1 is 'Correctorium biblie Roberti Grostegth C Maydesto[n]'. **2.** Stegmüller, no. 5815. The tables are: ff. 7^v–9, in the hand of Clement Cantyrbury, signed at the end 'Clemens Cantyrbury Anno domini 1491 in oct' assumptionis s. marie'; ff. 9^v–10^v, of the 131 chapters, and, at the end, the added words 'Nota tabulam super hunc librum secundum ordinem alfabeti In quaterno cum tabula super libros ysidori de summo bono'. **3** begins 'Iulius Cesar diuinis humanisque rebus': *CD* version, corresponding to edn. (RS), i. 40–396/12, ii. 2–4. 'C. Canterburi' is entered against this item in the 'register' of the St. Augustine's books compiled near the end of the fifteenth century (*Ancient Libraries*, p. 176). He had the book in his keeping, no doubt, when he compiled the table on ff. 7^v–9 and wrote on f. 2^v 'Hunc librum procurauit frater Iohannes Preston Monachus sancti Augustini Cant'. Et est liber de librario dicti monasterii sancti Augustini Cant'. D. (blank) G^a (blank) Clemens Cantyrbury. Anno domini 1491': cf. also f. 11^v and the arms of the abbey on f. 11, as in Clement Canterbury's book now Burney 11 (Emden, *Donors*, pl. ii). For John Preston, † after 1416, and Clement Canterbury, see Emden, *BRUO*, pp. 1518, 350, and Emden, *Donors*, pp. 14 and 8; also *BLR* vii. 151.

Lit. D. 17 (78). s. xv **(1)** and s. xiv/xv **(2–4)**. **1.** ff. 1–48^v Index of Nova Statuta, Accusacions–Worstedez. **2.** ff. 50–62^v Tables of chapters of Statutes of Edward III 1–50. **3.** ff. 63–182^v Statutes of Edward III 1–50, ending imperfectly: one leaf missing. **4.** ff. 183–224 Statutes of Richard II 1–11. **5.** f. i (flyleaf) A leaf of a service-book, s. xiii. ff. i+224. Written space 150×92 mm. 33 (art. 1) and 37–8 long lines. Collation: 1–6^8 7^{14} wants 14, blank, + 1 leaf before 1 (ff. 49–62) 8^{10} 9^{12} 10–15^{10} 16^8 17–19^{10} 20^{10} wants 1 before f. 183 21–22^{10} 23^{14} wants 14, blank. In **1** the quires are marked +, b–f: nothing is missing. A new series begins with 'a' at quire 8. **1** is in current anglicana. **2–4** are in anglicana (short *r*). Medieval limp parchment binding lined with a piece of linen. Written in England. 'Thomas Burgate me possidet', f. 1, s. xvi in.: cf. ff. 48^v, 224^v. 'Guliel' Kingsley Anno Dom: 1667', f. 1.

1. Cf. *MMBL* i. 18. **3** and **4** are in the same hand. In **4**, 8–11 Richard II may be contemporary additions to a collection which originally ended at 7 Richard II. ff. 206^v, 207^r, 208^v–209^v were left blank. **5.** Thirty forms remain in whole or in part, seventeen on the recto and thirteen on the verso. Mainly capitula and collects. Capitula of the common of a virgin are in col. 2 on the recto. Forms from the temporale, Advent to Stephen (Omnipotens sempiterne deus qui primicias . . .), on the verso.

Lit. E. 7, 8 (43). A.D. 1478. **1.** E. 7 ff. 3–92^v, E. 8 ff. 1–198^v Logica, under sixteen heads, anonymous, except (*g*), which is attributed to (William) Mylverley. **2.** E. 8 ff. 202–19. Mnemonic computistical verses, with explanations. **3.** E. 7

---

[1] Like five others of Preston's gifts.

f. 93 A binding leaf taken from a manuscript of logic written in s. xiii/xiv.
ff. 92 (E. 7)+220 (E. 8) and three medieval flyleaves of parchment (E. 7 f. 93)
and paper (E. 8 ff. 221–2). The division into two volumes may be ancient.
Stout paper. Written space c. 118×85 mm. c. 23 long lines. Frame ruling.
Collation: (E. 7) 1^{12} $2-9^{10}$; (E. 8) $1-9^{10}$ 10^6 $11-20^{10}$ 21^4 (ff. 197–200) 22–23^{10}. The
skilled, but not easy, secretary hand, the same throughout, is, no doubt, that of
William Ingram, who was professed at Christ Church, Canterbury, in 1483:
1c, f end 'quod W.I.'. 1a begins with an initial P, cut from some other book—
there is writing on the back—and pasted to f. 2: within it, a cock (?) bears a
scroll with the words 'Willelmus Ingram'. Secundo folio (E. 7 f. 3) *subicitur*.

'Iste liber constat Willelmo Ingram qui erat compositus Anno domini M° CCCC°
LXXVIII°', E. 7, f. 1.

1. (a) E. 7, ff. 2–27 De contradictoriis dandis.[1] Proposicio est oracio indicatiua congrua
et perfecta . . . (b) ff. 27^v–38 De commune tractatu. Terminus est in quem resoluitur
proposicio vt in subiectum . . . (c) ff. 38^v–50 De obligacionibus. Obligacio est quedam
ars mediante qua quis opponens . . . (d) ff. 50^v–71 De obieccionibus consequenciarum.
Vtilem quandam mixtionem de consequenciarum obieccionibus restat . . . (e) ff. 71^v–92
De obieccionibus iuxta hunc textum. Iuxta hunc textum tactum in libro periarmorum . . .
(f) f. 92^v, E. 8, ff. 1–18^v De obieccionibus insolubilium. Quatuor sunt diuisiones proposi-
cionum quarum prima . . . (g) ff. 19–48^v De materia de incipit. Quidlibet incipit esse
quod . . . apparet obuiare. Explicit tractatus Myluerley de incipit. (h) ff. 49–72^v De
materia de differt. Nulla differunt probatur sic . . . Expliciunt sophismata de differt.
(i) ff. 73–97^v De materia de scire. Scitum est non scitum probatur sic . . . Expliciunt
sophismata de scire. (j) ff. 98–124 De materia de contingentibus. Necessarium est
non necessarium probatur sic . . . Explicit sophisma de contingentibus. (k) ff. 124^v–156
De materia de proposicione ne equiuocacio . . . (l) ff. 156^v–162 De materia apparencie.
Circa materia aparencie multa concurrent dubia . . . (m) ff. 162^v–177^v De terminis
naturalibus. Natura est principium motus e quietis ipsius . . . (n) ff. 179–184^v De
materia proporcionum. Omnis proporcio aut est communiter dicta aut proprie dicta . . .
(o) ff. 185–8 De reduplicatiuis. Pro faciliori noticia ac instruccione iuuenum ostendo viam
probabilem . . . (p) ff. 188^v–198^v De materia motu(s). Ad materiam motus intellectui
imprimendam oportet plura scire . . . 2. (a) ff. 202–12 De materia que vocatur compown
manell. Filius Esto Dei Celum Bonus accipe grates. Compotus istius partes diuiditur in vi
partes quarum prima docet . . . (b) ff. 212–213^v Cisio ian ed ephi lucianus et hil fe ma mar
sulph / Pris wl fab . . . Isti vi^{ti} 4^{or} versus duodecim mensibus correspondent per ordinem
. . . (c) ff. 213^v–219 'Sep quadra pascha . . .' and other mnemonic verses, with explanations, ending abruptly. For Filius esto and Cisioianus see C. Wordsworth, *The Ancient
Kalendar of the University of Oxford*, 1904, pp. 6, 116–19.

Lit. E. 9 (12). s. xiv med. 1. ff. 1–8^v Incipiunt constituciones domini Othonis.
2. ff. 9–30 Incipiunt constituciones domini Ottoboni. 3. ff. 30–37^v Incipiunt
constituciones Oxonie. 4. ff. 37^v–43 Incipiunt constituciones Concilii Prouinc'
de Westmonasteria.' Et sunt constituciones domini Bonifacii archiepiscopi.
5. ff. 43–7 Incipiunt constituciones apud Reding. 6. ff. 47^v–59^v Incipiunt
constituciones de Lamehuht a domino Iohanne Cantuar' episcopo celebrate.
7. Prognostications of weather from the calendar, 'Si in die dominica kalende
ianuarii fuerint faciet yemen calidum . . .'. 8. ff. 60^v–61^v Prognostications from
nativities, and 'experimenta', 'Si vis scire ut stramina appareant . . .', partly in

---

[1] The titles of 1a–p, 2a are taken from the table of contents on f. 1.

French. ff. 61. Written space 140×83 mm. *c.* 36 long lines. Collation: 1–4⁸
5 seven (ff. 32–9) 6 six (ff. 40–5) 7–8⁸. Written in anglicana. Red initials.

1–6. Wilkins, *Concilia*, i. 649, ii. 1, i. 585, i. 736, ii. 33, ii. 50. For **3, 4** cf. C. R. Cheney
in *EHR* 50 (1935), 391, 402. **4** begins 'Uniuersis cristi fidelibus ad quos presens . . . Cum
ecclesia anglicana' and ends 'diximus (*sic*) apponenda'.

Lit. E. 10 (101). s. xiii/xiv. **1.** ff. 3–124 Testamenta duodecim patriarcharum.
2. ff. 124ᵛ–136 Narratio ex libro qui grece uocatur suda. **3.** ff. 136ᵛ–198
Incipiunt meditationes beati Bernardi abbatis. Multi multa sciunt . . . ff. 199.
Written space 105×67 mm. Collation of ff. 2–200: 1¹²+two leaves before
1 2–8¹² 9¹² wants 12 after f. 110 10–16¹² 17 six (ff. 195–200). Quires lettered a–r
on first rectos and last versos. Written in textura. Initials red or blue with
ornament of the other colour.

Written in England. From the Augustinian priory of Southwark, Surrey: 'Liber
beate Marie Ouerey', s. xvi in., ff. 2ᵛ, 198.

1, 2. Thomson, Grosseteste, pp. 43, 65. In 1 f. 2ʳ is blank, 2ᵛ has a table, 'T' Ruben de
hiis . . .' and f. 3ʳᵛ a heading, 'Hec abscondita et celata . . . in mente', in which it is said
that Grosseteste made this translation in 1242.

Lit. E. 11 (77). *Statuta Angliae, etc.*   s. xiv¹

Arts. 1–79. Statutes (etc.) up to 5 Edward III. At first the collection seems to
have ended at art. 62.

1. f. 6	Magna Carta. [E]dwardus dei gracia . . . Confirmation,	
	12 Oct. 1297.	*SR* i. 114
2. f. 10ᵛ	Incipit carta de Foresta.	i. 120
3. f. 12ᵛ	Incipiunt prouisiones de Merton'.	i. 1
4. f. 15	Incipit statutum de Marleberg'.	i. 19
5. f. 21	Incipit statutum Westm' primi. In French.	i. 26
6. f. 33ᵛ	Incipit statutum Gloucestr'. In French.	i. 45
7. f. 36ᵛ	Incipiunt explanaciones eiusdem.	i. 50
8. f. 37	Incipit statutum Westm' secundi.	i. 71
9. f. 61	Incipit statutum Westm' tercii. Quia emptores . . .	i. 106
10. f. 61ᵛ	Incipit statutum de finibus.	i. 128
11. f. 63	Incipit statutum Wyntonie. In French.	i. 96
12. f. 65	Incipit statutum de Mercatoribus. In French.	i. 98
13. f. 67	Incipiunt statuta de Religiosis.	i. 51
14. f. 67ᵛ	Incipit statutum de aportis Religiosorum. 'Statutum Karleoli'. Nuper ad noticiam . . .	i. 150
15. f. 69	Incipiunt statuta articuli cleri.	i. 171
16. f. 72	Incipit statutum de Cambi parti. [C]um contenu soit . . . Dated 20 Edw. I.	i. 216
17. f. 72	Incipit statutum de Bigamis.	i. 42
18. f. 73	Incipit statutum de scaccario. In French.	i. 197
19. f. 75ᵛ	Incipiunt districciones scaccarii. In French.	i. 197*b*

20. f. 76   Incipit statutum de escaetoribus 'apud Lincoln''.   i. 142
21. f. 77   Incipit statutum de coniunctim feoffatis.   i. 145
22. f. 78   Incipiunt articuli statuti Gloucestr'. Purueu est en-
             sement . . . la garauntie. Memorandum . . . concordat.
             9 Edw. II.   i. 52
23. f. 78ᵛ   Incipit statuta de visu francipleg'. In French.   i. 246
24. f. 79ᵛ   Incipit statutum de homag' et fidelitate faciend'.   i. 227
25. f. 79ᵛ   Incipiunt dies communes in Banco.   i. 208
26. f. 80   Incipiunt modus calumpniandi esson'.   i. 217
27. f. 80ᵛ   De circumspecte agatis. Rex talibus . . . licet porrigatur.   i. 101
28. f. 81   Incipit statutum de Iustic' assign'. In Latin.   Cf. i. 44
29. f. 81ᵛ   Incipit statutum de vocatis ad warant' 'forinsecis'.
             Cum tenens implicatus . . .   i. 108
30. f. 82   Incipit statutum quo waranto primo (sic). Anno Mille-
             simo cclxxviii . . . ex parte nostra. Cf. MMBL i. 252.
31. f. 83ᵛ   Incipit statutum nouum quo waranto. De le bref qest
             dist . . . auer brief.   i. 107
32. f. 84   Incipit vltimum statutum quo waranto. Quia breuia . . .   i. 107
33. f. 84ᵛ   Incipit statutum de vasto facto in custodia.   i. 109
34. f. 85   Incipiunt prerogatiua Regis.   i. 226
35. f. 87   Incipit statutum de conspiratoribus. In French.   i. 145
36. f. 87ᵛ   Incipit assisa panis.   i. 199
37. f. 87ᵛ   Incipit lucrum pistoris. In French.   i. 200
38. f. 88   Incipit assisa seruisie. In French.   i. 200
39. f. 88   Incipit de regia prohibicione et consultacione.   i. 108
40. f. 88   Incipit statutum de wardis et releuiis. In French.   i. 228
41. f. 88ᵛ   Incipit iudicium Pilorie.   i. 201
42. f. 89ᵛ   Incipit statutum de appellatis.   i. 141
43. f. 90   Incipit statutum de fragentibus prisonam.   i. 113
44. f. 90   Incipit de malefactoribus in parcis.   i. 111
45. f. 90ᵛ   De attornatis in finibus. Dated 'anno xxxv'.   i. 215
46. f. 91   Incipit super coheredes 'in hibernia'. Edwardus (sic) dei
             gracia . . . apud London' anno regni nostri quadragesimo
             nono. Cf. below, art. 69.   i. 5
47. f. 91ᵛ   Incipit exposicio vocabulorum. Sok hoc est secta . . .
             aueragio domini regis. Cf. MMBL i. 31.
48. f. 92ᵛ   Inquirendum est de Castris et aliis edificiis fossatis . . .
             in omnibus per annum. Called 'Statutum maneriorum'
             in art. 80.   i. 242
49. f. 93ᵛ   De hiis qui superuenerint ante iudicium. Cf. below,
             art. 71.   i. 110
50. f. 94   Incipit statutum Lincoln' de vicecomitibus. In French.   i. 174
51. f. 94ᵛ   Incipit iuramentum vicecomitis. Vous iuretz qe bien e
             loialment . . .   i. 247
52. f. 95   Incipit statutum de moneta. En countre les damages . . .
             soi e ses biens.   i. 219
53. f. 96   Incipiunt articuli de Moneta. Ces sount les choses . . .   i. 219a

54. f. 96ᵛ Incipiunt statutum de Ebor'. In French.   i. 177
55. f. 98ᵛ Edwardus dei gracia . . . (27 May 1306). Running title
            'Statutum nouum de foresta'.   i. 147
56. f. 100 Incipiunt articuli Oxon' (sic). [.]de primes fait a en-
            quere de chescune ville . . . perdaunt.   i. 211
57. f. 102ᵛ Incipit statutum de prisonibus. Statutum est de con-
            cilio domini . . . ponere voluerunt.
58. f. 103 Incipit statutum de Militi(bu)s.   i. 229
59. f. 103ᵛ Incipit statutum armatorum. A nostre seignur le Roi
            prient . . . santz plus.   i. 230
60. f. 104 Incipit Gauelet.   i. 222
61. f. 105 Incipit statutum de moneta nouum. Part of f. 105ᵛ was
            left blank.   i. 220
62. f. 106 Hic incipit sentencia lata super cartas. Dated 1254.   i. 6
63. f. 106ᵛ Hic incipit statutum de Karliolis. Dated at Carlisle,
            anno viii.   i. 215
64. f. 107 Statu(tu)m de ponendis in assisis. Quia dominus Rex
            per publicam . . . modo omittas T'.   i. 113
65. f. 108 Hic incipiunt Articuli Winton'.   i. 245
66. f. 108ᵛ Statutum de Ragman. In French. Cf. art. 28.   i. 44
67. f. 109ᵛ Articuli contra prohibicionem Regis. Sub qua forma . . .
            peccuniam.   i. 101/24
68. f. 110 Diffinicio conspiratorum. Dominus Rex mandauit . . .
            debeat T' etc.   i. 216/15
69. f. 110 Hic incipit Statutum Hibernie. Rex iustic' . . . Cum
            millites . . . Dated 9 May anno 8.   i. 5
70. f. 111 De proteccionibus calumpniandis. In French.   i. 217
71. f. 111ᵛ Incipit Statutum de hiis qui admittendi sunt ad de-
            fendendum ius suum. Cf. art. 49.   i. 110
72. f. 112 De magnis assisis in duellis iniungendis.   i. 218
73. f. 112ᵛ De feodis magnatum Anglie. Fe ferme est a tenir . . .
            come soun neif.
74. f. 113 Dies communes de dote sunt hic scripte. Si in octauis . . .
            In Crastino sancti Martini.   i. 208
75. f. 113ᵛ Incipiunt articuli Corone in Itinere Iusticiariorum. In
            primis de veteribus Placitis . . . columbar' destruantur.
            Ends at no. 55.   i. 233
76. f. 115 De terris felonum.   i. 230
77. f. 115ᵛ Hic incipit statut' officii coronatorum.   i. 40
78. f. 117 Incipit Statutum de anno et die bisextili. Edwardus dei
            gracia . . . teste me ipso apud. Expliciunt. f. 117ᵛ blank.   i. 7

79. Five statutes of Edward III: (a) f. 118 Hic incipiunt statuta edita tempore
Regis Edwardi Tercii anno primo. Al honour de dieu . . .; (b) f. 120ᵛ Hic
incipit statuta 'edit' tempore Hugonis Despenser'. Come Hugh' le Despenser . . .;
(c) f. 124 Hic incipit statutum editum apud Norhampton'. Nostre seignur . . .;
(d) f. 128 Hic incipit Westm' sextum. Au parlement . . .; (e) ff. 132ᵛ–136

Hic incipit Westm' septimum de Roberdesmen. Au parlement . . . est dit. Expliciunt noua statuta.

SR i. 255, 251, 257, 261, 265. ff. 136ᵛ–137ᵛ were left blank: seventeen names, the first 'Willelmus Holbourne', are on 136ᵛ.

80. Tables on a preliminary quire: (*a*) ff. 1–4, of chapters of arts. 1–6, 8; (*b*) ff. 4–5, 'Statuta in isto volumine', listing arts. 1–11 in one hand, arts. 12–61 in a second hand, and arts. 62–79 in a third; (*c*) f. 5ᵛ Dies communes in Cancellar'.

81. Additions, s. xv²: (*a*) f. 138ᵛ A table of all possible dates of Septuagesima; (*b*) ff. 139–43 A calendar in red and black: 'Erkenwal' in red, 30 Apr. and 14 Nov.; Osmund added at 4 Dec.; (*c*) on the right of (*b*) Tables of conjunction and opposition in two decennovenal cycles headed '1482' and '1501'; (*d*) f. 143 A table in red and black of months and the zodiacal signs applicable to each month, with columns for 'Blodeletyng', 'Medesyn', and 'Bathyng', and a table of moonlight, with place-names 'Bristow', 'Sandwich', 'Berwik', 'London', and 'Grauysende'; (*e*) f. 144ᵛ A compass with twenty-four divisions; (*f*) f. 145ᵛ An 'orlage' to calculate sunrise and moonrise, 'Furst set the sun on the day of the monthe and set the mone on the day of her age . . .'; (*g*) f. 146ʳᵛ Verses 'Ad mensem. mensisque diem . . .' (2 lines) and computistical memoranda in English and Latin. ff. 138, 143ᵛ, 145, 147–148ᵛ blank.

ff. ii + 148 + ii. 160 × 100 mm. Written space *c.* 120 × 65 mm. 33–6 long lines. Collation: 1⁶ wants 6, probably blank 2–11⁸ 12¹² 13¹² wants 9–12, probably blank, after f. 105 14–15¹² 16¹² wants 8–10 after f. 136 and 12 after f. 139, all blank 17⁶ 18 five (ff. 144–8). Arts. 1–79 in anglicana, current on ff. 1–62ʳ and in arts. 62–79. 4-line or 5-line spaces for coloured initials remain blank. Binding of s. xix, uniform with Lit. E. 7, E. 8. Secundo folio *debent*.

Written in England. 'Phillip Swallow', f. 138, s. xvi. Rather earlier scribbles include the names 'I. Appleton de Catewyke', f. 137, and 'Thwyng', f. 137ᵛ.

Lit. E. 12 (35). s. xv². **1.** ff. 1–23ᵛ Regule et rubrice in hoc opusculo sequenti contente cum magnis laboribus et deligencia fideliter collecte et excerpte sunt de vero ordinali ecclesie sar*um* per dominum clementem maydeston' quendam monachum et confratrem de monasterio ordinis sancti saluatoris iuxta Schene . . . (1ᵛ) et distinccione 13ᵃ q. 2ᵃ. Venerabili doctori et carissimo patri meo Thome Gasgayngne . . . valde diffuse. Quodcumque festum in dominica 2ᵃ . . . ut plangam. **2.** f. 24 Brito Celtes grece masculum generis . . . **3.** ff. 27–136 Regula de omnibus historiis inchoandis . . . Vidit Iohannes ihesum. deo gracias Explicit compendiosus tractatus de historiis inchoandis et responsoriis ferialibus et missis dominicalibus cantandis et de commemoracionibus faciendis per totum annum secundum usum Sarum per deuotum virum dominum Thomam Grantham dudum vicarium in capella regia sancti Stephani infra palacium Westm' utiliter compilatum Cuius anime propicietur deus. Amen. ff. 136. Written space 90 × 62 mm. 21–4 long lines. Frame ruling. Collation: 1–2¹⁰ 3⁶ 4–14¹⁰. Written in a secretary hand, with some anglicana forms.

1. Clement Maidstone's rules for the order of services according to the use of Sarum, called 'Crede michi'. Also in B.L., Add. 25456, ff. 94–103. Differs much from the text printed in HBS vii. 40/6–80/18. For the letter to Gascoigne, see there, p. xxxvi. Many notes in red in the margins refer to the readings of 'falsi libri'. **2.** At the end is the opinion of Richard 'Hampul super octauam leccionem mortuorum'. On the word at Job 19: 24

see *OED*, s.v. Celt. **3.** Also in B.L., Add. 25456, ff. 11–87, where the colophon is 'Explicit pica pro iii^bus commemoracionibus quod G.': the first section, 'Littera A', is partly printed in HBS vii. 119–26. The scribe wrote 'Osanna' in the upper margins, ff. 1, 27, before he began his work. ff. 24^v–26^v are blank.

Lit. E. 13 (56). s. xiv². **1.** ff. 7–16^v Tables of statutes of 1–50 Edward III. **2.** ff. 19–226^v Statutes of 1–45 Edward III. **3.** ff. 227–230^v Statutes of 47 and 50 Edward III. **4.** Additions to **2** in blank spaces on ff. 17–18^v, 60, 98–101^v, 231–232^v. **5.** Additions on flyleaves: (*a*) ff. 2–3^v Chronological notes of royal births, battles, etc. from 1312, ending with earthquakes, 21 May 1382 ('destruxit Campanill'': cf. HMC, *9th Rep.*, App., p. 128) and in 9 Richard II (1385–6); (*b*) ff. 4^v–5 'Taxacio bonorum Spiritualium et temporalium' of the province of Canterbury and other provinces totalling £20,875. 17*s*. 6*d*; (*c*) ff. 5^v–6 Kings of England from Alfred to Richard II and regnal years, except for Richard II. ff. 235. Written space 87 × 60 mm. 24 long lines. Collation of ff. 7–233 (the foliator missed a leaf after '201' and a leaf after '202'): 1^12 2^8 3^10 4–27^8 28 seven (ff. 227–33). Written in anglicana of a business kind, but not current.

Lit. E. 17 (62). s. xiv/xv. A 'monastic quire psalter not containing Mattins, with Collectar' (Frere). **1** (added). ff. 2^v–7 Antiphons at vespers of the Assumption of B.V.M., hymn of St. Bartholomew at vespers, 'Bartholomeus celi sydus . . .' (*RH*, no. 2318), and office at vespers of the Visitation of B.V.M. **2.** ff. 8–39^v Feria ii^a ad primam. Psalmus. Beatus vir . . .: order of prime, Monday to Saturday. **3.** ff. 40–52^v Penitential psalms. **4.** ff. 52^v–65^v Litany and prayers. **5.** ff. 66–85^v Psalm 118. **6.** ff. 86–122 Dominical and ferial office of vespers. **7.** ff. 122^v–140^v Collects and antiphons for Sundays after Trinity. **8.** ff. 140^v–144 Vespers at Epiphany. **9.** ff. 144–149^v Vespers of the common of saints, ending imperfectly. ff. 149. Written space 48 × 32 mm. 13 long lines. Collation: 1^6+1 leaf after 6 2–4^8 5^12 6–11^8 12^8 wants 6 after f. 96 13–15^8 16^4 (ff. 123–6) 17–18^8 19^8 wants 8. The additions are in anglicana (art. 1) and a sort of fere-textura (arts. 7–9).

Written in England, no doubt for Christ Church, Canterbury. 'Iste liber constat [. . . . .] monacho ecclesie cristi cant' ', f. 1, s. xv in.

Frere, no. 546. **1, 7–9** added in s. xv. **4.** The second martyr, following Stephen, was probably Thomas, but the name has been erased. Anne first of virgins. For the rest the names are the same as in Add. 6, in so far as they remain there.

Lit. E. 18 (55). s. xv/xvi. **1.** ff. 1–15 Index to **2**. **2.** ff. 17–50^v De creacione mundi et eius etatibus. In principio creauit deus celum et terram . . . peccata confitentibus parcat Amen. **3.** f. 51^rv Table of contents of **2**. ff. 52. A contemporary foliation of ff. 17–52, 'fo primo'—'fo xxxvi^to'. Paper. Written space 210 × 125 mm. 25–9 long lines. Only the vertical bounders are ruled and that with a hard point. Collation: 1–2^16 3 twenty. Written in a secretary hand.

Written in England (Lincolnshire?).

1, 3. In references the old leaf numbers are used: the recto is 'co(lumpna) 1^a' and the verso 'co(lumpna) 2ᵃ'. **2** consists of: ff. 17–38ᵛ a chronicle from the creation to 10 Henry VI (1431–2); ff. 38ᵛ–49 sections on prodigies and miracles, famous people, battles 'tardi temporis', the city of Lincoln to 1423, and a list of bishops of Lincoln to William Alnwick (1436–49); ff. 49–50ᵛ Quedam omissa in precedentibus et hic merito inserenda; f. 52 verses (8 lines), 'Hec supratacta patrum sunt dicta priorum . . .', giving 1438 as the date at which the chronicle was made.

Lit. E. 25 (47). s. xiv med. **1.** Short lections: (*a*) ff. 2–33ᵛ, of temporale; (*b*) ff. 34–68ᵛ, of sanctorale; (*c*) ff. 69–75, 'In octauis sancti Stephani', 'In octauis sancti Iohannis', 'In octauis Innocentium', of Edmund, king and martyr, 'In commemoracione sancte Margarete', 'In commemoracione sancti Nicholai', 'In commemoracione sancti Leonardi'; (*d*) f. 75, of Praxedes. **2** (added, s. xv). f. 76ᵛ Recipes for food in English: (*a*) Tak grene walnots xiiii nythis beforn medsomer . . .; (*b*) Tak iii vncis of comyn . . . ff. 74 (foliated 2–75) and three medieval end-leaves, 1, 76, 77. Written space *c.* 150 × 110 mm. Frame ruling in ink. *c.* 28 long lines. Collation of ff. 2–75: 1–8⁸ 9¹⁰. Written in current anglicana. Secundo folio *miscendam*.

Written in England, for monastic use. 'Ricardus Smyth of hoxisum (?)' among scribbles of s. xvi on f. 76.

Frere, no. 547. **1***a* begins 'Lecciones feriales prima ebdomada aduentus. Feria ii leccio prima. In illa die proiciet homo'. **1***b*. Andrew to Saturninus, including Austrobert, Cuthbert, Botulph, Romanus, and Osyth. Twelve lections for principal feasts.

Lit. E. 42 ff. 1–68, 75–81. + Maidstone, Kent County Archives Office, S/Rm Fae. 2 (*ff. 2*). *Passionale* s. xii¹

Seventy-seven leaves coming from four of the Passionalia listed in Eastry's catalogue of the Christ Church collection (*Ancient Libraries*, p. 52, nos. 359, 361, 364–5), thirty from vol. 1 (no. 359), fourteen from vol. 2 (no. 361), twenty-two from vol. 5 (no. 364), and eleven from vol. 6 (no. 365). ff. 7, 8, 47 are half-leaves only and ff. 66–8, 72, 73 are in bad condition. The condition of other leaves is fairly good, at least on one side, and some still have the complete written space, for example ff. 18–20, 54, 57, 58, 75.

The year was covered in seven volumes, beginning at 31 Dec., 1 Feb., 2 Apr., 29 June, 3 Aug., 21 Sept., and 11 Nov. A similar seven-volume set was at Glastonbury and probably at St. Augustine's, Canterbury, and at Rochester. The last two volumes of what seems to have been the St. Augustine's set remain (B.L., Arundel 91 and Bodleian, Fell 2) and part of a leaf of what may have been the sixth volume at Rochester survives in a binding at Worcester College, Oxford. B.L., Arundel 169 may be the fourth volume of a similar set: the lives run from 29 June to 2 Aug. Of the Christ Church set a second copy of vol. 2 survives (see below) and also 150 leaves of vol. 3 (*Ancient Libraries*, no. 362: cf. Ker, *MLGB*, p. 36). The latter resembles the fragments of vols. 5 and 6 fairly closely.

Vol. 1

Arts. 1–19 are from the volume listed in Eastry's catalogue as 'Vita sancti Siluestri continet uitas et passiones sanctorum quorum festa celebrantur a die Sancti Siluestri usque ad festum Sancti Ignacii'. The thirty remaining leaves are from eleven quires: ff. 1, 2, one sheet of quire 1; ff. 3, 4, one sheet (3)[1] of quire 2; ff. 5, 6, single adjacent leaves of quire 3; ff. 7, 8, single adjacent leaves of quire 4; ff. 9–12, two sheets (3, 4) of quire 5; ff. 13, 14, single adjacent leaves of quire 6; ff. 15, 16, one sheet (3) of quire 7; ff. 17–24, the whole of quire 8; ff. 25, 26, one sheet (1) of quire 9; ff. 27, 28, one sheet (2) of quire 10; ff. 29, 30, one sheet (2) of quire 11.

1. f. 1^{rv} Genovefa, *3 Jan.*[2] exiguitate census[3] . . . cristianis. *Acta Sanctorum*, Jan. I, 144–5 (sect. 15–21). *BHL*, no. 3336.

2. f. 2 Theogenes, *3 Jan.* Tunc beatus . . . in secula seculorum Amen. *AS*, Jan. I, 135 (sect. 9–13). *BHL*, no. 8107.

3. f. 2^{rv} Lucianus, 8 Jan. Incipit passio Sancti Luciani Mart' vi idus Ianuarii. Beatorum martirum sacra certamina . . . Talibus itaque. *AS*, Jan. I, 466 (sect. 1–5). *BHL*, no. 5010.

4. ff. 3–4^v Julianus, *9 Jan.* (f. 3^{rv}) quod ortamini . . . amator castitatis. (f. 4^{rv}) uisio ab oculis . . . Pro qua re dignum est. *AS*, Jan. I, 576–7, 578–9 (sect. 3–6, 14–18). *BHL*, no. 4529.

5. ff. 5–6^v Furseus, *16 Jan.* corporis egrotantis . . . illum ibi superare. *AS*, Jan. II, 37–8 (sect. 3–16). *BHL*, no. 3210.

6. ff. 7–8 Marius, Martha, Audifax, Abacuc, *19 Jan.* et multiplicaberis . . . in nimpha necata est. *AS*, Jan. II, 217–19 (sect. 8–19). *BHL*, no. 5543.

7. f. 8^v Agnes, *21 Jan.* S[er]uus cristi ambro[sius] . . . circundedit me. *AS*, Jan. II, 351 (sect. 1–3). *BHL*, no. 156.

8. f. 9 Patroclus, *21 Jan.* eligius qui erat prior et prepositus penarum eius . . . beatissimi patrocli martiris. qui . . . in secula seculorum amen. Explicit passio Sancti Patrocli Martiris. Cf. *AS*, Jan. II, 345 (sec. 10–12). *BHL*, no. 6520 (?).

9. ff. 9–12^v Vincent, 22 Jan. Incipit passio Sancti Vincentii Mart' xi kl. Febr. Probabile satis . . . duris ad molam funibus. *AS*, Jan. II, 394–7 (sect. 1–18). *BHL*, no. 8628.

10. f. 13^{rv} Asclas, *23 Jan.* nominis tui. et extende manum . . . uicesima prima in cristo . . . in secula seculorum amen. Explicit passio Sancti Ascli Martiris. *AS*, Jan. II, 456–7 (sect. 3–7). *BHL*, no. 722.

11. ff. 13^v–14^v Babylas, *24 Jan.* Incipit passio [. . . . .]. Numerianus rex cum immolasset . . . iniuste et. Mombritius, *Sanctuarium* (edn. 1910), i. 127/35–128/19. *BHL*, no. 890.

12. ff. 15–16^v Julianus, *27 Jan.* (f. 15^{rv}) si credis eum quem . . . celestibus disciplinis. (f. 16^{rv}) cereis abscessit . . . per eterna secula amen. Explicit uita

---

[1] I have presumed that quires were of four sheets (eight leaves) and call the outermost sheet 1 and the innermost sheet 4.

[2] Dates in italics are from *BHL*.

[3] I note the first and last words legible without difficulty.

Sancti Iuliani Episcopi. *AS*, Jan. II, 764, 766–7 (sect. 13–15, 26–30). *BHL*, no. 4544.

13. f. 16ᵛ Gregory, *12 Mar*. Incipit uita Sancti Gregorii Episcopi. Gregorius in urbe roma . . . memorię potius. Ed. Grisar in *Zeitschrift für katholische Theologie*, xi (1887), 162 (sect. 1, 2). *BHL*, no. 3639.
Art. 13 is an addition in a hand of s. xii².

14. ff. 17–19. Polycarp, *26 Jan*. cibi prebuit . . . colligat dominus iesus cristus . . . in secula seculorum amen. Explicit passio Sancti Policarpi Episcopi. *AS*, Jan. II, 706–7 (sect. 6–17). *BHL*, no. 6870.

15. ff. 19–25ᵛ Leucius, etc., 28 Jan. Incipit passio Sanctorum Martirum Leucii. Tyrsi. et Galenici. v kl' februarii. Eo tempore quo cristi membra . . . duabus ex numero. *AS*, Jan. II, 824–9 (sect. 1–30). *BHL*, no. 8280.

16. f. 26 Sabinianus, *29 Jan*. Domine parce . . . kalendas februarii . . . in secula seculorum amen. Explicit passio Sancti Sauiniani Martiris. *AS*, Jan. II, 941 (sect. 11, 12). *BHL*, no. 7438.

17. ff. 26–8 Aldegundis, *30 Jan*. Incipit uita Sanctę Aldegundis Virginis [. . . . .]. (f. 26ʳᵛ) Postquam omnipotentis dei . . . nuptię celebrentur. (f. 27ʳᵛ) angelus in uisu . . . qui coactus est. (f. 28) deprecantium peccatorum . . . secula seculorum amen. Explicit uita Sancte Aldegundis Virginis. *AS*, Jan. II, 1035–6, 1037, 1040 (sect. 2, 3, 6–10, 27). *BHL*, no. 245.

18. ff. 28–9 Balthildis. 30 Jan. Incipit uita Sanctę Balthildis Regine iii kl' Febr'. (f. 28ʳᵛ) Benedictus deus qui wlt omnes . . . deuotionem eius. (f. 29) patenter . . . incolumis ad suos est reuersus. Eius sollennitas celebratur tercio kalendas februarii. Explicit uita S' Balthil[dis]. Cf. *AS*, Jan. II, 739, 741– (sect. 2–4, 13–). *BHL*, no. 906(?).

19. ff. 29ᵛ–30ᵛ Honoratus, 16 Jan. Sermo Sancti Hilarii in Depositione . . . . xvii kl' Februarii. (f. 29ᵛ) Agnoscitis dilectissimi . . . non potest quisquam. (f. 30ʳᵛ) quotiens sibi in animo . . . decreuit metallis. *AS*, Jan. II, 17, 21–2 (sect. 1, 2, 23–8). *BHL*, no. 3975.

Vol. 2

Arts. 20–9 are from the volume listed by Eastry as 'Passionale sancti Ignacii secundum'. The fourteen remaining leaves appear to be from five quires: Maidstone leaves, one sheet of quire 1; ff. 31–4, two sheets (3, 4) of quire 2; ff. 36, 35 in that order, two single non-adjacent leaves of quire 3; ff. 37–40, two sheets (2, 3) of quire 3; ff. 41, 42, two single non-adjacent leaves of quire 5, probably sheet 1 of the quire cut in two. Running titles.

B.L., Cotton Otho D. viii, ff. 8–173 is a second copy of vol. 2 of the Christ Church passional.[1] Eastry called it 'Passionale sancti Ignacii primum'. It is rather later in date than arts. 20–9 and seems to have been less full, lacking the

---

[1] Two cols. 38 lines. Now shrunk and damaged by fire, but the script was no doubt always smaller and more compressed than that of E. 42.

lives of Dorothea and Theophilus and of Maximilianus (arts. 21, 25). The last life now is of Wulfran, 20 Mar., but there are perhaps signs of erasure on f. 173^v and the part of the table of contents which survives in Trinity College, Cambridge, 1155 has four erased lines after the last entry, 'Vita sancti Wlframni episcopi'. Arts. 20, 22–4, 26–9 occur in Otho D. viii at ff. 46–50^v, 96^v–100^v, 100^v–103, 103–139^v, 139^v–141, 141–145^v (corresponding to arts. 27, 28), 148–168^v.

20. Kent County Archives Office, Maidstone, S/RM. Fae. 2. Amandus, *6 Feb.* custodes iuxta . . . et in flumen. *AS*, Feb. I, 850, sect. 8/2–12/28. *BHL*, no. 332.

21. Kent County Archives Office, Maidstone, S/RM. Fae. 2. Dorothea and Theophilus, *6 Feb.* seculo homines qui sic mortui sunt ut animalia. qui . . . autem quia si. Not *BHL*, no. 2323.

22. f. 31 Perpetua and Felicitas, *7 Mar.* prior reddendo spiritum . . . ut testificetur omnipotentis dei . . . amen. Explicit passio sanctarum perpetue et felicitatis. *AS*, Mart. I, 638 (sect. 22, 23). *BHL*, no. 6633.

23. ff. 31–4 Quadraginta Milites, 11 Mar. Incipit passio Sanctorum Quadraginta Militum. Domiciani . . . et Clauicularii. v Idus Martii. In tempore licinii regis . . . credentes in cristo . . . amen. Explicit passio sanctorum Quadraginta . . . *AS*, Mart. II, 19D–21E (sect. 1–13). *BHL*, no. 7539. Complete.

24. ff. 34^{rv}, 36^{rv}, 35 Gregory, *12 Mar.* Incipit prefatio [. . . .]. Beatissimo ac felicissimo domino iohanni . . . humiliter parui. (f. 36^{rv}) Si delicioso cupitis . . . magisterio. (f. 35) fecundatur . . . infortuniis te. *AS*, Mart. II, 137B–E, 204D–206A, 210C–F. *BHL*, no. 3641.

25. f. 35^v Maximilian, *12 Mar.* Incipit passio Sancti Maximiliani Martiris iiii Idus Martii. Tusco et anolino consulibus . . . Cunque resisteret maximilianus respondit. *BHL*, no. 5813.

26. ff. 37–38^v Longinus, *15 Mar.* lateris sui gratiam . . . deum semper. Hec acta sunt in ciuitate cappadocie . . . in secula seculorum amen. Explicit passio Sancti Longini Martiris. *AS*, Mart. II, 385B–386C. *BHL*, no. 4965.

27. ff. 38^v–39 Gertrude, *17 Mar.* Incipit uita Sancte Geretrudis Virginis xvi kl' Apr'. Cum esset in domo parentum . . . *AS*, Mart. II, 594B– . *BHL*, no. 3490.

The verso of f. 38 and recto of f. 39 are almost wholly illegible.

28. ff. 39–40^v [Incipiunt miracula eiusdem] beate Virginis. Erat quedam . . . postulabat et. *AS*, Mart. II, 596F–598C. *BHL*, no. 3495.

29. ff. 41–42^v Cuthbert, *20 Mar.* (f. 41^{rv}) duxit ad uesperam . . . Uolens autem latius monstrare. (f. 42^{rv}) disposuit credo . . . At presbiter qui. The life by Bede, ed. B. Colgrave, pp. 236/27–244/6, 284/19–290/29.

Vol. 5

Arts. 30–50 are from the volume listed by Eastry as 'Inuencio sancti Stephani v^m'. ff. 43–57, 76–9 are probably from nine quires: ff. 43–6, two sheets (1, 2) of quire 1; f. 49, leaf 1 of quire 2; ff. 47, 48, one sheet of quire 3; ff. 50, 51, one sheet of quire 4; ff. 52, 53, one sheet of quire 5; ff. 76, 77, one sheet of quire 6; ff. 54, 55, one sheet (4) of quire 7; ff. 56, 57, one sheet (1) of quire 8; ff. 78, 79, one sheet of quire 9. Art. 40 (ff. 75, 62, 63, a singleton and a bifolium) may have been an insertion in its proper place after Bartholomew or an addition at the end.

30. ff. 43–6, 49 Stephen, *3 Aug.* (ff. 43–44ᵛ) adiuuante iesu . . . plurimum tempus. (ff. 45–46ᵛ, 49ʳᵛ) erubescere . . . subdiaconum nostrum nomine sennodum. *PL* xli. 836–9, 846–51 (bk. 1, ch. 3–11; bk. 2, ch. 2–4). *BHL*, no. 7861.

31. f. 47ʳᵛ Walburga, *25 Feb.* modis et blanditiis . . . debebis. Qui. *PL* cxl. 1096C–1098B. *BHL*, no. 8766.

32. f. 48ʳᵛ Oswald, *5 Aug.* diximus. Porro caput . . . et per annos uiginti octo laboriosissime tenuit. regnante . . . per immortalia secula seculorum amen. Explicit passio Sancti Oswaldi Regis et Martiris. From Bede, Historia Ecclesiastica, ed. Colgrave and Mynors, 1969, pp. 250–4.

33. f. 48ᵛ Cassian, *5 Aug.* Incipit uita Sancti Cassiani Episcopi. Non' Augusti. Sanctus ac bea[tissimus] cassianus uir genere egyptius fuit . . . cui se in pueritia. *Anal. Boll.* iv. 160/3–12 (as the text in footnotes). *BHL*, no. 1632.

34. f. 50 Taurinus, *11 Aug.* se quasi uiuus de fossa . . . a febribus tuis orationibus per . . . *AS*, Aug. II, 642F–643B. *BHL*, no. 7990.

35. f. 50ʳᵛ Hippolytus, etc., 13 Aug. Incipit passio Sancti Ypoliti martiris sociorumque eius Idus Augusti. Regressus beatus ypolitus post tertium diem . . . eadem hora. Mombritius (edn. 1910), ii. 29/14–30/1. *BHL*, no. 3961.

36. f. 51ʳᵛ Assumption of B.V.M., *15 Aug.* humanitatis induitur . . . sed ego honorifico patrem meum.

Marked for lections (within the octave?), 'Quinta die' and 'Sexta die': the latter begins 'Nulli dubium omnem illam'.

37. f. 52 Philibert, *24 Aug.* monasterii subripuerunt . . . suscepta est in gaudio cui est . . . in secula seculorum amen. Explicit vita sancti Filiberti Abbatis. *AS*, Aug. IV, 80D–F. *BHL*, no. 6805.

38. f. 52ʳᵛ Symphorianus, 22 Aug. Incipit passio Sancti Simphoriani martiris xi kl' Septembris. Cum aduersum cristianum nomen . . . sacrificauerint. *AS*, Aug. IV, 496B–D. *BHL*, no. 7967.

39. f. 53ʳᵛ Bartholomew, *24 Aug.* misit ad eum et rogauit . . . erat a me uinctus. *AS*, Aug. V, 34F–36A. *BHL*, no. 1002.

40. ff. 75ʳᵛ, 62–63ᵛ Miracles of Audoenus at Canterbury, 24 Aug. Printed from this copy: f. 75 by N. R. Ker in *Anal. Boll.* lxiv (1946), 51–3; ff. 62, 63 by A. Wilmart in *Anal. Boll.* li (1933), 288–92.

An addition, s. xii med.

41. f. 76 Genesius, *25 Aug.* luminibus ita a nobis . . . presens uirtus operata est? [. . . .] genesii martyris.
Miracles of Genesius. *PL* l. 1273C–1274B. *BHL*, no. 3307.

42. ff. 76–77ᵛ Georgius, Aurelius, Felix, et soc., *27 Aug.* (f. 76ʳᵛ) Fuit quidam iuuenis. temporibus abdiram regis nomine aurelius . . . illusorum [. . . .] ministerio. (f. 77ʳᵛ) sancti aurelii congregati . . . aggrauari decernit. *BHL*, no. 3408.

43. f. 54ʳᵛ Adrian, *8 Sept.* famule tue et non in uanum . . . cristo domino seruiant. cui est honor et gloria in secula seculorum amen. Explicit passio Sancti Adriani Martiris et aliorum uiginti [. . . .]. Cf. *BHL*, no. 3744b.

44. f. 54ᵛ Audomarus, 9 Sept. Incipit uita Sancti Audomari Episcopi v Idus Septembris. Dum sanctorum patrum ueneranda memoria . . . luxouium. *AS*, Sept. III, 402B–D. *BHL*, no. 767.

45. ff. 55–56ᵛ Protus and Hyacinthus, *11 Sept.* (f. 55ʳᵛ) cultura.talia... Credit factum pater. (f. 56ʳᵛ) moritur quasi homo . . . Explicit passio Sanctorum [. . . .]. Mombritius (edn. 1910), ii. 392/22–393/35, 397/11–58. *BHL*, no. 6975.

46. f. 56ᵛ Felix and Regula, *11 Sept.* Incipit passio Sancti Felicis et Germanę... die noctuque. *AS*, Sept. III, 772D, E. *BHL*, no. 2888.

47. f. 57ʳᵛ Exaltation of Holy Cross, *14 Sept.* palmarum cereis et lampadibus . . . plurimo incremento.donante domino nostro . . . per omnia secula seculorum amen. Explicit sermo in exaltatione Sanctę Crucis.

48. f. 57ᵛ Cornelius, 14 Sept. Incipit passio Sancti Cornelii [Pape]¹ xviii kl' Oct'. Temporibus decii cesaris . . . attulit ei. Accipiens autem. Mombritius (edn. 1910), i. 373/1–33. *BHL*, no. 1958.

49. f. 78ʳᵛ Lucia and Geminianus, *16 Sept.* autem non ualent... Et sedens in sede. Cf. Mombritius (edn. 1910), ii. 112/48–113/24. *BHL*, no. 4985.

50. f. 79ʳᵛ Euphemia, *16 Sept.* exhibere in conscientia . . . est et terribile. Mombritius (edn. 1910), i. 455/20–456/30. *BHL*, no. 2708.

Vol. 6

Arts. 51–62 are from the volume listed by Eastry as 'Passionale Sancti Mathei viᵐ'. The eleven remaining leaves are from five quires: ff. 80, 81, one sheet (4) of quire 1; ff. 58, 59, one sheet of quire 2; ff. 60, 61, one sheet of quire 3; ff. 66–8, three leaves of quire 4; ff. 64, 65, one sheet of quire 5.

B.L., Arundel 91 contains the same collection. The twelve pieces in E. 42 occur there on ff. 9ᵛ–12ᵛ, 12ᵛ–13ᵛ, 13ᵛ–16, 16ᵛ–20ᵛ, 23–26ᵛ, 81ᵛ–85, 86–99, 107–8, 108ᵛ–112, 190–5, 195ᵛ–198, 198–206ᵛ.

51. f. 80 Maurice, *21 Sept.* a sanctis factum... Explicit passio Sancti Mau[ricii]. *AS*, Sept. VI, 343E–F. *BHL*, no. 5737. As Ar., f. 12ᵛ.

---

¹ A deliberate erasure.

52. f. 80^{rv} Incipiunt Miracula eor[un]dem martyru[m]. Magne sunt uir[tu]tes.
. . . pondera trutinari. Expliciunt miracula. *PL* lxxi. 771–3. As Ar., ff. 12^v–13^v.

53. f. 81^{rv} Emmeram, *22 Sept.* Post passionem domini nostri . . . Vnde superno
inspiramine uenerabilis pontifex. *BHL*, no. 2539a. As Ar., ff. 13^v–14rb/1.

This abridgement, in which Emmeram is called Auitramnus, was known to Krusch only
in Arundel 91 (MGH, *Scriptores rerum Merov.* iv. 46).

54. f. 58^{rv} Firminus, *25 Sept.* sanctorum destruis . . . illius sollenitas. qui
perseuerans. *AS*, Sept. VII, 54D–55C. *BHL*, no. 3003. As Ar., ff. 19rb/23–
20va/19.[1]

55. f. 59^{rv} Cosmas and Damianus, *27 Sept.* nocuerunt eos . . . quomodo ei
ipsum. *AS*, Sept. VII, 477A–478B. *BHL*, no. 1970. As Ar., ff. 25va/3–26vb/7.

56. f. 60^{rv} Pelagia, 8 *Oct.* in prędicta ciuitate . . . Pueri fecerunt. *AS*, Oct. IV,
262–3 (sect. 2–11). *BHL*, no. 6605. As Ar., ff. 81vb/9–82vb/34.

57. f. 61^{rv} Denis, *9 Oct.* docente didicerant . . . affixus et sol sui domini.
Mombritius (edn. 1910), i. 394/20–395/41. *BHL*, no. 2175. As Ar., ff. 86rb/24–
87va/12.

58. f. 66^{rv} Demetrius, *8 Oct.*[2] Prędiisque . . . Explicit passio [. . .]. As Ar.,
f. 108rb/27–37.

59. ff. 66^v–68^v Miracles of Demetrius. Marin[ianus quidam genere ac opu-
lentia] clarus . . . Badly damaged text corresponding to Ar., ff. 108^v–110^v.

60. f. 64^{rv} Eustace, *1 Nov.* facie. ualde concupiuit . . . cibos [. . .] in tempore.
AS, Sept. VI, 127D–E. *BHL*, no. 2760. As Ar., ff. 192rb/9–193rb/28.

61. f. 65^r Rumwold, *1 Nov.* uniuerse carnis . . . cristo qui in unitate tri[. . . .]
Explicit uita Sancti Rumwoldi Confessoris. *AS*, Nov. I, 689–90 (sect. 10, 11).
BHL, no. 7385. As Ar., f. 198ra/7–198rb/7.

62. f. 65^{rv} Hubert, *3 Nov.* [. . . .] Post gloriosum bea[tissimi ac pre]cellentis-
simi landberti . . . preclusis nec non. *AS*, Nov. I, 808–809A. *BHL*, no. 3994.
As Ar. ff. 198–199ra/14.

Written space: (vol. 1) 277 × 190 mm (f. 18); (vols. 5, 6) 305 × *c.* 190 mm (ff. 54, 58). 2 cols.
35 lines (vol. 1), 36 lines probably (vol. 2: the full number nowhere remains), and 39 lines
(vols. 5, 6). Ruling with pencil. For the quiring see above. Several hands: the Christ
Church type is most marked in vol 1. Initials: (i) large (15-line, or so) and elaborate, in
more than one style, mainly blue and red, with purple, yellow, and green as ground colours,
and decorated with human and animal figures and interlace, ff. 2, 8^v, *9* (martyrdom of
Vincent), *13^v*, *16^v*, 26, 28, 29^v, *31*, 34, *35^v*, 38^v, 39, *48^v*, *50*, *52*, 54^v, *56^v* *57^v*, 65, *76*, 80,
81:[3] C. R. Dodwell, *The Canterbury School of Illumination*, 1954, refers to ff. 34, 35^v, 52

---

[1] At f. 20ra/26 Ar. omits what E. 42 has as two words, 'soma nobrica', after 'plebs iam'
(f. 58va/20: edn. 55C), so E. 42 cannot be derived from Ar. I owe this information to
Dr. William Urry.

[2] I follow Arundel in placing Demetrius after Denis.

[3] Initials which found themselves on the outsides of wrappers have been damaged more
or less seriously. Those on insides, shown here by italics, are usually in good condition,
but not always complete.

on pp. 66, 70, 75, 78 and reproduces part of the *T* on f. 35ᵛ in pl. 42d; (ii) 2-line, blue, red, green, or purple. Headings and explicits in alternate lines of red and green rustic capitals. First words of texts in blue, red, green, and purple. Running titles in vol. 2, but not apparently in vol. 1. Bound (except ff. 76–81) by P. Maple in 1952.

Written in England and no doubt at Christ Church, Canterbury. Typical late medieval Christ Church marking occurs on ff. 60, 65ᵛ, 81.[1]

Used in bindings and for the most part covers taken off by Dr. J. B. Sheppard in 1888. Two bifolia (5, 6, 13, 14) and five single leaves (49, 66–8, 75) are of unknown provenance. Most of the other thirty-four bifolia were used as covers of three series of business books, mainly of the archdeacon's court, written in the 1570s and 1580s, Comperta et detecta, Ad instantiam partium, and Depositiones, as appears from titles written on them. ff. 9, 12, 15, 16, 18–23, 25–34, 58, 59, 64, 65 are from Comperta et detecta, books 4, 13, 14, 16–24: five of these twelve books, 14, 17, 18, 20, and 21, are now X. 1. 12, 17, 14, 16, and 15 respectively. ff. 3, 4, 10, 11, 35–7, 40, 50–3, 56, 57, 60–3 are from Ad instantiam partium, books 21–3, 25–8, 49, 51: six of these nine books, 21, 26–8, 49, 51 are now Y. 4. 16, 19, 20, 21, and Y. 3. 17, 18² respectively. ff. 1, 2, 17, 24, 47, 48,[3] 54, 55 are from Depositiones, books 9,[3] 19, 21, 22: these four books are now PRC 39/9 and X. 10. 17, 18, and 21² respectively. Two bifolia, ff. 76–9,[4] are from books of visitation of exempt churches for 1580–5 and 1586–92 among the muniments of Lambeth Palace. The marks on six bifolia show that they come from other sources: ff. 7, 8 from 'Rental 1578', now R. 13; ff. 38, 39³ from an unidentified 'Booke of Rates'; ff. 41, 42³ from 'A inv. 6', now Maidstone, Kent County Archives Office, PRC 10/6, Liber inventariorum 1571–3; ff. 43, 46 from 'Constituciones 1578', now Z. 4. 17; ff. 44, 45 from an unidentified 'Liber licentiae 1578–9'; ff. 80, 81 from 'Eastry Rentals of Quitrents 1513 and 1596'.[5] The bifolium still at Maidstone wrapped the Common Expenditors Accounts, 1574–9, of the Commissioner of Sewers for Level of Romney Marsh.

Lit. E. 42, ff. 69–74. *Vitae Sanctorum* s. xv²

Three bifiolia which may have formed a supplement to one of the volumes of the twelfth-century 'Passionale': see E. 42, ff. 1–68, 75–81.

1. f. 69 Edward, *5 Jan.* me fratrum choris . . . commouit. Explicit uita beatissimi confessoris cristi Edwardi et gloriosi regis anglorum. *PL* cxcv. 788D–790B. *BHL*, no. 2423. The life by Aelred.

2. ff. 69ᵛ–72ᵛ Wulfstan, *19 Jan.* anglorum uirtute . . . (70ᵛ) quam cristum. (71ʳᵛ) spumas . . . auris. (f. 72ʳᵛ) incomoditatem . . . Profec-.

A copy of the late abridgement found in B.L., Harley 322 (which also contains art. 1) and Lansdowne 436. As *Vita Wulfstani*, ed. R. R. Darlington (Camden Soc., 3rd series, xl, 1928), pp. 68–73/26, 88/2–90/26, 96/10–98/31. Several leaves are missing after f. 70 and two after f. 71.

3. ff. 73–74ᵛ Seven Sleepers, *27 July.* in usum sed iussit incidi baltheos . . . speluncam miratus est. et non ascendit in cor.

Probably two leaves are missing after f. 73. The text on f. 74 seems similar to that of

[1] Cf. N. R. Ker in *British Museum Quarterly*, xiv (1940), 85.
[2] The books in X. 10 and Y. 3 are consistory court books.
[3] These three bifolia were sent back to Canterbury from the Kent County Archives Office, Maidstone, in 1951. Depositiones 9, from which ff. 47, 48 came, was itself returned in 1972: it keeps its old PRC number.
[4] Sent back to Canterbury from Lambeth Palace in 1955.
[5] Deposited at Canterbury by the Church Commissioners in 1966.

Huber's E (*Romanische Forschungen*, xxvi. 473–4): Malchus has sixty-two coins of the first year of Decius.

Written space 273 × 180 mm. 2 cols. 36 lines (f. 74). The script is influenced by twelfth-century models. Used as wrappers of business books, like the rest of E. 42. ff. 69, 70 are from 'Comperta et detecta, liber 15, 1576–7', now X. 1. 13. ff. 71, 72 are from 'Depositiones, liber 8, 1576–9'.[1] ff. 73, 74 are from 'Ad instantiam partium, liber 24, 1570–7', now Y. 4. 18 (1).

HH L. 3. 2 (39). *Horae*   s. xv in.

1. ff. 1–12^v Full calendar in French in gold, blue, and red, the two colours alternating for effect.

Feasts in gold include 'S'e Geneuiefue' (3 Jan.), 'S' Gile S'Leu' (1 Sept.), 'S' Denis' (9 Oct.), 'S' Marcel' (3 Nov.).

2. ff. 13–21 Sequentiae of Gospels. Antiphon, versicle, response, and prayer 'Protector in te sperantium' after John.

3. ff. 21–4 Passio domini nostri ihesu xpisti secundum iohannem.

John 19: 1–35 and prayer, 'Deus qui manus tuas . . .'.

4. ff. 24–9 Deuote oraison de nostredame. Obsecro te . . . michi famule tue . . .

5. ff. 29–32^v Oraison a nostredame. et a s't iehan lauangeliste. O intemerata . . . orbis terrarum. Inclina . . . ego misera peccatrix . . .

6. ff. 33–138 Hours of B.V.M. of the use of (Paris).

Nine lessons in matins. Hours of Cross and Holy Spirit are worked in.

7. f. 138^{rv} Memoire de saint germain.

8. ff. 139–160^v Penitential psalms and litany.

In the litany Denis is last of nine martyrs, Germanus sixth and Yvo last of eight confessors, and Genovefa fourth of twelve virgins.

9. ff. 161–219^v Office of the dead.

10. ff. 220–7 Les xv ioies de nostredame, the beginning missing. Sonet, no. 458.

11. ff. 227^v–231 Doulz dieu doulz pere saintte trinite . . . Sonet, no. 504.

12. ff. 231–40 Les heures de la conception.

13. Devotions to B.V.M.: (*a*) ff. 240–1 Antienne de nostre dame. Salue regina . . .; (*b*) f. 241^{rv} An*tienne*. Aue regina celorum aue domina angelorum. salue radix . . .; (*c*) f. 241^v–243 Inuiolata integra et casta es maria . . .; (*d*) f. 243^{rv} An*tienne*. Regina celi letare alleluia . . .; (*e*) ff. 243^v–244^v Alia oratio. Aue maria mater dei gloriosa. benedicta hora . . .; (*f*) ff. 244^v–245^v Des cinq ioies nostredame. Gaude uirgo mater xpisti. que per aurem concepisti . . .; (*g*) ff. 245^v–246^v An*tienne* Alma redemptoris mater que preuia celi porta . . .; (*h*) ff. 246^v–247 An*tienne*. O quam pulchra es et quam decora . . .; (*i*) ff. 247^v–249 Saluto te beatissima uirgo dei genitrix maria . . .; (*j*) ff. 249–50 Oraison. Glorieuse

[1] Recovered from the Kent County Archives Office, Maidstone, in 1951.

uierge marie. A toy me rendz . . .; (*k*) ff. 250–251ᵛ Memoire des cinq festes
nostredame. Aue cuius conceptio solenni plena gaudio . . .; (*l*) ff. 251ᵛ–252ᵛ
Deuote oraison a nostredame. Gaude dei genitrix uirgo immaculata . . .

(*a–d, g, h, k, l*) are memoriae. (*a–d, f, g, k, l*). *RH*, nos. 18147, 2070, 9094, 17170, 7017,
861, 1744, 6757. (*j*). Sonet, no. 675.

14. ff. 252ᵛ–253ᵛ Les vers saint bernard. Illumina . . . Omnipotens sempiterne
deus qui ezechie regi . . .

15. f. 254ʳᵛ Autre deuote oraison. Benedicat me hodie imperialis maiestas . . .

16. Devotions to God the Son: (*a*) ff. 254ᵛ–255 Autre oraison. O beatissime
domine ihesu xpiste respicere digneris super me miseram peccatricem . . .;
(*b*) ff. 255–6 Alia oratio. O bone et dulcissime ihesu per tuam misericordiam
esto michi ihesus . . .; (*c*) ff. 256–7 Autre oraison a nostresʳ. In manus tuas
domine deus meus . . .; (*d*) ff. 257–8 Oraison au corps ihesucrist. Ie te salue
ihesucrist parole du pere . . .; (*e*) f. 258ʳᵛ Oraison. Anima xpristi sanctifica
me . . . .

(*d*). Sonet, no. 875. (*e*). *RH*, no. 1090.

17. ff. 258ᵛ–259. Pour la paix . . . A memoria.

18. Hymns, memoriae, etc., from Advent to Corpus Christi: (*a*) ff. 259–60
Hymne en laduent nostreʳ. Conditor alme syderum . . .; (*b*) ff. 260–261ᵛ Sensuiuent les ix os que lon dit deuant noel. O sapiencia . . .; (*c*) ff. 261ᵛ–262ᵛ Le
iour de noel. Gloria in excelsis deo . . .; (*d*) ff. 262ᵛ–264 Hymne a complie par
toute la sainte quarantaine. Xpriste qui lux es . . .; (*e*) ff. 264–265ᵛ Hymne de la
passion. Vexilla regis . . .; (*f*) ff. 265ᵛ–268 Oraison tresdeuote a nostre dame.
estant soubz la croix. Stabat mater dolorosa . . . Oratio. Interueniat pro nobis
quesumus . . .; (*g*) f. 268ʳᵛ Oratio ad dominum ihesum. Ecce quomodo moritur
iustus . . .; (*h*) ff. 268ᵛ–269ᵛ En temps de pasques.hymne. Victime paschali
laudes . . .; (*i*) ff. 269ᵛ–270ᵛ Hymne du saint esperit. Veni creator spiritus . . .;
(*j*) ff. 270ᵛ–271 Memoire de la sainte trinite. Gloria tibi trinitas . . .; (*k*) f. 271ʳᵛ
Du saint sacrement. Ant'. O sacrum conuiuium . . .

19. ff. 272–273ᵛ Memoire de la sainte larme. Tremuit spiritu ihesus . . .

20. ff. 273ᵛ–301ᵛ Memoriae of angels and archangels (ff. 272ᵛ–273ᵛ) and of SS.
John Baptist, John Evangelist, Mark, Matthew, Luke, twelve apostles, Stephen,
Christopher, Sebastian (O quam mira . . .: *RH*, no. 30904), 'memoire des cinq
sains de grant merite' (Dyonisi radius grecie . . .: *RH*, no. 4707), 'Pris' (*Prejectus*),
10,000 martyrs, 'Merry' (*Medericus*), Leonard, Claude, Nicholas, Fiacre,
Anthony (hermit), Maur, Martin, Anne (Aue anna sanctissima aue deo dignissima . . .), Mary Magdalene, Margaret, Apollonia, Catherine, Genovefa, Barbara (O uirgo cuius magna deuotio . . .), memoria of 11,000 virgins, prayer 'De
ma dame Sainte Auoye', memoriae of Avia, 'des cinq vierges' (Katherina
tyrannum superans . . .: *RH*, no. 2691), All Saints, James the Great, Laurence.

21. ff. 301ᵛ–302 Agnus dei cristus immolatus est . . .

22 (added, s. xvi). f. 301ᵛ O meritum passionis Nati dei . . .

Five 4-line stanzas. Not as *AH* xv. 56.

ff. i+302+i. 175×115 mm. Written space 85×50 mm. 15 long lines. Collation: 1¹²
2–3⁸ 4⁴ 5–16⁸ 17¹⁰ (ff. 129–38) 18–27⁸ 29⁶ wants 2 after f. 219 29–37⁸ 38¹² wants 8–12.
Twenty competent 11-line pictures, four in art. 2, ten in art. 6, and 1 before each of arts.
3 (Gethsemane), 4 (B.V.M., crowned, with Child and angels), 5 (Christ descended from
the Cross; by him B.V.M., Mary, and St. John), 8 (David and Goliath), 9 (Job), 11
(Christ on the rainbow: bodies rising). Initials: (i–iii) 3-line, 2-line, and 1-line, in colour,
patterned in white, on decorated gold grounds, (i, ii) with sprays into the margin. Capital
letters in the ink of the text filled with yellow. Line fillers in blue and red on gold grounds.
Picture pages have continuous framed floral borders on grounds of gold paint. All
headings are in blue. Binding of s. xvi, much repaired: brown leather bearing a pattern
in gilt and central cartouche containing an erased name in gilt capitals (on the upper
cover the first four of 8 or 9 letters are MARI): rebacked and lettered 'MISSAL' on back.

Written in France for the use of a woman (arts. 4, 5, 16a). Bookplate of Benjamin Harrison. Bequeathed by Harrison, who was archdeacon of Maidstone, in 1887.

HH L. 3. 3 (40). *Horae*   s. xv med.

1. ff. 1–12ᵛ Full calendar in French in gold, red, and blue, the two colours
alternating for effect.

Entries in gold include Geneuiefue, Denis, Marcel, (3 Jan., 9 Oct., 3 Nov.). f. 13ʳᵛ blank.

2. ff. 14–19ᵛ Sequentiae of the Gospels.

Antiphon 'Te inuocamus . . .', versicle, response, and prayer 'Protector in te sperancium
. . .' follow John.

3. ff. 19ᵛ–22ᵛ Obsecro te.

4. ff. 23–5 O intemerata . . . orbis terrarum. Inclina . . . f. 25ᵛ blank.

5. ff. 26–84ᵛ Hours of B.V.M. of the use of (Paris).

6. ff. 85–100ᵛ Penitential psalms and litany.

Genovefa is first of thirteen virgins, and Lucia, sixth, repeated.

7. ff. 101–103ᵛ Hours of the Cross.

8. ff. 104–7 Hours of the Holy Spirit. f. 107ᵛ blank.

9. ff. 108–147ᵛ Office of the dead.

10. (a) ff. 148–152ᵛ Doulce dame de misericorde . . . (b) ff. 153–6 Doulx dieux
doulx pere . . . (c) f. 156 Saincte uraye croix aoree . . .

Sonet, nos. 458, 504, 1876.

11. ff. 156ᵛ–161 Memoriae of SS. Michael, John Baptist, James, Christopher,
Sebastian, Nicholas, Anthony (hermit), Katherine, Barbara. f. 161ᵛ blank.

ff. 161. 160×118 mm. Written space 90×55 mm. 17 long lines. Collation: 1¹² 2⁸+
a blank, f. 13, 3–9⁸ 10⁶: 1 leaf after 6 (f. 84) 11–12⁸ 13⁸+1 leaf after 6 (f. 107) 14–18⁸ 19⁴.
Fifteen mediocre 13-line pictures, 8 in art. 5 and 1 before each of arts. 2, 6–9, 10a (B.V.M.
seated, crowned, and Child: angels attend them), 10b (Trinity). Fourteen smaller pictures,
c. 37×35 mm, nine in art. 11, three in art. 2, one before art. 3 (B.V.M. in glory) and one
before art. 4 (wounded Christ in the lap of B.V.M.). Initials: (i) blue, patterned in white,
on decorated gold grounds; (ii, iii) 2-line and 1-line, gold on coloured grounds, patterned

in white. Line fillers in patterned red and blue, picked out with gold. Capital letters in the ink of the text are filled with pale yellow. Framed borders, usually compartmented, continuous on pages with larger pictures and in the outer margins of pages with smaller pictures. Red morocco binding, s. xvii.

Written in France. Book-plate of Benjamin Harrison. Given as HH L. 3. 2.

HH L. 3. 4 (61) *Preces, etc.*   s. xv²

1. A series of thirty (?) prayers taken from the Old Testament, each with a heading in English specifying the occasion for which it is suitable. The first prayer is from Exodus and Genesis, 'The praier of Loth. Iacob. and Moyses. And is for hem that takyn ony newe grete thing upon hem that thei wolde haue brought to good end. Oracio prima moisi legis latoris. E[xo] 34. Dominator domine deus misericors et clemens . . .'.

Prayer (27) is Daniel's and ends imperfectly at Dan. 3: 37 (f. 74ᵛ). The next prayer, (28?), begins imperfectly on f. 75, 'prophetis. qui locuti sunt' (Dan. 9: 6). Two leaves are missing at this point. Cf. Hoskins, p. 121.

2. ff. 81ᵛ–82 Spalterium abbreuiatum per sanctum Ieronimum debet hic inscribi . . . Verba mea auribus percipe domine intellige clamorem etc. Cf. art. 6.

3. (*a*) f. 82ʳᵛ Mathei 6. cristi institutio ad orandum. Pater noster . . . nomen tuum. (*b*) f. 82ᵛ Luce secundo veneracio angelica per diuinum consilium exibita beate marie. Aue maria . . . in mulieribus.

4. ff. 83–6 This praier folwinge is perteynynge for hem that haue atteyned a maner of parfitnesse . . . (f. 84) in blisse eternali. Hymnus laus et oracio iiii euangelistarum. xxiiii Seniorum et sanctorum angelorum et beatorum spirituum. Sanctus. sanctus. sanctus. dominus deus omnipotens . . . cum omnibus nobis. Amen.

5. f. 86ᵛ Oracio ad proprium angelum. Sancte angele dei minister celestis . . . (*ends imperfectly*).

6. ff. 87–106 Verba mea auribus percipe . . . (f. 105) Suscipere digneris domine sancte pater omnipotens eterne deus hos psalmos consecratos . . .

Psalter of St. Jerome and concluding prayer. ff. 106ᵛ–108ᵛ were ruled, but left blank.

ff. i+108+v. ff. 109–12 are medieval parchment end-leaves: 112 was pasted down. 115×80 mm. Written space 65×42 mm. 14 long lines. Collation: 1–3⁸ 4⁶+1 leaf after 2 (f. 27) 5–9⁸ 10⁸ wants 4, 5 after f. 74 11⁸ 12⁸ wants 2 after f. 86 13–14⁸. Quire 2 is signed with the sign for *-rum* (♃). Presumably a new series began with quire 5, but the mark on f. 32 has been cut off. The next six quires are marked b–g. A 5-line, or (f. 1) 6-line picture before each prayer of art. 1 and before arts. 2, 3*a*, *b*, 4, 5. Written in textura. Initials: (i) 2-line in colour on decorated gold ground; (ii) 1-line, gold on coloured grounds patterned in white, or (art. 6 only) alternately blue with red ornament and gold with slate-grey ornament. Continuous borders on picture pages and on three sides of all other pages. Binding of s. xix. Secundo folio *re ceruicis sit.*

Written in England. Apparently the end part of a much larger volume, perhaps a book of hours. Place-names scribbled on f. 111ᵛ, s. xvi, are Yorkshire ones, but widely scattered: 'ampleforde lx mark', 'frydaythorp xl mark', 'langtoft cˡⁱ', 'laghton in morthing [. . . .]'.

'wystowe c^{li}'. 'Robarte Walbanck' (?), f. 76, s. xvi. 'John Walker his booke', f. 106, s. xvi/xvii. Book-plate of Benjamin Harrison. Given as HH L. 3. 2.

HH N. 2. 1 (5). *Biblia* 1432–8

1. ff. 1^v–10 Incipit registrum de tempore et de sanctis. Dominica prima Epistola Ro 13 Scientes quia hora est finis Induimini dominum ihesum x . . .

Epistle and gospel lections of temporale, dedication of church, common of saints, sanctorale, the dead, and votive masses. Major feasts are in red, among them 'Alberti Episcopi' (April, after Tiburtius and Valerianus and before Mark), 'Sigismundi martiris' (1 May), 'Viti et sociorum eius' (15 June) and 'Venesclai martiris' (20 Sept.). f. 1^r and f. 10^v were left blank.

2. ff. 11–557 A Bible with the usual contents,[1] except for the presence of the Epistle to the Laodiceans after Colossians (f. 517) and the absence of the Prayer of Manasses. The order differs from the usual in that the two books of Maccabees follow Ecclesiasticus and Acts follows Catholic Epistles. The six ferial canticles, Benedicite, and Benedictus follow Psalms. At the end is 'Explicit vetus et Nouum testamentum Finitum Anno domini M° cccc° Tricesimo Secundo. etc.'.

The prologues are forty-three of the common set and sixteen others (shown here by *): Stegmüller, nos. 284, 285, 311, 323, 328, 330, 332, 335, 341+343, 344, 457, 462, 468, 551, 482, 487, 492, 494, 500, 510, 512, 516*, 522*, 525*, 527*, 529*, 532*, 535*, 540*, 545*, 590, 589, 607, 620, 624, 679* (headed 'Incipit prologus beati Ieronimi in epistola ad Romanos')+a variant of 674* ending 'ascribere simulacris', 651*, Ieronimi. Paulum apostolum proferam quem . . . vt occidat*, 670*, 680* (. . . lege ostendit), 677 and thirteen more as usual to 793 (765 . . . a Nicopoli), 809, 640, 834*. The psalms are numbered.

3. ff. 558–606^v Aaz apprehendens . . . consiliatores eorum. Expliciunt interpretaciones greco hebraico syriaco et latino sermone. Anno domini Mille° Quadringentesimo xxxviii°.

ff. 607^{rv}, i^{rv}, 608^{rv} are blank.

ff. 609, foliated i, 1–608 (for f. i see below, quire 52). 170 × 110 mm. Written space 122 × 77 mm. 2 cols. 47 lines. Collation: 1¹⁰ 2–46¹² 47¹² wants 8–12 after f. 557 48–51¹⁰ 52¹² (ff. 598–607, i, 608). Quires 2–38 are numbered at the end in roman or arabic figures. Admirably written in small clear cursiva. Initials: (i) 5-line or 6-line, patterned green, pink, or violet, usually on a ground of patterned colour; (ii) 3-line or 4-line, as (i), or blue with red ornament, or red without ornament; (iii) 2-line, blue or red, the blue often with red ornament; (iv) in art. 3, 1-line, blue or red. Capital letters in the ink of the text filled with pale yellow or touched with red: both colours are used together on capitals in the top line. In the bottom line the descending strokes of *x* and *m* and other descenders are elongated and curved and the curves are filled with yellow. Running titles in red between a pair of ruled lines. Binding of wooden boards covered with pink-stained leather and over it a cover of white—now dirty brown—leather. Clasped formerly at head and foot and on the side, but only the clasp at the foot now remains. Metal centre- and corner-pieces. Secundo folio *Abraham*.

Disfigured by coloured woodcuts pasted in the margins. The woodcuts are from a book of hours printed in France in s. xvi in. Two complete leaves from these hours are inserted loose. A piece of parchment pasted to one of them bears arms, for which see Woodruff's catalogue.

[1] See Bristol Public Library, 15.

Written probably in Bohemia (cf. art. 1). Bequeathed by Benjamin Harrison, as HH L. 3.2.

HH O. 9. 1. *N. de Lyra, Postilla super Psalmos*   s. xv. med.

[P]ropheta magnus surrexit in nobis luce vii. Quamuis liber psalmorum apud hebreos . . . (f. 213ᵛ) laudabunt te ad quam . . . Explicit postilla super librum psalmorum edita a fratre nycolao de lyra de ordine fratrum minorum sacre theologie doctore Anno domini Mᵒ. cccᵒ xxviᵒ.

Stegmüller, no. 5853. f. 214ʳᵛ blank.

ff. 214. Paper. 286 × 215 mm. Written space 210 × 150 mm. 2 cols. 39–44 lines. Frame ruling. Seventeen twelves and a final quire of ten leaves. Pieces of blank parchment as strengthening between and in the middle of quires. Written in cursiva. Initials: (i, ii) spaces remain blank on f. 1 and at the main divisions of the psalms; (iii) 2-line, red, a few only, most spaces being filled with letters in the ink of the text. Capital letters in the ink of the text marked with red on ff. 1–12 only. Contemporary binding of wooden boards covered with brown leather bearing fillets and one repeated ornament: two clasps missing, except for the metal pieces on the covers: a small early label inscribed 'lira super psalterium' on the spine. Secundo folio *et ideo*.

Written probably in the Netherlands. Armorial book-plate of Benjamin Harrison. Given as HH L. 3. 2.

HH O. 9. 2. *Commentary on parts of Exodus, etc., in Netherlandish*

s. xv

1. ff. 1–161ᵛ (*begins imperfectly*) men mogheste ende uerstaen . . . (f. 19ᵛ) Hier beghint dat prologus op die x gheboden. Salomon die wise man spreket aldus . . . (f. 132) op dat naeste des gonne in ons seluer. Amen. Nu hebbe ic di gheseit hoe die tien gheboden ghegheuen worden . . . in den seluen ghetal vindeste. Dat ons ende alle corsten menschen ghesci dat verleen ons die vader ende die soen ende die heilighe gheest Amen.

A dialogue between 'meester' and 'iongher' in three parts, (1) on the exodus of the children of Israel from Egypt, (2) on the ten commandments, and (3) on the children of Israel in the wilderness. (2) is printed from a rather different version by G. H. van Borssum Waalkes in *De Vrije Fries*, xvii (1888), 255–324. For other copies see *Des Coninx Summe*, ed. D. C. Tinbergen, 1900, p. 125. The first leaf is missing.

2. ff. 161ᵛ–213ᵛ Hier beghinnen somme sinne der heiligher scriften ghenomen wtten boec des heilighen leerres gregorius ghehieten moralia ouer iob . . . Gregorius in dat twijntichste boec. Al ist sake dat die heilighe scrift . . . daer hi van gloriert.

From Gregory, Moralia.

3. ff. 213ᵛ–220 Dat hier nauolghet is ghenomen wt sinte gregorius omelien op den propheet ezechiel van den vieren principalen duechden. Vier duechden sijn wtwelken . . . is van sijnre roepinghe. Deo gracias.

From Gregory on Ezekiel. f. 220ᵛ blank.

4. The pastedowns are parts of two parchment documents in Latin: (*a*) in front,

dated on the vigil of Simon and Jude, A.D. 1417 and signed 'W.Knoep'; (b) at the end, the last seven lines of a letter of confraternity in favour of fr. John Kersfloot, O.F.M., '. . . Dat' leyd' sub sigillo ministerii nostri maiori Anno domini M° cccc° xlix mensis [. . . .]'.

Eighteen words were added later to (b): Obiit fr' Iohannes Kersfloot ordinis minorum dignemini animam eius recommendare fratribus et sororibus vestris propter dulcissimum ihesum.

ff. 220. Paper. 215 × 140 m.. Written space c. 148 × 92 mm. 2 cols. 32–6 lines. Ruling with pencil. Collation: 1⁸ wants 1 2–9⁸ 10⁸ wants 5 after f. 75 11–15⁸ 16⁸ wants 8 after f. 125 17–27⁸ 28⁸ wants 8, blank. A strip of parchment as strengthening in the centre of each quire. In art. 1 the first and third leaves in each quire are signed 1 and 2 respectively after the quire letter: thus for example b1, b2, c1, c2 on ff. 8, 10, 16, 18. The second and fourth leaves have no signatures. Arts. 1, 2 by different hands in set hybrida. Initials: (i) metallic red and blue with red ornament touched or filled with green; (ii) in art. 2, 3-line or 2-line, blue or red; in art. 1 passages by 'die meester' begin with 3-line initials in blue and passages by 'die iongher' begin with 2-line initials in red. Capital letters in the ink of the text touched with red. Binding of wooden boards covered with brown leather bearing a pattern of fillets, repaired and rebacked in July 1930: two clasps missing.

Written in the Netherlands. Book-plate of Benjamin Harrison. Given as HH L. 3. 2.

Add. 6. *Breviarium* s. XIV²

Extensive remains of a breviary badly damaged by fire (in the audit room in 1674 ?) and now kept in two cardboard boxes. Well described by C. S. Phillips, *Canterbury Cathedral in the Middle Ages* (SPCK pamphlet, 1949), pp. 18–26. Box 1 contains: (a) the front board of the medieval binding; (b) in folder 1, parts of eighty-four leaves from the beginning of the manuscript (ff. 1–35, 35a, 36, 36a, 37–82); (c) in folder 2, parts of three leaves of the calendar (ff. 83–5) and of a bifolium containing writing of later date (ff. 86, 87). Box 2 contains: (a) in folder 3, parts of forty-one leaves of the psalter (ff. 1–21, 21a–h, 22–31, 31a, b); (b) the rest of the manuscript, still adhering to the sewing on the spine and still fastened by four out of eight bands to the back board of the medieval binding (ff. 32–153, 153a, 154–229, 229a, 230–307, 307a, 308–59). Throughout, the last twelve out of thirty-six lines are preserved on each page more or less completely. Many leaves in the folders have more text than this, but they rise to a point, so that on the few leaves where some part of the original first line remains it is no more than two or three letters wide (folder 1, ff. 22, 62–5, 81). The breviary seems to have been imperfect before it was burnt, leaves containing principal initials and borders having been removed and also leaves containing offices of St. Thomas of Canterbury: cf. below, arts. 1, 12.

MS. Add. 6* contains: (a) a reconstruction and abbreviated transcript of arts. 1, 2, 8–10, 12, 13 by Dr. Phillips, preceded by a 4-page introduction; (b) a transcript of art. 3 by Mr. Christopher Hohler.

1. Folder 1, ff. 1–80ᵛ Temporale from Advent to the twenty-fifth Sunday after Trinity.

The December office of St. Thomas of Canterbury was on three leaves missing after f. 15.

2. Folder 1, f. 81^{rv} Office of B.V.M.

Heading on f. 81^v 'Qualiter dicende sunt mat[utine] et hore de sancta maria sing[ulis die]-bus priuatim per totum annum.' hic se[quitur].' f. 82^{rv} blank.

3. Folder 2, ff. 83–5 Calendar in blue, red, and black, graded: July–December only, but all feasts in these months are complete or can be reconstructed.

No. 9 in Wormald's list of Christ Church calendars, *English Benedictine Kalendars after 1100* (HBS lxxvii, 1939, p. 65): 'a good, but damaged calendar', not collated. Entries in the main hand include 'Proscripcio monachorum Cant' Anno domini M° CC° VII' (15 July), 'Celebracio Oct' sancti dunstani', 26 Oct., the obit of Robert de Ludelawe (20 Oct.), 'Pro [papa] Innoc' quisque sacerdos memoria etc' (16 July), and similar notices at 17 July 'pro bonifacio', 25 Aug. 'pro Edm[. . . . .]', 17 Sept. 'pro lodowico rege francorum', and 25 Sept. 'pro Roberto abbate cistr'. Added obits of Edmund de Chert and of W. Sellyng, A.D. 149[.], at 15 Nov., 29 Dec. An entry 'Cuthwyne [. . .] Et Enswyth[. . . .]' at 31 Aug., added in s. xv. The word 'pape' erased; also the word 'Thome' in feasts of St. Thomas of Canterbury, 7 July (blue), 2 Dec. (red), and 29 Dec. (blue).

4. Folder 3, ff. 1–30^v Psalms.

Pss. 1–4, 95–117 are missing.

5. Folder 3, ff. 30^v–31^v, 31a, 31b; bound fragment, ff. 32–34^v Canticles, Confitebor–Quicumque vult, and Apostles' Creed.

6. Bound fragment, ff. 34^v–37 Litany.

In what survives, Elphege, Dunstan, and All Saints are doubled and the names are the same as and in the same order as in Lit. E. 17, art. 4, except for the absence of Anne among virgins.

7. Bound fragment, ff. 37–38^v Oraciones subs[equentes di]cende sunt pro diuersis neces[sita]tibus contingentibus. Pro ecclesia or'. Ecclesie tue domine preces . . .

8. Bound fragment, ff. 38^v–44^v Office for the sick.

This, except f. 38^v, and arts. 9, 10 are reconstructed in Add. 6*, ff. i–vi (pencil foliation).

9. Bound fragment, ff. 45–53^v Office of the dead.

10. Bound fragment, ff. 53^v–55^v Office of burial and rubric.

11 (added, s. xv). Bound fragment, ff. 55^v–57 Offices of SS. David, Augustine of England, Ethelbert, and Edward the martyr.

In the blank space after art. 10 and on an added bifolium.

12. Bound fragment, ff. 58–301^v Sanctorale, Andrew–Katherine.

Parts of the office of St. Thomas of Canterbury at 2 Dec. remain on ff. 63^v, 64: in between a leaf has been excised and f. 63 is only a corner of a leaf. Three leaves missing after f. 174 contained no doubt the July office of St. Thomas. For five other missing leaves see the collation, below.

13. Bound fragment, ff. 301^v–343 Common of saints. ff. 343^v–344^v blank.

14 (added, s. xv). Bound fragment, ff. 345–357^v Offices of SS. Ethelbert, David, Chad, Edward king and martyr, Adrian abbot, Wulfstan, Sebastian, Anne, and Frideswide. ff. 358–359^v blank.

15 (added, s. xv/xvi). Folder 2, ff. 86–87ᵛ (*a*) f. 86 A piece directed against disturbers of church and monks. (*b*) f. 86ᵛ A list of chapters (?). (*c*) f. 86ᵛ Nota bene istos iiii versus de vexilla Sancti [Thome]. Hoc est in signo Thome (*erased*) . . . preciosum sanguine signum. (*d*) f. 87 A text ending 'idus iunii'. (*e*) f. 87ʳᵛ Superscripcio litter[re Iohannis] Mandevylle peregrini. Viris venerabilibus Religiosis . . . dentur. Sequitur effectum littere illius Humili ac obsequiosa recommendacione premissa. Quoniam ab antiquo antequam mare transfretarem . . . augmentacione I. de Mandevylle Beati [Thome] Cantuar' humilis deuotus ac confidentissimus peregrinus.

The marks of sewing and the shape of this bifolium suggest that it is from the 'burnt breviary' and from the end of it. (*b*). The fourteenth entry is 'Versus Tamisii flumen iter capiunt'. (*e*). Not otherwise known. Printed by M. Seymour, *Notes and Queries*, ccxix (1974), 326–8.

ff. 461. For the foliation, see above, and for the height of the leaves originally, see below, binding. The width is 265 mm. Written space 262 (folder 1, f. 81)×177 mm. 2 cols. 36 lines (see above). All leaves in folders 1, 2 are now singletons, except: 13–21, a quire of 12 wanting 4–6 after f. 15; 22–31, a quire of 10; 49–60, a quire of 12; four bifolia, 33 and 37, 35a and 36, 41 and 46, and 86 and 87. The leaves in folder 3 and the bound fragment are collatable: 1¹⁰ 2¹⁰+1 leaf after 9 (f. 20) 3 eight (ff. 21a–h) 4¹² (ff. 22–31, 31a, b) 5–6¹² (ff. 32–55) 7² (ff. 56, 57) 8¹² wants 7 after f. 63 9–13¹² 14¹⁰ wants 10 after f. 137 15¹⁰ 16¹² wants 12 after f. 157 17¹² wants 10 after f. 166 18¹² want 7–9 after f. 174 19¹² 20¹² wants 1 before f. 190 21¹⁰ 22–26¹² 27¹² wants 1 before f. 270 28–32¹² 33⁸ wants 6–8, blank, after f. 344 34⁸ 35⁸ wants 8, blank, after f. 359. Initials: (i) all now lost (cut out or burnt), except folder 3, f. 21a, *S* of *Salvum* (Ps. 68), 5-line, blue patterned in white on pink and gold ground decorated with oak leaves in colour; (ii) f. 30ᵛ, beginning art. 5, 4-line, red and blue, with good outline ornament on a ground of hatched red lines; (iii, iv) 2-line and 1-line, blue with red ornament or red with violet ornament. In type (ii) initials the saw-pattern ornament in the margins runs nearly the full length of the pages and changes direction at the foot so as to run horizontally: the filling of the corner thus formed is distinctive. Part of the nearly continuous border on the first leaf of art. 12 remains. Capital letters in the ink of the text touched with red. The wooden boards (see above) are nearly complete, but bare of leather: the height is *c*. 400 mm.

Written for use in Canterbury Cathedral.

Add. 17. *Chronicle (in French)* s. XIII ex.

Nine leaves of a chronicle of English affairs, which probably began at the birth of Christ. The last date is 1087 (p. 18/28) and the last event the appointment of Guy (Wido) as abbot of St. Augustine's, Canterbury. The writing is very close, but quite good; hard to read, however, because of browning from exposure, especially on p. 1.

Dates which help one to find one's way are 995 (p. 7), 1035 (p. 10, near foot), 1070 (p. 14, 23 lines up), 1073 (p. 16/20), 1075 (p. 17/22), 1080 (p. 18/15). There is, perhaps, a special interest in Archbishop Lanfranc. On p. 18, ten lines from the foot, the author says that he is writing for people 'qui desirent sauoir et ne pount a les liures uenir' and that he is now going to turn from secular affairs to 'choses ke plus touchent seinte escripture.' Ore voil vn poy treter des choses ke touchent les obseruaunces de seinte eglise', beginning from the birth of Christ. The last words are 'la quarte none de feuerer de seint symeon ly veilz et de'.

ff. 9, paginated 1–18. 283 × 210 mm. Written space 273 × 170 mm. *c.* 70 long lines. Two bifolia (5–8 and 11, 12, 17, 18) and five singletons. Written in current anglicana. Kept in a folder.

Add. 18. *Prognostications (in French), etc.* s. XIII/XIV

1. pp. 1–28 [L]a table de la lune vous aprent en quele signe est la lune . . .

After the introduction there are three paragraphs under each sign, beginning respectively '[Q]uant la lune est', '[H]omme nee en', and '[F]emme nee en'. Ends imperfectly in the section on 'archer' (sagittarius).

2. p. 29 Last three lines of a recipe in French.

3. pp. 29–35 Sequitur de auro stellato et sic fit uel marmoratum vel granatum sume gipsum . . .

Recipes in French and Latin, ending abruptly(?) 'si le plumbez cum potier'. p. 36 blank.

ff. 18, paginated 1–36. 175 × 110 mm. Written space *c.* 120 × 77 mm. 31 long lines. Collation: 1¹⁴ 2⁴. Initials not filled in. Kept in a folder.

Probably used in binding. Each leaf is a little damaged, especially across the middle.

Add. 23. *Epistola Salvatoris; 'Signa', 'Litterae', 'Nomina cristi', Preces, etc.* s. XIII med.

A single sheet. The texts are on one side only and set out in eight columns, each about 50 mm wide, below a space 140 mm high and 427 mm wide, filled with magical patterns called 'signa', mostly in roundels and often inscribed, for example 'In quacumque die uideris hoc signum non peribis morte subitanea', 'Hoc signum porta tecum demon tibi nocere non poterit. set in omni loco saluus eris', 'Hoc est signum regis salomonis quo demones in puteo sigalauit qui super se . . .'. Twenty more roundels are on the dorse, which is otherwise blank.

1 (cols. 1, 2). Pieces beginning: (*a*) Cotidie uide hec signa greca et erit tibi gracia ad omnes et magnam leticiam habebis R c z o . . .; (*b*) Longinus miles perforauit . . .; (*c*) Iste littere uictoriam habent . . .; (*d*) Hos fer tecum caract' in lineo mundo Patrion. cecinoos . . .; (*e*) Ecce nomina cristi. adonay . . .; (*f*) Hii sunt lxxii nomina dei . . .; (*g*) Miserere mei domine fili dauid . . .; (*h*) Angelus domini dedit sancto columchille episcopo Gamata . . .

(*b*). To staunch blood.

2 (col. 3). Incipit epistola saluatoris domini nostri ihesu cristi ad abgarum regem quam dominus noster scripsit manu sua dicens Beatus es abagare rex qui me non uidisti et in me credidisti . . . in omnibus periculis fia(t) fiat amen.

Different from and longer than in *PG* xx. 123. Protects 'a grandine a pluuia a tonitruo a fulgure ab omni periculo . . .'.

3. Further pieces like art. 1 including: (col. 3) Hec sunt nomina domini . . .; Precor ut me saluare digneris ab omni malo . . .; On primum nomen domini . . .; (col. 4) Magical letters; Hoc nomen amandum et glorificandum et adorandum

est ERAGFRARI . . .; Eterne deus rex immortalis deus immensus . . .; Contra tempestates hec dices nomina et cessabit illico. Carado te benedicat . . .; (col. 5) Contra tempestatem hec dices nomina. Carado . . . : shorter than the preceding piece; A diagram and against it 'Hoc signum dedit angelus domini sancto columbano episcopo si quis fidelis hanc figuram . . .'; Hec nomina dei sunt apud hebreos . . .'; 'Dominus leo papa misit istas litteras karolo magno properanti ad bellum quas angelus domini sancto Gregorio detulit . . . . b. d. u. g. n. m. f. . . .'; A prayer for sore eyes, 'Lutum fecit dominus . . .'; (col. 6) A prayer for sleep invoking the seven sleepers of Ephesus; A string of prayers and charms to staunch blood, the first 'Sicut uere credimus quod sancta maria uerum infantem genuit . . .'; A long prayer, 'Adonay domine deus magne et mirabilis qui es iustus . . .', continuing into col. 7; (col. 8) Charms, badly rubbed.

One sheet, now flat, but once folded in thirty-two thicknesses. 512 × 427 mm. Written space 355 × 420 mm. 8 columns, with c. 84 lines each. Well written. Kept in a folder.

Written in England. 'Thomas Tymbyrden' de Sandwych' on the dorse, s. xv. Scribbles on two folds, s. xv, name 'Ric knyth' de Selling'' and others.

Add. 38. *Biblia* s. XIII med.

1. ff. 1–381ᵛ A damaged Bible with normal contents in the common order.[1]

The first leaf is missing, but was there in s. xix (before the Sotheby fire of 1865), when the historiated initials were listed on ff. vi, vii and in first place 'St Jerome writing in an ornamental *F* the length of the Page'. The scribe began Isaiah and Matthew on new quires (ff. 214, 306) after blank spaces. The prayer of Solomon (Ecclesiasticus, ch. lii) was added early in the first of the spaces, ff. 213ᵛ–214. I, II, III Ezra are so called in the running titles (EXDRE), not 1 Ezra, Nehemiah, 2 Ezra. Many corrections in darker ink over erasures.

The prologues, apart from two additions, are forty-eight of the common set and thirty-two others (shown here by *): Stegmüller, nos. 284, 285, 311, 307* (added), 323, 328, 330, 332, 'Thobias filius ananiel . . . iacet in niniue'* (added), 335, 341+343, 344, 357, 430*, 414* (. . . sacramentum), 'Liber psalmorum quamquam uno concludatur uolumine . . . ordinauit ut uoluit'*, 457, 455*, 462, 468, 482, 487, 490*, 486*, 491, 492, 494, 506*, 501*, 510, 512, 516*, 522*, 526, 525*, 528, 527*, 530*, 529*, 534, 532*, 538, 535*, 539, 540*, 543, 544*, 551, 552*, 590, 595*, 596*, 607, 620, 624, 677, 685, 697* (lacks the first five words), 699, 707, 715, 728, 736, 747, 752, 765 (. . . roma), 772, 780, 783, 793, 633*+631*, 640, 806*, 812*, 817*, 822*, 823*, 824*, 825*, 829*.

2. ff. 382–407 Aaz apprehendens . . .

The usual dictionary of Hebrew names. f. 407ᵛ blank.

ff. vii+407+v. 222 × 170 mm. Written space c. 167 × 120 mm. 2 cols. 54 lines. Collation impracticable. Added flex punctuation (?). Initials:[2] (i) in colour on coloured grounds, historiated; (ii) blue and red, with ornament of both colours or on grounds of blue and green; (iii) set outside the written space, blue or red with skilful ornament of the other colour; (iv) 1-line, blue or red. Capital letters in the ink of the text touched with red.

---

[1] See Bristol Public Library, 15.
[2] The Cathedral Library has a copy of C. Cotton's *Description of an Early Fourteenth Century 'Biblia Sacra'*, Press Mark Y. 12. 21, Chapter Library, Canterbury, printed in 1932, where the decoration is described in detail.

Rebound at the British Museum after 1930; previously in binding of s. xviii, the remains of which are kept separately.

Written in Spain (?). George Offor sale at Sotheby's, 27 June 1865, lot 158 (?).[1] Bought by E. L. Holland. Damaged in the fire at Sotheby's, 28 June 1865. Given by Mrs. E. L. Holland, The Paddock, St. Martin's Hill, Canterbury, 2 July 1930.

Add. 40. *Lectionarium* s. XIII med.

1. 'In aduentu lectiones et euangelia'. Incipit prologus sancti iheronimi presbiteri in ysaia propheta. Leccio prima. Nemo cum prophetis . . . insultarent. Explicit prologus. Incipit Ysaias propheta. Leccio ii. Visio Ysaie filii amos . . . (f. 116ʳ) deum clamant. Qui etiam ad dampnationis sue cumulum. eum quem na (*ends abruptly*).

Lessons of the temporale from Advent to Epiphany, twelve on Sundays and three on weekdays. The last words are in the lesson for Epiphany from Gregory, Hom. in Evangelia, i. 10. Christmas takes up thirty leaves (ff. 68–97ᵛ). Homilies are ascribed to Ambrose, Augustine, Bede, Fulgentius, Gregory, Leo, Maximus, and Origen. The beginning of the Gospel reading is given in front of each series of lessons and the full text after it.

2. A bifolium of a small service book (110 × 95 mm.), s. xii ex., is attached to the foot of f. 1.

The recto of the first leaf has the end of a prayer 'facimus in capite.sic in tua uirtute et hereditatem consequi mereamur Per' followed by 'Incipit ordo ad monachum benedicendum. Lecta . . .'.

ff. i+116+i. ff. i, 117 are modern parchment. 435 × 290 mm. Written space 300 × 195 mm. 2 cols. 24 lines. Collation: 1–14⁸ 15⁴. Quires 1–6 have numbers at the end and no catchwords, the rest catchwords and no numbers. The writing on ff. 105ᵛ–110 is between a pair of ruled lines. Changes of hand at f. 49 (7¹) and—for the worse—at f. 105ᵛ. Flex punctuation (?). Red initials patterned in white, with ornament of the same colour, 5-line and 2-line, the spaces on ff. 105–16 not filled. On ff. 1–31ᵛ the white spaces in the larger initials are sometimes filled with a yellow wash and throughout quires 1–13 capital letters in the ink of the text are filled with yellow. Binding of thick boards rebacked: a metal bar in the centre of the front cover: two clasps. Secundo folio *et post*.

Written in Italy for monastic use: the punctuation suggests that this is a Cistercian book. Given by Mrs. T. S. Frampton, 15 Mar. 1923.

Add. 66. *Comment. in Matthaeum* s. XIV²

(*begins imperfectly*) lexerunt dei filium causa humane salutis de celis descendisse . . . ad finem seculi. non deest seculi qui dominum merentur habere. Amen. Explicit liber tractatus super euangelium mathei. beati grisostomi Iohannis.

Begins at ix. 27. A verse-by-verse commentary, each section preceded by its text in red.

ff. iii+48+iii. 230 × 170 mm. Written space 187 × 125 mm. 2 cols. 49–50 lines and on ff. 47ᵛ–48 65 lines. Ink ruling. Six eights. Textura. 2-line blue initials with red ornament.

[1] According to the copy of the Offor sale catalogue in the Bodleian Library, lot 158 was bought by 'Howland' for seven guineas. Lots 157, 159 were also octavo-size Bibles.

Binding of s. xix in. for Sir William Betham, uniform with Lichfield Cathedral 14 and Fitzwilliam Museum, Cambridge, 134.

Written in England. Book-plate of Sir William Betham. His sale by Evans, 6 July 1830, lot 438, to Sir Frederic Madden, who recorded the provenance on f. ii. Madden's book-plate inside the cover and book-plate of the Revd. W. H. Pengelly on f. i^v. 'E. L. Holland 20 Sept. 1905', f. ii. 'In Memoriam E. L. H. Carolus Cotton Socius Regii Medicorum Collegii apud Edinburgum me jure tenet. A.D. 1930. Qui alienauerit anathema sit. Amen', f. ii. Given by Charles Cotton, O.B.E., F.R.C.P., 12 May 1936.

Add. 68. *Descriptio civitatis Romae, etc. (in Latin and English)*
s. xv^2

C. E. Woodruff, *A xvth century Guide-Book to the Principal Churches of Rome*, 1933, contains a translation of arts. 1–4, 10, 12 (pp. 1–79), an inaccurate tran-script of art. 11 (pp. 79–86), and an enlarged facsimile of f. 17^v. The author and compiler, William Brewyn, chaplain, names himself in arts. 2, 4, 10; he is prob-ably the scribe. He was in Rome in 1469 and in Canterbury in 1470.

1. ff. 5–37^v Ecclesia S. Iohannis Lateranensis. Sanctus Siluester . . .

Churches, relics, and indulgences at Rome. Woodruff, pp. 5–67. Memoranda for the scribe's own use (?) are in the margins here and there, for example on f. 21^v, 'prosam sancti petri quere in paruo libro tuo' (cf. Woodruff, p. 34).

2. ff. 38–39^v Excommunicaciones papales. Hic sequuntur quedam excommuni-caciones quas papa paulus . . . michi Willelmo Brewyn Capellano tunc temporis ibi existenti et audienti. Silicet in vrbe romana.ad portam ecclesie sancti petri apostoli. dedit . . .

Pronounced, says Brewyn, by Pope Paul (II) in 1469. Woodruff, pp. 67–70.

3. ff. 40–42^v Via de Calesia ad Romam.

The way to Rome from Calais. Woodruff, pp. 70–4.

4. ff. 42^v–43 Cambium monete diuerse. Ego Willelmus brewyn Capellanus habui pro ix s. in pecunia anglicana ii ducatos in vrbe Romana . . .

Woodruff, pp. 74–6.

5. ff. 43^v–44 Vie ciuitatis Romane . . . Porte. principales . . . Cimiterium Kalixti . . .

A list of roads, gates, and cemeteries in Rome.

6. ff. 44^v–49 In Ytalia in principio Tuscie situatur vrbs Rome. De cuius funda-cione . . . (f. 49) Gallus enim quamquam . . . (10 lines of verse). Hec in poli-cronica cestrie libro primo. Item gregorius in originali de mirabilibus rome et cetera. non intitulaui.

Extracts from Higden, Polychronicon, ed. RS, i. 206–38, and on ff. 44^v–46 about forty lines listing hills, bridges, palaces, and triumphal arches in Rome. The section on palaces begins 'Palacium maius erat in medio Rome'. Nothing is directly from Gregorius.

7. ff. 49^v–57^v Septimo kl' ianuarii. Rome via appia . . . sepultusque est in vaticano.

Martyrological entries for Rome, arranged topographically.

8. ff. 58–94 De natiuitate cristi. Rome cristi natiuitas ostensa est tali modo . . .

Extracts about Roman saints (etc.), in the order of the church year from Christmas to St. Clement. ff. 58–67ᵛ are from J. de Voragine, Legenda aurea, on Christmas, SS. Anastasia, Sylvester, Marcellus, Fabian, Sebastian, Agnes, Paula, Chair of Peter, Gregory, and De passione Domini, and it seems likely that all the rest is from this source.

9. f. 94ʳᵛ Miraculum sancti Egidii. Sanctus Egidius Romam adiit . . . remissum non dubitaret.

10. ff. 95ᵛ–96ᵛ Cantuaria. Ista habentur in ecclesia sancti thome martiris et archipresulis apud cantuariam . . . Item nota quod summa indulgenciarum tocius ecclesie est xxxviiᵐ anni cc et 1 dies perpet'. Anno domini mᵒ cccclxxᵒ videlicet anno iubeleo eiusdem thome martiris. Quod Willelmus Brewyn capellanus qui tunc temporis fuit ibi *scilicet* in festo translacionis eiusdem sancti thome martiris et scripsit hec. Deo Ihesu gracias ago et sancte marie et sanctis predictis.

Woodruff, pp. 76–9. Relics and indulgences at Christ Church, Canterbury. At the end the main hand added in red ink 'Nota de capite heretici coram sancto Anselmo in capella. Item de pomo sancti thome'.

11. English verses: (a) f. 98 Thow holy moder of god . . . (three 4-line stanzas); (b) f. 98ʳᵛ Ioy thu virgyn as it is ry3th The fader of hevyn . . . (five 4-line stanzas); (c) ff. 98ᵛ, 100 Ioy thu mary with virgyn flowers . . . (seven 4-line stanzas); (d) ff. 100–101ᵛ The Sterre shoon boþ . . . (twenty-four 4-line stanzas); (e) ff. 99ʳᵛ, 97ʳᵛ (*begins imperfectly*) The prince of prests to hym gan say . . . (line 88) Wher' evyr we may regne wᵗ Stevyn 'deo gracias'.

Woodruff, pp. 79–86. (*a–e*). *IMEV*, nos. 3675, 1808, 1807, 3810.3, 3448.8.

12. ff. 2–4 Tabula huius libri. Hoc in libello scribitur de vii ecclesiis principalibus . . .

Woodruff, pp. 1–4. A table of contents, excluding arts. 10, 11, and listing in the last thirteen lines two items which were formerly to be found on a quire or quires missing after f. 94: (1) Item de peregrinacione terre Sancte et de diuersis locis scilicet De Nazareth. De hierusalem. De Ecclesia sancti Sepulcri. De Monte Syon. De Acheldemach et De Valle Iosephat. De Templo Domini. De Betheleem. De Bethania. De Iordanis flumine. De Ierico. De Morte quarentina. De Galgala. De ciuitate kaer. De Alexandria. De Cesarea Palestine. De Acra ciuitate. De ciuitate Tybiriadis. De Arabia. De Tyro et Sydone.et Baruta.et aliis locis terre sancte et aliis. (2) Item de Stacionibus hierusalem et terre sancte in anglicis. pro illis qui volunt visitare terram sanctam spiritualiter in mente sua. adquirendum Indulg' ut inueni in rotula 'script''.

The table is on the 2nd-4th leaves of a preliminary quire. f. 4ᵛ is blank. f. 1 was pasted to the old binding and is blank, except for a note on the verso referring to 1469 'pastore summo existente paulo tunc [. . . .]'.

ff. ii+101+ii. 140×95 mm. Written space c. 105×72 mm. 23–5 long lines. Frame ruling in ink. Collation: 1⁴ 2⁶+1 leaf after 6 (f. 11) 3–5⁸ 6⁶ wants 5, 6 after f. 39 7–12⁸ 13⁸ wants 8 after f. 94 14 seven (ff. 95–101: 96–7 and 100–1 are bifolia and the right order is 95, 96, 98, 100, 101, 99, 97). In quires 7–13 (arts. 3–9) the first four leaves of each quire are numbered in a continuous series from 'a' on f. 40 to 'ē' on f. 91 (the four signs after z are 7, ɔ, ÷, ē). Written in a secretary-influenced anglicana. Initials 2-line or 1-line, blue with red ornament. Capital letters in the ink of the text touched with red. Binding of s. xviii. Secundo folio *virginis* (f. 6) or *Item de* (f. 3).

For the scribe and date see above. Belonged to Sir Henry Ingilby at Ripley Castle, York-shire (HMC, *Sixth Report* (1877), App., p. 361. 'N° 32', f. 1). Ingilby sale at Sotheby's, 21 Oct. 1920, lot 26. Bought in 1922.

Add. 75. *Breviarium* s. xiv²

1. ff. 1–84ᵛ Sanctorale, Saturninus–Maximus (29 Nov.–27 Nov.).

Includes proper offices for: f. 67, Piatus (of Tournai, 1 Oct.: hymn, Solemne festum precluit, *RH*, no. 19124); f. 79ᵛ Elizabeth (of Hungary, 19 Nov.: hymns, Nouum sidus and Pange lingua, *RH*, nos. 12372, 14452), and collects for Aldegundis (abbess of Mau-beuge, 30 Jan.), Eubertus (of Lille, 1 Feb., with octave), and Waldetrudis (of Mons, 2 Nov.).

2. ff. 84ᵛ–111 Common of saints.

3. ff. 113–30 Office of B.V.M.

4. In blank spaces: (*a*) ff. 111ᵛ–112, office of the Visitation of B.V.M.; (*b, c*) f. 130ᵛ, collects for Martha, virgin, and Livinus, martyr.

(*a*). Very current hand, s. xv/xvi. (*b, c*). s. xv.

ff. ii+130+ii. ff. 1–112 have a medieval foliation in red on versos. 125 × 95 mm. Written space 100 × 63 mm. 23 long lines. Collation : 1–15⁸ 16¹⁰. Initials: (i) ff. 1, 85, 4-line, red and blue with ornament of both colours; (ii) 2-line, blue or red, with ornament of the other colour; (iii) 1-line, red or blue. Capital letters in the ink of the text filled with yellow. Binding of s. xviii, rebacked in 1958. Secundo folio *Erat andreas*.

Written in the southern Netherlands or north-east France. Belonged in s. xix to Thomas Freston, if a letter now kept loose inside the cover refers to this manuscript. Given by Hugh Scott in 1958.

Add. 118. *Psalmi, etc.* s. xv²

1. ff. 1–141 Psalms 1–108.

Single leaves are missing where Pss. 52 and 80 begin. Headings, 'Secunda quinquagena' and 'Tercia quinquagena', before Pss. 51, 101.

2. ff. 141–55 Twenty-four hymns, (1–18) for feasts of temporale and sanctorale in one series, (19–24) for dedication of church and the common.

The saints for whom proper hymns are provided are Augustine (Celi cives applaudite, *RH*, no. 3471, between Passion Sunday and Easter), John Baptist, Peter and Paul, Mary Magdalene (Sidus solare, *RH*, no. 18975), Laurence (Conscendat usque sidera, *RH*, no. 3807), Anne (Festum nunc celebre, *RH*, no. 26607), Michael, and Elizabeth of Hungary (Hymnum deo, *RH*, no. 8263).

3. ff. 155–158ᵛ Incipit commendacio. Subuenite sancti dei . . .

Forms are feminine.

4. ff. 159–166ᵛ De sepultura. Non intres in iudicium . . .

Forms are feminine. f. 167ʳᵛ blank.

ff. i+167+iii. ff. 168–9 are medieval parchment flyleaves. ff. 1–18 are parchment and ff. 19 onwards paper, except four bifolia (28 and 33, 45 and 46, 79 and 80, 120 and 123) and two singletons (61, 107). 140 × 100 mm. Written space 80 × 55 mm. 17 long lines. Collation impracticable: mainly eights: many leaves mended at the foot. The single parchment leaves 61 and 107 were once no doubt conjugate with the leaves missing after 63 and 100. Well written in hybrida. The psalms are punctuated by the colon. Initials are skilful: (i) ff. 1, 28, 46, 79ᵛ, 120, 141, patterned gold on decorated coloured grounds, with red penwork in the margins; (ii) beginning Pss. 15, 18, 21, 51, 101, the hymns for Christmas, Easter, Corpus Christi and apostles, and arts. 3, 4, blue with red ornament or on decorated green grounds; (iii) 2-line, blue or red; (iv) for verses of psalms and hymns, 1-line, as (iii). A border in gold and colours in the lower margin of f. 1. Contemporary binding, much repaired, the lower cover entirely new, the upper bearing a pattern of lozenges and triangles, each containing a fleur-de-lis. Secundo folio *conuenerunt*.

Written in the Netherlands for female use. Given by Miss Joan Somerville, 27 July 1939.

Chart. Antiq. A. 42. *Vitae paparum et archiepiscoporum Cantuariae*
s. XIII ex.

Petrus apostolorum princeps Anno dominice incarnacionis secundum Ewangelium quadragesimo secundum Dyonisium xviii⁰ . . . et sanctus Oswaldus Wigorn' episcopus efficitur.

The last pope is John (XII, †964), 'centesimus xxxiiˢ papa post petrum', and the last archbishop, Dunstan (960–88). Oswald became bishop of Worcester in 961. A certain amount of English history is included, apparently from Florence of Worcester, whose dates are followed. Part only of the dorse was used for the text. For other pieces there see HMC, *Fifth Report*, App., p. 462.

A roll of six membranes. Written space c. 195 mm wide. Two columns, the second narrower than the first. Written in current anglicana.

Fragments[1]

Most of the fragments are either bound up as Lit. E. 42 (see above) or are loose in three boxes to which numbers were assigned in 1973, Add. 127 (formerly Box CCC), Add. 128 (formerly Box ABC in XYZ), and Add. 129. A few were separated out earlier and assigned low numbers in the 'Additional' series. A few are still *in situ* where pre-Dissolution or post-Dissolution binders put them.[2] A few, seen by me at Canterbury in 1949, are not at present to be found.[3]

[1] Items in the following lists preceded by * were used by binders before 1540. Items preceded by ** were used by binders after 1540.

[2] In references I have used letters to differentiate the binding fragments from the books inside them: thus X. 1. 10a, b are the covers and flyleaves of X. 1. 10.

[3] They are: (a) a leaf of Cassiodorus on Pss. 51–100, s. xii, which begins 'anticristi non inmerito' (Ps. 51: *PL* lxx. 373/2), is marked at the head of the recto 'Secunda Pars Cassiodori' and comes perhaps from the Christ Church copy recorded by Eastry, *Ancient Libraries*, p. 51, no. 329; (b) two leaves of Augustine on St. John, s. xii², 2 cols., 48 lines, containing the end of Homily 47 and the beginning of Homily 48; (c) a leaf of Aristotle: see below, list B, X. 1. 10b; (d) several leaves of Avicenna, Canon Medicinae, s. xiii ex., 2 cols., 69 lines; (e) two leaves of a commentary on Lamentations (ch. 2), written in a clumsy hand, s. xiv, not unlike that of Lit. B. 9. The Kent County Archives Office at Maidstone has other leaves of (b), (c), and (d). PRC 49/3 is six leaves of the same manuscript as (b) and contains parts of Homilies 4–7 on two single leaves, parts of Homily 14 on two single

The parchment leaves were for the most part either covers or flyleaves of business books of Canterbury Cathedral dating from the sixties, seventies, and eighties of the sixteenth century. Manuscript was used in binding both before this period and after it, but not extensively: many of the earlier and later books remain in their old covers and these are of plain parchment. It seems more likely than not that at any rate after the Dissolution business books were supplied to the cathedral ready bound by local stationers, who will have got their binding leaves from any convenient source. That unwanted Cathedral books were a main source is clear: there is no doubt about the provenance of Lit. E. 42 and there is a strong probability that the older fragments came either from the Cathedral or from the dispersed library of St. Augustine's. Later service books are perhaps more likely to be from local churches than from the monasteries.

The great series of Acta of the Archdeacon's Court and the Consistory Court with pressmarks ranging from X. 1. 1 to Z. 7. 7 present a very uniform appearance. Commonly they are not very thick books a little over 300 mm in height and about 215 mm in width. To wrap a book of this size the binder needed leaves from very large or fairly large books. He could take a single leaf of a very large book and lay it sideways to cover the whole of the blank book, front, back, and spine, or he could take a bifolium of a book about the same size as, or, better, a little larger than the blank book: in either case a little extra to fold in along the sides, if not along the top and bottom, would be welcome. A leaf laid sideways would have to measure about 450 × 300 mm to be useful and each leaf of a bifolium would have to measure about 305 × 235 mm, to allow for the part of it that went over the spine of the blank book. Antiphonals are the books most commonly met with in which the leaves are big enough to be used singly as wrappers. Thus, for example, four leaves of one antiphonal, list C, Add. 128/46, each measuring c. 460 × 305 mm were used for wrapping four books and a leaf probably from the same manuscript is still *in situ* as the cover of another book (X. 1. 10). In bifolia the great Christ Church passional was useful, but its leaves had to be cut down a bit at top and bottom to suit the size of the general run of business books. Their width, c. 275 mm, was ample and allowed a turn-in of about 55 mm.

About 1570 the binders used flyleaves or pastedowns taken from manuscripts as additional strengthening inside the covers. For these also two sizes of manuscripts came in useful, larger ones which were about the same size as the blank book or could be cut down to its size and smaller ones which could be used in

leaves and parts of Homilies 48, 49 on a bifolium: two of the single leaves are *in situ* as flyleaves of a Register of Wills in the Consistory Court 1560–3, PRC 32/29, and two were formerly flyleaves of a Liber detectionum et compertorum of the Archdeacon's Court 1565–6 and, starting from the other end of the book, an Index of Inventories of the same court 1569–85, now PRC 48/5; the bifolium was the cover of a Register of Inventories of the Archdeacon's Court 1564–6, now PRC 10/1. PRC 49/9 is four leaves of the same manuscript as (*c*). PRC 49/14 is four leaves of the same manuscript as (*d*): two are *in situ* as pastedowns in an Act Book of the Archdeacon's Court 1557–71, PRC 3/18, and two were flyleaves in PRC 10/2 (see below, p. 329, footnote). At Lambeth Palace, the pastedowns of a Visitation Book for 1569–70, VG 4/6, are two leaves of the same manuscript as (*d*).

bifolia laid sideways. Fortunately a few blank books with manuscript covers and end-leaves still remain as the binders left them and provide evidence of the methods used. X. 1. 9, Comperta et Detecta, lib. 10, 1567–9 is one of them. The cover is a bifolium of a fifteenth-century lectionary each leaf of which measures *c.* 302 × 290 mm: it has of course been much cut down in height. The quires of the blank book are sewn on three leather thongs which are taken through the cover in slits and project inside it at either end between cover and flyleaf. The function of the flyleaves—here leaves of a thirteenth-century breviary—was no doubt to protect the first and last leaves of the blank book from injury by the thongs. X. 1, 10, Comperta et Detecta lib. 11, 1570–1, is similarly bound: this time the cover is a leaf of the antiphonal mentioned above laid sideways—the leaf was not tall above to allow for any fold-in at the sides—and the flyleaves are from a thirteenth-century Aristotle. X. 1. 11, Comperta et Detecta, lib. 12, 1571–2, was no doubt similarly bound, but only the flyleaves, two leaves of a handsome Jerome on Minor Prophets, remain *in situ*: the present nineteenth-century cover takes the place of an antiphonal laid sideways, which has left clear offset on the flyleaves and can be identified as another leaf of the antiphonal used for X. 1. 10 (Add. 128/46, f. 4). At Maidstone, PRC 10/2, a Register of Inventories of the Archdeacon's Court 1566–7, was no doubt similarly bound. The cover, now PRC 50/15, was a bifolium of a fifteenth-century lectionary and the flyleaves were two leaves of the Avicenna referred to in the footnote on p. 312. The three volumes at Lambeth, now VG 4/5–7, are also good examples of this method of binding: the covers are from service books and the leaves inside them are from the Aristotle and the Avicenna.

When the manuscript fragments were taken off the business books in classes X, Y, Z, no record was made of where they came from. If they were covers, the failure to record the source does not matter much, because covers usually have old titles on them. If, however, they were end-leaves, there is no telling where they came from. The absence of information about Add. 127/16 is particularly unfortunate. How did this book, apparently from Ireland, come to be in Canterbury?

Manuscripts on paper do not seem to have been used in binding the business books in X, Y, Z.[1] Late medieval and sixteenth-century binders did, however, often use paper in the form of compressed pads which acted as pasteboards. Add. 129/25, 26 are pads still attached to their covers and Add. 127/3, 128/15,[2] 18,[2] 19,[2] 44, 45,[3] 129/20, 28, 36 are leaves taken, or probably taken, from pads.

Add. 127/9, 10, 13 and Add. 129/8 do not look like binding fragments. They are probably bits of books which have somehow or other escaped total destruction.

This is not of course a complete list of Canterbury fragments. I have left out some fragments which were difficult and seemed trifling, and I have probably

---

[1] A few end-leaves have been taken from books printed on paper.
[2] I have not listed these scraps.
[3] Add. 128/45 is, Mr. Nigel Wilson tells me, a stray leaf from Leiden, Voss gr. F. 2, the copy of Suidas which Grosseteste is believed to have used.

not seen all the fragments *in situ* inside bindings. At Lambeth Palace[1] and Maidstone[2] I have listed only such fragments as are parts of books of which other fragments are at Canterbury: all the fragments at Lambeth Palace—they come from five books only—are in this category, but not by any means all the fragments at Maidstone.[3]

A. Manuscripts written before 1200[4]

Add. 16. *Evangelia*   s. VIII ex.

f. 1. A stray leaf from B.L., Royal 1 E. vi (*CLA*, no. 214), containing John 11: 28–12: 34: cf. *CLA*, Suppl., p. 5. Bodleian, Lat. Bibl. b. 2 (P) (*Sum. Cat.* 2202*) is another leaf.

Add. 20. *Regula Chrodegangi (Latin and English)*   s. XI²

ff. 2. N. R. Ker, *Catalogue of Manuscripts containing Anglo-Saxon*, p. 138, no. 97.

Add. 25. *Gregory, Dialogues (in English)*   s. X ex.

ff. 4. Ibid., p. 138, no. 96.

Add. 32. *Gregorius, Dialogi*   s. XI in.

f. 1. Ibid., p. lxiii, no. 97*. Two Old English glosses.

**Add. 127/1. *Homeliae*   s. XI¹

Homilies from the summer part of a collection, probably generally like the Durham, Lincoln, and Bury St. Edmunds homiliaries now, respectively, Durham Cathedral, A. III. 29, Lincoln Cathedral 158, and Pembroke College, Cambridge, 24. In arranging the four bifolia I have followed Pem. 24 in placing homilies for the dedication, (*j-l*), after the common, but have taken (*h*) to be for a confessor, as Linc., no. 86. Only a small part of f. 6 remains.

Two leaves in the Kent County Archives Office, Maidstone, PRC 49/2 are probably also from this manuscript. They contain homily 90 and parts of homilies 89 and 91 of the

[1] The books of the Archdeacon's Court and the Consistory Court kept at Lambeth Palace are Visitation Books.

[2] The books of the Archdeacon's Court and the Consistory Court kept at Maidstone relate to probate: cf. *Guide to the Kent County Archives Office*, 1958, pp. 107–14. The chief series in which fragments occur as covers or end-leaves are PRC 2 (Registers of Accounts), PRC 3 (Act Books), PRC 10 and 28 (Inventories), PRC 17 and 32 (Registers of Wills), PRC 39 (Depositions), and PRC 48 (Indexes to Archdeaconry and Consistory Court Records).

[3] For fragments at Lambeth Palace see below, list B, X. 1. 10b, list C, Add. 128/46 and X. 1. 9a, and above, pp. 296, 313. For fragments at Maidstone see below, list A, Add. 127/1, 19, list B, X. 1. 10b, list C, Add. 3, Add. 128/37, 46/60, X. 1. 9a, and above, pp. 296, 312. The fragments at Maidstone are discussed in general by M. B. Parkes, *Guide* (op. cit.), pp. 227–30, and a typescript list of them by Mr. S. Freeth was issued in 1974. A two-leaf fragment of Cassiodorus on the Psalms (Pss. 41–3), s. xi, in a continental hand, came to light recently. It is now PRC 49/24 and was formerly in the binding of PRC 17/40, a Register of Wills for 1567–70. It has poor word-division and has been carefully corrected (in England, s. xii ?).

[4] For Lit. E. 42 see above, p. 289.

homiliary printed as Haymo's in *PL* cxviii (525B–529D: fifth Sunday in Lent, Rogation-tide): 28 out of probably 34 lines remain in each column. They formerly wrapped an index to an act book of the Archdeacon's Court, s. xvi².

(*a*) f. 1 iohannes qui . . . basilicę

(*b*) f. 1ʳᵛ VI idus sep' Nati[. . . .] Initium sancti eua[ngelii . . . .] Liber gen[era-tionis] dauid . . ., *as far as* in zara oriens.' ad nostram salutem

(*c*) f. 2ʳᵛ Vocat peccatores . . . in trono patris cum sancto spiritu uiuit . . . amen.

(*d*) f. 2ᵛ III kl' oct' dedicatio basilice sancti michaelis archangeli. Memoriam beati archangeli michaelis toto orbe uenerandam . . ., *as far as* Qui indicto

(*e*) f. 3ʳᵛ paruulos dominus suos uolebat . . . carnaliter uiuens se solum perdat

(*f*) f. 4 de continentia coniugali . . . dilectione fruuntur

(*g*) f. 4ʳᵛ Kl' Nouembris natale omnium sanctorum. Legimus in eclesiasticis historiis quod sanctus . . ., *as far as* angelorum agmina

(*h*) f. 5ʳᵛ ordo doctorum est . . . diligentius quesiturum

(*i*) f. 6ʳᵛ Et quamdiu haec . . .

(*j*) f. 7 . . . fixa constant ea quae continent.

(*k*) f. 7ʳᵛ Item ut supra Lectio sancti euangelii secundum Lucam. In illo tem-pore. Egressus iesus perambulat hiericho. Et ecce uir nomine zacheus . . . et reliqua. Quae inpossibilia . . ., *as far as* in humili credentium

(*l*) f. 8ʳᵛ aedificat supra fundamentum . . . templum dei estis

(*a*). Decollation of John Baptist, 29 Aug. (*b*). Nativity of B.V.M. (*c*). Matthew. (*d*, *e*). Michael. (*g*). All Saints. (*h*). Confessor. (*j–l*). Dedication of church.

(*b*) is partly as *PL* xciv. 413–14, but fuller at first. (*c–e*, *g*, *h*, *k*) are homilies of the homi-liary attributed to Paul the Deacon as set out in *PL* xcv, De tempore, nos. 55, 56, 58, 63, 88 and 202, the fragments here corresponding to: (*c*) *PL* xciv. 254D–256B; (*d*) *PL* cx. 60D–61B; (*e*) *PL* xcv. 1526D–1528B; (*g*) *PL* xciv. 452C–453C; (*h*) ibid. 472D–474A; (*k*) ibid. 439C–440D. Only the last eight words of (*j*) remain.

ff. 8. Written space of (*h*) 310 × 190 mm. 2 cols. 34 lines. Bifolia from four quires, 1+2, 3+4, 5+6, 7+8. In (*h*), f. 5ᵛᵇ/24, 31, the first word of a question has a mark of interroga-tion added above it.[1] 3-line metallic red initials.

Written in England. Used as wrappers in s. xvi², as appears from titles, dates, and scribbles: (ff. 1, 2) '1580'; (ff. 3, 4) 'Capitula celebrata 1582–1584'; (ff. 5, 6) 'Visitationes 1580–1582'; (ff. 7, 8) 'W. Cock notary public' and dates 1587, 1589. ff. 3–6, and perhaps the other leaves, are probably from volumes now put together as X. 2. 3.

Add. 127/12. *Homeliae*   s. xi in.

A central bifolium containing the whole of one homily and part of another: (*a*) f. 1 XV omelia. In purificatione sanctæ mariæ. Conueniendum est . . . domina-

[1] Cf. N. R. Ker, *English Manuscripts in the Century after the Norman Conquest*, p. 49. Add to the list there: B.L., Cotton Vespasian A. xiv, f. 115ᵛ and other leaves (s. xi in.); Oxford, Bodleian, Hatton 42 (s. ix, from Worcester), as an addition.

tur et regnat per omnia secula seculorum amen. (*b*) f. 2ʳᵛ Inquirendum est fratres karissimi et . . . et opus domini non respicitis (*ends imperfectly*).

The number XV on f. 1 shows that these homilies for the Purification of B.V.M. and Septuagesima are nos. 15, 16 of the collection called by Barré the 'Homéliaire de S. Père de Chartres' (H. Barré, *Les homéliaires carolingiens*, 1962, pp. 18–24). Pembroke College, Cambridge, 25, is an English copy, s. xi, from Bury St. Edmunds. Corrections, s. xiiⁱ, in a pointed hand, probably of Christ Church, Canterbury: the last six lines on f. 1ᵛ have been rewritten in this hand.

ff. 2. Written space 280 × 185 mm. 2 cols. 32 lines. Handsome black initials placed outside the written space.

Written in England. Used as a wrapper: 'Godmersham', f. 2.

Add. 127/15. *Ivo Carnotensis, Epistolae; etc.* s. xii in.

1. f. 1ʳᵛ begins in letter 106, has all letter 107 and ends in letter 108, *PL* clxii. 125C–127A. f. 2ʳᵛ begins in letter 125 (edn. 137B), has all letter 123, and ends in letter 126 (edn. 138A).

2. f. 3ʳᵛ genitos quorum conuersatio . . . Scripsistis nobis dilectissimi filii ut apostolica (*blank: a word left out or erased*) et compassionis uiscera aperi

The subject is monks who have become popes, beginning with Felix III, and bishops deposed and reinstated, for example 'Rothadum uero episcopum sanctę suessionis ęcclesię synodus . . . nicholaus papa ambos reconciliauit'.

ff. 3. Written space 197 × 126 mm. 27 long lines. Hand of Christ Church, Canterbury, type. 2-line initials, purple or green.

Written in England. Perhaps from the copy listed in Eastry's catalogue of the Christ Church library (*Ancient Libraries*, no. 126).

Add. 127/17. *Eusebius, Historia ecclesiastica* s. xii ex.

Two leaves from bk. 5: f. 1 has the last twenty-six entries in the table of contents and the beginning of the text 'Igitur Sotheri episcopo . . .' (*PG* xx. 406).

Two other leaves belong to Mr. M. B. Parkes: cf. *Guide to the Kent County Archives Office*, 1958, p. 229. They came from archives of the Kentish family of Hills.

ff. 2. Written space 285 × 140 mm. 2 cols. 39 lines. Handsome *I* of *Igitur* in colours, in a triple frame, green, red, and gold. Other initials 2-line, red or green with ornament. Written in England.

**Add. 127/19. *Priscianus* s. ix/x

This fragment, two separate leaves containing i. 21–5, 27–31, and the bifolium from the same manuscript in Maidstone, Kent County Archives Office, PRC 49/1a, b, containing i. 33–40, are included in M. Gibson's list of Priscian manuscripts, *Scriptorium*, xxvi (1972), 108, 115. The bifolium was the wrapper of PRC 10/15, a register of inventories of the Archdeacon's Court, 1583–7.

ff. 2. Written space 200 × 140 mm. 24 long lines.
Written probably in France.

Add. 127/20. *Usuardus, Martyrologium* s. xii[1]

A complete text from 1 Jan. to 6 Oct., ending at the words 'de antiquis pauli apostoli discipulis' (*PL* cxxiii. 602–cxxiv. 543; ed. J. Dubois, 1965, pp. 152–315). The beginning of a new month is shown by well-written red capitals in the margin, for example, f. 1ᵛ, 'Kalende mensis februarii'.

ff. 8. Written space 125 × 67 mm. 86 long lines. One quire, numbered xxii at the end. A hand of very small size. Written in England.

Add. 127/22. *Breviarium* s. xii med.

Consecutive leaves of the temporale for the eleventh to the twentieth Sundays after Pentecost.

ff. 6. Written space 145 × 92 mm. 34 long lines. Probably one quire lacking the outside bifolium. Well written. 1-line initials, green, red or blue.
Written in England for monastic use.

*(?) Add. 127/24. *Missale, cum notis* s. xii med.

1. ff. 1–10ᵛ Temporale for octave of Epiphany and from Septuagesima to the second Sunday in Lent.

Generally as *Missale Westm.* i, 68/35–70/13, 84/19–107/11, 131/1–31. The text is continuous over ff. 2–10.

2. ff. 11–12 Common of virgin martyr (cf. *Miss. Westm.*, ii. 1097–8) and virgin non-martyr.

Probably two leaves are missing after f. 11. f. 12 begins with the postcommunion in M. Rule, *The Missal of St. Augustine's Abbey, Canterbury*, 1896, p. 131, col. 2.

3. f. 12ʳᵛ De sancta trinitate.

As *M.W.* ii. 1110–11; Rule, pp. 131–2.

4. ff. 13–20 The last fifteen of a series of votive masses: (*a*) commemoration of relics; (*b*) Holy Cross; (*c*) B.V.M.; (*d*) B.V.M. in Advent; (*e*) All Saints; (*f*) *Pro prelatis et subditis*;[1] (*g*) Pro pace; (*h*) *Pro se ipso*; (*i*) Missa familiaris pro amico;

---

[1] Headings in italics in arts. 4–6 are illegible and derived from *Missale Westm.*

(*j*) Pro familiaribus; (*k*) *Pro familiaribus*; (*l*) *Pro infirmis*; (*m*) Pro iter agentibus; (*n*) Ad pluuiam postulandam; (*o*) Pro serenitate aeris.

(*d–o*) are collect, secret, and postcommunion only. (*a*) begins imperfectly in a gradual at the words 'uenite benedicti'. The secret is 'Suscipiat tua clementia . . .' and the postcommunion 'Diuina libantes misteria . . .', as in Rule, p. 139, but the formula after the word *per* in the secret and after the word *pro* in the postcommunion is 'sanctorum tuorum GREGORII AUGUSTINI ÆDBURGIS atque MILDRITHĘ. necnon et eorum quorum reliquię in ista continentur ęcclesia . . .'. (*b–o*) are the same or partly the same as masses in *Miss. Westm.* ii. 1115–62 and Rule, pp. 135–47: (*b*) *M.W.* 1115, Rule 135–6; (*c*) *M.W.* 1126, Rule 136–7; (*d*) Rule 137–8; (*e*) *M.W.* 1141, Rule 140; (*f*) *M.W.* 1143, Rule 140; (*g*) *M.W.* 1147, Rule 140–1; (*h*) *M.W.* 1152, Rule 142; (*i*) *M.W.* 1157, Rule 143; (*j*) *M.W.* 1145, Rule 141–2; (*k*) *M.W.* 1157, Rule 143–4; (*l*) *M.W.* 1162, Rule 146–7; (*m*) *M.W.* 1155, Rule 145; (*n*) *M.W.* 1159, Rule 145–6; (*o*) *M.W.* 1159, Rule 146.

5. Masses for the dead. (*a*) ff. 20–22 Pro defuncto a primo obitu [. . .]. Quesumus domine ut animę . . . (*b*) f. 22ᵛ *Pro patre et matre.* (*c*) ff. 22ᵛ–23 *Pro benefactoribus defunctis.* (*d*) f. 23 *Pro defunctis sororibus.* (*e*) f. 23 *Pro fratribus defunctis nostre congregationis.* (*f*) f. 23ᵛ *In anniuersariis defunctorum.* (*g*) f. 24 Pro *quiescentibus in cimiteriis.* (*h*) f. 24ᵛ Pro fidelibus de[functis].

(*a*). Collect, secret, preface 'Per quem salus mundi . . .', and postcommunion, the first two and last as Rule, pp. 148, 150, followed by lessons from Thessalonians and St. John (Omne quod dat . . .), the offertory Domine iesu criste rex glorie, and lessons from St. John (Ego sum panis . . . and Dixit martha . . .). The preface has been erased in Rule's manuscript. (*b–h*) are collect, secret, and postcommunion only: (*b*) *M.W.* ii. 1171–2; Rule, p. 155; (*c*) *M.W.* 1173; (*d*) *M.W.* 1176; Rule 155; (*e*) *M.W.* 1172–3; Rule 154; (*f*) *M.W.* 1174–5; Rule 153; (*g*) *M.W.* 1176–7; Rule 155; (*h*) *M.W.* 1177; Rule 155–6.

6. (*a*) ff. 24ᵛ–25 Missa generalis. (*b*) ff. 25–26ᵛ *Pro uiuis et defunctis generalis.* (*c*) f. 26ᵛ For the dead.

(*a, b*) are collect, secret, and postcommunion only: (*a*) *M.W.* 1179; Rule, 156–7; (*b*) *M.W.* 1177–8. (*c*) consists of Requiem . . ., Absolue . . ., De profundis . . ., Fiant . . ., Quia . . ., Vir fortissimus . . . and is, no doubt, an extra on the last page of the manuscript, supplementing 5*a*: Rule, 148, 151; cf. *M.W.* 1164, 1166, 1165.

ff. 26. Written space (ff. 3, 10) 165 × 100 mm. 21 long lines. Collation: 1 two (ff. 1, 2, the outside bifolium) 2⁸ (ff. 3–10) 3 two (ff. 11, 12, probably the third sheet of a quire) 4⁸ (ff. 13–20) 5⁴ (ff. 21–4) 6² (ff. 25, 26). 2-line green, red, or blue initials.

Written for use in Canterbury, probably at St. Augustine's, but possibly at St. Gregory's. The four bifolia, ff. 1+2, 4+9, 5+8, 6+7, have been laid flat and then folded across the middle to make four thicknesses at each end of a (medieval?) binding from which they have been removed with the six thongs of the binding still attached to them. ff. 3, 10, 14, 19 are bound in a modern wrapper with 127/22, 23, 25. The other fourteen leaves are cockled and distorted, but for the most part legible and complete.

Add. 128/10. *P. Comestor, Historia Scholastica*   s. XII ex.

As *PL* cxcviii. 1530A–1533B. A handsome manuscript.

ff. 2 (bifolium). Written space 308 × 200. 2 cols. 32 lines. 2-line red, green, or yellow-brown initials, with ornament.

Written in England. Used as the cover of a document of 1541/2.

Add. 128/12. *Lectionarium*   s. XII in.

Lections of the temporale from Christmas ('In principio . . .') to the Sunday within the octave of Christmas ('Erat ioseph . . .').

ff. 2 (bifolium). Written space 225 × 150 mm. 23 long lines. Initials: (i) 3-line, in gold and colours; (ii) 1-line, red with blue or green ornament.
Written in Germany, probably.

**Add. 128/14. *Collectarius*   s. XII/XIII

Collects and capitula for (pp. 1–4) Monday and Wednesday after Easter and (pp. 5–8) the fourth and fifth Sundays after Easter and Monday, Tuesday, and Wednesday in the fifth week.

On p. 1 the prayer 'Deus qui sollenitate . . .' (*Missale Westmonasteriense*, i. 304) is followed by commemorations of Holy Cross, B.V.M., St. Alphege (cues only), St. Dunstan (cues only), and All Saints. 128/14* is a transcript by W. P. Blore.

ff. 4, paginated 1–8. Written space 240 × 155 mm. 2 cols. 29 lines. Probably the outer bifolia of a quire, since there is a catchword on p. 8, but pp. 1, 2, 7, 8 are now singletons. 2-line and 1-line initials, red or blue with ornament of the other colour.
Written in England and presumably in Canterbury. pp. 3–6 formed the cover of Y. 2.19 ('Ad Instantiam Partium Lib. 37', 1556–9) and pp. 1, 2, 7, 8 were probably inside it at either end.

Add. 128/29. *Missale cum notis*   s. XII med.

1. ff. 1–11ᵛ Sanctorale from John Baptist (24 June) to Crisogonus (24 Nov.), with a gap after f. 9 between Jerome (30 Sept.) and Simon and Jude (28 Oct.).

2. ff. 12–18ᵛ Common of saints. A gap after f. 15.

3. ff. 19–20 Votive masses [Pro se ipso], Pro familiaribus, Contra [temptacionem carnis], [Pro pace], for rain (with lesson), for fine weather (a long prayer, imperfect at the beginning, and lesson, 'Factum est in una dierum . . .'), [Pro iter agentibus], Contra pestes aerias, Pro peste animalium.
The last nine of a series.

4. ff. 20–21ᵛ Masses for the dead, ending in the prayer Pro fratribus defunctis. Propiciare quesumus domine . . .

ff. 21. Written space 242 × 160 mm. 2 cols. 37 lines. Given quires of 8, the collation is probably 1⁸ 2⁸ wants 2, 3 after f. 9 and 6–8 after f. 11 3⁸ wants 1, 2 before f. 12 and 7, 8 after f. 15 4⁸ wants 4, 5 after f. 18. 2-line green or red initials, some cut out.
Written in England.

Add. 128/31. *Breviarium cum notis* s. XII ex.

Fragments of nine bifolia and three singletons, all fragmentary and torn. A fairly small book in long lines. Written space 115 mm wide. Initials red or blue with ornament of the other colour.

Written in England.

*Add. 128/48. *Officium mortuorum* s. XII ex.

ff. 3. Written space 137 × 85 mm. 20 long lines. 2-line red or blue initials with ornament of the other colour.

Written in England. These leaves, with others (see 128/47, 49, 50 in lists B and C), are stated to have been taken from the binding of a register of 1468.

Add. 128/52. *Missale* s. XI med.

Temporale in Lent, beginning 'et a cunctis' (*Sarum Missal*, p. 76/12) and ending 'Concede quesumus omnipotens deus ut qui ex merito' (ibid., p. 79/15). Many alterations, s. xiv.

Probably one leaf is missing after f. 1, which ends in the lesson from Numbers 20. f. 2 begins 'accenderet. Imploramus' in the secret for Feria vi post Oculi.

ff. 3 (singletons). Written space 232 × 148 mm. 33 long lines. Initials red or purple, set outside the written space.

Written in England.

**Add. 128/54. *Lectionarium* s. XII med.

Lessons from Jeremiah.

f. 1 begins in lesson 2 and ends in lesson 5. The last words of lesson 2 are 'regis sedechie'. Lessons 3–5 begin at Jeremiah 21: 1, 37: 3 and 37: 10 respectively. f. 2 has lessons 2, 3 on a weekday and lessons 1, 2 'feria sexta', beginning at Jeremiah 26: 1 and 25: 1 respectively.

ff. 2 (bifolium). Written space 285 × 180 mm. 2 cols. 34 lines. 2-line initials, brown, red, or green, with ornament.

Written in England. Formerly the cover of Y. 4. 23, 'Ad instantiam partium, lib. 29', 1581–3.

**Add. 128/58. *Augustinus, In Johannem* s. XII[1]

f. 1[r] begins at 'peruolat' (*PL* xxxv. 1895/32) and ends at 'pro nichilo' (1897/6). The end of Tract. ci and beginning of Tract. cii come on the recto: the *incipit* and *explicit* lines are alternately red and green. The verso is badly damaged.

f. 2[rv] runs from 'Nos diligimus' to 'ille mundum' (*PL*, 1898/37–1901/34).

Apparently one leaf of this manuscript contained nearly the same amount of text as three columns of *PL*.

ff. 2 (central bifolium). Written space *c.* 290 × 200 mm. 2 cols. 40 lines. A 3-line red initial *D.*

Written in England. Formerly the cover of X. 8. 12, 'Comperta et Detecta, liber 6', 1582–5.

X. 1. 11a. *Jeronimus, In Habbakuk* s. xii in.

Begins 'Et de quibus dicitur' and end 'ad tartarum' (*PL* xxv. 1319A–1324C). The text agrees almost letter for letter, abbreviation for abbreviation, and punctuation mark for punctuation mark with the Christ Church, Canterbury, copy now Trinity College, Cambridge, B. 3. 5, ff. 30/35–32/31.

ff. 2. Written space 255 × 170 mm. 2 cols. 44 lines. An excellent pointed hand of Canterbury (St. Augustine's?) type. 2-line initials, red or green.

Written in Canterbury and perhaps the St. Augustine's copy, *Ancient Libraries*, p. 220, no. 327. *In situ* as flyleaves of X. 1. 11, 'Comperta et Detecta, Lib. 12', 1571–2: the cover is modern and takes the place of Add. 128/46, f. 1, which has left offset traces on the Jerome.

B. Manuscripts written after 1200, other than service books

Add. 127/4. s. xv. Nigellus, Speculum stultorum. ff. 4. Written space 142 mm high. 36 long lines.

Add. 127/5. s. xv². A letter, 'Vellem hodierna die celeberrime presul . . .', and sixteen lines of verse, 'Cantuariensis aue cui dat cantaria nomen . . .'. f. 1. Paper.

Add. 127/6. s. xiii. Sermones. ff. 12. Written space 158 × 110 mm. 44 long lines.

Add. 127/7. s. xiii/xiv. Prosper, Sententiae. ff. 6. Written space 95 × 57 mm. 38 long lines.

Add. 127/8. s. xiii². Vita S. Thomae Cantuariensis. ff. 6. Written space 110 × 72 mm. 25 long lines.

Add. 127/9. s. xv. N. de Lyra, etc. ff. 6. Paper.

Add. 127/10. s. xiv. Sermones. ff. 2. Paper. Written space 280 × 180 mm. 2 cols. 63 lines.

Add. 127/13. s. xv. '. . . Explicit compendium de negotio naturali secundum albertum'. ff. 6. Paper. Written space 167 × 110 mm. *c.* 34 long lines.

Add. 127/14. s. xiv. Jus canonicum. ff. 6.

Add. 127/21. s. xiv². Registrum Cantuariense (?). f. 1.

** Add. 128/2. s. xv. Cassiodorus, Historia tripartita. f. 1. Written space 270 × 185 mm. 2 cols. 37 lines.

** Add. 128/13. s. xv². Casus matrimonialis.

Add. 128/26. s. xv. De propositionibus. ff. 4. Written space 148 × 110 mm.

* Add. 128/27a. s. xiii/xiv. G. Monemutensis, Historia Britonum. ff. 10 (5 bifolia). Written space 140 × 100 mm. 28–35 long lines.

* Add. 128/27b. s. xv. Constitutiones Symonis de Mepham, etc. Two fragments of one leaf.

* Add. 128/27c. s. xiv. Narrationes. f. 1. 2 cols.

* Add. 128/27d. s. xiii. Decretales Gregorii IX (I. vi. 56, 57). f. 1. 2 cols.

** Add. 128/33. s. xiv in. De officio missae. ff. 4. Written space 265 × 170 mm. 2 cols. 54 lines.

Add. 128/38. s. xiv. Epistolae Pharaonis ad Josephum. ff. 2. Written space 155 mm wide.

Add. 128/44. s. xv². Vocabularium Graeco-Latinum. f. 1. Paper.

* Add. 128/47. s. xiv. P. Pecham. Lumiere as Lais (in French). ff. 3. Written space 190 mm high. 2 cols. 49 lines.

** Add. 128/53. s. xiv. Augustinus, De civitate Dei. ff. 3. Written space 253 × 145 mm. 2 cols. 47 lines.

Add. 128/55. s. xiv. Jus canonicum. ff. 6. Written space 320 × 195 mm. 2 cols. 71 lines.

Add. 129/1. s. xiv². A. Nequam, De nominibus utensilium. f. 1. Written space 200 × 140 mm. 2 cols. 44 lines.

Add. 129/5. s. xv. Inventorium. f. 1. Paper.

Add. 129/8. s. xiv ex. Jus Canonicum. ff. 17. Paper.

Add. 129/20. s. xv. Tabula. ff. 2. Paper.

Add. 129/21. s. xv. Comment. in 1 librum Sententiarum P. Lombardi (?). ff. 8. Paper.

Add. 129/25, 26. s. xiv. Theologica. ff. 36 (?). Paper.

Add. 129/30. s. xiv. Carta fundationis prioratus de Maxstoke. f. 1.

** Add. 129/31. s. xiv. Orosius, De ormesta mundi. f. 1. Written space 290 × 195 mm. 2 cols. 69 lines.[1]

** Add. 129/32. s. xiii. Biblia (1 Paralip.). ff. 2. Written space 185 × 120 mm. 2 cols. 56 lines.

** Add. 129/35. s. xiii. Decretales. f. 1. Written space 185 × 105 mm. 2 cols. 48 lines.

Add. 129/36. s. xv. Theology (in English). f. 1. Paper.

** Add. 129/37. s. xiv. J. de Balbis, Catholicon. f. 1. Written space 325 × 220 mm. 2 cols. 70 lines.

Add. 129/40. s. xv in. Commentary on the mass (?: in English). ff. 2.

** X. 1. 10b. s. xiii. Aristoteles, De generatione et corruptione. ff. 2. Written space 163 × 90 mm. 27 long lines.

---

[1] Add. 129/31–4 are said to have been 'removed from Church Commissioners bundle 70416 7th August 1966' and Add. 129/35, 37, 38 were removed at the same time from bundles 70352, 70455, 70446. The marks on Add. 129/31, 32, 34 show, however, that they are not from bundle 70416, which is wholly concerned with Ickham. 129/34 is from 70395. For Add. 129/33, 34, 38 see below, list C.

* Y. 1. 6d. s. xiv. Instrumentum publicum. f. 1.

** Y. 2. 22a. s. xiv in. W. Durandus, Rationale divinorum. f. 1. Written space 262 × 171 mm. 2 cols. 54 lines.

Add. 127/4. Lines 490–550, 1172–1238, 3797–3852 of the edition by J. H. Mozley and R. R. Raymo, *Nigel de Longchamps, Speculum stultorum*, 1960. The fragments include line 1172: cf. edn., p. 189. Seven copies of the Speculum are in the Canterbury catalogues in *Ancient Libraries*: Christ Church, nos. 545, 709, 1434; St. Augustine's, nos. 485, 871, 1541, 1557.

Add. 127/6. Sermons on the gospels for the second to the twenty-fifth Sundays after Pentecost and, beginning the common of saints (f. 11ᵛ), the sermon 'Simile est regnum celorum sagene . . . Scitote fratres quid ista significant: quia perfectum . . .'.

Add. 127/7. *PL* li. 434C–488B, nos. 47–370, but with a big gap from no. 103 to no. 309 after f. 3.

Add. 127/8. The text is continuous and corresponds to *Materials for the History of Thomas Becket* (RS lxvii), ii. 457/32–458/27, 356/26–358/15, 323 *Dum igitur*—334/11 *dominio*.

Add. 127/9. Contra Judeum (Stegmüller, no. 5980), beginning imperfectly: '. . . Explicit libellus notabilis doctoris de lyra contra iudeum'. Also a question 'De celebracione missarum'.

Add. 127/10. English is scattered about in the first sermon, for example, f. 1ʳᵃ/1, 'Iste autem vii tube que blowyn sunt. ista 7 mirabilia . . .', and at the end 'þat were to man so kynd grant vs þi blys wyt oute hende ad quam . . .'.

Add. 127/13. Six chapters, the last beginning 'Ut nos igitur in hoc nostro compendio'.

Add. 127/21. A long headless piece on Christ Church business is followed by a letter in French of Archbishop Courtenay, Salisbury, 1 June 1384, headed 'A la garde de sarreines et de bois en Sussex grante par le Erceuesh' Willm Courtenay a Mathieu Kelly'.

Add. 128/2. From bk. 1 (*PL* lxix. 913B–915B). A handsome fere-textura.

Add. 128/13. Notice of appeal in a case between Richard St. Nicholas and Elizabeth Tooke of the parish of St. Margaret at Cliffe. The document records a conversation in English in which Richard promises to marry Elizabeth.

Add. 128/27a–e are from RE 6 and were extracted during repairs in 1932, no doubt. The binding is of brown calf, s. xv ex., and bears a small rectangular stamp of a dog and a floral stamp, neither, it seems, recorded by Oldham. (*a*) includes the beginning of bk. 6, ch. 15. (*b*) has the heading 'Incipiunt constituciones venerabilis patris domini Symonis de Mepham Cantuariensis Archiepiscopi' and the beginning of the text, 'Zelari oportet . . .' (Wilkins, *Concilia*, ii. 552). Constitutions of Archbishop Boniface followed, but only the heading remains. All the text is more or less faded, but the headings in red are clear. In (*c*) paragraphs begin 'Leo rex animalium semel', 'De caseo. Sicud narrat ysopus caseus', 'Bufo qui habitat in terra rogauit'. (*e*) is an unidentified fragment, s. xv.

Add. 128/38. Chapter xvi is 'Pharaonis ad io. super prestiti concilii prosecucione. Pharao diuina . . . salutem Et salubriter exposita salubrius . . .'.

Add. 128/44. English hand. Includes a list of thirty-eight Greek words, mainly prepositions, with their meanings, for example 'συν compono / ἐξ libero / προ eligo / ἁμα interficior recipio euertor aufero / κατα deicior / παρα attraho aufero euello . . .'. The leaf is not full.

Add. 128/47. From the same binding as 128/48 (list A). The text corresponds to MS. Bodley 399 f. 20ᵛ (bk. 2, dist. vi, ch. 75).

Add. 128/53. Bk. 22, ch. 3–8, 24, 25: *PL* xli. 754/4–761/9, 790/9–793/33. From 'Depositiones, Lib. 5', 1548–50.

Add. 128/55. Two of the leaves are complete and are from 'De verborum significatione'.

Add. 129/1. Text and commentary, the latter smaller. Begins in the commentary, 'hache de mache a quo pennatus'. On the verso a paragraph of text begins 'Aurifaber caminum habeat': cf. T. Wright, *A Volume of Vocabularies*, 1857, i. 117. Running title 'Alexander Nequam', s. xiv.

Add. 129/5. A narrow strip only. The inventory included books.

Add. 129/8. A quire of sixteen leaves and a singleton, half-burnt fragments of a commentary on Decretals (III. i) and Clementines (I. ix. 1) which refers often to the 'conclusio Io. (Andree?)'.

Add. 129/20. An index to a book, for example 'Vita breuis. via longa. virtus debilis partis 3ᵉ capitulo 14 a'.

Add. 129/25, 26. Pads taken from either end of the binding of some book. Each consists of some nine bifolia of paper laid open and pressed together and one leaf of parchment. The paper leaves contain notes, probably for sermons, written in current anglicana. The parchment leaves are blank, except for an Oxford pledge note (129/25): 'Caucio Magistri [. . . .] exposita in cista Wynton' 2° die Aprilis anno domini mᵒ ccccᵒ lxviᵒ et iacet pro[. . .]'.

Add. 129/30. Dugdale, *Monasticon Anglicanum*, vi. 524. Imperfect at both ends.

Add. 129/31. From bk. 6. A good example of anglicana script at its best. Marked 'Canterbury Rents. Collector's Book' and '70544'.

Add. 129/32. Marked 'Godmersham Rental 1600'.

Add. 129/35. Decretals (of Gregory IX?), bk. 5. Formerly the cover of 70352, a mid sixteenth-century rental (City of Canterbury) on nineteen leaves measuring 215 × 155 mm.

Add. 129/37. From the section De tropis of the Quarta pars. Formerly the cover of a rental of Monks Illeigh for 1599, now 70455 (2/53).

X. 1. 10b. Bk. 1. 4. *In situ* in binding of X. 1. 10: see below, list C, X. 1. 10a. From the same book as four leaves at Maidstone, Kent County Archives Office, PRC 49/9, which contain parts of bk. 3 of De anima and have been taken from PRC 39/6, a Depositions Book for 1568–73. Four leaves at Lambeth Palace, with part of bk. 2 of De anima, are also from this manuscript: they are pastedowns in Visitation Act Books for 1569–70 and 1570–1, now VG 4/5, 7. For another leaf now missing see above, p. 312, footnote.

Y. 1. 6d. *In situ* in binding of Y. 1. 6: see below, list C, Y. 1. 6a–c. A notarial instrument subscribed by Stephen de Pole, clerk of the diocese of St. Asaph and public notary by apostolic and imperial authority, who drew it up at the request (rogatus atque requisitus) of Master William Carleton. His notarial mark is on the left at the foot and on it 'S. de Pole'.

Y. 2. 22a. Inside the plain parchment cover of Y. 2. 22, 'Ad instantiam partium liber 39', 1559–62. Contains the section 'De sanctus' of bk. 4 (edn. Strasbourg 1493, f. 78).

C. Service-books written after 1200

Add. 3. s. xiv. Breviarium. ff. 16 (8 bifolia). Written space 196 × 123 mm. 2 cols. 26 lines.

Add. 127/2. s. xiii¹. Psalterium (Pss. 101–18). Written space 73 × 48 mm. 22 long lines.

Add. 127/3. s. xv. Tabula picae. ff. 6. Paper.

Add. 127/16. xiv. Breviarium. ff. 14. Written space *c.* 190 × 118 mm. 2 cols. 25 lines.

Add. 127/18. s. xiv/xv. Servitium B.V.M. f. 1. Written space 267 × 175 mm. 2 cols. 39 lines.

Add. 127/23a. s. xiv. Breviarium. f. 1. Written space 187 × 117 mm. 35 long lines.

Add. 127/23b. s. xiv. Breviarium. ff. 5. Written space 178×120 mm. 33 long lines.

Add. 127/25. s. xiii. Exorcismus aquae, etc. ff. 2.

Add. 128/1. s. xiii ex. Missale. ff. 2. Written space 253×135 mm. 13 long lines.

** Add. 128/3. s. xiv ex. Antiphonale. f. 1. Written space 440×275 mm. 2 cols. 20 lines and music.

* Add. 128/4. s. xv. Officium cum notis. f. 1.

* Add. 128/5. s. xiv in. Officium cum notis. f. 1.

* Add. 128/6. s. xv. Sequentia (?). f. 1.

** Add. 128/7. s. xv. Magnificat, cum notis. f. 1. Written space 365 mm wide.

** Add. 128/8. s. xiv. Graduale. f. 1.

Add. 128/9. s. xiv/xv. Antiphonale. f. 1.

** Add. 128/11. s. xv in. Gaude flore uirginali . . . f. 1. Written space 245× 260 mm. 22 long lines.

** Add. 128/28. s. xiv. Missale. ff. 2. Written space 280×160 mm. 2 cols. 30 lines.

Add. 128/30. s. xiii. Graduale. ff. 8. Written space 143×83 mm. 12 long lines and music.

Add. 128/32. s. xiv. Manuale. ff. 31. Written space 105×67 mm. 14 long lines.

Add. 128/34. s. xiv. Graduale. ff. 32. Written space c. 195×120 mm. 8 long lines and music.

Add. 128/35. s. xiv. Officium cum notis. f. 2.

** Add. 128/36. s. xiv/xv. Gloria in excelsis, etc. f. 2.

Add. 128/37. s. xv/xvi. Antiphonale. ff. 5. Written space c. 340×225 mm. 14 long lines and music.

** Add. 128/46. s. xv. Antiphonale. ff. 4. Written space 330×210 mm. 2 cols. 48 lines (or 16 lines and music).

* Add. 128/49. s. xiv. Breviarium. f. 1. Written space 120×82 mm. 2 cols. 39 lines.

* Add. 128/50. s. xv. Prayers in Netherlandish. ff. 2. Written space 67×48 mm. 15 long lines.

** Add. 128/51a+X. 1. 8a (flyleaf at the end). s. xiii. Breviarium cum notis. ff. 6. Written space 220×140 mm. 2 cols. 48 lines.

** Add. 128/51b+X. 1. 9b. s. xiii. Breviarium cum notis. ff. 4. Written space 230×145 mm. 2 cols. 42 lines.

Add. 128/51c. s. xiv. Breviarium (temporale) cum notis. f. 1. Written space 243×168 mm. 2 cols. 48 lines.

** Add. 128/56. s. xiv/xv. Missale. ff. 2. Written space 195 mm wide.

** Add. 128/57. s. xv. Missale cum notis. f. 1. Written space 290 × 190 mm. 2 cols. 38 lines.

** Add. 128/60. s. xv in. Lectionarium. ff. 5. Written space 334 × 225 mm. 2 cols. 42 lines.

** Add. 128/61. s. xiv. Calendarium. f. 1. Written space 305 × 185 mm.

** Add. 129/15+Y. 2. 22a. s. xv. Lectionarium. f. 1. Written space *c.* 290 × 190 mm. 2 cols. 43 lines.

Add. 129/16. s. xiii. Missale. f. 1.

Add. 129/19. s. xv ex. Psalmi et oratio 'pro Rege nostro Henrico Septimo'. ff. 2. Written space 195 × 148 mm. 21 long lines.

** Add. 129/33.¹ s. xiv/xv. Breviarium. f. 1. Written space 280 × 165 mm. 2 cols. 38 lines.

** Add. 129/34.¹ s. xiii in. Psalterium. ff. 4. Written space 247 × 163 mm. 2 cols. 37 lines.

** Add. 129/38. s. xv/xvi. Missale. f. 1. Written space 305 × 215 mm. 2 cols. 27 lines.

* Add. 129/39. s. xiv. Missale. ff. 2. 45 long lines. Written space 215 × 135 mm.

** X. 1. 8a. See above, Add. 128/51a.

** X. 1. 9a. s. xv. Lectionarium. ff. 2. 2 cols. 37 lines. Written space 255 × 170 mm.

** X. 1. 9b. See above, Add. 128/51b.

** X. 1. 10a. s. xv. Antiphonale. f. 1.

* Y. 1. 6a-c. Officia liturgica.

** Y. 2. 22b. s. xv. Lectionarium. f. 1. Written space 190 mm wide.

Add. 3. Temporale from Sexagesima to the first Sunday in Lent (pp. 1–16) and from Wednesday in Holy Week to lauds at Easter (pp. 17–32). Principal feasts are of twelve lessons. Some leaves damaged. 'Fragments of a breviary / Canterbury use' is stamped in gold on the cover.

The leaves were flyleaves: offset from the covers can sometimes be seen. Perhaps as many as thirty more leaves of this manuscript are in the Kent County Archives Office in Maidstone, PRC 50/2: here the cover is a large antiphonal and these much smaller leaves are pasted inside it as additional strengthening. They have been removed from a Register of Wills of the Archdeacon's Court, now PRC 17/26. One Maidstone leaf contains cues for the 'Regressio Sancti [Thome]' (2 Dec.).²

Add. 127/3. Each page contains calculations based on the number and letter referred to in its heading, for example, f. 1ᵛ, 'Primum G primacio 16. 13. 5. Domine ne in furore', (f. 4ᵛ) '6 A In principio 30 die Iulii'. Compare the section *Regula de historiis inchoandis*, HBS vii. 119–26; also above, Lit. E. 12.

¹ See above, p. 323, footnote.
² For this Christ Church feast see F. Wormald, *English Benedictine Calendars after A.D. 1100*, p. 65.

Add. 127/16. (*a*) ff. 1–10ᵛ Office of Corpus Christi, 'Sacerdos in eternum . . .': the lessons are not those in *Brev. ad usum Sarum*. (*b*) ff. 11–12 Mass of Corpus Christi. (*c*) ff. 12–14ᵛ In festiuitate sancti cannici abbatis. The hymns are *RH*, nos. 30796, 25732, 28591 and *AH* xxv. 185–7, xi. 95, known to Dreves from the breviary of the church of Clondalkin, near Dublin, now Trinity College, Dublin, B. 1. 3. These three consecutive short quires, 1⁴ 2⁶ 3⁴ were presumably additions at the end of a breviary used in a church with a special interest in St. Cannice of Clondalkin. (*c*) seems to be complete: f. 14ᵛᵇ is blank.

Add 127/23a. Part of the office of Corpus Christi.

Add. 127/23b. Part of the temporale for the period after Christmas.

Add. 127/25. A bifolium, perhaps once flyleaves at the beginning of a book. f. 2ʳ is blank, except for the title, s. xv, '[. . .] abbreuiatus Willelmi de Wenchepe'. Wincheap is a suburb of Canterbury and one of this name, s. xiii, gave two books to the cathedral library (*Ancient Libraries*, p. 62, nos. 518, 519).

Add. 128/1. Epiphany. A very large hand, the minims 10 mm high.

Add. 128/4 was inside the binding of MA 37, the journal of treasurer's accounts for 7–19 Edward IV.

Add. 128/5. Part of a leaf of polyphonic music.

Add. 128/6 is from the binding of Lit. C. 11, s. xviᶦ. A sequence begins (?) 'Aue miles triumphalis miles dulcis immortalis'.

Add. 128/7. The lower part of a very large leaf. Verses 2, 4, 6, 8 of Magnificat (Luke 1: 47, 49, 51, 53), verses 2 and 6 in black ink and verses 4 and 8 in red ink. The text is continuous from recto to verso. Presumably verses 1, 3, 5, 7 were on the upper half of the leaf. A large gold *E* of *Exultauit* (Luke 1: 47). Marked 'Decan: Cantuar. et Westbere 1560'.

Add. 128/9 was until 1937 the cover of 'G. 3. 34' ('Y. 15. 19'). Office for eighth Sunday after Pentecost.

Add. 128/11. A memoria of B.V.M., *RH*, no. 6809, and prayer following it, 'Domine ihesu criste fili dei uiui qui beatissimam genitricem Mariam . . .'. It is written in a very large hand as a broadsheet, the dorse blank.

Add. 128/28. Sanctorale, July–August. Cf. *Sarum Missal*, pp. 297–8, 302–4.

Add. 128/30. Three bifolia, the two outer sheets and the central sheet of a quire, and two singletons.

Add. 128/37. 128/37* is a transcript by W. P. Blore and a description by J. B. L. Tolhurst extracted from a letter he wrote to C. S. Phillips, 30 Dec. 1945. In Tolhurst's opinion 'The provenance of these fragments is indicated on page 2 where, following the commemoration of Christmas after the second vespers of St. Stephen, the three suffrages of St. Kenelm, St. Benedict and All Saints are indicated by the cues of their initials antiphons. These three suffrages correspond to the shorter services said on feasts; that of St. Kenelm standing "in loco patroni". The only monastery to which such a suffrage would be appropriate is Winchcombe where St. Kenelm was enshrined.' Nineteen more leaves of this antiphonal, nine bifolia and a singleton, are at Maidstone, PRC 50/1 and 50/2/1. Six of the bifolia in 50/1 were covers of PRC 3/13, an Act Book of the Archdeacon's Court 1552–4, PRC 17/27–9, Registers of Wills of the Archdeacon's Court 1549/50–1, 1552–3, and 1550–4, PRC 22/2, an Act Book of the Consistory Court 1550–7, and PRC 32/24, a Register of Wills of the Consistory Court 1551–2. PRC 50/2/1 is *in situ* as the cover of PRC 17/26, a Register of Wills of the Archdeacon's Court 1545–50 (cf. above, Add. 3).

Add. 128/46. Covers. f. 1 is from X. 1. 11, 'Comperta et Detecta, lib. 12' 1571–2: cf. above, list A, X. 1. 11a. f. 2 is from Y. 4. 14, 'Ad instantiam partium, lib. 43', 1567–8. f. 3 is from Z. 4. 12, 'Depositiones, lib. 15' 1567–8. f. 4 is from X. 1. 8, 'Comperta et Detecta, lib. 9', 1566–7: cf. below. Cf. also below, X. 1. 10a.

Cf. for the texts *Brev. ad usum Sarum*, i. dcxxxv–vi, and iii. 114–26, 655–8, 663–6.

Another leaf covers the Visitation Act Book for 1569–70, Lambeth Palace VG 4/6: the text is as *Brev. ad usum Sarum*, i. dcclii–vi. Four leaves are at Maidstone, PRC 50/9. One of them (50/9/2) has been removed from PRC 21/1, Register of Accounts and Inventories, Consistory Court, 1569–72 and one, cut in two (50/9/4, 5), is *in situ* in the binding of 48/13, the N–Y part of a two-volume Index of Wills of the Archdeacon's Court 1449–1564.

Add. 128/49, 50. From the same binding as list A, Add. 128/48.

Add. 128/51a+X. 1. 8a. Flyleaves. Temporale, fourth Sunday in Advent (f. 1), Stephen (f. 2), Ascension and octave (f. 3), Pentecost (X. 1. 8a), Trinity (f. 4), Sunday after Ascension (f. 5). Cf. above, Add. 128/46.

Add. 128/51b+X. 1. 9b. Two leaves were flyleaves of Y. 4. 14, Ad instantiam partium, lib. 43 (cf. above, Add. 128/46): sanctorale, Nativity of B.V.M. (f. 1), feast of relics (f. 2). Two leaves are *in situ* as flyleaves of X. 1. 9 (cf. below, X. 1. 9a): sanctorale, Agapitus (18 Aug.)—octave of Assumption of B.V.M. (22 Aug.), and (f. 2) Nativity of B.V.M. Probably one leaf came between X. 1. 9b, f. 2 and 128/51b, f. 1.

Add. 128/56. Temporale. Cf. *Sarum Missal*, pp. 47, 48, 57–9.

Add. 128/57. Sanctorale. Probably the outside sheet of the first quire. *Sarum Missal*, pp. 232–3, 248–51.

Add. 128/60. 'Die iii' begins with a sermon of Maximus, 'Audistis . . .' (*PL* lvii. 279). Titles show that these leaves were covers of Liber 41, 1563–6, Liber 43, 1564–6, and Liber Visitationis 1564 (now X. 1. 5). Another leaf is at Maidstone, PRC 50/14, removed from PRC 3/17, an Act Book (Probate) of the Archdeacon's Court 1563–6.

Add. 128/61. Calendar for May and June in blue, red, and black. Translation of Richard and memoria of Crispin and Crispinian, 16 June, in red. 'Sancti eligii episcopi et confessoris non sarum', 25 June. 'Dedicacio capelle de chomhope' added at 1 May, perhaps by the main hand, in red. Entries in blue are marked 'Duplex festum'. Francis Wormald, in a letter to Dr. Charles Cotton, 7 Sept. 1934, kept as 128/61*, says 'based upon Salisbury, but showing non Sarum features'.

Add. 129/15+Y. 2. 22b. The two halves of one leaf. Y. 2. 22b is inside the end cover of Y. 2. 22: see above, list B, Y. 2. 22a. As *Brev. ad usum Sarum*, i. dccclxxix–dcccxciv.

Add. 129/16. Votive masses. Cf. *Sarum Missal*, pp. 393, 410.

Add. 129/19. 'Isti Psalmi sequentes dicendi sunt statim post traditionem Hostie in missa Capitulari Pro Rege nostro Henrico Septimo videlicet Psalmi. Exaudiat te dominus. . . . Da quesumus deus famulo tuo regi nostro henrico septimo salutem . . .'. Cf. *Tracts of Clement Maydestone* (HBS vii), pp. 204–6.

Add. 129/33, 34, 38 came in 1966: see above, list B, Add. 129/31. 129/33 is from 70416, a rental of Ickham, 1600. 129/34 is a double thickness of parchment formerly covering 70395, a rental of Godmersham, 1434. 129/38, from the mass for the dead (cf. *Sarum Missal*, p. 432), was the cover of 70446, arrears of rents in London, etc., 1569.

Add. 129/39. A bifolium still *in situ* as part of the cover of a medieval binding now detached from the book to which it belonged. Office for Holy Thursday. Cf. *Sarum Missal*, pp. 103–4.

X. 1. 9a. Cover of 'Comperta et Detecta, lib. 10' 1567–9. A bifolium with lessons for (1) Mary Magdalene, 22 July, and (2) Anne and Seven Sleepers (26, 27 July), as *Brev. ad usum Sarum*, iii. 519–23, 550–7. For the flyleaves see above, list C, Add. 128/51b.

Three bifolia of this lectionary are at Maidstone. Two of them, PRC 50/15, are (1) the present cover of PRC 48/5, Index to Registers of Inventories of the Archdeacon's Court 1569–85, and (2) the former cover of PRC 10/2, Liber Blake Inventariorum, a register of inventories of the Archdeacon's Court 1566–7. Both were central bifolia of quires. The lessons are those in *Brev. ad usum Sarum*, iii. 99–105 (Vincent) and 499–505 (Margaret). The third bifolium was the cover of S/Rm SO 1 and is now bound inside it. S/Rm SO 1 has nothing to do with Canterbury diocesan business, but is a collection of 'Orders and

Decrees of Special Laths' of Romney Marsh made early in the seventeenth century: presumably it existed as a blank book for some forty years before this.[1]

Two more bifolia are at Lambeth Palace as covers of VG 4/5, 7: cf. above, list B, X. 1. 10b. They contain lessons for the Assumption of B.V.M. and were adjacent bifolia of one quire.

X. 1. 10a. Probably a leaf of the same manuscript as Add. 128/46. It wraps 'Comperta et Detecta, lib. 11' 1570–1. Third Sunday in Lent. For the flyleaves, X. 1. 10b, see above, list B.

Y. 1. 6a–c (for Y. 1. 6d, see above, list B) are *in situ* inside the limp parchment covers of 'Ad instantiam partium, lib. 13' 1463–8. Probably fragments of three different books: (a) a leaf of a noted breviary s. xiii in.; (b) a bifolium of a missal in a large hand, s. xiii, one leaf containing the story of the Passion and the other part of the Good Friday office, as *Sarum Missal*, p. 111; (c) a strip, s. xiii.

Y. 2. 22b. See above Add. 129/15.

CANTERBURY. ST. AUGUSTINE'S COLLEGE

Missale   s. xv med.

Fully described by F. C. Eeles, 'On a manuscript Sarum Missal of the fifteenth century, probably used in or near Canterbury, now in the library of St. Augustine's College, Canterbury', *Transactions of the St. Paul's Ecclesiological Society*, viii (1920), 72–84. The text of art. 1 often agrees with Canterbury Cathedral, Add. 128/29 (above, p. 320) against other missals.[2]

1. ff. 2–30^v, 1^{rv}, 31–58 Sanctorale, beginning imperfectly at 24 Feb.

2. ff. 59–79^v Common of saints, beginning imperfectly.

3. ff. 79^v–83 Missa de sancta maria.

4. ff. 83–91^v Votive masses: (a) ff. 83–8 Full offices of Holy Trinity, angels, 'Pro fratribus et sororibus', 'In commemoracione beati thome martiris' (ff. 84^v–85^v, not defaced), of Holy Spirit, 'Noue solennitatis corporis cristi ad missam', of Holy Cross and for peace; (b) ff. 88–91^v Collect, secret and postcommunion of All Saints and on fifteen other occasions, as listed by Eeles,[3] ending imperfectly in the second Missa generalis.

5. ff. 92–93^v Masses of the dead, beginning imperfectly and lacking a leaf or more after f. 92.

6. f. 93^{rv} Trentale sancti Gregorii pape.

7. ff. 93^v–94^v Later additions in several hands. Eeles, pp. 83–4.

---

[1] The pastedowns inside S/Rm SO 1 are from a missal in two columns of thirty-six lines. Two other leaves of it were used for the binding of PRC 10/4, a register of inventories of the Archdeacon's Court 1566–8, and are now PRC 50/12.

[2] Information from Mr. Christopher Hohler.

[3] Eeles lists a mass *Pro peccatoribus* before the mass 'Pro penitentibus', but I do not see it.

ff. iv+94+iii. 282×195 mm. Written space 200×120 mm. 2 cols. 36 lines. Collation: 1^8 (ff. 2–9) 2–3^8 4^8 (ff. 26–30, 1, 31, 32) 5–7^8 8^8 wants 3 after f. 58 9–10^8 11^6 12^8 wants 7 after f. 91 13 two (ff. 93, 94, a bifolium). Quires 4–11 signed a–h. A new hand at f. 26. Initials: (i) ff. 1, 52 (Assumption of B.V.M. and All Saints), blue patterned in white on decorated gold grounds; (ii) f. 38, 3-line or 2-line, gold on red and blue grounds patterned in white: sprays into the margin: (iii) 2-line, blue with red ornament; (iv) 1-line, red or blue. Continuous borders on ff. 1, 52 and a border on three sides of f. 38 (Nativity of B.V.M.). The text beside the initials on ff. 1, 52 has been rewritten. Binding of s. xviii.

Written in England. 'Alexander Herlekynden owyht this boke tha(t) wytnessyth the wryter', f. 94, s. xvi: a letter attached to f. iᵛ written by C. E. Woodruff, 7 Dec. 1918, notices one of this name of Woodchurch, Kent, in 1557, from a pedigree by G. S. Steinman in *Topographer and Genealogist*, i (1846), 229–58, and makes the point that Woodchurch was dedicated to All Saints. 'Hic liber Constat ad Thomam Thransam' and 'Richard Movntt' on f. 94 and 'John Collar' on f. 2 are of s. xvi. 'N⁰ 22', f. 2, s. xviii (?). Given anonymously in 1917: cf. *St. Augustine's College, Occasional Papers*, no. 33 (1917), p. 15.

CARDIFF. PUBLIC LIBRARY

The manuscripts in Welsh are described in HMC, *Report on MSS. in the Welsh language*, ii, pt. 2 (1903), 91–300 (Cardiff) and 301–45 (Havod).

1. 217. *Sermones, etc.*   s. xv med.

1. ff. 2–22ᵛ Incipiunt sermones dominicales per circulum anni. In aduentu. dominica 1ª. Uenit filius hominis . . . Lu.xii. Notandum quod triplex est aduentus domini primus est in mundum.

Brief sermons of the temporale.

2. ff. 22ᵛ–33 Incipit summa viciorum. Generaliter omne peccatum fugiendum est . . .

Forty-three chapters: a table of them precedes the text. Bloomfield, no. 368.

3. ff. 33–45 Incipiunt capitula in summam virtutum bre[uiatam] . . . (*table of 40 chapters*) . . . De fide capitulum 1. Fides generat victoriam. Iusticiam. gloriam . . .

f. 45ᵛ was left blank: see art. 6.

4. ff. 46–82 De s. andrea. Sanctus andreas post ascensionem domini apud siciliam predicauit . . .

Notes on feasts of the sanctorale, including on ff. 80–1, between Simon and Jude and Alexis, a 'Vita Pilati' beginning 'Tyrus rex moguncie dum iuxta mogun in opido vortheim in venacione'. f. 82ᵛ was left blank: see art. 6.

5. ff. 83ᵛ–114 Descendens ihesus de monte stetit etc. In presenti uita est quasi vigilia omnium sanctorum . . .

Brief sermons of temporale and sanctorale, beginning at All Saints and including six for St. Francis, ff. 100–1, 106ᵛ–108. The common of saints begins on f. 108. ff. 114ᵛ–115ᵛ, left blank, are partly filled with later notes.

6 (added). ff. 45ᵛ, 82ᵛ–83 Notes of the twenty-eight penitential canons which a priest should know and of cases in which 'tenetur homo confessionem iterare'.

7. Part of a leaf of a gradual is pasted inside the cover at each end.

Fourteenth–sixteenth Sundays after Trinity, the music not filled in. A handsome script, s. xiiⁱ.

ff. i+114+i, foliated 1–116. f. 1 is a medieval parchment flyleaf. 155 × 108 mm. Written space 120 × 83 mm. 31 long lines. Collation of ff. 2–115: 1¹² 2–5¹⁰ 6–7¹² 8¹⁰ 9–10¹⁴. Written in fairly small textura: black ink. 2-line red initials. Contemporary binding of wooden boards covered with stamped pigskin: lozenges, a stamp (three patterns) in each. Secundo folio *tatum.*

Written in Germany. From the Benedictine abbey of St. Godehard, Hildesheim: 'Liber monasterii sancti godehardi prope muros hilden[. . .] ordinis sancti Benedicti', f. 1, erased, but legible by ultraviolet light. '43' on the spine, s. xv (?). 'Thomas Chapman Esqʳᵉ July 26: 1843', f. 1. No. 19 in catalogue 48, Oct. 1925, of P. J. and A. E. Dobell, 8 Bruton St., London. Bought from Dobell, 14 May 1926.

1. 218. *Theologica*   s. xv²

1. ff. 2–18ᵛ (*begins imperfectly*) amabilis iuuenis istius quem . . . (f. 5) tam dilectam tibi liberet a morte eterna amen. Ecce aduocatus meus . . . (f. 7) sanguine voluisti qui . . . amen. Explicit prologus. Incipit tractatus beati bernardi abbatis de planctu virginis. Quis capiti meo aquam dabit . . . O vos sponse iherusalem filie dilecte dei vna mecum lacrimas fundite . . . (f. 17ᵛ) in secula seculorum. Sepulto domino a iudeis . . . et recommendo totaliter animam meam (*ends imperfectly*).

The prologue here is also in B.L., Royal 8 C. vii, art. 19, and is printed as far as *a morte eterna* in *PL* clxxxiv. 769. The 'tractatus', often ascribed as here to St. Bernard, is printed in *PL* clxxxii. 1133–42 from a copy which was incomplete at the beginning and which ended at *secula seculorum* (f. 17ᵛ).

2. ff. 19–42ᵛ (*begins imperfectly*) et ipsi sunt templum eius . . . Inimicus homo (*ends imperfectly*).

PL clxxxiv. 485/32–507/7, the meditations beginning *Multi multa sciunt*, often ascribed to St. Bernard. Single leaves are missing at beginning and end and after ff. 20, 27, and 38.

3. ff. 43–64 (*begins imperfectly*) species pulcras et illecebrosas inuenis . . . Hoc opto hoc desidero hoc totis viribus concupisco. Explicit.

A dialogue between Anima and Homo. Anima's words beginning 'Sicut amare non possum . . .' is the first complete piece here. A leaf is missing after f. 59.

4. ff. 64–104 Incipit augustinus de vera innocencia . . . (*numbered table of chapters, lacking 164–259 and ending imperfectly at 359*) . . . (f. 67, *begins imperfectly*) quia siue paruuli siue magni . . . si te ipsum prospexeris. Explicit deo gracias.

Prosper, Sententiae ex Augustino, *PL* li. 428/23–496, in 378 numbered sections. A leaf is missing after f. 65 and a leaf after f. 66. f. 104ᵛ, left blank, and the flyleaves, 105–8, contain scribbles and drawings of ships, birds, and beasts, s. xvi. The illuminator pencilled a costing note at the foot of f. 104ᵛ, 'De aureis litteris iiii prec' viii d'. De magnis litteris xxi prec' i d' '. Sixteen blue letters now remain and there was, no doubt, a gold letter on each of the leaves now missing before ff. 2, 19, 43, and 67.

ff. i+103+vi, foliated 1–110. ff. 105–8 are medieval end-leaves. 145 × 105 mm. Written space 102 × 70 mm. 25–8 long lines. Collation of ff. 2–104: 1–14⁸, lacking 1¹, 3³ after f. 18, 3⁶ after f. 20, 4⁶ after f. 27, 6² after f. 38, 6⁷ after f. 42, 9¹ before f. 60, 9⁸ after f. 65, 10² after f. 66. Quires numbered 1–14 and from quire 2 lettered in red a–n. Written in a secretary hand. Initials: (i) on missing leaves, see above; (ii) f. 7, 3-line, blue with red ornament; (iii) as (ii), but 2-line. The pigskin binding of s. xvi, with panels representing (1) 'Fides' and 'Spes' and (2) 'Charitas' and 'Paciencia', is Germanic and was not originally on this manuscript. Secundo folio *amabilis* (f. 2).

Written in England. 'Matthew Bradford his Booke 1701', f. 2. The nineteenth century book-plate of the Bibliotheca Elseghemensis may belong with the binding and not with the book on which it now is. Sale at Sotheby's, 30 July 1925, lot 294. No. 3 in P. J. and A. E. Dobell's catalogue 48 (8 Bruton St., London, Oct. 1925): the relevant slip is pasted to f. 1. Bought from Dobell, 14 May 1926.

1. 362 (Havod 1). Geoffrey of Monmouth and Dares Phrygius (in Welsh). s. xiv. *Report*, p. 301.

1. 363 (Havod 2). Geoffrey of Monmouth and Bonhed Seynt (in Welsh). s. xv. *Report*, p. 301.

In a modern binding by Eyre & Spottiswoode, preserving inside the covers the old leather of a mid sixteenth-century English binding with an ornament as centrepiece and corner-pieces and the letters *R* and *O* on each side of the centrepiece. A contemporary note on f. 213 says that this is a Cambridge binding of Aug. 1551. The old binding leaves have also been preserved: three complete leaves (ff. 1, 213, 214) and two fragments (ff. iv, 215) of a manuscript of logic (?), written in an informal English secretary hand, s. xv.

'Richardus O[. . . .] me sibi vendicat/Master', f. 1ᵛ, in the hand which wrote the note about the binding: cf. the initials on the covers. He annotated the text in Welsh and Latin, the latter in humanistic script.

1. 366. *Horae*   s. xiv/xv

1. ff. 1–10ᵛ Calendar in red and black, lacking January and June.

David, Chad, 'Wywaloi', 'Thome Herford' and Winefred are among additions, 1–3 Mar., 2 Oct., 3 Nov. 'Thome martyris' is crossed out at 29 Dec., but not 'Translacio thome' at 7 July.

2. ff. 12–59ᵛ, 120–128ᵛ, 60–96ᵛ Incipiunt hore beate marie uirginis secundum usum sarum.

Memoriae after lauds are of Holy Spirit, Holy Trinity, Holy Cross, SS. Michael, John Baptist, Peter and Paul, Andrew, Stephen, Laurence, Thomas of Canterbury (lightly cancelled), Nicholas, Mary Magdalene, Katherine, Margaret, All Saints, and for peace. Hours of the Cross are worked in.

3. ff. 97–119ᵛ, 129–136ᵛ Incipiunt septem psalmi . . . (f. 115ᵛ) Quindecim psalmi . . . (cues only of the first twelve), and (f. 129) litany.

4. Blank spaces on ff. 59ʳᵛ, 120, 60ᵛ, 61, 67ᵛ, 68, contain (*a*) six prayers in English, and (*b*, f. 68) seven lines each beginning 'wo worth'.

(*a*). A prayer for use at mass on each weekday, Monday–Saturday. The Monday prayer begins 'I beseche the swete ihesu that þᵘ vouchesaf of þⁱ souereyn goodnes'. (*b*) is hard to read. The fourth line is 'wo worth þᵗ iugement þᵗ hath non equite' and the seventh 'wo worth þᵗ Ryghte þᵗ may no fauour haue'.

ff. i+136+ii. 85×65 mm. Written space 48×35 mm. 11 long lines. Collation: 1⁶ wants 1 and 6, 2⁶ 3–17⁸ (ff. 12–136), together with six out of probably nine singleton leaves with pictures in front of quires 3 and 9, after 10¹, before 10⁸, after 12¹, and after 12⁶: quire 9 is misplaced after quire 16 (ff. 120–8). Full-page pictures with continuous borders precede matins, prime, terce, sext, vespers, and compline of art. 2 and form a passion series (ff. 11ᵛ, 120ᵛ, 61ᵛ, 68ᵛ, 79ᵛ, 85ᵛ: the rectos were blank: cf. art. 4). Pictures for lauds and none of art. 2 and before art. 3 are no doubt missing. Initials: (i) ff. 12, 29, 121, 62, 69, 74, 80, 86, 97, beginning each hour of art. 2 and art. 3, red or blue patterned in white on decorated gold grounds and with continuous borders; (ii) 2-line, gold on coloured grounds; (iii) 1-line, alternately gold with slate-grey ornament and blue with red ornament. Binding and leather case of s. xviii. Secundo folio (f. 13) *preoccupamus*.

Written in England. 'Thomas Biron was Born in the yeare of our lord God' is scribbled on f. 54ᵛ, s. xvii. Bought in 1923 from J. and J. Leighton.

1. 367. *Horae*   s. xv ex.

1. ff. 1–6ᵛ Calendar in blue and black.

Feasts in blue include two bishops of Angers, Maurilius, and Renatus, 13 Sept. and 12 Nov.

2. ff. 7–9ᵛ Sequentiae of the Gospels.

3. ff. 10–12 Oratio deuota. Obsecro te . . . For male use.

4. ff. 12–13 Alia oratio. O intemerata . . . orbis terrarum. Inclina . . .

5. ff. 13ᵛ–19ᵛ Adiutorium nostrum in nomine domini. Ad dominum cum tribularer . . . Oratio. Absolue domine animas . . .

Quindecim psalmi (Pss. 119–33) and final prayer. f. 20ʳᵛ blank.

6. ff. 21–49ᵛ Hours of B.V.M.

Antiphon and capitulum at prime are Assumpta est and Ab inicio and at none Pulcra es and Sicut cynamomum. The first leaf of each hour is missing and only vespers and compline end completely.

7. f. 50ʳᵛ Hours of the Holy Cross.

8. ff. 51–52ᵛ Hours of the Holy Spirit. f. 53ʳᵛ blank.

9. ff. 54–62ᵛ Penitential psalms, beginning imperfectly, and (f. 59) litany.

Thirteen martyrs: . . . (10) Priuate . . . (13) Eadmunde.

10. ff. 63–87ᵛ Office of the dead, beginning imperfectly. ff. 88–89ᵛ blank.

11. ff. 90–7 Hec quidem collecte illius preclarissime sancte brigide sicut quas ante istam crucem deuote docebat . . . Et tu lector dulcissime perlege deuote quia stupenda leges. O domine ihesu criste eterna dulcedo te amancium . . .

The fifteen Oes of St. Bridget and (f. 95ᵛ) Responsio saluatoris. Quicumque per circulum vnius anni suprascriptas oraciones . . . de profundo pelagi. Amen.

12. Prayers: (*a*) ff. 97–100 Domine deus omnipotens qui trinus es et unus . . . ; (*b*) ff. 100–1 Domine ihesu criste fili redemptor mundi defende me . . . perseuerare facias. quia tu es deus benedictus in secula seculorum. Amen. f. 101ᵛ blank.

13. ff. 102–104ᵛ Sensuiuent cinq belles oraisons que mons' sainct iehan leuange-liste fist en lonneur de la vierge marie. Mediatrix omnium . . . Auxiliatrix omnium . . . Reparatrix debilium . . . Illuminatrix peccatorum . . . Alleuiatrix peccatorum . . .

The word Maria is made up from the initial letters of the five prayers.

14. ff. 104ᵛ–109ᵛ Oraison tresdeuote a nostre dame . . . Missus est gabriel angelus ad mariam . . .

The long heading relates that Our Lady showed this prayer to Arnoul, 'chanoine regulier', in a vision and told him it should be said every Saturday. ff. 110–111ᵛ blank.

ff. ii + 111 + ii. Thin parchment, except ff. 90–7. 128 × 87 mm. Written space 76 × 46 mm. 27 long lines. Collation doubtful after f. 58: before this point it is 1⁶ 2⁸ 3⁶ 4⁸ wants 1 before f. 21 5⁸ wants 3 after f. 29 6 five (ff. 35–9) 7⁸ wants 3 after f. 41 8⁴ wants 2 after f. 47 9⁴ (ff. 50–3) 10⁶ wants 1 before f. 54. Written in good *lettre bâtarde*. The only surviving pictures are the small ones, 25 × 20 mm, four in art. 2 and one before art. 3 (B.V.M. with Child and angel). The larger pictures have been removed with the leaves on which they came. The surviving initials are: (i) 2-line, blue, patterned in white, on decorated gold grounds; (ii) 1-line, gold on dark-red grounds. Headings usually in blue. Line fillers in gold and red: the 'broken branch' filler occurs about once on every page. Capital letters in the ink of the text are filled with pale yellow. French red morocco binding, s. xix.

Written in France. 'Katharine Clarendon' on the pastedown, s. xix. Bought in 1923 from J. and J. Leighton.

1. 368. *Horae* s. xv med.

1. ff. 1–12ᵛ Full calendar in French in red and black.

Geneviève and Yves in red.

2. ff. 13–20ᵛ Sequentiae of the Gospels.

3. ff. 21–85ᵛ Hours of B.V.M. of the use of (Paris), the first leaf missing.

4. ff. 86–93 Hours of Holy Cross.

5. ff. 93ᵛ–99ᵛ Hours of Holy Spirit.

6. ff. 100–121ᵛ Penitential psalms and (f. 116ᵛ) litany.

Nine confessors: . . . (8, 9) germane benedicte. ff. 122–123ᵛ blank.

7. ff. 132–139ᵛ, 124–131ᵛ, 140–159ᵛ Office of the dead.

ff. ii + 159 + ii. ff. i, ii, 160 are medieval parchment end-leaves. 168 × 120 mm. Written space 90 × 60 mm. 12 or 13 long lines (14 on ff. 86–93). Collation: 1¹² 2⁸ 3⁸ wants 1 before f. 21 4–9⁸ 10¹⁰ 11⁸ 12⁶ 13–17⁸ 18⁴ 19–20⁸. Quire 16 is misbound after quire 17 as ff. 132–9. Fifteen lively pictures, 9-line or 10-line, with continuous floral borders and much gold ivy leaf, seven (out of eight) in art. 3, four in art. 2, and one before each of arts. 4–7. Initials: (i) 3-line, pink or blue, patterned in white, on decorated gold grounds; (ii, iii) 2-line, gold on coloured grounds. Line fillers of red, blue, and gold. Capital letters in the ink of the text filled with pale yellow. Binding of s. xix. Secundo folio (f. 14) *crederent*.

Written in France. 'M. Marsh' inside the cover, s. xix. Apparently the book of hours in manuscript bought from Henry Sotheran & Co. in 1923.

I. 369. *Horae*   s. xv²

1. ff. 1–7ᵛ Sequentiae of the Gospels.

The prayer 'Protector in te sperantium . . .' follows the extract from St. John.

2. ff. 7ᵛ–11 Oraison de nostre dame. Obsecro te . . . For male use.

3. ff. 11–15 Oraison deuote de nostre dame. O intemerata . . . orbis terrarum. De te enim . . . For male use.

4. ff. 15ᵛ–66ᵛ Hours of B.V.M. of the use of (Rouen).

The leaves with pictures in front of lauds and compline and one other leaf are missing. Memoriae after lauds of Holy Spirit, SS. Michael, John Baptist, Peter and Paul, Stephen, Laurence, Nicholas, Mary Magdalene, Katherine, Margaret, Barbara, Apollonia, and 'De la paix' (ff. 35ᵛ–42).

5. ff. 67–86ᵛ Penitential psalms and (f. 78) litany.

Martial last of apostles. Twenty-four confessors: . . . (7–11) mellone gildarde medarde romane audoene . . . Fourteen virgins: . . . (8–11) austreberta barbara anna honorina . . .

6. ff. 87–90ᵛ Hours of the Cross.

7. ff. 91–4 Hours of the Holy Spirit.

8. ff. 94ᵛ–123 Office of the dead.

9. ff. 123ᵛ–128ᵛ Douce dame de misericorde . . .

The Fifteen Joys, Sonet, no. 458.

10. ff. 129–31 The Seven Requests, in French, the first leaf missing.

Sonet, no. 504.

11. f. 131ʳᵛ Saincte vray croyx adoree . . .

Sonet, no. 1876.

ff. 131. 153 × 108 mm. Written space 93 × 58 mm. 17 long lines. Collation: 1–3⁸ 4⁸ wants 3 after f. 26 and 6 after f. 28 5–8⁸ 9 four (ff. 63–6) 10–16⁸ 17⁸ wants 7 after f. 128 18 two. Sixteen pictures, 11-line to 14-line, six (formerly eight) in art. 2, four in art. 1 and one before each of arts. 2 (pietà), 5–7, 8 (Death meets two richly dressed young men), 9 (pietà). Initials: (i, ii) 3-line and 2-line, mainly white on decorated grounds of gold paint; (iii) 1-line, gold paint on blue or dark-red grounds. Full-framed floral borders on grounds of gold paint on picture pages and a compartmented border the height of the written space in the outer margin of all other pages. Red or blue line fillers patterned in gold paint. Capital letters in the ink of the text touched with pale yellow. Binding of s. xix (?). Secundo folio *mundum*.

Written in northern France. Bought from G. E. Bullen in 1922.

I. 370. *Horae*   s. xv²

1. ff. 3–35ᵛ Incipiunt hore virginis gloriose.

Hours of Dominican use.

2. ff. 37–39ᵛ Incipiunt hore sancte crucis.

3. ff. 41–54 Incipiunt vii psalmi. Litany follows on f. 47ᵛ.

Eleven martyrs: . . . (10, 11) thoma petre. Seventeen confessors: . . . (9–17) dominice francisce thoma vincenti benedicte anthoni bernarde donacione ludouice.

4. ff. 55–70ᵛ Incipiunt Vigilie mortuorum secundum vsum Ordinis fratrum predicatorum.

5. ff. 70ᵛ–73 Oracio deuota de beata uirgine maria. Obsecro te . . . Et michi famule tue (*masculine forms interlined*) . . .

6. ff. 73–4 Oracio deuota de nomine ihesu. O bone ihesu. O dulcissime ihesu . . .

7. ff. 74–77ᵛ Sequentiae of the Gospels.

The order is Matthew, Mark, Luke, John, not as usual John, Luke, Matthew, Mark.

8. ff. 78–80 Gaude virgo barbara speculum honoris Temetipsam preparans . . .

Fifteen 4-line stanzas. Not in *RH*.

9. (added). Prayers in Netherlandish, s. xvi: (*a*) ff. 80ᵛ–82ᵛ O lieue here ihesu criste uw begheere ic . . .; (*b*) ff. 83–85 O myn here mij god ic gae toet vwer tefelen . . .

(*a*) is of the wounds of Christ and (*b*) for use before and after mass.

ff. ii+84+ii, foliated i, 1–87. f. 1 is a parchment flyleaf ruled like the rest of the manuscript. f. 85 was pasted to a former binding. 155 × 118 mm. Written space 93 × 65 mm. 19 long lines. Collation of ff. 2–85: 1⁸+ 1 leaf before 1 2–10⁸ 11²+ 1 leaf after 1. A full-page picture before arts. 1–4 (ff. 2ᵛ, 36ᵛ, 40ᵛ, 54ᵛ). Initials: (i) 5-line, in grisaille; (ii, iii) 4-line and 2-line, gold on coloured grounds; (iv) 1-line, gold with grey-blue ornament or blue with red ornament. Continuous framed borders of gold paint decorated with fruit and flowers on the four picture pages and on the pages with initials of type (i) opposite them: the initials look like extensions inward of the borders because the gold paint is taken round them. Borders on three sides of pages with initials of type (ii). Line fillers of blue and red in the litany only: many patterns. Capital letters in the ink of the text marked with red. Binding of s. xviii.

Written in the Netherlands. A large armorial achievement on f. 1ᵛ, s. xvi/xvii; the arms are 1 and 4 chequey argent and azure 2 and 3 a cross sable and or between 3 rampant lions crowned and spurred or and the motto 'Selon fortune lotins anno 1491'. 'a michel lotins' is on f. 1ᵛ and 'anno 1491' appears again on ff. 80, 83, 85 and 'selon fortune lotins' again on f. 85, s. xvi/xvii. English owners in s. xviii were successively Charles Lyttelton, dean of Exeter (†1768), Smart Lethieullier (†1760) by gift of Lyttelton (f. i), and Horace Walpole (†1797), whose armorial book-plate is inside the cover. No. 246 in J. and J. Leighton's *Catalogue of Manuscripts* . . ., issued in 1920: the relevant cutting is attached to f. i. Bought from Leighton in 1925.

1. 371. *Horae* (*in Netherlandish*) s. xv med.

1. ff. 5–16ᵛ Calendar in red and black.

Entries in red include 'Kermesse tongren', 'S. seruoes buscop', 'S. lambrecht buscop', 'S. matern buscop', 'S. hubrecht buscop' (9, 13 May; 17, 25 Sept.; 3 Nov.). Later entries record: at 3 Apr., the battle 'in sinte quintins heide anno xc . . . voer hasselt' (cf. J. Daris, *Histoire du diocèse . . . de Liège pendant le xvᵉ siècle*, 1887, p. 602); at 30 Aug., the murder of Ludovick van Boervon in 1482 (ibid., p. 501); at 13 Sept., the capture of Hasselt (in 1482: ibid., p. 559).

2. ff. 17–63ᵛ Prolog uan onser urouwen ghetijden. Dese ghetijden onser urouwen . . . (f. 17ᵛ) ghewoerden en can. Hier beghinnen die Mettenen . . .

Hours of B.V.M. of the use of (Utrecht), including some scholia in the text (in slightly smaller script) underlined in red and preceded by the word 'glose' in red. The prologue is Geert Groote's, edn. N. van Wijk, 1940, p. 36.

3. ff. 63ᵛ–82ᵛ Hier beghinnen die seuen psalmen uan penitencien in duytschen ghesat . . . Litanies follow on f. 73ᵛ.

4. ff. 83–103 Hier beghinnen die seuen ghetiden van der ewigher wijsheyt. ff. 103ᵛ–104ᵛ blank.

5. ff. 105–26 Hier beghinnen die vii ghetiden van den heilighen gheiste. Some glosses, as in art. 2. f. 126ᵛ blank.

6. ff. 127–158ᵛ Hier beghinnen des heylighen cruys ghetiden.

7. ff. 159–208ᵛ Hier beghint die vigilie in duytschen die gheordineert es . . . (f. 160) scriue die antiffenen. Inuitatorium. My hebben . . .

'Glose', sometimes lengthy, underlined in red. Van Wijk edn., p. 155.

ff. iv+204+iii, foliated 1–211. ff. 1–4, 209–11 are medieval parchment end-leaves, 1ʳ and 211ᵛ formerly pasted down. 145 × 100 mm. Written space 95 × 62 mm. 23 long lines. Collation: 1¹² 2–8⁸ 9¹⁰ 10–11⁸ 12⁶ 13–14⁸ 15⁶ 16–24⁸ 25¹⁰. Initials: (i) red or blue patterned in white and (art. 2) red and blue with red ornament; (ii, iii) 2-line and 1-line, red or blue. Some further decoration was attempted on ff. 17–27ᵛ: it is rough and garish. Capital letters in the ink of the text are stroked with red. Contemporary binding of wooden boards covered with brown leather bearing a rectangular border stamp, a fleur-de-lis stamp at each corner, and within the border—which is not continuous—diagonal fillets with a small round stamp at the intersections and a fleur-de-lis stamp in the lozenges: four bands: two clasps fastening on the front cover.

Written probably in the Liège region. Three ex-libris inscriptions: 'Dit boeck hoert tw katherina van floevertinghen et schoeyen et mobben', f. 5, s. xv/xvi; cf. ff. 2, 106; 'Dyt bock hooert toe suster crystyna brouwers . . . int yaer 95', f. 4, s. xvi ex.; 'Dit boeck hoert toe Anneken iaekaerts die ionghe dochter Anno 1620 den 2 noeuember', f. 3.

I. 372. *Horae*   1431

1. ff. iv–ixᵛ Calendar in red and black.

Includes, in red: Translacio s. augustini, 28 Feb.; Festum s. marie ad niues, 5 Aug.; Augustine, 29 Aug., with octave; Francis, 4 Oct.

2. ff. 1–91 Incipit officium gloriosissime uirginis Marie secundum consuetudinem romane curie . . . Explicit officium beate Marie virginis. Gratiam tuam domine mentibus nostris infunde . . .

The 'mutatum officium sancte Marie', for use in Advent begins on f. 79. ff. 78ᵛ, 91ᵛ blank.

3. ff. 92–125 Incipit officium sacratissime passionis domini nostri yhesu cristi.

The long Hours of the Cross. Hymn, 'In passione domini . . .'.

4. ff. 125ᵛ–119 Incipit officium sanctissime crucis. editum a papa iohanne xxii

in quo concessit in qualibet hora omni die quando dicitur. unum annum de . . . indulgentia uere penitentibus et confessis.

The usual short Hours of the Cross. ff. 129ᵛ–131ᵛ blank.

5. ff. 132–90 Incipit officium mortuorum.

6. ff. 190ᵛ–191 (a) Oracio pro patre et matre. Deus qui nos patrem . . . (b) Pro uno defuncto oracio. Inclina domine aurem tuam . . . f. 191ᵛ blank.

7. ff. 192–218 Incipiunt psalmi penitentiales . . . (f. 206) Incipiunt letanie . . . Explicit liber iste. Anno domini Mᵒ. ccccᵒ xxxiᵒ xiiᵒ die mensis Augusti. Deo gratias. Amen.

Nine martyrs: . . . (9) Gaii. Nine confessors: . . . (8, 9) Ludouice. Zenobi. Twelve virgins: . . . (9–12) Reparata. Margharita. Clara. Helisabeth.

8. ff. 218ᵛ–219ᵛ St. John 1: 1–14.

9. Prayers to B.V.M.: (a) ff. 220–1 Oracio pro omnibus gentibus. et pro parentibus. Sancta et inmaculata uirgo semper maria intercede pro me misera peccatrice. ancilla tua . . .; (b) f. 221ʳᵛ Oracio in necessitatibus et periculis. ualde deuota. O beata maria uirgo uirginum . . .

ff. iii+6+i+222+ii, foliated i–x, 1–87, 87*, 88–223. ff. ii, iii, x, 222 are medieval flyleaves. 115×80 mm. Written space 65×45 mm. 13 long lines. Collation of ff. iv–ix, 1–221: 1⁶ 2–8¹⁰ 9⁸ 10¹⁰ (ff. 88–91) 12–24¹⁰. Initials: (i) beginning arts. 2–5, 7, in colours on gold grounds, historiated (art. 2, B.V.M. and Child; art. 3, Christ crucified; art. 4, three crosses); (ii) 5-line, blue, pink, or green on grounds of decorated colours and gold; (iii) 2-line, red or blue with ornament of the other colour; (iv) 1-line, red or blue. Continuous borders on pages with initials of type (i). Binding of gilt red morocco, s. xviii.

Written in Italy in 1431: the date (art. 7) is in the main hand. A printed armorial bookplate, s. xviii attached to f. 1, is inscribed 'DEL MAR BELLISOMI' and bears the motto 'Tout iours prest'. Armorial book-plate of Frederick H. Sutton s. xix.

1. 373. *Horae, etc. (partly in Italian)* 1477

Hours of B.V.M. of the use of Rome and other devotions and doctrinal treatises.

1. ff. 1–48 Incipit offitium beate virginis Marie romano more.

2. ff. 48ᵛ–67 Penitential psalms and (f. 58) litany.

The litany includes Bernardine.

3. ff. 67–106 Office of the dead.

4. ff. 106ᵛ–134 Prayers: (a) f. 106 Oratio pro patre. Deus qui es uniuersorum creator . . .; (b) f. 106 Pro patre et matre. Deus qui nobis precepisti . . .; (c) f. 106ᵛ Oratio pro pluribus defunctis. Deus cui soli competit medicinam . . .; (d) f. 106ᵛ Item oratio pro pluribus defunctis. Inueniant quesumus domine anime . . .; (e) ff. 106ᵛ–111 Oratio ad confessionem peccatorum. Deus inestimabilis misericordie. deus inmense pietatis . . .; (f) ff. 111–112ᵛ Oratio pro peccatis. Deus piissime. deus clemens et misericors propitiare . . .; (g) ff. 112ᵛ–113 Domine yesu criste qui celum et terram fecisti . . .; (h) f. 113ᵛ Parce

domine quesumus parce populo tuo . . .; (*i*) f. 113^v Deus qui culpas nostras piis
uerberibus . . .; (*j*) ff. 113^v–114 Presta quesumus. omnipotens deus ut ad te
toto corde clamantes . . .; (*k*) f. 114^{rv} Deus qui mirabiliter cuncta condidisti
. . .; (*l*) f. 115 Domine deus omnipotens qui non dormitas . . .; (*m*) ff. 115–116^v
Domine yhesu criste filii (*sic*) dei uiui saluator mundi. Exaudi me . . .; (*n*) ff.
116^v–118 Oratio sancti ysidori. Succurre michi deus meus. cur spreuisti me
. . .; (*o*) ff. 118–20 Domine deus omnipotens sempiterne deus. Rex regum . . .
Qui unigenitum filium . . .; (*p*) ff. 120–3 Oratio sancti gregorii pape. Domine
exaudi orationem meam. quia iam cognosco . . .; (*q*) f. 123^{rv} Liberator clementissime rex et piisime liberator . . .; (*r*) ff. 123^v–128 Domine yesu criste uita
morientium.salus . . .; (*s*) ff. 128–9 Oratio pro tribulatione. Salua me domine
Rex eterne glorie qui potes saluare. et da michi . . .; (*t*) f. 129^{rv} Oratio ad crucem
adorandam. Domine yhesu criste fili dei uiui gloriosissime conditor mundi.
qui cum sis splendor . . .; (*u*) ff. 129^v–130^v Alia oratio ad crucem. Domine
yhesu criste adoro te in cruce ascendentem. deprecor te . . .; (*v*) ff. 130^v–131
Alia oratio ad crucem. Obsecro te yhesu filii dei uiui per crucem tuam. ut
dimittas . . .; (*w*) f. 131 Oratio pro fidelibus uiuis. Pretende domine fidelibus
tuis . . .; (*x*) ff. 131–3 Oratio ad virginem gloriosam. O inthemerata . . . orbis
terrarum. Inclina . . .; (*y*) f. 133 Deus uenie largitor. et humane salutis amator
. . .; (*z*) f. 133^v Oratio. Deus qui nos patrem et matrem . . .; (*aa*) f. 133^v
Presta quesumus omnipotens deus ut animas . . .; (*ab*) f. 134 Presta quesumus
animabus famulorum . . .; (*ac*) f. 134 Inueniant quesumus domine anime
fidelium . . . For male use.

5. ff. 134^v–140 Incipit offitium sancte crucis quod dominus Iohannes papa
xxii^{us} ordinauit qualibet hora deuote dicenti dies xl^a indulgentie per singulos dies
. . . Patris sapientia . . .

6. ff. 140^v–144^v Incipit offitium spiritus sancti. . . . Nobis sancti spiritus . . .

7. ff. 145–149^v Incipit offitium trinitatis.

The hymn is 'Quicumque uult animam firmiter saluare . . .', *RH*, no. 16566.

8. ff. 150–155^v Incipit offitium sacratissimi corporis domini nostri yhesu cristi
. . . Corporis misterium pange gloriosum . . .

Hours of Corpus Christi. *RH*, no. 3936.

9. ff. 155^v–60^v Incipit offitium beate uirginis Marie et angelorum . . . Sancta dei
genitris (*sic*) mater pietatis . . .

Hours of All Saints. The hymns are *RH*, no. 33290, *AH* xxx. 143.

10. ff. 161–7 St. Matthew, chapters 1, 2, 4: 1–11, 5: 1–12.

11. Offices of (*a*) ff. 167–173^v, Corpus Christi and (*b*) ff. 174–183^v, St. John
Baptist.

12. ff. 183^v–208^v Eighteen lections from the New Testament.

13. ff. 209–230^v Tria sunt hominum necessaria ad salutem silicet sciencia
credendorum . . . in prelio temptacionum subcumbere.

On the ten commandments, the twelve articles of faith and the Lord's Prayer.

14. ff. 230ᵛ–233 Incipit compendium de doctrina cristiana. Quilibet cristianus debet scire pater noster . . .

15. ff. 233–6 A calendar of sixty-six feasts, January–December.

'Theresia virgo' added at 15 Oct.

16. ff. 236ᵛ–244ᵛ Missa beate virginis Marie.

17. ff. 244ᵛ–245ᵛ Initium sancti euangelii secundum Iohannem. In principio . . . veritatis. Deo gracias amen. Per euangelica dicta delleantur nostra delicta amen.

John 1: 1–14.

18. ff. 246–248ᵛ The Athanasian Creed.

19. ff. 248ᵛ–249ᵛ Laus angelica. Te deum . . .

20. ff. 250–265ᵛ Quisti sono li septe psalmi penitentiali in vulgare. Considerando dauit profeta quanto e lo furore . . .

21. ff. 266–8 La zobia santa in anze che tu mangi . . .

Meditations on the Passion.

22. ff. 268ᵛ–289ᵛ Ars moriendi. Quamuis secundum philosophum tertio ethicorum . . . et sic anime morientium sepe miserabiliter periclitantur.

The QS version of Ars Moriendi: cf. M. C. O'Connor, *The Art of Dying Well*, 1942, p. 44 and for one of many manuscripts, University College, Oxford, MS. 53, ff. 212ᵛ–218ᵛ.

23. ff. 289ᵛ–290ᵛ Dies ire dies illa . . . Cf. art. 35 *d.*

24. ff. 291–6 Office of St. Katherine.

The hymn is Katerina mirabilis atque deo amabilis . . ., *RH*, no. 2687.

25. Prayers: (*a*) f. 296ʳᵛ Domine yesu criste qui hanc sacratissimam carnem . . ., followed by a notice in Italian of indulgence by Pope Boniface VI of 2,000 years; (*b*) ff. 296ᵛ–297 Omnipotens sempiterne deus qui uiuorum dominaris . . .; (*c*) f. 297ʳᵛ Domine deus pater omnipotens mitte in terram pacem . . .; (*d*) f. 298 Deus qui benedixisti uestigia apostolorum tuorum petri et pauli atque andree . . .

26. f. 298 In passione domini que datur salus homini . . .

RH, no. 8722.

27. ff. 298ᵛ–299 Augustinus. Fratres carissimi semper mementote in omnibus operibus nostris . . .

28. f. 299ʳᵛ O virgo virginum uirginitatis speculum . . .

29. ff. 299ᵛ–300 Lections from Philippians.

30. ff. 301–305ᵛ Oratio valde bona et perfecta ad quemcumque si quis eam dixerit deuotissime. Domine yesu criste qui in hunc mondum venisti propter nos peccatores redimere . . .

31. f. 306 Aue regina celorum mater regis angelorum O maria . . .

RH, no. 2072.

32. ff. 306ᵛ–312 The ten commandments, the five 'sentimenti del corpo', the seven mortal sins, the seven works of spiritual and corporal mercy, the seven sacraments, the three theological and four cardinal virtues, and the twelve articles of the faith (Apostles' Creed) in Italian.

33. ff. 312ᵛ–313ᵛ Omnipotens sempiterne deus miserere famulo tuo . . .

Prayers of the litany.

34. ff. 313ᵛ–320ᵛ Pss. 119–23 and prayer 'Absolue quesumus domine . . .', Pss. 124–8 and prayer 'Deus cui proprium est . . .', and Pss. 129–133 and prayer 'Pretende domine famulis . . .'.

35. (*a*) ff. 320ᵛ–321 Victime paschali laudes immolant cristiani. Agnus . . . (*b*) f. 321ʳᵛ Veni sancte spiritus et emite celitus. (*c*) f. 322 Virgo mater ecclesie eterna porta . . . (*d*) ff. 322–3. As art. 23.

(*a*–*d*). *RH*, nos. 21505, 21242, 21818, 4626.

36. ff. 323ᵛ–325 Salutations to B.V.M. in Italian, beginning 'Aue dio te salua dona senza guay de vergonia'.

37. ff. 325ᵛ–326ᵛ Cur mundus militat sub vana gloria . . .

Ten 4-line stanzas. Walther, no. 3934.

38. ff. 326ᵛ–330 O pater noster summo creatore De tuto quanto . . . A lo honore de cristo il pater nostro e finito.

Thirteen 8-line stanzas.

39. ff. 330ᵛ–334ᵛ Dulcissime domine yesu criste deus verus qui de sinu patris . . . et composuit eam beatus Augustinus.

Cf. *Lyell Cat.*, p. 380.

40. f. 335 A memoria of the Resurrection.

41. ff. 335ᵛ–337ᵛ Queste oratione se deuo dire dauante la effigie de cristo benedeto de la pieta . . .

The first five of the Seven Oes of St. Gregory in Italian, followed by all seven oes in Latin and a notice in Italian conveying indulgence of 14,000 years.

42. ff. 337ᵛ–338ᵛ Lection from 1 Corinthians 11: 23–9.

43. ff. 338ᵛ–339ᵛ Confessio Misse more carmelitorum.

44. ff. 340–1 Sempre sia regratiata la uergene maria luce de la stela . . .

45. ff. 341–2 Laus virginis alme. Maria mater lucis Que ad lumen cecos ducis . . . *RH*, no. 13201.

46. f. 342ʳᵛ El pater nostro de sancto Iuliano. El beato meser sancto Iuliano Venina de insul monte caluario . . . Ne da falsi testimonii. Amen.

Seventeen lines of verse.

47. ff. 343–346ᵛ Litany of B.V.M.

48 (added by the main hand). (*a*) ff. 347–50 A table of contents of arts. 1–47. (*b*) f. 352ᵛ Sancte Raynalde ora pro me ut omnes a terrenis cogitationes . . . (*c*) f. 353ʳᵛ Ogni di vedre la sancta messa . . .

(*c*). Go to mass, say devotions in praise of B.V.M., give alms, and say prayers for the dead daily.

ff. ii+353+ii. Paper. Medieval foliation. 138×98 mm. Written space *c.* 85×60 mm. 14–15 long lines. Collation: 1–13¹⁶ (ff. 1–208) 14–16¹² (ff. 209–44) 17–20¹⁴ (ff. 245–300). 21¹⁰ 22²⁰ 23¹⁶ (ff. 331–46) 24⁸ wants 8, probably blank. Written in small textura. A half-page picture of the Annunciation on f. 1. A few red initials. Handsome binding, s. xix ex., by Riviere.

Written by a named scribe at Milan in 1477: 'Ore roget cristum. librum qui viderit istum. Pro me scriptore. cum corde precetur et ore. Scriptor autem istius operis fuit Iohannes de schazexiis tqd (?) Moli (*sic*). qui scripsit in anno natiuitatis domini Mccccº lxxvii. et qui est notarius publicus *mediolani* et etiam notarius Mercatorum *mediolani* p[. .]ps carp̄ [. . . .]', f. 352ᵛ, in the main hand. Armorial book-plate of Willett Lawrence Adye. Bought in 1923 from Henry Sotheran & Co.

1. 375 ff. 149–53. '*La vie saint iohan baptiste*' (*in French*). s. xv med.

La vie saint iohan baptiste. Aue tres glorieux baptiste. De qui le saint euuange-liste . . . et a la fin saluation Amen.

Thirty-three 4-line stanzas. Not in Sonet.

ff. 5. 152×96 mm. Written space 88×60 mm. 16 long lines. ff. 151–2 are the central bifolium of a quire. A 12-line picture of St. John, f. 149: continuous framed floral border. Initials: (i) f. 149, 4-line, blue patterned in white on decorated gold ground; (ii) of each stanza after the first, 1-line, gold on red and blue grounds. The capital letter beginning each line of verse is filled with pale yellow.

Written in France. Probably removed from a book of hours. Now bound with a book of hours written in 1628, bought from L. Chaundy, 59 Davies St., London, in 1921.

1. 376. *Offitium mortuorum*   s. xv med.

Incipit offitium in agenda mortuorum. Ad vesperas. A'. Placebo . . .

For female use, as appears from the prayer 'Quesumus domine pro tua pietate miserere anime famule tue sororis nostre . . .' (f. 64).

ff. ii+64+iii. ff. ii, 65–6 are medieval end-leaves. 130×92 mm. Written space 62× 45 mm. 12 long lines. Collation: 1–6¹⁰ 7⁴. Initials: (i) f. 1, 7-line, red on a decorated gold ground: (ii, iii) 2-line and 1-line, gold with blue ornament or blue with gold ornament. f. 1 has a continuous border, in part damaged and in the outer margin renewed in a differ-ent style: a death's head in the inner margin and Christ blessing within a roundel sup-ported by angels at the foot. Binding of s. xix.

Written in Italy. The relevant slip from a sale catalogue, s. xix/xx, is attached to f. i.

1. 377. *Psalterium, etc.*   s. XII med.–XIV

A twelfth-century psalter, defective by s. xiv, when thirty-seven leaves were
supplied and now again defective through the loss of all but two of the leaves of
the first two quires. Many leaves are misbound.

1. ff. 75–76ᵛ, 3–74ᵛ, 83–109 Psalms, beginning imperfectly 'Conserua me
domine quoniam . . .' (Ps. 15. 1).

f. 75ᵛ ends 'tuę. custodi me' (Ps. 16. 8). f. 76 begins 'Quoniam domini est' (Ps. 21. 28). The
leaves supplied in s. xiv are 3–10, 43, 49–51, 58–74, 83–90. The ends of Pss. 51, 88, and
105 were obliterated when pictures were added before Pss. 52, 89, and 106: see below.

2. ff. 109–144ᵛ, 77ʳᵛ, 79–80ᵛ, 1–2ᵛ, 81–82ᵛ The six ferial canticles, followed by
Te deum, Benedicite, Magnificat, Benedictus, Nunc dimittis, Gloria in excelsis,
Credo in deum patrem, and Quicumque vult.

The Te deum is headed 'Ymnum sancti niceti episcopi dominicis diebus': cf. the Florentine psalter cited by P. Cagin, *Te Deum*, 1906, p. 176, and *Clavis*, no. 650. ff. 1, 2 were
supplied in s. xv: they contain all from 'in remissione' in Benedictus (Luke 1: 77) to 'deus
spiritus sanctus' in Quicumque vult.

3. ff. 82ʳᵛ, 78ʳᵛ Incipiunt letanię.

Fifty-seven martyrs: . . . (57) miniate cum sociis tuis. Nineteen confessors: . . . (9–19) sire
cerbone (*in red, added*), donate fridiane prosper zene felix nicholae iuste clemens octabiane.
Nineteen virgins, nos. 8, 9, 11–13, 18, 19 erased: . . . (16, 17) reparata nastasia.

ff. 114. 158 × 106 mm. Written space *c.* 115 × 70 mm. 22 or 23 long lines. The twelfth-
century leaves are ruled with a hard point. Collation: 1 two (ff. 75–6) 2–10⁸ (ff. 3–74)
11–14⁸ (ff. 83–114) 15⁸ (ff. 77, 79, 80, 1, 2, 81, 82, 78). Quires 3–6 are numbered IIII–VII.
All quires 2, 9–11, leaves 1, 7, and 8 of quire 7 and leaves 1 and 8 of quire 8 were supplied
in s. xiv. Leaves 4 and 5 of quire 15 were supplied in s. xv. The remaining twelfth-century
initials are red, '2-line' and '1-line', but set outside the written space. The 6-line initials
of Pss. 38, 52, 68, and 80 were tampered with later, probably in s. xvi, at the time that
13-line pictures of the Flagellation, Christ bearing His Cross, and the Annunciation were
set in front of Pss. 52, 89, and 106 (ff. 25, 54ᵛ, 69), borders were added on ten pages, and
the blank 5-line space for the initial of Ps. 143 was filled (f. 105). Initials on the leaves added
in s. xiv are (i) 2-line, red with red ornament and (ii) red. Binding of s. xviii.

Written in Italy and probably Tuscany, to judge from art. 3: Cerbonius was bishop of
Piombino. Bought in 1922 from G. E. Bullen.

1. 378. *Breviarium*   s. XV²

1. ff. 1–6ᵛ Kalendar in red and black.

Feasts in red are usually graded. They include Antony, Clare, and Louis (13 June, 12,
19 Aug.), the 'Impressio sacrorum stigmatum' (17 Sept.), and Francis, duplex maius
(4 Oct.).

2. ff. 7–187 Temporale from Advent, the first leaf missing.

ff. 18–20ᵛ, after the ferial office for the week after the third Sunday in Advent: Tabula de
antiphonis que ponuntur ante natiuitatem domini fiant sicut subscriptis tabulis continentur. In anno illo . . . orietur (cf. *SMRL* i. 246 and ii. 401–8). ff. 184–7: Aduentus domini
celebratur . . . antiphone maiores. scilicet O sapientia (*SMRL* ii. 114–21). f. 187ᵛ blank.

3. ff. 188–268 Liturgical psalter.

4. ff. 268–82 Incipit ymnarius.

The proper of saints begins on f. 274. Its twenty-eight hymns, cues apart, include three for Antony of Padua (*SMRL* ii. 143), three for the Transfiguration, Gaude mater pietatis, Exultet laudibus sacrata, Novum sydus (*RH*, nos. 6876, 5872, 12374: not in *SMRL*), three for Clare, Concinnat plebs fidelium, Generat uirgo filias, O clara luce clarior (*RH*, nos. 3718, 7200, 12809: not in *SMRL*), and four for Francis (*SMRL* ii. 166).

5. ff. 282^{v}–285^{v} Office of Holy Trinity.

6. ff. 286–471 Incipiu(n)t festiuitates sanctorum per anni circulum secundum ecclesiam . . . Explicit proprium sanctorum.

From Saturninus to Katherine and (f. 468) In anniuersario dedicationis ecclesie.

7. ff. 471–494^{v} Incipit commune sanctorum.

8. ff. 494^{v}–501 Incipit ordo officii beate marie virginis. ff. 501^{v}–503^{v} blank.

ff. i+503+i. 142×105 mm. Written space 92×65 mm. 2 cols. 28–30 lines. Collation: 1^{6} 2^{10} wants 1 before f. 7 $3–19^{10}$ 20^{2} (ff. 186–7) $21–29^{10}$ 30^{10} wants 9, 10, probably blank after f. 285, $31–43^{10}$ 44^{10} wants 8, 9, perhaps blank after f. 422 $45–52^{10}$. Initials: (i) at Christmas, Epiphany, Easter, Ascension, Corpus Christi (ff. 29, 47, 117^{v}, 135^{v}, 149^{v}) and beginning art. 6, in colours edged with gold on gold and coloured grounds, historiated: a pale-yellow lining bounds the historiation; (ii) ff. 43, 65, 98, 188^{v}, 312 (Chair of Peter), 418^{v} (In festo beati patris nostri Augustini), as (i), but the space within the yellow lining is blue patterned in white; (iii) 2-line, blue with red ornament or red with violet ornament; (iv) 1-line, blue or red. A continuous framed floral border on f. 188^{v}: David (?) in a roundel in the lower margin. Capital letters in the ink of the text are filled with pale yellow. Binding of wooden boards half covered with leather, s. xx. Secundo folio (f. 7) *unum*.

Written in Italy. Book-plate of Vernon, s. xix: sale at Sotheby's, 10 June 1918, lot 101. Catalogue 2 of P. J. and A. E. Dobell, Apr. 1921, item 22. Bought from Messrs. Dobell in 1925.

1. 379. *Breviarium* s. XIV/XV

Disordered fragments of the temporale of a breviary. ff. 14–25, 2–13, 26–8, 46–51, 29–35, 42–3, 1, 36–40, 52–61, 45 contain continuous text from Friday in Quinquagesima to the fourth Sunday after Pentecost, except for a gap of one leaf after f. 35. The seventh to tenth and fifteenth to eighteenth Sundays after Pentecost are on ff. 62 and 41 and the twenty-fourth Sunday after Pentecost and six lections for August from Proverbs 1 on f. 44.

ff. ii+62+ii. 150×106 mm. Written space *c.* 98×70 mm. 2 cols. 34 lines. Collation: $1–3^{12}$ (ff. 14–25, 2–13, 26–8, 46–51, 29–31) 4^{12} wants 5 after f. 35 (ff. 32–5, 42–3, 1, 36–9) 5^{12} (ff. 40, 52–61, 45) 6 three (ff. 62, 41, 44: ff. 41, 44 are a bifolium). 2-line initials, alternately red and blue. A picture over erasure of the original text on f. 1 and a tryptich of B.V.M. and Child, flanked by saints on the facing page (ii^{v}) are of s. xvii (?). Binding of thick polished wooden boards, bevelled inside and inlaid with ivory: see below.

Written in Italy. 'Tateono (?) Malatesta a Totio (?) Battaglia Accepit', the initials T. M., and three coats of arms are below the picture on f. ii^{v}. The arms in the middle appear to be of Malatesta of Bologna (Rietstap, ii. 136) and occur again as an ivory inset on the upper cover. The arms on the left, per fess argent and gules on the chief a sword gules, point to sinister, are surmounted by a cardinal's hat. They occur again as an ivory inset on the lower cover. Bought from Davis and Orioli in 1921.

1. 380. *Officia pontificalia, etc.* S. XIV

Occasional offices, lacking the first quire and imperfect at the end. ff. 1–9 and 46–51 are out of place; see below, arts. 9–11.

1. f. 10 (*begins imperfectly*) senciamus.' et qui nos . . .

Benediction of Palms.

2. ff. 10ᵛ–11ᵛ In uigilia pasche benediccio ignis. Dominus uobiscum7 Oremus7 Domine deus pater lumen indeficiens . . .

3. ff. 11ᵛ–18 Oracio in uestiario. Dominus uobiscum7 Oremus7 Omnipotens misericors deus qui sacerdotum ministerio . . .; followed by prayers 'in dormitorio', 'in domo infirmorum', 'in refectorio', 'in coquina', 'in promptuario', 'ante ianuam ecclesie', 'intus'.

Cf. A. Franz, *Die kirchlichen Benedictionen im Mittelalter*, i. 633–44.

4. Prayers on special occasions: (*a*) f. 18ʳᵛ Quando episcopus vel abbas fuerit suscipiendus. Deus fidelium omnium pastor et rector . . .; (*b*) ff. 18ᵛ–19 In creacione noui abbatis . . . Actiones nostras quesumus domine aspirando . . .; (*c*) ff. 19–22ᵛ Quando aliquis suscipitur in fraternitate congregacionis . . . Domine ihesu criste qui dixisti . . . (and four more); (*d*) ff. 22ᵛ–23ᵛ Ad minuendum sanguinem . . . Mediator dei et hominum . . . (Franz, i. 646); (*e*) ff. 23ᵛ–25 Quando tondetur infans primo. Domine saluator innocencie amator . . .; (*f*) ff. 25–6 Benediccio ad barbas iuuenum . . . Deus cuius spiritu creatura . . . (and another); (*g*) ff. 26–27ᵛ Ad clericum faciendum ex seculari habitu receptum. Oremus dilectissimi dominum nostrum ihesum cristum pro hoc famulo suo N . . . Oracio. Omnipotens s.d. propiciare peccatis nostris . . .

5. ff. 27ᵛ–28ᵛ Incipit ordo ad benedicendum monachum.

A form of profession, f. 28: Ego frater N promitto stabilitatem meam. et conuersionem morum meorum. et obedienciam secundum regulam sancti benedicti. coram deo et omnibus sanctis eius7 in hoc loco qui uocatur Oliua . . .'. Some alterations and additions. Plural forms interlined.

6. ff. 38ᵛ–40 Absolucio excommunicatorum . . . Oremus. Deus qui apostolo tuo petro . . .

7. ff. 40–5 Letania super vii psalmos.

The confessors are Martin, Nicholas, Wilhelm, Peter, Ethmund, Malachi, Benedict, Bernard, Robert.

8. f. 45ʳᵛ Quando exeunt fratres contra aliquem defunctum . . . Oremus. Tibi commendamus domine animam famuli tui . . .

Commendation of soul.

9. ff. 1–3 Benediccio baculi et pere peregrinorum. Deus inuicte potencie. pietatis inmense . . .

Andrieu, *Pont. Rom.* ii. 420.

10. ff. 3ᵛ–9ᵛ, 52–8 Incipit ordo ad inungendum infirmum.

11. ff. 58–65, 46–51ᵛ, 66–8 Office of burial.

12. ff. 78–79ᵛ Sequitur offitium defunctorum. Placebo. Dilexi. . . . Parce michi domine . . . non subsistam. Credo quod redemptor meus (*ends imperfectly*). The words 'Dilexi', 'Ad dominum', and 'Credo quod redemptor meus' are noted.

ff. 77+iii, foliated 1–19, 21–31, 33–79. 166×128 mm. Written space 130×90 mm. 12 long lines. Collation: 1¹⁰+1 leaf after 1 (ff. 10–21) 2¹⁰+1 leaf after 1 (ff. 22–33) 3¹⁰+1 leaf after 1 (ff. 34–44) 4¹⁰+1 leaf after 1 (ff. 45, 1–9, 52) 5¹⁰+1 leaf after 1 (ff. 53–63) 6¹⁰ (ff. 64, 65, 46–51, 66–7) 7¹². Quires 1–3, 5, 6 are signed at the beginning ii–iiii, vi, vii. A handsome large hand, the strokes unusually thick. Punctuation by point, punctus elevatus, and flex (., ⁝ 7). 2-line and 1-line red initials. Capital letters in the ink of the text are marked with red. Germanic binding of brown leather over wooden boards, s. xvi: two rolls, (1) of figures in four compartments, Christ blessing and legend 'DATA EST / MIHI OMN' David and initials W. R. and legend 'DE FRVCT / VENTRIS', Paul and legend APPARVIT / BENIGNIT', John Baptist and legend 'ECCE AGN / VS DEI QVI' (cf. Haebler, *Rollen und Platten-stempel des XVI Jahrhunderts*, i. 131), (2) incomplete, showing Adam and Eve at the tree and legend PECCATVM, the sacrifice of Isaac and legend FIDES, the crucifixion and legend SATISFACTIO.

Written for use in the Cistercian abbey of Oliva, diocese of Danzig: cf. art. 5.

1. 381, ff. 1–80. *Vita Sancti Winwaloi* s. XIII in.

Described, together with ff. 81–146, by A. Wilmart in *Anal. Boll.* lvi (1938), 24–5, by W. D. Macray in HMC, *Various Collections*, ii (1903), 24–7, and in *Catalogue of manuscripts . . . relating to St. David* (Cardiff Public Libraries), 1927, pp. 1–5.

Incipit vita et actus beati Wingualei abbatis Nonis Marcii cuius festum translatum est usque iiiiᵒ kl' Maii: (*a*) ff. 1–7 Ad exponendam uobis dilectissimi fratres . . . meritis subleuati ad regna celestia peruenire ualeamus. prestante . . . amen; (*b*) ff. 7–78 Incipit in uitam sancti Wingualoei cornugilensis abbatis. Vita breuis studii . . . (31 verses, followed by capitula of bk. 1). (f. 9) Auctores uero . . . Britannia insula de qua . . . uirtutes agerentur prestante . . . amen; (*c*) ff. 78–80ᵛ Incipiunt lecciones de eodem. Hanc autem rescripsimus . . . recedebat laus ihesus cristus qui . . . amen.

(*a*). Sixteen lections. *Acta Sanctorum*, March, vol. 1, pp. 254–5. (*b*). The long life of St. Winwaloe by Wurdestinus: *Anal. Boll.* vii. 172–249. (*c*). A summary of (*b*): cf. ibid. 169. The medieval Dover catalogue (see below) shows that 'Nomina paparum et archiepiscoporum' once followed (*c*) and that eight leaves are missing at the end.

ff. 80, bound with MS. 1. 381, ff. 81–146, q.v. Medieval foliation 1–70, 70–9. 172×125 mm. Written space 125×78 mm. 20 long lines. The first line of writing below the top ruled line. Collation: 1–4⁸ 5⁶ 6–9⁸ 10¹⁰. Initials red or blue. Secundo folio *forma egregium*.

Written in England. Book 6 on shelf 7 of class D in the library of the Benedictine priory of Dover in 1389, as appears from the inscription 'Ð : VII : Vita sancti Wingualei . . . . . forma egregium . . . . 88 . . . . 2' at the foot of f. 2: cf. *Ancient Libraries*, pp. 421, 460. An inscription at the head of f. 1 was read with the help of a reagent as an ex-libris of (Sir) Robert

Cotton (cf. Macray, loc. cit.): only the date '1600' is now legible. For a later owner see MS. 1. 381, ff. 81–146.

1. 381, ff. 81–146. *Vitae sanctorum*　　　　s. XII in.–XII med.

A collection of saints' lives. Sidenotes, running titles, and an intermittent foliation (see below) are in an unusual hand of s. xvi in. which occurs also in MS. 3. 833, q.v.

1. ff. 81–94 Mauricio summo sacrat hec Gozelinus ab imo. Beda uenerabilis qui de multis . . . triumphat et regnat in secula seculorum Amen.

The life of St. Ethelburga by Goscelin. *BHL*, no. 2630b. Collated as C by M. L. Colker, *Studia Monastica*, vii (1965), 398–417.

2. ff. 94–96ᵛ Berkinga monasterium . . . in sanctis suis qui regnat in secula.

Lections for St. Hildelitha, as in Capgrave, *Nova Legenda Angliae. BHL*, no. 3942. Printed by Colker, loc. cit., pp. 455–8.

3. ff. 97–102 Vita beati Ædwardi regis et martyris. Inclitus rex Eaduuardus . . . et amborum spiritu sancto uiuit . . . amen.

BHL, no. 2418.

4. ff. 102ᵛ–120 Regnabat regnorum pietas Edgarus . . . non solum quippe.

Goscelin's life of St. Edith, bk. 1 in its revised form and bk. 2 represented only by four poems. The prologue is omitted. Collated as C for Wilmart's edition in *Anal. Boll.* lvi. 39–98, 269–70, 277, 285, 293–4. f. 120ᵛ is blank.

5. ff. 121–129ᵛ Incipit historia sancti dauid. Dominus noster quamuis omnes . . . collocet qui est . . . amen.

The life by Ricemarch. *BHL*, no. 2107. Facsimile of f. 121 in *Catalogue of Manuscripts . . . relating to St. David* (Cardiff Public Libraries), 1927.

6. ff. 130–135ᵛ Sicut hyemps laurum . . . nil habeo melius. cape fructum muneris huius.

The metrical life of St. Mary of Egypt by Hildebert (Walther, no. 18159), ending imperfectly in Cantus VI, ed. *PL* clxxi. 1330B/11.

7. ff. 136–46 (*begins imperfectly*) cauta cogitatione . . . consolationes.' cui est . . . Amen.

BHL, no. 2377. The life of St. Ebrulfus ed. Mabillon, *Acta Sanctorum Benedictinorum*, i. 355–60, beginning at 355/9. f. 145ᵛ ends 'Hec et' (edn., 359/32) and f. 146 begins 'indubitanter' (edn. 359/56): one leaf is missing. f. 146ᵛ blank.

ff. 81–146 in a volume of ff. ii + 146 + i: see MS. 1. 381, ff. 1–80. Late medieval foliation i–xvi on ff. 81–96, i–vi on ff. 97–102, i–viii on ff. 103–10, vᵗᵒ, viᵗᵒ on ff. 134–5 and iiᵒ–viᵒ on ff. 136–40, each figure preceded by 'ffo.': cf. MS. 3. 833. 172 × 125 mm. Written space *c.* 145 × 90 mm. Ruling with a hard point. 26, 33 (ff. 97–134) and 19 (ff. 136–46) long lines: f. 135 was first ruled like f. 136 and then reruled in pencil with 34 lines.¹ Collation: 1–6⁸ 7⁴ + 1 leaf after 1 (f. 130) and 1 leaf after 4 (f. 134) 8¹⁴ wants 2 after f. 135 and

¹ ff. 135 and 146 are a bifolium: 135 was left blank before art. 7 and was made use of by the scribe of art. 6.

13 after f. 145. Arts. 1, 2 (quires 1, 2) in one and arts. 3, 4 (quires 3–5) in another good hand of s. xii in. Arts. 5 and 7 in different hands of s. xii med. The hand of art. 5 began art. 6 which is continued in several hands of varying size and appearance. Headings in red and green. Initials red, green, or, less commonly, blue. English binding of s. xvi/xvii, no doubt for Cotton: see above, MS. 1. 381, ff. 1–80. Secundo folio *de uisione*.

Written in England, arts. 1, 2 probably at or for the Benedictine nunnery of Barking. That arts. 1–7 were annotated and foliated at Barking, *c.* 1500, is likely: cf. MS. 3. 833. Belonged, together with ff. 1–80, to Robert Cotton and in 1903 to Sir G. O. Wombwell, Newburgh Priory, Coxwold, York: Wombwell sale at Sotheby's, 14 Apr. 1924, lot 136. Bought in 1925.

1. 382. *Biblia* s. XIII med.

1. ff. 1–246 Fragments—about half—of what may have been a normal small Bible.[1] (*a*) ff. 1–28, parts of 1 Chronicles (f. 1), Esther (ff. 2, 3), Judith (ff. 24–8), Psalms (ff. 4–13), Proverbs (ff. 14–23) (*b*) ff. 29–158ᵛ Song of Songs, Wisdom, Ecclesiasticus, Isaiah, Jeremiah, Lamentations, Baruch (these two books, ff. 48–49ᵛ, misbound before Isaiah), Ezekiel, Daniel, Minor Prophets, 1, 2 Maccabees, more or less complete (*c*) ff. 159–246 The New Testament in the usual order beginning near the end of the prologue to Mark.

The remaining prologues are 30 of the common set of 64,[1] Stegmüller nos. 468, 491, 500, 511, 510, 515, 512 (. . . vocem tuam etc.), 513, 519+517, 524, 521, 526, 528 (. . . demonstrabitur), 531, 534, 538, 543, 547, 553, 607, 620, 624, 728, 736, 747, 765 (a loadicea), 772, 780, 809. f. 246ᵛ was left blank. The top of nearly every leaf has been eaten away.

2. ff. 247–292ᵛ The usual dictionary of Hebrew names, Aaz apprehendens . . . (the first words are lost), ending 'consiliatiores eorum. Hic expliciunt interpretaciones'.

ff. 291+i. 115×85 mm. Written space 96×63 mm. Much cut down by a binder. 2 cols. 45 lines. Collation impracticable. Written in a small clear hand. Initials: (i) of books, in colour on coloured grounds touched with gold; (ii) of prologues, 3-line, red and blue, with ornament of both colours; (iii) of chapters, red or blue, with ornament of the other colour; (iv) of psalm verses and in art. 2, 1-line, red or blue. Binding of s. xix.

Written probably in France. Notes in an English hand, s. xvi, on f. 246. 'H. B. Green', s. xix, f. 202ᵛ and elsewhere. 'J. C. Orlebar Feb. 21 1828', f. 206ᵛ. 'James Goodson Febr. 28 1828', f. 207. Armorial book-plate of John M. Gray dated 1880. Bought from Edward Howell in 1920.

1. 384. *Weichbildchronik* (*in German*) s. XIV med.

f. 1ᵛ Nu horet vn' vornemet die zal der iare der si von der werlde begin bis an godes geburt . . . (f. 2ᵛ) von keyser Iulio. Iulius waz der erste kayser zu romen . . . (f. 3ᵛ) von der ersten keyser karle. Noch gotes geburt uber acht hundert iar . . . (f. 13ᵛ) von keyser Wyllikin dem letzten an dirre zal. Dor nach quam an das riche vnde wart zu keyser gelobet kunc willikyn (*William II, 1227–56*). vnde was an zwey vnde sechzik iar . . . (f. 14) Sint ir nu wol hat gehort die zal der keysere vn' de kunge dor zu der bebesce vn' der bysschoue von den daz godes

---

[1] See Bristol Public Library, 15.

hus vn' das recht zu meydeburc gestiften vn' bestetiget ist. Nu sult ir ouch horen wie mancherley recht si. vn' von wannen das recht ouch si. von gotes recht zum aller ersten. Nu horet vn' vornemet von des rechtes beginne . . . (f. 164ᵛ) vnde vber sin vnrechte volleyst (ends imperfectly).

Apparently a version of the Weichbildchronik for which see C. G. Homeyer, *Die deutschen Rechtsbücher des Mittelalters*, edn. 1931–4, p. *31, where thirty-six manuscripts are listed. The last of very numerous chapter headings is (f. 164ᵛ) 'von gewalde vn' roube do die hant hafte tat ist': cf. art. 110 in the editions, *Magdeburgisch Weichbildt* by (C. Zobel?) in 1589 (f. 99ᵛ) and *Das Sächsische Weichbild* by J. F. Ludovici in 1721.¹ f. 1ʳ blank.

ff. 164. 142×108 mm. Written space 90×80 mm. 2 cols. 19 long lines. Collation: 1–10⁸ 11⁶ 12–13⁸ 14⁸ wants 6 after f. 107 15–20⁸ 21⁸ wants 8 after f. 164. Quires numbered at the end in red. Textura. Red initials, 5-line (f. 1ᵛ) ,3-line and 2- line. Medieval binding of red leather over thin wooden boards. Metal centre-piece and cornerpieces on each cover. Central clasp missing. Secundo folio *is daʒ*.

Probably bought from G. E. Bullen in 1922.

1. 385. *Statuta Angliae; Leges et consuetudines de Montgomery*
s. xiv¹–xv med.

Arts. 1–45 are statutes (etc.) prior to 6 Edward III, preceded on ff. 1–16ᵛ by tables of chapters of arts. 7 (imperfect at the beginning), 16, 31–5. No doubt tables of chapters of arts. 1–6 were on a quire now missing before f. 1. A well-written pocket copy. Running titles throughout.

1. ff. 17–25 Magna Carta. The inspeximus of Edward I, 28 Mar. 1300, imperfect at the beginning. *SR* i, Charters, pp. 38/14–41. 36 chapters.

2. ff. 25–30 Incipit carta de Foresta. Edwardus dei gracia . . . *SR* i, Charters, i. 42–4, abbreviated. 16 chapters.

3. ff. 30–35ᵛ Incipit statutum de Merton'. *SR* i. 1.

4. ff. 35ᵛ–50ᵛ Incipit statutum de Marleberg'. *SR* i. 19.

5. ff. 50ᵛ–79ᵛ Incipiunt statuta de Westm' prima. In French. *SR* i. 26.

6. (*a*) ff. 79ᵛ–91 Incipiunt statuta Gloucestr'. In French. (*b*) f. 91ʳᵛ Iste articulus sequens in quadam billa scriptus consutus est statuto consignato in banco. Com contenu soit en nostre estatut . . . volunte le Roi. (*c*) ff. 91ᵛ–93 Sequitur articulus statuti Gloucestr' per dominum E. quondam Regem Anglie patrem dominum E R' nunc. anno regni sui nono et consilium suum correctus pro Ciuibus London' de forinsecis vocatis ad warantum in Hustengo London'. Purueu est ensement qe si homme . . .

(*a*). *SR* i. 45. There is a break in the writing at f. 83ᵛ (cf., below, collation) which ends 'ad liuere. Come auant ces houres etc.', after which five lines remain blank. f. 84 begins after five blank lines 'Come auant ces houres' (edn. 47/1). (*b*). *SR* i. 216/1–12 and cf. footnote. (*c*). *SR* i. 52. Cf. also art. 46*b*, *e*.

7. ff. 93–145ᵛ Incipit statutum Westm' secundi. *SR* i. 71.

¹ I owe the identification to Dr. Sigrid Krämer and Professor Krause.

8. ff. 146–149ᵛ Incipit statutum de finibus. *SR* i. 215.

9. ff. 149ᵛ–151 Incipit statutum de Religiosis. *SR* i. 51.

10. ff. 151ᵛ–152ᵛ Statutum de emptoribus terrarum. *SR* i. 106.

11. ff. 152ᵛ–157ᵛ Incipit statutum de mercatoribus. In French. *SR* i. 98.

12. ff. 157ᵛ–159ᵛ Incipit statutum de recognitoribus ponendis in assisis. *SR* i. 113.

13. ff. 159ᵛ–160ᵛ De homagio faciendo. Ri (*for* Qi) fra homage au Roi tendra . . . Different from and longer than *SR* i. 227.

14. ff. 160ᵛ–161 De conspiratoribus. In French. *SR* i. 216.

15. ff. 161–6 Incipit statutum Wynton'. In French. *SR* i. 96.

16. ff. 166–77 Incipiunt noui articuli super cartas. In French. *SR* i. 136.

17. ff. 177–180ᵛ Incipit statutum de coniunctim feoffatis. *SR* i. 145.

18. ff. 180ᵛ–185 Incipit addicio foreste. *SR* i. 147.

19. ff. 185–9 Incipit statutum de apportis (religiosis). *SR* i. 150.

20. ff. 189–90 Incipit sacramentum vicecomitis. *SR* i. 247.

21. ff. 190–192ᵛ Incipit statutum de escaetria. *SR* i. 142.

22. ff. 192ᵛ–193ᵛ Incipit assisa panis. *SR* i. 199.

23. f. 194 Incipit assisa ceruisis (*sic*). *SR* i. 200.

24. f. 194 Sequitur iudicium pillorie. *SR* i. 201/1–6.

25. ff. 194–195ᵛ Incipit commissio ordinacionum. Edward par la grace de dieu . . . Com nous al honour de dieu et pur le bien . . . cestres nos lettres patentes.
Westminster, 16 Mar. 3 Edward II.

26. ff. 195ᵛ–222ᵛ Incipiunt ordinaciones. 15 Oct., 5 Edward II. In French. *SR* i. 157. The running title is 'Noue ordinaciones'.

27. ff. 222ᵛ–229ᵛ Incipiunt articuli cleri. 24 Nov., 10 Edward II. *SR* i. 171. ff. 225, 226 damaged.

28. ff. 229ᵛ–231ᵛ Incipit statutum Lincoln' de Vicecomite. In French. *SR* i. 174.

29. ff. 231ᵛ–236 Incipit statutum Ebor'. 12 Edward II. In French. *SR* i. 177.

30. f. 236ʳᵛ Incipit statutum de composicione monete. *SR* i. 204.

31. ff. 236ᵛ–244 Incipit statutum de Hugone le Despenser anno primo R E tercii. In French. *SR* i. 251.

32. ff. 244–50 Incipit aliud Statutum factum apud Westm' anno primo domini Regis E tercii. In French. *SR* i. 255.

33. ff. 250–9 Incipit statutum Northampt'. In French. *SR* i. 257.

34. ff. 259–68 Incipit statutum factum apud Westm' Anno quarto R E' tercii. *SR* i. 261.

35. ff. 268–276ᵛ Incipit statutum factum apud Westm' anno regni regis E tercii post conquestum quinto. In French. *SR* i. 265.

36. ff. 276ᵛ–282 Incipit prerogatiua regis. *SR* i. 226.

37. f. 282ʳᵛ Incipiunt dies communes in Banco. *SR* i. 208.

38. ff. 282ᵛ–283 Incipiunt dies communes in Placito dotis. *SR* i. 208.

39. ff. 283ᵛ–285 Incipit statutum de vocatis ad War'. *SR* i. 108.

40. ff. 285–6 Incipit statutum de districcione scaccarii. In French. *SR* i. 197b.

41. ff. 286–290ᵛ Incipiunt peticiones illorum de querela Th' Comitis Lanc'. Fait a remembrer que le tierz iour de feuerer . . . en chescun bref. Explicit.

1 Edward III.

42. ff. 290ᵛ–291ᵛ Breue de reuocando ordinac'. *SR* i. 190.

43. ff. 291ᵛ–293ᵛ Incipit statutum inde factum apud Ebor'. 15 Edward II. In French. *SR* i. 189.

44. ff. 293ᵛ–297ᵛ Incipit statutum de terris Templariorum. 17 Edward II. *SR* i. 194.

45. ff. 297ᵛ–300 Incipit statutum de bigamis. *SR* i. 42.

46 (added). (*a*) ff. 300ᵛ–301 Incipit abiuracio latronum. (H)oc audis domine coronator . . . sic deus me adiuuet. (*b*) f. 301ʳᵛ Glouc' capitulo ix. Purueu est ensement que nul appel . . . (*c*) f. 301ᵛ Prouisum est insuper quod nullus religiosus feodum alicuius ingrediatur . . . tenetur. (*d*) ff. 301ᵛ–302ᵛ Nota quod vii modis fit diuorcium . . . (*e*) f. 302ᵛ Glouc' capitulo primo in fine Et la ou auaunt cez heures . . . (*f*) f. 303 Exposiciones vocabulorum. Sok. hoc est . . . (*g*) ff. 304–5 De esson'. Hic demonstratur quot modis essonium sunt (*sic*) calumpniand' . . . (*h*) ff. 305–306ᵛ Cum quis per breue domini petat . . . est quietus.

s. xiv² and (*f*) s. xv. (*b*). Cf. *SR* i. 49/9–14. (*c*). Cf. *SR* i. 51/1–4. (*e*). *SR* i. 47/18–22. (*f*). Explanations of Sok, Sak, Thol, Them only. f. 303ᵛ blank. (*g*). *SR* i. 217. (*h*). *SR* i. 110 (Statutum de defensione iuris).

47 (added, s. xv). ff. 307–345ᵛ Hee sunt leges et consuetudines libere Burgi de montgomery tentas et vsitatas a tempore Regis Henrici filii Regis Henrici primo. subscript'. In primis vtimur ad proximam Curiam ante festum sancti Michaelis eligere nobis Balliuos Coronat' et subballiuos de burgensibus nostris . . . ad exoneracionem tallag' nostrorum. Si quis sit inobediens (*ends abruptly in a*

section beginning Item nec vtimur inter nos leuare aliqua debita domino Rege).
f. 346^{rv} blank.

48. The heading of a charm for the falling sickness, 'Auamsapta id est medicina
. . .', is on the flyleaf, f. 349^v, s. xiv ex.

49. The pastedown inside the front cover is from the sanctorale of a 2-column
breviary, s. xiv, and contains part of the office of Blasius.

ff. 346+iii. ff. 347–9 are medieval parchment end-leaves. 87 × 60 mm. Written space
68 × 38 mm. Mainly in 23–5 long lines. Collation: 1^6 2^{10} 3^8 wants 1 before f. 17 and 8 after
f. 22 4–10^8 11^6 wants 6 after f. 83 12^8 wants 1 before f. 84 13–38^8 39 five (ff. 299–303) 40
four (ff. 304–7) 41–45^4 46^{12} 47^4 48^2+1 leaf after 1 (ff. 344–6). Arts. 1–45 are in a neat
anglicana. Art. 47 is in current anglicana influenced by secretary. Blue initials with red
ornament. Binding of s. xvi (?), much repaired. Secundo folio (f. 17) *scilicet heres*.

Probably in mid Wales in s. xv: cf. art. 47. 'Howell prichard owith this book god prosper
wth him for euer Amen', f. 347, s. xvi. 'DD 210' is a modern mark.

1. 704. *W. Lyndwood, etc.* s. xv med.

1. ff. 1–89^v Incipit liber primus constitucionum prouincialium. De summa
trinitate et fide catholica. Ignorancia sacerdotum et infra. Ne quis per ignoranciam se excuset . . . canonice compellendos etc. Explicit tractatus de Constitucionibus prouincialibus.

The Provinciale of William Lyndwood, the text without the commentary. Here anonymous. Fifty-two manuscripts are listed by C. R. Cheney in *The Jurist*, xxi (1961), 433–4.
An incomplete table of the five books on f. iii.

2. ff. 90^v–96^v Incipit tractatus qui vocatur regula decimarum pro presbiteris
omnium ecclesiarum cristi fidelium beneficiatis compilatus in insula maris
corsice per in theologia magistrum Andream hispan' ordinis sancti benedicti
pauperem episcopum Adiacen' olim ciuitaten' predicandus populis diebus
festiuis. [De]cimarum solucionem et premiciarum . . . priuilegiata preuilegio
dumtaxat domini pape (*ends imperfectly*).

The Regula Decimarum of Andreas Destarban, O.S.B., bishop of Ajaccio, †1427.

3 (added in s. xv in the space left blank between art. 1 and art. 2). (*a*) f. 89^v A
recipe in English 'ad destruendum fleumam'. (*b*) f. 90^{rv} Notes on the hours,
prime, terce, sex, none, vespers, and compline.

ff. iii+96. ff. i–iii are medieval parchment end-leaves. 148 × 105 mm. Written space
105 × 75 mm. Frame ruling in pencil. 21–6 long lines. Collation: 1–12^8. Written in
secretary script, not very carefully. 2-line blue initials. Contemporary binding of wooden
boards covered with pink leather: three bands: a central clasp missing. Secundo folio
sumptum ore.

Written in England. 'M. W. Colys' inside the front cover, s. xv: for persons of this name
see Emden, *BRUO*, pp. 465, 468, 472. Armorial book-plate of James Plunkett, Earl of
Fingall: 'a. d. 1725 empt. J. P.' is on the pastedown. Bought from Messrs. Robinson
in 1936.

2. 2. *Speculum Regis; De sacramentis ecclesiae; De sex principiis; Formularium*

s. xv med.–xv/xvi

Noticed in *Report*, p. 95, but the manuscript contains no Welsh.

1. ff. 1–14ᵛ O domine mi rex circa salutem anime [tue et de] periculis euitandis tuo ... Capitulum primum. O domine mi rex vtinam ... Ad quod te perducat ... Qui cum deo patre etc.

Speculum Regis, ed. J. Moisant, *De speculo regis Edwardi III*, Paris, 1891, pp. 127–69. J. Tait showed in *EHR* xvi. 110–15, that the author is likely to be Simon Langham, writing *c.* 1330. Cf. B.L., Royal 10 B. xi.

2. ff. 15–16ᵛ Hic incipit consecracio Electi In episcopum secundum Modum Anglicanum. Prouideat Electus cum suis ministris ... genuflectentes. Et sic finitur stallacio secundum modum Anglie.

David Yale put his own name as the bishop to be consecrated.

3 (filling the quire). (*a*) f. 16ᵛ Memoranda of rents of the bishop of Bangor from Dyffryn Clwyd: cf. art. 6*a*, *h*. (*b*) ff. 17–20ᵛ Miscellaneous notes on simony, the sacraments, confession, etc.: cf. art. 6*f*, 9*b*.

(*a*). Seventeen places, the first Llanruth.

4. ff. 21–59 Notandum est in sacramentis tria contigit reperiry secundum sanctum Thomam et secundum Petrum ... ad matrimonia illorum nobilium.

On baptism, confirmation (f. 25), the eucharist (f. 26), penitence (f. 34), confession (f. 36), and marriage (f. 48). f. 59ᵛ was left blank: see below.

5. ff. 60–74ᵛ Formulary pieces in which the name of the scribe, David Yale, often occurs.

A form of presentation to a benefice, 'porcionem in ecclesia de Llandinam', is addressed 'dilecto nobis in cristo magistro d. yale poet' laureato' and dated in 1503, f. 69. A form of restoration of goods is issued by Roger Horde, D.D., commissary of the bishop of Lincoln, Ruthin, 9 Sept. 1503, f. 70ᵛ. The formulary shows special interest in Ruthin and in Woodstock, Oxfordshire.

6 (filling the quire). (*a*) f. 75 Memoranda of rents of the bishop of Bangor from Dyffryn Clwyd: cf. art. 3*a*. (*b*) ff. 75ᵛ–76 In terra summus Rex est hoc tempore nummus ... Ergo patet cuique quod nummus regnat ubique. (*c*) f. 76 Hiis ideo metui Discere velle meum Vnde precor precibus Mitis adesto meis ... mille placebit opus. (*d*) f. 76 Memoranda in English about the Greys of Ruthin. (*e*) f. 76ᵛ Quando dies circumcisionis die dominica euenerit ... (*f*) f. 77ᵛ Notes like art. 3*b*. (*g*) f. 78 A continuation of (*a*). (*h*) f. 78ᵛ Two formulary letters purporting to be from David Yale, A.D. 1502 and 1501. (*i*) f. 78ᵛ A herb recipe in English.

(*b*). 35 lines. Walther, no. 9136. *Carmina Burana*, ed. A. Hilka and O. Schumann, 1930, no. 11. (*c*). 11 lines. (*d*). 32 lines. (*e*). Prognostications by weather according to the day of the week Circumcision (1 Jan.) falls on.

7. ff. 79–85ᵛ (*begins imperfectly*) proprietas relacionis mē (?) suscipere magis et minus ... et per posteria sed discripcio (*ends imperfectly*).

A commentary on Aristotle, *Categoriæ*, beginning in bk. 2 and ending in bk. 3. A section begins (f. 82) '[Q]ualitatem autem dico secundum quam. Hoc est 4^{tum} capitulum huius partis in quo determinatur de qualitate et dicit secundum hoc quod sunt due partes principales huius capituli . . .'.

8. ff. 86–99^v [F]orma est componi contingens. Iste liber intitulatur de sex principiis cum tamen fit de sex predictis . . . locatum ubi est (ends imperfectly).

A commentary on the De sex principiis (PL clxxxviii. 1257–70), ending in part 2, chapter 4, the first words of which are '[U]bi est circumscripcio corporis' (f. 99^v). Part 2 begins (f. 91^v) 'Accio uero est. Hec est 2^a pars principalis huius libri in quo auctor determinat de 6 principiis.de quibus promisit determinaturum se esse et continet in se sex capitula secundum numerum sex principiorum'. Albertus is quoted.

9. (a) ff. 100^v–104^v Nota quod licet omnes et singuli qui notantur . . . accusari in confessione (ends abruptly). (b) ff. 105^v–114 Pieces like art. 3b. (c) f. 114^v A table in English to show how much sums of money ranging from a farthing a week to a shilling a day amount to in a year. (d) f. 115 Two recipes in English for the 'Morffew'. (e) f. 115 A table of the 'Debita singulorum episcoporum In Reg(n)o anglie pontificio Romano soluenda'. (f) f. 115^v Two faded letters from David Yale.

(e). From twenty-one dioceses. ff. 100^r, 105^r left blank. On f. 100^r is 'Si quis habet quod habere decet sit letus habendo Ne sit alterius quod suum esse potest Quod M' dauid yale', repeated three times. Scribbles and 'Dauid Yale alias Tudyr de Rut[hyn]' follow (f).

ff. ii+115+ii. Paper and (ff. 1–14, 88, 89) parchment. 195 × 135 mm. Written space (art. 1) 155 × 85 mm. 34 long lines (art. 1). Collation: 1^{10} 2^6 wants 5, 6 3^6 (ff. 15–20) 4^{12} 5^8 6^4 7^{16} wants 16, probably blank; after this probably three quires, one ending at f. 78 and the next at f. 99, but their construction is doubtful. Art. 1 in set current anglicana. Arts. 2–9 in informal, mixed, but mainly secretary hands, partly—see below—by David Yale: changes at ff. 21, 45. Initials in red or in the ink of the text touched with red in arts. 1, 7, 8 only. 2-line spaces remain blank in art. 1. Binding of s. xix. Secundo folio Ecce domine.

Arts. 1, 7, 8 written probably in England and the rest in Wales. David Yale wrote his name on f. 1 and often later and wrote most of arts. 2, 3, 5, 6, 9 and memoranda about sheep and goats on the last page of art. 4. According to f. 115^v he was of Ruthin, Denbighshire: cf. arts. 5, 6d.[1] Belonged in s. xvi to his sons: 'Wyllyam ap Sir dauid yale os th(i)s boke god make hym a good man', f. 66; 'Thys buke doth pertene to me symon dauys pryst now a late ye yere of oure lorde mccccc and xvii^{ti} and alsoe thys bucke yn tyme past was yn ye possescyon of dauyt yale father to ye foresede symon dauys. And I desyre all yow y^t rede thys scrypture for ye loue of god to sey on pater noster and an auy for ye soules of ye foresede men', f. 105. Scribbled in by Thelwalls in s. xvi: Richard Thelwall, f. 47; Vnto Richard Thelwall, f. 90^v; John Thelwall, f. 99^v; Thomas Thelwall est verus possessor, f. 100^v. Phillipps MS. 6900. One of a number of manuscripts of Welsh interest acquired for Cardiff Public Library in 1895 from the Phillipps collection: cf. A. N. L. Munby, Phillipps Studies, v. 31.

2. 7. Welsh Laws (in Welsh)   s. xv^2

Report, p. 92. Phillipps 2743. Acquired as 2.2.

[1] Dr. A. B. Emden tells me that Yale was instituted vicar of Egham, Surrey, in 1500, portionary of Llandinam, Montgomeryshire, in 1503 (cf. art. 5), and prebendary of Bangor by 1504: resigned 1530.

2. 81. *The Book of Aneirin (in Welsh)* s. XIII[2]

Report, p. 91. Text printed by Ifor Williams, *Canu Aneirin*, 1938. K. Jackson in *Antiquity*, xiii (1939), 25–34, and C. A. Gresham, ibid. xvi (1942), 237–57, give the gist of Williams's Welsh introduction: on the manuscript see especially xiii. 29 and xvi. 237. Facsimile edition by J. G. Evans, Early Welsh Text Series, viii (1908). Cf. N. Denholm-Young, *Handwriting in England and Wales*, 1954, p. 44 and pl. 18. Phillipps 16614. Acquired as 2.2.

2. 385. *Apocalypsis cum glosa; Cantica Canticorum, cum glosa*
s. XII[1]

1. ff. 1–24[v] The Apocalypse spaced for interlinear glosses and with numerous but not continuous scholia in a small hand in the outer margins. The glosses are often brought down from or to a point and framed. No prologue.

2. ff. 25[v]–50 The Song of Songs glossed between the lines and with numerous comments in the margins, all four of them, if necessary.

3. Theological notes, mainly on the Sapiential Books, in several hand of s. xii in blank spaces: f. 25 Salomon filius dauid regis israhel iuxta numerum uocabulorum suorum . . . corporales conuerteret; f. 51 Notandum quod iste liber non canticum . . .; f. 51[v] Salomon pacificus quia in regno eius pax . . . perducunt; f. 51[v] Materia sponsus . . . finis dilectio dei.

ff. i+51+ii. 197 × 132 mm. Written space 140 high. The width of the column of text is 75 mm (art. 1) and 30 mm (art. 2). 21 lines (art. 1) and 17 lines (art. 2). No visible ruling, apart from an occasional vertical line in faint pencil. Art. 1 in a different hand from art. 2. Collation: 1–6⁸ 7⁴ wants 4, probably blank. Initials in art. 1 red or in black penwork with red, yellow, or green fillings. No ornament in art. 2: spaces for initials on f. 25[v] have not been filled. Continental binding, s. xix. Secundo folio *dicens. Noli.*

Written probably in France. Belonged to the Dominicans of Metz: 'Liber fratrum predicatorum Metensium', f. 24[v], s. xiii ex. William Bragge sale, 7 June 1876, lot 12. Book-plate of Thomas Brooke, Armitage Bridge: described in the *Catalogue of the Manuscripts and Printed Books collected by Thomas Brooke*, 1891, i. 23. Bought from P. H. Barnard in 1924.

2. 386. *Conradus de Saxonia, O.F.M., Speculum Beatae Mariae; etc.*
s. XIV med.

1. ff. 1–19 Pater noster etc. Scribit cantor Parisiensis in opere suo super psalmos. quod vice quadam . . . oraciones quibus inpediunt dyabolum. Exemplum de Iuliano.

A commentary on the Lord's Prayer. Vienna, Nationalbibliothek 1345, ff. 35–74, has the same incipit. Cf. art. 4.

2. f. 19[rv] Notula de Timore. Nota quod quadripartitus est timor . . . et iste timor erit in patria.

3. ff. 19[v]–64 Quoniam ut ait beatus Ieronimus. Nulli dubium est quin totum ad gloriam et laudem dei . . . benedictus fructus ventris qui est benedictus in secula.

A commentary on Ave Maria, called 'Speculum Marie virginis' in an added title (s. xv) on f. 21: eighteen chapters. Printed among the works of St. Bonaventura (edn. 1596, vi. 450–85), but by Conrad Holtnicker de Saxonia, O.F.M., †1279. Cf. *MMBL* i. 365.

4. ff. 64ᵛ–65ᵛ An alphabetical subject index of art. 1. References are to the leaves of art. 1 and the letters written in the margins there in three series, a-x, a-y, and a-(x).

5. ff. 66–69ᵛ An alphabetical subject index of art. 3. References are to chapter numbers and the letters written in the margins of each chapter.

6. ff. 69ᵛ–70ᵛ De Ascensione domini. vel generalis sermo. Signa eos qui in me cre. hec sequunter. Mʳ vltimo (Mark 16: 17). Quemcumque dominus habet pro uero cristiano . . . caro refloruit Ihesus cristus . . . Amen.

ff. vi+70+vi. Medieval foliation as far as '20'. 210×150 mm. Written space 155× 103 mm. 32 long lines. Textura. Collation: 1–7¹⁰. 3-line (f. 1) and 2-line red initials. Binding of s. xx. Secundo folio *eripere me*.

Written in Germany or Austria. '1⁰. 4⁰. 4⁰. 7⁰ vdalrici', f. 64, is in the hand of the title on f. 21. Belonged to the Augustinian house of Waldhausen in the diocese of Passau: 'Iste liber est Sancti Iohannis Ewangeliste Canonicorum regularium Monasterii In Walthausen Pat' dyoc'', f. 65ᵛ, s. xv ex. Sold at Sotheby's, 1 July 1925, lot 645. No. 22 in catalogue 48 of P. J. and A. E. Dobell, 8 Bruton St., London, Oct. 1925. Bought from Messrs. Dobell, 14 May 1926.

2. 611. *Galfredus Monemutensis, etc.*   s. XIII/XIV

1. ff. 1–9 *(begins imperfectly)* cessat de imperio agamemnonis . . . et alios quinque. Hactenus id dares frigius mandauit litteris. Explicit.

The first words are on p. 31/3 in the Teubner edition of Dares. Running title 'Hystoria grecorum et troianorum'.

2. f. 9ʳᵛ Notandum quod ciprus quidam filius yewan . . . Brutus uero Locrinum. Kambrium. Albanactum. a quibus tres partes britannie nomina sortita sunt.

Running title 'Genealogia troianorum'.

3. ff. 9ᵛ–10 Strenua cunctorum delectant gesta proborum . . . Frater Walensis madocus edeiruianensis (?). Ex libris densis collegit nos refouens his.

An introduction to art. 4 in twenty-six lines of verse printed hence by J. Hammer, *Geoffrey of Monmouth, Historia Regum Britanniae, A variant version* (Medieval Academy of America, 1951), p. 18.

4. ff. 10–130ᵛ Hystoria britonum. Cum mecum multa et de multis . . . in latinum sermonem transferre curaui. Explicit tractatus.

Described by Hammer, op. cit., p. 8. His C, 'the most complicated of all manuscripts of the Variant Version' and the basis of his text. No division into books and no break on ff. 20, 27, 35ᵛ, 46, 69ᵛ, 77ᵛ, 90ᵛ, 103ᵛ, 115ᵛ, 120ᵛ, at the points where in other copies bks. 2–11 begin. A leaf missing after f. 87. Some annotations of s. xv in English script, for example on f. 90ᵛ.

5. ff. 130ᵛ–132ᵛ (a) Prophecia merlini silvestris. Arbor sterilis a primo trunco

decisa . . . qui pacificato regno occidet. (*b*) In prophecia merlini . . . expectes. (*c*) Epitaphium arturi. Quem morum probitas . . . tumulata secunda.

(*a*). Cf. *Cat. of Romances*, i. 293, 313. (*c*). Four lines of verse. The prophecy of Merlin beginning *Sedente vortigerno* probably followed (*c*) on the first leaf of a new quire, but only the catchword 'sedente' remains.

ff. i+132+i. *c*. 190×150 mm, but the parchment is often short in width or length and has many holes. Written space 130–40×100 mm. 24 long lines. Collation: 1–7¹² 8¹² wants 4 after f. 87 9–10¹² 11¹²+1 leaf after 12 (f. 132). Written in textura of a slightly current sort, with little break between the main pieces. Initials red, 3-line and 2-line, on ff. 10ʳᵛ, 11, 70, 130ᵛ. Capital letters in the ink of the text filled with red. Binding of s. xix.

Written in Wales or perhaps England. In Wales in s. xvi when 'pullus aquile' in the text on f. 132 was glossed 'kiw yr eryr'. 'Powis' on the pastedown, s. xix. Earl of Powis sale at Sotheby's, 20 Mar. 1923, lot 99. Bought from Messrs. Quaritch in 1925.

2. 636. *'Livre des fortunes et infortunes'* s. XV/XVI

Cy commence vng petit liure des fortunes et infortunes de toutes creatures humaines tant hommes comme femmes selon les xii moys de lan et selon les xii signes lesquels sont colloques ou zodiaque et ce nous tesmoigne le tressaige philosophe et astrologie ptholome disant en telle maniere. Du signe du mouton My mars et my apuril. Personne qui est nee au signe du mouton . . . excepte de couleurs noires. Explicit. f. 36ᵛ was left blank.

ff. iii+36+iii. 177×120 mm. Written space 120×78 mm. Collation: 1–4⁸ 5⁴. Written in set cursiva. Pictures on ff. 1, 5, 9ᵛ, 13, 16, 19ᵛ, 21ᵛ, 24, 27, 29ᵛ, 32, 34ᵛ. Each picture is in two compartments of *c*. 32×40 mm showing the occupation of the month and the sign of the zodiac. Blue initials, 4-line, 3-line, and 2-line on grounds of red and gold paint. A continuous framed border on f. 1 and shorter framed borders on other picture pages. French binding, s. xix. Secundo folio *obtenir*.

Written in France. 'Iheremue Bryas Denis Regnault' and an ex-libris of 'Hierimy bryas', s. xvi, on f. 36ᵛ: cf. f. 23ᵛ. A description in French, s. xix, f. iiiᵛ. Armorial book-plate of Sidney Graves Hamilton, s. xix. Bought from Messrs. Ellis in 1922.

2. 637. *Breviarium* s. xv med.

1. ff. 1–178ᵛ, 195–7ᵛ Sanctorale from 26 Dec. (Stephen) to 21 Dec. (Thomas the apostle), preceded by three pages of rubric beginning 'Ordinato seruitio temporis dicendum est quod et quomodo agendum sit de festis sanctorum que ueniunt per annum. In primus igitur'.

Florentia, Maxentius, Junianus, Radegund, Leodegar, and Martin of Vertou are among saints for whom nine lessons are provided (1 Dec.; 26 June; 12, 13 Aug.; 3, 24 Oct.): cf. the Poitiers breviaries in V. Leroquais, *Les Bréviaires manuscrits des bibliothèques publiques de la France*, iii. 22, 62; iv. 41, 70. Leonius of Poitiers, usually 1 Feb., but here between Blasius, 3 Feb., and Agatha, 5 Feb., has three lessons. 'Pictauiis ciuitate depositio sancti fulgencii episcopi et confessoris', f. 130. There is no provision for the dedication of Poitiers cathedral at 17 Oct. Six leaves are missing.

2. ff. 197ᵛ–202ᵛ, 179–194ᵛ Incipit commune sanctorum. Imperfect at the end.

3. ff. 203–206ᵛ Offices of B.V.M., beginning imperfectly, and (f. 204ᵛ) Peter, with hymn 'Petrus beatus cathenarum laqueos . . .' (*RH*, no. 14885).

ff. ii+206+ii. 187×142 mm. Written space 115×85 mm. 2 cols. 32 lines (quires 1, 2) and 30 lines (quires 3–27). Collation: 1⁸ 2⁸ wants 4, 5 after f. 11 3–4⁸ 5⁸ wants 8 after f. 37 6⁸ wants 4, 5 after f. 40 7–14⁸ 15⁸ wants 5 after f. 111 16–23⁸ (ff. 115–78) 24⁸ (ff. 195–202) 25–26⁸ (ff. 179–94) 27 four (ff. 203–6). Hand and style of decoration change at f. 15. Initials: (i) patterned blue or (ff. 1–5ᵛ only) pink on decorated gold grounds; (ii) 2-line, blue with red ornament or gold with slate-grey ornament; (iii) ff. 1, 2 only, blue with red ornament. Borders continuous on ff. 1, 197ᵛ and in one or, rarely, two margins of other pages with initials of type (i): they are framed—and inferior in style—from f. 15 onwards. Capital letters in the ink of the text filled with pale yellow. Binding of s. xix. Secundo folio *p aut v*.

Written for use in the diocese of Poitiers. Book-plate of Frederic H. Sutton, s. xix.

2. 638. *Ordo sepeliendi mortuos* s. xv med.

1. ff. 1–18ᵛ Ordo offitii ad sepeliendum mortuos quando iacere debent in ecclesia . . . R'. Subuenite sancti dei . . .

Noted office. A heading on f. 18ᵛ includes the words 'Si uero fiat offitium pro papa uel archiepiscopo mediolanensi aut episcopo lauden'. 'tunc fiat . . .'. ff. iʳᵛ, 19ʳᵛ blank.

2. The pastedowns are a single sheet of parchment taken from a register of legal proceedings in the town and commune of Lodi, s. xiv. They are in a set form and cancelled; for example, in the matter of a black sow and her litter, 'Die mercurii v Iunii. in ciuitate laud' in domo habitacionis gir' calegarii qui habitat iuxta pontem cermon' (?). Presentibus [. . . .] bertolino garotta testibus reg'. manifestauit et confessus fuit betus de bergamo qui habitat in loco de luuir (?) . . .'. Line-ends are missing. The pasted-down sides can be seen to have writing on them.

ff. 20, foliated i, 1–19. 198×148 mm. Written space 122×97 mm. 20 long lines. Collation: 1¹² 2⁸ Initials 2-line and 1-line, blue with red, or red with pale-brown ornament. Capital letters in the ink of the text filled with pale yellow. Binding of wooden boards covered with white leather, s. xv: a now missing strap fastened to a pin on the back cover. Secundo folio *a luceat*.

Written in Italy for use in the diocese of Lodi. Book-plate of Edmund MᶜClure A.M. Bought from P. M. Barnard in 1927.

2. 641. *Legenda aurea* (*in Netherlandish*) s. xv med.

1. ff. 1–238ᵛ Forty-seven texts for feasts from 15 March to 24 July, preceded by a table headed (f. 1) 'Hier beghint die tafele van enen deele van den boeken es gheheiten aurea legenda of dat passionael beghinnende voer sinte benedictus dach tot sinte Iacobs dach'.

The texts correspond to chapters 47 (Longinus), 49–51, 53–61, 63, 65, 67–70, 72–98 (Christina) of the Legenda aurea of James of Voragine in the edition of T. Graesse, 1850. Seven Sleepers, not in Graesse, is here on ff. 169ᵛ–174ᵛ, after his chapter 87: it agrees with the text in the *Passionael*, edn. Gouda, 1478, f. lxxxiiᵛ.

2 (in another hand). ff. 238ᵛ–242 Hier beghint sancte Ierasimus passie des h. bisscops. In den tyde dyoclesiane . . . in deser legenden niet scryuen.

Erasmus, 24 June. Corresponds to the Latin printed by Graesse in his supplement, ch. 199, but not to the Netherlandish in the printed *Passionael* of 1478, where there is a different version. f. 242ᵛ blank.

ff. iii+242+iii. Paper and (for the outmost and inmost sheets of each quire) parchment. 208 × 140 mm. Written space 138 × 85 mm. 31 long lines. Collation: 1–11¹² 12¹² wants 7 after f. 138 13–16¹² 17–18¹⁴ 19¹² 20¹⁰ wants 6 after f. 236 21 two (ff. 241–2). Written in a formal hybrida: minims are not linked. Initials 2-line or more, red, sometimes with ornament in the ink of the text. Binding of s. xix ex. by the 'Guild of Women-Binders'. Secundo folio (f. 3) *si een*.

Bookplate inscribed 'Ex libris Robert Hall 1902'. No. 153 in cat. 2 (1921) of P. J. and A. E. Dobell, 8 Bruton St., London. Bought from Messrs. Dobell in 1921.

2. 801. *Pseudo-Cicero, Rhetorica ad Herennium*   s. xv med.

Etsi negotiis familiaribus . . . et exercitatione. Finis Amen. Explicit rethorica Marci tulli (*sic*) cicero(n)is ad herennium Deo Gracias.

Some interlinear glosses and marginal scholia.

ff. iv+107+iv, foliated 1–115. Paper. Paper flyleaves. 212 × 143 mm. Written space c. 145 × 75 mm. 18–23 long lines. Collation of ff. 5–111: 1–4⁸ 5¹⁶ 6⁶ 7¹⁰ wants 6–10, blank, after f. 63 8–13⁸. Written in rather poor fere humanistica and (ff. 72–99ᵛ) humanistica by several scribes who were at work at the same time, to judge from the blank pages at the end of quires 7 and 8 and the failure to use 7⁶⁻¹⁰. Ugly red initials with rough ornament at first: from f. 11ᵛ the spaces for initials remain blank. Contemporary binding of wooden boards covered with pink skin which extends only over the spine and one-third of each board: 'RETHOR. CIC. MANVSCRIT' on the spine and on the tail. Secundo folio *est quod*.

Written in Italy. 'Nº 38', f. 5 at the top. Libri sale, 28 Mar. 1859, lot 256. Phillipps 16299: sale at Sotheby's, 11 June 1896, lot 290, to F. S. Ellis (£1. 7s.). Bought from G. H. Last in 1920.

2. 874. *Pauline Epistles, etc.* (*in Netherlandish*)   1486

See C. C. de Bruin, *Middelnederlandse Vertalingen van het Nieuwe Testament*, 1934, pp. 477–86, and for another copy of arts. 2, 3, 5, *MMBL* i. 49.

1. ff. iv–vᵛ Dit es die tafel van den capitellen deser boeke. Op den iersten sondach in den aduent . . .

A table of epistle lections of the temporale.

2. ff. 1–137 Hier beghint dit prologus op sancte pauwels epistel totten romeynen. Pauwelus die apostel ons heren ihesu cristi heeft ghescreuen xiiii epistelen. Die x . . . (f. 3ᵛ) ende nederleit. Hier beghint sancte pauwels ierste epistel totten romeynen op kersauent. Pauwelus knecht cristi ihesu een gheropen apostel . . . Hier eynden die epistolen van sancte pauwels die voleyndet worden anno xiiiiᶜ ende lxxxvi op onser lieuer vrouwen hemeluaert auent . . . Amen.

Pauline Epistles, with general prologue. The prologue is printed by I. Le Long, *Boek-zaal der Nederduytsche Bybels*, 1732, pp. 281–4.

3. ff. 137–165ᵛ Catholic Epistles, with general prologue.

The prologue is printed by Le Long, op. cit., p. 288.

4. ff. 166–233ᵛ Acts, with prologue.

5. ff. 234–277ᵛ Apocalypse, with prologue and glosses.

Glosses written continuously with the text, preceded by the word 'glose' in red and underlined in red. The first 'glose' is on f. 235, 'der doot of des ordels esser nae bi . . .'.

In arts. 2–5 red headings show the occasion when each portion of the text should be read, and the word 'wtganc' marks the end of a lection. The only saints named in the headings are Andrew, Ursula, Ambrose, Matthew, Peter and Paul, Simon and Jude, Conversion of Paul, Peter and Paul (ff. 17, 35, 136, 167ᵛ, 171, 176, 185ᵛ, 193).

ff. iii+280+ii, foliated i–v, 1–95, 95*, 96–279. For f. iii see below. Paper (of good quality) and parchment: in quires 1–16 the parchment leaves are the outside bifolium in one quire and the central bifolium in the next quire; in quires 17–22 only the central bifolium is parchment; in quires 23–31 all leaves are paper and a narrow strip of parchment lines the central opening. 208 × 140 mm. Written space 148 × 83 mm. 2 cols. 26 lines. Collation of ff. iv, v, 1–277: 1 two (ff. iv, v), 2–23¹⁰ 24–30⁸ 31 two (ff. 276–7). Written in a good textura. A full-page frontispiece picture, f. iiiᵛ: St. Paul stands in a church. Initials: (i) f. i, 3-line red and blue with mauve ornament; (ii) 3-line, red patterned in white; (iii) 2-line, red or blue. Capital letters in the ink of the text are stroked with red. Contemporary Netherlandish binding of wooden boards covered with brown stamped leather, rebacked: stamps of four patterns outside and of five other patterns inside a panel formed by triple fillets and divided by triple diagonal fillets into lozenges and triangles: the largest stamp is a double-headed imperial eagle and the least usual an octagonal stamp bearing a trefoil. Secundo folio *maer si.*

Written in the Netherlands, art. 2 completed on 14 Aug. 1486 (see above) and art. 5 on 30 Sept. 1486: 'Dit boec wert volscreuen Anno xiiiiᶜ en' lxxxvi op sancte iheronimus dach deo graci', f. 277ᵛ. '1-1-0', f. iiiᵛ, is probably an English price-mark, s. xviii. In England in s. xix med.: 'Bought of Mʳ Jefferies Bookseller of Bristol 10 Augᵗ 1849 and paid him £7. 10 for it', f. iᵛ. Bought from Sotheran & Co. in 1929.

2. 878. *Nova Statuta Angliae*   s. xv in.

Statutes of Edward III and Richard II, etc. Arts. 1, 3, 5, 6 are in French.

1. ff. 2–140 Incipiunt statuta Ricardi secundi. Anno primo.

Statutes of 1–21 Richard II. A leaf containing the text in *SR* ii. 2/29–3/17 is missing after f. 2. f. 1ʳᵛ was left blank.

2. ff. 140–50 Statutum de hibernia apud Westm' editum anno xxxᵐᵒ. Edwardus dei gracia . . . Quia ex frequenti . . .

Nineteen chapters. *SR* i. 357 (1357).

3. ff. 150–152ᵛ Statutum apud Westm' editum anno xxviᵒ R.E. Edward par la grace . . . as meir' et baill' Deuerwyk salutz. Purceo que plusours foith . . . le dit roial et terrez.

The statute of the staple in five chapters, much shorter and different from *SR* i. 332 (1353). Shrewsbury and Cardiff are listed, as well as Carmarthen, as places in Wales where a staple shall be held. f. 152*ʳᵛ blank.

4. ff. 153–170ᵛ Capitula statutorum Reg. E. tercii.

Tables of statutes of 1–47 Edward III and (ff. 164ᵛ–170ᵛ) 1–17 Richard II. f. 170*ʳᵛ left blank.

5. ff. 171–80 Statutes of 28 and 34 Edward III.

Fifteen and twenty-two chapters. *SR* i. 345, 364.

6. f. 180ʳᵛ Incipit statutum editum anno xiiᵒ Regis Edwardi tercii. Pur ceo que plusourz pleyntz ent este faitz . . . plerra.

From the statute of York, 12 Edward II, *SR* i. 178, chapters 5, 6.

7. ff. 181–185ᵛ 'De puruiours'. Henricus dei gracia . . . vic' Bristoll' qui nunc est vel qui pro tempore fuerit salutem. Cum in statuto in parliamento domini E nuper R' Anglie progenitoris nostri Anno regni sui quarto tento edito inter cetera contineatur . . . Teste meipso apud Westm' xx die februarii anno regni nostri secundo.

Cf. *SR* ii. 124 (2 Henry IV, ch. 14). ff. 186–191ᵛ left blank.

ff. iv + 193 + iv, foliated i–iv, 1–152, 152*, 153–70, 170*, 171–95. ff. iv, 1–5, 191 damaged and repaired. Paper. 215 × 145 mm. Written space 150 × 85 mm at first and more later. 21–3 long lines at first, and more later. Faint frame ruling. Collation: 1²⁶ wants 1, probably blank, and 3 2²⁶ 3²⁴ 4²⁶ 5²⁸ 6–7²⁴ 8²⁰ three blanks missing in second half of quire. Arts. 1–4, 5–6, and 7 are in three different hands, all predominantly of secretary type. No coloured initials. Capital letters in the ink of the text touched with red. Binding of s. xx in. Secundo folio, now missing, was *face brief*.

Written in England. 'Iste liber constat Roberto Blake', f. 190ᵛ, s. xv/xvi. Armorial bookplate of Thomas Mostyn dated 1744. 'Nᵒ 178' and 'MS. Nᵒ 107', f. iv. Described in HMC, *Fourth Report*, App., p. 351. Mostyn sale at Sotheby's, 13 July 1920, lot 115, to Leighton (30s).

3. 46. Two leaves of Minor Prophets glossed, s. xii², formerly used in the binding of the extent of Nantconwy (*Report*, p. 92: Phillipps 18909) are now kept separately as MS. 5. 99, nos. x, xi.

3. 174. *Johannes de Bromyard abbreviatus; 'Sermones abbreviati'*

s. xv¹

1. ff. 5–236ᵛ In nomine patris et filii et spiritus sancti. Abstinencia suum inimicum scilicet carnem debilitat . . . deponens fertur remansisse. Explicit prima pars summe Brom3erd abbreuiat'.

An abbreviation of the first part, Abstinencia–Luxuria, of the long Summa Praedicantium of John de Bromyard, O.P., † probably by 1352. A table of the articles, Abstinencia–Luxuria, precedes the text on flyleaves (ff. 3ᵛ–4). English in the text on ff. 28ᵛ, 'wᵗ þys betyl be he smyte þᵗ al þys wyde world hyt wyte þᵗ to þᵉ vnkynde gyues al hˢ þyng 7 goth hym self a beggyng', and on f. 118 'horry beware by alleruch þᵗ þᵘ be nou3t yfounde al suche', is repeated, with variations, on f. 256ᵛ, s. xv/xvi: 'wyth this malle be he smytt that al the world hyt wytt that gyvyth away all his thinge and goeth hym selfe a beggynge'; 'hurry beware by alruth that thow be not yfound one such'. Another version of 'With this betyl . . .' is printed from a Bromyard manuscript by T. Wright, *Latin Stories* (Percy Society, viii, 1842), p. 29.

2. ff. 237–252ᵛ Dominica 1ª aduentus domini in ramis palmarum. Ecce rex tuus venit Mᵗ 21. Videmus quod in regis absencia . . . recipiant in eterna tabernacula. Amen. Qui me compleuit non tota nocte quieuit . . . Expliciunt quidam sermones abbreuiati pro quorum vlteriori processu recurre ad quemdam tractatum vocatum fasciculum morum secundum diuersas remissiones vel quotaciones in hiis sermonibus factas ad diuersa capitula illius libri.

Brief sermons from Advent to Trinity Sunday found in at least thirteen manuscripts of Fasciculus morum.[1] Schneyer, p. 204. References throughout are to the parts and chapters of Fasciculus morum.

3. ff. 252ᵛ–254ᵛ Ad missam celebrandam sex considero attendenda . . . o felix exercitium vbi cristus (*ends imperfectly*).

On the celebration of mass and (f. 254ᵛ) the dignity of the priesthood.

ff. iv+250+iv. Foliated 1–258. ff. 2–4, 255–7 are medieval end-leaves. 230 × 155 mm. Written space 155 × 85 mm. 33–5 long lines. Collation of ff. 5–254: 1–4¹² 5⁸ 6–20¹² 21⁸ 22⁸ wants 7, 8 after f. 254. Current hand of mixed, but mainly secretary, type. Initials: (i) f. 5, 4-line, brown-red and pink on a green ground with decoration in these colours forming a continuous border of unusual pattern; (ii) 2-line, blue with red ornament. Binding of wooden boards, perhaps medieval, recovered in s. xix. Secundo folio *quod fuerint denunciati*.

Written in England. Erased inscriptions, s. xv, on f. 257, 'Liber Iohannis [. . . . . .]' and two lines which have been read, almost certainly rightly, as 'Liber venerabilis in cristo patris et domini domini thome bekynton Well' et baton episcopi': in the name the letters *th*, *b*, and *y* are visible. Bishop Bekynton died in 1465. No. 133 in T. Thorpe's catalogue for 1836. Phillipps MS. 9419. Phillipps sale at Sotheby's 21 Mar. 1896, lot 102, to Tregaskis. Bought from William C. Elly in 1926.

3. 175. *Epistolarium* s. xv¹

1. ff. 4–137ᵛ 'Lectio epistule beati pauli apostoli ad romanos'. Dominica 1ª in aduentu domini leccio ep' ad romanos. Fratres.' Scientes quia . . .

Temporale for the year from Advent. Marked later for reading with 'grave' accents, ticks, and more or less boxed-in crosses: so too, arts. 2–5.

2. ff. 138–63 Sanctorale for the year, beginning imperfectly.

The catchword on f. 137ᵛ is 'In festiuitate sancti thome'. The present first words 'et ibi dicetur tibi quid te oporteat facere' are in a lesson for the Conversion of Paul. Proper lessons for a few principal feasts only. English saints have cues only: ff. 143–144ᵛ Dunstan, Edburga, Botulph, 'Translacio sancte bege virginis et reliquiarum', with provision for lessons both 'ad missam matutinalem' and 'ad magnam missam' (other cued feasts are not so provided), Alban, Etheldreda; f. 153ᵛ Oswin; f. 155 translation of Hilda, Aidan, translation of Cuthbert; f. 156 translation of Egwin, octave of Cuthbert; f. 159 Bee (next before Quintin); f. 161 octave of Bee; f. 161ᵛ Hilda and octave; f. 163 Egwin. The last entry is a cue for Silvester, 31 Dec. An added cue, 'De sancto Willelmo' (William of

[1] I owe this information to Professor Siegfried Wenzel.

York, 8 June) on f. 144. 'papa' erased where it occurs, for example on f. 143ᵛ. f. 163ᵛ blank.

3. ff. 164–80 Common of saints.

4. f. 180ʳᵛ In dedicatione ecclesie.

5. ff. 180ᵛ–190 Commemorations, beginning with Holy Trinity.

Lessons for thirty occasions, the last Pro defunctis', and a cue (f. 186ᵛ) 'De reliquiis epistola Redde deus mercedem. Quere in festo plurimorum confessorum'.

6 (added). f. 190ᵛ A lesson from Song of Songs (2: 8 sqq.), ending imperfectly.

7. Binding leaves: (a) f. 3, a leaf of bk. 46 of Digestum Novum, s. xiii, with very wide margins and many notes in them; (b) ff. 191–2, two bifolia from a commentary on logic written in current anglicana, s. xiv.

(b). 2 cols. A section begins 'Sequitur de cadenti posicione qualis est hic ponatur'.

ff. iii+187+iii. For three of the end-leaves see above, art. 7: ff. 1ʳ, 193ᵛ were formerly pasted to the binding. Thick parchment. A medieval foliation i–xxvii on ff. 164–90. 245×160 mm. Written space 160×90 mm. 20 long lines. Collation of ff. 4–190: 1–5⁸ 6⁶ 7–12⁸ 13¹⁰ 14–16⁸ 17⁶ 18⁸ wants 1 before f. 138 19–20⁸ 21⁴ wants 4, probably blank, after f. 163 22–24⁸ 25 three (ff. 188–90). Large hand. Initials: (i) red and blue, with ornament of both colours; (ii, iii) 2-line and 1-line, blue with red ornament. Capital letters in the ink of the text filled with pale yellow. Medieval binding of wooden boards covered with pinkish leather: five bands: central strap and pin now missing. Secundo folio cumcisionis.

Written for use in the north of England, in a church with a special interest in SS. Bee and Hilda and probably relics of Bee. 'Item yᵗ I thomas dal[. . .]' and 'John Bakehows for a pond of pepe[r]', f. 2ᵛ, s. xvi. 'Nᵒ 8' and 'E libris Nathaniel C: S: Poyntz', f. 1ᵛ: his sale at Sotheby's, 30 June 1921, lot 691. Bought from William C. Elly, 6 Apr. 1926.

3. 236. J. de Mandevilla, etc.   s. xv med.

1. ff. 1–10ᵛ (begins imperfectly) gatur accipitur catulus . . . Per rachel aue interpretatur videns (ends imperfectly).

Expositions of biblical texts, with interspersed 'narraciones'. A new biblical theme at each paragraph, e.g. f. 9ᵛ Hortamur vos ne in vacuum graciam dei recipiatis 2 cor' 6. Ille in vacuum graciam dei recipit. . . .

2. ff. 11–12ᵛ (begins imperfectly) primus vocatur physon vel ganges quod idem est . . . Quem bona nulla augent nec malum aliquid diminuit Qui in claritate viuit et Regnat per infinita secula seculorum Amen.

The beginning is in ch. 44 of Mandeville's Travels. Ch. 45 begins 'De insulis vero illis supradictis in terra presbiteri Iohannis' and ch. 46, the last, 'In redeundo autem de terra illa ad x dietas'. The text is of the 'Leiden version' of which three copies are listed by M. C. Seymour, Mandeville's Travels, 1967, p. 273.¹

ff. i+12+i. 242×170 mm. Written space 183×120 mm. 2 cols. 43–5 lines. Collation: 1¹⁰ 2². One hand of mixed but mainly secretary type. Red initials. Capital letters in the

¹ I owe this information to Mr. Seymour.

ink of the text filled with pale yellow or with red. Binding of s. xix marked on the spine
'Regula Sacerdotum'.

Written in England. Part of a larger book. Scribbles on f. 12ᵛ include the date 24 Nov.
1492 and 'Ista est dat' Indent' Dauyd phelpot de Ewias lacy (now Longtown, Heref.)',
s. xv ex. Phillipps MS. 4439: sale 6 June 1898, lot 967. No. 528 in catalogue 159 of
George Gregory, bookseller, 5 Argyle St., Bath (c. 1904): his label on the pastedown.
Bought from the Revd. D. C. Jones in 1925.

3. 242 + 5.99, nos. i–vi (Hafod 16). *Medical texts, etc. (mainly in Welsh)*   s. xiv/xv

Report, p. 318. Written space 285 × 120 mm. 27 long lines. Belonged in 1644
to William David Barry of Pencoed in the parish of Llangrallo: p. 49, 'Llyma
lyfyr William Dauid Barry obencoed i mlhwyf llangrallo'; 5.99, no. ii 'Hoc MS.
continet 53 folia. 1644. Ex dono Wᵐ Da. Barry'. 'Tho. Wilkins 1701', 5.99,
no. vᵛ, is no doubt the signature of Thomas Wilkins, rector of Llantrisant,
Glamorgan, 1684–97, for whom cf. I. Foster in *Proceedings of the British Academy*, xxxvi (1950), 198.

The Welsh is printed by I. Williams in *Bulletin of the Board of Celtic Studies*, iv. 34–6,
by M. Richards, ibid. xiv. 186–90, and by Ida B. Jones in *Études Celtiques*, vii (1955),
46–75, 270–339; viii (1958), 66–97, 346–93.

Latin occurs in 3. 242, pp. 2–8, 19, 20, 41, 49–59, and French on p. 7.

1. pp. 2–6 A Welsh–Latin herb vocabulary, Anetum—Yperikon. The A, B
entries are on p. 6.

2. pp. 6–8 Recipes: (p. 6) Potus optimus ad omnia vulnera . . .; (pp. 6–7) Hec
est ars confisiendi pilas medicinales ad plagas. Hec olus vrtica . . . in corpore
plagis (12 lines of verse); (p. 7) Auence. Consont. la menne Fenoyl rouge . . .;
(p. 7) Vnguentum ad plagas omnes et ad eas pertinentes recipe pigle. bugle . . .
Vnguentum preciosissimum ad plagam et scabium. Recipe fumum terre. plant'
. . .; (p. 8) Si vis ut dentes cadant. Accipe granum . . .

3. pp. 19, 20 Five charms, all with headings in Welsh and all using Christian
formulae and names and beginning 'In nomine patris+ . . .': (*a*) Rac clefyt
ymynyd . . . In nomine patris+et filii+et spiritus sancti amen . . . defende
ihesu criste animalia N ab omni malo . . . oues boues vaccas vitulos . . .; (*b*) . . .
fugite fugite febres terciane cotidiane quaterne. Crucifixus sub poncio pilato
fugite fugite febres . . .; (*c*) . . . Migranium uel migranam adiuro uos per patrem
. . . vt vermes commedere dentes huius famuli dei N non possent . . .; (*d*) . . .
Aue uirgo mater decus mundi+felix+appollonia . . ., against toothache; (*e*) . . .
sanet te N et protegat te . . . ab omni malo . . . Pater noster. Credo in deum.

4. p. 41 Charms and a recipe: (*a*) (*last five words remain*) qui hanc herbam usus
fuerit; (*b*) Ter dicatur pater noster et Aue maria . . . Sanctus nicasius maculam
habuit in oculo et deprecatus est dominum ut quicumque nomen suum scriptum
super se portauerit maculam non haberet . . . Cristus uincit. cristus regnat.
cristus imperat. Dominus ihesus cristus defendat oculos tuos ab omni malo per
uirtutem sancte crucis . . . amen; (*c*) Quicumque uiderit aliquem cadentem in

continenti trahat sanguinem digiti auricularis pacientis et hec tria nomina regum scribat in fronte . . et postea scribe hos versus in p*a*rgameno. Iaspar fert aurum. thus melchior. satropo myrram. Hec quicumque trium. fert secum nomina regum. Soluitur a morbo domini pietate. caduco. Nomina regum scribantur ex sanguine eiusdem pacientis. Versus vero in incausto; (*d*) Pro dolore uentris. Accipe quinque folium . . .

(*b*). For similar charms invoking St. Nicasius see B. Dickins and R. M. Wilson, 'Sent Kasi', *Leeds Studies in English*, vi (1937), 72–3. (*c*). The verses are Walther, *Sprichwörter*, no. 2456 (Caspar . . .).

5. pp. 49–60 Charms, prognostications and commonplaces: (*a*) pp. 49–52 Pro peste ouium et omnium animalium. In primis dicatur salis et aque exorcismus sicut consueuit ecclesia dominicis diebus . . . Oremus. Presta domine per huius aspersionem aque . . . Rogamus te domine sancte pater omnipotens. vt angelus tuus excludat uanos terrores . . . Benedictionem tuam domine populus fidelis accipiat . . . tua beneficia semper inueniatur per d'; (*b*) Legitur in uita sancti bernardi . . .: heading relating St. Bernard's encounter with the devil, followed by his verses, ending imperfectly in the third; (*c*) pp. 53–4 Charms: (i) Nota contra fantasmata. ✠ In nomine patris . . . Salua redemptor plasma . . . liberet hunc f. tuum Will' ab omni genere fantasmatis nocte die; (ii) Contra morbum caducum. Si aliquis ceciderit cum forcipe scinde parum de mollice auris dextere masculi . . .; (iii) for toothache, In nomine . . . Qui liberauit susannam . . .; (iv) for fever, In portu galilee iacebat sanctus petrus . . .; (v) Contra qualemcumque guttam . . .; (vi) Si uis sanare unum leprosum . . .; (vii) pro omni dolore: invoking the Cross: ends imperfectly; (*d*) p. 55 Queritur quare omne animal . . .; (*e*) p. 56 Si quis in prima die vniuscuiusque mensis . . .: prognostications of disease, according to the day of the month; (*f*) p. 56 The number of bones (219) veins (362) and teeth (man 30, woman 32) in the human body; (*g*) pp. 57–8 Demones gaudent quando quis mortaliter peccat . . ., and fourteen other short paragraphs, some beginning Quare, for example 'Quare ponitur uinum in calice ante aquam'; (*h*) pp. 58–9 Hoc carmen est contra qualemcumque guttam. ✠ In nomine . . . Coniuro te guttam . . .: the prayer 'Deus qui es sanctorum tuorum splendor . . .' follows; (*i*) p. 59 Clara dies pauli bona tempora . . . (4 lines: Walther, no. 28224); (*j*) p. 59 In manus tuas . . . Aue maria . . . et benedictus sit venerabilis Iohachim pater tuus . . . Quicumque predictam oracionem deuote cotidie dixerit uidebit mariam uirginem ante obitum suum in auxilium eius preparatam; (*k*) pp. 59, 60 Commonplaces, including 'Virgo iohannes auis . . .' (4 lines, Walther, no. 20508) and 'Sero rubens celum cras indicat esse serenum. Et quod mane rubet venturos denotat vmbres' (Walther, *Sprichwörter*, no. 28113b).

Arts. 6–8 formed the cover of MS. 3. 242. They are now kept separately as MS. 5.99, nos. i–vi.

6. Nos. i–iv. A complete leaf (iv), the upper and lower halves of a nearly complete leaf (i, ii) and the lower half of a leaf (iii) of a Passionale written in England, s. xii/xiii. The written space of (iv) is 303 × 192 mm.: 2 cols. 46 lines. Flex punctuation (?) perhaps all added. Initials green, red, or blue.

The contents are lives of Ursinus (*a, b*), followed immediately by Ebrulfus (*c*); then Egwin (*d*) and Savinianus and Potentianus (*e*). They are all (?) in Hereford Cathedral P. vii. 6. The order of (*c–e*) could be the same as there where the series runs (*c*), Sabinus, (*e*), (*d*).

(*a*) no. i, *recto* (*begins imperfectly*) ceps a beatissimo ursino instructus . . . repromisit ihesus cristus dominus (*ends imperfectly, a few words missing*).

(*b*) no. i, *recto and verso* Biturica urbs p[rimum] a sancto ursino qui ab apostolis . . . uirtutibus manifestans.

(*c*) no. i *verso–ii verso* Incipit uita sancti ebrulfi abbatis quarto kalendas ianuarii. Igitur fuit uir quidam nobilis ab illustribus parentibus ortus . . . obnoxii et reprobi (*ends imperfectly*).

(*d*) no. iii, *recto and verso* (*begins imperfectly*) Longe prorsus . . . demum quos edidit [. . .]s. Explicit prologus. Incipit uita . . . eguuini episcopi et confessoris. iii kl' ianuarii. Temporibus regum ethelredi atque kenredi . . . (*ends imperfectly*).

(*e*) no. iv, *recto and vero* (*begins imperfectly*) imperio. Cumque idem scelestissimus imperator . . . qui euangelium annuntiant de e [. . .] (*ends imperfectly*).

(*a, b*). 9 Nov. *BHL*, nos. 8413, 8411. *AS*, Nov. iv, p. 114 sect. 9, 10, and p. 108. Running title 'Episcopi' on the recto. (*c*). 29 Dec. Cf. *BHL*, nos. 2374, 2377–8. (*d*). 30 Dec. *BHL*, no. 2433. The verso is barely legible. (*e*). 31 Dec. *BHL*, no. 7416 (?). The running title is 'Sanctorum Sauiniani' on the verso and 'Potentiani martirum' on the recto.

7. No. v. Part of a large leaf, 210×250 mm. 2 cols. 32+ lines. Written in England, s. xii/xiii. (*begins imperfectly*) tione narratur. cum tam bona nobis annuntietur . . . quam cogitare (*ends imperfectly*).

Augustine, Contra Faustum, end of bk. 2 and beginning of bk. 3. The first remaining words are at *PL* xlii. 213/16 and the last at 216/7.

8. No. vi. A leaf of a large book formerly used as the outside cover of 3. 242. Written space 310×210 mm. 2 cols. 49 (?+) lines. Written in England. s. xii ex.

A harmony of the Gospels with commentary. The texts treated are those in chapters 14, 15 of part 3 of the Harmony of Clement of Lanthony (Bodleian MS. Hatton 61, f. 29ᵛ) and the text corresponds to that on ff. 288ᵛ–289ᵛ of the only known copy of part 3, Winchester College 17, which was copied *c.* 1435 in Gloucester, no doubt from an exemplar belonging to Lanthony Abbey.

3. 244. *Ubertinus de Casali* s. xiv med.

(*Preface*) Vivo ego iam non ego . . . non abicio gratiam cristi. Paulus apostolus. verus cristi immitator . . . (f. 1ᵛ) virginis gloriose. Amen. Capitulum primum de trinitate in quo probatur quod filius a patre procedit. Ihesus ex patre genitus. Cum ihesum audis ex patre genitum. scilicet . . . (f. 201) sue crucis similitudini conformantur. Explicit quartus liber de uita cristi. deo gracias Amen.

Ubertinus de Casali, O.F.M., Arbor vitae crucifixae Iesu. As compared with edn. 1485, this copy lacks bk. 5 and the last three chapters of bk. 4. The books are in 11, 8, 24, and 49 chapters: bk. 2, the first leaf missing, f. 32; bk. 3, f. 53ᵛ; bk. 4, f. 129ᵛ. f. 201ᵛ blank.

ff. ii+201+ii. A series of contemporary letters and numbers in red make a kind of foliation: they begin with a3 on f. 2 and, with some irregularities, run to f27 on f. 201: new letters begin on f. 41 (b), 89 (c), 118 (d), 143 (e), 162 (f). 247×185 mm. Written space 170×125 mm. 2 cols. 54 lines. Collation: 1–2¹² 3¹² wants 8 after f. 31 4–16¹² 17¹⁰. Small hand. Initials: (i) of the preface and books: shaded pink or grey on gold grounds historiated and with decoration into the margins: a kneeling friar is in the damaged *S* on f. 1; (ii) of chapters, 3-line, blue with red ornament or red with violet ornament, but larger initials are on f. 21 (bk. 1, ch. 10: red and blue, with blue, red, and violet ornament) and f. 53ᵛ (gold on decorated red and blue ground). Binding of s. xix. Secundo folio *personarum.*

Written in Italy. Phillipps MS. 4440: sale at Sotheby's, 29 Mar. 1895, lot 1141. Charles Butler sale, 19 July 1921, lot 527. Bought from William C. Elly in 1928.

3. 516. *Versus grammaticales*

s. xv²

(*begins imperfectly*) Certat agonizans sibi tot verbalia claudens . . . Atque fenestri per hec nunc [. . . .] (*ends imperfectly*).

More than 5,000 lines of verse in sections of varying length, each concerned with a word or a group of words arranged in alphabetical order, according to the first two letters. At present the first four sections are on Agonizo, Agrimonia, Agamus, and Agea (6, 2, 3, 1 lines) and the last on Speculum. On p. 213, in the section Po-, the names of eighteen kinds of apple are glossed by the main hand in English.

Later notes and scribbles: p. 229, s. xv/xvi, memoranda of monies received for masses, dirges, and obits, for example 'Item for to pray for a wife iiii d' ', 'Item a nobett at menhed ix d' ', 'Item a nobett at porloc vi d' '; p. 61, s. xvi, 'Nouerint uniuersi per presentes nos Morganum Pill' nauclerum . . . et miricke gregor'.

ff. iv+130 (paginated)+vi. Paper. 220×148 mm. Written space *c.* 160×90 mm. 22 long lines. Collation impracticable. A current mixture of secretary and anglicana. 2-line red initials. The contemporary parchment wrapper is included in a rebinding by W. H. Smith & Son, s. xx, as pp. (261–4).

Written in England. In north Somerset, s. xv/xvi. Bought from the Revd. D. C. Jones, Aberdare, in 1936.

3. 717. *Missale*

s. xiv/xv

1. ff. i–viii Calendar, 28 lines to the page. All entries in black.

Lyons is mentioned in ten entries: 24 Apr., 'Lu(g)d' Alexandri et sociorum eius'; 25 Apr., 'Marci euangeliste. Lugd' Rustici episcopi et confessoris'; 6 June 'Agobardi episcopi conf' Lugd' '; 28 June, 'Lugd' Hyrenei et soc' eius'; 12 July, 'Lugd' Viuentonli episcopi'; 4 Aug., 'Lugd' Aduentus sancti iusti de heremo'; 2 Sept., 'Translacio sancti Iusti episcopi Lugd' '; 12 Sept., 'Sacerdotis Lugd' episcopi'; 26 Sept., 'Lugd' Lupi episcopi et ancorite'; 29 Sept., 'Lugd' Annemundi episcopi'. 'Dedicacio S. Stephani', 15 Sept. f. viiiᵛ blank.

Additions in a current hand in French refer to damage to vines in 1543 'sur toutes les vignes du mandement' (f. i), in 1544 (f. iiiᵛ), and in 1549 'dans le mandement de St. Chamond' (f. ivᵛ).

2. ff. 1–137ᵛ, 143–82 Temporale from Advent to the Saturday after the octave of Pentecost.

Litanies on ff. 131, 134, 136: eight virgins, f. 136ᵛ, Petronilla, Anna, Simphorosa, Eugenia, Basilla, Domitilla, Emelia, Leonilla.

3. ff. 137ᵛ–143 Preface for Easter, ordinary, and canon of mass.

4. ff. 182ᵛ–228 Sanctorale from 14 Apr. (Tiburtius, Valerian, and Maximus) to 21 Dec. (Thomas Apostle).

Includes proper of Photinus et soc. and of Ireneus.

5. ff. 228–229ᵛ Lection for SS. Simon and Jude, office in commemoration of Holy Cross, two prayers 'ad cruces benedicendas', and office in commemoration of B.V.M.

6. ff. 229ᵛ–272 Temporale from the first Sunday after the octave of Pentecost to Friday before the first Sunday in Advent.

7. ff. 272–82 Common of saints.

8. Masses 'De trinitate' (f. 282), 'Ad sponsas' (f. 282ᵛ), 'In dedicatione ecclesie' (f. 284ᵛ) and 'In agenda mortuorum' (f. 285ᵛ).

9. ff. 287ᵛ–294 Collect, secret, and postcommunion of twenty-five votive masses.

10. ff. 294–7 Masses for the dead.

11. f. 297 Missa votiua.

Lections only from Isaiah (1: 16–19) and Mark (11: 22–6).

12. ff. 297ᵛ–298 Missa de corpore cristi. f. 298ᵛ blank.

ff. 306, foliated i–viii, 1–298. A medieval foliation, i–cclxxxxvii on ff. 1–288, repeats 'lxvii' and skips from 'lxxix' to 'lxxxx'. 245 × 185 mm. Written space 175 × 132 mm. 2 cols. 28 lines. Collation: 1–38⁸ 39². A picture of the Crucifixion, 75 × 55 mm, on f. 140. Initials: (i) f. 140, *T* of *Te igitur*, gold on coloured ground, with half-page border; (ii) red and blue: ornament on f. 1 only (red and the ink of the text); (iii, iv) 2-line and 1-line, red or blue. Capital letters in the ink of the text lined with red. Binding of s. xviii, labelled on the spine 'Missel de Lyon fin xiv siècle'. Secundo folio (f. 2) *tenti celestibus*.

Written in France for use in the diocese of Lyons. Probably in use in s. xvi¹ in or near St. Chamond, twenty miles south-west of Lyons: cf. art. 1. 'Yd. 7' inside the cover, s. xviii?; also a slip from an English sale catalogue, s. xix/xx. Sotheby sale, 22 Feb. 1921, lot 394. Bought in 1945 from the executors of F. E. Andrews of Cardiff.

3. 833. *Defensor, etc.*   s. XIII²

1. ff. 1–46 Huius libri qui bene poterit uocari scintillarius siue exortarius. primi capituli tractatus incipit . . . (*table of eighty-one chapters*) . . . (f. 1ᵛ) De caritate. Dominus dicit in euangelio. Maiorem caritatem nemo habet . . . nutritur ac pascitur.

Defensor of Ligugé, Scintillarium. *Clavis*, no. 1302. *CC* cxvii. 2–234, ed. H. M. Rochais: he lists many manuscripts, but not this one, in *Scriptorium*, iv (1950), 294. Probably twenty leaves are missing in gaps after ff. 8, 17, 19, 36. A tail of miscellaneous pieces, arts. 2–8, seems to be counted in with art. 1, to judge from the *explicit* of art. 8.

2. (*a*) f. 46 De sacramento altaris. Qui uero de sacramento altaris . . . (*b*) f. 46ᵛ De fide eiusdem sacramenti. Fides inquid nostras questio hec transcendit . . .

3. ff. 47ᵛ–48ᵛ De xv signis. Ieronimus in annalibus ebreorum . . . longe ante defunctis.

Cf. BL, Royal 7 D. xvii, art. 23.

4. f. 48ᵛ De x plagis egipti. Prima plaga egipti limphas in sanguine uertit . . . primordia truncat (10 lines).

Walther, no. 14585.

5. ff. 48ᵛ–50 Quedam apices: (a) Quicumque fidelium pro dei nomine . . .; (b) In nomine sancte et indiuidue trinitatis cum in procreacione . . .; (c) G. et A. karissimis fratribus et amicis suis G. in domino corporis et anime salutem. Auditu uestri lupi captu . . .; (d) Puer ille falsitatis et fraudis et turpitudinis nutritus . . .; (e) Quoniam te pater uenerabilis prelatu(m) et magistrum nostrum et esse scimus.ʹ et scientes corde letamur . . .

(a) and (b) are forms of manumission and dower. (c) is on a dispute between Comes and Episcopus.

6. ff. 50–5 Regule tyconii. Caute sane legendus est tractatus iste tyconii . . . Primo de domino et eius corpore . . . que dominus donauerit disseramus.

Augustine, De doctrina Christiana, iii. 30–7 (PL xxxiv. 82–90).

7. (a) ff. 55–56ᵛ De exposicione ciuitatis dei. Sanctus Iohannes qui supra pectus domini . . . et uiuunt in deo. (b) ff. 56ᵛ–58ᵛ De exposicione xii lapidum. Primus iaspis ponitur . . . inuisibiliter operante.

(a) and (b) on Apocalypse, 21.

8. Commonplaces: (a) f. 58ᵛ De locis predicacionum apostolicarum; (b) f. 59 De quibusdam ponderibus; (c) f. 59 De differenciis narracionum. Synalimpha est . . . Prosa est . . . Historia est . . . Fabule sunt . . . quia contra naturam est. Explicit liber exhortacionum feliciter.

9. ff. 61–149ᵛ Liber magistri iohannis belet de ecclesiasticis officiis. In primitiua ecclesia . . . tandem in celis coronemur. Amen. Explicit liber Magistri Iohannis beleth.

As Bodleian, MS. Bodley 196, ff. 82–116. A different version printed in PL ccii. 13–166. A quire missing after f. 124 contained the text in MS. 196, ff. 106–8ᵛ (cf. edn., cols. 126A–135D). A table of 182 unnumbered chapters stands before the text, ff. 59ᵛ–60ᵛ. A table of the seven deadly sins and their branches is in the blank space on f. 149ᵛ.

10. ff. 150–64 Summa magistri stephani de langedonʹ archiepiscopi de uiciis et virtutibus. Septem sunt peccata criminalia. gula Luxuria. Auaricia. Superbia. Inuidia. Ira. Tristicia. Et dicuntur criminalia.ʹ quia digna sunt uituperio et correpcione . . . Ad hec expectantur.ʹ de quibus nupcie impleantur.

Sections on the sins, Gula—Tristitia, are followed (f. 161) by others on the seven gates of death and of life, on the pains of hell and the joys of heaven.

11. ff. 164–6 Theological notes in six paragraphs, the first beginning Non numerositas operum. non diuturnitas temporum augent meritum. Set maior caritas et melior uoluntas. f. 166ᵛ left blank.

ff. iv+166+iii. ff. 61–80 have a late medieval foliation, 'ffo. primo'—'ffo. xix°'. 205 ×
145 mm. Written space 135 × 90–98 mm. 2 cols. 29 lines. Collation: 1–2⁸ 3 four (ff. 17–
20: the outermost and the innermost sheets) 4–5⁸ 6–7¹² 8–17⁸ 18¹⁰ wants 10, probably
blank, after f. 149 19¹⁰ 20¹⁰ wants 8–10, probably blank. Quires numbered at the beginning
in pencil. The numbers show that single quires are missing after ff. 8, 36, 124 and suggest
that arts. 10, 11 originally followed art. 8: i, iii–vi, viii, (ix) on quires 1–7 (ff. 1–60); i–viii,
x–xii on quires 8–18 (ff. 61–149); x, xi on quires 19, 20 (ff. 150–66). Initials: (i) beginning
arts. 1, 9, 10, red and blue, with ornament of both colours; (ii) red or blue, with ornament
of the other colour; (iii) 1-line, red or blue. Capital letters in the ink of the text marked
with red. Binding of s. xviii. Secundo folio *sine uia*.

Written in England. 'L[. . . . .] qui ipsum alienauerit.' Anathema
sit Amen', f. 1, s. xiii ex., partly erased. The presence both here and in MS. 1. 381, ff. 81–
146 (q.v.) of notes, pointers, and foliation in an unusual hand of s. xvi in. suggests that
the erased words were an ex-libris of the nunnery of Barking: traces of 'Liber sancte
Adelburge de' can be made out. 'Sum ex libris Ioannis Lewkenor Oxonii Anno Dom 1639',
f. 166ᵛ. 'Nathaniel C: S: Poyntz', f. iᵛ: his sale at Sotheby's, 30 June 1921, lot 555.

4. 234. *Ludolphus de Saxonia, Vita Christi* s. xv²

Twenty-two leaves, mainly bifolia in no order, of a copy of the Vita Christi of
Ludolph of Saxony, O.F.M.

'Incipiunt capitula secundi libri de vita ihesu cristi qui continet historiam ab anno xxxi°
usque ad annum tricesimum secundum inclusiue etc' ', f. 3: the chapters listed here are
nos. 62–92 of part 1 in the edition printed at Paris in 1509. A table of Sunday gospels 'in
libro de vita ihesu cristi expositorum et signatorum' follows the table of chapters.

ff. ii+22+iv, foliated 1–28. 300 × 210 mm. Written space 200 × 140 mm. 2 cols. 40 and
42 lines. ff. 3, 4, ff. 5, 6 and ff. 7, 8 are the outside bifolia of the first three quires of bk. 2,
as catchwords show. Ugly set hybrida. Initials: (i) f. 3, beginning bk. 2, 9-line, blue
patterned in white on a red and gold ground, with gold frame; (ii) 4-line, red or blue
patterned in white; (iii) 2-line, red. Capital letters in the ink of the text marked with red.
A border on three sides of f. 3. Binding of s. xix: cf. below.

Written in the Netherlands. Probably strengthening leaves inside the parchment wrapper
of a register of the Benedictine nunnery of Munsterbilsen in the diocese of Liège. The
wrapper, now ff. 25, 26, has on its first leaf the words 'Register von Kitmenden (?) Anno
1390' and 'Munsterbilsen pro Capitulo' in a hand probably of s. xvii.

4. 271. *Expositio in Psalterium; Opuscula Johannis Gerson; etc.*

1455

1. ff. 2–177 In primis considerandum est quod beatus Augustinus doctor
egregius in tractatus sui principio super psalterium hanc commendacionem . . .
(f. 4) Beatus vir . . . Impius est qui peccat in deum . . . post hanc vitam misera-
bilem consequi valeamus eternam. Ad quam nos perducat Ihesus cristus in
secula seculorum Amen. Et sic est finis huius operis. In die Vitalis martyris
Anno etc. lv etc. de quo sit deus benedictus in secula.

The attribution on the spine, s. xix, 'Jacobi Tarellay Exp. in Psalmos', is likely to be without authority.

Arts. 2–5, 8, 10, 11 are by or ascribed here to Jean Charlier de Gerson.

2. ff. 178–192ᵛ Prologus in tractatum De discrecione peccatorum quando

venalia sunt et quando mortalia. Qui quidem Tractatus originaliter a domino
Cancellario parisiensis ligwa gallica compillatus set a quodam alio aliter qualiter
in Latinum translatus etc. Qui attencius dei omnipotentis erga genus humanum
. . . eius misericordia Amen.

Apparently not the translation in edn. du Pin (1706), ii. 486–504. The French original is
no. 328 in the edition by Glorieux.

3. ff. 192ᵛ–208 Tractatus Cancellarii 'scilicet Parisiensis' de articulis fidei et
decalogo et confessione. Cristianitati suus qualiscumque zelator . . . laudabiliter
obseruatur et sic est finis. Explicit Tractatus seu opus Tripartitum de decem
preceptis et viciis capitalibus Editum a magistro Iohanne Gerson Cancellario
parisiensis.

Edn. du Pin, i. 427–50. The French original is no. 312 in the edition by Glorieux.

4. ff. 208–14 Sequitur nunc Tractatus de Veneracione ymaginum etc. Cum
nonnulli homines impii ymagines etc. et beate virginis et aliorum sanctorum non
solum negant esse venerandas . . . honoramus. Qui est benedictus in secula
seculorum Amen. Explicit Tractatus de veneracione ymaginum.

Attributed to Gerson by the main hand in the running title.

5. ff. 215–19 Sequitur Tractatus de arte audiendi confessiones hominum. Ne
si uirtus quam assuefacio . . . et perficiat. Et sic est finis huius tractatus de Arte
audiendi confessionem.

Edn. du Pin, ii. 446–53.

6. ff. 219ᵛ–221 Agamus nunc interim quod natura et ymitatrix nature Ars
solent nos . . . Expliciunt doctrine diffinitio. Secuntur alie doctrine secundum
alium modum.

7. ff. 221–48 De preceptis decalogi. Ea que precepit deus illa cogita . . . et
affectu dicenda est et sic est finis.

On the ten commandments, the seven deadly sins, the Lord's Prayer, etc.

8. ff. 248–50 Sequitur tractatus eiusdem cancelarii de Remediis contra reciduum
in peccata multum vtilis. Habet hoc proprium ars quelibet ut facilior compendio
ad finem ducit optatum . . . sciencia etas.

9. ff. 250ᵛ–256ᵛ Tractatulus de hoc nomine Ihesus vnicum habens partem. Et
vocabis nomen eius ihesus Luce primo. Hoc nomen ihesus . . . Et sic est finis
huius tractatus de hoc nomine ihesus etc.

10. ff. 256ᵛ–258ᵛ Tractatus Cancellarii Parisiensis de efficaci oracione Extractus
de quodam sermone eiusdem doctoris facti in concilio constanciensi etc. Sit
oracio vel obsecracio . . . et domina nature etc. Et sic est finis huius tractatuli etc.

From the sermon preached at Constance, 21 Apr. 1415: edn. Glorieux, v. 401/1–405/21
(part of no. 235).

11. ff. 258ᵛ–261 Sequitur Epistola doctrinalis et velud practica de modo orandi
quam misit Cancellarius sororibus suis in ydeomate gallico taliter introductam
in latinum. Sororibus meis in cristo dilectissimis Iohannes frater uester Salu-

tem in domino ... Non modice gauisus sum ... faciliter obtineat Quod prestare dignetur omnipotens amen. Explicit Epistola doctrinalis edita a reuerendo patre ac domino domino Iohanne de gersamio Cancellario Ecclesie Parisiensis In Sacra Pagina professore eximio. Sit timor in dappibus leccio benediccio tempus Sermo breuis wltus hylaris pars detur egenis Absint delicie murmur detraccio rixe finito cibo reddantur gracia cristo.

The French original is no. 1* in the edition by Glorieux. The verses are Walther, no. 18347.

ff. i+262+i, foliated 1–149, 149*, 150–263. Paper. 315×215 mm. Written space 215× 148 mm. 2 cols. 39–41 lines. Frame ruling. Collation of ff. 2–262: 1–9¹² 10¹⁰ 11–22¹². Ugly hybrida. Initials: (i) c. 12-line, blue with red ornament, f. 2: others of this size not filled in; (ii) 3-line, red. Capital letters in the ink of the text touched with red. Binding of s. xix. Secundo folio doctorem.

Written in Germany. 'Finitus est liber Iste Per manus Cunradi Nesselhauff Anno domini etc. lvᵗᵒ etc. In crastino bonifacii (6 June?) etc.', f. 261: cf. art. 1, finished by the same scribe on 28 Apr. of the same year. In P. M. Barnard's catalogue 141, item 189: bought from him in 1924.

4. 332. *Pontificale romanum* s. xv med.

1. ff. 1–15ᵛ (*begins imperfectly*) primam tonsuram debent habere parati sup-pellicia ... R'. Deus meus sperantes in te. V'. Esto (*ends imperfectly: catch-word* eis).

The order of conferring orders. The first leaf is missing and the first words now come in a long rubric before a formula read by the notary, 'Reuerendus in cristo pater et dominus N dei et apostolice sedis gratia episcopus talis mandat omnibus hic presentibus qui uenerunt pro ordinibus suscipiendis . . .' and the prayer 'Oremus dilectissimi fratres dominum nostrum [Iesum cristum] pro hiis famulis tuis qui ad deponendam . . .'. The end now is in cues following the direction 'Hiis itaque factis genuflectentibus omnibus episcopus bona uoce incipit ymnum sequentem. Veni creator...': cf. Andrieu, *Pont. Rom.* ii. 346.

The form of ordination of a deacon contains a litany, f. 10: ten confessors, Silvester Cerbone Leo Gregori Martine Benedicte Maure Bernarde Antoni Dominice. Two quires are missing between art. 1 and art. 2.

2. ff. 16–23 (*begins imperfectly*) orationem. Aufer a nobis domine iniquitates nostras . . . cum sanctis omnibus gloriemur.

Cf. ibid. ii. 432–40 (no. xxiii, Ordo ad benedicendam ecclesiam). The last form is the postcommunion 'Multiplica quesumus . . .' (ii. 440).

3. ff. 23–8 In Reconciliatione uiolate ecclesie sunt tantum necessaria ysopus sal cinis cribanus uinum et aqua. Primo veniat episcopus ... Oratio. [O]mnipotens sempiterne deus [qui sacerdoti]bus . . .

Cf. ibid. ii. 443 (no. xxvi).

4. ff. 28–30ᵛ Consecratio lapidis itinerarii. indutus episcopus. et cum mitra vel saltim cum rocheto et stola . . . [D]eum patrem omnipotentem [uotis exultantibus deprece]mur ut qui super omnem mundum . . .

Nearly as ibid. ii. 445–8 (βγ version). Ends 'Hac benedictione facta . . . in piscinam'.

5. Benedictions of vestments and vessels: (a) ff. 30ᵛ–31 Benedictio planete dalmatice stole et aliarum uestialium sacerdotum. [O]mnipotens sempiterne deus qui [per moysen famu]lum tuum . . .; (b) f. 31ʳᵛ Benedictio stole. Domine deus omnipotens qui ab initio in omnibus (sic) . . . immortalitate uestiri; (c) f. 31ᵛ Benedictio corporalium. Clementissime domine cuius . . .; (d) ff. 31–2 Benedictio patene. Consecramus domine et sancti+ficamus . . .; (e) f. 32ʳᵛ Consecratio calicis. Dignare domine calicem hunc in usum ministerii tui . . .

(a). Two prayers, as ibid. ii. 451 (no. xxxiii). (c–e). Ibid. 449–50 (nos. xxx, xxviii, xxix).

6. ff. 32ᵛ–37ᵛ Incipit ordo romane curie qualiter agendum sit feria quinta in cena domini. Statio ad sanctum iohannem lat'. Hac die sacrifitium . . . (f. 34) dicat plana uoce. Exorcizo te inmundissime spiritus . . . deinde diaconus dicat Ite missa est.

Cf. ibid. ii. 455–63 (no. xlii. 1–30). The 'Benedictio balsami. Deus misteriorum celestium . . .' (ibid. iii. 576) is added in a semi-humanist hand at the foot of ff. 34ᵛ–35.

7. ff. 37ᵛ–47ᵛ In consecratione virginum. In die precedenti consecrationis . . . archipresbiter dicat alta uoce. Reuerende pater postulat . . . (f. 47ᵛ) Uide amodo quod istas . . . uiuit et regnat deus per.

Cf. ibid. iii. 412–23 (I. xxiii. 7–56).

8. ff. 47ᵛ–51 Ordo ad benedicendum abbatem. et est sciendum quod abbates qui eliguntur per dominum papam . . . interrogat episcopus. Karissime frater quia gratia dei . . . cum baculo pastorali.

9. f. 51ʳᵛ Incipit benedictio abbatisse. omnia que dicuntur in abbate . . . Domine deus omnipotens qui sororem moysi . . . ad sedendum cum eisdem uerbis.

10. ff. 51ᵛ–54 Missa coniugi siue sponsi et sponse. Int'. Dominus sit vobiscum . . . in secula seculorum amen.

11. ff. 54–59ᵛ Ordo ad consecrandum cymiterium de nouo. In primis benedicat episcopus . . . et dicat hanc orationem, Benedicere digneris omnipotens deus piissime . . . (f. 59) Domine sancte pater omnipotens eterne deus locorum omnium . . . occurrant. Per eum. Hec idem oratio dicatur etiam in reconciliatione cimiterii.

12. ff. 59ᵛ–60ᵛ Incipit ordo ad reconsiliandum Cimiterium uiolatum. In primis benedicatur aqua uinum sal cinis . . . dicit orationem. Deus qui agrum figuli . . . super hoc cimiterium. Amen.

In Durand's pontifical the prayer begins Domine pie qui agrum (ibid. iii. 512).

13. f. 60ᵛ Benedictio ymaginis beate marie semper uirginis. Deus qui per moysen famulum tuum cherubin obumbrantia . . . consequatur. Qui uiuis.

14. (a) ff. 60ᵛ–63ᵛ Episcopus celebraturus cum peruenerit ad sacrarium sedens in sede sua dicat cum ministris infrascriptos psalmos. Quam dilecta tabernacula . . . Conscientias nostras . . . mansionem. Qui tecum. (b) ff. 63ᵛ–65ᵛ Quando episcopus induit se sacris indumentis dicat sequentes orationes. Ad calligas induendas. Indue me domine calligis rectitudinis . . . Ad tertia(m) lotionem.

Purum et mundum . . . me custodiat. Hec ultima oratio dicitur in qua(r)ta et ultima lotione manuum.

(*a*). Pss. 83, 84, 115, 129. (*b*). Seventeen prayers.

16. ff. 65ᵛ–66 De sacramento confirmationis paruulorum . . . . Omnipotens sempiterne deus qui regenerare . . . Pa+ter et fi+lius et spiritus + sanctus amen.

Cf. Andrieu, *Pont. Rom.* ii. 452–3 (no. xxxiv. 2–6).

17. f. 66ʳᵛ Benedictio lapidis primarii. Benedictio lapidis pro ecclesia hedificanda. Primo benedicatur . . . Benedic domine . . . percipiat.

Ibid., ii. 420–1 (no. xxii).

18. ff. 66ᵛ–67ᵛ Benedictio peregrinantium. Domine ihesu criste qui tua ineffabili . . . eternam acquirant. Per.

Ibid. ii. 418–20 (no. xx. 1–4).

19. f. 67ᵛ Benedictio cricis (*sic*) noue. Oratio. Benedic + domine hanc crucem . . . inimicorum. Per dominum.

Ibid. ii. 450 (no. xxxi. 1, 2).

20 (in a smaller hand). ff. 67ᵛ–72ᵛ Benedictions of things: (*a*) Benedictio ymaginis gloriosissime uirginis marie; (*b*) Benedictio armorum et uexilli belli; (*c*) Benedictio mapparum siue linteaminum sacri altaris; (*d*) Benedictio turibuli; (*e*) Benedictio capsarum petre (*cancelled*) 'pro' reliquiis et aliis sanctuariis conseruandis; (*f*) Benedictio baptisterii siue lapidis fontium; (*g*) Benedictio crucis imponende profisiscentibus in subscidium terre sancte; (*h*) Benedictio noue domus que hoc modo benedicetur; (*i*) Benedictio noui putei.

As bk. 2 of Durand's pontifical, chapters 13, 38, 10, 15, 18, 21, 30, 33, 35 (ibid. iii. 525–49), but usually without the introductory rubrics provided there.

f. 73ʳᵛ was left blank. The verso has a mnemonic, s. xv ex., 'Ad inueniendum pasc' Ebreorum et christianorum. Esse grauem nobis bello . . . cum religiosis' (eighteen words in three lines of verse), followed by eleven lines of explanation.

ff. vii+73+iv. ff. v–vii are medieval end-leaves. Traces of a medieval foliation 36–93 on ff. 16–73. 314 × 212 mm. Written space 185 × 128 mm. 2 cols. 26 lines. Collation: 1⁸ wants 1 2–9⁸ 10². Quires 1–9 signed a, b, e–l. Initials: (i) 6-line: a pink and green *R* edged with gold and historiated—a virgin kneels before her bishop—is on f. 38: initials probably of a similar kind have been cut from art. 1 (ff. 1ᵛ, 4, 5ᵛ, 6, 7ᵛ, 9ᵛ, 13ᵛ: *O, H,*[1] *E, A, S, D, S*) and from arts. 3–5 (ff. 23ᵛ, 28ᵛ, 30ᵛ: *O, D, O*); (ii) 2-line, red or blue, with ornament of the other colour. Rebound in 1957: the former binding was 'old yellow vellum'. Secundo folio (f. 1) *primam tonsuram.*

Written in Italy: Cerbonius, art. 1, suggests Tuscany. 'T. Hobart', f. v. 'Nᵒ 104', f. iii. HMC, *Fourth Report* (1874), Appendix, p. 349, no. 68 of the manuscripts of Lord Mostyn. Mostyn sale, 13 July 1920, lot 95, to J. and J. Leighton (£9. 9s.). Bought from Leighton in 1920.

---

[1] The *L* of *Lectorem* should follow the *H* of *Hostiarium*, but the usual form of words was omitted in the text on f. 4ᵛ, and added later in the margin: Lectorem opportet . . . Cum mitria dicat.

4. 333. *Cicero, De inventione rhetorica* s. XV med.

Incipit liber Rhetorice ueteris Tullii Marci Ciceronis. Sepe et multum hoc mecum cogitaui . . . que restant in reliquis dicemus. Explicit liber Rhetorice ueteris Ciceronis Marci Tillii (*sic*) Amen.

Scholia in the margins and interlinear glosses are fairly numerous.

ff. i+54+i. Paper. 305×218 mm. Written space 210×115 mm. 30 long lines. Collation: 1¹² 2–4¹⁴. Written in textura. Initials: (i) f. i, 7-line, red and blue; (ii) 2-line, red. Capital letters in the ink of the text filled with pale yellow at first, but marked with red from f. 16ᵛ. Binding of s. xix. Secundo folio *dacio*.

Written in Italy. Lot 254 and lot 48 in sales, s. xix and s. xix/xx; the relevant slips are attached to the pastedown and to f. i. Book-plate 'Henrici Alani', s. xix. Bought in 1920 from Leslie Chaundy.

4. 586. *Missale cum notis* s. XIV med.

The remains of a Sarum missal, lacking all before the Sanctorale and probably seventeen leaves thereafter. Rubrics differ from those in *Sarum Missal* and *Manuale Sarum*.

1. ff. 1–52ᵛ Sanctorale through the year from the vigil of Andrew to Katherine.

Probably eleven leaves are missing and the outer half of f. 9 has been removed. The word 'papa' erased, for example, on f. 31ᵛ. Collect, secret, and postcommunion for the translation of Thomas of Canterbury on f. 27: only the collect has been scratched out.

2. ff. 52ᵛ–74 Common of Saints. Two leaves missing.

3. ff. 74–84 Votive masses of Holy Trinity, Holy Spirit, Holy Cross, in commemorations of B.V.M., Pro fratribus et sororibus, De angelis, *In commemoratione omnium sanctorum* (three forms), *Pro papa* (this heading and the collect erased), *Pro uniuersali ecclesia*, Pro pace, *Pro episcopo, Pro prelatis et subditis, Pro rege, Pro rege et regina, Pro semetipso, Pro salute amici, Pro speciali amico, Contra temptationes carnis, Contra malas cogitationes, Ad inuocandam gratiam sancti spiritus, Pro petitione lacrimarum, Contra mortalitatem hominum, Pro penitente, Contra aereas potestates, Pro inspirante diuine sapiencie, Pro eo qui in vinculis tenetur, Pro tribulatione cordis, Ad poscendum donum trinitatis, Pro nauigantibus, Contra invasores ecclesie, Pro benefactoribus vel salute viuorum,* Ad pluuiam postulandam, Pro serenitate aeris, Pro peste animalium, Pro iter agentibus, Pro infirmo, Pro quacumque tribulacione, In tempore belli, Pro pace (*as above*), Pro peccatis, Pro salute amici, Pro semetipso, *De sanctis katerina margareta et maria magdalena, Missa generalis pro uiuis.*¹

4. ff. 84–85ᵛ Ordo ad faciendum sponsalia.

Four leaves (?) missing after f. 85.

5. f. 86 (*begins imperfectly*) de uinculis Amen. Sicut liberasti . . . ab omnibus angustiis animi.

The last words of the Commendatio animae in articulo mortis, *Manuale Sarum*, p. 118

¹ Italics show the texts consisting of collect, secret, and postcommunion only.

6. ff. 86–7 Hic incipit commendatio anime. R'. Subuenite . . .

Manuale Sarum, pp. 119–24.

7. ff. 92–4 Post missam dicant duo fratres . . . ant' Circumdederunt . . .

Office of burial, *Manuale Sarum*, pp. 152–61.

8. ff. 94–95ᵛ Omnibus dominicis quando de dominica agitur extra tempus pasche et tempus natalis usque domine ne in ira et nisi in dominica infra ascens' in hiis enim dicetur kyriel' ix leccionum pro disposicione cantoris dicitur unum istorum kyrie leyson . . .

Settings of Kyrie eleison for eleven occasions with some alternative forms, ending imperfectly in the kyrie at anniversaries and trentals and when the corpse is present.

ff. iii + 95 + iii. A pagination, s. xviii?, shows the disorder in which the leaves were formerly bound. 337 × 228 mm. Written space 258 × 165 mm. 2 cols. 39 lines. Collation: 1⁸ 2 five (ff. 9–13) 3–4⁸ 5⁸ wants 2 after f. 30 6⁸ 7⁸ wants 2–7 (ff. 45, 46) 8⁸ wants 1 9–10⁸ 11⁸ wants 4, 5 after f. 72 12⁸ 13 four (ff. 84–7) 14⁸: all leaves are now singletons. Well written. Initials: (i) ff. 1, 3ᵛ, 22, 35ᵛ, 43ᵛ, 52ᵛ (Andrew, Conception of B.V.M., John Baptist, Assumption and Nativity of B.V.M., and beginning art. 2), red or blue patterned in white on gold and coloured grounds with border ornament in red, blue, and a little gold, terminating in ivy leaves; (ii, iii) 2-line and 1-line, blue with red ornament; (iv) cadels with faint ornament. Capital letters in the ink of the text touched with pale yellow. A binding of 1958 replaced one of s. xix.

Written in England. The names 'Wisebeche' (s. xvi?: f. 4) and 'Thomas Carter' (s. xviii?) scribbled. The names 'P. Ranshaw' and 'G. G. Cook' in recent pencil and the armorial book-plate of Robert Chambers with motto Spero on f. iiiᵛ, s. xix. Bought from P. H. Barnard in 1929.

5.99. See 3.46 and 3.242.

CARDROSS. ST. PETER'S COLLEGE

1. *Horae* 1490

1. ff. 1–6ᵛ Calendar in red and black, rather empty.

Entries in red include Amandi et vedasti, Bonifacii martiris, Baselii archiepiscopi, Remigii et bauonis, Donaciani archiepiscopi, Nichasii episcopi (6 Feb., 5, 11 June, 1, 14 Oct., 14 Dec.). 'Maximiliani pont' et martiris' added at 12 Oct., s. xvi. 'Conceptio marie' in red at 8 Dec. has been scraped out.

2. ff. 7–11ᵛ Incipiunt hore sancte crucis. . . . Ymnus. Patris sapientia . . .

3. ff. 13–16ᵛ Incipiunt hore sancti Spiritus. . . . Ympnus. Nobis sancti spiritus . . .

4. ff. 17–20ᵛ Incipit missa de domina nostra. Et introibo ad altare dei . . .

5. ff. 21–24ᵛ Sequentiae of the Gospels.

6. ff. 25–6 Oratio deuota ad dominum ihesum cristum. O bone Ihesu. O dulcissime ihesu. o piissime ihesu . . . sanctum tuum. ihesum amen.

7. ff. 26–28ᵛ Oratio de domina nostra. Obsecro te . . . Et michi famulo tuo . . .

On f. 28ᵛ the words 'et in nouissimis diebus meis ostende michi faciem tuam et annuncies michi diem et horam obitus mei' have been crossed out.

8. ff. 28ᵛ–30 Oratio deuota ad dominam nostram. O intemerata . . . orbis terrarum. Inclina . . . et esto michi miserrimo peccatori . . .

On f. 30 the words 'Credo enim firmiter et fateor . . . dignitatis virtutem' have been crossed out.

9. ff. 30–32ᵛ Memoriae of SS. John Evangelist, Sebastian (heading only remains), Anthony hermit, Katherine, Barbara, Mary Magdalene.

A leaf missing after f. 30.

10. ff. 33–76ᵛ Hours of B.V.M. of the use of (Rome) beginning imperfectly.

Four leaves missing. A memoria of All Saints, 'Sancti dei omnes . . .', and a prayer for peace, 'Ut pacem tuam . . .', follow each hour. The 'Salutacio ad dominam nostram. Salue regina . . . Oratio. Omnipotens sempiterne deus . . .' follows compline (f. 69ʳᵛ). The office in Advent begins on f. 71.

11. ff. 77–89ᵛ Penitential psalms, beginning imperfectly, and (f. 83) litany.

Sixteen confessors: . . . (10–16) bernaerde francisce ludowice eligi egidi dominice liuine.

12. ff. 91–118ᵛ Incipiunt vigilie mortuorum.

Office of the dead. The prayer 'Partem beate resurrexionis . . .' at the end.

13. ff. 119–28 (begins imperfectly) ecclesie laudabo te . . . quoniam ego seruus tuus sum. Gloria. An'. Ne reminiscaris . . . Oratio. Omnipotens et misericors deus clementiam tuam . . . proficiat sempiternam. Per cristum dominum nostrum amen. 1490.

The Psalter of St. Jerome (Horae Ebor. 116–22), beginning at verse 17. f. 128ᵛ blank.

ff. 128. 170 × 115 mm. Written space 95 × 62 mm. 19 long lines. Ruling in red ink. Collation: 1⁶ 2–3⁸ 4⁸ wants 8 after f. 30 5⁸ wants 3 after f. 32 6–7⁸ 8⁸ wants 2 after f. 53 and 4 after f. 55 9⁸ wants 8 after f. 66 10⁸ 11⁸ wants 2 after f. 76 12–15⁸ 16⁸ wants 4 after f. 118+1 leaf after 8 (f. 123) 17⁶ wants 6, blank: together with three singleton picture pages, ff. 12, 70, 90. Three full-page pictures remain, f. 12ᵛ before art. 3, f. 70ᵛ before the Advent office in art. 10 (Annunciation), f. 90ᵛ before art. 12: rectos blank. Four 15-line pictures remain in art. 10; before lauds; before prime (f. 51ᵛ: a street scene, B.V.M., holding the ass on a string, the ox beside it, and Joseph, worried, carrying a basket, before a small entry gate; inside the gate a man in orange dress and blue turban holding a baby); before none (f. 59: death of B.V.M., five saints at her bed and a small tonsured figure with rosary facing out from it); before vespers (f. 62: ascension of B.V.M.). Fourteen smaller pictures, five in art. 9, four in art. 5 (St. Luke is painting a picture of B.V.M.) and one before each of arts. 4 (B.V.M. and Christ in glory), 6 (Christ, half length, with orb, blessing), 7 (Presentation in the temple), 8 (B.V.M. on temple steps, her parents below), and one before the Advent office in art. 10 (Mary and Joseph kiss). Initials: (i) ff. 7, 13, branchwork of gold paint and green, on pink grounds, historiated (Crucifixion and Ascension); (ii–iv) 4-line, 2-line, and 1-line, gold paint on blue or pink grounds, patterned in gold paint. Continuous framed borders of flowers, butterflies, birds (f. 30ᵛ), snails, strawberries on pages with full-page or 15-line pictures or initials of type (i): on f. 12ᵛ a man and a woman, she pushing a barrow on which is a basket of giant pinks: on f. 70^v three scenes from the life of B.V.M. Similar borders on three sides (not the outer margin) of pages with smaller pictures. Binding of red morocco, gilt, s. xvi: four ties missing. Secundo folio (f. 8) *Hora.*

Written in 1490, probably in western Flanders. Inside the cover are an erased inscription, a price-mark '£3. 3.', and an exhibition (?) label, 'On loan from *The Very Revd Monsignor Eyre June 6 1862*': the first three words and the first two digits of the year date are printed. Given by Charles Eyre (1817–1902, archbishop of Glasgow 1878). The college bookstamp, inscribed 'EX LIBRIS COLLEGII SANCTI PETRI GLASGUÆ' is on ff. 1, 3.[1]

CARLISLE. CATHEDRAL

Lives of Saints, etc. (in French) s. XIII med.

A legendary in French prose and verse—Picard dialect—described fully by R. Fawtier and E. C. Fawtier-Jones, 'Note sur un légendier français', *Romania*, l (1924), 100–10.

1. ff. 5–110 (quires 1–14) Lives in prose of the twelve apostles and St. Agnes, all known from other manuscripts (cf. especially B.N., fr. 686, ff. 449–525, where all but (*d*) and (*g–i*) occur): (*a*) f. 5 Disputacio sanctorum petri et pauli contra symonem magum (title from table of contents: first leaf missing); (*b*) f. 17^v Peter, imperfect owing to the loss of a quire after f. 19; (*c*) f. 21 Paul; (*d*) f. 30^v John the Evangelist; (*e*) f. 39 James the Greater; (*f*) f. 48^v Matthew; (*g*) f. 62^v Simon and Jude; (*h*) f. 77^v Thomas; (*i*) f. 92 Andrew (a leaf missing after f. 92); (*k*) f. 94 Philip; (*l*) f. 95^v James the Less; (*m*) f. 97^v Bartholomew; (*n*) f. 102^v Mark; (*o*) f. 104 Agnes; (*p*) f. 109^v 'piere as liiens'. ff. 110^v–111^v blank.

2. f. 112–133^v 'Vita sancti Alexis'. Collated by G. Paris in *Romania*, xvii (1888), 106–20.

3. ff. 134–139^v A version of the Dit de l'unicorne (Jubinal, *Nouveau receuil de contes*, 1842, ii. 113–23).

4. f. 139^v–144^v An extract from the Bestiaire Divin of Guillaume le Clerc, corresponding to lines 125–386 of the edition by C. Hippeau in *Mémoires de la Société des Antiquaires de Normandie*, xix (1852), 423–76 (Lion, Aptalos, Two stones).

5. f. 144^v–148 En lordre de Chistiaus estoit . . . ken paradis puissions aler. 171 lines of verse entitled in the table of contents 'Quod bonum est alta uoce in diebus sollempnibus in ecclesia decantare'.

6. ff. 148–164^v 'De s' Iehan bouchedor'. Used for the edition by H. Dirickx-van-der-Straeten, 1931. ff. 158–60 are damaged and fragmentary.

---

[1] The college, founded at Partickhill, Glasgow, in 1874, was moved to Bearsden in 1892 and to Cardross in 1948.

7. ff. 165–89 The first 1,404 lines of a life of St. Katherine, as in Arsenal MS. 3516 and other manuscripts: cf. E. C. Fawtier-Jones in *Romania*, lvi (1930), 81.

8. f. 3, a waste leaf from another manuscript, s. xiv, contains the first sixty-two lines of a verse romance in Picard dialect, telling the adventures of the son of Yolens, king 'en Gales', and his wife Andeluse, the daughter of the king of Denmark: Ki biaus mes set dire et reprendre . . .

A fragment of Durmant le Galois printed by J. Gildea in his edition (1965), p. 421, and in *Romania*, l. 103: cf. *Medium Aevum*, xxxvi (1967), 277–8.

f. 4ᵛ contains a table of contents in Latin, s. xiv. ff. 2, 191 are fragments of a never completed service-book, s. xiv.

ff. iv+185+iii, foliated 1–192. Medieval end-leaves: for ff. 2–4, 191 see above. ff. 1, 192 were formerly pastedowns. 165 × 120 mm. Written space *c*. 135 × 100 mm. Art. 1 in long lines and the rest in two columns. 24–8 lines to the page. Collation of ff. 5–189: 1⁸ want 1 2–11⁸ 12⁸ wants 2 after f. 92 13⁸ 14⁶ wants 6, probably blank, after f. 111 15¹⁰ 16–20⁸ 21⁴ (ff. 162–5) 22–24⁸. Quires 1–13 numbered at the end I, II, IIII–XIV in red. Quires 15–20 numbered at the beginning I–VI in black. Written in three hands: (1) art. 1; (2) arts. 2–6; (3) art. 7. Initials: in art. 1, red, sometimes with green ornament; in arts. 2–6, blue with red ornament, or red with green ornament; in art. 7, red with pale-brown ornament. Medieval binding of wooden boards covered with white leather, stained pink: central strap now missing, but the pin for it remains on the back cover. Secundo folio (f. 5) *vous estes*.

Written in northern France. In England by s. xvi, when someone scribbled on f. 110ᵛ 'he was not wyth a fley / he cald (?) hym wylkyn worddy'.

2. *Roman de la Rose (fragment: in French)* s. XIV in.

Eight leaves and 1,268 lines of the Roman de la Rose. In the edition by E. Langlois, Société des anciens textes français, 1914–24, they are lines 16653–828 (f. 1), 17795–954 (f. 2), 18755–19076 (ff. 3, 4), 19239–566 (ff. 5, 6) and 19891–20210 (ff. 7, 8).

Seems to agree with Langlois' *Ca*, for example at line 20145, 'Et fist tant as oisiaus de proie'. ff. 1–4, 6, 7 are complete. f. 5 lacks the top line and f. 8 the two top lines of text.

ff. 8. Written space 178 × *c*. 110 mm. 2 cols. 40 lines. Initials blue with red ornament or red with violet ornament. Kept in a folder.

Written in France. Formerly pastedowns in four volumes, apparently oblong in shape, *c*. 155 × 195 mm. Four of them bear the word 'Mercurius' (ff. 1ᵛ, 2ᵛ, 7ᵛ, 8) in a hand of s. xvii(?). 'James Pearson', f. 8, s. xvii/xviii. The folder bears the ex-libris of Carlisle Cathedral and the date 1866.

CARLISLE. ST. MARY'S CATHOLIC CHURCH, WARWICK BRIDGE[1]

Missale   s. xv med.

A Sarum missal described by Father Justin McCann in *Ampleforth Journal*, xxiv (1918), 1–10, 79–89, with much reduced facsimiles of pp. 49 and 220.

1. pp. 1–8 Graded calendar in red and black, lacking the first four months.
Includes the Visitation of B.V.M. The word 'pape' and feasts of St. Thomas have been blotted out.

2. pp. 9, 10 Benedictio salis et aque.

3. pp. 10–202 Temporale from Advent to Easter Eve.
The office of St. Thomas of Canterbury lined through, pp. 47–8.

4. pp. 202–30 Ordinary, prefaces, and canon of mass.

5. pp. 230–3 Rubrica de casibus diuersis et periculosis in missa contingentibus. Presbiter potest supplere missam . . . et vomitus eius comburetur ut supra dictum est.

6. (*a*) p. 233 Settings of Ite missa est. (*b*) pp. 233–4 De modo legendi lecciones ad missam. (*c*) pp. 234–5 In die pasche ante mat' et ante campanarum pulsationem . . .
(*a, b*) noted. (*c*). Directions for Easter procession.

7. pp. 235–328 Temporale from Easter to Sabbato quattuor temporum, ending imperfectly: one leaf missing.

8. pp. 329–31 Office of dedication of church, beginning imperfectly.

9. pp. 331–2 In reconsiliacione ecclesie officium.
As in edn., 1514.

9 (added in space left blank). p. 332 Lections of the common of saints (cf. art. 14)
Lections for a martyr, Wisdom 4: 7–11, 14, 15 and 2 Timothy 2: 8–10 and 3: 10–12.

10. pp. 333–432 Sanctorale, Andrew—Saturninus.
The office for the translation of St. Thomas of Canterbury has been crossed out on p. 380.

11. pp. 432–7 Ordo ad facienda sponsalia. No English.

12. pp. 437–9 Ordo ad seruicium peregrinorum faciendum.
pp. 440–4 were left blank at the end of quire 28 and were partly filled later with arts. 13, 14.

13 (added in s. xvi). pp. 440–1 Missa de commemoracione sancti Kentigerni.
In the hand which added to art. 15. Caldbeck was dedicated to St. Kentigern.

[1] On deposit at Ampleforth Abbey.

14 (added in s. xv). p. 444 Lections of the common of saints.

In the hand of art. 9. John 15: 12–16; Apocalypse 7: 13–17; 1 Corinthians 7: 25–34. References to these lections are in the margins of art. 15, pp. 447, 456, 474.

15. pp. 445–74 Incipit commune sanctorum.

Alleluia verses and 'Willelmus Robinson' were added on p. 471, s. xvi.

16. pp. 474–86 Commemorative masses of Holy Trinity, Angels, Holy Spirit, Holy Cross, Holy Name, Five Wounds, Corona Domini, and Corpus Christi.

The long heading to the mass of the Five Wounds (as in edn. 1514) has been crossed through.

17. pp. 486–91 Masses of B.V.M.

18. pp. 491–511 Forty-four votive masses.

Agrees with edn. 1514, ff. 30–40ᵛ, in contents and order, with one omission and one addition. The omission is of no. (26) in edn., the non-Sarum 'Pro se ipso', although there is a reference to it in the margin, p. 494, 'Item pro semetipso alia oracio non sarum Suppliciter te deus. ut sequitur in vii° folio'. The form not in edn. 1514 comes on p. 508 after Contra adversantes: 'Pro muliere pregnante quam fecit [papa] celestinus cum secr' et postco'. pro sorore sua pregnante et concessit c. dies indulgencie cuilibet sacerdoti eam dicenti deuote et infra missam oranti pro muliere pregnante' (this heading crossed through). As in edn. 1514, only collect, secret and postcommunion are provided for the masses after no. (17), Pro peste animalium.

19. pp. 511–19 Ad missam pro defunctis officium.

20. pp. 519–21 Oracio generalis.

Four forms as in edn. 1514 and Sarum Missal, pp. 442–5.

21. pp. 521–2 Trental of St. Gregory. As in edn. 1514.

22. p. 522 Missa pro mortalitate euitanda quam dominus papa clemens . . . (ends imperfectly).

As in edn. 1514, but the heading ends at 'indulgencie'.

ff. i+261+i, paginated (i, ii), 1–524. 505 × 340 mm. Written space 345 × 225 mm. 2 cols. 39–40 lines. Collation: 1⁶ wants 1, 2 2–14⁸ 15⁸+1 leaf after 7 (pp. 231–2) 16–20⁸ 21⁸ wants 8 after p. 328+2 leaves after 7 (pp. 329–32) 22–32⁸ 33⁸ wants 8. Several hands, changing at 21¹, 22¹, 25¹, 27¹, 29¹ (pp. 315, 333, 381, 413, 445) and elsewhere. A full-page crucifixion picture, p. 220: a man and a woman kneel in the lower border. Initials: (i) in colours on gold grounds, decorated in colours, including vermilion and green; (ii) pp. 212–17, for prefaces of mass, 2-line, gold on coloured grounds patterned in white, and, pp. 432, 437, 5-line and 4-line, gold on decorated coloured grounds: sprays into the margins; (iii) 2-line, blue or red, with ornament of the other colour; (iv) 1-line, blue or red. Cadels only in art. 11 (pp. 435–6). Floral borders, some continuous, on pages with initials of type (i) and on the picture page. Capital letters in the ink of the text filled or stroked with yellow. Binding of s. xix. Secundo folio (p. 11) erit iiiᵃ.

Written in England. Arms on p. 220: (i) to the left of the woman, gules on a chevron ermine a lion rampant sable; (ii) to the right of the man, sable on a bend gules between six mullets argent pierced of six points a tendril of the second. Given by Robert Cooke to the parish church of Caldbeck, Cumberland: 'Orate pro bono et salubri statu domini roberti Cooke et pro anima illius cum ab hac luce migrauerit. ac eciam pro animabus parentum suorum fratrum sororum et benefactorum qui dedit ecclesie paroch' de Cawlbek istud missale. Calicem argenteum. Paxillum argent'. duo pallia. vnum pallium lineum et superpellicium. Anno domini M°. D°. VI°', p. 219. 'This Missal belongs to St. Mary's Catholic Church, Warwick Bridge, Carlisle', f. i.

CARLISLE. TULLIE HOUSE

1. *Augustinus, Epistolae, etc.*   s. xiii[1]

1. ff. 1–149ᵛ Originally 139 letters of St. Augustine, the same collection as in Aberdeen 6, Eton College 105, q.v., and Merton College 3. Probably forty-three leaves are missing with the whole of letters XV, XXI–XXX, XXXVIII, and parts of nine other letters. A contemporary table of contents on ff. 1, 2 lists the whole collection as it originally was.

The letters are numbered I–CXXXVIII, because the number CXXXVII was repeated in error. The table of contents has, after the entry of letter VII, the words 'Epistole Augustini ad ieronimum et ieronimi ad augustinum' in epistolari ieronimi requirantur', as in the Aberdeen, Eton, and Merton manuscripts. 'scriptus' is written against no. XXXII–XXXIV, XLVI in the table of contents and against nos. XXXIV, XXXV, XLVI, CXXXVII in the text, s. xv.

For the order of the letters here as compared with the order in *CSEL* and *PL* and in the pre-Maurist editions see below, Eton College 105. The letters in the Aberdeen, Carlisle, Eton, and Merton manuscripts are set out by Römer, ii.

Arts. 2–4 follow art. 1 in Merton College 3. Art. 2 is also in Eton College 105.

2. (*a*) ff. 149ᵛ–151 Sermo s. augustini ad populum excusatorius pro clericis. Caritati uestre hodie de nobis . . . ibi regnemus. (*b*) ff. 151–3 Sermo sancti patris nostri augustini episcopi' de uita clericorum et moribus eorum. Propter quod uolui et rogaui . . . seruiam uobis.

(*a, b*). *PL* xxxix. 1574–81 and 1568–74 (sermons 356 and 355). Ed. C. Lambot, *Stromata patristica et mediaevalia*, 1950, pp. 132, 124. A leaf of (*a*) is missing after f. 149. 'scriptus', s. xv, on ff. 149ᵛ, 151: cf. art. 1.

3. ff. 153–7 Incipit liber sancti augustini episcopi' contra quinque hereses. Debitor sum fratres . . . custodit in secula seculorum amen. Explicit liber sancti augustini episcopi' contra quinque hereses.

PL xlii. 1101–16, sermon 10 of Quodvultdeus: cf. *Clavis*, no. 410. Three leaves are missing after f. 155.

4. ff. 157–76 Aurelii augustini doctoris ypponensis episcopi' contra aduersarium legis et prophetarum. liber primus incipit. Librum quem misistis . . . factas nunc in omnibus (*ends imperfectly*).

PL xlii. 603–56/51.

(5). 'Ad paulinam de uidendo deo in fine libri', according to the table of contents in front of art. 1. Now missing.

The letter to Paulina, Ep. 147 in *PL* xxxiii. In Merton College 3 this piece is separated from *Contra adversarium legis et prophetarum* by *De disciplina christiana*.

ff. iv+176+i. 360×260 mm. Written space 260×175 mm. 2 cols. 40 lines. Writing above top ruled line. Running titles, catchwords, and quire signatures on specially ruled lines. Pricks in both margins to guide ruling. Collation: 1⁸ 2⁸ wants 1 before f. 9 3⁸ wants 3, 4 after f. 17 4–19⁸ 20⁸ wants 1 before f. 150 and 8 after f. 155 21⁸ wants 1, 2 before f. 156 22⁸ wants 8 after f. 176. Quires numbered at the end and catchwords. The numbers run from I to XXVII (quire 21): IV, V, VI, X, XIIII are now missing. Admirably written. Punctuation includes the flex (?). Initials: (i) a 10-line *D* on f. 2 in red (patterned in white) and silver on a decorated blue and silver ground, with green edging; (ii) ff. 153, 157, blue with red and blue ornament; (iii) 3-line or 4-line, red or blue, plain or with ornament of the other colour, or, occasionally, brown with red or blue ornament. Binding of s. xviii, rebacked. Secundo folio (f. 2) CXXII *Item augustini*; (f. 3) *gustini ad.*

Written in England. Nothing now in the manuscript substantiates the nineteenth-century note on f. iv, 'A Manuscript Formerly belonging to the Monks of the Order of St. Agustin at the Priory of Conishead in Furness in the County of Lancaster'. Armorial book-plate of 'Wilson Braddyll Esq.' (of Conishead Priory). Given by E. R. G. Braddyll and his sisters to J. S. Estcourt in 1867 'as a Memorial of an Arduous Trust on their Behalf which I managed from 1846 to 1864'. Bought for £32 from a Leicester bookseller in 1926.

CARMARTHEN. CARMARTHENSHIRE RECORD OFFICE

Psalterium, etc. S. XIII med.

1. ff. 1–63ᵛ (*begins imperfectly*) De torrente in uia . . .

Psalms, beginning at 109: 7. A leaf missing after f. 7 contained the end of Ps. 117 and the beginning of Ps. 118. Each section of Ps. 118 begins with a coloured initial. A scribbler, s. xvi, rendered 'Benedictus dominus qui non' as 'Benedectus domynos qui none', f. 31ᵛ.

2. ff. 63ᵛ–79ᵛ, 89ʳᵛ, 81–87ᵛ, 88ʳᵛ, 90–92ᵛ The six ferial canticles, followed by Benedicite, Benedictus, Magnificat, Nunc dimittis, Te deum, Quicumque uult.

3. ff. 93–7 Audi domine hympnum et orationem 'quem famulus tuus' (*over erasure*) orat coram te hodie ut sint oculi tui aperti et aures tui intente ad orationem 'famuli' (*over erasure*) tu'i' (*over erasure of* -e) ad laudem et gloriam . . . miserere mei amen.

A prayer based on the opening words of the seven penitential psalms.

4. ff. 97ʳᵛ, 87aʳᵛ, 97aʳᵛ, 98–106 Fragments of a litany.

f. 97ʳᵛ has from the beginning to 'Sancte paule ora'. f. 87a is a small fragment from the list of confessors in which 'Leo' is followed by 'Rem[. . .]' (Remigius ?), Yr[. . .] and O[. . . .]. f. 97aʳᵛ is a very small piece with only the first letters of two successive lines, 'S' and 'S'. f. 98 begins at 'gradus' (*Brev. ad usum Sarum*, col. 252/40). The next three formulas are 'Vt regibus et principibus . . .', 'Vt episcopos et abbates . . .' and 'Vt 'heremite' (*over erasure*) nostr'i' (*over erasure of* -e) miserere et auxiliari digneris'. The rest of the series include 'Vt locum istum et omnes habitantes in eo . . .' and 'Vt regularibus disciplinis nos instruere . . .' between 'Vt miserias . . .' and 'Vt omnibus fidelibus . . .'. After 'Et ne nos' is 'Deus in adiutorium. Leuaui. Ad te leuaui. Iudica me. Emitte spiritum tuum. Salua nos criste. Post partum. Et ueniat super nos. Esto nobis. Memor esto congreg'. Domine saluum fac. Salua nos seruos tuos et ancillas tuas. Fiat pax in uir'. Oremus pro benefactoribus nostris. Domine exaudi oracionem meam', followed by nineteen prayers (ff. 100–106): (1) Omnipotens sempiterne deus dirige actus nostros . . .; (2) Inclina ergo o sancte spiritus in testimonia tua mentem meam . . .; (3) Deus cui omne cor . . .; (4) Ure igne . . . (5) Deus qui pro nobis filium tuum . . .; (6) Beate et gloriose semperque virginis dei genitricis marie quesumus omnipotens deus ut intercessio . . .; (7) Deus qui (sic) proprium est . . .; (8) Exaudi quesumus domine supplicum preces . . .; (9) Quesumus omnipotens deus ut famulus tuus rex noster atque regina . . .; (10) Omnipotens sempiterne deus qui facis mirabilia . . .; (11) Omnipotens sempiterne deus miserere famule tue et dirige eam . . .; (12) Pretende domine famulis et famulabus tuis . . .; (13) Da famulis et famulabus tuis quesumus domine in tua fide . . .; (14) Deus a quo sancta desideria . . .; (15) Adesto domine supplicationibus nostris . . .; (16) A domo tua quesumus domine spiritales nequitie . . .; (17) Absolue quesumus domine animas famulorum famularumque tuarum . . .; (18) Omnipotens sempiterne deus edificator et custos ierusalem . . . custodi istum locum . . .; (19) Deus qui es sanctorum tuorum splendor mirabilis atque lapsorum subleuator inenarrabilis . . . fac nos famulas tuas . . . Except nos. 2, 6, 18, 19, these prayers are in *Sarum Missal*. Nos. 10, 11, 13, 17 are for use by both sexes, and nos. 11, 19 by women only: 11 is in the feminine singular.

5. ff. 106–10 Commend' animarum. Subuenite sancti dei . . .

Manuale Sarum, pp. 119–21. Instead of *animam serui tui N.* (edn. 120/2), the reading here is 'animas seruorum tuorum et ancillarum tuarum'.

6. ff. 110–17ᵛ Pro fidelibus ad uesperas. Placebo . . .: ends imperfectly.

Office of the dead. A gap after f. 111. The responses to lessons 1–3, 9 are missing and those to lessons 4 and 6, Heu michi and Domine secundum, have been rewritten over erasure. The others are: (5) Heu michi; (7) Congregati sunt and Peccantem me (versicles Delicta iuuentutis and Deus in nomine tuo); (8) Libera me domine de viis inferni.

ff. iii + 119 (foliated 1–87, 87a, 88–97, 97a, 98–117) + ii. 180 × 125 mm. Written space 110 × 75 mm. 14 long lines. Collation of ff. 1–70: 1 ten (ff. 1–10) 2–6¹². After this ff. 71–90, 97, 97a are mounted separately and ff. 98–109 is a quire of twelve leaves. Well written. Initials: (i) all missing; (ii) 2-line, gold on grounds of red and blue patterned in white; (iii) 1-line, gold with blue ornament or blue with red ornament. Line fillers in red and blue or gold and blue. Capital letters in the ink of the text lined with red. Bound in blue levant morocco at the National Library of Wales, Aberystwyth, in 1923.

Written in England for female use in a religious community, but art. 3 was altered rather later to be used by a man. A formula in art. 4 is for God's help to a woman recluse (?) but the words were altered rather later to apply to a male hermit. Scribbled in, probably in Wales, in s. xviii: names of this date are 'John Bowen' (f. 37ᵛ), 'Mʳ Edward Thomas's Book' (f. 47) and 'Lewis Eva[ns] 1796' (f. 50). Belonged to the Venerable Archard Williams, Archdeacon of Carmarthen (†1879). Given in 1923 to the Carmarthenshire Antiquarian Society by Mrs. A. M. C. A. Soppitt in memory of her husband: cf. the Society's *Annual Report* for 1 Jan.–30 Sept., 1923, p. xii, and their *Transactions*, xviii (1923), 61–2. Their stamp is inside the cover. Acquired with their library in 1940.

CHELTENHAM. LADIES' COLLEGE

*Breviarium*¹   s. XIII ex.

A noted winter breviary described by C. Sayle in *Cheltenham Ladies' College Library*, 1914, pp. 17–20: f. 155ᵛ is reproduced ibid., p. 9, on a reduced scale.

¹ Deposited in the Bodleian Library.

1. ff. 1–6ᵛ Calendar in red and black, graded.

Among feasts in red are 'Relatio sancti Vedasti. Duplex' (15 July), 'Elevatio corporis sancti Vedasti. duplex' (1 Oct.), Amatus 'Duplex' (19 Oct.), Quintin 'Duplex' (31 Oct.), 'Leoniani abbatis. ix lect' ' (16 Nov.); in black are 'Oct' S' Vedasti. Missa' (13 Feb: no feast is entered on 6 Feb.), Vindicianus 'ix lect' ' (11 Mar.), Gaugericus 'ix lect' ' (11 Aug.), and, as an addition, s. xiv, 'Viriaci episcopi et martiris. Duplex' (29 Apr.). The hand is not that of arts. 2–9.

2. ff. 7–80ᵛ Liturgical psalter.

3. ff. 80ᵛ–81ᵛ Te Deum, Benedicite, Benedictus, Magnificat, Nunc dimittis.

4. ff. 81ᵛ–83 Litany.

Twenty-two confessors: (1) Vedaste ii . . . (13–22) Gaugerice Auberte Vindiciane Eligi Amande Amate Nicholae Seuerine Egidi Fursee. Twenty virgins: . . . (19, 20) Columba Elysabeth.

5. ff. 83–4 Sequuntur orationes quarum prima est de trinitate. Oratio. Omnipotens sempiterne deus qui dedisti nobis famulis tuis in confessione . . .

Prayers to Holy Trinity, Holy Spirit, B.V.M., Angels, John Evangelist, Peter, apostles, Stephen, martyrs, Vedast, confessors, virgins, 'Beate marie et omnium sanctorum. Concede quesumus omnipotens deus ut intercessio nos . . .', and the 'Oratio communis. Pietate tua . . .'.

6. f. 84ʳᵛ Feria iiiiᵃ in capite ieiunii et usque ad feriam quintam ante pascha dicuntur post hora diei . . .

Psalms, versicles, and prayers for use on weekdays, 'pro peccatis' after matins, 'pro episcopo' after terce, 'pro congregatione ecclesie' after sext, 'pro familiaribus' after none, 'pro pace' after vespers and 'contra tempestates' after compline.

The prayers are 'Exaudi quesumus . . .', 'Deus omnium fidelium . . .', 'Familiam huius ecclesie . . .', 'Prentende (sic) domine . . .', 'Deus a quo sancta desideria . . .', 'Omnipotens mittissime (sic) deus . . .'.

7. ff. 85–244 Sanctorale, Andrew–Mary of Egypt (30 Nov.–9 Apr.).

The office for the deposition of Vedast, 6 Feb., takes up eleven leaves, ff. 189–99. It appears to be complete, although the quiring is irregular at this point. The A of 'Aue presul gloriose . . .' (RH, no. 23766), beginning the office, has been cut out. Except at the three feasts of B.V.M., Conception, Purification, and Annunciation, and at the feast of Vedast, all main initials begin first lessons, Andrew, Eligius, Nicholas, Nicasius, Thomas apostle, Agnes, Vincent, Conversion of Paul, Blaise, Agatha, Matthias, Gregory, Mary of Egypt.

8. ff. 245–280ᵛ Common of saints, ending imperfectly in virgins.

9. ff. 281–390ᵛ. Temporale from Septuagesima Sunday, ending imperfectly in Friday after the fourth Sunday in Lent.

ff. iii+390+iii. 250 × 165 mm. Written space 175 × 115 mm. 2 cols. 33 lines. Collation: 1 six (ff. 1–6: 4, 5 are conjugate) 2–10⁸ 11⁶ (ff. 79–84) 12–15⁸ 16⁶+1 leaf after 3 (f. 120) 17–23⁸ 24⁶+1 leaf after 3 (f. 183) 25⁸ 26 ten (ff. 195–204: ff. 196, 203 and ff. 200, 201 are conjugate) 27–35⁸ 36 four (ff. 277–80) 37–39⁸ 40⁶ (ff. 305–10) 41–50⁸. Remains of quire numberings in three series, i–ix on quires 2–10, (i)–xiv, xvi–xxi on quires 12–31 and (i)–v on quires 32–6: in the third series only the numbers iii, iiii, v remain (ff. 268ᵛ, 276ᵛ, 280ᵛ). Initials: (i) red, pink, or blue, usually historiated, on coloured grounds framed in gold, and with borders in one or two margins containing jousting knights, grotesques, etc.: Sayle lists thirty-three of the thirty-four initials of this type, all but the *D* of Ps. 38: the initial at f. 189 (Vedastus) has been cut out; in art. 2 the initials mark the usual divisions and Ps. 114; (ii) of some feasts in art. 3 and to mark the beginning of Septuagesima and Lent in art. 5 (ff. 281, 311), red and blue with ornament of both colours and fillings of grotesques and animals in red penwork; (iii) 2-line, red or blue with ornament of both colours; (iv) 1-line, red or blue. Capital letters in the ink of the text are touched with red. Bound by F. Bedford, s. xix. Secundo folio (f. 8) *est in ore*.

Written in France for use in the diocese of Arras. Quaritch, catalogue 332 (1880), no. 20, at £100. 'To the Ladies' College Cheltenham John Ruskin 7th February 1887', f. iii: cf. the extracts from letters from Ruskin to Miss Beale in 1887 given in Cheltenham Ladies' College Library, pp. 12–15. Dearden, no. xix.

CHESTER. CATHEDRAL

1. *Biblia*   s. XIII med.

1. ff. 1–278 A Bible in the order Genesis–2 Chronicles, Ezra, Nehemiah, Tobit, Judith, Esther, Job, Psalms, Isaiah, Jeremiah, Lamentations, Baruch, Ezekiel, Daniel, Minor Prophets, 1, 2, Maccabees, Proverbs, Ecclesiastes, Song of Songs, Ecclesiasticus, Wisdom, Gospels, Acts, Catholic Epistles, Pauline Epistles, including the epistle to the Laodiceans, Apocalypse. Psalms are in parallel versions, Hebrew on the left and Gallican on the right. The Hebrew includes Ps. 151.

Books, except Psalms and Lamentations, are written continuously, the beginning of a new chapter being shown by a coloured initial in the text. There is a numbering of Psalms by a later, but medieval hand.

The prologues originally written include only thirty-one of the common set,[1] together with twenty-seven others, Stegmüller, nos. 349, 414, 430, 443, 529, 532, 535, 540, 544, 631, 635, 798, 803, and the following: a prologue to Wisdom, 'Hunc librum ieronimus asserit non a salomone ut putatur sed a philone . . . recipi scripturas' (cf. Southwell 5 and Stegm., no. 470); the first part of a prologue to Acts, 'Lucas medicus Antiochensis greci sermonis non ignarus . . . astiterunt etc. huiusmodi', the rest of which consists of Stegm., nos. 640, 631, and 635, and at the end a repetition of part of what has gone before, 'Primum quidem sermonem . . . astiterunt etc. huiusmodi'; prologues to each of the Pauline Epistles from 1 Corinthians to Philemon, each beginning with the words 'Hanc epistolam scripsit (*or* scribit) apostolus' and ending with the word 'dicens' cf. Bristol, Baptist College, Z. c. 18.

In s. xiv the common prologues to Wisdom and Maccabees (Stegm., nos. 468 and 551) and a prologue to Jonah (Stegm., no. 522) were added in the margins inside blue frames, and fourteen prologues, all of the common set, were added on ff. 278–80 in the following order and without indication of the books to which they belong: nos. 839, 327, 357, 507, 510, 512, 513, 531, 534, 538, 539, 543, 462, 521.

2. ff. 281–97 Aaz apprehendens . . . consiliatores eorum. Expliciunt interpretaciones. f. 297ᵛ is blank, except for notes added in s. xiv.

3. f. iiiʳ Thirteen lines of verse giving the names and order of the books of the

---

[1] See Bristol Public Library, 15.

Bible, added in an English humanist hand, s. xv: Genesis et exod leui numerus quoque deutro . . . Terminus est biblie clausus liber Apocalipsis.

4. Four sets of mnemonic verses were added in s. xiv on f. 297^v: (*a*) Occidit pueros . . . (3 lines); (*b*) Anna solet dici . . . (3 lines); (*c*) Prima parit cristus . . . (3 lines); (*d*) Deditus usure . . . (6 lines).

(*a, b, d*). Walther, nos. 13110, 1060, 4210.

ff. iii+297+ii. f. iii is a medieval flyleaf (cf. above, art. 3). 282 × 200 mm. Written space *c*. 185 × 120 mm. 2 cols. (4 cols. in art. 2). 67 lines. Collation: 1–12^{12} 13^{16} 14–23^{12} 24^{16}+1 leaf after 16 (f. 297). Small hand. Initials: (i) of books, *c*. 10-line, in colour on coloured grounds, with decoration in colours including green; (ii) of chapters of Lamentations, *c*. 6-line, blue with red ornament; (iii) of prologues, 4-line, blue with red ornament or red with green ornament; (iv) of Pss. 52, 109 in the Hebrew version, 3-line, as (iii); (v) of chapters, if they begin at the beginning of a line, and of psalms 2-line, as (iii); of chapters if they begin within a line and of verses of psalms, 1-line, blue or red. Capital letters in the ink of the text touched with red. Binding of s. xix. Secundo folio *hasta percutit*.

Written in England. Names: 'bartholomew mils', f. 297^v, s. xvi; 'Patty Batty', f. iii, s. xvii.

2. R. Higden, Polychronicon   s. xv med.

1. ff. 7–169 (*begins imperfectly*) sit molestus. Et iterum ait ad messores . . . dolendum est longam continuacionem diu postea habuerunt.

The Polychronicon in the AB text with the common continuation to 1377 (bk. 7, caps. 42–50): the first words now—the first leaf is missing—occur in the Rolls Series edition (ed. Babington, 1865) at p. 10/15 of vol. 1. Bk. 1, f. 7; bk. 2, f. 33; bk. 3, f. 51^v; bk. 4, f. 77; bk. 5, f. 97; bk. 6, f. 120; bk. 7, f. 137^v. The leaf on which five of the books began has been removed, f. 137 has been cut out, but not removed and an attempt was made to cut out f. 51. Chapter 44 of bk. 7 ends at 1342 'capitis interdixit. Vsque huc scripsit R' ': cap. 45 begins 'Hoc eodem anno non. Iunii natus regi E. Edmundus apud langlie'.

2. In front are: (*a*) ff. 1–6 the index to the Polychronicon, Abraham–Zerobabel, here beginning imperfectly 'Canutus rex'; (*b*) f. 6 a note of the five ages of the world from the beginning to the incarnation, 'Prima etas seculi . . . secundum verissimos V̄CXCVI', as in Magdalen College, Oxford, 97, f. 6^v, and B. L., Arundel 86; (*c*) on the pastedown, a vesica-shaped map of the world with Jerusalem in the middle. f. 6^v blank.

ff. 169. A foliation, s. xvii (?), begins at f. 7 and takes account of the leaves now missing. 415 × 280 mm. Written space 280 × 175 mm. 2 cols. 54 lines. Collation: 1^8 wants 1, 8 2–4^8 5^8 wants 3 after f. 32 6–9^8 10^8 wants 8 after f. 76 11–12^8 13^8 wants 5 after f. 96 14–15^8 16^8 wants 5 after f. 119 17^8 18 seven 19–21^8 22^{10} wants 3 after f. 163 and 10 after f. 169. Quires 1–13 signed a–n; quires 15–20 signed a–f. Three hands, changing at ff. 62 and 108 (beginning of quires 9 and 15). Initials: (i) ff. 51^v, 137^v (the others of this kind removed), in colour on gold grounds decorated in colours including green and with prolongations forming continuous borders; (ii) 3-line, blue with red ornament. Contemporary binding of wooden boards covered with sheepskin: two clasps. Secundo folio *Canutus* (f. 1) or *sit molestus* (f. 7).

Written in England. 'Humfrey Ridinge hous theis boke' (s. xvi, on pastedown). 'liber Iohannis Savile socii medii Templi London ex dono consaguinei sui henrici Savile de le bank Iuxta halifax' (f. 1, s. xvi ex.). A note about the missing leaves signed by Richard Gascoigne, Oct. 1650 (f. 169). Savile sale 6 Feb. 1861, lot 39 to Sir Thomas Phillipps: Phillipps 25063: sale, at Sotheby's, 27 Apr. 1903, lot 592 (to Sotheran, £55). E. Coates sale at Sotheby's, 9 July 1923, lot 248. Bought by the Friends of the Cathedral in 1924 or 1925.

3. *Horae*   s. xv med.

1. ff. 1–5ᵛ Incipiunt hore sancte crucis.

2. ff. 7–10 Hours of Holy Spirit, beginning imperfectly.

3. f. 10ʳᵛ Memore de saint nicholay.

4. ff. 11–57ᵛ Incipiunt hore beate marie virginis.
The antiphon and capitulum at prime are Assumpta est and Que est ista and at none Pulcra es and Sicut cynamomum. A memoria 'De sanctis' follows each hour from lauds to compline.

5. ff. 59–60 O intemerata . . . orbis terrarum. Inclina . . .
Imperfect at the beginning.

6. ff. 60–1 De sancta maria Ant'. Salue regina . . .

7. ff. 61–2 Ueni creator spiritus. *RH*, no. 21204.

8. ff. 62–3 Illumina oculos meos . . .
The verses of St. Bernard, here without heading.

9. ff. 63–4 Inicium sancti euuangelii secundum iohannem. John 1: 1–14.

10. f. 64ʳᵛ Memoriae of SS. Sebastian and Barbara (Aue trini lucifera . . .: *RH*, no. 23902).

11. ff. 66–83ᵛ Incipiunt septem psalmi penit'. Litany follows.
Seven confessors in the litany, Louis last. The order of doctors is Francis, Benedict, Anthony, Dominic, Bernardine.

12. ff. 84–121 Incipiunt uigilie mortuorum.

13 (added, s. xvi). f. 121ʳᵛ Leruefactus apprime te versus / Versus barbara condo tantillos . . . Ave philippam barbara caue (7 lines), and a similar stanza ending 'Ave symonem barbara caue'.
The last two syllables of each line are the same as the first two of the next line.

ff. i+117+i. The modern foliation 1–121 allows for the four missing leaves. 192 × 145 mm. Written space 110 × 80 mm. 16 long lines. Ruled in red. Collation: 15 quires of 8 leaves each, 1⁶, 5², 8¹, ⁸ missing, and a final leaf added to quire 7 (f. 57). Ten crude 11-line pictures: 7 in art. 4 (prime missing: massacre of innocents at compline) and 1 before each of arts. 1, 11, 12. Initials: (i) 4-line, in colour on gold grounds decorated in colours; (ii) 2-line, gold on coloured grounds, patterned in white and with short gold and blue sprays; (iii) as (ii) without the sprays. Continuous floral borders on picture pages. Line fillers in litany in red, blue, and gold. Capital letters in the ink of the text filled with pale yellow. Binding of s. xix lettered on spine 'MANVSCRIST (sic) SUR VELIN'. Secundo folio *tem tuam*.

Written probably in north-east France. 'Saint hubert' is in looking-glass writing on f. 64.

CHICHESTER. CATHEDRAL

Med. 1. *Augustinus*   s. xiii in.

1. ff. 1–60^v (*begins imperfectly*) spiritui sancto collecta . . . tu ignosce et tui.
De Trinitate, in fifteen books. *PL* xlii. 827–1098.

2. ff. 61–82^v Aurelii Aug' yponensis episcopi de libero arbitrio liber i^{us}. Incipit igitur (?) Adeo. Dic michi queso te . . . aliquando compellit. Explicit liber Beati Augustini yponensis episcopi De libero arbitrio.
De libero arbitrio, in three books (2, f. 65^v; 3, f. 73). *CSEL* lxxiv (1956): readings agree with the editor's C.

3. ff. 83–146^v Omnis diuina scriptura bipartita est . . . tandem fine concludimus. Explicit liber beati augustini de genesi ad litteram.
De Genesi ad litteram, in twelve books. *CSEL* xxviii (1895). In bk. 12, text corresponding to edn., pp. 409/25–416/1, 422/15–428/21 is missing, owing to the loss of a leaf after f. 144 and a leaf after f. 145. The relevant passage from the Retractationes, '[P]er idem tempus . . . bipartita est', is added in another hand on f. 82^v.

ff. 116. Parchment with many imperfections. 298 × 215 mm. Written space *c.* 200 × 140 mm. 42 long lines. Writing above top ruled line. Very wide lower margins. Collation: 1^8 wants 1, 2 2–7^8 8^8 wants 7, 8, blank after f. 60, 9^{12} 10^8 11^2 (ff. 81, 82) 12–18^8 19^6 20 two (ff. 145, 146). Pricks in both margins of quires 1, 2, 9 $^{2, 3, 10, 11}$, 11–20. Quires 1–3 numbered at the end. Several rather small hands. Initials: (i) blue and red, with ornament of both colours; (ii) 3-line or 4-line, blue or red, with ornament of the other colour; (iii) 2-line or 1-line, red or blue. Running titles in red. Contemporary binding of wooden boards covered with a double thickness of white leather: three bands: central strap and pin missing.

Written in England.

Med. 2. *Missale; Manuale*   s. xiii^2

1. (*a*) ff. 1–2^v Incipit exorcismus salis. (*b*) f. 2^v Ad mandatum faciendum.
Cf. *Manuale Sarum*, pp. 1, 18.

2. f. 3 In susceptione fratrum et familiarum 'et amicorum' in capitulo.

3. ff. 3^v–10 Ad uisitandum infirmum dicantur septem psalmi penitenciales.
Cf. ibid., p. 97. Litany, ff. 3^v–6. Twenty-three martyrs, Wulfhad eighteenth. Twenty-five confessors, Peter and Augustine, first and second, both doubled, Richard twentieth.

4. ff. 10–14^v Cum anima in exitu sui (*sic*) dissolucione corporis uisa feurit laborare . . .
Cf. ibid., p. 114.

5. ff. 14ᵛ–19 Post missam duo fratres stantes ad cap*ut* def*uncti* cant' Circumdederunt.

Burial office. Cf. ibid., p. 152.

6. ff. 19–25 Ordo ad cathecuminos faciendos.

Cf. ibid., p. 25.

7. f. 25ʳᵛ Ordo ad baptizandum infirmum infantem . . . Oratio. Medelam
tuam deprecor domine . . .

8. ff. 25ᵛ–26ᵛ Oracio sacerdotis antequam accedat ad altare. or. Deus qui de
indignis dignos . . . Ad collocandum calicem. Suscipe sancta trinitas hanc
oblacionem quam peccator quidem . . .

9. ff. 26ᵛ–32ᵛ Masses of Holy Trinity, Holy Spirit, Holy Cross, B.V.M., the
Incarnation (collect, 'Corda nostra quesumus domine sanctus splendor . . .'),
angels, martyrs, apostles, confessors, virgins, relics, All Saints.

10. ff. 32ᵛ–39 Prefaces (noted), ordinary (imperfect) and canon of mass.

11. ff. 39–43ᵛ Missa pro defunctis.

The mass, followed by collect, secret, and postcommunion on special occasions: In die
sepulture; Pro tricennalibus (two forms); Pro sacerdote; Pro patre et matre; Pro parentibus
defunctis; Pro defuncta femina; Pro familiaribus defunctis; Pro defunctis fratribus; In
die anniuersar'; Pro omnibus fidelibus defunctis. Nos. (1, 2, 12, 13, 5, 7, 8, 17, 15, 11,
10, 20) of the series of twenty masses in *Sarum Missal*, pp. 431–42.

12. ff. 44–5 Missa generalis pro fidelibus defunctis.

Three forms, as ibid., pp. 442–4, nos. (1, 3, 4).

13. f. 45 De sancto Ricardo officium.

Richard of Chichester. Nearly as *Missale de Lesnes* (HBS xcv, 1964), pp. 2–3.

14. ff. 45ᵛ–47ᵛ Collect, secret, and postcommunion (*a*) Pro religiosis, (*b*) Pro
tribulacione, (*c*) Contra aduersarios ecclesie, (*d*) Pro febricitantibus, and (*e*) complete office Pro infirmo morti proximo.

(*a*). The collect is 'Deus qui nos famulos tuos a seculi uanitate'. (*b*, *c*). The thirtieth and
third of the thirty-six masses in *Sarum Missal*, pp. 394–411. (*d*, *e*). Cf. ibid., pp. 406 n. 6
(Missa sancti Sigismundi), 410 n. 8.

15. ff. 47ᵛ–68 Temporale from Christmas to Pentecost.

Masses for Christmas, Stephen, Innocents, Thomas the Martyr (undamaged), Sunday
after Christmas, Circumcision, Epiphany, Purification, Annunciation, Easter, Ascension,
Pentecost.

16. ff. 68–84ᵛ Sanctorale, May–December.

Masses for Invention of Cross, Augustine of England (collect, secret, and postcommunion
only), Barnabas (c., s., p. only), Nativity of John Baptist, Peter and Paul, Commemoration
of Paul, Mary Magdalene, Assumption of B.V.M., Augustine (c., s., p. only), Nativity of
B.V.M., Exaltation of Cross, Michael, translation of Augustine, All Saints, Martin,
Edmund king and martyr, Edmund archbishop, Andrew, Nicholas, Thomas the apostle.

17. ff. 84ᵛ–101 Common of saints.

18. f. 101ʳᵛ De sancta maria magdalena Leccio libri sapientie. Mulierem fortem . . . (Proverbs 31: 10–31).

19. ff. 102–106ᵛ Ordo ad facienda sponsalia. Statuantur uir et mulier in ecclesia . . .

Cf. *Manuale Sarum*, p. 44.

20. ff. 106ᵛ–108 Ordo ad peregrinos benedicendos.

Cf. ibid., p. 60.

21. ff. 108–110ᵛ De nouitio suscipiendo. Statuto die professionis ueniant nouitii in capitulum . . .

The form of profession is 'Ego frater N offerens trado me ipsum diuine pietati in ecclesia sancte marie de Kenilleworth' seruiturum secundum Regulam sancti Augustini . . .'.

22. ff. 112ᵛ–113 De excommunicatione facienda.

23. f. 113ʳᵛ De absolutione facienda.

24. ff. 114–123ᵛ Benedictions of wax candles at the Purification, of ashes on Ash Wednesday, of palms on Palm Sunday, reconciliation of penitents on Holy Thursday and office 'In sabbato sancto pasche dum itur ad benedictionem noui ignis'.

Cf. *Manuale Sarum*, pp. 7, 9, 12, 15, 20.

25. ff. 123ᵛ–128 Incipiunt uigilie mortuorum. Placebo domino . . .

Responses as in *Sarum Missal*. Music for them was added in the lower margins by the hand which wrote art. 27.

26 (added, s. xiv). ff. 128–130ᵛ In die anniuersar' fundatorum Kenilworth. Pro fundatoribus dicatur Placebo in choro statim post gratias . . .

The litany is imperfect at the end, but identical, as far as it goes, with that in art. 3.

27 (added, s. xvi). f. 131ʳᵛ Prayers for the dead, the first 'Deus cui proprium est misereri semper et percere (*sic*) . . .'.

ff. i+131+i. ff. 1, 132 were pastedowns. 280 × 190 mm. Written space 180 × 105 mm. 24 long lines. Collation: 1⁴ 2–3¹² 4¹² wants 7 after f. 34 5–9¹² 10 two (ff. 100–1) 11–12¹² 13⁸ wants 6, 7 after f. 130. Several hands: a change for the worse at f. 78 and for the better at f. 100. Initials: (i) in art 10, especially, f. 35, *T* of *Te igitur*, and beginning art. 11, and (ii) beginning arts. 1, 19 and the mass of the Incarnation in art. 9, in colour on decorated gold grounds or on grounds of colour patterned in white; (iii) blue and red with ornament of both colours, prolonged sometimes as streamers in the margins; (iv) 2-line, blue with red ornament or red with lilac or blue ornament: the lilac is on ff. 6–99; (v) 1-line, blue or red. Capital letters in the ink of the text are filled with yellow on ff. 1–3ᵛ and from where the hand changes on f. 100 and with red elsewhere. Blue and red line fillers in the litany. Contemporary (?) binding of bevelled wooden boards, now bare of leather; seven bands secured to the boards by a combination of the groove method and the older tunnel method noticed by Graham Pollard:[1] two strap-and-pin fastenings missing. Secundo folio *in nomine*.

Written for the use of the Augustinian priory of Kenilworth, Warwickshire (cf. arts. 21, 26). 'Liber Roberti Baskett de Blandford Bryan Dorst.', ff. 1, 45, s. xviii.

[1] *The Library*, 5th series, xvii (1962), 1.

Med. 3. *'Distinctiones Groningen'* 1442

1. ff. 1–559[v] Predicandi officium amandum propter officii illius necessitatem . . .

A handbook for preachers set out in paragraphs and divided without reference to the paragraphs into 167 numbered sections each of which is subdivided by letters of the alphabet: numbers and letters are in the margins. The last paragraph begins 'Imitatores dei esse'. The title 'Distincciones Groningen' is on the tail: cf. art. 2. For other copies formerly in German libraries cf. *MBDS* ii. 136/20 (Erfurt University) and 423/33 (Erfurt Charterhouse): the latter is called 'Distinctiones magistri Petri Gruningen et est materia valens predicatoribus et volentibus facere collaciones ex diuersis collecta tractans moralia'.[1]

2. ff. 560–74 Registrum in distinctionibus gruningen . . . Opere completo laus sit altissimo in (secula) seculorum Amen. Finitus est ille liber a natiuitate domini M° cccc° xlii° vi[a] post Quasimodo ganti.

An index to art. 1, Abicere–Xpistus, with references to the divisions by numbers and letters. f. 574[v] blank.

ff. ii + 484 + i, foliated 1–309, 400–574. Paper. 285 × 210 mm. Written space c. 250–230 × 150–130 mm.: the larger measurements begin at quire 11. 2 cols. 47 lines. Frame ruling, quires 1–10 with a hard point and the rest with pencil. Collation: 1–38[12] 39–40[14]. A narrow strip of parchment cut from a manuscript of s. xiv lies down the centre of each quire. Written in hybrida, current from quire 11. Metallic red initials, 4-line or less. Contemporary binding of wooden boards covered with pink leather bearing a pattern of fillets: four bands: metal cornerpieces: two clasps and five bosses on each cover now missing: a chainmark at the head of the back cover. Secundo folio *dicens*.

Completed at Ghent on Friday, 7 Apr. 1442 (see above). Given to the Benedictine abbey of St. Peter, Erfurt, by the executors of Dr. Benedict Stendal, A.D. 1482: (a) inside the cover, '[Lib]er magistri benedicti stendal doctoris sacre pagine [qui] obiit anno domini 1482 cuius anima requiescat [in pace]'; (b) inside the cover, '[Hun]c librum prefati domini doctoris Testamentarii dederunt [. . . .]antis sancti petri Erfford'. 'Liber Bibliothecæ regalis Monasterii S. Petri Erfordiæ', f. 1, s. xvii. Pressmark 'S. 19', f. 1. '36' on a label on the upper cover. Item 45 at £1. 5s. in Stark's cat. 5 (1855): cf. Med. 4. 'G. Sumner, Woodmansey, 1855 / Case B/AG' inside the cover: his sale, Beverley, 31 Oct. 1877, lot 537. No. 657 in a nineteenth-century English sale catalogue: the relevant cutting is inside the cover.

Med. 4. *'Crispus de tempore et de sanctis'* s. xv med.

1. ff. 1–191 In aduentu 1[a] dominica. Dicite filie Syon ecce rex tuus . . . M[t] xvi. Quoniam quantum capit intellectus meus veritas eterna . . .

Sermons of temporale and sanctorale, with a few for unspecified occasions. The order is: temporale from Advent to Epiphany; Purification; Annunciation; temporale from Easter to Pentecost; John Evangelist (f. 51); sanctorale, 1 May to 1 Nov. (ff. 51–86); Assumption; George; Mark; Philip and James; Holy Spirit; Holy Cross; 11,000 virgins; Augustine; De paupertate; on Beati mites; temporale from Ascension to the twenty-fifth Sunday after Pentecost (ff. 99*[v]–163); first Sunday in Lent; Corpus Christi; dedication of church. At the end, ff. 190–1, is a list of the sermons, with leaf references, headed 'Registrum super Crispum de tempore. Item postea de sanctis' and there is a further note of the contents on f. 195[v]. ff. 99[v]–99*, 191[v]–195[v] blank.

Crispus is not listed by Schneyer and the present copy is the only one indexed in *MBDS*.

---

[1] The copy in the Bülow sale, 10 Oct. 1836, lot 191, is probably the one from the Charterhouse of Erfurt.

2. ff. i, ii, parchment leaves used in binding (f. i was pasted down), contain sermons in a hand of s. xii med.

The central bifolium of a quire. Two complete short sermons and parts of two others: (*a*) . . . quod preparauit deus diligentibus se quod n.p. etc' amen; (*b*) Hodie karissimi sollempnitatem huius ecclesie dedicationis annua deuotione recolimus. in quam uidelicet ad adorandum . . . ut per hec celestem et eternam mansionem ipsius habere mereamur. quod n.p. amen; (*c*, for common of apostles) Simile est regnum celorum segene (*sic*) . . . Saluator noster dilectissimi. sacram sue ueritatis cognitionem . . . nobis proponit. et ad fontem ueri boni . . . in eterna tabernacula quod n.; (*d*, for common of a martyr) Nisi granum frumenti . . . Dominus ac saluator noster dilectissimi et in paruis minimisque rebus nonnumquam nobis magnam doctrinam . . . Schneyer, p. 467, gives (*c*) as a sermon of Maurice de Sully.

ff. ii + 196, foliated (i, ii), 1–99, 99*, 100–95. For ff. i, ii see above. The medieval foliation ends at '189'. Thick paper. 206 × 145 mm. Written space *c*. 155 × 115 mm. 2 cols. *c*. 36 lines. Frame ruling. Collation: 1–22⁸ 23⁶ 24⁸ 25⁶. Quires numbered at the end. Strips of parchment from more than one manuscript in the central openings of quires and sometimes between quires. Written, not well, in the German equivalent of current anglicana. Binding of thick wooden boards covered with white leather: three bands: two clasps now missing: 'Crispus de tempore et de sanctis' on a label on the upper cover.

Written in Germany. 'Carthusien' prope Erffordia', f. 1, at top, and f. 86. Identifiable with O. 61 in the medieval catalogue of the charterhouse of Erfurt: *MBDS* ii. 499/41. No doubt lot 403 in the Bülow sale, 10 Oct. 1836. J. M. Stark, bookseller of Hull, catalogue 5 (1855), item 31 at 12*s*.; cat. 13 (1857), item 1010. Book-plate of Cecil Deedes inside the end cover.

Med. 5. *Ordo missae, etc.*   1481

1. ff. 1–2ᵛ Officium de sancto spiritu. Spiritus domini . . .

Missale Romanum, i. 239–42. 'Collecte generales in fine' is written in red at the foot of f. 1.

2. ff. 3–4 De sancta Trinitate.

Ibid. i. 252–4, but the sequence here is 'Benedicta semper sancta sit trinitas'.

3. f. 4ʳᵛ Gloria in excelsis . . .

The two forms of Gloria, the first headed 'Cantus angelicus' and the second 'De beata virgine maria'.

4. ff. 4ᵛ–5 Symbolum apostolorum. Credo in unum deum . . . uenturi seculi.

Ibid., i. 199.

5. ff. 5–20ᵛ Ordinary, prefaces, and canon of mass.

The ordinary ends imperfectly, f. 5ᵛ. Noted prefaces, ff. 6–9ᵛ. f. 10ʳ blank. Te igitur, f. 11.

6. ff. 21–22ᵛ Officium beate marie virginis.

The sequences are Ave preclara maris stella and Stabat mater.

7. ff. 23–27ᵛ Sequitur missa pro defunctis.

The mass is followed by collect, secret, and postcommunion Pro episcopo defuncto, **Pro** commemoracione episcopi, Pro sacerdote defuncto, Pro funere parentis, In deposicione defuncti, In anniuersario, Pro fratribus defunctis, Pro omnibus fidelibus defunctis, Pro Parentibus, Pro quolibet defuncto, Pro defunctis, Pro sepultis in cimiterio, Pro amicis defunctis, Pro amico, Pro Elemosinariis, Pro defunctis qui non sunt confessi.

8. ff. 27^v–28^v Lections: (*a*) Pro episcopis; (*b*) Feria iii. v et sabbato;(*c*) Tempore paschali usque ad Ascensionem domini; (*d*) Feria ii. iiii et vi; (*e*) In penitencia funeris cuiuscumque; (*f*) In xl^{ma}, ending imperfectly.

(*a*). From 1 Thessalonians 4. (*b*). Apocalypse 14: 13. (*c*). 1 Corinthians 15: 20–3. (*d*). 2 Maccabees 12: 42–6. (*e*). John 11: 21–7. (*f*). Begins at John 5: 21.

ff. 28. Thick parchment. 380 × 285 mm. Written space 258 × 170–190 mm. 16 long lines, ff. 6–20; 2 cols., 26 lines, ff. 1–5, 21–8. Collation: 1^6 wants 6 2^4 3^{10} 4^4 wants 4, blank, 5^6. Full-page crucifixion on patterned gold ground, f. 10^v. Initials: (i) ff. 1, 3, 11, 21, in colour on patterned gold grounds framed in green and red, or blue and green; (ii, iii) 2-line and 1-line, red. Capital letters in the ink of the text marked with red. Contemporary binding of thin wooden boards covered with pigskin bearing stamps of five patterns: metal centre-piece and corner-pieces: central clasp missing.

Written in Germany. The date 1481 is in the initial *S* on f. 23^v. Book-plate of Augustus Frederick, Duke of Sussex: not identifiable in his sale at Sotheby's, 31 July 1844. No. 2595 in a sale: a slip from the relevant catalogue is pasted inside the cover.

MS. Med. 6 is a large antiphonal from Spain, s. xvi. See Albert F. Seth, 'The Restoration of the Chichester Antiphonal', *Books and the Man, Antiquarian Booksellers' Association Annual, 1953*, pp. 38–46.

Binding fragments in the capitular archives[1]

Cap. I/23/4A. Two leaves and three scraps of a repertory of civil and canon law. s. xv[2].

Letter R: on one page the words discussed are Relacio, Relapsus, Relaxacio, Relegacio, Releuare, Religio. Paper. Written space 280 × 195 mm. 2 cols. 66 lines. A textura script in which *f* and *s* tend to fall below the line and *g* is humanistic, except in the head words. Written in Italy (?). Formerly used in binding Cap. I/23/4, a volume of accounts beginning in 1585 (Steer and Kirby, p. 21).

Cap. III/1/7. A bifolium of a summary of Pauline Epistles. s. xiv/xv.

One page has the end of the account of Galatians and the beginning of the account of Ephesians, 'Tunc accedit epistola ad ephesios. Et ostendit . . .'. Written space 205 + × 158 mm. 2 cols. 48 + lines. Written in current anglicana. Used as the cover of a copy of the Cathedral statutes of 1534 made in 1600 as a single quire of twelve leaves (Steer and Kirby, p. 68).

[1] The archives are kept in the Diocesan Record Office, County Hall, Chichester, and are catalogued by F. W. Steer and I. M. Kirby, *Diocese of Chichester, A Catalogue of the Records of the Dean and Chapter*, 1967. For the fragments in Cap. I/14/3a see below, p. 398.

CHICHESTER. DIOCESAN RECORD OFFICE

Binding fragments in the episcopal archives[1]

Nos. I–XII are the eleven or twelve manuscripts used in binding five of the Episcopal Registers, Ep. I/1/1–4, 6. These and other registers were rebound at the Public Record Office in 1936, when Ep. I/1/1a, 2a, 3a, 4a, 6a were created by separating the binding leaves, except a few, from the registers. The leaves in Ep. I/11a–3a were binding pads. Those in Ep. I/1/1a were formerly glued together. In all, 56 pieces are in Ep. I/1/1a, 33 pieces in Ep. I/1/2a and 93 pieces, some of them very small, in Ep. I/1/3a. Probably Ep. I/1/1–3 were bound at about the same time as Ep. I/1/6 began to be used: see below, nos. VII, XII.

I. Ep. I/1/1, f. i. Ep. I/1/1a, ff. 1–19, 20–6, 29, 31–43, 45–55. Ep. I/1/2a, ff. 61, 62.[2] Fifty-four leaves of Liber sextus decretalium. s. xiv.

Text with surrounding apparatus. Written space (text) *c.* 125 mm. wide. 2 cols. Apparatus in more than 87 lines to the column. Initials: (i) 3-line, pink on blue or blue on pink grounds; (ii) outside the written space, blue or red with ornament of the other colour. Written in Italy. Fifty-one leaves made pasteboards for the register of Bishop William Rede, 1397–1414 (Steer and Kirby, p. 1) and one leaf was used as a flyleaf. Two leaves were used in a later register: see below, no. VI.

II. Ep. I/1/1a, ff. 19a, 30. Ep. I/1/2a, ff. 57, 58. Four leaves of Justinianus, Institutiones. s. xiii.

Includes text from bk. 3, tit. xiii, De successionibus. Heavily glossed in the margins. Written space 145 × 80 mm. 2 cols. 40 lines. Used in the pads of two registers: see above, no. I, and below, no. VI.

III. Ep. I/1a, f. 27. Ep. I/1/2a, ff. 5, 6, 53, 54. Five leaves of a breviary. s. xiv.

Part of the office for Palm Sunday (*Brev. ad usum Sarum*, i. dccxlix–dcclxi) is on ff. 27, 54. Written space 198 × 138 mm. 2 cols. 33 lines. Initials not filled in. Used in the pads of two registers: see above, no. I, and below, no. VI.

IV. Ep. I/1/1a, f. 28. A leaf of a commentary on civil law. s. xv in.

On legacies. The words 'Secundo obstat quod determinaui in alia questione quam padue disputaui vbi dixi quod legatum . . .' are in the text on the verso, col. 2, line 4. Written space 290+ × 210 mm. 2 cols. 56+ lines. Written in England in a mixture of anglicana and secretary. Used in the pad of Ep. I/1/1: see no. I.

V. Ep. I/1/1a, f. 44. Ep. I/1/2a, ff. 7, 8,[3] 23, 24. Three bifolia of a civil law text. s. xiii.

Includes the headings 'De probacionibus' and 'De instrumentis'. Under 'De probacionibus' the second paragraph begins 'Causa que a diuo antonio patre nostro et que a nobis rescripte sunt'. Written space 147 × 80 mm. 2 cols. 41 lines. Written in Italy. Used sideways in the pads of two registers: see above, no. I, and below, no. VI.

[1] See F. W. Steer and I. M. Kirby, *Diocese of Chichester, A Catalogue of the Records of the Bishops, Archdeacons and Former Exempt Jurisdictions*, 1966.

[2] Ep. I/1/2a, f. 59, a blank leaf of thick parchment, was next in the pad to f. 62[v], as the offset shows.

[3] Offset on ff. 7, 8 is from Ep. I/1/2a, f. 60, a flyleaf of a copy of Bishop Sherburne's Donations (Steer and Kirby, p. 2).

VI. Ep. I/1/2, ff. i, ii, 124. Ep. I/1/2a, ff. 1–4, 9–22, 25–52, 55, 56. Ep. I/1/6a, ff. 2, 3. Ep. VI/4/1 (pastedowns). Fifty-seven leaves of Roffredus Beneventanus, De libellis et ordine iudiciorum. s. xiii.

Cf. Savigny ,*Geschichte des römischen Rechts*, v. 206. Part of the title and the beginning of the text, 'Si considerarem ingenium . . .', are on f. 41. The end of the text is on f. 3 of Ep. I/1/6a, '. . . ff. de acquirenda possessione in l. quamuis. Explicit libellus de iure canonico', as in edn. 1500, sign. (F. viiiᵛ). Most of the pieces consist of a nearly complete leaf and over half of the leaf conjugate with it. The three leaves in Ep. I/1/2 are complete.

Written space 288 × 163 mm. 2 cols. 75 lines. Initials: (i) pink or blue on decorated ground of both colours: the decoration includes a little gold; (ii) 3-line, blue with red ornament. The hand looks Italian and the decoration probably English. Twenty-four bifolia were cut down and laid sideways to make a binding pad for the Register of Bishop Richard Praty, 1438–45 (Steer and Kirby, p. 1) and three leaves, a bifolium and a single-ton, were used as end-leaves in the same volume. Two leaves were used in the binding of Ep. I/1/6: see below, no. XII. Ep. VI/4/1 is a parchment account book begun in 1521 (Steer and Kirby, p. 167), but bound in s. xvii ex.: probably its pastedowns were taken over from an older binding.

VII. Ep. I/1/3a, ff. 2, 12, 67, 71, 84. Ep. I/1/6a, f. 1. Six leaves of Codex Justiniani. s. xiii.

The last page of the text is now f. 1ʳ of Ep. I/1/6a, '. . . testem habeant. Finis libri 'codicis amen. Finito libro reddatur cena magistro' 'Iohanni Aluerton Anno domini Millesimo CCCCᵐᵒ Nono die xiiii Mensis Maii''. Wide lower margins. One of them, Ep. I/1/3a, f. 2, was used when the leaf was upside down and presumably a flyleaf of the Register, as a space for a collect, secret, and postcommunion headed 'pro grauida regina' and in-cluding the words 'famulam tuam Ianam reginam nostram': Jane Seymour's son was born on 12 October 1537.

Written space 215 × 118 mm. 2 cols. 41 lines (text). Written in England (?). Belonged to John Alverton in 1409. A pledge in an Oxford loan-chest in 1404 (?): 'Caucio '[. . . .]rerow' exposita in cista viene pro xxi (?) s' die proxima post festum omnium sanctorum [. . . c]-ccc[. .]ii'. Used in the binding pad of Ep. I/1/3, the Register of Bishop Story, 1478–1502 (Steer and Kirby, p. 2), and in the binding of Ep. I/1/6 (see below, no. XII).

VIII. Ep. I/1/3a, ff. 3, 4, 6, 16, 18, 20, 32, 33, 44, 47, 49, 50, *53, 56, 73, 79–81*.[1] Fragments of a commentary on the decretals. s. xiii.

A beginning is perhaps on f. 73ᵛ: 'In nomine patris etc'. Omnis sapiencia a domino. ut hic legitur in prouerbiis salomonis et alibi . . .'. On f. 56 the words 'Firmitur credimus. Hic titulus diuiditur in duas partes. in prima ponit articulos fidei. in secunda . . .' are preceded by seventeen (+) lines of verse ending 'Verba locis narrent populus indignus referri'. Written space 180 mm wide. 2 cols. 52+ lines. Written in Italy. Perhaps part of the same manuscript as no. IX. Marginalia in English hands, s. xiv and s. xv, include 'Loke al this', f. 73ᵛ. Used in the binding of Story's register: see no. VII.

IX. Ep. I/1/3a, ff. 5–94 (except the leaves listed above, nos. VII, VIII). 'Oculus decreti'; Thomas Aquinas, De articulis fidei; etc. s. xiii². The contents include: (1) ff. 13, 25, 55, 61, 63, 93, 94 An epitome of the Decretum of Gratian, ending (f. 93) 'ad destruccionem cuiusdam heresis. Explicit oculus decreti'; (2) Pseudo-Aquinas on the sacraments (Glorieux, no. 14ec), beginning on f. 93 immediately

---

[1] The larger pieces in no. VIII are shown by italics. They and the larger pieces in no. IX, ff. 58, 59, 62, 64, 65, 70, 75, 77, 78, 87, 88, 93, consist usually of most of a leaf together with a small piece of the leaf conjugate with it: three of these latter are referred to here as 46 (ii), 62 (ii), and 88 (ii). ff. 3–52, 61, 76, 79, 82, 83, 86, 89, 90 are half a leaf or less. Pieces of the old cover are laid down as Ep. I/1/3a, f. 1.

after (1), 'Quia sacerdotis officium circa tria principaliter uersatur': ff. 22, 60 are other leaves of this text; (3) Thomas Aquinas, De articulis fidei (Glorieux, no. 14*h*), beginning on f. 46 (ii) 'Postulat a me uestra deuocio ut de articulis fidei': the text continues from here on f. 88 (ii), which once formed part of the same leaf as f. 46, and other bits of it are on ff. 31, 62 (ii), 83; (4) a commentary on the Lord's Prayer beginning on f. 46ᵛ '[De ha]c oracione dominica per ysaiam dictum est' below a title in red in the margin 'Oracio dominica et simbolum apostolorum': presumably this ends on f. 85ᵛ, 'ut ego sum amen id est ueritas'; (5) immediately after (4), 'Prohemium ad simbolum. Notum sit dileccioni uestre quod milites seculi . . . (f. 69) tota uirtute perficiant prestante domino . . .'; (6) f. 86 begins 'Hic incipit liber de baptismate speculum ecclesie. Cum multa sint sacramenta noue legis vii tamen principalia': ff. 43, 54, 55, 62, 76, 88 may be other bits of this text, and the end of it on f. 88ᵛ, 'peccatorum nostrorum uulnera. amen. Explicit'; (7) ff. 14, 19, 27, 29, 57, 59, 64, 65, 72, 77, 82, 92 Fragments of a commentary on chapters of Decretum Gratiani.

5. Begins and ends as Ivo of Chartres, Sermo xxiii, De symbolo apostolorum, *PL* clxii. 604, 607, but the commentary in between, beginning on f. 85ᵛ, 'Credo . . . Primo uidendum est quo nomine hec doctrina', is not that printed as Ivo's: f. 69ᵛ is blank. 6. Cf. Vatican, Pal. Lat. 619, f. 1ᵛ. 7. Beginnings are (f. 65) 'Redintegranda (Causa 3, Q. 1). Hoc c. loquitur in rebus ecclesiasticis' and (f. 72) 'Cum enixa (Dist. 5, Cap. 1). Palea est secundum hug' '.

Written space 258+ × 170 mm. 2 cols. 60+ lines (ff. 46+88). Written in Italy. Marginalia in English hands, s. xiv/xv. Used in the same way as nos. VII, VIII.[1]

X. Ep. I/1/4a, ff. 1, 11+14, 16. Ep. IV/2/14. Three leaves and a strip of an antiphonal. s. xiv/xv.

The leaves in Ep. I/1/4a are from the common of martyrs and confessors: *Brev. ad usum Sarum*, ii. 403–7, 411–14, 421–9. The strip in Ep. IV/2/14 is from the common of a virgin martyr: ibid. 439–41. Written space 295 × 185 mm. 13 long lines and music. Written in England. The three leaves were used in the binding of Ep. I/1/4, a register containing documents of 1480–1506 and 1523–36 (Steer and Kirby, p. 2). The strip is strengthening inside the cover of an Act Book for 1629–36 (ibid., p. 147): possibly the binder got it from the register.

XI. Ep. I/1/4a, ff. 2, 3. Cap. I/14/3a, ff. 64–9. Eight leaves of a work on canon law. s. xiv.

Written space 265+ × 175 mm. 2 cols. 62+ lines. Written in anglicana. The two leaves in Ep. I/1/4a are from the binding of Ep. I/1/4: cf. no. X. The three bifolia in Cap. I/14/3a are from the binding of Cap. I/14/3, a copy of Bishop Sherburne's Donations made in 1526–31: cf. Steer and Kirby, *Records of the Dean and Chapter*, p. 14.

XII. Ep. I/1/6a, f. 6. A leaf of a commentary on St. John (20: 15). s. xiii.

Written space 245 × 145 mm. 2 cols. 56 lines. Written in informal textura: *s* is a descender. Used, together with leaves of nos. VI and VII, in binding a register containing documents of 1536–56 (Steer and Kirby, p. 3).

Nos. XIII–XXIV are *in situ* as covers or inside the covers of episcopal archives. They are ordered here according to the date of the volumes they cover.[2]

---

[1] Ep. I/1/3a, f. 37, is a flyleaf perhaps from no. VIII or no. IX. It is blank except for the titles 'Concordancie iuris ciuilis et canonici' and 'Concordia' in English hands, s. xv.

[2] Nos. XIV, XV, XXII, XXIII and five of the six pieces forming no. XXI cover single quires of fifty or less leaves and (Ep. I/11/17) 96 leaves.

XIII. Ep. II/9/1. A bifolium of a missal. s. xiv/xv.

Sanctorale, the first leaf for August (Ouen, Rufus, Augustine) and the second for September (Nativity of B.V.M.). Written space 235 × 150 mm. 2 cols. 28 lines. Written in England. The cover of a Detection Book for 1550–7 (Steer and Kirby, p. 105).

XIV. Ep. VI/2/1. A bifolium of a commentary on canon law. s. xiv.

A paragraph begins 'Causam. primo de intimacione facienda appellato presenti. 2° de ea facienda appellato absenti'. Written space 303 × 190 mm. 2 cols. 81 lines. Textura. Written in England. The cover of a rental for Jan. 1551/2 (Steer and Kirby, p. 164).

XV. Ep. III/4/4. A leaf of a gradual. s. xiv².

As *Sarum Missal*, pp. 148/25–150/16: fourth and fifth Sundays after the octave of Easter. Written space 260 × 175 mm. 13 long lines and music. Written in England. The cover of an Act Book for 1577–80 (Steer and Kirby, p. 140).

XVI. Ep. II/11/2. The upper half of a leaf of the commentary of Nicholas de Lyra on St. John (ch. 8). s. xiv.

A large manuscript. Written space *c.* 225 mm wide. Written in anglicana. Used as a pastedown (now raised) inside the front cover of a Register of Orders for 1606 and later years (Steer and Kirby, p. 112).

XVII. Ep. II/11/2. A leaf of a breviary. s. xv.

Sanctorale: lessons 7–9 for Cecilia, as *Brev. ad usum Sarum*, iii. 1086–9. Written space 260 × 160 mm. 2 cols. 35 lines. Written in England. Used as a pastedown (now raised) inside the back cover of the same register as no. XVI.

XVIII. Ep. V/3/1. A bifolium of a gradual. s. xiv.

The common of a martyr with the end of the sequence Clare sanctorum and the whole of the sequences Alleluia nunc decantet and Laus deuota: *Sarum Missal*, pp. 356–60. Written space 310 × 220 mm. 15 long lines and music. The central bifolium of a quire. Written in England. The cover of an Act Book for 1613–24 (Steer and Kirby, p. 155).

XIX. Ep. I/11/13. A strip from a bifolium of Tobit glossed. s. xiii.

Used inside the plain parchment cover of a Deposition Book for 1618–26 (Steer and Kirby, p. 19).

XX. Ep. I/17/20. A wide strip from a leaf containing canticles of the psalter. s. xi.

Begins in the last verse of Exultauit and ends in verse 15 of Cantemus domino. Written space 173 mm high. 26 (?) long lines. Open *a* fairly common. *ae*, not *ę*. Green 3-line C of *Cantemus*: other initials 1-line, red, green, or blue. Perhaps English. Strengthening inside the cover of a Detection Book for 1622–3 (Steer and Kirby, p. 25).

XXI. Ep. I/10/46. Ep. I/11/17. Ep. I/17/29. Ep. I/43/4. Ep. IV/2/18. Seven leaves of a large Bible. s. xii med.

Fragments of 2 Chronicles and Isaiah: 2 Chronicles 6: 39–8: 18 (Ep. I/11/17), 18: 2–20: 10 (Ep. IV/2/18), 27: 2–28: 18 (Ep. I/43/4); Isaiah 2: 8–4: 1 (Ep. I/43/4), 14: 32–17: 6 (Ep. I/10/46), 29: 11–34: 16 (Ep. I/17/29). Continuously written text. Section numbers in red in the margins. Running titles on specially ruled lines. An annotator, s. xiii, marked the margins of Isaiah with lection numbers: 'feria iiᵃ leccio iᵃ' at 2: 10, 'leccio iiᵃ' at 2: 20, 'leccio iiiᵃ' at 3: 5, 'leccio iiᵃ' at 15: 1, 'leccio iiiᵃ' at 16: 1, 'leccio iiiiᵃ' at 16: 8 (?). Within lections there are fairly numerous added stress marks as an aid to the reader.

c. 470 × 310 mm. Written space *c.* 332 × 205 mm. 2 cols. 46 lines. Ruling with a hard point, each column within a pair of lines. Perhaps in two good hands: in 2 Chronicles the backward slope is more marked than it is in Isaiah. The beginning of a new section is sometimes marked by a blue or red initial. Capital letters in the ink of the text sometimes stroked with red.

Written in England. Single leaves laid sideways were used as covers for an Instance Book for 1660–3, a Deposition Book for 1664–76, and an Act Book for 1666–74, all of which measure *c.* 320 × 205 mm (Ep. I/10/46, Ep. I/11/17, Ep. IV/2/18: Steer and Kirby, pp. 18, 19, 148). The central bifolium of a quire covers a Detection Book for 1667–9 which measures *c.* 350 × 230 mm (Ep. I/17/29: Steer and Kirby, p. 25). Two half leaves cut down the middle, one from 2 Chronicles and one from Isaiah, were tied together with string to make a cover of a tall narrow Account Book for 1660–8, which measures 385 × 150 mm (Ep. I/43/4: Steer and Kirby, p. 64).

XXII. Ep. IV/2/17. A bifolium of Gregory the Great, Moralia on Job. s. xiv.

Part of bk. 19: *PL* lxxvi. 131A–134C. Written space 228 × 143 mm. 2 cols. 35 lines. Written in England. Used as the cover for an Act Book for 1661–6 (Steer and Kirby, p. 147).

XXIII. Ep. I/15/1. Ep/I/18/51. Ep. I/43/5. Three bifolia of a commentary on Luke. s. xiii ex.

Parts of the commentary on chapters 2, 4–6. The commentary on Luke 6: 12 begins 'Factum est. Ecce secunda pars partis huius euangelii in qua agitur de uocacione discipulorum'. Written space 250 × 160 mm. 2 cols. 56 lines. Written in France (?). Used as covers: provenance unknown (Ep. I/15/1); of a 'call-book' for 1669–72 (Ep. I/18/51: Steer and Kirby, p. 30); of an Account Book for 1679 (Ep. I/43/5: ibid., p. 64).

XXIV. Ep. I/11/20. A bifolium of Concordantiae Maiores on the Bible. s. xiv ex.

Letter R. Quotations are in two columns and references to the Bible on the left of the first column and the right of the second column. Written space 315 + × 200 mm. 57 + lines. Used to wrap a Deposition Book for 1684–8 (Steer and Kirby, p. 19).

COLCHESTER. CASTLE SOCIETY

Evangelia[1]   s. XII[1]

1. ff. 3–94ᵛ Eusebian tables under arches (ff. 3–6ᵛ), letter of Eusebius (f. 7: Stegmüller, no. 581), and four Gospels, Matthew (ff. 11–33ᵛ), Mark (ff. 34–49), Luke (ff. 51–76), and John (ff. 77–94ᵛ), each preceded by a table of chapters and each, except now Mark, by a prologue or prologues.

Each Gospel is written continuously. Two leaves are missing, one before f. 34, with the prologue to Mark and the first thirty-five entries in the table of contents of Mark, and one after f. 93, with all between 'inclinasset' and 'inuenietis' (John 20 : 5–21 : 6). 2,700 verses in Matthew and 1,700 in Mark, according to stichometric notes on ff. 33ᵛ, 49. The margins contain: in black, Ammonian section-numbers (Matthew: i–cccxxxv; Mark: i–ccxxxiv; Luke: i–cccxxxix; John: i–ccxxxii); in red, immediately below the black numbers, numbers which refer to the ten canon tables on ff. 3–6ᵛ; in red, chapter-numbers, 77 in Matthew, 46 in Mark, 73 in Luke, and 35 in John.

The prologues are Stegmüller, nos. 595, 596, 590 before Matthew (Wordsworth and

[1] Deposited in the Colchester and Essex Museum.

White, pp. 1–4, 11–14, 15–17), no. 620 before Luke (W. and W., pp. 269–71) and no. 264 before John (W. and W., pp. 485–7).

The tables of chapters are on ff. 7ᵛ–8ᵛ, after the letter of Eusebius and before the prologues to Matthew, and on ff. 34, 49–50, 76ʳᵛ, after the prologues to the other Gospels. They agree with those printed by Wordsworth and White from Harley 2790 (Matthew), K, etc. (Mark, John), and D, etc. (Luke) on pp. 676, 175, 275, 493.

A hand of s. xvi added running titles and modern chapter-numbers and (ff. 2ʳᵛ, 8ᵛ) directions in English to find the Gospels from Advent to Lent.

2 (added, s. xii ex., on two preliminary leaves). ff. 1–2ᵛ (*begins imperfectly*) Surgit defunctus iuuenis quem suscitat unctus . . . (line 93) Tu petre me sequere. sis pastor ouesque tuere.

Each line gives the main theme of a section of the gospel story.

ff. iv+92+ii, foliated (i, ii), 1–94, (95–6). For ff. 1, 2 see above, art. 2. 240×150 mm. Written space 180×100 mm. 38 long lines. Ruling with a hard point: the vertical bounders double on quires 5–7 and single elsewhere. Collation of ff. 3–94: 1–3⁸ 4⁸ wants 8 after f. 33 5–11⁸ 12 five (ff. 90–4). At least three hands, one of them very good (ff. 7–30ᵛ). Initials: (i) f. 9, 15-line *B* of *Beatissimo*, knotwork, filled with curving branches on a yellow ground; (ii) of gospels and prologues, purple or red, usually with ornament in one or two colours; (iii, iv) 2-line and 1-line, red, purple, or rarely green. Human and animal figures and heads are in the decoration of the capitals and pedestals of the columns supporting the arches of the canon tables, ff. 3–6ᵛ: the style is Norman. Binding of s. xix. Secundo folio *a demonio* (f. 8) or *uolueris* (f. 10).

Written in England. 'Castle Society Colchester' on a stamp on the front cover.

COLCHESTER. COLCHESTER AND ESSEX MUSEUM

MSS. 213.32–216.32, 218.32–222.32 were given by Dr. L. S. Penrose in 1932 and are described in the *Colchester and Essex Museum Annual Report 1933*, pp. 20–3. MS. 217.32, also described there, and four other medieval manuscripts noticed on pp. 24, 25, were on loan from Dr. Penrose and were returned to his executors after his death in 1972.

213.32. Breviarium s. xv in.

1. ff. 1–275 Temporale from Advent to the twenty-fifth Sunday after Trinity.

2. ff. 275–284ᵛ 'In Dedicacione ecclesie', and octave of Dedication.

3. ff. 285–286ᵛ Benedictions. ff. 287–288ᵛ blank.

4. ff. 287–294ᵛ Sarum calendar in red and black, graded.

The word 'pape' and feasts of St. Thomas lightly cancelled. David and Chad added at 1, 2 Mar.

5. ff. 295–359 Liturgical psalter.

6. ff. 359–60 Te Deum, Benedicite, Benedictus, Magnificat, Nunc dimittis.

7. ff. 360–363^v Sarum litanies for each day of the week. f. 364^{rv} blank.

8. ff. 365–396^v Common of saints.

9. ff. 397–596 Sanctorale from Andrew to Saturninus. f. 596^v blank.

ff. iii+596+i. Two modern foliations: one of them counts in the flyleaves as 1–3 and is therefore three ahead. Thin parchment. 146×97 mm. Written space 90×60 mm. 2 cols. 35 lines. Collation: 1–36⁸ 37⁶ (ff. 289–94) 38–45⁸ 46⁴ 47² (ff. 363–4) 48–76⁸ Initials: (i) of main pages, including the usual eight psalms in art. 5, 6-line, in colours on coloured grounds, densely decorated and with prolongations in colours, blue and dark green pre-dominating: the prolongations form continuous borders of handsome work on ff. 1, 167^v (Easter), 193^v (Ascension), 200^v (Pentecost), 295, 365, 397; (ii) of Ps. 119 in art. 5, as (i), but 3-line; (iii) 2-line, gold on coloured grounds; (iv) 1-line, blue with red ornament or gold with violet ornament. Line fillers in gold and blue in art. 7. Binding of wooden boards covered with brown leather bearing stamps of two patterns, one a lozenge like Oldham, no. 284, damaged at the top, and the other a five-petal rose, s. xv ex. Secundo folio *versum loco*.

Written in England. 'Liber Ricardi Nykke episcopi Norwicen' 'quondam nunc autem Ioannis Yong Magistri Rotulorum domini Regis h octaui", f. 596: for Nykke, †1535, see Emden, *BRUO*. 'Liber Gulielmi Kymberlæi Bintoniæ ac Graftoniæ Rectoris [Binton and Grafton, Warwickshire], 1554', f. 596. 'Bought of Mrs E. G. of Sherstone Pinckney in the County of Wilts, widow 1° Mar. 1676°', f. i. A printed label inside the cover bears 'From the library of the Earl of Ashburnham. Appendix N° ccxv May 1897'. The armorial book-plate of Alexander, Baron Peckover of Wisbech, is pasted to f. i.

214.32. *Bartholomaeus de Sancto Concordio, Summa de casibus conscientiae* s. xv med.

ff. 5–250^v (*preface*) Quoniam ut ait gregorius . . . postulo correctorem. (*text*) Abbas. abbas in suo monasterio conferre potest . . . ut dictum est supra. Inuidia ¶2. Explicit summa de casibus consciencie quam edidit frater bartholomeus de Sancto Concordio pisanus ordinis fratrum predicatorum Qui obiit anno domini 1347 die 3 Iulii. Consummatum fuit hoc opus in Ciuitate Pisana anno domini 1338 de mense Decembris cum permissione sanctissimi patris et domini d. Benedicti pape duodecimi. Deo gracias.

In front are: ff. 1–4^v, a table of the articles, with leaf numbers added; f. 4^v, a notice about abbreviations, 'Iste sunt declaraciones supra breuiaturas in hac summa positas. Ac. Accursius . . . Item nota quod quamuis quis nesciat legere dictas breuiaturas non est magna uis. nam sufficere potest quod etiam sine illis inueniat ueritatem questionis et de allegacione non curet quia solum propter probacionem ponitur'.

SOPMA i. 157. Printed in 1473 (*GKW* 3450) and later.

ff. iii+250+iii. ff. 1–250 have an incorrect late-medieval foliation, 1–244. 228×160 mm. Written space 145×98 mm. 2 cols. 40 lines, lightly ruled with pencil. Collation: 1⁴ 2–25¹⁰ 26⁶. A small neat textura. A point as mark of abbreviation. Initials: (i) beginning each alphabetical section, pink on gold and blue grounds, decorated in colours and white and framed in black (cf. MS. 221.32); (iii) 3-line, blue with red ornament or red with violet ornament. A border in the inner margin of f. 5. French binding, s. xix in., for Monteil. Secundo folio (f. 6) *Vtrum abbatissa*.

Written in Italy. From St. Justina, Padua. 'Ista pisanella est Monachorum de obseruantia congregationis sancte Iustinæ. al' unitatis monasterio sancte Iustinæ paduane eiusdem congregationis deputata 'nᵒ undecimo'', f. 250ᵛ, s. xv ex. To the left of the inscription, the same hand wrote the number 252 within a frame and '.X. 11'. 'Institutio confessorum. Manuscrit du xivᵉ sᵉ appᵗ a Mʳ Monteil' is stamped on the front cover: cf. below, Edinburgh Univ. Libr. MS. 300. Small heraldic book-stamp of A(lexander) P(eckover) inside the cover. Given as MS. 213.32.

215.32. *Statuta Angliae*   s. xiv¹

1. ff. 1–6ᵛ Calendar in red and black.

2. ff. 7–13ᵛ Table of chapters of arts. 3–8, 11 and list of arts. 10, 12–17, 21, 18, 19, 22–36 in that order. f. 14ʳᵛ left blank: see below, art. 38.

3. ff. 15–23 Magna Carta.
Inspeximus of Edward I, ending 'valeat et pro nullo habeatur his testibus'. *SR*, Charters, i. 33.

4. ff. 23–7 Carta de Foresta.
Inspeximus of Edward I. *SR*, Charters, i. 42.

5. ff. 27–31ᵛ Prouisiones de Mertone. *SR* i. 1.

6. ff. 31ᵛ–44ᵛ Statut' de Marleberge. *SR* i. 19.

7. ff. 44ᵛ–68ᵛ Westminster I, in French. *SR* i. 26.

8. ff. 68ᵛ–74ᵛ Statute of Gloucester, in French. *SR* i. 45.

The title 'Incipit statutum Westmonasterii Secundi' is on f. 74ᵛ, immediately after art. 8. Arts. 9, 10 are an afterthought, no doubt, although in the main hand. They fill the central bifolium of a quire of ten leaves, instead of the usual eight.

9. f. 75ʳᵛ Explanaciones de Gloucestre. *SR* i. 50.

10. ff. 75ᵛ–76ᵛ Statut' de conspiratoribus. In French. *SR* i. 216.

11. ff. 77–121ᵛ Westminster II. *SR* i. 71.

12. ff. 122–3 Incipit statut' Religiosorum. *SR* i. 51.

13. ff. 123–4 Incipit statutum de emptoribus terrarum. *SR* i. 106.

14. ff. 124ᵛ–126ᵛ Incipit statutum Mercatorum. In French. *SR* i. 98. Ends imperfectly.

15. f. 127ʳᵛ Districciones scaccarii. In French. *SR* i. 197b.

16. ff. 127ᵛ–131 Incipiunt quia fines. *SR* i. 128. A leaf missing after f. 129.

17. ff. 131–2 Incipit modus calumpniandi esson'. *SR* i. 217.

18. f. 132ʳᵛ Incipiunt communes dies in banco. *SR* i. 208.

19. f. 132ᵛ Incipiunt communes dies de placito dotis. Heading only.

20. f. 133 (*begins imperfectly*) uel in scripto suo speciale ... The last six lines only.

21. ff. 133–135ᵛ Incipit s(t)atut' prerogatiue Regis. *SR* i. 226. Ends imperfectly.

22. ff. 136–9 Statut' de Moneta. In French, beginning imperfectly. *SR* i. 219.

23. ff. 139–142ᵛ Incipiunt Statuta de Scaccario. In French. *SR* i. 197.

24. ff. 142ᵛ–144 Incipiunt circumspecte agatis. *SR* i. 101.

25. ff. 144–146ᵛ Incipiunt Statuta de Bigamis. *SR* i. 42.

26. ff. 146ᵛ–147ᵛ Incipiunt Articuli Wynton'. *SR* i. 245.

27. ff. 147ᵛ–148ᵛ Incipit modus de homagio et Fidelitate facienda. In French. *SR* i. 227.

28. ff. 148ᵛ–150 Incipit visus franci plegii. In French. *SR* i. 246.

29. ff. 150–1 Incipit statutum de wardis et releuiis. In French. *SR* i. 228.

30. f. 151ʳᵛ Incipiunt districciones sokag'. Socag' put estre distinte en treys maners ... Cf. B.L., Royal 10 A.v, art. 30.

31. f. 151ᵛ Incipit composicio mensurarum. Per districcionem totius Regni sunt mensura ... octauam partem quarterii. Cf. B.L., Royal 9 A. vii, art. 22.

32. ff. 151ᵛ–152ᵛ Statutum de homagio inter sorores participes. Rex Iustic' salutem quidem de partibus nostris hibern' ... *SR* i. 5.

33. ff. 153–4 Statutum de admissis ante iudicium ad ius defendendum. *SR* i. 110.

34. ff. 154–5 Incipit statutum de Iurata et assisa. *SR* i. 113.

35. f. 155ʳᵛ Incipit statutum qualiter religiosi debent inpetrare tenementa. In French. *SR* i. 131.

36. ff. 156–63 Incipit Statutum de Norhamtone. In French. *SR* i. 257.

37 (added, s. xv). f. 163ᵛ Rex Balliuo Stannarie sue de Blakemore in Com' Cornub'. A writ on a complaint by Gentianus (Mattyngho), abbot of Hartland (1428–42).

38 (added in the same hand as art. 37). f. 14 A note of the six great-grandchildren of Lefardus de Bere, miles, and of their descendants through one or more generations.

Four descendants of Lefardus in the fourth and fifth generation of the male line bore the surnames Hudewyk, Bromford, Botteburgh, and Legh. A great-granddaughter married William Cheneston 'et habuit Th' Chenest[on] adhuc superstitem'.

For the family of de Bere, later Bromford, of Broomford in Jacobstowe, near Okehampton, Devon, see *Transactions of the Devonshire Association*, lxxii (1940), 122–41. Nicholas de Bere, great-grandson of Lefardus and grandfather of John Bromford appears in bishop Stapleton's register as patron of Jacobstowe, 1309–22.

ff. ii+163+iii. 103×68 mm. Written space *c.* 70×40 mm. 25 long lines. Collation: 1^6 2–9^8 10^{10} (ff. 71–80) 11–13^8 14^8+1 leaf after 8 (f. 113) 15^8 16^{10} wants 6 and 10 (ff. 122–9) 17 three (ff. 130–2: 131–2 are a bifolium) 18 three (ff. 133–5: 134–5 are a central bifolium) 19^{12} 20–21^8. Written in small sometimes current anglicana. Initials: (i) ff. 15, 77, pink on gold and coloured grounds, decorated (a seated king, f. 15) and with prolongations in colours and gold; (ii) gold on blue and pink grounds, with short prolongations in colours. Binding of s. xix in. Secundo folio (f. 16) *debuerit.*

Written in England after 1328 (art. 36). In Devonshire in s. xv (arts. 37–8). 'Alfred J. Horwood / Inner Temple', f. i^v: his sale, Sotheby's, 8 June 1883, lot 1296. Book-plate of Alexander Peckover, marked 'N° 70', inside the cover.

216.32. *Horae*   s. xv in.

1. ff. 1–2^v Hours of the Cross, beginning imperfectly.

2. ff. 2^v–6 Cy commencent les heures du saint esperit. Beginning imperfectly.

3. ff. 6–10^v Cy commencent les heures de la trinite. . . . Quicumque animam uult firmiter saluare . . . *RH,* no. 16566.

4. ff. 10^v–12 Cy commencent les heures du saint sacrement. Beginning imperfectly.

5. ff. 12–16^v Cy commencent les heures de tous sains. . . . Angelorum ordines deum qui laudare . . . *RH,* no. 35242.

6. ff. 16^v–56 Cy commencent les vigeles des mors. f. 56^v blank.

7. ff. 57–77^v Secuntur commendationes animarum. ff. 78–79^v blank.

8. Prayers: (*a*) f. 80 Oratio dominicalis. Pater noster . . .; (*b*) f. 80 Graces q*ue* on doit rendre a nostres' au matin. Gratias ago tibi omnipotens deus . . .; (*c*) f. 80^v Oroison a dire quant on se lieue. Mane cum surrexero intende ad me domine . . .; (*d*) f. 81^v Oroison deuote a la trinite. In manus tuas et misericordiam tuam. deus meus creator . . .; (*e*) f. 82^v Oroison deuote a nostre dame. Sancta uirgo maria que uerbum dei in carne genuisti . . .; (*f*) f. 83 Oroison deuote aux angeles. Sancti angeli et archangeli domini vobis supplico estote michi peccatori . . .; (*g*) f. 83^v Oroison deuote a nostres' pour aultruy. Domine deus omnipotens qui super cherubin sedes . . .; (*h*) f. 85 Oroison deuote pour aucun recommande. Domine deus qui non habes dominum sed omnia tue sunt . . . (*ending imperfectly*).

ff. iii+85+iii. 141×106 mm. Written space 77×46 mm and (quires 9–13) 80×55 mm. 14 and (quires 9–13) 16 long lines. Collation: 1 one (the last leaf of a quire) 2^8 wants 2 after f. 2 3 four (ff. 9–12) 4–8^8 9^4 (ff. 53–6) 10–11^8 12 8 wants 7 blank after f. 78 13^8 wants 7, 8 after f. 85. The hand changes at f. 53 (quire 9). A 10-line picture before arts. 3 and 5 (ff. 6^v, 12^v). Initials: (i) 4-line or 3-line, in colour on gold grounds, decorated and with prolongations forming continuous ivy-leaf borders in gold and colours; (ii) 2-line, like (i), but with short border sprays; (iii) 1-line, gold on coloured grounds. Line fillers in red, blue, and gold. From f. 53 (quire 9) there are no initials of type (i) and the initials of type (ii) have border sprays in a different style, the height of the written space. Binding of s. xix, labelled 'Missall'.

406 COLCHESTER. COLCHESTER AND ESSEX MUSEUM

Written in France. Probably part of a larger book. Armorial book-stamp of Alexander Baron Peckover of Wisbech inside cover.

218.32. *Missale* s. xv/xvi

1. ff. 1–61ᵛ Temporale from Advent to Corpus Christi.

2. ff. 62–63ᵛ Gloria and Credo.

3. ff. 64–85ᵛ Ordinary and canon of mass.

4. ff. 86–161ᵛ Sanctorale from Andrew to Katherine.

The thirty-nine feasts include 'Sancte marie pietatis' (f. 112, between 25 Mar. and 6 May), Desiderius, bishop of Langres (f. 115, 23 May), Claude (f. 117ᵛ, 6 June), feast of relics (f. 130, between 26 July and 1 Aug.), Mammes (f. 142, 17 Aug.), 'In dedicatione ecclesie' (f. 145, 26 Aug.), Lazarus (f. 147ᵛ, 1 Sept.), Valerius (f. 154, 22 Oct.).

5. ff. 161ᵛ–177ᵛ Common of saints.

6. ff. 177ᵛ–183 Secuntur misse peculiares.

Masses of Holy Spirit and B.V.M.

7. ff. 183–188ᵛ Secuntur orationes dicende ad deuotionem celebrantis.

Collect, secret, and postcommunion 'Pro congregatione', 'Pro familiaribus', 'Pro papa vel episcopo', 'Pro rege', 'Pro pace et libertate ecclesie', 'Ad graciam sancti spiritus postulandam', 'Contra carnis tentationem', 'Pro peccatis', 'Pro amico', 'Pro iter agentibus', 'Contra tempestatem', 'Ad pluuiam postulandam', 'De omnibus sanctis', 'Pro uiuis et defunctis', 'Oratio generalis que debet dici ultima'.

8. ff. 188ᵛ–194ᵛ Sequitur officium defunctorum.

9. ff. 194ᵛ–203ᵛ Masses 'Tempore pestis', 'Pro pace', 'Pro concordia et unitate ecclesie', 'Pro infirmo', 'Pro serenitate temporis'.

10. ff. 203ᵛ–205ᵛ Quinque plagarum christi missa.

11. ff. 205ᵛ–207ᵛ Holy water service.

12. ff. 207ᵛ–208 A mass 'pro infirmo' different from that on f. 199ᵛ.

13. ff. 208–214 'Benedictio fontium', noted. f. 214ᵛ blank.

ff. i+88+ii+124+i. Contemporary foliation of ff. 86–8, 91–207 in red i–iii, vi–viˣˣii. 300×200 mm. Written space 200×130 mm. 2 cols. 24 lines. Ruling in red ink. Collation: 1–4⁸ 5⁴+1 leaf after 4 (f. 37) 6–8⁸ 9¹⁰ 10⁸ 11⁶ (ff. 80–5) 12⁸ wants 4, 5, supplied in s. xix (?: ff. 89, 90) 13–26⁸ 27¹⁰ wants 10, probably blank. Initials: (i) for Mammes and sixteen other principal feasts in arts. 1 and 4, and *T* of *Te igitur* in art. 3, usually 5-line, in colour on gold grounds, historiated: framed floral borders in gold paint and colours, compartmented: the border on f. 1 includes a blank space for a shield; (ii) 2-line, gold paint, pink, or blue, on coloured grounds or grounds of gold paint decorated; (iii) 1-line, gold on coloured grounds. Capital letters in the ink of the text touched with yellow. Bound in France in blue morocco, gilt, s. xviii, the spine lettered 'MISSALE LINGDNEN' (*sic*). Secundo folio *cens eis*.

Written in France for use in the diocese of Langres. A 'Report from H. Grevel, 33 King Street, Covent Garden, London' kept with the manuscript, notes that it was in Quaritch's *General Catalogue of Books* for 1880 at £36.

219.32. (*A*) *Dieta Salutis* (*B*) *Pore Caitif* (*in English*)   s. xv¹

A. ff. 1–108 Hec est uia ambulate in ea . . . ductor illius coree ihesus uirginis filius qui cum eo . . . Amen. Explicit et cetera.

Dieta salutis, printed among the works of St. Bonaventure (ed. Rome 1596, vi. 285–342). Two leaves are missing.

For the author cf. the catalogue description of B.L., Royal 5 F. xiv, art. 3.

B. ff. 109–124ᵛ (*begins imperfectly*) sis. and anoon aftir wᵗ false glosyngis . . . for whi oonly suche shulen b[. .] (*ends imperfectly*).

Part of Pore Caitif, corresponding to Bodleian MS. Rawlinson C. 882, ff. 47/27–56ᵛ/10. Jolliffe, B.

ff. vi+124+iii. Two manuscripts made into one in 1875 to judge from the letter kept with it written by the binder, Francis Bedford, to Alexander Peckover, 15 Jan. 1875. The armorial book-plate of the Revᵈ Guy Bryan and the book-plate of Algerina Peckover are inside the front cover and the armorial book-plate of Jonathan Peckover is at the end.

(A). ff. 108. 165 × 110 mm. Written space 120 × 80 mm. 27 long lines. Collation: 1⁸ 2⁸ wants 3 and 6 (ff. 9–14) 3–10⁸ 11–12¹² 13⁶. Textura. Initials: (i) f. 1, red and blue, with red ornament; (ii) 3-line or 2-line, blue with red ornament. Capital letters in the ink of the text are touched with red. Secundo folio *igitur in nomine*. Written in England. 'Liber Arthuri Hearn ex dono [. . .] Bul[. . .] Armig.', f. 108ᵛ, s. xvii.

(B). ff. 16. 150 × 105 mm. Written space 108 × 70 mm. 23 long lines. Collation: 1–2⁸. Textura. 3-line blue initials with red ornament. Written in England. A slip from a book-seller's catalogue, s. xix², advertising (B) is attached to f. 125: '*Wyclyf*. Early English tracts . . . (12 mo) MS. on vellum'.

221.32. *Officia cum notis*   1462, s. xvi

1. The sung parts of the office of mass: f. 1, 'in honore sancti patris nostri benedicti'; f. 5ᵛ, of Holy Trinity; f. 9ᵛ, of Holy Spirit; f. 19ᵛ, of B.V.M.; f. 28ᵛ, 'In agenda mortuorum'; f. 41ᵛ, 'Pro peccatis'.

The text on ff. 41ᵛ–43ᵛ has been erased, but can be read. Two leaves missing after f. 41. f. 42 begins 'Alleluia. V'. Domine deus meus salutis mee in die clamaui'.

2. Sequences, (f. 44) Victime paschali, (f. 46) Sancte spiritus adsit nobis gratia, (f. 51ᵛ) Veni sancte spiritus et emitte celitus, and (f. 54ᵛ) Lauda syon saluatorem, for Easter, Pentecost, Monday, Wednesday, and Friday after Pentecost, and Corpus Christi.

3. ff. 62ᵛ–65ᵛ In visitacione uirginis marie.

Heading and text erased. New text written on ff. 63, 64–65ᵛ.

Arts. 4 (from f. 68), 5, 6 were added on three quires, s. xvi.

4. ff. 66–72ᵛ Kyries, Gloria in excelsis, Sanctus, and Agnus Dei 'In missis uotiuis de beata virgine'.

ff. 66–67ᵛ mostly over erasure, s. xvi (?).

5. Sequences: (a) f. 73 Homo natus in hoc mundo . . .; (b) f. 75 Uir dei benedictus mundi gloriam despexit . . .

(a). *RH*, no. 7977; *AH* xxxiv. 57. For the dead.

6. ff. 77–80ᵛ Mass of B.V.M. in Advent, ending imperfectly.

ff. 80. 620 × 455 mm. Written space 430 × 390 mm. 5 long lines and music. Collation:
1–5⁸ 6⁶ wants 2, 3 after f. 41 7–8⁸ 9⁸ 8 cancelled after f. 67 10² (ff. 68–9) 11⁴ (ff. 70–3)
12 three (ff. 74–6: ff. 75, 76 are a bifolium) 13⁴. Minims 18 mm high. Initials: (i) large,
3-line (f. 1) and 2-line, on ff. 1, 5ᵛ, 9ᵛ, 14ᵛ, 19ᵛ, 23ᵛ, 28ᵛ, in colour on gold grounds framed
in black: Benedict and his monks, f. 1; (ii) pink on blue and gold grounds, decorated in
colours and framed in black; (iii) red or blue with ornament in the other colour and green.
Contemporary binding of thick wooden boards covered with brown leather bearing a roll
with, *inter alia*, the letters *SB* within a roundel: heavy metal cornerpieces stamped with
lamb and flag, 'aue' 'ihesus', etc., and metal centrepiece and side-pieces. Large studs
project from the edges of the boards.

Written in the Benedictine abbey of Polirone in 1462: 'Iste liber est Monachorum congregationis sancte Iustine de obseruancia ordinis sancti Benedicti deputatus fratribus con[gre-
gation]is eiusdem habitantibus in monasterio sancti Benedicti de padoliron' mantuan'
diocesis scriptus in eodem monasterio de anno domini 1462 et signatus numero 792',
inside the front cover. 'signatus numero 792' again on f. 1, top right. Book-stamp of the
'Parrochia di S. Floriano Mantuæ' and below it the words, 'Felice Arieti Parroco 31 Agosto
1868' (as in Edinburgh, National Library of Scotland, Acc. 3822.1, q.v.), ff. 1, 80ᵛ. Ellis
and Elvey, catalogue 77, 1894, item 1 (£84).

222.32 *Antiphonale*   s. XIII ex.

1. ff. 1–204ᵛ Sanctorale from the Purification (imperfect at the beginning) to
Clement (2 Feb.–23 Nov.).

The twenty-four feasts include Anthony of Padua, who begins a new quire, f. 54, and
Francis. A further piece 'In festo sancti patris nostri Francisci' was added in s. xvii on
f. 204ʳᵛ.

2. ff. 205–255ᵛ Incipit commune sanctorum de antiphonario.

Ends imperfectly in the common of a virgin. At least one leaf missing after f. 251. The
last leaf of quire 1 (f. 10), between Agnes and Chair of Peter, was used by the scribe for
the beginning of the common of saints in error: as a result f. 10ʳᵛ has the same text as
f. 205ʳᵛ.

ff. i+255+i. 472 × 325 mm. Written space 395 × 245 mm. 7 long lines and music.
Collation: 1–5¹⁰ 6⁴ wants 4, probably blank (ff. 51–3) 7–11¹⁰ 12⁸+1 leaf before 1 (f. 104)
13¹⁰ 14–15¹² 16–18¹⁰ 19–21⁸ 22⁴ (ff. 201–4) 23–24¹⁰ 25⁸ 26¹⁰ 27 nine (ff. 243–51) 28 four
(ff. 252–5). Initials: (i) of seven feasts, Annunciation of B.V.M., Nativity of B.V.M., Michael, Francis (ff. 17ᵛ, 70, 84ᵛ, 123,
135, 148, 159ᵛ), pink on blue grounds, historiated; (ii) red and blue with ornament of
both colours; (iii) 1-line, red or blue with ornament of the other colour. Binding of wooden
boards covered with brown leather, s. xvii (?), and a velvet wrapper over all.

Written in Italy for Franciscan use. Item 6 in a catalogue of s. xix: 'Antiphonarium
Romanum thick large folio *most splendid*'.

COLCHESTER. PARISH CHURCH OF
ST. MARY

Biblia s. xiii med.

A Bible in the order Genesis–2 Chronicles, Prayer of Manasses, 1 Ezra, 2 Ezra (= Nehemiah), 1, 2 Maccabees, Esther 1–10: 3, Tobit, Judith, Psalms, the six ferial Canticles, Isaiah, Lamentations, Baruch 1–5, Jeremiah, Lamentations repeated, Baruch 1–5 repeated, Ezekiel, Daniel, Minor Prophets, Job, Proverbs, Ecclesiastes, Song of Songs, Wisdom, Ecclesiasticus, Baruch 6 (added on f. 294ᵛ), Esther 10: 4–13 and 11–16 (added on ff. 295ᵛ–296ᵛ), Matthew, Mark, Luke, Mark repeated, John, Catholic Epistles, Acts, Pauline Epistles, Apocalypse, ending imperfectly at 22: 1.

The prologues are 37 of the common set and 27 others, shown here by *: Stegmüller, nos. 284, 285, 328, 551, 341+343, prol. to Tobit* (Personam describens ostendit . . . conuersacione permansit), 335, 414*, 430*, 443* (marked 'vacat' in margin), 429*, 500, 503*, 511+510, prol. to Joel printed by de Bruyne, *Prefaces*, p. 144 (Iohel qui interpretatur . . . quando et micheas)*, 509*, 515, 512, 519+517+516*, 524+522*, 526, 525*, 528, 527*, 531*, 530*, 529*, 534, 532*, 539 (prologue to Zachariah, but placed before Haggai), 535*, prol. to Zechariah (Secundo anno darii filii hytaspis . . . regis imperium)*, 540*, 543, prol. to Malachi (Ultimum xii prophetarum . . . et in primo mensis quinti)*, 545*, 544*, 344+349*+350*, 482, 590, 620, 624 (these four added in the blank space on f. 295ʳᵛ after Baruch 6 and before the chapters of Esther), 607 (before the second copy of Mark), 624, 640, 670*, 674*, 676*, 707, 715, 728, 736, 748, 765, 772, 780, 783.

Gaps in the text after f. 28 where Exodus 38 : 2–Leviticus 21 : 21 is missing and after f. 99 where the end of the prologue to 1 Chronicles and 1 Chronicles 1–10: 3 are missing. 2 Kings, Proverbs, Matthew, and Catholic Epistles begin on new quires, ff. 75, 265, 297, 338. f. 264ᵛ is blank and ff. 294ᵛ–6ᵛ were originally blank.

Psalms in parallel versions, Gallican on the left and Hebrew, ending with Ps. 151, on the right. The earlier psalms are much abbreviated. The first canticle, Confitebor, is written opposite Ps. 151. The other five are in parallel versions, Gallican on the left and on the right a version which seems to be that of Mearns's MSS. B, C, O, P (J. Mearns, *Canticles Eastern and Western*, 1914, pp. 22–3): thus, the second canticle on the right begins 'Ego dixi in excessu' and the third 'Confirmatum est cor meum' (cf. Bodleian, MS. Kennicott 14, ff. 239ᵛ–242).

A stichometric note at the end of Ezekiel gives the number of verses as 3340. Luke 1: 1–4 is treated as part of the Gospel and not as a prologue: cf. *MMBL* i. 96, footnote.

2. Additions: (*a*) f. 242, margin, s. xiii, Cum fuerint anni completi mille ducenti / Et seni decies a partu virginis alme / Tunc anticristus nascetur demone plenus; (*b*) f. 378, s. xiii, a note on the senses of scripture; (*c*) f. iiiᵛ, s. xiv, a list of books of the Bible in the order and with the repetitions found here, headed 'Titulacio librorum iuxta ordinem bibliothece'; (*d*) f. ivʳᵛ, s. xiv ex., Nota breuissimum et utilem tractatum de biblia minus prouectis necessarium. Nota quod moyses . . . Explicit tractatus biblie breuis et vtilis valde sacerdotibus Deo gracias.

(*a*). Walther, no. 3717. (*b*). In a current hand. (*c*) ends with 'Nomina interpret' hebr' ', which is now missing after Apocalypse.

ff. iv+377+vi. ff. iii, iv, 378–80 are medieval flyleaves. 220×155 mm. Written space *c.* 160×100 mm. 2 cols. 45–59 lines. The first line of writing above the top ruled line. Collation: 1–2¹² 3 five (ff. 25–9) 4–6¹⁰ 7¹² 8 three (ff. 72–4) 9¹⁴ 10¹⁰ 11 two (ff. 99, 100, the outside bifolium) 12–15¹² 16⁶ (ff. 149–54) 17–21¹² 22¹⁴ wants 1 before f. 215 23¹² 24¹⁰+1 leaf after 5 (f. 245) 25¹⁶ wants 15, 16, probably blank, after f. 264 26¹⁰ 27¹² 28¹⁰ 29¹² 30¹⁰ 31¹² 32⁶+1 leaf after 6 (f. 337) 33–34¹² 35¹⁶. Quires numbered at the end in ink and quires 9–15 in pencil also, in another series i–vii. Several hands, changing at ff. 75, 149, 155, 203, 244, 316ᵛ, 338 (quires 9¹, 16¹, 17¹, 21¹, 24¹⁰, 30⁸, 33¹). Red initials. Binding of s. xix. Secundo folio *de petra deserti*.

Written in England. Pledged on eight occasions between 1452 and 1458 in the Chichester Chest at Oxford by master William Ketyll (rector of St. Mary at the Walls, Colchester, 1468–76: cf. Emden, *BRUO*, p. 1044): the entries are on ff. 376ᵛ–377 and the monogram of John Dolle, the university stationer, is on f. 376ᵛ. 'Robertus lynford' and 'William Norriche', f. 264, s. xv ex. and s. xvi. Armorial book-plate of F. Buddle Atkinson inside the cover. Sale at Sotheby's, 29 Nov. 1949, lot 1: bought for St. Mary's.

COVENTRY. CORPORATION RECORD OFFICE

Acc. 325/1. *Hoccleve, etc. (in English)*   s. xv med.

Poems by Hoccleve (arts. 1, 2) and Lydgate (arts. 3, 7), six short poems by Chaucer (art. 4), a verse version of Mandeville's travels (art. 5), and Titus and Vespasian (art. 6). The signatures (see below) suggest that there were originally over 180 leaves before art. 1. Probably these leaves were detached to make a separate volume (23 quires, signed a–z ?). Described by Doyle and Pace (cf. art. 4).

1. ff. 1–40 Musinge vppon the Restles besinesse . . . Doo bi thi rede his welthis shal witnesse. Explicit liber de Regimine principum.

Thomas Hoccleve, *De regimine principum*, ed. F. J. Furnivall (EETS, Extra series, lxxii, 1897), lacking the final stanza. ff. 1–4 are a replacement in the main hand, in place of leaves excised before f. 5. The upper part of f. 1 is occupied by a picture, 175×175 mm, of a man in round cap and long white gown standing in front of green hills.

2. ff. 40–70 (*a*) Et incipit prologus de Incendio Amoris. Affter þᵉ he(r)vest ynned had his sheves . . . (f. 43) And vnto þⁱ mercie and grace I call. Hic finit questus siue planctus Thome Occleue (*b*) Et Incipit quidam Dialogus inter eundem Thomam et quemdam amicum suum etc. And eendid my compleint in þis maner' . . . (f. 49) Shall purge as clene.as kerchief doþᵉ soope. Explicit dialogus (*c*) et incipit quedam fabula de quadam bona et nobile Imperatrice Romana Capº iijº. In þᵉ Romayn Gestis wreten' is thus . . . (f. 56) also adien shul wee. Here endithe the tale of a good woman which was sometime Emperice of Rome and nowe sueth the Prolog. Mi frende affter I trowe a weke or two . . . be knytte in feith. Here endeth the Prolog. And bigynnyth the Amoralizinge of þᵉ forsaide tale. The Emperour that I spak of bifor' . . . (f. 57) for oure Redempcioun Amen. Here endithe the Amoralisinge of þis tale. (*d*) Here beginnethe a processe to lerne to deie. Sethen all' men naturalli desiren . . . (f. 63ᵛ) the life þᵗ hath none eende. Here beginnith the prologe of the ixᵉ lesson' on all' hallowen daie. Thoo othir three partes which in þᵉ boke . . . (f. 64) ne tonge

expresse. Loo þis is seide ... (f. 64ᵛ) god graunte vs all' through his merciable grace amen. (e) Here beginnith þe prolog of þe tale of Ionathas. This boke to han eendid had I thouht ... (f. 69ᵛ) that wee do may. Here endith þe tale of Ionathas and of a wickid woman. And biginnyth þe moralizenge ther' of. etc. This Emperour ... to which bringe vs all' etc. Explicit.

The poems, all linked except (c) and (d), printed by F. J. Furnivall, *Hoccleve's Minor Poems*, EETS, Extra series, lxi (1892), pp. 95–110, 110–38, 140–78, 178–212, 212–42.

3. ff. 70–74ᵛ O yee folkis hardeherted as a stone ... her corious meetres in englissh to translate.

Lydgate, Dance of Death, ed. F. Warren, EETS, clxxxi (1931), 2–76. Follows art. 2 also in Bodleian MSS. Bodley 221, Laud misc. 735, and Selden supra 53.

4. Chaucer's ABC and five poems each called 'Balade': (a) ff. 75–6 Here biginneth a preiour of our ladie þᵗ Geffreie Chaucer made affter the ordre of the A.B.C. Almyghti and merciable Quene ...; (b) f. 76ʳᵛ Balade. Mi master boughton ...; (c) f. 76ᵛ Balade. To you my purs ...; (d) f. 76ᵛ Balade. The first stokke ...; (e) f. 76ᵛ Balade. Some time þe world ...; (f) f. 77 Balade de bon Counsail. Fle fro the pres ...

Ed. Skeat, *Works of Chaucer*, i. 261, 398, 405, 392, 394, 390 and from this manuscript by A. I. Doyle and G. B. Pace in *Publications of the Modern Language Association*, lxxxiii (1968), 26–9, (c), (e), (f) lack the *Envoy*. A reader, s. xvi, wrote on f. 77 'notabell wysdom for our dayes and happye ys he that imbraces the same'.

5. ff. 77ᵛ–95ᵛ Here biginnith the boke of Mawndevile. Almyghti god in trenite Oo god and persoones thre ... Though a man shulde bie hit of his brothere.

Printed from this the only known manuscript of a versification of Mandeville's Travels by M. Seymour, EETS 269 (1973), with a reduced facsimile of f. 77ᵛ.

The text is continuous to f. 89ᵛ and from f. 92. One bifolium of the intervening quire remains, the second or third—if the quire was of eight leaves—since the sense is broken at ff. 90ᵛ and 91ᵛ: Seymour presumes that it is the second bifolium. ff. 96–97ᵛ are blank.

6. ff. 98–129ᵛ Here biginnith the Sege of Ierusalem bi Vaspasian. Listeneth alle that ben a live ... And so longe hit forth gloode That xl yere he aboode (*ends abruptly at the end of a quire: catchword* Syn þᵗ he is so meke).

Ed. J. A. Herbert, *Titus and Vespasian* (Roxburghe Club, 1905), pp. 1–231. The last line here is line 5144 of the edition. Possibly a leaf which contained the remaining thirty-eight lines is missing, but probably, since ff. 130–136ᵛ are a quire of blank ruled leaves, the scribe meant to complete the poem on the first of these leaves and never did so.

7. ff. 137–67 Whan phebus passid was the Ram ... And of my tale thus I make an eende. Here endith the Sege of Thebes. God sende vs loue and Pees. Amen.

Lydgate, Siege of Thebes, ed. A. Erdmann, EETS cviii (1911).

8 (added in current hand, s. xv/xvi). ff. 167ᵛ–168 Behold we wrecches in this world present ... So þᵗ our soules wᵗ no spot be steyned. Twenty-four 4-line stanzas, each, except the last two, under a Latin heading. The first heading is 'Quando senex erunt (*sic*) sine sensu.' *IMEV*, no. 502.5. f. 168ᵛ blank.

ff. ii+168+i. 320×250 mm. Written space *c.* 245 mm high. Width of ruled space *c.* 190 mm. 2 cols. 40 lines. Pencil ruling. Collation: 1 four (ff. 1–4) 2⁸ wants 1–3 (ff. 5–9: no text missing, cf. above, art. 1) 3–12⁸ (ff. 10–89) 13 two (ff. 90–1) 14⁸ wants 6, 7 blank after f. 95 15–18⁸ 19⁸ wants 2 (ff. 130–6, blanks: see above art. 11) 20–23⁸. Quire 1 signed ꝛ in black. Quires 2–10 signed ꝛ, ꝯ, ≈, e, s, T, A, m, E in red: these are the abbreviations for et, con-, and est (?), the letters of the word est and the first three letters of the word amen. Quires 11–14 not signed. Quires 15, 16 signed aa, bb. Quires 17–23 not signed (signatures perhaps cut off). Two main hands, changing at f. 98: ff. 5–25ᵛ are perhaps in a third hand. The script is anglicana, with some influence from secretary: *r* is not a descender: from f. 98 ascenders are straight, not looped. A picture on f. 1: see above. Initials: (i) gold on coloured grounds patterned in white; (ii) 2-line, blue with red ornament; (iii) f. 1, and in art. 4*a*, 1-line, blue or red. Rebound in 1968: previously the binding was of plain brown leather over pasteboard, s. xvii. A chain of twelve links is attached to the middle of the back cover, as commonly on books from Coventry School Library. Secundo folio *So longe.*

Written in England. Described by Humfrey Wanley when in the public library of the city of Coventry housed in Coventry school, *CMA*, ii. 33, no. 12. Probably the 'Manuscript in English verse on Parchᵗ. fol.' in the catalogue made in 1697 (Cambridge, U.L., MS. Add. 4468, f. 16), the 'Chauceri Opera manuscript.' entered in the Donors' Book as the gift of Thomas Alforde gen.[1] (Cambridge, U.L., MS. Add. 4467, f. 5), and the 'Chaucer written upon Parchmᵗ wᵗʰ his effigies in his habitt at the beginning of the booke' in the list of 'Manuscripts in Coventry library' in Corpus Christi College, Oxford, MS. 390 (iii), f. 211. No doubt the 'manuscript copy of Lydgate's poems which the headmaster removed to his own house', mentioned in the 1834 *Report of the Charity Commissioners*, p. 131. As a result of this move it escaped the sale of the Coventry School Library in 1908. Rediscovered in 1950 and bought by the Corporation in 1962 for £300.

DOUAI ABBEY

3. *Biblia*   s. XIII med.

1. ff. 1–395ᵛ A Bible with usual contents in the usual order, as in Bristol, Public Library, 15. The prologues are the common set of sixty-four, together with a third prologue to Obadiah not recorded by Stegmüller, 'Esau filius ysaac frater iacob uocatus est etiam edom . . . Contra ydumeos loquitur hic propheta'. Capitula of Hebrews, 'Multipharie et multis modis . . . Deus autem pacis . . .' (nineteen chapters: ed. Wordsworth and White, pp. 682–8), follow the prologue without any indication that they are not part of it.

Haggai i is headed 'Item alius prologus'. After Apocalypse the scribe wrote 'Hic liber est scriptus. qui scripsit sit benedictus. amen'.

2. ff. 396–428ᵛ Incipiunt interpretaciones hebraicorum nominum. Aaz apprehendens . . . Zuzim. consiliantes eos. uel consiliatores.

The usual dictionary of Hebrew names.

3. A note at the foot of f. 3, s. xiii: Probra vxor adelphi proconsul in laude cristi uersificans conposuit virgiliocentonas id est carmen de cristo uirgilionis uersibus contextum sub nomine suo quia et ipse ut dicunt centona appelata est . . .

Cf. *Clavis*, no. 1480, and Stegmüller, no. 7009.

---

[1] One of this name was instituted rector of Allesley, Warwickshire, in 1643.

ff. ii+428+iii, foliated (i, ii), 1–297, 299–420, 420a, 421–31. ff. i, ii, 429–30 are medieval end-leaves. 158 × 105 mm. Written space 110 × 67 mm. 2 cols. 48–51 lines. Collation: 1–3²⁰ 4¹⁶ 5–6²⁰ 7²² 8¹⁸+1 leaf after 10 (f. 149) 10²⁰+1 leaf after 11 (f. 170) 11²⁴ 12–19²⁰ 20²⁴ 21²⁰ 22²⁴ wants 23, 24, probably blank. Initials: (i) of books and the eight divisions of the Psalter, in colours on coloured grounds, decorated or (ff. 1, 4ᵛ (Genesis), 184ᵛ (Psalms), 202 (Proverbs), 321 (Matthew)) historiated; (ii) of prologues, red and blue with ornament of both colours; (iii) of chapters, 2-line, blue or red with ornament of both colours; (iv) of verses of psalms and in art. 2, 1-line, red or blue. Binding of s. xx, but the leather of the old binding bearing a roll, a gilt centrepiece of fishes and small birds, and gilt corner-pieces, s. xvi, has been pasted over the front cover. Secundo folio *Abraham uidit*.

Written in France. Inscriptions on ff. iᵛ and 428ᵛ have been erased. "Fuit' Girardi Aurelii dono D. Iani Malerii viri doctissimi Humanissimike. 'Nunc est Regnardi florentini cui Idem Girardus dono dedit", on the front pastedown, s. xvi. 'Regnard', f. 1. 'John O'Sullivan, Listonell, County Kerry, Ireland', f. 429, s. xix in.

4. *Breviarium, etc.* s. XIII²

A breviary and other liturgical offices, described by D. D. Egbert, *The Tickhill Psalter and Related Manuscripts*, 1940, pp. 109–11, 205–8, with facsimiles of ff. 67, 164, 313 (pls. 108b, 109a, b). 'The text of the antiphons, responds, and hymns in the Breviary; the whole of the Missal as far as it goes; and the Litany are in close agreement with the corresponding parts of Add. MS. 35285, a Guis-borough book of somewhat earlier date, containing liturgical texts for the choir offices and the Missal.'[1] The wide separation of the different parts of the breviary (arts. 1, 9, 10) is also found in B.L., Add. 35285.

1. ff. 1–143 (a) Temporale of the breviary from Advent to the twenty-fifth Sunday after Pentecost, interrupted between the fifth Sunday after Easter and Ascension Day by (b) f. 97ᵛ the heading 'Incipit communi (*sic*) sanctorum a pascha usque pentecosten', followed by an abbreviated common of a martyr, martyrs, and a confessor (ff. 97ᵛ–98ᵛ) and (c) ff. 98ᵛ–106 the sanctorale for the month of May (cf. art. 9).

The scribe of art. 12 wrote 'Require dominica xviᵃ in fine istius libri' in the margin of f. 138ᵛ.

2. Masses: (a) ff. 145–153ᵛ, for first Sunday in Advent, vigil of Christmas, Christmas, Stephen, John, Innocents, Thomas the Martyr, Epiphany, Conversion of Paul, Purification of B.V.M., Annunciation of B.V.M.; (b) ff. 164–76, for Easter, Invention of Cross, Ascension, Pentecost, Trinity, Corpus Christi, John Baptist, Peter, Mary Magdalene, Laurence, Exaltation of Cross, Michael, All Saints, Andrew, Katherine, Nicholas; (c) ff. 176–81, for the common of saints; (d) ff. 181–186ᵛ, a votive series ending imperfectly in the postcommunion, Sumpta celestia, of the Missa communis (*Sarum Missal*, p. 443).

A leaf missing from (b) after f. 171.

3. ff. 154–63 Noted prefaces, and canon of mass. f. 158ᵛ blank.

4. ff. 187–245ᵛ Psalter, divided by larger initials into the usual eight liturgical divisions and into three fifties. f. 187 is damaged: thirteen lines remain in each column.

[1] I quote from a letter by Robin Flower at Douai Abbey: cf. Egbert, op. cit., p. 110.

5. ff. 245ᵛ–251 The six ferial canticles, followed by Te deum, Benedicite, Benedictus, Magnificat, Nunc dimittis, Quicumque vult.

6. ff. 251–3 Litany.

Apostles: (1) Petre *doubled*. Seventeen martyrs: . . . (14–17) Oswalde Dionisi cum so. Maurici cum so. Thoma. Nineteen confessors: (1) Augustine *doubled* . . . (12–19) Cuthberte Benedicte Leonarde Iohannes Wilfride Pauline Willelme Eadmunde. Fifteen virgins: . . . (14, 15) Hylda Brigida.

7. ff. 253–258ᵛ Office of the dead, with musical notes.

8. ff. 259–261ᵛ Burial office, ending imperfectly.

9. ff. 262–364ᵛ Sanctorale of the breviary, beginning imperfectly at 6 Dec. (Nicholas) and ending at 29 Nov. (Saturninus).

No entries between Vitalis (28 Apr.) and Marcellinus (2 June): cf. art. 1c. Nine lessons for —among others—Cuthbert, Wilfred, Oswald, king and martyr, Augustine of Hippo and Hilda (20 Mar., 24 Apr., 5 Aug., 28 Aug.—a daily memorial through the octave—and 18 Nov.). The translation of Wilfred occurs (12 Oct.). The Feast of Relics comes at a point agreeing with York use (19 Oct.).

10. ff. 364ᵛ–384 Common of saints of the breviary.

11 (added in the main hand in blank spaces). (*a*) ff. 143ᵛ–144 Holy water service. (*b*) f. 144ᵛ Days when 'Credo dicatur'. (*c*) ff. 153ᵛ–154 The Nicene Creed.

12 (added, s. xiv, in a blank space). f. 384ᵛ Breviary office for the sixteenth Sunday after Pentecost. Cf. art. 1.

13 (added on a flyleaf in a current hand, s. xiv). f. 385ᵛ [G]audeamus in domino. fratres dilectissimi. beatissime virginis marie . . . memoriam recolentes . . .'.

ff. i+384+iii. ff. 385–6 are medieval end-leaves. 210×118 mm. Written space 148× 80 mm. 2 cols. 33 lines (20 lines in canon of mass). Ruling with ink. Collation: 1–12¹² 13⁸ 14¹⁰+1 leaf after 5 (f. 158) 15¹² wants 9 after f. 171 16–22¹² 23 three (ff. 259–61) 24¹² wants 1–3 before f. 262 25–33¹² 34 six (ff. 379–84). The profuse and now badly damaged decoration by means of initials in colours, many historiated, or in gold, with border prolongations—continuous or nearly so on principal pages (118, 164, 187)—and grotesques, birds, and animals in the margins is described by Egbert, op. cit. The initials are: (i) larger historiated, now all cut out, except on f. 359ᵛ (Cecilia); (ii) smaller historiated, including the *P* of *Per omnia* beginning the common preface, f. 157ᵛ; (iii) punched gold on blue and red grounds patterned in white; (iv) 1-line, blue with red ornament or gold with violet ornament, except in quire 17 (ff. 187–98) where grey-blue takes the place of violet. Line fillers in red and blue in psalter and litany. Capital letters in the ink of the text are touched with yellow. Binding of wooden boards covered with modern leather: the remains of the leather of the former binding, stamped 'T.C.' in the centre, have been pasted to the new covers. Secundo folio *Aspiciens*.

Written in England for the use of Augustinian canons in the diocese of York. 'Thomas Kay[. . .] (*perhaps* Kayton)', f. 386, s. xv/xvi.

5. *Psalterium, etc.* s. XIV–XV

1. ff. 1–218ᵛ The Psalter, beginning imperfectly in Ps. 2: 11, (tre)more.

The leaves on which Pss. 1, 26, 52, 68, and 97 began and two other leaves are missing. Ps. 80 begins on a new quire, f. 119 (13¹): f. 118ᵛ is blank.

2. ff. 218ᵛ–240ᵛ Six ferial canticles, followed by Te deum, Benedicite, Magnificat, Benedictus, Nunc dimittis, Quicumque vult.

3 (s. xv). ff. 241–8. Antiphon, Ne reminiscaris . . . de peccatis nostris, and litany.

Eight pontiffs and confessors: . . . (8) ludouice. Six monks and hermits: 'benedicte' franscisse antoni 'bernardine' dominice ludowice. Nine virgins: . . . (8, 9) clara elyzabeth. f. 248ᵛ blank.

4 (s. xv). Antiphons for use with psalms, (a) ff. 249ʳᵛ, 271 at matins on Advent Sunday, (b) f. 271ʳᵛ at matins at Easter, (c) ff. 271ᵛ–277 throughout the week at matins and lauds, and (d) f. 277ʳᵛ throughout the week at vespers.

In (c) headings in French give the day of the week (dimenge, lundi, merdi, merquedi, ieudi, veredi, samedi). (d) ends imperfectly.

5 (s. xv). ff. 250–70 Dominical and ferial hymns, (1–4) at matins and lauds on Sundays, (5–16) at matins and lauds on weekdays, (17–23) at vespers on each day of the week, (24–7) at prime, terce, sext, and none.

ff. iv+278+iv, foliated (i–iv), 1–250, 250a, 251–77, (278–81). 108×78 mm. Written space 68×50 mm. 13 long lines in arts. 1, 2. Ruling with ink. Collation: 1¹² wants 1, 2 2⁸+1 leaf after 4 (f. 15) 3¹² 4¹² wants 3 after f. 33 5¹² 6¹⁰ 7¹² wants 8 after f. 71 8¹⁰ 9⁸+1 leaf after 4 (f. 90), wants 8 after f. 93 10–11¹⁰ 12⁶ (ff. 113–18) 13–14¹⁰ 15¹⁰ wants 1 before f. 139 and 3 after f. 140 16–18¹⁰ 19–22¹² 23¹⁰ 24⁶ (ff. 235–40) 25⁸ 26¹⁰ wants 9, 10 (ff. 249, 271–7) 27¹⁴ (ff. 250–62) 28⁸ (ff. 263–70). Initials: (i) of Pss. 38, 80, 101, 109 (but not Ps. 51) in colours on coloured grounds framed in gold, historiated (David points to his lips, David plays bells, David kneels at an altar, the Trinity): slight prolongations into the margins; (ii) gold or blue, with blue and red ornament; (iii) gold with blue ornament or blue with red ornament. Streamers of gold, blue, and red run the height of all pages with an initial of type (ii) and of all pages with an initial of type (iii) at the beginning of a line. Binding of s. xix/xx.

Written in France. 'Jacques Humbert Mirecurien' ' (Mirecourt, Vosges, ?), and other scribbles, ff. 255ᵛ–256. 'Ex Bibliotheca Ben. Anglorum D[ua]ci (?) Ciuit[atis]' (?), f. 1, s. xviii.

6. *Psalterium, etc.* s. xv med.

1. ff. 1–142ᵛ Pss. 1–150.

2. ff. 142ᵛ–155 The six ferial canticles, followed by Te deum, Benedicite, Benedictus, Magnificat, Nunc dimittis and Quicumque vult.

Audite celi is divided at Ignis succensus (Deuteronomy 32: 22).

3. ff. 156–63 Litany.

Twenty-two martyrs: . . . (3) Alexander . . . . (16–22) Albane Oswalde Edmunde Elphege Thoma Blasi Willelme. Twenty-six confessors: . . . (14, 15) Dunstane Cuthberte . . . (19, 20) Edmunde Benedicte . . . (26) Neote. Twenty-three virgins: . . . (21–3) Etheldreda Mildreda Osida.

4. ff. 163–9 Vespere pro defunctis.

The responses are Credo quod, Qui lazarum, Domine quando, Subuenite, Heu michi, Ne recorderis, Peccantem, Libera me, as in Tolhurst's group C (*Monastic breviary of Hyde Abbey*, ed. J. B. L. Tolhurst, vi (HBS lxxx, 1942), 110).

5. ff. 169–170ᵛ Missa de sancta Trinitate.

6. ff. 170ᵛ–172ᵛ Missa sancti Sebastiani contra pestilenciam. Egregie martir dei sebastiane . . .

7. ff. 172ᵛ–173 Benedictio sagittarum sancti Sebastiani contra pestilencia(m). . . . Deus qui beato gregorio famulo tuo . . . super has sagittas. Amen.

8. ff. 173–174ᵛ Missa de sancto Benedicto.

9. ff. 174ᵛ–175 Oraciones de sancto Iohanne euuangelista.
Collect, secret, and postcommunion.

ff. iv+175+iv. Thin parchment. 110 × 70 mm. Written space 78 × 40 mm. 20 long lines. Collation: 1–17¹⁰ 18 five (ff. 171–5). Initials: (i) of Pss. 1, 26, 38, 68, 80, 97, 109 and of arts. 2–5, 4-line or 3-line, in colours on decorated gold and coloured grounds, with prolongations in gold and colours forming borders on four, three, or two sides: green is used in the ornament; (ii) of art. 6, 2-line, gold on coloured ground, with sprays into the margin; (iii) of psalms and canticles, except as above, and in arts. 3–9, 2-line, gold with steel-grey ornament; (iv) of verses of psalms, 1-line, gold or blue. Gold and blue line fillers in the litany. Red morocco binding, s. xix/xx. Secundo folio *eodem*.

Written in England, for Benedictine use. A stamp, 'Ex Bibliotheca S. Edmundi Duaci', is mentioned by A. J. Collins in a description now kept with the manuscript, but I did not find it.

7. *Prick of Conscience (in English)* s. XIV/XV

Hic incipit liber qui vocatur stimulus consciencie. The might of ye fader almighty . . . yᵗ for us vouchid saue on rode to hyng. Explicit liber qui vocatur stimulus consciencie. Deo gracias amen.

Prick of Conscience, lacking lines 7316–77 of the edition by R. Morris for the Philological Society (1863), owing to the loss of a leaf after f. 115. The '5ᵗᵃ pars' begins on a new quire, f. 64: f. 63ᵛ is blank. The text begins on what seems to be the third leaf of the first quire. A blank leaf precedes it and a leaf originally in front of this is missing, unless it is f. ii.

ff. ii+150+ii. ff. ii, 151 are medieval end-leaves. 175 × 113 mm. Written space 125 × c. 60 mm. 30–2 long lines. Collation: 1¹² wants 1, perhaps blank, 2–4¹² 5¹⁶ (ff. 48–63) 6–9¹² 10¹² wants 5 after f. 115 11–13¹² 14 four (ff. 147–50). Written in one narrow pointed anglicana. Initials: (i) f. 1, 4-line, gold with red ornament; (ii) 2-line, red, plain or with ornament of the same colour. The first letter of each line is stroked with red. Contemporary binding of wooden boards covered with red leather, rebacked and repaired. Secundo folio *Monkynde*.

Written in England. 'Dan harri of beyston', verso of pastedown, s. xv/xvi. 'F. Thomas Woodhope Benedictinus Anglus 11 Julii 1630 . . . There is an other coppie of this booke in Doway Librarie¹ giuen by fa: Leander Pritchard', f. i: for Thomas Woodhope, monk of St. Gregory, Douai, †1654 or 1655 see *Memorials of Fr. Augustine Baker*, ed. J. McCann and H. Connolly (Catholic Record Society xxxiii, 1933), pp. 240–2. Still at Douai (St. Edmund's) in 1872 when seen by Edmund Bishop, as appears from Bishop's letter of 25 June 1872, now kept with the manuscript.² '*Δ*', f. 1, bottom left.

¹ Not known.
² Bishop went to Flanders and north-east France in May and June 'visiting St. Edmund's

8. *Horae*

1. ff. 1–6ᵛ Calendar in French, in red and black, not full.

2. ff. 7–11 Hours of the Cross, beginning imperfectly.

3 (filling quire 2). (*a*) ff. 11–12 Hymne du saint esperit. Veni creator spiritus . . .
(*b*) ff. 12–13 De nostre dame. ant'. Salue regina . . . (*c*) f. 13ʳᵛ De sainte barbe. ant'. Aue troni lucifera . . .

(*a–c*). *RH*, nos. 21204, 18147, 2148.

4. ff. 14–18 Les heures du saint esperit.

5 (filling quire 3). (*a*) ff. 18ᵛ–19ᵛ Les viii vers saint bernard. Illumina oculos
meos . . . (*b*) ff. 19ᵛ–21 Memoriae of SS. Nicholas, Sebastian, and Anthony
confessor and abbot.

6. ff. 22–61ᵛ Hours of B.V.M. of the use of (Tournai), beginning imperfectly.

7. ff. 62–76ᵛ Sensieuent les vii psalmes.
Penitential psalms and (f. 92ᵛ) litany.

8 (added, s. xvii). f. 76ᵛ Gaude virgo Catherina quam refecit lux diuina . . .
A memoria of St. Katherine, *RH*, no. 6993.

9. ff. 77–89ᵛ Sensieuent les vigilles.
Office of the dead, ending imperfectly.

10 (added on flyleaves, s. xvi¹). Records of births: (*a*) ff. 90–1, of Anette,
Adrienne, Jenette, Franchoise, Gilles, and Marguerite de Clerbois in 1522/3,
1525, 1529, 1532/3, 1534/5, and 1539; (*b*) f. 91ᵛ, of Barbette, Jenette, Ysabelet,
and Jean Capellin in 1504, 1505, and two unspecified years.

Godparents include in (*a*) 'Jacques de Clerbois mon pere', 'Guillaume gorret chanoine de
condet' (Condé-sur l'Escaut), and 'Gilles de le samen tresorier de Haynn' (Haine, Hain-
ault), and in both (*a*) and (*b*) members of the family of Fynes (Fine).

ff. i+89+iii. ff. 90, 91 are medieval end-leaves (see below). 185 × 130 mm. Written
space 97 × 77 mm. 14 long lines. Ruling with ink. Collation: 1⁶ 2⁸ wants 1 before f. 7
3⁸ 4⁸ wants 1 before f. 22 5–11⁸ 12 five (ff. 85–9): unnumbered leaves of modern parchment inserted after ff. 14, 62, 77. Initials: (i) ff. 14, 62, 77, 4-line, pink or blue patterned
in white on gold grounds; (ii, iii) 4-line and 2-line, gold on coloured grounds; (iv) 1-line,
blue with red ornament or gold with grey-green ornament. Sprays into the margin from
initials of type (ii). Capital letters in the ink of the text touched with yellow. Blue and
red line fillers in the litany. Of the continuous borders on the three pages with initials of
type (i) only the inner strips remain. Contemporary binding of wooden boards covered
with brown leather, rebacked: stamps of three patterns, the most distinctive a seated man,
form a border, which surrounds a rectangular panel containing three rows of the same
stamps: a fleuron and a hardly legible word-stamp, 'S[. . .]erlin' (?), are in the space above
and below the panel.

at Douai, where he . . . was allowed to look at books and MSS. in the monastery library.
He noted there (as a young friend found in 1888) certain linguistic peculiarities of a copy
of . . . *Prick of Conscience*' (Nigel Abercrombie, *Life and Work of Edmund Bishop*, 1959,
p. 42).

Written probably in French-speaking Flanders. The flyleaf records suggest ownership by the Capellin and Clerbois families, perhaps in or about Mons: Condé is a little to the east and Haine a little to the west of Mons.

9. *Officium mortuorum* s. xiv/xv

A fragment of a book of hours (no doubt), containing part of the office of the dead from the antiphon, 'Nequando rapiat' (f. 1) to verse 8 of Ps. 29 (f. 11ᵛ).

As *Manuale Sarum*, pp. 136–41, with three gaps. Six bifolia, probably from the last three quires of a manuscript. f. 12ʳᵛ is blank, except for scribbles, one of them in English, s. xvi.

ff. 12. 187 × 100 mm. Written space 103 × 70 mm. 21 long lines. Collation: 1⁸ wants 4, 5 after f. 3 2 four (the two central bifolia) 3 two (ff. 11, 12, a bifolium). Initials: (i) in gold on coloured grounds; (ii) 1-line, red with blue ornament or gold with blue-grey ornament. Capital letters in the ink of the text are touched with yellow. Binding of s. xx. Written in England. 'W. W. P.' on the cover.

10. *Antiphonale* s. xvi

The second volume of an antiphonal for Holy Week: Good Friday on ff. 1ᵛ–57 (Astiterunt reges . . .) and Holy Saturday on ff. 57–107 (In pace in idipsum . . .).

f. 1ʳ is blank. f. 107 is a waste leaf written in the main hand and reused later for the end of the Saturday office, after light erasure of the original text: the text on the verso is 'Tristis fuit anima eius usque ad mortem. R'. Mortem autem gladii acerbissimi doloris. Ad magnificat A'. Marie uirginis a[nima] que magnificauit dominum transfixa est gladio acerbissimi doloris [ui]dens transfigi filium'.

ff. 107. 685 × 525 mm. Written space *c.* 520 × 320 mm. 14 long lines or 5 long lines and music. Single sheets. Written in a very large hand: minims are 20 mm high. Initials: (i) ff. 1ᵛ, 57ᵛ, red and blue with red and violet ornament; (ii, iii) blue with red ornament or red with violet ornament in two sizes. Binding of thick wooden boards larger than the manuscript itself, covered with brown leather. Large metal corner-pieces and centre-pieces on each cover. A title on the upper cover 'Lᵒ Semana Sᵗᵃ 2ᵒ'. Written probably in Spain.

11. *Versarius* s. xii¹

A four-leaf fragment with noted responses and versicles for Sundays after Trinity, the tenth, eleventh, and twelfth Sundays on ff. 1–2ᵛ and the seventeenth to twenty-first Sundays on ff. 3–4ᵛ. The responses are abbreviated, only the first few words being given as a rule.

(Tenth Sunday). (V. De uultu tuo) beginning imperfectly at 'meum prodest'. V. Domine refugium . . . et progenie.

Dominica xi. R. In deo sperauit . . . V. Ad te domine clamaui . . . V. Venite exultemus domino . . . V. Preoccupemus faciem eius . . .

Dominica xii. R. Benedicam dominum. V. In domino laudabitur . . . mansueti (*ends imperfectly*).

(Seventeenth Sunday). (*Begins imperfectly*) nes populi.

Dominica xviii. R. Letatus sum. Alleluia. V. De profundis . . .

Dominica xix. R. Dirigatur . . . V. Confitebor tibi . . . psallam coram te.

Dominica xx. R. Oculi omnium. V. Aperis tu manum . . . V. Lauda anima mea . . .

Dominica xxi. R. Domine refugium. V. Priusquam montes . . . terra et or (*ends imperfectly*).

The Cluniac missal in the National Library of Scotland, Acc. 2710, has two versicles at the nineteenth Sunday, but otherwise agrees exactly with the eighteen forms here, one of which, *Confitebor*, is distinctively Cluniac.

ff. ii+4+ii. 200 × 125 mm. Written space 140 × 88 mm. 6 long lines and music. Ruling with a hard point. Probably two leaves are missing after f. 2. Well written. Blue, green, or metallic red initials. Bound in s. xx.

Written in England. The script is sufficiently like Bodleian MSS. Bodley 257 and Digby 158 and Corpus Christi College, Oxford, MS. 147 to make a Reading origin possible. Used in binding a medical manuscript or early printed book to judge from scribbles on f. 3, s. xvi: 'emerods fol. 14 fundament . . . fol. 22'. 'John Colthurst', f. 1ᵛ, s. xvi. Belonged to Sir John Lambert, K.C.B. Given by his granddaughter, Miss Lambert, of Bucklebury, Berks., in 1943.

DOWNSIDE ABBEY

21722. *Pontificale* s. xv med.

1. ff. 1–24ᵛ Incipit ordo ad faciendum clericum. quod potest fieri omni tempore. Oremus dilectissimi fratres . . .

The last form is an excommunication 'Autoritate . . . domini N. ecclesie paderborn' episcopi et nostri . . .'. A form of words spoken by the ordinand is written upside down on f. 18.

2. ff. 25–116ᵛ Orders for consecrating and blessing things: (*a*) f. 25 Incipit ordo consecrationis campane siue campanarum; (*b*) f. 33 Benedictio fenestre sacramentalis: litany, ff. 34–35ᵛ, in which the first four confessors are Sylvester, Gregory, Augustine, Martin; (*c*) f. 45 Incipit ordo consecrationis crucis; (*d*) f. 51 Incipit benedictio crucis metallizate; (*e*) f. 53 Incipit ordo consecracionis capsarum siue ymaginum; (*f*) f. 59 Benedictio muneris quod datur ecclesie; (*g*) f. 60 Sequitur ordo benedictionis lapidis primarii; (*h*) f. 63 Ordo in dedicacione ecclesie: the order of confessors in the litany is Martin, Nicolas, Sylvester: a form of excommunication on f. 92ᵛ begins 'In nomine domini. Nos fr. N. dei et apostolice sedis gracia ecclesie paderbornensis episcopus. excommunicamus . . .'; (*i*) f. 93ᵛ Incipit ordo in consecracione altaris; (*j*) f. 107 Benedictio cimiterii; (*k*) f. 111ᵛ Consecratio lapidis itinerarii; (*l*) f. 115ᵛ (added) Ordo reconciliacionis cimiterii violati. . . . (116ᵛ) Hic Episcopus potest pronunciare

prout in multis libris inuenitur de reconciliacione cimiterii Centum dies indulgenciarum et vnam karenam fidelibus ibi constitutis contritis.

3. (a) f. 117, begins imperfectly, as end of art. 2j above; (b) f. 117 Incipit ordo reconsiliacionis uiolate ecclesie; (c) f. 121ᵛ Cum excommunicatus uel anathematizatus reconsiliari postulat . . .; (d) f. 123ᵛ Benedictio in sabbato karitas dei; (e) f. 124 Benedictio in ordinacione clericorum; (f) f. 124 (added) De sancto spiritu. Introitus. Dum sanctificatus fuero . . .

4. ff. 125–44 Benedictiones episcopales Infra Missam. For principal feasts through the year, including St. Martin.

5 (added). Prayers at consecration of images (f. 144), '(in) imposicionem reliquiarum' (f. 144ᵛ) and at consecration of an altar. f. 145 is blank, except for an addition of s. xvii.

ff. iii+154+i. The medieval foliation—in red—stops at xl. 225 × 158 mm. Written space c. 165 × 100 mm and (art. 3) 185 × 128 mm. 18 long lines (arts. 1, 2), 20 or 21 (art. 3), and 19 (art. 4). Collation: 1–14⁸ 15⁴ (ff. 113–16) 16–18⁸ 19⁶ wants 6, probably blank. Several hands: black ink. Initials: (i) ff. 1, 107, 3-line, blue with red ornament and (f. 125) 4-line, red with blue ornament; (ii, iii) 2-line and 1-line, blue (arts. 1, 2 only) or red. Cadels introduce psalms in art. 2h–j: they have green ornament and, like the capitals in the ink of the text, are emphasized with strokes of red. Bound by Zaehnsdorf, s. xx.

Written in Germany for use in the diocese of Paderborn (cf. arts. 1, 2h). 'N. 64' at top of f. 1, s. xviii (?). 'Charles William Stanley Dixon Lord of the Manor of Newport 'To Geoffrey Gervase Hobson Matthews Downside 6 September 1928", f. i.

26524. *Missale*   s. xv med.

A Sarum missal described by Dom Aelred Watkin in *Downside Review*, lviii (1940), 444–6. The calendar and more than thirty other leaves are missing. The word 'pape' and feasts of St. Thomas of Canterbury have been erased or crossed out.

1. ff. 1–95ᵛ, 102ᵛ–126ᵛ Temporale through the year from Advent.
Art. 2 comes in after Corpus Christi.

2. ff. 95ᵛ–102ᵛ Gloria, Credo, prefaces, and canon of mass.

3. f. 127ʳᵛ Dedication of church.

4. ff. 128–156ᵛ Sanctorale, Andrew–Katherine.
The offices for David, Felix, translation of Edmund king and martyr, Dominic, and Thomas of Hereford are marked 'non sarum sed synod' '.

5. ff. 157–170ᵛ Common of saints.

6. ff. 170ᵛ–171ᵛ Ad missam sponsalium.

7. ff. 171ᵛ–172ᵛ Masses of Holy Trinity, Holy Spirit, and Angels.

8. ff. 172ᵛ–177ᵛ Masses of B.V.M.

The nine sequences ordinarily provided are supplemented by a series of seven, one to be said 'si placeat' on each day of the week: (10) Aue maris stella; (11) Ab arce siderea; (12) Saluatoris mater pia; (13) Salue mater saluatoris; (14) Salue porta cristallina; (15) Salue mater dolorosa; (16) Salue mater magne prolis. (10–13, 16) are in *Sarum Missal*, pp. 493, 490, 528, 521, 494. (14, 15) are *RH*, nos. 18126, 18018.

9. ff. 177ᵛ–184 Thirty-six votive masses: pro prelatis et subditis; pro parentibus et benefactoribus; pro uiuis et defunctis; of Holy Cross*; pro fratribus et sororibus*; of peace*; pro serenitate aeris*; ad pluuiam postulandam*; pro tempore belli*; pro quacumque tribulacione*; pro iter agentibus; ad poscendum donum sancte caritatis*; de omnibus sanctis; pro uniuersali ecclesia; pro pace; contra temptaciones carnis; ad inuocandam graciam spiritus sancti; pro semet-ipso (3 forms); pro papa nostro; pro episcopo; pro rege*; pro reg eet regina; pro penitente; contra mortalitatem hominis; pro femina; contra malas cogitaci-ones; pro tribulacione amici; pro quacumque tribulacione; contra aeris tempes-tatem; pro peste animalium; pro nauigantibus; contra temptaciones hostium; contra hereticos; pro infirmo.

The full offices are marked here by *.

10. f. 184ʳᵛ Memoria sigismundi regis et martyris contra febres. *Sarum Missal*, p. 406.

11. f. 184ᵛ Collect, secret, and postcommunion of St. John Evangelist.

Cf. Bodleian, MS. Hatton 1, f. 209.

12. f. 184ᵛ Mass of the dead, the beginning only.

ff. ii+185+ii, foliated 1–166, 166a, 167–84. 250×180 mm. Written space 180×113 mm. 2 cols. of 38–42 lines. Collation probably: 1⁸ wants 1, 2 (ff. 1–6) 2⁸ wants 3, 8 (ff. 7–12) 3–4⁸ 5 three (ff. 29–31), 6–10⁸ (ff. 32–71) 11 six (ff. 72–7) 12⁸ 13 six (ff. 86–91) 14 four (ff. 92–5) 15⁸ wants 4 (ff. 96–102) 16–18⁸ 19 one (f. 127) 20⁸ wants 1, 7 (ff. 128–33) 21⁸ wants 8 (ff. 134–40) 22 four (ff. 141–4) 23 six (ff. 145–50) 24 four (ff. 151–4) 25⁸ wants 3 (ff. 155–61) 26–28⁸. Initials: (i) all removed; (ii) 3-line, gold with lilac or pink ornament; (iii) 2-line, blue with red ornament; (iv) 1-line, blue or red. Capital letters in the ink of the text filled with pale yellow. Rebound in s. xx by W. H. S(mith).: the old cover, early s. xix, is kept separately.

Written in England. Many scribbles of s. xvii in the margins contain names which suggest that the manuscript was then in the hands of Beardemores, Erdiswicks, and Coynes: f. 41 Mathew Erdeswick . . .; f. 64 Isabella Erdiswick; f. 65 Francis Coyne; f. 65ᵛ Laurence Beardemore, Thomas Parker; f. 81 Thomas Coiney his Booke . . . 1632; f. 87 Agatha Coyn; f. 103ᵛ Thomas Coyne, Francis Coyne; f. 105ᵛ Thomas Coyney . . . 1632; Samp-son Coyney; f. 107 John Coyney . . . 1626; f. 111ᵛ John Beardemore of Kinesley; f. 113 Matthew Erdeswicke; f. 127 Jane Whithall; f. 139 Jane Coyne. 'Rowland Freeman 1817' is on f. 76 and 'R. M. Cooper's Bath 1831' on the old cover.

26525. *Missale* s. XIV in.

Incipit ordo missalis fratrum minorum secundum consuetudinem romane curie *(the last six words erased, but legible)*. Projecting tabs show the main divisions and the first four leaves of the canon of mass.

1. ff. 1–52ᵛ Temporale, first Sunday in Advent to Ash Wednesday.

2. ff. 53–54ᵛ Blessings of salt and water.

ff. 55–9 were left blank: see below, arts. 13, 14.

3. ff. 60–67ᵛ Temporale for Easter Eve, beginning imperfectly.

4. Prefaces and 'infra actionem' of mass (ff. 67ᵛ–71), Gloria and Credo in unum Deum (ff. 71ᵛ–72), and canon of mass (ff. 73–9).

In the creed an objector to *Filioque* erased the words 'Qui ex patre filioque procedit'.[1] ff. 72ᵛ, 79ᵛ–80ᵛ were blank and f. 72 was partly blank: see arts. 13, 14.

5. ff. 81–183ᵛ Temporale from Easter to the twenty-fourth Sunday after Pentecost.

6. ff. 184–282ᵛ Sanctorale, Andrew–Katherine.

The saints are those of *SMRL* ii. 271–305, together with Sother and Gaius (22 Apr.), Cletus and Marcellinus (26 Apr.), and Clare (12 Aug.), but without a vigil for Matthew: the omission was supplied on f. 58 (art. 13*b*).

7. ff. 282ᵛ–330ᵛ Incipit commune de missali.

8. ff. 330ᵛ–332 Dedication of church.

9. ff. 332–56 Votive masses.

The masses (collects, secrets, and postcommunions) in *SMRL* ii. 318–27, nos. 1–9, 37, 10, 11, 13–24, 26–36, 38–62. No. 25, Pro peccatis, occurs in its proper place, but is a full office.

10. ff. 356–366ᵛ In agenda mortuorum.

SMRL ii. 327–30, no. 63a–s, together with a Missa pro elemosinariis. Oratio. Deus cuius misericordie non est numerus . . ., after 63n. At 63l the heading is 'Missa in anniuersario famuli uel famule', but the mass has both singular and plural forms: feminine plurals follow the masculine plurals and feminine singulars are interlined above the masculine singulars.

11. ff. 366ᵛ–372 Votive masses.

SMRL ii. 331, nos. 64, 65, followed by full offices 'in honore sancti spiritus', 'in honore sancte crucis', and 'in honore beate uirginis' (cf. *SMRL* ii. 319–20). f. 377ᵛ was left blank. A now blurred text was added on it, s. xiv.

12. ff. 372–7 Mass of B.V.M.

13. Additions, s. xiv: (*a*) ff. 55–8 Officium de corpore cristi; (*b*, *c*) ff. 58–9 Offices on the vigil of Matthew and for Louis, king and confessor; (*d*) f. 72 Office for St. Helen.

(*a–c*) fill some of the gaps left blank in quire 5: cf. 14*b*, *c*.

14. Additions, s. xv: (*a*) ff. 19–21, lower margins, sequences for Christmas; (*b*, *c*) f. 59 Blessing of meat and sequence Victime paschali laudes; (*d*) f. 71 Sequences for feasts of B.V.M., Congaudent angelorum chori and Stirpe maria regia; (*e–g*) ff. 79ᵛ–80ᵛ Sequences: Omnes sancti seraphin . . ., for All Saints; Summi triumphum regis prosequamur laude . . ., for Ascension; Gaudeamus omnes in domino diem festum celebrantes . . ., for the Visitation of B.V.M.

---

[1] On *Filioque* cf. *Dictionnaire de Théologie Catholique*, v. 2309, a reference I owe to Dom Philip Jebb, O.S.B.

15. The binding leaves, ff. i, ii, 378, are from a breviary, s. xiv: f. i, Lent; f. 378, Passion week; f. ii, Holy week.

ff. ii+377+i. Soft parchment. For ff. i, ii, 378 see above, art. 15. A late medieval foliation of ff. 1–341 was made at a time when arts. 3, 4 (quires 6, 7) were bound in the middle of art. 6, after f. 218 (18¹²): the old numbers on these leaves, ciiic–ccxvii, have been erased. 182 × 130 mm. Written space 125 × 80 mm. 20 long lines. Collation: 1–4¹² 5¹² wants 12, blank, after f. 59 6¹⁰ 7¹² wants 12, blank, after f. 80 8–9¹² 10¹⁸ (ff. 105–22) 11–31¹² 32⁴ wants 4, blank (ff. 375–7). Quires 1–4 numbered at the end i–iiii. Quires 8–31 numbered at the end in red 1–24. The flex (?) is used as punctuation in arts. 6, 12. Initials: (i) ff. 1, 73, red and blue with ornament of both colours; (ii, iii) 2-line and 1-line, red or blue. Capital letters in the ink of the text lined with red. German pigskin binding over wooden boards, s. xv: two strap-and-pin fastenings missing.

Written in Germany. 'Diss hort geyn[. . . .]', f. 1, s. xv. Letters kept with the manuscript show that it belonged to the Revd. A. H. Payne in 1895 and was given by him in 1930.

26526. *Breviarium congregationis Sanctae Justinae*   s. XV ex.

1. ff. 1–6 Aduentus domini semper celebrari debetur . . .
Rubric. Placidus cum sociis and Justina are in the list of 'duplicia maiora'. f. 6ᵛ blank.

2. ff. 7–203 Incipit breuiarium monasticum a congregacione sancte iustine ordinatum et a papa eugenio quarto confirmatum . . . Explicit proprium temporis.

3. ff. 203–207ᵛ Office of the Transfiguration.

4. ff. 208–211ᵛ Table of anthems before Christmas.

5 (added, s. xvi). (*a*) ff. 211ᵛ–215 Hymns for Ascension, Pentecost, Corpus Christi, All Saints, Martyrs, dedication of church, and St. Martin. (*b*) ff. 215ᵛ–217ᵛ Prayers to B.V.M.

6. ff. 218–302 Liturgical psalter.

7. ff. 302ᵛ–305 Incipiunt psalmi penitenciales secundum curiam romanam.
Cues only of the psalms. A litany follows, in which Justina is third of virgins.

8. ff. 305–9 Incipit offitium mortuorum.

9. ff. 309–313ᵛ Incipit offitium beate marie virginis.

10. ff. 313ᵛ–314 Hymns for the Purification of B.V.M. ff. 314ᵛ–315ᵛ were left blank.

11. ff. 316–500ᵛ Incipit proprium sanctorum. Andrew–Katherine.

12. ff. 500ᵛ–503 In dedicatione ecclesie. f. 503ᵛ blank.

13. ff. 504–561ᵛ Incipit commune sanctorum. f. 562ʳᵛ was left blank.

14. A leaf of a psalter of s. xv, written in thirty-one long lines, lies at f. 217.

ff. 566, foliated 1–11, 11b, 12–82, 82b, 83, 83b, 84–182, 182b, 183–562. 138 × 100 mm. Written space c. 87 × 70 mm. 2 cols. 28–40 lines. Collation: 1⁶ 2–22¹⁰ 23¹⁰ wants 6–10, blank, after f. 217 24–32¹⁰ 33¹⁰ wants 9, 10, blank, after f. 315 24–48¹⁰ 49⁸ 50¹² 51¹⁰ 52¹⁰ wants 9, 10, blank, after f. 531 56–57¹⁰ 58¹² wants 11, blank, after f. 561. The hand changes often. 2-line and in art. 6 1-line initials, red or, less often, blue: many not filled in. Medieval (?) boards, rebacked: two clasps missing.

Written in Italy for use by a house of the congregation of St. Justina, O.S.B. A 3-line erasure at the foot of f. 7. Belonged in s. xvi to the family of de Peregrinis: 'Iste liber est mei andre peregrinis et leonardi et fratrum de peregrinis', f. 562ᵛ; 'Ego Petrus de Peregrinis scripsi hoc', f. 314 in capital letters. 'Breviarium / Ant. de Peccora' is on a label on the spine and 'Roma 1794 / Codex Francisci Buzzi' is inside the cover: cf. 'Buzzi', f. 561ᵛ. The printed 'E libris' of Edmund Bishop, 1846–1917, is inside the cover and his note of purchase, 26 Nov. 1869, signed E. B., is on f. 562ᵛ.

26527. *Breviarium*   s. XIV med.

1. ff. 1–6ᵛ Calendar, in which 'Cathedra Sancti Petri apostoli' is in red and all other feasts are in black. As a rule the only gradings are Duplex and Semi-duplex. The only entries in the original hand which do not occur regularly in thirteenth-century calendars of the papal court are the Perugian saints Constantius, Herculanus, and Ubaldus (29 Jan., 1 Mar., 16 May), 'Raptus helie prophete' (17 June), Margaret (13 July), and Cassian (13 Aug.). Pudentiana (19 May) is miswritten Prudentiana. Many later additions, including Louis of Toulouse (19 Aug. and translation, 14 May), William (de Malavalle, 10 Feb.), Petrus de Morrone (19 May), Dedicatio sen' ecclesie (18 Nov.), and after the main hand's entry of Saturninus (29 Nov.) 'et fit de eo totum duplex quia sunt hic de suis reliquiis'. The usual verses are at the head of each month, and at the foot of each month, except January and December.

The papal calendar is printed in *SMRL* ii. 365–76.

2. ff. 7–17ᵛ Sixty-two hymns of the temporale, sanctorale, and common of saints and for the dedication of a church, followed by the two Sunday hymns Primo dierum and Nocte surgentes. The sanctorale includes three hymns for St. Antony (En gratulamur, Laus regi, and Ihesu lux uera) and four for St. Francis (Proles de celo, In celesti collegio, Plaude turba, Decus morum). Trinity and Corpus Christi are passed over.

3. ff. 17ᵛ–73 Liturgical psalter.

4. ff. 73–7 Six ferial canticles, Te deum, Benedicite, Benedictus, Magnificat, Nunc dimittis, Pater noster, Credo, Quicumque vult.

5. ff. 77ᵛ–79 Litany. The order of doctors is Benedict, Bernard, Francis, Antony, Dominic. Clare is sixth and Elizabeth eighth (last) among virgins. In the versicle on f. 78ᵛ, 'Oremus ministro abbate (?) nostro . . .', the second and third words have been erased and *rectore* supplied in their place; similarly in the prayer on f. 79, 'Omnipotens sempiterne deus miserere famulo tuo abbate nostro . . .', *abbate* has been erased and *retore* (sic) written instead.

6. f. 79ᵛ Nicene creed.

7 (in another hand). ff. 80–5 Legenda de corpore cristi. (*a*) ff. 80–3 Lectio. [I]nmensa diuine largitatis . . . et illic plenus. (*b*) f. 83–5 Lectio sancti euangelii secundum iohannem. Lectio vii. [I]n illo tempore Dixit ihesus discipulis suis et turbis iudeorum. Caro mea . . . est potus (John 6: 55) Et rel'. Omelia sancti augustini episcopi. Cum enim cibo . . . a morte iam liberati.

Apart from the heading in red at f. 83, the text is written without break or indication of division into lections. It will be found in the following places in C. Lambot, 'L'Office de la Fête-Dieu', *RB* liv (1942), 61–123: (1) Inmensa–duraturam: L., pp. 76–7 (lines 1–76); (2) Huius sacramenti figura–elementorum: L., pp. 78–9 (lines 1–58); (3) In cristo –et illic plenus: L., p. 109 (lines 334–41); (4) Lectio santi euangelii–in semetipso: L., pp. 80–1 (gospel lection and lines 1–39); (5) Hic est panis–possumus: L., p. 104 (lines 64–6); (6) Cristus panis est–liberati: L., pp. 100–2 (lines 131–93).

8 (in another hand). ff. 85ᵛ–87ᵛ De specialibus antiphonis . . . continetur. Prima tabula. In anno illo . . . Explicit tabula aduentus.

SMRL ii. 401–8 (cf. i. 241–6).

9. ff. 88–475 In nomine domini amen. Incipit ordo breuiarii fratrum heremit- arum secundum consuetudinem curie romane.

The breviary of Haymo of Faversham: (*a*) f. 88, temporale; (*b*) f. 294ᵛ, general rubrics; (*c*) f. 296ᵛ, sanctorale; (*d*) f. 441ᵛ, common of saints; (*e*) f. 469ᵛ In dedicatione uel in anni- uersario ecclesie.

(*b*). Sects. 1–23 only: *SMRL* ii. 114–20. (*c*) includes Clare (f. 380. nine lessons, 'Admira- bilis femina . . . uulgabatur in populo'), Elizabeth of Hungary (f. 431ᵛ: nine lessons), and at the end, ff. 440–441ᵛ, the nine lessons for Clare, 'Venerabilis cristi sponse . . . sollicitius intendebat', printed by M. Bihl, 'Tres legendae minores S. Clarae', *AFH* vii (1914), 39– 42/7 (ch. 1 and ch. 2/1–9). Corpus Christi is absent.

10. ff. 473–477ᵛ Incipit offitium beate uirginis. *SMRL* ii. 185–91.

11. (*a*) ff. 477ᵛ–478ᵛ Ordo ad communicandum infirmum. (*b*) ff. 478ᵛ–480 Ordo ad ungendum infirmum. (*c*) ff. 480–482ᵛ Ordo commendationis anime.

Ibid. ii. 387–8, 388–90, 390–394/1 (cf. i. 231–40).

12. ff. 482ᵛ–488ᵛ Office of the dead and burial service, followed by rubrics, Notandum quod . . .

The rubrics are those printed in *SMRL* ii. 194/1–195/23 and 191/2–10.

13. ff. 488ᵛ–490 Incipit ordo ad benedicendum mensam per totum annum. Congregatis fratribus ad prandium . . . Oculi omnium.

SMRL ii. 199–203 (cf. i. 203–6).

14. Additions on ff. 490–491ᵛ include: (*a*) f. 490, a collect for St. Louis, O.F.M., 'Deus qui ecclesiam tuam . . . tribue quesumus ut qui . . . beati lodouigi con- fessoris tui atque pontificis . . .'; (*b*) f. 491ᵛ, a prayer invoking the aid of St. Bernard, 'Perfice quesumus domine pium nobis . . .'.

ff. i+490+i, foliated (i) 1–14, 16–491, (492). 280×205 mm. Written space *c.* 185× 130 mm. 32 long lines. Ruling with ink. Collation: 1⁶ 2–7¹² 8⁴ (ff. 80–3) 9⁴ (ff. 84–7) 10¹² 7, 8 cancelled after f. 93 11–35¹² 36¹⁰ 37–39¹² 40¹², the outside sheet (ff. 444, 455) supplied in s. xv ex. (?), 41–42¹² 43¹⁴ wants 13, 14, blank. Several hands. Punctuation includes the flex (?), even in an addition on f. 491ᵛ. Initials: (i) in colour on coloured grounds, patterned in white, historiated or (ff. 7, 32ᵛ, 61ᵛ) decorated in colours and gold: white-surpliced priests sing on f. 55 (Ps. 97); St. Francis, f. 410ᵛ; (ii) 2-line, blue or red with ornament of the other colour; (iii) 1-line, blue or red. Capital letters in the ink of the text touched with red. Binding of s. xix. Secundo folio (f. 8) *genario*.

Written in Italy (Perugia?): unusual spellings, especially in headings, e.g. *auentum* for *aduentum*, *octuber* for *october*, *settem* for *septem*. Belonged to a church with relics of St. Saturninus (art. 1). 'Johan: C. Jackson 1851' (f. 1): not identifiable in his sale, 13 Dec. 1895. 'ᴇ ʟɪʙʀɪs/ᴇᴅᴍᴠɴᴅɪ/ʙɪsʜᴏᴘ' on a printed label inside the cover.

26528. *Breviarium*   s. xɪɪɪ/xɪᴠ

1. f. 1ʳᵛ September and October of a calendar in red and black, graded. 11,000 virgins in red (21 Oct.).

2. ff. 2ᵛ–38 Pss. 1–150, without liturgical divisions and in part abbreviated.

3. ff. 38–42 Ferial canticles, followed by Benedicite, Benedictus, Nunc dimittis, Magnificat, Te deum, Quicumque uult.

4. ff. 42–53ᵛ Hymns for the week and for special occasions, ending imperfectly in the common of virgins, and with a gap after f. 51. The little of the sanctorale that remains includes Alma lux siderum for Denis the Areopagite, which Mearns, *Early Latin Hymnaries*, records only from German manuscripts.

5. ff. 54–5 Six sets of monastic canticles, the first, for Easter, beginning imperfectly in Hosea 6: 5. The other five sets are for Sundays (Mearns, *Canticles Eastern and Western*, p. 87, first set), Corpus Christi (Tu autem deus, Ecce quasi ros, Redemit dominus iacob), Apostles (Mearns, p. 91, set 9), Martyrs (Mearns, p. 90, set 1), and Virgins (Mearns, p. 92, third set).

6. ff. 55ᵛ–56 The hymns for Corpus Christi, Pange lingua gloriosi and Verbum superni.

7. ff. 56–57ᵛ The first words of prayers: (*a*) in ferialibus diebus ad omnes horas; (*b*) ad primam singulis diebus; (*c*) ad completorium per totum annum; (*d*) in aduentu domini et in quadragesima ad omnes horas; (*e*) in duodecim leccionibus et infra octauas.

8. ff. 57ᵛ–58 In quadragesima psalmi post laudes. Cues only.

9. f. 58ʳᵛ Incipit ordo de horis s. marie.

10. ff. 58ᵛ–59 Versus excerpti de hymnis in octauis precipuarum sollempnitatum per ebdomadam ad horas. Memento salutis auctor . . . In the extract beginning 'Sancti benedicti patris nostri' the fourth word has been erased.

11. ff. 59–60ᵛ Letania. Martin is fourth and Godehard, Odelric, Remigius, Willehad, Anscharius, Reymbertus, Brice, Felix, Basinus, Benedict are tenth to nineteenth of twenty-six confessors.

12. ff. 60ᵛ–61 Lecciones infra octauam assumpcionis. O felix maria . . .

13. Temporale (ff. 62–169ᵛ), sanctorale (ff. 170–239ᵛ), and common of saints (ff. 239ᵛ–251). The first leaf of the temporale, the first of the sanctorale, and

probably seven other leaves are missing. Corpus Christi, ff. 146ᵛ–149. Full office of St. Benedict, ff. 185ᵛ–187ᵛ, and of St. Martin, ff. 233ᵛ–236. The local German saints have collects only.

14 (added in blank spaces, s. xiv): (a) ff. 2ʳ, 251ᵛ Office of St. Anne; (b) f. 61 Collect for St. Paulinus; (c) f. 61 Prayer at terce 'in passione domini'; (d) f. 61ᵛ Memoria of 10,000 martyrs; (e) f. 61ᵛ prayers to St. Anne.

ff. ii+251+ii. 148×112 mm. Written space 120×90 mm. 30 long lines. Collation: 1 one 2–6¹⁰ 7¹⁰ (ff. 52–61) 8¹⁰ wants 1 before f. 62 and 10 after f. 69 9–10¹⁰ 11⁸ 12–13¹⁰ 14¹⁰ wants 2 after f. 118 15–18¹⁰ 19 six (ff. 167–72, three bifolia: gap after f. 169) 20–21¹⁰ 22¹⁰+1 leaf after 6 (f. 199) 23–26¹⁰ 27¹⁰ wants 3, 4 after f. 245. A new hand begins at f. 62. Initials: (iii) 2-line and 1-line, red or (art. 13 only) blue. Bound by Riviere, s. xx.

Written in northern Germany. '[. . . .] Phillips Ejus liber', f. 1. Edmund Bishop's printed 'E libris' is inside the cover and a note of purchase on 22 July 1869 signed 'E. B.' is on f. 1.

26529. *Horae* s. xv in.

A book of hours nearly of the common type produced abroad for the English market: cf. *MMBL* i. 46–8. Art. 4 may be out of place.

1. ff. 1–6ᵛ Calendar in red and black.

Feasts in red include John of Beverley (7 May, 25 Oct.) and Mildred (13 July). Spellings: Vunstani for Dunstani, Swithimi for Swithuni, Kenelini for Kenelmi. Feasts of Thomas of Canterbury and the word 'pape' erased.

2. f. 7ʳᵛ De sancta trinitate ant'. Domine deus omnipotens pater et filius et spiritus sanctus Da michi famulo tuo .N. uictoriam . . .

The prayer 'Libera me domine . . .' follows. *Lyell Cat.*, p. 373.

3. ff. 8–12ᵛ Memoriae, one to a leaf, of George, Christopher, Thomas of Canterbury (the name erased in all nine places and, except twice, replaced later), Katherine, and Mary Magdalene. The antiphons are *RH*, nos. 2742, 39618, 26999, 6991, 6985.

4. ff. 13–17 Summa uulnerum cristi secundum bernardum et coronatione flagellatione et crucifixione uidelicet quinque milia cccclxxv vnde versus Vulnera quatuor sunt cristi milia quinque . . . quod uulnera cristi(*four lines*). O domine ihesu criste eterna dulcedo . . .

The Fifteen Oes of St. Bridget. *Lyell Cat.*, p. 62. f. 17ᵛ blank.

5. Hours of B.V.M. of the use of (Sarum), the first leaf mostly gone. Memoriae after lauds of Holy Spirit, Holy Trinity, Holy Cross, Michael, John Baptist, Peter and Paul, Andrew, Laurence, Stephen, Thomas of Canterbury (crossed out), Nicholas, Mary Magdalene, Katherine, Margaret, All Saints, and for peace. Hours of the Cross are worked in.

6. ff. 44–46ᵛ Salve Regina and its farcing Salve virgo virginum (*RH*, no. 18318), the latter beginning imperfectly.

7. ff. 46ᵛ–47ᵛ Oracio bona. O intemerata . . . orbis terrarum. Inclina . . .

8. ff. 47ᵛ–49 Oracio. Obsecro te . . .

9. ff. 49–51 Virgo templum trinitatis . . .

The Seven Joys of B.V.M., with heading conveying an indulgence of 100 days 'a domino papa clemente proprio stilo composuit (sic)'. *RH*, no. 21899.

10. ff. 51–3 Ad ymaginem cristi crucifixi. Omnibus consideratis . . . *AH* xxxi. 87–9.

11. ff. 53–4 Oratio uenerabilis bede presbiteri de septem uerbis . . . preparatam. Oratio. O domine ihesu criste qui septem verba . . .

12. f. 54ʳᵛ Oracio. Deprecor te piissime domine ihesu criste . . .

13. ff. 54ᵛ–55ᵛ (*a*) Aue domine ihesu criste uerbum patris . . ., followed without break by (*b*) Aue uerum corpus natum . . ., (*c*) Aue caro cristi caro (*sic*) . . ., and (*d*) Anima cristi sanctifica me . . ., (*e*) Domine ihesu criste qui hanc sacratissimam carnem . . ., with heading conveying an indulgence of 2,000 years from pope Boniface 'ad supplicationem philippi regis francie'.

14. ff. 56–60ᵛ Incipiunt septem psalmi penitenciales.

15. ff. 60ᵛ–61ᵛ Incipiunt quindecim psalmi. Cues only of the first twelve psalms.

16. ff. 61ᵛ–68 Letania. Many Netherlandish as well as English saints. Spelling: ethmunde. f. 67ᵛ blank.

17. ff. 68–80ᵛ Office of the dead, beginning imperfectly.

18. ff. 81–88ᵛ Incipiunt commendationes animarum.

19. ff. 89–92 Psalmi de passione xpristi.

20. ff. 92–100ᵛ Psalter of St. Jerome, preceded by a long heading, 'Beatus uero iheronimus . . . regnum eternum amen', and the prayer 'Suscipe(re) digneris domine deus . . .'. Cf. *Lyell Cat.*, p. 72.

ff. i+100+ii. 212×158 mm. Written space 122×80 mm. 23 long lines. Collation: 1⁶ 2 six (ff. 7–12) 3⁶ wants 1 before f. 13, 5–6⁸ 7⁸ wants 4, 5, after f. 44 8–9⁸ 10⁸ wants 5 after f. 67 11–13⁸ 14⁶. Initials: (i) in colour on decorated gold grounds; (ii) 2-line, gold on coloured grounds patterned in white; (iii) 1-line, blue with red ornament or gold with blue-grey ornament. Continuous or part borders on the main pages. Line fillers only in the litany: red and blue and a gold ball. Capital letters in the ink of the text are emphasized with a stroke of red. Contemporary English binding of wooden boards covered with white leather, repaired: two strap-and-pin fastenings missing.

Written in the Netherlands for English use. In s. xvi Thomas Webbester of Doncaster, Yorks, 'uentener', noted on f. 102ᵛ that Mrs. Lucas of 'nvarke', widow of Richard Lucas, owed him money. 'Librum diuino farcitum dogmate præcum / Thomas Thomsonus uendicat ille tuus 1573' inside front cover. On 28 Sept. 1576 the same writer (?) entered an English prayer on f. 101 in which he asks that future owners of this book should 'com-mende to god*es* mercy Thomas Thomson scoller leiving or deade' and wrote on f. 100ᵛ 'As is specified on the other side obiect / for Thomas Thomson, so also is it ment / for the worshippfull William and / Susan Woollascott, for whom in god*es* behalf may it please the to indevour / the like, him, them, and the god graunt / goddes graic to see. Amen.' Sale at Puttick's, 5 July 1877, lot 700.

26530. *Horae*

A Sarum book of hours produced abroad for the English market (cf. MS. 26529 and *MMBL* i. 46–8). Described by Aelred Watkin in *Downside Review*, lviii (1940), 446–51.

1. ff. 3ᵛ–8ᵛ Calendar in red and black, lacking December. The word 'pape' and feasts of St. Thomas have not been cancelled. Spellings: Kenelini for Kenelmi, Fredeswiche for Fredeswide. f. 3ʳ blank.

2. ff. 9–10 Oratio ad sanctam trinitatem. Domine deus omnipotens pater et filius et spiritus sanctus Da michi famulo tuo uictoriam . . ., and collect, Libera me . . . f. 10ᵛ blank.

3. ff. 11–14ᵛ Memoriae, one to a leaf, of John Baptist, Thomas of Canterbury, Barbara, and Anne. The antiphons are *RH*, nos. 26987, 26999, 2126, 6773.

4. ff. 15–41 Incipiunt hore beate marie uirginis secundum usum anglie. Memoriae of Holy Spirit, Holy Trinity, Holy Cross, Michael, John Baptist, Peter and Paul, Andrew, John Evangelist, Stephen, Laurence, George, Thomas of Canterbury (Opem tuam nobis o thoma porrige . . .: not in *RH*), Nicholas, Mary Magdalene, Katherine, Margaret, All Saints, and for peace follow lauds. Hours of the Cross are worked in.

5. ff. 41–44ᵛ Salve Regina and its farcing, Salve virgo virginum (*RH*, no. 18318), the latter imperfect at the beginning.

6. ff. 44ᵛ–45ᵛ Oratio bona. O intemerata . . . orbis terrarum. Inclina . . .

7. ff. 46–7 Obsecro te, imperfect at the beginning.

8. ff. 47–48ᵛ Virgo templum trinitatis . . . (the Seven Joys: *RH*, no. 21899), preceded by a heading conveying an indulgence of 100 days 'a domino papa clemente qui hec septem gaudia proprio stilo composuit'.

9. ff. 49–50ᵛ Ad ymaginem cristi crucifixi. Omnibus consideratis . . . *AH* xxxi. 87–9.

10. f. 51ʳᵛ Bede's prayer of the seven words, imperfect at the beginning.

11. ff. 51ᵛ–52 Precor te piissime domine ihesu xpriste propter illam karitatem . . ., preceded by a heading: Dominus papa benedictus ordinis cisterciensis composuit orationem sequentem et dedit omnibus . . . eam . . . dicentibus tot dies indulgentiarum quot fuerunt uulnera in corpore xpristi. Summa uulnerum xpristi quinque milia ccc et xxᵗⁱ.

12. (*a–d*) ff. 52–3 The four prayers in MS. 26529, art. 13 *a–d*, but set out separately. (*e*) f. 53ʳᵛ Heading and prayer as in MS. 26529, art. 13*e*.

13. ff. 54–59ᵛ Incipiunt septem psalmi penitenciales.

14. ff. 59–61ᵛ Incipiunt xv psalmi. Cues only of the first twelve psalms.

15. ff. 61–65ᵛ A litany containing many Netherlandish as well as English saints. Spellings: eneline for Kenelme, zwithune for Swithune.

16. ff. 67–83ᵛ Incipiunt uigilie mortuorum.

17. ff. 84–92ᵛ Incipiunt commendationes animarum.

18. ff. 93–96ᵛ Sequuntur decem psalmi qui dicuntur ad honorem passionis domini nostri ihesu cristi. Pss. 21–30.

19. ff. 97–109ᵛ Incipit psalterium beati et gloriosi doctoris ieronimi abbreuiatum.

The same heading and prayer as in MS. 26529, art. 20, precede the psalms.

ff. vi + 104 + iii, foliated (i–iv), 1–109. ff. 1, 2, 107 are medieval parchment end-leaves. An older foliation of ff. 3–106 before leaves were cut out runs to 115. 135 × 110 mm. Written space 110 × 70 mm. 21 long lines. Collation of ff. 3–106: 1–2⁶ 3⁸ wants 6 after f. 19 4⁸ 5⁸ + 1 leaf inserted after 4 (f. 34) 6 three (ff. 39–41) 7 six (ff. 42–7) 8 three (ff. 48–50) 9 three (ff. 51–3) 10–13⁸ 14⁸ wants 8 after f. 92 15⁸ 16⁶. Two full-page pictures remain, ff. 34ᵛ (Flagellation), 66ᵛ: rectos blank. One 4-line picture, f. 96ᵛ: St. Jerome writing (cf. Watkin, loc. cit., p. 450). Initials: (i) in colour on gold grounds decorated with oak and ivy leaves: continuous borders of the same; (ii) 2-line, gold on coloured grounds patterned in white; (iii) 1-line, blue with red ornament or gold with slate-grey ornament. Binding of s. xx. Written in the Netherlands for English use. 'Hen. (?) Gosling of New Parke (near Harrogate?) Eboracensis 1699' on the stub of the leaf missing before f. 39. 'Edw. Parker N: 105', f. 3, s. xviii. Found in the hands of a 'very poor family' at Kelvedon Hatch, Essex, and given to the Revd. D. C. Nichols, priest at Ongar, in 1897 (cf. Watkin, loc. cit., p. 447).

26531. *Horae*   s. xv²

1. ff. 1–111ᵛ Hours of B.V.M. of the use of (Rome). Headings in French.

2 (added). ff. 111ᵛ–112ᵛ Apprehendit pilatus ihesum . . .

A brief catena from the Gospels, relating Christ's passion. See below, p. 480.

3. ff. 113–146 Penitential psalms and litany, the latter imperfect.

4. ff. 146ᵛ–148ᵛ Les vii vers s' bernard. Uias tuas domine . . . Illumina . . .

The series of seven verses is here preceded by Ps. 24: 4.

5. ff. 149–217ᵛ Office of the dead, imperfect at the end.

ff. ii + 217 + ii. 170 × 120 mm. Written space 95 × 65 mm. 13 long lines ruled in violet ink. Collation: 1–15⁸ 16⁶ 17⁸ 18⁸ wants 1, 2 before f. 135 19–27⁸ 28 five (ff. 213–17). Written in *lettre bâtarde*. Ten 10-line pictures, eight of them in art. 1: at compline, ascension of B.V.M., the Trinity above. Initials: (i) 3-line, in colours on gold grounds, decorated and (f. 97) historiated, an angel harping before B.V.M. and the Child; (ii) 2-line, gold on coloured grounds patterned in white and gold; (iii) 1-line, as (ii), but patterned in white only. Line fillers in red, blue, and gold. Capital letters in the ink of the text marked with yellow. Continuous framed borders on pages with initials of type (i) and framed borders the height of the written space in the outer margin of all other pages. Binding of s. xix, parchment over boards.

Written in France.

26532. *Liber precum* s. XVI in.

1. pp. 1–15 Hours of the Cross.

The heading conveys an indulgence of 3,000 days from Pope John XXII, A.D. 1330, 'in concilio dunensi'.

2. pp. 1–19 Hora matutina marie nunciatur . . .

RH, no. 8012. The heading states that Pope Clement VI composed these hours and granted indulgences 'xviii milia dierum venialium. Secunda vice totidem criminalia. Tercia vice consequitur eciam eodem modo totidem dies karenarum. Si nudus peregisset': cf. *AH* xxx. 106.

3. pp. 19–42 Oraciones cum mane surgis . . . Other prayers, graces, and recommendations follow.

4. pp. 42–4 Clemens papa vi^{us} contulit cuilibet legenti seu secum portanti has benedictiones vi annorum indul(gencias) et iii care(nas) Et securus erit a plaga pestilencie. Benedictio domini nostri ihesu christi cum suis sanctis apostolis sit semper mecum . . .

5. pp. 44–7 Oracio sancti Augustini a spiritu sancto ut dicitur sibi reuelata. Deus propicius esto mychi p(ec)c(a)tori . . .

6. pp. 47–8 Si quis fidem suam deo commendauerit hoc modo in fine vite numquam in vera fide temptetur. O summe omnipotens deus . . . commendo me . . .

7. pp. 48–53 Summa huius indulgencie est Centum milia sexaginta quatuor milia Centum et octo annorum Et possent eciam legi pro defunctis. Pater noster. O domine ihesu criste adoro te in cruce pendentem . . . Nine oes and concluding prayer.

8. pp. 53–7 Beatus gregorius fecit hanc oracionem contra plagam quondam mortalem romanos horribiliter affligentem deditque eam deuote dicentibus quingentos annos et vii carenas indulgenciarum et adiecit ut quicumque ad honorem quinque uulnerum cristi deuote legerit ab igne infernali liberabitur et mala morte non morietur. Aue manus dextera . . . *RH*, no. 1869: five aves, collect and prayer.

9. pp. 57–76 Sequuntur nunc quindecim oraciones de passione domini nostri ihesu cristi reuelate sancte Brigide regine Suecie . . . O Ihesu Criste eterna dulcedo . . .

10. pp. 76–80 Prayer to the five wounds, 'Salue tremendum caput . . .', with rubric conveying indulgence of three years from St. Peter and 140 days from each of thirty other bishops and confirmation by Pope Innocent.

11. pp. 80–2 Prayers at mass: (*a*) O verum corpus cristi salue . . .; (*b*) Anima cristi sanctifica me . . .

(*a*) indulgenced by Pope John XII with 1,000 years of venial sins and 1,000 days of mortal sins and (*b*) by Pope John XXII with 300 days.

12. pp. 82–6 Oracio coram ymagi(ne)m crucifixi dicenda quam qui deuote dixerit tot dies indulgenciarum meretur quot erant vulnera in corpore ihesu

tempore passionis eius quas indulgencias contulit Gregorius papa tercius ad peticionem regine Anglie. Precor te amantissime domine ihesu criste propter illam eximiam caritatem . . .

Cf. Leroquais, *Livres d'heures*, i. 336.

13. pp. 86–91 Qui hanc oracionem cotidie flexis genibus dixerit . . . mariam sibi in auxilium paratum. Oracio. Domine ihesu criste fili dei viui qui septem vltima verba . . .

14. pp. 91–3 Nycholaus papa concessit vnicuique hanc oracionem legenti continuatis diebus ore confesso omnium peccatorum suorum remissionem. Domine ihesu criste qui voluisti pro redempcione mundi . . .

15. pp. 93–8 Oracionem sequentem composuit sanctus Augustinus . . . Et sciet tres dies diem obitus sui. Domine ihesu criste qui in hunc mundum venisti . . .

16. pp. 99–101 Omnipotens et misericors deus rex celi et terre tuam clemenciam suppliciter deposco . . .

17. pp. 101–6 Confessio generalis de peccatis. O creator et domine celi et terre maris et omnis creature . . .

18. pp. 106–8 Inicium sancti ewangelii secundum Iohannem. Gloria tibi domine. In principio . . . veritate [John 1: 1–14]. Per ewangelica dicta Deleantur vniuersa nostra delicta Amen.

19. Sequuntur nunc oraciones de beata virgine.

(*a*) pp. 109–23 Et primo rosarium cum articulis vite cristi. Quod quicumque deuote dixerit maximas acquiret indulgencias . . . Suscipe rosarium virgo deauratum . . . Quem virgo carens vicio . . . *RH*, no. 32356.

(*b*) pp. 123–7 Oracio de doloribus septem beate marie virginis. Primus dolor. Aue dulcis mater cristi que dolebas . . . *RH*, no. 1783.

(*c*) pp. 127–30 Sequitur planctus beate marie virginis quem qui deuote corde recitauerit consequitur vii annos indulgenciarum et xl[a] karenas a Bonifacio papa. Stabat mater . . .

(*d*) pp. 130–3 Oracio ad beatam virginem de angustiis eius quas habuit quando cristus in cruce mortuus est. Memento obsecro dulcissima mater . . .

(*e*) pp. 133–6 Oracio ad beatissimam virginem de compassione et angustiis eius. Obsecro te domina mea sancta maria mater domini pietate plenissima summi regis filia . . .

(*f*) pp. 136–47 Quicumque subscriptam oracionem triginta diebus deuote dixerit . . . quecumque licita pecierit misericorditer obtinebit. Sancta maria perpetua virgo virginum . . . On p. 145 the direction in the text 'Et deuote hic pete quod vis' is in red.

(*g*) pp. 146–50 Oracio de septem gaudiis beate marie virginis corporalibus. Gaude virgo mater cristi . . . *RH*, no. 7017.

(*h*) pp. 150–1 Oracio aurea de beata virgine. Aue rosa sine spinis . . . *RH*, no. 2084.

(*i*) pp. 151–3 Quicumque oracionem sequentem deuote cotidie dixerit sine penitencia et misterio corporis cristi non decedet sic fertur reuelatum beato Bernardo cui ab angelo data est. Aue maria ancilla sancte trinitatis . . . *RH*, no. 1872.

(*j*) pp. 153–8 Oracio perpulchra ad virginem gloriosam ad quam Celestinus papa ccc dies indulgenciarum legentibus contulit. Aue mundi spes maria . . . *RH*, no. 1974.

(*k*) pp. 158–62 Oracio deuota ad beatam virginem Mariam. O excellentissima gloriosissima atque sanctissima . . .

(*l*) pp. 162–9 Subscriptam oracionem edidit beatus Sixtus papa quartus et concessit eam deuote dicentibus coram ymaginem beate marie virginis in sole undecim milia annorum indulgenciarum. Aue sanctissima maria mater dei regina celi . . . At the end are the fifteen liberations granted by B.V.M. to those who honour her conception and the prayer 'Gaude benedictissima dei genitrix . . .'. Cf. Leroquais, *Livres d'heures*, i. 336.

(*m*) pp. 169–72 Legitur in libro sancte mechtildis quod quodam tempore . . . Saluto te beatissima virgo nobillisima eterni patris filia. Orans . . . Three salutations.

(*n*) pp. 172–7 Sequens oracio vocatur aurea oracio ab angelo quodam sancto viro reuelatum quod qui eam deuote dixerit illo die nec dyabolus neque malignus homo ei nocere poterit. Et sciendum quod quidam propter eam de purgatorio fuerat liberatus. Eciam per eandem oracionem promerentur xl^a dies indulgenciarum. O intemerata . . . Orbis terrarum. Inclina . . .

(*o*) pp. 178–9 Oracio de domina nostra. O virgo virginum et pia domina . . .

(*p*) pp. 179–85 Fuit quidam monialis valde negligens et secularis . . . Iamque cum maria ad celos euolo. O mater cristi virgo dignissima . . . The long heading states that the nun, though worldly, recited five aves daily and so was saved from the pains of hell.

(*q*) pp. 185–7 Bonifacius papa concessit omnibus subscriptam oracionem feria sexta coram ymaginem commendacionis siue compassionis beate marie virginis dicentibus Sexies mille. sexcentos et sexaginta sex annos indulgenciarum. Oracio sequens. Aue maria dolore plena . . .

(*r*) pp. 187–8 Testamentum Iulii 2^i pape (1503–13) ad pulsum Aue maria octoginta milia annorum de quo firme papalium literarum habentur bulle. Aue maria. O gloriosissima regina misericordie . . .

20. J. H. Matthews filled the blank space on p. 188 with a prayer to SS. Benedict, Dunstan, and 'Walstan of Baver' and wrote a table of contents on pp. 189–91.

ff. 96, paginated 1–192. 98 × 76 mm. Written space 65 × 45 mm. 14 long lines Collation: 1–5⁸ 6⁸+1 leaf after 8 (pp. 97–98) 7⁴+1 leaf after 4 (pp. 107–8) 8⁸+1 leaf after 4 (pp. 117–18) 9⁸+1 leaf after 2 (pp. 131–2) 10–12⁸. Two small pictures: Veronica, p. 77; B.V.M. and Child, p. 163. Initials: (i) pp. 1, 111, in colour on gold grounds, decorated in colours and with borders; (ii) gold on coloured grounds patterned in white if the ground is blue and in gold paint if the ground is red: historiated on p. 58; (iii, iv) 2-line and 1-line, blue or red. Capital letters in the ink of the text touched with red. Parchment binding, s. xix: incised drawing of four saints on the front cover and of B.V.M. and Child on the back cover: 'Hore passionis' and 'J. H. M.' on the spine.

Written in the Netherlands (?). The ex-libris of John Hobson Matthews, s. xix, is on p. 192 and his arms are neatly inserted in a blank space on p. 98.

26533. *Horae, Psalterium, etc.* s. XIV med.

A book of hours and psalter described by Aelred Watkin in *Downside Review*, lviii (1940), 438–44.

1. ff. 1–6ᵛ Calendar in blue, red, and black. St. Edmund, king and martyr, in blue at 20 Nov. 'Ob. Isabelle filie I. de lindherst (*or* bundherst) vxoris henrici de harnhulle' added early at 9 Aug. 'pape' and feasts of St. Thomas of Canterbury erased.

2. f. 7 Table of a 532-year cycle.

3 (added, s. xiv). ff. 7ᵛ–8 Douce dame ieo vus pri. e humblement vus cri merci . . . Fourteen stanzas, varying in length, each beginning 'Douce dame'.

4. ff. 9–24 Hours of B.V.M. of the use of (Sarum), beginning imperfectly in matins. Memoriae of Holy Spirit, Holy Trinity, Holy Cross, Michael, John Baptist, Peter and Paul, John Evangelist, [. . .], [Thomas of Canterbury, Nicholas], Edmund confessor, Mary Magdalene, Katherine, Margaret, All Saints, and for peace follow lauds. Two leaves, the second containing memoriae of Thomas of Canterbury and Nicholas (traces remain on the stub), have been cut out after f. 15.

5. f. 24ʳᵛ Salve Regina.

6. ff. 25–226 Pss. 1–150. Ps. 109 begins on a new quire (f. 183).

7 (added in blank space before Ps. 109, s. xiv). f. 182 Ihesu nostra redempcio amor et desiderium . . . (RH, no. 9582). f. 182ᵛ blank.

8. ff. 226–44 Ferial canticles, Te deum, Benedicite, Benedictus, Magnificat, Nunc dimittis, Quicumque vult.

9. ff. 244–52 Litany.

Thirty-two martyrs: (1, 2) Stephane Edmunde . . . (14–16) Alphege Oswalde Edmunde . . . ff. 252ᵛ–254ᵛ blank and unruled.

10. ff. 255–266ᵛ Office of the dead and commendation of souls: cues of psalms only.

11. Additions, s. xiv: (a) f. 267 O sancta uirgo uirginum . . .; (b) f. 267ᵛ Ad cor tuum reuertere . . .; (c) f. 268 O mira cristi pietas . . .; (d) f. 268ᵛ Douce sire ihesu crist ke par vostre pleysir de femme . . .; (e) f. 270ᵛ Douce sire ihesu crist eyer merci de moy . . .

(a–c). RH, nos. 3694, 22341, 30733. (d, e). Sonet, nos. 541, 540.

ff. ii+271+ii. 129×90 mm. Written space c. 93×57 mm. 16 long lines. Ink ruling. Collation: 1⁸ 2¹² wants 8, 9 after f. 15 3⁶ (ff. 19–24) 4–8¹² 9¹⁰ 10–16¹² 17⁴ (ff. 179–82) 18–24¹² (ff. 183–266) 25⁶ wants 6, blank. Initials: (i) in colour, patterned in white, on grounds of punched gold and colour, the latter patterned in white, with prolongations into the margins in colours and gold ending in ivy leaves: fourteen are historiated (cf. Watkin, loc. cit.), four in art. 4 (Kings at lauds, Innocents at prime, Presentation at vespers, Flight into Egypt at compline: matins missing), nine in art. 6, including Ps. 51 (smaller than the others), but not Ps. 101, and one in art. 10; (ii) 2-line, blue with red ornament and streamers in both colours the length of the page; (iii) 1-line, blue with red ornament or red with green-blue ornament. Line fillers in red and blue in litany only. Binding of s. xvi, rebacked: gilt centrepiece and cornerpieces.

Written in England, probably for use in Suffolk, in view of the emphasis on St. Edmund, king and martyr, in arts. 1, 9. 'Willelmus Bury (?) de Colchestr' ', f. 271ᵛ, s. xv.

26534. *Officium mortuorum, etc.* 1439

1. ff. 1–62ᵛ Hic incipiunt exequie mortuorum. With music. The commendatory psalms begin on f. 46ᵛ. Sarum use.

2. ff. 62ᵛ–69ᵛ Oracio sancti augustini dicenda a sacerdote ante missam cum

celebrare intenderit. Summe sacerdos et uere pontifex . . . Cf. above, Newnham College, Cambridge, 7, art. 1, and Römer, i. 384.

3 (added). f. 70 Est primus tonus re. la. re fa. quoque secundus . . . Four lines of verse on the eight tones. Walther, no. 5814.

ff. ii+70+iv. ff. 71, 72 are medieval end-leaves. 142 × 98 mm. Written space 83 × 56 mm. 18 long lines. Collation: 1–4⁸ 5⁶ 6–9⁸. Initials; (i) ff. 1, 46ᵛ, 63, pink on gold grounds, decorated and with prolongations in gold and colours; (ii) 2-line, blue with red ornament; (iii) 1-line, blue or red. The ornament of the cadels is grey-green. Red morocco binding, s. xx. Secundo folio *prolongata est*.

Written in England. In the main hand at the end of art. 2: 'Scriptum et completum per manus domini thome [. . . . .] anno cristi ihesu 1439 die ipsa iunii mensis 9. Deo gracias'. Names were scribbled in s. xvi: Sprott (f. 71ᵛ), Willam lloyd (f. 67ᵛ), John Dauies (f. 27).

26536. *Pontificale* s. xiv²–xv med.

A pontifical described by Aelred Watkin, *Downside Review*, lix (1941), 84–92, and by Raymund Webster—from notes of Edmund Bishop, now bound up as ff. iii, iv—ibid. xliii (1925), 135–42 (thence in *Dictionnaire d'archéologie chrétienne et de liturgie*, x. 381–2). Used by Martène in s. xvii ex. for his *De ritibus ecclesiæ* (cf. arts. 27, 29, 50) and described by him among Lyon pontificals as 'Pontificale aliud quod usui etiam fuit ecclesiæ Tarentasiensi, annorum circiter 300. Ex bibliotheca V. Cl. Petri Menardi civis Turonensis'.

Thirty-one of the forty-four texts forming the older part of the manuscript, nos. 1, 5, 8–13, 15, 16, 18–26, 28, 29, 31, 33, 35, 37–44, agree substantially with texts in the three parts of the pontifical devised by Guillaume Durand, bishop of Mende, † 1396, ed. Andrieu, *Pont. Rom.* iii. The order is different from Durand's and there is no division into parts. In directions the subjunctive is usual, not, as in the printed edition, the indicative.

1. f. 1 Pontifex pueros . . .

Fuller and apparently an earlier form of the text than that printed *Pont. Rom.* iii. 333 (Durand, 1. i).

2. f.4ᵛ Ordo ad clericum faciendum. In primis queratur. si ordinandus sit confirmatus si libere sit condicionis Et de legitimo matrimonio . . .

3. f. 7 De sacris ordinibus celebrandis. Nota quod omnes prius debent peccata sua confiteri . . .

Hostiarii, f. 7ᵛ. Lectores, f. 9ᵛ. Exorciste, f. 11. Acoliti, f. 12ᵛ. Subdiaconi, f. 16. Diaconi, f. 25ᵛ. Presbyteri, f. 32ᵛ. The litany in the order for subdeacons lists martyrs in the order Stephane, Photine, Laurenti, Vincenti . . .

4. f. 43 Incipit ordo de consecracione calicis. Et primo de consecracione patene hoc modo incipit.

Nearly as the Roman pontifical of s. xii (*Pont. Rom.* i. 202–3).

5. f. 45 Benediccio corporalium fit hoc modo . . .

II. xi, but with an extra prayer, Domine deus qui iam sanctificare dignatus es hoc genus specierum . . . deus in unitate, between prayers 2 and 3.

6. f. 46 Benediccio planete dalmatice stole et aliarum vestium sacerdotalium atque leuitarum fit hoc modo . . . Omnipotens deus qui per moysen . . .

Cf. II. ix. Sect. 4 differs much.

7. f. 48 Benediccio lintheaminum maparum sacri altaris fit hoc modo . . . Domine deus omnipotens qui ab inicio . . .

8. f. 49ᵛ De benediccione sacrorum vasorum . . . II. xvi.

9. f. 49ᵛ De benediccione capsarum . . . II. xviii.

10. f. 52ᵛ Si quis proficisci desiderat in subsidium terre sancte . . . II. xxx.

11. f. 54 Si qui peregre proficisci velint . . . II. xxxi.

12. f. 56ᵛ Eis qui de peregrinacione redeunt hoc [. . .

No doubt II. xxxii, but only these six words remain and the catchword 'Officium' at the end of quire 9. A later hand has written in the margin 'Residuum quere in [*blank*]'.

13. f. 57 Qui ministri et que ornamenta pontifici missam sollempniter cele-branti sunt necessaria . . . III. xvii.

14. f. 57ᵛ Ordo ad vestiendum et deuestiendum episcopum pontificalibus. dum incipitur calciari sandaliis dicuntur isti psalmi . . .

15. f. 62 De barba tondenda . . . I. iv.

16. f. 62ᵛ De benediccione ymaginis beate marie virginis fit hoc modo . . . II. xiii.

17. f. 65 [D]e confirmacione et benediccione regularis abbatis canonicorum vel Monachorum (*this word over erasure*) vel abbatissarum. Confirmacio electi in abbatem regularem canonicum vel monachum vel abbatissam fit hoc modo . . .

Substantially as I. xx. The abbot is asked (f. 66ᵛ), 'Vis tuum sanctum propositum et sancti Benedicti vel augustini regulam obseruare . . .' (cf. edn. 401/27) and (f. 67) 'Vis huic sancte matri ecclesie lugdun' . . . fidem exibere' (cf. edn. 402/7).

18. f. 78 De benediccione abbatisse . . . I. xxi.

19. f. 80 De benediccione et consecracione virginum . . . I. xxiii.

20. f. 100ᵛ De benediccione vidue . . . I. xxiv.

21. f. 102ᵛ Incipit consecracio siue benediccio cimiterii . . . II. v.

22. f. 111 De ecclesie ac cymiterii reconciliacione . . . II. vi.

23. f. 124ᵛ De reconciliacione cymiterii per se sine ecclesie reconciliacione . . . II. vii.

24. f. 127 Benediccio noue crucis seu tabule . . . II. xii.

25. f. 132 De benediccione et imposicione primarii lapidis in ecclesie funda-tione . . . II. i.

26. f. 138ᵛ Ordo romanus ad benedicendum regem vel reginam. Imperatorem vel imperitricem . . .

I. xxv, ending abruptly on f. 152, 'esse debet' (edn. 434/12, middle of sect. 46). f. 152ᵛ was at first blank: cf. art. 45.

27. f. 153 [D]e examinacione ordinacione et consecracione episcopi . . .

Printed from this copy by Martène, De ritibus, edn. 1700, ii. 508–20. Substantially as I. xiv, but with a long piece in place of sect. 45, Sequitur benediccio . . . Respondeant episcopi Amen (Martène, 517/5–518/8). The bishop is asked (f. 161) 'Vis michi et ecclesie lugdun' . . . fidem . . . exibere' (cf. edn. 379/15) and swears (f. 187) 'Ego . . . promitto . . . quod . . . obediens ero perpetuo beato N. sancteque lugdunensis ecclesie . . .' (cf. edn. 392/9–11). At f. 161 (only) a handsome late hand has written 'tharentasiensi' in the margin opposite 'lugdun'.

28. f. 188 Sequitur edictum quod metropolitanus tradit in scriptura consecrato . . . I. xv.

29. f. 193ᵛ Feria quarta in capite ieiunii . . .

III. i. Printed from this copy by Martène, ii. 97–100.

30. f. 201ᵛ Item sequitur officium de dominica in ramis palmarum . . .

An order for use by the church of Bayeux who co-operate in processions with the monks of St. Vigor. The rubrics mentioning St. Vigor are printed by Leroquais from a Bayeux pontifical now at Lyon (Pontificaux manuscrits, i. 185).

31. f. 206 Ordo in quinta feria cene domini . . .

III. 2, sect. 1–36, followed by the long form of the prayer 'Deus humani generis . . .' (cf. edn. 567), the prayers 'Omnipotens sempiterne deus confitentibus tibi famulis tuis . . .', 'Domine sancte pater omnipotens deus respice propicius super . . .', and 'Exaudi quesumus omnipotens deus preces nostras quas . . .', and no more. Part of f. 219ᵛ and all ff. 220–4 remained blank at first: cf. art. 46.

32. f. 225 Dominica prima aduentus domini. Benediccio. Deus cuius vnigeniti aduentum et preteritum creditis et futurum expectatis . . .

The series of benedictions in the main hand extends only to Christmas, owing probably to loss of leaves at an early date after f. 227. The loss was made good later: cf. art. 47.

33. f. 262 Ecclesiarum dedicationes siue consecrationes . . . II. ii.

34. f. 292ᵛ Incipit consecracio altaris sine dedicacione. In primis paretur in ecclesia . . .

35. f. 320 Ad consecrandum tabulam siue altare portatile . . . II. iv.

36. f. 327ᵛ Ordo ad signum siue campanam ecclesie benedicendum. Antequam eleues campanam in altum lauabis aqua . . .

37. f. 332 De benediccione ymaginum sanctorum. Incipiat enim pontifex . . . II. xiv, omitting the first sentence.

38. f. 332ᵛ Benediccio generalis ad omne quod volueris benedicere . . . II. xxxix.

39. f. 33 De benediccione tabule ante vel post altare collocande . . . II. xx.

40. f. 333 De benediccio(ne) baptisterii siue lapidis foncium . . . II. xxi.

41. f. 333ᵛ De benediccione vasculi pro eucharistia condenda fabricati ... II. xvii.

42. f. 334 Sequitur benediccio thuribuli ... II. xv.

43. f. 334ᵛ Armorum et vexilli bellici benediccio fit hoc modo ... II. xxxviii.

44. ff. 336–9 In benediccione noui militis hoc modo procedatur ... I. xxviii.

Arts. 45–60 were added in s. xv. They fill blank spaces in quires 20, 29, 45, take up seven new quires (1, 31–5, 46), and supply a defect in quire 30. They are in three hands: (2) arts. 47, 48 to f. 242ᵛ; (3) arts. 45, 46, end of art 48 (from f. 242ᵛ), arts. 49–55; (4) arts. 56–60.

45, in blank space after art. 26 on f. 152ᵛ. Benedictio agni et aliarum carnium in pascha ... Durand, II. xxv.

46, in blank space after art. 31. (a) ff. 219ᵛ–222ᵛ De monacho vel alio religioso faciendo ... (b) ff. 222ᵛ–224ᵛ De professione monachorum ...

I. xviii, xix. The words 'talis quem precipuum huius sancte institutionis legislatorem dedisti' in the form of intercession 'Sancte spiritus qui te deum ...' have against them in the margin in another hand 'gloriossime (sic) uirginis marie ac benedicti abbatis'. In the later sixteenth century (?) 'stefani' was interlined above 'benedicti' (f. 221).

47, continuing art. 32 on ff. 228–41. Benedictions taking up the Christmas benediction which ended on f. 227ᵛ, continuing through the year, and ending with the common of saints. With art. 32 there are forty-seven in all. St. Anne is included.

48. ff. 241–4 Prayers for the dead and benediction of grave.

49. ff. 244–54 Incipit ordo ad baptizandum pueros et statuantur masculi ad dexteram cum duobus patrinis ... Insufflet in os puerorum Ita dicens Accipe spiritum sanctum N Recede inmunde spiritus de hac ymagine dei ...

50. ff. 254–259ᵛ Incipit ordo ad sponsam benedicendam.
Printed from this copy by Martène, ii. 630–2.

51. f. 259ᵛ Benedictio noue domus.

52. f. 260 Benedictio nauis. Durand, II. xxxiv.

53. f. 260ᵛ Benedictio noui putei. Durand, II. xxxv.

54. ff. 260ᵛ–261 Benedictio noue aree. Durand, II. xxxvi.

55. ff. 339–41 Table of contents of arts. 1–44, 46–54 and, as additions, 56, 60, 67.

56. ff. 261a–261hᵛ Feria quinta in cena domini hora sexta ingressus secretarium presul cum clericis ...
Office for blessing of oil on Holy Thursday.

57. ff. 341ᵛ–342 Anno domini Mᵒ iiᵒ xlix. In uigilia beate katherine ... Hoc habui a quondam (sic) libro auctentico reperto in conuentu montismeliani.

An account derived from a manuscript at Montmélian, Savoy, to the effect that the fall of part of a mountain was divine vengeance. Printed from this copy by Webster, loc. cit., pp. 141–2; also from a copy in the archives of Chambéry in *Revue des sociétés savantes*, 3rd series, iii (1861), 603–4. The mountain was Mont Granier, 1938 m, above Myans on the main road to Rome between Chambéry and Montmélian.

58. f. 343ʳᵛ Benedicto igne aspergatur aqua benedicta . . .
Rubric of the benediction of a wax candle.

59. ff. 343ᵛ–348 Incipit ordo ad catacuminum faciendum. In primis interroget sacerdos Quod est nomen eius et illi respondeant N . . .

60. ff. vii–ixᵛ Hic sequitur benedictio foncium post lectiones. dominus episcopus cum clero et populo procedit cum letania ad fontes . . .

Arts. 61–7 are additions in various hands of s. xv ex., xvi.

61, in blank space after art. 54 on f. 261ᵛ. Collect for St. Remy, Deus fundator fidei . . .

62, in blank space after art. 56 on f. 261hᵛ. Ordo benediccionis dyaconisse . . . Durand, i. xxii.

63, in blank space after art. 57 on f. 342ᵛ. Veni creator spiritus mentes tuorum uisita . . .

64, in blank space after art. 59 on f. 348ᵛ, s. xvi. Benediction of synod.

65, on f. vi, originally left blank. In degradatione clerici. Episcopus indutus supercilicio et pluuiali . . .
Cf. Watkin, loc. cit., 85.

66, added after art. 65 on f. viʳᵛ. Ita est forma absolucionis pro illis qui uerberant portatores literarum curie nostre officialatus tharen' et eciam qui capient et amouent de facto litere curie nostre off' tharen'. A' Parce domine parce . . .

67, added after art. 60 on ff. ixᵛ–xiiᵛ. Ordo s(e)peliendi clericos romane fraternitatis . . .
As the Roman pontifical of s. xiii (*Pont. Rom.* ii. 505–13).

ff. v+336+iii, foliated i–xii, 1–261, 261a–h, 262–351. Except i–xii, 1, 261a–h, 340–51, the foliation is medieval—but later than the loss of leaves after f. 56—running from II to CCCXXXIX, the even numbers in red and the odd numbers in blue. For ff. iii, iv see above. ff. v, 349 are medieval parchment leaves, formerly pastedowns. 227 × 160 mm. Written space 150 × 85 mm. 19 long lines, and 20 lines on ff. viᵛ–xiiᵛ, 228–61, 261a–h, 339ᵛ–348. Collation: 1 seven (ff. vi–xii), 2–29⁸ 30 eight (ff. 225–32), 31⁸ 32⁶ (ff. 241–6) 33⁸ 34⁶+1 leaf after 6 (f. 261) 35⁸ (ff. 261a–h) 36–44⁸ 45⁸+1 leaf after 8 (f. 342) 46⁶: in quire 37 the leaves are in the order 281, 278–80, 283–5, 282, through the binder's error. One main hand (arts. 1–44). The additions, arts. 45–60, are well written, especially those by the hands noticed above, before art. 45, as (2) and (4). Hand (3) is like (2), but less skilled. Initials of arts. 1–44: (i) f. 1, blue patterned in white, on gold and pink ground, decorated and with a border on three sides; (ii) gold and blue, with blue ornament; (iii) 2-line, red or blue, with ornament of the other colour; (iv) 1-line, blue or red. Line fillers in red and blue. Initials of arts. 46, 59, 2-line, blue with red ornament or red with olive-green ornament. Initials of arts. 47–54, 2-line, blue with red ornament or red with violet ornament. An historiated *F* (bishop at altar) begins art. 56. Bound in blue morocco, gilt, s. xviii. Secundo folio *tunc eleuatis* (f. 2).

Written in France. Arts. 3, 17, 27 suggest that arts. 1–44 are for use in the diocese of Lyons (but cf. art. 30). A shield, azure, but otherwise blank, surmounted by a cardinal's hat, is in the lower margin of f. 1. Later in the diocese of Moustiers en Tarentaise: cf. arts. 27, 57, 66. Inscriptions of ownership by Cardinal Guillaume Briçonnet, †1514, on f. 349: cf. Watkin, loc. cit., pp. 84–5 and Webster, loc. cit., p. 139. Later owners were the 'Oratorii Tolosani' (f. v^v, s. xvii), Pierre Menard of Tours (†1701), according to Martène, and 'Davin' (ff. v^v, 349). '18^m', f. v^v. Edmund Bishop's ex-libris is inside the cover, and his note of purchase, 22 May 1871.[1]

26537. *Hymnarium, etc.*   s. xv ex.; 1498

1. ff. 8–58^v Hymns of temporale and sanctorale in one series from Advent, of the common of saints and for the dedication of a church, 156 in all, preceded by a table (ff. 8–9, 'Registrum hympnorum'). Hymns for SS. Dorothea, Vitus, Achatius, Hermachora and Fortunatus, Affra, and Anthony (of Vienne) are included. ff. 1–6^v, 59–64^v are blank or were filled later (cf. art. 10).

2. ff. 65^v–106^v Forty-five sequences, preceded by a table (f. 65^v, 'Registrum super sequencias'). Nos. 1–37 are a regular series from Christmas to Nicholas (6 Dec.), followed by the common and In dedicatione: they include a sequence for Wenceslaus. The rest are (38) for Hedwig (Consurge iubilans: *RH*, no. 2843), (39–43, 45) commemorations of B.V.M., and (44) Margaret. f. 65^r blank.

3. ff. 107–10 Noted responses and antiphons from Advent, ending abruptly at Monday after the first Sunday after Epiphany. ff. 110^v–112^v are blank or were filled later (cf. art. 10).

4. ff. 113–115^v Egregius modus orandi rosarium matris marie. Munus valde gratum metrice compositum. Sacra canam nostre: que via certe salutis . . . campis in eliseis. Finis huius opusculi rosarii beate marie virginis precamur vt intercedat pro peccatis nostris ad dominum nostrum ihesum cristum filium eius. O mater dei memento mei amen. Walther, no. 17001. Widely spaced for an interlinear gloss.

5. f. 116 Ex gestis Anshelmi colliguntur forma et mores beate marie virginis gloriose. Maria dei genitrix didicit hebraycas litteras . . .

6. f. 116^v Istud carmen continet totam vitam cristi et canitur sub melodia patris sapientia valde deuotum et contemplatiuum in se. O crux frutex saluificus . . . *Opera Sancti Bonaventurae* (Quaracchi edn.), viii (1898), 86–7.

7. f. 117 Subscripte indulgentie sunt. quas quelibet persona ordinis Carth' omni die per totum annum consequi potest. An indulgence of Pope Sixtus IV, A.D. 1482, is followed by notes of indulgences attached to churches in Rome.

8. ff. 117^v–122^v Formam quam cristus tradidit viuend' in monasterio. Cristus

[1] Dr. David Rogers suggests to me that this may be the Roman pontifical sold in the Joseph Lilly sale, 15 Mar. 1871, lot 1801: it fetched £2. 12s. 6d. He suggests also that the binding is by Weir for Count MacCarthy-Reagh (1744–1811), whose library was sold in Paris in 1817.

nobis tradidit hanc formam viuendi . . . (fifty 4-line stanzas) . . . Hec sunt dicta
Egregii doctoris hainrici de hassia edita pro erudicione religiosorum. Scripta
per martinum ryeder de ferrea ciuitate tunc temporis studens alme vniuersitatis
Wiennensis ibidemque morans. In 4ª feria post festum Eph^e. Anno domini
1497. *RH*, no. 24568. Walther, no. 2772.

9. Pieces in honour of B.V.M.:

(*a*) ff. 123–126^v Sequitur Iubilus gloriose virginis marie semper. Gaude sedens
in decore . . . Corrected in green ink and many of the 134 4-line or 5-line stanzas
marked 'vacat'. *RH*, no. 6936.

(*b*) ff. 126^v–129 Sequens carmen nominatur Meritum gloriose virginis Marie.
Salue regina mater misericordie Mater spey et mater venie . . . One hundred
and one 4-line stanzas. *RH*, no. 18032. *AH* xxxii. 176–85.

(*c*) ff. 129–36 Incipit pulchrum dictamen atque oracio de beata virgine maria.
Illius assit gracia qui stricta cinctus fascia . . . arte proterua. Urbanus papa
quintus concessit omnibus contritis et confessis prescriptam oracionem in honore
beate virginis legentibus ccc^{os} dies indulgentiarum peccatorum venialium et
centum mortalium et 35 de peccatis oblitis cum 7tem carenis.

RH, no. 8378. Walther, no. 8730, listing seven manuscripts. *AH* xxx. 185–201 (sects. i–xi).
The place of sects. xii, xiii is taken here by fifteen lines beginning 'Hoc florum pratum'.
The initial letters of the first 111 stanzas should make the sentence 'I. Franco scolaster
Meschedensis seruitor alme uirginis mari*e* humilis *et* deuotus ista collegit et ea domino
Iohanni pape *xx*ii misit', but our scribe has *h*, *o*, *c*, *c*, respectively, for the four italicized
letters.

A hand of s. xvii notes 'descripsi et inserui parte prima deliciarum marianarum fol. 63
vocaui Triumphus marianum'. Similar notes on ff. 136, 137^v, 143^v refer to (*d*), (*e*), and
(*h*): the leaf references are respectively 'p. i, 599', 'fol. 419' and 'fol. 619'.

(*d*) ff. 136–7 Sequitur Triologus vel potius Quadrilogus per modum alphabeti
compositus Quem quicumque cum deuocione legerit in honore gloriose semper
virginis Marie habebit omni die xl^a dies indulgenciarum et 7tem karenas de
qualibet litera alphabeti hic posita quas indulgencias Innocencius papa 3us ad
hunc trilogum uel quadrilogum dedit. qui eundem composuit ad honorem
gloriose virginis marie (*all marked* vacat *and replaced by* Sequitur Alphabetum
gloriose semper virginis marie per modum Trilogi . . .). Aue maria sanctissima
dei creatura . . .

Twenty-five stanzas, the first twenty-three each beginning with a new letter of the
alphabet, A–Z, and the last two 'Et ob hoc' and 'Congaudendo'. The heading 'Recommendacio Innocentii pape ad beatam virginem Mariam' precedes stanza 2.

(*e*) ff. 137^v–138^v Oracio alia de gloriosa virgine Maria. Aue rosa speciosa Salue
candens lilium. . . . *RH*, no. 35714.

(*f*) ff. 138^v–139^v Letania gloriose semperque virginis Marie sequitur.

(*g*) ff. 139^v–143^v Incipit psalterium minus beate virginis compositum a sancto
Bonauentura . . . prima quinquagena. Aue virgo vite lignum . . . *RH*, no. 2276.

(*h*) ff. 143^v–148^v Laus beate virginis Marie dictata a sancto Bonauentura . . .
Aue celeste lilium . . . *RH*, no. 1726.

(*i*) ff. 148ᵛ–149 Alia letania de gloriosa virgine Maria sequitur.

(*j*) f. 149ᵛ Oracio hec que immediate sequitur Corone gloriose virginis Marie nominatur. O clementissima et excellentissima virgo Maria . . . defensatrix Amen. Addicio. Iam dictam oracionem hic inserere volui 'propter titulum ac nomen ipsius' licet versifice uel rithmice non sit conscripta vel composita. ff. 150–151ᵛ blank.

10 (additions on originally blank pages). (*a*) f. 5ᵛ Incipit breuiarium pro quacunque tribulacione . . .: table of thirty votive masses. (*b*) f. 6 Sequntur sex misse siue monachatus pro liberatione vnius anime . . . (*c*) f. 110ᵛ Lamentations, ch. 5 and ch. 4: 1–6. (*d*) f. 152ᵛ Recipes in German for healing a wound and for weak eyes.

11. ff. 1, 153 are flyleaves taken from a manuscript of meditations on paper, s. xv.

ff. v+150+v, foliated (i–iv), 1–153, (154–7). For ff. 1, 153 see above, art. 11. Paper, except ff. 65, 107, 112. 193 × 140 mm. Written space *c*. 140 × 92 mm. Frame ruling. Long lines: the number varies. Collation of ff. 2–152 impracticable: ff. 17–64 in eights. Initials: (i) ff. 10, 66, blue and red; (ii) red or blue and in art. 9 red or green. Written (arts. 1–8) in more or less current cursiva and (art. 9) in very current hybrida. Contemporary binding of wooden boards covered with stamped brown leather: stamps of five patterns, the largest an ovoid containing a dragon: rebacked: metal centrepiece and cornerpieces; two clasps missing: illegible title label on upper cover.

Art. 8 was written by Martin Rieder of Eisenstadt (near Vienna), when a student at the University of Vienna. Given in 1914 by Mr. and Mrs. James Weale.

26539. *Antiphonale* s. xv med.

In nomine domini. Amen. Incipit antiphonarium nocturnum sancte marie ordinis seruorum de uicentia secundum consuetudinem romane curie. In primo sabbato de aduentu domini. Ad vesperas. Versus Rorate celi desuper . . . The period covered is from Advent to the fifth Sunday after Epiphany. f. 239ᵛ blank.

ff. i+239+i. 520 × 375 mm. Written space 345 × 225 mm. 6 long lines and music. Minims 11 mm high. Collation: 1–21¹⁰ 22–23⁸ 24¹⁰ 25 three (ff. 237–9). Initials: (i, ii) pink, patterned in white, on gold and blue grounds, historiated, the larger size for Advent (Aspiciens, f. 3), Christmas (Hodie, f. 92), and Epiphany (Hodie, f. 153); (iii) as (i), (ii), but decorated in blue, red, green, and gold; (iv, v) 3-line and 1-line, red with blue or blue with red ornament. Capital letters in the ink of the text filled with yellow. Binding of thick wooden boards covered with brown leather, s. xix.

Written for the use of the Servites of Vicenza (see above). Armorial book-plate of John Mathew Gutch: his sale, 16 Mar. 1858, lot 299. Bequeathed by Edmund Bishop: his printed 'E libris' inside the cover.

26540. *Medulla grammaticae, etc.* s. xv med.

Described by Aelred Watkin, 'An English mediaeval instruction book for novices', *Downside Review*, lvii (1939), 477–88; lviii (1940), 53–66, 199–207.

1. ff. 1–52 (*begins imperfectly*) oriri sanitor spumancia reddit . . . Sadix. Interpretatur consolacio. Ex dei consolacione et gloriose virginis mediacione. omnia ad finem congruum dicuntur. Cui honor et gloria in secula seculorum Amen.

A work in three chapters, the first missing and the second on figures of Holy Writ, beginning near the end in an example of Methonomia. The rest is headed on f. 2ᵛ: Capitulum 3ᵐ secundum ordinem alphabeti de clausularum declaracione It expounds phrases and single words of ecclesiastical and especially biblical and liturgical texts and runs from Acceperunt triginta argenteos to Zetas, this last being followed by interpretations of the letters of the Greek alphabet and of some Greek words. There are northern English glosses, e.g. Hic poples tis . . . anglice a haym (f. 43ᵛ), Singularis ferus anglice ylk a wyld beyst (f. 45): cf. also Watkin, p. 479. Lincoln is given as an example of place: . . . determinate vt vado lincoln', f. 16. ff. 52ᵛ–54ᵛ blank.

2. ff. 55–100ᵛ O lux beata trinitas . . . Q(u)ando totus liber ympnorum est metrice compositus ut patet subtiliter intuenti. Ideo in principio videndum est quid sit metrum . . .

One hundred and fifteen hymns, not strictly ordered, each with interlinear glosses and followed by an exposition. Watkin, pp. 55–66, lists the hymns, except (5a) Ecce iam noctis, and discusses them, pp. 199–201. Ninety-seven are in the printed Sarum *Expositio hymnorum* of 1496 (for a list see *Brev. ad usum Sarum*, iii, pp. cvii–cxii) and eleven, not there (Nuntium vobis, Martyris ecce, Christe sanctorum, Iam christe sol, Rex aeterne domine, Beata nobis, Rex christe martini, Martine par, Aeterna christi munera . . . apostolorum, Felix per omnes, O Roma felix: nos. 41, 46–8, 56, 66, 78–9, 81, 109, 110), are in the printed *Expositio hymnorum* of 1488. The others are: (a) York hymns (Corde natus, Aeterna christi munera . . . martyrum, Proni rogamus, Iacobe iuste, Hymnum canamus, Iam ter quaternis: nos. 36, 85, 93, 95, 107, 115); (b) Preco benigne for St. Barnabas (no. 98). O lux beata trinitas occurs twice (nos. 1, 30), but at its first occurrence, the metre and not the text is expounded. The expositions are sometimes the same and sometimes not the same as those printed and in Cambridge, Peterhouse, MS. 215: cf. Watkin (1), p. 479, (2) p. 54, and H. Gneuss, *Hymnar und Hymnen im englischen Mittelalter* (Buchreihe der Anglia, xii), p. 201.

3. ff. 101–10 De accentu. Simplices plane in ecclesia legentes ab accentibus instruo . . . Breuis A ante B . . . Semper producis alius.

4. ff. 110ᵛ–111ᵛ Que non noscuntur. si non exempla sciuntur . . . Dufo cum rufo. sic nudus vnaque liquor.

195 lines. Walther, no. 15012.

5. f. 111ᵛ Strigilis et strigilis. repo repo rudo rudoque . . . tociensque sodalis.

9 lines. Cf. Thurot in *Notices et extraits*, xxii. 2, p. 509.

6. ff. 111ᵛ–113ᵛ Regula splendescit. qua sillaba prima patescit . . . excipe pluui.

Three hundred and sixteen lines. Walther, no. 16555.

7. ff. 114–15 Nomina propria. Adan atkyn and atkoc . . . Zebideus Zebide.

One hundred and fifty Latin Christian names, with from one to five English equivalents for each name. Watkin, pp. 480–3.

8. ff. 115ᵛ–119ᵛ Aduerbia. Vtinam Vt Vti Etsi Quatinus O si Wald god . . . Extrinsicus. Forinsicus. Wᵗ owtyn.

Adverbs with seventy and adjectives with 128 English equivalents.

9. ff. 119ᵛ–121ᵛ 'Nomina numeralia', roman and arabic, from 1 to 3000000,

'Et cetera usque millesies millia etcetera usque ad infenitum'. An explanation follows, f. 121ʳᵛ, 'Sciendum est quod omnis figura coniuncta cum aliis figuris . . .'.

10. ff. 122–252 Hec est regula generalis pro toto libro quod omnia nomina . . . sub breuitate do. Incipit liber intitulatus Medulla gramatice. Alma id est virgo abscondita . . . Zonico cas id est zona induere. Explicit liber intitulatus medulla gramatice.

Watkin, pp. 484–8. For other manuscripts of Medulla, see above, Bristol, University, DM 14.

11 (added). (*a*) ff. 252ᵛ–253 Expositions of the sequences Sancti baptiste preconiis (for John Baptist) and Laude iocunda (for Peter and Paul). (*b*) f. 253ᵛ Hic patent quedam proprietates auium et bestiarum. Leonum est rugire . . . Cicadarum fincare. (*c*) ff. 254–255ᵛ Verba difficiliora sacre scripture. Extum . . . Peculiaris. (*d*) ff. 256–258ᵛ Difficult words in the four parts of the psalter, Pss. 1–50, 51–100, 101–8, 109–50, and in other books of OT, book by book, ending imperfectly at 'Conclaue' (4 Kings 13: 10).

ff. i+255+iii. Paper, except three medieval parchment end-leaves, 256–8. f. i is a modern flyleaf. 285 × 210 mm. Written space 194 × 140 mm. 2 cols. 34–47 lines. Some ruling in red ink. Collation: 1⁶ 2–7⁸ 8¹⁰ (ff. 55–64) 9–14⁸ 15⁸+1 leaf after 8 (f. 121) 16–31⁸ 32 six (ff. 250–5). Quires 8–15 signed a–h and quires 16–28 a–m. Textura (except art. 11), mainly by one hand. Initials: (i) 2-line, blue with red ornament or red without ornament; (ii) 1-line, red. Capital letters in the ink of the text and the elongated letters in the first line on each page touched with yellow. Contemporary binding of wooden boards covered with white leather, rebacked: central strap and pin missing.

Written in England. 'ex spoliis D. O. G. Langdale Jan. 1934', f. i. Probably long in the Langdale family, since a sheet of paper bearing the names of jurors at a court baron of Sir Thomas Fairfax, lord of the manor of Holme upon Spalding Moor (between York and Hull), A.D. 1685, lies loose at the beginning: see Watkin, p. 204.

26542. *Pricking of Love, Pore Caitif, etc. (mainly in English)*

s. xv²

A full description by A. Watkin in *Downside Review*, lix (1941), 75–83.

1. ff. 1–90 In the Honoure and Worship of our Lord ihesu here begynnith the boke. callid Prickyng of Loue. and conteynith xxxviii chapitres. of þe whiche. The first is . . . (*table of 38 chapters*) . . . (f. 1*) Al forwoundred of our self ought us forto be . . . mote louen our lord in the blisse of heuene Amen. amen Deo gracias. Here endith the tretyse. that is called Pryckyng of loue. that was maad by a Frere Menour Bonauenture. that was a Cardynall of the Court of Rome.

2. ff. 90ᵛ, 92ᵛ, 92 How a man shal knowe. whiche is the speche of the flesshe in his hert. and whiche is of the world. and whiche is of the fende. and also whiche is of god almighty. our lord ihesu cryst . . . yt is spekyng of god. and not of thy self. Ihesu mercy. lady helpe. To whom I beseche. for me specialy praieth for grace And of my synnes amendement. tyme. wille and space.

Jolliffe, F. 12. Follows art. 1 also in Trinity College, Cambridge, B. 14. 19. The final couplet is in red. ff. 91, 92, the central sheet of quire 12, is upside down and back to front: ff. 91^{rv}, 93^{rv} blank.

3. ff. 94–168^v This tretyse sufficith to eche cristen man and womman. This tretyse compiled of a pore caityf. and nedy of gostly help of al cristen peple . . . and lastyng chastite. that we mown regne with the yn endeles blisse merciful lord. Amen. Explicit.

Jolliffe, B.

4. ff. 168^v–172 Quomodo verus cristi discipulus debet se configurare passionibus eius. et quod frequens memoria passionis cristi precipue valet ad tristiciam inordinatam repellendam etc. Nunc adest tempus ait sapiencia. vt omnis qui vult venire . . . vnde salubriter vulneratur. Hec in reuelacionibus predicte Matildis.

An extract from *Speculum spiritualium*: edn. 1510, ff. cxxxi, cxxxii.

5. ff. 172–173^v Sermo beati Augustini notabilis ad parachianos. Rogo vos fratres karissimi. vt attencius cogitemus quare cristiani sumus . . . et vos feliciter peruenietis ad regnum. Amen. Predicat actiua 'vita' dat egenis martirisatur. Contemplatiua 'uita' vigilat orat meditatur.

The interlined words in the final couplet are in red: cf. Walther, *Sprichwörter*, no. 22155a.

ff. iii + 174 + i, foliated 1, 1*, 2–173, (174). ff. ii, iii are parchment end-leaves: ii was pasted down. 233 × 172 mm. Written space 165 × 112 mm. 31 long lines. Collation: 1–11⁸ 12⁸ wants 6, 7, blank, after f. 93 13–22⁸: for 12⁴, ⁵ see above. Written in anglicana. If the scribe's writing did not reach the boundary of the written space he filled the vacant space with short wavy strokes as line fillers. Initials: (i) ff. 1, 2, in colour on gold grounds, decorated and with prolongations into the margins in gold and colours, including green; (ii) blue with red ornament. Calf binding, s. xvii. Secundo folio *that flesshe* (f. 2) or *Al forwoundred* (f. 1*).

From the nunnery of Dartford, O.P.: 'This book is youe to Betryce chaumbir'. And aftir hir decese to sustir Emme Wynter. and to sustir denyse caston' Nonnes of Dertforthe. And so to abide in the saam hous of the Nonnes of Dertforthe for euere. 'to pray for hem that yeue it", f. iii^v, s. xvi in. 'Ellen Haburlaie est verus possessor', f. iii, s. xvi; 'Marye Haburley', f. 53^v, s. xvi: the references to this family by H. Foley, *Records of the English Province of the Society of Jesus*, vols. 1, 5, 8 and in *Catholic Record Society*, li. 8, are noted by Edmund Bishop on a sheet of paper kept with the manuscript. The names 'William Richardson', f. ii, 'Richard Baxter', f. i, 'John Vavasour', f. i^v, and 'Ald: Metcalfe' on the strip conjugate with and in front of f. i are probably all of s. xvii.

26543. *Horae* s. xv med.

A damaged fragment of a book of hours for monastic use, described by A. Watkin in *Downside Review*, lxix (1951), 468–78 and called WI2 by J. B. L. Tolhurst, *The Monastic Breviary of Hyde Abbey*, vi (HBS lxxx, 1942), who used art. 1*e*.

1. ff. 1–16 Hours of B.V.M. The remains are: (*a*) ff. 1–6^v, fragments of matins and lauds; (*b*) f. 7, the end of a set of capitella at prime; (*c*) ff. 7–8^v, prayers at prime and an office to be said after prime; (*d*) ff. 8^v–9^v, hymns at terce;

(*e*) ff. 9ᵛ–13, Suffragia ad vesperas et ad laudes per totum annum; (*f*) ff. 13–16, compline.

(*a*). ff. 1–6 are half leaves only. (*b*). Printed by Watkin, p. 470. As Tolhurst, pp. 35–6, beginning at 'fac populum tuum'. (*d*). Nunc sancte nobis, Chorus noue ierusalem (at Easter) and Veni creator spiritus (at Pentecost). Cf. Tolhurst, p. 203. (*e*). Memoriae of Holy Trinity, Holy Cross, B.V.M., Peter and Paul, Thomas of Canterbury (the name erased), Birin, Swithun, and Athelwold, jointly, Benedict, Katherine, relics, for peace, and of All Saints. Printed by Watkin, pp. 471–6. Listed by Tolhurst, pp. 105–6.[1] (*f*). A leaf missing after f. 15.

2. f. 16ʳᵛ Salve regina as a memoria of B.V.M. The collect is 'Omnipotens sempiterne deus qui gloriose virginis . . .'.

Cf. Tolhurst, pp. 131–2.

3. f. 16ᵛ Memoria de passione.

At prime, terce, and sext (incomplete), 'Hora prima ductus est...'. Tolhurst, p. 136. Two leaves missing after f. 16.

4. f. 17ʳᵛ (*begins imperfectly*) Kyriel'. Cristel'. Kyriel' Pater noster. Et ne nos. Dispersit dedit pauperibus . . .

Graces, mostly printed by Watkin, pp. 477–8. Ends imperfectly in a form 'Post cenam'.

5. f. 18 (*the last eight words of a prayer*) et digni efficiamur gaudiis sempiternis. Per cristum dominum.

6. Prayers to B.V.M. and St. John: (*a*) ff. 18–19ᵛ Oratio deuota ad beatam uirginem mariam et ad sanctum iohannem euangelistam. O beata et intemerata . . . orbis terrarum. Inclina aures . . .; (*b*) ff. 19ᵛ–20ᵛ Sequitur alia oracio. O tu mater misericordie felix et incomparabiliter benedicta . . .; (*c*) f. 20ᵛ Alia oracio ad eandem uirginem. Obsecro te domina sancta maria et te sancte iohannes euangelista per dolorem. . . .

7. ff. 20ᵛ–30 Pss. 1, 2, 6, 7 (incomplete), 9 (headless), 10–19. Pss. 1, 2, 6, 7, 12 are abbreviated. Two leaves are missing after f. 33.

8. ff. 30–39ᵛ Seven penitential psalms and litany.

Two missing leaves contained all martyrs after Laurence and all confessors and virgins. On f. 36ᵛ is 'Ut dompnum apostolicum . . . conseruare digneris', with *apostolicum* lightly erased. ff. 34, 35, 37, 39 are half leaves only.

9. ff. 39ᵛ–50ᵛ Pss. 109–15, 131, 132, 134–41, 143–7 (incomplete).

Pss. 109–13 are abbreviated. ff. 42, 44, 46, 49 are half leaves only and a leaf is missing after f. 45.

10. f. 51ʳᵛ (*begins imperfectly*) ut non peream in tremendo iudicio.

A prayer to guardian angels.

11. ff. 51ᵛ–52 Hanc epistolam misit leo papa (*erased*) karolo regi dicens . . . Sequitur epistola uel oratio. Crux cristi sit semper mecum. Crux cristi est quam semper adoro . . .

12. Prayers at mass: (*a*) f. 52ʳᵛ Iohannes papa (*both words lightly cancelled*)

---

[1] The Winchester saints are commemorated together, not separately, as Tolhurst says.

vicesimus secundus concessit omnibus dicentibus subsequentem orationem inter eleuationem et tercium agnus dei tria milia dierum indulgencie. Anima xpristi sanctifica me . . . (*b*) f. 52ᵛ Quicumque dixerit hanc subsequentem orationem inter eleuationem et tercium agnus dei xii milia annorum conceduntur ei per bonefacium papam (*cancelled*) sextum ad supplicationem philippi regis francie. Domine ihesu criste qui hanc sacratissimam carnem et (*ends imperfectly*).

13. f. 53ʳᵛ Fragment of the Athanasian creed.

f. 53 is a half leaf only.

14. ff. 54–56ᵛ Fragments of the office of the dead.

The remains include *Confitebor*, *Verba mea*, and *Domine deus meus* (Pss. 137, 5, 7), the first lesson from Job, *Parce mihi*, and the response *Credo quod*. The last remaining words are 'Leccio iiᵃ'. Half leaves only.

ff. ii + 56 + i. All leaves have been cut across the middle[1] and eighteen of them, nine of the twenty-eight bifolia, are half leaves only, either the upper half (ff. 3, 4; 46, 49; 53, 56; 54, 55) or the lower half (ff. 1, 6; 2, 5; 34, 35; 37, 44; 39, 42). f. ii is the inner half of a parchment leaf, probably once a flyleaf. 110 × 83 mm. Written space 80 × 52 mm. 20 long lines. Collation: 1⁸ wants 4, 5 2⁸ (ff. 7–14) 3⁸ wants 2, 4, 5, 7 (ff. 15–18) 4⁸ wants 4, 5 (ff. 19–24) 5⁸ 6⁸ wants 2, 3, 6, 7 (ff. 33–6) 7⁸ 8⁸ wants 2, 7 (ff. 45–50) 9⁸ wants 1–3, 6–8 (ff. 51, 52) 10 four (ff. 53–6: 54–5 is the middle sheet of the quire). Initials: (i, ii) 4-line and 3-line, red and blue, with red ornament; (iii) 2-line, blue with red ornament; (iv) 1-line, red or blue. Bound at the Bodleian Library in 1962.

Written for use at Winchester Cathedral Priory. Bequeathed by F. J. Baigeant.

26547. *Bullarium franciscanum* s. XIV in.

Quoniam confusio scriptorum tam est memorie quam intelligencie inimica. et multe littere et priuilegia. sunt ordini nostro scilicet fratrum minorum ab apostolica sede concessa . . .

One hundred and thirty-four papal letters concerning the Franciscan order, many of them abbreviated, arranged in subject order in thirteen chapters. The introduction explains the arrangement: (1) 'que pertinent ad religionis ingressum'; (2) 'que ad habitus qualitatem'; (3) 'que ad diuinum officium'; (4) 'que ad paupertatem fratrum'; (5) 'que ad predicationis officium'; (6) 'que ad sepulturas'; (7) 'que ad euntes inter serracenos et alios infideles'; (8) 'que ad emunitatem ordinis et fratrum'; (9) 'que ad correcionem delinquentium'; (10) 'que ad absoluciones et dispensacionem penitencium'; (11) 'que ad ueneracionem et canonicacionem sanctorum'; (12) 'que ad indulgencias et remissiones benefactorum et loca fratrum uisitancium'; (13) 'que ad confirmacionem et collectionem omnium graciarum a sede apostolica memorato ordine concessarum'.

Celestis amor (*Bullarium Franciscanum*, ed. J. H. Sbaralea and C. Eubel, no. 399) has first place. The latest date in the thirteen chapters seems to be 18 Jan. 1283 (f. 10ᵛ, *Exultantes*: *Bull.*, no. 1524). The *Mare magnum* of Alexander IV and the *Mare magnum* of Clement IV form ch. 13, ff. 27–33ᵛ: *Bull.*, Supplementum, nos. XXXV, XLIII. They are followed by a miscellaneous tail of twenty-one pieces, ff. 33ᵛ–41ᵛ, the last of them *Cum hora undecima* of a Pope Nicholas dated at Rome 'apud sanctam Mariam maiorem. non' decembris pontificatus nostri anno ii': the place and date would suit a letter of Nicholas IV (cf. *Bull.*, no. 1744), but *Bull.* records a *Cum hora undecima* issued by him only at 13 Aug. 1291.

[1] A breviary now in the Hampshire County Record Office at Winchester has been treated in the same way.

An inserted quire of paper, ff. ii–viii, has the beginning of a table of contents, s. xvi: ff. iii^v–viii^v were left blank.

ff. viii+41+i. For ff. ii–viii see above. 180 × 130 mm. Written space 130 × 90 mm. 2 cols. 33 lines. Collation: 1–3¹⁰ 4¹⁰+1 leaf after 10. Red initials, 1-line. Capital letters in the ink of the text touched with red. Binding of s. xv, wooden boards covered with stamped brown leather, rebacked: five small bosses on each cover: a central clasp fastening from the front to the back cover is missing. Secundo folio *dam*.

Written in France. Erased inscription at head of f. 1. A paper leaf lying loose at the beginning bears the numbers 74 and 821 and a description of the manuscript in French, s. xix. No. 514 in an English sale catalogue: the relevant cutting is attached to the paper leaf. Edmund Bishop's 'E libris' inside the cover and 'Emptus 15° 'die' Decembris 1869 E. B.' on f. i.

26549. *Vitalis Blesensis, etc.*   s. XVI in.

1. ff. 1–18^v Grecorum studio nimium . . . se fore queque placent. 'Et sic est finis istius ouidii amphitrionis'.

The Amphitryo (or Geta) of Vitalis of Blois, ed. G. Cohen, *La 'Comédie' latine en France au xiie siecle*, 1931, i. 34–57. Interlinear glosses on ff. 1–13 and scholia in the margins of ff. 1–12. The first scholium begins imperfectly 'causa finalis et formalis cuilibet studioso considerandi Scias quod causa efficiens dicitur fuisse ouidius naso'.

2. ff. 19–48^v Pyerius me traxit amor iussitque camena . . . petendis. Hic dulces retinet fructus laborinthus In metrum rabis (?) dens dictare scolaris.

The Laborinthus of Everard 'Alemannus', ed. E. Faral, *Les Arts poétiques du xiie et du xiiie siècle*, 1924, pp. 337–77. Ends with two lines not in the edition. Some lengthy scholia. f. 49 blank.

3. ff. 49^v–50 [A]gedum precor nouene resonans chorus puellis . . . per astra gloria super eua amen.

Twenty-four 2-line stanzas. f. 50^v blank.

ff. 50. Paper. 195 × 140 mm. Written space 140 mm high. Frame ruling. 15–18 long lines. Collation: 1¹²+a slip after 2 2 six (ff. 13–18) 3–6⁸. Art. 2 in a set cursiva. Art. 1 in current and difficult cursiva. Red initials. Capital letters in the ink of the text stroked with red. Covers of marbled paper, s. xix.

Written in France (?). 'Pertinet Iohanni oberlinens' etc', f. 31^v, s. xvi in. Armorial bookplate of Henry Latham: his sale 31 Jan. 1872, lot 620. Earlier (?) no. 489 in the catalogue of an English bookseller, whose admirable description is pasted inside the end cover. Came to Downside with the collection of Edmund Bishop, †1917.

26619. (*J. de Guytrode*), *Lavacrum Conscientiae, etc.*   1476 (?)

1. ff. 1–12 Calendar in red and black. Feasts in red include 'Hugonis episcopi ordinis nostri' (Hugh of Grenoble) at 1 Apr., 'Commemoracio fratrum nostrorum' at 9 Nov., and 'Hugonis episcopi ordinis nostri' (Hugh of Lincoln) at 17 Nov. Feast of relics, 8 Nov.

2. ff. 13–19 Petis a me frater karissime In domino Ihesu ut aliquam formulam dignarem tibi transmittere . . . discretum sit obsequium vestrum. f. 19ᵛ blank.

3. ff. 20–113ᵛ Responsio cuiusdam fratris religiosi ad suum confratrem secularem dando sibi consilium quo potest uiuere uita bona et fyᵒ desaluand'. O mi frater multum preamande placet michi . . . conregnare et congaudere. Qui uiuit et regnat . . . amen. Explicit tractatus qui intitulatur lauacrum consciencie per me nicolaum schnider etc. sub anno domini 1476.

Jacobus de Guytrode, Lavacrum conscientiae, beginning in chapter 17. In the edition printed in 1489, the first words here occur on sig. i. 4. The scribe's name and the date may have been copied from the exemplar.

ff. i+113. Paper. 150×100 mm. Written space 108×70 mm. 17 long lines. No ruling. Collation: 1¹² 2¹² wants 8–12, perhaps blank, after f. 19 3¹⁰ 4–10¹². Written in a fairly current cursiva. Red initials. Capital letters in the ink of the text stroked with red. Contemporary binding of wooden boards covered with pink leather: central clasp inscribed 'maria', like the metal piece on the front cover to which it is attached: small bosses removed.

Written in Germany for Carthusian use (art. 1). From the Charterhouse of Buxheim, near Memmingen: 'Buxheim', f. 13. '100' in red on the backstrip.

33553. *Horae*   s. XV ex.

1. ff. 1–12ᵛ Calendar in red and black.

Includes: (in red) 'Sancte Anne matris marie', 'Festum niuis', 'Sancte Clare Virginis', 'Sancte Helysabeth regine' (27 May, 5, 12 Aug., 19 Nov.); (in black) translation of Clare, Francis and octave of Francis (2, 4, 11 Oct.). July is misplaced before June.

2. ff. 14–110 Incipit officium beate marie uirginis secundum consuetudinem curie romane. ff. 110ᵛ–111ᵛ blank.

3. ff. 113–74 Incipit officium mortuorum. f. 174ᵛ blank.

4. ff. 176–213 Incipit officium passionis domini nostri yhesu cristi. The long office (cf. art. 6). f. 213ᵛ blank.

5. ff. 215–244ᵛ Incipiunt septem psalmi penitentiales. sub una antiphona. Ne reminiscaris . . .

The litany begins on f. 231ᵛ. Zenobius is last of eight confessors and is followed by the 'doctores' Benedict, Francis, Dominic, Bernard, Leonard, and Antony. Reparata is last of eleven virgins.

6. ff. 246–51 Incipit officium crucis paruum . . . Patris sapientia . . .

7. ff. 252–267ᵛ Incipiunt psalmi graduales.

ff. iii+267+iv. f. 268 is a medieval parchment flyleaf. 202×93 mm. Written space 61× 44 mm. 11 long lines. Collation: 1¹² (the central sheet reversed) 2–16¹⁰ 17¹² (ff. 163–74) 18–20¹⁰ 21⁸ (ff. 206–13) 22–24¹⁰ 25⁶ (ff. 246–51) 26¹⁰ 27⁶: singletons inserted in front of quires 2, 12, 18, 22, 25 (ff. 13, 112, 175, 214, 245). Written in a very good hand, but the writing has sometimes faded on flesh sides. Five full-page pictures (65 × 44 mm) on versos of ff. 13, 112 (raising of Lazarus), 175, 214 (David and Goliath), 245 (the dead Christ in the arms of B.V.M.): rectos blank. Initials (i) beginning each of arts. 2–7, red and green or blue and green on gold grounds, all except the last (f. 252) historiated (B.V.M. and Child, Death with Scythe, Christ carrying the Cross, David, Christ rising from the Tomb); (ii) as (i), but smaller (4-line), and not historiated; (iii, iv) 2-line and 1-line, blue with red ornament or gold with blue ornament. Continuous floral borders on picture pages and on pages with initials of type (i): the ornament includes cherubs and framed portraits: erased arms in the lower borders, ff. 13ᵛ, 14, 214ᵛ. Borders in one margin of pages with initials of type (ii). Capital letters in the ink of the text touched with pale yellow. Binding of s. xix, lettered 'Missal' on the spine.

Written in Italy: art. 5 points to Florence and there are points of similarity with Cambridge, Fitzwilliam Mus., MS. 154. 'Presented to the Library by Mrs. Baxter, 1957'.

33554. *Horae*   s. xv in.

1. ff. 1–43ᵛ Hours of B.V.M. of the use of (Sarum), beginning imperfectly in matins and ending imperfectly in none. Hours of the Cross are worked in. Memoriae after lauds of Holy Spirit, Holy Trinity, Holy Cross, SS. Michael, John Baptist, Peter and Paul, Andrew, Stephen, Laurence, Thomas of Canterbury (Tu per thome sanguinem . . .), Nicholas, Mary Magdalene, Katherine, Margaret, All Saints, and for peace (but headed 'De tempore').

2. ff. 44–5 Salve regina, imperfect at the beginning, followed by the six stanzas, 'Virgo mater ecclesie . . .' (*RH*, no. 21818) and the prayer, 'Omnipotens sempiterne deus qui gloriose uirginis . . .'.

3. ff. 45ᵛ–46ᵛ Ad uirginem mariam. Gaude flore uirginali . . .   *RH*, no. 6809.

4. ff. 47–53 Salve virgo virginum stella matutina (*RH*, no. 18318), beginning imperfectly in the second stanza.

5. ff. 53–7 Ad uirginem mariam. Obsecro te . . .

6. ff. 57–59ᵛ O intemerata . . . orbis terrarum. Inclina . . .

7. ff. 59ᵛ–63 Virgo templum trinitatis (*RH*, no. 21899), beginning imperfectly in the third Joy.

The heading conveys an indulgence of 100 days 'a domino clemente qui hec septem gaudia proprio stilo composuit'.

8. ff. 63–65ᵛ Ad ymaginem cristi crucifixi. Omnibus consideratis . . .

RH, no. 14081. A leaf missing after f. 64.

9. ff. 65ᵛ–68 Oratio venerabilis bede presbiteri de septem verbis cristi in cruce pendentis. . . .

The heading is cancelled and the beginning of the prayer Domine iesu christe qui septem verba is missing with the leaf after f. 65. The prayer is followed, as commonly, by 'Precor te piissime . . .'.

10. ff. 68–71ᵛ Ad sanctum sacramentum: (*a*) Aue domine ihesu criste uerbum patris . . .; (*b*) Aue principium nostre creationis . . .; (*c*) Aue uerum corpus natum . . .; (*d*) Aue caro cristi cara immolata crucis ara . . .; (*e*) Anima cristi sanctifica me. (*f*) Domine ihesu criste qui hanc sacratissimam carnem . . .: the

heading conveys indulgence of 2000 years 'ad supplicacionem philippi regis francie'.

(*b*)–(*e*) are *RH*, nos. 2059, 2175, 1710, 1090. In s. xvii a reader wrote 'Idolatry' in the margin opposite (*c*).

11. ff. 72–82 Seven penitential psalms, beginning imperfectly.

12. ff. 82–84ᵛ Quindecim psalmi: cues only of the first twelve.

13. ff. 85–93ᵛ Litany. Swithun is in the form 'zwichine'.

14. ff. 94–127ᵛ Incipiunt uigilie mortuorum.

15. ff. 128–133ᵛ Commendatory psalms, beginning imperfectly at 118.9 and ending imperfectly at 118.82.

ff. ii + 133 + ii. 120 × 80 mm. Written space 68 × 48 mm. 16 long lines. Collation: 1 two (ff. 1, 2) 2⁸ 3 seven (ff. 11–17) 4–6⁸ (5² is a fragment) 7 three (ff. 44–6) 8⁸ 9⁸ wants 6 after f. 59 10⁶ wants 4 after f. 64 and 6 after f. 65 11⁶ (ff. 66–71) 12⁸ wants 1 (ff. 72–8) 13–18⁸ 19⁸ wants 2 after f. 127: single inserted leaves after 6² and 6⁵ (ff. 36, 40). Two full-page pictures of a passion series remain, Christ carrying the Cross before next and Christ Crucified before none. Three smaller pictures in art. 8. Initials: (i) in colour patterned in white on faded gold grounds, historiated, four in art. 1 (ff. 8 Visitation, 32 Shepherds, 37 Kings, 41 Presentation), and beginning arts. 5 (Pietà) and 8 (Adam and Eve and the tree and serpent); (ii) 2-line, gold on coloured grounds patterned in white; (iii) 1-line, gold with slate-grey ornament or blue with red ornament. Capital letters in the ink of the text filled with pale yellow. Continuous framed borders on pages with full-page pictures or historiated initials. Binding of s. xix.

Written in the Netherlands for English use (cf. MSS. 26529, 26530). 'John Bradshawe' (f. 60, s. xvii). Book-plate of Frederick George Lee, who had it in exchange from the Revd. Professor G. Bickell of Münster, 10 Feb. 1871 (f. iᵛ). 'Carissimæ filiæ Mariæ Ceciliæ Lee-Bond D.D. F. R. Benedictus Lee' (f. 134, s. xx). 'Presented to Library by Mrs. D. Bond 1957' (inscription on book-plate of F. G. Lee).

36212. *Breviarium, cum notis*   s. XII med.

1. ff. 1–233 Temporale from Advent to the twenty-fourth Sunday after Pentecost. The first two leaves and the eighth leaf are missing.

Office of St. Gregory (of Spoleto), 24 Dec., on f. 26. The forms of service for the week after the octave of Epiphany, ff. 59ᵛ–77, provide 'the complete framework of the office from matins to compline, including all the subsidiary devotions, suffrages, psalmi familiares, daily office of all saints and on the Sunday the procession "per officinas" in full and on the Monday in its place the seven penitential psalms and litany, and other matter said during the day'.[1] The Sunday office includes a collect for St. Benedict, 'Fac nos quesumus domine beati patris nostri benedicti hic imitari labores . . .' (f. 64ᵛ), a collect for St. Andrew (f. 64ᵛ), and a collect to be said 'In choro', 'Via sanctorum omnium . . . qui locum istum in honorem [. . . . .] consecrari uoluisti . . .' (f. 66ᵛ), in which the words 'cosme et damiani' have been written in a later hand over an erasure of about twenty letters. In the Monday litany Michael, John Baptist, and Andrew (who follows Peter and Paul) are doubled and also Benedict, but here the doubling is an addition: twenty-eight martyrs, Apollinaris, Vitalis, and Ursicinus seventh to ninth.

---

[1] So J. B. L. Tolhurst in a letter to S. J. P. van Dijk, 10 July 1961, the carbon copy of which is kept in a folder with other notes relating to MS. 36212.

The office for Passion Sunday, ff. 150–155ᵛ, is incomplete at both ends, owing to the loss of the outside sheet of quire 20: presumably more than one leaf is missing after f. 155, since f. 156 begins 'Incipiunt lecciones feriales De xl' and the next main heading is for Easter Saturday (f. 171).

Collects for Zeno, Gregory of Spoleto, Thomas of Canterbury, Cosmas and Damianus, and Anthony (abbot) added in the margins, s. xiii.

2. ff. 233–92 Sanctorale from 14 Apr. to 30 Nov.

The office of Tiburtius and Valerianus, 14 Apr., runs straight on from art. 1 without a break of even one line. Full twelve-lesson office of Apollinaris, ff. 252–254ᵛ. The feasts of Gervase and Protase, Peter, Assumption of B.V.M., Decollation of John Baptist, Nativity of B.V.M., Cecilia, and Andrew are distinguished by a larger initial letter (type i).

Collects for Cyric and Julitta, Mary Magdalene, Giles, and Francis added in the margins, s. xiii.

3. ff. 292ᵛ–306ᵛ Common of saints.

Lacks a leaf after f. 300 and ends imperfectly in confessors.

ff. i+306+i. ff. 1–306 were foliated incorrectly iii–cccxvi by a late medieval hand at a time when quires 1 and 20 were complete, but the first leaf of quire 40 was missing. 245 × 155 mm. Written space 185 × 110 mm. Ruling with a hard point. Long lines, usually 34. Collation: 1⁸ wants 1, 2, 8, 2–19⁸ 20⁸ wants 1 before f. 150 and 8 after f. 155 21–37⁸ 38⁴ 39⁸ 1–3 cancelled before f. 296 40⁸ wants 1 before f. 301 and 8 after f. 306. Catchwords by the main hand. Well written: *r* is usually a descender. The scribe made room for the music by writing the noted texts in smaller script. Initials: (i) 3-line, in red outline, sometimes zoomorphic (28ᵛ) on blue, green, and bistre grounds; (ii) 2-line and 1-line, red, filled with blue, green, and bistre. Capital letters in the ink of the text filled with bistre and stroked with red. Binding of modern wooden boards, rebacked: two clasps missing.

Written in Italy for Benedictine use, and probably, as Tolhurst thought, for the abbey of St. Apollinaris at Ravenna. Later apparently at a church of SS. Cosmas and Damianus. C. W. Dyson Perrins sale at Sotheby's, 11 Apr. 1961, lot 128, to Messrs. Maggs (£220). Book-plate of J. B. L. Tolhurst, †1961: bequeathed by him.

40190. *Collectarius, etc.*   1506

1. ff. 1–75ᵛ, 81–133ᵛ A calendar, ff. 4–9ᵛ, collects for the year, ff. 15ᵛ–75, and other texts. A book printed at Bamberg, *c.* 1481–4, for the use of the Congregation of Bursfeld (*GKW* 7160) has almost exactly the same contents.[1]

The manuscript differs from the printed book in having 'Remacli episcopi patroni nostri. Summum maius' in the calendar, 3 Sept. (f. 8), in naming Peter and Paul, Remaclus, and Benedict as the saints to be invoked in the Agenda mortuorum (f. 110ᵛ: the printed book has, instead, a rubric 'Hic exprimantur patroni loci et ordinis') and in having four forms of absolution on f. 132ʳᵛ after the heading 'Forma absolucionis in extremis plenaria': in the printed book the heading omits *plenaria* and is followed by a blank space. A valuable note on the manuscript by Dom Louis Brou, Quarr Abbey, 7 Apr. 1940, is attached to f. i.

2. ff. 76–9 Hec sunt extraordinarie posita de sanctis videlicet quorum festa in hoc loco aguntur soleniter.

Collects for Sigibertus, Remaclus, and Lambertus. f. 79ᵛ left blank.

[1] The Bodleian copy is Auct. 1 Q. 5. 50. I owe the date to Mr. L. A. Sheppard.

3. f. 80ʳᵛ A graded list of festivals in red and black, with a heading which says that some services have been cut down: 'De sanctis infrascriptis olim agebatur in hoc loco prout cuiuslibet dignitati congruebat. modo vero . . .'.

4. ff. 134–70 Noted hymns for the day, the proper of time from Advent to Corpus Christi, the common of saints (f. 152), the dedication of a church (f. 157) and the sanctorale (f. 158), seventy-five in all, excluding hymns for which cues only are given.

At the end the scribe wrote four lines of verse: Adde senos annos quinquagenis et habebis / Etatem qua me scripsit apollonius / Post annos mille quingentos sex super adde / Si tibi vis pateat data claudens fine libellum.

In the sanctorale, proper hymns are provided for Stephen, John Evangelist, Innocents (Que vox que poterit . . .), Purification of B.V.M., Benedict (Iesu corona celsior . . ., Te criste rex piissime . . .), Annunciation of B.V.M., Invention of Cross, Nativity of B.V.M., Peter and Paul, Mary Magdalene, Laurence, Assumption of B.V.M., Nativity of B.V.M., Michael, All Saints, Martin. According to Dom Brou (see above), the hymns are the same as in Trier MS. 436 from the Benedictine abbey of St. Matthias at Trier, which became a member of the Bursfeld Congregation in 1458. f. 170ᵛ blank.

5. f. 171 In solennitate Natalis beati Remacli ad vtrasque vesperas hymnus cui placet. Aule celestis consulem Remaclum dignum presulem . . .

RH, no. 23277. The first three lines noted. f. 171ᵛ blank.

6 (added, s. xvii) (*a*) f. 45ᵛ Suffrages of B.V.M., St. Remaclus, De patronis, and of St. Benedict. (*b*) Collects for Joseph, confessor, and for Abraham, Isaac, and Jacob, patriarchs.

ff. i+171+i. Paper. 260×190 mm. Written space *c*. 180×135 mm. 20–2 long lines. Only the vertical bounding lines are ruled. Collation impracticable. Written mainly by one scribe (see above) and for the most part in hybrida, but the calendar and f. 24ʳᵛ are in textura and ff. 1–3, 11ᵛ–14 in current cursiva. The marks of punctuation are the flex (?), punctus elevatus (:) and point (.). 1-line red initials. Contemporary, but rebacked binding of wooden boards covered with brown leather bearing a pattern of diagonal fillets in the centre and a fleuron in each of the lozenges so formed: the border is of two fillets lined on the inside with half-pineapple stamps: small corner ornaments: two metal clasps.

Written for use in the Benedictine abbey of Stavelot, diocese of Liège, where Remaclus was patron. The scribe Apollonius was fifty-six years old and wrote in 1506 (see above), a moment when Stavelot was considering becoming a member of the Bursfeld congregation.[1] Formerly no. 8405 in the Virtue and Cahill collection belonging to the Roman Catholic archbishopric of Portsmouth. The Virtue and Cahill book-plate inside the cover was defaced before the sale at Christie's, 5 July 1967, lot 175 (£170). Acquired in 1967.

45857. *Bernardus Ayglerius, Expositio Regulae Sancti Benedicti*

s. xv med.

Hic incipit exposicio Super regulam beati benedicti edita a bernardo abbate Cassinensis. Prohemium. Legitur in prouerbiis Doctrinam prudencium facilis. Ideoque qui sapientiam . . . peticionibus postulastis. Incipit prologus regule

---

[1] This observation comes from Dom Brou's note.

beati patris Benedicti abbatis. et exposicio eiusdem. Absculta. Aliqua littera
habet obsculta. quod quidem dicunt esse rectius. tenetur. . . .

The exposition of the Rule of St. Benedict by Bernardus Ayglerius, abbot of Monte Cassino, d. 1282, edited by Dom A. M. Caplet, *Bernardi I, abbatis Casinensis, in Regulam
S. Benedicti Expositio*, 1894. Complete as far as cap. 65, De proposito monasterii, which
ends imperfectly with the words 'abbatis sui dicens' (f. 168ᵛ). One leaf only remains after
this containing parts of chapters 71, 72 (f. 169).

ff. vi+169+x. ff. v, vi, 170–2 are blank parchment end-leaves. Thick parchment. 245 ×
162 mm. Written space 170 × 110 mm. 29–35 long lines. Frame ruling. Collation:
1–21⁸ 22 one (f. 169). Irregular hand of mixed type. Blue initials with red ornament.
Binding of s. xviii. Secundo folio *mea esse.*

Written in England. 'Anno domini Millesimo CCCC.lx° iiijᵗᵒ obiit Frater georgius
Donwton [*sic*] Monachus et sacrista in prima nocte sancti bartholomei hora xiiᵐᵃ'
is written at the foot of f. 1. Pricemark '1. 11. 6', f. ii, s. xviii. Armorial book-plate inscribed 'This Book belongs to / the Inner Library / bequeathed by the Will of / Thoˢ
Eyre Esqʳ deceased. / Wᵐ Wakeman and Vincent Eyre Esqʳˢ / Acting Executors 1792'.
The library was that at St. Mary's Catholic Church, Hassop, Derbyshire. Sold at Sotheby's,
7 Oct. 1974, lot 30.

48242–53, 58254. *Bishop of Clifton's Collection*

48242–53 (Clifton 1–12) and 58254, part of the library of the Catholic Bishopric
of Clifton, were given in 1976 by the Bishop of Clifton, Dr. Mervyn Alexander.
MSS. 4–10 were probably all the property of Canon John Williams passed on by
him to the Right Reverend the Honourable W. J. H. Clifford, bishop of Clifton,
†1893: cf. MSS. 5, 7. Other manuscripts from Canon Williams's collection are
now at St. Hugh's Charterhouse, Partridge Green. MSS. 5, 6, 8, 10 are Erfurt
manuscripts identifiable in the Bülow sale in 1836.

48242 (Clifton 1). *Missale romanum*   s. xv med.

1. ff. 1–6ᵛ Calendar in red and black.

f. 1 damaged at the foot. Additions include: 'Et consecratio ecclesie sancti Iohannis de
uaxano', 25 Apr.; 'Et sancti Grataliani Martiris', 12 August; 'Sancti Iodouici episcopi et
confessoris', 19 Aug.; 'Sanctorum martirum et pontificum tholomey et romani', 24 Aug.,
over erasure; 'Consecratio sancti Iodouicy de uassano', 13 Dec.

Arts. 2–12 are on ff. 7–197, headed 'Incipit ordo missalis secundum consuetudinem Romane curie' and ending 'Explicit liber missalis secundum consuetudinem romane curie. Amen deo gratias.'

2. ff. 7–90 Temporale from Advent to Easter Eve.

The music of Exultet not filled in, ff. 79ᵛ–83.

3. f. 90ʳᵛ Aduentus domini celebratur . . . in omnibus consecrationibus ecclesiarum et altarium. *SMRL* ii. 249–51.

4. ff. 90ᵛ–97 Paratus sacerdos . . .

Ordinary, prefaces, and canon of mass, lacking a leaf after f. 94.

5. ff. 97–131ᵛ Temporale from Easter to the twenty-fourth Sunday after Pentecost.

6. ff. 131ᵛ–164ᵛ Incipit offitium proprium sanctorum per circulum anni.

30 Nov. (Andrew)–25 Nov. (Katherine).

7. ff. 164ᵛ–181ᵛ Incipit comune sanctorum.

8. ff. 181ᵛ–182ᵛ In ipsa die dedicationis ecclesie.

The collect, secret, and postcommunion at the consecration of an altar follow the office of dedication. *SMRL* ii. 317–18.

9. ff. 182ᵛ–191ᵛ Votive masses. *SMRL* ii. 318–27, nos. 1–62.

10. ff. 191ᵛ–195 Missa in agenda mortuorum. *SMRL* ii. 327–31.

11. ff. 195–6 Missa pro sponso et sponsa.

12. ff. 196–7 Exorcisms of salt and water and immediately before the *explicit* a 'Benedictio ad omnia quecumque uolueris. Exorcizo te creatura florum vel erbarum et nomina cibaria que hic sunt posita. In nomine . . . per inuocacionem tui sancti nominis per intercessionem beate marie semper virginis et beati blaxii martyris tui . . . tutelam percipiant. Per cristum dominum nostrum amen'. f. 197ᵛ blank.

ff. ii+197+i. 320×225 mm. Written space 212×150 mm. 2 cols. 35 lines. Collation: 1⁶ 2–8¹⁰ 9¹⁰ wants 9 after f. 94 10–19¹⁰ 20 two (ff. 196–7). Initials: (i) an *I* historiated with the evangelist's figure and symbol begins each of the Holy Week lections from Matthew, Mark, Luke, and John, ff. 61ᵛ, 65ᵛ, 69ᵛ, 74ᵛ (where only John's eagle remains); (ii) 7-line (f. 7); (iii) 2-line, usually blue or red, plain or with ornament of the other colour, and filled sometimes with a wash of bistre, all rough work, except in quire 2 (ff. 7–16ᵛ) where lilac ornament is used with red initials. Initials of *Te igitur* (f. 95) and beginning art. 5 have been cut out. Capital letters in the ink of the text marked with red. Binding of s. xviii, covered with red velvet. Secundo folio (f. 8) *spei repleat*.

Written in Italy. Belonged to a church in Bassano (province of Vicenza: cf. art. 1) and in s. xviii (?) to Marius Marefuschus, whose armorial book-plate inside the cover bears a cardinal's hat above the shield and a scroll with his name below it: a pressmark 'F. v. 14' on the book-plate.

48243 (Clifton 2). *Missale*   s. xv in.

A missal for use in Herefordshire. Art. 21*a* and binding leaves (art. 24), are in the excellent and distinctive hand of the 'Graseley' who wrote Bodleian MS. Lyell 30 in 1441 and was identified by Dr. A. de la Mare as probably John Graseley, ordained priest in the diocese of Hereford between Sept. 1410 and Apr. 1412: cf. *Lyell Cat.*, p. 73 and pl. IVa. Arts. 2, 13, 17–19, 21*a* are in MS. Lyell 30: cf. also art. 24.

1. ff. 1–6ᵛ Calendar in red and black, graded.

Many feasts in red, including Wolstan, Milburga, David, Chad, Guthlac, 'Dedicacio ecclesie hereford', Ethelbert, Thomas of Hereford, Osith, Frideswide, Winefred (19 Jan., 23 Feb., 1, 2 Mar., 11 Apr., 11, 20 May, 2, 7, 19 Oct., 3 Nov.). Gradings for nine and three lessons, but not always. Feasts of St. Thomas of Canterbury not damaged.

2. ff. 7–11ᵛ Oracio deuota dicenda ante missam. Summe sacerdos et uere pontifex . . . neque siciam in eternum. Amen.

Ed. A. Wilmart, *Auteurs spirituels*, pp. 114–24. *Lyell Cat.*, p. 399.

3. ff. 12–14 Hoc modo fiat aqua benedicta.

4. ff. 14–38ᵛ Temporale and sanctorale from Christmas to Annunciation.

Proper offices for Christmas, Thomas of Canterbury, Epiphany, Purification of B.V.M., David, and Annunciation of B.V.M., ending with Gloria in excelsis for B.V.M., with her name in red, and Credo in unum deum. The sequence for Thomas of Canterbury is Mundo cristum oritur, as in *Missale Herfordense*, edn. 1874, p. 22. The sequence for David is Adest nobis dies alma, adapted from the common of a confessor.

5. ff. 39–41ᵛ Prefaces of mass.

6. ff. 42–44ᵛ Office of dedication of church.

7. ff. 45–50ᵛ Canon of mass.

8. ff. 50ᵛ–99 Temporale and sanctorale from Easter to St. Katherine.

Proper offices for Easter, Ascension, Pentecost, Trinity, Corpus Christi, John Baptist, Peter and Paul, translation of Thomas of Canterbury (mainly cues), Margaret (sequence, Exultemus in hac die), James, Anne, Assumption of B.V.M., Nativity of B.V.M., Michael, Thomas of Hereford, translation of Thomas of Hereford (partly cues), All Saints, Leonard, Katherine.

9. ff. 99–116 Masses of Holy Trinity, Angels, All Saints, Holy Spirit, Holy Cross, and B.V.M.

10. ff. 116–25 Collect, secret, and postcommunion of votive masses: Ad invocandam graciam spiritus sancti, Contra cogitaciones malas, Contra temptacionem carnis, Pro statu ecclesie, Pro sacerdote, Pro benefactoribus, Pro infirmo, Pro iter agentibus, Pro nauigantibus, Contra fulgura et tempestates, Pro pluuia postulanda, Pro serenitate aeris, Pro peticione lacrimarum, Pro penitentibus, De omnibus sanctis (at Advent and Easter), Oracio generalis de omnibus sanctis (three forms, the second 'pro uiuis et defunctis' and the third 'dominicis diebus et festis ix lc' '), Oracio generalis.

11. ff. 125–130ᵛ Missa pro defunctis.

12. ff. 130ᵛ–132 Hic incipit regula de trentali quod canonizatum est per gregorium papam et dicitur hoc modo . . .

13. ff. 132–133ᵛ Dominus papa iohannes composuit istud euangelium sequens apud auinionam iii die ante decessum suum . . . Passio domini nostri ihesu cristi. Secundum Iohannem. Non dicatur. Gloria tibi domine. In illo tempore. Apprehendit pilatus . . .

A catena from John and Matthew and prayer 'Deus qui manus tuas . . . et ueram scienciam (*sic*) usque in finem. per', with heading conveying an indulgence of 300 days, as in MS. Lyell 30, art. 10: cf. *Lyell Cat.*, pp. 65–6.

14. ff. 133–136ᵛ Quicumque dixerit uel audierit cotidie hec iiiiᵒʳ euangeliorum sequencia non morietur sine confessione et debent audiri cum bona deuocione . . .

Sequences of Gospels, Luke, Matthew, Mark, John.

15. ff. 136ᵛ–138ᵛ Office 'In visitacione beate marie. et sancte elizabeth'.

The hymn is Veni precelsa domina.

16. ff. 138ᵛ–141 Missa pro pestilencia cantanda. quam dominus papa Clemens sextus fecit et constituit in collegio cum omnibus cardinalibus . . . Recordare domine . . .

The heading conveys an indulgence of 260 days.

17. ff. 141–3 This prayer folewyng in englysch.' schal be seyde afore the receyuing of the holy sacrement goddis body. O benyng ihesu that woldiste suffre . . .

Cf. MS. Lyell 30, ff. 18ᵛ–21: *Lyell Cat.*, p. 365.

18. f. 143ʳᵛ This preyer on englysch folewyng. schal be seide aftur the receyueng of the holy sacrement goddis body. O thanked be ȝe holy fadur myȝthful god . . .

Cf. MS. Lyell 30, f. 36ʳᵛ: *Lyell Cat.*, pp. 365–6.

19. ff. 143ᵛ–146ᵛ Prayers in Latin and English for those journeying and against robbers.

The same seven pieces as in MS. Lyell 30, art. 13: *Lyell Cat.*, p. 66.

20. ff. 146ᵛ–151 Prayers invoking the persons of the Trinity, severally and together, B.V.M., Angels, Patriarchs, Apostles, Innocents, Martyrs, Confessors, Virgins, and All Saints. ff. 151ᵛ–152ᵛ left blank.

21 (in other hands). (*a*) f. 151ᵛ Oracio deuota contra pestilenciam. Stella celi extirpauit. . . . (*b*) f. 152 Oracio. Deus a quo sancta desideria . . .

(*a*). *RH*, no. 19438. In MS. Lyell 30, f. 258ᵛ: *Lyell Cat.*, p. 398. (*b*). The usual collect, secret, and postcommunion for peace.

22 (in another hand). (*a*) ff. 153–6 Officium misse de ueneracione supperni dominis (*sic for* nominis) ihesu cristi. (*b*) f. 156ʳᵛ Ihesu dulcis memoria dans vera cordis gaudia . . .

(*a*). Office of the Holy Name. (*b*). *RH*, no. 9542.

23. (on flyleaf). (*a*) f. 157 Clara dies pauli . . . (4 lines). (*b*) f. 157ᵛ Si prima tonitrua . . .

(*a*). Walther, *Sprichwörter*, no. 2788. (*b*). Significance of thunder, according to the day of the week.

24 (on flyleaves). ff. iii–ivᵛ, 158ʳᵛ are cancelled leaves, signatures [d. i], d. ii, and d. iiii of a book written by the scribe of art. 21*a*. They contain: (*a*) f. iii, the hardly legible end of a text; (*b*) ff. iiiʳᵛ, ivʳᵛ, first, directions in English for saying a prayer on occasions of special danger, for example on going a journey, in childbirth, on going before the king, and in a storm at sea, and, secondly, the prayer itself, 'Deus omnipotens pater et filius et spiritus sanctus da michi famulo tuo N. victoriam . . .'; (*c*) f. 158ʳᵛ, probably the end of the prayer beginning on

f. iv^r; (*d*) f. 158^v/12–20, a heading in English, apparently introducing a prayer against enemies ascribed to Pope Leo.

(*b*). The prayer, but not the directions, is in MS. Lyell 30, ff. 52–54^v, written by the same hand. The leaves have been crossed through with large X's, like Lyell 30, ff. vii, viii, 301, which are reject leaves of the main manuscript. ff. iii^r, 158^v have been pasted down and are hardly legible now. Written space 78 × 45 mm (as Lyell 30). 20 long lines (as Lyell 30).

ff. v + 156 + iv. For ff. iii, iv, 157–8 see above arts. 23, 24. f. v is parchment. 128 × 85 mm. Written space 80 × 45 mm. 22 long lines. Collation: 1^6 2^6 wants 6, blank 3–4^{12} 5^8 + 1 leaf after 8 (f. 44) 6^{10} + 2 leaves after 10 (ff. 55, 56) 7–14^{12} 15^4 (ff. 153–6). Initials: (i) *T* of *Te igitur*, f. 45, blue shaded to white on decorated gold ground, with prolongations forming a continuous border of colours and gold; (ii) ff. 12, 19, 7-line and 8-line, red and blue with red ornament; (iii) 2-line, red or green, with ornament of the other colour; (iv) 1-line, red or green. Capital letters in the ink of the text filled with pale yellow. Panel binding of s. xvi^1, rebacked: the panel on the back is a rose pattern not apparently recorded by Old-ham: the panel on the front is Oldham's HE 28 which was in use by a Hereford binder *c*. 1530 (cf. N. R. Ker in *Kunsthistorische Forschungen Otto Pächt zu seinem 70. Geburtstag*, 1972, p. 80). Secundo folio (f. 8) *mie. fornicacionis*.

Written in England (Hereford?: see above). 'P.S. I beseech you remember the soule of Edward Calife (?)', f. v, s. xvii.

48244 (Clifton 3). *Breviarium*   s. xv^1

Part of a Sarum breviary, imperfect and probably disarranged.

1. ff. 1–53 Liturgical psalter.

Imperfect at the beginning—the first words, 'iacob glorificate', are in Ps. 21 (*Brev. ad usum Sarum*, col. 38—and with gaps where leaves have been removed. Vespers ends on f. 43^v and is followed by prime, terce, sext, none (ending imperfectly at f. 51^v), lauds (beginning imperfectly at f. 52), and compline. At prime the rubric after Dirigere (edn., col. 55) begins (f. 48) 'His itaque peractis puer legat aliam leccionem de haymone Hoc Modo Iube Domine benedicere Sacerdos dicat benediccionem hoc modo Omnipotens sua gracia nos benedicat . . ., and the final direction, in place of *Excellentior* . . . (edn., col. 58) is (f. 48^v) 'Statim idem sacerdos dicat Benedicite . . . amen Et sic unusquisque se muniat signo crucis et sic statim a capitulo usque in chorum processionaliter reuertantur'.

2. ff. 53–56^v Sarum litanies for each weekday.

In the Tuesday litany 'Sancte Thoma or' ' is a contemporary addition marked for inser-tion in first place.

3. ff. 56^v–61 Office of the dead.

ff. 61^v–62^v, left blank, contain benedictions added in s. xv ex.: cf. art. 5.

4. ff. 63–89 Common of saints, beginning imperfectly.

5. ff. 89–90^v De benediccionibus dicendis ante leccionibus per totum annum . . .

f. 91^{rv}, left blank, contains three lessons for Thomas the Martyr in the same hand as the additions on ff. 61^v–62^v.

6. ff. 92–241^v Sanctorale, beginning imperfectly in Andrew, 30 Nov., and ending imperfectly in All Souls, 2 Nov.

Includes David and Chad. A reader noted in the margin of f. 164 in red 'Visitacio beate marie caret hic'.

ff. xiv+241+xii. Some margins cut off. 160×110 mm. Written space 112×75 mm. 2 cols. 33–6 lines. Collation impracticable. Initials: (i) missing; (ii) 2-line, blue with red ornament; (iii) 1-line, blue or red.

Written in England.

48245 (Clifton 4). *Preces, etc.* s. xv/xvi

Many of the verse pieces are recorded by Walther from manuscripts in Munich, especially Clm. 14793 from St. Emmeram, Regensburg, Arts. 1–3 are on quire 1.

1. ff. 1–3ᵛ Calendar in red and black, two months to a page.

Entries in red include Ruperti episcopi, Udalrici episcopi, Translacio corbiniani, Virgilii episcopi (27 Mar., 4 July, 20, 27 Nov.).

2. ff. 4–8ᵛ Seven penitential psalms.

3. ff. 8ᵛ–13ᵛ Incipit accessus altaris . . . Ymnus. Veni creator spiritus . . .

4 (quires 2, 3). (*a*) ff. 14–36ᵛ Formula communis pro simplicibus ad celebrandum seu communicandum se disponendis. Ad informacionem quorundam simplicium et ut indeuoti . . . (*b*) ff. 36ᵛ–37 Gracias tibi agimus omnipotens deus qui prima die . . . benigne ad omnium hominum fecit salutem Amen. f. 37ᵛ blank.

(*a*). Sections are ascribed to popes Urban IV and Innocent III, St. Bernard, M. de Cracovia, H. de Firmaria, Gerson, and Landolfus. Ends with six lines on the eucharist, 'Inflammat memorat . . .' (Walther, no. 9326).

5 (quires 4, 5). (*a*) Prayers before mass: (1) ff. 38–42 Oracio sancti Ambrosii episcopi ante missam. Summe sacerdos et vere pontifex . . . te miserante et donante . . . viuis etc.; (2) ff. 42–3 Oracio sancti Urbani pape ante missam. O uerbum incarnatum atque sacrosanctum misterium . . .; (3) f. 43ʳᵛ Oracio bonauenture ante missam. Eya ecce o celestis pater . . .; (4) ff. 43ᵛ–45 Oracio alberti magni ante missam. Omnipotens sempiterne deus fili vnigenite qui ex nostro . . .; (5) f. 45ʳᵛ Oracio ante missam. O preciosum et salutare sacramentum . . .; (6) ff. 45ᵛ–46 Oracio ante missam. Suscipe clementissime omnipotens eterne deus supplicaciones . . .; (7) ff. 46–9 Oracio sancti Ieronimi ante missam. O domine ihesu criste cuius tanta est magnificencia . . .; (8) ff. 49–51 Oracio sancti Augustini episcopi ante missam. O ihesu ihesu amor qui semper ardes . . .; (9) ff. 51ᵛ–52ᵛ Oracio domni Wilhelmi parisiensis ante Missam satis bona. O tu benedicte saluator misericordie . . .; (10) ff. 52ᵛ–53 Oracio de passione domini sequitur. Salue gloriosum capud . . .; (11) ff. 53–4 Oracio ante Missam. O claritas oculorum . . . (*b*) ff. 54–8 Secuntur oraciones. pro graciarum accione post Missam. Seven prayers: (1–4) to the three persons of the Trinity severally and together; (5) to B.V.M.; (6) f. 56ᵛ Oracio in suspiriis sancti Augustini pro graciarum accione in generali post missam. Gracias ago tibi domine sancte pater pro sancta incarnacione . . .; (7) f. 57ᵛ Post missam. Domine mi

rex mi pater nullatenus . . . (c) ff. 58–59ᵛ Notanda sunt hec decem documenta uniuscuiusque hominum pro erudicione sui ipsius. Sciendum quod quilibet cristifidelis et maxime religiosus . . .

(a, 1). Ed. Wilmart, *Auteurs spirituels*, pp. 114–24.

6 (quires 6–8). ff. 60–95ᵛ Vnum miserere dic stando . . . proficiendi. O susceptor et doctor bone voluntatis . . .

Twenty prayers, mostly 'ad sacramentum'. (19) is 'Oracio katherine . . . O Sapiencia dei et virtus altissimi ihesu bone . . .'.

Arts. 7–9 are on quires 9–11.

7. ff. 96–126ᵛ Twenty-eight prayers, mostly 'in sacramento'.

(1) is on Pater Noster. (2) contains the phrase 'Memento . . . sacrosancti Concilii': cf. (4), f. 100. (2, 3) are prayers 'cum duobus memoriis post officium dicenda'. (4), 'Memento mei domine . . .' is headed 'Sequitur memoria viuorum cuiusdam ydiote'. (24), f. 124ᵛ, 'Deus qui uoluisti pro redempcione mundi a iudeis . . .' conveys in its heading an indulgence of Pope Boniface VIII of forty years and as many quadragenes.

8. ff. 126ᵛ–132ᵛ Incipiunt quindecim gaudia quibus beata virgo Maria pre cunctis aliis fuit et est feliciter honorata. Gaude felicissima o celi et terre regina . . .

Fifteen paragraphs, each beginning with the same seven words.

9. ff. 132ᵛ–133ᵛ Verses: (a) Hic caput inclina presto mundo medicine . . . (8 lines); (b) Ad sacramentum panis. Aue caro iuncta verbo. vera vnitate . . . (4); (c) Ad sacramentum Calicis. Aue mundi precium sanguis redemptoris . . . (17); (d) Iussu diuino cum missa pie celebratur . . . (5: Walther, no. 9993); (e) Iste cibus deus est qui negat hic reus est; (f) Quisquis ad altare. cristo uis sacrificare . . . (4); (g) Epitaphium. Hic iacet Albertus preclarus in orbe dissertus . . . (4); (h) Aliud. Thomas de Aquino cuius doctrina fragrancior vino . . . (4).

10 (quire 12). (a) f. 134ʳᵛ Oracio pro fine bono ad beatam virginem. Eya mater misericordie virgo incomparabilis . . . (b) ff. 135–139ᵛ Incipit cursus bonus De passione domini Et primo ad Matutinum. Fons et origo tocius bonitatis . . . (c) ff. 139ᵛ–141 Short hours of the Cross, Patris sapiencia . . ., attributed to Pope John XXII and carrying an indulgence of 300 days. (d) ff. 141–145ᵛ Incipit Cursus de Compassione beate Marie virginis . . . O dulcissime ihesu dignare me . . . Mater sapiencie rosa sine spina . . .

(d). RH, no. 29539. AH xxx. 99.

11 (quires 13, 14). (a) ff. 146–62 Incipiunt centum meditaciones passionis cristi. Primus articulus. Eya dei sapiencia . . . piissime delecteris. (b) f. 162ʳᵛ Incipit prologus super centum meditaciones prescriptas. Venerabilis ille incarnate discipulus melodisoni illius sapiencialis horologii . . . consequatur. (c) ff. 162ᵛ–163 Prologus in centum meditaciones passionis domini nostri ihesu cristi. Amatorie passionis domini . . . presignatum. LAVS DEO. (d) ff. 163ᵛ–168ᵛ Hec infra collecta oramina et meditaciones sunt Sancte Brigitte quas ante crucem . . . (e) ff. 168ᵛ–169 Verses 'ex speculo consciencie circa cristi passionem': Quis qualis quantus cur . . . (3). Sequere conpaciens admirans . . . (2). (f) f. 169

Gradus ad dileccionem caritatis septem. Te quero. In te spero . . . . (*g*) Effigiem cristi qui transis . . . (6 lines). (*h*) Sancti cristofori faciem quicunque intuetur . . . (6).

(*a, c*). H. Suso. (*b*). In edn. Alost, sine anno (*BMC* ix. 128), sign. o. 2ᵛ–3, this prologue is ascribed to a canon of Groenendaal. (*d*). The Fifteen Oes of St. Bridget, with long heading. (*g*). Walther, no. 5256.

12 (quire 15). (*a*) ff. 170–9 Passio domini nostri ihesu cristi Quam beata virgo Maria reuelauit beato Anshelmo et de eius compassione quam habuit tempore passionis dilectissimi filii sui etc. Ascendam in palmam ut apprehendam . . . Hec verba poterat dicere beatus Anshelmus . . . sicut ipsi emerant cristum pro triginta etc. Laus deo. (*b*) ff. 179ᵛ–181ᵛ Meditacio bona et breuis Magni Alberti de passione domini nostri ihesu cristi. In nomine domini ihesu omne genu flectetur . . .

Arts. 13–18 are on quires 16–19.

13. (*a–j*) ff. 182–191ᵛ Ten salutations and prayers to B.V.M., including: (*a*) ff. 182–184ᵛ Incipit Rosarium gloriose virginis Marie . . . Aue maria . . . Ihesus cristus Quem de spiritu sancto angelo gabriele nunciante concepisti . . .; (*b*) ff. 184ᵛ–185ᵛ Item tria Aue maria valde deuota . . . Rogo te virgo polentissima . . .; (*h*) f. 190 O maria dei genitrix et omnium miseratrix . . .; (*i*) ff. 190ᵛ–191 Aue plena gracia virgo fecundata . . .; (*j*) f. 191ʳᵛ Deprecor te sanctissima virgo Maria mater dei omni pietate plena . . .

(*h*) is attributed here to St. Augustine, (*i*), *RH*, no. 2033, to Pope John XX, and (*j*) to Pope Celestine.

14. (*a–g*) ff. 192–6 A series of seven prayers: (*a*) Oracio sancti Augustini in suspiriis ad sanctam Trinitatem. Summa trinitas virtus vna et indiscreta . . .; (*b*) to the Father; (*c, e, f*) to the Son; (*d*) to the Holy Spirit; (*g*) f. 195 Oracio pro graciarum accione et beneficiis dei cottidie dicenda.

15. (*a–f*) ff. 196–198ᵛ Six prayers to the guardian angel and to angels, including (*e*) ff. 197–8 Suffragium deuotissimum ad proprium angelum. Veni creator spiritus et mentem tange celitus . . . .

(*e*). *RH*, no. 34377. *AH* xxxiii. 23, from a Tegernsee manuscript.

16. ff. 198ᵛ–215 Twenty-one memoriae of saints: Andrew, John Evangelist, Matthew, John Baptist, Peter, Paul, (*g*) De omnibus sanctis. Et canitur in tono sicut Aue uiuens hostia. O pater ingenite omnium creator . . ., Sebastian, Emmeram, Denis Rusticus and Eleutherius, Denis the Areopagite, (*l*) Wolfgang: Aue beatissime presul o wolfgange . . ., Benedict, (*n*) Jerome: Salue sancte Ieronime tu doctor veritatis . . ., (*o*) Barbara: Salue sancta barbara audi queso uota mea . . ., Apollonia, Scholastica, Margaret, Mary Magdalene, (*t*) Ursula: Aue virgo vrsula genere regalis . . ., Katherine.

(*g*). *RH*, no. 30802. *AH* xxxiii. 15. (*n*). *RH*, no. 18213. (*t*). *RH*, no. 2257.

17. ff. 215ᵛ–222 Prologus in carmen sequens quod philomena dicitur feliciter incipit et est valde deuotum et est in tono Aue uiuens hostia. Philomena preuia

temporis ameni . . . faciet repente. Explicit prologus. Incipit carmen. De hac
aue legitur . . . regi angelorum Amen.

Walther, no. 14071 (Johannes de Pecham).

18. (a) ff. 222ᵛ–226ᵛ In nomine domini Ego frater A. Confiteor tibi . . .
(b) ff. 227–9 Ego frater A. indignus monachus ordinis sancti benedicti Confiteor tibi . . . (c) f. 229ʳᵛ Sex condiciones considerande cuilibet uolenti bene
mori. Prima est quod infirmus moriturus . . .

19 (quire 20). (a) ff. 230–1 De parentela et origine sanctissimi Benedicti abbatis
patris nostri. Anno incarnacionis dominice quadringentesimo et octogesimo
natus fuit . . . (b) f. 231ʳᵛ Sub regula sancti Benedicti militant religiones infrascripte . . . (c) f. 232 Mitis et inuicte cristi verna Benedicte . . . (6 lines).
(d) ff. 232–241ᵛ Lists of popes (to 1407), cardinals, archbishops, and distinguished
bishops, abbots, monks, abbesses, and nuns of the order of St. Benedict.

(b). Twenty-three orders and the habit of each order are referred to. (c). Walther, no.
11128.

20 (quire 21). Verses: (a) ff. 242–243ᵛ Cum in nocte uideo in choro conuentum
. . . (94) lines); (b) f. 244 Metra quedam religioso meditanda et unicuique homini.
Religiosorum datur hec doctrina virorum . . . (13); (c) f. 244ʳᵛ De morte. Sepe
recorderis bone frater quod morieris . . . (19); (d) ff. 244ᵛ–245 De sui reputa-
cione. Sis quasi defunctus. quasi fetidus . . . (13); (e) f. 245 De memoria sepul-
chri. Hoc tibi sit menti . . . (15); (f) f. 245ᵛ Versus de armis domini nostri ihesu
cristi. Wlnera corona crux . . . (10); (g) ff. 245ᵛ–246 Ad crucifixum. Aspice
peccator. an non sim verus amator . . . (14); (h) f. 246 Iterum ad crucifixum.
Cultoresque crucis o crux fer . . . (16); (i) f. 246ʳᵛ Versus de extremo iudicio.
Vox marie ad cristum. O iudex iuste. cum omnibus dextera siste . . . (18);
(j) f. 247ʳᵛ Ad beatam virginem. Viuere si sine ve vis . . . (44); (k) ff. 247ᵛ–248
De beata virgine. Gaude virgo graciosa verbum verbo concepisti . . . (6);
(l) f. 248 Petrus comestor. de beata virgine. Si fieri possit quod arene puluis et
unde . . . (10); (m) f. 248ʳᵛ De assumpcione b. Marie. Scandit ad ethera virgo
puerpera . . . (13); (n) ff. 248ᵛ–249 De beata virgine. versus. Aue benignissima
pauperum matrona . . . (16); (o) f. 249 (of the Trinity) O pater ingenite rex
celice . . . (9); (p) f. 249 (of St. Peter) Petre princeps fidei et apostolorum . . . (4);
(q) f. 249 (of St. Paul) Paule doctor lux ecclesiarum . . . (4); (r) f. 249ʳᵛ (of St.
John Evangelist) Iohannes castissime. cui commendauit . . . (8); (s) f. 249ᵛ (of
St. James) Decollat vana iacobum fraus herodiana . . . (4); (t) f. 249ᵛ (of St.
Denis Areopagite) Hic martir gratus . . . (6); (u) f. 249ᵛ (of St. Wolfgang)
Wolfgange confessor alme . . . (2); (v) ff. 249ᵛ–50 (of St. Benedict) O pater
inuicte monachorum . . . (8); (w) f. 250 (of St. Anne) O felix anna te pascit . . . (2);
(x) f. 250 Priuilegia Sancte Dorothee virginis et martiris. In quacumque domo
. . . (7); (y) f. 250ᵛ Vos qui seruitis cristo seruire studete . . . (11); (z) f. 250ᵛ Tres
infelices sunt . . . vnde versus. Tres infelices in mundo dicimus esse . . . ;
(aa) f. 251ʳᵛ De mensa versus. Ad mensam residens. et panem . . . (37);
(ab) f. 252ʳᵛ Quedam metra pro religiosis consideranda ad horas canonicas.
Pulsatis nobis horas omittere nolis . . . (31); (ac) f. 252ᵛ Ligor et affligor sternor
spernorque flagellor . . . (4); (ad) f. 252ᵛ Nullus miretur si mundus flere iubetur

... (6); (*ae*) f. 253 Vita sancti Monachi versus. Germinant in claustro. pietas ut cedrum in austro ... (25); (*af*) f. 253ᵛ Aulam ingressuri venerantesque limina cristi ... (8); (*ag*) f. 253ᵛ Est nostre sortis transire per hostia mortis ... (6); (*ah*) f. 253ᵛ Sex operantur aqua per presbiterum benedicta ... (5); (*ai*) f. 253ᵛ Hic nullus tergat nisi missam psallere pergat ... (2).

(*a–g*). Walther, nos. 3634, 16572, 17041, 18282a, 8363, 20862, 1588. (*k*). *RH*, no. 7006. (*l*). Walther, no. 17728. (*o, p*). *RH*, nos. 13370, 14867. (*x*). *RH*, no. 8740. (*y, z, aa, ab*). Walther, nos. 20824, 19393, 388, 14930. In (*aa*) the headings after 'De mensa' are 'De lectore mense', 'De cella Prioris', 'De vestiaria', 'Locio vestimentorum', 'De hospitibus'. (*ag–ai*). Walther, nos. 5780, 17608, 8049.

21 (quire 22). Verses: (*a*) ff. 254–257ᵛ Tu qui vitam sempiternam cupis mortis et eternam ... (196); (*b*) ff. 258–61 Metra de xiiᶜⁱᵐ gradibus humilitatis. Primus gradus. Sit formido dei prefixa tue faciei ... (144); (*c*) f. 261ᵛ Sic per terrorem cristi venias ad amorem ... (4); (*d*) f. 261ᵛ Angelus. Scribo presentes. cantantes atque legentes ... (6); (*e*) f. 261ᵛ Fac tibi mente pari ... (6); (*f*) f. 261ᵛ Magister Serlo de exerci(ci)o et labore. Ista ne cesses. aderunt post semina messes ... (4); (*g*) f. 261ᵛ Idem de Tollerancia. Degeneri vita vitam corrumpere vita ... (4); (*h*) f. 261ᵛ Idem de sobrietate. Visne coronari vis deliciis saturari ... (2).

(*a*). Walther, no. 19513. (*b*). Twelve stanzas, Walther, nos. 5671, 18305. (*d*). Walther, nos. 17407, 17371. (*e*). Walther, no. 6207. (*g*). Walther, no. 4221. (*h*). Walther, no. 20648 and Walther, *Sprichwörter*, no. 33806. ff. 262–265ᵛ blank.

22. (*a*) ff. 266–71 Forma viuendi quam cristus religiosis tradidit in monasteriis degentibus. Cristus nobis tradidit hanc normam viuendi ... (*b*) f. 271 O bone claustralis. cristi protecte sub alis ... (14).

(*a, b*). Walther, nos. 2772, 12522. (*a*) is in fifty 4-line stanzas, each with its heading.

23. Benedictine pieces: (*a*) ff. 271ᵛ–272 Hec sunt dicta Egregii doctoris Hainrici de hassia edita pro erudicione religiosorum. Progenies et vita Sancti benedicti abbatis. Bis quadrageno quadragentenoque sub anno ... (39); (*b*) ff. 272ᵛ–273 Almi Benedicti uita Orbem illustrauit ita uelut sol irradians ... (60); (*c*) ff. 273ᵛ–274 Sacer ordo Benedicti Vtitur colore miti ... (60); (*d*) f. 274ʳᵛ Notantur capitula super regula beati patris nostri benedicti. Audi fili patrem de somno modo surge ...

(*b*) and (*c*) are each in ten 6-line stanzas. In (*b*), Walther, no. 824, *AH* xv. 192–3, stanza 9 begins 'Huius loci (*blank*) Gregem serua ne hunc ensis hosti(li)s confodiat': cf. *AH*, footnote. (*c*). Walther, no. 16988.

24. Prose pieces on death: (*a*) f. 275 Hec sequens oracio cuilibet cristiano est necessaria in extrema hora mortis. Deus meus deus meus misericordia mea refugium meum desidero te ...; (*b*) ff. 275–6 Alia oracio deuota pro peccatis et in extrema hora mortis. O domine pater tocius miseracionis non possum tibi satisfacere ...; (*c*) ff. 276–278ᵛ Incipit breuis tractatulus de quatuor nouissimis. Scriptum est Ecclesiastici 7ᵐᵒ capitulo. In omnibus operibus tuis ...

25. Short prose pieces: (*a*) ff. 279–82ᵛ Si veram catholicam fidem volumus habere debemus duo fundamenta in corda nostra ponere ...; (*b*) ff. 282ᵛ–283ᵛ Septem cause notande sunt de purgatorio igne. Prima causa est ...; (*c*) ff. 283ᵛ–285ᵛ De obediencia. Habet obediencia preconia multa que ipsam laudant ...;

(*d*) ff. 285–288ᵛ Vide ut omnes facias secundum exemplar quod tibi in mente monstratum est. Primo notandum est cuius hec sunt verba . . .; (*e*) ff. 288ᵛ–292ᵛ Sequitur Tractatus de cura pastorali. satis utilis. Pascite qui in uobis est gregem dei 1 petri 6ᵗᵒ. Apostolorum princeps vicarius . . .

(*e*). The eighteen points of a good pastor.

26. ff. 292ᵛ–297 Forma inquisicionis tempore visitacionis alicuius monasterii. Forma inquirendi in monasteria tam in capite quam in membris ex mero officio que seruata fuit per speculatorem in monasterio sancti proculi bonensis ut ponit in tytulo de inquisicionibus . . . Et primo vtrum monachi de spiritualibus . . . Item An sint conspiratores c. xxxviii.

121 heads, usually with a reference to the Rule. A text on f. 297ᵛ has been covered over with paper on which is the beginning of art. 27. St. Proculus, Bologna, was a member of the congregation of St. Justina from 1436.

27. ff. 297ᵛ–299ᵛ Ama dominum deum tuum . . .

Short paragraphs lettered (A), B–R, (S–Y, A–P), each consisting of a quotation from scripture, beginning with the appropriate letter and a related quotation from an author whose name begins with the same letter. The authors are Augustine–Ysidore, Ambrose–Prosper. f. 300ʳᵛ blank.

28. f. 301, the parchment pastedown, is part of a leaf of a noted service book, s. xii: six lines of text remain on each side.

ff. i+301+xi, foliated i, ii, 1–300, (301–11). Paper, except ff. 38, 49. 158×108 mm. Written space 108×72 mm. 25 long lines. Frame ruling. Collation of ff. ii, 1–300: 1¹⁴ 2–10¹² 11¹⁴ 12–24¹² 25 eleven (ff. 290–300). A strip of manuscript lies down the centre of each quire: the strip after f. 43 is from a medical manuscript, s. xiii. Cursiva, perhaps all by one hand, except art. 27 and a few other additions. Initials: (i) f. 38, blue *S*, with shaded patterning in white on a punched gold ground in a frame of red and green: a handsome floral border; (ii) red with green ornament; (iii, iv) 2-line or 3-line and 1-line, red. Capital letters in the ink of the text stroked with red. Contemporary binding of pink leather over wooden boards: three bands: metal cornerpieces and centrepiece on each cover missing: two clasps, the upper one missing. Parchment tabs show the main divisions.

Written for Benedictine use (arts. 18*b*, 19, 23, 26) in a south German area, probably Regensburg, but the calendar stresses Salzburg saints.

48246 (Clifton 5). *Miscellanea theologica*   s. xv¹

Arts. 1, 2 are on quires 1–6.

1. ff. 1–34 'Tractatus vnius Carthusiensis' (*these words cancelled*) De imitacione cristi et contemptu omnium vanitatum mundi. Qui sequitur me . . . vim intuleris. Tu autem domine miserere mei et sic est finis. 'Explicit tractatus de ymitacione cristi per vnum Carthusiensem cuius nomen in libro vite nunc et in eternum nominatur'.

Thomas à Kempis, De imitatione Christi, bk. 1. 25 chapters. Axters, p. 94.

2. Ars moriendi. (*a*) ff. 34ᵛ–60 Incipit tractatus de arte moriendi bonus. In nomine sancte et indiuidue trinitatis. amen. Cum de presentis exilii miseria . . . in tuo conspectu gaudeat in eternum. Qui viuis et r' etc. (*b*) ff. 60–1 Infrascripte

collecte pertinent ad letaniam ordinis cisterciensium. Domine ihesu criste fili dei viui tua sacrosancta . . . (c) ff. 61ᵛ–63ᵛ Sequitur alius modus disponendi se ad mortem quem practicauit quidam cellita(?) et est ordinis carthusiensium. Ego frater N indignus nomine carthus' confiteor . . . (d) ff. 64–65ᵛ Quidam egregius doctor in sermone publico predicauit quod qui deuota intencione infrascriptas sex missas legerit pro anima in purgatorio . . . nunquam reparetur in perpetuum amen Et sic est finis. 'Explicit tractatus de arte moriendi pulcherus scriptus 1428° circa festum sanctificacionis (erased) beatissime virginis marie'.

(a). GKW 2597–2614. Six chapters and prayers, etc. A reader noted at the head of f. 34ᵛ 'Istum tractatum melius et correctius [. . .] in Capella sancti Iohannis in libro qui intytulatur vocabularius luciarius', a reference to the volume listed as M. 15 primo in the medieval Erfurt catalogue, MBDS ii. 477 A reader, s. xv ex., noted of (d) 'Non est fide dignum nec ex scriptura sacra habet fundamentum'. ff. 66–70ᵛ blank.

3. (quires 7–9). ff. 71–103 Incipit Informacio meditacionis de passione domini et de profectu uite spiritualis Edita per dominum Heinricum Calcar pie memorie quondam priorem Maguncie et uisitatorem istius prouincie. Legitur in deuteronomio quod cum . . . In quo inestimabile gaudium nobis preparasti: ad quod . . . Amen. Anno domini 1424 complete sunt meditaciones suprascripte Sabbato ante dominicam xiᵃᵐ.

The dedication of St. Saviour's, Erfurt, in 1373 is on f. 106ᵛ among additions in the space left blank at the end of quire 9, ff. 103ᵛ–106ᵛ.

4 (quires 10–15). ff. 108–78 Incipit tractatulus deuotus de reformacione virium anime. Homo quidam descendit . . . Hiis uerbis mystice humane generis lapsus describitur . . . eterne beatitudinis inveniaris Amen. Deo gracias In omnibus respice finem.

For manuscripts and printed editions see J. van Rooji, Gerard Zerbolt van Zutphen, 1936, pp. 322–5, 359–60. Said in the medieval catalogue (cf. art. 2) to be part 2 of art. 3. ff. 107ʳᵛ, 178ᵛ blank.

Arts. 5, 6 are on quires 16–19, 21.

5. ff. 179–216ᵛ Capitula in subsequenti tractatu . . . (table of twenty chapters, with leaf numbers) . . . Intytulatur noster presens tractatulus. spiritualis phylosophia necessaria ac salubrius 'pro' sui ipsius cognicionis. pre oculis semper habenda. Iohannis Gerson Cancellarii parisiensis doctoris sacre theologii eximii. Cogitanti michi phylosophari de et super vera et profunda sui ipsius perfecta cognicione . . . applicauerit etc. Et sic est finis huius tractatuli boni et vtilis scriptus nuremberge per martinum bacc' Off' studii festinenter propter temporis defectum et occupacionem. Et est Cancellarius Parisiensis.

Johannes Castellensis, O.S.B., De cognitione sui ipsius, ed. C. Stroick, Ottawa, 1964, pp. 147–87. Cf. M. Grabmann, Mittelalterliches Geistesleben, i. 489–508.

6. ff. 217–226ᵛ, 238–46 Incipit libellus de perfectione filiorum dei. Quicumque vult viuere in perfectissimo statu alme matris ecclesie . . . Quod nobis prestare dignetur trinus et unus amen.

J. Ruysbroeck. No. 11, pp. 373–88, in the sixteenth-century Latin translation of his Opera, printed at Cologne in 1552. The text broke off at the end of quire 19 and was continued later on quire 21: 'residuum huius tractatus habetur in sequentibus foliis' is on a piece of paper pasted to f. 226ᵛ. ff. 246ᵛ–247ᵛ blank.

7 (quire 20). ff. 227–37 Tractatulus de laude scriptorum doctrine salubris ad celestinos et carthusienses ymmo totam ecclesiam generaliter ordinatus lugd' 1423 in apreli per magistrum Iohannem de gerson cancellarium parisiensem eximium sacre theologie professorem. Scrutare scripturas exhortabatur . . . speciosissimus deus benedictus in secula. amen. Explicit.

Edn. du Pin, ii. 694–703. A reader noted on f. 237, 'Effectum seu excerptum huius tractatuli fecit frater Iohannes Indag' cum aliquibus addicionibus Et habetur in libraria h 8 bis in declaracione statutorum antiquorum c⁰ 16': cf. *MBDS* ii. 381, H 8². f. 237ᵛ blank.

8. The pastedowns are two leaves of an Aristotelian text, s. xiii ex. A section begins 'Oracio autem est uox significatiua cuius partium alique . . .'.

ff. 247. Paper. A medieval foliation to 237; another, 71–100, on ff. 1–30. 150 × 105 mm. Written space *c.* 112 × 75 mm. *c.* 22 long lines. Frame ruling. Collation: 1–5¹² 6¹⁰ 7–17¹² 18¹⁶ wants 16, perhaps blank, 19¹⁰ 20¹² wants 12, blank, 21¹⁰. Quires 1–6 lettered a, bc, de, fg, hi, k: in quires 2–5 the first letter is at the beginning and the second letter at the end. A strip of parchment down the centre of each quire. Cursiva and (art. 4) hybrida by several hands. Flex punctuation (7) in art. 3. 2-line red initials. Capital letters in the ink of the text stroked with red. Contemporary binding of wooden boards covered with pink leather: central strap and pin missing. Secundo folio *sunt*.

Written in Germany, art. 2 in 1428 and art. 5 at Nuremberg by a scribe who calls himself a bachelor of the 'studium' of Off' (Offenburg, Baden ?).¹ 'Liber Carthusien*sium* prope Erford' ', ff. 106ᵛ, 237ᵛ, s. xv. Title, 'Calcar de reformacione virium . . .' and label with pressmark 'F. 11' ('F' in red) on the upper cover. F. 11 in the medieval catalogue (*MBDS* ii. 342). '55' on a label on the spine. Lot 529 in the Bülow sale, 10 Oct. 1836.

A loose piece of paper has on one side 'Written by Canon John Williams who died at Arno's Court [*Bristol*] and left these books to Bp. Clifford' and on the other the note to which these words refer: 'Nota bene the word here erased [*on f. 65ᵛ*] is sanctificacionis which was the title of the Feast of Our Lady's Conception till the Council of Basle anno 1439 commanded it to [*be*] called conceptionis. This a contemporary—John de Hagen— expressly states in the volume of MS. Sermons (page 279) which I possess.² This proves that the words 'Explicit' etc although by a different hand from the treatise itself were written before the council of Basle'. 'Codex Cliffordianus I' on a label inside the cover: cf. MS. 7.

48247 (Clifton 6). *Miscellanea theologica*   s. xv med.

1 (quires 1–3). ff. 1–36ᵛ Domino patri carissimo p. portuensis lotarius indignus dyaconus graciam in presenti et gloriam in futuro. Modicum ocii quod inter multas . . . liberet nos qui est benedictus in secula seculorum Amen Explicit liber de miseria humane condicionis 'Lotharii qui fuit romane ecclesie dyaconus cardinalis et postea electus in papam et dictus Innocencius papa 4ᵗᵘˢ'.

Ed. Maccarrone, 1955; *PL* ccxvii. 701–46. Bk. 2, f. 11ᵛ.

Arts. 2–5 are on quire 4.

2. ff. 37–39ᵛ Bernhardus de honesta vita. Petis a me mi frater . . . Et corona. In domino Ihesu Amen. Explicit formula uite beati Bernhardi ad fratrem suum gerhardum.

PL clxxxiv. 1167–70.

¹ I owe the suggestion to Dr. Sigrid Krämer.
² Now at St. Hugh's Charterhouse, Partridge Green.

3. ff. 39ᵛ–40ᵛ Bernhardus. Si quietum desideres o anima mea . . . hec iste bernhardus. Iubelus Beati Bernhardi. O ihesu dulcis memoria dans uera . . . sedibus amen. Explicit Iubilius b. bernhardi de nomine ihesu.

Written as prose. *RH*, no. 9542.

4. ff. 40ᵛ–43ᵛ Terret me tota uita mea Namque diligenter discusso . . . nomen tuum. Qui cum patre . . . et sic est finis libri anshelmi de consideracione humane miserie in nomine ihesu amen.

Notes follow, ff. 43ᵛ–44.

5. ff. 44–8 Ad honorem dei ac sanctorum apostolorum petri et pauli hanc exhortacionem scripsi. Hic introducuntur persone duorum uidelicet deflentis hominis et amouentis racionis. Homo. Anima mea inang ustiis cor meum . . . multis modis modo fiat finis (?) amen. f. 48ᵛ blank.

Arts. 6–8 are on quires 5–13.

6. (*a*) ff. 49–103ᵛ Incipit libellus de imitacione cristi et contemptu omnium vanita[tum]. Qui sequitur me . . . perpetue claritatis Amen. (*b*) ff. 106–18 Deuota exhortacio ad sacram cristi communionem. Venite ad me . . . ineffabilia dicenda.

(*a*). Thomas à Kempis, De Imitatione Christi, bks. 1–3. Bk. 1 in twenty-five chapters. Bk. 2 in twelve chapters, f. 52. Bk. 3 in sixty-one chapters, f. 69ᵛ: part of the text, equivalent perhaps to a quire of the exemplar, was left out on f. 72 and put in out of place on ff. 91–99ᵛ/5. A table of chapters of the three books, ff. 104–105ᵛ. (*b*) Imitatio Christi, bk. 4, in eighteen chapters, with a table at the end, f. 118ʳᵛ. A reader noted at the head of f. 106 that some think this is by the same author as (*a*) and to be reckoned its fourth book.

7. ff. 118ᵛ–132 Sequitur tractatus hugonis de humilitate obedientia et caritate. Cristus igitur cum in forma dei esset non rapinam arbitratus est . . . firmare concupiscit. Explicit hugo de . . . caritate etc.

PL clxxxiv. 793–212 and (f. 131, Duobus modis . . .), *PL* clxxvii. 565–7.

8. ff. 132ᵛ–149ᵛ Incipit tractatus de arte confessionis. Quoniam fundamenta et ianua uirtutum . . . gloria tua ad quam . . . benedictus amen.

Printed in editions of Aquinas and Bonaventura: cf. Glorieux, nos. 14 *fg* and 305 *dn*. The author is noted in the margin, f. 132ᵛ: Tractatus de puritate consciencie Mathei de Cracouia Episcopi Wormatensis doctoris egregii.

9 (quires 14, 15). ff. 150–75 Tractatus magistri Iacobi Carthusiensis sacre theologie professoris de arte 'bene' moriendi. Omnes morimur et quasi aque . . . Cum igitur condicio humane nature . . . et laudabimus. Quod nobis . . . Amen et finis est huius tractatus de arte bene moriendi 'fratris Iacobi carthusiensis et professi in domo erffordensi ordinis eiusdem. Sacre scripture professoris eximii Cracouiensis'.

Much corrected. A reader noted in the margin of f. 150 that C. 98 in the library (*MBDS* ii. 294) contained a text beginning 'O mors quam amara'. f. 175ᵛ blank.

10 (quire 16). (*a*) ff. 176–178ᵛ Queritur quando quodlibet peccatorum mortalium uel Capitalium sit peccatum mortale uel ueniale. Responditur secundum b. Augustinum peccatum mortale . . . non possum tibi dicere. (*b*) ff. 178ᵛ–188 Ad

utilitatem eorum qui curam gerunt animarum . . . a persona seculari. non inueni plus.

(*b*). A compendium in three parts. The last lines are on a slip after f. 188.

Arts. 11, 12 are on quires 17–21.

11. ff. 189–205 Secundum exiguitatem paru*um* [. . .]¹ acturi de cognicione differenciarum peccatorum ut quis valeat cognoscere . . . ut iam dictum est de histrionibus.

On the seven deadly sins. Slips added after ff. 189, 197. On the former is an introductory letter, 'In cristo sibi dilecto pirio de bunis de cremonia . . .', which gives the name of the author of this tract as Franciscus de Perusio, O.F.M.

12. ff. 205–74 Abbas et quilibet prelatus conuentualis requirere debet suos monachos fugitiuos . . .

The medieval catalogue (see below) calls this a *Collectorium valde prolixum . . . ex b. Thoma. ex decreto . . . sed sine omni ordine et confuse*. At first it is alphabetical. f. 274ᵛ blank.

13 (quire 22). (*a*) ff. 275–81 Litera confirmatorum ad priorem electum mittenda . . . (*b*) ff. 281ᵛ–283 Corrector librorum tam ab exemplaribus ordinis nostri quam a secularibus siue aliis . . .

(*a*). Formulary letters of the Carthusian order, thirty-six in all. (*b*). On the correction of books in a charterhouse. The corrector is advised not to mend errors of spelling: 'pocius toleret quam emendet. quia eandem diccionem sepissime in aliis et aliis locis inueniet aliter et aliter ortographizatam proper diuersa ydiomata linguas hominum habitudines aut patrie consuetudines. aut vicia scriptorum siue etiam propter vsum inueteratum'. f. 283ᵛ blank.

14. The pastedowns are from a manuscript of s. xiv written in the German equivalent of anglicana. They are partly covered by the turned-in leather of the covers.

ff. 282, foliated 1–76, 78–283. Paper, except ff. 181–2. Medieval foliations: 1–149 and, on ff. 189–265, 1–77. 215 × 150 mm. Written space varies: it is *c*. 165 × 110 mm at first and *c*. 190 × 120 mm later. *c*. 36 long lines at first and *c*. 49 long lines later: 2 cols., ff. 176–274. Collation: 1–12¹² 13¹² wants 5–12, blank, 14¹² 15¹⁴ 16¹²+1 leaf after 12 (f. 188) 17¹⁶ 18–20²⁰ 21¹⁶ wants 11–16 after f. 274 22¹² wants 10–12, blank. Quires 1–21 lettered at beginning and end, *a–x*. A fragment of a document on parchment is in the centre of each quire as strengthening. Cursiva by several hands. Red initials (and a few blue initials in art. 11), 3-line, f. 1, and 2-line. Capital letters in the ink of the text lined with red. Contemporary binding of wooden boards covered with greenish leather: three bands: central strap and pin missing: a partly illegible label on the upper cover gives '[Hugo] de humilitate . . .' (art. 7) as the main title: the catalogue (see below) follows it. Secundo folio *lutum*.

Written in Germany. 'Carthus' prope erfford' ', f. 1, s. xv. Identifiable with L. 101 in the late medieval catalogue of the Erfurt Charterhouse (*MBDS* ii. 467–8). Lot 319 in the Bülow sale, 10 Oct. 1836. 'W. Clifford' inside the cover.

48248 (Clifton 7). *De imitatione Christi, etc.*   s. xv med.

1. ff. 1–27 Flecto genua mea ad patrem domini nostri ihesu cristi. a quo omnis paternitas . . . donec intrem in gaudium domini mei qui . . . amen. Explicit

¹ A word I cannot read.

dyallogus hominis interioris et anime boneuenture 'vel alio nomine ym(a)go vite'. 'Explicit soliloquium boneuenture de quatuor exerciciis'.

Quaracchi edn., viii (1898), 28–67.

2 (filling quire 2). (*a*) ff. 27ᵛ–28ᵛ Prologus. Ad honorem nominis tui ihesu criste. Passionis ordinem liber tradit iste . . . milites locauit. Explicit passio breuis et rigmice composita et ordinata secundum ordinem geste rei prout ewangeliste coniunctim vel diuisim ea scripserunt que hic posita sunt nec preter ea que ewangeliste posuerunt aliquid additum est nisi de lacrimis domini in cruce quod ponit apostolus ad hebreos. In hac composicione semper quatuor versus sillabis sibi consonantibus terminantur. (*b*) f. 28ᵛ Nota sicut corpus humanum diuersa habet membrorum liniamenta . . . (*c*) f. 28ᵛ A prayer to B.V.M. beginning abruptly.

(*a*). Walther, no. 354. *AH* xxxi. 73–6. 116 lines in all.

3. (*a*) ff. 29–42ᵛ Incipit liber de imitacione cristi et contemptu omnium vanitatum. Qui sequitur me . . . vim intuleris. Et sic est finis libri primi de imitacione cristi. (*b*) ff. 43–49ᵛ Capitula libri secundi. i De exercicio compunctionis ut quis a deo purgetur . . . Uolens purgari a peccatis . . . et amaberis ab eo in eternum. Amen. Explicit exercitatorium hominis religiosi et deuoti. (*c*) ff. 49ᵛ– 57 Incipiunt capitula libri tertii . . . De interna conuersacione capitulum primum. Regnum dei intra vos . . . intrare in regnum celorum. Expliciunt ammoniciones ab interna trahentes. (*d*) ff. 57–88ᵛ Incipiunt capitula libri quarti sequentis . . . Audiam quid loquatur in me . . . perpetue claritatis amen. (*e*) ff. 91–102ᵛ Incipit exhortacio ad sacram cristi communionem. Venite ad me omnes . . . infallibilia dicenda et sic est finis.

(*a, c–e*). De imitatione Christi, bks. I–IV. (*a*) is in twenty-five chapters. Tables of the twelve and fifty-nine chapters of (*c, d*) precede them, and a table of the eighteen chapters of (*e*), 'Registrum precedentis materie', follows it. (*b*), in eleven chapters, is a work attributed to H. Calcar, Ord. Carth., which sometimes appears as bk. 2 of the Imitatio. It is printed by J.-B. Malou, *Recherches sur le véritable auteur de l'Imitatio de Jésus-Christ*, 3rd edn., 1858, pp. 402–13.

4 (filling quires 3 and 7). (*a*) f. 42ᵛ Scribbled notes including some words of German, 'Astucia id est calliditas uel sneydicheyt in malo . . .' (*b*) f. 88ᵛ Audi paucis verbis ordinem per quem scandere . . . possidetur. Hec Iohannes cassianus in libro de institucione monachorum. (*c*) f. 89 Oracio hominis obnubilati pro illuminacione cordis. Incommutabilis veritas lumen oculorum meorum . . . (*d*) ff. 89ᵛ–90ᵛ Quidam dixit beato Arsenio . . ., and other short pieces. (*e*) f. 90ᵛ Versus. Altaris sacri studeant meminisse ministri Qua racione fiant cruces in canone plures . . . (seventeen lines).

5 (quires 9–11). ff. 103–39 Consolacionis gracia aliquas sentencias deuotas in vnum coaceruaui libellum. quem meo pectori carius committere velim. et quasi quoddam delectabile pratum variis arboribus consitum . . . consolacionis graciam. Explicit prologus. Incipiunt capitula soliloquii anime . . . (table of twenty-five chapters) . . . Michi autem adherere deo bonum est. O breue et dulce verbum . . . (f. 138) equalis vna deitas: et in omnia secula nunc et in perpetuum Amen. Explicit soliloquium anime Amen.

An omission on f. 123 is supplied on ff. 138–9. ff. 139ᵛ–40ᵛ blank.

6 (quire 12). (*a*) ff. 141–51 Sex prohibet peccant abel . . . sponsam venio iam.
(*b*) ff. 151–2 [P]rima fides consti rescrip . . .

Mnemonic verses for (*a*) each chapter of each book of the Bible and (*b*) each titulus of the decretals. Walther, nos. 17610 (A. de Villa Dei) and 14575.

7. f. 154 is a bifolium laid sideways in the binding taken from a small ill-written breviary on parchment, s. xv.

ff. 152+ii. Paper. 208 × 142 mm. Written space *c.* 160 × 95 mm. 31–8 long lines. Frame ruling. Collation: 1–3¹⁴ 4–10¹² 11¹⁴ 12¹². Strips of a manuscript, s. xiii, down middle of quires as strengthening: rather larger pieces at ff. 43, 55 (between quires) and as book-markers (?). Hybrida (arts. 1, 2, 3*b*–*d*) and cursiva, art. 3*a, e* in one hand. 3-line (f. 1) and 2-line red initials. Capital letters in the ink of the text touched with red. Contemporary binding of wooden boards covered with brown leather: nine different stamps on the front cover, the largest a 'ihesus' stamp at the head and a 'maria' stamp at the foot and the most distinctive a pierced heart: seven different stamps on the back cover two of which do not occur on the front. Secundo folio *quo ordine*.

Written in Germany. The ex-libris of the Benedictine abbey of Huysburg, Saxony, is at the foot of f. 1, s. xvii: 'Liber B.M.V. in Huysburg'. A letter from W. H. Eyre, 9 Hill St., Berkeley Sq. (London), 6 June 1860, is kept with the manuscript: it is addressed probably to Canon John Williams (cf. MS. 5), who used space on it for a note about art. 3. 'Codex Cliffordianus III' (cf. MS. 5) on a label inside the cover; also '66'.

48249 (Clifton 8). *Sermones et Exempla ('Gesta Romanorum')*
1411 and s. xv[1]

A 'Collectorium quoddam de diuersis materiis' (so called on f. 1), a collection of sermons and stories useful for sermons begun by fr. Nicholas de Bunzenberg of the order of Servites in 1411 and written mainly in his hand.

1 (quire 1). ff. 1–8 Sermons: f. 1, Sermo bonus de fide. Amen dico uobis qui credit in me . . . In verbis istis facit dominus duo. Primo hortatur nos . . .; f. 4ᵛ, Sermo de circumcisione domini. Vocatum est nomen eius ihesus luce secundo. Bernhardus in soliloquio dicit . . .; ff. 7ᵛ–8ᵛ, quire fillers, an Advent sermon, etc.

2 (quires 2–10). (*a*) ff. 9–28ᵛ Incipit opus xlᵃˡᵉ. Cum autem ieiunas secundum scripturas et doctores tempus xlᵉ est tempus ieiunii . . . repudium Ihesum queritis etc. etc. Explicit opus pulcerimum et subtile sermonum 2ᵐ fratrem Nycolaum predicatorum ordinis. Scriptum per me fratrem Nycolaum de Bunzenberg ordinis seruorum Anno domini m° cccc° xi° quando eram in magnis infirmitatibus. (*b*) ff. 28ᵛ–32ᵛ A sermon for Cena Domini and four sermons for Christmas. (*c*) ff. 32ᵛ 56ᵛ Pieces on confession, simony (f. 42, 'Simonia est studiosa uoluntas emendi uel uendendi . . .'), matrimony, etc. (*d*) ff. 56ᵛ–90 Short sermons or notes for sermons. (*e*) ff. 90ᵛ–110 Incipit optimum xlˡᵉ maronis. Conuertimini ad me in toto etc. Ioelis 2°. Iste propheta inspiratus a spiritu sancto admonet nos quod si volumus quod deus . . . de inimicis possumus. Expliciunt sermones et contemplaciones super dominicalia et super xlᵃᵐ magistri maronis. (*f*) ff. 110–119ᵛ Sermons and notes, as quire fillers.

(*b–d*) and parts of (*e*) and (*f*) are in the same hand as (*a*). (*e*). Schneyer, p. 80, refers to Munich Clm. 26782, without author's name.

3 (quires 11, 12). (*a*) ff. 120–122ᵛ Nota signa quindecim contingencia . . . Erunt signa In sole . . . In hac dominica agitur de aduentu cristi . . . (*b*) ff. 122ᵛ– 143ᵛ Sequitur passio domini nostri ihesu. Iustus perit. Iustus perit . . . Hodie peragit sancta mater ecclesia . . . (*ends imperfectly*).

The scribe wrote 'Assit in principio' at the top of f. 120. (*b*). Annotated by the scribe of art. 2. 'Secunda pars', f. 135ᵛ; 'Tercia pars', f. 140ᵛ.

4 (quires 13, 14 and part of quire 27). (*a*) ff. 144–157ᵛ De humilitate cristi vel de passione. Allexander magnus pori regis indorum curiam intrauit . . . (*b*) ff. 157ᵛ– 158ᵛ Incipiunt probleumata aristotelis moralizata. Stateram non transsilies. Valerius maximus romanorum precipuus ac inter sapientes . . . (f. 158) 2ᵐ enigma. Secundum enigma est ignem gladio . . . (*c*) f. 159ʳᵛ Sermo bonus de Corpore cristi. (*d*) ff. 161ᵛ–162 Two stories like those in (*a*). (*e*) ff. 162–165ᵛ, 314–15 Est puer hic qui habet quinque panes. Primus panis est abstinencie . . .

(*a*), forty exempla, and (*d*) begin with words like 'Refert valerius', 'Rex quidam', 'Erat quidam imperator', 'Narrat Eusebius'. A *signe de renvoi* at the foot of f. 165ᵛ sends the reader to the continuation on f. 314 in blank space at the end of quire 27. ff. 160–1 blank.

5 (quires 15–18). (*a*) ff. 166–214ᵛ Sequitur aliqua gesta Romanorum. Hanibal multis annis regnauit . . . (*b*) ff. 214ᵛ–215ᵛ De remissione peccati in spiritum sanctum. (*c*) f. 216 De sepulturis.

(*a*). Forty-eight stories, each with an exposition 'mystice': cf. arts. 4*a*, *d*, 6*b*. (*b*) and (*c*) are quire fillers, (*b*) in the hand of art. 2. (*c*) is in German (17 lines). ff. 216ᵛ–217ᵛ blank.

6 (quires 19–22). (*a*) ff. 218–252ᵛ, 261–267ᵛ Sermo bonus de Caritate ad dilectum (?). Diligamus deum quoniam ipse . . . Quia 2ᵐ Aristotelem in 8º ethicorum . . .: other sermons follow on the epistle lessons for the second to the twentieth Sundays after Pentecost. (*b*) ff. 253–259ᵛ Six exempla like those in art. 5*a*.

The scribe of art. 2 took over on f. 249ᵛ and wrote to f. 257ᵛ and also ff. 261–267ᵛ. ff. 227ʳᵛ, 260ʳᵛ blank.

7 (quire 23). ff. 268–276ᵛ Sermo primus prime dominice in Quadragesima. Ductus est ihesus in desertum . . . Hic idem habentur Mᵗ . . . Appropinquante prelio omnes timent bellatores . . .: sermons on the text 'Nisi habundauerit' and for Advent follow.

The scribe of art. 2 wrote all but ff. 270–271ᵛ/19. ff. 273ᵛ, 277ʳᵛ blank.

8 (quires 24–8). Sermons, exempla, and notes fill ff. 278–330ᵛ.

The first piece and two others are sermons 'De festo visitacionis beate Marie' and the last piece is an exemplum of a famous preacher in Ireland. The scribe of art. 2 wrote the last leaf from line 24 on the recto and finished off art. 4*e* in blank space (see above). f. 318ʳᵛ remains blank.

9. The pastedowns at each end are parchment documents, s. xiv: (*a*) in front, nearly complete, a document issued by the nuns of Arnstadt, O.S.B.; (*b*) at the back, a notarial document.

(*a*). Nos Helmburgis Priorissa. Hyldegundis celleraria et Gysela Custrix necnon Totus conuentus cenobii sanctimonialium in opido Arnstete . . .'. About a debt of thirty-six pounds, Erfurt money. The names of witnesses remain, but the date has been cut off. Endorsed 'Domicelli Spinonis'. (*b*). The notarial subscription begins 'Ego vlricus quondam ma[. . . .]'. The scribe of art. 2 wrote in a blank space.

10. The flyleaf, f. 331, a paper leaf, contains the end of a list of persons in religion, for example 'Apud S. Odalricum in herbipoli Sorores margaretha . . .', 'In Osbruck dompnus albertus abbas'. Two of them had letters of confraternity. The scribe wrote 'Amen in gotes namen Iesus Maria Anna' at the end.

ff. i+330+i. Paper. 215×155 mm. Written space *c.* 160×120 mm. *c.* 38 long lines. Collation: 1⁸ 2¹² 3¹⁴ 4⁶+1 leaf after 3 (f. 38) 5¹⁰ 6–7¹⁴ 8–9¹² 10¹⁶ 11–13¹² 14¹⁰ 15–17¹² 18¹⁶ 19¹⁰ 20–21¹² 22¹⁶ 23¹² wants 10, 11, blank, 24¹² wants 11, 12, blank, 25⁶ 26 seventeen (ff. 294–310) 27¹⁴ wants 9–14, blank (ff. 311–18) 28¹². Frame ruling, if any. Strips from a parchment manuscript lie down the centres of quires. The main hand, N. de Bunzenberg's, is a sort of broken down fere-textura or hybrida. Arts. 1, 3, 4*c*, 5*a* are in cursiva. Initials: (i) f. 90ᵛ, red and blue; (ii) 3-line or less, red. Capital letters in the ink of the text marked with red. Contemporary binding of bevelled wooden boards covered with yellowish white leather: three bands: four of five bosses remain on each cover: two strap-and-pin fastenings missing: the front cover inscribed 'Opus quadragesimale Item opus quadragesimale Sermones de tempore et sanctis'.

Written in Germany (see above). Belonged in s. xv to the Benedictine abbey of St. Peter, Erfurt: 'Liber sancti petri in Erffordia', f. 1 (cf. f. 9), with pressmark 'C. 3' at the head of f. 1 and 'C III' on a label on the front cover. Bülow sale, 10 Oct. 1836, lot 376.

48250 (Clifton 9). *Libri Sapientiales; A. de Bellovisu, O.P.; etc.*

s. xv med.

1 (quires 1–7). ff. 1–80 Proverbs, Ecclesiastes, Song of Songs, Wisdom, and Ecclesiasticus.

Ecclesiasticus ends with the Prayer of Solomon, 'Et inclinauit salomon . . . vir in te. Explicit liber Ecclesiasticus'. The prologues are the three of the common set (see above, Bristol, Public Library, 15) and one to Song of Songs beginning 'Salomon filius dauid'. f. 80ᵛ blank.

2 (quires 8–16). ff. 83–193 Incipit epistola prohemialis in tractatu de declaracione difficilium dictorum et dictionum in theologia. Reuerendissimo in cristo patri ac domino suo specialissimo domino iohanni diuina ordinacione Episcopo bruxiensi frater armandus de bello uisu in ordine predicatorum . . . (f. 84ᵛ) famulari. Explicit prohemialis epistola . . . Incipit tractatus de declaracione dictorum diccionum difficilium que sunt superius apud theologos in occursu communium locucionum. Vt ergo circa dicenda ordinantius procedatur . . . Reuelat ut lux Cui honor et gloria in secula seculorum amen. Et sic est finis huius summule de declaracione difficilium dictorum et diccionum in theologia. ex hoc laus deo.

SOPMA i. 122 (no. 316). Printed often: *GKW* 2500–4. A table of chapters giving leaf numbers of art. 2 precedes it on ff. 81–82ᵛ. f. 193ᵛ blank.

3 (quire 17). ff. 194–201 Incipit Richardus de contemplacione. Modis tribus in graciam contemplacionis proficimus . . . tribuat qui cum patre et filio in celis regnat amen.

f. 201ᵛ, left blank, has added notes.

4 (quire 18). ff. 202–211ᵛ Hic incipit tractatulus de originali peccato Magistri Egidii ordinis fratrum heremitarum sancti Augustini. Ego cum sim puluis et cinis . . . te videre possimus qui es benedictus in secula seculorum Amen. Explicit tractatus de peccato originali editus a fratre Egidio de roma Ordinis fratrum sancti Augustini.

Glorieux, no. 400*h*. Printed in 1479 and later.

5. The pastedown at the beginning is a bifolium of a small copy of Boethius, De arithmetica.

s. xii¹: written space 128(+)×67 mm: 25+long lines. The text here is in edn. *PL* lxiii. 1123, 1135.

ff. i+211+i. Paper. Art. 2 has a medieval foliation 1–111. 213×145 mm. Written space *c.* 150×88 mm. 33–41 long lines. Frame ruling. Collation: 1¹⁰ 2¹²+1 leaf after 12 3–6¹² 7¹² wants 10, blank, after f. 80 8¹⁰+1 leaf after 10 (ff. 83–93) 9–15¹² 16¹⁶ (ff. 178–93) 17¹² wants 9–12, probably blank, after f. 201 18¹² wants 11, 12, probably blank, after f. 211. Art. 1 in hybrida and the rest in cursiva. Art. 3 ill written in haste. Initials: (i) 4-line, red and (f. 83) blue with red ornament; (ii, iii) 2-line and 1-line, red. Capital letters in the ink of the text stroked with red. Binding of wooden boards covered with brown leather, rebacked: the central clasp missing: chainmarks at the head of the back cover. Secundo folio *diuersus*.

Written in Germany. Belonged to the Franciscan convent of Hamm, Westphalia: 'Iste liber est pro conuentu hammon' ad usum fratris [. . . . .]' on the front pastedown, s. xv. 'No. ix. Bose. 1' is on the pastedown, s. xix.

48251 (Clifton 10). *Sermones Thomae Ebendorfer, etc.* s. xv²

A companion volume to Bodleian MS. Hamilton 5, which contains Ebendorfer's temporale sermons. Most of the spaces for headings remain blank.

1. ff. 2–204 Ambulans ihesus iuxta mare galilee . . . Mᵗ iiii°. Beatus ambrosius libro quinto super lucam . . .

Forty-six sermons of the sanctorale, beginning at Andrew and ending with a sermon on the subject of purgatory on the text 'Miseremini mei. miseremini mei'. Schneyer, p. 18 (T. Ebendorfer de Haselbach). The gospel texts are listed on f. 1ᵛ. f. 1 is blank except for the title 'Haselpach de sanctis'.

2. ff. 206–284ᵛ Corde creditur ad iusticiam . . . Roma. x°. Haymo. Non potest quis saluari . . .

Twenty sermons of the sanctorale, beginning at Andrew, twelve of the common of saints, six for feasts of B.V.M., and one for the Circumcision beginning 'In nouo anno noua cantilena'. The first sermon for the common is on the text 'Iam non estis hospites' and the first for feasts of B.V.M. on the text 'Ecce iste venit saliens'. The gospel texts are listed on f. 1ᵛ after those of art. 1. The list shows that a sermon on the text 'Vocatum est nomen eius ihesus' is missing at the end. f. 205ʳᵛ is blank.

ff. 284. Paper. 315×220 mm. Written space 220×140 mm. 2 cols. 41 lines. Ruling is with a hard point on versos. Collation: 1–23¹² 24¹² wants 9–12. A strip of parchment down the centre of each quire. Cursiva by two hands, the second and larger writing art. 2. Red initials: (i) ff. 1, 206; (ii) 3-line, but most of the spaces remain blank. Contemporary binding of wooden boards with leather over the spine and about 70 mm of each board. Secundo folio *Cris'*.

Written in Germany. 'Liber Bibliothecæ regalis Monasterii S. Petri Erfordiæ' at the foot of f. 2, s. xviii. '42' on a label on the spine. 'Bibl. Bülov. Beyern, G. H. Schr' ', f. 2, s. xix[1]: cf. below, p. 592. Bülow sale, 10 Oct. 1836, lot 23.

48252 (Clifton 11). *Horae*   s. xv med.

1. ff. 1–6ᵛ Calendar in red and black.

Feasts in red include Erkenwald, the Visitation of B.V.M. and the Transfiguration (30 Apr., 2 July, 5 Aug.). The two red feasts of St. Thomas of Canterbury and his octave, 5 Jan., have not been injured.

2. ff. 7–39ᵛ Hours of B.V.M. of the use of (Sarum).

Memoriae of Holy Spirit, Holy Cross, Holy Trinity, John Baptist, Andrew, Nicholas, Katherine, All Saints, and for peace follow lauds. Hours of the Cross worked in.

3. ff. 39ᵛ–40ᵛ Salue regina and Virgo mater ecclesie.

RH, nos. 18147, 21818.

4. f. 40ᵛ Gaude virgo mater cristi que per aurem . . . *RH*, no. 7017.

5. ff. 41–56ᵛ Penitential psalms, beginning imperfectly, (f. 48ᵛ) gradual psalms (cues only of the first twelve), and (f. 50) litany, ending imperfectly in the prayer 'Deus qui caritatis dona . . .'.

6. ff. 57–81ᵛ Office of the dead, beginning imperfectly.

7. ff. 82–93ᵛ Commendatory psalms, beginning imperfectly.

ff. iii + 93 + iii. 177 × 130 mm. Written space *c.* 112 × 80 mm and (arts. 6, 7) 105 × 77 mm. 18 and (arts. 6, 7) 17 long lines. Collation: 1⁶ 2–5⁸ 6² (ff. 39, 40) 7⁸ wants 1 before f. 41 8⁸ 9 one (f. 56) 10⁸ wants 1 before f. 57 11–12⁸ 13² (ff. 80, 81) 14⁸ wants 1 before f. 82 15⁶ wants 6. Initials: (i) shaded blue and pink on gold grounds decorated in colours, with prolongations forming a continuous border on f. 1 and borders on three sides of other main pages in art. 2; (ii) 2-line, blue with red ornament; (iii) 1-line, blue or red. Capital letters in the ink of the text filled with pale yellow. The style of decoration changes at f. 57. Contemporary binding of greenish leather over wooden boards: four bands: central clasp missing.

Written in England. 'Ex bibliotheca J. J. M[. . . .]', f. i, s. xviii.

48253 (Clifton 12). *Pseudo-Augustinus, Meditationes; etc.* s. xv med.

1 (quires 1, 2). ff. 2–15ᵛ (*begins imperfectly*) es deductus . . . in necessitatibus constitutis. pie (*ends imperfectly*).

H. Suso, Centum Meditationes, nos. 2 (last words only)—95. Cf. MS. 4 art. 11.

2 (quires 3–7). A series of nineteen prayers to the Father and the Son: (*a*) f. 16 (*begins imperfectly*) perpetuo recreari et in eternitate immutabiliter requiescere . . .; (*b*) f. 16ᵛ Aue nunc igitur o crucifixa . . .; (*c*) f. 16ᵛ Confiteor tibi domine pater celi et terre tibique bone et benignissime ihesu . . .; (*d*) f. 18 Deus

iustorum gloria et misericordia peccatorum qui dixisti nolo mortem peccatoris . . .; (*e*) f. 21 Altissime et mitissime deus amator creator . . .; (*f*) f. 23 Domine ihesu criste redempcio mea misericordia mea. salus mea. te laudo. tibi gracias ago . . .; (*g*) f. 26 Adesto suplicacionibus nostris domine deus quem quero. quem diligere cupio . . .; (*h*) f. 28 Criste domine uerbum patris qui venisti in hunc mundum peccatores soluere . . .; (*i*) f. 30 Obsecro domine et te nimis pium rogo in nomine dulcissimi filii tui . . .; (*j*) f. 33ᵛ Desertum ydumee cecus et morbidus possessor inhabitans clamo ad te . . .; (*k*) f. 34ᵛ Domine deus Sabaoth magne et admirabilis. terribilis et fortis . . .; (*l*) f. 36 Dominus de se ipso dicit. Ego sum alpha et oo. principium et finis. Quia sicut . . .; (*m*) f. 37 Domine ihesu criste fili dei viui qui expansis in cruce manibus propter mortalium omnium redempcionem. hausisti . . .; (*n*) f. 40 Si ante oculos tuos domine culpas quas fecimus . . .; (*o*) f. 41ᵛ Succurre michi domine deus meus antequam moriar . . .; (*p*) f. 44ᵛ Recordare domine ihesu. quia non auro uel argento. Sed proprii sanguinis tui me precio . . .; (*q*) f. 47 Rogo te immensa pietas deus meus. ne perdas me creaturam tuam ad tui similitudinem conditam . . .; (*r*) f. 49ᵛ Ad te dulcissime Ihesu et benignissime domine Ihesu qui fons pietatis es . . .; (*s*) ff. 53–4 Omnipotens sempiterne deus Rex regum et dominus dominancium. Creator . . . Exaudi me miserum . . . Exaudi. Exaudi. Exaudi. et miserere mei. Amen.

(*c*) is for the use of a religious. f. 54ᵛ blank.

3. ff. 55–67 Kyrieleyson. Cristeleyson. Criste audi nos . . .

Litany, with one or two prayers between each order, the first 'Omnipotens sempiterne deus qui dedisti famulis tuis in confessione . . .': Trinity, f. 55; B.V.M., f. 55; Angels, f. 56; Patriarchs, f. 56ᵛ; Apostles, f. 57ᵛ; Martyrs, f. 59ᵛ; Confessors, f. 61: Eadmunde, Richarde, Edwarde are the first three of five kings and pontiffs and Willelme, Roberte, Giralde, Columbane the last four of eleven monks and hermits; Virgins, f. 63: Etheldreda, Wendreda are sixteenth and seventeenth of twenty-one.

4. ff. 67–74 Spiritus sancte verus deus cum deo patre . . .

Prayers to the Holy Spirit in nineteen paragraphs and one prayer to Christ crucified (f. 72). Fourteen paragraphs begin 'O sancte spiritus'.

5. ff. 74ᵛ–110ᵛ Capitula meditacionum Augustini episcopi et Doctoris de spiritu sancto sequuntur . . . (*table of twenty-three chapters*) . . . Capitulum primum. Quomodo peccator inuocabit . . . Domine deus sancte spiritus time[o et]¹ desidero . . . permanes in secula seculorum. Amen. Spiritus sancti gracia⸴ illuminet dominus corda nostra. Expliciunt meditaciones beati Augustini de spiritu sancto.

Edited by A. Wilmart, *Auteurs spirituels*, pp. 427–51. His list of eighteen manuscripts, nearly all English, on pp. 419–25, does not include this one.

6. (*a*) f. 110ᵛ O sancte spiritus deus dileccionis et pacis . . . (*b*) f. 110ᵛ De sancto Iohanne Beuerlaci Arch' Eboraci. Inclite doctor Aue . . .

(*b*) added in blank space, s. xv². A memoria of John of Beverley with antiphon as *RH*, no. 28179 (*AH* xxviii. 284), except that the name John is substituted for Anselm.

7. ff. 111–18 (*begins imperfectly*) deuotas. visita desolatos. imple vacuos . . .

---

¹ *timeo et* appears to have been altered to *timens*.

inducuntur veritatem. prestante eodem spiritu sancto. qui . . . Amen. Explicit etc.

A meditation based on Veni creator spiritus. Mentes tuorum visita.

8. ff. 118–124ᵛ Que sequuntur excerpta sunt de libro Ricardi heremite qui dicitur melos amoris. O deus piissime penetrasti pectus pingendum profunda . . . liquidi langoris. Deo gracias.

Richard Rolle, Melos amoris. Cf. the edition by E. J. F. Arnould, 1957, p. 49, for the beginning of this extract.

9. ff. 124ᵛ–128 Contemplatiua uita est consideratiua. deum diligere . . . quod falso promittit inuitat.

10 (added, s. xv²). Prayers filling quire 17 and continued on two further leaves: (a) ff. 128ᵛ–131 Sancta maria virgo virginum dei mater et filiorum dei. Audi necessitatem meam . . .; (b) ff. 131–2 Summa sempiterna et benedicta trinitas pater et filius et spiritus sanctus deus omnipotens vniuersitatis conditor . . .; (c) f. 132ᵛ [D]omine ihesu criste qui stas in media via . . .; (d) f. 132ᵛ Dixit Abbas pastor qui querelosus est Monachus non est . . . (e) ff. 133–4 Suscipe confessionem meam vnica spes salutis mee domine deus meus. Nam gule ebrietatis . . . (f) ff. 134ᵛ–135 Adoro te digne o latens veritas . . . beata te in requie (28 lines). (g) f. 135 Aue ihesu criste uerbum patris filius virginis agnus dei salus mundi . . .

(f). RH, no. 519; AH l. 589 (Aquinas). (g). Five aves and prayer, 'Domine ihesu criste tu qui es panis . . .'. The scribe wrote 'ihesus' at the head of each page, ff. 133–5.

ff. v+134+iv, foliated (i–iv), 1–136 (137–9). For f. 1 see below. f. 136 is a medieval flyleaf. 182 × 128 mm. Written space 108 × 78 mm. 24 long lines. Ruling in red ink. Collation of ff. 2–135: 1 six 2⁸ 3⁸ wants 1 before f. 16 4–14⁸ 15⁸ wants 1 before f. 111 16–17⁸ 18 two (ff. 134–5). Arts. 1–5, 7–9 in poor textura. Art. 10 is in mixed, but mainly secretary hand, except (e) which is in a good hybrida. f. 1, an inserted frontispiece, s. xix?, shows a woman kneeling at an altar, her guardian angel behind her. Initials: (i) ff. 75ᵛ, 118, in colour, patterned in white, on decorated gold grounds and with ivy-leaf decorations into the margins; (ii) 3-line, blue with red ornament; (iii) in art. 1 only, 3-line and 2-line, blue with red ornament or gold with pale-green ornament; (iv) in art. 1 only, 1-line, red or blue. Binding of s. xix, lettered 'MISSALE M.S.': probably long without a cover to judge from the condition of f. 136ᵛ. Secundo folio (f. 2) es deductus.

Written in England. Two erased lines at the foot of f. 132ᵛ illegible except for 'Cartusienses ibi deo' at the beginning of line 2. Ex-libris of the London Charterhouse higher up the same page: 'Liber iste pertinet domui Salutacionis Matris dei prope Londonias iuxta Smyffeld' quem dompnus Willelmus Bakster attulit secum ad domum de Witham per licenciam Reuerendi patris dompni Willelmi Tynbyth prioris tunc existentis': Tynbyth was prior 1520–9. Other ex-libris inscriptions of the London Charterhouse on ff. 135, 135ᵛ, 136. Belonged to Lord Ashburnham: his sale at Sotheby's, 1 May 1899, lot 14. Item 119 in a bookseller's catalogue at £31. 10s.: the relevant slip is inside the cover. 'From the library of Gerald S. Davies Late master of the Charterhouse', f. iᵛ: his sale at Sotheby's, 20 June 1927, lot 441.[1]

58254, a *Missale Romanum*, Venice (N. de Franckfordia) 1484 (Weale-Bohatta,

[1] Untraced in the 1st edition of Ker, MLGB (p. 68). Entered wrongly in the 2nd edition as belonging to the Charterhouse of St. Hugh, Partridge Green.

Catalogus missalium, 1928, no. 892), has (1) fifteen parchment leaves of manuscript supplying a defect, (2) a mass of the Five Wounds added in the blank space at the end (quire 15, leaves 7, 8), (3) sixty-one sequences for the year from Christmas on thirty added leaves of paper and (4) a series of prayers on eight added leaves of paper. (4) is headed 'Sequitur modus orandi utilis sub missarum celebracionem cuique obseruandus. Quem Reuerendissimus pater dominus Vdalricus Episcopus Brixin' compilauit et de qualibet oratione specialiter usque ad prefationem . . .'.

The heading of (4) conveys an indulgence of 10+40+40 days. The text begins 'Cum autem sacerdos ascendit gradus altaris dicat O incomprehensibilis maiestas deus qui liberasti . . .'. The last prayer, 'Deus qui nobis sub sacramento inuincibili passionis tue . . .', is followed by 'In fine omnium dic cum presbitero Initium S. euangelii secundum Iohannem In principio erat uerbum ut infra'. There were two bishops of Brixen named Ulrich, Ulrich von Wien 1396–1417 and Ulrich von Putsch 1428–37, according to Gams, *Series episcoporum*.

DUNFERMLINE. PUBLIC LIBRARY

1. *Missale* s. xv med.

1. ff. 1–6ᵛ Calendar in red and black, not graded.

Nine main feasts are marked 'Communis elemosina'. Feasts in red include Ludger, Servatius, Boniface 'et socii', and Victorinus and Florianus (24 Apr., 13 May, 5 June, 2 Nov.); in black, 'Ludgeri episcopi mon' ', 'Aduentus sancte Walburgis virginis', 'Translacio sancti Ludgeri. Duorum ewaldorum', 'Aduentus duorum ewaldorum' (26 Mar., 4 Aug., 3, 29 Oct.). No entries for the Transfiguration, 6 Aug., the Holy Lance (cf. art. 14c), or the Presentation of B.V.M. (cf. art. 8), but the Visitation of B.V.M. is in red, with octave in black (2, 9 July) and St. Anne in black (26 July).

2. ff. 8–122 Temporale from Advent to the Sunday after Ascension Day, the first leaf missing.

Litany, f. 101ᵛ. Twenty-nine martyrs: . . . (21, 22) ponciane lamberte . . . (29) gereon. Twenty-one confessors: (1) augustine . . . (8–15) iheronime nycolae remigi ludgere hylari seruati willibrorde benedicte . . . (20, 21) lebuine odulphe. Seventeen virgins: . . . (9–11) scolastica walburgis gertrudis . . .

3. ff. 122–124ᵛ Kyrieleyson and Gloria in excelsis noted, Credo, and prayers before mass.

4. ff. 125–163ᵛ Prefaces and canon of mass.

Prefaces occur twice, first by themselves with music and then again without music before the appropriate form of Communicantes. Te igitur, f. 156. On f. 156ᵛ the red tail of the ornament of the initial *M* of 'Memento domine famulorum famularumque tuarum . . .' forms the words 'Orate pro fratre vestro hillando rubricatore propter ihesum', written beautifully in a minute hand.

5. ff. 7ʳᵛ, 164–202 Temporale from Pentecost to the twenty-fourth Sunday after Pentecost.

6. ff. 202–4 Benedictions of church and altar.

7. ff. 204–5 Benedictions of salt and water. f. 205ᵛ blank.

8 (added, s. xvi). f. 206ʳᵛ Office of Presentation of B.V.M.

9. ff. 207–18 Masses of Holy Trinity, Corpus Christi, Holy Spirit, Holy Cross, B.V.M., Angels, Eternal Wisdom, 'Pro peccatis', 'De sancto Paulo patrono nostro', 'Pro pace', 'Pro infirmis' and 'Contra pestilenciam'.

The sequence for St. Paul is 'Sancte paule merita tua colentes . . .', *RH*, no. 18493, *AH* xliv. 237 (from Münster service-books).

10. ff. 218–223ᵛ Collect, secret, and postcommunion of thirty-seven votive masses, the first 'Pro quacumque tribulacione'.

11. ff. 223ᵛ–228 In anniuersario seu commemoracione defunctorum.

12. ff. 228–42 Incipit commune sanctorum. The first leaf is missing.

13. ff. 242–310ᵛ Sanctorale through the year from Andrew to Katherine, the first leaf missing.

Ludger, f. 259, with sequence. Translation of Ludger, f. 299, with sequence, 'Cleri decantet concio . . .': *RH*, no. 3398. Feast of relics between Septem fratrum (10 July) and Translation of Benedict (11 July).

14. ff. 310ᵛ–313ᵛ Masses: (*a*) for St. Bridget, widow; (*b*) for the translation of St. Augustine; (*c*) 'De lancea domini'; (*d*) 'De uulneribus et passione domini nostri ihesu cristi'.

Sequences of (*a–c*): Gaude celum terra plaude nam birgitta . . .; De profundis tenebrarum . . .; Hodierne festum lucis . . . (*RH*, nos. 37509, 4245, 7944).

15. f. 313ᵛ De sancto lamberto Sequencia. Pange syon redemptori sub alterni forma chori . . .

RH, no. 14528. *AH* viii. 166, from a printed Münster gradual.

ff. i+313+i. ff. 8–122, 164–206 have a medieval foliation in black, ii–cxvi, cxviii–clx, and ff. 207–313 a medieval foliation in red, i–xxxv, xxxviii–cix. 425 × 300 mm. Written space 300 × 200 mm. 2 cols. 33 lines (17 and 19 lines in art. 4). Collation: 1⁶ 2⁸ wants 1 before f. 8 3–14⁸ 15¹² 16–17⁸ 18⁴+2 leaves before 1 (ff. 139, 140) 19⁸ 20²+1 leaf before 1 (f. 153)¹ 21⁸ 22⁸ (ff. 7, 164–70) 23–26⁸ 27⁴ (ff. 203–6) 28–31⁸ 32⁸ wants 4, 5, after f. 241 33–40⁸ 41⁸ wants 6–8, probably blank. Well written in admirably black ink. A skilful drawing of the Resurrection in the foot of the gold bar falling from the *R* of *Resurrexi* (f. 104, Easter). Handsome initials (cf. above, art. 4): (i) ff. 104 (Easter), 156 (*T* of *Te igitur*), 7 (Pentecost), 286 (Assumption of B.V.M.), in patterned blue on decorated gold grounds: floral borders; (ii) 4-line to 7-line, as (i), but no borders, or, in art. 4 only, gold and blue or red and blue, with ornament of red and violet on a green ground; (iii) 3-line, red and blue or one of these colours with ornament in green, violet, or red; (iv, v) 2-line and 1-line. Capital letters in the ink of the text touched with red. Germanic binding, s. xvi, of wooden boards covered with pigskin, bearing a floral roll and three stamps: two clasps. Projecting parchment buttons mark the principal divisions of the text and each leaf of the canon. Secundo folio (f. 8) *habemus abraham*.

Written for use in the diocese of Münster, Westphalia.² The rubricator Hillandus names

¹ Or 20⁴ wants 4, if there was once a Crucifixion picture facing *Te igitur*.
² Missals of Münster use are described by E. Lengeling, *Dona Westfalica*, *G. Schreiber zum 80. Geburtstage*, Münster, 1963, pp. 192–238. The cathedral possessed the bodies of SS. Victorinus and Florianus and their feast on 2 Nov. (art. 1) is peculiar to the diocese.

himself in the ornament of f. 156ᵛ.[1] 'Clare. Jersey. Sotheby' and 'Ridler' on the paste-down, s. xix. A description on a paper sheet pasted to the pastedown is signed 'G.R. 1897'. Given by George Reid in 1905.

2. *Antiphonale Cisterciense, Pars aestivalis*   s. XIII med.

1. ff. 1–56 Temporale from Pentecost. One leaf missing.

2. ff. 56ᵛ–133ᵛ Sanctorale from Benedict to Andrew (21 Mar.–30 Nov.). In natale sancti Bernardi, ff. 99ᵛ–103ᵛ. Cues for St. Robert added on f. 65.

3. ff. 134–161ᵛ Common of saints.

4. ff. 161ᵛ–166 In dedicatione ecclesie.

5. ff. 166–174ᵛ Office of the dead.

6. ff. 174ᵛ–176 Tonale, headed 'De prima differencia primi toni'.

7. ff. 176–195ᵛ Hymns with music: at the hours (1–10); of temporale and sanctorale from Easter to St. Andrew (11–36); of the common of saints (37–40); at the dedication of a church (41).

A normal Cistercian set (cf. C. Weinmann, *Hympnarium Parisiense*, 1905), except for the presence of Te deum laudamus in first place and the absence of hymns for St. Bernard (cf. art. 9*b*). A leaf missing before f. 182 contained all but the first three words of Chorus novae and nearly all Optatus votis (nos. 13, 14, Ascension).

8. f. 196ʳᵛ Cantica dominicis diebus et in festiuitate sancti michaelis. Domine miserere nostri . . . Audite qui longe estis . . . Miserere domine plebi tue . . . Cantica de resurrectione. Quis est iste qui uenit . . . Uenite et reuertamur . . . (*ends imperfectly*).

Only Mearns's first Sunday set and part of his first Easter set remain (*Canticles*, pp. 87–8).

9 (added in s. xiv). (*a*) ff. 197–203ᵛ In nat' xi milium uirginum . . . (*b*) ff. 203ᵛ–204 In festiuitate beati bernardi. Bernardus doctor inclite . . . (*c*) f. 204ᵛ Nouus abel cristus hostiam . . .

(*a, c*). Additions to art. 2. (*b*). An addition to art. 7 (*RH*, no. 2473), divided at 'Archana sacre pagine'.

11. Pieces of a three-column biblical concordance, s. xiii, and of a law book (?: f. 134) have been used to mend leaves.

---

ff. i+204+i. 355×240 mm. Written space 285×170 mm. 12 long lines, spaced for music. Collation: 1–5⁸ 6⁸ wants 1 before f. 41 7–11⁸ 12⁶ (ff. 88–93) 13–23⁸ 24⁸ wants 1 before f. 182 25⁶ 26¹⁰ wants a leaf or leaves after 2 (f. 196). Well written. Well-drawn initials: (i) ff. 1ᵛ, 56ᵛ, 100 (Bernard), red and blue, the blue patterned in white, with curving

---

[1] For the duties of the rubricator at the Fraterhaus in Münster see W. Oeser in *Archiv für Geschichte des Buchwesens*, v (1963), 219. Dr. Oeser tells me that this manuscript is certainly a product of the Fraterhaus and that its decoration is very like that of a breviary written 'pro . . . Hermanno von lancgen decano ecclesie maioris monasteriensis sancti pauli' in 1464, now in the Münster Staatsarchiv, Depositum Altertumsverein MS. 97, described loc. cit. 316–20.

interlace coloured green and pale brown; (ii) blue and red, or green and red, or brown and red, smaller than (i), with simpler ornament or none; (iii) red, blue, or brown, with a line of white; (iv) 1-line, red or blue, or, less often, brown or green. Capital letters in the ink of the text are touched with red. Medieval binding of wooden boards covered with light-brown leather, repaired: the back strip was lettered later 'Antiph' Cister.'. Secundo folio *et uidete*.

Written in Italy. '201' on upper cover. Given as MS. 1.

3. *Horae*　　　　　　　　　　　　　　　　　　　s. xv med.

1. ff. 1–95　Incipiunt hore sancte marie secundum usum romane ecclesie. A leaf or two missing at the end.

2. ff. 96–99ᵛ　Hours of the Cross, beginning imperfectly.

3. ff. 100–129ᵛ　Incipiunt septem psalmi penitentiales. Followed by a litany. f. 100 is misplaced before f. 1 and is back to front.

4. ff. 130–180ᵛ　Office of the dead, beginning imperfectly. ff. 181–183ᵛ blank.

ff. i+183+i. 152 × 105 mm. Written space 100 × 60 mm. 12 long lines. Collation: 1–6⁸ 7⁸ wants 8 after f. 55 8–12⁸ 13 four (ff. 96–9) 14–16⁸ 17⁸ wants 7 after f. 129 18–21⁸ 22⁶ 23⁸ 24⁸ wants 8, blank, after f. 183. Initials: (i) ff. 1, 68 (compline), 100, in colours on decorated gold grounds: full borders on ff. 1, 100, including hares and green birds; (ii, iii) 2-line and 1-line, blue with red ornament or red with violet ornament. Bound in Italy in s. xviii.

Written in Italy. A slip from p. 116 of an English auction sale catalogue in which this manuscript was lot 1461 is attached to f. (i). Book-plate of George Reid. Given as MS. 1

4. *Horae*　　　　　　　　　　　　　　　　　　　s. xv in.

1. ff. 1–12ᵛ　Calendar in French, in red and black.

Geneviève, Yves, Remy, Ursin (29 Dec.: first bishop of Bourges) in red.

2 (added, s. xv). (*a*) ff. 13–14ᵛ　St. John 1: 1–14, followed by the prayer, 'Protector in te sperancium . . .'. (*b*) ff. 15–17ᵛ Passio domini nostri ihesu cristi secundum Iohannem. In illo tempore. Apprehendit pylatus . . . est testimonium eius. Deo gracias. Deus (qui) manus tuas et pedes tuos . . . (*c*) f. 18ʳᵛ Aue cuius concepcio sollempni plena gaudio . . .

(*b*). Mainly from John 19: 1–35: see *Lyell Cat.*, p. 65. *Horae Ebor.*, pp. 123–4. (*c*). *RH*, no. 1744.

3. ff. 19–84ᵛ　Hours of B.V.M. of the use of (Bourges). The first leaf of matins and the first of none are missing.

4. ff. 85–104ᵛ　Penitential psalms and litany, lacking a leaf after f. 102 and ending imperfectly. f. 85 was supplied in s. xvi.

5. ff. 105–108ᵛ　Hours of the Cross, beginning imperfectly.

6. ff. 109–149ᵛ　Office of the dead. f. 109 was supplied in s. xvi.

7 (added, s. xv). (*a*) f. 150^{rv} Domine ihesu xpriste adoro te in cruce pendentem
. . . in cruce uulneratum . . . in sepulcro positum . . . pastor bone . . . Domine
ihesu criste; (*b*) f. 151 celos ascendisti . . . presentibus et futuris. amen.

Nos. 1, 2, 4, 7 of the Seven Oes of St. Gregory printed by Leroquais, *Livres d'heures*, ii.
346, followed by the first three words of another *O* and, after a missing leaf after f. 150,
by the concluding part of a prayer. f. 151^v was left blank.

ff. i+152+i, foliated (i), 1–125, 125*, 126–52. 131×98 mm. Written space 72×42 mm.
12 long lines. Collation: 1^{12} 2^8 wants 7, 8, perhaps blank, after f. 18 3^8 wants 1 before f. 19
4–8^8 9^8 wants 7 after f. 71 10^8 11^4 (ff. 81–4) 12^8 wants 1 (supplied later, f. 85) 13^8 14^8 wants 3
after f. 102 and 6 after f. 104 15 two (ff. 107–8) 16^8 wants 1 (supplied later, f. 109) 17–20^8
21 four (ff. 148–51). Initials: (i) ff. 42^v, 56, 63^v, 68^v, 75^v, 78^v, in colour patterned in white
on decorated gold grounds: ivy-leaf borders on three sides; (ii, iii) 2-line and 1-line, gold
on coloured grounds patterned in white: short sprays into the margins from the 2-line
initials. Line fillers in red, blue, and gold. Binding of s. xviii, covered with crimson velvet.

Written in France. 'Ce present Livre appartien a moi Gabriel Robin qui n'est ni Capusin
ni Prêtre ni a guère envie de l'être', f. 151^v, s. xviii. '£6/6/-' inside the cover. Book-plate
of George Reid. Given as MS. 1.

5. *Horae* s. XVI in.

1. ff. 1–128 Offitium Beate Marie Virginis secundum Consuetudinem R(omane)
C(urie). Salve regina after compline, f. 97.

2. ff. 128^v–129 Anima christi . . . *RH*, no. 1090.

3 (in another hand). (*a*) f. 129^v In eleuatione calicis. Aue vere sanguis . . .
(*b*) ff. 130–1 Salue sancta caro dei . . . (*RH*, no. 18175). (*c*) ff. 131^v–133 Gloria
in excelsis. (*d*) ff. 133–5 Credo in unum deum. (*e*) ff. 135–7 St. John 1: 1–14.
f. 137^v blank.

4. ff. 138–191^v Incipiunt septem psalmi penitenciales. The litany begins on
f. 168^v.

5. ff. 191^v–199 Simbolum athanasii.

6. ff. 199^v–203 Missa de beata vi(r)gine. Salue sancta parens . . . (*RH*, no.
18197). f. 203^v blank.

ff. iii+203+ii. The end-leaves are parchment: f. i was pasted down. 138×95 mm.
Written space 90–100×70 mm. 8–10 long lines. Collation: 1–8^8 9^6 10–17^8 18 three
(ff. 135–7) 19–25^8 26^8+1 leaf after 7 (f. 201) and 1 after 8 (f. 203). Initials: (i) f. 1, blue,
patterned in white, on decorated gold ground, and f. 138, gold with blue penwork ornament: continuous borders; (ii, iii) 2-line and 1-line, blue with red ornament, or red with
green ornament, or (ff. 138^v–152 only) gold with blue ornament. Gilt brown calf Italian
binding, s. xvi: the blurred centrepiece bears a shield, with the letters *S* and *N* at its base.

Written in Italy. From a monastery at Messina, according to a note by George Reid on
f. ii: cf. London, Victoria and Albert Museum, MS. Reid 71 (*MMBL* i. 384). '£5. 10. 0',
f. ii. Given as MS. 1.

6. *Graduale* s. xiv²

A handsome gradual, now damaged by the removal of forty-one leaves and the mutilation of three, cxcix, ccxli, and ccxliii. The medieval foliation of arts. 1–9— which I follow—takes the missing leaves into account. Texts and rubrics agree usually with *Missale Romanum*.

1. f. iʳᵛ Holy Water office, ending imperfectly.

2. ff. iii–ccxiiiᵛ Temporale from Advent to the twenty-third Sunday after Pentecost.

3. ff. ccxvi–ccliiᵛ Sanctorale from Andrew to Clement.

4. ff. ccliiᵛ–cccviiᵛ Incipit commune sanctorum de missali.

5. ff. ccviiᵛ–ccixᵛ In dedicatione ecclesie.

6. ff. cccixᵛ–cccxii In agenda defunctorum.

7. ff. cccxii–cccxxviiᵛ Kyries.

8. ff. cccxxviiᵛ–cccxliii Sequences at Christmas, Easter, Pentecost, at feasts of B.V.M., of the common of apostles, and of the dead: Letabundus exultet, Victime paschalis, Veni sancte spiritus, Missus gabriel de celis, Aue maria gratia plena, Verbum bonum et suaue, Iesse uirga(m) humidauit (*RH*, no. 9458), Celi solem inmitantes, Dies illa dies ire.

9. ff. cccxliii–cccxliiiiᵛ Nicene creed, ending imperfectly 'et per prophetas. Et unam sanctam'.

10 (added in s. xvii/xviii). (*a, e, f*) ff. 345, 352, 355 Supplements to arts. 2, 3: offices of the Transfiguration, Holy Trinity, and Holy Sacrament. (*b*) ff. 347–50 Index of incipits, with leaf references. (*c*) f. 351 'Index introitum ... Festorum huius Ecclesię'. (*d*) f. 351 'Festiuitates quę celebrantur in hac Ecclesia.'

(*b*) includes references to now missing leaves. (*c*). Sixteen feasts, among them George and 'Caroli confessoris et pontificis' (Carlo Borromeo, †1584).

11. f. cccxxxv is mended with a strip of a very large two-column manuscript in Beneventan script, s. xi (?). One line of each column can be read: Sępe au (?) ita mens accenditur ut quam / prius per morte pęnę suę debitum soluat.

12. f. 358, formerly pasted down, is a leaf of a missal, s. xiii/xiv, as *Missale Romanum*, i. 58 (Monday in first week of Lent).

In a question the mark of interrogation is written above the first word.

---

ff. i+305+i. The foliation of arts. 1–9 is medieval, in red, on versos: see above. Art. 10 (ff. 345–57) is paper. 310×210 mm. Written space 230×140 mm. 7 long lines spaced for music. Originally twenty-eight quires of 12 leaves and one quire of 10 leaves, ff. ccv–ccxiv. Thirty-nine leaves are now missing: 1², ¹¹, 2¹⁰, 3², ³, ⁷, 4⁵⁻⁸, 6¹², 7⁹, ¹⁰, 13⁶, ⁷, 14²⁻⁸, 15³, ⁵, ⁸, 17⁶, 18¹⁰, probably blank (f. ccxiv), 19¹, ¹², 20⁸, 21⁹, ¹², 22⁸, 23⁶, ⁷, 24¹, ², 29¹¹, ¹². Initials: (i) all removed with the leaves on which they came; (ii) of introits, 2-line, blue and red or blue and brown gold on a brown gold ground and with ornament in red and violet; (iii) 1-line, blue or red with ornament of the other colour. Binding of s. xvii (?), rebacked: stamps of two-headed eagle and fleuron: four bosses formerly on each cover.

Written in Italy. Belonged to a church of St. George in s. xvii/xviii, as appears from: (1) '[. . . .] Giorgio', f. i^v; (2) a note on f. xxiv^v that Giovanni Batta and [. . .] 'Presuito (?) sono sacristano nella chiesa di S^{to} Giorgio nell' anno 1703 entranto (?) 1704'; (3) 'Georgii vide fol. 265' in the margin of f. ccxxix^v, a reference to the common of saints.

DURHAM. CATHEDRAL

Thomas Rud, *Codicum manuscriptorum ecclesiae cathedralis Dunelmensis Catalogus classicus.* Durham, 1825.

Rud's fine catalogue was finished in 1727. The library owns the copy which he wrote in his own beautiful hand and to which he added the description of a Bible given in 1729 (A. IV. 30). It was not printed until 1825, when James Raine added an appendix in which he described the Dampier, Hunter, Randall, and Allan manuscripts acquired between 1776 and 1823 and gave an account of B. IV. 46–8, which Rud had excluded (pp. 319–437). Rud described 321 medieval and fifteen post-medieval manuscripts in his part of the *Catalogus* (pp. 1–316). All but twenty-five of the medieval manuscripts belonged to the cathedral priory before the Dissolution and are listed in Ker, *MLGB*, and the great majority of them are recorded in the medieval catalogues printed in *Catalogi Veteres*.

Three manuscripts came in after Rud's time, were added to the A and B presses, and were described in the 1825 catalogue: A. IV. 31, s. xvii, given in 1740; B. IV. 44, s. xiv, given in 1739 (*Catalogus*, p. 251: pp. 109–11 contain a copy of the Constitutions of Clarendon), and B. IV. 45, s. xv, given in 1768.

One gift to the cathedral in Rud's time (1724) was somehow missed by him and has now a Hunter number (Hunter 123, q.v.). For A. III. 36 and B. III. 34, see below.

R. A. B. Mynors, *Durham Cathedral Manuscripts to the End of the Twelfth Century.* 1939.

H. D. Hughes and J. M. Falkner, *A History of Durham Cathedral Library.* 1925.

I include here thirteen not-in-Rud manuscripts of the main series and fourteen manuscripts of the Hunter collection, which Raine described, but briefly. Four fragments, C. III. 25–8, were brought to my attention by Mr. A. J. Piper.

A. III. 36. *Petrus Cantor, etc.*   s. XII/XIII–XIII[1] (art. 4)

1. ff. 2–12 (*begins imperfectly*) et temptacionum. Vnde subdit . . . per omnia tempora. Expliciunt notule canonicarum epistolarum.

Petrus Cantor on the Catholic Epistles, Stegmüller, nos. 6524–30, beginning in James 1: 6. James is in 12, 1 Peter in 12, and 2 Peter in 7 divisions. Lemmata are only underlined on ff. 2–4^v.

2. ff. 12^v–13^v 'Sermo in dedicacione ecclesie'. Statuit Iudas Machabeus et fratres eius et uniuersa ecclesia israhel . . . dedicare possimus.' ut ad uitam eternam peruenire mereamur. Quod ipse . . . amen.

3. f. 13* Si quis diligit me sermonem meum . . . Legitur in prouerb' i⁰. Audiens sapiens . . . (*ends abruptly*). f. 13*ᵛ blank.

4. ff. 14–44ᵛ [P]ostquam dictum est de mundo archipo. dicendum est de mundo creato de quo dicit moyses . . . nec ipsa peccat neque secundum (*ends abruptly*).

William of Auxerre, †1231, Summa Sententiarum, bk. 2, ending at edn. Paris (P. Pigouchet) 1500, f. 66ᵛ. Glorieux, no. 129. Stegmüller, *Sent.* i. 124. f. 21ᵛ blank, but the text seems to be complete: 22 begins a new quire.

5. ff. 45–110ᵛ Verbum abbreuiatum f. dominus super terram. Si enim uerbum de sinu patris . . . crux et martirium. Item de cautela penitencie (*ends imperfectly*).

Petrus Cantor: Stegmüller, no. 6448. *PL* ccv. 23–330/43. Single leaves are missing after ff. 84 and 88 and a few leaves at the end.

6. Three scraps removed from the binding and now pasted to a stub after f. 110 are from a manuscript of grammatical verse, s. xiii. A section begins '[A]d sillogismum tres lector cerne figuras.' Quartum tu discas disposuisse modos. Hec sunt arma . . .'.

ff. ii+110+i, foliated i, 1–13, 13*, 14–110, (111). A medieval foliation of ff. 45–100 '1'– '68' takes account of the two leaves now missing from quire 12. 305 × 220 mm. Written space *c.* 265 × 150 mm on ff. 1–44, 235 × 135 mm on ff. 45–60 and 205 × 110 mm on ff. 61– 110. 2 cols. 59–65 lines (49 lines on ff. 61–110). Writing above the top ruled line, except in art. 4. Pricks in both margins. Collation of ff. 2–110: 1⁸ wants 1 2 six (ff. 9–13, 13*) 3–5⁸ 6⁸ wants 8, blank, after f. 44 7–11⁸ 12⁸ wants 1 before f. 85 and 5 after f. 88 13–14¹⁰. Quires 9–12 are numbered at the end II–V. Initials: 2 line in art. 1, red or yellow brown, with ornament of the other colour, and one in green with red ornament; (ii) 2-line spaces not filled in arts. 4, 5. Binding of s. xix. Secundo folio *et temptationum* (f. 2); *inuicem* (f. 46).

Written in England. 'Liber Iohannis Ruddi', f. iᵛ. 'Liber Ecclesiæ Cathedralis Dunelmensis ex dono Iohannis Rudd Armigeri', f. 1. Entered in Thomas Rud's autograph catalogue, but as an addition by another hand: 'Anonymi Glossæ in Epistolas Pauli'.

A. IV. 33. *Uthredus de Boldon*   s. xv¹

A collection of seven pieces by one hand listed in a contemporary table of contents on f. iii. An owner, s. xv, an admirer of Uthred of Boldon (†1397), wrote below the table 'Hec omnia per vthredum bolton, monachum dunelmensem. Egregium profecto theologum, et quod legentibus eius opera conspicuum est, acutissimi plane hominem ingenii, lege, et experieris' and above it 'Contra hostes ecclesię Wicliphistas pro eius libertate'. The same hand has added long notes on ff. 45ᵛ, 53ᵛ–54, 104ᵛ.[1] Arts. 1–7 are noticed by W. A. Pantin, 'Two treatises of Uthred of Boldon on the monastic life', *Studies in Medieval History presented to F. M. Powicke*, 1948, pp. 363–85. Bale, *Index*, p. 463, refers to a copy of arts. 3, 4, 7, without incipits, 'Ex Ioanne Pullano Oxoniensi'.

1. ff. 1–23 Dato quod progressus innocentie prime fuisset . . .

The table of contents calls this 'Tractatus de regalia et sacerdotio', but it seems to be an

[1] This scribe uses a comma, not a point, as punctuation.

unordered collection of notes intended for incorporation in arts. 2–7, as the cross-references show. A passage on f. 20ᵛ begins 'Obieccio contra dicta superius fo. 4 /: pro declaracione materie. Contra illud quod dicitur superius fo. 4 /: de saule': on f. 4ᵛ the passage to which this refers has /: against it.[1] Cf. Pantin, p. 364.

2. ff. 24–64ᵛ Incipit libellus de naturali et necessaria connexione ac ordine sacerdotalis officii et regalis. Sicut ex duobus spiritu scilicet et corpore . . . radix prodiit perdicionis.

The text on f. 24ʳᵛ is on a leaf added in the main hand to replace the text given in lines 1–15 on f. 24A which have 'va cat' against them: the heading on 24A is 'Incipit libellus magistri vthredi monachi Dunelm' ac sacre theologie professoris de naturali et necessaria connexione ac ordine sacerdotalis officii et regalis'. On f. 64 blank spaces have been left in the text for 'supra' and 'infra' references. Marginalia on f. 32 refer to art. 1. Cf. Pantin, p. 364. ff. 65–68ᵛ left blank.

3. ff. 69–99ᵛ Incipit tractatus Magistri vthredi monachi ecclesie cath' dunelm' ac sacre theologie professoris de dotacione ecclesie sponse cristi. Cf. Pantin, p. 365.

4. ff. 99ᵛ–110 Contra garrulos dotacionem ecclesie inpugnantes. [Q]uoniam propter quosdam falsos fratres . . . et honoribus preseruentur. Amen. Explicit contra garrulos dotacionem ecclesie inpugnantes. Cf. Pantin, p. 365.

5. ff. 110ᵛ–116 Ecclesia militans mater nostra . . . decipere sunt permissi.

Called 'Tractatus paruus de ecclesia militante etc' ' in the table of contents. Cf. Pantin, p. 365.

6. (a) ff. 116ᵛ–121 Incipit de perfeccione ecclesie graduali. Ad declaracionem huius materie planiorem oportet . . . Sicut in libro 4° historie ecclesiastice tripartite capitulo 2°. (b) f. 121 Anselmus de similitudinibus capitulo 131 diuidit mundum trifarie . . . hominis personaliter.[2]

Extracts from De perfectione vivendi in religione (Pantin, pp. 365–6): as Durham Cathedral, B. IV. 34, ff. 101/31–103ᵛ/35 and 100ᵛ/10–14. At f. 118/2 there is a reference back in the text, 'sic est superius dictum 26 o', which refers to f. 26/21, where 'O' is written in the margin. In the margin of f. 118 'et infra 121' refers to (b). f. 121ᵛ blank.

7. ff. 122–38 Tractaturus de supernaturali et preciosissimo eukaristie sacramento . . . de isto venerabilissimo sacramento. Explicit tractatus de preciosissimo eukaristie sacramento. Cf. Pantin, p. 365. ff. 138ᵛ–141ᵛ blank.

---

ff. ii+143+ii, foliated i–iii, 1–24, 24A, 25–141. A medieval foliator of ff. 1–120 numbered both 24 and 24A '24'. 170×120 mm. Written space c. 110×78 mm. c. 30 long lines. Frame ruling. Collation of ff. iii, 1–141: 1–2¹² 3¹²+1 leaf before 1 (f. 24) 4–5¹² 6⁸ 7¹² 8¹⁰ 9–10¹² 11⁸ 12¹² 13¹⁰ wants 9, 10, blank. Hair faces flesh within quires. A predominantly secretary hand, but with 8-shaped g and occasional long r. Red initials, 3-line or 2-line. Capital letters in the ink of the text filled or lined with red. Bound by C. Lewis, s. xix. Secundo folio *sicut in*.

---

[1] These words are difficult to understand if they are Uthred's own, unless the passage was written by a clerk to his dictation in the last year of his life, as is palaeographically possible, or is derived from a copy in Uthred's hand with the same leaf numbering.

[2] Cf. edn. *PL* clix. 679 (ch. 127) and Pantin, p. 376.

Written in England. Seen by George Plaxton at Trentham in 1715.[1] The binding bears the arms of the Duke of Sutherland and on f. i is 'This MS. is supposed to have come from the library at Stittenham. Sutherland': this is Stittenham, near Sheriff Hutton, Yorkshire. Duke of Sutherland (Trentham) sale at Sotheby's, 19 Nov. 1906, lot 1667, to Quaritch. J. M. Falkner sale at Sotheby's, 12 Dec. 1932, lot 476. Given by Sir John Noble.

A. IV. 34. *Notae in Cantica Canticorum* s. xii[1]

A medieval Durham book (*Catt. Vett.*, pp. 14, 90) which 'escaped the notice of Rud, and was rescued from a drawer in the library' by R. A. B. Mynors who described it in his *Catalogue*, p. 57, no. 74. 'Remarkable as a book which has survived for eight centuries without ever being bound.' On the construction of this book see A. I. Doyle, 'Further observations on Durham Cathedral MS. A. IV. 34', *Litterae Textuales, Essays presented to G. I. Lieftinck*, i (1972), 34–47, with facsimiles of ff. 6ᵛ–7, 44ᵛ–45, 52ᵛ–53.

A. IV. 35. *Beda, Vita Sancti Cuthberti* s. xii[2]

A medieval Durham book (*Catt. Vett.*, pp. 30, 107) alienated at some date, in a Sotheby sale, 27 June 1927, lot 606 (to Maggs for £360: the catalogue says it came from a library in the north of England), and bought back in 1936. Described by Mynors, p. 76, no. 131: pl. 46 shows four pages. Called Du in B. Colgrave's edition: described there, p. 32, and placed as a member of the large Bx group coming from Durham.

A. IV. 36. *Simeon Dunelmensis, etc.* s. xiii in.

Regnante apud northanymbros . . . (f. 4) renouante restituit. Exordium huius hoc est Dunelmensis ecclesie . . . non negligat. Aidanus . . . (f. 4ᵛ) Philippus. Gloriosi quondam Regis . . . (f. 107) susceptus est. Erat moribus insignis. statura et canicie uenerabilis . . . (f. 121ᵛ) assumeretur ad regnum.

The Historia Dunelmensis Ecclesiae, with continuation to 1144 (ff. 90–107) and, after a change of hand, the continuation by Geoffrey of Coldingham to 1199: cf. J. C. Davies in *Durham University Journal*, xliv (1951–2), 22–8. As far as f. 107, as edn. Arnold (RS lxxv, 1883), i. 7–11, 3, 17–160; from this point, as edn. Raine, *Historiae Dunelmensis Scriptores Tres* (Surtees Soc. ix (1839), 4–20). Bede's Death Song in English is at f. 25ᵛ. The list of bishops of Durham on f. 4ʳᵛ continues after Rannulfus in the main hand 'Gaufridus. Willelmus iiᵘˢ. Hugo. Philippus (1197–1207)'. f. 122ʳᵛ was left blank.

The text is in paragraphs, but without division into books. A table of 122 chapters was added on the flyleaves, ff. ivᵛ–vᵛ, in s. xiv. At the same time (?) numbers corresponding to the table were added in the margins of the text. A reader noted 'secundum librum P (?) prioris c. 133', f. 121, s. xv/xvi. Notes of this date and earlier, s. xiv–xv, are fairly numerous.

ff. v+122+i. ff. iii–v, 123 are medieval flyleaves: ff. iiiʳ, 123ᵛ were pasted down. 207 × 143 mm. Written space 135 × 88 mm. 23 long lines. Collation: 1⁸ 2⁶ 3–13⁸ 14⁶+1 leaf after 5 (f. 108) 15⁸ 16 five (ff. 118–22). Changes of hand at ff. 15, 107/10. Initials: (i) blue with red and green ornament, or (ff. 4ᵛ, 78ᵛ) green with red ornament: the 4-line space on f. 107 was long unfilled; (ii) 2-line, red, blue, or green, with ornament of one of

[1] Plaxton told Hearne about it: *Remarks and Collections of Thomas Hearne*, v (Oxford Historical Society, xlii, 1901, 31).

the other colours, or in the ink of the text: blue and green are not used in the same initial; (iii) in the list of bishops, f. 4ʳᵛ, 1-line, red, green, or blue. Continental binding, s. xix. *Secundo folio perlatum est.*

Written in England. Identifiable by the opening words of the second leaf with the 'Gesta Episcoporum Dunelmensium incomplete' listed in the medieval catalogue of Durham Cathedral priory (*Catt. Vett.*, p. 56 M: 2 fo prolatum (*sic*) est).[1] Erasures, ff. iiiᵛ, 121ᵛ, and a strip cut from the top of f. 1. 'liber sancti *chutberti*', f. 123, s. xv/xvi. Given to Matthew Parker by Robert Horne in 1569: 'Hunc Librum dedit Mattheo Cantuariensi Robertus Wintoniensis. vndecimo Mensis August. 1568 Quo tempore dedit M. Cant' R. Winton' historiam inpressam Matthei Westmonaster' ', f. 121ᵛ. 'Ex Museo H. Wijn', f. iv. 'bought at Leyden by Luchtman' and 'Thorpe 1836' inside the cover: no. 242 in Thorpe's catalogue for 1836, sold by him to Sir Thomas Phillipps. Phillipps MS. 9374. W. H. Robinson, catalogue 81 (1950), no. 43, with facsimile of f. 4ᵛ: bought by the Dean and Chapter.

B. III. 33. *Laurentius Dunelmensis, etc.* s. XII/XIII

1. ff. 1–22ᵛ Iponosticon laurentii monachi dunelmensis de ueteri et nouo testamento. Incipit de deo. Yponosticon id est memoriale. Principium rerum sine tempore . . . desinat hic in eum. Finit liber nonus. Explicit yponosticon Laurentii monachi de ueteri et nouo testamento.

Laurence of Durham, †1154, Hypognosticon, in nine books. Walther, no. 14729. This and fifteen other copies listed by A. Hoste in *Sacris Erudiri*, xi (1960), 255–8. Extracts only are in print in Surtees Society, lxx (1880), 62–71. Quires 1 and 3 are in disorder and the central bifolium of quire 3 is missing: the right order of leaves is 1, 3–8, 2, 9–16, 19, 20, 17, 18, 21, 22.

2. ff. 22ʳᵛ, 25–27ᵛ, 23 Incipit opusculum magistri Garnerii. capitulum primum. De adam sexto die creato . . . (*table of 36 chapters*) . . . Incipit prologus. Uersibus emensis his auctor basiliensis . . . si tenditis ad paradysum. [. . . . .] Amen.

Warnerius, Synodus, ed. P.-W. Hoogterp in *Archives d'histoire doctrinale et littéraire du moyen âge*, viii (1933), 374–97, from five manuscripts, not this. Walther, no. 20228. Apparently a CD text. The two last lines, ed. lines 589, 590, have been blotted out. Bk. 2 begins on f. 26 where there is a table of twenty-six chapters. f. 23ᵛ blank.

3. ff. 24ʳᵛ, 28 Quatuor eximias uirtutum proprietates . . . sicut ab hoste caue (*ends abruptly*).

Walther, no. 15311 (Hildebert). *PL* clxxi. 1055–61 col. 1/1, the first 230 lines only of the Libellus de quatuor virtutibus vitae honestae. f. 28ᵛ was blank, presumably: the lower half of the leaf has been cut off.

4 (added in s. xiii after art. 3). f. 28 [C]onuersus tristis sum forte diebus in istis. . . . Vt quod creatoris sim dignus et eius amoris (8 lines).

5. ff. 29–40ᵛ Opusculum Magistri Mathei Vindocin'. Spiritus inuidie cesset. non mordeat hostis. Introductiuum uindocinensis opus. Ne meas uiderer . . . De correctione. Sequitur de (*ends imperfectly*).

Matthew of Vendôme, Ars versificatoria. Ed. E. Faral, *Les arts poétiques du xiiᵉ et du xiiiᵉ siècle*, 1924, pp. 108–93, from five manuscripts, not this. The right order of leaves is

---

[1] A mistake for *perlatum*. The word *prolatum* does not occur near the beginning of Simeon's history.

29–34, 39, 35–8, 40. Four leaves are missing, two after f. 31 with edn. 127/4–139/last line, one after f. 34 with edn. 155/8–160/9, and one at the end with all after edn. 191/24. 'Secunda particula', f. 34, but the beginnings of parts 3 and 4 are not noticed on ff. 35, 37. The text here on f. 33ra/29–33va/1 is omitted in Faral's edition (p. 148).[1]

ff. iii+40+iii. 245 × 127 mm. Written space c. 188 × 95 mm. 2 cols. 54 lines. The first line of writing above the top ruled line. Collation: 1⁸ (ff. 1, 3–8, 2) 2⁸ 3⁸ wants 4, 5 (ff. 19, 20, 17, 18, 21, 22) 4 six (ff. 25–7, 23–4 (a bifolium), 28) 5⁸ wants 4, 5 (ff. 29–34) 6⁸ wants 1 and 8 (ff. 39, 35–8, 40). A very small hand changes at f. 39 to a slightly larger and less skilled one: punctuation includes the flex. Initials: (i) of art. 3, 15-line, handsome penwork Q, ornamented with foliage and small lions and—for the tail—a dragon; (ii, iii) 2-line (or more) and 1-line, blue or red, either plain or with ornament of the other colour. Binding of s. xviii, rebacked. Secundo folio (f. 3) Et male.

Written in France or the Netherlands. Ex-libris of the Cistercian abbey of Orval, Belgium (near the French frontier, east of Sedan): Liber sancte marie aureeuallis qui eum abstulerit anathema sit', f. 40ᵛ, s. xv. A later Orval ex-libris (s. xvii?), on f. 1 and mark 'MSS. d. 10' on f. 28. No. 88 in the 1675 Orval catalogue: cf. Scriptorium, xxvii (1973), 103. Acquired before 1918.

B. III. 34. *Kalendarium, etc.*　　　s. XIV/XV

A roll.

1. On the front, a calendar. Entries in red include 'Benedicti abbatis' at 21 Mar., and some fifteen English feasts, the least usual 'Fremundi regis' at 11 May. 'Machuti episcopi', 15 Nov.

2. On the dorse: (a) Wan þunder comes in ieniuer . . .; (b) In þe ȝer be iii daies 7 iii nyȝthes in þe wiche ȝif any man or woman ben geteþ (*sic*) withoute doute as seiþ seint bede. here bodys solden ben hoel . . .; (c) Post primam lunam epiphanie computa x dies . . .

(a) Prognostications from thunder, rubbed and in part revived by means of a reagent but still mostly legible by ultra-violet light. Four verses to a month—six for July—and six verses at the end, 'þank we ihesu þe heuene king . . . Amen amen for carite'; also, in the margin by another hand opposite the last nine lines, the couplet 'Wyne and mechel oþer good: and grete tempest in þe flod'.[2] *IMEV*, no. 4053: this copy noticed in the Supplement. (b). 29 Feb., 27 Mar., 13 Aug. (c). Rules for finding Easter and other feasts.

Four membranes. 2550 × 102 mm. Written in England. 'Tho: Rud' at the head of the roll. Presumably given by him.

C. III. 20. *Evangelia (fragm.)*　　　s. VII med.

See *CLA*, no. 147, Mynors, *Catalogue*, p. 17, no. 6, and T. D. Kendrick *et al.*, *Codex Lindisfarnensis*, 1960, p. 90.

C. III. 22. *Biblia*　　　s. XIII¹

A Bible with the usual books in the usual order, except that Psalms are in parallel versions, Gallican and Hebrew, Ecclesiasticus ends with the prayer of Solomon

---

[1] Information from Mr. A. J. Piper.
[2] þ is not distinguished from y in this couplet.

and Baruch (1-6) follows Jeremiah without heading on f. 291 as well as coming (1-5 only) after Lamentations, f. 295.

ff. 171ᵛ–172ᵛ, after Esther, were left blank. Job is on a quire of its own, ff. 173–82 (quire 19): the first three lines on f. 173 are 'Explicit liber Ecclesiasticus habens uersus duo milia sescentos. Incipit prologus . . . in librum Iob', so there seems to have been a change of order during the process of copying. f. 182ᵛ is blank after Job. Psalms are on four quires of their own, the Gallican version on the right on versos and on the left on rectos, as the running titles show, II PSAL I on versos and I PSAL II on rectos. f. 223ᵛ after Psalms is blank. Proverbs begins on a new quire, f. 224. 2 Maccabees ends imperfectly at 'semper aquam contrari' (15 : 40), f. 354ᵛ: one leaf is missing. Matthew begins on a new quire, f. 355. The capitula of 2 Peter end imperfectly, f. 435ᵛ. The two leaves remaining after this point contain Apocalypse 14: 4–18: 12 and Apocalypse 22: 4–21: the verso of f. 437 is blank.

Books are written continuously, except Ecclesiasticus which is in sixty-nine paragraphs, with headings in red. Corrections to the text in pencil, sometimes replaced by ink within a red frame. Marginalia are numerous in Matthew, but few elsewhere.

The prologues were originally fifty-two of the common set and thirty-two others noted here by *: Stegmüller, nos. 284 (the part of it on f. 1 has been mostly cut away), 285, 323, 328, 327 (to 1 Chronicles), 330, 332, Iudith uidua filia mesari . . . inter dothain balmon* (Isidore: PL lxxxiii. 147), 335+341, 342* (in red ink), 344+357+350*, 389*, 456*, 455*, 457, 468, 482, 487, 491, 492, 500, 504*, 510, 509*, 511, 515, 512, 519+517, 516*, 524, 522*, 526, 525*, 528, 527*, 530*, 529*, 534, 538, 535*, 539, 540*, 543, 545*, 551, 590, 607, 620, 624, 670*, 674*, 651* (paragraphs 1, 3, 4 in the order 3, 4, 1), 654*, 677, 661*, 676*, 685, 699, 707, 715, 734*, 728, 726*, 736, 737*, 742*, 747, 744*, 752, 765 (. . . ab urbe roma), 760*, 772, 770*, 780, 777*, 783, 793, 640, 631*, 809. Eight of them, nos. 677, 734, 728, 726, 742, 744, 777, and 631 are placed after, not before, the tables of chapters. Luke 1 : 1–4 is not treated as a prologue.

Further prologues were added at an early date: to Daniel, 494, continuing after 'aut odio', 'Sciendum autem nullum prophetam . . . et methodius sufficienter ei responderunt' +493*+In anno tertio regni ioachim qui . . . falsitatis*+Pater ioachim per m scribitur . . . et patri suo*, on f. 172ʳᵛ; 507 on an inserted slip of parchment, f. 321a; 532* in the margin of f. 332.

Capitula of OT books:[1] Genesis, Exodus, Joshua, Judges: series A forma a; Leviticus, Numbers: F; Deuteronomy: F forma a; Kings and Chronicles: unica forma b; Job: A; Ecclesiasticus, Wisdom, Isaiah: B; Maccabees: Ubi euersa ierusalem . . et in ierusolimam mitti. Capitula of NT books:[1] Matthew: as K;[2] Mark: a version of Cθ (etc.); Luke: as C(T); John: as PCθ; Romans: 'Scitis quia iudicium dei est. secundum ueritatem qui sine lege peccauerit . . . Obseruari debere ab eis qui hereses et scandala faciunt' (11 divisions); 1 Corinthians–Galatians: as R; Ephesians–Hebrews: as CH (etc.); Acts, 2 Peter: as BF (etc.); James, 1 Peter: as AB (etc.).

Stichometric notes after twelve books: Genesis (3700), Leviticus (2300), Numbers (5000), Joshua (6750), Judges (1750), 1 Kings (7300), 2 Kings (7200), 3 Kings (3000), 4 Kings (2250), Wisdom (1600), Ecclesiasticus (2600), Isaiah (3580).

Miscellaneous notes and scribbles include: 'Ego Iohannes de ho[. .][a3] Minor legi super hunc librum per totum annum integrum apud stanfordeam anno domini 1337 etc', pencilled on f. 26; 'W[i]llelmus Harlabi' (the r uncertain), pencilled on f. 223ᵛ, s. xiv; 'prior sancti leonardi', pencilled on f. 426ᵛ; 'Water Vachell' six times on f. 223ᵛ, s. xvi.

---

[1] The capitula of OT are printed in Biblia Sacra (in progress) and the capitula of NT by Wordsworth and White.
[2] C. III. 22 can be used to complete the text of K which is defective owing to the loss of a leaf: all from missa in mare (ch. 39) to et meretricibus (ch. 60) is missing.
[3] Hotona is likely.

Latin and English versions of proverbial sayings are on f. 401, s. xvi: 'scit(is) cito si scitis bene y^t thynge well done is twyse done; Canis in balneo A cowe in a cage; Asinus mauult stramen auro. A foole had rather have a bable than the tower of London'.

Six faded lines inside the cover, s. xv, appear to record a loan of four books by the prior of St. Leonard's (Stamford) to a Master Thomas: '[. . . . . . .] sancti leonardi et magister tho[. . . .] r[. . . . .] stat quod M' Thomas accepit de predicto priore libros infrascriptos [. . . .] sentenciarum 2 fo diapp[. . . . .] Item ex[posicionem super] epistolas pauli 2 fo prophetabant Item scriptum thome super primum sentenciarum 2 fo quin Item primam partem summe thome 2 fo cognicio'.

ff. 437+ii. ff. 438–9 are medieval binding leaves. *c.* 342 × 233 mm. Written space *c.* 220 × 137 mm. 2 cols. 51 lines. Pricks in both margins to guide ruling. The first line of writing above the top ruled line. Collation: 1–17^{10} 18^2 (ff. 171–2) 19–22^{10} 23^{12} wants 12, blank, after f. 223 24–34^{10} 35^{28} wants 22 after f. 354 36–42^{10} 43 seven (ff. 431–7). f. 321a is a slip inserted after 33^8. Traces of quire numbering: 'xvii cum ii foliis sequentibus' on f. 161, referring to ff. 161–72; 'xx' on f. 202^v; 'xxi' on f. 212^v; 'xxxii' on f. 323^v: the bifolium, quire 18, was not included in the numbering. Written by more than one scribe. Initials: (i) of books and principal psalms, and of Proverbs 25, red and blue, with ornament of both colours; (ii) of prologues, psalms, and the paragraphs of Ecclesiasticus, blue with red or green ornament or red with green or blue ornament; (iii) of chapters and psalm-verses and in lists of chapters, 1-line, red or blue. Capital letters in the ink of the text are stroked with red. The late medieval binding of thick bevelled boards, bare of leather, with one of two clasps remaining, was repaired and covered with new leather at the Bodleian Library in July 1947.[1] Secundo folio *occisione*.

Written in England. At the cell of Durham Cathedral Priory at Stamford, Lincolnshire, in 1337 and in s. xv (see above) and still in s. xvi[1], when ex-libris inscriptions were written on f. 439: 'Liber sancti leonardi Iuxta stanfo[. . .]'; 'Liber sancti Cuthberti cuius usus datur monasterio diui leonardi iuxta stanford[. . .] anno domini milesimo quingentesimo vice[. . . .]'; an inscription bearing the date 'mccccc(c)xxii'. 'D. 7. 32' and, later, 'XVIII. b. 3' in the library of the Brudenells of Deene Park, Corby, Northamptonshire: sold at Sotheby's, property of the late G. L. T. Brudenell, 12 Dec. 1966, lot 220, to Messrs. Maggs for £480. Bought by the Dean and Chapter in 1967.

C. III. 24. *Hermannus Contractus, Tabula arithmetica*   s. xii[1]

1. A sheet of parchment containing roman figures and symbols for fractions in twenty-six divisions horizontally and thirty-seven divisions vertically and at the foot six lines of partly illegible explanatory text, 'Ne [in] colligendis unciarum uel [m]inutiarum summulis ex pluralitate numerorum difficultas [minus] p[rompto] aliquando [cre]aretur [hęc quadri]latera ab ex[imio herimanno elaborata est figura] . . . [multi]plic[em si modo scriptum non fallat copulabis]'.

583 × 490 mm. Written space *c.* 570 × 460 mm. The dorse is blank. The same table for

[1] When I was at Deene Park a little before this time, a quire from the end of a copy of Petrus Comestor, Historia Scholastica, was lying loose in XVIII. b. 3. It was bound separately in 1947 and was lot 219 in the 1966 sale (to Maggs for £450, and now in Brussels, Bibliothèque Royale: the page with a sketch map of Jerusalem is reproduced in the sale catalogue). There is no reason to suppose that these leaves belong in any way with XVIII. b. 3: they had been put with it for safe keeping probably.

the multiplication of fractions is in St. John's College, Oxford, MS. 17 f. 48ᵛ (and also f. 57ᵛ) and the same text is on f. 49ᵛ there, whence the readings in square brackets are taken.

2. Three pieces kept with art. 1: (a) a photograph, reduced to c. 230×190 mm, of what seems to have been a companion sheet to that now at Durham, in which the rectangular space is divided into two triangles by a bar marked 'YPOTENVSA' culminating in a lion's head in the left-hand top corner: to the right of the head are five lines of text beginning 'In huius trigone' and at the foot are eight lines beginning 'Exigis a me', all written almost certainly by the same hand as the six lines in art. 1; (b) notes by J. T. Fowler dated 13 Nov. 1913; (c) eleven pages of typescript by Miss Frances Yeldham made in Apr. 1927.

(a). The same table is in St. John's College, Oxford, 17, f. 49 (and also f. 58), and the same texts are on ff. 49ᵛ–50 there, except that the first of them 'In huius trigone . . .' is shortened at the end by an 'et sic in ceteris' in place of some fifty words in (a). (b) is headed 'J. T. Fowler. Notes on framed MS. Chart of Weights and measures hanging in Loft near Librarian's desk'. It refers to the original of (a), not to art. 1. (c) refers to the original of (a) and to the tables and text in the St. John's manuscript, ff. 48ᵛ–50. Miss Yeldham did not know of art. 1. She says that the original of (a) 'when first found by Dr. (Charles) Singer in February, 1927, was pasted on linen and very roughly nailed to a wooden frame measuring 40″ by 24″ ', that it was sent to London for her use, and that she examined it in Apr. 1927. It is now missing.

C. III. 25. *Bernardus Dorna, etc.* s. XIII med.

1. ff. 1–9 Incipit libellus domini bernardi dorna. Quoniam nefanda subdolaque hominum caliditas appellauit. quod quasi penitus . . . dicere incipiamus. Tractaturi diuina fauente gratia de libellorum compositione . . . maliuole potiantur.

Printed by Wahrmund, *Die Summa Libellorum des Bernardus Dorna*, Quellen zur Geschichte des römisch-kanonischen Processes im Mittelalter, 1. i (1905). Dolezalek lists fifteen manuscripts, but none in Britain.

2. f. 9 De acusacionibus et commodo in criminibus puniendis sit procedendum. Quoniam rei pu. interest ut crimina non remaneant inpunita . . . uel alio modo l. ult'. Salarium aduocati iiiiᵒʳ modis petitur condic. certi. si certum est.

Five paragraphs following immediately on art. 1.

3. ff. 9ᵛ–10ᵛ Questio. In quadam ecclesia erant duo canonici eiusdem nominis . . .

Questions and answers in paragraphs headed 'questio', 'contra', 'solucio'. The second begins 'Quidam habens prebendam', the third 'Papa commisit potestatem talem archidiacono parisien'', the fourth 'Vacante quadam ecclesia', and the fifth 'Quidam episcopus impetrauit': this last ends imperfectly.

ff. 10. 297×202 mm. Written space 233×160 mm. 2 cols. 50–76 lines. One quire of 10 leaves: cf. C. III. 26. Written in France or, possibly, England.

C. III. 26. *Damasus, Brocarda* s. XIII med.

1. ff. 1–5ᵛ Solucio sentencie excommunicacionis late a suo iudice ante app. semper est obediendum . . . non posset aliter probari.

Cf. S. Kuttner, *Repertorium der Kanonistik*, pp. 419–22: 'zwischen 1210 und 1215 geschrieben'. The first leaf with the first seventeen brocarda is missing: the remaining text corresponds to Bodleian, Laud misc. 646 ff. 100ᵛ–110. f. 6 is blank.

2 (added, s. xiii). f. 6ᵛ Notes on Prescriptio and Negatoria.

3 (added, s. xiv¹). f. 6ᵛ Patris sapiencia. veritas diuina . . . (27 lines). *RH*, no. 14725.

ff. 6. 297 × 195 mm. 3 cols (f. 1) and 4 cols. Three bifolia, probably from the end of a manuscript and no doubt leaves 2–7 of a quire of eight leaves.

Written in France or England and (art. 3) England. C. III. 25, 26 are almost certainly two quires of one manuscript, possibly the 'Summa Tancredi cum aliis in uno quaterno' listed in *Catt. Vett.*, p. 36 H: cf. 36 I.¹

C. III. 27. *Dictionarium, etc.*   s. xiv med.

ff. 1–4 are from an alphabetical repertory (letter A), with references mainly to legal sources. f. 1, hard to read, begins in Alimenta. The entry for Anglia begins 'Anglia tenetur in feudum ab ecclesia romana nota hostiensis' and ends 'Anglici fortiter bibunt nota xxxii q. ii c.'. f. 4ᵛ ends in Argumentum. An addition under Anglia is 'In Anglia non bibitur temperate [. . . . .]'. f. 5 is a half leaf or wide strip with notes, mainly on confession. The text on the verso has been crossed out.

ff. 1–4 are two bifolia of paper, numbered in a medieval hand X–XIII. 275 × 190 mm. Written space 210 × 140 mm. 2 cols. *c.* 55 lines. Written in England in current anglicana.

C. III. 28. *Miscellanea*   s. xiv¹

A quire of a notebook of scholastic philosophy and theology, hard to read at both ends. The longer pieces are: ff. 5–7 Notandum quod proporcio est habitudo 2ᵃʳᵘᵐ rerum eiusdem generis ad inuicem in eo quod altera maior vel minor est . . . Ergo omnis modus est ex proporcione maioris inequalitatis. Expliciunt regule proporcionum; ff. 8ᵛ–10 Qualitas dicitur secundum quam quales dicimur qualitatis quatuor sunt species . . .; ff. 11ᵛ–12 [Questio] (?) est ista vtrum sciencia sacre scripture sit vtilis viatori ad beatitudinem prosequendam arguitur quod non quia sacra scriptura ex se sine caritate . . . f. 3ᵛ is mostly empty.

ff. 12. *c.* 208 × 125 mm. Written space *c.* 190 × 120 mm. 49 long lines (f. 5). One quire. Written in England in current anglicana.

Hunter 15, part 1. *P. Comestor, Historia scholastica*   s. xiii¹

(*begins imperfectly*) alioquin egrediatur ignis de rampno . . . et ierosolimite dis- (*ends imperfectly*).

The first words are in Judges 9 and the last in 2 Maccabees 1, edn. *PL* cxcviii. 1281/52 and 1521/6. One leaf is missing between these points. Red and blue running numbers in the margins in arabic figures probably contemporary with the text run from '123' on f. 1 to '259' on f. 51. Marginalia in anglicana, s. xiv.

¹ Laud misc. 646 begins with Tancred's De ordine iudiciario.

ff. 51. 305 × 225 mm. Written space 230 × 160 mm. 2 cols. 46 lines. Writing above top ruled line. Pricks in both margins to guide ruling. Collation: 1¹² wants 4 2–3¹² 4⁸ 5¹⁰ wants 9, 10. 2-line initials, blue or red with ornament of the other colour: many have been cut out. Running titles, chapter numbers, and running numbers in red and blue. Binding of s. xix.

Written in England.

Hunter 15, part 2. *Three Kings of Cologne, etc. (in English)*

s. xv in.

1. ff. 1–32ᵛ In the first chapitre of this booke . . . (f. 3) come ouer þe see. Incipit primum capitulum. Sithe of thise worshipeful kynges: all the worlde . . . with hem diuerse marchaundise and amonge (*ends imperfectly*).

The text in forty-four chapters is fuller and nearer to the Latin of John of Hildesheim than are the abbreviated English versions printed by C. Horstmann, *The Three Kings of Cologne* (EETS 85), 1886. It begins like the Latin with a synopsis of each chapter (ff. 1–3). After 'euery ȝere' (f. 31ᵛ col. 2/20: edn., p. 150/36) the text is unlike Horstmann's English versions, but renders the Latin printed by him on pp. 302/25–306/17.

f. 16ᵛ ends in chapter 22 'But whan', followed by the catchword 'they founde' and f. 17 begins in chapter 33 'And they supposen and verreily byleuen in al the Est' (cf. edn., pp. 71/19 and 115/1): probably eight leaves are missing. f. 27ᵛ ends 'and subdekenes haue wyues and the sey' and f. 28 begins 'good nyght' (cf. edn., pp. 284/2 (Latin) and 140/25): two leaves are missing.

2. ff. 33–34ᵛ (*begins imperfectly*) wykkede syknesses. ȝe though his merce were right good . . . but they leuen of: they shall not astirte the strook. Explicit.

A regimen of health in eight chapters. The first words are in ch. 5.

3. ff. 35–44ᵛ Redde Rationem villificationis tue. My dere frendes ȝe shullen vnderstonde . . . in the sighte of god. Cui honor et gloria in secula seculorum amen. This sermon' was preched at poules Cros of Mayster Thomas Wymbelton' the ȝere of grace M¹' ccc iiii×ˣ.

Fifteen manuscripts, not this, listed in the edition of Wimbledon's sermon by I. K. Knight, 1967. f. 37ᵛ ends 'ferthynge he' and f. 38 begins 'was pore' (cf. edn., lines 259 and 534: two leaves are missing). The outer half of f. 39 has been cut off with the text in edn., lines 673–713. Edn., lines 537–75 are not in this copy which reads (f. 38ʳᵃ/6) 'This seith the doctour. Here endeth . . .'. Some marginalia in the hand which wrote the table of contents on f. 3.

4. ff. 44ᵛ–48ᵛ A tretys made vpon the vii dedly synnes. in manere of a confession'. And euery synne is diuyded in iii parties. thought. speche. and dede. [E]uery-body that shal been confessed . . . taken in charge. by seruice (*ends imperfectly in a section beginning* In slouthe by dede: *catchword* or by office).

Jolliffe, C. 5.

5. Scribbles in the margins, s. xvi/xvii, include: f. 4, Gerald / the great hoast of the earle of Desmond. / The great power of / England. the hoast of / John fitz Thomas his hoast / did more harme than all / the rest John fitz Redmond / he was drowned himselfe; f. 18, [.]yoʳ loving son to comand 'This is michell is hand' Mʳ Forrest I Comend my vnto yoʷ and not forgetting yoʳ gente bed-fellowe my mother etc the case of my wrytting vnto yoʷ is that I want paper pen

and enke wherfore I must writte one this gent' booke I pray yoʷ Giue my that I want and will proue I cannott giue that I want; f. 27, Sound fourth / a balat / Sound fourth / trompettes / and stricke / vp your dromes / likewise sute / vp yoʷʳ cannons / heere comes a / noble Priste the Recheth prest that euer / Rodde . . .; f. 43, A mouse coullered garran wᵗʰ white heires in his forhead nowe of thadge of eight or nyne yeares or thearbouts gelded and stoullen from me at the last yeare of thinfection then by[ing] in the Contry at Balleclement nere Tollowsh (Tallow, co. Waterford).

ff. 48, bound after part 1. 303 × 215 mm. Written space 215 × 143 mm. 2 cols. 36 lines (44 lines on ff. 33–4). Every twelfth ruled line is extended into the margins. Collation: 1–3⁸ 4⁸ wants 4, 5 after f. 27 5 four (ff. 31–4, the two outer bifolia) 6⁸ wants 4, 5 after f. 37 and the outer half of f. 39 7⁸. Written in a good anglicana, the same throughout (secretary *r*). Spaces left for initials, 5-line down to 1-line. Long without binding, as appears from the rubbed state of ff. 1 and 48ᵛ. Secundo folio *goynge home*.

Written in England. A note of contents, f. 3, in a good hand of s. xvi includes as the last item 'A tract in French', now missing. Much scribbled on in Ireland in blue and brown inks, s. xvi/xvii, mainly, it seems, by James Forrest of Youghal, co. Cork, who describes himself as 'studient' in the margin of f. 42ᵛ. 'This indenture made at youghull the fiftinne day of december 1606 . . . Between James forest of youghull and Richard his brother . . .' is on f. 15, 'This is the book of Mary Benson of the' on f. 17ᵛ, and 'edmond forest' on f. 30ᵛ: see also above art. 5.

Hunter 30. *Defensor, Liber scintillarum; etc.*   s. xiv²

A collection of pieces useful to a priest.

1. pp. 1–51 Propicio cristo fratres karissimi. ita secundum . . . (p. 2) sicut stelle in perpetuas eternitates quod ipse . . . in secula seculorum . . . (*table of 82 unnumbered chapters*) . . . De caritate. Dominus dicit in euuangelio. maiorem caritatem nemo habet . . . nutritur et pascitur. Explicit liber scintillarum deo gracias.

Defensor, ed. H.-M. Rochais, *CC* cxvii (1957), 1–234. He lists this and 284 other copies in *Scriptorium*, iv (1950), 296–305. Chapters are numbered in the text to 81: ch. 33, De doctoribus, is not included in this numeration. Throughout, the sentences of each chapter are numbered in the margin and some of them are provided with a reference to the Bible, for example the first sentence of ch. 2 has '1 mᵗ v' against it. The sermon-like prologue is not one noticed by Rochais in *RB* lix (1949), 137–56.

2. pp. 51–61 Quia sacerdotis officium principaliter uersatur . . . quales descripti sunt . . . amen. Explicit summa de officio sacerdotis.

A summary 'ad omnium vtilitatem et maxime simplicium sacerdotum erudicionem' in ten paragraphs. Glorieux, no. 14*ec* (pseudo-Aquinas, ed. Vives, xxviii. 445).

3. pp. 61–70 Incipit speculum ecclesie compositum a fratre hug' de sancto victore iuxta parisius. Rubrica. Dicit apostolus ad ephesios ii induite vos armatura dei . . . recenta erunt. amen. Explicit speculum ecclesie (*etc.*).

Glorieux, no. 2*aw* (Hugh of St. Cher). Printed often.

4. pp. 71–4 Vir quidam extiterat dudum heremita Philbertus . . . Cum ipsius labii statim Amen Edat. Explicit disputacio corporis et anime.

Visio Philberti (Walther, no. 20421) in *c.* 382 lines. Twenty-three copies of the extended version, beginning *Vir quidam*, are listed by H. Walther, *Das Streitgedicht in der lateinischen Literatur des Mittelalters*, Quellen und Untersuchungen zur lateinischen Philologie des Mittelalters, v (1920), 213.

5. pp. 74–84 Incipit summa de trinitate et ordinacione mundi. De creacione rerum . . . De officio lamentacionis (*28 titles, in error for 29, the first*, De trinitate, *having been left out*). De trinitate Rubrica. De Trinitate hoc tenendum est quod in vna essencia . . . pro salute generis humani. Amen. Explicit summa (*etc.*).

Also in Cambrai 417 (393), f. 199ᵛ.

6. pp. 84–101 Incipit summa de foro penitenciali Breuis et vtilis et valde necessaria et maxime sacerdotibus super hiis noticiam non habentibus. In primis debet sacerdos interrogare penitentem . . . expugnauit amalech. Explicit summa de foro penitenciali.

Bloomfield, no. 429: this copy listed. Cf. Schulte ii. 533 and *MMBL* i. 238. Ends here with sections on the Creed, the Lord's Prayer, and the Gospels.

7. pp. 101–2 Tabula ad Canonem. Rubrica. Ut negligenciis circa sacramentum misse . . . sed quem direxit hec tabula. oret pro scribentis anima. Amen. Explicit tabula ad Canonem. deo gracias.

8. pp. 102–14 Incipit summa domini Berengarii Cardinalis Episcopi Tusculani et domini pape summi penitenciarii. Rubrica. Quoniam circa confessiones animarum pericula . . . cognoscere et non flere. Amen. Explicit summa (*etc.*).

Bloomfield, no. 804: this copy listed.

9. pp. 115–32 Incipit liber miserie condicionis humane editus a Lothario sanctorum Sergii et Bachi diacono Card' qui postea Innocencius tercius appelatus est. Rubrica. Domino patri karissimo P. dei gracia Portuensi Episcopo Lotharius . . . humilis exaltetur. De miseria hominis Rubrica. Quare de uulua . . . sulphur ignis in secula seculorum. Explicit liber miserie condicionis humane Amen.

Ed. M. Maccarrone, 1955; *PL* ccxvii. 701–46. The text is divided into unnumbered chapters, but not into parts. A table of unnumbered chapters on ff. 132–3 shows a division into three parts of 30, 40, and 19 chapters.

10. pp. 133–44 Incipit viridarium consolacionis de viciis et virtutibus. Rubrica. Quoniam ut petrus apostolus sit spiritu sancto . . . facie ad faciem. ad quam nos perducat . . . amen. Explicit viridarium consolacionis. deo gracias.

Bloomfield, no. 823 (Jacobus Beneventanus, O.P.): this copy listed. Printed in *Florilegium Casinese*, iv. 263–315.

11. p. 144 Incipit summa breuissima. composita per magistrum Iohannem andree in quarto libro decretalium. minimum doctorem decretorum. Cristi nomen inuocans . . . ex litteris.

Printed often: *GKW* 1742–56; *Tract. Univ. Juris*, ix, ff. 2–3ᵛ. Cf. *MMBL* i. 293.

12. pp. 145–50 Postulat a me vestra dileccio ut de articulis fidei et ecclesie sacramentis . . . Primus igitur articulus est . . . ad quam gloriam nos perducat.

Aquinas. *Opuscula*, ed. Mandonnet (1927), iii. 1–18.

13. (*a*) pp. 150–62 Credo in vnum deum . . . Primum et necessarium est cuilibet cristiano . . . Et quod venturus est ad iudicium Etc. Explicit symbolum de articulis et sacramentis Ec(clesie). (*b*) pp. 162–6 Incipit oracio dominica. Pater noster. Vt in summa exponatur sciendum est . . . a malo. Pater noster etc. Formam orandi breuem et utilem . . . pro peccato commisso per gladium.

(*a*). Aquinas. *Opuscula*, ed. Mandonnet, iv. 349–88, continuing for four lines after 'imprimatur'. (*b*). Only the first paragraph, 'Ut . . . a malo', is from Aquinas on Pater Noster, ed. Mandonnet, iv. 411.

14. pp. 166–9 Omelia de v regionibus. Rubrica. Negociamini dum venio verb' patris. Vnigenitus dei sol iusticie . . . decembris die lune.

15. pp. 169–82 Sequitur vivendi phil*osophice* ordo que qui seruauerit . . . Scribit enim venerabilis iohannes ispalensis caresie hyspanorum regine libellum breuem . . .

Fifty-seven paragraphs, the first, Aristotle's letter to Alexander, lifted from bk. 1, and the second, on quadrupeds, from bk. 4 of Thomas Cantimpratensis, De natura rerum. Other paragraphs are from bks. 10, 15, 17–19 of De natura rerum, and perhaps all are from this source, except para. 6, 'Alexander capta gasa . . .', para. 7, 'De reclusione xii tribuum et de morte alexandri. Rubrica. Itaque cum venisset alexander . . .', para. 53, on the signs of the zodiac, and para. 56, with two questions, the second of them 'Si potest deus omne impossibile'.

16. pp. 182–8 Incipiunt meditaciones Bernardi. Multi multa sciunt . . . vnum eundemque deo glorie ihesum cristum . . . per omnia secula seculorum amen. Expliciunt meditaciones sancti bernardi `deo gracias´.

Pseudo-Bernard. *PL* clxxxiv. 485–508. A couplet, s. xv, on p. 188, 'Nulla (*sic*) sanctorum sine pena glorificatur Ergo nil passis. gloria nulla datur': against it 'Salue' and below it in the same hand 'Hexham cognomen Willelmus nomen et omen'.

17. pp. 189–204 Incipit liber vii^us de compendio theologie . . . Septimus liber qui agit de finali Iudicio . . . fiducialiter expectamus. Explicit liber vii^us compendium theologie. Laus sit tibi criste quoniam liber explicit iste.

Thirty 'rubrice', the first 'de purgatorio' and the last 'de enumeracione celestium gaudiorum', a scholastic reworking of bk. 7 of the popular Compendium theologicae veritatis of Hugh of Strasbourg, O.P. (Glorieux, no. 6*dq*). The divisions are listed on pp. 205–6: . . . Explicit liber vii^us cum suis Rubricis Et cum articulis qui sunt numero Centum. Deo gracias qui incepit et perfecit. Some chapters are extended, for example that on indulgences, which contains a story of the value of the Portiuncula indulgence heard by the writer when he was at Assisi in the year 1301.

18. pp. 207–54 Do*min*e pondera fugere dilitiscendo uoluisse . . . manus leuet.

Gregory, Pastoral Care (inc. *Dum pondera*). *PL* lxxvii. 13–128. Headings not filled in after p. 216. Damage from damp at the top inner corner begins on p. 239 and gets worse.

19. pp. 254–5 De indumentis sacerdotalibus. Que cherubyn propiciatorium aspiciunt . . . vt quicumque ligaueris super t. etc.

20 (no break after art. 19). pp. 255/3 lines from foot–256 Quindecim singnis ante iudicium futuris que beatus Ieronimus dicit se reperisse in annalibus iudeorum . . . se fingunt nichil prosunt etc. pp. 257–8 left blank.

21. A binding leaf, pp. iii, iv, has on the verso the first fourteen lines of a docu-

ment of which not the least trace can be seen by ordinary light. By ultra-violet light '[. . .] S[. . .]uobis dilecti filii Capitulum ecclesie M[. . . .]' can be read in the first line, and some uncertain names further down which, like the hand, look Germanic. The blank recto was used later for a table of contents headed 'Hec sunt contenta in isto bag' ', but only arts. 1–3 were listed.

ff. ii+129+ii, paginated i–iv, 1–262. For pp. iii, iv see above, art. 21. 270 × 195 mm. Written space 230 × 150 mm, but less at first and more later. Frame ruling. 53–66 long lines (art. 4 in 2 cols.). Collation: 1–6¹² 7¹⁰ 8–10¹² 11¹² wants 11, blank. Several hands: changes at pp. 53, 87, 146, 189. Arts. 11–16 in textura and the rest in cursiva: r is a descender on pp. 87–144, 213–56. 4-line, 3-line, or 2-line red initials. Binding of s. xviii. Secundo folio *sectamini*.

Written probably in France. 'Iste liber est Monaldi degans archid' vesalin' (Vezaley?) sit in dei nomine amen', p. 258, s. xiv²: cf. p. iv, where a similar notice has been erased. In (northern) England not much later, when 'liber fratris Willelmi de bridlington' was written on p. iv, s. xiv/xv: see also, above, art. 16.

Hunter 57. *Augustinus* s. XII¹

1. ff. 3–98 Incipit liber Sancti Augustini episcopi super i'o'hanne'm' de caritate. Ab eo quod scriptum est. Quod erat ab initio . . . (f. 3ᵛ) precepta eius seruemus. Expliciunt capitulares. Incipit prologus. Meminit sanctitas uestra euangelium secundum iohannem . . . (f. 4) intelligatis loquamur. Explicit prologus. Incipit sermo primus . . . Quod erat ab initio . . . cristo prędicanti. Explicit sermo xᵘˢ aurelii episcopi in epistola sancti iohannis apostoli.

PL xxxv. 1977–2062. Many corrections and changes of punctuation in a good backsloping hand, s. xii: omissions are fitted in by erasing and rewriting on specially ruled pencil lines. On f. 98 the corrector wrote 'Explicit Tractatus sancti Augustini episcopi de caritate'. 'D.M.', f. 4, is a *nota bene* mark.

2. ff. 98–104ᵛ Incipit Augustinus contra v hereses. Debitor sum 'fratres' fateor non necessitate . . . et deus isáác. et deus iacob. (*ends imperfectly*).

PL xlii. 1101–5/30. Many corrections, as in art. 1.

3 (added in s. xii²). ff. 1–2ᵛ Sententi'a' beati Augustini de caritate. Diuinarum scripturarum multiplicem abundantiam . . . sed etiam breuis.

PL xxxix. 1533–5 (Sermo 350).

ff. ii+104+ii. 225 × 140 mm. Written space 170 × 95 mm. 26 long lines ruled with a hard point (ff. 1, 2 pencil). Collation: 1 two 2¹⁰ 3–12⁸ 13⁴ (ff. 93–6) 14⁸. Quires 2–14 numbered at the end i–xiiiᵘˢ. Arts. 1, 2 are in a fairly large but poor hand. Initials: (i) 2-line (3-line, f. 98), red (with green edging on ff. 3–4); (ii) 1-line, red or green. Binding of s. xviii. Secundo folio *dam sic* (f. 4) or *et in qua* (f. 2).

Written perhaps in England, but not by an English-trained scribe. In England in s. xii, as appears from the script of the corrections and art. 3. Belonged to the Augustinian abbey of Hexham, Northumberland: 'Liber sancti Andree de Hextildesham', f. 3, at the foot, s. xiv.

Hunter 58. *Exceptiones patrum, etc.*   s. xiv med.

1. ff. 1–29^v Indexes to art. 2*a–f*: (*a*) ff. 1–3^v Tabula super extractum de libris Alexandri Nequam de Naturis rerum secundum fratrem Oliuerum de Wakefeld iuxta litteras alphabeti; (*b*) ff. 4–6 Tabula super extractum (1) Remigii de anima (2) Rabani de laude crucis (3) decem omeliarum Cesarii. (4) Amonicionis Cesarii ad sororem suam et (5) octo omeliarum Eusebii ad monachos a 53 folio incipiens ad 96 folium; (*c*) ff. 6–10 Tabula super 81 epistolas Ambrosii. (2) Item de Nabute. (3) Item de excessu fratris sui. (4) Item de bono mortis. (5) Item in pastorali. (6) Item de ysaac et anima. (7) Item de fuga seculi. (8) Item de vita beata Iachob. (9) Item de paradyso. (10) Item in apologeticon dauid. (11) Item de sancta virginitate. (12) Item ad viduas. (13) Item de virginibus li. 4. (14) Item de exhortacione virginitatis. (15) Item de lapsu virginis consecrate. (16) Item de violatore. (17) de lamentacione super eis.¹ (19) Item de sacramentis. (20) Item ad ecclesiam vercell'. que tabula incipit a folio 99 et terminatur folio 200; (*d*) ff. 10–18 Tabula super extractum Ambrosii de incarnacione verbi. (2) Item Ambrosii de primo et 2° libro de penitencia. (3) Item eiusdem de tribus questionibus salomonis. (4) Item super exhortacionem ad pastores ecclesie. (5) Item super librum qui intitulatur annotaciones Augustini in iob. (6) Item super excepcionem ex libro Augustini de cathezizandis rudibus. (7) Item Cassiodori super psalterium. Et incipit hec tabula a folio 209 et terminatur ad folium 313; (*e*) ff. 18–24^v Incipit Tabula super extractum de verbis augustini super psalterium a folio 314 incipiens et terminatur ad folium 381² secundum ordinem alphabeti et vocalium 5; (*f*) ff. 25–29^v In ista tabula continentur cotaciones super dicta Ieronimi (1) in maiori breuiario et (2) in Minori super Psalterium secundum ordinem alphabeti et secundum ordinem 5 vocalium et incipit folio 423 et terminatur folio 459.

In each index the references are by page and by letter divisions corresponding to letters in art. 2: for example, 'Bonitas 449 h' refers to the present f. 221 and the passage opposite the letter H in its margin. (*f*) ends imperfectly in the letter X (Cristus). There was no doubt a now missing index to art. 2*g*.

2. ff. 30–128^v, 132–231^v Extracts from the works indexed in art. 1: see there for the titles of all but *c* (18) and *g* (1–3).

(*a*)	ff. 30–54	6.	ff. 96^v–98^v
		7.	ff. 98^v–100^v
(*b*) 1.	ff. 55–59^v	8.	ff. 100^v–103^v
2.	ff. 59^v–61^v	9.	ff. 103^v–106
3.	ff. 61^v–68^v	10.	ff. 106–8
4.	ff. 68^v–71	11.	ff. 108–113^v
5.	ff. 71–76^v	12.	ff. 114–16
(*c*) 1.	ff. 77–86	13.	ff. 116–17^v
2.	ff. 86–7	14.	ff. 117^v–119
3.	ff. 87^v–93	15.	f. 119^{rv}
4.	ff. 93–6	16.	ff. 119^v–120
5.	f. 96^v	17.	f. 120

¹ *c* (18) is omitted: cf. art. 2.
² In fact art. 2*e* ends on the page numbered 380.

(c) 18. f. 120^{rv}, from Ambrose, De mysteriis.

    19. ff. 120^v–122

    20. ff. 122–128^v

(d) 1. f. 132^{rv}

    2. ff. 132^v–135^v

    3. ff. 136–7

    4. f. 137^{rv}

    5, 6. Missing. They were on a quire (of 6 leaves?) after quire 12.

    7. ff. 139–177^v. Two leaves are missing.

(e)   ff. 177^v–207^v. Three leaves are missing.

(f) 1. ff. 208–224^v

    2. ff. 224^v–225^v

(g) 1. ff. 225^v–226^v, from 'Ieronimus Cypriano presbitero de Ps. 89'.

    2. ff. 227–8, from 'Ieronimus super ecclesiasten'.

    3. ff. 229–231^v 'Extraccio quedam beati Ambrosii super beati immaculati'.

d (7), *e*, and *f* (1) are ascribed to Thomas de Dockyng in headings: f. 139 'Non est continuacio verborum Cassiodori set fidelis excepcio quam compilauit fr' Th' de Dochr' (*?sic*, by misreading of Dock')'; f. 177^v 'Istam excepcionem compilauit fr' Th. de Dock' ex tractatu sancti Augustini super Psalterium'; f. 224^v 'Explicit excepcio de maiori breuiario Ieronimi. quam compilauit fr' Th' de dock' '. These three pieces begin: (f. 139) 'Cassiodorus in prefacione super Psalterium. Vt quidam de homero ait'; (f. 177^v) 'Tuncque apud constantinopolim prescianus grammatice artis'; (f. 208) 'Ieronimus in prefacione maioris breuiarii P'. Quamuis dauid omnes Psalmos cantasset.

Slips added after ff. 32, 213, 214, 229. f. 54^v blank. f. 138^v left blank at the end of art. 12 has an index to art. 2 like those in art. 1, added in s. xiv: page references range from 84 to 237.

The main hand (?) added a note in the margin of f. 118^v referring to 'lingua' in the text: Nota de sancta abba que labia superiora monialium suarum fertur abscidisse.

3. Pieces, other than the extracts forming art. 2 and the indexes to them, up to the point where the medieval pagination ends: (*a*) f. 129^{rv} (*begins imperfectly*: one leaf missing) peccata in ipso per mali^e frigiditatem latencia declarare . . . possidebit ad quam . . . ; (*b*) ff. 130–131^v Cum ieiunasset quadraginta diebus . . . M^t 4. Notandum autem est quod duplex est ieiunium . . . quadragesimale ieiunium est decime temporis solutum (?); (*c*) ff. 232–236^v Graciam dei recipiat. Ad corinth' 6. Karissimi domini caritas exigit et hortatur sacra doctorum professio vt qui iuxta gracias . . . ; (*d*) ff. 236^v–243 Short pieces (themes for sermons ?), ten in all, on texts from John 1: 7–12, Potestatem, Dedit (2), In propria venit, Venit, In propria venit, Vt testimonium perhiberet, Venit, Non, Erat lux; (*e*) f. 243 Erunt signa in sole . . . Luc' 21. Karissimi cristo domino in terris cum hominibus conuersante . . . (*ends abruptly*); (*f*) ff. 244^v–248 Placuit deo et translatus est. ecclesiastici 44. Sacrosancta racione ecclesie . . . quod nobis concedit etc.

(*a*, *b*) are lenten sermons. 'Ox' against the beginning of (*b*) indicates perhaps that it was preached at Oxford. (*c–f*) if not (*a*, *b*), are covered by the entry in the table of contents on f. 1, 'Item diuerse collaciones bone et vtiles. cum tabula'. (*e*, *f*) are in a smaller and more current hand than the rest. ff. 243^v–244, 248^v–249^v are blank.

4. ff. 250–72 Claro tam sancto quam meritis . . . non procedunt. Incipiunt

capitula huius libri . . . (*table of 76 chapters*) . . . (f. 251ᵛ) Incipit de capite. Fecit deus hominem ad ymaginem . . . nomine sociatur. Explicit rethorica moralis de officiis membrorum humani corporis edita a magistro Nicholao de sanctis cognomine et origine campanus.

The preface is addressed to Pope Clement (VI?). f. 272ᵛ blank.

5. Leaves extracted from the old binding have been assembled at the end: (*a*) ff. 274, 275, strips from a dictionary of canon law, letter A, s. xiv; (*b*) ff. 276–278ᵛ, leaves from a Psalter (Ps. 118) in a large English hand, s. xii/xiii: written space 195 × 125 mm: 18 long lines to the page: initials (i) 2-line, red or blue, with ornament of the other colour, or green with red ornament and (ii) 1-line, blue, red, or green.

Offsets, probably of (*b*), show on ff. iiiʳ, 273ᵛ.

ff. iv+272+viii. ff. 273–8 are medieval binding leaves: for 274–8 see art. 5. ff. 30–137, 139–248 have a contemporary pagination 3–200, 203–220, 233–56, 261–332, 337–8, 341–80, 423–77, 482–505, 510–18: the gaps come after ff. 128, 138, 150, 186, 187, 207, 231, 243. The slip inserted after f. 229 is numbered on the verso '473'. 225 × 160 mm. Written space *c.* 180 × 115 mm. Mostly in 36–44 long lines. Collation: 1–2¹² 3⁸ wants 6–8 after f. 29 4¹² wants 1 before f. 30 5–11¹² 12¹⁶ wants 5 after f. 128 and 16, blank(?), after f. 138 13¹² 14¹² wants 1, 2 before f. 151 15–16¹² 17¹² wants 3, 4 after f. 186 and 6 after f. 187 18–20¹² 21 two (ff. 230–1: the old pagination shows that two leaves are missing after f. 231) 22¹² 23⁶ (ff. 244–9) 24¹² 25¹² wants 12, blank, after f. 272. *Ad hoc* leaf signatures are partly cut off in the bottom right corner of versos and the bottom left corner of rectos of quires 4–8. They consist of numbers from 1 to 5 in matching pairs, beginning with 1 on the first verso and second recto through to 5 on the fifth verso and sixth recto. The numbers are plain in quire 4 and have one horizontal stroke through them in quire 5. After this, too much has been cut off by the binder for us to detect differences from quire to quire. Written in anglicana, sometimes current. A few 2-line blue initials with red ornament. Binding of s. xx in., by the same binder as the Durham Ritual, A. IV. 19, so probably about or after 1927. Secundo folio *Gracia* (f. 2) or *anhelans* (f. 30).

Written in England. Not in the old Durham catalogues, but almost certainly a Durham book by provenance, if not by origin. A letter-mark 'ff', f. 1, top right: a strip has been cut from the top of the opposing verso (f. ivᵛ), no doubt because it contained an ex-libris inscription. The leaf signatures are on the same system as in B. I. 34.[1] Cf. also above, art. 2, the reference to St. Abb of Coldingham, a cell of Durham.

Hunter 59. *J. Bury, Gladius Salomonis* s. xv²

1. (*preface begins imperfectly*) animalis homo cum suis pecoribus moram habet . . . (f. 2ᵛ) femur potentissime. Amen. Capitula sequentis operis . . . (*table of chapters: the last 6 of 42 are missing*) . . . (f. 5: *begins imperfectly in ch. 1*) were not grovnded in holy scripture. Also thus . . . (f. 112ᵛ) per scripturas suas dignetur efficere Ars sciencia et sapiencia patris Amen.

John Bury's anti-Pecock tract, which gives Pecock's Conclusions in English each followed by a 'Conclusio auctoris' in Latin. In the preface Bury speaks of 'opusculum meum quod gladius salomonis appellari potest' and refers to 'ille Reuerendus in cristo dominus meus. Frater Iohannes Lowe dominus Episcopus Roffensis' (1444–67): his own name comes in MS. Bodley 108 (*Sum. Cat.*, 1960) in the part of the preface missing here. A notice of the

[1] Information from Mr. A. J. Piper. In B. I. 34 the matching pairs are *ad hoc* signs.

Gladius Salomonis and extracts from the Bodleian copy are in C. Babington's edition of Pecock's Repressor (RS xix, 1860), i. xl–lxii and ii. 567–613. There the first words of the preface here are at p. 572/14, the table of chapters is on pp. 567–70, and the first words of the text here are at p. 575/24. In all, three leaves are missing. ff. 113–114ᵛ are ruled, but blank.

2. The first two of four binding leaves, ff. i–iv, contain a theological text in an upright secretary hand, s. xv. It ends abruptly on f. ii, line 12.

The subject is, in part, the Resurrection: for example, f. iᵛ, 'Dixi 2° quod nos habemus notare quomodo resurgemus cum cristo. quia cristus duobus modis surrexit. scilicet velociter et veraciter . . .'. ff. iiᵛ–ivᵛ are blank.

ff. iv+114. For ff. i–iv, two bifolia, see above, art. 2: f. i was pasted down. 212×153 mm. Written space 122×85 mm. 23 long lines. Collation: 1⁸ wants 1 and 6 2–7⁸ 8⁸ wants 6 after f. 59 9–14⁸ 15⁶ wants 6, blank. Written in a good set secretary hand. Initials: (i) missing; (ii) 2-line, blue with red ornament. Capital letters in the ink of the text stroked with red. Contemporary binding of wooden boards covered with pink leather, now dirty white, except on the turned-in pieces: four bands: a central clasp missing. Secundo folio (f. 1) *animalis.*

Written in England.

Hunter 67, item 10. *De oratione* s. xv ex.

Oracio omnis hoc primum proprium habet officium ut doceat aliquem . . . (f. 30) membrorum efficacior. Ista sunt de illa parte dyalectices quam inueniemur (?) vocant et quibusdam adiunctis que spaciosius dixi consulens legentium vtilitati que dixi non vt laudem quam minime habere . . . sed vtilitatis profectusque sui se coniunctum (?) esse racionem. τελοσ etcetera.

ff. 30ᵛ–38ᵛ were left blank and except 37ᵛ–38ᵛ were filled in s. xvi. A carefully written 'De sacris contionibus formandis Compendiaria formula Iohannis Hepini et cetera' was abandoned after thirteen lines on the recto of f. 31 and is followed on ff. 31ᵛ–33 by a piece on syllogisms in German.

ff. 38. 205×140 mm. Written space c. 160×95 mm. c. 40 long lines. Collation: 1¹² 2²⁸ wants 26, 27, blank. Written in current cursiva. No ornament: space for an initial only on f. 1.

Written probably in north-west Germany. Bound up with miscellaneous pieces of later date by the Durham binder Andrews, s. xix¹.

Hunter 97. *Registrum Brevium* s. xiv¹

1. ff. 1–61ᵛ A register of writs lacking sixty-two leaves, twelve (one quire) at the beginning, forty-seven (three quires and all but the last leaf of a fourth quire) after f. 12, one after f. 28, and two after f. 54, as appears from the medieval foliation xiii–xxiv, lxxii–iiiiˣˣvii, iiiiˣˣix–cxviii, cxxi–cxxix on ff. 1–63. 'Iste liber continet cxlii folia', f. 64ᵛ.

The main subjects are shown, except on ff. 35–43, by running titles added slightly later: Quare impedit, Quare non admisit, Prohibicio (including a letter to King E. from J., archbishop of York: de Haas and Hall, R. 137), Prohibiciones on ff. 1–12ᵛ; Nocument',

Diuise et perambulacio, Warantia carte, De compoto, De debito, De medio, De conuen-
cione, De custodia terre et heredis, De dote vnde nichil habet, Statuto, Noua disseisina,
Communa pastur' on ff. 13–34; De morte antecessoris, Nuper obiit, Quare Eiecit, De
Escaeta, Diem claus' extrem', De ydyota, Ingressum, De instrusione on ff. 44–53. The
order is on the whole like that in the register analysed in Holdsworth, ii. 617–36. ff. 55–7
are damaged.

2. Pieces were added later on the last quire: (a) f. 61ᵛ Et notandum quod omnia
breuia que incipiunt sic Precipimus . . .; (b) f. 61ᵛ De assisis (?) in com'. Fos
stang sepeque vi diuersi cursus aquarum . . . (4 lines); (c) f. 61ᵛ Dies communes
in banco. Mic oc quin tres . . . (5 lines); (d) ff. 62–3 Assisa de Foresta. Si quis
forestarius uel viridarius . . . Si Forestarius in dominico domini Regis consenciat
delicto capiat Rex suo superiori si superstes sit. Boys wast derra a checun eyre
dun Mark' au Roy; (e) f. 63ᵛ A list of thirty-seven counties with names in the
margin against six of them; (f) f. 64 A writ of King Richard 'De Leproso
remouendo'; (g) f. 64 A note of the total number of knights' fees (4021 5), of
knights' fees held by religious (1801 5), of towns (52080) and parish churches
(45011) in England.

(a–e). s. xiv. (f). s. xiv ex. (g). s. xiv. (b, c). Mnemonic verses.

(d). The names appear to be of judges in eyre, in the time of Edward III: (Northumberland) '[Ricardus] de Aldeburgh [Thomas] de heppescotes R[obertus] Parnyng'; (Notting-
ham) '[Ricardus] de Wylughby Rogerus de Bankwell Robertus de Sadynton'; (Norfolk)
'Iohannes de Shar[dl]ow Iohannes Clauer'; (Kent) '[. . . .]acoun Willelmus Scot [Ricardus]
de Kelleshull'; (Oxford) 'W. de Shareshull Iacobus de Wodestoke'; (Gloucester) 'Willelmus
de Shareshull [R]ogerus hillary Iohannes de Peyto [. . .] de mor (?)'.¹

ff. 64 + ii. For the medieval foliation see above. 200 × 125 mm. Written space c. 150 ×
70 mm. 48 long lines. Collation: 1¹² 2¹² wants 1–11 3¹² 4¹² wants 4 after f. 28 5⁸ 6¹² wants
11, 12 after f. 54 7¹⁰. Written in anglicana. Spaces left for initials on ff. 1, 1ᵛ, 4ᵛ, 15ᵛ,
22ʳᵛ, 25ᵛ. Contemporary binding of a double thickness of parchment, the surplus not
required as covers forming the two flyleaves, 65, 66.

Written in England. The scribbled beginning of a writ of King Henry addressed to the
sheriff of Suffolk is on f. 64ᵛ, s. xv. 'Iste liber constat Thome [.]ynningham (?) (erased and
H Geldryng or Seldryng substituted)', f. 64ᵛ, s. xv.

Hunter 98. *Horae*　　　　　　　　　　　　　　　　　　　　s. xv med.

Debris of a Sarum book of hours of the common continental-for-the-English-
market type (cf. *MMBL* i. 46): normally art. 9 precedes art. 8. Only thirty-
seven leaves are complete and only arts. 4–7.

1. ff. 1–6ᵛ Calendar in red and black, the top of each leaf damaged.

Ten added obits: John Euerad', 7 Jan., 8 Henry VI; Katherine Aker, 'matris mee', 27 Mar.,
20 Henry VI; Thomas Aker, 31 Mar., 8 Henry VI; William Aker, 24 May, 4 Henry VI;
Joan Aker, 'vxoris [mee]', 28 May 35 Henry VI; Jonet Aker, 4 June, 4 Henry VI; Margaret
Aker, 10 Aug., 12 Henry VI; Thomas Aker, 'patris mei', 19 Nov., 14 Henry VI; John
Bowre, 'fratris mei', 29 Nov., 6 Henry VI; 'Saio (?) Akyr Grocer (?) cognato meo', 29 Nov.,
21 Henry VI.

¹ Mr. A. J. Piper helped me with the elucidation of these names under the ultra-violet
lamp.

2. ff. 7–18^v Hours of B.V.M. of the use of (Sarum).

3. ff. 18^v–19^v Salve regina and the verses 'Virgo mater ecclesie . . .' and prayer 'Omnipotens sempiterne deus qui gloriose uirginis . . .'.

RH, nos. 18147, 21818.

4. ff. 20–23^v Has uideas laudes . . . Salve regina follows, farced with 'Salue uirgo uirginum . . .', and the prayer 'Deus qui de beate marie uirginis . . .'.

RH, nos. 7687, 18318.

5. ff. 24–5 O intemerata . . . orbis terrarum. Inclina . . . Masculine forms.

6. ff. 25–7 Oratio. Obsecro te . . .

7. f. 27^{rv} Oratio. Gaude uirgo mater xpristi que per . . .

RH, no. 7017.

8. ff. 27^v–29 Oratio uenerabilis bede presbiteri de septem uerbis . . . Domine ihesu xpriste qui septem uerba . . .

9. ff. 29–31 Ad ymaginem [. . .]. Omnibus consideratis . . .

RH, no. 14081 (etc.). *AH* xxxi, 87–9.

10. (*a*) f. 31^{rv} Omnibus confess[is . .] . . . duo milia annorum ad supplicationem philippi regis francie. Oratio. [D]omine ihesu xpriste qui hanc sacratissimam carnem . . . (*b*) Oracio. Aue caro cristi cara . . .

(*b*). *RH*, no. 1710.

11. ff. 32–39^v Penitential psalms, fifteen gradual psalms (cues only of the first twelve), and litany.

12. ff. 40–53^v Office of the dead.

13. ff. 54–58^v Commendatory psalms. f. 57 is a very small fragment of a leaf.

ff. iii + 57 + iii. 180 × 120 mm. Written space 105 × 70 mm. 20 long lines. Collation impracticable: a catchword (in hybrida?) marks f. 43 as the last of a quire (of 8 wants 4 after f. 39): after it 44–51 form a quire of 8. Initials: (i) removed; (ii) 2-line, gold on red and blue grounds patterned in white; (iii) 1-line, blue with red ornament or gold with violet ornament. Binding of s. xviii.

Written probably in the Netherlands for the English market. Belonged in the time of Henry VI to the son of Thomas and Katherine Aker (cf. art. 1).

Hunter 99. *Officium mortuorum, etc.* s. xv in.

1. ff. 1–31 Dilexi. A'. Placebo . . .

Office of the dead, noted, as also are arts. 2–4.

2. ff. 31–40 Commendacio animarum dicitur a choro si missa cuiuscumque anniuersarii uel pro corpore presenti in choro uel in capitulo fuerit celebranda et ubi missa ibi commendacio dicitur in superiori gradu incipiatur. Ant'. Beati immaculati. . . . Cf. *Manuale Sarum*, pp. 142–3.

3. ff. 40–5 Missa pro defunctis. Requiem eternam . . .

Cf. ibid., pp. 144–52.

4. ff. 45ᵛ–57ᵛ Post missam accedant clerici de iiᵃ forma ad caput defuncti et incipiant tribus uicibus antiphonam repetentes similiter cum toto choro sic. Circumdederunt me . . .

The burial office: cf. ibid., pp. 152–62. For male use.

5. Three lessons 'In commemoracione sancti Cuthberti' (ff. 57ᵛ–59), 'In commemoracione omnium sanctorum' (ff. 59–60ᵛ), in Advent (ff. 60ᵛ–62), at Christmas (f. 62ʳᵛ), of B.V.M. 'per estatem' (ff. 62ᵛ–64), and at Easter (f. 64ʳᵛ).

The lessons for St. Cuthbert are from ch. 39 of Bede's life of St. Cuthbert, Beatus pater cuthbertus cum circa finem . . . , In omnibus seruis cristi . . . , Catholica patrum statuta . . .

6. ff. 65–69ᵛ Hic incipiunt viiᵗᵉᵐ Psalmi penitenciales.

7. ff. 69ᵛ–79 A litany for each day of the week, as in *Brev. ad usum Sarum*. ii. 250–60.

f. 79ᵛ was left blank. A piece has been cut from the foot.

8. f. 80, a flyleaf, is part of an astronomical table, s. xv.

ff. ii+79+iii. For f. 80 see above, art. 8. 166 × 105 mm. Written space *c.* 125 × 72 mm. 21 long lines. Collation: 1¹⁰+2 leaves after 10 2⁸ 3–4¹⁰ 5–8⁸ 9⁸ wants 8, blank. Initials: (i) ff. 1, 65, 4-line and 3-line, dark blue with red ornament; (ii) 2-line, as (i); (iii) 1-line, blue or red. Cadels have pale-green ornament. Binding of s. xviii. Secundo folio *sanctum tuum*.

Written in England. 'Antho: Ovington', f. 78ᵛ, s. xvi.

Hunter 100. *Collectanea medica, etc.*   s. XII in.

A medieval Durham book (*Catt. Vett.*, pp. 33, 110) described by Mynors, *Catalogue*, pp. 49–50 (no. 57): pls. 35, 36 shows eight pages. Described also by F. Saxl and H. Meier, *Verzeichnis astrologischer und mythologischer illustrierter Handschriften des lateinischen Mittelalters*, iii (1953), 441–7.

Hunter 101. *Reginaldus Dunelmensis, Libellus de admirandis beati Cuthberti virtutibus*   s. XII²

Described by Mynors, *Catalogue*, no. 123. Perhaps autograph. Printed from this copy as the first publication of the Surtees Society (1835).

Hunter 102. *Sermones, etc.*   s. XIII¹

1. ff. 1–3ᵛ (*begins imperfectly*) datur non iam congrediens . . . qui regum baltheum dissoluit (*ends imperfectly*).

A new paragraph begins at the fourth line 'Iohel dicit. Residuum exute'. A leaf or more may be missing after f. 2. A paragraph on f. 3 begins 'Vrsarii similitudinem habere debemus'.

2. ff. 4–10 (*begins imperfectly*) hec est fides catholica . . . (f. 6ᵛ) Simile est regnum homini patrifamilias . . . Inclinatus ego patres ad parietem; intueor per cancellos . . . et inebriet iocunditatis uino. quod nobis conferat ihesus cristus Qui cum p.

An incomplete sermon followed by one for Septuagesima. The former includes the words (f.5ᵛ/24) 'fatuo quoque audire canticum de carolo uel arturo'. f. 10ᵛ blank.

3. ff. 11–40ᵛ In euangelio ad sanandum egrotum samaritanus profert uinum . . . videbimus enim eum sicuti est. Explicit.

A commentary on the Song of Deborah (Judges 5: 3–26). Breaks in the text after ff. 26, 32, where, probably, single leaves are missing.

4. (*a*) ff. 41–46ᵛ Quid existis in desertum uidere? Audi uerbum domini domus israhel. Vrbs fortitudinis . . . uelud ouem ioseph. Ihesum cristum qui cum patre et spiritu. (*b*) ff. 46ᵛ–48ᵛ Quid existis in desertum uidere? arundinem . . . Egressi patres ex egypto corpore mente . . . in fine inuenit (*ends imperfectly: probably a quire is missing*). (*c*) ff. 49–54 Uadam et uidebo eum. Eundem nobis fratres est . . . (on the four chariots of Ezekiel). (*d*) ff. 54–9 Cum audiret iacob quod iosep . . . Sapientis mos est ut turrim edificare uolens . . . . (*e*) ff. 59ʳᵛ, 63–5 Cum audisset iacob quod ioseph . . . . Cuius finis bonus est ipsum totum bonum est . . . premium. Quo nos perducat etc.

(*e*). A *signe de renvoi* on f. 59ᵛ in a later hand '4ᵗᵒ fo. sequenti'. The last 14 lines on f. 59ᵛ are blank.

5 (added early). ff. 60–62ᵛ 'In ascensione domini sermo'. Egrotauit ezechias usque ad mortem iuxta regulam naturalem. cui propheta . . . Quo nos perducat i. cristus.

In the blank space remaining on f. 62ᵛ a scribe of s. xiii¹ added memoranda of the seven things hateful to God and the virtues of the dove.

6 (added, s. xiii¹). (*a*) f. 65ʳᵛ The seven Advents of the Lord. (*b*) f. 66 Duo homines ascendunt in templum. . . . (*c*) ff. 66ᵛ–67ᵛ Non potest arbor mala . . . Verba sunt euangelica . . . (*d*) ff. 67ᵛ–69ᵛ [A]dcensiones disposuit in corde suo. . . . (*e*) ff. 69ᵛ–73 Anima que peccauerit ipsa morietur morte . . . Verba sunt prophete . . . . (*f*) f. 73ʳᵛ Cum immundus spiritus exierit etc. Nota eiectum demonium . . . (*ends imperfectly*).

(*d*). A sermon for Ascension Day on the 'septem gradus (*but there are eight*) quibus adcendere debemus'. f. 74ʳᵛ, left blank, has a few notes of s. xiii and s. xv.

ff. ii+74+ii. 130×115 mm. Written space *c.* 115×77 mm. 27–31 long lines. The first line of writing above the top ruled line. Collation: 1 three (ff. 1–3) 2⁸ wants 8, blank, after f. 10 3–4⁸ 5⁸ wants 1 before f. 27 and 8 after f. 32 6–7⁸ 8⁶ (ff. 49–54) 9⁸ 10⁸ wants 1, 2 before f. 63 11 six (ff. 69–74). Initials 2-line or 3-line, red or green, with ornament of the other colour. Binding of s. xviii, as on MS. 99, labelled 'Sermons M.S.'.

Written in England.

Hunter 103. *Officium mortuorum, etc.* s. xv med.

So far as they go, the texts and musical notation are those in Hunter 99, arts. 1, 2, 4, q.v. There is less rubric here than there.

1. ff. 1–51 Dilexi . . . Placebo . . .

2. ff. 51–64 Commendacio animarum dicitur solempniter hoc modo. A'.
Beati immaculati . . . (f. 64) Tibi domine commendamus . . .

The commendatory psalms (118, 138). f. 64ᵛ blank.

3. ff. 65–75ᵛ Post missam accedant ii clerici de iiᵃ forma ad caput defuncti et
dicant iii uicibus cum toto conuentu anth'. Circumdederunt me . . . transla
(*ends imperfectly at edn. 158/26*).

A leaf missing after f. 73.

ff. ii+75+ii. 138×85 mm. Written space 98×68 mm. 15 long lines. Collation:
1 seven (3–6 are two bifolia) 2–3⁸: then impracticable. Initials: (i, ii) 3-line (f. 1) and 2-line,
blue with red ornament; (iii) 1-line, blue or red. Binding of s. xviii, as on MS. 99. Secundo
folio *a labiis*.

Written in England.

Hunter 123. *L. Lazzarellus*   *c.* 1468

Ludouici Lazzarelli Liber de Apparatu Patauini Hastiludii ad reuerendum
dominum D. Ioh(a)nnem Chetvorth de Britannia archidiaconum Linchoniensem
et Iuristarum Pathauii Rectorem feliciter incipit. Qui regis astres diuini et
iuris alumnos: Me rege: nam presens hoc tibi surgit opus . . . (f. 27ᵛ) Corrige
iuditiis carmina linquo tuis.

Ten chapters. This copy is no. 86 in R. W. Hunt and A. de la Mare, *Duke Humfrey and
English Humanism in the Fifteenth Century*, Bodleian Library Exhibition Catalogue, 1970.
B.L., Arundel 212 is another copy. Printed in Padua in 1629. f. 28ʳᵛ blank.

Chedworth was archdeacon of Lincoln, 1464–71, and rector of the jurists at Padua,
1467–8: cf. Emden, *BRUO*, p. 402.

ff. 28. 188×118 mm. Written space 110×70 mm. 19 long lines. Ink ruling. Collation:
1–2¹⁰ 3¹⁰ wants 8, 9 after f. 27. Humanistic hand, nearly upright. 'Ludovici . . . incipit',
f. 1, is in eleven lines of capitals, a line of blue alternating with a line of red, within a frame
supported by two boys, one of them leaning on a shield. In the lower margin two boys
support a wreath containing a shield of arms of Chedworth. Initial *Q* on f. 1, 6-line, gold
on a decorated blue ground. A 2-line blue *I* on f. 26. Contemporary brown covers of soft
leather with slits in them for three leather bands on to which strings are tied and sewed.
The strings are then brought back through the covers and the pastedowns beneath them
and tied off on pieces of pink leather facing ff. 1ʳ, 28ᵛ. Two ties missing.

Written for presentation to John Chedworth, no doubt at Padua: Hunt and de la Mare,
op. cit., pp. 50–1. Belonged in s. xvii in. to William Orde of Wester Newbiggin, co. Durham, and rather later to John Orde: 'Wᵐ Ordei liber', motto 'Non est profectus ad virtutem, sine vitii diminutione' and date '160[.]', f. 1; 'Wᵐ Orde de Wester Newbigin', f. 26;
'Wᵐ Orde de Newbigin . . . MDCXXIII', f. 27ᵛ; 'Wᵐ Ourde 1622', f. 28ᵛ; 'John Orde of
Weetwood entered to his Demesne there yᵉ yeare 1647 att yᵉ Martin Masse', f. 28. Other
scribbled names, some perhaps earlier than 1600, are on f. 28ᵛ. '1724. Liber Ecclesiæ
Cathedralis Dunelm. viri reuerendi Tho. Drake, nuper minoris Canonici, nunc Vicarii
Norhamensis, donum', f. 1, in the hand of Thomas Rud.

Inc. 7, item 2. Thomas Aquinas, *In Ethica Aristotilis; etc.*[1] 1482.

1. ff. 2–74ᵛ Sicut dicit philosophus In principio metaphisice Sapientis est ordinare . . . terminacio scientie tocius libri ethicorum. Explicit summa Eximii doctoris Sancti Thome de aquino ordinis fratrum predicatorum Tocius ethice. Per me fratrem Iohannem lenglin ordinis eiusdem Scripta. anno 82 In die S. ignacii louanii existentem in falconis pedagogio. seu in collegio ad falconem. Orate pro scriptore. laborem legentis oro pensate. Laus tibi criste redimens nos mortis ab esu. criminis a fece demonis atque noce.

Glorieux, no. 14*at.* f. 1ʳᵛ was left blank.

2. ff. 75–6 Leonhardus Aretinus . . . Per multa michi . . . tamquam talpa quedam lucem a tenebris non discernis. Vale. Explicit epistola satis calumpniosa.

Letters 2 and 3 of bk. 9 in the edition of Leonardo Bruni's letters printed at Louvain in or after 1483 (*GKW* 5608; *BMC* ix. 161) and at Florence in 1741 (pt. 2, pp. 134–47). In the latter both letters are headed *Leonardus Lauro Quirino.*

ff. 76. Paper. 282 × 212 mm. Written space 207 × 150 mm. *c.* 60 long lines. Collation: 1–3¹² 4¹⁰ 5⁸ 6¹² 7¹⁰. Written in a small cursiva, the tops of ascenders sometimes looped or curved and sometimes straight. No coloured initials.

Written by a named South German scribe when a student at Louvain: 'frater Iohannes Lenglin conuentus Herbipoln (*changed to* franckfordensis) prouincie theutonice' is written below the *explicit* of art. 1. Bound between two printed books, the first Boethius, *De consolatione philosophiae*, Cologne 1482 (*GKW* 4531), bought by Lenglin in Cologne in 1483, and the other *Textus ethicorum aristotilis secundum Leonardi Aretini interpretationem*, Louvain 1476 (*GKW* 2360), bought by Lenglin in Louvain in 1480. The three pieces formed one volume in the library of the dominicans of Frankfurt whose ex-libris, 'Fratrum predicatorum franckf' ', and pressmark 'G. 47' is on f. 2 of the Aquinas and on the first and seventh leaves of the Boethius. The present binding is of s.xviii ex.

Fragments in Dean and Chapter Muniments

One leaf. 'Et in terra . . .'. s. xiv. med.

The Gloria from 'Et in terra', the text in four long lines to the page and the music in three tiers above each line. Written space 350 × 235 mm. *E* of *Et* blue with red ornament. In use as the cover of a Communar's cartulary, s. xv/xvi (Davis, *MC*, no. 344).

The class called 'Endpapers and Bindings' consists at present of a collection of fragments numbered from 1 to 46 and catalogued, except no. 46, by Elizabeth Fewster in 1968.[2] The items from known sources are listed here in the order in which they are likely to have been used by binders. All are probably English.

Nos. 21, 30, 31, 46 are from bindings of pre-dissolution records of Durham Cathedral Priory.[3]

---

[1] Mr. A. J. Piper told me of this manuscript. See Addenda, p. 998.

[2] No. 29, not a binding fragment, has been restored to MS. B. I. 13, Aquinas, Secunda secundae of the Summa, from which it had been separated before rebinding in s. xix. As bound, B. I. 13 ends with the tenth leaf of a quire. These two leaves are the eleventh and twelfth of the same quire.

[3] Besides fragments of books the collection contains: (37 A–C) two notarial instruments (1327 and 1329) and a mandate of the official of the court of York (1354), used in a double thickness as the cover of proceedings before the papal judge delegate, 1360–4; (38) a fair

30. Four bifolia. Digestum Novum, etc. s. xii/xiii.

Leaves from the last quire (?) of a copy of Digestum Novum containing: (1) ff. 1–2^v, part of bk. 50, tit. xvi, ending in ch. 120; (2) ff. 3^v–6, a series of legal dicta, each followed by references to the Code, Digest, and occasionally Institutes and 'Supra E. Bro'. The first dictum is 'Leges uel decretales epistole licet ad certas personas directe generalium constitutionum habent effectum' and the last 'Dictum in uno uidetur in alio repetitum'. The first reference is 'C. de nouo Codice confir. ¶ Sciant' and the last 'Digestum. de Iure do. L. post diuor. extra'. ff. 3, 6^v–8^v blank.

Written space (ff. 1–2) 200 × 110 mm. 2 cols. 47 lines. Used as the cover of the court book of the prior's official, 1487–98.

46. Two bifolia. Digestum Vetus. s. xiii[1]

From bks. 6, 7. Apparatus in a much smaller hand in the margins. Written space 240 × 130 mm. 2 cols. 54 lines. Used in a double thickness as the cover of a Repertory of deeds, etc., of Finchale Priory, drawn up by Thomas Swalwell, c. 1500–c. 1527.

31. A bifolium of Codex Justiniani, with surrounding commentary. s. xiii med.

From book 4. Written space 190 × 105 mm. 2 cols. 48 lines. Used for the Almoner's Rental, 1533–7.

21. A bifolium of a missal. s. xiv med.

Offices for Ember Saturday in June and the sixth and seventh Sundays after Trinity. Written space 260 × 163 mm. 2 cols. 28 lines. The outside bifolium of a quire. Used as a cover for the Bursar's Summary Account, 1535–6, etc.

Nos. 1–9, 11–16 come from seventeen of the twenty-seven Receiver's Books and ten of the nineteen Treasurer's Books for the period from 1541 to 1600. The volumes in question are RB 2, 7, 10–24 and TB 1, 6, 7, 9, 11, 14–18. Most of the pieces have been folded to make covers measuring usually rather more than 300 mm in height and 200 mm in width. Usually a double thickness of parchment was used for the Receiver's Books but only a single thickness for the thinner Treasurer's Books. 4B and 15B were additional strengthening inside the covers.

At least ten of the texts used to cover these records were to be found in more than one copy in the medieval cathedral library: cf. *Catt. Vett.*, pp. 21 B–D, 65 A–C, Isidore (4A); pp. 22 D, P, Q, 54 A–D, Sentences of Peter Lombard (6); pp. 36 X, Y, 48 X, Y, Summa Gaufredi (13); p. 46, Decretum (9); p. 47, Decretals (11, 12, 15: p. 47 B specifies 'Constitutiones Gregorii decimi'); p. 48 R–T, Hostiensis (14); p. 53, Concordantiae (1); p. 71 A–D, Summa de Vitiis, perhaps all, like 71 B, the Summa of Peraldus (8). Of Gorran on Corinthians (2) there was one copy, *Catt. Vett.*, p. 68 D, and of Peraldus on the Epistles (4B) at least one, *Catt. Vett.*, p. 27 I.

15A. Two bifolia (ff. 1, 3–5) and a single leaf (f. 2). Canon Law. s. xiii ex.

Five adjacent leaves (from additions to a copy of the Decretals of Gregory IX?) containing: (1) ff. 1–4^v, chapters 19–31 of the decrees of Gregory X at the

copy of Bursar-Granator indentures, 1464–5, used as a cover for the Bursar's Rental, 1507–10: the rough copy still exists among the muniments.

council of Lyons in 1274, accompanied by the commentary on chapters 15–31 of Garsias: '. . . Expliciunt gloseorum (? *sic*) nouarum constitucionum domini gregorii a domino garsio iuris ciuilis et canonici professore' (f. 4ᵛ); (2) f. 3, following on ch. 31 of (1), Velut fidei feruor deuocionis et compassionis pietas excitare dicitur corda fidelium . . .; (3) ff. 4ᵛ–5 Quia tractare intendimus de consanguinitate et eius gradibus . . .; (4) f. 5, added in another hand: (*a*) De supplenda negligentia clericorum. Idem Innocentius iiiiᵘˢ. Grandi non inmerito . . .; (*b*) De etate et qualitate. Item Gregorius ixᵘˢ. Nullum eorum quorum . . .; (*c*) De testibus. Item Innocentius iiiiᵘˢ. Mediatores . . .; (*d*) Idem. De eodem. Ad hec 'quia' per quamdam epistolam felicis recordacionis Gregorii pape predecessoris nostri . . .; (5) f. 5ᵛ, added in another hand: (*a*) Martinus episcopus seruus seruorum dei . . . Ad fructus uberes . . .; (*b*) [. . . .] fratribus ordinis [. . . .].

1. Text in P. Labbeus and G. Cossartius, *Sacrosancta concilia*, xi. 986–94. The text ends on f. 3, but the commentary continues until f. 4ᵛ. 3. Cf. B. L., Royal 11 D. i, f. 4. 4 *a, c*. Sextus liber decretalium, I. 8. 2, II. 10. 1. 5*a*. *Sacrosancta concilia*, xi. 1143–4. 5*b* is hardly legible.

The commentary is written more closely, but only a little smaller than the text. A full page of commentary (f. 4) has a written space of 380 × 230 mm and is in 2 cols. of 101 lines. Initials: (i) blue and red with ornament of both colours; (ii) 2-line, blue or red.

(1–3) written in Italy. Used for RB 2 (1542–3).

15B. A leaf with a list of tituli of the Decretals of Gregory IX in three columns on the recto and blank on the verso. Used inside 15A.

7. A bifolium and two single leaves of sermons on the gospels. s. xiv/xv.

The sermon on f. 1 on the text Querat et Iudicet (John 8: 50: fifth Sunday in Lent?) includes fifteen words of English, 'circa quod duo notantur in verbis thematis of hys owne leuyngg' a resonable sechingg' *querat* and of hys owne trespas a scherpe dressyngg' *iudicet*. Written space 210 × 140 mm. 46 long lines. Written in current anglicana. Spaces for initials not filled. Used for TB 1, 1557–8.

16. A membrane of an inspeximus of royal grants to the prior and convent of St. Bartholomew's, Smithfield, O.S.A. s. xvⁱ.

Incomplete: three grants of Henry I, two of Henry II and one of Richard I, as in *Calendar of Patent Rolls 1416–1422*, pp. 239–46 (1419) and in *Calendar of Patent Rolls 1422–1429*, pp. 171–2 (1424). Used for RB 7, 1559–60.

3. A bifolium and a single leaf from Historia Monachorum. s. xiii ex.

Parts of chapters 1, 6, 7 (*PL* xxi. 402D–406A, 409D–416A: cf. *Clavis*, before no. 199). Written space 243 × 147 mm. 2 cols. 49 lines. 2-line blue initials with red ornament. Used for TB 6, 1568–9.

5. Two bifolia from Smaragdus' commentary on the rule of St. Benedict. s. xii/xiii.

Parts of chapters 7, 9–13, 21, 22 (*PL* cii. 811D–815A, 821C–824D, 831C–834D, 841D–845A). Written space 255 × 170 mm. 2 cols. 40 lines. 4-line initials, blue or red with ornament of the other colour. Used for TB 7, 1569–70.

4A. A bifolium of Isidore, Etymologiae. s. xii[2].

Part of bk. 20: *PL* lxxxii. 708A–718A. Written space 250 × 160 mm. 2 cols. 42 lines. Pricks in both margins to guide ruling. The central bifolium of a quire. 2-line initials, red or green. Used for TB 9, 1571–2.

4B. Two bifolia of sermons of W. Peraldus on the epistles of the temporale. s. xiv med.

Printed in 1494 (Goff, P. 81) and later. Cf. A. Dondaine in *AFP* xviii (1948), 197–210. The beginnings of sermons for Sexagesima and Quinquagesima Sundays and the first and second Sundays in Lent remain. Written space *c.* 225 × 140 mm. 2 cols. 45 lines. Adjacent bifolia. Written in current anglicana. 2-line blue initials with red ornament. Used inside 4A.

12. Two bifolia of Decretals of Gregory IX. s. xiii ex.

Bk. 2, tit. xxvi–xxviii, with surrounding commentary. Written space of text 195 × 150 mm. 2 cols. 38 lines. The commentary in *c.* 91 lines to the column seems to be in the same hand as that in no. 15. Used for RB 10, 1574–5.

14/1, 2. Three bifolia of Hostiensis on the Decretals. s. xiii ex.

A smaller manuscript than C. I. 13. Commentary on bk. 5: tit. xvii and xx–xxii on 14/1, a bifolium; tit. xxxix on 14/2, two bifolia. Written space 330 × 207 mm. 2 cols. 68 lines. 2-line blue initials with red ornament. 14/1, the outside sheet of a quire, was used for TB 11, 1577–8, and 14/2 for RB 11, 1578–9.

6/1–3. Three bifolia and three single leaves of the Sentences of Peter Lombard. s. xiii med.

From bks. 3 and 4. Written space 218 × 110 mm. 2 narrow cols. 36 lines. 2-line blue initials with red and blue ornament running the height of the written space. 6/2, two bifolia, was used for RB 12, 1579–80, 6/1, a bifolium and a single leaf, for RB 13, 1581–2, and 6/3, two single leaves for RB 14, 1583–4.

11. A bifolium and a single leaf of Decretals of Gregory IX. s. xiii ex.

Bk. 1, tit. xxix, with surrounding commentary. Written space (text) 183 × 100 mm. (commentary) 298 × 175 mm. 2 cols. 40 lines (text). Up to 104 lines of commentary on a page. Blue initials with red ornament outside the written space. Used for RB 15, 1584–5.

2. Two bifolia of Nicholas de Gorran's commentary on the Pauline Epistles. s. xiv in.

2 Corinthians 12: 7–13: 14 (end). Each sentence of the text is followed by its commentary in smaller script: 2 lines of commentary to 1 line of text. Written space 295 × 180 mm. 2 cols. 60 lines (commentary). Used for RB 16, 1585–6.

9/1–4. Four bifolia and two single leaves of the Decretum of Gratian. s. xiii/xiv.

From pt. 1, dist. 34–7, 45–7 (9/1), pt. 1, dist. 50 (9/2, 3), and pt. 2, causa 5–7 (9/4). Written space 225 × 145 mm. 2 cols. 44 lines. Blue initials with red ornament. 9/2, a bifolium, was used for TB 14, 1588–9, 9/1, a bifolium and a single leaf, for RB 17, 1590–1, 9/4, two bifolia, for RB 18, 1592–3, and 9/3, part of a single leaf, for RB 19, 1593–4.

1/1–6. Ten bifolia of a biblical concordance. s. xiv med.

As Durham Cathedral A. I. 2 (Concordantiae maiores: Stegmüller, no. 3605):[1] Beatus–Bestia and Bonus–Calciamentum on 1/1; Egredietur–Electus and Esse–Evum on 1/2; Imperitia–Iudicium on 1/3; Lex–Leones and Machinas–Magnum on 1/4; Mors and Nequam–Nichil on 1/5, Opia–Orbis and Parvulus–Patiens on 1/6. Written space 305 × 195 mm. 3 cols. 64 and (1/1, 2) 66 lines. Written in anglicana. Large red and blue C with penwork decoration on a ground of hatched red lines. Used for RB 20 (1594–5), TB 15 (1594–5), RB 21 (1595–6), RB 22 (1596–7), TB 17 (1597–8), and RB 24 (1598–9) in the order 1, 4, 2, 6, 5, 3. Two bifolia were used on each Receiver's Book and single bifolia on each Treasurer's Book.

13/1, 2. Three bifolia of the Summa of Gaufredus de Trano on the Decretals. s. xiii ex.

13/1 has bk. 4, tit. xx–bk. 5, tit. iii: bk. 5 begins on f. 2. 13/2 has bk. 5, tit. xiii–xvi, xviii–xix. Printed in s. xv (Goff, T. 423–5). Written space 265 × 155 mm. 2 cols. 64 lines. Written in small textura: a reader disliked the triangular a and furnished it with an extra stroke at the top. Initials: (i) f. 2, red and blue with ornament of both colours; (ii) 2-line, blue with red ornament. Used for TB 16 (1596–7: 13/2, a bifolium) and for RB 23 (1597–8: 13/1, two bifolia).

8. A bifolium, a single leaf, and a strip from W. Peraldus, De vitiis. s. xiii ex.

See above, Birmingham University, 7/i/18. Part of Luxuria, including the beginning of the chapter 'Quod valde periculosum est coreas ducere'. Written space 257 × 155 mm. 2 cols. 46 lines. Incipient anglicana, current, but the ascenders still usually straight. Initials blue or red with ornament of the other colour. Used for TB 18 (1599–1600).

No. 45 was used as the cover of an Act Book of the Dean and Chapter's Officiality in Durham Diocese and Allertonshire, 1595–1606. It is a bifolium of a missal, s. xiii², with sanctorale for 25 Mar. and 1–3 May.

Two other pieces are of special interest.

No. 17. Two leaves of a calendar of Durham diocese. s. xiii in.

Two months to a page, July–Oct. on f. 1rv and Nov., Dec. on f. 2r. Not graded. Feasts in red include Oswald (5 Aug., with octave in black), 'Conceptio sancte marie' (8 Dec.) and an illegible entry, presumably the translation of Cuthbert at 4 Sept.; in black, 'Boisilii presbiteri' (7 July), 'Sancte Ebbe virginis' (25 Aug.), 'Aidani episcopi commemoratio reliquiarum' (31 Aug.), 'Sancte hilde uirginis' (17 Nov.). f. 2v contains a table of a great cycle, 19 × 28 years.

No. 22. Two leaves of a missal. s. xiv med.

A very handsome book. Includes cues for the office 'Sancti benedicti abbatis in Werem' ' between the offices of Silvester and Hilary. Written space 270 × 175 mm. 2 cols. 26 lines. Used as the wrapper of a book in the cathedral library. 'Liber ecclesiæ Cath. Dunelm' was written on it in s. xvi; also 'Rob. Pigot Book 1730': Pigot was librarian 1726–49.

[1] The concordance beginning 'Cuilibet volenti . . .': cf. R. H. and M. A. Rouse, 'The verbal concordance to the scriptures', AFP xliv (1974), 1–30.

DURHAM. ST. CHAD'S COLLEGE

1. *Antiphonale*   s. XIII med.

Incipit antiphonarium Romanum secundum 'quod' cisterciensis canit ecclesia.

1. ff. 1–96ᵛ Temporale from Advent to Easter Eve, beginning with the antiphon at vespers Custodit dominus.

2. ff. 96ᵛ–128 Sanctorale from 26 Dec. to 25 Mar.

Proper offices of Stephen, John, Innocents, Agnes, Purification of B.V.M., Agatha, Benedict, and Annunciation of B.V.M.

3. ff. 128–48 Common of saints.

4. ff. 148–151ᵛ 'Offitium defunctorum' and burial service.

5. ff. 151ᵛ–156ᵛ Seven settings of Venite exultemus domino.

6. ff. 156ᵛ–159 Incipit tonale. Discipulus. Quid est tonus? Magister. Regula naturam et formam canticum . . . responsurus diligentia. Quid est primus tonus? . . . ut subiecta docent.

PL clxxxii. 1153–64. Each of the eight tones is illustrated by a musical example. The last part of the *PL* text, *Memini te-doceri potens* (edn. 1163–6), does not occur here.

7. f. 159 Eight settings of 'Benedictus dominus deus israel . . . plebis sue'.

8. ff. 159ᵛ–160 Te deum.

9. f. 160ᵛ (*a*) Suffragia de sancta maria tempore paschali. (*b*) Sancti tui . . .

(*b*). Suffrage of All Saints.

10. ff. 161–206ᵛ Temporale from Easter to the twenty-fifth Sunday after Pentecost.

11. f. 207ʳᵛ (*a*) Quando festum s. Ambrosii post pasca celebratur dicitur ad utrumque magnificat hec ant'. Beatus uir . . . Cetera responsoria ut in unius confessoris pontificis. (*b*) In commemoratione unius martyris uel confessoris per resurrectionem. Beatus uir qui metuit . . . (*c*) In com' plur' Mar'. Filie hierusalem . . .

12. ff. 207ᵛ–275 Sanctorale from 25 Apr. to 30 Nov.

Proper offices of Mark, Philip, and James, Invention of Cross, Nativity of John Baptist, Peter, Paul, Mary Magdalene, Laurence, Assumption of B.V.M., Bernard, Justina, Martin, Cecilia, 'In natal' sanctorum theonisti. thabre. et thabrate' (ff. 267–269ᵛ), Clement, Andrew.

13. ff. 275–278ᵛ In natale euangelistarum. Ends imperfectly.

---

ff. iii+270+iii, misfoliated in s. xvii (?), (i–iii), 1–80, 89–278, (279–82). 365×265 mm. Written space *c.* 275×190 mm. 11 long lines and music, and (ff. 156ᵛ–157) 2 columns spaced for 66 lines. Music on coloured ruled lines, greenish brown (2 lines), yellow (1 line), and red (1 line): the order of colours varies, but two lines of the same colour are never together. Collation: 1–24⁸ 25⁶ (ff. 201–6) 26–34⁸. The ink did not take well on flesh sides. Punctuation with the flex is not used. Initials: (i) of the first response of each nocturn, patterned blue, red, or brown on coloured grounds, commonly pale yellow or brown, decorated; (ii, iii) red with blue ornament, in two sizes. Capital letters in the ink of the text are marked with red. Binding of s. xx¹. Secundo folio *et paries*.

Written for Cistercian use, presumably in the Veneto: Theonistus, Thabra, and Thabrata are local saints of the region between Venice and Treviso. Belonged in 1893 to the Revd. G. S. Richmond, Newburn, Newcastle: a letter to him from Robert Blair, secretary of the Society of Antiquaries of Newcastle upon Tyne, 28 June 1893, is attached to f. i.

2. *Horae*   s. xv med.

1. ff. 1–6ᵛ Calendar in red and black.

Most feasts in red graded maius duplex or minus (*or* semi) duplex, but a dozen are not graded, including 'Translatio sancte Brigide' (28 May), 'Sancte Brigide' (23 July), 'Canonizatio sancte Brigide' (7 Oct.), 'Sancte reparate' (8 Oct.).

2. ff. 7–98 . . . Explicit offitium beatissime uirginis marie secundum modum romane curie. Facto fine pie. laudetur uirgo maria.

The first leaf of the Hours is missing. The Advent office begins on f. 85 without any special break before it. f. 98ᵛ blank.

ff. ii+98+ii 120×90 mm. Written space 63×47 mm. 12 long lines. The ink has faded a bit on some leaves. Collation: 1⁶ 2¹⁰ wants 1 3–10¹⁰ 11⁴ wants 4, blank. Initials: (i) before f. 7, removed; (ii) 4-line or 5-line, blue with red ornament; (iii) 2-line, blue with red ornament or red with violet ornament; (iv) 1-line, blue or red. Capital letters in the ink of the text filled with pale yellow. English binding, s. xix². Secundo folio (f. 7) *Alleluya*.

Written in Italy. An erased round stamp (?) at the foot of f. 7.

DURHAM. UNIVERSITY LIBRARY

The catalogue by Thomas Rud, †1732, of the manuscripts in the library founded by John Cosin, bishop of Durham, in 1669 is printed in *Catalogi Veteres Librorum Ecclesiae Cathedralis Dunelm.* (Surtees Soc. (vii), 1838 (1840)), pp. 136–91. V. IV. 9 is not included as it was missing in Rud's time. The Cosin library was administered by the librarian of the University Library from 1832 and became part of it in 1937.

Cosin V. IV. 9. *Historia trium regum, etc.*   s. xv med.

1. ff. 3–106ᵛ, 108 Cum venerandorum trium Magorum . . . et tunc moriar. Quod et factum est. Explicit.

BHL, no. 5137 (John of Hildesheim, Ord. Carm., †1375). Ends like London, Law Society 4 (*MMBL* i. 119).

2. ff. 108ᵛ–111ᵛ In primordio itaque cum beata virgo Hilda Whitbiense cenobium quod tunc vocabatur Streneshalc cepit construere . . . patitur in dolore.

A quo nos liberet Iesus Cristus. qui nobis sit vbique propicius. Amen. Explicit. 'anno domini 1526'.

The miracle of St. Hilda turning snakes into stones (cf. *Nova Legenda Angliae*, ed. C. Horstman, ii. 30), with a moral application addressed to 'dilectissimi'.

3 (added in s. xviii²). (*a*) f. 107　A memorandum that 'Wm Jackson, a Roman Catholic and proscribed smuggler', attainted at Chichester, 16 Jan. 1748/9, died in prison and had a charm in his purse invoking the three kings, accompanied by a note in French that 'Ces billets' had touched the heads of the kings at Cologne and had various virtues: the writer refers to Spanheim, *Dubia evangelica*, ii. 289. (*b*) f. 108 'Gaspar fert myrrham . . .' (3 lines).

(*a*) and (*b*) in one hand, perhaps that of R. Harrison (cf. below). (*b*). Walther, *Sprichwörter*, no. 2456.

ff. v+104+i+4+v, foliated i–iii, 1–116. ff. ii, iii, 1, 2, 112–15 are medieval parchment end-leaves. For f. 107, paper, see above, art. 3. 163×113 mm. Written space *c.* 97× 66 mm. 19 long lines. Collation of ff. 3–106, 108–11: 1–13⁸ 14⁴. Written in anglicana (but *a* is in one compartment and *r* is short). Initials: (i) f. 3, 7-line, blue and red with red and blue ornament; (ii) 2-line, blue with red ornament. Binding of s. xix, like that of many Cosin manuscripts: the mark of the pin of a former strap-and-pin fastening can be seen as far back as f. 95. Secundo folio *de Israhel*.

Written in England. Scribbles and inscriptions bearing on the history of the manuscript, which seems to have gone to Cumberland from the south in s. xvi, are noticed by A. I. Doyle in *Transactions of the Cumberland and Westmorland Antiquarian and Archaeological Society*, lxvi (1966), 468–70: (*a*) '*Memorandum quod codex iste* [. . . . .] *Armigeri*' and '*Peto vt liber iste restituatur predicto domino Ricardo* (?)', f. 1, s. xv/xvi; (*b*) '*Iohanni ponde de Chelmersford*', f. 2; (*c*) '*Noueritis me fratrem Wyllelmum ponde ordinis minorum london*', f. 2ᵛ, s. xvi in.; (*d*) an erased inscription which appears to record purchase for 6*d.* by Nicholas Johnson at Sturbridge Fair, f. 114ᵛ; (*e*) 'Codex presens attinet Iohanni Grethed notario publico Carlii Registrario teste manu. I Gr. notarius', f. 114ᵛ, partly over (*d*), s. xvi med.; (*e*) the names Rychart Hareson and Bernardus Aglionby on f. 1ᵛ; (*f*) scribbles dated 1564 and naming 'Rychard Herryson of Edmonde Bridge', parish of Penrith, on f. 81ᵛ and Thomas Tutins of Carlisle 'offic' Curie cons' principalis' on f. 82; (*g*) 'Thomas Foster . . . July 16 1640', f. 83 (cf. f. 48); (*h*) 'Geo Davenport. Donum Johannis Tempest Armigeri. 1668', f. 2ᵛ; (*i*) 'Amissum reperit restituit R. Harrison 1778', f. 2ᵛ: the loss was probably between *c.* 1669, when other manuscripts were acquired for Cosin's library from Davenport, and s. xviii in., when the Cosin manuscripts, but not this one, were inscribed with an ex-libris in the hand of Thomas Rud. (*d*) and (*e*) are shown in the facsimile of f. 114ᵛ illustrating Doyle's note. The words in italics in (*a–c*) and part of (*d*) are legible by ultraviolet light.

Mickleton and Spearman 27. *Statuta Angliae*　　　s. XIV/XV

1. ff. ix–xivᵛ Sarum calendar in red and black, usually marked for nine and three lessons.

The words 'duplex festum' against Epiphany and Invention of Cross in red and against Gregory and Ambrose in black come probably from the exemplar: no other entries are so marked. In s. xv² David and 'Dedicacio ecclesie sancti andree' were added in one hand at 1, 9 Mar., 'Thomas Hawe anno quinto Edwardi iiii' was added at 16 Sept., and many feasts were marked 'non mo'. The entries of St. Thomas of Canterbury at 7 July and 29 Dec. erased, but the word 'pape' not erased. ff. i–viiiᵛ are a blank but ruled quire intended perhaps for tables of contents and chapters.

2. ff. 1–5 Magna carta. Henricus dei gracia . . . Pro hac autem . . . mobilium suorum. Hiis testibus domino M. Cant' Archiepiscopo. E London'. S Bathon' etc.

SR i, Charters, p. 26, but with the sentence before the witness clause as in *SR*, Charters, i. 118.

3. ff. 5–6 Incipit sentencia lata super trangressores predictarum libertatum. *SR* i. 6.

4. ff. 6–8 . . . Expliciunt Prouisiones de Mertoun. *SR* i. 1.

5. ff. 8ᵛ–14ᵛ Incipit statutum de Marleberg'. *SR* i. 19.

6. ff. 15–28 Incipit Westm' primum. In French. *SR* i. 26.

7. ff. 28–9 Et incipiunt districciones scaccarii pro debitis domini regis. Purceo ke la commune du realme ad grant damages . . . conu ke il eit receu. *SR* i. 197*b*/5–46, with differences.

8. ff. 29–32 Incipiunt statuta de scaccario. In French. *SR* i. 197.

9. (*a*) ff. 32–33ᵛ Incipiunt articuli monete. In French. *SR* i. 219. (*b*) ff. 33ᵛ–34 Per discrecionem tocius regni anglie ita fuit mensura . . . pars quarterii. Expliciunt articuli monete.

10. ff. 34–37ᵛ Incipiunt statuta Gloucestr'. Pur les granz meschefs . . . en tut son realme. Come auant ces heures . . . *SR* i. 47, with short preamble.

11. f. 37ᵛ Incipiunt explanaciones earundem. *SR* i. 50.

12. ff. 38–9 Incipiunt statuta de quo waranto. Rex vic' salutem. Cum in vltimo parliamento nostro apud Westm' per nos et consilium nostrum prouisum fuit et proclamatum quod archiepiscopi . . . inquisiciones inde factas.
Writs relating to franchises. Cf. *MMBL* i. 252.

13. ff. 39–40 . . . Expliciunt statuta de Rageman. In French. *SR* i. 44.

14. ff. 40–4 . . . Expliciunt statuta Exon'. In French. *SR* i. 210.

15. f. 44ʳᵛ Incipiunt statuta religiosorum. *SR* i. 51.

16. ff. 44ᵛ–47 Incipiunt statuta Mercatorum. In French. *SR* i. 53.

17. ff. 47–71ᵛ Incipiunt statuta apud Westm' edita. Anno regni Regis edwardi fil' Regis H xiiiᵒ. *SR* i. 71.

18. ff. 71ᵛ–74 Incipiunt statuta Wyntonie. In French. *SR* i. 96.

19. f. 74ʳᵛ Incipiunt statuta de quo waranto. Dated 18 Edward (I) at the end. *SR* i. 107.

20. ff. 74ᵛ–75 Incipiunt statuta Westm' tercii de ingressu feodorum. Quia emptores . . . *SR* i. 106.

21. ff. 75–6 Incipiunt statuta de ponderibus. Notandum quod carrata de

plumbo . . . et quodlibet conspicamen continet xxv. *SR* i. 205/1–49, with many differences.

22. ff. 76–7 Incipiunt capitula visus franciplegii. In French. *SR* i. 246.

23. f. 77^{rv} Incipit modus faciendi homagia et fidelitates. In French. *SR* i. 227.

24. ff. 77^{v}–78^{v} . . . et bene possunt. Explicit assisa panis et ceruisie. *SR* i. 199–200/33.

25. f. 78^{v} Incipiunt communes dies in banco. *SR* i. 208.

26. ff. 79–80^{v} Incipit ordinacio de seruientibus facta apud Westm' anno regni regis E tercii vicesimo tercio. *SR* i. 307.

27. ff. 80^{v}–84^{v} Incipit statutum de seruientibus. anno vicesimo quinto. quod dependet super ordinacionem proximam precedentem. In French. *SR* i. 311.

Arts. 28, 29 are early additions in the space left blank at the end of quire 13.

28. f. 84^{v} Incipit statutum de Chaumpatoribus. In French. Dated 20 Edward I. *SR* i. 216.

29. ff. 84^{v}–85 Incipit statutum de conspiratoribus. *SR* i. 216. ff. 85^{v}–88^{v} are blank and without ruling.

30. ff. 89–90 Richard par la grace de dieu . . . Sachetz que a nostre darrein parlement . . . lan de nostre regne secunde. *SR* ii. 13 (3 Richard II).

31. ff. 90–5 Pur commune profit . . . *SR* ii. 55 (12 Richard II). Running title 'Cantebrigge'.

32. ff. 95^{v}–97^{v} Pur releuacion et encresse . . . *SR* ii. 76 (14 Richard II). Running title 'Westm' '.

33. ff. 97^{v}–99^{v} Le Roi en son parlement . . . *SR* ii. 92. Running title 'Westm' Anno R. xx^{mo}'.

34. ff. 99^{v}–104 Au parlement tenuz a Westm' . . . *SR* ii. 78. Running title 'Westm' Anno R. xv^{mo}'. ff. 104^{v}–110^{v} ruled, but blank.

35 (added in s. xv in.). f. 111^{v} Iohanni de allnsley Maiori Iohanni Botener et Iohanni Parker Balliuis libertatis ville de Couentre Iohannes Sutton et Thomas Stretford de eadem villa salutem . . .

Sutton and Stretford, as auditors of account in a suit between Thomas Tenche and his bailiff Richard Warwike, have found Warwike £10 in arrears and by virtue of the relevant statute, unspecified, have arrested him and sent him to you, to be held until Tenche is satisfied. Coventry, Tuesday after St. James, 6 Henry IV.

ff. ii + 124 + iii, foliated (two unnumbered leaves), i–xiv, 1–113. For f. 111 see above, art. 35. 260 × 180 mm. Written space 175 × 115 mm. 26 long lines. On ff. 1–64^{v} lines 5, 10, 15, 20 on each page are usually more heavily ruled than other lines. Collation of ff. i–xiv, 1–110: 1^{8} 2^{6} 3–15^{8} 16^{6}. The signatures of quires 3–15, A–L, T, X, suggest that six quires are missing after f. 88. Written in anglicana, except art. 1. The hand of ff. 1–78^{v} is very like that of

ff. 13–20, 85–104 of the Lichfield manuscript now Bodleian, Rawlinson A. 389.[1] A new
hand begins on f. 79 and uses both single-compartment and double-compartment forms of
a. Initials: (i) ff. 1, 89, gold on red and blue grounds, patterned in white: prolongations
form continuous borders; (ii) 4-line, blue with red ornament. Line fillers in blue and red.
Binding of s. xviii/xix, like that on many Mickleton and Spearman manuscripts. Secundo
folio (f. 2) *quod illam*.

Written in England: the script and art. 35 suggest Coventry or its neighbourhood. 'John
Lightfoot', f. i, is beside and probably in the same hand as the words 'Le generall Table,
1641'. Given to Bishop Cosin's Library in 1817 by the Rev[d]. G. Wasey, together with
other Mickleton and Spearman manuscripts: cf. *Durham Philobiblon*, i (1951), 40–4.

Mickleton and Spearman 57. *Statuta Collegii de North Cadbury*
1428

Statutes of the collegiate church of N. Cadbury, Somerset, 26 Nov. 1428, certi-
ficated by Andrew Lanvyan, clerk of Exeter diocese and apostolic and imperial
notary: his mark has been cut out of f. 11.

Mickleton and Spearman 89. *De oculo morali*   s. XIII ex.

Incipit tractatus moralis de occulo. [Si diligenter] uoluerimus in le[ge domini] ...
nos perducat qui sine fine uiuit. AMEN. AMEN. AME(N).

Probably by Pierre de Limoges. Thomson, *Grosseteste*, pp. 256–8, lists forty-three manuscripts, but not this one, in British libraries. Fifteen chapters. An inscription, s. xv, at
the head of f. 1 has been cut off, except the last nine letters, 'e lymochia'. A couplet added
on f. 94, s. xiv: 'Sanis et non sanis est [sana refeccio panis] set cristi panis non est [sanus
nisi sanis]': cf. Walther, *Sprichwörter*, no. 595.

ff. iv+94+ii. ff. iii, iv are medieval parchment end-leaves. 175 × 120 mm. Written space
c. 125 × 75 mm. 26 long lines. 1–11[8] 12[8] wants 7, 8, probably blank. Initials: (i) f. 1, cut
out, except a small corner (gold?) and part of the border; (ii) 2-line, blue with red ornament
or red with green ornament. Binding of s. xviii. Secundo folio *duo nerui*.

Written in England. Belonged to Durham Cathedral Priory, *c.* 1500: 'Liber sancti Cuthberti et do*m*pni henricy Thew monachi Dunellm' ', f. iv[v]: for Thew cf. Emden, *BRUO*,
p. 1860. '9. V. g', f. 1, s. xv ex. (?), is not a form of pressmark found in other Durham
manuscripts: the ink is like that of the 'lymochia' inscription on f. 1. Acquired in 1817,
as MS. 27.

S.R. 2. B. 3 (Routh LXIX, C. 3), item 2. *Sermones, etc.*
1480; s. xv[2]

1. ff. 1–2 Incipit Miraculum preclarum de festo Purificacionis beate Marie
virginis. Temporibus beati bonifacii pape qui ut in ecclesiasticis historiis
legitur . . .

The main hand wrote the noted response 'Gaude maria virgo' against the reference to it
in the text on f. 2. f. 2[v] blank.

[1] I owe this observation to Dr. Doyle.

2. ff. 3-24ᵛ Incipiunt sermones nouiter collecti ex dictis sanctorum et katholi-
corum patrum de festo uisitacionis beate et gloriose semper virginis marie. Ad
ampliandum ac declarandum dominice incarnacionis . . . prout bulle eorum
recitate in refectoriis religiosorum clare commemorant. Incipit sermo primus . . .
Dignitatem festiuitatis hodierne dilectissimi diuinorum operum . . .
Twelve sermons on the feast of the Visitation of B.V.M. The preface refers to the council
of Basel and decrees of Popes Urban VI and Boniface (IX).

3. Sermons, etc.: (a) ff. 25-6 Ihesus. Sermo beati Maximi Episcopi. in Natali
Sanctorum Martirum. Sufficere nobis debent ad profectum . . .; (b) ff. 26-8
Sermo beati Maximi 'Episcopi' de Annunciacione beate Marie Virginis. Adest
nobis dilectissimi sanctissima dies dominice incarnacionis . . .; (c) ff. 28-9 Sermo
de Exordio festi Visitacionis Marie. Beatissima mater dei maria virgo virginum
domino consecrata propter beneficia . . .; (d) ff. 29-30 Sermo de Visitacione
b. marie virginis. collectus ex dictis sanctorum Patrum. Augustini. Ambrosii.
Ieronimi. Hilarii. Iohannis Crisostomi. Iohannis Damasceni. et aliorum
doctorum. Exquisita mundo gaudia. hodierne festiuitatis nouitas . . .; (e) f. 30ʳᵛ
Decretum sacri concilii Basiliensis De concepcione beate marie sine peccato
originali. Sacrosancta generalis synodus . . .
(a). PL lvii. 429-32. After (c) is a reference to another book in the library: Nota si placet
potest extunc continuari ulterius bulla Bonifacii pape et episcopi de festiuitate visitacionis
b. marie virginis. 'Que habetur in alio libro videlicet SS.v. numero cccxciiii circa finem
libri in lumbertica historia'. (e). Dated at the end 17 Sept. 1439. After (e) is a reference to
a book in another library: Nota si placet colligere vlterius aliquid de gloriosa virginis concepcione In monasterio Ilseneborgh (Ilsenburg, O.S.B., diocese of Halberstadt) habentur
sermones compilati a venerabili patre Iohanne hagen Carthusien'. prope Erffordiam vt
ore suo proprio michi idem pater retulit.

4. f. 31 Sequuntur Sermones de Vigilia Pasche. (a) f. 31 Sermo beati Augustini
Episcopi in Vigilia Pasche. Scimus fratres et fide firmissima . . . ydola paganorum. Explicit sermo. (b) ff. 31-2 Incipit alius eiusdem vnde supra. Sermo b.
Augustini Episcopi. Dicendum est cur tanta celebritate hodierna potissimum
nocte vigilemus . . . ut viueremus. Explicit sermo b. Augustini Episcopi de
Vigilia pasche. (c) f. 32ʳᵛ Sequitur alius eiusdem vnde supra. Cum vos dilectissimi ad vigilandum . . . lucis orate. Explicit etc.
(a-c). PL xxxviii. 1089, 1089, 1091 (Sermons 120-2).

5. ff. 32ᵛ-37ᵛ Incipit Passio Sancte Eugenie virginis et Sanctorum Prothi et
Iacincti martirum. Septimo igitur consulatus . . . benedicentes deum? cui est
gloria in secula seculorum Amen. Explicit.
Cf. BHL, nos. 2666-7. Contemporary additions in the margin. At the end a longer addition, 'Denique ante hos inquit paucos dies . . . et procidens ad pedes eius etc' ', marked
for insertion on f. 33 at a point where there is a signe de renvoi and a note (cut into by the
binder), beginning 'Nota si placet continuare'. Another note on f. 33 refers to the text
added in the margins of f. 32ᵛ: 'Nota passio presens sancte Eugenie longius ac diffusius
inuenitur in pargameno MM. vii. Ideo si placet legatur [. . .] de quo libro hec glosa in
circumferencia prioris folii exarata addita presenti passioni est que compensi'o'sior apparet.

6. Sermons for feasts of B.V.M.: (a) ff. 33-40ᵛ Sermo beati Augustini de
Assumptione beate Marie Virginis. 'Legatur in die Ass.' Adest dilectissimi
fratres dies valde venerabilis . . . potestas eternitas. et nunc et semper . . . Amen.
Explicit . . . Virginis; (b) ff. 40ᵛ-42ᵛ Sermo beati Ambrosii episcopi de Natiui-

tate (festiuitate *interlined in red*) beate Marie virginis. Qui eciam ad eius con-
cepcionem potest applicari. Approbate consue'tu'dinis est aput cristianos . . .
graciam filii tui . . . Amen; (*c*) ff. 42ᵛ–44ᵛ Sermo beati Ambrosii episcopi. In
purificacione sancte Marie. Si subtiliter a fidelibus . . . secundum carnem qui . . .
Amen. Explicit.

(*a*). *PL* xxxix. 2130–4 (Serm. supp. 208). (*b*). *PL* cxli. 320–4 (Fulbert of Chartres).
(*c*). *PL* lxv. 838–842c (Fulgentius). A note in red at the foot of the first page of (*a*): 'Quod
ille sermo sit beati Augustini confirmatur ex vita cristi parte secunda in sermone de
Assumpcione . . .'.

7 (contemporary additions in blank spaces after arts. 6, 8). ff. 44ᵛ, 46ᵛ–48ᵛ
Ex Tercia parte Vitaspatrum sequitur infra . . . (f. 48) Hec collecta ex Quarta
parte vitaspatrum anno lxxxº. Ex Secundo libro Isidori de summo bono capitulo viii sequitur. Necesse est omni conuerso . . . (f. 48ᵛ) consumant. Dicebat
senex . . . Hec in Vitaspatrum in 2ᵃ parte. Seneca. Moneberis libenter . . .
sed blanda verba timeas. Deo gracias.

Extracts from Vitas Patrum (several editions were printed by 1480), Isidore, and Seneca.

8. Two miracles: (*a*) ff. 45–6 Incipit Miraculum preclarum de Gloriosa Virgine
et Martire Katherina. Episcopus quidam Mediolanensis sabinus nomine . . .
anulus et cartha apud Mediolanum vsque hodie seruantur. Explicit Miraculum . . .; (*b*) f. 46ʳᵛ Incipit Miraculum de Institucione festi Concepcionis
beate Marie virginis. Tempore illo diuine placuit pietati anglicorum gente de
malis suis corrigere . . . mercede remuneremur: qui cum . . . Explicit Miraculum
. . . anno lxxxº.

(*a*). *BHL*, no. 1682.

9. Sermons for saints days. (*a*) ff. 49–53ᵛ Sermo in Natali sancti Martini episcopi beati Bernhardi abbatis. Iure sermonem a nobis expetit tam noster hic conuentus . . . sed non recuso laborem⁷ fiat voluntas tua. (*b*) ff. 53ᵛ–55 Sermo beati
Bernhardi abbatis In vigilia beati Andree apostoli. Sanctorum festa precipua . . .
fodiat et scrutetur. (*c*) ff. 55–8 Sequitur Sermo beati Bernhardi Abbatis In die
sancti Andree apostoli. Celebrantes hodie . . . euadimus . . . prestante amen.
(*d*) ff. 58ᵛ–62 De sanctis Iacobo vel Iohanne apostolis. Lectio sancti euangelii⁷
secundum Matheum. In illo tempore: Accessit ad ihesum mater filiorum zebe-
dei . . . Ex commentario beati Iohannis episcopi⁷ de eadem leccione. Tunc
accessit ad eum . . . sint contristati? Explicit etc.

(*a–c*). *SBO* v (1968), 399–411/5, 423–6, 427–33. (*c*) is followed by the words 'Sequitur
alius sermo eiusdem de b. Andrea qui sic incipit ut sequitur Beati andree apostoli solem-
nitas hodie celebratur etc. (*SBO* v. 434). Require in alio libro nostro papirio. T. vi'.
f. 62ᵛ blank.

10. ff. 63–72 Sermo beati Leonis pape de festiuitate omnium sanctorum.
Hodie virgo mater ecclesia per totum orbem . . . in vita viuencium qui . . . Amen.
Explicit Sermo etc. Deo gracias.

11. (*a*) ff. 72–74ᵛ Incipit passio beate Dorothee virginis et Martiris. In diebus
illis in prouincia capadocie . . . perrexit ad cristum⁷ cui est . . . Amen. (*b*) ff. 74ᵛ–
76 Igitur Theophilus aduocatus . . . sanctos suos⁷ cui honor . . . Amen. Explicit
passio beatorum Dorothee virginis ac Theophili martirum. Deo Gracias.

(*c*) f. 76 In quacumque domo nomen fu(er)it uel ymago Virginis egregie dorothee
. . . participetur amen. Fertur temporibus nostris . . . ab incendio illesa.
Deo gracias.

(*a, b*). Cf. *BHL*, nos. 2321–4. (*c*). The virtues of the image of St. Dorothy, with an added
note of its efficacy on the occasion of a fire in Brunswick.

12. (*a*) ff. 76ᵛ–80 In die dedicacionis ecclesie continuacio omelie venerabilis bede
ad Mensam in Refectorio sequitur vbi in choro finitur. Ex omelia . . . super
euangelio luce. Non est arbor . . . Et misericordia tua subsequetur me . . . in
terra viuencium: ihesus cristus . . . qui . . . Amen. Explicit omelia venerabilis
bede . . . (*b*) ff. 80–3 Sermo beati Maximi episcopi in dedicacione ecclesie.
Hodie dilectissimi fratres anniuersariam . . . inueniri mereamur per . . . Amen.
Explicit . . .

(*b*). *PL* lvii. 895–902.

13. Seventeen lines of verse inside the cover, 'Non hominem magnum terrent
quecumque labores Vt tandem absoluat quod bene cepit opus . . .'.

ff. 83. Paper. 305 × 215 mm. Written space *c.* 250 × 150 mm. From 29 to 55 long lines.
Frame ruling. Collation probably: 1¹⁰ 2¹⁴ (ff. 11–24) 3¹² + 1 leaf after 9 (f. 33) 4¹² (ff. 37–48)
5¹² wants 6 after f. 54 6–7¹². At least three hands, two writing current types of cursiva and
hybrida and one a square usually non-current hybrida. Punctuation by flex (?) throughout.
Initials: (i) 6-line or 7-line, metallic red; (ii) 2-line or 3-line, red. Capital letters in the ink
of the text stroked with red. Bound in 1488 after a printed book (see below): 'ligatus an[no
domini] MCCCC 88°' inside the cover. The binding is of brown stamped leather repaired
by Birdsall & Son Ltd., Northampton, in or about 1938: stamps of twelve patterns, five
lozenge shaped, two round, two square, two rectangular, and a rosette, seven used on the
back cover and the rest on the front.

Written in Germany, probably at Huysburg (O.S.B., diocese of Halberstadt, from 1444
a member of the Bursfeld congregation), arts. 7, 8 in 1480 and the rest about then, and
bound in 1488 after Boethius, *De Consolatione Philosophiae*, Nuremberg, 1486 (*GKW*
4537). The table of contents on a flyleaf at the beginning lists the Boethius and the manuscript pieces after it and ends 'Huisborch sancta tuus est liber iste Maria'. References
in arts. 3c, e, 5, 9c are to books with pressmarks SS. v, MM. vii, and T. vi in the library
of the writer's own house, presumably Huysburg, and to a book at Ilsenburg, some thirty
miles south-west of Huysburg. Annotated on the pastedown by Dr. M. J. Routh, †1854.
Part of his great bequest to Durham University.

S.R. 3. A. 4 (Routh II. C. 12). *Petrus Dorlandus, Viola animae*
1497

(f. 1) Prologus in subscriptum opus. Petrus Dorlandus carthusien' Dilecto
fratri domino Iohanni ecclesie beati Laurencii leodien' monacho S.p.d. Dixit
do*mpnus* prior sancti iacobi cupis te scire . . . Vale Ex domo nostra (que
est diui baptiste nomine insignita)¹ altera luce euangeliste anno 1497. (f. 1ᵛ)
Epygramma in laudem Elucidarii Cristiane religionis. Matheus Herbenus.
lectori salutem. Quisque breui cupias artis cunctas superare . . . (18 lines).
(f. 2) Prologus in dyalogos sequentes . . . Huc queso te lector. . . Incipit dyalogus
primus. Inter magistrum Raymundum Sebundium et dominum dominicum
seminiuerbium . . . (f. 2ᵛ) Ysagogicum seu introductorium in materiam sub-

---

¹ These brackets are in the manuscript.

sequentem. Raymundus. Vnde nunc venis mi dominice . . . (f. 49) . . . quem tam beniuolum in meis precibus sum expertus. Finit inter magistrum Raymundum sebondium . . . disputacio . . . Theologia naturalis finit feliciter.

Printed in 1499 (*GKW* 9046) and later, but without the prologue which Dorlandus addressed to someone who thought that Raymundus might be heretical: '. . . Stupeo nimis dilectissime scrupulos tuos . . . lege hominem atque iterum lege et non modo catholicum sed catholicorum vnum principem luce clarius deprehendes . . .'. A leaf missing after f. 36. The words 'Hic codex fuit scriptus in augusto anno 1497' in red and a list of the six dialogues were added on f. 49 in the same hand as the prologue (f. 1^r), three lines at the foot of f. 2, and marginalia in red ink throughout. ff. 49^v–50^v left blank.

ff. 50. Paper. 280×200 mm. Written space *c.* 220×140 mm. 46–52 long lines. Frame ruling. Collation: 1^{12} 2^{10} 3^8+1 leaf after 2 (f. 24) and 1 leaf after 8 (f. 32) 4^{10} wants 5 after f. 36 5^{10} wants 10, blank, after f. 50. Written in cursiva and hybrida by probably eight scribes collaborating to do a rapid job (for a ninth scribe see above): quire 1 by two scribes from f. 1^v; quire 2 by three scribes, two of them taking two bifolia each, ff. 14, 15, 20, 21 and ff. 16–19 and the third one bifolium, ff. 13, 22; and the three other quires each by one scribe. The distribution of the hands in quire 2 and inexact joins at ff. 15^v and 20^r ('Hic nichil deficit') shows that the exemplar was copied page for page: probably the same method was used in quire 1 where the first of the two scribes wrote ff. 1^v–2^v/12, 3^v/19–4/10 and ff. 11–12^v. 3-line or 2-line initials in red. Bound in s. xviii: cf. below.

Probably bound from an early date, as now, after *Dionysii Areopagitae Opera*, Paris, 1498 (*GKW* 8409), which has at the beginning the contemporary ex-libris of the Benedictine abbey of St. Jacques, Liège, 'Liber monasterii sancti Iacobi leodien' ' and at the end a note that it was acquired 'per fratrem iohannem diestemium blaerum priorem huius loci in anno millesimo quingentesimo In ianuario'. Old pressmarks B 38 and D. 56. The former is the pressmark given for this book in the catalogue of the library of St. Jacques by N. Bouxhon (1637–1703): cf. S. Balau in *Bulletin de la commission royale d'histoire*, lxxi (1902), p. 30.[1] Notes by M. J. Routh on the flyleaf in front. Acquired as S.R. 2. b. 3.

Add. 189. 4B7. *Bonaventura, Breviloquium* s. xv in.

(*begins imperfectly in the preface*) sunt quinque. Secundi x. Tercii v^{que} . . . delectaciones in rebus delectabilibus. qualis (*ends imperfectly: only a little missing*).

Bonaventura, Breviloquium, as edn. A. M. a Vicetia, Freiburg im Breisgau, 1881, pp. 6/6–652/14. Three leaves are missing between these points and some text on ff. 1–5 has been lost. Numbered tables of chapters of each of the seven parts follow the preface (ff. 5–6), but the chapters are not numbered in the text. pt. 2, f. 12; 3, f. 20; 4, f. 28^v; 5, f. 38; 6, f. 48^v; 7, f. 61^v.

ff. 67. 200×138 mm. Written space 155×90 mm. 41 long lines. Collation: 1^8 wants 1: 2–6 damaged 2^8 wants 5 after f. 19 3–8^8 9^8 wants 4, 5, 8. 2-line red initials. Capital letters in the ink of the text marked with red. Contemporary binding of bevelled wooden boards, bare of leather: five bands: blue and white thread for the headbands: central clasp missing. Secundo folio (f. 1) *sunt quinque*.

Written in England. 'F' carved on the front cover. 'Presented by Alice Edleston of Gainford from her family collection 1953'.

[1] I owe to Dr. Doyle the reference to Balau's article on the library of St. Jacques.

EASTBOURNE. PARISH CHURCH

Horae[1]   s. xv[2]

1. ff. 1–6 Sequentiae of the Gospels.

The antiphon Te invocamus and prayers 'Precor in te sperantium . . .' and 'Ecclesiam tuam quesumus domine benignus illustra . . .' follow the extract from St. John.

2. ff. 6–9 Oratio. Obsecro te . . . Masculine forms.

3. ff. 9–11ᵛ Oratio deuota. O intemerata . . . orbis terrarum. De te enim . . . (*ends imperfectly*).

4. ff. 12–50ᵛ Hours of B.V.M. of the use of (Bayeux), beginning imperfectly. Hours of the Cross and of the Holy Spirit are worked in.

5. ff. 591–64 Penitential psalms and (f. 61) litany.

Four confessors: siluester leo anthoni yuo. f. 64ᵛ blank.

6. ff. 65–92ᵛ Office of the dead.

ff. i+92+i. 190×130 mm. Written space 115×70 mm. 17 long lines. Ruling in red ink. Collation: 1⁸ 2⁸ wants 4, 5 after f. 11 3–5⁸ 6⁸+1 leaf after 5 (f. 44) 7 three (ff. 48–50) 8–12⁸ 13 two. Six 12-line or 13-line pictures remain, three in art. 4 (matins of Cross, prime and vespers (Presentation of B.V.M.), and one before each of arts. 1, 5, 6. Initials: (i) blue, patterned in white, on gold grounds decorated with flowers; (ii, iii) 2-line and 1-line, gold on red and blue grounds patterned in white. Red and blue line fillers, with blobs of gold. Capital letters in the ink of the text filled with pale yellow. Continuous borders on picture pages and pages with initials of type (i): compartmented, f. 1. English diced russia, gilt, s. xviii, the back lettered 'Missale M.S.'. Secundo folio *eum non*.

Written in France. 'R. Farmer', f. iᵛ, is the signature of Richard Farmer, master of Emmanuel College, Cambridge, †1797: his sale 7 May 1798, lot 8094, to T. Jones for £1. 5s.[2] '1831. July the 19ᵗʰ', f. iᵛ. 'Trelissick Library Compartment A Shelf 2', f. i. 'B shelf 2', f. iᵛ. Armorial book-plate of 'Davies Gilbert of Tredrea, Cornwall, and East Bourn, Sussex' inside the cover. Given in 1929 (?) by Miss Davies-Gilbert: cf. *Sussex Notes and Queries*, ii (1929), 61–2.

EDINBURGH. COLUMBA HOUSE, SCOTTISH CATHOLIC ARCHIVES

J. de Fordun, Chronicon, cum continuatione W. Bower s. xv ex.–1509

1. ff. 1–77ᵛ Incipiunt tituli Capitulorum libri primi gentis (*sic*) Scotorum . . . (*table of 35 chapters of bk. 1*) . . . (f. 1ᵛ) Incipies opus . . . (*6 lines of verse*) . . .

    [1] Deposited in the Bodleian Library, Oxford.
    [2] Lot 8094 is described as 'Another in fine preservation, bound in russia'. Lot 8093, described as 'Missale Romanum', is now Bodleian MS. Gough Liturg. 11 (*Sum. Cat.* 18326), a Book of Hours of the use of Rome. That the Eastbourne manuscript is not of the use of Rome is hardly an objection to the identification. 'Missale' was in s. xviii and s. xix the common term for a catholic service book.

(f. 2) De vetustate originis et gestis scotorum Et primo de mundo sensibili Capitulum primum. Ex variis quippe veterum scripturis . . . (f. 77^v) finaliter voluissem. 'Explicit liber quintus'.

The five books of the history of Scotland to the death of David I by John de Fordun, whose name is to be found from the initial letters of the first sixteen words of the verses on f. 1^v. Ed. W. F. Skene (*Historians of Scotland*, i), 1871, pp. 1–253, who collates this copy occasionally as F and describes it on p. xxviii. A table of chapters precedes each book. Chapter headings are in the hand of the text in quire 1 only.

2. ff. 77^v–210 'Incipiunt tituli libri noni. . . . (*table of chapters*) . . . De successione gratiose sobolis regis dauid Capitulum primum.' Antequam ad successorem nepotem et heredem . . . (f. 199^v) transmittamus. Explicit liber cronic' 'Anno domini m^o v^c nono'. Quoniam huius precedentis scoticronicon voluminis prolixitas . . . prefici regnis. Quo tempore ante incarnacionem cristi incepit scota a qua scocia. Quisque loqui gaudet . . . (f. 202^v) Quem deus exaltet. regnum regat atque gubernet.[1] (f. 203) Incipiunt tituli libri decimi . . . (f. 210) finit foel(i)citer'.

An abridgment of the abridgment of Bower's continuation of Fordun to 1437 found in N.L.S., Adv. 35. 1. 7, for which cf. Skene, pp. xviii, xli. The longer abridgment, apparently Bower's own work, divides the Scotichronicon into thirty-five books numbered 6–40 in continuation of Fordun, instead of into eleven, numbered 6–16. The shorter abbreviation found here begins (bk. 9, ch. 1, Antequam ad . . .) with bk. 8, ch. 8 of Adv. and after a chapter of eight lines on David's son Henry passes to Adv. bk. 9, ch. 20. From here to bk. 30, the book numbers of Adv. are followed, but bks. 16, 20–2, 25 are omitted. Bk. 31 corresponds to Adv. bks. 31, 32, bk. 32 to Adv. bks. 33, 34, bk. 33 to Adv. bks. 35, 36, bk. 34 to Adv. bk. 37, bk. 35 to Adv. bks. 38, 39 and bk. 36 to Adv. bk. 40. Throughout, Adv.'s chapters are shortened and many are omitted. The verses on ff. 199^v–202^v are 226 of the 500 verses printed in Goodall's edition of Fordun-Bower (1759), ii. 521–33.

Nine blank spaces in the text on f. 79^v suggest that the exemplar was damaged at this point. A few notes were added in the margins in s. xvi^1, among them: f. 150^v, that two horsemen appeared to the sacrist at Glastonbury on the eve of the battle of Bannockburn, saying that they were on their way to Bannockburn to deal vengeance for the unjust death of Simon de Montfort; f. 156^v, Testamentum Regis R. Brois. Scotica fit guerra peditis . . . (*7 lines of verse*); f. 157, One fuyt suld be all scottis weir . . . (*14 lines of verse*, rendering the Latin on the opposite page). Marginalia on ff. 26, 51^v, 77 suggest a special interest in St. Andrews. f. 210^v blank.

3, added on the flyleaf (f. vi) in the hand of the addition on f. 150^v. De quinque filiis Regis eduardi de Windsor. Notandum quod iste eduardus . . . Iste henricus rex deposuit predictum regem ricardum qui sepultus est apud sterling.

Seventeen lines nearly as *Liber Pluscardensis*, ed. F. J. H. Skene, p. 333: that Roger Mortimer was declared heir to the throne by King Richard at the parliament of Shrewsbury and that Henry IV destroyed a 'constitutio' in a Glastonbury chronicle 'que posuit filias rogeri Mortymar quod deberent succedere ad Coronam . . . et alteram pro se et suis fecit'.

ff. vi+211+ii. For f. (vi) see above. The foliation, s. xvii (?), starts with i on the first leaf of text and runs to ccx: two successive leaves are numbered lxxi.[2]. 325 × 235 mm (240 mm on leaves folded in by the binder in order to preserve marginalia). Written space *c.* 215 × 140 mm. Long lines, 32 on ff. 81–8, 42 on ff. 96–202, and a varying number up to 51 in art. 1. Frame ruling on ff. 1–77. Collation: 1–7^{10} 8^{10}+1 leaf after 10 (f. 80) 9–13^8 14^6

[1] The line before this gives James II's age as 17 at the date of writing.
[2] I follow this numbering, but use arabic figures.

(ff. 105–10) 15–22⁸ 23⁶+1 leaf before 1 (f. 173) 24⁸ 25–26⁶ 27² (ff. 201–2) 28² 29⁶. Art. 1 in skilled cursiva of a French type. Art. 2 in more or less textura-like hybrida by at least two hands (changes at ff. 81, 89). Red initials, (i) beginning books, (ii) beginning chapters, 4-line and (art. 2) 2-line: they appear to be by one hand throughout, probably the same hand as wrote the headings (except in quire 1), added the tables of chapters of art. 2, and wrote the date on f. 199ᵛ. Binding of s. xviii, rebacked. Secundo folio (f. 3) *deus et*.

Written in Scotland and annotated there in s. xviᶦ. Probably in France later in s. xvi, when 'Magister Robertus fournier 1567' was written on f. 108 and 'Lois fournier 1580' on f. 41 (cf. also ff. 16ᵛ, 17, 143ᵛ). A gift to the Scots College in Paris from James, fourth Earl of Drummond (†1716) in the year after he was forced to leave the kingdom: 'Ex libris Collegii Scotorum Parisien' Ex dono Illᵐᶦ et Nobᵐᶦ D.D. Jacobi Comitis de Drummond An. Dom. 1694', f. 1. 'P.A.', f. 210, bottom left.

Psalterium

s. XIII med.

A psalter now lacking all after Ps. 116 and ten leaves before this point. Nine of the missing leaves are those on which Pss. 1, 26, 38, 51 and 52, 68, 80, 97, 101 and 109 began. The other gap is in Ps. 105, after f. 83. The text begins now in Ps. 2: 4.

Marginalia in cursiva, mainly of s. xiv/xv. They include textual corrections, antiphons, the word 'Gloria' to mark the division of Pss. 36, 67, 77, 103, 104, and 106 and at f. 82 a gloss in German 'pfleger' above 'acola' (Ps. 104: 23); also, throughout, a numbering of the verses at intervals of fifty, for example 'cccl' on f. 21ᵛ and 'd' on f. 24.

ff. ii+82+ii, foliated (i, ii), 2–17, 19–29, 31–39, 41–50, 52–63, 65–75, 77, 79–83, 88, 84, 85, 87, 90–92 (93, 94). This foliation, s. xviii?, takes account of all the now missing leaves, except the leaf after f. 83, and passes in error from 85 to 87. 167 × 110 mm. Written space 125 × 88 mm. 19 long lines. Ruling in ink. Collation: 1–9⁸ (single leaves missing in quires 1, 3–5, 7, 8) 10 three (ff. 73–5) 11⁸ wants 8 after f. 83 12¹⁰ wants 6, 10 (ff. 84–7, 88 (now misplaced before f. 84), 90–2). Well written. *g* is 8-shaped. Little punctuation: the flex is used occasionally, for example after 'suo' (Ps. 13: 1). Initials: (i) removed; (ii) 3-line, red and pale blue (sometimes monochrome), with red ornament: the patterns are distinctive and effective; (iii) of verses, 1-line, red or blue. Each psalm is headed P S in coloured capitals. Binding of limp parchment, s. xx. Secundo folio *nabit eos*.

Apparently in Germany in s. xv and probably written there. Liturgical directions were added in s. xviii (in Britain ?).

EDINBURGH. FACULTY OF ADVOCATES

When the Faculty of Advocates gave their manuscripts to the National Library of Scotland in 1925 they retained ownership of most of the legal manuscripts listed in *Summary Catalogue of the Advocates' Manuscripts*, 1971, pp. 67–83, and among them twenty-one medieval manuscripts: Adv. 3.1.12; 10.1–1–3; 10.1.4(i); 10.1.4(ii); 10.1.5; 18.1.8; 18.4.15; 18.6.17; 25.4.10, 13–15; 25.5.6, 7, 10; 28.4.10; 28.6.1, 2; 28.7.5. These manuscripts are kept in the National Library of Scotland.

EDINBURGH. NATIONAL GALLERIES
OF SCOTLAND

The following manuscripts were deposited in the National Library of Scotland in 1957 and given numbers in the National Library series.

7122. Psalter written in France for Dominican use, s. xv med.

7123. Psalter written in the Netherlands, s. xiii².

7124. Hours of B.V.M. of the use of (Rome), written in France (?), s. xv¹.

7125. Hours of B.V.M. written in France, s. xv¹.

7126. Hours of B.V.M. of the use of (Rouen), s. xv¹.

7127. Hours of B.V.M. of the use of (Rouen), s. xv med.

7128. Hours of B.V.M. of the use of (Tournai), partly in Netherlandish, s. xv¹.

7129. Hours of B.V.M. of the use of (Utrecht) written in the Netherlands, probably for Augustinian canonesses, s. xv med.

7130. Hours of B.V.M. in Netherlandish and Latin. 1473 (?).
'Dit boeck hoert toe dirck borren wijf van ameronghen', in the main hand, f. 147ᵛ. The antiphons at prime and none are Quando natus es and Ecce maria. The capitulum at each of these hours is Ecce tu pulcra es.

7131. Prayers and meditations in Netherlandish and Latin, s. xv¹.

7132. Hours of B.V.M. of the use of (Utrecht) in Netherlandish, s. xv med.

7133. Hours (not now including hours of B.V.M.) in Netherlandish, s. xv med.

7134. Hours of B.V.M. of the use of (Utrecht) in Netherlandish, s. xv med.

7135. Hours (not now including hours of B.V.M.) in Netherlandish, s. xv¹.

7136. Devotions in Netherlandish, s. xv ex. Paper and parchment.

7137. Rule of St. Francis, 'Spiegel der volcomonheyt', papal privileges granted to the order of St. Francis, and rule of novices, all in Netherlandish, s. xv¹.

7138. Devotions in Netherlandish, s. xv med.

7140. De viris illustribus from Jerome (ff. 13–59ᵛ), Sigebert (ff. 63–101), Isidore (ff. 105ᵛ–118ᵛ) and Gennadius (ff. 120ᵛ–153ᵛ), preceded by an index, all 'scriptus per fratrem Iohannem petri delff', Ord. Carth., at the charterhouse of Utrecht, A.D. 1457–69.

7141. Fragments of three civil law books: (a) thirty-two leaves of Justinian, Institutes, written in England, s. xiii²; (b) nine leaves of Digestum novum written in England (?), s. xiii¹; (c) thirty-three leaves of Codex Justiniani written in Italy (?), s. xiii¹, but early in England. Respectively, the first four quires, the last quire, and the last four quires of manuscripts. (c) contains the explicit of bk. 9, and books 10–12.

7142. An abbreviation of Seneca's letters, with an introduction to each letter, scholia, and interlinear glosses, and a preface beginning 'Cum animus uirtuosus sit tamquam deus incarnatus ipse seneca', written in Germany in 1508. Paper. From the Kloss collection and Sotheby's sale, 7 May 1835, lot 4619.

EDINBURGH. NATIONAL LIBRARY OF SCOTLAND

I. Advocates' Manuscripts.

The Faculty of Advocates gave its manuscripts, apart from legal manuscripts,[1] to the National Library of Scotland in 1925.

Catalogues: (i) begun in the first half of s. xix and added to at intervals, according to subjects, in ten manuscript volumes, together with a two-volume typescript index; (ii) by Miss C. R. Borland in 1906–8, according to subjects, in four manuscript volumes, (1) Theology, (2) Law, History, Chartularies, (3) Poetry and Romance, Classics, Science, (4) Addenda; (iii) typescript, in progress; (iv) *Summary Catalogue of the Advocates' Manuscripts*, Edinburgh 1971; (v) I. C. Cunningham, 'Latin classical manuscripts in the National Library of Scotland', *Scriptorium*, xxvii (1973), 64–90.

(ii) includes all but twenty-one of the medieval manuscripts. (iii) is available in the manuscript room. In (iv) the section 'Mediaeval Manuscripts', pp. 100–12, has 179 entries. This figure includes the legal manuscripts, three manuscripts in Greek, and fourteen cartularies or registers, but not the seventeen medieval manuscripts listed in the section 'Gaelic Manuscripts', pp. 33–46.[2]

II. General Collection.

National Library of Scotland, Catalogue of Manuscripts acquired since 1925, 3 vols., contains descriptions of MSS. 1–1800 (vol. 1, 1938), MSS. 1801–4000 (vol. 2, 1966), MSS. 4001–4940 (vol. 3, 1968) A continuation in typescript available in the manuscript room covers MSS. 4941–11000. A volume of photographs, *Notable accessions since 1925*, Edinburgh, 1965, was produced to celebrate forty years of the National Library. It is referred to below as *NLS XL*. The medieval manuscripts are:[3]

651. s. xvi in. A. Wyntoun, Chronicle of Scotland. Paper.

652. s. xv². Psalterium. Flanders for a customer from Scotland.

F. C. Eeles in *PSAS* lxvi (1931–2), 426–41, with eight facsimiles, including one of the calendar for September which includes 'Dedicacio ecclesie de perch' (3 Sept.). McRoberts, no. 64.

2739. s. xvi¹. Sermones, etc. Germany (Erfurt, Ord. Carth.).

H. 140 at the Erfurt Charterhouse (*MBDS* ii. 428). Römer, ii. 116. Paper. Contemporary binding.

2799. s. xv med. Bartholomaeus de S. Concordio, Summa casuum. Italy.

---

[1] See above, Edinburgh, Faculty of Advocates.

[2] Add, as Miss Elspeth Yeo tells me, Adv. 34.4.16 (i), a parchment roll, s. xiii¹, containing (1) the end of a genealogy of Christ and (2) the first two chapters of the treatise on the mass beginning 'In virtute sancte crucis', ascribed sometimes to Richard of Wedinghausen, but here to Pope Innocent III.

[3] This list excludes the deposited manuscripts listed above under Edinburgh, National Galleries of Scotland and below under Society of Antiquaries of Scotland.

2808. s. xv ex. F. de Castillione, Oratio in Coena Domini. Italy.

Humanistic script.

3055. s. xiv med. Preces de Passione Christi in septem horas. Preces de novem angelorum ordinibus. France.

ff. 14. Probably once part of a book of hours.

3056. s. xv med. Augustinus, etc. Italy.

Römer, ii. 116. Paper.

3178. s. xv². Horae ad usum (Sarum).

5048. s. xiii¹. Kalendarium (fragm.). Scotland (Holyrood, O.S.A.).

ff. 2. July–October only. *PSAS* lxix. 471–9. McRoberts, no. 11.

5461. s. xiii med. Missale, cum notis (fragm.). Scotland (Jedburgh, O.S.A., ?).

ff. 8. Formerly the cover of a cartulary, 1542–1594, of the lordship of Jedburgh Abbey, now in the Scottish Record Office, CH. 6/6/3. *Trans. Edinburgh Bibliographical Soc.* iii (1952), 1–16. *NLS XL*, pl. 3. McRoberts, no. 18.

6121. s. xii ex. Augustinus, etc. England (Buildwas, O.C.; London, Ord. Carm.).[1]

Römer, ii. 116. Augustine is preceded by pseudo-Jerome on Mark and verses beginning 'Continuare volumus . . .'. These two texts occur together also in Emmanuel College, Cambridge, MS. 56, s. xv, and the verses were known to Dom Germain Morin only from that manuscript: cf. *RB* xxxi. 174–8. Contemporary binding. The bosses on the front cover only, four marks near the foot of the back cover, and the numbering of the pieces in arabic figures, s. xiii, are distinctive Buildwas features. Later at the Carmelite convent in London (Ker, *MLGB*, p. 124). Bodleian, MS. Bodley 730 has the same history.

6122. s. xii¹—xii/xiii. Miscellanea. England.

Six independent sections. (A) s. xii², (i) ff. 1–51 Part of P. Comestor, Historia Scholastica; (ii) ff. 52–64 A commentary on biblical books, as in the Christ Church, Canterbury, manuscript now Corpus Christi College, Cambridge, 288, ff. 111–24: begins 'Ozia lepro percusso'. (B) s. xii², (iii) ff. 65–77ᵛ Theological questions beginning 'Spiritus sanctus multiplex dicitur'; (iv) ff. 78–112ᵛ A mainly medical piece, apparently the same as that in New College, Oxford, 171, f. 89. (C) s. xii ex., (v) ff. 113–31 (P. Blesensis), Speculum Juris Canonici; (vi, vii) ff. 132ᵛ–171ᵛ Notes from the Digest, etc. (D) s. xii², (viii) ff. 142–9 A 'Summa de testibus' found also in B.L., Egerton 2819, f. 3ᵛ. (E) s. xii¹, in an admirable hand from the west of England (?), (ix) ff. 150–165ᵛ 'Sententie collecte de libris Ieronimi Ambrosii Augustini de corpore domini. Beatus Ieronimus in epistola ad Ephesios. Dupliciter inquit intelligitur caro cristi . . . mira non possunt'; (x) ff. 165ᵛ–166 Eight paragraphs, six of them 'De corpore canonum' on mass, the first beginning 'Missarum celebrationes ante horam diei terciam'; (xiii–xv) ff. 166ᵛ–181ᵛ, 181ᵛ–184, 184–6 Pieces by Odo of Cambrai and a letter of Ivo of Chartres (*PL* clx. 1053–70, 1119–22 and *PL* clxii. 285–8). (F) s. xii/xiii, (xvi) ff. 188–211ᵛ Seventeen paragraphs, identified in *PL* cxcvi (Richard of St. Victor), except the last five (ff. 197ᵛ–200ᵛ), followed by Richard of St. Victor, De statu interioris hominis, ending imperfectly. Binding perhaps contemporary with section F.

6123. s. xv med. Kalendarium. England.

<hr>

[1] 6121–31 were bought from the family of Borthwick of Crookston in 1946, 1960, and 1961. Other manuscripts from this source were sold at Sotheby's, 3 June 1946, lots 192, 193, 196, 198–210.

6124. s. xv in. Commentary on Matthew 3:16–17, 5:10–12, in English (fragm.).
ff. 2. Was the wrapper of a document relating to Swanton Abbot (Norfolk).

6125. s. xiv¹. Chronicon Angliae, etc. England (Norwich, O.S.B.).
Art. 1, a chronicle running to 1317, is 'per fratrem minorem compilatus' (of Yarmouth convent apparently), as the later Norwich monk owner noted in his table of contents. Ker, *MLGB*, pp. 138, 285.

6126. s. xv¹. W. Hilton, Scale of Perfection, bk. 1, in English.

6127. s. xv in. Pauline Epistles, in English.
Belonged to William Lambarde in 1596.

6128. s. xv med. Brut Chronicle to 1377, in English.

6129. s. xv². Horae B.V.M.: use of (Rouen).

6130. s. xv². Horae B.V.M.: use of (Rome). France.
The birth of Claude de Mailly, 22 May 1507, is in the calendar.

6131. s. xv ex. Horae B.V.M.: use of (Rouen).

8893. s. xv¹. Horae B.V.M.: use of (Amiens).

8899. s. xv/xvi. Horae B.V.M. (fragm.).
f. 1 from the same book as B.L., Royal 2 D. xl: cf. Janet Backhouse in *BMQ* xxxvii, 1973, 95–102, and pl. xli. *NLS XL*, pl. 15.

9153. s. xiii¹. Bernardus, etc. Germany (?), O.C. (?).
Bernard, De consideratione and sermons, Hugh of St. Victor, De arra animae, Drogo, De officiis divinis (*PL* clxvi. 1557–64), three pieces in verse, 'De natura filomene. De filomena legitur Quod cum deprehendit . . .' (ff. 137ᵛ–140ᵛ: stanzas 6–85 of the Philomena, *RH*, no. 14893, attributed to John de Pecham, *c.* 1230–92), 'Stans ad crucem filii uirgo cruciatur . . .' (68 lines, ff. 140ᵛ–141), 'Stabat iuxta cristi crucem . . .' (f. 141ᴵᵛ: *RH*, no. 19411), and a small collection of miracles, the first of them concerning Geoffrey, prior of Clairvaux (ff. 141ᵛ–143).
Philomena is in the main hand. Palaeographically it is perhaps just possible that this is an early work of Pecham, to which he later added stanzas 1–5, 86, 87.

9247. s. xii med. Boethius, De consolatione philosophiae (imperfect). England.
Written space 100 × 55 mm. 21 long lines.

9740. s. xiii/xiv. W. de Mandagoto, Libellus electionum; J. de Deo; etc. Italy.
This and MSS. 9741–3 were bought at Sotheby's, 2 Feb. 1960, lots 277, 284, 307, 314.

9741. s. xv med. Abbreviatio Sententiarum P. Lombardi; Pseudo-'Albertus Magnus de laude b. marie'; etc. Germany (Erfurt, Ord. Carth.).
Stegmüller, *Sent.*, no. 9; Stegmüller, no. 1061. H. 58 at the Erfurt Charterhouse (*MBDS* ii. 398).

9742. s. xv². Horae B.V.M.: use of Rome. Italy (Ferrara ?).
NLS XL, pl. 14. In 1948 T. de Marinis noted the provenance as almost certain.

9743. s. xv med. Horae: use of (Rome). Italy (Florence).
Humanistic hand. Arms of Ceruti.

9744. s. xv in. Ars dictaminis. Italy.

ff. 4 from a larger manuscript. Paper.

9998. s. xiii ex. Facetus; Speculum puerorum; De contemptu mundi. France.

Walther, nos. 3692, 3690, 2521. Nineteen leaves of a larger manuscript, foliated in a medieval hand 116–34. Item 13 in E. P. Goldschmidt's list 26 (1937), in which item 6 (Aesop) was another part of the same book.

9999. s. xv in. Adam Scotus, Sermones; Vita S. Hugonis; etc. England (London, Ord. Carth.).

MMBL i. 9–12. Bought at Sotheby's, 10 July 1972, lot 26.

10000. s. xiii in. Psalterium. England for a Scotswoman.

C. W. Dyson Perrins MS. 3 (*Catalogue*, 1920, pp. 9–11): his sale at Sotheby's, 3 Apr. 1957, lot 5. *Trésors*, no. 8. *NLS XL*, pl. 2. McRoberts, no. 9.

10981. s. xiii ex. Horae B.V.M.: use of (Paris).

Acc. 2710. s. xiii¹. Missale. Scotland (Lesmahagow, O.S.B.).

Cockerell sale, Sotheby's, 3 Apr. 1957, lot 5. McRoberts, no. 10. Three flyleaves containing additions, s. xiii², were left out of the binding made for Sydney Cockerell and are now kept separately, together with the former cover, s. xviii¹, and a flyleaf inscribed 'Dominus Petre 1725'.

Acc. 3037. s. xii¹. Biblia (fragm.). Italy.

A bifolium of a handsome and large Bible, used as a wrapper. 535 × 370 mm. Written space 405 × 245 mm. 2 cols. 44 lines. f. 1 contains Amos from 9: 7 and the common prologue and text of Obadiah as far as verse 20. f. 2 contains Micah 2: 4–5: 6. Obadiah is marked 'Liber xix' and Micah 'Liber xxi'.

Acc. 3502. s. xiv med. Gregorius, In Evangelia (fragm.: f. 1). England.

Acc. 3822.1. s. xv². Antiphonale (Sanctorale, etc.). Italy (O.S.B., in or near Mantua, perhaps Polirone).

Antiphons for feasts from 2 July (Visitation of B.V.M.) to 22 Nov. (Cecilia), for the common of saints (f. 86ᵛ), dedication of church, and 'Commemorationes communes', and for feasts from 30 Nov. (Andrew, f. 110), ending imperfectly at 29 June (Peter and Paul, f. 184). Includes 'In festo SS. Monacorum' in November, the Presentation of B.V.M. (21 Nov.), and 'In solemnitate S.P.N. Benedicti' (21 Mar., f. 151).

605 × 455 mm. Minims 20 mm high. For one of a few elaborate historiated initials see *Accessions of Manuscripts 1959–64*, pl. 1 Book-stamp of the 'PARROCHIA DI S. FLORIANO MAN[TVÆ]', s. xix, and below it the words '31 Agosto 1868 F. Arieti Parrᵒ'.[1] Alessandro Castellani sale, Rome, 29 Mar. 1884, lot 839 to the Edinburgh Museum of Science and Art. Given by the Royal Scottish Museum in 1964.

Acc. 3822. 2. s. xv ex.(?). Graduale (Sanctorale). Italy, O.P.

500 × 360 mm. A bifolium at each end from a very large and handsome homiliary in an Italian hand, s. xii ex., in which the initials have been drawn in in pencil, but not coloured: written space c. 440 × 200 mm: 2 cols. 43 lines. Lot 840 in the Castellani sale (cf. Acc. 3822. 1). Given as Acc. 3822. 1.[2]

Acc. 4118. A.D. 1499(?). Officium mortuorum, etc. Netherlands for John Brown, dean of Aberdeen Cathedral.

---

[1] Cf. above, Colchester, Colchester and Essex Museum, 221. 32.

[2] Acc. 3822 includes also some cut-out initials, s. xv and (one) s. xiii ex.

Described by D. McRoberts, 'Dean Brown's Book of Hours', *Innes Review*, xix (1968), 144–67, with facsimiles of six double opening. Bought at Christie's, 28 Apr. 1966, lot 162.

Acc. 4225, a small collection of fragments from bindings, pastedowns, etc., given by the Signet Library, includes two leaves of a handsome mid twelfth-century English copy of pseudo-Jerome, Breviarium in Psalmos, with lemmata in blue and red. Punctuation includes the flex (?).

Acc. 6236. s. xv ex. Preces, etc. Southern Netherlands (or Scotland ?) for Robert (Blackadder ?). Bought in 1974.

EDINBURGH. NEW COLLEGE[1]

J. Laing, *Catalogue of the Printed Books and Manuscripts in the Library of the New College, Edinburgh*. Edinburgh, 1868. The manuscripts are described on pp. 935–7.

Med. 1. *Jeronimus; Augustinus*   s. xv med.

1. ff. 1–29^v Ten letters of the correspondence between Jerome and Augustine printed in *PL* xxii and in *CSEL* liv–lvi: (*a*) ff. 1–3^v, Ep. 56; (*b*) ff. 4–6, Ep. 67, ending 'presumentis'; (*c*) ff. 6^v–8, Ep. 104; (*d*) ff. 8–20^v, Ep. 112; (*e*) ff. 20^v–21^v, Ep. 102; (*f*) ff. 21^v–26, Ep. 110; (*g*) f. 26^{rv}, Ep. 115; (*h*) ff. 26^v–27^v, Ep. 101, ending 'in domino gaudent'; (*i*) ff. 27^v–29, Ep. 105; (*j*) f. 29^v, Ep. 103.

(*a–c, f, h*) are Augustine's letters: Römer, ii. 117. In (i) the passage 'memor . . . frater' follows 'flagitem', as in Berlin, lat. 17. Greek is written boldly. 'IHS' at the head of f. 1.

2. ff. 29^v–31^v Incipit hieronimi presbiteri expositio litterarum hebraicarum in psalmo cxviii. Nudus tertius . . . calcare. Sit legenti letitia. audienti fides. credenti corona. Amen. Amen. Amen. domine.

Ep. 30, ending like Berlin lat. 17.

3. ff. 31^v–53 Incipiunt sancti hieronimi ad hibediam questiones. Quomodo esse . . . seruetur. Expliciunt indicia. Incipit liber primus. Ignota uultu . . . et extinguntur in nobis.

Ep. 120.

4. ff. 53^v–59 Incipit uita sancti pauli heremite edita a beato hieronimo. presbitero. Inter multos sepe . . . purpuras cum regnis suis. Explicit.

PL xxiii. 17–30.

5. ff. 59–64 Incipit uita sancti malchi captiui. monachi edita a beato hieronimo. Qui nauali . . . non posse superari. Explicit.

PL xxiii. 55–62.

[1] Besides the manuscripts described here, the library possesses a small manuscript of about 100 leaves containing prayers on the petitions of the Lord's Prayer and other prayers in Dutch and a calendar and the penitential psalms in Latin. It is well written and is dated 1555 at the end in the main hand.

6. (*a*) f. 64^{rv} Incipit damasi episcopi ad hieronimum. Dilectissimo filio . . . Dormientem te . . . errore benedixit? (*b*) ff. 65–72 Epistola Hieronimi ad damasum episcopum . . . Beatissimo pape Damaso Hieronimus in cristo salutem. Postquam epistolam . . . saluus erit.

Epp. 35, 36. The name Isaac is spelled 'ysahac'.

7. f. 72 Item hieronimi presbiteri in expositione euangelii secundum matehum (*sic*) inter cetera. Aue Rabi . . . interficeret eum.

PL xxvi. 207D, on Matthew 26: 49.

8. (*a*) f. 72^{rv} Epistola hieronimi ad rufinum. Iohannes apostolus et euangelista in epistola sua ait . . . me absoluet. (*b*) ff. 72^{v}–73 Alia eiusdem ad eundem. Dominus humilitatis magister. disceptantibus . . . impertias. Deo laus et gratia per infinita secula.

9. ff. 73^{v}–74 Ex libro officiorum Ysidori in regula canonicorum. Duo sunt genera clericorum . . .

Followed by further extracts on 'sacerdotes mali' attributed to Basil, Gregory, Augustine, and 'Albuinus' and from Malachi (2: 2).

ff. ii+76+i. ff. i, 77 are modern paper leaves. 242 × 165 mm. Written space 150 × 115 mm. 26 long lines. Collation: 1–9^8 10^4. Fere-humanistica by one good hand throughout: *r* is a descender in final position and often in other positions: *st* and *ct* ligatures widely spaced, but not actually joined. Initials: (i) f. 1, 4-line, in colour on decorated blue ground with red ornament in the margin, the height of the written space; (ii) 3-line, red with pink ornament or blue with red ornament. Capital letters in the ink of the text stroked with red. Conspicuous headings in large red rustic capitals. Contemporary (?) binding of wooden boards covered with red leather bearing a pattern of fillets, rebacked and repaired: two strap-and-pin fastenings from the upper to the lower cover missing. Secundo folio *Petrus*.

Written in Spain. 'N°. 114', f. ii, s. xviii (?). MS. 80 in Pettigrew's catalogue of the manuscripts of the Duke of Sussex, *Bibliotheca Sussexiana*, i (1827). Duke of Sussex sale, 31 July 1844, lot 29. 'Mr Sargent['s own]', inside the cover. Given by F. Sargent, probably before 12 Nov. 1844.[1]

Med. 2. *Athanasius; Vigilius Tapsensis* s. xv med.

1. ff. 1–66^v Athanasii Alexandrini Episcopi Contra Gentiles per Ambrosium Monacum Florentinum in Latinum Traductus. Liber Primus Incipit. Vere ac diuine religionis . . . deum et patrem in cristo iesu domino nostro cui . . . amen.

The translation by Ambrogio Traversari, general of the order of Camaldoli 1431–9, of the Contra Gentiles and (f. 32^v) De incarnatione verbi of St. Athanasius. Printed in *Athanasii Opera*, Paris, 1519.

2. ff. 67–97 Incipit liber primus beati Athanasii alexandrini episcopi de unita trinitate deitatis. Tu unus deus pater . . . et unitas et sempiternitas trinitatis. Explicit liber viii.

The eight books of Pseudo-Athanasius (Vigilius Tapsensis), De trinitate. *PL* lxii. 237–88.

[1] MSS. Med. 1–4 are not entered in the second Benefactors' Book begun on 12 Nov. 1844, but some of Mr. Sargent's many benefactions to the library were before this date. The first Benefactors' Book is missing.

Bk. 2, f. 72; 3, f. 75; 4 (ending 'distinguntur', edn., col. 267B), f. 81ᵛ; 5 (ending 'diuinitatis', edn., col. 276B), f. 85; 6 (ending 'uidebatur', edn., col. 282c), f. 89ᵛ; 7, f. 93; 8, f. 95ᵛ. There is no indication that the text here and in art. 5 is in question and answer form.

3. ff. 97–116 Incipit liber eiusdem athanasii episcopi de Spiritu Sancto. Hiis qui filium dei creatum . . . effici poterimus. Explicit liber de spiritu sancto.

Pseudo-Athanasius (Vigilius Tapsensis). *PL* lxii. 307–31.

4. ff. 116–24 Incipit professio arriana et confessio captholica Eiusdem Athanasii. Arriani dicunt filium dei non de substantia dei patris genitum . . . quam creatori qui est benedictus in secula seculorum amen. Explicit professio arriana et confessio captholica.

Pseudo-Athanasius (Vigilius Tapsensis). *PL* lxii. 297–308.

5. ff. 124–130ᵛ Incipit fides beati athanasii alexandrini episcopi. Credere iubemur in dei patris . . . cum omnibus nobis Amen.

Pseudo-Athanasius (Vigilius Tapsensis). *PL* lxii. 289–98.

ff. ii+130+i. f. ii is a parchment flyleaf with table of contents, s. xv. 233 × 170 mm. Written space 150 × 90 mm. 26 long lines. Ruling in ink. Collation: 1–6¹⁰ 7⁶ 8–13¹⁰ 14⁴. A neat and rather unusual humanistic script. Initials: (i) f. 1, 4-line, gold on ground of pink, green, and blue, edged with blue and decorated with white vine interlace and dots in groups of three: in the lower margins cupids hold a gold hoop; (ii) 3-line and 4-line, gold. Binding of s. xix. Secundo folio *neque iuxta*.

Written in Italy (Florence?). MS. 62 in Pettigrew's catalogue of the manuscripts of the Duke of Sussex, *Bibliotheca Sussexiana*, i (1827). Duke of Sussex sale, 31 July 1844, lot 28. 'Mʳ Sargent's own', f. i. Given as MS. Med. 1.

Med. 3. *Bonaventura, etc.*   s. XIII ex.

1. ff. 1–23 Itinerarium Bonauenture. Siue speculacio pauperis in deserto. Siue itinerarium mentis in deum. Primum de gradibus ascensionis in deum . . . (*table of 7 chapters*). Capitulum primum. De gradibus ascensionis in deum. Beatus uir cuius est auxilium abs te . . . et dicet omnis populus. fiat fiat. Amen.

Quaracchi edn., v. 296–313.

2. ff. 23ᵛ–43 Xpisto crucifixus sum cruci uerus dei cultor . . . graciarum actio. decus et imperium. per infinita secula seculorum. Amen.

Bonaventura, Lignum Vitae. Quaracchi edn., viii. 68–86.

3. ff. 43ᵛ–58ᵛ Incipit regula beati Basilii capadocie archiepiscopi. Audi fili admonicionem patris tui . . . rex glorie. Qui cum patre . . . Amen.

PL ciii. 683–700. ff. 59–60ᵛ blank.

4. ff. 61–70 Oratio siue meditatio sancti Augustini ad deum patrem omnipotentem. Domine deus meus da cordi meo te desiderare . . . crudelitatem. Amen.

PL clviii. 877–85+858–65 (Pseudo-Anselm, Oratio 10+Oratio 2). Römer, ii. 117.

5. Six paragraphs: (*a*) ff. 70–72ᵛ Quid tibi est o homo quod sic extolleris . . . affectionibus tuis et amore languentibus desiderius refice dulcoratam. Amen;

(*b*) ff. 72^v–73^v Da michi domine deus meus fidem rectam. spem . . . perpetualiter capiam. Amen; (*c*) ff. 73^v–76 Obsecro itaque domine . . . ac sempiternaliter uiuis et regnas deus per secula seculorum Amen; (*d*) ff. 76–78 O domine deus meus quomodo ausus sum te alloqui . . . vt sim unum cum cristo. Amen; (*e*) ff. 78–84^v O anima mea cogitemus quam sit breuis uita. quam lubrica uia . . . in omnibus erit deus; (*f*) ff. 84^v–86^v Quociens te sentis turpibus cogitacionibus pulsari . . . et digne laudare mereamur. Per dominum nostrum. et cetera.

6. (*a*) ff. 86^v–94^v Hugo de sancto uictore. De excitacione tepide mentis in amorem dei. Quoniam in medio laqueorum positi sumus . . . non erit finis. Cuius est honor et cetera. (*b*) ff. 94^v–95^v Item Idem Hugo de obliuione preteritorum malorum. et Ira. Insipientem doctus interrogas . . . intus extinguatur. (*c*) ff. 95^v–96^v Idem de quinque statibus mutabilitatis. Quinque status habet uita humana. per quos . . . in dolorem confusionis commitatur. Minor est labor malam concupiscenciam uincere. quam malam conscienciam tolerare.

(*a, b*). The same titles as here are ascribed to Hugh in the medieval catalogue of St. Augustine's, Canterbury (*Ancient Libraries*, p. 277, no. 777). (*a*), as far as 91/14 *quiesco*, is Pseudo-Anselm, Meditatio 14 (*PL* clviii. 779–81) and the whole is ch. 1–17 of Pseudo-Augustine, Manuale (*PL* xl. 951–9), as in Oxford, Bodleian, Laud misc. 325: cf. Römer, i. 122. (*b, c*). *PL* clxxvii. 509–10, 511–12 (Hugh of St. Victor, Miscellanea, i. tit. 74, 77).

7. ff. 97–141 Twenty-five prayers, all but four of them to named saints: (*a*) Ad angelos et archangelos.[1] Obsecro uos omnes sancti angeli . . .; (*b*) *John Baptist* Sancte Iohannes tu ille iohannes qui . . .; (*c*) *John Evangelist* Sancte et beate iohannes altissime . . .; (*d*) *John Evangelist* Sancte iohannes tu ille iohannes vnus . . .; (*e*) *Peter* Sancte et benignissime beate petre . . .; (*f*) *Paul* Sancte paule tu magne paule . . .; (*g*) *Andrew* Supplico tibi sancte andrea apostole dei qui syciam et achaiam prouincias . . .; (*h*) *All apostles* Domine ihesu criste qui dedisti potestatem apostolis . . .; (*i*) Exaudi me domine. adiuua me criste. trahe me post te . . .; (*j*) *Stephen* Sancte stephane. beate stephane . . .; (*k*) *Laurence* Laurea laudabilis laureate martyrii laurenti leuita . . .; (*l*) *Vincent* Miles cristi inuictissime et martir egregie leuita vincenti . . .; (*m*) *Nicholas* Peccator homuncule tu multum indigens . . .; (*n*) *Benedict* Sancte et beate Benedicte . . .; (*o*) *Gregory* Celestis ostensor tramitis . . .; (*p*) *Augustine of England* Omni laudis ueneracione. omni honoris preconio . . .; (*q*) Ad sanctum Eadmundum archiepiscopum. Dominici gregis pastor insignis . . .; (*r*) *Martin* Beatissime et sanctissime martine confessor . . .; (*s*) *Augustine of Hippo* Nobilissime doctorum ecclesie dei. et columpna . . .; (*t*) *Thomas of Canterbury* O beate et gloriose pontifex et martir Thoma qui iugi . . .; (*u*) Oracio episcopi uel abbatis ad sanctum sub cuius nomine regit ecclesiam. Sancte N. pie N. beate . . .; (*v*) *Mary Magdalene* Sancta maria magdalene que cum fonte . . .; (*w*) *Margaret* Gloriosa uirgo et martir preciosa beata margareta . . .; (*x*) *Katherine* Proles regum clarissima uirgoque deuotissima . . .; (*y*) *Katherine* Sancta katerina uirgo et martir gloriosa. plena misericordie . . .

Ten prayers, (*b*, *e*, *f*, *j–n*, *r*, *v*), are ascribed to Anselm in the headings. The rest are not ascribed. (*b–f*, *j*, *m*, *n*, *u*, *v*) are nos. VIII, XI, XII, IX, X, XIII–XV, XVII, XVI of the series of Anselm's prayers in *SAO* iii. 5–91. (*u*) is here for the use of an abbot.

[1] I omit further headings, except at (*q*, *u*). Only (*i*) is without heading.

8. f. 141ʳᵛ Memoriae of Adrian, abbot (of St. Augustine's, Canterbury), and of Mildred.

Follows art. 7 without break. The antiphons are 'Sancte adriane operator uirtutum . . .' and 'Mildretha uirgo celebris . . .'.

9. ff. 141ᵛ–145 Miserere mei deus.' secundum magnam misericordiam tuam. Non spero secundum meritum meum. siue secundum iusticiam meam . . . equalis una deitas. et ante omne seculum. et nunc et in perpetuum. Amen.

A meditation on Ps. 50. Also in B.L., Arundel 60, ff. 47–52.

10. ff. 145ᵛ–158ᵛ Incipiunt meditaciones beati augustini excitantes animam ad contemplandum deum. Eya nunc homuncio fuge paululum . . . Ergo misericors deus.' miserere miseri huius. Amen amen pie deus. Amen amen pie ihesu. Expliciunt meditaciones beati augustini excitantes animam ad contemplandum deum.

Römer, i. 377, ii. 117. A preface and twenty-five numbered chapters, a catena made up at first thus: preface and chs. 1–3, Anselm, Proslogion, chs. 1, 16, 17, 24; chs. 4, 5, Prosl., ch. 25; ch. 6, Prosl., ch. 26; ch. 7, Pseudo-Anselm, Or. 11. The rest beginning at ch. 8, 'Nichil certius morte . . .' is printed in PL xl. 943–950/21 (Pseudo-Augustine, De contritione cordis): the sources are prayers and meditations printed under Anselm's name in PL clviii.

ff. ii+158. f. i and the pastedown conjoint with it are medieval parchment leaves. 216 × 155 mm. Written space 150 × 100 mm. 24 long lines. 1–3, 12–14, 23–5 of the lines ruled on each page are prolonged into the margins and in three quires (5, 6, 13) prickings occur opposite these lines only. Collation: 1–7¹² 8¹⁰ 9–13¹² 14⁸. Initials: (i) ff. 23ᵛ, 43ᵛ, 70, 3-line, blue or red with ornament of the other colour; (ii), as (i), but 2-line; (iii) 1-line, blue or red. In art. 2 each I of Ihesus lies outside the written space. Capital letters in the ink of the text are stroked with red. Binding of s. xix. Secundo folio rerum existenciam.

Written in England. Arts. 6ab, 7p, 8 suggest a connection with St. Augustine's, Canterbury. MSS. 90+64+92+86+77 in Pettigrew's catalogue of the manuscripts of the Duke of Sussex, Bibliotheca Sussexiana, i (1827): his sale, 31 July 1844, lot 43. 'Mʳ Sargent's own' in pencil, f. i. Given as MS. Med. 1.

# Med. 4. *Augustinus, Soliloquia; Preces*	s. xv med.

1. ff. 1–39ᵛ Incipit liber soliloquiorum beati Aurelii Augustini anime ad deum de ineffabili laude dei. Rubrica prima Incipit. Agnoscas te domine cognitor meus . . . in eas confitebor (ends imperfectly).

Römer, ii. 117. PL xl 863–897/20. Thirty-seven chapters. Five leaves missing, two after f. 4, one after f. 18, one after f. 26, and one at the end.

2. (a) ff. 40–45ᵛ (begins imperfectly) Ista considerans non uehementissime gratulatur . . . Consideret diligenter unde ueniat quod fit et quo (ends imperfectly). (b) ff. 46–55 (begins imperfectly) ade: quos non emolit tanta dulcedo benignitatis . . . et fixa sit mens mea et cor meum amen. Finis Explicit.

(a). Römer, ii. 117. PL, xl. 985/20–989/10 from the foot (Speculum Peccatoris). (b). A meditation.

3. f. 55ʳᵛ (a) Scribe domine ihesu queso uulnera tua . . . (b) Crux michi sit

risus . . . (4 lines). (c) Qui cristum bene s(c)it . . . (2 lines). (d) Fratres carissimi non queo quem mente concupi . . . (*ends abruptly*).

(*b*). *RH*, no. 25087. (*c*). Walther, *Sprichwörter*, no. 28318.

4. Prayers to Father and Son: (*a*) f. 56ʳᵛ Oratio Sancti thome de acquino spetialissima completa et pulcherima ualde. Concede michi misericors deus que tibi placent et placita . . . frui per gloriam. Qui . . . amen; (*b*) ff. 56ᵛ–57 Oratio dicenda cum surgimus ad matutinum. Gracias tibi agimus . . .; (*c*) ff. 57–8 Oracio ad deum. Tibi dilectissimo creatori meo . . .; (*d*) f. 58ʳᵛ Oracio ad dominum ihesum[1] cristum dicenda. Precor te piissime domine ihesu criste propter illam eximiam caritatem . . .; (*e*) ff. 58ᵛ–59 Oratio pro desiderio compassionis domini nostri iesu cristi dicenda. Domine ihesu criste cor meum tuis uulneribus . . .; (*f*) f. 59 Oracio ad deum patrem omnipotentem. Domine sancte pater propter tuam largitatem . . .

(*a*). Cf. A. I. Doyle in *Dominican Studies*, i (1948), 229–38. (*f*) invokes St. Francis.

5. ff. 57–61 Oratio ad angelum qui custodit hominem ualde pulcra. O dulcissime Comes huius misere peregrinationis . . .

6. Prayers before and after mass: (*a*) ff. 61–64ᵛ Oratio dulcissima Sancti Ambrosii episcopi dicenda ante missam celebrandam ualde pulcra. Summe sacerdos et uere pontifex . . . neque siciam in eternum. amen; (*b*) f. 64ᵛ Oratio dicenda post celebratam missam. Gracias ago inmense maiestati et sempiterne pietati . . .; (*c*) f. 65ʳᵛ Oracio ad deum patrem dicenda. cum quis sumere uult corpus dominicum. Omnipotens et misericors deus ecce accedo . . .; (*d*) f. 65ᵛ Oratio ad beatam uirginem mariam post perceptionem heucaristie. Serenissima et inclita mulierum . . .

(*a*). A. Wilmart, *Auteurs spirituels*, pp. 114–24.

7. Orationes ad beatissimam uirginem mariam: (*a*) ff. 65ᵛ–66 Obsecro te sanctissima dei genitrix . . .; (*b*) f. 66ʳᵛ Oratio ad beatissimam uirginem mariam. Misericordissima domina dei genitrix virgo maria . . .; (*c*) f. 66ᵛ (*Heading as* (*b*)). Tibi supplico sancta et immaculata mater . . .; (*d*) ff. 66ᵛ–67 (*Heading as* (*b*)). Te deprecor domina mea mater domini . . .

(*a*). Masculine forms.

8. ff. 67–9 Oratio sancti Augustini quam fecit dictante angelo. Domine meus omnipotens qui es eternus et unus . . .

Römer, ii. 117. *PL* xl. 938–40.

9. ff. 69–77 Oratio quedam et aliqua utilissima ualde. que dicit et gessit gloriosus et eximius doctor Ieronimus cum circha finem uite presentis existeret. Pie ihesu uirtus mea et refugium meum . . . in longitudinem dierum in seculum seculi. amen. amen. amen.

---

[1] I have expanded the abbreviation in the heading of (*d*) and elsewhere as *ihesum*, but the scribe himself was in a state of confusion: in the heading of (*e*) he writes first *iesu* and then *ihesu* in full. See the next footnote.

10. ff. 77–79^v Oratio pro remissione peccatorum sancti Augustini. Domine ihesu criste qui in hunc mundum propter nos . . .

Römer, i. 376, ii. 117. *PL* ci. 476–9.

11. (*a*) ff. 79^v–81^v Incipit forma uiuendi beati bernardi abbatis in Rithimis. Hec michi uiuendi sit forma proficiendi . . . Omnia que dixi. ad laudem sint crucifixi Qui legis implora. pro me te deprecor ora. Explicit. (*b*) ff. 81^v–82 Si michi sint uires et prelia (*sic for* predia) magna quid inde? . . . quoniam satis? Bernardus.

(*a*). 115 lines. (*b*). 12 lines. Walther, no. 17797.

12. (*a*) f. 82^{rv} Apparuit temporibus nostris et adhuc est homo magni virtutis . . . inter filios hominum. (*b*) 'Verba Iosephi Hebrei de christo.'[1] Fuit hisdem diebus et temporibus ihesus sapiens . . . et genus. (*c*) ff. 82^v–83 Epistola pilati. Pontius pilatus thiberio cesari s.d. de ihesu cristo quem tibi plane . . . pati uel uenundari. Vale v° kl' aprilis.

(*a*). Stegmüller, no. 158. 1 (Epistola Lentuli). (*b*). Josephus, *Antiquitates*, bk. xviii, sects. 63, 64 (or xviii. 3. 3 in older editions), in the Latin version (edn. Paris, 1514, f. clxx). The heading is over erasure and not in the main hand. (*c*). Stegmüller, no. 187.

13 (added, s. xv). f. 83^v Oratio deuotissima Beatissimi aurelii augustini yponen' epyscopi. Domine sancte pater propter tuam largitatem et filii tui . . .

At first as 4*f*.

ff. ii+83+ii. 133×95 mm. Written space 87×55 mm. 30 long lines. Collation: 1^{10} wants 5, 6 2^{10} 3^{10} wants 1 before f. 19 and 10 after f. 26 4^{10} 5^{10} wants 4 after f. 39 6^{10} wants 1–3 before f. 46 7–9^{10} 10 one (f. 83). Quires 1–9 signed a–g in the usual later medieval way. The ink has not taken perfectly well on flesh sides. Written in a small round fere-humanistica: straight-backed and round-backed *d*. Initials: (i) f., 1 gold on a blue, red, and green ground; (ii) 3-line or 2-line, red or blue. Binding of s. xix. Secundo folio *in ore quia*.

Written in Italy. MSS. 75 and 140 in Pettigrew's catalogue of the manuscripts of the Duke of Sussex, *Bibliotheca Sussexiana*, i (1827). Duke of Sussex sale, 31 July 1844, lot 4. Given as MS. Med. 1.

Med. 5. *De tripartita domo Dei, etc.*   s. XIII[1]

1. (*a*) ff. 1–22^v 'De tripartita domo dei'. Nolite attendere fratres mei quid uobis promittit mondus iste. Set quid promittit conditor mondi . . . Mori uolunt set mori non possunt. Explicit liber. (*b*) ff. 22^v–23^v de tripartita domo dei. domus dei non inproprie neque abusiue . . . non gule set cordis. (*c*) f. 23^v audi illud. De trinitate que deus est. Sicut in sole tria sunt inseparabilia . . . illa magnificentia sublimis dei. Tu autem domine miserere nostri. Ricardus pesloe scripsit hunc librum.

(*a*). The author sets out his chapters at the end of his preface, first 15, beginning with De prelatis, then 'in secundo quaternione' 18 mainly on virtues, and 'in tertio quaternione' 19 mainly on vices, ending with 'De inferno'. In the present copy the chapters of the first quire are on ff. 1–7, those of the second on ff. 7–15, and those of the third on ff. 15–22^v. Spellings are normal, apart from a few words. (*b*) explains that the subjects of the first, second, and third quires of (*a*) are respectively 'mundus', 'paradisus', and 'infernus', the three mansions into which 'domus dei' is divided.

[1] So in full. The scribe of the text writes the word without *h*.

Holy Cross, B.V.M., Peter, Three Kings, for peace, and of All Saints for use 'In summis festis', 'In dupplicibus festis', and at feasts of nine and three lessons, and at the end the antiphon of a memoria of St. Alban, as at vespers on f. 51.

9. ff. 81ᵛ–83 Antiphons at vespers from Monday to Sunday.

10. ff. 83–84ᵛ In festo venerabilis sacramenti.

11. ff. 84ᵛ–85 Antiphons 'super nunc dimittis', Pacem tuam . . ., Vigila . . ., Salua nos . . .

12. Additions of s. xvii, xviii on ff. i, 85–89ᵛ, and in the margins.

ff. i, 89 are paper leaves: 89ᵛ is dated at the end '1766'. Marginalia include references to other service books: f. 17ᵛ 'in libro magno fol. 21'; f. 26ᵛ 'De S Anna officium inuenies in paruo libro proprium in quo habetur D. Albani officium'; f. 27ᵛ 'in paruo libro psalmorum'; f. 30ᵛ 'fol. 116 . . . in libro matutinorum'; f. 32 'in magno libro fol. 128'.

ff. ii+92+i, foliated (i–vi), 1–88, (89). The contemporary foliation in red begins with I on the fifth leaf and runs to LXXXV. 367×265 mm. Written space 282×210 mm. 10 long lines and music (11 lines, ff. 51–5). Collation: 1⁴ (ff. iii–vi) 2–6⁸ 7⁸+1 leaf after 8 (f. 49) 8⁶+1 leaf after 1 (f. 51) 9⁸ 10⁴ (ff. 65–8) 11⁶ (ff. 69–74) 12⁸ 13⁶. Ink of an admirable blackness. Initials: (i) blue (f. 1, red and blue) on decorated grounds of red or green, with sprays of red into the margins, which on ff. 1, 46 have green leaf terminals; (ii) blue, or red, or cadels. In some of the cadels there are inscribed scrolls: f. 50, AN 1535; ff. 56, 60, 67ᵛ, IA EM; f. 65, MA HE; f. 69, WO AR. ff. 51–5 (quire 8, except the outside sheet) differ from the rest of the book in script and decoration. Contemporary binding of wooden boards covered with decorated pigskin, the boards projecting 10 mm beyond the leaves at the head and 20 mm beyond them at the foot and on the side: two clasps: metal corner-pieces: 5 bosses removed from each cover.

Written probably in 1535 (cf. f. 50) for the use of a church of St. Alban of Mainz, probably in or near Cologne. Still in use as a service book in 1766. Referenced in 1907 together with other manuscripts of the 'Marr Musical Section', given in that year by the executrix of Robert Alexander Marr.[1]

EDINBURGH. ROYAL COLLEGE OF PHYSICIANS

Cursor Mundi; Northern Homily Cycle (in English) s. xiv¹

The manuscript is described and arts. 1, 2 are printed by J. Small, *English Metrical Homilies*, Edinburgh, 1862, with accurate facsimiles of a few lines on ff. 1, 16, 37.

1. (a) ff. 37–50ᵛ, 1–10 (*begins imperfectly*) In heuin on heie þan sale I scawe . . . Lauedi þaim help in al þair nedis. Amen. (b) ff. 10–14 'Incipiunt do[lores] beate Marie'. [S]pel yet I wald spek if I cuþe . . . To tore quen we sale turne.

---

[1] For Marr see *Musical Scotland*, ed. D. Baptie, 1894. I owe the reference to Mr. J. H. Stewart, reference librarian of the Public Library.

Amen. (*c*) ff. 14–15ᵛ [L]istnis nu god men wit yor lef . . . þat we be wit hir euir *and* a. amen.

(*a*). Cursor Mundi, lines 18989–23944, with two gaps, one of four leaves after f. 43 and one of three leaves after f. 45: f. 43ᵛ ends at line 20149, f. 44 begins at line 20801, f. 45ᵛ ends at line 21134, f. 46 begins at line 21601. Small fragments of two of the lost leaves remain, f. 48* with a few letters of lines 20633–53 on one side and of lines 20758–82 on the other, and f. 45* with a few letters of lines 21135–41 on one side and of lines 21259–66 on the other. f. 45 is damaged, with loss of text in 17 lines on each side. This copy printed, except f. 48*, in R. Morris's edition for the EETS, *Cursor Mundi*, pp. 1587–1608 (lines 18989–21264), 1237–51 (lines 21601–846), 1608–37 (lines 21847–23944). *IMEV*, no. 2153. 6. (*b*). Cursor Mundi, lines 23945–24359, 24520–730. This copy printed by Morris, pp. 1368–95, 1403–17. One leaf is missing after f. 12. *IMEV*, no. 3208. 3. (*c*). Cursor Mundi, lines 24733–968. This copy printed by Small, pp. xv–xxi and by Morris, pp. 1417–29. *IMEV*, no. 1885. 3. f. 15ᵛ col. 2 lines 3–40 left blank.

2. ff. 16–36ᵛ Fader and sun and hali gast þat anfald god es ay . . . prayed þaye (*ends imperfectly*: catchwords þat þe bischop suld).

Prologue, Ratio quare, and the first thirteen homilies of the 'Northern Homily Cycle', those for the four Sundays in Advent, Christmas, the Sunday after Christmas, Epiphany, the five Sundays after Epiphany, and the Purification. This copy printed by Small, pp. 1–63/16, 83/19–167/21. Three leaves are missing after f. 24, except for very small pieces, ff. 16*, 17*, 18*, originally, no doubt, conjugate with ff. 13–15. The first letter or two of the last three or four lines can be seen on the recto sides of these pieces and the last few letters of two lines on the verso side of f. 17*. The remains on the rectos can be identified in Small's text: p. 65/3–6 (f. 18*); p. 71/18–21 (f. 17*); p. 78/15–17 (f. 16*). *IMEV*, nos. 777, 323, 2996, 3790, 3018, 3789, 3857, 3556, 3492, 3395, 2930, 3012, 3021, 3740, 1464.

Thirty-four lines of verse in Latin on the fifteen signs before the Day of Judgement are part of the text on f. 19ᵛ: 'Unde versus de eiusdem signis. Signis ter quinis se prodet ad ultima finis . . . Iudicis ante pedes ueniet plebs tota resurgens. Isti uersus omittantur a lectore quando legit anglicum coram laycis'. They are not in the other copies, according to Small, p. vi. The language was studied in a dissertation by A. Wetzlar, *Sprache sowie Glossar der nordenglischen Homiliensammlung des Edinburger Royal College of Physicians*, Erlangen, 1907.

ff. 50, foliated 1–50, and five small fragments foliated 16*, 17*, 18*, 45*, 48*. Each leaf and fragment is mounted in a cardboard frame. Dimensions, as mounted, excluding the frame, *c*. 210 × 140 mm. Written space *c*. 190 mm high. 2 cols. Art. 1 in 40 lines (ff. 1–15ᵛ) and 41–3 lines (ff. 37–50ᵛ). Art. 2 in 43 lines. All leaves are now singletons: ff. 1–12 and 25–36 were no doubt twelves once (f. 36ᵛ has its catchword) and ff. 16–24 is almost certainly a twelve, with 10–12 represented now by the small fragments, 18*, 17*, 16* (in that order). Probably ff. 13–15 and the leaf missing before f. 13 formed a quire of two bifolia. Three hands: 37–50ᵛ, larger and less tidy than the others; 1–15ᵛ (not unlike Cotton Vespasian A. iii); 16–36ᵛ. Blank spaces: 14 lines on f. 39ᵛ and 13 lines on f. 41, perhaps for pictures; smaller spaces in art. 1 for headings; 3-line (f. 16 only) and 2-line spaces for initials. Mounted in cardboard and bound in s. xix².

Written probably in north-west Yorkshire.[1] The textura of the three hands is probably little, if at all, earlier than the anglicana, s. xivˡ, of notes and headings in art. 1 and Cursor Mundi, line 19226, which has been filled in in a space left by the scribe of the text. Bequeathed by Dr. John Drummond in 1741.

[1] As Professor Angus McIntosh kindly tells me.

EDINBURGH. ROYAL COLLEGE OF SURGEONS OF EDINBURGH

1. *Horae* s. xv¹

1. ff. 1–12ᵛ Calendar in red and black, rather empty.

Entries in red include 'Sancti euodi', 'Audoeni episcopi', 'Romani archiepiscopi roth' '
(8 July, 24 Aug., 23 Oct.). 'Audoeni episcopi', 'Reliquie ecclesie rothomag' ', in black,
5 May, 3 Dec. The names of the months in French.

2. ff. 13–17ᵛ 'Sequentia' of Luke, 'Inicium' of Matthew, 'Sequentia' of Mark,
and 'Inicium' of John, followed by the prayers 'Protector in te sperantium . . .'
and 'Ecclesiam tuam quesumus . . .'.

The usual Sequentiae of the Gospels, but not in the usual order which is John, Luke,
Matthew, Mark. ff. 18–19ᵛ blank.

3. f. 20ʳᵛ Memoria of St. Christopher. f. 21ʳᵛ blank.

4. ff. 22–57ᵛ Hours of B.V.M. of the use of (Rouen).

Memoriae after lauds of SS. Michael, John Baptist, Peter and Paul, Laurence, Nicholas,
Katherine, and All Saints. Single leaves are missing at the beginning of matins and lauds.
ff. 39ʳᵛ, 58–59ᵛ blank.

5. ff. 60–74 Penitential psalms and (f. 69ᵛ) litany.

Ursinus as disciple. Sixteen confessors: . . . (10, 11) romane mellone . . . (15) macute.

6. ff. 74ᵛ–77 Oratio ad uirginem mariam valde deuota. Obsecro te . . . For
male use.

7. ff. 77–80 O intemerata . . . orbis terrarum. De te enim . . . For male use.

8. ff. 80ᵛ–83ᵛ Hours of Holy Cross, Patris sapientia . . .

9. ff. 84–86ᵛ Hours of Holy Spirit, Nobis sancti spiritus . . . f. 87ʳᵛ blank.

10. ff. 88–111 Office of the dead. f. 111ᵛ blank.

11. ff. 112–116ᵛ Fifteen Joys in French, beginning imperfectly.

Sonet, no. 458.

12. ff. 116ᵛ–119 Cest ce que len dit en lonneur des v plaies nostre-*seign*ur.
Doulx dieu doulx pere saincte trinite . . .

Sonet, no. 504.

13. ff. 119ᵛ–123 La preere theophilus. Roine des cieulx glorieuse Fille et mere
de dieu precieuse . . . A toy me plaing noble roine.

Ten 12-line stanzas and a final four lines. Sonet, no. 1793.

14. ff. 123–124ᵛ Ci apres ensuient les sept vers Saint bernard. Illumina oculos
meos . . .

Eight divisions and final prayer.

ff. iii+124+iii. 200×140 mm. Written space 105×70 mm. 16 long lines. Collation: 1–2⁶ 3⁸ wants 8, blank, 4 two (ff. 20, 21) 5⁸ wants 1 before f. 22 6⁸ wants 1 before f. 29 7⁴ (ff. 36–9) 8–9⁸ 10⁴ (ff. 56–9) 11–13⁸ 14⁴+1 leaf after 2 (f. 86), wants 4, blank, after f. 87, 15–17⁸ 18⁸ wants 1 before f. 112 19⁶ (ff. 119–24). Twelve out of fifteen 12-line pictures remain, six in art. 4, and one before each of arts. 2 (St. Luke writing), 3 (a man and woman kneel, one on each side of the water St. Christopher is crossing), 5, 8, 9, 10. Initials: (i) 4-line, blue or red patterned in white on grounds of gold and the other colour; (ii) 2-line (4-line in art. 2 and on f. 116ᵛ), gold on blue and red grounds, patterned in white, with sprays of gold ivy leaf into the margins; (iii) 1-line, as (ii), but no sprays. Continuous borders on picture pages, with grotesques, etc., especially in the four corners, and effective bar ornament in gold and colours. Line fillers of red and blue, patterned in white and decorated with gold. Capital letters in the ink of the text filled with pale yellow. Red morocco binding, s. xix, lettered 'Missale romanum'. Secundo folio (f. 14) *cob in.*

Written in France for use in the diocese of Rouen. 'B.V.B.', f. iiᵛ. Item 229 in an English sale catalogue, s. xix. The relevant slip lies loose inside the cover.

2. *Horae*   s. xv²

1. ff. 1–12ᵛ Calendar in French, in gold, blue, and red, the two colours alternating for effect.

'Saint eloy' and 'Saint marcial' (25 June, 3 July) among feasts in gold.

2. ff. 13–17ᵛ Sequentiae of the Gospels.

The prayers 'Protector in te sperantium . . .' and 'Ecclesiam tuam . . .' follow John.

3. ff. 17ᵛ–20ᵛ Oratio deuota de beata maria. Obsecro te . . . For male use.

4. ff. 20ᵛ–23ᵛ De beata maria. O intemerata . . . orbis terrarum. De te enim . . .

5. ff. 24–73 Hours of B.V.M. of the use of (Rouen).

Memoriae after lauds of Holy Spirit, Holy Trinity, SS. Michael, John Baptist, Peter, Laurence, Nicholas, Romanus (Decus omne nunc romane . . .: *RH*, no. 4311), Vivianus, Katherine, All Saints, and of peace. ff. 47ᵛ (before prime), 73ᵛ blank.

6. ff. 74–89 Penitential psalms and (f. 84ᵛ) litany.

Twelve confessors: . . . (5, 6) mellone romane . . . (8) viuiane . . . (12) leobine . . . Fifteen virgins: . . . (11) austreberta . . .

7. ff. 90–95ᵛ Hours of Holy Cross, Patris sapiencia . . .

8. ff. 96–100ᵛ Hours of Holy Spirit, Nobis sancti spiritus . . . f. 101ʳᵛ blank.

9. ff. 102–138ᵛ Office of the dead.

10. ff. 139–143ᵛ Doulce dame de misericorde . . . Sonet, no. 458.

11. ff. 143ᵛ–146 Doulx dieu doulx pere sainte trinite . . . Sonet, no. 504.

12. f. 146ʳᵛ Saincte vraie croix auree . . . Sonet, no. 1876.

13 (in another hand). f. 146ᵛ (*a*) Domine ihesu criste cui data est omnis potestas in celo et in terra in mari et in omnibus abyssis tibi commendamus omnes cristianos nauigantes et benefactores nostros in galeis francie existentes . . . (*b*) Sanctificato diuino misterio . . . (*c*) Deus qui transtulisti patres nostros . . .

Collect, secret, and postcommunion for those 'in galeis francie existentes'. (*a*) asks for the intercession of B.V.M., SS. Peter and Paul 'ac dyonisii heranii nicolay claudii et cristofori. et beate katherine et sancte genouefe'.

ff. ii+146+xvii. The flyleaves are paper, except ff. i, ii, 147–8. 175×133 mm. Written space 100×70 mm. 16 long lines. Collation: 1^{12} 2^8 3^4 wants 4, blank, 4–9^8 10^2 (ff. 72, 73) 11–18^8 19^6 wants 6, blank, after f. 138 20^8 (ff. 139–46). Fourteen 13-line pictures, eight in art. 5 and one before each of arts. 2 (the evangelists in four compartments), 6–9, 10 (B.V.M. and Child: angels crown her: a women kneels on her left). Initials: (i, ii) 3-line (and in arts. 3, 4, 4-line) and 2-line, blue patterned in white on decorated grounds; (iii) 1-line, gold on blue and red grounds, patterned in white. Line fillers of red and blue, patterned in white and decorated with gold. A framed floral border on each page with an initial of type (i). A border the height of the written space in the outer margin of all other pages containing writing: the design on a verso side is usually the mirror image of the design on its recto. Binding of gilt calf, s. xvi: lozenges all over the covers contain letters, either S, or two Cs back to back and looped together, or conjoint M and C, arranged so that each letter occupies the whole of a row horizontally, beginning with S in the first row. Secundo folio (f. 14) *eum non.*

Written in France for use in the diocese of Rouen. 'Rt: Honble Lord Thurlow. F.S.A. 1844'. Printed book-plates of 'John Towneley Esqr',[1] of Henry John Bolland and, at the end, of Robert Kirk, M.D. 'N° 9', f. i.

EDINBURGH. ROYAL OBSERVATORY

Crawford Collection

The medieval astronomical and astrological manuscripts of James Lindsay (1847–1913: succeeded his father as 26th Earl of Crawford and 9th Earl of Balcarres in 1880) seem to have been bought during a few years in the 1870s and 1880s. Purchases were chiefly through Quaritch, particularly at the Bragge sale in 1876 and the Chasles sale in 1881. The manuscripts were kept with the rest of the astronomical library at the Dunecht Observatory, twelve miles west of Aberdeen, which had been built for Lindsay in 1872. In 1888 he gave his whole Dunecht collection, printed books and manuscripts, to the Royal Observatory.

The medieval and post-medieval manuscripts bought before 1877 and some of those which appear to have been bought in 1877 and 1878 were numbered from 1 to 41 and described by Lindsay in a sheaf catalogue now at the Observatory.[2] A little later the numeration was continued to 68 and the whole collection of manuscripts listed on a sheet of paper with single-line entries not in Lindsay's hand.[3] Here, the space remaining blank after 68 has not been filled except for entries numbered 101 and 102 at the foot of the verso after a space of thirty-seven lines. The space was left, no doubt, chiefly for the listing of the purchases at the Chasles sale in June 1881: thirteen Chasles numbers are noted in the margin. The manuscript to which the number 101 was assigned was bought later in 1881. R. Copeland, *Catalogue of the Crawford Library of the Royal Observatory,*

---

[1] Not identifiable in the Towneley sale at Sotheby's, 27 June 1883.

[2] Two medieval manuscripts, nos. 23 and 27, were excluded from the gift to Edinburgh and now form part of the John Rylands University Library in Manchester, MSS. 66, 67 (one manuscript in two volumes) and MS. 65.

[3] I owe my knowledge of these lists to Mrs. Mary F. I. Smyth.

Edinburgh, 1890, lists the manuscripts on pp. 485–97, but the arrangement by authors and subjects does not distinguish them individually. Descriptions of the collection are in *Isis*, liv. 482 (D. A. Kemp) and in *Publications of the Royal Observatory, Edinburgh*, ix (1973), 7–13 (E. G. Forbes).

The following table gives the present numbers, the numbers in use before the creation of the Crawford Room in 1973, the numbers assigned by Lord Crawford (sheaf catalogue and single-sheet), and such immediate provenances and dates of acquisition as are known to me.

Present number	Number before 1973[1]	Old Crawford number	Source
1.2	9.12.5.10	50	
1.27	9.13.4.2	1	? Weigel 1877
2.2	9.12.7.8	18	
2.3	9.10.7.7	28	
2.5	9.10.6.11		
2.20/1	9.12.7.7/1	7	
2.20/2	9.12.7.7/2	5	Bragge 1876
2.20/3	9.12.7.7/3	6	Bragge 1876
2.98	9.10.7.2	2	? Weigel 1877
2.119	9.10.6.13		
2.123	9.10.7.19		Chasles 1881[2]
3.2	9.11.5.7	25	? 1879
3.3	9.11.3.20	4	? 1878
3.4	9.10.7.6	26	Bragge 1876
3.9	9.11.5.16	66	? 1878
3.12	9.11.5.7	65	? 1878
3.13	9.11.5.2		
3.14	9.11.5.17		Chasles 1881[3]
3.23	9.11.3.18	8	
3.25	9.11.5.6		
3.28	9.11.3.19		Chasles 1881[4]
3.29	9.11.5.8		Chasles 1881[5]
4.3	9.11.5.5	101	Quaritch 1881
4.5	9.13.2.3	58	Quaritch 1877
4.6	9.14.5.14	16	
4.11	9.11.5.3	64	
5.10	9.21.5.1	3	
5.14	9.13.1.1	57	
7.76			Chasles 1881

[1] Before the pressmarks beginning with 9 came into use there were pressmarks beginning with 0: thus 2.2 is called 0.26.3 by Mrs. Singer, 3.14 was 0.26.9, and 5.10 is called 0.2.5 in *Trésors*, no. 25.
[2] 'Limit 75 francs. Bought for 30 francs.'
[3] 'Limit 80 francs. Bought for 40 francs.'
[4] 'Limit 70 francs. Bought for 70 francs.'
[5] 'Limit 175 francs. Bought for 50 francs.'

I owe thanks to the late Lord Crawford and to Dr. Taylor, librarian of the John Ryland University Library, Manchester, for permission to use accounts and letters from booksellers, mainly Bernard Quaritch, which relate to the formation of the libraries at Haigh Hall and Dunecht and are now deposited by Lord Crawford in the Rylands Library. After the Chasles sale Quaritch informed Lindsay of his purchases (18 Aug. 1881) and that he had spent in all 3,120 francs = £124. 16s. 6d. on 105 lots. A copy of the Chasles catalogue with the price of each of these lots against it is in the Crawford Room in the Royal Observatory.

Cr. 1.2. *J. de Sacrobosco, De sphaera; etc.* s. xv med.

1 (quires 1, 2). (*a*) ff. 1–3 (*begins imperfectly*) Causa dicitur quatuor modis scilicet causa materialis. formalis efficiens et causa finalis . . . (*b*) ff. 3ᵛ–16 Natura est principium motus et quietis eius in quo est primo et principaliter . . . Ignis est calidus et siccus etc.

(*a*). A quire missing before f. 1. Illustrated by drawings of rectangles, triangles, and other shapes, on ff. 2ᵛ–3, viiᵛ. (*b*). Thorndike and Kibre. Eight paragraphs. In New College, Oxford, 289, art. 4, called 'Termini naturales secundum M. Iohannem Garisdale'.

2 (quires 3–8). (*a*) ff. 17–31ᵛ Omnis proporcio aut est communiter dicta proprie. aut magis proprie dicta. Proporcio communiter dicta est duorum comparatorum . . . ex maiori velocitate in c quam b in c ergo etc. Expliciunt proporciones. (*b*) ff. 32–53 Corporum principalium mundanorum numerum figuram et motum intendo in presenti opusculo declarare. quantum sufficit . . . Climata igitur ad aquilonem sunt quasi infinita. Explicit commentum de Spera. (*c*) ff. 53ᵛ–57ᵛ Tullius. In oracione debet esse invencio. disposicio. elocucio. memoria. pronunciacio. Invencio est . . . conformacio. Explicit Tullius de coloribus rethoricis abreuiat'. f. 16ᵛ left blank.

(*a*). Sometimes verbally the same as Bradwardine's Tractatus proportionum breves, ed. H. L. Crosby, 1955. (*b*). J. de Pecham, De sphaera. Cf. L. Thorndike, *The Sphere of Sacrobosco*, 1949, pp. 445–50. (*c*). Notes and extracts from Rhetorica ad Herennium, bks. 1, 3–6. ff. 58–59ᵛ are blank.

3 (quires 9–12). ff. 60–87 Tractatum de spera 4ᵒʳ capitulis . . . aut mundana machina dissoluetur. Explicit tractatus spere.

J. de Sacrobosco, ed. Thorndike, op. cit., pp. 76–117. ff. 87ᵛ–90ᵛ are blank.

4 (quires 13, 14). ff. 92–107 Benedictus deus omnipotens qui machinam mundanam et creaturas absque exemplo condidit vniuersas. Que nobis . . . est corupta et non uirgo etc'.

Chiromancy. Thorndike and Kibre refer to six manuscripts in England and one manuscript at Montpellier. ff. 91ʳᵛ, 107ᵛ left blank.

5 (additions on flyleaves and in blank spaces). (*a*) f. iiᵛ Compotus iste diuiditur in 6 partes quarum . . . (*b*) f. viiᵛ Cf. art. 1a. (*c*) f. 16ᵛ A diagram showing the relation between the four elements and the four complexions. (*d*) f. 107 Mens cor cur cupiunt . . . (4 lines). (*e*) ff. 107ᵛ, 108 Drawings of hands.

(*a*). Thorndike and Kibre. Abandoned after six lines. (*d*). Walther, no. 10898. A prophecy.

ff. vii+108+iii. 163×115 mm. Written space *c.* 118×78 mm. 17–24 long lines. Frame ruling. Collation: 1–3⁸ 4⁶ 5–7⁸ 8⁸ wants 5, 6 blank after f. 58 and 8 blank after f. 59 9–10⁸ 11¹⁰ 12 five (ff. 86–90) 13¹⁰ 14¹⁰ wants 9, 10 probably blank after f. 108. 2 and 7 in quires 3, 9 and 2 and 5 in quire 4 are half sheets. Quires 1–12 signed at the beginning '2ᵘˢ qua'– '13ᵘˢ qua' in red. Written in anglicana under secretary influence (art. 4) and in secretary with occasional anglicana letter forms (arts. 1–3: in the hand of ff. 27/9–57ᵛ *a* is always in two compartments). Initials 4-line, 3-line, or 2-line, blue with red ornament. Capital letters in the ink of the text stroked with red. Contemporary binding of wooden boards covered with white leather, rebacked: two clasps. Secundo folio *latera*.

Written in England. 'Ex dono amici Mʳ Gulielmi Thwaytes 14 Novemb. 1581', f. vii. 'Ex dono amici Guliel. Thwayts' and 'H. Womock', f. viᵛ. 'S. Welles', f. viiᵛ, s. xvi/xvii. 'Plus vident oculi quam oculus. Henr' Dottin liber Henrici Dottin Ex dono Caroli Ballett Junioris 1688', f. 87 in a legal hand.

Cr. 1.27. *Jordanus de Nemore, etc.* s. XIII med.

1. ff. 1–13ᵛ Incipit liber phyloteig[ni] iordani de nemor[e] lxiiii proposiciones contine[ns]. Continuitas est indiscrecio rer' (*sic*) cum terminandi potencia. Cunctus fixio . . . constitutum est manifestum est. Explicit liber philotegni Iordani lxiiii pro*porciones* continens deo gracias.

Jordanus, De triangulis, ed. M. Curtze, 1887. Thorndike and Kibre. The propositions in larger and the proofs in smaller script. The propositions are numbered in red, i–lxiii. Diagrams in the margins.

2. ff. 14–21ᵛ Incipit pars prima libri iordani de nemore de ratione ponderum. Omnis ponderosi motum esse ad medium . . . trahere b. Explicit pars quarta. et cum eo finitur liber Iordani de racione ponderis.

Ed. E. A. Moody and M. Clagett, *The Medieval Science of Weights*, 1952, pp. 174–226. The postulates in larger and the theorems in smaller script. Diagrams in the margins. A 7-line addition below the text on f. 21ᵛ, 'Si fuerit aliquod corpus ex duobus mixtum . . . ponderis leuioris', circulated independently in many manuscripts.[1]

3. ff. 22–4 Si fuerit canonium si in metrum (*sic*) magnitudine . . . quod oportebat ostendere.

Liber de canonio, edn. op. cit., pp. 64–74. The propositions in larger and the proofs in smaller script.

4. (*a*) f. 24 Omne pondus cum quotlibet ponderibus ab eo continue sumptis . . . intercepti. Verbi gracia pondus unius marce . . . transposicio ponderum. (*b*) f. 24ʳᵛ Si trianguli tria latera coaceruentur . . . erit area trianguli.

(*a*). A separately floating proposition which commonly accompanies (*b*).[2] (*b*). Ed. M. Clagett, *Archimedes in the Middle Ages*, i. 642–7. A contemporary note in the side margin, as in Vat. Reg. Lat. 1261,[3] 'hec est pars phyloteigni et debet ei subiungi'. Another note in the lower margin, 'Hic sequatur de curuis superficiebus. scilicet (?) cuiuslib[. . . .]/rat in de pyramid'/et p[. . . .]'.

5. ff. 25–40 Ex quo mi papa presulum decus . . . consecrari. Quadratura circuli

---

[1] Information from Professor Clagett. To be printed in *Archimedes in the Middle Ages*, vol. 3.
[2] Information from Professor Clagett.
[3] Information from Professor Richard Rouse.

inter occultas . . . tue reuerencie apparere mereatur. Explicit. Respicit hic spaciis quadratus circulus equis / Nil quicumque probes plus minus inuenies.

Franco of Liège, De quadratura circuli, ed. Winterberg in *Abhandlungen zur Geschichte der Mathematik*, iv (1882), 142–90; also partly in *PL* cxliii. 1373–6.

6. (*a*) ff. 40ᵛ–41ᵛ Platonicam racionem quo pacto quadratus duplicari debeat edicam . . . qui in priore contemplari teduerit. (*b*) f. 41ᵛ Erat hostennes (*sic*) philosophus geometraque sagacissimus . . . multo plus dicat habere.

(*b*). Eratosthenes on the diameter of the earth. Thirteen lines.

7. ff. 42–52ᵛ Que magis recedunt a centro uel ab axe . . . neque maior neque minor. Explicit subtilitas magistri Gerardi de bruxella de motu.

Gerard of Brussels, De motu, ed. M. Clagett in *Osiris*, xii (1956), 112–48. The propositions in larger and the proofs in smaller script.

ff. ii + 52 + ii. 172 × 123 mm. Written space 117 × 70 mm. Long lines, 40 for the smaller script. Collation: 1–4⁸ 5⁸+1 leaf after 8 (f. 41) 6¹⁰ 7 one (f. 52). In quires 1–5 the first *five* leaves of each quire are signed a–e in red, followed by a quire mark: the quire marks are an *ad hoc* series r, v, q, z, y. Initials: (i) f. 25, red and blue with ornament of both colours; (ii) 2-line or 1-line, red or blue with ornament of the other colour; (iii) 1-line, red or blue. Binding of s. xviii with an armorial centrepiece (see below). Secundo folio *In triangulo*; penultimo folio (f. 51) *una sit*.

Written in France. A heavy erasure at the foot of f. 1. Identifiable as a manuscript bequeathed to the Sorbonne in 1271 by Gerard of Abbeville, archdeacon of Amiens, and listed in the Sorbonne catalogue of 1338 (lvi. 30): Philotheny Jordani de Nemore continens lxiiii propositiones. Liber eiusdem Jordani de ponderibus. Subtilitas Magistri G. de Brucella ex legato predicto (*G. of Abbeville*). Incipit in 2º fol. triangulo in pen. una sit. Precium x sol. (Delisle, *Cabinet des manuscrits*, iii. 68). Identifiable also with the manuscript containing arts. 1–3, 5, 7 belonging to Richard de Fournival, chancellor of Amiens, before 1260: cf. Delisle, op. cit. ii. 525, no. 43, R. H. Rouse in *Revue d'histoire des textes*, iii (1973), 260, and Clagett, loc. cit. (1956), pp. 104–6. The gilt centrepiece is the escutcheon of Pope Pius VI (1775–99), 'Gules a head of Boreas in the dexter chief blowing on a natural lily proper on a terrace vert, a chief silver with three molets of eight points gold' (D. L. Galbreath, *Papal Heraldry*, 1930, p. 103 and figs. 116 and 190: cf. Cr. 2.98). 'Leipzig, T. O. Weigel' inside the cover, as in 2.98. '77/GO', f. iᵛ. '10' on a label at the foot of the spine.

Cr. 2.2. *J. de Rupescissa, O.F.M.* 1476

(*a*) Primus liber de consideratione 5ᵗᵉ essentie omnium rerum transmutabilium. In nomine domini nostri yhesu cristi Incipit liber de famulatu philosophye euangelio domini nostri yhesu cristi et pauperibus euangelicis uiris. Dixit salomon sapiencie capitulo viiº deus dedit mihi . . . (f. 61ᵛ) et in eius absentia aqua ardens. (*b*) Incipiunt virtutes aque uite que sunt. Vt dicit Minadar qui primo . . . (f. 63) valet etiam hec aqua in infirmitatibus. Domine ad adiuuandum me festina. Amen. (f. 63ᵛ) Mccccºlxxviº die Sabbati xxᵐᵒ mensis Iullii. hora xxᵐᵃ Transcriptus et expletus fuit liber iste per me Nicolaum de regazola Ciuem cremon' et ad presens habitantem in Ciuitate Bude regni hungharie: ad honorem omnipotentis dei eiusque matris gloriose virginis Marie Totiusque Curie celestis Tempore et Regnante in prefato regno hungharie ac Bohemie etc' Serenissimo et Inuictissimo d. Principe et d.d. Mathia Rege gloriossisimo.

(*a*). Very many manuscripts and printed editions: cf. Singer and Anderson, no. 292. Bk. 2, f. 40ᵛ. (*b*). Singer and Anderson, no. 1040, referring to this copy and B.L., Add. 9751, f. 105ʳᵛ.

ff. 63. Paper. 200×150 mm. Written space 145×87 mm. 24 long lines. Collation: 1–6¹⁰ 7⁶ wants 4–6, blank. Written in current humanistica. 3-line (f. 1) and 2-line red initials. Contemporary binding of wooden boards, with dark-brown leather over the spine and some 40 mm of each cover: a central clasp from the front to the back cover missing. Secundo folio *Nam solis.*

Written by a scribe of Cremona in Budapest.

Cr. 2.3. *J. de Sacrobosco, etc.* s. xiv² (arts. 13, 14)–xv² and 1462 (art. 10*c*)

A table of contents, f. ii, s. xv, lists arts. 1–3, 4*a*, 5*a*, 6, 7*a*, *c*, *d*, 8, 9*b*, *g*, 11, 13; also 'Algorismus' after art. 2 and 'Item algorismus secundario' after art. 11. Paper tabs mark the main divisions. A loose slip with diagrams of the spheres and of the earth with its poles, circles, and tropics probably belongs with art. 1 or art. 2.

1 (quires 1, 2). ff. 1–18ᵛ [T]ractatum de spera distinguimus in quatuor capitula. dicens primo quid sit spera . . . mundi machina dissoluetur et sic est finis textus spere deo gracias.

J. de Sacrobosco, De Sphaera. Ed. L. Thorndike, 1943. Many glosses interlined at first. ff. 19–20ᵛ blank.

2 (quire 3). ff. 21–33ᵛ [C]irca tractatum de spera. Nota astronomia sic describitur. Astronomia est sciencia que considerat motum planetarum et figuram eorundem . . .

3 (quires 4, 5). ff. 34–57ᵛ Computus cirometralis. [C]ognicio veritatis de pausis temporum circa motum solis . . . si post addas explicit.

Thorndike and Kibre. GKW 7280 (Cologne, *c.* 1480/5). On f. 52ᵛ the year 1482 is referred to as in the future. Text corresponding to f. 53ᵛ is on the plate in D. E. Smith, *Rara Mathematica*, p. 472. Cf. art. 7*c*.

4 (quire 6). (*a*) ff. 58–64ᵛ [S]olaris ciclus an(n)os tenet octo viginti . . . (*b*) f. 65ʳᵛ Diagrams of a quadrant and (65ᵛ) text beginning 'Notandum quod quadrante habente duo latera . . .' (*c*) f. 67ʳᵛ Ex quo cantus regularis . . . fala cum sibi iungis ex' (?).

(*a*). Walther, no. 4000 (Computus Jacobi chirometralis). With a commentary beginning 'Iste liber qui intitulatur computus sacerdotalis metricus'. (*c*). On tones. f. 66ʳᵛ blank.

5 (quire 7). (*a*) f. 68 Me pudet audire iudeum talia scire . . . (20 lines). (*b*) ff. 68ᵛ–77ᵛ Qui virtutes vocabulorum sunt ignari de facili paloyzantur ut dicit aristoteles primo elencorum. Nos igitur in hoc breui compendio . . .

(*a*). Walther, no. 10842. (*b*). Text and commentary.

6 (quires 8–10). ff. 78ᵛ–108ᵛ Computus Iacobi. Quia ars computistica diuersorum autorum libr' multis perplexitatibus . . .

Thorndike and Kibre. The verses on which this is a commentary begin 'Ciclus solaris annos tenet octo viginti'. They differ from art. 4*a*. 'Secundus tractatus huius libri', f. 95. ff. 78, 109–110ᵛ were left blank.

7 (quires 11, 12). (*a*) ff. 111–18 Licet modo in fine temporum plures constat habere codices qui de arte calculatoria videantur sufficere . . . Aureus in iano numeris clauisque nouantur . . . Cum facit hunc locus ortum remiscere reus (?) . . . Explicit iste liber deo laus. (*b*) f. 119 Cisio ianus ephi sibi vendicat h(o)c feli mar an . . . (*c*) ff. 119ᵛ–131 Cognicio veritatis . . . si post prius addas. Explicit conpotus cyrometralis Completus. Sub anno domini millesimo quadringentesimo. decimo octauo mensis iulii octauo kalendas eiusdem. Scriptori pia requiem da virgo maria. (*d*) ff. 131ᵛ–134 [S]equitur de radicum extraccione et primo in numeris quadratis. vnde videndum est . . . in numeris quadratis et cubicis etc'. Et sic est finis . . . Et sic est finis.

(*a*). Alexander de Villa Dei, Massa compoti. Walther, no. 1835. (*b*). Walther, no. 2808. A common and variable mnemonic to remember saints days: cf. 8*d*. (*c*). As art. 3. Slips are tied in before f. 121 and before f. 122. (*d*). Thorndike and Kibre. ff. 118ᵛ, 134ᵛ blank.

8 (quires 13, 14). (*a*) ff. 135–139ᵛ Pro confectione astrolabii recipe tabulam aptam ad quantitatem . . . in quinque gradus sicut in limbo. (*b*) f. 140ʳᵛ A table of zodiacal signs and stars. (*c*) ff. 141–52 Quia plurimi ob nimeam acuitacionem et magnam scripturarum sentenciam canones vtilitates astrolabii declarantes . . . puncti tunc operare ut primus ostensum est etc. Et sic est finis. (*d*) f. 152ᵛ Cisioianus epi et hait vendicat oc veli . . . (*e*) f. 153 A table to show the sign of the zodiac at each new month and an accompanying text, 'In meridie 13 diei marcii sol intrat arietem . . .'. (*f*) ff. 154–157ᵛ Geometrie duo sunt species scilicet theorica et practica. Theorica est que solum mentis speculacione . . . inuenire. Fiat ergo quadrans . . . in iᵃ die et sequenciis. Et sic est finis huius.

(*a*). Thorndike and Kibre. A slip before f. 135 contains a table of distances, beginning on the recto 'Item hoc dicitur thonus 5625 miliaria' and on the verso 'Item a terra ad lunam sunt 15627'. Another slip after f. 136. (*b*) is under five heads, Nomina signorum, Longitudo stellarum, Latitudo stellarum, Declinacio, Nomina stellarum, and the first line reads across 'Aries, 22.0, 16.30, Meridionalis, Cornua arietis'. (*c*). Cf. Thorndike and Kibre. (*d*). Another version of Cisioianus: cf. art. 7*b*. (*f*). Thorndike and Kibre. Pseudo-Grosseteste on the quadrant: cf. Thomson, *Grosseteste*, p. 261. The text corresponds as far as f. 156ᵛ/15 'et ut prius' with that printed by Tannery in *Notices et extraits*, xxxv (1896), 593–617 (paras. 1–47). f. 153ᵛ blank.

9 (quire 15). (*a*) f. 158 Desiderans scire quot horas luna de nocte . . . horas inequales Et sic est finis huius. (*b*) ff. 158ᵛ–159ᵛ Sequitur tractatus de mensuracionibus Et primo de mensuracionibus rerum alciorum (*changed to* altitudinum). Si vis scire altitudinem rei alicuius accessibilis . . . capacitatem illius vasis. Et sic est finis. (*c*) f. 159ᵛ Item fiet quoddam lignum cum paruo stipite in sona . . . superficie illius operis. (*d*) ff. 160–161ᵛ Ad faciendum horalogium solare primo fiat vna linea . . . de vera plaga disteterint et cetera. Et sic est finis. (*e*) ff. 162–3 In composicione chilindri quod horalogium vocatur viatorum Accipe lignum durum buxum uel aliquid simile . . . (*f*) f. 163ᵛ Tables relating to (*e*). (*g*) ff. 164–5 Ad componendum horalogium Achas fiat dimidius circulus qui . . . vide ubi 2ᵃ linea tangit circulum.

(*b*). Thorndike and Kibre. *MMBL* i. 90. Corresponds to paras. 48–87 of the text printed by Tannery, loc. cit. 617–32. (*d*). Cf. Thorndike and Kibre. (*e, g*). Thorndike and Kibre.

10 (quire 16). (*a*) ff. 166–7 Mnemonics, mostly in verse, for finding days of fasting, dog days, etc. The verses are: (i) De ieiuniis quatuor temporum. Post crux post cineres . . . (5 lines); (ii) De diebus canicularibus. Iulius a nonis tibi diem caniculares . . . (4 lines); (iii) De quatuor temporibus anni. Ver petro detur . . . (3 lines); (iv) De conuersione pauli. Clara dies pauli bona tempora . . . (5 lines); (v) De festis habentes octauas. Octauas retinet assumpcio natque marie . . . (4 lines); (*b*) f. 167 Quid sit agendum in quolibet signo. Nil capiti facias aries cum luna refulget . . . (33 lines). (*c*) ff. 167ᵛ–168 Computus tables and their explanation: at the end 'Finis deo gracias per me Iodocum lumenshem (?) anno domini 1462 tunc temporis sco(larem) in hild' '. (*d*) ff. 169–72 Quadrantis noticiam 'cum gradibus tangendi' habere affectantes ex tribus premissis principaliter poterint contentari . . . Et tantum de scala altimetra (*ends abruptly*).

(*a*. i). Cf. Walther, no. 14312a; Walther, *Sprichwörter*, no. 21984. (*a*. ii). Cf. W., *S.*, no. 13169. (*a*. iii). W., no. 20134; W., *S.*, no. 33035. (*a*. iv). W., no. 2827. (*b*). Walther, no. 11780. (*d*). Thorndike and Kibre. ff. 172ᵛ–175ᵛ are blank, except for an unfinished circular diagram with the zodiacal signs on it.

11 (quire 17). (*a*) ff. 176–181ᵛ Tabula mediorum motuum ac conuencionum omnium planetarum ex tabulis alphoncii. (*b*) A volvel with five turning circles and five pointers inscribed (1) 'frigid' et hum' ', (2) 'calidum et humidum', (3) 'calidum et siccum', (4) 'calidum et humidum', (5) 'frigidum et siccum'. (*c*) ff. 182ᵛ–186ᵛ In nomine domini amen Ignorans motum necesse est ignorare naturam. Ita scribit philosophus 3° phisicorum . . . illius planete ad illud signum.

(*a*). Six tables of mean motion. (*c*). A calculation in the text on f. 185 is for 1460. f. 187ʳᵛ blank.

12 (quire 18). (*a*) ff. 188–90 A table of years, (14)60–(15)29, with entries under seventeen heads, the first 'Ciclus magnus' and the last 'Radix minutorum'. (*b*) ff. 190ᵛ–192 Tables of movable feasts, of solar and lunar motion, of conjunction and opposition and of the months. (*c*) ff. 192ᵛ–198 Circa noticiam et intellectum huius tabule prime septem laterum et trium cum medio foliorum . . .

(*a*). A new great cycle (of seventy-six years) begins at 1482. (*c*). Explanations of (*a*) and (*b*). f. 198ᵛ blank.

13 (quire 19). ff. 199–201ᵛ Incipit nouus algorismus per fratrem mathiam ord' pred' compilatus. Quia ars algoristica circa numeros versatur . . . multiplicacionis et iterum (?) figure redibunt. Explicit.

The bottom of f. 201 has been cut off. A slip after it supplies an omission in the text.

14 (quire 20). (*a*) ff. 203–205ᵛ De primis sillabis. Ab corripitur ut scabo . . . quere in katholicon 2 parte 22 et 23 capitulos. (*b*) ff. 206–208ᵛ About thirty paragraphs of miscellaneous matter, including verses in German. (*c*) ff. 202ʳᵛ, 209ʳᵛ Astronomical diagrams and (209ᵛ) eleven lines giving distances from earth to moon (etc.) in 'miliaria theutonicalia'.

(*a*). On short and long vowels in syllables ab–ut, at the beginning, in the middle, and at the end of words. (*b*) includes: ff. 206, 207ᵛ, calculations for A.D. '1364 completo' and '1366 incompleto'; f. 206ᵛ, three 6-line stanzas in German, 'Eyn kync ghebar tzu betlehem . . . den sy ghesunghen lobes schal'; f. 208, three 6-line stanzas in German, 'Grotze libe kan wol werken . . . sunder twybel mir verlan. Explicit cantus amoris'; f. 208 'Nobilis hunc

Bya de Regensteyn comitissa. Cui bona sancta pia fuerat mens celica missa. Fundat conuentum. Sit ei locus ille supernus. Pulcher et eternus melior quam milia centum. Quem Margareta de hezstede post renouauit. Petres (?) discreta lapidem primumque locauit. antistes gnarus albertus semine clarus. Sic conseruatus fuerat sic sanctificatus'.

15. The pastedowns are parchment, now raised and numbered i, 211. f. i is part of a leaf of a large noted service book, s. xiv. f. 211 is part of a leaf of the missal section of an ordinal, s. xiv, detailing offices of dedication of church and of saints days in the first week of November, including 'Commemoracio uel consecracio sancti Bernwardi episcopi et confessoris. . . . Eodem die dedicacio capelle sancti martini' and, as an addition in the margin, 'Pirminii con. et pon'.

ff. ii+209+ii. Paper, softer in arts. 13, 14 than elsewhere. For ff. i, 211 see art. 15. Medieval leaf numberings: (a) of the first halves of quires 13–15, 17, '1–5', '21–26', '31–34', '1–6' respectively; (b) of ff. 199–201, 203–5, 206–8, '68–70', '8–10', '13–15'. Written space: arts. 3–5, c. 120×83 mm; arts. 6–12, c. 165×100 mm. Long lines and (art. 2) 2 cols., varying in number. Collation: 1^{12} 2^{12} wants 8, 9, 11, 12, all probably blank, $3^{12}+1$ leaf after 10 (f. 31) 4–5^{12} 6^{12} wants 10, 11 after f. 66 7^{12} wants 11, 12, blank, after f. 77 8^{12} 9^{14} 10^8 wants 8, blank, after f. 110 $11^{12}+1$ leaf after 7 (f. 118) 12^{12} wants 12, blank, after f. 134 $13^{10}+1$ leaf after 10 (f. 145) 14^{12} 15^8 16^{10} 17^{12} 18^{12} wants 12, blank, after f. 198 19 three (ff. 199–201) 20^8 wants 4, 5 after f. 205+1 leaf before 1 and 1 leaf after 8 (ff. 202, 209). Many hands of various sizes: cursiva; current hybrida (arts. 8–12, probably all by the scribe who names himself in art. 10c); the German equivalent of anglicana, s. xiv² (arts. 13, 14). Initials: in arts. 8, 9, 12, 13, either 3-line (or more) or 2-line in red; elsewhere omitted or (a few) in the ink of the text. Capital letters in the ink of the text are stroked with red in arts. 8–12. Contemporary German (Hildesheim?) binding of wooden boards: white leather covers the spine and 60 mm of each board and is edged with a narrow strip of metal down the length of each board: two bands: strap and pin missing. Secundo folio *minime*.

Written in Germany, arts. 8–12 probably at Hildesheim. 'Liber Monasterii s. Michaelis', f. ii, s. xvii, is the ex-libris of the Benedictine abbey of St. Michael, Hildesheim. The binder, s. xv², used a leaf of a local service book as a pastedown (art. 15: St. Bernward was buried at Hildesheim in 1022) and incorporated nine earlier leaves, arts. 13, 14, which come presumably from a book belonging to a convent founded by countess Bya de Regenstein.

Cr. 2.5. *Tabulae astronomicae*

s. XIII med.

E. Zinner, 'Die Tafeln von Toledo', *Osiris*, i (1936), 747–74, analyses under 137 heads a manuscript of the tables of Arzachel which is to some extent the same as arts. 1–8.

1. Chronological tables: (a) f. 1^v Tabula ad inueniendum tempus nabugodonozor per tempus domini nostri ihesu cristi; (b) f. 2 Tabula inuentionis dierum annorum et mensium alexandri regis grecorum; (c) f. 2^v Tabula inuentionis dierum in annis et mensibus iezagar regis persarum; (d) f. 3 Extractio annorum persarum de annis arabum et e conuerso; (e) f. 3^v Tabula sequens ad inueniendum annos arabum per annos cristi; (f) f. 4 Tabula ad inueniendum inicium cuiusque mensis arabum; (g) f. 4^v Tabula ad inueniendum ferias kalendarum mensium latinorum; (h) f. 5 Tabula ad inueniendum ferias kalendarum mensium grecorum; (i) f. 5^v Tabula ad sciendum qua feria quisque mensis arabum ingrediatur;

(*j*) f. 6 Tabula inuentionis annorum arabum per annos domini nostri ihesu cristi; (*k*) f. 6ᵛ Tabula inuentionis dierum annorum cristi et mensium; (*l*) f. 7 Tabula inuentionis dierum annorum et mensium arabum.

In (*b*) the 'Anni collecti' begin at 1240 and in (*j*) the 'Anni cristi' at 1232. A note, s. xiii ex., on the pastedown refers to (*e*): 'In tabulam primam positam infra ad inueniendum annos arabum per annos cristi. sic intrabis. Sint anni cristi 1291 perfecti et uis inuenire annos arabum ad primam diem ianuarii anni 1292'.

2. Tables: (*a*) ff. 7ᵛ–8ᵛ Tabula arcus et corde; (*b*) ff. 9–10 Tabula sinus et declinationis; (*c*) ff. 10ᵛ–11ᵛ Tabula ascensionum signorum in circulo directo; (*d*) ff. 12–13 Ascensiones signorum in climate primo cuius latitudo est 16 gra et hore eius sunt 13; (*e–j*) ff. 13ᵛ–22 Similar tables, each on three pages, for the second to seventh climates; (*k*) f. 22ᵛ Tabula differentie ascentionum uniuerse terre; (*l*) f. 23 Tabula umbre.

(*b, c, k, l*). Cf. Zinner, nos. 25, 29, 26, 27.

3. (*a*) Tabula medii cursus solis in annis et mensibus arabum ad mediam diem ciuitatis toleti (ff. 23ᵛ–24), Tabula equationis solis (ff. 24ᵛ–27), and similar tables of mean course and equation and argumentum lune for moon, Saturn, Jupiter, Mars, Venus, and Mercury (ff. 27ᵛ–32, 33ᵛ–37, 37ᵛ–41, 41ᵛ–45, 45ᵛ–49, 49ᵛ–53) and of mean course for Caput draconis (ff. 32ᵛ–33). (*b*) Tabula accessionis et recessionis octaue spere in annis et mensibus arabum (f. 53ᵛ). (*c*) Tabula equationis motus octaue spere (ff. 54–55ᵛ).

(*a*). Cf. Zinner, nos. 33–98.

4. Tables: (*a*) ff. 56–58ᵛ Tabula binarii ad latitudines planetarum 5; (*b*) ff. 59–60 Tabula quaternarii ad latitudines 5 planetarum; (*c*) f. 60ᵛ Tabula apparitionis et occultationis 5 planetarum; (*d, e*) Tables of mean conjunction (f. 61) and opposition (f. 61ᵛ) 'solis et lune in annis arabum collectis ad meridiem ciuitatis toleti'; (*f, g*) Tables (f. 62) 'medie coniunctionis et oppositionis solis et lune in annis arabum expansis' and (f. 62ᵛ) 'in mensibus arabum'; (*h*) ff. 63–6 Tabula diuersi motus solis et lune in una hora; (*i*) f. 66ᵛ Tabula diuersitatis aspectus lune ad latitudinem toleti que est 39 gra et 54 minuta. hore uero eius 14 et 54 (*sic*) minuta: similar tables for each of seven climates follow on ff. 67–70.

Except (*c*), as Zinner, nos. 99–112.[1]

5. Eclipse tables: (*a–d*) Tables of eclipse of sun (ff. 70ᵛ–71) and moon (ff. 71ᵛ–72) 'in longitudine longiori' and 'in longitudine propiori'; (*e*) f. 72ᵛ Tabula equationis diametri umbre; (*f*) f. 72ᵛ Tabula quantitatis obscurationis solis et lune; (*g*) f. 72ᵛ Tabula conuersionis tenebrarum in utraque eclipsi.

(*a*). Cf. Zinner, nos. 113–21.

6. f. 73 Tabula ad inueniendum loca stellarum fixarum magis famosarum.
Forty stars, Alderaymira–Venebkartoz.

7. f. 73ᵛ Tabula longitudinum et latitudinum ciuitatum mundi magis famosarum.
Sixty-four cities, Tagea. Septa. Emerida. Corduba . . . Messie: Verona and Padua were added later.

---

[1] Zinner repeats his number 102 in error.

8. ff. 74–76^v Tabula proiectionum radiorum.

Zinner, no. 124.

9. f. 77 A rota to show the 'loca in orizonte in quibus principia signorum oriun-
tur in quolibet climate et occidunt'.

10. ff. 77^v–78 A table of latitudes 'trium superiorum planetarum' and another
of Venus and Mercury 'secundum ptholomeum'.

11. ff. 78^v–79 Tabula arcium et angulorum in climate quarto. cuius longior
dies est 14 horarum et dimidie et latitudo eius est 36 graduum: similar tables
for the fifth, sixth, and seventh climates follow on ff. 79^v–82.

12. ff. 82^v–83 Tabula diuersitatis aspectus solis et lune secundum ptholomeum
in circulo altitudinis in terminis quatuor longitudinum a centro terre et sunt 9
tabule.

13. ff. 83^v–91^v Tabula ad inueniendum tempus per altitudinem solis.

The hours and minutes are in columns numbered 15–80.

14. (a) ff. 92–6 Incipiunt tabule mediorum cursuum planetarum in annis et
mensibus domini nostri ihesu cristi ad meridiem ciuitatis marsilie. composite
a magistro willelmo anglico. (b) f. 96^v Tabula accessionis et recessionis octaue
spere in annis et mensibus cristi.

(a). Tables of mean course of sun, moon, argumentum lune, caput draconis, and the five
planets, beginning at 1160. Every twentieth year from then until 1620 is entered. The
heading is at the foot of f. 92. Cf. Zinner, loc. cit., p. 771. ff. 97–9 blank.

15. ff. 99^v–100 Tabula medie coniunctionis et oppositionis solis et lune in annis
cristi et mensibus ad meridiem ciuitatis nouarie. cuius longitudo ab occidente
est 30 gra et 50 minuta et latitudo eius est 45 gra.

Every seventy-sixth year is given from A.D. 77 to A.D. 1597. A cross opposite 1217 perhaps
suggests use in the seventy-six-year period 1217–92.

16 (added). (a) s. xv, ff. 100^v–101 Canon pro tabula longitudinis et latitudinis
Ciuitatum hic inferius positarum. Nota quod ista tabula . . . (b) s. xv, ff. 101^v–
102 Scire debes quod latitudo locorum uel ciuitatum quarumcumque . . . in
tabulis reperitur. (c) s. xiv (?), f. 102^v A table explained in a side note, 'Hii
sunt medii motus omnium planetarum ad unam horam et 18 puncta hore qui
debent subtrahi a mediis planetarum motibus super toletum. ut habeatur uere
medius motus eorum super mediolanum'. (d) f. i A table of the zodiacal signs.

(a). Seventy-eight places listed from west (Manna) to east (Antioch).

17 (added, s. xiv). f. 102^v Verses: (a) Annis quingenis decies annisque ducentis
. . . mille ter annos; (b) Annis millenis . . . cum ruit ense Thomas; (c) Virgo gens
(sic) uixit sexaginta tribus annis . . . (4 lines).

(a). Cf. Walther, no. 1119. Eight couplets, giving (1) the age of the world at the incarnation (5,199 years), (2) the length of Adam's stay in hell (43 for 4,304 years), (3–7) the years
from creation to incarnation, (8) the sum of (3–7), 'Complebit cristus cristo nascente
probatur / Quinquaginta duos nongentos mille ter annos', i.e. 3,952 years. (b). The year
of the murder of Thomas of Canterbury. (c). Walther, no. 20534 (Virgo parens).

ff. ii+100+ii. 220×155 mm. Written space *c.* 160×100 mm. Collation: 1⁴+1 leaf after 4 2–12⁸ 13⁸ wants 8, probably blank. Quires 1–12 are signed at the end o, 1–11. Italian binding, s. xv: wooden boards covered with brown leather: a rope pattern central ornament within a panel formed by repetitions of a floral stamp set sideways.

Written in northern Italy. Arts. 15, 16*c* suggest provenance from the Novara–Milan region. 'liber (?) PP' inside the cover. '£10. o. o' and '32' on a piece of paper inside the cover.

Cr. 2.20/1. *Kalendarium inrotulatum*   s. xiv med. (1339?)

1. Calendar in red and black.

January–November on the front, December on the back. Feasts of twelve lessons are marked: they include 'Roberti abbatis' and 'Barnardi abbatis' (29 Apr., 20 Aug.). 'Malachie episcopi', 5 Nov.

2, on the back. (*a, b*) Circular tables for finding the golden number and Sunday letter, both marked 1339. (*c*) Table to find Septuagesima and other movable feasts by means of the golden number and Sunday letter. (*d*) Tabula Magistri petri de dacia ad sciendum in quo signo sit luna et in quo gradu illius signi. (*e*) Dominus signorum. (*f*) Tabula ad sciendum quis planetarum regnat in qualibet hora diei. (*g*) Tabula eclipsis solis et lune usque ad annos domini 1364. Et sciendum est quod dies et hore incipiunt in meridie diei. (*h*) Canon supra tabula signorum. Ad locum lune habendum videas quota est dies . . .

(*d, h*). Thorndike and Kibre. (*h*) explains (*d*), which is the same as 2. 20/2, art. 2 (1, 2). (*e*). 'A man of signs', with explanatory text on each side of him, as in 2. 20/2, art. 4*a*. (*f*). As 2. 20/2, art. 2 (5). (*g*) lists twenty-five eclipses from 1339 to Mar. 1364/5. The last 100 mm are blank.

A roll of three membranes. *c.* 1030×73 mm. In art. 1 'KL' is gold on a blue ground. Written in France (?) for Cistercian use.

Cr. 2.20/2. *Almanac*   s. xv²

An almanac of seven sheets, each folded in eight to provide sixteen columns on each sheet or 112 columns in all.

1. Sheets 1–4 (cols. 1–64). A Sarum calendar in red and black.

Feasts in red are not numerous. They include: Translacio sancte Frideswide (11 Feb.); Translacio sancti Thome (erased, 7 July); Sancte Frideswide uirginis (19 Oct.); Sancti edmundi archiepiscopi (16 Nov.); Sancti hugonis episcopi (17 Nov.); Sancti Thome martyris (not erased, 29 Dec.: octave in black). 'pape' was erased at 31 Dec. where it was likely to catch the eye, but only there.

Each month with its accompanying tables takes up four columns, two of which contain indictions for four decennovenal cycles, 1463–1538. Three columns on each sheet are blank and a fourth column is blank except for the heading appropriate to the sheet, for example (sheet 1) 'Ianuarius Februarius Martius'.

2. Sheet 5 (cols. 65–80). 'Tabula signorum cum tabula lune et indiccionibus'.

Five tables with explanatory texts to show: (1, 2) the sign and degree of the moon 'omni die etatis sue' (cf. 20/1, art. 2*d*); (3) leap-year; (4) movable feasts; (5) 'quis planeta regnat in qualibet hora'. Four columns are blank.

3. Sheet 6 (cols. 81–96). A table to show lunar eclipses, twenty-nine in all, in the years 1461–81.

Three columns are blank. A fourth column bears the title 'Eclipses solis et lune diuis' in quattuor partibus'.

4. Sheet 7 (cols. 97–112). (*a*) A drawing of a 'man of signs', that is with the twelve signs of the zodiac on his body, and flanking text, 'Aries. Caue ab incisione in collo nec iucundas Venam capitalem . . .' (3 cols.). (*b*) A drawing of a 'man of veins', showing the positions of twenty-four veins, and flanking text in twenty-four paragraphs, 'Vena in medio frontis purgat emeroidas et frenesim iuuat . . .' (3 cols.). (*c*) Ad noticiam istius kalendarii est notandum quod in prima linea descendendo secundum longitudinem . . . (4 cols.).

(*a*). Thorndike and Kibre. (*c*). Twenty paragraphs, nos. 1–10 referring to art. 1, nos. 11–13 to art. 2, nos. 14–19 to art. 3 and no. 20, 'Vltimate manifestantur ymagines signorum et venarum cum scripturis conuenientibus', to art. 4. Five columns were left blank. One column bears the title 'Homo signorum cum homine venarum et cum canone tocius kalendarii'.

Seven sheets, each *c.* 232 × 160 mm, folded in eight to measure *c.* 120 × 40 mm. Well written in textura. Initials: (i) gold on blue and red grounds patterned in white for the *KL* at each month of art. 1 and the *A* of *Ad* in art. 4*c*; (ii) blue with red ornament; (iii) blue or red. The seven sheets and their covers, each double thicknesses of soft leather, are sewn together along one 40-mm edge: the covers were edged with strips of brown leather, but the sewing has come away and only one strip now remains.

Written in England. One of the blank columns of sheet 7 is inscribed (i) 'An ancient Almanack Wm Booth of Witton 'in Warw:shire' 1646', (ii) '90 Fothergill of Birmingham 1755', (iii) 'J. Ames of London FRS 30th June 1756. being the Gift of Dr Fothergill', (iv) three lines I cannot read. In his sheaf-catalogue Lord Crawford notes that 'It was bought by Mr Tutet at the Ames sale in 1779 whence it went to Mr J. B. Nichols'. William Bragge sale, Sotheby's, 7 June 1876, lot 54.

Cr. 2.20/3. *Almanac* s. xv²

An almanac of six sheets, each folded in eight to provide sixteen columns on each sheet, or ninety-six columns in all. The contents correspond to Cr. 2. 20/2, as follows: art. 1 as art. 1; art. 2*a–f* as arts. 4*b*, 2 (1–5); art. 3*a* as art. 4*c*; art. 3*b* as art. 3; art. 3*d* as art. 4*a*.

1. Sheets 1–4 (cols. 1–64). A Sarum calendar in red and black.

More feasts in red than in 20/2, but not Frideswide (black in October: no feast in February), nor Hugh. 'Translatio s' thome martyris' in red, 7 July: neither this, nor the December feast, nor the word 'pape' is erased.

Each month, with its tables of indictions, etc., takes up four columns, as in 20/2.

2. Sheet 5 (cols. 65–80). (*a*) Twenty-four paragraphs, alternately red and black, 'Vena in medio frontis incisa purgat emoroydas et frenesim iuuat . . .', set out in two columns, one on each side of a blank space, intended for a 'man of veins'. (*b–f*) Tables as in 20/2, but only the lunar tables are provided with explanatory text, 'Pro noticia tabule lune . . . pro precedentibus subtrahe'.

Three columns remain blank. A fourth column bears the title 'Indictiones. Festa mobilia. Homo venarum. Tabula planetarum. Tabula lune'.

3. Sheet 6 (cols. 81–96). (*a*) Ad noticiam istius kalendarii est notandum quod in prima linea descendente versus sinistram . . . (5 cols.). (*b*) A table of solar and lunar eclipses in the years 1473, 1478, 1479, 1480, and 1481 (3 cols.). (*c*) The mnemonic verse to find the Sunday letter over seven years 'Filius esto dei celum bonum accipe grates'. (*d*) Aries. Caue ab incisione capite . . .

(*a*) appears to be a revised form of the text in 20/2. Sixteen paragraphs, nos. 1–9 and no. 16, 'Tabula indictionum incipit anno domini 1463 . . .', referring to art. 1, nos. 10–13 to art. 2, and nos. 14, 15 to art. 3. (*c*) is below the first column of (*b*). (*d*) is in two cols., one on each side of a blank column intended for the 'man of signs'.

Three columns remain blank, besides that in (*d*). A fourth column bears the title 'Homo signorum. Canon. Eclipses'.

Six sheets, each *c.* 262 × 182 mm, folded in eight to measure *c.* 130 × 48 mm. Textura. Initials: (i) 2-line, gold with pale-red ornament; (ii) 1-line, gold with pale-red ornament or blue with dark-red ornament. Each sheet has a projecting rounded top over one fold (48 mm wide) and these six tops, sewn together, form a tab-like projection convenient to hold. Kept in a limp parchment case, like a slip-in spectacle case, to which a thong, 440 mm long, is attached: the parchment is inscribed, s. xvii, 'Calendarium perpetuum Wal[teri Elv]edon s[ocii] aulæ de Gonville'.[1]

Written in England. Acquired at the William Bragge sale, 7 June 1876, lot 55.

Cr. 2.98. *J. de Sacrobosco, De sphaera; Theorica planetarum* 1468

1. ff. 1–14ᵛ Iohannis.de sacro.busco.spera. Tractatum de spera Quatuor Capitulis distinguimus: dicentes primo . . . aut mundi machina dissoluetur. Finis.

Many manuscripts and printed editions. Cf. Cr. 3.29, art. 3. Another hand added after the last words 'Aut deus ens patitur. Aut Machina soluitur Orbis'.

2. ff. 15–29ᵛ Planetarum Theorica Incipit. Circulus ecentricus uel egresse cuspidis uel egredientis centri dicitur . . . et non corporaliter. Etsi planeta possent in hac materia explicari iuxta dicta tamen ea ipsa speculantibus relinquam. Finis. Scriptus per me b[. . . . . .] Anno domini M° cccc° lxviii°. secundo nonas februarii hora xxiiiᵃ. Finitus. Finis b[. . .] Monticulanus Finis.

The same common text as in Cr. 3. 12, q.v. An extra sentence here at the end. Some diagrams unfinished and others not started.

ff. ii+30+i. Paper. 210 × 155 mm. Written space 137 × 77 mm. 33–7 long lines. Frame ruling. Three quires of ten, marked a, b, c at the head of the first five rectos of each quire respectively. Upright current humanistica. Initials: (i) f. 1, 2-line, red *T* on blue and brown ground flourished into the margin in blue, red, green, and gold; (ii) 2-line, blue with red ornament or red with red ornament. A border below the written space on f. 1 includes a wreath: see below. Calf binding of s. xix, the backstrip, s. xviii, pasted on. Secundo folio *Vniuersalis*.

¹ Letters in brackets are taken from Lord Crawford's sheaf-catalogue. They are now illegible. There does not seem to be any evidence that this and 2/20/2 are copies of the perpetual calendar, 'cum tribus cyclis decemnoualibus', which Walter Elveden compiled, according to Leland (Emden, *BRUC*, p. 210).

Written in Italy by a named scribe. The arms of Pope Pius VI within the wreath on f. 1, the label of T. O. Weigel, and the mark '77 / WcG wo' inside the cover show that this book has the same history since s. xviii ex. as Cr. 1.27, q.v. '11' on a label at the foot of the backstrip.

Cr. 2.119. *J. de Muris*   1443

[E]t(si) bestialium voluptatum per quas gustus et tactus . . . sunt in hoc ordine consequentes. Et sic est finis musice Mur*is* Anno domini 1443 in capite ieiunii feria 5ᵃ.

Thorndike and Kibre (J. de Muris, De musica).

ff. 12. Paper. 202 × 155 mm. Written space 165 × 82 mm. 32 long lines. Only the vertical bounders are ruled. Cursiva. A 5-line space for an initial remains blank on f. 1. German binding, s. xvi[1]: see below.

Written in Germany. Bound in s. xvi[1] with a collection of written and printed pieces.[1] The chief and latest printed piece, the *Heptalogium* of Virgilius Wallendorfer of Salzburg, Leipzig, 1502, 4°, comes immediately after the J. de Muris. 'J. Lee Doctors Commons repaired June 1835' and the Lee of Hartwell book-plate inside the cover.

Cr. 2.123. *Johannes Dancko, Tabulae astronomicae; etc.*   1482?

1. ff. 1–18ᵛ Tabula horarum meridiei cum equatione dierum et noctium simul secundum horalogium integrum (ff. 1ᵛ–2), Tabula inuestigationis ascendentium ad latitudinem 51 graduum cuius dies longior 16 horarum 25 minutorum (ff. 2ᵛ–3), and other tables and explanatory notes.

A table begins 'Anno 1482 currente . . .' (f. 7). The words 'ex planckino' are in the text on f. 13 and ff. 15ᵛ–18ᵛ contain a 'Tabula domorum pro 7ᵐᵒ climate blanckini', one sign of the zodiac to a page, Taurus to Leo and Pisces missing: for the tables of Johannes Blanchinus see Thorndike and Kibre. Cf. art. 6.

2. ff. 19–87ᵛ . . . Explicit Equatorium magistri danckonis dictum Almanach.

Tables of planetary motion for the years 1340–80 by Johannes Dancko de Saxonia, lacking the canon 'Cum animaduerterem . . .' (cf. Thorndike and Kibre) and some tables at the beginning. The first table now, '[Tabula veri motus solis] In anno bisextili', comes at f. 17ᵛ in the copy in Bodleian, Rawlinson D. 1227.

3. ff. 88–95ᵛ A supplement to art. 2 for the years 1381 to 1400.

4. ff. 96–123ᵛ . . . Expliciunt tabule profacii.

Tables for 1360 to 1597.

5. ff. 124ᵛ–127ᵛ A 'Tabella ueri motus lune' and other tables of planetary motion, with explanatory notes.

[1] The other manuscript pieces are all by one scribe, s. xvi[1], who also annotated the *Heptalogium* and the other printed texts. His longest piece is at the end, 'Liber Hymnorum a Sanctis patribus Gregorio. Ambrosio. Hyeronimo. Prudencio. et ceteris diuersis metrorum generibus conscriptis', on forty-six leaves: the metre is noticed at the head of each hymn, sometimes in Greek capitals.

According to the table of contents inside the cover, 'Tabule ex quibus per simplicem addi-cionem habetur verus motus planetarum'. A calculation on f. 127ᵛ is for 1482. f. 124ʳ blank.

6. f. 1, left blank, contains tables and calculations for 1440 and 1468 and in what seems to be the main hand of arts. 1–5 a calculation, 'Hec est manus prouincialis ordinis predicatorum in Lipcz[k] doctoris theologie. Si vis . . . ut si vis habere ad annos 1481 scribe numerum 68 sub 81 et subtrahe. . . et habebis ad annum 1481. Si uero predictos introitus vis conuertere ad meridianum Nurenbergensem si tabulas non habes vide latitudinem regionum. nam nurem-berge in 49 gra. lipczk 51', referring to a table of houses 'planckini'.

7. Verses in German: (a) f. iii Sehe korn' egidii: habern' gersten' benedicti . . . (7 lines); (b) f. iii Aliter. Sehe korn' egidii . . . (9 lines); (c) f. iiiᵛ Snel auff in dy tabern' aurora lucis rutilat / Zwar (?) dy gesellen trincken gern' sicut ceruus desiderat / Hye ist ein guter wein aufgethan iam lucis orto sidere . . . (line 24) Horet auf gepott vnd von den sun paceque donans protinus.

(a–c) in one good hand, s. xv/xvi. (a). Cf. MMBL i. 161.

8 (added in 1555 and 1557). Horoscopes: (a) f. iii for a person unnamed, 24 Sept. 1555; (b) f. 128 for 'Georgius Spalatinus . . . filius M. Sebaldi Spalatini Noribergensis Ludimagistri Eystetensis', born 'Eystadii', 3 Mar. 1557.

ff. iii+127+iii. Paper. For ff. iii, 128, parchment flyleaves, see arts. 7, 8. 217×155 mm. Collation doubtful: the first quire is a 12 and ff. 96–127 are two 12s and an 8. Leaves are missing after f. 15 and before f. 19. Current pointed hybrida, very small outside the tables. No coloured initials. Rebound, s. xx, preserving the former brown leather covers, s. xv ex., on which is a floral border, diagonal fillets within the border, and stamps with the word 'maria' at head and foot outside it. A title on the tail, 'Tabule magne planetarum'.

Written probably in or near Nuremberg (art. 6). 'Sebaldus Spalatinus M.' inside the cover: art. 8 shows that he was from Nuremberg and schoolmaster at Eichstätt in 1557. Chasles book-plate, with number 3427, inside the cover. Michel Chasles sale, Paris (Claudin) 27 June 1881, lot 3427.

Cr. 3.2. *Alcabitius, Introductio in Astrologiam (in German)* 1474

In Gottes namen Amen Seich facht ann dy Capittel in dem Puch der eynfierung In dy Astrologey des Alkabicius vnd ist gesegt in funff vnderschaid . . . (*table of five parts*) . . . Der Erst vnderschaid von den wessen des Zodiacus. In den namen des herren Zodiacus das ist ain Circkel . . . (f. 31) das sie nicht vngelernet beleiben wan sie gehorend zu dysser kunst. Also endt sich der Tractat der eynfeurung in dy Astrologey des Maisters Alkabitius vnd hat zu Teutsch ge-macht Pruder Arnolt von freypurg predigre orden Anno domini 1312. Am andern tag des merczen vnd ist geschriben worden mit fleyssigem auffsechen vnd Corrigirn Durch purkhartten kekh zu Salczpurg. Anno domini 1.4.7.4 etc. Gott sey gelopt.

For the Latin cf. Thorndike and Kibre (Postulata . . .), Carmody, 1956, p. 144, and *GKW* 842–5, and for the German *SOPMA* i. 129, no. 332. A table of the Egyptian days follows, f. 31ᵛ. ff. 32–36ᵛ blank.

ff. i+36+i. Paper. 292×210 mm. Written space 210×140 mm. 36 long lines. Collation: 1–3¹². A careful cursiva. 1-line red initials. Capital letters in the ink of the text
touched with red. Binding of s. xix. Secundo folio *ling*.

Written at Salzburg by a named scribe. Lot 38 in a sale, s. xix: the relevant slip from the
catalogue (in German) is inside the cover. Below it a label, 'Ex bibliotheca K. Haiser
Mns. Nʳᵒ 20', printed, except the number. Also, top left, '79/WW'. 'Am 12/78 Zurcher
Auction R.T.' and 'NL. es' inside the back cover.

Cr. 3.3. *Alhacen, Optica; De crepusculo* s. XIII med.

1. ff. 2–186 Incipit primus tractatus libri alhacen filii alhaycen de aspectibus et
vii sunt differentie. Inuenimus uisum . . . est reflexio. Nunc autem terminemus
hunc tractatum qui est finis libri. `Explicit liber hal`h´acen filii halhaycen filii
aycen.´ de aspectibus.´

Alhacen, Optica, translated by Gerard of Cremona. Printed in 1572. Thorndike and
Kibre. Carmody, p. 139. Bk. 2, f. 22; 3, f. 63; 4, f. 84; 5, f. 94ᵛ; 6, f. 137. Diagrams and
many scholia in the wide margins. f. 136ᵛ blank.

2. ff. 186–9 Ostendere quid sit crepusculum et quid causa . . . et illud est quod
voluimus. `Explicit liber de ascensionibus nubium.´

Thorndike and Kibre refer to nine copies: in two, B.L., Royal 12 G. vii and Peterhouse,
Cambridge, 209, this short piece follows art. 1. Carmody, p. 140. The annotator wrote in
the margin of f. 186 that the 'uerus titulus est iste. Incipit liber abomadhi Malfagar id est
de crepusculo matutino et uespertino. et Safa[c] verba eius. ostendere quid sit crepusculum'.

A handsome inscription on f. 189 shows that arts. 1, 2 were corrected by 11 May 1269:
Ego Magister Guido dictus de Grana correxi diligenter Istos duos libros scilicet perspec-
tiuam Alhacen. et librum de ascensionibus nubium.´ Iuxta exemplar Magistri Iohannis
Lundoniensis quod ipsemet diligenter correxit ut dicitur.¹ Completa fuit correctio horum
librorum anno domini m° cc° lx° nono. quinto ydus maii scilicet in uigilia penthecostes.
The hand that wrote this occurs often in the margins, for example on f. 17.

f. 190ʳᵛ, left blank, contain notes of payments, hard to read, probably in the hand
of Andres: see below.

3. f. 1 A leaf of an Aristotelian text (?), s. xiii. Begins 'fit aer. Deinde quando
superfluit raritas fit ignis. et similiter raciocinantur qui putant quod aer est
elementum rerum'. Ends 'Sicut illud quod inuenit athaneus ex illis de athenis.
posuit enim quod elementa corporis hominis sunt frigidum et calidum et siccum
et humidum'.

Written space 223×150 mm. 2 cols. 53 lines.

ff. iii+190+ii, foliated (i, ii) 1–64, 64 i, 65–190 (191, 192). For f. 1 see above. 290×
198 mm. Written space 180×100 mm. 40 long lines. Collation of ff. 2–190: 1–9¹² 10⁸
11–12⁸ 13⁴ (ff. 133–6) 14–17¹² 18 six (ff. 185–90). Quires numbered at the beginning,
'1 quaternus' (f. 2) and then by numbers only. Two hands, changing at f. 137. Initials:

¹ Is the Master John of London in question the Master John of London whom Roger
Bacon praised for his skill in mathematics (*Opus Tertium*, ed. Brewer, xi. 34)? The John
of London who gave a now missing copy of Alhacen to St. Augustine's, Canterbury
(*Ancient Libraries*, no. 1138), is presumably the later John, for whom see A. B. Emden,
Donors of Books to S. Augustine's Abbey, Canterbury, 1968, pp. 11, 12 and pls. iii–v.

(i) f. 2, *I*, a man in blue and red gown holds an axe; (ii) 2-line, blue or red with ornament of the other colour. Capital letters in the ink of the text filled with pale yellow. 'Bound by F. Bedford', s. xix/xx. Secundo folio (f. 3) *illud corpus*.

Written in Spain (?). Sold by a citizen of Burgo de Osma to a Jewish doctor and citizen of Soria in 1424: 'Yo Iuan Andr*es* vezyno del Burgo de osma otorgo que vendo a vos rabi esua (?) fisyco vezyno del castillo de la cibdat de Soria esto libro de Espectibus e me otorgo por pagado e por que es verdat pus aqui mi nonbre. Fecha x dias de febrero anno de mill' e cuatrocientos e veynte e cuatro annos. Iuan Andr*es*', f. 189ᵛ.[1] '78. I. B.' at head of f. 2, s. xix.

Cr. 3.4. *Astrologica*   s. xv med.

1. ff. 1–2 [U]niuersa *astronomie*[2] iudicia a lunari ducata sumunt efficaciam. Venus et Iupiter vt est indorum autoritas fortunate sunt stelle . . . et ventos habet proprios. Explicit.

Thorndike and Kibre. Carmody, pp. 85–7.

2. f. 2 Quidam astrologus de domino anni. Vt singulis annis qualitates aeris . . . habet prouenire. Explicit.

Nineteen lines.

3. f. 2ʳᵛ De ventorum cognicione. Ventorum cognicio ex plura experiencia . . . et piscis locantur. Explicit.

Thorndike and Kibre. Carmody, p. 86, as part 2 of art. 1.

4. ff. 2ᵛ–6 [C]um omnis sciencia vel omnis ars propter vtilitatem suam naturaliter sit appetenda et vtilitas astronomie . . . in alia domo. Explicit liber de eleccionibus secundum haly et tholomeum.

Thorndike and Kibre refer to B.L., Sloane 332, ff. 59–70ᵛ. Pt. 2, f. 4ᵛ.

5. On the planets: (*a*) ff. 6–7 Incipit tractatus de dignitatibus planetarum. [S]unt autem in signis quedam fortitudines . . . a signis. Expliciunt fortitudines planetarum; (*b*) f. 7 Alie sunt fortitudines et debilitates quas planete ex esse diuerso . . .; (*c*) f. 7 In operibus lune . . .; (*d*) f. 7ᵛ Ad denotandam diuersam aeris dispositionem futuram . . .; (*e*) ff. 7ᵛ–8 Planetarum nature sunt hee. Saturnus est summe frigidus . . . pluuiosum tempus significat. Expliciunt nature signorum et planetarum.

Thorndike and Kibre refer to Bodleian, Ashmole 191, f. 9ᵛ, for (*a*) and to B.L., Harley 1612, f. 10, for (*d*), which is here only seven lines long.

6. f. 8 De 4ᵒʳ mensibus lune. Mensium lunarum sunt 4ᵒʳ species. et primus dicitur mensis paragracionis . . . in coniunccione. Explicit de mensibus lunaribus.

Cf. Thorndike and Kibre.

7. f. 8ʳᵛ De cursu solis et aliorum planetarum. Sol est calidus et siccus temperatus valde . . . motus cum sole. Expliciunt nature et cursus planetarum.

8. f. 8ᵛ Ad cognoscendum quando aliquis veniet ad te vtrum pro bono aut pro malo . . . (6 lines only).

---

[1] I am grateful to Professor Derek Lomax for helping me to read this inscription.

[2] The word is represented by the sign 'q'.

9. ff. 9–10ᵛ Zodiacal tables, Aries–Scorpio only.

A quire or more is missing between f. 10 and f. 11.

10. ff. 11–12 (*begins imperfectly*) sicut aqua et lac. Fortune quando aspiciunt malos . . . quod est ascensus etc. Explicit regule (*sic*) specialis.

Nos. 23–38 of a series of planetary signs of good and bad fortune.

11. ff. 12ᵛ–18ᵛ Omnia que a primeua rerum origine . . . quam in cubicis etc. Explicit algorismus de Integris.

J. de Sacrobosco, Algorismus. Printed often: cf. D. E. Smith, *Rara mathematica*, 1908, p. 32.

12. (*a*) ff. 18ᵛ–19 Omnia que a primeua rerum cognicione processerint . . . per ordinem. (*b*) ff. 19–23ᵛ Hec algorismus Ars presens dicitur in qua . . . Multiplicandorum de normis sufficiunt hec.

(*a*) differs from art. 11 after the fifth word and from Cambridge, U.L., Add. 6860, f. 118, after line 3. It is a 19-line introduction to (*b*), the verse arithmetic of Alexander de Villa Dei, Walther, no. 7470. Many marginalia.

13. f. 24ʳᵛ, left blank, has twenty-one currently written lines of mnemonic verse on the zodiacal signs and the planets, beginning with 'Sunt aries taurus...' (Walther, no. 18806).

ff. v+24+xxxiii. Paper and (ff. 1, 3, 5, 6, 8, 10–12, 16, 17, 21–4) parchment. 240 × 160 mm. Written space 160 × 110 mm. *c*. 37 long lines. Frame ruling. Collation: 1¹⁰ 2¹² 3 two. Quires 1, 2—there is a gap between them—are both signed 'b'. Secretary with some anglicana forms, by several hands. Spaces for 3-line and 2-line initials remain blank. Binding of s. xix, lettered on the spine 'LIB. MS / BIB. HALL.'. Secundo folio *grandes*.

Written in England. 'Nº 28' and 'J. O. Halliwell 1838', f. 1. No. 131 in Halliwell's 1840 catalogue, where it is said wrongly to be a folio. Halliwell sale, Sotheby's 27 June 1840, lot 138. Item 262 in an English bookseller's catalogue, s. xix: the relevant strip is inside the cover. Book-plate of William Bragge, 'at whose sale I bought it', as Lord Crawford notes in his sheaf-catalogue.

Cr. 3.5, ff. 17–25. 'Liber fatorum' s. xv²

(*a*) f. 18ʳᵛ Two circular diagrams. That on the verso is followed by 'Regule super prescriptam figuram. Sciendum est quod si numerus fuerit sumptus infra vii. sumendus est numerus . . .'. After these rules the last line on the page bears the heading 'Incipit liber fatorum. Capitulum primum'. (*b*) ff. 19–23ᵛ Nine circular diagrams furnished except the first with volvels.

(*a*). Thorndike and Kibre.¹ (*b*). Most of the circles have numbers and signs referring to months, days and the zodiac round the circumference. On ff. 20–22ᵛ the centre of the

¹ They refer to Vienna, Nationalbibliothek 3276, ff. 260ᵛ–274ᵛ. There the same heading as here, 'Regule . . .', and the same incipit, 'Sciendum est . . .', is followed by a text beginning 'Almogine 1. Hoc indumentum durabile fertur', which consists of answers by twenty-eight judges, each in twenty-eight lines. It seems certain that Cr. 3.5 originally contained this text, which differs a good deal from the version in Cambridge, Magdalene College, Pepys 911, q.v. Information about the Vienna manuscript was kindly supplied by Dr. Otto Mazal.

volvel contains two lines diverging from a point o and marked with numbers at intervals: the numbers along the lines are the same for each pair, for example on f. 20 they are 1, 2, 3, 4, 5, 6 both to left and to right of o and on f. 20^v they are 2, 4, 6, 8, 10, 11. The letter 'A' is in one part of this central space and the letter 'M' in another. ff. 17^{rv}, 19^v, 24–25^v blank.

ff. 9 bound after 16 and before 23 leaves of later paper, the former mostly blank and the latter containing 'Figuræ in librum de Reuolutionibus Copernici', according to the title, s. xvii, on f. 27. 217×163 mm. Collation: 1 three 2^6. Cursiva. A 3-line red S, f. 18^v. Parchment wrapper, s. xviii (?).

Written probably in France. 'N. 89 1833 Jan. Nby' in pencil, f. 2, and below in ink 'Martin v. Reider. 1833. Jan. Nbey (?) auction'. 'Martinus Jos: de Reider Bambergae 18 . . .' and, later 'Very Rare £1. 18. o' inside the cover.

Cr. 3.9. *Johannes Dancko de Saxonia, Canones in Tabulas Alphonsinas; Tabulae Alphonsinae* s. xv^2

1. ff. 1–13 Tempus est mensura motus . . . ad inuicem collige ut sciamur ad quam partem sit latitudo sicut in venere dictum est. Utrum stella eratica sit ascendens vel descendens . . . gra 2.4 Minuta 18. Ad laudem illius el qual mai non era.

Canons on art. 2, generally the text in edn. Venice, 1483 (GKW 1257), sign. a.2–b.8^v. The last paragraph, Utrum stella . . ., is not in the edition. f. 13^v blank.

2. ff. 14–40^v Tabula differenciarum vnius regni ad Aliud. Differencia dilluuii et alfoncii . . .

An imperfect copy of the Alphonsine tables, generally as edn. 1483, sign. c. 1 onwards. Leaves, perhaps six, are missing after f. 22: the text in edn. sign. d.7–e.3^v was presumably in the gap. f. 39^v has the table in edn., sign. g.5, after which all is missing except (f. 40) 'Tabula latitudinum quinque planetarum' (as edn., sign. g.8^v) and (f. 40^v) tables 'diuersi motus solis et lune in vna hora' and 'diuersi motus solis in vno m. diei'. The latitudes and longitudes of ninety-six cities (etc.) are given in a table on f. 19 next after the 'Tabula continens equationes accessus et recessus octaui spere' (f. 18^v: cf. edn. sign. d.3^v): Tangra Cepta Corduba . . . Alre. Saur. Nouaria. Mediolanum. In edn. a longer list of cities in a different order is on sign. m.5^{rv}. The tables on ff. 20–2 (edn. sign. d.4–d.6) have 'Radix ad cremonam' added at the head of each of them, s. xv ex.

f. 41^{rv} is blank, except for an unfinished 'Tabula radicum motuum . . .' (as f. 17 and edn. sign. c.8) on the verso: probably ff. 40–1 were at first intended as the central bifolium of quire 3 and scrapped at a time when the text in black had been written, but not the text in red.

3. f. vi is part of a document, s. xii ?, the text washed out. Twenty widely spaced lines. The word 'Mediolani' is legible in line 4 and 'Sancti Pauli' in line 14.

ff. vi+41+v. For f. vi see above. 225×175 mm. Written space 165×113 mm. 36 long lines (art. 1). Collation: 1^8 2^8 wants 6–8, probably blank, after f. 13 3^8 4 two (ff. 22, 23, the outside bifolium) 5–6^8 7^2. Initials in art. 1: (f. i), 5-line, blue with red ornament; (ii) 2-line, red, not filled in after f. 9. Bound like Cr. 3.12. '78 / -W. Wevi-42' inside the cover: cf. 3.12.

Written in northern Italy. Probably in the Cremona region in s. xvi (cf. art. 2). 'HANS MORABERGER', f. vi, s. xvi.

Cr. 3.12. *Messahala, De astrolabio; Theorica planetarum* s. xiv in.

1. ff. 4–10 In cristi nomine amen (*in the margin*). Scito quod astrolabium est nomen grecum . . . stature tue ad planitiem. Amen. Explicit astrolabium secundum Mesahalam.

Ed. R. T. Gunther, *Early Science in Oxford*, v. 195–231. Twenty-one diagrams. f. 10^v blank.

2. ff. 1–3^v In cristi nomine amen. Incipit theorica planetarum[1] (*in the margin*). Circulus ecentricus uel egresse cuspidis uel egredientis centri dicitur qui non habet centrum cum mundo . . . et non corporaliter. Amen. Explicit theorica planetarum.

Many manuscripts and printed editions, the last by F. Carmody, 1942. Cf. Thomson, *Grosseteste*, pp. 238–9. Another later copy in Cr. 2.98, q.v., has a final sentence after *corporaliter*.

ff. i+10+x. Hair sides much flecked. *c.* 280×205 mm. Written space: of art. 1, 195× 155 mm; of art. 2, 195×130 mm. 2 cols. 64–7 lines, art. 1. 54 long lines, art. 2. Collation: 1^{12} wants 1–3 (ff. 4–10, 1, 2: the missing leaves are perhaps those now in Cr. 3.29, quire 1) 2 one (f. 3). Worm-holes show that f. 1 once followed f. 10. Initials: of art. 1, 3-line and 2-line, red; of art. 2, not filled in. Binding of s. xix, uniform with Cr. 3.9.

Written in Italy. Once part of the same manuscript as 3.29, ff. 1–15. '78 / -Eel- / 21' inside the cover: cf. 3.9.

Cr. 3.13. *J. Charlier de Gerson, De vita spirituali animae*   1474

Incipit tractatus in sex lectionibus diuisus super differencia peccati mortalis a veniali editus a magistro Iohanne de (*cancelled*) gerson et missus ab eodem episcopo petro de aliaco cardinali cameracensi. Reuerendo in cristo patri . . . domino Petro episcopo cameracensi. suus discipulus iohannes cancellarius indignus ecclesie Parisiensis . . . Postulare dignata est beniuolencia tua . . . (f. 1^v) pro inuicem ut saluemur. Ego vos baptizaui aqua . . . ita finem huius operis dedicamus. Explicit anno domini M cccc lxxiiii in festo dominici confessoris quo die fratri iohanni de assindia qui hunc tractatum incepit eleccio conuentus sneken' ad prioratum est presentata. 'finitus per henricum de colonia priorem'.

The letter to Pierre d'Ailly, A.D. 1402, printed in *Œuvres complètes* (ed. Glorieux), ii (1960), 63–4, and the text which it introduces, ibid. iii. 113–202 (no. 97). The heading is muddled since the De differencia . . . is a different work of Gerson's (edn. 1606, ii. 283). The scribe wrote 'Ihesus' at the head of f. 1.

ff. i+30+i. Paper. 280×205 mm. Written space 200×140 mm. 2 cols. 43–7 lines. Frame ruling. Collation: 1–3^{10}. Written in textura by two hands (see above) changing at f. 11^v: the second hand is less upright and writes three or four more lines to the page. Initials: (i) f. 1, 5-line, red patterned in white; (ii) 2-line, red. Capital letters in the ink of the text touched with red. Binding of s. xix. Secundo folio *Istas dispositiones*.

Written by two named scribes, the first of whom was elected prior of the convent of

[1] A later hand which wrote headings also in Cr. 3.29 repeated 'Incipit Theorica plane-tarum' in red.

Sneken on 4 Aug. 1474 (see above). The name 'Orlando Bezzi' inside the cover, s. xix, and book-plate of interlaced O and B.

Cr. 3.14. *Astrologica, etc.* s. xv med.

1. ff. 1–5 Quadripartitus hermetis de 15 stellis lapidibus planetis et caracteribus. Dixit hermes Scito quod si luna fuerit cum aliqua fixarum stellarum quindecim . . . et est figura eius hec.

Under the headings 'Stelle fixe', 'Lapides', 'Herbe', 'Signa', 'Planete'. A table of the fifteen stars, Capud algor–Cauda capricorni, follows. Ed. L. Delatte, *Textes latins et vieux français relatifs aux Cyranides*, Bibliothèque de la Faculté de Philosophie et Lettres de l'Université de Liège, Fasc. xciii, 1942. Cf. L. Thorndike in *Mélanges Auguste Pelzer*, 1947, pp. 224–7.

2. ff. 5ᵛ–10ᵛ Liber de signis celi et ymaginibus in lapidibus exaratis. Dixit ptholomeus vultus huius mundi sunt subiecti vultibus celestibus . . . contra rabiem et fantasmata. Hec sufficiant de ymaginibus lapidum.

3. ff. 10ᵛ–13ᵛ Incipit liber thebith bencorath de ymaginibus astronomicis. Dixit aristotiles qui legit philosophiam . . . et proficuum regionum. Ipsi gloria in secula. Explicit liber thebith de ymaginibus astronomicis.

Erfurt Q. 189, listed by Thorndike, loc. cit., p. 235, ends in the same way: cf. *MMBL* i. 91.

4. ff. 14–15ᵛ Incipit libellus hali de significacione planetarum cum sole in duodecim signis. Saturnus in ariete sub radiis solis facit pluuias . . . bonam complexionem ostendit etc.

Thorndike and Kibre.

5. ff. 16–22ᵛ Iacobus alkindi de radiis. Omnes homines qui sensibilia sensu percipiunt . . . in vim oracionis perfecte (*ends imperfectly*).

Thorndike and Kibre.

6. (*a*) ff. 23–25ᵛ (*begins imperfectly*) totam missam et qualibet die da elemosinam . . . (*b*) ff. 25ᵛ–26ᵛ Sequitur de modo consecrandi figuram que est memorie et debet consecrari in septem missis . . . (f. 26) Sequitur de missis quibus consecranda est figura memorie. Salomon rex israel in cuius pectore dominus . . . notoria appellauit nam breuibus notis scienciam edocet . . . et laudet dei pietatem. (*c*) ff. 27–30 Hec est prima oracio de decem ad facundiam acquirenda. Omnipotens et incomprehensibilis et inuisibilis et indissolubilis deus . . . diligentia est cauendum. Explicit tractatus omnium oracionum generalium et specialium istius Artis.

(*a*). Prayers for wisdom for use in masses of Holy Trinity, Holy Spirit, John Evangelist, and B.V.M., and also (f. 24ᵛ) 'de nocte cum intraueris cubiculum' and (f. 25) when 'legere vel studere siue disputare volueris'. (*b*). Thorndike and Kibre, s.v. Salomon (Apollonius, Ars notoria). A table of fifteen chapters follows. (*c*). To be said 'ante notas arcium', that is 'ante (*or* super) primam (. . . quintam) figuram theologie (*or* astronomie)'.

ff. xvi+32+iii. ff. iii–xvi are of s. xviii (?). Paper. 290 × 212 mm. Written space *c.* 195 × 120 mm. 37 long lines. Frame ruling. Collation: 1¹² 2¹⁰ 3¹² wants 1 and 12 (12 blank).

Quires 1, 2 signed a, b. Quire 3 signed q (?). Written in current hybrida by a scribe who was able to keep a straight steady hand and the same number of lines to the page, with only the chain lines of the paper to guide him. Initials: (i) of arts. 1–4, blue patterned in white; (ii) 2-line, red or blue. Rebound in 1964. Secundo folio *significacione*.

Written in France. 'Domus probacionis. Paris. Societatis Iesu', f. 1, at top, s. xvi, and, top left, a large figure '2'. 'Ex bibliotheca Michaelis Chasles acad. scientiarum socii' is printed on a book-plate, f. iii^v: the number 2982 added in ink. Chasles sale 27 June 1881, lot 2982.

Cr. 3.23. *Michael Scotus, etc.* s. xiv²

1 (quire 1). Pieces on the influence of the planets, etc.: (*a*) f. 1^rv Dicit messahala de racione celi et stellarum et qualiter operantur in mundo. Primum capitulum. Deus altissimus fecit terram ad similitudinem spere Fecit circulum altiorem in circuitu eius . . . operanturque; (*b*) ff. 1^v, 16^rv Notandum est quod principatus planetarum in concepcione . . . Quia influit super talia; (*c*) ff. 16^v–18 Natus sub ioue Pulcram habet faciem . . . tamen et bone conscientie; (*d*) ff. 18–23^v Incipit 'liber ptholomei' de natiuitatibus hominum. Iste est liber de signis hominum. scilicet de ipsorum fortunis et infortunis . . . excepto in nigro. (*e*) f. 2^rv Sequitur de regionibus signorum per totum orbem. Nam (?) regio oriens est persa . . . bonum faceret ymmo malum.

(*a*). The first chapter of the Epistola Messahalae: cf. Thorndike in *Osiris*, xii (1956), 62–4. Art. 1 should perhaps follow art. 5: see below. (*b*) includes verses, 'Susceptum semen . . .' (7 lines; Walther, no. 18933).

2 (quires 2–4). ff. 3–15^v, 34–45^v (*begins imperfectly*) igitur ymagines 36 mixturate sunt inter signa . . . Aries habet stellas multas . . . Et in quolibet signo 10 hore.

Thorndike and Kibre. The section of Michael Scot, Liber introductorius, concerned with the judgement of nativities from the signs of the zodiac, the constellations and the planets, illustrated by fifty-three pen drawings roughly coloured in green, with the stars red: f. 3 Aries, Taurus; f. 3^v Gemini, Cancer; f. 4 Leo, Virgo; f. 4^v Libra, Scorpio; f. 5 Sagittarius, Capricornus; f. 5^v Aquarius, Pisces; f. 7^v Ursa maior, Ursa minor, and Draco in one drawing; f. 8 Hercules; f. 8^v Corona, Serpentarius, Boetes; f. 9 Agitator, Zepheus; f. 9^v Casephia, Equs vespertinus; f. 10 Andromeda, Perseus; f. 10^v Triangulus, Glocea vel clocea siue gallina; f. 11 Lira, Cignus, Vultur volans; f. 11^v Vultur cadens, Cetus; f. 12 Eridanus; f. 12^v Pulsans canonum, Delphinus; f. 13 Orion; f. 13^v Canis, Lepus; f. 14 Nauis, Austronotus; f. 14^v Demon meridianus, Piscis; f. 15 Puteus, Centaurus; f. 34 Serpens, with Coruus and Urna; f. 34^v Anticanis, Equs secundus; f. 35 Tarabellum, Vexillum; f. 35^v Saturnus, Iupiter, Mars; f. 36^v Venus, Mercurius; f. 37^v Sol; f. 39^v Luna drawn by four beasts, the two on the right oxen. For this set of illustrations see Saxl and Meier, iii. xxv–xliii, 85, 294–5; iv. 73. The text corresponds to Bodleian MS. Bodley 266 (*Sum. Cat.* 2466), ff. 105^v–114^v.

3 (quire 5). (*a*) ff. 24^v–25 Quicumque ceperit infirmari luna existente in principio signi arietis . . . Nil capiti facias aries dum luna refulget . . . (*b*) ff. 25–6 Si vis horas diei certissime cognoscere . . . (*c*) ff. 26^v–28 Sunt in unoquoque signo gradus qui proprie dicuntur masculini . . . vincentes in celo. (*d*) ff. 28^v–29 A double opening with a 'man of veins' and explanatory text on the left and a table of signs and parts of the body on the right. (*e*) ff. 29^v–33^v Incipit de impressione aeris. Nota de inuestigacione nature dicit Alanus in anticlaudiano.

Versus. Terrarum motus mugitum . . . (3 lines). Sentencia est quod natura scrutatur et conspicit terrarum motus . . . Et in isto (*ends imperfectly: catchword* habent fieri rores)

(*a*). The thirty-six lines of verse, three for each sign, are Walther, no. 11780. A full page 'man of signs' fills f. 24. (*b*). On the length of shadow, with a table. (*c*). Five tables and texts to show the zodiacal degrees 'qui dicuntur' (1) 'Masculini vel feminini', (2) 'lucidi', 'tenebrosi', 'fumosi', 'vacui', (3) 'putei', (4) 'azemena', (5) 'augmentantes fortunam'. (*e*). On earthquakes, thunder, coruscation, lightning, storms at sea, wind, 'turbo', the rainbow, clouds, dew, frost, mist, rain, snow, ice, and 'De regionibus aeris'.

4 (quire 6). (*a*) ff. 46–7 Fleobotomia vel minucio alia fit per metathesim Alia per antipasim . . . Unde dicit Auicenna Fleobotomia est vniuersalis euacuacio omnium humorum. (*b*) f. 47ᵛ Nota quod luna habet 4 humores secundum disposicionem . . . patent in figura quo dicitur Dominus signorum.

5 (quire 7). (*a*) f. 48 (*begins imperfectly*) eius ex substancia terre . . . patefeci tibi. Et cetera. (*b*) ff. 48–9 Liber zael de coniunccionibus. Coniunccio est quando due planete iunguntur . . . in coniunctione cum ioue. (*c*) ff. 49–50ᵛ Luminaria firmamenti sunt multa inter que septem planete noscuntur . . . in auinione est 46 graduum parisius vero 43. (*d*) ff. 51ᵛ–52ᵛ Diagrams and tables of solar eclipses, 1361–86 (f. 52), and of lunar eclipses, 1360–86 (f. 52ᵛ): f. 51ʳ is blank. (*e*) ff. 53–57ᵛ Sciendum quod in celo est quidem circulus qui vocatur zodiacus . . . in eis est decepcio super omnia. (*f*) ff. 57ᵛ–59ᵛ De domino anni. et de Elmanach solis. doctrina vtilis. Dicit albumasar oportet primo scire . . . (f. 58ᵛ) et maxime influere: tables follow naming the twenty-eight lunar mansions, Alnath . . . Albuaten, 'secundum quod proferunt arabes' (f. 59) and 'De Domino anni' for 1360–85 (f. 59ᵛ).

(*a*). The last eleven lines only. A section begins 'Mercurius significat scriptores'. (*c*) Thorndike and Kibre. A 'Tabula ad sciendum quis planeta regnat omni hora diei' fills f. 50. (*e*). On the signs of the zodiac and the planets. The catchword after (*f*) is 'Dicit messahalah': cf. art. 1*a*.

ff. iii+59+ii. 262×175 mm. Written space *c.* 192×115 mm. 39 long lines. Collation: 1¹² (ff. 1, 16–23, 2) 2 one (f. 3, the last leaf) 3¹² (ff. 4–15) 4¹² (ff. 34–45) 5¹⁰ (ff. 24–33) 6² (ff. 46, 47) 7¹² (ff. 48–59). Written in anglicana. Initials: (i, ii) 3-line and 2-line, red. Capital letters in the ink of the text filled with red. Bound in red morocco in 1964. Secundo folio (f. 16) *Mercurius.*

Written in England. 'John Clarke . . .' scribbled on f. 16, s. xvi/xvii. 'B[. . . . .] June 1847 (?)', f. 1.

Cr. 3.25. *Tabulae astronomicae*   s. xv¹

Three pieces bound together: ff. 1–46, 47–64, 65–77. The second and third, arts. 35, 36, were parts of larger books.

1. ff. 1–8ᵛ Almanach.

Planetary tables. Dates in the margins suggest use in 1435 (cf. art. 7) and later in s. xv: the latest date is 1490.

2. ff. 8–9 Tabula magnitudinis et paruitatis diei calculata in 6° climate.

3. f. 9 Tabula diuersorum motuum planetarum in vna die.

4. f. 10 Tabula Retrogradationis stacionum et directionum planetarum.

5. f. 10ᵛ Tabula directionis stationis et retrogradationis planetarum.

6. f. 11 Tabula obliquitatis solis.

An explanatory text follows.

7. f. 11ᵛ Tabula feriarum vel dierum in quolibet anno et mense occurente 1391 tunc erat numerus 1 et deinceps 1392 occurrebat numerus 2 . . .

In spite of the heading the table is for the twenty-eight year cycle 1415–42. 'Imcompleti 1435' in the margin. At the foot a text 'Tria requiruntur in plenilunari eclipsi . . .'.

8. ff. 12–13 Tabula lunaris eclipsis.

9. ff. 13ᵛ–14 [T]ria queruntur ad inueniendum coniunctionalem eclipsim . . .
A table follows on f. 14.

10. f. 14ᵛ Tabula diuersitatum solis in climate rodi . . .

11. f. 15 Tabula diuersitatis aspectus lune in climate 6°.

12. f. 15ᵛ The same 'in climate 7°'.

13. f. 16ʳᵛ Tabula solaris eclipsis in qua reperitur per quantum spacium sol eclipsatur.

14. ff. 16ᵛ–17 Reuolutionem cuiuslibet annorum nati . . . inuenire. Scias annum incarnationis . . .
Tables follow on f. 17.

15. ff. 17ᵛ–18 Vtrum planeta sit stacionarius. directus. uel retrogradus . . .
Five paragraphs on this and other questions of planetary motion.

16. f. 18ᵛ Tabula minutorum proporcionalium in partibus planetarum.

17. ff. 19–20 Tables of planetary latitude, Saturn–Mercury.

18. ff. 20ᵛ–21 Tabula recte spere eleuationis signorum in medio celi in circulo directo in qualibet regione. Two tables.

19. ff. 21ᵛ–28 Tabula ascensionum signorum. . . .
Tables for the sixth, seventh, fifth, fourth, third, second, and first climates, each on a double opening.

20. f. 28ᵛ Tabula equacionum dierum cum suis noctibus.

21. f. 29 Tabula motus solis et lune in vna hora.

22. f. 29ᵛ Tabula motus solis et lune in vno minuto diei.

23. f. 29ᵛ Tabula equationis diuersitatis longitudinis capitis arietis ab equatore.

24. ff. 30–31ᵛ Tabula multiplicationis.

25. ff. 32–34^v Tabula equationum domorum ad signum arietis super latitudine ciui(tatis) cremone gra 45.

For the Toledo table cf. J. Millás Vallicrosa, *Estudios sobre historia de la ciencia española*, 1949, p. 168.

26. ff. 35–6 Tabula equacionis sinus et declinacionis.

27. f. 36^v Tabula umbre.

As Cr. 2. 5, art. 2*l*.

28. f. 36^v Tabula augmentacionis equationum solis.

29. f. 37^{rv} Tabula differentie ascensionum uniuerse terre.

As Cr. 2. 5, art. 2*k*.

30. f. 37^v Tabula ad sciendum introitum solis in principia 12 signorum.

An explanation follows, 'Scias quod ista tabula facta est ad meridiem parisius anno domini 1330 ita quod . . .'.

31. ff. 38–39^v Table of planetary degrees, three zodiacal signs to a page.

32. f. 40^{rv} Tables of planetary conjunction.

33. ff. 43–42^v Tabula motus solis et lune in 1° minuto diei.

34. ff. 43–5 Tabula equacionum ad sciendum motum solis et lune in vna hora.

35. ff. 45^v–46 Item alia tabula de motu lune in 1° minuto diei.

36 (quires 5, 6). (*a*) ff. 47–61^v Tables of mean motion and of equation of Saturn, Jupiter, Mars, Sun, Venus, Mercury, Moon, and Argumentum lune. (*b*) f. 62 Tabula extraccionis cuiuslibet ere ex altera in annis collectis et expansis secundum alfontium. (*c*) f. 62 Tabula motus augium et stellarum fixarum sine *Radice*. (*d*) f. 62 Tabula motus ac et re 8^i circuli . . . reducta ad parisius. (*e*) ff. 62^v–64 Tables of mean motion 'reducta ad parisius'.

(*a*). The tables are preceded by an explanation, f. 47^{rv}, 'Medium motum seu equacionem augium et omnium planetarum inuenire cupiens . . .'. The 'Anni cristi collecti' are at intervals of sixty years, 1300–1660. A slip with calculations is inserted after f. 50. f. 64^v blank.

37 (quire 7). ff. 65–77 Tables of mean motion and equation of Saturn, Jupiter, Mars, Sun, Venus, Mercury, Moon.

Nearly as art. 36*a*.

---

ff. iii+77+iii.[1] Paper. 292×215 mm and, from f. 47, 280×200 mm. Collation: 1^{10} 2–4^{12} 5^{12} 6^6 7^{12}+1 leaf after 12 (f. 77). Written in hybrida, cursiva (ff. 47–64), and textura (ff. 65–77). Bound in 1964.

Written in Italy (ff. 1–46) and France (ff. 47–77). The inscriptions on f. 1, s. xvi, apply to ff. 1–46 only: 'Ad vsum P. D. Laurentii Guavenerii (?) Placentie' above erasure of 'Cleri Regulares Domus sancti Vincentii Placentie̜'.

[1] Excluding f. 78, a stray leaf from Cr. 5 10, q.v.

Cr. 3.28. *Prosdocimus de Beldomandis, etc.* s. xv²

1. ff. 1–22ᵛ Compositio astrolabii 'magistri' prosdocimi de beldemandis 'pataui'. Quamuis de astrolabii compositione tam modernorum quam veterum dicta . . . tunc operare ut superius ostensum est etc'. Et sic est finis ad laudem dei amen. Canones astrolabii feliciter expliciunt deo gratias amen.

The scribe wrote 'maria. yhesus. marie filius' above the title. Thorndike and Kibre. Not known to have been printed, but the intention of sending it to the press (at Padua?) is noted by a contemporary hand on a slip of paper before f. 1: 'Prosdocimi de beldemandis pataui viri clarissimi compositio et operacio Instrumenti dicti astrolabium 'reuisa et' tradita Impressioni propter bonum comune a domino federico 'delphino' artium et medicine doctore et mathematicarum disciplinarum in celeberrimo gimnasio patauino publico professore anuente deo feliciter Incipit'. Another slip with calculations for 1499 and 1503 lies after f. 19.

2. ff. 22ᵛ–30ᵛ 'Incipit algorismus de minutiis Ioannis de liueriis siculi'. Modum representacionis minutiarum uulgarium et fisicarum proponere 'institui'. Quia in fractione duo sunt numeri . . . a se elicere sed hec pro nunc dicta sufficiant amen. Explicit algorismus de minuciis hio'h'annis de liueriis siculi ad laudem dei amen.

Thorndike and Kibre (J. de Lineriis). Printed at Padua in 1483 after Prosdocimus de Beldomandis, Algorismus (*GKW* 3799).

3. (*a*) ff. 31–40 Incipit liber astrolabii editus a magistro io'h'ane yspano interprete quem translatauit de arabico in latinum ut sequitur. Dixit iohannes cum uolueris facere astrolabium accipe auricalcum optimum . . . quem admodum uides in hac figura. (*b*) f. 40ʳᵛ Recapitulacio tocius operis. Primum capitulum in mencione astrolabii et omnium super id cadencium . . . artici et antartici. 'Expliciunt Canones compositiui astrolabii quos Ioannes yspanus transtulit de arabico in latino. Et sequuntur hos: canones operatiui ut uides'. (*c*) ff. 41–48ᵛ In equacione solis qui est locus ex circulo signorum. Capitulum primum. Cum uolueris scire in quo signo sit sol . . . eodem anno ex 32 diebus. (*d*) f. 49ʳᵛ De diuisione septem climatum, with diagram. (*e*) f. 50 De difinicione astrolabii. Astrologie speculationis exercicium habere uolentibus . . . diligencia comprehendunt.

Messahala in the translation of John of Seville. Thorndike and Kibre. Carmody, p. 169. (*b*), (*c*) printed and (*a*) partly printed by J. Millás, *Traducciones orientales en los manuscritos de la biblioteca cathedral de Toledo*, 1942, pp. 2–84. (*b*). 'Usque huc corecti', f. 40ᵛ, in the hand of 'Expliciunt . . .'. (*c*) is preceded by a table giving positions of twenty-nine fixed stars, 'Venter murilegi . . . Cauda murilegi'.

4. ff. 50ᵛ–52 Diagrams and (f. 51) 'Tabulla declinacionis solis uerificata . . . secundum albategni'.

5 (added early). Two memoranda on f. 52ᵛ: (*a*) Memoria chome nostro padre fixe far in piu fiate quei lauorieri segondo che lui se sentiua poder spender in diuersi tenpi selui non auese auto a far per tuto el muro dalto e da baso . . .; (*b*) Adi 13 auosto 1492 'Io franc° delphin' me conuentai i testimonii maistro piero dei ponponaci mantuano e maistro vit° gabiano bresano e maistro clementino dei clementini de amera (?) paulo ronco bresano e salueto camotio bresano doctori de le arte tuti.

6. f. ii^rv Flyleaf notes, including mnemonic verses.

ff. ii+52+i. Paper. f. ii is a contemporary paper flyleaf. 290 × 220 mm. Written space *c*. 200 × 165 mm. The only ruling is a vertical bounder on the left of pages and sometimes horizontal lines for headings and the first line of a new text. Collation: 1^16 2^36 (f. 17 is not now conjugate with f. 52, nor f. 18 with f. 51). Current humanistic script. No coloured initials. Binding of stiff paper, s. xvii (?), with parchment over the spine and about 70 mm of each cover.

Written in Italy. Belonged to Francesco Delfini of Padua (?) in 1492 (art. 5*b*: cf. art. 1). '118' on the front cover. '289' and 'A/1/4' on paper labels on the spine. Michel Chasles book-plate, with number 3476. Chasles sale, 27 June 1881, lot 3476.

Cr. 3.29. *Thebit; J. Hispalensis; J. de Sacro Bosco* 1317, s. XIV in.

1 (quire 1). (*a*) ff. 1–2 'Incipit liber Thebit de ymaginacionibus planetarum' (*in red, in the same hand as a heading in 3.12*). Dixit Thebith.bencorath. et dixit aristotiles qui philosophiam et geometriam . . . si deus uoluerit. Expletus est liber thebith. bencorath. Sit laus et gloria deo. in sion. (*b*) ff. 2–3 Dixit alburahet. bonfelith. quia omnes homines orientalles . . . quod animus tuus desiderat. Amen.

(*a*). Thorndike and Kibre, who refer to edn., 1960. Carmody, p. 125; the introductory paragraphs ed. L. Thorndike in *Mélanges Pelzer*, 1947, p. 233. (*b*). Thorndike and Kibre. In forty-seven short paragraphs: the last but one, 'Cum uolueris prouocare aliquam puellam . . .', has been scratched through lightly. Thorndike prints the beginning and end of the text, loc. cit., pp. 256–7. f. 3^v blank.

2 (quires 2, 3). ff. 4–15^v 'Ysagoge Iohannis Yspalensis et primo de naturis signorum'. Cintura firmamenti in 12 equales distribuitur partes . . ad 1. tauri latitudo 27. Explicit quadripartitus Iohannis yspalensis. cum dei auxilio. die sabbati. iii die augusti. annis cristi curr. 1317. Amen.

Thorndike and Kibre. Carmody, p. 169.

3 (quire 4). ff. 16–22 Tractatum de spera quatuor capitulis distinguimus. dicente in primo . . . aut mondana machina disoluitur. 'amen Explicit tractatus de spera. secundum magistrum Iohannem de sacroboscho'.

Many manuscripts and editions, the last by L. Thorndike, *The Sphere of Sacrobosco and its Commentators*, 1949, pp. 76–117. Unfilled spaces for diagrams. f. 22^v blank.

ff. i+22+i. 272 × 200 mm. Written space: of arts. 1, 2, *c*. 198 × 155 mm; of art. 3, 195 × 130 mm. 2 cols. 62–3 lines, arts. 1, 2. 47 long lines, art. 3. Ruling with a hard point, art. 3. Collation: 1 three (ff. 1–3) 2^8 3 four (ff. 12–15) 4^8 wants 8 (ff. 16–22). Red initials, 3-line on ff. 1, 4, 16, and 2-line. Capital letters in the ink of the text are stroked with red. Binding of s. xix.

Written in Italy. The script shows that arts. 1, 2 were once part of the same volume as 3. 12, q.v. Art. 3 may be from another manuscript. Numbers, s. xix, top left of three leaves: f. 1, 11271; f. 4, 11269; f. 16, 11270. Chasles book-plate. Michel Chasles sale, Paris (Claudin), 27 June 1881, lot 2983.

Cr. 4.3. *Guido Bonatus* s. xv[1]

(*a*) ff. 1–39ᵛ Incipit tractatus 7ᵘˢ de ellectionibus secundum dicta sapientum Capitulum primum. Cum post iudicia pre ceteris astronomie partibus electionem indigemus . . . uel diminuere. Finis est tractatus de ellectionibus deo gracias amen. (*b*) ff. 40–2 Incipit introductorium sub breuiloquio ad iudicia stellarum secundum guidonem bonatum. Cum astronomie iudicia peruenire intenderis sit tibi cure . . . sequentes. (*c*) ff. 42–98ᵛ Incipit 8ᵘˢ tractatus de reuolucionibus annorum mundi secundum guidone bonatu. Quoniam 'post' tractatum electionum . . . regis et eius durabilitatem.

(*a*, *c*). Guido Bonatus de Forlivio, Liber introductorius ad iudicia stellarum, bks. 7, 8. The text corresponds to signatures z 3ᵛ–E 8 and F 1–R 6ᵛ of the edition of 1491 (*GKW* 4643). Chapters are not numbered in (*c*). (*b*). Sixteen paragraphs, the last beginning 'Et oportet te similiter scire significata'. A memorandum at the foot of f. 41 'Scrite carte xlvii tuto'.

ff. i+98+i. A contemporary foliation 1–103 takes account of the leaves missing from the end of quire 4. 283 × 220 mm. Written space 215 × 170 mm. 2 cols. *c.* 43 lines. Collation: 1¹² 2⁸ 3¹² 4¹² wants 8–12, perhaps blank, 5–8¹² 9¹² wants 12, blank. The signatures are k, q, y, v, e, 7, ɔ, I, x. Initials: (i) f. 40, 4-line, pink, patterned in white, on blue ground patterned in white and decorated in colour; (ii) 2-line, red or blue with ornament of the other colour. Paste-board binding of s. xviii/xix, rebacked: a chainmark from an older binding at the foot of f. 1. Secundo folio *stant*.

Written in Italy. The cover is inscribed 'Banco 1+' and 'A/Astrologia. De electionibus. Iudicia stellarum / secundum Guidonem Bonatum / Proibito'; also, later 'June 1818'. Quaritch, cat. 339 (1881), no. 4399, at £2. 16*s*.: bought thence by Lord Crawford.

Cr. 4.5. *Soloneus; Bartholomaeus de Usingen; etc.* s. xv/xvi

1 (quires 1, 2). ff. 1–25 Quamquam omnes homines natura scire desiderant vt in prohemio Metaphisice testatur Aristotiles Cum sciencia de numero bonorum est . . . (f. 21) de motu solis et lune in tabulis resolutis. finis.

A computistical work in fourteen chapters: Thorndike and Kibre (Soloneus, De temporum annotatione). Many tables and diagrams, including a Macrobian diagram of the world (f. 24ᵛ). One leaf missing after f. 3. On ff. 7ᵛ–8 a table of years 1457–1552 has against each year-number a word in red (counting prepositions in with the next word), the whole making a piece about the comet of 1456 and the death of King Ladislaus V in 1457: 'Percipite dilecti verba iohannis sedelli . . . principe sepulto probitatis spiritum in celis coniunget christus beatus amen'. The heading to the column in which this is written is 'Intervallum per dicciones ebdomodatim (?) per litteras designatum'. f. 25ᵛ blank.

A slightly later addition in a blank space on f. 2ᵛ: Hy deceptores fidei sunt sacreque scripture / Talomil Iudeus occam anglicus husque bohemus / Machmi paganus qui peior ceterisque primus.

2 (quire 3). ff. 26–34ᵛ Caput phisicum magistri virgilii de salczpurga. Tractatus de modo interpretandi hominis interioris et exterioris Incipit. (f. 27) Tractatus (*etc.*) . . . Homo cum secundum ysi. sit animal dei forme Natura mansuetum . . . Hec autem pro modica Iuuenum informacione collocata est pronunciata anno 92 in studio lipczm' gymnasii 1492 etc.

Virgilius Wallendorfer?. On the soul and (f. 31ᵛ) the body. f. 26 is a title-page, the verso blank. f. 35 contains a diagram of 'Specula immaterialia id est inorganica' and 'Specula materialia id est organica' and their interconnections and f. 35ᵛ a drawing of a human torso with some of the organs marked (Mackinney, p. 122).

3 (quire 4). ff. 37–45ᵛ Natura est principium et causa mouendi et quiescendi eius in quo est primum . . . deo autem nihil est simplicius.

Bartholomew de Usingen, M.A., Erfurt, 1491, †1532, Parvulus philosophiae, a tripartite abbreviation of the Physics, De generatione et corruptione, and De anima. Printed at Leipzig c. 1485 and later (GKW 3463–5). Many glosses in the margins and between the lines. Two slips added after f. 38. ff. 46–47ᵛ blank.

4 (quires 5, 6). (a) f. 48 Humano capiti ceruicem pictor equinam . . . rem prodigaliter vnam. (b) ff. 48ᵛ–63 Circa paruuli philosophie Moralis principium nonnullis annotabimus et primo de invencione . . . De invencione ac diuisione philosophie . . . viuit et regnat amen.

(a). Walther, no. 8556. 29 lines. (b). Apparently an abbreviation of the Ethics: cf. art. 3. ff. 63ᵛ–66ᵛ blank.

5 (quires 7, 8). On letter writing. (a) f. 67ᵛ Haud dubito nosci vix natos o genitor mi Nancisci posse finem studii sine patre . . . (23 lines). (b) ff. 68–83ᵛ Pervtilis epistolandi modus Wilhelmi Saphonensis ordinis Incipit. Quoniam quidam ducens trahimur ad cognicionem et sciencie cupiditatem . . . Conquestus mecum es Iohannes mi dilectissime in christo . . . Modus ep(isto)landi breuis et vtilis per fratrem gwil sapho or borᵘᵐ editus explicit foel(i)citer. (c) f. 84 A table setting out the different kinds of letters. (d) ff. 84ᵛ–86 On letter writing in prose and verse, the latter, fifty-seven lines in all, beginning 'Nate meum cupis auxilium tibi presto parari Vt ceptum studium possis sic concomitari'. (e) f. 86ʳᵛ Eight specimens of letters. (f) ff. 87–88ᵛ Epistola qua pene omnia precepta augustini daci clarent. Cogitanti mihi ac memoria repetenti . . .

(a). The various parts of a letter are shown. The name in the 'subscriptio' (line 20) is Conradus Coluich'. The hand is that of art. 4a. See Addenda p. 998. (d). Marked in the margins 'Causa', "Intencio', etc. The verses seem to be in reply to (a). f. 89ʳᵛ blank.

6 (added early). f. 67 Petitque humillime secum graciose dispensari . . .

Volk de Rogenbach 'nacionis bauerorum', an arts student at the University of Leipzig 'sub rectoratu venerabilis viri magistri Iohannis Reynhardt de zwicker (?) decretorum doctori(s)' asks to be excused for absences from lectures and exercises, in particular the exercises of the dean. He lists the nineteen courses he has attended, giving the name of each lecturer, the book he lectured on (Elenchi, De anima, Prior and Posterior analytics, Physics, Vetus ars, Parva logicalia, Nova logica, Spera materialis), and usually, but not in the case of exercises, the period, thus, 'Audiuit Lectiones gradubaccalariatus in artibus . . . A venerabili viro magistro Iohanne Liucke (?) de franckenfordis libros Elencorum quos incepit in vigilia Iohannis ante portam et finiuit in vigilia Margarethe . . . Stetitque in exerciciis . . . . Cum venerabili viro magistro gerhardo de osterburck pro tunc facultatis arcium decano benedigno in exercicio veteris artis . . .'.

ff. ii+94+ii, foliated (i, ii), 1–70, 73–89 (90, 91). Paper with several watermarks. 320 × 210 mm. Written space c. 220 × 110 mm. Collation: 1¹⁴ wants 4 2¹² 3¹² wants 12, blank, after f. 36 4¹² wants 12, blank, after f. 47 5¹⁰ 6¹² wants 9–11, blank, after f. 66 7¹⁰ (ff. 67–70, 73–8) 8¹² wants 12, blank. Cursiva of a stunted sort, except in arts. 1, 3. Initials: art. 1, blue or red with ornament of the other colour; arts. 2–5, red, unless the spaces remain blank. Binding of s. xix².

Written in Germany (Leipzig?: cf. arts. 2, 3, 6). Acquired in 1877: Quaritch's bill to James Lindsay, 31 Mar. 1877, included '1 Astronomia Vergilii 'MS' 1492 12s.'.

Cr. 4.6. *Astrological and other texts (in German)* s. xv²

A large collection, computistical (arts. 2–4), medical (arts. 7–10), and for the rest mainly concerned with the influence of the planets on human affairs.[1] The whole is written in one good hand, probably in or soon after 1478 (cf. arts. 3 c, 19), apart from a few additions in one hand, s. xvi, before art. 3 and after arts. 5, 13, and elsewhere. Arts. 5–11, 18, 27–9 are decorated with lively coloured drawings. Arts. 6, 14, 23 begin on new quires. The text appears to be complete, except for leaves at the end and one (?) leaf after f. 1.

For art. 11 and texts like arts. 3, 5 cf. the descriptions of B.L., Add. 17987 by Saxl and Meier, iii. 54–60, and O. Priebsch, *Deutsche Handschriften in England*, no. 193. At Munich, Cgm 328 and 349 contain texts like arts. 1, 8, 9, 11, 16, 17, 20.[2] Some of the matter in arts. 3, 5, 11, and very similar drawings, especially close to the drawings of the four complexions in art. 5, are in early printed calendars, starting with those printed by Blaubirer at Augsburg in 1481 and 1483 (Goff, K. 1 and Hain 9735—the Crawford copy of the 1483 *Kalendarium mit den figuren* is 7.75): these and later copies are listed by W. L. Schreiber, *Manuel de l'amateur de la gravure sur bois et sur métal*, 1926–30, v, between nos. 4415 and 4428.

1. f. 1ʳᵛ Hienach sagt es von den Newn Cometen daz sind stern mit schwanzen wann die an den hymel gesehen werden was die bedewtten. Der maister ptholomeus spricht daz der Cometen newn seyen . . . (*ends imperfectly*).

2. ff. 3–6 Hienach volget wie man ein yeglichen newen mone . . . annus ebolismalis. Ist daz du wilt vinden . . .
A table on f. 6 is headed 'Anno domini etc. 1457'.

3. (*a*) ff. 6ᵛ–9ᵛ Hienach volget wie du in dem nachgescriben Kalender vinden mugest . . . (*b*) f. 10 Tabula Radicum 7ᵗᵉᵐ planetarum In annis cristi. (*c–f*) ff. 12ᵛ–24 Planetary tables, (*c*), on versos facing a calendar, (*d*), on rectos, advice of a named authority for each month, (*e*), below (*c*), and verses on regimen for each month, (*f*), below (*d*).

(*b*). Table for 1459–99. (*c*). The first years of the third and fourth decennovenal cycles calculated from 1439 are noted as bases for calculations in columns between (*c*) and (*d*): Die dritt Iarczal 1477; Die vierd Iarczal 1496. (*d–f*). Cf. the Augsburg calendar for 1483 (see above), ff. (1–20). (*d*). Diocese of Konstanz. The small number of feasts in red include Ulrich, 'Auffra', 'Hilaria ir töchter', Magnus, Gallus, Othmar (4 July, 7, 12 Aug., 6 Sept., 16 Oct., 16 Nov.). (*e*) begins 'Es spricht der maister almansar daz man sol in dem Genner': cf. H. E. Sigerist in Sudhoff's *Archiv*, xvii (1925), 230–2. (*f*) begins 'Nit ensalbe deine bain': the couplet for October is 'Ich bitte dich Sand Galle daz er mir nüczlich valle'. The signs of the zodiac and occupations of the months are in roundels below (*d*).

[1] I have found it difficult to distinguish one piece from another, especially towards the end.

[2] Information from Dr. Sigrid Krämer.

The adding hand noted on f. 12 that Kaiser Maximilian was born 'in der newenstatt in Osterreych', 22 Mar. 1459, and, in another ink, 'Item der berwangerin mettlin ist geporen worden . . . in lansperg', 1 Feb. 1512.

4. ff. 24ᵛ–36ᵛ Tables and texts for finding the golden number, Sunday letter, movable feasts, etc., and a table of good, bad, and indifferent days for blood-letting (cf. *Horae Ebor.*, p. 22), and at the end weather lore based on the state of the weather on St. Paul's Day, 25 Jan.

5. ff. 37–50 Hienach sagt es Ettliche nüczliche vnnderschayde von dem firmament vnd von den Hymeln. vnd daz ist ze mercken. Got hiess abraham daz er ansehe den hymel . . .

Diagrams on ff. 40ᵛ, 43ᵛ. MacKinney reproduces the drawing of an astronomer at his desk on f. 37 (fig. 17). Drawings on ff. 44ᵛ, 45ᵛ, 46ᵛ, 48 show love-making, wife beating and burning, connubial boredom, and music making respectively, as illustrations of the four complexions: cf. the Augsburg calendar for 1483, ff. (49)–(53). ff. 50ᵛ–54ᵛ, left blank, were partly filled in s. xvi in.

6. ff. 55–60ᵛ Hienach sagt ez von dem Cristtag . . auff welichen tag der wochen der gefallen was . . . . Kumpt vnd gefellet der Cristtag an den Sunntag . . .

A drawing of the Christ Child on f. 55.

7. ff. 60ᵛ–78 Hie nach volget von dem aderlassen wenn vnd zu welicher czeit man in dem Iare zu auderlassen. vnd wie man sich dorinnen hallten sol. Man sol mercken daz der Mayster Auicenna . . .

Cf. Saxl and Meier, iii. 59, and Sudhoff in *Beiträge zur Geschichte der Chirurgie in Mittelalter*, i (1914), 190. A man of zodiacal signs on f. 73ᵛ and a drawing of a man bleeding a woman on f. 60ᵛ, as in the Augsburg calendar for 1483, f. (53ᵛ).

8. ff. 78ᵛ–80 Hienach stat ain lere geschrieben wie man die vintausen sol seczen an weliche stat vnd für was gepresten des leybes. Alles das lassen das man tut . . .

A drawing, f. 78ᵛ: two men in blue bathing trunks, one bleeding the other: MacKinney, fig. 57, reduced.

9. ff. 80–4 Hienach volget wie du dich vor dem bade . . . Nun gat ein Capittel an von den Bade . . .

On bathing. A drawing of a man and woman in an open-air bath, f. 80ᵛ. Cf. Munich, Cgm. 349, ff. 77ᵛ–82.

10. ff. 84–90 Hienach volget wie du an der buls zu greiffen . . . Ich han auch gesagt wie man baden . . .

Various medical lore. Drawings of a doctor standing by a woman in bed, taking her pulse, f. 84 (MacKinney, fig. 13), and of a doctor inspecting a urine bottle, f. 87ᵛ.

11. ff. 90–114ᵛ Hienach sagt es von den sieben planeten von irem lauff vnd gang . . . Saturnus ist der obrost planet vnd ist kalt und trucken . . .

Cf. Priebsch, p. 170, Saxl and Meier, iii. 56–8, and the Augsburg calendar for 1483, ff. (35)–(45). Two drawings before each section, one of the planet and the other of the occupation (etc.) appropriate to it: Saturn, f. 90ᵛ; Jupiter, f. 94; Mars, f. 96ᵛ; Sun, f. 99; Venus, f. 101ᵛ; Mercury, f. 104ᵛ; Moon, f. 106ᵛ: for three of these cf. Saxl and Meier, iii, pl. 89. In each section a drawing of a rayed man (on crutches, f. 91ᵛ; in chair, reading, f. 94ᵛ; soldier, f. 97ᵛ; king, f. 99ᵛ; conductor of music, f. 102; doctor, f. 104ᵛ; seated, f. 107) is accompanied by verses in Latin, the first set beginning 'Si quis nascatur cum saturnus dominatur' (Walther, no. 17938).

12. Lunar prognostications: (*a*) ff. 115–16 Hie nach sagt es wie man wissen vnd erkennen sol in einem yeden monat vnd besonder nach dem newen schön wetter oder regen. So wartt in welicher stunde ein newer mon . . .; (*b*) ff. 116ᵛ–121 Hienach sagt ez den vnderschayde eins yecklichen newen mons was in den xxx tagen an yegklichem tage zu thun ist . . .

(*b*) ends with a table in Latin under forty-one heads, 'Hospitacio hospiciorum . . . Radere caput et barbam'.

13. ff. 121ᵛ–124ᵛ Hienach volget die ausslegung was sey aspectus planetarum . . . Die czeit in den die planetten . . .

ff. 123–133ᵛ, left blank, were mostly filled in s. xvi with a text in German on the twenty-eight mansions of the moon.

14. ff. 134–6 Notandum quod ab anno domini mcccclⁱᵐᵒ usque ad annum domini 1550 inueniuntur hic notati singulis annis domini anni . . . vt patet intuenti.

A table to show the planet in the ascendent, the 'dominus anni', for each year, 1451–1550.

15. ff. 136–137ᵛ Hienach sagt es von den syben planeten vnd iren stunnden. Von nature vnd aigenschofft . . .

16. ff. 138–141ᵛ Hienach volget wie man ain Iudicium einer yedlichen fragen nach waren lauff dez Rechten astrolabiums seczen vnd machen sol. Wiltu ein iudicium seczen . . .

17. ff. 141ᵛ–175ᵛ Hienach sagt es von den zweliff zaichen des hymels . . . Das buch ist getailt in zway tail . . .

Prognostications by the sign of the zodiac, with a drawing of each sign from Aries, f. 149ᵛ, to Pisces, f. 173.

18. ff. 175ᵛ–188ᵛ Hienach sagt es von den zweliff monaten . . .

Prognostications from nativities, month by month, with drawings of the occupation of each month.

19. ff. 188ᵛ–219ᵛ Hienach volget wie du erkennen süllest oder mügest In welichem zaichen ain yeder planete alltag sey . . . Sequitur verus motus Saturni. Wann du wöllest wissen den rechten wauren lauff . . .

The tables on ff. 189ᵛ–215 are headed 'Incipit almanach omnium planetarum secundum prophacium Iudeum ad montem Pessulanum et primo Saturni'. Calculations for the year 1300 are adapted for the fifty-nine years from 1478. Also in Cr. 2.123, art. 4.

20. ff. 220–228ᵛ Hienach sagt es wie du den Ascendens daz ist das vffgandzaichen dez himels zu yeder zeit . . . Wiltu wissen zu vinden den graden dez ascendens . . .

Planetary tables on ff. 223–228ᵛ, the first headed 'Tabula ascensionis signorum in circulo recto'. According to the heading on f. 224ᵛ and following pages, the tables are for Vienna 'cuius latitudo est 47 graduum et 46 minutorum'.

21. ff. 229–230ᵛ Item in der nach geschriben tafeln vindestu die krefft vnd stercke der planeten . . .

22. ff. 231–51 Hienach vindestu geschriben den wauren lauff der planetten wie

du den selbst vinden vnd practicieren . . . Wiltu wissen zum ersten den mittlen lauff Saturni So leg zum ersten den Radix Wurcz Saturni. allz du den in der nachgeschriben taueln Saturni vindest ze vndrest geschriben In anno domini 1464 . . .

Includes: ff. 235–41, tables of mean motion in which the 'Radix . . . ad annum 1464 completum in meridie' is noted; f. 242, a table headed 'Auges planetarum huius anni' and marked at the side 'Anno 1464'; ff. 243–244^v, tables of equation; ff. 246^v–248^v, a section on eclipses; ff. 248^v–249^v, distances from earth to moon, 15,635 miles, and thence to the planets and 'a terra vsque ad celum', 109,390 miles. A hand of s. xvi, perhaps the usual hand, noted the 'Radix ad Straubingen tempore incarnacionis Ihesu cristi' at the foot of ff. 235–241, 250. ff. 251^v–254^v left blank.

23. ff. 255–279^v Hie nach volget die betuttung vnd ausslegung der Astronomey die geczogen ist vss den buchern der hohen mayster der Astronomi . . . Wan verenndrung (?) dez wetters in wissende da überlas ich vil bücher daz . . .

The influence of the planets on the weather and (ff. 270–272^v) the nature and complexions of the zodiacal signs, followed by tables and diagrams. Running title 'Astronomia' on ff. 267^v–277^v.

24. ff. 280–291^v Hienach volget der traktat den maister alchindus gemacht hat von der schickung des luffts vnd erkennung dez wetters . . . Wie man wissen sulle eines yedlichen luffts schickung . . .

The rather later annotator wrote in the margin of f. 284^v 'Item such am 147 plat in dem Schwarzen puch'.

25. ff. 291^v–323 Sections on the nine spheres, (f. 292^v) on the mean motion of the planets, (f. 293^v) von dem gang der himel vnd der sterren. Item Theodosius Ambrosius . . ., (f. 296) on the nine heavens, (f. 299) on the four parts of the earth and the seven climates, (f. 300^v) on the planets, (f. 305) on eclipses, (f. 310^v) on the signs of the zodiac and their (f. 316) houses and (f. 319^v) influence.

26. ff. 323–48 Hienach volget das 16 capitel von den Cometen . . . In disem buch da sind gesampnet vnd geschriben aller weyser mayster von der beteuttung der Cometten . . .

27. ff. 348–57 Hienach volget aber von den 12 zaichen dez hymels . . . In dem Capitel sind der howser der 12 zaichen . . .

Pictures of the signs.

28. ff. 357–72 Hienach volgend die 36 ymagines oder bildunge dez hymels . . . Ymagines der billde sind 36 wider septemtrione.

For a Latin text cf. above Cr. 3.23, art. 2. The thirty-five illustrations here are the same as there from Ursa to Vexillum, except for the presence of Draco in second place and the absence of Pulsans canonum, but they are vastly better.

29. ff. 372–9 Hienach volget von dem newnden hymel dorinnen got mit seinem ausserwelten wonet . . . Spera firmamentum. Ob dem firmament ist der newnd hymel Vnd der da haist die 9 spere . . . .

Decorative coloured drawings of Saturn, Jove, Mars, Sun, Venus, Mercury, and Moon: cf. Cr. 3.23, art. 2, but Moon here is a woman with torch, water bucket, and flag.

30. ff. 379–380^v Hienach volgend ettliche nüczliche vnderschayde waz sey

emisperium orizon zenith vnd polus . . . Emisperium ist der gancz hymel . . . (*ends abruptly*).

31. ff. 381–394^v In disen nachgeschriben figuren . . .
Planetary tables for use in prognosticating weather, etc.

32. ff. 395–429 Hienach volget von den erdbidem wassergussen vnd den grossen wynnden Die anfang von den plumen des tractats von den erdbidem . . .
Prognostications of all sorts from the planets.

33. ff. 429^v–455^v Hienach volget wie man den vffsteigenden grad der geburte vinden sol. . . .
On nativities and judicial astrology.

34. ff. 455^v–468^v Hienach volgennt manigerlay fragen vnd Iudicium der Astrologien . . . Ein frage is die ist geschehen von dez reichs wegen ob man die überkomen müge . . . in dem ascendens daz bedeutt über (*ends imperfectly*).
Directions for prognosticating the outcome of events in answer to questions, each in a paragraph. The last remaining paragraph, the twenty-seventh, begins 'Bistu gefraget von schacherey ob man in überchome oder nicht'.

ff. ii+463+i, foliated (i, ii), 1, 3–10, 12–143, 145–232, 234–53, 255–468 (469). The foliation is contemporary at first, but it is seldom visible after f. 84 and seems to have been one or two ahead of the present sixteenth-century foliation of ff. 85–468, for example ff. 134 was f. 136. Paper. 295 × 215 mm. Written space *c.* 225 × 145 mm. *c.* 42 long lines (ff. 255–85 mainly in two columns). Frame ruling. Written in cursiva by one good hand throughout. Collation: 1 nine (ff. 1, 3–10) 2–3¹² 4¹⁴ 5–9¹² 10¹²+1 leaf after 12 (f. 122) 11¹² wants 12, blank, after f. 133 12–20¹² 21¹² wants 11, 12, blank, after f. 253 22–38¹² 39¹² wants 11, 12 after f. 468. Quires numbered by the hand of the older foliation and immediately after it, but this numbering cannot be seen after f. 134 which is marked '136 12'. Many coloured drawings: see above. Initials: (i) f. 1, 17-line blue *D* on green ground, historiated (Ptolemy): continuous border; (ii) 4-line, or more, red and blue, or one of these colours; (iii) 3-line, mostly red or green. Capital letters in the ink of the text stroked with red. Binding of s. xix.

In an East Swabian dialect.[1] The drawings point to Augsburg: see above. The name Berwanger (art. 3) was common in Augsburg, *c.* 1500.[1] Straubingen (art. 22) is, presumably, Straubing, Bavaria. Belonged to the Vienna convent of discalced hermits of St. Augustine in s. xvii: 'Est conuentus Vienn: Erem: Disc: S. Augustini', f. 3.

Cr. 4.11. *J. de Ashenden, Summa judicialis de accidentibus mundi, Tractatus primus; etc.* s. xv med.

1. ff. 1–150 Incipit Summa Iudicialis magistri Iohannis de eschenden de accidentibus mundi . . . Mea contencio (*sic*) in hoc libro est conpilare sentencias astrologorum . . . pertractant satis diffuse. Et finitur hec distinccio. R. Conpleta est ergo hec conpilacio tractatus primi summe iudicialis de accidentibus mundi in ciuitate Oxonie per magistrum Iohannem de aschelden' 20 die mensis Iulii Anno cristi 1347 etc'. Explicit prima pars etc' huius summe.
Printed at Venice in 1489. For other copies see Emden, *BRUO*, p. 56, and *MMBL* i. 216.

[1] Information from Dr. Sigrid Krämer.

Only the first of the two 'tractatus' is here. A table of its twelve distinctions is on ff. iii[v]–iv[v]. Distinctions are marked by tabs and distinction numbers and chapter numbers shown in running titles. Annotations against distinctions 9–11 are fairly numerous. A piece of paper lying loose at f. 36 contains a calculation of an eclipse in 1471. A 'cedula' loose at f. 101 is referred to in the margin of that page, and another loose at f. 105 is referred to in the margins of ff. 103, 107: both are perhaps in the hand which wrote much of arts. 3, 4.

2. ff. 150[v]–152. Quicumque in iudicando peritus esse desiderat . . . ab acie viridis a terra.

3. Notes, diagrams, and tables for use in prognostication fill ff. 152[v]–154[v] and the pastedowns back and front. They include (front pastedown) a table of lunar mansions calculated for 1450 and (f. 153[v]) a zodiacal diagram marked 'Circa annos domini 1460'.

4. Pieces on the preliminary quire: (a) f. i, the beginning of a herb glossary, Latin–German, '[A]rthemisia eschlauch . . . Arillus druwenkerne'; (b) f. i, a table of the latitude and longitude of twenty-two cities, 'Iherusalem Roma Parisius . . . Magdeburg Brunswyck Monspessulanus'; (c) f. i[v], a table, and f. ii, a canon 'Verum motum solis et lune in vna hora . . . equacionem centri. Et sciendum quod hec tabula est facta super equaciones tabularum alfoncii per magistrum Iohannem de Ianua etc.'; (d) ff. ii[v]–iii, iv[v] Horalumen fit per tornatorem sicud figura docet et quomodo habeat . . . in vertice instrumenti etc.

(a). Cf. Thorndike and Kibre, s.v. Artemisia-biwuos. (d). On the working of a volvel. It was added after the table of art. 1 was written.

ff. 158, foliated i–iv, 1–154. The foliation 1–150, on rectos at the foot, is medieval. Paper. 285 × 210 mm. Written space c. 210 × 150 mm. 2 cols. c. 36 lines. Collation: 1[8] wants 1–4 (ff. i–iv) 2–5[12] 6[12]+2 leaves after 12 (ff. 61, 62) 7–13[12] 14[8]. Quires 2–14 numbered at the beginning 1–13. Strips of parchment, blank or cut from a document of s. xv, lie down some quire centres as strengthening. Cursiva by several hands. Initials: (i) f. 1, 11-line, red and black, with ornament of both colours; (ii, iii) 4-line or 3-line and 2-line, red. Contemporary binding of white skin over bevelled boards, repaired: five bosses formerly on each cover, but only the marks remain.

Written in Germany. '77/G.eg', a modern mark inside the cover, resembles marks in Cr. 1.27 and 2.98; also 'CS'.

Cr. 5.3A. *Kalendarium*   s. XV/XVI

ff. 2–7[v] Calendar in red and black. Added gradings.

Entries in black in the main hand include 'Festum patronorum' (lined through) and Sophia, widow (9, 13 May) and some German saints, Ludger, Godehard, Ulrich, Kilian, Wenceslaus. 'Festum reliquiarum' is added on seven days, each with a different Sunday letter, 20 July, 2, 4, 12 Aug., 17–19 Sept. Three feasts of St. Bridget added, each marked 'Totum duplex': 'Translacio', 28 May; 'Natale', 23 July; 'Canonizatio', 7 Oct. Other 'totum duplex' additions are Joseph, 'Locus dedicacionis' and the Presentation of B.V.M. (19 Mar., 30 July, 21 Nov.). 'Commemoracio beati Ioseph' added in red at 13 Jan. and 'Memoria anne ix l' ' in black at 9 Dec.

Added obits, s. xvi med.: 18 Feb., 'anno 155° (*sic*) do starff Gerdrud Vytinchoff vnd was [. . . .]'; 9 Mar., 'Anno 155 (*sic*) do starff broder Simon Janus. Oremus'; 23 Apr., 'Anno 1549 do sterff Birgitta holstuer abbatissa'; 3 May, '1549 starff Pater Ioannes Simonis'.

f. 1 may have been a flyleaf. The recto is blank and seems to have been pasted down. The verso contains tables 'pro aureo numero' beginning at 1501 and to find the Sunday letter beginning at 1504, and directions to find the movable feasts, etc.

ff. 7. 355 × 255 mm. From a Bridgettine house (in north Germany?) and probably once in front of a breviary.

Cr. 5.10. *Book of fate (in German)* s. xv med.

A handsome volume called 'Planetenbuch' in James Lindsay's catalogue.

1. The pastedown in front carries a circular turning chart with sun, moon, 'Polus articus' and 'Margensteren' in it and numbers in red, i–xxxii, round the edge. Above, two angels bear scrolls inscribed 'Reib vmb mit der hant' and 'Nicht gelaub es ist ein Tant'. Below, a figure in red labelled 'Antomel' points to 'Cometa', a star on the right.

2. f. 1 Coloured pictures of 'Katho', 'Aristotiles', 'Platho', and 'Virgilius', each with an inscribed scroll. Cato's has 'Aquilon vnd orient meridies vnd occident' on it.

3. f. 1ᵛ Thirty-two personal names, mainly from the Old Testament, David– Joseph, and against each a phrase, 'Von gotes huld'—'Von vil Mannen'.

4. ff. 2–3 Thirty-two heads in roundels labelled Zacharias—Nathon and in- scribed round the edges, (Zacharias) 'In Saturnus Puechen solt du Suden pald suechen'—(Nathon) 'Ic wil dich fristen in Iupiter suech westen'.

The names are those in art. 3, but in a different order. No. 21 is a black king, 'Morel'.

5. f. 4 Nort westen. Das kamlein such . . . Sud osten. Den hirssen.

The thirty-two points of the compass here are (1) Nort Westen, (2) Nort Osten, (3–30) Osten, Westen, Norden, Suden, each repeated as a group seven times, (31) Sud Westen. (32) Sud Osten. The animals (etc.) are those of art. 6.

6. ff. 4ᵛ–19 Gotes huld.vberal bis fro wann sy sir werden sol . . .

Thirty-two couplets on each page and in the middle a roundel containing a competent coloured drawing of one of the signs of the zodiac or one of twenty beasts and birds. Each couplet on f. 4ᵛ refers to the corresponding phrase in art. 3. The subject of each page is in red at the foot, 'Die wag, Gauch, Nachtigail, Esel, Valkch, Fuchs, Hierss, Per, Hunt, Krewss, Leb, Iunkchfraw, Zway, Vischs, Wassrar, Sparbar, Schutz, Kronich, Adlar, Han, Taub, Schorp, Ainhorn, Auf, Rab, Wider, Ochs, Chamel (two humps), Sitich, Has, Alster'. The verses and roundel for 'Gays' (capricorn) are missing at the end.[1]

ff. 19. 322 × 225 mm. Written space 225 mm high. 32 long lines. 1¹² 2 seven. Written in cursiva. Pictures in arts. 1, 2, 4, 6. Red initial, f. 4ᵛ, with ornament in the ink of the text. Capital letters in the ink of the text stroked with red or (f. 1ᵛ) green. Binding of modern wooden boards with the old leather over them and the old pastedowns (art. 1) inside: five modern bosses on each cover: cf. *Trésors*, no. 25.

[1] A leaf of paper, s. xix², bound at the end of Cr. 3.25, belongs here. It contains a list, '4 Die wag . . .': the numbers refer to the order of Camel (1)–Stag (32) in art. 5.

Cr. 5.14. *Aristoteles, etc.*   s. XIII[2]

1. ff. 1–6ᵛ 'Compotus communis. solaris et lunaris. fratris iohannis de sacro bosco.' Compotus est sciencia considerans tempora . . . . Annuat hec nobis huius sic capere fructum / Ecclesie cristi qui nos hinc fructificemus. Deo gracias amen. 'Explicit compotus communis (*etc.*).'

Printed in 1538 and later: J. de Sacrobosco, Computus. Cf. L. Thorndike, *The Sphere of Sacrobosco*, 1949, pp. 6–10.

2. ff. 7–8 Incipit tractatus de confeccione astrolabii. Astrologie speculationis exercitium habere uolentibus . . . stature ad totam planitiem. Explicit de operacione astrolabii.

Thorndike and Kibre (Johannes Hispalensis). Ed. Millás, 1942, pp. 316–21.

Arts. 3–5 are Aristotle's Physics, De anima, and De generatione in the 'Vetus translatio': *Aristoteles Latinus*, pp. 52, 58, 54. Annotations in the wide margins are heavy only on f. 9ʳᵛ. 'Liber physicorum et de anima', f. 9 and f. iiᵛ.

3. ff. 9–73 [Q]uoniam quidem intelligere et scire contingit circa omnes sciencias . . . nullam habens magnitudinem. Explicit liber octauus physicorum ar'. et cum eo totus liber. Deo Gracias. Amen. f. 73ᵛ blank.

4. ff. 74–98ᵛ [B]onorum honorabilium noticiam opinantes . . . aliquid alteri. Explicit liber de anima. Deo gracias amen.

5. ff. 99–119ᵛ [D]e generatione et corruptione. natura generatorum et corruptorum . . . ens corruptibile. Explicit liber de generatione et corruptione. Deo gracias.

ff. ii+119+i. 345 × 240 mm and (ff. 1–8) 315 × 225 mm. Written space 160 × 90 mm and (ff. 1–8) 235 × 165 mm. 27–31 long lines and (ff. 1–8) 2 cols., 54 lines. Collation: 1⁸ 2–6¹² 7⁴+1 leaf after 4 (f. 73) 8¹² 9¹²+1 leaf after 11 (f. 97) 10¹⁰ 11¹² wants 12, blank. Quires, except the first, numbered at beginning and end in a distinctive style, s. xiv: f. 9 is marked 'primus quaternus' and f. 20ᵛ 'primus': the other quires have roman numbers. Initials: a red *C* outside the written space, f. 1; in arts. 3–5 5-line and 2-line spaces remain blank, except for a red *D* added later on f. 111ᵛ. Thick bevelled boards bare of leather: in rebacking the front board was replaced upside down: a chainmark at the (present) head of this board: a parchment label on the front board, now upside down, has a paper label pasted over it on which appears to be 'Lectura cuiusdam [. . . . .] in quartum sent[. . .]', so perhaps the boards do not really belong to this book. Secundo folio *tobri libri* (f. 2) or *habebit* (f. 10).

Written in Italy. The quire marking shows that ff. 9–119 belonged to the Franciscan convent of Assisi.[1] They are identifiable in the 1381 inventory printed by L. Alessandri, 1906, p. 31, no. clviii of the Libraria publica: Libri fisicorum viii. De anima iii. De generatione et corruptione ii aristotilis. Cum postibus et cathena. Cuius principium est. Quoniam quidem intelligere . . . Finis vero . . . contigit non ens corruptibile. In quo libro omnes quaterni sunt X. B.' Price-mark 'iii flori' ', f. 120.

Cr. 7.76. *J. de Sacrobosco, Algorismus, cum commentario*   1496 (?)

(f. 1) Algorismus Prosaycus de Integris Magistri Ioannis de Sacro Busco de Sancto Sepulchro . . . (f. 3) Omnia que a primeua . . . (f. 35ᵛ) finis algorismi

---

¹ See above, Birmingham, Selly Oak Colleges, Lat. 2.

prosayci magistri Ioannis de sacro busco per me Iohannem de berck zabernia 5ta feria ante festum penthekost' argentine anno 1496. 'a magistro Ieorio tunc temporis rectore' (*these six words in red, the third altered in black to* Georgio).

Text and commentary, section by section, the commentary beginning (f. 4^v) 'Hic magister vult quod hec sciencia . . .'. Preceded by an introductory letter, (f. 1) 'Audiui a quibusdam viris . . . mater maria domino suo Heinrico de Heistenberck (?: *written over* We[. .]enberck) et humillimo domino ac fautori suo singularissimo Ieorio tinctoris tunc temporis rectore In ciuitate nostra argentine anno a natali cristiano 1496 Vale. Iohannes Zabernia', and an introduction, (f. 2) 'Circa initium algorismi Queritur Qualis sit sciencia presentis libelli . . .'. f. 36^{rv}, left blank, and six leaves added after it, were filled in s. xvi in. with a 'De modo conficiendi horalogium achas' (cf. Cr. 2. 3, art. 9g) and other short pieces, partly in German.

ff. 36, bound up in or before s. xviii after (1) a 12-leaf printed 'erclärung über den Almanach' in German and (2) J. Regiomontanus, *Kalendarium*, Augsburg 1492 (Goff, R. 98). 205 × 158 mm. Written space 160 × 95 mm. Text in 16 and commentary in 31 long lines. Collation: 1–3^{12}. Cursiva of two sizes. Binding of s. xviii.

Written at Strasbourg 'a magistro Ieorio' (see above), presumably in 1496 for J. de Berck Zabernia.

EDINBURGH. ST. MARY'S EPISCOPAL CATHEDRAL

Horae   s. XV/XVI

A book of hours like that described in *MMBL* i. 46 (Dulwich College, MS. 25). Noticed by F. C. Eeles, *Scottish Exhibition of Natural History, Art, and Industry*, Glasgow, 1911, p. 1061.

1. ff. 1–12^v Calendar in red and black.

'Remigii episcopi' in red, 1 Oct. Thomas of Canterbury, 29 Dec., is the only English saint. His name and the word 'pape' have been erased. An addition, f. 11^v: 'One sanct clement eyuff being the xxii day off nouember i th v^c lxiiii deceysit Ihone edmonstone off that ilk in ye morning at vii howres'. 'Susanna Recorfort' (?), f. 1 and 'Icolumkil 9ber 16 1192 Sister Sara Kircham', f. 12^v, are written in pointed insular script, s. xvii (?).

2. ff. 13–23 Incipiunt quindecim orationes. O domine ihesu criste eterna dulcedo . . .

The Fifteen Oes of St. Bridget.

3. ff. 23–7 [De sancta trini]tate oratio. [Do]mine deus [o]mnipotens [p]ater et fi[l]ius et spiritus [s]anctus da michi famulo tuo [N] victoriam . . . (f. 26) Libera me domine . . .

Includes Pss. 53, 66, 129.

4. ff. 27–37 Memoriae of eight Saints: John Baptist, John Evangelist, Thomas of Canterbury, Anne, Mary Magdalene, Katherine, Barbara, and Margaret.

The antiphons are *RH*, nos. 26988, 27075, 26999, 6773, 6895, 6991, 6714, 7011, as in Dulwich 25. f. 37^v blank.

5. ff. 39–95ᵛ Incipiunt hore uirginis marie secundum vsum anglie.

Memoriae in lauds of Holy Spirit, Holy Trinity, Holy Cross, of SS. Michael, John Baptist, Peter and Paul, Andrew, John Evangelist, Laurence, Stephen, Thomas of Canterbury (*cancelled*), Nicholas, Mary Magdalene, Katherine, Margaret, of All Saints, and of peace. Hours of the Cross are worked in. f. 49ᵛ is blank after matins. A leaf with the beginning of none missing.

6. (*a*) ff. 96–97ᵛ Salutacio virginis m(ari)e. Salve regina, followed by the set of versicles, Virgo mater ecclesie. (*b*) ff. 98–103ᵛ Has videas laudes . . . followed by the farcing of Salve regina with Salve virgo virginum.

(*a*). *RH*, nos. 18147, 21818. (*b*). *RH*, nos. 7687, 18318.

7. ff. 104–106ᵛ Deuotissima oratio ad sanctissimum uirginem mariam. O intemerata . . . orbis terrarum. Inclina mater misericordie . . . For male use.

8. ff. 106ᵛ–110ᵛ Oratio ad uirginem mariam. Obsecro te . . . For male use.

9. ff. 110ᵛ–113ᵛ Alia oratio de beata maria virgine. Aue mundi spes maria aue mitis . . . *RH*, no. 1974.

10. ff. 113ᵛ–118 Quicunque hec septem gaudia . . . Uirgo templum trinitatis . . . (f. 117) Te deprecor sanctissima maria . . .

RH, no. 21899: the Seven Joys. The heading gives indulgence of 100 days 'a papa clemente qui hec septem gaudia proprio stilo composuit. Expressions in the final stanza, Virgo mater pietatis . . ., induced R. Kirke to write 'Blasphem[ia] in Iesum Chr[istum]' in the margin of f. 117.

11. ff. 118ᵛ–124 Ad ymaginem domini nostri. Omnibus consideratis . . .
AH xxxi. 87–9. *RH*, no. 14081 (etc.).

12. ff. 124–127ᵛ Incipit oratio venerabilis bede presbiteri de qua fertur . . . preparatam. Oratio. Domine ihesu criste . . . (f. 126ᵛ) Precor te piissime . . .
Bede's prayer of the Seven Words.

13. Salutaciones domini nostri. (*a*) ff. 127ᵛ–128 Aue domine ihesu criste . . . (*b*) f. 128ᵛ Oratio dicenda in eleuacione cristi. Aue verum corpus natum . . . (*c*) f. 129 Aue caro cristi cara . . . (*d*) f. 129ʳᵛ In eleuatione calicis domini. Anima cristi sanctifica me . . . (*e*) ff. 129ᵛ–130 Alia oratio. Aue principium nostri creationis . . . (*f*) f. 130ʳᵛ Cuilibet dicenti . . . Domine ihesu criste qui hanc sacratissimam carnem . . .

(*a*). Fives aves. (*b–e*). *RH*, nos. 2059, 2175, 1710, 1090. The heading of (*f*) conveys an indulgence of 2,000 years granted by Pope Boniface VI 'ad supplicationem philippi regis francie'. f. 131ʳᵛ left blank: cf. art. 19*a*.

14. ff. 133–155ᵛ Seven penitential psalms . . . (f. 142ᵛ) Incipiunt quindecim psalmi . . . (cues only of first twelve) . . . (f. 145ᵛ) Letania sanctorum . . .
'zuithine birine' the last two confessors. 'edicha affra aldegundis' the last three virgins. On ff. 147ᵛ–148 the text has been partly rewritten.

15. ff. 156–202ᵛ Incipiunt vigilie mortuorum. An'. Placebo . . .

16. ff. 204–222ᵛ The commendatory psalms (Pss. 118, 138) and prayers.

17. ff. 224–233ᵛ Incipiunt psalmi de passione. Deus deus meus respice in me . . .

18. ff. 235–253^v Psalterium beati iheronimi. Verba mea auribus . . . Oremus. Oratio. Omnipotens sempiterne deus clemenciam tuam suppliciter deprecor ut me famulum tuum N . . .

19 (added in cursiva, s. xv/xvi). (*a*) f. 131^{rv} Gaude virgo mater cristi . . . (*b*) f. 155^v Illumina oculos meos ne vnquam obdormiam . . . (*c*) ff. 253^v–254^v Oracio deuota: ante celebracionem misse dicenda. Deus qui de indignis dignos facis . . . (*d*) ff. 254^v–255^v Alia oracio ad sanctam mariam ad missam dicenda. O serenissima et inclita uirgo maria . . . que et eundem creatorem . . . (*e*) f. 255^v Oracio valde deuota post misse celebracionem. 'Stella celi extirpauit . . .'

(*a*). *RH*, no. 7017. Five Joys. (*e*). *RH*, no. 19438. *AH* xxxi. 210, stanzas 1, 2, for use in time of plague. The heading does not apply to the text which is over erasure.

20 (s. xvii). (*a*) Robert Kirke wrote marginalia on ff. 18, 19, 21^v, 169, 254 and other leaves in Latin and on ff. 127, 154, 163^v in Gaelic: cf. also above, art. 10. (*b*) f. 223 Four lines of halting verse not wholly legible, ending 'yet as yor on yow may recken me. dorothe oxy[. . .]', beneath which Kirke wrote 'Dorothe Oxynford'.

ff. i+255. 100×75 mm. Written space *c*. 63×38 mm. 18 long lines. Collation: 1–2^6 3–4^8 5^8+1 leaf after 8 (f. 37) 6^8 7 three (ff. 47–9) 8^4+1 leaf before 1 9–12^8 13^8 wants 3 after f. 80 14^8 15^4 (ff. 94–7) 16–19^8 20^2 (ff. 130–1) 21–24^8 25^6+1 leaf after 5 (f. 170) 26–28^8 29^6+1 leaf after 6 (f. 202) 30–35^8 36 two (ff. 254–5), together with five inserted leaves, 38, 132, 203, 223, 234, with blank rectos and pictures on the versos. Full-page pictures in front of arts. 5, 15, 17 (Christ in judgement), 17 (the wounded Christ stands in the tomb: instruments of the Passion), 18 (St. Jerome before a crucifix). Twenty-two smaller pictures, *c*. 30×28 mm, seven (formerly eight) in art. 4, six (formerly seven) in art. 5 (slaughter of Innocents at vespers, flight into Egypt at compline), one before art. 7, and eight in art. 11. The picture before art. 3 and the picture of St. Katherine in art. 4 have been cut out of ff. 23, 33. Initials: (i) 5-line, pink on decorated grounds of gold paint; (ii–iv) 3-line, 2-line, and 1-line, gold paint on red grounds. Initials of type (iv) are included in the picture space, if possible. Continuous floral borders round picture pages and the pages facing them. Line fillers of red and gold paint in the litany. Binding of s. xviii. Secundo folio (f. 14) *nem et.*

Written in the Netherlands for the English market. In Scotland by s. xvi^2 (art. 1). Belonged to Robert Kirke, minister of Balquhidder and Gaelic scholar (1642?–95: see *DNB*): 'Liber R. Kirke 1676 Love and Live. Balquhidder', f. 90^v; 'Robert Kirke 1676', f. 37; '[. . .] Rob. Kirke Balquhidder Decr 7 1677', f. 211^v. Armorial book-plate of 'Sr Hugh Patersone of Bannockburn Barronet 1709'. 'Dean of Edinburgh 62/1' is on a small label inside the back cover.

EDINBURGH. SCOTTISH RECORD OFFICE

PA 5/1 ('Berne Manuscript'). *R. de Glanvilla, etc.*   s. xiii^2

Described in *Acts of the Parliament of Scotland*, i (1844), 177–8. The inner margins of ff. 46–63 are slightly damaged.

1. ff. 1–31 [Tractatus] de legibus et consuetudinibus [regni] anglie tempore Henrici regis secundi [compositus] iusticie gubernacula tenente illustri [uiro] Ranulfo de glanuilla et iuris [regni et con]suetudinarum eo tempore peritis[simo] illas solas leges continet et consuetudines secundum quas placitatur in curia regis ad scacarium et coram iusticiariis ubicumque fuerint prologus. Regiam potestatem non sol*is* armis . . . tractare non dedecuit.

A 'beta' text, called Be in G. D. G. Hall's edition of Glanvill, 1965. Fourteen books, with a table of chapters in front of each book. Passages on ff. 20ᵛ, 25, 27, 29 are marked 'vacat' in the margins.

2. ff. 31ᵛ–32ᵛ Primus normannie dux rollo qui et Robertus dictus.' regnauit annis xxx . . . cui successit Henricus filius eius 'et regnauit lviii annis'.

3. ff. 33–35ᵛ Anno gracie Mᵒ ccᵒ lxviiᵒ regni autem domini H Reg' fil' Iohannis Regis liiᵒ In octabis sancti martini prouidente ipso domino rege . . . per consilium regis prouidenda. Explicit.

Statute of Marlborough, 18 Nov. 1267. *SR* i. 19. An early copy.

4. ff. 35ᵛ–36ᵛ Hic incipiunt leges marchiarum inter scociam et angliam. Anno gracie Millesimo ccxlᵒ nono. ad festum sanctorum Tiburcii et Valeriani. Conuenerunt ad marchiam.Vicecomes Northumbrie . . . antequam transierit filum aque respon- (*ends imperfectly*).

Acts of Parliament of Scotland, i. 413–416, three lines from the foot: only twenty-one words are missing.

5. ff. 37–59ᵛ Breuia originalia de Cancelaria . De Recto. Henricus dei gracia . . .

A register of 323 writs beginning with a writ of right of 20 July, 21 Henry III, addressed to John de Vernon. Four other writs are dated: 26 Oct. 52, 15 Apr. 52, 5 Sept. 46 and 26 Oct. 54 Henry III (ff. 41, 50ᵛ, 57ᵛ). A writ De proteccione, f. 56, is in the name of Prince Edward.

The arrangement is not that of the registers analysed in Harmsworth, *History of English Law*, ii. 607–15: for example, at the beginning, ff. 37–40ᵛ, a group of nineteen writs of right and thirty-one writs of entry or intrusion under the heading 'Breuia originalia de ingressu' are separated by single writs, 'nuper obiit', 'de consanguinitate', 'quo iure', de auo', and 'indicauit'. The last writ is 'De resummonicione de iudicio. Rex vic' ebor' . . . T. G. de Preston'. No subject divisions. Such place-names as occur are mainly from the north of England, Yorkshire, Cumberland, and Northumberland: for the milieu cf. T. N. Cooper in *Scottish Historical Review*, xxvii (1948), 114–23 and his *Register of Brieves* (Stair Soc. x), pp. 4, 24. Gilbert de Preston figures several times. The ten writs of trespass are printed by G. D. G. Hall in *Law Quarterly Review*, lxxiii (1957), 69–73.

6. ff. 59ᵛ–61ᵛ Incipiunt leges scocie. et primo de catallo furato . . . De catallo furato (*expunged*) quod fuerit furatum . . .

Twenty-two paragraphs, all but three of which occur in *Acts*, pp. 372–8 (cf. the table on p. 220). The exceptions, nos. 18, 20, 22, occur elsewhere in *Acts*: no. 18 at p. 737, ch. 1; no. 20 at p. 398, ch. 3; no. 22 at pp. 663–5 from this copy (*Leges inter Brettos et Scotos*, in French). Facsimiles of ff. 59ᵛ, 61ᵛ in *Acts*, opposite pp. 178 and 177.

7. ff. 62–63ᵛ Leges et consuetudines quatuor burgorum Edinburg. Rokisburg Berewic.Striuelin. constitute per dominum Dauid Regem scocie. De redditibus domini regis in Burgagiis. In primis uidendum est quid sit redditus domini regis in Burgagiis . . . accomodauerit tenetur reddere. sed (*ends imperfectly*).

Acts, pp. 333–342/29.

8. Additions: (*a*) two memoranda in one hand in a blank space on f. 61ᵛ, the first beginning 'Memorandum quod W. bercator reddidit compotum [suum] dominica proxima ante festum sancti andree [anno] gracie m ccc vi', and the second 'Item eodem die Iohannes bercator de Malk[. . . . .] reddidit compotum suum'; (*b*) nineteen words scribbled, s. xiv(?), upside down on f. 26, 'vesterarii(?) þan was ve[. . . .] hi tak (?) vetenes of þe lauerd ihesu crist þat mykel of my blud was spilt'.

(*a*) is printed in *Acts*, p. 178, and is shown in the facsimile there of f. 61ᵛ. The editor suggests that the damaged place-name may have been Malkerston (now Makerston, Rox-burghshire).

ff. iii+63+iii. 268 × 175 mm. Written space *c.* 215 × 140 mm. 2 cols. 39 lines and, on ff. 1–4ʳ, 29 lines. Collation impracticable: probably two quires of twelve are followed by a quire of ten, wanting 9, 10, probably blank, after f. 32: many leaves and all from 46 have been mounted separately in the course of repairs. Probably all in one hand: for facsimiles see above, art. 6. Initials: (i, ii) 3-line and 2-line, red or blue, or, rarely, green, occasionally with ornament: red is the only colour on ff. 36–63. An ornate and heavy binding, s. xix, replaced a binding of 'modern parchment'. Secundo folio *Breue de.*

Written in northern England (or southern Scotland) in or after 1270 and probably before the death of Henry III in 1272 (art. 2). Probably in Roxburghshire in s. xiv in. (art. 8). Part of the library of J. Bongars, 1554–1612, which the Stadtbibliothek, Berne, acquired in 1632: noticed on p. 25 of the catalogue of the Bongars library made in 1634. Described by J. R. Sinner, *Catalogue Codicum MSS. Bibliothecae Bernensis*, Berne, 1772, iii. 56–70 (MS. 306). Given to the Register House by the Stadtbibliothek in 1814: a full account in H. Strahm, 'Ein englisch-schottischer Rechtscodex aus der Bibliothek Bongars', *Archiv des Historischen Vereins des Kantons Bern*, xliv (1958), 603–13.

PA 5/2 ('Ayr Manuscript'). *Leges burgorum Scotiae, etc.* s. xiv med.

Described in *Acts of the Parliament of Scotland*, i (1844), 179–81.

1. (*a*) f. 1 Qualiter quis probabit terram emptam infra Burgum. Ne [. . . . . .] (*b*) f. 1 Breue eiusdem. A[. . . . .]. (*c*) ff. 1–3 [. . . . . . .] . . . in altero statuto prenotate. (*d*) f. 3 Si homo Burgensis uel femina . . . (*e*) ff. 3–7 Si citaciones minus (*sic*) facte sunt.Si citaciones minus iuste facte sunt . . . dotem tunc amittere debet.

f. 1 is badly faded from exposure and, red headings and initials apart, hardly legible. Enough can be seen of (*a*) to show that it is as *Acts*, pp. 720–1 (Fragmenta Collecta, ch. 10). (*b*) was probably in seven lines. (*c*) becomes legible at the turn over to 1ᵛ and is at first a formulary dispute over land in court between Robertus and Iohannes. 2ᵛ/3–12, Item si quis calumpniauerit . . . calumpnie, and 2ᵛ/19–31, Si quis placitauerit . . . domini regis, are as *Acts*, p. 741, chs. 2, 3. (*d*) As Leges Burgorum, ch. 116 (*Acts*, p. 356). (*e*) Thirty-seven paragraphs, all but two of which are to be found in bk. 4 of Regiam maiestatem: cf. the table in *Acts*, pp. 238, 240. The fifth paragraph corresponds to *Acts*, p. 734, ch. 2, and the last to ch. xiv of bk. 2 of Regiam maiestatem (*Acts*, p. 612).

2 (added in current anglicana in the blank space at the end of quire 1). ff. 7ᵛ–8ᵛ Cest endenture fait a Rokesb' le xxxᵐᵉ iour doctobr' lan du grace mˡ ccc xlvi . . . et Lane susditz.

The border treaty of 1346. Printed from this copy in *Acts*, p. 180, footnote.

3 (added in s. xv in blank spaces of quires 1, 2, 7). ff. 8ᵛ–10, 77ᵛ Notices of proceedings of the Ayr Court of Guild in 1428, 1430, and 1431, and (ff. 9ᵛ–10) names of 'confratres Gilde'. Cf. art. 15.

4. f. 10ᵛ A table of contents in red in the main hand listing arts. 5–11, 14.

5. ff. 11–15ᵛ Assisa Reg' Dauid Rex Scottorum facta apud nouum castrum super tynam per totam communitatem suam Scocie tam Baronum burgensium quam aliorum De tolloneis et custumis burgorum. In primis de quadriga . . . et sic assendendo.

Sixteen paragraphs, nos. 1–10, 12 in *Acts*, pp. 667–72, under the headings Assisa de Tolloneis and Custuma Portuum (cf. the tables on p. 246). Nos. 11 and 13–16 are in *Acts*, pp. 673–9 (De Mensuris et Ponderibus; Assise Panis Vini et Cervisie).

6. ff. 15ᵛ–18ᵛ De articulis inquirendis in burgo In itinere Camerarii secundum vsum Scocie. In primis: Si Balliui faciant . . . de molendinis domini Regis.

Printed from this copy in *Acts*, pp. 680–2.

7. ff. 18ᵛ–30 Incipiunt capitula Capelle Regis Scocie tam de litteris in Curiis placitandis quam breuibus per Regem de Cancellaria mittendis . . . *(table of 81 writs numbered in red)* . . . (f. 20) Proteccio Regis Scoc' trium clausularum . . .

Printed from this copy by Lord Cooper, *Register of Brieves* (Stair Soc. x (1946), 33–52). Writs 25–58 are missing in the gap after f. 24. Facsimiles of parts of ff. 18ᵛ, 21 in *Acts*, opposite p. 179.

8. ff. 30ᵛ–42ᵛ Incipiunt capitula assisarum statutorum domini Dauid Regis Scocie In primis . . . *(table of 44 chapters numbered in red)* . . . (f. 32) Quomodo tenebuntur Curie prelatorum et Baronum et pro quanto homo debet suspendi. Assisa Regis Dauid facta apud Striuelyn . . .

For the order of printing of these chapters in *Acts* see there, pp. 212, 220, 222, 224. The scribe filled a space on f. 31ᵛ: Professio nunciorum / Accipe vasculum mendacii / Et vade per semitas seculi / Absque promocione negocii / Vt incurras indignacionem domini / Et sic capiet piecidem armorum / Per omnia secula seculorum.

9. ff. 42ᵛ–49ᵛ Mandatum Roberti Regis pro Statutis infrasciptis obseruandis. Robertus dei gracia Rex Scottorum[1] . . . in defectum.

Acts, pp. 466–73 (preface and chs. 1–26). Facsimiles of f. 42ᵛ (part) and f. 43 (part) in *Acts*, opposite p. 466.

10. ff. 49ᵛ–67ᵛ Incipiunt Capitula legis Burgorum Scocie . . . *(table of 105 chapters numbered in red)* . . . (f. 52) De annuali firma Domini Regis. Quilibet Burgensis domini Regis dabit domino Regi pro burgagio suo . . . et veteres diuisas Burgorum.

Acts, pp. 333–54 (chs. 1–105: cf. table, pp. 214–18).

11. ff. 68–76 Incipiunt statute Gilde apud Berwicum facte. In nomine Domini dei . . . vini ad Gildam nostram.

Preface and fifty-two paragraphs. *Acts*, pp. 431–8: cf. the table, pp. 226–8.

12. ff. 76–7 Qualiter infeodati per Baronem tenentur iurare. Quilibet infeodatus . . . pro munere capiendo.

Printed from this copy in *Acts*, p. 683 (Juramenta Officiariorum).

---

[1] *tt* is written *ct*, as commonly.

13. ɪ. 77 Titulus Inquisicionis secundum vsum Scocie. Inquisicio capta apud Raynfrew . . . ut patet per Breue.

A single formula. f. 77^v was left blank: cf. art. 3.

14. ff. 78–83^v Calendar in red and black, not graded.

Many English saints, but, St. Thomas of Canterbury apart, only Oswald king and martyr, 5 Aug., is in red. The Scotch saints are only two, Kentigern and Columba, 13 Jan. and 9 June, both in black: 'sancte keuoce' was added at 13 Mar. in s. xv. 'Dedicacio ecclesie de Iedd'', 9 July in red, and octave in red, in the main hand.

15. f. 84, a flyleaf, has faded writing of s. xiv on the recto (23 lines) and scribbles on the verso.

One scribbler, John Kenedy, wrote also on f. 9^v, where there is faint writing, perhaps like that on f. 84, below the Ayr additions.

ff. iii + 83 + v. ff. 84, 85 are medieval flyleaves. 195 × 130 mm. Written space 145 × 90 mm. 21–6 long lines and, in art. 1, 34 lines. Collation: 1^8 2^{10} wants 1 (blank?), a bifolium, ff. 10, 11, inserted after 2, 3 ten (ff. 20–9: five bifolia with a gap after f. 24) 4–5^{16} 6^{10} 7^{12}. Quires 2–6 signed I–V at the end. Written in anglicana and (arts. 1, 14) textura. 2-line red initials. Binding of s. xix. Secundo folio *ad Warentum*.

Art. 14 at least originated in or near Jedburgh. In Ayr, *c.* 1430 (art. 3). The name 'Michael Wallace' scribbled on f. 61^v is of s. xvi (?). 'Ebenezer Thomson Ayr Academy 1825' and, in faint pencil, 'Mr Thomson acquired it in 1824'. Acquired from Ebenezer Thomson: cf. *Memoir of Thomas Thomson* (Bannatyne Club, 1854), pp. 189–90.

EDINBURGH. SOCIETY OF ANTIQUARIES OF SCOTLAND

Three medieval manuscripts belonging to the Society were deposited in the National Library of Scotland in 1934. They have been given numbers in the National Library series and described in the *Catalogue of Manuscripts*, ii (1966), 15–17: MS. 1901, a thirteenth-century Bible, probably written in England; MS. 1902, Gregorius Magnus, Homiliae 40 in Evangelia, etc., s. xiv/xv, written in England; MS. 1903, hours of B.V.M. of the use of (Rome), s. xv^2, written in France.

MS. 1901 (ff. 439, written space 103 × 65 mm., 2 cols. 53 lines) was pledged in the Lyng chest at Cambridge: 'Caucio domini Iohannis Peynt*er* (the *n* doubtful) exposita ciste de lynk' xxiii die Ianuarii anno domini 1443 pro xxvi s' viii d' ', f. 1 The list of Hebrew names which follows the Bible begins 'Aad testificans': cf. *Sum. Cat.* vii. 213.

For these gifts to the Society see *Archaeologia Scotica*, iii. 67–8, 116.

EDINBURGH. UNIVERSITY OF EDINBURGH, REID SCHOOL OF MUSIC

D. 25. *Officia liturgica*

s. xv med.

Offices for the use of nuns. The forms in rubrics throughout are feminine. They have not been altered, but in phrases of the text on f. 14ᵛ, 'Pro fratribus *et sororibus* nostris' and 'seruos tuos *et ancillas tuas*', the words in italics have been crossed out.

1. (*a*) ff. 2–12 Domine labia mea aperies . . . Memor fui nocte . . . (*b*) ff. 12–13ᵛ Ad conpletorium. Iube domna benedicere. Ebdomedaria. Noctem quietam vitamque beatam . . .

Offices at matins and compline, all noted.

2. (*a*) ff. 13ᵛ–16ᵛ Sequntur preces maiores ad vesperas et ad matutinas. Ego dixi . . . (*b*) ff. 16ᵛ–19 Sequntur preces ad minores horas . . . Ego dixi . . .

Cf. *MMBL* i. 104. All noted. A leaf of (*a*) missing after f. 13.

3. (*a*) f. 19ʳᵛ Ad prandium quando ieiunatur ebdomadaria incipit more consueto. Benedicite Edent pauperes . . . (*b*) ff. 19ᵛ–20 Ad collacionem dicat lectrix. Iube domna benedicere Noctem quietam . . . (*c*) ff. 20–23ᵛ Infra ebdomadam paschalem Ebdomadaria more consueto dicat. Benedicite. Conuentus prosequitur. Hec dies quam fecit dominus . . . A litany follows on f. 21.

Mostly noted. Twenty-six martyrs: . . . (15) Ignati . . . (21–6) ponciane lamberte dionisi bonifati mauriti gereon. Twenty-three confessors: (1) Augustine . . . (9–11) godeharde epyphani berwarde . . . (22–3) libuine odulphe. Sixteen virgins: . . . (9, 10) walburgis gerdrudis. A capital letter and a stroke of red on it draw attention to Ignatius, Augustine, Jerome. Godehard, Epiphanius (of Pavia), and Bernwardus are Hildesheim saints.

4. ff. 24–31 Incipiunt vigilie. Placebo domine . . . (f. 28) Partem beate resurrexionis . . .

All noted, except part of f. 28.

5. (*a*) ff. 31–32ᵛ Prayers for the dead: pro anniuersario; pro tercennario; pro uno sacerdote; pro pluribus sacerdotibus; pro vno famulo; plurimorum famulorum; pro vna femina; plurimarum feminarum; pro benefactoribus; pro fratribus et sororibus; generalis (3 forms). (*b*) ff. 32ᵛ–33 (pro vno famulo); pro episcopo. Not noted.

6. f. 33ʳᵛ Settings of Gloria patri: eight tones.

7 (added early). ff. 33ᵛ–34 [H]omo quidam fecit cenam magnam . . .

Noted. f. 34ᵛ blank.

8. ff. 35–42ᵛ Lections from Lamentations on Thursday, Friday, and Saturday before Easter, three at each feast: (Thursday) Aleph. Quomodo sedet . . . in ecclesiam tuam. Iherusalem iherusalem. (Friday) Aleph. Quomodo obtexit . . . opidi. Iherusalem iherusalem; (Saturday) Alleph. Quomodo obscuratum est aurum . . . conuertere ad dominum deum tuum. All noted.

9. ff. 42ᵛ–46ᵛ In cena domini ad pedes locionum. Cena facta dixit ihesus discipulis suis . . . et hoc pane viuet in eternum. Hic est. Gloria patri et filio et spiritui sancto. Hic. All noted.

10. The pastedown at the beginning is a leaf of a handsome antiphonal (?) of s. xiiiᴵ, containing part of the office for the second Sunday after Pentecost.

Twelve long lines and music. Initials: (i) *L* of *Loquere*, red and green with ornament in the same colours; (ii) red or green.

11. The pastedown at the end is part of a leaf of an unfinished Missale plenum of s. xivᴵ, containing parts of offices of the Annunciation and of SS. Tiburtius and George: cf. *Missale Romanum*, i. 325–6.

Two cols. Music and rubrics not filled in. The leaf seems to have been used as scrap—as a flyleaf in some other book?—already in s. xiv when memoranda were written on it: (1) Nota post festum natiuitatis beate marie virginis feria quartaᴵ sunt mortui lxᵃ homines istius ecclesie porroga[. . . .]² vsque in natiuitatem cristi anno domini m ccc lº; (2) [. . .]n vigilia palmarum dedit domina hiburgis de osterloge [. . .]a et eo[dem] die tres cruces sunt depicte sub expensis.

ff. i+45+i, foliated 1–47. 250 × 170 mm. Written space 180 × 110 mm. 9 long lines and music (8 in quire 1). Collation of ff. 2–46: 1¹² 2¹⁴ wants 1 before f. 14 3⁸ 4¹². Punctuation with the flex (?), some of it original and some added.³ Initials in red, 2-line and 1-line, and cadels. Capital letters in the ink of the text marked with red. Contemporary binding of stamped pigskin over wooden boards: small fleur-de-lis and cinqfoil stamps: central strap and pin, the strap missing. Secundo folio *parabilis*.

Written in Germany. Belonged to the Augustinian nunnery of Marienberg, near Helmstedt, Brunswick: 'Liber monasterii beate marie virginis in [. .]hemb' (*cancelled*) 'Monte prope Helmestede Ordinis Canonicorum Regularium'', f. 1, s. xv.⁴ Stamp of the 'University of Edinburgh. Reid Bequest Chair of Music', f. 47ᵛ.

EDINBURGH. UNIVERSITY LIBRARY

C. R. Borland, *A Descriptive Catalogue of the Western Mediaeval Manuscripts in Edinburgh University Library*. Edinburgh, 1916. MSS. 1–230. Twenty-four plates.

300. *Decretales Gregorii IX et Innocentii IV*   s. xiii²

1. ff. 1–273ᵛ Gregorius episcopus seruus seruorum dei dilectis filiis doctoribus et scolaribus bon' (*over erasure*) commorantibus . . . Rex pacificus . . . homagium compellatur. Expliciunt decretales.

Bk. 2, f. 65; 3, f. 122; 4, f. 185ᵛ; 5, f. 209. The last leaf of bk. 2 is missing. An apparatus,

---

¹ 8 Sept. was a Wednesday in 1350.
² The first letter not quite certain.
³ The flex is used in art. 5 as a mark of punctuation within a sentence and in arts. 1, 2 as a mark at the end of a sentence, where the pitch falls, for example, after 'Pro rege nostro', as against the punctus elevatus after 'Exurge domine adiuua nos', where the pitch rises.
⁴ The whole ex-libris seems to be in one hand, but written at more than one time.

'*Gregorius etc seruus*. Imperator appellat se seruum . . .', in a hand different from that of the text, extends only to f. 6. After this the wide margins contain only occasional notes in ink and pencil. At first f. 273 was followed by a blank leaf, 282: see art. 2. The first leaf of quire 11 is misplaced at the end of the quire (f. 121).

2. ff. 274–82 De rescriptis. Cum in multis . . . derogari. Expliciunt noue constituciones.

Thirty-seven of the forty-two decrees of Innocent IV, printed by Mansi, *Concilia*, xxiii. 652–74 after the bull Cum nuper of 1245. The decrees absent from this copy are nos. (7) Grandi non, (23) Ad apostolicae, (24) Abbate sane, (30) Non solum, (41) Dilecto . . . Praeterea cum. No. (33) precedes no. (32). No. (27), Cum suffraganeorum, is much longer than in edn., continuing after *appellandum*, 'ad archid*iaconos* uero aliisque inferioribus prelatis . . . remittere non postponat'. No. (28), Quia cunctis, is addressed 'Dilecto filio andree capellano nostro'.

Art. 2 is written in several hands, one of them probably the main hand, on a quire, 28, inserted after f. 273, and on the leaf left blank at the end of quire 27. f. 282ᵛ remained blank.

3. Verses added in the margins and in blank spaces, s. xiii, include: f. 65 Errans. falsator. et presulis insidiator . . . (4 lines); f. 282 Casibus hiis senis mulier . . .; f. 282 Quanto dignior es . . . (2 lines); f. 282ᵛ Tu qui multa potes . . . (2 lines); f. 282ᵛ Inconstans animus . . . (2 lines).

The verses on f. 282ʳᵛ are Walther, *Sprichwörter*, nos. 2454a, 23585, 31721, 12215.

4 (added, s. xiii). f. 282ᵛ A poem of twenty-one long lines in French, hard to read: Ior cheuauchei baitier (?) par delez le buisson damor Si troue sanz deloyer pucele qui . . . par deux et par la douce dame.

ff. ii+282+ii. 260×165 mm. Written space 125×77 mm. 2 cols. 42 lines. Collation: 1–10¹² 11⁶ wants 6 (ff. 121, 117–120) 12⁸ 13⁴ (ff. 130–3) 14–17¹² 18¹⁰+1 leaf after 6 (f. 188) 19¹² 20⁴ (ff. 205–8) 21–23¹² 24–26⁸ 27⁶ (ff. 269–73, 282) 28⁸ (ff. 274–81). *Ad hoc* pencil signatures. Written by several hands. Initials: (i) of books, blue and red with ornament of both colours, blue predominating; (ii) of tituli, outside the written space, and as fancy lettering for the first word or two of each book, blue or red with ornament of the other colour. Binding of blue morocco, s. xix. The marks of five bosses and of a chain attachment (?) on a former binding show on ff. 280–2. Secundo folio (text) *mentum*, (apparatus) *in terra*.

Written in France. Damaged inscriptions of ownership and price: [. . . . .] de gofanis [. . . .] tur' et quatuor denarios', f. 282, s. xiii ex.; 'Has decretales dati (?) sunt (?) pro sexaginta decem sol' et sunt iohannis de kaer capellani [in] ecclesia and' ', f. 282ᵛ, s. xiv¹; 'Iste liber est [. . . . . . .] de C[. . . .] clerici parochie de [. . . .] Et detur [. . .] libris tor' ', f. 282, s. xiv²; also of use by a member of a convent of Friars Minor of the custody of Rodez: 'Isti decretales sunt ad vsum fratris [. . . . .] ordine fratrum minorum [. . . . .] pro[uincie] aquitanie de custodia ruthen' ', f. 273ᵛ, s. xiv; also of price only, 'detur s' xl tur' and 'detur pro xl sol' turon' et [. . . .]', f. 282ᵛ, s. xiii. Stamped 'Manuscrit appᵗ a Mᵗ Monteil' in blind on the front cover, as regularly on manuscripts belonging to A.-A. de Monteil, 1769–1850. Phillipps MS. 1324. Phillipps sale at Sotheby's, 15 June 1908, lot 338. Bequeathed by James Cathcart White in Jan. 1943, together with MSS. 301–13.

301. *Psalterium*   s. xv in.

1. ff. 1–6ᵛ Calendar in red, black lined through with red, and black, graded and with many additions and erasures.

Major feasts are marked 'Cand' ', or 'Cap' '; other feasts, 'Cap' sed non conuersis', 'xii l' ', 'Missa'. The Feast of Relics and Hugh (of Lincoln) in red (8, 17 Nov.). The Conception, 8 Dec., is called 'Sanctificacio beate marie virginis in utero'. The Visitation (in red) and its octave (2, 9 July), Anne (26 July), Eobanus, bishop and martyr (26 July), and Elizabeth of Hungary (in red, 19 Nov.) are among additions; also, on the October page, 'Prima dominica post festum dionisii et sociorum eius erit dedicacio ecclesie nostre'.

Probably all erasures are of entries made by monks who treated the calendar as though they owned it. Some of these entries can still be read: 26 Jan., 'dies professionis mee 1418', 15 Mar., 'obiit Pater domni Iohannis franckenfeld[1] 1397'; 9 Apr., 'obiit domnus gofredus de bugbach auunculus domni iohannis franckenfeld[1] 1392'; 10 July, 'Obiit Prior domnus albertus (?) harh' anno 1416'; 6 Dec., 'Anno 1407 frater Iohannes francken[. . . .] monachus fecit professionem [. . .] xxiii'.

2. ff. 7–98 Psalms, with noted antiphons, etc.

Larger initials show the principal psalms, 1, 26, 32, 38, 45, 51, 52, 59, 68, 73, 79, 85, 101, 105, 109, and tabs the ferial divisions (Pss. 32, 45, 59, 73, 85, 101).

3. ff. 98–106 Six ferial canticles and Benedicite, Benedictus, Magnificat, Nunc dimittis, Te deum (headed 'Cant' Augustini et Ambrosii'), Quicumque vult.

4. ff. 106ᵛ–113 Cantica dominicis diebus . . .

Mearns, *Canticles*, pp. 87–92: Sunday, first set; Advent, second set; Christmas, first set, here 'in natiuitate domini. in circumcisione. in epyphania domini. in purificatione beate marie uirginis'; Lent; Easter, first set, here 'in resurreccione. ascensione. et penth' '; common of saints, ninth set (in the order 1, 3, 2), here for apostles and martyrs, and first set, here for a martyr or confessor; common of virgins, second set.

5. ff. 113ᵛ–120ᵛ Twenty-six hymns, not counting divisions: Conditor alme, Veni redemptor gencium, Audi benigne, Vexilla regis, Hic est dies, Optatus votis, Veni creator, Iam cristus astra, Pange lingwa, Sacris sollempnis, Verbum supernum, Ut queant laxis, Aue maris stella, Mysterium ecclesie, Vere gracia plena es, Crux fidelis, Criste redemptor omnium, Ihesu saluator seculi, Deus creator omnium, Eterne rerum conditor, Splendor paterne, Iam lucis orto, Nunc sancte nobis, Rector potens, Rerum deus, Criste qui lux es.

A normal collection of Carthusian hymns, as Bodleian Canon. liturg. 271, 378, and Rawlinson G. 19.[2] The hymns for the hours here follow the series from Advent to All Saints.

6. ff. 120ᵛ–122ᵛ Letania.

Twelve virgins: . . . (7–12) Anastasia Blandina Scolastica Eufemia Petronilla Maria magdalena. Additions: to apostles, Barnabas at the end; to confessors, Jerome in third place and Hugh at the end; to virgins, Katherine in fifth place.

7. ff. 122ᵛ–127ᵛ In agenda defunctorum.

Ends imperfectly. The last remaining page has been erased.

ff. 126+i (paper). Medieval foliations on versos in roman figures and on rectos in arabic figures. They begin with art. 2 and are therefore six behind the present foliation. 275 × 190 mm. Written space 210 × 130 mm. 26 long lines. Collation: 1⁶ 2–16⁸. Quires 2, 3 numbered at the end i, ii. Punctuation in the psalms is by colon (:). The flex (?) is used only in arts. 6, 7. Initials: (i) f. 7, 6-line, red with red ornament; (ii) of Ps. 109, 4-line, red;

---

[1] The last four letters are uncertain.
[2] The manuscript used by Mearns, *Hymnaries*, Canon. liturg. 370 (I. 4), does not have Crux fidelis or Criste qui lux es.

(iii) of other principal psalms and beginning arts. 3–5, 3-line, red; (iv) 2-line, red; (v) of verses, 1-line, red. Binding of stamped pigskin, s. xvi: rosette and fleur-de-lis on the front cover, within a border; rosette (larger) and eagle on the back cover: five bosses on each cover now missing. Secundo folio (f. 8) *Cum inuocarem*.

Written in Germany for Carthusian use. The ex-libris of the Erfurt Charterhouse, 'Sum Carthusię Erfort' is on the flyleaf, f. 127, s. xvi. 'Fol. 120 d. 1 April. 1835 / Beyern G. H. Sch^r¹ inside the cover shows that this is one of the many Erfurt manuscripts rescued by F. Gottlieb Julius von Bülow of Beyernaumburg: cf. *Sum. Cat.* v. 11, 24, 660 and *Serapeum*, xviii (1857), 149; also, for the form of inscription here, Bodleian Add. A. 373 (*Sum. Cat.* 29624). Probably the Psalter of 120 leaves, lot 1556 in the Bülow sale, 10 Oct. 1836. In a Sotheby sale, s. xx: the relevant slip from the catalogue is pasted inside the cover. Given as MS. 300.

302. *Horae*   s. xv in.

1. ff. 1–12ᵛ Full calendar in French in red and black.

In red: 'Sainte geneuieue', 3 Jan.; 'Saint more saint bon', 15 Jan.; 'Saint yues', 19 May; 'Saint loys roy', 25 Aug.; 'Saint denis', 9 Oct.

2. ff. 13–17ᵛ Sequentiae of the Gospels.

No prayer after John. f. 18ʳᵛ blank.

3. ff. 19–77 Hours of the B.V.M. of the use of (Paris).

ff. 77ᵛ–78ᵛ left blank: for an addition see art. 16.

4. ff. 79–100ᵛ Penitential psalms and litany.

The last nine of twenty-three confessors are Lambert, Louis, Armagil, Antony, Fiacre, Maur, Yvo, Eloy, Maglore. Geneviève is fourteenth of twenty-three virgins.

5. ff. 100ᵛ–107 Cy commencent les heures de la croix.

Begins imperfectly.

6. ff. 107–13 Incipiunt hore de sancto spiritu.

7. ff. 113–144ᵛ Office of the dead.

The second and third nocturns of matins are omitted.

8. ff. 144ᵛ–148 Oratio de nostra domina. Obsecro te . . . Feminine forms.

9. ff. 148–52 Oroison de nostre dame. O intemerata . . . orbis terrarum. De te enim . . . Feminine forms. ff. 152ᵛ–153ᵛ blank.

10. ff. 154–159ᵛ Doulce dame de misericorde mere de pitie . . .

The Fifteen Joys. Sonet, no. 458.

11. ff. 159ᵛ–163 Yci sensuiuent les sept requestes de nostre seingneur. Douls dieu doulz pere sainte trinite . . . Sonet, no. 504.

12. f. 163 Sainte uraye croix aouree . . . Sonet, no. 1876. f. 163ᵛ blank.

13. ff. 164–82 Memoriae of Holy Trinity, Holy Spirit, B.V.M. (Salue regina . . .),

¹ No doubt Georg Heinrich Schäffer, the author of the catalogue, *Bibliotheca Büloviana*, prepared for the sale in 1836.

Holy Cross, SS. Michael, John Baptist, Peter, Paul, Andrew, John Evangelist, James the great, Bartholomew, Matthew, Stephen, Vincent, Laurence, Denis, Christopher, George, Sebastian, Cosmas and Damian, Martin, Nicholas, Anthony hermit, Maur, Fiacre, Maturin, Louis king, Anne (Anna pia mater aue . . .: *RH*, no. 1109), Mary Magdalene, Katherine, Margaret, Geneviève, Avia, Elizabeth (Illa regis filia hec contemptibilia . . .: not in *RH*).

14. ff. 182–5 Quiconques ceste oroison dira chacun iour deuotement a genoulx lannemy ne mal homme . . . Cest loroison que fist bede lonnorable prestre des sept derrenires paroles que nostre seigneur ihesu crist dist en la croix. Or'. Biau sire dieux ihesu crist qui le derrenier iour . . .

15. Form of commendation: (*a*) 185^{rv} Sancta maria mater domini nostri ihesu xpisti in manus eiusdem filii tui et in tuas commendo hodie . . .; (*b*) ff. 185^{v}–187^{v} Domine sancte pater omnipotens eterne deus in illa sancta custodia in qua commendasti . . .

16. A hand of the later s. xvi added prayers and devotions in French on the pages left blank after art. 3 and on ff. 188–190^{v}.

ff. i+187+iv. 165 × 122 mm. Written space 80 × 53 mm. 14 long lines. Collation: 1^{12} 2^6 3–9^8 10^4 (ff. 75–8) 11–12^8 13^8 wants 7 after f. 100 14–19^8 20^4 (ff. 150–3) 21^8 22^2 (ff. 162–3) 23–25^8. Thirteen attractive 10-line pictures, 8 in art. 3 and 1 before arts. 4, 6, 7, 10 (B.V.M. and Child: angels in the air hold a crown above her), 11 (Christ on the rainbow: B.V.M. and St. John below). The picture before art. 5 is missing. Initials: (i, ii) 3-line and 2-line in colours patterned in white on decorated gold grounds; (iii) 1-line, gold on coloured grounds patterned in white. Line fillers in red and blue touched with gold. Capital letters in the ink of the text filled with pale yellow. Floral borders, with much gold ivy-leaf, on three sides of picture pages and as prolongations in the left margin of all pages with initials of type (ii), the height of the written space. Binding of s. xix. Secundo folio (f. 14) *tate uiri*.

Written in France (Paris?). 'From the Ashburnham Col.' according to a note inside the cover. Given as MS. 300.

303. *Horae*   S. XV

A book of hours very like Dulwich College 25 (*MMBL* i. 46). When both books were complete the differences in contents and arrangement were probably only— details apart—the presence here of art. 6c and there of arts. 10 and 13.

1. ff. 1–6^{v} Calendar in red and black.

Feasts in red include: Patrick, Edward, and Cuthbert, 17, 18, 20 Mar.; Swithun, 15 July; Cuthbert, 4 Sept.; Hugh of Lincoln, 6 Oct. and 17 Nov. Feasts of Thomas of Canterbury erased, 7 July and 29 Dec., but not the word 'pape'.

2. ff. 8–14^{v} Incipiunt quindecim oraciones ad passionem ihesu cristi.

The Fifteen Oes of St. Bridget.

3. ff. 16–17^{v} De sancta trinitate. Domine deus . . . da michi famule tue N. uictoriam . . . Oremus. Oracio. Libera me domine . . . N. famulam tuam . . .

Pss. 53, 66, 129 between the prayers.

4. ff. 19–35ᵛ Memoriae of nine (formerly ten) saints: John Baptist, John Evangelist, George, Christopher, Anne, Mary Magdalene, Katherine, Barbara, Margaret.

Each memoria takes up one leaf and is preceded by a leaf with a picture. Presumably the missing one, formerly in third place, as the quiring shows, was of Thomas of Canterbury. The first seven and ninth antiphons are *RH*, nos. 26988, 27075, 7242, 18445, 6773, 6895, 6991, and 7002 (Gaude virgo gloriosa margarita preciosa . . .). The eighth is 'Gaude virgo barbara gloriosaque generosa . . .': six 4-line stanzas.

5. ff. 37–74ᵛ Incipiunt hore beate marie uirginis secundum usum sarum. Memoriae after lauds of *Holy Spirit, Holy Trinity, Holy Cross,* SS. *Michael,* John Baptist, *Peter and Paul, Andrew, Stephen, Laurence,* Thomas (of Canterbury: Tu . . . *erased), Nicholas,* Mary Magdalene, Katherine, Margaret, *All Saints* and peace (headed 'De tempore'). Hours of the Cross are worked in. At the end, 'Has horas canonicas cum deuocione . . .'.

6. (*a*) ff. 74ᵛ–75ᵛ Salve regina, followed by the set of six versicles, 'Virgo mater ecclesie . . .' and prayer 'Omnipotens sempiterne deus qui gloriose uirginis . . .'. (*b*) ff. 75ᵛ–77 Ad gloriosam uirginem mariam. Gaude flore uirginali . . . Oremus. Oracio. Dulcissime domine ihesu criste qui . . . (*c*) ff. 77–81 Has uideas laudes . . ., followed by the farcing of Salue regina with Salve virgo virginum.

(*a*). *RH*, nos. 18147, 21818. (*b*). *RH*, no. 6810. (*c*). *RH*, nos. 7687, 18318.

7. ff. 81–83ᵛ Ad virginem mariam. Obsecro te . . . Feminine forms.

8. ff. 83ᵛ–85 Oracio de sancta maria. O intemerata . . . orbis terrarum. Inclina mater . . . Feminine forms.

9. ff. 85–87ᵛ Quicumque hec septem gaudia . . . Uirgo templum trinitatis . . .

RH, no. 21899: the Seven Joys. The heading gives indulgence of 100 days 'a domino papa clemente qui hec septem gaudia proprio stilo composuit'.

10. ff. 88–91 Ad ymaginem xpristi crucifixi. Omnibus consideratis . . . (f. 91) Oremus, Oracio. Omnipotens sempiterne deus qui vnigenitum filium tuum . . .

AH xxxi. 87–9. *RH*, no. 14081 (etc.).

11. ff. 91ᵛ–93ᵛ Oracio venerabilis bede presbiteri de septem verbis . . . sibi preparatam. Domine ihesu criste qui septem verba . . . Oracio. Precor te piissime domine ihesu criste . . .

12. ff. 93ᵛ–95ᵛ (*a*) Salutaciones ad sanctum sacramentum. Aue domine ihesu criste verbum patris . . . (*b*) Oracio. Aue principium nostre creationis . . . (*c*) Ad sanctum sacramentum. Aue verum corpus natum . . . (*d*) Oracio. Aue caro cristi cara . . . (*e*) Oracio. Anima cristi sanctifica me . . . (*f*) Omnibus confessis . . . francie (*this heading erased*). Domine ihesu criste qui hanc sacratissimam carnem . . .

(*b–e*). *RH*, nos. 2059, 2175, 1710, 1090.

13. ff. 97–110ᵛ Incipiunt septem psalmi . . . (f. 103ᵛ) Incipiunt quindecim psalmi . . . (f. 106) litany.

Cues only of the first twelve gradual psalms. In the litany Swithun is spelled Zwichine: Gertrude is among virgins, but not Edith.

14. ff. 112–131ᵛ Office of the dead.

15. ff. 133–144ᵛ Incipiunt commendationes animarum . . . (*Pss. 118, 138*) . . .
Oremus. Oratio. Tibi domine commendo . . . Oremus. Oracio. Misericordiam
tuam domine sancte pater . . .

16. ff. 146–150ᵛ Incipit psalterium de passione domini. Deus deus meus . . .
Oremus. Oracio. Respice quesumus domine super hanc familiam tuam . . .

17. ff. 151–64 Beatus vero iheronimus in hoc modo disposuit psalterium . . .
regnum eternum Amen. Oracio. Suscipere digneris. domine . . . (f. 153) Incipit
psalterium beati iheronimi. Uerba mea auribus percipe . . . Oremus. Oracio.
Omnipotens sempiterne deus clemenciam tuam . . .

The two prayers are for use by a woman. f. 164ᵛ blank.

ff. ii+164+ii. 190×125 mm. Written space 115×72 mm. 21 long lines. Collation:
1⁶ 2⁸ (ff. 8–14, 16) 3⁴ wants 4 (ff. 17, 19, 21) 4⁴ (ff. 23, 25, 27, 29), 5⁴ (ff. 31, 33, 35, 37) 6⁸
(ff. 38–42, 44–6) 7⁸ 8⁸ (ff. 55, 57–9, 61, 62, 64–5) 9⁸ (ff. 67–70, 72–5) 10–11⁸ 12⁴ (ff. 92–5)
13⁸ 14⁸ (ff. 105–10, 112–13) 15–16⁸ 17⁸ (ff. 130–1, 133–8) 18⁸ (ff. 139–44, 146–7) 19⁸
(ff. 148–50, 152–6) 20⁸, together with twenty-three inserted leaves with blank rectos and
full-page pictures on the versos. The twenty-three pictures are: one before art. 2 (Christ
stands holding orb, blessing); one before art. 3 (Trinity); nine in art. 4; seven in art. 5 (a
passion series), and one before each of arts. 13–17 (13, Christ on the rainbow: bodies
rising: B.V.M. and St. John kneel; 14, raising of Lazarus; 15, angels carry two haloed
figures in a sheet; 16, instruments of the Passion; Christ stands in the tomb; 17, St.
Jerome). One picture is missing in art. 4 (see above) and one, before vespers, in art. 5.
Nineteen smaller pictures, eight illustrating the memoriae in art. 5, as shown by italics,
nine in art. 10 (three crosses; Holy Face; each of the Five Wounds; B.V.M., Child, and
angel; John Evangelist), one before art. 6c (B.V.M. and Child in glory), and one before
art. 9 (B.V.M. kneels before a church: Joachim and Anne: priest).¹

Initials: (i) historiated, to art. 7, 10 (Adam and Eve and the serpent), 11 (B.V.M., St. John,
and the crucified Christ); (ii) facing the full-page pictures, 6-line, in colours patterned in
white on decorated gold grounds; (iii) 2-line, gold on red and blue grounds patterned in
white; (iv) 1-line, gold with blue-grey ornament, or blue with red ornament. Line fillers
in the litany only: blue or gold. Capital letters in the ink of the text filled with pale yellow.
Binding of s. xvii, rebacked: a rayed IHS centrepiece. Secundo folio (f. 9) *ne in capite*.

Written for the use of a woman (arts. 3, 7, 8, 17), perhaps in England, but if so, copied
from one of the many Sarum hours produced in Flanders for the English market. In a
Sotheby sale, s. xx: the relevant cutting from the catalogue is inside the cover. Given as
MS. 300.

304. *Horae*   s. xv/xvi

1. ff. 1–12ᵛ Calendar in French in gold, blue, and red, the two colours alternating
for effect.

In gold: Gervais, Eloy, Marcial, Denis, Rommain (19, 25 June, 3 July, 9, 23 Oct.).

2. ff. 14ᵛ–17ᵛ Sequentiae of the Gospels.

Prayer, 'Protector in (te) sperantium . . .', after John.

¹ Cf. M. R. James's description of the large and small pictures in a closely similar book
of hours, Fitzwilliam Museum, Cambridge, MS. 54, which has twenty large pictures now,
but probably had twenty-five originally.

3. ff. 17^v–19^v Oratio de beata maria virgine. Obsecro te . . . Masculine forms.

4. ff. 19^v–21^v Oratio de beata maria. O intemerata . . . orbis terrarum. De te enim . . . (*ends imperfectly*). Masculine forms.

5. ff. 23^v–60 Hours of B.V.M. of the use of (Rouen). Memoriae of Holy Spirit, Nicholas, Michael, John Baptist, and Katherine after lauds.

6. f. 60^{rv} Memoria of Margaret.

7. ff. 60^v–64 Hours of Holy Cross. Patris sapientia . . .

8. ff. 64–8 Hours of Holy Spirit. Nobis sancti . . .

9. ff. 68–81^v Penitential psalms and litany.

The list of apostles ends with Martial, all apostles and evangelists, Ursinus, 'Omnes sancti discipuli domini'. Confessors: . . . (8–12) mellone gildarde et medarde romane audoene euode. . . . Virgins: . . . (9–11) katherina austreberta columba.

10. ff. 81^v–101 Incipit officium mortuorum.

11. ff. 101–108^v Les quinze ioyes nostre dame. Et les Sept requestes de nostre seigneur. (*a*) Doulce dame de misericorde . . . (*b*) f. 106^v Doulx dieu doulx pere . . . Sonet, nos. 458, 504. f. 109^{rv} blank.

12. ff. 111^v–113 Three memoriae of Mary Magdalene: (*a*) O Magdalena nobilis Insignita miraculis . . .; (*b*) O mundi lampas . . .; (*c*) Gaude pia magdalena spes salutis . . .

(*a*). Six couplets. (*c*). *RH*, no. 6895.

13. ff. 113–114^v Memoria of Claude.

ff. ii+99+ii, together with fourteen blank leaves put in by the binder before picture pages (ff. 13, 22, 30, 39, 42, 47, 50, 53, 61, 65, 69, 82, 102, 110). 185 × 130 mm. Written space 105 × 62 mm. 22 long lines. Collation, excluding insertions: 1^{12} 2^8 3^8 wants 1 before f. 23 4–11^8 12–13^4. Written in set non-current hybrida: cf. MS. 306.[1] Sixteen full-page pictures, all but one on rectos, set in gold-paint frames, with saints in niches on the sides: 8 in art. 5, 2 before art. 9 (f. 68^v, David and Bathsheba; f. 70, David in prayer and Nathan standing), and 1 before each of arts. 7, 8, 10 (Job), 11 (B.V.M., Child, and 4 angels), 12 (assumption of Mary Magdalene, supported by angels). A 12-line picture before art. 13. For the pictures in art. 1, see below. Initials: (i, ii) 3-line and 2-line, red, blue, and white on decorated grounds of gold paint; (iii) 1-line, gold paint on grounds of blue or red decorated with gold paint. Capital letters in the ink of the text touched with pale yellow. Framed floral borders on grounds of gold paint, strewn with black dots, dashes, and roundels, and including monkeys, birds, etc.: they lie all round f. 1 and on three sides of ff. 1^v–12^v, where they include the occupations of the month on rectos and the signs of the zodiac on versos of the lower border, and in the outer margin of all other pages, the height of the written space. Line fillers blue or red decorated in gold paint, strewn as in the borders. Binding of s. xix by F. Bedford. Secundo folio (f. 15) *eum non.*

Written in France (Rouen?). 'Ex musæo Huthii' label inside the cover. Huth sale, 2 June 1913, lot 3805 to Maggs (£230). Later in the same sale as MS. 306, q.v. Given as MS. 300.

[1] In both manuscripts initial *t* is distinguished from medial and final *t* by a short projecting horn stroke at the base of the upright.

305. *Horae* s. xv²

No. 21 in *Trésors*, with enlarged facsimile of f. 60ᵛ.

1. ff. 1–12ᵛ Calendar, not very full, in red and black.

In red, Amandus, Boniface, Basil, Remigius and Bavo, Donatian, Nichasius (6 Feb.; 5, 14 June; 1, 14 Oct.; 14 Dec.); in black, octave of Thomas (of Canterbury), David, translation of Thomas (of Canterbury) (5 Jan., 1 Mar., 7 July).

2. f. 14ʳᵛ Ad salutandum faciem ihesu xpristi. Salue sancta facies . . . Memoria of Holy Face, *RH*, no. 18189.

3. ff. 15–19 Hours of Holy Cross (Patris sapientia . . .). f. 19ᵛ blank.

4. ff. 21–24ᵛ Hours of Holy Spirit (Nobis sancti spiritus . . .).

5. ff. 26–29ᵛ Missa beate marie virginis.

6. ff. 30–33ᵛ Sequentiae of the Gospels.

7. ff. 35–85ᵛ Incipiunt hore beate marie virginis secundum vsum romanum.

Salve Regina after compline, f. 78ᵛ. The special office for Advent begins on f. 80. f. 47ᵛ blank.

8. ff. 86–88ᵛ Deuota oracio ad mariam virginem. Obsecro te . . . Masculine forms.

9. ff. 88ᵛ–90 Alia oracio ad mariam virginem. O intemerata . . . orbis terrarum. Inclina mater . . . Masculine forms. f. 90ᵛ blank.

10. ff. 91–104 Incipiunt septem psalmi penitenciales. Litany, f. 98ᵛ. f. 104ᵛ blank.

11. ff. 106–130ᵛ, 132–135ᵛ Office of the dead.

12. ff. 135ᵛ–139ᵛ, 131ʳᵛ, 140ʳᵛ Memoriae of twelve saints: John Baptist, Peter, James, Sebastian (O quam mira refulsit . . .: *RH*, no. 30904), Christopher (O martir cristofore . . .: *RH*, no. 29471), Nicholas, Anthony (hermit), Francis (Salue sancte pater patrie . . .: *RH*, no. 40727), Anne, Mary Magdalene, Katherine, Barbara (O pulcra precipuum . . .: *RH*, no. 30857). f. 141ʳᵛ blank.

ff. iii+141+v. 200×140 mm. Written space 110×72 mm. 20 long lines. Ruling in red ink. Collation: 1–2⁶ 3–9⁸ 10⁴ (ff. 76–9) 11⁸+2 leaves after 8 (ff. 89, 90) 12–16⁸ 17⁶ (ff. 133–8) 18 four (ff. 139, 131, 140–1), together with nine singleton leaves with blank rectos and pictures on the versos, ff. 13, 20, 25, 34, 48, 60, 67, 80, 105. Written in set cursiva. Nine full-page pictures: five (originally nine?) in art. 7, before matins, lauds, terce, none, and the advent office (Coronation of B.V.M.); one before each of arts. 2 (Christ holding orb and blessing), 4, 5 (B.V.M. and Child and four angels playing music), 11 (burial service: a cripple in the foreground receives alms). Initials: (i) 8-line, gold, patterned in white, historiated; f. 86, B.V.M., St. John and a haloed male figure hold the dead Christ; f. 88ᵛ, B.V.M. and Child in glory; beginning each memoria of art. 12; (ii), as (i), but 7-line and on decorated gold grounds, not historiated; (iii, iv) 3-line and 2-line, gold on red and blue grounds patterned in white; (v) 1-line, blue with red ornament or gold with slate-grey ornament. Line-fillers in litany only: blue and gold. Capital letters in the ink of the text filled with pale yellow. Continuous framed floral borders, with figures, animals, and grotesques in them, on the nine main double openings now left and on ff. 15, 57, 64, 71, 76, 91 which once had pictures facing them, no doubt. Similar borders at head and foot of pages with initials of type (i). English binding, s. xix in. Secundo folio (f. 15) *Incipiunt*.

Written in the southern Netherlands. The border in the lower margin of f. 13ᵛ contains arms: per pale (1) or a chevron gules with five fleur-de-lis argent between three cockatoos vert, (2) azure a turretted mansion or. The owner in s. xix in. was English and recorded the number—the present number—of leaves of 'Miniatures' and of 'Blooming letters' (that is the type (ii) initials) in gothic script on f. iiiᵛ.[1] Lot 3809 in the Huth sale, 2 June 1913, to Tregaskis (£200). The relevant cuttings from a later sale catalogue and bookseller's catalogue (item 80 at £350) are attached to ff. i, ii. Given as MS. 300.

306. *Horae*   s. xv/xvi

1. ff. 1–12ᵛ Full calendar in French in gold, blue, and red, the two colours alternating for effect.

The saints in gold in MS. 304 are in gold here, except 'eloy'.

2. ff. 13–16ᵛ Sequentiae of the Gospels.

Prayer, 'Protector in te sperantium . . .', after John.

3. ff. 16ᵛ–18ᵛ Oraison a nostre dame. Obsecro te . . . Masculine forms.

4. ff. 18ᵛ–21 Aultre oraison a nostre dame. O intemerata . . . orbis terrarum. De te enim . . . Masculine forms.

5 (added, s. xvi in.). f. 22 Memore de la transfiguration nostre seigneur. *antifona*. [C]hristus splendor patris . . . f. 22ᵛ blank.

6. ff. 23ᵛ–47 Hours of B.V.M. of the use of (Rouen).

Leaves, probably four, missing after f. 40 contained sext, most of terce, and the first words of none. Memoriae of Holy Spirit, Nicholas, Katherine, and Margaret after lauds.

7. ff. 47–49ᵛ Hours of Holy Cross. Patris sapientia . . .

8. ff. 49ᵛ–52 Hours of Holy Spirit. Nobis sancti . . . f. 52ᵛ blank.

9. ff. 53–64 Penitential psalms and litany.

Apostles: . . . (17) marcialis. Confessors: . . . (8–12) mellone gildarde et medarde romane audoene ansberte . . . Virgins: . . . (9–11) Katherina austreberta honorina . . .

10. ff. 64–82ᵛ Office of the dead. f. 64ᵛ blank.

11. ff. 82ᵛ–86ᵛ Les quinze ioyes nostre dame. Doulce dame de misericorde . . . Sonet, no. 458.

12. ff. 86ᵛ–89 Les sept requestes a nostre seigneur. Doulz dieu doulz pere . . . Sonet, no. 504.

13. f. 89 Saincte vraye crois adoree . . . Sonet, no. 1876. f. 89ᵛ blank.

ff. iii+89+iii. 185 × 125 mm. Written space 105 × 62 mm. 23 long lines. Collation: 1¹² 2⁸ 3² (ff. 21, 22 inserted in s. xvi in.) 4–5⁸ 6⁸ wants 3–6 after f. 40 7⁸ 8² (ff. 51, 52)

[1] Dr. Munby suggested to me that John Trotter Brockett might have made this note.

9–12⁸ 13⁶ wants 6, blank. Script as MS. 304, but less good. A full-page picture before art. 6 (f. 23: Annunciation and in the margins, four small scenes and single figures: Adam and Eve and the serpent above B.V.M.'s canopy) and before the added art. 5 (f. 21ᵛ). Ten 20-line pictures, some rectangular and some arched, five in art. 6 (at prime, f. 37, God appears to Abraham in the lower margin; at terce, f. 40ᵛ, the shepherds have a woman with them) and one before each of arts. 2 (St. John and, in the border at the foot, SS. Luke, Matthew, and Mark, each in a compartment) 7, 8, 9 (David and Nathan: in the border at the foot, David and Goliath), 10 (the three living and the three dead: in the border at the foot, Death's arrow pierces a man). Initials, borders, and line fillers as in MS. 304, but less good: in plan the only differences are that some picture pages here have continuous borders, the pictures themselves being smaller, and that the occupations of the months and signs of the zodiac in art. 1 are in side borders. Capital letters filled as in MS. 304. Binding of s. xix: according to the Huth sale catalogue it is by Bedford. Secundo folio (f. 14) *Qui non.*

Written in France (Rouen?). 'Ex musæo Huthii' label inside the cover. Huth sale, 2 June 1913, lot 3811, to Tregaskis (£170). Lot 336 in the same sale as MS. 304. Given as MS. 300.

307. *Horae*   s. xv med.

1. ff. 1–12ᵛ Full calendar in French in gold, blue, and red, the two colours alternating for effect.

In gold: Remy Hylaire, Anthoine, Sauinian, Helene, Mastie, Loup (13, 17, 24 Jan., 4, 7 May, 29 July).

2. ff. 13–18 Sequentiae of the Gospels.

Prayer, 'Protector in te sperantium . . .', after John.

3. ff. 18ᵛ–21ᵛ Alia oracio. Obsecro te . . . Masculine forms.

4. ff. 21ᵛ–25ᵛ Alia Oratio. O intemerata . . . orbis terrarum. De te enim . . . Masculine forms. f. 25ᵛ blank.

5. ff. 26–28ᵛ Hours of Holy Cross. Patris sapientia . . .

6. ff. 29–31ᵛ Hours of Holy Spirit. Nobis sancti . . .

7. ff. 31ᵛ–76 Incipiunt hore beate marie uirginis secundum vsum trecensem.

8. ff. 76–80 Memoriae of SS. Michael, Laurence, Sebastian (O quam mirra (*sic*) . . .: *RH*, no. 30904), Nicholas, Barbara (Gaude barbara beata summo polens . . .: *RH*, no. 6711), Apollonia, Anthony hermit.

9. ff. 80–81ᵛ Deuote contemplacion. Stabat mater . . . Oratio. Interueniat pro nobis quesumus . . .

10. ff. 82–96ᵛ Penitential psalms and litany.

Twelve martyrs: (1–3) lazare stephane benigne . . . Eleven confessors: . . . (5–11) iuliane emonde lupe remigi medarde claudi huberte. Fifteen virgins: . . . (7–9) radegundis iuliana martha . . .

11. ff. 97–135 Office of the dead.

The ninth lesson is Audiui vocem (Apocalypse 14: 13). f. 135ᵛ blank.

ff. iii+135+iii. 188×135 mm. Written space 95×72 mm. 16 long lines. Ruled in red ink. Collation: 1–2⁶ 3⁶+1 leaf before 1 (f. 13) 4–10⁸ 11⁶ (ff. 76–81) 12⁶+1 leaf before 1 (f. 82) 13–17⁸ 18⁸ wants 8, blank. The singleton, f. 13, is not in the main hand. Thirteen 13-line pictures, 8 in art. 7 (Innocents at vespers) and 1 before each of 2, 5, 6, 10 (Christ seated in judgement: bodies rising), 11 (Job). Five 8-line pictures, 3 in art. 2, 1 before art. 3 (B.V.M. holds the dead Christ), 4 (B.V.M. and Child). An historiated 4-line initial begins art. 9 (B.V.M.). Other initials: (i, ii) 3-line and 2-line, blue patterned in white on gold grounds decorated in colours; (iii) 1-line, gold on blue and red grounds patterned in white. Line-fillers blue and red patterned in white and picked out with gold roundels. Capital letters in the ink of the text filled with pale yellow. A framed floral border, the ground partly of gold paint, lies round each picture page. A similar border, usually without gold paint as ground, in the outer margin of all other pages, except 25ᵛ (but including 135ᵛ): it is separated from the written space by a narrow border of oak leaves or flowers on a gold ground. English binding, s. xix. Secundo folio (f. 14) *beret de lumine.*

Written in France for use in the diocese of Troyes. Belonged to Sir John Trelawny in 1868 and lent then by him to the National Exhibition of Works of Art at Leeds (label on f. 1). Trelawny library book-plate inside cover. In a Sotheby sale, s. xx: the relevant slip from the catalogue is pasted to f. i. Given as MS. 300.

308. *Horae*   s. xv¹

No. 16 in *Trésors*, with facsimile of ff. 50ᵛ–51.

1. ff. 1–6ᵛ Calendar in red and black.

No erasure of St. Thomas of Canterbury or of 'pape'.

2. ff. 8–46 Hours of B.V.M. of the use of (Sarum).

The memoriae after lauds are of Holy Spirit, Holy Trinity, Holy Cross, SS. Michael, John Baptist, Peter, John Evangelist, Laurence, Stephen, Thomas of Canterbury (*untouched*), Nicholas, Katherine (Aue gemma claritatis . . .: *RH*, no. 1808), Margaret, All Saints, and for peace. Hours of the Cross are worked in. A piece of paper attached to f. 41ᵛ contains an alternative form of the antiphon at vespers of Holy Cross, 'De cruce depositum hora vesperarum mater cum aspiceret . . .'.

3. ff. 46–7 Salve regina, followed by the verses 'Virgo mater ecclesie . . .' and the prayer 'Omnipotens sempiterne deus qui gloriose uirginis . . .'.

RH, nos. 18147, 21818. ff. 47ᵛ–49ᵛ blank.

4. ff. 51–66 Hic incipiunt septem psalmos (*sic*) penitenciales . . ., (f. 58) Incipiunt xv psalmi . . ., (f. 59ᵛ) litany.

Cues only of the first twelve of the gradual psalms.

5. ff. 67–96 Office of the dead.

6. ff. 97–108ᵛ Hic incipiunt commendaciones animarum. Beati immaculati . . . Pss. 118, 138.

7. ff. 110–19 Hic incipiunt psalmi de passione domini nostri ihesu xpisti. Deus deus meus . . .

8. ff. 120–122ᵛ Oracio deuota ad sanctam trinitatem. Domine deus omnipotens pater et filius et spiritus sanctus da michi N. famulo tuo uictoriam . . . Oracio. Libera me domine fili dei uiui . . .

Pss. 53, 66, 129 between the prayers.

9. Prayers to B.V.M.: (*a*) f. 124^{rv} Oracio ad beatam uirginem mariam. O maria piissima stella maria (*sic*) clarissima . . .; (*b*) f. 124^v Item ad mariam. Oracio. Commendo tibi sancta maria . . . extremum diem . . .; (*c*) ff. 124^v–125 Item ad mariam Oracio. Per tuum uirgo filium. per patrem per paraclitum . . .; (*d*) f. 125 Item ad mariam Oracio. Succurre michi uirgo maria intercessionibus tuis apud dominum . . . et saluum me faciat N. famulum tuum . . .

(*a*). *RH*, no. 13213. (*c*). 10 lines.

10. ff. 125^v–127 Three memoriae of Holy Cross, the third (*c*) 'O Crux salue preciosa o crux salue gloriosa . . .'.

(*c*) is *RH*, no. 30332, referring to M. R. James's catalogue of the Fitzwilliam collection in Cambridge, where (p. 139) three stanzas and part of a fourth are printed from the page of MS. 55 on which the Rood of Bromholm is depicted. Here there are four 5-line stanzas.

11. f. 127^{rv} Item de eodem Oracio. Domine ihesu criste fili dei uiui spes mea misericordia mea . . .

12. ff. 127^v–129 Oracio deuota. Concede michi queso misericors deus que tibi placita sunt . . .

13. ff. 129–30 Oracio deuota ad nomen ihesu. O bone ihesu. O piissime ihesu. O dulcissime ihesu. O ihesu fili marie uirginis . . .

Cf. H. E. Allen, *Writings ascribed to Richard Rolle*, 1927, p. 314. ff. 130^v–132^v blank.

ff. iii+132+ii. f. (134) was pasted down. 165 × 110 mm. Written space 87 × 58 mm. 18 long lines. Collation: 1^6 2–16^8, together with six singleton leaves with blank rectos and pictures on the versos (7, 36, 39, 42, 109, 123). Fourteen full-page pictures on versos, eight in art. 2 and 1 before each of arts. 4–9 (6, God the Father raises a nude figure in a sheet; 7, Christ stands in the tomb; 8, the Trinity, Christ crucified; 9, B.V.M., crowned, and Child). Art. 2 has a passion series from lauds to compline: lauds, the Agony in the garden; prime, Betrayal; terce, before Pilate (the usual terce scene, the Scourging, is omitted); after this, normal. The first picture of art. 2 and the pictures before arts. 8, 9 have captions (instructions for the illuminator?) lightly written at the foot of the page in English: 'the salutacion'; 'the trinite'; 'a image of oure ladey'. Other picture-pages have Latin words in this position, for example 'In conuertendo' (compline), 'Domine ne in f' (art. 4), 'Beati immaculati' (art. 5).

Initials: (i) 5-line, shaded pink and blue on gold grounds, decorated in colours, including green, the decoration forming a complete or (ff. 110, 120, 124) partial border; (ii) 2-line, gold on red and blue grounds patterned in white, with sprays of green and gold into the margins; (iii) 1-line, gold with grey-green ornament or blue with red ornament. Blue and gold line fillers in art. 4 only. Binding of wooden boards covered with pink leather, s. xv: five bands: two strap-and-pin fastenings, the straps missing. Secundo folio (f. 9) *opera mea*.

Written in England. On ff. ii^v–iii and again on iii^v is an entry recording the birth, 16 Sept. 1553, 'about vii of the clocke at afternoone' of Francis Palmis 'at Lindeleye in the countie of Yorke in the parishe of Otleye', son of Margaret Palmis and her husband Francis 'of the same Towen and parishe esquire. Teste Gualterus Corbett vnius susceptorum predicti Frauncisci Palmis' and roundels showing that Francis and Isabel Palmis were the children of Francis Palmis and his wife Margaret, sister of Sir Andrew Corbett Kt. of Morton Corbett, Shropshire. 'John [. . . . . . .] July the 27th 1772. This Book was given to him by his Aunt Ursula [. . . . . .] of Mansfield in Nottinghamshire, July 29th 1771', f. ii. A slip from a Sotheby sale catalogue, s. xx, is attached to f. i.

309. *Horae*   s. xv ex.

A *de luxe* book of hours.

1. ff. 1–6ᵛ Full calendar in French in gold, blue, and red, the two colours alternating for effect.

In gold: Loys, Leu Gille, Denis (25 Aug., 1 Sept., 9 Oct.).

2. ff. 7–10ᵛ Sequentiae of the Gospels.

Prayer, 'Protector in te sperancium . . .', after John.

3. ff. 11–13ᵛ Obsecro te . . . Masculine forms.

4. ff. 13ᵛ–15 O intemerata . . . orbis terrarum. Inclina . . .

5. (*a*) f. 15ʳᵛ Oraison deuote a dire au matin quant on se lieue. In manus tuas domine . . . (*b–k*) ff. 15ᵛ–18 Prayers on setting out for church (Vias tuas domine . . .), on passing a cemetery, on entering church, on taking holy water, before the crucifix, before the image of B.V.M. (. . . Gaude virgo mater cristi . . .: *RH*, no. 7017), on sitting down in church, on going to communion, when the priest turns, on adoring the body of Christ (Corpus domini nostri ihesu cristi nazereni . . . . Aue salus mundi verbum patris. . . . Aue verum corpus natum (*RH*, no. 2175)). Cf. art. 27.

6. f. 18ʳᵛ Oroison a nostreseigneur. O bone ihesu per tuam piissimam misericordiam esto michi ihesus . . .

7. ff. 18ᵛ–20 De nostredame. Stabat mater . . . Oratio. Interueniat pro nobis . . . f. 20ᵛ blank.

8. ff. 21–3 Dulcissime domine ihesu criste verus deus. qui de sinu patris . . . Cf. Leroquais, i. 163.

9. ff. 23–24ᵛ Sensuit Oroison moult deuote contre toute mortalite. maladie. mort subite tempeste famine. guerre et contre tous ses ennemis. Recordare domine testamenti tui sancti . . . Oremus. Omnipotens sempiterne deus factor celi et terre . . .

10. ff. 24ᵛ–28ᵛ Sancta maria dei genitrix piissima per amorem . . .

11. ff. 29–31 En nom du pere. et du filz. et du saint esperit. sensuit le liure de Ihesus. Et premierement (*a*) la sai[n]cte oroyson quil a fait. Nostre pere qui es ez cieulx . . . (*b*) La Salutation angelique. Ie te salue marie . . . (*c*) Le credo. ou sont douze articles de la foy. Saint pietre. Ie croy en dieu . . . (*d*) Sensuiuent les dix commendemens de la loy. Vng seul dieu tu adoreras . . . (*e*) Les cinq commandemens de saincte eglise. Les dimenches messe orras . . . (*f*) Qui habet mandata mea . . . (*g*) Tout ainsi que descent en la Fleur la Rousee . . .

(*a–e*). Sonet, nos. 1252, 881, 794, 2287, 1060.

12. ff. 31–32ᵛ Memoriae: (*a*) Deuote salutation a nostredame. Aue cuius conceptio . . . (*RH*, no. 1744); (*b*, *c*) of Augustine and Nicholas of Tollentino.

13. ff. 32ᵛ–33ᵛ Passio domini nostri ihesu cristi secundum Iohannem. In illo

tempore. Apprehendit . . . testimonium eius Deo gratias. Oremus. Oratio. Respice quesumus domine super hanc familiam tuam . . .

The catena mainly from John 19: 1–35. Printed in *Horae Ebor.*, p. 123, but with a different prayer following it: cf. *Lyell Cat.*, pp. 65–6.

14. (added, s. xv/xvi). f. 33ᵛ Pape boniface a donne a tous ceulx . . . Domine ihesu xpriste qui hanc sacratissimam carnem . . .

The heading conveys an indulgence of 2,000 years. ff. 34–36ᵛ blank.

15. ff. 37–94 Hours of B.V.M. of the use of (Rome), with hours of Holy Cross and Holy Spirit worked in and Salve regina after compline of Holy Spirit (f. 89). The Advent office begins on f. 89ᵛ. f. 94ᵛ blank.

16. ff. 95–106ᵛ Penitential psalms and litany.

Ten confessors: . . . (8–10) ludouice francisce dominice. Eleven virgins: . . . (9) genouefa . . .

17. ff. 107–137ᵛ Office of the dead.

18. ff. 137ᵛ–138ᵛ En passant par le cymitiere. deuez dire. A'. Auete omnes anime fideles . . . Oremus. Oratio. Domine ihesu criste salus et liberatio . . .

Leroquais, ii. 341.

19. Texts in French: (*a*) ff. 138ᵛ–140 Protestation. Mon treschier seigneur ihesu crist voyez cy la foy . . .; (*b*) f. 140ʳᵛ Protestacion. Sire dieu tout puissant tout voyant . . .; (*c*) ff. 140ᵛ–142ᵛ Cy comment (*sic*) les trois verites salutaires. Vray est que dieu nostre bon pere . . .; (*d*) ff. 142ᵛ–143ᵛ Deuote oroyson a la vierge marie. Ie vous remercie tres glorieuse vierge marie mere de dieu des tresgrans graces et aydes . . .

(*b*). Sonet, no. 2007. Printed by Leroquais, ii. 339. (*c*). Sonet, no. 2372. Leroquais, ii. 28.

20. ff. 143ᵛ–158 Memoriae of: (1) Holy Trinity; (2) *Michael*; (3) John Baptist; (4–9) John Evangelist, Peter and Paul, James, Andrew, Bartholomew, all apostles; (10–17) Innocents, Stephen, Laurence, *Christopher*, *Sebastian* (Ant'. O quam mira . . .), Denis, Cosmas and Damianus, all martyrs; (18–26) Martin, *Nicholas*, Anthony (hermit), *Francis*, De Saint francois. de Saint Loys et de Saincte Claire. Salue sancta progenies. Francisci patris minorum . . ., Anthony of Padua (Gaude quondam seculi . . .), Maur, Fiacre (Ant'. Gaude parens ymbernia . . .), confessors; (27–31) SS. Mary Magdalene, Katherine, Margaret, Genovefa, (31) Barbara. Ant'. Virgo fide sana de stirpe creata prophana . . .; (32) Des v sains a qui dieu a donne grace especiale. Dyonisi radius grecie . . .; (33) Oraison des cinq sainctes a qui dieu a donne grace especiale. Katherina tyrannum superans . . .; (34) All Saints.

(14) *RH*, no. 30904. (22) Not in *RH*. (23) *RH*, no. 6923. (25) Not in *RH*. (31) *RH*, no. 34601. (32) Denis, George, Christopher, Blaise, Giles. *RH*, no. 4707. (33) Katherine, Margaret, Martha, Christina, Barbara. *RH*, no. 2691. f. 158ᵛ blank.

21. ff. 159ᵛ–177 Sensuiuent les comendaces. Subuenite sancti dei . . .

22. ff. 177–8 Sensuiuent les sept vers Saint Bernard. Illumina . . . Oremus. Oratio. Omnipotens sempiterne deus qui ezechie regi . . . f. 168ᵛ blank.

23. ff. 179ᵛ–185ᵛ Passio domini nostri ihesu cristi secundum Iohannem. In illo tempore. Egressus est ihesus . . . monumentum posuerunt ihesum (John 18–19).

24. ff. 185ᵛ–186 Deus qui uoluisti pro redemptione mundi . . .

25. f. 186ʳᵛ De Reliquiis palacii. Ant. Cruci corone spinee . . .
Memoria of three Instruments of the Passion. *RH*, no. 3986.

26. ff. 188–191ᵛ Hore de conceptione beate marie.
The hymns are printed in *AH* xxx. 94–5.

27. ff. 192–4 Prayers at mass: (*a*) Quant le presbitre monstre le corps nostre-seigneur. Aue salus mundi verbum patris . . .; (*b*) Autre oroison. Aue verum corpus natum . . .; (*c*) Entre le leuacion et le communion. oratio. In manus tuas domine commendo . . .; (*d*) Deus pius et propicius agnus . . .; (*e*) Salutacion au corps nostres'. Aue preciosissimum et sanctissimum corpus . . .; (*f*) Dittes deuotement quant vous vouldrez confesser. Per angelorum sanctorum omnium . . .; (*g*) Quant vouldrez receuoir nostres'. Domine ihesu criste. fili dei viui. te supplex queso . . .; (*h*) Apres ce que on a Receu nostres'. Vera perceptio corporis et sanguinis tui domine . . .

(*a*, *b*). *RH*, no. 2175. (*d*, *f*, *g*, *h*). Cf. Leroquais, i. 158, 151, 156, 174. (*e*). Printed by Leroquais, ii. 341.

28. ff. 194ᵛ–195ᵛ Memoriae of SS. Mathurin, Apollonia, and Avia.

29 (a contemporary addition). (*a*) ff. 196–7 Oroison tresdeuote quant on veult recepuoir nostre seigneur. Tout puissant et misericor dieux seigneur voyci ie viens . . . (*b*) f. 197ʳᵛ Oraison de nostre dame. Sancta et immaculata uirginitas . . . (*c*) ff. 197ᵛ–198 Prosa. Beata es uirgo et gloriosa . . . (*d*) ff. 198–9 Oraison de saint gregoire. O domine ihesu criste adoro te . . . (*e*) ff. 199–201 Memoriae of SS. Claude, Lazarus, and Martha. (*f*) f. 201ʳᵛ Oroison a nostre seigneur. Benedictio dei patris cum angelis suis sit super me amen . . . (*g*) ff. 201ᵛ–202ᵛ Six prayers: (1) Contre la tempeste. A domo tua quesumus . . .; (2) Pour impetrer grace de ses peches. Exaudi quesumus domine supplicum . . .; (3) Pour quelque tribulacion. Ineffabilem misericordiam tuam . . .; (4) Pour ceulx qui vont en voyaige. Adesto domine supplicationibus . . .; (5) Pour nos bienfaicteurs. Pretende domine famulis et famulabus . . .; (6) Pour ses amys qui sont en necessite. Omnipotens sempiterne deus salus eterna credencium . . .

(*a*). Sonet, no. 2115. (*c*). *RH*, no. 2330. (*d*). The Seven Oes of St. Gregory. (*g*). 1–4, 6 are collects of votive masses in *Missale Romanum*: i. 472, 467, 468, 461, 462, and 5 occurs there, ii. 308.

ff. i+203+iii. Parchment of fine quality. 140×96 mm. Written space 85×45 mm. 25 long lines. Collation: 1⁶ 2⁸ 3⁶ (ff. 15–20) 4–11⁸ 12⁸+2 leaves after 8 (ff. 93, 94) 13–22⁸ 23⁴ (ff. 175–8) 24⁸ 25⁸+1 leaf before 1 (f. 187) 26⁸. Written in *lettre bâtarde*. Three full-page pictures: f. 159, Christ on the rainbow: bodies rising: the heavenly congregation, among them Justice with sword and scales; f. 179, Christ carrying the Cross; f. 187ᵛ (a singleton, the recto blank) Joachim and Anne kiss before the Golden Gate and in three smaller compartments, Joachim and the angel, offering of kid, Anne and the Angel.

Twelve 21-line pictures, ten in art. 15 (Innocents at vespers), one before art. 16 (raising of Lazarus) and one before art. 17 (Job). Fifteen 10-line pictures, five in art. 20, as shown by italics, four in art. 2, three in art. 29e, and one before each of arts. 3 (B.V.M. crowned, Child and angels), 4 (B.V.M. and St. John), and 7. Five figures in the margins: David, f. 97; James, f. 145; Andrew, f. 145ᵛ; Katherine, f. 157; Barbara, f. 157ᵛ. Art. 1 has the occupation of the month in the side margin of each page and the sign of the zodiac at the foot of each page.

Initials: (i) 3-line or 4-line, gold-paint or white or blue on decorated grounds of colour or gold paint; (ii) as (i), but 2-line; (iii) 1-line, gold paint on red grounds. Gold and red line fillers. Capital letters in the ink of the text filled with pale yellow. Headings in blue. Framed floral borders all round or on three sides of picture pages and the height of the written space in the outer margins of pages of art. 1 and of pages with initials of type (i): the grounds are wholly or partly of gold paint: in them, animals, birds, and insects. French brown calf binding, probably of 1560–80.¹ Secundo folio (f. 8) *Oremus*.

Written in France (Paris?). Armorial book-plate of Edward Southwell Trafford, s. xix, inside the cover. Sale at Sotheby's, 19 June 1914, lot 137: plates in the catalogue show the binding and ff. 95, 187ᵛ.

310. *Horae*   s. xv¹

1. ff. 1–12ᵛ Full calendar in French in gold and blue, which alternate for effect.

2. ff. 13–18 Sequentiae of the Gospels.

No prayer after John.

3. ff. 18–21ᵛ De nostra domina oratio. Obsecro te . . . Feminine forms.

4. ff. 21ᵛ–25ᵛ Alia oratio. O intemerata . . . orbis terrarum. De te enim . . . Feminine forms.

5. ff. 25ᵛ–26ᵛ Passio domini nostri ihesu xpisti secundum iohannem. In illo tempore. Apprehendit pylatus . . . testimonium eius. Deo gracias.

6. ff. 27–93 Hours of B.V.M. of the use of (Paris). f. 93ᵛ blank.

7. ff. 94–112ᵛ Penitential psalms and litany.

Maturinus is first of fourteen confessors.

8. ff. 112ᵛ–120 Hore de cruce . . . Patris sapientia . . .

9. ff. 120–125ᵛ Hore de sancto spiritu . . . Nobis sancti . . .

10. ff. 125ᵛ–173 Office of the dead.

11. ff. 173ᵛ–179 Doulce dame de misericorde . . . .

The Fifteen Joys. Sonet, no. 458.

12. ff. 179–183ᵛ Les cinq plaies nostreseigneur. Quiconques ueult estre bien conseillie . . . Doulx dieu doulx pere saincte trinite . . .

The Seven Requests. Sonet, no. 504.

¹ I owe the date to Mr. Giles Barber.

13. A quotation from St. Bernard 'super missus homelia iiii^ta' is on f. ii^v, s. xv/ xvi.

ff. ii+183+ii. The flyleaves are parchment from an older binding. 187×135 mm. Written space 90×60 mm. 15 long lines. Collation: 1^12 2–10^8 11^8+1 leaf after 8 (f. 93) 12–22^8 23^2. Fourteen pictures by an artist delighting in movement, eight in art. 6 and one before each of arts. 7–12 (11, B.V.M. and Child attended by angels; 12, Christ on the rainbow: bodies rising). Initials and line fillers as in MS. 302. Floral borders, including figures, on three sides of picture pages and, without figures, on three sides, not the inner margin, of all other pages, including the blank page, 93^v. Rebound in 1958 by D. Cockerell and Son: the former binding was 'red velvet over millboards'. Secundo folio (f. 14) *ex sanguinibus*.

Written in France (Paris?). 'The Gift of the Revd Edward Thorold', f. i^v, s. xviii, below a pressmark (Syston Park?) '1 Cab. T (?). 5. B. 6'. 'Syston Park' book-plate inside the cover and above it a label with monogram 'JHT' (J. H. Thorold of Syston Park). Not in the catalogue of the Thorold sale at Sotheby's, 12 Dec. 1884. Given as MS. 300.

311. *Horae*   s. xv/xvi

1. ff. 1–2^v Memoriae of St. Regulus, 11,000 Virgins, and St. Maurice 'sociisque eius'. f. 3^rv blank.

2. ff. 4–15^v A rather empty calendar in blue, red, and black, the blue and red alternating for effect.

3. ff. 17–23^v Sequentiae of the Gospels.

The prayer 'Protector in te sperancium . . .' after John.

4. Devotions to B.V.M.: (*a*) ff. 24–28^v Obsecro te . . .; (*b*) ff. 28^v–29^v Or' ad beatam mariam. Gaude virgo mater xpristi que per aurem . . . Ore(mus). Oratio. Deus qui beatissimam virginem mariam . . .; (*c*) ff. 29^v–30 Aue regina celorum aue domina angelorum Salue radix sancta . . .; (*d*, added in s. xvi) f. 30^rv Te o virgo virginum . . . Inuoco . . .

(*a, d*). Masculine forms. (*b*). RH, no. 7017. Five Joys. (*c*). RH, no. 2070.

5. ff. 31–91^v Hours of B.V.M. of the use of (Beauvais).

6. (*a*) ff. 91^v–94 An anthem of B.V.M. for each day of the week, Aue regina celorum (as art. 4c), Felix namque, Virgo prudentissima, Anima (*but the scribe wrote* Eimcta) mea, Tota pulcra, O beata dei, Salue regina misericordie. (*b*) f. 94^rv Deus qui salutis eterne beate marie . . . (*c*) ff. 94^v–95^v Regina celi letare . . . Oremus. Omnipotens sempiterne deus qui gloriose virginis et matris marie corpus . . .

(*c*). RH, no. 17170.

7. ff. 96–115 Penitential psalms and (f. 109) litany.

Eighteen martyrs: . . . (6–18) Firmine Quintine Cymphoriane Iuste Cosma Damiane Fabiane Sebastiane Luciane cum sociis Maurici cum sociis Ypolite cum sociis Clare Thoma.

8. ff. 115^v–118^v Hours of Holy Spirit. Domine labia . . . Nobis sancti spiritus . . .

9. ff. 119–122ᵛ Hours of Holy Cross. Domine labia . . . Patris sapiencia . . .

10. ff. 123–157* Office of the dead.

The ninth lesson is Scio quod redemptor meus (Job 19: 25–7).

11. ff. 157*–176 Memoriae: of *Holy Trinity*; of *Michael*, Peter and Paul, James, *Stephen*, Laurence, *Christopher*, Sebastian (O quam mira . . .), *Denis, Claude, Francis, Nicholas, Cosmas and Damian*; Or' ad angelum. Angele qui meus es custos pietate . . .: ends imperfectly, f. 169ᵛ; of Symphorian (*begins imperfectly*, f. 170), *Emiremondus* abbot, Medard, Barbara (Aue trium lucifera . . .), *Restituta* (O celestis regni rosa restituta gloriosa . . .), Genovefa, *Katherine*; Or' pro deffunctis. Auete omnes anime fideles . . .[1]

RH, nos. 30904 (Sebastian), 22954 (angel), 23902 (Barbara).

12. ff. 176ᵛ–178 Domine iesu christe adoro te in cruce pendentum . . . adoro te in cruce uulneratum . . . . adoro te in sepulcro positum . . . . pastor bone . . . adoro te propter illam amaritudinem . . .

Five of the Seven Oes of St. Gregory.

13 (added, s. xvi). f. 178ʳᵛ (*a*) Domine deus omnipotens qui ad principium . . . (*b*) Domine deus meus si feci ut essem reus tuus . . .

14 (added in s. xvi in the same hand as arts. 4*d*, 13). (*a*) f. iiiᵛ Three 8-line stanzas, signed Le Bel, describing the arms 'En lescusson de ce premier fermant' and 'En lautre escu dembas', i.e. on the two clasps of the former binding. The first two lines of the third stanza are 'En lautre escu dembas a du suaire / De saint Ricule protecteur de senlis'. (*b*) f. iv Notes from Seneca and Boethius.

ff. iv+180+ii, foliated i–iv, 1–157, 157*, 158–74, 174*, 175–8, (179, 180). For ff. iii, iv see above: iii was pasted down. 140×102 mm. Written space 73×45 mm. 17 long lines. Collation: 1 three 2–3⁶ 4⁸ wants 8, blank, after f. 23+1 leaf inserted before 1 (f. 16) 5⁸ wants 8, blank, after f. 30 6–12⁸ 13⁸+1 leaf after 8 (f. 95) 14–22⁸ 23⁸ wants 4 after f. 169 24⁶ (ff. 173–8). Written in *lettre bâtarde*. Fourteen 13–15 line pictures, five in art. 11 (SS. James, Sebastian, Medard, Barbara, Genovefa) and one before each of arts. 1 (St. Regulus), 3, 4 (B.V.M. and Child in glory), 5, 7–9, 10 (Dives in flames), 12 (vision of St. Gregory). Twelve smaller (7-line) pictures in art. 11. In art. 2, only January has its occupation and sign of the zodiac. Initials: (i–iv) 4-line, 3-line, 2-line, and 1-line, gold paint on blue or red grounds patterned in gold paint. Line fillers in the litany only: red or blue ornamented with gold paint. Capital letters in the ink of the text filled with yellow. Continuous floral borders on picture pages: grounds are gold paint or plain, compartmented. A border the height of the written space on ff. 4ᵛ, 17ᵛ, and where each hour begins in art. 5. Binding of red velvet, s. xix. Secundo folio *gia sunt*.

Written in France, for use, probably at Senlis, by the persons whose initials, *G* and *M*, linked by a love knot, are in the border below the picture of St. Regulus on f. 1: the arms of Senlis and *S* are to the right of the picture. Belonged rather later to the Le Bel who wrote arts. 4*d*, 13, 14. 'D. Chastellain. Anthoinette Le Bel 13 Januier 1592', f. iiiᵛ. 'René Chastellain 1682', f. ivᵛ. The arms of Le Bel (cf. H. J. de Morenas, *Grand armorial de France*, no. 3880) impaling another in the border, f. 1, and quartering another in the border, f. 31, are probably additions of s. xvi. f. 16 is an inserted leaf containing

[1] Italics show that there is a picture.

well-drawn arms on the verso, s. xvii, argent a chevron sable between three martlets of the same (Chastelain of Senlis: de Morenas, no. 3710) and gules on a fess azure three fleurs-de-lis or; they are accompanied by headings 'Castellan. Insign. et Primog.' and 'Fuzell. Insign.' and five names, 'Nicolaus. Daniel. Iacobus. Carolus. 'Ludouicus''. Lot 10 in a French sale, s. xix: the relevant slip from the sale catalogue is pasted to f. i.[1] 'From the Dynely collection', f. i: lot 303 in the sale of Capt. Dynely of Bramhope Manor, near Otley, Yorkshire, at Christie's, 13 Feb. 1865. Armorial book-plate of Frederick Collins Wilson and 'Leeds. March 1865' inside the cover. In a Sotheby sale, s. xx: the relevant slip from the catalogue is pasted to f. i.

312. *Horae*   s. xv[2]

1. ff. 1–12ᵛ A rather empty calendar in red and black.

Entries in red include 'Vedasti et Amandi', 'Bonifacii episcopi', 'Basilii episcopi', 'Donatiani episcopi' (6 Feb., 5, 15 June, 15 Oct.).

2. ff. 14–21ᵛ Incipiunt hore de sancta cruce. Domine labia . . . Patris sapientia . . .

3. ff. 23–29ᵛ Incipiunt hore de sancto spiritu. Domine labia . . . Nobis sancti spiritus . . .

4. ff. 31–37ᵛ Incipit missa beate marie.

5. ff. 37ᵛ–44ᵛ Sequentiae of the Gospels.

6. ff. 46–129ᵛ Incipiunt hore beate marie uirginis secundum usum romanum.

Salve regina after compline. The Advent office begins on f. 121.

7. ff. 130–140ᵛ Twelve memoriae: 'De sancta ueronica. Ant'. Salue sancta facies . . .' (*RH*, no. 18199) and of SS. Michael, John Baptist, Peter and Paul, Nicholas, Sebastian (O quam mirra (*sic*) . . .: *RH*, no. 30904), Anthony (hermit), Mary Magdalene, Katherine, Barbara, Margaret, Apollonia (Virgo cristi egregia . . .: *RH*, no. 21744).

8. ff. 140ᵛ–145 Ad beatam uirginem mariam. Obsecro te . . . Masculine forms.

9. ff. 145–8 Alia oracio. O intemerata . . . orbis terrarum. Inclina . . . Masculine forms. f. 148ᵛ blank.

10. ff. 150–172ᵛ Penitential psalms and litany.

Bernardine last of five 'monachi Et heremite'.

11. ff. 174–222ᵛ Office of the dead.

'Partem beate resurrectionis . . .' at the end.

ff. iii+222+iii. 130×90 mm. Written space 85×40 mm. 14 long lines. Ruling in red ink. Collation: 1–2⁶ 3–17⁸ 18⁴ (ff. 145–8) 19–27⁸, together with 14 single leaves with blank rectos and pictures on the versos, ff. 13, 22, 30, 45, 66, 80, 86, 92, 98, 104, 113, 120, 149,

---

[1] According to this catalogue the arms on f. 31 are of Noel le Bel, governor of Creil under Charles VIII: he was enobled in 1493.

173. Handsome textura. Full-page pictures of good quality on the versos of the single leaves: nine in art. 6 (Innocents at vespers, Flight into Egypt at compline, Coronation of B.V.M. before the Advent office) and one before each of arts. 2, 3 (an unusual composition), 4 (B.V.M., Child, and two angels), 10, 11 (raising of Lazarus). Initials: (i) usually 8-line, pale purple, patterned in white, historiated: twelve in art. 7, four in art. 5, and one before art. 8 (B.V.M. and the dead Christ); (ii) 5-line, gold paint on decorated blue and red grounds; (iii, iv) 2-line and 1-line, white on grounds of gold paint. Continuous framed floral borders on pages with pictures and with initials of type (ii): these pages form double openings and the ground colours of the borders are the same on the verso and its facing recto. Similar borders the height of the written space in the outer margins of pages with initials of type (i). Line fillers in the litany only, white on grounds of gold paint. Capital letters in the ink of the text filled with very pale yellow. Bound by Douglas Cockerell and Son in 1958, when the clasps of the previous purple velvet binding, s. xix, were retained. Secundo folio (f. 15) *mortis mee*.

Written in Flanders. Friends wrote for the owner in s. xvi on f. 45: (i) 'Ie vous aime et sy aimeray / tant quen ce monde viueray / 1569[1] Raison le veult / Halewin'; (ii) '1568 / Maintenir faut / Charles de Croy / A vous faire / tres humble Seruiteur'. 'Iusti van Horne. In Deo Iesu meo', ff. ii, 224. Armorial book-plate of Philip Carteret Webb, f. ii[v]: not idenfiable in his sale, 25 Feb. 1771. A pressmark, O. 7, s. xviii (?), f. i. 'Hon. B. C. Maxwell' pencilled on f. i[v], s. xix.

313. *Biblia* s. XIII med.

1. vols. 1, 2; vol. 3, ff. 1–88 A Bible in the usual order and with the common set of sixty-four prologues (cf. above, pp. 210–12), now bound in three volumes, Genesis–Psalms, Proverbs–Maccabees, New Testament.

Matthew begins on a new quire (16[1]), Proverbs on a new leaf (10[10]). Two leaves of 1 Maccabees are missing after f. 131. The words '[B]ooz ducit ruth in uxorem. Et ex ea suscepit obetz patrem ysai patris dauid' precede Ruth. The prologue to 1 Timothy ends, as usually in regular Bibles, with the words 'a laodicia'. vol. 3, f. 88[v] blank.

In the margin of vol. 1, f. 1[v] is 'Credo in deum patrem . . . hoc modo recitat Aug' sinbolum prout habetur in sermone eius de fide qui incipit credimus in vnum deum vnum patrem etc' ', s. xv.

2. vol. 3, ff. 89–126. Aaz apprehendens . . . zuzim consiliantes eos uel consiliatores eorum.

The usual dictionary of Hebrew names. f. 126[v], originally blank, has the prayer '[S]umme sacerdos et vere pontifex . . .' as an addition, s. xv.

One manuscript bound in three volumes: ff. iii+225+iii; ff. iii+139+iii; ff. iii+126+iii. 155 × 110 mm. Written space 107 × 74 mm. 2 cols. 50 lines. Collation: 1–14[24] 15[30] wants 21, 22 after vol. 2, f. 131 16–18[24] 19[16] (vol. 3, ff. 73–88) 20[24] 21[14]: the last 15 leaves of quire 10 are now the first 15 of vol. 2. Well-written initials: (i) of books, 6-line or 7-line, red and blue with ornament of both colours; (ii) of prologues, as (i), but 4-line or 5-line; (iii) of chapters, 2-line, red or blue with ornament of the other colour; (iv) of psalm verses and in art. 2, 1-line, red or blue. On f. 3[v] of vol. 1 the *I* of *In principio* runs the height of the written space. English bindings, s. xviii/xix: speckled calf, the cover of the spine gilt: gilt edges. Secundo folio *hanc uniuersi*.

Written in France and there in s. xv. 'Hearne, Bookseller, Binder, and Stationer. 81 Strand' is on a label inside each front cover. In a sale, s. xx: the relevant slip from the catalogue is inside vol. 1.

---

[1] The letter *P* between the figures 5 and 6.

314. *A. de Cermisono, Tractatus in arte cirurgiae*   s. xv²

Tractatus nobilem et excelentissimum virum dominum Antonium de cermisono in artis cirurgie. Solus deus sanat lang[uidos] sua mirabili potencia Et ex suma benignissima virtute. 14[. .]. De lacumine que nascitur in capite puerorum. In capite puerorum nascitur quedam crusta que . . . .

Recipes for the cure of diseases of the head and other parts of the body in descending order, in 170 numbered chapters. Up to about f. 45 the margins have been damaged by damp and some text has been lost on ff. 1–18: repairs were done in Italy, s. xix. As far as ch. 71 a male or female figure is drawn in the margin against the beginning of each chapter and points to or touches the part of the body with which the chapter deals: on ff. 1–9 nearly all these figures have been lost. The feet are reached by ch. 90 and from ch. 93 the recipes are in no particular order. Chs. 154, 159–61, 165, 167 (part), and 168–70 are in Italian and added recipes in Italian are in the margins of ff. 39ᵛ, 41ᵛ, 81. Persons are named in ch. 156 (f. 80ᵛ), 'Modus faciendi pillulas magistri hilarrandi que valent ad omnes egritudines . . .' and in ch. 168 (f. 86ʳᵛ), 'Ceroto perfectissimo el quale vsa maestro zanino barbero in bologna . . . et sic est finis huius ceroti expertissimi in quo Ego girardus de Auerolodis de brixia vidi experiencia'. Probably chs. 154–70 are an early addition to the original collection, 168–70 and perhaps also 154–67 by Girardus.

For printed Consilia of A. de Cermisono, beginning with diseases of the head, see *GKW* 6514–15.

ff. ii+87+ii. Paper. A medieval foliation in red, (11)–(98), remains here and there: it included the leaf now missing after f. 62. 197 × 150 mm: on f. 84 a further 5 mm of the lower margin has been preserved and folded in. Written space 145 × 95 mm. 28 long lines. Collation: 1⁸ 2–6¹⁰ 7¹⁰ wants 5 after f. 62 8–9¹⁰. The strips of thin parchment strengthening the fold of the innermost sheet of each quire have been removed, except in quires 8, 9. Mainly in two current hands, one frequently taking over from the other: neither of them occurs after ch. 153 (f. 80). Chapters 154–70 may be all in one hand: see above. 2-line metallic red initials. Capital letters in the ink of the text are filled with pale yellow and stroked with red. Bound in Italy, s. xix. Secundo folio *Aliquando*.

Written in northern Italy. An early owner is named on f. 86ᵛ: see above. 'This book, or rather manuscript, was purchased at Trieste in the year 1849, and is presented to Dʳ Cumming as a token of respect and gratitude by the Revᵈ Buchan. W. Wright 1856.' Belonged to A. S. Cumming, 2 Nov. 1910, when John L. Comrie, 25 Manor Place, Edinburgh, wrote a letter to him which is now kept loose inside the cover.

315. *Statuta Edwardi III, etc.*   s. xiv²

Forty-one statutes, probably assembled by the writer for his own use. All but no. 3 are printed in *SR*. The series begins at 1 Edward III and ends at 38 Edward III, but some earlier statutes are included, without indication that they are earlier (nos. 9, 15–17, 19, 32). Nos. 9, 15, 16, 24 are in Latin. Preceded on ff. 2–7ᵛ by tables of chapters headed 'Hec sunt capitula nouarum Stat' regis Edwardi tercii' (ff. 2–7ᵛ) and by tables of 'Dampna in triplo' and 'Dampna in Duplo' (f. 1ʳᵛ).

1, 2. ff. 8, 11. *SR* i. 255, 251.

3. f. 15ᵛ Cum nadegeres en temps le Roi Edward . . . plousours grantz du Roialme Dengleterre surueissent a Hugh' le Despenser . . . assent et estatut a touz iours.

Statute of 1 Edward III concerning followers of the Despensers, as in B.L., Royal 19 A. xiv, ff. 24^v–25^v. Refers to the statute of (7) Mar., anno 1 (*SR* i. 251).

4–7. ff. 18, 22^v, 27^v, 32^v. *SR* i. 257, 261, 265, 269.

8. f. 36^v. *SR* i. 275. After '*come* desus est dit' (edn., p. 275 *ad fin.*) it continues 'Come en lestat' fait a Westm' . . . osteil le Roi' (edn., pp. 276, col. 2, para. 3–277, col. 1/12).

9. f. 39. *SR* i. 171 (Articuli Cleri, 9 Edward II).

10–14. ff. 43, 44, 57^v, 60^v, 63^v. *SR* i. 280, 281, 292, 295, 273.

15. f. 65^v. *SR* i. 140 (28 Edward I).

16. f. 66. *SR* i. 113 (23 Edward I).

17. f. 66^v *SR* i. 180 (14 Edward II).

18. f. 67^v Incipit statutum de cibis. Nostre s' le Roi desirant . . . *SR* i. 279/2.

19–23. ff. 68^v, 69^v (Incipiunt prerogatiua angl' anno xiiii^{mo}), 70, 71^v, 73^v. *SR* i. 274, 282, 343, 300, 302.

24. f. 74^v *SR* i. 307. Addressed to W., archbishop of York.

25–7. ff. 77, 81 (Incipit sacramentum Iustic'), 81^v. *SR* i. 311, 305, 324.

28. f. 85. *SR* i. 316. A piece of coloured thread, sewn in, and a cross on f. 87^v draw attention to the word 'Rome' (edn. 318, col. 2/23).

29, 30. ff. 88, 89. *SR* i. 310, 303.

31. f. 91^v. *SR* i. 324.

At the end, f. 94, two mnemonic couplets, headed 'Offic' Vic' ' and 'Assisa': (1) Fabrica. furca. porta. domus . . . traduntur hec vicecomitibus; (2) Fos. stag. sepe. que . . . Poscunt assisam . . .'.

32. f. 94^v Incipit sacramentum abiurantis regnum. *SR* i. 250.

33–41. ff. 94^v, 100, 104, 110^v, 115^v, 123^v, 132^v, 135, 143. *SR* i. 319, 329, 345, 349, 364, 371, 376, 378, 383.

An orderly run, 25–38 Edw. III. ff. 146^v–147^v blank.

ff. i+147+i. 128×90 mm. *c.* 95×65 mm. 23–30 long lines. Frame ruling. 1^8 wants 1, perhaps blank, 2–18^8 19^4. Quires 2–18 lettered at the end A–R. Written in current anglicana by a scribe who tried sometimes not to link his minims (see, e.g., f. 24). 2-line spaces left for initials, but not filled. Binding of s. xix. Secundo folio (f. 9) *come il puisse*.

Written in England. 'Franciscus Palgrave Int' Templi Soc. 1823', f. 146. 'Fredk York Powell 1892 Ch Ch Oxford', f. 147.

318. *De Musica*   s. xv/xvi

1. ff. 1–6^v Circa noticiam musice sciencie Queritur primo quid sit musica et 2° vnde dicatur. quantum ad primum Musica est ars arcium . . . In quibus omnis comprehenditur cantus.

ff. 7–8^v blank.

2. ff. 9–19ᵛ [H]ic sequitur libellus continens in se aliqua breuia documenta ad artem cantandi pertinencia que pro iuuenum informacione multum videntur valere . . . Primo est notandum quod musica sic describitur . . . eo quod non vni soni cantus.

On keys and tones, the latter illustrated by noted liturgical texts. f. 20ʳᵛ left blank: a pen and ink sketch of 'Santa Katerina' with sword and wheel added on the recto, s. xvi.

3. ff. 21–31ᵛ De musica tracturi que inter septem artes liberales connumeratur occurrit in primis dictum principis philosophorum arestotelis . . . Octo sunt beatitudines. Per me sebastianum fabri de cuchach (or crichach).

On tones in ten chapters, illustrated in the same way as art. 2. f. 32ʳᵛ blank.

ff. ii+32+ii. Paper. 207 × 140 mm. Written space c. 155 × 100 mm. 8 long lines and music in art. 2, 5 in art. 3. Collation: 1⁸ 2–3¹². Written in cursiva, each article in a different hand. Binding for Edinburgh University, s. xix.

Written in Germany, art. 3 by a named scribe.

320. *P. de Pergula, Logica*   1455

1. ff. 1–58ᵛ Omnes qui aliquid memoria dignum suis posteris relinquerint . . . et hęc de Insolubilibus dicta sufficiant. Deo gratias. Amen. Explicit feliciter Tractatus logice magistri Pauli de la pergula peritissimi viri die sancto Epiphanie sexto Ianuarii per me Mariᵐ de sanctonazᵒ Canonicum Regularem. 1454.

Printed often (Hain, nos. 12622–8), last in 1961.

2. ff. 59–65 Cum sepenumero cogitarem non mediocrem iuuenibus fructum afferre si composicionis et diuisionis materiam clarissime intellegerent. Hanc horam Petre de Guidizoᵇᵘˢ Hodie institui . . . ex te repperies. Deo gratias. Amen. die martis. Explicit Tractatus de sensu composito et diuiso edito a preclarissimo viro Magistro Paulo pergulensi doctissimo et famosissimo. die octauo Ianuarii 1454.[1] In monasterio sancti Io. de Viridario padue. Deo sit laus. et gloria. Amen. Deo gratias. Amen.

Printed after art. 1, but without the last ten lines here, 'Habes mi petre tractatum breuissimum . . . ex te repperies', which are taken in edn. 1961 from Bodleian Canon. misc. 22, f. 80. Edn. Ven. 1481 gives Peter's surname as de Guidonibus.

3. ff. 65ᵛ–68ᵛ Sophismata asinina magistri Pauli pergulensis clarissimi [. . . .]. Hec est uera tu es asinus . . . hoc est aliquod de ly. b. cᵐ. Expliciunt sophismata Asinina Arcium doctoris Magistri Pauli pergulen' eximii viri.

Cf. edn. 1961, p. xii. ff. 70–73ᵛ blank. f. 69 does not belong here. It is a paper leaf with B, C entries from an alphabetical index to a manuscript with 411 or more leaves.

ff. ii+73+ii. Paper. 145 × 102 mm. Written space c. 105 × 70 mm. 22–6 long lines. Frame ruling. Collation: 1–6¹⁰ 7¹⁴ wants 13, 14, probably blank (ff. 61–8, 70–3: for f. 69 see above). Written in a small clear and unpretentious humanistic script. 1-line red initials. Capital letters in the ink of the text are marked with red. Binding of s. xix for Edinburgh University. Secundo folio *Continua.*

[1] A Tuesday in 1455.

Written by Marinianus de Sanctonazario (?), O.S.A., in the monastery of St. John de Viridario, Padua. Art. 1 was completed on the 6th and art. 2 on the 8th of January, 1454/5: for the colophons (in red ink) see above. A number '746' at the head of f. 1. Acquired probably in s. xix.

321. *P. de Pergula, Logica; etc.* s. xv²

1. ff. 2–41 Incipit prologus in loica magistri Pauli de pergula. eximii doctoris. Omnes qui . . . Et hec de insolubilibus dicta sufficiant ad laudem yesu cristi. et sue dulcissime uirginis matris marie. Amen. Finis.

As MS. 320, art. 1, q.v.

2. ff. 41ᵛ–44ᵛ Incipit tractatus de sensu composito et diuiso diligentissime compilatus per magistrum Paulum pergulensem. Cum sepenumero . . . ex te reperies. Explicit tractatus sensus compositi et diuisi per eximium doctorem magistrum paulum pergulensem limpidissime declaratus.

As MS. 320, art. 2, q.v. As there, the Peter to whom the work is addressed is called Peter 'de guidizonibus'.

3. (*a*) f. 45ʳᵛ Incipit tractatus de inuentione medii termini. sa(n)cti Thome de Aquino. Quoniam principium silogizandi . . . cum quibus sunt conuertibiles. Et hec de inuentione medii termini dicta sufficiant. (*b*) f. 46 Nota quod regule inueniendi medium . . . Nota tamen quod alique istarum regularum fallunt interdum.

(*a*). Pseudo-Aquinas. *Opuscula*, ed. Mandonnet, 1927, v. 174–5 (Opusc. 49). (*b*). Nine rules for finding the mean term, six 'constantes' and three 'inconstantes'.

4. ff. 46–61 Propositio resolubilis debet resolui hoc modo . . . scies alicam. Finis.

ff. 61ᵛ–63ᵛ were left blank.

5. ff. 64–105 Incipit Metaphisica Alexandri. Quot modis dicitur simplex duo mo' quod non habet partes actuales nec essentiales nec uirtuales . . . secundum corpus quia corruptibile. Explicit liber distinctionum que fuerunt apte parisius. Laus tibi criste.

Cf. *Traditio*, xxiii. 354 (? Alexander Fassitelli de S. Elpidio, O.E.S.A., †1326). One hundred and eight chapters, listed on ff. 105–6. ff. 106ᵛ–108ᵛ were left blank.

6 (added). Additions of s. xvi in the margins of ff. 2–8ᵛ and in blank spaces include (f. 61ᵛ) twenty-six 'Versus breues super omnes regulas suppositionum. A. pre. confundit. distribuit. sub. Destruit . . .'

7 (binding leaves). ff. 1, 109–10 (f. 1ᵛ) cupiditati subiecit . . . (f. 110ᵛ) conputrescunt in sterquilinio [consu]etudinis praue. Sit ergo.

Three adjacent leaves (f. 1 is the wrong way round), fairly well written, s. xii¹, presumably taken over from a former binding. The first section seems to be on rulers, the second (f. 1) is 'De claustralibus. Ad claustrales loquens scriptura ait . . .', and the third (f. 110) is 'De sacerdotibus. Ad sacerdotes dominus ait. Vos estis sal terre . . .'. The third has 'xlvii' against it. Written space 120 × 73 mm. 29 long lines.

ff. iii+107+iv, foliated (i, ii) 1–108 (109–12). Paper, except ff. 68, 69, 74, 75 (and ff. 1, 109–10). 150×98 mm. Written space 94×65 mm. 39 long lines and (ff. 64–106) 2 cols. of 28 lines. Collation of ff. 2–108: 1–5¹⁰ 6¹² 7¹² wants 1, perhaps blank, before f. 64 8–9¹² 10¹⁰. Initials of arts. 1–4: (i) f. 2, 6-line, blue with red and pale-purple ornament; (ii, iii) 4-line and 3-line, red. Initials of art. 5: (i, ii) 4-line and 2-line, red. Binding of s. xix with centrepiece of the arms of the University of Edinburgh and 'University Library Edinburgh' around them. Secundo folio *Relatio*.

Written in Italy. Acquired in s. xix.

322. *R. de Sancto Victore, Beniamin minor*   s. xv²

Incipit liber Riccardi de sancto Victore de duodecim patriarchis. Beniamin adolescentulus . . . Dum igitur dina in aliis (*ends imperfectly*).

PL cxcvi. 1–38a, about one-fifth of the text only. Stegmüller no. 7325. The catchword on f. 15ᵛ is *animarum statum*.

ff. ii+15+ii. 250×175 mm. Written space 192×120 mm. 2 cols. 36 lines. Collation: 1⁸ wants 1 2⁸. Initials: (i) 4-line, blue; (ii) 2-line, red or blue. Binding of s. xix.

Written in Italy. A fragment of a manuscript, another part of which is Edinburgh U.L. 67, Testamenta duodecim patriarcharum in Grosseteste's translation, with book-plate of the Duke of Sussex, s. xix: since MS. 67 is two quires of 8 followed by a singleton it may have preceded MS. 322 immediately. A pencilled number '4141' at the head of f. 1: cf. '4169' in MS. 67.

324. *Gesta Alexandri Magni, etc.*   s. xv²

1. (*a*) ff. 1–39ᵛ Incipit liber de Natiuitate Vita et morte omniumque gestorum Alexandri. Sapientium quippe egiptii scientes mensuram terre undasque maris . . . (f. 39) et obiit iiii kl' aprilis. fabricauit autem A. ciuitates xii que omnes continuo habitantur quarum nomina sunt hec . . . (f. 39ᵛ) Duodecima A. quę dicitur Egyptus. Explicit hystoria gestorum A. pueri magni Regis phy. macedon' de natiuitate sua et actibus suis et morte ipsius. (*b*) ff. 39ᵛ–40 Post mortem siquidem augustissimi Alex. macedonis . . . Scripsit itaque dotomeus in piramida huiusmodi uersus. Hos uersus scripsit dotomeus phyllosophus impyramide Gestorum Regis Alexandri. Hic iacet infectus . . . (30 couplets). (*c*) ff. 40ᵛ–41 Posuit itaque demostenes uersus in persona A. reprehendentis se ipsum . . . En ego qui totum . . . (28 lines). (*d*) f. 41 Quibus uitiis uictus fuerat A. hic exponitur. Alexander qui puer magnus dicebatur . . . morbo. (*e*) f. 41ʳᵛ Versus exortatorii (?) ad uitia expellenda. Si tua uolueris(*sic*). neque publica iura uereri . . . (12 lines). (*f*) ff. 41ᵛ–43ᵛ Forma epistole quam mardoceus princeps iudeorum missit Alexandro ipsum a cultura ydolorum cupie(n)s reuocare. Postquam phy. macedonus uniuersas regiones mundi . . . et de greco in latinum translata. Summo principum A. phy. Mardocenus Iudeorum minimus . . . retinet et conseruat. Finis deo gratias Amen.

(*a*), De praeliis, printed in s. xv (*GKW* 874–9) and by O. Zingerle, *Die Quellen zum Alexander des Rudolf von Ems* (Germanistische Abhandlungen, iv), 1885, pp. 129–65. Here in 130 paragraphs and at the end a list of twelve cities founded by Alexander. For this version of (*a*) followed by (*b–f*) see Zingerle, pp. 66–7, and F. Pfister in *Münchener*

and a final couplet, 'Nomine Matheus tulit hoc carmen medicine Cui miserere deus et
viuere dat sine fine'. (*d*). Verses on the months: cf. Follan, loc. cit., pp. 41–3. (*e*). Walther, no. 17274. (*f*). A rhyming prologue and ninety numbered chapters, Arthemisia–
Cerimboletis, each subdivided by letters in the margins: O. Priebsch, *Deutsche Handschriften in England*, ii. 167, describes the copy in B.L., Add. 17527. (*h*). Arranged by
parts of the body, with references by chapter-numbers and letters, for example 'zu den
augen 2 g.'. (*i*). A Latin–German vocabulary of herbs, A–O: cf. above, p. 578. (*j*). Medical
recipes uniformly written under various heads and partly (ff. 115–17) in Latin. (*k*). Cf.
Follan, loc. cit., p. 45. (*m*). The pestilence recipes noticed by Follan, loc. cit., p. 44.

3 (quires 13–18). (*a*) ff. 132–93 Hie vindestu gescriben in diszem bůch gar gůt
ertzenei nach des registers sag dy meister ortlof von wirczburg geboren v̇z bey-
eren zůsamen pracht hat ausz krichiszer czungen in latin vnd ausz latin in deutsche
czungen . . . Von ersten got hat iiii element beshaffen . . . (f. 192ᵛ) dy heiligen v
vonden gesegen dich sechstund' amen. In nomine p. et f. et s.s. amen. (*b*) ff.
193–201ᵛ Recipes and other pieces in the same hand as (*a*). (*c*) f. 201ᵛ [S]ume
dei pontifex erharde pro tibi famulantibus iugiter intercede . . . (*d*) f. 201ᵛ
[D]omine ihesu criste verus deus noster per oracionem serui tui blasii . . . (*e*) f.
201ᵛ A prayer to St. James.

(*a*) differs greatly from the printed text of Ortolf von Bayerlant, ed. J. Follan, 1963.
Follan describes it on pp. 35–6. Some of the chapters in the edition are recognizable here,
for example nos. 74–5, 100–1, 94–7, 156 in that order on ff. 153–60. On f. 151ᵛ a charm
headed 'Ein segen contra glantes' has been crossed out. So too on f. 170 a 'Benedictio
contra maculos'. The seventeen lines of (*a*) on f. 193 are part of a recipe omitted in error
from f. 192. (*b*) ends with a piece on the five sorrows of B.V.M. (*c–e*) are early additions.

4 (quires 19, 20). ff. 202–17 Mainly prognostics: (*a*) ff. 203–204ᵛ Wer an dem
Ersten tag des monds so er new ist sich wurt der sicht lang . . .; (*b*) ff. 204ᵛ–206ᵛ
Hie wil ich dir schriben von den moneten wie sich ein ieklicher mensch halten
sol. Aristoteles spricht . . .; (*c*) ff. 207–12 Von den zwelff zeychen. Der wider
ist ein zeichen von Orient . . .; (*d*) f. 212ʳᵛ De complexione hominum. Die erst
heysst Colera . . .; (*e*) ff. 213ᵛ–217ᵛ Herbarius appcdecario virtusque (?).
Alleluia sawerampfer . . .

For (*a–c*), prognostics according to the age of the moon, the month, and the zodiacal sign
at birth, and (*d*) see Follan, pp. 34–6. (*e*) is a table of herb-names in Latin and German.

ff. i+217+i. Paper, except ff. 1, 4, 5, 7, 10, 11, 14. 207 × 155 mm. Written space *c.* 135–
155 × 85–100 mm. 20–35 long lines. Collation: 1²⁰ wants 16, 17, 20 2¹²+1 leaf after 12
(f. 30) 3¹⁸+1 leaf after 18 (f. 49) 4¹⁸ wants 10–18 after f. 58 5 five (ff. 59–63) 6 seven (ff. 64–
70) 7⁶ (ff. 71–6) 8–9¹⁴ 10¹⁰ wants 9, 10, perhaps blank, after f. 112 11¹² 12⁸ wants 8 after
f. 131 13¹² wants 12 after f. 142 14–17¹² 18 eleven (ff. 191–201) 19 eight (ff. 202–9) 20⁸.
Quires 5–11 numbered at the end 1–7. Quires 14–18 numbered at the beginning ii–vi.
Written in cursiva. 2-line red initials in arts. 2, 3, 4. Capital letters in the ink of the text
touched with red. Binding of s. xix.

Written in southern Germany or Austria. The inscription in red ink at the foot of the first
leaf of quire 2 can refer only to art. 1: 'Das buch ist vnd hat gescriben Balthasar Smyt
von Sweinfurt (*Bavaria*) Im Mᵒ ccccᵒ 63ᵒ Zu der Newenstat vff der Steyermark In hern
[. . . . . .]'. Another inscription in red ink in two lines at the foot of f. 10 has been erased,
except for the last words, 'Anno domini etc. 1464ᵗᵒ in die Sancte appolonie virginis'.
No. 187 (?) in an English sale catalogue, s. xix. The relevant slip is inside the cover and
also the number.

331. *Miscellanea theologica*   1431, 1433, and s. xv med.

The title on the label on the front cover, 'Liber pro nouellis militibus Cristi. Hic multa doctrinalia deuocionalia et moralia collecta sunt', and the words 'Liber nouiciorum' in red on f. 1 show that this was a collection of use to young monks especially. Many of the pieces are common in manuscripts of this date (2*a*, 3*a*, 6*b*, *c*, *e*, 7*a*, 12*a*, *b*). A nearly contemporary scribe made the volume even more miscellaneous than it was by adding short pieces in blank spaces (art. 16). Notes by him are dated in 1431 and 1434: cf. arts. 7*c*, 16*e*.

The title on the front cover, now partly illegible, and the table of contents on f. 1 are copied in the medieval Erfurt catalogue (*MBDS*, ii. 343). The table lists arts. 1, 3*a*, 4, 5, 6*a–e*, 7*a*, 8*a*, *b*, 10*a*, *d*, *e* (ff. 167ᵛ–168), 11*a*, *c*, 12*a*, *b*, 13, 14 *b*, *c*, and eight of the other short pieces on quires 21–3; also 16*c*. Parchment tabs show where arts. 2*a*, *b*, 3*a*, 5, 6*d*, 7*a*, 8*a*, 12*a*, 15*g* begin.

1 (quires 1–3). ff. 2–39ᵛ Tractatus magistri Hugonis de Professione Mona-chorum. Tractatus iste qui est de professione monachorum tres habet partes . . . (f. 2ᵛ) Capitulum primum. Cum displicat deo infidelis et stulta promissio. Ecc' v. Promissio vero stulta . . . animaduertunt omnia etc. Explicit tractatus magis-tri Hugonis de professione monachorum. 1433.

Gulielmus Peraldus: cf. A. Dondaine in *AFP* xviii, 210–15.[1] Divided into three parts of 9, 4, and 12 chapters. f. 40ʳᵛ was left blank.

2 (quires 4, 5). A 'Compendium religiosorum' against religious who hold property, sermons, and letters: (*a*) ff. 41–51 Venerabilissimo in cristo patri ac domino domino Cistercii ceterisque doctoribus . . . Sacro concilio generali Anno domini 1415. Constancie celebrato congregatis. Pro euidenti et necessaria salute animarum nostrarum . . . et hec omnia adicientur vobis etc. Terminatur hic compendium religiosorum moderni temporis de anno videlicet domini 1415 In concilio Constancien' promulgatum; (*b*) ff. 51ᵛ–53ᵛ Sermo de sancto Iohanni Baptista. Ecce elongaui . . . Ita scribitur psalmo '54' et beatus Ieronimus . . .; (*c*) ff. 53ᵛ–54ᵛ Sermo de Sanctificacione b. Marie virginis. Sancti estote . . . Exodi. Dicut b. Bernhardus. Sanctos eos dicimus . . .; (*d*) ff. 54ᵛ–55ᵛ Epistola beati Bernardi ad Magistrum Walterum. Sepe meum animum . . . est me dignus; (*e*) ff. 55ᵛ–56ᵛ Ad R Romane ecclesie Subdiaconum. Bene fecisti karissime mi . . . nos esse confidito; (*f*) ff. 56ᵛ–57 Ad illustrem iuuenem de Perona. Sermo qui insonuit . . . fero scitientibus; (*g*) f. 57ʳᵛ Ad parentes G. consolatoria. Si filium vestrum facit deus suum . . .; (*h*) ff. 57ᵛ–59 Ex persona helye monachi. Sola causa qua liceat non obedire parentibus . . . viuamus. per omnia secula seculorum. Amen; (*i*) ff. 59ᵛ–62 Epistola cuiusdam egregii magistri Parisiensis de vicio proprietatis quam scripsit ad quemdam canonicum regularem . . . Cris-tus ihesus dei eterni filius. qui est fons et origo . . .; (*j*) f. 62 A note on the same subject headed 'Clemens iii de statu monachorum'; (*k*) ff. 62ᵛ–64ᵛ Extracts from the Fathers, etc.: cf. art. 9.

(*a*). Another copy from the Erfurt charterhouse in Bodleian, Hamilton 30 (*SC* 24448), art. 7. Cf. E. Jørgensen, *Catalogus codicum latinorum medii aevi Bibliothecae Regiae Hafniensis*, i. 142 (Tractatus contra religiosos proprietarios), 165. The scribe wrote

[1] I owe the reference to Professor Richard Rouse.

'Principium medium finem. rege uirgo maria' at the head of f. 41. (*d–h*). *PL* clxxxii, letters 104, 105, 109, 110, 111. A new hand begins at (*d*).

3 (quire 6). (*a*) ff. 66–77ᵛ 'Quoniam fundamentum et Ianua virtutum . . . apparuerit gloria tua ad quam . . . 'Explicit Tractatus de consolacione bonus et utilis pro religiosis. M. mathei de Cracouia Finitus anno domini 1431 . . . Sabbato dominice letare . . .'. (*b*) on a bifolium wrapped round (*a*), 'Bernhardus et dicitur prosa b. Bernhardi. Cum reuoluo toto corde . . . Ad quem anxius suspiro Amen'.

(*a*). Usually called De puritate conscientie. (*b*). Walther, no. 3742. The first 124 lines are on f. 65ʳᵛ and the last 20 on f. 78: a signe de renvoi on f. 65ᵛ. f. 78ᵛ blank.

4 (quire 7). ff. 79ᵛ–82 Sequencia extracta sunt de confessionali magistri Iohannis Kusyn ad habendam noticiam peccatorum. Sciendum igitur quod aliqua sunt peccata . . .

ff. 79ʳ, 82ᵛ–87ᵛ were left blank.

5 (quire 8). ff. 88–97ᵛ In nomine domini Amen. In cristo sibi dilecto P. frater vester franciscus de perusio ordinis fratrum minorum . . . Devocionis vestre sinceritas . . . omnibus aliis etc. et sic est finis. Explicit tractatus Francisci Curialis. et optimus de Septem peccatis mortalibus et eorum speciebus et remediis etc.

6 (quires 9, 10). (*a*) ff. 98–102ᵛ Si vis in spiritu proficere . . . nec ullam ei reuer-enciam exhiberi. Explicit formula vite compendiosa. (*b*). ff. 103–4 'formula b. Bernhardi de vita et ho. clericorum religiosorum.' Petis a me frater karissime . . . et gloria mea in domino. 'Explicit formula honeste vite beati bernhardi'. (*c*) ff. 104–11 'Incipit formula siue summa nouiciorum composita a fratre dauid ordinis sancti francisci de exterioris hominis conuersacione'. Primo semper considerare . . . Castus esto in omnibus etc. Terminatur formula beati Bernhardi abbatis de vita et honestate. (*d*) ff. 111ᵛ–113ᵛ Formula perfeccionis spiritualis. Ut homo in sui creatoris cognicione . . . tota deuocione commendo Amen. (*e*) ff. 113ᵛ–119 Speculum peccatoris beati Bernhardi abbatis. Quoniam karissimi in via huius seculi . . . vitam eternam possideas. Quod tibi concedat ille qui est in secula seculorum Benedictus Amen. Explicit speculum peccatoris Beati Bern-hardi abbatis.

(*b*). The title in the hand of art. 16. *PL* clxxxiv. 1167–70c. (*c*). Dauid de Augusta, O.F.M. Printed in *Maxima bibliotheca veterum patrum* (1677), xxv. 869. (*d*). Cf. Jørgensen, op. cit., p. 130. (*e*). *PL* xl. 983–92. ff. 119ᵛ–120ᵛ blank.

7 (quire 11). (*a*) ff. 122–32 Speculum amatorum mundi. Videte quomodo caute ambuletis non quasi insipientes . . . possideat. Quod nobis concedet Qui . . . amen. (*b*) ff. 133–134ᵛ Dicta beati Augustini de virtutibus psalmorum. Canticum psalmorum corpus sanctificat . . . . (*c*) Short pieces before and after (*a*)—f. 121ʳᵛ was left blank—include (f. 121ᵛ) verses 'In cruce sudauit dominus. Serue ne quiesces . . .', headed 'Ramfreydus', and against them in the hand of art. 16 'Anno 1434 Sabbato die post undecim m. virginum Recordare consolacionis tue etc'.

a). Henricus de Hassia: cf. Jørgensen, op. cit., pp. 114, 160. (*b*). Cf. Stegmüller, no. 369. (*c*). Walther, no. 8885.

8 (quire 12). (*a*) ff. 137–141ᵛ Sunt autem multe condiciones quare mundus est fugiendus . . . cordis oris et operis conseruantes. (*b*) ff. 141ᵛ–143ᵛ Short pieces, including three 'similitudines', the first ascribed to Anselm, and a question 'Vtrum religiosus eodem genere peccati grauius peccet quam secularis. Et videtur quod non . . .' which the table of contents ascribes to Anselm. (*c*) ff. 135–6 Vado mori. res certa quidem. nil cercior illa . . . Vt vitare queam deuia. vado mori.

(*a*). Fifteen heads. (*c*). Cf. Jørgensen, op. cit., p. 151, and Walther, no. 19965. The scribe who wrote (*a*, *b*) left f. 135ʳᵛ blank. Sixty-one lines of (*c*) were added by another hand on f. 135ʳᵛ and the remaining thirteen on an inserted slip, f. 136.

9 (quire 13). ff. 144–53 Leaves laid out for 'Auctoritates', that is extracts from the fathers, especially Augustine, Bernard, Gregory, Jerome, and Ambrose, but of Ambrose only five lines were written, f. 153. ff. 153ᵛ–157ᵛ were left blank.

10 (quire 14). (*a*) ff. 158–62 Excerpta de dictis Innocencii super miseriam condicionis humane. De iniqua possessione diuiciarum. Sapiens protestatur . . . (*b*) ff. 163ᵛ–166 Mundus odiendus et fugiendus est. Tria sunt que hominem principaliter ab amore seculi . . . (*c*) f. 166 Bernhardus ad Thomam prepositum de Beuerla. Generositas sangwuinis. proceritas corporis . . . (*d*) f. 166ᵛ Bernhardus de accel(er)anda conuersione. Ecce nos reliquimus . . . (*e*) ff. 162–3, 167–8 Short pieces.

(*c*). PL clxxxii, Ep. 107, beginning at col. 243ᴀ: cf. art. 2*d–h*. ff. 168ᵛ–169ᵛ were left blank.

11 (quire 15). (*a*) ff. 170ᵛ–179ᵛ Sequuntur scripta beati Ieronimi et primo. Exhortacio de timore dei. Hortor vos karissimi mei . . . sine quo nichil penitus sumus. (*b*) f. 180ʳᵛ Schemes of virtues, etc. (*c*) f. 181ʳᵛ Sixteen 'Virtutes misse', etc. f. 170ʳ was left blank.

12 (quires 16–18). (*a*) ff. 183–91 Incipit tractatus de arte bene moriendi. Cum de presentis exilii miseria . . . delinquere. sicut fecit Ihesus cristus . . . (*b*) ff. 191–213ᵛ Incipit tractatus de quatuor nouissimis. Memorare nouissima tua et in eternum non peribis. Ecclesiastici viiᵒ. Sicut dicit Augustinus . . . ac nouissima prouiderent etc'. Explicit cordiale et tractatus de quatuor nouissimis etc'.

(*a*). Printed often (*GKW* 2597–2614). For the authorship see M. C. O'Connor, *The Art of Dying Well*, 1942, pp. 48–60. (*b*). Printed often (*GKW* 7469–7514). f. 214ʳᵛ blank.

13 (quires 19, 20). ff. 215–39 'Meditaciones circa cerimonialia misse pro deuocione excitanda'. 'Caue'. Exigis a me frater dulcis in domino vt circa canonem misse aliquas tibi meditaciones compendiosas depingam . . . Ante omnia scire volo tuam caritatem . . . percipite regnum. Ad quam nos . . . amen. Explicit libellus 'qui intitulatur Caue' de preparacione misse.

f. 226ᵛ was left blank and a new hand begins on f. 227. f. 239ᵛ was left blank.

14 (quire 21). ff. 240–58 contain many short pieces headed, aptly, 'Exhortaciones doctorum et multa alia hinc inde collecta'. Among them are: (*a*) f. 243ᵛ Si seruire cupis altare respice caute . . .; (*b*) ff. 246–7, in larger script than the rest, 'Incipit lilium uirginitatis. Quodlibet lilium habet plurima folia . . .'; (*c*) ff. 248–

50 De septem miraculis que fiunt in consecracione venerabilis sacramenti. Reuela oculos meos. Ammirabo mirabilium . . . Reuela oculos meos etc.

(*a*). Ten lines of verse, Walther, no. 19790. (*b*). Cf. Jørgensen, op. cit., p. 148. (*c*). Cf. ibid., p. 109 (Albertus de Colonia). The words 'Deus assit inceptum meum' head ff. 248, 253.

15 (quires 22, 23). (*a*) ff. 259–262ᵛ Lists of chapters of books of the Old Testament. (*b*) ff. 262ᵛ–263ᵛ A chronologically arranged subject list from the Gospels, beginning 'Luce 1 a solus. [D]e concepcione precursoris'. (*c*) f. 264 Incipiunt expositores librorum biblie. (*d*) f. 264 The words 'Per studium' and in a bracket against them five lines of verse, 'Viget ingenium precor ut studeatis . . .'. (*e*) ff. 264ᵛ–265ᵛ Expositio oracionis dominicalis. (*f*) ff. 265ᵛ–270 Extracts from the Fathers. (*g*) ff. 275–277ᵛ Collacio de sancto Iohanne baptista. Imitatores mei estote fratres Ad phill' iii c. Pro impetranda gracia dicimus cum deuocione Aue maria. Venerabiles patres licet sanctissima patriarcha scilicet patronus et legifer noster Beatus iohannes baptista cuius natiuitatem . . .

(*c*). The commentators on Genesis come first, Alcuin, Origen, Bede, Isidore, Rabanus, Gregory. ff. 271–274ᵛ, 280–283ᵛ were left blank.

16. Many blank spaces were filled or partly filled by a scribe whose hand occurs in corrections and marginalia throughout and also in a note on the binding leaf (art. 17). He writes in German on ff. 147, 148ᵛ, 155ᵛ. His additions include: (*a*) f. 87ᵛ Casus prioris; (*b*) 153–4, 270ᵛ Extracts 'Ex reuelacionibus b. Trute'; (*c*) f. 155ᵛ Aspice serue dei. Sic me posuere Iudei . . .; (*d*) f. 157 Nouus predicator. Primo super omnia nullus predicator verecundetur de Reuerencia exhibenda nomini domini nostri Iheu cristi et b. Marie. Sit eis in exemplum quod nuncii principum faciunt. dicunt enim vnser gnediger her' und forste et similia . . .; (*e*) f. 170 Anno domini 1431 festum natiuitatis tercia feria fuit. et sic dominico die ante vigiliam post nonam fuit recordacio leccionum que in vigiliis legebantur. Similiter proxima dominica post festum natiuitatis fuerunt recordate lecciones que in uigilia circumscisionis legebantur. Ita quod perfecta ebdomada singulis diebus fuit recordacio facta; (*f*) f. 239ᵛ De taciturnitate metra. Qui raro fatur. fatusque suus moderatur . . . De loquacitate. Vere turbatur nimis hic qui plurima fatur . . .; (*g*) f. 243 Respice qui transis cum sis michi causa doloris . . .; (*h*) f. 243 Ad mortem pergo dure premor . . .; (*i*) f. 243 Alligor affligor spernor . . .; (*j*) f. 243 O plebs ingrata per adam patrem viciata . . .; (*k*) f. 252 Optinet in celis oracio munda fidelis . . .; (*l*) f. 283ʳᵛ Incipiunt capitula per anni circulum . . . In capitulo . . . Benediccio ad prandium . . . Sequuntur collecte nocturnales . . .

(*a*). Offences with which the prior could deal, under six heads. (*b*). St. Gertrude. (*c*) 10 lines. Walther, no. 1601. (*d*). Don't repeat yourself and Don't go too fast are other pieces of advice. (*f*). 24+24 lines. Walther, nos. 15628, 20185. (*g–k*). 12, 6, 8, 12, 10 lines. (*g*). Walther, no. 16671. (*k*) is spaced for a gloss. (*l*). The first section, capitula, ceases after nine lines when the scribe wrote 'et cetera scribendo capitula cum suis accentibus et rubricis per omnia a principio usque ad finem sicud habentur in diurnali'.

17. f. 284 is part of a leaf of a handsome glossed copy of Antiqua Compilatio Decretalium III, s. xiii¹, and a strip from the same leaf lies between f. 13 and f. 14.

Parts of 4. xiv. 2, 3 and 4. xv. 2, 3 remain (edn. Friedberg, pp. 129–30), but the piece immediately before 4. xv. 2 ends 'et adulterium fit utrimque commissum', not *excitandum*.

18. ff. i, 285, pastedowns, now raised, are from a two-column manuscript of s. xv in. containing names of people cited to appear on particular days before a court (?). Thus the first entry for Wednesday in the fourth week of Lent (f. 285) is 'Item rursus (?) citatus henricus greben s contra Iohannem costorf prorogatur secunda post palmas'. ff. i^r, 285^v are hard to read.

ff. ii+282+ii, foliated i, 1–285. Paper, except the end-leaves, arts. 17, 18. A medieval foliation of ff. 2–283 begins with '1' and ends with '288', '301', '302', '304': it takes into account leaves now missing, some of which were probably blank. 215 × 150 mm. Written space *c.* 160 × 110 mm. Partly in 2 columns and partly in long lines. 27–39 lines. Frame ruling. Collation of ff. 2–283: 1–2^{12} 3^{14}+1 leaf after 14 (f. 40) 4–5^{12} 6^{14} 7^{12} wants 9–11 after f. 86 8^{12} wants 11, 12, perhaps blank, after f. 97 9^{12} 10^{12} wants 11, blank, after f. 119 11^{14} 12^8+a slip inserted after 1 (f. 136) 13^{14} 14–15^{12} 16^{12}+1 leaf before 1 (f. 182) 17^{12} 18^{12} wants 9–12, perhaps blank, after f. 214 19^{12} 20^{12}+1 leaf after 12 (f. 239) 21^{20} wants 20 after f. 258 22^{12} 23 ten (ff. 271–80) 24 three (ff. 281–3).

Quires numbered at the beginning. Cursiva and (art. 16) hybrida. Punctuation with the flex (?) is used only in the liturgical piece on f. 283. Red initials in several sizes, a few with muddy ornament. Capital letters in the ink of the text are filled with red or yellow and sometimes with both red and yellow in the same letter. Contemporary binding of thick wooden boards cut flush with the edges of the leaves and covered with pigskin: three bands: two clasps missing: a title-label on the front cover.

Written in Germany, probably at the Charterhouse of Erfurt, and partly in the years 1431, 1433, and 1434 (arts. 1, 3*a*, 16). 'Ad carth' prope Erfford' pertinet hic liber' (f. 284: cf. ff. 1, 1^v, 2). Listed as F. 13 in the catalogue compiled *c.* 1475 (*MBDS* ii. 343). Lot 430 in the Bülow sale, 10 Oct. 1836: cf. MS. 301. Bought at the (W. A. Cragg) sale at Sotheby's, 10 Dec. 1962, lot 143 (£85).

ELY. CATHEDRAL

Liber Eliensis[1]   s. XII ex.

1. ff. 2–188^v Incipit prologus de historia Eliensis insule . . . Cum animaduerterem . . . et triumphat de sanctis suis.

Printed from this copy, (F), by E. O. Blake, *Liber Eliensis* (Camden Soc., 3rd series, xcii, 1962), pp. 1–394: cf. there, p. xxiv and HMC, *Twelfth Report*, App., pp. 393–4. Each book begins on a new quire: 2, f. 39 (6^1); 3, f. 109 (14^1). A prologue and unnumbered table of chapters before each book: those of bks. 2, 3 fill the ends of quires 5 and 13. A singleton (or a bifolium with the second leaf blank) is missing after f. 108 (13^{10}) which ends in the table of bk. 3 with the catchword 'Carta Herfordensis episcopi de p' ' (edn., p. 243). Additions to the account of abbot Brihtnoth on ff. 59^v, 61^v (edn., pp. 123, 127) are contemporary. Later additions, s. xiv, include bk. 2, chs. 16, 128 on ff. 47, 92^v. The word 'papa' and the name of St. Thomas of Canterbury have been erased where they occur.

2. Additions on a flyleaf and in the blank space on f. 188^v: (*a*) f. 1, s. xiv in. 'Isti sunt confessores cristi quorum corpora iacent ex parte aquilonali chor

---

[1] On deposit in Cambridge University Library, EDC 1.

ecclesie Eliensis in locellis separatis in pariete lapideo. Wlstanus Eboracensis archiepiscopus . . .'; (b) f. 1ʳᵛ, s. xv, 'In cronicis anglicis et latinis reperitur quod monasterium apud Ely . . .'; (c) f. 1ᵛ, s. xiv, 'Hic liber insignis etheldrede memoratur/ Qui monachis dignis eliensibus attitulatur. / Rex edmunde fouens semper monachos berienses / Regraciando regens esto monachos elienses'; (d) f. 188ᵛ, s. xii/xiii, 'Hugo prior Elyen' ecclesie et totus conuentus eiusdem loci Omnibus . . .; (e) f. 188ᵛ, s. xiv, 'Memorandum quod domus militum templi de Denya . . .'.

(c). These verses appear to be in the hand of Henry de Kirkestede, monk of Bury St. Edmunds, s. xiv², for whom see R. H. Rouse in *Speculum*, xli (1966), 471–99. They are perhaps his thank-you for the loan of this copy of Liber Eliensis to Bury: the Liber was used for the Bury compilation, MS. Bodley 240, begun in 1377.[1] (d). Grant to Stephen, son of Humphrey [C]arnifex. (e) is rubbed, but legible by ultra-violet light. It is a memorandum of the Templars' holding 'de feodo ecclesie Eliensis' at Waterbeach, etc.

ff. vii+189+ii. An incorrect modern foliation which counts the parchment flyleaf as 1 and repeats the numbers 78 and 84 has taken the place of a correct late medieval foliation. 267×185 mm. Written space c. 188×130 mm. 2 cols. 30 lines. Pricks in both margins to guide ruling. Collation of ff. 2–188: 1–4⁸ 5 five (ff. 34, 35, 37, 38, 36) 6–7⁸ 8–9¹⁰ 10–11⁸ 12–13¹⁰ 14–16⁸ 17¹⁰ 18⁸ 19–21¹⁰ 22⁸. Quires 14–20 are numbered at the end, beginning with i, and have catchwords. Well written by four hands, changing at ff. 21ᵛᵃ/19, 109, 112: the first hand is the best. Initials: (i) f. 1, an 11-line *C* in pencil outline containing a pencil historiation, a kneeling monk giving a book to St. Etheldreda (?); (ii) 2-line, red or green (both colours sometimes) and, f. 109, blue, with ornament in red and green: on f. 5ᵛ the red and green initial is ornamented with gold dots. Binding of s. xviii, repaired by Gray, Cambridge, in 1930. Secundo folio (f. 3) *Sed ne*.

Written at the Benedictine abbey of Ely. The late medieval Ely pressmark '6.60', at the head of f. 1: cf. *MMBL* i. 403, footnote.[2]

Fragments in the capitular archives[3]

1. A bifolium of notes on Psalms. s. xiii[1]

The notulae on Ps. 5 begin at verse 10, 'Quoniam non est in ore eorum ueritas. Facta oracione deliberacione ab imeditis profectus. hic notatur'. Written space c. 215×125 mm. 2 cols. 74 long lines. Small hand. Used as the front flyleaf inside the cover of EDC 1/A/3, the 'Registrum dompni Edwardi Walsyngham Prioris Eliensis' (c. 1424–8: Davis, *MC*, no. 376).[4]

2. A leaf of Thomas Aquinas, Commentary on the Meteora of Aristotle. s. xiii ex.

Includes the beginning of the text, 'Sicut in rebus naturalibus nichil est perfectum'. Written space c. 285×160 mm. 2 cols. 76 lines. Small hand. Used as the back flyleaf of the same book as no. 1.

[1] Cf. C. Horstmann, *Nova Legenda Angliae*, i (1901), lix.
[2] In Ker, *MLGB*, p. 78, I mistook the figure 6 here and in Bodley 762 for a *G*.
[3] The capitular archives (EDC) are deposited in Cambridge University Library.
[4] The cover itself is a bull of Pope Gregory XI, 13 Mar. 1372, addressed to Thomas Arundel, archdeacon of Taunton (bishop of Ely, 1374–88). Cf. M. Aston, *Thomas Arundel*, p. 7, a reference I owe to Professor C. R. Cheney.

ELY. DIOCESAN RECORD OFFICE[1]

EDR F/5/32. *Formularium Juris Canonici*   s. xv[2]

1. ff. 1–88 A north of England collection of formulary documents, beginning with citations. Cf. A. W. Gibbons, *Ely Episcopal Records*, p. 127, and Owen, p. 30.

One of the few dated pieces is a form of assignation of proctors by John Arundell, M.A., attested by William Munteyn, notary public, diocese of Bath and Wells, at Durham College, Oxford, 1 May 1467 (f. 85ᵛ). Other named notaries are Thomas Mynskipp' alias Driffeld', diocese of York, William Westerdale, diocese of York, and Robert Bartram, diocese of Coventry and Lichfield (ff. 83ᵛ, 84ᵛ, 87). Two pieces at the end are in the name of William Langton, B.L., receiver general of the treasury of York (ff. 87ᵛ, 88).

2. ff. 89ᵛ–96ᵛ Twenty-two added pieces fill the last quire. Seven of them bear dates between 1467 and 1479. They include: (v) ff. 89ᵛ–90, an indenture between Richard Andrew, dean of York, and the rector of Kilham, Yorkshire, 30 Apr. 1477; (viii) f. 91, a letter from Laurence (Booth), archbishop of York (1476–80), on the election of Robert Bothe as dean of York, 14 Aug. 1477; (xxii) f. 96ᵛ, a letter of Gilbert, prior of Bolton in Craven, to dean Bothe, 10 Oct. 1479.

All these pieces may be in the same hand as art. 1.

ff. 96. Paper. 305 × 220 mm. Written space *c.* 210 × 145 mm. *c.* 41 long lines. Frame ruling with a hard point. Collation: 1¹⁸ 2¹⁶ 3¹⁸ 4¹⁶ 5¹² 6¹⁶. Quires numbered at the beginning 1–6. Art. 1 in a small clear secretary hand, becoming looser towards the end. Limp parchment cover, with paper over it, s. xviii (?).

Written in England and probably at York, *c.* 1470–80. Belonged slightly later (s. xv–xvi) to the 'Iohn Newsam' whose name, with paraph, is on f. 96ᵛ and ('I. Newsam') on f. 1.

EDR F/5/33. *Formularium Juris Canonici, etc.*   s. xv in.

1. ff. 1–3ᵛ A table of contents of art. 2, except f. 22, before leaves were lost.

Leaf references given. The unnumbered leaf after 3 is blank.

2. ff. 4–25 Forms of citation, letters testimonial, dimission, sequestration, prohibition, etc., apparently the collection of an official of the ecclesiastical court of York. Cf. Owen, p. 30.

Two quires. Four leaves are missing from the first quire and fifteen from the second: see below. Begins with a 'Litera citacionis'. 'in dies' is glossed 'ilkaday' on f. 12. Later additions are in the name of Henry, bishop of Worcester (H. Wakefield, 1375–95) (f. 15) and a letter of Thomas, bishop of Worcester (? T. Peverel, 1407–19), at Henbury (f. 22ᵛ). ff. 15ᵛ, 16ʳ blank.

3. Memoranda of purchases, etc., added in blank spaces: (*a*) ff. 13ᵛ, 14, 30 Jan.– 7 July, 14–15 Henry IV; (*b*) ff. 18ᵛ, 19ᵛ–20, 22ᵛ, 24, 25ᵛ and inside the end cover.

(*a*) begins with expenses of a journey to London (by the bishop of Worcester?), 30 Jan.–

---

[1] The Diocesan Record Office is in Cambridge University Library. For the archives (EDR) see D. M. Owen, *A Catalogue of the Records of the Bishop and Archdeacon of Ely*, 1971.

6 Feb. 1415: 'Memorandum quod dominus recessit de Breodon' versus london' . . .'. The account was made up 'in presencia Magistri Thome preceptoris sancti Wolstani Wygorn' Nicholai Trentham et Iohannis Bawsey' (f. 14). (*b*). Hartlebury and 'Brymescros' are mentioned on f. 25ᵛ and expenses at Chipping Norton, Enstone, Islip, and Tetsworth (all on the London road from Worcestershire) inside the end cover.

ff. 26, foliated 1–3, (3*), 4–25; formerly ff. 45. A contemporary foliation of ff. 4–25 by quires, 'Primus quaternus primo folio', etc., shows which leaves are missing. Paper. 210 × 140 mm. Written space *c.* 160 × 110 mm. Collation: 1⁴ 2²² wants 7, 9, 14, 16+1 leaf after 22 (f. 22) 3¹⁸ wants 1, 4–16, 18 (ff. 23–5). Written in current anglicana. Contemporary limp parchment cover.

Written in York or from a York exemplar. In 1415 probably in the possession of a servant of Thomas Peverel, Bishop of Worcester.

Fragments in the diocesan archives.

EDR L/3/1/. Two leaves from the end of Archbishop Stratford's statutes for the Court of Arches. s. xiv ex.

1. ff. 1–2 appellationis causa probare . . . iii id' Maii anno domini M° ccc° xlii°. Wilkins, *Concilia*, ii. 692–5. 2. f. 2ʳᵛ In tuitoriis negociis introducendis . . . ut maliciose deferret eam [. . . .]. The text ends at the foot of the first column on the verso: the second column is blank. Written space 272 × 160 mm. 2 cols. 66 lines. A bifolium with continuous text. 2-line red initials. In use as an end-leaf inside the plain parchment cover of an Induction Book for 1427 to 1519 (Owen, p. 71).

EDR O/19/1/1, 2. Two bifolia of Jerome on Minor Prophets. s. xiii ex.

One leaf has the end of Amos and the beginning of Obadiah. Written space 258 × 170 mm. 2 cols. 55 lines. Formerly end-leaves inside the plain parchment cover of B/2/5, a visitation book for 1565–7 (Owen, p. 8), as appears from the offset.

EDR D/2/11. Parts of two leaves of a breviary. s. xiv/xv

From the sanctorale for May, as *Brev. ad usum Sarum*, iii. 286 (John Evangelist), 289 (Nereus and Achilleus), 294–5 (Dunstan). A cue for John of Beverley (7 May) in red on the first leaf. Written space 220 mm wide. 2 cols. The first six lines remain on each leaf. In use as strips inside the cover of an instance-book for 1574–81 (Owen, p. 21).

EDR F/5/51. Part of a bifolium of St. Bernard on the Song of Songs. s. xii ex.

Part of the text in *SBO* i. 136/20–142/30. The beginning of sermon 23 remains. The last sixteen lines of the central bifolium of a quire. Written space 145 mm wide. 2 cols. Pricks in the inner margin to guide ruling. Punctuation includes the flex (?). In use as a broad strengthening strip inside the cover of a precedent-book compiled *c.* 1580 (Owen, p. 34).

EDR O/19/2/1, 2. Two leaves of an antiphonal. s. xv

First Sunday in Advent and Servitium beate Marie per Adventum (*Brev. ad usum Sarum*, i. xix–xxv, ii. 283–5). Written space *c.* 340 × 230 mm. 2 cols. 51 lines (17 lines and music). Covers, one marked '19 Januarii 1571–28 Julii 1578' and the other '6 Octob. 1604–15 Aug. 1605'. The former was presumably the cover of EDR D/2/9 (Owen, p. 24).

EDR O/19/3/1–4. Four leaves of a gradual. s. xv

(1) Trinity Sunday. (2, 3) Corpus Christi. (4) second to fourth Sundays after Trinity. Written space *c.* 275 × 220 mm. 11 long lines and music. (1) is marked 'Acta expedita coram domino Delegato et Commissario etc domini Archiepiscopi Cantuarien' durante Visitatione sua Metropolitica in Dioces' Elien' 1608', (2) 'Visitatio Metropolitica Domini

Archiepiscopi Catuarien., anno etc. 1608', (3) 'Act' super presentacionem . . . 1608', (4) 'K. 1610'. Cf. B/2/29 (Owen, p. 65).

In Register of Wills, 1610–14 (Liber Y). A bifolium and two strips from a homiliary. s. xii[2]

The homily of Haymo of Auxerre for the third Sunday after the octave of Epiphany begins on f. 1, 'Cum descendisset . . . Superius . . .', and his homily for the fourth Sunday on f. 2, 'Ascendente . . . In huius lectionis . . .' (PL cxviii. 137, 147). The former is preceded by a homily ending 'cogit iusticia ad retribuendum' and the latter by a homily ending 'in cordibus nostris per sanctum spiritum qui datus est'. The strips are from the same quire as ff. 1, 2 and contain part of the text in PL, cols. 139, 140, 145, 146.

Written space 267 × 170 mm. 2 cols. 41 lines. Pricks in inner margin to guide ruling. Handsome English hand. The two initials are (1) green and red, (2) blue and red. The bifolium was the pastedown in front and the strips were laid down at the end of the Register, which was until 1974 in a plain leather binding, s. xvii: this has been preserved.[1]

In Consistory Court Register of Wills, 1703–8. Two bifolia and a strip from a volume of sermons (?). s. xiv/xv

A piece begins 'Maria Magdalene etc. Maria magd' pertinet ad statum'. The number 98 is in the corner of one leaf. Written space c. 235 × 150 mm. 2 cols. 62 lines. Pastedowns in a binding bearing Oldham's rolls HE. a. 1, HM. a. 3, and SW. b. 2, work of s. xvii in.: apparently the book was not used for one hundred years after it was made.

EDR O/19/4. A bifolium of Tacuinum sanitatis. s. xiii/xiv

Cf. Thorndike and Kibre. From the end of the text: f. 2ʳ has 'Explicit tacuinum dei excelsi adiutorio neapoli 11 marcii viii indiccionis per manus magistri faragii supradicti ad opus regis excellentissimi akakoli supradicti et laus sit deo excelso'. f. 2ᵛ, left blank, was filled with a sermon on 'Altissimus de terra creauit' (Ecclesiasticus 38: 4). Written space 277 × 215 mm. 62 long lines. English hands, f. 2ᵛ current. Folded to make a cover 300 × 190 mm.

EDR O/19/5. A leaf of an antiphonal. s. xv[2]

Brev. ad usum Sarum, i. cccxxxiii–v (Octave of Epiphany). Written space 335 × 220 mm. 2 cols. 45 lines (15 lines and music). Folded to make a cover 305 × 215 mm. Marked '9.19.21' and 'Procurationes Episcopi Eliensis' (cf. Owen, p. 74).

ETON COLLEGE

M. R. James, A Descriptive Catalogue of the Manuscripts in the Library of Eton College. Cambridge, 1895.

Covers MSS. 1–193. Before 1895 the manuscripts were referred to by their shelfmarks, for which James substituted a continuous series of numbers: Bk. 1.1–13: MSS. 1–13; Bk. 2.1–11: MSS. 14–24; Bk. 3.1–12: MSS. 25–36; Bk. 4.1–12: MSS. 37–48; Bk. 5.1–11: MSS. 49–73;[2] Bk. 6.1–18: MSS. 74–91; Bl. 1.1–10: MSS. 92–101; Bl. 2.1–9, 9*, 10–12: MSS. 102–14; Bl. 3.1–13: MSS. 115–27; Bl. 4.1–16: MSS. 128–43; Bl. 5.13,

---

[1] Information from the University binder. The registers of wills of the Consistory of Ely are in the care of the Cambridge University Archivist (cf. Owen, p. 29).

[2] MSS. 49–73 were transferred to Peterhouse, Cambridge, in 1946.

14: MSS. 144, 145; Bl. 6.1–26: MSS. 146–71; Bl. a. 1–5: MSS. 172–6; Bp. 3.7, 11, 13–15: MSS. 183–7; Bp. 4.18: MS. 188; Bp. 5.16, 18: MSS. 189, 190.[1]

Catalogus Manuscriptorum Angliae et Hiberniae (ed. E. Bernard), ii. 46–8. Oxford (1697).

Numbered 1–126 and in the continuous series of pt. 2, 1799–1924. Probably all the manuscripts recorded in *CMA* are now in the library. I have referred to *CMA* only if there is no earlier evidence that a manuscript was at Eton. James provided a concordance of *CMA* numbers with those now in use, *Catalogue*, pp. xiii–xv.[2]

R. Birley, 'The history of Eton College Library', *The Library*, 5th series, xi (1956), 231–61: referred to below as 'Birley'.

R. Birley, *The History of Eton College Library*. Eton, 1970.

Bindings

Most of the medieval Eton manuscripts were rebound in calf by three binders, Andrew Lisley, Williamson, and Slatter. Lisley's and Williamson's bindings are discussed by Birley.[3] In rebinding, a few composite manuscripts were made: MS. 32 and probably MS. 108 by Lisley; MSS. 48 and 101 by Williamson; MS. 76 by Slatter or Williamson, one of whom presumably detached MS. 82 (now in a Slatter binding) from MS. 76 ff. 1–40.

Lisley was paid over three years, 1519–20,[4] 1520–1, and 1521–2, and possibly over a longer period: the accounts for 1518–19 and 1522–3 are missing. In 1520–1 and 1521–2 he received commons for forty-six weeks. Probably he bound many manuscripts which have since been rebound.

The unnamed binder who bound twenty specified books in 1600–1[5] can hardly be anyone but Williamson. Eighteen of the bindings survive,[6] fifteen of them on manuscripts, and most of them bear the 'Herculis and Vena' roll, Oldham's HM.b. 2. This same roll occurs on a copy of college statutes bound in 1601–2[7] and on a collection of transcripts of college charters bound in 1602–3.[8] At the latter date the binder is named as 'Williamson'. He is named again in the accounts for 1608–9 when he bound fourteen specified manuscripts.[9] Eleven of them are still in his bindings[10] and all but one bear the 'Herculis and Vena' roll. Williamson used wooden boards when he used his roll, but his leather is over

---

[1] MSS. 177–82, 191–3 have no shelfmarks.
[2] On p. xiii MSS. 21 and 25 are identified wrongly with entries in *CMA*.
[3] Birley, pp. 235, 246–8 and pls. iv–vii, and R. Birley, *The History of Eton College Library*, Eton, 1970, pp. 8, 9, 22–5, where (p. 25) Birley suggests that Williamson is likely to be Vincent Williamson, citizen, stationer, and bookbinder of London. For Lisley see also N. R. Ker in *The Library*, 5th series, xvii (1962), 79.
[4] Birley, pl. iii, shows a page of these accounts.
[5] Accounts 1591–1602, p. 640.
[6] 'Hieronymus in Danielem' (MS. 76) was later rebound by Slatter and 'Hieronymi Catalogus vir illustr' has not been found.
[7] Accounts 1591–1602, p. 683. Roll (*a*) and stamps (*d–g*) shown by Birley, pl. vi.
[8] Accounts 1603–21, p. 37. Roll (*a*) and stamps (*b*, *e–h*): stamp (*f*) is on the spine.
[9] Accounts 1603–21, p. 317.
[10] The rebound manuscripts are 9, 74, and either 45 or 125, probably the latter and larger, in view of the price.

pasteboards when it is decorated merely with a pattern of triple fillets, as on MSS. 15, 46, 48, 98, which are identifiable in the 1600–1 accounts, and on MS. 43 which is identifiable in the 1608–9 accounts. The style of binding and the pastedowns suggest that MSS. 7, 13, 97, all three in pasteboards, are also of his binding, but they are not mentioned in the accounts. The roll usually extends over the leather covering the broad bevel on the inside of the boards, visible when the book stands with its fore-edge facing outwards. There is usually hatching on the spine, and sometimes cross-hatching.[1]

Ten of the medieval manuscripts are still in Lisley bindings[2] and twenty-eight of them are still in Williamson bindings. A much larger number of them, sixty-one in all, are in bindings by Slatter, who was paid over £11 in 1715 for binding eighty-eight 'manuscripts etc. belonging to College Library'.[3] Slatter used pasteboards covered with light calf, plain except for an ornament at each corner of a rectangular panel formed by fillets. No gilding is used. The ornaments are five, larger or smaller according to the size of the book. As a binder Slatter has the great merit that he tended to keep old flyleaves and pastedowns when he rebound a book.[4]

Traces of an old numeration of the manuscripts are to be seen on the fore-edge of the board on two Lisley bindings, '9' on MS. 99 and '10' on MS. 108 and on the bevel of three Williamson bindings, '2' on MS. 6, '5' on MS. 127 and '43' on MS. 8.

The following list is of bindings by L(isley), W(illiamson), and S(latter). The number i, ii, iii, iv, or v after S indicates the ornament used by Slatter. The figure 1 or 9 before W shows that the manuscript in question is listed in the accounts for 1600–1 or 1608–9. The letter a, b, c, or d, after W shows the presence of the roll (a) or of a stamp shown by Birley, pl. vi. (P) indicates that Lisley or Williamson used pastedowns taken from medieval manuscripts or that Slatter took such pastedowns over from the older binding: these pastedowns are noted in the descriptions, below.[5] Eighteen Williamson bindings are priced individually in the accounts. These sums are noted. There were also three lump payments in 1600–1: 18s. 8d. for MSS. 5, 8, 18, 104, 114 and three printed books; 15s. for MSS. 98, 101, and a printed book; 9s. 4d. for MSS. 6, 17, 19, 106.

MS.	Binding	MS.	Binding	MS.	Binding
1	Si	5	1Wa (P)	8	1Wa
2	Si	6	1Wab	9	Sii (9W: 3s. 6d.)
4	Sii	7	W (P)	10	Sii

[1] Most of the bindings between 5 and 106 have been rebacked recently by Mr. R. L. Day, who has preserved as much old work as possible. Of Williamson's, 42, 48, and 101 have not been repaired.

[2] I exclude MSS. 30 and 103 for which see Birley, p. 235.

[3] In all seventy-three manuscripts are now in Slatter bindings.

[4] Cf. also p. 745, footnote.

[5] For pastedowns and flyleaves used by Williamson when he bound two printed books and the volume of transcripts of charters see under MSS. 5 and 14+16+19. The pastedowns he used when he bound the college statutes are two bifolia of a handsome copy of Nicholas de Lyra on Deuteronomy in an English hand, s. xiv².

MS. Binding	MS. Binding	MS. Binding
12 Sii	74 (9W: 2s. 2d.)	124 Si (P)
13 W (P)	76 Si (1W: 14d.) (P)	125 Si (?9W: 3s. 6d.).
14 L	77 Sii (P)	Cf. 45
15 1W 2s. 4d. (P)	79 Siii (P)	126 Si
16 L	80 9Wa 16d.	127 9Wad 3s. 6d.
17 1Wa (P)	81 Siii	129 9Wa 2s. 2d.
18 1Wa (P)	82 Siii	130 Si
19 1Wa (P)	83 Siii (P)	131 Sii
20 L	87 Siv (P)	132 9Wa 2s. 2d.
21 Si	88 Siv	134 Si (P)
22 Si	97 W (P)	135 Siv (P)
23 Si	98 1W	136 Si
24 Sii	99 L	137 Si (P)
27 Si	101 1Wa (P)	140 Siv (P)
28 Sii	102 9Wa 6s.	145 Sii (P)
29 Sii	104 1Wa	149 Sv
32 L (P)	105 Sii (P)	150 Siv
33 9Wa 2s. 2d.	106 1Wacd (P)	151 Siii
34 L (P)	107 L (P)	152 Siv
35 Si	108 L (P)	153 Sv (P)
36 Si	109 9Wab 6s. (P)	154 Siv
37 L (P)	110 Si	155 Siii
38 Sii	112 Si	156 Siii (P)
39 Sii	114 1Wa (P)	157 Siii
41 Sii (P)	115 Sii	158 Siii
42 9Wa 2s. 2d. (P)	116 L	160 Siii
43 9W 16d.	117 Sii	165 Siii
44 Si	118 Si	169 Siii
45 (?9W: 3s. 6d.). Cf. 125	120 9Wa 3s. 6d.	170 Siii (P)
46 1W 20d. (P)	122 9Wad 3s. 6d.	171 Siii (P)
48 1W 20d. (P)	123 Si	172 Si

Robert Elyot

The Lisley and Williamson bindings are evidence that certain manuscripts were at Eton by 1520, 1601, and 1609. Robert Elyot's marginalia provide evidence of the same kind. Elyot—for whom see Emden, *BRUO*, p. 638—died as vice-provost of Eton in Jan. 1499, so any Eton manuscript with his hand in it was at Eton by this time. To the best of my knowledge, twenty-two manuscripts have in them either his distinctive *nota bene* heads or notes in his hand, or both. They are MSS. 5, 13, 17, 18, 22, 23, 34, 35, 36, 38, 41, 76+82, 81, 83, 99, 102, 103, 105, 108, 117, 125, 219 pp. 91–118. MS. 5 was his own book and it seems likely that the five books with the largest amount of annotation in them, 17, 18, 34, 36, 76, were his, especially 34, which he seems to have had at Oxford in the time, 1450–61, when he and Thomas Wych were both there. On the other hand, four books with only a little of his writing in them were certainly college books and not his own; 22 and 103 were at Eton by 1465, and 99 and 105 were gifts in 1476 and 1489 respectively. For further details see N. R. Ker, 'Robert Elyot's Books and Annotations', *The Library*, 5th series, xxx (1975), 233-7.

1,2. *Biblia*   s. XIII²

1. vol. 1, ff. 1–5ᵛ (*begins imperfectly*) eorum uel lumen uel illuminacio. Arody stupor vel ammiracio . . . Aroez . . . Arphath . . . Arphazach . . . Zusym. preparati uel terribiles in acie. vel que est hec aqua.

A dictionary of Hebrew names, the first leaf missing. A few more interpretations and the names of the three kings follow Zusym. ff. 6–9ᵛ blank.

2. vol. 1, ff. 10–176ᵛ; vol. 2, ff. 1–160ᵛ A Bible with the usual contents in the usual order,¹ ending imperfectly at Acts 3: 10, 'quoniam ipse erat qui ad'.

Nehemiah begins (vol. 1, f. 133) with an initial of type (ii) but is run together with 1 Ezra as one book of eighteen chapters. Joshua and Proverbs begin on new quires, vol. 1, f. 62 and vol. 2, f. 1. Within books the text is continuous: the beginning of a new chapter, as set out in the tables of chapters, is shown by a coloured initial, not by paragraphing. The chapter numbers in the margins agree with those now in use.

The prologues are the common set,¹ except for the absence of Stegmüller, no. 327 before 2 Chronicles, no. 468 before Wisdom, no. 677 before Romans, and no. 765 before 1 Timothy, but the common prologues to Ephesians, Philippians, Colossians, and 1 Thessalonians are additions in a contemporary hand.

A table of chapters precedes every book but 3 Ezra, Song of Songs, Lamentations, and Baruch.²

Gen., Ex., Josh., Judic.	Series Δ, forma B
Lev., Num., Deut., Ruth	Series K
1–4 Reg.	Series E
1, 2 Paralip.	Series unica, forma b
Ezra+Neh.	Series B
Job, Is.	Series A
Tob., Jud., Esth.	As Am.³
Eccles.	Series A, forma b
Sap., Ecclesiasticus, Parab., Jer.	Series A, forma a⁴
Eze.	Visio quatuor animalium . . . hereditate accepit israel.
Dan.	De filiis captiuitatis . . . prandium abacuc prophete.
1 Macc.	Ubi euersa ierusalem . . . perdere eum.
2 Macc.	Ubi occisus est anthiocus . . . et ierosolimam mitti.

In NT the capitula seem to be those printed by Wordsworth and White from C (etc.), except of John, as ₣ (etc.), of Philemon, as A (etc.), and of Acts, as B (etc.), but Philippians, 1 Thessalonians, and Titus have a final sentence after *circa se corpus*, and *deuitet*, 'Sanctorum commemorat . . . uictoribus suis', 'Quos sanctorum commemorat . . . et thimotheus', and 'Quorum in epistola . . . et appollo', respectively. A slightly later hand added an explanation of the word anathema to the capitula of 1 Corinthians.

¹ Cf. above, Bristol Public Library 15.
² For the tables of chapters of OT I follow *Biblia Sacra*, which reaches at present to Baruch and for the tables of NT, Wordsworth and White.
³ *Biblia Sacra* prints no capitula for Tobit, Judith, Esther. The capitula here are those in Amiens 1, as shown by de Bruyne, *Sommaires*.
⁴ In the table before Jeremiah the readings are those of MS. K (Casinensis 508, s. xiii).

Contemporary corrections in the margins throughout in a business hand. The longer corrections have usually been erased—not, however, at f. 129ᵛ of vol. 1—after being taken into the text in the usual twelfth-century manner or after being rewritten in textura in the margin, as, for example, on ff. 46 and 130 of vol. 1 and f. 103 of vol. 2. The shorter corrections have not been taken into the text or rewritten in the margin. The corrections stand out well, because of the absence of later annotations in this Bible.

One volume bound in two, ff. iv+176+ii and ff. ii+160+iv. Vol. 1, ff. iii, iv and vol. 2, ff. 161–2 are medieval pastedowns and flyleaves. 420 × 295 mm. Written space 240 × 160 mm. 2 cols. 58 lines. The first line of writing is above the top ruled line. Collation: 1⁴ wants 1 2² 3⁴ 4–5¹⁰ 6⁸ 7–8¹⁰ 9⁴+1 leaf after 4 (f. 62) 10–20¹⁰ 21⁴ (ff. 173–6) 22–37¹⁰: quires 22–37 form vol. 2. Catchwords and numbers at the end i–xxviiii for quires 4–32. Many quires have *ad hoc* signatures on the first five leaves in red, for example quires 28–31 are marked thus: vol. 2, ff. 71–5 v . . a, v . . b, v . . c, v . . d, v . . e; ff. 81–5, iiia, iiib, iiic, iiid, iiie; ff. 91–5, xva, xvb, xvc, xvd, xve; ff. 101–5 . . . . a, ... b, ... c, ... d, ... e. Art. 1 in a business hand. Initials: (i) beginning the general prologue, Genesis, Pss. 1, 109, Matthew, in colour patterned in white, on gold grounds historiated (cf. James, *Catalogue*, for details), within a frame of colour or gold, edged often with black; (ii) beginning books and principal psalms, including Pss. 51, 101, as (i), but decorated, sometimes with animals, not historiated; (iii) of prologues and Nehemiah, as (ii), but smaller (usually 6-line); (iv) of psalms and tables of chapters, 2-line, red or blue, with ornament of the other colour; (v) of chapters within books, and verses of psalms, and within tables of chapters, 1-line, red or blue, and (art. 1) red or green. Bindings by Slatter. Secundo folio *tia sacramenta*.

Written in England (?). 'Ex dono Magistri Spenser anno domini 1496', f. iiiᵛ.[1]

3. *Bible Historiale (in French)* s. xiv²

Ci commencent les paraboles salemon. Les paraboles salemon fils dauid . . . soit auec tous vous. Explicit apocalipsis. Ci fine la pocalipse monseignour saint iehan apostre et euuangeliste. Deo gracias.

The second volume of a 'Bible Historiale Complétée': cf. S. Berger, *La Bible française au moyen âge*, 1884, pp. 187–99. Six leaves are missing, with Song of Songs 1: 1–v: 11, Wisdom 7: 12–Ecclesiasticus 1: 2, Amos 8: 10–Micah 2: 11, Matthew 1: 1–3: 7, Ephesians 5: 4–Philippians 2: 13. Only Baruch and Romans have prologues. The translation of Titus is the second version, as usual, but the translation of Apocalypse (by hand 3, ff. 235ᵛ–41) is the rare 'Version A': cf. Delisle and Meyer, *L'Apocalypse en français au 13ᵉ siècle* (Société des Anciens Textes Français), 1901, p. ccxxxvii.[2] Matthew began on a new quire (quire 13). f. 241ᵛ blank.

ff. iii+241+iii. ff. ii, iii, 242 are medieval end-leaves: f. ii was pasted down. 435 × 305 mm. Written space 285 × 203 mm. 2 cols. 50 lines. Collation: 1¹² 2¹² wants 3 after f. 14 and 10 after f. 20 3–9¹² 10¹² wants 6, 7 after f. 111 11¹² 12¹⁰ (ff. 129–38) 13¹² wants 1 before f. 139 14–17¹² 18¹² wants 11 after f. 207 19¹² 20⁸ 21¹²+1 leaf after 12 (f. 241). *Ad hoc* leaf signatures. Mainly by one hand. A second hand completed quire 10 and wrote quires 13–14 (ff. 104ᵛ col. 1/17–106ᵛ, 139–61) and a third begins at f. 224ᵛ col. 2/42 and continues to the end. One large four-compartment picture, 180 × 200 mm on f. 1 and twenty-seven smaller pictures, a column wide and 17 lines or less in height: see James, *Catalogue*. Initials: (i) of books, 12-line or less, blue or pink, patterned in white, on decorated grounds

---

[1] John Spenser, vicar of Huntingdon, seems to be the only person of this name recorded by Emden (*BRUC*, p. 544) who might be this donor. He died by Oct. 1501.

[2] I owe this information to Mr. C. R. Sneddon.

of the other colour and gold; (ii) 2-line, blue or pink, patterned in white, on gold grounds and with short oak-leaf or ivy-leaf sprays into the margins. Capital letters in the ink of the text filled with pale yellow. A nearly continuous frame on f. 1: dogs chase hares along the lower horizontal bar. Shorter borders on other pages with initials of type (i). The letters of running titles are like 1-line initials, gold with blue ornament and blue with red ornament alternately. Binding of s. xviii, repaired in 1963. Secundo folio *mal et.*

Written in France. A motto 'Une sans Plus', f. 242^v, s. xvi. 'Time of Richard 2nd Saml R. Meyrick L.L.D.', f. ii^v: for Meyrick, 1783–1848 see *DNB*. *CMA* 89.

4. *Dictionarium;* (*ff. 86–126^v*) *P. Comestor, Allegoriae*[1] s. xiv/xv–xv in.

1. ff. 1–12^v (*begins imperfectly*) celare . . . uespertilio (*ends imperfectly*). An index to art. 2.

2. ff. 13–85^v Abba secundum papiam sirum nomen est . . . Vath quandoque est interieccio gaudentis (*ends imperfectly*).[2]

Stegmüller, no. 1159 (cf. 1159, 1). A 'Reportorium Biblie'—so the added title in Laud misc. 30—Abba to Zizania, attributed 'cuidam canonico regulari' in a preface which does not occur in this copy. Fuller than the other copies I have seen, B.L., Royal 8 E. vii and Harley 2270, and Bodleian, Bodley 863 and Laud misc.30, where the first three words in the list are Abba, Abdicare, Abducere. Here Abacus, Abalienati, Abat' follow Abba and Abdo follows Abdicare. At least nineteen leaves are missing in gaps after ff. 21, 24, 64, 73: at these points the text passes from Athacus to Bitallassum, from Cancer to Cauteriatus, from Lupanar to Mitulo, and from Pardus to Salpiga.

ff. ii + 126 + ii. 267 × 180 mm. Written space *c.* 180 × 118 mm (arts. 1, 2); 200 × 130 mm (art. 3). 2 cols. (3 cols. in art. 1). 45 lines (art. 2), 51 lines (art. 3), and *c.* 70 lines (art. 1). Collation: 1^8 wants 1–3 2^8 wants 8 after f. 12 3^{12} wants 10–12 after f. 21 4 nine (ff. 22–30) 5–6^{12} 7^{12} wants 11, 12 after f. 64 8^{12} wants 1, 2 before f. 65 and 12 after f. 73 9^{12} 10^8 11^8 wants 1, 2 before f. 94 12^8 13^8 wants 5–8 after f. 111 14^8 wants 1 before f. 112 15^8. Quires 10–15 (art. 3) signed a–d, f, g in the usual late medieval manner. Art. 3 is in anglicana, s. xiv/xv: current and secretary forms occur mainly on the first twelve leaves. Art. 2 is in a current mixture of anglicana and secretary, s. xv in. Art. 1 is like it, but rather later. Initials: (i) f. 86, red and blue with red and violet ornament; (ii) 3-line in art. 3, 3-line or 2-line in art. 2, blue with red ornament. Binding by Slatter. Written in England. The word 'West' at the head of f. 86, s. xv/xvi. *CMA* 121.

5. *Ambrosius, In Ps. 118*   s. xii^2

1. ff. 1–159^v Incipit tractatus beati ambrosii archiepiscopi mediolanensis ciuitatis super beati immaculati. Licet mistica queque . . . in hortis passus est cristus. Explicit expositio beatissimi ambrosii archiepiscopi mediolanensis ciuitatis super psalmum centesimum octauum decimum: id est beati immaculati.

PL xv. 1261–1604. Annotations, for example on ff. 60, 62, are in the hand of the donor, Robert Elyot.

2. The flyleaves, i, 160, are two leaves from letter E of the Concordantiae

---

[1] See Addenda, p. 998.

[2] I owe the identification of art. 2 to Professor Richard Rouse. Bale lists it as a work of Alexander Nequam (*Index*, p. 25), as Powicke noticed when he described the Merton copy (*Medieval Books of Merton College*, pp. 173–4).

maiores (Stegmüller, no. 3605),[1] written in England, s. xiv², and used by William-son in 1600–1 and other years in binding nine manuscripts and two printed books.

In all, twenty-four more or less complete leaves and four strips survive of what may perhaps be the 'concordaunce of ii partes' listed in the Eton inventory of 1465 (*Etoniana*, series 1, no. 28 (1921), p. 443). The written space of the leaves in MS. 17 measures 320 × 200 mm in 3 cols. of 75 lines. Nos. 2 and 5 are conjoint and so too are nos. 7 and 8, nos. 11 and 14, nos. 12 and 13, and nos. 19 and 22. Probably, therefore, nos. 9–24 are two complete and adjacent quires of eight leaves and nos. 1–6 are a quire of eight leaves lacking the central bifolium. Blue initial *F* with red ornament in *Faba*, the first word of letter F.

1.	MS. 7, f. i	Captiuus–Carcer
2.	MS. 97, f. i, formerly pastedown	Carcer–Carnes
3.	MS. 13, f. i	Carnes–Causa
4.	MS. 13, back pastedown	Certamen–Cessare, on the exposed side
5.	MS. 97, f. ii	Cibus–Circumdatus
6.	MS. 7, f. 193	Circumdatus–Cito
7.	MS. 104, f. v, formerly pastedown	Digitus–Diligere
8.	MS. 104, f. vi	Discedere–Discumbens
9.	MS. 106, f. i	Effeminatus–Egestas
10.	MS. 17, ff. v, vi	Egestas–Egressus
11.	MS. 5, f. 160	Egressus–Eleuare
12.	MS. 106, f. 136	Eleuans–Emaus
13.	MS. 106, back pastedown	Emanuel–Emortuus, on the exposed side
14.	MS. 5, back pastedown	Enutrire–Equus, on the exposed side
15.	MS. 17, f. 323	Errare–Erudire
16.	MS. 106, front pastedown	Eruditor–Eramentum, on the exposed side
17.	MS. 19, f. v, formerly pastedown	Esse–Euaginare
18.	Ge. 1. 5, flyleaf at back	Euaginare–Exaltare
19.	Ge. 1. 5, front pastedown, now raised	Exaltatus–Exceptorum
20.	Ga. 2. 3, front pastedown, now raised	Excitare–Exhortari
21.	MS. 5, f. i	Exhortari–Expandere
22.	Ge. 1. 5, front flyleaf	Expectare–Expuere
23.	Ge. 1. 5, back pastedown, now raised	Expuens–Extollens
24.	MS. 19, f. 282, formerly pastedown	Extollens–Fabricator

The strips in a volume of transcripts of charters, s. xvi ex., bound by Williamson, are from a leaf with words beginning Com-. Of two strips in MS. 97 one is from letter B and the other from letter C.

ff. i+159+i. For ff. i, 160 see above. 350 × 235 mm. Written space 250 × 145 mm. 2 cols. 32–4 lines. Pricks in both margins to guide ruling. Collation: 1–19⁸ 20⁶+1 leaf after 6. Hair sides are often heavily flecked. Written in an unstable and at times ugly hand, probably the same throughout: *g* is flat topped in the first quire only and 8-shaped first in the first column of f. 8ᵛ and regularly from f. 9: two forms of *t*: a tag on *i* at the foot: tailed *ę* represents *æ*: punctuation includes the flex (?). Initials: (i) f. 1, red, yellow, and green, with plait-work infilling; (ii) 4-line, or less, or set outside the written space, red and green, with ornament of both colours, or red, or in the ink of the text; (iii) 1-line, red or green. Capital letters in the ink of the text filled with bistre on ff. 1–3 and with green on ff. 16ᵛ–17 and elsewhere touched with red. Binding by Williamson. Secundo folio *per uinum.*

Not in an English hand, but in England by s. xv ex., if not before. A 2-line erasure follows the explicit on f. 159ᵛ. A large red V at the foot of f. 1. 'Liber Collegii de Eton ex dono Magistri Roberti Elyo[t] anno domini 1501⁰' on the pastedown in front, which, was as worm-holes show, taken over from the old binding: for Elyot, see p. 631.

[1] See above, p. 511.

6. *Augustinus, In Psalmos 1–50* s. xv[1]

Beatus uir . . . De domino nostro . . . de illo eriget (*sic*) suam. Aurelii doctoris exposicionis super psalmos prima pars. Explicit.

PL xxxvi. 67–599. ff. 154ᵛ–155ᵛ blank.

ff. ii+155. 425×290 mm. Written space *c.* 310×190 mm. 2 cols. 47 lines. Collation: 1–19⁸ 20 three (ff. 153 and 155 conjoint). Quires signed a–v in the usual late medieval manner. Textura. Initials: (i) ff. 1, 37ᵛ, 38ᵛ, 101ᵛ (Pss. 1, 26, 38), red and blue with ornament of both colours (saw pattern in the margins); (ii) 4-line or 5-line, blue with red ornament; (iii) beginning tituli and for *I* of *In finem*, 2-line, red or blue; (iv) beginning verses, 1-line, red or blue. The initials of types (ii), (i), and (iii, iv) are referred to in that order in a costing note on f. 155ᵛ: 'cxvii capitales littere xiiᵈ et iiii grosse littere viiᵈ xiᶜ xvi parue littere et ❡ⁱ xiᵈ. pro ligatura xxxiiiiᵈ'. Capital letters in the ink of the text filled with pale yellow. Binding by Williamson. Secundo folio *Quam montem*.

Written in England. 'Prima pars Augustini super psalterium et incipit in 2° fo quam montem', f. i, s. xv, in the same hand as the similar inscriptions in MSS. 22, 97, 101.

7. *Augustinus, In Psalmos 51–100* s. xii[2]

1. ff. 1–191 Aurelii [Augustini] do[ctoris in psalm]o quinqua[gesimo] primo sermo incipit. [P]salmus breuis est . . . uenturum est iudicium.

PL xxxvi. 599–1293. A medieval numbering of psalms, top right of rectos and top left of versos, but most of the numbers have been cut off by the binder. f. 191ᵛ blank.

2. ff. i, 193. For these flyleaves see MS. 5, art. 2.

3. The pastedowns are parts of two leaves of a large missal in big writing, s. xiii ex. They contain part of the advent office (cf. *Missale Romanum*, i. 10). Coloured initials not filled in.

ff. ii+191+ii. For the parchment flyleaves i, 193 see above. 408×290 mm. Written space 305×200 mm. 2 cols. 45 lines. Pricks in both margins to guide ruling. Collation: 1–14⁸ 15 seven (ff. 113–19: no text missing) 16–24⁸. Quires, except the last, numbered at the end [Iᵘˢ]–XXIIIᵘˢ. Probably all in one rather poor hand. Initials: (i) f. 1, cut out; (ii) usually 4-line, red, blue, or green, with ornament in one **or** more of the other colours; (iii) 1-line, red, green, or blue. Binding no doubt by Williamson, in view of art. 2. The opening word of the second leaf is lost, but was probably *auferetur*.

Written in England.

8. *R. Grosseteste, In Psalmos 1–100* s. xv med.

1. ff. 1–203ᵛ Psalmorum liber grece psalterium ebrayce . . . conuersacio perfecta.

Cf. M. R. James in *Journal of Theological Studies*, xxiii (1922), 181–5, and Thomson, *Grosseteste*, p. 75. The attribution to Grosseteste is on f. 1 in a hand of s. xvii which noted the contents of many Eton manuscripts. Small gaps occur fairly often, presumably because the scribe could not read his exemplar. f. 204ʳᵛ blank.

---

[1] There are not any paragraph marks, however.

2. ff. 205–16 Abierunt . . . yemis proprietates que? 85 C.

An index to art. 1 in another hand. References are to the leaf numbers of art. 1 and to the letters, A, B, or C, entered in the margins of art. 1. f. 216ᵛ blank.

ff. iii+216+iii. Medieval foliation. f. 217 is a medieval flyleaf. 385 × 250 mm. Written space 255 × 155 mm. 2 cols. 52 lines. Collation: 1–27⁸. Quires 1–19 lettered a–v. After this the scribe seems to have gone back to 'a' and to have written the quire letter after as well as before the leaf number, but most signatures have been cut off, not, however (for example) 'f 2 f' on f. 194 (quire 26, leaf 2). Written in informal textura, with some influence from secretary. Initials: (i) ff. 1, 1ᵛ, 205, gold on coloured grounds patterned in white, with sprays of gold and green into the margins: 't. ihc. b' in gold within the letter on f. 1, as in Lambeth Palace 59, f. 191;¹ (ii) 6-line, or less, blue with red ornament; (iii) ff. 1–26ᵛ only, 1-line, blue. Bound by Williamson. Secundo folio *et venit*.

Written in England. At Eton by 1600–1.

9. *P. Lombardus, In Psalmos* s. xiii¹

Incipit liber ymn[orum] uel soliloquiorum prophete de cristo. Cum omnes prophetas sancti spiritus reuelatione . . . omnis spiritus laudet dominum. Amen. hic ex.

PL cxci. 55–1296. The commentary follows the text, psalm-verse by psalm-verse, in smaller script. Large initials emphasize the division into three fifties as well as into the eight liturgical divisions. Many marginalia.

ff. iv+183+ii. 342 × 240 mm. Written space 262 × 165 mm. 2 cols. 53–60 lines for the commentary: 2 lines of commentary take up the space of 1 line of text. Pricks in both margins to guide ruling. At first both sizes of script are written above the top ruled line: the larger size drops below at f. 91ᵛ and the smaller size at f. 105. Collation: 1–22⁸ 23⁸ wants 8, blank. Several hands: the script is more expert from f. 85ᵛ and has a crossed instead of an uncrossed sign for *et* from this point. Initials vary in style and colouring, but are commonly: (i) of principal psalms, red and blue or red and green with ornament of these three colours or of two of them; (ii) 4-line, blue or red with ornament of the other colour, or green with red ornament; (iii) of verses and in the commentary, 1-line, blue or red. No green is used on ff. 1–96. Binding by Slatter. Earlier in a Williamson binding. Secundo folio *quantur laudanda*.

Written in England. 'Iste' begins an erased inscription in two long lines on f. 183ᵛ.

10. *R. Rolle, On the Psalms and Canticles (in English)* s. xv med.

Gret habundance of gasteli comforth . . . (f. 158ᵛ) for yi² ilke spirit loue ye lorde. Explicit psalterium dauid. Incipit canticum ysaye. Confitebor tibi. I sal schrife til ye lorde . . . (f. 168ᵛ) in ye Ioy of heuen Amen.

Rolle's commentary on the psalms, the six OT canticles, and Magnificat. Ed. H. R. Bramley, 1884. H. E. Allen, *Writings of Richard Rolle*, p. 172, lists this copy and thirty-seven others. Extracts from this copy printed by D. Everett in *Modern Language Review*, xvii. 218–19. She notes that the text is uninterpolated.

¹ As M. R. James noted in an interleaved *Catalogue*, where he refers also to a King's College, Cambridge, manuscript, but without giving its number.

² *y* stands for both thorn and *y* in this manuscript.

ff. iv+170+ii. ff. iii, iv, a parchment bifolium, were used as pastedown and flyleaf in a former binding. 352 × 240 mm. Written space 260 × 180 mm. 2 cols. 40 lines. Collation: 1–5¹² 6¹⁰ 7–13¹² 14¹⁶ (16 was pasted down). Quires signed a–o. Written in sloping current anglicana by the same hand throughout. Initials: (i) ff. 1, 2, red and blue, with red and violet ornament; (ii, iii) 2-line and 1-line, red or blue. Slatter binding: the rustmark from the chain attachment of an earlier binding is near the foot of the side of f. iii. Secundo folio *witte of*.

Written in England. A 2-line mostly illegible erasure, f. 170: 'pro salu[. . . . .] thome [. . . . .] defunctorum / orate pro animabus [. . . .]'. *CMA* 10.

12. *Gregorius Magnus, Moralia in Job, pars 2*   s. XIII¹

1. ff. 1–232ᵛ Hec exponuntur in sequenti libro. Non sit in recordatione. sed conteratur quasi lignum infructuosum . . . magnitudinis eius intueri? Moralia beati Gregorii pape per contemplacionem sumpta Libri sex. pars iiiiᵃ incipit. Incipit liber septimus decimus. Quotiens in sancti uiri hystoriam . . . ne forte in uitio murmurationis excedat memoretur quod timeat (*ends imperfectly*).

Moralia, bks. 17–33, xvii. *PL* lxxvi. 9–697/26. As in Bodleian, MS. Bodley 253, the words 'Hec exponuntur in sequenti libro' followed by the relevant section of Job are in front of each book. The division into parts is noted at bk. 17 (see above), at bk. 23 (Libri vᵉ Pars vᵃ incipit), and at bk. 28 (Libri viii pars ultim(a) incipit). Lemmata are doubly underlined in red. Some marginalia, s. xiii² and later. Chapter numbers of Job were added in s. xiv.

2. ff. ii, 235, end-leaves (formerly pastedowns) are two leaves of a commentary on the Decretals of Gregory IX in a handsome round Italian hand, s. xiv in.: 2 cols., 69 lines.

On bk. 2. xxv. 9–12 and bk. 2, xxvi. 17. 18. The commentary on 2. xxv. 9 begins '*Apostolice uobis*. qui interesse debebatis eleccioni uel eleccionem celebrare *ammonicionis* temporalem'. The contemporary running titles, 'De sentencia et re iudicata' and 'De excepcionibus' are in an English hand. Presumably taken over by Slatter from the old binding.

ff. iv+232+iv. For ff. ii, 235 see above. 362 × 240 mm. Written space 288 × 175 mm. 2 cols. 38 lines. The first line of writing above the top ruled line. Pricks in both margins to guide ruling. A ruled line for the book number in the upper margin. Collation: 1–29⁸. Quires numbered at the end. Catchwords in anglicana. A handsome tall black hand. Punctuation includes the flex (?). Initials: (i) of bk. 17, f. 1, in colours patterned in white on gold and coloured ground decorated in colours; of bk. 18, f. 11, historiated, Christ blessing; of bk. 28, f. 152, gold on coloured ground, decorated in colours; (ii) of other books, blue and red, with ornament of both colours; (iii) of the sections of Job, 4-line, blue with red and blue ornament. Binding by Slatter. Secundo folio *intentione omnique*.

Written in England.

13. *Gregorius Magnus, Moralia in Job*   s. XIII med.

1. ff. 1–213ᵛ Incipiunt capitula primi libri iob. Inter multos. De qua stirpe . . . (f. 8) oracionem lectoris. Expliciunt capitula xxxv librorum Mor' que prenotauimus. et huic uolumini apposuimus. ut per ea diligens lector cicius inuenire possit sentencias quibus edificari desiderat. Hec uisio per totam hyspaniam scripta inuenitur in principio moralium. Beatus Gregorius papa librum iob petente sancto Leandro spalense episcopo exposuit . . . et prescribi instituit.

(f. 9) Incipit prefacio reuerentissimo ac sanctissimo fratri leandro episcopo. Gregorius seruus seruorum dei. Dudum te frater beatissime . . . (f. 9ᵛ) fulciatur. Explicit prologus. Incipiunt moralia beati gregorii pape per contemplacionem sumpta in libro sancti Iob libri xxxv Prima pars incipit. Inter multos . . . lacrimas reddat Amen. Laus tibi sit criste quoniam liber explicit iste.

PL lxxv. 509–lxxvi. 782. This copy discussed by N. R. Ker, 'The English Manuscripts of the Moralia of Gregory the Great', *Kunsthistorische Forschungen Otto Pächt zu Ehren*, 1972, p. 82: facsimile of part of f. 71ᵛ. Preceded by a table, as in B.L., Harley 3112, giving the first words of each chapter and a brief summary of its contents (ff. 1–8) and by the vision of Taio (f. 8). Chapter numbers on more than one system and letters a–g subdividing chapters are in the margins; also distinctive pointing hands and annotations of various dates, including some English by Robert Elyot (f. 121: see p. 631) and 'Nota pro lollardis' (s. xv) on f. 100 against the mention of heretics in the text, near the end of bk. 16.

2. f. i and the pastedown at the end are from the biblical concordance found also in MS. 5, q.v.

ff. iii+213+iii. For f. i and the pastedown at the end see above. f. 216 and the pastedown at the beginning are leaves of medieval parchment. 410 × 275 mm. Written space 310 × 190 mm. 2 cols. 70 lines. First line of writing below top ruled line. Collation: 1⁸ 2–17¹² 18¹²+1 leaf after 12. Quires 2–18 numbered at the end I–XVII and with catchwords. A 10-line initial, red and blue with ornament of both colours, begins each book. Binding no doubt by Williamson, in view of art. 2. Secundo folio *filius cuius* or (f. 10) *uoluntati*.

Written in England. At Eton by s. xv ex.: see p. 631. 'prec' istius libri Cˢ', f. 216.

14, 16, 19. *Petrus Cantor; Gilbertus Autissiodorensis*   s. XII/XIII

Commentaries on thirty-eight books of the OT bound in three volumes, all of which have suffered from damp at beginning and end: in MS. 16 one or both sides of ff. 1–8, 203, 205–11 are covered with transparent paper as a preservative. The commentaries are on the Octateuch, 1–4 Kings, Tobit, Judith, Esther, Ezra, Nehemiah, 1, 2 Chronicles, 1, 2 Maccabees, Isaiah, Jeremiah, Lamentations, Daniel, the twelve Minor Prophets, and Wisdom. All are by and some are here attributed to Petrus Cantor, except the commentary on Lamentations, art. 19, which is by and here attributed to Gilbert of Auxerre. Arts. 1–3 (Genesis–Leviticus) and arts. 19–21 (Isaiah–Malachi) correspond to B.L., Royal 2 C. viii ff. 1–108, 132–232; arts. 4–8 to Balliol College 23.

Contemporary numbers in the margins (in MS. 14 in red) show the following chapter divisions: Genesis, 81; Exodus, 139; Leviticus, 86+; Numbers, 74; Deuteronomy, 153; Joshua, 33; Judges, 18; Ruth, 4; 3+4 Kings, 90; Tobit, 15; Judith, 21; Esther, 14; Ezra, 10; Nehemiah, 13; 1 Chronicles, 26; 2 Chronicles, 36; 1 Maccabees, 23; Isaiah, 66; Daniel, 13. Chapter numbers agreeing with those now in use were added later.

Hormanian(?) tables of contents, s. xvi in., headed 'Contenta' (MS. 14, f. iᵛ; 16, f. iiᵛ; 19, f. iiᵛ): cf. below, p. 651. The table in MS. 19 lists after art. 22 'Summa Io. Wallensis ad omne genus hominum / Albertanus de arte dicendi et tacendi / Melybeus et prudentia de consolatione et consilio / Imago mundi / Parisiensis de prebendis / De pluralitate beneficiorum / De conuersione peccatoris ad deum': probably these now missing pieces were only bound here at Eton, *c.* 1500. A slightly earlier table in MS. 16, f. ii, attributes arts. 4–12, 16 to Rabanus.

1. MS. 14, ff. 1–69ᵛ Principium uerborum . . . in *egypto huius uite*.[1] Explicit tractatus super Genesim.

Stegmüller, no. 6454.

2. MS. 14, ff. 69ᵛ–121ᵛ Incipit super Exodum. Fecit moyses primum operimentum . . . flamma per noctem. Explicit tractatus super Exodum.

Stegmüller, no. 6455.

3. MS. 14, ff. 121ᵛ–200ᵛ Incipit super Leuit'. Ezechiel pari'e'tem perfodit . . . sunt precepta etc' pro quibus et ceteris omnibus [. . . .] gracias dei agimus. Explicit tractatus Cantoris super Genesim. Exodum et Leuiticum.

Stegmüller, no. 6457. 'explicit leuiticus. Incipit super num'' in a small hand at the foot of f. 200ᵛ: this leaf and 199 are damaged. Some long scholia in margins. f. 201ʳᵛ was left blank. Mnemonic verses were added on the recto in s. xiii: Quinque libros Moysi . . . Apocalipsis (5 lines); Hagiographia sunt . . . canonicauit (3 lines); Quinque libros Moysi . . . atque Tobias (4 lines).

4. MS. 16, ff. 1–38 (*begins imperfectly, the first quire missing*) [. . . .] dire resonet . . . iudicia sicut et mandata.

On Numbers, beginning at 5: 6. Stegmüller, no. 6458.

5. MS. 16, ff. 38–73ᵛ Incipit tractatus super Deutron'. Fasciculus mirre michi dilectus. Tria solent in mirra . . . oleum unctionis est super eum. Expliciunt glose super Deutronomium.

Stegmüller, no. 6459.

6. MS. 16, ff. 74–84 Incipit prologus Ieronimi in iosue. *Tandem finito* etc' *uelut grandi fenore.* Hoc enim pro magno habebat debito . . . non illis imputetur. Expliciunt notule super Iosue.

Stegmüller, no. 6460.

7. MS. 16, ff. 84–94 Incipit Iudicum. Primo in genesi exigentibus meritis . . . uel aliis de filiis israel. Explicit Iudicum.

Stegmüller, no. 6461.

8. MS. 16, ff. 94–6 Incipit ruth. Sicut in testa parua nucleus . . . usque inclusumque (?) ad dauid. Explicit Ruth.

Stegmüller, no. 6462.

9. MS. 16, ff. 96–141ᵛ Incipit Regum. Surgens dominus a cena . . . saul. et filios eius . . . de hoc iere. capitulo ultimo. Expl. Reg' iiiiᵘˢ.

2 Kings, f. 106ᵛ. 3 Kings, f. 118ᵛ. 4 Kings, f. 131ᵛ. Stegmüller, nos. 6466, 1 (1–3 Kings, as in MS. Bodley 371) and 6466 (4 Kings).

10. MS. 16, ff. 142–147ᵛ Incipit tractatus super thobiam. Sagitte tue acute . . . in terra uiuentium in secula seculorum. Explicit tractatus super thobiam.

Stegmüller, no. 6471.

11. MS. 16, ff. 148–53 Incipiunt Glose in libro Iudith. *Apud hebreos.* etc'. Hystoriam iudith transtulit Ieronimus . . . Dum durat presens seculum. Expliciunt Notule in libro Iudith.

Stegmüller, no. 6472.

---

[1] These and other words in italics are underlined in the manuscripts.

12. MS. 16, ff. 153–157^v Incipit prefatio Beati Ieronimi in Libro Hester. Frater fratrem adiuuans . . . Post tenebras spero lucem. Expl' Glose super Hester.

Stegmüller, no. 6473.

13. MS. 16, ff. 158–66 Incipit tractatus Cantoris super esdram. Reuertere Reuertere sunamitis etc'. Per sunamitem.' Sinagoga . . . in melius conuerterit. Expl' esdr'.

Stegmüller, no. 6469.

14. MS. 16, ff. 166–172^v Verba neemie filii elchie. *Et factum est.* Huc usque uerba esdre . . . in corde ardet. Expliciunt note super esdram.

Stegmüller, no. 6470.

15. MS. 16, ff. 172^v–195^v Incipit tractatus cantoris super paralipomenon. Incipit prologus. Liber iste censetur paralipomenon grece . . . (f. 185^v) ad inferna descendunt. Incipit liber secundus. *Confortatus est* cristus scilicet eterna. quia *in se.* Expliciunt notule in Paralipomenon.

Stegmüller, nos. 6467–8. ff. 196–197^v are blank and without ruling.

16. MS. 16, ff. 198–213^v Liber Machabeorum. *Et factum est.* Inicium huius libri simile est . . . (f. 211^v) magister in historiis. Explicit [. . . . .]. Incipit [. . . .] *Fratribus.* Iste secundus liber . . . interpretatur humiles siue occidentales (*ends imperfectly*).

Stegmüller, nos. 6502–3. Ends at 2 Maccabees 12: 10.

17. MS. 19, ff. 1–104^v Incipit Prologus in Ysaiam prophetam. Habemus firmiorem propheticum sermonem . . . agant uiui (*sic*) mali de quo supra. Expliciunt Notule Super Ysaiam.

Stegmüller, no. 6485.

18. MS. 19, ff. 105–55 Cantor super Ieremiam prophetam. Uidit daniel uirum indutum lineis . . . et honori restituit.

Stegmüller, no. 6486.

19. MS. 19, ff. 155–175^v (*no break after art. 18*)[1] O Vos omnes . . . Ite maledicti etc' cum iam nec paciencie (*sic*) nec uenie locus erit. Gilibertus autisiodorensis ecclesie diaconus exposiciones lamentacionum ieremie ordinauit. Expliciunt glose super Lamentationes.

Stegmüller, no. 2544 (cf. 6487). Annotations in the margins by a skilled hand. f. 176^{rv} blank and without ruling.

20. MS. 19, ff. 177–184^v (*begins imperfectly*) dei et con[silium] salomon[is] . . . cognomento balthasar. *Anno primo.* Hec pericope et sequens . . . nec a perfectis laudabile. Expliciunt glose super danielem prophetam deo gracias amen.

Stegmüller, no. 6489. Begins in Daniel 6: 12 (Royal 2 C. viii, f. 189^v col. 1/8 up) and ends on *res turpis,* 13: 63.

---

[1] Similarly, B.L., Royal 2 C. viii has no break at f. 174.

21. 19, ff. 185–263^v Incipit prologus in Osee. Triplex funiculus . . . sapientes cum insipientibus. Explicit Malachias cum duodecim prophetis.

Stegmüller, nos. 6490–501. f. 264^{rv} is blank and without ruling.

22. MS. 19, ff. 265–280^v Quecumque scripta sunt ad nostram doctrinam et utilitatem scripta sunt. Aperiat ergo nobis . . . et de omnibus liberauit e.d. Explicit.

On Wisdom. Stegmüller, no. 6483.

23. Binding leaves: (a) MS. 14, f. 202, a bifolium of the same manuscript as is used in MS. 20, q.v.; (b) MS. 19, ff. vi, 281, two leaves of a well-written copy of Origen on Genesis, s. xii^1; (c) MS. 19, ff. v, 282, formerly pastedowns, two leaves of the biblical concordance used in MS. 5, q.v.

(b). Written space 255 × 150 mm. 2 cols. 40 lines. The running title is 'Omelia ii^a in Gen''. f. 281 begins 'malia quorum uescentes' and ends 'paucos habet proximos'. f. i begins 'cauit. Nisi enim remissionem' and ends 'uideantur. tamen que ad'. *PG* xii. 163A–168C, 171C–174C.

MS. 14. ff. i+200+ii. ff. i, 201, 202 are medieval endleaves: 202 was pasted down. 375 × 265 mm. Written space *c.* 265 × 175 mm. 2 cols. 42 lines. Pricks in both margins to guide ruling, except in the two first quires. Collation: 1–25^8. Quires numbered at the end and catchwords. Several hands, none expert. Initials: (i) mainly red or green with green-filled penwork ornament on pale-purple grounds; (ii) 2-line or 1-line, red or green. Capital letters in the ink of the text touched with red. Binding by Lisley. Tertio folio *secundum.*

MS. 16. ff. ii+214+i. f. ii is a medieval leaf, formerly pasted down. 375 × 265 mm. Written space *c.* 265 × 175 mm. 2 cols. 42 lines. Pricks in both margins to guide ruling. Collation: 1–8^8 9^8+1 leaf after 8 (f. 73) 10–17^8 18–20^{10} 21^{12} 22^8 23–24^{10} 25^8 wants 7 after f. 213. Quires numbered at the end, beginning with II, and catchwords. Several hands, none expert. Initials: (i) at first as in MS. 14, later red or green with ornament of the other colour and occasionally blue; (ii) 2-line or 1-line, red or green. Capital letters in the ink of the text touched with red. Binding by Lisley.

MS. 19. ff. vi+280+v. For ff. v, vi, 281–2 see above. 375 × 265 mm. Written space *c.* 265 × 175 mm. 2 cols. 39–46 lines. Pricks in both margins to guide ruling. Collation: 1–2^{10} 3–5^8 6–13^{10} 14^8 15–17^{10} 18 four (ff. 173–6) 19^8 (ff. 177–84) 20–27^{10} 28–29^8. Quires numbered at the end and catchwords. Several hands, not expert. Initials: (i) red, sometimes with black penwork ornament (filled in green, f. 1); (ii, iii) 2-line and 1-line, red, sometimes with ornament of the same colour. Capital letters in the ink of the text stroked with red on ff. 105–214 only. Binding by Williamson. Tertio folio *pacionem.*

The three volumes were written in England and belonged in s. xiii to the Cistercian abbey of Quarr, Isle of Wight, as appears from verses of that date on the pastedown of MS. 14: 'Est de Quadraria liber iste tuusque^1 Maria / Sit reus ante deum qui tibi tollat eum'. MSS. 16 and 19 have no inscriptions now, but the blank bifolium inserted by Williamson in front of a copy of College Statutes^2 may have been removed by him from MS. 19, when he rebound it, since it bears the words 'Est de quarraria liber tuus iste Maria', s. xiv,

^{1} M. R. James read 'crucisque'. The right reading is pointed out by fr. S. F. Hockey in a letter of 9 Nov. 1964.

^{2} See above, p. 620. The four blank bifolia at the end of the Statutes may be from this or some other volume rebound by Williamson. One of them bears a note of pledging in the Gotham chest at Cambridge, 'Caucio M' Iohannis Marshall exposita ciste Gotham in festo sancti Grisogoni martiris (*24 Nov.*) pro v marcis anno domini millesimo cccc x^o. Supplementum cuius principale est pupilla oculi'.

followed by an erased line. Nos. 9, 22 and 8 in the list of 'Bokys of the liberary' at Eton in 1465, 'Item Cantor uppon Genesim iii fo secundum', 'Item an exposicion uppon Numeri and other ii fo set accidere', 'Item Cantor uppon Isaiae and Jeremye iii fo pacionem' (M. R. James in *Etoniana*, series 1, no. 28 (1921), 444).[1]

15. *Radulphus Flaviacensis, In Leviticum* s. XII ex.

'Incipit prologus domni'. [Cum inter socios] aliquando sermo de iudeorum . . . (f. 3) perfidia iudeorum. Incipiunt capitula libri primi . . . (*table of ten chapters*) . . . (f. 3ᵛ) Item alius prologus. Tercius in moysi libris . . . dispensanda. Incipit liber primus leuitici cum explanatione. De holocausto bouis. Capitulum I. Docauit (*sic: initial* D *entered instead of* U) autem dominus . . . Huius libri initium . . . in monte synai. Explicit liber vicesimus explanationis super leuiticum domni Radulfi monachi flauiacensis.

Maxima Bibliotheca Patrum, xvii (1677), 48–246. Stegmüller, no. 7093. Twenty books, each preceded by a table of chapters. The *nota bene* sign 'D.M.' on f. 52 is in the main hand. f. 253ᵛ blank.

ff. ii+253+ii. 350×250 mm. Written space 250×160 mm. 2 cols. 37 lines. Pricks in both margins to guide ruling. Collation: 1¹⁰ 2⁸ 3¹⁰ 4–13⁸ 14–17¹⁰ 18–19⁸ 20–27¹⁰ 28¹⁰ wants 10, blank. Catchwords and (quires 1–6 only) numbers at the end. Punctuation includes the flex (?). Initials: (i) f. 1, on a special piece of parchment pasted on and later peeled off and lost: one edge, with blue ground and green frame remains; (ii) of each book, in colour on coloured grounds, decorated in colours: green, blue, red, brown, and purple occur, with fine effect: some zoomorphic shapes, including 'little white lions' on f. 3ᵛ; (iii) 3-line, blue, green, and red, with ornament of one of the other colours; (iv) 1-line, green, red, or blue. Williamson binding: the mark of the chain attachment of an older binding shows near the foot of the side of ff. 1–5. Secundo folio *etur. et fame.*

Written in England. A pressmark, s. xiv (?), '1ª partis 2ᵉ graduˀ et in sinistro', f. 253ᵛ. Identifiable by the opening words of the second leaf with the copy at Eton in 1465, no. 6 in the list of 'Bokys of the liberary' printed by M. R. James in *Etoniana*, series 1, no. 28 (1921), 444.

16. See above, MS. 14.

17. *Hugo de Sancto Caro, In libros Salomonis* s. XIII²

1. ff. 1–76ᵛ 'Notule M Hugonis de Vyenna Magni theologi de ordine predicatorum. lectoris paris'. qui postea extitit cardinalis. ac penitenciarius principalis domini pape super parabolas ecclesiasten librum Sapiencie. ecclesiasticum et cantica canticorum'. Dicit ecc' xxxix b occulta prouerbiorum . . . inspicere uolenti. 'Expliciunt prouerbia. siue parabole salomonis' (*these five words over erasure*).

2. ff. 77–114ᵛ Beatus uir cuius est auxilium abste . . . quod factum est suple. Explicit ecclesiastes.

---

[1] The use of tertio instead of secundo folio references suggests that the second leaves of MSS. 14 and 19 were already damaged by 1465. The secundo folio of MS. 14 can still be read, 'deserta', but the secundo folio of MS. 19 is illegible.

3. ff. 115–53 Fili concupiscens sapienciam . . . eis liberans et saluans. Expliciunt glose super librum sapiencie a fratre hugone confecte.

4. ff. 155–288ᵛ Summi regis palatium.' in quatuor . . . proponimus nos lecturos.
Explic' ecc'.

5. ff. 289–321 Deus in gradibus eius . . . ueni de libano.

1–5. Stegmüller, nos. 3677, 3679, 3684, 3686, 3682. He notes the ending of art. 5 found
here (Cant. Cant. 4: 8) also in Cambridge, U.L., Kk. 1. 16 and in Paris, Ste Geneviève 62.
Robert Elyot, †1499 (see p. 631) glossed some words in English, for example 'hinnulus
an hynde', f. 307ᵛ, and 'ferculum. a restyng place', f. 314ᵛ, and dated his final piece of
writing, 'deo gracias legi totum anno 1493. 18 die iunii claudo', f. 321. ff. 153ᵛ–154ᵛ were
ruled but left blank after one of the scribes had finished his work: cf. the inexact join where
a new hand begins at f. 91 and two leaves, now removed, were left blank at the end of
quire 12. ff. 321ᵛ–322ᵛ are blank.

6. The former pastedowns, now ff. v, 323, and f. vi are from the biblical concordance used in MS. 5, q.v.

ff. vi+322+v. For ff. v, vi, 323 see above art. 6. ff. 2–179 are foliated incorrectly in
a medieval hand 1–181 and the first fourteen columns of art. 5 are numbered. 310×
225 mm. Written space c. 245×150 mm. 2 cols. 46–58 lines. Collation: 1–4⁸ 5⁶ 6–9⁸
10⁶ (ff. 71–6) 11⁸ 12⁸ wants 7, 8, blank, after f. 90 13–35⁸ 36¹⁰ 37⁴ (ff. 285–8) 38–40⁸ 41¹⁰
(ff. 313–22: f. 322 was pasted down to the medieval binding). Some ad hoc pencil signatures. Five scribes wrote at the same time: (i) ff. 1–76ᵛ, 115 (quire 16¹)–153; (ii) ff. 77
(quire 11¹)–90ᵛ; (iii) ff. 91–114ᵛ; (iv) ff. 155 (quire 21¹)–288ᵛ; (v) ff. 289–321. Initials:
(i) blue and red with ornament of both colours; (ii) 2-line, red or blue with ornament of
the other colour. Binding by Williamson. Secundo folio est sicut equus.

Probably written in England. An erasure on f. 322ᵛ. 'Iste est Iohannes Sydeberne et sic
dixit Tomas Sugete', f. 322, s. xiv/xv. At Eton before 1500.

18. R. Holcot, In Sapientiam Salomonis   s. xiv/xv

1. ff. 9–222 Dominus petra mea et robur meum R̄e 22 (3 Kings 22). Artes et
sciencie . . . (f. 221) de omni angustia. quod nobis concedat qui . . . amen.
Explicit liber holcot super sapiens etc. 'Os iusti meditabitur sapienciam p' 36.
Omnis sciencia siue humanitus adinuenta . . . perducat qui sine fine viuit et
regnat. Quamuis ista sapiencia . . . informantur. Deo gracias'.

Stegmüller, no. 7416. Two hundred and twelve numbered chapters. A final chapter '213'
and note 'Quamuis . . . informantur' (for the note, cf. B. Smalley in AFP xxvi (1956), 10)
have been added by another hand at the end. Added letters in the margins in red, A–F
or A–G, divide each chapter into sections of about thirty-two lines: they are used for
reference purposes in art. 2b, c, e, f. Marginalia by Robert Elyot, †1499 (see p. 631) include
some words of English on f. 38ᵛ. f. 222ᵛ blank.

2. Six lists and indexes relating to art. 1 fill a preliminary quire and two quires
at the end: (a) ff. 1–8ᵛ A littera quid significat. 195 . . . Zone quattuor in sacra
scriptura. 24; (b) f. 8ᵛ Iste sunt questiones litterales et non litterales in libro
holcott; (c) ff. 223–36 A dicitur quandoque essencialiter quandoque nocionaliter
sicut patet. 195. e. f . . . Zoroastes vide in risus. 90. Explicit tabula lecture
Holcote super librum sapiencie scripta per magistrum Nicholaum Kempston'

Anno domini millesimo quadringentesimo septuagesimo quinto etc'; (d) ff.
236ᵛ–237 Quamuis autem ista sapiencia . . . informantur. 1. Iusticiam simulant
se diligere 4ᵒʳ genera hominum . . . 212. Rane loco piscium nunc in scola et
3ᵇᵘˢ generibus; (e) f. 237ʳᵛ 1. An salamon fuerit auctor libri sapiencie 28 . . . 64.
An diuinacio per sompnia sit licita 202; (f) ff. 237ᵛ–240ᵛ 1. Ambicio est summa
caritatis '5 C' (over erasure) . . . (540) Cristus fecit triplex argumentum '110 E'
519. Explicit tabula fratris Roberti Holcoti super librum sapiencie de ordine
fratrum predicatorum doctoris sacre theologie conuentus norhamtonie.

(a, c, f) are alphabetical indexes, (a) nearly contemporary with art. 1. (b)—in the same hand
as (c)—lists sixty-seven questions and (e) sixty-four questions. (d–f) are in one hand. In
(f), each entry, except the last of all, is numbered. The reference numbers and letters,
5 C, etc., replace older numbers, mostly erased, except on f. 240ʳᵛ, which appear to
correspond to pencilled numbers at the head of the leaves. The highest of the old numbers now remaining in (f) is '988' against Timor bonus.

3. On the pastedown at the end: (a) Consulo quisquis eris qui pacis federa
queris . . . (2 lines); (b) Plurima cum soleant hominum corrumpere mores . . .
(2 lines); (c) Memorandum, s. xv, of an obit for the vicar of All Saints, Bristol.

(a, b). Walther, Sprichwörter, nos. 3250, 21633. (c). 'Memorandum quod xiiᵒ die mensis
Augusti decretum est per Cancellar' Episcopi Wygorn' in ecclesia parochialis sancti
Augustini quod vicarius ecclesie omnium sanctorum faceret solempniter celebrare exequias
et missam cum aliis expensis ordinatis per philippum Morgan Episcopum quondam
Wygorn (1419–26) Crastino Epiphanie annuatim pro anima T Marchall quondam vicarium
ecclesie omnium sanctorum supradict' et benefactorum eiusdem sub pena excommuni-
cacionis Et hoc factum est in presencia M' Roberti Peuesy vic' sancti Leonardi M W
Parkar vic' sancti Nicholai¹ et Iohannis famuli eiusdem. Ac Willelmi famuli Magistri
Roberti Peuesy M' Iohannis Harnham et Iohannis Whytsyde'. Pevesy became vicar of
St. Leonard's, Bristol, in 1427 (BRUO, p. 1473). In the All Saints records Marchall is
last mentioned as vicar in 1433: he was no longer vicar at Easter 1442.²

ff. i+240. f. i is a parchment leaf taken over from an earlier binding. 362 × 232 mm.
Written space 278 × 170 mm. 2 cols. 56 lines. Collation: 1⁸ 2–18¹² 19¹² wants 11, 12,
blank, after f. 222 20⁸ 21⁸+two leaves after 8 (ff. 239, 240). Quires 2–19 lettered a–s in
the usual late medieval manner. Art. 1 in textura of two sizes, the larger for the text of
Wisdom, and (ff. 221–2 only) anglicana. Kempston's hand, art. 2b, c is mainly secretary.
Initials: (i) f. 9, red and blue, with red, blue, and violet ornament; (ii) 3-line, blue with red
ornament. Binding by Williamson. Secundo folio cognomen habeo (f. 10) or Cibus (f. 2).
Written in England. At Bristol in s. xv: see above. 'dryfeld' in red, f. 238ᵛ. Belonged to
Nicholas Kempston (†1477) in or before 1475 (cf. art. 2c). 'Liber quondam magistri
Nicholai Kempston anno domini 1477 numquam vendendus secundum vltimam voluntatem defuncti sed gratis et libere occupandus a sacerdotibus instructis in lege domini ad
predicandum verbum dei successiue ab vno sacerdote ad alterum sacerdotem absque omni
precio quamdiu durauerit. Orate igitur pro anima eius', f. i. Similar inscriptions are in
MSS. 36, 77, and 117, and Longleat MS. 9 went from Kempston to M. William Meny-
man, fellow of Whittington College, on the same terms. For these and other books belonging to Kempston see Emden, BRUO, p. 1034, and MMBL i. 155. At Eton before c. 1500:
see above.

19. See above, MS. 14.

¹ These three words repeated twice.
² I owe these references to the Bristol City Archivist.

20. *Haimo, In Isaiam; Alexander de Essebie, Liber festivalis*

s. XII ex.

1. ff. 1–165ᵛ [Incip]it expositio hamon[is super Ysaiam] prophetam [. . .]. Ysaias propheta nobili prosapia ortus? filius fuit amos . . . sita est. Explicit prologus. Uisio isaie filii amos . . . dampnatione? sed de sua liberatione. Deo gracias. Explicit expositio hamonis super Ysaiam prophetam.

PL cxvi. 715–1086. Stegmüller, no. 3083.

2. ff. 166–175ᵛ Incipit prologus libri festiualis ab alexandro priore de essebie compositus. Duo preclara diuine pietatis dona . . . in margine notabitur. Incipit prologus metricus libri festiualis. Omnia cum nequeam sanctorum scribere gesta . . . Ordine quo subeunt amodo musa. Explicit liber primus.

Book 1 only. Walther, no. 13254. Russell, *Writers*, p. 12. After the *explicit* the scribe left a blank space—filled early with miscellaneous notes—and then wrote the words 'Incipit tractatus de trinitate'. The first note begins 'Sacerdos dum benedicit tribus digitis', then on Triclinium, Lenticula, etc.

3. ff. 176, 177 (formerly pasted down) are a bifolium from Decretals of Innocent IV in an English hand, s. xiii². Some of the texts are followed by the commentary of Bernard of Compostella, junior (cf. Schulte, ii. 119).

These leaves (written space 305 × 170 mm.: 2 cols., with 78 lines of commentary or 60 lines of text) and the two incomplete leaves in MS. 14 are adjacent bifolia of the same quire once in the order (1) MS. 14, f. 202, upper part, (2) MS. 20, f. 176, (3) MS. 20, f. 177, (4) MS. 14, f. 202, lower part. Two or more leaves are missing between (2) and (3). The pieces *a* (end)–*e* (beginning) are on (1), *e* (end) –*g* on (2), *h–l* (beginning) on (3), *l* (end)–*r* on (4).

(*a*) . . . non fuerint inde assecuti.
(*b*) [P]ia consideratione . . .
(*c*) [C]um debitorum onera . . .
(*d*) . . . prefigentibus *parti*. diem etc.
(*e*) De sentencia et re iudicata. [C]um eterni tribunal . . .
(*f*) [A]d apostolice dignitatis et infra. Sane cum dura . . .
(*g*) [A]bbate sane et infra. Abbas de benef. pro se . . .
(*h*) [N]on solum in fauorem . . .
(*i*) [G]rauis et dolore non vacua . . .
(*j*) [R]omana ecclesia et infra. Statuimus ut quilibet . . .

(*k*) [. . .] inpetrata [. . .] derogante.
(*l*) [A]d memoriam et . . . manentibus semper saluis.
(*m*) [N]ullum eorum . . .
(*n*) [P]ro humani generis . . .
(*o*) [V]olen[tes libertatem . . .
(*p*) . . .] uesti[. . .] . . . expensis computare.
(*q*) [Ard]uis mens nostra . . . plenarie tribuemus.
(*r*) [R]omana ecclesia et infra. Licet . . .

(*b*), (*e–g*), (*j*), (*n, o*), (*r*) are Collectio III. 21–4, 30–3. Except (*n*), Pro humani generis, they are followed by the commentary. When he came to (*f*) the scribe began copying the commentary before the text, but at a certain point he saw his mistake and stopped and began the text, and he or another wrote warning notes on f. 176, 'textus est ex alia parte folii', and on f. 176ᵛ, 'glosa est ex alia parte folii . . . redeas huc'. (h), Non solum, is preceded by the last fifty-nine lines of the commentary on Collectio III. 29.

The extravagants have no commentary. (a)—only the last four lines of Mediatores remain —, (c), (h, i), (l, m), (q) are listed by J. P. Kessler, 'Untersuchungen über die Novellen-Gesetzgebung Papst Innocenz IV', *Zeitschrift der Savigny-Stiftung für Rechtsgeschichte*, lxii (Kan. Abt. xxxi, 1942), 200–2, 282–5. The three others are:

(d). This occurs in Vatican, Ottob. lat. 3089, ff. 211ʳᵇ–211ᵛᵃ, where it begins 'Venerabilium fratrum nostrorum Rothomagensis episcopi et lexouiensis episcopi'. It concerns tithes in dispute between Rouen and Luxeuil: see above p. 254.

(k) is in Ottob. lat. 3089, f. 221ᵛᵃ, where it begins 'Cum debitor'.

(p) is evidently the text in Ottob. lat. 3089, f. 221ʳᵇ–221ᵛᵃ, beginning 'Sane quia iusto iudicio celestis imperatoris uestigiis' and ending 'expensis necessariis computare'. The last part of the text is complete in col. 2 on f. 202ᵛ, but of the first part only the extreme ends of lines survive in col. 1, including 'uesti-' at the end of line 1.

(o), Volentes, is in the second column on f. 202. Only a few letters at the beginning of each line survive, enough to show that the text in print, 'Volentes . . . possunt', was followed here by the supplement 'Sane quia de huiusmodi . . . competat speciali' which occurs in some manuscripts, for example Munich, Clm. 14032, where it is an early addition at the foot of f. 275. The text which follows Sane quia is the commentary on Volentes, but only a few letters of it are legible in the first column on f. 202ᵛ.[1]

Where assassins are mentioned in (m) a reader noted in the margin 'Tales habet quidam baro saracenorum. qui credunt se saluari. si preceptum domini sui perficiant. talis wlnerauit regem Angl' Edwardum in terra sancta'.

ff. i+176+ii, foliated 1–120, 120*, 121–77. For ff. 176, 177 see above, art. 3. 330×240 mm. Written space 240×170 mm. 2 cols. 37 lines. Pricks in both margins to guide ruling. Collation: 1–22⁸. Quires numbered at the end: the numbers have been cut off, except XXᵘˢ on f. 151ᵛ, where we might have expected XIXᵘˢ. Ill written. Punctuation includes the flex (?). Initials: (i) f. 1, red and blue, with green and purple ornament; (ii) 3-line or 2-line, red or blue with ornament of the other colour. Bound by Lisley. Secundo folio [transire fe]cerit.

Written in England. At Eton by 1521.

21. *Jeronimus, In Danielem et Prophetas Minores; etc.*   s. xii med.

1. ff. 1–42ᵛ (*begins imperfectly*) ualla ea tantum que obscura sunt . . . contineri. Explicit prologus. Incipit expositio beati Ieronimi in librum danielis prophete ad pammachium et marcellam. Anno tertio regni ioachim . . . respondere debeamus. Quomodo susanna uxor . . . inculpabant.

PL xxv. 494/6–584. The last four lines on f. 42ᵛ, Quomodo . . ., are in red. Two leaves missing before f. 1. 'Nota bene' marks by 'r' and 'A' in the margins are perhaps in the main hand.

2. ff. 42ᵛ–322ᵛ Incipit explanationum in oséé prophetam beati ieronimi presbiteri liber primus ad pammachium. Si in explanationibus . . . iohannem intelligens. Explicit liber explanationis beati ieronimi presbiteri in malachiam prophetam.

[1] I am grateful to Professor Stephan Kuttner for reference to the Ottoboni and Munich manuscripts and other help; also to Dr. Sigrid Krämer, who sent me a photograph of Clm. 14032.

PL xxv. 815–1578. Probably eleven leaves are missing after f. 47 with the commentary on
Hosea 1: 10–4: 15 (edn., 828/6 lines from foot–853/34): a reader, s. xvii, noticed the gap.
One leaf is missing after f. 301 with part of the commentary on Zechariah 13 (edn., 1517/
5 lines from foot–1520/34).

3. ff. 322ᵛ–326ᵛ Incipit sermo uenerabilis ambrosii mediolanensis episcopi de
obseruantia episcoporum. Si quis frater oraculum domini reminiscatur . . . dare
promisisti AMEN. Explicit sermo uenerabilis ambrosii (*etc.*).

Pseudo-Ambrose, De dignitate sacerdotali. *PL* xvii. 567–80.

4. ff. 326ᵛ–336. Incipit questio sancti ieronimi presbiteri de induratione cordis
pharaonis. et de aliis iiiiᵒʳ questionibus. Perfectorum est ea quę affluentissimo
. . . pro littera. Explicit prologus. Incipit liber questionis. Optimus dispensator
humani generis . . . comprehendatis AMEN. Questio sancti ieronimi presbiteri
de induratione cordis pharaonis. et de aliis quattuor questionibus explicit.

Stegmüller, no. 6370 (Pelagius). Cf. G. Morin in *RB* xxvi (1909), 163–88. The basis
of the edition by G. de Plinval, *Essai sur le style et la langue de Pélage*, 1947, pp. 137–203:[1]
thence *PLS* i. 1506–39. Carefully corrected in orthography, for example, 'abundauit'
instead of 'habundauit' and 'comprehendatis' instead of 'conprehendatis'.

5. f. 336ʳᵛ Ieronimus in annalibus ebreorum de quindecim signis quindecim
dierum precedentium diem iudicii. Signum primi diei. Mária omnia . . . longe
ante defunctis. Finis ádest diei iudicii.

6. f. 336ᵛ P.P.P. . . . ruit Roma.

A prophecy of the fall of Rome printed in James's *Catalogue*. Cf. P. Lehmann, *Erforschung
des Mittelalters*, i. 138.

ff. ii+336+i. f. ii is a medieval parchment flyleaf. 385×285 mm. Written space 285×
182 mm. 2 broad cols. 37–45 lines. Pencil ruling. Pricks in both margins to guide ruling.
On ff. 111–280ᵛ the writing is between a pair of ruled lines. Double bounders between the
columns, the space between them ruled on ff. 1–110ᵛ only. Collation: 1¹⁰ wants 1, 2
2–4¹⁰ 5¹⁰ wants 10 after f. 47 6–30¹⁰ 31¹⁰ wants 4 after f. 301 32–34¹⁰. Catchwords. One
hand, except ff. 281–283ᵛ, which are admirably written, perhaps by the corrector, for
whose writing see, for example, f. 229. Hyphens in the main hand are horizontal. Initials:
(i) red, green, or brown, with ornament in one, two, or three colours; (ii) 2-line, red, green,
brown, or (ff. 101, 325ᵛ–326 only) blue. Slatter binding.

Written in England. As M. R. James saw, this is almost certainly the manuscript listed as
'C' in the catalogue of the library of the Benedictine abbey of Peterborough, s. xiv ex.:
'Pastorale Ambrosii. Questio Ieronimi de induracione cordis Pharaonis et de aliis quatuor
questionibus. Item de xv signis ante diem iudicii' (M. R. James, *Lists of Manuscripts
Formerly in Peterborough Abbey Library*, 1926, p. 30).[2] 'Sum liber Iohannis Rogers [. . . .]
Elitzur (?) 1594', f. 1. 'Thomas Horn', f. 333ᵛ. '1713. Dedit Collegio B.M. de Etona Tho.
Horne Soc.', f. i.

22. *Jeronimus, In Prophetas Minores*   s. XIII med.

Incipit explanationum in osee prophetam Beati Ieronimi presbiteri liber primus
ad pammachium. Si in explanationibus . . . iohannem intelligens. Explicit liber

---

[1] But his date, s. xi/xii, is too early.
[2] This catalogue regularly omits the first item in each manuscript.

explanationis beati ieronimi presbiteri in malachiam prophetam ad mineruum et alexandrum. amen.

PL xxv. 815–1578. Lemmata are shown by large black dots on the outer of the two bounding lines. 'A' here and there in the margins as a 'nota bene' sign. f. 210ᵛ, left blank, and flyleaves, ff. v, vi, 211–13, are more or less full of pencilled notes, mainly of s. xiii and all probably theological. Thomas Gascoigne wrote in the margins, for example on f. 43 and on f. 55 where he notes that it is customary with St. Jerome to write *quo* for the conjunction *quod* in his commentaries; this apropos of the commentary on Amos 2: 14, 'Non quo fortis sit: sed quo fortius esse se iactet' (edn., 1012/5 lines from foot). The words 'handyl of a plow stivam' opposite 'stibam' in the text, f. 77, and other marginalia are in the hand of Robert Elyot; see p. 631.

ff. vi+210+v. ff. iii–vi, 211–13 are medieval parchment end-leaves: iiiʳ and 213ᵛ were pasted down. 385×285 mm. Written space 275×165 mm. 2 cols. 46 lines. Writing below top ruled line. Pricks in both margins to guide ruling. Collation: 1–2¹² 3¹⁰ 4–7¹² 8¹⁰ 9–17¹² 18¹⁰. Quires numbered at the end. Initials: (i) red and blue, with ornament of both colours; (ii) rarely, 1-line, blue or red. Capital letters in the ink of the text filled with yellow, but not beyond f. 3. Slatter binding. Secundo folio *tue prudencie*.

Written in England. 'L. Ieronimus super xii prophetas [. . . . .]', f. 1, at foot, s. xiv; also, above the title and in the same ink, 'P' (?) and in pencil 'xxx'. No. 4 in the Eton inventory of 1465, 'Item Saint Jerome uppon smale prophetis iiᵈᵒ fo *tue prudencie*' (M. R. James in *Etoniana*, series 1, no. 28 (1921) p. 444).

23. *Prophetae Minores glossatae* s. XIII med.

Minor prophets, Non idem est ordo . . . anathemathe amen, in a central column, with commentary on either side in smaller writing. The first two paragraphs of commentary are 'Ordo xii prophetarum. secundum lxx . . . composita' and 'Ier. Materia oséé triplex est . . . permansit' and the last paragraph is 'Vel cor patris ad filium . . . consentient'.

The prologues are the eighteen of the common set in their usual order (see p. 210) and eight others: to Obadiah 'Esau filius ysaac . . . loquitur hic propheta' after Stegmüller, nos. 519+517; to Micah, 'Semper dei qui semper . . . imposita sunt', after 526; to Habak-kuk, 530 after 531; to Zephaniah, 532 after 535; to Haggai, 'Cum cyrus rex persarum . . . prohibentibus' after 538; to Zechariah, 540 and 'Cirus rex persarum . . . tempore inter-missam' after 539; to Malachi, 545 after 543. The general prologue (500) and the prologue to Hosea (507) are in the larger size of script; the other prologues in the smaller.

Lines drawn from the text lead the reader to the commentary. Many notes in ink and pencil, s. xiii, in the margins, on the blank verso of f. 110 and on the flyleaf, f. 111ᵛ. Mnemonic verses on f. ivᵛ, 'Ose Ioel Amos . . .' (2 lines) and 'Osee saluans . . . ultimus horum' (6 lines), s. xv/xvi seem to be in the hand of Robert Elyot (see p. 631).

ff. iv+110+iv. ff. iii, iv, 111, 112 are medieval parchment end-leaves: iiiʳ, 112ᵛ were pasted down. 355×235 mm. Written space 220×143 mm across text and commentary. 24 lines of text and 48 of commentary. Writing below the top ruled line. Collation: 1⁸ 2¹⁰ 3⁶ 4¹⁰ 5–6⁸ 7¹⁰ 8¹² 9⁸ 10¹² 11¹⁰ 12⁸. Quires numbered at the beginning in pencil, I–XII. *Ad hoc* pencil signatures. Initials: (i) red and blue, with ornament of both colours; (ii) of prologues usually, red or blue with ornament of the other colour;[1] (iii) within books, red or blue. Slatter binding: the mark from the chain attachment (?) on a former binding

---

[1] Coloured initials are not used in the commentary, except on f. 32 where a type (ii) initial was used by mistake: a reader, s. xiii, noted here 'glos' est non prologus'.

shows at the head of ff. iii, 1. Secundo folio (text) *per heliseum* or (commentary) *ne contionem*.

Written in England. A slip has been cut from the top of f. iv. Erased inscriptions, ff. iii^v, 1: the former begins 'Iste liber constat domino' and M. R. James has noted in an interleaved copy of his *Catalogue* that the last word is 'perhaps Quarreria' (cf. MS. 14). At Eton by 1500, if the hand on f. iv is Elyot's.

24. Apocalypsis (Latin and English); Berengaudus, In Apocalypsim; Sermones Odonis

1455

1. ff. 1–78^v (a) Apocalipsis ihesu cristi quam dedit illi deus . . . septem ecclesie sunt. (b) Apocalips of ihesu criste. whiche god 3afe to hym . . . (f. 1^v) ben seuene churchis. (c) Beatum Iohannem apostolum et euangelistam hunc librum . . . in melius commutandum. etc. Explicit exposicio Belengarii Super Apoc'.

The order is chapter by chapter, (a) Latin text, (b) English text, (c) the commentary by Berengaudus, *PL* xvii. 765–970, Stegmüller, no. 1711. The English is the later Wycliffite version.

2. ff. 78^v–234 (a) Dominica prima aduentus domini. Mathei xxi°. Cum appropinquasset ihesus Ierosolimis . . . Presens euangelium bis in anno legitur quia causa vtriusque aduentus . . . (f. 181^v) perueniamus amen. Expliciunt Omelie bone memorie Magistri odonis de Cancia super euangelica (*sic*) dominicalia . . . (b) Sermo de inuencione sancte Crucis. Sicut fulgur exit ab oriente . . . Sampson tollens mandibulam azini . . . (f. 211^v) et omnia in omnibus ad quam cellam etc'. (c) Vnius Euangeliste. Designauit dominus . . . Qui familiaritatem alicuius desiderat . . . (f. 234) eterne glorie recipiamus amen. Gloria sit altissimo patri et domino nostro ihesu cristo et spiritui sancto. Expliciunt Omelie Odonis de Cancia quondam Archiepiscopi Cantuariensis scripte per dominum Robertum Edyngtone infra hospicium strenui Militis Iohannis Lysle apud Wodehousse iuxta Arden' in vigilia sancti laurencii martiris per ipsum dominum Robertum finaliter conscripte anno domini millesimo cccc^mo quinquagesimo quinto litera dominicali E etc'.

Sermons on the Sunday Gospels by Odo of Cheriton, †1247: cf. Russell, *Writings*, p. 92, P. Meyer in *Romania*, xiv. 389–90 and the references given by Mynors, *Catalogue of the Manuscripts of Balliol College, Oxford*, p. 27; also Schneyer, pp. 100, 126, and G. Antolin's listing of the sermons of Escorial O. ii. 7 in his catalogue (1913), iii. 198–204.[1] The sermons are not numbered. Letter-marks, beginning with *a*, at intervals of less than a column in the margins of each sermon: cf. art. 2b.

(a) Sixty-six sermons of the temporale from Advent. The correspondence with Esc. appears to be:

Eton 1–22	Esc. T. 1–11, 14, 12, 15–23
Eton 22 (Sat. in 1st week of Lent)	Esc. S. 1 (Transfiguration)
Eton 24–7	Esc. T. 24–7
Eton 28 (Annunc. of B.V.M.)	Esc. S. 3 (Annunc. of B.V.M.)
Eton 29–66	Esc. T. 28–65

(b) Sermons for feast days from 3 May to 2 Nov. and for the dedication, fifteen in all. Eleven of them are in Esc.

[1] Antolin's list is not numbered. It consists of a prologue and sixty-five sermons of the temporale (T), and a prologue and twenty-five sermons of the sanctorale, common of saints, and dedication (S).

1. f. 181ᵛ *Inv. Crucis.* Sicut fulgur . . . Sampson tollens . . . (Esc. S. 5).

2. f. 184 *Joh. Bapt.* Elizabeth impletum . . . In Marco dominus apprehendit . . . (Esc. S. 8).

3. f. 187ᵛ *Cath. Petri.* Beatus es Symon bariona . . . Caro dicitur vita carnalis . . .

4. f. 190 *Maria Magd.* Rogabat ihesum . . . In 4° libro regum . . . (Esc. S. 17).

5. f. 192 *Assump. B.V.M.* Intrauit ihesus . . . Cum in hoc euangelio . . . (Esc. S. 4).

6. *Nat. B.V.M.* (*a*) f. 194 Liber generationis . . . Rorare (*sic*) celi desuper. Messis ecclesie . . . (*b*) f. 195ᵛ Contextus genealogie et interpretaciones. Liber generacionis . . . Prefacio tocius operis premisit . . . (Esc. S. 2).

7. f. 196ᵛ *Exalt. Crucis.* Cum exaltatus . . . Sicut enim ceruus . . . (Esc. S. 6).

8. f. 198ᵛ *Michael.* Quis putas maior . . . Paruulus non perseuerat in ira . . .

9. f. 201 *Simon et Judas.* Legitur in exodo . . . Surgentesque mane . . .

10. f. 201ᵛ 'Institutio festi omnium sanctorum'. Legimus in historiis apostolorum . . .

11. f. 202 *Omn. SS.* Videns ihesus . . . Hodie nos miseri . . . (Esc. S. 21).

12. f. 205ᵛ *Omn. SS.* Gaudeamus . . . Dominus sic dirigat . . . (cf. Esc. S. 22).

13. f. 206ᵛ 'Dies animarum'. Dixit martha . . . Numquam magis gauise sunt anime . . . (Esc. S. 24).

14. f. 208ᵛ 'De memoria mortis et sacramentorum fructu'. Dixit ihesus d.s. et turbis iudeorum Ego sum panis viuus . . . Fratres dilectissimi si mortuus loqueretur . . . (Esc. S. 25).

15. f. 210 *Ded. Eccl.* Ingressus Iesus . . . Publicanorum id est illorum . . . (Esc. S. 23).

(*c*) Nine sermons of the common of saints, as Esc., S. 12, 10, 13–16, 18–20.

3. (*a*) f. 234ʳᵛ A list of the sermons of art. 2, with leaf numbers. (*b*) ff. 235–6 Repertorium plurium notabilium in homiliis Odonis . . .

(*b*) For this index, added in s. xviᴵ, and other indexes in books belonging to William Horman, see N. R. Ker in *The Library*, 5th series, xvii (1962), 79–82. It is provided with leaf numbers and letter marks. ff. 236ᵛ–238 are ruled, but blank.

ff. iii+238+ii. ff. ii, iii, 239 are parchment leaves, s. xv. ff. 1–238 have a medieval foliation 1–78, 1–1[60]. 363×242 mm. Written space 265×152 mm. 2 cols. 53–4 lines. Frame ruling in ink, supplemented, sometimes at least (see ff. 79–97), by faintly pencilled horizontal lines within the frame. Collation: 1–12¹² 13¹⁴ (ff. 145–58) 14–19¹² 20⁸. Quires marked a–v in the usual late medieval manner; some, also, 'finis quaterni' or with a number, for example, f. 206ᵛ, 'finis vndecimi quaterni' and f. 207, '12 quaternus', by someone who was leaving art. 1 out of his calculations. All in one ugly, but clear and competent, mixture of anglicana and secretary. Initials: (i) ff. i, 78ᵛ, blue with red ornament; (ii) 3-line, red. Capital letters in the ink of the text marked sometimes with red. Binding by Slatter. Secundo folio *facere nesciunt.*

Written by a named scribe working for Sir John Lisle (1405–71) at Woodhouse (Isle of Wight).¹ 'Liber Willelmi Horman', and table of contents headed 'Contenta', f. iiiᵛ. Presumably given by Horman.

¹ I owe the identification to Mr. Mark Booth of the Warwickshire County Record Office, who referred me to the Inquisitio Post Mortem of 11 Edward IV (Records Commission, iv. 354) where Wodehouse, Chute, and Throxton are given as holdings of Sir John Lisle in Hampshire and the Isle of Wight, and to J. C. Wedgwood, *History of Parliament, Biographies 1439–1509* (1936), where it is said that a Robert Edyngton was one of Sir John Lisle's executors: cf. *VCH. Hampshire*, v. 200.

25. *Biblia*   s. XIII[2]

1. ff. 2–457[v] A Bible with the usual contents in the usual order (cf. Bristol Public Library, MS. 15), except that the Prayer of Manasses does not occur after 2 Chronicles.

The layout is admirably contrived so that the end of Apocalypse and the end of quire thirty-eight coincide exactly. 'DAVID' is the running title of Psalms.[1]

The prologues are sixty of the common set of sixty-four—Stegmüller, no. 327 to 2 Chronicles, no. 512, the second prologue to Amos, no. 589 to Matthew, and no. 839 to Apocalypse are the only absentees, together with fifteen others, Stegmüller, nos. 514 (as second prologue to Amos, preceded by the words 'Amos interpretatur honustus'), 530 (after 531), 596 and 595 (before 590), 670 and 674 (before 677), 633 (after 640), 806, 816, 818, 822, 823, 824, 825 to the seven Catholic Epistles, and 835 to Apocalypse. 'Multorum nobis' before Ecclesiasticus and 'Quoniam quidem' before Luke are duly assigned to their authors in headings.

Red underlines here and there and letters, usually *h* and/or *a*, in red above the words underlined, for example, at 1 Kings 15: 3 'et non concupiscas ex rebus ipsius aliquid' is underlined and the letters *h* and *a* are written above *concupiscas*, at Proverbs 3: 9 'da pauperibus' is underlined with *r* and *a* above *pauperibus*, and at Proverbs 9: 12 'et proximis tuis' is underlined with *c* above *proximis*: for the meaning of these letters (but not *r*) cf. art. 3*b*. Superior letters, but not just the same ones as here, are, above these words of Proverbs 3: 9 and 9: 12 quoted from 'Correctorium E' by H. Denifle in *Archiv für Literatur und Kirchengeschichte des Mittelalters*, iv (1888), 485, 492.

2. ff. 458–97 Hee sunt interpretationes hebraicorum nominum incipientium per A litteram. Aaz apprehendens . . . Zuzim consiliantes eos. uel consiliatores eorum. Deo Gratias Amen. ff. 497[v]–498[v] blank.

3 (added in a nearly contemporary hand). (*a*) f. 1 Incipit doctrina ad cognitionem correctionis biblie. Qwoniam super omnes scripturas uerba sacri eloquii . . . confusa translationibus continentur. (*b*) f. 1[rv] Alia doctrina magis nota. Sciendum etiam (?) quod in biblia inuenies . . . Et sic de singulis poterit tua discretio iudicare. Explicit doctrina.

(*a*). W. Brito, Correctorium Bibliae (Stegmüller, no. 856, 2 = 2817). Printed by Denifle, loc. cit., 293–4. (*b*). Three paragraphs, the third explaining what the red letters (see above) mean, *h* hebrei, *a* antiqui, *g* greci, *i* ieronimus (cf. Denifle, p. 310) and *c* correccio. This last is further explained in the margin: 'Si autem aliquando ita inueneris. dic̃it ẽi.′ significat quod correccio ita habet. siue super diccionem siue super punctum sit C. Si autem ita dic̃it ei. significat quod correccio non habet neque cum linea supposita. neque sine ea'.

ff. i+498+i. Soft good parchment. 330×235 mm. Written space 210×142 mm. 2 cols. (3 cols. in art. 2). 49 lines. Collation: 1¹²+1 leaf before 1 (f. 1) 2–41¹² 42 five (ff. 494–8). Quires numbered at the end (but most of the numbers have been cut off) and catchwords. Punctuation with the flex (?) added throughout. Initials: (i) of books, in colour on coloured grounds, historiated (cf. James, *Catalogue*) or decorated: gold is used as a ground colour only on ff. 2, 4, 5 (Genesis), 357 (Matthew); (ii) of prologues, red or blue, with ornament of both colours; (iii) of chapters, outside the written space, blue or red, with ornament of the other colour; (iv) of psalm verses and in art. 2, 1-line, blue or red. Capital letters in the ink of the text filled with pale yellow. Red morocco binding, s. xviii, rebacked by R. L. Day in 1966. Secundo folio *astrologis* (f. 3).

As James noted, the script, including art. 3, appears to be Italian and the decoration French.

---

[1] The psalter has usually no running title in Bibles.

Given by William Hetherington, fellow, in 1773: a book-plate inside the cover is to this effect.

26. *Biblia*   s. xii/xiii

1. 'The byble in laten' (f. vii, s. xv) in the order Genesis–2 Chronicles, Isaiah, Jeremiah, Baruch, Lamentations, Ezekiel, Daniel, Minor Prophets, Job, Ezra, Nehemiah, Esther, 3 Ezra (Stegmüller, no. 94, 1), Proverbs, Ecclesiastes, Song of Songs, Wisdom, Ecclesiasticus, Prayer of Solomon (Ecclesiasticus lii), Tobit, Judith, 1, 2 Maccabees, Psalms (Gallican, Roman, and Hebrew in parallel columns, with Ps. 151 at the end of each version), Gospels, Acts, Catholic Epistles, Apocalypse, Pauline Epistles, including the Epistle to the Laodiceans in last place: Colossians follows 2 Thessalonians. A closely similar Bible from St. Albans is at Corpus Christi College, Cambridge, MS. 48.[1]

Ezra and Nehemiah are written as one book in a single series of chapters numbered 1–35, with 'Explicit liber ezre' at the end, after which comes 'Hic post incensam a caldeis . . . doctissimo salutem et reliqua' (cf. de Bruyne, *Préfaces*, v. 3). The Hebrew alphabet with the meaning of the letters precedes Lamentations. Proverbs and Psalms begin on new quires, ff. 185, 229. Most books begin on a new leaf. The Prayer of Manasses is an early addition in the margin of f. 111ᵛ, the page on which 2 Chronicles ends. Running titles in red on lines ruled specially.

Prefaces, argumenta,[2] and other preliminary matter include forty-six prefaces of the common set of sixty-four[3] and many other pieces shown here by *.

(*Genesis–1 Chronicles*). Stegmüller, nos. 284, De interpretatibus sacre historie ex hebreo in grecum qui quibus successerint. Ante incarnationem domini nostri iesu cristi ccc° xli° . . . pleniter nouerant*, 285, 311, *312** (Iesus filius naue in typum domini . . .), *313**, *315**, 323, *321**, *319**, 328, 327 (as second preface to 1 Chronicles), *326**.

(*Isaiah–Daniel*). 482, *478** (. . . sed euangelium), 487, *478** (Ysaiam. ieremiam . . . nescit alfabetum), 491, 492, *478** (Ysaiam. ieremiam . . . non legantur), 494, *495**.

(*Minor Prophets*). 500, 507, *510*, Iohel qui interpretatur . . . quando et Micheas*, *509**, *515*, *512* (. . . audiendum uerbum dei), *519+517*, *516**, *524*, *522**, *526*, *525**, *528*, *527**, *531*, *530**, *529**, *534* (*divided at* Iosiam regem: *the rest headed* Item aliud argumentum), *532**, *538* (Moriente dario . . .: Ieremias . . . deus eduxit *omitted*) *535**, *539*, *540**, Secundo anno darii . . . regis imperium*, *Ultimum xii prophetarum . . . uenit in ierusalem**, *545**, *544**.

(*Job–2 Maccabees*). 344, 357, *350**, *349**, *330**, *341+343*, 457, *456** (. . . usque perducant), 468, *455** (. . . commodare: as prologue to Wisdom), 332, *Tobias filius annanihil . . . claritatis promeruit** (between Tobit and Judith), 335, *551*.

(*Psalms*, ff. 229–42). *430**, *414**, *389** (. . . octoginta octo), *443**, *410**+Psalmi chore sunt . . . tricesimus tercius*, *394** (. . . dubitaret in fine cessatum), *405**, *451** (Jerome, Ep. 106:

---

1 The Bible at Corpus is partly in three columns and partly in four. It does not contain 3 Ezra or Psalms, places Proverbs, Ecclesiastes, and Song of Songs between Job and Ezra, and has all four Gospels with their prologues in parallel columns, but in all other respects its contents and arrangements are closely similar to those in Eton 26. The only differences in the prologues, etc., seem to be that Corpus has Stegmüller, nos. 674 and 676 at Romans, instead of the seven prologues 651 . . . 679 and does not have Stegmüller, no. 319 at 1 Kings, that it has the letter of Senatus in first place before the Gospels, and that the capitula are grouped instead of being placed before each book.

2 The argumenta are carefully noted as such in the headings. They are shown here by italics.

3 See Bristol, Public Library, 15.

Biblia Sacra, ix, Liber Psalmorum, 8–42), 434* (. . . donec omnia complentur), 418, c. 2*, Notandum sane quod quattuor erant notarii . . . numerus intelligatur*, 450*, 382*, Est igitur alleluia . . . tegeris ullo*, Quidam dicunt hunc psalmum . . . Laudate dominum in sancto eius laudate* (ff. 235ᵛ–241, on the psalm titles), Prophetia est inspiratio . . . dicit quinque libros*.

(*Gospels, Acts, Catholic Epistles, Apocalypse*). 595*, Quatuor in primo . . . quilibet horum* (8 lines of verse), Canon Tables (ff. 295ᵛ–296), 596* (. . . uiuis canendas), *590*, 606, 620, 624, 640, *631*, 809, 807*, 808*, 806*, 815*, *812*, *818*, 820*, *822*, *823*, *824*, *826*, 825*, *829*.

(*Pauline Epistles*). 670* (headed 'Incipit prefacio pelagii de corpore epistolarum beati pauli apostoli), *651* (Omnis textus . . . factus est), 662*, 661* (. . . discrepare uidetur legunt quidam epistolam ad laodicenses set ab omnibus exploditur), 674*, *651* (Epistle pauli . . . appositas), *678*, *679*, 654* (headed 'Uersus damasi pape in sanctum paulum apostolum. meritorum predicatio'), *683*, *688*, *701*, *706*, *721*, *730*, 747, *753*, *736*, *765* (. . . roma)+*760*, *772*+*770*, *780*, *783*, *793*.

A table of chapters is in front of forty-nine books.[1]

Genesis–Judges. Series *A*a.[2]

1 Kings. i. De helcha et uxoribus eius anna et fenenna. ii. De anna immolatione . . . xlviii. De uiris israhel et saule et filiis eius in gelboe occisis.

2 Kings. xlix. De dauid reuertente á cede amalech et de homine nunciante ei mortem saulis. et quod dauid preceperit eum occidi . . . xcviii. De dauid numerante . . . iebusei oblato.

3 Kings. i. De senectute dauid. et de adonia usurpante sibi regnum. et de abisag . . . lviii. De ochozia filio achab regnante super israhel.

4 Kings. lix. De ochozia cadente. et idola . . . xci. De enilmerodach subleuante iochim de carcere.

1, 2 Chronicles. Series unica, forma a.

Esther. De conuiuio assueri regis . . . pro iudeis directe (18 chapters). As Am. in de Bruyne, *Sommaires*.

Proverbs. i. Ad sciendam sapientiam et disciplinam patris audiendam . . . lix. De muliere forti et de precio eius.

Ecclesiastes. Series A, forma b.

Wisdom. i. De diligendo iusticiam et de non temptando deum . . . xlv. De noua creatura auium et de hospitalitate.

Tobit. De tobia quomodo captiuus . . . in sancta conuersatione permansit. 15 chapters.

Judith. Arfaxad rex medorum superans . . . fine optimo uitam conclusit. 22 chapters. As Am. in de Bruyne, *Sommaires*.

1 Maccabees. De alexandro multos reges superante . . . qui uenerant eum perdere. 61 chapters.

2 Maccabees. Ubi occisus est antiochus rex . . . et ierosolimam mitti. 55 chapters.

Psalms 1–150 (ff. 241–2). Primus psalmus ostendit quod ipse erit lignum uite . . . Quod ipse per spiritualem armoniam sit in sanctis omnibus collaudandus.

Matthew. As Wordsworth and White, C. 28 chapters.

Mark. De iohanne baptista et uictu . . . et sepultura et resurrectio eius. 14 chapters.

Luke. As Wordsworth and White, C (etc.). 21 chapters.

John. De uerbo in principio . . . ac petro dicit pasce oues meas. 14 chapters.

Acts. Ubi precepit iesus discipulis ab ierusalem ne discederent. et ubi reuersi . . . Vbi paulus romam uenit. 63 chapters.

James. De inimicorum . . . astricti. 12 chapters.

1 Peter. De regenerationis inuicta potentia . . . petri apostoli. 13 chapters.

2 Peter. De sanctis quod . . . euerti. 8 chapters.

1 John. De uerbo uite . . . cultura. 15 chapters.

2 John. De diligendis . . . reseruauit. 3 chapters.

[1] See footnotes 1, 2, above, p. 632. The writing is crowded in the tables of 1 Kings, Proverbs, and elsewhere.

[2] References in this form are to *Biblia Sacra*.

3 John. De filiis . . . aduentum. 4 chapters.

Jude. De falsis . . . epistole. 4 chapters.

Apocalypse. Quod beatus sit qui seruauerit . . . De perfectione bonorum et malorum. 56 chapters.

Romans. De natiuitate domini secundum carnem. De fide . . . Salutatio pauli ad fratres. 53 chapters.

1 Corinthians. Gratias agit apostolus . . . qui non credunt in dominum iesum. 69 chapters.

2 Corinthians. De passionibus et consolationibus apostoli . . . et pacem habere commonente. 29 chapters.

Galatians. De resurrectione domini . . . stigmata iesu portante. 12 chapters.

Ephesians. De sanctis quod ante . . . caritas cum fide. 31 chapters.

Philippians. De omnibus in iesum cristum . . . . et quod domus cesaris persecutoris facta est ecclesia cristi redemptoris. 8 chapters.

1 Thessalonians. De apostolo et siluano . . . epistola legeretur. 10 chapters.

2 Thessalonians. De persecutione quod exemplum . . . ut reuereantur. 6 chapters.

Colossians. De spe reposita sanctis . . . et laodicensium. colosenses. 12 chapters.

1 Timothy. De fabulis et genealogiis . . . et de custodiendo deposito. 12 chapters.

2 Timothy. De loide auia et euniche . . . et fratribus uniuersis. 7 chapters.

Titus. De domino patre . . . et salutatione apostoli. 7 chapters.

Philemon. De philemone et appia . . . adiutoribus pauli. 4 chapters.

Hebrews. De cristo quod deus sit . . . quod cum timotheo commendat. 23 chapters.

In Catholic Epistles and Pauline Epistles agreement seems to be usually with Wordsworth and White's A (etc.), but with many differences. Corrections (which often reduce the number of chapters) tend to increase the amount of difference. Sometimes there is much correction. Chapter numbers in the margins of books are those of the tables of chapters: there is often a double numbering, for example in Exodus, 1–139, as in the table, and 1–40.

Stichometric notes in the form 'Explicit liber prouerbiorum. habet uersus septingentos quadraginta' are provided at the end of twenty-six books: Genesis, 3700; Exodus, 3000; Deuteronomy, 2600; Joshua, 1700; Judges, 1750; Ruth, 250; 3 Kings, 2400; 4 Kings, 2250; 1 Chronicles, 2040; 2 Chronicles, 2100; Tobit, 900; Judith, 1100; Esther, 700; Proverbs, 1740; Ecclesiastes, 800; Song of Songs, 280; Wisdom, 1800; Ecclesiasticus, 2900 (the note is before the prayer of Solomon); Isaiah, 3580; Jeremiah, 4450 (the note follows Lamentations); Ezekiel, 3340; Daniel, 850; Minor Prophets, 3800; 2 Maccabees, 1800; Mark, 1800; Acts, 3600.

2. (*a*) ff. 291–2 Five ferial canticles: (1) Canticum ezechie. Ego dixi in excessum dierum meorum . . . domus dei mei; (2) Canticum anne. Confirmatum est cor meum . . . cornu cristi sui; (3) Canticum moysi. Cantemus domino . . . in medio mari; (4) Domine audiui auditionem . . . in claritatem eius; (5) Attende celum et loquar . . . terram populi sui. (*b*) ff. 292ᵛ–293ᵛ Epistle and gospel lections of the temporale and 'in anniuersario dedicationis ecclesie'.

(*a*) follows Ps. 151 immediately. Not the common versions: cf. Mearns, *Canticles*, p. 77. The sources are noted in the margin in very small writing: (1) Ys. cvii; (2) primo Re. iiii; (3) Exo. xxiiii; (4) abachuc; (5) Deu. cli.

ff. vii+362+vii. ff. viiʳ, 363ᵛ were pasted down to a former binding. 335×230 mm. Written space 238×160 mm. 3 cols. 62 lines. Pricks in both margins to guide ruling. Collation: 1 seven (ff. 1–7) 2¹⁰+1 leaf after 7 (ff. 8–18) 3¹⁰+1 leaf after 6 (ff. 19–29) 4¹⁰+1 leaf after 2 (ff. 30–40) 5¹² 6¹⁰+1 leaf after 5 (ff. 53–63) 7¹⁰ 8¹⁰+1 leaf before 1 (ff. 74–84) 9¹⁰+1 leaf after 4 (ff. 85–95) 10–17¹⁰ 18¹⁰ wants 10, blank, after f. 184 19¹⁰+1 leaf before 1 and 1 leaf after 5 (ff. 185–96) 20⁸+1 leaf after 1 (ff. 197–205) 21¹⁰ 22¹⁰+1 leaf after 4 (ff. 218–28) 23–28¹⁰ 29⁸ 30–35¹⁰ 36⁸ wants 7, 8, blank. 3 and 8 in quire 19, 5 and 8 in quire 21 and 4 and 5 in quire 29 are half-sheets. Quires numbered at the end, in pencil;

also in ink I–XXI, eight unnumbered quires, XXII–XXVII, one unnumbered quire; also catchwords. An excellent square upright hand. A little punctuation with the flex (?), for example on ff. 164ᵛ–165. Initials: (i) gold on blue and pink grounds, patterned, framed in green; (ii) red or blue, with ornament of the other colour; (iii) 1-line, red or blue. Binding of s. xviii. Secundo folio *fornicariam*.

Written in England. A gift to St. Albans from prior Matthew: 'Hunc codicem dedit domnus mathias prior sancto albano quem qui ei abstulerit aut titulum deleuerit anathema sit. amen' in red, f. 1, s. xiii; 'Biblia Mathei prioris Sancti Albani de armario B', f. 191, erased. 'Iohannes Sybley', f. 1, s. xv. 'Edwarde Seymour 27 August: 1582', f. vii. 'Eton Colledg book', f. 1, s. xv/xvi.

27. *Biblia*   s. XIII in.

1. ff. 1–359ᵛ A Bible beginning at f. 14, before which are two quires of capitula and prologues. The order of books is Genesis–2 Chronicles+Prayer of Manasses, Esther, Ezra+Nehemiah, Tobit, Judith, 1, 2 Maccabees, Isaiah, Jeremiah, Lamentations, Ezekiel, Minor Prophets, Job, Proverbs, Ecclesiastes, Song of Songs, Wisdom, Ecclesiasticus+Prayer of Solomon, Daniel, Psalms, Gospels, Pauline Epistles, Catholic Epistles, Apocalypse. Baruch is absent.

Within books the text is continuous—except for a little paragraphing in Matthew—the beginning of a new chapter being shown only by a number in the margin and sometimes by a coloured letter in the text. The chapter numbers are the modern ones, except in Genesis and Deuteronomy where there is a double numbering (80 and 50; 156 and 34). Ezra and Nehemiah are one book of twenty-three chapters under the heading 'Incipit Esdras propheta', paragraphed at ch. 'xi', Nehemiah 1: 1, against which 'Incipit secunda distinctio' is written in the margin. The division of the psalms into three fifties is marked by initials of type (iii) at Pss. 51 and 101, but smaller than those used to mark the liturgical divisions. Isaiah and Psalms begin on new quires (f. 174, 22¹; f. 270, 33¹). Matthew begins on a new leaf, f. 301 (f. 300ᵛ is blank), but not on a new quire.

Scattered marginalia in ink and pencil. A corrector wrote 'Cor' at the end of quires 23 and 30 (ff. 189ᵛ, 247ᵛ).

Only five prologues are in the body of the Bible, all to NT, four of the common set, Stegmüller, nos. 624 (*after* John) 677 (Quoniam (!) sunt . . .), 809, and 640, and 834 to Apocalypse. Forty-nine more are on the two quires at the beginning, 32 of the common set and 17 others shown here by *: on ff. 1–3, Stegmüller, nos. 284, 285; on ff. 6ᵛ–13ᵛ, Stegmüller, nos. 311, 323, 315*, 321*, 319*, 482, 487, 492, 491 (. . . temporibus indicant. Hec interpretatio ieronimi est. Si quid in ea mouerit . . . obseruanda est), 494, 500, 503*, 506*, 507, 511, 510, 515, 512, 516*, 519+517, 524, 522*, 526, 525*, 528, 527*, 529*, 532* +Iosiam regem iude . . . denunciauit (*this is the end of* 534), 535*, 538 (. . . uniuersa esse completa), 540*, 544*, 344, 357, 349*, 355* (Terra illa hus . . .), 350*, 457 (. . . erat ecclesiastes), 328, 332, 335, 341+343, 330, 513, 531: 513, 531 were added rather later than the others.

Capitula of Genesis–4 Kings are on ff. 3–8ᵛ and capitula of Job on f. 12 after prologue 350.¹

Genesis–Judges	Series lambda, forma a.
Ruth	Series lambda.
1–4 Kings, Job	Series A¹

The only stichometric note is after Ruth, 'Habet uersus 1 M. ccl' (*sic*).

2. ff. 359ᵛ–377ᵛ Aaz apprehendens . . . Zuzim consiliantes etc.

The usual alphabetical dictionary of Hebrew names.

¹ See footnote above, p. 632.

3. ff. iii, iv, 378–9 are binding leaves taken from a copy of the Decretals of Gregory ix.

From bk. 4. No apparatus. 2 cols. 45 lines. English hand, s. xiii/xiv.

ff. v+377+vi. ff. iii–v, 378–80 are binding leaves of medieval parchment (cf. art. 3): iii^r and 380^v were pasted down. 310×215 mm. Written space 213×132 mm. 2 cols. (3 cols. in art. 2). 54 lines. The first line of writing above the top ruled line. Pricks in both margins to guide ruling. Collation: 1^8 2 five (ff. 9–13) 3–18^8 19–20^10 21^10+2 leaves after 10 (ff. 172–3) 22–29^8 30–31^10 32^10+2 leaves after 10 (ff. 268–9) 33–41^12. A continuous series of pencil signatures, a–x, Ɔ, Λ, > is on verso sides of the first three leaves of each quire from 1^1 (f. 1^v) to 8^3 (f. 56^v) and the same signatures are repeated on the facing rectos: thus, in quire 1 ff. 1^v, 2 are marked 'a' and in quire 2 ff. 9^v, 10 are marked 'd'. The hand changes at f. 174 (22^1). Initials: (i) ff. 1, 2^v, 14, in colours on gold grounds, historiated (see James's *Catalogue*) and edged in green; (ii) of Exodus, in colours on a decorated gold ground; (iii) of Leviticus and most other books and the ten main divisions of the psalter, blue and red ornamented in colours including green and pale yellow and often with purple linings and grounds; (iv) of prologues on ff. 6^v–9, psalms, and where a new paragraph begins in St. Matthew or a new letter in art. 2, 2-line, blue or red with ornament of the other colour; (v) of prologues on ff. 9–12, 2-line or 3-line, blue or red; (vi) of psalm verses, in capitula on ff. 8–12, and to mark chapters in some books, especially Maccabees, Matthew, and Acts, 1-line, blue or red.[1] Slatter binding. Secundo folio *Inpromptu est*.

Written in England. 'Liber M' hyle vicarii collegii sancti georgii infra castrum de Windesor super quo ego Io Esterfeld' canonicus ibidem exposui domino Thome petyt capellano x s' de pecunia magistri stokes', f. v, s. xv/xvi: for Esterfeld, canon of St. George's Chapel, Windsor, 1500–13, and John Stokes, canon there 1486–1503, see Emden, *BRUO*. Presumably one of the four Bibles covered by *CMA* 31, the others being 1+2, 26, 28+29.

28, 29. *Vetus Testamentum, cum commentariis Hugonis de S. Caro*
s. xiii²

1. The OT in two volumes, breaking after Psalms, the text in the central space on each page and the commentary fitted round it as convenient, the pattern varying from page to page.

Text. The forty-seven books in the usual order and with the usual prologues: see p. 210.

Leviticus, Proverbs, and Minor Prophets begin on new quires, MS. 28, f. 102; MS. 29, ff. 1, 399. The two prologues to Joel are not in the usual order, Stegmüller, no. 510, preceding no. 511. The two prologues to Jonah, nos. 524, 521, are run together as one. The running title of Lamentations 5 is 'Prologus'.

Commentary. The commentary, here anonymous, is that attributed to Hugh of St. Cher. It is absent throughout 2 Ezra (Stegmüller, no. 94, 1) and Esther xi–xvi, but is elsewhere continuous; (Genesis–2 Chronicles) Stegmüller, nos. 3632, 3634, 3636, 3638, 3640, 3642, 3644, 3646, 3648, 3650, 3652, 3655, 3657, 3659; (1 Ezra–Psalms) nos. 3662, 3664, 3668, 3670, 3672, 3674, 3676; (sapiential books) nos. 3678, 3680, 3683, 3685, 3687; (Isaiah–Daniel) nos. 3689, 3691, 3693, 3695, 3697, 3699; (Minor Prophets) nos. 3701–2, 3704, 3706–14; (1, 2 Maccabees) nos. 3715–6.[2]

[1] On f. 8 the rubricator put in the blue initials, but not the red ones.
[2] Stegmüller refers to Paris, B.N. lat. 59 (Genesis–Ezekiel) and lat. 156 (Daniel–2

A commentary on the Prayer of Manasses is included in no. 3659 (2 Chronicles). No. 3693 (Lamentations) occupies MS. 29, ff. 242–69: many of these leaves are wholly filled by commentary. MS. 28, f. 101^v and MS. 29, ff. 398^{rv}, 516^{rv} are blank.

2. Contemporary additions in the margins of MS. 28, ff. 428–510 (Psalms) and MS. 29, ff. 59^v–71 (Ecclesiasticus) consist of (*a*) an author's name or initial in red, (*b*) a sentence in red beginning 'Quod', and (*c*) a commentary on the sentence in black; for example, MS. 28, f. 438, opposite Ps. 17: 1, Diligam te domine, (*a*) Weiricus, (*b*) Quod multiplicibus ex causis. dominus sit amandus, (*c*) Diligam te domine fortitudo . . . nocere proficiat.

The names are: (in the margins of Psalms) Adam de Persen' (f. 488), Balduinus (Bald'), Bernardus, Cassianus, Gaufridus, Gilebertus (Gislebertus), Hugo de Foill' (Foll'), Hugo de Sancto Victore, Petrus Cantor, Petrus Ravennas, Richardus, Weiricus; also the initial B; (in the margins of Ecclesiasticus) Bald', Bern', Gaufr', Rad', Weiricus.

(MS. 28) ff. vi+519+iii: ff. iii–vi, 520–1 are medieval binding leaves: iii^r was pasted down. (MS. 29) ff. ii+516+iii: f. 517 is a medieval flyleaf. Thin parchment. 272 × 185 mm. Written space *c.* 172 × 115 mm. Text in 48 lines. Commentary in 55–9 lines. Collation: (MS. 28) 1–6^{16} 7^6 wants 6, blank, after f. 101 8–32^{16} 33^{18}. (MS. 29) 1–16^{16} 17–19^{12} 20–25^{16} 26^{10} (ff. 389–98) 27–33^{16} 34^6. *Ad hoc* signatures in pencil in MS. 29 and in red ink (traces only) in MS. 28. In s. xv, probably, the leaves in the first half of each quire were numbered i–viii. Initials: of books and the usual eight psalms, in colour on grounds of colour and a little gold, expertly decorated and (MS. 28, ff. 1, 8, 428^v) historiated (Jerome writing, Creation, David); (ii) of prologues, as (i), but smaller; (iii) of commentaries, blue and red with ornament of both colours; (iv) of chapters, 2-line blue or red with ornament of the other colour; (v) of verses of psalms, 1-line, blue or red. Bindings by Slatter, repaired by R. L. Day in 1966. Marks of the eight bands and the chainplate of an older binding show on ff. iii, iv of MS. 28. Secundo folio: (MS. 28) *euangelium* (text) and *energie* (commentary); (MS. 29) *tat. In foribus* (text) and *dei facta* (commentary).

Written probably in France. Given by William Ayscough, bishop of Salisbury, †1450: 'Liber Collegii Regalis beate Marie de Etona. iuxta Wyndesor ex dono Willelmi Episcopi Sar' ', MS. 28, f. 1, and MS. 29, f. 1.

30. *J. de Athon, Septuplum* s. XIV/XV

(*Text*) Subnectiuam tabulam fragilitatis humane . . . absortus uorticibus. (*Commentary*) Cum illius non sim auctoritatis . . . sicque materia viciorum in generali. Deo gracias. Explicit per hoc septuplum commentatum.

The first part of the Septuplum on the seven deadly sins: for the author, † by Nov. 1349, see Emden, *BRUO*, p. 12 (Acton). Bloomfield, no. 963. Gonville and Caius College, Cambridge, 282 (both parts: written in 1355) gives the date of composition as 1346. The author's text is surrounded by his commentary. Some annotation in the margins, including 'Nota bene contra religiosos', f. 21^v, in red ink.

ff. 105. 355 × 240 mm. Written space *c.* 252 × 155 mm. 2 cols. 57 lines (commentary). Collation: 1–13^8 14 one (f. 105). Text in large and commentary in fairly small textura: not good. Blue initials with red ornament all of one size, taking up 2 lines of text and 4 lines or 5 lines of commentary. A continuous saw-pattern border in blue, red, and green on f. 1.

Maccabees), and other Paris manuscripts. 59 + 156 is a two-volume bible, breaking after Baruch, with Hugh's commentaries fitted round the text.

Contemporary binding of wooden boards covered with white leather: eight bands: two strap-and-pin fastenings now missing: a missing label near the head of the back cover was secured by six nails: a chainmark near the foot of the side of the front cover. Secundo folio (text) *perhennis*, (commentary) *me dominus*.

Written in England. The marks of label and chain on the binding suggest that this book was at Eton by *c*. 1500. *CMA* 115.

32, ff. ii, 1–96. *Miscellanea theologica*   s. xiii[2]

Miscellaneous devotional pieces, most of them by or attributed to St. Bernard and St. Anselm and (arts. 4, 6) compendia of Gregory's Moralia and of Vitas Patrum. The contemporary titles of arts. 2, 4–10, shown here within carets, are written in a small current hand. A fifteenth-century table of contents on f. ii is headed 'In isto libro continentur isti tractatus' and lists arts. 1–10, 13, with leaf references.

1. ff. 1–3 Quo studio et quo affectu . . . in ara cordis adoletur.

Hugh of St. Victor, De modo orandi. *PL* clxxvi. 977–88.

2. ff. 3–9 'Meditaciones beati bernardi'. Multi multa sciunt . . . vnum eundemque dominum glorie. qui . . . amen.

Pseudo-Bernard. *PL* clxxxiv. 485–508.

3. ff. 9ᵛ–11 Anima cristiana. anima de graui morte . . . solus benedictus in secula seculorum amen.

Anselm, Meditatio III. *SAO* iii. 84–91.

4. ff. 11–19 'Notabilitates moralium beati gregorii pape super librum iob extracte sub compendio'. Temptancia quippe uicia que inuisibili circa nos . . . et sepe alia succedunt.

Fifty-one paragraphs, not in book order. Many pointing hands in the margins and on f. 15ᵛ the words '[ʒ]ef þu seche non' ese [þu] dredust no disese', s. xv in.

5. ff. 19–21ᵛ 'Meditacio beati bernardi de diligendo deo'. Vigili cura 'mente' sollicita. summo conatu . . . tu es domine deus meus.

PL xl. 847–54 (chapters i–ix).

6. ff. 22–35 'Vitas patrum sub compendio'. Liber primus de prouectu patrum . . . (*titles of the 18 books*). Dixit abbas antonius. Si uis placere deo quocumque uadis . . . filium suffocauit. Explicit liber de prouectu patrum.

7. ff. 35–6 'Meditacio ad concitandum timorem'. Terret me uita mea . . . diligunt nomen tuum. qui . . . amen.

Anselm, Meditatio I. *SAO* iii. 76–9.

8. (*a*) ff. 36–7 'Deploracio amisse virginitatis'. Anima mea. anima erumpnosa . . . misericordia tua qui es . . . amen. (*b*) ff. 37–8 Amans nos deus . . . deus in eternum. (*c*) f. 38ʳᵛ Tota anima diligendus est deus . . . a cupiditate mala. (*d*) ff. 38ᵛ–39 Audite celi et auribus percipe terram quam . . . celestia et terena amen.

(*a*). Anselm, Meditatio II: *SAO* iii. 80–3. 'he wold not here: nov lett him feele' is at the head of f. 36ᵛ.

9. ff. 39–41ᵛ 'Meditacio 'beati' bernardi de planctu virginis marie. quem fecit in morte filii sui'. Quis dabit capiti meo aquam. et oculis meis . . . benedictus sit filius eius dominus noster . . . Amen.

Cf. B.L., Royal 7 A. vi, art. 16. Printed as St. Bernard's in early editions and partly in *PL* clxxxii. 1133.

10. ff. 42–46ᵛ, 49 'Liber beati bernardi edditus abati cluniacensi de dissiplina monacorum'. Uenerabili patri Willelmo frater bernardus . . . Usque modo si qua me scriptitare insistis . . . ne precipitentur.

SBO iii. 81–107/16. In s. xv the part of the text on f. 49 was recopied on f. 47 and the further section 'Scio quippe nonnullos . . . precor et supplico valete. Explicit apologeticon Ber.' (iii. 107/19–108) added. f. 47ᵛ blank.

11. (*a*) ff. 48ʳᵛ, 49ʳᵛ [S]umma questionis fuit cur deus homo factus sit ut per mortem suam . . . hoc deo debebat non diabulo. (*b*) f. 49ᵛ Paragraphs beginning 'Misericordiam uero dei que tibi parue', 'Diaboli uero reconciliacioni', and 'Racionabilia et quibus nichil'.

(*a*). A compendium of Anselm, Cur deus homo, the latter part of it written immediately after the part of art. 10 on f. 49.

12. ff. 49ᵛ–50 Domino et patri uniuerse ecclesie . . . urbano . . . anselmus . . . Quoniam diuina prouidencia . . . auctoritate reboretur. Cum adhuc in beati (*sic*) monasterio abbas essem . . . Presumptori ubique (*ends abruptly*).

Anselm, De incarnatione verbi: ed. Schmitt, ii. 1–5/9.

13. ff. 50–72ᵛ Anselmus de similitudinibus. Uoluntas tripliciter. uoluntas enim dicitur . . . in quantum uolunt. 'Explicit Anselmus de similitudinibus'.

PL clix. 605–702 (ch. 1–192). In paragraphs numbered later from 1 to 203. To avoid running on to a new quire the scribe wrote the last sixteen words of para. 202 and all para. 203, 'Uerba defuncti osberti . . .' (edn., ch. 192), in the lower margin of f. 72ᵛ.

14. ff. 73–96ᵛ Subit animum dictare aliquid . . . set non finis querendi.

Bernard, De consideratione, in five books. *SBO* iii. 393–493.

15. Miscellaneous pieces on the flyleaf, f. ii, include charms on the recto and verses and a French prayer on the verso: (*a*)+a.p. petrus super petram sedebat . . .; (*b*) Quicumque habuerit dolorem dencium dicat cotidie deuota mente. pater noster et aue maria et statim sanabitur pro animabus patris et matris sancti laurencii martiris; (*c*) Quicumque patiens fluxum sanguinis per nasum. scribat bironix si fuerit masculus . . . si fuerit femina. scribat bironixa . . .; (*d*) In mundo duo sunt que nil . . . (2 lines); (*e*) Nullius rei possessio iocunda erit sine socio; (*f*) Duce dame saynt marie virgine et pucele Raynge des aungeles mere au Roy de cunsail mercy vous cry . . .; (*g*) In sacco sord[e]t qui regum . . .; (*h*) Cor prauum velat sub verbi . . . (2 lines); (*i*) Non est prudentis propter mala . . . (3 lines).

(*a–f*) are of s. xiii ex. and (*g–i*) of s. xv. (*a–c*), for toothache and nose-bleeding, are probably in the hand which wrote the inscription containing dates 1261 and 1265 (see below). (*d, g, h, i*). Walther, *Sprichwörter*, nos. 11880, 12024a, 3425a, 17699.

ff. i+96. An incorrect late medieval foliation ends at '52' (f. 50). 292 × 200 mm. Written space *c.* 215 × 145 mm. 2 cols. 49 lines. Collation: 1¹⁰ 2–4¹² 5² (ff. 47, 48) 6–9¹². *Ad hoc* signatures in pencil. The part of art. 10 copied in s. xv is in non-current hybrida. Initials: (i, ii) 4-line and 2-line, blue with red ornament. Capital letters in the ink of the text filled with pale yellow. Bound in s. xvi¹ with MS. 32, ff. 97–216, q.v. Secundo folio *aliquando*.

Written in England. An owner or reader wrote at the head of f. ii, 'iii idus octobris anno domini m° cc° lx° i° fui admissus cum custode. Anno domini m.cc.lxv fui institutus [. . .]' and at the head of f. 1, 'Edewardus de valle scolarium ordine fecit quandam su[m]mam sermonum [. . .] et incipit. Letabor ego super eloquia et thema est Sicut letancium omnium habitacio'.[1] 'Prec' v⁸', f. 94ᵛ. '4', f. ii. At Eton by 1521: see MS. 32, ff. 97–216.

32, ff. 97–216. *Thomas Wallensis, In Psalterium*   s. xv med.

1. ff. 97–212 Beatus qui custodit verba . . . apoc' 22. Crisostomus omelia 36 super matheum in imperfectum dicit . . . (f. 98) Cetera nota in glosa. Incipit opus vallensis super ps' sequentes. Beatus vir . . . Psalmista in principio sui libri pulcre et racionabiliter . . . per graciam set etiam per naturam etc.

Stegmüller, no. 8246, 3. T. Waleys, O.P., *fl.* s. xiv¹, on Pss. 1–20: 2: for this and other copies and the printed editions see B. Smalley in *AFP* xxiv (1954), 50–107. Numbers in the margins divide the text into 376 sections.

2. ff. 212–216ᵛ Amaritudo peccatorum 2bc . . . De urso 212bc Hic finis etc.

A table of art. 1 using the section numbers in the margins there and also subdivisions of these numbers by letters a–c.

3. A conjoint pair of leaves form the pastedown and flyleaf at either end of MS. 32: (*a*) in front, the first bifolium of a quire of a theological manuscript, s. xv med.; (*b*) at the end, a bifolium of Justinian, *Institutes*, i. 5, 6, with surrounding apparatus, s. xiii ex.

(*a*). 2 cols. *c.* 43 lines. Frame ruling. Written in England in secretary hand. '24' at the head of f. iᵛ is a leaf number. Other leaves are in the bindings of MSS. 34, 107, q.v.

ff. 120, bound after an earlier manuscript (ff. ii, 1–96). For ff. i, 217 see above, art. 3. 292 × 200 mm. Written space *c.* 220 × 145 mm, 2 cols. *c.* 45 lines. Frame ruling. Collation: 1–7¹² 8–9¹⁰ 10¹⁶. Secretary hand. Initials: 3 line (f. 97) and 2-line, not filled in. Bound with ff. ii, 1–96 by Lisley who removed the previous limp parchment cover and used it as the wrapper of building accounts of Eton College for 10 Henry VIII. This cover, still in use as a wrapper, is inscribed on the front 'Wallensis super psalterium partim usque ad Psalmum 20 Domine in virtute tua'. Secundo folio (f. 98) *verbum psalmiste.*

Written in England. At Eton by 1521.

33. *Gregorius, Dialogi; etc.*   s. xii/xiii

1. ff. 1–97 Incipit dialogus beati Gregorii pape. de miraculis sanctorum patrum. Quadam die nimis . . . ipsi fuerimus. Explicit dialogus beati Gregorii pape urbis rome de miraculis sanctorum patrum.

[1] For these sermons see Schneyer, p. 348. There are copies in Worcester Cathedral, MS. F. 16 ('Sermones de valle Scolarium') and MS. Q. 87.

PL lxxvii. 149–429. Bk. 2, f. 19; 3, f. 39; 4, f. 68. f. 97ᵛ blank. 'Post hunc librum sequencia leguntur' is in the margin opposite the end of the text.

2. ff. 98–101ᵛ Incipit prologus beati Ieronimi presbiteri⸴ in actus captiui monachi. Qui nauali prelio . . . posse superari. Expliciunt actus captiui monachi.

PL xxiii. 53–60. For this and arts. 4, 6 see *Clavis*, nos. 617–19.

3. ff. 101ᵛ–103ᵛ Incipit de sancto frontonio. Qui homo dei et cristi esse . . . delicta donentur.

BHL, no. 3192 and, for the *explicit* here, the supplement to *BHL*, no. 3192a.

4. ff. 103ᵛ–108 Incipit prologus beati Ieronimi presbiteri⸴ in uita sancti Pauli primi heremite. Inter multos sepe . . . moratus est.

PL xxiii. 17–28.

5. ff. 108–147ᵛ Incipit prologus in uitam beati Antonii. Presbiter euagrius⸴ carino (*sic*) filio salutem. Ex alia in aliam linguam . . . corruptionis artifices. Explicit uita Sancti Antonii abbatis.

PL xxvi. 834–976. The 'versio Evagrii'.

6. ff. 147ᵛ–159ᵛ Incipit prologus in uita sancti hylarionis. edita a beato Ieronimo. Scripturus uitam beati hylarionis . . . locum dilexerat. Explicit uita sancti hylarionis.

PL xxiii. 29–54.

7 (added). f. 159ᵛ Notification by the prior and convent 'Syreburn'', A.D. 1256, that they have granted Hugh de Beaumont, burgess of Winchester, and Archibald and their wives Alice and Matilda 'plenariam participationem omnium bonorum spiritualium que fuerint seu facta sunt et de cetero fient in Monasterio nostro et in aliis ecclesiis nostris' and have caused their names to be inscribed 'in nostro Martilogio'.

ff. i+159+iii. 272 × 170 mm. Written space 205 × 108 mm. 35 long lines. Collation: 1–10⁸ 11⁶ 12⁸ 13⁴ wants 4, probably blank, after f. 97, 14–19⁸ 20⁴. Flex punctuation (?), except in art. 1. Initials: (i) green, red, or blue, plain or with ornament. The ornament is red with the green and blue initials and green much more often than blue with the red initials. Pale-yellow fillings sometimes to initials of types (i) and (ii). *Incipits* and *explicits* commonly in red and green capitals. Williamson binding: no chainmark. Secundo folio *liter inuenienda*.

Written in England. Presumably at the Benedictine alien priory of Monk Sherborne, Hants., by 1256: cf. art. 7. At Eton by 1608–9 and doubtless earlier: cf. Birley, p. 233.

34. *Gregorius, Homiliae in Ezekielem; Fasciculus Morum*

s. xv med.; 1443

1. ff. 1–103 Incipiunt omelie beati gregorii pape in ezechielem prophetam numero xxii. dicte in patriarchio lateranensi in basilica que appellatur aurea. Prologus eiusdem operis. Dilectissimo fratri Marnilino (? *sic*) episcopo Gregorius seruus seruorum dei. Omelias que in beatum ezechielem . . . redeatur. Omelia iᵃ. Dei omnipotentis aspiracione . . . erudit. Sit itaque gloria . . . amen.

PL lxxvi. 785–1072. Pt. 2, f. 52^v. The scribe wrote 'Per te gregori celeste intrar honori' at the head of f. 1. Robert Elyot, †1499, wrote marginalia beginning 'Nota', glossed 'inhiant' with 'gape' and 'oriens' with 'est' on f. 100^v and noted on f. 103 that 'hec pars 2^a gregorii super ezechielem corrigitur secundum librum M T Wich': for Thomas Wyche, fellow of Oriel College, Oxford, 1435–6, † by Sept. 1475, and his books, see Emden, *BRUO*, p. 2102.

2. ff. 104–91 (also foliated 1–88) Abstinencia quid sit. particule 6 capitulo 3. A. A quibus . . . (f. 107) sexto decimo E. Incipiunt narraciones. Narracio ad bene loquendum particule 1 capitulo 1 H . . . (f. 107^v) diabolo ibidem . . . (*table of the seven 'particule'*) . . . (f. 108) Prima particula. De peccato in generali. Capitulum primum. Frater noster dilecte . . . sine defectu Ad quod . . . Amen. Finis sermonum est hec colleccio morum. Hic explicit liber qui vocatur Fasciculus morum scriptus per Willelmum Gybbe capellanum parochie de Wysebech. cuius anime Ihesus filius uirginis marie propicietur et perducat ad gaudia eterne vite. Anno domini Millesimo CCCC^{mo} quadragesimo tercio.

This and other copies of Fasciculus morum are listed by A. G. Little, *Studies in English Franciscan History*, 1917, pp. 139–40. 'Assit principio sancta Maria meo Presens huic operi sit gracia neumatis almi', f. 104, in the main hand. Many pointing hands in the margins.

3. A tale and a sermon: (*a*) f. 191^{rv} (88^{rv}) Legitur in miraculo beate marie quod erat quondam parisius quidam Ribaldus qui vocabatur Gobardeys . . .; (*b*) ff. 191^v–192 (88^v–89) Diues mortuus est. Marcus. In hiis verbis 2° video. Primo hominem consolacionis magne . . .

Some English in both pieces. (*a*) is printed from this copy, the only one known, by S. Wenzel in *Neuphilologische Mitteilungen*, lxxii (1971), 83–5.

4. ff. 192–199^v (also foliated 89–96) Abstinencie 3^x est species Prima ciborum et potuum moderacio . . . sicut granum sinapis. dicite. Huic (*ends imperfectly*).

Extracts from Speculum Laicorum (*Cat. of Romances*, iii. 408). The last words here are on Fides.

5. The pastedowns and two flyleaves (ff. i, 200) are: (*a*) in the front, the central bifolium of a quire in a hand of mainly secretary type, s. xv^2: a meditational piece in which a section numbered 133 begins 'Data est tibi o domine ihesu omnis potestas in celo et in terra'; (*b*) at the end, parts of two bifolia in a current hand of mainly secretary type, s. xv: apparently a commentary on the Psalms (Pss. 9, 10). Cf. above, p. 661.

ff. i+199+i. For ff. i, 200 see above, art. 5. ff. 104–99 have a modern foliation of their own 1–96. 270×227 mm. Written space 210–25×140–55 mm. 2 cols. in art. 1; then long lines. 33–53 lines. Frame ruling from f. 27 where the hands changes. Collation: 1–3^8 4^6+1 leaf after 2 (f. 27) 5–10^8 11^{10} 12^{14} 13–24^8 (ff. 104–99). Quires 1–4 signed a–d and quires 13–24 signed+, a–l. Several hands varying much in size. In art. 1 the change from fere-textura to (mainly) secretary is at f. 27. Arts. 2–4 by Gybbe are in an untidy current anglicana, with some secretary forms mixed in. Initials: in art. 1, 3-line or 2-line, blue with red ornament; in arts. 2–4, 3-line, 2-line, and 1-line metallic red. Capital letters in the ink of the text marked with red in arts. 2–4. Binding by Lisley. Secundo folio *tus est*.

Written in England. Gybbe, who wrote arts. 2–4 in 1443, was the scribe of Bodleian, MS. Bodley 152 (*Sum. Cat.* 1945) and, as Dr. Ian Doyle has kindly told me, of Bodleian, MS.

Rawl. poet. 118 (*Sum. Cat.* 14611) and Vatican, MS. Ottoboni 334. Probably belonged to and the gift of Robert Elyot: see above, p. 631.

35+219 pp. 51–4. *Thomas Aquinas* s. XIII ex.

Arts. 1–4 are nos. 806 and 811, 3 in Dondaine and Shooner.

1. ff. 1–16 Questio est de spiritualibus creaturis . . . supra dictum est.

Ed. L. W. Keeler, 1946; Marietti edn., ii. 367–415. The space left blank on f. 16^{rv} is filled with a table of questions of arts. 1–3. Many marginalia.

2. ff. 17–94^v Questio est de potencia dei . . . sentencie damasceni.

Marietti edn., ii. 7–270. Ends with q. 10, art. 4. The blank space on f. 94^v is filled with a 'questio', 'utrum deus possit esse principium creature productum absque emanacione personarum'. Not many marginalia after f. 40. A typical head by Robert Elyot on f. 61: see p. 631.

3. ff. 95–166^v, MS. 219 pp. 51–4 Questio est de malo . . . (f. 166^v) posterius in tempore ut dicitur in quarto (*ends imperfectly in q. 16 art. 4: catchword* phisicorum). Of the next quire there are two leaves in MS. 219, containing parts of q. 16 arts. 6, 7 on pp. 51, 52 and parts of q. 16 arts. 10, 11 on pp. 53, 54.

Marietti edn., ii. 445–671 col. 1/47; 679 col. 2/53–683 col. 2/15; 693 col. 2/40–696 col. 1/18.

4. ff. 167–78 [S]icut philosophus dicit in x ethicorum . . . qui est principium omni causa. Explicit liber causarum. amen.

Ed. H. D. Saffrey, 1954: he consulted this copy of the 'famille universitaire' and called it V (p. xliii). Four leaves are missing after f. 170^v, which ends 'quo multiplicantur intelligentie' (edn. 39/14): f. 171 begins 'signanter autem dicit' (edn. 73/4). f. 178^v, left blank, was once pasted down. It contains a table of contents and other writing all much rubbed: at the top, 'lib . . . . continet xvi (*or* xv) pecias'.

5. ff. vi, vii, two conjoint leaves taken over from an older binding (f. vi^r was pasted down) are from a treatise on the Trinity, s. xiii med.

Sections begin on f. iii, '[N]unc post testimonia ueteris T' de fide sancte trinitatis et unitatis ad noui T' auctoritates accedamus' and on f. iv '[H]ic oritur questio satis necessaria. Constat et irrefragabiliter uerus est quod deus pater genuit filium'. The author calls his opponents 'garuli racionatores' and 'ueritatis aduersarii'. 2 cols. 27+ lines. A fine large hand between double ruled lines. The leaves were used in binding by s. xv: see below.

ff. vii+178+iv in MS. 35 (for ff. vi, vii see above, art. 5) and ff. 2 in MS. 219. 325 × 235 mm. Written space 245 × 170 mm. 2 cols. 60 lines (46 lines in art. 4). Collation: 1–2^8 3–8^{12} 9^6 (ff. 89–94) 10–15^{12} 16 two (MS. 219, pp. 51–4, a bifolium) 17^{12} wants 5–8 after f. 170 18 four (ff. 175–8). A new hand at art. 4 writes Aristotle's text in textura and Aquinas's commentary smaller in incipient book-hand anglicana. 3-line and 2-line blue initials with red ornament: omitted in art. 4. Binding by Slatter. Secundo folio *adueniens*.

Written in England. 'liber M. I. Grene.[1] prec' [. . . .] (*altered to* x^s)' and a table of contents, f. iv^v, s. xv. At Eton before 1500: cf. art. 2. The leaves now in MS. 219 were used to bind the 'rough copy' of the bursar's accounts for 1646.

[1] Perhaps the John Grene, † by 1484, who owned Magdalen College, Oxford, MSS. 121–32: Emden, *BRUO*, p, 815.

36. *Martinus, Tabula in Decreta et Decretales; Aquinas; etc.*

s. XIII/XIV

1. ff. 1–132ᵛ Inter alia que ad fidelium cristi doctrinam scripta sunt ius canonicum . . . Aaron. Quod aaron sacerdocium approbatur discordiam facit . . . extra i. t. vi de elect' licet. . . . Explicit liber scriptus.ʲ qui scripcit sit benedictus. Explicit tabula Martini super decreta et decretales.

The alphabetically arranged index of canon law made by Martin of Troppau, O.P., †1279. Schulte, ii. 137. Many manuscripts and printed editions. ff. 133–135ᵛ were left blank. The fairly numerous marginalia of an early annotator include 'contra Wal' ' on f. 16 and 'Dunelm' on f. 17 where the text—on Bellum—is concerned with warlike bishops. The same man added a table of words, Aaron–Zizannia, on ff. 133–5. The words under each letter of the alphabet in this table are numbered continuously from 1: corresponding numbers in red are in the margins of the text.

Arts. 2, 3 are no. 807 in Dondaine and Shooner.

2. ff. 136–218ᵛ Questio est de malo et primo . . . in anima sunt ergo etiam cogitaciones (*ends imperfectly in q. 16, art. 8*).

De malo. *Quaestiones disputatae*, (Marietti edn.) ii. 445–687/17. The gap after f. 218 is noticed by a hand of s. xiv. Some marginalia in the hand which annotated art. 1. Others are by Robert Elyot (see p. 631), including some words of English on f. 155, 'the fynd leyth before mannys mynd or vnderstandyng hys inward wyth and hys wystys (?) thyngyſ þᵗ aperit gode' and 'styryt and entysyt a man to yvyl' against q. 3, art. 4 (edn. p. 502), the latter translating *instigat hominem ad peccandum*.

3. ff. 219–234ᵛ (*begins imperfectly*) in 6 ph' corpus autem est per aliquam formam . . . reducit se in actum quantum ad ea que sunt ad finem.

De spiritualibus creaturis. The first words are in Marietti edn., ii. 378, col. 2/19. The reader who noticed the gap after f. 218 wrote on f. 219 'Hic deficiunt duo articuli et principium tercii'. 'Nichil deficit sed verte folium', s. xv, f. 232ʳ: f. 232ᵛ was left blank and the final question, 'utrum potencie anime . . .' (ff. 233–234ᵛ), is in another hand.

4. ff. 235–238ᵛ Et factum est cum consummasset ihesus. etc' cᵐ 26. A principio huius ewangelii ostendit ewangelista primo cristum esse regem . . .

A commentary on Matthew 26: 1–28: 20. The scribe wrote 'per passionem et crucem tuam adiuua me domine' at the head of f. 235.

5 (added). (*a*) f. 132ᵛ, in the main hand, between the last words and the explicit of art. 1, 'Nobilitas hominis . . . iura tenere'. (*b*) f. 238, in pencil, s. xivᵢ, in a blank space before the beginning of the commentary on Matthew 28: 'Al oþer loue is lych þe mone . . .'.

(*a*). Three couplets, Walther, no. 11860. (*b*). Seven 4-line stanzas. *IMEV*, no. 196. Printed from this manuscript by C. Browne, *Religious Lyrics of the Fourteenth Century* (2nd edn., 1957), pp. 65–6.

ff. iv+238+i. ff. iii, iv, 239 are medieval parchment endleaves: iiiʳ was pasted down. 300×205 mm. Written space 205×145 mm (art. 1) and 232×150 mm (arts. 2, 3). 2 cols. 39–55 lines. Collation: 1–11¹² 12⁴ wants 4, blank, after f. 135 13–15¹² 16–17¹⁰ 18–19¹² 20 six (ff. 216–21: three bifolia) 21¹² wants 12, blank, after f. 232 22 six (ff. 233–8). Textura in several hands, except ff. 133–5, 233–8, where the writer of marginalia to arts. 1–3 supplied art. 1 with a table, finished off art. 3, and added art. 4, all in a more or less current anglicana little if at all later than the rest of the book. Initials: (i) f. 136, red and blue with ornament of both colours; (ii) 2-line, blue or red with ornament of the other colour, or—the red initials in art. 1—no ornament: spaces remain unfilled on ff. 9ᵛ–132ᵛ and after f. 171ᵛ. Slatter binding. Secundo folio *auditis*.

Written in England. An erased inscription and a table listing arts. 1–3 are on f. ivᵛ, s. xiv in.: the former probably ends 'ordinis predicatorum'. Belonged later to Nicholas Kempston (cf. MS. 18): 'Liber Magistri Nicholai Kempston'', f. iiiᵛ; 'Liber quondam Magistri Nicholai Kempston' qui obiit anno domini 1477. numquam vendendus secundum vltimam voluntatem debitoris eiusdem defuncti set libere occupandus a sacerdotibus eruditis in lege domini ad predicandum verbum dei successiue ab vno sacerdote ad alterum sacerdotem gratis et absque omni precio quamdiu durauerit liber iste. Orate igitur pro anima eius', f. ivᵛ. At Eton by 1500 (cf. art. 2).

37. *Gregorius, Dialogi; etc.* s. xii/xiii

1. ff. 1–116 Incipit liber primus Dialogorum beati Gregorii pape. Quadam die nimis . . . ipsi fuerimus. Explicit liber iiiiᵘˢ dial(og)orum.

PL lxxvii. 149–429. Bk. 2, f. 29; 3, f. 44; 4, f. 77. A table of chapters before bks. 2–4: 39, 38, 61 chapters, not numbered.

2. ff. 116ᵛ–130 Incipit liber decem cordarum beati augustini episcopi. Dominus et deus noster misericors...ibi inueniemus. amen. Explicit liber decem cordarum beati augustini episcopi.

PL xxxviii. 75–91. f. 130ᵛ was left blank.

3. A bifolium of a manuscript used at either end as pastedown and flyleaf contains closely written 'notulae' on books of OT written in an English hand of s. xiii¹ (2 cols. 65 lines): Judges, Ruth, Tobit, Judith, Esther, Ezra, Nehemiah, 1 Kings on the exposed side of the pastedown at the beginning; 1–4 Kings on f. 131ʳᵛ; Proverbs, Ecclesiastes, Song of Songs on the exposed side of the pastedown at the end; Wisdom, Maccabees, Psalms on f. iʳᵛ.¹

The author is mainly concerned with hard words. He begins on Esther with 'De libro hest' paucula excipiam', on Ezra with 'Ad hesdram filium uerto', on Maccabees with 'Adest liber machabeorum id est bellatorum', quotes Comestor, and gives some interpretations in French, for example 'Scorpionibus in gallico. escurges', f. 131ᵛ.

ff. i+130+i. 265×180 mm. Written space 198×115 mm. 27 long lines. Pricks in both margins to guide ruling in quire 1 only. Collation includes the flex (7). Initials: (i) 5-line, yellow-brown, sometimes with red ornament; (ii) 1-line, yellow-brown or red. Lisley binding: the mark of the strap-and-pin fastening of an earlier binding shows on ff. 1, 127–30. Secundo folio *tem patrie*.

Written in England (or Wales). The ex-libris of the Cistercian abbey of Valle Crucis, Denbighshire, on f. 130 was read by M. R. James, who used a reagent, and is legible by ultra-violet light: 'Iste liber constat *Abbatie de Valle Crucis*',² s. xv. At Eton by 1521.

38. *Sermones, etc.* s. xii med.

1. ff. 1–136ᵛ Eighty-four sermons and short pieces, the first seventy-eight for the church year from Advent, temporale and sanctorale, in one series. Most of

---

¹ See Addenda, p. 998.   ² The letters in italics are not legible by ordinary light.

them are ascribed to their authors by initials or other abbreviations in red in the margins, commonly A. C. or B. A. C. for Abbas Clarevallensis or Bernardus Abbas Clarevallensis and A. R. for Abbas Rievallensis. Nearly the same collection in a different order is in Jesus College, Oxford, MS. 6, and Lambeth Palace, MS. 497.[1] The sermons marked A. R. are printed, except the two in *PL*, nos. 3, 35, by C. H. Talbot, *Sermones inediti B. Aelredi Abbatis Rievallensis*, Series scriptorum S. Ordinis Cisterciensis, i, 1952. Most of the sermons marked A. C. or B. A. C. are extracts only from sermons of St. Bernard. I give here occasions, ascriptions, and incipits, but not headings, generalizing variants of 'A. C.', 'B. A. C.', 'A. R.' to these forms. A hand of s. xv, Robert Elyot's, I think, numbered the pieces in the margins—the numbering goes wrong after '56'—and listed most of them on f. iii^{rv}. Elyot's hand occurs also in the margin of f. 62^v and elsewhere: see p. 631.

1–6. Advent. 1. f. 1 B. A. C. Hodie fratres celebramus aduentus initium . . . 2. f. 2 Id. Saluatorem expectamus . . . 3. f. 2^v A. R. Tempus est fratres karissimi ut . . . 4. f. 8 Al'. In die illa inquit propheta . . . 5. f. 9^v Omne caput languidum . . . Vulnus et liuor . . . 6. f. 11^v Amal. Rorate celi desuper . . . Duo sunt ordines iustorum . . .

Jesus, nos. 7, 8, 1, 4, 5, 2. 1. *SBO* iv. 161.[2] 3. *PL*. clxxxiv. 817.

7. D. 4 in Adv. f. 12^v Montes israhel . . . Sunt montes. sunt campi . . .
Jesus, no. 3.

8. Vig. Nat. f. 15^v B. A. C. Iesus cristus filius dei nascitur . . .
Jesus, no. 9. *SBO* iv. 197.

9–12. Nat. 9. f. 15^v B. A. C. Legitur in euangelio quod pastores . . . 10. f. 16^v B. A. C. Cum sederis inquit salomon . . . 11. f. 17^v A. R. Aliis quidem temporibus officium meum . . . 12. f. 19 Propter nimiam caritatem suam . . .
Jesus, nos. 10, 18, 6, 17, 11. Talbot, p. 37 (no. 2).

13, 14. Circ. 13. f. 19^v A. C. Postquam consummati sunt . . . Magnum et mirabile . . . 14. f. 20^v Idem. Postquam consummati sunt . . . Ab initio deus . . .
Jesus, nos. 11, 12. 14 is *SBO* iv. 273.

15. D. infra Nat. f. 21 Dum medium silentium Fratres. est bonum . . .
Jesus, no. 19.

16–18. Epiph. 16. f. 22 B. A. C. Apertis thesauris suis . . . Necessarium nobis . . . 17. f. 23 A. R. In illa dulcissima festiuitate . . . 18. f. 28 Cum creator omnium formam . . .
Jesus, nos. 14, 21, 13. 16. *SBO* iv. 304. 17. Talbot, p. 39 (no. 3). 18. *PL* clxxi. 413 (Hildebert).

19. D. 1 post oct. Epiph. f. 28 Cum esset iesus . . . Sicut mundus iste . . .
Jesus, no. 15.

---

[1] Lambeth is in nearly the same order as Jesus.
[2] References to *SBO* are given only if an *incipit* here agrees with one there.

20. D. 2 post oct. Epiph. f. 29 B. A. C. Nuptie facte sunt . . . Omnes enim nos ad spirituales . . .

Jesus, no. 16.

21, 22. Conv. S. Pauli. 21. f. 30 B. A. C. Saule saule . . . Merito quidem . . . 22. f. 30ᵛ Saule saule . . . Vereor dilectissimi ne quis . . .

Jesus, nos. 71, 72. *SBO* iv. 327, 330. 22 is marked 'bonus sermo', s. xv.

23, 24. Purif. f. 31ᵛ A. C. Postquam impleti sunt . . . Purificationem beate uirginis . . . 24. f. 32 B. A. C. Suscepimus deus misericordiam tuam . . . Gratias redemptori nostro qui tam copiose preuenit nos . . .

Not in Jesus. *SBO* iv. 341, 338.

25. Epiph. f. 32ᵛ A. R. Hodie fratres karissimi sermo nobis habendus est de amore . . .

Jesus, no. 22. Talbot, p. 47 (no. 4).

26. D. 1 Quad. f. 35ᵛ Amb'. Ductus est iesus . . . Tria sunt; que ad usum salutis . . .

Not in Jesus.

27, 28. Quad. 27. f. 36ᵛ A. R. Suscepimus hodie fratres solempne ieiunium . . . 28. f. 39ᵛ A. R. Sicut nouit caritas uestra tria nobis . . .

Jesus, nos. 23, 24. Talbot, pp. 52, 57 (nos. 5, 6).

29, 30. S. Benedictus. 29. f. 42ᵛ A. R. Notum est omnibus quod nemo . . . 30. f. 48 A. R. Benedictus deus et pater . . .

Jesus, nos. 25, 26. Talbot, pp. 62, 71 (nos. 7, 8).

31. Annunc. 32. 'In Assumptione sancte Marie'. 33–8. Annunc. 31. f. 51ᵛ A. C. Ut inhabitet gloria in terra nostra . . . Gloria nostra hec est . . . 32. f. 53 A. C. Signum magnum apparuit . . . Vehementer quidem . . . 33. f. 54 A. R. Festiuitas illa sicut nouit . . . 34. f. 57ᵛ A. R. Hodierna festiuitas principium est . . . 35. f. 61 Idem. Ecce ascendet . . . Recedens á nobis . . . 36. f. 65 Idem. Ve michi quia vir pollutis labiis . . . 37. f. 68 B. A. C. Missus est angelus . . . Auctor integritatis . . . 38. f. 69ᵛ Egredietur uirga . . . Hodie fratres karissimi impletum est quod . . .

Only 31, 33–5, 38 are in Jesus, nos. 31, 27, 28, 30, 29. 32 is in Lambeth 497, f. 38ᵛ. 31. *SBO* v. 13. 33, 34, 36. Talbot, pp. 77, 83, 89 (nos. 9–11). 35. *PL* cxcv. 251.

39–42. Ram. Palm. 39. f. 70ᵛ Uenite filii . . . Audite fratres karissimi quam dulci uoce . . . 40. f. 71ᵛ Amal'. Maria ergo accepit . . . Notandum est quod ea . . . 41. f. 72 Amal'. De significatione eiusdem diei. Habet ecclesiastica . . . consuetudo ut . . . 42. f. 72 A. C. Non sine causa spiritum . . .

Jesus, nos. 32–4, 39.

43. Passio domini. f. 73ᵛ A. C. Isti sunt dies quos obseruare . . .

Jesus, no. 38.

44, 45. Cena Domini. 44. f. 74ᵛ A. C. Audistis fratres in euangelio . . . 45. f. 75 Quicumque manducauerit . . . In quinta feria quam uocamus . . .

Jesus, nos. 40, 35.

46. Parasc. f. 76ᵛ Amal'. Cristus passus est pro nobis . . . Hec dies dilectissimi parasceue . . .

Jesus, no. 36.

47–50. Pasch. 47. f. 77ᵛ A. C. Ecce uicit leo . . . Vicit plane malitiam sapientia . . . 48. f. 78ᵛ A. R. Desiderio desideraui . . . malitiam. 49. f. 81 A. R. Desiderio desideraui . . . consortio ad quam nos . . . cristus. 50. f. 83 Hec est dies . . . Possidebat dilectissimi diabolus . . .

Jesus, nos. 41, 37, 42, 43. 47. *SBO* v. 73. 48, 49. Talbot, p. 94 (no. 12, the version printed in the footnotes).

51, 52. Asc. 51. f. 84ᵛ A. R. Satis nouit dilectio uestra fratres karissimi . . . 52. f. 87 Au. Regna terre cantate deo . . . Hortatur propheta omnes gentes . . .

Jesus, nos. 44, 45. 51. Talbot, p. 100 (no. 13).

53–9. Pent. 53. f. 87ᵛ A. C. Emitte spiritum tuum . . . Sicut per faciem . . . 54. f. 88 Difficile adquiescat animus meus . . . 55. f. 89 A. R. Hodierna die fratres karissimi audire mallem . . . 56. f. 92ᵛ A. R. Assum fratres mei dilecti assum . . . 57. f. 95ᵛ Spiritus domini repleuit . . . Quid mirum si . . . 58. f. 96ᵛ Amal'. Accipite spiritum sanctum . . . Non solum hoc operatur . . . 59. f. 97ᵛ Quoniam apostoli ituri erant ad omnes gentes . . .

Jesus, nos. 48, 46 (attributed to A. R.), 47, 49–52. 54–6. Talbot, pp. 104, 106, 112 (nos. 14–16). 54 and 56 are marked for eight lessons: 'usque huc', ff. 88ᵛ, 94.

60. Joh. Bapt. f. 98 A. R. In domo patris mei . . . Cur tibi queso te . . .

Jesus, no. 53. Talbot, p. 117 (no. 17).

61–4. Petr. et Paul. 61. f. 100ᵛ A. R. Presentem diem fratres karissimi beatissimorum . . . 62. f. 105 A. R. Licet nobis dilectissimi fratres ex ipsa consuetudine . . . 63. f. 109 A. C. Gloriosi principes terre . . . Tria sunt que in festiuitatibus . . . 64. f. 110 Idem. Petrus et Paulus duo sunt luminaria . . . Gloriosa nobis solempnitas . . .

Jesus, nos. 54, 55, 57, 58. 61, 62. Talbot, pp. 122, 129 (nos. 18, 19). 64. *SBO* v. 188.

65. 'In Festiuitate 'id est Natiuitate' (*interlin., s. xiv*) beate Marie De Throno Eburneo'. f. 110ᵛ A. R. Memoria beatissime virginis quam . . .

Jesus, no. 56. Talbot, p. 136 (no. 20).

66, 67. Mich. 66. f. 116 A. C. Ascendit fumus . . . Angelorum hodie memoria . . . 67. f. 117ᵛ Idem. Audistis fratres euangelicam lectionem aduersus eos . . .

Jesus, nos. 59, 60. *SBO* v. 294, 299.

68, 69. Ded. Eccl. f. 118 A. C. Si dedero sompnum oculis meis . . . Olim rex gloriosus . . . f. 119 Idem. Urbs fortitudinis . . . Domus hec fratres eterni regis opidum . . .

Jesus, nos. 61, 62. *SBO* v. 375, 379.

70–2. Omn. SS. f. 119ᵛ A. C. Scimus quoniam diligentibus deum . . . Festiua nobis est . . . 71. f. 120ᵛ A. C. Timete dominum . . . Tota interim fratres beatitudo nostra est . . . 72. f. 121 A. R. Hodie apparet . . .

Jesus, nos. 63, 64, 73. 70, 71. *SBO* v. 361, 363. 72. Talbot, p. 144 (no. 21).

73, 74. Martinus. 73. f. 125 A. C. Martinus hic pauper et modicus celum diues ingreditur . . . et meritis beati MARTINI prestare dignetur qui cum . . . deus. 74. f. 125ᵛ Idem. Domine si adhuc . . . Ó uere sanctissimam animam . . .

Jesus, nos. 65, 66. 74. *SBO* v. 411/4.

75, 76. Clemens. 75. f. 126 A. C. Pretiosa in conspectu . . . Audiat peccator . . . 76. f. 126ᵛ Idem. Tradiderunt corpora sua ad supplicia . . . Quid ad hec dicemus fratres? Congratulamur martiribus . . .

Jesus, nos. 67, 68. 75. *SBO* v. 412. 76. *SBO* v. 414/9.

77, 78. Andreas. 77. f. 127 A. C. Uenite post me . . . Beati Andree apostoli festiuitas hodie . . . 78. f. 128 Idem. Uidens andreas crucem cum gaudio . . .

Jesus, nos. 69, 70. 77. *SBO* v. 434.

79, 80. Synod. 79. f. 128ᵛ A. R. Supersedeo excusationi . . . 80. f. 132 A. R. Non sum sapiens. non sum legis peritus . . .

Jesus, nos. 74, 75. Talbot, pp. 150, 156 (nos. 22, 23).

81–3. 81. f. 135 De oleo triformi. Reges sunt et sacerdotes . . . 82. f. 135 De officio sacerdotali. Quadripartitum est officium sacerdotale . . . 83. f. 135 De ueste sacerdotali. Vestis qua sacerdos uti debet triplex est . . .

Jesus, nos. 76–8.

84. ff. 135–136ᵛ B. A. (C). Dixit symon petrus ad iesum. Ecce nos reliquimus omnia . . . Verba lectionis huius fratres ea arbitror esse de quibus psallit ecclesia . . . perfectione secura. prestante domino nostro iesu cristo.

Jesus, no. 79. Ends three columns short of the end of the copy in MS. 39, art. 5 (II, 9), q.v. Not assigned to any particular occasion.

2. ff. 136ᵛ–151ᵛ Five sermons ascribed to Robert Pulleyn: (1) f. 136ᵛ Prefatio Magistri Roberti pull' De Obsidione Sirie. Legimus in libro regum quod rex syrie . . .; (2) f. 139 Sermo eiusdem cuius supra. Apud veteres in libro numeri . . .; (3) f. 141ᵛ Sermo Magistri Roberti Pul'. Postquam israhel de terra . . .; (4) f. 145ᵛ Item eiusdem de pugna Amalech contra israhel. In exodo. Venit autem amalech . . .; (5) f. 149ᵛ Sermo eiusdem cuius supra. Heri fratres karissimi de bono conscientie . . .

Nos. 16–19, 2 in the list of Pulleyn's sermons by F. Courtney in *Analecta Gregoriana*, lxiv (1954), 33–5. All five are in Lambeth Palace MS. 458 and nos (1–4) are in the same order there as here. For three more Pulleyn sermons see below, arts. 6, 10.

3. f. 151ᵛ Magister Hugo. Tempus flendi . . . Prius flere debet . . . letificetur.

From Hugh of St. Victor on Ecclesiastes, hom. 16: *PL* clxxv. 229–30.

4. ff. 152–154ᵛ Libellus beati Augustini de quattuor uirtutibus karitatis. Inter ceteras uirtutes . . . non folia laudis.

PL xlvii. 1127–34. Römer, i. 197.

5. ff. 154ᵛ–162 Incipit liber de conflictu uitiorum atque uirtutum beati pape leonis. Apostolica uox clamat . . . (f. 161) fidem prebeto. Cuiusdam relatione nuper cognoui quod dico . . . tradere debes.

Opposite 'fidem prebeto' Robert Elyot noted that this is 'finis libri augustini de conflictu viciorum et virtutum secundum alios libros': cf. Römer, i. 49–51. *PL* xl. 1091–1106.

6. ff. 162–8 Two sermons ascribed to Robert Pulleyn: (1) f. 162 Sermo Magistri Roberti Pull'. Quattuor reges aduersus quinque . . .; (2) f. 164ᵛ Eiusdem sermo. cuius supra. Dicit dominus. Ecce ego demetam . . .

Nos. 5 and 4 in Courtney's list (above, art. 2).

7. ff. 168–203ᵛ Incipit tractatus Magistri Hugonis parisiacensis super Lamentationes Ieremie non tamen continue. Quomodo sedet sola ciuitas . . . miseria consequatur.

Hugh of St. Victor on Lamentations. *PL* clxxv. 255–322. Stegmüller, no. 3823.

8. ff. 203ᵛ–210ᵛ Quod nusquam inueniatur dominus nisi in Cruce id est fide. Caritate. Spe. et Timore. Circumire possum domine celum et terram . . . cotidie manum mittere.

Drogo, Meditatio in Passionem et Resurrectionem Domini. *PL* clxxxiv. 751/7 from foot–768 (sect. 15 (pt.), 16–17, 19–25, 27–37, 39–41). Shorter than the printed text in several places, omitting, for example, all between 'ministerium' (sect. 37/20) and 'Data est michi' (sect. 39/1). Cf. *Recueil*, i. 105, and L. Gjerløw in *RB* lxxxii (1972), 316–17.

9. ff. 210ᵛ–212ᵛ Five short sections: (*a*) f. 210ᵛ De uita et morte cristi. Desideremus uitam . . . plus amandus est; (*b*) f. 211 De humanitate cristi. Cum omnibus modis . . . que ille sustinuit; (*c*) f. 211ᵛ De gaudio domini et gaudio seculi. Gaudere nos apostolus precipit . . . bono letatur eterno; (*d*) f. 212 De desiderio sancto. Tota uita cristiani boni . . . ab amore seculi; (*e*) f. 212 De humilitate cristi. Intelligamus ergo preter effusionem . . . in cordibus nostris caritatem.

10. ff. 212ᵛ–214 Exortatio De Egressione huius seculi. Egredimini filie ierusalem . . . Adhuc infirmis et delicatis . . . in diademate patris.

No. 11 in Courtney's list of Pulleyn's sermons (above, art. 2).

11. ff. 214ᵛ–215 De superedificantibus lignum fenum stipulam. Nusquam securitas fratres . . . utique super omnia benedictus. et laudabilis et gloriosus in secula amen.

'A.C.' in red against the title. In *Opera Bernardi*, edn., Paris, 1517, f. 90ᵛ. f. 215ᵛ was left blank.

---

ff. iii+215+ii. For f. iii see above, art. 1. 285 × 193 mm. Written space 225 × 140 mm. 2 cols. 38 lines. Ruled with pencil. Pricks in both margins of quire 2 (only, ?) to guide ruling. Of the ruled lines, 1, 3, 35, 37, 38 are usually extended into the margins. Collation: 1⁸ wants 1 (blank?), 2–27⁸. Quires numbered at the end. Well written. 'Line' punctuation in the curly form found in Cirencester manuscripts[1] occurs on ff. 84ᵛ, 85, where the hand is perhaps different from that elsewhere. Initials: (i) f. 1, green patterned in white, with red and green ornament; (ii) 3-line or 2-line, red, green, or blue, often with a line of white; (iii) in arts. 8–11, as (ii), but 1-line. Slatter binding. Secundo folio *Et hec quidem*.

Written in England, perhaps in the Gloucester region, to judge from the script.[2] Pledged at Oxford in 1460 by Robert Selby: 'Caucio domini Roberti Selby exposita in Cista exonie Anno domini mᵒ ccccᵒ lxᵒ vᵒ die mensis Octobris et habet 3ᵃ supplementa 2ᵒ fo primi exire 2ᵒ fo 2ⁱ diffidenciam 2ᵒ fo 3ⁱ demedet et iacet pro xxviˢ viiiᵈ', f. 215ᵛ. Another

---

[1] Cf. N. R. Ker, *English Manuscripts in the Century after the Norman Conquest*, p. 47 and pl. 20*a, b*.

[2] For the West of England circulation of art. 8 see Gjerløw, loc. cit.

pledging entry on the same leaf, 'C cum tribus supplementis . . . (*as above, but* demedat)', is over erasure. It is followed by the mark of the stationer, probably John Doll, and 'xxvi s' viii d' and, in a later hand, 'pret' x s'. At Eton by 1500: cf. art. 1.

39. *Bernardus (etc.)* s. XIII in.

1. ff. 1–29 Incipit prephacio exortacionum beati bernardi abbatis clareuall'. ad eugenium papam. Subit animum dictare . . . set non finis querendi.

De consideratione. *SBO* iii (1963), 393–493. The title here is like that in Bodley 168 and other English manuscripts.

2. ff. 29–46 Incipit liber Beati Bernardi abbatis de amore dei. Venite ascendamus ad montem domini . . . et nouissimi primi. Explicit liber Sancti Bernardi abbatis de amore dei.

PL clxxxiv. 367–408. 'D.M.' in the margin, f. 46.

3. ff. 46ᵛ–48 Sermo magistri Serlonis de Iusto homine bene uiuente. Dicite iusto quoniam bene 'ys' 3 c''. Simplicitas dicti sine determinatione . . . in hoc maxime. Dicite iusto quoniam bene.

Not one of the sermons of Serlo of Savigny, O.C., printed by B. Tissier, *Bibl. Patr. Cisterc.* vi. 107–29.

4. ff. 48–59 In illo tempore.' Missus est angelus gabriel . . . Omelia lectionis Eiusdem.' Beati Bernardi abbatis clareuall'. Quid sibi uoluit euangelista . . . set specialiter fiat michi secundum verbum Tuum. Explicit omelia beati bernardi abbatis.

SBO iv. 13–57. Divided by headings 'De eodem' and 'Item de eodem' at 'Libenter' and 'Non est dubium', but not at 'Novum quidem'. 'D.M.' in the margin, f. 54, probably in the main hand.

5. ff. 59ᵛ–211ᵛ Sermons and short pieces nearly all of them ascribed in headings to St. Bernard and most of them printed in vols. iv–vi of *SBO*: cf. iv. 146. The selection is like than in B.L. MS. Add. 4899, but with differences.

I. ff. 59ᵛ–127 Sermons of the temporale, Advent–Pentecost.

1–7. ff. 59ᵛ, 61ᵛ, 62ᵛ, 64ᵛ, 65ᵛ, 66, 67 Adv. 1–7.[1]

8–13. ff. 67ᵛ, 69, 70ᵛ, 73, 75, 76ᵛ Vig. Nat. 1–6.

14. f. 79 Nat. 2, ending 'nec ipse malleus 'frangere possit'' (edn. iv. 254/4): cf. Add. 4899 where the last words 'nec ipse malleus' are followed by a blank space of forty-one lines.

15. f. 79ᵛ Epiph. 1, as far as 'set agnosci' (iv. 296/6), followed by (De) D(iversis) 54, as in Add. 4899. The running title is 'in die natalis domini'.

16, 17. ff. 80ᵛ, 82 Nat. 3, 4.

18, 19. ff. 82ᵛ, 83ᵛ Circ. 2 (= *PL*, Circ. 1), 3.

20. f. 85ᵛ In Epiphania domini. Hodie fratres magi ab oriente . . . propter nature societatem. The first half is mainly Epi. 1, sect. 5, and Epi. 2, sect. 1–3.

21. f. 86ᵛ Qui in plenitudine . . . iusticia. *SBO* iv. 312/2–313/2 (Oct. Epi., parts of sects. 4, 5).

22. f. 86ᵛ Deficiente uino . . . proueharis in filium. The first quarter is *SBO* iv. 315 (1 Post Epi., sects. 2–4).

[1] I follow, but extend slightly, the sigla in *Recueil*, ii. 204–5 and *SBO* iv. 126–7.

23. f. 88 Obsecramus uos . . . in syon. Quad. 6, ending at *SBO* iv. 379/22.

24–6. ff. 88ᵛ, 90ᵛ, 91 QH 1–3 (as one) 4, 5.

27–31. ff. 93, 94, 95, 95ᵛ, 96 Quad. 1–5.

32, 33. ff. 97ᵛ, 98ᵛ D. 25, 107. 2.

34. f. 99 Quad. 6 in *PL*: cf. *SBO* v. xi.

35, 36. ff. 99ᵛ, 101 Ram. Palm. 1, 2.

37. f. 101ᵛ Dixi sepius. nec mente . . . necessariam experimur. V. Hebd. Maj., beginning at *SBO* v. 69/18.

38. ff. 102–110ᵛ Noli timere filia syon . . . cotidie manum mittere in xpistum dominum. *PL* clxxxiv. 741–68, sects. 1–41: cf. *Recueil*, i. 106, where this copy is mentioned, but classified wrongly—it belongs to Leclercq's 'premier groupe'—and MS. 38, art. 8, where the paragraphing is different.

39. f. 110ᵛ Sermo sancti Bernardi abbatis. Hec est dies quam fecit dominus . . . Ista dies est non dies . . . per predestinationem.

40–2. ff. 111ᵛ, 113, 115 Pasc. 2, 1, 3.

43. f. 116ᵛ Pasc. 4 (= D. 44).

44. f. 117 D. 111.

45, 46. ff. 117, 119ᵛ Oct. Pasc. 1, 2.

47. f. 120 Rog.

48, 49. ff. 120ᵛ, 121 Asc. 1, 4.

50, 51. ff. 123, 123ᵛ D. 60, 61.

52. f. 124 Asc. 6 (= *PL*, Asc. 5).

53. f. 125ᵛ Pent. 1.

54, 55. ff. 126ᵛ, 127 D. 88, 45.

II. ff. 128–64 Sermons of the sanctorale, vigil of Andrew–All Saints, and Dedication of Church.

1. f. 128 Vig. And.

2, 3. ff. 128ᵛ, 130ᵛ And. 1, 2.

4. f. 132 Conv. Pauli.

5. f. 133ᵛ D. 51.

6–8. ff. 133ᵛ, 134, 134ᵛ Purif. 2, 3, 1.

9. f. 135ᵛ Dixit symon petrus ad iesum. Ecce nos reliquimus . . . Verba leccionis huius fratres ea arbitror . . . habeamus iesus cristus dominus noster qui . . . . The running title is 'In festo sancti Benedicti'. The text is partly the same as *PL* cxliv. 548–53 (Nicholas of Clairvaux: cf. *Recueil*, i. 52 and above, MS. 38, f. 135).

10. f. 137 Ben., beginning at 'Plantatus secus' (*SBO* v. 4/3), like Add. 4899, f. 56.

11. f. 138ᵛ D. 47.

12. f. 138ᵛ Annunt. 2.

13. f. 139ᵛ Sermo S' B' abbatis.' de cruce cristi et cruce diaboli. Uolumus scire ut sciamus . . . mercedem glorie. Cf. *ASOC* xviii. 87.

14. f. 140ᵛ Joh. Bapt.

15, 16. ff. 142, 143ᵛ Petr. et Paul. 2, 3.

17. f. 144ᵛ D. 87. For Mary Magdalene.

18. f. 146 Assump. 1.

19. f. 147 *PL* clxxxiv. 1001–10. Cf. *Recueil*, ii. 261–70.

20–2. ff. 149ᵛ, 151, 152 Assump. 2–4.

23, 24. ff. 154, 155 D. 91, 92.

25, 26. ff. 155ᵛ, 156 Michael 1, 2.

Z

27. f. 158 Omn. SS. 4, sects. 3–6.

28. f. 158ᵛ Omn. SS. 1, sect. 7 (from 'Vere apertum est os'): *SBO* v. 332/7–15.

29. f. 160ᵛ Distinctio pertinens ad eundem sermonem. D. 99.

30. f. 161 D. 66.

31–3. ff. 161ᵛ, 162ᵛ, 163ᵛ Ded. Eccl. 1–3.

III. ff. 164–203ᵛ Sermons and short pieces, mostly of the De Diversis collection. Cf. the analysis in *ASOC* xxi (1965), 20, where nos. 1 and 25 are wrongly given as D. 64 and D. 81.

1, 2. ff. 164, 164ᵛ D. 63, 62.

3. f. 164ᵛ Iustum deduxit . . . Est iustus qui in principio . . . gratiam et gloriam dominus dabit amen. *Opera*, edn. Paris, 1517, f. 86ᵛ.

4, 5. ff. 165, 165ᵛ D. 53, 52.

6. f. 166 Sapientia uincit malitiam. cristus diabolum . . . sapientia cibat.

7. f. 166ᵛ Prima gratia est timor domini . . . ante thronum dei. *PL* clxxxiv. 1113: cf. *ASOC* xviii. 45.

8–16. ff. 167ᵛ, 168, 169, 169ᵛ, 171, 171ᵛ, 173, 174, 174ᵛ D. 93, 6, 10, 8, 31, 16, 23, 24, 4.

17. f. 175ᵛ In labore messis, 2 (*SBO* v. 220 = D. 39).

18. f. 176 De altitudine et bassitudine cordis (*SBO* v. 214 = D. 36).

19. f. 176ᵛ Disponit ratio castigare . . . seruire iusticie. *Recueil*, ii. 92–3.

20. f. 176ᵛ Parab. ii: cf. *ASOC* xviii. 36.

21–31. ff. 178, 179ᵛ, 180, 181, 181, 181ᵛ, 181ᵛ, 182, 182ᵛ, 183, 184 D. 22, 12, 5, 85, 82, 83, 7, 32, 69, 19, 9.

32. f. 184 In labore messis, 1 (*SBO* v. 217 = D. 38).

33, 34. ff. 184ᵛ, 185ᵛ D. 29, 67.

35–37. ff. 185ᵛ, 186, 186ᵛ VI post Pent. 1, VI post Pent. 2 (in *PL*), VI post Pent. 2.

38. f. 189ᵛ IV post Pent.

39–41. ff. 190, 190ᵛ, 191 D. 13, 104, 26.

42. f. 191 Ad exercitium humilitatis . . . quid meditetur. *Recueil*, ii. 193–4.

43–52. ff. 191ᵛ, 192, 192, 192ᵛ, 193ᵛ, 193ᵛ, 194, 194, 194ᵛ, 194ᵛ D. 71, 95, 94, 72, 73+74, 75, 77, 49, 76, 79.

53. f. 194ᵛ Annunt. 1 in the P version (*SBO* v. 13–29/22).

54–66. ff. 196ᵛ, 197ᵛ, 198, 198, 199ᵛ, 201, 201ᵛ, 201ᵛ, 202, 202, 202ᵛ, 203, 203 D. 35, 64, 80, 96, 3, 108, 65, 59, 98, 102, 103, 101, 105.

67. f. 203ᵛ IS. 12.

68. f. 203ᵛ D. 84.

69. f. 203ᵛ Tria sunt loca . . . solos malos. In the Maurist edition of St. Bernard (1690), between D. 103 and D. 104.

IV. ff. 204–11ᵛ Rerum quarumdam numeralis distinctio ex dictis s' Bernardi.

1. f. 204 Quattuor sunt iudicia. Secundum prescienciam . . . et firmabit prescienciam. *Analecta monastica*, i. 160.

2. f. 204 Mors anime obliuio . . . per dileccionem (4 lines). *Opera*, edn. 1517, f. 112.

3. ff. 204–11 (*a*) Racionalis creatura ad hoc se debet diligere . . . proprium diuinum. (*b*) Bona prouidere . . . contraria. (*c*) Preciosam . . . Samuel. (*d*) f. 210ᵛ Vsque hodie in ciuibus babilonie . . . fruc. suum. (*e*) Spiritus sanctus arguit . . . iudicat. (*f*) Reuertere . . . (*g*) Tres sunt quibus reconcilari debemus . . . cor lu. erit. (*h*) Non est speciosa laus . . . et dulcis labor. Sententiae, not set off in paragraphs, but distinguished by a red or blue initial for each separate piece. (*a*–*c*) are nos. 1–175, 178–88 of the series in *PL* clxxxiv.

1135–56, in the order (*a*) 1–89, (*b*) 178–88, (*c*) 90–175. (*f*) is IS. 10. (*g*). Cf. edn. Paris,
1517, f. 110ᵛ.

4. f. 211 D. 78.

5. f. 211 D. 100.

6. f. 211 D. 64. 1.

7. f. 211ʳᵛ Quot sunt status anime. Tres sunt status anime . . . poterit optinere salutis.
Edn. Paris, 1517, f. 111ᵛ.

8. f. 211ᵛ S. 1.

ff. ii+210+iv, foliated in a medieval hand (i, ii), 1–43, 45–211, (212–15). ff. 212–13 are
late medieval parchment end-leaves: 213ᵛ was pasted down. 305×205 mm. Written
space *c.* 205×130 mm. 2 cols. 37 lines. Pricks in both margins of at least some quires.
The first line of writing above the top ruled line. Collation: 1–24⁸ 25¹⁰ 26⁸. Quires numbered at the end and sometimes also at the beginning. Catchwords. Mainly in one hand:
punctuation includes the flex (ʔ). Initials: (i) blue or red with ornament of the other
colour, or green with red ornament; (ii) as one, but smaller—3-line or 2-line; (iii) on
ff. 204–11, 1-line, red or blue. Slatter binding. Secundo folio *ratio est.*

Written in England. 'Liber Magistri Ricardi Hopton quem emit ab executoribus Petri
Bylton' pro xx s' ', f. 213: Hopton gave books (cf. MSS. 101 and MS. 114) in or before
1492–3 when the audit roll, EA 24, contains a payment 'pro scriptura super libros quos
doctor Hopton dedit collegio'.[1]

41. *Homiliae in Evangelia*   s. XI/XII

Ninety-three homilies on the Gospels, numbered in s. xv from 1–92: the homily
after no. 79 was missed. Except at no. 49 there are no authors' names. The
scribe seems to have begun by copying an incomplete copy of the homiliary of
Haymo of Auxerre, and then to have used other homiliaries to fill up gaps, but
they are not all filled and there are no homilies here for Christmas, Easter, or
Pentecost. Six groups may be distinguished (I–VI), followed by a short miscellaneous tail (VII). A *nota bene* head by Robert Elyot (see p. 631) in the margin,
f. 2ᵛ.

I. ff. 1–123. Nos. 1–43. Homilies in the order of the church year from Advent
to the twenty-fourth Sunday after Pentecost, but the occasion is only shown by
the Gospel text. Nos. 1–40 (first Sunday in Advent to the nineteenth Sunday
after Pentecost) are homilies of Haymo printed in *PL* cxviii and listed by H.
Barré, *Les Homéliaires carolingiens de l'école d'Auxerre* (Studi e Testi, 225,
1962), pp. 147–57: I give Barré's numbers in brackets. Nos. 41–3 occur in the
homiliary of Smaragdus (*PL* cii).

1. (I. 1). f. 1 Cum appropinquasset . . .[2] Spiritualiter autem (edn. 12c) . . .

2. (I. 9). f. 4 Postquam consummati . . . Quia mediatoris . . .

3. (I. 12). f. 8 Era'n't Ioseph et maria . . . Si superiora . . .

---

[1] Emden, *BRUO*, p. 961. Only MS. 114 now contains a Hopton *ex dono*—on the flyleaf facing the first leaf of text: the corresponding leaf in MS. 39 is missing.

[2] The gospel texts are preceded by headings like 'Secundum lucam . . .' and by the
words 'In illo tempore' or, where appropriate, 'In illo tempore dixit iesus discipulis suis'.
These I omit.

4. (I. 13). f. 12 Cum factus esset . . . Rationabiliter magistri . . .

5. (I. 14). f. 15 Vidit Iohannes . . . In huius lectionis breuitate . . .

6. (I. 15). f. 17 Nuptię factę . . . Miracula domini et saluatoris nostri (edn. 127C) . . .

7. (I. 16). f. 21ᵛ Cum descendisset . . . Superius euangelista . . .

8. (I. 17). f. 25 Ascendente 'iesu' in nauicula . . . In huius lectionis serie . . .

9. (I. 22). f. 26ᵛ Post dies sex . . . Dominus iesus cristus per . . .

10. (I. 23). f. 28ᵛ Egressus Iesus . . . Supra refert euangelica lectio . . .

11. (I. 24). f. 31ᵛ Erat Iesus eiciens . . . Dicturus euangelista . . .

12. (I. 25). f. 36 Abiit Iesus . . . Mare galileę . . .

13. (II. 2). f. 41 Duo ex discipulis . . . In exordio huius lectionis . . .

14. (II. 3). f. 44ᵛ Stetit Iesus . . . Herent sibi diuinę lectiones . . .

15. (II. 6). f. 47ᵛ Undecim discipuli . . . Domini iussionem . . .

16. (II. 10). f. 49 Modicum et iam . . . Quotiens euangelicam lectionem . . .

17. (II. 11). f. 52 Vado ad eum. . Frequenter ab initio . . .

18. (II. 12). f. 54ᵛ Amen amen dico uobis si quid petieritis . . . Largitor uirtutum . . .

19. (II. 15). f. 57ᵛ Cum uenerit Paraclitus . . . In multis locis euangelii . . .

20. (II. 13). f. 59ᵛ Quis uestrum . . . Sciens dominus iesus cristus post . . .

21. (II. 17). f. 62 Erat homo ex pharisaeis . . . Sicut unius ignorantia . . .

22. (II. 21). f. 65ᵛ Elisabeth impletum est . . . Non solum opera . . .

23. (II. 22). f. 67ᵛ Venit Iesus in partes . . . Cesareas tres legimus . . .

24. (II. 23). f. 70 Estote misericordes . . . Inter ceteras uirtutes . . .

25. (II. 24). f. 73ᵛ Cum turbe inruerent . . . De piscibus quos apostoli . . .

26. (II. 25). f. 76ᵛ Amen amen dico uobis nisi habundauerit . . . Qui putant precepta . . .

27. (II. 26). f. 79ᵛ Cum multa turba . . . Dominus iesus cristus ante . . .

28. (II. 27). f. 83 Attendite a falsis . . . Preuidens dominus doctrinam . . .

29. (II. 28). f. 86ᵛ Homo quidam erat dives . . . Usus sacrę scripturę . . .

30. (II. 29). f. 90 Cum appropinquaret . . . In huius lectionis serie . . .

31. (II. 30). f. 91ᵛ Duo homines . . . In multis locis sacra scriptura . . .

32. (II. 31). f. 93ᵛ Exiens 'Iesus' de finibus . . . Supra retulit euangelica lectio . . .

33. (II. 32). f. 96 Beati oculi . . . In exordio huius lectionis . . .

34. (II. 33). f. 99ᵛ Dum iret . . . Qui iudeę terrę . . .

35. (II. 34). f. 102^v Amen amen dico uobis. Nisi granum frumenti . . . Ortaturus dominus discipulos . . .

36. (II. 35). f. 104 Intrauit Iesus . . . Conditor et redemptor humanę naturę . . . Marked for lections, I–IIII.

37. (II. 36) f. 106 Nemo potest duobus . . . Cum ad unius dei . . .

38. (II. 37). f. 108^v Ibat Iesus in ciuitatem . . . Mediator dei et hominum . . .

39. (II. 38). f. 111. Cum intraret . . . Quotiens legimus dominum . . .

40. (II. 39). f. 114. Accesserunt ad Iesum . . . Predicante domino . . .

At the end, f. 119, there is a reference back to no. 39: Expositionem istius sententie quere superius ebdomada octaua decima post pentecostem.

41. f. 119 Quis putas maior . . . Superius enim scriptum est . . . (PL cii. 477).

42. f. 121 Ascendens Iesus . . . Marcus non hoc in ciuitate . . . (PL cii. 482).

43. f. 122^v Abeuntes Pharisaei . . . Nuper sub cesare . . . (PL cii. 504).

II. ff. 123–46. Nos. 44–9. Homilies for Lent. All except no. 49 occur in Smaragdus's Homiliary. Nos. 45–8 were added by the scribe as an afterthought on an inserted quire. Notes in red on ff. 136^v and 145 help the reader to find his way to the last two leaves of no. 44.

44. ff. 123–36^v, 145–6 Incipit passio . . . Post duos dies clarissimi luminis . . . (PL cii. 174).

45. f. 137 Feria vi ebd. ii(i) in quadragesima . . . Iesus fatigatus . . . Iesus fatigatus ab itinere quid est . . . (PL cii. 141).

46. f. 138^v Sabbato ebdomade in quadragesima . . . Perrexit Iesus . . . Mons quippe oliueti sublimitatem . . . (PL cii. 145).

47. f. 140^v Feria ii post vicesim' . . . Prope erat Pascha . . . Quod autem appropinquante pascha . . . (PL cii. 155).

48. ff. 143–144^v Feria vi post xx . . . Erat quidam languens . . . Inter omnia miracula quę . . . (PL cii. 161). The last fourteen lines on f. 14^v remain blank.

49. f. 146 Incipiunt dicta sancti augustini de cena domini. Ante diem festum paschę . . . Ecce pascha ecce transitus . . . soluatur in cęlo.

III–VI. Thirty-seven homilies, all to be found in a South German homiliary, seven manuscripts of which are listed by Barré, pp. 26–7. Barré refers to this collection as B and lists the individual homilies in his table of initia, pp. 239–344, whence my numbers in brackets are taken: cf. also the full list in the catalogue description of Reims MS. 1407. Occasions are specified in III–V and sometimes in VI.

III. ff. 147–152^v Homilies for the twenty-third to twenty-sixth Sundays after Pentecost.

50. (B II. 63). f. 147 Simile est regnum celorum homini regi . . . Pręsens lectio sancti euangelii . . .

51. (B II. 64). f. 148 Abeuntes pharisei . . . Quantis remediis et medicaminibus.

52. (B II. 65). f. 149ᵛ Ecce princeps unus . . . Fratres karissimi audistis in lectione euangelica . . .

53. (B II. 66). f. 150ᵛ Accedens unus . . Accessit ad iesum quidam de scribis . . .

IV. ff. 152ᵛ–157ᵛ Homilies for Monday, Tuesday, Wednesday, and Thursday in the week of Pentecost.

54. (B II. 5). f. 152ᵛ Sic Deus dilexit . . . Saluator noster fratres karissimi. quia . . .

55. (B II. 6). f. 153ᵛ Amen amen dico uobis. qui non intrat . . . Verba sancti euangelii fratres karissimi ita . . .

56. (B II. 7). f. 155 Nemo potest uenire . . . Dominus ac redemptor noster ait . . .

57. (B II. 8). f. 156ᵛ Conuocatis Iesus . . . Modo fratres cum euangelium . . .

V. ff. 158–176ᵛ Thirteen homilies for the common of saints.

58. (B II. 33). f. 158 Facta est contentio . . . (Apostles). Bonis moris esse. solet . . .

59. (B II. 39). f. 159ᵛ Ecce ego mitto uos . . . (Martyrs). Attendamus dilectissimi fratres quemadmodum . . . Marked in red for eight lections.

60. (B II. 40). f. 160ᵛ Qui amat patrem . . . (Martyr). Gaudeamus dilectissimi gaudio spiritali . . .

61. (B II. 41). f. 162 Amen amen dico uobis nisi granum frumenti . . . (Martyr). Saluator noster dilectissimi discipulorum . . .

62. (B II. 53). f. 163 Ve vobis qui . . . (Martyr). In presenti lectione sancti euangelii . . .

63. (B I. 16). f. 164 Qui uos audit . . . (Martyr). Cum dominus et saluator noster fideles . . .

64. (B I. 78). f. 165 Hec mando uobis . . . (Apostles). Euangelicam lectionem quę modo . . .

65. (B II. 37). f. 166 Homo quidam nobilis . . . (Confessor). Homo nobilis qui abire dicitur . . .

66. (B II. 45). f. 168 Sint lumbi uestri . . . (Confessor and bishop). Audistis karissimi quomodo dominus . . .

67. (B II. 47). f. 169ᵛ Si quis uenit . . . (Martyr). Si consideremus karissimi fratres . . .

68. (B II. 10). f. 171 Vigilate . . . (Confessor and bishop). Sermonem euangelicum fratres karissimi oportet . . .

69. (B I. 81). f. 173 Nolite arbitrari . . . (Martyrs). Admonet nos dilectissimi euangelicus sermo . . .

70. (B II. 28). f. 174ᵛ Videns turbas Iesus . . . (Martyrs). Cum dominus ac saluator noster circuiret . . .

A blank space of 3½ lines at the foot of f. 176ᵛ.

VI. ff. 177–200ᵛ A series of seventeen homilies headed on f. 177 'Incipiunt euangelia priuatis diebus in xl'. They are for (Ash Wednesday) and the following Friday, the first Sunday in Lent and the following Monday, Tuesday, Wednesday, and Friday, for (Tuesday), Friday (two homilies) and Saturday in the second week of Lent, for (Tuesday and Thursday) in the third week, for (Wednesday) in the fourth week, for (Wednesday and Friday) in the fifth week, and for Palm Sunday.

71. (B I. 30). f. 177 Cum ieiunatis . . . Clemens et pius dominus . . .

72. (B I. 31). f. 178 Attendite ne iustitiam . . . Lectio ista quam audistis . . .

73. (B I. 32). f. 178ᵛ Ductus est iesus . . . Sollemne ieiunium quadraginta dierum . . .

74. (B I. 34). f. 180 Cum uenerit filius . . . Dominus et saluator noster dilectissimi discipulis . . .

75. (B I. 35). f. 181ᵛ Cum introisset iesus . . . Cum ingressus fuisset . . .

76. (B I. 36). f. 182ᵛ Accesserunt ad iesum scribę et pharisei dicentes. Magister uolumus a te . . . Incredulam iudeorum gentem . . .

77. (B I. 37). f. 184ᵛ Erat dies festus . . . Quia dominus et saluator noster homo factus est . . .

78. (B I. 40). f. 185ᵛ Super cathedram . . . Mansuetus et pius dominus . . .

79. (B I. 42). f. 187 Homo erat paterfamilias . . . Multis ac diuersis parabolis . . .

79a. (B I. 43). f. 188ᵛ [U]nde supra. Quod ex hesterna lectione sancti euangelii . . .

80. (B I. 44). f. 190 Homo quidam habuit . . . Euangelica lectione fratres karissimi audistis filiorum . . .

81. (B I. 46). f. 192 Si peccauerit . . . Frequenter fratres karissimi in euangelio . . .

82. (B I. 47). f. 193ᵛ Surgens Iesus . . . Cum intrauit iesus in domum petri . . .

83. (B I. 51). f. 195 Preteriens Iesus . . . De homine cęco nato . . .

84. (B I. 54). f. 196 Facta sunt encenia . . . Audistis ex lectione euangelica fratres karissimi quia facta sunt encenia in (sic). Encenia enim festiuitas est . . .

85. (B I. 56). f. 198 Collegerunt pontifices . . . In uerbis sacris euangelicę lectionis . . . .

86. (B I. 57). f. 199 Desiderata nobis dilectissimi et uniuerso . . . .

VII. Nos. 87–92. Six homilies, of which no. 87 is for Palm Sunday, like no. 86, nos. 88, 89 are assigned to the common of martyrs, and no. 90 is 'in xl ii ebdomada sabbato'. Nos. 91, 92 are on the gospel text for the nineteenth Sunday after Pentecost (cf. no. 40). Nos. 88–90, 92 are in Barré's list of *initia*, from B.

87. f. 200 Vnde supra. Quod dominus et saluator noster dei filius ante omnia secula genitus . . .

88. (B II. 14) f. 201ᵛ Attendite a fermento phariseorum . . . Presciuit ergo dominus et saluator noster multos in sancta ęcclesia . . .

89. (B II. 17) f. 203 Cum audieritis bella . . . Domino deo nostro laudes lęti . . . scientia coronatur. Per . . . Pseudo-Maximus (*PL* lvii. 715–16).

90. (B I. 38) f. 204 Post dies sex.᾿ assumpsit iesus . . . Misericors dominus et saluator noster fratres dilectissimi electos suos per huius uitę labores . . .

91. f. 206 Accesserunt saducei ad iesum . . . Magistrum uocauit. cuius noluit esse discipulus. Dominus autem sic . . .

92. (B II. 58). ff. 207–208ᵛ Item de eadem lectione. Postquam dominus et saluator noster impios sacerdotes super se irruentes quasi feras bestias . . .

Two tables were added in s. xv to make the collection easier to use: (*a*) ff. iii–iv, of the homilies in their order here and with the numbers assigned to them in s. xv; (*b*) ff. 209–10, of the same homilies, with their numbers, in the order of the church year, in four series, temporale, sanctorale, common of saints, octave of dedication.

(*b*). The order indicated by the second table is: (temporale), 1, 3, 2, 5, 4, 6–8, 73, 71, 74–7, 92 and 90, 10, 78 and 92, 79, 80, 11, 81, 45, 46, 12, 47, 83, 48, 84, 85, 44, 49, 86, 13–18, 20, 19, 54–7, 82, 21, 24, 53, 25–34, 37–9, 91, 42, 50, 43, 52; (sanctorale) 23 for Cathedra S. Petri, 62 for Vitus and Modestus,[1] 89 for Gervase and Protase, 22 for John Baptist, 35 for Laurence, 60 for octave of Laurence, 36 for Assumption of B.V.M., 58 for Bartholomew,[2] 41 for Michael; (common) 59, 64 for apostles, 61, 63, 65, 67 for a martyr, 69, 88, 77 (*sic for* 70) for martyrs, 68 for a confessor, 66 for confessors; 84 for octave of dedication. Unexpected assignments are 92 for both Saturday in the first week and Monday in the third week of Lent, 53 for Wednesday after the fourth Sunday after Pentecost, 86 for Good Friday, and 84 for the octave of the dedication. 9, 40, 72, and 87 are not included.

ff. vi+208+vi. Parchment of poor quality, with holes and tears avoided by the scribe. ff. iii–vi, 209–12 are medieval pastedowns and flyleaves: for ff. iii, iv, 209–10 see above. 277 × 185 mm. Written space 220 × 133 mm. 32–7 long lines (less on the first few leaves). Ruling with a hard point: double vertical bounders, but the scribe wrote up to the outer of the two lines. Collation: 1–26⁸: 26⁴,⁵ are singletons. Quires numbered at the end as far as 'XVI'. Ill written, mainly by one hand, whose *y* with wavy first limb is distinctive (f. 196/30, *Ierosolymis*). The *I* of *In illo tempore* beginning each homily, red with red ornament, lies outside the written space. Capital letters in the ink of the text touched with red or (ff. 89–109) pale yellow: both colours are on the capitals on ff. 108ᵛ–109. Slatter binding. Secundo folio *et bene*.

Written on the Continent (France?) and, to judge from marginalia, still there in s. xii. In England by s. xv when the tables and some annotations were added and the homilies were numbered. 'Myles', f. 212, s. xv. A strip cut off the foot of f. 2: there may have been an ex-libris here. At Eton by 1500: see above p. 631.

[1] In homiliary **B** for Cornelius and Cyprian.
[2] In homiliary **B** for Apollinaris.

42. *Pseudo-Chrysostomus, Homiliae in Matthaeum* s. xv in.

1. ff. 1–297 Sicut referunt matheum conscribere . . . in loco sancto. Expliciunt omelie Iohannis Crisostomi. patriarche constantinopolitani super Matheum operis imperfecti etc'. Quod Wodewarde.

Stegmüller, no. 4350. The edition in *PG* lvi. 611–946 is arranged differently and makes fifty-four homilies instead of fifty-seven, which is the usual number in the manuscripts: cf. the catalogue description of B.L., Royal 3 B. vii. The last words here, as in other manuscripts, come in edn. at col. 908/11. Marginalia by the same hand as in MS. 17.

2. Indexes to art. 1: (*a*) ff. 297^v–300^v Abraham quare dicitur cristus habrahe filius . . . Item omelia 54 per totum de aduentu (*ends imperfectly on* Dies iudicii); (*b*) ff. 301–311 (*begins imperfectly*) Dies insciencia dicitur que obscurabitur in fine mundi 56 b. Dignitas . . . Zelus nascitur ex amore magno 1 l zelus sapere nescitur et ira non potest habere consilium 2 p.

Parts of two indexes to art. 1 put together to make a complete index, A–Z. (*a*) is in the hand of the text and fills the space which remained blank in quire 25. (*b*), an index on a different principle referring to subdivisions of the homilies by letters, looks like the remains of another manuscript: there are no letters in the margins of art. 1, but they occur in Bodleian MSS. Bodley 709 and 743, both of which have the same index as (*b*). ff. 311^v–313^v were left blank. A reader began a list of the homilies of art. 1 on f. 311^v, but only got to no. 23.

3. The pastedown at the end is a leaf of a noted breviary, s. xiii^2: 2 cols. 36 lines. The exposed side contains part of the offices for lauds and vespers at Epiphany.

Cf. *Brev. ad usum Sarum*, cols. cccxxix–cccxxxi, but the use is not Sarum. The last anti-phon in lauds is Stella ista sicut flamma and the hymn (cue only), Hostis herodes. Another fragment of the same manuscript used in the binding of MS. 43, q.v., may be from the leaf before this one, since it contains part of the office for the vigil of Epiphany (cf. edn., cols. cccxviii–cccxx).

ff. iii+313. ff. ii, iii are medieval parchment flyleaves. 255×175 mm. Written space *c.* 175×115 mm. 29 long lines. Collation: 1^{12} 2^{10} 3^{14} 4–25^{12} 26^{16} wants 1–3 before f. 301. Quires 1–9 (only) signed in the usual late medieval way, except that the quires are num-bered (in arabic figures) and the leaves lettered (a–f) instead of vice versa.[1] Written in current anglicana, which looks strange from about f. 95 because minims are not linked but made in separate unfooted strokes, so that *m* resembles 111 and *n* and *u* 11. Art. 2b is in a mixture of anglicana and secretary, the latter predominating. Initials 3-line (4-line, f. 1; 2-line, ff. 297^v–311), blue with red ornament. Bound by Williamson. Secundo folio *scilicet rex*.

Written in England, arts. 1, 2a by a scribe named Wodewarde. Two inscriptions of gift: (i) f. iii^v 'Liber Collegii Regalis beate Marie de Eton' ex dono M' Thome Weston' socii eiusdem Collegii xxiii° die Aprilis anno domini m° ccccliii° Et Anno Regni Regis Henrici Sexti xxxi°'; (ii) f. 313^v 'Ex dono Magistri Willelmi Wey quondam socii istius collegii regalis beatissime marie Eton', above which is 'E.C.' and to the left of these letters 'Eton' (cf. MSS. 76, 99). Perhaps the explanation of the two inscriptions is that copies of the homilies on Matthew were given by both Weston and Wey and that Wey's copy was scrapped in or before 1608–9, except for the last thirteen leaves kept for the sake of the index which was already imperfect in Weston's copy.[2]

[1] A series of quire and leaf signatures beginning with 1a–f, seems to me rather better than one beginning with a1–6, but it did not catch on with scribes or printers.

[2] Birley has another suggestion, p. 232. ff. ii, iii were in their present position before Williamson's time, as they have the same pattern of worm-holes as f. 1. Similar holes do not occur on f. i, a paper flyleaf added by Williamson.

43. *Matthaeus glosatus*   s. XII/XIII

1. ff. 1–84ᵛ Matheus ex iudea . . . (f. 1ᵛ) Liber generationis . . .

A central column of text widely spaced for interlinear glosses and flanked by discontinuous apparatus in a much smaller hand. The first three paragraphs of apparatus are 'Matheus cum primo . . . sacramentum' (prologue to Matthew, Stegmüller, no. 589), 'Hec causa matheum scribere . . . dauid natum', 'Modus tractandi talis est, Primus genealogiam . . . in hoc euangelio tractat'. The apparatus ends, f. 84ᵛ, 'Sic ueniet quemadmodum uidistis eum euntem in celum'.

2 (added). (*a*) ff. 84ᵛ–85 [L]ibros omnes quos edidit beatus augustinus hic breuiter enumeramus. [C]ontra paganos uel ad achademicos libri tres . . . [I]tem ad quos supra de correctione et gratia li. vii. (*b*) f. 86 Si azorium fuerit bonum: mole donec sencias lenitatem in malacione. et tunc pone in album cornu uel in conkam offree. et accipe gummam arabicam et distempera in aqua et quando dissoluta fuerit: cola per medium pannum et inde distempera azorium. (*c*) f. ivᵛ Versus Sibilli de cristo. quos ponit Augustinus in libro quem composuit contra incredulitatem Iudeorum Paganorum et Arrianorum. Iudicii signum tellus . . . et sulphuris amnis. Hec de cristi natiuitate . . . potuit obseruari. Item alii versus Sibillini de Passione domini. In manus inquit (*sic for* iniquas) infidelium postea ueniet . . . reuocatur ostenso.

(*a, b*) fill part of the blank space in the last quire. (*a*), s. xii/xiii, is the usual list of Augustine's works, based on his Retractationes. (*b*). A recipe for blue, s. xiiiᴵ. (*c*). s. xiii. Walther, no. 9907. *PL* xlii. 1126, 1127.

ff. iv+86+iii. ff. iii, iv are medieval parchment end-leaves from an older binding: for iii, see below. 262 × 188 mm. Written space *c.* 170 mm high. Ruling for 53 lines of apparatus, but on no page are all the lines written on. Pricks in both margins to guide ruling which provides for both text and apparatus on a single grid. Writing below the top ruled line, except for the apparatus in quire 1. Collation: 1–10⁸ 11⁸ wants 6, 7, blank. Quires numbered at the end, I–XI. Initials: (i) ff. 1, 1ᵛ, 4, red and blue with ornament of both colours on a ground of yellow-brown wash; (ii) blue or red, with ornament of the other colour; (iii) red or blue. Binding of s. xvii/xviii, plain except for a fillet round the edges, no doubt Eton work by Williamson, since the strips of parchment used in binding are: (*a*) at the beginning, from the same book as Williamson used a leaf of when binding MS. 42, q.v.; (*b*) at the end, from a flyleaf with Horman's inscription of gift on it, '[. . . . . .] Hormani quondam [. . . . .]nii' (cf. MS. 48): no chainmark: the strap and pin of an older binding have left marks on the leaves at beginning and end. Secundo folio *culus*.

Written in England. The ex-libris of the Premonstratensian abbey of Otham, Sussex, prior to its removal to Bayham, Sussex, is on the recto of f. iii, which was pasted to a former binding: 'Hic liber est Canon' de Otteham', s. xiii. At Eton by *c.* 1600.

44. *Albertus Magnus, In Lucam et Marcum*   *c.* 1481

A page for column copy of Balliol College, Oxford, MS 187, written in Oxford and probably in New College by many scribes not earlier than 1479 and probably a year or two later: described by N. R. Ker, 'Eton College 44 and its exemplar', *Litterae Textuales, Essays presented to G. I. Lieftinck*, i (1972), 48–60, with facsimiles of ff. 32 and 362.

ff. iv+623+iv. ff. iii, iv, 624-5 were pastedowns and flyleaves of a contemporary binding. Paper, except ff. iii, iv, 624-5. 305×220 mm. Written space varies and is sometimes as much as 265×185 mm. Faint ruling with a hard point or by making a crease to show the scribe where he should begin his writing. Collation: 1–25²⁴ 26²⁴ wants 24, blank: in quire 16 1, 2 are missing and have been replaced by the present ff. 362, 363 (cf. ibid. 56). Written in a current mixture of anglicana and secretary, except ff. 362, 363 which are in fairly skilful secretary by a scribe who made many corrections throughout (cf. ibid. 56, 59). 2-line spaces for initials not filled. Binding by Slatter. Secundo folio *actus incidens*.

Written in England (Oxford). Probably came to Eton through William Horman: cf. ibid. 59. *CMA* 3.

45. *P. Comestor, Historia Scholastica; Allegoriae in Bibliam*

s. XIII[1]

1. ff. 1-193ᵛ [Imperatorie] maiestatis est: tres in palatio . . . Incipit hystoria scolastica theologie discipline. De creatione quatuor celorum et de empireo. [In principio] erat uerbum . . . scilicet in cathacumbis. 'Explicit historia actuum'.

PL cxcviii. 1053–1722. Stegmüller, nos. 6543–65. Inset pieces are usually headed 'Magister' or 'Incidentia'. A contemporary chapter numbering in red and blue and a later one in brown ink.

2. ff. 193ᵛ–244ᵛ 'Incipiunt allegorie super vetus testamentum'. In precedentibus prescripta descriptione originis . . . et summus bonus deus conuertitur (*sic*) et non peribit.

PL clxxv. 634–828. Stegmüller, nos. 3847–8. Thirteen books. The arrangement of the New Testament (bks. 11–13) differs from edn. (cf. above, MS. 4): the last words here come at edn. 810/4.

3 (added). (*a*) f. 244ᵛ Petrus eram . . . (4 lines). (*b*) ff. 244ᵛ–245 Aaron . . . (*c*) f. 247ᵛ (flyleaf) Ascalonica necat . . . (2 lines).

(*a, c*). s. xv. (*a*) Walther, no. 4050. In (*c*) 'herodes' is written above 'Ascalonica'. (*b*). The beginning of an index to art. 1, s. xiv, with references to the brown-ink chapter numbers. It ends abruptly at Amon. ff. 245ᵛ–246ᵛ blank.

ff. iv+246+v. f. 247 is a medieval parchment flyleaf. 295×200 mm. Written space 175× 115 mm. 2 cols. 43 lines. First line of writing above top ruled line. Collation: 1–18¹² 19¹⁰ 20¹² 21¹² wants 8–11, blank, after f. 245. Quires numbered at the end. ff. 1ᴵⱽ, 12ᴵⱽ (i.e. the first sheet) are in a better hand than the rest: it uses crossed *x*. Initials: (i) the words *Imperatorie* and *In principio* were on now missing pieces of parchment pasted in spaces left for them on f. 1;[1] (ii) red and blue with ornament of both colours; (iii) of chapters and of the first word of each book after the initial letter, 2-line, red or blue with ornament of the other colour; (iv) of inset pieces in art. 1, as (iii), but 1-line. Binding of s. xix. Secundo folio *primo enim*.

Written in England. The pressmark 'H. xvii' at the foot of f. 1 shows ownership by an institution in the late Middle Ages.[2] The scribble 'Chicsan', s. xv, on f. 247ᵛ is poor evidence that the institution was the Gilbertine priory of Chicksands in Bedfordshire. Probably *CMA* 41 covers both this and MS. 125.

---

[1] Cf. *MMBL* i. 266.
[2] In an interleaved Eton catalogue M. R. James has noted of the pressmark 'a tall narrow hand, like those of St. Mary's, York'. The expected form at St. Mary's, York, would be, however, 'In H. xvii'.

46. *Ambrosius; Faustus Reiensis*   s. XV

A collection of pieces by or attributed to St. Ambrose. Arts. 1, 9–12 are listed by
the main hand in red ink on f. ii, under the heading 'Hi libri in prẹsenti conscri-
bitur uolumine': leaf numbers are given.[1]

1. ff. 1–146ᵛ, 178ᵛ–215ᵛ The collection of letters in ten books (*Clavis*, no. 160),
but the beginnings of bks. 3 and 4 are not shown. Bks. 1–6 contain the 35 letters
printed in *CSEL* lxxxii (1968). Bk. 7 consists of 18, bk. 8 of 9, and bk. 9 of 7
letters, nos. 44–77 in the Erasmian and other early editions.[2] Erasmus's no. 78
begins bk. 10 and is followed by no. 30, Relatio Symmachi (f. 122ᵛ), 31, 29, 32,
Contra Auxentium de basilicis tradendis (f. 136ᵛ), 33, 82, 28, 83, 80, 81, 26, 84,
85 (=*PL*, Epist. 22, divided at 'Helyseum scripture', with heading 'Alia eiusdem').

On f. 215 the passage of *PL*, Ep. 22, Notus homo . . . sed quero etc. (edn., *PL* xvi, 1024C–
1025B (1067C–1068A)), is added in the margin. Spaces for Greek were left blank and filled
later only on ff. 21ᵛ–22.

Arts. 2–7 lie between the seventy-seventh and seventy-eighth items of art. 1, nos.
33 and 82 in Erasmus's edition.

2. ff. 146ᵛ–156ᵛ De obitu Theodosii imperatoris epytaphius sermo habitus ad
populum die xlᵐᵒ á sancto Ambrosio. Hoc nobis motus terrarum . . . tenebis
hospicio. Ambrosio fleris Theodosi maxime cesar: Te dicente pium sanctæ
quoque lægis amicum.

Clavis, no. 159. *PL* xvi. 1385–1406 (1447–68).

3. ff. 156ᵛ–161 Ambrosius seruus cristi. Virginibus sacris. Diem fẹstum
sacratissime uirginis . . . ualeat inuenire. Passa est beatissima martir agnes
duodecimo kalendas februarii regnante domino nostro ihesu cristo. cui . . . Amen.

Pseudo-Ambrose. *Clavis*, no. 2159. *BHL*, no. 156. *PL* xvii. 735–42 (813–21).

4. ff. 161–162ᵛ Ambrosius seruus cristi. fratribus per omnem Italiam in
domino eternam salutem. In diuinis uoluminibus . . . consequi misericordiam
. . . Amen. Martirizati sunt autem sancti martires Ceruasius et Protasius . . . in
secula seculorum Amen.

Pseudo-Ambrose. *Clavis*, no. 2195. *BHL*, no. 3514. *PL* xvii. 743–7 (821–5).

5. ff. 162ᵛ–164 Ambrosius seruus cristi uocatus episcopus. Dilectissimis
fratribus et uniuersis plebibus in domino eternam salutem. Magna martirum
et precælsa testimonia . . . pridie nonas nouembris. regnante domino nostro
ihesu cristo.

Pseudo-Ambrose on SS. Vitalis and Agricola. *Clavis*, no. 2244. *BHL*, no. 8690. *PL* xvii.
747–9 (825–7).

6. ff. 164–176ᵛ Qui ad conuiuium magnum . . . seruare digneris.

Clavis, no. 149. *PL* xvi. 336–64 (351–80: Exhortatio virginitatis).

---

[1] The references show that the double opening is the unit: f. '2' is what we should call
ff. 1 verso and 2 recto.

[2] The order in *PL* xvi. 876–1286 (913–1342) is different. The *PL* numbers may be
found from the concordance in vol. xvi. 867–74 (906–10).

7. ff. 176ᵛ–178ᵛ Seruus cristi Ambrosius episcopus. cristum uerum deum colentibus. fratribus per uniuersam Italiam in domino perhennem salutem. Omnia que á sanctis dei . . . illi placuerunt. Passi sunt autem beatissimi cristi martires. Cantius. Cantianus. et Cancianillus . . . in secula seculorum.

Pseudo-Ambrose. *Clavis*, no. 2175. *BHL*, no. 1547.

8. ff. 215ᵛ–227ᵛ Epistola ambrosii de consolatione Valentiniani imperatori. Etsi incrementum . . . compenses. Amen.

Clavis, no. 158. *PL* xvi. 1357–84 (1417–44).

9. ff. 227ᵛ–263ᵛ Incipit liber beatissimi ambrosii doctoris eximii mediolanensis episcopi de morte satiri fratris sui siue de resurrectione Lege feliciter. Liber primus. Deduximus fratres dilectissimi . . . timere nequeamus. Amen. Explicit liber beati ambrosii de morte fratris sui sancti satiri.

Clavis, no. 157. *PL* xvi. 1289–1354 (1345–1414).

10. ff. 264–268ᵛ Oratio pulcerrima deuotissima sancti Ambrosii. Summa et incomprehensibilis natura . . . ipse inspiraueris: Qui æternitate perhenni . . . Amen. Deo gratias.

Pseudo-Ambrose. *PL* xvii. 755–62 (833–42).

11. ff. 269–83 Liber sancti ambrosii episcopi de incarnatione uerbi incipit. lege feliciter. Debitum fratres cupio soluendum: sed hesternos . . . intelligibilium. Deo gratias.

Clavis, no. 152. *PL* xvi. 818–46 (853–84).

12. ff. 283ᵛ–306 Incipit liber beati ambrosii episcopi de spiritu sancto. Capitula . . . (*table of 13 chapters*) . . . Fides catolica in uniuersum mundum . . . gloria sublimare. Amen. Deo gratias.

Clavis, no. 962 (Faustus Reiensis). *CSEL* xxi. 101–57. Bk. 2, f. 294ᵛ: a table of twelve chapters in front of it. ff. 306ᵛ–308ᵛ were left blank.

ff. ii+305. The foliation, (i, ii), 1–306, (307–8) is medieval: numbers are skipped after ff. 153, 221, and 302. f. i is a contemporary flyleaf. 278 × 195 mm. Written space *c.* 185 × 120 mm.[1] 30 long lines.[1] Ruling with a hard point. Collation: 1–22¹⁰ 23⁶ (ff. 223–8) 24–30¹⁰ 31¹⁰ wants 10, blank: 10 is pasted to the binding. Upright humanistic script by a named scribe (see below): he wrote 'ihesus', not 'iesus', and often misused *æ*: the addition in the margin of f. 215 (see above, art. 1) is perhaps in his non-humanistic hand. Initials: (i) 8-line (f. 1) and 3-line, gold on blue, red, and green grounds, decorated with white vine interlace and dots in groups of three, in the Florentine style of *c.* 1435–40;[2] (ii) 3-line, blue. A gay bird in the margin, f. 1. Binding by Williamson. Secundo folio *ergo mensura*.

Written in Italy by the same scribe as Magdalen College, Oxford, MS. 59 (Ambrose, De fide) and MS. 76: 'Si vis scire lector: quis astitit litteræ scriptor. Alamanum signa. Iohannem de Rodenberga', f. 268ᵛ.[3] At Eton by 1601.

---

[1] The dimensions of the written space and the number of lines are the same as in Magdalen College, MS. 76.

[2] As in Magdalen College, MS. 76. I owe the dating to Dr. A. de la Mare.

[3] Dr. de la Mare tells me that Vat. Lat. 1801 is signed 'Ioannes Lamperti de Rodenberg' and dated Rome 1452 and that Vat. Lat. 1812 is signed 'Iohannes Rodenbergh'. A reduced facsimile of the last page of Vat. Lat. 1801 is reproduced by Fava in *Academie e Biblioteche d'Italia*, vi (1931–2), 112.

47. *Augustinus, etc.*　　　　　　　　　　　s. xv med.

A collection of writings mainly by or attributed to St. Augustine (arts. 1, 2, 6, 8–10) and by anti-Wycliffites (arts. 3–5) written in the distinctive hand of John Malberthorp, fellow of Lincoln College, Oxford, and later (1445 or 1446–1455) of Eton College, † after 1471: cf. Emden, *BRUO* (Mabulthorpe). Lincoln College, Oxford, 6 and 101, ff. 1–24, 49–167, St. John's College, Cambridge, 254, Cambridge University Library Ii. 6. 15, and B.L., Harley 635 are also in his hand. Arts. 5*a, b* occur also in Harley 635, ff. 202ᵛ–205, 205–10, and arts. 3*b*, 4*a, b,* and 5*c* are extracts from the full texts in Harley, ff. 179–192ᵛ, 192ᵛ–198, 198–202ᵛ, 65–179. Malberthorp's marginalia occur throughout. They are often exclamations, for example, 'o ecclesie olim continencia' (f. 153), 'o fallaces heretici' (f. 169ᵛ).

1. ff. 1–39 De libro '50' retractacionum beati augustini. Capitulum 4ᵐ. Libros de doctrina cristiana . . . Sunt precepta quedam. Prologi in libros beati augustini de doctrina cristiana. capitulum primum. Sunt precepta quedam tractandarum scripturarum . . . disserui. adiuuante domino. qui . . . amen. Deo gracias. semper.

PL xxxiv. 15–122. Prologue of five numbered chapters and four books of 41, 43, 39, and 30 numbered chapters. Preceded by the relevant extract from Retractationes.

2. ff. 39–108 Incipit prologus in libros confessionum beati Augustini yponensis episcopi. Confessionum mearum . . . Magnus es domine. Explicit prologus. incipit liber primus . . . Magnus es domine . . . sic aperietur. Explicit liber xiiiᵘˢ confessionum beati Augustini episcopi. Laus tibi ihesu. dulcedo mi. semper. M' I.M'.

PL xxxii. 659–868. Preceded by the relevant extract from Retractationes. The division of each book into chapters is shown only by numbers in the margins, not by spacing. f. 108ᵛ blank.

3. (*a*) ff. 109–15 Questio de adoracione ymaginum. Numquid domini nostri ihesu cristi crucifixi . . . in claritatem visionis beate. Ad quam visionem . . . Amen Deo gracias. (*b*) ff. 115–16 Excerpta sunt hec sequencia ex tractatu doctoris Wodeford' contra Wicliff. de adoracione ymaginum. Cultus dei prout denotat actum . . . Vt dicit martinus in cronica sua.

Letter-marks A–G in the margins of (*a*) and H, I in the margins of (*b*). (*a*). Cf. J. Russell Smith in *Dominican Studies*, vii (1954), 188. (*b*) and art. 4*a* are pseudo-Woodford, as Dr. Catto tells me.

4. (*a*) ff. 116–118ᵛ Excerpta de tractatu Wodeford' contra Wycliff. de peregrinacione ad loca sancta. Circa peregrinaciones ad loca sancta . . . vt in ierusalem fieret peregrinis. Amen. Deo gracias. (*b*) ff. 118ᵛ–119 Sequitur de oblacionibus fiendis in locis sanctorum. Licitum est et meritorium cristi fidelibus . . . vbi hec miracula exercent. Explicit. Deo gracias.

(*a*). Letter-marks A–C in the margins.

5. (*a*) ff. 119–121ᵛ Opinio et confessio M' iohannis Wycliff. de sacramento altaris. vt recitat eum doctor nicholaus radecliff de sancto albano in libro suo. qui incipit. Vniuersis cristi fidelibus capitulo 27. Sepe confessus sum et adhuc

confiteor . . . veritas vincet eos. Finis opinionis M' I. Wicliff. Hec est confessio perfidie huius heretici M' I. Wycliff . . . (b) ff. 121ᵛ–126ᵛ Contra quam . . . arguit nobilis doctor nicholaus radecliff monachus de sancto albano . . . subita infirmorum. Expliciunt notabilia excerpta de libro doctoris nicholai de sancto albano contra Wicli'f'istas edito de diuinissima eukaristia. Deo gracias. (c) ff. 126ᵛ–131ᵛ Incipiunt quedam notabilia excerpta de questionibus Doctoris Wodeford contra eosdem Wiclifistas de eadem eukaristia diuinissima. De questione prima eiusdem doctoris. Eukaristia est nomen grecum . . . mutauit opinionem.

(a), printed in *Fasciculi Zizaniorum* (RS, 1858), pp. 115–32, is, like (b), extracted from Nicholas Radclif against Wyclif: cf. Royal 6 D.x, art. 2, and Emden, *BRUO*, p. 1539. In Harley 635 the heading 'Opinio . . . 27' and the words 'Finis opinionis W.' are marginalia. The running title on ff. 119ᵛ–120 is 'Opinio Wicliff. de sacramento altaris Obscura. perplexa. et multum erronea'. (c) is from the seventy-two questions on the eucharist of William Woodford, composed in 1383 or 1384: cf. Little, *Grey Friars in Oxford*, 1892, p. 246. In art. 14 Malberthorp calls it 'Item questio doctoris Wodeford' contra Wyclifistas et pauonistas de sacramento eukaristie'. It is followed by three lines on the calling of the apostles, 'Prima vocacio . . . ad apostolicam dignitatem'. f. 132ʳᵛ blank.

Letter-marks A–E in the margins of each of (a–c).

6. ff. 133–44 Incipit liber beati Augustini de cognicione vere vite. Sapientia dei que os . . . ad summum bonum perducat. amen. Explicit liber beati Augustini de cognicione vere vite. Deo gracias.

Letter-marks A–K in the margins. *PL* xl. 1005–32. Attributed to Honorius.

7. f. 144ᵛ Cassiodorus libro de institucionibus diuinarum litterarum. Numquam inquit potest occultum inueniri꞉ quod non per viam suam queritur . . . cuncta festinat. Hec ille.

Extracts from bk. 1, chs. xxviii–xxxiii, the first at edn. Mynors, 70/18, 19 and the last, 84/22–24.

8. ff. 145–54 Liber beati augustini de vtilitate credendi. scriptus ad honoratum. Si michi honorate . . . in ceteris prom'p'tior. Explicit liber 'beati augustini' de utilitate credendi.

Letter-marks A–K in the margins. *PL* xlii. 65–92.

9. ff. 154–6 Incipit sermo beati augustini. de assumpcione beate marie virginis. Quia profundissime 'et' sua dignitate altissime . . . tu et tui. qui cum . . . amen. Deo gratias. Explicit sermo beati augustini de assumpcione beatissime marie semper virginis.

Letter-marks A–C in the margins. *PL* xl. 1143–8. f. 156ᵛ blank.

10. ff. 157–169ᵛ In nomine sancte trinitatis Aurelii Augustini liber incipit de moribus ecclesie contra manicheos Capitulum primum. In aliis libris opinor . . . aliquando veniamus. conuersi ad deum. Explicit liber beati augustini de moribus ecclesie. Deo gracias.

Bk. 1 only. Forty numbered chapters. *PL* xxxii. 1309–44.

11. ff. 169ᵛ–182 'Tabula elaborata super contenta in hoc libro' (so the title in art. 14), an alphabetical table of contents of arts. 1–10 compiled by

Malberthorp, no doubt: cf. Lincoln College, Oxford, 101, art. 18, and Harley 635 ff. 271ᵛ–276ᵛ.

A longish hostile entry under 'Wicliff'. Letters used in references to arts. 3–6, 8, 9 correspond to letters entered in the margins of these pieces.

12. ff. 182–6 Questio 2ᵃ doctoris subtilis. super prologum primi libri sentenciarum. notabilis valde pro stabilimento fidei catholice. ecclesie sacrosancte. Vtrum cognicio supernaturalis necessaria viatori . . . periculo exponendo. Explicit. Deo gracias.

Sect. 95–123 of Ordinatio I: J. Duns Scotus, *Opera omnia*, i (1950), 59–87: cf. 124*–125*.¹

13. ff. 186–189ᵛ Contra gentiles libri primi capitulo 4° Quod veritas diuinorum ad quam naturalis ratiocinacio pertingit conuenienter hominibus credenda proponitur. Duplici igitur veritate . . . opera eius. Deo gracias.

Aquinas, Contra Gentiles, bk. 1, chs. 4–8, and bk. 2, ch. 2. Dondaine and Shooner, no. 808.¹

14. f. 189ᵛ Contenta in hoc libro. sunt hec in ordine . . . Deo gracias semper. M' I. M'. f. 190ʳᵛ blank.

ff. i+190. From f. 37 the foliation used by James is 12 beyond that now in use. 300 × 200 mm. Written space 220 × 130 mm. 51 and 52 long lines. Collation: 1–15¹² 16¹⁰. The first leaf of quire 3 is signed b 1, so the series of quire marks probably began with +, not with *a*, as is not uncommon in English manuscripts.² Modified textura: anglicana forms of, *d*, *f*, and *s*: a mark of punctuation used within and at the end of sentences is shaped like a short comma. Initials: (i) ff. 1, 39, gold on grounds of red and blue, patterned in white, with prolongations into the margins; (ii, iii) 5-line and 4-line, blue with red ornament. Binding of s. xvii: the binder took over two end-leaves of the medieval binding as pastedowns. Secundo folio *misit*.

Written by John Malberthorp (see above) for his own use: 'Liber M' Iohannis Malberthorp' ' is on the pastedown at the end. *CMA* 22, 23.

48, ff. 1–96. *Augustinus* s. xii¹

Works by or attributed to Augustine and (5) the Sermo Arrianorum.

(1) ff. 1–17ᵛ Aurelii augustini doctoris hypponensis episcopi. De adulterinis coniugiis. Liber primus incipit. Prima questio est frater dilectissime pollenti . . . occasio castitatis. Explicit de adulterinis coniugiis. (2) ff. 17ᵛ–28ᵛ Aurelii Augustini doctoris. De natura et origine animę ad renatum Liber incipit. Sinceritatem tuam erga nós³ renáte . . . dilatione conscripsi. Explicit ad renatum de natura et origine animę. (3) ff. 28ᵛ–37 Incipit ad petrum presbiterum De eadem Ré. Domino dilectissimo fratri et conpresbitero petro. agustinus episcopus in domino salutem. Peruenerunt ad me . . . uel fecerit. Explicit ad petrum

---

¹ These modern descriptions follow the foliation given by James: see below.

² The first quire is marked + also in St. John's College, Cambridge, 254, Lincoln College, lat. 6, and B.L., Harley 635. In Lincoln College, lat. 101, the first quire has no serial number and the second is marked +. In Ii. 6. 15 the first quire has no serial number and the second is marked a. Cf. above, p. viii.

³ The stress-marks are not, perhaps, by the main hand.

presbiterum De natura et origine ánimae. (4) ff. 37–55 Incipit ad uincentium uictorem de eadem re liber primus. Quod michi ad te scribendum . . . plausibus alienis. Explicit liber secundus ad vincentium de natura et origine animae. (5) ff. 55–7 Incipit sermo arrianorum. Dominus noster iesus cristus. deus unigenitus . . . habens om(n)ium. Cui . . . Amen. Explicit sermo arrianorum. (6) ff. 57–69ᵛ Aurelii augustini doctoris. contra istam arrianorum perfidiam liber incipit. Eorum precedenti disputationi . . . hoc fine concludimus. Explicit liber aurelii augustini doctoris respondentis contra arrianorum perfidiam. (7) ff. 69ᵛ–96 Incipit eiusdem contra aduersarium legis et prophetarum liber primus. Librum quem misistis . . . explicare curabo. Aurelii augustini doctoris contra aduersarium legis et prophetarum liber secundus explicit.

1. *PL* xl. 451–86. 2–4. *PL* xliv. 475–548. 5, 6. *PL* xlii. 677–85, 683–708. 7. *PL* xlii. 603–66. (1–7) occur in this order in Salisbury Cathedral 128, s. xi ex. For (2–7) cf. also B.L., Royal 5 A. xiii from Worcester Cathedral. f. 96ᵛ blank.

ff. 1–96 in a composite volume of ff. iv+240+ii. For f. iv, a medieval parchment flyleaf, see below. Strong parchment. 280 × 195 mm. Written space 225 × 115–130 mm. 34–9 long lines. Ruling with a hard point. Twelve quires of 8. Written in a good narrow hand, the same throughout: hyphens are nearly horizontal: the flex (?) is occasionally used as a mark of punctuation (f. 9/27, 30), but has perhaps been added. Initials: (i) red or green, the latter sometimes with a little ornament in red; (ii) 1-line, red or green. Capital letters in the ink of the text sometimes filled with red. Binding by Williamson, who added ff. 97–240. Secundo folio *Cum hec*.

Written in England. 'Donum Guilielmi Hormani quondam socii huius colle (*sic*: cancelled) contubernii', f. iv, below a 'Contenta' in the same hand covering ff. 1–96 only.

48, ff. 97–106. '*Augustini de uera innocentia liber*' s. XII/XIII

Aurellii Augustini de uera innocentia liber incipit.

Prosper of Aquitaine, Sententiae ex operibus Sancti Augustini, in 390 chapters. *Clavis*, no. 525; Römer, i. 192. *PL* xlv. 1859–98 and li. 427–96. The scribe wrote 'In nomine patris et filii et spiritus sancti' at the head of f. 97.

ff. 10. 280 × 195 mm. Written space 198 × 122 mm. 49 long lines. A quire of ten leaves. Initials blue or red, placed outside the written space.

Written in England. Belonged perhaps with ff. 107–240 in the Middle Ages, but if so the order was then 107–240, 97–106: f. 106ᵛ shows marks of rust from a former binding. At Eton by 1601.

48, ff. 107–240. *Notulae in Bibliam* s. XII ex.

Notes on the Bible: (*a*) f. 107, Notule super Genesin. Materia moysi in hoc opere. est creatio mundi . . . (f. 120ᵛ) texerat eum. Expliciunt Notule geneseos; (*b*) f. 121, on Matthew, 'Matheus primo ponit unde oriundus . . .'; (*c*) f. 126, on Mark, 'Omnibus legitime certantibus corona . . .'; (*d*) f. 155, on Luke, 'De paradiso uoluptatis' unde primus homo . . .'; (*e*) f. 186, on John, 'Omnia poma noua et uetera . . .'; (*f*) f. 197ᵛ, on Catholic Epistles, 'Iuxta tertium euangelistarum iiiiᵒʳ cognouimus . . .'; (*g*) f. 219ᵛ, on Jerome's preface to Genesis,

'Desiderius proprium nomen est . . .'; (h) f. 220, Fourteen paragraphs, the first beginning 'Lectores diuinarum scripturarum primum instruere oportet'; (i) f. 222ᵛ, Glose super Genesim . . . Expliciunt note ad literam Genesi; (j) f. 227ᵛ, on Exodus; (k) f. 230, on Leviticus; (l) f. 231ᵛ, on Judges; (m) f. 233ᵛ, on Kings.

The margins of (a) contain sigla, M C, M G, M e R, M O, M.P.e, M.P.M. On their significance see B. Smalley in *RTAM*, vii (1935), 256–9. (c–f) have longish introductions, ff. 126ʳᵛ, 155ʳᵛ, 186–7ᵛ, 197ᵛ. In (c) there is a blank space on f. 135ᵛ after which the gloss begins again with the first words of Jerome's prologue: the words 'Expliciunt congrua notularum addicio hec est. Et baptizabuntur . . .' are on f. 139, and another 'Expliciunt . . .' is on f. 142. In (d) a fresh beginning follows a blank space on f. 156 and f. 159ᵛ was left blank because the parchment was too poor to write on. (m) continues the history of the Jews to the time of Christ, ending 'Secundus patruus qui iacobum interfecit'. f. 240ᵛ blank.

The space on f. 135ᵛ contains an addition in a contemporary hand, 'Statuit terminos moyses iuxta montem domini . . .'.

ff. 107–240 in a composite volume. 280 × 195 mm. Written space 212 × 145 mm. 2 cols. 45–50 lines. Collation: 1⁸ 2⁸ wants 7, 8, probably blank after f. 120 3–17⁸. Probably all in one hand and written in the order (b–l), (a). Initials 2-line or 1-line, red or blue, with ornament of the other colour: the terminals are sometimes small human or animal heads (ff. 155, 221) and the I on f. 197ᵛ is a delicate blue and red dragon. Bound with ff. 1–96 in s. xvii in. and with ff. 97–106 then or earlier: wormholes on f. 107 and later leaves, decrease in size and number. Secundo folio (f. 108) *fusione*.

Written in England. Inscriptions of ownership by the cell of St. Albans at Belvoir, Lincolnshire, on f. 107, s. xiii/xiv, in red: (a) at head, 'Liber beate marie de Beluero'; (b) at foot, 'Hunc librum dedit frater Willelmus de Beluero prior eiusdem ecclesie deo et beate Marie de Beluero quem qui alienauerit uel fraudem aliquam inde fecerit indignacionem dei incurrat. Anima dicti Willelmi et anime omnium fidelium defunctorum requiescant in pace amen'. Another ex-libris, s. xiv, on f. 145ᵛ. At Eton by 1601.

74. *Jacobus de Voragine, Sermones dominicales*   s. xv med.

1. Humane vite labilis decursus salubri erudicione nos monet . . . (f. 182) qui est principium et finis. Qui sine fine . . . Amen. Explicit liber Ianuensis. Incipit Tabula eiusdem. (f. 182ᵛ) Abstinencie sex sunt species 42 a 2 . . . (f. 190) Zorastes fuit interfectus a vino 83 b. Explicit tabula super sermones dominicales Ianuensis. Summa sermonum istius libri. 159. Amen.

Sermons, three for each Sunday, from Advent to the twenty-fifth Sunday after Pentecost. Printed early and often. Schneyer, p. 324. The table on ff. 182ᵛ–190 refers to sermon numbers and the subdivision of sermons by letters and numbers placed in the margins.[1] The stories in the sermons are listed at 'Narracio' under seventy-three heads.

In sermon 7 (f. 6ᵛ) an interpolated passage, shown here by italics, comes presumably from the margin of the exemplar: 'Hylarius autem et Cris' aliter dicunt. *similiter Notyngam . . . et Rabanus dicunt vt dicit Repingdon* et verius vt videtur quod Iohannes non dubitauit'. This misled a reader, s. xv, who observes in the margin: 'Hic nota quod Notyngam et repyngdon erant ante Ianuensis'. 'Nota contra fratres pred[icatores]', f. 61, margin. f. 190ᵛ was left blank.

[1] In lettered subdivisions numbers are often employed doubly, the leading number being placed in a circle or underlined for distinction: thus, at 87d, ① ② 1 2 3 ③ 1 2 3 and at 95b, 1̲ 1 2 3 2̲ 1 2 3 4 5.

2. Additions on the blank page at the end and on the flyleaves, s. xv: (*a*) f. iii, extracts from De animalibus, De celo et mundo, etc., beginning '[C]um omnis desiderii compos creatura racionabiliter appetat suam perfeccionem' and headed 'secundum Aristotelem et alios philosophos in libro et tractatibus de naturis rerum precipue aristotelis'; (*b*) f. iii^v 'Nota secundum sentenciam doctorum . . .', on the twelve 'effectus' of the eukarist, according to G. de Baysio on the Decretum, De consecratione, distinctio 2; (*c*) f. iii^v, from 'Paris' in opere 40^li *sermo* 53' on Sapientia dei; (*d*) f. 190^v, from 'Ianuensis in opere 40^li dominica 4^a *sermo* 54. Inuenit ihesus in templo vendentes . . . vt serui'; (*e*) ff. 191–2, a list of the pericopes of the sermons in art. 1. A reader's note on f. iii^v, in the margin of *c*, begins 'I loue better terrestria quam celestia . . .'.

ff. iii+190+iv. ff. iii, 191–2 are medieval parchment flyleaves. 260 × 182 mm. Written space *c*. 192 × 130 mm (but less at first). 2 cols. 32–45 lines. Frame ruling. Collation: 1–3^12 4–7^8 8–18^10 19^8, but quires 4–7 have a ninth leaf placed in each of them after leaf 2 (ff. 39, 48, 57, 66). Quires lettered from *a* in the usual late medieval manner. ff. 1–7 in a neat hand in which secretary predominates: after this a mixture of current anglicana and secretary, mainly by one hand. Initials: (i) f. 1, blue patterned in red; f. 182^v, red patterned in white; (ii) 3-line, blue (ff. 1–7 only), and 2-line, red. Plain calf binding, s. xviii: previously in a Williamson binding: see p. 629. Secundo folio *animam suam*.

Written in England. 'Pertinet ad M' Walterum Smyth', ff. 1, 192, s. xvi; probably therefore the gift of Walter Smyth, † 1524 (Emden, *BRUO*, p. 1720), but not either of the books referred to in his will. At Eton by 1608–9.

76, ff. 1–40, +82. *Jeronimus in Danielem; W. de Monte*

s. XII med.–XIII in.

1. 76, ff. 1–39^v Incipit prefatio beati Ieronimi presbiteri super danielem prophetam. Contra epistolam (prophetam *interlined*) danielem duodecimum librum . . . quod ei respondere debeas. Explicit liber sancti hieronimi presbiteri super danielem prophetam.

PL xxv. 491–584. 'Ieronimi (?) percurri librum transiui historiam Anno gracie 1497 7 die septembris', f. 39^v, in the hand of Robert Elyot, who wrote also some marginalia: see p. 631.

2. 76, ff. 39^v–40^v Vnus deus. Vnus dominus . . . De duodecim prerogatiuis Beate Marie. Expliciunt capitula.

The table of chapters of art. 3. Printed from B.L., Harley 325 by B. Smalley and G. Lacombe, *The New Scholasticism*, v (1931), 148–50.

3. 82, ff. 1–64 Incipit liber numeralis Magistri Willelmi de Monte. Audi israel. Deus tuus deus unus est. Ysaias . . . copiosius sunt (ex)arata. Explicit Numerale.

Smalley and Lacombe, loc. cit. 147, list this and eleven other manuscripts. Many additions of s. xiii in the margins. One of two longer pieces is on a scrap of parchment tied to f. 40^v of MS. 76, 'Vnus est deus et hoc natura docet . . . comprehendi potest' (cf. the incipit of Merton College, MS. 257, art. 2) and the other is on a slip nearly as big as a page inserted after f. 13 of MS. 82. Verses in the margins are: f. 14, s. xiii, 'Turpe referre pedem

. . .' (2 lines: Walther, *Sprichwörter*, no. 31945); f. 14, s. xiii, 'Cautius euitat pugnam gladiator et idem . . .' (4 lines); f. 57, s. xv ex., in the hand noticed above, art. 1, 2 lines on the plagues of Egypt, 'Sanguis Rana culex . . .' (Walther, *S.*, no. 27492c).

4. 82, ff. 64ᵛ–65ᵛ Amor quasi Viscus . . . Xristus trahit omnia. De domin(i)o. Expliciunt capitula libri Similitudinarii Magistri Willelmi de Monte secundum Alphabetum.

A list of the pieces in art. 5.

5. 82, ff. 66–88 Incipit liber similitudinarii Magistri Willelmi de monte. Amor terrenus inuiscat animam . . .

The last piece in the alphabetical series is 'Xristus trahit omnia. Omnia ad me traham . . . populi multi'. It is followed by a piece 'De dominio. Apostoli in uia . . . nudus egreditur. Explicit'. Cf. Balliol College, Oxford, 222.

Many additions in the margins, as in art. 3, among them one from 'Virgilius in Copa', f. 75ᵛ, and one beginning in French 'Ki bon morsel met a sa buche: enueiot a sun quor', f. 71ᵛ; also references 'Supra' and 'Infra' to leaves or letters of the alphabetical series of art. 5 and to art. 6. Longer additions are on slips added after ff. 75, 81, 84, 87 and on a leaf which has been included in the foliation as '80'. Verses in the margins of f. 74, s. xiii, are 'Vltra sauromatas fugiam scrutabor ubique Expers inuidie si locus ullus erit' and 'Ve michi nascenti ve nato . . .' (2 lines: Walther, *S.*, no. 32825).

6. The principal annotator of arts. 3, 5 filled the space remaining blank at the end of quire 15, ff. 88ᵛ–90ᵛ with twenty-three paragraphs headed (i) De Raptoribus et diabolo, (ii) De morum honestate, (iii) De penitentiam agente, (iv) De parentibus honorandis (from Solinus), (v) De Tinea, (vi) De Inuidia, (vii) De lilio, (viii) Peccatores, (ix) Negotiator, (x) Passiones, (xi, xii) Vsurarius, (xiii) Cupiditas, (xiv) Prudencia, (xv) *no heading*, (xvi) Cupidus prelatus, (xvii) Cupiditas, (xviii) De prelatis cupidis, (xix) Omnia communia esse debent, (xx) Vsurarius, (xxi) De diuitibus quod sint miseri, (xxii) Commercium cristi, (xxiii) Spes videndi deum.

(i) begins 'Aiunt scriptores historiarum tam bestiarum quam volucrum . . . quorum Principes sunt apud Grecos Aristotiles et Teofrastus apud Latinos Plinius secundus hanc perdicis esse naturam'. (viii) begins 'Qui facit actus porcinos porcus est'. (xv) is the story of the philosopher who spat in the emperor's beard, (xvi) of the mouse crossing a ford, (xviii) of the fool and his cheese. There are references back to art. 5. Verses, 'Sis mundus. verus . . .' (3 lines: Walther, *S.*, no. 29747), were added in the margin of f. 89ᵛ.

MS. 76: ff. 40 (for further details see MS. 76, ff. 41–132). MS. 82: ff. ii+89+ii, together with five slips (see above, arts. 3, 5), one of them numbered 80. 235 × 160 mm. Written space: of arts. 1, 2, 180 × 110 mm in 33 long lines; of arts. 3–6, *c.* 158 × 83 mm in 36 long lines. Collation: (MS. 76, ff. 1–40) 1–5⁸; (MS. 82) 6–8¹⁰ 9–11⁸ 12¹⁰+1 leaf after 10 (f. 65) 13⁸ 14⁸ (ff. 74–9, 81, 82) 15⁸. Quires 6–11 are numbered at the end, i–vi, and have catchwords. Art. 1 in a good small hand, s. xii. Arts. 2, 4 in one hand, probably a little later than arts. 3, 5, s. xiii in. The additions on slips are in charter hands of s. xiii¹, one of them (after f. 75) current. Initials in art. 1: (i) f. 1, blue and metallic red; (ii) 2-line, metallic red and once (f. 15) blue. Initials in arts. 2–6: 2-line, blue or red, or, once only (f. 89), green, and in art. 3 only, black and red in handsome style. Bindings by Slatter, but MS. 76, ff. 1–40 at least were previously in a Williamson binding: see above, p. 629. Secundo folio (MS. 76, f. 2) *autem extremam*.

Written in England. At Eton before 1500.

76, ff. 41–132. *Berengaudus, In Apocalypsin* s. XIV ex.

1. ff. 41–130ᵛ Hic incipit liber apocalipsis id est reuelacionis ihesu cristi cum sua exposicione secundum barenguidum quam reuelacionem . . . annos. Explicit prefacio expositoris. Hic incipit textus apocalipsis. Apocalipsis ihesu cristi . . . seruis suis et cetera vsque ad Post . . . apertum. Incipit exposicio prime visionis. Beatum iohannem apostolum . . . esse mereamur. Qui cum patre . . . amen.

Stegmüller, no, 1711. *PL* xvii. 765–970 (843–1057), but the preface, one sentence giving dates—St. John died A.D. 102, 'plenus dierum', is not printed in *PL*. Many notas in the margins (f. 110, 'Nota pro archideaconis' against 'Nam ab adulteris presbiteris precium accipiunt . . .'), perhaps by William Wey, since they are in the same hand as those in MS. 42.

2 (added, s. xv). ff. 131–132ᵛ Euangelium in die sancto pasche. vt patet Marci vltimo. Maria magdalene et secundum Mattheum vltimo altera maria . . . patriam ad quam nos perducat qui . . . amen.

A 'Moralis exposicio' on the gospel for Easter Day. 'Nota bene per totum' at the head of f. 131 in red.

ff. 41–132 in a volume of ii + 132 + iv leaves. ff. 133–4 are medieval parchment end-leaves, the flyleaf and pastedown of a former binding. 230 × 160 mm. Written space 175 × 120 mm. 2 cols. 38 lines. Collation: 1–11⁸ 12⁴. Quires signed in the usual late medieval way. The script is an anglicana-influenced textura and (art. 2) current anglicana. Initials: 4-line (f. 41), 3-line, and 2-line, blue with red ornament. Capital letters in the ink of the text filled with red. Bound with ff. 1–40 by Slatter or Williamson: the marks of the strap-and-pin fastening of a former binding show on ff. 133–4. Secundo folio *scripto diriguntur*.

Written in England. 'Ex dono Willelmi Wey. quondam socii istius Collegii Regalis Etone', f. 133ᵛ, and above these words, 'Eton' and 'E.C.' as in MS. 42, q.v.

77. *'Glosule Mathei'* s. XII ex.

1. ff. 1–86 Fecit deus duo luminaria in firmamento celi . . . (f. 86) quasi a'r'ra future mercedis. Expliciunt glosule Mathei.

Stegmüller, no. 6575: attributed to P. Comestor. A solid block of text. Lemmata are underlined, including lemmata of the two prologues, Matheus ex iudea, f. 1ᵛ, and Matheus cum primus, f. 2ᵛ (Stegmüller, nos. 590, 589). Chapter numbers added in the upper margins, s. xv. A few marginalia in a sloping hand, s. xv, which occurs in other books belonging to Nicholas Kempston: see, especially, f. 14ᵛ.

2. ff. iv, v, 87–8. Four leaves used as flyleaves in binding, taken from a copy of the Metaphysics in the 'old' translation, s. xiiiᶦ.

Aristoteles Latinus, no. 280. Written space 175 × 85 mm. 48 closely written long lines. Many side notes in a very small hand. ff. 87, 88 were the first two leaves of the text, '[O]mnes homines natura scire desiderant. Signum autem est sensuum dilectio . . .'. f. iv begins 'Pitagorici autem in numerorum mutacione res esse dicunt. plato autem'. A section begins on f. vᵛ '[D]e veritate consideratio partim quidem difficile est'. The same page ends abruptly at line 22 'a discordia et huiusmodi', so these were abandoned leaves: f. iii, conjoint with f. v, is blank.

ff. v + 86 + v. ff. iii–v, 87–9 are parchment end-leaves taken over from an older binding:

iii, 89 were pastedowns: for iii–v, 87–8 see above art. 2. Parchment of poor quality, with holes and splits. 235 × 172 mm. Written space 190 × 130 mm. 45–6 long lines. Pricks in both margins to guide ruling. Collation: 1–10⁸ 11⁶. Quires numbered at the end in pencil. The 2-line space for an initial on f. 1 was not filled. Binding by Slatter. Secundo folio *quia hec duo*.

Written in England. 'Liber sancte [. . . . .] Glose super matheum', f. 1, at the head: 'Liber sancte marie de [. . . .]', followed probably by an anathema, was read by M. R. James. A pressmark, a large red '14', is on the binding leaf, f. vᵛ. 'Liber magistri Nicholai Kempston' ', f. iiiᵛ. 'Liber quondam Magistri Nicholai Kem'p′ston' qui obiit anno domini 1477. numquam vendendus secundum voluntatem defuncti sed gratis et libere occupandus a sacerdotibus instructis in lege domini ad predicandum verbum dei successiue ab vno sacerdote ad alterum sacerdotem absque omni precio quamdiu durauerit. orate igitur pro anima eius', f. iiiᵛ (cf. MS. 36). *CMA* 60.

78. *Psalterium, etc.*   s. XIII in.

1. ff. 1–2ᵛ March, April, November, December of a calendar in gold (Christmas), blue, red, badly faded green, and black, with added gradings 'III', 'II', 'In cappis', 'In albis', 'xii lc'', 'iii lc''. Leonard (8 Nov.) is 'quasi in albis. xii l''.

Cf. E. Bishop and F. A. Gasquet, *The Bosworth Psalter*, 1908, pp. 69, 171, 177, where the gradings are listed. Odd and untidy. Apparently two very different hands took turns at writing the March and April entries. 'Passio sancti Elfegi archiepiscopi' in blue, 19 Apr. 'Obitus Iohannis Bokyngham' added at 10 Mar., s. xv. Both leaves have pieces cut out of them at the top and in the middle.

2. ff. 3–113 Pss. 1–151, beginning imperfectly 'abiit in consilio impiorum'.

Gallican psalter. Benedictine divisions. Seven of the principal leaves are missing: see below.

3. ff. 113–23 Six ferial canticles, Te deum, Benedicite, Benedictus, Magnificat, Nunc dimittis, Quicumque uult.

4. ff. 123–7 Litany.

Very like the litany of B.L., Arundel 155. Twenty-nine martyrs: . . . (2) Thoma (*erased*) . . . (10) *erased* (11–17) Ælphege Salui Blasi Pancrati Albane Oswalde . . . Thirty-two confessors. . . . (10–20) Augustine cum sociis tuis Odo Dunstane Audoene Nicholae Uulgani Remigi Cuthberte Suithune Fursee Uulfride . . . Twenty-seven virgins: . . . (10) Baþtildis . . . (20, 21) Aeldrida Mildrida . . . (27) Osyþa. 'II' in a later hand against Thomas, Aelphege, Dunstan, Benedict, and All Saints. Two martyrs, Erasmus (in the erasure) and Yreneus, seven confessors, Edmund, 'Vlstan' (Wulfstan), Richard, Hugh, Bertin, Julian, and Ethelbert, and two virgins, Anne and Edburga, added in s. xv.

5. ff. 128–153ᵛ Hymns.

Mearns, *Hymnaries*, lists the twelfth-century Christ Church, Canterbury, collection in Arundel 155 (E 1). Eton 78 differs from it only by the absence of Iste confessor and hymns for the dedication and by the presence at the end of two hymns for St. Mary Magdalene, Lauda mater ecclesia, and Eterni patris unice, which are among later additions in Ar.: cf. H. Gneuss, *Hymnar und Hymnen im englischen Mittelalter*, 1968, p. 100. As in Ar. there are three hymns for Benedict, Festa presentis, Panditur mundus, Magno canentes, three for Dunstan, f. 139ʳᵛ, printed by Gneuss, pp. 241–3 (this copy collated as Et), and three for Mary Magdalene, Festum colentes, Letus hoc festum, Largitas cristi (cf. Gneuss, p. 245).

6. ff. 153ᵛ–161ᵛ Incipiunt cantica in festis duodecim lectionum canenda.

Twenty-four monastic canticles, nos. (1, 3, 5, 8, 9) of the sets listed—but not numbered—

by Mearns, *Canticles*, for respectively Sundays, Advent, Christmas, Lent, Easter, his sets 9 and 1 for the common of saints and his second set for the common of virgins, ending imperfectly in Non vocaberis at the words 'amplius desolata' (Mearns, pp. 87–92).

ff. iv+161+iv. 262×200 mm. Written space 190×125 mm. 22 long lines. Pricks in both margins to guide ruling. The first line of writing above the top ruled line. Collation: 1 two (ff. 1, 2) 2⁸ wants 2 after f. 3+1 leaf now missing before 1 3⁸ 4⁸ wants 2 after f. 19 5⁸ wants 6 after f. 31 6⁸ wants 8 after f. 38 7⁸ 8⁸ wants 3 after f. 48 9–10⁸ 11⁶+1 leaf after 3 (f. 73) 12⁸ 13⁸ wants 4 after f. 87 14–17⁸ 18⁴ (ff. 124–7) 19–22⁸ 23 two (ff. 160–1). The hand changes for the better at f. 152. Initials: (i) *B* of *Beatus* and the words 'uir qui non' were or were intended to be on a singleton leaf before f. 3; (ii) of Pss. 80, 97 and beginning art. 5, red on ground of gold and patterned blue or blue on ground of gold and patterned red, with spiral decoration: the initials of Pss. 26, 38, 52, 101, 109, probably of this type, are on now missing leaves; (iii) of all other psalms, including Ps. 51, 3-line, red or blue, at first with ornamental frills in both colours and green on a brown ground, but from f. 85 with simpler ornament of the other colour, the ground not coloured; (iv) of verses, 1-line, blue or red (not after f. 84ᵛ). Plain calf binding, s. xviii. Secundo folio (f. 3) *abiit.*

Written in England, for use in the Benedictine cathedral priory of Christ Church, Canterbury: cf. arts. 1, 4, 5.[1] 'Dedit Collegio B.M. de Etona Tho: Horne Soc. 1713', f. 1. Earlier, Horne lent his manuscript to Samuel Woodford (1636–1700) for his collation of psalters completed in 1688: Woodford's manuscript is now at St. Deiniol's Library, Hawarden.

79. *P. de Palma, Moralitates super Proverbia Salomonis*

s. xiv/xv–xvi[1]

1. ff. 1–86 'Moralitates super prouerbia salomonis'. Iungat epistola. Prologus Ieronimi super libros salomonis quem scripsit . . . sine fatigacione laudabitur. Ad quem finem nos perducat cristus deus noster amen.

'Postilla fratris petri de palma' (Pierre de Baume, O.P., †1345), f. 1, s. xv ex. The author names himself in the text on f. 26, 'Ego frater Petrus de Palma'. For him see *Histoire littéraire de la France*, xxxvi. 180–90, and B. Smalley, *English Friars and Antiquity*, 1960, pp. 249–51: she used this copy (cf. p. 395), the only one listed by Stegmüller, no. 6735. 'Mor' 1ᵃ super prouer' ' is written across each double opening. f. 86ᵛ blank.

2 (added). ff. 87–122 Canon ad vsum huius repertorii in Petrum palmensem . . . (f. 122) Exerpsit Guilielmus Hormanus. Scripsit Darellus.

On this table to art. 1 and its scribe see N. R. Ker in *The Library*, 5th series, xvii (1962), 83. References are by leaf number and line number and between them either 'a' for the verso, or 'b' for the recto facing it. f. 122ᵛ blank.

3 (added on flyleaves, s. xv/xvi). (*a*) f. iv A table of the 'Capitulorum loca in parabolis Solomonis', with leaf numbers. (*b*) f. vʳᵛ Ex Rodulpho Flauiacensi in leuiticum. Paucis est concessa . . . martirum comprobatur. (*c*) ff. vᵛ–viᵛ Beda quomodo in manibus computari debet. Centesimus sexagesimus . . . Cui scripsit deo viuat.

(*b*). From the preface: cf. MS. 15, f. 1ʳᵛ.

ff. vi+122+ii. ff. iii–vi are the pastedown and flyleaves from the medieval binding. Art. 1

[1] But Bishop considered that the calendar was of St. Augustine's, adapted later for use at Christ Church.

has a medieval foliation in the top right corner of each recto. After the book had been cropped by a binder this foliation was repeated, lower down, in a hand probably of s. xvi in. 210 × 140 mm. Written space 160 × 102 mm. Art. 1 in 46 long lines, numbered by fives in red in the outer margin. Collation: 1–7¹² 8² (ff. 85, 86) 9–10¹⁰ 11–12⁸. The script of art. 1 is essentially textura, but with linked minims and minims linked to a following letter, for example *i* to *l*. Initials 2-line, blue with red ornament or red with dark-blue ornament. Binding by Slatter. The chainmark from an older binding shows on f. iii. Secundo folio *tria milia*.

Art. 1 written probably in France. Art. 2 added for William Horman, s. xvi¹. 'Donum Guilielmi Hormani quondam socii huius contubernii', f. iii^v and in a different hand, f. iv^v.

80. *Jeronimus, Contra Jovinianum; etc.* s. XII in.

1. ff. 1–132^v Incipit liber beati ieronimi presbiteri contra iouinianum hereticum. Pauci admodum dies sunt. quod sancti . . . luxuriam susceperunt. Explicit liber secundus beati ieronimi presbiteri contra iouinianum hereticum.

PL xxiii. 211–338 (221–352). Bk. 2, f. 76^v.

2. Space fillers in the main hand in the last quire: (*a*) ff. 132^v–133 Tres sorores fuerunt . . . natus est xpistus; (*b*) f. 133^v De notis litterarum. Notas litterarum inter se ueteres faciebant . . .; (*c*) f. 134^rv (*begins imperfectly ?*) Iohannes autem cum audisset in uinculis opera xpisti . . . scandalizatus in me; (*d*) ff. 134^v–135^v Luna. Mercurius. Venus. Sol. Mars. Iouis. Saturnus. Spera cęlestis ex diapente diatessaronque . . . parte una epiophda. Gloria seculorum amen. Sex sumus qui ludimus qui solem nunquam uidimus . . . Simphoniis pariterque tonis. diascismate bino. Diapente et diatessaron . . . consonam reddunt. Omnis cantus regularis secundum boetium . . . pulchreque distinguitur.

(*a*). A commonplace on the three Marys: cf. Vatican, Reg. lat. 340, f. 140^v. (*b*). On cyphers, with *b* for *a* (etc.), or with points, one to five in number, or the next consonant standing for the vowels, *a, e, i, o, u*. (*c*). A noted office of St. John Baptist, consisting of Matthew 11: 2–4, Mark 7: 17–29, and Matthew 11: 5, 6. (*d*). On chanting and tones, noted, except 'Omnis cantus . . . distinguitur', and other brief explanatory notes on tones. ff. 136^v–138^v were left blank.

3 (added, s. xii²). (*a*) ff. 136^v–137^v Aue uirginum gemma Katerina salue sponsa regis . . . sponsoque tuo satiata. Gloria patri et filio et spiritui sancto. (*b*) f. 137^v Eterne uirgo memorie. Quam sibi despondit rex glorie . . . Atque nostra clementer suscipe 'vota'.

(*a*) RH no. 23938, and (*b*) are spaced for music, but only a few notes were entered.

ff. v + 138 + ii. f. v, a medieval leaf, was the pastedown in a former binding. 228 × 145 mm. Written space 162 × 90 mm. 23 long lines. Ruling with a hard point. Collation: 1–16⁸ 17¹⁴ wants 6 after f. 133, and 11, 12 (these two probably blank): 13, 14 are pasted together (f. 138) and were the pastedown in a former binding. Quires 7–17 lettered at the end, g–r. Initials: (i) red (f. 1), or green (f. 76^v), with ornament of the other colour; (ii) 2-line or 1-line, red or green. Capital letters in the ink of the text are filled with red and green on f. 1^r only. Binding by Williamson. The chainmark from an earlier binding shows on f. v and the marks of a central strap-and-pin fastening on ff. v, 138. Secundo folio *uano*.

Arts. 1, 2 are in the same hand as the Textus Roffensis and other Rochester manuscripts: cf. N. R. Ker, *English Manuscripts in the Century after the Norman Conquest*, 1960, p. 31.

An erased inscription at the foot of f. 1 is illegible: a reagent has been used on it. According to M. R. James in an interleaved copy of his *Catalogue* there was a Rochester Cathedral priory ex-libris here and 'per H precentorem'. Entered in both the medieval Rochester catalogues: cf. Ker, *MLGB*, p. 161. 'Liber Willelmi Barett', s. xv/xvi, f. 138: he wrote ∴ IHC ∴. above his name. 'Donum Guilielmi Hormani quondam huius contubernii socii', f. v^v.

81. *Gregorius, Liber Pastoralis; etc.* s. XII med.

1. ff. 1–28 Incipit prologus. Opus subditum propter quosdam . . . non despiciat. Incipiunt capitula . . . (*tables of chapters of 2 books, 24 and 20*) . . . Incipit cur deus homo liber anse'l'mi archiepiscopi cantuariensis. Sepe et studiosissime . . . attribuere debemus. Qui est benedictus in secula s(e)c(ul)orum.

SAO ii. 42–133. Bk. 2, f. 16^v The text on f. 10^v is spaced to admit a long scholium on *natura* (edn. 72/2), 'Natura generale nomen est . . . quia terra est'. 'Legi hunc libellum 'totum' anselmi primum et 2^m vocatum cur deus homo primo die decembris anno gracie 1485. deo gracias', f. 27^v, in the hand of Robert Elyot: see p. 631.

2. (*a*) ff. 28–30^v Ibo michi ad montem myrrę et ad colles libani. Et loquar sponsę meę. Sponsus quidam hic loquitur qui sponsam habet.' et . . . tanto magis in unum congregamur. Amen. (*b*) ff. 30^v–31^v Dum medium silentium tenerent omnia. Tria sunt silentia. Primum silentium est ignorantia languoris . . . preparatum est ab initio seculi. Amen. Amen. Amen. (*c*) f. 32^rv Cor etenim nostrum simile est molendino. semper molenti . . . Unde et in fine panę uitę ęternę carebunt. ue illis.

(*b*). *PL* xcv. 1177–9: cf. *Lyell Cat.*, p. 333. (*c*). *Similitudines Anselmi*, nos. 41, 42: *PL* clix. 621–2.

3 (another hand). ff. 33–36^v [T]rina uirtus suffragetur. ut sincere predicetur. trinitatis gloria . . . rem ut est intueamur. nos def' in [. . .].

Fourteen 6-line or 8-line stanzas, rhyming aabccb or aaabcccb. Widely spaced in continuous writing, ten lines to the page.

4. ff. 37–94 Liber regule pastoralis Gregorii pape. Scriptus ad iohannem episcopum. Gregorius seruus seruorum dei. Quia melius fuerat bona non incipere . . . dilectissimi filii . . . (*table of 65 chapters*) . . . (f. 38^v) Prologus in libro pastorum. Gregorius urbis romę episcopus . . . id est uigilate. Incipit liber pastoralis cure editus a sancto gregorio papa urbis rome. (f. 39) P(astoralis cure pondere)^1 fugere . . . manus leuet.

No division into books. Only the first forty-eight chapters are numbered. The editions, *PL* lxxvii. 13–128, etc., do not include the preliminaries here. According to the 'prologus' on f. 38^v (also in St. John's College, Oxford, MS. 28, f. 6^v, s. x) Gregory began the Pastoral Care 'in gallia longounensis'^2 and finished it 'in gallia belgica . . . in ciuitate que dicitur brigalis': the scribe left a gap of a dozen letters between 'quia' and 'imperatoris', where the St. John's copy has a gap of 12 mm.

'Post hunc librum Minores collationes', f. 94, s. xiii. f. 94^v blank.

---

¹ Probably the intention was to have an initial *P* and alongside it these twenty-two absent letters in fancy script. The decorator, however, used the whole space for the *P*.
² *lugdunensis* altered to *lugdunensi*, St. John's.

ff. iii+94+iii. 210×140 mm. 165×100 mm. 37 long lines. Collation: 1–3⁸ 4⁶ (ff. 31–6) 5–12⁸ 13 two. Fairly well written. The 'semi-colon' is used as a mark of punctuation at the end of a sentence. Initials: (i) f. 1, gold on a ground of brown and blue, the blue decorated in colours: f. 37, gold on a ground of blue decorated in white: f. 39, a handsome *P* in blue and red on a ground of light brown and gold, the gold decorated with an interlace of branches; (ii–iv) 4–line, 2-line or 3-line, and 1-line, red, blue, green, or brown. Binding by Slatter. Secundo folio *et magnitudini*.

Written in England. At Eton by 1500.

82. See above, MS. 76

83. (*A*) *Paschasius Radbertus; etc.* (*B*) *P. Cantor*   s. XII in.–XIII in.

1. (*a*) ff. 1ᵛ–2 Incipiunt capitula libri paschasii de corpore et sanguine domini. i. Cristi communionem uerum corpus . . . xxii Quod immolatio agni paschalis ad corpus domini pertineat. Item alia capitula extra librum. i. Quid digne uel indigne sumentibus . . . xxi. Epistola sancti augustini ad consentium de corpore domini post resurrectionem. (*b*) ff. 2ᵛ–43ᵛ Incipit liber paschasii de corpore et sanguine domini. (f. 3) Dilectissimo filio. et uice cristi presidenti magistro monasticę disciplinę alternis successibus ueritatis condiscipulo. P. paschasius episcopus. Noui igitur nec ambigo . . . (f. 4) monui deuotus. amen. i. Quisquis catholicorum . . . quantotius uenire ualeamus. amen. (*c*) Twenty-three chapters, numbered i–xxii, xxi, beginning: (i) f. 43ᵛ Postquam typicum pascha fuerat impletum; (ii) f. 44 Omnia uobis diuinorum eloquiorum; (iii) f. 47 Instruens beatus apostolus corinthios de dominici corporis et sanguinis sacramento; (iv) f. 48ᵛ Cum itaque ipse filius dei dicat caro mea; (v) f. 49ᵛ In cęlebratione autem tanti mysterii; (vi) f. 50ᵛ Confessionem autem dare; (vii) f. 51 Hęc namque dominici corporis et sanguinis gratia; (viii) f. 52 Non inconuenienter edere arbitror; (ix) f. 54 Matrona quędam beato gregorio per stationes publicas; (x) f. 56 Quidam nobilissimus uir secundum carnis prosapiam; (xi) f. 57 Miror autem satis unde hoc usurpatum sit; (xii) f. 58 Diximus in superioribus de sacramento satis dominici; (xiii) f. 61 Paschę autem huiusmodi obseruantiam; (xiv) f. 62 Postquam in superioribus de sacramento dominici corporis et sanguinis plura iam diximus . . . in occulto; (xv) f. 64 Eclesia beatę uualburgę in qua miracula plurima fieri solebant; (xvi) f. 64ᵛ In ea uia quę aruennensis monasterii ducit ad forum.' est ecclesia sancti petri que dicitur ad salas in cuius uicinia manebat quidam latro; (xvii) f. 65 Qui ita helemosinam tribuit uel aliquid opus bonum agit; (xviii) f. 66 Quidam namque presbiter in pago abrincatino de continentia; (xix) f. 67ᵛ Legimus in ystoria gentis anglorum quod quidam episcopus duos fratres palatinos; (xx) f. 67ᵛ Theodosius quondam famosus imperator quedam uice a quodam monacho; (xxi) f. 68ᵛ Quidam uassus nomine racherius ad quoddam monasterium; (xxii) f. 69 Quidam rex longobardorum sicut in eiusdem gentis ystoria legitur. in cimiterio cuiusdam ęcclesię sancti iohannis sepeliri se fecit hereticus tamen perseuerauit; (xxiii) ff. 69ᵛ–75 Augustinus de corpore domini. Dilectissimo fratri consentio augustinus. Quantum ad oculos . . . dilectissime fili. Explicit.

(*a*). Table of (*b*) and (*c*). ff. 1ʳ, 2ᵛ left blank. (*b*). *PL* cxx. 1263–1345. This copy listed in edition of B. Paulus, *CC, Cont. Med.* xvi (1969), xxviii. (*c*) has a reference at (xii), f. 58, to ch. xxii of (*b*): De quo nimirum iam aliquid in superioribus in xx° ii° capitulo breuiter diximus. (xv–xxii) are miracles, some with little or no bearing on the eucharist. (xxiii) is *PL* xxxiii. 942–9 (Ep. 205).

The copy of *a+b+c* in MS. Bodley 859 (*Sum. Cat.* 2722), ff. 227–259ᵛ, is probably derived directly or indirectly from Eton 83, with the substitution of St. Milburga for St. Walburga in *c*(xv).

2. ff. 75–83 Sixty-three brief extracts from canons of councils, 'canones aposto-lorum', 'sinodus ybernensis', Augustine, Jerome, and decrees of early popes, Anacletus, Clement, Gregory, Innocent, John, Julius, Leo, Nicholas, Symma-chus, Stephen.

The first piece is a decree of Anacletus on the primacy of the Roman church, 'De prima-tibus super quibus me quidam uestrum consuluerunt . . .'. The last four are: 'Ex concilio cabillionensi. Si quis precantauerit . . .'; 'Ex eodem. Si aliquis manducat aut bibit . . .'; 'Gregorius. Omnino metuenda et cauenda est antiqui hostis astutia . . .'; 'Ex concilio africano. His qui penitentiam in infirmitate petit . . . dedit probauerit'.

3. ff. 84–197ᵛ Incipiunt distinctiones. per alphabetum disposite. Abel dicitur ecclesie principium propter innocentiam . . . ales summa petendo. Expliciunt distinctiones per alphabetum disposite.

Petrus Cantor, Distinctiones Abel, beginning with Abel and ending with Cristus, which is taken, as usual, under the letter X. Stegmüller, no. 6451, lists thirty-nine manuscripts, not this: cf. also A. Wilmart in *Mémorial Lagrange*, 1940, p. 336. Like many copies, this one ends with the verses on the evangelists, 'Virgo iohannis auis . . .' (Walther, *Initia*, no. 20508). Marginalia in an English hand, s. xiii, on ff. 187ᵛ–188.

4. Added pieces: (*a*) ff. 197ᵛ–198, in the main hand, including (f. 198) a 'Nota quod parisiensis ecclesia hanc habet consuetudinem quod in uigilia natalis domini maiores implent officium puerorum in omnibus horis ad significandum curam ioseph quam habebat in partu uirginis'; (*b*) ff. 198–9, s. xiii, notes on Palma and Tabernaculum; (*c*) f. 197ᵛ, s. xv, a quotation from Holcot on Wisdom which seems to be in the hand of Robert Elyot (see p. 631). f. 199ᵛ is blank.

5. ff. ii, iii, are a folded leaf of the Institutes of Justinian (bk. 3, tit. xii, xiii) in an English hand, s. xiii ex., used in binding.

Tit. xiii ends on the first column of the verso. The rest of the page was left blank.

ff. iii+199+ii. For f. ii, formerly pasted down, and f. iii, see above, art. 5. ff. 1–83 and ff. 84–199 are two originally separate manuscripts, (A) s. xii and (B) s. xiii, bound together in or after s. xiii. The present binding is by Slatter. The mark of a chain attached to an earlier binding shows on f. iii. in the usual position near the foot of the fore-edge.

(A). ff. 1–83. Poor, flecked parchment, with tears and irregularities. 230 × 153 mm. Written space *c.* 195 × 115 mm. 2 cols. 26 lines. Ruling with a hard point. Collation: 1 two 2–10⁸ 11⁸+1 leaf after 8. 3 and 6 in quires 3 and 8 and 2 and 7 in quire 7 are half sheets. Quires 2–10 numbered at the end I–VIIII. Large sloping ugly writing, probably by one hand throughout. The mark of abbreviation for *-ur* is often used to denote omission of *r*. Elaborately shaped 2-line (f. 3, 3-line) initials in unfilled outline in the ink of the text on a red ground. Capital letters in the ink of the text filled with red. Secundo folio *ditur*.

Probably written in Germany. Writing on f. 1ᵛ is in an English hand, s. xv/xvi.

(B). ff. 84–199. 230 × 153 mm. Written space *c.* 170 × 105 mm. 40 long lines. The first line of writing above the top ruled line. Pricks in both margins of quire 1. Collation: 1–7⁸

8^6 9–14^8 15^6. The hand changes at f. 132 (7^1). Blue *A* with red ornament, f. 84: no other coloured initial. Secundo folio *Aduersa*.

Probably written in England. Marginalia to art. 3 and art. 4*c* are in English hands.

(A)+(B) were at Eton by s. xvi, if 'Aeton Colledge' on f. iv^v may be taken to apply to both manuscripts. (A) was among the books found in 'Mr Belfeldes Chambre after his death', in 1558 (Birley, p. 241). Robert Elyot seems to have used (B): see above.

84. *Alanus de Insulis, Distinctiones theologicae* s. xiv^2

1. Incipit liber Magistri Alani qui quot modis intitulatur de diuersis vocabulorum significacionibus secundum ordinem alphabeti. Incipit prologus. Quoniam iuxta aristotilice autoritatis . . . subsidio. Incipit prologus magistri Alani ad Hermengaldum sancti Egidii abbatem. Reuerendissimo patri . . . A. dictus magister. Sic in presenti multiplici . . . (f. 1^v) valeas in eternum. Prologus explicit. Et liber incipit. Incipiunt capitula . . . (*table of words beginning with A*) . . . Quot modis sumitur hoc nomen anima. in sacra scriptura Anima proprie spiritus racionalis . . . id est imiteris.

Distinctiones, Anima–Zelare, each heading beginning 'Quot modis dicitur (*or* ponitur, *or* sumitur)'. Stegmüller, no. 950. PL ccx. 685–1012. Sources are in red in the margins. They are mainly the Bible, with a few classics, for example, f. 2^v under Anima, 'In asclepia mercurii virgilius'. f. 248^v was left blank.

2. The pastedown at the beginning is from the fifth leaf and the pastedown at the end from the second leaf of a calendar in red and black, written in England, s. xiii^1. The exposed sides contain October and March. (See Addenda, p. 999.)

Entries in red include: 1 Mar., 'Sancti dauid archiepiscopi'; 12 Mar., 'Gregorii pape et anglorum apostoli'; 20 Mar., 'Cuthberti et Wlfranni episcoporum'. No gradings.

ff. ii+248+iv. 250 × 180 mm. Written space 180 × 128 mm. 34 long lines. Collation: 1^{12} 2^{10} 3–4^8 5–25^{10}. Quires are marked in the usual later medieval fashion with signatures running a–z, 7, Ɔ. Written in anglicana. Initials: (i) f. 1, 3-line, blue; (ii) 1-line, red or blue. Red and blue scrolling down the margins shows the limits of each head word: it does not go beyond the last page of quire 8, f. 78^v. Contemporary binding of wooden boards covered with pink leather: two clasps and a label formerly attached by nails to the back cover are missing: a chainmark near the foot of the side of the front cover. Secundo folio *Angelus*.

Written in England. A title—illegible to me—and the number 87 in a medieval hand on the back cover. One of the 'Bookes of the Colledge found in Mr Belfeldes Chambre after his death' in 1558 (Birley, p. 241).

87. *Plautus* s. xv med.

f. 1 Plauti pœte comici clarissimi prima comœdia. Amphitrio incipit . . . 'Asinaria' begins on f. 22^v, 'Captiui' on f. 39^v, 'Curculio' on f. 58, 'Cassina' on f. 70^v, 'Cistellaria' on f. 83^v, 'Aepidicus' on f. 90^v and 'Aulularia' on f. 100.

The same eight plays as in B.L., Royal 15 A. xviii and in the same order. Preceded, as there, by the 'Epigramma Plauti. Postquam est morte captus . . .' (3 lines), from Aulus Gellius, Noct. Att. i. 24. ff. 112^v–116^v were left blank. On f. 115^v Bernardo Bembo added 'Segidius in libro quem scripsit de Poetis . . . his versibus suis demonstrat. Multos incertos certare hanc rem vidimus . . .', thirteen lines on the ten comic poets from Noct. Att. xv. 24. They also are in the Royal manuscript.

ff. iv+116+ii. ff. iii, iv are the pastedown and conjugate flyleaf taken over from the medieval binding. 250×175 mm. Written space 160×100 mm. 28–37 long lines. Ruling partly with pencil and partly with hard point. The first line of writing is above the top ruled line. Collation 1–11¹⁰ 12⁶. Unstable humanistic hand: on f. 15 the scribe began to change one odd form of g for another, and from f. 17/5 the new form is always (?) used: rounded instead of upright d and biting of d and a following letter begin to appear about f. 54. Initials outside the written space: (i) gold on red, green, brown, and blue grounds, decorated with twining white branches and white dots in groups of four or more: a man with sword and shield in the S on f. 70ᵛ; (ii) blue or red. The catchwords of quires 7–11 are on elaborate backgrounds of birds, beasts, etc. Binding by Slatter. Secundo folio *Propterea pacem.*

Written in Italy. 'Emptus patauii dum studerem leg. 1456 idibus Ianuariis', f. iv, in Bernardo Bembo's hand. 'Codex [. . .] bernardi bembi' partly erased, f. ivᵛ. Bequeathed by Henry Wotton in 1639, no doubt.[1] *CMA* 106.

88. *Germanicus Caesar, Aratea, cum commentario* s. xv²

Fragmentum Arati cum armento (*sic for* commento) nouiter repertum in sicilia. (*a*) Aratus quidem fuit athinodori patris filius . . . (f. 2) mathematice reperimus. (*b*) Celum circulis quinque distinguitur . . . (f. 3) Antepositis deformia. (*c*, f. 4) Hic est Stellarum ordo utrorunque circulorum . . . (f. 4ᵛ) connexio uero piscium communem habet stellam. (*d*, f. 5) M. T. Ciceronis Traductio Arati cilici poete clarissimi de Signis celestibus incipit foeliciter. Ab ioue principium . . . (f. 24ᵛ) hydraque lucet. (*e*, ff. 4ᵛ–17ᵛ, 19–24, in the margins, except on f. 4ᵛ) Ab ioue . . . Queritur quare a ioue ceperit . . . In tyrso stellas tres. Sunt omnes xxxi. (*f*, f. 24ᵛ, in the margin) Idra super cuius caudam . . . per singula latera. (*g*, f. 25, after twelve blank lines) Ethereum uenit taurus . . . (f. 27ᵛ) non irrita pisces. (*h*, f. 28) Solem per se ipsum constat moueri . . . (f. 29ᵛ) pronus incumbat. (*i*, f. 30) Luna terris uicinior . . . (f. 32ᵛ) certissimus auctor. (*j*, f. 33) A Bruma in fauonium . . . (f. 36) dicimus fieri. (*k*) Ante omnia autem duo esse nomina . . . (f. 39) noxias tempestates. (*l*) Vertices extremos circa quos spera uoluitur polos . . . (f. 39ᵛ) Sunt omnes xx. (*m*, f. 40) [P]rimum a Sole capiemus presagia purus oriens manu sinistra . . . (f. 48ᵛ) impleat lumine. Si quis. (*eleven lines left blank*) Plura deficiunt: que propter uetustatem: et quinternionum fractionem colligi nequaquam potuerunt.

(*d*, *g*) are lines 1–430 and Fragm. IV, lines 52–163 of the Aratea of Germanicus, ed. A. Breysig, 1867 (2nd edn., 1899) and Bährens, *Poetae Latini Minores*, i. 148–72, 193–9. (*a–m*) are in the same order in the Vatican, Madrid, Berlin, and Palermo manuscripts called V, Vᶜ, Vᵈ, and F by the editors and in B.L., Add. 15819: for V see Breysig (edn. 1), p. xxi, and for F see R. Sabbadini, 'Sallustius, Ovidius . . .', *Museo Italiano di Antichità Classica*, iii (1888), 87–95. Breysig (edn. 1) prints (*b*, *c*), (*e*), (*h–l*) and the first seven words of (*m*) as follows: (*b*) pp. 105–107/13; (*c*) pp. 107/14–109/10; (*e*) pp. 109/12–179/13; (*h*) pp. 193/5–196/8; (*i*) pp. 197–202; (*j*) pp. 203–9; (*k*) pp. 210–15; (*l*) p. 112, footnote; (*m*, first seven words) p. 215; these scholia are largely from Isidore and Pliny. For (*f*) cf.

[1] For the Wotton bequest see Birley, p. 249, and for a fuller account his *History of Eton College Library*, pp. 26, 27, 72, 73. None of the manuscripts bear Wotton's name or *ex dono*.

Breysig, p. xxi. (*m*), from the eighth word is an excerpt from Hyginus, Astronomica, IV, beginning near the end of ch. 6 and ending in the middle of ch. 14 (ed. Bunte, 1875, pp. 105/3–116/19).

(*a*) has gaps in it and the scribe wrote in the margins 'In ueteri exemplari erant delete pene littere' (f. 1ᵛ) and 'Hic idem in ueteri exemplari erat defectus: qui et supra' (f. 2). Against the space in front of (*g*) he wrote 'Tantum deerat in exemplari'. On ff. 7–24ᵛ there are blank spaces for pictures and captions in the margins, for example (f. 11) 'hic ponitur herictonius cum curru'. ff. 3ᵛ, 49–52ᵛ blank.

ff. iv+52+ii. Paper. ff. ii–iv are blank leaves of the same paper as ff. 1–52. 235 × 165 mm. Written space 120 × 70 mm. 22 long lines. Ruling with a hard point on versos in the first half of each quire and on rectos in the second half. Collation: 1⁴ 2–5¹⁰ 6⁸. Written in sloping humanistica: a change of scribe at f. 40. Intitials: (i) f. 5, 3-line gold *A* on a green and red ground; (ii) 2-line, dark blue. Binding by Slatter. Secundo folio *mathicis*.

Written in Italy. 'nᵒ 22', f. iii. *CMA* 120.

89. *Seneca*   s. XIII[1]

A collection of pieces by or attributed to Seneca. At the time of M. R. James's *Catalogue* the present arts. 1 and 3 came between arts. 5 and 6. On rebinding, *c.* 1900, art. 3 was put in the place indicated by the old quire numbers and art. 1 at the beginning, a position suggested by 1*a*. The many nearly contemporary scholia in red ink and pencil in the margins of arts. 2–5, 7 include a pencilled Germanic gloss on f. 21, 'non exorant id est verbidden'.

1. (*a*) f. 1 Ieronimus in libro de viris illustribus sic scribit de seneca. Lucius anneus . . . interfectus est. (*b*) ff. 1–2ᵛ Fourteen letters between Seneca and St. Paul. (*c*) f. 2ᵛ Epytaphium quod fecit seneca de se ipso cum moreretur. Cura labor meritum . . . ossa tibi (6 lines).

(*a*)–(*c*). Cf. MS. 135. (*a*). PL xxxiii. 629. (*b*). In the same order as edn. Haase (Teubner series), iii. 476–81. (*c*). *Anthologia Latina*, ed. Riese, no. 667.

2. ff. 3–39ᵛ (*begins imperfectly*) cias amamur . . . perdere et dare. Expliciunt libri septem lucii. annei. Senece. de beneficiis ad eburtium liberalem amicum suum.

The first words are in bk. 4, ch. 5.

3. (*a*) ff. 40–1 Incipiunt capitula epistolarum senece ad lucilium. Vt omne . . . disputat habundanter. (*b*) ff. 42–143ᵛ Incipiunt epistole senece ad lucilium. . . . Ita fac mi lucili . . . ad hunc peruenire. mansueta sunt. Vale.

(*a*). Eighty-nine numbered chapters. The division into twelve books is by a much later hand. f. 41ᵛ blank. (*b*). Eighty-nine numbered letters with Epist. 85 of the editions in last place: cf. L. D. Reynolds, *The Medieval Tradition of Seneca's Letters*, 1965, p. 74. The total number is eighty-nine and not eighty-eight, because Epist. 48 is counted as two letters, 48 and 49, the latter beginning at *Mus sillaba est*. Scholia in red explain the subject of each letter.

4. ff. 144–163ᵛ Incipit liber senece de naturalibus questionibus 'vel causis rerum ad lucilium'. Grandines hoc modo fieri . . . (f. 152ᵛ) et leui manu querimus. (f. 153) 'Incipit iiᵃ particula huius operis'. Epistola. Quantum inter philosophiam . . . (f. 159ᵛ) nisi qui effug'. Sen' lucil'. salutem. Epistola. Non preterit

me lucili . . . uitia discutuntur. Explicit seneca de naturalibus questionibus 'vel causis rerum huius mundi. ad lucilium'.

Used for Gercke's edition (Teubner, 1907: cf. pp. xxvi, xxxiv). Said to be closely related to Montpellier, H. 116. The first of the three 'particule' here corresponds to bks. 4B–7, the second to bks. 1, 2, and the third to bk. 3. 4A, De Nilo, is absent.

5. ff. 164–175ᵛ Lucii. annei. Sen'. ad neronem imperatorem. discipulum suum. De clemencia liber iᵘˢ incipit. Scribere de clementia . . . praua flectantur. Explicit liber iiᵘˢ sen'. de clementia. ad neronem.

6. ff. 176–178ᵛ Incipit liber senece De copia uerborum. siue de quatuor uirtutibus. qui dicitur formula uiuendi. 'ad paulum'. Quatuor uirtutum species . . . puniat ignauiam.

Ed. Haase, iii. 468–75; PL lxxii. 23–8 (Martin of Braga).

7. ff. 179–81 Incipit liber Senece de remediis fortuitorum malorum ad callionem. Licet cunctorum poetarum . . . ista felicitas. Amen.

Ed. Haase, iii. 446–57. f. 181ᵛ blank.

8. ff. 182–7 'Excerpta de epistolis Senece'. Primum argumentum composite mentis existimo . . . que per negligentiam fit.

The added title is in an English hand, s. xv. f. 187ᵛ blank. Ten paragraphs, also in Exeter Cathedral 3549 B, art. 12b: (2) Ita uiue.' ut nichil . . .; (3) Sic utrosque reprehendas . . .; (4) Cum rerum natura delibera . . .; (5) Ait quidam philosophus . . .; (6) Inimica est multorum conuersatio . . .; (7) Sapientie seruias oportet . . .; (8) Inmodica ira . . .; (9) Satis multum temporis . . .; (10) Initium est salutis noticia peccati . . . Cf. C. J. Herington, 'A thirteenth-century manuscript of the Octavia praetexta in Exeter', Rheinisches Museum für Philologie, n.f., ci (1958), 376, f. 187ᵛ blank.

ff. i+187+i. 252×170 mm. Written space c. 170×108 mm. 2 cols. 37 lines. Writing above top ruled line. Collation: 1 two (ff. 1, 2) 2–3¹² 4¹²+1 leaf after 12 (ff. 27–39) 5² (ff. 40–1) 6–12¹² 13¹⁸ (ff.126–43) 14⁸ 15–16¹² 17²+1 leaf after 2 (f. 178) 18²+1 leaf after 2 (f. 181) 19⁶. Quires 2–18 numbered at the end V–XXI. Initials: (i) ff. 21, 176, red and blue with ornament of both colours; (ii) 4-line, red or blue with ornament of the other colour; (iii) in arts. 1, 6–8, as (ii), but smaller and outside the written space; (iv) 1-line, red or blue. Capital letters in the ink of the text filled with red. Running titles in red and blue. Binding of s. xix/xx.

Probably a German manuscript (see above) in England by s. xv, when some marginalia were added, among them the '·:·IH̄C·:·mᵃ·:·' characteristic of Thomas Gascoigne (f. 2ᵛ). CMA 114.

90. Cicero, etc. s. XII/XIII

1. (a) ff. 1–4ᵛ Animaduerti brute sepe catonem . . . [existiman]di [sunt]. (b) ff. 5–12 Quintus Mutius Augur Sceuola . . . prestabilius putetis. Explicit [. . . .] amicicia. (c) ff. 12ᵛ–18ᵛ Incipit maior cato de senectute. O tite si quid ego . . . impendentem timens quis (ends imperfectly). (d) ff. 19–48ᵛ Marci tullii ciceronis de officiis liber primus incipit. Quamquam te marce fili . . . preceptisque letabere. M. Tullii Ciceronis de officiis liber explicit. (e) f. 48ᵛ Incipiunt epitaphia ciceronis edita a xii sapientibus basilio. asmenio. volamio. Euforbio. Iuliano.

hilasio.Palasio. asclepiadeo. Eustenio. Pompeliano. Maximino. Vitale. Hic iacet
arpinas . . . gloria restituit. (*f*) f. 49ʳᵛ Four short introductory paragraphs, 'Supra
tullium de amicicia', 'Supra tullium de senectute', 'Circa tullium de paradoxis',
'Circa tullium de officiis'.

(*a–c*). Three works of Cicero which commonly go together and sometimes with (*d*), as in
B.L., Royal 15 A. viii and 15 A. xx: ff. 3–4 of (*a*) are much damaged, a leaf is missing after
f. 11 of (*b*), and (*c*) ends at xix. 67. (*e*). *Anthologia Latina*, ed. Riese, 603–9, only the first
seven of the twelve epitaphs.

2. ff. 50–62 Incipit thimius platonis. Socrates in exortacionibus suis uirtutem
laudans . . . ex leui admonitione perspicuo. Explicit.

This copy collated as *Et* by J. H. Waszink, *Corpus Platonicum Medii Aevi, Plato Latinus,*
iv (1962), 5–52: for the type of text see edn., p. clxi.

3. ff. 64–82ᵛ (*begins imperfectly*) tacula tinnitusque . . . retrogradari facit.
Explicit astrologia marciani.

Bks. 1, 2, 8 of M. Capella, De nuptiis Philologiae et Mercurii. This copy listed by C.
Leonardi, 'I Codici di Marziano Capella', *Aevum,* xxxiv (1960), 35–6. Begins in sect. 7
and lacks all between *et ipsum to-* in sect. 65 and *plenitudo. An aliud* in sect. 108, owing to
the loss of the first leaf and of three leaves after f. 67.

4. (*a*) ff. 83–5 Incipit sompnium scipionis quod macrobius exponens . . . et de
septem planetis. Cum in africam uenissem . . . solutus sum. Explicit sompnium
scipionis. (*b*) ff. 85–123ᵛ Macrobii ambrosii de scipionis sompnio liber primus
incipit. Inter platonis et ciceronis libros . . . nec principium motus ad deprecan
(*ends imperfectly*).

All between *sensuum celebrantur* in I. 6. 81 and *uiros in numerum deorum* in I. 9. 6 is missing
owing to the loss of two leaves after f. 93. The last words are in II. 15. 26. Neat drawings
in the margins and on ff. 106–7, 114, 116, 117ᵛ in the text space.

5. At f. 50 the margins become very wide and from this point many of them,
together with blank spaces, were filled by one hand with medical recipes and
accounts in English, s. xvi². Accounts are dated 1577 (f. 59ᵛ) and 1581 (f. 48ᵛ)
and entries on f. 62 are of small day-to-day payments between 17 Oct. and 17
Nov. 1574. An entry on f. 48ᵛ shows who the writer was: 'Memorandum yᵗ I
Raphe savyowʳ parson of robeston and curate in tendbe have passed accownt wᵗ
nicolas trafford alias Ihon Wyll*i*ams prisoner att yᵉ svte off Elizabeth Lloyd and
so agreed and there restethe vnto me viˡⁱ xiiiˢ iiiiᵈ yᵉ iiii daye off awguste 1574':
cf. also ff. 74ᵛ–75.

Saviour was presented to Robeston, Pembrokeshire, 27 Feb. 1564 (*Bulletin of the Board of
Celtic Studies,* xiv (1950–2), 133).[1]

ff. viii+123+v. 230×140 mm. Written space *c.* 170×90 mm and, from f. 50 onwards,
75 mm. 42 long lines. The first line of writing above the top ruled line. Collation: 1⁸ 2⁸
wants 4 after f. 11 3⁶ wants 4–6 after f. 18 5–7⁸ 8⁸ wants 8, perhaps blank, after f. 49 9⁸
10⁶ 11⁸ wants 1 before f. 64 and 6–8 after f. 67 12⁸ 13⁸ wants 8, probably blank, after f. 82
14⁸ 15⁸ wants 4, 5 after f. 93 16–18⁸ 19 three (ff. 121–3).² Initials: (i) blue and red with

¹ Information from Dr. B. C. Barker-Benfield.
² The collation is based on Sir Sydney Cockerell's, dated 5 Mar. 1894. No doubt
Cockerell saw the manuscript before it was rebound and before the damp-damaged
leaves at the beginning were mounted separately.

ornament of both colours; (ii) 2-line, blue or red, with ornament of the other colour. 'Bound by Wilson Cambridge', f. i^v: James saw the manuscript before it was rebound and says in his *Catalogue* (1895), 'Original binding of white skin over boards now replaced by a new morocco binding'. Secundo folio *certe non potuit*.

Written in England. Belonged to the Dominican convent of Haverfordwest, Pembroke-shire: 'Iste liber est de communitate fratrum hauerford mutuatus fratri hug' de thoresby', f. i, s. xiv. Later owners were Ralph Saviour (see above, art. 5) and 'W. Bathon' (William Bourchier, Earl of Bath, 1557–1623).[1] 'Dedit hunc librum Collegio Etonensi Thomas Richardson S.T.P. eiusdem Collegii Socius 1722': he also gave MS. 133.

91. *Ovidius* s. XIII[1]

Arts. 1–6, 8–10, 12–15 are pieces by or here attributed to Ovid and listed in a fifteenth-century table of contents on f. iv^v under the heading 'Libri Ouidii'. The same pieces in the same order under the heading 'Omnes libri Ouidii' were in a Christ Church, Canterbury, manuscript, one of thirty-three 'Libri Ade prioris' (cf. above, Canterbury Cathedral, Lit. D. 11) listed in the early four-teenth-century catalogue (*Ancient Libraries*, p. 72, no. 632). The writer of the table of contents included art. 7 in his numeration from 1 to 14, but made no entry opposite the number. Quire signatures (see below) suggest that arts. 13–15 originally followed art. 11, but the table shows that the present order is medieval. Scholia in pencil, s. xiii, mostly in art. 1. Marginalia in an English hand, s. xiv. Typescript notes by Professor E. H. Alton are pasted to f. ii.

Arts. 1–9 are on quires 1–4.

1. ff. 1–18 Hanc tua Penelope . . . ne uelit esse michi. Explicit liber heroydum. siue opus epistolarum.

Collated as Ea by H. Dörrie, 1971. Bks. 5, 11, 20 are preceded by couplets, 'Nympha suo . . .', 'Eolis eolide . . .', and 'Accipe cydippe . . .': for these 'Eingangs-Disticha' see H. Dörrie in *Nachrichten der Akademie der Wissenschaften in Göttingen*, Phil.-Hist. Klasse, 1960, pp. 208–14.

2. ff. 18–30^v Qui modo nasonis . . . superstes opus. Expliciunt epygramata amorum. siue opus sine titulo.

Amores. Collated as Ea by E. J. Kenney, Oxford, 1961.

3. ff. 30^v–42 Si quis in hoc artem . . . naso magister erat. Explicit liber o. de arte amatoria.

Collated as Ea by Kenney, op. cit.

4. ff. 42^v–46^v Legerat huius amor . . . femina virque meo. Explicit liber o. de remedio amoris.

Collated as E 1 by F. W. Lenz, 1965 and as Ea by Kenney, op. cit.

5. ff. 46^v–47^v Nux ego iuncta uie . . . perficiatis iter. Explicit libellus ouidii de nuce.

Ed. Bährens, *Poetae latini minores*, i. 90–6.

---

[1] I owe the identification to Dr. B. C. Barker-Benfield, who compares the signature in E. Doyle, *Official Baronage of England*, i. 108. The same man owned MS. 133 and B.L., Royal 8 F. xvi.

6. f. 47^v Nox erat et sompnus . . . nox stetit alta meos. Explicit libellus ouidii de sompnio.

Walther, *Initia*, no. 13342.

7. ff. 47^v–48 Uer erat et blando . . . sic properare tuum.

Walther, *Initia*, no. 20127. Riese, *Anthologia latina*, no. 646. Patrick Young added the title 'Rosa Ausonii' on f. 47^v.

8. f. 48 Parue pulex et amara lues . . . quam sibi me socium. Explicit libellus ouidii de pulice.

Walther, *Initia*, no. 13752. Printed before 1500 (Hain 12255).

9. f. 48^{rv} Conueniunt cuncti subito . . . cuculus per secula salue. Explicit libellus ouidii de cuculo.

Walther, *Initia*, no. 3288. Riese, *Anthologia latina*, no. 687.

Arts. 10, 11 are on quires 5, 6.

10. ff. 49–66^v, 91–92^v, 67–71^v Tempora cum causis . . . increpuitque lira. Explicit liber ouidii Fastorum.

In bk. 1 line 658 consists only of the first two words, Nec semen. and in bks. 4, 5 a dozen lines are unfinished (4.939, 940, 945, 946, 953–4; 5.83, 85, 87, 89, 90 and some others): presumably the exemplar was damaged.

11. f. 72^{rv} Kl Ian'. festum iani. consecratio templorum iouis et esculapii . . .

A Roman calendar, Jan.–June only. It differs often from the calendar printed in Burmann's edition of Heroides, Amsterdam, 1727.

12. ff. 73–90^v, 93–134^v (quires 7–11) In noua fert animus . . . presagia uiuam. Explicit liber ouidii methamorphoseos.

No. 91 in the list of 390 copies by F. Munari, *University of London, Institute of Classical Studies, Bulletin*, Suppl. 4, 1959. The error in binding quire 9 is old: a medieval hand wrote 'a' on f. 102^v, 'b' on f. 103, 'a' on f. 107, and 'b' on f. 108 to show the correct order. A note by 'R. O' about the dislocation, dated 29 Jan. 1842, is on a slip lying loose after f. 101: Henry Bradshaw added the words 'Sheet 3 is bound inside sheet 4 March 6 1878 H. B.' and numbered the leaves of the quire 99, 100, 102, 101, 103, 104, 105, 106, 108, 107, 109, 110, to show the order in which they should be read.

Arts. 13–15 are on quires 12–14.

13. ff. 135–152^v Parue nec inuideo . . . comprobat acta suo. Explicit liber o. de tristibus.

Collated as ϵ in S. G. Owen's edition, Oxford, 1889: cf. there, p. xxvii.

14. ff. 153–69 Naso thomitane . . . iam noua plaga locum. Explicit liber ouidii de ponto.

Collated as E in Owen's edition, Oxford, 1915: cf. there, p. ix.

15 (added early). f. 169^{rv} [.]ic serpens uentis pernitior atque sagittis . . . uehit inde rapinam. Explicit ouidius de mirabilibus mundi.

126 lines. Walther, *Initia*, no. 8095 (Hic semper . . .), and no. 18131 (Sic serpens . . .). Edited by M. R. James, 'Ovidius, De mirabilibus mundi', *Essays presented to W. Ridgeway*, Cambridge, 1913, pp. 286–98: he calls this copy 'ludicrously bad'. See also P. Lehmann, *Pseudo-Antike Literatur des Mittelalters*, 1927, p. 7.

ff. iv + 169 + iii. The foliation is by Henry Bradshaw: see above, art. 12. f. iv is a medieval flyleaf. 270 × 195 mm. Written space *c.* 180 × 112 mm. 2 cols. 50 lines. The first line of writing is below the top ruled line. Collation: 1–5¹² 6¹⁴ (ff. 61–6, 91, 92, 67–72) 7¹² 8¹² (ff. 85–90, 93–8) 9¹² (bound wrongly: see above, art. 12) 10–13¹² 14¹² wants 12, blank. Quires 1–6, 12, 13 numbered at the end I–IIII, VI–IX; quires 2–14 marked at the beginning in pencil, s. xiv, a–r. Arts. 1–14 in very small hands: the scribes spread out their writing of pentameters to make them take up the space of hexameters. Initials: (i) f. 1, pink on a blue ground, decorated; (ii) 4-line or less, red and blue with ornament of both colours; (iii) 2-line, ranged with the capital letters 2 or 3 mm outside the written space, red or blue with ornament of the other colour. Binding of spotted calf, s. xviii, rebacked. Secundo folio *Quisquis ab.*

Written in France perhaps, rather than in England, but art. 15 looks English, s. xiii, and marginalia of s. xiv are in an English hand. Probably this is the 'Omnes libri Ouidii' once at Christ Church, Canterbury (see above). Erasures, f. iv. An ex-libris at the head of f. 1. '[. . . . .] ex liberalitate [. . . .] parcat deus amen', s. xiv, partly erased and the ex-libris of Winchester College, 'Liber collegii beate Marie prope Winton' ', written over the erasure in s. xv. 'Liber vii^us', f. 1, s. xiv. 'Iohannes Savage his booke ex dono patrui Willelmi Savage Maii die 7. 1602' in a legal hand, f. iv. Belonged presumably to Patrick Young,†1652, who wrote notes on f. 18 and elsewhere: loaned by him to Nicholas Heinsius in 1639 (cf. F. W. Lenz in *Eranos*, li (1953), 76, and lxi (1963), 115).[1] '1650 26 Octob. Barth. van Wouw', f. iv. '1695 Liber Collegii Regalis de Etona ex dono Domini . . . . (*sic*) Moyle', f. iv: there was a Moyle in the school in 1678.

96. *Chronicon* s. XIII med.

ff. 2–24^v Incipit compendium veteris testamenti editum a magistro petro pictauensi. et cancellario parisiensi. Considerans ystorie prolixitatem nec non et difficultatem scolarum . . . ad propriam patriam sunt reuersi.

Roundels and connecting lines show the descent from Adam to Christ and after Christ (ff. 10–24^v) the succession of popes (red line), Roman emperors (blue line), British and English kings (red line), and French kings (blue line) in parallel columns. Accompanying notes, some headed 'Incidentia', are concerned with general and, especially latterly, English history. The work attributed to Peter of Poitiers (Stegmüller, no. 6778) is the main source as far as f. 9^v. The last words on f. 24^v refer to the Tartars in Hungary, A.D. 1241, and the latest event mentioned is the death of Walter Marshall, A.D. 1245 (f. 24). A long 'Incidentia de subuersione monasterii glastonie' in the time of bishops Savaric and Joscelyn of Bath and the minority of Henry III is on f. 24^rv and there are references to Glastonbury in the notices of St. Patrick and King Arthur on ff. 14, 15: in the latter the 'Insula Auallonie' is equated with Glastonbury and it is said that Arthur (arcturus) was in his burial place there 'inter duas piramides lapideas' for 648 years until after a fire Abbot Henry de Soili (1189–93) 'regium corpus ad maiorem ecclesiam transtulit et in quodam mausoleo in petra nobiliter exciso ante quoddam altare collocauit'.

Six leaves are missing: two between f. 2^v, which ends (in the first column) 'iosedech quem interfecit rex babilo-', and f. 3, which begins 'eneas. tempore ian. rapuit paris helenam'; three between f. 9^v, which ends in a passage on Hannibal at the words 'ptholomei philopatoris', and f. 10, which begins with Pope Linus on the left and in mid sentence of a passage on Nero, 'tes eum*?* fecerunt ut ranam emitteret uomitum', in the second column; one between f. 17^v, where a passage in the first column breaks off 'doctissimus et tam liberalium quam ec-', and f. 18, which begins 'Temporibus leonis pape obiit remigius'. A small part of f. 23 is torn off.

The illustrations are described in James's *Catalogue.* The big roundels, *c.* 90 mm in

---

[1] It is Heinsius's *Junianus.* In Dörrie's edition of Heroides, p. 14, the previous owner is said wrongly to be Hadrianus Junius, 1511–75.

diameter, are on ff. 1 (tripartite: Christ in glory; Adam and Eve and the serpent; Adam and Eve cast out of Paradise), 4 (anointing of David), 7 (Habakkuk and the angel), 7ᵛ (Judith and Holofernes), 8 (Mardocheus, Esther, and Aman), 8ᵛ (Alexander). Plans of the ark are on f. 2ᵛ and a plan of Jerusalem on f. 7ᵛ. Figures and scenes not in roundels include Galen (f. 11), Paul, first hermit (f. 12), Nicholas (f. 12ᵛ), Bernard (f. 22ᵛ), the murder of Thomas of Canterbury (f. 23), and Francis preaching to the birds (f. 23ᵛ: reproduced by A. G. Little, *Franciscan History and Legend*, 1937, pl. 11).

ff. vi+23+vi, foliated i–v, 1–25, (26–30). ff. 1, 25 are medieval flyleaves. ff. 3–24 have a medieval foliation at the foot, 4–10, 14–21, 23–9. 485 × 335 mm. Ruled space *c.* 400 × 310 mm. Columns vary in number: six at most. 94 ruled lines, but not all lines are used on any one page. The first line of writing below the top ruled line. Collation: 1¹² wants 2, 3, 9, 10 (ff. 2–9) 2¹⁰ wants 1, 10 (ff. 10–17) 3⁸ wants 8, probably blank. For the pictures see above. 1-line red initials. Binding by B. H. Smith, s. xx. The secundo folio must have been *nie*: the leaf is now missing.

Written in England, perhaps at the Benedictine abbey of Glastonbury, in which the writer of the text was particularly interested. Names, s. xvi/xvii, on ff. 7ᵛ, 25: 'Elizabeth Flovern'; 'William Hardine'. Probably no. 342 in Patrick Young's catalogue of the manuscripts of Worcester Cathedral, A.D. 1621–2, ed. I. Atkins and N. R. Ker, 1944, p. 59: 'Compendium veteris testamenti editum à Magistro Petro Pictaviensi cancellario Parisiensi. Initium 'Considerans historiæ prolixitatem' et cæt. usque ad annum 1242. fol. large'. Not in *CMA*.

97. *Decreta Romanorum Pontificum, etc.* s. XII in.

A copy of the decretals of Pseudo-Isidore noticed by Z. N. Brooke, *The English Church and the Papacy*, 1952, pp. 85–8, 236, and by Schafer Williams, *Codices Pseudo-Isidoriani*, Monumenta Juris Canonici, Series C, Subsidia iii (1971), 20, 21. Closely related to St. Omer 189 and, as Brooke saw, to the much later copy of English provenance now B.L., Royal 11 D. iv, where arts. 1–11 here are in the order 11, 12, 4, 1, 5, 6, 2, 7–10.[1] Arts. 3–7, 8 *a, b,* 10*b,* 11 are in *Decretales Pseudo-Isidorianae et Capitula Angilramni*, ed. P. Hinschius, 1863.

1 (added, s. xiv). f. iii Ordo epistolarum uel decretorum. Romanorum pontificum in hoc libro. Beati clementis Petri discipuli . . . Beatissimo Siluestro. etc.

A table of contents of art. 6. The heading and the hand are the same as in Exeter Cathedral 3512, art. 4, q.v. Royal, art. 11. f. iiiᵛ blank.

2. ff. ivᵛ, 1 Incipiunt nomina xi Regionum. continentium infra se prouintias CXIII . . . In Italia. prouintie sunt numero xvii . . . id est uentio. Royal, art. 12. f. ivʳ blank.

3. (*a*) ff. 1–2ᵛ In nomine domini nostri iesu cristi. Incipit prefacio Sancti Isidori episcopi 'yspalensis' libri huius. Isidorus mercator . . . ordinem suum. (*b*) f. 2ᵛ Epistola aurelii carthagin'i'ensis episcopi. ad damasum papam. Beatissimo pape damaso . . . Gloriam apostolice sedis . . . amantissime pater. Data . . . (*c*) ff. 2ᵛ–3 Rescriptum beati pape damasi aurelio archiepiscopo directum. Reuerentissimo fratri . . . Scripta sanctitatis tue . . . cooperatores ostendat. Data . . . Explicit. (*d*) ff. 3–4 Incipit ordo de celebrando Concilio. Hora diei prima ante solis ortum . . . cum omni fiducia loqui. Explicit.

(*a–d*). Royal, art. 4. Hinschius, pp. 17–24.

[1] Art. 3 of Royal, tables of chapters, is not in Eton 97.

4. ff. 4–5 Incipit breuiarium Canonum apostolorum et primorum a sancto clemente . . . subiectis capitulis suis.

Tables follow the heading in two numbered series, (*a*) I–LXXX, (*b*) I–L. Royal, art. 1. Hinschius, pp. 25–7. (*a*), nos. II–XXXII, is capitula of art. 6, but with omissions, and from no. XXXIII, Canones niceni concilii . . ., capitula of art. 11. (*b*) is repeated below, art. 10a. After no. L of (*b*), 'Quod non debeat una mersio in baptismate quasi in morte domini promoueri' (cf. art. 10*a*) is a sentence, '[P]lura capitula ab apostolis constituta in decretis apostolorum ut superius continetur legimus. sed adhuc ea minime reperire quiuimus. et ideo illa hic non inseruimus. fidelibus inuestigatoribus hęc inseranda conseruantes committimus', which in Royal precedes art. 5.

5. f. 5 De canonibus apostolorum quod non sint respuendi . . . testatur. Beatissimo papę dámaso. ieronimus. Gloriam sanctitatis tuę . . . Ora pro nobis beatissime papa. Data v kl' mai. accepta romę.

Royal, art. 5. Hinschius, p. 27.

6. ff. 5–86ᵛ Incipiunt aecclesiastice regule sanctorum apostolorum prolate per clementum . . . Incipit epistola clementis ad iacobum fratrem domini. Clemens Iacobo . . . Notum tibi facio domine . . . protestatur acturum. Explicit pręfatio.

Royal, art. 6. Hinschius, pp. 27, 30–257. Eight leaves are missing after f. 54 with the text in edn., p. 171/5 lines from foot–p. 194/last line.

7. ff. 86ᵛ–87ᵛ Item. incipiunt capitula decretalium venerabilium apostolicorum sanctę romanę sedis aeclesiae. I. Primum excepta quędam . . . CXXXVIII'I' Decreta pape Nicholai. '235'.

Table of 138 (altered to 139) chapters, much added to and emended in s. xv. It gives the contents of art. 8*a–c*, with—as additions—leaf references. Royal, art. 2. Hinschius, pp. 445–8, lists only chapters 1–116 (117).

8. (*a*) ff. 88–232 Incipiunt excerpta quedam ex synodalibus gestis sancti siluestri papę capitulo primo. Temporibus sancti siluestri . . . Et responderunt omnes tercio anath' sit. (*b*) ff. 232–5 Ex grecis et latinis canonibus et synodis Romanis . . . causa agebatur. Dei ordinationem accusat . . . permiserit uiolandum (*altered to* -dam). (*c*) f. 235ʳᵛ Synodale decretum nicholai papae. Nicholaus episcopus . . . Vigilantia uniuersalis . . . atque benedictione gaudere. Cuius supra. Domnus papa nicolaus synodo in basilica constantiniana pręsidens dixit . . . dignitate persistat. Nichilominus auctoritate apostolica . . . inthronizatus sit. (*d*) ff. 235ᵛ–236 Iusiurandum quod in eadem synodo fecit Beringarius. Ego Beringarius indignus diaconus . . . sponte subscripsi. (*e*) f. 236ʳᵛ Anno ab incarnatione sempiterni principii m. lxxº ixº mense Februario . . . sicut in consequentibus continetur. Ego beringarius corde credo . . . ab ea recesserant. Expliciunt decreta romanorum pontificum.

(*a*, *b*). Royal, art. 7. (*c*). Royal, art. 8*a*, *b*. (*d*, *e*). Royal, art. 8*c*, *d*.

(*a*). Papal decrees, Silvester I–Gregory I: Hinschius, pp. 449–694. Single leaves missing after ff. 201, 204. On f. 226ᵛ Grandisson noted that Pope Gregory was the first to style himself 'seruus seruorum dei'. (*b*). Capitula Angilramni: Hinschius, pp. 757–69. On f. 234 a contemporary note in the margin opposite 'Delatori aut lingua capuletur aut conuicto caput amputetur': 'Hoc capitulum non est canonicum sed a secularibus legibus sumptum'. (*c*, *d*). Council of Rome, A.D. 1059: Mansi, *Consilia*, xix. 897–900. (*d*, *e*). Berengarius' retractions at the councils of Rome in 1059 and 1079. Headings apart, they are part of Lanfranc's De corpore et sanguine Domini in PL cl. 410D–411C.

9. f. 237 Incipit liber canonum pars secunda. (a–c) ff. 237^v–239^v Prima est synodus nicena . . . Ciuitates numero cxv. (d) ff. 239^v–241 In nomine domini nostri iesu incipit ordo de celebrando Concilio. Hora diei prima . . . fiducia loqui. (e) f. 241^{rv} Canones generalium conciliorum á temporibus constantini coeperunt . . . multorum in unum. Explicit prefacio. (f) ff. 241^v–242 Incipiunt capitula conciliorum grecię. Canones apostolorum. Canones Niceni concilii . . . Synodus toletana lxviii episcoporum. (g) f. 242^{rv} Prima epistola papę damasi ad paulinum anthiocenum. Confessio fidei . . . (h) f. 242^v Decreta romanę sedis de recipiendis et non recipiendis. Expliciunt capitula.

(a–f). Royal, art. 9a–f. (g, h). Royal, art. 9g. The double opening, 236^v–237, contains the 'Expliciunt . . .' of art. 8 and the 'Incipit . . .' of art. 9 in large capitals. (a–c). Lists of 47 synods and councils, of provinces, and of 115 cities in 17 provinces. (d) repeats art. 3d. (e). PL lxxxiv. 91. (f) gives the contents of art. 11 and at the end three titles of pieces not in art. 11 and therefore here marked 'va cat': 'Sententię quę in ueteribus exemplaribus conciliorum non habentur sed a quibusdam insertę sunt. Decreta quorundam pręsulum romanorum ad fidei regulam et disciplinam aecclesiasticam constituta. Synodus Toletana lxviii episcoporum'. Like art. 7 it has been much added to and corrected in s. xv. (g) is a list of 101 papal letters, nearly the same list as in art. 7, nos. 14, 15, 24–116 (117), except for the last five items, 'Uigilii papę ad profuturum episcopum. Epistola Gregorii papę ad leandrum spalensem episcopum. Cuius supra ad eundem leandrum. Cuius supra ad recaredum regem gothorum. Cuius supra ad pędictum antistitem'.

10. (a) f. 242^v [I]ncipiunt capitula canonum apostolorum. I De ordinatione episcopi . . . L. Quod non debeat una mersio in baptismate quarte (sic) in morte domini prouenire. (b) ff. 243–4 Incipiunt canones apostolorum numero L. I cap. Episcopus a duobus aut tribus episcopis . . . et spiritus sancti. Expliciunt canones apostolorum numero L^{ta}.

Royal, art. 10. (a). The table of (b): cf. art. 4b. (b). Hinschius, pp. 27–30.

11. ff. 244^v–364 Canones sancti et magni concilii niceni quod conditum est . . . era cccxiii. Incipiunt capitula . . . . (20 numbered chapters) . . . Incipit pręfacio sancti concilii. [C]oncilium sacrum . . . dulcia mella fluit (10 lines). Explicit praefacio. Prologus. Cum conuenisset hoc sanctum . . . Honorius episcopus subscripsi. Explicit ispalense concilium secundus.

Royal, art. 10. Canons of councils from Nice i to Seville ii. Hinschius, pp. 257–444. ff. 364^v–366^v blank.

12. For f. i, formerly pasted down, and f. ii, a bifolium, and other fragments used in binding see MS. 5, art. 2.

ff. iii + 358 (excluding four paper leaves added at each end in 1973), foliated i–iv, 1–21, 21, 22–54, 63–98, 100–201, 203–4, 206–325, 325, 326–66: the foliation from 1 to 366 follows the medieval foliation in its three errors and takes into account the quire missing after f. 54 and the two leaves missing from quire 25. f. iii is a medieval flyleaf. 430 × 325 mm. Written space 322 × 217 mm. 2 cols. 43–5 lines. Ruling with a hard point. Collation of ff. iv, 1–366: 1–24^8 25^8 wants 3 after f. 201 and 6 after f. 204 26–30^8 31^6 (ff. 248–53) 32–37^8 38^6 39–45^8 46^4 (4 was pasted down). Quires 1–45 numbered at the end I–[VII], [VIIII]–XLVI. Initials of various sizes, green or red, the largest—7–12 lines—on ff. 5^{rv}, 88, elsewhere usually 4-line, and on ff. 2^v–4, 2-line or 3-line. The same two colours are used for headings and for incipits which are often in alternate lines of red and green capitals. Binding of s. xvii in., no doubt by Williamson, in view of art. 12: repaired by

R. L. Day in 1973.[1] Marks on ff. iv, 1–4 show that a former binding had bosses. Secundo folio *tes viii* (f. 1).

Written in a hand of Norman type, probably at Exeter.[2] Identifiable with the Breviarium canonum apostolorum beginning 'In Ytalia' (cf. art. 2) listed in the 1327 catalogue of Exeter Cathedral library (Oliver, *Lives*, p. 304). Annotated by Bishop John Grandisson: see especially the note signed 'I. Ex.', f. 137ᵛ. At Eton in s. xv when 'Liber Decret' Romanorum Pontificum et incipit in 2° fo tes viii' was written on f. ivᵛ in the same hand as the similar entry in MS. 22.

98. *W. Lyndwood, Provinciale glosatum* s. xv[1]

1. ff. 1–27 A. hec monasilliba quandoque . . . Zenodochium . . . loci ordinario. Explicit Tabula quod M. B(?).

An index to art. 3. Leaf and letter references were added later in the margins.

2. ff. 27ᵛ–29ᵛ Per tabulam sequentem potest lector . . . in compilacione noua quam fecit et glosauit magister Willelmus linwode vtriusque iuris doctor que vocatur prouinciale. . . . Finis sit libro reddatur gracia cristo.

Tables of chapters and (f. 29ᵛ) tituli of art. 3. f. 30ʳᵛ blank.

3. ff. 31–331 Reuerendissimo in cristo patri . . . A titulo siue Rubrica de summa trinitate et fide catholica. Ignorancia sacerdotum et infra ne quis . . . et quiescere mereamur. Amen. Explicit tabula (*altered to* liber) qui intitulatur prouinciale editus a Willelmo linwode vtriusque iuris doctore cuius anime propicietur deus amen.

The Provinciale, with commentary. This copy listed by C. R. Cheney in *The Jurist*, xxi (1961), 433. Bk. 2, f. 90ᵛ; 3, f. 115ᵛ; 4, f. 253; 5, f. 259. Ten leaves are missing after f. 100. The scribe wrote 'Assit principio sancta maria meo' at the head of f. 31.

4. (*a*) ff. 331ᵛ–332 Sequitur constitucio henrici Chichele archiepiscopi Cant'. super articulis summe excommunicacionis ad minus ter in anno . . . Nuper in concilio nostro . . . (*b*) f. 332ʳᵛ Sequitur constitucio eiusdem henrici Chichele . . . super augmentacione exilium vicariarum. [C]um propter nimiam . . . (*c*) f. 332ᵛ Sequitur constitucio Iohannis Stratforde (*sic*) archiepiscopi Cant' de festo sancti Edwardi regis et confessoris solemniter celebrando . . . Quanquam admonicione diuina . . .

(*a*) Printed 'ex MS. Ætonensi' (this copy) in the 1679 edition of Lyndwood, pp. 73–4. The form of excommunication is in English, Fyrste yei be acursyd . . . (*b, c*). Printed ibid., pp. 74–5.

5. Articles of enquiry: (*a*) f. 333 Articuli inquirendi in causa heresis. Primo inquiratur an aliqui sint heretici seu lollardi in genere . . . et qualia sint et quibus; (*b*) ff. 333–4 In primis in singulis ecclesiis paroch' post pronunciacionem verbi dei petatur certificatorium execucionis mandati citatorii directi archidiacono london' pro visitacione predicta . . . et si sic quibus personis. Cetera suppleat prouida discrecio inquirentis (*these five words in red*).

---

[1] The repairs brought to light not only two strips of the Concordance, but also a small piece of a law-book in Italian rotunda, s. xiv.

[2] Or so I think. But whether Exeter manuscripts in writing like this were produced locally or in France has still to be investigated.

(*a*). Twenty-eight heads, mainly on heresy. (*b*). Thirty-three heads at a visitation, on residence and other matters, some coinciding with (*a*). f. 334ᵛ blank.

6 (added, s. xv ex.). (*a*) f. viʳᵛ Extracts from Duns Scotus on distinctio 2 and distinctio 35 of bk. 2 of the Sentences of Peter Lombard, on mortal and venial sin and on whether sin 'actuale et mortale sit per se corrupcio boni'. (*b*) f. vᵛ Ther was þe deyn and þe offyciall Wᵗ ii fayc*es* lyke a dyall þ*er* hode*s* were furryd wᵗ catt They had of fine (?) er I wentt þᵗ wold pay for my qwyt rentt. I schrew þᵉᵐ lith for þᵗ.

(*b*). According to M. R. James, *Catalogue*, from an English version of Mapes, Apocalypsis Golie. In the same hand as the names on f. vᵛ: see below.

ff. vi+334+v. ff. v, vi, 335 are medieval parchment endleaves: vʳ, 335ᵛ were pasted down.[1] The medieval foliation of art. 3, 1–311, takes account of the quire missing after f. 100. 403×275 mm. Written space 275×180 mm. 2 cols. 39–56 lines. Collation: 1–20¹⁰ 21¹² 22–25¹⁰ 26¹² 27–33¹⁰. The Provinciale in textura and the commentary on it in anglicana modified by secretary. Initials: (i) ff. 31, 115ᵛ, red and blue with red and violet ornament (and a little green on f. 31); (ii, iii) 4-line and 2-line, blue with red ornament or red with violet ornament. Binding by Williamson rebacked by R. Day in 1974. Secundo folio *sue. Anime.*

Written in England. Scribbled names, s. xv ex.: f. iiiᵛ 'W Butler Raff Ferysch' and beside art. 6b 'Karulus Thornhyll Willelmus Butler Radulfus Ferysch decanus Radulfus both archidiaconus';[2] f. 335 'Willelmus Butler ys a knaue'. 'Donum Guilielmi Hormani quondam socii huius collegegii (*sic: cancelled*) contubernii', f. ivᵛ.

99. *Petrus Calo de Clugia, O.P., Legenda, Pars II*   s. xiv/xv

1. (*a*) ff. 1–229 Conuersio beati pauli apostoli propter tria solemniter ab ecclesia celebratur. Primo propter gaudium immensum . . . (*b*) f. 229 Eusebii pape nacione greci festum agitur 6° non' octobris . . . (*c*) f. 229ʳᵛ Flora virgo sanctimonialis romana capta est similiter cum lucilla virgine . . . Passi sunt autem 4° kalendas augusti.

(*a*). Three hundred and fourteen lives of saints in the order of the church year from 25 Jan. to 17 Mar. (ff. 1–65) and from 29 Apr. to 31 July (ff. 65ᵛ–229). They correspond to nos. 119–212, 289–522 of the sanctorale of the legendary of Petrus Calo (†1348) in Venice, Marciana ix. 15–ix. 20, as set out in *Anal. Boll.* xxix (1910), 56–83, with a few omissions and one addition, and a few differences in order. The large gap is not due to loss of leaves: cf. art. 2. Half the other omissions are of lives which are given in duplicate in the Venice manuscript.

The contents and order here as compared with *Anal. Boll.* are nos. 119–24, 126–36, 138–9, 143–82, 184–200, 202–12, 289–385, 387, 386, 388–407, 410–36, 446, 437–40, 409, 441–5, 447–50, 452–76, 478–81, 484–91, 493–503, 505–6, 504, 507–12, 514–19, 521–2, followed by a life not in the legendary as listed in *Anal. Boll.*: ff. 227ᵛ–229, 'Germanus autisiodorensis oppidi indigena fuit. parentibus splendidissimis . . . episcopatus sui 30°. pridie kl' augusti'.[3] Only the first seventeen lines of no. 493 are here (ff. 201ᵛ–202), marked 'vacat' and with the note at the head 'scripta est superius 204 folio', a reference presumably to

---

[1] Recent repairs brought to light part of a leaf in a good current English hand, s. xiv/xv. The running title is 'De temporibus [anni]'.

[2] Emden, *BRUC*, records Ralph Bothe, archdeacon of York in 1478.

[3] But see *Anal. Boll.*, no. 694 for a reference to it. Presumably Marciana ix. 17 is defective at the end.

the exemplar and not to this copy which has this life of St. Julia on f. 117. Cross references are many and include references to subdivisions of the lives by letter marks not given in this copy, for example, after no. 438, 'Quarto kl' Iulii fuit victoria cristianorum de turchis. de qua exultacionis crucis N. O' (f. 176). (*b*). 26 Sept. Not in the list in *Anal. Boll.* (*c*). 27 July. *BHL*, no. 5017. Not in the list in *Anal. Boll.*

A note on f. 145 is in the hand of Robert Elyot: see p. 631.

2. ff. 230–231ᵛ A table of the lives in art. 1. Leaf numbers were added later. Three added titles in the margin of f. 231ᵛ seem to be in Elyot's hand: two repair omissions and the third is 'Vita sancti lazari nota in prima parte huius operis 197'.[1]

The table includes all but sixteen of the pieces listed in *Anal. Boll.* between no. 119 and no. 522. The absentees are nos. 183, 213–23, 258, 408, 451, 520.

ff. i+232+i. The pastedown and flyleaf at each end have been taken over from an older binding. A medieval foliation throughout the text, 1–231, may be in Robert Elyot's hand. It repeats the number 37 and misses three leaves after '60' and three numbers after '64'. It has been revised on ff. 61–7, but is the present foliation elsewhere. 400 × 310 mm. Written space *c.* 290 × 190 mm. 2 cols. 57 or 58 lines. Collation: 1–29⁸. Written in skilled current hybrida. Initials: (i) f. 1, 9-line, blue patterned in white on a ground of decorated gold and of red patterned in white: a border of flowers and gold ivy leaves on three sides of col. 1; (ii) 3-line, blue with red ornament or red with blue-grey ornament. Capital letters in the ink of the text filled with pale yellow. Binding by Lisley: Birley, pl. iv, shows the back cover and the inscription there, '2ᵃ pars cathalogi sanctorum', once protected by a now missing piece of transparent horn attached to the cover by sixteen nails. Two strap-and-pin fastenings missing. Secundo folio *dignissime*.

Written in France, perhaps for Benedictine use, in view of the scribal slip on f. 119 (no. 359, translation of St. Dominic), 'Translatio sancti benedicti patris nostri . . .'. 'Ex dono magistri Willelmi Wey socii istius collegii' (*the last five words erased*) and near it the mark E͡C, f. 232ᵛ. In view of the note on f. 231ᵛ it is likely that the now missing first volume was at Eton once.

101, ff. i, 1–182. *Augustinus, In Johannem* s. XIV²

Aurelii augustini doctoris yponiensis episcopi. omelie in euangelium domini ihesu secundum Iohannem quas ipse colloquendo prius ad populum habuit. et inter loquendum a notariis exceptas. eo quo habite sunt ordine uerbum ex uerbo postea dictauit. Intuentes quomodo audiuimus . . . meum terminare sermonem. Explicit.

PL xxxv. 1379–1976. *CC* xxxvi (cf. p. xiii for the heading). Letter marks in the margins. f. 181ᵛ blank. f. 182ʳᵛ, blank, has prickings, but no ruling.

ff. i, 1–182 in a composite volume of ff. i+327+i. 380 × 260 mm. Written space 285 × 185 mm. 2 cols. 49 lines. Collation: 1–22⁸ 23⁴ 24² (ff. 181–2: f. 182ᵛ was pasted to a former binding). Initials: (i) f. 1, letter *I*, a scaly blue and pink dragon on a gold ground: his tail turns into a continuous blue, pink, and gold border; (ii) 4-line, blue with red ornament. Bound by Williamson with ff. 183–328. The marks of the pins of two strap-and-pin fastenings of a former binding and of its thongs placed as four sideways v's show on f. 182ᵛ. Secundo folio *dum ad dominum*.

[1] It is no. 43 in *Anal. Boll.*

Written in England. 'Istum librum ego 'M. Ric' Hopton' emi ab executore petri Bylton pro lvi s' viii d' anno domini m°cccc° lv', f. 182: cf. MS. 39. 'Liber Augustini super Iohannem et incipit in 2° fo dum ad dominum', f. i, in the same hand as the similar inscriptions in MSS. 22 and 97. Probably given by Hopton: see MS. 39.

101, ff. 183–328. *Gregorius Magnus, Homiliae in Evangelia, etc.*

s. XIII ex.

Four works of Gregory the Great. The table of contents listing them is now upside down as f. 328, but was presumably once in front of f. 183. It is headed 'Contenta' and is in the same hand as the table in MS. 19, q.v., p. 639.

1. ff. 183–226 Incipit prologus xl omeliarum beati Gregorii pape. per contemplacionem sumptarum. Reuerentissimo et sanctissimo fratri secundino . . . cerciores fiant. Explicit prologus. Incipit liber primus . . . . (*table of the 40 homilies*) . . . Incipit omelia 1ª. leccio sancti ewangelii secundum lucam. In ill' . . . Erunt signa . . . mentibus loquatur. cui . . . amen.

PL lxxvi. 1075–1312. Bk. 2, f. 199ᵛ.

2. ff. 226–275ᵛ Incipiunt Omelie beati Gregorii pape super Ezechielem. Per contemplacionem sumpte. Incipit prologus. Dilectissimo fratri mariniano episcopo.' Gregorius . . . auidius redeatur. Liber. Dei omnipotentis aspiracione . . . perpetuam erudit. Sit itaque gloria . . . amen. Explicit feliciter.

PL lxxvi. 785–1072.

3. ff. 275ᵛ–296ᵛ Incipiunt capitula cure pastoralis secundum Gregorium. ro. pon. . . . (*table of chapters of two books, 21+42*) . . . Gregorius urbis rome episcopus hunc librum cure pastoralis scripsit per excusacionem episcoporum . . . in occidentales plagas gallorum fugerat. In hoc libro narrat opus esse difficile principium ecclesie. Hic incipit liber primus . . . Pastoralis cure me pondera . . . tui meriti manus leuet.

PL lxxvii. 13–128.

4. ff. 296ᵛ–327 Incipiunt capitula libri Dialogorum . . . (*table of 35 chapters of bk. 1*) . . . Incipit Dialogus Gregorii pape urbis Rome. [Q]uadam die nimis quorundam . . . deo hostia ipsi fuerimus. Explicit Dialogus Beati Gregorii pape urbis rome. de uita et uirtutibus uirorum sanctorum in italia commanencium.

PL lxxvii. 149–429. Bk. 2 (36 chapters), f. 302ᵛ; 3 (38 chapters), f. 309; 4 (62 chapters), f. 318. f. 327ᵛ blank.

ff. 183–328 in a composite volume. For the flyleaf, f. 328, see above. 380 × 260 mm. Written space 305 × 205 mm. 2 cols. 57–60 lines. Collation: 1–11¹² 12¹²+1 leaf after 12 (f. 327). *Ad hoc* pencil signatures. Initials: (i) ff. 183, 226, 276, blue and red with ornament of both colours, extending in saw pattern nearly the height of the page; (ii) 2-line, blue with red ornament and shorter lengths of blue and red saw pattern. Bound in 1600–1 with ff. i, 1–182, q.v. Secundo folio (f. 184) *bit. Ignis*.
Written in England.

102. *Nicholaus de Gorran, In Lucam* 1450

1. ff. 1–328^v Disciplina medici exaltabit . . . ecclesiasticus 38. Inter figuras animalium celestium . . . custodientibus disciplinam. Lucas syrus nacione. Huius operis duplex prohemium premittitur . . . more duracionem continuam. Deo gracias amen. Maria. IS (*as monogram*). Explicit opus super euangelium luce per egregium doctorem M. Nicholaum Gorram. ordinis predicatorum. Scriptum anno 1450.

Stegmüller, no. 5780. Letters in the margins subdivide chapters. The *explicit* is followed by two lines of verse in the same hand, 'Sit propter scripta semper trinitas benedicta Huncque letificet qui michi bona prebet'. Below are a paraph and monogram (?) and the words 'Per cistolam'. The scribe copied marginalia from his exemplar, for example, f. 255, 'Nota pro isto passu S. Bedam Monachum Giruensem in partibus borialibus anglie. super lucam li. 6'. On f. 3^v Robert Elyot points out a dislocation: cf. below, collation.

2. ff. 329–346^v Abscondita erat mater ihesu in salutacione angelica . . . Zachei constancia . . . et saluacio 19b.

An index to art. 1. References are by chapter numbers and letters. The entry under 'Questiones' occupies nine columns, ff. 341–3.

ff. ii + 346 + ii. 392 × 253 mm. Written space *c*. 260 × 135 mm. *c*. 50 long lines. Frame ruling in pencil. Collation: 1^8 (ff. 1–3, 5, 4, 6–8, the central bifolium having been folded the wrong way round) 2–40^8 41^{10} 42–43^8. Quires 1–41 signed a–z, aa–ss, top right of rectos. Ugly textura for the gospel text and cursiva for the commentary: from f. 129 the loops on ascenders, *b*, *h*, *l*, characteristic of cursiva, give place to straight strokes or strokes which bend over backwards. Initials: (i) f. 1, 11-line, gold on decorated blue, green, and red ground in imitation of the Italian style: a handsome floral border beside it; (ii) 9-line blue with red ornament. Capital letters in the ink of the text stroked with red. Binding by Williamson. Secundo folio *Quod per*.

Written in 1450, probably by a Netherlandish scribe, but one working in England, to judge from the style of the smaller initials. At Eton by 1500: see p. 631.

103. *Pseudo-N. de Gorran, In Epistolas Pauli* s. xv^1

1. ff. 1–31 Qui docet filium suum in zelum . . . Ecclesiastici xix. Finis et est causa causarum . . . est determinatum. Explicit epistola prima ad thimotheum. **2.** ff. 31–51 Incipit prohemium in epistolam secundam ad eundem. Argumentum. Machabeus primus sumptis armis . . . et nobilior erat. Explicit epistola secunda ad thymotheum. **3.** ff. 51–63 Incipit argumentum in epistola ad tytum. Erudit filium suum . . . gulosi exemplo. Explicit epistola ad tytum. **4.** ff. 63–7 Incipit argumentum in epistola pauli ad philemonem. In tempore iracundie . . . iste demas. Explicit epistola ad philemonem. **5.** ff. 67–150^v Incipit argumentum in epistola pauli ad hebreos. Narrabo nomen tuum . . . dabit dominus. cuius . . . Amen.

1–5. Petrus de Tarentasia. Stegmüller, nos. 6891–5. Not ascribed here, but considered, as commonly, to be Gorran's in the St. Albans and Eton inventories: see below. At ch. 4 of art. 2, f. 46^v, the scribe left a space for an initial like those beginning arts. 1–5 and the running title on ff. 46^v–50 is 'Super Epistolam Pauli ad Tymotheum terciam'. A note by Robert Elyot (see p. 631) on f. 32.

ff. iii+150+iii. Thick parchment. 368×267 mm. Written space 250×160 mm. 2 cols. 45 lines. Collation: 1–5⁸ 6⁶ 7–8⁸ 9⁶ 10⁸ 11⁶ 12–16⁸ 17⁶ 18–19⁸ 20⁸ wants 7, 8, blank. Quires signed a–v. The text of the Epistles in larger and the commentary in smaller textura— but g is flat topped and s may be round or kidney-shaped, probably by a foreign scribe working for Whethamstede (see below). Initials: (i) f. 1, gold and blue, with ornament in red and blue forming a border: at each corner a roundel, two of them containing a lamb and flag and two an eagle in white with gold halos on blue grounds; (ii) ff. 1, 68, blue and red, with ornament of both colours; (iii) 2-line, blue with red ornament. Contemporary wooden boards: eight bands: two clasps missing: formerly covered with pink leather, and, over it, a white chemise, of which a small fragment remained until 1964 when the boards were re-covered: a piece of the pink leather has been preserved and is pasted inside the front cover. Secundo folio *edificacionem*.

Probably written in England. The ex-libris of the Benedictine abbey of St. Albans is on f. 150ᵛ: Hunc librum ad usum Conuentus Monasterii sancti Albani assignauit venerabilis pater dompnus Iohannes Whethamstede olim Abbas Monasterii antedicti. vinculoque anathematis innodauit illos omnes qui aut titulum illius delere curauerint; aut ad usus applicare presumpserint alienos'. No. (8) in the list of books made for Whethamstede (abbot 1420–40, 1452–65) printed in *Annales J. Amundesham* (R.S.), ii. 268: 'Item in factura eiusdem super quasdam Epistolas Pauli lˢ'.[1] Alienated, in spite of the anathema, and at Eton by 1465 when listed as no. (xv) in the inventory (cf. MS. 14): 'Item Goram vppon dyuers episteles ii fo edificacionem'.

104. *Pseudo-Hugo de Sancto Caro* s. xv med.

1. (a) ff. 1–27ᵛ Galathe sunt greci etc. Incipit argumentum in epistolam ad galathas. Et dicuntur tria in hoc argumento . . . ab epheso. Paulus etc. Hec epistola diuiditur in 3 partes. Primo premittit . . . Per hoc verbum hebreum vera esse que locutus est ostendit etc. Explicit hugo de vienna super epistolam Pauli ad Galathas. (b) ff. 28ᵛ–51ᵛ Paulus Apostolus. Incipit epistola ad ephesyos de qua dicit hay. in orig' sic. Sciendis (*sic*) quod hec epistola . . . et in hiis omibus (*sic*) duobus terminat epistolam. Explicit . . . ad Ephesios. (c) ff. 52–70ᵛ Philipenses. Incipit argumentum in epistolam ad philipenses que habet partes iii . . . in odorem suauitatis. Paulus. Hec epistola in partes d(uas). In prima premittit . . . aut peccatum est ex racione secundum viam fantasie. amen. Explicit. . . ad Philipenses. (d) ff. 71ᵛ–87ᵛ Paulus. Epistola hec ad Colocenses habet partes duas. In prima p. premittit . . . ac remissio peccatorum maneat semper vobiscum. Amen. Explicit . . . ad Colocenses. (e) ff. 88–105ᵛ Tessalonicenses etc. Incipit argumentum in epistolam ad tess'. In quo . . . in nomine ipsius etc. Paulus. Hec epistola diuiditur in 3 partes. In prima . . . proficiatis. Gracia domini nostri ihesu cristi sit vobiscum amen. Explicit . . . super primam epistolam Pauli ad thessalocenses. (f) ff. 106ᵛ–117 Paulus etc. Incipit argumentum in epistolam 2ᵃᵐ ad thessalocenses etc. Paulus et Siluanus etc. Hec epistola diuiditur in partes 3 . . . Sic exponit hay. Explicit . . . super 2ᵃᵐ epistolam pauli ad Thessalonicenses. (g) ff. 117–54 Incipit argumentum . . . . a macedonia per tyticum diaconum. Sequitur textus. Paulus etc. (f. 117ᵛ) Paulus etc. Diuiditur hec epistola in partes duas. In primum (*sic*) premittit . . . . seruare doctrinam. Amen. Confirmacio est. Explicit . . . super primam epistolam ad Thimotheum. (h) ff. 154ᵛ–171ᵛ Paulus Apostolus etc. Notandum quod in primis nouem epistolis . . . largiuntur sint vobiscum etc. Explicit . . . super 2ᵃᵐ

[1] Nos. (6) and (7) are also Gorran.

epistolam Pauli ad Thimotheum. (*i*) ff. 172–80 Paulus seruus dei. In prima ad thim. informabat prelatum . . . dicens gracia dei cum omnibus vobis. Amen. Explicit . . . super epistolam Pauli ad Tytum. (*j*) ff. 180ᵛ–183 Paulus vinctus ihesu cristi. In tribus precedentibus epistolis habetur informatio prelatorum . . . quia homines sunt. etc. Explicit . . . super epistolam pauli ad philemonem. (*k*) ff. 183ᵛ–264 Multiphariam multisque modis. Ro. xi c. Quamdiu sum gentium apostolus . . . sic inuenietur sic aperietur Amen. Explicit . . . super Paulum ad hebreos.

Each explicit, (*a*)–(*l*), ascribes the commentary to Hugh of Vienne. (*a*–*g*) appear to be the same set of commentaries as occur in Turin, Bibl. Naz. 542 (D.V. 29), ff. 256–318, s. xiii (Stegmüller, nos. 11159–65): as there, the prologues of Ephesians, Colossians, and 2 Thessalonians are not commented upon. Reference letters in the margins: cf. art. 2. ff. 28ʳ, 71ʳ, 106ʳ blank.

2. ff. 164ᵛ–187 Abrahe facte sunt promissiones . . . Ysaac figurabat cristum. Et aries inter spinas cristi carnem et(c)' hebr. 1.

A table of art. 1, furnished with chapter and letter references. f. 287ᵛ blank.

3. ff. v, formerly pasted down, and vi, are conjoint leaves of the concordance used in MS. 5, q.v.

ff. vi+287+iv. For ff. v, vi, see above. 390 × 240 mm. Written space *c.* 257 × 145 mm. 52 long lines. Ruling with pencil. Collation: 1⁸ wants 1–3 2–35⁸ 36¹⁰. Two series of quire signatures, the first on quires 1–14, h⁺–v⁺, and the second on quires 15–33, a–v, with a horizontal stroke through each letter. Written in textura influenced by cursiva. Initials: (i) *c.* 11-line, in colours on gold grounds decorated in colours, including green, in the common effective mid-fifteenth-century English style; (ii) 6-line and in art. 2 4-line, blue with red ornament. Binding by Williamson. Secundo folio *natus animus*.

Written in England, perhaps by a foreign scribe. Evidently the second volume of two: the quires of the first volume were marked probably from *a* onwards, followed by *a⁺–g⁺* and the first three leaves of *h⁺*, and contained probably the commentaries on Romans and 1, 2 Corinthians listed by Stegmüller from the Turin manuscript (nos. 11156–8). At Eton by 1601.

105. *Augustinus, Epistolae, etc.* s. XIII in.

1. ff. ivᵛ–vᵛ, 1–172 Incipiunt capitula voluminis huius.' numero centum triginta nouem. I. Epistola augustini ad uolusianum 'fo. primo' . . . (f. vᵛ) CXXXIX Item epistola eiusdem ad Probam de orando deo 'fo. 167'. (f. 1) Epistola Augustini ad uolusianum. Domino illustri et merito . . . aut intelligimus.

Closely related to the copy in the Tullie House Museum, Carlisle, q.v., and to Merton College, Oxford, 3 which have the same collection of 139 letters in the same order and arts. 2, 3 after them (but in reverse order); also to Aberdeen University, 6, which breaks off in letter cxxxviii.[1] All four manuscripts have the same red-ink notice after letter vii in the table of contents, 'Epistole augustini ad Ieronimum. et Ieronimi ad Augustinum in epistolari Ieronimi requirantur'.[2] In both table and text two letters seem to have been

[1] Römer lists this collection at ii. 2, 100, 121 (Eton) and 298.

[2] The commoner collection of 143 or 144 letters has the same letters together with two from Jerome, one to Jerome, and one to Boniface (*PL*, Epp. 81, 82, 165 and App. 16) and Ep. 147 complete as well as in an excerpt: cf. Römer, i. 281–2. Some of these manuscripts omit Ep. xxviii of the present collection (*PL*, Ep. 215).

numbered cxxvi: to correct the error, the numbers from the second cxxvi were raised by one, perhaps at the same time, s. xv, as leaf references were added to the table.

The following table shows the numbers of the letters here, as compared with (col. 2) pre-Maurist printed editions and (col. 3) *PL* xxxiii and *CSEL* xxxiv, xxxv.

	Pre-Maurist	PL and CSEL		Pre-Maurist	PL and CSEL		Pre-Maurist	PL and CSEL
i	1	132	xlv	99	164	lxxxix	153	46
ii	2	135	xlvi	122	111	xc	154	47
iii	3	137	xlvii	123	257	xci	155	258
iv	4	136	xlviii	124	96	xcii	156	131
v	5	138	xlix	125	259	xciii	157	190
vi	6	92	l	127	100	xciv	162	43
vii	7	143	li	129	97	xcv	166	105
viii	77	41	lii	108	265	xcvi–	182–8	App. 1–7
ix	20	233	liii	130	144	cii		
x	21	234	liv	131	101	ciii–	192–6	App. 11–
xi	22	235	lv	80	199	cvii		15
xii	23	98	lvi	132	266	cviii–	189–91	App. 8–
xiii	31	25	lvii	133	99	cx		10
xiv	32	27	lviii	134	58	cxi	197	189
xv	33	30	lix	135	110	cxii	168	34
xvi	34	31	lx	136	77	cxiii	169	35
xvii	35	24	lxi	137	78	cxiv	170	52
xviii	36	32	lxii	138	122	cxv	171	76
xix	37	109	lxiii	73	245	cxvi	68	88
xx	38	243	lxiv	139	260	cxvii	172	51
xxi	39	26 (i)	lxv	140	261	cxviii	173	66
xxii	40	26 (ii)	lxvi	141	264	cxix	174	238
xxiii	41	26 (iii)	lxvii	143	188	cxx	175	239
xxiv	43	16	lxviii	144	145	cxxi	176	240
xxv	44	17	lxix	145	248	cxxii	177	241
xxvi	45	127	lxx	146	205	cxxiii	179	150
xxvii	46	214	lxxi	147	33	cxxiv	180	228
xxviii	47	215	lxxii	148	21	cxxv	181	147
xxix	48	93	lxxiii	149	38			(extr.)
xxx	49	102	lxxiv	128	112	cxxvi	158	139
xxxi	50	185	lxxv	42	232	cxxvii	160	134
xxxii	51	154	lxxvi	150	242	cxxviii	159	133
xxxiii	52	155	lxxvii	151	3	cxxix	92	176
xxxiv	53	152	lxxviii	63	18	cxxx	161	49
xxxv	54	153	lxxix	126	20	cxxxi	164	87
xxxvi	55	117	lxxx	84	19	cxxxii	163	44
xxxvii	56	118	lxxxi	113	15	cxxxiii	165	53
xxxviii	57	187	lxxxii	114	5	cxxxiv	167	89
xxxix	58	121	lxxxiii	71	6	cxxxv	111	148
xl	59	149	lxxxiv	72	7	cxxxvi	199	262
xli	201	90	lxxxv	115	9+14	cxxxvii	200	196
xlii	202	91	lxxxvi	116	10	cxxxviii	65	80
xliii	203	23	lxxxvii	117	4	cxxxix	121	130
xliv	204	173	lxxxviii	152	141			

Later annotations include a numbering of the letters based on the collection of 143 letters and the division of the longer letters by numbers in the margins (s. xv ?); also drawings and notes, s. xv, for example on f. 7 a head and 'Correctio' and on f. 65 the upper part of a cowled figure at a desk, with scroll, 'Nota questionem et responsum'. Some of the notes seem to be by Robert Elyot, one of whose typical heads is on f. 109: see p. 631.

2. ff. 172–4 Sermo sancti augustini de uita et moribus clericorum. Propter
quod uolui . . . In uerbo dei seruiam uobis.

PL xxxix. 1568–74 (Sermo 355). Edited by G. Lambot in *Stromata Patristica et Mediaevalia*, i (1950), 124–31. Notes by Robert Elyot on f. 172ᵛ, 'Legant processum hunc
moderni episcopi et erubescant', and on f. 173, 'Notent hoc episcopi' against 'Non est
episcopi seruare aurum'.

3. ff. 174–6 Sermo augustini ad populum excusatorius pro clericis. Caritati
uestre hodie de nobis . . . et tamen uobiscum ibi regnemus.

PL xxxix. 1574–81 (Sermo 356). Edited by Lambot, ibid. 132–43. f. 176ᵛ blank.

ff. iii+178+ii, foliated i–v, 1–176. f. iii was pasted to a former binding. Medieval foliation, 1–176. 376×265 mm. Written space 255×180 mm. 2 cols. 40 lines (as in the
Carlisle manuscript). The first line of writing is above the top ruled line. Pricks in both
margins to guide ruling. Collation of ff. iv, v, 1–176: 1² 2–23⁸. Quires 2–22 numbered at
the end I–XXI. No flex punctuation: where Carlisle has the flex (?) Eton has either the
punctus elevatus (⁖) or a point. Initials: (i) f. 1, 8-line, blue with handsome ornament in
red and blue externally and red and green internally; (ii) 4-line, blue with red ornament,
or red with blue ornament, or green with red ornament: all roughish work after quire 2.
On ff. iv, v a line of yellow wash covers the capital letter beginning each entry. Slatter
binding. Marks from an older binding of the chain attachment near the foot of the side
and of the metal piece for a central strap can be seen on f. iii. Secundo folio (f. 2) *de me
opinionem*.

Written in England. Belonged in s. xv² to three Kentish churchmen in succession,
Thomas Chichele, Thomas Mareys, and John Mocer (Emden, *BRUO*, pp. 412, 1221,
1326 Mower): 'Liber magistri Thome Mareys Rectoris de Sturmowth in Comitatu
Kancie emptus de executoribus M' Thome Checheley Archidiaconi Cantuariensis anno
domini 1468⁰. vltimo die mensis Aprilis'; f. iiiᵛ; 'Liber magistri Iohannis Mocer vicarii
de tenterden. Emptus cantuarie ab executoribus magistri Thome maris et a magistro
Symone hogges officiali pro xxxiii s' iiii d' ', f. iiiᵛ. In Mocer's will, PCC Milles 20 ff.
164ᵛ–165ᵛ, A.D. 1489, this manuscript, MS. 106, 'omelias Originis super Matheum', and
'Rabanum de Ludowicum' (Rabanus on Maccabees, with his preface to Louis I?) were
bequeathed to Eton. The Origen and Rabanus are now missing.

106. *Augustinus, De Verbis Domini et Apostoli; etc.*   s. xii¹

1. ff. iiᵛ–iiiᵛ Hęc sunt quę ut obseruetis precipimus . . . non inducatur. Explicit
regula sancti augustini.

PL xxxii. 1377–84. Cf. Römer, i. 160–3. f. iiʳ, left blank, contains the couplet, s. xii ex.,
printed by James, *Catalogue*, 'Unde supperbimus . . .' (Walther, *Sprichwörter*, no. 32162).

2 (added: perhaps leaves out of another book). ff. ivᵛ–vᵛ (s. xiv²) Hic est sermo
beati Ieronimi presbiteri de omnipotencia et inuisibilitate atque eternitate dei
et de membris dei variisque affectibus more prophetico figuraliter ei assignatis.
Omnipotens pater et filius . . .

PL xlii. 1199–1206/8, *manifestum demonstrare*, but the text here continues for twenty-one
lines, 'Ieremias. Nouum creauit dominus super terram . . . . et hostibus fortis appareret.
Amen'.

3. ff. 1–125ᵛ Incipiunt capitula sancti augustini de verbis domini et de quibusdam sententiis pauli apostoli . . . (*table numbered incorrectly* 1–93) . . . (f. 1ᵛ)

De uerbis euangelii . . . C (*for* E) 'uangelium' audiuimus et in eo . . . ẹtiam in fine mutare.

PL xxxix, in another order. Ninety-eight sermons—numbered correctly in the upper margin, s. xv—corresponding to nos. 1–37, 98, 38–97 in the list by P. Verbraken in *RB* lxxvii (1967), 27–46: he notes that this copy is of 'Type B 1'. The table lists the thirty-eighth sermon here (Verbr., no. 98) twice, as no. XXXVIII and again as no. XCIII. The lower part of f. 64ᵛ was left blank before the change of hand. On f. 115ᵛ 18½ lines of text have been crossed through, because the ink took badly, and recopied and two leaves later the scribe, mistrusting his parchment, left f. 117ᵛ partly blank. Letter references (cf. art. 5) and a few marginalia in English hands, s. xv, added in the margins. At the end is the couplet 'En (*not* Est) labor est finis' printed in James's *Catalogue*.

4. ff. 125ᵛ–130ᵛ Incipit uita sancti augustini. (*a*) Beatus itaque augustinus ex prouincia affricana . . . (f. 129ᵛ) in hanc uitam quemadmodum Nescio. (*b*) Hic posuit cineres . . . felicior sobolis (6 lines). (*c*) Post mortem igitur matres naui-gantes . . . (f. 130) enumerare queat. (*d*) Sane beatus ieronimus . . . curare non desinit. Hic igitur augustini terminus. hic uitẹ excursus fuit. 'Augustine vale'.

BHL, no. 788. Römer, i. 204. The verses are Walther, no. 21115.

5 (added in s. xv). ff. 131–135ᵛ Abba pater . . . Zizannia id est mali in v*erbis* de Semine.

A table of art. 3, referring to the sermon numbers and to the letters which subdivide each sermon.

6. The pastedowns and ff. i, 136 are bifolia of the biblical concordance: see MS. 5.

ff. i+139+i, foliated i–v, 1–136.[1] 390 × 290 mm. Written space *c.* 310 × 236 mm. 2 cols. 47 lines. Ruling with a hard point. Collation: 1² (ff. ii, iii) 2 two (ff. iv, v) 3–16⁸ 17⁶+1 leaf after 2 (f. 115) 18⁸ 19 three (ff. 128–30) 20⁶ wants 6, blank. Quires 3–19 numbered I–XVII at the end (quires 3–9) or at the beginning (quires 11–19). Probably three hands, changing at ff. 57 (10¹) and 65 (11¹), where there is an inexact join, which suggests simul-taneous writing by two scribes. Initials: (i) ff. 1ᵛ, 125ᵛ, in outline edged with red and green on coloured grounds decorated with green and white circling branches: a dragon head at each end of the C on f. 1ᵛ; (ii) 3-line, red with ornament of the same colour. Binding by Williamson. Secundo folio *esse maliuolos* (f. iii) or *tis suẹ* (f. 2).

Written in France (?).[2] A 2-line erasure, f. 130ᵛ. Arts. 2, 5 are later and English. 'xxxviiᵘˢ', f. 130ᵛ, s. xiv (?). A table of contents like those in Horman's books, headed 'Contenta' and an inscription of gift (to Eton), 'Donum M' Ioannis Moyer', f. iiiᵛ, s. xv/xvi. One of four books bequeathed to Eton by John Moyer or Mocer or (Emden) Mower: see MS. 105.

107. *Augustinus, De Civitate Dei*   s. XIII in.

1. (*a*) Incipiunt capitula libri XI. De ea parte operis . . . (f. 5ᵛ) deum uidebunt. (*b*) Incipit prologus in librum beati augustini de ciuitate dei sumptus de libro retrac(ta)tionum eiusdem. Interea cum roma gothorum . . . (f. 6) filii israhel. (*c*) Aurelii augustini doctoris eximii contra aduersarios gloriose ciuitatis dei. de ipsa ciuitate primus liber incipit. Gloriosam ciuitatem dei . . . (f. 229) Gracias gratulantes agant. Amen.

(*a*). Tables of chapters of bks. 11–22, as in *CC* xlvii (1955), xxi–xlv, ending with bk. 22, ch. xxix. Chapter numbers were added later. (*b*). ibid. i–ii and *PL* xxxii. 647 (II. 43). (*c*). *CC* xlvii, xlviii. *PL* xli. 3–804. In bks. 1–10 the paragraphing does not agree with the

---

[1] See Addenda, p. 999.   [2] Verbraken says 'italien?'.

chapter numbers added in the margins in s. xiv (?): for example, bk. 1 is in twenty-seven paragraphs, but is marked for thirty-six chapters. Bks. 11–22 have an inconspicuous early, but not original chapter numbering in roman figures and a later chapter numbering in the margins in large arabic figures: the earlier and later numbers do not always agree. There are more paragraphs in bks. 11–22 than in bks. 1–10. ff. 229ᵛ–230ᵛ were left blank.

2. f. i is a bifolium of the manuscript used in MS. 32: see above, p. 661. One leaf is numbered 43.

ff. i+230. For f. i see above. 400 × 265 mm. Written space 280 × 180 mm. 2 cols. 46 lines. The first line of writing above the top ruled line. Pricks in both margins to guide ruling. Collation: 1–11¹⁰ 12¹² 13–20¹⁰ 21–22¹² 23⁴ (4, f. 230, is pasted down). Only quires 1–5 are numbered—at the end. A new hand begins at f. 46ᵛ and the ruling changes from three vertical lines between the columns to two vertical lines between the columns when the new hand begins a new quire (f. 51). Initials: (i) f. 6, 9-line, red on gold and pink ground, historiated: Augustine writing; (ii) red and blue, or one of these colours, with ornament of both colours or of one colour or without ornament: of bk. 7, red on a ground of decorated brown and blue; of bks. 19–22, unfinished; (iii) 3-line, red or blue; (iv) 1-line, red, in art. 1a. Lisley binding. Secundo folio *naturali pondere*.

Written in England. At Eton by c. 1520.

108. (A) *Augustinus, De Trinitate;* (B) *Tabula in N. de Lyra, etc.*

s. xiii/xiv–xv in.

1. ff. 1–110ᵛ Incipit [.....] D[a nobis Domine in uia hac qua te duce ingredimur intellectum atque in te inspira in]reprehe[nsibiliter . . . et ignoran]tie teneb[ras remoue a me Qui . . . amen]. Epistola aurelii augustini ad aurelium carthaginensem episcopum. Domino beatissimo et sinceristissima caritate uenerando . . . in domino salutem. De trinitate . . . (f. 2) anteponi. Incipiunt capitula . . . De triplici causa . . . (f. 4ᵛ) et processionis spiritus sancti (*numbered tables of chapters of the fifteen books*). In nomine domini nostri ihesu cristi aurelii augustini episcopi de trinitate. Incipit liber primus. prohemium. C 1. De triplici erroris causa. falsa de deo opinantium. Lecturus hec que de trinitate . . . et tu ignosce et tui. amen. Explicit liber de trinitate.

PL xlii. 817–1098. *CC* xvi. The introductory letter to Aurelius is preceded by a damaged copy of the prayer printed by G. Morin in *RB* xxi. 129–32 (*Clavis*, no. 328: Römer, i. 185) and followed by the lists of chapters printed in *CC* xvi. 3–23. f. 1 was mended, but not well mended, in s. xiv.

2 (added). f. 111 Incipit tabula super libros beati aug' de trinitate. contra achademicos qui de singulis . . . vt facit omnis (*ends abruptly*).

An alphabetical subject index which got only as far as *Bonum*. References are by book, chapter number and, sometimes, letter division of chapter. f. 111ᵛ blank.

3. ff. 112–185ᵛ Abacuk prophetauit destruccionem caldeorum . . . olei nota zac' pᵒ f. Explicit tabula super doctorem de lyra. compilata et scripta per fratrem Willelmum Morton de sacro ordine fratrum Minorum in conuentu Couentrey Anno domini mᵒ ccccᵐᵒ tercio. et c'.

Copies of the table in Oxford are in Bodley 42 (1846), Exeter College 16, Lincoln College 69 and Merton College 12. All of them call the author William Norton. References to Lyra's postils are by book of the Bible, chapter number and letter division of chapter.

Notes by Robert Elyot (see p. 631) include 'a seeler or a keuer of gold' as a gloss to *propiciatorium*, f. 164.

4. ff. 186–7 *Incipiunt questiones Fratris Nicholai de Lira super Bibliam Hic contente vel tacte preter punctatas in capite . . . Expliciunt questiones Fratris Nicholai de lira super Bibliam.*

A list of 207 questions in alphabetical order. The first is 'Utrum Apocalipsis liber conuenienter ponitur . . . in prologi exposicione super Euangelium Iohannis', and the last 'Utrum yris sit signum federis genesis 9'.

5. f. 187^{rv} Notes: (*a*) of three quodlibets of Nicholas de Lira in a manuscript which Dr. (Thomas) Gascoigne gave to Lincoln College, Oxford;[1] (*b*) on measures 'De quadam veteri biblia extracta de Cant' ' (perhaps a Bible at Canterbury College, Oxford), 'Cal*culus* quarta pars oboli . . . Momentum est quarta pars hore'; (*c*) Nota hugonem de vienna magnum theologum super prou' capitulo 14 . . .

(*a*), (*b*) in the same hand as the notes to art. 3. James, *Catalogue*, prints (*a*). (*c*) lists seventeen critical marks, the first 'astericus' and the last 'phietro'.

6. The pastedown and flyleaf at each end, ff. i, 188, are bifolia from bk. 4 of the Institutes of Justinian in an English hand, s. xiv med.: 2 cols., 35 lines.

ff. i+188+i. For ff. i, 188 see art. 6. ff. 1–111 and ff. 112–87 are two originally separate manuscripts, (A) s. xiii/xiv and (B) s. xv in., in a Lisley binding (see p. 629): they were probably put together by him. A label on the back cover is now missing.

(A) ff. 1–111. 338×225 mm. Written space 215×150 mm. 2 cols. 40 lines. Collation: 1–9^{12} 10 three (ff. 109–11). Initials: (i) red and blue with violet and red ornament and also blue where the ornament is 'saw pattern'; (ii) 2-line, blue with red ornament or red with violet ornament. Capital letters in the ink of the text marked with red. Secundo folio [*o*]*mnia si uoluerint*.

Art. 1 is probably French, but nearly contemporary and later marginalia are in English hands. Art. 2 was added in s. xiii/xiv in current anglicana. A 2-line erasure on f. 110^v contained a date.

(B) ff. 112–87. 338×225 mm. Written space 220×140 mm. and in art. 4 253×185 mm. 2 cols. 46–55 lines. Frame ruling on pages where the writing is current. Collation: 1–3^8 4^4+1 leaf before 1 (f. 136) 5^{10} 6^{10}+1 leaf before 1 (f. 151) 7^8+1 leaf before 1 (f. 162) 8^{12} 9^4 wants 4, blank, 10^2 (ff. 186–7). Several hands writing anglicana and current mixtures of anglicana and secretary; also (art. 4) secretary and (ff. 142–144^v) a continental (?) cursiva. Initials: (i) f. 112, 6-line, blue, patterned in white, on ground of punched gold, decorated in colours: prolongations form a continuous border; (ii) 3-line or 4-line, blue with red ornament. Secundo folio 2^a *ut* (f. 113). Written in England.

(B) was at Eton before 1500 (cf. art. 3), (A) possibly not before *c*. 1520.

109. *Eusebius, Historia ecclesiastica; J. de Forda; R. Miledunensis*

s. XIII in.

1. ff. 1–80^v Incipit epistola sancti ieronimi presbiteri ad cromatium episcopum super librum ecclesiasticum editum ab eusebio episcopo. Peritorum dicunt

[1] Thirteen volumes of Gascoigne's gift to Lincoln College are listed in the 1474 catalogue (*BQR* viii. 343–59), nos. 31, 34, 37, 50–3, 90, 96, 104, 119, 120, 126, and Lincoln College MSS. 8, 33, and 54 were also of his gift.

esse medicorum . . . ad obitum theodosii augusti. Explicit epistola. Incipiunt capitula libri primi. I. De diuinitate cristi . . . translata sunt (*table of 16 chapters of bk. 1*). Successiones sanctorum apostolorum . . . premia meritorum.

PL xxi. 461–540. A table of chapters is in front of each of the eleven books.

2. ff. 81–102ᵛ Incipit prologus uenerabilis Iohannis prioris de forda. ad domnum Bartholomeum exoniensem episcopum.¿ in uitam beati Wulurici anachorete haselbérgie. Reuerendo patri et domino Bartholomeo . . . (f. 81ᵛ) qui pie audierint hec. Valete. Explicit prologus. Incipit alius ad domnum Baldewinum cantuariensem archiepiscopum. Reuerentissimo domino et patri in cristo karissimo baldewino . . . (f. 82) paternitas uestra. Explicit prologus. Incipit uita beati uulrici anachorete haselberie edita a uenerabili iohanne priori de forda. De uocatione eius et conuersione. Beatus uulricus de mediocri anglorum gente . . . dicat esse assum. Explicit uita beati uulrici anachorete.

The life of St. Wulfric of Haselbury, *BHL*, no. 8743, edited by M. Bell (Somerset Record Society xlvii, 1933), with use of this copy. Bk. 2, f. 89; 3, f. 96.

3. ff. 103–82 Quoniam homo peccando tam uoluntate quam opere . . . disiuncta nec esse necesse.

Parts 1 and 2 of bk. 2 of the Sententiae of Robert of Melun: cf. *Œuvres de Robert de Melun*, iii.i (Spicilegium Sacrum Lovaniense, Études et Documents xxi, 1947), ed. R.-M. Martin, p. viii. Chapters are numbered in the margin in roman figures from 'i' to 'lxxxiii' on ff. 103–123ᵛ and in arabic figures from '1' to '68' on ff. 131ᵛ–148ᵛ: '1' is written where the text begins 'Ipsum namque nouum testamentum . . .'. f. 182ᵛ blank.

ff. iii + 184 + iii, foliated (i–iii), 1–145, 145*, 146–53, 153*, 154–82, (183–5). 390 × 290 mm. Written space *c*. 290 × 195 mm and (art. 3) *c*. 270 × 175 mm. 2 cols. 45 lines and (art. 3) 48–57 lines. Pricks in both margins to guide ruling. Collation: 1–12⁸ 13⁶ (ff. 97–102) 14–23⁸ 24². Quires 1–24 numbered at the beginning and quires 1–10 also at the end. A change of hand at f. 103 (art. 3). Flex punctuation (7) was added to art. 2, but only on the first two pages. Initials on ff. 1–102: (i) blue with red ornament, or, sometimes, green and red ornament; (ii) 3-line, green or red, or, rarely, and not in art. 2, blue. Initials on ff. 103–82: (i) blue with red ornament; (ii) 2-line, red with blue ornament, or green with red ornament, or, rarely, blue with red ornament. Binding by Williamson. Secundo folio *didisse*.

Written in England. John Bale saw art. 2 at Eton, *c*. 1550 (*Index*, p. 202).

110. *Seneca, Tragoediae decem*   s. xiv med.

1. ff. 1–52 Soror tonantis hec enim solum michi . . . Fulmina mictes. Lucii annei. se her. etheus. explicit. deo gracias.

Hercules Furens, f. 1; Thyestes, 5; Thebias, 10ᵛ; Hippolytus, 13ᵛ; Oedipus, 19; Troades, 24; Medea, 29ᵛ; Agamemnon, 34; Octavia, 38ᵛ; Hercules Oetoeus, 43. Interlinear glosses and scholia in the margins. Bernardo Bembo wrote against the words of 'Chorus' at the end of Hercules Oetoeus 'Nota et iterum nota suauissimum notandum'. This copy collated as e by G. C. Giardina, *Senecae Tragoediae*, Studi pubblicati dall'istituto di filologia classica, xx (1966). Cf. also A. P. MacGregor in *Proc. American Philological Ass.* cii (1971), 327–56, who lists it among the 'conflati'.

2. f. 52ᵛ (*a*) Omne peccatum est actio. actio autem . . . fecisse peniteat. (*b*) Seneca paulo. Tulit priscorum . . . licuit.

(*a*). *Clavis*, no. 1090 (Pseudo-Martinus de Braga, De moribus). *PL* lxxii. 29–32. *Senecae Opera*, ed. Haase, iii. 462–7. (*b*). An extract from the letter beginning '*Aue mi paule carissime. putasne me*', ed. Haase, iii. 480/9–11.

3. Flyleaf notes and scribbles include: f. ii^v, 'Mccclxxxxi die Iouis xvi Febr' de nocte venientie (? *sic*) dies veneris hora quinta Carolus natus' and 'Mccclxxxxv die tertio augusti [. . . .] filium nomine dominicus[. . . .]'; f. 54^v, three lines in the hand of Bernardo Bembo.

ff. iii+52+iii. ff. ii, iii, 53, 54 are medieval end-leaves: ii was pasted down. 396×278 mm. Written space 275 mm high. 2 cols. (ff. 1–4^r, 3 cols.) 56 lines. Collation: 1–6⁸ 7⁴. Initials: (i) 3-line, blue with red ornament; (ii) 2-line, blue with red ornament, or red with pale-green or slate-blue ornament. Binding by Slatter. Secundo folio *Non uetera*.

Written in Italy. An inscription on f. 54, s. xiv, is partly legible by ultra-violet light: 'Iste tragedie Senece sunt mei [. . . .] 'de nouaria' empte prec' [. . .] ducatorum [. . .]'. The same hand wrote lower down the page 'Si quis furatur uel redat uel moriatur Ad talem mortem quod ad furcas suspendatur'. Bought by Bernardo Bembo in 1450: 'Hoc senece volumen tragiedalle quod meum est emi ego [bernardus bembo] (*almost certain by ultra-violet light*) ducatis quinque cum dimidio id est ducatis v ÷. Quo tempore uincentie in domo eximii arcium ac theologie doctoris magistri Iohannis franzigine morabar anno natiuitatis milesimo quadragintessimo. quinquagessimo. anno Iubelei', f. 53; 'Ego b[ernardus bembo] emi has tragidias duc' 6', f. 53^v. Given by Wotton, no doubt: see MS. 87. *CMA* 113.

112. *Dante, Divina commedia* (*in Italian*) s. XIV med.

Incomincia la conmedia di dante alleghieri di firenze. nella quale tracta delle pene et punimenti de uitii et de meriti et premii delle uirtu. Canto I de la prima parte la qual si chiama inferno nel qual lautore fa prohemio ad tucta lopera. Nel mezo del cammino . . . (f. 28) Et quindi uscimo a riueder le stelle. (f. 29) Chomincia la seconda parte della commedia di dante . . . et contiene xxxiii canti. Qui nel primo canto sono quelli chesperano di uenire quando chesia a le beate genti. Per correr miglior acque . . . (f. 56) Puro et disposto a salire alle stelle. (f. 57) Comincia la terza cantica de la comedia di dante . . . chiamato paradiso . . . et diuidesi in noue parti si come linferno. Canto primo . . . di sapienza . La gloria di colui . . . (f. 84) Lamor che muoue il sole et laltre stelle.

Entered on p. 497 of the list of Dante manuscripts by G. Petrocchi, *La Commedia secondo l'antica vulgata*, i (1966), 481–563, but misdated early fifteenth century. ff. 28^v, 56^v, 84^v were left blank. The last bears a difficult eight-line inscription, 'Nota che [que]sto Dante . . . Summa in tuto *lire* lviii *solidi* xiii so. . .', recording apparently expenses in some connection with this copy.[1] From f. 40 onwards marks in brown ink occur in the bottom right-hand corner of most leaves: I do not know what they mean.

ff. i+84+i. 400×265 mm. Written space 293 mm high. 2 cols. 45 lines. Collation: 1¹⁰ 2⁸ 3–4¹⁰ 5⁸ 6–7¹⁰ 8⁸ 9¹⁰. Written in 'cancellaresca toscana', the Italian equivalent of non-current anglicana: as James Wardrop noted inside the cover, the script is like that of Milan, Trivulziana, 1080 (facsimile edition, 1921), written by Ser Francesco di Ser Nardo

[1] 'Spese' is in line 2 and 'spexe' in line 5, 'pagadi a piero nerodo (?) d*e* adam d*e*' in line 6, and, after an illegible word or two, 'Ciuidal' as the first word in line 7. Dr. A. de la Mare has kindly helped me with this inscription. Ultra-violet light is of no avail.

in 1337. A capital letter begins each stanza: C, D, E, F, G, O, Q, S, T are ornamented with a pair of thin vertical lines and A, B, N, P, R, V with a pair of thin horizontal lines and I and L have no ornament. Initials: (i) ff. 1, 29, 57, pink on blue and red grounds, historiated: cf. James, *Catalogue*; (ii) 3-line, blue or red with ornament of the other colour. A border all round f. 1 and on one side of ff. 29, 57. Binding by Slatter, rebacked. Secundo folio *Per questa*.

Written in Italy. The arms of Alighieri, per pale or and sable a fess argent, at the foot of f. 1.[1] *CMA* 44.

114. *P. Lombardus, Sententiae* s. XIII[2]

Cupientes aliquid . . . .

The four books of the Sentences, each preceded by a table of chapters. Bk. 2, f. 79; 3, f. 140^v; 4, f. 193. ff. 78^{rv}, 191^v-2^v, 265^v-268^v were left blank. Interlinear glosses and many annotations in the broad margins and in blank spaces. s. xiii[2], xiii/xiv. 'Hec sunt 7 que mulierem obseruare decet vt sit silicet Casta tacens residens humilis operans pia prudens', f. 267^v, s. xiv.

ff. i+268. bks. 1 and 3 have a medieval page numbering. f. i is a medieval flyleaf. 360 × 248 mm. Written space 215 × 130 mm. 2 cols. 35 lines. Collation: 1–6^{12} 7^6 (ff. 73–8) 8–16^{12} 17^6 (ff. 187–92) 18–23^{12} 24^4 (4, f. 268, is pasted down). *Ad hoc* pencil signatures. Initials: (i) red and blue with ornament of both colours; (ii) 2-line, blue with red ornament. Williamson binding. Secundo folio in textu (f. 5) *sustinemus*; in tabula (f. 2) *De inmutibilitate*.

Written in England. 'Beaufort' in small writing, s. xiv ?, at the head of f. 1. '[. . . . .] nonagesimo quinto', f. 267^v, probably a Cautio note of A.D. 1395. 'Donum M' Richardi hopton sacre theologie professoris et quondam socii huius collegii', f. i^v.

115. *Jacopo della Lana, Commentary on Dante (in Italian)* s. XV[2]

Nel mezo . . . vita. Ad inteligencia de la presente chomedia si chome usano li espositori in le sciencie . . . (f. 44^v) del ultimo chapitolo. amem. Qui chompie le esposicion dela prima parte de dante chiamata inferno. 'per Iacomo dala lana fata'. Poscia che dito et tocado breuemente . . . la ueritade. deo gracias amen. (f. 46) Per chorer miglior aqua . . . etc. In questa seconda parte . . . lo qualle viue et regna per infinita sechula seculorum. amen. Qui chompie le esposizion de la segonda chanticha zioe del purgatorio del libro de dante deo gragias.

The commentary on the Inferno and Purgatorio by Jacopo della Lana, first printed in 1477 (*GKW* 7964: ascribed to Benvenuto da Imola). Edn. Bologna, 1866, i. 103–518, ii. 7–403. The passage 'Poscia che . . .' (edn. i. 517–18), is squeezed in as an afterthought in the second column of f. 44^v. f. iii^{rv} is ruled but blank, except for an 11-line note about Dante on the verso. f. 45^{rv} is blank and without ruling.

ff. ii+97+i, foliated in a medieval hand (i–iii), 1–96, (97). Paper. 293 × 220 mm. Written space *c.* 230 × 175 mm. Frame ruling. 2 cols. *c.* 65 lines. Collation of ff. iii, 1–96: 1^{14}

[1] Four other manuscripts with these arms have been noted, Braidense, AG xiii. 41, Strozziano 151, Laurenziano 40, 14, and Riccardiano 1010: cf. M. Barbi, *Per il testo della Divina Commedia*, Rome, 1891, pp. 46–7 (reprinted from *Rivista critica della letteratura italiana*, vi and vii). These are manuscripts of the 'Dante del cento' group.

2–4^{10} 5 one (f. 44) 6^{12} 7–10^{10}. Cursiva by more than one hand. Initials: (i) f. 1, 6-line, blue with red ornament; (ii) 3-line or 2-line, blue or red. Binding by Slatter.

Written in Italy. 'Io Delphini', f. iii, s. xvi: cf. MS. 124. Part of the Henry Wotton bequest in 1639, no doubt: cf. MS. 87. *CMA* 45.

116+219, pp. 27–50. *T. Aquinas, Prima pars Summae*   s. XIII/XIV

1. MS. 116, ff. 1–144^v, MS. 219, pp. 39–46, 35–8, 27–34, MS. 116, ff. 145–9. Incipit summa de theologia edita a fratre thoma de aquino ordinis predicatorum. libri primi questio prima de necessitate huius doctrine. Quia catholice ueritatis ... decebat eum qui est super omnia benedictus deus in secula amen. Explicit liber primus summe fratris thome de aquino ordinis fratrum predicatorum Magistri in theologia.

584 numbered sections. f. 144^v ends in Q. 91 a 2 (sect. 455). f. 145 begins in Q. 117 a 1 (sect. 576). Ten of the thirty-six leaves missing in this gap are in MS. 219, where parts or all of sect. 455–8, 466–8, 479–83, 490–7, 533–8, 549–57, 560–4, 572–6 survive: see below, collation. Dondaine and Shooner, *Codices Manuscripti operum Thomae de Aquino*, i (1967), nos. 809, 811.2. Contemporary marginalia in English hands.

2. MS. 116, ff. 149^v–153^v Incipiunt rubrice summe de theologia fratris thome de aquino ordinis fratrum predicatorum. I. Questio prima de ipsa sciencia theologica. et queruntur x ...

A table of the 119 questions of art. 1. f. 154^v was left blank and pasted down.

3. MS. 219, pp. 47–50 Fragments of an alphabetical index to art. 1, once perhaps in front of it. p. 47 begins in A, '204 appropriare'. p. 48 ends in D, '549 vtrum demones ...'. p. 49 begins in P, '395 vtrum memoria fit alia potentia ab intellectu'. p. 50 ends in S, '95 vtrum scientia dei ...'. The numbers are the section numbers of art. 1.

ff. i+154 in MS. 116. ff. 12 in MS. 219. 330 × 220 mm. Written space 225 × 140 mm. 2 cols. 51 or 52 lines. Line numbering by fives between the columns on ff. 1–46^r. Collation: 1 two (a bifolium: MS. 219, pp. 47–50) 2–13^{12} (ff. 1–144) 14 four (the outside bifolium and another: MS. 219, pp. 39–46) 15 two (the outside bifolium: MS. 219, pp. 35–8) 16 four (the outside bifolium and another: MS. 219, pp. 27–34) 17^{12} wants 10, 11, blank: 12 pasted down (ff. 145–54). *Ad hoc* signatures in pencil. Initials: (i) f. 1, 5-line, pink patterned in white on blue and red decorated ground: a gold frame; (ii) 2-line, blue with red ornament or red with pale-green ornament. Lisley binding. The mark of a label secured by six nails is on the back cover. Secundo folio *vnde manifestum*.

Written probably in England. At Eton by *c*. 1520. Partly dismembered in s. xvii^1 when six bifolia were used in the bindings of Eton college accounts: see below, MSS. 219+221.

117. *R. Grosseteste, etc.*   s. XIV med. –XIV/XV

1 (s. xiv). ff. 1–104^v 'Dict' Lincoln'.' Amor multipliciter ... (f. 103) iusticie et misericordie etc. Explicit.

One hundred and forty-seven dicta. Thomson, *Grosseteste*, pp. 215–32. Dictum 127 is omitted in its place, f. 86^v, and added by another hand on ff. 103–4, together with a second copy of Dictum 134. f. 92^r was left blank: the verso contains a scheme of linked words to illustrate 'non reddentes malum pro malo'. A loose leaf (61*) after f. 61 has diagrams illustrating Dictum 96 (f. 62). f. 104ᵛ blank.

2 (quire 11, added in s. xv). Tables, etc., of art. 1: (a) ff. 105–111ᵛ Abstinencia. require in dicto 36 . . . ysopus calidus est; (b) ff. 111ᵛ–112ᵛ A list of the 147 dicta. (c) f. 112ᵛ In hoc libello sunt capitula . . . ad populum feci. Explicit tabula super dicta Lyncolniensis.

An earlier copy of (b) is on f. vʳᵛ.

Arts. 3–6 are of s. xiv/xv.

3. ff. 113–55 'Lincoln' de Cessacione legalium.' Fuerunt plurimi in primitiua ecclesia . . . et infirmitatis medicinam. 'Explicit Lincoln' de Cessacione legalium.'

Ibid., p. 122. f. 155ᵛ blank.

4. ff. 156–165ᵛ 'Lincoln' de venenis.' Racio veneni potissime . . . et merces qui cum . . . deus. Explicit tractatus qui dicitur 'de venenis secundum Lincoln'' (the addition over erasure). 'Explicit Lincoln' de venenis'.

Pseudo-Grosseteste: ibid., p. 270.

5. ff. 166–182ᵛ Caᵐ 24 Ulterius restat iuxta promissa discutere differenciam inter peccatum venale et mortale . . . non sit necesse procuratorie sic orare amen.

Chapters 24–6 of pt. 5 of a summa of theology. Ch. 25 begins 'Ex istis patescit. ut dictum est in principio 23ⁱⁱ huius 5ᵗⁱ quod necessitati sumus peccare saltem venialiter'. Ch. 26 begins 'Ulterius iuxta promissa videndum est de suffragio existencium in purgatorio'. 'Lincolniensis' and William of Auxerre are quoted. ff. 174ᵛ, 175ʳ left blank after ch. 24.

The decoration is the best evidence that art. 5 was part of MS. 117 from the first: cf. f. 179 with f. 145.

6. ff. 183–201ᵛ, 212ʳᵛ, 202–11 (a) Intencio venerabilis viri fulgentii in sua methelogia est sub tegmine fabularum . . . (f. 193ʳᵃ/54) ut augustinus et anselmus et alii. sic igitur finita est 6 mithologia ful de virtute prouidencie. (b) Sequitur 7ᵃ mithologia ful de apolline. Dei iouis prole fingunt namque poete apollinem primum filium et principium . . . (f. 204) plus valet quam omnes virtutes sic igitur finitur 12ᵃ mithologia fulgencii et commentarium super primum librum mithologiorum eiusdem. Liber secundus mithologiorum fulgencii incipit de pictura paridis . . . ex tali glorificacione sequitur finalis dampnacio. Sic ergo finiuntur mithologie primi libri et secundi. etc.

(a). The commentary on Fulgentius by John Ridevall, ed. H. Liebeschütz, Fulgentius Metaforalis, pp. 65–114. The text 'enim notandum . . . incidentem' (edn., pp. 108/11–111/17) was left out at f. 191ʳᵇ/56, and supplied on the recto of an inserted leaf, f. 192: 192ᵛ is blank. For Ridevall and his commentaries cf. B. Smalley, English Friars and Antiquity, 1960, pp. 109–32. (b) appears to continue (a). It is not in Cambridge, U.L., Ii. 2.20 and Mm. 1.18, nor in B.L., Royal 7 C. i and seems to have been unknown to Liebeschütz. It is in Pembroke College, Cambridge, 230, ff. 97–126ᵛ.

ff. v+212+iii. ff. 1–104 and 113–65 were paginated in s. xvii. ff. iii–v, 213 are medieval end-leaves: for v cf. above, art. 2. ff. iiiʳ, 213ᵛ were once pasted down. 330 × 230 mm. Written space c. 250–230 × 155 mm. 2 cols. 57–60 lines. Collation: 1–4⁸ 5¹²+1 leaf before

1 (f. 33) 6–7¹² 8¹⁰ (ff. 70–9) 9¹²+1 leaf, now inserted after 12 as f. 92, but formerly before 1, as the page numbering shows, 10¹² (ff. 93–104) 11⁸ (ff. 105–12) 12¹² 13–14⁸ 15¹² 16¹⁴, blank, after f. 165 17¹² wants 10, 11, blank, after f. 174 18¹² wants 12, blank, after f. 182 19¹²+1 leaf inserted after 9 (f. 192) 20 six (ff. 196–201) 21¹² wants 12 (21¹ is misplaced after 21¹¹). Quires 1–10 numbered a–k in red ink and quires 12–15 l–o in pencil: the rest of the manuscript seems to have been in confusion when signatures were put in, c (in red ink) on quire 16, p, q (in pencil) on quires 17, 18, b (in red ink) on quire 19, a (in red ink) on quire 20. Anglicana by several hands. Initials: (i) f. 1, 4-line, gold on blue and red ground patterned in white: short sprays into the margin; (ii) 4-line or 5-line, blue and red with red ornament and on f. 94 red and blue saw-pattern ornament; (iii) 2-line or 3-line, blue with red ornament. Slatter binding. Secundo folio *et nobilis*.

Written in England. 'Liber [. . . .]', f. iv: M. R. James, helped by a reagent, read 'Liber magistri Iohannis de Rau*erton*' Canonici', but the name is now illegible. 'Caucio magistri Richardi [. . .]ord Exposita in cista de Duncan [. . .] die mensis [. . . . .] mccccl[. . .] et habet supplemetum 2° fo ingreditur et iacet pro [. . .]', f. 211ᵛ; also higher on the page, 'Caucio cum Supplemento 2° fo ingreditur', initials, and 'xx⁸ Duncan': the initials are I inside a D or a G standing either for John Doll or John Godsond, the Oxford stationers. Belonged to Nicholas Kempston (cf. MS. 18), whose hand occurs in marginalia, for example on f. 48: 'Liber quondam Magistri Nicholai Kempston Anno domini 1477 numquam vendendus set libere occupandus a sacerdotibus instructis ad predicandum verbum dei successiue quamdiu durauerit secundum vltimam voluntatem defuncti. Orate igitur pro anima eius', f. ivᵛ. At Eton by 1500: cf. f. 72 for a typical head by Robert Elyot (see p. 631).

118. *Bartholomaeus de Pisis* s. xv²

1. ff. 1–299ᵛ In nomine domini nostri yhesu cristi. et beatissime uirginis marie matris sue. ac beati patris nostri francisci. Incipit opus quod intitulatur de conformitate uite beati francisci ad uitam domini nostri yhesu cristi redemptoris nostri. editum a fratre Bartholomeo de pisis ordinis minorum. sacre theologie magistro ob reuerentiam sui patris precipui beati francisci. anno domini M CCC°lxx xv°. Incipit primus prologus pro opere prefato. Sanctorum uita. probis fulta operibus . . . et perfruendum me perducere digneris. Qui cum patre tuo . . . Amen. Finis arboris et operis. Francisce iesu typice dux norma minorum . . . (4 lines). Francisce sequens dogmata superni creatoris . . . (2 lines).

BHL, no. 3134. Three books: 2, f. 163ᵛ; 3, f. 253ᵛ. Quaracchi edn., *Analecta Franciscana*, iv (1906), v (1912).

2. f. 300 Documents relating to art. 1: (*a*) Copia litere a magistro bartolomeo directe generali ministro et capitulo generali pro approbatione operis precedentis. Reuerendis in cristo patribus henrico . . . Data in loco prefato assisii die prima mensis augusti; (*b*) Litera responsiua capituli generalis istud opus approbantis. In christo sibi carissimo . . . Frater henricus . . . Deo gratias Amen.

(*a*, *b*). *Anal. Fran.* v. 503–4. f. 300ᵛ is blank.

ff. iii+300+ii. f. iii is a medieval flyleaf. 315 × 230 mm. Written space *c*. 227 × 165 mm. 2 cols. 53 lines. Collation: 1–30¹⁰. Quires signed, except quire 9, a–h, i–z, aa–ff. A small neat hand. Initials: (ii) f. 1, 13-line, red patterned in white on historiated gold ground: St. Francis receives the stigmata; (ii) f. 1, 4-line, gold on blue ground patterned in white; (iii) ff. 1ᵛ, 163ᵛ blue with red ornament, or, f. 253ᵛ, red without ornament; (iv, v) 7-line and 2-line, blue or red. Capital letters in the ink of the text filled with pale yellow. Slatter binding. Secundo folio *nis in medio*.

Written in Italy. 'Iste liber Competit loco sancti Appolonii extra brixiam', f. iii^v, s. xvi. *CMA* 59.

119. *Gregorius, Registrum; V. Bellavacensis, etc.* s. XIII in.–XV

ff. 2–182 (s. xiii in.) and ff. 183–248 (s. xv med.) are two independent manuscripts put together for William Horman and furnished with indexes by him (arts. 1, 9). A table of contents for Horman on f. 1 lists arts. 4–8, with leaf references.

1 (added, s. xv/xvi). ff. iii–v^v Index alphabeticus in potiora registri diui Gregorii In quo indice numerus algorithmicus seruit numero foliorum in dextro cornu signatorum A.B.C. et D seruiunt quatuor columnis eiusdem folii. Verbum subnexum indicat principium epistole. Ade anima in peccato mortua est 75b. charitas . . .

An index to art. 4. For this and other indexes in manuscripts belonging to William Horman see N. R. Ker in *The Library*, 5th series, xvii (1962), 77–85. f. vi^rv blank.

2. ff. 2–4^v Tables of chapters of each of the fourteen books of art. 4.

f. 1^rv was left blank: see above. Lines of music on f. ii^v (see art. 10) offset onto f. 1 before ff. iii–vi were in their present place.

3. f. 5 Simbolum fidei dictum (*in margin* editum) a beato gregorio papa. Credo in unum deum omnipotentem patrem et filium et spiritum sanctum tres personas . . . laxari peccata. in nomine patris et filii et spiritus sancti.

4. ff. 5–182^v Registri beati Gregorii pape liber primus. Incipit mense septembri Indictione nona. Gregorius seruus seruorum dei⸴ uniuersis episcopis⸴ per siciliam constitutis. Ualde necessarium . . . (f. 182) moribus seruare concedat. Amen. Duodecima. Data kalendis nouembris⸴ Indictione. Explicit liber Registri beati Gregorii pape. deo gracias.

MGH, *Epist.* i–ii (1891–9). *PL* lxxvii. 441–1328. Three letters of bk. 1 (nos. xv, xxii, xxiii) omitted in their places are on f. 182^rv. They should come on ff. 7^v, 8, where the scribe noted in red in the margins, 'Quere in fine libri'.

5. ff. 183–201^v Epistola consolatoria de morte amici. Dilecto deo et hominibus. illustrissimo domino. in cristo sibi carissimo. diuina fauente clemencia francorum principi ludouico. frater vincencius beluacensis de ordine predicatorum salutem . . xvi tantummodo capitula continentem. . . . (*table of 16 chapters*) . . . In primis igitur aduertere debet . . . regie maiestatis Amen.

Vincent of Beauvais. Printed in 1481 (Goff, V. 277).

6. ff. 201^v–235 Incipit prologus sequentis opusculi. De puerorum nobilium condicione. Serenissime ac reuerentissime domine sue francorum dei gracia Regine margarete. frater vincencius de ordine predicatorum qualiscumque lector in monasterio suo de regali monte . . . per capitula subiecta distinctum . . . (*table of 51 chapters*) . . . (f. 202) Filii tibi sunt. erudi illos . . . virginitas honorari. Amen. Explicit liber de puerorum erudicione.

Vincent of Beauvais. Printed in 1477 and later; last by A. Steiner, Cambridge, Mass., 1938, who lists three copies in England, but not this one.

7. ff. 235ʳᵛ, 238ʳᵛ Incipit breuiloquium de virtutibus antiquorum principum ac philosophorum. Quoniam misericordia et veritas . . . Secunda pars principalis de prudencia et 1° quod debet esse in principibus. Hiis breuiter premissis de *(ends abruptly)*.

Johannes Wallensis, O.F.M., Breviloquium, printed in 1496 and later: cf. A. J. Little, *The Grey Friars in Oxford*, 1892, p. 144. The last words here are at the beginning of pt. 2 (edn. 1496, f. 245). The text is continuous. Evidently something else intervened on the two now missing leaves, 236, 237, since a reader noted on 235ᵛ at the foot 'vertatis ad tercium folium quod sic incipit seccabit'.

8. ff. 239–48 Quis dabit capiti meo aquam . . . Oportunius multo a me nunc? quam tunc a propheta dei dicitur . . . alia non queras. Explicit liber sancti iohannis crisostomi de reparacione lapsi.

Printed in s. xv (Goff, J. 294–5). Cf. *PG* xlvii. 277–308 (De reparacione lapsi, bk. 1).

9 (added, s. xv/xvi). ff. 248ᵛ–249 Repertorium breue in Vincentium Beluacensem de consolatione super morte amici . . .

Brief indexes to arts. 5, 6 by one of Horman's scribes. ff. 249ᵛ–250ᵛ blank.

10. ff. i, ii, 251, 252 and the pastedown inside the front cover are five leaves from near the end of the temporale of a (Sarum ?) gradual.

English hand, s. xiv. 11 long lines and music. The leaves in the order pastedown, 251, ii, i, 252 contain text for the fifteenth and the eighteenth–twenty-first Sundays after Trinity and Friday and Saturday 'quattuor temporum septembris', with some differences, especially in the versicles from that in *Sarum Missal*, pp. 186–7, 189–92, 198–201. The last four leaves are two bifolia with continuous text.

11. The pastedown inside the back cover is a bifolium of a two-column theological manuscript written in anglicana, s. xiv/xv.

ff. ii+252+ii, foliated in s. xv/xvi (i–vi), 1–235, 238–250, (251–2); also from f. 183 in s. xv, 1–53, 56–68. For ff. i, ii, 251–2 see above art. 10. 358×250 mm. Written space on ff. 5–182ᵛ 255×165 mm and from f. 183 270×170 mm. Art. 4 in 2 cols. of 41 lines: pricks in both margins to guide ruling. Arts. 5–8 in 55–64 long lines: frame ruling. Collation of ff. iii–vi, 1–250: 1⁴ (ff. iii–vi) 2 four (ff. 1–4: 1, 2 a bifolium) 3–14⁸ 15⁶ (ff. 101–6) 16–24⁸ 25 four (ff. 179–82) 26–31⁸ 32⁸ wants 6, 7 after f. 325 32⁸ 33⁴. Quires 3–24 are numbered at the end I–XXII and have catchwords. Quires 26–32 are lettered a–g. Art. 4 in a good back-sloping hand: a little flex punctuation (?) added at first. Arts. 5–8 in secretary hand, good, except at first. Initials of arts. 2–4: (i) 6-line, usually in two colours, red and green, or red and purple, or green and purple, with curled leaf and other ornament in one or more colours, red predominating; (ii) 3-line, red, green, or purple. Initials of arts. 5–8: (i) f. 183, 6-line, red; (ii) f. 239, 4-line, blue with red ornament; (iii) 2-line, metallic red. One of three known bindings by the Bat Binder (Oldham, *EBSB*, p. 28 and pl. xxii), the others being on printed books of 1486 and 1489: the evidence from this manuscript suggests that he was a Winchester binder: rebacked: a now missing label was attached to the back cover by twelve nails. Secundo folio (f. 6) *multum tuum*.

The Registrum (arts. 2–4) is from the Cistercian abbey of Ford: 'Liber sancte marie de fforda Quicumque illum alienauerit anathema sit', f. 182ᵛ, s. xiii, erased, but legible by ultra-violet light and read by M. R. James with the help of a reagent. It was alienated and in s. xv² pledged by Henry Eryvin, (i) in Oxford (?) and (ii) as vicar of St. John's, Winchester (1468–72): (i) 'Registrum Gregorii. Caucio [. . .] h. [Eryuin]¹ Exposita m. Ricardo

¹ Illegible, but traces of descenders leave no doubt that this or 'Eryvin' was the word.

Swan xii die octobris anno domini m° cccc° xlvi° pro x marcis et habet supplementa
Iosephum in antiquitatibus. Sanctum Thomam super 4 sententiarum et Augustinum de
ciuitate dei', f. 182ᵛ, below the Ford ex-libris; (ii) 'Caucio henrici Eryvin vicarii Ecclesie
sancti Iohannis Wynton' Reuerendo in cristo patri et domino. domino Henrico Abbati
de hyda. pro libris inscriptis. In primis. pro regula Sancti benedicti 2° fo. dirigatur.
Item (no more), f. 66: for Eryvin and Swan see Emden, BRUO, pp. 646, 1828. Probably
the manuscript remained in Winchester and was acquired there by William Horman,
who had close Winchester connections before he became headmaster of Winchester
College (1495–1501). Horman added arts. 1, 5–9 and had the whole bound (see above):
'Liber Willelmi Horman', f. 1, written before binding, as it has been partly cut off;
'Donum Guilielmi Hormani quondam socii huius contubernii', f. 1ᵛ. A title on the tail,
as usually on Horman's books: 'Registrum Gregorii'.

120. *Augustinus, etc.* s. XIV med.

A large corpus of Augustinian and Anselmian pieces (all but six of arts. 1–49),
followed by texts attributed to Boethius (50–4), Hugh of St. Victor (55), Chrysostom (58), John Damascene (59, 60, 74), Dionysius (61–6), Bernard (67, 69–72);
the rest unattributed. It is mostly ill written and has many scribal errors:
a reader noted the need for correction (art. 55). A nearly contemporary table of
contents, f. iii: the last item, 'Sentencie damasceni per quatuor libros distinctos',
is followed by an erased line.

1. ff. 1–3 Incipit liber aurelei augustini episcopi de dialetica. Dialetica est
bene disputandi sciencia . . . defluxum est. Explicit . . .

Pseudo-Augustine. *Clavis*, no. 361. *PL* xxxii. 1409–20.

2. ff. 3–7 Incipiunt cathegorie id est predicamenta augustini episcopi. Continet
iste decem nature vera libellus . . . manifestius erudire. Explicit.

Pseudo-Augustine. *Clavis*, no. 362. *PL* xxxii. 1419–40. The prologue is Alcuin's.

3. ff. 8–11ᵛ (*begins abruptly, after a blank space, f. 7ᵛ and f. 8ʳᵃ/1–29*) inueniuntur
uel reprehendi non possunt . . . ut possitis sustinere.

PL xl. 492/36–518 (De mendacio).

4. ff. 11ᵛ–25ᵛ Aurelii augustini doctoris preclarissimi de 83 questionibus . . .
Omne uerum a ueritate . . . ambo essent. Explicit.

PL xl. 11–98.

5. (a) ff. 25ᵛ–28 Incipit liber sancti augustini de penitencia. Quam sit utilis et
necessaria . . . mors eterna uitatur. (b) f. 28 Penitentes penitentes . . . dimitte
incertum et tene certum. (c) ff. 28–31ᵛ Quantum sit appetenda . . . in odorem
suauitatis amen.

(a). *PL* xxxix. 1535–49, Sermo 351. Cf. *Clavis*, no. 284 (p. 75). (b). *PL* xxxix. 1713–15,
Sermo 393. Cf. *Clavis*, no. 285. (c). *PL* xl. 1113–30. (a–c) are treated as one piece, (a) in
four, (b) in one, and (c) in ten paragraphs. A later hand wrote against the beginning of
(c) 'Aug. de vera et falsa penitencia capitulum 1 secundum alium librum hic incipit etc' '.

6. ff. 31^v–48$^{v\,1}$ Incipit prologus beati augustini in libro de doctrina cristiana. Sunt precepta quedam . . . facultate deserui. Explicit . . .

PL xxxiv. 15–122.

7. ff. 48^v–49 Incipit hic de decem plagis. Non sine causa est . . . ad terram promissionis poteritis peruenire.

CC ciii. 413–16, 412–13 (Sermo c(a) of Caesarius of Arles). *Clavis*, no. 1008: cf. no. 368.

8. ff. 49–54^v Incipit liber augustini de correpcione legis et gracie. Domino dilectissimo . . . ualentino . . . Uenerunt ad nos duo iuuenes . . . multitudinem peccatorum. Explicit de correpcione.

PL xliv. 875–9; 915–46. In edn. the two letters to Valentine (Epp. 214, 215) precede De gratia et libero arbitrio.

9. ff. 54^v–55 Incipit liber augustini de laude caritatis. Diuinarum scripturarum . . . etiam breuis.

PL xxxix. 1533–5, Sermo 350. Cf. *Clavis*, no. 284 (p. 75) and no. 698.

10. ff. 55–57^v Aurelii augustini episcopi yponensis liber incipit qui appelatur vnde malum. Dic michi queso . . . libentissime adiungo.

PL xxxii. 1221–40: De libero arbitrio, bk. 1.

11. ff. 58–68 Incipit primus liber de libero arbitrio uoluntatis. Iam (si) f(i)eri potest . . . aliquando compellit.

PL xxxii. 1240–1310: De libero arbitrio, bks. 2, 3. f. 68^v blank.

12. ff. 69–74 Incipit liber augustini de uera innocencia. Innocencia vera est . . . respexeris. Explicit liber augustini de vera innocencia siue de sentenciis prosperi.

Clavis, no. 525. *PL* xlv. 1859–98.

13. ff. 74–9 Incipit liber augustini de opere monachorum. Iussioni tu(e) sancte frater . . . fratribus et filiis nostros propinquos (*sic*).

PL xl. 549–82.

14. ff. 79–84 Incipit liber de singularitate clericorum. Promiseram quidem . . . erit uobiscum amen.

Pseudo-Cyprian. *Clavis*, no. 62. *PL* iv. 835–948.

15. ff. 84–89^v Incipit liber augustini de natura et origine anime. Quod michi arte (*sic*) scribend' . . . in diluuii uastitate ita scriptum est.

PL xliv. 509–46/32 (De anima et eius origine, bks. 3, 4). Two books, the second ending abruptly. Towards the end the scribe left blanks, where he could not read his exemplar.

16. (*a*) ff. 90–92^v Incipit liber augustini ad dulticium de 8 questionibus. Quantum michi uidetur . . . discere quam docere. Explicit . . . (*b*) f. 92^v Ferunt autem philosophici natum leonis catulum tribus dormire diebus . . . exurgam diluculo. (*c*) f. 92^v Notum quidem miraculum nostri (?) saluatoris . . . de sepulcro leuauit.

(*a*). *PL* xl. 147–70. (*b*, *c*). Single paragraphs on the resurrection.

17. ff. 92^v–94 Incipit liber augustini de disciplina cristianorum. et cetera. Locutus est sermo dei ad nos . . . conuersi ad dominum amen. Explicit . . .

PL xl. 669–78.

---

^{1} The foliation given by Römer, ii. 122–3, is one behind from f. 48 and two behind from f. 74.

18. ff. 94–96ᵛ Incipit liber augustini de agone cristiana. Corona victorie . . . corona(m) victorie mereamur.

PL xl. 289–310.

19. ff. 96ᵛ–97ᵛ Incipit sermo augustini de assumpcione beate virginis. Ad interrogata . . . regnas deus per secula seculorum amen.

PL xl. 1141–8.

20. ff. 98–101 Incipit liber augustini contra quinque hereses. Debitor sum fratres . . . custodit in secula seculorum amen.

PL xlii. 1101–16. *Clavis*, no. 410 (Quodvultdeus).

21. ff. 101–104ᵛ Aurelii augustini doctoris eximii liber primus incipit ad inquisicionem ianuarii. Dilectissimo filio ianuario . . . De hiis que . . . daturam atque locuturam.

Two books. *PL* xxxiii. 200–23, Epistolae 54, 55.

22. ff. 105–106ᵛ Incipit liber augustini de uisitacione infirmorum. Assit principio sancta maria meo. Visitacionis gracia . . . iustificatus ab ipso qui . . . Amen.

PL xl. 1147–58. Attributed to Baldricus Dolensis (Baudry de Bourgeuil) in Lambeth Palace, 363, f. 94: cf. *PL* clxvi. 1211.

23. ff. 106ᵛ–108 Liber augustini de cognicione uere uite. Sapiencia dei . . . columbe condidit.

Pseudo-Augustine (Honorius). *PL* xl. 1005–1016/56: the 'versio graeca' ends at this point.

24. f. 108ʳᵛ Liber augustini de gaudio electorum et supplicio dampnandorum. Tria sunt sub manu . . . misericordem. Cuius est . . . amen.

The De tribus habitaculis of Patrick, bishop of Dublin 1074–84. A. Gwynn, *The Writings of Bishop Patrick*, 1955, pp. 104–24.

25. (a) ff. 108ᵛ–120 Liber augustini de retractacionibus. Iam diu istud facere cogito . . . retractare cepissem. Explicit. (b) f. 120 De achademicis libri iii . . . Ad quos de correpcione et gracia i'.

(a). *PL* xxxii. 583–656. (b). The titles of the ninety-five works referred to in (a). f. 120ᵛ blank.

26. ff. 121–122ᵛ Incipit liber beati augustini de diffinicionibus recte fidei siue de ecclesiasticis dogmatibus. . . . Credimus unum deum esse patrem . . . in moribus inueniri. Explicit.

PL lviii. 979–1000 (Gennadius). Cf. *Clavis*, no. 958a.

27. ff. 123–33 Monologion anselmi. Reuerendo amando et amico . . . lamfranco. frater anselmus reccensis (*sic*) vita peccator habitu monachus. Quoniam agenda sunt . . . trinus et unus.

SAO i. 5–87.

28. (a) ff. 133–6 Incipit prologus in prosologion anselmi. Postquam opusculum

. . . trinus et vnus deus benedictus in secula seculorum amen. (*b*) f. 136 Ergo domine . . . non intelligere.

(*a*). *SAO* i. 93–124. (*b*) Three paragraphs headed in red 'sumptum ex eodem libello'. They repeat three sections of (*a*) copied on f. 133ᵛ.

29. ff. 136–8 Anselmus contra insipientem. Dubitanti vtrum sit . . . reprehendisti.

SAO i. 125–39.

30. ff. 138–41 Anselmus de veritate. Incipit prefacio anselmi cantuariensis archiepiscopi in subditum opus. Tres tractatus . . . vel rectitudo.

SAO i. 173–99.

31. ff. 141–143ᵛ Incipiunt capitula in libro anselmi de libertate arbitrii . . . (*table of 14 unnumbered chapters*) . . . Incipit tractatus . . . Quoniam liberum arbitrium . . . de illis interrogare.

SAO i. 205–26. Annotated in s. xv.

32. ff. 144–149ᵛ Incipiunt capitula eiusdem de casu dyaboli . . . (*table of 28 unnumbered chapters*) . . . Incipit tractatus . . . Illud apostoli . . . potestate loquendi. Explicit.

SAO i. 231–76. Many corrections. 'loke' in margins, ff. 145ᵛ, 146ᵛ, s. xv.

33. ff. 149ᵛ–153 Incipit epistola de incarnacione verbi. Domino et patri . . . urbano frater anselmus uita peccator . . . Quoniam omnia promouencia . . . aperte inueniet.

SAO ii. 1–35.

34. ff. 153–158ᵛ Hic incipit liber anselmi de processione spiritus sancti. Legatur (*sic*) a grecis . . . non sensui Latinitatis. Explicit.

SAO ii. 177–219.

35. ff. 159–170ᵛ Meditationes beati anselmi. (i) Terret me . . . diligunt nomen tuum. (ii) Anima mea erumpnosa . . . ad confortacionem misericordiam tuam. (iii) Deus piissime propiciare peccatis nostris . . . exspecta exspectamus. (iv) Domine iesu criste compleat tua potentissima bonitas . . . redemptor meus benedictus amen. (v) Sancta maria inter sanctos . . . fructus ventris tui. (vi) Virgo mundo venerabilis . . . te laudaturus. (vii) Maria te uul[t] cor meum amare . . . benedictus dominus in eternum fi. f. (viii) Sancte iohannes . . . cuius est sanare. (ix) Sancte fidelis petre . . . in beatitudinem rengni celorum. (x) Sancte paule qui omnes . . . consolacio miserorum qui sis benedictus in secula seculorum amen. (xi) Sancte et beate iohannes altissime euangelistarum . . . que intra me sunt benedicte amen. (xii) Sancte stephane . . . dilectus amicus eius qui est benedictus in secula amen. (xiii) Cum enim insani . . . requiescamus domino qui uiuit . . . amen. (xiv) Peccator homuncule . . . et mei creatoris qui es benedictus in secula amen. (xv) Sancte benedicte et beate gileberte quem tam . . . ecce beate benedicte gisberte . . . gloriemur coram deo qui viuit . . . amen. (xvi) Sancta maria magdalene que cum fonte . . . contemplacionem qui cum patre . . . (xvii) Dulcis et beningne domine iesu criste qui . . . securitatem qui viuis. (xviii) Omnipotens et pie domine iesu criste . . . exaudias saluator mundi

qui cum p. (xix) Sancta crux per quam nobis . . . qui sit benedictus in secula seculorum. (xx) Anima cristiana anima de graui morte . . . deus solus benedictus in secula seculorum amen. (xxi) Domine iesu criste rex glorie qui es verus angnus pro nobis in ara crucis . . . saluator mundi qui cum patre . . . amen. (xxii) Domine deus meus da cordi meo . . . proximos duriciam. (xxiii) Deus meus misericordia mea oro per dilectum . . . loquaris qua(si) parturiens. (xxiv) Deus dominorum domine prestabi(li)s . . . per iesum cristum saluatorem meum qui . . . amen. (xxv) Ad te deus meus et creator meus . . . indulge per eundem. (xxvi) Ad te domine lacrimabiliter ingemisco . . . merear per te domine qui (xxvii) Da nobis omnipotens deus velle cogitare . . . per eundem dominum (*8 lines*). (xxviii) Domine deus pater omnipotens sensuum illuminator . . . vsque perficiam (*6 lines*). (xxix) Deus qui es lux vera . . . michi ear per dominum (*5 lines*). (xxx) Deus cuius oculi respiciunt vias hominum . . . non presumit. (xxxi) Miserator et misericors deus magne et terribilis tibi confiteor . . . et sicud scis miserere mei domine deus amen. (xxxii) Domine iesu criste da cordi meo . . . crudelitatem amen. (xxxiii) Omnia diuini amor munus . . . saluatorem meum qui . . . amen. (xxxiv) Domine iesu criste filii (*sic*) dei viui miseri peccatoris . . . post hanc vitam qui cum patre etc' amen. (xxxv) Summe sacerdos et vere pontifex qui te optulisti . . . ut non exuriam neque sciciam in eternum amen.

(i, ii), (v–xx). *SAO* iii. 5–91, Meditationes I, II, Orationes V–XVI, XVIII, X, IX, IV, Med. III, with some abbreviation and other differences: Med. II ends at line 111 and Or. VIII at line 102, (xi) is Or. XI+XII, (xii, xiii) are Or. XIII, (xv), Or. XV, is for St. Gilbert (of Sempringham ?).

(iii) begins as Pseudo-Anselm, Or. 7 (*PL* clviii. 875), but lacks the last eight lines there and is in a different order at the end. (xxii–xxiv) are the same as (xxxii, xxxiii) and as Pseudo-Anselm, Or. 10+14+2 (*PL* clviii. 877–85, 888, 858–65). (xxxi) is *PL* ci. 1386–7. (xxxv) is Pseudo-Anselm, Or. 29 (*PL* clviii. 921), printed by Wilmart, *Auteurs spirituels*, pp. 114–24, and attributed to Jean de Fécamp.

36. ff. 170ᵛ–173 Hic incipit vita beati anselmi Cant' Episcopi. Osbernus[1] quidem nomine etate adolescentulus . . . consuetudinis dirumpatur.

An abbreviation of part of the life by Eadmer: cf. edn. R. W. Southern, 1962, pp. 16–91, for the beginning and end.

37. f. 173ʳᵛ Epistola venerabilis Anselmi ad dom*p*num Willelmum abbatem fiscan'. Domino abbati et patri reuerendo Willelmo frater Anselmus . . . felicitatem ex quo uestra probietas (*sic*) . . . nobis retribuat.

Ep. 65, lines 1–113 (*SAO* iii. 181–5).

38. ff. 173ᵛ–175ᵛ Incipit disputacio inter cristianum et gentilem secundum anselm' Cant'. Maiestas cur ad dolores . . . interim faciente.

Other copies in B.L., Royal 5 E. xiv, f. 70, and in Magdalen College, Oxford, 56, ff. 136ᵛ–139.

39. ff. 175ᵛ–178 Sermo anselmi de concepcione gloriose virginis Marie. Principium quo salus . . . hominem genuisse amen.

Pseudo-Anselm: *PL* clix. 301–18. Identified as Eadmer's and printed by H. Thurstan and T. Slater, *Eadmeri monachi Cantuariensis tractatus de Conceptione sanctae Mariae*, 1904.

[1] MS. Osbernui.

40. f. 178 Ad dominum papam Innocencium pro fulcono lugd' archiepiscopo. Qui malorum (*sic*) negociis . . . eflagitat.

Ep. 171 of St. Bernard: *PL* clxxxii. 331–2.

41. f. 178^{rv} Ad canonicos lugd' ecclesie de concepcione beate virg' marie. Inter ecclesias gallie constat . . . iudicio emendari (*sic*).

Ep. 174 of St. Bernard: *PL* clxxxii. 332–6.

42. (*a*) ff. 178^v–179^v De sacrificio azimi et fermentati. Anselmus seruus ecclesie cantuariensis uualletanno (*sic*) vnenburgensi (*sic*) episcopo. Scienti breuiter loquor. Si certus essem . . . iudicatur. (*b*) f. 179^v Alia epistola anselmi. Dilecto et amico uualeranno . . . Gaudeo et gratias ago . . . olim quandam epistolam.

SAO ii. 223–32, 239–42.

43. (*a*) ff. 180–189^v Incipiunt sermones *domp*ni Anselmi archiepiscopi per quasdam similitudines disti(n)cti. Voluntas tripliciter intelligitur . . . (*b*) ff. 191^v–192 Dum quietum siliencium (*sic*) . . . agendum intermittere. (*c*) f. 192^{rv} Mediatoris dei et hominum . . . salutare dei nostri. cui est . . . amen. (*d*) f. 192^v Legitur in libro regum quod saul . . . nephando euocaret.

(*a*). Chapters 1–191 of Similitudines in the order 1–46, 72–191, 47–71: *PL* clix. 605–701. (*b–d*) are three paragraphs of which (*b*) and (*c*) follow the Similitudines also in B.L., Royal 8 D. viii (arts. 39, 40).

44. ff. 192^v–200^v Incipit liber anselmi cur deus homo. Opus subditum quod propter quosdam . . . quod est benedictus in seculorum secula amen.

SAO ii. 42–133.

45. ff. 200^v–202^v Hic incipit liber anselmi de gramatico et gramatica. De gramatico peto . . . proficisse non negabis.

SAO i. 145–68.

46. ff. 202^v–206^v Hic incipit liber de concordia predestinacionis et presciencie. De tribus illis questionibus . . . petentibus inpendere. Explicit.

SAO ii. 245–88.

47. f. 207 De altercacione inter Augustinum et pellagianum. Annotacio interrogacionum scelesti pelagiani . . . ingerit penam. Explicit.

Ten paragraphs.

48. f. 207^{rv} De lamentacione Anselmi pro virginitate amissa. Anima mea erumpnosa . . . misericordia tua. qui benedictus es in secula.

Med. II, as above, art. 35 (ii), but continuing to the end.

49. ff. 207^v–211^v Incipiunt capitula libri de conceptu virginali et originali peccato . . . (*table of chapters*) . . . Incipit liber de conceptu virginali. Cum in omnibus . . . probari poterit. Explicit.

SAO ii. 137–73.

For arts. 50–3 cf. M. Cappuyns in *Dictionnaire d'histoire et géographie ecclésiastique*, ix (1937), 371–4 and for art. 54 (Dominicus Gundisalvinus), ibid. 362.

50. ff. 212–213^v Incipit liber boecii de trinitate ad I archidiaconum. Inuestigatam diutissime questionem . . . inicium. Explicit prologus. Incipit tractatus boecii de trinitate. Tristiane (*sic*) religionis . . . racionemque coniunge. Explicit . . .

Loeb edn. 1918, 2–30, 32–6. Two books.

51. ff. 213^v–214 Incipit boecius de ebdomatibus. Postulas ut ex ebdomadibus nostris . . . omnia bona etc. Explicit . . .

Ibid. 38–50.

52. ff. 214–15 Incipit liber eiusdem de professione fidei catholice. Cristianam fidem . . . Laus perpetua creatoris.

Ibid. 52–70.

53. ff. 215–18 Incipit liber boecii de duabus naturis et vna persona in cristo. Anxie te quidem diuque . . . perscribit. Explicit . . .

Ibid. 72–126.

54. f. 218^{rv} Incipit liber boecii de vnitate et vno. Vnitas est res vnaqueque . . . id quod est etc. Explicit . . . amen. benedicamus domino.

PL lxiii. 1075–8.

55. ff. 218^v–234^v Incipit tractatus Hug' de archa noe. Cum sederem aliquando . . . prouocet. Sit deus benedictus per cuncta seculorum secula amen. Explicit tractatus de significacione arche. Hugonis de sancto victore. amen deo gracias.

PL clxxvi. 617–704. Forty paragraphs. 'loke', s. xiv, in the margins of ff. 219, 220. 'Ecce optimus processus si liber esset bene correctus', f. 233^v, s. xv^2.

56. ff. 234^v–235^v Cum in omni aere angelorum multitudo uersetur . . . perfruamur. quam omnes nos liceat p[. . .]eri. gracia domini nostri iesu cristi qui . . . amen.

57. ff. 235^v–237 Hodierna die dominus noster pependit in cruce et nos festiuitatem nimia leticia celebremus ut discamus crucem totius spiritualis . . . Igitur domini imitatores simus. Estote namque ait similes patris vestri qui in celis est et ut celorum regna mereamur. per cristum dominum n. amen.

A version of the sermon in *PL* xxxix. 2047 (Augustine, Serm. Suppos. clv). Cf. *PG* xlix. 399–407 (Chrysostom) and *Clavis*, no. 368.

58. ff. 237–9 Sermo Iohannis crisostomi de prodicione Iude. Hodie dilectissimi fratres dominus noster iesus cristus traditus est . . . ad mensam cristi accedamus. cum quo deo patri . . . amen.

Cf. *PG* xlix. 373–89.

Arts. 59–61 are in Grosseteste's translation, as in Bodleian, e Mus. 134, pp. 459–516. Cf. Thomson, *Grosseteste*, p. 45, for art. 59, and p. 50, for arts. 60, 61.

59. ff. 239–47 Incipit logica damasceni. Sermo de philocosmis id est amatoribus mundi . . . (f. 240) dei gloriam aspiciens et ineffabili gaudeo astans. Sanctissimo et deo honorabili patri consm̄e (? *sic*) . . . Augustini (*sic*) quidem necessitate (*sic*) . . . retribuite . . . (*table of 50 chapters*) . . . Primum capitulum de ente. Ens commune nomen est . . . inconfusum et inuertibilem. Explicit.

60. ff. 247–8 Introduccio dogmatum elementaris a uoce Sancti Iohannis damasci. ad Iohannem sanctissimum episcopum Loadocie. Liber incipit. In nomine patris et f. et spiritus s. vnius trisy. potestate (*sic*) deitatis . . . possumus et opposita ipsis. 'Explicit elementarium dam''.

61. ff. 248–53 De hiis que in cristo duabus voluntatibus et operacionibus et reliquis naturalibus proprietatibus ex compendio et de duabus naturis. et de vna ypostasi. Cum duas naturas . . . semper cum ipso esse et frui ipsius gloria et regno nunc et semper et in secula seculorum amen. Explicit.

Twenty chapters.

Arts. 62–6 are treatises of the Pseudo-Areopagite in the translation of J. Sarazenus.

62. ff. 253–258ᵛ 'liber dyonisii de angelica Ierarchia'. Quoniam prudencie serenitatem nostre . . . uersibus exametris comprehensum. Angelorum scripturarum . . . astrum . . . (*table of 15 chapters*) . . . Omne datum bonum et omne donum perfectum . . . silencio venerantes.

Dionysiaca, i. lxxv, cix; ii. 727–1039.

63. ff. 258ᵛ–265 Hic incipit dyonisius de ecclesiastica Ie. Post translacionem angelice ierarchie . . . raciones ostendisse . . . (*table of 7 chapters*) . . . Quod nostra quidem ierarchia . . . accendam scintillas.

Dionysiaca, i. cxiv; ii. 1071–1476.

64. ff. 265–274ᵛ Memor hospicii . . . referendam. Hic incipit liber dyonisii de diuinis nominibus . . . (*table of 13 chapters*) . . . Nunc autem o beate . . . duce deo transibimus.

Dionysiaca, i. cxii, 5–561. The prologue, 'Memor . . .', is treated as though it were part of art. 63.

65. ff. 274ᵛ–275ᵛ 'Liber dyonisii de mistica theologia'. Ante misticam theologiam. simbolica theologia . . . interpretatur. Trinitas supersubstancialibus . . . ab omnibus simpliciter absoluti supra tota.

Dionysiaca, i. cix, 565–602.

66. ff. 275ᵛ–277ᵛ 'Epistola dyonisii ad gaium monachum'. Tenebre occultantur lumine . . . et hiis qui erunt post te trades.

Dionysiaca, i. 605–69; ii. 1501–78.

67. ff. 278–82 Incipit hic libellus beati Bernardi de gracia et libero arbitrio. Domino W. abbati sancti Theodorici frater b. opusculum . . . habebunt. Loquente me . . . hos magnificauit.

SBO iii. 165–203. Twenty-two chapters.

68. ff. 282–286ᵛ De duodecim gradibus humilitatis. In hoc opusculo cum euangelio . . . quam in nostro codice leges.

SBO iii. 15–59. Forty-three chapters.

69. ff. 286ᵛ–289 Incipit liber bernardi ad cluniacenses monachos. Venerabili patri W frater bernardus fratrum qui in claraualle sunt . . . scatet pauimentum.

SBO iii. 81–106/4 (Apologia ad Guillelmum). Seventeen chapters.

70. ff. 289–95 'Liber bernardi super dixit symon petrus ad iesum'. Ut tibi dilectissime presentes exortationis scedulas . . . fastidium non admittat. Dixit symon petrus ad iesum Ecce nos relinquimus omnia . . . Fidelis sermo et dignum . . . et habundancius habeamus iesus cristus dominus noster Amen. Explicit.

PL clxxxiv. 437–76 (Geoffrey of Auxerre: cf. *Recueil*, i. 16–20). Fifty-eight chapters.

71. ff. 295–300 Incipit hic bernardus super missus est gabriel. Scribere me aliquid . . . deuotissime destinaui. Explicit liber de laudibus virginis.

SBO iv. 13–58. Homilies 1–4, divided into seven, seven, five, and eight chapters respectively.

72. ff. 300–3 Incipit liber bernardi de diligendo deo. Viro illustri domino a. ecclesie romane dyacono cardinali et cancellario b. alias dictus de clareualle domino uiuere et in domino mori. Oraciones a me et non questiones . . . quam noua iterum dictare. Illa uero et sincera est caritas etc.

SBO iii. 119–148/9. A blank space of twenty-one lines follows.

73. ff. 303–13 Hic incipiunt allegorie quedam super aliquos libros biblie ut in legendo patebit. Primus liber tractat de misteriis rerum gestarum . . . Moralis sentencia de eodem. In principio creauit deus celum et terram. Celum significat summa terra ima . . . set etiam mori parati sum.

P. Comestor, Allegoriae in Sacram Scripturam, bks. 1–5 only. Stegmüller, no. 3847. *PL* clxxv. 633–90. Nineteen, nineteen, twenty-two, ten, and eighteen chapters. f. 313ᵛ blank.

74. ff. 314–33 Iohannis Damasceni qui in assur (*sic*) liber incipit in quo est vera Tradicio ortodoxe fidei capitulis diuisa O (*sic*) a burgundione iudice que visa est (*sic*) de greco in latinum domino meo (*sic*) Eugenio Pape beate memorie translatus. capitulum primum . . . Deum nemo uidit . . . fructificantes amen.

De fide ortodoxa. This copy mentioned, but not used by the editor, E. M. Buytaert, in 1955. f. 333ᵛ blank.

ff. iii + 333 + ii. ff. ii, iii are medieval flyleaves. 333 × 230 mm. Written space 270 × 170 mm. 2 cols. 67 or 68 lines and (arts. 27–34) 55–60 lines. Collation: 1–5¹² 6⁸ (ff. 61–8) 7–9¹² 10–11⁸ 12⁴ wants 3, 4, blank after f. 122 13–18¹² 19¹² wants 9 after f. 202 20⁶ (ff. 206–11) 21–25¹² 26⁶ (ff. 272–7) 27¹² 28⁸ 29¹² 30⁴ (ff. 310–13) 31¹² 32⁸. Quires 13–15 (arts. 27–34) in anglicana; the rest in small and difficult textura by probably two hands: in the main hand *f*, *r*, and *s* descend a little below the line. Initials: (i) red and blue with ornament of both colours; (ii) 2-line, blue with red ornament. Williamson binding. Secundo folio *aut consuetudine*.

Written in England. 'Liber fratris *Iohannis de Burgo* prio/ris de la[. . . . . . .]*tralibus* / [. . . . . .] *istum librum uendiderit* absque / *mera voluntate nostra Nos frater* Iohannes / *prior de la* . . . . *eum uel eos in hiis scrip/tis excommunicamus*[[. . . . .]/[. .] anno gracie m ccc octauo decimo', f. iii, in seven lines: probably *quem dedit claustralibus* or the like was in line 2. M. R. James helped by a reagent saw more than can be seen now—his readings in italics—and identified the owner with J. de Burgo, prior of Launde, Leicestershire, O.S.A., in 1306: cf. Dugdale, *Monasticon*, edn. 1846, vi. 188. Given to Eton by Mag. John Bonour (†1467: Emden, *BRUO*, p. 219): 'Donum M. Iohannis Bonour quondam socii huius regalis collegii', f. iiᵛ, over erasure. A price, 'viii marke', on f. 333.

122. *Eustrathius (et al.), In Ethica Aristotelis* s. XIII ex.

Eustracii metropolitani nikee enarracio.' in primum aristotelis moralium ad nicomachum. Philosophia in duas partes diuisa dico . . . et dei formissimis.

Aristoteles Latinus, no. 281. Grosseteste's translation of the Ethics and of the commentaries on it by Eustrathius, Michael of Ephesus, Aspasius, and others. Bk. 2, f. 34; 3, f. 41; 4, f. 53ᵛ; 5, f. 64ᵛ; 6, f. 98; 7, f. 134; 8, f. 153ᵛ; 9, f. 171; 10, f. 193ᵛ. The 'Enarracio ephesii domini Michaelis' on bk. 5 begins at f. 82. The commentary on bk. 5 which precedes it ends imperfectly, near the end, 'ut intemperato est videre', f. 81ᵛ. f. 221ᵛ blank.

Bks. 1–4 are printed in *The Greek Commentaries on the Nicomachean Ethics of Aristotle in the translation of Robert Grosseteste*, i (Corpus Latinum Commentariorum in Aristotelem Graecorum, VI, 1), Leiden, 1973, and bks. 8, 9 in *Verhandelingen van de koninklijke Vlaamse Academie voor Wetenschappen, Letteren en Schone Kunsten van Belgie, Klasse der Letteren*, no. 45 (1963). The editor of bks. 8, 9, W. Stinissen, listed this copy, and the editor of bks. 1–4, H. P. F. Mercken, collated it as E and noted that it is one of the best, pp. 91*, 127*.

No divisions within books, except by later chapter numbers and sub-divisions of chapters by letters in the margin, and in some books, divisions by numbers: thus, bk. 1 is divided into 139 sections. Scholia, some beginning 'Ordina sic' (e.g. f. 101), in neat current anglicana, s. xiii ex., in the margins of many pages: note especially 'Alius liber habet . . .' (f. 26: printed by Mercken, p. 151), 'Hic errat commentator. sicut infra dicit episcopus qui comentum transtulit a *principio*' (f. 41ᵛ: bk. 3. 2), 'In libro episcopi. sic . . .' (f. 106ᵛ), 'Aliquod exemplar habet . . .' (f. 108ᵛ), 'Aliquis liber habet . . .' (f. 219ᵛ). Two scholia are headed 'Linc'', f. 37 (at edn. 213/38), and f. 93. 'Hoc creditur esse dictum Lync'' against a passage on f. 41ᵛ (bk. 3.2) is in a later hand. Cf. J. Dunbabin in *Traditio*, xxviii (1972), 467–72.

ff. ii+223+ii, foliated (i, ii), 1–122, 122*, 123–203, 203*, 204–21, (222, 223). 335×230 mm. Written space 242×155 mm. 2 cols. 50 lines. Collation: 1–6¹² 7¹⁰ wants 10 after f. 81 8–18¹² 19 ten. *Ad hoc* signatures in pencil in the *left* bottom corner of rectos. Initials: (i) f. 1, 4-line, blue and red with ornament of both colours; (ii) 2-line, blue with red or blue and red ornament. Capital letters in the ink of the text filled with pale yellow. Williamson binding. Secundo folio *est hominis*.

Written in England. An early inscription on f. 1, at the foot, erased, so that only the last letter, a capital *A* standing by itself, can be read. The form suggests that this book may be from a Franciscan convent: cf. Ker, *MLGB*, p. xix. 'Liber Willelmi Horman', f. 1, beside a note of the contents headed 'Contenta', as in other Horman books. No doubt given by him.

123. *Flores historiarum* s. XIII ex.–XIV. in.

Incipit prologus in librum qui flores hystoriarum intitulatur. Temporum summam lineamque descendentem . . . Circa festum cathedre sancti petri uenit quidam Cardi (*ends imperfectly*).

Flores historiarum, from the Creation, ending in the annal for 1306 (ed. H. R. Luard (RS, xcv), iii. 327/11). Luard described this copy in i. xv, xvi, collated it as E, and printed it where it differs from Chetham 6712 (iii. 239–92, 294–312, 313–27). Matthew Parker used it (only ?) for his first edition of 1567 (*STC* 17652). A new quire begins with William the Conqueror, f. 158. Cf. R. Vaughan, *Matthew Paris*, 1958, pp. 92–102.

Written by one hand and at one time to 'celebrarunt' near the end of the annal for 1284 (f. 240ᵛᵃ/14: edn. iii. 62/18). From this point to 'regno', four words from the end of the annal for 1294 (f. 247^r, end) seems to be all in one hand, the same as before, but changes in ink and appearance suggest that the events of these years may have been recorded on twelve occasions; edn. iii. 62/19–63/9; 63/9–66/18; 66/18–22; 66/22 *Cuius ossa* –67/22; 67/22–74/18; 74/19 *Nam*- 30; 74, footnote; 83/23–84/13; 84, footnote (*Hoc anno -papatus*); 85/17–86/26; 268/8–272/6; 272/7–278, last line. A second hand took over at the turn of the leaf and wrote from 'per dies' to 'transfretauit' (ff. 247^v–250^v), and a third hand went on from 'Hic tempore' to 'redemptis' (ff. 250^v–251^v): edn. 278, last line–288/1; 288/1–292/10. The rest from 'Et statim post hec redierunt quidam nuncii de uasconia referentes qualiter in quodam conflictu inter anglos et gallos' (f. 251^v: cf. edn. iii. 292/10–12; 100/3–4) may be all in hand 2, but there is a change in appearance after 'non debet exigi uel imponi' (edn. 103/3: annal for 1297).

Erased marginalia, s. xiv in., include notes of the succession of priors of Merton on ff. 168, 172, 175, 176^v, 177^v, 183^v, 196, 197^v, 203^v, 211, 225, 227, 243, 251^v, 262^v, some of them read by Sir Frederic Madden and printed by Luard, i. lii.[1] Two notes of Merton interest escaped notice, one on f. 243, because it was added in the text space, and one in red ink, s. xiv, on f. 251^v (A.D. 1296): edn. iii. 84, footnote, and 292. Thomas Gascoigne, †1458, wrote notes on ff. 85, 86, 96^v against passages in the text mentioning St. Ermenburga, St. Ebba, and Bede (edn. i. 333/5, 336/6, 16, and 374) and there are some other marginalia of s. xv. Much more was added in the margins in s. xvi by a writer whom Luard took to be Matthew Parker: he was at work in London in 1562, as appears from a reference to the flooding of the Thames in that year (f. 182, A.D. 1195: edn. ii. 113).

ff. ii + 265 + ii. A late medieval foliation 1–110 is continued to 265 in a hand of s. xvi. 272 × 193 mm. Written space 202 × 142–150 mm. 2 cols. 37 lines (36 lines on f. 243^r: 34 lines on ff. 243^v–265^v). Collation: 1^{12} + 1 leaf after 12 2–4^{12} 5 three (ff. 50–2) 6^{12} (misbound in the order 56–8, 53–5, 62–4, 59–61) 7–13^{12} 14^{10} wants 10, blank, after f. 157 15^{10} 16–22^{12} 23^{10} 24 four (ff. 262–5). Nine pictures c. 80 mm high and as wide as the column, one where each new reign begins from William I, f. 158. Initials: (i) blue (f. 1) or red and blue (f. 27^v), patterned in white on grounds of gold and blue, decorated (f. 1) or historiated (f. 27, Nativity: cf. James, *Catalogue*); (ii) 2-line, blue or red with streamer decoration of both colours: the style changes at f. 242, *A* of *Anno eodem*, and only one colour is used after this: it changes again at f. 245 (1294): the last two initials, ff. 257^v, 262^v, have not been filled in; (iii) on ff. 1–27 only, 1-line, as (ii). Slatter binding, Secundo folio *lamech*.

'Liber [. . . . .]' at the head of f. 1, where M. R. James read 'Liber sancte Marie de [. . . . . .]', is no doubt the ex-libris of the Augustinian priory of Merton, Surrey, where the manuscript belonged in s. xiv (see above). Used by Thomas Gascoigne in s. xv. Probably removed from Merton before the Dissolution, since a deliberate effort was made to conceal the evidence that it belonged there. In the hands of Matthew Parker in s. xvi and possibly no. (33) in the list of John Parker's books at Beakesborne (Lambeth Palace MS. 737): Florilegi historia siue Matheus Westm'.[2] *CMA* 58.

124. *Johannes Diaconus, Vita S. Gregorii*   s. XI/XII

1. ff. 1–137^v In nomine domini nostri iesu cristi incipit epistola Domni Iohannis Leuite de uita beati Gregorii. Beatissimo ac felicissimo domno iohanni . . . Nuper

[1] The notes are illegible by ordinary light, except for a few words on f. 176^v. They are easier to read by ultra-violet light, even though Madden used a reagent. The note on f. 227 was missed by Madden and can still be read easily by ultra-violet light: '+Obiit Eustachius prior xii i Kalend' febr' anno prioratus sui xiii° cui successit Gilbertus Aycte viii kl' Marcii in cathedra sancti Petri installatus'. I am grateful to Mr. Derek Turner for help in dating the erasures.

[2] But no. (33) is more likely to be Chester Beatty MS. 70 (Sotheby's, 8 Dec. 1975, lot 55), which has John Parker's name in it.

ad uigilias . . . (f. 2) liberari per iesum cristum dominum nostrum. Explicit epistola Incipit capit' libri i . . . (*table of 43 chapters*) . . . Explic[it] cap' libri primi vitae beati gregorii romani pontificis. Incipit textus eiusdem. Gregorius genere romanus. arte phylosophus . . . denegasse cognoscar. Explicit liber quartus uitę beati gregorii romani pontificis. Deo gratias.

BHL, no. 3641. *PL* lxxv. 59–242. Bk. 2, f. 20ᵛ; 3, f. 49ᵛ; 4, f. 83ᵛ. A table of chapters precedes each book. Facsimiles: of f. 122, the greater part of which contains a picture of the funeral of St. Gregory, in the catalogue of the Burlington Fine Arts Exhibition, 1908, pl. 14, and, reduced, by Birley, pl. 8; of ff. 3, 83ᵛ in *New Palaeographical Society*, ii, pl. 169. 'Gregorii Legenda', f. 138, s. xv.

2 (added in another hand). f. 137ᵛ Gregory's letter to Queen Teudelinda of the Lombards.

Registrum, ix. 67 (Jaffé, *Regesta*, no. 1592).

3. Thirteen documents added in s. xii on flyleaves, in blank spaces, and in margins relate, so far as they are legible, to the affairs of the abbey of Farfa.

The eight legible pieces are printed by P. Kehr in *Quellen und Forschungen aus Italienischen Archiven und Bibliotheken, herausg. vom. koenigl. Preuss. Hist. Inst. in Rom*, IX (1906), i. 177–84. His texts are from f. iiiᵛ (nos. 2, 3: Pope Anastasius), f. iv (nos. 1, 5: Pope Eugenius, the Emperor Frederick), f. ivᵛ (no. 4: the Emperor Frederick), ff. 3ᵛ–4 across the foot (no. 6: Hugh, bishop of Ostia), f. 3ᵛ at the head (no. 7: provost and prior of St. Salvator), and f. 137ᵛ (no. 8: St. Bernard). Four pieces on f. iii, which was formerly pasted down, are hardly legible. A piece on f. ivᵛ has been erased and has a note of a law case 'die xviii decembr' ' written over it, s. xv.

4. f. 138, a flyleaf cut from a bull of Pope Eugenius IV, Florence 1440, concerning the see of Sisteron and one Gaucherius.

Bernardo Bembo wrote a note on the recto referring to art. 1, ff. 80 and 125. The verso is blank, except for later scribbles.

ff. iv+137+iii. For ff. iii, iv, 138 see above, arts. 3, 4: ff. iiiʳ, 138ᵛ were pasted down. 315×200 mm. Written space 220×125 mm. 30 long lines. Collation: 1–6⁸ 7⁶ 8–17⁸ 18 three (ff. 135–7). Contemporary catchwords, for example on f. 102ᵛ. For the script, of Roman type, see G. Brugnoli in *Rivista di cultura classica e medievale*, iii (1961), 332–41. Initials: (i) f. 1 and beginning each book, handsome red penwork on grounds filled with green, pale yellow, and, twice only, magenta; (ii, iii) 2-line and 1-line, red filled with green and pale yellow. Capital letters in the ink of the text filled with pale yellow. Slatter binding. Secundo folio *temporum*.

Belonged to and probably written at the Cluniac abbey of Farfa, near Rome: cf. art. 3. 'Explicit liber Mey Iohannis de pl[. . . .]', f. ivᵛ, s. xv. Belonged to Bernardo Bembo: cf. art. 4. 'Io: Delphini' f. iv, as in MS. 115 and a printed Juvenal and Persius of 1476, now Eton College MS. 138, and Bodleian e Mus. 25 (*Sum. Cat.* 3495).[1] Given by Wotton, no doubt: cf. MS. 87. *CMA* 70.

125+219, pp. 71–78. *P. Comestor, Historia Scholastica* s. xii/xiii

1. ff. 1–90ᵛ, MS. 219, pp. 71–8, ff. 91–166 Incipit Historia Scolastica Geneseos Epilogus. Imperatorię maiestatis est . . . scilicet in cathacumbis. Explicit his-

---

[1] The editors of *NPS* identified him, no doubt rightly, as Cardinal Giovanni Delphini, †1622: cf. *Das Konzil von Konstanz, Festschrift für Hermann Schaüfell*, 1964, p. 494.

toria ecclesiastica magistri P manducatoris. Epitaphium eiusdem. Petrus
eram . . . quod hic est.

PL cxcviii. 1053–1722. The Epitaph (in red ink) is Walther, *Initia*, no. 14050. Many
contemporary marginalia. Notes in English hands, s. xv. include some by Robert Elyot
(ff. 46, 90: see p. 631). ff. 166ᵛ–169ᵛ were left blank.

2. A neat hand of s. xii/xiii wrote many notes in the wide margins, among them
at least eighty-four pieces of verse from 2 to 14 lines in length. The verses are:

(*a*) Thirty-two of the biblical pieces listed by A. Wilmart in *RB* xlviii. 256–8 as almost
certainly by Hildebert of Le Mans (cf. B. Scott in *Sacris Erudiri*, xvi. 404–24): f. 6ᵛ
Arca noe, Vt 4; f. 8ᵛ Est abrahe dictum, Vt 6; f. 10 Vult intrare nequit, Vt 8; f. 11 Patrem
significat, Vt 10²; f. 11ᵛ Spelunca duplici, Vt 12; f. 11ᵛ Cum sponsum rebecca, Vt 11;
f. 12ᵛ Est certum, Misc. 69; f. 13 Plenus ager florum, Vt 13; f. 15 Exiit ignotas, Vt 14;
f. 17ᵛ, Accepit fruges, Vt 51 = Nt 12; f. 20 Israel est moyses, Vt 16; f. 22ᵛ Egyptus,
Vt 17; ff. 27ᵛ, 28 Aurea pontificis, Vt 22 (two copies); f. 29 Accinctus gladio, Vt 19; f. 30ᵛ
Hostia tuturis, Nt 14; f. 32ᵛ Mactatam uitulam, Vt 23; f. 36 Exploratores, Vt 24; f. 40
Cum pecudes multas, Vt 25; f. 42 Vestem contextam, Vt 26; f. 45ᵛ Axa caleph, Vt 27;
f. 53 Sanson significat, Vt 29; f. 57 Quare ter, Vt 30; f. 70ᵛ Abner, Vt 32; f. 77 Terram
miphiboseth, Vt 34; f. 83ᵛ In base sunt, Vt 21²; f. 133ᵛ Cur voluit, Nt 1; f. 137ᵛ Sunt
ydrie, Nt 19; f. 140ᵛ Petra capit, Nt 3; f. 141ᵛ Panes quinque, Nt 21; f. 144ᵛ Mens mala,
Nt 23 = 25; f. 145 Exit de iericho, Nt 5¹; f. 147ᵛ Traduntur seruis, Nt 7.

(*b*) Eight similar pieces listed by Wilmart, loc. cit. 157: f. 3 Denotat ecclesiam, Vt 2; f. 73
Bersabee lex est, Vt 33; MS. 219, p. 74 Defuncto puero, Vt 35; f. 93 Regi precepit, Vt 36;
f. 134 Dat magus, Nt 2; f. 139ᵛ Quinque uiros, Nt 20; f. 142ᵛ Cum tribus assumptis,
Nt 8; f. 143 Pastor⸴ ouem, Nt 16.

(*c*) Forty-five other pieces, mostly like (*a*) and (*b*).

f. 2 Ponte caret pontus . . . (2).
f. 2 Non pede sed pennis . . . (2: Walther, *Sprichwörter*, no. 18209).
f. 2 Est pecus id quod arat . . . (2: W., *S.*, no. 7772).
f. 6ᵛ Siria producit bitumen. et anglia stagnum. Nutritur atramentum gallia sola suum.
f. 9 Melchissedec domino panem . . . (2).
f. 14 Lya rachelque iacob . . . (8). Vt maiora metas . . . (8: *PL* clxxi. 1410).
f. 15 Ad domini verbum . . . (3).
f. 16 Cura paterna iosep . . . (8).
f. 21ᵛ E regione decet . . . (4).
f. 21ᵛ Prima rubens unda . . . (5: Walther, *Initia*, no. 14595).
f. 21ᵛ Sanguis rana culex . . . (2: W., *I.*, no. 17276).
f. 22ᵛ Mane legunt rorem . . . (4).
f. 23ᵛ Percussit petram moyses . . . (4).
f. 24 Lex fuit in binis . . . (6).
f. 25 Ad mensam domini . . . (4).
f. 26ᵛ Iacinctus designat . . . (4).
f. 30 Turturis abscissam . . . (6).
f. 36 Dicitur vuarum collectio . . . (3).
f. 37 Bis silicem . . . (3: W., *I.*, no. 2202: cf. *RB* xlviii. 22).
f. 37 Aspice serpentem . . . (5).
f. 39 Ymbra scenos . . . (3).
f. 41 Dissona sunt animus . . . (2: W., *S.*, no. 6019).
f. 48ᵛ Edum mactauit . . . (7).
f. 48ᵛ Primo madet . . . (7: W., *I.*, no. 14621).
f. 52ᵛ Femina nulla bona uel si bona . . . (2: W., *S.*, no. 9140).
f. 52ᵛ Femina fraude quidem . . . (2: W., *S.*, no. 9077).
f. 52ᵛ Femina dulce suum . . . (2: W., *S.*, no. 9039).
f. 62 Mel notat (*sic*) illecebrem . . . (6: W., *I.*, no. 10863).
f. 63 Te parere docent . . . (4).

f. 80^v Has certatrices salomon . . . (6).

f. 82 Sunt tereces cocclee . . . (4).

MS. 219, p. 75 Burdonem producit equus commixtus asello . . . (6: W., *I.*, no. 2259).

f. 133 Virgo deum peperit . . . (4: W., *I.*, no. 20503).

f. 134 Me(l)chio fert aurum . . . (2).

f. 134 Iure fleo de te . . . (2).

f. 138^v Tres tribus anna viris . . . Quas duxere . . . (8: cf. W., *I.*, no. 19420).

f. 138^v Tres tribus anna viris . . . Que nupsere . . . (10: cf. W., *I.*, no. 19420).

f. 138^v Anna viros habuit . . . (5: W., *I.*, no. 1068).

f. 139 Nupta fuit ioachim . . . (12: W., *I.*, no. 12499).

f. 139^v Quinque modis presens contingit . . . (6).

f. 140 Fletque rigatque . . . (5).

f. 140^v Terdenum fructum . . . (2).

f. 145 Albentis lapidis . . . (3).

f. 147^v Lectus ager mola . . . (6: cf. Scott, loc. cit. 419).

3. Further pieces of verse, about 170 lines in all, were added in s. xiii on f. 167^v and on flyleaves, nos. 1–30 on f. 167^v, nos. 31–3 on f. 168, nos. 34–41 on f. 169, nos. 42, 43 on f. iii^v, and nos. 44, 45 on f. v^v.

1. Mundat. fecundat. conseruat. deinde coronat . . . (3 lines).
2. Hic homo despiciens mundum . . . (2).
3. Arta uia est uere . . . (4: Walther, *Sprichwörter*, no. 1457).
4. Bis medicus lucas . . . (3).
5. In petra cristo . . . (3: W., *S.*, no. 11926).
6. Qui cecidit.' stabili . . . (1: W., *S.*, no. 23923).
7. Surge ferens lectum . . . (2).
8. Cristus acus caput . . . (2).
9. Est pars longa crucis . . . (3).
10. Non fuit in mendo mens fixa . . . (2).
11. Debilis et uacua. leuis . . . (3).
12. Est fidei. fraudis. ueri . . . (1).
13. Egris et sanis est sana . . . (2: W., *S.*, no. 595).
14. Qui prope me transis uideas . . . (2).
15. Bestia. fel. virus. tinea . . . (2).
16. Quam miseri sunt presbiteri. qui pro muliere . . . (2).
17. Est carni cognata uenus. iactancia. fastus . . . (8).
18. Fallitur egregio . . . (2: W., *S.*, no. 8790).
19. Brutus erat stulti sapiens . . . (2).
20. Est orientalis babilon subiecta seleuco . . . (4).
21. Frigida letifere uis est concessa . . . (9).
22. Cum tibi dona petas. equi . . . (2).
23. Cum dare non posses olim . . . (2: W., *S.*, no. 4087).
24. Cum duo contingant . . . (2: W., *S.*, no. 4134).
25. Omne solum forti . . . (2: W., *S.*, no. 19878).
26. Vbicunque bene es.' in patria tua est (*sic*).
27. Militis uxorem clamidis . . . (7: W., *Initia*, no. 11032).
28. Quid iuuat ad surdes si cantet sisiphus aures (1: W., *S.*, no. 25052A).
29. Pocula ne bibulus . . . (2).
30. Corpore deformes edicunt iussa tiranni . . . (8).
31. [. . . . .] . . . nouus heres imperat eri (4: line 1 cut off: W., *S.*, no. 4680a).
32. Me piget hic esse. quoniam . . . (4).
33. Digne reuera meretrix est dicta . . . (5: W., *I.*, no. 4473).
34. Hec tria doctorum sunt nomina sacra magorum . . . (9).
35. Matheum signat vir . . . (18).
36. Fons stillabit ad hoc. uerborum consule uenas . . . (4).
37. Ieiunans facies pallori iuncta uaganti . . . (3).
38. Credimus in cristum. cristo . . . (2).

39. Sit tibi diuicie nec amor . . . (2: W., *S.*, no. 29241).
40. Illic inuenies quicquid mare . . . (2).
41. Nobilitas sine re . . . (2: W., *S.*, no. 17029).
42. Sanguis rana culex . . . (3: W., *S.*, no. 27492C).
43. Est homo sanguineus . . . (10: W., *I.*, no. 5693).
44. Primus in orbe dies . . . (7: W., *I.*, no. 14669A).
45. Prima facta die . . . (6: P. Riga, Aurora, lines 1–6).

4. Prose pieces on the flyleaves include: (*a*) f. iii, Liber methodii. episcopi. ecclesie. paterensis. et martiris cristi Quem de hebreo et greco in latinum transferre curauit id est de principio rerum. interregna gencium. et fine seculorum. Sciendum (?) nobis est fratres karissimi quomodo in principio deus creauit . . . eripere dignetur. Qui . . . Amen; (*b*) f. iv^{rv}, notes from 'Ysidorus', 'Beda', 'Strabo', and others; (*c*) f. v^v, De rerum figuris. Uerum (*sic*) figure aut allegorice . . . desipuerunt. Hec de rerum figuris quibus sacre plene sunt pagine.' dicta sufficiant: definitions of Historia, Allegoria, Anagoge, Tropologia follow; (*d*) f. 168, [. . .] Barlaam. Iosaphat. [Quoniam] (?) liberum arbitrium est anime racionalis uoluntas sine prohibicione . . . (*e*) f. 168, Has notulas inueni super psalterium Glosatum magistri petri. De historia sumpsit esdras . . .; (*f*) f. 168^v, Aleph doctrina . . .

(*a*). Printed in 1475 and later, last by E. Sackur, *Sybillinische Texte und Forschungen*, 1898, pp. 60–96. (*d*). Two paragraphs, the first on free will and pre-election and the second on 'Imago cristi'. (*e*). Interpretations of the Hebrew alphabet.

ff. v+167+iv in MS. 125 and ff. 4 in MS. 219. ff. iii–v, 168, 169, are medieval flyleaves. 310×230 mm.¹ Written space *c.* 230×165 mm. 2 cols. 49–51 lines. Collation: 1–11⁸ 12⁸ (ff. 89, 90; MS. 219, pp. 71–8; ff. 91, 92) 13–21⁸ 22 three (ff. 165–7). A new scribe, writing a closer hand, begins at f. 30^v. Initials: (i) f. 1, *I* of *In principio*, gold on a blue ground; (ii) f. 1, *I* of *Imperatorie*, blue and red with ornament of both colours; (iii) f. 152^v, beginning Acts, 6-line, blue with red ornament; (i) 2-line, blue, red, or rarely, green, sometimes with red ornament. Slatter binding. Secundo folio *terra herbam.*

Written in France (?). In England by s. xv at latest and at Eton by 1500: a typical head by Robert Elyot, (see p. 631) is on f. 48. Two bifolia of quire 12 were used in binding college accounts for 1638 and 1648: see below, MSS. 219+221 (XV).

126. *Johannes filius Serapionis*　　　　　　　　　　s. XIII ex.

1. ff. 1–116 [T]ractatus primus iohannis filii serapionis medici (?). Innuit (?) iohannes. Incipiamus cum ausilio dei et bonitate inspiracionis eius librum abreuiatum in causis egritudinum et significationibus earum et ipsarum curacionibus. Huius autem tractatus sunt capitula xxxii° . . . (*table of 32 chapters*) . . . Capitulum de caluicio primum de allopicia et tyria. [E]gritudines iste accidunt . . . est i et s. Completum est postremum agregati ex libro medicine edicione Iohannis filii serapionis.

Thorndike and Kibre. The translation by Gerard of Cremona, printed in 1479 and later. Seven books, each preceded by a table of chapters.

¹ The leaves in MS. 125 and MS. 219 are the same size, so Slatter did not take anything off the edges in rebinding.

2. ff. 116–118ᵛ Hic incipiunt sinonima. Iohannis filii serapionis. [A]lasef id est punctus rubeus . . . Zezi id est uitriolum. Expliciunt nomina sinonima.

Thorndike and Kibre (Aliasef, Incipiunt). Printed with art. 1 in editions of 1497 and 1530.

3 (added, s. xvi in.). ff. vi–viiᵛ Tabula alphabetica . . .

An index to art. 1, tractatus 1–6, made for William Horman: cf. N. R. Ker in *The Library*, 5th series, xvii (1962), 84.[1]

ff. vii+118+iv. ff. v–vii, 119–22 are medieval flyleaves. The foliation of arts. 1–2 '1–118' is of *c.* 1500: traces of an earlier foliation remain on ff. 4–21. 345×245 mm. Written space *c.* 218×150 mm. 2 cols. 52 lines. Collation: 1–14⁸ 15⁶. Spaces for initials, (i) 4-line or 5-line and (ii) 2-line remain blank. Slatter binding. Secundo folio *huius egritudinis*.

Written probably in France. 'Donum Guilielmi Hormani quondam socii huius contubernii', f. vᵛ.

127. *Articella, etc.*   s. XIII ex.

Arts. 1–7 are the seven texts forming an Ars Medicinae which circulated together in the Middle Ages and were printed as Articella, *c.* 1476 (*GKW* 2678) and later. Four of them (4–7) are accompanied here by commentaries: cf. the similar 'Articella' manuscript in the Wellcome Historical Medical Library (*Catalogue*, p. 59). Fairly numerous marginalia, some in the hand of art. 8*d* and some earlier.

1. ff. 1–7 Incipiunt ysagoge Ihoa[n]nicii. Medicina diuiditur in duas partes . . . boni maliue discretione.

Johannicius, Isagoge.

2. ff. 7ᵛ–9 Prohemium libri pulsuum philareti. Intentionem habuimus in presenti conscriptione . . . Et hec nobis sufficiant ad presentia. Explicit liber pulsuum philareti.

Philaretus, De pulsibus.

3. ff. 9ᵛ–14 Incipit liber Theophili de urinis. De urinarum differencia negocium . . . conuenienter exposuimus.

Theophilus, De Urinis. ff. 14ᵛ–15ᵛ were left blank.

4. ff. 16–80 Prefacio domini constantini affricani montis cassiani monachi ad glauconem . . . delectantur. (*text*) Vita breuis ars uero longa . . . (*commentary*) Plurimi interpretes huius libri . . . (f. 79ᵛ) et irochidus et rochicus. Expliciunt aphorismi ypo. cum commento Gal'.

Hippocrates, Aphorismi, in seven 'particulae', in the translation of Constantinus Affricanus, with Galen's commentary. A piece of text was left out on f. 79 and added on f. 80 in a slightly later hand. f. 80ᵛ blank.

5. ff. 81–125 (*text*) Omnis qui medicine artis studio . . . (*commentary*) Videtur michi quod ex melioribus . . . in sexagesima finitur. Explicit liber pronosticorum ypocratis.

---

[1] The date there assigned to MS. 126, s. xv, is wrong; so too is James's date.

Three particulae. f. 125ᵛ blank.

Hippocrates, Prognostica, with Galen's commentary, in the translation of Gerard of Cremona (?).

6. ff. 126–75 (*text*) Qui de egrotancium accidentibus . . . (*commentary*) Illi qui sentencias de absidis (*altered to* assidis) . . . ei dicat ipsas. Explicit regimentum acutarum ypocratis cum comento Galieni deo gracias. Finito libro sit laus et gloria cristo. Qui scripsit scribat semper cum domino uiuat.

Hippocrates, Regimen acutarum, with Galen's commentary. f. 175ᵛ blank.

7. ff. 176–265ᵛ (*preface*) Intendimus edere sermonem exponentem . . . et non egrediens. Tegny Gal'. (*text*) Tres sunt omnes doctrine . . . (*commentary*) Et in omnibus doctrinis que secundum . . . secundum quod magis completum est. Explicit comentum hali supra tegni Galieni. Hostia que deus es que cunctis sola salus es Sanes infirmos serues ad premia firmos.

Galen, Ars parva, with commentary of Hali Abnrudianus.

8. Medical notes on the flyleaves and in a blank space of art. 2 in English hands, s. xiv, include: (*a–c*) f. iii, verses, 'Largus amans hillaris . . .' (8 lines), 'A nona noctis donec sit tercia lucis . . .' (5 lines), 'Gaudet epar spodio . . .' (2 lines); (*d*) ff. iiiᵛ–vᵛ, 14ᵛ–15, a medical dictionary, A–E; (*e*) ff. 266ᵛ–276 Medical verses from one to six lines in length, 59 lines in all, beginning with four couplets on the humours, 'Succo marcelli malue cum mercurialis Sanguis purgetur tibi si superesse videtur . . .'.

(*a–c*). Walther, *Initia*, nos. 10131, 56, 7098. (*c*) is also Walther, *Sprichwörter*, no. 10190b. (*d*) begins 'Ars primus insurgit' and has references to authorities, especially 'Parysiensis' on the Aphorisms of Hippocrates: others are 'Petrus de yspania', Avicenna, Isidore, Averroes, Ysaac, Gilbertus, Gerardus, Cardinalis. (*e*). Headings at intervals.

ff. v+265+v. ff. iii–v, 266–8 are medieval flyleaves. The medieval foliation of ff. iii–v, 1–268, '1–18', '22–131', '133–275', followed in James's *Catalogue*, takes into account the blank leaves now missing after ff. 15 and 125, as well as the six old flyleaves. 343 × 243 mm. Written space 207 × 145 mm. 2 cols. 35 lines in arts. 1–3. 21 lines (text) and 42 lines (commentary) in arts. 4–7.

Collation: 1¹⁰ 2⁸ wants 6–8, blank, after f. 15 3–7¹⁰ 8⁸ 9⁸ wants 8, blank, after f. 86 10–12¹⁰ 13⁸ 14⁸ wants 8, blank, after f. 125 15–28¹⁰. A professional-looking piece of writing, the text in much larger script than the commentary and spaced so that every other ruled line is blank. Initials: (i) blue and red with ornament of both colours in saw pattern the height of the written space; (ii) 2-line, blue or red with ornament of the other colour. Running titles in blue and red. Williamson binding. Secundo folio *Operaciones*.

Written probably in France. Annotated in England in s. xiv¹ and pledged then in Oxford loan chests. Parts of ten pledge notes, all erased or crossed through, can be read with the help of ultra-violet light, one (no. 5) on f. iii and the rest on f. 268ᵛ: (1) almost entirely illegible; (2) a caution of Master Thomas Corbet, other details illegible; (3) only 'Thome apostoli pro' and 'et tradatur' legible; (4) at the foot of f. 268ᵛ, Caucio M' Nicholai de Holebourne' exposita in antiqua cista [. . . . .]; (5) Caucio m' Iohannis Giffard exposita in cista Wintonye pro xx s' die martis proxima post festum translacionis sancti Thome Anno domini m° ccc° xxx°; (6) Caution of two persons, the name of the first illegible, the second John de Hameldon, in the Vaughan chest for 20 shillings, Wednesday before Chair of St. Peter, A.D. 1331; (7) partly over (1) and partly over (6), C' m' Gregorii Waterden (?) exposita in cista de g[. . . . . .]d pro xx (?) s' die mercurie proxima post festum sancti Iohannis Baptiste m ccc° xliiᵒ et habet supplementum spera (?); (8) Caucio Magistri Iohannis Nikelyn Exposita in Cista Wynton' pro vna marca die martis proxima post festum

Translacionis sancti Thome Anno domini M° ccc^mo li et tradatur M' Iohanni de landreyn; (9) as (8), but the date is Tuesday after the feast of St. Benedict, A.D. 1351[/2]; (10) partly over (2), Caucio magistri Iohannis [. . . . . .] exposita in cista vyennye pro xiii [. . . . .] petronille virginis Anno domini Millesimo [ccc] Nonagesimo primo. 'vii^a' is written against (10). For Nikelyn, who appears to have pledged his book both in July 1351 and in Mar. 1352 see Emden, *BRUO*, p. 1361 and for Landreyn, Emden, p. 1090, *MMBL* i. 343, and Talbot and Hammond, p. 160. 'Liber M' Willelmi [. . . .] pro xviii s' ', f. 268^v, s. xiv. 'Donum Guilielmi Hormani', f. 1.

128. L. B. Albertus, De re aedificatoria   s. xv²

1. ff. iii–v^v, 1–221^v Leonis baptiste alberti de re aedificatoria incipit. Lege feliciter. Multas et uarias artes . . . (f. v^v) architectus in negotio. (f. 1) Leonis baptiste alberti de re aedificatoria liber primus incipit lege feliciter. Lineamentum. De lineamentis aedificiorum . . . elegantiores habeantur. Deo gratias *(these two words expunged)* Deo saluatori meo gloria et gratiae.

Printed in 1485 and often later. Ten books. This MS. described by C. G. Grayson, 'Un Codice del 'De re aedificatoria' posseduto da Bernardo Bembo', *Studi letterari. Miscellanea in onore di Emilio Santini*, 1955, pp. 181–8 and plate showing parts of ff. 1, 70^v, 231^v. Bernardo Bembo wrote the whole of f. 70^v, a few notes in the margins and one longish note on f. 208, printed by Grayson, p. 182, and by James, *Catalogue*; also a table of contents on f. i^v and the book number at the head of each recto. ff. 222–227^v were left blank.

2. ff. 229–235 *(begins imperfectly)* primus cuius radix unitas . . . his studiis litterati.

A fragment of the same text as art. 1, corresponding to ff. 182/14–190/31 (end of bk. 9: edn. 1512, f. cxlv). It is no doubt the exemplar of art. 1, since the catchword 'mar.' written in the margin of f. 231^v (see Grayson's plate) has been copied into the text of f. 186/29: cf. Grayson, p. 185, who shows that the writing of these thirteen pages, a strong humanistica of a personal kind, is by Alberti himself. ff. 235^v–238^v were left blank. ff. 228 and 239, blank unruled leaves of parchment, served as a wrapper for ff. 229–238.

ff. ii+242+i. foliated i–v, 1–240. f. ii^r was formerly pasted down. Paper, except the end-leaves and ff. 228, 239. 320×215 mm. Written space (art. 1) 208×102 mm. and (art. 2) 245×135 mm. 30 long lines in art. 1 and 41 in art. 2. Ruling with a hard point, the horizontals very faint in art. 1 (see f. 221). Collation of ff. iii–v, 1–239: 1–23^10 24^12 (see above). Strips of parchment as strengthening in the middle of quires. Quires numbered at the beginning: '24' is on the blank leaf, f. 228. Art. 1 in current sloping humanistica. For art. 2 see above. Initials of books, 6-line to 11-line, gold on grounds of blue, pink, and green, decorated with white vine ornament and white dots in groups of three. Rope-patterned red leather over wooden boards: four clasps now missing: '·LEO· BAPT· ALBERTVS· ARCHITECTVS·' in good capitals flanked by leaves on the fore-edge. Secundo folio *completis*.

Written in Italy. Belonged to Bernardo Bembo, whose arms, azure a chevron or between three four-petalled flowers or, are in the lower margin of f. 1. Given by Wotton, no doubt: cf. MS. 87. *CMA* 4.

129. Aristoteles, Ethica, etc.   s. XIII ex.

Described in *Aristoteles Latinus*, no. 282.

1. ff. 1–67^v Omnis ars et omnis doctrina. Similiter autem et actus . . . Dicamus igitur incipientes. Explicit.

Ethics. Among many nearly contemporary marginalia in English hands are two couplets from Ovid on f. 46, beginning 'Est deus in nobis' (Fasti, 6. 5, 6 and Ars amatoria, 3. 349–50). More notes were added in s. xv.

2. ff. 68–150ᵛ Quoniam omnem ciuitatem . . . et quod possibile et quod decens.

Politics, bks. 1–8, in the translation of William de Moerbeka.

3. ff. 150ᵛ–152ᵛ Habitum autem utique erit hiis dicere . . . quam uocamus kalokaganthiam. et cetera.

De bona fortuna.

4. ff. 153–4 Postulas ut ex ebdomadibus n(ost)ris eius questionis . . . omnia bona. Explicit liber de ebdomadibus boecii. deo gracias.

Cf. MS. 120, art. 51. f. 154ᵛ blank.

5. ff. 155–206ᵛ Rethorica assecutura dyaletice est . . . Dixi. audistis. habete. iudicate. Aristotelis de arte Rethorica. Liber tertius et ultimus finit. alleluia.

Rhetorica in the translation of William de Moerbeka. Some marginalia in bk. 3 refer to the Greek, for example, f. 199, 'Non ex toto consonant hec greco. sed translatio non [. . .] consonanciam. immo etiam aliqua mutaui ut esset [. . . .]', f. 200, 'non erat capitulum in greco'. A facsimile of bk. 3 is in the Bodleian Library, Oxford, MS. Facs. d. 31.

6. ff. 206ᵛ–217ᵛ De poetica ipsaque et speciebus ipsius quam uirtutem habet . . . et solutionibus dicta sunt tanta. Primus Aristotelis de arte poetica liber explicit. Alleluia.

One of two known copies: cf. Aristoteles Latinus, i. 79. Annotations, s. xiii ex., on f. 207ᵛ.

ff. iii+217+iii. 270×190 mm. Written space c. 180×112 mm. 33 and (arts. 2–6) 32 long lines. Collation: 1⁶ 2–3⁸ 4–6¹² 7¹⁰ wants 10, blank, after f. 67 8–15¹⁰ 16⁸ wants 8, blank, after f. 154 17–21¹² 22⁴ wants 4, blank. Ad hoc signatures in pencil in art. 1. Three hands, changing at ff. 68, 155. Initials in art. 1: (i) f. 1, 4-line, blue patterned in white on blue and pink ground decorated in gold and colours; (ii) of each book, red or blue with ornament of both colours; (iii) 2-line, red or blue with ornament of the other colour. Initials of arts. 2–6: (i) ff. 68, 155, 173ᵛ, 193ᵛ, pink, violet, or red, patterned in white, on coloured grounds, historiated, except f. 173ᵛ, (1) Aristotle, (2) teacher and scholar: in the margin a bearded man and a trumpeting angel emerge from either end of a piece of ornament, (3) an orator; (ii) 3-line or 2-line, red or blue with ornament of the other colour; (iii) 1-line, red or blue. Capital letters in the ink of the text marked with red in art. 1 and with pale yellow in art. 5. Williamson binding. Secundo folio fortassis est.

Written in Italy (arts. 2–6) and perhaps in England (art. 1). Art. 1 was in England by s. xiii/xiv: see above. At Eton by 1609.

130. *Porchetus; Petrus, prior S. Trinitatis; Aquinas*   s. xiii²–xiv¹

1 (s. xiv¹). ff. 1–91ᵛ In nomine domini altissimi qui est trinus et unus . . . Libellum autem istum victoriam nuncupamus eo quod per eum iudei facile conuincuntur . . . sequar litteram codicum hebraycorum veteris scilicet testamenti secundum quod translata est a fratre Raymundo martino hyspano de partibus sachalonie ordinis predicatorum a quo sumpsi huius libelli materiam . . . (f. 1ᵛ) Hucusque frater Raymundus. Huius autem libelli tenor . . . alteret proprietatem. Capitula quidem prime partis hec sunt . . . (table of 24 chapters) . . .

Capitulum primum de diuisione iudeorum tempore cristi in iudeos et cristianos. Rubrica. Quemadmodum domino contingit . . . quod totum est sabbatum vt predictum est. ad quam quidem vitam et requiem sempiternam nos inducat dominus noster ihesus . . . amen.

Porchetus Januensis, Ord. Carth., Victoria contra Judeos. Bk. 2, in sixteen chapters, begins on f. 56.

2 (s. xiv¹). (a) ff. 92–224 Dilectissimo domino et patri in cristo Stephano dei gracia cantuariensi archiepiscopo . . . Petrus seruus eius deuotus et prior sancte trinitatis Londonie dictus cum salute corporis . . . pater venerande. Ego et quidam iudeus . . . (f. 92ᵛ) disputacionem nostram exorsi sumus . . . (*tables of the 56, 18, and 31 chapters of bks. 1–3*) . . . (f. 94) Quod cristus siue messias iam venit.' probatur per verba danielis et per verba iacob in genesi. Capitulum primum. Ad probandum autem quod Messias iam venerit . . . tractauimus et disputauimus domino nostro . . . amen. (b) ff. 224–226ᵛ Contra eos qui negant resurrexionem . . . Petrus. Post aliquot dies predictus Symon . . . ad gaudium cuius non erit finis. Explicit liber tercius disputacionis Symonis et Petri de confutacione iudeorum.

The only known copy of a work written in 1208: cf. R. W. Hunt, 'The disputation of Peter of Cornwall against Symon the Jew', *Studies in Medieval History presented to F. M. Powicke*, 1948, pp. 143–56: Peter's preface addressed to Stephen Langton is printed on pp. 153–6. (a). Bk. 2, f. 157ᵛ; 3, f. 191ᵛ. (b) is a supplement to (a) in four chapters, the first without number and the three others numbered 33–5 in continuation of bk. 3. The *explicit* includes it with bk. 3, but it belongs to the period immediately after Simon's conversion to the Christian faith. ff. 227–230ᵛ blank.

3 (s. xiii²). (a) ff. 231–94 Sunt autem. o beate etc. Ad intellectum librorum beati dyon' . . . bonorum omnium largitori qui est trinus et unus deus uiuens et regnans per omnia secula seculorum. Amen. (b) ff. 294–8 Precurre prior in domum tuam . . . et in hoc terminatur exposicio huius libri. benedictus deus per omnia. Amen.

(a) and (b) are covered by the title pencilled at the foot of f. 231: 'Scriptum fratris thome de alkino super librum Dionisii de diuinis nominibus et super librum de eb[domadibus]'. (a). *Opera*, ed. Mandonnet, ii. 220–654. (b). ibid. i. 165–92. Dondaine and Shooner, no. 810. f. 298ᵛ blank.

ff. iv+302+vi, foliated i, ii, 1–113, 113a, 114–88, 188a, 189, 189a, 190–6, 196a, 197–262, 262a, 263, 263a, 264–304. ff. 1, 2, 299–302 are medieval endleaves. 315 × 215 mm.

Arts. 1, 2. Written space 245 × 145 mm. 2 cols. 63–7 lines. Frame ruling reinforced by horizontals at intervals of about 8 lines. Collation of ff. 3–230: 1–2¹² 3⁸ (ff. 27–34) 4–19¹² 20⁸. Written in anglicana. *Ad hoc* signatures. Initials: (i) red and blue with ornament of both colours and violet; (ii) mainly 2-line, blue with red ornament or red with blue, or, from f. 98 onwards, violet ornament; (iii) 1-line, blue or red. Secundo folio (f. 4) *Ista. Quemadmodum.*

Art. 3. Written space 220 × 150 mm. 2 cols. 48–51 lines. Collation of ff. 231–98: 21–25¹² 26¹⁰. *Ad hoc* signatures. Initials: (i) f. 231, blue patterned in red, with blue and red ornament; (ii) 2-line, blue with red ornament or red with violet. Secundo folio (f. 232) *tellectum.*

Slatter binding. Rust marks from the metal on a former binding show on ff. 1, 297–302: one at head, one at foot, and two on the side of each leaf.

Two manuscripts written in England, probably bound together in the Middle Ages. 'Precium istius libri iiii^{or} nobilia', f. 300^v, s. xiv. *CMA* 55.

131. *Cassiodorus, Historia tripartita; Martinus Polonus, Chronicon; Vegetius*   s. xiv med.–xiv ex.

1 (s. xiv ex.). ff. 1–141^v In hoc corpore continentur historie ecclesiastice ex socrate. sozomeno. theodorico. in vnum collecte et nuper de greco in latinum translate.' libri xii^{cim}. Prefacio cassiodori senatoris serui dei. Vtiliter nimis in capite . . . esse cognoscit. Incipiunt tituli libri primi ecclesiastice historie cum opere suo ab epiphanio scolastico domino prestante translati . . . (*table of 19 chapters*) . . . Incipit liber primus. Aiunt antiquis principibus . . . imperatoris theodosii. Historie ecclesiastice liber xii^{us} explicit. Explicit ecclesiastica historia tripartita.

PL lxix. 879–1214. *CSEL* lxxi. No. 105 in the list of 138 copies by W. Jacob, *Die handschriftliche Überlieferung der sogenannten Historia Tripartita des Epiphanius-Cassiodor*, Texte und Untersuchungen zur Geschichte der altchristlichen Literatur, lix (1954), 44, 127–32: Jacob makes it and St. John's College, Cambridge, 169, his group Vc. A table of chapters in front of each book.

2 (s. xiv ex.). ff. 141^v–200^v Incipit cronica fratris Martini domini pape penitenciarii et capellani de ordine predicatorum. Quoniam scire tempora . . .

The chronicle of the popes is on verso sides and the chronicle of the emperors on recto sides from f. 150^v to f. 197^r which ends with the annal for 1270 and the death of the king of Navarre: 'in domo fratrum ordinis carmeli est defunctus'. After this the chronicle of the popes continues for another seven pages, ending at 1285 (Honorius IV), 'sollicite prosequenda. etc.'. Additions and corrections in the margins are many and include a mention of St. Francis at 1238, f. 194^v, where the text refers to St. Dominic. Printed in 1574 and later.

3 (s. xv). ff. 201^v–202 A 'Tabula de Cronicis Martini', with leaf references to art. 2.

'1479' on f. 202 probably gives the date of writing. ff. 201^r, 202^v–205^v blank.

4 (s. xiv med.). ff. 206–217^v Flauii vegecii Renati viri illustris epotoma institutorum rei militaris de commentariis catonis augusti . . . prestare victoriam. Incipiunt capitula primi libri . . . (*table of chapters of five books*) . . . (f. 206^v) Incipit prologus vegecii renati ad iustinianum imperatorem. Bonarum arcium studia . . . vetus doctrina monst(r)auerat. Explicit vegecius de re militari etc.

The preliminary notice, indicating five books, is also in B.L., Royal 7 C. i, f. 281. According to the table, bk. 5 begins at 'Precepto maiestatis tue' (4. 31), but there is no indication of a new book in the text. The chapters are not numbered. f. 218^{rv} blank.

ff. iii+218+ii. f. iii is a medieval end-leaf, formerly pasted down. ff. 1–141, 151–200 have a medieval foliation 1–141, 1–50. 305 × 205 mm. Written space of arts. 1, 2, 225 × 130 mm.: 2 cols., 49 lines; of art. 4, 253 × 172 mm: 2 cols., *c.* 63 lines, frame ruling. Collation: 1–11^{12} 12^8+2 leaves before 1 (ff. 133–4) 13–16^{12} 17^{14} wants 12–14, blank, after f. 200 18^4+1 leaf after 4 (f. 205) 19^8 20^6 wants 6, blank, after f. 218. Red-ink signatures on quires 1–15 are of the usual late medieval kind—except that the series begins with

+ :[1] it runs +, a–o. Quires 1–17, 19, 20 numbered at the beginning I–XVII, XVIIII, XX: since art. 3 (quire 18) is later than the numeration this suggests that a quire is missing after art. 2. Written in anglicana, art. 3 more or less currently. Initials of arts. 1, 2: (i) ff. 1, 142, red and blue, with blue, red, and violet ornament, extended on f. 1 to form a continuous border; (ii) as (i), but 4-line; (iii) 3-line, blue with red ornament. Initials of art. 4, 3-line and 2-line, blue with red ornament: the style is unusual and unattractive. Slatter binding. Secundo folio *et agere*.

Written in England. 'Donum M. Rogeri Lupton (†1540) Iuris canonici Professoris et huius Collegii quondam Prepositi', f. iii^v: he wrote some notes in the margins, for example on f. 116.

132. *Galenus* s. XIII[2]

Arts. 1–11, 12a, 13, 15–19 are works by or attributed to Galen in the Latin of various translators. Thorndike and Kibre give references to the similar collections in Montpellier 18, Paris University 125 and other manuscripts and to the printed editions of 1490 and 1515. Peterhouse 33 has all but arts. 9, 11, and Edinburgh, Univ. Libr. 166 all but arts. 12, 13. Arts. 6–11 occur together and in the same order as here in Vatican, Pal. lat. 1094, Chartres 284, and the Edinburgh manuscript.[2] Running titles in red by a careless writer who misunderstood the still visible pencilled instructions. They are usually more or less full on their first occurrence and by first letters afterwards, for example 'DCD' for art. 1 after f. 2, which has 'DE CERENTIS DIOB'.

1. ff. 2–19 Ut egritudinum que non ... auxilio dei et eius adiutorio. Completus est tractatus libri Ga. de diebus creticis. tercius.

The scribe began on f. 1, but wrote only one column there and began again on a slightly larger scale on f. 2: the column on f. 1 has sixty-five more words in it than the corresponding column on f. 2. f. 1^v was blank until s. xv, when the table of contents printed in James's *Catalogue* was entered there.

2. ff. 19–40^v Ego non intendo in hoc meo libro . . . et non est eis necessarius tractatus quartus.

De crisi.

3. ff. 41–56^v Initio huius libri diffiniri morbum oportet . . . sepe alia sequantur et que non.

De accidenti et morbo.

4. ff. 56^v–83^v Medicorum non solum moderni . . . Que quidem in suo loco dicemus.

De interioribus.

5. ff. 83^v–110 Quamuis karissime fili Iohannes ingenium acutissimum . . . suauiter percutiatur. Explicit megategni.

6. ff. 110–60 Librum de sanitatis ingenio a te et a multis . . . aqua marina mixta cum sale. que videlicet ydropicis et carnosis.

---

[1] See above, MS. 47.

[2] Chartres 284 was partly destroyed in 1944. I owe details about it and my reference to the Vatican manuscript to Professor Richard Rouse.

Bks. 1–13 and part of bk. 14 of De ingenio sanitatis: the last words here are in the 1515 edition at bk. 14, ch. 15. The Edinburgh manuscript ends at the same point. In the margin, f. 110, apropos of drinking, 'Nota de norwegis et ghelrensibus. De vernicali pleno semper'.

7. ff. 160–3 Cum in arte medicine studerem . . . et fortassis in eo sentitur distensio uene facil*iter*.

Thorndike and Kibre (Cum iam in arte). De tactu pulsus.

8. ff. 163–5 Dixit G. oportet nos inspicere pulsus . . . uia ad id quod in hoc libro [diximus].

De utilitate pulsus. The last word is probably concealed by the initial letter of art. 9.

9. ff. 165–168ᵛ Gal inquit Quoniam illi quorum proprium est . . . valde intenditur. et superat.

De motibus liquidis.

10. ff. 168ᵛ–170 Dixit G. si neruis qui sunt . . . inter uoluntatem et naturam. Explicit tractatus G. de voce et anelitu (*these seven words in the lower margin*).

11. ff. 170–179ᵛ Medicorum anathomicos necesse est . . . proximum est epar. Et ita [patet diuersitas inter Galenum et Aristotelem].

Anatomia vivorum. Running title 'ANATHO G'. Cf. G. W. Corner, *Anatomical Texts of the Earlier Middle Ages*, 1927, pp. 35–43, who reproduces a page of Chartres 284 on which there is almost exactly the same amount of text as here, since it corresponds to f. 170ʳᵃ/31–170ᵛᵃ/27. The text appears to end abruptly, but probably the last line, *patet . . . Aristotelem*' has been erased (cf. art. 8).

12. (*a*) ff. 179ᵛ–184 Rogasti me amice monthee ut describerem tibi . . . transferam ipsum. Explicit 'Gal' de secretis'. (*b*) f. 184 Recipes in ten short paragraphs, the first beginning 'Pillule ante cibum et post cibum'.

(*a*). The title 'liber de secretis Galieni' is over erasure, s. xv.

13. ff. 184–8 Sperma hominis descendit ex omni humore . . . per naturam sui corporis. Explicit liber de xii portis.

The title 'Liber de spermate uel de 12 portis Galieni' is in the margin of f. 184, s. xv. ff. 188ᵛ–190ᵛ were left blank.

14 (added, s. xiii/xiv). (*a*) f. 188 Cum scire uolueris de aliqua questione . . . nisi error fuerit in scriptore. Oracio. O intelligencia prima mouens . . . es tu in manibus tuis sortes mee (?) et tunc prohice. (*b*) f. 188ᵛ Thirty-two questions, four in each of eight roundels lettered A B G D E O Z T. The first question in roundel A is 'An erit bonum ire extra domum uel non'. (*c*) f. 189 A table divided into sixteen compartments is headed by one letter from the A B G D series of (*b*) and by one from the E O Z T series. The first compartment under AE has 'aquila auis' in it and the last under DT 'baccelari. S'. (*d*) ff. 189ᵛ–190ᵛ Twelve roundels, four to a page, each divided into twelve sections. The roundels are 'specierum' (2), 'fructuum' (2), 'bestiarum' (1), 'volatilium' (3), 'ciuitatum' (4). Each section contains a question: 144 questions in all. (*e*) ff. 188ᵛ–190ᵛ, below (*b*) and (*d*). Answers to the questions in (*d*) arranged under the names of sixteen kings (turcorum, yspanie . . . romanie), each of whom answers nine questions.

(*a–e*). Manuscripts of the Pronosticon Socratis Basilei are listed by L. Thorndike, *History of Magic and Experimental Science*, ii. 117, note 1. For another, see above, p. 235. R. Vaughan, *Matthew Paris*, notes this copy at p. 258 and reproduces the Spera bestiarum of (*d*) from MS. Ashmole 304 as pl. xxi *b*. (*a*) consists of directions for the use of (*b*) and a prayer 'ut dirigas me in hac sorte'. The first answer in (*e*) is 'Quod uis erit et bonum tibi inde eueniet' and the last 'Grauida pariat filiam de qua magnum bonum sibi eueniet'.

15. ff. 191–235 Incipit tractatus primus libri Galieni de simplici medicina. Non est michi necesse hic ostendere . . . si deus voluerit. Finitus est tractatus quintus libri galieni in medicinis singularibus.

Bks. 1–5 only.

16. ff. 235–7 Incipit liber Galieni de malicia complexionis diuerse. Malicia complexionis diuerse . . . de ingenio sanitatis. Explicit liber Galieni de malicia complexionis diuerse.

17. ff. 237–257ᵛ Incipit primus tractatus libri Galieni de iuuamentis membrorum. Inquit G. quod corpora animalium . . . Similiter enim uidimus anothomicos uocantes eas. Explicit octaua pars de iuuamentis membrorum.

f. 258ʳᵛ blank and without ruling.

18. ff. 259–269 Quoniam cum sit elementum minor pars . . . attrahit violenter. Bk. 2, f. 267.

19. ff. 269–84 Incipit primus tractatus libri Gal' de conplexionibus. Quoniam insignes antiqui . . . in medicinis ipsis. Explicit liber Gal' de conplexionibus. Deo gracias.

Thorndike and Kibre, s.v. *Quoniam* and *Insignes*. Preceded by thirteen lines, 'Summe . . . hominis', a summary under eight heads, as in Edinburgh 166, f. 125ᵛ, but here written without break after art. 18.

20 (added). (*a*) ff. 284ᵛ–285 Ego omnium artium magister merito noncupatus cui liberalium doctrina . . . (*ends abruptly*). (*b*) f. 285ᵛ Quoniam quidam de melioribus amicis . . . incipiam a digestiuis. Medicine igitur [. . .] simplices sunt . . . (*ends imperfectly*).

(*a*) of s. xiii/xiv. Thorndike and Kibre (Apollonius, Ars notoria). In a 10-line prologue a 'tractatus de cognicione astronomie siue astrologie' and excerpts 'ex antiquissimis libris' are announced: '. . . Ego siquidem de prepositis tractaturus primo in me miratus sum . . . De notoria arte igitur quedam notule . . .'. (*b*). s. xiv. Thorndike and Kibre (John of Parma, De medicinis simplicibus).

ff. iii+285+iv. 270×190 mm. Written space 178×120 mm. 2 cols. 51–3 lines (45 lines, ff. 259–70). Collation: 1–14¹² 15¹⁴ 16⁸ (ff. 183–90) 17⁸ 18–21¹² 22⁸ 23⁴ (ff. 255–8) 24–25⁸ 26¹² wants 12 after f. 285, except for a narrow strip. The first line of writing below the top ruled line. Written in several small hands, expert, but not easily legible. Initials: (i) pink or blue patterned in white on decorated coloured grounds: some animal heads in the decoration and on ff. 237, 269, a dog and a hare; (ii) 2-line, blue or red, with ornament of the other colour. Bound by Williamson in 1608–9. Secundo folio *quod omne*.

Written probably in France. Marginalia of s. xv in an English hand. No. xxxiii in the Eton inventory of 1465, 'Item a boke of Fesyke ii fo. quod omne'.

133. *Orosius, De ormesta mundi; Epistola Alexandri*   s. XII med.

1. ff. 1–85 [O]rosius presbiter hispanus genere. uir eloquens . . . imperium tenente. Ecce uenit ad me religiosus iuuenis . . . pernitiosasque doctrinas. Orosium uirum eruditissimum . . . miraque breuitate ordinauit. Preceptis tuis parui beatissime pater . . . per te iudicata si deleas.

Clavis, no. 571. *PL* xxxi. 663–1174. J. M. Bately and D. J. A. Ross list this and many other manuscripts in *Scriptorium*, xv. 329–34. Bk. 2, f. 12; 3, f. 21ᵛ; 4, f. 32ᵛ; 5, f. 45; 6, f. 57; 7, f. 69ᵛ. Bk. 1 is preceded by the same preliminary matter as B.L., Royal 13 A. xx. Three leaves are missing. A space on f. 2ᵛ was perhaps intended for a map. On ff. 15ᵛ and 16ʳᵛ the script is spread out, as though the scribe wanted to begin quire 3 at a particular point. Some marginalia and the running book numbers were entered in s. xiv.

2. ff. 85–87ᵛ Semper memor fui tui etiam inter dubia . . . dentibus in signi onustus preda in castris (*ends imperfectly*).

Alexander's letter to Aristotle, ending at edn. Kübler, 1888, p. 206/20. D. J. A. Ross lists this and 112 other manuscripts in *Scriptorium*, x. 129–32.

ff. iii + 87 + iii. Paper flyleaves, s. xviii (?). 280 × 195 mm. Written space 190 × 110 mm. 2 cols. 39 lines. Collation: 1–6⁸ 7⁸ wants 2 after f. 49 8⁸ wants 8 after f. 62 9⁸ 10⁸ (3 and 6 half sheets) 11⁸ wants 1 before f. 79 12 two (ff. 86–7): quires numbered at the beginning in pencil: catchwords added in s. xiii (?). A neat backward-sloping hand, the same throughout. Initials: (i) at first, in one, two, or three of the colours blue, red, and green, with ornament in the same colours, but from bk. 5 monochrome and in bks. 5, 6 without ornament; (ii, iii) 2-line (or more) and 1-line, blue, or red, or, at first, green: two colours in one initial sometimes: the 5-line O on f. 1 has been excised. Medieval binding of wooden boards covered with dirty white leather, rebacked: the old back strip, lettered 'OROSIUS' pasted on: central strap and pin missing. Secundo folio *tam apud*.

Written in England. 'W. Bathon', f. 1, at the top: cf. MS. 90. 'Dedit hunc librum Collegio Etonensi Thomas Richardson S.T.P. eiusdem Collegii socius 1722', f. iiiᵛ: cf. MS. 90.

134. *Robertus Crikeladensis*   s. XII²

Tranquillus in catalogo uirorum illustrium de plinio. Plinius secundus nouem menses (*sic*) . . . maturaret orauerit. Proemium Roberti crikeladensis prioris oxenefordie super excerptis naturalis historie librorum plinii secundi. Studiosis et precipue claustralibus et scolasticis Robertus . . . (f. 1ᵛ) Et gratias agite illustrissimo regi anglie henrico secundo (*over erasure ?*) cuius nomini hoc opus dedicare presumpsi. Incipit prologus Rodberti crikeladensis prioris oxinefordie in deflorationem naturalis historie plinii secundi. Regi anglorum. Tibi illustrissime Rex anglorum henrice . . . (f. 2) hic et in eternum. Amen. Explicit prologus supradicti prioris. (f. 12ᵛ) Incipiunt Capitula libri primi . . . (*tables of chapters of nine books*) . . . (f. 12ᵛ) De mundo. Mundi extera indagare. nec interest hominum . . . (f. 164ᵛ) modo relucentibus.

Robert of Cricklade's excerpts from the Natural History of Pliny the Younger in nine books, preceded by the relevant extract from Suetonius (cf. Teubner edn, 1898, pp. 300–1): bk. 2, f. 32; 3, f. 51ᵛ; 4, f. 78; 5, f. 104; 6, f. 130; 7, f. 141; 8, f. 147ᵛ; 9, f. 156ᵛ. A later hand, s. xiv, has noted where each book of Pliny begins 'in mangno volumine': 'li. 26' on f. 147ᵛ, where bk. 8 begins is the latest note of this kind. The last chapter but one is on stones, ending 'imagines deorum' (cf. bk. 37 of Pliny, near the end) and the last of all two sentences 'De adulteratione gemmarum'. Robert's scholia in the margins, referred to in his preface, are at first in small script by the main hand and later, from f. 46, in a hand of s. xii/xiii: there are none after f. 63ᵛ. Thomas Gascoigne wrote his characteristic 'IH̄C mᵃ' (ihesus maria) on f. 1ᵛ.

ff. ii+164+v. ff. 165–7 are medieval end-leaves and f. 167ᵛ was pasted to a former binding. 295×205 mm. Written space 205×130 mm. 2 cols. 69 lines. Collation: 1–20⁸ 21⁴. Quires 1–8 are numbered at the end and quires 1–9 have catchwords. Handsome initials: (i) f. 12ᵛ, gold on blue and red decorated ground, edged in green; (ii) of bks. 2–9, red, together with one or both of the colours green and blue; (iii) f. 1, red patterned in white, with red, blue, and green ornament; (iv) 2-line, green, red, or blue. Slatter binding. Secundo folio *extraxi*.

Written in England. Used by Thomas Gascoigne, †1458. Seen at Eton by John Bale (Bale, *Index*, p. 368).

135. *Seneca, Epistolae* s. XII med.

1. ff. 2–5 Ieronimus in cathalogo uirorum illustrium. Lucius anneus (*over erasure*) seneca cordubensis . . . interfectus est. Explicit prologus beati ieronimi presbiteri. Incipiunt epistole ad sanctum paulum transmissę á seneca. Seneca paulo salutem. Credo tibi paule . . . (f. 5) Epitaphium senecę. Cura. labor. meritum . . . (6 lines).

The extract from Jerome, the fourteen letters between Paul and Seneca and the epitaph of Seneca, as in MS. 89, art. 1, q.v. f. 1, a singleton, is blank on the recto and has the words 'In hoc uolumine continentur epistole senece ad lucilium octoginta nouem' on the verso in large red and green capitals within a handsome penwork frame, s. xii.

2. ff. 5–166ᵛ Seneca lucilio suo salutem. Ita fac mi lucili . . . reliquerunt. nichil scire. uale.

Letters numbered 1–89, letter 48 being divided in two, as in MS. 89, q.v. This copy noticed by L. D. Reynolds, *The Medieval Tradition of Seneca's Letters*, 1965, p. 74, as one of the common b type of the δ text. No division into books. Many marginalia by Bernardo Bembo, some with dates attached to them, 27 Feb. 1478 (f. 105ᵛ), 22 Jan. 1484 (f. 72ᵛ), 12 Oct. 1488 (f. 71ᵛ), 24 June 1491 (f. 99ᵛ).

3. f. 167ʳᵛ (*a*) Versus de rerum mutabilitate. Nuper eram locuplex . . . digerat eius ero. (*b*) Si cubat incumbit . . . (3 lines). (*c*) Si rogat addideris . . . (3 lines). (*d*) Si quatio fiat cutio . . . (3 lines). (*e*) Scando conpositis dedit . . . (3 lines). (*f*) Angor formido defensor amor ligo palpo . . . (3 lines). (*g*), as (*f*) lines 1, 2. (*h*), as (*b*), (*c*).

(*a*). 88 lines, s. xii. Walther, *Initia*, no. 12488. *PL* clxxi. 1418–20 (Hildebert). (*b–h*). Grammatical mnemonics in several hands, s. xii ex.

4. Flyleaf notes, ff. iiiᵛ, ivʳᵛ, 168ʳᵛ, 169ʳ, by Bernardo Bembo, mainly on Seneca's letters, including: f. 168, Surge patre Francisce tuos insulsus honores Dissipat: heu magne dillacerentur opes. Hęc tua quis credat? profert dum rauce Gerardus Carmina? Quę mallem dum canit esse sua. Hec petrus meus inter equitandum cum romam profisisceremur. ad innocentium viiiᵐ Pontificem anno salutis 1484. 'Matheo gerardo recitante petrarce rithmos et vulgaria'; f. ivᵛ, Solus cum solo in colloquio vberrimo affatim omnia. 1488 xxii octobr' Ro. opitulante Altissimo; f. 168ᵛ, a note containing the date 'xviii Ian' 1484'.

5. A letter of Nicolaus Sagundinus to his son Mark, Venice, 23 Aug. 1463, copied by Bembo on a scrap of paper attached to f. iii^v.

Printed by James, *Catalogue* (read *inerter* for *forte* in the last line but one).

ff. iv+167+iv. ff. iii, iv, 168–9 are medieval end-leaves: iii^r, 169^v were pasted to a former binding. 292×197 mm. Written space *c.* 210×132 mm. 26 long lines: the writing is between a pair of ruled lines in quires 5–8. Collation: 1^8+1 leaf added before 1 2–8^8 9^6+1 leaf before 1 (f. 66) 10–20^8 21^8 wants 8, probably blank. Quires numbered at the end. In handsome large round script, mainly by one scribe: the scribe of ff. 72^v/6–88^v uses tailed *e* and a distinctive form of *g*: the flex (?) is much used as a mark of punctuation, but most of it is probably not original. Initials: (i) f. 2, 6-line, red with red ornament; (ii) 2-line, blue, green, red, or brown. Slatter binding. The fore-edge is lettered 'EPISTOLE SENECE'. Secundo folio (f. 3) *ueteri*.

Written in Italy. Belonged to Bernardo Bembo in s. xv². Given by Wotton, no doubt: cf. MS. 87. *CMA* 112.

136. *Seneca, Letters, etc.* (*in Italian*)   s. XIV/XV

1. ff. 1–4^v Qui chomincia le Robriche delle pistole di tutto i libro di senecha vniuersalmente.

A table of art. 3 divided by books, each preceded by a short summary.

2. ff. 4^v–7 Qui Comincia Il prolagho de llibro de liberali istudii di Senecha . . . Liberali studii desideri di sapere . . . ne vna cosa sapere sia sano et allegro. Amen Amen Amen.

Letter 88 of Seneca's Letters: cf. art. 3.

3. ff. 7^v–131^v Qui comincia il prolago del libro di senecha Il quale contiene capitoli cxxiiii°. Senecha fue vno sauio humo Disciepolo duno filosafo chebe nome fozion . . . trouate. (*text*) Cheluomo dee Racogliere . . . Ita fac mi lucilli etc. primo. Cosi fae amico mio lucillo . . . Et intra quelli chelmodo chiama beati. Deo gratias. Finiscie i libro delle pistole di senecha deo gratias Amen Amen.

Letters 1–87, 89–124 divided into twenty-two books, 'le quali pistole e insengnamenti e adornamenti fecie traslatare in lingua fiorentina Richardo petri cittadino di firenze', as appears from the preface, f. 7^v. Books 1–15 contain letters 1–87. Letter 89 is counted as two letters 'lxxxviii' and 'lxxxix', the second beginning at the words 'Hec Lucile virorum optime'. No marginalia.

4. f. 131^v Nel nome del nostro singnore giesu cristo. Santo Ierolimo scriue di senecha nel catalago de santi. Luccio armeo (*sic*) senecha . . . fu morto.

Cf. MS. 89, art. 1*a*.

5. ff. 131^v–132^v Lettere di senecha maestro di nerone a paolo apostolo e di paolo a senecha. Senacha a paolo salute. O paolo io credo . . . valentemente. Qui finiscono lepistole di paolo a senacha e da senacha a paolo. Scritto per me lorenzo di stefano sambarducci popolo san filicie Impiazza deo gracia.

The first thirteen of the fourteen letters in MSS. 89, art. 1*b*, and 135, art. 1.

ff. ii+132+ii. 305×230 mm. Written space 230×180 mm. 2 cols. 45 lines. Ruling with pencil. Collation: 1–15⁸ 16¹². Well written in the Italian equivalent of anglicana. Initials: (i) ff. 1, 7ᵛ, 6-line and 3-line, in colour on gold and coloured grounds (a man's head in the *Q* on f. 1), with prolongations in gold and colours, including green, which form a continuous border; (ii) 2-line, blue with red ornament or red with violet or, rarely, blue ornament. Capital letters in the ink of the text filled with pale yellow in quire 1 only. Binding by Slatter. Secundo folio *solitudine*.

Written by Lorenzo di Steffano Sambarducci of the parish of San Felice in Piazza (Florence): cf. art. 5. *CMA* 111.

137. *Vitruvius* s. XIV/XV

Cum diuina tua mens et numen. Imperator . . . discipline rationes . . . (*table of 11 chapters of bk. 1*) . . . Architecti est sciencia pluribus disciplinis . . . (f. 62) in dicem voluminibus explicata. Grates omnipotenti. Victruuii liber decimus et ultimus explicit. amen.

Listed by C. H. Krinsky, 'Seventy-eight Vitruvius Manuscripts', *Journal of Warburg and Courtauld Institutes*, xxx (1967), 36–70. Marginalia by Bernardo Bembo and others. ff. 62ᵛ–64ᵛ blank.

ff. iii+64+i. ff. 1–62 have a medieval foliation. ff. ii, iii are end-leaves from the medieval binding, pastedown and flyleaf. 310 × 205 mm. Written space 210 × 120 mm. 47–50 long lines. Frame ruling in pencil: the first line of writing is above the frame line. Collation: 1¹⁰ 2⁸ 3–6¹⁰ 7⁸ wants 5, 6, blank. Initials: (i) of books, 9-line or more, pink, edged in metallic red and patterned in white, on grounds of dark blue patterned in white: historiations at bk. 1, Vitruvius, and bk. 2, Hercules; (ii) in bk. 1 only, 4-line, blue or red with ornament of the other colour. Slatter binding. Secundo folio *titudinis*.

Written in Italy. A long inscription by Bernardo Bembo on f. iii shows that this book was acquired by him at the auction of Jacopo Langusci in 1453 and that it went astray later and was returned to him by Luigi Regii's son in 1493: Vetruuius Nobilis Archytectus exactissimi vir ingenii: Olim ex bibliotecha Clarissimi Mathematici Iacobi Langusci Veneti Post eius casum patauii: sub astatione multis cum aliis in nostratium cętum deductus est. Anno saluatoris M. cccc. liiiᵒ. Tandem multiplici amicorum 'vsu': et indulctu prębito: quod raritas tunc librorum effecerat: veluti transfuga xx ferme annos nobis delituit nescio ne obscurus in ulna. vt poeta diceret. Demum hodie Paulus Cornelius Ludouici filius: quem de Arrigis dictitant: id certior factus ex nostratibus hunc fuisse nobilem 'Archytectum:' bonam mentem indutus veteri domino destinandum curauit. Quod bono omine xvi Iunii 1493 factum est. Quo die opportune sermo est diuinus in missarum solenniis quanti habenda sit deperditorum recuperatio. et quam celebri gaudio exilarandum sit mentibus dominorum: cum redemptio est deperditarum rerum insperato facta. his qui iacturam optatissimarum quidem et usu suauissimorum magni pensandam esse statuerunt. Iuxta illud petrarce nostri Che piu gloria é nel regno degli ellecti: Dun spirito conuerso: et piu si stima. Che de nouanta noue altri perfecti. Idibus noʳ Bernardi Bembi doctoris manus. A no doubt earlier inscription by Bembo on f. iii has 'been erased: Codex patricii Veneti Bernardi Bembi olim D. Jac. Langusci. 'Ludouici Rigii Cornarii' and 'N. 76 Vetruvio de architetura' are in one hand on f. iiᵛ: after the name Bembo added 'Obiit dignus uir. xᵒ Octobris 1492'. Given by Wotton, no doubt: cf. MS. 87. *CMA* 125.

140. *Claudius Ptolemaeus, Cosmographia* s. XV ex.

(f. 1ᵛ) Claudii Ptholomei liber primus cosmographie incipit. In quo differt cosmographia a corographia. Cosmosgraphia imitatio est totius cogniti orbis . . .

(f. 138) Omnes prouintie nostre habitabilis sunt nonaginta et quatuor. finis.
Laus deo.

The translation by Jacopo d'Angelo, printed in 1475 and later. Thorndike and Kibre.
Bk. 2, f. 12; 3, f. 37^v; 4, f. 61; 5, f. 78; 6, f. 100^v; 7, f. 114^v; 8, f. 127. Eleven paragraphs
on ff. 12^v–16, the first beginning 'Quod qui gentes subiacent' and the last ending 'parti
contraria. finis', are headed 'Hoc quod scriptum est inferius non est de opere ptholomei'.
f. 1 has a table of chapters of bk. 1 and each of bks. 2–8 is preceded by a table. A corner
of f. 16 is missing. ff. 138^v–139^v blank.

The picture on f. 1 is described by J. J. G. Alexander, 'Notes on some Veneto-Paduan
illuminated books of the Renaissance', *Arte Veneta*, xxiii (1969), 9–20, and attributed by
him to Leonardo Bellini: reduced facsimile.

ff. iv+139. ff. iii, iv are medieval binding leaves, pastedown and flyleaf. 280 × 210 mm.
Written space 200 × 135 mm. 38 long lines. The first line of writing above the top ruled
line. Collation: 1^{10} 2^{10}+1 leaf before 1 (f. 11) 3^8 4–7^{10} 8^8 9–13^{10} 14^{10}+2 leaves after 9
(ff. 137, 138): 10 (f. 139) was pasted down. Humanistic script. On f. 1 a 19-line picture,
95 × 135 mm, of Ptolemy giving his book to a king: see above. Initials: (i) of books, 8-line
or less, gold on blue grounds patterned in white and decorated in green and pink; (ii)
3-line or 4-line, as (i), except that at first pink alternates with blue as the colour for the
ground. A border of green and pink interlace and gold in the margins of f. 1 and a floral
border in one margin of other pages with initials of type (i). Binding by Slatter. *Secundo
folio De his.*

Written in Italy. At the foot of f. 1 cherubs support a wreath containing the arms of
Molini of Rovigo, per fess a wheel gules and argent counterchanged (Rietstap, pl. ccxxiv).
CMA 107.

145. *Ambrosius* s. XII^1

1. ff. 1–18 Liber beati Ambrosii De Isaac et anima. In patre nobis sancti
isaac . . . debet et custodire. Explicit de Isaac. et anima.

PL xiv. 501–34 (527–60). The running title by the main hand, as in arts. 2–6.

2. ff. 18^v–32 Liber Primus Beati Ambrosii de fuga seculi. Frequens nobis est . . .
hauserint? per dominum . . . amen. Explicit de fuga seculi.

PL xiv. 569–96 (597–624).

3. ff. 32^v–54 Liber Beati Ambrosii De Iacob et uita beata. Necessarius ad
disciplinam . . . peremptus est morte. Explicit de Iacob et vita beata.

PL xiv. 597–638 (627–70).

4. ff. 54^v–75^v Liber Beati Ambrosii De paradyso. Et plantauit deus para-
disum . . . quę sunt spiritualia. Explicit liber Beati Ambrosii episcopi de
paradyso.

PL xiv. 275–314 (291–332).

5. ff. 75^v–90 Liber Apologeticus Beati Ambrosii episcopi In regem dauid.
Apologian prophetę dauid . . . mercarentur. Cui est honor . . . amen. Explicit
apologia feliciter.

PL xiv. 851–884 (891–926) f. 90^v was left blank.

ff. iii+90+ii. f. iii is a parchment binding leaf: see below. 295 × 190 mm. Written space
225 × 117 mm. and in quire 10 225 × 132 mm. 33 and in quire 10 37 long lines. Ruling
with a hard point. Collation: 1–11⁸ 12 two. Well written. Initials, 6-line, or less: of arts.
1, 5, green and red with ornament of both colours; of arts. 2, 3, green or red, with ornament of the other colour; of art. 4, red. The first line and the explicit of each text and the
running titles are in capitals. Binding by Slatter, 'mended April 1894'. Secundo folio
nantem.

Written in England. 'Liber Guilelmi Horman', 'Contenta . . .' and 'Donum Guilielmi
Hormani quondam socii huius contubernii', f. iii°.

147. *Apuleius* s. xv in.

1. ff. 2–106 [. . . . .] Incipit metamorpheos [. . . .]. A[t] ego tibi sermone isto . . .
gaudens obibam.

Collated as E by D. S. Robertson, *Apulée. Les Métamorphoses*, Paris, 1940, and noticed
at i. 49; cf. also D. S. Robertson in *Classical Quarterly*, xviii (1924), 27–42, 85–99, and the
edition of bks. iv. 28–vi. 24 by P. A. Grimal ('*Erasme*' ix, 1963).

Books numbered i–xi. Annotations by Bernardo Bembo. Damaged by damp, especially
ff. 50–70.

2. ff. 106–120ᵛ iᵘˢ liber floridorum. Ut ferme religiosis . . . efficit condicione.
Explicit liber floridorum. Finito libro sit laus et gloria cristo Amen.

Three books, numbered xii–xiv in continuation of the numbering in art. 1. Ed. R. Helm,
1910. Damaged by damp: part of each leaf from f. 110 onwards has been lost and was
repaired, no doubt at the time of rebinding, s. xix ex. ff. 121–124ᵛ left blank.

ff. v+123+iv, foliated i–iv, 1–124, (125–8). f. 1 is a medieval flyleaf. 220 × 155 mm.
Written space c. 147 × 100 mm. 30 long lines. Collation of ff. 2–124: 1–4¹⁰ 5⁸ 6–12¹⁰
13⁶ wants 6, blank. Written in more than one hand: a change at f. 7/22. 2-line red initials
begin books. Capital letters in the ink of the text stroked with red. The drawings on f. 1ᵛ
and in the margins of forty-seven pages are described in detail in James's *Catalogue*,
pp. 76–80. Bound by Wilson, Cambridge, in 1894. Secundo folio *nodosum*.

Written in Italy. 'Codex Bernardi Bembi patricii Veneti', f. 123ᵛ. Another inscription,
f. 1, is hardly legible: it includes the words 'die x Iulii'. Given by Wotton, no doubt:
cf. MS. 87. *CMA* 12.

149. *Cicero, De officiis* 1497/8

M. T. Ciceronis Officiorum lib. i ad m. filium. Quanquam te m. fili . . . (f. 126)
præceptisque lætabere. M. T. Ciceronis officiorum lib. finit. Romæ die martis
xiv februar. MCCCCLXXXXVII. B.S.

For this copy and other copies of De officiis written by Bartolomeo Sanvito in 1494, 1495,
and 1498 see J. Wardrop, *The Script of Humanism*, 1963, pp. 24, 29–31, and *MMBL* i.
391–2, and for the scribe and illuminator, J. J. G. Alexander and A. C. de la Mare, *The
Italian Manuscripts in the Library of Major J. R. Abbey*, 1969, pp. 105, 107, 109. Bk. 2,
f. 54ᵛ; 3, f. 86ᵛ. Facsimile of f. 1 in *Burlington Fine Arts Club, Exhibition of Illuminated
MSS.*, 1908, pl. 161; of ff. 1, 126, slightly reduced, by Wardrop, op. cit., pl. 19. Marginalia
by the scribe in red. ff. 126ᵛ–128ᵛ blank.

ff. ii+128+ii.[1] An old foliation ceases at 50. 153 × 102 mm. Written space 100 × 53 mm. 25 long lines. Ruling with a hard point: double vertical bounders. Collation: 1–12^{10} 13^8 (7, 8 pasted together). Quires lettered at the end, A–N. Written in skilled sloping humanistica: f. 1^r has 13 lines only, all in capitals, a line of gold alternating with a line of blue, red, black, purple, blue, red, in that order: on f. 126 the capitals of the explicit are in four lines, respectively pink, gold, blue, and red. Initials: (i) f. 1, green, historiated (Cicero and his son); (ii) ff. 54^v, 86^v, in colour on decorated coloured grounds; (iii) of paragraphs, blue, set outside the written space. A continuous border on f. 1: four sages are seated in the lower margin. Short side borders on ff. 54^v, 86^v. Binding by Slatter. Secundo folio *impedio*.

Written by Sanvito. Perhaps belonged to Bernardo Bembo, who owned other manuscripts written by Sanvito.[2] A scribble on f. 120^v is perhaps in a French hand, s. xvi. *CMA* 119.

150. *Theodulus, etc.* s. XI

1. ff. 1–6^v (*begins imperfectly*) Si uictus fueris . . . ne desperatio ledat.

Theodulus, Ecloga, lines 23–344, collated as δ by J. Osternacher, 1902, with reduced facsimile of f. 1.

2. ff. 6^v–18^v Emula quid cessas . . . uiuere parte puto.

Maximianus, Elegiae, collated as A by Bährens, *Poetae Latini Minores*, v (1883), 316–48. Interlinear glosses are probably in the same hand as the text, as in arts. 3–6. 'BAXLE DAMA IACN USNANSA' between art. 1 and art. 2 has been interpreted as 'ABEL ADAM CAIN SUSANNA'. 'Hoc item in alio Codice peruetusto paruulo', f. 6^v, opposite the first line of the text, s. xvii.

3. ff. 18^v–37^v Magnanimium eaciden . . . scit cetera mater. 'Aura silet puppis currens ad littora venit' (*the addition, s. xv*).

Statius, Achilleis, collated as E by H. W. Garrod, 1906. f. 18^v reproduced in *New Pal. Soc.* i. 110.

4. ff. 37^v–52 Legerat huius amor . . . femina uirque meo.

Ovid, Remedia amoris, collated as E by F. W. Linz, 1965: cf. pp. xviii–xx.

5. ff. 52–70^v Hanc tua penelope . . . de gente reportas.

Ovid, Heroides, i. 7–vii. 159, collated as E by H. Dörrie, 1971.

6. ff. 70^v–81 Domino sancto et in cristi gratia specialiter erudito floriano abbati arator subdiaconus. Qui meriti florem . . . tempore sanctos (*ends imperfectly*).

Arator, Historia Apostolica (*Clavis*, no. 1504), collated as N by A. P. McKinlay, *CSEL* lxxii (1961). Ends at i. 521.

ff. iv+81+iv. Some of the parchment defective, for example ff. 20, 79. 227 × 165 mm. Written space *c.* 177 × 110 mm. 29 long lines. Collation: 1 one 2–11^8: 3 and 6 in quires 7, 8, 9 are half sheets. Beneventan script, ff. 74–80^v/16 in a better hand than the rest: E. A. Lowe, *The Beneventan Script*, 1914, p. 338. Initials in the ink of the text: (i) ff. 6^v, 18^v, 52, 3–5 line, in more or less elaborate outline; (ii) 2-line. Binding by Slatter, rebacked. Written in southern Italy: the script is of the Bari type. *CMA* 101.

[1] A parchment flyleaf of MS. 160 (f. iii), blank, except for 'Script. 1497' on the verso (s. xvii?), belonged here no doubt and was misplaced by Slatter.

[2] According to Wardrop, p. 29, there are annotations by Bembo, but I am unable to find them.

151. *Baptista Mantuanus, Ord. Carm.* s. XV/XVI

1. (*a*) ff. 3–44ᵛ Clarissimo Viro D. Bernardo Bembo Patricio Veneto iure consulto Frater Baptista Mantuanus Carmelita. S.P.D. Beatissime virginis et martyris Catharine . . . (f. 5ᵛ) ab angelis. Fratris Bap. Mant. Carmelitæ theologi ad magnificum D. Bernardum bembum patricium Venetum et iureconsultum peritissimum secunda Parthenice incipit. Fratris . . . incipit (*as above, repeated in red*). Costidis agressi pugnam . . . honor iste sepultis. Finis. (*b*) ff. 44ᵛ–45 Francisci Careti Parmensis Iuris Pontificii Scholaris Studiosissimi in Inuidum Lectorem Carmen. Inuide quid tantum . . . Virgiliique nepos. Secundæ par- thenices opus diuinum Bononie impressum solerti animaduersione Francisci Cereti permensis: communibus impensis Benedicti Hectoris Bibliopolæ Platonis- que eiusdem impressoris acuratissimi: ciuium bononiensium Anno natiuitatis dominicæ M.CCCC.LXXIX (*sic*). Quinto idus Februarias.

Copied from the edition of 1489, *GKW* 3290. ff. 45ᵛ–48ᵛ blank.

2 (added on a preliminary bifolium). (*a*) f. 1 Salue Magniloqui . . . (*b*) f. 1ᵛ Sancti Hieronymi ad Demetriadem virginem. Ama scripturas sacras . . . (*c*) f. 2ᵛ De Fratre Baptista Mantuano. Carmen Petri Bembi Bernardi filii. Pecte tuos iterum. iam tandem pecte capillos . . .

(*a*), 2 lines and 4 lines of verse and a maxim, and (*b*) in the hand of Bernardo Bembo. (*c*). Ten lines of verse by Pietro Bembo, 1470–1547.

ff. ii+48+ii. 210×140 mm. Written space 138×88 mm. 27 long lines. Horizontals ruled in ink and vertical bounders in pencil. Collation: 1² 2–6⁸ 7⁶. Textura: the scribe used both upright *d* and rounded *d*, the latter chiefly in bitings with a following *e*. Initials, ff. 3, 15ᵛ, 44ᵛ, purple and white on grey-blue grounds. Capital letters in the ink of the text filled with pale yellow. Binding by Slatter. Secundo folio (f. 4) *strare putat*.

Written in Italy. Belonged to and probably made for Bernardo Bembo. His arms are in a wreath at the foot of f. 3: 'VIRTVS ET HONOR' on a scroll beneath them. Given by Wotton, no doubt; cf. MS. 87. *CMA* 94.

152. *Juvenalis* s. XV med.

1. ff. 1–65 Semper ego auditor . . . et torquibus omnes. Y͞HS MARIA

The sixteen satires, not divided into books. Marginalia by Bernardo Bembo, some damaged by a binder. ff. 65ᵛ–66ᵛ were left blank.

2 (added). (*a*) f. 65ᵛ Materiam et causas Satyrarum hac inspice prima. Carpitur hac Satyra . . . probra notantur. (*b*) f. 66 Notes and verses including three lines in Italian.

In Bembo's hand. (*a*), 19 lines, summarizes the satires: cf. MS. 153, art. 3.

ff. ii+66+ii. 203×130 mm. Written space 140 mm high. 30 long lines. Ruled in ink. The first line of writing is above the top ruled line. Collation: 1–6¹⁰ 7⁶. Humanistic script. Initials: (i) f. 1, 8-line gold *S* on a handsome ground of blue, green, and pink, decorated with dots in groups of three and curving white branches; (ii) 4-line, blue or red. Binding by Slatter. Secundo folio *Ius nullum*.

Written in Italy. Belonged to Bernardo Bembo. Given by Wotton, no doubt: cf. MS. 87.
CMA 85.

153. *Juvenalis; Persius* s. xv med.

1. ff. 1–77ᵛ Iunii decii iuuenalis satiri: liber primus. Semper ego auditor . . . et
torquibus omnes. I. DECII. I. AQVINATIS. FINIS.

Satires 1–16, divided into five books. f. 78ʳᵛ blank.

2. ff. 79–92 Nec fonte labra . . . finitor acerui. PERSII FINIS.

Satires 1–6. f. 92ᵛ blank.

3 (added). (*a*) f. 93 Prima docet Satire causas: formamque libelli . . . (*b*) ff. 93ᵛ–
94ᵛ Ó curas hominum: Ó quantum . . ., and other verses and notes.

On the flyleaves, (*b*), in Bernardo Bembo's hand. (*a*) lists the satires of art. 1 in sixteen
lines of verse, each with a leaf reference.

ff. iv+92+iii. ff. iii, iv, 93, 94 are medieval pastedowns and flyleaves. An early foliation
ends at 77. 170 × 100 mm. Written space 130 mm high. 25 long lines. Ruling with a hard
point. The first line of writing above the top ruled line. Collation: 1–9¹⁰ 10². Current
humanistica. Throughout, the first two or three letters of each line are in red. Initials; (i)
3-line, gold on blue, green, and red grounds decorated with dots in groups of three and
white interlacing branches; (ii) 2-line, gold on blue, green, and red grounds patterned in
white. A border in the lower margin of f. 1. Elsewhere decoration in the margins—white
vine-stem on a blue ground—springs from the initial or is beside it, but separate. Binding by Slatter. Secundo folio *Iratis*.

Written in Florence by a scribe working for Vespasiano da Bisticci.[1] Belonged to Bernardo
Bembo, whose arms, supported by an angel, are in the border on f. 1. 'Nº 4', f. iv, s. xvi (?).
Given by Wotton, no doubt: cf. MS. 87. *CMA* 86.

154. *Commentarium in Persium* s. xv/xvi

[A]ulus. Persius Flaccus natus est pridie nonas decembris . . . (f. 2) aliud uero
significet. Nec fonte labra . . . ut qui auaritię eius finem voluerit imponere
facile uideatur etiam syllogismum Chrysippi deffinire.

A life of Persius (ff. 1, 2) and commentary on the six satires: 1, f. 2; 2, f. 19ᵛ; 3, f. 28;
4, f. 38; 5, f. 43ᵛ; 6, f. 56ᵛ. f. 62ᵛ blank.

ff. ii+62+ii. An old foliation is 1–48, 41–54. Paper. 210 × 145 mm. Written space
170 × 110 mm. 22–7 long lines. Collation: 1–7⁸ 8⁶. Written in sloping humanistica. No
decoration. Bound by Slatter. Secundo folio *utramque*.

Written in Italy. *CMA* 105.

155. *Eutropius et Paulus Diaconus* s. xv

Primus in ytalia ut quibusdam placet regnauit Ianus . . . (f. 46ᵛ) diligentiam
reseruamus. Huc usque historiam Eutropius conposuit. Cui tamen aliqua.

[1] As Dr. A. de la Mare tells me.

Paulus diaconus addidit. Anno ab urbe condita millesimo c xviii° . . . (f. 79ᵛ) Anastasius presbiter ordinatus est. Pauli diaconi addicionum ad Romanam hystoriam Eutropii hystoriagraphi Liber explicit.

The additions carry the history as far as A.D. 729, but from f. 68ᵛ, 'Cum iam ut premissum est . . .', they consist of excerpts from Paulus Diaconus, Historia Langobardorum. Ed. H. Droysen, MGH, Auct. Antiq. ii (1879), 6–182 (Eutropius), 185–224 (Paulus), 396–405 (ex Pauli Historia Langobardorum). Spaces for headings of books not filled. f. 80ʳᵛ left blank: only the inner half remains.

ff. ii+80+i. Paper. Foliated in s. xv or s. xvi. 200 × 145 mm. Written space 145 × 98 mm. 35 long lines. Collation: 1–6¹² 7⁸. Quires signed a–g on the usual late medieval system. Textura. Initials 7-line (f. 1), 5-line, and 1-line, not filled in, except a rough P in the ink of the text on f. 1. Bound by Slatter. Secundo folio *siluius*.

Written in the Netherlands. *CMA* 52, 103.

156. *P. Marsus* s. xv²

P. Marsi. Pierii. Piscinatis. Bembice. Peregrine. Et primo librum alloquitur suum. O mihi non latis proles educta sacello . . . (*prologue of 88 lines*) . . . (f. 3ᵛ) Ad Bernardum Bembum in hispania legatum Paulus Marsus Ex Argolica profectione 'uocatus ac demum' inuitatus ad Hispalicam Feliciter incipit. Soluere ab Adriaco . . .

Twenty-one pieces on ff. 3ᵛ–35, one of them (f. 15ᵛ) bearing the date of composition, 28 Aug. 1467, when Paolo Marsi was on a visit with Bernardo Bembo to the temple at Hippo. Annotations by Bembo. ff. 35ᵛ–40ᵛ left blank: on 40ʳ Bembo wrote a memorandum, printed in James's *Catalogue*, of the names of six people and the votes they received (?) in an election, 13 July 1494.

ff. iii+40+i. ff. ii, iii are a contemporary pastedown and flyleaf. Excellent parchment. 220 × 120 mm. Written space c. 132 mm high. 18 long lines. Ruling with a hard point. Collation: 1–4¹⁰: 4¹⁰ (f. 40) was pasted down. Written in current humanistica. 2-line purple initials, most of them outside the written space. Binding by Slatter. Secundo folio *Est etiam*.

Made for Bernardo Bembo, no doubt: his motto, 'Virtus et honor', is on f. iiiᵛ in purple ink, surrounded by bay and palm, and his arms are in the lower margin of f. 1. Given by Wotton, no doubt: cf. MS. 87. *CMA* 95.

157. *Naldus Naldii* s. xv²

1. f. vᵛ Naldi naldii florentini epigramma ad clarissimum Virum bernardum bembum Legatum Venetum. Bembe siracusio . . . τέλοσ.

Ten lines. No. 31 in Naldus Naldius Florentinus, *Epigrammaton Liber*, ed. A. Perosa, Budapest, 1943, p. 10. Below it Bernardo Bembo wrote 'Id est Poetę manibus ingenium'. ff. ii–v blank.

2. ff. 1–26 Naldi de Naldis (*altered to* Naldi Naldii) Bucolica in Laurentium Medicen Iuuenem clarissimum. Daphnis. Aegloga in L. eundem. Daphnis pastor erat . . . non aspernatus Apollo. τέλοσ.

Eleven eclogues. Cf. W. L. Grant in *Manuscripta*, 6 (1962), 144–54, and 11 (1967) 155–8:[1]
he notes (pp. 153–4) that Eclogue xi, Pimeneus . . . ad Laurentium Medicen, which is
known only from this manuscript, ff. 23–25ᵛ, is in a different hand from the others, but
the hand seems the same to me. ff. 26ᵛ–28ᵛ blank.

ff. i+32+i. 208×127 mm. Written space 122 mm high. 20 long lines. Collation of
ff. ii–v, 1–28: 1⁴ 2–3¹⁰ 4⁸. Upright current humanistic hand. Initials: (i) f. 1, 4-line, gold *D*
on blue ground patterned in white and historiated: Daphnis chasing a nymph; (ii) 2-line,
gold on grounds coloured blue, pink and green, blue and green, or blue patterned in
white. A border on two sides of f. 1. Binding by Slatter, rebacked in 1974. Secundo
folio *En dure*.

Written in Italy. The Medici arms are in the lower margin of f. 1, but this copy was
designed by Naldi for Bernardo Bembo by the addition of a preliminary quire on which he
wrote an 'epigramma' asking Bembo to read his verses. Given by Wotton, no doubt:
cf. MS. 87. *CMA* 99.

158. *J. Boccaccius, De mulieribus claris* s. xv²

[P]ridie Mulierum Egregiarum paulum . . . dentibus inuidorum depereat.
Iohannis Bochacii de Certaldo de mulieribus claris liber explicit. Finis.

Printed in 1473 (*GKW* 4483) and later. ff. 94ᵛ–96ᵛ were left blank.

ff. ii+96+ii. Paper. Nearly contemporary foliation. 210×140 mm. Written space
143×85 mm. 31 long lines. Pencil ruling: the top horizontal, but not the bottom one,
prolonged into the margins: double vertical bounders. Collation: 1–9¹⁰ 10 six. Upright
humanistic hand. Spaces for 4-line (f. 1) and 3-line initials left blank. Binding by Slatter.
Secundo folio *et animi*.

Written in Italy. *CMA* 33.

160. *W. de Conchis* s. xiii med.

MS. 160 and 161 were the last two pieces in a volume of over 250 leaves, which
belonged to Master John of London in s. xiv¹ and, by his gift, to St. Augustine's,
Canterbury (*Ancient Libraries*, p. 340, no. 1222). The rest of the volume is now
Bodleian, e Mus. 223. The quires of MS. 160 are numbered at the foot of versos
towards the left xxii–xxiv in continuation of and by the same hand as the series
in e Mus. which ends with 'xix' on the verso of f. 186, formerly '194'. MS. 160,
art. 2, appears to be in the same hand as part of e Mus. Leaf numbers were
added to the table of contents, e Mus., f. iiiᵛ: they show that the William of
Conches began on 'fo 195' and the Adelard of Bath on 'fo 228': the latter number
is still just legible on MS. 161, f. 1.

1. ff. 1–22ᵛ (*begins imperfectly*) modo siccum ex vicinitate estatis. modo eadem
ratione calidum . . . Non enim extincto naturali calore diu potest homo viuere.

---

[1] See now *Naldi Naldii Florentini Bucolica, Volaterrais, Hastiludii, Carmina varia*, ed.
W. L. Grant, 1974. This manuscript, *E*, is taken as the basis of the text of the eclogues.

William of Conches, De philosophia mundi, lacking nine leaves[1] at the beginning. The first words now are in edn. *PL* clxxii. 68/11. Particula 3, f. 5^v; particula 4, f. 12^v. Ends at edn. 99/14 from foot. A. Vernet lists sixty-seven copies in *Scriptorium*, i. 252–5, but not this one, nor any ending at this point, but some copies of the parallel Dragmaticon do not continue further than this (Vernet, p. 246). Verses added in the margin of f. 16^v by the hand of art. 2: Humanum semen sex primis . . . (4, Walther, no. 18933, *Susceptum* . . .); vii^{tem} in lacte dies . . . (2).

2 (filling the quire). (*a*) f. 23 Omnipotens. dominus. ihesus. cristus. deus altus . . . aures prebe pietatis. (*b*) f. 23 Sequentiae of the four gospels. (*c*) ff. 23^v–24 Deus magnus et immensus Et quem . . . deus eterne glorie. (*d*) f. 24 D[. . . .] . . . fiat fiat fiat. (*e*) f. 24^v Verses 1–20 of Ps. 108.

(*a*). On the names of Christ in twenty-two lines of verse. (*b*) consists of the first four words of John and Matthew, the words 'Recumbentibus cristi discipulis' from Mark (16:14) and the words 'Surgens iohannes de sinagoga' from Luke (4: 38). (*c*). Twenty-three couplets, *RH*, no. 25424, *AH* xv. 268. (*d*). A protective charm, the first words blotted out: M. R. James read them as 'Deus abraham deus ysahac deus iacob deus aaron deprecor te rex immortalis', using probably the reagent which now stains the page.

ff. iii+24+ii. ff. 1–24 are numbered in pencil in a medieval hand '204'–'227'. f. iii, a parchment flyleaf, belongs to MS. 149, q.v. 168×105 mm. Written space 108×70 mm. Collation: 1–2^{10} 3^4. For the quire numbering and hand of art. 2 see above. Art. 1 in a small hand, probably rather earlier than e Mus. 223. 2-line and 1-line initials, blue with red ornament or red with blue-green ornament. Binding by Slatter.

Written in France. Belonged to John of London: see above. At Eton by 1697 (cf. MS. 161), but not recorded in *CMA*.

161. *Adelardus Bathoniensis, Quaestiones naturales*   s. xii med.

'Incipit liber Adelardi Batoniensis ad nepotem suum de solucione questionum naturalium'. Cum in angliam nuper redierim henrico Willelmi anglis imperante . . . (f. 1^v) nepoti respondebo. Qua ratione . . . vtrum stellę animate sint (*table of chapters, numbered later from 1 to 76*). (f. 3) Meministi nepos quod . . . Quidam autem altius uel intelligentes uel furentes (*ends imperfectly*).

Thorndike and Kibre. Collated as E for the edition by M. Müller, *Beiträge zur Geschichte der Philosophie des Mittelalters*, xxxi (1934): the last words correspond to edn. 68/17. The text is written without breaks: chapter numbers are in the margins by the main hand. The leaves, especially the last five, are damaged by damp. In chapters 1–62 questions are preceded by ⊃– and answers by ⊃–C: after this N and A are used.

Two lines of verse in a business hand in the lower margin of f. 13^v: Cum tibi sint nati . . . uitam (Walther, *Sprichwörter*, no. 4531).

ff. ii+37+ii. Traces of a pencil foliation like that in MS. 160 can be seen on some leaves, for example 9–14, where the first two digits are 24: a number in ink on f. 1 is 'fo 228'.[2] 167×110 mm, but the width rises to 117 mm where the binder has spared marginalia and is raised throughout to 125 mm by means of a strip of modern paper. Written space

---

[1] To judge from the foliation, s. xiv. If the quire numbers are right, two quires are missing between e Mus., f. 186 and 160, f. 1.

[2] In e Mus. 223 the pencil foliation has been renewed here and there in ink. It is not renewed in MS. 160 and only on f. 1 of MS. 161. Probably a few leaves, four or more, were lost between MS. 160, f. 24 and MS. 161, f. 1, after the leaves were foliated in pencil and before they were foliated in ink.

127 × 82 mm. 29 long lines. Collation: 1–4⁸ 5 five (ff. 33–7, mounted separately). Initials: (i) f. 1, 4-line, red; (ii) f. 3, 2-line space not filled. Binding of s. xix/xx, imitating a Slatter binding: presumably the leaves were mended at this time.

Written in England. Put after MS. 160, q.v., by s. xiv in. *CMA* 1.

165. *M. Vegius, De liberis educandis, etc.* s. xv²

1. ff. 1–84 Maphei Vegii de liberis educandis. Si tantum nobis ingenii esset . . . Perpetuo tenentes obseruent. Deo gratias. Ex libris clarissimi viri Vehii laudensis de liberorum educatione Epithoma feliciter finis adest. Rome apud sanctum petrum Nono kal. Ianuarii MCCCCXLIIII. tempus quo Mafeus librum feliciter edidit.

An abbreviation of the text printed in 1491 (Hain 15920) and later. Six books. Headings, usually in red: Epithoma libri secundi, f. 18; Epithoma libri tertii feliciter lege, f. 29; and ff. 35ᵛ, 54ᵛ, 69ᵛ. f. 84ᵛ blank.

2. ff. 85–119 Contentio inter terram Aurum et Solem de prestantia coram Ioue per Mafeum. Cum decertarent inter se aliquando . . . manifeste declarauit. Finit.

Printed in 1497 (Hain 15933) and later. f. 119ᵛ blank.

ff. iii+119+ii. Paper. f. iii is a contemporary paper flyleaf. 220 × 145 mm. Written space 140 × 75 mm. 23–6 long lines. Vertical bounders made by folding the leaf on each side of the written space. Collation: 1–9¹² 10¹² wants 12, unless it is the present f. iii. Current hybrida under humanistic influence. Red initials in the margins of ff. 1, 18; none elsewhere. Binding by Slatter. Secundo folio *sub te*.

Written in Italy. *CMA* 96.

169. *Petrus Riga, Aurora* s. XIII in.

1. ff. 1–177 A copy of the Aurora in its third edition, according to P. E. Beichner, *Aurora, Petri Rigae Biblia Versificata* (Publications in Mediaeval Studies, University of Notre Dame, xix, 1965), p. xix, but the last two of the three texts, Acts, Job, Song of Songs, whose presence distinguishes the third from the second edition, are here not in the main hand. The order is the usual one, except that the Recapitulationes (no heading here, f. 106ᵛ: edn., pp. 605–25) comes after OT, not Gospels.

'Incipit prologus super auroram'. Incipit aurora et primo agit de vi diebus. Omnis scriptura diuinitus inspirata . . . interfectionem diaboli a cristo. Frequens sodalium meorum peticio . . . (f. 2) patenter illuxit. Primo facta die꞉ duo celum terra leguntur . . . (f. 106ᵛ) cesar in aure tua. Principio rerum . . . (f. 112) hii docuere fidem. Explicit uetus testamentum. Incipit prologus super quatuor euangelia. Post legem . . . (f. 159) terminat ecce metrum (*as Beichners's P*). Finito libro sit laus et gloria cristo. (*new hand*) Incipit prologus in libro iob. Librum Iob moysi . . . (f. 177) palma figurat. 'qui mundum uincit ne cura cor eius adurat. Explicit etc''.

Ed. Beichner, pp. 4–8, 21–417, 605–25, 421–535, 626–739 (Cant. Cant., line 793). No break at f. 166ᵛ between Job and Song of Songs. In Song of Songs the headings often differ from edn.: many begin 'Sequitur'.

A corrector put in some Aeg. 1 additions in the margins, for example the two last lines of the six after line 286 of 2 Kings (edn., p. 282) and the lines of 3 Kings printed in edn., pp. 287 (headed, f. 74, 'scribe hoc totum ante quartas adonias'), 297, and 302. He wrote 'non debet hic esse spatium uel littera capitalis' on f. 19ᵛ and 'non est hic (s)patium uel capitellum' on f. 20: these appear to be directions to the rubricator not to put in coloured letters where Genesis, line 1517, is repeated after line 1522 (cf. Beichner's footnote), and at Genesis, line 1539. And on f. 36 he wrote 'vacat' and 'non scribas hos iiiiᵒʳ', to draw attention to Exodus lines 1291-2, 1301-2, which in this copy are written after line 1300, but separated from it by a space of three lines: the corrector copied them again in their proper places.

2. Brief pieces on flyleaves and at the end include: (*a*) f. 177, verses 'Si rogo conponas . . .' (3 lines), 'Vescio poto cibo textum do visito soluo . . .' (2 lines: cf. Walther, *Sprichwörter*, no. 33805), 'Tres celebrat missas natali presbiter unus . . .' (4 lines); (*b*) f. 177ᵛ Isti sunt xii dies ueneris De quibus clemens papa inuenit in canonibus et in a[ct]ibus apostolorum dominum dixisse discipulo suo petro. Si quis ieiunauerit in pane . . .; (*c*) f. iii Conditor en rerum statuit sine semine clerum . . . (4 lines).

(*a*, *b*) of s. xiii, probably in a French hand. (*c*) of s. xv in an English hand.

ff. iii+179+ii. ff. ii, iii are medieval flyleaves. 227×140 mm. Written space 149 mm high and in the prose on ff. 1, 2 50 mm wide. Wide margins. The first line of writing above the top ruled line. Collation: 1-22⁸ 23⁴ wants 4, blank. Quires 1-14 numbered at the end. The first scribe sometimes wrote a whole line of verse as catchword. Mainly in one small distinctive hand: a second scribe began at f. 159 (Job) and a third at f. 169. Initials blue or red with ornament of the other colour: as far as f. 33 the scribe indented for 2-line initials, but, throughout, the initials are 1-line and placed in the same way as the capital letters beginning each line of verse: a space of 4 mm separates the capital beginning a line from the letter following it, except in the line after one beginning with a coloured initial on ff. 1-33, where the scribe was forced by the indent to write the capital in with the rest of the verse. Binding by Slatter. Secundo folio *uoluminis*.

Written probably in France. 'Iste liber est Ioanni de [. . . .] clerico', f. 178, s. xiv. In England by s. xiv/xv, when 'Willelmus permissione diuina Cantuar' Episcopus Ang' et apostolice sedis legatus Walterus' and 'Theos ymon nostri pie Eleyson', three times repeated, were scribbled on f. iiᵛ. *CMA* 32.

170. *Pharetra Sacramenti* s. xv¹

1. Incipit prologus in libellum editum contra lollardos. qui dicitur pharetra sacramenti. Quis dabit capiti meo aquam . . . populi mei. ait ieremias propheta deflens . . . (f. 130ᵛ) ad lumen quod est cristus pertingere mereamur. Cui sit . . . amen.

Two parts, each of three 'particulae'. Part 1 ends on f. 68ᵛ, 'Explicit tractatus de sacramento eukaristie'. Its third particula (ff. 36-68ᵛ) consists of forty-eight 'miracula' in four sets of twelve: no. 7 in the fourth set happened in the church of St. Mary Magdalene 'in suburbio Oxonie', on St. James's Day 1262. Part 2 begins on f. 68ᵛ, 'Incipit tractatus de sacramento penitencie'. Its third particula (ff. 109-130ᵛ) consists of miracles taken mainly from 'Cesarius' (of Heisterbach). A few begin 'Refert gerardus barri' (Giraldus Cambrensis). Cambridge, Univ. Libr., Ff. 6. 44, ff. 57-135, and Lambeth Palace, 392, ff. 59-111 are other copies.

2. Binding leaves: (*a*) ff. iii–iv, two leaves in small current anglicana, s. xiv, partly at least on burning-glasses, quoting Alacen, with diagrams; (*b*) ff. 132ᵛ–133, the latter part of a Franciscan letter of fraternity, dated from Boston 'circa festum natiuitatis Beate Marie Virginis', 1372; (*c*), below (*b*) and written the other way up, a conveyance (?) of a messuage 'cum duobus croftis', dated from 'Leek in festo sancti Michaelis', no year (s. xiv²: current anglicana); (*d*) on the dorse of (*b*) fragments of a theological text in English, s. xiv².

(*a*). A passage begins 'Ad primum articulum ipse Respondet sic dicit proposicio alecen incenditur de certa distancia speculorum ad inuicem propter reflexiones eorum'. (*b*). No. 12 in the list by A. G. Little, 'Franciscan Letters of Fraternity', *BLR* v (1954–6), 13–25. (*d*) in a hand like (*c*) is hard to read. The layout is: (i) 29 lines centred, each line incomplete at the end; (ii) 4 lines above (i), beginning incompletely further to the left and ending incompletely; (iii) 8 faded lines to the left of the upper part of (i); (iv) 2 lines in Latin below (iii); (v) 12 lines below (iv). I note: in (i), . . . to 3ᵉ discendyng of 3e processe forseyd. it is to wyth. 3at . . .; in (ii), . . . wythstodytz 3e sensualite. stered be [. . . . .] and harn ecause 3at skyle asse iccitz to sensualite . . .; in (v), . . . dywerse and sondry yernys. is 3er sondry maner [. . .] and 3at yernyng is callyd kyndly. als [. . . .] and bestial mene . . .

ff. iv+130+vi. For ff. iii, iv, 132, 133 see above. ff. 131, 134 are blank medieval end-leaves, flyleaf and pastedown. 187×115 mm. Written space 135×85 mm. 22–6 long lines. Ruling with pencil. Collation: 1–8¹⁶ 9². Signatures in the common late medieval form. Written in current anglicana. 3-line blue initials with red ornament. Binding by Slatter. Secundo folio *suis nefandis*.

Written in England. Art. 2*b* suggests provenance from the east of England: 'Leek' (2*c*) is probably Leake, near Boston. *CMA* 92.

171. *N. de Gorran, Fundamentum aureum*   s. XIII/XIV

Incipiunt themata de dominicis edita per fratrem Nycholaum de Gorram ordinis fratrum predicatorum. Dominica prima in aduentu epistola Ro. xiii. Hora est iam nos de sompno surgere . . . Sicut dicit sapiens ecclesiastes iii. Omnia tempus habent . . . (f. 118) Incipiunt themata de festis . . . In festo sancti andree. In baculo meo . . . Sicut dicitur sap' ii Vmbre transitus . . . (f. 228ᵛ) (*De uno apostolo*). Vox turturis . . . Sicut transeunte . . . (f. 245) In die cinerum et in sequenti xvᵃ. Dabo eis coronam . . Dicitur communiter quod . . . (f. 259ᵛ) uerbum et spiritus sanctus et hii tres vnum sunt.

Sermons of the temporale, sanctorale, common of saints and for Lent by Nicholas de Gorran, printed in 1509 and later (Fundamentum aureum). Schneyer, pp. 318, 330, 546, 121. Three leaves are missing after f. 2. ff. 116ᵛ–117ᵛ blank.

As compared with edn. Antwerp, 1620, the order differs at two points, after f. 77, where a temporale series ends at the twenty-fifth Sunday after Pentecost, and after the end of the common saints. With three exceptions the sermons on ff. 77–116 and 245–259ᵛ are to be found in the edition:

ff.		
77ᵛ–79ᵛ	210–12	Ad religiosos
79ᵛ–81	207–8	In visitationibus
81–4	203–6	In synodo
84–6	90–3	In dedicatione
86–88ᵛ	208–10	In electione prelati
88ᵛ–93ᵛ	93–7	In ordinibus

94–8	212–15	In ingressu religionis . . . De cruce
99	69	In capite ieiunii
99^v–113^v	71–83	Lent
113^v–114^v	85–6	Post ramos palmarum
114^v–115^v	27–8	In cena domini
115^v–116	89	In sabbato sancto
245–7	69–71	In capite ieiunii
247–9	83–5	In ramis palmarum
249–53	86–9	Feria quinta
253–5	29–31	Easter
255–7	39–40	Ascension
257–9	42–3	Pentecost
259^{rv}	44–5	Trinity

The three sermons not in the printed edition are De cruce on ff. 98–9: Si quis vult venire . . . Saluator noster inuitans nos ad penitenciam . . .; Verbum crucis . . . Sicut dicit beatus augustinus palato non sano pena est panis . . .; Deponente esse pondus . . . Sicut aquila prouocat. . . . Some sermons are cues only, as in the printed edition, but the references provided here make no sense, for example, f. 228^v, 'Domine in uoluntate . . . supra viii': this sermon is on f. 122^v. 'xix p^a' low down in the margin of f. 68 suggests some connection with manuscripts copied on the pecia system.

2 (added in a good small current hand, s. xiv). ff. 260–266^v An index to art. 1, with references to the leaf numbers of this manuscript: it ends imperfectly.

ff. iv+266+iii. ff. iii, iv, 267 are medieval end-leaves: 267^v was pasted down. A medieval foliation on ff. 1–259, 1, 2, 6–262 takes account of the three leaves now missing from quire 1. On ff. 1–8 the columns on rectos are marked a, b and the columns on versos c, d. 173 × 118 mm. Written space c. 125 × 82 mm. 2 cols. 36 lines. Collation: 1^{12} wants 3–5 after f. 2 3–14^{12} 15^{10} (ff. 166–75) 16–22^{12} 23^{10} wants 8–10. Signatures, where they occur, are ad hoc. Initials: (i) f. 1, 6-line, red and blue with ornament of both colours; (ii) 2-line, blue with red ornament or red with blue-green ornament. Binding by Slatter. Once chained: the mark shows at the foot of f. iii and as far as f. 4. Secundo folio sum est cecum.
Written in England. CMA 63.

172. J. de Dondis, Opus Planetarii   s. xv med.

1. ff. 1–57 Diagrams to explain the construction of planetary clocks.

Versos are blank, except f. 19^v. Headings and captions in clear upright humanistica. The diagrams on ff. 1–20 numbered 1–51. H. A. Lloyd, Giovanni de Dondi's Horological Masterpiece, 1364 (Limpsfield, 1955) reproduces twenty-five diagrams from the closely similar copy now Bodleian MS. Laud misc. 620. They occur on the following leaves of MS. 172: 5, 6, 7, 8, 12, 16 (Lloyd, pls. 1–6); 24, 21, 23, 29 (Lloyd, pls. 11–14); 36, 33, 35, 45, 41, 42 (Lloyd, pls. 16–21); 42, 43, 50, 47, 49, 51, 53, 52, 55 (Lloyd, pls. 23–31). ff. 57^v–58^v blank.

2. ff. 59–144 Opus planetari Ioanis de dondis fisici paduani ciuis. Capitulum prohemiale de intencione auctoris intencionis cauxa et modo procedendi. Astronomorum priscorum eximii qui prestantibus . . . ut suo modo apparent in celo. . . . Finito libro frangamus ossa magistro. Si non sunt fracta frangamus cum vna staga Finito adi 12 Aprilis hora 21 e meza.

Thorndike and Kibre. Part 1 in twenty-five chapters. Pt. 2, f. 135, in two chapters. Pt. 3, f. 138^v. Spaces for diagrams in the text remain blank: the decision to have the diagrams separately on ff. 1–57 instead of mixing them in with the text of part 1 seems to have been made after the text was written. On ff. 60–84 the spaces have numbers in them from 1 to 51, corresponding to the numbers on ff. 1–20. Many corrections in a hand like the second of those which wrote the text. On f. 135 scribe (4) copied a passage which scribe (3) had already copied on f. 134ᵛ: it is marked 'vacat' and 'Istud vacat qui(a) bis scriptum est'. The guide for the rubricator in the margin of f. 143ᵛ is 'ordinatio quam feci berto de Padua pro communi horologii'. A table of Auges and Signa phisica lies between the last word of the text and 'Finito . . .'. ff. 102ᵛ, 144ᵛ blank.

ff. iii + 144 + ii. f. iii is a medieval paper flyleaf. ff. 59–144 have an old foliation (s. xvi?), 2–87. Paper. 350 × 240 mm. Written space 255 × 155 mm and on ff. 59–67 225 × 155 mm. 51–3 long lines and on ff. 59–68 2 cols. of 45–8 lines. No ruling on ff. 59–67, other than faint vertical bounders; full ruling from f. 68. Collation: 1–5¹⁰ 6⁸ 7 ten, the first leaf missing (ff. 59, 64, 65, 60–3, 66, 67) 8¹⁰ 9⁶ 10¹⁰ 11 nine (ff. 94–102) 12–15⁸ 16¹⁰. Quires 2–6 signed a–e. Art. 2 is written by five scribes who seem to have been working contemporaneously, except in quire 16: (1) ff. 59–67ᵛ (quire 7); (2) ff. 68–83ᵛ, 103–26 (quires 8, 9, 12–14), 136–138ᵛ, 143ʳᵛ; (3) ff. 84–102, 127–134ᵛ (quires 10, 11, 15); (4) ff. 135–6; (5) ff. 138ᵛ–142ᵛ, 144. Notes, 'hic nichil deficit' on f. 83ᵛ, 'hic nichil deficit vsque ad finem quinterni' on f. 102 and 'hic nichil deficit usque in finem etc' on f. 134ᵛ draw attention to inexact joins at points where there is a change of scribe. Hands 2–5 are current humanistica in strong contrast with the ugly current hybrida of hand 1. Hands 1–3 use only the 2-shaped r. Spaces for initials and headings left blank. Binding by Slatter.

Written in northern Italy. *CMA* 54.

176. *H. de Bracton*   s. XIII ex.–XIII/XIV

Incipit liber Henrici de Bractone. Que sunt Regi necessaria. In Rege qui recte regit.' necessaria sunt duo hec . . . (f. 294ᵛ) habuerint siue non. Explicit liber henrici de bractone.

Editions by T. Twiss, 1878 (RS lxx) and by G. E. Woodbine, 1915–42 (4 vols.). Woodbine's LC (edn. i. 15). Bk. 2, f. 53; 3, f. 79ᵛ; (4), f. 199; (5), f. 258. Bk. 2 begins at 'Cum autem', ed. Woodbine, ii. 304 (as OB). Bk. 3 begins at edn. iii. 18. The points at which bks. 4, 5 begin are shown only by headings of s. xvi. ff. 2–97/1 are in an earlier hand than the rest. f. 1ʳᵛ, in the later hand, is not conjugate with f. 12 and is no doubt a supply: the last part of the text on the verso has been squeezed in. The text written by the earlier hand has been corrected and added to by the later hand in the margins and (the longer additions) on slips attached to ff. 7, 9, 11, 12, 14ᵛ. Only these longer additions are noted by Woodbine, i. 374–7. The first paragraph on f. 34, 'De heredibus qui succedunt . . . ut liquere poterit', is by the later hand over erasure. On f. 6 the corrector changed 'Cipewik' to 'Schipewich' (edn. ii. 51). ff. ii–xiᵛ, in the later hand, contain a table of titles 'Que sunt Regi necessaria 'fo primo' . . . priuilegium actoris 'cclxxxix'', with leaf numbers added later: ed. Woodbine, ii. 1–18, iii. 1–12, iv. 1–20. A list of headings is on a slip attached to f. 170ᵛ. A running title covers bk. 1 only.

ff. i + 304 + i, foliated i–xi, 1–295. An incorrect medieval foliation begins with 'fo. i' on f. 1 and ends with 'fo. cclxxxix' on f. 294; the foliator's troubles came at 100, 200, 240, and 250: he wrote 'lxxxxx' on f. 100 and 'c' on f. 101 and made similar errors at ff. 201–2, 242–3 and 253–4. 285 × 205 mm. Written space 235 × 165 mm and on ff. 2–96 (scribe 1) c. 240 × 170 mm. 2 cols. and on ff. ii–xi 3 cols. 46–7 lines by scribe 1 (more on ff. 31–33ᵛ). 42–3 lines by scribe 2. The vertical ruling between the columns is with three lines by scribe 1 and with two lines by scribe 2. The ruling of f. 97 by scribe 1 was adapted to suit scribe 2, who preferred a wider space between the columns (13 mm, instead of 9 mm). Collation of ff. ii–xi, 1–294: 1¹⁰ 2¹² wants 1, supplied by scribe 2 (f. 1) 3¹² 4¹⁴ + a bifolium after 9 (ff. 34, 35) 5–25¹² 26 two (ff. 293–4): also six slips (see above). Anglicana by two scribes (see above): the earlier wrote a current business hand of a slightly formal kind and the later a book-hand which is only occasionally current. Initials: (i) f. 1, an 18-line *I* in blue patterned in white, with pink and gold ornament prolonged into the margins; (ii) ff. 53, 79ᵛ, 4-line and 3-line, blue patterned in white, with red ornament; (iii) 2-line, blue or red; (iv) ff. ii–xi, as (iii), but 1-line. All the initials of type (iii) appear to be of one date, after scribe 2 had written his portion. Binding of s. xix. Secundo folio *precipit* (f. 2) or *primus partus* (f. iii).

Written in England. The name of 'Lewes Imery de Greys [Inn]', s. xvi, can be read on f. 294ᵛ by ultra-violet light. Not in *CMA*.

177, part 1. *Figurae Bibliorum*   s. XIII²

Twelve pictures, one to a page, numbered I–XII in s. xix. Each picture contains five medallions and two half medallions. James listed their subjects in his *Catalogue*, pp. 95–104, and showed later, 'On two series of paintings formerly at Worcester Priory', *Cambridge Antiquarian Society, Proceedings*, x (1904), 99–110, that pictures III–XII are closely related to the now lost glass paintings in the Chapter House of Worcester Cathedral.

Cf. also J. M. Wilson in *Associated Architectural Societies, Reports and Papers*, xxxii (1913), 132–8, and pls. 1–10 (pictures III–XII on a reduced scale) and *Burlington Fine Arts Club, Exhibition Catalogue*, 1908, pl. 72 (pictures VIII, IX). Each picture from III to XII has below it one of the ten commandments, in the order 2–10, 1. A page before picture I, a page after picture II, and two pages after picture XII were left blank.

ff. 8. 275 × 188 mm. The pictures measure *c.* 200 × 150 mm. Collation: 1 two (ff. 1, 2) 2⁶ (ff. 3–8). Bound in s. xvii ex. with MS. 177, part 2: the binding is English, rebacked in 1894.

English. 'The gift of Sʳ John Sherard of Lobthorp in Lincolnshire. Stuart Bickerstaffe 1690', f. 8ᵛ. Seen by Wanley in 1725, together with MS. 177, part 2, q.v.

177, part 2. *Apocalypsis cum figuris*   s. XIII²

Ninety-eight pictures, *c.* 150 × 160 mm, including the frames, and below each a portion of text in French, from two to nine lines in length, abbreviated from the Apocalypse: (p. 1) Seint Iohan preche al puple et lur mustre la parole ihesu crist. en ki il deiuont creare . . . (p. 98) del liure de vie. La grace ihesu crist seit on nus. Amen. '+Le pocalips ce demise'.

All pictures described by James, *Catalogue*, pp. 104–8. The text is referred to by L. Delisle and P. Meyer, *L'Apocalypse en français au xiiiᵉ siècle* (Société des Anciens Textes Français), 1901, p. lxxxvi. Listed and noticed by M. R. James, *The Apocalypse in Art*, 1910, pp. 4–5 (no. 10) and p. 55: 'a sister book to Lambeth 434'. The middle sheet of quire 5 is misbound as the second sheet: the right order of the pages is 33–4, 37–40, 35–6, 45–6, 41–4, 47–8.[1] pp. 99, 100 are blank.

ff. 50, paginated 1–100. 275 × 188 mm. Bound with MS. 177, pt. 1, q.v., probably for Stuart Bickerstaffe. On 11 Aug. 1725 Humfrey Wanley 'waited on Mʳˢ Bickerstaffe at Chelsea' and saw this manuscript which he thought 'not unfitt' for the Harleian library:

[1] As Mr. C. R. Sneddon noticed, 8 Nov. 1969.

of the pictures he noted that 'they seem to be about as old as the Reign of our King Henry II, and are explained in old French; which was then the Court Language' (*The Diary of Humfrey Wanley*, ed. C. E. and Ruth C. Wright, 1966, ii. 371). Book-plate of G. Pitt. 'The Gift of George Henry Pitt Esqr to Eton College May 28th 1817' inside the cover.

178. '*The Eton Choirbook*'
s. XVI in.

1. 126 leaves of a volume which once contained probably 225 leaves and nearly one hundred pieces, most of them in honour of B.V.M., set to music by twenty-six named English composers. All the pieces are printed by F. Ll. Harrison, *The Eton Choirbook*, Musica Britannica x–xii (1956–60), with much reduced facsimiles in vol. x of ff. 1^{rv} (pls. i*a*, ii*a*), 2 (pl. ii*b*), 14 (pl. i*b*), 26^v–27 (pl. iii), 38^v–39 (pl. iv). A table in vol. xii supplies the place of the manuscript index on f. 1, which is printed—with errors—in James's *Catalogue*, pp. 109–11. The index lists ninety-five pieces and notes the signature of the leaf on which each piece began. It is alphabetical as far as x. 7 (f. 109), after which all indexed pieces are settings of Et exultavit, except Davy's Passio Domini which begins imperfectly on f. 126 (sign. ee. 4). Two unindexed pieces are a Salve Regina on ff. 26^v–29 (sign. f. 3^v–6), no doubt by Robert Wilkinson (see below) and a Creed by Wilkinson on f. 126^v (sign. ee. 9^v): these are not in the main hand and are per-haps, as Dr. Harrison suggests (vol. x, p. xvii), in Wilkinson's hand. A second index below the Creed on f. 126^v repeats sixty of the entries on f. 1.

All pieces now complete at the beginning begin at the top of a verso side: references by signature in the index are to the recto and the verso facing it, so that, for example, 't. 5' is the reference for the piece beginning on t. 4^v (f. 92^v). The setting of O domine celi by Richard Davy (master of the choristers at Magdalen College, Oxford, 1490–2) ends on f. 59 with the words 'Hanc antiphonam composuit Ricardus Davy vno die collegio magdalene Oxoniis' and has arms in four of its initials, (1) England, (2) Westminster Abbey, (3) Magdalen College, (4) Bost (provost of Eton 1477–1504), sable a fess or between three stags heads couped argent: a fifth coat is entirely defaced.[1] 'Robertus Wilkynson' is in the cadel O of *Ostende*, f. 28, 'Robertus Wylkynson cuius anime propicietur deus' in the cadel O of O *pia*, f. 29, and 'Wylkynson' in the last line of music on f. 29. Fairfax's *Et exultauit* (missing) is marked 'Regale' in the index. ff. 92, 123^v blank.

2. ff. v, vi, 127–8 Four bifolia of a Bible written in a good early twelfth-century English hand are sideways at each end as binding leaves. They make a whole quire, the text extending from 'ut confundat sapientes' in titulus 5 of the table of capitula of 1 Corinthians to 'et beniuolentia dei et de domino' in titulus 3 of the capitula of Ephesians. 1, 2 Corinthians and Galatians are complete between these points.

The capitula of 1 Corinthians (73 chapters) and of 2 Corinthians (28 chapters) are those printed by Wordsworth and White from AF (etc.), but the capitula of Galatians (12 chapters) are, surprisingly, those of Wordsworth and White's N, a Pauline Epistles in Anglo-Saxon minuscule, s. viii^2, now Colmar 38 (*CLA*, no. 750). The capitula of Ephesians, so far as they go, are also close to N. The old chapter numbers in red in the text, agreeing with these divisions, have been cancelled sometimes in favour of new numbers in black, which agree usually with those now in use. The 'argumentum' to 1 Corinthians, Stegmüller, no. 685, and the 'argumentum' to Galatians, no. 707, follow the capitula, but the

---

[1] 'Eton College' against it in modern pencil in the margin. There are also arms on f. 90 in the initial of a setting by John Browne, sable a chevron between three lilies argent, on a chief gules three owls of the second.

'argumentum' to 2 Corinthians, no. 699, precedes them. A stichometric note at the end of 1 Corinthians, 'habet versus dccclxx'.

Written space 390×220 mm. 2 cols. 51 lines. Ruling with a hard point. It includes two pairs of vertical bounders between the columns. f. v was the outermost, f. vi the second, f. 128 the third, and f. 127 the innermost sheet of the quire. Monochrome red or green initials: (i) 5-line or 6-line; (ii) 1-line. The running title is on a specially ruled line.

ff. vi+126+vi. For ff. v, vi, 127–8 see above, art 2. 590×420 mm. Written space 440× 330 mm. 13 long lines and music. The 126 extant leaves are all signed with letter and number a. 1–ee. 9 and show that there were originally 27 quires of eight leaves each (aa. 1–dd. 8) and a final quire of nine leaves (ee. 1–9): the missing leaves are a. 8, b. 3–6, c. 4, 5, e. 1–8, f. 1, 2, 7, 8, n. 1–8, o. 1–8, p. 1–8, r. 4, 5, s. 1–8, t. 1–3, 6, 7, y. 1–8, aa. 1–8, bb. 2–7, cc. 1–8, dd. 1–8, ee. 4, 5, 6. A foliation of s. xvi ex.(?)[1] runs from 1 to 145, missing f. 42 after '50', and suggests that twenty now missing leaves were still extant at that time. The leaves in question are b. 3–6, c. 4, 5, one leaf between d. 8 and f. 3, f. 7, 8, two leaves between m. 8 and q. 1, one leaf between r. 8 and t. 4, t, 6, 7, two leaves of quire aa, two leaves between b. 8 and ee. 1 and two of the three leaves now missing from quire ee. These leaves bore the numbers 10–13, 19, 20, 32, 37, 38, 86, 87, 102, 105, 106, 132, 133, 136, 137, 141, 142. Written in script distinguished from textura only by the descenders of f and s and the kidney-shaped form of final s: for two additions, see above. Initials: (i) f. 38v, the S of Walter Lambe's Salve regina, pink on a gold ground, historiated (John Baptist, lamb, and scroll inscribed 'Ecce agnus dei') and with a short framed border in the side margin; (ii) in colour and gold paint on coloured grounds patterned in gold paint, or, as far as f. 54, brown with ornament of the same colour: birds, animals, and some human figures form initials or parts of them now and then or are used in the decoration; (iii) blue with red ornament—but not beyond the gap after f. 77 (sign. m. 8); (iv) on f. 1 and from f. 78 onwards, 1-line, blue or red. Type ii initials are used on the double openings on which new pieces begin and type iii initials on other double openings: the two types are used together on a double opening only on ff. 1v–2 and 4v–5. Cadels are used on pages with type ii initials. In the added Salve regina, ff. 26v–27, the nine orders of angels are shown in pasted-on initials. Binding of s. xvi², wooden boards covered with brown leather bearing Oldham's roll HE. g. 2: rebacked.[2] Secundo folio tum cuncta.

Arms of Eton college in initials on f. 41: see above for other arms. Probably acquired for use in college chapel when Robert Wilkinson was master of the choristers (1500–14: cf. above). Identifiable by the opening words of the second leaf with 'a grete ledger of prick song 2 fo tum cuncta' entered in the college inventory of 1531 (?): Etoniana, no. 28, 4 June 1921, p. 447.

179. *Biblia* s. XIII med.

1. ff. 1–507 A Bible in the order Genesis–2 Chronicles, Ezra, Nehemiah, 3–6 Ezra (Stegmüller, nos. 96, 94.2, 95, 97), Esther, Tobit, Judith, Job, Psalms, and thence as usual, except that Catholic Epistles precedes Acts. 2 Chronicles is followed by 'Oratio ẹzẹchiẹ 'sedechie'. Domine omnipotens deus patrum . . . gloria in secula seculorum amen'. Pss. 109–32 are abbreviated.

Proverbs begins on a new quire, f. 257 (18¹). The prologues are forty-nine of the common set in Bristol Public Library 15, and 7 others shown here by *: Stegmüller, nos. 284, 285, 311, 323, 328, 330, 341+342*, 332, 335, 344; 430* before Psalms and Cum omnes

---

[1] This foliation has been repeated in modern pencil, top right. The true foliation is in pencil bottom right.

[2] This roll is not known to have been used on books printed before 1545 nor after 1574. A date in Mary's reign (1553–8) is likely.

prophetas . . . secundus est beatus* (Peter Lombard) and 414* after Psalms; 457, 468, 487, 491, 492, 494, 500, 511, 509*, 515, 519+517, 524, 521, 526, 528, 531, 534, 538, 539, 540*, 543, 551, 590, 677, 685, 699 (Post acceptam . . .), 707, 715, 728, 736, 747, 752, 765 (. . . ab urbe roma), 772, 780, 783, 793, 809, 640, 835*. The general prologue (284) is not divided into chapters.

Marginalia in an English hand, s. xiii², perhaps the same as wrote 'Occidit pueros herodes . . .' (3 lines: Walther, no. 13110) on f. iii.

2. f. 256^{rv}, by the main hand in the space remaining blank in quire 17. Collect, secret, and postcommunion of nine votive masses.

The sets, except the second, are in *Sarum Missal*: pp. 385–6, Holy Spirit; 389–91, B.V.M.; 331–2, Francis; 392–3, Pro fratribus et sororibus; 400, Contra temptaciones cordis; 394, All Saints; 445, Missa generalis; 438, Pro defunctis fratribus et sororibus. The second set is headed 'In commemoracione cristi': (*collect*) Corda nostra quesumus domine sanctus splendor . . .; (*secret*) In mentibus nostris quesumus domine uere fidei sacramenta confirma . . .; (*postcommunion*) Presta quesumus omnipotens pater ut qui filii tui . . .

3. ff. 507–541^v Aaz apprehendens . . . consiliatores eorum.

The usual dictionary of Hebrew names.

ff. v+531+v. ff. viii, 532–3 are medieval end-leaves: 533^v was pasted down. A medieval foliation in pencil 1–540 on ff. 1–529: 12 numbers were left out after 256—unless, as seems unlikely, a quire is missing here—and one number after 376. 164×115 mm. Written space 115×c. 73 mm. 2 cols. 44 lines. Collation: 1–3^{16} 4^{12} 5–12^{16} 13^{14} 14–15^{16} 16^{14} 17^8 (ff. 249–56) 18^{16} 19^{12} 20^{10} 21–33^{16} 34^{12} 35^8 36^{10} wants 10, blank. Initials: (i) ff. 4, 231, 455^v (Genesis, Psalms, Romans), blue or red and blue on blue grounds, historiated: see James's *Catalogue*; (ii) ff. 101, 413^v (1 Kings, Matthew), as (i), but decorated, not historiated, and on green or dark-red grounds; (iii) of other books and of divisions of Psalms, including Pss. 51, 101, 5-line or more, blue and red with ornament of both colours; (iv) of prologues, 5-line, and (v) of chapters, 2-line, blue or red with ornament of the other colour; (vi) of verses of Psalms and in art. 3, 1-line, blue or red. Capital letters in the ink of the text marked with red. English binding, s. xvi², of pasteboard covered with brown leather bearing a gilt centrepiece and cornerpieces: two clasps missing: the mark of the clasp of an older binding shows on f. 533. Secundo folio *sanctus uir*.

Written in England. An illegible erasure, f. v^v. In two other faint inscriptions, s. xv, the words here within brackets were read by M. R. James with the help of a reagent: (i) 'Ista biblia constat [magistro ricardo] pede doctore quem emebat apud hereford pro iii^{li} vi^s viii^d', f. 533; (ii) 'Iste liber est fratris R[icardi Lynke] ex dono magistri Ricardi [Pede]', f. 531^v: for Pede, dean of Hereford 1463–80, see Emden, *BRUO*. 'Jo. Walter 1625', f. v^v. 'Liber collegii B.M. de Etona d.d. Edw. Betham Socius 1776', f. v. Samuel Meyrick, L.L.D. (1783–1848) wrote his estimate of the date, 'Time of Henry 3rd', and his name inside the cover.

181. *Horae*   s. xv med.

1. ff. 1–12^v A rather empty calendar in French, in red and black.

Sauinien, Helene, Mastie, Loup in red, 24 Jan. 4, 7 May, 28 July.

2. ff. 13–18 Sequentiae of the Gospels. 'Protector in te sperantium . . .' after John.

3. ff. 18^v–21^v Hours of the Cross . . . Patris sapientia . . .

4. ff. 22–24^v Hours of the Holy Spirit . . . Nobis sancti spiritus . . .

5. ff. 25–68 Hours of B.V.M. of the use of (Troyes). f. 68ᵛ blank.

6. ff. 69–84ᵛ Penitential psalms and (f. 80) litany.

Sixteen martyrs: . . . (9) Sauiniane . . . Fourteen confessors: . . . (2) Frodoberte . . . (6–10) Auentine Blasi Victor Nicete Lupe . . . Fourteen virgins: . . . (7) Sauina . . . (11–13) Helena Mastidia Syria . . .

7. ff. 85–126 Office of the dead.

The ninth lesson is 'Fratres. Audiui uocem de celo . . . secuntur illos' (Apocalypse 14: 13).

8. ff. 127–130ᵛ Obsecro te . . . Et michi famule tue . . .

9. ff. 130ᵛ–132ᵛ Alia de beata maria uirgine. O intemerata . . . orbis terrarum. Inclina . . . michi peccatori . . .

10. ff. 132ᵛ–134ᵛ De beata maria. Stabat mater dolorosa . . .

11. ff. 134ᵛ–136ᵛ Five prayers: (*a*) Quant on se veult confesser on doit dire ceste oroison. Per sanctorum omnium angelorum . . .; (*b*) Quant on veult recepuoir dieu. Domine ihesu xpiste fili dei uiui te suppliciter ut (*sic*) hodie . . .; (*c*) Aultre orison quant on veult recepuoir nostreseigneur. Domine non sum dignus ut intres sub tectum meum sed tantum dic uerbo . . .; (*d*) Quant tu recepuras dy ceste orison. Domine ihesu xpiste non sum dignus ut intres sub tectum meum. sed propicius esto michi peccatori. Amen; (*e*) Quant tu auras receu. Uera preceptio (*sic*) corporis et sanguinis . . .

12. ff. 136ᵛ–140ᵛ Memoriae of Sebastian (O sancte Sebastiane semper uespere et mane Horis cunctis . . .: 40 lines, *RH*, no. 13708), Nicholas, Pantaleon, Agnes, Barbara.

ff. ii+140+ii. Parchment flyleaves. 163 × 117 mm. Written space 90 × 65 mm. 15 long lines. Ruling in red ink. Collation: 1–2⁶ 3–16⁸ 17² (ff. 125–6) 18⁶+1 leaf after 3 (f. 130) 19⁸ wants 8, probably blank. A full-page pietà before art. 8 (f. 126ᵛ) and 11-line pictures before arts. 2–7, described in James's *Catalogue*, except the burial picture on f. 85. Initials: (i) 4-line, blue patterned in white, either on gold grounds decorated in colours or in a later style (ff. 22, 25, 55, 58, 127) employing gold paint and dark red as grounds and naturalistic flowers, pansies, etc., as decoration; (ii, iii) 2-line and 1-line, gold on grounds of blue and red patterned in white. Continuous borders on picture pages, borders on three sides of pages with initials of type (i) and sprays into the margins from initials of type (ii). Capital letters in the ink of the text filled with pale yellow. Line fillers in blue and red, patterned in white, and with infillings of gold. Gilt red morocco binding, English work, s. xviii.

Written for the use of a woman (art. 8, but cf. art. 9) in the diocese of Troyes. 'E Libris Antonii Storer Donum Frederici Comitis Carliolensis Anno Domini 1776', f. i. Part of the Storer bequest in 1799. S. R. Meyrick wrote an estimate of the date, 'close of reign of Henry VI', inside the cover: cf. MS. 179.

191. *Chronicon Angliae inrotulatum*　　　　　s. xv¹

A descent from Adam to Henry V, headed by a pair of roundels, one showing Christ in judgement, sitting on the rainbow, blessing, and the other Adam and Eve and the serpent at the tree. On the left is the introduction, 'Considerans

historie Britonum. Pictorum. Scottorum. Anglorum. Danorum et Normano-
rum prolixitatem nec non et difficultatem . . . per Reges Britanie. Anglie.
Archiepiscopos Cantuarie et Principes Wallie eis contemporaneos vsque ad
Regem nostrum 'Henricum post conquestum Normannorum quintum . . .
ordinem historie sic produxi', and on the right the text begins 'In agro damas-
ceno'. From here notices on either side of a central green bar extend to the
coronation of Henry V 'nono videlicet die Aprilis. Anno domini Millesimo
CCCCᵐᵒ xiiiᵒ Etatis sue vicesimum septimum agens annum'.

For the form of the introduction 'Considerans . . .', cf. above MS. 96 and *MMBL* i. 94.
It says that Henry V was the first king to be anointed with the holy oil given by B.V.M. to
St. Thomas of Canterbury. Events of Christian history are few and confined to the left
margin: here the promised list of archbishops of Canterbury ends opposite Edward II
with Robert (Winchelsey, 1294–1313) and the words 'Hic desunt nomina archiepiscoporum
Cant''. The Norman dukes from Rollo are also on the left. On the right are Welsh kings
from Kambrius, son of Brutus: the stemma divides at Rodriware. Of Sweyn it is recorded
that St. Edmund appeared to him at Bury, said 'haue þis swayne kyng to þyn eskyng', and
pierced his body with a lance. A writer, s. xvi, with perhaps a special interest in Wales
has made some additions. The dorse is blank.

A roll of nine membranes measuring *c.* 6300 × 345 mm. Written in anglicana. Six
roundels are historiated, the largest of them 77 mm across; they show, after the two heading
the roll, Noah and the ark, Brutus and his three sons, the Nativity of Christ, and St.
Thomas of Canterbury, a sword through his mitre. Many others contain shields: see
James's *Catalogue*. From Edward the Confessor on, the kings bear individual arms. Shields
in twenty-four roundels show the arms of descendants of Edward I and Edward III. The
three initials are blue with red ornament.

Written in England. Not in *CMA*.

196. *Beda, In Lucam (fragm.)* s. XII ex.

Seven leaves of Bede on Luke, six from bk. 4 and one from bk. 6.

As *PL* xcii. 477/26–479/18 (f. 1), 483/6–492, last line but one (ff. 2–6) and 628/22–630/31
(f. 7). The number of the book is in red at the head of each recto and the number of the
chapter of Luke, xi, xii, xxiiii, at the foot of each recto. There is also a chapter numbering
in red ink in the text, li (f. 4), lii (f. 6) and xciiii (f. 7), at the head of paragraphs beginning
'Attendite', 'Ait autem quidem', and 'Dum hec autem' (edn. 487/20, 491/4, 628/32).

ff. iii + 7 + iii. 340 × 240 mm. Written space 263 × 168 mm. 2 cols. 38 lines. Pricks in
both margins to guide ruling. No visible ruling on ff. 1–6. f. 1 was the last leaf of quire
XII: this number on the verso. ff. 2–6 are five adjacent leaves of the next quire. 2-line
initials, blue with red ornament on ff. 4, 7, and red with green ornament on f. 6. Binding
of s. xxⁱ.

Written in England, f. 5 was the pastedown of a book with the pressmark D. d. 1. 10, an
unidentified old Eton mark.

202. *Alexander de Villa Dei, Doctrinale* s. XIV med.

1. [S]cribere clericulis paro doctrinale nouellis . . . (f. 93ᵛ) Quas tres personas
in idem credo deitatis. Magistri alexandri de uilla dei doctrinalis liber explicit.
Gracias deo. Amen.

Printed often and last in 1893, *Das Doctrinale des Alexander de Villa-Dei*, ed. D. Reichling. f. 94^{rv} blank.

2. ff. i–iv Two leaves of Prosper, Epigrammata, folded to make four and used in binding. They contain ix/3–xv (ff. i, iv) and xxix–xxxv/2 (ff. ii, iii).

PL li. 502–3, 507–9. A tall narrow Italian hand, s. xiii ex. 32 long lines.

ff. iv+94. For ff. i–iv see above. 123×95 mm. Written space 80 mm in height. 14 long lines. Collation: 1–11^{8} 12^{6}. Initials: (i) f. 1, 4-line, not filled in; (ii) 2-line, red or blue, plain or with ornament of the other colour. Binding of thick boards cut square and flush with the edges of the leaves: five bosses on each cover: a central strap attached to the front cover fastened on to a pin on the back cover, but both are missing: rebacked. Secundo folio *Inde leget*.

Written in Italy. Given by W. J. Myers in 1896.

203. *J. de Voragine, Legenda aurea* s. XIV med.

1. Uniuersum tempus presentis uite . . . (f. 1^{v}) usque aduentum. De aduentu. Aduentus domini per iiii^{or} septimamas . . . (f. 368) cum eo habitare dignetur per gloriam Quod ipse . . . amen. Explicit legenda de sanctis. De sancto prorso (*sic for* furseo) episcopo. Prorsus episcopus cuius hystoriam . . . (f. 379^{v}) gloriam perueniamus. prestante domino nostro ihesu cristo. Amen.

Originally probably the 182 pieces from Advent to De dedicatione ecclesiae printed in Graesse's edition (1845), together with a supplement of six pieces in the main hand. According to the table of contents (ff. 379^{v}–380^{v}), G., nos. 174–6, 176–80 were on the two quires missing after f. 360: perhaps no. 177 was passed over in error. The contents and order differ from G., nos. 1–173, 181–2 only in that G., nos. 131–9 are here in the order 131, 134–8, 132, 139, 133. The running title of G., no. 181 (Pelagius) is here 'De sancto beda'. In one of its margins, f. 361^{v}, a reader noted 'Item apparuerunt tres soles Anno domini M^{o} CCC^{o} lxviii^{o} et apparuerunt in occidente ix^{a} die Iunii et erat verus sol in medio'.

The supplement is: f. 368, De sancto prorso (see above); f. 369, De sancto martiale. Sanctus martialis cum esset . . .; f. 370^{v}, De sancto saturnino. Anno quintodecimo imperii cesaris . . .; f. 375, De sancta eulalia. Anima que peccauerit . . .; f. 376, De sancta columba. Cum aurelianus imperator . . .; f. 376^{v}, De sancto iuliano. Beati pacifici . . . Hac gracia spiritus sancti beatus iulianus . . .

2. The pastedowns are two fragments of a document in a French hand s. xv, still mostly fastened down: the blank dorse is exposed. The words 'guillielmo houssaye bachelar' ', 'predictus Religiosus vir frater Iohannes de la plan', and 'sigillo curie andeg' et petiit ab eodem domino offic' ' can be read in successive lines on an unstuck corner at the back.

ff. i+380. A medieval foliation 1–360, 385–403 takes account of two missing quires. 212×155 mm. Written space *c.* 150×103 mm. 2 cols. 39 lines. The ruling is unusual in that double vertical lines are used to bound the left side of the first column on versos and the right side of the second column on rectos and single vertical lines elsewhere. Collation: 1–30^{12} 31–32^{10}. Quires 1–5 marked 'cor' at the end (for *correctum?*). Initials: (i) f. 1, 4-line red *U* on a blue and gold decorated ground: a dragon in the margin; (ii) 3-line, blue or red with ornament of the other colour and tails of both colours the height of the book. The letters of *Uniuersum* following the initial *U* on f. 1 are in capitals on a patterned red ground. Capital letters in the ink of the text stroked with red. Contemporary binding of white skin over wooden boards: five bands: a central strap and pin from the front to the back cover is missing: a hole towards the foot of the front cover may be for the metal piece to which a chain was attached. Secundo folio *bus erat*.

Written in France. An erasure, f. 380ᵛ, where J. A. Herbert, helped by a reagent, read 'Iste liber est domini abbatis sancti albini [ande]g' ': of the place-name 'albini' can be read under ultra-violet light and [ande]g' is confirmed by art. 2, so provenance from the Benedictine abbey of St. Aubin, Angers, seems certain. Given by W. J. Myers in 1896.

204. *Apuleius Barbarus, etc.* s. XII med.

Arts. 1–5a, 6–11 correspond to arts. 1, 2, 4–11 and the beginning of art. 12 of B.L., Harley 4986, a closely related German manuscript described by A. Beccaria, *I codici di medicina del periodo presalernitano*, 1956, pp. 252–4 (no. 77). For the piece once here in the gap after f. 51, see ibid, p. 253. Contemporary glosses in German are fewer than in Harl., but both manuscripts have 'fascha' above 'malagma' (f. 12ᵛ, Harl., f. 8).

1. ff. 3–5 Incipit erbarius apulei platonici. Antonii. Musa. Marco. Agrippe. Salutem. Cesari Augusto prestantissimo omnium mortalium sed et iudicibus ipsius. Scitote ... (f. 3ᵛ) sic uteris. Nomina herbe uettonice Greci PRIONITEN ... experti affirmant.

Antonius Musa, De herba vettonica. Ed. E. Howald and H. E. Sigerist, *Corpus Medicorum Latinorum*, iv, 1927, 3–10 (line 174).

2. (*a*) ff. 5–20ᵛ, 25–51ᵛ Incipit Apulei platonici de medicaminibus herbarum. Apuleius Platonicus Madaurensis Ciuibus suis salutem. Ex pluribus paucas ... profuisse uideatur. Finit prefatio. Nomina herbe arnoglosse . . . sicque cum eo hominibus subuenies (*ends imperfectly in* Mandragora). (*b*) ff. 21–24ᵛ Ysopum est herba maritima . . . prodere.

(*a*). Edn. cit., pp. 15–225. Illustrated by coloured drawings of the herbs, many of which have German names against them, s. xiii, for example, f. 12, 'brachwurz' against 'dracontea'. The picture of artemisia monoclos has been cut from f. 11. The leaf missing after f. 48 contained the text between 'ad loca mulierum si dolent' and 'urinam mouent' (edn., pp. 208–213/11). At the end the picture of mandragora is missing. 'Heribulbum' is pictured on a slip of parchment, f. 37a. (*b*) on inserted leaves, s. xii. Descriptions of twenty-two herbs, the first Hyssop and the rest alphabetically from Asphodel to Pyrethrum. Spaces for illustrations remain blank or are filled with sketchy drawings. In order to make an apparent connection with f. 21, the scribe erased the last word on f. 20ᵛ, presumably *eliotrope*, and substituted 'ysopi', so that the heading runs 'Nomina herbe ysopi'.

3. f. 53 (*begins imperfectly*) nuto commixto cum equis et mulabus . . . per triduum emendabit.

Medicina de taxone. Edn. cit., pp. 230–1 (lines 35–73). Ed. H. J. de Vriend, *The Old English Medicina de Quadrupedibus* (Groningen diss., 1972), pp. 4/17–16: Harl. is collated. The picture of the badger was no doubt on the missing leaf.

4. ff. 53–8 Ad omnes homines ceruinum cornu . . . plagas mundabit.

Edn. cit., pp. 235–70. Ed. de Vriend, pp. 12–52/9, 56/21–60/18, 25/10–56/20: Harl. is collated. As in Harl. the sections on lion, bull, and elephant come at the end. Nine

coloured drawings of the animals, the last the elephant, in the space on f. 58ᵛ left blank
after art. 5. The hare has been cut from f. 54.

5. f. 58ᵛ De menta. Est suaui odore . . . que fide a te posco.

6. ff. 59–66 Incipit epistola anthimii viri illustrissimi comitis ad gloriosum
regem francorum. Theodericum. De obseruatione ciborum. Racio obserua-
tionis uestre pietatis secundum precepta auitorum (*sic for* auctorum) medicinalium . . . similiter uua passa et ipsa bona est.

Anthimus, De observatione ciborum. Ed. E. Liechtenhan, *Corpus Medicorum Latinorum*,
viii (1963). 'agabuh' glosses 'perca', f. 63.

7. ff. 66–75 De rafano. Rafanum calidam inesse uirtutem . . . necesse sit purget.

Gargilius Martialis, De oleribus et pomis. Ed. V. Rose, 1875, pp. 133–203/15 (chapters 1–56).

8. ff. 75–7 De natura ordei frumenti. Ordei natura est frigida . . . Hęc omnia
et medicaminibus constant.

Diaeta Theodori. Ed. K. Sudhoff in *AGM* viii (1914–15), 381–403.

9. ff. 77–78ᵛ De clisteribus. Ad clistrem quod greci apoteon . . . id est auripig-
mento.

Six paragraphs on enemas.

10. ff. 78–80 (*a*) De leone et eius remedio. Qui h(ab)uerit carnes leonis . . .
Grilli puluis cum butrio sumendus est. (*b*) Incipit de uolucribus. De aquila.
Aquilę partem qui in domo sua . . . aut foris inungues. probatum est.

Virtues of lion and other animals and of birds. Beccaria notes that a fuller form of the same
text is in St. Gall MS. 217.

11. ff. 80–2 Citonus purgatis . . . et melius coagulatur.

Receipts found also in Harl., ff. 68ᵛ/18–70ᵛ/12. f. 82 is pasted to a leaf of art. 12. The last
seventeen words of the text are at the head of the recto of f. 82: the rest of the leaf, probably
blank, has been cut off.

12. The pastedowns at either end and the flyleaves, ff. i, 82* (pasted to f. 82), 83,
are five leaves of a copy of Major Prophets in an Italian hand, s. xii.

Isaiah 13: 10–14: 1, Jeremiah 2: 9–3: 19. Written space 230 × 105 mm. 25 long lines.

ff. i+80+ii. Thick parchment. A foliation of s. xvi (?), 1–82 (followed here) was made
before the loss of two leaves of quire 7. 276 × 190 mm. Written space *c.* 200 × 137 mm.
29 long lines. Ruling with a hard point. Collation: 1² 2–3⁸ 4⁸ (ff. 19, 20, 25–30) +2
bifolia inserted after 2 (ff. 21–4) 5⁸+a slip after 7 (f. 37a) 6⁸ 7⁸ wants 3 and 6 (these
leaves were numbered 49 and 52) 8–10⁸ 11⁴. Probably all in one large hand, apart from
the nearly contemporary insertion on ff. 21–24ᵛ. Two full-page pictures of men gathering
herbs and preparing medicines, ff. 1ᵛ (reduced facsimile by MacKinney, fig. 20), 2ʳ:
1ʳ and 2ᵛ are blank. For the illustrations of arts. 2 and 4 see above. Initials: (i) ff. 3, 5,
5-line, in red outline, filled with green and blue; (ii) 2-line or 1-line, red. Binding of wooden
boards covered with fifteenth-century Italian rope-patterned leather, repaired and
rebacked, but most of the old spine has been preserved: two clasps, one missing, fastened
from front to back.

Written in Germany, J. A. Herbert, helped by a reagent, read part of an erased inscription at the head of f. 3, s. xv, as 'Iste liber pertinet ad librariam ecclesie et capituli ecclesie': I cannot read beyond 'librariam' by ultra-violet light. Given as MS. 202.

208. *J. de Clerk, Dietsche Doctrinale (fragm., in Netherlandish)*
s. xiv[1]

Fragments described and printed by J. Priebsch, 'Zwei neue fragmente aus Jan de Clerk's *Dietsche Doctrinale*', *Tijdschrift voor Nederlansche Taal-en-Letterkunde*, xxi (1902), 227–37.

The lower half of a bifolium, formerly a strip in the binding of J. Driedo, De redemptione et captivitate humani generis (etc.), Louvain 1548 (etc.), in a contemporary Germanic binding. Cf. G. Lyunggren, *Leyen Doctrinal*, Lund Germanische Forschungen, xxxv (1963). Each leaf measures c. 112 × 180 mm. Bound by Spottiswoode & Co. Ltd.

209+220, no. II. *Ambrosius, De bono mortis (fragm.)* s. xii med.

Fragments of De bono mortis. The two leaves in MS. 209 contain the text from 'a sanctis suis' to 'melius que mouent' (edn. *CSEL* xxxii(1), 707/13–712/22). The two leaves in MS. 220 contain the text from 'reamur illum debitum' to 'infideles sunt' (edn. 746/18–752/6): they are bound in the wrong order. 'A' and 'R' in the margins are contemporary 'nota bene' signs.

ff. 4. The written space is complete on one leaf, 195 × 103 mm. 30 long lines. Pencil ruling. MS. 209 was bound by Wilson & Co.

Written in England. Formerly pastedowns in Gg. 4. 14, J. Simancas, etc., Venice, 1569, etc. (MS. 209) and in Ff. 5. 12, Cicero, Paris, 1549 (MS. 220, no. II), both of them books bound in Oxford, perhaps by Christopher Cavey, c. 1570: cf. N. R. Ker, *Pastedowns in Oxford Bindings*, nos. 1375, 1377, and p. 216.

210. *Breviarium (fragm.)* s. xiii[1]

Fragments of the temporale of a breviary from Wednesday to Saturday in the week after Easter (f. 1) and for the second and third Sundays after Easter (f. 2): cf. *Brev. ad usum Sarum*, i. dcccxxxv–dcccxlv, dcccxcvii–dccccxiii. The capitulum of the office for the third Sunday after Easter is Advocatum habemus.

A bifolium. Written space 155 × 110 mm. 2 cols. 30 lines. 2-line and 1-line initials, blue or red with ornament of the other colour. Bound like MS. 209.

Written in England. Used as binding strips.

211. *Breviarium (fragm.)* s. xvi/xv

A fragment of the sanctorale of a small breviary. The feasts are Invention of the Cross, John before the Latin Gate, Gordianus and Epimachus, Nereus and Achilleus (3–12 May): cf. *Brev. ad usum Sarum*, iii. 281–9.

A leaf cut in two, but nearly complete. Written space 82 mm wide. 2 narrow cols. Blue initials with red ornament. Bound like MS. 209.

Written in England. Formerly pastedowns in 'Da. 8. 18', probably a duodecimo: the mark is obsolete and unidentified.

212. *Jus canonicum (fragm.)*   s. XIV med.

Part of a leaf of an unidentified text.

The script is an ugly anglicana. Bound like MS. 209.

Formerly the wrapper of a small book.

213. *R. Higden, Polychronicon*   s. XV[1]

1. ff. iii–ix Index, Aaron–Zorobabel, covering art. 3, bks. 1–6 and bk. 7, chapters 1–44.

References are by book, chapter, and letter. The letters agree with those entered in the margins of the text.

2. (*a*) ff. ix–x^v, col. 1 Eggebertus Rex Westsaxonum filius Alcimundi . . . sepultus apud West' anno domini 1422. (*b*) f. x^v A drawing of Windsor Castle and below it a scene identified as the consecration of Thomas Bekyngton in Eton College chapel, 13 Oct. 1443. (*c*) f. x^v, below (*b*), a roundel inscribed 'Edwardus iiii^{tus} rex potentissimus' and about it four points of the compass, east at the top, with the names of English districts and notes of them in each of the four directions. (*d*) f. x, in the margin, s. xv ex., the descent of Henry VII from Edward III.

(*a*). A genealogical descent of English kings from Egbert to Henry VI illustrated by skilful pen-and-ink pictures in roundels of Egbert, Alfred, Athelstan, Edgar, Canute, Edward 'confessor et virgo', William I, Richard I, Henry III. A roundel for Henry V was not filled. A large half roundel at the foot of the column on f. x^v is inscribed 'Henricus VI^{us}'. (*b, c*) are later than (*a*) and in a less skilled hand. A facsimile by W. H. St. John Hope, *Windsor Castle*, 1913, pl. xixd.

3. ff. 1–268^v Presentem cronicam conpilauit frater Ranulphus Cestrensis monachus. Post preclaros arcium scriptores . . . (f. 237^v) capitis interdixit. 'Hucusque Ranhohus (*sic: a stroke through the head of the first* h) secundum librum Regium' (*in red*). Capitulum 45. Hoc anno Non' Iunii natus est regi . . . (f. 239) steriliora esse ceperunt. 'Hucusque compilauit Ranulfus' (*in red in the margin*). Hoc eciam anno dominus Walterus berkeley . . . (f. 245) continuacionem postea habuerunt. (*2 lines blank*). Ricardus de Burdegalia filius Edwardi principis Wallie coronatur . . . Peueneseye. Anno gracie m cccc xx° et regni regis Henrici quinti septimo.' dominus humfredus frater regis fit locum tenens et regni anglie rector loco fratris sui Iohannis ducis Bedfordie. Hoc anno dum Thomas Comes Sarum obsideret villam de Freyny.' (*ends abruptly: the last two lines on the page are blank*).

A copy of the AB text, said by J. Taylor, *The Universal Chronicle of Ranulf Higden*, Oxford, 1966, p. 116, to be a sister manuscript to Harvard College 116. Bk. 2, f. 36; 3. f. 62; 4, f. 101; 5, f. 131; 6, f. 169; 7, f. 197. Bk. 7 is in forty-four chapters to 'capitis interdixit', where the RS edition ends (viii. 338). Chapters 45–52 cover 1342–77 in the common continuation called (C) by Taylor (pp. 114–17). From the coronation of Richard II to the end at 1420 the text is in annalistic paragraphs, year by year, not in chapters.

The very many marginalia, most of them in the beautiful hand of art. 2a, include some neat drawings, for example the tower of Babel (f. 6ᵛ) and Romulus and Remus (f. 58). Of the fifteen I note here, nos. 2, 3, 8, 9, and perhaps no. 6 show interest in the south-west of England. Nos. 1, 2, 5, 6, 13 are by the principal annotator. No. 15 is, as Mr. Roger Lovatt notes in a letter of 25 May 1964, in the same hand as Lambeth Palace MS. 436 and B.L., Sloane 2515, and so may be assigned confidently to John Blacman. Part of no. 4 is also in this hand and no. 3 may be.[1] Nos. 8, 9 are referred to and no. 2 is printed by J. A. Robinson in *Journal of Theological Studies*, xx (1919), 105–6.

1. f. 35ᵛ (bk. 1, against the text in edn. RS, ii. 160): 'Lingua nostra vocatur saxonica et contra opinionem Georg' '.

2. f. 156 (bk. 5, ch. 20): on St. Congar of Congresbury, Somerset.

3. f. 157ᵛ (bk. 5, ch. 22): the inscription on a bell at Malmesbury.

4. f. 196 (bk. 6, ch. 29): on the claims of William I to the throne of England.

5. f. 201 (bk. 7, ch. 4): on Carthusian customs.

6. f. 214 (bk. 7, ch. 18, apropos of Stephen's coronation 'contra iuramentum suum', edn. vii. 478): 'argumentum pro forskew', i.e. Sir J. Fortescue, a Somerset man, *c.* 1394–76.

7. f. 229 (bk. 7, ch. 35): in favour of Edmund (Crouchback), earl of Lancaster, †1296.

8. f. 230 (bk. 7, ch. 36): the 'cimbalum sancti andree Wellie' with music on a 3-line stave.

9. f. 230ᵛ (bk. 7, ch. 36): on Joscelin, bishop of Bath and Wells.

10. f. 231ᵛ (bk. 7, ch. 37): on the visit of Henry III to Oxford in 1264, '. . . Hec in crono-graphia sancti Albani quam compilauit vnus de monachis ibidem'.

11. f. 231 (bk. 7, ch. 37): on the foundation of Merton College, Oxford.

12. f. 232ᵛ (bk. 7, ch. 38): 'Istius Edwardi erat tibiarum longa dimissio. ex cronica sancti albani'.

13. f. 240ᵛ (bk. 7, ch. 48, the reference to the great wind of 1362): 'The grete wynde is ny owte of mynde'.

14. f. 252, A.D. 1397: the prophecy 'Vulpes cum cauda . . .' and its explanation, ending 'hec in cronic' S. Albani. 1397'.

15. f. 257ᵛ, A.D. 1399, on the words spoken in English by Henry IV before his coronation, 'Syres I thank god . . .', with a reference back to f. 229 and no. 7: 'Magnificum verbum regis . . . vide plus supra libro 7° c° 35. b. Et eciam in margine ibidem inferiori'.

Other brief notes in the margins pick out and explain difficult words in the text, for example (f. 1) 'quadrafidus. in quatuor partes fissus'. Most of them are in the hand of the principal annotator. There are often two or three to a page. A careful erasure at the foot of f. 241.

In nine places the scribe went wrong, in the opinion of a corrector, by beginning a new paragraph and leaving space for a 2-line initial where the text should have run straight on. The corrector filled these spaces by writing in them before the initials were put in: on f. 92 he wrote 'nichil deest set hec scriptura est suplen' vacuum nam scriptor hic errauit' and on f. 117 'hic nichil deest set scribo hic pro vacuo suplendo. neque hic in istis duabus vel tribus lineis', but on ff. 109, 111, 137, 141, 143, 144, 151 he filled the space by repeating a portion of the text. All the letters he wrote are cancelled by expunction.

ff. vi+276+iv, foliated (4 unnumbered leaves) i–x, 1–270, (271–2). Fairly thin smooth parchment. ff. i, ii, 269, 270 are medieval flyleaves. 303 × 225 mm. Written space 197 × 130 mm. 40 long lines and (ff. iii–x, 23ᵛ–24ᵛ) 40 lines in 3 cols. Collation of ff. iii–x, 1–268: 1–4⁸ 5¹⁰ 6–9⁸ 10¹⁰ 11–34⁸. Quires 1–34 signed + (a)–z 7 aᵒ–gᵒ a⁺ b⁺. Art. 3 in

---

[1] Blacman's hand is also in the margins, ff. 100ᵛ, 195ᵛ. He makes much use of the punctus elevatus (⸵), even in brief notes. As a notary he attested documents in the earliest Eton College lease book, ff. 62, 63ᵛ, 64ᵛ, 65ᵛ, 66ᵛ, as Mr. Patrick Strong kindly told me.

a mainly secretary hand, the same throughout: 8-shaped *g* is regular, long-tailed *r* occasionally used, two compartment *a* common. Art. 1 is in a hand of the same type. Art. 2*a* and many marginalia are in skilful secretary by one hand. Initials: (i) of books, shaded blue and pink on gold grounds: in them the (added) arms of Eton College: prolongations into the margins formed of green branches, pale-lilac lily flowers and gold and green leaves; (ii) of chapters, 3-line and 2-line, blue with red ornament. A crimson morocco binding by C. Lewis was replaced in s. xx¹ by a W. H. Smith morocco binding. Secundo folio *adhibere*.

Written in England. In Somerset in s. sv¹. Perhaps once intended as a gift to Eton from John Blacman, fellow 1443–53, †1485 (cf. Emden, *BRUO*, p. 195), but in fact his gift to the charterhouse of Witham where he became a religious in or after 1459: 'Liber domus beate marie de Witham ordinis Cartus' ex dono M. Iohannis Blacman', f. 1, at foot.¹ No. 4 in the list of Blacman's books printed by M. R. James, *Henry the Sixth*, 1919, p. 55: 'Item librum policronicon 2 fo adhibere'. 'John France (?) his book', f. iᵛ, s. xvi. 'Mʳ Edward Griffiths', f. 270, s. xvi. Bought by Lord Ashburnham from the bookseller Rodd: Ashburnham Appendix 105 (HMC, *Eighth Report*, App. III, p. 105): sale at Sotheby's, 1 May 1899, lot 91. George Dunn sale at Sotheby's, 11 Feb. 1913, lot 515 (£330), and bought for Eton College: cf. *Eton College Chronicle*, 27 Feb. 1913, p. 314.

218. *Bernardus, Sermones in Cantica Canticorum (fragm.)*

s. XII med.

Nineteen leaves of St. Bernard on the Song of Songs, containing—a 1-leaf and a 4-leaf gap apart—consecutive text from 'in te. Si manum' in sermon 24 (*SBO* i. 160/11) to 'spiritualia comparantes' in sermon 31 (i. 223/5).

Noticed in *SBO* I. lv. Ker, *Pastedowns in Oxford Bindings*, no. 1121. One volume of the set of Aristotle in the bindings of which these leaves were used is now in the Bodleian Library, 8° A. 14 Art. Seld., and its pastedowns, now MS. Selden supra 102*, ff. 9, 10 (*Pastedowns*, no. 1141), are two of the leaves missing in the gaps: presumably the binder took twenty-two consecutive leaves and one leaf has disappeared. The text is complete on ff. 1, 6, 7, 9, 11, 12, 15, 16, 19. Each leaf contained about seventy-two of the lines of the text in *SBO*.

The text is closely similar to *R* (Bodleian, Rawlinson C. 118), a contemporary manuscript written almost certainly at Reading: cf. *SBO* I. lii–liii. Like *R* (f. 61) and *O* it contains in sermon 26 a passage on Saul and Jonathan not noticed in the apparatus to *SBO*.² The passage is marked 'vacat' in the margin of *R* and 'discerne diuersas sententias' in the margin here, f. 7ᵛ.

The fifty-eight leaves of this copy at present known in Oxford libraries and at Eton (cf. *Pastedowns*, no. 1062) are from sermons 5–9, 16–31, 37, 38, 76, 77, 78, 80, 81. Twenty-five leaves are singletons, or, sometimes, bifolia, still *in situ* in the bindings of printed books at Merton College and in the Bodleian—four bifolia were used for one book, Savile Q. 5. The rest have been collected in guard-books (Eton, Merton E. 3. 32, Corpus Christi).

1–8	Bodleian, Savile Q. 5	*SBO* i.	25/2–47/4
9, 10	Merton College, A9 B82		89/14–94/13
11–14	E. 3. 32, ff. 1–4		94/13–105/10

¹ Blacman came originally from the diocese of Bath and Wells (Emden).

² Between the words *criminis* and *Merito* (i. 179/15): Nota multis ignota⸴ de saul et ionatha. Beatus tamen ieronimus circa finem libri quem edidit contra iouinianum. ionathan fidenter saluare uidetur dicens. Inter dauid uirum sanctum. et saul regem pessimum⸴ ionathas medius fuit. Quem nec inter hedos ponere possumus. quia prophete amore dignus est⸴ nec inter arietes. ne parem eum facimus dauid⸴ maxime cum et ipse interfectus sit. Erit igitur inter oues⸴ sed in inferiori ordine. *R* reads *criminis multis ignota*, omitting *Nota*, so Eton cannot be derived from Rawl. In *O* (Merton College 46) the passage 'Nota multis . . . ordine' is written by the main hand in the margin of f. 69ᵛ.

15, 16	A9 B82	105/10–110/18
17	E. 3. 32, f. 5	110/18–112/24
18	67. e. 4	113/6–116/1
19	E. 3. 32, f. 6	116/1–118/16
20, 21	E. 3. 32, ff. 7, 8	121/5–126/21
22	67. e. 4	126/22–129/3
23	E. 3. 32, f. 9	129/12–131/28
24	31. g. 42	131/28–134/16
25	E. 3. 32, f. 10	134/19–137/10
26	81. a. 8	137/17–140/18
27	95. i. 20	140/19–143/4
28	31. g. 42	143/4–145/16
29	81. a. 8	145/16–148/4
30, 31	81. a. 7	148/11–155/8
32	95. i. 20	155/8–160/11
33–48	Eton College 218, ff. 1–16	160/11–204/4
49	Bodleian, Selden supra 102*, f. 10	204/4–206/21
50	Eton College 218, f. 17	206/24–209/12
51	Bodleian, Selden supra 102*, f. 9	214/26–217/12
52, 53	Eton College 218, ff. 18, 19	217/17–223/5
54	Merton College, 74. c. 2	*SBO* ii. 12/12–15/10
55	Corpus Christi College 487, no. 67 (2)	257/23–260/10
56	67 (1)	265/22–268/21
57, 58	68	283/4–289/3

ff. 19. Written space 157 × 97 mm. 33 long lines. Ruling in pencil. Initials 3-line, red or green, or (but not on the Eton leaves) blue, sometimes with ornament in another colour. Bound in 1919.

Written in England. Removed from the bindings of Gi. 6. 1–10 (earlier, Dg. 7. 1–10 and Fd. 7. 1–10), ten volumes of an octavo set of Aristotle in Latin, Venice, 1560–2, bound in Oxford by Dominic Pinart in or soon after 1590.

219 + 221. *Fragmenta* s. XII–XV

Leaves of manuscripts were used as covers of the 'rough copies' of the annual college accounts for some years of s. xvi and most years from 1598 to 1648. From 1609 onwards, if not earlier, they were often leaves of manuscripts from college library: see below, X, XIV–XVI. These old covers were preserved when this series of accounts was rebound in white vellum in s. xviii.[1] In 1920 they were put together in a bound volume (219) and—the larger ones—loose in

[1] In rebinding, several of these thin yearly volumes, measuring about 310 × 205 mm, were often put together: thus for the years 1575–1633 there were originally thirty-six, but now seventeen, separate volumes. The 'rough copies' for some years are missing. On the other hand, there are two of them for some years, one arranged under leaf numbers and the other under Tituli: the latter formed the basis of the final copy of the account. Twenty-four volumes (as originally bound) survive for the years 1607–19 when Thomas Allen was bursar, many of them written in his admirable hand. His memoranda on the covers provide the firm evidence that the leaves forming MSS. 219 + 221 come, except XVII and, perhaps, XVIII, from this series of accounts. The evidence is clearest on one cover, now MS. 219, pp. 47–50, on which Allen wrote 'Ian 31 anno 1609° my layengs out for this yeare weare on these pages of this booke viz\^t', followed by page references with sums of money against them. The page references are to the white-vellum volume now numbered '8' on the spine.

a portfolio (221). Forty-seven of the forty-nine pieces in these two volumes have the date of the account on them and are arranged here in the order of these dates. Sixteen different manuscripts were used (I–XVI).

I. 221, nos. 1, 2. Two leaves from the temporale of a handsome noted breviary—the music not filled in—written in England in s. xv med.

Brev. ad usum Sarum, i. xc–xcv, cxxvi–cxxxv (Advent). The written space is complete on no. 2, 380 × 247 mm. 2 cols. 54 lines. Headings in red, but coloured initials not filled in. Elaborate cadels.

No. 1 is marked 'Ed 6^{ti} 3°' and '3 to 4'. No. 2 is marked 'Ed 6^{ti} 6to to 1 Mariæ'.

II. 221, no. 3 One leaf from the sanctorale of a missal written in England in s. xv in.

Offices of Scholastica, Valentine, Juliana, Chair of Peter, and Matthew, 10–24 Feb.: cf. *Sarum Missal*, pp. 253/3–255/16. A scribbler wrote 'Hampshier in Harlinge the dampshier', s. xvi. 410 × 270 mm. Written space 270 × 175 mm. 2 cols. 36 lines. Initials: (i) 2-line, blue with red ornament; (ii) 1-line, blue or red.

Marked '5 to 6' (Edward VI or perhaps Elizabeth I).

III. 221, no. 4. Two leaves of the calendar of a service book written in England in s. xv in.

May–August in red and black, graded, with added obits which show provenance from St. George's Chapel, Windsor, including Henry VI at 21 May and Henry VII at 11 May: payments against some names. The feast of St. Thomas of Canterbury has been cancelled at 7 July and his name is cancelled in a list of feasts at which a memoria is said at vespers 'in ecclesia Sarum', entered in a blank space of May. Written space 290 × 205 mm. The central bifolium of a quire.

Marked '1 Mar. to 1 et 2 Phil. et Mar.'.

IV. 221, no. 5. One leaf from the temporale of a gradual written in England in s. xv in.

The leaf begins in the sequence Resonet and ends in the sequence Eya musa (Monday and Tuesday after Pentecost): *Sarum Missal*, pp. 163–4. Written space 320 × 210 mm. 2 cols. 14 lines and music.

Marked 'Anno domini 1576 to 1577'.

V. 221, nos. 6, 7. Two bifolia of a handsome copy of Gregory, Moralia in Job, written in England in s. xii med.

The text is continuous from *PL* lxxv. 1135/3 si superna—1145/14 crescat (part of bk. 16). Contemporary running titles. 'Lib' ' on versos and 'XVI' on rectos. The chapter numbers of bk. 16 are in a large hand in the margins, s. xiv (?), and the chapter numbers of Job in the top right corner of each page, s. xv. 395 × 265 mm. Written space 272 × 170 mm. 2 cols. 37 lines. Pencil ruling. The two central bifolia of a quire.

Marked '1586 to 1587'.

VI. 219, pp. 79–86. Two bifolia of a commentary on the Apocalypse (?) written in England in s. xv in.

A passage on p. 79 runs 'sicut ergo color yridis est principium omnium colorum sic pater simpliciter est principium omnium tam creatorum quam increatorum': the Son is compared to sardis. 'nota secundum Ioachim', p. 80. No breaks in the text. Written space 260 × 160 mm. 2 cols. 57–9 lines. Written in a secretary hand.

One bifolium (pp. 81–4) is marked 'Anno 1598', the other 'Anno 1599'.

VII. 219, pp. 119–22. A bifolium of theological distinctions, letter S, written in England in s. xiv².

Running titles in red on rectos, 'De spiritu sancto 156', 'De superbia 157'. The piece on pride begins 'Ut dicit hugo de sancto victore superbia est elacio'. Written space 267 × 150 mm. 2 cols. 43 lines. Large square textura. 2-line blue initials with red ornament. Marked 'Anno 1603'.

VIII. 219, pp. 19–26, 55–70. Six bifolia of a copy of Aquinas, De veritate, written in England in s. xiii ex.

Fragments of questions 1–3, 15, 16, 18, 19, 29. Dondaine and Shooner, no. 811.1, 4. The right order of the pages is 59–70, 55–8, 19–26. A medieval foliation shows that pp. 59–70 were ff. 2, 5, 6, 7, 8, 11 and that pp. 19–22 were ff. 109, 120 of the original manuscript. By calculation, pp. 55–8 were ff. 14 and 21. p. 26 contains the last words of the text, 'non sufficienter', followed by a numbered table of contents, '1. Quid sit veritas . . .', ending imperfectly at '47' (= De prouidentia Dei, q. 5, art. 4). Numbers in the margins of the text corresponded no doubt to those in the table, for example, '30' (p. 57), '145' (p. 19, at the beginning of q. 15), '161' (p. 22, at the beginning of q. 19): the highest number is '253' (p. 24). Written space 250 × 155 mm. 2 cols. 50 lines. Quires in twelves, no doubt: the remains here are 1², 5–8, 11, 2³, 10, 10¹, 12, and the central bifolium of the last quire. 2-line initials, blue or red, with ornament of the other colour. Secundo folio *et falsum* 'nisi' in mente.

The markings are: (pp. 19–22) "Anno 1605 to' Anno 1606'; (pp. 23–6) 'Anno 1606 to 1607'; (pp. 59, 60, 69, 70) '1614'; (pp. 55–8) 'Anno 1615'; (pp. 61, 62, 67, 68) '1615' and 'continet 80ᵗᵃ schedulas'; (pp. 63–6) '1617' and 'continet schedulas 80ᵗᵃ et tres'.

IX. 221, nos. 8–17. Five complete leaves—three of them cut in two—and two half leaves from the temporale of a large antiphonal written in England in s. xv.

No. 12 is the first leaf of the text and almost entirely rubric: cf. *Brev. ad usum Sarum*, i. i–iv. After this the order is 15+16, 14+17, 13, 11, 9+10, 8: edn. i. ccxcix–cccxiii, cccxiii–cccxxv, cccxxv–cccxxix, cccxl–ccclxvi, ccccxi–ccccxx, ccccxxv–ccccxxix. 14+17 is a principal page with the beginning of the Epiphany office. Cues of memoriae of St. Thomas of Canterbury have been erased on nos. 15+16. Written space 395 × 265 mm. 2 cols. 60 lines.

Marked: (no. 8) 'Anno domini 1607, Decemb. 23° pro anno proximè sequente'; (no. 9) 'Anno domini 1608 Decemb. 20ᵐᵒ pro anno proxime sequente usque ad finitum computum anno Domini 1609'; (no. 10) 'Anno domini 1609° et anno regni Regis Iacobi septimo. et 21° die Decembris, pro anno proximè sequente, usque ad finitum computum anno Domini 1610'; (no. 11) '1610 to 1611'; (no. 12) '1613'; (no. 16) '1717 to 1718' (*sic*) and 'continet schedulas 80ᵗᵃ et duas (*altered to* octo) et duas et unam'; (no. 17) '1618'.

X. 219, pp. 27–50. Six bifolia of MS. 116, art. 1, q.v.

The markings are: (pp. 47–50) 'Anno 1609' and '1608 to 1609'; (pp. 27, 28, 33–4) '1626'; (pp. 29–32) '1627'; (pp. 35–8) 'Anno domini 1630'; (pp. 39, 40, 45, 46) 'Winsore Anno 1640 et 41'; (pp. 41–4) '1642'.

XI. 221, nos. 18, 19. Two bifolia of sequences from the sanctorale and common of saints of a noted missal written in England in s. xiv med.

Begins with a headless sequence (1), 'sere da puros mentis oculos in te defigere cristianissimi fidem operibus redimere beatoque fine. Ex eius incolatu seculi auctor ad te transire'. (2–11) are Alle celeste, Ad celebres, Odas hac in die, Sacrosancta, Alleluia nunc, Laus deuota, Organicis, Virginis venerande, Exultemus, Ierusalem (*Sarum Missal*, pp. 482, 483, 485, 475, 486, 486, 487, 489, 489, 473). (1–3) are on the first leaf of no. 19. (4, 5) are on the first leaf of no. 18. (6–8) are on the second leaf of no. 18. (9–11) are on the second sheet of no. 19. Only (2), (7), (10) are complete.

No. 18 is marked 'Anno 1610 to 1611'. No. 19 is marked 'Anno 1614'.

XII. 219, pp. 15–18. A bifolium of a medical manuscript written in England in s. xiv med.

The text is divided into Tractatus, Doctrinae, and Capitula, in the same way as the Chirurgia of Guy de Chauliac, but the text is different. Tr. 2, Doctr. 2, Cap. 4 is 'De apostemate quod fit in radice anis. Apostema quod fit . . .', and Cap. 6 is 'De apostemate sub titillico'. Two consecutive leaves, numbered 34 and 35. Written space 205 × 145 mm. 2 cols. 47 lines. The central bifolium of a quire. Written in current anglicana. 2-line blue initials with red ornament.

Marked 'Anno domini 1619'.

XIII. 219, pp. 1–14. Three bifolia and a singleton (pp. 1, 2) of a copy of Revelationes Sanctae Birgittae written in England in s. xv².

Printed in 1492 and later. These leaves are from bk. 7, chs. 2, 3, 6, 9–12, 23–8. pp. 7–10 are a consecutive pair and so are pp. 11–14. Written space 198 × 145 mm. 41–3 long lines. No visible ruling. Written in a secretary hand influenced by anglicana. 2-line blue initials with red ornament.

The markings are: (pp. 3–6) 'Anno domini 1621'; (pp. 1, 2) 'Anno domini 1622. Recepta'; (pp. 11–14) 'Anno domini 1623'; (pp. 7–10) 'Anno domini 1623 et 1624'.

XIV. 219, pp. 91–118. Seven bifolia of a copy of 1, 2 Chronicles with gloss, written in England in s. xiii.

The text runs with gaps from 'tempore percussit dauid' (1 Chronicles 18: 3) to 'et offerentur' (2 Chronicles 35: 12). It takes up most of the page. The gloss fitted in beside it in smaller writing is scanty. Marginalia by Robert Elyot (see p. 631) include (p. 98) 'hoc inpendium cost' and (p. 106) above 'stibinos', 'id est coloris stibii id est albi sterche'. Written space 220 mm high. Probably leaves 1, 2, 4, 5, 8, 9, 11, 12 of one quire, two bifolia of a second quire, and one bifolium of a third.

The markings are: (pp. 93, 94, 103, 104) '1631'; (pp. 91, 92, 105, 106) 'Anno 1632'; (pp. 107, 108, 113, 114) 'Anno domini 1632'; (pp. 95, 96, 101, 102) 'Anno 1633'; (pp. 109–12) 'Anno domini 1633'; (pp. 97–100) 'Anno domini 1634'. pp. 115–18 are not dated.

XV. 219, pp. 71–8. Two bifolia of MS. 125, art. 1, q.v.

pp. 73–6 are marked '1638' and pp. 71, 72, 77, 78 'Anno MDCXLVIII'.

XVI. 219, pp. 51–4. A bifolium of MS. 35, art. 3, q.v.

Marked '1646'.

XVII. 219, pp. 87–90. A bifolium of Codex Justiniani, s. xii/xiii, written probably in Italy.

From bk. 1, tit. 48–51 and bk. 2, tit. 4–6. Many early marginalia. Written space 250 × 135 mm. 2 cols. 51 lines.

Marked 'Fysshers et Brimfast. Ro de Cur' in annis Henrici VIII . . . .' (a good many years of Henry VIII, Henry VI, and Edward (IV) are listed in this heading).[1]

XVIII. 221, no. 20. A leaf of the commentary on Psalms by Nicholas de Lyra, O.F.M., written in England in s. xv².

[1] A manor in North Mundham, Sussex, formerly belonging to Eton. Its deeds, once at Eton, are now deposited in the West Sussex Record Office, Chichester, Add. MSS. 1735–1801. The biofolium was probably the wrapper of Add. 1737.

The end of the commentary on Ps. 23, '... glorie tue', and the beginning of the commentary on Ps. 24, '[A]d te domine leuaui animam meam. Titulus in fine Ps. dauid supra egit propheta de redditu ...'. 428 × 285 mm. Written space 305 × 195 mm. 2 cols. 60 lines. Written in a current mixture of anglicana and secretary, the ascenders not looped.

No mark, but scribbles suggest that this leaf wrapped accounts.

220. *Fragmenta*   s. XI ex.–XV

Most of the pastedowns and strips of parchment used in binding books in the library are happily still *in situ*. A few pastedowns and strips were collected into a guardbook, MS. 220, in 1920.[1] For nos. I, II, XVII, XVIII, XXIII, XXIV below, cf. Ker, *Pastedowns in Oxford Bindings*, p. 270. All the writing is probably English, except in nos. VI, XIII, XV(?), XVIII.

(I) Pastedowns, two bifolia of Gaudentius, Tractatus, s. xi ex.[2] (II) See MS. 209. (III) Two strips from a noted service book, s. xii. (IV) A strip, s. xiv. (V) A strip, s. xii. (VI) Two strips of a service book, s. xii.[2] (VI) Two strips of a service book, s. xii/xiii. (VII) A bifolium of Ovid, Fasti, s. xiii[1]. (VIII) Pastedowns, parts of two leaves of a commentary on Genesis (?), s. xii[2]. (IX) Two leaves of a small Bible, s. xiii. (X) A pastedown, part of a leaf, s. xiii[2]: Aristotle.[3] (XI) Pastedowns, two fragments of one leaf of Aquinas, Prima pars Summae, Q. 54–5, s. xiii ex. (XII) Pastedowns, two bifolia of sermons, s. xiii/xiv. (XIII) Two tiny scraps in Netherlandish, s. xiv. (XIV) A pastedown, the upper part of a leaf, s. xv. (XV) Two strips of a verse text in French, s. xiii. (XVI) A strip from the same membrane as MS. 280, no. 5a, q.v. (XVII) A pastedown, one leaf of Petrus Comestor, Historia Scholastica, s. xii/xiii. (XVIII) A pastedown, part of a leaf of the Decretals of Gregory IX (bk. 1, tit. ix, x), with surrounding apparatus, s. xiii ex. (XIX) A strip from a service book, s. xiv. cf. MS. 280, art. 2. (XX) A strip, scholastic theology, s. xiii ex. (XXI) A strip from a noted service book (common of virgins), s. xiv. (XXII) A pastedown, part of a leaf of a missal, s. xii. (XXIII) A pastedown, a leaf of a missal, s. xiv/xv. (XXIV) Pastedowns, two leaves of a gradual, s. xiv. (XXV, XXVI) Two strips, making one leaf of Decretals of Gregory IX: bk. 2, tit. 25, 26. s. xiii[2].

(I). Parts of Tractatus XV–XVII (edn. *CSEL*, lxviii (1936), 134/12 *fratribus*—139/24 *sacerdotum*, 145/2 *orasse*—150/6 *exustorum*). Written space 195 × 115 mm. 33 long lines. English hand. Removed from Ea. 3. 6, an Oxford binding (Ker, *Pastedowns*, no. 1688).[2] (IV). Biblical history. (V). A commentary on Romans. Removed from Ec. 8. 21,

---

[1] Others were bound separately: see MSS. 196, 208–12, 218, 223.

[2] Eight other leaves of this manuscript are in Oxford libraries (*Pastedowns*, nos. 1209, 1220). One of the two bifolia *in situ* as pastedowns of Merton College 2 f. 10 fills the gap between *sacerdotum* and *orasse* here. The other forms the outside sheet of the next quire: one leaf has from *in multo* to *nouimus* (edn., pp. 153/4–155/17) and the other is blank, except for the quire number XXII at the foot of the verso. One of the two bifolia *in situ* as pastedowns of All Souls College 80. g. 8 contains the end of Origen's homily on Leviticus, De sacrificiis propitiationis (*PG* xii. 508–25: in front of Gaudentius also in the Reims manuscript, as the editor notes, p. xxi) and the words 'Incipit praefacio' of the heading of Gaudentius' preface. The other has the end of Gaudentius' preface from edn. p. 12/25 *meritorum*, the list of the nineteen treatises (edn., pp. 16, 17) and the beginning of Tractatus I, as far as edn., p. 19/1, *sabbatum*.

[3] See Addenda, p. 999.

Bellarminus, *Tertia controversia generalis*, sine anno. (VI). 2 cols. Quire numbered 'X^us' on the second strip. Netherlandish hand (?). Removed from Ee. 7. 28, *Rituale Romanum*, Lyon, 1616, where a small piece of one of the two strips still remains. (VII). Fasti iii. 269–369, 573–672. Long narrow format. Written space 195 mm high. 50 long lines. (VIII). A good English hand. Punctuation includes the flex (?). Removed from Fa. 9. 3, Diodorus Siculus (in Latin), Lyon, 1552, with stag centrepiece.[1] (IX). 1 Kings 7–14. Written space 110×75 mm. 2 cols. 55 lines. Removed from Fi. 8. 21, C. Hubertus, Strasbourg, 1561. (X). Removed from Ff. 7. 3, Cicero, *Ad Herennium*, Cologne, 1563, in a centrepiece binding: bought at Oxford by William Chetwynde, s. xvi, 'Teste Roberto Astono qui nebulo est ut ita loquor'. (XI). The columns on the recto numbered 377 and 378. Removed from G. 436/1 (formerly Gi. 8. 4), Cicero, *De philosophia*, *Prima pars*, Venice (Aldus), 1555, in a Cambridge centrepiece binding: the title-page is inscribed 'Sum Gulielmi Charki 1563'. (XII). Written space 130×95 mm. Removed from Eh. 5. 1, *Actiones et monumenta martyrum*, Geneva, 1560. (XIII). The written space is 40 mm wide. (XIV). Partly on the Dies mali. (XV). The text is written in couplets, every second line indented by one letter. Thirty-four lines in a written space 205 mm high, but only a word or two remains in each line. One strip has paragraphs beginning 'Walwan' and, seven lines further down, 'Ider (?)' and the other a paragraph beginning 'Beduer'. 'Petreim' (twice), 'Bretun' and 'Gerin' are other names at the beginning of lines. Removed from Ff. 4. 11, Synesius, etc. (in Greek), Paris, 1553, one of many books bearing Oldham's roll HM. a. 14: cf. below, MS. 280. (XVII). Written space 240×155 mm. 2 cols. 40 lines. Removed from Ed. 2. 8, an Oxford binding, *Pastedowns*, no. 1443. (XVIII). The hand is Italian. Removed from Eh. 4. 1, an Oxford binding (*Pastedowns*, no. 783). (XXII). From the end of a missal for monastic use. The recto has the collect, secret, and postcommunion of the masses in *Missale Westm.* ii. 1177, 1181–2, *Pro omnibus fidelibus defunctis* and *Pro vivis atque defunctis*. The verso has the collect, secret, and postcommunion of two masses, the first the *Pro vivis atque defunctis* in *M.W.* ii. 1179, but with a second secret, 'Suscipe clementissime pater has oblationes quas ego indignus . . .', and the second 'Pro priore' in which the collect and postcommunion are nearly those in *Missale Romanum*, i. 487 (*Pro episcopo*) and the secret is 'Offerimus tibi domine hostias placationis . . . gaudere, per'. All that remains after this is the beginning of the collect 'Pietate tua . . .' (*Missale Westm.* ii. 1177, *Pro vivis atque defunctis*). (XXIII). Commemorations of B.V.M., Holy Trinity, and Holy Spirit. Written space 248×153 mm. 2 cols. 42 lines. Removed from Ed. 2. 8, like no. XVII (*Pastedowns*, no. 1444). (XXIV). One leaf has part of the Easter sequence *Fulgens praeclara*, the other part of the office for Monday after Easter (*Sarum Missal*, p. 138), ending with the first lines of the sequence Zyma vetus. Written space 277× 160 mm. 36 long lines. Removed from Fc. 2. 14, an Oxford binding, *Pastedowns*, no. 1683. (XXV, XXVI). Removed from Bm. 1. 2, Ben Jonson, *Works*, 1616.

223. *Breviarium* (*fragm.*) s. XIV in.

Fragments of the sanctorale of a breviary. The right order of the leaves is 2, 1, 4, 3. f. 2^rv contains part of lesson 3, lessons 4–7 and part of lesson 8 for St. Michael (29 Sept.), and on the verso a commemoration of St. Jerome (30 Sept.), Sancti nos domine. f. 1^rv has an office of St. Michael (for the octave ?). f. 4 begins in the office of the ordination of St. Dunstan (21 Oct.) followed by Crispin and Crispinian (25 Oct.) and Simon and Jude (28 Oct.). f. 3^rv has lessons 1–4 and part of lesson 5 for All Saints.

The importance of St. Dunstan is stressed by four rubrics on f. 4^rv in which provision is made for the octave of the ordination: (1) 'at the end of the office, 'Nota quando predicta fest' habet oct' per totam ebdomadam et ultima die octauarum. Inuitat'. Regem confessorem . . . Et nota quod iste octaue semper debent celebrari in proxima die ante uigiliam symonis

---

[1] Perhaps an Oxford binding. The stag is larger than centrepiece xxix in *Pastedowns* and faces right.

et iude. tamen si ista uigilia dominica euenerit. Tunc ibi celebrari debent. et tunc ad primas vesperas'; (2) Nota quod si ordinatio sancti Dunstani oct' habuerit: Tunc dicantur duo N° de dominica. cetera de sancto Dunstano; (3) Tamen si oct' sancti Dunstani ista die celebrare fuerint. Tunc erit ant' super ps' . . .; (4) Si oct' sancti Dunstani hic celebrate fuerint . . . Another rubric follows the feast of Crispin and Crispinian: Si ista fest' dominica euenerit: duo Nocturna dicantur de Sancto Dunstano. et responsoria per ordinem de hystoria . . .

ff. 4. Written space (only f. 4 is complete) 215×145 mm. 2 cols. 28 lines. Two bifolia from one quire, no doubt the first and third sheets of the quire: ff. 2, 3 formed the outermost sheet, as appears from the catchword 'arche' on f. 3ᵛ: probably one leaf is missing between f. 2 and f. 1 and between f. 4 and f. 3. Initials: (i) 2-line, alternately in colour on decorated grounds of gold and colour and in gold on grounds of pink and blue, the latter patterned in white; (ii) 1-line, blue with red ornament or red with violet ornament. Capital letters in the ink of the text are touched with red. Bound in s. xx^{1}.

Written in England, perhaps for use at the Benedictine abbey of Glastonbury.[1] Formerly pastedowns of Bd. 2. 17, P. Jovius, *Historiae*, Paris, 1558–60, in contemporary English binding: the gilt centrepiece is of a fairly common type, but has not hitherto been localized.

225. *Jeronimus, In Prophetas Minores* (*Nahum–Malachi*) *et Danielem* s. XII med.

1. ff. 1–82 Incipit liber explanationum beati Ieronimi presbiteri super Naum prophetam ad paulam et eustochiam. filiam eius. In ordine duodecim prophetarum . . . iohannem intellegens. Explicit liber malachię prophetę.

PL xxv. 1231–1578. Very imperfect. Besides the four leaves missing after f. 11 and the single leaf missing after f. 24, single quires are missing after ff. 8, 12, and 35 and two quires after f. 20, probably a total of forty-five leaves, or over half the text. ff. 10, 11 are torn at the top and initials have been cut from ff. 34, 69, and 70.

2. ff. 82–91ᵛ Incipit prologus in danielem prophetam. Contra prophetam danielem . . . persarum et (*ends imperfectly*).

PL xxv. 491–522/25. The initial *A* has been cut from f. 83.

ff. 91. Soft parchment of good quality. 360×265 mm. Written space 267×170 mm. 2 cols. 44 lines. Ruling with a hard point. Collation: 1^{8} 2^{8} wants 4–7 after f. 11 3^{8} 4^{8} wants 5 after f. 24 $5–12^{8}$. Quires 4–12 numbered at the beginning VII, VIII, X–XVI.

[1] I should like to take this opportunity of quoting from the last letter Francis Wormald wrote to me, 16 Oct. 1971, in reply to my question to him whether MS. 223 might be a fragment of a Glastonbury breviary: '. . . I think that the reason for this fuss about the Ordination of St. Dunstan arises from the fact that the Octave fell on the rather important feast of SS. Simon and Jude. The Christ Church Canterbury practice seems to have been to defer it to the day after SS. Simon and Jude, i.e. 29th October, when it is called Celebratio Oct. Sancti Dunstani, see E. Bishop, *Bosworth Psalter*, p. 111. The Glastonbury calendar does not give us any information really. The Ordination of St. Dunstan appears there as a feast of 4 copes on 21 October and SS. Simon and Jude have a rather high grading of two copes; quite enough to interfere with an octave. My guess is for Glastonbury rather than Canterbury which apparently deferred rather than anticipated the feast. I doubt whether any other house would have kept the Ordinatio S. Dunstani on such a high level as to keep it with an Octave'.

Well written. Initials: (i) of books, all removed; (ii) of prologues, removed, except *A* in green and red on f. 14, *A* in red on f. 39, *U* in blue on f. 54ᵛ, and *C* in red on f. 82; (iii, iv) 2-line and 1-line, red, green, purple, or blue. Contemporary binding of wooden boards covered with once white leather: two bands: central strap and pin missing: marks of a label, *c.* 40 × 80 mm, attached by six nails, are near the top of the back cover. Secundo folio *mundi esse.*

Written in England. 'George Manly' scribbled on f. 57, s. xvi. 'James Bowen Anno 1745' on the pastedown at the end.¹ Phillipps MS. 3610. Sir Thomas Phillipps sale, 21 Mar. 1895, lot 86, to Quaritch (£17 10s.). Given by Sir J. H. B. Noble in 1921.

226. *Gregorius, Moralia in Job, lib. 1–16*   s. XII med.

[R]euerentissimo [a]tque sanctissimo [f]ratri Leandro . . . (f. 1ᵛ) ex utraque fulciatur. Explicit proemium. Incipit prefatio subsequentis operis. Inter multos sepe queritur . . . deo latius disserantur. Explicit liber XVI.

PL lxxv. 509–1162. f. 207ᵛ blank. Two leaves are missing. This copy discussed by N. R. Ker, 'The English manuscripts of the Moralia of Gregory the Great', *Kunsthistorische Forschungen Otto Pächt zu Ehren*, 1972, p. 82. Facsimile of part of f. 142ᵛ shows the initial *Q* of bk. 11. There are pencilled caricatures in the margins of ff. 63, 131.

ff. iv+207+iv. 385 × 290 mm. Written space 280 × 190 mm. 2 cols. 43 lines. Ruling with a hard point, the horizontal lines often reinforced in pencil. Collation: 1–20⁸ 21⁸ wants 1, 2 before f. 161 22–25⁸ 26¹⁰ wants 10, blank. Probably in two hands, changing for the better at f. 120 (16¹): the punctuation by point has often been altered to a short horizontal line. Initials of books 1–16 in a handsome style used at Reading (cf. J. R. Liddell in *Bodleian Quarterly Record*, viii (1935), 49), mainly blue with ornament in green and red: the initial of the introductory letter (f. 1) has been cut out. Binding of s. xx. Secundo folio *accepta.*

Written in England and probably at Reading (see above). A strip has been cut from the foot of f. 1. Identifiable by the opening words of the second leaf with no. (21) in the list of books 'que per anni circulum legende sunt siue in ecclesia priuatim noctibus siue in refectorio' at Reading in s. xiv (Liddell, p. 49). Inscribed 'Liber Clementis burdett prec' xxxˢ iiiiᵈ' on f. 94, 'Francis Englefyld knight' on f. 138 and 'Thomas Reynolde prec. iiiˢ' on f. 1: for Englefield and Burdett and a J. Reynoldes, whose name occurs in three other manuscripts from Reading, see Liddell, pp. 49–51. Phillipps MS. 3616: sale 21 Mar. 1895, lot 356, to Nichols (£39). Given to Eton by Sir J. H. B. Noble in Nov. 1921.

246. *G. Monemutensis, Historia Britonum*   s. XIII²

1. ff. 1–60ᵛ Eneas post traianum bellum excidium cum ascanio . . . sermonem [transferre curaui].

Ed. A. Griscom, 1929. This copy noticed by J. Hammer, in *Modern Language Quarterly*, iii (1942), 240. A gap in the text near the end, since nearly all f. 60 is missing. The prophecies of Merlin end 'Transibit terminos furor' (f. 35: edn. 397/8). Some nearly contemporary marginalia. Summaries of the text are at head and foot of many pages in a hand of s. xv. 'Historia Bruti', f. 1.

2. Additions on flyleaves and in blank spaces. (*a*) f. iʳᵛ, a poem in Welsh, s. xvi; (*b*) f. iᵛ Nulla valet tantum. virtus . . . (2 lines of verse); (*c*) f. iiiᵛ Cronica nulla

---

¹ Bowen had some Reading manuscripts (cf. de Ricci and Wilson, *Census*, p. 1671), but there is no evidence that this book is from Reading.

canit britonica bella peracta . . . (6 lines of verse); (*d*) f. iii^v Rethorice referam regi regalia reddam . . . (5 lines of verse). (*e*) f. 60, medical recipes.

(*a*). Part of a *cywydd* describing the misfortunes of the lover in the rain. Not otherwise known. The beginning and possibly the end are wanting.[1] (*b*). Walther, *Sprichwörter*, no. 18971. (*c*). In a strange hand, probably s. xv ex. (*d*). Every word begins with the letter *r*.

ff. iii+60. 185×130 mm. Written space 150×100 mm. 35–6 long lines. Collation: 1–5^12 (5^12 a small fragment). Initials: 3-line (f. 1) and 2-line, red or blue with ornament of the other colour. Medieval binding of wooden boards covered with pink leather: four bands: central strap and pin missing. Secundo folio *libus muniuit*.[2]

Written in England or Wales. In Wales in s. xvi: cf. art. 2*a*. A name, perhaps 'cadwaler', f. 1, s. xvi, and above it the rather later number 134. '27' on a paper label on the spine. Savile sale at Sotheby's, 6 Feb. 1861, lot 6. Phillipps MS. 25145: sale at Sotheby's, 27 Apr. 1903, lot 1213, to W. E. Tyldesley Jones, K.C. Given by his son, J. E. Tyldesley Jones, 7 July 1940.

265. *Horae B.V.M.*   s. xv/xvi

1. ff. 1–12^v Full calendar in red and black.

Feasts in red include 'Amandi et uedasti', 'Bonifacii episcopi', 'Eligii episcopi', 'Remigii et bauonis', 'Donaciani archiepiscopi', 'Eligii episcopi', 'Nychasii episcopi' (6 Feb., 5, 25 June, 1, 14 Oct., 1, 14 Dec.). 'Frederici episcopi' in black, 18 July.

2. ff. 14–15 Salutatio beate ueronice cristi a'. Salue sancta facies . . . *RH*, no. 18175. f. 15^v blank.

3. ff. 17–21^v Incipiunt hore de sancta cruce. . . . Patris sapiencia . . .

4. ff. 22–25^v Incipit offitium de sancto spiritu. . . . Nobis sancti spiritus . . . f. 26^rv blank.

5. ff. 28–31^v Incipit missa beate marie uirginis.

6. ff. 32–6 Sequentiae of the Gospels. f. 36^v blank.

7. ff. 37–89^v Incipiunt hore beate marie uirginis secundum consuetudinem romane ecclesie. Advent office, f. 83.

8. ff. 90–104^v Incipiunt septem psalmi penitenciales . . . (f. 97^v) Incipiunt letanie.

Nine pontiffs and doctors: . . . (9) ludouice. Seven monks and hermits: (1) francisce . . . (5–7) elziarii dominice ludouice. Twelve virgins: . . . (12) gertrudis.

9. ff. 106–136^v Incipiunt uigilie mortuorum.

Office of the dead. f. 137^rv blank.

10. Passio domini nostri ihesu cristi . . .

The Passion according to the four evangelists: ff. 139–149^v Matthew 26, 27; ff. 151–159^v

---

[1] Information from Mr. B. G. Owens of the National Library of Wales, where there are photographs of these two pages.

[2] The scribe broke the word *militibus* after the first syllable and fell into error. A contemporary hand wrote in 'uel militibus'.

Mark 14, 15: 1–46; ff. 161–169ᵛ; Luke 22, 23: 1–53; ff. 171–8 John 18, 19. Paragraphed in Matthew at 27: 62, in Mark at 15: 42, in Luke at 23: 50, and in John at 19: 38. Gold crosses in the text before Matthew 27: 35, 51, 57, 59, Mark 15: 37, Luke 23: 6. ff. 178ᵛ–179ᵛ blank.

11 (added in s. xvi). ff. iiᵛ–iii Te adoro deum meum et benedico . . . Miserere michi peccatrici . . . et electis tuis amen. f. iiiᵛ blank.

ff. iii+179+i. ff. ii, iii are old flyleaves; see art. 11. 206×150 mm. Written space 110×75 mm. 20 long lines. Ruling with pale-red ink. Collation: 1–2⁶ 3² (ff. 14, 15) 4⁸ 5⁸+1 leaf after 2 (f. 28) 6–8⁸ 9⁸+1 leaf after 6 (f. 66) 10–13⁸ 14² (ff. 103–4) 15–21⁸ 22¹⁰ 23⁴, together with eleven singletons with pictures on versos and blank rectos. Italianate hand: catchwords written vertically (f. 113ᵛ). Eleven out of probably nineteen full-page pictures remain, four in art. 10 (Betrayal, Crowning with thorns, Scourging, Carrying the Cross, ff. 138ᵛ, 150ᵛ, 160ᵛ, 170ᵛ), three in art. 7 (shepherds and a woman dance to bagpipes before sext,¹ Christ in the temple before compline,¹ Christ with Mary and Martha before the Advent office, ff. 65ᵛ, 78ᵛ, 82ᵛ: the rest missing) and one before each of arts. 2 (The Holy Face), 3, 5 (the wounded Christ appears to his Mother), 9. Four smaller pictures, c. 50×50 mm in art. 6. Initials: (i) usually blue patterned in white on grounds of gold and dark-red patterned in gold paint, but on ff. 17, 22 part of the border design and made up of grisaille logs; (ii) 2-line, blue, patterned in white on decorated gold grounds; (iii) 1-line, gold on grounds of blue or red patterned in white. The pages with pictures and the pages facing them have continuous framed borders on coloured grounds bearing flowers, birds, beasts, insects, and grotesques, and a few figures and framed scenes; also on ff. 62 (terce) and 83 scenes of country life, stag and boar hunting, bears, monkeys, etc., and the same castle in the background. The pages with smaller pictures have borders on three sides (not the *outer* margin). Line-fillers in red, few and inconspicuous: nearly always the scribe managed to fill his line with text. Handsome binding of dark-brown gilt leather over thin wooden boards, s. xvi/xvii: fan pattern ornament and two eagles displayed and crowned on each cover.

Written in the Netherlands. Belonged to a woman in s. xvi (art. 11). Armorial book-plate of Joseph Whatley, s. xix. Belonged to Brigadier H. A. Tyler, The Old Rectory, Dalham, Newmarket, Suffolk: sold by him at Sotheby's, 3 June 1946, lot 191. Bought by J. Hely-Hutchinson from Quaritch in Nov. 1946. Given by him in June 1954.

266. *Horae B.V.M.*　　　　　　　　　　　　s. xv med.

1. ff. 2–13ᵛ Full calendar in French in gold, blue, and red, the two colours alternating for effect.

Feasts in gold include 'S' leu S' gile', 'Saint denis', 'Saint eloy' (1 Sept., 9 Oct., 1 Dec.).

2. ff. 14–19 Sequentiae of the Gospels.

3. ff. 19–22ᵛ Obsecro te . . . Michi famulo tuo . . .

4. ff. 23–25 O intemerata . . . orbis terrarum. Inclina . . . ego peccatrix . . .

5. ff. 26–93 Hours of B.V.M. of the use of (Paris).

Nine lessons at matins. A leaf missing after f. 76 contained the beginning of none. f. 93ᵛ blank.

¹ Probably misplaced leaves. They are as a rule the pictures before terce and none respectively. The double opening, sext and the picture of the shepherds, is illustrated in the 1946 sale catalogue.

6. ff. 94–111ᵛ Penitential psalms and (f. 107) litany.

Seven confessors: . . . (6, 7) germane maglori. Eleven virgins: . . . (6) oportuna . . . (10) genouefa . . .

7. ff. 112–115ᵛ Hours of the Cross. . . . Patris sapientia . . .

8. ff. 116–19 Hours of the Holy Spirit. . . . Nobis sancti spiritus . . . f. 119ᵛ blank.

9. ff. 120–164ᵛ Office of the dead.

10. ff. 165–70 Doulce dame de misericorde . . .

The Fifteen Joys: Sonet, no. 458.

11. ff. 170ᵛ–173 Doulx dieu doulx pere . . .

The Seven Requests: Sonet, no. 504.

12. f. 173ʳᵛ Saincte uraie croix adoree . . . Sonet, no. 1876.

13. ff. 174–6 Dame ie te rens le salut Qui fist enfer rompre et destruire . . .

Nine 8-line stanzas. Sonet, nos. 318, 320.

14. ff. 176ᵛ–181ᵛ Memoriae: (a) Saint sebastien de cueur piteux Qui par la uoulente de dieux . . . (20 lines); (b–d) of SS. Katherine, Geneviève, Apollonia; (e) Memoire de pluseurs uierges; (f) of St. Margaret; (g) Memoire de tous sains.

(a). Sonet, no. 1511.

ff. ii+1+180+iii, foliated (i, ii), 1–181, (182–4). For f. 1, see below. 193 × 135 mm. Written space 95 × 62 mm. 15 long lines. Ruling in red ink. Collation of ff. 2–181: 1¹² 2⁸ 3⁴ (ff. 22–5) 4–7⁸ 8⁴ (ff. 58–61) 9⁸ 10⁸ wants 8 after f. 76 11⁸ 12⁴ (ff. 85–8) 13⁶ wants 6, blank, after f. 93 14–16⁸ 17² (ff. 118, 119) 18⁸ 19⁶ 20–22⁸ 23⁸ wants 8, blank, after f. 164 24¹⁰ wants 10, blank, after f. 173 25⁸. *Lettre bâtarde* is used for catchwords. Fifteen pictures, 11-line and (f. 14) 12-line: seven (formerly eight) in art. 5 (at terce one of the shepherds is a woman: none missing); one before each of arts. 2, 6–9, 10 (B.V.M. and Child), 11 (Trinity), 14a. Initials: (i) blue or red patterned in white on decorated gold grounds; (ii) 2-line, as (i); (iii) 1-line, gold on blue and red grounds patterned in white. Picture pages have continuous framed borders. All other pages have a border the height of the written space in the outer margin: the pattern on versos is a mirror image of the pattern on rectos. Line fillers of blue and red patterned in white, with gold infilling. Capital letters in the ink of the text filled with pale yellow. Binding of red morocco covered with fleur-de-lis and other gilt ornament, s. xvii.

Written in France. Three obliterated shields in the lower border, f. 26. f. 1 is a parchment frontispiece added in s. xvii, blank on the verso and bearing on the recto the title 'LOFFICE DE LA / VIERGE MARIE / POVR TOVS LE TEMPS / DE LANNEE' in a panel below the arms of Anne of Austria (1601–66) held by putti. Another armorial shield (?) has been cut from the foot of f. 1. Numbers and marks inside the covers include, in front, '1418' (cancelled) and '1389' and, at the back, 'Axa+', 'Pp. Yy' (cancelled) and 'Aa Pxp+'. A pasted-down strip of an English bookseller's catalogue, s. xviii, inside the back cover. 'Nº 2 Roche mss', f. 1. Phillipps MS. 3898.¹ Sold by W. H. Robinson Ltd. to J. Hely-Hutchinson in Feb. 1947. His gift to Eton in June 1954.

¹ MSS. 3898–3901 are marked in the Phillipps catalogue as 'Roche MSS.': 'Possibly James Roche of Cork: he sold Add. MS. 19869 to the British Museum in 1854' (A. N. L. Munby, *Phillipps Studies*, iii. 154).

267. *Horae B.V.M.*   s. XV/XVI

1. ff. 1–6ᵛ Full calendar in French in gold, red, and blue, the two colours alternating for effect.

Feasts in gold include 'Saint leu. S' gille' and 'Saint denis', 1 Sept., 9 Oct.

2. ff. 7–10ᵛ Sequentiae of the Gospels.

'Protector in te sperancium . . .' after John.

3. ff. 10ᵛ–13ᵛ Oratio valde deuota ad beatissimam uirginem mariam. Obsecro te . . . Et michi famulo tuo . . .

4. ff. 13ᵛ–16ᵛ Oratio deuota beatissime uirginis marie. O intemerata . . . orbis terrarum. De te enim . . . Masculine forms.

5. ff. 16ᵛ, 25–79 Secuntur hore beatissime uirginis marie. secundum vsum Romanum.

Hours of the Cross and of the Holy Spirit worked in. No break before the Advent office, f. 74.

6. ff. 80–91ᵛ Penitential psalms and (f. 87ᵛ) litany.

Twelve martyrs: . . . (12) eutropi. Fourteen confessors: . . . (14) guillerme. Twelve virgins: . . . (9) genouefa . . .

7. ff. 92–119ᵛ Office of the dead.

8. ff. 17–24 Passio domini nostri ihesu cristi secundum Iohannem. Egressus est dominum . . . posuerunt ihesum. Deo gratias.

John 18, 19. Paragraphed at 18: 28, 19: 5, 13, 25. These leaves, one complete quire, are misplaced. Their proper place is either here or before art. 2.

9. f. 120ʳᵛ A memoria of Holy Trinity.

10. ff. 120ᵛ–122 Sensuiuent les oroisons saint gregoire.

Seven Oes.

11. ff. 122–30 Memoriae of SS. Michael, John Baptist, John Evangelist, Peter and Paul, James, Laurence, Nicholas, Anne, Mary Magdalene, Katherine, Margaret, Barbara (Gaude barbara beata summe polens . . .: *RH*, no. 6711), Apollonia, Genovefa, Maria Jacobi and Maria Salome jointly (O sorores egregie . . .).

12. ff. 130ᵛ–131ᵛ Stabat mater dolorosa . . .

13. f. 132ʳᵛ Aue cuius conceptio . . . *RH*, no. 1744.

ff. i+132+iv. 165×110 mm. Written space 90×55 mm. 23 long lines. Collation: 1⁶ 2⁸ 3² (ff. 15, 16) 4–9⁸ (ff. 25–72) 10⁸ wants 8, blank after f. 79 11–15⁸ 16⁸ (ff. 17–24) 17⁸ 18⁶. Written in *lettre bâtarde*. Two full-page rectangular pictures in art. 5, before matins of Holy Cross (f. 44ᵛ: Christ carries his Cross) and matins of Holy Spirit (f. 46ᵛ: the disciples meet one another?). Nineteen 18–20-line pictures, ten in art. 5, two of them before matins of Cross and Holy Spirit, and one before each of arts. 2–4, 6 (David and Uriah), 7–11. Twenty smaller pictures, fifteen in art. 12, four at the paragraphs in art. 8

(Betrayal, Crowning with thorns, Scourging, and the wounded Christ), and one before art. 13. Occupations of the months and signs of the zodiac in the lower border of each page of art. 1. Initials: (i) 3-line or 2-line, pink, violet, or blue and white on grounds of gold paint and red patterned in gold paint; (ii) either as (i), but without gold paint as a ground, or of gold paint on a blue or a red ground, patterned in gold paint. Line fillers treated like initials of type (ii). Capital letters in the ink of the text filled with pale yellow. A continuous framed border of rich decoration on every page: the borders vary in colour and design, but are devised usually so that the pattern and the colour scheme match on facing pages: a forest full of monkeys is on the double opening where lauds begins (ff. 35^v–36). Inscribed scrolls in the ornament on five double openings: ff. 8^v–9, Espoir en dieu; f. 11^v, Aue regina celorum . . .; f. 12, Alma redemptoris mater . . .; ff. 27^v–28, Alma redemptoris mater . . .; f. 30^v, Regina celi letare . . .; f. 31, Aue gracia plena . . .; f. 45^v, Adoramus te criste . . .; f. 46, Veni sancte spiritus . . . Binding of s. xvi ex., tooled all over in blind: cf. G. D. Hobson, *Les Reliures à la fanfare*, 1935, pl. xxiib for a binding of rather similar pattern and the same Oiseau passant, Papillon, and Grande marguerite stamps.

Written in France. A conjoint *A* and *R* (?) in a blue shield at the foot of ff. 25, 33, and 80. 'N° 100 De la bibliotheque de feu M^r de foille (?) 'ancien chevalier et homme de lettres' achetee en 1796 par B . . . .', inside the end cover. 'N° 100', f. i^v. 'Francis Fry / Bristol' and the relevant slip from a sale catalogue, s. xix, inside the front cover: the catalogue says this is from the 'choice collection of the late Mr Scarisbrick'.[1] Bought by John Hely-Hutchinson from Messrs. Maggs in Nov. 1946: his gift to Eton in 1954.

268. *Julius Caesar* s. xv^2

[G]alia est omnis diuisa in partes tres . . . quarum laudibus et uirtute. Finis.

Book 2, f. 13; 3, f. 20; 4, f. 25^v; 5, f. 31^v; 6, f. 42^v; 7, f. 51; 8, f. 67^v; 9, f. 76^v; 10, f. 92; 11, f. 102; 12, f. 125^v; 13, f. 142^v; 14, f. 162. The passage[1] '[E]xceptus est Ce. aduentus . . . facile obtineri' (sect. 51, 52. 1–3 of bk. 8) is misplaced as the beginning of bk. 9, as in Florence, Laur., Plut. lat. 68. 8 and very many later manuscripts: 'Litteris', properly the first word of bk. 9, begins a new paragraph. Except at this point there is no paragraphing within books. 'Gaii' expunged at the end of bk. 6. f. 171^v blank.[2]

ff. i+171+i. Fine smooth parchment at first; later it is flecked on hairsides. 335 × 235 mm. Written space 220 × 125 mm. 36 long lines. Vertical bounders are double and ruled with hard point (quire 2, pencil). The horizontal lines to guide the scribe are in light-brown ink. Collation: 1–7^{10} 8^8 9–16^{10} 17^8 18^6 wants 6, blank. Quires 1–17 signed at the end A–R. Upright humanistic script. Initials and headings to books omitted: the space for the initial on f. 1 is 9-line and for other initials normally 6-line. Binding of brown morocco gilt on the spine and round the edges, with '.C.IVL.CAES. / .COMMENT. / .IO.BAP.AEGN. / .MANV. / SCR.' on the front and '.INIMICI. MEI. MEA. / .MICHI.NON.ME. / .MICHI.' on the back: no. xx in the list of bindings done for Thomas Maioli in G. D. Hobson, *Maioli, Canivari and others*, 1926, p. 73, and described by H. M. Nixon, *Twelve Books in Fine Bindings from the Library of J. W. Hely-Hutchinson*, Roxburghe Club, 1953, pp. 20–1.

Written in Italy. The script is probably Ferrarese.[3] The binding appears to record that the owner before Thomas Mahieu (Maioli, †c. 1585) was the Venetian humanist Giovanni

---

[1] Not in the sale of Charles Scarisbrick at Christie's, 26 Nov. 1860.

[2] Not examined by Virginia Brown, *The Textual Transmission of Caesar's Civil War* (Mnemosyne, Suppl. xxiii), 1972, but listed there on p. 64. Professor Brown saw the manuscript in 1972 and kindly allows me to quote from her letter of 9 July to the librarian, that this is a 'conflated text of M and N . . . unique in that it shows neither the omission at 2. 17. 2 nor the transposition at 2. 18. 5'; probably therefore 'copied from a contaminated exemplar which had been corrected'.

[3] Information from Dr. A. de la Mare.

Baptista Egnazio, 1470–1553. Armorial book-plate inside the cover of Guy de Sève de Rochechouart, 1640–1724, bishop of Arras. Sold in June 1750 after the death of his nephew Guy de Sève, to the Paris bookseller, Prault. Bought (from him?) by the Marquis de Migieu:[1] 'Demigieu 1752' inside the back cover. No. 44 *bis* in his catalogue, A.D. 1760, printed by H. Omont in *Revue des Bibliothèques*, xi (1901), 235–96 (cf. p. 256). Armorial book-plate inside the front cover of the Richard family of Dijon, dated 1809. Landau-Finaly sale at Sotheby's, 12 July 1948, lot 33 (the sale catalogue, pl. iv shows the front cover and spine), to John Hely-Hutchinson. Given by him to Eton in June 1954.

280. *Fragmenta* s. XIII–XV in.

A guard-book put together in 1972 contains pieces removed from bindings bearing Oldham's roll HM. a. 14. These were used by a binder in the last years of s. xvi: cf. Birley, p. 245. The books in question are Fe. 1.4, 5, 7, Fg. 1.4, 5, 6, Fh. 1.3, 4, 6.

1. Nos. 1a–d, 2b, 5b, 6a–d, 7a, b, 8a–d, 9 are part of the Berkshire assize file of Hugh Huls.

Probably all the pieces are near in date to no. 7a, a writ dated at Westminster, 2 Oct. 10 (Henry IV), bidding Hugh Huls and Roger Norton, justices, take an assize of novel disseisin: cf. *Calendar of Patent Rolls 1408–13*, p. 479 (24 Oct. 1408). Nos. 6c and 8c are two parts of one piece 'anno 5', mentioning Old Windsor. No. 6a is 'anno 5' and no. 6b 'anno 7'. No. 1a is a list of twenty-four jurors, the first of them Mr. Henry Fetiplace. No. 1c may be the bottom part of no. 5b, which is headed 'Assisa de ten' in Esthanney' and lists nearly the same jurors as no. 1a. No. 2b is a list of thirty-two jurors headed 'Assisa de ten' in Abyndon'. No. 8a is a list of jurors in Woolhampton and no. 8d is headed 'Assisa de Ten' in Wolham[pton]'. No. 9 is an Abingdon document. The clerk's name appears at the end of five pieces: 1b, 'Haseley; 1d, 'Lynster'; 6a, d, 'Roderham'; 7a, 'Byllynf''.

Nos. 1d, 6a, b, 6c+8c, 7a, b are complete or nearly complete pieces.

2. No. 2a is a strip of a handsome noted breviary, s. xiv. MS. 220, no. XIX, is another piece of the same book and other pieces still remain in bindings, for example in Fb. 1.8 and Fe. 1.6.

3. Nos. 3a+3b, 4a+4b, 5a+MS. 220, no. XVI, form three more or less complete membranes of rolls, s. xiii[1].

No. 3a+3b. A membrane of the coram rege roll for Hilary term, 1238, containing nos. 148c–149a in *Curia Regis Rolls*, xvi (at press). The two other membranes 'come from the Bench essoin roll for 1224 Mich.'.[2]

---

[1] The note by de Migieu (?) on f. i has no authority probably, apart from the final entry that 'Mr Prault libraire a Paris 'en 1751'' was the last owner.

[2] Information from Mr. C. A. F. Meekings, who tells me that the assize files for Henry IV and Henry V, the roll for 1238 and the essoin rolls for the 1220's were among records kept in the Chapter House at Westminster and not in the Tower of London. 'It looks therefore as if the parchment was in a lot got from Westminster not long before Agarde began his labours which were in part designed to guard against this sort of thing by extensive listing.'

EVESHAM. ALMONERY MUSEUM

Psalterium s. xiv¹

1. ff. 2–7^v Calendar in blue, red, and black, of the Benedictine abbey of Evesham.

Collated by F. Wormald, *English Benedictine Kalendars after A.D. 1100*, ii (HBS lxxxi, 1946), 27–38. The word 'pape' and feasts of St. Thomas of Canterbury erased. The outside sheet of quire 1, ff. 1, 8, was perhaps left blank at first, but only a very small portion of f. 8 remains. The recto of f. 1 contains: in eleven lines, probably by the main hand, an abbreviated office ending with the collect 'Deus qui pro nobis filium tuum crucis patibulum . . .'; scribbles of s. xvii, including the name John Bone and a quotation from Chrysostom in Greek.

2. ff. 9–140 Psalter, beginning imperfectly at Ps. 2: 13, Cum exarserit.

Two leaves are missing besides the first, one after f. 18 with part of Ps. 17 and one after f. 111 with Pss. 109: 1–111: 1.

3. ff. 140–53 Six ferial canticles, Te deum, Benedicite, Benedictus, Magnificat, Nunc dimittis, Quicumque vult.

4. ff. 153–157^v Litany.

Thirty-nine martyrs: . . . (30–6) Alban, Edmund, Oswald, Kenelm, Kanute, Edward, Wistan (doubled). Forty-four confessors: . . . (12–16) Dunstan, Edmund, Egwin (doubled), Cuthbert, Odulf . . . (29) Ethelwold . . . (33) Benedict (doubled) . . . (35) Credan. Ends imperfectly in the prayer 'Deus qui es sanctorum splendor . . .'.

5. Nearly all the text is missing on the seven leaves after f. 157, but ff. 159, 160 are identifiable as fragments of the office of the dead.

6. Binding leaves: (*a*) formerly the wrapper, a leaf of the chronicle of Florence of Worcester, s. xii¹; (*b*) part of a leaf of Thomas Aquinas, Catena aurea, s. xiv.

(*a*) agrees closely with the Worcester copy, now Corpus Christi College, Oxford, 157, pp. 248/28–250, col. 2/16: A.D. 532, here entirely derived from Marianus Scotus, *PL* cxlvii. 736/25–739/10. 375×280 mm. Written space 270×180 mm. 2 cols. 39 lines. Ruled in pencil with double vertical bounders and three lines between columns. Purple *D* of *Dionysius*. (*b*). Luke 15: 19–22 and commentary.

ff. v+164+v. 160×103 mm. Written space 113×67 mm. 22 long lines: 2 cols., ff. 153–7. Collation: 1⁸ 2¹² wants 1 and 12 3–4¹² 5¹⁴ 6¹² 7¹⁰ 8¹² 9¹⁰ 10¹⁰+1 leaf after 9 (f. 110) 11¹² wants 1 before f. 112 12–14¹² 15⁶: less than half 15¹,² (ff. 159, 160) and only very small portions of 1⁸, 14¹², 15³⁻⁶ (ff. 8, 158, 161–4) remain. Initials: (i) beginning Pss. 26, 38, 51, 52, 68, 80, 97, 101, in colour, historiated, on gold and coloured grounds, with prolongations into the margins which form continuous borders: ivy-leaf terminals: some grotesques in the borders; (ii) 2-line, in colour on gold and coloured grounds, decorated and with prolongations as (i), but round three sides of the page only; (iii) 1-line, blue with red ornament or gold with pink ornament. Bound at the British Museum in 1960: the former wrapper is bound in (art. 6*a*). Secundo folio (f. 9) *Cum exarserit*.

Written in England for use in the abbey of Evesham. Deposited in the British Museum in 1938 by the trustees of the Prideaux-Brune (St. Austell) estate: sold by them at Sotheby's, 2 Feb. 1960, lot 256.

EXETER. CATHEDRAL

Catalogues: (i) *CMA* ii. 55–6; (ii) of 1811, printed by R. Botfield, *Notes on Cathedral Libraries*, 1849, pp. 132–7. The numbers on the manuscripts at the head of the spine and inside the cover are the Botfield numbers.

The following in *CMA* are now missing: 3, Dictionarium, seu Glossarium Latinum, mutilum; 5, Ciceronis Rhetorica, Liber elegantissime scriptus; 6 (ii), Breve Compendium super octo Libros Physicorum Aristotelis;[1] 7, Cicero de Fato / Somnium Scipionis / Macrobius in Somnium Scipionis / Timaeus Platonis / In calce Libri adjicitur tractatus quidam de Morte Apostoli, seu de Pomo;[2] 10, SS. Bibliorum Lat. ex versione B. Hieronymi duo Volumina, nonnihil mutilata; 11 (i), Collectanea Liber Gallicus, per Anonymum.

Manuscripts 'which in one way or another have an historical interest' are noticed in HMC, *Report on Manuscripts in Various Collections*, iv (1907), 27–34, especially 3508, 3509, 3512, 3514, 3533. Schenkl notices 3507 and 3525.

L. J. Lloyd and A. M. Erskine, *The Library of Exeter Cathedral*, 1967, includes facsimiles of MS. 3500, f. 108, MS. 3501, f. 76ᵛ, MS. 3505, f. 1, MS. 3507, f. 65, and MS. 3508, f. 11.

3500. *Exon Domesday*   1086 (?)

'The senior survivor of the mass of original documents produced in connection with' the Domesday inquest of 1086 (R. W. Finn, *Domesday Studies, The 'Liber Exoniensis'*, 1964, p. 1).[3] Printed by the Record Commissioners in 1816, *Libri censualis vocati Domesday-Book, Additamenta ex codic. antiquiss.*, pp. 1–494, and described there briefly on p. ix. Ralph Barnes wrote on f. (ii) 'In the Year 1816 This Book was printed . . . from a transcript made by me Ralph Barnes Chapter Clerk' and 'Bound 29 May 1816'. Facsimiles of ff. 103 and 313 in *Pal. Soc.*, 2nd series, ii, pls. 70, 71; of ff. 47, 531 in *VCH. Wiltshire*, ii (1955), pls. opposite pp. 169, 217; also of f. 108 (see above) and as noted below in the notes on sections *a–c*.

Before 1816 Exon Domesday was in two volumes of 258 and 275 leaves and had an early sixteenth-century foliation, i–xii, 1–520.[4] The leaves were then in wild confusion. Barnes, aided by David Casley and by notes written in the manuscript itself mainly by Charles Lyttelton, dean of Exeter 1748–62, put them in better order, renumbered them,[5] and wrote a serial letter on the first leaf of each of the 103 sections into which the manuscript appeared to fall.[6]

---

[1] The Breve Compendium is set down wrongly in *CMA* as the second item in no. 6 (now MS. 3526). It is in fact the first item in the Trinity manuscript (see footnote 2).

[2] Now Trinity College, Cambridge, O. 2. 11, as Dr. B. C. Barker-Benfield tells me.

[3] Referred to below as Finn.

[4] Notes by Barnes on ff. 537, 541 dated 1810, refer to the old division into two volumes and the old foliation. He says that f. 221 is missing. It was recovered a little later, numbered 347, and printed in edn., pp. 326*, 327*.

[5] Up to 494 the numbers at present in use have been underlined.

[6] The present order was arrived at gradually. The stage Barnes had reached in 1812 is shown by his account of Exon Domesday made in that year and now in the Chapter Library, by purchase in 1974. One adjustment to the numbering took place after the

The following table shows the Barnes letter-mark, the subject, and the make-up of each of these sections, new and (in brackets) old leaf numbers, and blank pages. An asterisk shows that the section is referred to in the notes which follow. Braces against letter-marks show that the sense runs on from one section to the next. The sections which do not or probably do not correspond to quires of the original manuscript are referred to in the notes: see *f, h, k, n, 2b, u, 4d, o*.[1]

Letter-mark	Subject	Make-up	New and old leaf numbers	Blank pages
a*	Wiltshire Geld A	6	1–6 (240–5)	4–6^v
b*	(a) Wiltshire Geld B (7–9^v)	6	7–12 (288–93)	10^{rv}
	(b) Dorset boroughs (11–12^v)			
c*	Wiltshire Geld C	4	13–16 (276–9)	16^v
d	Dorset Geld	8	17–24 (294–301)	24^v
e	'Dominicatus regis in Dorseta'	four	25–8 (247–50)	
f*	(a) Queen Matilda and king (29, 30)	see note	29–35 (251–7)	32^v, 33^v, 34–35^v
	(b) Knights holding from queen (31, 32)			
	(c) Ida, countess of Boulogne (33)			
g	Cerne	4 wants 4	36–8 (258–60)	
h*	(a) Abbotsbury (39–40^v)	see note	39–46 (261–8)	41^v, 42^v, 45^v–46^v
	(b) Athelney (41)			
	(c) Tavistock (42)			
	(d) Milton (43–5)			
i	William of Mohun	4 wants 4	47–9 (269–71)	
k*	(a) Roger Arundel (50–2)	see note	50–3 (272–5)	52^v, 53^v
	(b) Serlo of Burcy (53)			
l }	Widow of Hugh fitz Grip	4	54–7 (280–3)	
m }	,,	4	58–61 (284–7)	
n*	Walter of Claville	one	62 (204)	
o	Lists of hundreds	4 wants 3	63, 64, leaf without modern number (302, 303, 306)	Leaf without modern number
p	Devon Geld	8 wants 8	65–71 (311–17)	71^v
q*	Cornish Geld	two	72, 73 (304, 305)	73^v
r	Somerset Geld	8	75–82 (i–viii)	
s }	King, in Devonshire	8	83–90 (113–20)	
t }	,,	2	91, 92 (121–2)	92^{rv}
u	,,	8 wants 7, 8	93–8 (422–7)	98^v
w }	King, in Cornwall and Somerset	8	99–106 (141–8)	
x }	,,	one	107 (183)	
y	Queen Matilda	8 wants 6–8	108–12 (438–42)	112^v
z	Queen Edith	4 wants 4	113–15 (187–9)	115^v
2a	Wulfweard Wite	one	116 (26)	
2b*	Exeter	four	117–20 (307–10)	
2c	Coutances	4	121–4 (318–21)	
2d }	,,	8	125–32 (322–9)	
2e* }	,,	6	133–8 (135–40)	137^v–138^v

book was bound, when it was seen that seven leaves after f. 494 were out of place: the next thirty-one leaves are foliated 519–25, 495–518.

[1] I have used the word section as a term for divisions indicated by Barnes and the word quire when referring specifically to quires of the original manuscript.

Letter-mark	Subject	Make-up	New and old leaf numbers	Blank pages
2f	Coutances	8	139–46 (123–30)	
2g	,,	4	147–50 (131–4)	
2h*	,,	4 wants 3	151–3 (52–4)	152^v–153^v
2i	Bishop Osmund	one	154 (25)	
2k*	Bishop Giso of Wells	6	155–60 (231–6)	155^{rv}, 160^v
2l	Glastonbury	8	161–8 (330–7)	
2m*	(a) Glastonbury (169–73)	see note	169–75 (106–12)	
	(b) Winchester (173^v–5^v)			
2n*	Tavistock	6 wants 6	176–81 (341–6)	
2o	Buckfast	two	182–3 (347–8)	
2p	Horton	one	184 (338)	
2q	Bath	three	185–7 (49–51)	187^v
2r*	Muchelney	4	Leaf without modern number, 188–90 (102–5)	Leaf without modern number, 190^{rv}
2s	Athelney	2	191–2 (41, 42)	192^{rv}
2t*	Shaftesbury	one	193 (27)	193^r
2u*	Terrae elemosinarum	two	194–5 (339–40)	
2w*	,,	4 wants 4	196–8 (14–16)	
2x*	Bishop of Exeter in Cornwall	three	199–201 (393, 428–9)	201^v
2y	Various Cornish churches	8	202–9 (430–7)	207^v–208^r, 209^{rv}
2z	Robert of Mortain	8	210–17 (348–55)	
3a	,,	8 wants 7, 8	218–23 (378–9, 374–7)	223^v
3b	,,	10	224–33 (356–65)	
3c	,,	8	234–41 (366–73)	
3d	,,	8 wants 5–7	242–6 (388–92)	246^{rv}
3e	,,	8	247–54 (380–7)	
3f	,,	20	255–74 (66–85)	
3g	,,	8 wants 8	275–81 (86–91, 93)[1]	281^v
3h	Eustace	4	282–5 (37–40)	283^v–285^v
3i*	Hugh	two	286–7 (35, 36)	
3k	Baldwin	8	288–95 (394–401)	
3l	,,	8	296–303 (402–9)	
3m	,,	8	304–11 (410–17)	
3n	,,	4	312–15 (418–21)	
3o	Juhel	8	316–23 (451–8)	
3p	,,	8	324–31 (462–9)	
3q	,,	three	332–4 (459–61)	
3r	Ralph of La Pommeraye	8	335–42 (470–1, 473–8)	
3s	,,	two	343–4 (479–80)	344^v
3t	Walter (Walscinus) of Douai	8	345–52 (219–26)	
3u	,,	4 wants 4	353–5 (184–6)	
3w	William of Mohun	8	356–63 (196–203)	
3x	,,	two	364–5 (217–18)	365^v
3y*	William of Falaise	6 wants 2	366–70 (61–5)	370^{rv}
3z	Alfred d'Epaignes	4 + 1 leaf after 4	371–5 (9–12, 8)	375^v

[1] There is no number 92.

Letter-mark	Subject	Make-up	New and old leaf numbers	Blank pages
4a	Odo fitz Gamelin	6	376–81 (43–8)	380^v–381^v
4b	Thurstan fitz Rolf	6	382–7 (55–60)	385^{rv}, 386^v–387^v
4c ⎫	Goscelm and Walter	4	388–91 (481–4)	
4d* ⎬	,,	two	392–3 (485, 499)	
4e* ⎭	,,	4 + 1 leaf after 4	394–8 (486–9, 13)	398^v
4f* ⎫	W. Capra	four	399–402 (495–8)	
4g* ⎭	,,	4	403–6 (517–20)	406^v
4h* ⎫	Tetbald fitz Berneric	one	407 (502)	
4h2* ⎬	,,	one	408 (472)	
4h3* ⎭	,,	2	409–10 (493–4)	
4i*	Ruald Adobed	four	411–14 (503–6)	
4k	W. de Poilleau	4	415–18 (513–16)	418^v
4l* ⎫	Robert of Albemarle	one	419 (492)	
4l2 ⎭	,,	two	420–1 (490–1)	
4m	Roger of Courseulles	8	422–9 (94–101)	
4n	,,	8 wants 8	430–6 (1–7)	436^{rv}
4o*	(a) Edward of Salisbury, sheriff of Wilts. (437) (b) William of Eu (438–9)	4	437–40 (ix–xii)	437^v, 439^v–440^v
4p	Roger Arundel	6 wants 6	441–5 (172–6)	445^v
4q	Gilbert fitz Thorald and four others	4	446–9 (177–80)	446^v, 448^r, 449^v
4r	Matthew of Mortagne	2	450–1 (181–2)	451^{rv}
4s	Serlo of Burcy	4	452–5 (213–16)	454^v–455^v
4t	Franci taini	8	456–63 (17–24)	
4u	,,	4	464–7 (227–30)	467^v
4w	Nicholas, Godebold, etc.	8 wants 7	468–74 (28–34)	474^{rv}
4x	Servientes regis	8 wants 7, 8	475–80 (190–5)	
4y ⎫	Angli taini	8	481–8 (500, 507–12, 501)	485^v–486^r
4z ⎭	,,	6	489–94 (208, 207, 209–12)	494^{rv}
5a ⎫	Terrae occupatae	8	495–502 (443–50)	
5b ⎬	,,	8	503–10 (149–56)	
5c ⎬	,,	8	511–18 (157–64)	
5d ⎭	,,	8 wants 8	519–25 (165–71)	525^v
5e*	Geld in Somerset, and holdings of Glastonbury and St. Petrock	four	526–9 (237–9, 246)	529^{rv}
5f*	Various holders	two	530–1 (205–6)	530^r, 531^v
(5g)*	Table	one	532	

Summary account of the sections

Quire of 20 leaves. *3f.*

Quire of 10 leaves. *3b.*

Quires of 8 leaves. *d, r, s, 2d, f, l, z, 3e, k–m, o, p, r, t, w, 4m, t, y, 5a–c.*

Quires of 8 leaves with leaves missing.[1] *p, u, y, 3a, d, g, w, x, 5d.* See also below the notes on *2u, b, m, w, 4d, e.*

Quires of 6 leaves. *a, b, 2e, k, 4a, b, z.*

Quires of 6 leaves with leaves missing.[1] *2n, 3y.* See also below the note on *4h.*

Quires of 4 leaves. *c, l, m, 2c, g, r, 3h, n, 4c, g, k, o, q, s, u.* See also below the note on *f.*

Quires of 4 leaves with single leaves added. *3z, 4e.*

[1] Except in *3y* all these leaves were probably blank leaves.

Quires of 4 leaves with leaves missing.[1] *g, i, o, z, 2h, 3u.* See also below the notes on
k, 2w.
Quires of 2 leaves. *t, w, 2s, 4h3* (?).
Sections of uncertain construction. *e, f, h, k, q, 2o, q, u, x, 4d, f, h, i, l, 5e, f.* See the
notes for most of these.
Sections consisting of one leaf. *x, 2a, i, p, t.* See also below the notes on *f, h, n, 4h, l.*
Sections in the same order now as before Barnes's rearrangement. *e–k; s, t; 2f, g; 2n, o;
3b, c; 3f, g; 3k–n; 3r, s* (except that before 1816 *4h2* came between the second and third
leaves of *3r*); *4p, q, r.*

Notes on the sections

Eleven quires are marked 'E' in an early and careful hand at the foot of the first recto:
w, 2f, 3f, h, t, w, y, 4a, m, o,[2] x.

In ten quires an otherwise blank leaf has on it the words 'Consummatum est' (f. 155^r 'Consummatum est [. . . .] Wite', the last word erased, but legible; f. 494^v 'Comsumatum est').
The leaves in question are the last versos of *2y, 3y, 4b, q, r, s, u, w, z* and the first recto of
2k. Probably the words show that all the matter for the quire had been gathered in and
that the blank space was to remain blank.[3] In one quire, *4z,* 'Consummatum est usque
huc' is written in the margin of f. 490 opposite a blank space of three lines, which lies
between the accounts of the holdings of English thanes in Devon and in Somerset.

At the beginning of some quires linked by subject with the preceding quire the scribe
took care to be more specific than usual: 'Episcopus constantiensis' instead of 'Episcopus'
(*2d, f*); 'Rogerus de curcella' instead of 'Rogerus' (*4n*); headings 'Cornubia' (*3c, e*) and
'Cornugallia' (*3f*); 'Abbas glastingeberiensis' instead of 'Abbas' (*2m*); heading 'Mansiones
de comitatu' (*x*).

a. Much smaller format and script than elsewhere: cf. the facsimile of f. 1^v in *VCH.
Wiltshire*, ii, pl. opposite p. 180. Poor thin parchment, a hole on f. 2. Written space
c. 148 × 105 mm. 40 long lines. Frequent 'd.m.' in the margins of ff. 1–3. This *nota bene*
sign, meaning probably *dignum memoria*, occurs twice in quire *b*, but not elsewhere in
Exon Domesday. It is a not unusual sign in manuscripts of s. xi ex. and s. xii and is particularly common in Salisbury Cathedral manuscripts of the late eleventh and early
twelfth century. f. 529 followed *a* before 1816 and to judge from its size belongs with it
and not with *5e.*

b, c. See N. R. Ker, 'The beginnings of Salisbury Cathedral Library', *Medieval Learning
and Literature, Essays presented to R. W. Hunt*, 1975, p. 35, for these two quires which
are largely in the hand of a professional (?) scribe employed in making the early collection
of books at Salisbury Cathedral. In *b* his hand appears to precede writing in a hand which
occurs elsewhere in Exon Domesday, but it does not necessarily have precedence: the
quire may have been turned round and have been originally in the order 10–12, 7–9, with
10 left blank. The 'Salisbury scribe' and the scribe or scribes working with him had much
more matter than they could fit into the leaves as ruled with 20 lines and, except on f. 7^r,
they did not attempt to follow the ruling. Quire *b* has a crease down its length, as though
it had been folded at some time. A similar crease can be seen on ff. 50–2: cf. the note on
section *k.*

Facsimiles of ff. 8, 14 are in *VCH. Wiltshire*, ii, opposite pp. 181, 216, and of f. 9 by Ker,
loc. cit., pl. IIIa.

f. ff. 29, 30, 34, 35 are a quire of 4 leaves. Probably ff. 31–3, like some at least of the single
leaves now in other quires, were the first halves of bifolia originally, ff. 31, 32 the first two
leaves of a quire of 4 and f. 33 the first leaf of a quire of 2. Later someone in need of parchment cut off the blank leaves and the now single leaves were put inside the quire of 4 leaves
for safe keeping.

[1] Except in *3y* all these missing leaves were probably blank leaves.
[2] See below the note on *4o.*
[3] So the editors of *Pal. Soc.* But Finn thought (p. 28) that the words probably referred
to the activities of a corrector.

h. ff. 43–6 are a quire of 4 leaves. There is no reason to suppose that the single leaves for Abbotsbury, Athelney, and Tavistock (ff. 39–42) preceded them or were in this order.

k. ff. 51, 52 are a bifolium and probably ff. 50–2 and a (blank) leaf missing after 52 formed a quire of 4 leaves. There is no reason to suppose that f. 53 belongs here. It shows no sign of the crease visible on ff. 50–2.

n. Evidence from ruling, supported by pricking, shows that this single leaf (f. 62) belongs to the same quire as *5f* (ff. 530–1). It came immediately before f. 530 before 1816.

q. Finn, p. 33, refers to ff. 72–4, but there is no f. 74.

2b and *2x* may have formed one quire of 8 wants 8: cf. Finn, p. 34.

2e. The recto of f. 138 has five erased lines on it, 'Mansiones episcopi [co]nstant[. . . .]': see Finn, p. 29.

2h. A scribe used part of the blank space on f. 153ᵛ to add an account of a holding of the bishop of Bayeux: Finn, p. 131. The same scribe wrote an addition on a blank page of *4n* (f. 436ᵛ). His hand is very like and may well be the same as the main hand of Exchequer Domesday: cf. R. W. Finn in *EHR* lxvi (1951), 561, and V. H. Galbraith, *The Making of Domesday*, 1961, pp. 109–12.

2k. The prickings suggest that the quire began as two bifolia, ff. 156–9. When it was full the scribe took another bifolium for the remaining Wells text and folded its blank second leaf so that it came before f. 156, so converting a 4 into a 6.

2m. Three bifolia and a singleton, f. 171. Probably the singleton was conjoint with a leaf after f. 173 which was discarded because of an error in copying. The text on ff. 173ᵛ– 175ᵛ appears to be a fair copy, unlike the rest of Exon Domesday: see below.

2n. f. 176 is also numbered 177.

2r. This quire of 4 is very obvious because the scribe failed to prick for the third line of writing. The unnumbered leaf has six erased lines on the verso.

2u, w. The prickings show that these sections are really one quire, an 8 with the last three (blank) leaves missing.

2x. The error in binding is noted on ff. 199ᵛ and 200 in a hand of s. xv/xvi or xvi in.

3i. f. 286 has been cut out and then tied on again with string.

3y. The stub of the missing leaf remains after f. 366. The first line began with *T* and the second with *W*.

4d, e. Probably these were one quire of 8 leaves with a now missing (blank) last leaf.

4f. These four leaves should be in the order 399, 401, 402, 400. The correct order is shown by Lyttelton's notes on ff. 399ᵛ, 400ʳᵛ, 401, but was not adopted in the 1816 rebinding or in the edition: cf. *VCH. Devonshire*, i. 376.

4g. These leaves came at the end of the manuscript before 1816. There are worm-holes and the pinmark from a former binding on all of them. The pinmark can be traced back as far as f. 510 of the old foliation, now f. 485.

4h. Probably a quire of 6 leaves with the last two (blank) leaves missing.

4i. A leaf is missing after f. 414: cf. *VCH. Devonshire*, i. 512.

4l. Probably a quire of 6 leaves with the last three (blank) leaves missing.

4o. No doubt this section is really two quires, a 2 (ff. 437, 440) and a 2 (ff. 438–9). f. 438 is marked 'E' at the foot: cf. above.

5e. ff. 526–8 are larger than ff. 1–6 (above, *a*), 529, but much smaller than the rest of the manuscript. 215 × 130 mm. Written space 160 × 115 mm. 19–24 long lines. The continuation of the Somerset geld, above, *r*, is on f. 526ʳᵛ: see *VCH. Somerset*, i. 536–7.

5f. See above the note on *n*.

(5g). Not marked by Barnes. Ruled with 18 long lines. See below.

Exon Domesday is arranged by fiefs and within fiefs by counties, Devon in first place, and the guiding rule for making it seems to have been to provide at least one quire for each holder, the minimum size of quire being probably a single bifolium. The exceptions to this rule are: (1) *4q, t–z, 5f*, where minor holders are grouped together; (2) *2m*, where Glastonbury is in the first half of the quire and the Winchester holdings in Somerset in the second half. *2m* may not be the exception it seems to be, however. The Winchester entry was all written at one time and is in a good small hand which does not seem to occur elsewhere in Exon Domesday. The writing is closer than in other sections—apart from *a–c, 5e*—and is in 21 or 22 lines to the page. Probably the entry was added in a convenient blank space after the rest of Exon Domesday had been completed.

The uniformity of the ruling with twenty widely spaced lines shows that the quires were prepared to a single plan: the variations are in the quality of the ruling, not in its scale.[1] The many hands show that the entries were made in a large centre.[2] The continual changes of hand within fiefs suggest that the material became ready for inscription in the book at different times and was entered by any scribe who happened to be available.[3] The construction of the quires and their ruling show that the scribes sometimes knew beforehand about how much space they would need for a fief.[4] On the other hand, the large number of blank leaves, probably many more once than now, suggests a wait-and-see policy and that the scribes were acting as a rule on some such instructions as these: take a bifolium; when you have filled the first leaf do not go on to the second leaf, but take another bifolium and continue on that; and so on, up to four bifolia.

The order of the quires does not matter much. They are not likely to have been put into a permanent cover until after they had been used for Domesday. Some order then became necessary. It may be indicated for about half the volume by the table on f. 532^{rv} (edn., p. 493). Here the twenty-four heads appear to correspond to the contents of ff. 17–30, 33–46, 65–112, 117–281, 286–7 in the following order: (1) Dominicatus S. Regis:[5] ff. 25–8, 83–107; (2) Terrę Reginę Mathildis: ff. 29, 30, 108–12; (3) Terra Boloniensis comitissę: f. 33; (4) Hugonis comitis: ff. 286–7; (5) Comitis de Moritonio: ff. 210–81; (6) Terrę aeclesiarum in cornubia: ff. 202–9; (7) Terrę Episcopi constantiensis: ff. 121–53; (8) Terrę Osmundi episcopi in Sommerseta: f. 154; (9) Terra Abbatissę Sancti Eduuardi in Sommerseta: f. 193; (10) Terra Gisonis episcopi: ff. 155–60; (11) Terra Walchelini

---

[1] *3l* (ff. 296–303) is poorly ruled, without vertical bounders.

[2] Cf. Finn, pp. 30–2, and his article in *Bulletin of the John Rylands Library*, xli (1959), 363–8, where he distinguishes the work of two main scribes, A (about 700 entries) and G (about 550 entries), and ten minor scribes.

[3] For example, the holdings of Odo fitz Gamelin in Devonshire are set out in the first twenty-four paragraphs of *4a* (edn., pp. 352–7) by eight different scribes, as follows: (1) para. 1; (2) paras. 2, 3, 22; (3) paras. 4, 6, 7, 10–13; (4) para. 5; (5) paras. 8, 9, 15, 16, 19, 21, 23, 24; (6) para. 14; (7) paras. 17, 18; (8) para. 20.

[4] For example, when the scribe came to rule f. 41 he knew that the Athelney entry would take up less than a page. He ruled his lines on the usual scale, but did not bother to go beyond line 13. The entry took up only nine lines in fact.

[5] Stephen?

episcopi in Sommerseta: ff. 173–5; (12) Terra exoniensis episcopi: ff. 117–20, 199–201; (13) Inquisitio Gheldi In Deuenesira. In Cornubia. In Sommerseta. In Dorseta: ff. 65–82, 17–24; (14) Terrę elemosinarum in Deuenesira et Sommerseta: ff. 194–8; (15) Terra Abbatis hortonensis: f. 184; (16) Terrę Cerneliensis abbatię: ff. 36–8; (17) Terrę Mideltonensis abbatię: ff. 43–5; (18) Terrę Abbodesberiensis Abbatię: ff. 39–40; (19) Adeliniensis abbatię in dorseta et somerseta: ff. 41, 191–2; (20) Terra Abbatię de Bada: ff. 185–7; (21) Tauestochensis Abbatię: ff. 42, 176–81; (22) Bulfestrensis Abbatię: ff. 182–3; (23) Glastiniensis Abbatię: ff. 161–72; (24) Micheleniensis Abbatię: ff. 188–90. This can only represent a real order throughout, if an original entry for Winchester between Wells and Exeter was replaced by the present entry on ff. 173–5.[1] Otherwise it is a possible order for forty-nine of the 110(?) quires.

ff. xiv + 532 + xxi. The foliation 1–532 (see above) misses single blank leaves after ff. 64 and 187 and skips the numbers 74 and 177. ff. 533–4 are medieval flyleaves once at the beginning. 280 × 165 mm. Written space c. 187 × 135 mm. 20 long lines to the page, except on ff. 1–16, 526–9, for which see above. The parchment varies in thickness. Collation: see above. Many rather poor hands of Norman type. The only good hands are in sections *b, c, 2m, 5e*, and are probably additions: see above. No coloured initials, apart from a red *I* in *2m* (f. 173ᵛ). Bound in 1816: rebacked.

Presumably at Exeter in the Middle Ages. Borrowed by Brian Duppa: 'Maii: 1669 This Booke was taken forth of the lybrary of the Deane and Chapter of Exeter and by them sent unto the Lord Bᵖ of Sarum. T. Wright' (f. 534ᵛ). Borrowed also by Charles Lyttelton and shown by him to the Society of Antiquaries of London on 22 Jan. 1756, when he read a paper about Exon Domesday to the Society. Lyttelton's notes on the manuscript dated in 1750 and now bound with it as ff. 538–9 were in front of vol. 1 before 1816, as Barnes recorded in the volume referred to above, p. 800, footnote 6.[2]

3501, ff. o, 1–7. Leaves from either end of a gospel book, s. xi², which Bishop Leofric, † 1072, gave to his cathedral, and which was given—except these eight leaves—by the dean and canons of Exeter to Archbishop Matthew Parker in 1566 and by Parker to Cambridge University Library, where it is now Ii. 2. 11. The eight leaves were bound at some later date with MS. 3501, ff. 8–130. For details of the manumissions and other texts on these leaves, s. xi²–xii, see *The Exeter Book of Old English Poetry*, 1933, and N. R. Ker, *Catalogue of Manuscripts containing Anglo-Saxon*, 1957, pp. 28–31 (no. 20).

3501, ff. 8–130. The 'Exeter Book' is reproduced in facsimile and fully described by R. W. Chambers, Max Förster, and Robin Flower, *The Exeter Book of Old English Poetry*, 1933: cf. also Ker, op. cit., p. 153 (no. 116).

The collation in Ker, *Catalogue*, is defective. It should read: 1⁸ wants 1 2⁸ wants 2 after f. 15 3–4⁸ 5⁸ wants 1 before f. 38 6–8⁸ 9⁸ wants 2, 7 after ff. 69, 73 10–11⁸ 12⁸ wants 8 after f. 97 13⁸ 14⁸ wants 1 before f. 106 and 8 after f. 111 15⁸ wants 8 after f. 118 16⁸ wants 8 after f. 125 17 five (ff. 126–30). 2 and 6 in quire 16, and 3 and 7 in quires 6 and 15 are half-sheets. 6 is a half-sheet and the now missing 2 was a half-sheet in quire 2.[3] The

---

[1] See above, pp. 802, 805.

[2] This volume also contains a copy of Lyttelton's paper to the Society of Antiquaries.

[3] In Anglo-Saxon manuscripts the half-sheets are usually the second and seventh or the third and sixth in a quire. Asymmetrical arrangements occur occasionally: Ker, p. xxiv.

fact that a leaf is missing from quire 2 after f. 15 was first firmly established by J. C. Pope, 'The Lacuna in the text of Cynewulf's *Ascension* (*Christ* II, 556b)', *Studies in Language, Literature, and Culture of the Middle Ages and later in honor of Rudolph Willard*, 1969, pp. 210–19. For the leaf missing from quire 15 see A. Bliss and A. J. Frantzen, 'The integrity of *Resignation*', *Review of English Studies*, N.S., xxvii (at press). For the leaf missing from quire 16 see J. C. Pope in *Speculum*, xlix (1974), 615–22.

The borrowers' book of Exeter Cathedral records the loan of the Exeter Book to Edward Lye, 1694–1767, in 1759: 'June 30 1759. The Saxon MSS. Nº 1 was lent to Dʳ Lye for a twelfmonth, the editor of Junius'.

3502. *Ordinale Ecclesiae Exoniensis*   s. xv²

A copy of the ordinal which John de Grandisson, bishop of Exeter 1327–69, drew up for his church in 1337, as appears from the introductory sentences on f. 7. Used by J. N. Dalton in *Ordinale Exon.* i, ii (HBS xxxvii, xxxviii, 1909): I. viii–ix, description; I. ix, text of the 'Iuramentum pro Ministris Ecclesie' added on f. 105ᵛ; I. xxviii–l (even numbers), text of calendar on ff. 1–6ᵛ; I. 1–369, text of ordinal on ff. 7–102; ii. 463–71, text on ff. 103–5, 'Ad sciendum quod kyrie . . . Agnus de dominicis. Explicit ordinale secundum usum Exon' '; ii, pls. i, ii, facsimiles of parts of ff. 12ᵛ, 78ᵛ. Dalton omitted the text on ff. 102–3, 'In Ecclesia Exonie Distinguntur festa. seu Officia diuina per septem gradus. scilicet per Maiora duplicia . . . Ferialia. Maiora duplicia principalia . . .', which differs only slightly from that on f. 11ʳᵛ (edn. i. 15–17). A leaf after f. 91 and nearly half f. 97 are missing: cf. edn. i. 333, 352.

f. v is a leaf of a gradual, s. xiv, with part of the office for the fourth Sunday in Lent. 8 long lines and music.

ff. v+105+iv, foliated (i–v), 1–91, 93–106, (107–10). ff. i, ii, 109, 110 are modern paper. ff. iiiʳ, 108ᵛ were pastedowns and f. v was once pasted to f. iii, as the offset shows. 342 × 240 mm. Written space 250×158 mm. 51 long lines. Collation: 1⁶ 2–11⁸ 12⁸ wants 6 after f. 91 13⁸ 14⁴. Quires 2–4 signed a–c. Written in a non-current upright secretary. Initials: (i) f. 7, 10-line, blue on gold ground, with oak-leaf decoration in colours, including green, and prolongations forming a continuous border: a blank shield in the lower border; (ii) f. 7, 5-line, gold on blue and red ground patterned in white; (iii, iv) 4-line and 2-line, blue with red ornament; (v) 1-line, red or blue. Capital letters in the ink of the text and the heads of tall letters prolonged in the first line on a page are filled with yellow. Contemporary binding of wooden boards covered with brown leather bearing a pattern of fillets, repaired: two strap-and-pin fastenings missing. Secundo folio (f. 8) *familiarem*.

3503. *Euclides, etc.*   s. xiii²

1. ff. 1–96ᵛ Punctus est illud cui non est pars . . . figuraliter componere. Explicit liber euclidis philosophi de arte geometrica continens cccc. lxv proposita et propositiones. et xi porismata preter anxiomata singulis libris premissa. proposita quidem infinitiuis propositiones indicatiuis explicans. Deo gratias.

Propositions in larger and proofs in smaller script, as in Bodleian Auct. F. 3. 13 and Royal Society 28 (*MMBL* i. 232). An omission from the text on f. 31 was added on a slip of parchment now kept in an envelope inside the front cover.

2. ff. 96ᵛ–163ᵛ 'Arismetica Iurdani.' (f. 97) Incipit liber primus arismetice. (*Text*) Unitas est esse rei per se discretio . . . sit possibile. (*Commentary*) Aut enim minor numerat . . . et hoc est quod ostendi debuit.

Jordanus Nemorarius, Arithmetica, in ten books. Thorndike and Kibre. For other manuscripts see *MMBL* i. 231. The added title is in pencil, s. xiii, repeated in ink, f. 97, at foot. Text in larger and commentary in smaller script.

3. ff. 164–217ᵛ 'Musica Boetii.' Prohemium in quo ostenditur musicam naturaliter nobis esse coniunctam. et mores honestare uel euertere. Omnium quidem perceptio . . . non ei coequatur quod monstrat presens descriptio.

PL lxiii. 1167–1300. Scholia in the margins. The added title is in pencil, s. xiii.

ff. iii+218+iii, foliated (i–iii), 1–30, 30*, 31–217. A fragment of a medieval flyleaf with a note of contents on it, s. xiii, 'Continentur in hoc volumine . . .', has been pasted to f. ii. 350×250 mm. Written space 232×138 mm. 2 cols. 22 lines of larger and 44 lines of smaller script. Collation: 1–27¹² 28² (ff. 216–17). Initials: (i) 2-line, red and blue with ornament of both colours; (ii) 1-line, red or blue with ornament of the other colour. 'Bound by White Exeter', f. iᵛ, s. xix. Secundo folio *recte linee*.

Written in England. 'Liber magistri Iohannis Pyttys titulo empcionis prec' duorum marcarum 1455' on a parchment strip pasted to the modern flyleaf, f. ii. 'Hunc librum legauit et dedit Ecclesie Cathedrali Exon'. Magister Iohannes Pyttys. eiusdem Ecclesie Canonicus et Prebendarius remansurum in libraria eiusdem Ecclesie Cathenatum quamdiu durauerit', f. 1, s. xv. Listed in the cathedral inventory of 1506: Oliver, *Lives of the Bishops of Exeter*, p. 367. In 1662 John Wolston and Baldwin Rowcliffe wrote their names in pencil on f. 216. *CMA*, no. 8. 'Nº 5', f. iᵛ.

3504. *Legenda de tempore 'de usu Exoniensis ecclesie'*   s. XIV med.

The first volume of a contemporary copy of the lectionary drawn up by Bishop John de Grandisson for the use of the cathedral church of Exeter. It is annotated by Grandisson himself. The upper margin has been injured by damp. f. 1 begins 'Incipit legenda de usu Exoniensis ecclesie. secundum ordinacionem et abreuiacionem Iohannis de Grandissono episcopi. Et diuiditur in tres partes. Prima pars. continet quicquid legitur de biblia . . . Secunda pars. continet sermones et omelias que pertinent ad temporale . . . Tercia pars. in alio uolumine. continet lecciones proprias sanctorum . . .'.

Part 1 (ff. 1–92ᵛ) and part 2 (ff. 93–279ᵛ) are printed by J. N. Dalton, *Ordinale Exon.* iii (HBS lxiii, 1926), pp. 13–176, and the manuscript is described there on pp. 1–8. The words 'Explicit legenda de tempore. De Sanctis. in alio libro' on f. 279ᵛ (edn., p. 176) are in Grandisson's hand. f. 280 was left blank. A leaf is missing after f. 176 (edn., p. 113). Each leaf and sometimes each page is marked 'ex', bottom right, probably to show that it has been checked (examinatur): cf. edn., pp. 3, 7, 8.

ff. ii+279+iv, foliated (i, ii), 1–175, 177–284. ff. 281–4 are medieval end-leaves. 365× 230 mm. Written space 250×150 mm. 34 long lines. Collation: 1–11⁸ 12⁴ (ff. 89–92) 13–22⁸ 23⁸ wants 4 after f. 175 24–35⁸ 36⁴. For the quire signatures—partly in red ink— see edn., pp. 2, 3. Initials: (i) f. 1, 4-line, blue patterned in white on gold and pink ground, decorated with Grandisson's arms (cf. edn., p. 3) and with prolongations into the margins; (ii) 3-line or 2-line, as (i), but the prolongations are short; (iii) 2-line, blue with red ornament. Bound in wooden boards, s. xx: for the old binding still existing in 1926 see edn., p. 1. For a bookmarker see edn., p. 2. Secundo folio *lex. et uerbum*.

Written for John de Grandisson and given by him to his cathedral church, together with MS. 3505, on 25 Mar. 1366: '[Ego I. de G. Exon' Do ecclesie Exon' librum istum cum pari suo de Sanctis.] Anno consecracionis mee xxxix In festo Annunciacionis dominice Ma[nu mea]' is in Grandisson's hand at the head of f. 1: the words in brackets, lost apparently in the course of recent repairs, are recorded in edn., p. 4. The fifth of nine books entered in the inventory of various things 'que nouo scaccario continentur' in 1506 (Oliver, *Lives*, p. 350): the secundo folio agrees. 'No 3' on a paper label inside the cover.

3505. *Legenda de sanctis de usu ecclesiae Exoniensis*   s. XIV med.

A companion volume to MS. 3504 and written in the same hand. It is annotated by Grandisson himself. f. 1 begins 'Incipit tercia pars legende Exon' usus de sanctis. compilate per Iohannem de Grandissono episcopum'.

Printed by J. N. Dalton, *Ordinale Exon*. iii (HBS lxiii, 1926), pp. 177–470 and described on pp. 1, 2, 8–12. A leaf is missing after f. 65 (edn., p. 258). Many leaves are and probably all were marked 'ex', as in MS. 3504, q.v.: cf. edn., pp. 9–11.

ff. iv+231+iii, foliated (i–iv), 1–64, 66–235. Dimensions and number of lines as in MS. 3504. Collation: 1–8⁸ 9⁸ wants 1 before f. 66 10–28⁸. For the quire signatures—partly in red ink—see edn., p. 9. Initials as in MS. 3504: the initial on f. 1 contains Grandisson's arms. Medieval binding of wooden boards covered with white leather, with a chemise over all (cf. edn., p. 1): six bands: two strap-and-pin fastenings. Three bookmarkers: cf. edn., p. 2 ('four'). Secundo folio *lum non possent*.

Written for and given by Bishop Grandisson, like MS. 3504: 'Ego I. de G. Ex. Do ecclesie Exon' librum istum cum pari suo. Manu mea', in Grandisson's hand at the head of f. 1. The sixth of nine books in the new exchequer in 1506: cf. MS. 3504: the secundo folio agrees.[1] 'No 4' inside the cover.

3505B. *Legenda de sanctis secundum usum ecclesiae Exoniensis*
s. XIV ex.

1. ff. 1–221ᵛ Incipit legenda de sanctis secundum usum Exon'. Compilata per Iohannem de Grandissono Episcopo. In sollempnitate sancti andree apostoli et de eius passione . . . Leccio prima. Proconsul egeas . . .

A copy of MS. 3505, ff. 1–228ᵛ (edn., pp. 177–466/16), together with nine lessons for St. Anne not in MS. 3505 (ff. 92–94ᵛ) and nine lessons from Job for All Souls (ff. 181–182ᵛ) instead of the nine lessons from 1 Corinthians 15: 12–58 in MS. 3505 (edn., pp. 401/16–402/6: cf. edn., pp. 469–470/16, where the lessons from Job are printed from MS. 3505, ff. 230ᵛ–232). Two leaves missing after f. 211 contained the text in edn. 445/29–449/35. The text of the leaf missing from MS. 3505 is here on ff. 63ᵛᵃ/10–64ᵛᵃ/8. f. 1 in facsimile in the 1927 sale catalogue.

2. ff. 221ᵛ–222 Three lessons 'In festo apparicionis beati michaelis octauo idus Maii'.

3. ff. 222ᵛ–223 Three lessons 'In festo reliquiarum secundum usum Exon' ecclesie celebrando die lune post ascensionem domini'.

4. ff. 223–4 Three lessons of St Sativola printed from this copy by P. Grosjean in *Anal. Boll.* liii (1935), 363–5.

[1] Presuming that Oliver's '*Cum non possint*' is his error: the inventory itself has gone astray since his time.

5. ff. 224–6 In festo sancti Gabrielis quod celebratur in ecclesia Exoniensi. prima secunda feria mensis Septembris. scilicet in crastino incepcionis historie. Si bona . . .

Nine lessons and a lesson after prime. *Ordinale Exon.* iii. 165–9. Cf. the office on ff. 127ᵛ–129, where there are no proper lessons.

6. f. 226ʳᵛ Three lessons 'In commemoratione beate marie per aduentum secundum usum Sar' '.

The 'Lectio prima' in *Brev. ad usum Sarum,* i. lxxiii–lxxiv, divided at Multas ob causas and Maria autem.

7. ff. 226ᵛ–232 Lecciones cotid' de sancta maria.

Lessons of B.V.M. at Advent, Christmas, from Purification to Advent, and at Easter, as *Brev. ad usum Sarum,* ii. 287–314, with some differences of division, in particular seven sets, instead of six, for the period from Purification to Advent. f. 232ᵛ is blank.

ff. iii+230+i. The modern foliation is 2 ahead from f. 214, having left out the numbers 212 and 213. f. iii, medieval, was pasted down. 390×270 mm. Written space *c.* 280× 172 mm. 2 cols. 33 lines. Collation: 1–26⁸ 27⁸ want 4, 5, after f. 211 28–29⁸. Initials: (i) blue or pink, patterned in white, on punched gold and coloured grounds, with prolongations into the margins; (ii) f. 226, 3-line, gold on blue and pink ground, patterned in white; (iii) 2-line, blue with red ornament or red with violet ornament; (iv) 1-line, blue. Capital letters in the ink of the text marked sometimes with red. Binding of s. xx, with the old brown leather covers bearing Oldham's rolls HE. c. 1 and RP. b. 2 (s. xvi²) pasted on. Secundo folio *do. in ista uoce.*

Written in Exeter (?), probably at the same time as the now missing companion volume containing the Temporale which is entered in the 1506 inventory of the new treasury of the cathedral (Oliver, p. 350). Both were the gift of William Poundestoke (†1414: Emden, *BRUO,* p. 1509): 'Istam legendam de sanctis cum una legenda de temporali in alio volumine que incipit in secundo folio in textu. Do in ista uoce.¹ Magister Willelmus Povndestoke quondam canonicus ecclesie Cathedralis Exon' dicte ecclesie Cathedrali in testamento suo legauit cuius anime propicietur deus. Amen', f. 232. The present volume was probably alienated before 1506, since it is not in the inventory of that date. Book-plate of (Heneage of) Coker Court inside the cover. Sale at Sotheby's, 11 Apr. 1927, lot 279. Bought by the Dean and Chapter for £250.

3506. *J. de Gadesden, Rosa medicinae; etc.* s. xiv²

This copy of the Rosa is described by N. Capener in *Annals of Surgery,* cliv (1961), Supplement, pp. 13–17, with facsimiles of f. 1, reduced, and of the initials and drawing on f. 236ᵛ, both enlarged and reduced.

1. ff. 1–239 Galienus primo de ingenio sanitatis . . . in generali. Explicit prohemium libri qui nominatur Rosa medicine quem Magister Iohannes de Gatesdene compilauit ad profectum medicorum et aliorum discipulorum. Incipiunt libri primi capitula . . . Quia ergo primi libri erunt de morbis communibus . . . Set non vacat michi modo. Explicit Rosa medicine Magistri I. de Gadesdene deo igitur sint gracie infinite qui ad hunc perduxit Amen . . . (f. 239ᵛ) I. Grenstede me scripsit.

¹ These four words over erasure. Presumably the original secundo folio was that of the other volume, 'am iudices'.

Bks. 2–5 begin on ff. 39, 190ᵛ, 232, 236ᵛ. Each has a table of chapters in front of it. Emden, *BRUO*, p. 739, lists this and fourteen other manuscripts. Printed in 1492 (Goff, J. 326) and later. ff. 221, 227 are out of place: see below, collation. f. 240ʳᵛ blank. 'Iohannes Shaxton Artium Magister' describes the centipede, 'Centumpedes anglice Sowes' (also called 'Chestworme') mainly in English, s. xvii, in the margin of f. 212.

2. f. 239ᵛ (after *perduxit Amen* in art. 1) De urina. In vitreo uase totalem collige mane . . . concipiatur.

Seventeen lines of verse, the last five, 'In muliere patens . . .', below a heading 'Signa si mulier conciperit masculum vel feminam'.

3. ff. 240ᵛ–241 Vrina ruffa significat salutem . . . uenenose signum est mortis 1381.

A text on reading urines set round an unfinished circular diagram: ff. 240ʳ, 241ᵛ were left blank. Thorndike and Kibre.

4. ff. 242–7 Solucionem febris acute mediante fluxu san. a naribus significat . . . cum fluxu sanguinis per nares.

In short paragraphs according to the seventeen colours of urine, the 'circulus' to which the urine belongs, etc.

5. f. 247 Hec est ars medicinarum laxatiuarum tam simplicium quam compositarum in genere . . . hec sufficiant de quantitate laxacionis medicinarum secundum M. Io. stephani. Explicit de laxatiuis.

Thorndike and Kibre. A copy in Bodleian, Canon. misc. 455, ff. 223–225ᵛ.

6. ff. 247–250ᵛ Incipit M. P. limouic' de medicinis. Medicina alia subtilis alia grossa. subtilis autem potest diuidi . . . Item fiat circulus illinitus tiriaca uel (*ends imperfectly*).

More than half f. 249 is missing.

ff. v+251. ff. i, ii are inserted leaves of paper. The late medieval foliation, 1–239, on the right of rectos towards the foot is later than the dislocation in quire 20. 312×220 mm. Written space *c.* 230×140 mm. 2 cols. 50 lines. Collation: 1¹⁰ 2–18¹² 19⁴ (ff. 215–18) 20¹² (sheet 4 is bound the wrong way round) 21¹² wants 12 after f. 241, perhaps blank, 22¹² wants 10 after f. 250 and 12. Leaves in the first halves of quires 1–6, 8–17 are marked in pencil or in blue ink with a regular series of letter and figure signatures from a i to q vi. Initials in art. 1: (i) f. 1, 7-line, blue *G*, patterned in white, on a decorated gold and red ground, with prolongations forming a continuous border: a dragon bites the letter; (ii) red and blue with ornament in red or in red and blue: the *Q* on f. 236ᵛ contains a seated reader, his open book inscribed 'venite ad me omnes languentes'; (iii) 2-line, blue with red ornament, or, after f. 203, plain blue. Binding of s. xv/xvi of wooden boards covered with white leather: six bands; two clasps now missing: a chain clip on the side of the front cover, near the top. Secundo folio *illo sanguine exibunt*.

Written in England by a named scribe. Pledged in a Cambridge loan chest, *c.* 1400: 'Caucio M. Thome Mordon (†1416: Emden, *BRUC*, p. 409) exposita ciste de Derlyngton pro iii li' in festo sancti leonardi et habet tria supplementa ysiderum cum aliis Manipulum florum et zonam argenteam', f. 241ᵛ. Identifiable by the opening words of the second leaf with a Rosa Medicinae which belonged to All Souls College, Oxford, from soon after the foundation of the college in 1438 until *c.* 1600: six inventories and T. James's *Ecloga Oxonio-Cantabrigiensis*, 1600, record it (N. R. Ker, *Records of All Souls College Library*, 1971, pp. 130, 182). The names John Woolton and Richardus Ackworth, s. xvii in., accompany notes on ff. i and v respectively. Woolton, of All Souls College 1584–5, D.M.

1599, in practice in Exeter, was the eldest son of John Woolton, bishop of Exeter (cf. *DNB* xxi. 911). For Ackworth, see Foster, *Alumni Oxonienses*, p. 5. 'This booke was given to ye Liberary of Exon by me John Mongwell Senr January 1658/9', f. v^v. *CMA*, no. 4.

3507. *Rabanus Maurus, etc.* s. x²

Described by R. Derolez, *Runica manuscripta*, 1954, pp. 220–1. The contents are nearly the same as ff. 10^v–65 of Cotton Vitellius A. xii, ff. 4–77, a manuscript of s. xi/xii by a Salisbury scribe,[1] which contains everything here, except art. 3c, but with enough differences to make it unlikely that Vit. is copied from 3507 (as I suggested it was in *Wiltshire Magazine*, liii (1949), 156).

1. ff. 1, 3, 2, 4–58 Incipit prologus hrabani peritissimi uiri. Dilecto fratri machario monacho hrabanus peccator in christo salutem. Legimus scriptum . . . (f. 1^v) et mihi remittas. Explicit prologus. Incipiunt kapitula libri sequentis. i. De numerorum potentia . . . (f. 3^v) xcvi. De ætatibus. Expliciunt kapitula. (f. 2) Incipit ipse liber hrabani de compoto. Quia té uenerande preceptor . . . qui est benedictus in secula amen.

Rabanus Maurus, De computo. *PL* cvii. 669–728.

2. (*a*) f. 58^rv Versus de duodecim mensibus anni. Id circo certis . . . (9 lines). (*b*) Tetrasticon autenticum. de singulis mensibus. Hic iani mensis sacer . . . (48 lines). (*c*) f. 59^v Versus de singulis mensibus. Primus romanas ordiris . . . (12 lines). (*d*) f. 59^v Versus de mensibus et signis xii. Dira patet iani . . . (12 lines). (*e*) ff. 59^v–60 Versus de duodecim signis. Primus adest aries . . . ludere pisces (12 lines). (*f*) f. 60 Versus de cursu anni. Bissena mensium uertigine . . . (17 lines). (*g*) f. 60^rv De octo tramitibus circuli decennouenalis. Linea christe tuos . . . (8 lines). (*h*) f. 60^v Versus de septem dierum uocabulis. Prima dies phoebi . . . (7 lines).

(*a–c, e–h*). Walther, nos. 8654, 7988a, 14678, 14646, 2187, 10329, 14566. (*c, f, h*). *Anthologia Latina*, nos. 639 (Ausonius), 680, 488. (*e*). Cf. *Anth. Lat.*, no. 615 (six lines ending *lumine pisces*). (*g*). *PL* cxxxix. 578.

3. (*a*) ff. 60^v–61^v De septem miraculis manu factis. Primum capitolium romę . . . mirabilis ædificii. (*b*) ff. 61^v–63^v Duo sunt extremi uertices mundi. quos appelabant polos . . . decurrit accipiens. (*c*) f. 63^v Incipiunt dies egyptiaci qui debeant obseruari. Non interscias . . . die quinto. (*d*) ff. 63^v–64 Item dies ægyptiaci. Quos maxime obseruare debemus . . . obseruandi sunt. (*e*) f. 64^rv Incipit ordo librorum catholicorum in circulo anni legendorum. In primis in lxx ponunt eptaticum . . . usque in lxxam. (*f*) f. 64^v Omnes uero litteræ a similitudine uocis caracteras acceperunt. A. Subhiato . . . Z. Vero appius claudius testatur. dentes moti. Dum exprimitur imitatur. (*g*) f. 65^rv A alfa. agricola . . . ω oo. finis. א aleph interpretatur doctrina . . . τ tau. errauit uel consummauit. (*h*) f. 65^v Λ (*sic*) mia. i . . . ψ niacusin. dccc(c). chile dischile . . . CHRISTVS XPS. alfa . . . eneacoses. (*i*) f. 66 Three runic alphabets, A–Z, and extras, followed by the words 'Pax uobiscum et salus pax' in runes, with the Latin letters above them in

---

[1] The same scribe wrote Salisbury Cathedral 25, ff. 176^v–203, and 128, ff. 25–116, Bodley 765, f. 1/16–19, and Keble College 22, ff. 3–4^v, 5^v–7, 10.

rustic capitals. (*j*) f. 66ᵛ De concurrentibus. Si uis scire concurrentes . . .
eodem anno. (*k*) f. 66ᵛ De epactis. Et qualem lunam . . . habetur. (*l*) f. 66ᵛ In
octauo anno x et vii epactas . . . concurr' ii. (*m*) f. 66ᵛ De sex ætatibus nominis
(*sic*). Prima infantia vii annos tenet . . . annorum tenet.

(*b*). Thorndike and Kibre. *PL* xc. 368–9: cf. A. van de Vyver in *RB* xlvii (1935), 140.
(*g*). Greek and Hebrew alphabets, with interpretations. (*h*). Numbers with the Greek
words for them. (*i*). Derolez, pp. 221–36.

4. ff. 67–97ᵛ Incipit liber isidoris psalensis episcopi. de natura rerum. Domino
et filio sisebuto esidorus (scilicet ego *interlined*) salutem (scilicet mitto *interlined*).
Dum te prestantem . . . (f. 67ᵛ) efficiat. Explicit prefatio. Incipiunt capitula-
tiones. i. De diebus . . . xlviii. De partibus terra (*sic*). Alii autem prologum
cuius initium tu fortem loculentis uaga carmina gignis in hunc locum introducunt.
Alii autem isidori esse respuunt sed gilde. De diebus. Dies est solis . . . stadiorum
estimauerunt. Cuius terre expositionem in medio ociano subiecto declarat formula. Finiunt expositiones numero quadraginta Nouem. Explicit liber isidori
psalensis episcopi de natura rerum.

PL lxxxiii. 963–1018. Thorndike and Kibre. 48 (not 49) chapters. Ascribed to Gildas in
the heading of Vitellius A. xii. F. Barlow (and others), *Leofric of Exeter*, Exeter, 1972, pl.
vii, shows f. 68, reduced. The two Old English glosses on f. 92ᵛ are noted by Derolez,
op. cit., p. 220: cf. N. R. Ker, *Catalogue of MSS. containing Anglo-Saxon*, p. 153, no. 116*.
The same two glosses are also in the copy from St. Augustine's, Canterbury, B.L., Cotton
Domitian i, f. 34ᵛ (Ker, no. 146), whence A. S. Napier printed them (*Old English Glosses*,
1900, no. 41).

5. f. 97ᵛ Tres filii noę diuiserunt orbem . . . Iaphet in europa.

An Isidorian world diagram follows, inscribed in the top compartment 'In asia . . . libia',
in the lower left compartment 'In affrica . . . et minores', and in the lower right compartment 'In europa . . . austraicias'.

ff. iii+97+iii. Slightly damaged by damp. 312 × 195 mm. Written space 228 × 130 mm.
29 long lines. Collation: 1⁸ wants 1, probably blank (ff. 1–7 now misbound in the order 1,
3, 2, 5, 4, 6, 7) 2–12⁸ 13 two (ff. 96, 97). Quires 1–12 lettered at the end a–m. Hair outside
all sheets. Written in handsome square Anglo-Saxon minuscule, apparently by the same
scribe as Bodleian, MS. Bodley 718 (*Sum. Cat.* 2632), and Paris, B.N., lat. 943: cf. *New
Pal. Soc.*, pl. 111. Initials: (i) f. 1, green; (ii) 1-line, alternately metallic red and in the ink
of the text. Capital letters in the ink of the text filled with yellow. Binding of s. xviii:
a slight rustmark from the chain attached to a former binding shows on f. 1 at the foot.
Secundo folio *xxv de speciebus* (f. 3) or *ex multitudine* (f. 5).

Written in England. At Exeter in 1327 (Inv., p. 303) and no doubt much earlier. 'Nº 25'
inside the cover; also 'Nº 2'. *CMA*, no. 25.

3508. *Psalterium, etc.*   s. XIII¹

1. ff. 5–10ᵛ Calendar in blue, red, and black, graded.

Cf. HMC, *Report*, pp. 29, 30, and J. K. Floyer in *Associated Architectural Societies' Reports
and Papers*, xxxii (1913), 149–50. In the main hand: in large red and blue capitals, 'Sancti
Gregorii pape anglorum apostoli ix lc' (12 Mar.) and 'Ordinatio beati gregorii pape
anglorum apostoli ix lc' ' (3 Sept.); in red, 'Dedicatio ecclesie beate marie uirginis in
Wigorn' a pontifice siluestro (*1216–18*)' (7 June). Early additions: in red and blue capitals,
'Dedicacio ecclesie s' helene wigorn' ix lc' ' (9 May) and 'Sancte helene regine' (18

Aug.); in green, 'Sancti Godewali Episcopi et confessoris iii lc' ' (6 June); in blue, 'Festum reliquiarum ix lc' ' (15 Sept., the Sarum date); in black, 'Obitus Reg' decani Wigorn' ' (18 Aug.). Additions made at Exeter include: in s. xiii², 'Sancti Gabrielis' (24 Mar.); 'Obitus Rogeri de Winkligh' decani' (13 Aug.: he died in 1252), 'Dedicacio Exon' Ecclesie' (21 Nov.); in s. xv, 'Obitus Magistri Henrici Webber huius ecclesie Decani' (13 Feb.: he died in 1477) and at the foot of the April page an 8-line notice of the great wind on St. Brice's day, 1467, and the couplet 'Ecce tonat Bricius . . .'.

2. ff. 11–169ᵛ Pss. 1–150 and noted antiphons.

The psalms in each liturgical division are numbered, a fresh number being given to each psalm after an antiphon: thus, in the first division, the numbers are ii–ix, each preceded by Parˢ, against Pss. 7, 11, 15–20. As usual in psalters each verse begins on a new line, but here the scribe often filled his line by running over and so produced a text which can hardly be read: for example, on f. 31 the first nine words of Ps. 21, verse 5, fill line 12 and the last five words fill spaces at the ends of lines 11, 9, and 6. Ps. 109 begins on a new quire, f. 134.

3 (in the space left blank at the end of quire 18). (a) f. 133, in red, Tres quinquagenos dauid canit ordine psalmos. Uersus ter mille. sexcentos sex canit ille. Numero psalmorum dauid. centum. quinquaginta. et uersus quinque milia centos quinquaginta unus. (b) f. 133 Canticum psalmorum. animas decorat . . . in celo collocabit. (c) f. 133ʳᵛ De sancta maria in aduentu secundum quod canit salesburiensis ecclesia. atque Wellensis ecclesia. Vespere usque ad vigiliam natalis domini . . .

(b). Römer, i. 196. PL cxxxi. 142/29–57. (c). Cf. Brev. ad usum Sarum, ii. 283. A reference to Hereford use on f. 133ᵛ.

4. ff. 170–185ᵛ. Six ferial canticles, Te Deum, Benedicite, Benedictus, Magnificat, Nunc dimittis, Quicunque vult, Pater noster, Credo in unum Deum.

At the end the scribe wrote 'Animam scribentis. benedicat lingua legentis'. After Quicunque vult he wrote the alphabet, a to z, followed by '& ÷ amen. Ecce labor uictus. sit scriptor a. benedictus'.

5. f. 186. A list of thirty prayers, 'Pater noster . . . Dominus vobiscum'.

The first six, 'Pater noster . . . Domine auerte', and the last eight, 'Deus tu conuersus . . . Dominus vobiscum', are listed in Ordinale Exon. i. 36, 28. f. 186ᵛ, left blank, bears a note made in 1541, 'These are the names of the secondariis anno domini 1541. Ex parte decani John Come. Ex parte cantoris John partridge Thomas peteven John amerry Thomas Wylliams'.

6. ff. 188–194ᵛ Litany.

Apostles: Petre, doubled. Twenty-two confessors: . . . (4) Gregori, doubled, . . . (14–18) Cuthberte, Cedde, Oswalde, Egwine, Swithune . . . Twenty-one virgins: . . . (2) Helena, doubled, an addition over erasure, . . . (17–21) Editha, Wereburga, Eadburga, Milburga, Wenefreda. The last three prayers are 'Deus qui es sanctorum tuorum splendor . . .', 'Omnipotens et misericors deus clementiam tuam suppliciter deprecor. ut me famulum tuum N . . .', and (added early) 'Omnipotens s.d. qui per beatam helenam . . .' (ends imperfectly).

7 (on the preliminary quire). (a) f. 1ʳᵛ Dominica prima post octabas epiphanie cap'. Benedictus deus . . . (b) f. 1ᵛ Prayers: Presta quesumus domine ut a nostris mentibus . . .; O. et misericors deus confitenti michi famulo tuo . . .; O.s.d. qui gloriose uirginis et matris . . . (ends imperfectly) (c) ff. 2–3ᵛ Collects of the second to the twenty-fifth Sunday after Pentecost, beginning imperfectly.

(*d*) f. 4 Salue lignum triumphale. inter ligna nullum tale. arbor salutifera . . . perfruamur gloria. (*e*) f. 4^v Sanctus iohannes xxii volens diuinum cultum ampliare et mentes fidelium . . . (*f*) f. 4^v Non solum autem cristus lauit nos . . . in salutem.

(*a–d*) are nearly contemporary additions. (*e, f*) are of s. xv. (*a*). Sunday and Monday capitula at the hours. (*d*). Sixteen 3-line stanzas. (*e*). Indulgences of Pope John XXII, Avignon, 1 Nov. 1317. (*f*). Said in the margin to be from Bede 'dominica infra oct' epiphanie'.

8. ff. ii, 195, 187, the pastedowns and a flyleaf, are three leaves of Casus decretalium in 2 cols. of 64 lines, s. xiii ex.

The lemmata on f. 187, the only leaf in good condition, are from Decretals, bk. 5, tit. 31, 32, and the cases appear to be those of Bernardus de Botono Parmensis, as in printed copies of the glossed decretals.

ff. ii+186+i+7+ii. For ff. ii and 195, pastedowns, and f. 187 see above, art. 8. 305 × 210 mm. Written space 206 × 135 mm. 16 long lines. Writing above the top ruled line. Collation of ff. 1–186, 188–94: 1 four(2 bifolia: a gap after f. 1) 2^6 3–12^8 13^8 wants 8, blank, after f. 97 14–17^8 18^4 (ff. 130–3) 19 four (ff. 134–7) 20–24^8 25^8+1 leaf after 8 (f. 186) 26^8 wants 8 (ff. 188–94). Large ugly script: a 'sine pedibus' type begins at f. 29^v. Initials: (i) f. 11, a 13-line *B* of curling branches and beasts biting them, blue, red, and green on a pale-yellow ground: facsimile in *Archaeologia*, ciii (1971), pl. lii; (ii) for principal psalms, including Pss. 51, 101, in colours on gold and coloured grounds, the gold decorated with concentric circles and small white lions twining in them, or historiated (four psalms), ff. 52^v, 66, 115, 117: Pss. 38, 51 (David and Goliath), 97,[1] 101 (a kneeling queen); (iii) ff. 150^v, 170, 3-line and 4-line, gold; (iv, v) 3-line and 1-line, red or blue; also, in quire 3 only, (vi) 3-line, blue, red, green, or purple, with ornament in red and blue, and (vii) 1-line, blue or purple with red ornament, or red with blue ornament. Repaired medieval binding of wooden boards covered with brown leather: five bands: central strap and pin missing. In repairs the boards have been turned round and the pastedowns bound in back to front: the mark of a four-nail chain staple shows at what is at present the foot of the front cover. Secundo folio (f. 2) *nunquam*, or (f. 12) *ges terre*.

Written in England (Worcester ?), perhaps for use at an altar of St. Gregory. In use apparently at the church of St. Helen, Worcester, in s. xiii^1. In Exeter in s. xiii. Identifiable in the inventory of 1506 (Oliver, *Lives*, p. 333): Psalterium de secunda forma 2 fo *ges terre*. '10' on a label at the head of the spine and 'N° 10' inside the cover. Frere, no. 576.

3509. *R. Higden, Polychronicon*   s. XIV^2

(f. 9) Prologus primus in historiam policronicam. Post preclaros arcium scriptores . . . (f. 10^v) conscribetur. (f. 11^v) De orbis dimensione pres*cianus* in cosmographia sua. Ex senatus consulto . . . (f. 180^v) et ecclesia libertatem. Explicit historia. Et cito post hoc . . . (f. 181) utrinque discessum est.

A copy of the 'AB' form of the Polychronicon, ending at 1341 (edn. RS viii. 336). Preceded on ff. 1–8^v by an index, 'Abraham . . . De Zorobabel. de quatuor rebus fortis'. ff. 11^r, 181^v, 182^{rv} are blank.

[1] At Ps. 97 a man is carrying what looks a bit like a sledge. Is it Samson with the gates of Gaza? G. Haseloff notes that an English psalter, s. xiii, Paris, B.N., lat. 1315, has this subject at Ps. 97 (*Die Psalterillustration im 13 Jahrhundert*, 1938, p. 12). The initials of Pss. 1, 97, 101 are reproduced in colour as the frontispiece of G. Oliver, *Monasticon Dioecesis Exoniensis*, 1846.

ff. iii+182. 312×215 mm. Written space 235×150 mm. 43 long lines. Ruled in
yellowish-brown ink. Collation: 1–22⁸ 23⁸ wants 6, 7, blank, after f. 181. Quires 2–22
signed a–v in the usual later medieval manner. The middle of each quire is marked by
a red cross at the foot of the outer margin of the recto of leaf 5. Written in anglicana.
Initials: (i) 4-line and 3-line, blue and red with ornament of both colours; (ii) 2-line, blue
with red ornament; (iii) 1-line, blue. Contemporary binding of wooden boards covered
with white leather, repaired: six bands: formerly covered with a chemise, a fragment of
which is now stuck to f. 182: two clasps missing: chainmarks at head and foot of the back
cover. Secundo folio in textu (f. 10) *in historia romana.*

Written in England. A copy of the Polychronicon, '2° folio in textu In historia romana',
was lent by Baldwin Schillyngforde (Emden, *BRUO*, p. 1689) to John Schepways, 7 June
1392, with consent of the Dean and Chapter of Exeter, and returned on 15 Oct. (HMC,
Report, p. 40).

3510. *Missale*   s. XIII²

1. ff. 3–8ᵛ Sarum calendar in blue, red, and black, graded.

Not in *Sarum Missal* are: in blue, 'Primus dies ascensionis' (30 Apr.), 'Descendit spiritus
sanctus super apostolos' (16 May), 'Concepcio S. Marie nichil apud Sar' ' (8 Dec.); in red,
'Sancti Botulphi abbatis iii lc'. nichil apud Sarum' (7 June); in black, 'Pierani episcopi'
(5 Mar., no grading), 'Ricardi episcopi' (3 Apr., no grading), 'Petroci confessoris' (4 June,
9 lessons), 'Sancti Hugonis lincoln' episcopi. Memoria' (17 Nov.). 'Ob' Ade le Yunge'
added at June 11. St. Thomas and the word 'pape' have not been blotted out.

2. ff. 9–65ᵛ Temporale for the year from Advent.

Abbreviated: cues only, except for collects, secrets, and postcommunions. The secret
for the second Sunday after Epiphany is Ut tibi grata. A tab made by slit and knot shows
Pentecost, f. 51.

3. ff. 65ᵛ–66ᵛ In dedicatione ecclesie.

4. ff. 67–70ᵛ Noted prefaces, ending imperfectly, and canon of mass, beginning
imperfectly.

What remains is in *Sarum Missal*, pp. 211/19–212/30, 223/26–229.

5. ff. 71–144ᵛ Sanctorale, Andrew to Saturninus.

Offices for Richard (of Chichester, †1253, f. 86ᵛ) and Gabriel, archangel (f. 121ᵛ) are in
the main hand; so too the office 'Sanctorum martirum quinquaginta oratorum', which
follows Saturninus on f. 144ʳᵛ. ff. 73–4 should follow f. 82. ff. 145–148ᵛ were left blank:
see art. 12.

6. ff. 149–157ᵛ Common of saints. f. 158ʳ blank.

7. ff. 158ᵛ–161ᵛ Masses of Holy Trinity, Holy Cross, B.V.M., 'Pro fratribus et
sororibus' and of All Saints.

8. ff. 162–4 Collect, secret, and postcommunion of masses (Pro tribulatione
cordis, beginning imperfectly), Pro nauigantibus, Pro infirmo, Pro benefactoribus
uel pro salute amicorum, Contra aduersarios, Pro peste animalium, In tempore
belli.

As *Sarum Missal*, pp. 409/13–412. f. 164ᵛ blank.

9. ff. 165–72 Pro defunctis.

As *Sarum Missal*, pp. 431–436/28, 437/17–442/14.

10. ff. 172–5 Missa communis.

As *Sarum Missal*, pp. 442/15–445/33. f. 175ᵛ was left blank.

11. ff. 176–192ᵛ Lections of B.V.M., Holy Cross, Angels, at Easter, Ascension, Pentecost, and Christmas, of the common of saints and for the dead. ff. 193–196ᵛ were left blank: see art. 12*f–h*.

12. Additions on flyleaves and in blank spaces: (*a*) ff. 1–2ᵛ, s. xiii/xiv, Office of the Transfiguration and collects, secrets, and postcommunions of SS. Gabriel, Raphael, Edmund confessor and bishop, Hugh confessor and bishop, and, in another ink, Peter and Paul 'in tempore paschali'; (*b*) f. 66ᵛ, s. xiv, Credo in unum deum . . .; (*c*) ff. 145–6, Office of Corpus Christi; (*d*) ff. 146–147ᵛ, Office of St. Gabriel; (*e*) f. 175ʳᵛ, s. xiv, Three masses of All Saints and a mass for parents and benefactors; (*f*) ff. 192ᵛ–193 Lections for the dead and at Epiphany; (*g*) f. 193ᵛ, s. xiii/xiv, Collect, secret, and postcommunion of All Saints in Advent; (*h*) ff. 193ᵛ–195 Lections of the Assumption and Nativity of B.V.M.; (*i*) f. 196ᵛ, s. xiv in., A list of ornaments at the altar of St. Gabriel 'in ecclesia Exon' '.

(*a, c, d, g*) supplement art. 5. (*f, h*) supplement art. 11. (*d*). The hymn is *RH*, no. 12532. (*e*), (*f*), (*g*). *Sarum Missal*, pp. 457–8 and 436; pp. 432/26–28 and 38/23–25; p. 458.

ff. vi+194+iv, foliated (i–iv), 1–197 (198–200). ff. iv, 1, 2, 197 are medieval end-leaves: iv was pasted down and 197 once followed 2, as worm-holes show. 308×212 mm. Written space *c*. 228×150 mm. 16 long lines (2 cols., ff. 176–95). Writing between a pair of ruled lines. Collation of ff. 3–196: 1⁶ 2–3¹² 4¹⁰ 5⁶ 6⁶+1 leaf after 4 (f. 53) 7¹⁰ 8 five (ff. 66–70: 67, 68 are a bifolium)¹ 9¹² (now misbound as a 4 and an 8 in the order 9¹, ², 9¹¹, ¹², 9³⁻¹⁰) 10–12¹² 13¹⁰ 14¹² 15⁸ (ff. 141–8) 16¹² 17 two (ff. 161–2, the outside bifolium of a quire) 18¹² 19¹⁰ 20⁶ 21⁸ wants 7, 8, probably blank, after f. 196. Initials: (i) 3-line, red and blue with ornament of both colours; (ii) red or blue, with ornament of the other colour; (iii) 1-line, red or blue. Bound in s. xx. Secundo folio (f. 10) *et hostiis*.

Written in England and probably at the time when Walter de Bronescombe was bishop of Exeter (1258–80: Emden, *BRUO*, p. 279): his special devotion to St. Gabriel (art. 5: cf. art. 12*a*, *d*) is noted by Dalton, *Ordinale Exon.* iii, p. xiii. At Exeter Cathedral and probably at the altar of St. Gabriel there (art. 12*i*) in s. xiv¹ when the words 'Pro anima Thome de Walsham patris magistri Benedicti de Paston et Beatrice Matris eius' were written at the head of f. 196ᵛ. A little later 'Pro anima Benedicti de Paston' canonici Exon' ' was written further down the same page: Paston was canon of Exeter in 1314 and died in 1331 (*BRUO*, p. 1433). 'Nᵒ 6' inside the cover. 'Nᵒ 12' on f. ivᵛ. *CMA*, no. 12. Frere, no. 579.

3511. *J. de Voragine, Sermones dominicales et festivales*   s. xiv med.

1. ff. 1–8ᵛ (*begins imperfectly*) Gradus ecclesie tres xvi. b. c . . . Zizannia quos designat xxx. a.

An alphabetical table of art. 2. Numbers refer to sermons and letters a–d to quarter lengths of sermons: the letters are not actually entered in the margins of art. 2.

2. ff. 9–193ᵛ Incipiunt sermones dominicales fratris Iacobi ordinis fratrum predicatorum archiepiscopi Ianuensis super euangelia per circulum anni.

---

¹ 'Oportet quod istud folium iungatur sextario. in quo est principium sanctorum', is at the foot of f. 70, s. xiv in.

Humane labilis uite . . . vita erit communis. Ad illum benedictum finem perducat . . . amen. Expliciunt sermones dominicales per circulum anni a fratre
Iacobo Ianuensi archiepiscopo editi ordinis fratrum predicatorum.

Often printed. Schneyer, p. 324. Three sermons for each Sunday, numbered later i–clix.
Single leaves missing after ff. 58, 78, 153.

3. (a) ff. 194–195ᵛ A table of pericopes of art. 4 in the order in which they occur.
(b) ff. 196–205ᵛ An alphabetical table of art. 4, Abbas–Xpistus.

The scribe wrote 'Maria Ihesus Iohannes' at the head of f. 194. (b). References as in art. 1.

4. ff. 206–387ᵛ Incipiunt sermones festiuales per circulum anni fratris Iacobi
archiepiscopi Ianuensis ordinis fratrum predicatorum. de sancto andrea. Ves-
tigia eius secutus est . . . Tria sunt necessaria . . . consequi set tamen post (ends
imperfectly).

Often printed. Schneyer, p. 516. Sermons numbered i–cclxxxv. A leaf missing after
f. 241 and at least fourteen leaves at the end. The last sermon now is the fourth for All
Saints. Art. 3a shows that there were eighteen more of the sanctorale, followed by three
for dedication of a church, three for consecration of an altar and three 'In noua missa', the
last of all on the text 'In sono eorum dulces fecit modos', as in printed editions. The
number 'cccxii' (of the last sermon) is entered under the word 'Missa' in art. 3b.

ff. ii+387. 300×185 mm. Written space c. 212×125 mm. 2 cols. 45 lines. Collation:
1¹² wants 1–4 2–5¹² 6¹² wants 3 after f. 58 7¹² wants 12 after f. 78 8–13¹² 14¹² wants 4 after
f. 153 15–16¹² 17⁸ (ff. 186–93) 18¹⁰+2 leaves before 1 (ff. 194–5) 19–21¹² 22¹² wants 1
before f. 242 23–32¹² 33⁶ (ff. 373–8) 34¹² wants 10, 11, and all but a small fragment of 12
(f. 387): after this there are stubs of eleven more leaves. Signatures in pencil or red ink,
sometimes ad hoc. An early systematic series c–e covers quires 7–9 and another begins
with a at f. 313. Written in several small hands, changing at ff. 139, 206, 349, 379.
Initials: (i) f. 9, gold on coloured ground, historiated (a Dominican friar preaching);
f. 206, blue on gold and pink ground, decorated in colours; prolongations into the margins;
(ii) 2-line, blue with red ornament. Contemporary binding of wooden boards covered
with white leather: five bands: two clasps missing: a label once on the lower cover was
attached to it by six nails. Secundo folio (f. 10) ecce quia.

Written in England. Notes on ff. 126ᵛ, 173ᵛ, the last pages of quires 11 and 15, date from
a time when the manuscript was still unbound: 'magister habet sequens'; 'Rokesle habet
sequentem vnum'.[1] Belonged perhaps to Bishop John de Grandisson (†1369), whose
distinctive hand is on f. 76 and elsewhere. Given to the hospital of St. John at Exeter by
Canon John Westcote, canon of Exeter, †1418: 'Istum librum dat et concedit magister
Iohannes Westecote Canonicus Ecclesie Cathedralis Exon' custos Hospitalis Sancti
Iohannis Baptiste infra portam orientalem Ciuitatis Exon' Magistro et Fratribus eiusdem
hospitalis in puram et perpetuam elemosinam et eorum successoribus imperpetuum et
eisdem liberauit possessionem dumtamen eorum consensu et assensu habeat vsum eiusdem
ad terminum vite sue Dat' Exon' xiiii die Mensis Februarii Anno domini Millesimo
ccccᵐᵒ xviiᵐᵒ',[2] f. iiᵛ. 'Liber Hospitalis S.I. Exon' ', f. iiᵛ, s. xv. 'Nᵒ 42', f. i. CMA, no. 42.
'Nᵒ 8' inside the cover.

3512. 'Excerpta ex decretis romanorum pontificum', etc.　　s. XII in.

Art. 1 corresponds to B.L., Royal 9 B. xii, arts. 7, 8. Arts. 2, 3 correspond to

[1] Cf. 'W[. .]dewer' habet ii [. . .]', f. 151.
[2] The date has been changed, wrongly, to 1317, by erasure of one c.

9 B. xii, art. 9, and to Eton College 97, art. 8*b–d*, q.v. A note of contents on f. 3ᵛ, s. xii, is in a hand which occurs in other Exeter manuscripts.[1]

1. ff. 4–214 Incipiunt excerpta ex decretis romanorum pontificum. Epistola clementis pape ad iacobum hierosolimorum episcopum. Clemens urbis rome . . . Et responderunt omnes 'teio' anathema sit.

Papal letters, Clement I–Gregory II, numbered i–lxii by the hand of art. 4. The first part of Lanfranc's abbreviation of pseudo-Isidore. The companion volume containing the councils is Oxford, Bodleian, Bodley 810 (*Sum. Cat.* 2677). For the manuscripts, except this one, and Lanfranc's authorship, see Z. N. Brooke, *England and the Papacy*, pp. 57–83, 231–5. Annotated throughout by Bishop Grandisson.

2. ff. 214–220ᵛ Ex grecis et latinis canonibus et synodis romanis . . . agebatur. Dei ordinationem . . . permiserit uiolandum.

Capitula Angilramni, printed in *Decretales Pseudo-Isidorianae et Capitula Angilramni*, ed. P. Hinschius, 1863, pp. 757–69. Numbered lxiii, in continuation of art. 1.

3. ff. 220ᵛ–222ᵛ (*a*) Nicholaus episcopus . . . benedictione gaudere. (*b*) Cuius supra. Dominus papa nicholaus . . . intronizatus sit. (*c*) Iusiurandum quod in eadem synido (*sic*) fecit beringerius. Ego beringerius . . . sponte subscripsi.

Proceedings of the council of Rome, A.D. 1059, and Berengar's oath at the council: Mansi, *Concilia*, xix. 897–900. Numbers lxiv against (*a*, *b*) and lxv against (*c*), in continuation of arts. 1, 2.

4 (added, s. xiv/xv). ff. 1ᵛ–2ᵛ Ordo epistolarum uel decretorum Romanorum pontificum in hoc libro. i. Beati clementis petri discipuli.' tres prolixe epistole. quarum due.' ad beatum iacobum Ierosolimorum episcopum. tercia.' ad omnes status uniuersalis ecclesie. . . . lxv. Beringarii retractatio.

A table of arts. 1–4 under sixty-five numbered heads. The heading and the hand are the same as in Eton College 97, art. 1, q.v.

ff. iv+221+ii, foliated (i), 1–226. ff. i, 3 are probably blank leaves of quire 28 moved here to make a pastedown and flyleaf: they are ruled for 27 lines. 295 × 183 mm. Written space *c.* 195 × 120 mm. 32 long lines in quires 1–16, 31 or less in quires 17–26 and 27 in quires 27, 28. Ruling with a hard point. Collation of ff. 4–224: 1–27⁸ 28 five. Quires 1–20 numbered at the end and quires 21–7 at the beginning. The hand changes at f. 164 (21¹). The first hand writes hyphens both at the end of one line and at the beginning of the next line. Initials: (i) f. 4, blue with green and red ornament; (ii, iii) 3-line and 1-line, blue, green, or red. Binding of s. xiv (?), wooden boards covered with white leather and a white chemise over all: four bands: two strap-and-pin fastenings missing: marks of a large label, 75 × 120 mm, formerly on the back cover: the loop for a chain is attached by four nails at the foot of the back cover and projects below it. A bookmarker at f. 66. Secundo folio *sensus*.

Written in England and perhaps at Exeter. Certainly at Exeter in s. xii, when the table of contents was written on f. 3ᵛ. 'Liber Ecclesie Cathedralis Exoniensis' in the hand of Bishop Grandisson at the head of f. 4. Identifiable in the Exeter inventories of 1327 and 1506 (Oliver, *Lives*, pp. 304, 369). Apparently alienated between these dates and, like Bodley 810, which is similarly inscribed, returned to Exeter under the will of Walter Gybbys, †1413: 'Hunc librum legauit magister Walterus Gybbys ecclesie Cathedralis

---

[1] This hand wrote a table of contents in eleven Exeter manuscripts now in the Bodleian Library, Bodley 97, 147, 148, 193, 229, 707, 717, 739, 808, 810, 813. Here and in Bodley 148 and Bodley 810 the table is preceded by a paragraph mark.

Exon' canonicus dum vixit in testamento suo ad vsum eiusdem ecclesie ibidem perpetuo remansurum quem quidem librum executores dicti defuncti deliberarunt Decano et Capitulo ecclesie Cathedralis predicte tercio die mensis Septembris Anno domini millesimo cccc xiiii', f. 3ᵛ.¹ 'Nº 24', f. i. *CMA*, no. 24. 'Nº 9' on a paper label inside the cover.

3513. *Pontificale* s. XIV/XV

1. ff. 1–104 Printed, with many errors, by Ralph Barnes, *Liber Pontificalis of Edmund Lacy*, Exeter, 1847, pp. 1–288/8.

The contents include, ff. 57–74ᵛ, a series of 194 'benedictiones per anni circulum edite a venerabili Patre Fratre Iohanne de Pecham archiepiscopo Cantuariensi' (edn., pp. 152–205). They are not mentioned by D. Douie, *Archbishop Pecham*, 1952.² Passages added in the margins by other hands—contemporary, except no. 12—are not noted by Barnes as additions or (nos. 13, 17) are omitted by him: (1–11) ff. 30–33ᵛ, in the order for conferring orders, the passages about the duties of each class of ordinand, spoken by the bishop, sitting, 'et episcopus sedens . . . manibus', 'Et episcopus . . . nouos', 'Sedendo . . . fundere', 'Et dicat . . . ministrare', 'Et sedens . . . Tunc', 'Redeant . . . surgens', 'Sedens episcopus . . . tunc' (edn., pp. 79/20–24, 80/13–15, 81/6–9, 28–30, 83/12–14, 84/2 up–85/2, 87/17–19), the passage between 'leuatas' and 'Et rediens' (edn., p. 87/21–28), and three short passages before the consecration, 'Submisse . . . eiusdem', 'Pax tecum . . . tuo', 'Stola . . . in fine' (edn., p. 89/4, 7–8, 10–12); (12, 13), f. 46, at the blessing of a widow, the English form of vow, s. xv/xvi, printed in edn., p. 123, footnote, and the corresponding French form, s. xiv/xv, 'Ie N veue avowe a dieu . . .'; (14–17) f. 94ʳᵛ, in the order of marriage, the words 'Admoneo . . . confiteatur', 'to hauen . . . manum retrahendo', 'Wyth þys ryng . . . dowe' (edn., pp. 257 last line–258/2, 258/22–32, 259/27, 28), and the words 'Tunc inclinatis eorum capitibus dicat episcopus benedictionem . . . Benedicat vos deus etc.' after edn., p. 259/30.

2. Additions: (*a*) on the pastedown at the beginning, s. xiv, a prayer for use at the dedication of an altar, 'Dignare igitur dominator domine hoc quesumus altare . . .'; (*b*) f. iiiᵛ, s. xv, a table of contents with leaf references, headed 'In isto pontificali subscripta continentur'; (*c*) f. 104ᵛ, s. xv in., a collect of St. Raphael; (*d*) ff. 104ᵛ–105, s. xv, an order of admission to a confraternity.

(*b*). edn., pp. xvii, xviii, but with the page numbers of the edition in place of the leaf numbers of the manuscript; (*c*, *d*) edn., pp. 288–90.³

ff. iii+104+ii. ff. 1–104 have a contemporary foliation in red roman figures. 273 × 190 mm. Written space 185 × 115 mm. 40–2 long lines. Collation: 1–9⁸ 10⁶ 11¹⁰ 12–13⁸. Quires signed +, a–l. Two hands, the second writing ff. 57–74ᵛ. Initials: (i) blue and red, with red and lilac ornament; (ii) 3-line, blue with red ornament; (iii) 1-line, red or blue. Medieval binding of wooden boards covered with white leather stained pink and with a white leather chemise over all: six bands: two strap-and-pin fastenings (one pin missing). Secundo folio *ueritatem*.

Written in England. Given by the executors of bishop Edmund Lacy (†1455): 'Hunc librum pontificale dederunt Executores bone memorie Edmundi lacy. nuper dum vixit

¹ The inscription is damaged, but evidently identical with that in Bodley 810. Gybbys does not mention these manuscripts in his will, Reg. Arundel, ii. 167ᵛ, but he asks his executors to bestow 'in pios usus' the residue of his goods not specifically bequeathed. Perhaps he borrowed both books and forgot that they were not his own: Emden notes (*BRUO*, p. 760) that he was mentally unstable in 1410.
² Another copy is in the pontifical at Bangor Cathedral, art. 16, q.v.
³ The first word of the English passage in (*d*) is *Lo* not *So*.

Exonien'. Episcopi. de bonis eiusdem. Ecclesie Cath' Exonien'. ibidem remansurum quamdiu durauerit ad laudem dei pro salute anime dicti Edmundi. ita quod nullo modo alienetur a dicta Ecclesia Cathedrali', f. iᵛ. Entered in the 1506 inventory (Oliver, *Lives*, p. 331). 'Nº 12' inside the cover and '12' on a label at the head of the spine. 'Nº 41', f. 1. *CMA*, no. 41.

3514. *Galfredus Monemutensis; Henricus Huntendonensis; etc.*

s. xiii med.–xiii²

A miscellany mainly of English history described in HMC, *Report*, pp. 30–3 and by T. Jones (below, art. 13), p. 28: for arts. 13, 15, see K. Hughes in *Proceedings of the British Academy*, lix (1975), 246–50. A table of contents, f. ii, s. xiv in., 'In isto volumine continentur libri subscripti . . .', has twenty-two heads. It shows that the gap after art. 5 contained 'Item de nominibus regum a bruto ad kadwaladrum. Item Beda de concordia maris et lune'. Arts. 9, 10 are earlier than the rest.

1 (quire 1). (*a*) pp. 1–6 Sciendum namque est nobis . . . penam pacientur. Vnde nos perducat . . . Amen. (*b*) p. 6 Anni ducenti milleni ter duodeni . . . (3 lines). (*c*) p. 8 Four added lines headed 'Pictoribus atque poetis'.

(*a*). Pseudo-Methodius, De fine saeculi. Cf. above, Eton 125, art. 4*a*. (*b*). On antichrist. Printed in HMC, *Report*. (*c*). The lines begin 'Quidlibet audendi', 'Nolo pater' (Walther, *Sprichwörter*, no. 17136), 'Mille Rates', 'Ioce tue'. pp. 7, 8 were left blank.

2 (quires 2, 3). (*a*) pp. 9, 10 [A]dam genuit seth . . . qui in minoribus premature descesserunt. (*b*) pp. 10–18 'De aduentu anglorum in Britanniam.' Anno ab incarnacione domini ccccº xlviii. Martianus cum Valentiniano . . . et sanctus beda uenerabilis presbiter. (*c*) pp. 19–21 Incipit epilogium de obitu beati atque eximii doctoris bede . . . Dilectissimo in cristo collectori cuthuuino cuthbertus . . . Munusculum quod misisti . . . ineruditio lingue facit. (*d*) pp. 21–30 Primus omnium regum francorum qui apud illos more regio . . . regis nauarre.

(*a*). A genealogical table, ending with the sons of Edward I, John, Henry, and Alphonso, who died young. (*b*). A summary history to the death of Bede in 734. (*c*). The 'insular version' of Cuthbert's letter edited by E. van K. Dobbie, *The Manuscripts of Caedmon's Hymn and Bede's Death Song*, 1937, pp. 119–27. Like Dobbie's Tr3 (p. 90), to judge from the heading and the Old English death song. (*d*). To Philip IV (miscalled Louis), 1285–1314. pp. 31, 32 blank.

Arts. 3–8 are on quires 4–11.

3. (*a*) pp. 43–52 'Beda de ymagine mundi'. [S]peculum mundi ad instruccionem eorum quibus deest copia librorum . . . reperitur. Mundus dicitur quasi undique motus . . . Insulas circumiuimus et cetera. Explicit liber qui dicitur ymago mundi. (*b–g*) pp. 36–40, 53 Diagrams and a map illustrating (*a*).

(*a*). PL clxxii. 119/4 up–133/4. Thorndike and Kibre. (*b, c*), pp. 36–7, 39. The nine spheres. (*d*), p. 39. A circular tail-biting dragon and around it the words 'En annus Ego sum sic sol se circuit in quo qui fluxit pridem status nunc temporis Idem'. (*e*), p. 40. The winds, with verses 'Euro vulturnus subsolanusque sodales . . .' (4 lines). (*f*), p. 40. Phases of the moon, accompanied by the words 'coniunct(i)o, Monoydes, Dyathomos, Amphitritos, Pansellenor: a head labelled Sol above 'coniunct(i)o'. (*g*), p. 53. A map, Jerusalem in the middle, east at the top, wind-names round it, and in the four corners outside the circle a text, 'Ventorum quatuor principales species sunt . . . et cetera hiis similia'. pp. 33–5, 38, 41, 42 blank.

4. Genealogies: (*a*) pp. 54–6 Incipit genealogia uirorum ab adam usque ad brutum. Adam pater generis humani . . . anno ab incarnacione domini dclxxxix. Finit genealogia regum britannie successiue regnancium a primo ad ultimum. id est a bruto usque ad calawadrium. (*b*) p. 56 'Genologia ad probandum quod lewlinus princeps Wallie fuit cognatus dei'. Lewelinus fi. griffini . . . fi. adam. fi. dei. (*c*) pp. 56–7 Cyprius quidam filius ieuan . . . a britonibus preda nominatur. (*d*) pp. 57–8 Genealogia anglorum. [E]thelwldus fuit egbricti . . . a noe genitus reperitur. (*e*) p. 58 Incipit genealogia normannorum et unde originem ducunt. Normanni origine dani dcccvi[to] ab incarnacione domini . . . Iohannes frater eius Iunior. Henricus iiii[us] filius. (*f*, *g*) pp. 54, 55, lower margins, Genealogia romanorum . . . Hee due genalogie. vel due aduersitates. secundum diuersos libros ouidii et aliorum auctorum confirmantur.

(*b*). Marginalia, s. xiv, show interest in the descent of Welsh families from Rodri maur, Belimaur and Japhet. (*d*) contains the story of Sceaf. (*e*) ends with the kings of England to Henry III, called here Henry IV, Henry, son of Henry II, king 'per sex menses', being counted as Henry III.

5. pp. 58–60 Hec est mensura anglie . . . et uixit xxxiiii annis (*ends imperfectly*).

Dimensions of England, followed by lists of two archbishoprics, fifteen bishoprics, thirty-two shires, and (p. 60) kings from 'Kynegilfus' to Henry II and their burial places.

6. pp. 61–6 'Genealogia regum francie'. Anno primo Graciani et Valentiniani . . . rotam fortune expertus est.

From the Conquest this becomes an English history. It ends with mentions of the imprisonment of Falkes de Breauté at Bedford (1224) and of Hubert de Burgh at Devizes (1233).

7. pp. 67–93 Daretis frigii entellii hystoria de vastacione troie incipit a cornelio nepote salustii de greco in latinum sermonem translata. Incipit prologus. Cornelius nepos salustio crispo suo salutem. [C]um multa uolumina legerem . . . et alios quinque. Actenus id dares frigius mandauit litteris. 'Explicit historia daretis'.

Ends with the casualties of the Trojan war. Cf. *Catalogue of Romances*, i. 12–25.

8. pp. 94–218 Cum mecum multa de multis . . . interno congratulatur affectu. Incipit historia britonum a galfrido arturo (*cancelled*) monemutensi. de britannica lingua in latinum translata. [B]ritannia insularum optima . . . in nostram transferre curaui. Explicit.

J. Hammer mentions the marginalia, s. xiv, on p. 158, bk. 7, chs. 1, 2 of Historia Britonum, omitted from the text, and extracts from Augustine, De Civitate Dei, and prints the marginalia on pp. 159, 160, a commentary on Merlin's prophecy, in *Hommages à J. Bidez et à F. Cumont* (Collection Latomus, ii), 1949, pp. 112, 113–17. pp. 219–22 are blank.

Arts. 9–15 are on quires 12–25.

9. pp. 223–6 Lists of archbishops of Canterbury to Hubert (†1205) and of Sens and Tours, of bishops of Le Mans and eight other French sees, and of abbots of Jumièges and St. Wandrille.

Cf. HMC, *Report*. The scribe wrote in the upper margin of p. 223 'Dares frigius [. . . .]s gildas. Beda presbiter. Galfr' monomut'. Henr' huntund'. Walt' Oxenford Warinus Brito. Willelmus Malmesbir' Marria[nus]'.

10. pp. 226–450 In hoc volumine continetur hystoria anglorum nouiter edita ab henrico huntendunensi archidiacono libri x. Primus liber est.' de regno romanorum . . . notificaremus. Incipit prologus hystorie anglorum contexte ab henrico huntendunensi archidiacono anno gracie millesimo centesimo tricesimo quinto. Cum in omni fere litterarum studio . . . Te nunc intrante reuixi. 'Explicit hystoria . . .'.

Ed. Arnold (RS lxxiv), 1879, pp. 1–292. Book numbers in red, top right. The hand changes at p. 442 (14 Stephen). Some marginalia probably by Russell, e.g. on p. 275; others on pp. 229–31 by a reader, *c.* 1500, who noted *inter alia* 'In Com' Bark' olim fuit sedes episcopalis apud Sonnyngg' vbi quinque fuerunt episcopi. prout habetur in certis tabulis in domo Capitulari Sarum appositis'.

11 (added, s. xiv). p. 450 Apres cestui Roy Estephene regna henri le filz Emperice . . . et la conquist le viime (*ends imperfectly*).

A chronicle of the reign of Henry II.

12. pp. 450–504 Incipiunt capitula in historia normannorum. et tendentem in reges anglorum. De Ricardo primo . . . (p. 452) De rege henrico quarto (*altered later to* iii). Postquam Willelmus lungespee filius Rollonis . . . Venit Pandulphus legatus Norwicensis electus (*ends abruptly at 1215*).

Cf. HMC, *Report.* pp. 505–6 blank.

13. pp. 507–19 'Cronica de Wallia'. Annus M'C' nonagesimus ab incarnacione domini. In hoc anno . . .

Annals 1190–1266, printed from here by Thomas Jones in *Bulletin of the Board of Celtic Studies*, xii (1946), pp. 29–41: facsimile of p. 507. The hand changes at 1255 (p. 518, col. 2/27: edn., p. 40/21). pp. 520–1 blank.

14. pp. 522–3 Resus filius Griffini . . . qui fuit episcopus Meneuensis.

On the seven sons and seven daughters of Rhys ap Gruffudd ap Rhys and the seven sons of his daughter Nest. Printed ibid. 41–2, except for nine lines on p. 522, 'Hec sunt regna que mare deleuit . . . regheth' (cf. ibid. 41, footnote) and marginalia of s. xiii ex. which supply some facts not in the text, for example about the Caunvile and Martin families.

15 (another hand). pp. 525–8 Cronica ante aduentum domini. Anno ccccxl . . . Cui sucessit (*ends abruptly*).

Annals to 1285. 1254–85 (pp. 527–8) printed ibid. 42–3. pp. 529–34 were left blank: 529 (see below), 530, 532, 533 have notes in Russell's hand.

ff. ii+266, paginated (rectos only) (i–iv), 1–(454), 457–(534). 252 × 187 mm. Written space *c.* 180 × 130 mm. 2 cols. 33–42 lines. Pricks in both margins of quire 12. Writing above top ruled line, pp. 223–442. Collation: 1⁴ (pp. 1–8) 2⁸ 3⁴ (pp. 25–32) 4¹⁴ wants 13 after p. 60 + a bifolium after 3 (pp. 39–42) 5¹⁶ (pp. 63–94) 6–10¹² 11⁴ (pp. 215–22) 12–20¹² 21⁶ (pp. 439–50) 22–23¹² 24¹²+1 leaf before 1 (pp. 501–2) 25⁴ (pp. 527–34). pp. 1–66 and 507–18 in one hand. Initials: (i) pp. 227, 228, 4-line, red and blue with ornament of both colours; (ii) 2-line and 3-line, red or blue with ornament of the other colour or (quires 1–11) not filled in; (iii) pp. 451–2, 1-line, blue or red. No initials in arts. 13–15. Medieval binding of wooden boards covered with white leather: four bands: central clasp. A book-marker at pp. 484–5. Secundo folio (p. 3) *Ex tunc.*

Written in England or Wales. 'Adam de F[. . . .]herd', p. iv. 'Iohannes Braye' inside the end cover, s. xiii ex.; also there 'Henmarssh Anno domini etc' lxiiii^to', s. xv. 'F' twice at the top of p. 1. Belonged in s. xv² to John Russell (bishop of Lincoln, †1494: Emden,

BRUO, p. 1609): 'Stirpe parum clarus magis aptus quam bene doctus / Fraudis inexpertus facto sermoneque veRus celluy Ie suis', p. 529, as in B.L., Royal 15 A. xxi and other books. 'Nº 15' inside the cover and on p. i. '[1]5' on a label at the head of the spine. *CMA*, nos. 15–20.

3515. *Missale, cum notis* s. XIII in.–XV

1. ff. 1–133 Dominica iᵃ aduentus domini. Ad te leuaui animam . . . dono curetur per.

Temporale through the year from Advent. The secret for the second Sunday after the octave of Epiphany is *Oblata domine*. Many alterations and additions, s. xiii–xv. Thus, the collect for Stephen, Omnipotens sempiterne deus. qui primitias . . . (f. 11), was cancelled, s. xiv, in favour of the Sarum form, Da nobis . . . Among additions in the margins are: f. 13, the office of Thomas of Canterbury, s. xiii/xiv; f. 15, the collect, secret, and postcommunion of St. Hilary, s. xv; f. 87ᵛ, 'Benedictio panys in pask', s. xiii/xiv. These are as *Sarum Missal*, pp. 31, 237, 454. Music omitted after f. 119.

2. (*a*) ff. 133ᵛ–134 De sancta Maria. (*b*) f. 134ʳᵛ Benedictio salis et aque.

As *Sarum Missal*, pp. 390–1, 10–12. No music.

3. (*a–e*) f. 135ʳᵛ In purificatione sancte Marie Benedictio candelarum. Oremus Dominus uobiscum. Adesto domine supplicationibus nostris et has candelas . . .: followed by prayers and absolution on Ash Wednesday and benedictions of ashes, palms, and new fire on Ash Wednesday, Palm Sunday, and Easter Saturday respectively. (*f–m*) ff. 135ᵛ–137ᵛ Offices of Paul, Chair of Peter, Mark, Holy Cross (*h, i, l, m*) and collect, secret, and postcommunion of Agnes, Vincent, George, and Blasius.

The script looks rather earlier than in art. 4, but the texts here seem to be a supplement to art. 4, where, for example, cues only are provided for the collect, secret, and postcommunion of Mark and Holy Cross. Differs much from *Sarum Missal*. No music.

4. ff. 138–51 (*begins imperfectly, lines 1–4 erased*) Feasts from 2 Feb. to 21 Dec.

Full offices (shown by italics) or collect, secret, and postcommunion of thirty-seven feasts: *Purification of B.V.M.*, Chair of Peter, Matthew, Gregory, *In capite ieiunii* (partly erased), *Easter*, Mark, Philip and James, Invention of Cross, *Rogation, Ascension, Pentecost, Trinity, John Baptist, Peter and Paul*, Margaret, Mary Magdalene, James, Chains of Peter, Laurence, *Assumption of B.V.M.*, Bartholomew, Decollation of John Baptist, *Nativity of B.V.M., Exaltation of Cross*, Matthew, *Michael*, Luke, Simon and Jude, *All Saints*, Leonard, Martin, Katherine, *Andrew*, Nicholas, Conception of B.V.M. (marginalia, s. xiii, make up a full office), Thomas apostle.

5. ff. 151ᵛ–159ᵛ Common of Saints.

6. ff. 159ᵛ–160 In dedicatione ecclesie. *Sarum Missal*, pp. 202–4.

7. ff. 160–1 De sancta cruce. *Sarum Missal*, pp. 386–7.

8. ff. 161–3 Missa de sancta maria.

Sarum Missal, pp. 389/35–391, 387/15–389/30. From 388/3 is in the hand of arts. 9–12.

Arts. 9–13 and the end of art. 8 are on two added quires, s. xv.

9. ff. 163–166ᵛ 'Missa pro pace' and collect, secret, and postcommunion of

fourteen votive masses, Pro serenitate aeris, Ad pluuiam postulandam, In tempore belli, Pro quacumque tribulacione, Contra pestilenciam, Pro papa, Pro semetipso, Contra temptacionem carnis, Pro speciali amico, Pro iter agentibus, Pro peste animalium, Pro semetipso, Contra cogitaciones malas, Ad poscendum donum.

All as *Sarum Missal,* except Contra pestilenciam (Deus qui nobis, Subueniat nobis, Exaudi nos).

10. ff. 166ᵛ–169 Prefaces of mass, the first for Christmas and the last the common preface. *Sarum Missal,* pp. 211–15, 220.

11. ff. 169ᵛ–173 Canon of mass.

12. (*a*) ff. 173–174ᵛ Missa pro defunctis. (*b*) ff. 174ᵛ–177ᵛ Collect, secret, and postcommunion In die sepulture, In anniuersariis, Pro trigintali, Pro fratribus et sororibus, Pro patre et matre, Pro benefactoribus, Pro trigintalibus euoluendis, Pro parentibus et benefactoribus, Pro omnibus fidelibus and Oracio generalis (two forms).

(*a*). *Sarum Missal,* pp. 431–3. (*b*). ibid., pp. 434, 437–8, 438–9, 438, 436, 437, 439, 436–7, 442, 442–3, 445.

13 (added in current hand). (*a*) f. 177ᵛ Gloria in excelsis deo . . . (*b*) f. 178 Credo in vnum deum patrem . . . f. 178ᵛ blank.

14 (added in s. xiii¹). f. 137ᵛ Carta de Welesford Mane die sancti Nicholai . . .

Twenty-seven entries in several hands follow the heading. Each entry appears to refer to a household and a very small sum of money. Usually two dots precede each entry, with a cancelling stroke through them and—further left—what looks like a reversed *c* or the sign for *con,* but 'leg' is twice in this position. The first three entries are (1) 'Phelipus de Luccumbe alic'. et simon. et sib'. sib'. p' et p' d'. (2) Hur' de Loueston et angn' et Ioh'. alic'. wat' Ioan. et Ioan' alpays et felic'. d'. (3) Nich' doling. ux' p' o'.¹ Many crossings out and additions.

ff. iii+177+iv. f. 181 was pasted down. 243 × 175 mm. Written space *c.* 185 × 120 mm. 2 cols. and, ff. 138–45, long lines. 40 lines (quire 18). 34 lines (quires 1–16, 19–21). 30 lines (quire 17). 28 lines (quires 22, 23). Pricks in both margins of quires 1–13, 18–21. In arts. 1–3 the first line of writing is above the top ruled line, except in three quires, 15–17, where the top ruled line looks like an afterthought. Collation: 1–10⁸ 11¹⁰ 12–13⁸ 14⁴ (ff. 107–10) 15–17⁸ 18 three (ff. 135–7) 19–23⁸. Quires 1–11 numbered II–XII. Arts. 1, 2, 4–8 (to f. 161ᵛ) mainly in one poor hand. A better hand wrote three quires, 15–17. Initials, ff. 1–161ᵛ: (i) f. 1, red and blue *A* with ornament of both colours; (ii) 2-line, red, blue, or green, plain or with ornament in one of the other colours. Initials, ff. 162–177ᵛ: 2-line, red. Capital letters in the ink of the text filled with red. Binding, s. xv: wooden boards covered with white leather and a chemise over all: five bands: central strap and pin: the binder damaged marginalia in art. 1. The book includes a five-tailed leather bookmarker. Secundo folio *credendo.*

Written in England. Used presumably in the Devon (?) parish in which Welesford lies (art. 14). 'liber I. hyett' and 'liber domini I. hyett precii xxvi s' viii d' ', f. 181. His gift to the chapel of St. Anne in the parish of St. Sidwell, Exeter: 'Dominus Iohannes Hyotte Anniuellarius in Ecclesia Cath' Exon' contulit hunc librum Missale deo et capelle sancte Anne in paroch' sancte Satiuole situat' ob honore sancte anne et beati Iohannis Euang'

¹ p' for penny, d' for halfpenny, o' for farthing.

ibidem pro celebrant' quamdiu durauerit remansurum', f. 169, s. xv. 'N° 14' and 'n° 9' inside the cover. *CMA*, no. 9.

3516. *W. Woodford; R. Ullerston* s. xv[1]

Two originally separate English manuscripts bound together in s. xv.

1. ff. 2–63ᵛ [Uenerabili] in cristo patri ac illustri domino thome Cantu' archiepiscopo tocius anglie primati et sedis apostolice legato humilis suus seruitor. frater Willelmus Woford deuotissimus . . . Reuerendissime pater mandatis uestris . . . traxatum fuit nimis breue. Scripta in castro de framlynham in vig' pasch'. Paternitatem vestram . . . per tempora longiora. amen.

Woodford's tractate against Wyclif written in 1396. Emden, *BRUO*, p. 2081. Printed in the *Fasciculus rerum expetendarum* of O. Gratius (ed. E. Brown, 1690, i. 191–265), but the last sentence before the colophon, in which the author explains that his time was too short for a full discussion, is not in the printed text.

2. ff. 64–111 Reuerendi magistri patres et domini alias ut audistis eram pertractando textum . . . iuxta scienciam michi datam domino concedente. etc. Explicit tractatus Magistri Ricardi Vllerston' Magistri in theologia qui intitulatur defensorium dotacionis ecclesie editus ab eodem Oxon' Anno domini M°. cccc^mo primo.

Cf. A. Hudson in *EHR* xc (1975), 10; Emden, *BRUO*, p. 1928. Thirty chapters. f. 111ᵛ blank.

ff. i+110, foliated 1–111.

Art. 1. 257×170 mm. Written space 200×125 mm. 2 cols. 40 lines. Collation: seven quires of 8 and a quire of 6 (ff. 58–63). Textura. A 3-line space for an initial, f. 2, remains blank.

Art. 2. 225×160 mm. Written space 168×105 mm. 32 long lines. Frame ruling. Collation: six quires of 8. Signatures a. i–f. viii. Written in non-current secretary. 2-line red initials.

Binding, s. xv: white leather over wooden boards and a chemise over all: four bands: central clasp: remains of a staple for the chain on the back cover near the foot: a label on the back cover under horn secured by six nails, inscribed 'Continentur in hoc libro conclusiones Willelmi Woford contra conclusiones Wykclyff. Item defensorium dotacionis ecclesie Magistri Ricardi Hollerston. doctoris in theologia Oxon' '. Secundo folio *pietas*.

Art. 1 (if not art. 2) was the gift of Henry Webber (Emden, *BRUO*: † by Feb. 1477): 'Liber M' Henrici Webber decani ecclesie Cath' Exon' ', f. 63ᵛ; 'Hunc librum disposuit Magister Henricus Webber Decanus Ecclesie Cathedralis Exon'. Magne Librarie Ecclesie Cath' predict' de bonis suis propriis', f. 1ᵛ. Art. 1 is entered in the 1506 inventory, p. 370. Presumably art. 2 was then with it. 'N° 56' inside cover; also, on a label, 'N° 13'. '13' at head of spine. *CMA*, nos. 45–6.

3517. 'Catholicon' 1431

Aaron propre [nom] interpretatur mons fortis masculum generis. Ab preposicion qui sert a lablatif . . . (f. 148) Zucarum. ri. idem. ne. generis. Explicit catholicon, quod completum fuit anno domini M° iiii^mo. xxxi° die xiiii^a mensis februarii. Deo gracias.

The Latin–French dictionary called Aalma (after the first word in Paris, B.N. lat. 13032), printed in *Recueil général des lexiques français du moyen âge*, ii (Bibliothèque de l'Ecole des Hautes Etudes, cclxix, 1938), ed. M. Roques, who lists this and eleven other copies, all differing much from one another (p. xvii). The text is followed (f. 148^{rv}) by six couplets and a triplet and the name 'R. Lugon' written very large (f. 148^v). The first couplet is 'Tu prece sacrifica pro lugon tancito librum/Scribere qui fecit non sine versiculis' and the next three all name Lugon. The word 'Retro' is written after each couplet, and the triplet begins 'Tu metra retrogrado cum sensu suscipe'. ff. 149–151^v left blank.

ff. iii+150+ii, foliated i, ii, 1–153. f. 1 is a medieval flyleaf. 245×175 mm. Written space 170×128 mm. 2 cols. 36 lines. Collation of ff. 2–151: 1–18^8 19^6 (6 was pasted down). Written in textura. Initials: (i) f. 2, 3-line *A* in red and blue; (ii) 2-line, blue or red. Binding of s. xviii.

Written in France in 1431 for R. Lugon. 'E. C. Harington 1825' f. ii. His armorial bookplate inside the cover. 'This Book was presented to the Chapter of Exeter by the Revd E. C. Harington, Incumbent of St David's. 28th April 1842', f. i^v.

3518. *Martyrologium ecclesiae Exoniensis* s. XII[1]

(*begins imperfectly*, 8 *Febr.*) cum illa execrans . . . (*31 Dec.*) actus cl[ari].

Usuard's martyrology, with English and local Exeter additions in the main hand and many later additions and obits in the margins. Printed from a later revised copy by J. N. Dalton, *Ordinale Exon.* ii (HBS xxxviii, 1909), 371–459. Description of MS. 3518 in *Ord. Ex.* i (HBS xxxvii, 1909), xxv, xxvi; facsimile of f. 22^v in ii, pl. viii; variations from the printed text, obits apart, listed by G. H. Doble in iv (HBS lxxix, 1940), 3–39. The parts of the text missing here at the beginning and between the present quires 7 and 8 are in edn. 371–381/16, 439/10 (9 Oct.)–453/2 (6 Dec.).

The obits, many of them dated, have not been printed. The dates range from 1072 (Leofric) to 1258.[1]

ff. 62. 220×162 mm. Written space 180×100 mm. 27 long lines. Ruling with a hard point. Collation: 1–7^8 8 six (ff. 57–62). Quires 2, 4–7 numbered at the end III, V–VIII. 2-line red or blue initials. Medieval binding of bevelled wooden boards, bare of leather: four bands; central strap-and-pin fastening missing: a red leather loose cover (s. xix ?) over the boards.

Written at Exeter. 'N° 21' inside the cover. *CMA*, no. 27.

3519. *Medica, etc.* s. xv in.

1. ff. 2–40^v (*begins imperfectly*) Et sic sub diuo si sit frigidata bibatur . . . Dicitur ictericum potata repellere morbum (*ends imperfectly in the section* Vulgago).

Macer, De viribus herbarum, ed. Choulant, 1832, ll. 56–1539.

2. ff. 49–51^v (*begins imperfectly*) nigri et albi corticum citri . . . coctum ad ignem. Ista sunt prescripta de simplici aqua vite et de composita et de perfectissima ad exemplar originalis extracta ex diuersorum dictis philosophorum medicine artis.

Cf. Singer and Anderson, no. 1000. Attributed in some copies to Theodoricus (Borgognoni), bishop of Cervia (1270–98).

[1] A transcript by Canon Doble is in the Cathedral Library.

3. ff. 52–61ᵛ Absinthium amarum calidum . . . wermot. Absinthium ceutonica . . . Zima fermentum idem sunt.

A Latin–English vocabulary of herb names, etc. Cf. B.L., Royal 12 E. i, f. 69.

4. ff. 62–63ᵛ Vnguentum quod dicitur diacacio multum habet contra omnem guttam . . . Pernetz de grece de cat . . .

Recipes in French.

5. (a) ff. 63ᵛ–64 Chescun homme ad quatre humours . . . et la vrine molt clere. (b) f. 64ʳᵛ Corpus hominis ex quatuor constat humoribus . . . non modica egritudo.

(b). Cf. Thorndike and Kibre, *Corpus humanum ex quatuor constat* . . .

6. ff. 65–67ᵛ De planetis et eorum virtute. legite que sequuntur. Sciendum est ergo quod si aliquis nascitur in aliqua hora diei . . . a bono deo suscipiet. scilicet vitam eternam. Amen.

7. ff. 67ᵛ–116ᵛ Incipit liber graduum secundum constantinum. Quoniam disputacionem simplicis medicine . . . sompnus prouocabitur.

Thorndike and Kibre. Arranged alphabetically, Absinthium–Viola.

8. ff. 117–21 Oportet te alexander. Alexander cum sit homo corpus corruptibile . . . non possunt. Oportet te alexander cum a sompno surexeris . . . sanitatem ministrat. Debilitant . . . opus est homicidis.

Aristotle to Alexander, De sanitate servanda. Thorndike and Kibre. Preface and fourteen sections, most of them followed by verses, fifty-nine in all, the first 'Lumina mane manus . . .' (Renzi, v. 6) and the last 'Debilitant siccant . . .' (18 lines).

9. ff. 121–233 Oua formicarum trita surdarum aurium licet . . . In medicando has passiones (*ends abruptly*).

A large mass of recipes partly in French, among them some charms, including one 'Pur le cancre' (f. 128ʳᵛ), which invokes among others Edmund king and martyr; also a long 'ordo' for exorcizing an evil spirit, ff. 127ᵛ–128, a prayer against all ills, 'Duce dame seint marie pucele pure reigne des angeles . . .', with directions for reciting it (f. 160ʳᵛ), and a list of the twelve fasting Fridays, 'Ioe clement apostoille de Rome . . .' (ff. 160ᵛ–161). The lower right corner of many leaves has been eaten away, with slight loss of text on ff. 129–144 and some later leaves. ff. 233ᵛ–235ᵛ were left blank.

10. Additions in the space after art. 9 include (f. 233ᵛ) a 'Carmen propter febres. Coniuro te cr(e)atura salis per deum viuum . . .', s. xv, and (f. 234) a long recipe in English for the 'ache yn a mannys arme'.

ff. i+226+i, foliated i, 2–40, 49–199, 201–36. The foliation, medieval except on ff. 234–6, takes account of leaves now missing and repeats the number 'cciii' in error. 220 × 158 mm. Written space c. 160 × 120 mm. 26–9 long lines. Collation: 1⁸ wants 1 2–23⁸ 24⁸ wants 8 after f. 199 25–28⁸ 29⁴. Quires 1–23 numbered in the usual late medieval manner a–e, g–z, 7. Written in current anglicana: a change of hand at f. 137. Initials 2-line, red or green: none in art. 9. Contemporary binding of wooden boards covered with pink-stained leather: five bands: two strap and pin fastenings now missing. Secundo folio (f. 2) *Et sic.*

Written in England. An erasure, f. iᵛ. Names 'William herde' and 'Edwarde eliott(?)' on

f. 233, s. xvi. 'N⁰ 2' and 'N⁰ 18' inside the cover and '18' on a label at the top of the spine. *CMA*, no. 2.

3520. (*A*) *Anselmus, Opera;* (*B*) *Ambrosius, etc.;* (*C*) *Misc. theol.*
s. XII in.–XII[1]

An early collection (s. xii in.) of works of St. Anselm, not used for *SAO*, forms arts. 1–11 (A). It was bound with arts. 12–16 (B) after 1327 and before 1506: see below.

1. pp. 1–22 Incipit prefatio anselmi cantuariensis archiepiscopi in opus subditum. Tres Tractatus pertinentes . . . ord[inari]. Ex[plicit] prefacio. Incipiunt capitula in tractatu de ueritate. [i]. Quod ueritas . . . in omnibus ueris. Expliciunt capitula. Incipit tractatus de ueritate editus ab anselmo cantuariensi archiepiscopo. Discipulus. Quoniam deum . . . uel rectitudo. Explicit tractatus de ueritate. *SAO* i. 173–99.

2. pp. 22–39 Incipiunt capitula in tractatum de libero arbitrio. i. Quod potestas . . . xiiii. Diuisio eiusdem libertatis. Incipit tractatus de libero arbitrio. Discipulus. Quoniam liberum arbitrium uidetur repugnare . . . de illis interrogare. *SAO* i. 205–26.

3. pp. 39–75. Incipiunt capitula in tractatum de casu diaboli. i. Quod etiam . . . quantum ad esse. Expliciunt capitula. Incipit tractatus de casu diaboli. editus ab anselmo cantuariensi archiepiscopo. D'. [I]llud apostoli . . . loquendi. Explicit tractatus de casu diaboli. *SAO* i. 232–76.

4. pp. 75–98 Incipit epistola de incarnatione uerbi. Domino et patri . . . aperte inueniet. 'Explicit Epistola de incarnatione verbi' (*these five words added, s. xiv*). *SAO* ii. 3–35.

5. pp. 99–169 Incipit prefatio cur deus homo. Opus subditum . . . despiciat. Explicit prologus. Incipiunt capitula primi libri. Questio de qua totum opus pendet . . . probata sit (*capitula of two books*). Expliciunt capitula. Incipit cur deus homo liber A' c' a'. Sepe et studiosissime . . . benedictus in secula Amen. Explicit cur deus homo liber 'beati' anselmi cantuariensis archiepiscopi. *SAO* ii. 42–133.

6. pp. 69–76 Incipit meditatio animę cristianę. Anima cristiana anima de graui morte . . . benedictus in secula seculorum. Amen. Explicit meditatio animę cristianę. *SAO* iii. 84–91 (Med. 3).

7. pp. 176–203 Incipiunt capitula de conceptu uirginali et originali peccato. i. Quę sit originalis . . . post baptisma. Incipit liber anselmi de conceptu uirginali et originali peccato. Cum in omnibus . . . probari poterit. Explicit de conceptu uirginali et de originali peccato. *SAO* ii. 137–73. Twenty-nine chapters.

8. pp. 202–9 Incipit epistola anselmi archiepiscopi de sacrificio azimi et fermentati. Anselmus seruus ęcclesię cantuariensis.' Waleramno nuemburgensi episcopo. Scienti . . . iudicatur. Explicit de sacrificio azimi et fermentati. *SAO* ii. 223–32.

9. pp. 209–27 Quomodo gramaticus sit substantia et qualitas. Discipulus. De grammatico peto ut me certum facias . . . non negabis. *SAO* i. 145–68.

10. pp. 228–30 Oratio episcopi uel abbatis ad sanctum sub cuius nomine regit ecclesiam. Sancte N. pie N. beate N. unus de gloriosis . . . fiat fiat. *SAO* iii. 68–70 (Or. 17).

11. pp. 230–2 Oratio propria monachorum ad sanctum benedictum. Sancte et beate benedicte . . . secula seculorum. Amen. *SAO* iii. 61–4 (Or. 15).

A scribble, s. xii, in the blank space on p. 232 'H' rex angl' et dux normannie'.

Arts. 12–16 (B) are mainly on the eucharist, s. xii in. Headings and explicits were not filled in. pp. 233–68 are injured by damp.

12. pp. 235–53 'Ambrosius de Misteriis'. 'Ex' moralibus . . . operetur.

PL xvi. 389–410 (405–26). pp. 233, 234 were left blank.

13. pp. 253–93 [D]e sacramentis . . . peruenire possitis. Per . . . amen.

PL xvi. 417–62 (435–82). Ambrose, De sacramentis. Only a small fragment remains of pp. 275–6.

14. pp. 294–301 [M]agnitudo cęlestium beneficiorum . . . piis nos operibus preparare dignetur. qui regnat in secula seculorum amen.

The direction for the rubricator, '[. . . . . .] episcopi de corpore et sanguine cristi in pascha Eusebii emiseni', is partly cut off in the upper margin. *Clavis*, no. 966: Faustus Reiensis (Pseudo-Eusebius Emesenus), sermo 16. In *PL* among the works of Jerome, Caesarius, and Isidore (xxx. 280–4, lxvii. 1052–6, lxxxiii. 1225–8).

15. pp. 303–58 Lanfrancus misericordia dei catholicus. Berengario catholicę ecclesię aduersario. Si diuina pietas . . . et uerus est sanguis quem potamus.

PL cl. 407–42. Lanfranc, De Corpore et Sanguine Domini. Directions for the rubricator partly cut off: in the upper margin of p. 303, 'Incipit epistola do[. . . . .]'; in the lower margin of p. 358, '[. . . . .] Lan' cantuariensis ecclesie archiepiscopi ad Berengarium Turonensem'.

16. pp. 359–477 [A]d rem his temporibus . . . Cui pro tanta caritate gratias referamus ęternas. regnanti cum deo . . . amen. Explicit liber domni Guimundi auersani episcopi. de corpore et sanguine domini.

Guitmund, bishop of Aversa, against Berengar. *PL* cxlix. 1427–94. The direction for the rubricator, 'Incipit liber Guimundi (*etc.*)', in the upper margin of p. 359. p. 478 blank.

Arts. 17, 18 (C) were written in s. xii[1].

17. pp. 479–86 [I]ndubitanter credo unum esse deum et non plures . . . prebet experimentum.

Eleven paragraphs.

18. pp. 486–94 Coniugium quod et matrimonium appellatur . . . Vnde manifestum est quod (*ends abruptly*).

PL clxxvi. 153–67/29, as tractate 7 of Hugh of St. Victor, Summa sententiarum. Cf. A. Wilmart in *RTAM* xi (1939), 144 (Gautier de Mortagne).

ff. ii+247+iii, paginated (i–iv), 1–500. p. 500 was pasted down. 225 × 135 mm. Binding of thick bevelled boards covered with thin and now tattered white skin: four bands: central strap. The work appears to be late medieval, reusing older boards by turning them round. A chainmark, a single round hole, at the foot of the back cover. Secundo folio *quid sit ueritas.*

A. pp. 1–232. Written space c. 170 × 95 mm. 30–1 long lines. Ruling with hard point. Collation: 1–8¹² 9–10¹⁰. Quires numbered at the end. Several hands, all probably French. 4-line, 3-line, and 2-line initials, red, blue, or green.

B. pp. 233–478. Written space c. 148 × 80 mm. 30 long lines. Ruling with hard point. Collation: 11–17⁸ 18⁸ wants 8, blank, after p. 358 19–25⁸ 26⁴. Quires numbered at the end or the beginning. Signatures of the usual late medieval type were added probably in s. xv. All in one hand of Norman type, resembling hands in other Exeter manuscripts of this period. Initials not filled in.

C. pp. 479–94. Written space 185 × 125 mm. 2 cols. 42 lines. Ruling with hard point. Collation: 27⁸. Initials not filled in.

A was written probably in France and B probably at Exeter. They are listed separately in the Exeter catalogue of 1327 and together in the Exeter catalogue of 1506 (Oliver, *Lives*, pp. 303, 371). The damage to the beginning of B must have taken place before A was bound with it, since there is no similar pattern of damp on the last leaves of A. The status of C is unclear: 'Rogeri de Sidbir' ' (Sidbury, Devon) is on its last page, s. xii. 'N° 16' inside the cover. *CMA*, no. 1.

3521. *J. Seward, etc.* s. XIV med. (art. 3), XV¹

Described by J. N. Dalton, *The Collegiate Church of Ottery St. Mary*, 1917, pp. 1–8. Miscellaneous pieces lie on either side of seven quires (8–14) containing statutes of Ottery and Crediton.

1 (quire 1). pp. 1, 2 De omnibus obitibus gradatim sequentibus per annum in ecclesia de Otery. In primus . . . iohannis 22ⁱ pape.

Printed by Dalton, op. cit., p. 218. pp. ix, x, 3, 4 blank.

2 (quires 2–6). The Ludicra and Invectiva of John Seward (1364–1435 or 1436: Emden, *BRUO*, p. 1364): (a) pp. 5–28 Argumentum in ludicra Iohannis Segvard. Presumptuosos et erraces (sic) in metricis.' oblatratus . . . faciat in commune.' Valete. Expliciunt ludicra Iohannis Segvard; (b) pp. 29–81 'Hic incipiunt [. . . . . inu]ectiue Iohannis Segvard in Willelmum Reli[k et magistrum] Willelmum Scheffeld.' Omnes gaudete metriste . . . redarguit ipsum. Vt Relik vt Scheffel in Seward inuehit vsque Iam premissa breuis pagina quenque docet; (c) p. 82 Epitafium Magistri I. Bacun. Hic fuit anglorum decus et flos philosophorum . . . (7 lines); (d) pp. 83–6 Epistola Iohannis Segvard ad perspicacissimam et disertissimam vniuersitatem Oxonie. Reuerendissimi in cristo . . . mancipatum. Script' primo london' . . . anno regni regis Henrici quarti post conquestum anglie terciodecimo. 'Explicit Epistola Iohannis Segvard ad perspicacissimam (etc.)'. Incipiuntque ludicra eiusdem Iohannis.

See V. H. Galbraith, 'John Seward and his Circle', *MARS* i. 85–104, and for this copy V. H. Galbraith in *Trans. Edinburgh Bibl. Soc.* iii (1946), 385–6. Quire 6, the bifolium containing (d), should precede quire 2. In (b) the ten epigrams to John Leylond are on a leaf sewn to p. 75 and are marked by a *signe de renvoi* to follow the epigrams addressed to Richard Attham on pp. 72–5. p. 82 was left blank after (b), and (c) was added on it. 'ii c let*ter* prise xii d' at the head of p. 83 cannot be a rubricator's charge for art. 2, which has only three coloured initials.

3 (quire 7). pp. 87–110 Iste liber quem pre manibus habemus vocatur secretum philosophorum et intitulatur isto nomine . . .

At first the same intriguing piece as in B.L., Add. 18752, 32622, and Sloane 2579. Bk. 1, 'de grammatica', is mainly on inks ('De incausto lumbardie', p. 87), colours, the preparation of parchment, and secret writing'. 'liber 2us de retorica. Retorica docet etiam ornate loqui . . .' comes on p. 92 and 'Dialectica docet discernere verum a falso . . .' on p. 93/12. Shortly after p. 96/24, 'Arsmetrica docet de numero . . .', the text diverges from that of the other manuscripts and turns into recipes and charms, etc., among which are: p. 102, a charm to get rid of rats; p. 105, 19 lines in English headed 'fpr tp tbkkn rbtpxnbs'; p. 108, 'In ye monyt of march figis et reyses and oder swetemetys vse . . .' and other advice in English on food, drink, and bloodletting, etc., month by month, March–December; p. 108, Ieronimus fecit istam loricam contra demones . . .; p. 109, A charm 'pro furibus', beginning with the verses 'Disparibus meritis pendunt tria corpora ramis Dismas et Iesmas . . .' (Walther, no. 4582); p. 110, in last place, eight 'Medecynys for hors' written sideways to save space.

4 (quires 8–14). (*a*, *b*) pp. 111–286 Statutes of Ottery and (p. 225) Crediton. (*c*) pp. 287–8 Six recipes, two of them in English in the same hand as (*a*, *b*). (*d*) p. 288 An added recipe in English 'For to make fysheglue. Take the sawle of a mywelfyshe that is to say a whyte skyn that lyeth by the chynebone . . .'.

(*a*). pp. 114–21, 135–224 printed by Dalton, op. cit., pp. 81–115, 133–258.

5 (quires 15–19). (*a*) pp. 291–416 Hic incipiunt medicine pro dolore membrorum ad ex^m et primo pro pedum locione . . . (*b*) p. 362, in the same hand as (*a*), a list, crossed through, of eleven books under the heading 'De accepcione librorum Magistri Iohannis Excetre secum a camera sua londoniis ad curiam'.

(*a*). Recipes and other pieces in the same hand as art. 4, partly in Latin and partly in English, including: pp. 311–12, De diebus in quibus est sanguinem minuere et in quibus non. et in omnibus mensibus. In Ianuario sunt octo dies . . . Explicit kalendare mensium pro sanguinis minucione; p. 312, Sunt ii(i) dies et noctes in quibus qui natus fuerit corpus eius integrum erit usque in diem iudicii . . .; p. 312, Isti sunt dies mali . . .; p. 316, Hic incipit tractatus aureus de medicinis et pro laicis in lingua materna. The man þat wil of lechecraft lerne . . . in diuerse place: this appears to be an introduction to the collection of recipes in English beginning on p. 317 'For þe heed ache. Take and sethe verueyne' and continuing to about p. 350; pp. 368–71 De 4^{or} temporibus anni . . .; pp. 372–92, a regimen, 'Bonum est ut unusquisque seruet calorem naturalem . . . in suo ascensu. Ista sunt quamuis pauca a secretis secretorum Aristotelis extracta. et sufficiunt ad commune regimen generis utriusque humani. Expliciunt abstracta a libris Aristotelis pro sanitate corporis humani'; p. 400, Galienus de signis mortis. F(r)ons rubet . . .; p. 403, . . . Expliciunt fata infantum sub diuersis natorum signis et hoc singulis mensibus. (*b*). Printed by Dalton, op. cit., p. 2. The incipit of each book is given, or the incipit of the table in front of it and the leaf on which the incipit comes. John Exeter bequeathed 'omnes libros meos c. xxxvi in numero quod manu mea propria scripsi pro maiori parte ad cathenandum in libraria de Otery' (Registrum Lacy, f. 513^v: will, 28 July 1445).

Recipes were added in other hands on pp. 298–300, 420. pp. 289, 290 were left blank. The former contains musical notes on a five-line stave and the names Robertus Crook, Thomas Argulas, and Rogerus Kendale and against them 'De comitatu Barwyci'.

6. pp. i–viii, 423–30 Four leaves of Digestum vetus, bk. 8, laid sideways as binding leaves.

English hand, s. xiv. pp. i, 430 were pasted down.

ff. iv+211+v, paginated (i–x), 1–430. A medieval foliation of pp. 135–288 'i' to '77'.
The leaf attached to p. 75 is unnumbered. Paper and (art. 2) parchment. 223 × 150 mm.
Written space: art. 3, 205 × 133 mm in 65 long lines; art. 5, *c*. 165 × 97 mm in 24 long
lines; art. 2, 145 × 85 mm in 26 long lines. Collation of pp. ix, x, 1–420: 1 three (pp. ix, x,
1–4) 2¹² 3 seven (pp. 29–42) 4⁶+1 leaf before 1 (pp. 43, 44) 5¹² 8 cancelled after p. 70 and
replaced by a leaf sewn to the stub (pp. 71, 72), 9 cancelled, +2 leaves inserted after the
stub of 9 (pp. 73–6) and a leaf (unnumbered) sewn to p. 75 6² (pp. 83–6) 7–12¹² 13¹⁴ (pp.
231–58) 14¹⁶ wants 16, perhaps blank, after p. 288 15–16¹² 17¹⁴ 18¹⁶ 19¹². Quires 2–5
signed a–d and quires 15–19 m–q. Strips of parchment taken from a manuscript lie
between and down the middle of the paper quires. Arts. 1–3 in current anglicana, 2*b* of
a set type, 3 earlier than the rest. Arts. 4*a*–*c*, 5*a*, *b* in one hand, tall, narrow, and upright,
a mixture of anglicana and secretary. Blue initials with red ornament. Binding of wooden
boards covered with white leather: four bands: central strap and pin, the strap missing.
Secundo folio (p. 85) *quam reformari*.

Written in England, arts. 1, 4, 5 in Devon, and probably at Ottery St. Mary. Presumably
one of the books given by John Exeter to the collegiate church of Ottery St. Mary in
1445. 'Sum liber Thomæ Drake ex dono amici mei W M', p. 421, s. xvi/xvii. 'Nᵒ 17'
inside the cover. 'Nᵒ 23', p. ix. *CMA*, nos. 22, 23.

3522, 3523, 3524, 3549A are fifteenth-century copies of the constitutions of
Bishop Peter de Quivil (Emden, *BRUO*, p. 2208: †1291).[1] 3522 was given by
John Snow, precentor, in 1763. 3523 belonged to John Anstis and Sir Jonathan
Trelawny, †1721, and was given by Sir Harry Trelawny, 2 October 1817. 3549A
was bought in 1887.

3522 and 3549A end with the words 'Orate pro Episcopo Petro uiuo et mortuo et
quicunque hoc fecerit gaudebit Quadraginta dierum Amen'. 3523 and 3524 are
in contemporary white-leather bindings.

3525. *Miscellanea theologica*   s. XII in.

1. pp. 1–49 Licet multi et probatissimi . . . non prodesse. Explicit ad Orosium.
Beati augustini.

PL xl. 735–52 (Pseudo-Augustine). *Clavis*, no. 373. Römer, i. 61.

2. pp. 49–52 Item sententię ex libris eiusdem excerptę aduersum manicheos.
Interrogatio. Quare fecit deus hominem . . . uidebantur exposui. Explicit.

Bk. 2, chs. 28, 29, of Augustine, De genesi contra manicheos (*PL* xxxiv. 218–20); ch. 28
is cast into question and answer form.

3. (*a*) pp. 52–70 Questiones partim in genesim partim alię. Interrogatio. Queritur quid in cęli terręque nomine significatur quando dicitur. In principio
creauit deus cęlum et terram . . . ueritate adueniente cessauit umbra. Explicit.
(*b*) pp. 70–9 Item alię questiones. Int'. Quomodo ut ait apostolus omnes sunt
administratorii . . . uel carie defecerunt consumpta. (*c*) pp. 79–93 Item alię questiones. Int. Quid est quod in libro geneseos legitur. quia cum esset moyses in
diuersorio . . . adiuuari potentiam suam.

Quotations from Jerome and Sallust in (*a*) and from Jordanes in (*b*).

---

[1] Mr. Daniel Huws tells me that N.L.W., Peniarth 162 i, another fifteenth-century
copy of these constitutions, is inscribed 'Constat Honynton'. He suggests that a fifteenth-

4. pp. 93–120 Responsiones prosperi contra Impugnationes hereticorum. quas contra libros beati augustini de predestinatione opposuerunt. Doctrinam quam . . . ex prescientia ducentur.

PL li. 155–74.

5. pp. 121–51 Sermo de ęcclesiastico ordine et figura. Legitur in ęcclesiastica historia. quod nabuchodonosor . . . et secundum ea non uiuere. (*b*) pp. 151–74 Sermo de dedicatione ęcclesię. Ecclesia autem domus dominica metonomice dicitur . . . Erit enim deus omnia in omnibus.

(*a*) and (*b*) together form a 'Summa de diuinis officiis' in Cambridge, Fitzwilliam, MS. Maclean 101, ff. 169–174ᵛ. In Salisbury Cathedral 135 they are on ff. 7–13ᵛ and 17–23. Cf. my description of Lambeth Palace 1229, nos. 14, 15, in E. G. W. Bill, *A Catalogue of Manuscripts in Lambeth Palace Library, MSS. 1222–1860*, 1972, p. 59.

6. pp. 174–5 Ideo in aqua et non in alio liquore baptizatur homo . . . vi.ʲ elemosina. vii.ʲ martirium.

Sentences on baptism, Christ's birth in the winter, 'carnis integritas', horn neither flesh nor bone, despairing of pardon, and the seven ways to redemption.

7. (*a*) pp. 175–9 Sermo exceptus de libello augustini de pęnitentia. Pęnitentes. pęnitentes. pęnitentes. si tamen estis pęnitentes . . . dimitte incertum et tene certum. (*b*) p. 179 Augustinus. Quicumque adorant et colunt aues celi . . . cum diabolo punientur.

(*a*). *PL* xxxix. 1713–15 (Sermo 393). Römer, i. 144.

8. pp. 179–92 Paradisus in quo fuit adam positus. in quo erat uarietas arborum et fructuum.ʲ significat ęcclesia . . . Helias panem quem mulier fecit comedit.

Significations from the Old Testament, Genesis–Kings.

9. Nearly contemporary additions: (*a*) p. 192 Anna et emeria . . . mater domini; (*b*) p. 193 Ex testimoniis iiiiᵒʳ euangeliorum et epistola ieronimi contra heluinium. Sancta maria mater domini . . . est inseparabilis; (*c*) pp. 194–6 Incipiunt exceptiones amalarii. [I]n septuagesima cantatur . . . thesaurus esse promeruit; (*d*) p. ii Aue maria gratia plena dominus tecum benedicta tu in mulieribus et benedictus fructus uentris tui.

(*d*) is in a charter hand, with long ascenders and descenders.

ff. i+99, paginated i, ii, 1–24, 24*, 24**, 25–196. 195 × 120 mm. Written space 130 × 70 mm. 25 long lines. Ruling with a hard point. Collation: 1–5⁸ 6–7¹⁰ 8⁸ 9–10¹⁰ 11¹⁰+1 leaf after 10 (f. 99). Metallic red or (p. 94) green initials set outside the written space: within the written space only a one-letter width was reserved. Capital letters in the ink of the text filled with red. Contemporary binding of white skin over wooden boards cut flush with the edges of the leaves: projecting ears at head and foot of the spine: two bands: central strap and pin missing. Secundo folio *natura est*.

Written in England. A title on the back cover, s. xv: 'Augustinus ad orosium discipulum suum et prosper contra eiusdem sancti augustini impugnationes. thomson';[1] also

century bishop of Exeter tried to make good Quivil's intention that every parish should have its copy.

[1] In Syon Abbey books the donor's name was written in this position on a label under horn.

'Precium [. . .] viii^d. 'W.A.S. m.d.' at the top of p. 1, s. xvii (?). 'N° 20' inside the cover and '20' on a lozenge-shaped label on the spine. 'N° 30', p. i.

3526. *Johannes de S. Paulo, Breviarium*   s. xiii[1]

1. ff. 1–47 Assiduis peticionibus me karissimi . . . uero de febribus . . . (*table of chapters of bk. 1*) . . . Quoniam longitudini in hoc opere parcere destinauimus . . . opera dirigente deo omnipotente.

Thorndike and Kibre (John of St. Paul, Breviarium). Five books: 2, f. 10^v; 3, f. 21; 4, f. 30^v; 5, f. 35^v. A table of chapters before each book. A running title in red and blue capitals gives title (BRE IO DE SP) and book number. Marginalia in various hands, s. xiii, xiv, and a few English glosses and notes, s. xvi.

2. f. 47^{rv} Gynaecological recipes in twenty-four paragraphs added in a hand nearly contemporary with art. 1.

One recipe is 'ad concipiendum masculum'; another (magic ?) has been rubbed and is hardly legible.

ff. i+47+i. 190 × 130 mm. Written space 162 × 100 mm. 2 cols. 33–8 lines. Writing above top ruled line. Collation: 1–2^8 3^8 wants 1 before f. 17 4–6^8. Initials: (i) of preface and bks. 2–5, 3-line, blue and red with ornament of both colours and violet: saw pattern down the side; (ii) of bk. 1, 3-line, red with violet ornament; (iii) of chapters, 2-line, red with violet ornament or blue with red ornament; (iv) of tables of chapters, 1-line, blue or red. In a limp vellum cover, s. xvii (?). Secundo folio *fectio*.

Written probably in England. 'N° 22' inside the cover. 'N° 6' on f. i is the *CMA* number.

3529. *Johannes Boccaccius, Genealogiae Deorum*   s. xv[2]

1. (*a*) ff. 1–166^v [G]enealogie deorum gentilium. Iohannis Bocacii Cerdaldensis. Ad hugonem hierusalem. Et Cipri Regem. Liber primus Incipit F.E.L.I.C.I.T. E.R. Qui primus apud gentiles. deus habitus sit. [M]are magnum et dissuetum . . . prosapia finem. ego eque libello conficiam. Deo gracias. Alleluya. Explicit xiii boccasii de genealogia deorum gentilium subtiliter ac compendiose abbreuiat'. hiis que ad cognicionem poematum minus necessaria sunt reiectis. Et reliquis duobus libris quia de genealogia deorum non sunt. omissis. (*b*) f. 167 Versus dominici siluestri super quindecim libris genealogie deorum gentilium B.O.C.C.A.C.I.I. Que narrat ter quinque libris . . . Epigramma dominicus addit (17 lines). (*c*) ff. 167^v–174 [D]e Antheo libro primo . . . de zezio. libro ix. Deo gracias.

Probably (*a*–*c*) are copied from the edition printed at Cologne *c.* 1473 (*GKW*, no. 4480). A scroll below the last words on f. 166^v bears 'Prandez en gre. moun cur', perhaps a Grey motto, in the main hand. f. 174^v blank.

2 (end-leaves). (*a*) ff. i–iv Four leaves of the romance of Tristan in French prose, s. xiii ex. (*b*) f. 175 Part of a receipt and expense roll of an abbey in Kent, under the heading 'Compotum d*om*pni Thome (?) Elham superuisoris ibidem a festo [sancti michaelis] ar[changeli . . .] xx vsque [ad . . .] ex tunc prov' per vnum annum integrum reuolutum', s. xiv med.

(*a*) is two bifolia of one quire, the central bifolium and the bifolium next but one to it. The text, part of the story of the tournament of Louvezerp, is printed from this manuscript by P. E. Bennett in *Romania*, xcv (1974), 94–104. Written space 195 × 125 mm. 2 cols. 35 lines. 2-line initials, red or blue, with ornament of the other colour. (*b*). The first section, one line only, concerns hens and the next three sections give receipts from sales of wood and expenses of cutting wood, etc. The fifth section begins 'Et in liberacione *domp*no abbati citra festum Sancti Petri quod dicitur ad vincula viii li' vi s' viii d' Et in solucione Willelmo Gryme': only six lines remain. The place-names Faversham, Ostwode, Godemannys occur. The dorse is blank.

ff. v + 173 + ii. Paper, except ff. i–v, 175. Foliation : one unnumbered leaf, i–iv, 1–121, 123–76. 277 × 200 mm. Written space 175 × 110 mm. 27–40 long lines. Collation: 1–2¹² 3¹⁰ 4–5¹² 6–8¹⁰ 9–14¹² 15¹² + 1 leaf after 12. Strips of a manuscript in the central openings of quires, but little can be seen of the writing. Art. 1 is in a skilled and mannered secretary script, with some anglicana letter-forms mixed in and the two-compartment *a* regularly on ff. 1–10: the appearance changes, for example on ff. 47, 101, but the hand is probably the same throughout: ascenders usually have straight tops on ff. 1–46ᵛ. Headings and initials not filled in. Contemporary (Oxford?) binding of brown leather over wooden boards: patterns are made by fillets, small roundels, and a small triangular stamp (S. Gibson, *Early Oxford Bindings*, stamp 6) which is used as a border on the back cover and as a centrepiece within lozenges on both covers: five bands: two clasps missing: rebacked: for the binding leaves see art. 2: no chainmark: a title in ink and '1627' scratched on the back cover. Secundo folio *Est spelunca*.

Written in England. A gift to the Benedictine abbey of St. Augustine's, Canterbury: 'Bocacius de Geneologia deorum de adquisicione D' patricii Grey.[1] de librario sancti Augustini extra Cant'. D' [*blank*] Gradu [*blank*]', f. 1 at the top. 'Sum Tho: Mas: Anno Christi MDCXIIII', f. 1. *CMA*, no. 11 (2).

3533. *Formularium, etc.*   s. xv med.–xv ex.

Described in HMC, *Report*, pp. 33, 34. Arts. 2–12 are late fifteenth century. Arts. 1–3 are on quires 1–4.

1. ff. 1–39ᵛ Tria sunt que pertinent ad cartas silicet scriptura sigillacio et seisina . . . Carta feodi simplicis facta perquisitori. Sciant presentes et futuri quod ego Iohannes Langeston de Oxon' . . .

Also in B.L., Harley 773, 3352 and 5240 (where it is ascribed to David Penkayr: cf. G. Pollard in *Oxoniensia*, xxxi (1966), 73) and in the Brudenell manuscript sold 10 July 1967, lot 51, to B. M. Rosenthal, New York. Names are mainly of Oxford townspeople. William Brandon, master of Balliol College (1440–50?) is mentioned on f. 35. The last piece is an 'Acquietancia facta per ordinarium alicui administranti bonorum alicuius. Omnibus ad quos presentes littere peruenerint Iohannes Kerkeby in decretis Bacalarius . . .': he describes himself as sequestrator and commissary of William (Heyworth or Booth) bishop of Lincoln (cf. Emden, *BRUO*, p. 1078, Kyrkby). The first piece is dated 20 Henry VI and the latest date seems to be 36 Henry VI. The preface ends with four lines of verse, 'Will' con Will' rufus . . . Henricus sextus regnat filici (*sic*) tempore viuat' (f. 2: Walther, no. 20887).

2. (*a*) f. 39ᵛ Indentura apprenticii. (*b*) f. 40 Two paragraphs, the first 'Inquiratur pro domino Rege . . .' concerning a burglary 'in com. de G.', 1 Aug. 4 Edward IV.

[1] 'P. Grey' had the keeping of no. 841 in the St. Augustine's catalogue, *c.* 1500 (*Ancient Libraries*, p. 183).

(*a*). John, son of Simon Mersburgh of Rotherham is bound to John Dolfyn, baxter of Rotherham, for seven years from Michaelmas 1436. (*b*). An addition on a blank page.

3. ff. 41–42ᵛ In itinere Iustic' non admittatur esson'. Cur ceste estatut fuist reherc' . . .

On essoins, in French.

Arts. 4–8 are on quires 5, 6.

4. ff. 43–46ᵛ [T]enur per seruice de cheualere est tenur per homage . . . deuers ambideux. Et nota quando breue de natiuis habendis.

The Old Tenures printed by Pynson and later (*STC* 23878–84). As compared with *STC* 23878 there are some differences in order and the last six sections, Tenur per elegir–Rent sek, do not occur here.

5 (added). f. 46ᵛ Six lines of verse, 'Anna solet dici . . . volucremque Iohannem'. Walther, no. 1060.

6. ff. 47–8 Prescripcion est si come vn home preign' title . . . etc' non plus.

Definitions of terms, forty-three in all, the last Warnot.

7. ff. 48ᵛ–58ᵛ Saches que en Cort de Baron'. si home poet pleder par pleynt . . . rez plegg' a pair.

Most sentences on ff. 48ᵛ–53ᵛ begin 'Et sachez'. From f. 53ᵛ, 'Ore fair a dire de dettes . . .' the form is a dialogue between Querens and Defendens. f. 59ʳᵛ left blank contains an addition, s. xvi, two forms addressed to the authorities in Devonshire, the first 'A warrant for the good behavyor', 20 Oct. 11 Elizabeth.

8. (*a*) f. 60ʳᵛ Lez Estatut' laborers. Edwardus dei gracia . . . capitalibus (Constabulariis) septem hundredorum Cirenc' in Com' Glouc' . . . salutem. Vobis precipimus quod vos . . . iuxta formam statutorum predictorum. T. W. Notyngham apud Glouc'. xxi die Aprilis anno regni nostri decimo septimo. (*b*) ff. 60ᵛ–86 Rules for labourers in English, 'Fyrst hyt is ordeyned that euery seruant reteyned in the labour of husbandry preposyng for to depart . . . accordyng to þᵉ sayd statute'.

(*b*). Thirty-six paragraphs, 2–15 about wages. f. 65ᵛ blank.

9 (quire 7). Legal forms: (*a*) ff. 66–8 Presentacio de fraccione prisone . . .; (*b*) ff. 68ᵛ–74ᵛ Forms of supersedeas, warrant and attachment, eighteen in all; (*c*) ff. 75–6 Officium coronatoris. Hec sunt inquirenda de Coronatoribus domini Regis. In primis Coronatores habent mandatum . . . (*d*) ff. 76ᵛ–78 Modus Tenendi Curiam cum Vic' Franc'. In primis preceptum factum balliuo . . .

(*a*). Seventeen forms of presentment, followed by the heading 'Presentacio pro non reparacione pont' ', but no form follows. (*b*). A Gloucestershire collection. (1, 2) are issued by Richard Pole, J.P., of the county of Gloucester and (3, 6) by Richard (Clyve), abbot of Cirencester, J.P., 2 Aug. 2 Richard III 'apud D' and 'apud Dryffeld' (5), f. 70 is of 10 Jan. 2 (Richard III) 'Teste Lymeryk apud C'. (8–16, 18) are in the name of or name John Langley (or J. L.), J.P. of the county of Gloucester: the date where given is 5 Richard III. (*c*). On killings, woundings, breakings in, hidden treasure. (*d*). Court at Merden, Shropshire, 36 Henry VI. The form of oath is in English; also the charge (77–78ᵛ) 'Fyrst serys ye shall goo and enquere . . . and do vs to wete'. A further article of inquiry is fitted in on f. 79, with a reference to f. 78ᵛ.

Arts. 10–13 are on quires 8–10.

10. ff. 79^v–83^v Ye shull vndyrstand that armes began at the sege of Troy . . . a chefren goulez.

A treatise on heraldry. The arms of the king of England, five dukes, York–Norfolk, and ten earls, Salisbury–Shrewsbury, are listed on the last three pages.

11. ff. 84–101 Coats of arms, three to a page and four on ff. 98^v, 101, in all 107.

The arms are described on the left in English, except nos. 78, 81, 82, 85–91, 93, 94, 104–6. The person who bore the arms is named on twenty-nine occasions: (1–12) St. George, King of England (old), King of England, Queen of England, jointly and alone, St. Denis, King of France, Duke of Gloucester, Emperor of Rome, Kings of Jerusalem, Aragon, and Tharsis, (17) Haryngton, (18) le count Vrum*e*nde, (19) le Roy Marne, (38, 39) Le Count de Stafford, Le Count de Arundell, (43–5) Emperor of Constantinople, Kings of Greece and Hungary, (46) King Arthur, (47, 48) Kings of Portugal and Navarre, (49) Le Count de Oxinford, (52) Le syr de zouch, (56) Le syr de Wylby, (69) Le yerle de deuyn-shere, (86) byshopp cheddeworth of lyncole (†1471), (87) yerle of Kyme (?).

12. ff. 101^v–103^v For to kepe haukys. To helpe an hauke of dyuerse sykenesse. For the Ree . . . and comenly they be horyst. Explicit.

13. ff. 104–106^v, left blank, contain (*a*) f. 105^v, a form of indenture between William Chaberleyn de Aresfeld and Robert Darell of the same, brewer, relating to the Horne on the Hoppe, parish of St. Mary, Oxford, and (*b*) f. 106^v, a recipe 'for the fflyx' in English. (*c*) The couplet 'Sancti swithuni translacio si pluuiam det Quadraginta dies continuare solet' is on a flyleaf of parchment pasted to f. 108.

ff. ii + 106 + ii. Parchment and (quires 6–10) paper. 212 × 135 mm. Written space 155 × 90 mm. *c*. 36 long lines (art. 1). Collation: 1^{10} wants 1, 2 2^{10} 3–4^{12} 5^{10} + 1 leaf after 10 (ff. 43–53) 6^{12} 7^{14} + 1 leaf after 5 (f. 71), wants 13, 14, perhaps blank, after f. 78 8^4 (ff. 79–82), 9–10^{12}. A red *T* on f. 1 is the only initial. Capital letters in the ink of the text are touched with red in quires 1–3 only. Textura for the headings and secretary for the text of art. 1. Arts. 2–12 in current anglicana of a legal sort, mainly in one hand. Binding of s. xix. Secundo folio *vel vicineto*.

Written in England and perhaps in Gloucestershire.

3548A. *Sacramentarium* (*fragm.*) s. x

Eighteen small fragments of a sacramentary described by E. Lega-Weekes in *Devon and Cornwall Notes and Queries*, ix (1916), 33–35, with a reduced facsimile of most part of no. 6; also very fully, with a transcript, in MS. 3548A/1, where fragments marked 1–12, 14, 15 are identified as coming from eight leaves. No. 16 was not known to Miss Lega-Weekes. No. 13 is blank, except for an offset from no. 11.

ff. 1, 2 Second Sunday and (f. 2) fourth Sunday in Advent and (f. 2^v) vigil of Christmas. No. 1, the top five lines of a bifolium, and No. 14.

f. 3 Sexagesima Sunday. No. 6i–iv, four pieces joined together and making in all about half a leaf.

f. 4 Friday and (f. 4ᵛ) Saturday before Quinquagesima. No. 2.

f. 5 Wednesday and (f. 5ᵛ, col. 2) Thursday after the third Sunday in Lent. Nos. 5, 10, 12, 15, 16.

The office for Thursday begins with the collect 'Media nocte [. . .] angelum tuum . . .'.

f. 6 Easter Eve. Nos. 3, 4, 11.

f. 7 Easter Eve and (f. 7ᵛ) Easter Day. Nos. 8, 9.

f. 8 Sabbatum quattuor temporum and (f. 8ᵛ) seventeenth Sunday after Pentecost. No. 7.

f. 3 has a written space 220 mm wide and 23 out of probably 29 lines in two columns. The initial *I* of *In illo tempore*, plaitwork and dragon head, is shown in the facsimile.

Written in France (?). Used, probably at Exeter, in the same bindings as 3548F, q.v.

3548B. *Missale (fragm.)*   s. XIII in.

Eight leaves of a missal. A full description made by F. E. Brightman in 1927 is kept with it as 3548B/1. Three blocks of text remain: (i) f. 1, vigil of Epiphany and Epiphany; (ii) ff. 2–4, first to fourth Sundays after the octave of Epiphany; (iii) ff. 5–8, Easter Eve.

(iii) runs from the adjuration 'Audi maledicte' to the lection 'In principio creauit' and includes most of the litany, which here comes after the order of making catechumens. Thirty-three confessors: . . . (8–13) Taurine Germane Nicholae Audberte Audoene Romane. The only English saint is Wereburga, thirteenth of seventeen virgins. In 3548B/1 Brightman lists each form and its agreement on ff. 1–4 with Sarum, Westminster, and Roman forms, and on ff. 5–8 with the Remiremont missal printed by Martène, *De antiquis ecclesiae ritibus*, I. 1, art. vii, ordo vi (edn. 1783, i. 17).

Written space 235 × 155 mm. 2 cols. 30 lines. Pricks in both margins to guide ruling. Two quires, one consisting of a bifolium ff. 1, 4, and two singletons immediately preceding f. 4, and the other of the two middle bifolia of a quire (ff. 5–8). 2-line initials, red, green, or blue.

Probably English. Used in binding 3779, a cathedral account book, 'Liber solutionum', running from 1499 to 1561: cf. FMS/3, below.

3548C. *Benedictionale (fragm.)*   s. X

Two consecutive leaves described and printed by S. F. H. Robinson, 'On a fragment of an Anglo-Saxon Benedictional preserved at Exeter Cathedral', *Trans. St. Paul's Ecclesiological Society*, v (1905), 221–8, with a facsimile of f. 1ʳ. The remains are for the first to third Sundays after the octave of Easter, beginning 'lit et bonum redemptionis' and ending 'regenerationis su[ę]', as in the Benedictional of St. Æthelwold, ff. 58/19–60/2, ed. Warner and Wilson (Roxburghe Club, 144), pp. 22, 23.

Written space 210 × 140 mm. 16 long lines. Large caroline minuscule, rather of the type of the Benedictional of St. Æthelwold, but larger,[1] and the *g* is different. 2-line red initials.

---

[1] The Benedictional of St. Æthelwold has nineteen lines in 205 mm.

Written in England. The pressmark, K. 4.5, on f. 1ᵛ shows that these leaves covered (not quite completely), L. Krentzheim, *Observationes chronologicæ*, 1606. Stains, a worm-hole, and a chainmark support the evidence from the pressmark.

3548F. *Breviarium (fragm.)* s. XIII/XIV

Thirty leaves of a handsome breviary recovered from bindings.

1. ff. 1–5 Dominical and ferial lections from Daniel and Minor Prophets.

Three fragments (2–4 are consecutive leaves): f. 1ʳᵛ, lections 2–5 from Daniel, i, ii; ff. 2–4ᵛ, lections 2, 3 on (Friday) and 1–3 on Saturday from Daniel ii, lections 1–6 on 'Dominica xxvii' from Hosea i, ii, and lections 1–3 on Monday from Hosea iv; f. 5ʳᵛ begins in lection 1 and ends in lection 5 from Joel i.

2. (*a*) f. 6ʳᵛ Lections within the octave of Pentecost from Amos i, ii. (*b*) ff. 6ᵛ–26 Lections from the Gospels and 'Gregorius' and antiphons on Sundays after the octave of Pentecost.

Ten fragments: leaves are missing after ff. 9, 11, 12, 14, 15, 16, 20, 22, 23, 26. (*b*). The lections and antiphons remaining in whole or part are for: 1st–3rd Sundays (ff. 6ᵛ–9); antiphon Nolite iudicare for 4th Sunday and lections for 5th and 6th Sundays (ff. 10, 11); 6th and 7th Sundays (f. 12); 8th–10th Sundays (ff. 13, 14); antiphon at vespers on 10th Sunday and lections for 11th Sunday (f. 15); 14th Sunday (f. 16); 15th–18th Sundays (ff. 17–20); 19th–21st Sundays (ff. 21, 22); 22nd, 23rd Sundays (f. 23); 24th, 25th Sundays (ff. 25, 26). Mainly as *Brev. ad usum Sarum*, cols. mcccxcix–mccccxlix, but lections 7–9 often differ and are nearer Hereford use. They are almost all attributed to Gregory, often wrongly, for example Idropsis . . . and Conuenerunt . . . (17th and 18th Sundays). Where 'Gregorii pape' occurs in headings, 'pape' has been erased.

3. ff. 27–30 Part of the office of dedication of church, corresponding usually to *Brev. ad usum Sarum*, cols. mcccclviii–mcccclxiv.

Four consecutive leaves. The capitulum at lauds is Vidi civitatem as in *Ordinale Exon.*

ff. 30. 410 × 260 mm. Written space 300 × 185 mm. 2 cols. 23 lines. All leaves are now singletons. Handsome script and decoration. 2-line initials, blue or red with ornament of the other colour and prolongations running the height of the page in red, blue, and, some-times, gold. Bound in 1930.

Written in England. Used in binding. A note in the library refers to the source as the edition of Galen in 5 vols., Venice 1541 (cf. 3548A), and the smaller leaves, cut down to *c.* 370 × 240 mm, 1–5, 19, 20, 24–6, are no doubt from these volumes, which are in plain and perhaps local Exeter bindings of s. xvi. The pressmark R. 1.2 on f. 10 shows that this leaf is from vol. 2 of the Biblia Polyglotta of Arias Montanus, Antwerp, 1569–72, and fifteen other leaves of this size are likely to be from this volume and the seven other volumes of the Bible, all of which were rebound in s. xix. Four leaves remain unaccounted for.

3549B. *Isidorus, Etymologiae; Seneca; etc.* s. XIII med.

1 (added, s. xiv). ff. 1–23ᵛ A est prior littera litterarum. eth' li. 1 capitulo iiii . . . Zorobabel 1' vii 'd' xxxvii'.

An index to art. 2, headed by an explanatory note, 'Primus numerus istius tabule significat librum. secundus uero significat capitulum. tercius distinctiones capitulorum (*sic for* librorum: cf. art. 2). An addition in the margin, f. 10ᵛ, ends 'Hec Gillelmus Nouiomen' '.

2. ff. 24-135^v Epistola sancti ysidori spalensis episcopi ad braulionem cesar-augustanum episcopum ... (f. 25) Vt ualeas que requiris euo (?) in hoc corpore inuenire. hec tibi lector pagina subsequens monstrat de quibus rebus in singulis conditor huius codicis disputauit (*these 24 words in red*). En tibi sicut pollicitus sum ... conscriptum maiorum. In libro primo de gramatica ... instrumentis equorum. Incipit liber sancti ysidori iunioris spalensis episcopi ad braulionem cesaraugustanum episcopum scriptum qui uocatur ethimologiarum ... (*table of 28 chapters*) ... Expliciunt capitula. Incipit liber primus. i. De disciplina arte. Disciplina*.*' a discendo ... ardore sicetur. Explicit ysidorus ethimologiarum.

PL lxxxiii. 73-728, preceded by five letters between Isidore and Bravlio, PL lxxxiii. 908-14, Epp. ix-xiii. Each of the twenty books has been divided into distinctions by numbers in the margins, probably in Grandisson's hand: thus in the margins of bk. 1, numbers preceded by 'd' ' run from i to xcvii. Corresponding numbers, preceded by 'd' ', were added to art. 1, probably very soon after it was written, and make the chapter referen-ces there unnecessary for finding purposes.

3. ff. 135^v-136^v Lotium est urina ... Sillogismus consermocinatio*.*' uel con-clusiua ratio. Dicitur enim absolute*.*' arta conclusio.

Notes on words beginning with the letters L–S in alphabetical order. Also in Douai MSS. 318, 319, and 320, all from Marchiennes.[1]

4. ff. 136^v-137^v Incipit fabri plantiadis fulgentii vc (?) Expositio sermonum antiquorum cum testimoniis. Ne de tuorum preceptorum domine ... tam delenifica.

Fabius Planciades Fulgentius, Sermones antiqui. Ed. R. Helm (Teubner), 1898, pp. 111-26.

5. ff. 138-69 Incipiunt capitula in libro sententiarum Sancti ysidori episcopi. Capitula primi libri ... (*table of 31 chapters*). ... Quod deus incommutabilis sit et de cetera creatura dei quod sit bona set mutabilis. Summum bonum deus est ... securius transeatur. Explicit liber sentenciarum beati ysidori episcopi.

PL lxxxiii. 537-738. Bk. 2, f. 145^v: 44 chapters. Bk. 3, f. 156: 67 chapters. A table of chapters before each book. 3.67, 'De penitentibus', is an addition to the table and the chapter is perhaps an addition to the text by the main hand: it begins 'Penitentibus exemplum iob primus ...' (f. 168^v) and is not in PL.

6 (added, s. xiv). f. 169^{rv} Sermo beati augustini. Supplico fratres karissimi. et paterna pietate commoneo ... confidam*.*' tamen quia (*ends abruptly*).

Perhaps in Grandisson's hand. PL xxxix. 2284 (Serm. App. 285).

7. ff. 169^v-174. Incipit liber differenciarum seu diffinitionum sancti ysidori. Inter deum et dominum ... secunda geometria. etc. (*ends abruptly*).

Part of bk. 2 of De differenciis rerum, PL lxxxiii. 69-94/4. f. 174^v blank.

Arts. 8-13, 17 are in Eton College 89, arts. 1-8.

8. f. 175^{rv} (*a*) Iheronimus in libro de uiris illustribus sic de seneca scribit. Lucius anneus seneca ... interfectus est. (*b*) Incipiunt epistole senece ad paulum

---

[1] Information from Professor Richard Rouse.

et pauli ad senecam. Anneus seneca paulo salutem. Credo tibi paule . . . (*c*) Cura labor . . . ossa tibi.

The extract from Jerome, the fourteen letters between Paul and Seneca, and the epitaph of Seneca, as in Eton College 89, art. 1, q.v.

9. ff. 175ᵛ–221 Epistola prima senece ad lucilium. De tempore. Ita fac lucili mi . . . (f. 220) mansueta sunt. Vale. (f. 221) Expliciunt epistole senece ad lucilium.

The eighty-eight letters arranged and numbered as in Eton College 89, art. 3, q.v. f. 220ᵛ blank.

10. ff. 221–247ᵛ Incipit eiusdem liber primus de beneficiis ad eburtium liberalem amicum suum. Inter multos ac uarios . . . perdere et dare. Explicit liber vii lucii annei senece de beneficiis (*etc.*).

11. ff. 247ᵛ–252ᵛ Incipit eiusdem liber primus de clementia ad neronem imperatorem. Scribere de clementia . . . praua flectantur. Explicit liber secundus senece de clementia.

12. ff. 252ᵛ–256 Incipit eiusdem de copia uerborum. siue de iiiiᵒʳ uirtutibus ad paulum. (*a*) Quatuor uirtutum species . . . (f. 254) puniat ignauiam. (*b*) Incipit liber senece de copia uerborum. Primum argumentum composite mentis . . . negligentiam fit.

(*a*). ed. Haase, iii. 468–75; *PL* lxxii. 23–8 (Martin of Braga). (*b*). The same ten paragraphs as in Eton College 89, art. 8.

13. ff. 256–7 Incipit liber senece de remediis fortuitorum malorum. Licet cunctorum poetarum carmina . . . ista felicitas.

14. ff. 257–9 Incipit ludus senece de morte claudii cesaris. Quid actum sit in celo . . . ut a cognitionibus abesset.

Apocolocyntosis Divi Claudii, printed in 1513 and often later, last by R. Waltz, 1961.

15. (*a*) ff. 259–61ᵛ Incipiunt prouerbia senece. et primo de hiis que per a litteram incipiunt. Alienum est? quicquid optando euenit . . . Zelari autem hominibus uiciosum est. (*b*) ff. 261ᵛ–262 Auida est periculi uirtus . . . ex quo petatur ultio.

(*a, b*). Cf. B.L., Royal 8 E. xvii, art. 9. (*a*), an alphabetical collection, A–Z, is printed in early editions of Seneca, for example in the Erasmian edition of 1529, pp. 685–90. As far as 'Negandi causa . . .', no. 9 under the letter N, it is the collection of Publilius Syrus. The rest, from 'Nondum felix . . .', is extracted from pseudo-Seneca, De moribus. (*b*). An alphabetical collection, A–V (Ultio).

16. f. 262 De memoria Senece. Seneca sic scribit de se ipso. in libro de causis. ostendens . . . Cum multa iam michi ex me desideranda . . . quantum uobis satis sit superest.

A quotation from the elder Seneca, Controversiae, 1 praef., sects. 2–3 and the first nine words of sect. 4.

17. ff. 262–290ᵛ Incipiunt libri Senece de Naturalibus questionibus. De grandine liber primus. Grandinem hoc modo fieri . . . flumini dulcior gustus.

Eight books in the order IVb, V–VII, I–III, IVa.

18. ff. 290ᵛ–294 Incipit octauia Senece. Iam uaga celo sidera fulgens . . Cuius gaudet Roma cruore. Explicit Octauia Senece.

On this copy see C. J. Herington in *Rheinisches Museum für Philologie*, n. f. ci (1958), 354–69.

19. f. 294 Incipiunt quedam sumpta de Tragediis Senece. Quod nimis miser uolunt . . . non quod licet. Hec qui legerit. de tragediis senece Sumpta esse Nouerit.

Fifty-three items. Collated loc. cit., 369–71.

20. ff. 294–5 Hoc est finis cuiusdam epistole precedentis. Quomodo molestus est . . . esse utilem? quam presentiam. Vale.

Letter 102. f. 295ᵛ blank.

ff. iv+295+iv. f. iv is a medieval parchment flyleaf. 225 × 168 mm. Written space 160 × 108 mm. 2 cols. and (ff. 291–293ᵛ) 3 cols. 53–6 lines. Pricks in both margins to guide ruling from f. 24. Collation: 1¹² 2¹² wants 12 blank 3–11¹² 12⁶ (ff. 132–7) 13–14¹² 15¹²+1 leaf after 7 (f. 169) 16–18¹² 19¹⁰ (ff. 211–20) 20–25¹² 26 three (ff. 293–5: 293–4 are a bifolium). Quires 3–12 numbered at the end i–ix. Written like a Bible of the period. Flex punctuation (?) in arts. 19, 20 only. Initials: (i) red and blue with ornament of both colours; (ii) 2-line, red or blue, with ornament of the other colour; (iii) 1-line, red or blue. Initials in art. 1: blue, with elaborate penwork ornament. Capital letters in the ink of the text sometimes marked with red. Binding of s. xix. Secundo folio (f. 25) *veni ad* or (f. 2) *Anceps*.

Arts. 1, 6 are English and the rest probably English. Belonged to John de Grandisson, bishop of Exeter, † 1369: 'Liber I. de Grandissono', ff. 137ᵛ, 174; 'Iste liber est [. . . . .] de grandissono Episcopi Exon' ', erased, f. 24. 'R. Foxton', f. 24, is probably a later owner (s. xiv²).[1] 'Est nicolai horsley', partly over the erasure on f. 24, is in the same hand as a table of contents on f. 296, s. xvi: one of this name matriculated at Corpus Christi College, Cambridge, in 1544. Belonged to Thomas Kerslake, bookseller of Bristol: his catalogue of 1858, item 3380. His gift to the Dean and Chapter in 1889.

3549G. *Horae B.V.M.* s. xv in.

1. ff. 1–36ᵛ Hours of B.V.M. of the use of (Sarum).

Begins imperfectly in matins. Hours of the Cross worked in. Memoriae of Holy Cross, Michael, John Baptist, Peter, Laurence, Thomas of Canterbury (Tu per thome sanguinem . . .), Nicholas, Mary Magdalene, Katherine, Margaret, All Saints, and for peace follow lauds (ff. 7–13ᵛ).

2. ff. 36ᵛ–37ᵛ Salve regina and prayer 'Omnipotens sempiterne deus qui gloriose uirginis . . .'.

3. ff. 38–52 Fragments of the penitential psalms and (f. 47) gradual psalms and (f. 48) litany.

All confessors after Augustine and all virgins are missing in a gap after f. 48. f. 52ᵛ left blank: a prayer to St. Roche added on it, s. xv/xvi.

4. ff. 53–86ᵛ Office of the dead, beginning imperfectly.

Manuale Sarum, pp. 133–42.

[1] There is a Robert Foxton in Emden, *BRUC*, at the right date. His signature in the Ely consistory register, 1373–81, f. 25, is very like the signature here.

5. ff. 87–100ᵛ Commendatory psalms (118, 138), ending imperfectly in Ps. 138.

Manuale Sarum, p. 143.

ff. 100. 120×75 mm. Written space 68×40 mm. 17 long lines. Collation: 1⁸ wants 1 (2, 3 are small fragments not included in the foliation) 2 two (ff. 5, 6) 3⁸ wants 8 after f. 13 4⁸ wants 6, 7 after f. 18 5⁸ 6¹⁰ 7⁸ wants 1 before f. 38 8 three (ff. 45–7) 9 three (ff. 48–50) 10⁴ wants 1, except a corner, and 4, probably blank, 11⁶ 12 four (ff. 59–62, two bifolia) 13⁸ wants 7 after f. 68 14⁸ 15⁸ wants 5 after f. 81 16⁸ 17⁶ wants 3, 4 after f. 94 18 four (ff. 97–100: 99, 100 are a bifolium). Initials: (i, ii) 3-line and 2-line, blue with red ornament; (iii) 1-line, red or blue and, in the litany only, gold instead of red. No binding: kept in a box.

Written in England.

FMS/1, 2, 2a. *Orosius (fragm.)* s. x

Three strips. No. 2 is 57 mm wide, from the middle of a leaf, with part of a handsome initial *S* of 'Sufficien[tia]', the first word of bk. 7 of Orosius' history, in colours on a purple ground fifteen lines deep. 'expediam. EXPL' ' and 'Incipit liber' are in the two lines above it. The leaf contained *PL* xxxi. 1059/12–1062/7.

Written space 232 mm high. 36 lines. Written on the Continent. Removed from a binding.

FMS/3. *Vita S. Basilii (fragm.)* s. x in.

Eight small stained pieces. No. 1 contains part of a heading in red, '[. . . .] caesarea [. . .]otione innotuit' in the first two lines and 'caesariensium ciuitatem [. . . .]sionem' in line 6. No. 2 has 'in iordane fluuio' in line 2 and 'Basilius autem' in line 4.

BHL, no. 1023. The text agrees with Trinity College, Cambridge, 717, f. 45ᵛᵃ/28–31 (no. 2) and f. 45ᵛᵇ/26–30 (no. 1). No. 1 is 155 mm wide and contains the full height of five lines of text and parts of two other lines. The script is insular minuscule: *r* uncial, but the first stroke descends below the line: *a* rounded.

Written in England. Removed from the spine of 3779: cf. 3548B.

Misc. 1/2. *Missale (fragm.)* s. xiv med.

A bifolium containing: (1) f. 1ʳᵛ, part of an office for use at Easter from 'Nisi dominus. Psalmus. Beati omnes. Paululum cum pertransissem . . .' to 'Quando mestis' in the sequence beginning (the first word or two missing) 'per quam data. noua mun[. . . . .] Et aperta fide certa. regna sunt celestia'; (2) f. 2ʳᵛ, part of the office of St. Anne from the collect 'Deus qui beatam annam diu sterilem' to 'in celis est ipse meus fra' in the communio 'Quicumque fecerit uoluntatem'. These are noted offices, probably supplementary to a missal.

Headings in the hand of John de Grandisson, bishop of Exeter 1328–69: f. 1, top margin, 'Ad missam⸴ in paschali [tempore]'; f. 2, top margin, 'De sancta Anna' and, further to the right, 'I. ex.'; f. 2, the words 'vel ut in dominica' after the heading 'Sequencia aliqua de sancta maria ad placitum'.

Only f. 2 is complete. Written space 200 × 130 mm. 30 long lines. 2-line blue initials with red ornament.

Written in England. At Exeter Cathedral (?) in s. xiv. Used in binding. Scribbled on in s. xvii 'per me Iohannem Bickley (?)' and the date 27 Mar. 1625. On loan from Ilsington Church, Devon, since 1935.

FORT AUGUSTUS ABBEY

Rat. 1. *Patristica* 1080, 1083

A book written for the most part by Marianus, founder of the Irish community at Regensburg. Described by A. P. Forbes soon after its arrival in Scotland, 'Account of a manuscript of the eleventh century by Marianus of Ratisbon', *PSAS* vi (1841–6), 33–40. *Trésors*, no. 3.

M. Dilworth, 'Scribe and monastic founder', *Scottish Gaelic Studies*, x (1968), 125–48, prints the inscriptions found in the lower margins of thirteen leaves, which record the scribe's progress, usually in the form of an invocation of the saint on whose day he was writing, for example (f. 23) 'Sancte uite pro missero mariano intercede'. The thirteen dates are: f. 1, 7 (?) June 1080; f. 4, 9 June 1080; f. 11, 11 June; f. 23, 15 June; f. 41, Friday, 19 June 1080; f. 48ᵛ, 20 June; f. 59, 26 June; f. 65, 29 June; f. 68, 1 July 'in nocte'; f. 84, 4 July; f. 96ᵛ, 8 July; f. 106ᵛ, 11 July 'in hac sabbati nocte', 1080; f. 122, 13 July 1080. The scribe calls himself Marianus on ff. 11, 23, 96ᵛ, 106ᵛ. He wrote in Irish in six inscriptions, using insular letter-forms.

Another scribe, John, began work on f. 122. Inscriptions by him are on f. 136ᵛ, 'Domine iesu criste propter tuam magnam misericordiam missero iohanni propitius esto', and on f. 141, 'Tertia kl' aprilis hodie in quinta feria. Anno domini millesimo octogessimo tertio (Thursday, 30 Mar. 1083). meę autem peregrinationis pene septimo. et huius loci habitationis ab scottis octauo. Regnante quarto henrico. Miseri iohannis[1] anima requiescat in pace amen': cf. also art. 8.

Arts. 2, 3, 4, 7, 8 correspond to arts. 1–5 of Munich, Clm. 13080, a twelfth-century book from the abbey of Prüfening, near Regensburg.

Vienna, Nationalbibliothek 1247 (Theol. 287) is another manuscript written by Marianus (in 1079): for a facsimile see *Pal. Soc.* i. 191. Another, now apparently lost, was written in 1074: see J. F. Kenney, *Sources for the early history of Ireland*, p. 617.

A statement that the manuscript is the autograph of Marianus and a table of contents are in a good italic hand, s. xvi, on the pastedown.

1. ff. 1–11 Incipiunt dicta sancti basilii episcopi ad exhortandos monachos. Audi

---

[1] Letters in italics have been renewed.

fili mi admonitionem patris tui . . . deus diligentibus se. Expliciunt dicta sancti basilii episcopi ad exhortandos monachos. Sit nomen domini benedictum. ex hoc. nunc. et usque in (seculum) a quo est omne datum optimu(m) et omne donum perfectum.

Twenty-five numbered chapters. *PL* ciii. 683–700.

2. ff. 11ᵛ–56 Incipit liber sancti effrem diaconi. de iudicio dei. et resurrectio*ne* et de regno celorum et de munditia anime. Gloria omnipotenti deo: qui ós nostrum superno nutu . . . qui renouauit nos. Per infinita. secula seculorum amen. Explic' libri effrem. Sit nomen domini benedictum ex hoc nunc et usque in seculum: a quo est omne datum optimum et omne donum perfectum. Domine miserere miseri scriptoris. suis fratribus peregrinis. hec dicta scribentis causa tui amoris.

The six sermons attributed to Ephraem, here called 'libri', the sixth, De compunctione cordis, being divided as two: f. 15ᵛ, De beatitudine animę; f. 18ᵛ De penitentia; f. 22ᵛ De luctaminibus; f. 26 De die iudicii; f. 31ᵛ De compunctione cordis; f. 51 Incipit liber vii sancti effrem. Venite karissimi michi. venite patres et fratres . . . (*Clavis*, no. 1143). Printed in the order 6, 1–5 at (Freiburg im Breisgau), sine anno (*GKW* 9334), and in the Froben reprint of this edition; also in *Ephraemi Syri opera omnia*, iii (1746), 553–60, 579–81, 589–99.

3. ff. 57–73 Incipiunt omelię sancti cesarii episcopi ad monachos. Nine sermons: (*a*) f. 57 Inter reliquas beatitudines . . . ; (*b*) f. 58ᵛ Sicut a nobis dominus pro suscepti officii necessitate . . . ; (*c*) f. 60ᵛ Ad locum hunc carissimi. non ad quietem . . . ; (*d*) f. 62ᵛ Scimus quidem fratres karissimi: spiritali militię . . . ; (*e*) f. 65 Ad hoc fratres karissimi ad istum locum conuenimus . . . ; (*f*) f. 66 Videte uocationem uestram fratres karissimi . . . ; (*g*) f. 67ᵛ Quid nos uobis dicturi sumus fratres . . . ; (*h*) f. 69ᵛ Quod fraternitati uestrę karissimi qualemcumque sermonem profero . . . ; (*i*) f. 71ᵛ Sancta caritas ac sollicitudo . . .

(*a*). Caesarius of Arles, Sermo 4 (*CC* ciii. 21). (*b–f*). Hom. vi–ix in *PL* lxvii. 1056–69: for their authorship cf. Morin in *CC* civ, pp. 988, 955, 987, 955, 990.

4. ff. 73–84 Incipit libellus autperti presbiteri de conflictu uitiorum atque uirtutum. missus ad landefredum presbiterum et abbatem in baioaria constitutum. Apostolica uox clamat per orbem . . . et aliis tradere debes. Explic'. Deo gratias.

The De conflictu vitiorum et virtutum of Autpertus, abbot of St. Vincent on the Volturno, near Benevento, †781. The heading here occurs also in two Munich manuscripts, Clm. 13080 from Prüfening and Clm. 14500 from St. Emmeran, Regensburg: cf. G. Morin in *RB* xxvii (1910), 204–12.

5. ff. 84ᵛ–106ᵛ In subsequenti hoc libro qui nuncupatur sinonima id est multa uerba in unam significationem coeuntia, sanctę recordationis isidorus . . . sed eternis premiis remuneratus uiuat cum cristo qui . . . Incipiunt sinonima isidori. Anima mea in angustiis est . . . Tu michi super uitam meam places. Explic' deo gratias. Sit nomen domini benedictum. a quo est omne donum perfectum.

PL lxxxiii. 825–68.

6. ff. 107–22 Incipit prefatio alcuini. Dilectissimo filio huitoni comiti: humilis leuita alcuinus salutem. Memor 'sum' petitionis tuę . . . dignus efficietur: domino miserante qui regnat in sęcula sęculorum amen. Sit nomen domini benedictum.

a quo est omne datum optimum et omne donum perfectum. Domine miserere miseri scriptoris. qui hec scripsit suis fratribus peregrinis.

Alcuin, De virtutibus et vitiis. *PL* ci. 613–38.

7. ff. 122–125ᵛ Incipit libellus de quatuor uirtutibus. Prudentia fortitudine. temperantia. iustitia. qui pretitulatur formula uitę honestę. editus a quodam martino episcopo ad mironem Regem. Quatuor uirtutum species . . . aut deficientem contempnat ignauiam. explicit.

Martin of Braga, Formula vitae honestae. *PL* lxxii. 23–8. *Clavis*, no. 1080.

8. ff. 125ᵛ–137 Hunc libellus smaragdus abbas de diuersis uirtutibus collegit. et ei nomen diadema monachorum imposuit. quia sicut diadema gemmis. Ita hic fulget uirtutum ornamentis. De oratione. Hoc est remedium eius . . . et deus pacis et dilectionis erit uobiscum. Sit nomen domini benedictum in quo est omne datum optimum et omne donum perfectum. Sanctissima maria. et sancti dei omnes pro misero iohanne apud dominum nostrum iesum cristum intercedite ut sua ei demittantur peccata.

An abbreviation of the Diadema, chapters 1–6, 9–11, 13, 26, 27, 29, 37–40, 97, 98 of the text printed in *PL* cii. 594–687. f. 137ᵛ is blank, except for discontinuous erased writing, partly in red ink.

9. ff. 138–41 In cena domini ad mandatum. Ante diem autem festum paschę . . . et ego in ipsis.

John 13: 1–17: 26.

10. ff. 18ᵛ–29ᵛ (lower margins) [Con]stantinopolitanus. Dicamus fratres quod ait propheta. Miserere mei deus. secundum magnam misericordiam tuam. Ó portus omnino tempestate carens . . . ab illis inferioribus sunt blasfemant.

Usually eight or nine lines on each page.

11 (added, s. xii). f. 141 A record of the gift to the Irish convent at Regensburg of a vineyard and other properties by 'domina Liukardis aduocatissa mater friderici ratisponensis aduocati'.

Printed by Forbes, loc. cit., pp. 38–9.

12 (added, s. xii). f. 141ᵛ A list of about 150 persons, presumably those for whom the convent was to pray, beginning with Henry, duke of Bavaria and 'Liutkarth aduocatissa'.

In several hands. Printed by Forbes, loc. cit., pp. 39–40.

ff. 141. Thick parchment originally much holed and cracked, but before the scribes wrote defects were repaired with pieces of parchment sewn on with dark thread. 270 × 198 mm. Written space 202 × 135 mm. 32–3 long lines. The ruling is on two or three leaves at a time. Collation: 1–2¹⁰ 3⁸ 4–10¹⁰ (4 and 7 are half-sheets in quire 6) 11⁸ + 1 leaf after 5 (f. 104) 12 ten (ff. 108–17: 112, 113 are a bifolium) 13–15¹⁰ 16 four (ff. 138–41). Written in caroline minuscule of German type: for the scribes see above. The notes in Irish on ff. 41, 48ᵛ are in Irish minuscule. Red initials. Capital letters in the ink of the text filled with red. Binding of wooden boards half-covered with stamped pigskin, executed in 1524. Secundo folio *Nam terrenę*.

Written by Marianus (arts. 1–6, 10 and the headings of arts. 7, 8) and John (arts. 7–9) in

the Irish Benedictine house at Regensburg, founded by Marianus in 1075. 'Liber monasterii diui iacobi scotorum ratisponen' quem conuentus fecit denuo ligari 'anno domini
1524'' inside the front cover, s. xvi[1]. 'Ex lib: Monasterii S. Iacobi Scotorum Ratisbonæ
redemit ex alienis manibus post centum circiter annos Bernardus Baillie abbas an. 1737'[1]
on f. 1, at the top and down the side, partly over an inscription of s. xvi in faded brown
ink. Erasure at foot of f. 1. Believed to have been brought to Fort Augustus when the
Scottish abbey of St. James, which had taken the place of the Irish abbey in the second
decade of the sixteenth century, was suppressed in 1862.

Rat. 2. *Regula S. Benedicti, cum expositione Bernardi abbatis Casinensis*
s. xv med.

1. ff. 3–201[v] Legitur in prouerbiis doctrina prudentum facilis. Ideoque qui
sapienciam . . . quod assiduis uobis edidi peticionibus postulatis. Obsculta o
fili . . . Obsculta aliqua litera habet ausculta . . . cum sanctis suis ad gloriam regni
sui perueniamus Amen. Qui me scribebat Iohannes fuchstayn' sacerdos nomen
habebat. Explicit exposicio regule Sancti Benedicti secundum Bernhardum
Abbatem Monasterii Cassinensis doctoris sacre theologie necnon et vtriusque
iuris.

The Rule of St. Benedict with the exposition of Bernardus Ayglerius, abbot of Monte
Cassino, †1282, edited by A. M. Caplet, *Bernardi I, abbatis Casinensis, in Regulam S.
Benedicti Expositio*, 1894. ff. 1[v]–2[v] contain a table of seventy-four numbered chapters.
f. 1[r] is blank.

2 (added, s. xv). (*a*) f. 201[v] A form of absolution, 'Et ego auctoritate dei . . .
auctoritate domini nostri pape vrbani sexti qua fungor in hoc casu spetialiter et
expresse commissa absoluo te Matheum ab omni uinculo excommunicacionis . . .'.
(*b*) f. 201[v] A copy of the form of words used in the election of an abbot of the
Irish Benedictine abbey of St. Giles, Nuremberg. The elector is described as
'abbas Mon' sancti Iacobi ybern*icorum* Ratisbone'. (*c*) f. 1[v] Note of the death
of Thomas, abbot 'monasterii S. *Iacobi Scotorum* extra muros . . . Herbipolen',
14 Jan. 1494/5.

(*b*). The Irish at Nuremberg were replaced by Germans in 1418. The word 'ybern*icorum*'
has been altered to 'scotorum' and the italicized letters are illegible. (*c*) has been partly
rewritten, including the words in italics. The Irish were replaced by Germans at St.
James, Würzburg, in 1497.

ff. 202. 265 × 185 mm. Written space 190 × 132 mm. 2 cols. 17 lines of text and 35 of
gloss. Collation: 1–7⁸ 8⁸ wants 7 after f. 61 9–12⁸ 13⁸ wants 2 after f. 96 14⁸ wants 6 after
f. 107 15⁸ 16⁸ wants 8 after f. 124 17–25⁸ 26⁶. Quires numbered at the end. Written in
two sizes of textura. A new hand begins at f. 167[v]. Initials red or blue or, occasionally,
in both colours. Bound in thick wooden boards covered with pigskin bearing a pattern
of fillets, s. xvi in. (?): a central boss on each cover and metal cornerpieces: two strap-
and-pin fastenings now missing: 'Regula diui Benedicti' written on the back cover.
Secundo folio *Si equaliter* (f. 2) or *sapientissimum* (f. 4).

Written in Germany. The second scribe, Fuchstayn, wrote a poor hand. 'Iste liber est
monasterii sancti Iacobi [. . . . .] rat' ', f. 202, s. xv ex.: 'Scotorum Ratisponen' is written
over the erasure. 'Hunc librum sibi vendicant scoti rat' religiosi 1526. sancta brigida ora
pro nobis', f. 202. 'Ex libris Monasterii S. Iacobi Scotorum Ratisbonæ', f. 1, s. xvi.
A 3-line erasure, f. 202. Presumably brought from Regensburg in 1862: cf. Rat. 1.

[1] For Baillie see *Innes Review*, ix. 188.

A. 2. *Horae*

A book of hours described by M. Dilworth in *Innes Review*, xix (1968), 77–81, where there are further details of arts. 1, 6, 7 and (pl. i) a reproduction of the coloured print of the Five Wounds (s. xvii?) pasted inside the cover. No. 39 in *Trésors*.

1. ff. 1–12ᵛ Calendar in red and black.

Entries in red include 'Translacio sancti francisci', 'Natalis beati Antonii' and 'Natale beati francisci' (25 May, 13 June, 4 Oct.), the two last with octaves in black.

2. ff. 13–19 Sequentiae of the Gospels, beginning imperfectly.

3. ff. 19–21ᵛ Apprehendit pilatus ihesum . . . testimonium eius. . . . Deus qui manus tuas . . .

A catena consisting mainly of John 19: 1–35, abbreviated: cf. *Lyell Cat.*, p. 66.

4 (in another hand, filling the quire). ff. 21ᵛ–22ᵛ O bone ihesu per tuam piissimam misericordiam . . .

5. ff. 23–82 Hours of B.V.M. of the use of (Rome), beginning imperfectly.

6. ff. 82ᵛ–85ᵛ Litany of B.V.M. and prayers. f. 86ʳᵛ blank.

7. ff. 87–108ᵛ Penitential psalms, beginning imperfectly, and (f. 98ᵛ) litany.

Benedict is before Francis, Anthony, Dominic, and Louis. Ten virgins: . . . (7) clara . . . (9, 10) genouepha radegundis.

8. ff. 110–13 Hours of the Cross. f. 113ᵛ blank.

9. ff. 114–16 Hours of the Holy Spirit, beginning imperfectly. ff. 116ᵛ–119ᵛ blank.

10. ff. 120–166ᵛ Office of the dead, beginning imperfectly.

Arts. 11–17 were added, early, in other hands.

11. ff. 167–170ᵛ Obsecro te, beginning imperfectly. Masculine forms.

12. ff. 170ᵛ–174ᵛ Oracio valde deuota ad beatam uirginem mariam ad remissionem peccatorum impetrandam. O intemerata . . . orbis terrarum. de te enim . . .

In the hand of art. 11. Masculine forms.

13. ff. 174ᵛ–175ᵛ Oracio beati bernardi ad beatam uirginem. O uirgo uirgo uirga sublimis o uere celestis planta . . .

In the hand of art. 11.

14. ff. 176–8 Stabat mater dolorosa . . .

15. ff. 178–9 De nostra domina oratio. Inuiolata integra et casta es maria . . .

RH, no. 9094, with following prayer. In the hand of art. 4.

16. ff. 179ᵛ–180ᵛ O domine ihesu criste adoro te in cruce pendentem . . .

The Seven Oes of St. Gregory. f. 181ᵛ blank.

17. ff. 182–183ᵛ Oracio ad sanctam trinitatem. Tres equales et coeterne persone . . . f. 184ʳᵛ is blank.

ff. i+184+ii. 129×92 mm. Written space 76×53 mm. 15 long lines. Ruling in red
ink. Collation: 1¹² 2¹² wants 1 before f. 13 and 12 after f. 22 3–10⁸ 11⁸ wants 1 before f. 87
12–13⁸ 14⁶ wants 1 before f. 110 and 6 after f. 113 15⁶ 16⁸ wants 1 before f. 120 17–21⁸
22⁸ wants 1 before f. 167 23⁸ 24 three (ff. 182–4). Written in *lette bâtarde.* Initials:
(i) 3-line, in colour on gold grounds; (ii, iii) 2-line and 1-line, plain red or blue. Capital
letters in ink of text touched with pale yellow. Line fillers in red in litany. Pages with
initials of type (i) have a side border the height of the written space. Binding of s. xviii.
Written in France. 'a guillaume Saumaire' (ff. 72ᵛ, 108ᵛ, 126ᵛ, s. xv/xvi). 'Marie R' (f. 1,
at foot) is the signature of Marie de Guise, wife of James V, king of Scotland, †1560.[1]
'Seton 102', s. xix, on a label inside the cover. Given by Lord Ralph Kerr, †1916.

A. 3. *Horae*   s. XV in.

1. ff. 1–10ᵛ Calendar in French in red and black, lacking January and February.
'S' thumas de cantorbie', 29 Dec., is the only saint in red who is not of the early church.
'S' ysabiel vesue', 19 Nov.

2. ff. 11–51ᵛ, 135–138ᵛ, 83–7, 52–69. Hours of B.V.M. of the use of (Thérou-
anne).
Sext and none are misplaced. Five leaves of the text are missing, including the first.
Each hour begins on a new quire. ff. 87ᵛ, 69ᵛ blank.

3. ff. 70–81 (in another hand) Sensieuent les heures de le crois.

4. ff. 81–2 (in the hand of art. 3) Les dix commandemenҭs de la loy. In French.

5. f. 82ʳᵛ (in the hand of art. 3) Les v commandent (*sic*) de sainct eglise. In
French.

6. ff. 88–114ᵛ Penitential psalms, beginning imperfectly, and (f. 104) litany.
Twenty-five confessors: . . . (20–5) gaugerice maure anthoni fiacri aychadre francisce.
Twenty-three virgins: . . . (14–17) waldetrudis aldegundis gertrude ursula.

7. ff. 115–122ᵛ Chi sensieuwent les xv ioie de le glorieuse vierge marie. Douche
dame de misericorde. mere de pitie . . . Sonet, no. 458.

8. ff. 123–128ᵛ Chi sensieuwent les vii requestes. Quiconques welt estre bi̯en
conseillies . . . Douls dieux douls peres sainte trinites . . . Sonet, no. 504.

9. ff. 129–134ᵛ, 139–163ᵛ (in another hand) Office of the dead, beginning imperfectly.

10. ff. 164–170ᵛ (in another hand) Missus est angelus gabriel . . .
Ends imperfectly in the final prayer, Te ergo precor . . .

11. ff. 171–2 (in the hand of art. 10) Memoriae: (*a*) of five martyrs, Denis,
George, Christopher, Blaise, Giles, beginning imperfectly; (*b*) of five virgins,

[1] Cf. Dilworth, loc. cit., p. 77, and *Trésors*, no. 39.

Katherine, Margaret, Martha, Christina, and Barbara, 'Katherina tyrannum superans . . .'.

(a). *RH*, no. 4707. (b). *RH*, no. 2961. The version printed in *Innes Review*, xix. 146–7 omits Christina. f. 172ᵛ is blank.

12. (a) ff. 173–175ᵛ . . . ceste protestacion pour fiable et ferme a ma mort et au iugement ou siecle des siecles amen. (b) f. 176 Deus qui beatos tres magos . . . (c) ff. 176ᵛ–177 'Orison de saint barbe' in French. (d) ff. 178–179ᵛ Ceste orison qui sens' fu trouuee deriere le grand autel s' pierre a romme et s' grigore donna a tous ceulz qui deuotement le diront autant de iours de pardon quil y ara eult de corpz enterres en le chymentiere ou on le dira . . . Auete omnes anime fideles quarum corpora hic . . .

Added in different hands, s. xv and (b) s. xvi in. (?). The first page of (a) has had a later prayer written over it and is illegible.

ff. vii+179+vi. 115×80 mm. Written space 70×50 mm. 13 long lines. Collation: 1¹² wants 1, 2 2⁸ wants 1 before f. 11 3⁶ 4–6⁸ 7⁶ wants 1, 2 before f. 48 8⁶ wants 1 and 6, 6 blank (ff. 135–8) 9⁶ wants 1 (ff. 83–7) 10⁸ (ff. 52–9) 11² (ff. 60, 61) 12–13⁸ 14⁴+1 leaf after 4 (f. 82) 15–16⁸ 17⁸ wants 1 before f. 104 19⁸ 20⁶ (ff. 123–8) 21⁸ wants 1 and 8 (ff. 129–34) 22⁸ (ff. 139–46) 23⁶ 24⁸ wants 7 after f. 158 25 four (ff. 160–3) 26⁸ wants 1 before f. 164 27 nine (ff. 171–9). Initials: (i) 5-line, in colour on gold and coloured grounds, decorated and with continuous borders; (ii) 2-line, gold on coloured grounds, with short border sprays; (iii) 1-line, blue with red ornament or gold with grey-blue ornament. Line fillers in gold, blue, and red. Binding of s. xvii, the spine gilt.

Written in north-eastern France. 'H. P. Heneage given by Dr. FitzGerald', f. i, s. xix.

A. 4. *Bernardus, etc.*   s. xv med.

1. ff. 1–9 Incipit epistola beati bernardi ad quend[am sa]cerdotem de dignitate eucharistie ac b[. . . . . .] sacerdotum. Cristus qui dedit se vobis primo in redempcionis precium . . . dabit in premium. Amen. Explicit.

PL clxxxiv. 779–90 (Instructio sacerdotis, Secunda pars). The right order of the leaves is 1, 2, 4, 3, 5, 6, 8, 7, 9. f. 10ʳᵛ blank. f. 1 torn.

2. ff. 11–12ᵛ Notes: (a) Corona clericalis est signum caracteris . . .; (b) Ad debitam ministri preparationem principaliter quatuor requiruntur. Primum est lotio manuum . . .

3. ff. 13–65 Introitus misse in duᶜⁱ sunt differencia. Aliqui sunt regulares. Aliqui sunt irregulares . . . quoque terminemus ut in eternum laudemus eum qui viuit et regnat in secula seculorum Amen.

An exposition of mass. Quotations are in larger script and underlined. f. 65ᵛ blank.

4. ff. 66–70ᵛ Six moralized tales: (a) De tribus ymaginibus per quas tria genera hominum intelliguntur. Rex quidam leo dictus fecit fieri tres ymagines . . .; (b) De vacca alba cornuta per quam anima humana intelligitur. Legitur in fabulis quod quidam habebat vaccam candidam . . .; (c) De muliere secretum reuelante. Laycus quidam probus dum sepius audisset mulieres . . .; (d) De fabro iusto et eius octo denariis. Virgilius ad instantiam titi imperatoris arte

magica ymaginem . . .; (*e*) De gratitudine qualiter remunerat et de ingratitudine qualiter finaliter condempnat. Henricus imperator quendam pauperem sibi occurrentem . . .; (*f*) De anima quam deus maxime diligit et in die iudicii requirit. Troianus imperator miro modo dilexit vineas et ortos . . .

(*b*). Argus and Mercury. (*d*). Focas the smith. (*e*). Steward and Guy. (*f*). Boar in vineyard.

5 (added). f. 70ᵛ Four lines of verse: Egregius labor est cum magno principe castra . . . miseri qui castra sequuntur.

Walther, *Sprichwörter*, no. 7013.

ff. i+70+i. Paper. 122 × 92 mm. Written space 96 × 70 mm. 26–9 long lines. Frame ruling. Collation: 1–7¹⁰. In quire 1 the third and fourth sheets are reversed. Written in a small cursiva, art. 3 in two sizes. No coloured initials. Capital letters in the ink of the text are touched with red. Continental binding, s. xix.

Written in Germany. A cutting from an English bookseller's catalogue in which this MS. was no. 472 is attached to the pastedown. 'From Mr. Ellice. 1893' (f. i).

GLASGOW. ART GALLERY AND MUSEUM

Psalterium, etc.[1]   s. XIV med.

1. ff. 1–100ᵛ Incipit psalterium ordinatum secundum ordinem minorum fratrum. et consuetudinem Romane ecclesie. Inuitatoria subscripta dicuntur singula singulis diebus dominicis . . . exclusiue. Primum inuitatorium Venite exultemus . . .

A liturgically arranged psalter, with noted invitatories, antiphons, and hymns, and the ferial canticles in their places. Psalms and canticles were numbered from 1 to 164 in s. xvi, each section of Ps. 118 being included in the series: cf. art. 7a.

2. ff. 100ᵛ–103 Te Deum, Benedicite, Benedictus, Magnificat, Nunc dimittis, Pater Noster.

Numbered, except Pater Noster, 165–9 in continuation of art. 1.

3. ff. 103–106ᵛ Litany.

4. ff. 106ᵛ–112ᵛ Incipit officium defunctorum secundum consuetudinem romane curie. Nota quod . . . letentur per. Explicit officium mortuorum.

5. (*a*) ff. 112ᵛ–119 Incipit officium recolende passionis et debet dici sicut in duplici festo et semper in inceptione horarum debet dici per signum crucis de inimicis. V'. Per signum crucis . . . Ymnus. In passione domini qua datur salus homini . . . Explicit officium passionis. (*b*) ff. 119–10 Incipiunt orationes ipsius. Obsecro te domine ihesu criste ut passio tua sit michi uirtus . . . Oracio. Totius bonitatis fons in (*sic*) origo . . . Oracio ad ihesum. Domine ihesu criste filii (*sic*) dei uiui qui tuas sanctissimas manus . . . Expliciunt oraciones passionis.

[1] Deposited in the Mitchell Library, Glasgow.

6. ff. 120–1 Feria quarta caput ieiunii. Ab ista feria quarta cynerum usque in cenam domini et nullo alio tempore ante inchoationem matutini . . . Postea dicitur officium beate marie.

Directions for special psalms, prayers, etc., to be said during Lent.

7. Additions: (a) ff. ii–v^v Tabula psalmorum psalterii. secundum ordinem Alphabeti; (b) ff. 121–2 Hymns of the common of saints, Deus tuorum militum, Sanctorum meritis, Eterna cristi munera, Iste confessor; (c) f. 123 Notes in Italian of times when the Bible is read.

(a). s. xv. A table of arts. 1, 2, with numbers added in red by the hand which numbered arts. 1, 2. (b). s. xvi. (c). s. xvii.

8. (a) f. i and the pastedown at the beginning are a folded leaf of Digestum Novum (bk. 42, tit. vi) surrounded by commentary: s. xiii: 2 cols. 47 lines. (b) The pastedown at the end bears a text in German, s. xv/xvi, set to music polyphonically: Myn ogen sagen sagen dat myn . . .

ff. v+122+i. Foliation of s. xvi (?). For ff. i–v see above. 232 × 165 mm. Written space 153 × 100 mm. 29 long lines. Collation: 1–6¹² 7–9¹⁰ 10⁸ 11¹⁰ 12² (ff. 121–2). Seven 7-line pictures in art. 5a, at matins the Betrayal and Scourging in two compartments, at prime before Pilate, at terce carrying the Cross, at sext the Crucifixion and drink of vinegar, with B.V.M. and St. John by the Cross, at none the Crucifixion, B.V.M. and St. John, at vespers the Descent from the Cross, at compline the Entombment: B.V.M. kisses the Face and St. John the Feet: backgrounds of deep blue. Initials: (i) in colour on coloured grounds, historiated (Ps. 1, David; Ps. 109, Christ blessing) or ornamented in colours (Pss. 26, 38, 52, 68, 80, 97); (ii) as (i), but smaller (Pss. 118, 121, 126, 131, 137); (iii) 3-line, blue, with red and blue ornament; (iv) 2-line, blue or red, with ornament of the other colour; (v) 1-line, as (iv), or without ornament. Binding of wooden boards covered with brown leather: a central panel containing a small square floral ornament carelessly set in groups of four is enclosed by two borders, each with a different rope pattern: two clasps from the front to the back cover. Secundo folio *Primo dierum*.

Written in Italy. 'Liber psalterii mei [. . . .]', f. 123^v, s. xvi. 'Iacopo Martino' is pencilled on f. 123.

Burrell Collection, 1.¹ *P. Lombardus, Sententiae*   s. xiii¹

Incipiunt capitula primi libri sentenciarum. Omnis doctrina est . . . (f. 3) debeamus uelle. Cupientes aliquid . . . (f. 3^v) premisimus. Incipit primus liber. Ueteris ac noue legis . . . usque uia duce peruenit. Explicit liber sentenciarium (*sic*).

Bk. 2, f. 82; 3, f. 146; 4, f. 196. Each book begins with an unnumbered table of chapters (as Quaracchi edn., 1971, I, ii. 5–53) and bks. 3, 4 have brief introductions after the tables, 'Huius uoluminis continencia . . . accedat' and 'Hiis tractatis que ad doctrinam . . . accedamus'. The scribe wrote nothing in the wide margins, which contain only distinction numbers of bks. 1, 2, 4 added in large black roman figures, and some later notes. ff. 6, 7 are supply leaves, s. xv²: the writer failed to get all his text in and overflowed on to a slip inserted after f. 7. f. 269^v left blank.

¹ The manuscripts of the Burrell Collection are at present in store.

ff. 269. 350×227 mm. Written space 175×98 mm. 2 cols. 42 lines. Collation: 1¹²
wants 6, 7 (supplied) 2–11¹² 12¹⁴ wants 14, blank, after f. 145 13–21¹² 22¹⁰ 23⁶. Initials:
(i) ff. 1, 3ᵛ, beginning table and text of bk. 1, 4-line and 6-line, blue or red, patterned in
white on grounds of blue, red, and gold, decorated (a dragon head on f. 1 and a bird on
f. 3ᵛ); (ii) of bks. 2–4 and their tables, red and blue with ornament of both colours; (iii)
of paragraphs, 2-line, blue or red, with ornament of the other colour; (iv) of subdivisions
of chapters and in tables, 1-line, blue or red. Binding of brown leather over wooden
boards, s. xvi, rebacked: fillets frame a large panel and within it broad diagonal bands bound
large lozenges: stamps of four patterns on the bands, in the lozenges, and on three edges,
outside the panel: two clasps missing: five bosses formerly on each cover: the mark from
the chain (?) of an older binding shows on f. 269 at the foot. Secundo folio *que unitatem*.

Perhaps French, but marginalia, supply leaves, and the binding look Netherlandish.
Belonged to a Dominican convent in s. xviii: (i) 'Litera/E / Scr. 5 Nº 3 / Ex Bibliotheca
Conuentus[. . . .] / O.P.' inside the cover; (ii) 'Co[. . . . .] Ordin. Praedicator' stamped
on f. 1 at the top. A pressmark of this date, 'N. 4 [. . . .]', and a circular stamp with faint
inscription inside the cover. '529/200' there and '529' on f. 1, in pencil, s. xix. Part of the
gift of Sir William Burrell (†1958) in 1944: inventoried at Hutton Castle in 1948 (no. 2)
and the Art Gallery in Mar. 1954.

Burrell Collection, 2. *Horae B.V.M.* s. xv med.–xv²

1. ff. 1–12ᵛ Full calendar in red and black.

Feasts in red include 'Translatio sancti nicholay', 'Yuonis confessoris', 'Michaelis in
monte gargano', 'Michaelis in monte tumba', 'Nicholay episcopi et confessoris' (9, 19
May, 29 Sept., 16 Oct., 6 Dec.). Many Breton saints in black: 'Guillermi episcopi',
'Gilde confessoris' (24, 29 Jan.); 'Guyngaloy abbatis', 'Diochonii abbatis', 'Sumorani
regis' (3, 9, 29 Mar.); 'Senigui confessoris' (3 Apr.); 'Nerecii episcopi' (5 May); 'Gategrani
episcopi', 'Iudicaeli martyris', 'Meuali (*sic*) episcopi', 'Aroni' (6, 7, 21, 22 June); 'Sa(m)-
sonis dolensis episcopi' (28 July); 'Pauli episcopi leonensis' (10 Oct.); 'Maudeti abbatis'
(18 Nov.); 'Corentini episcopi', 'Iudicaeli regis' (12, 17 Dec.). Additions in the lower
margins of ff. 2, 9, s. xvii (?), have been erased.

The calendar shares the errors 'Veri (*for* Seueri) et securi' (2 Dec.) and 'Anguli' (*for*
Auguli) with the Nantes hours described by Leroquais, ii. 298.

2. ff. 21–28ᵛ, 13–20ᵛ, 29–50ᵛ Hours of B.V.M.

The antiphon and capitulum at prime are O admirabile commercium and Virgo uerbo,
and at none, Ecce maria and Per te dei. Hours of the Cross and of the Holy Spirit are
worked in.

3. ff. 50ᵛ–52 Inicium sancti euangelii secundum iohannem. Gloria tibi domine.
In principio . . . ueritatis (John 1: 1–14). . . . Oremus. Protector in te sperancium . . .

4. f. 52 Antifona de beata virgine maria. Salue regina . . .

5 (added, s. xv). f. 52ᵛ De saint eustache. antiphona.

A memoria of St. Eustace, martyr.

6. ff. 53–66 Penitential psalms and (f. 61ᵛ) litany.

Twenty-six confessors: . . . (9) Yuo . . . (20–6) Brioce Guillerme Tugduale Corentine
Paule Paterne Sanson.

7. ff. 66ᵛ–69 Obsecro te domina . . . Et michi famule tue . . .

8. ff. 69–73 In commemoracione defunctorum ad vesperas.

Office of the dead, vespers only: cf. art. 11.

9. ff. 73–74ᵛ Siensuyuent les douze articles de la foy en franczois. Ge croy en vng dieu fermement . . . Ge tendroy iucque a la mort.

Thirteen 4-line stanzas.

10. ff. 75–6 Hoc scriptum repertum fuit rome retro altare beati petri apostoli. Iohannes papa xiiᵘˢ concessit omnibus dicentibus hanc antifonam . . . qua dictum cimiterium intrauerint. Antifona. Auete omnes anime . . . Oremus. Domine ihesu xpiste salus et liberatio fidelium animarum . . .

Cf. Leroquais, i. 140, 176, 243 for the ascription to John XII. f. 76ᵛ blank.

11. ff. 77–95ᵛ In commemoracione defunctorum. Inuitator'. Regem cui . . .

Office of the dead, matins and lauds: cf. art. 8.

12 (added, s. xv). ff. 95ᵛ–99ᵛ In ii° nocturno antifona . . . In iii° nocturno antifona . . .

Nocturns of B.V.M.: (2) Antiphon Specie tua and psalms Eructauit, Deus noster and Fundamenta (44, 45, 86); (3) Antiphon Gaude maria and psalms Cantate . . . cantate, Dominus regnauit and Cantate . . . quia (95, 98, 97). A reference back at the end of each nocturn, 'Querez les leczons au commancement du liure'.

Arts. 13–18 are on four quires added in s. xv², perhaps a little later than arts. 5, 12.

13. ff. 100ᵛ–112ᵛ Memoriae of SS. John Baptist, John Evangelist, Peter and Paul, James, all apostles, Stephen, Laurence, Christopher (. . . michi famulo tuo N. sis propicius . . .), Sebastian, Denis, all martyrs, Nicholas, Claud, Anthony hermit (Anthoni pastor inclite . . .: *RH*, no. 1203), Anne, Mary Magdalene, Katherine, Margaret, Barbara (Gaude barbara beata. summe pollens . . .: *RH*, no. 6711), Apollonia.

14. ff. 112ᵛ–114 Sensuiuent plusieurs deuotes louenges peticions oraisons et requestes qui a toute personne ayant entendement sont necessaires a dire a nostre seigneur ihesucrist. Primierement tu diras au matin quant tu te leueraz de ton lit. In matutinis . . . Quant tu ystras hors de ta maison. dy. Vias tuas . . . Quant tu prendras leau benoite dy. Asperges . . . Quant tu seras deuant le crucifist. Salua nos criste saluator . . .

Cf. Leroquais, ii. 196, 224.

15. Memoriae: (*a*) ff. 114–15 De sancto bonauentura. Doctor optime ecclesie sancte lumen beate bonauentura . . . ; (*b*) f. 115ʳᵛ De sancto anthonio de paduano. Gaude quondam seculi. transiens viator . . . ; (*c*) ff. 115ᵛ–116ᵛ De sancto francisco. Salue sancte pater patrie. lux forma minorum . . .

(*b, c*). *RH*, nos. 6923, 40727.

16. ff. 116ᵛ–120 Sensuyuent cinq belles oraisons que monseigneur sainct iehan leuangeliste fist en lonneur de la vierge marie . . . Mediatrix . . .

The first letter of each prayer makes the word MARIA. The heading notes the 'benefices' attached to each of them. Cf. Leroquais, i. 280.

17. Prayers: (*a*) f. 120^{rv} Oraison a dieu le pere la quelle se doibt dire par maniere de protestation. O dieu createur redempteur conseruateur . . . ; (*b*) f. 121 Oraison a ihesucrist. Doulx ihesucrist ie proteste . . .; (*c*) ff. 121^v–122^v Les douze articles de la foy en franzoys. Ie croy en dieu le pere tout puissant . . . Mon dieu mon createur ie proteste et confesse que en ceste foy . . .; (*d*) ff. 122^v–124 Mon benoist dieu ie croy de cueur et confesse de bouche . . .; (*e*) ff. 124–5 Alia. Sire dieu tout puissant. tout voyant. toutes choses cognoissant . . .

Sonet, nos. 1314, 524, 794, 1150, 2007. (*d*) is printed by Leroquais, ii. 339.

18. ff. 125–128^v Obsecro te . . . Et michi famulo tuo . . . Cf. art. 7.

ff. i+128+i. 180×120 mm. Written space 103×80 mm. 16 long lines. Ruling in red ink. Collation: 1–2^6 3–12^8 13^8 wants 8, probably blank, after f. 99 14–16^8 17^6 wants 6, blank. The hand changes at f. 100. Nine 12-line pictures in the part before f. 100, seven in art. 2 (no picture at lauds; two shepherds at terce have abandoned a game with sticks and a ball to look up at an angel bearing a scroll with 'Puer Natus est Nobis' on it: all white kings at sext) and one before art. 6 and art. 8: continuous floral borders. Twenty-three pictures on and after f. 100, three of them full page (f. 100 John Baptist); f. 114^v Bonaventura; f. 116 Francis: each with border containing repetitions of 'MIEVLX OV LA MORT M', or the same without the final 'M', one, 70×58 mm, on f. 115 (Anthony of Padua), and nineteen, 40×33 mm, in art. 13. Initials: (i) f. 125, 4-line O of *Obsecro*, historiated (B.V.M. at prayer); (ii) 4-line, red or blue patterned in white on decorated gold grounds; (iii) 2-line, blue or red with ornament of the other colour; (iv) 1-line, blue or red. Capital letters in the ink of the text filled with pale yellow. Binding of purple velvet, s. xix. Secundo folio (f. 22) *omnes fines*.

Written in France (Brittany) for a woman (art. 7), but in the supplement art. 18 has masculine forms. An obliterated shield of 4 quarters, 1 and 4 vair, f. 12^v. '£65', f. i^v. Given as MS. 1.

Burrell Collection, 3. *Horae*   s. xv med.

A book of hours, probably of the use of Rome (cf. arts. 1, 7), but very imperfect and misbound so as to bring art. 6 into first place.

1. f. 65 The last ten lines of hours of B.V.M.

The last part of a heading '*que* ad aduentum domini. Item a pascha resurrectionis . . .' remains, but the antiphon after it, 'Regina celi letare . . .', has been erased: a few letters are legible.

2. ff. 65–9 Oracio de (*cancelled*) beate marie virginis. Obsecro te . . . Et michi famulo tuo . . .

3. ff. 69–71^v Oracio bona et deuota. O intemerata . . . orbis terrarum inclina . . . michi peccatori . . .

4. f. 71^v Versus. Aue regina celorum Mater regis angelorum. O maria . . .

5. ff. 72–4 Domine ihesu criste qui septem verba . . .

The Seven Words. f. 74^v blank.

6. ff. 1–16 Incipiunt vii psalmi pe'. Litany, f. 11^v.

Twelve confessors: . . . (10–12) Blasii Bricte Amande. f. 16^v blank.

7. ff. 17–47 Incipiunt vigilie mortuorum.

Office of the dead, the responses of the nine lessons as in Roman use. f. 47ᵛ blank, except for scribbles.

8. ff. 48–64ᵛ Psalterium sancti Ieronimi. Verba mea . . . Oremus. Omnipotens sempiterne deus clementiam tuam . . . ut me famulum tuum N. . . .

ff. i+74+ii. 112 × 77 mm. Written space 62 × 40 mm. 16 long lines. Collation: 1 four (ff. 65–8) 2⁶ (ff. 69–74) 3⁶+1 leaf after 1 (ff. 1–7) 4¹⁰ 5⁶+1 leaf after 2 (ff. 18–24) 6–10⁸ (ff. 25–64). Initials: (i) 4-line and (f. 72) 2-line, red or blue patterned in white on decorated blue grounds; (ii) 2-line, gold on grounds of blue and red patterned in white; (iii) 1-line, blue with red ornament or gold with blue ornament. Continuous floral borders on first pages of arts. 2, 3, 5–7 (ff. 66, 69, 72, 1, 17). Capital letters in the ink of the text filled with pale yellow. Binding of red morocco, s. xviii: gilt spine.

Written in France. 'Ex libris Leonis S. Olschki Bibliopolae Veneti. Nº 14966 Scrin. 279' inside the cover. Given as MS. 1: no. 21 in a Kelvingrove inventory, 1 May 1948.

GLASGOW. MITCHELL LIBRARY

185666. *'Gratie . . . congregationi sancti Georgii in Alga concesse'*
s. XV ex.

1. ff. 1–5 Summarium priuilegiorum gratiarum et immunitatum summorum pontificum concessorum congregationi sancti Georgii in alga. Et primo: Quod status nostre congregationis . . .

A summary of the graces (etc.) in art. 2, under forty heads, each beginning with the word *Quod.* f. 5ᵛ blank.

2. ff. 6–46 Infrascripte sunt gratie et immunitates et exemptiones congregationis sancti Georgii in alga concesse a diuersis summis pontificibus ut infra uidelicet. Et primo. Gregorius episcopus . . .

Letters, (1) of Gregory XII, 27 June 1407, (2–5) of Eugenius IV, (6–8) to Eugenius IV, all 'Datum Florentie . . . anno decimo', (9–15) of Eugenius IV, (16, 17) of Nicholas V, (18) of Paul II, (19) to Sixtus IV, 21 May 1464, (20) of Innocent VIII, 18 Mar. 1486. f. 46ᵛ blank.

3 (added in s. xvi²). (*a*) ff. 47–53ᵛ Three papal letters: from Pius V, sine anno; from Eugenius IV, A.D. 1437; from Innocent VIII, A.D. 1494 (*sic*), 'Idus Decembris Pont. nostri anno septimo'. (*b*) ff. 55ᵛ–56 Comparuit et se personaliter presentat coram uobis D. Vicº eiusque locumtenente D. Raphael de cremona . . . (*c*) f. 57ᵛ Beatissime pater. Quando per ordini . . . desideratio felicita.

(*a*) is the decree under which the secular canons became regular canons. (*b*) and (*c*) record a dispute following on (*a*) between the canons of the congregation and the canons of the order of St. Augustine concerning precedence in processions (etc.), in which Dom Raphael de Cremona, abbot of Santa Maria de Pace, O.S.A., was spokesman for the Augustinians. (*c*) is in Italian. ff. 54–5, 56ᵛ–57, 58ʳᵛ blank.

ff. iii+58+ii. f. iii is a medieval flyleaf. ff. 6–46 were foliated 1–41 in s. xvi (?). 170×120 mm. Written space 115×70 mm. 27 long lines. Collation: 1–4¹⁰ 5⁸ 6¹⁰. 2-line blue or red initials. Binding of s. xix. Secundo folio *officia*.

Written in Italy.

308857. *Horae* s. xiv²

1. ff. 1–12ᵛ Calendar in gold, blue, and black.

Includes: in blue, 'Amancii episcopi ruth' ' (4 Nov.); in black, 'Dalmacii episcopi' (13 Nov.).

2. ff. 13–16 Sequentiae of the Gospels. ff. 16ᵛ–22ᵛ blank.

3. ff. 23–92 Hours of B.V.M. of the use of (Rome).

A leaf missing in lauds. The Advent office begins on f. 82. 'Regina celi letare . . .' (*RH*, no. 17170) at the end, f. 92. Headings throughout in Provençal, for example, f. 81ᵛ, 'Lo sapde deuan la premiera dominica dels auens entro a la vigilia de nadal se muda lo orde de nostra dona e disem lo en la forma que seensec. E comensam a uespres'.

4. ff. 92–99ᵛ La messa de la natiuitat de Ihesuxpist.

5. ff. 100–3 Hours of Holy Cross. Patris sapiencia . . .

6. ff. 103–14 Passio domini nostri iesu cristi Secundum Iohannem. Egressus est iesus . . . posuerunt iesum. John 18: 1–19: 42.

7. ff. 114ᵛ–117 Hours of Holy Spirit. Nobis sancti spiritus . . . f. 117ᵛ blank.

8. ff. 118–20 Regem cui omnia viuunt. Venite adoremus. Uenite exultemus domino . . . Ps. 94.

9. ff. 120–65 Anti'. Dirige . . . (f. 158) Vespras dels morts antifena. Placebo . . . Vespers of the dead after matins. No lessons.

10. ff. 165ᵛ–182ᵛ Penitential psalms and (f. 177ᵛ) 'Las letanias', ending imperfectly.

A brief litany. 'sancte philiberte' added, s. xv/xvi.

ff. iii+183+iv, foliated (i–iii), 1–49, 49*, 50–183 (184–6). f. 183 is a medieval flyleaf, see below. 175×115 mm. Written space 110×54 mm. 14 long lines ruled in red ink. Collation: 1–2⁸ 3⁶ (ff. 17–22) 4–5⁸ 6⁸ wants 7 after f. 44 7–12⁸ 13⁶+1 leaf after 6 (f. 99) 14⁸ 15⁸+2 leaves after 8 (ff. 116–17) 16–22⁸ 23 nine (ff. 174–82). The ink has often taken badly on flesh sides. Ten pictures in rectangular frames, 10-line, 9-line (f. 165ᵛ), and 6-line (f. 82): f. 23, a kneeling congregation and priest at altar, holding a candle; f. 82, Annunciation; f. 94ᵛ, Manger: an angel places the Child on Mary's lap; f. 100, Crucifixion; f. 115, Descent of Dove; f. 118, shrouded corpse on bed, clergy and mourners, an angel at the back holds the soul; f. 120, burial service; f. 165ᵛ, the last trump, bodies rising. Initials: (i) 5-line or 6-line, in colour on gold grounds, historiated, 7 in art. 3 (shepherds at lauds; visitation at prime; birth of B.V.M. (?) at terce; B.V.M. reads to an old man at sext; B.V.M. holds a green frame at none; B.V.M. at altar at vespers; marriage of B.V.M. and Joseph at compline) and one on f. 158 (kneeling singers); (ii) as (i), but 3-line and decorated; (iii, iv) 2-line and 1-line, gold on blue and red grounds, patterned in white. Light borders on pages with pictures. Capital letters in the ink of the text filled with yellow. Bound by Zaehndsdorf, s. xx.

Written for use in the diocese of Rodez. The arms of the counts of Rodez, gules a lion rampant or, are in the lower margin of f. 23. 'Ipheton (?) de burges. Ce sont les heures de la grant mere de ton pere qui les tenuoye auiourduy ce 27 mars lan venant 1552 que feust le moy suyuant que tu feus mariee nayant finis tes 17 ans Ie te prie et qui a*n*que (?) ententes tes entreprinses Regarde la fin Et aye la crainte de dieu deuant tes yeux Ton pere [. . . . .]', f. 183. Book-plate of J. Cresswell. The relevant cutting from a (Quaritch ?) catalogue is kept with the book. Bequeathed by John Cowie in 1965.

308858. *Horae* (*in Netherlandish*)   s. xv med.

1. ff. 1–12ᵛ Full calendar in red and black.

2. ff. 13–48ᵛ Dit is die vrouwe ghetide: of the use of (Utrecht).

3. ff. 49–62 Dit sijn die seuen salm dauid. Litany, f. 57ᵛ. f. 62ᵛ blank.

4. ff. 63–66ᵛ Dit is die cruus getide domine. The short hours of the Cross.

5. ff. 67–87ᵛ Dit is die Wijsheit ghetide.

6. ff. 87ᵛ–88 Prayers to SS. Katherine and Barbara. f. 88ᵛ blank.

7. ff. 89–102ᵛ Dit sijn die Vigilien Placebo . . .
Office of the dead. Three lessons in matins.

ff. ii + 102 + ii. f. 103 is a parchment flyleaf. 192 × 130 mm. Written space 90 × 63 mm. 18 long lines. Collation: 1⁸ 2⁴ 3⁸ 4⁶ 5⁸ 6⁶ 7–8⁸ 9⁶ (ff. 57–62) 10⁴ (ff. 63–6) 11–12⁸ 13⁶ (ff. 83–8) 14⁸ 15⁶. Initials: (i), blue on decorated gold grounds; (ii) 3-line, gold on dark-red and blue grounds; (iii) 2-line, blue with red ornament; (iv) 1-line, blue or red. Line fillers in litany only, gold and blue. Light borders (flowers, fruits and birds) on three sides of pages with initials of type i and the height of the written space on pages with initials of type ii, and on each page of the litany: gold in many small roundels and in the tails of peacocks. Binding of s. xixᴵ.

Written in the Netherlands. 'Dit boeck is gekomen uijt de Rariteijt Camer van Christoffel Plantijn. wiens dochter was getrouwt aen Iustus Raphelengius Professor tot Leijden van de Hebreeiche en Orientaelse taalen. van wiens soon francois Rapheleng dit boeck met twee silbere vergulde sloten verciert aen mijn Moeder Zal': Agatha van Velden is gelegateert int Iaer 1642. a 43. met en opschrift in dorso: Dit boeck is over de driehondert Iaer out. Pieter van Weesp', f. 103. 'Piter van Weesp heest in sijn leeve dit boek gegeve tot een gedachtenis int jaer 1714 an Anna Marija van Leeuwen vrouw van johan versijde', f. 103ᵛ. 'Mountstuart. E. Grant Duff bought this book in Amsterdam in Decʳ 1862 and gave it to John Webster Esqʳ Advocate 31 King St. Aberdeen Decʳ 1872'. No. 1521 in Rough List no. 49 of Wilson Ross & Co. Ltd. at £30: the relevant leaf with their admirable description is kept loose inside the cover. Bequeathed as 308857.

308859. *Horae*   s. xv/xvi

1. ff. 1–6ᵛ Calendar in French, in gold, red, and blue, the two colours alternating for effect. 'Saint romain' in gold, 23 Oct.

2. ff. 7–10ᵛ Missus est gabriel . . . et seculum per ignem Amen. Oratio. Te deprecor ergo mitissimam piissimam misericordissimam . . . Cf. below, art. 9.

3. ff. 10ᵛ–14ᵛ Memoriae of Holy Trinity, Michael, John Baptist, John Evangelist, Peter and Paul, James, Stephen, Laurence, Sebastian, Nicholas, Romanus, Anne Mary Magdalene, Katherine, Barbara (Gaude barbara beata summe pollens . . .: *RH*, no. 6711).

4. ff. 15–18 Sequentiae of the Gospels. Prayer, 'Protector in te sperancium . . .' after John.

5. (*a*) ff. 18–20 Oratio deuotissima ad beatissimam virginem mariam. Obsecro te . . . (*b*) ff. 20–2 Alia oratio de beata maria. O intemerata . . . orbis terrarum. De te enim . . . (*c*) f. 22ʳᵛ Alia salutatio Ad beatam virginem. Aue cuius conceptio solemni plena gaudio . . . Oratio. Deus qui nos conceptionis natiuitatis . . .

(*a, b*). Masculine forms. (*c*). *RH*, no. 1744.

6. ff. 23–50ᵛ Hours of B.V.M. of the use of (Rouen), with hours of Holy Cross and Holy Spirit worked in.

7. ff. 50ᵛ–58ᵛ Sequuntur septem psalmi penitentiales. Litany, f. 55ᵛ.

Ursinus as a disciple, after apostles. Twenty-two confessors: . . . (7–13) Mellone Gildarde et Medarde Romane Audoene Ausberte Seuere Laude . . . Twelve virgins: . . . (7) Austreberta . . .

8. ff. 58ᵛ–74ᵛ Office of the dead.

9. f. 74ᵛ Heading 'Oraison de nostre dame a dire au samedi'.

Almost certainly the heading refers to art. 2, which with art. 3 (quire 2) should come here and not in their present position: cf. Leroquais, i. 95, 250.

---

ff. iv + 74 + viii. ff. iii, iv, 75–80 are blank leaves ruled like the rest of the manuscript. 177 × 100 mm. Written space 130 × 57 mm. 31 long lines. Collation: 1⁶ 2–6⁸ 7⁴ (ff. 47–50) 8–10⁸. Written in set round hybrida. Fourteen 18-line pictures, ten in art. 6 and one before each of arts. 2 (B.V.M. and Child, kneeling woman, and angel), 4, 7, 8. Initials: (i, ii) 4-line and 2-line, mauve and white on grounds of gold paint, decorated with flowers, etc.; (iii) 1-line, gold paint on red, blue, or deep-purple grounds. Line fillers in the same three colours decorated with gold paint. Capital letters in the ink of the text filled with gold paint. Compartmented borders of conventional decoration all round picture pages and in the outer margin of all other pages. Gilt binding, French, s. xviii.

Written for use in the diocese of Rouen. 'PRYTANEE BIBLIOTHEQVE' round the edge and 'R. F.' flanking the fascia of the French Republic in the centre of an oval stamp on f. 1 show ownership by the Collège de Clermont in Paris, now the Lycée Louis le Grand.[1] The relevant strip from a bookseller's catalogue, s. xix, is pasted to f. i. 'Purchased from a London bookseller' by J. B(lackwood) G(reenshields) who wrote a note about the manuscript at 'Kerse, Lesmahagow, 1876' on f. ivᵛ: his book-plate inside the cover: his sale at Sotheby's, 18 July 1916, lot 496. Bequeathed as 308857.[2]

[1] Information from Mr. Jean Vezin, who told me that the college was called Prytanée français from 31 July 1798 until 1803 and referred me to A. Franklin, *Les Anciennes bibliothèques de Paris*, ii (1870), 262, where the stamp is reproduced.
[2] The words 'An odd bookplate stuck on' are pencilled, evidently as a warning, on the book-plate of John, Earl of Roxburghe, dated 1703, pasted inside the cover.

308876. *J. de Fordun, Chronicon, cum continuatione*

s. XV/XVI (after 1491)

1. ff.–1 250ᵛ Prefacio scriptoris. Honorabilium antecessorum gesta laudabilia . . . et regnat amen. Sequitur adhuc de eodem. Insuper vt demus . . . propono. Incipit prologus. Cum ad seriem cronicarum . . . (f. 1ᵛ) interfui etc'. Incipiunt capitula primi libri . . . (*table of 34 chapters*) . . . (f. 2) Ex variis quippe veterum scripturis . . . (107ᵛ) autoribus approbatur. Sicut in ewangelio ihesu cristi vna et eadem historia per quatuor ewangelistas approbatur. Sequitur genealogia . . . (250ᵛ) and forfatis bath to god and yine office.

A history of Scotland to 1436 in eleven books. The preliminary matter, 'Honorabilium . . . interfui etc', is printed from this copy in W. F. Skene's edition of Fordun (Chronicles of Scotland, i), pp. lii–liv and in F. J. H. Skene's *Liber Pluscardensis* (Chronicles of Scotland, vii), pp. 3–4. ff. 2–107ᵛ contain an abbreviation of Fordun's history, and the passage linking it with the continuation, ed. W. F. Skene, pp. 4–253, 387–401, xx. The rest (f. 107ᵛ, Sequitur genealogia . . .) is printed by F. J. H. Skene, pp. 6–400, from this copy, which he describes on pp. xiv–xvi (cf. also W. F. Skene's edition, pp. xxiii, xxiv) and says is closely similar to Bodleian, Fairfax 8 (*Sum. Cat.* 3888) and Brussels 7396 and by the same scribe as part of the Brussels manuscript: all three manuscripts have the date 1489 at bk. 8, ch. 17.

Each book is preceded by a table of the first words of its chapters. ff. 243ᵛ–244ᵛ are blank after bk. 10, which ends abruptly, as in other manuscripts, 'proximorum relacione'. ff. 251–252ᵛ were left blank. Letters from W. F. Skene to Milne Home, 22 Aug. 1878 and 20 Aug. 1879, are pasted to ff. iᵛ, iiʳ.

2. ff. 253–62 Tabula librorum.

A table of chapters of the eleven books of art. 1.

3. (*a*) ff. 262–267ᵛ In dei nomine amen. Per hoc presens publicum instrumentum . . . (f. 262ᵛ) Sane diligenter hec attendentes Nos Guillermus capel. Rector . . . (*b*) ff. 267ᵛ–268 Secunda appellacio. In nomine domini Amen. Tenor(e) huius presentis . . . (*c*) f. 268 Monicio vniuersitatis parisiensis. Nos guillermus capel . . . sic signatum *per* Mesnart etc.

(*a–c*) are contemporary copies of documents issued by the University of Paris, 13, 18, and 20 Sept. 1491. Also in Fairfax 8, ff. 192–196ᵛ, in a hand of about the same date. Printed by C. Égasse du Boulay, *Historia Universitatis Parisiensis*, v (1670), 795–806.

4. ff. 268–269ᵛ Sequntur nomina monasteriorum in Scocia.

Printed from this copy by F. J. H. Skene, ed. cit., pp. 403–7.[1] ff. 270–1ᵛ were left blank.

5 (added in s. xvi on blank pages of quires 13, 14). (*a*) f. 251 Rex sum Regnorum bina . . . (4 lines). Responsio ab anglo (*altered much later to* Gallo) facta. Predo Regnorum qui dicitis esse duorum . . . (2 lines). Qui tenet teneat possessio valet. (*b*) f. 251ᵛ Metra magni thurci a papa Alexendro. Roma diu tutibans (*sic*) . . . (4 lines). Responsum pape A. Fata silent Stelleque tacent . . . (6 lines). De dicto papa A. Thiberus vitulum. Galia taurum. Inferna bouem. (*c*) f. 252 Lilia Quisquis amat francorum . . . (4 lines). (*d*) f. 269ᵛ Tu proprios radios sol fuderit orbe leonis . . . (10 lines).

(*a, b*) in one hand which wrote 'Vostre bon amy MONTIOYE. R' ' at the foot of f. 251ᵛ.

[1] The copy in Fairfax 8, ff. 198–199ᵛ, was made by Adamson in 1650 from an exemplar in 'Edinburgh College'.

(a). 'Rex sum . . .' is Walther, no. 16784, the first four of five lines printed by T. Wright, *Political Songs* (RS), i. 26. (b). Walther, nos. 16845, 21070, the latter printed in *Neues Archiv*, xxxiii. 106. (d) celebrates the marriage of James IV of Scotland and Margaret Tudor in 1503.

6 (added in s. xvi on flyleaves). (a) f. v^{rv} Heir followis ye causis and occasionis of ye conuentioun of ye nobill men yat conuenit in Linlithq^w ye xxii day of Iulii anno etc xliii^o to be schawin to every man yat war no^t yair in credence. In the first thair grund and fundatioun is . . . (b) ff. v^v–vi^v Ane ballat of ye cuming of crist and of ye annunciatioun of o^r Ladye Compylit be maister Iohne ballenden. Quhen goldin phebus . . . Finis amen Imprentit be Iohne Scot etc.

(a). Report of a meeting at Linlithgow, 22 July 1543, and mention of later meetings at Winchburgh, 24 July, and at Linlithgow, 2 Aug., followed by three paragraphs rehearsing 'part of ye handis and articulis In ye contract of mariage and peax' between the infant Queen Mary and Prince Edward of England, Cf. Rymer, *Foedera*, xiv. 792–6 and *Hamilton Papers*, i. 630–2. Apparently a preliminary stage of the 'secret band'. (b). Twenty-two 8-line stanzas apparently copied from an unknown printing of Bellenden's 'The Benner of Pietie', no. 1 of the pieces in the Bannatyne Manuscript: Hunterian Club edition, ii. 3–8.

7 (added in s. xvii). f. 271^v (a) A piece about King Robert and the Scone pastures in 1390, printed by F. J. H. Skene, ed. cit., p. 408, from this copy. (b) Bruce's epitaph, 'Hic iacet . . . polorum' (4 lines), 'ex Scotichron. lib. 15 c. 14'.

ff. vi+271+ii. An old foliation is book by book. Paper and parchment, the latter for the outside of each quire and the middle sheet of each quire, except quire 13. 270×170 mm. Written space c. 200×130 mm. 2 cols. 39–44 lines. Frame ruling: sometimes pencil and sometimes ink is used. Collation: 1–8²⁰ 9¹⁸ 10–12²⁰ 13¹⁴ (ff. 239–52) 14²⁰ wants 20, blank. Quires lettered at beginning and end. Written in cursiva, arts. 1–4 in one hand. Initials: (i) red, the ornament red or in the ink of the text; (2) 2-line, red. Binding of s. xviii: centre-piece of the Marchmont arms, with motto 'Fides probata coronat': 'FORDONI SCOTICHRONICON' on a label on the spine. Secundo folio *Tandem*.

Written in Scotland. A gift to the Cistercian abbey of Newbattle, Midlothian: 'Liber sancte marie de Neubotill ex dono virorum venerabilium domini henrici et domini Iacobi herculi de linlithq^w', f. 1, s. xv/xvi.[1] 'Liber Ricardi Bruni et amicorum', f. 1, s. xvi ex. 'J. Gilmour' (?), f. 1, at top, crossed out.[2] Passed to the family of Hume of Polwarth. Sale of Sir J. Home-Purves-Hume-Campbell at Marchmont House, Berwickshire, 1913. Old marks D. 29.26, for which A. l.15 was substituted, f. ii, and XXI on a paper label on the front cover, s. xviii (?). Bequeathed as 308857.

308892. *Institutiones patrum Praemonstratensium* s. XIII¹–XIV²

1 (s. xiii¹). ff. 1–47 Incipiunt instituciones patrum premonstratensium. Quoniam ex prececto (*sic*) regule iubemur habere cor . . . (f. 1^v) sine difficultate

---

[1] For a bequest to Trinity altar in St. Michael's, Linlithgow, by James and Henry Erkill (or Arkill), priests, in 1496, see John Ferguson, *Ecclesia Antiqua*, 1905, pp. 308, 312: I owe this reference to Dr. John Durkan, who also tells me that 'Lioin albinic', written above and rather earlier than the inscription of Richard Brown, suggests ownership by Lyon King of Arms.

[2] Read as Gilmour by F. J. H. Skene and identified by him with Sir J. Gilmour, †1671.

repperiatur . . . (*table of 21 chapters*) . . . Incipiunt capitula prime distinctionis. De matutinis. Audito primo signo ad matutinas festinent surgere fratres . . .

Four distinctions, the first three (ff. 1ᵛ, 13ᵛ, 22ᵛ) in 21, 17, and 9 numbered chapters. The fourth distinction is in 22 numbered chapters—the table in front of it lists only the first 16—after which there follow, without break, 95 unnumbered paragraphs, all but the last three with headings. f. 47ᵛ blank.

Apparently statutes of Prémontré intermediate between the statutes of *c*. 1174 printed by Martène, *De antiquis ecclesiae ritibus*, edn. 1737, iii. 890–926 (MA), and the statutes of probably 1236–8 printed by P. Lefèvre, *Les Statuts de Prémontré réformés sur les ordres de Grégoire IX et d'Innocent IV au xiiiᵉ siècle* (Bibliothèque de la Revue d'histoire ecclésiastique, xxiii, 1946), pp. 1–126 (HT). The numbered chapters as far as D. 4.16 are nearly those of MA, the only new one being D. 1.17 (= HT, D. 1.15). D. 4.17–22 and the unnumbered paragraphs following it contain much of the material which distinguishes HT from MA, for example paras. (66) and (90) are both to be found in the long chapter of HT 'De annuo capitulo' (D. 4.1), the former as lines 68–71 and most of the latter, 'Quomodo abbates intrantes ad capitulum generale intrare debeant premo(n)stratum', as lines 7–23, 28–31. The preface is that of MA.[1]

2 (s. xiv²). ff. 52–89 Incipit quinta distinctio in qua continentur quedam additamenta de nouo ordinata. Quolibet sabbato in vesperis beate marie quando cantantur . . .

Forty-five paragraphs. Paras. 25–40 (ff. 66–84) correspond to chapters 6, 7, prologue, chapters 1–5, 8–14, 19 of the Quinta Distinctio printed in J. Lepaige, *Bibliotheca Praemonstratensis ordinis*, Paris, 1633, pp. 832–40. Para. 45, 'Petrus permissione diuina . . .', about oaths of obedience, etc., required from office holders and administrators, is dated at Prémontré, 10 Oct. 1374.

3 (added). ff. iiᵛ, viiᵛ, 47*ᵛ, 51*ᵛ, 96. Historiated initials cut from a large servicebook, s. xvi, in which minims were 11 mm in height, are pasted to paper leaves at the beginning and end of the manuscript and between art. 1 and art. 2.

(i) The Trinity. (ii) Andrew. (iii) Peter and Paul. (iv) David. (v) B.V.M. and Child in glory; angels crown her. ff. 48–51ᵛ are blank.

ff. vii+47+vi+40+vi, foliated i–vii, 1–47, 47*, 48–51, 51*, 52–97. For the inserted leaves see above, art. 3. 125 × 88 mm. Written space *c*. 95 × 60 mm. Long lines, 29 (art. 1) and 21 (art. 2). The first line of writing in art. 1 is above the top ruled line. Collation: 1¹⁰ 2¹² 3⁸ 4¹⁰ 5⁶+1 leaf after 6 (f. 47) 6–10⁸ (ff. 52–91). Red initials, 6-line (f. 1), 3-line (f. 52), and 2-line. Binding of s. xvi with gilt centrepiece in the style of Ker, *Pastedowns*, centrepieces vii, viii, flanked by F and II: rebacked. Secundo folio *Et cum in chorum*.

Written in France. 'francoys' in tall letters, f. 1, s. xvi. Ownership by the French boy king, Francis II (1544–60), seems unlikely. Bequeathed as 308857.

308893. *Statuta Angliae* s. XIV[1]

1. ff. 1–5ᵛ E. dei gracia . . .

The great charter of 6 Nov. 1217 (cf. *EHR* xxii. 514–18), with *E* instead of *H* as the first letter.

2. ff. 5ᵛ–8 Incipit de Foresta. H. dei gracia . . . et bene obseruentur. *SR* i, Charters, p. 20.

[1] An edition for publication in *Analecta Praemonstratensia* is being prepared by H. Thomas, O.P. I thank him for help with this description.

3. ff. 8–11 Incipiunt prouisiones de Merton'. *SR* i. 1.

4. ff. 11–18 Incipit Marleberg'. *SR* i. 19.

5. ff. 18–21ᵛ Incip*it* statut*um* Glouc'. In French. *SR* i. 45.
Corrections in lighter ink.

6. ff. 21ᵛ–22 Incipiunt explanaciones. Quedam explanaciones facte sunt . . . de vastis factis post statutum. Dat' apud Gloucestr' Anno Regni Regis E. vi etc'. Cf. *SR* i. 50.

7. ff. 22–37 Incip*it* statut*um* Westm' primi. In French. *SR* i. 26.

8. ff. 37–66 Incipiunt statuta West' secundi. *SR* i. 71.

9. ff. 66–7 Incipit tercium. *SR* i. 106.

10. ff. 67–69ᵛ Incip*it* statut*um* Wynton'. In French. *SR* i. 96.

11. ff. 69ᵛ–70 Incipiunt Inquisiciones. Modus inquirendi de statutis Wynton' quando obseruantur. *SR* i. 245.

12. ff. 70–2 Incip*it* statut*um* de Mercatoribus. In French. *SR* i. 53.

13. ff. 72–74ᵛ Hic incipiunt statuta Ebor'. In French. *SR* i. 177.

14. ff. 74ᵛ–78 Incip*it* statut*um* scaccarii. In French. *SR* i. 197.

15. f. 78ʳᵛ Incipiunt districciones eiusdem. In French. *SR* i. 197b.

16. ff. 78ᵛ–79ᵛ Incip*it* statut*um* de Reli(gi)osis. *SR* i. 51.

17. ff. 79ᵛ–80 Incip*it* statut*um* de Militibus. *SR* i. 229.

18. ff. 80ᵛ–81 Incipit statutum de ponendo in assis' et iur'. *SR* i. 113. A writ on the statute follows.

19. ff. 81–2 Incipit statutum de bigamis. *SR* i. 42.

20. ff. 82–83ᵛ Incip*it* statut*um* Lincolnie. *SR* i. 142.

21. (*a*) ff. 83ᵛ–84 Incipit Circumspecte agatis. Rex talibus . . . porrigatur. (*b*) f. 84ʳᵛ Incipit statutum de regia prohibicione. Sub qua forma . . . Parisius Anno xiiiiᵗᵒ.
(*a*). *SR* i. 101/1–23. (*b*). *SR* i. 101/24–102/13. Cf. Graves in *EHR* xliii. 18.

22. ff. 84ᵛ–85ᵛ Incipit statutum de Iusticiariis assignatis. In French. *SR* i. 44.

23. ff. 85ᵛ–86 Incipiunt dies communes in Banco. *SR* i. 208.

24. f. 86ʳᵛ Incipiunt dies communes in Banco de placito dotis. *SR* i. 208.

25. ff. 86ᵛ–87 Incipit statutum conspiracionis facte apud Berwic'. Cum il soit apertement defendu . . . Donee a Berwik en lan xx. Cf. *SR* i. 216.

26. f. 87 De conspiracione et eius pena. Dominus Rex mandauit per Gilbertum de Botheby . . . Cf. *SR* i. 216.

27. ff. 87–8 Incipit statutum de vocatis ad Warantum. *SR* i. 108.

28. f. 88^{rv} Incipit modus calumpniandi essonia. Non iacet qui(a) terra capta est . . . *SR* i. 217.

29. ff. 88^v–89 De homagio. Kaunt fraunc homme fra homage a son seign*our* . . . seignorages. *SR* i. 227.

30. f. 89 De fidelitate facienda. Kaunt fraunc homme fra feute a son seignour. il tendra . . . *SR* i. 227.

31. ff. 89–90^v Incipiunt capitula visus francorum pleg'. Hec sunt capitula que debent inquiri . . . Debet iuratus in primo iurare . . . thes' inuentoria. Cf. *SR* i. 246 (in French).

32. ff. 90^v–91^v Incipit assisa panis. *SR* i. 199.

33. f. 91^v Incipit assisa ceruisie. *SR* i. 200.

34. ff. 91^v–92 Incipit de quo waranto. De breui quod vocatur quo waranto. statuit dominus Rex . . . constitucionis presentis. Cf. *SR* i. 107 (Quo warranto novum, in French).

35. ff. 92–94^v Incipiunt noui articuli super cartam foreste. *SR* i. 147.

36. ff. 94^v–98 Incipiunt articuli cleri. *SR* i. 171.

37. ff. 98–100^v Incipit statutum de finibus. Quia fines . . . *SR* i. 128.

38. ff. 100^v–101. Incipit statutum de attorn' et finibus. *SR* i. 215.
Dated in 35 Edw. I.

39. f. 101^{rv} Incipit statutum de wardis et releuiis. In French. *SR* i. 228.

40. f. 102 De anno et die in anno bisextili. *SR* i. 7, but in the name of King Edward, not King Henry.

41. f. 102^{rv} De proteccionibus non allocandis. In French. *SR* i. 217.
Dated 18 Nov., 34 Henry (III).

42. f. 102^v Incipit statutum de prisonibus. *SR* i. 113.

43. ff. 102^v–103^v Statutum de antiquo dominico corone. Dicit quod antiquo . . . secundum consuetudinem manerii. etc.
Cf. the text in *Year Books 20–21 Edward I* (RS, 1866), pp. xviii–xix.

44. ff. 103^v–106^v Incipit statutum Prerogatiua Regis. *SR* i. 226.
Dated at Westminster, 27 May, anno 13 Edwardi.

45. ff. 106^v–112 Incipit statutum de Northt'. In French. *SR* i. 257.

46. ff. 112–14 Incipit statutum de coniunctim feoffatis. *SR* i. 145.

47. ff. 114–16 Incipit statutum scaccarii vltimi (*sic*). *SR* i. 69.
Dated 'apud Rochel', 23 Mar., anno 12 Edwardi.

48. (a) ff. 116ᵛ–119ᵛ Tables of chapters of arts. 3, 4, 7, 5, 8. (b) f. 119ᵛ Summa statutorum in hoc libello contentorum . . . (ends imperfectly).

Only arts. 1–5, 7–9 are listed in (b).

49. On flyleaves, s. xiv: (a) ff. ivᵛ–v 'Le serment de vic' ' and other legal formulae in French; (b) f. 120ʳᵛ Sequitur pena super pistorem. Si panes quadrantales . . . De Tolneto . . . De assisa ceruisie . . . De Carnificibus . . . De Mensuris . . . De vendicione bladi . . . De forstalleriis . . . De diuisione auar' . . . De vendicione farine . . .

ff. v+119+iii. For ff. iv, v, 120 see above, art. 49. 140×85 mm. Written space c. 110×60 mm. 28–32 long lines. Collation: 1–14⁸ 15⁸ wants 8 after f. 119. Written in one clear business hand in or soon after 1328 (art. 45). A contemporary two-compartment drawing in blue ink on f. vᵛ: above, Crucifixion, with B.V.M. and St. John; below, B.V.M. and Child: she holds a branch on which a bird perches. Initials: (i) f. 1, gold E on pink and blue ground patterned in white: a single spray into the margin; (ii) 2-line, blue with red ornament. Binding of s. xx. Secundo folio viuarios.

Written in England. Bought by Charles Cowie for £5. 5s. in 1911 from Alexander W. MacPhail, bookseller, Edinburgh. A letter from MacPhail is loose inside the cover. Bequeathed as 308857.

308894. *Antiphonale* s. XV ex.

1. ff. 1, 1*, 2–5ᵛ Graded calendar: blue is used for 'Duplex maius' feasts, red for 'Duplex minus' feasts and feasts of twelve lessons, and black for commemorations.

The twenty-three 'Duplex maius' feasts include: 15 Jan., Sancti Mauri abbatis; 10 Feb., Sancte Scolastice Virginis; 21 Apr., Transitus sanctissimi patris nostri Benedicti; 29 July, Sanctarum Flore et Lucille Virg. et Mart.; 5 Oct., Sanctorum Placidi et sociorum eius; 7 Oct., Sancte Iustine Virginis et Martiris. Many additions of s. xvi and s. xvii, including 'Anniuersarium Patris Ludouici Barbo primi fundatoris huius nostre congregacionis' at 19 Sept. and 'Dedicatio Ecclesie duplex maius' at 9 Nov.; Gregory, 12 March, and Holy Innocents, 28 Dec., were upgraded to 'Duplex maius'.

2. ff. 6–10 Tabula parisina. De specialibus annis laudum quo ponuntur ante natiuitatem domini fiat sicut in subscriptis tabulis continetur . . .

A table of Advent antiphons according to the day of the week on which Christmas falls.

3. Incipit antiphonarium monasticum secundum consuetudinem Monachorum congregationis de obseruantia Sancte Iustine. (a) ff. 10–53ᵛ Temporale; (b) ff. 53ᵛ–85 Incipit proprium sanctorum; (c) ff. 85–90ᵛ Incipit commune sanctorum.

Initials over 3-line in size show the principal feasts, including in (b) Flora and Lucilla, f. 71 (7-line) and 'In festo sancti Donati episcopi et patroni huius ciuitatis', f. 74 (4-line).

4. ff. 91–92ᵛ Incipit officium beate Marie Virginis.

5. ff. 92ᵛ–94ᵛ Incipit officium defunctorum secundum ordinem romane curie.

6. ff. 94ᵛ–96ᵛ Incipiunt viiᵗᵉᵐ psalmi penitenciales (cues only). The Litany follows.

Thirteen martyrs: . . . (11) Placide cum sociis tuis . . . Added names are Laurentius and Pergentinus among martyrs and Mustiola and Flavia among virgins.

7. (a) f. 96ᵛ Antiphona pro peste. Beatissime cristi miles et martyr sebastiane . . . (b) f. 96ᵛ Antiphona pro tempore Capituli. Emitte domine obsecro . . . ff. 97–98ᵛ were left blank.

8 (added in s. xvii). ff. 97ᵛ–98 Office 'In Festo S. Coronę Domini' and several antiphons.

9. The pastedown at each end is part of a leaf of a very large and handsome twelfth-century copy of Augustine on the Psalms, written in Italy.

The *E* of *Exaudi* (Ps. 63) is pale yellow and red on a ground of red and dark blue decorated with white vine stems.

ff. i+99, foliated (i), 1, 1*, 2–98. 235×175 mm. Written space 160×120 mm. 2 cols. 33 lines. Collation: 1–9¹⁰ 10¹⁰ wants 10, blank. Initials: (i) blue, sometimes with red ornament; (ii) 3-line, blue or red. Binding of wooden boards (old ?), covered in s. xx.

Written in Italy for the use of the Benedictine abbey of SS. Flora and Lucilla at Arezzo, a member of the congregation of St. Justina from 1474: cf. arts. 1, 3, 6. In an English bookseller's catalogue, s. xxᴵ, at £8. 8s.: the relevant cutting is inside the cover. Acquired in 1966 as part of the Robert Davidson Main bequest.

309758. *Registrum brevium*   s. xiv in.

A register of writs near in date to the Bodleian register called 'R' by de Haas and Hall, which they print, pp. 108–311. Imperfect at both ends. The medieval foliation shows that forty leaves (five quires, no doubt) are missing at the beginning, two leaves after f. 75, and single leaves after ff. 54, 106, 128, 131. f. 106 should follow f. 102. Statutes are occasionally referred to in red in the margins, for example at f. 18ᵛ, against de Haas and Hall, R. 136, Westm. I, c. 19. ff. 7ᵛ–8ᵛ blank.

Coloured initials break the text into sections. Fifty-nine of them remain. I give the first title in each section and the de Haas and Hall number of the first writ following it.

f. 1 De vi laica amouenda. R. 136
f. 4ᵛ De vasto in dote. R. 162
f. 9 De recapione aueriorum ante le Pone. R. 217
f. 16 Ne quis distringatur ad respondendum de contractibus etc. extra balliuam factis. R. 234
f. 18 De homine replegiando. R. 236
f. 24ᵛ De natiuis habendis. R. 244
f. 26ᵛ De minis. R. 253
f. 27ᵛ De transgressione in Comitatu.ᴵ R. 283
f. 41ᵛ Audita querela in 5 portubus. R. 273
f. 43ᵛ Aud' et terminand'.²
f. 47 De conspiracione.

ᴵ Many writs of trespass.

² Cf. R. 340–4. R. 344 is here on f. 45, a complaint of mag. W. de Langtone, master of the hospital of St. Leonard, York. In two writs, ff. 45ᵛ, 46, mag. W. Germeyn, parson of Scrivelsby (Lincs.), is named as complainant.

f. 49ᵛ Quando vicecomes recusat dare billam petenti. R. 351

f. 51ᵛ Inquisitio de escaeta. R. 360

f. 53ᵛ De etate probanda.[1]

f. 54ᵛ Si sit ad dampnum. R. 876

f. 60ᵛ Carta de licencia post inquisicionem. Rex . . . Licet de communi consilio regni nostri statutum sit quod non liceat viris religiosis . . .

f. 62 De compoto in Comitatu. R. 418

f. 66ᵛ De debito in Comitatu. R. 478

f. 69ᵛ De plegio acquietando in Comitatu. R. 512

f. 73ᵛ De annuo reditu in Comitatu. R. 476

f. 74 De cartis reddendis in Comitatu. R. 515

f. 76 Scrutatis pedibus finium. R. 553[2]

f. 77 De medio in Comitatu. R. 471

f. 78ᵛ De dote in Londoniis. R. 594

f. 80 De amensuracione dotis. R. 595

f. 81 De pontibus et stagnis reparandis. R. 441[3]

f. 85ᵛ De comunia pasture in Comitatu. R. 461

f. 86 De superoneracione pasture. R. 463

f. 88 Ne fiat secta que fieri non debet. CC. 118

f. 89 De secta facienda ad molendinum in Comitatu. R. 412

f. 92ᵛ De turnis Vicecomitis pro Religiosis. Cf. R. 612

f. 93ᵛ De custodia terre et heredis habenda in Comitatu. R. 556

f. 96 De herede rapto in socagio. R. 584

f. 98 Quod barones non ponantur in assisis. R. 632

f. 101 Quod nullus placitetur de libero tenemento suo sine precepto Regis. R. 411

f. 101ᵛ Quod proximus heres propinquior sit ad hereditatem emendam.[4]

f. 103ᵛ De nocumento. R. 656

f. 105 De disseisina. R. 645

f. 111ᵛ De associacione. R. 672

f. 117ᵛ Certificacio no. disseisine. R. 666

f. 118ᵛ De attincta no. disseisine. R. 709

f. 121 De reddiseisina. R. 695

f. 125. De iudicio festinando quod diutinam cepit dilacionem. Rex . . . Quia reddicio iudicii loquele . . . Cf. R. 685, etc.

f. 126 De morte antecessoris. R. 736

f. 128 Attincta de morte antecessoris. R. 745

f. 130 Quare eiecit. R. 753

f. 131 De ingressu ad terminum qui preteriit in primo gradu sine titulo. R. 767

f. 132ᵛ De ingressu per intrusionem post mortem tenentis ad vitam sine titulo. R. 805

f. 134ᵛ De ingressu per illam que tenuit in dotem in primo gradu. R. 802

f. 138 De ingressu de dote alienata contra Statutum Glouc'. R. 833

f. 141ᵛ De ingressu cui in vita quando mulier clamat tenere ad vitam. Cf. R. 793

f. 141ᵛ De ingressu sine assensu capituli[5]

f. 143 Cessauit per biennium in primo gradu sine titulo. R. 825

f. 145 Forma donacionis in le descendere. R. 861

f. 147 Aliter in le reuerti. R. 868

f. 147ᵛ Aliter in le remanere. R. 863

f. 148ᵛ Contra Relig' ingredient' contra Statutum.[6]

[1] Cf. de Haas and Hall, p. cxviii, note 9.

[2] Here a case of 9 Henry III about common pasture in Campden, the justice Martin de Pateshull, querent Ralph, Earl of Chester, deforciant Gervase, abbot of Pershore.

[3] Here about the repair of the road between Huntingdon and Godmanchester.

[4] Custom in the town of Northampton.

[5] Seventeen writs of entry for ecclesiastics, the first for a friar of the hospital of St. John of Jerusalem.

[6] A single writ to the sheriff, 'Si A fecerit te etc' tunc summone etc' abbatem . . .', to summons an abbot in breach of the statute of Marlborough.

f. 148ᵛ De attornatis. Cf. R. 599, etc.
f. 153ᵛ Proteccio patens.¹

2. ff. 154–5 are from a small service-book, s. xv in.

Cf. *Brev. ad usum Sarum*, i. ccxliii, ccxliv and ii. 49–52. Perhaps abandoned leaves. f. 154ᵛ is partly blank.

ff. i+154+iii, foliated i, 1–123, 123*, 124–56. For ff. 154, 155 see above, art. 2. ff. 1–148 have a medieval foliation xli–clxxxxv made before the loss of 46 leaves. 113×75 mm. Written space 83×46 mm. 26 long lines. Ruling in ink. Collation: 1–6⁸ 7⁸ wants 7 after f. 54 8–9⁸ 10⁸ wants 5, 6 after f. 75 11–13⁸ 14⁸ wants 2 (ff. 106, 102–5, 107, 108) 15–16⁸ 17⁸ wants 6 after f. 128 18⁸ wants 2 after f. 131 19–20⁸. Well written in anglicana. Fifty-nine initials, mostly 6-line or 7-line, in colours on decorated gold and coloured grounds and with prolongations in colours, picked out with gold, to form almost continuous borders: some crowned heads in the initials and some dragons and grotesques in the margins. Binding of s. xvi (?), repaired.

Written in England. Said by Mason to be of Walter Stirling's gift, but not in the inventory of 1792: cf. 309759.

309759. *Psalterium* s. XII²

1. ff. 5–104 A psalter beginning imperfectly at 'michi sine causa' (Ps. 3: 7). About thirty leaves are missing after this point in ones, twos, and threes, and a larger gap after f. 61 contained Pss. 75: 1–88: 20. All the leaves on which principal initials probably occurred are missing (Pss. 1, 26, 38, 51, 52, 68, 80, 97, 101, 109). The psalms were numbered in s. xv in., when, also, a sentence beginning 'quod iste' was added at the foot of many pages on which a new psalm begins, for example, (f. 87ᵛ, Ps. 125) 'quod iste nos eterni gaudii exultacione repleat', (f. 88, Ps. 126) 'quod iste in nobis que bona sunt edificat et edificata conseruat'.

2 (added, s. xv in.). Prayers: (*a*) f. 1 Domine ihesu criste fili dei uiui qui uoluisti . . .; (*b*) ff. 1ᵛ–2ᵛ Oracio ad beatam mariam de pite. Stabat mater dolorosa . . .; (*c*) ff. 2ᵛ–4ᵛ Oracio de sancta maria. Aue uirgo uirginum . . .; (*d*) f. 4ᵛ Oracio de sancta anna matris matre. Anna sancta ihesu cristi matris mater protulisti . . .

(*b*, *c*). *RH*, nos. 19416, 2271. (*d*). A memoria of St. Anne, ending imperfectly. Cf. *RH*, no. 1105.

ff. ii+104+ii. 110×78 mm. Written space 71×39 mm. 20 long lines. Mainly in quires of eight. Initials: (i) see above; (ii) 3-line, gold with blue and red ornament; (iii) of verses of psalms, 1-line, blue or red. Small red or blue roundels fill out lines. Binding of green morocco, s. xix ex., by Fleming of Glasgow.

Written in England. Bequeathed to Stirling's and Glasgow Public Library by the founder, Walter Stirling, †1791. No. 436 in the catalogue made in 1792: see T. Mason, *Public and Private Libraries of Glasgow*, 1885, p. 60.

¹ The first few lines of the writ only.

GLASGOW UNIVERSITY. HUNTERIAN MUSEUM

The collection of manuscripts and printed books is deposited in the University Library and administered by its officers. The manuscripts are fully described by J. Young and P. H. Aitken, *A Catalogue of the Manuscripts in the Hunterian Museum in the University of Glasgow*, 1908, and listed briefly by G. Haenel, *Catalogi librorum manuscriptorum*, 1830, cols. 786–98; thence in Migne, *Dictionnaire des manuscrits*, ii (1853), 95–110.

GLASGOW UNIVERSITY. UNIVERSITY LIBRARY

The General Collection contains manuscripts acquired between the late seventeenth century and the twentieth century, in so far as they do not form part of collections of books named after their donors (Euing, Ferguson, Hamilton, Hepburn, Murray). A catalogue of the books in the library, with pressmarks, was begun in 1691 and includes some manuscripts. A catalogue of the manuscripts was made in Apr. 1805 (MS. Gen. 329) and is printed in an abbreviated form by Haenel, op. cit., cols. 784–6. In Haenel's time the manuscripts were kept in case BD. 1 and he gives their shelf numbers.[1] Later catalogues with different pressmarks were made in 1828 (MS. Gen. 332) and 1836 (MS. Gen. 330). The named collections were acquired at the following dates: Euing in 1874: cf. Euing 1; the Euing Musical Collection in 1936 by transfer from Anderson's College; Ferguson in 1921: cf. Ferguson 13; Hamilton in 1879: cf. Hamilton 8; Hepburn in 1971: cf. Hepburn 1; Murray in 1910: cf. Murray 504.

Euing 1. *Biblia*   s. XIII[2]

1. ff. 1–361ᵛ A Bible lacking Prayer of Manasses and Psalms, but otherwise with the usual contents in the usual order.[2]

Proverbs begins on a new quire, f. 163. Stichometric notes: after Proverbs, 'habet uersus numero m̄dccxi'; after Ecclesiastes, 'Versus numero dccc'; after Song of Songs, 'habet uersus numero cclxxx'; after Wisdom, 'habet uersus numero īdcc'. The running title of Genesis is 'Yenesis' or 'Ienesis'.

The prologues are 35 of the common set of 64[2] and 31 others shown here by *: Stegmüller, nos. 284, 285, 311, 323, 328, 332, 335, 341+343 (Rufini in libro hester . . .), 349*, 344, 357, 457, 462, 468, 482, 480*, 487, 490*+486*, 492, 494, 500+501* (. . . refertur), 504*, 508*, 511, 510, 515, 512, 519+517, 516*, 524, 522*, 526, 525*, 528, 527*, 530*, 529*,

---

[1] Haenel lists BD. 1. a. 13, now Gen. 1227, as a fifteenth-century copy of a French translation of Boethius, De consolatione philosophiae. I think it sixteenth century and have not included it.

[2] See above, Bristol Public Library, 15.

534, 532*, 538, 535*, 539, 540*, 543, 544*, 552*, 550*, 551, 596*, 590+601*, 595* (last sentence only), 670*, 674*, 677, 633*+631*, 807*, 806*, 816*, 822*, 834*.

2. f. 362 A table of texts from the New Testament to illustrate eighteen theological positions, the first of them 'Quod fit unus deus probatio'.

3 (added in s. xv). ff. 362ᵛ–364ᵛ A table of lections of temporale, sanctorale, and common of saints.

ff. ii+365+ii, foliated (i, ii), 1–133, 133*, 134–364 (365–6). 200×142 mm. Written space 136×86 mm. 2 cols. 57 lines. Collation: 1–13¹² 14⁸ wants 8, blank, after f. 162 15–30¹² 31⁸ 32². Admirably written and decorated. Art. 3 is in cursiva (German ?). Initials: (i) to Genesis, historiated with the Creation in seven compartments; (ii) to other books and some prologues, in colour, usually reddish brown, on deep-blue decorated grounds—human figures and dragons occasionally; (iii) red and blue with ornament of both colours; (iv) to some prologues, red or blue with ornament of the other colour; (v) to chapters, as (iv), but almost always outside the written space. Binding of s. xix. Secundo folio *cramenta*.

Written in Italy. A heavy erasure at the foot of f. 1. In German hands in s. xix to judge from '365 Blätter', f. iiᵛ. Bequeathed by William Euing, underwriter in Glasgow, †1874. Formerly BD. 19. h. 16.

Euing 2. *Petrus Riga, Aurora*   s. xiii¹

(f. 3) Primo facta die duo celum terra leguntur ... (f. 216ᵛ) Descendens patrum ueterum de germine natus.

The Aurora of Petrus Riga, originally without title or name of author, but 'Aurora uocatur liber iste' was added on f. 1, s. xiii. Ed. P. E. Beichner, 1965. Stegmüller, nos. 6823–5. This copy has the same books as Beichner's 'third edition' in the usual order, Pentateuch, Joshua, Judges, Ruth, 1–4 Kings, Tobit, Daniel, Judith, Esther, Maccabees, Gospels, Acts, Job, Song of Songs. It does not have the prose preface, 'Frequens sodalium . . .', the Recapitulationes, or the prologue to Job, edn., pp. 7–8, 605–25, 669. ff. 129–131ᵛ are blank after Maccabees and the Gospels begin on a new quire, f. 132: they end after Beichner, line 2900, with 'Explic' uetus et no. t.'. f. 217 has nine mnemonic verses in the main hand, 'Quinque libros moysi. iosue. iudi. samuelem . . . Hii quia sub (*sic*) dubii sub canone non numerantur' (Walther, no. 16027). f. 217ᵛ blank. Notes in an English hand on f. 1ʳᵛ, s. xiii, include definitions of Hystoria, Allegoria, Tropologia, and Anagoge, with examples.

ff. v+216+ii, foliated (i–iii), 1–64, 64*, 65–217, (218–19). ff. 1, 2 (a bifolium) and f. 218 are medieval flyleaves. 218×150 mm. Written space 155×65 mm. 35 long lines. The first line of writing above the top ruled line. Pricks in both margins to guide ruling. Collation of ff. 3–217: 1–20¹⁰ 21–22⁸. Quires 1–8 numbered at the end in front of the catchword, for example 'IIIIᵘˢ Grande tab''. Initials: (i) 2-line, red or blue with ornament of the other colour; (ii) 1-line, red or blue. A binding of 1970, red morocco by Douglas Cockerell & Son, replaces a binding of s. xix. Secundo folio *Dulcia*.

Probably written in England. 'Liber domini Thome dackomb Rectoris de Tarent Gunevylle prec' iii s' iiii d' ',¹ f. 1, s. xvi: for Dackomb, † *c.* 1572, and his books see A. Watson, in *The Library*, 5th series, xviii. 204–17. '75' at the foot of f. 3 on the right, s. xvi. Armorial book-plate of 'The Revᵈ Michˡ Becher. King's College, Cant.' (fellow of King's College,

¹ Or so I read in 1950. It is now very difficult to read, having been thoroughly cleaned, and from 'Rectoris' onwards I cannot read anything.

Cambridge, † 1809). 'George Reading Leathes', f. iii, s. xix. Given as Euing 1. Formerly BD. 19. h. 14.

Euing 3. *Horae*   s. x²

1. ff. 2–13ᵛ Calendar in red and black.

Not full. Amandus and Vedastus, Basil, Remigius and Bavo, Donatianus, Livinus are among entries in red (6 Feb., 14 June, 1, 14 Oct., 12 Nov.).

2. ff. 15–20 Hours of Holy Cross.

3. ff. 21–25ᵛ Hours of Holy Spirit.

4. ff. 27–31ᵛ Incipit missa beate marie virginis.

5. ff. 32–36ᵛ Sequentiae of the Gospels.

6. ff. 37–40 Oratio de domina nostra. Obsecro te . . . Masculine forms.

7. ff. 40–2 Oratio de domina nostra. O intemerata . . . orbis terrarum. Inclina . . . Masculine forms.

8. ff. 42ᵛ–47ᵛ Memoriae of Holy Trinity, SS. Michael, John Baptist, Peter and Paul, Andrew, Laurence, Christopher, Katherine, and Barbara.

9. ff. 49–96ᵛ Hore beate marie virginis secundum usum Romanum.

10. ff. 98–113ᵛ Penitential psalms and litany.

11. ff. 115–138ᵛ Office of the dead.

ff. ii+138+ii, foliated (i), 1–94, 94a, 95–140. 117×87 mm. Written space 60×44 mm. 18 long lines. Collation of ff. 2–138: 1–2⁶ 3–11⁸ 12⁶ 13–17⁸; together with eight inserted singletons with pictures, ff. 14, 26, 48, 58, 73, 92, 97, 114. Written in set cursiva. Twelve full-page pictures on versos, seven in art. 9 (Innocents at vespers; Flight into Egypt at compline), and one before each of arts. 2–4, 10, 11. Fourteen small pictures, 25×25 mm, four in art. 5, nine in art. 8, and one before art. 6 (Pietà). Initials: (i) blue on gold grounds decorated in colours; (ii) 2-line, gold on coloured grounds patterned in white; (iii) 1-line, blue with red ornament, or gold with blue-grey ornament. Line-fillers in litany in blue or gold. A continuous border on pages with full-page pictures or initials of type (i). A binding of 1961 by D. Cockerell & Son replaces a binding of s. xix by Spachman.

Written in the southern Netherlands. '26.5.53' inside the cover, the date of acquisition by William Euing, is followed by a name (of a bookseller?),[1] which I cannot read. Given as Euing 1. Formerly BD. 19. h. 31.

Euing 4. *Horae*   s. xv med.

No. 17 in *Trésors*, with facsimile, pl. 12, of f. 55. No 571 in *Flemish Art, 1300–1700*, 1953. No. 32 in *La miniature flamande*, 1959.

1. ff. 2–13ᵛ Full calendar in French in red and black.

Among entries in red: Saint omer en fleurs, 8 June; Saint bertin, 5 Sept.; Saint omer, 9 Sept.

[1] Cf. Euing 7, 9, 10.

2. ff. 14–16ᵛ Hours of the Cross.

3. ff. 17–19ᵛ Hours of the Holy Spirit.

4. ff. 20–21ᵛ Sequentiae of the Gospels, John and Luke only.

5. ff. 22–64ᵛ Hours of B.V.M. of the use of (Thérouanne).

6. ff. 65–67ᵛ Obsecro te . . . Masculine forms.

7. ff. 68–70ᵛ Deuote orison de nostre dame. O intemerata . . . orbis terrarum. De te enim . . .

8. f. 71ʳᵛ Salve regina. ff. 72–73ᵛ blank.

9. ff. 74–88 Penitential psalms and litany. f. 88ᵛ blank.

10. ff. 89–122 Office of the dead. f. 122ᵛ blank.

11. (a) ff. 123–127ᵛ Douche dame de misericorde mere de pite . . . (b) ff. 127ᵛ–130ᵛ Quiconques uelt estre bien consillies . . . Douls dieus dous pere . . .
Fifteen Joys and Seven Requests. Sonet, nos. 458, 504. ff. 131–134ᵛ blank.

ff. i+133, foliated 1–134. f. 1 is a medieval flyleaf. 226 × 157 mm. Written space 105 × 65 mm. 16 long lines. Collation: 1–2⁶ 3–9⁸ 10⁴ (ff. 70–3) 11–17⁸ 18⁶ wants 2, probably blank, after f. 130. Twelve 12-line pictures, ff. 14, 17, 22, 31ᵛ, 40ᵛ, 45ᵛ, 49, 52, 55, 61, 74, 89. Initials: (i) blue or red patterned in white on decorated gold grounds; (ii, iii) 2-line and 1-line, gold on coloured grounds. Line-fillers in red and blue touched with gold. Continuous borders on picture pages. A binding of 1961, red morocco by D. Cockerell & Son, replaces a binding of s. xix by Nelson, Glasgow.

Written in north-east France. Bequeathed as Euing 1. Formerly BD. 19. h. 12. Exhibited at the Royal Academy of Arts, Winter Exhibition 1953, and in Brussels in 1963.

Euing 7.   *Officium missae, etc.*   s. xv ex.

1. ff. 1–11ᵛ Masses of: (a) Holy Trinity; (b) Corpus Christi; (c) Holy Spirit; (d) Holy Cross; (e) the Passion; (f) the Five Wounds; (g) B.V.M.; (h) the Compassion of B.V.M.; (i) St. Anne; (j) St. Anthony hermit; (k) St. Augustine.
(f) is preceded by a heading, 'Sanctus bonifacius papa egrotauit usque ad mortem . . .', and is followed by a notice of forty days indulgence from Pope Innocent IV. The sequences of (h–j) are *RH*, nos. 9813, 11850, 883.

2. ff. 11ᵛ, 13–15ᵛ Eleven votive masses, the first 'Contra mortalitatem'.

3. ff. 15ᵛ–18 Masses of the dead.

4. f. 18ᵛ Gloria and Credo in unum deum.

5. ff. 19–23ᵛ Ordinary, prefaces, and canon of mass. A leaf missing.

6. ff. 24–30 Masses of the common of saints. f. 30ᵛ blank.

ff. i+30+i. 173 × 127 mm. Written space 118 × 86 mm. 2 cols. 31 lines. 28 long lines on ff. 21–3. Collation: 1¹⁰ 2¹⁰ wants 9 before f. 21 3¹⁰ wants 10, probably blank, after f. 30:

together with singleton picture pages after 2¹ and 2⁸. Written in a round hybrida. Two full-page pictures on rectos, the versos, blank: f. 12, a seated boy bishop; f. 20, the Trinity: Christ, wounded, on the Father's lap, the Dove between them. Initials: (i) ff. 1, 6ᵛ (at art. 1g), 21, in colours on decorated gold grounds; (ii) gold, with blue or pink ornament; (iii, iv) 2-line and 1-line, red or blue. A floral border on three sides of f. 1 and on one side of f. 6ᵛ. Binding of s. xix. Secundo folio *panem*.

Written in the Netherlands. Names 'Lisette Grimberg' (twice), 'Balthasar', 'Stephan Kripo', f. 20ᵛ, s. xviii. Euing's note '27.4.64 ic/Boone' inside the cover. Given as MS. Euing 1. Formerly BD. 19. h. 12.

Euing 9. *Psalterium, etc.* s. xv med.

1. ff. 2–13 Calendar in blue, red, and black, the blue and red alternating for effect.

Graded Totum duplex, Duplex, Missa, Memoria. 'Totum duplex' feasts include 'Relatio sancti Vedasti', 15 July, and 'Auberti episcopi et confessoris', 13 Dec. 'Duplex' feasts include: 'Depositio sancti vedasti', 6 Feb.; 'Quiriaci martyris', 29 Apr.; 'Ludouici regis francie', 25 Aug.; 'Ieronimi presbiteri et confessoris', 30 Sept.; 'Eleuacio corporis sancti uedasti', 1 Oct.; 'Leodegarii episcopi et martyris', 2 Oct.; 'Amati episcopi et confessoris', 19 Oct.; 'Quintini martyris', 31 Oct.

2. ff. 15–196ᵛ Liturgical psalter.

3. ff. 196ᵛ–214 Six ferial canticles, Te deum, Benedicite, Magnificat, Benedictus, Nunc dimittis, Quicumque uult.

4. ff. 214–220ᵛ Litany.

Twenty-seven confessors: (1–4) Vedaste (doubled) Silvester Leo, Ieronime (doubled) . . .

5. ff. 220ᵛ–224ᵛ Collects of Holy Trinity, Holy Spirit, B.V.M., angels, John Baptist, Peter and Paul, John Evangelist, apostles, Stephen, martyrs, Vedast, Jerome, confessors, Mary Magdalene, Katherine, virgins, Communis oratio, Oratio generalis (Pietate quesumus domine nostrorum solue uincula . . .: for male use). ff. 225–9ᵛ left blank.

6 (added, s. xvi). ff. 225–8 A note in French of the profit of reading the psalter.

ff. i+229+i, foliated 1–195, 195*, 196–230. Flyleaves and pastedowns are medieval. 158 × 109 mm. Written space 87 × 57 mm. 17 long lines. Ruling in red ink. Collation of ff. 2–229: 1–2⁶ 3⁸+1 leaf inserted before 1 (f. 14) 4–29⁸. f. 14 is blank on the recto and has a full-page drawing on the verso: a woman in black kneels before St. Peter. Initials: (i) of the usual eight psalms and Pss. 51, 101 and of art. 3, red or blue patterned in white on gold grounds: Ps. 1 historiated (St. Jerome); (ii) 2-line, gold on coloured grounds patterned in white; (iii) 1-line, blue with red ornament or gold with blue ornament. Borders on four sides of f. 15 and on three sides of other pages with initials of type (i). Line fillers in blue and red. Binding of s. xviii.

Written for use in the diocese of Arras and probably in a church of St. Jerome. '21.6.60 ie/Knight', inside the cover, records the date, the price, and the bookseller, Knight, from whom William Euing bought this manuscript. Given as MS. Euing 1. Formerly BD. 19. h. 26.

Euing 10. *Psalterium, etc.* 1502

1. ff. 2–147^v, 149–85 A liturgical psalter, beginning imperfectly at Ps. 13.

2. ff. 185–201^v Six ferial canticles, Benedicite, Benedictus, Te deum, Credo in deum patrem, Quicumque uult.

3. ff. 201^v–208^v Litany.

Nine confessors: . . . (8, 9) Louis, Bonaventura. Monks and hermits: Benedict, Francis, Anthony, Bernardine, Dominic, Bernard, Sebald. Ten virgins: (1, 2) Mary Magdalene, Clare . . . Prayers on f. 27 contain the words 'miserere famulo tuo ministro nostro' and 'respice propicius super famulam tuam abbatissam nostram'.

4. f. 208^v Six advent invitatories.

5. ff. 209–24 Hymns of the temporale from Advent to the Transfiguration, twenty-three in all, if we include the Advent capitulum, Venite ascendamus . . . de ierusalem, which follows Verbum supernum and is headed 'Ymnus'.

Hymns for De lancea domini, between Pentecost and Trinity, are Pange lingua gloriose lancee and Eterna cristi munera nos sacient (*RH*, nos. 14444, 604); those for the Transfiguration, Exultet laudibus and Novum sidus (*RH*, nos. 5872, 12374). The second hymn for Trinity Sunday (after O lux beata trinitas) is Festi laudes hodierni ritu (*RH*, no. 6151).

6. ff. 224–227^v Versicles of principal feasts of the temporale.

7. ff. 227^v–260^v Antiphons and collects of the temporale.

8. ff. 260^v–262^v Suffragia.

(i) Holy Cross. (ii) Peter and Paul. (iii) Francis. (iv) Otto et socii, Clare, Louis, Bonaventura, Anthony, Bernardine. (v) Francis and saints following him. (vi) For peace.

9. ff. 262^v–263^v In i^o nocturno benedictio. Exaudi domine ihesu criste preces seruorum tuorum . . . In ii^o nocturno benedictio. Ipsius pietas et misericordia . . . In iii^o nocturno benedictio. A uinculis peccatorum nostrorum . . . Benedictio. Cuius festum colimus . . .

In all, seventeen forms of benediction.

10. f. 148^{rv} Part of the office of prime on Sunday.

A single leaf from a missing part of the book, inserted into quire 15.

ff. i+262, foliated 1–263. 134×90 mm. Written space 89×59 mm. 16 long lines. Collation of ff. 2–147, 149–263: 1^{10} wants 1–3, 2–26^{10} 27 four (ff. 260–3): for f. 148 see above, art. 10. Written in a good hand and admirably black ink. Initials: (i) to the usual seven psalms (Ps. 1 is missing), blue on gold grounds in red and green frames; (ii, iii) 2-line and 1-line, blue or red. Capital letters in the ink of the text are touched with red. Binding of wooden boards over brown leather, bearing a narrow roll, a centrepiece and angle-pieces, s. xvi.

Written in Germany, apparently for Franciscan nuns: 'Scriptum per Iohannem Seydenfaden et finitum feria v^a post andree. 1502', f. 263^v. The date of acquisition, the price and the bookseller are recorded by William Euing in a note inside the cover, '6.5.61 Knt/38'. Given as MS. Euing 1. Formerly BD. 19. h. 28.

Euing 26. *Fragmenta missalis ad usum fratrum Carmelitarum*

s. XIV ex.

'This Collection of various small Alphabets and Letters in different colours with curious small miniature figures and devices in many of them—and ornaments— was selected and made by my dear relative Esther Cory from a large folio *imperfect* Missal which I purchased at a sale for £7. 7. The Larger Miniatures, Initial Letters, and Ornaments in the same Missal, were collected and bound in 2 volumes folio and were sold at my Sale in 1833 for £28. 10—P. A. H.', on a flyleaf. 'Finis Anno Domini 1800 28', on a slip at the end.

The two volumes referred to in this note by P. A. Hanrott were acquired by the British Museum in 1874 and are now B.L., Add. 29704–5: see M. Rickert, *The Reconstructed Carmelite Missal*, 1952. Another volume is Add. 44892.

Initials in red and blue with penwork historiations, initials in gold on decorated coloured grounds, initials in gold with violet ornament, initials in red with red penwork ornament, cadels with elaborate olive-green penwork historians, whole words in gold, blue or red, sometimes with two colours in one word and even in one letter, and often with penwork ornament round each letter, line fillers in gold and blue, and border sprays, all mounted on 140 leaves of paper measuring 163 × 123 mm and bound handsomely.

Lot 14 in the Hanrott sale, 31 Jan. 1857, as Euing noted inside the cover, where he wrote also 'if Knt' (cf. Euing 9). Given as Euing 1. Formerly BD. 19. h. 9.

Euing 29. *Missale, pars autumnalis*

s. XVI in.

1. ff. 1–59ᵛ Temporale from the sixth Sunday after Pentecost to Friday after the twenty-fifth Sunday after Pentecost.

2. ff. 60–1 De venerabili sacramento corporis et sanguinis cristi ie. ff. 61ᵛ, 62 blank.

3. (a) f. 62ᵛ Settings of the words 'Gloria in excelsis' and 'Credo in unum deum'. (b) ff. 63–4 Gloria, Credo. (c) f. 64ʳᵛ John 1: 1–14 and prayer 'Protector in te sperantium . . .'.

4. ff. 65–78ᵛ Noted prefaces and (f. 71) canon of mass.

5. ff. 79–87ᵛ Collect, secret, and postcommunion of twenty-nine votive masses, beginning with Holy Trinity. and ending with 'Pro principe'.

'De sancto Adriano' is in fifth place and 'De sanctis ecclesie' in seventh. The latter's collect has the phrase 'per sanctorum tuorum Adriani Georgii et beate Natalie. atque ceterorum quorum reliquie in presenti continentur ecclesia. merita gloriosa'.

6. ff. 87ᵛ–94 Masses of Holy Trinity, Holy Spirit, Holy Cross, B.V.M., SS. Peter and Paul, and St. Adrian.

7. ff. 94–9 Pro defunctis.

8. ff. 99–101ᵛ Feria ii. Leccio isaie prophete. Hec dicit dominus deus. Orietur in tenebris lux . . .

Epistle and gospel lections of masses of the dead, one pair assigned to each day of the week, Monday to Saturday.

9. ff. 102–162ᵛ Sanctorale, 1 Aug.–29 Nov., Chains of Peter–Saturninus.

Includes offices for Philibert and Bernard, jointly (20 Aug.), Adrian (8 Sept., with vigil), Leonard and Winnoc, jointly (6 Nov.), Theodore and Ragnulf, jointly (9 Nov.).

ff. vi+162+vi. Thick parchment. 330×235 mm. Written space 230×155 mm. 2 cols. 23 lines and (ff. 71–78ᵛ) 18 lines. Collation: 1⁸ wants 1, 2 2–12⁸ 13⁸+1 leaf after 8 (f. 101) 14–20⁸ 21⁸ wants 6–8, blank, after f. 162. 4⁴,⁵, 15³,⁶, 17¹,⁸, 17³,⁶, and 20¹,⁸ are half-sheets: four of these leaves, 15³, 17¹, 17³, and 20¹, are historiated (ff. 112, 126, 128, 157). A full-page crucifixion, with an evangelist's symbol at each corner of the border, f. 70ᵛ. Initials: (i) in colour, historiated, ff. 71 (Mass of St. Gregory), 112ᵛ (Assumption of B.V.M.), 126ᵛ (Nativity of B.V.M.), 128ᵛ (St. Adrian), 150ᵛ (All Saints); (ii) ff. 1, 65, in colour on coloured grounds patterned in gold; (iii, iv) 3-line and 2-line, blue with red ornament or red with violet-blue ornament; (v) 1-line, blue or red. Continuous framed floral or architectural borders on f. 1 and the six other main pages and a shorter border on f. 65. Binding of s. xix in. Secundo folio *us erit*.

Written for use in a church where St. Adrian was principal patron and where there were relics of Adrian, George, and Natalia, no doubt the Benedictine abbey of Grammont, Flanders. The arms in the initials on ff. 1, 65 are quarterly 1 and 4 azure a cross gules, 2 and 3 vert three escallops argent (de l'Esclatière ?). Given as Euing 1. Formerly d. 3. a. 16.

Euing Music Collection, R. d. 56. *Antiphonale, etc.*   s. xv med.

1. ff. 1ᵛ–177ᵛ In aduentu domini dominica prima ad Magnificat anth*iphona*. Ecce nomen domini . . .

Antiphons (only): (*a*) ff. 1–111, of the temporale to the twenty-fourth Sunday after Pentecost, and (f.102ᵛ) the ferial antiphons for August, September, October, November, as set out in *SMRL* ii. 109–12; (*b*) ff. 111–162ᵛ, of twenty-nine feasts of the sanctorale, Andrew–Clement; (*c*) ff. 162ᵛ–163ᵛ In dedicacione; (*d*) ff. 163ᵛ–173ᵛ, of the common of saints; (*e*) ff. 173ᵛ–177, of the Festum nivis; (*f*) f. 177ᵛ An*tiphona* de Sancta Maria. Sub tuum presidium . . .

(*b*) includes antiphons for the Franciscan saints Anthony of Padua, Clare, and Francis, 'Aue gemma virtuosa . . .' for Dorothy (*RH*, no. 1824; *AH* v. 163), and antiphons for the common of saints 'in Pasca' between Annunciation and Philip and James, as set out in *SMRL* ii. 133–5.

The scribe began (*a*) on the recto of f. 1, wrote a line and a half and decided that it would be better to begin on the verso. The rest of the recto contains: (*g*) in the main hand 'A'. Media vita in morte sumus . . . tradas nos', noted; (*h*) a prayer against plague, added in the same hand as art. 2*f*, 'Omnipotens sempiterne deus qui inter[cessione] gloriosi martiris tui sancti sebastiani generalem pestem . . .'.

ff. 178–179ᵛ were ruled, but left blank.

2. ff. 180–205ᵛ In dominicis y*mpnus* ad Nᵒ. Primo dierum omnium . . .

Hymns: (*a*) at matins and vespers on Sundays; (*b*) f. 182, of the temporale from Advent to Corpus Christi; (*c*) f. 193, of the sanctorale; (*d*) f. 200ᵛ, of the common of saints; (*e*) f. 205, for the dedication of a church; (*f*) f. 205ᵛ, added, for Clare, 'in secundis vesperis. ymnus. Decus clarum feminarum . . . iam 'lucys' orto sydere' (*ends imperfectly*).

Musical notes above the first line or two of each hymn. In (*c*) proper hymns are provided for twelve feasts, Anthony of Padua, Conversion of Paul, Chair of Peter, John Baptist, Peter and Paul, Mary Magdalene, Chains of Peter, Clare (Concinat plebs . . .; Spretis natiuo . . ., Clarum lumen effunditur . . .), Assumption of B.V.M., Michael, Francis, All Saints. A leaf missing after f. 200 which ends in Plaude turba for Francis. (*f*). *RH*, no. 4307. Stanzas 1, 2 of the hymn printed in *AH* iv. 119 from a Prague manuscript.

ff. i+205+i. 142×105 mm. Written space 110×75 mm. 7 long lines and music and (art. 2) 17 long lines. Art. 1 ruled in red ink. Collation: 1⁶+1 leaf before 1 (f. 1) 2–25⁸ 26⁸ wants 1 before f. 200 and 8. Written in ugly textura. Red initials. Capital letters in the ink of the text stroked with red. Binding of boards covered with yellow pigskin, s. xvi, bearing a roll of musical instruments.

Written in Germany for Franciscan use. 'Iohan. C. Jackson. 1840 (the third figure doubtful)', f. 1: the owner is presumably the Revd. John C. Jackson from whom the Bodleian bought some manuscripts in the years from 1864 to 1877 (*Sum. Cat.*, Index of Owners). Part of the Music Collection bequeathed by William Euing (for whom cf. MS. Euing 1) to Anderson's College, Glasgow, and transferred thence in 1936.

Euing Music Collection, R. d. 57. *Hymnale, etc.* s. xv/xvi

1. ff. 2–113ᵛ Eterne rerum conditor . . .

Hymns: (*a*) at the hours (9); (*b*) f. 13, Quem terra pontus, for feasts of B.V.M.; (*c*) f. 14, of the temporale, Advent to Pentecost (21), followed by Criste cunctorum for the dedication of a church and three hymns for Corpus Christi; (*d*) f. 55ᵛ, of the sanctorale (22); (*e*) f. 95, of the common of saints; (*f*) f. 101ᵛ, a supplement (6).

(*c*). The Corpus Christi hymns are Pange lingua, Verbum supernum, and Magister cum discipulis (*RH*, no. 10918; *AH* iv. 31). (*d*). For fifteen feasts, Stephen–Andrew, including Anne (A solis ortus cardine, Salue sancta parens, Clara diei gaudia moduliset: *RH*, nos. 24, 18201, 3305) and Bernard (Bernardus doctor).(*f*). Parts of two hymns were copied twice, first on f. 103 and then again on f. 104. The first copy ends a few words earlier than the second and has no glosses. The last hymn is Iam regina discubuit for Bernard (*RH*, no. 9365). ff. 1ʳᵛ, 114ʳᵛ blank.

Widely spaced, as for music, but the interlinear space contains only glosses in a neat small hand, probably that of the scribe of the text, except on eight occasions when music was entered later on top of the glosses. On ff. 2, 3, 68ᵛ–69 a later hand added letters, a, b, c, etc., above words to show the order in which they should be taken.

2. ff. 115–24 Populus qui ambulabat . . .

Twenty-one monastic canticles for Christmas, Easter, Sundays, the common of apostles, martyrs, and virgins, and Corona spinea.

The same seven Cistercian sets as in Mearns' E. 1 and I. 3 (Mearns, *Canticles*, pp. 87–92) and in St. Paul's Cathedral 15 (*MMBL* i. 257). f. 124ᵛ blank.

ff. i+124+xvi. 130×95 mm. Written space 85×65 mm. Six long lines. Collation: 1–3¹² 4–7¹⁰ 8¹² 9⁸ 10 ten (ff. 97–106) 11⁸ 12¹⁰. Written in two sizes of hybrida, the smaller (for the glosses) current. The flex is used in art. 2, if more than one mark of punctuation was needed in a sentence. The 'punctus elevatus' is made like a semi-colon, but with the comma above the point. 2-line and 1-line red initials. Contemporary (?) Germanic binding of dark-brown leather, rebacked: a heads-in-medallions roll as border and within it horizontal and vertical fillets enclosing a space of *c*. 67 × 30 mm. in which a panel stamp is inserted: on the front the Annunciation and below it 'ECCE VERGO CO[NC]IPIET LVCE I'; on the back the baptism of Christ and below it '[HIC] EST FILIV[S M]EVS DILE[CT]'.

Written for Cistercian use, probably in north-west Germany or the Netherlands. 'Iste liber pertinet Sorori dederadis De (*erased*) borken', f. 1, s. xv/xvi. '8.11.56' and 'E. K.', f. 1, give the date of acquisition by Euing and perhaps the initials of a bookseller: cf. above, Euing 3, 7, 9, 10. Bequeathed and transferred as R.d. 56.

Ferguson 13. *Ludovicus Rigius, Decem libri*   1492?

1. ff. iv^v–v^v Ludouicus Rigius Bene esse 'Francisco Bollano'. Patrię Venetoque generi dicit: . . . Si apud maiores nostros est conseruatum . . . quiefactę animę. Finis argumenti primi vniuersalis originis operę Ludouici Rigii [. . . . .]. Item argumentum secundum [. . . . .] commentorum quę sunt fundamenta operum naturę et artis.

An introduction, evidently copied last. It is mainly in praise of Lull and to show that Rigius attempts in art. 2 to condense the teaching of Lull's forty books into ten books of his own. What these ten books are is set out in art. 4. The words *Francisco Bollano* were added later in a space left blank. The text has been emended, especially near the end, mainly by erasing words like *tibi* and *tuas*, for example *que tibi traddo* becomes *que traddo*.

2. (*a*) ff. 1–27^v [U]trum difficilius sit facere quod poscis an negare: necdum statui . . . moritur nec extinguitur. Finis commenti Aphorismorum rote corruptionis.

(*b*) ff. 27^v–62 Incipit commentum Aphorismorum rote generationis. [T]edium opus in operando . . . Itaque iis breuibus uerbis perfecimus Comentum Anno gratie dei saluatoris nostri yhesu Chrysti Millesimo quadringentesimo octuagesimo. Cui honor et gloria. Finis.

(*c*) ff. 63–99 [C]omentum apertum lucidumque fecimus . . . Anno gratie Millesimo quadringentesimo octuagesimo primo: mense Martii: dieque primo. Finis Voythię.

(*d*) ff. 100–113^v Chaos uniuersale principiorum Voythię: et aliorum in theorica. [S]i fixellam iunco texerem: . . . rotę ignitę nostrę perfectionis. τελωσ.

(*e*) ff. 114–157^v Prologus primus in indiuiduis inueniendis et preparandis: et in fructu huius operis foculi. [L]ibellum yconomum Centum Aphorismorum . . . est potentia. inde actus. τελωσ. Inueni fontes regis simul arui coloni . . . (4 lines of verse). Laus deo.

(*f*) ff. 159–74 Trialogus: Interloqutores Ludouicus: Franciscus et Mapheus. Ludouicus. [E]n primus et secundus: utinam tertius adesset . . . preite filii achademie nostre.

(*g*) ff. 174^v–249^v 'Practica Quatripartita'. [S]epe et multum mecum consideraui . . . cui in perpetuum debemus. τελωσ.

(*h*) ff. 250–68 Principium libri secretorum. [N]umquid sit et qualiter et quomodo habeatur Ars et opus theoricale prathicaléque alchimicum . . . scrutante corda. cui honor et gloria. τελωσ.

(*i*) ff. 269–272ᵛ Gubernaculum currus. [E]x hortatu et precibus tuis reiteratis . . . recte intelligis. τελωσ.

(*j*) ff. 272ᵛ–282ᵛ Hysterologia. [O]pus in sex libellis diuisum. uel currum ignitum sex rotarum . . . Finis Gubernaculi.

(*a*, *b*) are two sets of fifty aphorisms each. f. 62ᵛ blank. (*c*). Seventy chapters and many diagrams. f. 99ᵛ blank. (*d*). Two parts of nine and eight chapters. (*e*). Four parts of eleven, twenty-eight, twenty-six, and fifty-three chapters. f. 158ʳᵛ blank. (*f*). Seventeen chapters. (*g*). Four parts of eighty-eight, fifty-three, twenty-two, and thirty chapters. (*h*). Seven short parts of eighteen, eight, eighteen, nine, two, six, and eleven chapters. In chapter 1 of part 1 the author says he has written six books and this is 'librum finalem'. f. 268ᵛ blank. (*i*) consists of a preface, index under the letters B to R, referring to Lull's works, and a final note 'Terminata sunt elementa posita sub forma alphabeti . . .'. (*j*) consists of a preface and table of chapters of (*a–i*).

3. Short pieces: (*a*) f. 283 Interrogationes; (*b*) ff. 283ᵛ–284ᵛ De magisterio terrarum nigrarum. Corpora defuncta mortuorum . . . in corpore viuo; (*c*) ff. 284ᵛ–285 De magisterio auri potabilis. Restaureatur humanum genus . . . hoc lumine aperto. (*d*) ff. 285ᵛ–286 Aperitio trianguli voythię. Litterę primę quadrangulorum . . . decem et octo enumerauimus.

(*a*). Twenty heads.

4. f. 286ʳᵛ Ludouicus Rigius Francisco Bollano (*these two words erased*) salutem dicit. Opus dedicatum nomini tuo in conspectu habes fili mi diuisum in decem codiculos . . . Porrho libri terminati in numero decem sunt: fundamentum primum yconomus est Centum Aphorismorum: Secundum Comenta: Tertium voythia: Quartum cahos: Quintum foculus: Sextum trialogus: Septimum operatiua prathica: Octauum secretorum liber: nonum gubernaculum currus: Decimum nouissimúmue histerologia . . . Mons uero deus est cui honor et gloria. Anno gratię quadringentesimo octuagesimo quinto et anno primo motus ecclesię. Finis.

5. ff. 287–99 Proprietarium sulphureorum Trianguli magni Voythię. Ludouic [. . . . .]. [S]uprema fermenta seu librum fermentorum . . . et maxime harum. τελωσ.

Three parts.

6. ff. 299ᵛ–305ᵛ Hermofroditus collericorum et collericarum. Me ad scribendum fili dietim impellis . . . vincente omnia secreta. Die x oct'. Anno gratie Mcccc° lxxxv. hora xᵃ noctis: gratia eius qui omnia concedit. τελωσ.

Two parts, a general introduction and an introduction to six tables for which the space remains blank on ff. 300–302ᵛ.

7. ff. 305ᵛ–306ᵛ De optasis optatesis et dulphuc igne lapillorum. Ne decipiaris petitione tua fili mi . . . absque vigilantia in rebus externis. τελωσ. `die 6 octobris 1492: opus per me subscriptum ex ordine auctoris quintionum 31'.

The added words are in another hand.

ff. iii+308+iii, foliated i–v, 1–306 (307–9). The foliation from 1 to 286 may be contemporary. 235 × 148 mm. Written space 143 × 80 mm. 35 long lines. Collation of ff. iv, v, 1–306: 1² (ff. iv, v), 2–6¹⁰ 7⁸ (ff. 51–8) 8–29¹⁰ 30⁸ (ff. 279–86) 31–32¹⁰. Written in good current humanistica. Spaces for 4-line (f. 1), 3-line (ff. iv^v, 1), and 2-line initials not filled. Binding of diced russia gilt, s. xviii, with repeated gilt elephants on the spine, as on MS. 14 which was N° 60 in the same collection.

Written in Italy. 'N°. 62', f. iii^v, s. xviii. 'N°. 29', f. iv. Belonged to John Ferguson, Professor of Chemistry in the University of Glasgow, †1916. The chemistry and alchemy section of his library was bought by the University for £7,000 in 1921.

Ferguson 32. *Macer, etc.* s. xv med.

1. ff. 2–76^v Las (*for* Sal) commune est clauiger huius artis et claudit et aperit omnia . . . quia talis fistula est incurabilis.

Only the first page agrees with Albertus Magnus, *De alchemia*, beginning 'Sal commune est clauiger' (ed. Zetzner, 1659, ii. 433). The text is followed on ff. 76^v–79^v by a table of the 120 chapters, the first 'De sale communi' and the last 'Aqua mercurii'. ff. 80–1 contain three paragraphs, the first beginning 'Tellus namque cum aqua'. ff. 1^rv, 81^v were left blank.

2. ff. 83–172 Herbarum quasdam dicturus carmine uires . . . sic apta solucio fiet.

Macer, De viribus herbarum, often printed. Walther, no. 7711.

3. ff. 172–9 Alleluya est herb(a hab)ens folia tria uel duo rotunda . . . Cristiana folia habet rotunda aliquantulum ut pisa Et vnum habet stipitem et paruulos stipites exeuntes.

A list of herbs, A–X, with brief descriptions and, often, English names.

4. f. 179^v Medicina pro gutta. Anser sumatur veteranus qui videatur . . .

Fifteen lines. Walther, no. 1278.

ff. iv+81+i+97. 95 × 60 mm. Written space 60 × 33 mm. Mainly in 18 or 19 long lines. Collation: 1–2¹⁰ 3¹² 4–7¹⁰ 8¹⁰ wants 10, blank, after f. 81: f. 82 is a blank inserted in 1968 9–17¹⁰ 18 seven (ff. 173–9). Written in a secretary-influenced textura, occasionally current and with a long-tailed r now and then. 2-line red initials. Capital letters in the ink of the text sometimes touched with red. '. . . paper-thin tawed skin over oak boards . . . dilapidated beyond repair' replaced by goat-skin over oak boards by Anthony Gardner in 1968. Secundo folio *tam uel plus*.

Written in England. 'Cuthbart Younger', f. 81^v, s. xvi. 'A treatise of chemistry and medicine [. . . .] Cambridge' inside the cover, s. xvii.

Ferguson 39. *Geber, etc.* s. XIII/XIV

1. ff. 1–30 Liber primus de lxx de alchimia. liber diuinitatis. Laudes sint deo habenti graciam . . . in quocumque uolueris.

Geber, Liber divinitatis. The chapters are not numbered consecutively and are not in the same order as Singer and Anderson, nos. 74–8, 80–3, 85–102. The following table shows the order here (on the left) and in Singer and Anderson (on the right).

1	74, 75	63	101
2	76	28	90
23–7[1]	85–9	30	92
31–8	93–100	29	91
no number	100B	64–70	101A–F, 102
40	100A	12	82
13	83	5	77
41	78	9, 10	80, 81

2. ff. 30–32ᵛ Prologus in libro administrationum. Inter omnia negociorum genera nullum post alkimie disciplinam . . . (f. 31) suscepti operis debitum absoluam. Aurum itaque aureum generat colorem . . . quoniam faciem reddit quasi defuncti. Explicit liber iste deo gracias.

As far as 'abluendum erit' (f. 32ᵛᵃ/10) this is sections 108, 77–81, 32–8, 54–76, 84 of the *Liber sacerdotum* printed by P. E. M. Berthelot, *La Chimie au moyen âge*, 1893, i. 187–228: cf. Singer and Anderson, no. 499, sect. 1–10 and beginning of sect. 11. Four sections follow here: 'Item de eodem Coques lardum . . .'; 'De generibus almisadir . . .'; 'Sandaraca in insula rubri maris . . .'; 'Genera sulphuris 4 sunt . . .'.

3. ff. 32ᵛ–33ᵛ De basilisco. Incipit experimentum probatum et uerissimum ac memorie dignum de faciendo puluere manerei basilisci. ad conficiendum crisim . . . et preciosissimum efficitur. deo gracias.

Derived, it is said, from 'Mulena babylonicus' and his eunuchs.

4. ff. 33ᵛ–34 Expositio secunda. Incipit expositio secunda ex uerbis Morieni quam h' ait cum k. rege f. zezib. f. maccia. dixit enim sume fumum album . . . attribuit.

Singer and Anderson, no. 66 IV. Ed. Manget, *Bibliotheca chemica curiosa*, 1702, i. 518.

5. (a) f. 34 Incipit expositio specierum. Dixit morienus quod corpus inmundum secundum philosophos quod interpretatur asrob . . . nisi dei altissimi uoluntate. (b) ff. 34–9 Aurum sic fit. set non accedas ad experimentum. donec discas parum. Accipe cipri eris posios . . . de grano masticis. Liquefit (*sic*) tardius. (c) ff. 39–40ᵛ Argenti confectio. Sume alumen nigrum. semen bombacis . . . et ad ignem coquitur. facit rubicundum.

(a–c) are written as though one piece. (a). Cf. Singer and Anderson, no. 66 V, and Manget, op. cit., pp. 518–19. (b). As sections 3–79, 82–98 of Mappae Clavicula, as printed in *Archaeologia*, xxxii (1847), 193–209: for manuscripts, but not this one, see *Speculum*, x. 70–81. (c). Recipes for silver and gold, a piece on the origin of metals (f. 40ʳᵛ), and a piece beginning 'Capsores salerni' (f. 40ᵛ).

6. ff. 40ᵛ–41 Alkereisan id est bruscus . . . Duenec.

Interpretation of names. Recipes were added in s. xiv in the space remaining blank on f. 41 and f. 41ᵛ, left blank, has a piece beginning 'In rosario in capitulo auicenne quod incipit soluimus sane aurum dicitur'.

7. ff. 42–56ᵛ Recipes beginning imperfectly 'Lincar sic fit accipe sal alkali'.

8. ff. 57–58ᵛ (*begins imperfectly*) ideo expedit nos cum medicina fundente illum dealbare . . . verissimam tamen et omnino certam.

---

[1] Chapters 25 and 27 are misnumbered XXX and XXXVIII.

Geber, Summa perfecti magisterii. Leaves are missing between f. 57ᵛ which ends 'aut palliando decoret' and f. 58 which begins 'medicine multiplicatur'. The remains corres-pond, with considerable differences, to Manget, op. cit. i. 550–1 (from near the beginning of ch. 5 to the middle of ch. 7) and 557 (Recapitulatio, except the last lines). f. 58/1–21 are not in the edition.

9. f. i has diagrams, s. xv, one on the recto headed 'De peregrinantibus' and the other on the verso headed 'De matrimonio contracto'.

ff. i+58. 197×150 mm. Written space 145×92 mm on ff. 1–41 and *c.* 152×105 mm thereafter. 2 cols. 40 lines on ff. 1–41 and *c.* 40 lines thereafter. Pricks in both margins to guide ruling of arts. 1–6. Collation: 1–3¹⁰ 4¹⁰+1 leaf after 10 (f. 41) 5⁶ 6⁶+1 leaf after 6 (f. 54) 7² 8 two (ff. 57–8, a bifolium). Arts. 1–6 in textura, the rest in textura changing in places to cursiva. Initials in arts. 1–4, in the margins or between the columns, red with violet ornament: 2-line spaces remain blank in art. 8. Binding of thick wooden boards, one-third covered with dirty white leather. A heavy chainmark at the head of the back cover. Secundo folio *inhumetur.*

Written in France (?). Formerly Bi. 16. e. 26.

Ferguson 63.   *Turba philosophorum, etc.*   1470, 1495, s. xv²

One of four uniform notebook-like volumes of alchemy in the Ferguson collec-tion written by a north Italian scribe who names himself in MS. 76 as John Visto 'lo paringone'. The other two volumes are MSS. 135 and 192. MSS. 63 and 76 were once bound together—cf. MS. 76 art. 5*a*—and probably all four were one volume until the early nineteenth century. Ferguson obtained them at various dates between the 1880s and 1908.

1 (quires 1–3). ff. 1–50 Incipit liber Turbe philosophorum. Arisleus philoso-phus. Inicium libri Turbe philosophorum. Qui dicitur Codex veritatis . . . Huius autem codicis principium est. Arisleus gręcus genitus pitagore . . . in nummis imponatur. Explicit liber turbe philosophorum.

Singer and Anderson, no. 1. Seventy-three chapters. f. 50ᵛ blank.

2 (quire 4). (*a*) ff. 51–62 De quibusdam vegetabilibus gelatiuis et induratiuis. Quedam vegetabilia preterea saturnum et iouem indurant . . . (*b*) ff. 64ᵛ–65 Infrascripta (?) recepta data fuit michi per magistrum Iohannem teutonicum compatrem meum et experta per ipsum quam verissimum rem dixit . . .

(*a*). Mainly on hardening of metals. ff. 62ᵛ–66ᵛ were left blank. (*b*) is an addition in the main hand. An addition of s. xvi on f. 66ᵛ refers to art. 4 which began originally on the facing page: see below.

3 (quire 5). (*a*) ff. 67–71ᵛ Subscripta extracta a pratica Magistri Iohannis de nanis de viterbo fratrum predicatorum 1470. Solis calcinacio sic fit . . . (*b*) ff. 72–82ᵛ Liber secretissimus secretorum Geberis de ordine in proiectione agregationis omnium corporum liquabilium purgatorum seu preparatorum in primo ordine sine medicina solum fermentat' prout supra continetur in libro suo paruo de inuestigacione perfecti magisterii Et in libro testamenti sui. Iste sunt operationes et actiones que occultate fuerunt a philosophis . . .

4 (quire 6). ff. 83–9 Rosa nouella Magistri Arnoldi de Villa noua. Diuina

potentia composuit mundum . . . posse creari preciosissimum ex re vilissima. Deo gratias amen. Explicit Rosa Nouella Magistri Arnoldi de Villa nouella. 1495.

Thorndike and Kibre. Preface addressed to 'Nobili Marcho petro et comes (*sic*) flandrensis' and four chapters. ff. 89ᵛ–90ᵛ blank.

5 (quire 7). ff. 91–98ᵛ Incipiunt questiones Arnoldi de villa noua super opus maius. Ad questiones quas michi fecistis vobis respondebo per ordinem. Primo queritur quot furnelli sunt necessarii . . . et perfectius operatur. Finis.

A preface and thirty-six paragraphs, all but the last two beginning with the words 'Item queritur'. The text seems to differ much from that printed by Zetzner, iv. 544–53 (Singer and Anderson, no. 235). ff. 99–100ᵛ are blank.

ff. iii+100+iii. Art. 1 has an old foliation 1–50. The same hand numbered ff. 51–8 '17–24', ff. 67–74 '1–8' and ff. 91–5 '1–5'. Paper. 167 × 80 mm. Written space *c*. 130 × 60 mm. *c*. 30 long lines. Collation: 1–2¹⁶ 3¹⁸ 4–5¹⁶ 6⁸ 7¹⁰. Quire 5 once followed quire 3, no doubt: cf. the old foliation and the note on f. 66ᵛ. Written in good sloping current humanistica. Red initials, 7-line (f. 1) and 2-line or 3-line. Binding of s. xix.

Written probably in the Veneto: cf. MS. Ferguson 76, art. 5. Art. 3*a* is dated in 1470 and art. 4 in 1495. Belonged to Paul Barrois, whose number '635' is on a round green label at the foot of the spine and on f. iᵛ. (Barrois-)Ashburnham sale, 10 June 1901, lot 480, to Ellis for 16*s*. Bought by Ferguson, 29 Mar. 1902. Formerly Bi. 16. e. 20.

Ferguson 76. *R. Bacon, etc.* s. xv², 1492

A notebook by the same hand as MS. Ferguson 63 and formerly part of it.

1 (quires 1, 2). (*a*) ff. 1–4ᵛ, 6–26 Incipit Tractatus Rug'i'erii baconis medici. et fundamentum suum summarium est perfecta putrifactio rei sine qua nichil generatur nec augmentatur. Cum enim prima corpora metalorum post preparationem ipsorum . . . et studiis liberalibus eruditi. Finis. Explicit liber fratris R. de bachonis gallici ordinis minorum liber 2ᵘˢ in pratica. (*b*) ff. 4ᵛ–6 Set hic prius interpono tractatulum breuem discipuli hermetis necessarium multum 2° libro Rugierii sequenti Et animaduerte. Distinctiones secretorum sapientum in quibus . . . Aqua permanens . . . a corruptione. Et hanc viam sequitur Rugerius. (*c*) ff. 26ᵛ–28ᵛ Tractatus Marie prophetisse. Conuenit Aron cum Maria prophetissa . . . ignoranciam vasis. Explicit tractatus Marie prophetisse. Maria mira sonat . . . (6 lines).

(*a*). Theorica on ff. 1–4ᵛ and Practica on ff. 6–26. (*b*). Thorndike and Kibre, s.v. Distinctio (Morienus). Singer and Anderson, no. 69. (*c*). Thorndike and Kibre. Singer and Anderson, no. 9. Zetzner, v. 83–86, where the verses (Walther, no. 10687) are printed.

2 (quire 3). ff. 29–33 Opus lunare prima sublima mercurium . . . in oleum capitulo 34. Finis.

Recipes. ff. 33ᵛ–40 blank.

3 (quire 4). (*a*) ff. 41–49ᵛ Aqua nostra philosophica siue acetum acerimum ac fortius naribus. cui nulla res nigrior. nulla res fetidior . . . solutionis et soluti. (*b*) ff. 50ᵛ–51ᵛ Per Magistrum Iohannem lust compatrem meum expertum.

Fixacio salis uitrioli . . . Et hec a Iohanne lust compatre meo per litteras michi traditas uel missas. die 23 madii 1491. (*c*) ff. 51ᵛ–52 Si autem decoquitur arseni-cum . . . (*d*) f. 52ᵛ A recipe for salt meat in Italian.

(*a*). Not as Singer and Anderson, no. 259. (*b*). Lust occurs also in MS. Ferguson 192, art. 5: cf. also MS. 63, art. 2*b*. f. 50ʳ blank.

4 (quire 5). (*a*) ff. 53–6 Et primo in Diccione 37 ubi loquitur Cinon super verbo quod incipit quousque puluis fiat. glosa ibi dicit quod rosarius ait . . . (*b*) ff. 57ᵛ–64ᵛ Pratica concordans Gebro in M'. solo. . . .

(*a*). The reference in a hand of s. xvii (?) at the head of f. 53, 'vide ante p. 27 ubi Cinon ait' is to the copy of Turba philosophorum in MS. Ferguson 63, art. 1, and the section there on ff. 26ᵛ–27, beginning 'Cinon ait'. (*b*). Miscellaneous alchemical recipes, including (f. 58ᵛ) a 'Sermo philosophicus' in Italian verse, 'Prediti corpi. disoluiti in aqua . . .' (12 lines), and a piece beginning (f. 64ᵛ) 'Claudus de francia ad faciendum argentum bonum', above which is 'Hec recepta posita est iustior in alio libello'. ff. 56ᵛ–57 blank.

5 (quires 6, 7). ff. 65–77 Recipes, partly in Italian, including several derived from mag. Johannes Petrus of Feltre (near Venice), 'physicus' (ff. 70ᵛ, 73, 75ᵛ, 76), one of which, in Italian, ends with the words 'et per mi zohannem visto lo paringone (*or* -goue) in vno sigillo del dicto mʳᵒ zohan piero. bello et (?) belis-simo'. The next heading is 'Recepte parati per mi Mᵒ zohani*tio* . . .'. ff. 77–80ᵛ blank.

The script resembles the last part of MS. Ferguson 135.

ff. i+80. ff. 41–55 have an old foliation '1–15'. Paper. 172×80 mm. Written space *c*. 130×60 mm. *c*. 30 long lines. Collation: 1–2¹⁴ 3–5¹² 6–7⁸. 2-line red initials in art. 1. Carton binding, s. xix in. (?), uniform with that of MS. Ferguson 135.

Formerly part of MS. Ferguson 63, q.v. A strip from a catalogue of s. xix¹, 'Tractatus Rogerii Baconis, cod. chart. in 8ᵛᵒ. Saec. xv', is pasted inside the cover. '6335 Ph.' from the collection of Lord Guilford: Phillipps sale, 19 June 1893, lot 24. Bought by John Ferguson on 3 Sept. 1893. Formerly Bi. 16. e. 30.

Ferguson 80. *Geber, Summa perfecti magisterii*   s. xv²

(*begins imperfectly*) modum permiscendi . . . perquisicionem hec dicta sufficiant. Explicit liber geber regis persarum.

Geber, Summa perfecti magisterii, beginning near the end of the preface of bk. 1. Cf. MS. Ferguson 135, art. 1. f. 66ᵛ, left blank, contains an alchemical fragment in Italian, s. xv/xvi, which probably continued on the now missing last leaf of quire 7.

ff. ii+66+ii. Paper. A foliation beginning at 5 on f. 4 takes account of the three now missing leaves. 180×108 mm. Written space 138×70 mm. 29 long lines. No ruling. Collation: 1¹⁰ wants 1 and 10 2–6¹⁰ 7¹⁰ wants 1 and 10. Current humanistic writing. Initials and headings not filled in. Binding of s. xix¹ by the same English binder as MS. Ferguson 192.

Written in Italy. 'Phillipps 1336', f. i. Phillipps sale 17 May 1897, lot 333, to Quaritch for £1. 2*s*. Ferguson notes inside the cover that he bought this manuscript from Quaritch on 22 June 1897.

Ferguson 83. *R. Lullius*   1469

1. ff. 1–148 In christi nomine. Incipit theorica Raimundi lulii. In arte maiori. quę est prima pars testamenti. Deus qui gloriose (*altered to* gloriosus) . . . (f. 4ᵛ) per capitulum succedens. (f. 6) Incipit secunda pars theoricę testamenti. in alkimia quę dicitur forma minor. Cum determinatum sit de forma maiori . . . (f. 90ᵛ) post considerationem capituli nostrę Alkimie Amen. Explicit primus liber testamenti domini Raymundi lulii in arte Alkimię Deo gratias. (f. 91) Incipit secundus liber siue secunda pars testamenti magistri remundi lulii qui dicitur practica alkimię. et primo de diffinitione. quid sit alkimia. Alchimia est vna pars celata . . . (f. 148) cum cantilena quę sequitur presentialiter. Explicit practica quę dicitur secunda pars testamenti magistri remundi. Sit laus iesu christo et marię.

Singer and Anderson, no. 244: cf. iii. 1148. The text in Zetzner, iv. 156/8–158/20 was not copied, but space was left for it on ff. 102–103ᵛ. The Practica is in eighty-one chapters numbered in the main hand. In the colophon on f. 148 'endoardo de ulzidescoth' represents Edward of Woodstock. The scribe wrote 'Iesus. Marię filius' at the head of f. 1. ff. 5ᵛ, 148ᵛ blank.

2 (quire 16). ff. 149–61 Diagrams with accompanying texts in illustration of art. 1. ff. 161–161*ᵛ blank.

3. ff. 162–212 Thesaurus infinitus raimondi vel codicillum vel uade mecum de numero philosophorum. Deus in virtute trinitatis . . . dum tamen intelligas magisterium. Explicit thesaurus infinitus. deo gratias. 1468 mense februarii die nona omnibus incompletis hora 21ª. Amen.

Singer and Anderson, no. 252. Many side notes.

4 (in the space remaining in quire 21). (*a*) ff. 212ᵛ–214 Incipiunt afforismi. Aurum philosophorum lapis est . . . Amita est turpitudini omnis pars quę non conuenit suo toto. Gloria sit christo qui laudetur ab omnibus. Amen. Explicit pratica raimundi lullii in arte alchimię. Hii afforismi erant post praticam testamenti in exemplari. (*b*) f. 214ᵛ An alphabet with reference back to art. 3, ch. 10 (f. 167). (*c*) f. 215 A diagram labelled 'Tabula ista est codicilli'. f. 215ᵛ blank.

(*a*). Divided into three 'regimina' of 13, 19, and 4 heads.

5. ff. 216–31 Pratica magistri raimundi de compositione lapidis philosophorum nec non lapidum preciosorum per principia lapidis vegetabilis. In nomine sanctę trinitatis . . . Iam sæpe et sæpius . . . et unus essentialiter. R. per o.s.s.A. Explicit liber siue compendium excellentissimi uiri raimundi lulii. de composicione lapidum preciosorum per lapidis principia numeralis.

Singer and Anderson, no. 253 (Anima artis transmutacionis). f. 231ᵛ contains a table of the significance of the letters used in the text on f. '219 a tergo'. ff. 232–233ᵛ blank.

6 (added in s. xv ex. in part of the space remaining in quire 22). (*a*) ff. 234–5 Rainaldus de uilla noua in speculo medicine Capitulo de medicina subtiliatiua quod incipit Incohantes igitur . . . (*b*) Extracts from 'Rainaldus de spermate et lacte'. f. 235ᵛ blank.

7. ff. 236–240ᵛ Incipit epistula magistri raimundi in uirtute sanctę trinitatis

ipsiusque infinitę bonitatis. Cum ego raimundus de insula maioricarum ... ex ea intentum. Laudemus deum semper. Explicit. Factum est quod iussisti. Laus deo. An 'Alphabetum testamenti' follows: 'A significat deum ... R. Ignem'.

Singer and Anderson, no. 250. ff. 241–247ᵛ are blank, except for added recipes on ff. 244–6 beginning 'Tincar est quedam species boracis cuius uirtus est facere cito fundi omne metallum durum ...'.

ff. iii+247+i, foliated i–iii, 1–161, 161*, 162–99, 201–47 (248). A contemporary foliation on ff. 1–90. Paper. ff. ii, iii are contemporary flyleaves. 202 × 145 mm. Written space c. 135 × 85 mm. 28–9 long lines. Frame ruling. Collation: 1–10¹⁰ 11⁸ 12–15¹⁰ 16¹⁴ 17–19¹⁰ 20⁸ 21¹⁶ wants 1 before f. 201 22–23¹⁰ 24¹². Written mainly by one hand in current humanistica. Red initials, 4-line, 3-line, and 2-line. Capital letters in the ink of the text stroked with red. Binding of s. xix.

Written in Italy. Art. 3 was completed on 9 Feb. 1469. 'Old No. 1657 in a Sale' and 'Phillipps 2318' on f. iii. Phillipps had it from Thorpe in 1824: his sale, 6 June 1898, lot 964, to Quaritch for £3. 8s. 'John Ferguson June 14. 1898'. Formerly Bi. 16. e. 18.

Ferguson 104. *'Dicta bartholomei', etc.*   1364 or 1365

1. ff. 3–25ᵛ Dicta bartholomei. Necessarium vndequodque peruemiant. vnde omnes magistri antiquarum erudiciones scienciarum non de suis solis instituebant. sed veterorum imitebantur ... Et sic editor huius voluminis. magister scilicet bartholomeus facit qui volumen illud greco quod nomen fuit ydyomate transtulit in latinum ... nominatur. In primis notandum de iiiiᵒʳ Elementis ... Basilita pleuresi.

ff. 1–2ᵛ were left blank: see art. 10.

2. ff. 25ᵛ–32 Incipit liber de Coytu. Creator volens animalium genus firmiter ... aqua sit solutum apium. Explicit liber de coitu.

Thorndike and Kibre (Constantinus Affricanus). *Constantini opera*, Basel, 1539, pp. 299–307.

3. ff. 32–57 Hic incipit liber secretorum alchimie. In hoc libro veridico et autentico et ex pluribus experimentis experto a magistro constantino ... (f. 35) medicus sed non e contrario. Explicit prologus. Incipit tractatus alchimie et primo de operacionibus ... que notatur per istum versum. Calcino sublimo. texo. fingo. coagulo soluo.

Partly cosmographical, with diagrams. A leaf is missing after f. 51.

4. ff. 57–66 Hic incipit primum capitulum huius tincture. Acci. ergo in nomine domini unam partem aque uitrioli ... et habebis alexir album quod vsui reserua. Explicit primus liber. f. 66ᵛ blank.

5. ff. 67–82 Isti sunt tituli capitulorum cuiusdam tractatus. qui est de extractis. siue compilat' quibusdam magis necessariis. de libro Geber. et est diuisus in duas partes ... collocato ... (*table of tituli of the two parts*) ... Capitulum 1. Qui querit sulphur calcinare ... perquisicio. hec dicta sufficiant. Deo summo.

gracias summas reddamus. Amen. Explicit summa Geber perfeccionis magisterii. Amen.

An abbreviation of Geber, Summa perfecti magisterii, beginning in bk. 1, tit. 13.

6. ff. 82–4 Hec sunt extracta de libro geber. siue zeber. siue abutari. filii machumeti. Nota quod in decoctione . . .

7. ff. 84–91 De elixir albo. In nomine domini amen. Recipe sal alkali libram . . . Explicit iste liber in nomine domini nostri ihesu cristi et sanctissime virginis matris marie. amen. Iste liber completus est per manus nicolai altsmer sacerdotis. licet indigni. Anno domini m° ccc° lxiiii° sabbato proximo mane ante dominicam Letare etc.[1]

Recipes, including one headed 'Elixir comitis henrici de phauber (?)' (f. 88ᵛ).

8 (added in the main hand, but in darker ink). ff. 91–3 Oleum benedictum sic conficitur. Recipe Lateres rubeos. quos non tetigit aqua . . .

Cf. Thorndike and Kibre. Medical recipes. Nineteen lines on f. 92ʳᵛ are in German. f. 93ᵛ blank.

9 (added in s. xv). ff. 95–108ᵛ (begins imperfectly: two leaves missing) Vidi alios qui cum diligencia non faciebant quasdam sublimaciones et vlterius procedere . . . tantum apponas ad aquas puluerum. Sed nota aqua auri pertinet (ends abruptly).

Pseudo-Albertus Magnus, Semita recta, ed. Zetzner, ii. 424/19–452/5, with many differences. The scribe left f. 101ᵛ and part of f. 101ʳ blank, but nothing is missing. ff. 109–110ᵛ, left blank, contain recipes, s. xv/xvi.

10 (added in s. xiv). (a) f. 1 Faded text, evidently a table of numbers. (b) f. 1ᵛ [Est l]apis in mundo que non reperitur eundo . . . (17 lines). (c) f. 2ʳᵛ Charms 'Ad furem probandum', 'Ut aliquid cito discas et numquam obliuiscaris', etc.

(b). Cf. Singer and Anderson, no. 793 X, XVII. (c). Some directions in German have been crossed out.

11 (inside the cover, s. xv). (a) In front, recipes. (b) At the back, herb-names, some with German equivalents.

ff. 110. A medieval foliation of ff. 32–90, 'I–LX' is older than the loss of a leaf in quire 5. Greyish thick paper. 198 × 140 mm. Written space c. 170 × 110 mm. c. 30 long lines. Frame ruling. Collation: 1¹² 2¹⁰ 3¹² 4¹⁰ 5¹⁰ wants 8 after f. 51 6–9¹⁰ 10²⁰ wants 3, 4: 2, now mostly cut off, was blank. Quires 1–9 numbered at the end. Two pieces of parchment at each central opening strengthen the paper at the string-holes. Written in a modified textura. 3-line and 2-line initials in the ink of the text: they and capital letters are stroked with red. Contemporary limp parchment wrapper, the back strip covered by a piece of brass, 25 mm wide, in which are twenty-eight small round holes to carry the strings, set in four horizontal rows of seven, two rows above and two below a central raised brass button. The strings from the upper two rows, 47 mm apart, are plaited together, as are the strings from the lower two rows, 42 mm apart. A piece of string attached to the wrapper was probably meant to loop on to the central button, but it does not now reach so far.

Written in northern (?) Germany and finished, except for additions, in Mar. 1364 or 1365: cf. art. 7. Formerly Bi. 16. d. 26.

[1] The day before the fourth Sunday in Lent fell on 2 Mar. in 1364 and on 22 Mar. in 1365.

Ferguson 106. *J. de Rupescissa, etc.*   1469/70, s. XV ex.

1. ff. 1–60 Primus liber de consideratione quinte essentie omnium rerum transmutabilium. In nomine domini nostri yhesu cristi. Incipit liber de famulatu philoxophie . . . Dixit salomon . . . aqua ardens. Expletus fuit liber iste per me. Iohanem die decimooctauo mensis februarii. Millesimo quadrigentesimo sexagesimo nono laus deo.

J. de Rupescissa. Singer and Anderson, no. 292.

2. ff. 60–68ᵛ Cum ego Raymundus . . . aleuiat membra ʼhominis agrauata. Explicit ars operatiua magistri Raymundi. deo gratias Amen.

R. Lull. Singer and Anderson, no. 1004.

3. f. 69ʳᵛ Medical recipes.

4. ff. 69ᵛ–79ᵛ Humanum corpus cum sit compositum per ingressionem contrariorum . . . item aliquid in eo positum non putrefacit.

Arnoldus de Villanova, De aqua vitae. Singer and Anderson, no. 1003.

5. ff. 79ᵛ–81 [C]orpus namque humanum ex 4ᵒʳ humoribus . . . dolorem capitis. Et dicta de urinarum tractatu sufficiant.

6. ff. 81–2 Seven recipes, the first 'Aqua iuuentutis de libris secretis secretorum. [R]ecipe lignum aloes . . .' and the last 'Ad timorem et terrorem', ending 'principes deberent in bello istam aquam pugillibus suis ministrare'.

7. ff. 82–4 Questo sie lo secreto dela incognita herba Celidonia. La quale lo omnipotente idio. . . . f. 84ᵛ blank.

ff. i+84+i. Paper. 220×165 mm. Written space 145×95 mm. 26 long lines. Collation: 1–7⁸ 8⁶ 9–10¹⁰ 11 two (ff. 83, 84). Written in round fere-humanistica and (arts. 2–7) a good sloping humanistica. Initials: (i) f. 1, 6-line, blue with red ornament; (ii) 3-line, blue with red ornament or red with violet ornament. Binding of s. xix¹. Secundo folio *inferunt*.

Written in Italy. Formerly Bi. 16. d. 28.

Ferguson 116. *J. Platearius*   s. XIII¹

1. ff. 1–47 Amicum induit qui iustis amicorum . . . in ultimo die iouis lune decrescentis.

Johannes Platearius, Practica. f. 1 is rubbed from exposure. An 'Elect*uarium* de succo rosarum . . .' added on f. 47, with side note, 'Istud elect' est in Antidotario'. f. 47ᵛ blank.

An English hand, s. xiii/xiv, noted in the margin of f. 21ᵛ, 'Contra tussim secundum Magistrum Symonem de Witeby Recipe . . .'.

ff. 47+ii. ff. 48, 49 are medieval end-leaves: 49ᵛ was pasted down. 205×128 mm. Written space 150×87 mm. 2 cols. 36 lines. The first line of writing above the top ruled line. Collation: 1–4⁸ 5⁶+1 leaf after 2 (f. 35) 6⁸. The spaces for 3-line (f. 1) and 2-line initials not filled. Binding of s. xix for Sir Thomas Phillipps: the marks of the four bands of the former binding show on f. 49ᵛ. Secundo folio *hec balneo*.

In England in s. xiii and probably written there. 'Incipit liber de medicinis 'fratris georgii fraunceys", f. 1, s. xv. Numbers 5 (?) and 54 on f. 1, the former on a paper label. Tenison sale at Sotheby's, 1 July 1861, lot 59, to Boone for 19s. Phillipps MS. 15748: his sale, 10 June 1896, lot 561. 'J. Ferguson Oct. 1896' inside the cover.

Ferguson 135. *Geber*   s. xv²

Uniform with MS. 63, q.v., and in the same hand.

1 (quires 1–5). (*a*) ff. 1–75 Incipit feliciter Summa alkimie perfectionis Geberis regis Arabum. peritissimi philosophorum. Totam nostram scienciam . . . perquisicionem hec dicta sufficiunt. et sic est finis Deo gracias amen. Explicit summa alchimie (*as above*). (*b*) ff. 75–77ᵛ Hic inferius annotantur quedam glose super Geberem ut magis elucescat ignorantibus . . .

(*a*). Singer and Anderson, no. 105. Manget, *Bibliotheca chemica curiosa*, i. 519–57. (*b*). Leaf references in the margins refer to the leaves of (*a*).

2 (quires 6, 7). (*a*) ff. 78–87ᵛ Inicium 2ⁱ libri Geberis videlicet comentum suum super sumam suam de inuestigatione perfectionis magisterii. Inuestigatione huius nobilis sciencie Ex continuo . . . Quam ex libris antiquorum Abreuiauimus. Deo gracias. Explicit secundus liber Geberis Comentum suum de investigacione perfecti veritatis. super sumam suam. (*b*) f. 87ᵛ Ars Rotacionis elementorum. Lapis . . . in lapidem. (*c*) ff. 88–92ᵛ Liber fornacuum Geberis. Sublimatur autem ipse mercurius . . . uel roborauit et confortauit. Deo gracias amen. Explicit 3ᵘˢ liber furnacuum Geberis. (*d*) f. 93ʳᵛ In proporcione requiritur . . . per nouem aquilas hermetis et nouem stellas. (*e*) ff. 94–100ᵛ 4ᵘˢ liber Testamenti Geberis. Ex omnibus rebus vegetabilium . . . apposito arsenico. Deo gracias amen. Explicit liber Testamenti Geberis 4ᵘˢ. (*f*) ff. 101–2 Dissolucio ferri. Sume limaturam . . . in opere veritatis.

(*a*). Cf. Singer and Anderson, no. 73 iii, iv. The text in Manget, op. cit., i. 558–62 differs much. (*b*). The conversion of stone to stone in eight operations. (*c*). Singer and Anderson, no. 72. Twenty-one chapters. (*e*). Thorndike and Kibre. Ed. Manget, op. cit., i. 562–4. ff. 102ᵛ–103ᵛ blank.

3 (quire 8). (*a*) ff. 104–119ᵛ Iesus. Maria. Liber quintus Geberis compendiosum de inuestigatione perfectionis magisterii pratice . . . Considerauimus in nostris voluminibus . . . alibi est narratum. Explicit quinta pars siue quintus liber compendii Geberis super sumam suam vbi theorice . . . ut supra explicit. (*b*) f. 119ᵛ A recipe for 'Oleum album'.

(*a*). The introduction, ff. 104–6, is that of Singer and Anderson, no. 73. After this point the text is in four particulae, the first of them beginning 'Amplius considerauimus'.

4 (quire 9). ff. 120–121ᵛ Recipes. ff. 122–123ᵛ blank.

ff. i+123. Paper. 172 × 80 mm. Written space *c.* 130 × 60 mm. *c.* 30 long lines. Collation: 1–3¹⁶ 4¹² 5¹⁶+1 leaf after 16 (f. 77) 6¹² 7¹⁰+two bifolia, 95–6, 97–8, bound in after 5 as independent sheets, each with its own string, 8¹⁶ 9⁴. Red initials: (i) 3–6 line; (ii) 2-line.

Written in Italy: cf. MS. Ferguson 63. A strip inside the cover is from the same sale catalogue as the strip in MS. Ferguson 76: it reads 'Summa Alkimiæ profectionis Geberis Regis Arabum. cod. chart. in 8ᵛᵒ. Sæc. xv'. '1025' in red on the spine. Ferguson got this manuscript in about 1880, according to his note in MS. Ferguson 76, f. i. Formerly B1. 17. a. 26.

Ferguson 147. *Antidotarium Nicholai, etc. (in English)* s. xv in.

1. ff. 1–55ᵛ I Nichollas ypᵣeiede of summe men yn practisye of medycyne studye to hem þᵗ woleþ . . . (f. 2) dispensacyon. Aurea alexandria . . . of coldnesse.

A translation of the alphabetically arranged Antidotary of Nicholas, Aurea alexandrina–Zinzeber. ff. 52ʳ, 56ʳᵛ, left blank, contain recipes in English and Latin, s. xvi.

2. ff. 57–62ᵛ Sarum calendar in Latin, in red and black.

'Sancti fretamundi', May 11. No erasures. Notes on fast days added in s. xvi; also some recipes in Latin and English, one ending 'quoth Mʳⁱˢ Walker' (f. 57ᵛ).

3. ff. 63–91 Medicyn for scabbis oþer for peyne. Take þe rote of horsehese . . .

Medical recipes. A charm 'to make a man slepe' is crossed out on f. 81. f. 91ʳᵛ has added recipes, s. xvi.

4. ff. 92–158 Here a man may se the vᵢrtuys of the erbis wyche be the hote . . . take yt ouȝt and drye it.

Medical recipes. A leaf missing after f. 121. Additions of s. xvi are a charm on f. 158ᵛ and recipes for conserves and a charm on the flyleaf, f. 159ʳᵛ: of the latter 'the vowels must be scrapt out and chewed and swallowed'.

ff. i+158+iii. f. 159 is a medieval paper flyleaf. Paper and parchment, the latter for the outside and middle sheets of each quire. 165 × 113 mm. Written space 122 × 80 mm. 27 long lines. Collation: 1¹⁰ wants 1 2–5¹⁰ 6¹⁰ wants 8–10, probably blank, after f. 56 7⁶ (ff. 57–62) 8⁸+1 leaf after 4 (f. 67) 9–12¹⁰ 13¹⁰ 8 cancelled and supplied in parchment (f. 119) 14⁸ wants 1 before f. 122+1 leaf after 4 (f. 125) 15–16¹⁰ 17⁸+1 leaf after 4 (f. 154). Quires 12–16 marked B–F at the end. Written in anglicana (short *r* and, often, single compartment *a*) by one hand throughout. 2-line red initials. Binding of s. xviii/xix. Secundo folio *of þe pacient*.

Written in England. 'Conyers Purshull', ff. 1, 158. 'Montague Durlacher Given to me by J. Carpenter Esqʳ 1841', f. iᵛ.

Ferguson 153. *Guielmo Sadacense, De alchimia (in Italian)*

s. XVI in.

1. ff. 1–224ᵛ Incomenzia sadacina di tuta larte de alchimia composita da Frate Guielmo sadasense de lordine de frati di sancta maria del carmino indigno mᵒ perusino de sacra theologia existente in exilio dil suo sacro ordine e lecta de medecini veracissimi de aprobati philosophi et alchimisti dignissimi . . . . . . (*two lines erased*). Ogni dato perfecto et ogne dono optimo e desendente di sopra . . . et cosi se finisse questo tardo libro nel capitulo de la galina. grazie infinite a lo optime creatore et a la sua gloriosa madre et orazione sian fate per frate guielmo carmelita compositore de questo libro Amen. Fr' patricius de disenzano carmelita scripsit hunc librum feriarie ibi studentem cum maximo labore et precio. Quoniam dominus Nicholaus a quo habuit copiam misus fuerat tunc a principe hercule. ad ungarie regem et statim reuersurus festinauit ipse patricius tradu-

cere. nam lingua theutonica scriptus erat. Non Mireris ergo lector si incompositus (?) sit. Quoniam laborauit patricius quantum potuit. De aliis autem libris duobus sequentibus quere alibi. et stude cogita et recogita (?) si eum inteligere cupis. Laus deo Amen.

Thorndike and Kibre (Omne datum optimum). Cf. L. Thorndike, *History of Magic and Experimental Science*, iii. 628–32. Singer and Anderson, no. 381. Bk. 1, thirty-six chapters: at the end it is said that it is 'reducto et composto per frate guielmo sedazerio de lo seraphino ordine de frati de sancta gloriosa maria de monte carmelo et in exilio existente'. Bk. 2, nineteen chapters, begins on f. 165. Ercole I was Duke of Este 1471–1505.

2. ff. 224ᵛ–240 Recipes in Latin and Italian.

Begins with six lines of verse, 'Calcina disolue . . .', and ends with sixteen lines of verse, 'Soluiti li corpi in aqua atuti el dico . . . In his enim carminibus continetur totum magisterium et sic concludimus hunc librum gratia dei cristi et virginis. Amen'.

ff. i+240+iii. Paper. 142 × 100 mm. Written space 115 × 65 mm. 16 long lines. Current humanistica. 2-line red initials, but spaces were not filled after f. 29. Headings omitted after f. 83. Binding of s. xvi: a winged dragon below crossed keys as centrepiece.

Written in Italy. Book-plate of Frederick North, 5th Earl of Guilford, inside the cover. Part of the library sold in 1830 and bought then and later by Sir Thomas Phillipps (A. N. L. Munby, *Phillipps Studies*, iii. 56). Phillipps 5712: his sale at Sotheby's, 27 Apr. 1903; lot 14.

Ferguson 192.   *R. Lullius, etc.*   s. xv²

A companion volume to MSS. 63, 76, 135.

1. ff. 1–19ᵛ De inuestigacione artis secreti occulti super totum opus maius in compendio. Quia homo est magis nobile animal de mundo . . . uel secretorum. Adonay propter tuum amorem et multiplicacionem fidei chatholice et ad honorem beate marie semper virginis perfecit magister Raymondus in Aueniam (?) in cenobio fratrum predicatorum istum tractatum de inuestigacione secreti occulti. Celestino suo discipulo in anno mᵒ cccᵒ ixᵒ.

Thorndike and Kibre.

2. ff. 19ᵛ–23ᵛ Incipit tractatus margaritarum. Opus namque margaritarum sic condies. Primo quod accipies . . . Other operations follow to f. 27ᵛ.

3. ff. 28–38 In nomine sancte trinitatis et eterne veritatis Incipit compendium artis magice transmutacionis metallorum. Accipe nigrum nigrius nigro . . . reperitur in arte alchimie.

Thorndike and Kibre (Lull, Ars Magica).

4. ff. 38ᵛ–41 Pratica fratris eliẹ. Recipe libram 1 artⁱ vitrioli . . . tamen semper cum nouis maᵇᵘˢ. Explicit pratica fratris Elye ordinis Sancti Francisci.

5 (in part of the space remaining at the end of quire 3). ff. 41ʳᵛ, 42ᵛ, 43ʳᵛ Recipes, one of which ends (f. 41ᵛ) with the words 'Ista Recepta data per magistrum Iohannem lust compatrem meum quam dixit esse verum credeᵐ suo (?)': cf. MS. Ferguson 76, art. 4b, and MS. 63, art. 2b.

6 (quire 4). (*a*) ff. 44–51ᵛ 1. Accipe ergo ipsam inmundiciam scoc' (?) quia habet
virtutem igneam . . . tocius perfectionis magisterii. Et cum compleueris Lauda
deum. (*b*) ff. 52–56ᵛ Recipes, headed on f. 52 'De tinctis albis et ru' '.

(*a*). As far as f. 49ᵛ in paragraphs numbered 1–10.

7 (quire 5). (*a*) ff. 57–65 Hic ponentur alique glose inuente. que fuerunt per
volumina Raymondi lulii super certis capitulis. Et primo super capitulo. Ordina-
mur namque tibi et cetera . . . (*b*) ff. 65ᵛ–68ᵛ In nomine do. incipit tractatus de
dono dei occulto. Capitulum 1. calcinacionis auri et argenti et eius ablucione.
Accipe 5 partes solis puri . . . (*c*) f. 68ᵛ Fermento iunge. volatum calcinaque
solue . . . (7 lines).

(*a*). Cf. Thorndike and Kibre (Ordimur). (*b*). Paragraphs on f. 68ᵛ are headed 'Hec
Geber' and 'Hec Morienus ad discipulum'.

8 (quire 6). (*a*) ff. 69–70 Sumarius alkimie. Obmissis cunctis argumentacionibus
. . . (*b*) ff. 70ᵛ–71, 74–75ᵛ, 76ᵛ Miscellaneous notes. (*c*) ff. 71ᵛ–73 De mineralibus tractatus in more (?) consurgens. Ceterorum philosophorum rebus
mineralibus omnibus . . .

(*a*) lists twelve 'operationes'. (*c*) quotes Plato and Turba philosophorum. f. 76ʳ blank.

ff. ii+76+ii. The old foliation '1–74' repeated two numbers in error. Paper. 172×80
mm. Written space *c.* 130×60 mm. *c.* 30 long lines. Collation : 1¹⁰ 2¹⁴ 3¹⁸ (ff. 25–42)
4¹⁴ 5¹² 6⁸. Spaces for 2-line initials not filled. Binding of s. xix, like that of MS. Ferguson
80.

Written in Italy: cf. MS. Ferguson 63. 'Phillipps 2674': Phillipps sale, 27 Apr. 1903,
lot 16. 'J. Ferguson 18 Dec. 1908', f. i. Formerly Bi. 17. a. 24.

Ferguson 205. *J. de Rupescissa, etc. (in English)*   s. xv²

1. ff. 1–71 A translation into English of three alchemical pieces, set out as three
books: (i) ff. 1–33ᵛ The first boke of the consideracion of quynte essence of alle
thinges that mowe bee changid from oone kynde to an other . . . The furst decre
is þᵗ by the vertue the whiche god hath yeue to nature . . . and praising of alle
holy churche Amen quod Rogier bacon; (ii) ff. 33ᵛ–54ᵛ Hic incipit secundus
liber de generalibus remediis. In the name of oure lord . . . (f. 49ᵛ) in his absence
laus deo. Alaxus affrike disciple of Robert Claddere . . . shewid to noon maniere
man. Here endith the secund boke the whiche is callid the general remedies ayens
diuerse infirmitees; (iii) ff. 54ᵛ–71 And here bigynneth the thrid boke of the
werkes of alkymys with his chapitres alle here foloweng. Alle wisedame is of
god . . . and þe tyncture shal be loste aftre þe furste examinacion or the secunde.
Explicit semita secundum Albertum in alkamia.

Agrees closely with B.L., MS. Sloane 353, another copy by the same scribe, which ends
imperfectly at the words 'waisshing and decoction', here on f. 59ᵛ. Singer and Anderson's
references to Sloane are: for (i) and (ii) as far as f. 49ᵛ, no. 292. xxxviii; for (ii) from f. 49ᵛ,
p. 772 (Alexis); for (iii), no. 293. xii (J. de Rupescissa). The reference to (iii) is, however,
misplaced, since it is a translation, not of J. de Rupescissa, but of Pseudo-Albertus
Magnus, Semita recta, Singer and Anderson, no. 177 (ed. Zetzner, ii. 423–55).

2. ff. 71ᵛ–75ᵛ Hic incipit opus bonefacii 14 cum sequentibus capitulis albis et

rubiis. Alle thees parfite writingʒ here after . . . and here we shall bigynne atte dissolucion of lune and congelacion of mercury and of þe fixion of hym . . . and to high plaisance of god amen. Finito libro reddatur gracia cristo.

For the Latin cf. Thorndike and Kibre (Ut primo dicamus) and Singer and Anderson no. 158. Five chapters.

3. ff. 75ᵛ–84 For to purge Iubiter. Take 3 li' or as muche as þᵘ wilte þereof . . . abidyng the fire and perisshing.

Recipes. A paragraph on f. 82ᵛ ends with the words 'this is werke of Maister Parys' and one on f. 83 contains the words 'this werke maister boleyne hydde in his boke'.

4. ff. 84ᵛ–86 Sophisticaciones. De cupro solem facere. Accipe cuprum lamina-tum . . . sauf oonely of wyne.

Recipes.

5 (added). f. 86ᵛ Notes of events in 1489, written in very current script and end-ing imperfectly, because the lower half of the leaf has been cut off: 'Anno iiiiᶜ iiiiˣˣ ix whas sente a grete harmy in to breton' the xvi day of Marste and to calys xv C more hall so the s[ame] her. Anno iiiiᶜ iiiiˣˣ ix whas sclan the herell of n[ort]homberlonde the xxviii day of haperel the same her folyng whente the keyng t[o the] nort contrey wᵗ a grete hoste of pep[ell] the xii day of May that her' whas gaderyd of hewerey leylode men [. . .] of hewerey nobell viii d' þᵗ made the pepell worte (?) for to areys. Item þᵉ nor[. . .] broke the gateys of cworkeys ga[. . . . .]'.

ff. iii+86+iii. Foliated 1–86 in s. xvi. 210×140 mm. Written space c. 158×95 mm. 35 long lines. Collation: 1–10⁸ 11⁶. Quires marked in the usual late medieval manner, but with 'fo.' between letter and number, as in Sloane 353: thus f. 19 is marked 'c fo. 3'. Arts. 1–4 by one hand in an odd mixture of set textura and secretary in two sizes, larger for the headings and smaller for the text. The smaller size is current and has long tailed r occasionally. Few abbreviations. Initials: (i, ii) 3-line and 2-line, blue with red ornament; (iii) 1-line, blue or red. Binding of red morocco, gilt, s. xviii/xix, lettered 'Mirror of light'. Secundo folio thingʒ that been.

Written in England. '[. . .] Kyngstone', f. 1, s. xvi. 'Dekyngstone (?) whose Booke of fower score leaves and fyve and a halfe this is', f. 86. Formerly Bi. 16. d. 45.

Ferguson 209. *Isaac Judeus, etc.*   s. XIV in.

1. ff. 3–39ᵛ Incipit tractatus urinarum Isaac translatus a quonstantino africano in latinam linguam. In latinis quidem libris . . . dolorem renum significat. Deo Gratias Amen.

Thorndike and Kibre. *Omnia Opera Ysaac*, 1515, ff. clvi–cciii. ff. 1–2ᵛ left blank. Recipes added on f. 1.

2. (a) ff. 39ᵛ–45ᵛ Incipiunt uersus Egidii de urinis. Dicitur urina quoniam fit renibus una . . . Egidius doctor fecit hec metra salerni. Expliciunt uersus egidii de urinis. (b) ff. 45ᵛ–52 Incipiunt uersus egidii de pulsibus. Ingenii uires . . . facit colectio pulsum. (c) f. 52 Sunt subsolanus uulturnus . . . (4 lines). (d) f. 52 Dat scropulus numerum . . . (2 lines). (e) f. 52ᵛ Hec lapidem frangunt . . . (4 lines). (f) f. 52ᵛ Vtraque spica. tunus . . . menstrua ducunt (4 lines). (g) f. 52ᵛ

Thus. maxtix. mirtus . . . menstrua stringunt. (*h*) f. 52^v Armoniach. maxtix . . .
(2 lines). (*i*) f. 52^v Ruta uiris uenerem . . . (1 line). (*j*) f. 52^v Lac anabula parit . . .
(2 lines). (*k*) f. 52^v Paruus enutriteus . . . (3 lines). (*l*) f. 52^v Disuia se cellat
canit . . . (4 lines). (*m*) f. 52^v Squiria nil. stranguria . . . (2 lines). (*n*) ff. 52^v–53^v
Res aloes lignum . . . cogit amare iecur (67 lines). (*o*) ff. 53^v–54 His signis
moriens . . . nichil aufert utilitatis (14 lines). (*p*) f. 54 De certicis (*sic*) signis.
Sanguis et urina . . . (2 lines). (*q*) Largus. amax (*sic*). illaris . . . (8 lines).

(*a, b*). Aegidius Corboliensis. 347 and 377 lines. Walther, nos. 4432, 9332. *GKW* 269,
268. (*c*) Walther, no. 18872. (*n*) Walther, no. 16604. (*o–q*) Walther, nos. 8211, 17273,
10031. Probably much of (*e–m*) is in *Flos medicinae scholae Salernitanae*: cf. ed. Renzi, v,
lines 2592–2603 for (*e–g*), line 1092 for (*i*), and lines 1176–7 for (*j*).

3. ff. 54–5 Vena frontis ualet Doloribus capitis . . . dolori femorum. dorsique.
On the veins and 'ventosae'.

4 (added early). f. 55 Dicitur ungue(n)tum mollis confectio pinguis . . .
Twenty-one medical verses. f. 55^v blank.

5. ff. 56–72^v (*begins imperfectly*) De simplicibus febribus. Post tractatum simplicium febrium interpolatarum. agendum est de compositis. Febris composita
. . . et uentositatem consumat.
Four leaves have been cut out before f. 56.

6. (*a*) ff. 72^v–73 Urina alba et te(nuis) sumam indigestionem significat . . .
amistionem significat. (*b*) f. 73 Short paragraphs on tastes (Sapores tribus
modis . . .) and on the nineteen colours of urines.
(*a*). Urso, De urinis, ed. P. Giacosa, *Magistri Salernitani nondum editi*, 1901, pp. 283–9.

7. ff. 74^v–106^v Macer id ex herbis siccis loquitur uel acerbis . . . apta solucio
fiet. et cetera.
Macer, De viribus herbarum: 2,271 lines. Walther, no. 10550.

8. f. 107 A table of the seventy-eight chapters of art. 7, 'Arthemisia . . . Aloe Et
sic est finis'. f. 107^v blank.

9 (added). f. 1 Recipes.

ff. iii+105+i, foliated (i), 1–107, (108). ff. 1, 2 are a bifolium of parchment ruled like
arts. 1, 3–6. 185×138 mm. Written space 150×100 mm. 2 cols. and for arts. 2, 7, 8,
long lines. Collation of ff. 3–107: 1–6^8 7^8 wants 6–8 blank after f. 55 8^8 wants 1–4 (ff. 56–9)
9–10^8 11^6 12–14^8 15 two (ff. 106–7). 2-line red initials and in art. 7 3-line spaces left blank.
Binding of green buckram, s. xviii. Secundo folio *Fel enim*.
Written in Italy. 'Libro donato del sig' [. . . . .] de [. . . . .]', f. 2, s. xviii. Book-stamp of
'Comes Donatus Silva', f. i^v. Bought by Ferguson on 28 Nov. 1896. Formerly Bi. 16. e.
22.

Ferguson 234. *Bartholomaeus Anglicus*   s. xv med.

1. ff. 4–99 Cum proprietates rerum sequantur . . . vt dicit ysidorus libro xv°.
Fifteen books. Printed often. A table was added in s. xv^2 on ff. 1–3^v: 'Incipit tabula et

incipiunt tytuli librorum et capitulorum venerabilis bartholomei anglici de proprietatibus rerum . . . Expliciunt tytuli . . . Et hic inferius secuntur auctores de quorum scriptis in hoc volumine tractatur. Augustinus . . . Stephanus strabus. Inter philosophos autem. Aristoteles . . . Zoroastes magnus'.

2. f. 99ᵛ Infirmus qui patitur penitentiam beati Cornelii primo petat . . . et confidat in dominum et in beatum Cornelium et saluabitur.

Directions for performing the penitence of St. Cornelius. f. 100ʳᵛ blank.

3. (*a*) A piece beginning 'Nota 2ᵐ dionisium In demonibus . . .', s. xv, is written on the blank dorse of (*b*) and inserted after f. 6. (*b*) A parchment document. Most of the text remains, 'Ich herman van Boidberch Sanderssoen laet allen den goenen weten . . . Die in den gericht van xancken gheerft en' gheguet sijn . . .', s. xv.

(*b*). H. van Boidberch invites all persons having claims on his estate to come at 10 a.m. on the third Sunday in Lent to his house at Xancken 'tot wilhems huys van bemel myt alsulken brieuen en' sedulen als sy hebben dat mynen guede angeet'.

ff. iii+100+iii. Paper. 288×210 mm. Written space 210×150 mm. 2 cols. *c.* 55 lines. Frame ruling. Collation: 1 three 2–3¹² 4¹⁰ 5¹⁴ 6–8¹² 9¹⁴ wants 14, blank. Quires 2–6 numbered at the end iᵘˢ–vᵘˢ. Written in cursiva. 6-line, 5-line, and 2-line red initials. Binding of s. xix. Secundo folio (f. 5) *verbis*.

Written in the Netherlands. Label of 'J. L. Beijers Librairie ancienne et moderne Neudeg. 56 Utrecht' and a slip from a Dutch sale catalogue (in French), in which this book was item 70, are inside the cover.

Ferguson 241. *Dialogue of Placides and Timeo, etc.* (*in French*)
s. XV ex.

1. ff. 1–65 Aristotes dist en son liure de naturez. au commenchement dun liure . . . (f. 1ᵛ) touttes choses et singuleres. Chy commenchent les secres des philosophes. Sy deuons sauoir que philosophes . . . sans Rubriche. Iadis fust 1 tamps que chil . . . a Raison Et ly dist Placides. Maist*re* che dist placides a tymeo dites moy car . . . seroient a dieu soies atant mentais. Explicit de placides et tymeo et cet'.

For printed editions of 1514 and 1520 in B.L. see their *Catalogue*, s.v. Coeur. A long letter from John Holmes of the British Museum to Lord Ashburnham, 2 Mar. 1853, loose inside the cover, is mainly about art. 1. f. 65ᵛ blank.

2. ff. 66–73 Che sont les secres des femmes translates de Latin en franchois. Et est deffendu de Reueler a femme par nostre saint pere le Pappe sur paine descumemeint en la decretale Ad meam doctrinam. Au commenchement vne damoisielle me pria par loialle courtoisie . . . Car chest chosse humaine et naturelle etc'. Explicit les secret des femmes.

Secres des dames, ed. A. Colson, Paris, 1880, from a copy in his possession and Paris, B.N. fr. 631, 2027, 19994. f. 73ᵛ blank.

ff. i+73+i. Contemporary foliation. Paper. 270×205 mm. Written space *c.* 212×145 mm. *c.* 39 long lines. Frame ruling in pencil. Collation: 1¹⁴ 2²⁰ 3¹⁶ 4¹⁶ wants 16, blank, after f. 65 5⁸. Written in cursiva. Initials: (i) red and black penwork on pale-brown grounds, decorated in penwork; (ii) 2-line, red. Binding of s. xix¹. Secundo folio *anchien.*

Written in France. 'A Charle de beaulie', f. 73ᵛ, s. xv ex. (Barrois–) Ashburnham sale, 10 June 1901, lot 152, to Ellis for £5. 10s. 'John Ferguson Oct. 15 1901'.

Ferguson 259.   *Recepta alchimica, etc.*   s. xv², 1474

1 (quire 1). (*a*) pp. 1–7 Quid lapis est scitis flos eris et aurea vitis . . . (*b*) p. 8 'Figure (12) signorum' and of the planets. (*c*) pp. 9–12 Sequitur fixacio uzifur et aliorum spirituum. Recipe de calce viua . . . (*d*) p. 13 A table of 'Digestiue'. (*e*) pp. 14–23 Recipes.

(*a*). 205 lines of alchemical verse, beginning with Walther, no. 15826, here in forty-four lines. The paragraphing suggests that there are fifteen separate pieces, but, apart from the first, Walther records only 'In mundo lapides . . .' (p. 4: 11 lines: Walther, no. 9009). pp. 24–8 were left blank.

2 (quire 2). pp. 29–44 Recipes, etc.

Includes 'Vna phares mire per metra tibi do scire . . . .' (p. 29): 6 lines, Singer and Anderson, no. 837. pp. 37–42 were left blank.

3 (quires 3, 4). Recipes, etc., including: (*a*) p. 45 Ad faciendam medicinam penetratiuam . . . et superfluis practicis 1474; (*b*) pp. 46–50 Ad extrahendam quintam essenciam ab antimonio . . . ; (*c*) p. 52 Operacio lune probata. Mercurii vine lune pars vna parate . . . (7 lines); (*d*) p. 52 Alphabetum philosophorum. A forma . . . Z Venus; (*e*) p. 52 Termini philosophorum. Cor ignem et solem significat . . . Vinum aquam solis et lune; (*f*) pp. 60–4 Aduerte carissime que secuntur quia vera sunt intelligentibus. Prima preparacio . . . in septem pro-posicionibus notum et laudet deum. Explicit rosarius abbreuiatus; (*g*) p. 66 Cogitur exire spiritus de corpore iouis . . . nam talia posui pro te 1474 decembris; (*h*) pp. 73–8 Recipes 'Ad faciendum lazurium'; (*i*) pp. 82–3 Medical recipes 'In pestilencia', 'In febribus. Recipe herbam collectam infra festiuitates beate virginis que dicitur eybisch . . .', 'In dissenteria', 'In ictericia', 'Contra pestilen-ciam summum remedium. Recipe in mayo radicem herbe que dicitur huff-pleter . . .'.

(*b*). Not as Singer and Anderson, no. 589. (*f*). Thorndike and Kibre. Zetzner, iii. 650–3. (*g*) Twenty-four lines of verse. Thorndike and Kibre (Conradus de Hildensee). Singer and Anderson, no. 801. pp. 79–81, 84 were left blank.

ff. 42, paginated 1–84. 132 × 93 mm. Written space *c.* 112 × 75 mm. *c.* 34 long lines. No ruling. Collation: 1¹⁴ 2⁸ 3¹⁴ 4⁶. Written in current hybrida. No ornament. Stitched, but no binding.

Written in Germany, 3*a*, *g* dated in 1474. Probably taken out of a larger book.

Ferguson 263.   *Albertus Magnus, etc.*   s. XIII ex.

1. ff. 1–37ᵛ Mineralia alberti. De commixcione et coagulacione similiter . . . secundum hunc modum dictum sit. Explicit liber mineralium domini Alberti magni.

Opera, ed. Borgnet, v. 1–103. A note in the margin of f. 29 is dated 1492.

2. ff. 37ᵛ–38 Dubium apud multos esse solet . . . saluatur enim virtus ipsorum. Explicit liber de commixcione elementorum Fratris Thome de Aquino. Deo gracias.

Opera, xvi (1869), 353.

3 (added, s. xiv). ff. 38ᵛ–40ᵛ, 57ᵛ [A]d pronosticandum diuersam aeris disposicionem futuram . . . fuisse creduntur. Explicit liber de pronosticacione aeris astronomicus.

Grosseteste, De impressionibus aeris. Ed. L. Baur, *Die philosophischen Werke des Robert Grosseteste*, Beiträge zur Geschichte der Philosophie des Mittelalters, ix (1912), 41–51. Thomson, *Grosseteste*, p. 103, lists seventeen copies, not this. Here the text continues for a dozen lines after the last words of edn. *in signis aquosis*, 'Nota quod luna moratur in signo quolibet . . .'. When the scribe came to the date (edn., p. 49/23) he wrote 'Mᵒ çccᵒ 1249ᵒ'. He ran out of space on f. 40ᵛ, and continued on f. 57ᵛ, which contains, after the end of the text, a diagram of twelve concentric circles, divided into twelve parts, one for each sign of the zodiac.

4. (*a*) ff. 41–52 Quoniam quidem ars alchimica quamplures viros doctilogos videntibus oculis excecauit et in mediis fluctibus erroris in profundum facto naufragio dimersit . . . cum sapienti insipiens equauiter (?) Amen. (*b*) ff. 52–7 Practica. Supposito ex insinuacione veridica sapientum Quod artis nostre duo sint principia . . . Marcos. Lucet enim ut rubinus per animam tingentem quam acquisiuit virtute ignis. De residuis require superius in fine questionis etc.

(*a*). References in the margins to Albertus (often), Aristotle, Hermes, Geber, etc. (*b*). f. 53 is a supply leaf in a different, but contemporary hand. Before its first paragraph (recto, col. 1/27) a hand of s. xv wrote 'Hic debent stare versus' and the same hand wrote in the lower margin 'Hec est expositio versuum stancium in eiusdem folii latere secundo. ergo verte'. The verses in question are the last fifteen lines on f. 53ᵛ: 'Es quod nigrescat. massetur. sole calescat . . .'. The exposition of the verses begins on f. 53, 'Ft.¹ Dico . . .', and continues to the end: the last words on f. 57, 'Aureus ut' are a comment on the beginning of verse 15. The lemmata on ff. 54–7 are in 'secret' writing¹ over erasure, in the hand which wrote the supply leaf, 53. The exposition is in four 'regimina' on lines 1–3, 4–8, 9–13, and 14, 15 respectively, the second beginning on f. 54, 'Sequitur secundum regimen operis secundum Hermetem', the third on f. 55ᵛ and the fourth on f. 57. Quotations are largely from Turba philosophorum. For f. 57ᵛ, left blank, see art. 3.

ff. 57. 172×130 mm. Written space *c.* 133×95 mm. 37–9 long lines for arts. 1, 2; 2 cols., 36 lines for art. 4. Ruling in ink. Collation: 1–6⁸ 7⁴+four leaves after 2 (ff. 51–4: for f. 53, see above art. 4) and one leaf after 8 (f. 57). Well written in small current script with two-compartment *a* and almost always straight ascenders. Art. 3 is cursiva. 2-line red initials. A cover of thin parchment now over the front and spine only may be contemporary: the strings were brought through the parchment on the spine and fastened on to three pieces of thick leather, one of which, the highest, is now missing, and the strings with it. Boxed by E. Riley in 1969. Secundo folio *cernitur*.

Written in Germany.

Gen. 1. *Horae*   s. xv²

1. ff. 1–12ᵛ Calendar in French, in red and black. St. Gervais in red (20 Dec.).

2. ff. 13–60ᵛ Hours of B.V.M., with Hours of the Cross and of the Holy Spirit

---

¹ Substitution of the next letter of the alphabet: thus 'Ft' stands for *Es*.

worked in. The antiphon and capitulum at prime are *Quando natus* and *Ab inicio*; at none *Ecce maria* and *Paradisi porta*. ff. 61–62ᵛ blank.

3. ff. 63–82 Penitential psalms and litany. St. Gervais is twelfth out of twenty-four martyrs.

4. ff. 82–117ᵛ Sequitur seruicium mortuorum.

5. ff. 118–122ᵛ Douce dame de misericorde mere de pitie . . . Sonet, no. 458. The Fifteen Joys.

6. ff. 122ᵛ–125 Chy sont les vii requestes. Biau sire dieu doulz dieu doulz pere . . . Sonet, no. 504.

7. f. 125 Sainte uraye crois aouree . . . (8 lines). Sonet, no. 1876. f. 125ᵛ blank.

ff. i+125+i. 160×112 mm. Written space 88×59 mm. 16 long lines. Collation: 1¹² 2⁸ 3⁶ 4–7⁸ 8⁴ 9–12⁸ 13⁸ 1 canc. after f. 94 14–16⁸. Four 12-line pictures, not good, on ff. 13, 36ᵛ, 63, 82ᵛ (Job and two friends). Initials: (i) blue on red ground or gold on blue ground, decorated; (ii) 3-line, red and blue, with red and green-grey ornament; (iii) 2-line, blue with red ornament or red with green-grey ornament; (iv) 1-line, red or blue. Capital letters in the ink of the text filled with yellow. Line fillers in red and blue. Floral borders, compartmented and framed, on picture pages: parts of the border are on grounds of gold paint. A binding by D. Cockerell & Son in 1966 replaces a binding of s. xix by Carss, Glasgow.

Written in France. 'Ex libris Bibliothec[æ] universitatis Glasguens[is]' and 'Ex dono Juvenum Humanissimorum Johannis Smith et Gulielmi Bruce A.M. Academ[. .] alumn: Neil Campbell Principal', f. 1: Campbell was principal from 1728 to 1761. F. 8. 34 in the catalogue of 1828 and F.10.11 in the catalogue of 1836. Later BD. 1. i. 11 and BE. 7. f. 8.

Gen. 2. *Horae* (*partly in Netherlandish*)   s. xv med.

1. ff. 1–12ᵛ Calendar in Netherlandish, in red and black.

'S' Denijs. S' Fikier' in red, 9 Oct. Thomas of Canterbury, erased at 29 Dec., is the only English saint.

2. ff. 13–55ᵛ Hours of B.V.M. of the use of (Sarum). Hours of the Cross worked in. Memoriae after lauds of Holy Spirit, Holy Trinity, Holy Cross, Michael, John Baptist, Peter and Paul, Andrew, Laurence, Stephen, Thomas of Canterbury (erased), Nicholas, George, Christopher, Anne, Mary Magdalene, Katherine, Margaret, All Saints, and for peace (ff. 28–36ᵛ).

The leaves on which matins, lauds, prime, and sext began are missing. Rhymed antiphons of the memoriae of George, Christopher, and Anne: *RH*, nos. 7242, 18445, 6773.

3. ff. 56–69ᵛ Penitential psalms and litany.

The first leaf missing. No English saints in the litany. Fourteen virgins: . . . (6) Anna . . . (9) Anna . . . (12–14) Walburgis Juliana Amplonia.

4. ff. 70–6 (*begins imperfectly*) Deel my vrauwe an dat gheual . . . Des van adaem niet meer en quam. Paues innocent heest gheset . . .

Begins with the last line of a stanza. Twenty 9-line stanzas follow, each beginning 'Dii biddic'. A final 8-line stanza in red conveys an indulgence of Pope Innocent of 100 days. f. 76ᵛ blank.

5. ff. 77–81 Van onser lieuer vrauwen een ghebet. Aue god grues vch vrauwe reyn . . . Des viant in das ewich licht. Amen.

120 lines of verse. f. 81ᵛ blank.

6. f. 82 Oratie. Porrige nobis domine dexteram tuam . . .

Arts. 7–11 were added in England.

7. ff. 82ᵛ–83 Oratio dicenda quodlibet die pro bono statu regis [. . .] anglie. Antª. Qui celorum continet thronos . . .

The king's name, probably Henry, has been erased the three times it occurs.

8. f. 83 Aue uerum corpus natum . . . *RH*, no. 2175.

9. ff. 84–106ᵛ Office of the dead.

10. ff. 106ᵛ–118 Commendatio animarum.

Pss. 118, 138 and prayer 'Tibi domine commendamus . . .'. *Manuale Sarum*, p. 143.

11. ff. 118ᵛ–120 'xv psalmos': cues only of the first twelve. f. 120ᵛ blank.

ff. i+120+iii. ff. 121–2 are medieval flyleaves. 148×110 mm. Written space *c.* 97×65 mm. 15 long lines and, on ff. 84–120, 16–18 lines. Collation: 1¹² 2⁸ wants 1 3⁸ wants 1 before f. 20 4⁸ 5 three (ff. 35–7) 6⁸ wants 1 and 8 (ff. 38–43) 7⁸ 8⁴ (ff. 52–5) 9⁸ wants 1 before f. 56 10⁸ wants 8, probably blank, after f. 69 11⁸ wants 1 before f. 70 12⁸ wants 6, probably blank, after f. 81 12–14⁸ 15⁶ 16 seven (ff. 114–20). Initials of arts. 2–5: (i) ff. 34, 77, in colours on gold grounds or gold with slate-grey ornament; (ii, iii) 5-line, gold on coloured grounds patterned in white; (iv) 1-line, blue with red ornament. Initials of arts. 8–11: (i, ii) 3-line and 2-line, blue with red ornament; (iii) 1-line, red or blue. Continuous borders on f. 34 for the memoria of Anne, on the four remaining principal pages of art. 2 (terce, none, vespers, compline) and on f. 77. A binding of 1967 by D. Cockerell & Son replaces one of s. xix by Carss, Glasgow.

Written in the southern Netherlands and (arts. 7–11) in England. The flyleaves bear names written in s. xvi: 'Ionker Martyn fan beay perroy', f. 121; 'Iacob van der gavere', f. 122; 'Elyzabeth burdet', f. 121. A hand of s. xvii entered on f. 69ᵛ the names of husband and wife in seven generations of the Orell family from Robert and Agnes to George and Anabil. 'Barre whit field sables hyves ore' is written beside an uncoloured shield of arms on f. 55ᵛ, s. xvii. 'Ex libris Bibliothecæ Universitatis Glasguensis 1727', f. 1. Once 'By. 6. 3', f. 1. F. 8. 35 in the catalogue of 1828 and F. 10.5 in the catalogue of 1836. Later BD. 1. i. 12 and BE. 7. f. 23.

Gen. 6. *Vegetius, etc.*   s. xv med.

1. ff. 1–111, 121, 130 (*Begins imperfectly*) precedant. Ita autem seuere apud maiores . . . (f. 110ᵛ) doctrina monstrauerit. Expliciunt libri quinque scilicet flauii uegecii renati uiri illustris comitis etylii de re militari siue arte bellica. Expliciunt feliciter tracti de commentariis augusti traiani adriani fortiniani catonis cornelii celsii frontini paterni et aliorum.

The first words are in bk. 1, rubrica 13, Teubner edn., 1885, p. 17/5. Bk. 2, f. 11ᵛ; 3, f. 37; 4, f. 86; 5, f. 102, Precepta belli naualis: edn., bk. 4, 31–46. The right order of leaves is 1–89, 121, 130, 90–109, 111, 110.

2. ff. 112–15 Incipit alius tractatus de re militari. Possumus ad presens alia

enumerare per que marini pugnatores hostes impugnare debent . . . continetur sub prudencia.

Three topics: naval warfare; the humours in war; 'commune bonum' in war. The right order of leaves is 112, 113, 115, 114.

3. ff. 114ᵛ, 116–119ᵛ, 122–3 Aristotilis in libro de secretis secretorum . . . Proceres sunt addicio . . . maius est signum.

Chapters De ordine et multitudine bellatorum and De cornu: edn. Paris, 1520, ff. lii–lv.

4. (a) ff. 120, 123–9, 131 Informacio breuis supe(r) hiis que videntur ex nunc fore prouidenda quantum ad passagium diuina fauente gracia faciendum. In dei nomine amen. Super facto passagii ad laudem dei et exultacionem (sic) ortodoxe fidei . . . confirmetur in secula seculorum amen amen. (b) ff. 129ʳᵛ, 132–138ᵛ Informacio alia de pertinentibus ad passagium et primo de domino rege Ierosolimitani et de passagiis hactenus factis et per quos et per quas partes et quid ibi profecerint. Rubrica. Dominium regni ierosolimitani sic processit a tempore cristi . . . valde enim necessarium est adiutorium cicilie pro passagio nec vitari potest.

On how to achieve a successful crusade. (a) is addressed to the king (of France) as appears from the wording on f. 129. (b) begins with a historical account of expeditions to the Holy Land up to the capture of Acre in 1290 and ends with a plea for 'pax et concordia . . . inter cristianos principes', to be achieved by marriages particularly. The right order of leaves is 123–5, 120, 131, 126–9, 132–8. ff. 139–142ᵛ blank.

ff. iii+142+iii. 136×90 mm. Written space 93×62 mm. 24–5 long lines. Collation: 1–11¹² 12¹² wants 11, 12, probably blank: 8⁶,⁷ is misplaced in quire 11, 11¹,¹² has been put in the middle of quire 11 and 10 ⁴,⁹ has changed places with 10⁵,⁸ (for the leaves in question, see above, arts. 1–4). Written in cursiva. Initials: (i) ff. 112, 113, red and blue with red and grey-blue ornament; (ii) 3-line, blue with red ornament or red with grey-blue ornament. Binding of s. xviii.

Written in France. An old Glasgow University pressmark CL. f. 6 n. 2 on f. ii. F. 8.37 in the catalogue of 1828 and F. 10.2 in the catalogue of 1836. Later BD. 1. i. 18 and BE. 7. f. 29.

Gen. 7. *Biblia*   s. XIII med.

1. ff. 3–413 A Bible with the usual books in the usual order and with all but one of the common set of sixty-four prologues: cf. above, Bristol Public Library, 15. The absent prologue is that to 2 Chronicles. Tobit begins a new quire, f. 169: f. 168ᵛ is partly blank.

2. ff. 414–52 Aaz apprehendens . . . consiliatores eorum.

The usual dictionary of Hebrew names, here written in paragraphs, all words beginning with the same two letters being in one block: thus paragraph 2 begins at Abba, 3 at Achab, 4 at Ada.

3 (added in s. xvi). f. 2ʳᵛ Scona mesta dolo propria iam perdita probo . . . Scona tu tibi plaude et pate frui.

Forty-eight lines of verse, followed by 'quod Gildas'. Now hard to read, partly as a result of recent cleaning.

ff. iii+450, foliated (i), 1–452 (453–4). f. 1, formerly the pastedown, and ff. 2, 453 are medieval parchment end-leaves. 152×113 mm. Written space 108×70 mm. 2 cols. 56 lines. Collation of ff. 3–452: 1¹⁶ 2¹⁸ 3–6¹⁶ 7–8²⁴ 9²⁰ (ff. 149–68) 10–13²⁴ 14²² 15–19²⁴ 20²⁴ wants 8, probably blank. Initials: (i) of books, the usual eight psalms and Ps. 51 (but not Ps. 101), red and blue with ornament of both colours; (ii) of prologues, as (i), but smaller, or as (iii), but larger; (iii) of chapters, 2-line, red or blue with ornament of the other colour, or of green, instead of blue; (iv) of verses of psalms, 1-line, blue or red. Capital letters in the ink of the text filled with red. A binding by D. Cockerell & Son in 1970 replaces a binding of s. xix by Carss, Glasgow. Secundo folio *finibus mundi*.

Written probably in England. 'Liber patrici Ramsay' (f. 1ᵛ) and 'Codex Patrici Ramsay', (f. 413), s. xvi, accompanied in both places by an uncoloured shield bearing a displayed eagle: on f. 1ᵛ a stag's head and the motto 'Forthe is ay' are above the shield and the words 'A meschope (?)' and 'Huris al men devoris P R' below it. 'Ex libris Bibliothecæ Universitatis Glasguensis Will: Dunlop. Principall' (principal, 1690–1700), f. 3. Old pressmark A. f 5 n: 3, f. 3: under this mark in the shelf catalogue of 1691. F. 8. 32 in the catalogue of 1828 and F. 10.8 in that of 1836. Later BD. 1. i. 7 and BE. 7. f. 10.

Gen. 193. *Diodorus Siculus*   s. xv med.

Prohemium in libros Diodori siculi: quos Poggius florentinus Latinos fecit ad Nicholaum V summum pontificum. Nullus antea . . . Sed iam ipse Diodorus Loquatur. Diodori siculi historiarum priscarum a poggio in latinum traducti incipit liber primus: in quo hec continentur . . . (table of chapters of bk. 1) . . . Magnas merito gratias . . . scribetur a nobis. FINIT.

Printed in 1472 (*GKW* 8374) and later. Bk. 1, f. 2; 2, f. 19; 3, f. 43; 4, f. 66; 5, f. 93; 6, f. 126. A table of chapters in front of each book, but there are no breaks in the text within books.

ff. iv+152+iv. ff. iii, iv, 153–4 are medieval end-leaves: iiiʳ and 154ᵛ were pasted down. 244×168 mm. Written space *c*. 150×110 mm. 2 cols. 30–4 lines. Ruled in ink. On ff. 1–130 the scribe ruled for 36 lines, but he did not use the last three or so. Writing above the top ruled line. Collation: 1–15¹⁰ 16 two. Humanistic hand. A gold initial on a blue, purple, and green ground ornamented with dots and white vine-stem patterning begins the preface and each book. The margins of ff. 1, 19, 93 have decoration, including winged cherubs, who support an empty shield. Red morocco binding, English work, s. xviii: each corner contains a shell enclosed in a wreath, gilt. Secundo folio *uersatur*.

Written in Italy. 'Bibliothecæ Collegii A[tre]bat: Louan:', ff. 1, 152ᵛ, 153ᵛ, s. xvii.[1] In England in s. xviii: the price-mark of this date, 2-2-0 has been changed to 1-1-0. An old Glasgow pressmark Ff. 4. n. 2 is offset on f. i. F. 6. 16 in the catalogue of 1828 and F. 6. 18 in that of 1836. Later BD. 1. c. 20 and BE. 8. d. 1.

Gen. 212. *Florus*   s. xv med.

Incipit Lucius Florus Pater Lucani et Frater Senece de historia Romano(r)um. Populus Romanus a rege romulo . . . consacraretur. Finis.

The epitome of Livy by Lucius Annaeus Florus. Bk. 2, f. 15ᵛ; 3, f. 35ᵛ. Marginal scholia only on f. 1. f. 78ʳᵛ blank.

[1] The College of Arras at Louvain was founded in 1508: cf. F. Claeys Bouuaert, *Contribution à l'histoire économique de l'ancienne Université de Louvain* (Bibliothèque de la Revue d'histoire ecclésiastique, fasc. 32), 1932, p. 23, a reference I owe to Mr. E. van Balberghe.

ff. ii+78+ii. 228×152 mm. Written space 160×94 mm. 25 long lines. Collation: 1–4⁸ 5–6¹⁰ 7–8⁸ 9¹⁰. Humanistic hand. Initials: (i) of books, gold on coloured grounds, with white-vine ornament, like MS. Gen. 193, but less good; (ii) 2-line, red or blue. Bound in olive morocco, s. xviii in. Secundo folio *agitabant*.

Written in Italy. The binding bears the arms of Karl Heinrich von Hoym, 1694–1736, whose library was sold in Paris, 2 Aug. 1738: cf. MS. Gen. 216. Old Glasgow pressmark CL. f. 5. n. 2. F. 6. 20 in the catalogue of 1828 and F. 7. 19 in that of 1836. Later BD. 1. d. 9 and BE. 8. d. 20.

Gen. 216. *Juvenalis; Persius*   s. xv²

1. ff. 1–85 [S]emper ego auditor . . . omne legumen.

Satires of Juvenal. XVI precedes XV. In IX. 37 the scribe left out the Greek words.

2. ff. 85ᵛ–100 [N]ec fonte labra . . . finitor acerui.

Satires of Persius. f. 100ᵛ blank.

ff. ii+100+ii. 222×145 mm. Written space 147×80 mm. 23 long lines, ruled with a hard point. Writing above the top ruled line. Collation: 1–10¹⁰. Good humanistic hand. Spaces for titles and initials remain blank. Binding of s. xviii, with the Hoym arms. Secundo folio *Aut lugdunensem*.

Written in Italy. From the library of Count Hoym, like MS. Gen. 212. Old Glasgow pressmark CL. f. 5. n. 3. F. 6. 19 in the catalogue of 1828 and F. 7. 21 in that of 1836. Later BD. 1. d. 18 and BE. 8. d. 24.

Gen. 223. *Clement of Lanthony, etc. (in English)*   s. xv in.

1. Preliminaries to art. 2: (*a*) ff. 1–6ᵛ Here bigyneþ a kalender of þe gospel þat ben radd in þe chirch . . .; (*b*) ff. 7–13 In þe bigynnyng of holy chirche it was forboden . . . for þee and for þy lawe. Amen ihesu for þy mercy; (*c*) ff. 13–14 þe prologe on a book maad of þe foure gospeleris. Clement a prest of þe chirche of lantony . . . and in what place of þe bible; (*d*) ff. 14–23ᵛ Here bigynnen þe chapitris of þe first part . . .

(*a*). Divided into temporale, 'sanctorum', and 'commemoraciouns'. Refers to art. 2 by part, chapter, and subdivisions of chapters by letters of the alphabet. (*b*). Three paragraphs, the first, fifteen lines, on the 'gode maner in holy chirche in summe cuntrees' of translating the gospel and expounding it to the congregation 'in her comyne langage'; the second (ff. 7–10ᵛ) beginning 'Seynt austyn seiþ'; the third (ff. 10ᵛ–13) beginning 'Oure lord ihesu crist very god'. The two latter are printed by Forshall and Madden, i. 44 and xiv–xv.

2. ff. 24–189 In þe bigynnyng oþer first of alle þyngis . . . schul ben writen. Here endiþ oon of foure. þat is a boke of alle foure gospellers gaderid schortly into o storye. by Clement of lantony.

The translation of the Gospel harmony of Clement of Lanthony (s. xii), in twelve parts: cf. Wells, *Manual*, p. 407. Red letters in the margins subdivide chapters. f. 189ᵛ blank.

3. ff. 190–212ᵛ Here bigynneþ þe prologe of þe smale pistlis. Not þe same ordre is at grekis . . . into alle worldis.

The Catholic Epistles in the earlier Wycliffite translation: ed. Forshall and Madden.

4. ff. 213–23 (a) Here bigynnen þe ten comaundementis þat god hym self wrote . . . to þe puple. Alle maner of men schulden holde goddis comaundementis . . . (f. 217) he doiþ þe dede wiþoute for þe. Here enden þe ten comaundementis.' þt eche man schulde kepe and (b) her bigynnen þe seuen dedly synnes. The first synne is pride . . . (f. 221) and moost for to kepe. Here enden þe seuene dedly synnes.' and (c) bigynnen þe seuene workis of bodily mercy. þe first is this þat crist schal seye . . . as þe gospel telliþ. Here enden þe seuene workis of mercy bodily.' and (d) bigynnen oþere seuene of gostly workis of mercy. The first is to teche vnkunnyng men goddis lawe . . . (f. 221v) and resoun nediþ þerto. Here enden þe seuene werkis of gostly mercy.' and (e) begynnen þre gode vertues. Feiþ is þe first . . . (f. 222v) loue fayleþ not. (f) Fyue wittis bodily ben þes . . . þes ben fyue wittis gostly . . . þes ben þe seuene ʒiftis of þe holy goost . . . þes ben þe seuene sacramentis . . . (f. 223) sixe maner of consernyng [. . .] (g) foure þyngis neden to eche man if þe word of god schal profite to hym . . . þanne it profitiþ hym not to his saluacion.

Cf. B.L., Royal 17 A. xxvi, arts. 1–7. (e). Jolliffe, G. 11. f. 223v blank.

ff. iii + 223 + iii. 205 × 145 mm. Written space 147 × 96 mm. 26–30 long lines. Collation: 1⁶ 2⁸ 3⁸+1 leaf after 8 (f. 23) 4⁸ 5⁶+1 leaf after 3 (f. 34) 6–20⁸ 21⁶+1 leaf after 3 (f. 162) 22–26⁸ 27⁶+1 leaf after 6 (f. 212) 28⁸ 29⁴ wants 4. Written in a poor textura. Initials 4-line (ff. 7, 24) and 2-line, blue with red ornament. Parchment binding, s. xviii. Secundo folio (f. 8) bi þis.

Written in England. 'Henry FitzSimons', f. 223, s. xvi. Bought for £66 Scots in 1697: see Munimenta Alme Universitatis Glasguensis, iii (1854), 436. F. 6. 22 in the catalogue of 1828 and F. 7.22 in that of 1836. Later BD 1. d. 22 and BE 8. e. 4.

Gen. 235. Juvenalis   s. xv²

Materiam et causas satyrarum hac inspice prima. Iunii iuuenalis aquinatis satyrarum liber primus incipit. Semper ego auditor . . . omne legumen.

XVI precedes XV. In IX. 37 the scribe omitted the Greek words. I–VII are preceded by a line or two of verse in red, not in the main hand, V, for example, by the line 'Quot mala sustineat parasithica uita notabis'.

ff. iii + 76 + iii. 207 × 130 mm. Written space 130 × 73 mm. 26 long lines. Collation: 1–2⁸ 3–8¹⁰. Slightly current humanistic hand. Initials omitted, except the S on f. 1, gold on a ground of colours and gold. A binding of 'diced brown calf', s. xviii (?), like that formerly on MS. Gen. 338, was replaced by a binding by D. Cockerell & Son in 1969.

Written in Italy. F. 8. 23 in the catalogue of 1828 and F. 7.29 in that of 1836. Later BD. 1. f. 12 and BE. 8. e. 17.

Gen. 288. Psalterium, etc.   s. xv med.

1. ff. 1–6v Full calendar in red and black.

Giles, Remigius and Bavo, and Eligius in red (1 Sept., 1 Oct., 1 Dec.).

2. A series of hours, each assigned to a day of the week and followed by its appropriate mass: (a) ff. 8–14v In die dominica: hore de sancta trinitate; (b)

ff. 16–22^v In die lune hore pro fidelibus defunctis; (c) ff. 24–29^v In die martis hore de sancto spiritu; (d) ff. 31–37^v In die mercurii hore de omnibus sanctis; (e) ff. 39–45^v In die iouis hore de sancto sacramento; (f) ff. 46–51^v In die ueneris hore sancte crucis;(g) ff. 52–58^v In die sabbato hore beate marie uirginis.

The hymns of (a–g) are *RH*, nos. 16566, 4335, 12022, 18373, 3936, 14275, 4496; printed in *AH* xxx. 10, 173, 15, 143, 29, 32, 123. Each set of hours ends with a 4-line metrical 'Recommendacio': (a) Has horas sit (sic) uercolo (sic) ut in trinitate . . .; (b) Has horas cristi metricas cum deuocione . . .; (c) Has horas canonicas cum deuocione . . .; (d) Has horas sic recolo cum deuocione . . .; (e) Has horas sic recolo pia racione . . .;(f) Has horas canonicas cum deuocione . . .; (g) Tue matris in honore corde deuoto et ore . . . (a, c, e, f) are *RH*, nos. 37827, 7681, 37826, 7680.

3. ff. 59–60^v Incipit missa de aduentu domini.

4. ff. 61–83^v Incipit officium beate marie uirginis quod dicitur per totum aduentum.

The order is vespers, compline, matins–none. A memoria of All Saints follows each hour.

5. ff. 87–107^v In dedicacione sancti michaelis.

Vespers, matins (nine lessons), and lauds.

6. ff. 108–11 Incipit missa sancti michaelis archangeli. f. 111^v blank.

7. ff. 113–239^v Liturgical psalter.

Vespers begins on a new quire, f. 213.

8. ff. 239^v–250^v Six ferial canticles, Benedicite, Benedictus, Te deum, Magnificat, Nunc dimittis, Quicumque uult.

9. ff. 251–256^v Hic incipiunt letanie sanctorum.

25 martyrs: . . . (7) erasme . . . (25) mauri (sic) cum sociis tuis. 14 confessors: . . . (11–14) ghislene willerme egidi eligi. 19 virgins: . . . (19) rosiana.

10. ff. 257–265^v Incipit psaltherium beati iheronimi doctoris.

The prayer 'Liberator animarum mundi redemptor . . .' follows and ends imperfectly: it is for male use.

11. ff. 267–296^v The Passion according to each of the evangelists, assigned respectively to Palm Sunday, and Tuesday, Wednesday, and Thursday in Holy Week.

ff. iv+296+iii. 221 × 155 mm. Written space 125 × 82 mm. 21 long lines. Collation: 1^6 2–6^8 7^8 wants 8, probably blank, after f. 58 8–10^8 11^8 wants 8, probably blank, after f. 83 12–26^8 27^4+1 leaf after 4 (ff. 207–11) 28–33^8 34^6 wants 6 after f. 265 35–37^8 38 three (ff. 294–6). The collation excludes the eighteen singleton leaves with blank rectos and pictures on the versos: f. 7^v, Trinity, God the Father holding the Cross, on which is the Son; f. 15^v, raising of Lazarus; f. 23^v, Pentecost; f. 30^v, All Saints; f. 38^v, the Host in a golden ciborium, an angel with lighted taper on each side of it; f. 84^v, Michael kills a human-headed monster; ff. 112^v, 131,^{v} 144^v, 156^v, 168^v, 183^v, 197^v, 212^v, before Pss. 1, 26, 38, 52, 68, 80, 96, 109 (Trinity); ff. 266^v, 275^v, 283^v, 291^v, Matthew, Mark, Luke, John writing. Probably arts. 2f, g, 3–5, 10 were illustrated with now missing pictures. Initials: (i) blue or red patterned in white on decorated gold grounds; (ii, iii) 4-line and 2-line, gold on coloured grounds patterned in white; (iv) 1-line, gold with iron-grey ornament, or blue with red ornament, and short sprays into the margin. Line fillers in art. 10 only: blue and gold. Continuous borders on picture pages and on pages with initials of type (i). Capital letters in the ink of the text filled with pale yellow. A red morocco binding by D. Cockerell & Son in 1969 replaces a binding of s. xix with gilt and patterned fore-edges.

Written probably in north-east France. Given by Lord Rosebery in 1918: his book-plate inside the cover. Exhibited at the Royal Academy of Arts Winter Exhibition 1953–4, no. 575 in the catalogue, *Flemish Art 1300–1700*, where it is noted that the style of one of the two artists is near to that of William Vrelant. Formerly BE 9. c. 16.[1]

Gen. 324. *Ambrosius, De officiis* s. xv ex.

Eximii et melliflui doctoris sancti Ambrosii Episcopi de Offitiis liber incipit ad filios. Non arrogans videri arbitror . . . instructionis conferat. Beatus uir qui ista bona . . . et quantum coctidiano dono (*ends imperfectly?*).

The text in *PL* xvi. 25–184 ends *conferat*. The rest, 'Beatus uir . . .', is eight lines on f. 92^v. Bk. 2, f. 45; 3, f. 69^v.

ff. x+92+xiv. Paper. 248 × 175 mm. Written space 177 × 95 mm. 31 long lines. Colla-tion: 1–8^{10} 9^8 10 four. Mainly in one humanistic hand: a second hand begins at f. 88/5. Initials: (i) ff. 1, 45, 69^v, red or blue with ornament of the other colour; (ii) 2-line, red or blue. Binding of s. xix in.

Written in Italy. 'Sum M. Bartholi M', f. 1, s. xvii. F. 6.11 in the catalogue of 1828 and F. 6.5 in the catalogue of 1836. Later BD. 1. c. 12 and BE. 7. b. 13.

Gen. 327. *Lactantius* s. xv[2]

1. ff. 1–265 Firmiani Lactantii diuinarum institutionum liber primus incipit feliciter. Magno et excellenti ingenio uiri . . . a domino consequamur. Firmiani Lactantii institucionum liber septimus et vltimus explicit feliciter.

Clavis, no. 85. The main hand put alternative readings in the margins here and there and marked them 'al'.

2. ff. 265–293^v Firmiani Lactantii tractatus de Ira dei incipit feliciter. Animad-uerti sepe donate . . . mereamur (*sic*) iratum. Firmiani Lactancii tractatus de Ira dei explicit.

Written in thirty-two paragraphs, without headings or numbers. The scribe left blank spaces on ff. 287^v and 288, where passages corresponding to edn. *CSEL* xxvii. 115/19–116/4 and 116/15–117/2 have been left out.

3. ff. 293^v–319^v Incipit tractatus de opificio hominis ab eodem feliciter. Quam minime sim quietus . . . celeste direxerit. Firmiani Lactancii tractatus de opificio hominis explicit feliciter.

Written in thirty-five paragraphs, without headings or numbers.

ff. iii+317+iii, foliated 1–323. The flyleaves are parchment, s. xv (?). 250 × 184 mm. Written space 165 × 110 mm. 27 long lines. Collation of ff. 4–320: 1–24^{12} 25^{10} 26^{12} 27^{10} wants 8–10, probably blank. Written in expert set cursiva. The scribe did not use the last

---

[1] My description, made before the manuscript was rebound, records a now missing pastedown with a note on it about the number of miniatures written in the same hand as the note on the pastedown of Gen. 1111.

(twenty-eighth) ruled line on a page. Initials: (i) gold and blue, with ornament in red and blue-grey; (ii) 2-line, blue with red ornament or red with blue-grey ornament. Line fillers in red and blue. Continuous borders of gold and blue in a strongly marked style on ff. 1, 266, 294. Binding of s. xviii. Secundo folio *prestabilius*.

Written in France. 'Ex libris Ioan. Bapt. Des Marettes' and 'Ex libris adr. L'archevêque medici Rothemag. 1738' inside the cover. Old Glasgow pressmarks 'CL. f. 4 n. 1' and 'Ff. 4. n. 5'. F. 6.9 in the catalogue of 1828 and F. 6.6 in that of 1836. Later BD. 1. c. 17 and BE. 7. b. 16.

Gen. 333. *J. de Fordun, Chronicon, cum continuatione*   s. xv²

Ex variis quippe veterum scripturis . . . (f. 110) ewangelistas approbatur.¹ Hiis sic expeditis . . . (f. 299ᵛ) compilauit vt sequitur. Cest tout.

A history of Scotland to 1436 in eleven books. ff. 2–110 contain an abbreviation of Fordun's history and the passage linking it with the continuation: ed. W. F. Skene (Chronicles of Scotland, i), pp. 4–253, 387–401, xx. The rest is collated as C by F. J. H. Skene, *Liber Pluscardensis* (Chronicles of Scotland, vii), pp. 6–391: he describes it on pp. x, xi, xvi, xvii.

Peculiarities are the omission of edn. 169/28–174/1 on f. 185 and the omission of the verses in the vernacular forming chapters 8 and 11 of bk. 11. ff. 43ᵛ, 51ᵛ, 200ᵛ, 201, 297ᵛ blank.

ff. ii+298+i, foliated i, 1–299, (300). Paper. 261 × 195 mm. Written space c. 190 × 125 mm. Frame ruling in pencil. c. 30 long lines usually, but c. 57 on ff. 44–79. Collation of ff. 2–274: 1¹⁰ 2 thirteen 3⁴ 4¹⁰ 5 five (ff. 39–43) 6–7⁸ (ff. 44–59) 8–9¹⁰ (ff. 60–79) 10¹⁴ 11¹⁴ 12 canc. after f. 104 12–13¹² (ff. 107–30) 14–25¹². The quiring of ff. 275–99 is uncertain. Written in cursiva, mostly by two scribes, (1) ff. 2–6ᵛ, 80–130ᵛ, (2) ff. 7–43, 131–299. Two others, more expert, were responsible for two quires each, (3) ff. 44–59ᵛ, (4) ff. 60–79. Scribe (2) wrote 2-line decorated initials in the ink of the text: elsewhere the spaces left for initials were not filled. Binding of s. xix by Carss, Glasgow. Secundo folio *Deinde est*.

'Iste liber scriptus fuit apud dunfermlin Willelmo Sanctiandr' archiepiscopo (William Schevez, archbishop 1478–97) de mandato dompni Thome monimelle monachi et sacriste eiusdem loci', in hand (2), f. 299ᵛ. 'Scheuez', f. 2. 'Liber Willelmi Gaderar [. . . . .] Anno 154[. . . . .]', f. 2, in purple ink.² 'Guilielmus Hammiltoune est huius libri possessor', f. 299ᵛ: cf. f. 118ᵛ. 'Ex libris Bibliothecæ Vniuersitatis Glasguensis Will Dunlop princ' ' (principal, 1690–1700), f. 3. 'AB f. 4 n. 15', f. 3: under this mark in the shelf catalogue of 1691, no. 15 of shelf (forulus) 4 of case AB. F. 5. 18 in the catalogue of 1828 and F. 6.14 in that of 1836. Later BE. 7. b. 8.

Gen. 334. *Cicero*   s. xv²

Cicero's Orator, Brutus, and De oratore, copied from a manuscript in which the leaves were disarranged. The correct order is given in a note of s. xviii/xix on f. iii, signed 'G.R.'. There are no headings on ff. 1, 27, 63.

1. (*Orator*). ff. 1–1ᵛ col. 2/33 media philosophia; 64 col. 1/14 repetitam—69ᵛ col. 2/3 quam nobis; 8 col. 1/13 faciendorum—27 suscepisse. M. T. Ciceronis de paruo oratore ad B. Liber explicit.

Listed among the *integri non mixti* in Heerdegen's edition of Orator (1884).

---

¹ As Glasgow, Mitchell Library, 308876, q.v. In edn., Skene omitted the thirteen words 'Sicut . . . approbatur' by accident.
² Burgess of Elgin, s. xvi. Cf. J. Durkan and A. Ross, *Early Scottish Libraries*, 1961, pp. 46, 99, 103, 112.

2. (*Brutus*). ff. 27–32 col. 2/37 non loquuntur sed; 97 col. 2/1 est ea laus—102ᵛ col. 2/38 et grecis licteris; 38 col. 2/28 eruditus—48ᵛ col. 1/5 quamquam; 113 col. 1/8 hoc quidem—118ᵛ col. 2/33 hec omnia; 54 col. 2/29 uite decorabat—62ᵛ oportunorum. M. Tullii Ciceronis de claris oratoribus liber Explicit.

3. (*De oratore*). ff. 63–4 col. 1/14 atque ab; 1ᵛ col. 2/33 ditis e—8 col. 1/13 Oratorem; 69ᵛ col. 2/3 autem nisi qui—97 col. 1/38 aliquot horas; 32 col. 2/37 de imperatoris officio—38 col. 2/27 non omnia que; 103 col. 1/1 sunt in natura—113 col. 1/7 lacessiti; 48ᵛ col. 1/5 dicimus—54 col. 2/29 hercule; 118ᵛ col. 2/33 inquit—149ᵛ curamque laxemus. Et sic finis totius libri.

ff. ii+151+ii. 262×186 mm. Written space 168×116 mm. 2 cols. 38 lines. Collation: 1–18⁸ 19⁸ wants 8, blank. Well written in textura. Initials: (i) ff. 1, 27, 63, 89, 127, 7-line, blue on decorated gold or (f. 27 only) pink grounds; (ii) 3-line, as (i). Partial floral borders in gold, gold paint, and colours on pages with initials of type (i). Binding of s. xviii in., uniform with MS. Gen. 216. Secundo folio *id maxime*.

Written in France. On f. 1, lower margin, an angel holds a shield bearing sable a Latin cross or and upon it a crown of thorns. A black and white shield is on f. 149ᵛ: quarterly 1 and 4 argent a lion rampant sable, 2 and 3 checky argent and sable: a crozier behind the shield. 'quatre vingt sous', f. 1. Belonged to Count Hoym, whose arms are on the binding: cf. MSS. Gen. 212, 216. Old Glasgow pressmarks CL. f. 4. n. 8 and Ff. 4. n. 6. Later F. 6.8 (in 1828), F. 6.16 (in 1836), BD. 1. c. 14 and BE. 7. b. 9.

Gen. 335. '*Abstraccio super octo libros phisicorum*', etc. s. xv ex.

1. ff. 1–54 Incipit compendiosa abstraccio super octo libros phisicorum aristotilis. Prologus. Quoniam liber phisicorum aristotilis ad sciencie naturalis cognicionem tendenti ceteris est vtilior . . . habens magnitudinem. Et sic terminat philosophus communem consideracionem de rebus naturalibus in primo principio tocius nature. qui est super omnia deus benedictus in secula. amen. Deo gracias. Explicit compendiosa abstraccio super octo libros phisicorum Aristotilis.

2. ff. 54ᵛ–89ᵛ Incipit compendiosa abstraccio super tres libros de anima. Prologus. Quoniam post librum phisicorum . . . vel amarum. Et sic finis. Deo gracias.

3. ff. 90–5 Tunc vnumquodque arbitramur cognoscere cum causas cognoscimus . . . per modum recipientis.

Notes and definitions.

4. ff. 95–102ᵛ Deus enim et natura nichil operantur frustra . . . generari et eleuari. Et sic patent soluciones 16 questionum.

Sixteen questions 'De causis naturalibus', attributed to Richard Lavenham, Ord. Carm. (Emden, *BRUO*, p. 1109). B.L., Royal 12 E. xvi, art. 3, and Sloane 3899 are other copies.

ff. ii+103+iii. End-leaves of thick parchment: ff. i, 106 were pastedowns. 173×107 mm. Written space 98×65 mm. 26 long lines. Collation: 1–12⁸ 13⁸ wants 7, probably blank. Written in a small textura. Initials: (i) f. 1, gold paint and green on a blue ground patterned in white; (ii) gold with blue-grey ornament; (iii) 2-line, blue or red. Contemporary binding of wooden boards covered with brown leather bearing small stamps of three patterns, two of them apparently nos. 10 and 21 in S. Gibson, *Early Oxford Bindings*, and the third like, but larger than, Gibson, no. 6. Four small bosses on each cover. Secundo folio *non sit*.

Written in England. 'Liber Monasterii Radingensis' in a humanistic hand, s. xvi in., on a scroll at the top of f. 1. 'John Palmer', f. 104ᵛ, s. xvi. The relevant slip from a nineteenth-century sale catalogue is pasted inside the cover. Acquired in 1870. Formerly BD. 1. i. 8 and BE. 7. e. 24.

Gen. 336. *Statuta Angliae* s. xiv[1]

A pocket copy.

1. ff. 1ᵛ–9 Kalendar' statutorum et cartarum.

Lists arts. 2–24 and provides tables of chapters of arts. 2–6, 8–9.

2. ff. 10–20ᵛ 'Henricus dei gracia . . . Dat' per manum venerabilis patris domini R. Dunelmensis Episcopi Cancellarii nostri apud sanctum Paulum', 6 Nov. 1217.

On this version of Magna Carta see H. J. Lawlor in *EHR* xxii. 514–18.

3. ff. 20ᵛ–26 Incipit carta de Foresta. Henricus dei gracia . . . Dated 6 Nov. 1217.

4. ff. 26–32 Incipit prouis' de Merton'. *SR* i. 1.

5. ff. 32–49 Incipiunt statuta Marleberg'. *SR* i. 19.

6. ff. 49–82ᵛ Incipiunt Stat' Westm' primum. In French. *SR* i. 26.

7. ff. 82ᵛ–84ᵛ Incipit statutum Religiosorum. *SR* i. 51.

8. ff. 84ᵛ–95 Incipiunt statuta Gloucestr'. In French. *SR* i. 45.

9. ff. 95–161ᵛ Incipit Westm' secundum. *SR* i. 71.

10. ff. 161ᵛ–164 Incipit statutum de transgr'. In French. *SR* i. 44.

11. ff. 164–6 Incipit statutum de militibus. *SR* i. 229.

12. ff. 166–172ᵛ Incipit statutum Winton'. In French. *SR* i. 96.

13. ff. 172ᵛ–174ᵛ Incipit Westm' tercium. Quia emptores . . . *SR* i. 106.

14. ff. 174ᵛ–181ᵛ Incip' statut' de mercatoribus. In French. *SR* i. 98.

15. ff. 181ᵛ–182ᵛ Incipit prouisio de anno bissextili. *SR* i. 7.

16. ff. 182ᵛ–185ᵛ Incipit statutum de quo warranto. Rex vic' salutem. Cum in vltimo parliamento nostro . . . et secundum inquisicionem inde factam. Cf. *MMBL* i. 187.

17. ff. 186–193ᵛ Incipiunt statuta de scaccario. In French. *SR* i. 197.

18. ff. 193ᵛ–195 Incipiunt Dies communes in banco. *SR* i. 208.

19. ff. 195–6 Incipit calumpnia esson'. *SR* i. 217.

20. ff. 196–198ᵛ Incipit visus franc' pleg'. Hec capitula debent inquiri . . . bis per annum In festo sancti Mich' et Pasch'. Et debet eciam primus Iuratus iurare quod verum dicet . . . (1) Si omnes liberi tenentes venerunt sicut sumoniti sunt . . . (31) Si uigilie fuerunt seruate secundum quod prouisum erat in regno per totum. Hec autem capitula debent inquiri pro pace . . . et thesaurus inuentus. Thirty-one heads. Cf. *SR* i. 246 (in French).

21. f. 199 Incipit composicio mensurarum. Per discrecionem tocius regni Anglie . . . partem quarterii. Cf. *MMBL* i. 252 and *SR* i. 204.

22. ff. 199–201 Incipit Assisa panis et Ceruis'. *SR* i. 199.

23. ff. 201ᵛ–204 Incipit extenta manerii fac'. *SR* i. 242.

24. ff. 204–5 Incipit modus faciendi homagium. In French. *SR* i. 227.

Arts. 25–8 were added in s. xiv¹.

25. ff. 205ᵛ–207ᵛ Articuli de iudicio pillorie. Si pistor . . . *SR* i. 201.

26. ff. 207ᵛ–209ᵛ Iudicium pillorie. Pistor non debet . . . deliberetur.

27. ff. 209ᵛ–210ᵛ Statutum de Champatoribus. In French and Latin. *SR* i. 216.

28. ff. 210ᵛ–213 Statutum de coniuncto feoffamento super cartas. *SR* i. 145.

29 (added in s. xiv). ff. 213ᵛ–214ᵛ Statutum London et aliarum Ciuitatum. Acorde est et assenti que tote manere draps vendable . . . (*ends imperfectly*). *SR* i. 314 (25 Edward III). The writing has faded.

30 (added in s. xv²). f. ivᵛ Wil con. Wil rufus . . . Four verses on the kings of England, ending with Edward IV. Walther, no. 20887.

ff. vi+214+iii. ff. ii–vi, 215–16 are medieval end-leaves: ii, 216 were pastedowns in a former binding. 105×70 mm. Written space 72×40 mm. 20 long lines. Collation: 1⁸+1 leaf after 8 2¹⁰ 3¹² 4¹⁰ 5–14¹² 15¹⁰ 16–17¹² 18⁸ 19⁸+3 leaves after 8 (ff. 212–14). Written in anglicana. A full-page, 72×42 mm, picture of the Crucifixion on f. 9ᵛ. Initials: (i) pink or blue on decorated gold grounds, with prolongations into the margins which contain some animals and birds: the *H* on f. 10 has the seated figure of a king in it; (ii) 2-line, blue with red ornament and bars of red and blue running the height of the written space. A brown morocco binding by D. Cockerell & Son, 1965, replaces a binding of s. xix. Secundo folio (f. 11) *nostrorum*.

Written in England. 'Peter Bales', f. iii, s. xvi/xvii, followed by a note in pencil suggesting that this is the hand of 'Peter Bales the English Writing master' (1547–1610?). 'Bibliothecæ Universitatis Glasguensis dono dedit Æneas Macleod Armig. de Cadbole MDCC-LXXXVI', f. iiᵛ. F. 8.38 in the catalogue of 1828 and F. 10.1 in that of 1836. Later BD. 1. i. 19 and BE. 7. g. 4.

Gen. 337. *Boethius, De consolatione philosophiae*   s. xv²

Anitii Mallii Seuerini Boeti . . . phylosophicæ consolationis liber primus incipit. Carmina qui quondam . . . cunta cernentis. Deo gratias amen. Explicit liber Boetii de consolatione phylosophica. deo gratias. amen. f. 56ᵛ blank.

ff. iii+56+iii. Medieval foliation in the lower right corner of rectos. 215×145 mm. Written space 142×95 mm. 25 long lines. Collation: 1–7⁸. Humanistic hand, except for long-tailed *r*: the final round *s* falling far below the line is conspicuous. Initials: (i) f. 1, 9-line, blue patterned in white, with red and blue ornament; (ii) 2-line, blue with red ornament or red with yellow-brown ornament; (iii) 1-line, red. Binding by D. Cockerell & Son in 1970, replacing a 'red-brown diced sheep' binding of s. xix. Secundo folio *verum dulcibus*.

Written in Spain(?). F. 8.19 in the catalogue of 1828 and F. 7.11 in that of 1836. Later BD. 1. d. 19 and BE. 8. d. 25.

Gen. 338. *Lactantius*   1444

1. ff. 3–42 Lactantii firmiani de ira dei ad donatum incipit. Animaduerti sepe donate . . . uereamur iratum. Explicit dei (*sic*) ira dei.

Cf. Gen. 327. Twenty-two numbered chapters. f. 42ᵛ blank.

2. ff. 43–80ᵛ Lactantii firmiani de opificio dei. siue formatione hominis ad demetrianum incipit. Quam minime sim quietus . . . celeste direxerit. Finis. Finiui Basilee vi kl' Maii MCCCC xl iiiiᵒ.

Twenty-one numbered chapters.

3. ff. 80ᵛ–82 (*a*) Augustinus. De his libris dici potest . . . ueritatis astipulantur. (*b*) Idem. Nimis peruerse se ipsum . . . non fuisse. (*c*) Idem. Lactantius quasi quidam fluuius . . . destruxit. (*d*) Idem. Lactantium propter eruditionem . . . excerptum reperies. (*e*) Idem. Firmianus qui est Lactantius Arnobii discipulus . . . a patre interfectus est.

Cf. B.L., Royal 6 A. xv, art. 6. (*e*) is Jerome, De viris illustribus, ch. 80. f. 82ᵛ blank.

ff. iii+80+i, foliated i, 1–82, (83). ff. 1, 2 are medieval flyleaves. 182×126 mm. Written space 120×75 mm. 25 long lines. Collation of ff. 3–82: 1–8¹⁰. Humanistic script. Initials: (i) ff. 3, 43, gold on purple, green, and blue grounds, patterned in white; (ii) red, set in the margins. Capital letters in the ink of the text touched with yellow. A binding of 1970 by D. Cockerell & Son replaces a binding of s. xix: ff. 1, 82 bear marks of the bosses of a medieval (?) binding. Secundo folio *esset omnium*.

Written at Basel in 1444. Script and decoration are Italian in style. The book-plate of 'Nicholaus de la Place Sancto Stephaniˢ Abbas', s. xviii, with arms, azure three mullets or, and a crozier behind the shield, is now pasted inside the cover, but was formerly on f. 2ᵛ: for it see R. H. Rolland's *Supplément* to Rietstap, *Armorial Général*, ii. 345. F. 6. 29 in the catalogue of 1828 and F. 9.42 in the catalogue of 1836. Later BD. 1. h. 1 and BE. 7. e. 22.

Gen. 339. *Summa Reymundi, etc.*   s. xiii med.

1. ff. 10–40 Quoniam in foro penitenciali . . . a communi stipite toto gradu inter se Iohannes.

The Summa de Matrimonio which commonly goes with art. 4. On f. 40ᵛ God the Father, two men, and two women support a table of consanguinity.

2. ff. 41ᵛ–42 Coloured diagrams of vices facing virtues. f. 41ʳ was left blank.

3. ff. 43–51 . . . Expliciunt omnes tituli summe remundi et matrimonii.

A table of chapters of arts. 1 and 4. ff. 51ᵛ–52ᵛ were left blank.

4. ff. 53–278 Incipit summa de penitencia. Quoniam ut ait ieronimus . . .
Venite benedicti percipite regnum. amen.

Reimundus de Peniaforti, †1275, Summa de poenitentia, in three books. Printed very often.

5. ff. 278–88 Conuertimini ad me . . . Non est mirum fratres si seruus rogat
dominum . . . conseruet uestimenta sua ne nudus ambulet.

The 'utilis tractatus de confessione', B.L., Royal 8 F. vii, art. 6, ends differently.

6. f. 288 Audiens sapiens sapientior erit . . . non acquiescas eis. Five lines.

A preliminary quire and blank spaces of quires 5–7, 30 contain additions of
s. xiii, mainly in one hand.

7. ff. 2–6ᵛ Aspiciebam et ecce . . . concrepantes. Que est ista etc. Explicit.

An explanation of the 'Arbor amoris' which fills f. 7.

8. f. 8ʳᵛ [A]ffinitas est propinquitas . . . in sponsa de futuro. Iohannes.

An explanation of the diagram of the degrees of consanguinity on f. 7ᵛ.

9. ff. 8ᵛ–9ᵛ A table of tituli of bks. 1–4 of the Decretals of Gregory IX.

10. (a) f. 40 Veni creator spiritus et in me robur insere . . . (b) f. 41 Planctus
ante nescia . . . (c) f. 42ᵛ Prayers. (d) f. 42ᵛ Nititur ignotum mea mens expellere
uotum . . .

(a, b, d). RH, nos. 21198, 14950, 11981.

11. (a) f. 51ʳᵛ Isti sunt casus quos ad episcopum debes mittere . . . (b) f. 52ʳᵛ
Nota si aliqua negligencia fit de sacramento circa altare quomodo satisfaciendam
. . .: seven paragraphs.

12. ff. 288ᵛ–290 Theological notes, now rubbed and torn. ff. 290–1 may be a
cancelled sheet of art. 1 or art. 3: the original text has been erased.

ff. i+290, foliated 1–291. f. 1 is a medieval flyleaf. 105 × 72 mm. Written space 80 × 45
mm. 30–3 long lines. Writing above top ruled line, except on ff. 15–40. Collation of
ff. 2–291: 1–2⁸ 3¹⁰ 4⁸ 5⁴+1 leaf after 4 (f. 40) 6² (ff. 41–2) 7¹⁰ 8¹² 9⁸ 10–25¹⁰ 26–28¹² 29¹⁴+1
leaf after 14 (f. 283) 30 eight. A small clear hand. Initials: (i) red and blue with ornament
of both colours; (ii) 2-line, red, with ornament in blue or red. Capital letters in the ink
of the text are stroked with red. Binding of wooden boards covered with pink leather,
probably Germanic and fifteenth-century: metal clasp: five small bosses on each cover.
Written probably in France. Formerly BE. 7. g. 5.

Gen. 482. *Horae*   s. xv med.

A mutilated book of hours which once probably had all the pieces normally
found in books of hours produced abroad for the English (and Scotch?) market:
arts. 1–3, 9 in Edinburgh University 303, (q.v.), are missing here and arts. 1–11
here correspond to arts. 4–8, 10–15 there. Most pieces are imperfect, leaves
having been cut out before ff. 1, 2, 5, 11, 13, 14, 15, 16, 17, 19, 21, 23, 26, 27, 32,
34, 45 and after f. 45.

1. f. 1ʳᵛ Memoriae of Anne (Gaude felix anna que concepisti . . .) and Mary Magdalene (Gaude pia magdalena spes salutis . . .).

RH, nos. 6773, 6895.

2. ff. 2–18ᵛ Hours of B.V.M. of the use of (Sarum), with hours of the Cross worked in. Memoriae after lauds of Holy Spirit, Holy Trinity, Holy Cross, Michael, John Baptist, Peter and Paul, Andrew, Laurence, Stephen, Thomas of Canterbury (Tu per thome sanguinem . . .), Nicholas, Mary Magdalene, Katherine, Margaret, All Saints, and for peace.

3. ff. 19–20ᵛ Salve regina, farced with Salve virgo virginum. *RH*, no. 18318.

4. f. 21ʳᵛ O intemerata . . . Masculine forms.

5. ff. 21ᵛ–22ᵛ Oratio deuota. Obsecro te . . . Masculine forms.

6. ff. 23–4 Omnibus consideratis . . .

AH xxxi. 87–9. *RH*, no. 14081 (etc.).

7. (*a*) ff. 24–25 Oratio uenerabilis bede presbiteri de septem uerbis . . . preparatam. Oratio. Domine ihesu criste qui septem uerba . . . (*b*) f. 25ʳᵛ Oratio bona. Precor te piissime domine ihesu criste propter illam caritatem . . .

8. f. 25ᵛ (*a*) Oratio. Aue domine ihesu criste uerbum patris . . . (*b*) Oratio. Aue uerum corpus domini nostri ihesu cristi . . . (*c*) Oratio. Aue caro cristi cara . . .

(*a*). Five aves. (*b*). Cf. *RH*, no. 2175. (*c*). *RH*, no. 1710.

9. ff. 27–33ᵛ Penitential psalms, (f. 30ᵛ) gradual psalms, headed 'Incipiunt quindecim psalmi' (cues only of the first twelve), and (f. 31ᵛ) litany.

10. ff. 34–44 Office of the dead.

11. f. 45ʳᵛ Commendatory psalms.

12 (added, s. xvi in.). f. 26 (*begins imperfectly*) Rorans ymber meritum hora vespertina . . . Salua nos et libera mortis in agone. Ora pro nobis et cetera. Deus qui populos pictorum et britonum (*ends abruptly*).

Vespers and compline of hours of St. Ninian. In Edinburgh, Univ. Libr. 42 these hours (beginning 'Niniane presul hora matutina . . .': not in *RH*) are on ff. 73–5 and the prayer 'Deus qui . . .' on f. 35ᵛ.[1]

13 (added by 'Georg Sinclar', s. xvii). (*a*) f. 15ᵛ Com loue let us walk in younder Spreing . . . this to my loue content will bring (6 lines of verse). (*b*) f. 26ᵛ In the begening of this year in breaten shal great things apear . . . (10 lines of verse).

ff. ii+45+ii. 209 × 147 mm. Written space 127 × 80 mm. 23 long lines. Ruling with violet ink. 2 and 6, 3 and 5, 8 and 13, 10 and 12, and 34 and 35 are the only remaining bifolia. Well written. Pictures removed, no doubt. Initials: (i) removed, (ii) 2-line, gold on red and blue grounds, patterned in white; (iii) 1-line, blue with red ornament, or gold with blue-grey ornament. Capital letters in the ink of the text are touched with red. A binding of 1971 by Ernest Riley replaces one of s. xix by Carss, Glasgow.

[1] I owe the reference to Monsignor David McRoberts.

Written in the Netherlands. In Scotland by s. xvi in. 'Georg Sinclar', ff. 15ᵛ, 26ᵛ, 38ᵛ, s. xvii: he wrote art. 13. 'Robertus Cleland est huius libri possessor 1681', f. 12ᵛ. 'James Graham Writer', f. 13ᵛ. Old Glasgow pressmark 'Append. AT. 5. 2', f. 1. F. 8. 17 in the catalogue of 1828 and F. 7. 28 in the catalogue of 1836. Later BD. 1. f. 31 and BE. 8. e. 10.

Gen. 999. *Graduale romanum (fragm.)* s. XV

Parts of the offices for Palm Sunday and the following week.

The text agrees closely with that indicated in *SMRL* ii. 234/9–235/7 (f. 1ʳᵛ), 236/8–9 (f. 2ʳᵛ), 237, Feria 2/5—Feria 3/9 (ff. 4–6ᵛ), 237, Feria 4/2–11 (ff. 7–8ᵛ), 238, Feria 4/16—239/29 (ff. 9–10ᵛ, 3ʳᵛ). f. 3 should follow f. 10.

ff. i+10+i. A medieval foliation in red, except on f. 3, cxxxiii, cxxxviii, cxli–cxliii, cxlv, cxlvi, cxlviii, cxlix. 540 × 390 mm. Written space 415 × 270 mm. 7 long lines and music. Collation: 1 two (ff. 1, 2, bifolium) 2¹⁰ wants 4 and 7 (ff. 4–10, 3). A picture of Christ's entry into Jerusalem in the lower margin of f. 1, partly cut off by the binder. Initials red or blue with ornament of the other colour. Cadels lined with green or pale yellow. Capital letters in the ink of the text filled with pale yellow. Binding of s. xx.

Written in Italy (?). 'Miss Cooper with W.(?) Booth's Compliments', f. 2ᵛ.

Gen. 1053. *Processus Scotiae (in Latin and French)* s. XIV/XV

Documents about the 'Great Cause' of Scotland described by E. L. G. Stones, 'The Records of the Great Cause', *Scottish Historical Review*, xxxv (1956), pp. 89–109, where its relation to the missing leaves of the exchequer register Liber A is discussed (p. 99).[1]

'It seems highly probable that this manuscript, together with British Museum manuscript Cotton Vitellius E. xi, ff. 178–255, was compiled by the royal clerks, early in the reign of Henry IV, when Henry was reasserting the English claim to the suzerainty of Scotland'. Stones printed (pp. 108–9) the reply of the Scots to Edward's demand for recognition found here on f. 5ʳᵛ. f. 27ᵛ blank.

ff. iii+27+ii. 358 × 250 mm. Written space c. 255 × 150 mm. c. 40 long lines. Frame ruling. Collation: 1–3⁸ 4 three (ff. 25–7). Written in expert small secretary and (ff. 9–14ᵛ and marginalia on ff. 1–6ᵛ) in anglicana of a rather legal sort: the two hands are probably contemporary. No coloured initials. Bound in 'Hermitage Calf' by D. Cockerell and Son in 1955: previously in 'parchment over handmade blackboard'. Secundo folio *Anno domini*.

Written in England. Perhaps part of a larger book, excerpted because of its Scotch interest. 'Marie R', f. 1, is taken to be the signature of Mary of Guise, 1515–60, queen of James V of Scotland. Belonged probably to William Cecil, Lord Burghley (1520–98): lot 11 of the Latin manuscripts in the (Cecil) sale, 21 Nov. 1687, to Anthony, Earl of Kent (1645–1702). Listed when at Wrest Park, Bedfordshire, in *CMA*, II. i. 391, item 5, and catalogued when there in HMC, *Second Report* (1874), Appendix, p. 5, no. 8. Wrest Park Sale at Sotheby's, 21 June 1922, lot 629, to Oppenheim (£3. 10s.). Bought soon afterwards by Charles R. Cowie (1851–1923), Woodend House, Partickhill, Glasgow: cf. *Glasgow Herald*, 30 Sept. 1922, p. 6, and *Burns Chronicle*, xxiii. 110. Belonged to his son, John

---

[1] A detailed account of the contents of MS. Gen. 1053 is in Professor Stones's forthcoming volume on the Great Cause. A reduced facsimile of the upper part of f. 1 accompanies his note on the manuscript in *The College Courant*, xi (1958), no. 21.

Cowie (†1963) in 1930, as appears from the description in MS. Gen. 1054 made by Dr. D. W. Hunter Marshall. Formerly BE. 10. y. 3.

Gen. 1060. *Biblia, pars prima*   s. xv med.

The first volume of a large Bible, Genesis–Ecclesiasticus, with the usual books, including the Prayer of Manasses, and in the usual order.[1]

Ecclesiasticus ends imperfectly at 'deprecabitur. Si enim' (39: 8). Psalms are numbered in the main hand, i–clxxi, the twenty-two divisions of Ps. 118 being taken into account. The prologues are sixteen of the usual set[1] and four others, shown here by *: Stegmüller, nos. 284, 285, 311, 323, 328 ('Tantus et talis est liber iste . . . euangelii questiones. Sed' precedes the normal opening 'si septuaginta'), 327 (as a second prologue to 1 Chronicles: 2 Chronicles has no prologue), 330, 332, 335, 341+343, 357, 344, 349*, 430*, 457, 456*, 455*, 462, 468.

ff. i+278+iii. 430×305 mm. Written space 270×177 mm. 2 cols. 50 lines. Ruling in red ink. Collation: 1–27¹⁰ 28⁸. Well written. Jerome's general preface, Genesis, Exodus, and Leviticus have large (*c.* 15-line) historiated initials and full borders, pictorial, except to the preface (ff. 1, 4, 23ᵛ, 39). Decoration on the same elaborate scale was begun on ff. 50, 65, 199ᵛ, 211, 222 (Numbers, Deuteronomy, Judith, Job, Psalms), but was not completed. Elsewhere the spaces for larger and smaller (3-line) initials remain blank. No running titles. Binding by D. Cockerell & Son, 1962, replacing a binding of s. xix. Secundo folio *die putant.*

Written in Italy. An armorial shield, nebule sable and argent (Fregosi of Genoa), is in the lower border on f. 1. It stands on a wolf and below a pair of compasses. Armorial bookplate of John Callander of Craigforth, Advocate, s. xviii. Presumably F. 1.18 in the catalogue of 1828. Old pressmarks are O. 3.11 and BD. 19. c. 9.

Gen. 1111. *J. de Voragine, Legenda sanctorum, cum supplemento*   s. xv²

1. (*a*) ff. 1–4 Tabula ad inueniendum omnes legendas sanctorum que in isto uolumine continentur. (*b*) ff. 4–5ᵛ Tractatus de perfectione penitencie. In per fectione penitencie tria obseruanda sunt . . . et ad ruinam tocius operis.

(*a*). An alphabetical table of the 254 pieces in arts. 2, 3, with references in red to the leaf numbers of this manuscript.

2. ff. 6–268ᵛ In nomine domini nostri ihesu cristi feliciter amen. Incipit prologus super legendam auream scilicet legendas et flores sanctorum. Quas compilauit frater iacobus natione ianuensis. ceterique doctores. Uniuersum tempus presentis uite . . .

Parts 1–4 begin at Advent, Christmas, Septuagesima, and Easter respectively: ff. 6ᵛ, 22, 52ᵛ, 76. Part 5 runs from Urban, 25 May, who here follows Petronilla, f. 100ᵛ. Four missing leaves contained lives of Gordianus and Remigius—as appears from art. 1*a*— and parts of nos. 58, 59, 70, 73, 145, 146 of the pieces in Graesse's edition (1890) derived from the Basel (M. Wenssler) edition printed in or before 1474. This manuscript lacks also Graesse's nos. 48,[2] 52, 64, 95,[3] 138,[2] and 168[3].

---

[1] See Bristol Public Library, 15.
[2] See art. 3, nos. 13 and 21.
[3] See below Praxedis and Elizabeth.

Eighty-two of the pieces printed by Graesse are preceded here by a picture: Advent (Christ as judge), Andrew, Nicholas, Ambrose, Lucy, Thomas apostle, Christmas, Stephen, John Evangelist, Innocents, Thomas of Canterbury, Silvester, Circumcision, Epiphany, Paul, Anthony hermit, Sebastian, Agnes, Vincent, Conversion of Paul, Julian hospitaller, Purification of B.V.M., Blaise, Agatha, Chair of Peter, Matthias, Gregory, Benedict, Annunciation of B.V.M., Passion of Christ, Resurrection of Christ, Secundus, George, Mary of Egypt, Peter Martyr, Philip, James the less, Invention of Cross, John Evangelist, De letaniis maioribus et minoribus (Clergy in procession), Barnabas, John Baptist, Peter, Paul, Margaret, Alexius, Mary Magdalene, Christina, James, Christopher, Seven Sleepers, Martha, Chains of Peter, Dominic, Laurence, Assumption of B.V.M., Bernard, Bartholomew, Augustine, Decollation of John Baptist, Giles, Nativity of B.V.M., Adrian, Matthew, Maurice, Justina, Cosmas and Damianus, Michael, Francis, Denis, Leonard, Luke, 11,000 Virgins, Simon and Jude, Eustace, De commemoratione defunctorum, Martin, Cecilia, Clement, Katherine, James intercisus, Barlaam and Josaphat. Probably the missing leaves had pictures of Mark, Ascension of Christ, Holy Spirit, and Remigius.

Between Advent and De dedicatione ecclesiae seventeen pieces are not among those printed by Graesse.

f. 11^v, after edn., no. 2. Barbara. *Inc.* Regnante maximiano imperatore, as *BHL*, no. 915.

f. 49^v, in addition to the five pieces forming edn., no. 30. (1) Julian and Basilissa. *Inc.* Iulianus apud Antiochiam nobili fuit ortus. (2) Julian of Le Mans. *Inc.* Iulianus fuit alius Romane urbis ex magna progenie.

f. 54^v, after edn., no. 35. Bridget. *Inc.* Brigida virgo beata in scotia.

f. 64, after edn., no. 45. Anastasius. *Inc.* Anastasius de quadam persidis regione.

f. 72^v, after edn., no. 51. Quadraginta milites. *Inc.* Quidam milites tempore lumii (*sic*) regis.

f. 89, after edn., no. 63. Basilides. *Inc.* Cum paganorum persecutio famulos, as *BHL*, no. 1018.

f. 119, instead of edn., no. 95. Praxedis. *Inc.* Praxedis et potentiana virgines.

Six pieces after edn., no. 172:

f. 225^v *Eligius*.[1] *Inc.* Eligius lemouecas galliarum urbe . . . expirauit.

f. 230^v Victoria. *Inc.* Victoria sub persecutione decii.

f. 231 *Nichasius*. *Inc.* Post constantini cesaris augusti regenerationem.

f. 232^v Affra. *Inc.* Apud prouinciam retia in ciuitate augusta.

f. 233 Pantaleon. *Inc.* Pantaleon filius eustorgii senatoris defuncta.

f. 233^v Evaristus. *Inc.* Euaristus natione grecus.

f. 237^v, after edn., no. 179. *Louis*, bishop. *Inc.* Ludouicus fidelis cristi famulus humilisque, as *BHL*, no. 5055.

f. 257^v, instead of edn., no. 168. *Elizabeth of Hungary*. *Inc.* Elizabeth filia regis vngarorum in palatio et in purpura, as *BHL*, no. 2510a.

f. 263, after Elizabeth. Clare. *Inc.* Clara uirgo beata claris orta natalibus.

3. ff. 268^v–374^v Fifty-one lives of saints in no order, a continuation of art. 2, without break. The longest pieces are nos. 14, 32, 40, 41, 47, 50.

1. f. 268^v Isidore. *Inc.* Ysidorus natione carthaginensis filius seueriani.

2. f. 270^v Leander. *Inc.* Leander beatissimus duce seueriano patre.

3. f. 271^v Hildefonsus. *Inc.* Illefonsus ex hyspania. ciuitate toletana, as *BHL*, no. 3921.

4. f. 272^v Dominic of Silos. *Inc.* Dominicus ex patre nobili ac religioso, as *BHL*, no. 3921.

[1] Here and in art. 3 italics show that a piece is preceded by a picture.

5. f. 273ᵛ Facundus and Primitivus. *Inc.* Tempore Marchi et Antonii imperatorum preses: cf. *BHL*, no. 2821.

6. f. 274 Felix of Scillis. *Inc.* Felix de Scillitana ciuitate oriundus fuit.

7. f. 275 Narcissus. *Inc.* Sicut affrica direxit ad nos beatum felicem. Ita alamania.

8. f. 276ᵛ Columba, virgin. *Inc.* Crudelis aurelianus imperator de partibus.

9. f. 277 Fronto. *Inc.* Fronto ex partibus petragoricensibus extitit oriundus. Hunc mater eius.

10. f. 278ᵛ Emeterius and Celidonius. *Inc.* Emeterius et Celidonius apud legionensem urbem.

11. f. 279 Zoilus. *Inc.* Zoylus autem ex parentibus clarissimis cordube.

12. f. 279ᵛ *Lazarus. Inc.* Lazarus in terra iudee oriundus nobilibus.

13. f. 281 John Chrysostom. *Inc.* Iohannes cognomento crisostomus antiochenus filius secundi. As *Legenda Sanctorum*, ed. Graesse, no. 138.

14. f. 283ᵛ *Thomas Aquinas. Inc.* Thomas de aquino ordinis predicatorum doctor egregius. nobilibus ortus. Cf. *BHL*, nos. 8155, 8157–8.

15. f. 295ᵛ *Alban* of Hungary, king and martyr. *Inc.* Erat olim in partibus aquilonis homo, as *BHL*, no. 201.

16. f. 298ᵛ Augustine of England. *Inc.* Augustinus tempore mauricii augusti missus est.

17. f. 299 Boniface. *Inc.* Postquam gens anglorum inclita, as *BHL*, no. 1404.

18. f. 300ᵛ Richarius. *Inc.* Temporibus gloriosissimi regis francorum Dagoberti, as *BHL*, no. 7224.

19. f. 302ᵛ Medardus. *Inc.* Medardi sancti pater de forti francorum genere.

20. f. 304 Germanus. *Inc.* Germanus parisiorum pontifex territorii augustidunensis, as *BHL*, no. 3468.

21. f. 304ᵛ 'De sanctis Spe. Fide. et Caritate sororibus. et matre earum Sapientia'. *Inc.* Mulier quedam nomine sapientia, as *BHL*, no. 2970.

22. f. 306ᵛ Servatius. *Inc.* Seruatius regimen tenebat episcopalis cathedre . . . urbis tungrensis.

23. f. 307ᵛ Quiriacus. *Inc.* Post uenerabilis constantini finem, as *BHL*, no. 7023.

24. f. 309 Amalberga. *Inc.* Amalberga virgo cristi gloriosissima huius uite.

25. f. 311 *Walburga. Inc.* Postquam deo cara anglorum natio, as *BHL*, no. 8766.

26. f. 314 Agapitus. *Inc.* Agapitus puer sub rege antiocho pagano, as *BHL*, no. 125.

27. f. 315ᵛ Magnus. *Inc.* Magnus cum fuisset unicus parentibus suis in partibus apulie: cf. *BHL*, no. 5169.

28. f. 317 Omer. *Inc.* Audomarus pontifex ex nobilibus et inclitis, as *BHL*, no. 768.

29. f. 319 Bertin. *Inc.* Bertinus abbas post beati audomari obitum multis.

30. f. 320 Firminus. *Inc.* Temporibus priscis quibus fides cristiana, as *BHL*, no. 3003.

31. f. 323 *Bavo. Inc.* Bauo genere nobili. parentibus inclitis hasbalniense editus.

32. f. 325ᵛ Martial. *Inc.* Predicante domino nostro ihesu cristo apud iudeam, as *BHL*, no. 5552.

33. f. 334ᵛ Benedicta. *Inc.* Benedicta uirgo nobili ex prosapia religione.

34. f. 337 Justa and Rufina. *Inc.* Iusta et Ruffina sexu fragiles humiles, as *BHL*, no. 2569.

35. f. 337 Leocadia. *Inc.* Leocadia uirgo deo dedicata. toleti incola.

36. f. 337 Eulalia of Merida. *Inc.* Eulalia uirgo beatissima filia liberii.

37. f. 337ᵛ Eulalia of Barcelona. *Inc.* Eulalia genere nobili ciuis barchinonensis.

38. f. 338 Mammes. *Inc.* Mames puer annorum duodecim in cesarea.

39. f. 338 Aemilianus cucullatus. *Inc.* Emilianus pastor ouium portans secum cytharam.

40. f. 338ᵛ *Nicholas of Tolentino, O.E.S.A. Inc.* Ethimologia nominis. Nicholaus dicitur a nychos . . . Gloriosus deus in sanctis suis qui suos ad gloriam, as *BHL*, no. 6232.

41. f. 347 *Livinus.* *Inc.* Tempore igitur quo colomagnus inclitus rex scotorum, as *BHL*, no. 4960.

42. f. 352 Maurus. *Inc.* Maurus clarissimo senatoris genere patre euticio: cf. *BHL*, no. 5773.

43. f. 354ᵛ *Donatian.* *Inc.* Temporibus aurelii principis qui post augustum, as *BHL*, no. 2282.

44. f. 358 Alban of England. *Inc.* Albanus de britannia anno domini cc° lxxx° vi° adhuc paganus, as *BHL*, no. 210.

45. f. 358 *Victor.* *Inc.* Maximianus imperator cum uenisset ad urbem massiliam.

46. f. 358ᵛ Tecla. *Inc.* Cum paulus apostolus de antyochia yconium uenisset.

47. f. 359ᵛ *Anthony of Padua.* *Inc.* Est namque in regno portugalie ciuitas quedam, as *BHL*, no. 589.

48. f. 367ᵛ Romanus. *Inc.* Romanus monachus antiochie primus et nobilis.

49. f. 367ᵛ Felix and Fortunatus. *Inc.* Felicis ac fortunati martirum natale apud acquilegiam.

50. f. 368 Antoninus of Piacenza. *Inc.* Antoninus. athleta cristi. fortissimus apamie opido oriundus

> Identifies Antoninus as of Apamea and one of the Theban legion under St. Maurice. Numerous miracles at Piacenza are related and the invention of his body in the time of Bishop Savinus and its translation to the tomb of St. Victor in the church of Piacenza on 13 Nov.: cf. *BHL*, no. 580, a shorter text, without miracles and B.L., Harley 3683, ff. 133–51ᵛ.[1]

51. f. 374 Cassianus. *Inc.* Cassianus episcopus ex nobili genere in alexandria.

> The main hand wrote in red on f. 374ᵛ: Benedicamus domino. / Deo gratias amen. / Amen trino numini gloriam canamus. / Amen deo homini gratias agamus. / Amen matri uirigini laudes referamus.

ff. i+374+i. ff. 6–374 were numbered in a medieval hand from i to ccclxxiii before the loss of four leaves. 318×230 mm. Written space 231×151 mm. 2 cols. 53 lines. Collation: 1⁴+1 leaf after 4 (f. 5) 2–7¹² 8¹² wants 5 after f. 81 9¹² wants 8 after f. 95 and 10 after f. 96 10–16¹² 17¹² wants 1 before f. 183 18–30¹² 31¹⁰ 32¹² 33⁴ wants 4, probably blank. One hundred and two pictures, most of them *c.* 75×65 mm, on grounds of red, or, from f. 257ᵛ, blue, patterned in gold. Initials: (i) beginning the preface and each of the five parts of art. 2 and the life of St. Antoninus in art. 3 (f. 368), pink or blue on decorated gold grounds and with prolongations into the margins and into the space between the columns; (ii) 3-line, blue with red ornament or red with violet ornament. Capital letters in the ink of the text are filled with yellow. Binding of s. xviii, probably German. Secundo folio (f. 7) *domus israel*.

'Executed in the region of French Flanders, *c.* 1400–10', according to the catalogue of the Winter Exhibition 1953–4 at the Royal Academy of Arts, London (*Flemish Art 1300–1700*, no. 563). 'Iste liber est [. . . . . .]' in red at the foot of f. 5ᵛ, probably in the main hand. The long life of St. Antoninus (art. 3, no. 50), with its special initial, suggests a connection with Piacenza from the first. Memoranda on f. 374ᵛ are in Italian, s. xvii (?). A note of the number of pictures and initials is in German inside the cover.[2] Book-plate of Archibald Philip, Earl of Rosebery: his gift in 1918. Formerly BE. 8. x. 6.

Gen. 1115. *Euclides, etc.* 1480

Euclid's geometry in Latin and other texts mainly on geometry. Arts. 11–16 are concerned with squaring the circle. Arts. 2, 4–9, 11 are also in the Dresden

---

[1] I owe the reference to Harley 3683 to Guy Philippart, S.J.

[2] The same hand wrote a similar note in MS. Gen. 288, q.v.

manuscript fully described by M. Curtze in *Zeitschrift für Mathematik und Phisik*, xxviii (1883), Hist. Lit. Abt., 1–13: cf. *Bibliotheca Mathematica*, Dritte Folge, x (1909–10), 232.

1. ff. 8–172ᵛ Euclidis philosophi socratici Incipit liber elementorum artis geometrice translatus ab arabico in latinum per adelardum goth' bathoniensem sub comento magistri campani nauarriensis. Punctus est cuius pars non est. Linea est longitudo sine latitudine . . . propositum erat inscripsisse. Et sic est finis geometrie euclidis perscripte manu die 4ª decembris 1480. Explicit 15ᵘˢ et ultimus geometrie euclidis cum commento Magistri campani. With diagrams in the margins.

2. ff. 173–175ᵛ Tractatus ysoperimetrorum. Ysoperimetorum (*sic*) ysopleurorum rectilineorum et circulis contentorum . . . et solidum poliedrum minus spera. Explicit tractatus de ysoperimetris.

Thorndike and Kibre. The first four words, 'Prelibandum vero primum qui', have been left out.

3. ff. 175ᵛ–177 Tractatus de eadem materia secundum intencionem magistri thome brarbardun. Nunc tractum subiungam ysoperimetrorum quem euclides pretermisit . . . In hoc ergo nostrum tractatum expediamus. Expliciunt ysoperimetra secundum magistrum thomam brarbardun.

Thomas Bradwardine, Geometria: edn. Paris, 1530, ff. 9ᵛ–10 (tract. 2, cap. 5).

4. ff. 177ᵛ–188 Incipit liber de visu. Ponatur ab oculo eductas rectas lineas . . . quemadmodum in circularibus. Explicit liber de visu.

Euclid, Optica. Thorndike and Kibre.

5. ff. 188ᵛ–193 Incipit tractatus de speculis. Visum rectum 'esse' cuius media . . . in eis. stupa posita accenditur. Explicit tractatus speculorum.

Pseudo-Euclid, Catoptrica. Thorndike and Kibre.

6. ff. 193ᵛ–197ᵛ De sublimiori quod geometre adinuenerunt . . . ad punctum vnum. Explicit liber speculorum combu.

Alhasen, De speculis comburentibus. Thorndike and Kibre. Ed. J. L. Heiberg and E. Wiedemann, *Bibl. Math.*, Dritte Folge, x (1909–10), 218–31.

7. ff. 197ᵛ–198ᵛ Ista sunt que sequuntur. In principio libri appollonii de piramidibus. Et sunt anxiomata que premittuntur in libro isto. Cum continuatur inter punctum aliquod . . . secundum ordinem. Expliciunt anxiomata in librum precedentem extracta a libro appollonii de pyramidibus.

Edited from other manuscripts in Heiberg's edition of Apollonius Pergaeus (Teubner ser., 1891–3, II. lxxv–lxxx). Precedes art. 6 in Paris, B.N. lat. 9335: cf. *Bibl. Math.*, Dritte Folge, iii (1902), 71.

8. f. 199 Incipit liber euclidis de graui et leui. Corpora sunt equalia in magnitudine . . . que est g. Explicit liber euclidis de graui et leui et comparacione corporum ad inuicem.

Pseudo-Euclid. Thorndike and Kibre. Ed. E. A. Moody and M. Clagett, *The Medieval Science of Weights*, 1952, pp. 26–30.

9. ff. 199ᵛ–201 Incipit liber de canonio. Si fuerit canonium simmetrum magnitudine et substancie . . . quod oportebat ostendere.

Edn. ibid., pp. 64–74.[1] The running title on ff. 200ᵛ–201 is 'Archimenides (de) canonio'.

10. f. 201ʳᵛ Omnis ponderosi motum esse ad medium . . . leuitatis b super a.

The suppositions and first proposition and proof of Elementa Jordani super demonstrationem ponderum, edn. ibid., pp. 128–9.

11. ff. 202–203ᵛ Incipit liber archimenidis de quadratura circuli. Omnis circulus ortogonio triangulo . . . quod declarare uoluimus.

Archimedes, De mensura circuli, in the translation of Gerard of Cremona, ed. M. Clagett, *Archimedes in the Middle Ages*, i (1964), 40–54: a copy of Traditio II.

12. ff. 203ᵛ–207ᵛ Omnis corda minor est arcu suo . . . Si non est equalis sine ipsis proueniret.

A paraphrase of another version of art. 11.

13. ff. 208–9 Incipit 4ʳᵃ circuli secundum magistrum campanum cum commento eidem ascripto. Aristotiles in eo qui de cathegoriis libro inscribitur . . . et tanto quadrato. Explicit quadratura circuli edita a magistro campano cum commento eidem ascripto.

Thorndike and Kibre (Campanus de Novara, De quadratura circuli). Edited from other copies by Clagett, op. cit., i. 588–606. Followed as in other copies by eight lines of verse:

Rem nouam mira		quadraturam circ
Velut inscripti	bilem	apud doctos sec
Olim licet sci		plures cernunt oc
Vere demonstra		hoc in fine sec

uli

14. ff. 209ᵛ–210 Quadracio circuli est hec. Sit circuli quadrandi . . . quod est quod intendimus. Explicit quadratura circuli secundum alium doctorem.

A version of the Quadratura per lunulas: cf. op. cit. i. 618–25.

15. (a) ff. 210–11 Incipit 4ʳᵃ circuli secundum alardum. Quelibet media proporcionalia earundem quantitatum sunt equalia. Esto exemplum b. et c. . . . medio loco proporcionalem. Explicit quadratura circuli secundum magistrum alardum in maiori commento. (b) ff. 211–212ᵛ Sequitur quedam extracta a commento eiusdem. Propositum duobus quadratis alterum . . . circumscribere. Esto exemplum a.d. . . . a b diuisa per equalia in d.

(a) three and (b) twelve paragraphs. Cf. Clagett, ibid., p. 569, and Jordanus Nemorarius, De triangulis (ed. M. Curtze, Thorn, 1887), bk. 3, sect. 14 sqq.

16. ff. 213–214ᵛ Extractum a commento Io. de muris capitulo octauo ut facilius intelligantur que dicta sunt supra textum archimenidis. Proporcionem circumferencie circuli . . . necessario inclusa est. Hec sufficiant pro quadratura circuli.

17. ff. 214ᵛ–222ᵛ Si a medio alicuius lateris trianguli ducta linea super aliud eius latus . . . ex d in c.

Twenty-three propositions and proofs, the thirteenth to twentieth (ff. 218ᵛ–221) numbered from 16 to 24. The paragraph marked 17 begins 'Cubum datum dupplare. Lineam vnius basis cubi dati dupla'. ff. 223–225ᵛ blank.

[1] I am grateful to Professor Clagett for help with arts. 9–12, 14–17.

18 (added, probably in the main hand). ff. 226–229^v Planam tersam et politam habeas ex latone tabulam. In cuius medio sit centrum signatum C. eritque dicta tabula mater nominata . . .

Directions to make an astronomical instrument. A table, 'Auges planetarum anno 1450 completo', follows.

19. ff. 1–6, 232 (flyleaves) contain, inter alia: (*a*) f. 1^v Conclusiones astronomie misse Regi francie karolo septimo per Iohannem de Monte arcino de villa senis in ytalia . . .; (*b*) f. 2 Nomina autorum insignium artis matheseos; (*c*) f. 3^v Magia de vita et morte. Sphera apuleii platonici ex doctrina Zoroastris pythagore et democriti philosophorum.

(*a*). A prophecy about Joan of Arc sent to Charles VII in 1429. (*b*). The first name is Thales milecius. (*c*). A diagram to forecast the length and outcome of an illness. Christ (Vita) stands on the devil (Mors). Cf. Thorndike and Kibre.

ff. viii+224+ii, foliated i, 1–233. Paper, except ff. 1, 232 (probably once pastedowns). For ff. 1–6, 232 see above art. 19. 283×203 mm. Written space 190×110 mm. Long lines, about 33 for propositions and about 47 for proofs and commentary. Frame ruling with pencil. Collation of ff. 8–231: 1–21^{10} 22^6 23^8. Propositions in textura and proofs in small current cursiva by one hand throughout. Initials: (i) f. 8, blue on gold ground, decorated; (ii) beginning arts. and the several books of art. 1, 4-line, gold and blue with blue and red ornament; (iii) beginning propositions, 1-line, blue or red. Capital letters in the ink of the text filled with pale yellow. Binding by Carss, Glasgow. Secundo folio (f. 9) *circulum c. b. d. f.*

Written in France, art. 1 in 1480. 'Ff. 3. n. 5' and another earlier Glasgow mark 'G (?). f. [.] n. 9' on f. 1^v. F. 5.11 in the catalogue of 1828 and F. 5.3 in that of 1836. Later BD. 1. c. 2 and BE. 8. y. 18.

Gen. 1116. *Palladius*   s. xv^1

1. ff. 6–71 Palladii. Rutulii. Tauri. Emiliani auri (*sic*) illustris opus agriculture incipit feliciter . . . (*table of chapters*) . . . De preceptis rei rustice. Primo. Pars est prima prudencie . . . ora xi. pedes xxix. Palladii Rutilii . . . opus de agricultura. Explicit deo gracias.

Marginalia in elaborate frames. ff. 1–5^v, 72–83^v were left blank.

2. ff. 74–78^v. Payments for medicines in Spanish in current writing. They include the dates 1442 on f. 74, 1446 on f. 75 and 1447 on ff. 76^v, 78.

ff. 83. Paper. ff. 6–71 have a contemporary foliation in red, I–LXVI. 282×210 mm. Written space 210×155 mm. 2 cols. 29–33 lines. Frame ruling in pencil. Collation impracticable. Written in an upright semi-cursive hand. 4-line, 3-line, and 2-line red initials. Red morocco binding, s. xviii, uniform with that of MS. Gen. 1184. Secundo folio *nosus atque.*

Written in Spain. Old Glasgow pressmark 'CL. f. [. . .]' partly covered by a later bookplate. F. 5.19 in the catalogue of 1828 and F. 5.2 in that of 1836. Later BD. 1. c. 3 and BE. 8. y. 17.

Gen. 1119. *Biblia, pars secunda* 1446

The second part of an Old Testament, containing Proverbs, Ecclesiastes, Song of Songs, Wisdom, Ecclesiasticus, Job, Tobit, Judith, Esther, Isaiah, Jeremiah, Lamentations, Baruch, Ezekiel, Daniel, Minor Prophets, 1, 2 Maccabees.

The prologues are thirty-four of the common set[1] and sixteen others, shown here by *: Stegmüller, nos. 457, 468, 344, 357, 332, 335, 341+343, 337*, 482, 480*, 486*, 487, 491, 492, 494, 495*, 500, 507, 504*, 506*, 511, 510, 515, 513, 512, 519+517, 516*, 524, 521, 526, 525*, 528, 527*, 531, Abacuc propheta in principio voluminis sui describit dyabolum cum membris suis . . .* (ends as 530*), 529*, 534, 532*, 538, 535*, 539, 540*, 543, 544*, 545*, 547, 553, 551.

Isaiah begins on a new leaf, f. 58. At the end of 1 Maccabees is 'Explicit liber machab' primus versus duo milia trecenti'. ff. 168–169^v blank.

ff. ii+168+i, foliated i, 1–170. f. 1 is a parchment flyleaf, probably post medieval. 302 × 210 mm. Written space 220 × 140 mm. 2 cols. *c.* 53 lines, the number varying from column to column. Frame ruling. Collation of ff. 2–169: 1–21^8. Written in good hybrida. The flex (?) is a common mark of punctuation throughout. Initials: (i) of books, red and blue, with ornament in red, blue, green, and sometimes violet; (ii) of prologues, at first like (i), but smaller: later, usually monochrome, blue with red ornament or red with violet ornament; (iii) of chapters, 2-line, red or blue. Capital letters in the ink of the text stroked with red. A red morocco binding of 1969 by D. Cockerell & Son replaces a binding of s. xix by Carss, Glasgow. Secundo folio *quiesces*.

Written in the Netherlands, no doubt: the scribe gives his name and the date of writing at the end, f. 167^v: 'Deo gracias. Explicit liber iste per manus Alberti de heenvliet presbiteri. Anno domini 1446 in profesto praxedis virginis (20 July). Orate pro eo'. 'Ex libris La^n Campbell Trajecti ad Rhen^m 15 Apr: 1702. The gift of the Right Honble The Lord Archibald Campbell', f. 1.[2] 'Ex dono Lauchlani Cambell. Jo: Stirling Principal', f. 2: Stirling was principal from 1701 to 1727. For the gift cf. *Munimenta Alme Universitatis Glasguensis* (1854), iii. 447. 'BM. f. 2, no. 1', f. 2: under this number in the catalogue begun in 1691. F. 4.1 in the catalogue of 1828 and F. 5.22 in the catalogue of 1836. Later BD. 1. b. 20 and BE. 8. y. 8.

Gen. 1125. *Terentius* s. xv med.

1. The six plays: f. 3, 'Andria'; f. 39, 'Eunuchus'; f. 75, 'Eaphtontumerumenos'; f. 113, 'Adelphis'; f. 149^v, 'Hechira'; f. 179^v, 'Phormio', ending, f. 217^v, 'Vos valete et plaudite. Calliopius recensui. Terencii affri liber comediarum sextus explicit'.

Many interlinear glosses to the first two plays and a few later. The argumenta are those usually printed and, in addition, 'Orto bello . . .' and 'Meretrix . . . illuditur' (ff. 2, 39^v), as in Gen. 1189. Andria and Eunuchus are preceded by scholia, ff. 1^{rv}, 2^v—the scribe began on f. 2^v and went back to f. 1—, 37^v–38^v. In front are, besides the Andria scholia and argumenta: f. 2, 'Reuertente autem scipione . . . uocabatur uenit'; f. 3, 'Natus in exelsis . . . cautus erit' (6 lines). Both pieces are also in Gen. 1189, q.v.

2. ff. 218–20 Nobilis natura. sed padi ortu nobilissimus . . . passa est. Historia Galteri et griseldis coniugum composita a francisco petrarcha poeta laureato.

---

[1] See Bristol Public Library, 15.

[2] *DNB* records that Archibald Campbell, 3rd Duke of Argyll, 1682–1761, studied law at Utrecht.

de mirabili et virtuosa paciencia et perseverancia Griseldis in tribulationibus sibi illatis per Galterum eius virum. Explicit. Deo gracias Amen.

Francisci Petrarchae Opera, ed. Bas. 1581, pp. 541–6; thence in *Originals and Analogues of some of Chaucer's Canterbury Tales*, Chaucer Society, 1875, pp. 153–70. This copy described by N. Mann in *Italia mediœvale e umanistica*, xviii (1975), 189.

3. f. 220ᵛ (*a*) Epitaphium Regis Karoli septimi. Rex karolus fueram . . . anglia tota timet. (*b*) Epitaphium domini chy. de pistorio qui sepultus est in ecclesia kathedrali pistorien'. Hic cynus in cineres sua busta reliquid accuta . . . fluentibus orbe.

Fifteen lines and six lines of verse on Charles VII of France, †1461, and Cino da Pistoia, †1336. Walther, nos. 16707, 7865.

ff. iv+221+v. Paper. 305 × 217 mm. Written space 160 × 110 mm. 16 long lines. Frame ruling in pencil. Collation: 1¹⁰ 2⁸ 3–19¹². Large round hybrida. ff. 1–2, 37ᵛ–38ᵛ, 218ᵛ–220ᵛ are in the same good hand, but smaller. Initials: (i) f. 3, blue on a decorated gold ground; (ii) gold on patterned coloured grounds; (iii) 2-line, red with blue-grey ornament, or blue with red ornament. Binding of s. xviii. Secundo folio (f. 4) *ssent fabulas*.

Written in France. 'Ce liure a este de messʳ Iehan du chastel euesque de Carcassonne. Bertaud Not'', ff. 1, 220ᵛ, as in MS. Gen. 1189. F. 1.16 in the Glasgow catalogue of 1828 and F. 5.23 in that of 1836. Later BD. 1. b. 23 and BE. 8. y. 6.

Gen. 1126. *Biblia* s. XIII²

1. ff. 1–315ᵛ A Bible with the usual contents in the usual order and the common set of sixty-four prologues (as in Bristol Public Library 15), with gaps due to damage.

Ten or eleven leaves are missing (see below) and initials have been cut out of twenty-six leaves. f. 249ᵛ ends in 2 Maccabees 13: 9: Matthew begins a new quire, f. 250.

2. ff. 316–343ᵛ Aaz apprehendens . . .

The usual dictionary of Hebrew names, ending imperfectly in Zechri.

ff. i+343+i. 308 × 205 mm.: the shaving of the running titles shows that the upper margin was once a good deal wider. Written space 188 × 122 mm. 2 cols. of 61–3 lines. Collation: 1¹⁶ wants 3 after f. 2 2–7¹⁶ 8¹² wants 2 after f. 112 9¹⁶ wants 10 after f. 131 and 16 after f. 136 10–11¹⁶ 12¹⁶ wants 16 after f. 183 13–15¹⁶ 16¹⁶ wants 1 before f. 232 and 8, 9 after f. 238+1 leaf after 6 (f. 237) 17 four (ff. 246–9) 18–20¹⁶ 21¹⁶+2 leaves after 16 (ff. 314–15) 22¹⁴ 23¹⁶ wants 15, 16. Initials: (i) of books and the usual eight divisions of the psalter, in colour on decorated gold grounds; (ii) of prologues, in colour on decorated grounds, usually blue; (iii) of chapters, 2-line, blue or red, with ornament of the other colour; (iv) of psalm-verses, 1-line, blue or red. The blue morocco binding by D. Cockerell & Son, 1969, replaces a nineteenth-century binding by Carss of Glasgow. Secundo folio *corporum*.

Written perhaps in England. From the Augustinian abbey of Cambuskenneth, near Stirling: 'Cambouskyneth' in large letters, s. xv, at the foot of f. 3 and in smaller letters on f. 1. 'Ex libris Bibliothecæ Universitatis Glasguensis. Will Dunlop', ff. 2, 169ᵛ: Dunlop was principal, 1690–1700. 'A. f. 2 n: 1', f. 2: entered as no. 1 of Forulus 2 of Case A in the catalogue begun in 1691. Later Glasgow marks are Ff. 3. n. 2, F. 4.7 (in 1828), F. 2.17 (in 1836), BD. 1. b. 19, and BE. 8. y. 7.

Gen. 1130. *Nicholas Love, Mirror (in English); etc.*   s. xv med.

1. ff. 1–132 (*Prologue*) Quecumque scripta sunt . . . (f. 4, *text*) After ye tyme yat man was exilede . . . where he souereyne kynge w^t ye fad^r and ye holigost one god in trinite lyuey and regney w^t oute ende amen. þus endey ye contemplacion' of ye blessed life of oure lorde ihesu . . . lollardes and heretikes. amen. Blessed be ye name of oure lorde ihesu and his moder Marie nowe and euer wythe oute ende Amen. Explicit speculum vite cristi.

Love's translation of Speculum vitae Christi, printed in 1488 by Caxton, and later, last in the edition of L. F. Powell, *The Mirrour of the Blessed Lyf of Jesu Christ*, 1908, pp. 7–301. Sixty-three chapters. A leaf missing after f. 29 contained parts of chs. 10, 11.

2. ff. 132–42 A shorte tretice of ye hiest and most woryi sacrament of cristes blessede body and ye merueyles yer of. Memoriam fecit mirabilium . . . confort our' wretchede life amen. Explicit speculum vite cristi complete.

A treatise on the sacrament which usually follows art. 1. Printed by Powell, op. cit., pp. 301–24.

3. ff. 142–145^v Dominis suis reuerendis et amicis in cristi visceribus dilectis viro illustri domino priori et fratribus vniuersis in ecclesia sancti Andree in Scocia seruicio mancipatis. Frater adam dei et seruorum dei seruus . . . Soliloquium de instruccione anime . . . uobis o uiri uenerabiles transmitto . . . absolutus. Explicit prologus. Incipit liber Magistri Ade Cartusiensis de instruccione anime. Capitulum primum. Secretis interrogacionibus pulsabo animam meam . . . tu temere suspicaris (*ends imperfectly*).

PL cxcviii. 843–848/40.

ff. i+145+i. 294 × 200 mm. Written space *c.* 200 × 125 mm. 30 long lines. Collation: 1^8 wants 1, 2 2–3^8 4^8 wants 8 after f. 29 5–18^8 19^8 wants 5–8. Written all by one hand in a large anglicana, with short *r* and broken minim strokes: *y* is used in place of þ. Initials: (i) ff. 132, 142, gold on coloured grounds patterned in white; (ii) 3-line, blue with red ornament. A binding of green morocco by D. Cockerell & Son, 1969, replaces a binding of s. xix by Carss, Glasgow. Secundo folio *after in yis buke*.

Written in England. The arms in the initial on f. 142, 1st and 4th a cross engrailed or, 2nd and 3rd gules a cross moline argent, agree with those of William, Lord Willoughby d'Eresby, †1409, reproduced by W. H. St. J. Hope, *The Stall Plates of the Knights of the Garter, 1348–1485*, 1901, pl. xx. Listed under the mark AY. 5. 14 in the catalogue begun in 1691. Old Glasgow pressmarks 'Append. AT. 5.1' and 'Ff. 3.4' on f. 1. Later F. 5.14 (in 1828), F. 5.5 (in 1836), BD. 1. b. 25, and BE. 8. y. 10.

Gen. 1184. *Seneca, Tragoediae*   s. xv ex.

The ten plays: f. 1, 'Hercules furens'; f. 37, 'Thiestes'; f. 67, 'Thebays'; f. 83, 'Yppolytus'; f. 116, 'Edippus'; f. 142^v, 'Troas'; f. 173, 'Medea'; f. 200^v, 'Agamenon'; f. 226, 'Octauia'; f. 252, 'Hercules ohetheus'.

One leaf containing Thebais, lines 397–434, is missing. f. 303^{rv} blank.

ff. vi+303+vi. Paper. The foliation (contemporary) takes account of the missing leaves after 75 and 303 and runs to 306. 262 × 205 mm. Written space 175 × 100 mm. 20 long lines. Collation: 1^{16} 2^{14} $3-4^{16}$ 5^{14} 6^{16} wants 1 before f. 77 $7-12^{16}$ $13-15^{14}$ $16-18^{16}$ 19^{14} 20^{16} wants 12, 13, 15, 16, probably blank. Written in textura. Initials: (i) beginning each play, blue and red, with red and violet ornament; (ii) 2-line, blue with red ornament or red with violet ornament. Binding of s. xviii.

Written in Italy. Former Glasgow pressmark CL. f. 4 [n.   ] partly obscured by a later book-plate. F. 6.7 in the catalogue of 1828 and F. 6.13 in that of 1836. Later BD. 1. c. 9 and BE. 7. b. 6.

Gen. 1189. *Terentius*   s. xv med.

The six plays: f. 4, 'Andria'; f. 35, 'Eunuchus'; f. 70^v, 'Heuteron Timorumenos'; f. 103, 'Adelphos'; f. 135, 'Echira'; f. 162^v, 'Phormio', ending, f. 194, 'Vos valete et plaudite cali'o'pius recensui. Terencii liber explicit phormionis. Nouissimi terencii phormio explicit'.

Some interlineations and marginal scholia. An omitted passage is supplied by another hand on ff. 152–154^v. The verse argumenta are those usually printed. There are also prose argumenta to Andria, 'Orto bello . . . sodali illius' (ff. 1^v–2) and to Eunuchus 'Meretrix . . . illuditur', the latter as in Prete's edition, Heidelberg, 1954, p. 178: it precedes the verse argumentum to Eunuchus.

In front are: f. 1, 'Terencius genere extitit affer ciuis cartaginensis reuertente . . . uocabatur uenit'; f. 2, 'Epitaphium supra terencium', but nothing follows; f. 4, the epitaph 'Natus in excelsis . . . cautus erit' (6 lines), ed. Baehrens, *Poetae Minores*, v. 385. ff. 2^v, 3^{rv} blank.

ff. i+195+i. Paper. 276 × 198 mm. Written space 172 × 115 mm. 21 long lines. Ruling with a hard point. Collation: 1^{22} $2-4^{24}$ 5^{26} 6^{24} $7^{24}+3$ leaves inserted after 7 (ff. 152–4) 8^{24}. Clumsy semi-humanistic script. Spaces left for initials remain unfilled. Bound in s. xix by Carss, Glasgow. Secundo folio *et ibi*.

Written in Italy. 'Ce liure a este de feu mess^r Iehan du chastel euesque de Carcassonne (1456–75). Bertaud Not' ', ff. 1, 194: the other Terence, Gen. 1125, is similarly inscribed. F. 5.15 in the catalogue of 1828 and F. 5.1 in the catalogue of 1836. Later BD. 1. c. 4 and BE. 7. b. 1.

Gen. 1228. *Alexander Trallianus*   s. xv^2

Incipit primus liber Alexandri yatros sophiste . . . Capitulum primum de allopicia et ophiasi. Contingit hec duplex passio . . . (f. 413) cum oleo Roseo ungito et uteris.

Alexander Trallianus, Practica, in three bks (1, f. 5; 2, f. 154; 3, f. 370), with a numbered list of chapters (149, 271, 66) before each book. Thorndike and Kibre. Ed. Lyon, 1504. Fairly numerous marginalia and interlineations in a good upright hand.

ff. ii+413+ii, foliated i, 1–415 (416). ff. 1, 415 are medieval parchment flyleaves. ff. 5–413 have a medieval foliation i–ccccix. 305 × 215 mm. Written space 190 × 110 mm. 25 long lines. Collation of ff. 2–414: $1-51^8$ 52^6 wants 6, blank and probably now f. 1. Written in a large ugly set hybrida, with split tops to *a, i, u* and the final down-stroke of *m* and *n*. 3-line red initials. A binding by D. Cockerell & Son, 1970, replaces one of s. xix. Secundo folio *frenesis* or (f. 6) *diuturna*.

Written probably in France. An erasure, f. 1. F. 5.5 in the catalogue of 1828 and F. 2.16 in the catalogue of 1836. Later BD. 1. b. 22 and BE. 7. a. 16.

Gen. 1357. *Pseudo-Aristoteles, Secreta secretorum; etc.*   s. xv med.

1. ff. 1–4 Dilectissimo filio. flauiano. leo lectis dileccionis tue epistolis. quas miramur . . . sensus sui prauitate saluetur.

Letter 28 of Pope Leo I in *PL* liv. 755–81. Cf. *Clavis*, no. 1656/28.

2. ff. 4–5ᵛ Perdidit absalon sceleratissimus . . . exicium uoluit intulisse. Deo gracias. Amen.

PL lvi. 1151–4 (sermo 8: Pseudo-Leo). Cf. *Clavis*, no. 1661.

3. ff. 6–21 Domino suo excellentissimo In cultu religionis cristiane strenuissimo guidoni de ualencia ciuitatis tripolis glorioso pontifici. philipus . . . misit ad aristotilem unam epistolam sub hac forma. Magister reuerende. intimare dignum duxi . . . occidere omnes. Cui aristotiles sic rescripsit. O fili gloriosissime . . . sicut dictum fuit de ipso superius.

Thirty-six paragraphs. An abbreviation of the translation of Secreta secretorum by Philip of Tripoli (*GKW* 2481–7). Six lines for a heading on f. 6 remain blank. ff. 21ᵛ–22ᵛ blank.

ff. i+22+i. Paper. ff. i, 23 and the pastedowns with which they are conjugate are leaves of the original manuscript, ruled but otherwise blank. 298×214 mm. Written space c. 190×150 mm. 2 cols. 29–35 lines. Ruling with violet ink. Collation: 1¹² 2¹⁰. Written in textura: *f* and *s* descend slightly below the line; final *t* is sometimes superior, especially at the end of a line. 2-line blue initials with red ornament on ff. 1, 4; elsewhere the spaces remain blank. Capital letters in the ink of the text filled with pale yellow, but only on ff. 1–5ᵛ. Limp parchment binding, s. xx.

Written probably in Spain. Probably part of a larger manuscript. Obtained in 1975 from Bernard M. Rosenthal Inc., San Francisco: his *Bulletin* 18 (1975), no. 7, with facsimile of f. 6.

Hamilton 8. *Leonardo Bruni Aretino (in Italian)*   s. xv²

Proemio del primo bello punico traslatato uulgare per miss' Leonardo aretino il quale mando aun suo amico. E parra forse a molti che io uada dietro a cose troppo antiche . . . achi glimolestaua. Deo gratias. Amen.

The translation into Italian of the Commentaria tria de primo bello Punico of Leonardo Bruni printed *c.* 1471 (*GKW* 5604) and in *Scelta di curiosita letterarie*, fasc. 165 (1878).

ff. i+83+i. Paper. 238×170 mm. Written space 152×95 mm. 26 long lines. Writing above top ruled line. Collation: 1–8¹⁰ 9 three. Written in a current humanistic hand. A gold initial on f. 1. Other initials in outline only. Binding of s. xviii. Secundo folio *La ghuerra*.

Written in Italy. Erased inscription, f. 83. Probably no. 2554 in Thorpe's catalogue for 1828 and no. 12111 in his catalogue for 1830. Bought in 1879 from the representatives of Professor Sir William Hamilton, †1856. Formerly BC. 10. a. 9.

Hamilton 11. *'Commentum super Macrobium'*   s. xii²

(*Preface*) [V]t irrefragabilia philosophantium asseuerant examina p. philosophorum donatus laurea.' philosophia in luculentam erexit consonantiam . . . .

(*text*) Macros longum bios uia (*sic*) uel ponitur ibi b pro u . . . quando agitur de controuersia de scripto et sententia. si ita inquam dixisset unum etc'. (*ends abruptly*).

A commentary on Macrobius's commentary on Cicero's Somnium Scipionis, ending at 2.5.6. After the end of the text two lines written in s. xv (?) have been erased. 'Commentum super Macrobium', f. 1, s. xv.

ff. iii+25+iii. 233 × 153 mm. Written space *c.* 200 × 140 mm. 2 cols. 61–70 lines. Collation: 1–2⁸ 3⁸+1 leaf after 8 (f. 25). Written in a very small hand. No ornament. Binding of s. xix. Secundo folio *Sed licet.*

Written in France. Probably part of a larger manuscript. 'Magistri T.' is at the head and, in another hand, 'Herman ded" at the foot of f. 1, s. xii; 'Magistri T.' and 'Herman' in the same positions on ff. 9, 17. Hamilton (?) wrote on f. ii 'One of the Dorville MSS. written by the same scribe if the most exact resemblance of the writing may prove it'.[1] Acquired like MS. Hamilton 8. Formerly BC. 10. a. 12.

Hamilton 22. *Ambrosius, De officiis*   s. xv²

1. Ambrosii ecclesie doctoris sapientissimi Mediolanorum presulis sacratissimi ad suos quos in cristo per ewangelium genuit filios carissimos officiorum liber primus . . . Non arrogans videri . . . instructionis conferat. Ambrosii doctoris sancti et eximii Officiorum liber tercius finit.

PL xvi. 23–184.

2. The pastedowns are two bifolia of a small manuscript on parchment, s. xii/xiii, written in small hands (2 cols. 55 lines) and containing on three of its four leaves a commentary on canon law and on the fourth extracts from the Fathers. Headings of the commentary are De gradu consan(guinitatis) and De inpedimento uiolentie: the latter begins 'Circa inpedimentum uiolentie notandum quod ex sui natura'.

ff. 126. Paper. 223 × 152 mm. Written space 170 × 105 mm. 25 long lines, ruled with a hard point. Writing above top ruled line. Collation: 1–12¹⁰ 13⁶. Written in a round sloping hybrida. 3-line, 2-line, and 1-line red initials. Capital letters in the ink of the text marked with red. Contemporary Netherlandish binding of boards covered with brown leather bearing stamps of four patterns within 2-line fillets and small roundels where the fillets intersect: central clasp. Secundo folio *quisque profecerit.*

Written probably in the Netherlands. Acquired like MS. Hamilton 8. Formerly BC. 10. b. 1.

Hamilton 26. *R. Lull, etc. (in French)*   s. xv/xvi

1. ff. 1–180 Sequitur. Incipit prima pars testamenti magistri Raymundi lullii In qua (*these two words cancelled*) Reuerendissimi doctoribus (*altered to* doctoris) que dicitur theorica. Pour celuy dieu de nature (?) louer benistre et adourer . . . (f. 94) Alkemye est vne partie celee . . . ne bouter a hors de sein fruit. Nous

---

[1] Bodleian MS. D'Orville 207 (*SC* 17085) is perhaps meant, but there is no close resemblance.

auons fait nostre testament par la voullente de A. nostre seignur en lhylle dengleterre en leglise saincte katherine en pres londres vers la partie du chatel deuent
la Riuiere de lacamise Regnant le roy Edouard de bloid destoh par la grace de
dieu Roy Dengleterre et lauons mis es mains de qualmetem en garde En lan
apres l'incarnation nostre seignur mil ccc. trente dulx aueucque tous ses volumes
qui nommes sont en dy testament. Explicit.

This copy described by Singer and Anderson, no. 244 and pp. 1143–7. The colophon
corresponds with that in Catalan in Corpus Christi College, Oxford, MS. 244, f. 80ᵛ:
cf. above MS. Ferguson 83, art. 1. Some notes have been added in French, s. xviii, e.g.
on f. 167ᵛ.

2. ff. 180ᵛ–191ᵛ Tables and diagrams in illustration of art. 1, with accompany-ing
text, mainly in red and blue, ending (f. 191) 'Et atant preuue lacheuement des
figures instrumentalles de nostre testament En rendant graces . . . Amen.
Explicit testamentum preclarum magistri Ramondi'. f. 190 is a double thickness
of paper: the scribe drew a diagram on the verso and then substituted another
for it on a pasted-down leaf. ff. 192–194ᵛ blank.

3. ff. 195–199ᵛ Du vert lion moult a noter. Operacio solis et lune et notetis
diligenter. Et cest assauoir que ceste pratique est parolle tres vraye . . . vraye
lune etc. Explicit loperacion de la pierre des philosophes la quele operacion
est pou congnue. Leo viridus et nota.

R. Bacon, De leone viridi, in French. Singer and Anderson, no. 193. x, and p. 1136.

4. ff. 199ᵛ–200 Recipes for Greek fire, etc., one beginning 'Recipe auripimenti'
headed 'Maistre Ihan le bourguegnon' (f. 200).

ff. i+198+ii, foliated (i), 1–160, 162–75, 177–200 (201–2). Paper. 220 × 150 mm. Written
space c. 150 × 105 mm. 35–40 long lines. Frame ruling at first: none after f. 93. Collation:
1 ten 2–7¹² 8⁴ wants 4, probably blank, after f. 85 9–13⁸ 14⁸+1 leaf after 8 (f. 134) 15⁸ 16¹⁰
17–19⁸ 20 eight (ff. 179–86) 21⁸ 22⁶. Current cursiva and (ff. 185ᵛ–191) larger hybrida.
2-line blue initials: none after f. 94. Up to f. 81ᵛ titles are in red on strips of paper pasted
over titles in yellow-brown ink. Binding of s. xviii/xix. Secundo folio *en quel*.

Written in France. A small label inside the front cover contains a printed *B* within
a border of flower petals and in manuscript the number 3018². 'Nº 3505', f. i. Acquired
like MS. Hamilton 8. Formerly BC. 10. b. 5.

Hamilton 79. *Paulus de Pergula, Logica*   1431

Omnes qui aliquid memoria dignum suis posteris reliquerunt . . . . . . (f. 42ᵛ) Et
hec de insolubilibus dicta sufficiant ad laudem virginis Marie Amen. post
originale. Me Iacobus philippus de fagedis scripsit 1431 die 23 nouembris.
(f. 43, lightly erased) Explicit clarum compendium in facultate logice ac intro-
ducio iuuenum per humilem ac [in] ar[te]m artium doctorem magistrum paulum
de pargula post originale.

Printed often: see above, Edinburgh, University Library, 320. The *explicit* on f. 43 has
been erased, but is legible by ultra-violet light. ff. 1ʳ, 43ᵛ were left blank. The latter has
a note at the top, 'simon scriptor fratigena uenit stare nobiscum die 12 madis 1438',
and lower down two lines of verse, 'Huc properet quisquis. lacrimis . . .'.

ff. 43+i. 210×142 mm. Written space *c.* 160×90 mm. 39–40 long lines. Vertical bounding lines, but no horizontal ruling. Collation: 1¹⁰+1 leaf before 1 2–4¹⁰ 5 two (ff. 42–3). Written in a current textura. A red initial, f. 1ᵛ. The binding of wooden boards covered with brown patterned leather is probably contemporary Italian work: rebacked.

Written in Italy: see above. Listed in three Thorpe catalogues: in (1827), no. 10; in 1828, no. 2556; in 1830, no. 12115. Acquired like MS. Hamilton 8. Formerly BC. 10. d. 12.

Hamilton 137. *Johannes Dorp*   s. xv med.

1. ff. 1–246 Iste est tractatus summularum maiistri Iohannis Buridani qui prima sui diuisione diuiditur in nouem partes principales. In prima parte determinat... Et sic patet solucio huius dubitacionis etc' etc'. Et sic habetur finis tractatuum venerabilis magistri Iohannis dorp et summularum eius in cuius completione deus gloriosus sit benedictus cum matre sua gloriosa in secula seculorum Amen.

John Dorp's commentary on Buridan's Summulae de dialectica, printed in 1487 and later (*GKW* 5759–64). Pt. 2, f. 44ᵛ; 3, f. 60; 4, f. 87ᵛ; 5, f. 126ᵛ; 6, f. 151; 7, f. 181; 8, f. 203. Spaces for lemmata filled only on ff. 2ᵛ–22ᵛ, 60–64ᵛ. f. 246ᵛ blank.

2. ff. 247–9 [D]ialetica est ars artium ad omnium methadorum . . . quasi suppositio uel (*ends abruptly*).

Buridan's text, ending in the first part in the section beginning 'Propositio ypothetica'. ff. 249ᵛ–278ᵛ blank.

ff. 279, foliated 1–96, 96A, 97–278. Paper. 298×220 mm. Written space *c.* 220×140 mm. Frame ruling. 2 cols. *c.* 55 lines at first, *c.* 40 later. Probable collation of ff. 1–252: 1¹² wants 1 2–8¹² 9² (ff. 96, 96A) 10¹² 11²⁰ wants 1–3 before f. 109 12¹² 13¹² wants 1 before f. 138+2 leaves after 12 (ff. 149–50) 14 eighteen (probably a 12, with a 6, ff. 161–6, inserted into it after leaf 10) 15–21¹². A strip of parchment lies down the centre of each quire: in the opening after f. 142 it is cut from a document of s. xv. Written in current hybrida in several difficult and ugly hands, varying in size. Spaces for initials have not been filled. Contemporary binding of wooden boards covered with white leather bearing a pattern of fillets and the marks of five bosses formerly on each cover: two clasps missing. Secundo folio *in sciencie.*

Written in Germany. Inside the cover are: 'Iohannes p[. .]berch est huius libri possessor', s. xv; the mark '1 R 2. gl.' in red pencil; a cutting from a bookseller's catalogue, s. xix, 'Johannis Buridani metaphysica . . .'. Acquired like MS. Hamilton 8. Formerly BC. 10. x. 18.

Hamilton 138. *Ars moriendi*   s. xv ex.

Probably part of a larger manuscript.

1. ff. 1–10ᵛ Incipit prohemium de arte moriendi. Cum de presentis exilii miseria . . . expelli foras. A quo vos custodiat qui sine fine . . . Amen. Explicit.

Often printed, but the ending here is different from that of *GKW* 2597–2614, since after the usual final paragraph beginning 'Cum autem tota salus' there is another beginning 'Diceret quis quomodo'. Cf. M. C. O'Connor, *The Art of Dying Well*, 1942, pp. 48–112, for manuscripts and editions: she refers on p. 112 to Notre Dame MS. 3, which ends in the same way.

2. ff. 10ᵛ–12 Miscellaneous notes in the hand of art. 1, including: (*a*) f. 11, a form of confession, '[E]go frater N indignus nomine Carthusien' confiteor tibi clementissime deus pater . . .'; (*b*) f. 12 Incipiunt quedam attentica salomonis. Ego ecclesiastes fui super israhel in Iherusalem et proposui in animo meo (Ecclesiastes 1: 12) . . . nec vidit mala. que sub celo sunt. Gloria mundana non est nisi visio vana.

ff. 12. Paper. 305 × 220 mm. Written space *c.* 230 × 150 mm. 2 cols. 38 lines. Frame ruling. The first line of writing above the top line. A single quire taken from a larger manuscript. Written in round hybrida. Initials: (i) f. 1, red; (ii) 3-line and 2-line spaces not filled. Binding of s. xix.

Written in Germany or the Netherlands, perhaps in 1440, if this number written at the end of art. 2 (1444 altered to 1440) may be taken as a date. Presumably written for Carthusian use. Acquired like MS. Hamilton 8. Formerly BC. 10. x. 19.

Hamilton 141. *Aegidius Romanus, De regimine principum* s. xv med.

1. Incipit liber de regimine principum editus a fratre Egidio romano ordinis fratrum predicatorum (*sic*). Ex regia ac sanctissima prosapia . . . (f. 172ᵛ) promisit fidelibus qui est benedictus . . . amen. Explicit liber de regimine principum editus a fratre egidio romano ordinis fratrum heremitarum sancti augustini. Deo gracias. ff. 173–6 contain capitula of the three books.

Printed in 1473 and later (*GKW* 7217–9). f. 176ᵛ blank.

2 (on the back pastedown, s. xv). Senhors e donas escotatz / et auriretz meruillia / Io [. . . .] de paradis . . . .

Four 8-line stanzas, two of them on the pasted-down side. The beginning of a vision of paradise.

ff. i + 176 + i. The foliation on ff. 1–60 is medieval. 287 × 200 mm. Written space *c.* 180 × 115 mm. 2 cols. 37–47 lines. Frame ruling. Collation: 1–10¹⁶ 11¹² wants 12 after f. 173 + 2 leaves after 10 (ff. 171–2) 12 three (ff. 174–6). Quires 1–11 signed a–l. In quires 1–10 the first nine leaves are numbered. Catchwords consist of the last word or two of the page already written as well as the first word or two of the page to come. Written in cursiva. Initials: (i) f. 1, 6-line, blue and red, with ornament of both colours; (ii) 2-line, blue with red ornament or red with blue-grey ornament. Contemporary binding of wooden boards covered with brown leather: stamps of three patterns, lamb and flag, lily, fleuron: five bosses missing from each cover: central clasp. Secundo folio *Cum ergo*.

Written and bound in France (art. 2 suggests the south). In England by s. xv ex. when the words 'Caro suo congnato cristofero Forster (?) committantur hii 2° libri. sub assecuracione Magistri been. Hic liber cum alio tabulorum est michi pignus pro viˢ viiiᵈ' were written on the pastedown at the beginning.¹ 'Clayton meus verus possessor est', f. 176, s. xvi¹. 'Thys booke est me [. . .] Thomas Eden', f. 1, s. xvi. 'Liber Iohannis Eden de Wendelburye' (Oxon.), f. 1, s. xvii in. Acquired like MS. Hamilton 8. Formerly BC. 10. x. 22.

¹ One Christopher Forster was at Oxford at the time (1481–2) when Thomas Benne, M.A., was keeper of the Guildford chest (Emden, *BRUO*, pp. 168, 707).

Hepburn 1. *Biblia*   s. XIII med.

A Bible with the usual contents, except for the presence of the creed 'Quicumque uult . . .' after Psalms, and in the usual order: cf. Bristol Public Library 15. In OT the prologues are of the common set, except that, as sometimes in regular French Bibles, there is no prologue to Wisdom. In NT the prologues are, all but one (589, the second prologue to Matthew), of the common set, together with six others shown here by *: Stegmüller, nos. 596*, 590, 607, 620, 624, 677, 685, 699, 707, 715, 728, 736, 747, 752, 765 (1 Timothy: . . . a Laodicia), 772, 780, 783, 793 (made into two, with heading 'Incipit prologus Pauli ad Hebreos' before 'Hec est causa'), 640, 809, 807*, 812*, 818*, 822*, 834* (before Apocalypse), 839 (after Apocalypse). There are no prologues to the last three Catholic Epistles.

f. 355^{rv}, the last leaf of quire 15, was left blank: NT begins on a new quire, f. 356. ff. 448–449^v blank. Currently written notes on the first leaf of Luke.

ff. i+449+i. 125×88 mm. Written space 95×65 mm. 2 cols. 48 lines. Collation: 1^{24} 2 nineteen (ff. 25–43) 3–4^{24} 5^{26} 6^{22} 7^{24} 8 twenty-five (ff. 164–88) 9–10^{24} 11 twenty-five (ff. 237–61) 12^{22} 13–16^{24} 17 twenty-five (ff. 380–404) 18 nineteen (ff. 405–23) 19 twenty-six (ff. 424–49). Initials: (i) of books, in colour on blue or pink grounds, historiated in good style: a few touches of gold; (ii) of prologues, as (i), but decorated, sometimes with beasts (the letter *I* is a dragon), or birds; (iii) of chapters, 2-line, blue or red with ornament of the other colour; (iv) of verses of psalms, 1-line, blue or red. Binding of black morocco, s. xx^1. Secundo folio *deserto fonte*.

Written in France. Ownership notes: f. 449^v, '+I^{hus} Foyraci procurauit hanc Bibliam suo natiuo Exidelii anno domini millesimo Quingentesimo trigesimo nono, mense aprili. Signabat Foyraci; Consumptum est Folium'; f. 1, at foot, '[. .] F. Cardinalis de Sourdis Arc. Bur[degalensis]. Catalogo inscriptus', s. xvi/xvii. François d'Escoubleau de Sourdis was archbishop of Bordeaux, 1599–1628. Letters at the head of f. 1, 'M' on the left and 'O' on the right: a late medieval pressmark (?). 'N° 16' inside the cover and bookplate of James Stewart Geikie, M.D. The relevant cutting from a Sotheby (?) sale catalogue, s. xx^1, attached to f. i. Bequeathed in 1971 by Dr. C. A. Hepburn.

Murray 504. *A. de Butrio, Reportorium iuris civilis et canonici*   s. xv^1

A. De diccione a vide . . . facit guido de Suza. Explicit Reportorium Excellentissimi doctoris vtriusque iuris domini Anthonii de Botrio deo gracias.

The index, A–Uxor, of the Bolognese lawyer, Anthonius de Butrio, †1408 (cf. Schulte, ii. 293). Bartholus, Cynus, and Guido de Suza are commonly quoted, besides the Digest and Code.

ff. ii+430+ii. Paper. Remains of a medieval foliation, but 'CCCCV' is the only complete figure, f. 407. 376×262 mm. Written space 272×175 mm. 2 cols. 60–2 lines. Frame ruling. Collation: 1–6^{10} 7^8 8–31^{10} 32^{12} 33^{10}+1 leaf after 10 (f. 331) 34–38^{10} 39^{12} wants 5 after f. 386 40–42^{10} 43^{10} wants 7–10, probably blank. Single leaves inserted after 28^3, 39^5, 41^4, 41^6 (ff. 271, 387, 407, 410). Fairly small round hands changing at f. 332 and perhaps elsewhere. Initials: (i) of each alphabetical section, blue with red ornament or red with mauve ornament; (ii) 1-line, blue or red. Binding of s. xviii (see below). Secundo folio *uide*.

Written in Italy (Bologna ?). Two inscriptions follow the *explicit*, both in the same very current hand: (*a*) MCCCCXXVII dexe(m)bris suappar de libris; (*b*) Ego Suappar Andree de libris ziuis bononiensis vendidi d*o*m*i*no Iachopo [. . .] picxente (?) reportorium d*o*mini ant' de butrio continens zircha zentum paginas pro [. . . .] f' de [. . . . .] anno domini mccccxxviii de mense ianuarii'. The pressmark of the Premonstratensian abbey of Parc, near Louvain, 'k. theca 3', is inside the cover and the defaced arms of the abbey are outside, s. xviii. 'Nº 213', 'Nº 5', and '92', f. ii. Lot 92 in the sale of Parc manuscripts in 1829. Book-plate of John Lee, 'Doctors Commons. Repaired Nº 3/94 London': his sale at Sotheby's, 7 Apr. 1876, part of lot 2073, which consisted of eight volumes of A. de Butrio. Sale at Sotheby's, 10 Nov. 1888, lot 135. Given by David Murray in 1910. Formerly BE. 8. x. 8.

Murray 657. *Sextus liber decretalium; Apparatus Johannis Andreae in Sextum* s. xiv med.

1. ff. 1–38ᵛ Bonifacius episcopus seruus seruorum dei dilectis filiis doctoribus et scolaribus uniuersis salaman'ti'ce commorantibus salutem . . .

The Sext, with preliminary letter of Pope Boniface VIII addressed to the university of Salamanca.

2. ff. 39–154ᵛ Quia preposterus est ordo . . . licet nouiter inchoantes. Iohannes an. Explicit apparatus domini Iohannis Andree super sexto Libro decretalium deo gracias amen.

The commentary on the Sext commonly printed with it. Nearly contemporary marginalia and a few of later date.

ff. 154. 400 × 275 mm. Written space 310 × 195 mm. 2 cols. 53 lines (art. 1) and 55 lines (art. 2). Collation: 1–2¹⁰ 3⁸ 4–15¹⁰ 16⁶. Catchwords below the space between the columns: those on ff. 10ᵛ, 20ᵛ are written vertically. Some quires have *ad hoc* signatures in red ink: the marks distinguishing one leaf from another are preceded by *di* on ff. 119–23, by *ma* on ff. 129–33, by *da* on ff. 139–43. Initials of art. 1: (i, ii) 3-line and 2-line, blue with red ornament or red with violet ornament; (iii) for the 'Regule iuris', f. 38ʳᵛ, 1-line, red or blue with ornament of the other colour. Initials of art. 2: (i) f. 39, 6-line, blue with red ornament; (ii) 3-line (and on ff. 39–48ᵛ, 2-line), as (i) in art. 1. Medieval binding of wooden boards covered with red leather now worn and torn: borders formed by vertical and horizontal fillets contain stamps of two patterns, an amphisboena in a frame with rounded base in the outermost and innermost borders and a larger rectangular floral stamp in the border between them; roundels singly or in groups of three are outside, between, and inside the borders: four bands: five small bosses on each cover: two clasps, now missing, fastened from the back to the front cover: remains of paper labels on the back cover and on the spine. Secundo folio *necessitas*.

Written perhaps in Spain and certainly there in s. xiv, as appears from the script and spellings of marginalia. A number in ink '1383' on a round label at the foot of the spine and another in pencil '1427' inside the cover. Given as MS. Murray 504.

GLOUCESTER. CATHEDRAL

W. H. Stevenson provided a fairly full description of MS. 34 and very brief, but accurate notes on the medical and astrological manuscripts (6, 16–18, 25, 7, 19,

28, 15, 21 in that order), on the theological manuscripts, except 27 (23, 1, 3, 14, 2, 29, 12, 22 in that order), on the Lydgate (5) and on the register of writs and collection of statutes (33) in HMC, *Twelfth Report*, Appendix ix (1891), 397–9. The present descriptions appear in an abbreviated form in S. M. Eward, *A Catalogue of Gloucester Cathedral Library*, 1972, pp. 1–5. MS. 15, astrology, s. xvi¹, and the fragments forming MS. 36 are noticed there, pp. 5–7, but not here.

When Canon C. Y. Crawley was librarian (1849–64), most of the manuscripts and many early printed books were admirably rebound in light calf. A notebook records '1858 September. Sent 49 vols. of MSS and Early printed Books to Oxford to be bound' and under Nov. 1860 'Sent to Mr. Omash to be bound 51 vols, To Mr. Nest 54 vols and 76 of College School. All returned by Feb. 18 1861 except the School Books'. A list of the books sent to Omash in 1860 is inserted loose in the notebook and shows that MSS. 9, 20, and 23 were bound at this time. The Dean and Chapter accounts show that Omash was paid £143. 0s. 6d. in 1859 and £46. 13s. 6d. in 1861. The style of the bindings suggest that the manuscripts sent to Oxford in 1858 were nos. 1, 3, 5–7, 14–18, 21, 22, 25–9, 32, 33. They differ from the 1860 bindings by bearing fillets only, not a roll. The inscription in MS. 33 shows that the binder was Omash. Many Omash bindings with and without a roll as ornament are in the Bodleian Library. His work was of high quality.

1. *Vitae sanctorum* 　　　　　　　　　　　　　　　　　　　　s. XIII in.

The third volume of a three-volume collection of lives of the saints covering the church year from 30 Nov. The first volume is now Lincoln Cathedral MS. 149 and the second perhaps Lincoln Cathedral MS. 150.¹ The third volume has lives from 17 Sept., Lambert (art. 1), to 1 Dec., Eligius (art. 33), followed by lives in no particular order. A contemporary table of contents on f. ii is headed 'Hoc ordine scriptus est liber iste sed non legitur per ordinem circa finem libri' and has notes against the lives of Andrew and Eligius (arts. 32, 33), 'miracula eius quere in alio volumine' and 'Ex hoc transponitur lib' ' respectively: the reference is to Lincoln Cathedral MS. 149, art. 1, but the intention to transfer art. 33 to its place after art. 1 there seems not to have been carried out. The contemporary table of contents of Lincoln Cathedral 149 (f. 1ᵛ) has two early additions referring to Gloucester Cathedral 1, arts. 34, 35, 40, 41: (1) 'Kl' ianuarii. Post euangelium Legitur in Ref. Vita sancte Eufrosine. Require in alio volumine post uitam sancti hugonis abbatis cluniacensis'; (2, after 'Vita sancti siluestri [pape]') 'Translationem sancti Iacobi Require in alio volumine post festum sancti kenelmi'.

Art. 42 and parts of arts. 46 (James) and 48 (Aldhelm) appear not to be found elsewhere.

1. f. 1ʳᵛ *17 Sept. Lambert, bishop, M.*² Gloriosus uir lambertus pontifex. opido

---

¹ MS. 150 is perhaps as much as fifty years older than the other two volumes. It may be mere coincidence that it exactly fills the gap between them.

² 'Incipit . . .' precedes all texts but art. 47 and 'Explicit . . .' follows all but arts. 2, 5,

traiectense oriundus fuit . . . Tunc agmina clericorum et uulgus (*ends imperfectly*). Cf. *BHL*, nos. 4677–80.

2. ff. 2–3 *21 Sept. Matthew, E.* (*begins imperfectly*) et nuptiarum bonarum coniugia cum a deo benedicantur . . . et superauerint in dei nomine sequens libellus ostendit. *BHL*, no. 5690. f. 3ᵛ is blank.

3. ff. 4–6 *22 Sept. Maurice et soc., M.* Temporibus diocleciani . . . dei seruientibus 'ore persoluunt' illi . . . amen. Cf. *BHL*, no. 5743.

4. ff. 6–8ᵛ *27 Sept. Cosmas and Damian, M.* Licet omnium sanctorum ueneranda solempnia . . . prestat fieri usque in hodiernum diem . . . amen. *BHL*, no. 1970.

5. ff. 8ᵛ–9ᵛ *29 Sept. Michael.* Incipit dedicatio basilice sancti michaelis archangeli. Memoriam beati archangeli michaelis . . . capiant salutis auxiliante . . . amen. *BHL*, no. 5948.

6. ff. 9ᵛ–12ᵛ *30 Sept. Jerome, presbiter.* Ieronimus presbiter in oppido stridonis quod a gothis . . . (f. 12) impleuit annis octoginta octo et mensibus sex auxiliante . . . amen. Contigit autem huiusmodi miraculum in monasterio sancti ieronimi fieri . . . asserendo narrantur. Cf. *BHL*, no. 3869.

7. ff. 12ᵛ–22 *1 Oct. Remigius, archbishop.* Post uindictam scelerum que facta sunt . . . per orbem nationibus predicare sufficerent. Begins as *BHL*, no. 7155.

8. ff. 22–30 *2 Oct. Leodegarius, bishop, M.* Gloriosus igitur ac preclarus leodegarius urbis augustudunensis episcopus . . . Translatio uero sancti corporis medio marcii mensis. *BHL*, no. 4853.

9. ff. 30–35ᵛ *9 Oct. Denis et soc.* Post beatam ac salutiferam . . . ut par erat amisit regnante . . . amen. *BHL*, no. 2175.

10. ff. 35ᵛ–39 *7 Oct. Sergius and Bacchus, M.* Imperante maximiano . . preceptum dei.' cui . . . amen. *BHL*, no. 7599.

11. ff. 39–40ᵛ *14 Oct. Calixtus, pope, M.* Temporibus macrini et alexandri incendio diuino concremata est . . . sub die duodecimo kalendarum nouembris in pace amen. *BHL*, no. 1523.

The word 'pape' has been erased from heading and colophon.

12. ff. 40ᵛ–42ᵛ *18 Oct. Luke, E.* Incipit prefacio in vita sancti luce ewangeliste. Lucas hebraice latine ipse consurgens . . . (*prologue*) Cum in diuersis voluminibus . . . (*text*) Igitur gloriosissimus apostolus . . . quem predicauit. qui cum . . . amen. *BHL*, no. 4973.

13. ff. 42ᵛ–43ᵛ *18 Oct. Justus, M.* Incipit passio sancti iusti martyris que est xv kl' nouembris. Cum deus omnipotens sanctorum numerum . . . in quem credunt gentes.' cui est . . . amen. *BHL*, no. 4590.

34, 38, 42, 43, 45–48. To save space I omit these formulae, if they conform to type: Incipit (*or* Explicit) passio (*or* vita) sancti . . ., followed sometimes by the rank, e.g. bishop, and usually, but not always, by the class, A(postle), E(vangelist), M(artyr), C(onfessor), or V(irgin), but not by the date. Dates occur only in the headings of arts. 13, 18, 31, 32.

14. ff. 43ᵛ–45 *25 Oct. Crispin and Crispinian, M.* Cum sub maximiano et diocleciano qui simul . . . largitur infirmis. cui . . . *BHL,* no. 1990.

15. ff. 45–8 *28 Oct. Simon and Jude, A.* Symon chananeus et iudas zelotes apostoli . . . et ultima de decimo. Gloria deo . . . amen. *BHL,* nos. 7749, 7751.

16. ff. 48–51 *2 Nov. Eustace et soc.* Incipit vita et exilium sancti Eustachii sociorumque eius. In diebus traiani imperatoris demonum . . . captiuos plurimos ducentes. Explicit uita (*etc.*) Begins as *BHL,* no. 2760.

17. f. 51ʳᵛ Incipit passio eorum. Contigit autem antequam reuerteretur . . . gubernat in celo et in terra . . . amen.

18. ff. 51ᵛ–53ᵛ *31 Oct. Quintin, M.* Incipit passio sancti Quintini Martyris pridie kl' nouembris. Sanctum atque perfectum et gloriosum triumphum . . . octauo kalendas iulii. post gloriosam resurrectionem . . . *BHL,* nos. 6999, 7000.

19. ff. 53ᵛ–56 *6 Nov. Leonard, C.* Beatus igitur leonardus temporibus anastasii imperatoris in prouintia galliarum . . . ibidem curantur.' prestante . . . amen. *BHL,* no. 4862.

20. ff. 56–57ᵛ Inc' Mir'. Preterea post transitum sancti leonardi per miracula . . . alteram ad sanctum leonardum. Cf. *BHL,* nos. 4863–71.

21. ff. 57ᵛ–60 *8 Nov. Quatuor Coronati.* Temporibus quibus dioclecianus perrexit pannonis . . . eorum recoleretur. regnante . . . amen. *BHL,* no. 1836.

22. ff. 60–61ᵛ *9 Nov. Theodore, M.* Temporibus suis maximus et maximianus imperatores miserunt . . . usque in presentem diem ad laudem . . . amen. *BHL,* no. 8077.

23. ff. 61ᵛ–63 *11 Nov. Menna, M.* Anno secundo imperii sui dioclecianus augustus ad obseruandum . . . nominis sui usque in presentem diem. cui est . . . amen. *BHL,* no. 5921.

24. ff. 63–81 *11 Nov. Martin, bishop.* Incipit prefatio seueri episcopi in uita sancti martini episcopi. Plerique mortali studio . . . (*text*) Igitur martinus Sabarie pannoniarum oppido . . . (f. 68) crediderit. Incipit epistola seueri ad eusebium presbiterum. Hesterna die cum ad me . . . (f. 68ᵛ) probatum. Incipit alia epistola sulpitii ad aurelianum diaconum. Postea quam a me . . . (f. 69ᵛ) solatium. Incipit liber primus dialogorum seueri sulpitii. Cum in unum locum ego et gallus . . . dolore discessum est. *BHL,* nos. 5610–12, 5614–16.

25. ff. 81–84ᵛ *20 Nov. Edmund, king, M.* Incipit prologus in passione sancti eadmundi Regis et Martyris. Domino sancte metropolitane dorouernensium ecclesie archiepiscopo dunstano . . . (*text*) Asciti aliquando in britanniam . . . quibus meremur supplicium.' per eum . . . amen. *BHL,* no. 2392.

26. ff. 84ᵛ–89ᵛ *22 Nov. Cecilia, V. M.* Incipit prologus in passione sancte cecilie uirginis et martyris. Humanas laudes et mortalium infulas . . . (*text*) Omnibus patent uestigia . . . ad memoriam beate cecilie usque in hodiernum diem.' Regnante . . . amen. *BHL,* no. 1495.

27. ff. 89ᵛ–91 *23 Nov. Clement, pope, M.* Secundus romane ecclesie prefuit episcopus clemens . . . et benedicitur ibi cristus filius dei.' qui . . . amen. *BHL,* no. 1848.

The word 'pape' has been erased from heading and colophon.

28. ff. 91–2 Incipiunt miracula. In diuinis uoluminibus refertur quod . . . implere dignatus est cristus dominus noster. cui . . . Expliciunt miracula. *BHL,* nos. 1855, 1857.

29. ff. 92–7 *24 Nov. Chrisogonus, M., and Anastasia, V. M.* Incipit prologus in passione sancti chrisogoni martyris et sancte anastasie virginis et martyris. Omnia que a sanctis gesta sunt . . . *(text)* Pretextati illustris uiri filiam anastasiam . . . dominus beneficia sua ad laudem . . . amen. *BHL,* no. 1795.

30. ff. 97–105ᵛ *25 Nov. Katherine, V.M.* Incipit prologus in passione sancte katerine uirginis et martyris. Cum sanctorum fortia gesta ad memoriam . . . *(text)* Tradunt annales hystorie quod . . . ad passionem properauit.' cui . . . amen. *BHL,* no. 1663.

31. ff. 105ᵛ–106 *29 Nov. Saturninus, M.* Incipit passio sancti saturnini martyris. iii kl' decembris. Tempore quo maximianus augustus rediens . . . sub die tercio kalendarum decembrium.' in laudem . . . amen. *BHL,* no. 7493.

32. ff. 106–108ᵛ *30 Nov. Andrew, A.* Incipit passio sancti andree apostoli. ii kl' Decembris. Passionem sancti andree apostoli quam oculis nostris . . . operari non desinit.' ad laudem . . . amen. Begins as *BHL,* no. 428.

33. ff. 108ᵛ–113 *1 Dec. Eligius, bishop.* Igitur eligius lemouicas galliarum urbe . . . a superis emisit spiritum. Begins as *BHL,* no. 2474.

34. ff. 113–115ᵛ *17 July. Kenelm, M.* Incipit prologus in passione beati kenelmi martyris. De beato kenelmo in tota anglia . . . *(text)* Kenulfus. gloriosissimus et piissimus rex merciorum . . . infixos habuerat.' per omnia benedictus deus amen.

Cf. Hardy, *Materials for British History* (RS), i. 508.

35. f. 116ʳᵛ Incipit translatio corporis beati iacobi apostoli a ier' ad hisp'. Postea uero discipuli eius collegerunt ossa apostoli . . . prope locum sancti iacobi apostoli domini nostri iesu cristi.' cui . . . amen. Explicit . . . *(as above)* . . . ab ierosolimis ad hispanias.

The first leaf of quire 15. The heading begins on the second line of the first column on the recto. The line above is blank, perhaps as a result of erasure.

36. ff. 116ᵛ–118 Incipiunt miracula eiusdem apostoli. Tres militi dioceseos lugdunensis ecclesie sibi condixerunt . . . peruenire ualeamus amen. Expliciunt *(etc.).*

The three miracles printed in *Liber Sancti Jacobi, Codex Calixtinus* (ed. W. M. Whitehill, 1944, i. 276–83, miracles XVI–XVIII) derived from Dicta Anselmi, chs. 21–3, ed. R. W. Southern, *Memorials of St Anselm,* 1969, pp. 196–209: cf. ibid., p. 29, and Southern in *Mediaeval and Renaissance Studies,* iv (1958), 207.

37. ff. 118–135ᵛ *5 Jan. Edward, king.* Incipit prologus in uita reuerentissimi

Regis eadwardi. Multis ueterum studio . . . (*letter*) Dilecto et diligendo . . . (*text*) Gloriosi ac deo dilecti regis ea(d)wardi . . . corda commouit.

The life by Ailred, *BHL*, no. 2423: cf. for twenty-nine copies, not this, A. Hoste, *Bibliotheca Aelrediana*, 1962, pp. 123–5. A table of forty-five unnumbered chapters before the text.

38. ff. 135ᵛ–138 Incipit relatio de ymagine domini. Apud cesaream capadocie urbem . . . nec in perditione morientium letatur. Qui cum . . .

Begins as *BHL*, nos. 4228–9.

39. ff. 138–42 *1 Dec. Chrysantus, M., and Daria, V. M.* Incipit prologus in passione sancti crisanti m' et Darie vir. Hystoriam priorum sanctorum . . . (*text*) Pollemius uir illustrissimus alexandrine urbis . . . corone suscepit . . . amen. Explicit passio (*etc.*). *BHL*, no. 1787.

40. ff. 142–5 *29 Apr. Hugh, abbot.* Incipit 'prologus in' uita sancti hugonis abbatis cluniace(n)sis. Patrum cluniacensium conuentui sancto.' seruus hugo . . . (*text*) Hugo iste quem debitus sermo . . . anno uerbi incarnati millesimo centesimo nono. Explicit uita (*etc.*) *BHL*, no. 4012.

41. ff. 145–147ᵛ *11 Feb. Euphrosyna, V.* Fuit uir in alexandria nomine paphnutius . . . glorificantes deum patrem et filium et spiritum sanctum.' cui . . . amen. Begins as *BHL*, no. 2722.

42. ff. 148–50 *17 Mar. Patrick, bishop, C.* Patricius qui sulcat uocatur brittoni natione . . . et est in dun lethgles.

Printed by L. Bieler, 'Eine Patriksvita in Gloucester', *Festschrift Bernhard Bischoff*, 1971, 347–59, with a facsimile of part of f. 148.

43. ff. 150–3 *26 June. Salvius, bishop, M.* Regnante in perpetuum domino et saluatore nostro iesu cristo tempore gloriosissimi ducis francorum . . . et unus in trinitate. Ipsi honor . . . amen. *BHL*, no. 7472.

44. ff. 153–62 *19 Jan. Wulfstan, bishop, C.* Gesta sanctorum patrum . . . indulsit sanitate.

BHL, no. 8757. *Vita Wulfstani*, ed. R. R. Darlington, (Camden Soc., xl), pp. 68–108. The text show signs of use and was marked in pencil for nine lessons.

45. ff. 162–163ᵛ Incipiunt miracula post obitum ipsius. Si salutifere fidei nostri rudimentum . . . rediuiuum receperunt. *BHL*, no. 8758. f. 163ᵛ, col. 2 is blank.

46. ff. 164–175ᵛ *James, A.* Incipit prefacio beati calixti pape in miracula beati iacobi apostoli. Calixtus episcopus seruus seruorum dei uenerabilibus filiis Gilielmo . . . (*argumentum*) Summopere precium . . . (*text*) Beatus iacobus apostolus qui sub obedientie feruore . . . et mirabilia eius filiis hominum.

Paragraphs 1–3, 5–20 agree with *Codex Calixtinus*, i. 261 sqq. (caps. 1–15, 19–22: for caps. 16–18 see above, art. 36), with some differences in order, and most of paras. 21–38 are to be found in Pseudo-Turpin and in *Acta Sanctorum*. Paras. 39–64 (ff. 171ᵛ–175ᵛ) are an English collection otherwise unrecorded, it seems, mostly about people who sought help from the hand of St. James at Reading. Para. 64 concerns Peter, son of Richard de Leuns of Wavercurt, near Banbury, A.D. 1197.

47. ff. 175ᵛ–182 *22 June. Alban et soc., M.* Reuerendo patri et domino karissimo

Symoni Willelmus in domino salutem. Cum liber anglico sermone conscriptus
. . . (*prologue*) Quisquis beatorum martyrum . . . commendare curaui. Passio
beati albani anglorum prothomartyris et sancti amphibali sociorumque eius.
Cum persecutio que sub diocletiano mota est . . . commutare dominus iesus
cristus.' qui uiuit . . . amen. *BHL*, no. 213.

48. ff. 182–92. *25 May. Aldhelm, bishop, C.* Hoc opus osmundus nulli probitate
secundus Presul sanciuit canonisque sub ordine misit. Incipit commendatio
sequentis operis. Dignum aliquid cognitione uestra . . . habeatis seruitium.
Incipit prefatio in uita sancti aldelmi episcopi et confessoris eximii. Sanctorum
patrum pia certamina studio recolentes . . . pro posse nostro cupimus. (*text*) Ad
sancti igitur genealogiam flectamus ingenium . . . deuote permansit seruicium.

The life by Faricius, *BHL*, no. 256. Printed in *PL* lxxxix. 63–84, from B.L., Cotton
Faustina B. iv, ff. 141–58, but the 'commendatio' does not occur there nor the matter in
the last eleven paragraphs here, from the words 'Decursis autem non plus duobus annis'
(ff. 188ᵛ–192), in which there are, among other things, a vision of Aldhelm vouchsafed
to the writer (f. 189) and miracles concerning women, one 'in uico culchertune' (f. 190ᵛ)
and another about forty miles from Malmesbury at 'galingáán' (f. 191ᵛ). A table of
twenty-nine unnumbered chapters precedes the text. ff. 192ᵛ–194ᵛ were left blank.
Scribbles here include (f. 194) 'þᵗ ys soþ þᵗ alle men seyn in hope ys help þᵗ ys my tryst
þer of iᶜ am fayn in hope ys help so seyd y ferst', s. xiv ex.

ff. ii+194+i. f. ii is a medieval flyleaf: see above. Thick parchment. 393 × 280 mm.
Written space 305 × 195 mm. 2 cols. 48 lines (39 lines on ff. 1–3). Pricks in both margins
to guide ruling. The first line of writing is above the top ruled line. Collation: 1 three
(ff. 1–3) 2–24⁸ 25⁸ wants 6, probably blank, after f. 192: f. 194ᵛ was once pasted down.
Mainly in one clear hand. Initials: (i) green and red or blue and red, with ornament in
two or three of these colours; (ii) 2-line, blue, sometimes with red ornament, or red,
always without ornament. Capital letters in the ink of the text are touched with red.
Running titles in red. Binding of s. xix. Secundo folio *et nuptiarum*.

Written in England. The interest shown in St. James and in Reading (arts. 35, 36, 46),
the presence of a life of Hugh, abbot of Cluny (art. 40), and the seventeenth-century
provenance suggest that the three-volume collection, of which this is the third volume,
may have belonged to the cell of Reading at Leominster, some twenty miles north-west of
Hellens. 'Ex dono Foulki Wallwyn Armig. de Hellens in Comitat. Hereford', f. ii, presumably records a gift to the cathedral by Fulk Walwyn of Hellens, Much Marcle, near
Ledbury, †1660.

2. *Pseudo-Athanasius, etc.* s. XII², XV/XVI

1 (s. xii²). ff. 1–71ᵛ Nine texts on the Trinity and the Creed which form a single
unit in Bodleian, Canon. Pat. Lat. 112 in Corbie *ab* script, s. ix in., and in a dozen
later manuscripts mostly of Norman or English origin: cf. A. Wilmart, 'La lettre
de Potamius à Saint Athanase', *RB* xxx (1913), 257–85. (*a*) f. 1 Incipit liber
primus Athanasii episcopi de unitate trinitatis. Unus deus pater et unigenitus
dei filius . . . et unitas trinitatis. Explicit liber octauus fidei patris. et filii. et
spiritus sancti. Hos libellos octo transcripsi. qui multa addita et immutata continent. (*b*) f. 23 Incipit libellus fidei patris . . . uestras ante porcos. Credimus
patrem omnipotentem . . . pro peccatis eternam. Hoc placuit. amen. Explicit
expositio fidei catholicẹ. (*c*) f. 23ᵛ Incipit De trinitate et de spiritu sancto. His

qui filium dei creatum esse . . . effici poterimus. Amen. Explicit . . . (*d*) f. 35 Incipit prologus in Altercatione Sancti Athanasii episcopi et Confessoris contra Arrium. Sabellium. uel fotinum hereticos. Cum in manus strenui lectoris . . . (f. 61) ualeat peruenire. Explicit Altercatio Inter Athanasium Alexandrinum episcopum et Arrium hereticum. Incipit Sententia. Iudicis Probi. Probus. Amore ueritatis . . . forte capessant. Explicit sententia iudicis probi . . . (*e*) f. 65 Incipit epistola Potamii ad Athanasium . . . subscripserunt. Domino fratri gloriosissimo ac beatissimo . . . (*f*) f. 66 Epistola Athanasii ad Luciferum. Domino beatissimo ac merito . . . Etsi credo . . . desiderantissime. (*g*) f. 67 Solutiones obiectionum Arrianorum. Prima enim obiectio est . . . creatum ostendere. (*h*) f. 71ᵛ De fide Sancti Ieronimi. Credo in unum deum patrem . . . ad uitam eternam. amen. (*i*) f. 71ᵛ Eiusdem de fide apud Bethleem. Credimus in unum deum . . . quod est. unius cum patre (*ends imperfectly*).

(*a*). *PL* lxii. 237–88. *Clavis*, no. 105 (Eusebius Vercellensis). Wilmart, loc. cit., p. 270. (*b*). *PL* lxii. 287–8. *Clavis*, no. 552 (Gregorius Illiberitanus). Wilmart, p. 271. (*c*). Ed. Simonetti, Bologna, 1956. *PL* lxii. 307–34. Wilmart, p. 271. (*d*). *PL* lxii. 179–238. *Clavis*, no. 807 (Vigilius). Wilmart, p. 272. (*e*). Ed. Wilmart, pp. 280–3 (cf. p. 272). *Clavis*, no. 542. (*f*). *PL* lxii. 515–17. Wilmart, p. 273. (*g*). *PL* lxii. 469–72. *Clavis*, no. 812. Wilmart, p. 274. (*h*). Ed. Morin, *RB* xxi. 3. *Clavis*, no. 553. Wilmart, p. 274. (*i*). Ed. A. E. Burn, *An Introduction to the Creeds*, 1899, pp. 245–6. *Clavis*, no. 554. Wilmart, p. 274. Two leaves of (*a*) are missing after f. 16 and one leaf of (*d*) is missing after f. 51.

Arts. 2–12 were written *c*. 1500. Römer notices arts. 2, 3 (ii. 125).

2. ff. 72ᵛ–74ᵛ Diui Aurelii Augustini hipponensis Episcopi Omelia in illud quod scribitur in Canticis Canticorum capitulo 4° licet sub veteri translatione. Ibo michi ad montem . . . sponse mee. Sponsus quidam hic loquitur . . . in vnum congregamur. Finis.

PL cxcviii. 1784 (P. Comestor, sermo 29). f. 72ʳ blank.

3. f. 74ᵛ Augustinus de secreto gloriose incarnationis domini nostri iesu christi. Inter cetera hunc locum lege . . . cum timore et secrete sunt exponenda. Explicit transcriptum ex quodam veteri codice in biblioteca Wyndesore lege caute et catholice.

Attributed to Augustine in Bodleian, Laud misc. 436, s. ixᴵ (Römer, i. 380). Gloucester Cathedral D. 3.14, Augustine, *Confessiones*, Deventer 1483 (*GKW* 2896) has at the end copies of arts. 3, 4 in the hand of William Horman and headed by him 'Ex vetusto volumine in libraria Wyndesore sicut et quod sequitur': cf. below on binding and ownership.

4. f. 74ᵛ Fides gregorii episcopi gneocestirie et martiris. illius qui stagnum piscibus copiosum in arentem campum conuertit et montem prece transtulit . . . Vnus deus pater verbi viuentis sapientie . . . et sempiternus ex sempiterno.

The creed of Gregory, bishop of Neo-Cesarea, in the translation of Rufinus (*PG* x. 983–7). Cf. art. 3.

5. ff. 75–76ᵛ Planctus siue lamentum Origenis per diuum hieronimum presbiterum e greco traductum. Errores vero quos hic deplangit Origenes recitat beatus Hieronimus in epistola secunda siue libro contra Ruphinum post medium qui sic incipit Scedule quas. In afflictione et dolore animi incipio loqui . . . mihi ecclesie.

Also in Bodleian, Fairfax 25 (*Sum. Cat.* 3905), ff. 116–119ᵛ and in Vatican, Reg. lat. 121, ff. 316ᵛ–319.

6. ff. 76ᵛ–77ᵛ Leodrisius Crebellus ad Eneam siluium Cardinalem senensem (1448–58) in epistolam Ioannis Chrisostomi prologus incipit. Ad patrem reuerentia cultuque . . . Mediolani xiii kal. septembris. Ioannis Chrisostomi . . . ad Cyriacum episcopum . . . Epistola e greco in latinum traducta a Leodrisio Crebello.

For the original cf. *PG* lii. 681–5. Another copy of this translation, but with a preface by Crebelli addressed to P. C. Decembrio, is Florence, Bibl. Riccardiana, MS. 827, ff. 121ᵛ–124. Cf. also L. Cribellus, *De expeditione Pii II adversus Turcos*, ed. C. Zimolo (Rerum Italicarum Scriptores xxiii, pt. 5), 1948–50.[1]

7. ff. 77ᵛ–79ᵛ Sentencia sancti Hieronimi de essentia et inuisibilitate et immensitate dei. et attributis eidem. Omnipotens deus pater et filius . . . se manifestum demonstrare. Explicit.

Pseudo-Jerome, De membris domini, *PL* xlii. 1199–1206/8.

8. f. 80 Remigius in Matheum capitulum cccli. Si anni recte . . . manducarent pascha.

That the new moon was on 8 Mar. in the year of Christ's Passion. Manuscripts of the commentary are listed by Stegmüller, nos. 7226–7.

9. ff. 80–82ᵛ Epistola roberti Grosthedde episcopi lincolniensis de intelligentiis. Dilecto sibi in cristo magistro sude (*sic*) rufo . . . errorem meum corrigas etc. Explicit.

Grosseteste, De forma prima omnium and De intelligenciis. Cf. Thomson, *Grosseteste*, pp. 98, 104.

10. ff. 82ᵛ–83 (*a*) A note about Bede and his works. (*b*) An extract from Vincent of Beauvais, Speculum historiale, lib. 14, caps. 163, 175, about Alcuin and other English scholars and Charlemagne. (*c*) Epistola Sergii pape ad Ceolfridum abbatem pro venerabili beda. Hortamur deo dilectam . . . presentiam impertitum.

(*b*). Extracts from bk. 23, caps. 173, 175 (edn. 1591, f. 331).
(*c*). *PL* lxxxix. 33.

11. ff. 83–4 Notes and extracts: (*a*) from Eusebius, Historia ecclesiastica, bk. 3, ch. xi, Post iacobi martirium . . . est sub traiano; (*b*) on the seventy-two apostles, chs. 11, 20, 32; (*c*) from Jerome against Vigilantius on the translation of the bones of the prophet Samuel; (*d*) on the Assumption of B.V.M.

(*a*). Cf. *PG* xx. 246, 251, 282.
(*c*). *PL* xxiii. 343.

12. ff. 84ᵛ–86 Beatus Fulgentius episcopus de assumptione beate Marie Virginis et matris domini. Adest dilectissimi fratres dies valde venerabilis . . . per inmortalia secula seculorum Amen. τελωσ (*in red*).

Pseudo-Augustine, Sermon ccviii in *PL* xxxix. 2130–4. *Clavis*, no. 368/208 (Ambrosius Autpertus). ff. 86ᵛ–87ᵛ blank.

---

[1] I owe these two references to Professor P. O. Kristeller.

13. f. i^v A table of contents in a hand which first listed art. 1 and then arts. 2–10a in another ink.

The hand is William Horman's, since it is the same as that in the table of contents in the Deventer Augustine, D. 3.14 (see above, art. 3).

14. The pastedowns are two bifolia of a manuscript of sermons written in long lines in a current and difficult English hand, s. xiv in.

A heading is 'Dominica in passione'. There are references to Anselm, Aristotle, Augustine, Avicenna, Cicero, Gesta Britonum and Juvenal.

ff. i+87. 325×230 mm. **Art. 1.** Written space 240×160 mm. Pricks in both margins to guide ruling. 2 cols. 36 lines. Collation: 1–2^8 3^8 wants 1, 2 before f. 17 4–6^8 7^8 wants 5 after f. 51 8–9^8 10^2. Initials: (i) blue, red, or green, with ornament in two or three of these colours; (ii, iii) 2-line and 1-line, red, blue, or, rarely, green. **Arts. 2–12.** Written space 238×153 mm. 2 cols. 46–62 lines. Collation: 11–12^8. Several small secretary hands. Red initials.

Binding of wooden boards covered with brown leather bearing stamps of the 'Virgin and Child' binder, no. IV in the list by N. R. Ker in *The Library*, 5th Series, xvii (1962), 80–5: two clasps missing. Secundo folio *deitate patris*.

Written in England. Art. 1 belonged to and arts. 2–12 were probably made for William Horman, *c*. 1458–1535: cf. arts. 3, 13, MS. 3 and Ker, loc. cit. One of a group of three manuscripts (MSS. 2, 3, 23) and six printed books (D. 3.14 (formerly D. 3.20), D. 3.16 (formerly D. 3.18), E. 7.5, G. 5.2, H. 6.6, 11.2.15), all belonging to Horman, which were given to the Cathedral Library by Henry Brett and his sisters Margaret and Joyce, as appears from the Benefactors' Book, pp. 22, 26.[1] The fact that five shillings were paid in 1674 to 'Mr Bretts servant Howell bringing several books given to ye library'[2] suggests that the donor was the Henry Brett who died on 31 Mar. 1674 aged 87, but the Henry, Margaret, and Joyce of the Benefactors' Book were his grandchildren: cf. *Visitation of the County of Gloucester, 1682–3*, ed. T. Fitzroy-Fenwick and W. C. Metcalfe, 1884. The younger Henry Brett (of Dowdeswell), †8 Apr. 1682, aged 25. The elder Henry Brett married Margaret, daughter of Thomas Seames, alderman of Gloucester,[3] and it is probably through Seames that Horman's books came to the Bretts: 'Thomas Semys' is at the beginning of both D. 3.16 and 11.2.15. 'N°. 4', f. i.

3. *Augustinus, De Civitate Dei*   s. XIII ex.

1. ff. 11–241^v Incipiunt capitula primi libri doctoris augustini de ciuitate dei.... Sentencia de libro retractacionum beati augustini de ciuitate dei. Interea cum roma . . . (f. 11^v) ciuitatem dei. Aurelii Augustini doctoris yponensis episcopi de ciuitate dei liber primus incipit contra paganos in nomine domini. Gloriosissi-

---

[1] These books are listed in Miss Eward's catalogue, pp. 17, 214, 12, 125, 14, 39. Professor Hellinga noticed the Deventer Augustine, D. 3.14, in the Benefactors' Book, when he and I visited Gloucester Cathedral Library with the Oxford Bibliographical Society on 15 July 1967. His discovery adds five more to the four Horman books at Gloucester which I described in *The Library*. All five have the distinctive titling on the tail and one of them, E. 7.5, an index to the works of St. Ambrose printed in 1506, has a typically Hormanian note explaining how it works. A tenth book of the gift, 'Variorum Authorum Medicinam', has not been found.

[2] Account Book 3, p. 279. I owe this reference and other help to Miss Suzanne Eward.

[3] Thomas Semys, clothier, was mayor of Gloucester in 1565 and the same name occurs in the mayoral list at 1578 and 1599.

mam ciuitatem dei . . . congratulantes agant. Gloria et honor . . . amen. Explicit liber vicesimus secundus de ciuitate dei.

PL xli. 13–804. Of the twenty-two books, 1 and 11–22 are preceded by numbered tables of chapters. A pencil note on f. 47, the first leaf of quire 5, refers to the copying of this quire: 'Pro isto quaterno xiiii sol'. Die sabbati ante festum beati Eadmundi. Item ii sol' '. Many contemporary marginalia in a good current hand. The text has been corrected carefully and ff. 156* and 166* are slips of parchment on which passages omitted by the scribe on ff. 157 and 165ᵛ have been supplied: 'Quere super cedulam' is written at the appropriate point on f. 157.

2 (added in s. xvi¹). ff. 1–10ᵛ Aaron non consensit populo idolotranti li.14 c. 11f . . .

An alphabetical index to art. 1, ending imperfectly at 'Pulcritudo'. For more exact reference, chapters are subdivided by letters of the alphabet from *a* to *k*: corresponding letters have not been entered in the margins of art. 1. For this and similar indexes in books belonging to William Horman see N. R. Ker in *The Library*, 5th series, xvii (1962), 77–85.

ff. ii+241+i. f. ii is a medieval flyleaf. 335 × 240 mm. Written space *c.* 245 × 150 mm. 2 cols. 51 lines. Collation: 1¹⁰ 2–8¹² 9¹⁰+1 leaf after 1 (f. 96) 10–20¹² 21⁴, together with two inserted slips (see above). Initials: (i) red and blue with ornament of both colours; (ii) 1-line, red or blue. Capital letters in the ink of the text are filled with red. Binding of s. xix. Secundo folio *recte saperent*.

Written in England. An erased inscription, s. xiii (?), at the head of f. iiᵛ. Bequeathed to Eton College by William Horman, headmaster 1486, fellow 1501, †1535: 'Donum Guilielmi Hormani quondam socii huius contubernii', f. iiᵛ.¹ Given to Gloucester Cathedral by Henry Brett: Benefactors' Book, p. 22, no. 6 (cf. MS. 2).

5. *J. Lydgate, Siege of Troy (in English)* s. XV

Lydgate's Troy Book, beginning imperfectly in line 56 of the prologue and ending imperfectly in line 14 of the Envoy (f. 372ᵛ).

Described in detail as G in H. Bergen's edition, EETS, Extra Series, cxxvi (1935), 38–40. Probably fifty-three leaves are missing between f. 1 and f. 372 with bk. 1, lines 4213–424 after f. 64, bk. 2, lines 5329–6592 after f. 145, bk. 3 lines 2251–3492, 3761–4164, and 4303–852 after ff. 207, 211, and 213. Corners only remain of f. 52* which contained bk. 1, lines 3291–3360, and of f. 373, which contained the Envoy from line 15. The first leaf of the text and the other missing leaves existed when a pagination was made in s. xvii. The seventh sheet of quire 2 is bound the wrong way round: the pagination of ff. 25–8, '57–58', '53–56', '51, 52' shows the right order. The third and fourth sheets of quire 20 were supplied in s. xv (ff. 316–17, 330–1). Bk. 2 begins on a new quire (quire 5) at f. 68; bk. 3, f. 176. ff. 65ᵛ–67ᵛ are blank.

ff. i+374+i, foliated i, 1–52, 52*, 53–373 (374). ff. 52* and 373 are small fragments: see above. Paper and (the outside and middle sheets of each quire) parchment. 290 × 205 mm. Written space *c.* 225 × 115 mm. 34–42 long lines. Frame ruling. Collation: 1²⁰ wants 1, 2 2¹⁶ 3²⁰ 20 cancelled+1 leaf after 19 (f. 53) 4²⁰ wants 12–14 after f. 64, 17, 18, probably blank, after f. 66 and 20, probably blank, after f. 67 5²⁰+1 leaf after 20 (f. 88) 6–7¹⁸ 8²⁰ 9²⁰ wants 2–19 after f. 145 10–12²⁰ 13²⁰ wants 2–19 after f. 207 14²⁰ wants 4–9 after f. 211 and 12–19 after f. 213 15–16²⁰ 17¹⁸+1 leaf after 1 (f. 256) 18–21²⁰ 22²² wants 21, 22 after f. 373.

¹ This inscription is also in Eton College MSS. 48, 79, 80, 98, 119, 126, 145, q.v.

In each quire the first two parchment leaves are marked with a serial capital letter and the first eight paper leaves with the letters a–h, for example (quire 3), C, a–h, C. A fairly clear current anglicana, probably all by one scribe, except for the four supply leaves, which are in a mixed, but mainly secretary hand. 4-line and 3-line spaces for initials have not been filled. Binding of s. xix.

Written in England. 'Iohn Risdon', f. 272, s. xvi. Listed in the catalogue of Gloucester Cathedral manuscripts made in 1671, Bodleian MS. Tanner 268, f. 8. Probably identifiable with 'An old English manuscript' listed in the Benefactors' Book, p. 6, as the gift of John Donne of Gloucester.

6. *Gilbertus Anglicus, Compendium Medicinae*　　　　s. XIII/XIV

Incipit liber morborum tam uniuersalium quam particularium a magistro gilleberto anglico compilatus ab omnibus auctoribus et practicis magistrorum extractus et exceptus qui compendium medicine intitulatur . . . (*table of chapters*) . . . Morbis vniuersalibus propositi nostri intencio est . . . fabarum (*ends imperfectly*).

The Compendium Medicinae of Gilbertus Anglicus, edn. Lyons, 1510. The foliation shows the correct order of ff. 5–47 which are misbound in the order 37–46, 5–10, 47, 11–36. The last words on f. 84ᵛ are 'uel ii. ut dictum est' (end of chapter De esora magna, edn., f. ccclviii). The rest of f. 84ᵛ was left blank. The text continues on f. 85 in another hand with 57 lines to the column. The last words on this leaf are near the end of the chapter De incendio ignis uel aque, four chapters from the end (edn., f. ccclxi).

Blank spaces contain a list of herbs (f. 47ᵛ, s. xiii/xiv) and a method 'ad detrahendos cuniculos de vno loco ad aliud per spacium de j mil' (f. 84ᵛ, s. xv).

ff. i+85+iv. ff. 86–8 are blank medieval end-leaves. 314×210 mm. Written space 240×150 mm (ff. 1–10, 215×150 mm). 2 cols. 48–53 lines. Collation: 1¹⁴+1 leaf after 14 2¹⁰ 3⁸ 4 three (ff. 34–6) 5¹⁰+1 leaf after 9 (f. 46) 6⁸ 7⁸+1 leaf after 2 (f. 58) 8¹⁰ 9⁶ 10⁴ 11 one (f. 85). Initials: (i) f. 37, 7-line, red and blue with ornament of both colours; (ii) 2-line, blue or red, the former ornamented in red, the latter in violet or not at all. Binding of s. xix. Secundo folio *Hic queritur*.

Written probably in England. 'Mortonbagot iuxta emlaye Robertus rector' is scribbled on f. 7ᵛ, s. xv: the place is Mortonbagot, near Henley in Arden, Warwickshire. Identifiable with the 'De Morbis. fol. MS.', no. (6) in the list of gifts of Henry Fowler in the Benefactors' Book, p. 25. His benefaction was in 1677 to judge from the entry in Account Book 4, p. 341: 'Given Dʳ Fowlers man bringing books for yᵉ library 5.0'.[1] Fowler, a doctor and alderman of Gloucester, †1685, was son of Henry Fowler, rector of Minchinhampton, who owned MS. 12, q.v.

7. *Guido de Cauliaco, Chirurgia*　　　　s. xv med.

In dei nomine Incipit inuentarium seu collectarium in parte cirurgicali medicine compilatum et completum anno domini millesimo cccᵒ lxiiiᵒ per guidonem de caulhiaco cyrurgicum magistrum in medicina in preclaro studio montispessulani. Postquam prius gratias ago . . . vrinam et ideo iuxta (*ends imperfectly*).

The Chirurgia of Guy de Chauliac, printed in 1490 and later. Five leaves of the first quire are missing and two leaves of the last quire. The last words now are in pt. 7, doct. 2,

---

[1] I owe the reference to Miss Eward.

ch. 6: cf. edn., 1513, f. 73ᵛ col. 2/7 from foot, and (in English translation) EETS cclxv (1971), 636/36. ff. iiᵛ, 169 contain recipes, s. xv ex.

ff. ii+161+ii. ff. ii, 169 were pastedowns in the medieval binding. Medieval foliation 1, 5–12, 15–100, 102–53, one leaf unnumbered, 154–68, before leaves were lost from quire 1. The outside and middle sheets in each quire are parchment and the rest paper. 295 × 220 mm. Written space 212 × 150 mm. 2 cols. *c.* 48 lines. Frame ruling. Collation: 1¹⁶ wants 2–4 after f. 1 and 13, 14 after f. 12 2–10¹⁶ 11⁸ wants 7, 8. Written in a clumsy hand based on secretary. Red initials, without ornament. Binding of s. xix. Secundo folio, now missing, should be *quedam ad.*

Written in England. 'Iste liber constat [. . . . . .]', f. 169; over the erasure is 'Magistro Waltero knyghtley¹ prec' in valore tractatu (?) xxxiii s' iiii d' et vltra', s. xv ex. '*domino* laurencio okylta', s. xv ex., f. 169. Perhaps no. (4), 'Collectorium Medicum fol. MS.', in the list of Henry Fowler's gifts in the Benefactors' Book, p. 25: cf. MS. 6. 'Nᵒ 9', f. iiᵛ.

12. *Legenda Sanctorum (in English)*   s. xv med.

Seint andrewe and othir of þe dissipulis weren callid þre tymys of oure lord . . . neuer founde harme in his body (*ends imperfectly*).

A translation of the Legenda Sanctorum of Jacobus de Voragine: cf. Wells, *Manual*, ch. v. 25 (and *First Supplement*) and Pierce Butler, *Legenda Aurea*, 1899, pp. 50–75. Ninety-three lives at present, corresponding to nos. 1–93 of MS. Harley 4775, as set out by Butler, but a quire (of twelve leaves, probably) is missing after f. 168 which will have contained lives not in Harl.: B.L., Add. 35298 has at this point lives of Edward the Confessor, Winefred, and Erkenwold. f. 168ᵛ ends in the life of Gervase and Protase 'Emperour and a grete' and f. 169 begins in the life of Alban 'vois was contynewelly hurd'. The last words now in the manuscript come near the end of the life of St. James, 25 July (cf. Bodleian, Douce 372, f. 78ᵛ/32). f. 1 is damaged and quire 18 is disordered.²

ff. ii+214+ii. Paper. 256 × 200 mm. Written space *c.* 210 × 140 mm. 33–41 long lines. Collation: 1–17¹² 18¹² wants 11, 12 after f. 214 (ff. 211–13, 205–10, 214). Quires signed a–o, q–t. Written by one hand throughout, a mixed anglicana-secretary. Initials: (i) ff. 1, 12 (Christmas), gold on grounds of red and blue, patterned in white, from which feathery sprays project into the margins; (ii) 3-line or 2-line, gold with blue-grey ornament; (iii) 2-line, blue with red ornament. Binding of s. xvii ex. Secundo folio *achaia.*

Written in England. Belonged in 1626 to Henry Fowler, rector of Minchinhampton, Gloucestershire (f. 1).³ No. 14 in the list of his son's gifts in the Benefactors' Book, p. 25: cf. MS. 6.

14. *Sermones, etc.*   s. XIII/XIV

1. ff. 1–20ᵛ Twenty-two brief sermons, the first 'De natali. Quoniam pater meus et mater mea etc. Istud thema potest diuidi in duas partes. In prima parte facit propheta mencionem de primis parentibus . . .'. All, but the last, 'De caritate', are for specified occasions.

¹ No doubt Walter Knyghtley, † by May 1501: see Emden, *BRUO*, p. 1064.

² It is probably no accident that the missing leaves come at the points where the lives of English saints are inserted in Add. 35298 and Lambeth Palace 72.

³ Fowler also owned MSS. 19, 21, B.L., Royal 5 F. ii, 12 C. xv, 12 D. vi, 12 G. iv, 15 B. ix and Bodleian, Auct. D. 3.14, Auct. D. 4.8, Hatton 63, Gough Missals 173, Wood empt. 4.

2. ff. 21–27ᵛ Incipit liber aurelii augustini de vera innocencia. Innocencia uera est . . . si te ipsum bene respexeris. Explicit liber de uera Innocencia.

The Sententiae from Augustine collected by Prosper of Aquitaine. *PL* li. 427–96.

3. ff. 28–9 Qui bene presunt presbiteri duplici honore digni sunt scilice, sustentacione et reuerencia . . .

A potted version of the first part of the popular priests' guide, Qui bene presunt, preserving chiefly the verses, of which some 102 lines have been copied from 'Hec sunt precipue sermonibus insinuanda . . .' (6 lines: Walther, no. 7598) to 'Iacta te semina. Noua fac . . .' (14 lines: Walther, no. 9678). Most of the verses, if not all of them, occur on ff. 222–8 of the copy of Qui bene presunt in B.L., Royal 4 B. viii. ff. 29ᵛ–32ᵛ are blank.

4. ff. 33–130 Heads of sermons through the year, the first of the temporale, Dominica prima aduentus domini. Quasi diluculum preparatus est egressus eius Osee 6. Tria notantur in uerbis istis. Dignitas venientis et vtilitas ipsius aduentus . . ., and the first of the sanctorale (f. 113), De sancto andrea. Omnis quicunque . . . Nota tria scilicet quod omnis . . .

Schneyer, p. 428, referring to Paris, B.N. lat. 16473, f. 144ᵛ and Durham, U.L., Cosin V. v. 4, f. 3.

5. ff. 130ᵛ–138 Five sermons: (*a*) Da michi intellectum et scrutabor le. t. et custodiam etc. Sacre legis diuine expositori . . .; (*b*) Eloquia domini . . . In uerbis istis dauid prophetarum eximius . . .; (*c*) Uerba que ego locutus sum uobis . . . In istis uerbis ueritas summa que deus est . . .; (*d*) Dom. 21 post trinitatem. Induite uos armaturam dei Eph. 6c. Quia teste beato Iob 7 Milicia est . . .; (*e*) Dominica 3 aduentus. Sic nos existimet homo Cor. 4. Differencia ministrorum dei et hominis . . .

6. ff. 138ᵛ–140ᵛ 'Sermo in tempore penitencie'. Conuertimini sicut in profundis . . . ys' 31. Verba sunt saluatoris ad animas peccatrices . . .

7. ff. 141–154ᵛ Ante omnia fratres karissimi diligatur deus deinde proximus . . . in monasterio constituti. Ad hoc nobis diuina precepta leguntur . . . in illo glorietur.

The rule of St. Augustine and the commentary on it by Hugh of St. Victor. *PL* clxxvi. 881–924.

8. ff. 154ᵛ–155ᵛ Articles to be considered: (*a*) In Electione et Examinatione pastoris. De die obitus pastoris. An ante dictum obitum tractatum fuit de aliqua persona eligenda . . .; (*b*) In visitacione inter regulares sacerdotes Inquiretur. An omnes sint regulariter obedientes suis superioribus . . .; (*c*) In visitacione inter moniales inquiretur et statuatur. Quod abbatissa frequens sit in claustro . . . et quod nulla femina secularis (*ends abruptly*). f. 156ʳᵛ blank.

9. ff. 157–162ᵛ Tractatus de septem sacramentis ecclesie. Actiuus contemplacio. R.A. Que sursum sunt contemplari sapere et intelligere . . . id est ante quem nullum nec post quem alium.

10. ff. 163–181ᵛ Exposicio Canonis Misse. Loquimur dei sapienciam in misterio. Cor. 2. Quoniam opera ihesu cristi qui est dei virtus et dei sapiencia . . . Soli deo honor et gloria Tymo. 1° Amen secula. Explicit exposicio Canonis Misse. ff. 182ʳᵛ, 184ʳᵛ blank.

11. f. 183 (should follow f. 184) A torn binding leaf taken from an early thirteenth-century medical manuscript with text (in red) and commentary. Fifty-one long lines, hard to read.

ff. i+182+i+1+i. For f. 183 see above. 292 × 190 mm. Written space *c.* 210 × 138 mm. 2 cols. 45–6 lines. Writing above top ruled line, ff. 1–140. Collation: 1¹⁴ 2¹² 3⁶ (ff. 27–32) 4¹² wants 2 after f. 33 5–10¹² 11¹⁰ 12¹² 13 three (ff. 138–40) 14¹² 15 nine (ff. 153–61) 16¹² 17¹² wants 9, 11 (ff. 174–82, 184). Written in a good current anglicana, not yet bookhand. Initials 2-line, red or blue without ornament. Binding of s. xix. Secundo folio *deus cum.*

Written in England, probably by an Augustinian canon. 'Liber thome woodehows ex dono magistri smyth 1507', f. 183. An erasure after art. 10, f. 181ᵛ.

16. *Medica*   s. XIII ex.–xv in.

1 (s. xiii ex.). ff. 1–38 Intendimus edere sermonem exponentem . . . in duobus tractatibus quos nominauit.

The translation of the commentary of Haly Abenrudianus on Galen, Ars parva, printed in various editions of *Articella*, e.g. Venice 1523. Thorndike and Kibre. f. 38ᵛ blank.

2 (s. xiv²). ff. 39–52ᵛ Miscellaneous medical notes, including some names of herbs in English. Ends imperfectly.

3 (s. xiii ex.). ff. 77–83ᵛ, 53–72ᵛ [V]idetur michi quod ex melioribus rebus . . . in die lxᵒ. Explicit Comentum Galieni super librum pronosticorum finito libro Laus et gloria cristo. Amen.

A translation of Galen's commentary on Hippocrates, Prognostica. Thorndike and Kibre.

4 (s. xiii ex.). ff. 98–105ᵛ, 92–97ᵛ, 84–91ᵛ, 73–76ᵛ Prefacio *domini* constantini affricani monti cassianensis monachi ad othonem discipulum suum. Licet peticionibus tuis . . . confirmare ponunt. Expliciunt commenta afforismorum ypocratis.

The translation by Constantinus Africanus of Galen's commentary on Hippocrates, Aphorismi. Two leaves are missing.

5 (s. xv in.). ff. 106–109ᵛ Secundum quod vult auicenna consideracio que attenditur in pulsu . . . et quando etc. Explicit pulsus M. Bernardi de Sordi*na*.

Bernardus Pictaviensis, De pulsibus. Thorndike and Kibre. Wickersheimer, p. 78, refers only to Paris, B.N., MS. lat. 6957, ff. 26–34ᵛ.

6 (s. xv in.). ff. 109ᵛ–113ᵛ Doctrinam de gradibus intendimus . . . plures sapores etc. Explicit opus Bernardi de Gordion de gradibus.

Bernardus de Gordonio, De gradibus. Thorndike and Kibre.

7 (s. xv in.). ff. 113ᵛ–115ᵛ Regimen acutorum consistit in tribus . . . lecturam nostram etc. Explicit tractatus M. Bernardi de Gordonio super regiment' acutorum.

Thorndike and Kibre.

8 (s. xv in.). ff. 115ᵛ–118ᵛ Dicit autem Iohannes de sancto amando super antitod' de fleobotomia . . . 5ᵃ regula est quod non debent (*ends imperfectly*).

A commentary on the Phlebotomy of Johannes de Sancto Amando: cf. Thorndike and Kibre.

9 (s. xv in.). ff. 119–120ᵛ (*begins imperfectly*) temperata relata est ista . . . perfecte sunt in eis virtutes.

On complexions, humours, etc.

10 (s. xv in.). ff. 121–142ᵛ De diffinicione medicine ac primarum eius parcium et subdiuisione. Theorice introducciones appellantur . . . calido et sicco in gra (*ends imperfectly: catchword* du vnde patet).

Arnaldus de Villanova, Medicinalium introductionum speculum. Thorndike and Kibre, cols. 773, 1572.

ff. i+142+iv. ff. 143–5 are medieval end-leaves: 145ᵛ was pasted down. ff. 39–52 (art. 2) are paper. *c.* 294×200 mm. Written space *c.* 240×155 mm. 2 cols., except ff. 39–52. Varying number of lines. Writing above top ruled line on ff. 1–35, 73–6, 84–97. Frame ruling for arts. 2, 5–10. Collation: 1–4⁸ 5⁶ (ff. 33–8) 6¹⁴ (ff. 39–52) 7⁶+1 leaf after 5 (ff. 77–83) 8⁸ (ff. 53–60) 9¹² (ff. 61–72) 10⁸ (ff. 98–105) 11⁸ wants 1, 2 (ff. 92–7) 12⁸ (ff. 84–91) 13⁴ (ff. 73–6) 14⁸ 15⁸ wants 6 after f. 118 16–17⁸ 18⁶: quires 7–13 are misbound in the order 8, 9, 13, 7, 12, 11, 10. Small textura (arts. 1, 3, 4), current anglicana (art. 2), and mixed but mainly secretary script (arts. 5–10). Spaces for initials filled only on f. 1 (ink of the text) and f. 98 (blue or red, with ornament of the other colour). Binding of s. xix. Secundo folio *carum. nam.*

Written in England. 'John Shakespeare 1623. de. 22' is scribbled on f. 50. Probably the 'Comment. Gal. prognost, fol. MS.', no. (8) in the list of Henry Fowler's gifts in the Benefactors' Book, p. 25.

17. *Galenus, Pantegni; etc.*   s. XIII ex.

1. ff. 1–52 Galienus loquturus de medicina libellum suum composuit . . . translatus sic incipit. Cum tocius sciencie generalitas . . . ad intelligendum. Explicit liber pantegni amen.

Galen, Liber Pantegni, in the translation of Constantinus Africanus.

2. ff. 56–71ᵛ Ysaac filius salomonis israelita seggregauit sibi . . . Iam igitur remouetur ab elementaritate proculdubio.

Isaac, Liber de elementis. Printed in 1515.

3. ff. 71ᵛ–96ᵛ Summe que sunt in sermone primo libri galieni de complexione . . . operantur in corpore uniuersaliter quidem (*ends imperfectly in bk. 3: catchword* duo corpora).

Galen, De temperamentis, in the translation of Gerard of Cremona. Thorndike and Kibre. A leaf is missing after f. 85.

4 (s. xiv in.). Recipes and notes closely written in current hand in the space left blank at the end of quire 5. Notes on the divisions of the sciences are headed (f. 54ᵛ) 'Diuisio musice secundum intencionem alfarabii libro de ortu scienciarum'.

5 (s. xiv). The margins of ff. 55^v, 57, 58^v, 59, 60^v, 64^v, 65, 74 bear pencilled arrangements of dashes in sixteen lines and of roundels in fifteen groups, for use in geomancy. Some of these schemes are labelled: f. 59, 'de parliamento vtrum ad pacem vel guerram proueniet'; f. 60^v, 'de aduentu Rothwell die martis qu(e) est ante carnipriuium'; f. 65, 'de Iohanne hlaurberg' (?); f. 74^v, 'de nuncio die veneris ante sanctum Cutbertum'.

6. ff. ii, 97, the old pastedowns, have theological and philosophical notes in small current English script, s. xiii.

ff. ii+96+ii. For ff. ii, 97, see above. 225 × 190 mm. Written space: of art. 1, c. 220 × 155 mm; of arts. 2, 3, c. 190 × 115 mm. Two cols. of 53–68 lines (art. 1) and 38 lines (arts. 2, 3). Collation: 1^{12} 2^{12}+1 leaf inserted after 6 (f. 19) 3–4^{12} 5^6 (ff. 50–5) 6–8^{10} 9^{12} wants 1 before f. 86. Art. 1 in very small textura. Arts. 2, 3 larger and with some cursive forms (d, h). Initials: (i) ff. 1, 47^v, red and blue: (ii) 2-line, red or blue. Binding of s. xix. Secundo folio *non nobis necesse est.*

Written in England. The words 'Liber pantegni Galieni' and 'prec' librorum x s'' are at the head of f. 1, s. xv.

18. *Medica*   s. XIII in.–XIII ex.

Arts. 1–6 (quires 1–6: s. xiii in.) are a standard collection of medical texts found for example in Bodleian, MS. Laud lat. 106, and All Souls College, MS. 71, and printed in *Articella* (1476 and later editions: *GKW* 2678–83): Isagoge Iohannicii, Aphorismi Hippocratis, Tegni Galieni, Theophilus de Urinis, Philaretus de Pulsibus, Prognostica Hippocratis.

1. ff. 1–7^v Incipiunt ysagoge Iohannicii ad tegni Galieni. Medicina in duas diuiditur partes . . . maliue discrecio.

f. 8^{rv} was left blank: see art. 17a.

2. ff. 9–16^v Incipit prima particula afforismorum ypocratis. Vita breuis ars uero longa . . . et deglutire non possit mortale.

3. ff. 17–32 Tres sunt omnes doctrine . . . inscripcionem habituris. Explicit. The running title is 'Tegni'.

4. ff. 33–40 Incipit liber urinarum a voce theophili. De urinarum differencia negotium multi ueterum medicorum . . . conuenienter exposuimus.

5. ff. 40–2 Intencionem habemus in presenti conscripcione . . . sufficiant ad presentia.

6. ff. 42^v–47 Omnis qui medicine studio . . . ordine preceptorum. Explicit liber pronosticorum ypo.

7 (added, s. xiii^1, at the end of quire 6). ff. 47–51 Qui de egrotancium egritudinibus . . . et illis conueniens. Explicit regimen acutarum ypocratis.

Printed in *Articella*.

8. ff. 52–77ᵛ Compleuimus in libro primo . . . in renibus creant. Expliciunt diete particulares.

Isaac, Dietae particulares, in the translation of Constantinus Africanus. ff. 73–7 are in a slightly later looking hand.

9. ff. 80–199ᵛ Quoniam quidem ut in rhetoricis tullius ait . . . multum valent. Explicit viaticus.

Constantinus Africanus, Viaticus.

10 (added, s. xiii, in the blank space at the end of quire 19). (*a*) ff. 200–201ᵛ Galienus testatur in tegni quod quicumque interiorum membrorum connitor esse desiderat eum in anathomia esse oportet diligentem . . . vel tantum feminas generat. (*b*) ff. 201ᵛ–202ᵛ Notes and recipes. (*c*) f. 206ᵛ Quis color. et que sit substancia. quanta sit. et quid . . .

(*a*). A very small hand. Apparently an abbreviation of the anatomy edited by Sudhoff in *AGM* xix (1927), 212–39: cf. Thorndike and Kibre. (*c*). s. xiii ex. Verses on urines in 134 lines. For ff. 202ᵛ–205 see below, art. 17*b*.

11. ff. 207–225ᵛ Dicitur urina quoniam fit renibus una . . . (*commentary*) Vrina dicitur vna renibus . . .

Aegidius Corboliensis, De urinis, in verse (ed. Choulant, 1826, pp. 3–18), together with a commentary. The prologue, 'Liber iste est noue translacionis . . .', is added at the foot of f. 207ᵛ. ff. 225ᵛ–228ᵛ, left blank at the end of quire 22, were filled with medical notes in s. xiii ex., some of them written over art. 16*c*, *d*.

12. ff. 229–266ᵛ Begins imperfectly with the explanation of the first of the forty diagrams of Tacuinum Sanitatis.

The introduction, 'Tacuinum sanitatis . . .' (Thorndike and Kibre) and first diagram were, no doubt, on the now missing first leaf of quire 23. Diagrams are on versos and their explanations on rectos. f. 266ᵛ contains diagram 39, so at least two leaves are missing after f. 266 to complete the text. Printed at Strasbourg in 1531.

13 (s. xiii ex.). f. 267ʳᵛ Hic incipit paruum compotum. (*a*) In principio creauit deus . . . (*b*) Fallit amor cautos . . . pasca tenet. (*c*) Circumcisus adam . . .

(*b*). Thorndike and Kibre refer to St. John's College, Oxford, MS. 188, f. 21ᵛ. Walther, no. 6236. (*c*). Thirty lines of verse on the festivals of the church, Walther, no. 2805. Thorndike and Kibre.

14 (s. xiii ex.). ff. 268–272ᵛ Res aloes lingnum . . . sudanda milueam sonat.

Materia medica in 391 lines of verse. Cf. Walther, no. 16604; Thorndike and Kibre. (*a*). The first 138 lines are the text printed by Sudhoff in *AGM* ix (1916), 236–42, but in the order 1–11, 131–3, 12–14, 134, 141, 137–8, 129–30, 15–19, 22, 20, 21, 23, 25–8, 24, 135–6, 139–40, 67–73, 78, 74–7, 29–36, 43, 44, 52–4, 48–51, 45–7, 57–9, 55, 56, 60–6, two lines 'De colofonia', 114, 98, 117, 115–16, 119, 120, 118, 142–3, 122–4, 80–2, 88, 89, 84–7, 90, 91, 83, 92–5, three lines 'De lapide lazuli', 96, 97, 100–1, 79, 128, 102–4, 110–11,[1] 99, 112–13, 37–42. (*b*). Lines 139–391 are the greater part of the text printed by S. de Renzi, *Collectio Salernitana*, v (1859), 39–44, lines 1233–1585, but in a different order: thus the first twenty lines are de Renzi, lines 1278–80, 1237–41, 1233–4, 1268–70, 1243–5, 1258–60. Both (*a*) and (*b*) are full of fantastic errors of which the last three words (de Renzi, line 1581 . . . *siccanda uulnera sanat*) are a good example.[2] In several hands.

---

[1] Sudhoff missed the numbers 105–9.

[2] Probably these verses go back to an early exemplar in a difficult or strange script. The texts printed by de Renzi and by Sudhoff are in alphabetical order.

15 (s. xiii ex.). f. 273ʳᵛ Incipit anatomia membrorum. Quoniam interiorum membrorum humani corporis composiciones . . . qui uenit ad aures dicitur pusticus.

Copho, Anatomia Porci, ed. Renzi, ii. 388.

16. Margins and blank spaces have many notes in ink and pencil of s. xiii and later, including: (a) f. 273ᵛ, a recipe 'secundum magistrum H. de Eveham contra phisim'; (b) f. 74ᵛ, the draft of a letter in faded pencil, s. xiii, 'abbd' kilborne (?) dilectissime amice sue . . . ter proposui infra festum pentecosten ipsam uisitasse et de sua promocione cum magistro galfrido collocucione habuisse'; (c) f. 225ᵛ, in pencil, a note of the contents of arts. 1–9, 11, in a hand of s. xiii: 'Ars medicine. Diete particulares. Viaticus. Versus egidii'; (d) f. 225ᵛ, in pencil, in the same hand as (c), a note of payments, '[. . .] xxviii d' apud berkingham (?) [. . .] galfrid' ij d' et ob' '; (e) f. 272ᵛ, charms.

(a). Perhaps Hugh of Evesham, †1287, for whom see Emden, BRUO, p. 656, and Talbot and Hammond, p. 92. (b). Mentions 'sorores mee' and that master Geoffrey's counsel had been withdrawn.

17 (added in blank spaces, s. xv). (a) f. 8ʳᵛ Quando in facie infirmi . . . desiderio vehementer. τελοσ libri prescientie ypocratis qui in eius sepulcro in pixide eburnea inuentus est et est 24 propositionum. Moreyn. (b) ff. 202ᵛ–205 Ingenii vires . . . philaretus vomeris horret Telos quod W. Moreyn.

(a). Printed by Karl Sudhoff in AGM ix (1916), 90–104. (b). The verses of Aegidius Corboliensis, De pulsibus. Ed. L. Choulant, 1826, pp. 28–43. Walther, no. 9332.

ff. i+274+i. Art. 9 is foliated in a medieval hand 1–120. 240×165 mm. Written space 147×85 mm in art. 9 and rather more elsewhere. 29–30 long lines (art. 9); 32 long lines (arts. 1–6). In arts. 1–6, 8 and the first quire of art. 9 the first line of writing is above the top ruled line. Pricks in both margins to guide ruling in art. 11. Collation: 1–5⁸ 6⁸+3 leaves inserted after 8 (ff. 49–51) 7⁸ 8¹⁰ 9⁶ 10⁴ (ff. 76–9) 11–12¹² 13¹⁴ 14–15¹⁶ 16¹⁴ 17¹⁶ 18¹⁸ 19⁸+1 leaf after 4 (ff. 198–206) 20–21⁸ 22⁶ (ff. 223–8) 23⁸ wants 1 before f. 229 24–27⁸ 28⁸ wants 8. Arts. 1–12 and part of art. 14 in various small textura hands. Arts. 13, 14 (part), 15 in current hands. Art. 17b is more or less humanist, but 17a by the same scribe is not. Initials: (i) red and blue, with ornament of both colours; (ii) 2-line or 1-line, red or blue, with ornament of the other colour. Binding of s. xix. Secundo folio Sunt et composite.

Written in many hands, probably in England, except art. 12 which is perhaps Italian. Certainly in England in s. xiii (cf. art. 16) and in the hands of W. Moreyn in s. xv (art. 17). Given by Henry Fowler, according to a modern note on f. i, but not identifiable in the list of his gifts in the Benefactors' Book, p. 25 : it might be no. (7), 'Instructio Medici. fol. MS.', which is otherwise unaccounted for.

19+23 f. 1. *Henry Daniel, O.P., Liber uricrisarum (in English)*
s. xv med.

(*prologue*) Dilecto socio in cristo Waltero Turnour de Ketene . . . et habet capitula 20. (*text*) Urine is als myche to say in Englyssh' as on the reynes . . . (f. 180ᵛ) hunc conseruare digneris. Amen. Explicit liber uricrisarum ex latino in vulgare translatus a fratre henrico Daniell ordinis fratrum predicatorum omnium doctrinarum et scripturarum etc'. A table of contents follows after a blank leaf (ff. 182–7).

Three books of judgements of urines, with a Latin preface addressed to Walter Turnour and at the end twenty-four lines of Latin verse which give 1379 as the year of compilation. Talbot and Hammond, p. 79, list fourteen manuscripts, but not this one. Isaac Judeus, De urinis, seems to be a main source. The first leaf, containing the Latin preface, is misbound at the beginning of MS. 23. Many leaves are tattered, e.g. 71, 79, 80, 132, and seven are missing after f. 79. f. 25, beginning bk. 2, has a picture of a doctor holding a bottle of urine in front of three students; a similar picture on f. 125^v, beginning bk. 3. ff. 187^v–192^v were left blank.

Early in s. xvii Henry Fowler of Minchinhampton wrote many notes in the margins, including the names of eight persons known to him, the condition of whose urine corresponded to a condition mentioned in the text: for example, f. 31^v, 'that was the evill Crisis of M^r Jo: Crosley bookeseller in Oxf: 1612. Oct. 12 his payne did lessen wch did signifie that his maladye had the masterie of nature illuminatio mortis. sparks shine brightest when they goe out'.[1] Fowler refers to the authority of Friar Narburgh, a Franciscan living in 1464, on ff. 24^v, 35, and elsewhere. According to him, f. 191^v, notes on urines written in another hand on ff. 187^v–191 are 'Written by my true frende Mr Alexander Ramsey att Hales Howse in parochia de Stroude in Com: Gloucest: 1616: febr: 24'.

ff. 193 in MS. 19, foliated 1–21, 21*, 22–192, and f. 1 in MS. 23. Paper. A medieval foliation chapter by chapter. 210 × 140 mm. Written space c. 150 × 90 mm. 29–31 long lines. Frame ruling. Collation: 1^{12} (1^1 is misbound as the first leaf of MS. 23) 2^{12} 3^{10}+1 leaf after 10 (f. 33) 4–6^{12} 7^{12} wants 11, 12 after f. 79 8^8 wants 1–5 before f. 80 9–19^8 20^{10} 21^{14} wants 13, 14, probably blank. Written in anglicana. Initials: (i) MS. 23, f. 1, blue with red ornament; (ii) 3-line, red. Contemporary binding of pink leather over wooden boards: two strap-and-pin fastenings missing. Secundo folio *Vnde dicitur*.

Written in England. 'anno 1540' and 'per me Robertum Iordanum anno predicto', f. 181^v Belonged to Henry Fowler of Minchinhampton: his name and the date 6 Dec. 1614 on f. 25 and a note in his hand on f. 180^v referring to Dominican friars 'of which order this daniell munke of Glastonburie was from whence I had this boke originaliter'. No. (9) in the list of his son's gifts in the Benefactors' Book, p. 25: 'An old Translat. by H. Daniel 4° MS.': cf. MS. 6.

21. *Astrologica, astronomica, meteorologica*   s. xv^2

A collection mainly of astrological and astronomical pieces noticed briefly by D. E. Rhodes, 'Provost Argentine of King's and his Books', *Transactions of the Cambridge Bibliographical Society*, ii (1956), 211. The whole manuscript is probably in Argentine's hand, except ff. 1–4/8, 5^v–6, 10^{rv}, 12^{rv}, 115^v/15–134^v, 203^v/18–219, 229^v–232. For him see also Talbot and Hammond, p. 112.

1. ff. 1–12^v Two quires of miscellaneous notes, including a piece beginning 'Considera signum ascensus' (ff. 1–4) and one headed 'Geomantia' (f. 7^v), a note 'Arturus rex obiit anno christi 540 12 calend' Iunii' (f. 9), a note of the longitudes of Cambridge, Norwich, Oxford, and London (f. 9) and horoscopes of Edward V 2 Nov. 'anno domini 1470 imperfecto' and of Edward IV, 27 Apr. 1442,

---

[1] Crosley's will is dated 5 Sept. 1612 and was proved on 12 Feb. 1612/13 (Univ. Reg. GG, f. 107).

'secundum calculacionem M. Ioh' Arg' set calculabat secundum tabulas Norwici' (f. 9ᵛ: cf. arts. 10, 11). 'quod Argentem', f. 11ᵛ.

2. ff. 13–16 Astrolabii circulos et membra nominatim . . . profunditatem. Explicit Tractatus optimus conclusionum Astrolabii.

Included among the *spuria* of Grosseteste by Thomson, *Grosseteste*, p. 243, who notes three manuscripts: another is MS. Bodley 790, f. 108. Argentine wrote 'Argentem pimpe' in Greek capitals on f. 13: cf. arts. 3, 14.

3. ff. 17–33 Circulus eccentricus circulus egresse cuspidis et circulus egredientis . . . et non retrog(r)aditur. Finit theorica planetarum. etc.

Ascribed to Walter Brit in Bodleian MS. Digby 15, f. 58, and to Simon Bredon in MS. Digby 48, f. 96. 'Argent' and (in Greek capitals) 'pimpe' in red ink at the end.

4. ff. 33ᵛ–37 Notes and tables, including the description of a 'Nocturnale' and a list of towns with their latitudes and longitudes.

5. ff. 37ᵛ–68 Sex sunt signa . . . in libro fructus finit. Hunc librum edidit Habraam Amenesire quod interpretatur magister adiutorii. quod Argentem.

Abraham ibn Ezra, Introductorius. Printed in 1507. 'Hic deficit principium introductorii', f. 37ᵛ.

6. ff. 69–99ᵛ Mundus iste duodecim signis regitur . . . reuerti ei deterius et e conuerso. Finit tractatus optimus et certissimus. 'Argentyn'.

'liber iste intitulatur liber sapientie Alii dicunt quod est liber zael', f. 69, in the margin.

7. (a) ff. 100–104ᵛ Incipiunt capitula de naturis 12ᶜⁱᵐ domorum secundum Magistrum Rogerum Bultynbroke in sua geomancia. Si questio fiat de vita . . . in peiore ponetur etc. Finit tractatus de 12 domibus secundum m. R.B. (b) ff. 104ᵛ–105ᵛ Incipit secundum eundem. Aries est signum masculinum mobile calide . . . et de similibus. Explicit capitulum de qualitatibus signorum secundum magistrum Rogerum Bultyngbroke in opere tripartito.

For Roger Bollyngbroke, convicted of necromancy and hung at St. Paul's Cross, 18 Nov. 1441, cf. Emden, *BRUO*, p. 214. His Geomancy and Opus tripartitum are not known.

8. ff. 107–109ᵛ Sicut dicit commentator super 60 verbo centiloquii . . . in vno signo tantum Finit feliciter de diebus creticis etc.

Cf. L. Thorndike, *History of Magic*, iii. 217, for the De diebus criticis of Hugo de Civitate Castellis, *fl.* 1350, which begins thus.

9. ff. 110ᵛ–134ᵛ Dixit Messahallah quod inter omnes libros astronomie . . . non habere inimicos. Explicit liber natiuitatum etc'. 'secundum Messahalla etc'.'

Thorndike and Kibre.

10. (a) ff. 136–138ᵛ Canones tabularum sequentium. et sunt tabule Willelmi Norwich et eciam canones sui. Horas et minuta de die transacta in ascensiones reducere. Cum numero horarum . . . in proposito. (b) ff. 140–161ᵛ Astronomical tables, one of them (ff. 156–160ᵛ) headed 'Tabula reperiendi principia domorum calculata ad latitudinem ciuitatis norwici. que latitudo est 52 gra et 42 minuta et

est tabula Willelmi Norwiche monachi sancte fidis'. (*c*) f. 162 A canon referring to the tables on ff. 156–160ᵛ.

To (*c*) Argentine added a note at the foot of f. 162 which ends 'Hanc lineam horarum et minutorum addidit Ioh' Argenten ad tabulas Willelmi Norwhich' et hunc canonem edidit anno domini 1477 imperfecto'. On the verso, radices of planets for 1476 are in his hand.

11. (*a*) ff. 163–70 Tabule Magistri Iohannis Holbroke fundate super verissimam anni quantitatem et facte erant graui diligencia cantebrig' Anno domini 1433°. (*b*) f. 170ʳᵛ Tables 'alfonsi'. (*c*) f. 171ʳᵛ Tables ascribed to William Norwich, monk of (Horsham) St. Faith. (*d*) ff. 172–81 Tables of equations of planets. (*e*) ff. 181ᵛ–182ᵛ Tables of John Holbroke.

(*a, d*). For Holbrook, master of Peterhouse, Cambridge, †1437, see Emden, *BRUC*. (*d*) appears to go with (*c*).

12. (*a*) f. 183ʳᵛ Rules for calculating conjunctions 'secundum Willelmum monachum sancte fidis iuxta Norwichum'. (*b*) ff. 184–7 Rules 'Pro locis planetarum querendis per tabulas Holbroke siue Alfonsi'. f. 187ᵛ is blank.

13. (*a*) ff. 188ᵛ–195 Tables 'minutorum proporcionabilium secundum arzachelem'. (*b*) ff. 195–196ᵛ Canon tabule precedentis. Volumus istam tabulam exponere que est de parte proporcionali habenda . . . quod extrahitur. Finit canon.

(*b*) is the canon referring to (*a*).

14. ff. 196ᵛ–201 Incipit composicio astrorum speculi generalis. Ad laudem et honorem summi dei nostri et ad preces quorundam sociorum meorum ac nostrorum opus incepi astrorum speculi generalis secundum principia et questiones ptholomei et composui nouariensis. Hoc autem opus . . . Habeatur lamina rotunda . . . situacio perpendiculi a C datur. Finit feliciter.

Thorndike and Kibre. A copy in Cambridge University Library, Ii. 1.13, ff. 26ᵛ–28. 'Composicio huius instrumenti est in libro spisso in libraria aule gunuyle' in red ink, f. 199ᵛ: cf. art. 15. 'Argentem pimpe' in Greek capitals, f. 197ᵛ: cf. arts. 2, 3. Diagrams on ff. 199ᵛ, 200 have not been filled in.

15. ff. 201ᵛ–219 Incipit tractatus de saphea. Siderei motus et effectus motuum . . . 2arum horarum si deus voluerit. Explicit liber tabule que nominatur Saphea et vocatur Astrolabium arzachelis. Argentem.

Arzachel, Astrolabium, in the translation of Willelmus Anglicus (L. Thorndike, *History of Magic*, iii. 201). Sixty-one chapters. A red-ink note on f. 202ᵛ refers to another copy at Gonville Hall, Cambridge (cf. art. 14): 'Composicio instrumenti in libro quodam pendente in libraria aule gunuyle'. The diagrams on ff. 202ᵛ–203 are unfinished.

16. ff. 220–4 Incipit tractatus extractus de libro perscrutatoris de pluuia et gelu et tonitruo et ceteris huiusmodi. Nota secundum perscrutatorem . . . et hec sunt pro maiori parte secundum perscrutatorem eboracensem. Finit feliciter.

Cf. Thorndike, op. cit. iii. 678, and *MMBL* i. 159.

17. (*a*) ff. 224ᵛ–227 Flores alkabucii. Ad pronosticandam diuersam aeris disposicionem futuram propter diuersitatem motuum superiorum . . . aspexerunt se in signis aquosis. (*b*) ff. 227–228ᵛ Astrological notes, '[S]et in signis sunt gradus qui dicuntur putei . . . et caudam eius in 7° signo ab eo etc. Expliciunt flores alkabicii de astronomia'.

(*a*). R. Grosseteste, De impressionibus aeris, ed. L. Baur, 'Die philosophischen Werke des Robert Grosseteste', *Beiträge zur Geschichte der Philosophie des Mittelalters*, ix (1912), 42–51. Thomson, *Grosseteste*, pp. 103–4, lists seventeen manuscripts, but not this one. (*b*) follows (*a*) without break.

18. ff. 228ᵛ–232 Incipit liber Saphar de mutacione temporis qui dicitur deazar babilonensis. Superioris discipline inconcussam . . . ascribitur efficacie.

Thorndike and Kibre (Albumazar, Liber imbrium, in the translation of Hugo Sanctallensis).

19. ff. 232ᵛ–235 Incipit liber Messahalach quem edidit propter vnum de amicis qui erat mercator cum quo fecit societatem et lucrati sunt in paruo tempore magnam pecuniam. Attendendum 'est' ergo ad hoc quod dicam . . . vtile venditori. Finit.

Thorndike and Kibre (Liber super anona).

20. ff. 236–239ᵛ Notes and tables mainly in Argentine's hand, including: (*a*) f. 236ʳᵛ Lists headed 'Fortuna planetarum', 'Infortuna planetarum', 'Fortitudines planetarum', 'Debilitates planetarum', with the additions of Eschendon and Zael; (*b*) f. 238ᵛ A 'rota paschalis'; (*c*) f. 239ᵛ Lists showing the 'Motus stellarum fixarum' and the 'Distancia capitis arietis 8ᵉ spere a capite arietis 9ᵉ spere' in degrees and minutes, according to Ptolemy and later calculators: the last two are Simon Bredon and William Worcester; (*d*) f. 239ᵛ Astronomical notes made 'ad meridiem Cantebrigie' in 1480.

21. Blank spaces after arts. 2, 5, 7–9, 10*a*, 16, 19 and before art. 13 were filled with miscellaneous pieces: (*a*) f. 16ᵛ; (*b*) f. 68ʳᵛ; (*c*) ff. 105ᵛ–106 Figura ptholemei . . . pro scienda quando et qualiter morbi habere debeant suas determinaciones; (*d*) f. 110; (*e*) f. 135ʳᵛ Notes from 'Messahalla in libro de Receptione' and from Roger of Hereford; (*f*) ff. 138ᵛ–139ᵛ Cum volueris scire vtrum aliqua res est cara vel vilis . . .; (*g*) f. 188 Tables with 'quod Argentem' at the end; (*h*) f. 224; (*i*) f. 235ᵛ.

ff. i+240+i, foliated (i), 1–157, 157*, 158–239 (240). 212 × 150 mm. Written space *c.* 150 × 100 mm. 29–36 long lines. Frame ruling. Collation: 1⁸ 2⁴ 3–12⁸ 13⁶+1 leaf after 5 (f. 98) 14–21⁸ 22⁸+1 leaf after 8 (f. 171) 23–30⁸ 31⁴. Written in several secretary hands: Argentine's shows some humanistic influence and has the spelling 'christi'. Initials mainly red, plain or with green or pale-brown ornament, but also gold (f. 13), purple (for example, ff. 49ᵛ, 69), and green with purple ornament (f. 17). As far as f. 75 capital letters in the ink of the text are touched with red. Purple ink for some headings. Binding of s. xix. Secundo folio *in eo toto*.

Written in England, mostly by and partly, perhaps, for John Argentine, provost of King's College, Cambridge, †1508. 'Questo libro e mio Zoan Argentem', f. 238ᵛ, is nearly the usual form of his ex-libris: cf. Rhodes, loc. cit., p. 208. 'Henricus Fowler: 1627', f. 1. Presumably the 'De Planetis, etc. 4° MS.', no. (10) in the list of his son's gifts in the Benefactors' Book, p. 25: cf. MS. 6.

22. *Sermons, etc. (in English)* s. xv med.

Sermons and a fragment of Gesta Romanorum, all in English, described by D. S. Brewer, 'Observations on a fifteenth century manuscript', *Anglia*, lxxii

(1955), 390–9. Arts. 1, 3 are imperfect fragments of a manuscript used perhaps as a protective pad in front of and after art. 2.

1. pp. 1–44 Four sermons for Advent, a semon 'pro anima' (pp. 24–33), and two sermons for Septuagesima, the last ending imperfectly, 'eskape deth but'.

The sermon on pp. 24–33 is 'largely composed of a long translated extract from the . . . *Sermones Dominicales* of John Felton'. The others correspond to sermons at or near the beginning of B.L., Royal 18 B. xxv.

2. pp. 45–722 Sixty sermons of the temporale, beginning at Christmas and ending at the twenty-fifth Sunday after Pentecost, 'throughout closely similar to the great sermon collection of Lincoln Cathedral', MSS. 50, 51.

3. pp. 723–87 (*begins imperfectly*) Charite. The byrde þ^t was schet . . . to þ^e brownne dowȝtur (*ends abruptly*).

A fragment of Gesta Romanorum (twenty tales) in a translation independent of that in the three other manuscripts and in de Worde's edition, according to Brewer, who shows the order of the tales here and in the other manuscripts by means of a table. Printed by K. I. Sandred, *A Middle English version of the Gesta Romanorum edited from Gloucester Cathedral MS 22* (Acta Univ. Upsaliensis, Studia Anglistica Upsaliensia 8), 1971: pp. 45–82 (text); pp. 11–24 (description); pp. 171–76, reproductions of thirteen varieties of watermark occurring in arts. 1–3.

4. pp. 787/6–796 were left blank until s. xvi, when they were filled with notes which include (p. 795) references to pp. 615–26 of art. 2, (p. 792) jottings from a sermon headed 'fylpps notations at powles', and (p. 796) the name 'Master pendilton doctor of deuinite'.

Pendleton, †1558, became vicar of Todenham, Glouc., in 1554: Emden, *BRUO 1501–40*; *DNB*.

ff. i+395+i, paginated (i, ii), 1–79, 79*, 79**, 80–277, 288–439, 439*, 439**, 440–796 (797–8). Paper. 218 × 150 mm. Written space *c.* 145 × 85 mm. 27–8 long lines. Frame ruling (in arts. 1, 3 with a hard point). Collation of pp. 45–722: 1–42^8. Art. 2 is in current anglicana under secretary influence. Arts. 1, 3 are by one scribe in a hand of mainly secretary type. 2-line red initials. Capital letters in the ink of the text filled with red. Binding of s. xix. Secundo folio *mankynde*.

Written in England. Belonged in s. xvi perhaps to the 'Iohn Cox of Haddon' whose name is on p. 785. Ralph Willet and Rowland Willet who scribbled their names on p. 308 are likely to be the Gloucestershire people so named who matriculated at New College, Oxford, Ralph in 1598 and Rowland in 1604. Probably the 'Postills English' in the list of manuscripts given by prebendary Hugh Nash, †1675, entered in the Benefactors' Book, p. 16.

23, ff. 2–238. *Harmonia Evangeliorum, etc.*   s. XVI in.

1. ff. 2–95^v (*begins imperfectly: four leaves missing*) rum eorum. Per viscera . . . et sermonum confirmante sequentibus signis.

A harmony of the Gospels, the first remaining words from Luke 1: 78 and the last from Mark 16: 20. Written in paragraphs—176 remain—which perhaps represent chapters, but the only chapter numbers entered in the text are 7 (f. 3 Capitulum 7^m. Et postquam consummati sunt . . . Iesus. Quod vocatum est ab angelo), 8 (Cum natus esset iesus . . .), and 23 (Et circuibat Iesus totam galileam . . .).

2. ff. 96–132ᵛ Oratio prologi in librum de vita christi. Domine ihesu christe fili dei viui concede michi fragili . . . corporis et anime singulorum.

The 181 prayers in the Vita Christi of Ludolphus of Saxony (printed often: Hain, nos. 10288–393), in which each chapter is followed by a prayer.

3. ff. 133–135ᵛ A list of feasts of the temporale, sanctorale, and common of saints, with references to book numbers and chapter numbers which agree with the books and chapters of the Vita Christi of Ludolphus.

4. Prayers and meditations: (a) f. 136ʳᵛ Clementissime ihesu gratias tibi ago ex omnibus viribus meis . . . et vera matrem mi- (ends imperfectly); (b) f. 137 Adoramus te christe rex israel lux gencium . . . cogitaciones pacis et redemptionis; (c) f. 137 Oratio sancti Anselmi. Domine deus meus.ʲ si feci ut essem reus tuus . . .; (d) f. 137ᵛ Prayers to Father, Son, and Holy Spirit: Domine deus omnipotens paterque consubstancialis . . .; Domine Iesu christe fili dei viui creator . . .; Domine sancte spiritus qui equalis . . .; (e) f. 138ʳᵛ Domine deus noster credimus in te patrem et filium et spiritum sanctum. Neque enim diceret . . .; (f) ff. 138ᵛ–140 Domine deus omnipotens qui es trinus et vnus qui es semper in omnibus . . .; (g) ff. 140–142ᵛ Meditacio sancti Anselmi. Summe sacerdos et vere pontifex . . .; (h) ff. 142ᵛ–143ᵛ O intemerata . . . orbis terrarum. De te enim . . .; (i) f. 143ᵛ Meditacio beati Bernardi ad gloriosam virginem. Mentem et oculos pariter cum manibus . . . (ends imperfectly).

(f–h). Edited by A. Wilmart, Auteurs spirituels, pp. 573–7, 114–24, 494.

5. ff. 144–53 Orationes anime saluti maxime salutares et castigatissime in veram formam redacte secuntur. (a) f. 144 Omnipotens sempiterne deus trinitas sancte tibi gratias ago . . . (b) f. 144ᵛ Domine Iesu criste fili dei viui gratias tibi ago ex omnibus viribus . . . (c) f. 145 Veni sancte spiritus et emitte celitus . . . (d) f. 145 Deus lumen cordium te videntium . . . (e) f. 145ᵛ O crux gloriosa o crux adoranda o lignum preciosum et admirabile signum per quod et diabolus est victus et mundus . . . (f) f. 145ᵛ O intemerata . . . orbis terrarum inclina . . . (g) f. 146ᵛ O sincerissime castitatis type . . . (h) f. 147 Auete omnes celi ciues eterna pace . . . (i) f. 148 Omnipotens sempiterne et misericordissime deus per omnium sanctorum . . . (j) f. 148 Ad petitionem lachrimarum. Deus qui omnia ex nihilo creasti . . . (k) f. 148ᵛ Domine et deus meus Iesu criste qui recens natus . . . (l) f. 148ᵛ O rex omnium seculorum et eterni triumphator . . . (m) f. 150 O decus o ipsa pulchritudo rogo te per illam sanctissimam effusionem . . . (n) f. 150 O sacratissima dei genitrix virgo maria dignare me adorare laudare et benedicere sacrosancta membra tua. Adoro et benedico . . . pedes tuos et benedico . . . (o) f. 151 Expergiscere tandem o miserrime hominum qui securus . . . (p) f. 151ᵛ Planctus anime compuncti. Hei mihi infelix anima in tantis peccatis . . . (q) ff. 152ᵛ–153 Domine Iesu Christe molesta est mihi vite mee conscientia . . .

(f). The shorter form of O intemerata: cf. art. 4h and Wilmart, p. 488. (n). Ten paragraphs, the last beginning 'Adoro. benedico animam tuam'. (p). Not the same as art. 9. ff. 153ᵛ–155ᵛ blank.

6. ff. 156–82 Prefaces of temporale, sanctorale, common of saints, and the dead. The English saints in the sanctorale are Cuthbert, Swithun (three feasts), Hedda,

Athelwold (two feasts), Birin (two feasts): a Winchester missal is probably the source. The prefaces for Swithun are (f. 175) Eterne deus. per christum Qui seruilem formam . . ., (f. 175ᵛ) Eterne deus. Cuius doctrine dulcedine et amoris magnitudine . . ., (f. 178ᵛ) Eterne deus. Et te in tuis fidelibus collaudare . . .: the first, between Paul and Hedda, suits the Deposition; the second between Benedict and Mary Magdalene suits the Translation; the third between Faith and Simon and Jude should be for an occasion earlier than the usual date of the Ordination, Oct. 30. f. 182ᵛ is blank.

7 (in the hand of ff. 214–237ᵛ). f. 183ʳᵛ De merito orationis. Sciendum quod duplex est orationis meritum . . . Prohemium in capite orationis. Domine deus pater misericordiarum qui scis . . . apud misericordiam tuam domine.

8. ff. 184–185ᵛ Exhortatio salutaris terrorem iudicii ac timorem diuine vltionis incutiens et compunctionem. Expergiscere o miserabilis homo iamiamque moriture . . . fetentem de monumento uocauit.

9. ff. 185ᵛ–189 Deploratio peccatoris iam compuncti deique misericordiam flagitantis. Hei michi infelix anima in tantis peccatis . . . meorum vincula peccatorum Amen.

From Isidore, Synonyma: PL lxxxiii. 840–4, sect. 57–74.

10. ff. 189–237ᵛ Exordium a confusione propria. Deus glorie et pater misericordiarum. audeo ne apparere . . . et alligatura tua.

According to a nearly contemporary note in the margin of f. 189 this series of 13 prayers, petitions, etc, ending with an 'Oratio luctans cum deo. Domine deus et saluator meus quem non reputares . , .', is from the Rhetorica divina of William of Auvergne: 'Omnia que secuntur excerpta sunt a Rhetorica diuina Willelmi Parisiensis'. I have not been able to find them in the edition printed in 1674. A leaf is missing after f. 211.

11. f. 238ʳᵛ Preparatoria ad rem diuinam facienda. This heading is followed by a listing of arts. 4, 5, 7, 10, with leaf references.

ff. i+238+i. Paper. The contemporary foliation 5–253 includes the leaves now missing from arts. 1 and 10: it repeats the number 114. 208 × 147 mm. Written space c. 150 × 90 mm. 19–32 long lines. Collation: 1¹⁴ wants 1–4 (ff. 2–11) 2¹⁶ 3¹² 4–5¹⁶ 6–11¹² 12¹² wants 11, probably blank, after f. 153 13¹⁴+1 leaf before 1 (f. 155) 14¹⁶ wants 14–16, probably blank, after f. 183 15¹⁶ 16¹⁶ wants 13 after f. 211 17–18¹². Several hands, art. 1 and ff. 189–214 predominantly humanistic, the rest secretary, more or less under humanist influence. 2-line red initials. Bound by Omash of Oxford in 1861.¹

Written in England, art. 6 probably at Winchester for William Horman who himself appears to have written one double opening (162ᵛ–163). Belonged, no doubt, to Horman, whose books regularly have a well-written title on the tail: the title in this position here is 'Historia euangelica' (see above on MS. 2). Identifiable with no. (4), 'Historiam evangelicam', in the list of Henry Brett's gifts in the Benefactors' Book, p. 22: for details see above, MS. 2.

25. *Medica, etc.* s. XIII¹

1. f. 1 (*begins imperfectly*) quantitatem existentem. aliquociens . . . uidentur equalia.

On vision. For the first words—but not the rest—cf. Euclid, Optica (ed. Heiberg, Teub-

¹ See above, p. 934.

ner series, p. 91/10). The propositions are in larger and the proofs in smaller script. f. 1ᵛ is blank.

2. ff. 2–4ᵛ Uisum rectum esse. cuius media . . . phylosophorum. forte non uacat.

Pseudo-Euclid, Catoptrica, but the translation is not identical with that in Corpus Christi College, Oxford, MS. 251, and other manuscripts, from which Heiberg gives specimens, op. cit., pp. li–liii. The propositions are in larger and the proofs in smaller script.

3. ff. 5–6 (*begins imperfectly*) excessus a.b. ad f.g. tantus est f.g. ad d.e . . . est maior d.c. et ita de aliis.

Part of a treatise in apparently nine chapters on the making of an astrolabe and volvel. The six remaining chapters are lettered D–I. A space for a diagram was left at the end of each chapter, but only some of the spaces have been filled.

4. ff. 6–7 Incipit Heremannus de astrolabio componendo. Heremannus cristi pauperum peripsima et philosophie tyronum asello . . . debet notificari.

PL cxliii. 381–90. Ten chapters.

5. ff. 7–9ᵛ De vtilitatibus astrolabii. Quicumque astronomice discipline periciam . . . fabricare horologia.

Gerberti Opera mathematica, ed. N. Bubnov, 1899, pp. 114–47. *PL* cxliii. 389–404. The seventeen chapters are listed in front of the text.

6. f. 9ᵛ De composicione horologii doctrina. (*a*) Vt scias an horologium congruat illi prouincie in qua es. Vt scias de quolibet orologio in astrolapsu . . . latitudo ipsius climatis in quo es. (*b*) De composicione horologii uiatorum. Componitur quiddam simplex et paruulum . . . corausto usque (*ends imperfectly*).

PL cxliii. 405–407/4.

7. f. 10 (*begins imperfectly*) solis. Sic ubi eum tangat . . . et inuenies te esse in xvᵒ die aprilis.

The last ten lines only of, apparently, instructions for using an astrolabe.

8. f. 10 Directions for taking measurements: (*a*) Ad sciendam maris uel fluuii profunditatem. Vt scias profunditatem . . . septimi xliii; (*b*) Si uis scire latitudinem campi uel fluuii. adcipe lignum . . . triplum. et sic deinceps.

9. f. 10ʳᵛ Two tables giving the position of twenty-five stars.

The first table agrees generally with that in *PL* cxliii. 385–8.

10. ff. 11–23ᵛ Incipiunt afforismi ursonis de effectibus qualitatum. Quoniam phisicalis sciencie inuentores aut negligencia thediosi . . . substanciam eius. Explicit.

Thorndike and Kibre. Ed. in 1924 and 1936. f. 22 should precede f. 21.

11. ff. 23ᵛ–27 Incipit physionomia. Ex tribus auctoribus quos pre manus habeo loro scilicet medico aristotele philosopho et palemone declamatore . . . prope modum secuti sumus.

Ed. R. Foerster, *Scriptores physiognomici*, ii (1893), 3–145.

12. ff. 27–31 Incipit tractatus de spermate intitulatus et primo quomodo sperma in sanguine conuertitur. Sperma hominis descendit ex omni humore corporis . . . secundum naturam sui corporis.

Galen, De semine. Thorndike and Kibre.

13. ff. 31–3 Incipit libellus ursonis de effectibus qualitatum. Cum questionum fere omnium soluciones . . . efficitur. Et hec de effectibus qualitatum dicta sufficiant. Explicit urso de ef. qualitat.

Thorndike and Kibre. Ed. C. Mathaes, Leipzig diss., 1918.

14. f. 33^{rv} Incipit epistola Galieni ad glauconem nepo. s. Indigestionem abstinencia et concupiscenciam uirtus sapiencie amputat. Si diligenter animaduertis . . . atque feruor minuet.

Galen, De medendi methodo.

15. ff. 34–9 Tractatus de naturalibus quorundam phylosophorum questionibus inuicem coniocantibus. Epulis sobrietatis philosophis . . . lunari repugnat humor.

Macrobius, Saturnalia, bk. 3, sects. iv–xvi. Cf. B. Lawn, *The Salernitan Questions*, 1963, p. 15.

16. f. 39 Qui uocem claram uult frater semper habere . . . Hac de materia nunc expedit ergo tacere.

Twenty lines of verse, 'De modo curandi', according to a title in the margin. Walther, no. 15736.

17. f. 39^{rv} Medicina est sciencia sanorum. egrorum et neutrorum . . . esse quod est.

18. f. 39^{v} Septem sunt cara. quia sunt bona uel quia rara . . .

Ten lines of verse. Walther, no. 17537.

19. ff. 40–5 Incipit tractatus de crisi. Galienus in libro de crisi. Sex inquit sunt alterationes . . . in eadem dispositione. malum est.

20. ff. 45–6 Cogitanti michi uotum uestrum uotum bonum . . . si fieri potest. petita licencia. uade in pace. Amen.

Archimatheus, Practica. Thorndike and Kibre. Two leaves missing after f. 45, with half the text. f. 46^{v} is blank.

According to the table of contents on f. iii, written in the same skilled semi-humanistic hand as the ex-libris of Thomas More (see below), art. 20 was followed by 'Tractatus alcantari caldeorum philosophi'. Possibly the missing text is now New York, Columbia University, Plimpton 161: cf. de Ricci and Wilson, *Census*, p. 1782, and Thorndike and Kibre. The table was used no doubt by the Worcester label writer, whose version of it is printed by Stevenson in his HMC account, p. 398.

ff. iii+46+i. ff. ii, iii are medieval flyleaves, a bifolium. In art. 10 the columns are numbered in a medieval hand. *c.* 190 × 130 mm. Written space *c.* 137 × 90 mm. 2 cols., except for arts. 1, 2. 60–1 lines. The first line of writing above the top ruled line. Collation: 1^1

wants 10 after f. 9 2¹²+1 leaf after 11, at present misbound after 10 (f. 21) 3¹² 4¹² wants 10, 11 after f. 45. Written in minute textura by a remarkably skilled scribe, apparently the same person as wrote in an even smaller script, arts. 1, 2 (ff. 1–34) of Bodleian, MS. Bodley 679 (*Sum. Cat.* 2596). Initials: (i) f. 45, red and blue; (ii) 2-line, red or blue. 'Bound 1859'.

Written in England. From Worcester Cathedral Priory: 'Liber fratris Thome Mor' monachi monasterii Wygorn' ', f. iii, s. xv. The label with table of contents is now pasted to f. ii.¹ 'Thome Arderni liber', f. iii, s. xvi. Identifiable with 'Tho. Wigorn. de speculo etc.', no. (2) in the list of gifts of Hugh Nash, prebendary, †1675, in the Benefactors' Book, p. 16.

27. *Theologica*

s. XIII ex.–XV med.

A miscellany written at various dates, s. xiii ex. (arts. 1–6), s. xiv med. (arts. 7–13) and s. xv med. (art. 14).

1. ff. 1–12 Quia sacerdotis officium circa tria principaliter . . . quo potero describam. Incipit tractatus de ordine sacerdotalium indumentorum. [D]iuina quidem officia in septem horas canonicas distinguntur . . . quales descripti in ultimo diccio cuius regnum et imperium . . . amen. Explicit tractatus de ordine numero et significacione sacerdotalium indumentorum. de misteriis. amen.

Glorieux, no. 14*ec* (Pseudo-Aquinas, ed. Vives, xxviii. 445).

2. ff. 12ᵛ–16ᵛ [Q]uam sit appetenda gracia penitencie omnis auctoritas clamat . . . qui confitentur peccata in uitium (*ends imperfectly: catchword* amore boni).

3. ff. 17–19 [Q]uatuor uirtutum species multorum sapiencium sentenciis diffinite sunt . . . ignauiam uel condempnat.

Martin of Braga, Formula vitae honestae: cf. *Clavis*, no. 1080. *PL* lxxii. 23–7.

4. ff. 19–20ᵛ Inmensa est duplex custodia discipline ibi enim debet homo . . . quia sicut iam supra diximus alius sic et alius sic. Hec uobis fratres de sciencia et disciplina interim nos diximus bonitatem uero orate ut eam det nobis deus amen.

5. ff. 20ᵛ–21 [A]postolica uox clamat per orbem . . . uenerabilis ab omnibus (*ends abruptly*).

Ambrosius Autpertus: cf. above, Fort Augustus, Rat. 1. Ends here at *PL* xvii. 1059 (chapter 3, line 3).

6. ff. 21ᵛ–22ᵛ Cum ad sacerdotem pro peccatis confitendis peccator . . . uel ex fabulacione.

7. ff. 23–47 Incipit liber lotharii cardinalis qui lotharius postea dictus fuit innocencius papa (*erased*) iiiᵘˢ. De contemptu mundi De miseria hominis De vilitate humane condicionis. Incipit prologus. Domino patri dei gracia Portuen. episcopo . . . sulphur et ignis ardens in secula seculorum.

PL ccxvii. 701–45.

¹ Stevenson writes as though the label was then (*c.* 1890) *in situ* on the back cover 'protected by a covering of horn' (HMC *Report*, p. 398), but it must have been in its present position since 1859. The Worcester labels (cf. Ker, *MLGB*, p. 205) were not usually protected by horn.

8. ff. 47ᵛ–57ᵛ Incipit tractatus qui dicitur speculum ecclesie et ordo misse et eius significatum. Dicit apostolus ad eph. 6 Induite uos . . . in bonis operibus. Explicit tractatus qui dicitur speculum ecclesie de ordine misse et eius significato.

Hugh of St. Cher, Speculum Ecclesiae. Printed often.

9. ff. 57ᵛ–65ᵛ Incipiunt meditaciones beati augustini episcopi. Eya nunc homuncio fuge paululum . . . nec detestor bonitatem tuam. Expliciunt meditaciones beati augustini episcopi.

Twenty-four paragraphs. See above, Edinburgh, New College, Med. 3, art. 10, and Römer, i. 377.

10. ff. 66–70 Lamentaciones beate uirginis. Quis dabit capiti meo aqua . . . O uos filie ierusalem . . . sit filius eius dominus noster . . . amen. aue maria.

Printed in early editions of St. Bernard's works, for example edn. Paris (Rembolt), 1517, sign. EE viᵛ. The text in *PL* clxxii. 1133–42 is incomplete at the beginning.

11. ff. 70ᵛ–71 Hugo super hunc ps' miserere. Miserere . . . Audite peccatores orantem peccatorem . . . in misericordiam tuam.

A commentary on Ps. 50.

12. ff. 71–73ᵛ Hugo de 5 septenis. Quinque septene in sacra scriptura . . . inspexeris memento mei. amen. amen.

Hugh of St. Victor, De quinque septenis, chapters 1–4. *PL* clxxv. 405–10.

13 (added in the blank space at the end of quire 8). (*a*) ff. 73ᵛ–75 Quatuor uirtutum species . . . (*b*) f. 75 Nota de stilo gregorius. Si tetrasillabice penultima longa notatur . . . (*c*) ff. 75–6 Extracts 'De utili prouidencia dei libro vᵒ capitulo xiᵒ', 'De mercede temporali capitulo xvᵒ', 'De mercede sanctorum capitulo xviᵒ'. (*d*) f. 76ᵛ Quindecim figuras refert Ieronimus de libris anialibus (? *sic for* annalibus) iudeorum. Prima die eriget se mare . . . resurgent omnes.

(*a*), so far as it goes, repeats art. 3. (*b*) was inserted after (*c*) was written. (*d*). The fifteen signs before the Day of Judgement.

14 (s. xv). ff. 77–127 [S]icut dicit apostolus . . . in istis vi mandatis. Explicit lyncoln' de opere mandatorum.

Thomson, *Grosseteste*, p. 131, lists twenty-three manuscripts, but not this one.

15. ff. iiᵛ, iii, ivᵛ Notes on grammar, s. xv.

ff. iv+127+iv. ff. i–iv are medieval end-leaves: iiʳ and 130ᵛ were pasted to a former binding. 160×117 mm. Written space c. 125×80 mm. 2 cols. of 31–4 lines in arts. 7–14 and 22 long lines in arts. 1–6. Collation: 1–2⁸ 3⁸ wants 7, 8, perhaps blank, after f. 22 4–5¹² 6–8¹⁰ 9–14⁸ 15⁴ wants 4, probably blank: a quire or more missing after f. 16. Art. 14 is in a current and mainly secretary hand, apart from a patch of textura in the middle of f. 103ᵛ. Initials of arts. 7–12: (i) 2-line, red or blue, with ornament of both colours; (ii) 1-line, red or blue, sometimes with ornament; spaces for initials of arts. 1–6 remain blank. Secundo folio *enciam passionis*.

Written in England. The fifteenth-century table of contents on f. ivᵛ, listing arts. 1, 7–9, 14, is followed by '[. . . . .] beate marie'. 'January ii 1636 Memorandum I bought this booke the day and yere aboue named of John Mather bookeseller in Shrosbury by me foulke Jorden (?)', f. iii. Identifiable with the first of three manuscripts entered in the Benefactors' Book, p. 16, as the gift of Hugh Nash, prebendary, †1675: 'Lincoln de Opere Mandat.'.

28. *W. de Conchis, De philosophia mundi; etc.* s. xv med.

A miscellany. The order of arts. was at first 5–7, 1, 3, 4, 2, 8.

1. ff. 1–55ᵛ Quoniam ut ait tullius . . . longitudinem terminemus. Explicit philosophia de conchis. 'verius credo sit philosophia boycii dasci'.

William of Conches, De philosophia mundi: *PL* clxxii. 41–102. A. Vernet lists sixty-seven manuscripts, but not this one, in *Scriptorium*, i (1946–7), 252–5: for others see *MMBL* i. 284 and above, Eton College 160. The addition to the *explicit* is of s. xv.

2. ff. 56–71ᵛ Hic dicendum est de quibusdam per que poterit homo melius intelligere difficultates naturalium philosophorum et aliorum philosophorum per dei graciam qui est dator omnis sapiencie et sciencie. Natura⸴ quedam est naturans. quedam naturata. Natura naturans est deus. Natura naturata est quelibet alia . . . qui est finis omnium creaturarum amen.

3. ff. 72–92 Tractatum de spera 4 capitulis distinguimus. Dicentes primo quid sit spera. quid axis spere . . . aut tota machina mundana dissoluitur. Explicit tractatus de spera.

J. de Sacrobosco. Ed. L. Thorndike, *The Sphere of Sacrobosco and its commentators*, 1949, p. 76.

4. ff. 92ᵛ–119ᵛ Vna sciencia est alia nobilior . . . per qualitat' elementarium operacionum ut idem patet. Finita est ista compilacio super materia de spera celesti ad maiorem introduccionem scolarium in monte pessulano studencium quam compilauit Magister Robertus anglicus et finiuit anno domini mᵐᵒ ccᵐᵒ lxxᵐᵒ 2º sole existente in primo gradu tauri scorpione existente in ascencione. Qui scripsit carmen sit benedictus amen. q. Io. C. Explicit compilacio super materia de spera celesti.

Robertus Anglicus on the Sphere of Sacrobosco, ed. Thorndike, op. cit., pp. 143–98, but without the words here after 'patet'. Cf. J. C. Russell, *Writers of Thirteenth Century England*, p. 129.

5. ff. 120–33 Tractatus de ymagine mundi siue de spera editus a M. Roberto quondam episcopo Lincoln'. Intencio huius tractatus est describere figuram machine mundi . . . ymaginanda occurrunt. Explicit tractatus breuis de ymagine mundi.

Cf. Thomson, *Grosseteste*, pp. 115–16, but the present copy ends differently.

6. ff. 133ᵛ–138 Debes scire quod circulus solis 2 habet medietates . . . qui ex sexto geometrie habetur. Explicit quadrans Magistri Campani.

Thorndike and Kibre do not ascribe to J. Campanus.

7. ff. 138ᵛ–143ᵛ Omnia que a primeua rerum origine processerunt . . . Intercisa est siue discontinua quando omittitur (*ends imperfectly*).

J. de Sacrobosco, Algorismus. Thorndike and Kibre.

8. ff. 144–153ᵛ (*begins imperfectly*) fuissent et quasi appareat . . . Iohannes vero ponens se super hos (*ends imperfectly*).

A fragment of pseudo-Bonaventura, Meditationes de Passione Christi. As edn. 1596, vi. 404*b*D–409*a*A (Friday).

ff. i+153+i. 172×122 mm. Written space *c.* 120×70 mm. 26–34 long lines. Frame ruling. Collation: 1⁸ wants 1, 2 2⁸ 3¹⁰ 4–6⁸ 7⁸ wants 8, probably blank, after f. 55 8–18⁸ 19¹² wants 1 before f. 144 and 12 after f. 153. The quire signatures are in the order e–l, s, t, m–r, a–c, x, so ff. 120–43 once stood at the beginning and were followed by ff. 1–55, 72–119, 56–71, 144–53 in that order, and single quires marked d and v are missing after f. 143 and before f. 144. The script is current anglicana mixed with secretary, changing at art. 8. Two sizes of blue initials with red ornament. Secundo folio *angustiis* (f. 2) or *et grauium* (f. 121).

Written in England. No. (12) in the list of Henry Fowler's gifts in the Benefactors' Book, p. 25: 'Rob. Anglicus de Sphæra. Rob. Lincoln, de Imag. mundi 8° MS'.

29. *Michael de Hungaria, Tredecim Sermones* s. xv med.

1. ff. 1–113 Sequitur. Humiliat. dominus. filius. voca. seruit. Stans. moritur. diligit. venit. ambula. surge. resurge. Intencio Magistri Michaelis de Vngaria auctoris huius operis in hiis duobus versibus est ista . . . operis subsequentis. Sermo primus. Sequitur. Karissimi dicit Nicholaus de Lyra . . . ad gloriam perueniemus. Quam nobis concedat qui sine fine viuit et regnat amen. Expliciunt quatuordecim sermones.

The two sections of sermon 8 are counted here as two sermons, 8 and 9, making fourteen sermons in all, as in the edition of 1481: no. 8 begins with the word *Mori* and no. 9 with the word *Moritur*.

2. Three originally blank leaves, 114–16, contain charms, a recipe 'for a canker', notes of moneys received, and scribbles, including the name 'thomam gardiner', all in English, s. xvi.

ff. i+116+i. 152×107 mm. Written space 105×68 mm. 25 long lines. Frame ruling. Collation: 1–4¹² 5¹² wants 1–3 before f. 37 6–9¹² 10¹² wants 9 blank after f. 113. Written in a clear current hand of mixed but mainly secretary type. Coloured initials not filled in. Binding of s. xix. Secundo folio *vade fides tua*.

Written in England.

33. *Registrum brevium; Statuta Angliae; etc.* s. xv in.

1. ff. 1–47ᵛ A register of writs in 316 paragraphs, beginning with a judicial writ of 1375: Quando vic' mand' quod non inuenit pleg' de pros' (*this heading in the margin*). Edwardus dei gracia . . . vic' Ebor' salutem . . . T. R. de Bealknapp' apud W secundo die Marcii anno r.r. nostri Angl' xlix . . .

All writs begin *Rex* or (the first) *Edwardus* or (once) *Aliter*, except two in the names of justices, (f. 5ᵛ) W de H et socii, justices in eyre 'in Com E . . . dat' apud Ebor' ', 20 July 49 Edward III, and (f. 23ᵛ) Thomas de Ingilby and Roger Fulthorp, justices of the Lord Bishop of Durham 'ad omnes assisas . . . in Com' Dunelm' et Sadbryg' ', at Stockton, 20th day, etc. There are headings throughout in the margins, but no obvious divisions other than the paragraphs. For R. de Bealknap in the printed register of judicial writs see de Haas and Hall, pp. lxxiv, lxxv.

2. ff. 48–55ᵛ (1) Primo Arrerag' Redditus assis' firmar' Consuetudines . . . acquietancie. Summa summarum tocius expenc' et sic debet etc'. (2) Rotulus compoti de tali Manerio in forma subscripta disponatur. Idem reddit compotum de tot. scilicet . . . communiter xl quart' (*ends imperfectly*: *catchwords* 'Quod si grang').

(1) Headings for and (2) model of a manorial account, ending in the section headed 'Ad estimacionem Grang' '. Printed from this copy by D. Oschinsky, *Walter of Henley*, 1971, pp. 469–75.

Arts. 3–46 are statutes, etc., of known date in or before 1305 (art. 27) or of uncertain date.[1]

3. ff. 56–57ᵛ Statuta de scaccario. In French. *SR* i. 197.

4. ff. 57ᵛ–58 Districciones Scaccarii. In French. *SR* i. 197*b*.

5. ff. 58–9 Statuta de Exonia. In French. *SR* i. 210.

6. ff. 59–60 Articuli de Exonia. In French. *SR* i. 211.

7. f. 60ᵛ Statut' de Ragemon. In French. *SR* i. 44.

8. ff. 61–4 Noui articuli. In French. *SR* i. 136.

9. f. 64ʳᵛ Statuta de itinere. Ade primes deit le Iustice lire deuant toutz de la Countee Le breue le Roy . . . par cheson de le heir.

10. ff. 64ᵛ–65ᵛ Statuta de finibus. Quia fines . . . *SR* i. 128.

11. ff. 65ᵛ–66ᵛ Statuta de presentibus vocatis ad Warrantum. *SR* i. 108.

12. f. 66ʳᵛ Statutum de quo Warranto primum. Anno gracie mcclxxviii . . .

A Latin version of the French in *SR* i. 45/1–21 *usent*, followed after 'utantur' by the words 'in forma breuis subscripti' and three writs, 'Cum nuper in parliamento nostro . . .', 'Precipimus tibi quod . . .', and 'Summone per bonos summonitores talem quod sit coram iusticiariis nostris . . .'.

13. ff. 67ᵛ–68 Statutum de iuratis et assisis extra Comitatum. *SR* i. 113.

14. f. 68ʳᵛ Statutum de Antiquo dominico Corone. Licet in antiquo dominico non currat . . . alii facient ignoro etc.

Ed. A. J. Horwood, *Year Books 20–21 Edward I* (RS 1866), pp. xviii–xix.

15. ff. 68ᵛ–69 Statutum Circumspecte agatis. *SR* i. 101.

16. f. 69 Statutum de Regia prohibicione. Sub qua forma important laici . . . licet Regia prohibicio porrigutur (*sic*). Dat' parisius anno xiiii. *SR* i. 101/24.

On arts. 15, 16 cf. E. B. Graves, 'Circumspecte agatis', *EHR* xliii (1928), 14.

17. f. 69ʳᵛ Statutum de vasto facto in custodia. *SR* i. 109.

18. ff. 69ᵛ–70 Statutum de Gaueleto in London. *SR* i. 222.

---

[1] I omit the word *Incipit* or *Incipiunt* which begins arts. 3–6, 8–27, 30–5, 37–50, 52, 53.

19. f. 70^{rv} Statutum de Anno et die bisextili. *SR* i. 7.

20. ff. 70^v–72 Consuetudines Kancie. In French. *SR* i. 223.

21. f. 72^{rv} Statuta de moneta. In French. *SR* i. 219.

22. ff. 72^v–73 Articuli de tonsura monete. In French. *SR* i. 219*a*.

23. f. 73^{rv} Statuta de coheredibus. *SR* i. 5.

In name of Edward (I) and addressed to master Gerard, justice of Ireland.

24. ff. 73^v–74 Statuta de Militibus faciendis. Rex concessit quod omnes qui milites esse debe(n)t et non sunt . . . fines admittant.

25. f. 74^{rv} Statuta armorum in Torneamentis. In French. *SR* i. 230.

26. ff. 74^v–75 Statuta de conspiratoribus cum Breue. In French. *SR* i. 216.

27. f. 75 Statutum de Conspiratoribus aliter. In French. *SR* i. 145.

28. ff. 75–7 Modo incipiunt Capitula Itineris que tangunt Coronam. Inquirendum est de Castris et aliis edificiis circumdatis . . . consilia per annum etc. Fifteen heads.

29. f. 76^{rv} Modo incipit Officium Coronatoris. Primes doit le Coroner demander si le quatre villes soient venuz . . . des chateux le felon.

30. ff. 76^v–77 Officium Coronatoris Aliter. *SR* i. 40.

31. f. 77^v Statutum de petentibus admitti. Cum quis per breue domini Regis petat aliquod ten' versus ten' . . . eat quietus.

32. ff. 77^v–78 Statutum de Terris mortuandis. In French. *SR* i. 31.

33. f. 78^{rv} Statutum de proteccionibus domini Regis. In French. *SR* i. 217.

34. f. 78^v Visus franciplegii. In French. *SR* i. 246.

35. f. 79 Modus faciendi homagium et fidelitatem. In French. *SR* i. 227.

36. f. 79^{rv} Modo incipit Assisa panis. In French. Cf. *SR* i. 199.

37. f. 79^v Assisa Ceruisie. In French. Cf. *SR* i. 200.

38. ff. 79^v–80 Lucrum Pistoris. In French. Cf. *SR* i. 200.

39. f. 80^{rv} Iudicium Pillorie. *SR* i. 201.

40. ff. 80^v–81 Modus Calumniandi Essonia. *SR* i. 217.

41. f. 81 Dies communes in Banco. *SR* i. 208.

42. f. 81^{rv} Dies communes de dote. *SR* i. 208.

43. ff. 81^v–82 Composicio facta ad puniendum infringent' Assisam. *SR* i. 202.

44. f. 82^{rv} Tractatus de forstallariis et huiusmodi. *SR* i. 203.

45. f. 82ʳᵛ Quot modis dicitur excepcio. Notandum quod quatuor modis dicitur excepcio . . . ad aliam responsionem.

Cf. B.L., Royal 10 A. v, art. 20; *MMBL* i. 39.

46. ff. 82ᵛ–83 Composicio Monete et mensura terre. *SR* i. 204.

47. ff. 83–88ᵛ Summa que vocatur cadit assisa. Edwardus dei gracia . . . salutem. Si A. fecerit te securum . . . et hoc breue etc. Modo dicendum est que raciones et excepciones cassant Breue Mortis Antecessoris. Cadat assisa si petatur . . . Modo possessio loco suo ut predictum est.

48. ff. 88ᵛ–92 Summa que dicitur Bastardia. Si bastardus se clamando legitimum heredem . . . sicut superius dictum est etc.

49. f. 92ʳᵛ Officium Seneschalli. Ceo est loffice du Seneschall coment il deit vers sceus . . . et la Court prochien. ou nul homme fuist fors le Seignour. Baillif fait le Seneschall . . . et la Court prochien. In dialogue form.

50. ff. 92ᵛ–93 De Releuio et de distinctione Socagii. Nous (*sic*) deuez sauer que la . . . en le Regestre pleinement. Cf. *SR* i. 228.

51. f. 93 Modo incipit quid sit homagium. Sciendum quod homagium est iuris vinculum . . . tamen in persona heredis (13 lines).

52. f. 93ʳᵛ Distincio villanorum et de eorum sequela. Vn home deit suyte a la Court son Seignour de tres semaignes . . . le villenage son Seignour (23 lines).

53. ff. 93ᵛ–94 Libertates Anglie. Soka idem est quod secta . . . et pro auxilio ad hoc dando finito.

Explanations of thirty Anglo-Saxon law terms, the last 'Bordelpeni'.

54. ff. 94ᵛ–95 Bastard Baignard Braisard . . . Parlebien.

Surnames arranged for the most part according to their endings, those in -ard, -el, -et, -i, -le coming first. f. 95ᵛ is blank.

55. ff. 96–119ᵛ Tables of chapters of statutes, 1 Edward III–17 Richard II, in French, numbered 'cxxix' to 'ccxi'.[1]

56. ff. 120–249 Statutes of 1–50 Edward III and 1–21 Richard II.

A numbering corresponding to that in art. 55 begins at 'cxxix' but goes no further than 'clv'. 'quod S' at the end.

57. ff. 249ᵛ–283 Statutes of 1–13 Henry IV, in French. *SR* ii. 111–69.

58. ff. 283ᵛ–287 Statute of 1 Henry V, in French. *SR* ii. 171–4, but with an eleventh chapter at the end, 'Item que toutz Priours Aliens . . . de lez possessions dicelles etc' '. f. 287ᵛ blank.

59. ff. 288–95 (quire 38). Statute of 2 Henry V, in French. *SR* ii. 175–87. f. 295ᵛ blank.

---

[1] In late collections, for example Bodleian, Douce 362, and Lincolns Inn, Hale 74, the 'vetera statuta' are numbered 1–128, statutes of 1–50 Edward III, 129–188, and statutes of 1–21 Richard II, 189–213.

ff. i+296+i, foliated i, 1–22, 22*, 23–295 (296). *c.* 293 × 200 mm. Written space *c.* 195 × 118 mm. 42 long lines. Collation: 1–12⁸ 13–14⁴ 15–38⁸. Signatures: of quires 1–6 (art. 1), M–R; of quire 7 (art. 2), a; of quires 8–12 (arts. 3–54), g–l; of quires 13–16 (art. 55), c–f; of quires 17–38 (arts. 56–9), h–z, 7, ɔ, ÷, est, a, b. ff. 96–135ᵛ are in a legal type of anglicana and all the rest in one good secretary hand. Initials: (i) ff. 1, 48, 96, 249ᵛ, 283ᵛ, gold on coloured grounds, with continuous or partial borders; (ii) mostly 4-line, blue with red ornament. 'This book was re-bound by Omash, Binder to the Bodleian Library in Oxford, A.D. 1858. F(rancis) J(eune) Ecc. Glouc: Thes:', f. i.¹ Secundo folio *ex illis qui.*

Written in England, in the north, to judge from art. 1. 'Jo: Br:', f. 295ᵛ, s. xvi.

34. *Historia Monasterii Gloucestriae; Macer; etc.*   s. xv in.

1. (*a*) ff. 1–24ᵛ Sequitur hic de prima fundacione Monasterii sancti petri Glouc' ab Osrico subregulo de licencia regis. Anno ab incarnacione domini DC. lxxxi . . . in Bullis papalibus inde confectis. (*b*) ff. 25–43ᵛ Hic incipiunt donaciones omnium bonorum Monasterii sancti Petri Glouc' tam temporalium quam Spiritualium. Ethelbaldus Rex Merciorum dedit . . . tempore Reginaldi abbatis.

(*a, b*) edited as *Historia et Cartularium Monasterii Gloucestriae*, by W. H. Hart (RS 1863–7), 1–58, 58–121. They are together also in Queen's Coll., Oxford, MS. 367 and in B.L., MS. Cotton Domitian viii, both of s. xv. f. 44ʳᵛ blank.

2. ff. 45–58 Abecedarium diuersarum herbarum secundum ordinem alphabeti. Alleluya panis cuculi . . . Zipperis id est Galla.

English as well as Latin names are usually given. Cf. Trinity College, Cambridge, MS. 1109, art. 36, and Stevenson's description in HMC.

3. ff. 58ᵛ–62ᵛ Cum ea que in curacione sunt vtilia inueniri non possunt recipere duximus quid pro quo. A. Pro aristologia rotunda Ruta domestica . . . Pro zinzibero Piretrum.

An alphabetical Quid pro quo. Cf. Thorndike and Kibre.

4. ff. 63–89 (*begins imperfectly*) Et prodest lumbis sic vulnarumque querelas . . . Pellit frigorem reuocabit et ipsa calorem.

Macer, De viribus herbarum, lacking the first leaf. Lines 17–1917 of the edition by L. Choulant, 1832. ff. 89ᵛ–91ᵛ blank.

5. ff. 92–96ᵛ A 'tabula super librum subsequentem' covering the contents of arts. 6–9 leaf by leaf, including the leaves numbered i and lxxxxi, now missing before f. 97 and after f. 185.

6. ff. 97–161ᵛ (*begins imperfectly*) aqua vite contra paralisim . . . aristologie lonurre.

Recipes for making waters, oils, ointments, etc., mainly in Latin, but with passages in English. Cf. Stevenson, loc. cit.

7. ff. 161ᵛ–165. Ere² begynneth þe makyng of Watres for Steynours. To make steyning wat*ur* Sic incipies. Wan þᵘ schalt diȝt þo cloþ . . .

In English except the last recipe.

   ¹ See above, p. 934.
   ² Doubtless 'Here' was intended, but the rubricator put in a paragraph mark instead of an initial *H*.

8. ff. 165ᵛ–172 Incipit tractatus bonus de vrinis cognoscendis vt lucide valeat medicus intueri cui infirmitati vnusquisque subiceat. et sic morbo conuenientem medicinam poterit tucius adhibere. Vrina alba in colore tenuis in substancia . . . vel caloris ebullicionem. Explicit.

Thorndike and Kibre. Fifty-nine lines of verse on urines come near the end. They begin 'Si lapis est solidus epatis si coctio cruda'.

9. ff. 172ᵛ–185ᵛ A farrago of recipes and charms, beginning with a recipe for scabies, 'Radices elene campane bene parata . . .'. Ends imperfectly.

A few passages in English. A charm, 'Si vis esse knxkskbklks', f. 175ᵛ: cf. *MMBL*, i. 207.

10. Medical notes of s. xvi on ff. ivᵛ, ii include seven lines in Welsh.

ff. iii+185+i. ff. ii, iii are medieval end-leaves. ff. 63–89, 97–185 are foliated in a medieval hand ii–xxviii, ii–lxxxx. 180 × 122 mm. Written space *c.* 135 × 90 mm. 30 long lines. Collation: 1–5⁸ 6 four (ff. 41–4) 7–8⁸ 9⁸ wants 3 after f. 62 10–12⁸ 13⁸ wants 6–8 after f. 96 14⁸ wants 1 before f. 97 15–24⁸ 25 two (ff. 184–5). Written in a good square anglicana, probably by the same scribe throughout. 3-line, 2-line, and 1-line red or blue initials. Limp vellum binding, s. xix. Secundo folio *et urbis*.

Written in England (Gloucester ?). Perhaps in Wales in s. xvi: cf. art. 10. A short erasure at the head of f. 1 is preceded by the date 1556. Bought for £150 in 1879 from S. Calvary & Co., booksellers, Berlin, who had it from a Naples bookseller in Oct. 1878 (letter in D. and C., Rec. 139/5, and Chapter Act, 27 Mar. 1879).

35.

For these fragments of homilies and lives of saints in Old English, s. xi, see N. R. Ker, *Catalogue of Manuscripts containing Anglo-Saxon*, 1957, p. 154, no. 117. They were used in the bindings of the Register of Abbots Braunch and Newton (1500–10, 1510–14) and another book.

36.

See above, p. 934.

GLOUCESTER. DIOCESAN RECORD OFFICE

Fragments of manuscripts at present kept in the Gloucester City Library were sent there by Miss Hockaday, daughter of F. S. Hockaday, who for many years before his death in 1924 had the records of the diocese in a fire-proof building at his home.[1] Some of nos. 1–23, 30–2 come from and others almost certainly come from the long series of 'Act Books', eighty-seven of which are earlier than 1600[2]. All the bifolia were covers. The single leaves and the strips were

---

[1] I. M. Kirby, *Diocese of Gloucester. A Catalogue of the Records of the Bishop and Archdeacons*, 1968, pp. x, 127.

[2] Ibid., pp. 1–8, GDR 1–87. These 'Act Books' and the other records listed by Miss Kirby are housed at present in the City Library.

presumably inside plain parchment covers like those still on many of these books. The only piece of manuscript still *in situ* seems to be that in GDR 10 (1554–6). Some of the plain parchment covers, for example those on GDR 16, 38, 58, 71, 80, 89, have attached to them small pieces of paper which are probably the remains of labels (see especially GDR 71). Similar pieces of paper are or were on some of the manuscript covers (nos. 4, 5, 13, 22(?), 23).[1] A small fragment of the same manuscript as no. 13 was formerly in use as strengthening to the spine of GDR 5 (episcopal visitation, 1551).[2] Some fragments have a title or date on them which shows or suggests where they come from: 'Visitacion' (no. 3); '1567' (no. 4); 'Old Visitacion Bookes' (no. 14); 'Visitacions Anno 1600' (no. 16). Others were scribbled on in the later s. xvi: 'Meredithe contra be[. . .]one in causa diffamacionis . . .' (no. 23); 'Iohannes horne de Sain birin con[. . .] William harwode ibidem causa diff' ' (no. 10); 'Richard Gwillem of beamesbarowe' (no. 13); 'Richard Hands' (no. 22).[3] All these pieces, except no. 5 and perhaps nos. 2, 6, 7, 12, appear to have been written in England.

1. A bifolium of a Sarum ordinal. s. xiv.

The first leaf contains the end of the temporale, dedication of church and the common of an apostle, the second, saints days from Julian to Valentine (27 Jan.–14 Feb.). Written space 192 × 140 mm. *c.* 34 long lines. Written in anglicana.

2. A leaf of Decretum Gratiani written in England (?) in s. xii/xiii.

Part 1, D. xxxiv, xxxv, including Friedberg's paleae 22–4. The apparatus is contemporary, in a neat hand. 305 × 225 mm. Written space 228 × 150 mm. 2 cols. 49 lines.

3. A bifolium from a copy of Parvum volumen. s. xiv.

Liber feudorum, tit. lxx. Full apparatus in the same hand. The sheet was folded at the edges so that each leaf measures 305 × 220 mm.

4. A bifolium of a commentary on Sextus liber Decretalium. s. xiv.

Bk. 3, tit. xv. 300 × 210 mm. Written space 185 mm wide. 2 cols. 81 + lines. Blue initials with red ornament.

5. A bifolium of the Decretals of Gregory IX written in France (?) in s. xiii/xiv.

Bk. 1, tit. vi, caps. 35–40. From a handsome book, with apparatus in the same hand as the text and wide margins containing notes in an English hand, s. xiv. The sheet was folded at the edges so that each leaf measures 303 × 205 mm. Written space (text) 220 × 130 mm. Initials red or blue with ornament of the other colour.

6, 7. Two single leaves from the commentary of Bonaventura on the Sentences of Peter Lombard written in England (?) in s. xiv.

Bk. 2, d. 1: cf. edn. 1596, pp. 17, 18. Written space 230+ × 135 mm. 2 cols. 62+ lines. Small hand. Blue initials with red ornament. The leaves were perhaps used as flyleaves.

8. A strip from a bifolium of a Bible in English. s. xiv/xv.

[1] The piece of paper stuck on no. 13 was removed in 1974. String was used to attach the paper to no. 23 and to the cover mentioned in the footnote to no. 23.

[2] I rely on a note I took twenty years ago. The book has been rebound and the fragment is no longer to be found.

[3] The cover mentioned in the footnote to no. 23 has 'Iohannes [. . . .]' and 'I Ethering' (?) on it.

Exodus 34 in the later Wycliffite translation. The full width of one leaf remains and a little of the leaf conjugate with it.

Written space 130 mm wide. 2 cols. Blue initials with red ornament.

9. A strip from a leaf of a noted breviary. s. xv in.

Sanctorale for early November (All Souls, Winefred–Martin). Initials blue with red ornament or red with greenish-brown ornament.

10. Part of a leaf of a large noted breviary. s. xiv².

First Sunday after Epiphany. Written space 255 mm wide. Handsome script. Blue initials with red ornament.

Probably once a normal-sized wrapper, but the lower part has been torn off.

11. A bifolium of a noted breviary. s. xiv.

Sanctorale for January (Fabian and Sebastian). 295 × 185 mm.

12. One leaf of a missal written in England (?) in s. xii/xiii.

Common of martyrs. 295 × 200 mm. Written space 223 × 150 mm. 2 cols. 32 lines. Plain red or blue initials.

13. One leaf of a commentary on civil law. s. xiii.

A section begins 'Restat uidere de preiudicialibus actionibus et primo de ea'.

300 × 200 mm. Written space 265 × 170 mm. 2 cols. 56 lines.

14. A bifolium of an antiphonal. s. xiv.

Sanctorale for October (Thomas of Hereford; 11,000 virgins): cf. *Hereford Breviary*, ii (HBS xl), 348–53, 378–9.

Written space 255 × 160 mm. 2 cols. 10 lines and music.

15. A bifolium of a noted missal. s. xiii in.

Lent and Palm Sunday: cf. *Sarum Missal*, pp. 82, 96. The sheet was folded at the edges so that each leaf measures 300 × 230 mm.

Written space 265 × 183 mm. 2 cols. 36 lines. Initials: 2-line, blue or red with ornament of the other colour.

16–19. Two bifolia and two single leaves of a book containing sequences and (17ii, 18, 19) settings of Agnus Dei and Sanctus. s. xiv.

16i. (*a*) A headless piece which ends 'in celesti patria decantemus omnia alleluya'. (*b*) Sabbato. Sequencia. Benedicta es celorum regina et mundi tocius domina...(*York Missal*, ii (Surtees Soc., 1874), 87). (*c*) In exaltatione sancte crucis. Laudes crucis attolamus .... (*Sarum Missal*, p. 482).

16ii. (*d*) End of Christo inclita (*S.M.*, p. 484: All Saints). (*e*) Sequence for Martin, 'Sacerdotem cristi martinum . . .' (*S.M.*, p. 484).

17i. (*f*) End of sequence Clare sanctorum (*S.M.*, p. 486: Apostles). (*g*) Alleluia nunc decantet . . . (*S.M.*, p. 486: Apostle or Apostles).

295 × 200 mm. Written space 235 × 140 mm. 10 long lines and music. Nos. 18, 19 were probably once joined together.

20, 21. Two strips of a liturgical psalter. s. xiv.

Psalms 115–17, 137–8. Noted antiphons. Height of written space 265 mm. 2 cols. 30 lines. Initials: (i) of psalms, blue with red ornament or red with violet ornament; (ii) of verses, 1-line, blue or red.

22. A bifolium of Augustine on Psalms (57, 58). s. xii.

The sheet was folded at the edges, so that each leaf measures 310 × 235 mm: the full height before folding was 390 mm.

Written space 293 × 185 mm. 2 cols. 49 lines. Ruling with a hard point. Lemmata in capitals.

23. A bifolium of a missal, s. xii[1].[1]

23i is marked 'cxliii' on the recto (the number is a later addition in red) and begins in the preface for the Sunday before Advent at the word 'interriti'. The office 'In dedicatione ecclesie' follows, ending 'tristis mestusque' in the preface 'Uere dignum aeterne deus. Pro annua dedicatione . . .'.

23ii is marked 'i' on the recto (this early number in red was repeated later, s. xiv?, with the addition of the words 'Incipit numerus de s' ' in front of it) and 'ii' on the verso.[2] It begins in the office for Felix (14 Jan.) at the words '(ma)nentem ciuitatem'. Offices for Maurus, Marcellus, Prisca, and Fabian and Sebastian (15–20 Jan.) follow.

On both 23i and 23ii the cues for the sung parts of the mass are usually in a hand of s. xiv over erasure.

Written space 247 × 145 mm. 2 cols. 35 lines. A handsome round hand. 3-line and 2-line initials, red, green, blue, or purple. The script and decoration of Bodleian MS. Bodley 210 from the abbey of Gloucester are generally similar.[3]

24–9. Fragments of nine leaves of Gregory, Moralia. s. xii[1].

No. 24 is from bk. 27: *PL* lxxvi. 433B–435B. No. 25, a fragment of a bifolium, is from bk. 30 (edn., cols. 532–3, 549). No. 26 (i, ii), two fragments of a bifolium, is from bk. 30 (edn., cols. 536–9, 544–6). No. 27 is from bk. 30 (edn., cols. 539B–541B). No. 28 is from bk. 30 (edn., cols. 541C–543D). No. 29, a fragment of a bifolium, is from bk. 31 (edn., cols. 578–81). The leaves have 'LIBER' at the head of versos and the book number at the head of rectos.

Written space 255 × 172 mm. 2 cols. 40 lines. Ruling with a hard point. From three quires: (1) no. 24; (2) nos. 25–8; (3) no. 29. No. 24 is in a different hand from the others: the enlarged, now damaged tail of *g* in the last line on the recto may have been of the 'bow and arrow' type.[4] The leaves have been cut into symmetrical shapes for some purpose. They are not binding fragments.

30. A strip from a law book. s. xiii.

The running title 'COL' ' suggests Parvum volumen; cf. Corpus Christi College, Oxford, 73, ff. 57–165.

31. Two strips forming a complete leaf of Medulla Grammaticae. s. xv in.

[1] Another bifolium of this missal was in the hands of a Gloucester antique dealer in 1951, when I saw it through the kindness of F. W. Potto-Hicks, rector of Elkstone, Gloucestershire. It belongs now to Mrs. Gent, 24 Grove Terrace, London, NW 5. The leaves are marked in red, 'xxxi' on 1[r], 'xxxii' on 1[v], 2[r], and 'xxxiii' on 2[v]. They contain the sanctorale for 15–24 Aug.: Assumption of B.V.M., octave of Laurence, Agapitus, Helen, Magnus, octave of the Assumption, Timothy and Symphorian, Timothy and Apollinaris, Bartholomew. In 1951 f. 2[r] had, like no. 23ii, a paper label tied on to it with string.

[2] In this manuscript the same number is used to mark each side of a double opening, not the recto and verso of a leaf.

[3] Cf. especially the three forms of initial *A* used on the Gent bifolium and on f. 86[v] of MS. Bodley 210. In both manuscripts they are used in the same order in successive paragraphs.

[4] Cf. N. R. Ker, *English Manuscripts in the Century after the Norman Conquest*, 1960, p. 7.

End of St- and beginning of Su-. Written space 212 × 135 mm. 36 long lines. The script is a current mixture of anglicana and secretary.

32. A strip from a manuscript of scholastic philosophy. s. xiv.

On matter and form. The full height of the written space, 247 mm, and 60 mm of the width remain. 55 lines.

A strip from an antiphonal, s. xiii ex., is inside the binding of GDR 10 (responsions and depositions, 1554–6).

Expositiones ewangeliorum for the tenth to sixteenth Sundays after the octave of Pentecost (*Ordinale Exon.* i (HBS xxxvii), 191–2). The full height of the written space, 225 mm, and 63 mm of the width remain. 42 long lines (14 lines of text and music).

GUILDFORD. SURREY ARCHAEOLOGICAL SOCIETY

8/5. Registrum brevium[1]   s. xiv[1]

Edwardus dei gracia . . . balliuis suis de Notyngham salutem . . .

A register of writs in general agreement at first (ff. 1–47ᵛ, after which a leaf is missing) with the Bodleian register called R by de Haas and Hall, *Early Registers of Writs*, Selden Society lxxxvii, 1970, nos. 1–360, except at ff. 17ᵛ–20, where there are a dozen forms of Prohibicio formata: R. 133 is here on f. 16ᵛ and R. 135–7 on f. 20ᵛ; five forms on ff. 18ᵛ–19 are CC. 72–6 in that order. f. 49 begins with a writ Ad inquirendum de ydiota. After this the order is (f. 49) Ad quod dampnum, (f. 51ᵛ) account, (f. 54ᵛ) debt and detinue, (f. 57ᵛ) warranty of charter, (f. 59ᵛ) mesne, (f. 60ᵛ) dower, (f. 61ᵛ) sections generally in the order of R. 433–70, (f. 65ᵛ) suit, (f. 68) wardship, (f. 71) exemption from tourn, (f. 71ᵛ) electing coroner and verderer, (ff. 72–73ᵛ) sixteen miscellaneous writs including service on assizes, respite of military service, beaupleder, and prohibitions of distress, (f. 75, after a missing leaf) novel disseisin (the first piece on f. 75 is R. 645), (ff. 82–85ᵛ) record and process, beginning with R. 682 and ending imperfectly. The only leaf remaining after this, f. 91, is torn and stained. It contains a dozen forms of Precipe quod reddat.

The first writ (of right) bears no date. Many forms in the ecclesiastical group, ff. 14–21, are in the name of the bishop of Lincoln or an official of the bishop: on f. 19, De separatis decimis is CC. 76 in the RC/T version (de Haas and Hall, p. li). R. 239, 240 are addressed to Hugh le Despenser, justice of the king's forest on this side Trent. Trespass is a large section, ff. 36–44, beginning with R. 283.

There are at least thirty-five forms of record and process, most of them addressed to the king's treasurer and chamberlains, two to his treasurer and barons of exchequer, and one (f. 84ᵛ) 'De recordo et processu loquele et errore corrigendo' to R. de Grey, his justice of C(hester).[2] There are no writs of consultation.

For eight missing leaves see below. Four leaves, 12, 45, 58, 91, are fragmentary. After f. 1 provision was made for coloured initials at nine points: f. 26ᵛ at R. 182; f. 28ᵛ at R. 215; f. 30 at R. 219; f. 34 at R. 244; f. 36 at R. 283 (new leaf); f. 49 at Ad inquirendum de ydiota; f. 51ᵛ at R. 418 (new page); f. 57 at R. 518 (new page); f. 59ᵛ at R. 471, after a blank space. R. 357 begins a new page, f. 46ᵛ, but does not have a coloured initial: the last fifteen lines on the recto are blank.

[1] On deposit in the Guildford Muniment Room, Castle Arch, Guildford. Mr. Derek Hall told me of this manuscript and helped me with the description.
[2] This is presumably the R. de G. of R. 764.

ff. ii+82. The medieval foliation i, iii–xlvii, xlix–lxiii, lxv–lxxiii, lxxv–iiii^{xx}v, iiii^{xx}xi takes account of eight now missing leaves and jumps in error from lxiii to lxv. 250×170 mm. Written space *c.* 185×112 mm. 34 long lines. Collation: 1^{12} wants 2: 12 is a small fragment 2–3^{12} 4^{12} wants 12: 9 is a fragment 5^{12} only a corner of 10 remains 6^{12} (ff. 61–3, 65–73) 7^{12} wants 1 before f. 75 8 one (f. 91). Written in anglicana. Spaces for 2-line initials not filled. Only the upper cover of the medieval limp parchment binding remains: five bands.

'Constat (?) W^{o} B.', f. ii^{v}, s. xv. 'Ri. hutton', f. 1, at foot, s. xv/xvi. Bequest of A. R. Bax to the Surrey Archaeological Society before 1934.

HARROW SCHOOL

11AA. *Cicero, Epistolae*   s. xv med.

Cicero's letters to (1) Quintus and (2) Atticus and (3) his letters to Brutus and Brutus' to him, followed by (4), pseudo-Cicero, letter to Octavianus. Edited by W. S. Watt, (1, 3, 4) Oxford 1958, pp. 20–103, 112–46, 213–19, (2) Oxford, 1965, 2 vols.

1. ff. 1–34^{v} M.T.C. sal[. . .] Quinto Ciceroni fratri. Primus liber. [E]tsi non dubitabam . . . et optime frater Vale. Liber tertius ad Q. fratrem explicit.

2. ff. 37–251^{v} M. T. Ciceronis epistolarum ad Atticum liber primus incipit feliciter. Cicero Attico salutem dicit. Petitionis nostrae quam . . . atque etiam rogo. M. T. Ciceronis epistolarum ad atticum liber xvi et ultimus explicit. Deo laus semper.

3. ff. 252–265^{v} M. T. Ciceronis ad brutum epistolarum liber incipit. Publius clodius tribunus . . . arbitrabor vi kl' sextil'.

4. ff. 265^{v}–267^{v} Cicero Octaui(an)o S. Si per tuas legiones . . . fugere decreui.

The Greek is supplied in spaces left for it in pale-red ink by another hand, the same perhaps as put in translations of it in the margins. Many corrections and alterations between the lines and in the margins, for example in art. 1 'uel lætitiam' opposite 'licentiam' (edn., p. 23/13) and in art. 2 'uel conciuncula', 'uel Sampsicer à me' and 'uel cum sim' opposite 'contumelia', 'Sampsicerame' and 'consumi' (edn. i. 68/19, 69/5, 71/8). Art. 1 has the words 'priusquam Trebatius ueniret uicem imperatoris subire' after 'posset' (edn., p. 74/18) and three of the six other readings of VORP noted by Watt, p. 2. Its first letter is divided into eleven sections by red initials at *Ac, At, Nequaquam, Sint, In, Iam, Hoc, Atque, Unum, Ac* (edn., pp. 21/9, 22/12/ 23/17, 24/22, 25/20, 26/19, 27/21, 32/21, 34/23, 36/13) and has 'correcta' at the end. ff. 35–36^{v} and 268^{rv} were left blank.

ff. ii+268+ii. Strong paper: it is particularly thick and stiff on ff. 1–36, 73, 84, 267. 265×195 mm. Written space 210×110 mm. 36 long lines. Ruling with a hard point, the writing between a pair of lines, the vertical lines in the outer margins triple. Collation: 1–22^{12} 23 four (ff. 265–8). Written in a clumsy upright humanistica by one hand throughout. Spaces for initials, 6–7 line and 2-line, not filled, except for a 2-line *S* in red on f. 252. 1-line red initials in art. 1, I. i. Binding of s. xix^{1} by Charles Lewis: see below. Secundo folio *sit magnum*.

Written in Italy. Erasures on ff. 1, 34^v, 267^v. Belonged to Henry Drury: 'H. Drury. Epistolæ . . . corio Russico quas sepsit C. Lewis', f. i: his sale 19 Feb. 1827, lot 1201. 'This book for many years in the library of the late J. B. Yates Esq. of West Dingle Liverpool was presented to the Harrow School Library by his grandson H. Y. Thompson some time head of the School. Jany 1st 1872'.

Horae s. XV^2

1. ff. 1–12^v Calendar in French in gold, red, and blue, the two colours alternating for effect, as often in Rouen hours.

Feasts in gold include 'Nostre dame des neges', 'La transfiguration' and 'Sainct romain' (5, 6 Aug., 23 Oct.).

2. ff. 13–19 Sequentiae of the Gospels.

'Protector in te sperantium' and 'Ecclesiam tuam quesumus domine . . .' after John.

3. ff. 19^v–23^v Orison de la uierge marie. O intemerata . . . orbis terrarum. De te enim . . .

4. ff. 24–27^v Obsecro te . . . f. 28^{rv} blank.

5. ff. 29–92 Hours of B.V.M. of the use of (Rouen).

Memoriae after lauds of Holy Spirit, Holy Cross, Michael, John Baptist, Peter and Paul, Laurence, Nicholas, Katherine, Margaret, Barbara (Virgo fide sana . . .: *RH*, no. 34601), Mary Magdalene, Anne, and a 'Memore de la pais'. f. 92^v blank.

6. ff. 93–115 Penitential psalms and litany.

Victricius, Romanus, Mellonius, and Audoenus are seventh to ninth and eleventh of sixteen confessors. Austroberta is twelfth of virgins. ff. 115^v–116^v blank.

7. ff. 117–120^v Hours of Holy Cross.

8. ff. 121–124^v Hours of Holy Spirit.

9. ff. 125–172^v Office of the dead.

10. ff. 173–9 Doulce dame de misericorde . . .

The Fifteen Joys of B.V.M. Sonet, no. 458.

11. ff. 179–83 Doulx dieu doulx pere saincte trinite . . .

The Seven Requests. Sonet, no. 504.

12. ff. 183^v–188^v Royne dez cieulx glorieuse . . .

Twelve 12-line stanzas. Sonet, no. 1793.

13. ff. 189–96 Domine labia mea aperies . . . Artes[1] docta regis nata . . .

Hours of St. Katherine. *RH*, no. 23129. *AH* xlvi. 282. f. 196^v was left blank.

ff. ii+196. 220×160 mm. Written space 100×67 mm. 15 long lines. Collation: 1^{12} 2–24^8. Fifteen handsome 12-line pictures, eight in art. 5 and one before each of arts. 6–9, 10 (B.V.M. and Child attended by angels), 12 (Pietà) and 13 (a couple kneel before St. Katherine, who treads on a man wearing a turban and holding a scimitar). Initials: (i)

[1] The illuminator put in a *P* instead of an *A*.

5-line or 4-line, blue or red on gold grounds, decorated and, if on rectos, with sprays into the margins; (ii) as (i), but 3-line or 2-line; (iii) 1-line, gold on blue and red grounds patterned in white. Line-fillers in blue, red, and gold. Capital letters in the ink of the text filled with yellow. Each picture has a continuous border framed in gold, that on f. 29 (Annunciation) including five scenes from the life of B.V.M. All other pages have a border the height of the written space in the outer margin. Contemporary binding of wooden boards covered with brown stamped calf: a double border of larger stamps, (1) unicorn and (2) lamb and flag, encloses (3-7) five rows of smaller stamps, (3) lamb and flag, (4) stag, (5, 6) two rows of hare (?) pursued by dog, each in its compartment, (7) stag. Two strap-and-pin fastenings from the front to the back are missing. Secundo folio (f. 14) *lios dei*.

Written for use in the diocese of Rouen. 'Feuilles non comprises les figures quy sont 15 Kernaud (?) le 15 Juillet 1692 Fauart age de 80 ans', f. 196ᵛ. An engraved black and white armorial shield inside each cover, s. xvii/xviii (?): a fess wavy, with crescent above and anchor below the fess.[1] The copy in front has 'Labbe [. . . .] Sauué' on its upper edge. The copy at the back has 'Ce liure a été vendu onze cent vingt deux livres a la vente de Mᵒ de la Valliere' on its lower edge.[2] Given by A. H. Bright in 1942.

HARTLEBURY CASTLE, HURD EPISCOPAL LIBRARY

Biblia   s. XIII med.

Eleven complete and five incomplete quires of a Bible beginning at 3 Kings 2: 45 and ending at 2 Peter 2: 17. The text missing between these points is from 3 Kings 20: 42 to 4 Kings 1: 15 after f. 6, from 1 Ezra 9: 3 to Judith 8: 32 after f. 30, from 1 Maccabees 7: 16 to the end of 2 Maccabees after f. 38, from Job 42: 10 to the end of Job after f. 45, from Isaiah 30: 31 to Jeremiah 15: 8 after f. 50, a leaf of Zechariah after f. 90, the whole book of Psalms and all five Sapiential books.

The points that can still be made about contents and order of books as compared with a 'normal' Bible (cf. above, Bristol Public Library, 15) are: the absence of the prayer of Manasses after 2 Chronicles—a reader, s. xiv, noticed it and wrote 'Hic deficit oracio manasse'; that Maccabees follows Esther (as in B.L., Royal 1 E. i); that Catholic Epistles follow Pauline Epistles and not, as usual, Acts: presumably Pauline Epistles were at the end, before Apocalypse. Job and Isaiah begin on new quires (ff. 39, 46). On the other hand, Matthew follows Minor Prophets on the same page (f. 93). Job (ff. 39-45: quire 6) is associated by running titles, script, signatures, and ruling (see below) with the part of the manuscript beginning on f. 79, which suggest that it may have followed Minor Prophets in the scribe's exemplar, as it does in Royal 1 B.viii and 1 E. i.[3] The scribe wrote 'Finit hic' at the end of Malachi (f. 93), perhaps to show that no more of the Old Testament was to follow here.

Within books the text is written continuously as a rule, the beginning of a new chapter being shown by a coloured initial. Chapter numbers and running titles in red and blue occur regularly only on ff. 39-45 (Job) and from f. 79. Elsewhere they are, for the most part, additions in ordinary ink, s. xiv in. Textual corrections are in the margins of ff. 1-30, but seldom after this point.

---

[1] de Morenas gives the arms of Favart as azure a fess wavy or.
[2] The Duc de la Vallière sale was in 1783.
[3] I am grateful to the librarian, Mr. Leonard Greenwood, for information about quire 6.

The remaining prologues are twenty-five of the common set and four others, shown here by *: Stegmüller, nos. 328, 330, 341+343, 551, 344+349*, 482, 491, 492, 494, 495* (. . . manifestior prophetarum), 500, 510+509* (placed *after* Joel), 512, 519+517, 524, 526, 528, 530*, 534, 538, 590, 607, 620 (followed immediately and without break by Luke 1: 1–4), 624, 809. On f. 39 spaces were left for words of the prologues to Job which the scribe could not read in his exemplar: the missing words have been supplied in the margins in contemporary pencil.

ff. 141. Thick parchment. 432×290 mm. Written space 290×170 mm. 2 cols. 61–3 lines. The first line of writing above the top ruled line in quires 1–5, 7–10. Pricks in both margins in quires 1–5, 7–11. From f. 82, where Minor Prophets begin, no horizontal lines are prolonged into the margins; so too in quire 6. Collation: 1⁸ wants 1 and 8 (ff. 1–6) 2–4⁸ (ff. 7–30) 5⁸ (ff. 31–8) 6⁸ wants 8 (ff. 39–45) 7 five (ff. 46–50) 8⁸ 9–10¹⁰ 11¹² (ff. 79–90) 12¹² wants 1 before f. 91 13–15¹² 16⁴ (ff. 138–41). From quire 11 each page in the first half of a quire is marked as a rule with a letter in pencil, except the first page and the last page; so too in quire 6. ff. 39–45 (quire 6), 79–141 in one hand. The script changes also at ff. 52, 72. Initials: (i) to books, red and blue, with ornament of both colours (and green, f. 46), sometimes streaming the full height of the book; (ii) to prologues, usually 4-line, blue with red ornament; (iii) to chapters (see above), 1-line, blue or red, the red plain and the blue usually ornamented in red: on ff. 39–45, 79–141 all the initials are blue. Capital letters in the ink of the text are touched with red on most pages from f. 79. Loosely tied in cardboard covers, s. xix (?): the medieval sewing remains.

Written in England. 'Thomas Lewis de glawdesbrie in' is scribbled on f. 71 and 'Thomas Smyth' on f. 77, s. xvi. The Hartlebury Castle book-stamp and 'Drawer 10' are inside the cover. Belonged, presumably, to Richard Hurd, bishop of Worcester 1775–1808.

HARTLEPOOL. PUBLIC LIBRARY

Psalmi, hymni, etc.   s. XV/XVI

1. ff. 1–64ᵛ In Dominicis diebus ad primam. hym. Iam lucis . . . ps. cxviii. Beati immaculati . . .

Liturgical psalter, with hymns for the week at (1) f. 1, prime, terce, sext, none, (2) f. 27ᵛ, vespers, and (3) f. 61, compline. The text on f. 29 has been rewritten over erasure and ff. 1, 28 are substituted leaves, s. xviii (?).

2. ff. 64ᵛ–69 Three sets of canticles: (*a*) for apostles, Vos sancti domini, Fulge-bunt, Reddidit deus; (*b*) at matins, Beatus vir qui in sapientia, Benedictus, Beatus vir qui inuentus; (*c*) for feasts of B.V.M. and for the common of virgins, Audite me, Gaudens gaudebo, Non vocaberis.

Mearns, *Canticles*, pp. 91 (set 9), 90 (set 1), 92 (second set).

3. ff. 69ᵛ–143 Hymns through the year: (*a*) thirty-one of the temporale, for Advent, Christmas, Epiphany, Lent, Easter, Ascension, Pentecost, and Corpus Christi; (*b*) f. 98, two 'In dedicatione ecclesie'; (*c*) f. 99ᵛ, three 'In omnibus festiuitatibus uirginis marie'; (*d*) f. 102, twenty-seven of the sanctorale; (*e*) f. 132ᵛ, twelve of the common of saints.

(*a*). The parts of the hymn for Sundays in Lent, 'Ad preces nostras deitatis . . .', on ff. 75ᵛ, 77 are over erasure, except for the initial *A*, and the rest of the hymn is on the substituted leaf, f. 76. The hymn originally written was 'Aures ad nostras deitatis . . .', that is to say *RH*, no. 234 has been substituted for *RH*, no. 1612. (*b*). The second and third words of the hymn Urbs ierusalem beata have been changed, so that *Urbs beata hierusalem* became *Urbs ierusalem beata*: cf. *RH*, nos. 20918, 20920. (*d*). The hymns are: (1–3) 'In festo sanctissimi patris nostri benedicti', Criste[1] sanctorum, Signifer inuictissime, Aurora surgit (*RH*, nos. 3006–7, 18984, 1664); (4, 5) for Michael, Tibi christe splendor, Christe sanctorum; (6–8) for John Baptist, Ut queant laxis, Antra deserti, O nimis felix; (9, 10) f. 110, for Prosper, Ista dies eximia, Carnem longis ieiuniis (*RH*, nos. 9124, 2642; *AH* xxii. 233); (11, 12) ff. 112–119ᵛ, for Peter and Paul, Felix per omnes and Aurea luce, both noted throughout; (13, 14) for Mary Magdalene, Nardi maria and Huius obtentu; (15, 16) f. 120ᵛ, for Venerius, Deus creator omnium custos tuorum militum. qui beatum venerium, and its *Divisio* for use at lauds, Cuius uoces et carmina (*RH*, no. 36645; *AH* xliii. 303, where no medieval source is recorded); (17–19) for the Transfiguration, O nata lux, O sator rerum, Deus manens primordium; (20) for Laurence, Martiris christi colimus; (21) f. 126ᵛ, for Justina, Phebus astris cum omnibus (*RH*, no. 14899) and cues to art. 6; (22, 23) for All Saints, Christe redemptor omnium conserua, Iesu saluator seculi; (24, 25) for Martin, Rex christe martini decus, Martine par apostolis; (26, 27) f. 131ᵛ, for Jocunda, Iocunda virgo nobilis (*RH*, no. 9381; *AH* xxii. 150, where no manuscript source is recorded) and its *Divisio* Age iam precor domina in remota (not printed in *AH*). The changes to (*a*, *b*) were probably made in s. xviii.

4. ff. 143–8 Hymnus sanctorum ambrosii et augustini. Te deum . . . Noted throughout.

5. f. 148ʳᵛ Post euangelium . . . Te decet laus te decet hymnus . . .

6. ff. 148ᵛ–150ᵛ Hymns for Justina of Padua, Iustina beatissima and Iustina que christi martir (*RH*, nos. 9917, 9918): cf. art. 3*d*, no. 21. f. 151ʳᵛ was left blank.

7 (added, s. xvii ?). f. 151 Suscepit deus israhel puerum suum . . . Euouae.

8. ff. 152–63 Four sets of canticles: (*a*) for Advent, Ecce dominus, Cantate domino, Hec dicit dominus; (*b*) for Christmas, Populus gentium qui sedebat, Letare hierusalem, Urbs fortitudinis; (*c*) for Lent, Deducant oculi, Recordare domine, Tollam quippe; (*d*) for the period from Easter to Pentecost, Qui est iste, Venite reuertamur, Expecta me.

Mearns, *Canticles*, pp. 87–8.

9. ff. 163ᵛ–195 Incipit antiphonarium de commune sanctorum.

The first leaf is missing.

10. ff. 196–209ᵛ Antiphons for feasts of Scholastica, Gregory, B.V.M. ad Nives, the Transfiguration, and (f. 206ᵛ) Justina.

A leaf is missing after f. 207.

11 (added early). ff. 210–211ᵛ Hymns for Benedict, Laudibus ciues resonent, Quicquid antiqui cecinere, Rusticum solo benedicte.

RH, nos. 10443–4, 16689, 17599 (only from a Douai hymnal of 1611). Art. 11 is referred to in a cross reference on f. 102.

ff. i+209+i, foliated (i), 1–163, 165–207, 209–11 (212): except on ff. 1, 28, 76, 210, 211,

[1] The scribe writes Cristus and Christus in full, but commonly the abbreviation *xp-* which I have expanded as *chr-*.

the foliation is in a contemporary hand in red half-way down the outer margin of rectos. 540 × 370 mm. Written space 390 × 245 mm. 16 long lines (18 on ff. 210–11) or six long lines and music. Minims about 14 mm high. Collation: 1⁸ wants 1 (f. 1 is a substituted leaf) 2–3⁸ 4⁸ wants 4 (f. 28 is a substituted leaf) 5–9⁸ 10⁸ wants 4 (f. 76 is a substituted leaf) 11–18⁸ 19⁶ (ff. 145–50) 20⁸ 21⁸ wants 6 after f. 163 22–25⁸ 26¹⁰ wants 10 after f. 207 27⁴ wants 4, probably blank (ff. 209–11). Initials: dark red picked out with blue and green on gold grounds decorated in all three colours; (ii, iii) 2-line and 1-line, blue with red or red with either blue or violet framing lines and patterned infilling of green, red, blue, and pale yellow, or some of these colours: a few of the smaller initials are purple. The second letter of words beginning with an initial of types (i, ii) is a 2-line or 1-line cadel filled or lined with yellow. Massive binding of wooden boards covered with brown leather, rebacked: metal corner-pieces and centre-pieces decorated with stamps of five patterns, (i) B.V.M. and Child, (ii) yh̄s, (iii–v) fleurons: bosses at the corners and in the centre of each cover; forty-four studs project from the sides: two strap-and-pin fastenings from front cover to back cover are missing.

Written in Italy for use in the Benedictine abbey of San Prospero at Reggio d'Emilia after it became in 1481 a member of the congregation of St. Justina.

HAWARDEN. ST. DEINIOL'S LIBRARY

1 (34588). *Breviarium* 1514

1 (quires 1, 2). (*a*) f. 1ʳᵛ Responses and versicles for SS. Lucy, Barbara, Agnes, and Agatha. (*b*) ff. 2–13ᵛ Calendar in red and black, graded. (*c*) f. 14 A table of the 'literae dierum' in 27 lines and 19 columns. (*d*) f. 15 Prayers to SS. Joseph and Anthoninus. (*e*) ff. 15ᵛ–16ᵛ Magnificat, Pater noster, Credo in deum patrem, Salve regina, and prayer 'Ecclesie tue domine . . .'.

(*a, d, e*) are additions in spaces left blank. (*b*). The few feasts in red include: 'Dominici patris nostri totum duplex' 5 Aug. (octave, 'simplex', in black); 'Georii martiris simplex', 23 Apr.; 'Elyzabeth vidue semiduplex', 19 Nov.; 'Sanctificacio marie virginis totum duplex', 8 Dec. Feasts in black include 'Udalrici episcopi et confessoris simplex', 'Wenczeslai martiris iii lc'', 'Galli confessoris simplex' (4 July, 28 Sept., 16 Oct.). A column beside that for the Sunday letters contains the 'literae dierum' running in series of 27 from 'a' at 1 Jan. to 'k' at 31 Dec.: cf. *Horae Ebor.*, p. 22 and below, (*c*). (*c*). For use in bloodletting. The columns are alternately red and black. The letters used are the alphabet and four extras 7, ÷, ,, and reversed c. Each line begins with the name of one of the signs of the zodiac in German and ends with one of the words Gut, Böss, Mittel. The first two lines are:

> wider 7 p e y m b t i ÷ q f z n s u k ɔ r g Gut
> wider ɔ q f z n c u k 7 r g 7 o t x l a s h Gut

Cf. the table in *Horae Ebor.*, p. 22.

2. ff. 17–154ᵛ Temporale from Advent to the twenty-fifth Sunday after Trinity.

3. ff. 154ᵛ–158ᵛ In dedicacione ecclesie et in anniuersario eiusdem.

4. ff. 158ᵛ–309. Sanctorale, Andrew-Saturninus.

Includes proper offices for: Thomas Aquinas, 28 Jan. (translation) and 7 Mar.; translation of Mary Magdalene, 19 Mar.; Vincent (Ferrer), 4 Apr.; Petrus Martyr, 29 Apr.; Katherine of Siena, 30 Apr.; Corona Domini, 7 May; translation of Dominic, 24 May; Anne, 26

July; Dominic, 5 Aug.; Transfiguration, 6 Aug.; Elizabeth, widow, 19 Nov.[1] Prayers only for Udalric, Wenzeslas, and Gall.

5. ff. 309–325ᵛ Incipit officium in communi sanctorum.

6. ff. 325ᵛ–329ᵛ De officio beate virginis.

7. ff. 329ᵛ–390 Ad longam primam. Deus in adiutorium . . . Ymnus. Iam lucis orto . . . Anno domini m vᶜ xiiii ipsa die Galli confessoris finitum est istud diurnale.

Office for prime on Sundays and terce, sext, none, vespers, and compline on each day of the week. Vespers on Saturday ends with 'Sorores sobrie estote . . . fortes in fide' (1 Peter 5: 8, 9). The hymn for compline, Te lucis, is followed by (f. 387ᵛ) 'Oracio. Visita quesumus domine habitacionem istam . . .', (f. 388) Sequencia. Aue preclara maris stella in lucem (*RH*, no. 2045), and (f. 390) 'Oracio. A cunctis nos quesumus domine mentis et corporis defende periculis: et intercedente beata dei genitrice maria et beatis apostolis tuis petro et paulo atque beato dominico. beata maria magdalena cum omnibus sanctis? salutem nobis tribue . . .'. ff. 390ᵛ–392ᵛ blank.

8. A scrap of parchment pasted to the inside of the upper cover contains a text in German, s. xv: 'statt oder dorff gericht' can be read.

ff. 392. 115 × 83 mm. Written space 70 × 55 mm. 14 long lines. Collation: 1¹⁰ 2⁶ 3–49⁸. Punctuation includes the flex (?). Initials: (i) in shaded colour on gold and coloured grounds; (ii, iii) 2-line and 1-line, blue or red. Continuous framed floral or (f. 117ᵛ) diaper borders show where the offices for Advent, Christmas, Easter, Ascension, and Pentecost begin and the beginning of art. 4. Neat, but unorganized acanthus scrolls, flowers, gold leaves, and gold balls in the margins mark other principal feasts, including the translation of Mary Magdalene, f. 196. The front cover is a contemporary wooden board covered with pink-stained leather: a border of fillets containing 'Iesus Maria' and 'Maria Iesus' stamps at head and foot encloses a panel in which are floral and rosette stamps of five patterns: the back cover is missing: three bands: two clasps missing.

Written in (southern?) Germany for the use of Dominican nuns: finished on 16 Oct. 1514. A loose scrap of paper at f. 384 is inscribed 'Schwester Anna Rosina Knallerin', s. xvii. No doubt part of the library formed by W. E. Gladstone, 1809–98, in the last decades of s. xix as a foundation collection for St. Deiniol's Library, which he set up by trust in 1896.

2 (34589). *Horae eternae sapientiae, etc.*   s. XV/XVI

1. ff. 1–102ᵛ Flecto genua mea ad deum patrem domini nostri iesu xpristi ex quo . . .

Hours of the Eternal Wisdom, of great length: lauds, f. 12; prime, f. 23ᵛ; terce, f. 32ᵛ; sext, f. 45; none, f. 58; vespers, f. 70; compline, f. 82ᵛ. The hymn is 'Ihesu dulcis memoria dans vera cordis gaudia . . .'. Each hour begins with: (1) Flecto genua . . .; (2) Gracias ago tibi domine iesu criste pro uniuersis beneficiis . . .; (3) Gracias ago tibi domine iesu criste cuius gracia sum . . .; (4) Suscipe confessionem meam . . . Each hour, except matins and terce, ends with 'Obsecro te domina . . .', which, repeated six times, fills in all twenty-four leaves. Each hour, except matins, includes a prayer of the Passion, the first, f. 13ᵛ, 'Domine ihesu xpriste filii (*sic*) dei viui qui hora matutina stans ligatus . . .'. Forms in Obsecro te and elsewhere are for male use.

[1] My dates are those in art. 1*b*.

2. ff. 103–10 Prayers before mass: (a) ff. 103–4 Omnipotens et misericors deus
Ego reus et indignus peccator accedo ad sacramentum . . .; (b) ff. 104–5 Oracio.
Gracias ago tibi domine ihesu xpriste qui me indignum peccatorem per graciam
tuam . . .; (c) f. 105ʳᵛ Oracio. Serenissima et inclita mater domini nostri ihesu
xpristi sancta maria. Regina mundi . . .; (d) f. 106ʳᵛ Domine ihesu xpiste fili dei
viui corpus tuum pro nobis crucifixum . . .; (e) ff. 107–8 Sanctissima maria
virgo perpetua spiritus sancti cultura . . .;(f) ff. 108–10 Aue ihesu xpiste verbum
patris virginis filius . . . in vita mea peregi.

3. ff. 110–125ᵛ Hic incipiunt septem psalmi. Litany, f. 121.

Eighteen martyrs: . . . (4–7) Geori vite wenczeslae stanislae . . . Fourteen confessors: . . .
(13, 14) vdalrice procopi. Twelve virgins: . . . (11) affra cum sodalibus tuis . . .

4. ff. 125ᵛ–155 Incipiunt vigilie mortuorum.

The responses after lessons are (1) Redemptor meus, (2) Manus tue, (3) Memento queso,
(4) Quomodo confiteor, (5) Rogamus te, (6) Ne tradas, (7) Absolue domine, (8) Deus eterne,
(9) Libera me domine de morte. f. 155ᵛ blank.

5. ff. 156–164ᵛ Prayers to the Three Persons of the Godhead (a–c) and to the
Trinity: (a) Domine sancte pater omnipotens deus qui consubstancialem. . . .;
(b) Domine ihesu criste fili dei viui qui es verus . . .; (c) Domine sancte spiritus
omnipotens deus . . .; (d) Domine deus meus omnipotens eterne et ineffabilis . . .;
(e) Benediccio dei patris et filii et spiritus sancti venerande trinitatis . . .;(f) ff.
159–164ᵛ Ad sanctam trinitatem. O domine pater piissime ihesu criste dulcissime . . .

(a–c). Cf. Horae Ebor., p. 124.

6. Nine main paragraphs: (a) ff. 164ᵛ–165 Omnipotens et misericors deus qui
nobis rectam et dignam . . .; (b) ff. 165–167ᵛ O alpha et o deus omnipotens
principium rerum . . .; (c) ff. 167ᵛ–168ᵛ Auribus percipe domine oracionem
meam et intende . . .; (d) ff. 168ᵛ–170 Non est similis tui in diis domine . . .;
(e) f. 170ʳᵛ Confiteor tibi domine deus meus in toto corde meo et glorificabo . . .;
(f) ff. 170ᵛ–172ᵛ Omnipotens eterne deus et misericors pater ante omnia secula
benedicte . . .; (g) ff. 172ᵛ–173ᵛ O alme deus cuius inerrabilis est virtus . . .;
(h) Dulcissime domine ihesu criste verus deus qui de sinu patris omnipotentis
missus es in mundum peccata hominum relaxare . . .; (i) ff. 177ᵛ–179 Domine
rex omnipotens in illa sancta custodia . . .

(h). Cf. Lyell Cat., p. 380.

7. ff. 179–82 Gaude gaude dei genitrix virgo maria . . .: followed by six other
short prayers to B.V.M.

8. (a) f. 182ʳᵛ Aue ihesu criste uerbum patris filius virginis . . . (b) ff. 182ᵛ–
183 Dirigere et sanctificare regere et custodire dignare domine sancte pater . . .
(c) f. 183ʳᵛ Salue lux mundi uerbum patris hostia vera . . .

(a). Five aves: cf. Horae Ebor., p. 70.

9. ff. 183ᵛ–185ᵛ Oracio de quinque vulneribus. Domine ihesu criste rogo te
per sanctissima quinque vulnera . . .

Three prayers of the wounds. ff. 186–91 are ruled, but blank.

ff. iv+192 (or 191). ff. i–iv are ruled blank leaves. 152×120 mm. Written space 97×75 mm. 16 long lines. Collation : 1–18¹⁰ 19¹² (11 is pasted down and probably 12 is beneath it). 11¹, ¹⁰ are half sheets, the original 11¹⁰ having been replaced by a contemporary hand (f. 110). Initials: (i) patterned gold or shaded colours, including green on coloured grounds, historiated or with figures: ornament springs into the margin from one or two points; (ii) 3-line, in colour on gold grounds or in gold on coloured grounds; (iii, iv) 2-line and 1-line, red or blue. Type (i) initials number 136, 119 of them in art. 1. The largest, 7-line or 8-line, are the F of *Fac mecum* (f. 4) and begin the prayers of the Passion: f. 13ᵛ, Christ before Pilate; f. 27ᵛ, *cut out*; f. 36, Christ before Herod; f. 48ᵛ, Denudation before the Cross; f. 61ᵛ, Christ crucified; f. 74ᵛ, Last Supper; f. 92ᵛ, Gethsemane. A suppliant figure in black, with white hair and white moustache, appears in many initials on ff. 1–106 and on f. 158. Binding of wooden board covered with leather, s. xvii: decoration in blind; the centre-piece on the front cover includes 'IHS' and that on the back cover 'MARIA'.

Written in south-eastern Germany or Bohemia. 'An: 1670 die 8 Aprilis Has precatorias Orationes dono accepit Adm Rdus Religiosus P. Seraphinus à Spiritu Sancto Ordinis Carmelitarum tunc temporis Monachii per infrà scriptum M. Matthæum Carl Parochum (?) in Raunblzhausen et Schwabhausen¹', f. iv. 'M.C.P.C./P.F.' stamped on the front cover. Belonged, no doubt, to W. E. Gladstone: cf. MS. 1.

5 (34592). *Horae* s. xv med.

1. ff. 1–12ᵛ Full calendar in French in red and black.

The few feasts in red include: S' leu S' gile, 1 Sept.; S' denis, 9 Oct.; S' marcel, 3 Nov.

2. ff. 13–16ᵛ Sequentiae of the Gospels, imperfect: two leaves missing after f. 15.

3. ff. 16ᵛ–23ᵛ Oratio deuota. Obsecro te . . . michi famule tue N . . .

4. ff. 23ᵛ–27ᵛ Alia oratio. O intemerata . . . orbis terrarum. De te enim . . .

5. ff. 28–90 Hours of B.V.M. of the use of (Paris). f. 90ᵛ blank.

6. ff. 91–110ᵛ Penitential psalms and (f. 104ᵛ) litany.

Seventeen martyrs: . . . (2) saturnine . . . Seventeen confessors: . . . (8) maturine . . .

7. ff. 110ᵛ–118 Hore de sancta cruce. . . . Patris sapiencia . . .

8. ff. 118–124ᵛ Hore de sancto spiritu. . . . Nobis sancti spiritus . . .

9. ff. 124ᵛ–130 Hore de sancta Katherina. f. 130ᵛ blank.

10. ff. 131–178ᵛ Office of the dead.

11. ff. 179–207 Commendationes animarum. Subuenite sancti dei . . . numeren-tur. Per. Fidelium deus omnium. etc.

As *Manuale Sarum*, pp. 119–20. f. 207ᵛ blank.

12. ff. 208–210ᵛ Salutacio ad sanctum iohannem bapt'. Salue limes legis mosaice. salue preco regis clemencie . . .

Memoria of John Baptist. Thirteen 4-line stanzas. The last stanza begins O Iohannes salua peccatricem.

---

¹ Schwabhausen is 25 km. north east of Munich and, as Dr. Sigrid Krämer tells me, Rumeltshausen is near by.

13. ff. 210ᵛ–211ᵛ Ante corpus cristi deuota oracio. Aue domine ihesu criste uerbum patris filius uirginis . . .

Five aves.

14 (a) ff. 211ᵛ–213ᵛ De nostra domina deuota oracio. Stabat mater dolorosa . . . (b) ff. 213ᵛ–214ᵛ De nostra domina salutacio. Aue cuius concepcio solenni plena gaudio . . .

RH, nos. 19416, 1744.

15. (a) ff. 214ᵛ–215 Oratio. Domine ihesu xpiste creator et saluator mundi da michi per tuam gratiam hodie . . . (b) ff. 215–217ᵛ Deuota oratio quam compilauit sanctus thomas de aquino. Concede michi misericors deus que tibi placita sunt . . . (c) ff. 217ᵛ–218 Deus cognoscens hominem antequam nascatur. tu famule tue . . .

16. ff. 218–219ᵛ Dominica. A'. Alma redemptoris mater que peruia celi porta . . .

A memoria of B.V.M. for each day of the week. RH, no. 861.

17. f. 220ʳᵛ Veni creator spiritus mentes tuorum uisita . . .

18. ff. 220ᵛ–222ᵛ De maria magdalena. (a) Gaude et (sic) uenerabilis sancta maria magdalena que cunctis mortalibus . . . inclina aures tue pietatis ad me indignam ancillam tuam . . . (b) Gaude pia magdalena spes salutis uite uena . . .

(b). RH, no. 6985.

19. ff. 222ᵛ–223 Memoria of Margaret.

20. ff. 223–5 O bone ihesu. o piissime ihesu. o dulcissime ihesu . . .

21. ff. 225–7 Memoriae of Christopher and Maturinus.

22. f. 227ʳᵛ (a) Salue regina . . . (b) Aue regina celorum. aue domina angelorum. salue radix . . .

RH, nos. 18147, 2070.

23. ff. 228–229ᵛ Memoriae of Agnes and Genovefa.

24. ff. 230–4 Hours of All Saints.

The antiphon at each hour is from Sancta dei genitrix mater pietatis . . . : RH, no. 33290; AH xxx. 143.

25. ff. 234ᵛ–235 A memoria of Martha. f. 235ᵛ blank.

ff. i+235+i. 167 × 130 mm. Written space 88 × 58 mm. 15 long lines. Ruling in red ink. Collation: 1¹² 2⁸ wants 4, 5 after f. 15 3–25⁸ 26 five (ff. 203–7) 27⁸ 28⁴ (ff. 216–19) 29⁸ 30² (ff. 228–9) 31 six (ff. 230–5). Arts. 11, 24, 25 less well written than the rest. Seven 11-line pictures, one before each of arts. 5–8, 9 (B.V.M. seated, the Child on her lap: Katherine stands before her, her right hand on the shoulder of a kneeling woman in black), 10, 23 (SS. Agnes, John Baptist, and Margaret). Initials: (i) 3-line, blue patterned in white on gold grounds decorated in colours; (ii–iv) 3-line, 2-line, and 1-line, gold on grounds of red and blue, patterned in white. Floral borders, continuous on picture pages and on three sides of pages with initials of type (i). Binding of olive-brown morocco, s. xvii: gilt fillets and small cornerpieces.

Written in France (Paris ?) for the use of a woman, who had probably a special devotion to SS. Saturninus and Mathurinus. An armorial book-plate inside the cover, s. xviii: gules a saltire argent: 'de Madaillon' is written in the space at the foot of the plate. An erasure, f. 236. A foolish inscription, 'hures d'hery trois Roy de france', f. 1, s. xvi/xvii. 'W. E. G(ladstone) 1880' inside the cover. Given as MS. 1.

HEREFORD. CATHEDRAL

Two hundred and twenty-seven medieval manuscripts. A. T. Bannister, *A Descriptive Catalogue of the Manuscripts in the Hereford Cathedral Library, with an Introduction by M. R. James*. 1927. A catalogue by Professor Sir Roger Mynors is in preparation. See also F. C. and P. E. Morgan, *Hereford Cathedral Libraries and Muniments*, 1970.

Fragments in the capitular archives.

1. A bifolium of Digestum Novum. s. xiv.

No apparatus. Written space 250 (?+) × 125 mm. 2 cols. 44(?+) lines. English textura. Spaces for 2-line and 1-line intitials not filled. In use as the cover of R. 585, Clavigers' accounts for 1490–1512.

2. Two bifolia of Huguitio, Derivationes. s. xiv.

L, M words on the sheet in front (cf. Lambeth Palace 80, ff. 79, 88) and N words on the sheet at the back. Written space 255 × 175 mm. 2 cols. 72 lines. The sheet in front was the outside one of a quire. The sheets are laid sideways as pastedowns inside the plain parchment cover of R 2 D, Dean and Chapter Act Book, vol. 1, 1512–66.

3. A bifolium of a noted breviary. s. xiv.

From the temporale for the fourth and fifth Sundays after the octave of Epiphany and for Septuagesima Sunday: *Hereford Breviary*, i (HBS xxvii), 233–6. Written space 282 × 180 mm. 2 cols. 42 lines. The central bifolium of a quire. 2-line initials, blue with red ornament or red with pink (?) ornament. Folded at the edges to make the cover, 312 × 230 mm, of Cap. 41 (4), a copy of 'Iniunctiones siue Statuta Ecclesiæ Cathedralis Hereford', 1583, which bears the name of Thomas Thornton (canon of Hereford 1573–1629).

HEREFORD. DIOCESAN RECORD OFFICE

1/1, 2. *Two bifolia of a missal*   s. XIV

Badly damaged. Legible pieces are for Monday and Tuesday in the first week of Lent and Tuesday in the second week. Written space 245 × 150 mm. 2 cols. 38 lines. A double thickness of parchment covering Misc. 1, a volume mainly of wills for the year 1552.

2/1–6. Six strips of a breviary (Hereford use ?). s. xiii/xiv.

The text corresponds to *Hereford Breviary*, i (HBS xxvii), 5 (strips 1, 2), 23–4 (strips 3, 4), 24 (strips 5, 6): 3 and 4 together and 5 and 6 together make nearly complete leaves. Strip 6 has the beginning of the litany, in which Ethelbert follows Stephen as second of martyrs

and has 'ii' added against his name. Written space 270+ × 240 mm. 2 cols. 26+ lines.
1, 2 are inside the cover of Instance Book I, 10 (1570–1573); 3, 4 inside the cover of
Instance Book I, 11 (1574–1578/9); 5, 6 inside the cover of Office Book 56 (1570–1579).

3/1, 2. Two leaves of a missal. s. xiii².

One leaf from near the end of the temporale, twentieth to twenty-second Sundays after
the octave of Pentecost, and the other from near the beginning of the sanctorale, Nicholas,
Octave of Andrew, Conception of B.V.M., Damasus, Lucy, Vigil of Thomas (6–20 Dec.).
2 cols. 30+ lines. Pastedowns inside the plain parchment cover of Office Book 62 (1579–
80).

HODNET. PARISH CHURCH

Horae   s. xv¹

An imperfect book of hours of the common abroad-for-England type (see above,
Blackburn 091.21035, and *MMBL* i. 46), with one difference, that the Oes of
St. Bridget come before Bede's prayer of the Seven Words instead of immediately
after the calendar.

1. ff. 1–6ᵛ Calendar in red and black.

The English saints in red are Wolstan, Edmund, 'Riquardi episcopi' (3 Apr.), Dunstan,
Aldhelm, translation of Edmund, 'Translacio riquardi' (16 June), and Thomas of Canterbury (7 July, 29 Dec., neither erased). The calendar of Bodleian, Liturg. 400 seems to
be almost identical and has the same spelling of the name of St. Richard of Chichester.

2. ff. 7–19 Hours of B.V.M. of the use of (Sarum), with hours of the Cross
worked in. Memoriae after lauds (f. 12ᵛ, 'Incipiunt suffragia sanctorum') of
Holy Spirit, Holy Trinity, Holy Cross, Michael, John Baptist, Peter, Andrew,
Stephen, Laurence, Thomas of Canterbury (Tu per thome sanguinem . . .:
not erased), Nicholas, Mary Magdalene, Katherine, Margaret, All Saints and
for peace. None, vespers and compline are missing.

3. ff. 19–21ᵛ Salve regina, followed by the five verses 'Has videas laudes . . . sic
collaudando mariam' (*RH*, no. 7687) and by Salue virgo virginum . . . (*RH*, no.
18318).

4. ff. 21ᵛ–22ᵛ O intemerata . . . orbis terrarum. Inclina mater . . .

5. ff. 22ᵛ–24ᵛ Obsecro te . . .

6. ff. 24ᵛ–25ᵛ Virgo templum trinitatis . . .
The Seven Joys of B.V.M. *RH*, no. 21899.

7. ff. 26–27ᵛ Omnibus [considera]tis parad[isus uolu]ptatis . . .

RH, no. 14081 (etc.). *AH* xxxi. 87–9. Cf. *Lyell Cat.*, p. 391.

8. ff. 28–31 The fifteen Oes of St. Bridget, beginning imperfectly in the second.

9. ff. 31–2 Incipit oracio venerabilis bede presbiteri de septem ultimis uerbis
cristi in cruce pendens (*sic*). Domine ihesu xpriste qui septem uerba . . .

10. f. 32 Precor te piissime domine ihesu xpriste propter illam caritatem . . .

11. f. 32ᵛ Incipiunt oraciones ad sacramentum. Aue domine ihesu xpriste uerbum patris . . . (*ends imperfectly*).

12. ff. 33–40ᵛ Seven penitential psalms, beginning imperfectly, and litany in which the only English saints are Oswald, Botulph ('Botulpe'), and Milburga. The litany of Liturg. 400 is different.

13. ff. 41–52ᵛ Office of the dead, imperfect at both ends.

14. ff. 53–59ᵛ Commendations of souls (Pss. 118, 138), imperfect.

15. ff. 60–61ᵛ Psalms of the Passion, beginning imperfectly at Ps. 21: 25. Pss. 25, 27, 28 follow, the last ending imperfectly.

16. ff. 62–6 Psalter of St. Jerome, beginning imperfectly in Ps. 24: 20. Followed by 'Omnipotens sempiterne deus clementiam tuam suppliciter deprecor . . . proficiat sempiternam'.

17. f. 66ᵛ Blank, except for additions, s. xv/xvi: (i) A prayer in English, 'O swet blyssyd lady os þᵘ art þe most mygty . . .'; (ii) 'Benedictum sit dulce nomen domini nostri ihesu cristi . . .', with heading conveying an indulgence of three years 'quos clemens papa concessit ob rogatum ludouici sancti regis francie. Anno domini 1264. hoc habetur in libro qui dicitur fasciculus temporum'.

ff. ii+66+ii. 215×150 mm. Written space 128×75 mm. 24 long lines. Collation: mainly quires of eight (1⁶, 4 three, 6¹⁰), with the following leaves missing: 2¹ before f. 7, 2⁵ after f. 9, 3⁴, ⁵ after f. 15, 3⁷, ⁸ after f. 16, 5¹ before f. 20, 6² after f. 27, 6⁸, ⁹ after f. 32, 7⁸ after f. 40, 8¹ before f. 41, 9⁶ after f. 52, 10⁶ after f. 59, 11¹ before f. 62, 11⁷, ⁸, probably blank, after f. 66. ff. 17, 19 are the outer bifolium of quire 4. Well written. All pictures and 'type i' initials removed, either the whole page having been cut out or—ff. 17, 18, 24ᵛ, 26—the initial. The remaining initials are: (ii) in gold on coloured grounds, with floral sprays projecting into the margins; (iii) blue or gold with ornament in red or blue-grey. Capital letters in the ink of the text stroked with red. Line-fillers in red, blue, and gold. Each page with a 'type i' initial had no doubt a floral border in gold and colours at head and foot, the width of the written space: these remain on ff. 17, 18, 24ᵛ, 26. Rebound by Roger Powell in 1956. Secundo folio *cio fecunda* (f. 7).

Written for English use, probably in NE. France.[1] In England by s. xv/xvi (cf. art. 17).

HORNBY, LANCS. ST. MARY'S CATHOLIC CHURCH

1. *Breviarium*	s. XIV/XV

The sanctorale of a Sarum breviary, Andrew–Martin (11 Nov.), ending imperfectly.

---

[1] But Dr. J. J. G. Alexander tells me that such decoration as remains is English.

Cues for John of Beverley, translation of Osmund, Etheldreda, and Frideswide, added in the margins of ff. 44ᵛ, 70, 125, 126, refer to the common. A memoria of Agapitus, as *Brev. ad usum Sarum*, iii. 710, is in the margin, f. 93ᵛ.

ff. i+50+i+2+i+11+i+72, foliated i, 1–138. ff. 51, 54, 66 are inserted leaves of blank parchment. 173 × 118 mm. Written space 130 × 83 mm. 2 cols. 40 lines. Collation: 1–4¹² 5¹² wants 3 after f. 50 and 6–8 after f. 53 6¹² wants 6, 7 after f. 63 and 10 after f. 65 7¹² wants 6, 7 after f. 73 8–12¹². Initials: ff. 1, 89ᵛ (Assumption of B.V.M.), 116 (Michael), 128 (All Saints), red and blue with ornament of both colours extending the height of the written space; (ii) 2-line, blue with red ornament. No covers, but sewn.

Written in England. 'Liber Iohanis Iones. Na werth nef er benthic byyd', f. i, s. xvi.[1] A label inscribed 'St. Mary's, Hornby', s. xix, is pasted to f. i.

2. *Breviarium* s. xiv med.

Part of the temporale of a Sarum breviary running from Thursday in the second week of Advent to Monday in the third week of Lent (*Brev. ad usum Sarum*, i. xcv–dclxx). The two missing leaves contained the office of St. Thomas of Canterbury.

ff. 70+ii. 165 × 110 mm. Written space 123 × 80 mm. 36–7 long lines. Collation: 1¹² 2¹² wants 9, 10 after f. 20 3–6¹². Initials: (i) 2-line, blue with red ornament; (ii) 1-line, red or blue. Capital letters in the ink of the text filled with pale yellow. Part of the old limp parchment cover remains. A label inscribed 'St. Mary's, Hornby' is pasted to the spine.

HULL. UNIVERSITY

F. 1300. *Paulus Venetus, O.E.S.A., Logica* 1434

Conspiciens in circuitu librorum . . . compendium utile construxi . . . Terminus est signum oracionis . . . asserendo promisi. Et sic est finis obiectionum consequenciarum Deo gratias Amen. Explicit breuis logica octo tractatibus principalibus compilata per sacre pagine celeberrimum magistrum paulum fratrem de veneciis 1434. Completa per me fratrem antonium de vulpis die 13 Augusti. Amen.

Printed often: Goff, P. 219–31. For the author, †1429, see Emden, *BRUO*, p. 1944. The title 'Loyca magistri pauli de uenetiis' is on f. vᵛ.

ff. v+122+i. Paper. 209 × 140 mm. Written space c. 140 × 95 mm. 25 long lines. Collation: 1–9¹² 10¹⁴. Red initials, the first historiated (Paulus Venetus ?) and with ornament in red and green. Stamped pigskin binding over wooden boards, s. xvi in.: the leather extends only over part of the sides. Secundo folio *Terminus prime*.

Written in Italy by a named scribe in 1434. Three inscriptions: 'Iste liber est mei fratris

[1] Professor Idris Foster refers me to the maxim printed in *Myvyrian Archaiology*, ii (1872), 851, 'Na werth nev er benthyg byd', 'Do not sell heaven for the loan of the world'.

Iacobi de Ricardis ordinis predicatorum', f. 122ᵛ, s. xv; 'Iste liber est conuentus soncinensis', f. 123ᵛ, s. xv; 'Iste liber constat (?) sancti iacobi de soncino' (Soncino, Lombardy), f. 1, crossed through. Item 73 in Blackwell's catalogue 323. Acquired in 1933.

HUNTINGDON. ARCHDEACONRY LIBRARY

Biblia[1]   s. XIII med.

1. ff. 1–472 A Bible with the usual contents in the usual order,[2] imperfections apart: it begins at Genesis 50: 11 and Titus (from 3: 13), Philemon, Hebrews, and Acts (to 8: 10) are missing after f. 448. The prologues are fifty-nine of the common set of sixty-four[2] (five being absent owing to loss of leaves), together with a third prologue to Obadiah, Esau filius ysaac . . . loquitur hic propheta, and a second prologue to Habakkuk, Stegmüller, no. 530.

The many pencilled marginalia are mainly corrections which were afterwards incorporated into the text in ink in the painstaking manner common in the twelfth century: cf. N. R. Ker, *English Manuscripts in the Century after the Norman Conquest*, pp. 50–1. A good example is on f. 439ᵛ where the scribe missed the words *regnum dei non consequenter* (Galatians 5: 21) and to fit them in four whole lines have been erased and rewritten. The headings and colophons of books and prologues were not corrected and are often wrong. f. 472ᵛ blank.

2. ff. 473–515ᵛ Hic incipiunt interpretaciones hebraicorum nominum. Aaz apprehendens . . . Zuzim consiliantes eos. vel consiliatores eorum. Hic expliciunt Interpretaciones hebraicorum nominum.

3. The pastedowns are two leaves of a copy of the gospel harmony of Victor of Capua with the commentary of Zacharias Chrysopolitanus, s. xii ex. The text here corresponds to Bodleian MS. Bodley 209, ff. 130, 134ᵛ.

ff. iii + 515 + iii. ff. ii, iii, 516–17 are bifolia of thick paper of the date of binding and ff. i, 518 are parchment leaves of the same date. 245 × 165 mm. Written space 155 × 105 mm. 2 cols. (art. 2, 3 cols). 49 lines. Collation: 1–8²⁴ 9²² 10¹⁰ (ff. 215–24) 11–18²⁴ 19²²+2 leaves after 6 (ff. 423–4) 20 sixteen (eight bifolia: leaves missing after f. 448) 21¹⁶ (ff. 457–72) 22²⁴ 23²⁰ wants 20, blank. Initials: (i) of books and principal psalms, usually 7-line, in colour on coloured grounds, historiated, framed in gold; (ii) of prologues, usually 3-line, in colour on coloured grounds, decorated in colours and gold; (iii) of chapters, 2-line, red or blue with ornament of both colours extending the height of the page; (iv) of verses of psalms and in art. 2, 1-line, red or blue. Capital letters in the ink of the text filled with red. Binding of s. xv ex.: wooden boards covered with brown leather bearing a pattern of fillets and a fleur-de-lis stamp: metal centrepieces and cornerpieces: two now missing clasps ran from the back cover to the front cover.

Written in France. 'Anthonius de Labroye me possidet', f. ii, s. xvii ?: cf. f. 515ᵛ. 'Buckden Library. Presented by the Revᵈ. Chris: Anstey prebendary of Asgarby 1774'. The diocesan library for the use of the clergy of the diocese of Lincoln, formerly at Buckden Palace, Hunts., was moved to Huntingdon when the present library was built in 1891.

[1] Deposited in Cambridge University Library, MS. Add. 7801.
[2] See above, Bristol Public Library, 15.

Formularium[1] s. xv[1]

A formulary for use in the diocese of Lincoln based probably on a collection made by an official of Philip Repingdon, bishop of Lincoln 1405–19, most of the forms on ff. 5–128 being in his name. They include: f. 93, De litteris ad predicandum contra lollardos. Cum pertinenciis etc. Philippus etc. Ad solum pastoralis officii licet immerito . . .; f. 93ᵛ, Commissio ad procedendum contra lollardos. Philippus . . . Ad inquirendum in forma iuris . . . Documents copied rather later, but in the main hand, are on ff. 1–4ᵛ, 128ᵛ, among them: f. 1, an appointment of proctors by J. de K., All Saints Church, Oxford, 30 Sept. 1419; f. 2, the condemnation of Juliana Bothurwyk or Butterwyk by the chancellor of Oxford (R. Rugge), A.D. 1386; f. 128ᵛ, 'Copia dispensacionis ad scolas', a dispensation to Thomas Clyffe, rector of Islip, from John (Kemp), bishop of London. The latest date seems to be 1430 (f. 4).

Most of the forty-two flyleaves are blank, but ff. ii–ivᵛ, xvᵛ, 129–33, 154ᵛ contain copies of documents, some of which suggest that the manuscript was in the diocese of Norwich in the later part of s. xv: f. 131ᵛ, the constitution concerning first fruits of Bishop Walter Southfield, A.D. 1255; f. 132, Bishop William Bateman's 'Declaracio dicte constitucionis'; f. ivʳᵛ, a citation by James Goldwell, commissary (of Archbishop Kemp, 1452–4), to the vicar of St. Paul's, Canterbury, citing James Downe of his parish to appear 'ad obiciendum . . . contra purgacionem . . . Iacobi Sevenoke', monk of St. Augustine's, Canterbury (abbot 1457–64); f. 154ᵛ, an address by James Goldwell, bishop of Norwich, king's orator at the Roman curia, 'ante fores mansionis sue' in Rome to those 'qui eum in ingressu ciuitatis comitabuntur qum (*sic*) missus erat ab Excellentissimo rege Edwardo iiii ad obedienciam faciendam sixto iiiiᵗᵒ Anno cristi Millesimo cccc lxxii'. A form of safe conduct from King Louis for the legates of the King of Aragon, 2 May 1474, is on ff. 130ᵛ–131ᵛ.

ff. xv + 128 + xxix. Paper, except ff. i–iii, 155–7. ff. i, 157 were pastedowns. ff. 1–133 have a medieval foliation 2–4, 7–36, 38–103, 105–38, which takes account of the leaves now missing from quires 1, 3, 9. 215 × 145 mm. Written space 145 × 90 mm. *c.* 33 long lines. Frame ruling in ink. Collation: 1¹² wants 4, 5 after f. 3 2¹² 3¹² wants 12 after f. 33 4–8¹² 9¹² wants 7 after f. 99 10–11¹². Quires 1–10 signed a–k. Strips of blank parchment between and in the middle of quires as strengthening. Written in a mixed but mainly secretary hand: ascenders are straight, not looped. No ornament. Contemporary binding of wooden boards covered with white leather: the clasp missing. Secundo folio *Condempnacio*.

Written in the diocese of Lincoln (?), but probably in Norfolk in the later fifteenth century. 'T. Godsalve', ff. iᵛ, xvᵛ, 23, and elsewhere, s. xvi, may be the Thomas Godsalve of Norwich in whose library Bale saw manuscripts (*Index*, p. 576). 'Sa: Rooper', f. iᵛ, s. xvii.

[1] Deposited in Cambridge University Library, MS. Add. 7802.

IPSWICH. PUBLIC LIBRARY

MSS. 1–9 are catalogued by M. R. James, 'Descriptions of the Ancient Manu-
scripts in the Ipswich Public Library', *Proceedings of the Suffolk Institute of
Archaeology and Natural History*, xxii (1934), 86–103. The Benefactors' Book
'made and given by William Saires Bookbinder of Ipswich A: 1615' records that
MSS. 1–8 were the gift of William Smart, portman. They are listed in the order
4, 6, 1, 5, 7, 3, 8, 2. Smart had many manuscripts which had belonged to the
Benedictine abbey of Bury St. Edmunds and are now, by his gift, at Pembroke
College, Cambridge. Ipswich MSS. 4, 6, 8 are from Bury and MS. 2 may be
from Bury. His bequest to Ipswich, 8 Nov. 1598 (will proved 2 Nov. 1599)[1]
included a number of early printed books. It was 'made a part of the library
anno 1612'. The bindings of MSS. 1–9 are of s. xix by W. J. Scopes, Ipswich.

1. s. xiv/xv. Concordantiae Bibliorum, the version of the Concordantiae
Sancti Jacobi attributed wrongly to Conrad of Halberstadt, senior, O.P.
(*GKW*, nos. 7418–21: *SOPMA*, no. 755): cf. R. H. and M. A. Rouse in *AFP*
xliv (1974), 17. The first leaf is missing and the end and there are other gaps.

ff. 301. Written space 310 × 190 mm. 3 cols. 73 lines. Written in England in rather poor
anglicana. Secundo folio *ii c percussit*.

2. s. xii/xiii. Beda, In Lucam.

Begins in chapter 5, the first two quires (16 leaves?) missing. The text is in 94 numbered
chapters.

ff. 130. Written space 237 × 168 mm. 2 cols. 40 lines. Pricks in both margins to guide
ruling. Well written. Initials: (i) of books, red or blue with curled-leaf ornament on pale
red grounds; (ii) of chapters, 2-line or 3-line, green with red ornament, or red with green,
or blue with red. Written in England and perhaps the copy listed in the part of the Bury
St. Edmunds catalogue written in s. xii/xiii.[2]

3. s. xii med. Exodus glosatus.

Text ruled independently from the gloss which flanks it. f. 3/8 begins 'qui ingressi sunt'
below a space of seven lines, left blank for 'Hec sunt nomina filiorum israel', words which
were not in the end placed here but on the recto of the second leaf of a bifolium in front
of f. 3. The *H*, 100 × 100 mm, is pink and green and contains spiral decoration and small
white lion-dogs on a gold and blue ground. Below it, 'ec sunt nomina' is a line of green
and red letters and 'filiorum israel' another line of blue and red letters.

ff. 130. Written space 180 mm high and *c*. 185 mm wide across the three columns. Pencil
ruling.

4. s. xiv med. Mariale.

Set out under 151 rubrics, the first 'Quomodo lux id est spiritus sanctus vel virgo beata
in nobilitate speciositate bonitate precellit' and the last 'Quomodo ipse dominus noster
Ihesus cristus matrem suam semper perhonorificauit et honorari fecit et facit'. The prologue begins 'Exordium salutis nostre dicit b[. . . .]'.

ff. 133. Written space 220 × 138 mm. 2 cols. 44 lines. Textura. Written in England.

---

[1] M. R. James, *On the Abbey of S. Edmund at Bury*, 1895, p. 4.
[2] The marks at head and foot of f. 1 can hardly be taken as evidence for chaining in the
medieval Bury library, as f. 1 was originally the first leaf of quire 3.

A gift to Bury St. Edmunds, probably by John de Brinkele, abbot 1361–79: 'Mariale sancti edmundi per I abbatem. M. xi'.

5. s. xv med. **1.** ff. 1–81ᵛ . . . Explicit Pabulum vite. **2.** ff. 82–191ᵛ Jacobus de Voragine, Sermones quadragesimales.

1. Distinctiones, now Gloria–Vita eterna. A table at the end, f. 81ʳᵛ, shows that there were 133 chapters (not numbered) and that the first 41, Abstinencia, Adulacio, Ambitio, Amicicia dei, Amor sui corporis . . . Gaudium, are missing. Another table, ff. 78–81, is divided under temporale, sanctorale, and De mortuis, with references to material in art. 1 suitable to each occasion. **2.** Schneyer, p. 278. Ninety-eight sermons: some gaps. A scribble on f. 37ᵛ, 'The sayd tomas smyth of Woodbys'.

ff. 192 (82 is double). Written space *c.* 215 × 145 mm. Written in current anglicana.

6. s. xiii¹ (ff. ii–vii, s. xv). Compilationes theologicae, fully described by James, pp. 90–95.

James gives twenty articles, which he divides 1–10 and for the short pieces on ff. 177–82, a–k. The main pieces are: (2) ff. 1–51ᵛ, a compilation called Flos rami from Gregory, Moralia on Job; (5) ff. 57–64ᵛ, a compilation from Gregory on Ezekiel; (6) ff. 64ᵛ–98, a work called Paratum 'super euangelium Mathei et Luce . . . a viginti et vi voluminibus sanctorum studiose compilatum'; (9) ff. 104–53, a compilation called Palma penne excerpted 'ab ethimologiis Rabani et a Warnerio Gregoriano' and from 'Modernus' (the running title is 'R' on ff. 104–25, 'G' on ff. 125–32, and 'M' on ff. 132–53); (10) ff. 155–75, tabular 'distinctiones super psalterium secundum petrum Pict' cancellarium par' et secundum alios quosdam'. Short pieces include; (3) f. 52, a sermon of Richard Fishacre ('fishakel'); (*a*) f. 177, acrostics on the name Edmundus; (*b*) f. 177, verses 'De Innocentio' and 'De predicatoribus' (printed by James: Walther, nos. 6281, 2838); (*c*) f. 177ᵛ, a piece in English, 'Ailredus rex. Wanne king is radles . . . .', *IMEV*, no. 1820(6); (*f*) f. 178ᵛ, includes verses in French against ill-behaved monks; (*i*) ff. 180–1, a bifolium of a commentary on psalms in the hand of arts. 2–10, used for (*h*) and (*k*).[1]

ff. 189, foliated ii–vii, 1–182 (a leaf in quire 20 was not numbered). ff. 1–176 have a medieval foliation 25–201 and ff. ii–v a medieval foliation 49–52. Written space 210 × 140 mm. 2 cols. 67 lines. The first line of writing above the top ruled line. The mark of a chain on a former binding shows on ff. i (parchment flyleaf), ii–vii, 1, 2. Written in England.

The table of contents inside the cover of Pembroke College, Cambridge, 101, in the hand of the Bury St. Edmunds monk Henry de Kirkestede (s. xiv²) shows that in his time ff. 1–176 of MS. 6 were ff. 25–201 of a volume of 288 leaves, pressmarked S. 65 in the Bury library.[2] The rest of the manuscript, apart from eighteen leaves,[3] is now Pembroke College 101, ff. 1–93: the medieval foliation is 1–24, 203–23, 225–34, 236–48, 250–65, 267, 280, 281, 283–8. The leaves now at Ipswich seem to have been made into a separate volume in s. xv, when ff. 49–54 of another book were added in front of them.

7. s. xvi in. 'Hore beate virginis marie secundum vsum Sarum' (ff. 97–135) and other devotions, fully described by James, pp. 95–99.

Many headings, nine prayers (ff. 18ᵛ–19, 173–5, 273ᵛ, 276ʳᵛ), and a form of confession (ff. 282–7) are in English. The contents include: ff. 43ᵛ–44, a rubric in English (printed by James) in the main hand, which conveys an indulgence of Ave maria dated 26 Mar. 1492; f. 169ᵛ, a prayer 'de revelacione diuina transmissa vni monacho de bynhym circa anno domini mcccc et lxxxv'; f. 252, hours of the Holy Name in which vespers and compline are said to be 'edite a deuoto Ricardo de hampole': cf. H. E. Allen, *Writings Ascribed*

---

[1] Cf. Pembroke College, Cambridge, 101, art. 5.

[2] Information from Dr. R. M. Thomson.

[3] According to Kirkestede's table, the missing leaves contained 'Proprietates verborum pro sermonibus' and 'Summa Lincoln (*R. Grosseteste*) Templum domini'. They were no doubt ff. 268–79.

to Richard Rolle, 1927, pp. 9–10; f. 277^{rv}, a direction in English to saye the Psalter of Our Lady indulgenced by William (Waynflete), bishop of Winchester (1447–86), Edward (Story), bishop of Chichester (1478–1503), James (Goldwell), bishop of Norwich (1472–99), John (Morton), bishop of Ely (1478–86), and John (Marshall), bishop of Llandaff (1478–86). The calendar with two feasts of Erkenwold in red and Angulus (7 Feb.) in black suggests London. In the hours of B.V.M. the memoriae at lauds are repeated at vespers. In the litany, f. 188^v, Edward is first and Erkenwald twentieth of twenty-four confessors. The long form of confession in English, ff. 282–287^v is set out according to the seven sins, the ten commandments, the five wits, the seven works of bodily and seven works of spiritual mercy, the seven gifts of the Holy Spirit, the seven sacraments and the eight beatitudes: it begins 'Fyrst I knowledge myself gylty': cf. Jolliffe, C. 21. Some English headings have been erased or crossed out; also the words 'pape' and 'pope' and in the litany 'Sancte Thoma', first among martyrs.

ff. 290. Written space 143 × 105 mm. 19 long lines. Written in England. 'Anne Wythypoll owth thys boke', f. 97, s. xvi.

8. s. xiii in. and (art. 2) s. xii/xiii. **1.** ff. 4^v–135^v Incipit breuis expositio psalterii. A quibusdam fratrum diu rogatus . . . prior se ipso fiat. Introitus. Apud hebreos opus istud intitulatur liber ymnorum . . . in laudem eius erupit dicens. Incipit breuis expositio psalterii secundum magistrum Ricardum de Sancto Victore. Psalmus primus. Beatus uir . . . Mediator dei et hominum . . . (f. 125^v) ut deum laudare possit. Explicit expositio psalterii. Incipiunt cantica. Canticum ysaie prophete. Cum in precedentibus prophecie sue . . . saluus esse non poterit. Explicit. **2.** ff. 137–229 Libri Iosue et Iudicum glosati.

Cf. James, pp. 99–102. The incipit of (**1**) is that assigned by Stegmüller, nos. 7326, 7377, to Robert of Bridlington's Breviarium super Psalmos.[1] In front of it (ff. 2–4) and in the margins are many pieces in a hand 'marvellous in its minuteness, beauty and regularity' (James), which writes up to 102 lines to the page. These pieces include the Romana series of Psalter collects (cf. *The Psalter Collects*, ed. L. Brou, HBS lxxxiii (1949), 57), extracts from W. de Montibus and O(do) Cluniacensis, and glosses on St. Matthew and other books of the Bible.

1. Written space 123 × 75 mm. 2 cols. 40 lines. Written in England.

2. Written space *c.* 155 × 115 mm. Text and glossed ruled on one grid. Written in England.

Two originally distinct manuscripts bound together by s. xv, when the ex-libris of Bury St. Edmunds and the pressmark B. 240, referring to (**1**), and B. 55, referring to (**2**), were added on f. ii^v: there are similar two-in-one ex-libris pages in the Bury manuscripts now Pembroke College, Cambridge, 85, and London, Wellcome Historical Medical Library, 5867.

9. s. xiii. **1.** ff. 1–338^v Biblia. **2.** ff. 339–55 Interpretationes nominum. Aaron mons fortis . . .

1. Acts is before instead of after Pauline Epistles, 3 Ezra is absent, and Esther 10: 4, Dixit que mardocheus–16: 24 et inobediencie, is an addition. Otherwise order and contents are as usual: see Bristol Public Libr., 15. The chapter numbering through Ezra and Nehemiah is continuous, 1–36. 48 prologues of the common set (see Bristol 15) and 6 others shown here by *: 330, 332, 335, 341 + 343, 344, 357 (added), 349*, 430*, 457, 462, 468, 455* (as a prologue to Wisdom), 482, 487, 492, 500, 507, 511, 515, 513, 519 524, 526, 528, 531 (the beginning only), 534, followed by Prophetatur de euersione . . . profertur a domino*, 538, 539, 545*, 543, 551, 590, 607, 620, 624, 674*, 677 and thirteen more as usual to 793 (685 is missing with the beginning of 1 Corinthians; 765, . . . ab urbe roma; 793 after instead of before Hebrews), 809, 839.

[1] Information from Dr. R. M. Thomson.

2. For copies in the Bodleian see *Sum. Cat.*, Index. It is followed by a further thirteen interpretations, Astaren–Carthach, headed 'Hec nomina non inueni in interp' '.

Written space 138 × 85 mm. 2 cols. 55 lines. Secundo folio *archam*. Written in England. At Ipswich by, at latest, the last years of the sixteenth century and used then and for over a hundred years as a place for entering, sometimes handsomely, the names of citizens, especially sergeants and bailiffs of the town. The earliest dated entry seems to be 'Rychard beamont sargant in Anno 1595', f. 164^v. One of the fullest entries is 'Philipp Courtnall elected Seriant the xxix September anno domini 1608 Tho Sicklemore and William Acton Bayliffs', f. 162. 'Donum thesau[. . . . .] cognomine Roberti', on the flyleaf.

Suffolk collection, 1. *Albertus de Saxonia, Sophismata*   1402

1. Ob rogatum quorundam meorum paruulorum . . . (f. 71^v) et sic patet ad sophisma. Benedictus deus in donis suis. Finito libro frangamus capud magistri. Expliciunt sophismata Reuerendissimi Alberti de Saxonia. Scripta a Fratre Petro cathalonie nacionis Ordinis Fratrum Heremitarum sancti Augustini studente senarum. Anno domini M° CCCC° ii In purificacione beate marie die completa et c'.

Albert of Saxony, Sophismata, printed in 1489 (*GKW* 799) and later. f. 72^{rv} is blank.

2. The pastedowns, now raised from the boards, are two parts of one leaf of a missal in an English hand, s. xii med., containing: (*a*) the end of an office with hymn, Criste sanctorum decus angelorum, versicle, Domus mea, antiphon, Sanctificauit; (*b*) office of mass 'In anniuersario dedicacionis ecclesie'; (*c*) the beginning of a mass of Holy Trinity. Some notes on logic were added on the back pastedown, s. xv.

(*b*). As *Sarum Missal*, pp. 202/25–204/6, except that the gradual Locus iste is here followed by the versicle Vox leticie et exultacionis. (*c*). As *Sarum Missal*, p. 384/2–11 *ab omnibus semper mu*.

Written space 135 mm wide. 2 cols. 33 lines. Ruling with a hard point (?). Initials blue, red, or green.

3. The flyleaf, f. i, contains on the recto a list of sixteen names of donors of books and the names of the books they gave, s. xiii/xiv.

A Franciscan list, almost certainly of donors to the Franciscan convent at Ipswich. Reproduced in facsimile in *Ipswich Library Journal*, xlvi (1939), and, better, in *Friends of the National Libraries Annual Report, 1938–9*, pl. xi: in the plate letters of a dozen line-ends are missing. The list appears to be complete except for the heading, of which traces remain, but half the last line of a three-line note at the foot of the page, 'Recomendentur eciam omnes alii qui contulerunt libros communitati . . .' has been cut off. The names of the last two donors, fr. Laurence Bretoun and fr. Oliver de Stanewey are additions, s. xiv[1]: cf. Emden, *BRUO*, p. 261, and *BRUC*, p. 551. The verso is blank except for some notes of small payments 'Willelmo le pulter' and to others.

4. Strips of a thirteenth-century theological manuscript lie between the quires as strengthening.

ff. i+72+vi. Paper. ff. 73–8 are paper flyleaves. For f. i see above, art. 3. 215 × 145 mm. Written space 158 × 100 mm. 2 cols. 40–8 lines. Collation: 1–6^{12}. Written in a small cursiva: the tops of ascenders are sometimes looped and sometimes straight. Red initials, sometimes with ornament in the same colour. English binding of wooden boards covered with pink-stained leather, s. xv: a central strap and pin missing. Secundo folio *tum hec est uera.*

Written by a Catalan scribe at Siena in 1402. f. 29 bears this date, as well as f. 71ᵛ. Owned by or in use by Franciscan friars, two of them belonging to the Mantua convent, in s. xv: 'Ista sophismata sunt fratris pasquini de [................] Roma que ego emi a quodam studente[...........]', f. 71ᵛ; 'Ista sophismata sunt ad vsum fratris bartholomei (*cancelled and* simonis *substituted*) ordinis minorum de mant' ', f. 71ᵛ; 'Ista sophismata sunt ad vsum fratris Simonis de mantua ordinis fratrum Minorum de Eadem Capelani Magnifice domine paule de malatest' Consortis domini domini Francisci de gonzaga (†1407) mantue. Illustrissimy Alme Ciuitatis domini. que tribus libris in portu gruario redemit', f. 78ᵛ; 'Ista sophismata sunt ad Vusum (*sic*) fratris Simonis de mantua ordinis Sancti Francisci studentis in loycalibus', f. 78ᵛ. The name 'pasquinus' is written after the catchword, f. 12ᵛ. Bound in England, s. xv, by a binder who used as a flyleaf a document belonging almost certainly to the Franciscan convent in Ipswich: possibly the book belonged at this time to a foreign friar studying in England, since the notes on the back pastedown (above, art. 2) do not seem to be in an English hand. E. P. Goldschmidt, catalogue 30, item 1 (£27. 10s.). Acquired in 1938.

KEELE. UNIVERSITY

1. *Hugo de Sancto Victore, etc.*　　　　　　　　　s. XIII¹–XIV

1. ff. 1–91 De fidei sacramento. De fide que in nobis 'est' omni poscenti rationem reddere debemus esse parati. ut ait petrus in epistola sua . . . per inuocationem trinitatis. Restat de coniugio et ordinibus.

Hugh of St. Victor, Summa sententiarum, tractatus I–VI. *PL* clxxvi. 41–154. The scribe wrote 'Sancti spiritus adsit michi gratia' at the head of f. 1. The last eleven lines on f. 91 were left blank.

2. ff. 91–9 Nine paragraphs, with headings: (*a*) In deo solo dispositio bonorum et malorum consistit; (*b*) Ex deo sunt omnia et per ipsum omnia subsistunt; (*c*) De angelorum creatione; (*d*) De eterna dei dilectione; (*e*) Peccauimus omnes in adam; (*f*) De capite ueteris hominis; (*g*) De quibus arboribus fuit crux cristi facta; (*h*) De refectione diuina; (*i*) ff. 97–9 Expositio multarum dubitabilium questionum.

Incipits: (*a*) Disponit deus bona que uult fieri . . .; (*g*) Sancta et diuina eloquia . . .; (*h*) Venite filii ad me . . .; (*i*) Inter rationale et rationabile quit inter. R' Rationale est quod rationis utitur intellectu . . . (*i*) ends abruptly 'sapientia ualere non potest. Philosophie nomen' in the reply to the question 'Inter sapientiam et eloquentiam qualiter distinguitur'.

3. ff. 99ᵛ–102ᵛ De morali philosofia. Moralium dogma phylosoforum per multa dispersum uolumina contrahere disposui et quasi in artem colligere primum quia fragilis est memoria . . . iudicis cuncta cernentis.

An abbreviation of the Moralium dogma philosophorum (ed. J. Holmberg, 1929; *PL* clxxi. 1007–56).

4. ff. 103–125ᵛ Hic oritur questio satis necessaria. Constat et inrefragabiliter uerum est quod deus pater genuit filium . . . nisi in hac uita. nec erit eis meritum supplicii. sed supplicium mali meriti.

A catena from the Sentences of Peter Lombard, the first piece from i. 4.1 and the last from iv. 50.1, with some additions, for example the last nine words and on f. 122^v six lines of verse on the hindrances to marriage, 'Uotum condicio. violentia . . . subire thori' (Walther, no. 20845).

5 (s. xiv). ff. 126–137^v Brief notes on lections, mostly from the gospels and epistles, beginning imperfectly.

The notes on any one lection take a page or two pages usually, beginning at the top, thus 'Ex sion species decoris eius . . .' (f. 126^v), 'Si linguis hominum loquar et angelorum . . .' (f. 128^v). On ff. 129^v–133 they are on lections for the fifteenth to eighteenth Sundays after Pentecost, on ff. 134–136^v for the second to fifth Sundays after Pentecost, and on f. 137 on 'A uoce tonitrui formidabunt'.

6 (s. xv). f. 138 Summe sacerdos et uere pontifex . . . ueritatem. profundum quippe nimis etc.

The first nineteen lines of this well-known prayer before mass, pp. 114–15 in Wilmart's edition in *Auteurs spirituels*. f. 138^v is blank, except for 'Ab', perhaps a pressmark.

ff. i+139+i, foliated (i), 1–44, 44*, 45–138. Medieval foliations 1–126 on ff. 1–44, 45–125, 138, and 61–72 on versos of ff. 126–37. 167 × 132 mm. Written space 120 × 87 mm between double vertical bounders. 25 long lines in arts. 1, 2; 30 lines usually in arts. 3, 4. The first line of writing above the first ruled line. Pricks in both margins of quires 14–16. Collation of ff. 1–125, 138: 1–12^8 13^6+1 leaf after 6 (f. 102) 14–16^8 (ff. 103–25, 138). Several fairly good hands. Initials (not filled in, art. 4): (i) f. 1, 6-line, blue with red ornament; (ii) 2-line, red or blue, with ornament of the other colour; (iii) 1-line, red or blue. The three initials and part of the text on f. 9^v are shown by Edward Johnston, *Writing, Illuminating and Lettering*, 1906, fig. 79.

ff. 61–72 are a single quire, probably the sixth, of a smaller book (157 × 117 mm.) inserted between 16^7 and 16^8. No ruling. Current hand. No ornament.

Binding of s. xix^1, parchment over pasteboard, lettered 'De fidei sacramento' on the spine. Secundo folio *mentum habet*.

Written in Italy. A small oval stamp, s. xix in., pasted to the foot of f. 1, bears the name 'P. M. DE ANGELIS'. Inside the front cover are: (1) 'William Grace Siena 1837'; (2) a slip from an English bookseller's catalogue, s. xix, in which this was item 3; (3) 'Ex libris Gualteri Sneyd' on a round bookstamp; (4) 'Edward Johnston' on a cut out rectangle of paper (cf. above: he died in 1944). Lot 705 in the Walter Sneyd sale at Sotheby's, 16 Dec. 1903, to Peach for £2. 10s. Bought from Days Ltd., 96 Mount Street, London, in 1956.

ADDENDA

BRAILES. PRESBYTERY LIBRARY

118 (2). *Gregorius Magnus, Homiliae in Evangelia; etc.*   s. xv ex.

1. ff. 1–75 In illo tempore. Dixit ihesus discipulis suis. Erunt signa in sole et luna . . . Dominus ac redemptor noster paratos nos . . . mentibus loquatur. Qui viuit . . .

Gregory, Homiliae in Evangelia. *PL* lxxvi. 1077–1312.

2. ff. 75–7 In vigilia natalis domini Lectio sancti Euangelii secundum Matheum. In illo tempore cum esset desponsata . . . Omelia Origenis de eadem Lectione. [Q]ue fuit necessitas ut desponsata . . .

PL xcv. 1162: Homiliary of Paulus Diaconus, De tempore, no. 17.

3. ff. 77ᵛ–78 In principio erat uerbum. Oportet nos fratres karissimi de illa diuinitate disputare . . . homo factum est.

4. ff. 78–82 Expositio Bede super dicta Salomonis. [S]apientissimus regum Salamon laudes sancte ecclesie versibus sed plenissima . . . Mulierem fortem . . . in presenti vita collaudare seruiciis. Amen.

PL xci. 1039–52 (De muliere forti), preceded by a fifteen-line introduction. Stegmüller, no. 1609.

5. ff. 82ᵛ–86 Maria stabat ad monumentum . . . Audiuimus mariam ad monumentum . . . et hec dixit michi. cui est honor et gloria . . . Amen. Poscamus veniam lacrimis imitando mariam. Hec Origenes.

Pseudo-Origen, De Maria Magdalena. *Opera,* 1522, iii, f. 129.

6. ff. 86–102 Sermo beati Augustini episcopi de Ieiunio quadragesimali. Rogo vos et ammoneo fratres karissimi ut in isto legitimo . . . glorie preparemur.

The same series of sermons or extracts from sermons attributed to Augustine, Leo, Maximus, Ambrose and John (Chrysostom) for use on weekdays in Lent occurs in Exeter Cathedral 3504, ff. 254–279ᵛ (see p. 809), under the heading 'Ad collacionem ante completorium'. It is set out in *Ordinale Exon.* iii (HBS lxiii, 1926), 169–76.

7. ff. 102–3 Sermo beati iohannis episcopi. Hodie nobis iohannis virtus . . .

Pseudo-Petrus Chrysologus, Sermo 127: *PL* lii. 549. *Clavis,* nos. 227, 930.

8. ff. 103–5ᵛ Heu me quid agam. vnde sermonis exordium faciam? . . .

PL xcv. 1508, Homiliary of Paulus Diaconus, De sanctis, no. 50 (St. John Baptist). *Clavis,* no. 931.

9. ff. 105ᵛ–8 Sermo beati iohannis episcopi de Pentecost'. Hodie nobis terra factum est celum non stellis de celo in terram descendentibus sed apostolis . . .

10. ff. 108–11   Sermo beati ambrosii episcopi de purificacione beate marie. Si subtiliter a fidelibus . . . secundum carnem qui est benedictus in secula amen.

PL lxxix. 1291 (Ambrosius Autpertus), but ends differently. *Clavis*, no. 842. ff. 111ᵛ–12ᵛ blank.

ff. 112. Paper: change of watermark at quire 5. 283 × 200 mm. Written space 220 × 145 mm. 2 cols. 39–49 lines. Frame ruling with a hard point. Collation: 1–14⁸. Written by more than one hand in neat non-current hybrida, with occasional use of long-tailed *r*, for example, f. 44ᵛᵃ/13. 2-line red initials on ff. 82ᵛ–105ᵛ: elsewhere spaces are left blank. Bound after (1), Eusebius, *Historia ecclesiastica*, and Bede, *Historia ecclesiastica gentis anglorum*, printed at Strasbourg in 1514: the binding of wooden boards covered with brown leather bearing Oldham's rolls AN.g.1. and ornament I (2) is English and contemporary with the printed book: pastedowns are from an ordinal in secretary hand.

Written in England. The title page of (1) is inscribed '2 Jan 1617 h Hayere (?)' and rather earlier (?) and crossed through 'Bossevile'.

pp. 314, 324. On Canterbury Cathedral Add. 128/44, 45 see N. G. Wilson in *Scriptorium*, xxx (1976), 46–7.

p. 507. Durham Cathedral, Inc. 7. Lenglin wrote at the foot of f. 1 in textura 'Textualia sancti thome de aquino doctoris tocius ethice.Exemplar ualde incorrectum erat etc.'. At the end of bk.7, f. 54ᵛ, he wrote 'Scriptor huius. bonitate libri tractus. ipsumque scribere decreuerat set bonum exemplar sibi deerat ut plene vides qua propter rogat de praua scripcione legentibus veniam. si promeruit culpam. Per me fratrem Iohannem Lenglin ordinis predicatorum de preit. In anno quinto sui sacerdocii. dominice incarnacionis octuagesimo 2°'.

He headed art. 2 'Sequens hec epistola a leonardo aretino de ethicis uirtutibus cuidam `est' scripta. In qua multa bona prospicies ideo hic eam depinxi. Ex epistolario ipsius habeo'. Probably he used the copy for the printer at Louvain.

p. 572. Edinburgh, Royal Observatory, Cr. 4. 5. Wilhelmus Saphonensis. Professor P. O. Kristeller has kindly given me the reference to his notice of L. G. Traversagnus, Savonensis O.F.M. (1425-1503), in his *Medieval Aspects of Renaissance Learning*, 1974, p. 155.

p. 634. Eton College 4.

Art. 3 was missed from the description:

ff. 86–126ᵛ   In precedentibus premissa descripcione . . . beatus ergo seruus ille. Vigilias (*ends imperfectly: catchword* uocat ad similitudinem).

Petrus Comestor, Allegoriae in Sacram Scripturam: *PL* clxxv. 633–817/16, but the arrangement of NT there is not that found in the manuscripts; Stegmüller, nos. 3847–8. Two leaves are missing after f. 93, with bk. 3, chs. 11–21, and probably thirteen leaves after f. 111, with the end of bk. 8, all bks. 9–11, and the beginning of bk. 12. The last words are in bk. 13, ch. 19, which begins 'Sint lumbi uestri precincti' (as MS. 45, f. 243): only one leaf of the text is missing here.

p. 666. Eton College 37. After rebacking there are now four paper leaves at each end. The pastedowns have been raised, revealing notes on Numbers and Deuteronomy at the beginning and on Ecclesiasticus and Wisdom at the end.

p. 700. Eton College 84. Now rebound and with new clasps. Part of the old leather from the back cover has been pasted inside the front cover, two paper flyleaves have been added at each end, and the pastedowns have been raised, to reveal September and April, the latter including 'Passio S. Ælphegi' in red on the 19th.

p. 720. Eton College 106. After rebacking there are now four paper leaves at each end. The pastedowns have been raised.

p. 726. Eton College 116. After rebacking there are now four paper leaves at each end. The pastedowns have been raised.

p. 789. The fragment numbered X contains the end of bk. 1 and the beginning of bk. 2 of De generatione et corruptione.

Bristol Baptist College. MSS Z.c.23, Z.d.5, Z.d.39, Z.d.41 and Z.e.38 have been sold. The first of these was lot 56 in Sotheby's sale, 13 December 1976.